# BIBLIOGRAPHY OF
# BRITISH HISTORY

1851-1914

# BIBLIOGRAPHY OF
# BRITISH HISTORY

## 1851–1914

ISSUED UNDER THE DIRECTION OF
THE AMERICAN HISTORICAL ASSOCIATION
AND THE ROYAL HISTORICAL SOCIETY
OF GREAT BRITAIN

COMPILED AND EDITED BY

## H. J. HANHAM

OXFORD
AT THE CLARENDON PRESS
1976

*Oxford University Press, Ely House, London W. 1*

OXFORD LONDON GLASGOW NEW YORK
TORONTO MELBOURNE WELLINGTON CAPE TOWN
IBADAN NAIROBI DAR ES SALAAM LUSAKA ADDIS ABABA
KUALA LUMPUR SINGAPORE JAKARTA HONG KONG TOKYO
DELHI BOMBAY CALCUTTA MADRAS KARACHI

ISBN 0 19 822389 7

*Printed in Great Britain
at the University Press, Oxford
by Vivian Ridler
Printer to the University*

# PREFACE

THIS book has been an excessive time in preparation. When it was begun in 1960 the state of nineteenth-century historical scholarship was still at a relatively low ebb. In whole fields there was sometimes not a single work whose standards of scholarship were at all adequate. There were few reproductions of up-to-date library catalogues. And many of the appropriate classes of records in the Public Record Office were still either only partly open, or in such a confused state that they were extremely difficult to use. The instinct of the bibliographer was inevitably to drag his feet a little in the hope that times would change for the better. And change they did. The *British Union Catalogue of Periodicals* of 1955 was followed by the complete library catalogue of the British Museum (5), by a new guide to the Public Record Office (44), and by a spate of bibliographical guides. In 1968 a thirty-year limit on the opening of public documents replaced the old fifty-year rule. The number of high-level studies and monographs multiplied rapidly. Now at last it has become possible to see fairly clearly what is important for scholars and what is not. This bibliography, consequently, attempts to sum up the state of scholarship after a ten-year renaissance of nineteenth-century studies.

The greatest single problem which the bibliographer of the nineteenth century faces is the vast proliferation of printed matter that took place during this period. The daily newspapers (some of them by the end of the century were down in price to a halfpenny), the local newspapers, the memoirs of the great and the far from great, the innumerable biographies, the records of churches and chapels, the local handbooks, the popular journals bound up in volume form, the novels and volumes of verse, by their sheer volume threaten to overwhelm the reader. To examine the literature of even quite a small religious denomination leads one to feel that any minister competent to preach, any chapel with the backing of a moderately wealthy congregation, must have had to fight really hard to avoid commemoration in a series of more or less worthless hagiographies in verse and prose. One result of this proliferation of the printed word was that the library system proved unable to take the strain. The British Museum collected only those books which came to its notice or which it deemed important. Local libraries were extremely unsystematic about what they collected. For minor items (particularly pamphlets) it is therefore often necessary to hunt far and wide. Few items seem to have disappeared altogether, but to track them down is often laborious in the extreme.

The intention of this bibliography, as of the others in the series, is to list the major works which a student is likely to wish to consult, a selection of other works which makes clear the scope of contemporary printed materials, and a selection of biographies and autobiographies. Where it has seemed useful to do so, books have been grouped by category: first works of reference, secondly histories, thirdly contemporary works and biographies. Contemporary works have, where appropriate, been arranged in chronological, and biographies in alphabetical, order. The text was revised late in 1970 to include books and articles published up to the end of that year. Further entries were added while the book was going through the press, so that the present text also includes many works published in 1971 and 1972, and some published in 1973.

The method of selection has been as follows. A fairly complete listing of books was made using the subject catalogue of Manchester Central Library as a basis, the work being undertaken by Mrs. Julie Bartle. Four sections were then arranged in provisional order and expert opinion was sought on them. The section on the churches was discussed with Dr. J. F. S. Kent, that on the law with Dr. C. H. S. Fifoot, that on Wales with Mr. I. G. Jones and Dr. Kenneth Morgan, and that on local history with Dr. W. H. Chaloner. The provisional drafts of these four sections were then revised, and provided the model for the arrangement of other sections. These have all been compiled in such a way as to keep a balance between them, and inevitably reflect the personal predilections of the compiler. Where possible, however, given a rather awkward timetable, I have asked fellow scholars to comment on particular sections as they were produced, and have taken their advice as to revisions. For help in this way I am grateful to Professor W. R. Ward, Professor Tapan Raychaudhuri, Professor J. H. Parry, Professor J. R. English, Professor F. M. Leventhal, Professor Mark Roskill, and Professor John Clive.

I cannot conclude without offering my special thanks to those scholars named above who so generously helped me at various stages, the Chief Librarian and staff of Manchester Central Library who for three years housed my card catalogue, Mrs. Julie Bartle, the research assistant who first got the project off the ground, and Mrs. Francey Kyte who typed the entire manuscript with exceptional skill and dispatch.

H. J. HANHAM

*Cambridge, Mass.,*
*January 1975*

# CONTENTS

# ABBREVIATIONS

An attempt has been made to use abbreviations that are immediately recognizable, such as *Amer. Hist. Rev.* for *American Historical Review*, *Econ. Hist. Rev.* for *Economic History Review*, and *Eng. Hist. Rev.* for *English Historical Review*. Parliamentary papers are indicated by their command number, e.g. [3214], [C. 3214], [Cd. 3214], [Cmd. 3214], or their sessional number, e.g. H.C. 321 (for a House of Commons paper), H.L. 321 (for a House of Lords paper), plus their year, volume, and page number, e.g. H.C. 321 (1851–2). XX, 123, as recommended by the Royal Historical Society.

| | |
|---|---|
| Acad. | Academy |
| add. | additions, additional |
| admin. | administration |
| agric. | agriculture, agricultural |
| Ala. | Alabama |
| Amer. | American |
| antiq. | antiquarian |
| app. | appendix |
| arch. | archaeological |
| Ark. | Arkansas |
| assoc. | association |
| Aust. | Australian |
| Balt. | Baltimore |
| Bd. | Board |
| bibliog. | bibliography, bibliographical |
| biog. | biography, biographical |
| Birm. | Birmingham |
| Bost. | Boston, Mass. |
| bull. | bulletin |
| *c.* | *circa* |
| C., Cd., Cmd. | command paper |
| Cal. | California |
| Camb. | Cambridge |
| cent. | century |
| ch. | chapter |
| coll., colls. | collection, collections |
| comp. | compiler, compiled, compilation |
| Conn. | Connecticut |
| cont. | continued |
| corresp. | correspondence |
| cumul. | cumulated |

| | |
|---|---|
| dept. | department |
| *D.N.B.* | *Dictionary of National Biography* |
| doc., docs. | document, documents |
| eccles. | ecclesiastical |
| econ. | economic |
| ed. | editor, edited |
| Edin. | Edinburgh |
| edn., edns. | edition, editions |
| educ. | education, educational |
| Eng. | English |
| enl. | enlarged |
| Ga. | Georgia |
| H.C. | House of Commons |
| H.L. | House of Lords |
| H.M.S.O. | Her [His] Majesty's Stationery Office |
| hist. | history, historical |
| Ill. | Illinois |
| inst. | institute |
| instn. | institution |
| intro. | introduction |
| j., journ. | journal |
| Kans. | Kansas |
| Ky. | Kentucky |
| lang. | language |
| libr. | library |
| lit. | literary, literature |
| Lond. | London |
| mag. | magazine |
| Manch. | Manchester |
| Mass. | Massachusetts |
| Md. | Maryland |
| med. | medical |
| Mich. | Michigan |
| misc. | miscellaneous, miscellany |
| Mo. | Missouri |
| mod. | modern |
| MS., MSS. | manuscript, manuscripts |
| N.B. | New Brunswick |
| n.d. | no date |
| N.J. | New Jersey |
| n.s. | new series |
| N.Y. | New York |
| N.Z. | New Zealand |

| | |
|---|---|
| no. | number |
| Oxf. | Oxford |
| Pa. | Pennsylvania |
| parl. | parliamentary |
| P.E.I. | Prince Edward Island |
| Phila. | Philadelphia |
| phil. | philosophical, philosophy |
| pol. | politics |
| priv. pr. | privately printed |
| P.R.O. | Public Record Office |
| proc. | proceedings |
| pseud. | pseudonym |
| pt., pts. | part, parts |
| publ. | published |
| publs. | publications |
| quart. | quarterly |
| rec. | record |
| repr. | reprint, reprinted |
| res. | research |
| rev. | review, revised |
| Scot. | Scottish |
| sec. | secretary |
| ser. | series |
| soc. | society |
| stat., stats. | statistical, statistics |
| stud., studs. | study, studies |
| suppl., suppls. | supplement, supplements, supplemented |
| trans. | translated, transactions |
| univ. | university |
| v., vol., vols. | volume, volumes |
| Va. | Virginia |
| *V.C.H.* | *Victoria County History* |
| W.A. | Western Australia |
| Wash. | Washington |

# I

## GENERAL

### A. BIBLIOGRAPHIES AND OTHER REFERENCE BOOKS

#### I. GENERAL

1  COLLISON (ROBERT LEWIS WRIGHT). Bibliographies, subject and national: a guide to their contents, arrangement and use. 1951. 3rd edn. 1968.
Useful for unfamiliar topics.

2  BESTERMAN (THEODORE). A world bibliography of bibliographies . . . 2 v. Lond. 1939–40. 4th edn. 5 v. Lausanne. 1965–6.
The fullest work of its kind. New bibliogs. are listed in *The bibliographic index: a cumulative bibliography of bibliographies*, 1937+, N.Y. 1938+.

3  WALFORD (ALBERT JOHN) *and others, eds.* Guide to reference material. Libr. Assoc. 1959. Suppl. 1963. new edn. 3 v. 1966–70.
Lists currently standard works. The American counterpart is Constance Mabel Winchell, *Guide to reference books*, 8th edn., Amer. Lib. Assoc., Chicago 1967, suppls. 1968+. An early and wider-ranging venture was William Swan Sonnenschein, *The best books: a reader's guide and literary reference . . .*, 3rd edn., 6 v. 1910–35, repr. Detroit 6 v. 1969. Its most recent counterpart is Lionel Roy McColvin and others, *The Librarian subject guide to books*, 3 v.+, 1959+. Lionel Madden, comp., *How to find out about the Victorian period: a guide to sources of information*, 1970, is a useful handbook to the reference books for the Victorian period.

4  THE ASLIB DIRECTORY: a guide to sources of specialised information in Great Britain and Ireland. Assoc. of Special Libraries and Information Bureaux. 3rd edn. Ed. by Brian John Wilson. 2 v. 1970.
A guide to library collections. The Libr. Assoc. also publishes guides to regional library resources. For American libraries consult Anthony Thomas Kruzas, ed., *Directory of special libraries and information centers*, 2nd edn. Detroit 1968, and Lee Ash [and Denis Lorenz], *Subject collections: a guide to special book collections and subject emphases as reported by university, college, public and special libraries in the United States and Canada*, N.Y. 1958, 3rd edn. N.Y. 1967.

5  BRITISH MUSEUM. General catalogue of printed books: photolithographic edition to 1955. 263 v. 1960–6. Suppl. for 1956–65. 50 v. 1968. Suppl. for 1966–70. 26 v. 1971–2.
The main list of British books used by scholars. The British Museum libr., is now styled the British Libr.

6  THE NATIONAL UNION CATALOG, pre-1956 imprints: a cumulative author list representing Library of Congress printed cards and titles reported by other American libraries. Comp. and ed. with the cooperation of the Library of Congress and the National Union Catalog subcommittee of the Resources

committee of the Resources and Technical Services Association, Amer. Libr. Assoc. [Chicago] 1968+. In progress.

To be the most comprehensive finding list in existence. Will replace the earlier catalogues prepared by the Library of Congress. Cont. by U.S. Library of Congress, *The national union catalog: a cumulative author list . . . 1953–1957*, 28 v. Ann Arbor, [Mich.]. 1958, . . . *1958–1962*, 54 v. N.Y. 1963, and . . . *1963–1967*, 59 v. Ann Arbor 1969, cumul. in *The national union catalog, 1956–1967*, 120 v., Totowa, N.J. 1971–2.

7 THE BRITISH NATIONAL BIBLIOGRAPHY . . . a subject list of the new British books published in [1950+] based upon the books deposited at the Copyright Office of the British Museum . . . 1951+.

Standard for post-1950 British books. Publ. in parts, with annual cumulative vols.

8 THE ENGLISH CATALOGUE OF BOOKS . . . 1835–1968. 1864–1969.

Until 1950 the standard list of British books issued by major publishing houses. Cumulates four-yearly. For its provenance see Graham Pollard, 'General lists of books printed in England', *Inst. Hist. Res. Bull.* xii (1934–5), 164–74. It may be usefully suppl. by Joseph Whitaker, publisher, *A reference catalogue of current literature . . .*, 1874–1961+, which appeared at irregular intervals, by *Whitaker's cumulative book list*, 1924+, and by Bertram Dobell, *Catalogue of books printed for private circulation*, 1906.

9 UNITED STATES CATALOG: books in print, 1899. Minneapolis. 1899. 4th edn. N.Y. 1928. Suppls.

Suppls. appear as *Cumulative book index*, 1928–32+.

10 BAER (ELEANORA A.). Titles in series: a handbook for librarians and students. 2nd edn. 2 v. N.Y. 1964. Suppl. 1967, 1971.

Lists publishers' series.

11 THE NEW CAMBRIDGE BIBLIOGRAPHY OF ENGLISH LITERATURE. Vol. III 1800–1900. Ed. by George Watson. Camb. 1969. Vol. IV 1900–1950. Ed. by Ian Roy Willison. Camb. 1972.

Replaces the *Cambridge Bibliography of English Literature*, ed. by Frederick Noel Wilse Bateson, 4 v. Camb. 1940, with suppl. ed. by George Watson, Camb. 1957, which has a wider coverage. Lists in subject order. For major authors *The concise Cambridge bibliography of English literature, 600–1950*, ed. by George Watson, 2nd edn. Camb. 1965, is much more convenient. It is one of those books to be owned by all scholars.

12 LONDON LIBRARY. Catalogue of the London Library. New edn. 2 v. 1913–14. Suppl. 3 v. 1920–53.

To be used with *Subject index of the London Library*, 1909, suppl. 3 v. 1923–55. Together the two ser. constitute a very useful starting-point for research. May be suppl. by the new subject catalogue of Manchester City Reference Library, which is being issued in parts.

13 BRITISH LIBRARY OF POLITICAL AND ECONOMIC SCIENCE. A London bibliography of the social sciences, being the subject catalogue of the British library of political and economic science at the London School of Economics, the Goldsmiths' library of economic literature at the University of London, the libraries of the Royal Statistical Society and the Royal

Anthropological Institute . . . Compiled under the direction of Bertie Mason Headicar and Clifford Fuller. 4 v. 1931–2. Suppls. to 1968. Monthly accession lists.

Much less convenient to use than the London Libr. catalogue, but has wide coverage.

14  PEDDIE (ROBERT ALEXANDER). Subject index of books published before [up to and including] 1880. 4 v. 1933–48.

No set plan: each of the 4 v. must be consulted for any subject. Succeeded by the British Museum, *Subject index of the modern works added to the library . . . in the years 1881–1900*, ed. George Knottesford Fortescue, 3 v. 1902–3, with supplements for periods of five years. For most purposes the *Subject index of the London Library* (**12**) is more convenient. For recent books, *The Library of Congress catalog: books, subjects*, Wash. etc. 1950–4+, Ann Arbor [Mich.]. 1955+, quart. with annual and 5-year cumulations, is convenient. The Assoc. of Res. Libr. has produced *A catalog of Great Britain entries represented by Library of Congress printed cards . . . to July 31, 1942*, 2 v., Ann Arbor, Mich. 1944.

15  HALKETT (SAMUEL) *and* LAING (JOHN). Dictionary of anonymous and pseudonymous English literature. New and enl. edn. by James Kennedy, William Allan Smith, and Alfred Forbes Johnson. 8 v. Edin. and Lond. 1926–56.

First edn. 4 v. Edin. 1882–8. The standard work. For a list of dictionaries of anonyms and pseudonyms, see Archer Taylor and Fredric J. Mosher, *The bibliographical history of anonyma and pseudonyma*, Chicago 1951.

## 2. HISTORICAL PUBLICATIONS

16  HISTORICAL ASSOCIATION, LONDON. Annual bulletin of historical literature, 1911+. 1912+.

Highly selective annotated lists covering both British and world history. More used by British historians than the annual *International bibliography of historical sciences*, 1926+, Paris 1930+.

17  FURBER (ELIZABETH CHAPIN) *ed.* Changing views on British history: essays on historical writing since 1939. Camb., Mass. 1966.

In effect an annotated bibliog. Geoffrey Rudolph Elton, *Modern historians on British history, 1485–1945: a critical bibliography, 1945–1969*, 1970, is an annotated handlist which incl. articles. There are also a number of pamphlet guides of which Robert Kiefer Webb, *English History, 1815–1914*, Amer. Hist. Assoc. Wash. 1967, is the best. Most general guides to historical literature are too wide-ranging to be fully satisfactory, but it may sometimes be useful to consult George Frederick Howe and others, eds., *The American Historical Association's guide to historical literature*, new edn. N.Y. 1961, John Roach, ed., *A bibliography of modern history*, Camb. 1968, Edith Margaret Coulter and Melanie Gerstenfeld, eds., *Historical bibliographies . . .*, Berkeley 1935, repr. 1965, and Pierre Caron and Marc Jaryc, eds., *World list of historical periodicals and bibliographies . . .*, Internat. Committee of Historical Sciences, Oxf. 1939. For historical miscellanies there is Internat. Committee of Historical Sciences, *Bibliographie internationale des travaux historiques publiés dans les volumes de 'mélanges': international bibliography of historical articles in festschriften and miscellanies*, 2 v. Paris 1955–65.

18  ROYAL HISTORICAL SOCIETY. Writings on British history, 1901–1933: a bibliography of books and articles on the history of Great Britain from

about 400 A.D. to 1914, published during the years 1901–1933 inclusive, with an appendix containing a select list of publications in these years on British history since 1914. 5 v. in 7. 1968–70.

The two parts of vol. V cover 1815–1914. Publs. of socs. listed in Mullins (**24**) are omitted. Both works are cont. by the ser. of annual vols. comp. by Alexander Taylor Milne for 1934–9, with 2 vols. for 1940–5, and by Donald James Munro for 1946–8. Subject order. Louis B. Frewer, comp., *Bibliography of historical writings published in Great Britain and the Empire, 1940–1945,* 1947, has been overtaken by the Milne vols.

19 LANCASTER (JOAN CADOGAN) *comp.* Bibliography of historical works issued in the United Kingdom, 1946–1956. Inst. Hist. Res. 1957.

Cont. by William Kellaway as *Bibliography of historical works . . . 1957–[1970],* 3 v. Inst. Hist. Res. 1962–72. Lists books only, in subject order.

20 ALTHOLZ (JOSEF LEWIS). Victorian England, 1837–1901. Conference on British Studies bibliographical handbooks. Camb. 1970.

A convenient checklist of books and articles.

21 TEMPLEMAN (WILLIAM DARBY) *ed.* Bibliographies of studies in Victorian literature for the thirteen years, 1932–1944. Urbana, Ill. 1945.

Cont. for 1945–54 by Austin Wright, Urbana 1956, and for 1955–64 by Robert C. Slack, Urbana 1967. Reprints annual bibliographies from *Modern Philology,* 1933–57, and *Victorian Studies,* 1957–8 +. Gradually broadens in scope in later years.

22 VICTORIAN BIBLIOGRAPHY for 1957+. Incl. in *Victorian Studies,* 1957–8+.

An indispensable list of books and articles with references to selected reviews. At first chiefly literary, now general. Cumulative vols. are publ. at 10-yearly intervals (see **21**).

23 MULLINS (EDWARD LINDSAY CARSON). Texts and calendars: an analytical guide to serial publications. Roy. Hist. Soc. 1958 [1959].

Robert Somerville, *Handlist of record publications,* British Records Assoc. 1951, and Peter Gouldesbrough and others, *Handlist of Scottish and Welsh record publications,* British Records Assoc. 1954, are useful subject indexes, which incl. some material not in Mullins.

24 MULLINS (EDWARD LINDSAY CARSON). A guide to the historical and archaeological publications of societies in England and Wales, 1901–1933. Inst. Hist. Res. 1968.

Cont. by the Milne series of *Writings on British history* (**18**), for post-1933 period.

25 MILNE (ALEXANDER TAYLOR). A centenary guide to the publications of the Royal Historical Society, 1868–1968, and of the former Camden Society, 1838–1897. Roy. Hist. Soc. 1968.

26 BOEHM (ERIC H.) *and* ADOLPHUS (LALIT). Historical periodicals: an annotated world list of historical and related serial publications. Santa Barbara & Munich. 1961.

The chief general periodicals for British history in the period 1851–1914 are *Victorian Studies,* Bloomington, Ind. 1957+, *English Historical Review,* 1886+, *[Cambridge]*

*Historical Journal*, 1925+, *History*, Hist. Assoc., 1916+, *Bulletin of the Institute of Historical Research*, 1923+, *Journal of British Studies*, Conference on British Studs., Hartford, Conn. 1961+, *Past and Present*, 1952+, *Transactions of the Royal Historical Society*, 1872+, *Journal of Modern History*, Chicago 1929+, *American Historical Review*, N.Y. 1895+, *History Today*, 1951+, and *Historical studies: papers read before the . . . Irish Conference of Historians*, 1958+. More specialized periodicals are listed under the appropriate subject heading.

27  ASSOCIATION OF SPECIAL LIBRARIES AND INFORMATION BUREAUX: Index to theses accepted for higher degrees in the universities of Great Britain and Ireland, 1950–51+. Aslib. 1953+.

The American equivalent publ. by the Assoc. of Research Libr. is *Doctoral dissertations accepted by American Universities* [now *American doctoral dissertations*], 1933–4+, Assoc. of Res. Libr., N.Y., now Ann Arbor, [Mich.] 1934+. Abstracts of American dissertations on microfilm are printed in *Dissertation abstracts . . .*, Ann Arbor, 1938+, which was styled *Microfilm abstracts*, 1938–51.

28  INSTITUTE OF HISTORICAL RESEARCH (University of London). Historical research for university degrees in the United Kingdom. Part I Theses completed—Part II Theses in progress. 1967+.

Earlier lists are in *History*, 1920–9, *Inst. Hist. Res. Bull.*, 1930–2, and in the *Theses supplement* to *Inst. Hist. Res. Bull.*, 1933–66.

29  KUEHL (WARREN FREDERICK) *comp.* Dissertations in history: an index to dissertations completed in history departments of United States and Canadian universities, 1873–1960. Univ. of Kentucky Pr. 1965.

Suppl. by American Historical Association, *List of doctoral dissertations in history in progress or completed at colleges and universities in the United States . . .*, Wash. 1902+.

### 3. OFFICIAL PUBLICATIONS

30  FORD (PERCY) *and* FORD (GRACE). A guide to parliamentary papers: where they are, how to find them, how to use them. Oxf. 1955, new edn. 1956.

Very useful for beginners. The parl. papers are the most important single printed ser. of papers for 19th-cent. British hist. House of Commons papers, 1731–1900, are available in Readex microprint. For U.S. holdings of originals see Winifred Gregory, ed., *List of the serial publications of foreign governments, 1815–1931*, N.Y. 1932. For specialized lists of particular classes of papers see the indexes at **33–6**. For non-parl. papers H.M.S.O. lists are the only guide. A reprinting programme on a subject-by-subject basis is described in *Checklist of British parliamentary papers in the Irish University Press 1000-volume series, 1801–1899*, Shannon 1972.

31  FORD (PERCY) *and* FORD (GRACE). Select list of British parliamentary papers, 1833–1899. Oxf. 1953. Repr. Shannon 1970.

A useful finding list for papers relating to domestic affairs. Largely supersedes Hilda Vernon Jones, ed., *Catalogue of parliamentary papers, 1801–1900 . . .*, [1904], with suppls. for 1901–10, 1911–20, [1912, 1922].

32  FORD (PERCY) *and* FORD (GRACE). A breviate of parliamentary papers, 1900–1916: the foundation of the welfare state. Oxf. 1957. Repr. Shannon 1970.

Summarizes papers. Cont. by *A breviate . . . 1917–1939*, Oxf. 1951, repr. Shannon 1970.

**33** GENERAL ALPHABETICAL INDEX to the bills, reports, estimates, accounts, and papers, printed by order of the House of Commons, and to the papers presented by command, 1852–1899. 1909.

Succeeded a 3-vol. index for 1801–52. Gives references to bound vols. only. Must, therefore, be suppl. by the sessional lists and indexes, publ. each year, or by the *General alphabetical index* for 1852–3 to 1868–9, [H.C. 469–II. (1870). LXXI, 1], and subsequent decennial vols. if working with unbound papers.

**34** GENERAL INDEX to the bills, reports, and papers printed by order of the House of Commons and to the reports and papers presented by command, 1900 to 1948–49. H.M.S.O. 1960.

**35** GABINÉ (BERNARD LUTHARD) *comp.* A finding list of British royal commission reports, 1860–1935. Camb., Mass. 1935.

One of a number of useful working tools. Others incl. Edward Di Roma and Joseph A. Rosenthal, comps., *A numerical finding list of British command papers published 1833–1961/62*, N.Y. Public Libr. 1967, and K. A. C. Parsons, *A checklist of British parliamentary papers (bound set), 1801–1950*, Camb. Univ. Libr. 1958.

**36** A GENERAL INDEX to the sessional papers printed by order of the House of Lords or presented by special command. 3 v. 1860–90. Vol. I repr. 1938.

Covers 1801–85. Later years are covered by annual indexes. Most Lords papers were also publ. as Commons papers. Unduplicated papers are in the British Museum or the library of the House of Lords.

### 4. MANUSCRIPT COLLECTIONS

**37** HISTORICAL MANUSCRIPTS COMMISSION. Record repositories in Great Britain; a list prepared by a joint committee of the Historical Manuscripts Commission and the British Records Association. 3rd edn. H.M.S.O. 1968.

Lists all repositories of manuscripts.

**38** HISTORICAL MANUSCRIPTS COMMISSION (NATIONAL REGISTER OF ARCHIVES). List of accessions to repositories . . . 1954+. 1955+. Annual. Index for 1954–8. 1967.

Lists all new MS. accessions in repositories incl. in **37**. Issues for 1954–6 issued gratuitously by National Register of Archives as *Bulletins*. Later numbers publ. by H.M.S.O.

**39** HISTORICAL MANUSCRIPTS COMMISSION. The twenty-third report of the Royal Commission on Historical Manuscripts, 1946–1959. H.M.S.O. 1961.

This report (followed by the 24th on 1960–2 and the 25th on 1963–7) marked a new departure. The main emphasis is now on listing the reports on individual MS. collections made by the National Register of Archives. These reports are to be consulted in a small number of major British libraries. It is hoped eventually to compile a complete national record of MS. collections.

40   HISTORICAL MANUSCRIPTS COMMISSION. Guide to the reports of the Royal Commission on Historical Manuscripts, 1870–1911. 3 v. H.M.S.O. 1914–38. Suppl. for 1911–54. 3+ v. H.M.S.O. 1966+.

Few collections listed have post-1850 material. There is a complete list of publs. in *Reports of the Royal Commission on Historical Manuscripts*, government publs. sectional list 17, H.M.S.O. 1972. A 'location list' of MSS. listed has been publ. in the 24th and subsequent reports of the commission. For the commission's work generally see Historical Manuscripts Commission, *Manuscripts and men . . .*, H.M.S.O. 1969, which includes a history.

41   HEPWORTH (PHILIP). Archives and manuscripts in libraries. Libr. Assoc. pamphlet 18, 2nd edn. 1964.

Lists printed catalogues of British libraries and county record offices.

42   BRITISH NATIONAL ARCHIVES. Government publications sectional list 24. H.M.S.O. 1969 and revisions.

Lists all record material printed under official auspices and some of the official indexes on sale to the public.

43   LIST AND INDEX SOCIETY. Vol. 1+. 1965+.

The society exists to print indexes of papers in national repositories for the use of members. It publishes approx. 12 vols. a year, incl. reports on non-official records in the P.R.O.

44   PUBLIC RECORD OFFICE. Guide to the contents of the Public Record Office. Vol. I. legal records, etc. Vol. II state papers and departmental records. Vol. III documents transferred to the P.R.O., 1960–1966. 3 v. H.M.S.O. 1963–8.

Suppl. by *Classes of departmental papers for 1906–1939*, P.R.O. handbook 10, H.M.S.O. 1966, and by a list of maps (**132**). Printed guides to particular classes of papers are listed below (**373, 909, 1218, 2660**). Working lists are printed by (a) Kraus Reprint Corporation in conjunction with H.M.S.O. and are listed in **42**, and (b) by the List and Index Society **43**. Up-to-date reports on the work of the office are publ. in the annual *Report of the [Deputy] Keeper of the Public Records*, 1840+.

45   BOND (MAURICE FRANCIS). Guide to the records of parliament (House of Lords Record Office). H.M.S.O. 1971.

One of the major collections of official papers.

46   BRITISH MUSEUM. Catalogue of additions to the manuscripts . . . 1836+. 1843+.

Early vols. entitled *List of additions*. Other catalogues are listed in Theodore Cressy Skeat, *The catalogues of the manuscript collections in the British Museum*, rev. edn. 1962.

47   JOHN RYLANDS LIBRARY, MANCHESTER. Handlist of the collection of English manuscripts in the John Rylands Library, 1899–1928. By Moses Tyson. 1929. Suppls.

Additions are listed initially in *The bulletin of the John Rylands Library*, Manch. 1903+.

48   CAMBRIDGE UNIVERSITY LIBRARY. Summary guide to accessions

of western manuscripts (other than medieval) since 1867. Comp. by Arthur
E. B. Owen. Camb. 1966.

49  HAMER (PHILIP MAY) *ed.* A guide to archives and manuscripts in the
United States. Comp. for the National Historical Publications Commission.
New Haven, [Conn.]. 1961.

Comprehensive.

50  U.S. LIBRARY OF CONGRESS. The national union catalog of manuscript collections, 1959–1961, based on reports from American repositories
of manuscripts. Ann Arbor, [Mich.]. 1962. In progress. Annual vols. now
produced.

An invaluable guide and finding list, kept admirably up to date.

## 5. PERIODICALS AND NEWSPAPERS

51  BRITISH UNION CATALOGUE OF PERIODICALS: a record of the
periodicals of the world, from the seventeenth century to the present day, in
British libraries. Ed. by James D. Stewart and others. 4 v. 1955–8. Suppl. to
1960. 1962. Annual suppls.

Commonly known as Bucop. Invaluable for location of periodicals and (usually) for
dates of publication. Suppl. by various regional lists prepared under the auspices of
the Library Assoc., e.g. *The London union list of periodicals: holdings of the municipal
and county libraries of Greater London*, 1951, new edn. 1958. For current periodicals
there is David Woodworth, ed., *Guide to current British periodicals*, Libr. Assoc. 1970.

52  UNION LIST OF SERIALS in libraries of the United States and Canada.
Ed. by Winifred Gregory and others. 3 v. N.Y. 1927–33. 3rd edn. 5 v. N.Y.
1965.

The U.S. equivalent of Bucop (**51**). For new periodicals suppl. by *New serial titles:
a union list of serials commencing publication after December 31, 1949*, 1950–60 cumulation, 2 v. Wash. 1961, 1961–5 cumulation, 2 v. N.Y. 1966, 1966–8 cumulation, 2 v.
Wash. 1969. Monthly suppls.

53  HOUGHTON (WALTER EDWARDS) *ed.* The Wellesley index to
Victorian periodicals, 1824–1900: tables of contents and identification of
contributors, with bibliographies of their articles and stories. v. 1+. Toronto.
1966+.

Sets a new standard for bibliog. Indispensable when complete. Will index *c.* 40 major
periodicals, identifying anonymous writers. The progress of this and other indexing
projects may be followed in *The Victorian periodicals newsletter*, 1+, Bloomington,
Ind. 1968+.

54  POOLE (WILLIAM FREDERICK) *and* FLETCHER (WILLIAM
ISAAC) *eds.* Poole's index to periodical literature [1802–1906]. 6 v. Boston
& N.Y. 1882–1908. Repr. Gloucester, Mass. 1958.

Awkward to use but indispensable. For guidance on use see Wayne Somers, 'Aids to
the use of *Poole's index*', *Victorian periodicals newsletter*, 8 (1970), 15–22, Marion V.
Bell and Jean C. Bacon, eds., *Poole's index: date and volume key*, A.C.R.L. Monographs
No 19, Chicago 1957, and C. Edward Wall, ed., *Poole's index to periodical literature:
author index*, Ann Arbor, Mich., 1971. For an author index see William Isaac Fletcher

and Richard Rogers Bowker, *Annual literary index, 1892–1904, including periodicals, American and English, essays, book chapters,* etc., *with author-index, bibliographies, necrology and index to dates of principal events,* 13 v. N.Y. 1893–1905, cont. as *Annual library index, 1905–1910,* 6 v. N.Y. 1906–11. *The essay and general literature index, 1900–1933: an index to about 40,000 essays and articles in 2144 volumes of collections of essays and miscellaneous works,* N.Y. 1934, continued in cumulative vols., and Helen Grant Cushing and Adah V. Morris, eds., *Nineteenth-century readers' guide to periodical literature, 1890–1899, with supplementary indexing, 1900–1922,* 2 v. N.Y. 1944, are also useful. Daniel Carl Haskell, comp., *A check list of cumulative indexes to individual periodicals in the New York public library,* N.Y. 1942, is a handy guide to an elusive type of index.

55   THE SUBJECT INDEX TO PERIODICALS . . . 1915–16+. [Styled British humanities index, 1962+.] Libr. Assoc. 1919+. Quart. with annual cumulations.

Preceded by *The Athenaeum subject index to periodicals, 1915,* 1916. Much fuller than its American rivals, *The [annual] magazine subject-index,* 1907+, Boston, 1908+, the *International index to periodicals,* N.Y. 1916+, and the *Reader's guide to periodical literature,* Minneapolis & N.Y., 1905+.

56   STEAD (WILLIAM THOMAS) ed. *The review of reviews*: the annual index of periodicals & photographs for 1890–[1902]. 13 v. 1891–1903.

Title varies. Arrangement clumsy. But useful for English magazines of which 100–200 indexed.

57   THE TIMES. Tercentenary handlist of English & Welsh newspapers, magazines & reviews, 1620–1919. [Comp. by Joseph George Muddiman.] 1920. New edn. 1933.

Arranged chronologically by date of foundation of paper, with alphabetical index. Not as easy to use as the *Newspaper press directory* (58). The main newspaper collection is in the British Museum newspaper library at Colindale, where arrangement is by place of publ. The main holdings are listed in a suppl. to the old British Museum *Catalogue of printed books* called *Newspapers published in Great Britain and Ireland, 1801–1900,* 1905.

58   THE NEWSPAPER PRESS DIRECTORY. Ed. by Charles Mitchell. 1846+. Annual.

The best guide. Arranged under place of publication. Microfilm edn. available. Some-times referred to as *Mitchell's newspaper press directory.* More convenient to use than *May's British and Irish press guide* . . ., 1874–89, cont. as *Willing's press guide* . . ., 1890+. Additional information is sometimes incl. in advertising manuals, such as *The Advertiser's A.B.C.* . . ., 1891–1925.

59   UNITED STATES, LIBRARY OF CONGRESS. A checklist of foreign newspapers in the Library of Congress. Wash. 1929.

For U.S. microfilm holdings of newspapers see **62**.

### 6. MICROFORM PUBLICATIONS

60   PHILADELPHIA BIBLIOGRAPHICAL CENTER AND UNION LIBRARY CATALOGUE. Union list of microfilms: rev. and cumul. edn. Ann Arbor, [Mich.]. 1951. Cumul. for 1949–59. 2 v. Ann Arbor. 1961.

Repl. by a number of separate publs.

61  UNITED STATES. LIBRARY OF CONGRESS. National register of microform masters. 1966+. Wash. 1965+. Irregular.

A union list of negatives.

62  UNITED STATES. LIBRARY OF CONGRESS. Newspapers on microform. Wash. 6th edn. 1967.

Gives source and location in North American libraries.

63  TILTON (EVA MAUDE) *comp.* A union list of publications in opaque microforms. 2nd edn. N.Y. 1964.

64  GUIDE TO MICROFORMS IN PRINT. 1961+. Wash. 1962+. Annual.

Suppl. by the biennial *Subject guide to microforms in print.*

65  HALE (RICHARD WALDEN, Jr.) *ed.* Guide to photocopied historical materials in the United States and Canada. Amer. Hist. Assoc. Ithaca, N.Y. 1961.

## 7. DIRECTORIES

66  NORTON (JANE ELIZABETH). Guide to the national and provincial directories of England and Wales, excluding London, published before 1856. Roy. Hist. Soc. Guides and Handbooks No. 5. 1950.

To be used in conjunction with, Charles William Frederick Goss, *The London directories, 1677–1855: a bibliography with notes on their origin and development,* 1932. See also **9380–1.**

67  HENDERSON (GEORGE POLAND) *comp.* Current British directories: a comprehensive guide to the local, trade and professional directories of the British Isles. 1952. 6th edn. 1970.

Useful for the older directories. Good subject index.

## 8. COLLECTIVE BIOGRAPHY

68  RICHES *afterwards* SUTTON (PHYLLIS M.) *comp.* An analytical bibliography of universal collected biography, comprising books published in the English tongue in Great Britain and Ireland, America and the British dominions. Libr. Assoc. 1934.

Includes a useful index of persons. Max Arnim, *Internationale personalbibliographie, 1800–1943,* 2 v. Leipzig & Stuttgart 1944–52, suppl. for 1944–59 (vol. III), Stuttgart 1963, is chiefly German in scope. There is a useful list of general biogs. in Robert Bigney Slocum, *Biographical dictionaries and related works . . .,* Detroit 1967.

69  BIOGRAPHY INDEX: a cumulative index to biographical material in books and magazines. N.Y. 1946+. Quart. with cumulations.

70  MATTHEWS (WILLIAM). British autobiographies: an annotated bibliography of British autobiographies published or written before 1951. Berkeley & Los Angeles. 1955.

Very useful. His *British diaries: an annotated bibliography of British diaries written between 1442 and 1942*, Berkeley and Los Angeles, 1950, is fuller on the 18th cent. than on the 19th.

**71 DICTIONARY OF NATIONAL BIOGRAPHY.** Ed. by Sir Leslie Stephen and Sir Sidney Lee. 63 v. 1885–1901. Repr. with minor revisions. 22 v. 1908–9. 7 suppls., 1901–70, with biographies to 1960.

*The Concise Dictionary*, vol. I (Index and Epitome) to 1900, vol. II 1901–50, 2 v. 1903–61, doubles as an index and a short handbook. Suppl. vols. and a revised *Concise D.N.B.* are to be issued at 10-year intervals. Corrections are printed in *Inst. Hist. Res. Bull.* A consolidated list of corrections to date was publ. as University of London: Inst. of Hist. Res., *Dictionary of national biography: corrections and additions*, Boston 1966.

**72 BOASE (FREDERIC).** Modern English biography: containing many thousand concise memoirs of persons who have died since the year 1850. 3 v. Truro. 1892–1901. Suppl. 3 v. Truro. 1908–21. Repr. Lond. 6 v. 1965.

Indispensable for those not in *D.N.B.* Based on newspaper obituaries.

**73 WHO'S WHO.** 49th+ edn. 1897+. Annual.

Dates from 1848, but until 1896 was only a list of office holders. Biographies supplied by subjects. Final entries repr. on death in *Who was who*, vol. I. 1897–1916, vol. II. 1916–28, vol. III. 1929–40, vol. IV. 1941–50, vol. V. 1951–60. Very valuable as scope wide.

**74 PRATT (ALFRED T. CAMDEN).** People of the period: being a collection of the biographies of upwards of six thousand living celebrities. 2 v. 1897.

One of the best biographical dictionaries. Broader in scope than *Men of the time*, 15 edns. 1852–99 (13–15 edns. entitled *Men and women of the time*), to which there was a suppl. composed of biographies withdrawn because of death, *Men of the reign*, ed. by Thomas Humphry Ward, 1885. Other useful biographical works were *The biograph and review*, 7 v. 1879–82, *Eminent persons: biographies reprinted from the Times*, 5 v. 1870–82, Lloyd Charles Sanders, *ed., Celebrities of the century, being a dictionary of men and women of the nineteenth century*, 1887, new edn. 1890.

Until 1868 the *Gentleman's magazine* publ. a good deal of biographical material. An attempt was made to continue it in *The register and magazine of biography, a record of births, marriages, deaths and other genealogical and personal occurrences*, 2 v. 1869, and in Henry Benjamin Wheatley, *Index of Obituary notices for the year* [1878–82], Index Soc. 1880–4.

**75 ROYAL SOCIETY OF LONDON.** Obituary notices of fellows of the Royal Society. 9 v. 1932–54.

Earlier obituaries are in the *Proceedings* or *Yearbook*. Later obituaries in *Biographical memoirs of fellows of the Royal Society*, 1955+. Good for scientists and non-scientists. For members of the British Academy there are full obituaries in *Proceedings of the British Academy*, 1903+.

**76 KUNITZ (STANLEY JASSPON)** *and* **HAYCRAFT (HOWARD).** British authors of the nineteenth century. New York. 1936.

Illustrated. 1,000 biogs. with bibl. of each author. Incl. scientific authors. Suppl. by the same authors' *Twentieth century authors*, 1942, with supplement, 1955.

77  COKAYNE (GEORGE EDWARD). The complete peerage. New edn. rev. and much enl., ed. by the Hon. Vicary Gibbs, H. Arthur Doubleday, and others. 14 v. 1910–59.

Standard. Vol. XIII deals with peerages created between 1901 and 1938. Footnotes contain many references to out-of-the-way sources. Comparable in scope is James Balfour Paul, *The Scots peerage*, 9 v. Edin. 1904–14, of which vol. 9 is an index. The transformation, migration, and extinction of peerages and baronetcies may be traced in Edward Solly, *An index of hereditary English, Scottish and Irish titles of honour*, Index Soc. v. 5, 1880, James William Edmund Doyle, *The official baronage of England* [confined to peers of the rank of viscount and above], 3 v. 1886, and an appendix to Whitmore's *Genealogical guide* (**92**).

78  COKAYNE (GEORGE EDWARD). The complete baronetage [1611–1800]. 5 v. 1900–6. Index. Exeter. 1909.

Deals only with baronetcies created before 1800. Scottish baronetcies are dealt with in Riddell's MS in the National Library of Scotland. Since 1914 the Standing Council of the Baronetage has published *The roll of the baronetage* (from 1925 *The Roll of baronets*) which lists all officially recognized baronets.

79  BURKE (JOHN) *and others*. A genealogical and heraldic dictionary of the peerage and baronetage of the British Empire. 1826+.

Earliest vols. have the title *A general and heraldic dictionary . . .*; later vols. have the title *Burke's genealogical and heraldic dictionary*. 1st–9th edns. publ. at irregular intervals 1826–47, 10th–98th edns. publ. annually 1847–1917, 1921–40, 99th edn. 1949, 100th edn. 1953, then at intervals of three years. From 1885 an appendix includes Privy Councillors, knights, and a selection (varied from time to time) of other notables. *Burke's handbook to the most excellent Order of the British Empire*, ed. A. Winton Thorpe, 1921, is a useful supplement.

80  DEBRETT (JOHN) *and others*. Debrett's peerage . . . 1715+.

Bound with *Debrett's baronetage . . .* (1808+) as *Debrett's peerage, baronetage, knightage and companionage*, 1878+. Titles vary. After *c.* 1860 much more informative than Burke about the education and careers of those included. For 1869–72 there is also a shortened version of *Debrett's peerage* and *Debrett's House of Commons* (**499**), entitled *Debrett's titled men: a pocket companion to the peerage, baronetage, the House of Commons, and the orders of knighthood*.

81  DOD (CHARLES ROGER PHIPPS) *and others*. The peerage, baronetage and knightage of Great Britain and Ireland. 1841+.

Title changed to *Dod's peerage . . .*, 1866. Dod spelt his name 'Dodd' until 1847. Sometimes much better informed than Burke and Debrett, but restricted more closely to holders of titles.

82  LODGE (EDMUND). The peerage of the British Empire . . . 81 v. 1832–1912.

From 1859 *The peerage and baronetage of the British Empire*. Much more clearly arranged than *Dod* and *Debrett*. Absorbed Joseph Foster, *The peerage, baronetage and knightage of the British Empire for 1880* [–1883], 4 v. 1879–82, genealogically the best of the lesser peerages. Lodge also publ. a genealogical vol. as a companion to the peerage in order to cut down the labour of revision.

83  WALFORD (EDWARD) *ed.* The Windsor peerage. 1890–4.

Continued as *Whittaker's Windsor peerage, baronetage and knightage*, 1895–7.

84  WHITAKER (JOSEPH) *publisher*. A directory of titled persons . . . designed as a companion to Whitaker's almanack . . . 1897–99.

Continued as *Whitaker's peerage for the year 1900* . . ., 1899–1940. A suppl. ed. by Douglas Sladen and W. Wigmore, *The green book of London Society*, was publ. 1910–11, comprising an alphabetical directory of titled persons and an official list similar to that in *Whitaker's almanack*.

85  SHAW (WILLIAM ARTHUR). The knights of England. 2 v. 1906.

Lists all creations to 1904 with a brief note to assist identification. Since 1912 the Imperial Soc. of Knights Bachelor has issued at intervals a *Knightage: a complete list of the existing recipients of the honour of knighthood* . . ., sometimes known as *Bull's knightage* after its first editor, Sir William Bull.

86  BURKE (JOHN) *and others*. A genealogical and heraldic dictionary of the landed gentry of Great Britain and Ireland. 17 edns. 1833–1952.

1st edn. entitled, *A genealogical and heraldic dictionary of the commoners of Great Britain and Ireland*, 4 v. 1833–8, recent edns are entitled *Burke's genealogical and heraldic dictionary of the landed gentry*. Indexed by Marshall and Whitmore (**92**). Considerable turnover of families between editions. Possession of land not a necessary qualification for inclusion. Suppl. by *Burke's landed gentry of Ireland* (**10,245**) and Arthur Charles Fox-Davies, ed., *Armorial families* . . ., Edin. 1895, 7th edn. 2 v. Lond. 1929.

87  WALFORD (EDWARD) *ed*. The county families of the United Kingdom; or, a royal manual of the titled and untitled aristocracy . . . 60 v. 1860–1920.

From 1894 styled *Walford's county families* . . . Gradually supplanted by *Kelly's handbook to the titled, landed and official classes*, 1875+, which began its career as *The upper ten thousand* . . ., 1875–7, and *Kelly's handbook to the upper ten thousand*, 1878–9. *Walford* is superior in quality but less comprehensive than *Kelly*.

88  HAYS (FRANCES) *ed*. Women of the day: a biographical dictionary of notable contemporaries. 1885.

Incl. women of all countries. *The ladies' court book*, 1908–18, continued as *The ladies' who's who*, 1919–27, and later incorp. in *Hutchinson's women's who's who*, 1934+, was at first little more than an address book.

## 9. GENEALOGY

See also the genealogical dictionaries under collective biography (**77–87**).

89  KAMINKOW (MARION J.). A new bibliography of British genealogy with notes. Baltimore. 1965.

Suppl. by her *Genealogical manuscripts in British libraries: a descriptive guide*, Baltimore 1967. The best libr. cat. of genealogy is Manchester Public Libraries, *Reference library subject catalogue, section 929: genealogy*, ed. by George Eric Haslam, 3 pts. Manch. 1956–8. Audrey Hamsher Higgs and Donald Wright, comps., *West Midland genealogy: a survey of the local genealogical material available in the public libraries of Herefordshire, Shropshire, Staffordshire, Warwickshire and Worcestershire*, Libr. Assoc., West Midlands branch, 1966, is also useful.

90  WAGNER (*Sir* ANTHONY RICHARD). English genealogy. Oxf. 1960. 2nd edn. 1971.

A masterly introduction. Gerald Kenneth Savery Hamilton-Edwards, *In search of ancestry*, 1966, rev. edn. Chichester, 1969, publ. in N.Y. as *Tracing your British ancestors: a guide to genealogical sources*, 1967, is useful for tracing the humbler members of society. For the local historian and beginner concerned chiefly with the 19th century, David E. Gardner and Frank Smith, *Genealogical research in England and Wales*, 3 v. Salt Lake City [Utah]. 1956–64, is sometimes more useful. Leslie Gilbert Pine, *The genealogist's encyclopaedia . . .*, Newton Abbot, 1969, is a miscellany rather than an encyclopedia.

91   GALTON (*Sir* FRANCIS). Hereditary genius: an enquiry into its laws and consequences. 1869.

Deservedly famous. Links genealogy with genetics. Includes much biographical information. William Townsend Jackson Gun, *Studies in hereditary ability*, 1928, and Paul Bloomfield, *Uncommon People*, 1955, are less successful exercises in the same field. See also Annan (**8296**) and Sir Francis Galton and Edgar Schuster, *Noteworthy families (modern science): an index to kinships in near degrees between persons whose achievements are honourable, and have been publicly recorded*, Eugenics Record Office, Univ. of Lond., Publs. Vol. I, 1906.

92   MARSHALL (GEORGE WILLIAM). The genealogist's guide to printed pedigrees. 1879. 4th edn. Guildford. 1903. Repr. Baltimore. 1967.

Continued by John Beach Whitmore, comp., *A genealogical guide: an index to British pedigrees in continuation of Marshall's Genealogist's Guide (1903)*, 1953 (also Harleian Soc. vols. xcix, ci, cii, civ, 1947–53). An index under surnames of pedigrees in local hist. and genealogical books and periodicals. Invaluable. A useful supplement is William Phillimore Watts Phillimore, *An index to changes of name . . . 1760–1901*, 1905.

93   CAMP (ANTHONY JOHN). Wills and their whereabouts: being a thorough revision and extension of the previous work of the same name by B. G. Bouwens. Soc. of Genealogists. Canterbury. 1963.

94   WAGNER (*Sir* ANTHONY RICHARD). The records and collections of the College of Arms. 1952.

95   WAGNER (*Sir* ANTHONY RICHARD). Heralds of England: a history of the Office and College of Arms. H.M.S.O. 1967.

Lavish. See also Walter Hindes Godfrey and Sir Anthony Richard Wagner, *The College of Arms, Queen Victoria Street*, Survey of London, 1963, an architectural hist. Arthur Charles Fox-Davies, *A complete guide to heraldry*, 1909, rev. edn. by J. P. Brooke-Little, 1969, is a convenient guide.

96   HOWARD (JOSEPH JACKSON) and CRISP (FREDERICK ARTHUR) *eds.* Visitation of England and Wales. 21 v. priv. pr. 1893–1921. Notes in 14 v. 1896–1921.

Carefully comp. modern pedigrees. Suppl. by the same authors' *Visitation of Ireland*, 6 v. 1897–1918.

97   HUNTER (JOSEPH). Familiae minorum gentium. 5 v. 1894–1936. Publ. as Harleian Soc. vols. 37–40 (ed. by John William Clay) and v. 88 (ed. by John William Walker).

Mostly north-country families. A related work bringing many pedigrees down to 1940 is John William Walker, *Yorkshire Pedigrees*, 3 v. 1942–4, Harleian Soc. v. 94–6. It supersedes Joseph Foster, *Pedigrees of the County Families of England [Yorkshire]*, 5 v. 1873–5.

98  WARRAND (DUNCAN). Hertfordshire families. 1907.

Other good vols. of modern county pedigrees are Arthur Roland Maddison, ed., *Lincolnshire pedigrees*, 4 v. 1902–6, Harleian Soc. v. 50–2, 55, Walter Rye, *Norfolk families*, 2 pts. Norwich 1911–13 (Index by Charles Nowell, Norwich 1915), Arthur Oswald Barron, *Northamptonshire families*, 2 v. 1906, William Phillimore Watts Phillimore, comp., *County pedigrees: Nottinghamshire*, 1910, and John Comber, comp., *Sussex genealogies*, 3 v. Camb. 1931–3.

99  MISCELLANEA GENEALOGICA ET HERALDICA and the British Archivist, 1866–1938. 31 v. 1866–1938.

Other valuable genealogical periodicals were *The topographer and genealogist*, 1846–58, *The herald and genealogist*, 1863–74, *The genealogist*, 1877–1922, and *The ancestor*, 1902–5. *The genealogist's magazine*, 1925+, the j. of the Society of Genealogists, is the chief contemp. j.

## 10. OFFICE HOLDERS

100  HAYDN (JOSEPH TIMOTHY) *comp.* The book of dignities. 1851. 2nd edn. by Horace Ockerby 1890. 3rd edn. 1894.

The fullest list of office holders.

101  POWICKE (*Sir* FREDERICK MAURICE) *and* FRYDE (EDMUND BOLESLAW) *eds.* Handbook of British chronology. 2nd edn. Roy. Hist. Soc. 1961.

Lists bishops and chief ministers of the Crown.

102  BUTLER (DAVID EDGEWORTH) *and* FREEMAN (JENNIE). British political facts, 1900–1960. 1963. 3rd edn. 1969.

103  THE ROYAL KALENDAR AND COURT AND CITY REGISTER. Annual. 1767–1893.

Title varies.

104  THE BRITISH IMPERIAL CALENDAR [and civil service list]. 1809+. Irregular; later annual and official.

Suppl. by *The Foreign Office list*, 1852+, *The Colonial Office list*, 1862+, *The army list*, 1756+, *The navy list*, 1805+.

105  WHITAKER (JOSEPH) *publisher*. Almanack for the year of our Lord ... 1869+.

After a shaky start became the main list of office holders and source of misc. information. Other lists of office holders are to be found in *Who's who*, 1849–1903, and the *Who's who yearbook*, 1904–17.

## 11. ENCYCLOPEDIAS

106  WALSH (JAMES PATRICK). Anglo-American general encyclopedias: a historical bibliography, 1703–1967. By Seamus Padraig Walsh. N.Y. 1968.

107 THE ENCYCLOPAEDIA BRITANNICA . . . 8th edn. 21 v. Edin. 1853–60. 9th edn. 24 v. Edin. 1875–89. 11th edn. 29 v. Camb. 1910–11.

The 11th edn. was the best British encyclopedia ever produced and is a must for all students of the period.

108 KNIGHT (CHARLES). The English cyclopaedia: a new dictionary of universal knowledge. 25 v. 1854–70.

Much used: based on the *Penny Cyclopedia*, 27 v. 1833–43. Suppls. 2 v. 1851–1858.

109 CHAMBERS (W. & R. Ltd.), *publisher*. Chambers' encyclopaedia: a dictionary of universal knowledge. Ed. by Andrew Findlater. Edin. 10 v. 1860–8. Rev. edn. 10 v. 1874. New edn. 10 v. 1888–92. Further edns, 1895, 1901, etc.

110 BEETON (SAMUEL ORCHART) *and others*. Beeton's illustrated encyclopaedia of universal information . . . ed. by George Rose Emerson. 4 v. 1879–81.

Brings together Beeton's previous encyclopedias.

111 THE POPULAR ENCYCLOPAEDIA: or Conversations lexicon . . . 7 v. Glasgow 1841. Five edns. Rev. edn. publ. as *The new popular encyclopaedia*, 14 v. 1900–3.

112 THE NATIONAL CYCLOPAEDIA OF USEFUL KNOWLEDGE. Comp. by Charles Knight. 12 v. 1847–51, rev. edn. 1856–9.

Rev. edn. publ. as *The national encyclopaedia: a dictionary of universal knowledge*, 14 v. 1867–8, new edn. 14 v. 1884–8.

113 THE POPULAR EDUCATOR. 6 v. 1852–5. 6th edn. 1884.

A general course in self-education. Cover reads *Cassell's popular educator*. Rev. edn. publ. as *The new popular educator*, 8 v. 1888–92, 4th edn. 1905. Cassell also publ. *Cassell's encyclopaedia of general information*, 10 v. 1908.

114 TOMLINSON (CHARLES). Cyclopaedia of useful arts. 2 v. 1854.

In the same tradition is *The technical educator* (title on wrapper: *Cassell's technical educator*) 4 v. 1870–2. Other edns. 4 v. 1879–81, 1884–6, 1888–90, 6 v. 1897. Also publ. as *The new technical educator*, 6 v. 1892–5.

115 THE HARMSWORTH ENCYCLOPAEDIA. 8 v. [1905]. 10 v. 1906.

Much used. Publ. in America as *Nelson's encyclopaedia*, 12 v. [1906]. Became *Nelson's perpetual loose-leaf encyclopaedia*, 12 v. 1909. A related work is Arthur Mee, ed., *Harmsworth self-educator*, 8 v. 1905–7.

116 THE EVERYMAN ENCYCLOPAEDIA. 12 v. 1913.

The most famous of all pocket encyclopedias.

## 12. DICTIONARIES

For a list of dictionaries see the *New Cambridge bibliography of English literature* (11).

117  MURRAY (*Sir* JAMES AUGUSTUS HENRY), *and others*. A new English dictionary on historical principles founded mainly on the materials collected by the Philological Society. 10 v. Oxf. 1888–1928. Reissued as The Oxford English Dictionary. 12 v. with Suppl. 1933. Repr. 1961, 1970. New suppl. 1972.

Cover has *The Oxford English Dictionary*. Superseded all other hist. dictionaries.

118  WRIGHT (JOSEPH). The English dialect dictionary, being the complete vocabulary of all dialect words still in use, or known to have been in use during the last two hundred years . . . 6 v. 1898–1905.

Remains a standard work. For slang, etc., see Eric Partridge, *A dictionary of slang and unconventional English*, 1937, 7th edn. 2 v. 1970, and *A dictionary of the underworld, British & American* . . ., 1949, 3rd edn. 1968.

119  WEBSTER (NOAH). An American dictionary of the English language. 2 v. N.Y. 1828. New edns. publ. at various places 1841, 1847, 1859, 1864, 1879, 1884, etc.

Also publ. in England under different titles. The best English edn. of the period is *Webster's international dictionary of the English language*, 1890.

120  WRIGHT (THOMAS) *and others*. The universal pronouncing dictionary and general expositor of the English language. Lond. & N.Y. 5 v.+1 v. of plates [1852–6].

121  HUNTER (ROBERT) *and others*. The encyclopaedic dictionary: a new and original work of reference to all the words in the English language . . . 7 v. 1879–88.

Also publ. as *The imperial dictionary* . . ., 1897 and 1900, *The people's dictionary* . . ., 1900, *The American dictionary* . . ., 1899, *The international dictionary* . . ., 1901, *The modern world dictionary*. . ., 1911.

122  WHITNEY (WILLIAM DWIGHT), *and others*. The century dictionary. An encyclopedic lexicon of the English language. N.Y. & Lond. 6 v. 1889–91. Suppl. 2 v. 1909.

### 13. GENERAL STATISTICS

123  LANCASTER (HENRY OLIVER). Bibliography of statistical bibliographies. Internat. Stat. Inst. Edin. & Lond. 1968.

Chiefly concerned with technical studies.

124  KENDALL (MAURICE GEORGE) *ed*. The sources and nature of the statistics of the United Kingdom. Roy. Stat. Soc. 2 v. Edin. & Lond. 1952–7.

For 20th-cent. statistics. For these see also Interdepartmental Committee on Social and Economic Research, *Guides to official sources*, H.M.S.O., 5 v. 1948–61: No. 1. *Labour statistics*, 1948, rev. edn. 1950, 1958; No. 2. *Census reports of Great Britain, 1801–1931*, 1951; No. 3. *Local government statistics*, 1953; No. 4. *Agriculture and food statistics*, 1958; No. 5. *Social security statistics*, 1961.

125 MITCHELL (BRIAN REDMAN) *and* DEANE (PHYLLIS). Abstract of British historical statistics. Camb. 1962.

Indispensable.

126 MULHALL (MICHAEL GEORGE). Mulhall's dictionary of statistics. 1884. 4th edn. 1899. Suppl. by Augustus Duncan Webb, *The new dictionary of statistics; a complement to the fourth edition of Mulhall's 'Dictionary of statistics'*, 1911.

A useful compendium.

127 STATISTICAL ABSTRACT for the United Kingdom in each year, 1840 to 1854 (to be continued annually). [1743] H.C. (1854). XXXIX, 131. Annual to 1939–40.

Suppl. by similar vols. for the empire (**1222**) and for India (**998**).

128 MISCELLANEOUS STATISTICS of the United Kingdom. [2427] H.C. (1857–8). LVII, 41. Annual to 1882.

### 14. MAPS, ATLASES, AND GAZETTEERS

For county maps see **9374.**

129 BRITISH MUSEUM. Catalogue of printed maps, charts and plans: photolithographic edition complete to 1964. 15 v. 1967.

The most important single collection.

130 AMERICAN GEOGRAPHICAL SOCIETY (MAP DEPARTMENT). Index to maps in books and periodicals. 10 v. Boston. 1968.

131 NATIONAL COUNCIL OF SOCIAL SERVICES. The historian's guide to Ordnance Survey maps. Comp. by J. B. Harley and others. 1965.

The Ordnance Survey maps are the basic tools for the historian. On them see also the Ordnance Survey Department's *Catalogue of 6-inch and 25-inch county maps and town plans of England and Wales and the Isle of Man, and the one-inch and smaller scale maps and other publications of the Survey*, 1906, and *A description of Ordnance Survey large-scale plans*, Chessington. 1954. Many of the older Ordnance Survey maps have recently been reprinted.

132 PUBLIC RECORD OFFICE. Maps and plans in the Public Record Office. I. British Isles, *c.* 1410–1860. 1967.

133 CHUBB (THOMAS). The printed maps in the atlases of Great Britain and Ireland; a bibliography, 1579–1870. 1927.

Indispensable. But see also Harold Whitaker, comp., *The Harold Whitaker collection of county atlases, road-books & maps, presented to the University of Leeds: a catalogue*, Leeds. 1947.

134 MAP COLLECTORS' CIRCLE. Map collectors' series. 1+. 1963+.

Invaluable for pre-1850 maps. It is to be hoped that post-1850 maps will be covered in due course.

135  UNITED STATES LIBRARY OF CONGRESS. A list of geographical atlases in the Library of Congress with bibliographical notes. Comp. by Philip Lee Phillips. 4 v. Wash. 1909–20. Cont. by Clara Egli Le Gear in 2 v. (nos. 5 & 6) Wash. 1958–63.

136  LEWIS (SAMUEL). A topographical dictionary of England. 7th edn. 4 v. & atlas. 1848.

Companion vols. are *A topographical dictionary of Wales*, 3rd edn. 2 v. & atlas 1848, *A topographical dictionary of Scotland*, 2nd edn. 2 v. & atlas 1851, *A topographical dictionary of Ireland*, 2nd edn. 2 v. and atlas 1850. Gives an account of the hist. and present state of each town or parish, with statistics from the 1841 census. The fullest and best of the gazetteers, with larger towns receiving up to 10 pages. Later works like *The national gazetteer . . .*, 3 v. 1868, *The imperial gazetteer . . .*, 2 v. 1872, *The comprehensive gazetteer . . .*, 6 v. 1893–5, and *Cassell's gazetteer . . .*, 6 v. 1893–8, are of little value apart from the census figures they include.

137  BARTHOLOMEW (JOHN) *ed.* Gazetteer of the British Isles. 1887. New edn. [1893].

Rev. by John Bartholomew and reissued as *The Survey gazetteer of the British Isles*, 1904, 1914, and (rev. by John Bartholomew, the younger) 1921. The best of the concise gazetteers. Occasionally useful is the *Railway and commercial gazetteer of England, Scotland and Wales*, 1868, 17th edn. 1917.

138  MURRAY (JOHN) *publisher.* Murray's English handbooks. Numerous edns. throughout the period.

Collectively these handbooks form the most comprehensive and up-to-date gazetteer of the day. For a list see *Catalogue of the London Library* (12).

### 15. PICTURES, PHOTOGRAPHS, SOUND ARCHIVES, AND MUSEUMS

139  CORBETT (EDMUND VICTOR) *ed.* The libraries, museums and art galleries year book, 1968. 1968.

A useful directory. Publ. irregularly.

140  NUNN (GEORGE WALTER ARTHUR) *ed.* British sources of photographs and pictures. 1952.

141  STANDING COMMISSION ON MUSEUMS AND GALLERIES. Survey of provincial museums and galleries. H.M.S.O. 1963.

142  UNITED STATES, LIBRARY OF CONGRESS. A.L.A. portrait index: index to portraits contained in printed books and periodicals. Ed. by William Coolidge Lane and Nina E. Browne. Wash. 1906. Repr. 3 v. N.Y. 1965.

143  NATIONAL PORTRAIT GALLERY. Catalogue of the National Portrait Gallery, 1856–1947, with a supplement, 1948–1959. 1960.

Some of the better-known portraits are reproduced in *British historical portraits*, Camb. 1957. There is some relevant material in British Museum, Dept. of Prints and Drawings, *Catalogue of engraved British portraits*, 6 v. 1908–25.

**144 THE VANITY FAIR ALBUM.** 44 v. 1869–1912.

The best series of caricatures.

**145 PORTRAITS OF MEN OF EMINENCE** in literature, science and art, with biographical memoirs. The photographs from life, by E. Edwards. 6 v. 1863–7. Vols. 1 and 2 by Lovell Augustus Reeve, vols. 3–6 by Edward Walford.

One of the earliest and best of the biog. magazines whose main feature was a ser. of high-quality photographs. Others in the same class were, *Men of Mark: a gallery of contemporary portraits . . . photographed from life by Lock and Whitfield, with brief biographical notices by Thompson Cooper*, 7 v. 1876–83, and *Men and Women of the day: a picture gallery of contemporary portraiture*, 7 v. Jan. 1888–July 1894. Much larger portraits were used for A. J. Albery, *Our Conservative and Unionist statesmen*, 6 pts. 1893–8.

**146 NATIONAL FILM ARCHIVE.** Catalogue. Pt. I. Silent news films, 1895–1933. British Film Inst. 1951. 2nd edn. 1965. Pt. II. Silent non-fiction films, 1895–1934. British Film Inst. 1960. Pt. III. Silent fiction films, 1895–1930. 1966.

**147 SOUND ARCHIVES.** No catalogue of historic recordings is at present available. But see Henry F. J. Currall, ed., *Gramophone record libraries, their organisation and practice*, 1963, and Association for Recorded Sound Collections, *A preliminary directory of sound recordings collections in the United States and Canada*, N.Y. Public Libr. 1967. The British Inst. of Recorded Sound gives occasional lists in its j. *Recorded sound*, 1961+.

## B. GENERAL HISTORIES AND STUDIES

### I. COLLECTIONS OF DOCUMENTS

**148 YOUNG (GEORGE MALCOLM)** *and* HANDCOCK (WILLIAM DAY) *eds*. English historical documents, 1833–1874. 1956. Vol. XII, pt. 1. of English historical documents ed. by David Charles Douglas.

To be completed. Herman Ausubel, *The late Victorians: a short history*, N.Y. 1955, is a short paperback which fills some of the gap after 1874.

**149 BRIGGS (ASA)** *comp.* They saw it happen. Vol. IV. 1897–1940. Oxf. 1960.

**150 REYNOLDS (REGINALD ARTHUR)** *ed.* British pamphleteers. Vol. II. From the French Revolution to the nineteen-thirties. 1951.

**151 GOODWIN (MICHAEL)** *ed.* Nineteenth-century opinion: an anthology of extracts from the first fifty volumes of *The Nineteenth Century*, 1877–1901. 1951.

One of the best of a number of collections from newspapers and journals. Others of use are Yvonne Ffrench, ed., *News from the past, 1805–1887: the autobiography of the nineteenth century . . . being a miscellany of newspaper accounts . . .*, 1934; Harry Findlater Bussey and Sir Thomas Wemyss Reid, eds., *The newspaper reader: the journals of the*

*XIXth century on the events of the day*, 1879; Francis Hereward Maitland, ed., *One hundred years of headlines, 1837–1937*, [1938]; Sir James Marchant, ed., *History through 'The Times': a collection of leading articles on important events, 1800–1937*, 1937; John Douglas Woodruff, ed., *Dear sir: a selection of letters to the editor of The Times*, 1936; Alice Clay, ed., *The agony column of The Times, 1800–1870*, 1881; Marion Miliband, ed., *The Observer of the nineteenth century, 1791–1901*, 1966; Robert James Cruikshank, *Roaring century, 1846–1946*, [from the *Daily News*], 1946; Raymond William Postgate and Aylmer Vallance, *Those foreigners: the English people's opinion on foreign affairs as reflected in their newspapers since Waterloo*, 1937; and Charles Larcom Graves, ed., *Mr Punch's history of modern England*, 4 v. 1921–2.

**152  LAVER (JAMES). Victorian vista. 1954.**

Cont. in his *Edwardian promenade*, 1958. One of a considerable number of scrapbook collections. Cp. Leslie Baily, *Scrapbook, 1900 to 1914*, 1957, *Leslie Baily's BBC scrapbooks*, Vol. I, *1896–1914*, 1966, and Alan John Bolt, *This was England: manners and customs of the ancient Victorians . . . between 1870 and 1900*, 1931.

**153  VRIES (LEONARD DE)** *comp.* Panorama, 1842–1865; the world of the early Victorians as seen through the eyes of the *Illustrated London News*. 1967.

*The Illustrated London News* is an important source. The publishers produced many special numbers, incl. vols. commemorating the reigns of Victoria and Edward VII.

## 2. GENERAL HISTORIES

**154  WOODWARD (*Sir* ERNEST LLEWELLYN). The age of reform, 1815–1870. Oxf.1938. 2nd edn. 1962.**

Vol. XIII of the *Oxford History of England*. Woodward, Ensor, Halévy, and Briggs (**155–7**) are the best group of hists. available.

**155  ENSOR (*Sir* ROBERT CHARLES KIRKWOOD). England, 1870–1914. Oxf. 1936.**

Vol. XIV of the *Oxford History of England*. An unusually strong book. There is also much stimulating matter of relevance to pre-1914 in Alan John Percivale Taylor, *English History, 1914–1945*, Oxf. 1965, which is vol. XV of the *Oxford History*.

**156  HALÉVY (ÉLIE). A history of the English people in the nineteenth century . . . Trans. by E. I. Watkin and D. A. Barker. 5 v. 1924–34. 2nd edn. 6 v. 1949–52.**

A famous work, strongest on the early 19th cent. and on 1895–1914.

**157  BRIGGS (ASA). The age of improvement [1783–1867]. 1959.**

Vol. VIII of *A history of England* ed. by William Norton Medlicott.

**158  GRETTON (RICHARD HENRY). A modern history of the English people [1880–1922]. 3 v. 1913–29.**

Has worn better than most such hists.

**159  WEBB (ROBERT KIEFER). Modern England: from the eighteenth century to the present. N.Y. 1968.**

A good American general textbook. May be compared with Alfred Freeman Havighurst, *Twentieth-century Britain*, Evanston, Ill., 1962, 2nd edn. 1969, for the latter part of the period covered. Norman Frank Cantor and Michael S. Wertham, eds., *The English tradition: modern studies in English history*, vol. II, N.Y. 1967, is a selection from the works of British historians. Most foreign countries have their textbooks of British hist.; few are of any more lasting value than their British counterparts. At one time Carl Brinkmann, *Englische Geschichte, 1815–1914*, Berlin 1924, 2nd edn. [*England seit 1815*] 1938, was highly thought of.

160  WOOD (ANTHONY CAMERON). Nineteenth-century Britain, 1815–1914. 1960.

A solid British school textbook. For the 20th cent. there is also Lewis Charles Bernard Seaman, *Post-Victorian Britain, 1902–1951*, 1966.

161  THOMSON (DAVID). England in the nineteenth century, 1815–1914. 1950.

A widely-read paperback, popular and not always accurate, but stimulating. Walter Leonard Arnstein, *Britain, yesterday and today: 1830 to the present*, Boston 1966, is an American equivalent. Sir James Ramsay Montagu Butler, *A history of England, 1815–1918*, Home Univ. Libr. 1928, 2nd edn. [1815–1939] 1960, is still helpful. Derek Edward Dawson Beales, *From Castlereagh to Gladstone, 1815–1885*, 1969, and Henry Mathison Pelling, *Great Britain, 1885–1955 . . .*, 1960, are good brief hists.

162  TREVELYAN (GEORGE MACAULAY). British history in the nineteenth century, 1782–1901. 1922. 2nd edn. 1937.

Fuller than his *A history of England*, 1926, 3rd edn. 1945, and his *English social history* (**6864**), but not one of his better works. Other general hists. in use in the first half of the 20th cent. are now of little value. They incl. Sir Sidney James Mark Low and Lloyd Charles Sanders, *The history of England during the reign of Victoria (1837–1901)*, 1907; Gilbert Slater, *The making of modern England*, 1913, rev. edn. [*The growth of modern England*], 1932, 2nd edn. 1939; Octavius Francis Christie, *The transition from aristocracy, 1832–1867 . . .*, 1927, cont. as *The transition to democracy, 1867–1914*, 1934; John Alfred Spender, *A short history of our times*, 1934, 2nd edn. 1935, and *Great Britain: empire and commonwealth, 1886–1935*, 1936; Sir John Arthur Ransome Marriott, *England since Waterloo (1815–1900)*, 1913, 10th edn. 1932, and *Modern England, 1885–1932*, 1934, 3rd edn. 1946; and Esmé Cecil Wingfield-Stratford, *The Victorian trilogy*, 3 v. 1930–3. Sir Winston Leonard Spencer-Churchill, *A history of the English-speaking peoples*: vol. IV, *The great democracies*, 1958, is likewise of little value.

163  NEW CAMBRIDGE MODERN HISTORY. 12 v. Camb. 1957+. X. The zenith of European power, 1830–70. Ed. by John Patrick Tuer Bury. Camb. 1960. XI. Material progress and world-wide problems, 1870–1898. Ed. by Francis Harry Hinsley. Camb. 1962. XII. (1st edn.) The era of violence, 1898–1945. Ed. by David Thomson. Camb. 1960. XII. (2nd edn.) The shifting balance of world forces, 1898–1945. Ed. by Charles Loch Mowat. Camb. 1968.

Includes sections on Britain. For a single-author coverage see Harry Hearder, *Europe in the nineteenth century, 1830–1880*, 1966, and John Morris Roberts, *Europe, 1880–1945*, 1967. There are some good essays in Martin Gilbert, ed., *A century of conflict, 1850–1950: essays for A. J. P. Taylor*, 1966.

164  THE ANNUAL REGISTER . . . 1758+.

An invaluable year-by-year hist. The bias changes from generation to generation. Much superior to *The British almanac and companion*, 1828–1914. Joseph Irving, *The annals of our time: a diurnal of events, social and political, which have happened in, or had relation to, the kingdom of Great Britain, from the accession of Queen Victoria . . ., 1869,* rev. edn. 1871, suppls. to 1891, 1879–92, is a sort of epitome of the *Annual register.*

**165  MOLESWORTH (WILLIAM NASSAU).** The history of England from the year 1830. 3 v. 1871–3. New edn. 1874.

Once highly regarded.

**166  WALPOLE (*Sir* SPENCER).** The history of twenty-five years [1856–1880]. 4 v. 1904–8.

Still the fullest account of the period. Intended to suppl. his *A history of England from the conclusion of the great war in 1815,* 5 v. 1878–86, new edn. 6 v. 1890.

**167  SMITH (JOHN FREDERICK) *and* HOWITT (WILLIAM).** John Cassell's illustrated history of England. 8 v. [1856]–64. Numerous editions.

A generally accurate, blow-by-blow account of events.

**168  BRIGHT (JAMES FRANCK).** A history of England, 1837–1880. 1888.

Occasioned a famous review by Lord Acton, *Eng. Hist. Rev.* iii (1888), 798–809.

**169  McCARTHY (JUSTIN).** A history of our own times: from the accession of Queen Victoria to the Berlin Congress. 4 v. 1879–80. 4th edn. [down to 1905] 7 v. 1908.

Excessively popular and uncritical, but useful as reflecting a shrewd journalist's version of events.

**170  PAUL (HERBERT WOODFIELD).** A history of modern England [1845–95]. 5 v. 1904–6.

The fullest and best of a ser. of violently partisan hists. by Liberal journalists using *Hansard* as their main source. Earlier works of a similar character were Peter William Clayden, *England under Lord Beaconsfield* [1873–80], 1880, and *England under the coalition* [1885–92], 1892, 2nd edn. 1893, George Carslake Thompson, *Public opinion and Lord Beaconsfield, 1875–1880,* 2 v. 1886, and Justin Huntly McCarthy, *England under Gladstone, 1880–84,* 1884, the latter written from the viewpoint of the Parnellites. There is a quaint attempt at a more Whiggish version of this type of hist. in Sir Algernon Edward West, *Political England: a chronicle of the nineteenth century told in a letter to Miss Margot Tennant,* 1922.

## 3. Interpretative Studies

**171  KITSON CLARK (GEORGE SIDNEY ROBERTS).** The making of Victorian England. 1962.

An up-to-date survey, widely praised. Suppl. by his *An expanding society: Britain 1830–1900,* Camb. & Melb. 1967.

**172  YOUNG (GEORGE MALCOLM).** Victorian England: portrait of an age. 1936. 2nd edn. 1953.

Deservedly celebrated. See also his *Victorian essays,* ed. by William Day Handcock, 1962.

**173  BUCKLEY (JEROME HAMILTON).** The Victorian temper: a study in literary culture. Camb., Mass. 1952. Repr. 1969.

174  WILLEY (BASIL). Nineteenth-century studies: Coleridge to Matthew Arnold. 1949.

Cont. by his *More nineteenth-century studies: a group of honest doubters*, 1956. Literary in emphasis.

175  IDEAS AND BELIEFS OF THE VICTORIANS: an historical re-valuation of the Victorian age. 1949.

Short radio talks.

176  WILLIAMS (RAYMOND). Culture and society, 1780–1950. 1958.

Bold generalizations about English culture.

177  ROBSON (ROBERT) *ed*. Ideas and institutions of Victorian Britain: essays in honour of George Kitson Clark. 1967.

A valuable scholarly symposium.

178  EVANS (JOAN). The Victorians. Camb. 1966.

Photographs and text. Cp. Nicolas Bentley, *The Victorian scene: a picture book of the period 1837–1901*, 1968. Sir Charles Alexander Petrie, *The Victorians*, 1960, is in the same vein, but lacks the superb illustrations.

179  YOUNG (GEORGE MALCOLM) *ed*. Early Victorian England, 1830–1865. 2 v. 1934.

180  HOUGHTON (WALTER EDWARDS). The Victorian frame of mind, 1830–1870. New Haven [Conn.]. 1957.

Themes in Victorian literature.

181  HOUSE ([ARTHUR] HUMPHRY). The Dickens world. 1941. 2nd edn. 1942.

182  BURN (WILLIAM LAURENCE). The age of equipoise: a study of the mid-Victorian generation. 1964.

183  APPLEMAN (PHILIP), MADDEN (WILLIAM A.), *and* WOLFF (MICHAEL) *eds*. 1859: Entering an age of crisis. Bloomington, Ind. 1959.

184  LYND (HELEN MERRELL). England in the eighteen-eighties: toward a social basis for freedom. Lond. & N.Y. 1945. Repr. 1968.

A first-rate work, not as well-known as it should be.

185  AUSUBEL (HERMAN). In hard times: reformers among the late Victorians. N.Y. 1960.

186  WARD (THOMAS HUMPHRY) *ed*. The reign of Queen Victoria: a survey of fifty years of progress. 2 v. 1887.

An interesting symposium. There is also some useful material in Thomas Hay Sweet Escott, *England: its people, polity and pursuits*, rev. edn. 1885, and in William Henry Whitrow, and others, *The nineteenth century series* [also known as the Library of modern progress], 25 v. and index, 1900–5.

187  NOWELL-SMITH (SIMON HARCOURT) *ed.* Edwardian England, 1901–1914. 1964.

The most sumptuous of the many products of the cult of Edwardiana. See also Sir Charles Alexander Petrie, *The Edwardians*, N.Y. 1965, and Robert Cecil, *Life in Edwardian England*, 1969. Among older books there are Thomas Hay Sweet Escott, *King Edward and his court*, 1903, and Fossey John Cobb Hearnshaw, ed., *Edwardian England, A.D. 1901–1910: a series of lectures delivered at King's College, University of London, during the session 1932–3*, 1933.

188  HYNES (SAMUEL LYNN). The Edwardian turn of mind. Princeton. 1968.

Comparable with Houghton (**180**), but takes Dangerfield (**295**) as his starting-point.

189  ADAMS (WILLIAM WHEEN SCOVELL). Edwardian heritage: a study in British history, 1901–1906. 1949.

Donald Read, *Edwardian England, 1901–15: society and politics*, 1972, is fuller.

190  PLAYNE (CAROLYN ELISABETH). The pre-war mind in Britain: an historical review. 1928.

A general analysis. Geoffrey Marcus, *Before the lamps went out*, 1965, is popular.

191  MARWICK (ARTHUR J. B.). Britain in the century of total war: war, peace and social change, 1900–1967. 1968.

192  READ (DONALD). The English provinces, *c.* 1760–1960: a study in influence. 1964.

### 4. Outsiders' Views of England

There is a seemingly inexhaustible travel literature, little or none of it incl. in Edward Godfrey Cox, *A reference guide to the literature of travel . . .*, Vol. 3: *Great Britain*, Seattle 1949. Only a selection of books of general interest is incl. here, in alphabetical order.

193  WILSON (FRANCESCA MARY) *ed.* Strange island: Britain through foreign eyes, 1395–1940. 1955.

An anthology. There is little in Frederick Charles Roe, ed., *French travellers in Britain, 1800–1926: impressions and reflections*, 1928, Harry Ballam and Roy Lewis, eds., *The visitors' book: England and the English as others have seen them, A.D. 1500 to 1950*, 1950, and Edward Smith, *Foreign visitors in England and what they have thought of us . . .*, 1889. Robert Charles Leclair, *Three American travellers in England: James Russell Lowell, Henry Adams, Henry James*, Phila. 1945, is a brief thesis.

194  BAILEY (JAMES MONTGOMERY). England from a back window: with views of Scotland and Ireland. Boston & N.Y. 1879.

195  BERNSTEIN (EDUARD). My years of exile: reminiscences of a socialist. Trans. by Bernard Miall. 1921.

196 BLANC ([JEAN JOSEPH] LOUIS). Letters on England. Trans. by James Hutton. 2 v. 1866. 2nd ser. trans. by James Hutton and L. J. Trotter. 2 v. 1867.

197 BULTEAU (AUGUSTINE). The English soul. Trans. by Helen Tracy Lowe Porter. 1914.

198 CAZAMIAN (LOUIS). Modern England. 1911.

199 COLLIER (PRICE). England and the English from an American point of view. N.Y. & Lond. 1909. Repr. 1911.

200 DALLAS (GEORGE MIFFLIN). A series of letters from London written during the years 1856, '57, '58, '59, and '60. Ed. by Julia Dallas. Phila. 1869.

See also Susan Dallas, ed., *Diary of George Mifflin Dallas, while United States Minister to Russia, 1837 to 1839, and to England, 1856 to 1861*, Phila. 1892.

201 DANA (RICHARD HENRY). Hospitable England in the seventies: the diary of a young American, 1875–1876. Lond & Camb., Mass. 1921.

202 DAVIS (RICHARD HARDING). Our English cousins. N.Y. 1894.

203 DIBELIUS (WILHELM). England. Trans. from the 5th German edn. by Mary Agnes Hamilton. 1930.

204 EMERSON (RALPH WALDO). English traits. Lond. 1856. Boston 1857. many edns.

205 ESQUIROS (ALPHONSE). L'Angleterre et la vie anglaise. 5 v. Paris. 1860–9.

Versions were publ. in English as *The English at home*, ed. by Sir Frederick Charles Lascelles Wraxall. 2 v. 1861, 2nd ser. 1862, 3rd ser. 1863; and as *Religious life in England*, 1867.

206 FONTANE (THEODOR). Journeys to England in Victoria's early days, 1844–1859. Trans. by Dorothy Harrison. 1939.

207 HAWTHORNE (NATHANIEL). The English notebooks: based upon the original manuscripts . . . ed. by Randall Stewart. Mod. Lang. Assoc. N.Y. & Lond. 1941.

Covers 1853–8. The section on Lincoln is reproduced in Hawthorne's *Our old home*. 2 v. 1863.

208 HERZEN (ALEXANDER). My past and thoughts: the memoirs of Alexander [Ivanovich] Herzen. Trans. by Constance Garnett. 6 v. 1924–7.

Herzen's life in England, 1852–5, is covered by section 4 in vols. V and VI.

209 HOPPIN (JAMES MASON). Old England: its scenery, art and people. Camb., Mass. 1867. 6th edn. Boston. 1879.

210 JAMES (HENRY). English hours. Boston & Lond. 1905.

211 KELLNER (LEON). Ein Jahr in England, 1898–1899. Stuttgart. 1900.

212 LENIN (VLADIMIR IL'ICH). On Britain. Trans. by Tom Dexter and I. Lasker. Comp. by C. Leiteizen. Moscow. 1959.

213 MARX (KARL) and ENGELS (FRIEDRICH). On Britain. Moscow. 1953.
A useful selection of articles and letters.

214 MILLER (HUGH). First impressions of England and its people. Edin. 1858.
Cp. William Johnston, *England as it is: political, social and industrial, in the middle of the nineteenth century*. 2 v. 1851.

215 MONTALEMBERT (CHARLES FORBES RENÉ DE), *Comte de Montalembert*. The political future of England. Ed. by John Wilson Croker. 1856.

216 MORAN (BENJAMIN). The journal of Benjamin Moran, 1857–1865. Ed. by Sarah Agnes Wallace and Frances Elma Gillespie. 2 v. Chicago. 1948–9.
Moran was Sec. of the U.S. Legation in London. See also his *The footpath and highway: or, wanderings of an American in Great Britain in 1851 and '52*. Phila. 1853.

217 OLIVEIRA MARTINS (JOAQUIM PEDRO). The England of to-day. Trans. by C. J. Willdey. 1896.

218 O'RELL (MAX) *pseud. of* BLOUET (LEON PAUL). John Bull and his island. 1883. 20th edn. 1884.
One of a series of humorous books which achieved an enormous popular success and are now unjustly neglected.

219 PETERS (CARL FRIEDRICH HUBERT). England and the English. 1904.

220 RAJARAMA CHHATRAPATI, *Maharajah of Kolhapoor*. Diary of the late Rajah of Kolhapoor, during his visit to Europe in 1870. Ed. by Edward W. West. 1872.
An early example of a type that seems to parody itself.

221 RECOULY (RAYMOND). En Angleterre. Paris. 1910.

222 RÉMO (FÉLIX). La vie galante en Angleterre. Paris. [1888.]
Careless and fatuous, but interesting as an example of a curious French genre. Rémo also publ. *L'égalité des sexes en Angleterre*, Paris 1886.

223 SCHLESINGER (MAX). Saunterings in and about London. Trans by O. Wenckstern. 1853.

224 TAINE (HIPPOLYTE ADOLPHE). Taine's notes on England [1860–70]. Trans. by Edward Hyams. 1957.

225 TICKNOR (GEORGE). Life, letters and journals of George Ticknor. Ed. by George Stillman Hillard. 2 v. Lond. 1876. New edn. Boston & N.Y. 2 v. 1909.

Incl. letters written in England in the 1850s.

226 DE TOCQUEVILLE ([CHARLES] ALEXIS [HENRI MAURICE CLÉREL]). Journeys to England and Ireland. Trans. by George Lawrence and K. P. Mayer. Ed. by Jacob Peter Mayer. 1958.

For Tocqueville's ideas see also Seymour Drescher, *Tocqueville and England*, Camb., Mass. 1964.

227 VASILI (*Count* PAUL) *pseud. of* LAMBER (JULIETTE). The world of London. 1885.

228 WEY (FRANCIS ALPHONSE). Les anglais chez eux. Paris. 1854. Enl. edn. 1856.

Engl. version by Valerie Pirie publ. as *A Frenchman sees the English in the fifties*, 1935, and *A Frenchman among the Victorians*, New Haven, [Conn.]. 1936.

229 WHITE (RICHARD GRANT). England without and within. Boston & Camb., Mass. 1881.

## 5. GENERAL BIOGRAPHICAL STUDIES

230 BRIGGS (ASA). Victorian people: some reassessments of people, institutions, ideas and events, 1851–1867. 1954. Rev. edn. 1965.

231 HIMMELFARB (GERTRUDE). Victorian minds. N.Y. 1968.

232 BAGEHOT (WALTER). Biographical studies. Ed. by Richard Holt Hutton. 1881. 3rd edn. 1914.

Suppl. by his *Literary studies*, 2 v. 1879, 4th edn. 2 v. 1891. New edn. 3 v. 1895.

233 BRYCE (JAMES) *Viscount Bryce*. Studies in contemporary biography. 1903.

234 CHURCHILL (*Sir* WINSTON LEONARD SPENCER-). Great contemporaries. 1937. Rev. edn. 1938.

See also his *Thoughts and adventures*, 1932.

235 KEYNES (JOHN MAYNARD), *Baron Keynes*. Essays in biography. 1933. New edn. 1951. Repr. 1961.

236 MACCARTHY (*Sir* DESMOND). Portraits. Lond. & N.Y. 1931.

237 MASSINGHAM (HAROLD JOHN) *and* MASSINGHAM (HUGH) *eds*. Great Victorians. 1932.

238 RUSSELL (BERTRAND ARTHUR WILLIAM), *Earl Russell.* Portraits from memory and other essays. 1956.

239 STRACHEY (GILES LYTTON). Eminent Victorians: Cardinal Manning, Florence Nightingale, Dr. Arnold, General Gordon. 1918.

The symbol of the reaction against Victorianism. For his methods see Anthony Edward Dyson, 'The technique of debunking', *Twentieth Cent.* clvii (1955), 244–56.

240 WALPOLE (*Sir* SPENCER). Studies in biography. 1907.

See also his *Essays: political and biographical,* ed. by Francis Holland, 1908.

241 WEST (*Sir* ALGERNON). Contemporary portraits: men of my day in public life. 1920.

See also his *One city and many men,* 1908.

242 McCARTHY (JUSTIN). Portraits of the sixties. 1903.

One of a ser. incl. George William Erskine Russell, *Portraits of the seventies,* 1916, Horace Gordon Hutchinson, *Portraits of the eighties,* 1920, E. T. Raymond (pseud. of Edward Raymond Thompson), *Portraits of the nineties,* 1921. Thompson also publ. *Portraits of the new century (the first ten years),* 1928, *Uncensored celebrities,* 1918, and *All & sundry,* 1919.

243 ESCOTT (THOMAS HAY SWEET). Personal forces of the period. 1898.

Escott publ. many similar vols. of which *Politics and letters,* 1886, *Platform, press, politics and play: being pen and ink sketches of contemporary celebrities,* Bristol [1895], *City characters under several reigns,* 1922, and *Club makers and club members,* 1914, are the best.

244 RUSSELL (GEORGE WILLIAM ERSKINE). Collections and recollections, by one who has kept a diary. 1898.

A storehouse of anecdotes, like his *An onlooker's notebook,* 1902, *Social silhouettes,* 1906, *Sketches and snapshots,* 1910, *One look back,* 1912, *Politics and personalities,* 1917, and *Prime ministers and some others,* 1918. Similar collections of anecdotes for American readers were publ. by George Washburn Smalley in *Studies of men,* 1895, *Anglo-American memories,* 2 v. 1911–12, and the first vol. of his *London letters and some others,* 2 v. 1890.

245 BAUMANN (ARTHUR ANTHONY). The last Victorians. 1927.

See also his *Persons & politics of the transition,* 1916, and the selection ed. by Humbert Wolfe, *Personalities,* 1936.

246 LESLIE (*Sir* [JOHN RANDOLPH] SHANE). Men were different: five studies in late Victorian biography: Randolph Churchill, 1849–1895, Augustus Hare, 1834–1903, Arthur Dunn, 1860–1902, George Wyndham, 1863–1913, Wilfrid Blunt, 1840–1922. 1937.

247 MILNER (VIOLET GEORGINA), *Viscountess Milner.* My picture gallery, 1886–1901. 1951.

248  INGE (WILLIAM RALPH) *and others*. The post Victorians. 1933.

249  ADAMS (WILLIAM WHEEN SCOVELL). Edwardian portraits. 1957.
May be suppl. by Dudley Barker, *Prominent Edwardians*, 1969.

250  GARDINER (ALFRED GEORGE). Prophets, priests & kings. 1908.
Cont. in *Pillars of society*, 1913, *The war lords*, [1915], and *Certain people of importance*, [1926].

251  SMITH (FREDERICK EDWIN), *Earl of Birkenhead*. Contemporary personalities. 1924.

# II

# POLITICAL AND CONSTITUTIONAL HISTORY

## A. GENERAL

### 1. Works of Reference

For lists of office holders see **100–5, 256.**

252 HANHAM (HAROLD JOHN) *ed.* The nineteenth-century constitution, 1815–1914: documents and commentary. Camb. 1969.

253 COSTIN (WILLIAM CONRAD) *and* WATSON (JOHN STEVEN) *eds.* The law and working of the constitution: documents 1660–1914. 2 v. 1952. 2nd edn. 1961–4.

Replaced Sir Charles Grant Robertson, ed., *Select statutes, cases and documents to illustrate English constitutional history* . . ., 1904, 9th edn. 1949. More useful than David Oswald Dykes, ed., *Source book of constitutional history from 1660,* 1930, and Carl Stephenson and Frederick George Marcham, eds., *Sources of English constitutional history: a selection of documents from A.D. 600 to the present,* N.Y. 1937. Eugene Charlton Black, ed., *British politics in the nineteenth century,* N.Y. 1969, is less constitutional.

254 EMDEN (CECIL STUART) *ed.* Selected speeches on the constitution [1719–1932]. 2 v. 1939.

255 PAUL (HERBERT WOODFIELD) *ed.* Famous speeches. 2 v. 1910–12.

See also Leopold Wagner, ed., *Modern political orations* [1838–88], 1896, Alsager Hay Hill, *The oratorical year book for 1865* . . ., 1866, Joseph Hendershot Park, *British prime ministers of the nineteenth century: policies and speeches,* N.Y. 1950, *Hansard's extra-parliamentary debates* [Feb.–Nov. 1890], 1890, and *The extra-parliamentary Hansard* [Oct. 1899–Sept. 1901], 2 v. 1900–1.

256 THE CONSTITUTIONAL YEAR BOOK [and politician's guide] for 1885[–1939]. Repr. 54 v. Brighton. 1971.

Publ. by the Conservative Central Office. Includes lists of office holders, brief biographies of M.P.s and peers, election results, a summary of the events in parliament during the previous year, and numerous statistical tables. By far the most useful political handbook ever published. *The Liberal year book,* 1905–39, repr. Brighton 1971–2, an imitation published by the Liberal Publications Department, is less useful.

257 MONTGOMERY (HUGH) *and* CAMBRAY (PHILIP GEORGE) *comps.* A dictionary of political phrases and allusions. 1906.

258 [REDGRAVE (SAMUEL)]. Murray's official handbook of church and state . . . 1852. 2nd edn. 1855.

An encyclopedia of official institutions. A similar work, not as well arranged, is Charles

Roger Phipps Dodd (afterwards Dod), *A manual of dignities, privilege, and precedence: including lists of the great public functionaries, from the revolution to the present time*, 1842.

**259** BUXTON (CHARLES). The ideas of the day on policy. 1866. 3rd edn. 1868.

Cont. by his son, Sydney Charles Buxton, Earl Buxton, as *A handbook to political questions of the day: being the arguments on either side*, 1880, 11th edn. 1903. Sets out the pros and cons of debate.

**260** NATIONAL LIBERAL CLUB (GLADSTONE LIBRARY). Catalogue. 1908.

A useful checklist of political literature.

**261** THOMAS (ERNEST CHESTER). Leading cases in constitutional law. 1876. 8th edn. 1947.

Sir David Lindsay Keir and Frederick Henry Lawson, *Cases in constitutional law*, Oxf. 1928, 5th edn. 1967, is also useful.

## 2. GENERAL WORKS

The indispensable books are Bagehot (**278**), Todd (**279**), and Lowell (**286**).

**262** SMELLIE (KINGSLEY BRYCE SPEAKMAN). A hundred years of English government. 1937. 2nd edn. 1950.

Much wider in scope than the title suggests. The best general political history of the period.

**263** KEITH (ARTHUR BERRIEDALE). The constitution of England from Queen Victoria to George VI. 2 v. 1940.

Useful, but needs revision.

**264** BIRCH (ANTHONY HAROLD). Representative and responsible government: an essay on the British constitution. 1964.

A useful study of the development of constitutional theory.

**265** BEER (SAMUEL HUTCHISON). Modern British politics: a study of parties and pressure groups. 1965. 2nd edn. 1969.

Title of the American edn. *British politics in the collectivist age*, N.Y. 1965, 2nd edn. 1969. Good.

**266** GRAINGER (JOHN HERBERT). Character and style in English politics. Camb. 1969.

Discursive. Cp. Archibald Paton Thornton, *The habit of authority: paternalism in British history*, 1966.

**267** GUTTSMAN (WILHELM LEO). The British political elite [since 1868]. 1963.

A sociological study.

**268** EMDEN (CECIL STUART). The people and the constitution: a history of the development of the people's influence in British government. Oxf. 1933. 2nd edn. 1956.

A quaint earlier attempt at the same sort of history is Arthur Crump, *A short enquiry into the formation of political opinion from the reign of the great families to the advent of democracy*, 2nd edn. 1888.

**269** LASKI (HAROLD JOSEPH). Parliamentary government in England: a commentary. 1938.

Not a history, but incorporates much historical material. Another analysis of the same date is Harold Richard Goring Greaves, *The British constitution*, 1938, 3rd edn. 1955.

**270** SOMERVELL (DAVID CHURCHILL). British politics since 1900. 1950. 2nd edn. 1953.

A similar short history is Neville Penry Thomas, *A history of British politics from the year 1900*, 1956.

**271** HERTZ *afterwards* HURST (*Sir* GERALD BERKELEY). The Manchester politician, 1750–1912. 1912.

The only attempt so far at a regional political history. Written too close to events to have lasting value.

**272** KEIR (*Sir* DAVID LINDSAY). The constitutional history of modern Britain, 1485–1937. 1938. 9th edn. 1969.

The best of the general constitutional history textbooks. The later editions of Thomas Pitt Taswell-Langmead, *English constitutional history: a textbook for students and others*, 1875, 11th edn. 1960, and Dudley Julius Medley, *A student's manual of English constitutional history*, Oxf. 1894, 6th edn. 1925, are fuller at some points. For a brief guide see Stanley Bertram Chrimes, *English constitutional history*, 1947, 3rd edn. 1965.

**273** JENNINGS (*Sir* WILLIAM IVOR). Cabinet government. 1936. 3rd edn. 1959.

Forms, with his *Parliament* (**421**) and *Party politics* (**506**), a full lawyerly account of the development of the 20th-cent. constitution as revealed in histories, biographies, and legal textbooks. Not based on original research.

**274** CLOKIE (HUGH McDOWALL) *and* ROBINSON (JOSEPH WILLIAM). Royal commissions of inquiry: the significance of investigations in British politics. Stanford, [Calif.] 1937.

See also *Report of the departmental committee on the procedure of royal commissions* [Chairman: Lord Balfour of Burleigh], [Cd. 5235] H.C. (1910). LVIII, 371.

**275** GNEIST (HEINRICH RUDOLPH VON). Das heutige englische Verfassungs- und Verwaltungsrecht. Berlin. 1857.

There is an interesting account of this and Gneist's other works in Sir George Walter Prothero, 'Gneist on the English constitution', *Eng. Hist. Rev.* iii (1888), 1–33. See also Reinhard Josef Lamer, *Der englische Parlamentarismus in der deutschen politischen Theorie im Zeitalter Bismarcks (1857–1890)* . . ., Historische Studien 387, Lübeck & Hamburg 1963. Eduard Fischel, *The English constitution*, trans. by Richard Jenery Shee, 1863, is another German work of the same type as Gneist's. See also **8512**.

**276 MAY (THOMAS ERSKINE),** *Baron Farnborough.* The constitutional history of England since the accession of George the Third, 1760–1860. 2 v. 1861–3. 3rd edn. 3 v. 1871. New edn. [down to 1911] by Francis Holland. 1912.

Whig history at its best. John Russell (Earl Russell), *An essay on the history of the English government and constitution . . .,* 1821, new edn. 1865, and Henry Brougham, Baron Brougham and Vaux, *The British constitution: its history, structure and working,* 1861, 3rd edn. 1862, are more partisan.

**277 HEARN (WILLIAM EDWARD).** The government of England: its structure and its development. Lond. & Melb. 1867. 2nd edn. 1887.

A mixture of legal and political analysis, with the legal predominating. Dicey's avowed starting-point is *The law of the constitution* (**281**). Better than Herbert Broom, *Constitutional law viewed in relation to common law . . .,* 1866, 2nd edn. 1885, or Homersham Cox, *The institutions of the English government . . .,* 1863.

**278 BAGEHOT (WALTER).** The English constitution. 1867. 2nd edn. 1872.

A series of brilliant essays which give the most perceptive account of the constitution to date.

**279 TODD (ALPHEUS).** On parliamentary government in England: its origin, development and practical operation. 2 v. 1867–9. 2nd edn. 1887–9. Abridged and rev. edn. by Sir Spencer Walpole. 2 v. 1892.

A painstaking, descriptive work, still of the greatest value.

**280 CRAIK (***Sir* **HENRY)** *ed.* The English citizen: his rights and responsibilities. Original edn. 13 v. 1881–5. Suppl. 5 v. 1885–1904.

A useful set of short monographs, the majority by recognized authorities. The original 13 v. consisted of: 1. Henry Duff Traill, *Central government,* 1882, rev. edn. 1908; 2. Sir Spencer Walpole, *The electorate and the legislature,* 1881, 2nd edn. 1892; 3. Sir Mackenzie Dalzell Edwin Stewart Chalmers, *Local government,* 1883; 4. Frederic William Maitland, *Justice and police,* 1885; 5. Alexander Johnstone Wilson, *The national budget, the national debt, taxes and rates,* 1882; 6. Sir Henry Craik, *The state in its relation to education,* 1884, 3rd edn. 1914; 7. Thomas Welbanke Fowle, *The poor law,* 1881, 2nd edn. 1890; 8. Thomas Henry Farrer, Baron Farrer, *The state in its relation to trade,* 1883; 9. William Stanley Jevons, *The state in relation to labour,* 1881, 4th edn. by Francis Wrigley Hirst, 1910; 10. Sir Frederick Pollock, *The land laws,* 1883, 3rd edn. 1896; 11. Arthur Ralph Douglas Elliot, *The state and the church,* 1882, 2nd edn. 1899; 12. Sir Spencer Walpole, *Foreign relations,* 1882; 13. *Colonies and dependencies*: part I 'India' by James Sutherland Cotton, part II 'The Colonies' by Edward John Payne, 1883.

To these were added: Sir Edmund Frederick Du Cane, *The punishment and prevention of crime,* 1885; Sir [John] Frederick Maurice, *National defences,* 1897; Thomas Mackay, *The state and charity,* 1898; William Blake Odgers, *Local government,* 1899, 2nd edn. 1907; Edward John Payne, *Colonies and colonial federations,* 1904.

**281 DICEY (ALBERT VENN).** Lectures introductory to the study of the law of the constitution. 1885. 10th edn. 1959.

The most influential book of its kind since Blackstone. There are good commentaries by the eds. of the recent edns. and in Sir William Ivor Jennings, *The law and the constitution,* 1933, 5th edn. 1959.

282 MAITLAND (FREDERIC WILLIAM). The constitutional history of England: a course of lectures. Camb. 1908.

Includes a brilliant account, running to 200 pages, of the state of public law in 1887–8.

283 ANSON (*Sir* WILLIAM REYNELL). The law and custom of the constitution. 2 v. Oxf. 1886–92. 3rd edn. 3 v. Oxf. 1897–1908. Vol. I. 5th edn. 1922, vol. II in 2 pts. 4th edn. 1935.

Long standard, and still the fullest, account of many subjects. There is a parallel French work of much less erudition, Amable Charles, Comte Franquet de Franqueville, *Le gouvernement et le parlement britannique*, 3 v. Paris 1887.

284 COURTNEY (LEONARD HENRY), *Baron Courtney of Penwith*. The working constitution of the United Kingdom and its outgrowths. 1901. Abridged edn. 1905.

285 LOW (*Sir* SIDNEY JAMES MARK). The governance of England. 1904. 5th edn. 1918.

286 LOWELL (ABBOTT LAWRENCE). The government of England. 2 v. N.Y. 1908. New edn. 2 v. N.Y. 1912. Repr. 1920.

One of the major landmarks of political science during the period.

287 HATSCHEK (JULIUS). Englisches Staatsrecht mit Berücksichtigung der für Schottland und Irland geltenden Sonderheiten. 2 v. Tübingen. 1905–6.

Comparable in scope with Lowell (286), but much more legalistic. Hatschek also published a short text-book, *Das Staatsrecht des vereinigten Königreichs Grossbritannien-Irland*, Tübingen 1914.

288 RIDGES (EDWARD WAVELL). Constitutional law of England. 1905. 8th edn. 1950.

A 20th-cent lawyer's textbook. Cp. Dalzell Henry John Chalmers, *Outlines of constitutional and administrative law*, 1910, 5th edn. 1936.

### 3. Studies of Special Periods and Events

289 GASH (NORMAN). Reaction and reconstruction in English politics, 1832–1852. Oxf. 1965.

290 CONACHER (JAMES BLENNERHASSET). The Aberdeen coalition, 1852–1855: a study in mid-nineteenth-century party politics. Camb. 1968.

Monumental. See also his *The Peelites and the party system, 1846–52*, Newton Abbot 1972, and Wilbur Devereux Jones and Arvel Benjamin Erickson, *The Peelites, 1846–1857*, Columbus, Ohio 1972.

291 ANDERSON (OLIVE). A liberal state at war: English politics and economics during the Crimean War. 1967.

An important pioneering work. For the Crimean War see also **2420–44**.

292 COWLING (MAURICE JOHN). 1867: Disraeli, Gladstone and revolution: the passing of the second Reform Bill. Camb. 1967.

Uses the crisis of 1867 as an opportunity to analyse the political forces at work: good. On this subject see also **665**.

293 SHANNON (RICHARD THOMAS). Gladstone and the Bulgarian agitation, 1876. 1963.

Excellent. Shows how wide-ranging were the groups interested in the 'Bulgarian horrors'. Links politics and religion.

294 MASTERMAN (CHARLES FREDERICK GURNEY). The condition of England. 1909. Repr. ed. by J. T. Boulton. 1960.

A minor classic of social and political analysis.

295 DANGERFIELD (GEORGE). The strange death of liberal England [1910–14]. N.Y. 1935. Lond. 1936. Repr. N.Y. 1961.

Stimulating and important. Peter Rowland, *The last liberal governments:* Vol. 1, *The promised land, 1905–1910*, 1968, vol. 2, *Unfinished business, 1911–1914*, 1972, is/a partisan Liberal polemic. Colin Cross, *The Liberals in power (1905–1914)*, 1963, is a very conventional outline.

296 DONALDSON (FRANCES). The Marconi scandal. 1962.

For further details see **5657**.

297 HAZLEHURST (CAMERON). Politicians at war: July 1914 to May 1915. 1971.

## 4. JOURNALS OF POLITICAL EVENTS

298 CHARLES GREVILLE. The Greville memoirs, 1814–60. By Charles Cavendish Fulke Greville. Ed. by Giles Lytton Strachey and Roger Fulford. 8 v. 1938.

The definitive edn. Suppl. by Arthur Henry Johnson, ed., *The letters of Charles Greville and Henry Reeve, 1836–1865*, 1924. The *Memoirs* originally appeared in 8 v. ed. by Henry Reeve, 1874–87: additional material was included in *The Greville diary*, ed. by Philip Whitwell Wilson, 2 v. 1927. *Leaves from the Greville diary*, ed. by Philip Morrell, 1929, is a useful selection.

299 GLADSTONE. The Gladstone diaries. Ed. by Michael Richard Daniell Foot and others. 10 v. Oxf. 1968+. In progress.

300 HENRY GREVILLE. Leaves from the diary of Henry [William] Greville [1832–72]. Ed. by Alice Byng, Viscountess Enfield, later Countess of Strafford. 4 v. 1883–1905.

Useful, but inferior to his brother's diary (**298**). Sir Mountstuart Elphinstone Grant Duff, *Notes from a diary* [1851–1901], 14 v. 1897–1905, suppl. by his *Out of the past: some biographical essays*, 2 v. 1903, is the work of a raconteur rather than a diarist. The best stories are brought together in Arthur Tilney Bassett, ed., *A Victorian vintage*, 1930.

301 BRIGHT. The diaries of John Bright [1837–87]. Ed. by Robert Alfred John Walling. 1930.

302  HAMILTON. The diary of Sir Edward Walter Hamilton [1880–5]. Ed. by Dudley Ward Rhodes Bahlman. 2 v. 1972.

303  WEBB. My apprenticeship [1858–92]. By Beatrice Webb [Baroness Passfield]. 1926.

Followed by *Our partnership* [1892–1911], ed. by Barbara Drake and Margaret Isabel Cole, 1948; *Beatrice Webb's diaries, 1912–1924*, ed. by Margaret I. Cole, 1952; and *Beatrice Webb's diaries, 1924–1932*, ed. by Margaret I. Cole, 1956. The first two autobiography based on diaries, the other two extracts from diaries only. By far the best journals of the period. The originals are in the British Libr. of Political and Econ. Science.

304  ESHER. Journals and letters of Reginald [Baliol Brett], Viscount Esher. [1870–1930]. Ed. by Maurice Vyner Baliol Brett and Oliver Silvain Baliol Brett, Viscount Esher. 4 v. 1934–8.

A fuller version of the journals for 1872–95 is in *Extracts from journals*, 2 v. priv. pr. Camb. 1908–14. (Publ. by Lord Esher in his lifetime.)

305  BLUNT. My diaries: being a personal narrative of events, 1888–1914. By Wilfrid Scawen Blunt. 2 v. 1919–20. 1-vol. edn. 1932.

The well-informed and incisive journals of a Radical poet and country gentleman. Particularly strong on the Near East and Ireland. His earlier diaries are largely reproduced in his *Secret history of the English occupation of Egypt* [1879–82], 1907, 2nd edn. 1907, *Gordon at Khartoum* [1882–6], 1911, *India under Ripon* [1883–4], 1909, and *The land war in Ireland* [1885–8], 1912.

306  WEST. Private diaries of Sir Algernon West [1892–8]. Ed. by Horace Gordon Hutchinson. 1922.

Mainly about Gladstone. Earlier diaries form the basis of West's *Recollections, 1832–1886*, 2 v. 1899.

307  FITZROY. Memoirs [1898–1923]. By Sir Almeric William FitzRoy. 2 v. [1925].

Clerk to the Privy Council and the confidant of statesmen.

308  RIDDELL. More pages from my diary, 1908–1914. By George Allardice Riddell, Baron Riddell. 1934.

A companion to *Lord Riddell's war diary*, 1933, and his *Intimate diary of the peace conference and after*, 1933. Riddell was proprietor of the *News of the World*. Cp. Ralph David Blumenfeld, *R. D. B.'s diary* [1887–1914], 1930, the jottings of a journalist.

309  SCOTT. The political diaries of C. P. Scott, 1911–1928. Ed. by Trevor Gordon Wilson. Lond. & Ithaca, N.Y. 1970.

310  ADDISON. Four and a half years [June 1914–Jan. 1919]. By Christopher Addison, Viscount Addison. 2 v. 1934.

The diary of a minister in wartime. His memoirs of the period are in his *Politics from within, 1911–1918 . . .*, 2 v. 1924.

## 5. POLITICAL CARTOONS

*Punch, Judy,* and the *Westminster Gazette* were the periodicals most noted for their cartoons.

311  TENNIEL (*Sir* JOHN). Cartoons (from "Punch") 1871–1881 [and 1882–1891]. 2 v. 1895.

312  FURNISS (HARRY). Pen and pencil in parliament. 1897.

> More elaborate, but in many ways less successful than his *M.P.s in session, from Mr. Punch's parliamentary portrait gallery,* 1889.

313  GOULD (*Sir* FRANCIS CARRUTHERS). The elector's picture book. *Pall Mall gazette* extra no. 63. 1892.

314  GOULD (*Sir* FRANCIS CARRUTHERS). The Westminster cartoons. Nos. 1–7. 1895–1903.

> Paper bound. Succeeded by *Political caricatures,* 4 v. 1903–6, much more elaborately produced. The 2 ser. include the best of Gould's cartoons for the *Westminster Gazette.* Gould also produced *Cartoons of the campaign: a collection of political cartoons made during the general election of 1895,* 1895.

315  LAWSON (*Sir* WILFRID) *and* GOULD (*Sir* FRANCIS CARRUTHERS). Cartoons in rhyme and line. 1905.

316  GOULD (*Sir* FRANCIS CARRUTHERS). Froissart's modern chronicles. 3 v. 1901–4.

317  BEGBIE ([EDWARD] HAROLD) *and* GOULD (*Sir* FRANCIS CARRUTHERS). The political Struwwelpeter. 1899.

> Begbie and Gould also publ. *The Struwwelpeter alphabet,* 1900, and *Great men,* 1901.

## B. THE MONARCHY

### 1. GENERAL

318  HARDIE (FRANK MARTIN). The political influence of the British monarchy, 1868–1952. 1970.

> See also the decidedly antipathetic [Basil] Kingsley Martin, *The crown and the establishment,* 1962, repr. 1963, and, for eulogies, Henry Hector Bolitho, *A century of British monarchy,* 1951, new edn. 1953; Angus William Holden (Baron Holden), *Four generations of our royal family,* 1937; Sir Charles Alexander Petrie, *Monarchy in the twentieth century,* 1952, and many others. Christopher Hibbert, pseud. of Arthur Raymond Hibbert, *The court at Windsor: a domestic history,* 1964, is the best of the social hists.

319  KEITH (ARTHUR BERRIEDALE). The king and the imperial crown: the powers and duties of his majesty. 1936.

> A legalistic study. Cp. Richard Henry Gretton, *The king's majesty: a study in the historical philosophy of modern kingship,* 1930.

320  LINDSAY (WILLIAM ALEXANDER). The royal household. 1898.

Lists of office holders, 1837–97. For other royal officials see Paul Herman Emden, *Behind the throne*, 1934, the life of Sir Henry Ponsonby (**333**), and Sir John William Fortescue, *Author and curator*, 1933. For the records of the Lord Chamberlain's department see [P.R.O.,] *Lord Chamberlain's department: class list, 1499–1902*, List & Index Soc. 47, 1969.

321  WILLIAMS (NEVILLE). The royal residences of Great Britain: a social history. 1960.

Brief. See also Sir Owen Frederick Morshead, *Windsor Castle*, 1951, 2nd edn. 1957; Harold Clifford Smith, *Buckingham Palace*, 1931; Ivor Brown, *Balmoral*, 1955; Derek Hudson, *Kensington Palace*, 1968; and Helen Cathcart, *Sandringham . . .*, 1964.

322  BRADLAUGH (CHARLES). The impeachment of the house of Brunswick. 1871. 10th edn. 1891.

A celebrated but not very impressive republican onslaught. See also Norbert J. Gossman, 'Republicanism in nineteenth-century England', *Int. Rev. Soc. Hist.* vii (1962), 47–60.

## 2. The Royal Family

323  PAKENHAM (ELIZABETH), *Countess of Longford*. Victoria R.I. 1964.

American title: *Queen Victoria: born to succeed*, N.Y. 1965. Largely repl. the older biogs. Of these Giles Lytton Strachey, *Queen Victoria*, 1921, new edn. 1948, is the best, but there are quite good ones by Sir Sidney Lee, 1902, rev. edn. 1904, Edward Frederic Benson, 1935, and Roger Thomas Baldwin Fulford, 1951. Dame Edith Sitwell, *Victoria of England*, 1936, is interesting. Henry Hector Bolitho, *Victoria and Albert*, 1938, and *Victoria the widow and her son*, 1934, are popular. An interesting book is disguised under a bad title in Tom Cullen, *The empress Brown: the story of a royal friendship*, 1969, which deals with the same topic as Evelyn Ernest Percy Tisdall, *Queen Victoria's John Brown . . .*, 1938, and *Queen Victoria's Private Life . .*, 1961. Cecil Blanche Woodham-Smith, *Queen Victoria . . .*, 1+v. 1972+, will be a full biog.

324  HARDIE (FRANK MARTIN). The political influence of Queen Victoria, 1861–1901. 1935. Repr. 1963.

A pioneer study. See also Corinne Comstock Weston, 'The royal mediation in 1884', *Eng. Hist. Rev.* lxxxii (1967), 296–322. There is little further in Algernon Cecil, *Queen Victoria and her prime ministers*, 1953, and Sir John Arthur Ransome Marriott, *Queen Victoria and her ministers*, 1933.

325  GERNSHEIM (HELMUT) *and* GERNSHEIM (ALISON). Queen Victoria: a biography in word and picture. 1959.

A magnificent collection of photographs.

326  LETTERS OF QUEEN VICTORIA. 9 v. 1907–32.

These invaluable volumes are arranged in 3 ser., each of 3 vols., ser. 1 covering 1837–61, ed. by Arthur Christopher Benson and Viscount Esher, 1907, Ser. 2 covering 1862–85, ed. by George Earle Buckle 1926–8, and Ser. 3 covering 1886–1901, ed. by G. E. Buckle, 1930–2. Henry Hector Bolitho also ed. *Further letters of Queen Victoria from the archives of the House of Brandenburg-Prussia*, 1938.

327  CONNELL (BRIAN) *ed.* Regina vs. Palmerston: the correspondence between Queen Victoria and her foreign and prime minister, 1837–1865. 1962.

**328  GUEDALLA (PHILIP)** *ed.* The Queen and Mr. Gladstone. 2 v. 1933–4.
Correspondence.

**329  FULFORD (ROGER THOMAS BALDWIN)** *ed.* Dearest child: letters
between Queen Victoria and the Princess Royal, 1858–1861. 1964.

Cont. in his *Dearest mama: letters between Queen Victoria and the Crown Princess of
Prussia, 1861–1864*, 1968, and *Your dear letter, 1865–71*, 1971. See also **349.**

**330  VICTORIA (QUEEN).** Leaves from the journal of our life in the Highlands. 1868.

Characteristically ingenuous and direct. Suppl. by *More leaves from the journal of our
life in the Highlands*, 1884. A condensed version of the 2 vols. was publ. by David
Skene Duff as *Victoria in the Highlands: the personal journal of Her Majesty Queen
Victoria*, 1968. This contains supplementary information. Another 1-vol. condensation
was also publ. in 1968 as Queen Victoria, *Our Life in the Highlands*.

**331  VICTORIA (QUEEN).** Leaves from a journal: a record of the visit of the
Emperor and Empress of the French to the Queen and of the visit of the Queen
and HRH The Prince Consort to the Emperor of the French, 1855. Intro.
by Raymond Mortimer. 1961.

See also Edith Saunders, *Distant summer*, 1947.

**332  EYCK (FRANK).** The Prince Consort: a political biography. 1959.

But see also Roger Thomas Baldwin Fulford, *The Prince Consort*, 1949, and Henry
Hector Bolitho, ed., *The Prince Consort and his brother*, 1933. Kurt Jagow, ed., *Letters of
the Prince Consort, 1831–61*, trans. by E. T. S. Dugdale, Lond. & N.Y. 1938, is a
convenient selection. A characteristic 19th-cent. life is Charlotte Mary Yonge, *Life of
H.R.H. the Prince Consort*, 1890; a popular modern one is Evelyn Ernest Percy Tisdall,
*Restless Consort . . .*, 1952. The official life was Sir Theodore Martin, *The life of H.R.H.
the Prince Consort*, 5 v. 1877–80.

**333  PONSONBY (FREDERICK EDWARD GREY),** *Baron Sysonby.* Sidelights on Queen Victoria. 1930.

Episodes in court and political life from the papers of Sir Henry Ponsonby, the Queen's
private secretary. There is further material in Arthur Augustus William Harry Ponsonby (Baron Ponsonby of Shulbrede), *Henry Ponsonby, Queen Victoria's private
secretary: his life from his letters*, 1942, and Magdalen Ponsonby, *Mary Ponsonby: a
memoir, some letters and a journal*, 1927.

**334  WATSON (VERA).** A queen at home: an intimate account of the social
and domestic life of Queen Victoria's court. 1952.

Covers the period 1837–85. Based on the records of the Lord Chamberlain's department
(**320**).

**335  LUTYENS (MARY)** *ed.* Lady Lytton's court diary, 1895–1899. 1961.

**336  MALLET (VICTOR)** *ed.* Life with Queen Victoria: Marie Mallet's
letters from court, 1887–1901. 1968.

337  BUCHANAN (MERIEL). Queen Victoria's relations. 1954.

A useful account of a difficult subject. See also Edward Frederic Benson, *The Kaiser and his English relations*, 1936, Geoffrey Malden Willis, *Ernest Augustus, Duke of Cumberland and King of Hanover*, 1954, and Edward Frederic Benson, *Queen Victoria's daughters*, 1938.

338  MAGNUS[-ALLCROFT] (*Sir* PHILIP MONTEFIORE). King Edward the seventh. 1964.

A good modern life. Largely replaces the official life, Sir Sidney Lee, *King Edward VII: a biography*, 2 v. 1925–7. There are a number of other interesting studies: Virginia Cowles, *Edward VII and his circle*, 1956; Hugh Evelyn Wortham, *The delightful profession: Edward VII, a study in kingship*, 1931; Edward Frederic Benson, *King Edward VII*, 1933; George Dangerfield, *Victoria's heir: the education of a prince*, N.Y. & Lond. 1941, and Sigmund Münz, *Edward VII at Marienbad: political and social life at the Bohemian spas*, 1934.

339  GERNSHEIM (HELMUT) and GERNSHEIM (ALISON). Edward VII and Queen Alexandra: a biography in word and picture. 1962.

An enormous improvement on earlier collections such as William Henry Wilkins, *Our king and queen . . .*, 2 v. 1902–3.

340  LEGGE (EDWARD). King Edward in his true colours. 1912.

The earliest of a series of personal reminiscences by Edward's associates. Legge also publ. *More about King Edward*, 1913, and *King Edward, the Kaiser and the war*, 1917. Other works of the same type are Algernon Bertram Freeman-Mitford, Baron Redesdale, *King Edward VII*, 1915, Reginald Baliol Brett, Viscount Esher, *The influence of King Edward*, 1915, and Sir Lionel Cust, *King Edward VII and his court*, 1930. John Percy Claude Sewell, ed., *Personal letters of King Edward VII, together with extracts from correspondence of Queen Alexandra, the Duke of Albany, and General Sir Arthur and Lady Paget*, 1931, also belongs to the same category. Lower in the social scale are the memoirs of the King's servants of which only Charles William Stamper, *What I know: reminiscences of five years' personal attendance upon his late majesty King Edward the seventh*, 1913, is of any value.

341  WATSON (ALFRED EDWARD THOMAS). King Edward VII as a sportsman. 1911.

342  BURDETT (*Sir* HENRY CHARLES). Prince, princess, and people: an account of the social progress and development of our own times, as illustrated by the public life and work of their Royal Highnesses the Prince and Princess of Wales, 1863–1889. 1889.

343  BATTISCOMBE (GEORGINA). Queen Alexandra. 1969.

See also Hans Roger Madol, *The private life of Queen Alexandra, as viewed by her friends*, 1940. William Rutherford Hayes Trowbridge, *Queen Alexandra: a study of royalty*, 1921, Evelyn Ernest Percy Tisdall, *Unpredictable queen: the intimate life of Queen Alexandra*, 1953, and Sir George Compton Archibald Arthur, *Queen Alexandra*, 1934, are useful popular lives.

344  VINCENT (JAMES EDMUND). His Royal Highness Duke of Clarence and Avondale: a memoir. 1893.

The heir to the throne who died young. See also Michael Harrison, *Clarence: the life of H.R.H. the Duke of Clarence and Avondale (1864–1892)*, 1972.

**345  NICOLSON (*Sir* HAROLD GEORGE). King George the fifth: his life and reign. 1952.**

Absolutely first rate. There is some additional material in John Francis Gore, *King George V: a personal memoir*, 1941, and James Wentworth Day, *King George V as a sportsman* . . ., 1935. Of earlier lives the only one of any merit is Sir George Compton Archibald Arthur, *King George V*, 1929. There are several collections of speeches.

**346  POPE-HENNESSY (JAMES). Queen Mary, 1867–1953. 1959.**

There is also an official life of her mother: Clement Kinloch Cooke, *A memoir of H.R.H. Princess Mary Adelaide, Duchess of Teck, based on her private diaries and letters*, 2 v. 1900.

**347  EDWARD VIII. A king's story: the memoirs of H.R.H. the Duke of Windsor, K.G. 1951.**

The King also publ. *The crown and the people, 1902–1953*, 1953, and *A family album*, 1960. There is a straightforward life by Henry Hector Bolitho, *King Edward VIII*, 1937, new edn. 1954.

**348  WHEELER-BENNETT (*Sir* JOHN WHEELER). King George VI: his life and reign. 1958.**

Incl. much on George V.

**349  BARKELEY (RICHARD). The Empress Frederick, daughter of Queen Victoria. 1956.**

See also Princess Catherine Radziwill, *The Empress Frederick*, 1934, and Egon Caesar Corti, Conte Corti, *The English Empress*, trans. E. M. Hodgson, 1957. There are two good selections of letters in addition to those at **329**: Frederick Edward Grey Ponsonby, Baron Sysonby, ed., *The letters of the Empress Frederick* [to Queen Victoria], 1928, and Arthur Stanley Gould Lee, ed., *The Empress Frederick writes to Sophie: letters 1889–1901*, 1955. Some letters of her youngest daughter have also been publ. in James Pope-Hennessy, ed., *Queen Victoria at Windsor and Balmoral: letters from her grand-daughter, Princess Victoria of Prussia, June 1889*, 1959.

**350  ASTON (*Sir* GEORGE GREY) *and* GRAHAM (EVELYN), *pseud.* of LUCAS (NETLEY) H.R.H. the Duke of Connaught and Strathearn: a life and intimate study. 1929.**

See also Mary Howard M'Clintock, *The Queen thanks Sir Howard* [Elphinstone], 1945. Sir Howard was a member of the Duke's household, 1859–90.

**351  ALICE, Grand-Duchess of Hesse, Princess of Great Britain and Ireland: biographical sketch and letters. Comp. by Carl Sell. Trans. by Princess Christian. 1884. Popular edn. 1885.**

On Princess Alice see also David Skene Duff, *Hessian tapestry*, 1967.

**352  DUFF (DAVID SKENE). The life story of H.R.H. Princess Louise, Duchess of Argyll. 1940.**

**353  DUFF (DAVID SKENE). The shy princess; the life of Her Royal Highness Princess Beatrice, the youngest daughter and constant companion of Queen Victoria. 1958.**

See also M. E. Sara, *The life and times of Princess Beatrice*. 1945.

## C. CENTRAL GOVERNMENT

### 1. GENERAL

**354** PARRIS (HENRY WALTER). Constitutional bureaucracy: the development of British central administration since the eighteenth century. 1969.

See also Francis Michael Glenn Willson, *The organization of British central government, 1914–1956 . . .*, ed. by Daniel Norman Chester, Roy. Inst. Public Admin., 1957, 2nd edn. 1968, William James Millar Mackenzie and Jack William Grove, *Central administration in Britain*, 1957, Sir John Arthur Ransome Marriott, *The mechanism of the modern state . . .*, 2 v. Oxf. 1927, and Sir Ernest Barker, *The development of public services in Western Europe, 1660–1930*, 1944. There is much material in Todd (**279**), and Lowell (**286**).

**355** BREBNER (JOHN BARTLET). 'Laissez-faire and state intervention in nineteenth-century Britain'. *J. Econ. Hist.* viii (1948). Suppl. 59–73. Repr. in Carus-Wilson, *Essays* (**4066**), III, 252–62.

**356** MACDONAGH (OLIVER ORMOND GERARD MICHAEL). 'The nineteenth-century revolution in government: a reappraisal'. *Hist. J.* i (1950), 52–67.

With reply by Henry Walter Parris, *Hist J.* iii (1960), 17–37, marks the beginning of historians' attempts to move beyond Dicey (**357**). See also Valerie Cromwell, 'Interpretations of nineteenth-century administration—an analysis', *Victorian studs.*, ix (1966), 245–55, and Gillian Sutherland, ed., *Studies in the growth of nineteenth-century government*, 1972.

**357** DICEY (ALBERT VENN). Lectures on the relation between law & public opinion in England during the nineteenth century. 1905. 2nd edn. 1914. Repr. 1962.

The most influential book on the developing role of the state during the first half of the 20th cent. To be used with caution.

**358** ANDERSON (OLIVE). 'The Janus face of mid-nineteenth-century English radicalism: the Administrative Reform Association of 1855.' *Victorian Studs.* viii (1965), 231–42.

See also the *Official papers* of the Administrative Reform Assoc., 1855, and **388**.

**359** HELPS (*Sir* ARTHUR). Thoughts upon government. 1872.

A general discussion of government. Inferior to Sir Henry Taylor, *The statesman*, 1836.

**360** BOYLE (*Sir* COURTENAY EDMUND). Hints on the conduct of business, public and private. 1900.

A guide to official business by the Sec. of the Board of Trade.

**361** HALDANE COMMITTEE REPORT. Report of the machinery of government committee [Chairman: Viscount Haldane]. Ministry of Reconstruction. [Cd. 9230] H.C. (1918). XII, 1.

The only official attempt to consider the whole structure of government. Suppl. by Ministry of Reconstruction, *Reconstruction Problems: No. 38: the business of government*, 3 pts. H.M.S.O., 1919.

362 ABRAMOVITZ (MOSES) *and* ELIASBERG (VERA F.). The growth of public employment in Great Britain [1890–1950]. Nat. Bureau Econ. Res. Princeton. 1957.

See also J. Veverka, 'The growth of government expenditure in the United Kingdom since 1790', *Scottish J. Pol. Econ.* x (1963), 111–27.

363 WRIGHT (MAURICE). Treasury control of the civil service, 1854–1874. Oxf. 1969.

Important. See also Sir Horace Perkins Hamilton, 'Treasury control in the eighties', *Public Admin.* xxxiii (1955), 13–17, and Roy Malcolm Macleod, *Treasury control and social administration: a study of establishment growth at the Local Government Board, 1871–1905*, 1968.

364 BEER (SAMUEL HUTCHISON). Treasury control: the co-ordination of financial and economic policy. Oxf. 1956. 2nd edn. 1957.

Confined to mid 20th cent., but the only reliable account of the subject. See also Sir Ralph George Hawtrey, *The exchequer and the control of expenditure*, 1921.

365 FITZROY (*Sir* ALMERIC WILLIAM). The history of the Privy Council. 1928.

See also his diary as Sec. of the Council (307). For a previous Sec. see *Correspondence of Sir Arthur Helps, K.C.B., D.C.L.*, ed. by his son, Edmund Arthur Helps, 1917.

366 HARRIS (JOHN SHARP). British government inspection: the local services and the central departments. 1955.

367 WILLIS (JOHN). The parliamentary powers of English government departments. Camb., Mass. 1933.

368 CHIAO (WAN-HSUAN). Devolution in Great Britain. Columbia Studies in history, economics and public law, vol. CXXIV, no. 1. N.Y. 1926.

369 HANDOVER (PHYLLIS MARGARET). The history of the *London Gazette*, 1665–1965. H.M.S.O. 1965.

370 PUGH (RALPH BERNARD). The crown estate. 1960.

371 DUGDALE (GEORGE STRATFORD). Whitehall through the centuries. 1950.

## 2. MINISTERS

372 MACKINTOSH (JOHN PITCAIRN). The British cabinet. 1962. 2nd edn. 1968.

Standard. Replaced Arthur Berriedale Keith, *The British cabinet system, 1830–1938*, 1939, 2nd edn. 1952. See also Hans Daalder, *Cabinet reform in Britain, 1914–1963*, Stanford, Calif., 1964, and Samuel Edward Finer, 'The individual responsibility of ministers', *Public Admin.* xxxiv (1956), 377–96.

373 PUBLIC RECORD OFFICE. List of Cabinet papers, 1880–1914. P.R.O. handbooks 4. H.M.S.O. 1964.

The working papers printed for use by the cabinet. See also P.R.O., *The records of the Cabinet Office to 1922*, P.R.O. handbooks 11, H.M.S.O. 1966.

374 [PUBLIC RECORD OFFICE.] Cabinet letters at Windsor, 1868–1916. List and Index Soc. Vol. 5. 1965.

A list of the Prime Ministers' reports to the sovereign on cabinet business—the only official record until 1916.

375 WILLSON (FRANCIS MICHAEL GLENN). 'Ministries and boards: some aspects of administrative development since 1832'. *Public Admin.* xxxiii (1955), 43–58.

376 SCHAFFER (B. B.). 'The idea of the ministerial department: Bentham, Mill and Bagehot'. *Aust. J. of Pol. & Hist.* iii (1957), 60–78.

377 CARTER (BYRUM E.). The office of prime minister. 1956.

See also R. M. Punnett, 'The parliamentary and personal backgrounds of British prime ministers, 1812 to 1963', *Quart. Rev.* 301 (1964), 254–66, and Lucille Iremonger, *The fiery chariot: a study of British prime ministers and the search for love*, 1970. For the prime ministers' private secretaries see Sir Charles Alexander Petrie, *The powers behind the prime ministers*, 1958.

378 WILLSON (FRANCIS MICHAEL GLENN). 'The routes of entry of new members of the British cabinet, 1868–1958'. *Political Studs.* vii (1959), 222–32.

See also Harold Joseph Laski, *The British cabinet: a study of its personnel, 1801–1924*, Fabian Tract No. 223, 1928, and Guttsman (**267**).

379 WILSON COMMITTEE ON THE REMUNERATION OF MINISTERS. Report from the select committee on remuneration of ministers [Chairman: John William Wilson]. H.C. 241 (1920). VIII, 429.

The only serious work on the subject.

### 3. THE CIVIL SERVICE

380 COHEN (EMMELINE WALEY). The growth of the British civil service, 1780–1939. 1941. Repr. 1965.

Largely replaced by Parris (**354**). There is little more in Sir John Craig, *A history of red tape . . .*, 1955, and William Charles Bryant, *The civil service of the crown: its rise and constitution*, 1876.

381 KITSON CLARK (GEORGE SIDNEY ROBERTS). ' "Statesmen in disguise": reflexions on the history of the neutrality of the civil service'. *Hist. J.* ii (1959), 19–39.

A useful starting-point for the role of the civil service. To be suppl. by John Donald Kingsley, *Representative bureaucracy: an interpretation of the British civil service*, Yellow Springs, Ohio 1944, Herman Finer, *The British civil service: an introductory essay*,

1927, rev. and enl. edn. 1937, and Sir Cecil Harcourt-Smith, and others, *The civil-servant and his profession* . . ., 1920.

382  KELSALL (ROGER KEITH). Higher civil servants in Britain from 1870 to the present day. 1955.

A sociological study. For the work of the higher civil service see Harold Edward Dale, *The higher civil service of Great Britain*, 1941, and Geoffrey Kingdon Fry, *Statesmen in disguise: the changing role of the administrative class of the British home civil service, 1853–1966*, 1969, neither of which is strong on hist.

383  EMDEN (CECIL STUART). The civil servant in the law and the constitution. 1923.

384  MARTINDALE (HILDA). Women servants of the state, 1870–1938: a history of women in the civil service. 1938.

Fuller than Dorothy Elizabeth Evans, *Women and the civil service* . . ., 1934.

385  ROUTH (GUY). 'Civil service pay, 1875 to 1950'. *Economica*, n.s. xxi (1954), 201–23.

386  NIXON (JOHN). The authentic history of civil service superannuation. 1930.

See also Herbert D. Brown, *Civil service retirement in Great Britain and New Zealand*, Wash. 1910, and Marios Raphael, *Pensions and public servants: a study of the origins of the British system*, Paris 1964.

387  HUGHES (EDWARD). 'Civil service reform, 1853–5'. *History*. xxvii (1942), 51–83. Repr. in *Public Admin*. xxxii (1954), 17–51.

Cont. in his 'Sir Charles Trevelyan and civil service reform, 1853–5', *Eng. Hist. Rev.* xliv (1949), 53–88, 206–34, and 'Postscript to the civil service reforms of 1855', *Public Admin*. xxxiii (1955), 299–306, and in Harold John Hanham, 'Political patronage at the Treasury, 1870–1912', *Hist. J.* iii (1960), 75–84.

388  LEWIS (RICHARD ALBERT). 'Edwin Chadwick and the administrative reform movement, 1854–6'. *Univ. of Birmingham Hist. J.* ii (1949–50), 178–200.

See also Chadwick's own 'On the economical, social, educational and political influences of competitive examinations as tests of qualifications for admission to the junior appointments in the public service', *Stat. Soc. J.* xxi (1858), 18–51, and **358**.

389  NORTHCOTE-TREVELYAN REPORT. Report on the organisation of the permanent civil service [by Sir Stafford Northcote and Sir Charles Trevelyan], together with a letter from the Rev. B. Jowett. [1713] H.C. (1854). XXVII, I. Repr. *Public Admin*. xxxii (1954), 1–16.

The fundamental document for civil service history. Suppl. by *Papers relating to the reorganisation of the civil service*. [1870] H.C. (1854–5). XX, 1, *Reports of committees of inquiry into public offices, and papers connected therewith* [1715] H.C. (1854). XXVII, 33, and Sir Charles Edward Trevelyan, and others, *Papers originally printed in 1850, respecting the emoluments of persons in the permanent employment of the government* . . ., 1856. There is a considerable literature, both pro and con. See in particular George Charles Brodrick, *Promotion by merit in relation to government and education*, 1858, and Horace Mann, *Civil service competitions considered as a means of promoting popular education*, 1857. See also *Report from the select committee on civil service appointments* [Chairman: Sir George Cornewall Lewis]. H.C. 337 (1856). IX, 1.

390 TROLLOPE (ANTHONY). The three clerks. 3 v. 1858. Numerous edns.
The best of the Victorian civil service novels.

391 MARVIN (CHARLES). Our public offices: embodying an account of the disclosure of the Anglo-Russian agreement and the unrevealed secret treaty of May 31st, 1878. 1879. 2nd edn. 1880.
The revelations of a disgruntled ex-official.

392 EATON (DORMAN BRIDGMAN). Civil service in Great Britain: a history of abuses and reforms and their bearing upon American politics. N.Y. 1880.
First issued as a House of Representatives report.

393 MOSES (ROBERT). The civil service of Great Britain. N.Y. 1914.
An excellent analysis by an American admin. reformer. Cp. Francis George Heath, *The British civil service: home, colonial, Indian and diplomatic*. 1915.

394 PLAYFAIR COMMISSION ON THE CIVIL SERVICE. First report of the civil service inquiry commission [Chairman: Lyon Playfair]. [C. 1113] H.C. (1875). XXIII, 1. Appendix [C. 1113–I] H.C. (1875). XXIII, 31. Second report. [C. 1226] H.C. (1875). XXIII, 451. Third report. [C. 1317] H.C. (1875). XXIII, 569. Index. [C. 1444] H.C. (1876). XXII, 561.
The first of three major inquiries into the civil service during the period.

395 RIDLEY COMMISSION ON CIVIL ESTABLISHMENTS. First report of the royal commission appointed to inquire into the civil establishments of the different offices of state at home and abroad [Chairman: Sir Matthew White Ridley]. [C. 5226] H.C. (1887). XIX, I. Second report. [C. 5545] H.C. (1888). XXVII, I. Third report. [C. 5748] H.C. (1889). XXI, I. Minutes of evidence. [C. 5748–I] H.C. (1889). XXI, 17. Fourth report. [C. 6172] H.C. (1890). XXVII, I. Minutes of evidence etc. [C. 6172–I] H.C. (1890). XXVII, 17.

396 MACDONNELL COMMISSION ON THE CIVIL SERVICE. Royal commission on the civil service: first report of the commissioners [Chairman: Lord MacDonnell]. [Cd. 6209] H.C. (1912–13). XV, 109. Appendix to 1st report. [Cd. 6210] H.C. (1912–13). XV, 113. Second report. [Cd. 6534] H.C. (1912–13). XV, 255. Appendix to 2nd report. [Cd. 6535] H.C. (1912–13). XV, 259. Third report. [Cd. 6739] H.C. (1913). XVIII, 275. Appendix to 3rd report [Cd. 6740] H.C. (1913). XVIII, 279. Fourth report. [Cd. 7338] H.C. (1914). XVI, I. Appendices to 4th report. [Cd. 7339–40] H.C. (1914). XVI, 165. Fifth report. [Cd. 7748] H.C. (1914–16). XI, 673. Appendix to 5th report. [Cd. 7749] H.C. (1914–16). XI, 725. Sixth report. [Cd. 7832] H.C. (1914–16). XII, I. Appendix to 6th report. [Cd. 8130] H.C. (1914–16). XII, 91.

**397** PARKINSON (JOSEPH CHARLES). Under government: an official key to the civil service. 1859. 5th edn. 1869.

A useful guide to employment. See also the *Handbook to government situations*, 1866, etc., and other guides listed by Wright (**363**).

**398** CIVIL SERVICE COMMISSION. First report of her majesty's civil service commissioners. [2038] H.C. (1856). XXII, 361. Annual. 1856+.

The main source for details of civil service recruitment.

**399** THE CIVIL SERVICE YEAR BOOK and official calendar. 1873–1917. Annual.

See also the lists in **103–5**.

**400** CIVIL SERVICE GAZETTE. 1853–1926.

The most important civil service newspaper. But see also *The civilian*, 1869–1925.

## 4. INDIVIDUAL OFFICES

For departmental records see **42–4**. Public health is treated at **7395–7493**. The service departments and the India and Colonial Offices each have separate entries.

**401** ROSEVEARE (HENRY). The Treasury: the evolution of a British institution. 1969.

See also Jenifer Margaret Hart, 'Sir Charles Trevelyan at the Treasury', *Eng. Hist. Rev.* lxxv (1960) 92–110, Edward Bridges, Baron Bridges, *The Treasury*, New Whitehall ser. 12, 1964, 2nd edn. 1966, and J. C. Sainty, comp., *Treasury officials, 1660–1870*, 1972.

**402** SOMERVILLE (*Sir* ROBERT). History of the Duchy of Lancaster. Duchy of Lancaster. 2 v. 1953–70.

Suppl. by his *Office-holders in the Duchy and County-Palatine of Lancaster from 1603*, Chichester 1972.

**403** PROUTY (ROGER WARREN). The transformation of the Board of Trade, 1830–1855: a study of administrative reorganization in the heyday of laissez faire. 1957.

**404** MACDONAGH (OLIVER ORMOND GERARD MICHAEL). A pattern of government growth, 1800–60: the Passenger Acts and their enforcement. 1961.

**405** CRAIG (*Sir* JOHN HERBERT McCUTCHEON). The mint: a history of the London mint from A.D. 287 to 1948. Camb. 1953.

**406** LAMBERT (ROYSTON JAMES). 'Central and local relations in Mid-Victorian England: the Local Government Act Office, 1858–71'. *Victorian Studs.* vi (1962), 121–50.

407 [PUBLIC RECORD OFFICE.] Subject index and box list to Home Office papers, 1879–1900. List and Index Soc. Vol. 22. 1967.

Suppl. by a similar list for 1900–9 (List & Index Soc. Vol. 23, 1967), and by *Home Office Registered Papers* (List & Index Soc. Vol. 30, 1967). Covers the main stream of domestic affairs not assigned to subject departments.

## 5. BIOGRAPHIES OF OFFICIALS

Confined to those whose work was not so specialized that they appear in one of the subject categories below (e.g. Public Health, Education). See also the works of Sir Algernon West (**306**).

408 ANDERSON. The lighter side of my official life. By Sir Robert Anderson. 1910.

Head of the Secret Service and sec. of the Prison Commission.

409 BUTLER. The confident morning. By Sir Harold Beresford Butler. 1950.

410 COLE. Fifty years of public work of Sir Henry Cole, K.C.B., accounted for in his deeds, speeches and writings. Ed. by Alan S. Cole and Henrietta Cole. 2 v. 1884.

Cole was sec. of the Science and Art Dept., 1853–73.

411 CUNYNGHAME. The unconventional civil servant: Sir Henry H. Cunynghame. By Charles Humble Dudley Ward and C. B. Spencer. 1938.

412 KEMPE. Reminiscences of an old civil servant, 1846–1927. By Sir John Arrow Kempe. 1928.

413 MALLET. Sir Louis Mallet: a record of public service and political ideals. By Sir Bernard Mallet. 1905.

414 MORANT. Sir Robert Morant: a great public servant. By Bernard Meredith Allen. 1934.

415 PRESTON-THOMAS. The work and play of a government inspector. By Herbert Preston-Thomas. 1909.

416 RIVERS WILSON. Chapters from my official life. By Sir Charles Rivers Wilson. Ed. by Everilda MacAlister. 1916.

417 SALTER. Memoirs of a public servant. By Arthur Salter, Baron Salter. 1961.

418 TREMENHEERE. 'A Whig inspector'. By Robert Kiefer Webb. *J. Mod. Hist.* xxvii (1955), 352–64.

On Hugh Seymour Tremenheere. See also the inadequately edited, *I was there: the memoirs of H. S. Tremenheere*, ed. by E. L. and O. P. Edmonds, Eton 1965.

# D. PARLIAMENT

## I. PARLIAMENT AS A WHOLE

### (a) *General*

419  MACDONAGH (MICHAEL). The pageant of parliament. 2 v. 1921.

A full-scale description of parliament at work. His earlier works, *The book of parliament*, 1897, and *Parliament: its romance, its comedy, its pathos*, 1902, are pot-boilers. So too is Duncan Schwann, *The spirit of parliament*, 1908.

420  DICKINSON (GOLDSWORTHY LOWES). The development of parliament during the nineteenth century. 1895.

421  JENNINGS (*Sir* WILLIAM IVOR). Parliament. Camb. 1939. 2nd edn. 1951.

Not a hist. but includes much useful hist. material. May be suppl. by *Government and opposition: a quarterly of comparative politics*, 1+, 1965+.

422  WALPOLE (*Sir* SPENCER). The electorate and the legislature. 1881. 2nd edn. 1892.

423  JENNINGS (GEORGE HENRY) *comp*. An anecdotal history of the British parliament, from the earliest periods to the present time. With notices of eminent parliamentary men, and examples of their oratory. 1880.

A rev. edn. of G. H. Jennings and William Steven Johnstone, *A book of parliamentary anecdote*, 1872. The best collection of parliamentary anecdotes, John Aye (pseud. of John Atkinson), *Humour of parliament and parliamentary elections*, 1931, is amusing but slight.

424  STONE (*Sir* JOHN BENJAMIN). Sir Benjamin Stone's pictures: records of national life and history reproduced from the collection of photographs made by Sir Benjamin Stone, M.P., with descriptive notes by Michael MacDonagh. 2 v. 1906. Vol. 2: Parliamentary scenes and portraits.

425  CURZON (GEORGE NATHANIEL), *Marquess Curzon of Kedleston*. Modern parliamentary eloquence. The Rede lecture . . . 1913.

### (b) *Debates and Procedure*

For parl. papers see **30–6**.

426  A BIBLIOGRAPHY OF PARLIAMENTARY DEBATES OF GREAT BRITAIN. Comp. by John A. Woods. House of Commons Library Document No. 2. 1956.

H. Donaldson Jordan, 'The reports of parliamentary debates, 1803–1908', *Economica*, xi (1931), 437–49, discusses the merits of *Hansard* and the other reports, but is weak on newspapers.

**427  ROSS (CHARLES). The parliamentary record. 1861–1939.**

Styled *Ross's parliamentary record*, 1876–9. A useful summary of the work of parliament, giving an account of the progress of bills and notes on parl. papers. Issued weekly during the parl. session. Superseded Joshua Toulmin Smith, *The parliamentary remembrancer*, 8 v. 1857–65, which pioneered the field.

**428  HANSARD'S PARLIAMENTARY DEBATES. Third series. 365 v. 1830–91.**

Succeeded by *The parliamentary debates (authorised edition), fourth series*, 199 v. 1892–1908. Then by *The parliamentary debates (official report)*, 1909+, which has separate vols. for Lords and Commons. The Lords ser. is numbered as a new series. The Commons ser. ranks as the fifth ser. of *Hansard*. Until 1909 there was no verbatim report of proc. and newspaper reports, particularly those of the *Daily News* and *The Times*, are often as full as those in *Hansard*.

**429  LAW (WILLIAM). Our Hansard: or, the true mirror of parliament: a full account of the official reporting of the debates in the House of Commons. 1950.**

Deals with Commons reporting since 1909. There is a history of the office of shorthand-writer to the Commons in *Second report from the select committee on publications and debates' reports* [Chairman: Sir George Toulmin]. H.C. 398 (1914–16). IV, 781. There is no adequate account of 19th-cent. reporting.

**430  THE TIMES PARLIAMENTARY DEBATES. 38 v. 1886–94.**

Separate vols. for Lords and Commons. The only reports which rivalled *Hansard* during the period. The *St Stephen's Chronicle*, 4 v., 1867, contains comparable reports but only for a single session.

**431  MAY (THOMAS ERSKINE), *Baron Farnborough*. A treatise on the law, privileges, proceedings, and usage of parliament. 1844. 11th edn. 1906. 18th edn. 1971.**

Standard.

**432  WITTKE (CARL FREDERICK). The history of English parliamentary privilege. [Columbus, Ohio]. 1921.**

**433  CLIFFORD (FREDERICK). A history of private bill legislation. 2 v. 1885–7.**

Clifford was the leading expert on private bills in his own day and the founder of the *Locus standi reports*, **436**.

**434  WILLIAMS (ORLANDO CYPRIAN). The historical development of private bill procedure and standing orders in the House of Commons. 2 v. 1948–9.**

Vol. I incl. a calendar of select committee reports and debates. Vol. II incl. a full analysis of standing orders in force and repealed.

**435  BRISTOWE (SAMUEL BOTELER). Private bill legislation: comprising the steps required to be taken by promoters or opponents of a private bill before and after its presentation to parliament . . . 1859.**

436  CLIFFORD (FREDERICK) *and* STEPHENS (PEMBROKE SCOTT). Practice of the court of referees on private bills in parliament; with reports of cases as to the locus standi of petitioners . . . 2 v. 1870–73.

Used in conjunction with James Mellor Smethurst, *A treatise on the locus standi of petitioners against private bills in parliament,* 1866, 3rd edn. 1876.

437  MACASSEY (L. LIVINGSTONE). Private bill legislation and provisional orders: handbook for the use of solicitors and engineers engaged in promoting private acts of parliament and provisional orders for the authorization of railways, tramways . . . 1887.

438  DODD (CYRIL) and WILBERFORCE (HERBERT WILLIAM WRANGHAM). Private bill procedure . . . 1898.

## 2. HOUSE OF LORDS

### (a) *General*

439  PIKE (LUKE OWEN). A constitutional history of the House of Lords from original sources. 1894.

There is no more up-to-date hist., apart from an article by Arthur Stanley Turberville, 'The House of Lords and the advent of democracy, 1837–67', *History,* xxix (1944), 152–83, repr. in his *The House of Lords in the age of reform, 1784–1837 . . .,* 1958.

440  SAINTY (J. C.). Leaders and whips in the House of Lords, 1783–1964. House of Lords Record Office memo. 31. 1964.

441  ANDERSON (OLIVE). 'The Wensleydale peerage case and the position of the House of Lords in the mid nineteenth century'. *Eng. Hist. Rev.* lxxxii (1967), 486–502. Comment by Robert Francis Vere Heuston. Ibid. lxxxiii (1968), 777–82.

For details see John Fraser MacQueen, *Discussion and judgment of the Lords on the life peerage question,* 2 pts. 1856–7.

442  PUMPHREY (RALPH E.). 'The introduction of industrialists into the British peerage: a study in adaptation of a social institution'. *Amer. Hist. Rev.* lxv (1959–60), 1–16.

443  BROMHEAD (PETER ALEXANDER). The House of Lords and contemporary politics, 1911–1957. 1958.

444  ROGERS (JAMES EDWIN THOROLD) *ed.* A complete collection of the protests of the Lords [1624–1874], with historical introductions. 3 v. Oxf. 1875.

445  PALMER (*Sir* FRANCIS BEAUFORT). Peerage law in England. 1907.

446  PEERAGE CREATIONS. Return of all the peerages created during the tenure of each government from the year 1880 down to the present time. H.L. 2 (1920). VIII, 235.

Unfortunately does not cover all creations since the last major return: *Return of all peerages of the United Kingdom . . . created since the 1st day of January 1830*, H.C. 81 (1871). LVI, 757.

447 REPRESENTATIVE PEERS. Report from the select committee of the House of Lords on the representative peerage of Scotland and Ireland. H.L. 140 (1874). VIII, 209.

For the names of representative peers see J. C. Sainty, *A list of representative peers for Scotland, 1707 to 1963, and for Ireland, 1800 to 1961*, House of Lords, Record Office memo 39, 1968.

For the Scottish peers see Fergusson (**9809**).

### (b) *Journals and Procedure*

For debates see **426–30**.

448 THE JOURNALS OF THE HOUSE OF LORDS. 1509+.
Indexed decennially.

449 MINUTES OF THE HOUSE OF LORDS. 1824+.
The daily notes on public business issued to peers.

450 LORDS COMMITTEE ON THE DESPATCH OF PUBLIC BUSI-NESS. Report from the select committee of the House of Lords appointed to consider and report, whether, by any alterations in the forms and proceedings of this House, the despatch of public business can be more effectually promoted [Chairman: Viscount Eversley]. H.C. 321 (1861). XI, 417.

Followed by a further committee on the hours of sitting, H.L. 259 (1867). XXVII, 1, and a joint committee with the Commons [Chairman: Earl Granville]. H.C. 386 (1868–9). VII, 171.

### (c) *Lords Reform*

451 ALLYN (EMILY). Lords versus Commons: a century of conflict and compromise, 1830–1930. Phila. 1931.

The best book so far, with a useful bibliography of articles and pamphlets. See also Harry Jones, *Liberalism and the House of Lords: the story of the veto battle, 1832–1911*, 1912.

452 WESTON (CORINNE COMSTOCK). 'The Liberal leadership and the Lords' veto, 1907–1911'. *Hist. J.* xi (1968), 508–37.

453 JENKINS (ROY). Mr. Balfour's poodle. An account of the struggle between the House of Lords and the government of Mr. Asquith. 1954.
Entertaining but thin.

454 ROSEBERY COMMITTEE ON LORDS REFORM, 1908. Report from the select committee on the House of Lords [Chairman: the Earl of Rosebery]. H.L. 234 (1908). X, 111.

455 BRYCE CONFERENCE. Conference on the reform of the second chamber: letter from Viscount Bryce to the Prime Minister. [Cd. 9038] H.C. (1918). X, 569.

456 BROOKES (HENRY). The peers and the people and the coming reform. 1857. 3rd edn. 1884.

A typical Radical pamphlet.

457 PRIMROSE (ARCHIBALD PHILIP), *Earl of Rosebery*. The reform of the House of Lords: three speeches delivered in that House on June 20, 1884, March 19, 1888, and March 14, 1910. 1910.

458 MACPHERSON (WILLIAM CHARTERIS). The baronage and the senate: or, the House of Lords in the past, the present, and the future. 1893.

A conservative reply to the case for reform made in Liberal speeches. A similar work is Sir William Thomas Charley, *The crusade against the constitution: an historical vindication of the House of Lords*, 1895.

459 REID (ANDREW) *ed*. The House of Lords question. 1898.

A Liberal symposium.

460 CLAYTON (JOSEPH). The bishops as legislators: a record of votes and speeches delivered by the bishops of the established church in the House of Lords during the 19th century. 1906.

George Hadfield, *The expediency of relieving the bishops from attendance in parliament illustrated by episcopal speeches and votes in the Irish Church debates of 1868 and 1869*, 1870, states the case from the point of view of the older nonconformists.

461 EDGCUMBE (*Sir* EDWARD ROBERT PEARCE). The House of Lords and the unjust veto. 1907.

A good Liberal pamphlet. Fuller are Thomas Alfred Spalding, *The House of Lords: a retrospect and a forecast*, 1894; Joseph Clayton, *The truth about the Lords: our new nobility, 1857–1907*, 1907; and Howard Evans, *Our old nobility*, 1879, 5th edn. 1907.

462 McKECHNIE (WILLIAM SHARP). The reform of the House of Lords: with a criticism of the report of the Select Committee of 2nd December, 1908. Glasgow. 1909.

A scholarly discussion of the issues at stake.

463 MUIR (JOHN RAMSAY BRYCE). Peers & bureaucrats: two problems of English government. 1910.

464 TEMPERLEY (HAROLD WILLIAM VAZEILLE). Senates and upper chambers: their use and function in the modern state, with a chapter on the reform of the House of Lords. 1910.

Compares the Lords with other second chambers. So too does Sir John Arthur Ransome Marriott, *Second chambers: an inductive study in political science*, Oxf. 1910.

465 WONTNER (ADRIAN). The Lords: their history and powers with special reference to money bills and the veto. 1910.

### 3. HOUSE OF COMMONS

#### (a) *General*

466 FRASER (PETER). 'The growth of ministerial control in the nineteenth century House of Commons'. *Eng. Hist. Rev.* lxxv (1960), 444–63.

See also Valerie Cromwell, 'The problem of supply in Great Britain in the nineteenth century', *Études présentées à la Commission Internationale pour l'Histoire des Assemblées d'États*, xxix (Paris 1966), 1–12, 'Changing parliamentary attitudes to income tax in the nineteenth century', ibid. xxxi (Louvain & Paris 1966), 35–42, and 'The private member of the House of Commons and foreign policy in the nineteenth century', ibid. xxvii (Louvain & Paris 1965), 193–218.

467 BERRINGTON (HUGH). 'Partisanship and dissidence in the nineteenth-century House of Commons'. *Parl. Affairs.* xxi (1967–8), 338–74.

Important.

468 CHESTER (DANIEL NORMAN) *and* BOWRING (NONA). Questions in parliament. Oxf. 1962.

From 1902. See also Patrick Howarth, *Questions in the house: the history of a unique British institution*, 1956, and Colin Leys, 'Petitioning in the nineteenth and twentieth centuries', *Political Studs.* iii (1955), 45–64.

469 BROMHEAD (PETER ALEXANDER). Private members' bills in the British parliament. 1956.

470 MARSDEN (PHILIP). The officers of the Commons, 1363–1965. 1966.

471 LAUNDY (PHILIP). The office of speaker. 1964.

There are also two popular books, Arthur Irwin Dasent, *The speakers of the House of Commons from the earliest times to the present day*, 1911, and Michael MacDonagh, *The speaker of the house* [1914].

472 ARNSTEIN (WALTER LEONARD). The Bradlaugh case: a study in late Victorian opinion and politics. Oxf. 1965.

A celebrated case involving the expulsion of an atheist from the Commons. See also **4008**.

473 HERBERT COMMITTEE ON OFFICES OF PROFIT. Report from the select committee on offices or places of profit under the Crown [Chairman: Sir Dennis Herbert]. H.C. 120 (1940–1). III, 487.

Includes a hist. of the disqualification of members for accepting an office of profit. Alfred Beaven Beaven, 'List of opposed elections on taking office', *Eng. Hist. Rev.* xxvi (1911), 139–48, deals with the re-election of ministers who had vacated their seat on accepting office. *Report from the select committee on House of Commons (vacating of seats)* [Chairman: H. H. Asquith]. H.C. 278 (1894). XII, 397 and H.C. 272 (1895). X, 561, deals with vacating of seats by ordinary members.

474 THOMAS (JOHN ALUN). The House of Commons, 1832–1901: a study of its economic and functional character. Cardiff. 1939.

Cont. in his *The House of Commons, 1906–1911: an analysis of its economic and social character*, Cardiff. 1958. Concerned solely with the 'interests' represented in the House.

Earlier ventures in the same style are in the *Financial reform almanack and year book* [Liverpool 1851–1912], from 1872; *The parliamentary directory of the professional commercial and mercantile members of the House of Commons*, 1874; and Harold Richard Goring Greaves, 'Personal origins and interrelations of the Houses of Parliament (since 1832)', *Economica*. ix (1929), 173–84.

475 WANG (CHI KAO). Dissolution of the British parliament, 1832–1931. N.Y. 1934.

476 WITMER (HELEN ELIZABETH). The property qualifications of members of parliament. N.Y. 1943.

### (b) *Journals*

477 JOURNALS OF THE HOUSE OF COMMONS. 1547+

The official minutes of the House, giving membership of committees. Indexed decennially. Ross (**427**), is often more useful in tracing the progress of a bill. *The votes and proceedings of the House of Commons*, 1680+, are excessively brief. There is a useful memorandum on the Commons *Journals* in *Report from the select committee on publications and debates' reports* [Chairman: Sir George Toulmin]. H.C. 321 (1914–16). IV, 665. But the best guide is David Menhennet, *The Journal of the House of Commons: a bibliographical and historical guide*, House of Commons Libr. doc. 7, 1971.

### (c) *Reports of Proceedings*

Arranged in chronological order. For debates see **426–30**.

478 WHITTY (EDWARD MICHAEL). St Stephen's in the fifties: the session 1852–3: a parliamentary retrospect. 1906.

Originally publ. as *History of the session 1852–1853 . . .*, 1854. His *The governing classes of Great Britain: political portraits*, 1854, 2nd edn. 1859, deals mainly with the following session.

479 WHITE (WILLIAM). The inner life of the House of Commons (1856–71). Ed. by Justin McCarthy. 2 v. 1897.

White was doorkeeper to the House.

480 DENISON (JOHN EVELYN), *Viscount Ossington*. Notes from my journal when Speaker of the House of Commons [1857–72]. priv. pr. 1899.

481 JEANS (WILLIAM). Parliamentary reminiscences [1863–86]. 1912.

The memoirs of an indifferent journalist. Sir Alexander Mackintosh, *From Gladstone to Lloyd George: parliament in peace and war* [1881–1921], 1921, and *Echoes of Big Ben: a journalist's parliamentary diary, 1881–1940*, [1945], are works in the same class. So are Sir Thomas Wemyss Reid, *Cabinet portraits . . .*, 1872, and *Politicians of today . . .*, 2 v. 1879–80.

482 LUCY (*Sir* HENRY WILLIAM). Men and manner in parliament. 1874. 2nd edn. 1919.

The first of Lucy's justly famous reports. Deals with the 1874 session. Later chronicles are *A diary of two parliaments: the Disraeli parliament, 1874–1880*, 1885, 2nd edn. 1885, *A diary of two parliaments: the Gladstone parliament, 1880–1885*, 1885, 2nd edn. 1886, *A diary of the Salisbury parliament, 1886–1892*, 1892, *A diary of the Home Rule parliament, 1892–1895, 1896, A diary of the Unionist parliament, 1895–1900,* Bristol 1901, and *The Balfourian parliament, 1900–1905,* 1906. Lucy also publ. two retrospective vols: *Peeps at parliament taken from behind the Speaker's chair* [1893–5], 1903, and *Later peeps at parliament . . .* [1896–1902], 1904, as well as vols. of reminiscences (**5440**).

483 O'CONNOR (THOMAS POWER). Gladstone's House of Commons [1880–5]. 1885.

O'Connor also publ. *Sketches in the House: the story of a memorable session* [1892], 1893.

484 LOWTHER (JAMES WILLIAM), *Viscount Ullswater.* A Speaker's commentaries. 2 v. 1925.

M.P. 1883–5, 1886–1921. Speaker 1905–21. A good account of his years in the House before and after he became Speaker.

485 TEMPLE (*Sir* RICHARD). Letters & character sketches from the House of Commons: Home Rule and other matters in 1886–1887. Ed. by Sir Richard Carnac Temple. 1912.

Much better than his *Life in parliament . . .,* 1893, and *The House of Commons,* 1899. Cp. Charles Wallwyn Radcliffe Cooke, *Four years in parliament* [1885–9] *with hard labour,* 1890, 3rd edn. 1891.

486 GRIFFITH-BOSCAWEN (*Sir* ARTHUR SACKVILLE TREVOR). Fourteen years in parliament [1892–1906]. 1907.

See also his *Memories* (**847**).

487 HOPE (JAMES FITZALAN), *Baron Rankeillour.* A history of the 1900 parliament. vol. 1 1900–1901. 1908.

No more publ.

488 ERSKINE (BEATRICE CAROLINE), *Mrs Steuart Erskine, ed.* The memoirs of Sir David Erskine of Cardross, K.C.V.O. 1926.

Serjeant-at-arms, 1885–1915. Thin.

### (d) *Procedure*

489 REDLICH (JOSEF). The procedure of the House of Commons: a study of its history and present form . . . Trans. by A. Ernest Steinthal. Suppl. by Sir Courtenay Peregrine Ilbert. 3 v. 1908.

Standard.

490 CAMPION (GILBERT FRANCIS MONTRIOU), *Baron Campion.* An introduction to the procedure of the House of Commons. [1929]. 3rd edn. 1958.

The best modern work on the subject.

491 HUGHES (EDWARD). 'The changes in parliamentary procedure, 1880–1882'. In Essays presented to Sir Lewis Namier. Ed. by Richard Pares and Alan John Percivale Taylor. 1956. 289–319.

**492  ADDISON (WILLIAM GEORGE CLIBBENS).** 'The parliamentary oath'. Theology xlii (1941). 217–24.

For fuller treatment see Arnstein (472).

**493  BOURKE (ROBERT),** *Baron Connemara.* Parliamentary precedents: being decisions of the Right Honourable Charles Shaw Lefevre, Speaker of the House of Commons, on points of order, rules of debate, and the general practice of the House. 1857. 2nd edn. [Decisions . . .] 1857.

**494  BLACKMORE (EDWIN GORDON).** The decisions of the Right Hon. John Evelyn Denison, Speaker of the House of Commons (April 30, 1857–February 8, 1872), and of the Right Hon. Sir Henry Bouverie William Brand, G.C.B., Speaker of the House of Commons (February 9, 1872–February 25, 1884), on points of order, rules of debate, and the general practice of the House. Adelaide. 1892.

For Speaker Brand's papers see D. J. Johnson, comp., *The letters and diaries of Speaker Brand, 1855 to 1892: a list,* House of Lords Record Office memo 43, 1970.

**495  BLACKMORE (EDWIN GORDON).** The decisions of the Right Hon. Arthur Wellesley Peel, Speaker of the House of Commons, from his election to the Speakership, February 26, 1884, to his retirement from the chair, April 9, 1895, on points of order, rules of debate, and the general practice of the House . . . Adelaide. 1900.

### (e) *Members of Parliament*

Monographs on Welsh, Scottish, and Irish members will be found in the appropriate national section.

**496  MEMBERS OF PARLIAMENT.** Return of the names of every member returned to serve in each parliament from the year 1696 up to the present time . . . Pt. II [1801–74] H.C. 69-1 (1878). LXII. Pt. II. Index and Lists for 1880–5 H.C. 169 (1890–1). LXII, 281.

Known as *The official return of members of parliament.* Suppls. carry the return down to 1929: [1885–1900] H.C. 365 (1901). LIX, 231. [1900–6] H.C. 334 (1908). LXXXVII, 853. [1906–10] H.C. 250 (1911). LXII, 639. [1910–18] H.C. 183 (1919). XL, 767. [1919–22] H.C. 97 (1923). XIX, 201. [1922–3] H.C. 134 (1924). XVIII, 869. [1923–4] H.C. 123 (1924–5). XXII, 525. [1924–9] H.C. 56 (1929–30). XXIV, 1.

**497  VACHER'S PARLIAMENTARY COMPANION. 1833+.**

Gives names and addresses of members of both Houses. Publ. monthly during session.

**498  DOD (CHARLES ROGER PHIPPS).** The parliamentary companion. 1832+. Annual.

Styled *The parliamentary pocket companion,* 1832–42, and *Dod's parliamentary companion,* 1865 +. Justly celebrated. Edward Walford publ. a poor man's *Dod* with a bare minimum of biographical information as [*Hardwicke's*] *shilling House of Commons,* 1856–99.

**499 DEBRETT'S HOUSE OF COMMONS AND THE JUDICIAL BENCH. 1867–1931.**

Prints arms claimed (often quite wrongly) by members and includes information not in *Dod*. Handsomely produced.

**500 THE TIMES. The new House of Commons. 1880+.**

Title changed to *The Times House of Commons*, 1910. Edns. for 1880, 1885, 1886 publ. by *The Times*; 1892, 1895, 1900, 1901 repr. from *The Times* by Macmillans, 1910+ again published by *The Times*. No issue for the 1906 election. Contains a useful introduction on the events leading up to the election. Biographies of M.P.s very brief. Superseded *The New Parliament: guide to the House of Commons*, publ. by P. S. King, the parliamentary printers, in 1857, 1859, 1868. Outlived *The popular guide to the [new] House of Commons . . .* publ. by the *Pall Mall Gazette* as an *Extra*, irregularly 1885–1910, with pen and ink sketches and maps, and rather more information about some M.P.s.

**501 SAUNDERS (WILLIAM). The new parliament, 1880. 1880.**

Includes an excellent introduction on the election. *Ward and Lock's guide to the House of Commons*, 1880, 1881, 1882, 1886, prints biographies of members in much the same way and may be regarded as a companion to it.

**502 COX (HAROLD). Parliamentary pictures and personalities: 'Graphic' illustrations of parliament, 1890–1893, containing one hundred and thirty-five character sketches by Reginald Cleaver, Sydney P. Hall, Paul Renouard, H. W. Brewer, and other artists, and over six hundred portraits of members of the present House of Commons. 1893.**

**503 ROBERTS (THOMAS NICOLLS). The parliamentary buff book. 1866–81. Annual.**

An analysis of the division lists of the House of Commons.

**504 THE PARLIAMENTARY GAZETTE. February 1905–July 1942. Thrice yearly.**

Title *The premier parliamentary record and review* for first two numbers, *The premier parliamentary gazette and review* for Nos. 3 and 4. Like the earlier *The parliamentary chronicle . . .*, 1882–3, gives a concise account of proceedings in both houses, votes of members, and misc. information similar to that in *The constitutional year book* (**256**). Chiefly useful for the voting behaviour of M.P.s.

**505 BEAN (WILLIAM WARDELL). The parliamentary representation of the six northern counties of England . . . and their cities and boroughs. From 1603, to the general election of 1886. With lists of members and biographical notices. Hull. 1890.**

Useful for local connections of members and election results which are often given in great detail for pre-1872 elections. Other studies of English constituencies are:

*For counties:*

Cornwall. William Thomas Lawrance, *Parliamentary representation of Cornwall . . . 1295 to 1885 . . .*, Truro [1926].

Cumberland and Westmorland. Richard Saul Ferguson, *Cumberland and Westmorland M.P.s from the Restoration to the Reform Bill of 1867*, 1871.

Essex. George Caunt, *Essex in parliament*, Chelmsford 1969.

*Gloucestershire.* William Retlaw Williams, *The parliamentary history of the county of Gloucester* . . ., *1213–1898* . . ., Hereford 1898. Cont. to 1929 by Sir Francis Adams Hyett, *Members of parliament for Gloucestershire and Bristol, 1900–1929* . . ., [1930].

*Herefordshire.* William Retlaw Williams, *The parliamentary history of the county of Hereford* . . ., *1213–1896* . . ., Brecknock 1896.

*Lancashire.* William Duncombe Pink and Alfred Beaven Beaven, *The parliamentary representation of Lancashire, county and borough, 1258–1885* . . ., 1889.

*Lancashire, Eccles Div.* J. Brierley Watson, *The member for Eccles*, Eccles 1964.

*Oxfordshire.* William Retlaw Williams, *The parliamentary history of the county of Oxford* . . ., *1213–1899* . . ., Brecknock 1899.

*Worcestershire.* William Retlaw Williams, *The parliamentary history of the county of Worcester* . . ., *1213–1897* . . ., Hereford 1897.

*For boroughs:*

*Ashburton.* Harold John Hanham, 'Ashburton as a parliamentary borough, 1640–1868', *Devonshire Assoc. Trans.* xcviii (1966), 206–56.

*Coventry.* Thomas Walker Whitley, *The parliamentary representation of the city of Coventry from the earliest times to present date*, Coventry 1894.

*Dewsbury.* Christopher J. James, *M.P. for Dewsbury: one hundred years of parliamentary representation*, the author 1970.

*Honiton.* W. H. Wilkin, 'Notes on the members for Honiton, 1640–1868', *Devonshire Assoc. Trans.* lxvi (1934), 253–78.

*Horsham.* See **644**.

*Hythe.* George Wilks, *The barons of the Cinque Ports and the parliamentary representation of Hythe*, Folkestone [1892].

*Lambeth.* George Hill, *The electoral history of the borough of Lambeth* . . ., 1879.

*Preston.* William Dobson, *History of the parliamentary representation of Preston*, 2nd edn. Preston 1868.

*Reading.* Arthur Aspinall and others, *Parliament through seven centuries: Reading and its M.P.s*, 1962.

*Rochester.* Frederick Francis Smith, *Rochester in parliament, 1295–1933* . . . *also the borough of Chatham, 1832 to 1918*, 1933.

*Tiverton.* See **644**.

For the functioning of the electoral system in particular constituencies see **652**.

## E. POLITICAL PARTIES

### 1. GENERAL

506   JENNINGS (*Sir* WILLIAM IVOR). Party politics. 3 v. Camb. 1960–2.

A general history of British politics written from a lawyer's point of view, rather than a hist. of party.

507   BULMER-THOMAS (IVOR). The growth of the British party system. 2 v. 1965. 2nd edn. 2 v. 1967.

A convenient summary of the literature of the subject. Alan Beattie, ed., *English party politics*, 2 v. 1970, is a coll. of docs.

508   OSTROGORSKI (MOISEI). Democracy and the organization of political parties. Trans. by Frederick Clark. 2 v. 1902.

A famous attack on machine-politics, including a description of the rise of the 'caucus' in Britain in the 1870s and 1880s. For a modern account of the same process, see Hanham (**643**).

509  McKENZIE (ROBERT TRELFORD). British political parties: the distribution of power within the Conservative and Labour parties. 1955. 2nd edn. 1963.

Primarily concerned with post-1945 parties, but includes much background information on the Conservative and Labour parties.

510  BELLOC ([JOSEPH] HILAIRE [PIERRE RENÉ]) and CHESTER-TON (CECIL EDWARD). The party system. 1911.

A pungent attack. Best read with Belloc's political novels, *Emmanuel Burden*, 1904, and *Mr Clutterbuck's election*, 1908, and with Chesterton's *Gladstonian ghosts*, 1905, an attack on Liberal nonconformity, and *Party and people: a criticism of the recent elections and their consequences*, 1910.

511  CAMBRAY (PHILIP GEORGE). The game of politics: a study of the principles of British political strategy. 1932.

512  CRAWSHAY (W. S.) *and* READ (F. W.). The politics of the Commons: compiled from the election addresses, speeches, etc., of the present members. [1886].

513  HANHAM (HAROLD JOHN). 'The sale of honours in late Victorian England'. Victorian Studs. iii (1959–60), 277–89.

## 2. THE LIBERAL PARTY

514  BULLOCK (*Sir* ALAN LOUIS CHARLES) and SHOCK (MAURICE) *eds*. The Liberal tradition from Fox to Keynes. 1956.

Docs. Suppl. by Simon MacCoby, ed., *The English radical tradition, 1763–1914*, 1952, also a vol. of docs.

515  McCALLUM (RONALD BUCHANAN). The Liberal party from Earl Grey to Asquith. 1963.

Recent, but does not replace Walter Lyon Blease, *A short history of English liberalism*, 1913, or Henry Hamilton Fyfe, *The British Liberal party: an historical sketch*, 1928. Sir Henry Herman Slesser, *A history of the Liberal party* [1944], is of little value. Roy Douglas, *The history of the Liberal party, 1895–1970*, Lond. and Cranbury, N.J. 1971, is partisan but fuller for its period.

516  MACCOBY (SIMON). English radicalism 1853–1886. 1938.

Companion vols. are *English radicalism, 1886–1914*, 1953; *English radicalism, 1786–1832*, 1955; and *English radicalism, 1762–1785*, 1955. Covers a very wide range of radical activities not very coherently. Older books are John Morrison Davidson, *Eminent radicals in and out of parliament*, 1880, William Harris, *The history of the radical party in parliament*, 1885, and Clement Boulton Roylance Kent, *The English radicals: an historical sketch*, 1899.

517  SOUTHGATE (DONALD GEORGE). The passing of the Whigs, 1832–1886. 1962.

Biographical in emphasis.

518  VINCENT (JOHN RUSSELL). The formation of the Liberal party, 1857–1868. 1966.

A stimulating work of the greatest interest. See also William Evan Williams, *The rise of Gladstone to the leadership of the Liberal party, 1859 to 1868*, Camb. 1934, and J. M. Prest, 'Gladstone and Russell', *Roy. Hist. Soc. Trans.*, 5 ser. 16 (1966), 43–64. For another good modern study, of a later period, see Shannon, *Gladstone and the Bulgarian agitation* (**293**).

519  HAMER (DAVID ALAN). Liberal politics in the age of Gladstone and Rosebery: a study in leadership and policy. Oxf. 1972.

See also Henry Colin Gray Matthew, *The Liberal imperialists: the ideas and politics of a post-Gladstonian elite*, 1973, and Hugh Vincent Emy, *Liberals, Radicals and social politics, 1892–1914*, Camb. 1973.

520  STANSKY (PETER [DAVID LYMAN]). Ambitions and strategies: the struggle for the leadership of the Liberal party in the 1890s. Oxf. 1964.

See also Kenneth Owen Morgan, 'John Morley and the crisis of Liberalism, 1894', *Nat. Libr. Wales J.* xv (1967–9), 451–65.

521  CLARKE (PETER FREDERICK). Lancashire and the new Liberalism. 1971.

An important and wide-ranging study of the end of the 19th cent. and the early 20th cent. There is a shortage of books on the early 20th cent. But see Michael Craton and Herbert William McCready, *The great Liberal revival, 1903–6*, Hansard Soc. 1966, John Frederic Glaser, 'English nonconformity and the decline of Liberalism', *Amer. Hist. Rev.* lxiii (1957–8), 352–63, Dangerfield (**295**), Masterman (**294**), and Trevor Gordon Wilson, *The downfall of the Liberal party, 1914–1935*, Lond. & Ithaca, N.Y. 1966.

522  BARDOUX (JACQUES). L'Angleterre radicale: essai de psychologie sociale (1906–1913). Paris. 1913.

A sequel to his *Essai d'une psychologie de l'Angleterre contemporaine:* Vol. I. *Les crises belliqueuses* [1815–1900], Paris, 1906; vol. II. *Les crises politiques: protectionnisme et radicalisme* [1900–5], Paris, 1907, both of which deal extensively with Radical attitudes.

523  QUESTIONS FOR A REFORMED PARLIAMENT. 1867.

An able symposium by a group of young Liberals. See also *Essays on reform*, 1867, by the same group. Some of the essays were repr. in Wilhelm Leo Guttsman, ed., *A plea for democracy: an edited selection from the 1867 essays of reform and questions for a reformed parliament*, 1967.

524  REID (ANDREW) ed. Why I am a Liberal: being, definitions and personal confessions of faith by the best minds of the Liberal party. [1885].

525  THE RADICAL PROGRAMME: with a preface by the Rt. Hon. Joseph Chamberlain. 1885. New edn. ed. by David Alan Hamer. Brighton. 1971.

For the background of this most famous of all Radical programmes see Christopher Henry Durham Howard, 'Joseph Chamberlain and the "unauthorized programme"', *Eng. Hist. Rev.*, lxv (1950), 477–91. Cp. Sir Charles Wentworth Dilke, *A radical programme*, 1890.

526 BUXTON (SYDNEY CHARLES), *Earl Buxton, ed.* The Imperial parliament. 10 v. 1885–8.

This useful series deals with the problems foremost in the minds of moderate Liberals before the Home Rule split in 1886. The vols. are: 1. John Douglas Sutherland Campbell, Marquess of Lorne, later Duke of Argyll, *Imperial federation*, 1885; 2. Sir John Lubbock, Baron Avebury, *Representation*, 1885, 2nd edn. 1890; 3. William Rathbone, Albert Pell [a Tory] and Francis Charles Montague, *Local government and taxation*, 1885; 4. William Edward Baxter, *England and Russia in Asia*, 1885; 5. Margaret Mary Dilke [Mrs. Ashton Dilke] and William Woodall, *Women's suffrage*, 1885; 6. William Sproston Caine, William Hoyle, and Dawson Burns, *Local option*, 1885, 6th edn. 1909; 7. Henry Broadhurst and Robert Threshie Reid, Earl Loreburn, *Leasehold enfranchisement*, 1885; 8. Henry Richard and John Carvell Williams, *Disestablishment*, 1885; 9. Joseph Firth Bottomley Firth, *Reform of London government and of city guilds*, 1888; 10. Albert Grey, Earl Grey, and William Henry Fremantle, eds., *Church reform*, 1888.

527 BELLOC ([JOSEPH] HILAIRE [PIERRE RENÉ]) *and others.* Essays in Liberalism, by six Oxford men. 1897.

Essays by Belloc, F. W. Hirst, J. A. Simon (Viscount Simon), J. S. Phillimore, J. L. Hammond, and P. J. Macdonel. Followed by Francis Wrigley Hirst, Gilbert Murray, and J. L. Hammond, *Liberalism and the empire: three essays*, 1900, an anti-imperialist tract.

528 SAMUEL (HERBERT LOUIS), *Viscount Samuel.* Liberalism: an attempt to state the principles and proposals of contemporary Liberalism in England. 1902.

529 HOBSON (JOHN ATKINSON). The crisis of Liberalism: new issues of democracy. 1909.

An attack on the complacency and imperialism of the Liberal leaders. See also **8486**.

530 HOBHOUSE (LEONARD TRELAWNEY). Liberalism. Home Univ. Libr. 1911.

531 ROBERTSON (JOHN MACKINNON). The meaning of Liberalism. 1912. 2nd edn. 1925.

Samuel (**528**), Hobhouse (**530**), and Robertson, although differing in their approach, contain the 'classical' exposition of post-Gladstonian Liberalism. The Conservative reaction to it is most strongly expressed in Al. Carthill, [pseud. of Bennet Christian Huntingdon Calcraft Kennedy], *The legacy of Liberalism*, 1924.

532 FAGAN (LOUIS). The Reform Club, 1836–1886: its founders and architect. 1887.

Histories of other Liberal clubs are, Robert Steven, *The National Liberal Club: politics and persons* [1925], Christopher John Laurence Brock and Sir Gilbert Hollinshead Blomfield Jackson, *A history of the Cobden club*, 1939, Henry Turner Waddy, *The Devonshire Club and 'Crockford's'*, 1919, and William Haslam Mills, ed., *The Manchester Reform Club, 1871–1921 . . .*, priv. pr. Manch. 1922. *Memorials of Brooks's from the foundation of the club, 1764, to the close of the nineteenth century, compiled from the records of the club*, 1907, consists chiefly of annotated lists of members of the main citadel of Whiggism.

**533** WATSON (ROBERT SPENCE). The National Liberal Federation: from its commencement to the general election of 1906. 1907.

Watson was president of the Federation 1890–1901. Percy Corder, *The life of Robert Spence Watson*, 1914, gives further details. See also Francis H. Herrick 'The origins of the National Liberal Federation', *J. Mod. Hist.* xvii (1945), 116–29, and Barry McGill, 'Francis Schnadhorst and Liberal party organisation', ibid. xxxiv (1962), 19–39. The main sources are *Proceedings attending the formation of the national federation of Liberal associations*, Birmingham 1877, the *Annual report*, 1879–88, and *Proceedings in connection with the . . . annual meeting*, 1889–1930.

**534** THE LIBERAL AND RADICAL YEAR BOOK and statesman's encyclopaedia. 1887–9. Repr. Brighton. 1971.

The 1889 edition was styled *The political world yearbook*. With *The Liberal year book*, 1887–9, rept. Brighton 1971. an indispensable source of information about Liberal political organizations in the 1880s. There is no connection between them and the later *Liberal year book* (**535**).

**535** THE LIBERAL YEAR BOOK. 1905–39. Repr. Brighton. 1971–2.

An official directory publ. by the Liberal Publication Dept.

**536** THE LIBERAL MAGAZINE. 1893+. Monthly.

A handbook for Liberal speakers and candidates equivalent to the Conservative *National union gleanings* (**556**). The bound annual vols. were accompanied by an invaluable vol. of *Pamphlets and leaflets*, 1894–1924. *The Liberal monthly*, 1906–20, was also issued by the Liberal Publication Dept.

**537** HUDSON. Sir Robert Hudson: a memoir. By John Alfred Spender. 1930.

Hudson was a full-time official of the National Liberal Federation from 1886 and head of the party organization, 1893–1927.

**538** HOWES. Twenty-five years' fight with the Tories. By Joseph Howes. Leeds & Morecambe. 1907.

The political record of an agent of the National Reform Union, a Liberal body.

**539** TWEEDIE. Yesterday: retrospect and rumination. By George Richard Tweedie. [1932].

The memoirs of a professional science lecturer who became a Liberal party agent.

### 3. THE LIBERAL UNIONISTS

There is no history. The lives of the Chamberlains and Hartington, (**749–50, 778**), are the nearest substitute.

**540** FRASER (PETER). 'The Liberal Unionist alliance: Chamberlain, Hartington and the Conservatives, 1886–1904'. *Eng. Hist. Rev.* lxxvii (1962), 53–78.

**541** LIBERAL UNIONIST COUNCIL. Memoranda. 1893–1912.

Suppl. by leaflets. Similar in character to *National union gleanings* (**556**), with which it was merged in 1912. The Liberal Unionist Association also publ. many pamphlets, 1886–92, and a short-lived journ., *The Liberal Unionist*, 1887–92, ed. by John St. Loe Strachey of the *Spectator*.

4. THE CONSERVATIVE PARTY

542  BLOCK (GEOFFREY DAVID MAURICE). A source book of conservatism. Conservative Political Centre. 1964.

Includes full bibliog. Suppl. in *Swinton Journal*, xiv (1968–9), pt. 4, 32–6. See also the *Constitutional year book* (**256**).

543  WHITE (REGINALD JAMES) *ed*. The Conservative tradition. 1950.

Documents.

544  BLAKE (ROBERT), *Baron Blake*. The Conservative party from Peel to Churchill. Lond. 1970. N.Y. 1971.

545  CORNFORD (JAMES PETERS). 'The transformation of Conservatism in the late nineteenth century', *Victorian Studs*. vii (1963–4). 35–66.

See also his 'The parliamentary foundations of the Hotel Cecil', in Robson, *Ideas and Institutions* (**177**), 268–311, 'The adoption of mass organization by the British Conservative party' in Erik Allardt and Yrjö Littunen, *Cleavages, ideologies and party systems*, Westermarck Soc. X, Helsinki 1964, pp. 400–24, and 'Aggregate election data and British party alignments, 1885–1910', in Erik Allardt and Stein Rokkan, eds., *Mass politics: studies in political sociology*, N.Y. & Lond. 1970, pp. 107–16.

546  McDOWELL (ROBERT BRENDAN). British conservatism, 1832–1914. 1959.

An analysis of the views of Conservative journalists and writers. Fossey John Cobb Hearnshaw, *Conservatism in England: an analytical, historical and political survey*, 1933, is an older work, thin on the 19th cent. Thomas Edward Kebbel, *A history of Toryism from the accession of Mr. Pitt to power in 1789 to the death of Lord Beaconsfield in 1881*, 1886, and *Lord Beaconsfield and other Tory memories*, 1907, are fuller at some points, but add little. Maurice Woods, *A history of the Tory party . . .*, [1924], has only a single chapter on the 19th cent.

547  CECIL (*Lord* HUGH RICHARD HEATHCOTE GASCOYNE-). Conservatism. Home Univ. Libr. 1912.

One of a number of thoughtful books, resulting from the rethinking forced on the Conservative party by the defeats of 1910. The best of the others are Sir [George] Geoffrey Gilbert Butler, *The Tory tradition: Bolingbroke, Burke, Disraeli, Salisbury*, 1914, repr. 1957, Sir Keith Grahame Feiling, *Toryism: a political dialogue*, 1913, and John McFarland Kennedy, *Tory democracy*, 1911. *Unionist policy and other essays*, by Frederick Edwin Smith, Earl of Birkenhead, 1913, also belongs to the same period, but is less coherent as a statement of the Conservative viewpoint.

548  FEUCHTWANGER (EDGAR JOSEPH) Disraeli, democracy and the Tory party: Conservative leadership and organisation after the second Reform Bill. Oxf. 1968.

Good. For Conservative organization after 1885 see Chilston, *Chief Whip* (**736**), and R. B. Jones, 'Balfour's reform of party organization', *Inst. Hist. Res. Bull*. xxxviii (1965), 94–101.

**549   SMITH (PAUL). Disraelian Conservatism and social reform. Lond. & Toronto. 1967.**

A good study of an important subject. See also Robert Trelford McKenzie and Allan Silver, *Angels in marble: working-class Conservatives in urban England*, 1968.

**550   GORST (HAROLD EDWARD). The fourth party. 1906.**

A history of the activities of Lord Randolph Churchill, Arthur Balfour, Sir Henry Drummond Wolff, and John Gorst in the parliament of 1880–5. See also Francis H. Herrick, 'Lord Randolph Churchill and the popular organization of the Conservative party, *Pacific Hist. Rev.* xv (1946), 178–91, William John Wilkinson, *Tory democracy*, N.Y. 1925, and Standish O'Grady, *Toryism and the Tory democracy*, 1886.

**551   BLEWETT (NEAL). 'Free fooders, Balfourites, whole hoggers: factionalism within the Unionist party, 1906–10'. *Hist. J.*, xi (1968), 95–124.**

See also Peter Fraser, 'The Unionist debacle of 1911 and Balfour's retirement', *J. Mod. Hist.* xxxv (1963), 354–65 and Richard A. Rempel, *Unionists divided: Arthur Balfour, Joseph Chamberlain and the Unionist Free Traders*, Newton Abbot 1972.

**552   ROBB (JANET HENDERSON). The Primrose League, 1883–1906. N.Y. 1942.**

Based on the records of the League and the *Primrose League Gazette*, 1887+. Useful bibliog.

**553   PETRIE (*Sir* CHARLES ALEXANDER). The Carlton club. 1955.**

See also Philip George Cambray, *Club days and ways; the story of the Constitutional Club, London, 1883–1962*, 1963. The only full history of a provincial conservative club is Frederick Stancliffe Stancliffe *John Shaw's, 1738–1938*, Manch. 1938.

**554   THE CAMPAIGN GUIDE . . . a handbook for Unionist speakers. Edin. 1892. 14th edn. 1922.**

Major revisions were 5th edn. 1894, 8th edn. 1900. An official Conservative publication. Suppl. by *The Unionist record: a fighting brief for Unionist candidates and speakers, 1895–1900*, [1900], 2nd edn. *1895–1905*, [1910].

**555   NATIONAL UNION [OF CONSERVATIVE AND CONSTITUTIONAL ASSOCIATIONS]. Publications. 1868+.**

The only complete set is in the Conservative Res. Dept. Libr. The reports of the annual conference were not publ. until 1947.

**556   NATIONAL UNION [OF CONSERVATIVE AND CONSTITUTIONAL ASSOCIATIONS]. National Union gleanings. 1893–1939.**

Title changed to *Gleanings and memoranda*, 1912–33, then *Politics in review*. Mainly extracts from speeches and the press. The Liberal counterpart was *The Liberal magazine* (**536**). Suppl. by *The Conservative*, 1905–14 (entitled *The Conservative and Unionist*, 1907–12, *Our flag*, 1912–14) and by *Notes for speakers*, 1904+.

**557   ASSOCIATION OF CONSERVATIVE CLUBS. Conservative clubs gazette. 1895+.**

First 33 nos. entitled *Monthly circular*.

## 5. SOCIALISM, THE LABOUR PARTY, AND WORKING-CLASS POLITICS

### (a) *General*

558 INTERNATIONAL INSTITUTE OF SOCIAL HISTORY LIBRARY, AMSTERDAM. Alfabetische catalogus van de boeken en brochures van het Internationaal Instituut voor Sociale Geschiedenis. 12 v. Boston. 1970.

The main library specializing in socialism.

559 SOCIETY FOR THE STUDY OF LABOUR HISTORY. Bulletin. 1+. Sheffield. 1960+.

Incl. an annual bibliog. and retrospective bibliogs. to 1945. The main source for articles is *Int. Rev. Soc. Hist.* 1+, Amsterdam 1956+. For biography see **6592 a.**

560 BROPHY (JAQUELINE). 'Bibliography of British labor and radical journals, 1880–1914'. *Labor Hist.* iii (1962). 103–26.

561 EDWARDS (JOSEPH). The Labour annual, 1895 [–1900]: a year book of industrial progress and social welfare. Manch. 1894–9.

Cont. as *The reformer's year book for* 1901[–9], 1900–8 and *The Daily News year book*, 1910–13. The ser. was repr. Brighton 1971.

562 COLE (GEORGE DOUGLAS HOWARD). A history of socialist thought. 5 v. in 7. 1953–60.

The standard British history of socialism in all countries. Useful bibliogs. As informative on organizations as on ideas. But see also Adam Bruno Ulam, *Philosophical foundations of English socialism*, Camb., Mass. 1951. Harry Wellington Laidler, *A history of socialist thought*, 1927, is still useful at some points.

563 BEER (MAX). A history of British Socialism 2 v. 1919. Rev. edn. 1929.

Largely supplanted by Cole (**562**) but still useful. See also Joseph Clayton, *The rise and decline of socialism in Great Britain, 1884–1924*, 1926, an account of the gradual move away from socialism in the labour movement, and two Marxist works: Arthur Leslie Morton and George Tate, *The British labour movement, 1770–1920: a history*, 1956, and Theodore A. Rothstein, *From Chartism to Labourism, historical sketches of the English working-class movement*, 1929.

564 ENSOR (*Sir* ROBERT CHARLES KIRKWOOD) *ed.* Modern socialism, as set forth by socialists in their speeches, writings and programmes. 1904. 3rd edn. 1910.

A useful collection. See also Henry Mathison Pelling, ed., *The challenge of socialism* [1954], James Bavington Jefferys, ed., *Labour's formative years . . . 1849–1879 . . .*, and Eric John Ernest Hobsbawm, ed., *Labour's turning point . . . 1880–1900 . . .*, vols. II and III of the History in the making series, ed. by Dona Torr, 1948, and Cole and Filson (**6592**).

565 COLE (GEORGE DOUGLAS HOWARD). British working-class politics, 1832–1914. 1941.

Extremely useful. Like Keith Hutchison, *Labour in politics*, 1925, which was a pioneer short handbook, relies heavily on Arthur Wilfrid Humphrey, *A history of labour representation*, 1912, which, although rather out of date, is still useful.

566  BRIGGS (ASA) *and* SAVILLE (JOHN) *eds.* Essays in Labour history in memory of G. D. H. Cole, 25 September 1889–14 January 1959. 1960. 2 ser. [1886–1923] 1971.

567  GILLESPIE (FRANCES ELMA). Labor and politics in England, 1850–1867. Durham, N.C. 1927. Repr. N.Y. 1966.

For the later years of the Chartist movement see also the lives of Harney and Jones (**595–6**). The Chartist movement generally is dealt with in the previous vol. of this bibliog.

568  HARRISON (ROYDEN). Before the socialists: studies in labour and politics, 1861–1881. 1965.

569  COLLINS (HENRY) and ABRAMSKY (CHIMEN). Karl Marx and the British labour movement: years of the First International. 1965.

See also Chimen Abramsky, 'Survey of literature on the First International since 1945', *Soc. Study of Labour Hist. Bull.*, no. 9 (1964), 11–23, suppl. by A. M. Johnstone, ibid., no. 11 (1965), 76–81, *Documents on the First International . . .*, 5 v. Moscow, 1962–8, and Julius Braunthal, *History of the International, 1864–1914*, trans. by Henry Collins and Kenneth Mitchell, 1967. On Marx's daughter see Chushichi Tsuzuki, *The life of Eleanor Marx, 1855–1898: a socialist tragedy*, 1967. On Engels there is a good study, Siegfried Bünger, *Friedrich Engels und die britische sozialistische Bewegung, 1881–1895*, Berlin 1962.

570  GRENDI (EDOARDO). L'avvento del laburismo: il movimento operaio inglese dal 1880 al 1920. Milan. 1964.

Chiefly concerned with the differences between English and continental labour movements.

571  PELLING (HENRY MATHISON). The origins of the Labour party, 1880–1900. London. 1954. 2nd edn. Oxf. 1965.

Indispensable. Good bibliog. Pelling and Poirier (**572**) replace John Hotchkiss Stewart Reid, *The origins of the British Labour party*, Minneapolis, 1955, and Godfrey Elton, Baron Elton, *England, Arise! a study of the pioneering days of the labour movement*, 1931.

572  POIRIER (PHILIP PATRICK). The advent of the [British] Labour party. Lond. & N.Y. 1958.

Covers much the same ground as Pelling (**571**).

573  PELLING (HENRY MATHISON). Popular politics and society in late Victorian Britain: essays. 1968.

Largely concerned with Labour politics.

574  THOMPSON (PAUL RICHARD). Socialists, Liberals and Labour: the struggle for London, 1885–1914. 1967.

Important. S. Bryher, *An account of the labour and socialist movement in Bristol*, Bristol 1929, is much more limited in scope.

575  DOWSE (ROBERT EDWARD). Left in the centre: the Independent Labour party, 1893–1940. 1966.

Little before 1914, on which see A. E. P. Duffy, 'Differing policies and personal rivalries in the origins of the Independent Labour Party', *Victorian studs.* vi (1962–3), 43–65.

The main sources for the history of the I.L.P. are the *Report of the annual conference*, Glasgow, 1893+; *I.L.P. News*, 1893–1903; *The labour leader*, 1891–1922; *The socialist review*, 1908–34; *The socialist annual*, 1906+; and *The socialist year book and labour annual*, Manch. 1911+(title varies). See also James Keir Hardie, *The I.L.P.: all about it*, 1909, and Frank Herbert Rose, *The coming force: the labour movement*, I.L.P., Salford 1909.

576  BEALEY (FRANK) and PELLING (HENRY MATHISON). Labour and politics, 1900–1906: a history of the Labour representation committee. 1958.

Standard. Since 1900 there has been a *Report of the annual conference*, first of the L.R.C., and from 1906 of the Labour party.

577  McKIBBIN (R. I.). 'James Ramsay MacDonald and the problem of the independence of the Labour party, 1910–1914'. *J. Mod. Hist.* xlii (1970), 216–35.

578  LEE (HENRY WILLIAM) *and* ARCHBOLD (E.). Social-democracy in Britain: fifty years of the socialist movement. Ed. by Herbert Tracey. 1935.

A history of the Social-Democratic Federation, mainly by Lee, its secretary, 1885–1913. The main source for its history is *Justice*, 1884–1925. For ideas see Henry Myers Hyndman and William Morris, *A summary of the principles of socialism*, 1884.

579  MORRIS (WILLIAM) *and* BAX (ERNEST BELFORT) *eds.* The manifesto of the Socialist League. 1885.

The opposition to Hyndman. Morris and Bax also publ. *Socialism, its growth and out-come*, 1893. Their organ was *Common weal*, 1885–94.

580  BESANT (ANNIE). Modern socialism. 1890.

For Mrs. Besant's life see **4023**.

581  WOODCOCK (GEORGE). Anarchism: a history of libertarian ideas and movements. Cleveland [Ohio], 1962. Repr. Lond. 1963.

There is no systematic account of British anarchism, but see Max Nettlau, *Bibliographie de l'anarchie . . .*, Brussels, 1897; *Der Anarchismus von Proudhon zu Kropotkin . . . 1859–1880*, Berlin, 1927; and *Anarchisten und Sozial-Revolutionäre . . . 1880–1886*, Berlin, 1931; Rudolf Rocker, *The London years*, trans. by Joseph Leftwich, 1956; Peter Alekseevich Kropotkin, *Memoirs of a revolutionist*, N.Y., 1899; Guy Alfred Aldred, *Dogmas discarded . . .*, Glasgow, 1940; and *No traitor's gait . . .*, Glasgow 1955, repr. in his *Essays in revolt*, 2 v. Glasgow, n.d.; and W. C. Hart, *Confessions of an anarchist*, 1906.

582  MACBRIAR (ALAN MARNE). Fabian socialism and English politics, 1884–1918. Camb. 1962.

Full bibliog. The pioneer hist. of the movement was Edward Reynolds Pease, *The history of the Fabian Society*, 1916, rev. edn. 1925, 3rd edn. 1963. It is still important. Margaret Isabel Cole, *The story of Fabian socialism*, 1961, and Anne Fremantle, *This little band of prophets: the story of the gentle Fabians*, 1960, add little, but are pleasant reading.

583   FABIAN SOCIETY. Fabian tracts. 1884+.

These famous tracts, the annual reports of the Society, 1889+, and *Fabian news*, 1891+, are the main sources for the history of the Fabians. For a list of the tracts see MacBriar (582). The *new statesman*, 1913+, was at first an organ of the Fabian Society.

584   SHAW (GEORGE BERNARD) *ed.* Fabian essays in socialism. 1889. Jubilee edn. 1948.

The first major statement of Fabian ideas.

585   GREGORY (ROY). The miners and British politics, 1906–1914. Oxf. 1968.

586   PELLING (HENRY MATHISON). A short history of the Labour party. 1961. 3rd edn. 1968.

A short sketch. The American equivalent is Carl Fremont Brand, *The British Labour party: a short history*, Stanford, [Conn.], 1964. Among older introductory histories Francis Williams, Baron Francis-Williams, *Fifty-years' march: the rise of the Labour party*, 1949, and Herbert Tracey, ed., *The book of the Labour party: its history, growth, policy and leaders*, 3 v. [1925], new edn. [*The British Labour party . . .*] 1948, are still of use. For official party publications see *Labour party bibliography*, Labour party, 1967. For early Labour party ideas see 'Character sketches: the Labour party and the books that helped to make it', *Review of reviews*, xxxiii (1906), 568–82.

587   THE LABOUR PARTY FOUNDATION CONFERENCE and annual conference reports, 1900–1905. Hammersmith reprints of scarce documents no. 3. Foreword by Henry Mathison Pelling. 1967.

588   BARRY (E. ELDON). Nationalisation in British politics: the historical background. 1965.

589   KENDALL (WALTER). The revolutionary movement in Britain, 1900–21: the origins of British communism. 1969.

Good on the Social Democratic Federation, the Socialist Labour party, the British Socialist party, and other related groups.

590   CLAY (*Sir* ARTHUR TEMPLE FELIX). Syndicalism and labour: notes upon some aspects of social and industrial questions of the day. 1911.

For the syndicalist point of view see Tom Mann, *The industrial syndicalist*, 1911, *Socialism*, Melbourne 1905, and *From single tax to syndicalism*, 1913: also Mann's journal *The syndicalist*, 1912–14. J. E. F. Mann, N. Sievers, and R. W. T. Cox, *The real democracy: first essays of the Rota club*, 1913, is a syndicalist manifesto. For labour opposition to syndicalism see James Ramsay MacDonald, *Syndicalism: a critical examination*, 1912, Sidney and Beatrice Webb, *What syndicalism means*, Letchworth 1912, and Philip Snowden, Viscount Snowden, *Socialism and syndicalism*, 1913.

591   PENTY (ARTHUR JOSEPH). The restoration of the gild system. 1906.

The first coherent account of guild socialism. Stanley Thomas Glass, *The responsible society: the ideas of the English guild socialist*, 1966, is a recent account. See also Penty's *Old worlds for new . . .*, 1917, Samuel George Hobson and Alfred Richard Orage, *National guilds . . .*, 1914, S. G. Hobson, *National guilds and the state*, 1920, and George

Douglas Howard Cole, *Self-government in industry*, 1917, 3rd edn. 1918. See also the lives of Hobson and Orage (**606–7**). The nearest equiv. to a history is Niles Carpenter, *Guild socialism: an historical and critical analysis*, 1922.

### (b) *Biographies*
#### (i) *General*

**592** COLE (MARGARET ISABEL). Makers of the Labour movement. 1948.

**593** THE LABOUR WHO'S WHO . . . a biographical directory to the national and local leaders in the labour and co-operative movement, 1924. 1924.

Useful for pre-1914 leaders. Cont. as an irregular ser. See also **6592a**.

**594** HULSE (JAMES WARREN). Revolutionists in London: a study of five unorthodox socialists. Oxf. 1970.

Shaw, Morris, Stepniak, Kropotkin, Bernstein.

**595** HARNEY. The chartist challenge: a portrait of George Julian Harney. By Albert Robert Schoyen. 1958.

An interesting study of a chartist who outlived the chartist movement. For Harney's correspondence see Frank Gees Black and Renée Métivier Black, *The Harney papers*, Assen [Netherlands] 1969. There is an interesting comparison with the *Life of Thomas Cooper, written by himself*, 1872, and Robert Josiah Conklin, *Thomas Cooper the chartist (1805–1892)*, Manila 1935.

**596** JONES. Ernest Jones, chartist: selections from writings and speeches. By John Saville. 1952.

Jones lived to become an official Liberal candidate for Manchester in 1868 and 1869.

**597** HOWELL. Respectable radical: George Howell and Victorian working-class politics. By Fred Marc Leventhal. Lond. & Camb., Mass. 1971.

The first good life of a Victorian working-class politician. Howell's contemporary, Applegarth is by contrast badly served by Arthur Wilfrid Humphrey, *Robert Applegarth . . .*, [1913].

**598** BURT. Thomas Burt, M.P., D.C.L., pitman & privy councillor: an autobiography with supplementary chapters by Aaron Watson. 1924.

Watson also publ. *A great labour leader: being a life of the Right Hon. Thomas Burt, M.P.*, 1908. Burt was one of the first two working-man M.P.s elected in 1874.

**599** BROADHURST. Henry Broadhurst, M.P. The story of his life from a stonemason's bench to the Treasury bench. Told by himself. 1901.

The first working-class man to become a minister.

**600** SOUTTER. Recollections. By Francis William Soutter. 1923.

Followed by *Fights for freedom: the story of my life*, 1925. A prominent early Lib.-Lab.

**601** CUNNINGHAME GRAHAM. Don Roberto: being the account of the life and works of R. B. Cunninghame Graham, 1852–1936. By Aimé Felix Tschiffely. 1937. Abridged edn. [Tornado cavalier]. 1955.

See also Herbert Faulkner West, *A modern conquistador: Robert Bontine Cunninghame Graham, his life and works*, 1932, and Hugh MacDiarmid [Christopher Murray Grieve], *Cunninghame Graham: a centenary study*, Glasgow 1952.

602  SNELL. Men, movements and myself. By Harry Snell, Baron Snell. 1936.

603  BARNES. From workshop to war cabinet. By George Nicoll Barnes. 1924.

604  CLYNES. Memoirs. By John Robert Clynes. 2 v. 1937.

See also Edward George, *From mill boy to minister: an intimate account of the life of the Rt. Hon. John Robert Clynes, M.P.*, 1918.

605  CARPENTER. My days and dreams. By Edward Carpenter. 1916.

A socialist dreamer, whose work has had great influence, notably *Towards democracy*, 1883, completed 1905, and *Civilisation, its cause and cure . . .*, 1889. Sheffield City Libr. publ. *A bibliography of Edward Carpenter* in 1949. See also Stanley Pierson, 'Edward Carpenter: prophet of a socialist millennium', *Victorian Studs.* xiii (1969–70), 301–18.

606  ORAGE. A. R. Orage: a memoir. By Philippe Mairet. 1936. Rev. edn. N.Y. 1966.

Orage edited the *New Age* which took up guild socialism (**591**). Orage's main independent work was *An alphabet of economics*, 1917. See also Wallace Martin, *The New Age under Orage: chapters in English cultural history*, Manch. 1967.

607  HOBSON. Pilgrim to the left: memoirs of a modern revolutionist. By Samuel George Hobson. 1938.

### (ii) *Fabians*

608  WEBBS. The Webbs and their work. By Margaret Isabel Cole. 1949.

A useful introduction. See also Kitty Muggeridge and Ruth Adam, *Beatrice Webb: a life, 1858–1943*, 1968, Mary Agnes Hamilton, *Sidney and Beatrice Webb*, 1933, and Margaret I. Cole, *Beatrice Webb*, 1945. Beatrice Webb's diaries (**303**) are one of the chief sources for Fabian and Labour history.

609  SHAW. Shaw: his life, work and friends. By St. John Greer Ervine. 1956.

There is no fully adequate account of Shaw as a Fabian. But see also Gilbert Keith Chesterton, *George Bernard Shaw*, 1909, Archibald Henderson, *George Bernard Shaw: man of the century*, N.Y. 1956, and Dan H. Laurence, ed., *Bernard Shaw: collected letters, 1874–1897*, 1965; *1898–1910*, 1972, and **8412**.

610  WELLS. Experiment in autobiography. By Herbert George Wells. 2 v. 1934.

See also **8426**.

611  DAVIDSON. Memorials of Thomas Davidson, the wandering scholar. Ed. by William Angus Knight. 1907.

612  CLARKE. William Clarke: a collection of his writings and a biographical sketch. Ed. by Herbert Burrows and John Atkinson Hobson. 1908.

613 NESBIT. E. Nesbit: a biography. By Dorothy Langley Moore. 1933. Rev. edn. Phila. 1966.

See also Edith Nesbit Bland, ed., *Essays by Hubert Bland. . .*, 1914.

614 OLIVIER. Sydney Olivier: letters and selected writings, with a memoir. Ed. by Margaret Olivier, Lady Olivier. 1948.

*(iii) Social Democrats*

615 HYNDMAN. The record of an adventurous life. By Henry Mayers Hyndman. 1911.

Hyndman also publ. *Further reminiscences*, 1912. The best life is Chushichi Tsuzuki, H. M. *Hyndman and British socialism*, 1961, but see also Frederick James Gould, *Hyndman: prophet of socialism, 1842–1921*, 1928, and Rosalind Travers Hyndman, *The last years of H. M. Hyndman*, 1923. Hyndman's chief works were *England for all*, 1881; *The historical basis of socialism in England*, 1883; *The economics of socialism*, 1896; *The future of democracy*, 1915; and *The evolution of revolution*, 1920.

616 MORRIS. William Morris: romantic to revolutionary. By Edward Palmer Thompson. 1955.

The chief book for Morris's politics, but see also Philip Henderson, *William Morris: his life, work and friends*, 1967, and Lloyd Eric Grey [pseud. of Lloyd Wendell Eshleman], *William Morris: prophet of England's new order*, 1949. John William Mackail, *The life of William Morris*, 2 v. 1899, is important for his non-political activities. Other lives incl. May Morris, *William Morris: artist, writer, socialist*, Oxf. 1936, [William Howard] Aymer Vallance, *William Morris, his art, his writings and his public life: a record*, 1897, John Bruce Glasier, *William Morris and the early days of the socialist movement*, 1921, and Hector V. Wiles, *William Morris of Walthamstow*, 1951. There is also John Goode, 'Gissing, Morris and English socialism', *Victorian Studs.* xii (1968–9), 201–26. Philip Henderson, ed., *The letters of William Morris*, 1950, and Eugene D. Lamire, ed., *The unpublished lectures of William Morris*, Detroit 1970, are based on the Morris MSS. in the British Museum. There is a collected edn. of his works, ed. by his daughter May Morris, 24 v. 1910–15, plus 2 v. suppl. 1936. Of the political works the best are *News from nowhere*, 1890, *A dream of John Ball . . .*, 1888, *Architecture, industry and wealth*, 1902, and three pamphlets, *How I became a socialist*, 1896, *Art and socialism*, 1884, and *Chants for socialists*, 2 pts., 1884–5.

617 MANN. Tom Mann's memoirs. 1923.

Suppl. by the unfinished Dona Torr, *Tom Mann and his times*, vol. 1. '1856–1890', 1956, which was carried to 1892 in History Group of the Communist party, *Tom Mann and his times 1890–92*, Our history pamphlet no. 26–7, 1962.

618 QUELCH. Literary remains of Harry Quelch. Ed. by Ernest Belfort Bax. 1914.

619 BAX. Reminiscences and reflections of a mid and late Victorian. By Ernest Belfort Bax. 1918.

Bax's chief works were *The religion of socialism . . .*, 1887, *The ethics of socialism . . .*, 1889, *Outlooks from the new standpoint*, 1891, *Outspoken essays on social subjects*, 1897, and *Essays in socialism . . .*, 1906.

620 CHAMPION. 'H. H. Champion: pioneer of Labour representation'. By Henry Mathison Pelling. *Camb. J.* vi (1952–3). 222–38.

621   LANSBURY. The life of George Lansbury. By Raymond Postgate. 1951.

By Lansbury's son-in-law. Lansbury himself published *My life*, 1928, *Looking backwards . . .*, 1935, *My quest for peace*, 1938. See also Edgar Lansbury, *George Lansbury: my father*, 1934.

622   SANDERS. Early socialist days. By William Stephen Sanders. 1927.

### (iv) *The I.L.P.*

623   KEIR HARDIE. J. Keir Hardie: a biography. By William Stewart. 1921.

Suppl. but not replaced by lives by Emrys Hughes, 1956, David Lowe, 1923, and Henry Hamilton Fyfe, 1935, Kenneth Owen Morgan, 1967, and others. Hardie's main works are incl. in Emrys Hughes ed., *Keir Hardie's speeches and writings, 1888–1915*, 3rd edn. 1928.

624   MACDONALD. The life of James Ramsay MacDonald, 1866–1919. By Godfrey Elton, Baron Elton. 1939.

Standard. Other useful works are Iconoclast [Mary Agnes Hamilton], *The man of tomorrow: J. Ramsay MacDonald*, 1923, rev. edn. 1929; Hubert Hessell Tiltman, *James Ramsay MacDonald: Labour's man of destiny*, 1929; Herbert Tracey, *From Doughty Street to Downing Street: the Rt. Hon. J. Ramsay MacDonald*, 1924; and Lauchlan Macneill Weir, *The tragedy of Ramsay MacDonald: a political biography*, 1938. For MacDonald's views see his *Socialism and society*, 1905, and *The socialist movement*, 1911.

625   BLATCHFORD. Robert Blatchford: portrait of an Englishman. By Laurence Victor Thompson. 1951.

Blatchford himself wrote *My life in the army*, 1910 and *My eighty years*, 1931. Albert Neil Lyons, *Robert Blatchford*, 1910, is also useful. Blatchford's main achievements were the creation of the Clarion movement, centred on his paper *The clarion*, 1891–1934, and his *Merrie England*, 1894. Blatchford's changes of view are reflected in *Dismal England*, 1899, *Britain for the British*, 1902, *God and my neighbour*, 1903, *Not guilty . . .*, 1906, and *The sorcery shop*, 1907.

626   ALLEN. Clifford Allen: the open conspirator. By Arthur Marwick. Edin. 1964.

See also Martin Gilbert, *Plough my own furrow: the story of Lord Allen of Hurtwood as told through his writings and correspondence*, 1965.

627   BROCKWAY. Inside the left: thirty years of platform, press, prison and parliament. By Archibald Fenner Brockway, Baron Brockway. 1942.

628   GLASIER. The enthusiasts: a biography of John and Katharine Bruce Glasier. By Laurence Victor Thompson. 1971.

Wilfrid Whiteley, *J. Bruce Glasier: a memorial*, Manch. 1920, is inadequate.

629   HENDERSON. Arthur Henderson: a biography. By Mary Agnes Hamilton. 1938.

630   JOWETT. Socialism over sixty years: the life of Jowett of Bradford. By Archibald Fenner Brockway, Baron Brockway. 1946.

631   PATON. Proletarian pilgrimage: an autobiography. By John Paton. 1935.
Cont. in *Left turn!*, 1936.

632   SMILLIE. My life for Labour. By Robert Smillie. 1924.

633   SNOWDEN. An autobiography. By Philip Snowden, Viscount Snowden.
2 v. 1934.

Colin Cross, *Philip Snowden*, 1966, is good on the pre-1914 period. Snowden's most
important pre-war writings were *The socialist's budget*, 1907, and *Socialism and the
drink question*, 1908.

634   THOMAS. My story. By James Henry Thomas. 1937.

See also William Gregory Blaxland, *J. H. Thomas: a life for unity*, 1964, and Henry Roy
Stewart Phillpott, *The Right Hon. J. H. Thomas (impressions of a remarkable career)*,
[1932].

635   THOMPSON. Here I lie. By Alexander Mattock Thompson. 1937.

A co-founder of *The clarion*.

## F. THE ELECTORAL SYSTEM

### 1. WORKS OF REFERENCE

636   McCALMONT (FREDERICK HAYNES). The parliamentary poll
book of all elections, from the passing of the first Reform Act in 1832 . . . .
1879. 7th edn. 1910. New edn. with election results to 1918 by John Russell
Vincent and M. Stenton. Brighton. 1971.

Superseded Edward Walford, *Hardwicke's electoral representation of the United Kingdom from the Reform Act of 1832 down to the present time*, 1856, James Acland, *The
imperial poll book . . . 1832–67*, 1867, and similar publs. The standard list of results for
1885–1918 is now F. W. S. Craig, *British parliamentary election results, 1885–1918*,
1974. For comparative data see Stein Rokkan and Jean Meyriat, *International guide to
electoral statistics*, The Hague & Paris 1969.

637   KINNEAR (MICHAEL). The British voter: an atlas and survey since
1885. Ithaca, N.Y. & Lond. 1968.

638   BOUNDARY COMMISSION 1867–68. Representation of the People
Act, 1867 . . . Boundary commission: report of the boundary commissioners
for England and Wales, 1868. [3972] H.C. (1867–8). XX, 1.

Maps show municipal, 1832, and proposed boundaries for all boroughs and some counties. The report of the commission was considered by a select committee [*Report from
the select committee on boundaries of boroughs* [Chairman: Spencer Walpole]. H.C. 311
(1867–8). VIII, 1.] along with petitions from objectors, which are printed in H.C.
318 (1867–8). LVI, 183. The final boundaries, which varied slightly from those recommended by the boundary commission, are printed in *Philips' atlas of the counties of
England*, rev. edn. 1875.

639   BOUNDARY COMMISSION, 1885. Boundary commission (England
and Wales): report of the boundary commissioners for England and Wales,

1885. Part I. Counties [C. 4287] H.C. (1884–5). XIX, 1. Part II. Boroughs [C. 4287–I] H.C. (1884–5). XIX, 297.

Supplementary report [C. 4382] H.C. (1884–5). XIX, 473. Details of 1885 constituency boundaries.

640  STANFORD'S PARLIAMENTARY COUNTY ATLAS and handbook of England and Wales . . . with . . . particulars relating to county statistics, local administration, and the new parliamentary constituencies. 1885.

Useful descriptive notes. For maps of constituencies see George Washington Bacon, ed., *Bacon's popular atlas of the British Isles*, 1904.

## 2. GENERAL

641  HANHAM (HAROLD JOHN). The reformed electoral system in Great Britain, 1832–1914. Hist. Assoc. G 69. 1968.

A pamphlet guide to be suppl. by the detailed bibliog. notes in his edn. of Dod's *Electoral facts* (**642**) and **662–3**.

642  GASH (NORMAN). Politics in the age of Peel: a study in the technique of parliamentary representation, 1830–1850. 1953.

Indispensable for the system in 1850. The best contemp. guide was Charles Roger Phipps Dod, *Electoral facts, from 1832 to 1852, impartially stated . . .*, 1852, 2nd edn. 1853, new edn. of the 2nd edn. by Harold John Hanham, Brighton 1972. Recent sociological studies of the period incl. T. J. Nossiter, 'Aspects of electoral behavior in English constituencies, 1832–1868', in Erik Allardt and Stein Rokkan, eds., *Mass politics: studies in political sociology*, N.Y. & Lond. 1970, pp. 160–89, and 'Voting behaviour, 1832–1872', *Political Studs.* xviii (1970), 380–9, and D. C. Moore, 'Political morality in mid-nineteenth-century England: concepts, norms, violations', *Victorian Studs.* xiii (1969–70), 5–36.

643  HANHAM (HAROLD JOHN). Elections and party management: politics in the time of Disraeli and Gladstone. 1959.

Full for 1868–81. See also Arthur Frederick Thompson, 'Gladstone's whips and the general election of 1868', *Eng. Hist. Rev.* lxiii (1948), 189–200; John Paul Delacour Dunbabin, 'Parliamentary elections in Great Britain, 1868–1900: a psephological note', *Eng. Hist. Rev.* lxxxi (1966), 82–99; John Vincent, 'The effect of the second Reform Act in Lancashire', *Hist. J.* xi (1968), 84–94; William Henry Maehl, 'Gladstone, the Liberals and the election of 1874', *Inst. Hist. Res. Bull.* xxxvi (1963), 53–69; and Robert Kelley, 'Midlothian: a study in politics and ideas', *Victorian Studs.* iv (1960–1), 119–40.

644  JEPHSON (HENRY). The platform: its rise and progress. 2 v. 1892. Repr. 1968.

Of little value. Joseph Grego, *A history of parliamentary elections and electioneering in the old days . . .*, 1886, has only a few paragraphs on post-1850 elections. For local elections before 1885 there are two detailed accounts: Frederick John Snell, *Palmerston's borough* [Tiverton] *a budget of electioneering anecdotes . . .*, 1894, and William Albery, *A parliamentary history of the ancient borough of Horsham, 1295–1885*, 1927. But see also Barrie Stuart Trinder, ed., *A Victorian M.P. and his constituents: the correspondence of H. W. Tancred, 1841–1859*, Banbury Hist. Soc. 8, 1969.

645 NICHOLAS (HERBERT GEORGE) *ed.* To the hustings: election scenes from English fiction. 1956.

646 VINCENT (JOHN RUSSELL). Pollbooks: how Victorians voted. Camb. 1967.

Uses pre-1872 lists of how people voted. See also his 'The electoral sociology of Rochdale', *Econ. Hist. Rev.* 2 ser. xvi (1963-4), 76-90.

647 GWYN (WILLIAM BRENT). Democracy and the cost of politics in Britain [1832-1918]. 1962.

648 THOMAS (JOHN ALUN). 'The system of registration and the development of party organisation, 1832-1870'. *History*, xxxv (1950). 81-98.

On this topic see also *Report from the select committee on registration of county voters* [Chairman: J. G. Dodson]. H.C. 203 (1864) X, 403, the report of a similar Commons committee in 1870, [H.C. 360 (1870) VI, 191], and *Report from the select committee on Registration (Occupation Voters) Bill* [Chairman: Sir Henry James]. H.C. 162 (1884-5). XI, 1.

649 O'LEARY (CORNELIUS). The elimination of corrupt practices in British elections, 1868-1911. Oxf. 1962.

650 MARTIN (JOHN BIDDULPH). 'Electoral statistics: a review of the working of our representative system from 1832 to 1881 in view of prospective changes therein'. *Journ. Statistical Soc.* xlvii (1884). 75-124.

To be read in conjunction with two of his other articles in the same journal: 'The elections of 1868 and 1874', xxxvii (1874) 193-229, and 'The electoral "swing of the pendulum" ', lxix (1906), 655-707. See also Alfred Frisby, 'Voters *not* votes: the relative strength of political parties as shown by the last two general elections', *Contemporary Rev.* xxxviii (1880), 635-46, Trevor Owen Lloyd, 'Uncontested seats in British general elections, 1852-1910', *Hist. J.* viii (1965), 260-5, and Neal Blewett, 'The franchise in the United Kingdom, 1885-1918', *Past and Present*, 32 (Dec. 1965), 27-56, suppl. by a note by Grace A. Jones, ibid. 34 (July 1966), 134-8.

651 LLOYD (TREVOR OWEN). The general election of 1880. 1968.

652 PELLING (HENRY MATHISON). Social geography of British elections, 1885-1910. 1967.

A detailed region-by-region survey. For detailed local studies see Janet Howarth, 'The Liberal revival in Northamptonshire, 1880-1895 . . .', *Hist. J.* xii (1969), 78-118, R. J. Olney, *Lincolnshire politics, 1832-1885*, 1973, Richard W. Davis, *Political change and continuity, 1760-1885: a Buckinghamshire study*, Newton Abbot 1973, and P. F. Clarke, 'British politics and Blackburn politics, 1900-1910', *Hist. J.* xii (1969), 302-27. A. W. Roberts, 'Leeds Liberalism and late Victorian politics', *Northern History*, v (1970) 131-56, is more general.

653 BLEWETT (NEAL). The peers, the parties and the people: the general election of 1910. 1972.

For the 1906 election see A. K. Russell, *Liberal landslide: the general election of 1906*, Newton Abbot 1973.

654 LORDS COMMITTEE ON THE ELECTIVE FRANCHISE. Report from the select committee of the House of Lords appointed to inquire what would be the probable increase of the number of electors in the counties and boroughs of England and Wales from a reduction of the franchise, and whether any or what change is likely to be made in the character of the constituencies by such increase . . . [Chairman: Earl Grey] H.C. 455 (1860). XII, I.

655 HARTINGTON COMMITTEE ON PARLIAMENTARY AND MUNICIPAL ELECTIONS. Report from the select committee on parliamentary and municipal elections [Chairman: the Marquess of Hartington] H.C. 352 (1868–9). VIII, 1. Further report H. C. 115 (1870). VI, 131.

The only full-scale inquiry into elections during the period. Led directly to the Ballot Act.

656 DILKE COMMITTEE ON PARLIAMENTARY AND MUNICIPAL ELECTIONS. Report from the select committee on parliamentary and municipal elections [Chairman: Sir Charles Dilke] H.C. 162 (1876). XII, 359.

One of three select committees appointed to examine the arrangements made under the Ballot Act, 1872. The other two dealt with the hours of polling [*Report from the select committee on parliamentary and municipal elections (hours of polling)* [Chairman: W. E. Forster, Sir Charles Adderley, Sir M. W. Ridley]. H. C. 320 (1877). XV, 1. Further report H.C. 325 (1878). XIII, 405], and the charges made by returning officers [*Report from the select committee on the Parliamentary Elections (Returning Officers) Bill.* [Chairman: Spencer Walpole]. H.C. 280 (1874). XI, 1].

657 CAVENDISH COMMISSION ON SYSTEMS OF ELECTION. Report of the royal commission appointed to enquire into electoral systems [Chairman: Lord Richard Cavendish]. [Cd. 5163] H.C. (1910). XXVI, 295. Minutes of evidence [Cd. 5352] H.C. (1910). XXVI, 363.

658 MAURICE (FREDERICK DENISON). 'On the means of checking bribery and corruption in the election of members of the House of Commons'. Papers read before the Juridical Soc. iii, (1863–70). 208–18.

Part of a considerable literature on the subject. See also William Dougal Christie, *The ballot and corruption and expenditure at elections . . .*, 1872, and Lewis Emanuel, *Corrupt practices at parliamentary elections*, 1881. Details of corruption are given in the reports of the trials of election petitions published as parliamentary papers and in the evidence taken by the various committees of parliamentary elections (655, 659–61).

659 BOUVERIE COMMITTEE ON CORRUPT PRACTICES PREVENTION ACT, 1854. Report from the select committee on the Corrupt Practices Prevention Act (1854), &c. [Chairman: Edward Pleydell Bouverie]. H.C. 329 (1860). X, 1.

660 LOWE COMMITTEE ON CORRUPT PRACTICES PREVENTION AND ELECTION PETITIONS ACTS. Report from the select committee on Corrupt Practices Prevention and Election Petitions Acts [Chairman: Robert Lowe.] H.C. 225 (1875). VIII, 437.

661 FINLAY COMMITTEE ON ELECTION PETITIONS, 1897–8. Report from the select committee on parliamentary election petitions [Chairman: Sir Robert Finlay]. H.C. 347 (1897). XIII, 1. Further report. H.C. 340 (1898). IX, 555.

### 3. FRANCHISE REFORM

662 SEYMOUR (CHARLES). Electoral reform in England and Wales: the development and operation of the parliamentary franchise, 1832–1885. New Haven, Conn. 1915. New edn. Newton Abbot. 1970.

Standard. Homer Lawrence Morris, *Parliamentary franchise reform in England from 1885 to 1918*, N.Y. 1921, which purports to be a continuation of Seymour, is totally inadequate.

663 CONACHER (JAMES BLENNERHASSET) *ed.* The emergence of British parliamentary democracy in the nineteenth century: the passing of the Reform Acts of 1832, 1867 and 1884–5. N.Y. 1971.

A source book. Of contemp. books James Murdoch, *A history of constitutional reform in Great Britain and Ireland; with a full account of the three great measures of 1832, 1867 and 1884*, Glasgow 1885, is a badly-proportioned summary of the debates in parliament. Shorter works on the same lines are William Heaton, *The three reforms of parliament: a history, 1830–1885*, 1885, and Alexander Paul, *The history of reform: a record of the struggle for the representation of the people in parliament*, 1884, 5th edn. 1885. Paul was an advocate of shorter parliaments and also publ. *Short parliaments: a history of the national demand for frequent general elections*, 1883.

664 HERRICK (FRANCIS HERKOMER). 'The second reform movement in Britain, 1850–1865', *Journ. Hist. of Ideas*, ix (1948). 174–92.

See also Herbert C. F. Bell, 'Palmerston and parliamentary representation', *J. Mod. Hist.* iv (1932), 186–213.

665 SMITH (FRANCIS BARRYMORE). The making of the second Reform Bill. Camb. & Melb. 1966.

An admirable study. But see also Cowling (**292**). Replaces Joseph Hendershot Park, *The English Reform Bill of 1867*, N.Y. 1920. Francis Herkomer Herrick, 'The Reform Bill of 1867 and the British party system', *Pacific Hist. Rev.* iii (1934), 216–33, is still worth consulting. So is Hans Krieger, *Die englische Wahlreform von 1867 im spiegel der deutschen Presse*, Saalfeld [for Berlin] 1936. Homersham Cox, *A history of the Reform Bills of 1866 and 1867*, 1868, is now of merely antiquarian interest.

665a JONES (ANDREW). The politics of reform, 1884. Camb. 1972.

666 HARE (THOMAS). The machinery of representation. 1857.

Followed by his best-known work, *A treatise on the election of representatives, parliamentary and municipal*, 1859, 4th edn. 1873. Both advocate the abandonment of the existing system of representation in favour of proportional representation, for which see also **674**.

667 GREY (HENRY GEORGE), *Earl Grey*. Parliamentary government considered with reference to a reform of parliament: an essay. 1858. New edn. 1864.

The ablest Whig account of the problem of reform.

668  MILL (JOHN STUART). Considerations on representative government. 1861. Rev. edn. 1865.

One of the most influential books on representation ever written.

669  LOWE (ROBERT), *Viscount Sherbrooke*. Speeches and letters on reform. 1867.

The most famous speeches of the day. See also Benjamin Disraeli, Earl of Beaconsfield, *Parliamentary reform: a series of speeches* . . . (*1848–1866*), ed. by Montagu William Lowry-Corry, Baron Rowton, 1867, and William Ewart Gladstone, *Speeches on parliamentary reform in 1866*, 1866. For an interpretation of these speeches see Francis Barrymore Smith, ' "Democracy" in the second reform debates', *Hist. Studs. Aust. & N.Z.* xi (1963–5) 306–23.

670  ESSAYS ON REFORM [Ed. by A. O. Rutson.] 1867.

A brilliant Liberal symposium on the consequences of electoral reform. See also **523**.

671  CARLYLE (THOMAS). 'Shooting Niagara: and after?' *Macmillan's Mag.* xvi (1867), 319–36.

The picturesque case against reform.

672  BAGEHOT (WALTER). Essays on parliamentary reform. 1883.

A collection of penetrating essays of various dates.

673  ELLIS (ARTHUR). 'The parliamentary representation of the metropolitan, agricultural, and manufacturing divisions of the United Kingdom, with suggestions for its redistribution'. *Stat. Soc. j.* xlvi (1883), 59–100.

One of a series of articles showing the growing sophistication of electoral studies. See also Robert Arthur Talbot Gascoyne-Cecil, Marquess of Salisbury, 'The value of redistribution: a note on electoral statistics', *Nat. Rev.* iv (1884–5), 145–62. There is additional matter in John Noble, *Parliamentary reformers' manual*, Manch. 1883.

674  LUBBOCK (*Sir* JOHN), *Baron Avebury*. Representation. 1885. Rev. edn. 1906.

A staunch advocate of proportional representation. On this subject see also **666**, Henry Richmond Droop, *On the political and social effects of different methods of electing representatives*, 1869, and John H. Humphries, *Proportional representation: a study in methods of election* . . ., 1911.

675  ROSENBAUM (SIMON). 'The general election of January, 1910, and the bearing of the results on some problems of representation'. *Roy. Stat. Soc. J.* lxxiii (1910), 473–528.

### 4. WOMEN'S SUFFRAGE

#### (a) *General*

676  ROVER (CONSTANCE). Women's suffrage and party politics in Britain, 1866–1914. Lond. & Toronto. 1967.

The only scholarly book on the subject. Useful bibliog. Helen Blackburn, *Women's suffrage: a record of the women's suffrage movement in the British Isles* . . .' 1902, Agnes Edith Metcalfe, *Women's effort: a chronicle of British women's fifty years' struggle for citizenship (1865–1914)*, Oxf. 1917, and Elizabeth Cady Stanton and others, *History of woman suffrage*, 6 v., Nat. Amer. Woman Suffrage Assoc., N.Y. 1881–1922, give some additional material.

677 FULFORD (ROGER THOMAS BALDWIN). Votes for women: the story of a struggle. 1957.

The most readable account to date, but weak on the earlier phases of the movement. There are a number of earlier short histories still worth looking at: Dame Millicent Garrett Fawcett, *Women's suffrage: a short history of a great movement*, 1912, Bertha Mason, *The story of the women's suffrage movement*, Manch. 1912; Phyllis Crawhall Challoner and Dame Vera Laughton Mathews, comps., *Towards citizenship: a handbook of women's emancipation*, 1928; and Ray Strachey [i.e. Rachel Costelloe], 'The cause': *a short history of the women's movement in Great Britain*, 1928.

678 PANKHURST (ESTELLE SYLVIA). The suffragette movement: an intimate account of persons and ideals. 1931.

A full history written from the militant suffragette point of view. See also her *The suffragette: the history of the women's militant suffrage movement, 1905–10*, N.Y. 1911, written in the heat of the struggle. A similar work is Frederick William Pethick-Lawrence, Baron Pethick-Lawrence, *Women's fight for the vote*, [1910]. For an attack on militancy see Teresa Billington-Greig, *The militant suffrage movement: emancipation in a hurry*, [1911]. For a survey of views on militancy see Huntly Carter, ed., *Women's suffrage & militancy*, [1912]. For the Pankhursts generally see David John Mitchell, *The fighting Pankhursts: a study in tenacity*, 1967.

679 MILL (JOHN STUART). The subjection of women. 1869. Rev. edn. 1870.

The most famous of contemp. pleas for women's emancipation. Support was also given in Barbara Leigh Smith (afterwards Bodichon), *Reasons for the enfranchisement of women . . .*, 1866, *Objections to the enfranchisement of women considered*, 1866, and *Reasons for and against the enfranchisement of women*, 1872; Annie Besant, *The political status of women*, [1885]; Margaret Mary Dilke, *Women's suffrage*, 1885; Brougham Villiers, ed., *The case for women's suffrage*, 1907; Lady Constance Lytton, *No votes for women: a reply to some recent anti-suffrage publications*, 1909; and Sir [Robert] Arthur Arnold, *Women's suffrage*, 1872.

680 DICEY (ALBERT VENN). Letters to a friend on votes for women. 1909.

Probably the best pamphlet against women's suffrage. See also Frederick Augustus Maxse, *Woman suffrage, the counterfeit and the true: reasons for opposing both*, [1877], 2nd edn. 1884, and *Objections to woman suffrage*, 1874, Harold Owen, *Woman adrift: the menace of suffragism*, [1912], and Sir Almroth Edward Wright, *Unexpurgated case against woman suffrage*, 1913. For Gladstone's equivocal views see William Ewart Gladstone, *Female suffrage: a letter to Samuel Smith, M.P.*, 1892.

681 WOMEN'S SUFFRAGE JOURNAL. Manch. 1870–90.

The best of the women's suffrage journals. Other important ones were *Votes for women*, 1907–18, *The common cause*, Manch. (later Lond.) 1909–33 [title became *Women's suffrage* 1913–14, *The common cause of humanity*, 1914–20, etc.], *The vote: the organ of the Women's Freedom League*, 1909–33, and *The suffragette: the official organ of the Women's Social and Political Union*, 1912–15. The opposition is represented by *The anti-suffrage review*, 1908–18.

## (b) *Biography*

**682  BALFOUR.** Ne obliviscaris: dinna forget. By Lady Frances Balfour. 2 v. 1930.

**683  FAWCETT.** What I remember. By Dame Millicent Garrett Fawcett. 1924.

Dame Millicent also publ. *The women's victory—and after: personal reminiscences, 1911–1918.* 1920. There is a full life by Ray Strachey [i.e. Rachel Costelloe], *Millicent Garrett Fawcett* [1931].

**684  KENNEY.** Memories of a militant. By Annie Kenney. 1924.

**685  LYTTON.** Letters of [Lady] Constance Lytton: selected and arranged by [Lady] Betty Balfour. 1925.

Lady Constance Lytton herself publ. *Prisons & prisoners: some personal experiences* [1914].

**686  PANKHURST.** Unshackled: the story of how we won the vote. By Dame Christabel Pankhurst. Ed. by Frederick William Pethick-Lawrence, Baron Pethick-Lawrence. 1959.

**687  PANKHURST.** My own story. By Emmeline Pankhurst. 1914.

See also Estelle Sylvia Pankhurst, *The life of Emmeline Pankhurst*, 1935.

**688  PETHICK-LAWRENCE.** My part in a changing world. By Emmeline Pethick-Lawrence, Baroness Pethick-Lawrence. 1938.

Her husband, Frederick William Pethick-Lawrence, Baron Pethick-Lawrence, in *Fate has been kind*, 1943, also deals with the suffragette campaign.

**689  ROBERTS.** Pages from the diary of a militant suffragette. By Katherine Roberts. 1911.

**690  SWANWICK.** I have been young. By Helena Maria Swanwick. 1935.

Ed. *The common cause.*

## 5. ELECTION LAW

**691  ROGERS (FRANCIS NEWMAN).** The law and practice of elections . . . . 1820. 17th edn. 3 v. 1894–1909. In progress.

Name changed to *Rogers on elections . . .*, 12th edn. 1876. Standard throughout the period. Gerald Augustus Robert Fitzgerald, *The Ballot Act, 1872*, 1872, 2nd edn. 1876, Sir Ernest Arthur Jelf, *The Corrupt and Illegal Practices Prevention Act, 1883*, 1894, 3rd edn. 1905, and Miles Walker Mattinson, *The franchise acts, 1884–5*, 1885, are useful suppl. works. Rival textbooks by Sir Edward Chandos Leigh and Sir Henry Dennis Le Marchant, 1870, 4th edn. 1885, John Cunningham, 1877, 3rd edn. 1885, and Sir Hugh Fraser, 1906, 3rd edn. 1922, were all popular in their day.

**692  COX (EDWARD WILLIAM).** The law and practice of registration and elections . . . with instructions for the management of elections. 5th edn. 1847. 14th edn. 2 v. 1885.

From 10th edn. 1868 by Cox and Standish Grove Grady and styled *The new law* . . . . Intended mainly for solicitors acting as election agents. Deservedly popular. Succeeded by Frank Rowley Parker, *The powers, duties and liabilities of an election agent* . . ., 1885, 2nd edn. 1891, in progress, which reflects the decline of corrupt practices and the appointment of increasing numbers of professional election agents.

693  LEWIS (*Sir* CHARLES EDWARD). The election manual for England and Wales . . . . 1857. 3rd edn. 1865.

An unpretentious work by a practising agent. Similar works were publ. by Charles Favell Forth Wordsworth, 1832, 6th edn. 1868; Henry Jeffreys Bushby, 1857, 5th edn. [*Bushby's manual*] 1880; James Broughton Edge, 1874; J. B. Edge and William Hardy, 1885; William Leader, 1879; Sir John Eldon Gorst, 1883, 2nd edn. 1884; John Charles Shaw, 1884; and Daniel Ward, 1885, 3rd edn. 1906.

694  GLEN (WILLIAM CUNNINGHAM). The parliamentary registration manual. 1868. 4th edn. 1885.

Title varies. Succeeded by Montague Johnstone Muir Mackenzie and Sydney George Lushington, *The parliamentary and local government registration manual* . . ., 1888, 3rd. edn. 1909. Other registration manuals of note are those of Edward Bretherton, 1863; Eugene E. Street, 1878, 3rd edn. 1880; Alexander Charles Nicoll and Arthur John Flaxman, 1876, 3rd edn. 1885; and Michael Moloney, 1903, 2nd edn. 1907.

695  SHARKEY (P. BURROWES). Handbook of the practice of election committees. 1859. 2nd edn. 1866.

After 1868 the trial of election petitions passed to judges of the common law courts. The new procedure is given in Henry Hardcastle *The law and practice of election petitions* . . ., 1874, 3rd edn. 1885. The first of the long series of vols. of *Election cases* falling within the period is David Power, Benjamin Bridges Hunter Rodwell, and Edward L'Estrange Dew, eds., *Reports of the decisions of committees of the House of Commons in the trial of controverted elections* . . . [1847–56], 2 v. 1853–7. Later vols. were ed. by Francis Stafford Pipe Wolferstan and E. L. Dew [1857–8], 1859; F. S. P. Wolferstan and Samuel Boteler Bristowe [1859–64], 1865; and Edward Loughlin O'Malley and Henry Hardcastle and their successors [1869+], 7 v. 1869–1929+.

# G. POLITICAL THEORY

This brief section is confined to books on political theory *per se*. For social theory and other types of thought consult the index.

696  HARRISON (WILFRID). Conflict and compromise: history of British political thought, 1593–1900. N.Y. 1965.

Suppl. by his *Sources in British political thought, 1593–1900*, N.Y. 1965. There are some additional docs. in Thomas Edwin Utley and John Stuart Maclure, eds., *Documents of modern political thought*, Camb. 1957.

697  BOWLE (JOHN EDWARD). Politics and opinion in the nineteenth century: an historical introduction. 1954.

698  BRINTON (CRANE). English political thought in the nineteenth century. 1933. 2nd edn. 1949.

Good.

699 BARKER (*Sir* ERNEST). Political thought in England from Herbert Spencer to the present day. 1915. 2nd edn. [Political thought in England, 1848 to 1914] 1928. New edn. 1947.

700 HEARNSHAW (FOSSEY JOHN COBB) *ed.* The social and political ideas of some representative thinkers of the Victorian age . . . . 1933. Repr. N.Y. 1950.

701 MURRAY (ROBERT HENRY). Studies in the English social and political thinkers of the nineteenth century. 2 v. Camb. 1929.

There are also some passages in William Graham, *English political philosophy from Hobbes to Maine*, 1899.

702 LETWIN (SHIRLEY ROBIN). The pursuit of certainty: David Hume, Jeremy Bentham, John Stuart Mill, Beatrice Webb. Camb. 1965.

703 SEARLE (GEOFFREY RUSSELL). The quest for national efficiency: a study in British politics and political thought, 1899–1914. Oxf. & Berkeley, [Calif.]. 1971.

704 RITCHIE (DAVID GEORGE). The principles of state interference: four essays on the political philosophy of Mr. Herbert Spencer, J. S. Mill, and T. H. Green. 1891. 4th edn. 1902.

705 MACKINTOSH (ROBERT). From Comte to Benjamin Kidd: the appeal to biology or evolution for human guidance. 1899.

See also positivism (**8434**) and evolution (**8615–41**).

706 MACCUNN (JOHN). Six radical thinkers: Bentham, J. S. Mill, Cobden, Carlyle, Mazzini, T. H. Green. 1907.

707 HAMBURGER (JOSEPH). Intellectuals in politics: John Stuart Mill and the philosophic radicals. New Haven, [Conn.]. 1965.

708 PANKHURST (RICHARD KEIR PETHICK). The Saint Simonians, Mill and Carlyle: a preface to modern thought. 1957.

709 LIPPINCOTT (BENJAMIN EVANS). Victorian critics of democracy: Carlyle, Ruskin, Arnold, Stephen, Maine, Lecky. Minneapolis. 1938.

710 LECKY (WILLIAM EDWARD HARTPOLE). Democracy and liberty. 2 v. 1896.

More random comments on events than a work of theory. But there are interesting parallels with Dicey, *Law and opinion* (**357**).

711 HARRIS (FREDERICK PHILIP). The neo-idealist political theory: its continuity with the British tradition. N.Y. 1944.

712 HSIAO (KUNG-CHUAN). Political pluralism: a study in contemporary political theory. 1927.

Henry Meyer Magid, *English political pluralism: the problem of freedom and organization*, N.Y. 1941, adds little.

713 MILL. The improvement of mankind: the social and political thought of John Stuart Mill. By John Mercel Robson. Toronto. 1968.

Sympathetic. For an attack on Mill's politics see Maurice Cowling, *Mill and Liberalism*, Camb. 1963. For Mill's philosophy see **8461**. His major political works were *On liberty*, 1859, and *Considerations on representative government*, 1861.

714 MAINE. From status to contract: a biographical study of Sir Henry Maine, 1822–88. By George A. Feaver. 1969.

See also **1157**.

715 STEPHEN. Liberty, equality, fraternity. By Sir James Fitzjames Stephen. Ed. by Reginald James White. Camb. 1967.

Reprints an important work 1st publ. in 1873. For Stephen's career see **3132**.

716 BAGEHOT. Walter Bagehot: a study of his life and thought, together with a selection from his political writings. By Norman St. John Stevas. 1959.

See also Alastair Buchan, *The spare chancellor: the life of Walter Bagehot*, 1959, and Emilie Isabel Barrington, *Life of Walter Bagehot*, 1914. Bagehot's most theoretical study of politics is in *Physics and politics: or, thoughts on the application of the principles of 'natural selection' and 'inheritance' to political society*, 1872, 8th edn. 1887.

717 NEWMAN. The political thought of John Henry Newman. By Terence Kenny. 1957.

A sketch. Needs to be suppl. by the books at **3944**.

718 GREEN. The politics of conscience: T. H. Green and his age. By Melvin Richter. Lond. & Camb., Mass. 1964.

An illuminating study of a key thinker. The works of T. H. Green were ed. by Richard Lewis Nettleship (3 v. 1885–8), who also publ. *Memoir of Thomas Hill Green . . .*, 1906.

719 BOSANQUET. Bernard Bosanquet's philosophy of the state: a historical and systematic study. By Bertil Pfannenstill. Lund. Sweden. 1936.

For Bosanquet's philosophy see **8447**. His main political work was *The philosophical theory of the state*, 1899, 3rd edn. 1920.

720 PEARSON. Professor of democracy: the life of Charles Henry Pearson, 1850–1894. By John Tregenza. Melb. &c. 1968.

721 SIDGWICK. Henry Sidgwick & later utilitarian political philosophy. By William Clyde Havard. Gainesville, Florida. 1959.

Sidgwick's principal political work was *The elements of politics*, 1891, 3rd edn. 1908. For his life see **8467**.

**722 AUBERON HERBERT.** Auberon Herbert: Crusader for liberty. By S. Hutchinson Harris. 1943.

A consistent libertarian.

**723 GOLDWIN SMITH.** Goldwin Smith: Victorian Liberal. By Elisabeth Wallace. Toronto [1957].

Smith's secretary [Theodore] Arnold Haultain published *Reminiscences by Goldwin Smith*, Lond. & N.Y. 1910, *A selection from Goldwin Smith's correspondence*, Lond. & N.Y. 1913, and *Goldwin Smith: his life and opinions*, N.Y., Toronto, & Edin. 1913.

A sage rather than an independent thinker.

**723a WALLAS.** Between two worlds: the political thought of Graham Wallas. By Martin J. Wiener. Oxf. 1971.

## H. INDIVIDUAL POLITICIANS

There is a vast literature, to which there is no convenient guide. For the unpublished papers of the politicians concerned see Brooke (**724**), and Cameron Hazlehurst and Christine Woodland, comps, *A guide to the papers of British Cabinet ministers, 1900–1951*, 1974.

### I. PRIME MINISTERS

**724 BROOKE (JOHN).** The Prime Ministers' papers, 1801–1902: a survey of the privately preserved papers of those statesmen who held the office of Prime Minister during the 19th century. Hist. Manuscripts Commission. H.M.S.O. 1968.

**725 ABERDEEN.** The Earl of Aberdeen. By Arthur Hamilton Gordon, Baron Stanmore. 1893.

Lady Frances Balfour, *The life of George, fourth Earl of Aberdeen*, 2 v. 1923, is fuller, but no more satisfactory. Wilbur Devereux Jones, *Lord Aberdeen and the Americas*, Athens, Georgia, 1958, and Thomas Macknight, *Thirty years of foreign policy: a history of the secretaryships of the Earl of Aberdeen . . .*, 1855, deal with one aspect of his career.

CORRESPONDENCE: Lord Stanmore pr. priv. much of the *Correspondence of the Earl of Aberdeen*, of which 13 v. are in the British Museum. See also *The correspondence of Lord Aberdeen and Princess Lieven, 1832–1854*, ed. by Ernest Jones Parry, Roy. Hist. Soc., Camden 3 ser. LX and LXII, 2 v. 1938–9.

**726 ASQUITH.** Life of Herbert Henry Asquith, Lord Oxford and Asquith. By John Alfred Spender and Cyril Asquith, Baron Asquith of Bishopstone. 2 v. 1932.

A good official life. But the newer life by Roy Jenkins, *Asquith*, 1964, is much more readable, and there is also Cameron Hazlehurst, 'Asquith as prime minister 1908–1916', *Eng. Hist. Rev.* lxxxv (1970), 532–59. There is some additional material in the potboilers written by Asquith in retirement: *The genesis of the war*, 1923, *Studies and sketches*, [1924], *Fifty years of parliament*, 2 v. 1926, and *Memories and reflections, 1852–1927*, 2 v. 1928. Sir Desmond MacCarthy, ed., *H.H.A.: Letters . . . to a friend, 1915–27*, 2 ser. 1933–4, show Asquith at his best. There is much on the Asquith circle in Margot [Emma Alice Margaret] Asquith, Countess of Oxford and Asquith, *The autobiography of Margot Asquith*, 2 v. 1920–2, new edn. 1962; *Places & persons*, 1925; *More memories*, 1933; *More or less about myself*, 1934; and *Off the record*, 1943. Also in Herbert Asquith, *Moments of memory: recollections and impressions*, 1937, and in Frances Horner, Lady Horner, *Time remembered*, [1933].

SPEECHES: The standard edition of Asquith's political speeches is *Speeches by the Earl of Oxford and Asquith*, ed. by Jesse Basil Herbert, 1927. Earlier vols. are *Speeches . . . [1892–1908] selected and reprinted from* The Times, [1908]; *Trade and the empire: Mr. Chamberlain's proposals examined in four speeches . . .*, 1903; *The justice of our case . . . four speeches*, 1914; *The war, its causes and its message: speeches . . . August–October 1914*, 1914; *The pocket Asquith*, comp. by E. E. Morton, 1914; and *The Paisley policy*, 1920. *Occasional addresses, 1893–1916*, 1918, is standard for the non-political speeches.

727  BALFOUR. Arthur James Balfour, first Earl of Balfour. By Blanche Elizabeth Campbell Dugdale. 2 v. 1936.

Sydney Henry Zebel, *Balfour: a political biography*, Camb. 1973, is fuller than Kenneth Young, *Arthur James Balfour: the happy life of the politician, prime minister, statesman and philosopher*, 1963. For his early years the main account is Balfour's own *Chapters of autobiography*, ed. by Blanche E. C. Dugdale, 1930. For the tariff reform controversy see Alfred Manuel Gollin, *Balfour's burden: Arthur Balfour and imperial preference*, 1965. For Balfour and the empire see Judd (**1252**).

SPEECHES ETC.: *Opinions and argument from speeches and addresses of the Earl of Balfour . . . 1910–1927*, [ed. by Blanche E. C. Dugdale], [1927], *Fiscal reform: speeches . . . from June 1880 to December 1905*, 1906; *Aspects of Home rule*, ed. by Laurie Magnus, 1912, *Essays and addresses*, 1893, 3rd edn. 1905; *Essays speculative and political*, 1920.

728  CAMPBELL-BANNERMAN. The life of the Right. Hon. Sir Henry Campbell-Bannerman, G.C.B. By John Alfred Spender. 2 v. 1923.

See also John Wilson, *C.B.: a life of Sir Henry Campbell-Bannerman*, 1973, and José F. Harris and Cameron Hazlehurst, 'Campbell-Bannerman as prime minister', *History*, lv (1970), 360–83. The only other biography is by Thomas Power O'Connor, 1908. *Early letters of Sir Henry Campbell-Bannerman to his sister Louisa, 1850–51*, ed. by John Sinclair, Baron Pentland, 1925, are childish trifles. There is only one short collection of speeches, *Speeches . . . 1899–1908, selected and reprinted from* The Times [1908].

729  DERBY. Lord Derby and Victorian conservatism. By Wilbur Devereux Jones. Oxf. 1956.

Based mainly on printed sources, as is George Edward Bateman Saintsbury, *The Earl of Derby*, 1892, a good short life. A new life by Robert Blake has not yet appeared.

730  DISRAELI. The life of Benjamin Disraeli, Earl of Beaconsfield. By William Flavelle Monypenny and George Earle Buckle. 6 v. 1910–20. 2-v. edn. 1929.

Monumental. Robert [Norman William] Blake, Baron Blake, *Disraeli*, 1966, is a better book but does not entirely replace Monypenny and Buckle. Blake has also publ. *Disraeli and Gladstone*, Camb. 1970. There is additional material on his early life in Bernard Robert Jerman, *The young Disraeli*, Princeton 1960, but other lives are only commentaries. The best are James Anthony Froude, *Lord Beaconsfield*, 1890, and Thomas Power O'Connor, *Lord Beaconsfield: a biography*, [1878], one of the sharpest attacks on Disraeli's character and policy. On Disraeli's wife there is James Sykes, *Mary Anne Disraeli: the story of Viscountess Beaconsfield*, 1928, Frances Evans Baily, *Lady Beaconsfield and her times*, 1935, and Daniel Hope Elleston, *Maryannery . . .*, 1959.

SPEECHES: The standard edition is *Selected speeches of the late Right Honourable the Earl of Beaconsfield*, ed. by Thomas Edward Kebbel, 2 v. 1882.

POLITICAL WRITINGS: *Whigs and Whiggism: political writings*, ed. by William Hutcheon, 1913. Disraeli is at his best in *The letters of Disraeli to Lady Bradford and Lady Chesterfield* [1873–81], ed. by Lawrence John Lumley Dundas, Marquess of Zetland, 2 v. 1929. See also **899**.

731   GLADSTONE. The life of William Ewart Gladstone. By John Morley, Viscount Morley. 3 v. 1903. 2-v. edn. 1907.

A political life of the first rank, but needs to be suppl. by Sir Philip Montefiore Magnus [-Allcroft], *Gladstone: a biography*, 1954, which has new material, and the personal reminiscences in *The life of William Ewart Gladstone*, ed. by Sir Thomas Wemyss Reid 1899; Williams and Prest (**518**); *The personal papers of Lord Rendel* (**874**); Lord Kilbracken's *Reminiscences* (**1150**); Herbert John Gladstone, Viscount Gladstone, *After thirty years*, 1928; Lionel Arthur Tollemache, *Talks with Mr. Gladstone*, 1898; and Auguste Schlüter, *A lady's maid in Downing Street*, ed. by Mabel Duncan, 1922. Erich Eyck, *Gladstone*, trans. by Bernard Miall, 1938, repr. 1966, is interesting because of its author. Richard Deacon, *The private life of Mr Gladstone*, 1965, adds little. For monographs consult the index to this bibliography. There are two major collections of cartoons, William Thomas Stead, *Gladstone in contemporary caricature*, [1898], and [E. J. Milliken], *The political life of the Right Hon. W. E. Gladstone illustrated with cartoons and sketches from 'Punch'*, 3 v. [1897]–8, 6 v. 1898.

All the major figures in the Gladstone family have lives. There are lives of Mrs. Gladstone by Mary Drew, 1919, and Georgina Battiscombe, 1956, of Herbert Gladstone by Sir Charles Mallet (**766**), of Henry Gladstone by Ivor Thomas, 1936, of Mary Gladstone by Lucy Masterman, 1930, of her husband Harry Drew, by George William Erskine Russell, 1911, and of Gladstone's grandson and heir William Gladstone, M.P., by Herbert John Gladstone, Viscount Gladstone, 1918. Mary Drew also publ. *Acton, Gladstone and others*, 1924. Some of her best letters are in *Some Hawarden letters, 1878–1913*, ed. by Lisle March-Phillipps and Bertram Christian, 1917.

CORRESPONDENCE: Daniel Conner Lathbury, ed., *Correspondence on church and religion of W. E. Gladstone*, 2 v. 1910; Philip Guedalla, ed., *The Palmerston papers: Gladstone and Palmerston . . . correspondence . . . 1851–1865*, 1928, and *The Queen and Mr. Gladstone*, 2 v. 1933; Agatha Ramm, ed., *The political correspondence of Mr. Gladstone and Lord Granville, 1868–1876*, Roy. Hist. Soc. Camden 3 ser. lxxxi–lxxxii, 2 v. 1952; *1876–1886*, 2 v. Oxf. 1962. Slighter are Arthur Tilney Bassett, ed., *Gladstone to his wife*, 1936, and Paul Knaplund, ed., *Gladstone–Gordon correspondence, 1851–1896: selections from the private correspondence of a British prime minister and a colonial governor*, Amer. Phil. Soc. Trans., n.s. v. 51, pt. 4, Phila. 1961. For the chief collection of Gladstone letters see British Museum, Dept. of Manuscripts, *Catalogue of additions to the manuscripts: the Gladstone papers, Additional Manuscripts 44086–44835*, 1953. For the Gladstone library see Saint Deiniol's Library, *Materials for the study of the Rt. Hon. W. E. Gladstone and his times at St. Deiniol's Library*, Hawarden [1969].

SPEECHES: Arthur Tilney Bassett, *Gladstone's speeches: descriptive index and bibliography*, 1916, prints some speeches and lists the remainder. The most important collections of speeches are *Speeches and addresses delivered at the election of 1865*, 1865, *Speeches on parliamentary reform in 1866*, 1866, *Speeches in South-west Lancashire, October 1868*, Liverpool 1868, *Political speeches in Scotland, November and December, 1879*, Edin. 1880, *Political speeches in Scotland, March and April 1880*, Edin. 1880, *Political speeches delivered in November 1885*, Edin. 1885, *Speeches on the Irish question in 1886*, Edin. 1886. The speeches of 1886–91 were issued in 2 v. by Arthur Wollaston Hutton and Herman Joseph Cohen as *The speeches and public addresses of the Right Hon. W. E. Gladstone, M.P.*, vols. IX and X, 1892–4. Vols. I–VIII never appeared. Most of the vols. listed above were reissued, sometimes under different titles. There are two pocket edns.: *Speeches on great questions of the day . . . 1870*, and *The pocket Gladstone*, comp. by Joseph Aubrey Rees, 1911. The Midlothian speeches of 1879 and 1880, ed. by Michael Richard Daniell Foot, were repr. in one vol. in 1971.

WRITINGS: Gladstone himself prepared the only collected edition, *Gleanings of past years*, 7 v. 1879, and *Later gleanings*, 1897, 2nd edn. 1898. The former includes the important, *A chapter of autobiography*, 1868. *The Gladstone diaries* are in course of publication: see **299**.

732  PALMERSTON. 'The most English minister . . .'. The policies and politics of Palmerston. By Donald George Southgate. 1966.

There is a monumental but incomplete official biography, *The life of Henry John Temple, Viscount Palmerston, with selections from his diaries and correspondence*, by Henry Lytton Bulwer, Lord Dalling and Bulwer, 3 v. 1870–4, cont. for 1846–65, by Anthony Evelyn Melbourne Ashley, 2 v. 1876. Herbert C. F. Bell, *Lord Palmerston*, 2 v. 1936, repr. 2 v. 1966, is a useful alternative to Southgate. Philip Guedalla, *Palmerston, 1784– 1865*, 1927, Noel William Baring Pemberton, *Lord Palmerston*, 1954, and Jasper Ridley, *Palmerston*, 1970, are more popular lives. Anthony Trollope, *Lord Palmerston*, 1882, and John Douglas Sutherland Campbell, Marquess of Lorne, later Duke of Argyll, *Viscount Palmerston, K.G.*, 1892, 3rd edn. 1906, both contain some useful interpretations. See also Karl Marx, *The story of the life of Lord Palmerston*, ed. by Eleanor Marx Aveling, 1899, repr. Moscow 1968, and [Basil] Kingsley Martin, *The triumph of Lord Palmerston* (**2424**). See **902** for Lady Palmerston.

CORRESPONDENCE: Philip Guedalla, ed., *The Palmerston papers: Gladstone and Palmerston: being the correspondence of Lord Palmerston and Mr. Gladstone, 1851–1865*, 1928, B. Connell, *Regina vs. Palmerston* (**327**), and Arthur Paul John Charles James Gore, Viscount Sudley, *The Lieven–Palmerston correspondence, 1828–1856*, 1943.

733  ROSEBERY. Rosebery: a biography of Archibald Philip, fifth earl of Rosebery. By Robert Rhodes James. 1963.

Replaced the Marquess of Crewe, *Lord Rosebery*, 2 v. 1931, the official life. The other lives are of no importance. There is one selection of speeches, *Lord Rosebery's speeches (1874–1896)*, 1896. *Miscellanies, literary & historical*, ed. by John Buchan, Baron Tweedsmuir, 2 v. 1921, brings together Rosebery's non-political speeches and essays, many of them already included by Charles Geake in *Appreciations and addresses delivered by the Earl of Rosebery*, 1899.

734  RUSSELL. The life of Lord John Russell. By Sir Spencer Walpole. 2 v. 1889.

The official life. John Prest, *Lord John Russell*, 1972, replaces the older lives by Stuart Johnson Reid, 1895, and Alexander Wyatt Tilby, 1930. Russell himself publ. *Recollections and suggestions, 1813–1873*, 1875, while he was in retirement. *Lady John Russell: a memoir*, 1910, new edn. by Sir Desmond MacCarthy and Agatha Russell, 1926, and *Recollections of Lady Georgiana Peel*, ed. by Ethel Peel, 1920, are useful for Russell's family life.

CORRESPONDENCE: George Peabody Gooch, ed., *The later correspondence of Lord John Russell*, 2 v. 1925; *Selections from speeches of Earl Russell, 1817 to 1841, and from despatches, 1859 to 1865*, 2 v. 1870.

735  SALISBURY. Life of Robert, Marquis of Salisbury. By Lady Gwendolen Gascoyne-Cecil. 4 v. 1921–32.

Incomplete. Some fragments of a further vol. were priv. pr. as *Biographical studies of the life and political character of Robert, third Marquis of Salisbury*, [?1953]. The only complete modern life is Aubrey Leo Kennedy, *Salisbury, 1830–1903: portrait of a statesman*, 1953. See also Michael Pinto-Duschinsky, *The political thought of Lord Salisbury, 1854–68*, 1967, and works on foreign policy at **938–9**.

SPEECHES: There is no adequate edn. Frederic Sanders Pulling, *Life and speeches of the Marquis of Salisbury*, 2 v. 1885, and Sir Henry William Lucy, ed., *Speeches of the*

*Marquis of Salisbury, with a sketch of his life,* 1885, are both too early to include Salisbury's speeches while premier.

ESSAYS: *Essays . . . foreign politics* [1861–4], 2 v. 1905; Paul Smith, ed., *Lord Salisbury on politics: a selection from his articles in the* Quarterly Review, *1860–1883,* Camb. 1972.

## 2. CABINET MINISTERS

(Except Lord Chancellors for whom see **3098–107**.)

736 AKERS-DOUGLAS. Chief whip: the political life and times of Aretas Akers-Douglas, Ist Viscount Chilston. By Eric Alexander Akers-Douglas, third Viscount Chilston. Lond. 1961. Toronto 1962.

737 ARGYLL. George Douglas, eighth Duke of Argyll (1823–1900): autobiography and memoirs. Ed. by Ina Erskine Campbell, dowager Duchess of Argyll. 2 v. 1906.

738 ARNOLD-FORSTER. The Right Honourable Hugh Oakeley Arnold-Forster: a memoir. By his wife, Mary Arnold-Forster. 1910.

739 BALFOUR OF BURLEIGH. A memoir of Lord Balfour of Burleigh. By Lady Frances Balfour. 1925.

740 BIRRELL. Things past redress. By Augustine Birrell. 1937.

Slight. The 3 v. of *The collected essays and addresses of the Rt. Hon. Augustine Birrell, 1880–1920,* 1922, are mainly literary. See also **10288**.

741 BRIGHT. The life of John Bright. By George Macaulay Trevelyan. 1913. 2nd edn. 1925.

See also Herman Ausubel, *John Bright: Victorian reformer,* N.Y. 1966; Donald Read, *Cobden and Bright: a Victorian political partnership,* 1967; *Diaries of John Bright* (**301**); Mills, *John Bright and the Quakers* (**3886**); and Sturgis, *John Bright and the empire* (**1245**). *The Rt. Hon. John Bright, M.P. From the collection of 'Mr. Punch',* 1878, is a book of cartoons.

SPEECHES: The standard edn. is that of James Edwin Thorold Rogers in 3 v.: *Speeches on questions of public policy . . .,* 2 v. 1868, and *Public addresses . . .,* 1879. There are also two popular edns., *Speeches on public affairs of the last twenty years . . .,* ed. Richard Herne Shepherd, 1869, and *Selected speeches . . .,* Everyman's Libr., 1907. Many important public statements are included in *Public letters of the Right Hon. John Bright, M.P.,* ed. by H. J. Leech, 1885, 2nd edn. with memoir, 1895. The American Civil War speeches are gathered together in *Speeches of John Bright, M.P., on the American question,* Boston 1865.

742 BRODRICK. Records & reactions, 1856–1939. By William St. John Fremantle Brodrick, Earl of Midleton. 1939.

Also partly autobiographical is his *Ireland, dupe or heroine,* 1932.

743 BRUCE. Letters of the Rt. Hon. Henry Austin Bruce, G.C.B., Lord Aberdare of Duffryn. 2 v. priv. pr. Oxf. 1902.

Suppl. by a vol. of *Lectures and addresses,* priv. pr. *c.* 1900, repr. 1917.

744   BRYCE. James Bryce, Viscount Bryce of Dechmont, O. M. By Herbert Albert Laurens Fisher. 2 v. 1927.

See also Edmund Ions, *James Bryce and American democracy, 1870–1922*, 1968. Bryce's *Essays and addresses in war time*, 1918, belong outside the period.

745   BULWER-LYTTON. The life of Edward Bulwer, first Lord Lytton. By Victor Alexander George Robert Bulwer-Lytton, second Earl of Lytton. 2 v. 1913.

Earlier lives were attacked by William Alfred Frost in *Bulwer Lytton: an exposure of the errors of his biographers*, 1913, and are incomplete and inaccurate.

746   BURNS. John Burns: Labour's lost leader: a biography By William Richard Gladstone Kent. 1950.

See also Joseph Burgess, *John Burns: the rise and progress of a Right Honourable*, Glasgow 1911.

CANNING. For Earl Canning see **1131**.

747   CARDWELL. Edward T. Cardwell: Peelite. By Arvel Benjamin Erickson. *Amer. Phil. Soc. Trans.* n.s. xlix, pt. 2. Phila. 1959.

Inadequate. For his career as an army reformer see Biddulph, *Lord Cardwell at the War Office* (**2703**).

748   CARNARVON. The life of Henry Howard Molyneux Herbert, fourth Earl of Carnarvon, 1831–1890. By Sir Arthur Henry Hardinge. 3 v. Lond. & Edin. 1925.

Suppl. by a ser. of *Essays, addresses . . .*, priv. pr. 3 v. 1896. See also Cornelis Willem de Kiewiet and Frank Hawkins Underhill, eds., *Dufferin–Carnarvon correspondence, 1874–1878*, Champlain Soc. xxxiii, Toronto 1955.

749   AUSTEN CHAMBERLAIN. The life and letters of the Rt. Hon. Sir Austen Chamberlain. By Sir Charles Alexander Petrie. 2 v. 1939–40.

Sir [Joseph] Austen Chamberlain himself publ. an important collection of letters to his stepmother, *Politics from inside: an epistolary chronicle, 1906–1914*, 1936, a vol. of essays on men and affairs, *Down the years*, 1935, and a travel book, *Seen in passing . . .*, 1937. The only collection of speeches to be publ., *Peace in our time: addresses on Europe and the Empire*, 1928, has only one pre-1914 speech.

750   JOSEPH CHAMBERLAIN. The life of Joseph Chamberlain. v. 1–3 by James Louis Garvin. 1932–4. v. 4–6 by Julian Amery. 1951–69.

Mainly docs. but indispensable. A useful suppl. is Chamberlain's *A political memoir, 1880–92*, ed. by Christopher Henry Durham Howard, 1953. Peter Fraser, *Joseph Chamberlain: radicalism and empire, 1868–1914*, 1966, is a useful ser. of essays. Michael Charles Hurst, *Joseph Chamberlain and Liberal reunion: the round table conference of 1887*, Lond. & Toronto 1967, 'Joseph Chamberlain, the Conservatives and the succession to John Bright, 1886–89', *Hist. J.* vii (1964), 64–94, and *Joseph Chamberlain and west Midland politics, 1886–95*, Dugdale Soc., Oxf. 1962, and Elsie E. Gulley, *Joseph Chamberlain and English social politics*, Columbia Univ. studies in Political Science vol. 123, no. 1, N.Y. 1926, are useful monographs. There were numerous contemporary lives. Of controversial pamphlets see William Thomas Stead, *Joseph Chamberlain: conspirator or statesman* [1900], and John Mackinnon Robertson, *Chamberlain: a study*,

1905. Daniel Hope Elletson, *The Chamberlains*, 1966, gives basic information about the family.

SPEECHES: The standard collection is *Mr Chamberlain's speeches*, ed. by Charles Walter Boyd, 2 v. 1914. Other anthologies are *Speeches of the Rt. Hon. Joseph Chamberlain* ed. by Sir Henry William Lucy, 1885, *The radical platform* [1885], *Home rule and the Irish question* . . ., [1881–7], 1887, *Speeches on the Irish question* . . ., [*1887–90*], 1890, *Foreign & colonial speeches*, 1897, *Imperial union and tariff reform*, 1903, 2nd edn. 1910.

751  CHAPLIN. Henry Chaplin: a memoir. By his daughter Edith Vane-Tempest-Stewart, Marchioness of Londonderry. 1926.

752  CHILDERS. The life and correspondence of the Right Hon. Hugh C. E. Childers, 1827–1896. By Edmund Spencer Eardley Childers. 2 v. 1901.

On his Australian career there is also Edward Sweetman, *The educational activities in Victoria of the Rt. Hon. H. C. E. Childers* . . ., Melb. 1940.

753  LORD RANDOLPH CHURCHILL. Lord Randolph Churchill. By Sir Winston [Leonard Spencer-] Churchill. 2 v. 1906. rev. 1-v. edn. 1952.

A splendid biog. Holds its own against Robert Rhodes James, *Lord Randolph Churchill*, 1959. Lord Randolph publ. only *Men, mines and animals in South Africa*, 1892. Early biogs. are of little value, but Lord Rosebery's *Lord Randolph Churchill*, 1906, is a perceptive sketch. *The reminiscences of Lady Randolph Churchill*, 1908, René Kraus, *Young Lady Randolph: the life and times of Jennie Jerome, American mother of Winston Churchill*, N.Y. [1943], and Anita Leslie, *Lady Randolph Churchill; the story of Jennie Jerome*, N.Y. [1969], have some useful information, but they are not as full as Ralph Guy Martin, *Jennie: the life of Lady Randolph Churchill* . . ., 2 v., Englewood Cliffs, N.J. 1969–71, publ. in London as *Lady Randolph Churchill: a biography* . . ., 2 v. 1969–71.

SPEECHES: Louis John Jennings, ed., *Speeches of the Right Honourable Lord Randolph Churchill, M.P., 1880–1888*, 2 v., 1889, is preferable to the early, Henry William Lucy, ed., *Speeches of Lord Randolph Churchill, with a sketch of his life*, 1885.

754  WINSTON CHURCHILL. My early life: a roving commission. By Sir Winston [Leonard Spencer-] Churchill. 1930.

Good. Other autobiog. works relating to the pre-1914 period are *The story of the Malakand Field Force*, 1898; *The river war*, 1899, rev. edn. 1902; *London to Ladysmith via Pretoria*, 1900; *Ian Hamilton's march*, 1900; *My African journey*, 1908; *Thoughts and adventures*, 1932. Also partly autobiog. is *The world crisis, 1911–1914*, 1923. The official biog. was started by Randolph Spencer-Churchill with *Winston S. Churchill*, 2 v. London. & Boston 1966–8, covering the life to 1914, and has been cont. by Martin Gilbert for 1914–16 in vol. III of the life, Lond. & Boston, 1971. Each vol. of this biog. has a *Companion volume* of docs. in several parts, v.1 +, 1967 +. The most attractive account of Churchill as a young cabinet minister is Violet Bonham-Carter, Baroness Asquith, *Winston Churchill as I knew him*, 1965, publ. in N.Y. as *Winston Churchill: an intimate portrait*, 1965. There are many 1-v. lives, notably those by Charlie Lewis Broad, 1941 and revisions, and Virginia Cowles, 1953. See also John Marsh, *The young Winston Churchill*, 1955; Peter De Mendelssohn, *The age of Churchill: heritage and adventure, 1874–1911*, 1961; Mary Cogan Bromage, *Churchill and Ireland*, Notre Dame, Ind. 1964; Robert Rhodes James, *Churchill: a study in failure, 1900–1939*, 1970; Maurice Percy Ashley, *Churchill as historian*, 1968; Charles Eade, ed., *Churchill by his contemporaries*, 1953; Sir John Wheeler-Bennett, *Action this day: working with Churchill*, 1968; and Alan John Percivale Taylor and others, *Churchill: four faces and the man* [N.Y. ed. *Churchill revised* . . .], 1969. Ben Tucker, *Winston Churchill; his life in pictures*, 1945,

3rd edn. 1955, Randolph Spencer-Churchill and Helmut Gernsheim, comps., *Churchill: his life in photographs,* 1955, and Fred Urquhart, *W.S.C.: a cartoon biography,* 1955, are all useful. For Churchill at the Colonial Office see Higham (**1251**), and at the Admiralty see Gretton and Dawson (**2869**).

SPEECHES (TO 1914 ONLY): *Mr Brodrick's army,* 1903, *For free trade,* 1906, *Liberalism and the social problem,* 1909, *The people's rights,* 1910, new edn. ed. by Cameron Hazlehurst, 1970.

BIBLIOGRAPHY: Frederick Woods, *A bibliography of the works of Sir Winston Churchill,* 1963. The literature about Churchill is excessively voluminous and needs a bibliog.

755  CLARENDON. The life and letters of George William Frederick, fourth Earl of Clarendon. By Sir Herbert Eustace Maxwell. 2 v. 1913.

A shorter life by George J. T. H. Villiers, *A vanished Victorian: being, the life of George Villiers, fourth Earl of Clarendon, 1800–70,* 1938, adds little. Aubrey Leo Kennedy, ed., '*My dear duchess': social and political letters to the Duchess of Manchester, 1858–1869,* 1956, has many Clarendon letters. His niece, Maria Theresa Earle (Mrs. C. W. Earle), publ. *Memoirs and memories,* 1911, with useful reminiscences.

756  CREWE. Lord Crewe, 1858–1945: the likeness of a Liberal. By James Pope-Hennessy. 1955.

757  CROSS. A political history. By Richard Assheton Cross, Viscount Cross. Priv. pr. 1903.

758  DERBY (15th EARL OF). Speeches and addresses of Edward Henry, XVth Earl of Derby, K.G. Ed. by Thomas Henry Sanderson, Baron Sanderson, and Edward Stanley Roscoe. 2 v. 1894.

Includes a brief memoir. No author could be found for a projected official biography because of restrictions imposed by Lady Derby. Another selection of *Speeches and addresses on political and social questions, 1870–1891,* was publ. priv. in 1893. Some rather thin letters to Lady Derby are printed in Lady Burghclere (Winifred Anne Henrietta Christina Gardner), *A great lady's friendships: letters to Mary, Marchioness of Salisbury, Countess of Derby, 1862–1890,* 1933.

759  DILKE. The life of the Rt. Hon. Sir Charles W. Dilke, Bart., M.P. By Stephen Lucius Gwynn and Gertrude Mary Tuckwell. 2 v. 1917. Abridged edn. by Gertrude M. Tuckwell (A short life . . .). 1925.

The official life. Roy Jenkins, *Sir Charles Dilke: a Victorian tragedy,* 1958, rev. edn. 1965, is the first to deal fully with the Dilke divorce, which provoked, *inter alia,* William Thomas Stead, *Has Sir Charles Dilke cleared his character?,* 1891. For his wife see Betty Askwith, *Lady Dilke: a biography,* 1969.

760  ELGIN. Letters and journals of James, eighth Earl of Elgin . . . . Ed. by Theodore Walrond. 1872.

Nothing on home politics, but Sir John George Bourinot, *Lord Elgin,* Toronto, 1903; George McKinnon Wrong, *The Earl of Elgin,* 1905; William Paul McClure Kennedy, *Lord Elgin,* 1926; and John Lyle Morison, *The eighth Earl of Elgin,* 1928, are little better. For his Canadian career see Sir Arthur George Doughty, ed., *The Elgin–Grey papers, 1846–52,* 4 v., Ottawa, 1937. For his Chinese mission, Laurence Oliphant, *Narrative of the Earl of Elgin's mission to China and Japan . . .'* 1859, is still useful.

ELGIN. For the ninth Earl of Elgin see **1135** and **1251**.

761 ELLENBOROUGH. Lord Ellenborough: a biography of Edward Law, Earl of Ellenborough, Governor-General of India. By Albert Henry Imlah. Camb., Mass. 1939.

Mainly concerned with his Indian career, 1842–4, as are other, earlier, lives.

762 FORSTER. Life of the Right Honourable William Edward Forster. By Sir Thomas Wemyss Reid. 2 v. 1888. 1-v. edn. 1895. Repr. Bath. 1970.

763 FORTESCUE. '. . . and Mr Fortescue': a selection from the diaries from 1851 to 1861 of Chichester Fortescue, Lord Carlingford, K.P. Ed. by Osbert Wyndham Hewett. 1958.

Another selection is Alistair Basil Cooke and John Russell Vincent, eds. *Lord Carlingford's journal: reflections of a cabinet minister*, 1885, Oxf. 1971.
See also the life of his wife, Lady Waldegrave (**904**).

764 FOWLER. Life of Henry Hartley Fowler, first Viscount Wolverhampton. By Edith Henrietta Fowler. 1912.

For Fowler's partner and fellow-Wesleyan see Denis Crane, *The life-story of Sir Robert W. Perks, baronet, M.P.*, 1909.

765 LLOYD GEORGE. Lloyd George, 1863–1914. By William Watkin Davies. 1939.

Suppl. by William George, *My brother and I*, 1958, which has many pre-1914 letters, and David Lloyd George, *War memoirs*, 6 v. 1933–6, 2-v. edn. 1938. For Lloyd George's Welsh career see also **9608**. General biogs. of note are Malcolm Thomson and Frances Louise, Countess Lloyd-George, *David Lloyd George: the official biography* [1948]; Thomas Jones, *Lloyd George*, 1951; Frank Owen, *Tempestuous journey: Lloyd George, his life and times*, 1954; and Richard Lloyd George, Earl Lloyd-George, *Lloyd George*, 1960. Most other books on Lloyd George concentrate on the period after 1914, notably Frances Louise, Countess Lloyd-George, *The years that are past*, 1968, and *Lloyd George: a diary*, ed. by Alan John Percivale Taylor, 1971. But see Martin Gilbert, comp., *Lloyd George*, Englewood Cliffs, N.J. 1968. Two books of cartoons are *Lloyd George by Mr Punch*, 1922, and David Low, *Lloyd George & Co.: cartoons from 'The Star'* [1921]. A. J. P. Taylor, ed., *Lloyd George: twelve essays*, 1971, and Kenneth Owen Morgan, ed., *Lloyd George: family letters, 1885–1936*, Cardiff and Lond. 1973, are two useful addns. to the lit.

SPEECHES: *Better times: speeches* [1903–1910], 1910; *The people's budget*, 1909; *The people's insurance*, 1911; *Through terror to triumph: speeches and pronouncements since the beginning of the war*, ed. by Frances Louise Stevenson, afterwards Lloyd-George, 1915; *Slings and arrows: sayings chosen from the speeches of David Lloyd George*, ed. by Philip Guedalla, 1929.

766 HERBERT GLADSTONE. Herbert Gladstone: a memoir. By Sir Charles Edward Mallet. 1932.

Gladstone also publ. a vol. of reminiscences, *After Thirty Years*, 1928, chiefly designed to vindicate his father.

767 GOSCHEN. The life of George Joachim Goschen, first Viscount Goschen, 1831–1907. By Arthur Ralph Douglas Elliot. 2 v. 1911.

Percy Colson, ed., *Lord Goschen and his friends: the Goschen letters*, 1946, and Thomas

J. Spinner, jr., *George Joachim Goschen: the transformation of a Victorian Liberal*, Camb. 1973, add little to Elliot.

There are 3 v. of speeches: *Reports and speeches on local taxation*, 1872, *Political speeches delivered during the general election*, *1885*, Edin. 1886, and *Essays and addresses on economic questions* (*1865–1893*), 1905.

768   GRAHAM. Sir James Graham. By John Trevor Ward. 1967.

Charles Stuart Parker, *The life and letters of Sir James Graham, second baronet of Netherby, P.C., K.C.B., 1792–1861*, 2 v. 1907, is a useful quarry. See also William Torrens McCullagh Torrens, *The life and times of . . . Sir James R. G. Graham*, 2 v. 1863, and Arvel Benjamin Erickson, *The public career of Sir James Graham*, Oxf. & Cleveland [Ohio], 1952.

769   GRANVILLE. The life of Granville George Leveson-Gower, second Earl Granville, K.G. By Lord Edmond Fitzmaurice, Baron Fitzmaurice. 2 v. 1905.

Granville's close friendship with Gladstone is chronicled in *The political correspondence of Mr. Gladstone and Lord Granville, 1868–1876*, ed. by Agatha Ramm, Camden 3 ser. lxxxi–lxxxii, 2 v. 1952, cont. for *1876–86*, 2 v. Oxf. 1962. Some of Granville's official letters are in Paul Knaplund, *Letters from the Berlin embassy, 1871–1874, 1880–1885: selections from the private correspondence of British representatives at Berlin and Foreign Secretary, Lord Granville . . .*, Annual Report Amer. Hist. Assoc. 1942, Vol. II. Wash. 1944.

770   Sir EDWARD GREY. Grey of Fallodon: being, the life of Sir Edward Grey, afterwards Viscount Grey of Fallodon. By George Macaulay Trevelyan. 1937.

The official biog. Grey's own *Twenty-five years, 1892–1916*, 2 v. 1925, is much more distinguished. His *Fallodon papers*, 1926, and *The charm of birds*, 1927, are two of many books and speeches devoted to his hobbies. Keith Robbins, *Sir Edward Grey*, 1971, is a good modern biog. Sydney Charles Buxton, Earl Buxton, *Edward Grey, bird lover and fisherman*, 1933, and Seton P. Gordon, *Edward Grey of Fallodon and his birds . . .*, 1937, are personal sketches.

SPEECHES: *Speeches on foreign affairs, 1904–1914*, ed. by Paul Knaplund, 1931.

771   Sir GEORGE GREY. Memoir of Sir George Grey, Bart., G.C.B. By Mandell Creighton. priv. pr. Newcastle. 1884. Repr. 1901.

772   HALDANE. Haldane of Cloan: his life and times, 1856–1928. By Dudley Sommer. 1960.

Not fully satisfactory but easier to use than Sir Frederick Barton Maurice, *Haldane: the life of Viscount Haldane of Cloan*, 2 v. 1937–9. *Richard Burdon Haldane: an autobiography*, 1929, and Haldane's *Before the war*, 1920, are readable. A good recent study is Stephen Edward Koss, *Lord Haldane: scapegoat for liberalism*, N.Y. 1969. There is still some interest in *The Daily Chronicle, Lord Haldane and the army: what he did to thwart Germany . . .*, 1915, Robert Stevens, *The vindication of Lord Haldane . . .*, Rotterdam etc. 1917, and Edward Grey, Viscount Grey of Fallodon and others, *Viscount Haldane of Cloan, O.M.: the man and his work*, repr. from *Public Administration*, 1928.

SPEECHES: *Army reform and other addresses*, 1907; *Universities and national life*, 1910, rev. edn. 1911; *Selected addresses and essays*, 1928.

773   HAMILTON. Parliamentary reminiscences and reflections. By Lord George Francis Hamilton. 2 v. 1916–22.

774   HARCOURT. The life of Sir William Harcourt. By Alfred George Gardiner. 2 v. 1923.

775   HARDWICKE. Charles Philip Yorke, fourth Earl of Hardwicke, Vice-Admiral, R.N. A memoir. By Elizabeth Phillipa Biddulph, Baroness Biddulph. 1910.

Primarily a naval biog.

776   HARDY. Gathorne Hardy, first Earl of Cranbrook: a memoir. By Alfred Erskine Gathorne-Hardy. 2 v. 1910.

Based on an extensive diary. Tampers with the text of the diary without acknowledgement.

777   HARROWBY. Reminiscences. By Dudley Ryder, 2nd Earl of Harrowby. Priv. pr. 1891.

778   HARTINGTON. The life of Spencer Compton, eighth Duke of Devonshire. By Bernard Henry Holland. 2 v. 1911.

Supplanted the popular Henry Leach, *The Duke of Devonshire: a personal and political biography* [1904]. The only vols. of speeches are *Election speeches in 1879 and 1880, with address to the electors of North-east Lancashire,* 1880, and *Speeches delivered during the election period of 1886, in favour of the Unionist cause . . . reprinted from The Times,* Dublin 1887.

779   HERBERT. Sidney Herbert, Lord Herbert of Lea: a memoir. By Arthur Hamilton Gordon, Baron Stanmore. 2 v. 1906.

780   HERRIES. Memoir of the public life of the Rt. Hon. John Charles Herries, in the reigns of George III, George IV, William IV and Victoria. By Edward Herries. 2 v. 1880.

There is a suppl. by Edw. Herries, *A letter . . . in reply to an article on a 'Memoir of the public life of . . . J. C. Herries',* 1881.

781   HICKS BEACH. Life of Sir Michael Hicks Beach, Earl St. Aldwyn. By Lady Victoria Alexandrina Hicks Beach. 2 v. 1932.

782   ISAACS. Rufus Isaacs, first Marquess of Reading, 1860–1935. By Gerald Rufus Isaacs, 2nd Marquess of Reading. 2 v. 1942–5.

See also Harford Montgomery Hyde, *Lord Reading: the life of Rufus Isaacs, First Marquess of Reading.* 1967, and Walker-Smith (**3159**).

783   JAMES. Lord James of Hereford. By George Ranken Askwith, Baron Askwith. 1930.

784   KIMBERLEY. A journal of events during the Gladstone ministry, 1868–1874, by John, first Earl of Kimberley. Ed. by Ethel Drus. Roy. Hist. Soc., Camden miscellany 21. Camden 3 ser. xc. 1958.

KITCHENER. See **2814**.

785  3rd MARQUESS OF LANSDOWNE. Lord Lansdowne: a biographical sketch . . . By Abraham Hayward. 1872.

786  5th MARQUESS OF LANSDOWNE. Lord Lansdowne: a biography. By Thomas Wodehouse Legh, Baron Newton. 1929.
A fine biog. For his Indian career see **1137**.

787  LEWIS. Letters of the Right. Hon. Sir George Cornewall Lewis, Bart. to various friends. Ed. by Sir Gilbert Frankland Lewis. 1870.

788  LONG. Walter Long and his times. By Sir Charles Alexander Petrie. 1936.
Preferable to Long's own *Memories*, 1923.

789  LOWE. Life and letters of the Right Honourable Robert Lowe, Viscount Sherbrooke. By Arthur Patchett Martin. 2 v. 1893.
Massive and ill-organized, but better than James Francis Hogan, *Robert Lowe, Viscount Sherbrooke*, 1893. Lowe's best speeches were pr. as *Speeches and letters on reform*, 1867. On Lowe's Australian career see Ruth Knight, *Illiberal liberal: Robert Lowe in New South Wales, 1842–1850*, Melb. & Camb. 1966.

790  LYTTELTON. Alfred Lyttelton: an account of his life. By his widow, Dame Edith Sophy Lyttelton. 1917. Abridged edn. 1923.
His letters to Mary Gladstone were publ. priv. as *Letters of Alfred Lyttelton, c.* 1915.

791  McKENNA. Reginald McKenna, 1863–1943: a memoir. By Stephen McKenna. 1948.
Deplorable. The only vol. of speeches is the very late *Post-war banking policy: a series of addresses*, 1928.

792  MALMESBURY. Memoirs of an ex-Minister. By James Howard Harris, 3rd Earl of Malmesbury. 2 v. 1884. 3rd edn. 1884. 1-v. edn. 1885.
Valuable but inaccurate.

793  MANNERS. Lord John Manners and his friends. By Charles Whibley. 2 v. 1925.

794  MARLBOROUGH. The later Churchills. By Alfred Leslie Rowse. 1958.
Mainly devoted to Lord Randolph and Sir Winston but includes an account of Lord Randolph's father, the 7th Duke.

795  MASTERMAN. C. F. G. Masterman: a biography. By Lucy Masterman. 1939.

796  MOLESWORTH. Life of the Right Hon. Sir William Molesworth, Bart., M.P., F.R.S. By Dame Millicent Garrett Fawcett. 1901.
See also Hugh Edward Egerton, ed., *Selected speeches of Sir William Molesworth . . . on questions relating to colonial policy*, 1903.

797 MORLEY. Recollections. By John Morley, Viscount Morley of Blackburn. 2 v. 1917.

A projected life by Francis Wrigley Hirst never got beyond *Early life & letters of John Morley*, 2 v. 1927. Hirst, however, publ. Morley's tendentious *Memorandum on resignation, August 1914*, 1928. David Alan Hamer, *John Morley: Liberal intellectual in politics*, Oxf. 1968, is a fine study of Morley's ideas. An edn. of *The works of Lord Morley* were publ. in 15 v. 1921, and repr. in 12 v. 1923. For his career at the India Office see **1061–2**. For his intellectual circle see **4006**.

798 MUNDELLA. A. J. Mundella, 1825–1897: The Liberal background to the Labour movement. By Walter Harry Green Armytage. 1951.

NAAS (EARL OF MAYO). See **1140**.

799 NEWCASTLE. The life of Henry Pelham, fifth Duke of Newcastle, 1811–1864. By John Martineau. 1908.

NORTHBROOK. See **1142**.

800 NORTHCOTE. Life, letters and diaries of Sir Stafford Northcote, first Earl of Iddesleigh. By Andrew Lang. 2 v. Edin. 1890. 1-v. edn. 1891.

There is a collected edn. of his *Lectures and essays*, Edin. 1887.

801 PANMURE. The Panmure papers: being a selection from the correspondence of Fox Maule, second Baron Panmure, afterwards eleventh Earl of Dalhousie, K.T., G.C.B. Ed. by Sir George Brisbane Scott Douglas and Sir George Dalhousie Ramsay. 2 v. 1908.

802 PLYMOUTH. Robert George, Earl of Plymouth, 1857–1923. Priv. pr. Camb. 1932.

803 RIPON. Life of the first Marquess of Ripon. By Lucien Wolf. 2 v. 1921.

For Ripon's Indian career see **1143**.

804 SAMUEL. Memoirs. By Herbert Louis Samuel, Viscount Samuel. 1945.

The official biog. is John Edward Bowle, *Viscount Samuel: a biography*. 1957. Samuel's main political writings are *Liberalism: an attempt to state the principles and proposals of contemporary liberalism in England*, 1902, *The war and liberty*, 1917, and *An unknown land* [an utopia], 1942. His other works are philosophical. For his papers see H. S. Cobb, comp., *The political papers of Herbert, First Viscount Samuel: a list*, House of Lords Record Office memo 35, 1966, and *The personal and literary papers . . .*, memo 41, 1969.

805 SEELY. Adventure. By John Edward Bernard Seely, Baron Mottistone. 1930.

Seely also publ. another vol. of reminiscences, *Fear and be slain: adventures by land, sea and air*, 1931.

806 SINCLAIR. The Right Honourable John Sinclair, Lord Pentland, G.C.S.I.: a memoir. By his widow, Marjorie Adeline Sinclair, Baroness Pentland. 1928.

807  SMITH. W. H. Smith. By Eric Alexander Akers-Douglas, Viscount Chilston. 1965.

Repl. Sir Herbert Eustace Maxwell, *Life and times of the Right Honourable William Henry Smith, M.P.*, 2 v. Edin. 1893. For Smith's firm see *The story of W. H. Smith & Son*, priv. pr. 1921, 5th edn. 1955.

808  SOMERSET. Letters, remains and memoirs of Edward Adolphus Seymour, twelfth Duke of Somerset, K.G. Ed. by William Hurrell Mallock and Lady Guendolen Ramsden. 1893.

809  STANSFELD. James Stansfeld, a Victorian champion of sex equality. By John Lawrence Le Breton Hammond and Lucy Barbara Hammond. 1932.

810  TREVELYAN. Sir George Otto Trevelyan: a memoir. By George Macaulay Trevelyan. 1932.

811  TWEEDMOUTH. Edward Marjoribanks, Lord Tweedmouth, K.T. 1849–1909: notes and recollections. By Ishbel Maria Gordon, Marchioness of Aberdeen. 1909.

812  VILLIERS. The free trade speeches of the Right Hon. Charles Pelham Villiers, M.P. With a political memoir. Ed. by a member of the Cobden Club. 2 v. 1883. People's edn. 1884.

WOOD (VISCOUNT HALIFAX). See **1053**.

813  WYNDHAM. Life and letters of George Wyndham. By John William Mackail and Guy Wyndham. 2 v. [1925].

Earlier works were Guy Wyndham, comp., *Letters of George Wyndham, 1877–1913*, 2 v., priv. pr., Edin. 1915, and Charles T. Gatty, *George Wyndham, recognita*, 1917, both containing many letters. Charles Walter Boyd, *George Wyndham*, 1913, is an essay from the *Cornhill Magazine*. John Biggs-Davison, *George Wyndham: a study in Toryism*, 1951, is jejune.

### 3. OTHER MAJOR POLITICAL FIGURES

(Excluding those whose careers were chiefly Indian or colonial.)

814  ABERDEEN. 'We twa'. Reminiscences of Lord and Lady Aberdeen. [By John Campbell Gordon and Ishbel Maria Gordon, Marquess and Marchioness of Aberdeen.] 2 v. 1926.

Suppl. by *More cracks with 'we twa'*, 1929, and Lady Aberdeen, *The musings of a Scottish granny*, 1936. Aberdeen was Lord-Lieutenant of Ireland, 1886, 1906–15. There is a life of Lady Aberdeen by Marjorie Adeline Sinclair, Baroness Pentland, *A bonny fechter . . .*, 1952.

815  BROUGHAM. Lord Brougham and the Whig party. By Arthur Aspinall. Manch. 1927.

The most recent life is Frances Hawes, *Henry Brougham*, 1957. The most spirited life is by Lord Campbell (**3100**). Brougham also publ. a carelessly-written autobiog., *The*

*life and times of Henry, Lord Brougham: written by himself*, 3 v. Edin. & Lond. 1871.
Brougham's works were issued in 11 v., Glasgow 1855–61, and Edin. 1872–3. Brougham
was chiefly concerned with educational and judicial questions after 1852. See Amy
Margaret Gilbert, *The work of Lord Brougham for education in England* . . ., Chambers-
burg, Penn. 1922.

816   COBDEN. The life of Richard Cobden. By John Morley. 2 v. 1881.

Formal, and lacks an index. *The political writings of Richard Cobden*, 2 v. 1867, 4th edn.
2 v. 1903, and *The American diaries of Richard Cobden*, ed. by Elizabeth Hoon Cawley,
Princeton, [N.J.] 1952, are necessary suppls. See also Donald Read, *Cobden and Bright*
. . ., 1967. Of the numerous other general lives only Lewis Apjohn, *Richard Cobden
and the free traders*, 1881, and Sir Edward William Watkin, *Alderman Cobden of Manchester*, 1891, are still useful. The Cobden Club essays, *Richard Cobden and the jubilee
of free trade*, 1896, demonstrate the position Cobden had obtained in Liberal mythology.
William Harbutt Dawson, *Richard Cobden and foreign policy*, 1926, and John Atkinson
Hobson, *Richard Cobden, the international man*, 1918, new edn. by Neville Masterman,
1968, are important monographs. Carl Brinkmann, *Richard Cobden und das Manchestertum*, Berlin 1924, gives a German, and Charles Taquey, *Richard Cobden, un révolution-
naire pacifique*, Paris 1939, a French view of his influence.

SPEECHES: *Speeches on questions of public policy* . . ., ed. by John Bright and James Edwin
Thorold Rogers, 2 v. 1870, final edn. 1907.

PAPERS: Francis William Steer, ed., *The Cobden papers*, Chichester 1964.

817   COURTNEY. Life of Lord Courtney. By George Peabody Gooch. 1920.

Courtney himself publ. *The diary of a church-goer*, 1904, new edn. 1918. *Cornish
granite: extracts from the writings and speeches of Lord Courtney* . . ., [ed. by E. C. M.
Stewart and E. Satterthwaite], 1925, includes his principal works.

818   COWEN. Life of Joseph Cowen, M.P. for Newcastle, 1874–86.
With letters, extracts from his speeches . . . . By William Duncan. 1904.

There is also Evan Rowland Jones, *The life and speeches of Joseph Cowen, M.P.* . . . .
[1886].

SPEECHES: *Speeches on public questions and political policy* . . ., [1873], Newcastle, 1874,
and *Speeches* . . . *at the general election, 1885*, Newcastle, 1885, are less useful than
*Joseph Cowen's speeches on the near eastern question, foreign and imperial affairs, and on
the British Empire*, rev. by his daughter Jane Cowen, Newcastle, 1909.

819   COWPER. Earl Cowper, K.G. A memoir. By Katrine Cecilia Cowper,
Countess Cowper. Priv. pr. 1913.

Has valuable letters.

CURZON. See **1132**.

DUFFERIN. See **1134**.

820   FAWCETT. Life of Henry Fawcett. By Sir Leslie Stephen. 1885. 5th
edn. 1886.

Political economist turned political radical. Had he not been blind he would have been
in the cabinet. Postmaster-General, 1880–4. Winifred Holt, *A beacon for the blind:
being, a life of Henry Fawcett, the blind Postmaster-general*, 1915, is a convenient short
life.

821 LABOUCHERE. The life of Henry Labouchere. By Algar Labouchere Thorold. 1913.

Hesketh Pearson, *Labby*, 1936, is entirely derivative. See also **1246**.

822 BONAR LAW. The unknown prime minister: the life and times of Andrew Bonar Law, 1858–1923. By Robert Norman William Blake, Baron Blake. 1955.

Publ. in N.Y. as *Unrepentant Tory* . . ., 1956. Supplants Henry Archibald Taylor, *The strange case of Andrew Bonar Law* [1932].

823 PLAYFAIR. Memoirs and correspondence of Lyon Playfair, first Lord Playfair of St. Andrews. By Sir Thomas Wemyss Reid. 1899.

824 RAIKES. The life and letters of Henry Cecil Raikes, late Her Majesty's postmaster-general. By Henry St. John Raikes. 1898.

825 F. E. SMITH. Frederick Edwin, Earl of Birkenhead. By his son, Frederick Winston Furneaux Smith, Earl of Birkenhead. 2 v. 1933–5. Rev. edn. publ. as F. E. The life of F. E. Smith . . . . 1959.

Better than William Newton Alexander Camp, *The glittering prizes: a biographical study of F. E. Smith* . . ., 1960, and the earlier lives by Ephesian [pseud. of Carl Eric Bechhofer Roberts], 1936, and Henry Archibald Taylor, 1931. Smith's essays, *Points of view*, 2 v. 1922, *Contemporary personalities*, 1924, *Law, life and letters*, 2 v. 1927, and *Last essays*, 1930, have much on politics.

SPEECHES: *The speeches of Lord Birkenhead*, 1929. *Speeches delivered in the House of Commons and elsewhere, 1906–1909*, 1910.

## 4. OTHER POLITICIANS

826 ACLAND. Memoir and letters of the Right Honourable Sir Thomas Dyke Acland. Ed. by Sir Arthur Herbert Dyke Acland. Priv. pr. 1902. [Peelite country gentleman: friend of Gladstone.]

827 ADDERLEY. Life of Lord Norton (Right Hon. Sir Charles Adderley, K.C.M.G., M.P.) 1814–1905: statesman & philanthropist. By William Shakespear Childe-Pemberton. 1909. [Junior minister with colonial and local government interests.]

828 AMBERLEY. The Amberley papers: the letters and diaries of Lord and Lady Amberley. Ed. by Bertrand Russell, Earl Russell, and Patricia Helen Russell, Countess Russell. 2 v. 1937. New edn. 1966. [An excellent account of an aristocratic Radical.]

829 AMERY. My political life. By Leopold Charles Maurice Stennett Amery. 3 v. 1953–5. [Imperialist.]

830 ATHERLEY-JONES. Looking back: reminiscences of a political career. By Llewellyn Archer Atherley-Jones. 1925. [Liberal: legal representative of miners' unions.]

831 BALDWIN. Stanley Baldwin. By George Malcolm Young. 1952. [Inadequate, like the other lives of Baldwin, especially on the pre-1924 period. There is a little more in Arthur Windham Baldwin, Earl Baldwin, *My father: the true story*, 1955. Keith Middlemas and John Barnes, *Baldwin: a biography*, 1969, is a compilation rather than a biog.]

831a BEAVERBROOK. Beaverbrook. By Alan John Percivale Taylor. Lond. & N.Y. 1972.

832  BERNAL OSBORNE. The life of Ralph Bernal Osborne, M.P. By Philip Henry Dudley Bagenal. Priv. pr. 1884. [Independent Liberal buffoon, *c.* 1840–70.]

833  BOTTOMLEY. Bottomley's book. By Horatio William Bottomley. 1909. [The basis for all subsequent lives, the best of which is Julian Symons, *Horatio Bottomley: a biography,* 1955.]

834  BOWLES. The irrepressible Victorian: the story of Thomas Gibson Bowles, journalist, parliamentarian and founder editor of the original *Vanity Fair.* By Leonard Edwin Naylor. 1965.

835  BRASSEY. T. A. B. A memoir of Thomas Allnutt, second Earl Brassey. By Frank Partridge. 1921. [Imperialist.]

836  BROOKFIELD. Annals of a chequered life. By Arthur Montague Brookfield. 1930. [Conservative back-bencher in the 1890s.]

BRUNNER. See **5272.**

837  CECIL. All the way. By Lord [Edgar Algernon] Robert [Gascoyne-] Cecil, Viscount Cecil. 1949. [Mainly concerned with the pre-1914 period. His *Great experiment: an autobiography,* 1941, is chiefly about the League of Nations.]

838  CHANNING. Memories of Midland politics, 1885–1910. By Francis Allston Channing, Baron Channing. 1918. [Liberal back-bencher].

839  COLLINGS. Life of the Rt. Hon. Jesse Collings. By Jesse Collings and Sir John Little Green. 1920. [Joseph Chamberlain's henchman. Specialized in land reform, for which see also **4217.**]

840  COLMAN. Jeremiah James Colman. By Helen Caroline Colman. Priv. pr. 1905. [Leading Nonconformist M.P. 1871–95.]

841  COWPER-TEMPLE Memorials [of William Francis Cowper-Temple, Baron Mount-Temple]. [By Georgina Cowper-Temple, Baroness Mount-Temple]. 1890. [A prominent Whig.]

842  CREMER. Sir Randal Cremer: his life and work. By Howard Evans. 1909. [International arbitration movement, *c.* 1870–1908, and Inter-Parliamentary Union.]

843  ELLIS. The life of the Rt. Hon. John Edward Ellis, M.P. By Arthur Tilney Bassett. 1914. [Quaker and Radical. M.P. 1885–1910.]

844  FARQUHARSON. In and out of parliament. 1911. The House of Commons from within. By Robert Farquharson. 1912. [Scottish doctor: popular House of Commons figure 1880–1906.]

845  FOWLER. Sir Robert N. Fowler, Bart., M.P. By John Stephen Flynn. 1893. [Lord Mayor of London. Conservative.]

846  GOOCH. Under six reigns. By George Peabody Gooch. 1958. [Liberal historian. M.P. 1906.]

847  GRIFFITH-BOSCAWEN. Memories. By Sir Arthur Sackville Trevor Griffith-Boscawen. 1925. [Conservative M.P. from 1892. See also **486.**]

848  HARVEY. Alexander Gordon Cummins Harvey: a memoir. Ed. by Francis Wrigley Hirst. [1925.] [Young Lancashire Liberal.]

849 HEATHCOTE. A country gentleman of the nineteenth century: being a short memoir of the Right Honourable Sir William Heathcote, Bart., of Hursley, 1801–1881. By Frances Awdry. Winchester & Lond. 1906. [M.P. for Oxford Univ.]

850 HENNIKER HEATON. The life and letters of Sir John Henniker Heaton Bt. By Rose Henniker Porter. 1916. [Author of the Imperial penny post.]

851 HEWINS. The apologia of an imperialist. By William Albert Samuel Hewins. 2 v. 1929. [Director of L.S.E., tariff reformer, Conservative M.P.]

852 HIBBERT. Memories of the Right Honourable Sir J. T. Hibbert, K.C.B. By his wife, Eliza Ann Hibbert. Priv. pr. Glasgow. 1911. [Devoted Liberal junior minister. A weak life.]

853 HOARE. The unbroken thread. By Samuel John Gurney Hoare, Viscount Templewood. 1949. [Chiefly about the author and his father, both Conservative M.P.s.]

854 JOYNSON-HICKS. Jix, Viscount Brentford. By Henry Archibald Taylor. 1933. [Defeated Churchill in Manchester, 1906].

855 KENYON-SLANEY. Memoir of Colonel the Right Hon. William Slaney Kenyon-Slaney, M.P. Ed. by Walter Durnford. 1909. [Tory country gentleman, author of the Kenyon-Slaney clause in 1902 Education Act.]

856 LEVESON-GOWER. Bygone years: recollections. By Edward Frederick Leveson-Gower. 1905. [Whig M.P., brother of Lord Granville.]

857 LEVESON-GOWER. Years of content, 1858–86. 1940. Years of endeavour, 1886–1907. 1942. Mixed grill. 1948. By Sir George Granville Leveson-Gower. [Whig M.P. and Whip in 1880s and 1890s. Son of preceding.]

858 LINCOLN. The autobiography of an adventurer. By Ignatius Timothy Trebich Lincoln. Trans. by Emile Burns. 1932. [Hungarian adventurer who demonstrated how easy it was for a spy to become a Radical M.P. See also David Lampe and Laszlo Szenasi, *The self-made villain: a biography of I. T. Trebitsch-Lincoln.* 1961.]

859 LOYD-LINDSAY. Lord Wantage, V.C., K.C.B. A memoir. By his wife Harriet Sarah Loyd-Lindsay, Baroness Wantage. 1907. 2nd edn. 1908. [Soldier, volunteer, Red Cross pioneer, agriculturalist, Financial Sec., War Office].

860 LUBBOCK. Life of Sir John Lubbock, Lord Avebury. By Horace Gordon Hutchinson. 2 v. 1914. [There is also a symposium *The life work of Lord Avebury, 1834–1913*, ed. by Ursula Grant Duff, 1924. An all-rounder; banker, politician, philanthropist, writer.]

861 MACLEAN. Recollections. By James Mackenzie Maclean. Manch. 1902. [Journalist and associate of Lord Randolph Churchill.]

862 MAXWELL. Evening memories. By Sir Herbert Eustace Maxwell. 1932. [Conservative Whip and writer.]

863 MELLY. Recollections of sixty years (1833–1893). By George Melly. Priv. pr. Coventry. 1893. [Liverpool Liberal.]

864 MITFORD. Memories. 2 v. 1915. Further memories. 1915. 2nd edn. 1917. By Algernon Bertram Freeman-Mitford, Baron Redesdale. [Mainly diplomatic: a well-connected Tory.]

865　MOND. Alfred Mond, first Lord Melchett. By Henry Hector Bolitho. 1933. [Liberal industrialist who turned to politics. Mond publ. 2 v. of essays, *Questions of today and tomorrow*, [1912], and *Industry and politics*, 1927.]

866　MONTAGU. Edwin Montagu: a memoir an an account of his visits to India. By Sir [Sigismund] David Waley. Bombay, London., & N.Y. 1964. [Liberal under-secretary under Asquith.]

867　MORLEY. The life of Samuel Morley. By Edwin Hodder. 1887. Numerous edns. [Hosier, philanthropist, Nonconformist spokesman.]

868　MOWBRAY. Seventy years at Westminster. By Sir John Robert Mowbray. Edin. 1900. [M.P. for Oxford Univ.]

869　MURRAY. Master and brother: Murrays of Elibank. By Arthur Cecil Murray, Viscount Elibank. 1945. [A life of Lord Murray of Elibank who, as Master of Elibank, was Liberal Chief Whip 1910–12. A bad book.]

870　NEWTON. Retrospection. By Thomas Wodehouse Legh, Baron Newton. 1941. [One of the few notable back-bench peers in early 20th cent.]

871　PEASE. Elections and recollections. By Sir Alfred Edward Pease. 1932. [Whig. Good.]

872　PELL. The reminiscences of Albert Pell . . . . Ed. by Thomas Mackay. 1908. [Tory agriculturalist and philanthropist: spokesman of Poor Law Guardians.]

873　RATHBONE. William Rathbone: a memoir. By Eleanor Florence Rathbone. 1905. [The philanthropist-politician *par excellence*.]

874　RENDEL. The personal papers of Lord Rendel: containing his unpublished con-versations with Mr. Gladstone . . . . Ed. by Frederick E. Hamer. 1931. [Friend of Gladstone, engineer, Welsh land reformer.]

875　RIBBLESDALE. Impressions and memories. By Thomas Lister, Baron Ribbles-dale. 1927. [Liberal Whip in the Lords.]

876　ROEBUCK. Life and letters of John Arthur Roebuck, P.C., Q.C., M.P.; with chapters of autobiography. By Robert Eadon Leader. 1897. [Radical critic turned elder statesman.]

877　RYLANDS. Correspondence and speeches of Mr. Peter Rylands, M.P. By Louis Gordon Rylands. 2 v. Manch. 1890. [Radical, exponent of economy in administration, Radical Unionist.]

878　SALVIDGE. Salvidge of Liverpool: behind the political scene, 1890–1928. By Stanley Salvidge. 1934. [The ablest local party manager of his day, and the only one to have a good biography.]

879　SIMON. Retrospect . . . . By John Allsebrook Simon, Viscount Simon. 1952. [Lawyer and rigid Liberal.]

880　SMITH. My life work. By Samuel Smith. 1902. [Liverpool philanthropist, non-conformist Radical.]

881　STANLEY. Lord Derby, 'King of Lancashire' . . . . By Randolph Spencer-Churchill. 1959. [Junior minister 1895–1903.]

882  STUART. Reminiscences. By James Stuart. 1911. [Middle-of-the-road Nonconformist, pioneer of technical and adult education.]

883  THOMPSON. General T. Perronet Thompson, 1783–1869. By Leonard George
Johnson. 1957. [Antique Radical.]

884  TORRENS. Twenty years in parliament. By William Torrens McCullagh Torrens.
1893. [Important but crotchety Radical, who fell out with the caucus in the 1880s.]

885  URQUHART. David Urquhart: some chapters in the life of a Victorian knight-
errant of justice and liberty. By Gertrude Robinson. Oxf. 1920. [Eccentric, specialized
in foreign affairs.]

886  VINCENT. The life of Sir Howard Vincent. By Samuel Henry Jeyes and Frederick
Douglas How. 1912. [Soldier, director of criminal investigation, protectionist M.P.
1885–1908.]

887  WEDGWOOD. The last of the Radicals. By Cicely Veronica Wedgwood. 1951.
[Josiah Clement Wedgwood, Baron Wedgwood himself publ. *Essays & adventures*,
1924, and *Memoirs of a fighting life*, 1940. M.P. from 1906.]

888  WILLIAMS. The life and work of William Williams, M.P. . . . . By Daniel Evans.
Llandyssul. 1939. [Welsh Radical M.P. 1835–47, 1850–65.]

889  WILLOUGHBY DE BROKE. The passing years. By Richard Greville Verney,
Baron Willoughby de Broke. 1924. [Conservative M.P. 1895–1900: organizer of 'Die-
hards', 1910–11.]

890  WILSON. Henry Joseph Wilson, fighter for freedom, 1833–1914. By Mosa Anderson. 1953. [Nonconformist Radical of the most vigorous type. See also William Stewart
Fowler, *A study in radicalism and dissent: the life and times of Henry Joseph Wilson,
1833–1914*, 1961.]

891  WINFREY. Leaves from my life. Priv. pr. King's Lynn. 1936. Great men and others
I have met. Kettering. 1943. By Sir Richard Winfrey. [Liberal agent, land reformer,
Holland county councillor, M.P. 1906–24.]

892  WINTERTON. Pre-war. 1932. Orders of the day . . . . 1953. Fifty tumultuous years.
1955. By Edward Turnour, Earl Winterton. [Active young Tory M.P.]

893  WOLFF. Some notes on the past. 1892. Rambling recollections. 2 v. 1908. By Sir
Henry Drummond Wolff. [Diplomat: member of the Fourth Party.]

## 5. POLITICAL HOSTESSES

894  LADY BATTERSEA. Reminiscences. By Constance Flower, Baroness
Battersea. 1922.

895  LADY HORNER. Time remembered. By Frances Jane Horner, Lady
Horner. 1933.

896  LADY JERSEY. Fifty-one years of Victorian life. By Margaret Elizabeth
Child-Villiers, Countess of Jersey. 1922.

897  LADY JEUNE. Memories of fifty years. By Susan Elizabeth Mary Jeune, Lady Jeune, afterwards Baroness St. Helier. 1909.

Her *Lesser questions*, 1894, deals mainly with social changes.

898  LADY KNIGHTLEY. The journals of Lady Knightley of Fawsley, 1856–1884. Ed. by Julia Cartwright. 1915.

899  LADY LONDONDERRY. Frances Anne: the life and times of Frances Anne, Marchioness of Londonderry and her husband Charles, third Marquess of Londonderry. By Edith Helen Vane-Tempest-Stewart, Marchioness of Londonderry. 1958.

See also *Letters from Benjamin Disraeli to Frances Anne, Marchioness of Londonderry, 1837–61*, ed. by Edith, Marchioness of Londonderry. 1938.

900  LADY OTTOLINE MORRELL. Ottoline: the early memoirs of Lady Ottoline Morrell. Ed. by Robert Gathorne-Hardy. 1963. Publ. in N.Y. as Memoirs of Lady Ottoline Morrell. 1964.

901  LADY DOROTHY NEVILL. The life & letters of Lady Dorothy Nevill. By Ralph Henry Nevill. 1919.

Ralph Nevill also ed. *Leaves from the note-books of Lady Dorothy Nevill*, 1907; *The reminiscences of Lady Dorothy Nevill*, 1906; *Under five reigns*, 4th edn. 1910, and *My own times*, [1912].

902  LADY PALMERSTON. Lady Palmerston and her times. By Mabell Frances Elizabeth Ogilvy, Countess of Airlie. 2 v. 1922.

See also Lady Airlie, *In Whig Society, 1775–1818* . . ., 1921, Francis Evans Baily, *The love story of Lady Palmerston*, 1938, Abraham Hayward, *Lady Palmerston* . . ., 1872, and Sir Tresham Lever, ed., *The letters of Lady Palmerston*, 1957.

903  LADY SOUTHWARK. Social & political reminiscences. By Selina Mary Causton, Baroness Southwark. 1913.

904  LADY WALDEGRAVE. Strawberry fair: a biography of Frances, Countess Waldegrave, 1821–1879. By Osbert Wyndham Hewett. 1956.

For her husband see **763**.

905  LADY WARWICK. Life's ebb and flow. By Frances Evelyn Greville, Countess of Warwick. [1929].

See also Margaret Blunden, *The Countess of Warwick: a biography*, 1967, and Theo Lang, *My darling daisy* . . ., 1966, publ. in N.Y. as *The darling daisy affair*, 1966. Her husband, Francis Richard C. G. Greville, Earl of Warwick, publ. *Memories of sixty years*, 1917.

906  LADY WESTMORLAND. The correspondence of Priscilla, Countess of Westmorland, 1813–1870. Ed. by Lady Rose Sophia Mary Weigall. 1909.

# III

## EXTERNAL RELATIONS

### A. GENERAL

#### 1. REFERENCE

907 FOREIGN OFFICE LIBRARY. Catalogue of printed books in the library of the Foreign Office. H.M.S.O. 1926.

A useful subject catalogue.

908 RAGATZ (LOWELL JOSEPH) *comp.* The literature of European imperialism, 1815–1939: a bibliography. Wash. 1944. Repr. 1947.

See also his *Bibliography for the study of European history, 1815 to 1939*, Ann Arbor [Mich.] 1942, suppls. 1943–56. To be suppl. by Alfred von Wegerer, ed., *Bibliographie zur Vorgeschichte des Weltkrieges*, Berlin 1934.

909 PUBLIC RECORD OFFICE. The records of the Foreign Office, 1782–1939. P.R.O. handbooks 13. H.M.S.O. 1969.

An excellent guide which will be suppl. by a *List of Foreign Office confidential print to 1914*. The records of the Foreign and Colonial offices overlap considerably for this period. For the latter see 1218. Foreign Office papers printed for the use of the cabinet are listed in 373.

910 PUBLIC RECORD OFFICE. List of Foreign Office records to 1878. P.R.O. Lists and Indexes LII. H.M.S.O. 1929. Repr. N.Y. etc. 1963.

Suppl. by P.R.O. Supplementary Lists and Indexes XIII, *List of Foreign Office records*, Vols. 1–8 [1879–1913], N.Y. etc. 1964–5.

911 PARRY (CLIVE) *ed.* Law officers' opinions to the Foreign Office, 1793–1860. 97 v. Farnborough. 1970.

912 TEMPERLEY (HAROLD WILLIAM VAZEILLE) *and* PENSON (*Dame* LILLIAN MARGERY) *comps.* A century of diplomatic blue books 1814–1914: lists, edited with historical introductions. Camb. 1938. Repr. 1966.

Indispensable for publ. official papers.

913 BOURNE (KENNETH) *ed.* Foreign policy of Victorian England, 1830–1902. Oxf. 1970.

An attempt to cover the same ground as the well-known work of Harold William Vazeille Temperley and Dame Lillian Margery Penson, eds., *Foundations of British foreign policy from Pitt (1792) to Salisbury (1902): or, documents, old and new, selected and edited with historical introductions*, Camb. 1938, repr. 1966. Joel H. Wiener, ed., *Great Britain: foreign policy and the span of empire*, 4 v. 1972, covers the 18th, 19th, and 20th cents.

914  JONES (EDGAR REES) *ed.* Selected speeches on British foreign policy, 1738–1914. 1914.

915  GOOCH (GEORGE PEABODY) *and* TEMPERLEY (HAROLD WILLIAM VAZEILLE) *eds.* British documents on the origins of the war, 1898–1914. 11 v. in 13. 1926–38.

Monumental. Parallel collections have been publ. for the other great powers. For a discussion of their value see Taylor (**925**).

916  UNITED NATIONS. List of treaty collections. N.Y. 1956.

Largely repl. Denys Peter Myers, *Manual of collections of treaties and of collections relating to treaties*, Camb., Mass. 1922.

917  PARRY (CLIVE) *ed.* The consolidated treaty series. 1+. Dobbs Ferry, N.Y. 1969+.

Intended to cover all treaties from 1648.

918  BRITISH AND FOREIGN STATE PAPERS, 1812–14+. Compiled by the librarian and keeper of the papers, Foreign Office. 1832+.

Treaties and agreements of all sorts. Suppl. by Foreign Office, *Treaty series*, 1892+, publ. as part of the parl. papers, but also available as a separate series. There is a useful index to treaties, Clive Parry and Charity Hopkins, comps., *An Index of British treaties, 1101–1968*, 3 v. H.M.S.O. 1970.

919  FOREIGN OFFICE. Treaties containing guarantees or engagements by Great Britain in regard to the territory or government of other countries. [C. 9088] H.C. (1899). CIX, 1.

See also Valerie Cromwell, 'Great Britain's European treaty obligations in March 1902', *Hist. J.* vi (1963), 272–9.

920  HERTSLET (LEWIS) *and others, comps.* A complete collection of the treaties and conventions and reciprocal regulations at present subsisting between Great Britain and foreign powers, and of the laws, decrees and orders in council concerning the same; so far as they relate to commerce and navigation; to the repression of the slave trade; and to the privileges and interests of the subjects of the high contracting parties. 30 v. 1840–1924. Indexed.

Later vols. styled *Hertslet's commercial treaties*.

921  HERTSLET (*Sir* EDWARD). *comp.* Treaties and tariffs regulating the trade between Great Britain and foreign nations; and extracts of treaties between foreign powers, containing most-favoured-nation clauses applicable to Great Britain. 6 v. 1875–9.

Covers Austria, Turkey, Italy, China, Spain, Japan.

922  BERNHARDT (GASTON DE) *ed.* Handbook of treaties, etc., relating to commerce and navigation between Great Britain and foreign powers. 1908. New edn. 1912.

923  GEISS (IMANUEL) *ed.* July 1914: the outbreak of the First World War: selected documents. N.Y. 1967.

Originally publ. as *Julikrise und Kriegsausbruch, 1914,* 2 v. Hanover 1963–4.

924  MOLHUYSEN (PHILIP CHRISTIAAN) *and* OPPENHEIM (ELSA RACHEL) *comps.* Bibliothèque du Palais de la Paix: catalogue. Leyde. 1916. Suppl. and index. 2 v. 1922.

See also Fred L. Israel, ed., *Major peace treaties of modern history, 1648–1967,* intro. by Arnold Toynbee, 4 v. N.Y. 1967.

## 2. BRITAIN IN WORLD POLITICS

925  TAYLOR (ALAN JOHN PERCIVALE). The struggle for mastery in Europe, 1848–1918. Oxf. 1954.

The nearest thing to a satisfactory general history of international politics, though Europe-based. Must be suppl. by Langer (**926–7**). For a different emphasis see René Albrecht-Carrié, *A diplomatic history of Europe since the Congress of Vienna,* N.Y. 1958, Lond. 1959, and Frederick Samuel Northedge and M. J. Grieve, *A hundred years of international relations,* 1971.

926  LANGER (WILLIAM LEONARD). European alliances and alignments, 1871–90. N.Y. 1931. 2nd edn. 1950.

With **927** the greatest diplomatic history ever produced: unrivalled for range, though German-oriented.

927  LANGER (WILLIAM LEONARD). The diplomacy of imperialism, 1890–1902. 2 v. N.Y. 1935. 2nd edn. 1 v. N.Y. 1951.

928  HEADLAM-MORLEY (*Sir* JAMES WYCLIFFE). Studies in diplomatic history. 1930.

A series of essays. Valuable essays on the period are also incl. in George Peabody Gooch, *Recent revelations of European diplomacy,* 1927, 4th edn. 1940, and *Studies in diplomacy and statecraft,* Lond. & N.Y. 1942; Arshag Ohan Sarkissian, ed., *Studies in diplomatic history and historiography in honour of G. P. Gooch,* 1961; William Norton Medlicott, ed., *From Metternich to Hitler: aspects of British and foreign history, 1814–1939: essays,* 1963; Kenneth Bourne and Donald Cameron Watt, eds., *Studies in international history: essays presented to W. Norton Medlicott,* 1967.

929  WARD (*Sir* ADOLPHUS WILLIAM) *and* GOOCH (GEORGE PEA-BODY) *eds.* The Cambridge history of British foreign policy, 1783–1919. 3 v. Camb. 1922–3.

Now very dated, but not replaced by any more recent work. Useful bibliogs.

930  PLATT (DESMOND CHRISTOPHER ST. MARTIN). Finance, trade, and politics in British foreign policy, 1815–1914. Oxf. 1968.

A valuable pioneering study.

931  TAYLOR (ALAN JOHN PERCIVALE). The trouble makers: dissent over foreign policy, 1792–1939. 1957.

A sprightly survey of the opponents of official policy. Andrew Rothstein, *British foreign policy and its critics, 1830–1950*, 1969, is a series of 4 Marxist lectures, 3 of them on W. S. Blunt, E. D. Morel, and Robert Dell. For the 1850s and 1860s see also Valerie Cromwell, 'The private member of the House of Commons and foreign policy . . .', *Liber memorialis Sir Maurice Powicke: studies presented to the International Commission for the History of Representative and Parliamentary Institutions*, xxvii, Louvain and Paris 1965, 193–218.

932   PHELPS *afterwards* GRANT (CHRISTINA). The Anglo-American peace movement in the mid-nineteenth century [1835–54]. N.Y. & Lond. 1930.

933   ROBSON (MAUREEN M.). 'Liberals and "vital interests": the debate on international arbitration, 1815–72'. *Inst. Hist. Res. Bull.* xxxii (1959), 38–55.

For the development of arbitration see Jackson Harvey Ralston, *International arbitration from Athens to Locarno*. Stanford, Cal., 1929.

934   KNAPLUND (PAUL). Gladstone's foreign policy. N.Y. & Lond. 1935.

Largely replaced by Medlicott (**2270**) and (**2406**).

935   LOWE (CEDRIC JAMES). The reluctant imperialists: British foreign policy, 1878–1902. 2 v. Lond. 1967. lv. N.Y. 1967.

A general introductory work making no great claims to originality. Vol. 2 is a short vol. of documents. Cont. by C. J. Lowe and M. L. Dockrill, *The mirage of power: British foreign policy, 1902[–22]*, 3 v. 1972.

936   CHIROL. Fifty years in a changing world. By Sir Valentine Chirol. 1927.

The memoirs of one of the best-informed British journalists specializing in foreign (particular eastern) affairs.

937   FOOT (MICHAEL RICHARD DANIELL). British foreign policy since 1898. 1956.

A useful brief summary.

938   GRENVILLE (JOHN ASHLEY SOAMES). Lord Salisbury and foreign policy: the close of the nineteenth century. 1964.

Important. See also Dame Lillian Margery Penson, *Foreign affairs under the third Marquis of Salisbury*, 1962, and Lowe, *Salisbury and the Mediterranean* (**2349**).

939   HOWARD (CHRISTOPHER HENRY DURHAM). Splendid isolation: a study of ideas concerning Britain's international position and foreign policy during the later years of the third Marquis of Salisbury. 1967.

An interpretative essay.

940   PENSON (*Dame* LILLIAN MARGERY). 'The new course in British foreign policy, 1892–1902'. *Roy. Hist. Soc. Trans.* 4 ser. xxv (1943), 121–38. Repr. in Ian R. Christie, ed., Essays in modern history . . ., Lond. & N.Y. 1968. 308–28.

941   MONGER (GEORGE W.). The end of isolation: British foreign policy, 1900–1907. 1963.

Good. Johan Marius Goudswaard, *Some aspects of the end of Britain's 'splendid isolation' 1898–1904*, Rotterdam 1952, is also well worth consulting.

942 CONWELL-EVANS (THOMAS PUGH). Foreign policy from a back bench, 1904–18: a study based on the papers of Lord Noel-Buxton. 1932.

See also Howard S. Weinroth, 'The British radicals and the balance of power, 1902–1914', *Hist. J.* xiii (1970), 653–82.

943 MADDOX (WILLIAM PERCY). Foreign relations in British Labor politics: a study in the formation of party attitudes on foreign affairs, and the application of political pressure designed to influence government policy, 1900–1924. Camb., Mass. 1934.

944 COLLINS (DOREEN). Aspects of British politics, 1904–1919. Oxf. & N.Y. 1965.

Useful, but less thorough than Williamson (**2669**).

945 ALBERTINI (LUIGI). The origins of the war of 1914. Trans. and ed. by Isabella Mellis Massey. 3 v. 1952–7.

A good introduction. See also Sidney Bradshaw Fay, *The origins of the World War*, 2 v. N.Y. 1929, long the standard account. Goldsworthy Lowes Dickinson, *The international anarchy, 1904–1914*, 1926, new edn. 1937, is a stimulating essay that should not be overlooked. Henry Ralph Winkler, *The League of Nations movement in Great Britain, 1914–19*, New Brunswick, N.J. 1952, deals with the reaction of those who wanted to prevent future wars by collective agreement.

946 CHURCHILL (*Sir* WINSTON LEONARD SPENCER-). The world crisis, 1911–1914. 1923.

The first v. of 6. The opinionated, but stimulating account of a cabinet minister. Cp. Asquith's *The genesis of the war* (**726**), Grey's *Twenty-five years* (**770**), Lloyd George's *War Memoirs* (**765**), Haldane's *Before the war* (**772**), Morley's *Memorandum on resignation* (**797**), and Robert Threshie Reid, Earl Loreburn, *How the war came*, Lond. 1919, N.Y. 1920. See also Ernst Anrich, *Die englische Politik im Juli 1914: eine Gesamtdarstellung der Julikrise*, Stuttgart & Berlin 1934, Keith G. Robbins, 'Lord Bryce and the First World War', *Hist. J.* x (1967), 255–77, and Sir Herbert Butterfield, 'Sir Edward Grey in July 1914', *Hist. Studs.* v (1963), 1–25.

947 INTERNATIONAL POLICY: essays on the foreign relations of England. Edited by Richard Congreve. 1866. 2nd abridged edn. 1884.

A positivist symposium covering India as well as foreign countries. Comparable in conception with *Essays on reform*, etc. (**523**).

948 SEELEY (*Sir* JOHN ROBERT). The expansion of England: two courses of lectures. Boston & Lond. 1883.

Famous and influential. For other imperialist works see **1272–82**.

949 DILKE (*Sir* CHARLES WENTWORTH). The present position of European politics: or, Europe in 1887. 1887.

Dilke also wrote extensively on imperial problems. See **1273**.

950 WILKINSON ([HENRY] SPENSER). The great alternative: a plea for a national policy. 1894. New edn. 1902.

A demand for a positive foreign policy. See also his *The nation's awakening: essays towards a British policy*, 1896, 2nd edn. 1897, *Britain at bay*, 1909, and **2664**. The idea that Britain was in danger is also stressed by [Arthur] George [Villiers] Peel, in *The enemies of England*, 1902, *The friends of England*, 1905, and *The future of England*, 1911.

951 ANGELL (*Sir* NORMAN). The great illusion: a study of the relation of military power in nations to their economic and social advantage. 1910.

A famous attack on the 'armed camps' before 1914. Suppl. by his *Arms and industry: a study of the foundations of international polity*, N.Y. 1914, publ. in London as *The foundations of international polity*, 1914. Cp. Henry Noel Brailsford, *The war of steel and gold: a study of the armed peace*, 1914, 3rd edn. 1915.

952 JOHNSTON (*Sir* HARRY HAMILTON). Common sense in foreign policy. 1913.

By a famous proconsul.

## 3. IMPERIALISM

Books in this section should be read in conjunction with the lives of the great imperialists, Chamberlain (**750**), Milner (**1305**), Cromer (**1673**), Curzon (**1132**), Lugard (**1626, 1771, 1868, 1870**), and Johnston (**1625**).

953 FIELDHOUSE (DAVID KENNETH). The colonial empires: a comparative survey from the eighteenth century. 1966.

A useful general survey. For facts and figures Grover Clark, *The balance sheets of imperialism: facts and figures on colonies*, N.Y. 1936, 2nd edn. 1967, is useful.

954 GOLLWITZER (HEINZ). Europe in the age of imperialism, 1880–1914. Trans. by David Adam and Stanley Baron. 1969.

A short but valuable study, well illustrated. Much better than Carl G. Wingenroth, *Deutscher und englischer 'Imperialismus' vor dem Weltkrieg*, Bottrop 1934.

955 KIERNAN (VICTOR GORDON). The lords of human kind: European attitudes towards the outside world in the imperial age. 1969.

Very perceptive, written from a Marxist viewpoint.

956 MOON (PARKER THOMAS). Imperialism and world politics. N.Y. 1926.

Long the most widely-consulted book on the subject. Now outdated.

957 KOEBNER (RICHARD) *and* SCHMIDT (HELMUT DAN). Imperialism: the story and significance of a political world, 1840–1960. Camb. 1964.

One of the few really good books in the field.

958 FIELDHOUSE (DAVID KENNETH) *ed.* The theory of capitalist imperialism. 1967.

A useful summary of the literature of the subject. One of a number of books intended to aid undergraduates. Others incl. Harrison Morris Wright, ed., *The 'new imperialism': analysis of late nineteenth-century expansion*, Boston 1961; George Hans Nadel and Lewis Perry Curtis Jr., eds., *Imperialism and colonialism*, N.Y. 1964; and Louis Leo

Snyder, ed., *The imperialism reader: documents and readings on modern expansionism*, Princeton [N.J.] 1962.

959 MAUNIER (RENÉ). The sociology of colonies: an introduction to the study of race contact. Ed. and trans. by Emily O. Lorimer. 1949.

An early attempt at a general theory. Should be read with **960–1**.

960 SCHUMPETER (JOSEPH ALOIS). Imperialism and social classes. Trans. by Heinz Norden and ed. by Paul M. Sweezy. N.Y. & Oxf. 1951. Many edns.

961 MANNONI (DOMINIQUE OTARE). Prospero and Caliban: the psychology of colonization. Trans. by Pamela Powesland. N.Y. 1956. 2nd edn. 1964.

962 MASON (PHILIP) and others. Man, race and Darwin . . . 1960.

Useful for racial aspects of imperial expansion. See also Mason's *Prospero's magic: some thoughts on class and race*, 1962.

963 THORNTON (ARCHIBALD PATON). Doctrines of imperialism. N.Y. 1965.

An introductory survey.

964 KEMP (TOM). Theories of imperialism. 1967.

Marxist.

965 BENNETT (GEORGE) *ed.* The concept of empire: from Burke to Attlee, 1774–1947. 1953. 2nd edn. 1962.

Docs. Robin William Winks, ed., *British imperialism: gold, God, glory*, N.Y. 1963, gives brief extracts from controversial writings on the nature of British imperialism.

966 CREIGHTON (DONALD GRANT). 'The Victorians and the empire'. *Canadian Hist. Rev.* xix (1938), 138–53.

A good statement of the old scholarly orthodoxy, on which see also William Leonard Langer, 'A critique of imperialism', *Foreign Affairs*, xiv (1935–6), 102–19. A new approach began with John Andrew Gallagher and Ronald Robinson, 'The imperialism of free trade', *Econ. Hist. Rev.*, 2 ser. vi (1953–4), 1–15, their *Africa and the Victorians*, (**1621**), and their contribution to the *New Cambridge Modern History*, vol. XI (**163**). To this Oliver MacDonagh, 'The anti-imperialism of free trade', *Econ. Hist. Rev.* 2 ser. xiv (1961–2), 489–501, Desmond Christopher St. Martin Platt, 'The imperialism of free trade: some reservations', *Econ. Hist. Rev.* 2 ser. xxi (1968), 296–306, and Eric Stokes, 'Late nineteenth-century colonial expansion and the attack on the theory of economic imperialism: a case of mistaken identity', *Hist. J.* xii (1969), 285–301, were responses. See also Samuel Berrick Saul, 'The economic significance of constructive imperialism', *J. Econ. Hist.* xvii (1957), 173–92, David Saul Landes, 'Some thoughts on the nature of economic imperialism', ibid. xxi (1961), 496–512, and Richard J. Hammond, 'Economic imperialism: sidelights on a stereotype', ibid. xxi (1961), 582–600. For attempts to sum up the debate see David Kenneth Fieldhouse, ' "Imperialism": an historiographical revision', *Econ. Hist. Rev.* xiv (1961–2), 187–209, Alan George Lewers Shaw, 'A revision of the meaning of imperialism', *Australian J. Pol. & Hist.* vii (1961), 198–213, and Jean Stengers, 'L'impérialisme colonial de la fin du XIXe siècle: mythe ou réalité', *J. African Hist.* iii (1962), 469–91.

967 THORNTON (ARCHIBALD PATON). The imperial idea and its enemies: a study in British power. 1959. 2nd edn. 1966.

A perceptive general survey. Suppl. by his *For the file on empire: essays and reviews*, 1968. See also Eric Stokes, *The political ideas of English imperialism*, 1960, an inaugural lecture, and Donald Craigie Gordon, *The moment of power: Britain's imperial epoch*, Englewood Cliffs, N.J. 1970.

968 FABER (RICHARD). The vision and the need: late Victorian imperialist aims. 1966.

969 SEMMEL (BERNARD). Imperialism and social reform: English social-imperial thought, 1895–1914. Lond. & Camb., Mass. 1960. Repr. Garden City. [N.Y.] 1968.

An important pioneering work. See also Ernst Wiegner, *Der britische Imperialismus: eine kritische Betrachtung des Chamberlain-Programs*, Zurich 1938.

970 MOMMSEN (WOLFGANG JUSTIN). 'Nationale und ökonomische Faktoren im britischen Imperialismus vor 1914'. *Historische Zeitschrift* ccvi (1968), 618–64.

971 PORTER (BERNARD). Critics of empire: British radical attitudes to colonialism in Africa, 1895–1914. 1968.

Good.

972 TSIANG (TINGFU FULLER). Labor and empire: a study of the reaction of British labor, mainly as represented in parliament, to British imperialism since 1880. Columbia Studs. in Hist. Econ. and Public Law, vol. CVI. No 1. N.Y. 1923.

973 BRIE (FRIEDRICH WILHELM DANIEL). Imperialistische Strömungen in der Englischen Literatur. 2nd edn. Halle 1928.

See also Greenberger (**1018**).

974 ROBERTSON (JOHN MACKINNON). Patriotism and empire. 1899.

One of the first and best attacks on imperialism.

975 HOBSON (JOHN ATKINSON). Imperialism: a study. 1902. 3rd edn. 1938, and reprs. New edn. Ann Arbor [Mich.] 1965.

Taken up by Lenin (**983**). Famous as the first popular attack on imperialism. Summarizes his arguments in *Capitalism and imperialism in South Africa*, N.Y. 1900, *The psychology of jingoism*, 1901, and 'The scientific basis of imperialism', *Pol. Sci. Q.* xvii (1902), 460–89.

976 HOBHOUSE (LEONARD TRELAWNEY). Democracy and reaction. Lond. 1904. N.Y. 1905. 2nd edn. Lond. 1909.

Includes a carefully measured Liberal attack on imperialism.

977 CRAMB (JOHN ADAM). Reflections on the origins and destiny of imperial Britain. Lond. & N.Y. 1900. New edn. N.Y. 1915.

978  MACKINDER (*Sir* HALFORD JOHN). Britain and the British seas. 1902. 2nd edn. Oxf. 1907.

Geopolitics brought to the aid of imperialism.

979  GOLDMAN (CHARLES SYDNEY) *and others.* The empire and the century: a series of essays on imperial problems and possibilities, by various writers. 1905.

A confident imperialist symposium.

980  BÉRARD ([EUGÈNE] VICTOR). British imperialism and commercial supremacy. Trans. by H. W. Foskett. 1906.

One of a great number of foreign works prompted by imperial rivalries. See also Bardoux (**522**), Gerhart von Schulze-Gaevernitz, *Britischer Imperialismus und englischer Freihandel zu Beginn des zwanzigsten Jahrhunderts,* Leipzig 1906, Erich Marcks, *Die imperialistische Idee in der Gegenwart,* Dresden 1903, and Achille Viallate, *La crise anglaise: impérialisme et protection,* Paris 1905.

981  MACDONALD (JAMES RAMSAY). Labour and the empire. 1907.

982  CROFT (HENRY PAGE), *Baron Croft.* The path of empire. With an intro. by Joseph Chamberlain. 1912.

983  LENIN (VLADIMIR IL'ICH). Imperialism: the highest stage of capitalism . . . Numerous English trans. Orig. edn. 1916.

Much the most influential treatment of the subject. For the differences between Lenin and Hobson see Stokes (**966**).

984  WOOLF (LEONARD SIDNEY). Empire & commerce in Africa: a study in economic imperialism. 1919. Repr. Lond. & N.Y. 1968.

One of the most influential left-wing attacks on imperialism. Established a sort of orthodoxy. See also his *Economic imperialism,* Lond. & N.Y. 1920.

## B. THE INDIAN EMPIRE

There is a fast-growing literature on the subject which is increasingly concerned with the social and economic life of the people of India rather than with their transitory British rulers. The emphasis here is inevitably on the British in India and Indian reactions to them, rather than on India in general.

### I. REFERENCE

(Additional reference works are entered under Asia)

985  SUTTON (STANLEY CECIL). A guide to the India Office library, with a note on the India Office records. H.M.S.O. 1952. 2nd edn. 1967.

Suppl. by the Librarian's *Annual report* and Joan Cadogan Lancaster, *A guide to lists and catalogues of the India Office records,* 1966. The biggest and best specialist library for Indian history, with all the official records of the British administration of India.

986 INDIA OFFICE LIBRARY. Catalogue of European printed books. 10 v. Boston. 1964.

Suppl. by *Index of post-1937 European manuscript accessions,* Boston 1964. Vol. 10 is a catalogue of periodicals. For a subject catalogue consult the *Library catalogue* of the School of Oriental and African Studies (**2506**), and vol. 4. of Lewin (**1213**).

987 FOSTER (WILLIAM). A guide to the India Office records, 1600–1858. 1919. Repr. 1966.

The records of the East India Company. See also Mildred Archer, ed., *British drawings in the India Office library*: Vol. 1. *amateur artists*; Vol. 2. *official and professional artists*, 2 v. H.M.S.O. 1970.

988 WAINWRIGHT (MARY DOREEN) *and* MATTHEWS (NOEL) *comps.* A guide to western manuscripts and documents in the British Isles relating to South and South-East Asia. 1965.

A magnificent work, absolutely indispensable. Does not cover the India Office records.

989 LOW (DONALD ANTHONY) *and others.* Government archives in South Asia: a guide to national and state archives in Ceylon, India and Pakistan. Camb. 1969.

A great boon to researchers, replacing a series of outdated and ill-organized handbooks.

990 CAMPBELL (FRANCIS BUNBURY FITZGERALD) *comp.* Index-catalogue of Indian official publications in the library, British Museum. [1900.]

A very useful subject catalogue whose range is wider than the title suggests, since it includes works publ. by public bodies and about them. For British parliamentary papers see *Annual lists and general index of parliamentary papers relating to the East Indies published during the years 1801 to 1907 inclusive.* H.C. 89 (1909). LXIV, 757. For recent govt. pubs. see Rajeshwari Datta, ed., *Union catalogue of the central government of India publications held by libraries in London, Oxford and Cambridge,* Centre of South Asian Studs., Camb. Univ., Lond. 1970, and *Union catalogue of government of Pakistan publications . . .,* 1967.

991 SELECTIONS FROM THE RECORDS OF THE GOVERNMENT OF INDIA. 450 nos. Calcutta. 1853–1912.

A tantalizing series of miscellaneous official papers, almost all post-1851, many of them listed in Campbell (**990**). Suppl. by provincial government *Selections,* also listed in Campbell. There is an index to some of the earlier vols. of both Indian and provincial records in Meredith Townsend, *The Indian official thesaurus: being introductory to 'Annals of Indian administration',* Serampore 1858. The annual reports to Parliament by the India Office (**1103**) and the annual reports of the provincial administrations constitute a running series of records. There is also a good deal of semi-record material in *The annals of Indian administration,* 19 v. Serampore 1856–75.

992 PATTERSON (MAUREEN L. P.) *and* INDEN (RONALD B.) *eds.* Introduction to the civilization of India: South Asia: an introductory bibliography. Chicago. 1962.

A useful guide, which is usually more valuable for historians than J. Michael Mahar, *India: a critical bibliography,* Tucson, Ariz. 1964. New publs. are listed annually in the *Journal of Asian studies* (**2505**), and in *The Indian national bibliography,* Calcutta 1957+. Sachchidananda Bhattacharya, *A dictionary of Indian history,* N.Y. 1967, is a useful compilation of facts for beginners. Useful specialist bibliogs. incl. Norman Gerald Barrier, *Punjab history in printed British documents: a bibliographic guide to parliamentary papers and select, nonserial publications, 1843-1947,* Univ. of Missouri Studs. L, Columbia, Mo. 1969, and *The Punjab in nineteenth-century tracts: an introduction to the pamphlet collections in the British Museum and India Office,* East Lansing, Mich. 1969, and Frank Newton Trager and others, eds., *Annotated bibliography of Burma,* New Haven, Conn. 1956.

993  CASE (MARGARET H.). South Asian history, 1750-1950: a guide to periodicals, dissertations and newspapers. Princeton, [N.J.] 1968.

994  PHILIPS (CYRIL HENRY) *ed.* Historians of India, Pakistan and Ceylon. 1961.

A study of South Asian historiography.

995  [ROYAL] ASIATIC SOCIETY OF BENGAL. Journal. 1+. Calcutta. 1832+.

The principal Indian j. of scholarship and opinion during the period. The form of publ. changed from time to time. From 1865 to 1904 the *Proceedings* of the Soc. were publ. apart from the j. and there were further reorganizations in 1935 and 1959. The Bombay equivalent was Royal Asiatic Soc. (Bombay Branch), *Journal,* 1841-4+, Bombay 1844+. The chief js. for Anglo-Indians were *The Asiatic quarterly rev.,* 1886+ [title changed to *The imperial and asiatic rev.,* 1891-1912, *Asiatic rev.,* 1914-52, *Asian rev.,* 1953+] and *The Calcutta rev.,* Calcutta 1844+.

996  HUNTER (*Sir* WILLIAM WILSON) *ed.* The imperial gazetteer of India. 9 v. 1881. 2nd edn. 14 v. 1885-7.

The first attempt at a comprehensive survey of British India. Based on local reports, many of them incl. in Hunter's *A statistical account of Bengal,* 20 v. 1875-7, and *A statistical account of Assam,* 2 v. 1879. A 1-v. account (v. 6 of *The imperial gazetteer*) was also publ. by Hunter for popular use as *The Indian empire: its history, people and products,* 1882, 3rd edn. 1893. For an account of the local surveys used in compiling this survey and its successor (**997**) see Sashi Bhusan Chaudhuri, *History of the gazetteers of India,* New Delhi 1964, and Henry Scholberg, *The district gazetteers of British India: a bibliography,* Zug, Switz. 1970. There is no convenient summary of census materials, except for the 20th cent. which is covered in Kingsley Davis, *The population of India and Pakistan,* Princeton [N.J.] 1951, repr. N.Y. 1968.

997  COTTON (JAMES SUTHERLAND) *and others, eds.* The imperial gazetteer of India . . . new edition published under the authority of His Majesty's Secretary of State for India in council. 26 v. Oxf. 1907-9.

The fullest work of reference on pre-1914 India. Based on extensive provincial and district surveys, many of which were printed separately.

998  STATISTICAL ABSTRACT relating to British India, from 1840 to 1865. [3817] H.C. (1867). LXXII, 1. Annual to 1942-3.

A useful statistical series. Needs to be suppl. by the detailed annual statistics publ. by the government of India.

999  GRIERSON (*Sir* GEORGE ABRAHAM). Linguistic survey of India. 11 v. Calcutta. 1903-28.

Important for Indian languages. Grierson also wrote extensively on modern vernacular literature.

1000  YULE (*Sir* HENRY) *and* BURNELL (ARTHUR COKE). Hobson-Jobson: being a glossary of anglo-indian colloquial words and phrases, and of kindred terms, etymological, historical, geographical and discursive. 1886. 2nd edn. 1903. Repr. Delhi etc. 1968.

1001  WILSON (HORACE HAYMAN). A glossary of judicial and revenue terms, and of useful words occurring in official documents relating to the administration of the government of British India . . . 1855. Repr. Calcutta 1940.

1002  BUCKLAND (CHARLES EDWARD). Dictionary of Indian biography. 1906.

A useful outline, but no substitute for an Indian *D.N.B.* See also Sir Roper Lethbridge, *The golden book of India: a genealogical and biographical dictionary of the ruling princes, chiefs, nobles and other personages, titled or decorated, of the Indian empire,* 1893, new edn. 1900, and *Who's who in India: containing lives and portraits of ruling chiefs, notables, titled personages and other eminent Indians,* Lucknow 1911, suppl. 1912.

1003  PHILIPS (CYRIL HENRY) *and others, eds.* The evolution of India and Pakistan, 1858 to 1947: select documents. 1962.

For constitutional documents see also **1096**.

1004  NATIONAL ARCHIVES OF INDIA. Selections from educational records of the government of India. 1+. New Delhi. 1960+.

Vol. I covers educational reports 1859–71, vol. II, ed. by J. P. Naik, covers university education, 1860–87. Continues the work of Sir Henry Sharp and James Alexander Richey who publ. 2 vols. of *Selections from educational records of the government of India,* 2 v. Calcutta 1920–2, covering the period down to 1859.

## 2. GENERAL

### (a) *Histories and Descriptive Works*

1005  SPEAR ([THOMAS GEORGE] PERCIVAL). India: a modern history. Ann Arbor, [Mich.] 1961.

The best western one-vol. hist. Spear's *The Oxford history of modern India, 1740–1947,* Oxf. 1965, and *A history of India,* vol. II, Harmondsworth 1965, are also good. Michael Edwardes, *British India, 1772–1947: a survey of the nature and effects of alien rule,* 1967, and Sir Percival Joseph Griffiths, *The British impact on India,* 1952, add little but detail.

1006  MAJUMDAR (RAMESH CHANDRA), RAYCHAUDHURI (HEM-CHANDRA) *and* DATTA (KALIKINKAR). An advanced history of India. 1946. 3rd edn. 1967.

The best Indian one-vol. hist. Sir Rustom Pestonji Masani, *Britain in India: an account of British rule in the Indian subcontinent,* Lond. & Calcutta 1960, presents a somewhat different viewpoint, but adds little. Should be suppl. by Swaminath Natarajan, *A century of social reform in India,* Bombay & Lond. 1959, 2nd. edn. 1963. There is an older nationalist account in Baman Das Basu, *India under the British crown,* Calcutta 1933.

1007 THE CAMBRIDGE HISTORY OF INDIA. 6 v. Camb. 1922–37. New edn. Delhi. 1958–62.

Out of date, but useful on British administration and other topics. Good bibliogs. Vol. VI covers 1858–1918. There is a summary of the 6 v. in Henry Herbert Dodwell, ed., *The Cambridge shorter history of India*, Camb. 1934, new edns. Delhi 1958, 1969. Dodwell also publ. a useful study, *India*, 2 v. 1936, the second vol. of which covers 1858–1936.

1008 MAJUMDAR (RAMESH CHANDRA) *ed.* Bharatiya Vidya Bhavan's history and culture of the Indian people. *c.* 12 v. Bombay 1953+. In progress.

The only Indian multi-vol. hist. Vols. IX to XI cover 1818–1914 and are all by Majumdar, whose standpoint is that of a Bengali and Hindu nationalist of the time of the independence movement. Intended to be suppl. by Majumdar's *History of the freedom movement*, 3 v. Calcutta 1962–3. On cultural hist. Sri Ramakrishna Centenary Committee, *The cultural heritage of India*, 3 v. Calcutta 1937, 2nd edn. 5 v. Calcutta 1953 etc., is a useful reflection of Hindu ideas. Sheikh Mohamad Ikram and Thomas George Percival Spear, eds., *The cultural heritage of Pakistan*, 1955, covers Muslim hist. For interpretative studies of Indian culture see Dhurjati Prasad Mukerji, *Modern Indian culture: a sociological study*, Bombay 1942, 2nd edn. 1948, Wilfred Cantwell Smith, *Modern Islam in India: a social analysis*, Lahore 1943, 2nd edn. 1947, repr. 1963, and Pramatha Nath Bose, *A history of Hindu civilisation during British rule*, 3 v. Calcutta 1894–6.

1009 THE INDIAN ECONOMIC AND SOCIAL HISTORY REVIEW. 1+. Delhi. 1963+.

The only Indian scholarly j. to print consistently good articles on the period. Good articles also appear in *J. of Asian Studs.*, *Modern Asian Studs.*, and *J. Asian Hist.* (**2505**), good reviews in *South Asian Rev: the j. of the Royal Society for India, Pakistan and Ceylon*, 1+, 1967+, and less good articles in *J. of Indian Hist.*, 1+, Dept. of Hist., Univ. of Allahabad, 1921+, *J. of the Pakistan Hist. Soc.*, Karachi 1953+, and *Bengal Past & Present: j. of the Calcutta Hist. Soc.*, 1+, Calcutta 1907+.

1010 THOMPSON (EDWARD JOHN) *and* GARRATT (GEOFFREY THEODORE). Rise and fulfilment of British rule in India. 1934. Repr. Allahabad. 1962.

Long one of the best and most informative books on the British in India. Now dated. Needs to be read with the attack on the British record in Reginald Reynolds, *The white sahibs in India*, 1937, 3rd edn. 1946.

1011 PRASAD (BISHESHWAR). The foundations of India's foreign policy. Vol. I. 1860–1882. Bombay. 1955.

Neither accurate nor adequate. A hist. of Indian foreign policy is badly needed. For the Indian frontiers see 1173–5. Among contemp. works note James Talboys Wheeler, *Summary of affairs of the government of India in the foreign department from 1864 to 1869*, Calcutta 1868, John William Shaw Wyllie, *Essays on the external policy of India*, ed. by Sir William Wilson Hunter, 1875, and Sir Orfeur Cavenagh, *Reminiscences of an Indian official*, 1884.

1012 MEHROTRA (SRI RAM). India and the commonwealth, 1885–1929. 1965.

A very good book.

1013  KONDAPI (CHENCHAL). Indians overseas, 1838–1949. New Delhi. 1951.

A useful survey. Should be suppl. by Ina Mary Cumpston, *Indians overseas in British territories, 1834–1854,* 1953, repr. 1969, and 'A survey of Indian migration to British tropical colonies to 1910', *Population Studs.* x (1956–7), 158–65, Ramesh Chandra Majumdar, *Hindu colonies in the Far East,* Calcutta 1944, 2nd edn. 1963, and the studs. of Indian migrants in East Africa (**1733**), Fiji (**1423**), Guiana (**1583**), Malaya (**2215**), Mauritius (**1794**) and South Africa (**2032**). For further details see *Report of the committee on emigration from India to the crown colonies and protectorates* [Chairman: Lord Sanderson]. [Cd. 5192–4] H.C. (1910). XXVII, 1+.

1014  O'MALLEY (LEWIS SYDNEY STEWARD) *ed.* Modern India and the west: a study of the interaction of their civilizations. 1941. Repr. 1968.

Useful because there is so little else on the subject. May be suppl. by another symposium, Sir John Ghest Cumming, ed., *Political India, 1832–1932: a co-operative survey of a century,* 1932.

1015  BEARCE (GEORGE DONHAM). British attitudes towards India, 1784–1858. 1961.

A useful general survey. See also Stokes (**1050**), and Hutchins (**1051**).

1016  TREVELYAN (*Sir* GEORGE OTTO). The competition wallah. Camb. 1864. 2nd edn. 1866.

A deservedly famous satire on the British in India. Charles Thomas Buckland, *Sketches of social life in India,* 1884, is an urbane Bengal official's account. Most modern works are of little value, among them Hilton Brown, ed., *The sahibs: the life and ways of the British in India, as recorded by themselves,* 1948, Dennis Kincaid, *British social life in India, 1608–1937,* 1938, Michael Edwardes, *Bound to exile: the Victorians in India,* 1969, and John Keith Stanford, ed., *Ladies in the sun: the memsahib's India, 1790–1860,* 1962. There are a few agreeable reminiscences in Sir Stanley Reed, *The India I knew, 1897–1947,* 1952, but they are of little account.

1017  COTTON (*Sir* HENRY JOHN STEDMAN). New India: or, India in transition. 1885. New edns. 1904, 1907.

A perceptive study of changing relations between Britons and Indians. Cp. Sir Valentine Chirol, *India,* 1926, a famous account of 20th-cent. British India, and Lovat Fraser, *India under Curzon & after,* 1911.

1018  GREENBERGER (ALLEN JAY). The British image of India: a study in the literature of imperialism, 1880–1960. 1969.

A study of British writers.

1019  LEE-WARNER (*Sir* WILLIAM). The protected princes of India. 1894. 2nd edn. [The native states of India.] 1910.

See also *The British crown & the Indian states: an outline sketch drawn up on behalf of the standing committee of the Chamber of Princes by the directorate of the Chamber's special organisation,* 1929, and Panikkar (**1114**).

1020  CADY (JOHN FRANK). A history of modern Burma. Ithaca, N.Y. 1958. Suppl. 1960.

Other general hists. incl. Dorothy Woodman, *The making of Burma,* 1962, and Htin Aung, *A history of Burma,* N.Y. 1967. For external relations see Daniel George Edward

Hall, *Europe and Burma: a study of European relations with Burma to the annexation of Thibaw's kingdom, 1886,* 1945, and *Burma,* 1950, 2nd edn. 1956. Godfrey Eric Harvey, *British rule in Burma, 1824–1942,* 1946, is perceptive but of little value for the period. Colonial admin. is dealt with at **1129**. Aspects of British rule are covered by Sir Henry Yule, *A narrative of the mission sent by the governor-general of India to the court of Ava in 1855 ...,* 1858, new edn. by Hugh Tinker, Kuala Lumpur etc. 1968, *The Dalhousie-Phayre correspondence* (**1133**), Sir Charles Haukes Tod Crosthwaite, *The pacification of Burma,* 1912; Sir Herbert Thirkell White, *A civil servant in Burma,* 1913; [George Eustace] Riou Grant Brown, *Burma as I saw it, 1889–1917,* 1926; John Nisbet, *Burma under British rule—and before,* 2 v. 1901; John Frank Cady, *The problem of law and order in Burma under British administration,* Wash. 1944; Ma Mya Sein, *Administration of Burma: Sir Charles Crosthwaite and the consolidation of Burma,* Rangoon 1938; Thaung Blackmore, 'Dilemma of the British representatives to the Burma court after the outbreak of a palace revolution in 1866', *J. South East Asian Studs.* x (1969), 236–52; and Ernest Chew, 'The withdrawal of the last British residency from upper Burma in 1879', ibid. 253–79.

1021   MORRIS (MORRIS DAVID). 'Towards a reinterpretation of nineteenth-century Indian economic history'. *J. Econ. Hist.* xxiii (1963), 606–18.

Repr. with important dissenting comments by Toru Matsui, Bipan Chandra, and Tapan Raychaudhuri, in *Ind. Econ. & Soc. Hist. Rev.* v (1968), 1–101 and as a separate vol., Delhi 1969. See also Morris D. Morris and Burton Stein, 'The economic history of India: a bibliographic essay', *J. Econ. Hist.* xxi (1961), 179–207.

1022   DUTT (ROMESH CHUNDER). India in the Victorian age: an economic history of the people. 1904. 2nd edn. [The economic history of India in the Victorian age] 1906. New edn. 2 v. Delhi. 1960.

Still the best general econ. hist. May be suppl. by V. B. Singh, ed., *Economic history of India, 1857–1956,* Bombay 1965; Sir Theodore Morison, *The economic transition in India,* 1911, and *The industrial organisation of an Indian province,* 1906; Daniel Houston Buchanan, *The development of capitalistic enterprise in India,* N.Y. 1934; Palamadai Samu Lokanathan, *Industrial organization in India,* 1935; Simon Smith Kuznets, ed., *Economic growth: Brazil, India, Japan,* Durham, N.C. 1955; Vera Powell Anstey, *The economic development of India,* 1929, 3rd edn. 1949; Balmokand Bhatia, *Famines in India: a study in some aspects of the economic history of India, 1860–1945,* Bombay etc. 1963, 2nd edn. 1967; and two attacks on the British economic record, Dadabhai Naoroji, *Poverty and un-British rule in India,* 1901, and William Digby, *'Prosperous' British India: a revelation from official records,* 1901. For the pre-mutiny period there is also Manmathnath Das, *Studies in the economic and social development of modern India, 1848–56,* Calcutta 1959.

1023   WATT (*Sir* GEORGE). The commercial products of India: being, an abridgment of 'The Dictionary of the Economic Products of India'. 1908.

An invaluable handbook on all aspects of the Indian economy.

1024   KUMAR (RAVINDER). Western India in the nineteenth century: a study in the social history of Maharashtra. Lond. & Toronto. 1968.

Combines social and economic hist. Cp. Ira Klein, 'Utilitarianism and agrarian progress in western India', *Econ. Hist. Rev.* 2 ser. xviii (1965), 576–97; Gordon Johnson, 'Chitpavan Brahmins and politics in western India in the late nineteenth and early twentieth centuries', in Edmund Leach and Soumyendra Nath Mukherjee, eds., *Elites in South Asia,* Camb. 1970, pp. 95–118; and Rustom Dinshaw Choksey, *Economic life in the Bombay–Deccan, 1818–1939,* Bombay 1955, *Economic life in the Bombay–Gurarat ...,*

Bombay 1968, *Economic life in the Bombay–Karnatak* . . ., Bombay 1963, and *Economic life in the Bombay–Konkan* . . ., Bombay 1960.

1025  BADEN-POWELL (BADEN HENRY). The Indian village community, examined with reference to the physical, ethnographic and historical conditions of the provinces, chiefly on the basis of the revenue-settlement records and district manuals. 1896.

Important for the structure of Indian rural life. See also his *The origin and growth of village communities in India*, 1899, 2nd edn. 1908, and for an earlier view, Sir Henry James Sumner Maine, *Village communities in the east and west*, 1871. For a modern analysis see Sir Manilal Balabhai Nanavati and Jashwantrai Jayantilal Anjaria, *The Indian rural problem*, Bombay 1944, 6th edn. 1965.

1026  BLYN (GEORGE). Agricultural trends in India, 1891–1947: output, availability and productivity. Phila. 1966.

See also Dharm Narain, *Impact of price movements on areas under selected crops in India, 1900–1939*, Camb. 1965.

1027  NEALE (WALTER CASTLE). Economic change in rural India: land tenure and reform in Uttar Pradesh, 1800–1955. New Haven [Conn.]. 1962.

See also two important books, Elizabeth Whitcombe, *Agrarian conditions in Northern India*: Vol. I. *The United Provinces under British rule, 1860–1900*, Berkeley 1971, and I. J. Catanach, *Rural credit in Western India: rural credit and the co-operative movement in the Bombay presidency, 1875–1930*, Berkeley 1970. There is also G. R. S. Hambly, 'Richard Temple and the Punjab Tenancy Act of 1868', *Eng. Hist. Rev.* lxxix (1964), 47–66, and Binay Bhushan Chaudhuri, 'Rural credit relations in Bengal, 1859–1885', *Indian Econ. & Soc. Hist. Rev.* vi (1969), 203–57.

1028  KUMAR (DHARMA). Land and caste in South India: agricultural labour in the Madras presidency during the nineteenth century. Camb. 1965.

Opens up an important topic.

1029  RUNGTA (RADHE SHYAM). The rise of business corporations in India, 1851–1900. Camb. 1970.

See also Dhananjaya Ramchandra Gadgil, *The industrial evolution of India in recent times*, 1924, 5th edn. 1970, and **5702**.

1030  MORRIS (MORRIS DAVID). The emergence of an industrial labor force in India: a study of the Bombay cotton mills, 1854–1947. Berkeley. 1965.

1031  SILVER (ARTHUR WISTAR). Manchester men and Indian cotton, 1847–1872. Manch. 1966.

Important. See also Dwijendra Tripathi, 'Opportunism of free trade: Lancashire cotton famine and Indian cotton cultivation', *Indian Econ. & Soc. Hist. Rev.* iv (1967), 255–63, and P. Harnetty, 'The Indian cotton duties controversy, 1894–1896', *Eng. Hist. Rev.* lxxvii (1962), 684–702.

1032  HAMILTON (CHARLES JOSEPH). The trade relations between England and India (1600–1896). Calcutta. 1919.

Only a sketch. To be suppl. by Parimal Ray, *India's foreign trade since 1870*, 1934, and Yeshwant Sakharam Pandit, *India's balance of indebtedness, 1898–1913*, 1937.

1033   SANYAL (NALINAKSHA). Development of Indian railways. Calcutta. 1930.

The only book on the subject. For background see Daniel Thorner, *Investment in empire: British railway and steam shipping enterprise in India, 1825–1849*, Phila. 1950, and Percy Stuart Attwood Berridge, *Couplings to the Khyber: the story of the North-Western railway*, Newton Abbot & N.Y. 1969.

1034   MAYHEW (ARTHUR INNES). Christianity and the government of India: an examination of the Christian forces at work in the administration of India and of the mutual relations of the British government and Christian missions, 1600–1920. 1929.

Opens up the subject, but no more. United Theological College Library, Bangalore, *Indian church history archives*, rev. edn. 1968, reports on the holdings of the main record repository in India.

1035   GRIMES (CECIL JOHN). Towards an Indian church: the growth of the church of India in constitution and life. 1946.

Deals with the constitution of the established Anglican Church of India. See also Eyre Chatterton, *A history of the Church of England in India since the early days of the East India Company*, 1924, and William Ashley-Brown, *On the Bombay coast and Deccan: the origin and history of the Bombay diocese, a record of 300 years' work for Christ in Western India*, 1937.

1036   RICHTER (JULIUS). A history of missions in India. Trans. by Sydney H. Moore. Edin. & Lond. 1908.

Outdated, but comprehensive. Hilko Wiardo Schomerus, *Indien und das Christentum*, 3 v. Halle-Saale, 1931–3, adds little. For mission history see **3412–42** and Sharpe (**1041**). One modern monograph touches on the period (most deal with pre-1850 events), Muhammad Mohar Ali, *The Bengali reaction to Christian missionary activities, 1833–1857*, Chittagong 1965. John Charles Pollock, *Shadows fall apart: the story of the Zenana Bible and Medical mission*, 1958, is interesting on Indian women. See also G. A. Oddie, 'Protestant missions, caste and social change in India, 1850–1914', *Indian Econ. & Soc. Hist. Rev.* vi (1969), 259–91.

1037   FARQUHAR (JOHN NICOL). Modern religious movements in India. N.Y. 1915.

A valuable outline, not yet replaced. See also Sir Sarvepalli Radhakrishnan, *Eastern religions and western thought*, Oxf. 1939.

1038   SUNDKLER (BENGT GUSTAV MALCOLM). Church of South India: the movement towards union, 1900–47. 1954.

See also Hans Rüdi Weber, *Asia and the ecumenical movement, 1895–1961*, 1966.

1039   COTTON. Memoir of George Edward Lynch Cotton, D.D., bishop of Calcutta, and metropolitan, with selections from his journals and correspondence. Ed. by Mrs. Cotton. 1871.

A useful life of an important bishop. See also the life of his successor, Frances Maria Milman, ed., *Memoirs of the Right Rev. Robert Milman, D.D., lord bishop of Calcutta & metropolitan of India, with a selection from his correspondence and journals*, 1879. Other useful Anglican biographies are Herbert Alfred Birks, *The life and correspondence of*

*Thomas Valpy French, first bishop of Lahore*, 2 v. 1895, Charles Edwyn Gardner, *Life of Father Goreh*, ed. by Richard Meux Benson, 1900, Carol Graham, *Azariah of Dornakal*, 1946, and James Edward Cowell Welldon, Bishop of Calcutta, *Recollections and reflections*, 1915.

1040   DUFF. The life of Alexander Duff. By George Smith. 2 v. 1879.

See also William Paton, *Alexander Duff: pioneer of missionary education*, 1923, D. H. Emmott, 'Alexander Duff and the foundation of modern education in India', *Brit. J. Educ. Studs.* xiii (1964–5), 160–9, and Lal Behari Day, *Recollections of Alexander Duff, D.D., LL.D., and of the mission college which he founded in Calcutta*, 1879. Duff was the leading Scots missionary in India.

1041   FARQUHAR. Not to destroy but to fulfil: the contribution of J. N. Farquhar to Protestant missionary thought in India before 1914. By Eric J. Sharpe. Lund [Sweden]. 1965.

An important study of missionary ideas, not confined to Farquhar. See also Sharpe's *John Nicol Farquhar: a memoir*, Calcutta 1963.

1042   GREAVES (MONICA ALICE). Education in British India, 1698–1947: a bibliography and guide to the sources of information in London. London Univ. Inst. of Educ. 1967.

For published docs. see also **1004**.

1043   NURULLAH (SYED) *and* NAIK (J. P.). History of education in India during the British period. Bombay. 1943. 2nd edn. 1951.

Probably the best general history. Bhagwan Dayal Srivastava, *The development of modern Indian education*, Calcutta 1955, rev. edn. Bombay 1963, Shridhar Nath Mukerji, *History of education in India: modern period*, Baroda 1951, 5th edn. 1966, and D. P. Sinha, *The educational policy of the East India Company in Bengal to 1854*, Calcutta 1964, are also useful. Syed Mahmood, *A history of English education in India . . . 1781 to 1893 . . .*, Aligarh 1895, is a factual compilation.

1044   JAMES (HENRY ROSHER). Education and statesmanship in India, 1797 to 1910. 1911. 2nd edn. 1917.

A discussion of British policy. Other useful works of the same general type are Frederick William Thomas, *The history and prospects of British education in India*, Camb. 1891; Arthur Innes Mayhew, *The education of India: a study of British educational policy in India, 1835–1920, and its bearing on national life and problems in India today*, 1926; Gerta Hertz, *Das britische Erziehungswesen in Indien*, Berlin 1932; Ellen E. McDonald, 'English education and social reform in late nineteenth-century Bombay . . .', *J. Asian Studs.* xxv (1966), 453–70; and Sir Philippe Joseph Hartog, *Some aspects of Indian education, past and present*, Univ. of London Inst. of Educ. Studies & Reports VII, 1939.

1045   INDIAN EDUCATION COMMISSION, 1882. Report with appendixes . . . [Chairman: Sir William Wilson Hunter]. 11 pts. Calcutta. 1883–4.

The appendixes consist of reports on indiv. provinces and a hist. of educ. in each province. For a commentary and summary of recommendations see James Johnston, *Abstract and analysis of the report of the Indian education commission . . .*, 1884. See also *Report of the Indian Universities Commission* [Chairman: Sir Thomas Raleigh], Simla 1902, and *Report of the commission appointed by the government of India to enquire into the conditions and prospects of the University of Calcutta* [President: Sir Michael Sadler.] [Cmd. 386–90] H.C. (1919). XIV–XVI.

For the hist. of the main 19th-cent. university institutions see [Pramathanath Banerjee and others, eds.,] *Hundred years of the University of Calcutta: a history of the university issued in commemoration of the centenary celebrations*, Univ. of Calcutta 1957, suppl. 1957; Sonderrao Ramrad Dongerkery, *A history of the University of Bombay*, University of Bombay 1957; [Kolappa Pillay Kanksabhapathi Pillay], *History of higher education in south India: University of Madras, 1857–1957*, 2 v., Madras 1957; James Fawthrop Bruce, *A history of the University of the Panjab*, Lahore 1933; Herbert Leonard Offley Garrett, *A history of Government College, Lahore, 1864–1964*, Lahore 1964; and Shyam Krishna Bhatnagar, *History of the M.A.O. College, Aligarh*, Bombay 1969.
For the publ. educational records of the government of India see **1004**.
There is an excellent ser. of general reports on Indian education publ. by the Indian Bureau of Education beginning with *Review of education in India in 1886, with special reference to the report of the Education Commission; by Sir Alfred Croft*, Calcutta 1888. The ser. cont. with *Progress of education in India, 1887–88 to 1891–92*, by A. M. Nash, Calcutta 1893, and then became a ser. of parl. papers beginning with the *Third quinquennial review* by James Sutherland Cotton [C. 9190] H.C. (1899). LXV, 501. This series was cont. to the 7th quinquennial report publ. in 1919.
In addition each of the provincial administrations publ. reports on the state of education.

**1046 CHATTERJEE (*Sir* ATUL CHANDRA) *and* BURN (*Sir* RICHARD). British contributions to Indian studies. 1943.**

**1047 CHATTERJI (SUNITI KUMAR). Languages and literatures of modern India. Calcutta. 1963.**

See also Vinayak Krishna Gokak, ed., *Literatures in modern Indian languages*, Delhi 1957, Syed Abdul Latif, *The influence of English literature on Urdu literature*, 1924, and Bhupal Singh, *A survey of Anglo-Indian fiction*, 1934.

**1048 ARCHER (MILDRED) *and* ARCHER (WILLIAM GEORGE). Indian painting for the British, 1770–1880: an essay. 1955.**

See also Mildred Archer, *Indian architecture and the British*, Feltham, Middx. 1968, and Roderick William Cameron, *Shadows from India: an architectural album*, Bombay etc. 1958.

**1049 BARNS (MARGARITA). The Indian press: a history of the growth of public opinion in India. 1940.**

See also Swaminath Natarajan, *A history of the press in India*, Bombay 1962, and Ram Ratan Bhatnagar, *The rise and growth of Hindi journalism (1826–1945)*, Allahabad n.d.

(b) *British Policy*

**1050 STOKES (ERIC). The English utilitarians and India. Oxf. 1959.**

An important pioneering work, chiefly on the pre-1850 period.

**1051 HUTCHINS (FRANCIS GILMAN). The illusion of permanence: British imperialism in India. Princeton [N.J.]. 1967.**

Tendentious, but interesting.

**1052 METCALF (THOMAS RICHARD). The aftermath of revolt: India, 1857–1870. Princeton [N.J.]. 1964.**

1053  MOORE (ROBIN JAMES). Sir Charles Wood's Indian policy, 1853–66. Manch. 1966.

Thorough. See also Sir Algernon Edward West, *Sir Charles Wood's administration of Indian affairs from 1859 to 1866*, 1867.

1054  GOPAL (SARVEPALLI). British policy in India, 1858–1905. Camb. 1965.

Unsatisfactory, as is B. L. Grover, *A documentary study of British policy towards Indian nationalism, 1885–1909*, Delhi 1967.

1055  MOORE (ROBIN JAMES). Liberalism and Indian politics, 1872–1922. 1966.

A useful short introduction.

1056  KNIGHT (L. A.). 'The Royal Titles Act and India'. *Hist. J.* xi (1968), 488–507.

1057  BLUNT (WILFRID SCAWEN). India under Ripon: a private diary. 1909.

Not reliable, but a useful source.

1058  MARTIN (BRITON) *Jr*. New India, 1885: British official policy and the emergence of the Indian National Congress. Berkeley etc. 1969.

1059  SINGH (HIRA LAL). Problems and policies of the British in India, 1885–1898, 1963.

1060  EDWARDES (MICHAEL). High noon of empire: India under Curzon. 1965.

A pleasant suppl. to Dilks (**1132**).

1061  WOLPERT (STANLEY A.). Morley and India, 1906–1910. Berkeley etc. 1967.

Good. But needs to be suppl. by Stephen E. Koss, *John Morley at the India Office, 1905–1910*, New Haven [Conn.] 1969, a good study of Morley's attitudes. Morley's papers have been catalogued: Molly C. Poulter, comp., *A catalogue of the Morley collection (Mss. Eur. D. 573): the private papers of John, Viscount Morley of Blackburn, 1838–1923*, 2 v. India Office Libr. 1965. There were a number of contemp. works of little value, such as E. Major, *Viscount Morley and Indian reform*, 1910. There are two collections of Morley's Indian speeches: *Speeches on Indian affairs*, Madras 1908, new edn. 1917, and *Indian speeches, 1907–1909*, 1909. See also Das (**1062**), and the works on Minto (**1141**). For Morley's career see also **797**.

1062  DAS (MANMATH NATH). India under Morley and Minto: politics behind revolution, repression and reforms. 1964.

1063  McLANE (JOHN R.). 'The decision to partition Bengal in 1905'. *Ind. Econ. & Soc. Hist. Rev.* ii (1965), 221–37.

See also Frederic Augustus Eustis and Z. H. Zaidi, 'King, Viceroy and cabinet: the modification of the partition of Bengal, 1911', *History* xlix (1964), 171–84.

1064  FISCHER (GEORGES). Le parti travailliste et la décolonisation de l'Inde. Paris. 1966.

### (c) *Indian Movements and the British*

There is a vast Indian literature on the subject, much of it quasi-biographical in character. For details consult the library catalogues listed above.

1065  DE BARY (WILLIAM THEODORE) *ed.* Sources of Indian tradition. N.Y. & Lond. 1958.

Primarily concerned with Indian movements.

1066  MISRA (BANKEY BIHARI). The Indian middle classes: their growth in modern times. 1961.

The first attempt to tackle a difficult problem. Needs reconsideration.

1067  McCULLY (BRUCE TIEBOUT). English education and the origins of Indian nationalism. N.Y. & Lond. 1940. Repr. Gloucester, Mass. 1966.

An important pioneering work, though in need of revision.

1068  GUPTA (ATULCHANDRA) *ed.* Studies in the Bengal renaissance: in commemoration of the birth centenary of Bipinchandra Pal. Jadavpur. 1958.

See also Nemai Sadhan Bose, *The Indian awakening and Bengal* [1800–1911], Calcutta 1960, 2nd edn. 1969; there is some useful background material in John H. Broomfield, *Elite conflict in a plural society: twentieth-century Bengal*, Berkeley 1968.

1069  CHAUDHURI (SASHI BHUSAN). Civil disturbances during the British rule in India (1765–1857). Calcutta. 1955.

Like his *Civil rebellion in the Indian mutinies, 1857–59*, Calcutta 1957, part of a fast-growing literature on agrarian protest movements. See also Blair Bernard Kling, *The blue mutiny: the indigo disturbances in Bengal, 1859–1862*, Phila. 1966, I. J. Catanach, 'Agrarian disturbances in nineteenth century India', *Ind. Econ. & Soc. Hist. Rev.* iii (1966), 65–84, Suresh Singh, *The dust storm and the hanging mist: a study of Birsa Munda and his movement in Chhotanagpur, 1874–1901*, Calcutta 1966, Kalikinkar Datta, *The Santal insurrection of 1855–57*, Calcutta 1940, the official reports on riots such as those in Deccan in 1874, and works on the mutiny and rebellion of 1857 (**1189–1211**).

1070  SHARMA (JAGDISH SARAN). Indian National Congress: a descriptive bibliography of India's struggle for freedom. Delhi etc. 1959.

Covers 1885–1958.

1071  CHAND (TARA). History of the freedom movement in India. 2+ v. Delhi. 1961+.

A bad official hist. sponsored by the Indian government. Ramesh Chandra Majumdar, *History of the freedom movement in India*, 3 v. Calcutta 1962–3, is a better (but Bengal-oriented) account. Prem Narain, *Press and politics in India, 1885–1905*, Delhi 1970, surveys the nationalist press. There are also a number of regional official hists., such as Kalikinkar Datta, *History of the freedom movement in Bihar*, 3 v. Patna, 1957–8, and a number of official collections of docs., notably Uttar Pradesh Advisory Board for the

History of Freedom Movement [S. A. A. Rizvi and M. L. Bhargava, eds.], *Freedom struggle in Uttar Pradesh: source-material*, 6 v. 1957–61.
[For contemp. British reactions see Sir Valentine Chirol, *Indian unrest*, 1910, Charles Freer Andrews, *The renaissance in India*, 1912, James Campbell Ker, *Political trouble in India, 1907–1917*, Calcutta 1917, and *Report of committee appointed to investigate revolutionary conspiracies in India* . . . [President: Sir Sidney Rowlatt] [Cd. 9190] H.C. (1918). VIII, 423.]

1072 SEAL (ANIL). The emergence of Indian nationalism: competition and collaboration in the later nineteenth century. Camb. 1968.

Covers *c.* 1870–88. A good modern account, though not always accurate. There is useful background material on Britain in Ina Mary Cumpston, 'Some early Indian nationalists and their allies in the British parliament, 1851–1906', *Eng. Hist. Rev.* lxxvi (1961), 279–97.

1073 TRIPATHI (AMALES). The extremist challenge: India between 1890 and 1910. Bombay. 1967.

Important. See also Biman Behari Majumdar, *Militant nationalism in India and its socio-religious background, 1897–1917*, Calcutta 1966, Argov and Wolpert (**1077–8**).

1074 MAJUMDAR (BIMAN BEHARI). Indian political associations and reform of legislature, 1818–1917. Calcutta. 1965.

For spokesmen for Indian interests see P. N. Singh Roy, ed., *Chronicle of the British India Association, 1851–1952*, Calcutta [1965], and Jogesh Chandra Bagal, *History of the Indian Association, 1876–1951*, Calcutta [1953].

1075 CHANDRA (BIPAN). The rise and growth of economic nationalism in India: economic policies of Indian national leadership, 1880–1905. New Delhi. 1966.

See also A. P. Kannangara, 'Indian millowners and Indian nationalism before 1914', *Past and Present*, no. 40 (1968), 147–64.

1076 SITARAMAYYA (BHOGARAJU PATTABHI). The history of the Indian National Congress. Allahabad. 1935. Rev. edn. 2 v. Bombay. 1946–7.

The official hist. now replaced for the early years of Congress by Sri Ram Mehrotra, *The emergence of the Indian National Congress*, Delhi etc. 1971. There is useful additional information in Pansy Chaya Ghosh, *The development of the Indian National Congress, 1892–1909*, Calcutta 1960, and Biman Behari Majumdar and Bhakat Prasad Majumdar, *Congress and congressmen in the pre-Gandhian era, 1885–1917*, Calcutta 1967.

1077 ARGOV (DANIEL). Moderates and extremists in the Indian nationalist movement, 1883–1920: with special reference to Surendranath Banerjea and Lajpat Rai. Bombay etc. 1967.

1078 WOLPERT (STANLEY A.). Tilak and Gokhale: revolution and reform in the making of modern India. Berkeley etc. 1962.

1079 QURESHI (ISHTIAQ HUSAIN). The Muslim community of the Indo-Pakistan subcontinent, 610–1947: a brief historical analysis. The Hague. 1962.

See also Aziz Ahmad and Gustave Edmund von Grunebaum, comps., *Muslim self-*

*statement in India and Pakistan, 1857–1968,* Wiesbaden 1970, and Aziz Ahmad, *Islamic modernism in India and Pakistan, 1857–1964,* 1967.

1080 PAKISTAN HISTORICAL SOCIETY. A history of the freedom movement (being the story of Muslim struggle for the freedom of Hind-Pakistan) 1707–1947. 4 v. in 7. Karachi. 1957+. In progress.

An attempt at a thorough Pakistani account of Muslim political movements. See also Khursheed Kamal Aziz, comp., *The historical background of Pakistan, 1857–1947: an annotated digest of source material,* Karachi 1970, Ram Gopal, *Indian Muslims: a political history, 1858–1947,* Bombay 1959, and Henry Hector Bolitho, *Jinnah: creator of Pakistan,* 1954.

1081 BAHADUR (LAL). The Muslim League: its history, activities & achievements. Agra. 1954.

See also Matiur Rahman, *From consultation to confrontation: a study of the Muslim League in British Indian politics, 1906–1912,* 1970.

1082 AZIZ (KHURSHEED KAMAL). Britain and Muslim India: a study of British public opinion vis-à-vis the development of Muslim nationalism in India, 1857–1947. 1963.

See also Azizur Rahman Mallick, *British policy and the Muslims in Bengal, 1757–1856,* Asiatic Soc. of Pakistan, Public. no 9, Dacca 1961.

1083 AHMAD (QEYAMUDDIN). The Wahabi movement in India. Calcutta. 1966.

A popular Muslim movement against the regime.

1084 SINGH (KHUSHWANT). A history of the Sikhs. Vol. II. 1839–1964. Princeton [N.J.]. 1966.

1085 AHMED KHAN. The life and work of [Sir] Syed Ahmed Khan [K.C.S.I.] By George Farquhar Irving Graham. Edin. 1885. Rev. edn. 1909.

The leading Muslim spokesman in India. See also Johannes Marinus Simon Baljon, *The reforms and religious ideas of Sir Sayyid Ahmad Khan,* Leiden 1949; Bashir Ahmad Dar, *Religious thought of Sayyid Ahmad Khan,* Lahore 1957; Hafeez Malik, 'Sir Sayyid Ahmad Khan's doctrines of Muslim nationalism and national progress', *Modern Asian Studs.* ii (1968), 221–44, and 'Sir Sayyid Ahmad Khan's contribution to the development of Muslim nationalism in India', ibid. iv (1970), 129–47; Aziz Ahmad, *Islamic modernism;* **1079**; and Yusuf Husain, ed., *Selected documents from the Aligarh archives,* Aligarh Muslim Univ., Bombay 1967.

1086 BANERJEA. A nation in the making: being the reminiscences of fifty years of public life. By Sir Surendranath Banerjea. Bombay. 1925. New edn. Bombay. 1963.

1087 GANDHI. The story of my experiments with truth. By Mohandas Karamchand Gandhi. Trans. by Mahadev Desai. 2 v. Ahmedabad. 1927–9. Numerous edns. publ. under the title Autobiography.

Gandhi's *Collected works* are being issued in Delhi by the Indian government in a vast ser. There is an enormous Gandhi literature, for which see Jagdish Saran Sharma,

*Mahatma Gandhi: a descriptive bibliography*, Delhi 1955. The fullest life is Dinanath Gopal Tendulkar, *Mahatma* . . ., 8 v. Bombay 1951–4, rev edn. 8 v. Delhi 1960–3. Much the best work on Gandhi's early life and British connections is Chandran David Srinivasagam Devanesen, *The making of the Mahatma*, Madras 1969. But see also **2032**.

**1088   NAOROJI.** Dadabhai Naoroji: the grand old man of India. By Rustom Pestonji Masani. 1939. Repr. Mysore. 1957.

See also Naoroji's *Speeches and writings* . . ., Madras 1909, and *Essays, speeches, addresses and writings*, ed. by Chunilal Lallubhai Parekh, Bombay 1887, and also Birendranath Ganguli, *Dadabhai Naoroji and the drain theory*, Bombay 1965.

**1089   NEHRU.** The Nehrus: Motilal and Jawaharlal. By Bal Ram Nanda. 1962.

See also Jawaharlal Nehru, *An autobiography: with musings on recent events in India*, 1937, numerous edns., Beatrice Pitney Lamb, *The Nehrus of India: three generations of leadership*, 1967, and Michael Brecher, *Nehru: a political biography*, 1959. There is a useful collection of Nehru's work in Dorothy Norman, ed., *Nehru: the first sixty years* . . ., 2 v. N.Y. 1964, Lond. 1965.

**1090   PAL.** Memories of my life and times. By Bipin Chandra Pal. 2 v. Calcutta. 1932–51.

See also his *Swadeshi & Swaraj: the rise of new patriotism*, Calcutta 1954.

**1091   RAMAKRISHNA.** The gospel of Sri Ramakrishna. Trans. by Swami Nikhilananda. N.Y. 1942. 4th edn. Mylapore. 1964.

There is a useful life by Romain Rolland, *Prophets of the new India: Book I Ramakrishna, Book II Vivekananda*, trans. by E. F. Malcolm-Smith, 1930.

**1092   RANADE.** Mahadev Govind Ranade: a biography. By Trimbak Vishnu Parvate. Bombay etc. [1963].

See also Ramabai Ranade, *Ranade: his wife's reminiscences*, Delhi 1963.

**1093   TAGORE.** My reminiscences. By Sir Rabindranath Tagore. 1917.

Much the most influential literary man in India during the period, and the subject of innumerable studies. For his father, also very influential, see Devendranath Tagore, *Autobiography*, trans. by Satyendranath Tagore and Indira Devi, 1916.

**1094   VIVEKANANDA.** The master as I saw him: being pages from the life of the Swami Vivekananda, by his disciple Nivedita . . . [Margaret Elizabeth Noble]. Calcutta. 1910.

See also Vivekananda's *Complete works, original and translated*, 7 v. Advaita Ashran 1922–6, with index vol. 1926, numerous edns. There are numerous works on Vivekananda incl. **1091**.

## 3. ADMINISTRATION

### (a) *General*

The major contemporary works listed (particularly **1120–9**) were for the most part more thorough than their successors, and should always be consulted. Much detailed information is incl. in the reports of the debates of the legislative council of India (1854–1947) and of the legislative councils of Bengal, Bombay, and Madras, 1862+.

1095 WILSON (PATRICK). Government and politics of India and Pakistan, 1885–1955: a bibliography of works in western languages. Berkeley. 1956.

1096 BANERJEE (ANIL CHANDRA) *ed.* Indian constitutional documents, 1757–1947. 3rd edn. 4 v. Calcutta. 1961–5.

Largely replaces Arthur Berriedale Keith, ed., *Speeches & documents on Indian policy, 1750–1921*, 2 v. 1922, and Jatindra Kumar Majumdar, ed., *Indian speeches and documents on British rule, 1821–1918*, Calcutta 1937. See also Philips (1003). For diplomatic documents (chiefly pre-1851) there is Sir Charles Umpherston Aitchison, ed., *A collection of treaties, engagements and sunnuds relating to India and neighbouring countries*, 7 v. Calcutta 1862–5, new edns. 8 v. 1876–8, 11 v. 1892, 13 v. 1909.

1097 ILBERT (*Sir* COURTENAY PEREGRINE). The government of India: being, a digest of the statute law relating thereto . . . Oxf. 1898. 3rd edn. 1915.

The introduction has been repr. as *The government of India: a brief historical survey of parliamentary legislation relating to India*, Oxf. 1922.

1098 KEITH (ARTHUR BERRIEDALE). A constitutional history of India, 1600–1935. 1936.

Still the only comprehensive study. But see also Cecil Merne Putnam Cross, *The development of self-government in India, 1858–1914*, Chicago 1922, Sir Reginald Coupland, *The Indian problem, 1833–1935* . . ., 1942, Donovan Williams, 'The Council of India and the relationship between the home and supreme governments, 1858–1870', *Eng. Hist. Rev.* lxxxi (1966), 56–73, and Robin James Moore, 'The twilight of the Whigs and the reform of the Indian councils, 1886–1892', *Hist. J.* x (1967), 400–14. Most recent monographs have been disappointing; among the best are S. N. Singh, *The Secretary of State for India and his council, 1858–1919*, Delhi 1962, Parmatma Sharan, *The imperial legislative council of India [from 1861 to 1920]* . . ., Delhi 1961, and Ranbir Singh Jain, *The growth & development of Governor-General's executive council (1858–1919)*, Delhi 1962.

1099 MISRA (BANKEY BIHARI). The administrative history of India, 1834–1947: general administration. Bombay. 1970.

1100 WOODRUFF (PHILIP) *pseud. of* MASON (PHILIP). The men who ruled India. 1. The founders. 2. The guardians. 2 v. 1953–4.

A splendid account of British officialdom. To be suppl. by John Beames, *Memoirs of a Bengal civilian*, 1961, which has an intro. by Woodruff.

1101 O'MALLEY (LEWIS SYDNEY STEWARD). The Indian civil service, 1601–1930. 1931. Repr. 1965.

Not nearly comprehensive enough. Sir Edward Arthur Henry Blunt, *The I.C.S.: the Indian civil service*, 1937, is even thinner. There is a useful account of civil service recruitment, 1600–1860, by Bernard S. Cohn in Ralph Braibanti, ed., *Asian bureaucratic systems emergent from the British imperial tradition*, Durham, N.C. 1966. For the new system of recruitment introduced in the 1850s see Robin James Moore, 'Abolition of patronage in the Indian civil service and the closing of Haileybury college',

*Hist. J.* vii (1964), 246–57, and J. M. Compton, 'Open competition and the Indian civil service, 1854–1876', *Eng. Hist. Rev.* lxxxiii (1968), 265–84. Naresh Chandra Roy, *The civil service in India*, Calcutta 1958, 2nd edn. 1960, though chiefly concerned with the post-1947 service, is interesting on the development of the I.C.S. There is much useful material in *The selection and training of candidates for the Indian civil service* [C. 1446] H.C. (1876). LV, 277, which is a collection of docs. For the political service see **1114**. For the medical service see Dirom Grey Crawford, *A history of the Indian medical service, 1600–1913*, 2 v. 1914, and *Roll of the Indian medical service, 1615–1930*, 1930, and Donald McDonald, comp., *Surgeons twoe and a barber: being some account of the life and work of the Indian medical service, 1600–1947*, 1950.

**1102  BADEN-POWELL (BADEN HENRY).** The land systems of British India: being a manual of the land tenures and of the systems of land-revenue administration prevalent in the several provinces. 3 v. Oxf. 1892.

See also his *A short account of the land revenue and its administration in British India, with a sketch of the land tenures*, Oxf. 1894, 2nd edn. 1907, and **1204**.

**1103  INDIA OFFICE.** Statement exhibiting the moral and material progress and condition of India, during the year 1859–60. [In 4 pts.] H.C. 265 & 265-I-III (1861). XLVII, 1.

Full. Cont. as an annual report on the administration of British India publ. as a parl. paper down to 1918. There are also administrative reports of each of the provincial administrations publ. in India.

**1104  THE INDIA OFFICE LIST . . . 1886–1947.**

Title varies. Lists all types of officials. Absorbed *The East-India register and army list*, 1803–60, which became *The Indian army and civil list*, 1861–76, and *The India list, civil and military*, 1877–95.

**1105  BARING COMMITTEE ON INDIAN TERRITORIES.** First report from the select committee on Indian territories [Chairman: Thomas Baring]. H.C. 426 (1852–3). XXVII, 1. Second to sixth reports, appendix and index pr. in vols. XXVIII–XXIX of 1852–3.

Along with **1106** provides a valuable survey of Indian administration under the East India company.

**1106  LORDS COMMITTEE ON INDIAN TERRITORIES.** Report from the select committee of the House of Lords appointed to inquire into the operation of the Act 3 & 4 Will. 4, c. 85, for the better government of Her Majesty's Indian territories . . . [Chairman: Marquess of Salisbury]. H.C. 41 (1852–3). XXX, 1. Further reports H.C. 627 and H.C. 627–I and II (1852–3). XXXI–XXXIII.

**1107  HOBHOUSE COMMISSION ON DECENTRALISATION.** Report of the royal commission upon decentralisation in India [Chairman: Charles E. H. Hobhouse]. [Cd. 4360] H.C. (1908). XLIV, 1. Evidence in 9 v. [Cd. 4361–9] H.C. (1908). XLIV–XLVI.

On Indian administration after Curzon: chiefly valuable as a source of information.

**1108  ISLINGTON COMMISSION ON PUBLIC SERVICES.** Royal commission on the public services of India: report of the commissioners [Chairman: Lord Islington.] Report. [Cd. 8382] H.C. (1916). VII, 87. Appendixes in 19 v. [Cd. 7293-6, 7548-83.] H.C. (1914). XXI-XXIV. [Cd. 7900-8] H.C. (1914-16). XV-XVII.

Another important source.

1109  THOMAS (PARAKUNNEL JOSEPH). The growth of federal finance in India, being a survey of India's public finances from 1833 to 1939. 1939.

Not up to the standards of contemp. economics, but the only general hist.

1110  BHATTACHARYYA (SABYASACHI). Financial foundations of the British raj: men and ideas in the post-Mutiny period of reconstruction of Indian public finance. Indian Inst. of Advanced Study. Simla. 1971.

The structure of public finance established by James Wilson. See also Ira Klein, 'Wilson vs Trevelyan: finance and modernization in India after 1857', *Indian Econ. & Soc. Hist. Rev.* vii (1970), 179-209.

1111  COYAJEE (*Sir* JEHANGIR COOVERJEE). The Indian currency system (1835-1926). Madras. 1930.

1112  KEYNES (JOHN MAYNARD), *Baron Keynes*. Indian currency and finance. 1913. Repr. 1971.

See also Dietmar Rothermund, 'The monetary policy of British imperialism', *Indian Econ. & Soc. Hist. Rev.* vii (1970), 91-107.

1113  WELBY COMMISSION ON INDIAN EXPENDITURE. First report of the royal commission on the administration of the expenditure of India [Chairman: Lord Welby.] [C. 8258] H.C. (1896). XV, 1. Evidence & Appendixes. [C. 8259] H.C. (1896) XVI, 1; [Cd. 130] H.C. (1900). XXIX, 1. Final report [Cd. 131] H.C. (1900). XXIX, 553.

The main source for Indian finances.

1114  PANIKKAR (KAVALAM MADHAVA). An introduction to the study of the relations of Indian states with the government of India. 1927. 2nd edn. 1932.

See also Lee-Warner (1019), Sir Terence Creagh Coen, *The Indian Political Service: a study in indirect rule*, 1971, and I. F. S. Copland, 'The Baroda crisis of 1873-77: a study in governmental rivalry', *Modern Asian Studs.* ii (1968), 97-123.

1115  PRASAD (BENI). The origins of provincial autonomy: being, a history of the relations between the central government and the provincial governments in British India from 1860 to 1919. Allahabad. 1941.

An inadequate book on an important subject.

1116  TINKER (HUGH RUSSELL). The foundations of local self-government in India, Pakistan and Burma. 1954.

Good. See also S. W. Goode, comp., *Municipal Calcutta: its institutions in their origin and growth*, Corporation of Calcutta, Edin. 1916, Christine Dobbin, 'Competing élites in Bombay city politics in the mid-nineteenth century, 1852-83', in Edmund Leach and

Soumyendra Nath Mukherjee, eds., *Élites in South Asia*, Camb. 1970, pp. 79–94, and 'The Parsi panchayat in Bombay city in the nineteenth century', *Modern Asian Studs.* iv (1970), 149–64.

1117 RANKIN (*Sir* GEORGE CLAUS). Background of Indian law. Camb. 1946.

A good introduction.

1118 DERRETT (JOHN DUNCAN MARTIN). Religion, law and the state in India. 1968.

Much the most thorough work on the subject. See also Shankar Vinayak Gupte, *Hindu law in British India*, Bombay 1945, 2nd edn. 1947, and Whitley Stokes, ed., *The Anglo-Indian codes*, 2 v. Oxf. 1887–8.

1119 INDIAN POLICE COMMISSION. Report of the Indian police commission [President: A. H. L. Fraser] and resolution of the government of India. [Cd. 2478] H.C. (1905). LVII, 657.

Includes a handy short hist. See also Sir Percival Joseph Griffiths, *To guard my people: the history of the Indian police*, 1971, Salig Ram Nigam, *Scotland Yard and the Indian police*, Allahabad 1963, Sir Edmund Charles Cox, *Police and crime in India*, 1911, and *My thirty years in India*, 1909, and Stephen Meredyth Edwardes, *The Bombay city police: a historical sketch, 1672–1916*, 1923.

1120 CAMPBELL (*Sir* GEORGE). Modern India: a sketch of the system of civil government . . . 1852.

A full guide. There is some additional material in Arthur Mills, *India in 1858: a summary of the existing administration . . . of British India . . .*, 1858, 2nd edn. 1858, and Thomas John Hovell-Thurlow, Baron Thurlow, *The company and the crown*, 1866.

1121 PRICHARD (ILTUDUS THOMAS). The administration of India from 1859 to 1868: the first ten years of administration under the crown. 2 v. 1869.

1122 BUCKLAND (CHARLES EDWARD). Bengal under the lieutenant-governors: being a narrative of the principal events and public measures . . . from 1854 to 1898. 2v. Calcutta. 1901.

1123 CHESNEY (*Sir* GEORGE [TOMKYNS]). Indian polity: a view of the system of administration in India. 1868. 3rd edn. 1894.
Good.

1124 STRACHEY (*Sir* JOHN) *and* STRACHEY (*Sir* RICHARD). The finances and public works of India from 1869 to 1881. 1882.

1125 HUNTER (*Sir* WILLIAM WILSON). Bombay, 1885 to 1890: a study in Indian administration . . . 1892.

1126 PHILLIPS (HENRY ARTHUR DEUTEROS). Our administration of India: being a complete account of the revenue and collectorate administration in all departments . . . 1886.

1127 STRACHEY (*Sir* JOHN). India. 1888. 4th edn. 1911 [later edns. styled India: its administration & progress].

A major work on all aspects of Indian admin. Cp. Joseph Chailley, *Administrative problems of British India*, trans. by Sir William Meyer, 1910.

1128 MORISON (*Sir* THEODORE). Imperial rule in India: being an examination of the principles proper to the government of dependencies. 1899.

1129 IRELAND (ALLEYNE). Colonial administration in the far east: the province of Burma. A report prepared on behalf of the Univ. of Chicago. 2 v. Boston. 1907.

Monumental. See also Frank Siegfried Vernon Donnison, *Public administration in Burma: a study of development during the British connexion*, 1953, and John Sydenham Furnivall, *Colonial policy and practice: a comparative study of Burma and Netherlands India*, Camb. 1948, N.Y. 1956.

(b) *Viceroys and Governors-General*

(In alphabetical order)

1130 General works on the viceroys such as Clive Bigham, Viscount Mersey, *The viceroys and governors general of India, 1756–1947*, 1949, and Venkatesh Balkrishna Kulkarni, *British statesmen in India*, Bombay 1961, give only biog. outlines and are of little use. George Nathaniel Curzon, Marquess Curzon of Kedleston, *British government in India: the story of the viceroys and government houses*, 2 v. 1925, is chiefly about buildings and patterns of life.

1131 CANNING. 'Clemency' Canning: Charles John, 1st Earl Canning, Governor-General and Viceroy of India, 1856–62. By Michael Maclagan. 1962.

See also Sir Henry Stewart Cunningham, *Earl Canning*, Oxf. 1891, and Augustus John Cuthbert Hare, *The story of two noble lives: being memorials of Charlotte, Countess Canning, and Louisa, Marchioness of Waterford*, 3 v. 1893.

1132 CURZON. Curzon in India. By David Dilks. 2 v. 1969–70.

Good. Does not entirely replace the official life, Lawrence John Lumley Dundas, Earl of Ronaldshay, later Marquess of Zetland, *The life of Lord Curzon: being, the authorized biography of George Nathaniel, Marquess Curzon of Kedleston, K.G.*, 3 v. 1928. The best 1-vol. life is Kenneth Rose, *Superior person: a portrait of Curzon and his circle in late Victorian England*, Lond. & N.Y. 1968, which is much better than Leonard Oswald Mosley, *Curzon: the end of an epoch*, 1960, publ. in N.Y. as *The glorious fault: the life of Lord Curzon*, 1960. On Curzon and foreign affairs see also Sir Harold George Nicolson, *Curzon: the last phase, 1919–1925 . . .*, 1934. His widow (Grace Elvina Curzon, Marchioness Curzon) publ. an attractive v. of *Reminiscences*, 1955. For his Indian career there are many minor works, and many colls. of speeches. Most convenient is *Lord Curzon in India: being, a selection from his speeches . . . 1898–1905 . . .* intro. by Sir Thomas Raleigh, 1906. Fullest is the official *Speeches by Lord Curzon . . .*, 4 v. Calcutta, 1900–6.

1133 DALHOUSIE. The Marquis of Dalhousie's administration of British India. By Sir Edwin Arnold. 2 v. 1862–5.

See also Daniel George Edward Hall, ed., *The Dalhousie–Phayre correspondence, 1852–1856*, 1932 [on Burma]; J. G. A. Baird, ed., *Private letters of the Marquess of Dalhousie*,

1910; Sir William Wilson Hunter, *The Marquess of Dalhousie*, 1890; Sir William Lee-Warner, *The life of the Marquis of Dalhousie, K.T.*, 2 v. 1904; George Douglas Campbell, Duke of Argyll, *India under Dalhousie and Canning* . . ., 1865; and Sir Charles Robert Mitchell Jackson, *A vindication of the Marquis of Dalhousie's Indian administration*, 1865.

**1134** DUFFERIN. Helen's tower. By Sir Harold George Nicolson. 1937.

The only attempt to view his career in perspective. Most of the relevant facts and letters are printed in Sir Alfred Comyn Lyall, *The life of the Marquis of Dufferin and Ava* . . ., 2 v. 1905, and Charles Edward Drummond Black, *The Marquess of Dufferin and Ava* . . ., 1903. On his Canadian career see **1476**. There are two collections of speeches: *Speeches and addresses*, ed. by Henry Milton, 1882, and *Speeches delivered in India, 1884–8*, ed. by Sir Donald Mackenzie Wallace, 1890.

**1135** ELGIN. Speeches by the Earl of Elgin, Viceroy and Governor-General of India, 1894–1899. Calcutta. 1899.

For his later career see **1251**.

**1136** HARDINGE. My Indian years, 1910–1916: the reminiscences of Lord Hardinge of Penshurst [by Charles Hardinge, Baron Hardinge]. 1948.

See also *Speeches of his excellency the Right Hon'ble Baron Hardinge of Penshurst*, 2 v. Madras 1914–19, and *Speeches* . . ., comp. by H. H. Sir Bhavsinhji, K.C.S.I., Maharaja of Bhavnagar, Madras 1915. For Hardinge's unpubl. papers see N. J. Hancock, *Handlist of Hardinge papers at the University Library, Cambridge*, Camb. 1968.

**1137** LANSDOWNE. The administration of the Marquis of Lansdowne as Viceroy and Governor-General of India, 1888–1894. By Sir George William Forrest. Calcutta. 1894.

See also Lansdowne's *Speeches* . . . *1888–1894*, Calcutta, 1895, and **786**.

**1138** LAWRENCE. The necessary hell: John and Henry Lawrence and the Indian empire. By Michael Edwardes. 1958.

Popular. See also Dharm Pal, *Administration of Sir John Lawrence in India, 1864–1869*, Simla 1952, Reginald Bosworth Smith, *Life of Lord Lawrence*, 2 v. 1883, 7th edn. 1901, Sir Richard Temple, *Lord Lawrence*, 1889, and Sir Charles Umpherston Aitchison, *Lord Lawrence and the reconstruction of India under the crown*, Oxf. 1892.

**1139** LYTTON. The history of Lord Lytton's Indian administration, 1876–1880 . . . By Lady Betty Balfour. 1899.

**1140** MAYO. A life of the Earl of Mayo, fourth Viceroy of India. By Sir William Wilson Hunter. 2 v. 1875.

Hunter also publ. *The Earl of Mayo*, 1890. A vol. of *Speeches in England and India*, ed. by Gosto Behary Mullick, Calcutta 1873, is the most valuable of a number of works publ. in India soon after Mayo's assassination.

**1141** MINTO. Lord Minto: a memoir. By John Buchan, Baron Tweedsmuir. 1924.

Suppl. by Mary Caroline Elliot Murray Kynynmound, Countess of Minto, *India, Minto and Morley, 1905–10: compiled from the correspondence between the viceroy and the secretary of State*, 1934, Syed Razi Wasti, *Lord Minto and the Indian nationalist movement, 1905–1910*, Oxf. 1964, *Speeches by the Earl of Minto, Viceroy and Governor-General of India*, Calcutta 1911, and Wolpert and Das (**1061–2**).

**1142** NORTHBROOK. Lord Northbrook's Indian administration, 1872–1876. By Edward C. Moulton. Bombay etc. 1968.

See also Sir Bernard Mallet, *Thomas George, Earl of Northbrook, G.C.S.I.: a memoir,* 1908, and Goshthavihari Mallika, *Lord Northbrook and his mission in India . . . with an appendix containing all the important speeches of Lord Northbrook,* Calcutta 1873.

**1143** RIPON. The viceroyalty of Lord Ripon, 1880–84. By Sarvepalli Gopal. 1953.

See also **803**. There are 2 v. of publ. speeches which deal only with Indian problems, one ed. by Ram Chandra Palit, Calcutta, 1882, the other ed. by Kali Prasanna Sen Gupta, 2 v., Calcutta 1883.

### (c) *Biography*

**1144** LAURIE (WILLIAM FERGUSON BEATSON). Sketches of some distinguished Anglo-Indians, with an account of Anglo-Indian periodical literature. 1875. New edn. 1887. 2nd ser. 1888.

**1145** AMEER ALI. Ameer Ali: his life and work. By Khursheed Kamal Aziz. Lahore. 1968.

Lawyer, judge, privy councillor, and spokesman of Indian Muslims.

**1146** BURNE. Memories. By Sir Owen Tudor Burne. 1907.

Served in India and the India office in London.

**1147** CAMPBELL. Memoirs of my Indian career. By Sir George Campbell. Ed. by Sir Charles E. Bernard. 2 v. 1893.

**1148** CARSTAIRS. The little world of an Indian district officer. By Robert Carstairs. 1912.

**1149** DARLING. Apprentice to power: India, 1904–1908. By Sir Malcolm Darling. 1966.

**1150** GODLEY. Reminiscences. By Arthur Godley, Baron Kilbracken. 1931.

Permanent Under-Secretary of State for India.

**1151** HODGSON. Life of Brian Houghton Hodgson, British resident at the court of Nepal . . . By Sir William Wilson Hunter. 1896.

**1152** HUME. Allan Octavian Hume, C.B., 'father of the Indian National Congress', 1829 to 1912. By Sir William Wedderburn. 1913.

**1153** HUNTER. Life of Sir William Wilson Hunter, K.C.S.I., M.A., LL.D., a vice president of the Royal Asiatic Society . . . By Francis Henry Bennett Skrine. 1901.

**1154** JACOB. John Jacob of Jacobabad. By Hugh Trevor Lambrick. 1960.

1155   KISCH. A young Victorian in India: letters of H. M. Kisch of the Indian Civil Service. Ed. by Ethel A. Waley Cohen. 1957.

1156   LYALL. Life of the Right Hon. Sir Alfred Comyn Lyall, P.C., K.C.B., G.C.I.E., D.C.L., LL.D. By Sir [Henry] Mortimer Durand. Edin. & Lond. 1913.

1157   MAINE. Sir Henry Maine: a brief memoir of his life by . . . Sir Mountstuart Elphinstone Grant Duff . . . with some of his Indian speeches and minutes . . . ed. by Whitley Stokes. 1892.
Chiefly docs. See also 714.

1158   MEADE. General Sir Richard Meade and the feudatory states of central and southern India: a record of forty-three years' service as soldier, political officer and administrator. By Thomas Henry Thornton. 1898.

1159   O'DWYER. India as I knew it, 1885–1925. By Sir Michael O'Dwyer. 1925. 3rd edn. 1926.

1160   RIVETT-CARNAC. Many memories of life in India, at home and abroad. By John Henry Rivett-Carnac. Edin. & Lond. 1910.
Typical of the more discursive type of civil service memoirs. Covers Bengal, 1857–94.

1161   SMITH. Servant of India: a study of imperial rule from 1905 to 1910 as told through the correspondence and diaries of Sir James Dunlop Smith. Ed. by Martin Gilbert. 1966.

1162   SYDENHAM. My working life. By George Sydenham Clarke, Baron Sydenham. 1927.

1163   TEMPLE. Men and events of my time in India. By Sir Richard Temple. 1882.
See also his *India in 1880*, 1880, 3rd edn. 1881 and *The story of my life*, 2 v. 1896.

1164   WEDDERBURN. Sir William Wedderburn and the Indian reform movement. By Samuel Kerkham Ratcliffe. 1923.
See also his *Speeches and writings*, ed. by G. A. Natesen, Madras 1918.

(d) *Defence*

1165   COCKLE (MAURICE JAMES DRAFFEN) *comp.* A catalogue of books relating to the military history of India. Simla. 1901.
See also John Henry Leslie and David Smith, comps., *A bibliography of works by officers, non-commissioned officers and men who have ever served in the Royal, Bengal, Madras or Bombay artillery*, 9 pts. [A–L] Sheffield and Dartford 1909–20. The War Office Library issues lists of works about Indian forces of the Crown.

1166  THE ARMY IN INDIA, 1850–1914: a photographic record. National
Army Museum. 1968.

On the leaders of the Indian army see Sir George William Forrest, *Sepoy generals:
Wellington to Roberts*, Edin. & Lond. 1901, and Sir Owen Tudor Burne, *Clyde and
Strathnairn*, Oxf. 1891. The Victorian cult of Mutiny heroes resulted in such works as
Lionel James Trotter, *The life of John Nicholson, soldier and administrator . . .*, 1897,
9th edn. 1904, and *A leader of light horse: life of Hodson of Hodson's Horse*, Edin. &
Lond. 1901, George Hewitt Hodson, ed., *Hodson of Hodson's horse . . .*, rev. edn. 1883
[orig. publ. as *Twelve years of a soldier's life in India . . .*, 1859], Barry Joynson Cork,
*Rider on a grey horse: a life of Hodson of Hodson's horse*, 1958, and Sir Hugh Henry
Gough, *Old memories*, Edin. & Lond. 1897. William Young Carman, *Indian army
uniforms under the British from the 18th century to 1947*, vol. I *Cavalry*, 1961, vol. II
*Artillery, engineers, infantry*, 1969, is a useful handbook.

1167  REDDY (K. N.). 'Indian defence expenditure, 1872–1967'. *Indian Econ.
& Soc. Hist. Rev.* vii (1970), 467–88.

1168  PEEL COMMISSION ON THE INDIAN ARMY. Report of the commissioners appointed to inquire into the organization of the Indian army . . .
[Chairman: Jonathan Peel]. [2515] H.C. (1859–Sess. 1). V, 1. Minority report
by Major-General Hancock. [2516] H.C. (1859–Sess. 1). V, 601. Papers.
[2541] H.C. (1859–Sess. 2). VIII, 647.

See also *Report from the select committee on army (India and the colonies)* [Chairman:
Viscount Cranborne]. H.C. 478 (1867). VII, 197. Further report. H.C. 197 (1867–8).
VI, 789, which deals with the possible use of Indian forces in the colonies.

1169  KITCHENER MEMORANDUM ON THE ARMY IN INDIA.
Return of the memorandum recently issued by General Lord Kitchener of
Khartoum and the local commander-in-chief in India upon the organisation
and training of the army in India. H.C. 200 (1904). LXIII, 527. Correspondence etc. regarding the administration of the army in India. [Cd. 2572] H.C.
(1905). LVII, 471. [Cd. 2615] H.C. (1905). LVII, 539. [Cd. 2718] H.C.
(1906). LXXXI, 439. [Cd. 2842] H.C. (1906). LXXXI, 463.

The chief publ. docs. in a great controversy that led to the resignation of the Viceroy,
Lord Curzon.

1170  CADELL (*Sir* PATRICK ROBERT). History of the Bombay army.
1938.

The only comprehensive hist. of one of the major units of the Indian army. For the
training of army cadets in East India company times see Henry Meredith Vibart,
*Addiscombe: its heroes and men of note*, 1894. For a minor army scandal see Arthur
Hawkey, *Last post at Mhow*, 1969.

1171  SANDES (EDWARD WARREN CAULFEILD). The military engineer in India. 2 v. Chatham. 1933–5.

Vol. II is a history of irrigation and other engineering projects constructed by army
engineers.

1172  MACGREGOR (*Sir* CHARLES METCALFE). The defence of India:
a strategical study. Government of India. Simla. 1884.

The most important work on Indian strategy. For Macgregor see also **1183**. For Indian
strategy see Hoskins, *British routes to India* (**2394**), Hermann Oncken, *Die Sicherheit*

*Indiens: ein Jahrhundert englischer Weltpolitik*, Berlin 1937, and Beryl J. Williams, 'The strategic background to the Anglo-Russian entente of August 1907', *Hist. J.* ix (1966), 360–73. There was a good deal of contemp. writing on the Indian frontier question, incl. Sir John Miller Adye, *Indian frontier policy: an historical sketch*, 1897, John Dacosta, *A scientific frontier: or, the danger of a Russian invasion of India*, 1891, and Henry Bathurst Hanna, *Can Russia invade India?* 1895, *India's scientific frontier: where is it? what is it?* 1895, and *Backwards or forwards?* [1896].

1173 ELLIOTT (JAMES GORDON). The frontier, 1839–1947: the story of the north-west frontier of India. 1968.

Good. But does not replace Cuthbert Collin Davies, *The problem of the north-west frontier, 1890–1908, with a survey of policy since 1849*, Camb. 1932, repr. 1963, which needs to be suppl. by Horst Jaeckel, *Die Nordwestgrenze in der Verteidigung Indiens, 1900–1908, und der Weg Englands zum russisch-britischen Abkommen von 1907*, Cologne 1968, which is better than Peter Carl O'Moole Stearns Braun, *Die Verteidigung Indiens, 1800–1907: das Problem der Vorwärtsstrategie*, Cologne 1968. Sir Robert Warburton, *Eighteen years in the Khyber, 1879–1898*, 1900, repr. Karachi & Lond. 1970, gives useful background material. For the north-west frontier see also 2487–504. For the north-east frontier see 2545 and 2562–5.

1174 ALDER (GARRY JOHN). British India's northern frontier, 1865–95: a study in imperial policy. 1963.

1175 INDIA ARMY, INTELLIGENCE BRANCH. Frontier and overseas expeditions from India. 2 v. Calcutta. 1908.

On frontier warfare see Sir George John Younghusband, *Indian frontier warfare*, 1898.

1176 BROWNE. The life and times of General Sir James Browne, K.C.B., K.C.S.I. By James John Macleod Innes. 1905.

1177 CHAMBERLAIN. Life of Field-Marshal Sir Neville Chamberlain, G.C.B., G.C.S.I. By Sir George William Forrest. Edin. & Lond. 1909.

1178 CLYDE. The life of Colin Campbell, Lord Clyde: illustrated by extracts from his diary and correspondence. By Lawrence Shadwell. 2 v. Edin. & Lond. 1881.

See also Archibald Forbes, *Colin Campbell, Lord Clyde*, 1895.

1179 CREAGH. The autobiography of General Sir O'Moore Creagh. [1924].

1180 EDWARDES. Memorials of the life and letters of Major-General Sir Herbert B. Edwardes . . . By Emma, Lady Edwardes. 2 v. 1886.

1181 GRANT. Life of General Sir Hope Grant: with selections from his correspondence. Ed. by Sir Henry Knollys. 2 v. Edin. & Lond. 1894.

See also 2537 for Grant's work in China.

1182 HAVELOCK. Havelock. By Leonard Cooper. 1957.

See also John Clark Marshman, *Memoirs of Major-General Sir Henry Havelock, K.C.B.*, 1860.

1183 MACGREGOR. 'Sir Charles MacGregor and the defence of India, 1857–1887'. By Adrian Preston. *Hist. J.* xii (1969), 58–77.

MacGregor was the leading thinker of his generation on problems of Indian defence. See also Lady MacGregor, ed., *The life and opinions of Major-General Sir Charles Metcalfe MacGregor*, 2 v. Edin. 1888, and 1172.

1184 NAPIER. Field-Marshal Lord Napier of Magdala, G.C.B., G.C.S.I.: a memoir by his son Henry Dundas Napier. 1927.

See also H. D. Napier, ed., *Letters of Field Marshal Lord Napier of Magdala, concerning Abyssinia, Egypt, India, South Africa, etc.*, 1936, and the works on the Abyssinian campaign at 1746–7.

1185 NORMAN. Memoirs of Field Marshal Sir Henry Wylie Norman, G.C.B., G.C.M.G., C.I.E. 1908.

1186 OUTRAM. James Outram: a biography. By Sir Frederic John Goldsmid. 2 v. 1880. 2nd edn. 2 v. 1881.

See also Lionel James Trotter, *The Bayard of India: a life of General Sir James Outram, Bart*, 1903.

ROBERTS. For Lord Roberts's Indian career see 1195 and 2825.

1187 STEWART. Field Marshal Sir Donald Stewart, G.C.B., G.C.S.I., C.I.E.: an account of his life, mainly in his own words. Ed. by George Robert Elsmie. 1903.

1188 TAYLOR. General Sir Alex Taylor, G.C.B., R.E.: his times, his friends, and his work. By Alicia Cameron Taylor. 2 v. 1913.

### (e) *The Sepoy Mutiny and the 1857 Rebellion*

The Indian Mutiny has become the centre of a great historical controversy, turning on the question of whether or not it was a national movement against the British overlords. Only a selection of the fast-growing literature of the subject can be incl. here. Nor is there room for the many vols. of recollections of events.

1189 LADENDORF (JANICE M.) *comp.* The revolt in India, 1857–58: an annotated bibliography of English language materials. Zug, Switz. 1966.

1190 IMPERIAL RECORD DEPARTMENT. Press-list of 'mutiny papers', 1857: being, a collection of the correspondence of the mutineers at Delhi, reports of spies to English officials and other miscellaneous papers. Calcutta. 1921.

See also Krishna Dayal Bhargava, ed., *Descriptive list of mutiny papers in the National Archives of India, Bhopal*, 2 v. National Archives of India, New Delhi 1960–3.

1191 FORREST (*Sir* GEORGE WILLIAM) *ed.* Selections from the letters, despatches and other state papers preserved in the Military Department of the Government of India, 1857–58. 4 v. Calcutta. 1893–1912.

Forrest used the same material in his *A history of the Indian mutiny*, 3 v. 1904–12.

1192 MUIR (*Sir* WILLIAM) *ed*. Records of the intelligence department of the north-west provinces of India during the mutiny of 1857 . . . 2 v. Edin. 1902.

1193 ROWBOTHAM (WILLIAM BEVILL) *ed*. The naval brigades in the Indian mutiny, 1857–58. Navy Records Soc. vol. LXXXVII. 1947.

See also Gerald Lloyd Verney, *The devil's wind: the story of the naval brigade at Lucknow: from the letters of Edmund Hope Verney and other papers* . . ., 1956.

1194 RUSSELL (*Sir* WILLIAM HOWARD). My diary in India in the year 1858–9. 2 v. 1860. New edn. by Michael Edwardes. [My Indian mutiny diary.] 1957.

Probably the best of a very considerable number of diaries publ. after the mutiny.

1195 ROBERTS (FREDERICK SLEIGH), *Earl Roberts*. Letters written during the Indian mutiny . . . Ed. by his daughter. 1924.

1196 KAYE (*Sir* JOHN WILLIAM). A history of the sepoy war in India, 1857–1858. 3 v. 1864–76.

Cont. by George Bruce Malleson, *History of the Indian mutiny, 1857–58: commencing from the close of the second volume of Sir John Kaye's history of the sepoy war*, 3 v. 1878–80, with index vol. by Frederic Pincott, 1880. The two ser. were combined and ed. by Malleson as *Kaye's and Malleson's history of the Indian mutiny* . . ., 6 v. 1888–9. Still the standard hist. of the mutiny.

1197 DUFF (ALEXANDER). The Indian rebellion: its causes and results, in a series of letters. Edin. & Lond. 1858.

The reports home of the leading Scottish missionary in India.

1198 AHMED KHAN (*Sir* SAYYID). An essay on the causes of the Indian revolt. Agra. 1859. English trans. [The causes of the Indian revolt] Benares. 1873.

Much the most perceptive account of the origins of the mutiny.

1199 MAJUMDAR (RAMESH CHANDRA). The sepoy mutiny and the revolt of 1857. 2nd edn. Calcutta. 1963.

One of the few books that attempt a careful interpretation of the mutiny. For comment on it see Sashi Bhusan Chaudhuri, *Theories of the Indian mutiny (1857–59)* . . ., Calcutta 1965.

1200 SAVARKAR (VINAYAK DAMODAR). The Indian war of independence 1857. By an Indian Nationalist. Lond. [1909]. Repr. Bombay. 1947.

The first work (written in 1908) to suggest that the Sepoy mutiny was a war of independence.

1201 SEN (SURENDRANATH). Eighteen fifty-seven. Delhi. 1957.

An attempt at an 'impartial' hist. publ. by the government of India. Only partly successful.

1202 JOSHI (PRAKASH CHANDRA) *ed.* Rebellion, 1857: a symposium. New Delhi. 1957.

Communist. Incls. some perceptive essays.

1203 STOKES (ERIC). 'Traditional resistance movements and Afro-Asian nationalism: the context of the 1857 mutiny rebellion in India'. *Past & Present* 48 (1970), 100–18.

See also his 'Rural revolt in the great rebellion of 1857 in India: a study of the Saharanpur and Muzaffarnagar districts', *Hist. J.* xii (1969), 606–27, and 'Traditional elites in the Great Rebellion of 1857: some aspects of rural revolt in the upper and central Doab', in Edmund Ronald Leach and Soumyendra Nath Mukherjee, eds., *Elites in South Asia*, Camb. 1970, pp. 16–32.

1204 RAJ (JAGDISH). The mutiny and British land policy in North India, 1856–1868. Bombay. 1965.

1205 PALMER (JULIAN ARTHUR BEAUFORT). The mutiny outbreak at Meerut in 1857. Camb. 1966.

1206 SRIVASTAVA (KUSHHALILAL). The revolt of 1857 in central India: Malwa. Bombay. 1966.

1207 GUPTA (PRATUL CHANDRA). Nana Sahib and the rising in Cawnpore. Oxf. 1963.

1208 TAHMANKAR (DATTATRAYA VISHWANATH). The ranee of Jhansi. 1958.

Poor, but Sir John George Smyth, *The rebellious rani*, 1966, is little more than a consolidated ser. of regimental histories.

1209 INNES ([JAMES JOHN] McLEOD). Lucknow and Oude in the mutiny: a narrative and a study. 1895.

See also his *The sepoy revolt: a critical narrative*, 1897.

1210 EDWARDES (MICHAEL). Battles of the Indian mutiny. 1963.

Popular. Cp. Richard Collier, *The sound of fury: an account of the Indian mutiny*, 1963, publ. in N.Y. as *The great Indian mutiny . . .*, 1964.

1211 SHERRING (MATTHEW ATMORE). The Indian church during the great rebellion: an authentic narrative of the disasters that befell it . . . ed. by R. C. Mather. 1859.


## C. THE COLONIAL EMPIRE

### 1. REFERENCE

1212 COLONIAL OFFICE LIBRARY. Catalogue. 15 v. Boston. 1964.

Much the fullest catalogue. Suppl. in preparation.

1213  LEWIN (PERCY EVANS) *comp*. Subject catalogue of the library of the Royal Empire Society, formerly the Royal Colonial Institute. 4 v. 1930–7. Repr. 1967. Suppl. 7 v. Boston. 1971.

A fine subject catalogue to a libr. badly damaged by bombs. The fullest historical subject bibliogs. are in *The Cambridge history of the British empire* (**1237**).

1214  SIMPSON (DONALD HERBERT) *comp*. Biography catalogue of the library of the Royal Commonwealth Society. 1961. Cont. by suppl. to **1213**.

A splendid work, fully indexed and incl. country-by-country sections. For biog. see also Sir John Bernard Burke, *A genealogical and heraldic history of the colonial gentry*, 2 v. 1891–5.

1215  FLINT (JOHN EDGAR). Books on the British empire and common-wealth: a guide for students. 1968.

See also William Parker Morrell, *British overseas expansion and the history of the Common-wealth: a select bibliography*, Hist. Assoc. Helps for Students 63, 1961, new edn. 1970; Arthur Reginald Hewitt, *Guide to resources for commonwealth studies in London, Oxford and Cambridge, with bibliographical and other information*, Inst. Commonwealth Studs. 1957; and Dame Margery Freda Perham, *Colonial government: an annotated reading list on British colonial government . . .*, Oxf. 1950.

1216  WINKS (ROBIN WILLIAM) *ed*. The historiography of the British empire-commonwealth: interpretations and resources. Durham, N.C. 1966.

1217  MAXWELL (LESLIE F.). A bibliography of the law of British colonies, protectorates and mandated territories. Vol. 7 of A Legal bibliography of the British Commonwealth of Nations. 1949. Suppl. 1954.

1218  PUGH (RALPH BERNARD). The records of the Colonial and Dominions offices. P.R.O. handbooks no. 3. H.M.S.O. 1964.

An admirable survey. Suppl. by P.R.O., *List of Colonial Office confidential print to 1916*, P.R.O. handbooks no. 8, H.M.S.O. 1965, and *List of Colonial Office Records* P.R.O. Lists and Indexes XXXVI, 1911, repr. N.Y. etc. 1963. For non-official records see Bodleian Libr., Oxford, *Manuscript collections in Rhodes House library*, comp. by Louis Benson Frewer, 2 pts. Oxf. 1968–70.

1219  ADAM (MARGARET ISABELLA), EWING (JOHN), *and* MUNRO (JAMES) *comps*. Guide to the principal parliamentary papers relating to the dominions, 1812–1911. Edin. 1913.

See also the lists in *The Cambridge history of the British empire* (**1237**).

1220  THE COLONIAL OFFICE LIST . . . Annual. 1862–1966.

Lists of officials and official papers, plus misc. data. Retrospective lists of papers in 1878 issue for 1864–77, in 1914 issue for 1877–1913. For governors see David P. Henige, comp., *Colonial governors from the fifteenth century to the present: a comprehen-sive list*, Madison, Wis. 1970. For 1903 Edgar G. Wall, *The British empire year book, 1903: an annual statistical volume of reference, compiled with the assistance of H.M. imperial and colonial governments*, 1903, is a handy suppl.

1221 COLONIAL OFFICE. Reports made to the Secretary of State by the governors of the colonies. 1845+.

The annual report of each colony was normally publ. as a parl. paper. These reports are a major source of data.

1222 STATISTICAL ABSTRACT for the several colonial and other possessions of the United Kingdom, in each year, 1850 to 1863. [3508] H.C. (1865). LV, 433 [Title varies]. Annual to 1936–45.

Suppl. by *Statistical abstract for the British empire in each year from 1889 to 1903: first number*. [Cd. 2395] H.C. (1905). XCIV, 319. Annual to 1913. See also *Statistical tables relating to the colonial and other possessions of the United Kingdom*. [2127] H.C. (1856). LVII, 289. Irregular to 1912.

1223 COLONIAL AND INDIAN EXHIBITION, 1886. Official catalogue. 1886.

Suppl. by a ser. of reports and handbooks covering the greater part of the empire. They are listed in The British Museum catalogue (5), and are a valuable but little-used source.

1224 ROYAL COMMISSION ON LABOUR. Foreign reports vol. II. The colonies and the Indian empire, with an appendix on the migration of labour. [C. 6795–XI] H.C. (1892). XXXVI, pt. V, 61.

A colony-by-colony survey.

1225 BOARD OF EDUCATION. Special reports on educational subjects. Vol. 4. Educational systems of the chief colonies of the British empire (Dominion of Canada, Newfoundland, West Indies) [Cd. 416] H.C. (1900). XXI, 1.

The first of an extraordinarily comprehensive ser. of educational reports. Cont. for the self-governing colonies by vol. 5. [Cape Colony, Natal, Commonwealth of Australia, New Zealand, Ceylon, Malta] [Cd. 417] H.C. (1900). XXII, Pt. 1. Then cont. for the non-self-governing colonies in *Special reports on educational subjects. Vol. 12. Educational systems of the chief crown colonies and possessions of the British empire, including reports on the training of native races. Part I. West Indies and Central America, St Helena, Cyprus and Gibraltar* [Cd. 2377] H.C. (1905). XXV, 325. *Part II [Vol. 13]. West Africa, Basutoland, Southern Rhodesia, East Africa protectorate, Uganda, Mauritius, Seychelles* [Cd. 2378] H.C. (1905). XXVI, 1. *Part III [Vol. 14]. Federated Malay States, Hong Kong, Straits Settlements, Fiji, Falkland Islands* [Cd. 2379] H.C. (1905). XXVI, 385.

1226 D'ABERNON COMMISSION ON RESOURCES OF THE DOMINIONS. First interim report of the royal commission on the natural resources, trade and legislation of certain portions of his majesty's dominions [Chairman: Sir Edgar Vincent, afterwards Lord D'Abernon] [Cd. 6515] H.C. (1912–13). XVI, 91. Evidence etc. I. Migration [Cd. 6516] H.C. (1912–13). XVI, 95. II. Natural resources, trade and legislation [Cd. 6517] H.C. (1912–13). XVI, 393. Other evidence taken in London [Cd. 7173, 7351] H.C. (1914). XVIII, 1, 213; [Cd. 7710] H.C. (1914–16). XIII, 865. Memoranda: Food & raw materials [Cd. 8123] H.C. (1914–16). XIV, 371; Trade statistics [Cd. 8156] H.C. 1914–16). XIV, 499; Harbours and canals [Cd. 8461] H.C. (1917–18). IX, 523. Papers [Cd. 8460] H.C. (1917–18). IX, 475. Second interim report on Australia and New Zealand [Cd. 7210] H.C. (1914). XVIII, 137; New Zealand evidence [Cd. 7170] H.C. (1914). XVII, 101; Australian evidence [Cd. 7171-2] H.C. (1914). XVII, 361, 731. Third interim report on South Africa [Cd. 7505] H.C. (1914). XVIII, 447; South African evidence [Cd. 7706-7] H.C. (1914-16). XIII, 279, 657. Fourth interim report on Newfoundland [Cd. 7711] H.C. (1914-16). XIV, 1; Newfoundland evidence [Cd. 7898] H.C. (1914-16). XIV, 29. Fifth interim report on Canada [Cd. 8457] H.C. (1917-18). VIII, 159; Canadian evidence [Cd. 7971] H.C. (1914-16). XIV, 173; [Cd. 8458-9] H.C. (1917-18). VIII, 229, IX, 1. Final report [Cd. 8462] H.C. (1917-18). X, 1.

The commission was established at the request of the 1911 imperial conference and incl. representatives of the dominions.

1227   LUCAS (*Sir* CHARLES PRESTWOOD) *ed.* A historical geography of the British colonies [empire]. 7 v. in 11. Oxf. 1888–1923.

Covers each colony in turn, incl. India, in 2 v. An authoritative pocket encyclopedia. Much better than Edgar Sanderson, *The British empire in the nineteenth century: its progress and expansion at home and abroad: comprising a description and history . . .*, 6 v. 1898–9, new edn. 1901.

1228   HERBERTSON (ANDREW JOHN) *and* HOWARTH (OSBERT JOHN RADCLIFFE) *eds.* The Oxford survey of the British empire. 6 v. Oxf. 1914.

A survey of the empire in 1914, which tries to avoid covering the same ground as Lucas (**1227**). Arranged geographically.

1229   GUNN (HUGH) *ed.* The British empire: a survey . . . 12 v. 1924.

A comprehensive ser. by first-rate authors. Vol. I is a general survey of the colonies, vol. II a hist. by Sir Charles Lucas, vol. III a study of constitutional development by Arthur Berriedale Keith, vol. IV a study of resources by Percy Evans Lewin, vol. V a history of health problems by Andrew Balfour and H. H. Scott, vol. VI a study of the press and communications by John Saxon Mills, vol. VII a study of trade and commerce by Sir Charles McLeod and A. W. Kirkaldy, vol. VIII makers of the empire by Hugh Gunn, vol. IX the native races of the empire by Sir Godfrey Lagden, vol. X the universities and educational systems by Arthur Percival Newton, vol. XI literature and art by Edward Salmon and A. A. Longden, vol. XII migration within the empire by Ernest Albert Belcher and J. A. Williamson.

1230   SIMMONS (JACK) *ed.* From empire to commonwealth: principles of British imperial government. 1952.

Docs. See also Bennett (**965**).

1231   BELL (KENNETH NORMAN) *and* MORRELL (WILLIAM PARKER) *eds.* Select documents on British colonial policy, 1830–1860. Oxf. 1928.

On economic policy see also Alan George Lewers Shaw, ed., *Great Britain and the colonies, 1815–1865*, 1970.

1232   KEITH (ARTHUR BERRIEDALE). Selected speeches and documents on British colonial policy, 1763–1917. 2 v. [1918]. Suppl. by Albert Frederick Madden [Imperial constitutional documents, 1765–1965]. Oxf. 1953. Repr. 1966.

1233   OLLIVIER (MAURICE) *comp.* The colonial and imperial conferences from 1887–1937. 3 v. Ottawa. 1954.

Docs. See also **1248**.

1234   EGERTON (HUGH EDWARD) *ed.* Federations and unions within the British empire. Oxf. 1911. 2nd edn. Oxf. 1924.

Federal constitutions. See also Arthur Percival Newton, ed., *Federal and unified constitutions: a collection of constitutional documents for the use of students*, 1923, and Martin Wight, ed., *British colonial constitutions, 1947*, Oxf. 1952, which is useful, though post-1914.

1235   COLONIAL OFFICE. Colonial [office] journal. 1907–20.

For unofficial views of empire see *Empire review*, 1901+, and *The round table: a quarterly review of the politics of the British empire*, 1910+, and the js. at **1268**.

## 2. GENERAL

1236   CARRINGTON (CHARLES EDMUND). The British overseas: exploits of a nation of shopkeepers. Camb. 1950. 2nd edn. 2 v. 1968+.

The best short hist. of the British empire. The following are also useful: Godfrey Elton, Baron Elton, *Imperial commonwealth*, 1945; Eric Anderson Walker, *The British empire, its structure and spirit*, 1943, 2nd edn. Camb. 1953; William David McIntyre, *Colonies into commonwealth*, 1966; Alfred LeRoy Burt, *The evolution of the British empire and commonwealth from the American revolution*, Boston 1956; Paul Knaplund, *The British Empire 1815–1939*, 1941, and *Britain: commonwealth and empire, 1901–55*, 1956; Arthur Percival Newton, *A hundred years of the British empire (1840–1940)*, 1940; Sir Ernest Barker, *The ideas and ideals of the British empire*, Camb. 1941; Denis Judd, *The Victorian empire, 1837–1901*, 1970, and Gerald Sandford Graham, *A concise history of the British empire*, 1970.

Older books, such as Hugh Edward Egerton, *A short history of British colonial policy*, 1897, 9th edn. 1932, and James Alexander Williamson, *A short history of British expansion*, 1922, 4th edn. 1953, are now out of date.

1237   THE CAMBRIDGE HISTORY OF THE BRITISH EMPIRE. Vol. II. The growth of the new empire, 1783–1870. Vol. III. The empire-commonwealth, 1870–1919. Camb. 1940–59.

The best comprehensive survey of all aspects of imperial hist. Excellent bibliogs. The national vols. that form part of the ser. are out of date and not to be relied on, though they, too, have good bibliogs. There is useful suppl. material in Kenneth Ernest Robinson and Albert Frederick Madden, eds., *Essays in imperial government presented to Margery Perham*, 1963.

1238   SWINFEN (DAVID BERRIDGE). Imperial control of colonial legislation, 1813–1865: a study of British policy towards colonial legislative powers. Oxf. 1970.

1239   KNOWLES (LILIAN CHARLOTTE ANNE). The economic development of the British overseas empire. 3 v. 1924–36.

Badly out of date, but not entirely repl. See also Edmond Carton de Wiart, *Les grandes compagnies coloniales anglaises du XIX$^e$ siècle*, Paris 1899.

1240   SCHUYLER (ROBERT LIVINGSTON). The fall of the old colonial system: a study in British free trade, 1770–1870. N.Y. 1945. Repr. Hamden, Conn. 1966.

1241   MORRELL (WILLIAM PARKER). British colonial policy in the mid-Victorian age: South Africa, New Zealand, and the West Indies [1853–72]. Oxf. 1969.

Good. See also his *British colonial policy in the age of Peel and Russell*, Oxf. 1930.

1242   BODELSEN (CARL ADOLPH [GOTTLIEB]). Studies in mid-Victorian imperialism. Copenhagen. 1924. 2nd edn. Lond. etc., 1960.

Long indispensable; now dated. See also J. H. Davidson, 'Anthony Trollope and the colonies', *Victorian Studs.* xii (1968–9), 305–30.

1243   McINTYRE (WILLIAM DAVID). The imperial frontier in the tropics, 1865–75: a study of British colonial policy in West Africa, Malaya and the South Pacific in the age of Gladstone and Disraeli. 1967.

Very perceptive. Colin C. Eldridge, *England's mission: the imperial idea in the age of Gladstone and Disraeli, 1868–1880*, 1973, also covers new ground.

1244   KNAPLUND (PAUL). Gladstone and Britain's imperial policy. 1927. Repr. Hamden, Conn. 1966.

Useful. There is also a short guide, Richard Henry Gretton, *Imperialism and Mr Gladstone, 1876–1887*, 1923. See also Ina Mary Cumpston, 'The discussion of imperial problems in the British parliament, 1880–85', *Roy. Hist. Soc. Trans.*, 5 ser. 13 (1963), 29–48.

1245   STURGIS (JAMES LAVERNE). John Bright and the empire. 1969.

1246   HIND (R. J.). Henry Labouchere and the empire, 1880–1905. 1972.

1247   TYLER (JOHN ECCLESFIELD). The struggle for imperial unity, 1868–1895. 1938.

See also his section of *The Cambridge history* (**1237**); Seymour Ching-Juan Cheng, *Schemes for the federation of the British empire*, N.Y. 1931; Alfred LeRoy Burt, *Imperial architects: being, an account of proposals in the direction of a closer imperial union, made previous to the opening of the first colonial conference of 1887*, Oxf. 1913; Berger, *The sense of power* (**1494**), and John Donald Bruce Miller, *Richard Jebb and the problem of empire*, Commonwealth papers 3, 1956.

1248   KENDLE (JOHN EDWARD). The colonial and imperial conferences, 1887–1911: a study in imperial organization. 1967.

Good. See also his 'The Round Table movement and "Home Rule all round"', *Hist. J.* xi (1968), 332–53, Richard Jebb, *The imperial conference: a history and study*, 2 v. 1911, and Richard H. Wilde, 'Joseph Chamberlain's proposal of an imperial council in March 1900', *Canadian Hist. Rev.* xxxvii (1956), 225–46. For docs. see **1233**.

1249   TRAINOR (LUKE). 'The British government and imperial economic unity, 1890–1895'. *Hist. J.* xiii (1970), 68–84.

See also S. M. Hardy, 'Joseph Chamberlain and some problems of the "under-developed estates"', *Univ. of Birmingham Hist. J.* xi (1967–8), 170–90, Vincent Ponko, 'The

Colonial office and British business before World War I: a case study', *Business Hist. Rev.* xliii (1969), 39–58, and **1290**.

**1250  BELOFF (MAX).** Imperial sunset: Britain's liberal empire, 1897–1921. 1969. N.Y. 1970.

There is a ser. of attractive impressionistic sketches in James Morris, *Pax britannica: the climax of an empire*, 1968. See also Donald Craigie Gordon, *The moment of power: Britain's imperial epoch*, Englewood Cliffs, N.J. 1970.

**1251  HYAM (RONALD).** Elgin and Churchill at the Colonial Office, 1905–1908: the watershed of the empire-commonwealth. 1968.

A good study of Churchill.

**1252  JUDD (DENIS).** Balfour and the British empire: a study in imperial evolution, 1874–1932. 1968.

Fuller than Hans E. Bärtschi, *Die Entwicklung vom imperialistischen Reichsgedanken zur modernen Idee des Commonwealth in Lebenswerk Lord Balfours*, Aarau 1957.

**1253  GOLLIN (ALFRED MANUEL).** Proconsul in politics: a study of Lord Milner in opposition and power. 1964.

For Milner's colonial career see **1305**.

**1254  NIMOCKS (WALTER).** Milner's young men: the 'Kindergarten' in Edwardian imperial affairs. Durham, N.C. 1968. Lond. 1970.

**1255  MANSERGH ([PHILIP] NICHOLAS [SETON]).** The Commonwealth experience. 1969.

Urbane and comprehensive. Deals chiefly with the 20th-cent. commonwealth, but has coverage back to 1839. Better than Sir Percival Joseph Griffiths, *Empire into commonwealth*, 1969, and Hessel Duncan Hall, *Commonwealth: a history of the British commonwealth of nations, 1900–1957*, 1970.

**1256  HANCOCK (*Sir* WILLIAM KEITH).** Survey of British commonwealth affairs. 2 v. 1937–42.

Concerned with the post-1918 commonwealth, but full of useful *aperçus* on earlier periods.

**1257  JENKYNS (*Sir* HENRY).** British rule and jurisdiction beyond the seas. Oxf. 1902.

A legal survey. See also **1238**.

**1258  SCHUYLER (ROBERT LIVINGSTON).** Parliament and the British empire: some constitutional controversies concerning imperial legislative jurisdiction. N.Y. 1929. Repr. 1963.

**1259  WIGHT (MARTIN).** The development of the legislative council, 1606–1945. 1946.

1260 TODD (ALPHEUS). Parliamentary government in the British colonies. 1880. 2nd edn. 1894.

An encyclopedia of institutions, comparable with his famous work on Britain (279).

1261 KEITH (ARTHUR BERRIEDALE). Responsible government in the dominions. 3 v. Oxf. 1912. 2nd edn. 2 v. Oxf. 1928.

1262 DAWSON (ROBERT MACGREGOR). The development of dominion status, 1900–1936. Lond. & N.Y. 1937. Repr. 1965.

1263 EVATT (HERBERT VERE). The king and his dominion governors: a study of the reserve powers of the crown in Great Britain and the dominions. 1936. 2nd edn. 1967.

1264 KEITH (ARTHUR BERRIEDALE). Imperial unity and the dominions. Oxf. 1916.

The limitations on colonial self-government.

1265 LIVINGSTON (WILLIAM SAMUEL) *ed.* Federalism in the commonwealth: a bibliographical commentary. 1963.

A useful series of bibliographic essays.

1266 SHAW (ALAN GEORGE LEWERS). Convicts and the colonies: a study of penal transportation from Great Britain and Ireland to Australia and other parts of the British empire. 1966.

See also Alan Frederick Hattersley, *The convict crisis and the growth of unity: resistance to transportation in South Africa and Australia, 1848–1853,* Pietermaritzburg, 1965.

1267 MORRELL (WILLIAM PARKER). The gold rushes. Lond. 1940. N.Y. 1941. 2nd edn. Lond. 1968.

1268 REESE (TREVOR RICHARD). The history of the Royal Commonwealth Society, 1868–1968. 1968.

Founded as the [Royal] Colonial Institute, which publ. *Proceedings,* 1869–1909, and *United Empire,* 1910+, under various titles. On the history of the society see also Avaline Folsom, *The Royal Empire Society, formerly the Royal Colonial Institute: formative years,* 1933, and James Rufus Boosé, *Memory serving: being, reminiscences of fifty years of the Royal Colonial Institute,* 1928.

1269 ELTON (GODFREY), *Baron Elton ed.* The first fifty years of the Rhodes Trust and the Rhodes scholarships, 1903–1953. Oxf. 1955.

1270 RUSSELL (JOHN). The schools of Greater Britain: sketches of the educational systems of the colonies and India. Lond. & Glasgow. 1887.

1271 GREY (HENRY GEORGE), *Earl Grey.* The colonial policy of Lord John Russell's administration. 2 v. 1853. 2nd edn. 1853.

An important exposition of Grey's views. See also Charles Bowyer Adderley, Baron Norton, *A review of 'The colonial policy of Lord John Russell's administration . . .',* 1869, and *Our relations with the colonies and crown colonies,* 1870.

1272 SMITH (GOLDWIN). The empire: a series of letters, published in *The Daily News*, 1862, 1863. Oxf. 1863.

1273 DILKE (*Sir* CHARLES WENTWORTH). Greater Britain: a record of travel in English-speaking countries during 1866 and 1867. 2 v. 1868. 8th edn. 1885.

Suppl. by *Problems of Greater Britain*, 2 v. Lond. & N.Y. 1890, 4th edn. 1890, and *The British empire*, 1899.

1274 FORSTER (WILLIAM EDWARD). Our colonial empire: an address . . . Edin. 1875.

1275 FREEMAN (EDWARD AUGUSTUS). Greater Greece and greater Britain . . . 1886.

1276 FROUDE (JAMES ANTHONY). Oceana: or, England and her colonies. 1886. New edn. 1886.

1277 HÜBNER (JOSEPH ALEXANDER von), *Count*. Through the British empire. Trans. from the French. 2 v. 1886.

1278 DE LABILLIÈRE (FRANCIS PETER). Federal Britain: or, unity and federation of the empire. 1894.

1279 WHITE (ARNOLD). Efficiency and empire. 1901.

1280 GOLDMAN (CHARLES SYDNEY) *ed.* The empire and the century: a series of essays on imperial problems and possibilities. 1905.

Essays by well-known authors. See also Carl Johannes Fuchs, *The trade policy of Great Britain and her colonies since 1860*, trans. by Constance H. M. Archibald, 1905.

1281 JEBB (RICHARD). Studies in colonial nationalism. 1905.

1282 AMERY (LEOPOLD CHARLES MAURICE STENNETT). Union and strength: a series of papers on imperial questions. 1912.

3. THE COLONIAL OFFICE AND THE COLONIAL SERVICE

1283 CELL (JOHN W.). British colonial administration in the mid-nineteenth century: the policy-making process. New Haven [Conn.]. 1970.

Good on the structure of the Colonial office and its attitudes. Henry Lindsay Hall, *The Colonial office: a history*, 1937, covers 1830–85, but is largely out of date. There is an excellent short history of the Colonial office, 1801–1925, by Ralph Bernard Pugh in the *Cambridge history* (**1237**), vol. III, 711–68. John Arthur Cross, *Whitehall and the commonwealth: British departmental organisation for commonwealth relations, 1900–1966*, 1967, deals with a minor aspect of Colonial office administration. See also B. A. Knox, 'The provision of legal advice and Colonial Office reorganization, 1866–7', *Inst. Hist. Res. Bull.* xxxv (1962), 178–97.

1284 BLAKELEY (BRIAN L.). The Colonial Office, 1868–1892. Durham, N.C. 1972.

1285  KUBICEK (ROBERT VINCENT). The administration of imperialism: Joseph Chamberlain at the Colonial office. Durham, N.C. 1969.

1286  TAYLOR. Autobiography of [Sir] Henry Taylor, 1800–1875. 2 v. 1885.

A minor classic. Incl. much comment on his work at the Colonial Office up to 1872. Edward Dowden, ed., *Correspondence of Henry Taylor*, 1888, is more concerned with Taylor's literary work.

1287  MERIVALE. Herman Merivale, C.B. By Charles Merivale. 1884.

Merivale was Perm. Under-Sec., 1848–59.

1288  BLACHFORD. Letters of Frederic [Rogers], Lord Blachford, Under-Secretary of State for the Colonies, 1860–1871. Ed. by George Eden Marindin. 1896.

1289  PARKINSON. The Colonial Office from within, 1909–1945. By Sir [Arthur Charles] Cosmo Parkinson. 1947.

See also Sir John Bramston, 'The Colonial office from within', *Empire Rev.* i (1901), 279–87, Sir William Alexander Baillie-Hamilton, 'Forty-four years at the Colonial office', *Nineteenth century* lxv (1909), 599–613, and Sir Edward Howard Marsh, *A number of people: a book of reminiscences*, 1939.

1290  PONKO (VINCENT). 'Economic management in a free trade empire: the work of the Crown Agents for the Colonies in the 19th and early 20th centuries'. *J. Econ. Hist.* xxvi (1966), 363–77.

See also *Report of the committee of enquiry into the organization of the Crown Agents' office* [Cd. 4473] H.C. (1909). XVI, 377. Minutes of evidence etc. [Cd. 4474] H.C. (1909). XVI, 403.

1291  HITCHINS (FRED HARVEY). The Colonial Land and Emigration Commission, [1840–78]. Phila. 1931.

Useful, but largely replaced by Macdonagh (**404**).

1292  HEUSSLER (ROBERT). Yesterday's rulers: the making of the British Colonial Service. Syracuse, N.Y. & Lond. 1963.

Chiefly on the 20th-cent. African service. Sir Charles Joseph Jeffries, *The colonial empire and its civil service*, Camb. 1938, and Sir Alan Cuthbert Burns, *Colonial civil servant*, 1949, are occasionally useful.

1293  FURSE (*Sir* RALPH DOLIGNON). Aucuparius: recollections of a recruiting officer. 1962.

The memoirs of the man who recruited the colonial service after 1910.

1294  BRUCE (*Sir* CHARLES). The broad stone of empire: problems of crown colony administration, with records of personal experience. 2 v. 1910.

See also Sir Charles Lucas, *British colonial administration*, publ. as vol. VI of the *Oxford survey* (**1228**).

1295  BARKLY. Sir Henry Barkly: mediator and moderator, 1815–1898. By Mona Macmillan. Cape Town. 1970.

1296 BELL. Glimpses of a governor's life: from diaries, letters and memoranda. By Sir Henry Hesketh Joudou Bell. 1946.

1297 BOWEN. Thirty years of colonial government: a selection from the despatches and letters of the Right Hon. Sir George Ferguson Bowen. Ed. by Stanley Lane-Poole. 2 v. 1889.

1298 DENISON. Varieties of vice-regal life. By Sir William Thomas Denison. 2 v. 1870.

1299 DES VŒUX. My colonial service in British Guiana, St. Lucia, Trinidad, Fiji, Australia, Newfoundland and Hong Kong: with interludes. By Sir George William Des Vœux. 2 v. 1903.

1300 EYRE. The hero as murderer: the life of Edward John Eyre, Australian explorer and governor of Jamaica, 1815–1901. By Geoffrey Dutton. 1967.
See also **1590**.

FRERE. For Sir Bartle Frere see **2091**.

1301 GLOVER. Life of Sir John Hawley Glover. By Elizabeth Rosetta Glover. Ed. by Sir Richard Temple. 1897.

GORDON. For Sir Arthur Gordon see **1307**.

1302 GREY. Sir George Grey, K.C.B., 1812–1898. By James Rutherford. 1961.
Good on the Cape and New Zealand.

1303 GRIMBLE. A pattern of islands. By Sir Arthur Francis Grimble. 1952.
A classic of colonial administration: on the Gilbert and Ellice Islands.

LUGARD. For Lord Lugard see **1626, 1771, 1868,** and **1870**.

1304 MACGREGOR. Sir William MacGregor. By Roger B. Joyce. Melb. 1971.

1305 MILNER. Lord Milner and the empire: the evolution of British imperialism. By Vladimir Halpérin. 1952.
See also Sir John Evelyn Wrench, *Alfred Lord Milner: the man of no illusions, 1854–1925,* 1958, Edward Crankshaw, *The forsaken idea: a study of Viscount Milner,* 1952, Alfred Manuel Gollin, *Proconsul in politics: a study of Lord Milner in opposition and in power,* 1964, and, for Milner's South African career, **2059**. There are two good collections of speeches, *Constructive imperialism . . .,* 1908, and *The nation and the empire: being, a collection of speeches and addresses,* 1913.

1306 POPE-HENNESSY. Verandah: some episodes in the crown colonies, 1867–1889. By James Pope-Hennessy. 1964.
A life of Sir John Pope-Hennessy, governor of Mauritius, etc.

1307 STANMORE. The career of Arthur Hamilton Gordon, first Lord Stanmore, 1829–1912. By James Keith Chapman. Toronto. 1964.

For his correspondence see J. K. Chapman, ed., *A political correspondence of the Gladstone era: the letters of Lady Sophia Palmer and Sir Arthur Gordon, 1884–1889,* Amer. Phil. Soc. Trans. lxi, pt. 2, Phila. 1971, and **731**, and for his Fijian career **1423**.

1308 WELD. The life of Sir Frederick Weld, G.C.M.G., a pioneer of empire. By Alice Mary [Fraser], Lady Lovat. 1914.

1309 WOOLF. Sowing: an autobiography of the years 1880–1904. By Leonard Sidney Woolf. 1960.

Cont. in *Growing . . . 1904–1911,* 1961 and *Beginning again . . . 1911–1918,* 1964. One of the most distinguished of modern autobiogs. His colonial career is excellently dealt with in *Growing* and in his *Diaries in Ceylon, 1908–1911: records of a colonial administrator, being the official diaries maintained by Leonard Woolf while Assistant Government Agent of the Hambartota District, Ceylon,* and *stories from the east: three stories in Ceylon, Ceylon Hist. J.* ix, Dehiwala, 1962, repr. Lond. 1963.

### 4. COLONIES IN AUSTRALASIA AND THE PACIFIC

#### (a) *Australasia Generally*

1310 GRATTAN (CLINTON HARTLEY). The Southwest Pacific . . . a modern history: Australia, New Zealand, the islands, Antarctica. Vol. I to 1900. Vol. II since 1900. Ann Arbor. [Mich.]. 1963.

1311 WARD (JOHN MANNING). Empire in the antipodes: the British in Australasia, 1840–1860. 1966.

One of the few attempts to cover the hist. of both Australia and New Zealand.

1312 COGHLAN (Sir TIMOTHY AUGUSTINE) and EWING (Sir THOMAS THOMSON). The progress of Australasia in the nineteenth century. Nineteenth Century Series v. 11. 1902.

See also Coghlan's *Statistics of the seven colonies of Australasia, 1861 to 1896,* Sydney 1897.

1313 ALLIN (CEPHAS DANIEL). Australasian preferential tariffs and imperial free trade: a chapter in the fiscal emancipation of the colonies. Minneapolis. 1929.

1314 REEVES (WILLIAM PEMBER). State experiments in Australia and New Zealand. 2 v. 1902. New edn. by John Child. 2 v. 1970.

1315 SWEET & MAXWELL LTD. A legal bibliography of the British Commonwealth of Nations. Vol. 6: Australia, New Zealand and their dependencies . . . 2nd edn. 1958.

#### (b) *Australia*

1316 FERGUSON (Sir JOHN ALEXANDER) ed. Bibliography of Australia, 1784–[1900]. 7 v. Sydney & Lond. 1941–69.

For current books see *Australian national bibliography*, Canberra 1961+. Dietrich Hans Borchardt, *Australian bibliography: a guide to printed sources of information*, Melb. etc. 1963, 2nd edn. 1966, is a handy guide. For theses see *Union list of higher degree theses in Australian university libraries: cumulative edition to 1965*, Hobart 1967. There is a good hist. bibliog. in *The Cambridge history of the British empire*, vol. VII, pt. I, *Australia*, Camb. 1933. Specialized bibliogs. incl. John Greenway, *Bibliography of the Australian aborigines and the native peoples of Torres Strait to 1959*, Sydney 1963, and Jean Craig, *Bibliography of public administration in Australia, 1850–1947*, Sydney 1955. *The dictionary catalog of printed books* of the Mitchell Libr. of the Public Libr. of New South Wales, 38 v. Boston 1968, is a fine subject catalogue.

**1317  NATIONAL LIBRARY OF AUSTRALIA.** Guide to collections of manuscripts relating to Australia. Canberra. 1965 and suppls.

To be suppl. by Phyllis Mander-Jones, ed., *Manuscripts in the British Isles relating to Australia, New Zealand and the Pacific*, Canberra 1973, an important guide.

**1318  CLARK (CHARLES MANNING HOPE)** *ed.* Select documents in Australian history, 1851–1900. Sydney. 1955.

See also his *Sources of Australian history*, 1957, John T. Gilchrist and William J. Murray, *Eye-witness: selected documents from Australia's past*, Adelaide etc. 1968, and Peter Coleman and Les Tanner, *Cartoons of Australian history*, Melb. 1967.

**1319  THE AUSTRALIAN ENCYCLOPEDIA.** 10 v. Sydney & East Lansing, Mich. 1958.

For additional data consult *The official directory and almanac of Australia for 1883[–1916]*, styled *The year-book of Australia*, 1885–1916, Sydney 1882–1916, and the official year-books of the states and the commonwealth.

**1320  AUSTRALIAN DICTIONARY OF BIOGRAPHY.** Ed. by Douglas Pike. 12 v. Melb. etc. 1966+.

Arr. in 3 ser.: the 1st covered 1788–1850 in 2 v., the 2nd will cover 1851–90 in 4 v., and the 3rd will cover 1891–1939 in approx. 6 v. To be authoritative. See also Percival Serle, *Dictionary of Australian biography*, 2 v. Sydney 1949.

**1321  WRITINGS ON AUSTRALIAN HISTORY.** Publ. in Historical studies [Australia and New Zealand]. Melb. 1940+.

*Historical studies* is the leading hist. j. in Australia. But see also *The Australian j. of politics and history*, Brisbane 1955+, Royal Australian Hist. Soc., *Journal and proceedings*, Sydney 1901+, and the various js. publ. in the indiv. states.

**1322  HANCOCK (*Sir* WILLIAM KEITH).** Australia. 1930.

Still the best general study. For more up-to-date works see Raymond Maxwell Crawford, *Australia*, 1952, rev. edn. 1960; Alan George Lewers Shaw, *The story of Australia*, 1955, 3rd edn. 1967; Douglas Pike, *Australia: the quiet continent*, Camb. 1962; Gordon Greenwood, ed., *Australia: a social and political history*, Sydney 1955; and Charles Manning Hope Clark, *A short history of Australia*, N.Y. 1963, Lond. 1964, new edn. 1969.

**1323  EASTWOOD (JENNIFER JILL)** *and* SMITH (FRANCIS BARRY-MORE)** *eds.* Historical studies: selected articles. Melb. 1964.

1324 WARD (RUSSEL BRADDOCK). The Australian legend. Melb. 1958. 2nd edn. 1965.

A study of national myths.

1325 ALLEN (HARRY CRANBROOK). Bush and backwoods: a comparison of the frontier in Australia and the United States. Sydney and East Lansing, Mich. 1959.

Cp. the earlier Frederick Alexander, *Moving frontiers: an American theme and its application to Australian history*, Melb. 1947. Geoffrey Blainey, *The tyranny of distance: how distance shaped Australia's history*, Melb. 1966, gives an alternative view.

1326 NADEL (GEORGE HANS). Australia's colonial culture: ideas, men and institutions in mid-nineteenth century eastern Australia. Melb. and Camb., Mass. 1957.

An important pioneer study.

1327 TROLLOPE (ANTHONY). Australia. Ed. by P. D. Edwards and R. B. Joyce. St. Lucia, Queensland. 1968.

A shrewd contemp. estimate, well edited. First publ. in Trollope's *Australia and New Zealand*, 2 v. 1873. Cp. Albert Gordon Austin, ed., *The Webbs' Australian diary, 1898*, Melb. 1965.

1328 FITZPATRICK (BRIAN). The Australian commonwealth: a picture of the community, 1901–1955. Melb. 1956.

Disappointing, but there is no better study of 20th-cent. Australia.

1329 NEW SOUTH WALES ARCHIVES AUTHORITY. Guide to the state archives of New South Wales. Sydney. 1963+.

There is no general hist. On Sydney see Alan Birch and David Stirling Macmillan, eds., *The Sydney scene, 1788–1960*, Melb. 1962. For politics etc. see **1339–40, 1342**.

1330 SERLE (GEOFFREY). The golden age: a history of the colony of Victoria, 1851–1861. Melb. 1963. The rush to be rich . . . 1883–1889. Melb. 1971.

Good. See also Geoffrey Winthrop Leeper, ed., *Introducing Victoria*, Melb. 1955; Henry Gyles Turner, *A history of the colony of Victoria from its discovery to its absorption into the commonwealth of Australia*, 2 v. 1904; [Royal] Hist. Soc. of Victoria, *The Victorian historical magazine . . .*, Melb. 1911+; and James Alexander Grant and Geoffrey Serle, comps., *The Melbourne scene, 1803–1956*, Melb. 1957. For politics see **1341**.

1331 CROWLEY (FRANK KEBLE). South Australian history: a survey for research students. Adelaide. 1966.

Douglas Pike, *Paradise of dissent: South Australia, 1829–1857*, 1957, 2nd edn. Melb. etc. 1967, is an admirable study. Edwin Hodder, *The history of South Australia: from its foundation to the year of its jubilee . . .*, 2 v. 1893, is a useful quarry. The principal hist. j. is *South Australiana . . .*, Adelaide 1962+.

1332 BOLTON (GEOFFREY CURGENVEN). A thousand miles away: a history of north Queensland to 1920. Brisbane. 1963.

For Queensland see also Queensland Parliament Libr., *Royal commissions held in Queensland, 1860–1966*, Brisbane 1966.

**1333**  CROWLEY (FRANK KEBLE). Australia's western third: a history of Western Australia from the first settlements to modern times. 1960.

See also his *The records of Western Australia*, Perth 1953; Francis G. Steere, *Bibliography of books, articles and pamphlets dealing with Western Australia* . . ., Perth 1923; *University studies in history* . . ., Univ. of Western Australia, Nedlands, 1934+; [Royal] Western Australian Hist. Soc., *Journal and proceedings* [*Early days*], Perth 1927+; Alexandra Hasluck, *Unwilling emigrants: a study of the convict period in Western Australia*, Melb. 1959; James Sykes Battye, *Western Australia: a history* [to 1900], Oxf. 1924; and Douglas Lockwood, *The front door: Darwin, 1869–1969*, Adelaide 1968.

**1334**  FLINN (ELIZABETH). The history, politics and economy of Tasmania in the literature, 1856–1959. Hobart [Tas.]. 1961.

See also Peter Ross Eldershaw, comp., *Guide to the public records of Tasmania*, 3 v. Hobart, Tas. 1958-. Tasmanian Hist. Res. Assoc., *Papers and proceedings*, Hobart 1+, 1951–2+, is good. For Tasmanian politics etc. see **1339–40, 1342**.

**1335**  BURROUGHS (PETER). Britain and Australia, 1831–1855: a study in imperial relations and crown lands administration. Oxf. 1967.

**1336**  WARD (JOHN MANNING). Earl Grey and the Australian colonies, 1846–1857: a study of self-government and self-interest. Carlton, Victoria. 1958.

Important for constitutional hist. See also his *Australia's first governor-general: Sir Charles FitzRoy, 1851–1855*, Sydney 1953.

**1337**  HALL (HENRY LINDSAY). Australia and England: a study in imperial relations. 1934.

Early, but not replaced by the brief, unreliable Sir Archibald Grenfell Price, *Australia comes of age: a study of growth to nationhood and of external relations*, Melb. 1945. Needs to be suppl. by Charles S. Blackton, 'The dawn of Australian national feeling, 1850–1856', *Pacific Hist. Rev.* xxiv (1955), 121–38, and 'Australian nationality and nationalism: the imperial federationist interlude, 1885–1901', *Hist. Studs. Aust. & N.Z.* vii (1955), 1–16; R. A. Shields, 'Australian public opinion and imperial federation . . ., 1884–1891', *Canadian J. of Hist.* i, no. 2 (1966), 57–66; Luke Trainor, 'British imperial defence policy and the Australian colonies, 1892–96', *Hist. Studs.* xiv (1969–70), 204–18; Charles Grimshaw, 'Australian nationalism and the imperial connection, 1900–1914', *Aust. J. Pol. & Hist.* iii (1957–8), 161–82; Barbara R. Penny, 'Australia's reactions to the Boer War: a study in colonial imperialism', *J. Brit. Studs.* vii (1967–8), pt. 1, 97–130; and Richard H. Wilde, 'The Boxer affair and Australian responsibility for imperial defence', *Pacific Hist. Rev.* xxvi (1957), 51–65.

**1338**  HUGHES (COLIN ANFIELD) *and* GRAHAM (BRUCE DESMOND) *eds*. A handbook of Australian government and politics, 1890–1964. Canberra. 1968.

A compendium of facts and figures.

**1339**  MELBOURNE (ALEXANDER CLIFFORD VERNON). Early constitutional development in Australia: New South Wales, 1788–1856: Queensland, 1859–1922: with notes to 1963 by R. B. Joyce. St. Lucia, Queensland. 1963.

See also Edward Sweetman, *Australian constitutional development* [to 1901], Melb. 1925; Frederick Lloyd Whitfield Wood, *The constitutional development of Australia*,

1933, W. A. Townsley, *The struggle for self-government in Tasmania, 1842–1856*, Hobart 1951, Frank Clifton Green, ed., *Tasmania: a century of responsible government, 1856–1956*, Hobart 1956, and Gordon Desmond Combe, *Responsible government in South Australia*, Adelaide 1957.

**1340** LOVEDAY (PETER) *and* MARTIN (ALLAN WILLIAM). Parliament, factions and parties: the first thirty years of responsible government in New South Wales, 1856–1889. Melb. etc. 1966.

See also Allan William Martin and P. Wardle, *Members of the Legislative Assembly of New South Wales, 1856–1901: biographical notes*, Canberra 1959; Brian Dickey, ed., *Politics in New South Wales, 1856–1900*, Melb. 1969; and Joan Rydon and Richard Neville Spann, *New South Wales politics, 1901–1910*, Melb. 1962. For Queensland there is Charles Arrowsmith Bernays, *Queensland politics during sixty years, 1859–1919* . . ., Brisbane 1919, and for Tasmania, Carrel Inglis Clark, *The parliament of Tasmania: an historical sketch*, Hobart 1947.

**1341** JENKS (EDWARD). The government of Victoria (Australia). 1891.

See also Henry Lindsay Hall, *Victoria's part in the Australian federation movement, 1849–1900*, 1931 [Government of Victoria], *One hundred years of responsible government in Victoria, 1856–1956*, Melb. 1958, and Ambrose Pratt, *David Syme: the father of protection in Australia*, 1908.

**1342** KNIBBS (*Sir* GEORGE HANDLEY). Local government in Australia. Melb. 1919.

See also Herbert Edward Maiden, *The history of local government in New South Wales*, Sydney 1966, and Karl Rawdon von Stieglitz, *A history of local government in Tasmania* . . ., Launceston, Tas. [1958].

**1343** QUICK (*Sir* JOHN) *and* GARRAN (ROBERT RANDOLPH). The annotated constitution of the Australian commonwealth. Sydney. 1901.

A full contemp. guide incl. a careful account of the hist. of federation. On federation see also Alfred Deakin, *The federal story: the inner history of the federal cause*, ed. by Herbert Brookes, Melb. 1944, new edn. by John Andrew La Nauze, Parkville 1963; Bernhard Ringrose Wise, *The making of the Australian commonwealth, 1889–1900: a stage in the growth of the empire*, 1913; Hall (**1341**); J. A. La Nauze, *The Hopetoun blunder: the appointment of the first prime minister of the Commonwealth of Australia*, Carlton 1957; and the works cited in the extensive biblio. to Crisp (**1344**). The issues at stake were debated in a series of conferences: *Victoria: official record of the proceedings and debates of the Australasian federation conference, Melbourne* . . . *1890*, Melb. 1890; *New South Wales: official report of the National Australasian convention debates, Sydney* . . . *1891*, Sydney 1891; *South Australia: official report of the National Australasian convention debates, Adelaide* . . . *1897*, Adelaide 1897; *New South Wales: official record of the debates of the Australasian Federal convention, second session, Sydney* . . . *1897*, Sydney 1897; *Victoria: official record of the debates of the Australasian Federal convention, third session, Melbourne* . . . *1898*, 2 v. Melb. 1898.

**1344** CRISP (LESLIE FINLAY). The parliamentary government of the Commonwealth of Australia. Lond., Adelaide, & New Haven [Conn.]. 1949. Rev. edn. Lond. & N.Y. 1961. New edn. [Australian national government.] Melb. 1965.

**1345** SAWER (GEOFFREY). Australian federal politics and law, 1901–1929. Carlton. 1956.

Primarily a legal survey: good. See also Sir George White Cross Paton, ed., *The Commonwealth of Australia: the development of its laws and constitution*, 1952, and Sir Arthur Dean, *A multitude of counsellors: a history of the bar of Victoria*, Melb. etc. 1968.

1346  ELLIS (ULRICH RUEGG). A history of the Australian Country party. Parkville. 1963.

See also his *The Country party: a political and social history of the party in New South Wales*, Melb. 1958, and Bruce Desmond Graham, *The formation of the Australian country parties*, Canberra 1966.

1347  GOLLAN (ROBIN). Radical and working class politics: a study of eastern Australia, 1850–1910. Parkville. 1960.

See also Robert Noel Ebbels, comp., *The Australian labor movement, 1850–1907: extracts from contemporary documents*, ed. by Lloyd G. Churchward, Sydney 1960, and Patrick Ford, *Cardinal Moran and the A.L.P.: a study in the encounter between Moran and Socialism, 1890–1907: its effects upon the Australian Labor party: the foundation of Catholic social thought and action in modern Australia*, Carlton 1966.

1348  CRISP (LESLIE FINLAY). The Australian federal Labour party, 1901–1951. 1955.

1349  BARTON. Edmund Barton. By John Reynolds. Sydney. 1948.

1350  DEAKIN. Alfred Deakin: a biography. By John Andrew La Nauze. 2 v. Melb. 1965.

A good biog. of the most notable Australian statesman. Alfred Deakin himself wrote a good deal, incl. *The crisis in Victorian politics, 1879–1881: a personal retrospect*, ed. by J. A. La Nauze and Raymond Maxwell Crawford, Carlton 1957, and *Federated Australia: selections from letters to the* Morning Post, *1900–1910*, ed. by J. A. La Nauze, Carlton 1968.

1351  GLYNN. Patrick McMahon Glynn: a founder of Australian federation. By Gerald O'Collins. Carlton. 1965.

1352  HOLMAN. Australian labour leader: the story of W. A. Holman and the labour movement. By Herbert Vere Evatt. Sydney & Lond. 1940. Abridged edn. Sydney. 1954.

1353  HUGHES. William Morris Hughes: a political biography: Vol. I, that fiery particle, 1862–1914. By Laurence Frederic Fitzhardinge. Sydney. 1964.

1354  PARKES. Fifty years in the making of Australian history. By Sir Henry Parkes. 2 v. 1892.

See also his letters in *An emigrant's home letters*, ed. by A. T. Parkes, Sydney 1897, his *Australian views of England* . . ., 1869, *Speeches* . . . *1848–1874*, Melb. 1876, and *The federal government of Australasia: speeches* . . ., Sydney 1890. There is no good biog., but see Charles E. Lyne, *Life of Sir Henry Parkes* . . ., 1897.

1355  BORDER (ROSS). Church and state in Australia, 1788–1872: a constitutional study of the Church of England in Australia. 1962.

See also Arthur de Quetteville Robin, *Charles Perry, bishop of Melbourne: the challenge of a colonial episcopate, 1847–76*, Nedlands, W.A. 1967.

1356 O'FARRELL (PATRICK JAMES) *assisted by* O'FARRELL (DEIR-DRE) *eds*. Documents in Australian Catholic history. 2 v. 1969.

See also his *The Catholic church in Australia: a short history, 1788–1967*, Melb. 1968; Timothy Lachlan Lautour Suttor, *Hierarchy and democracy in Australia, 1788–1870: the formation of Australian Catholicism*, Carlton 1965; and John Neylon Molony, *The Roman mould of the Australian Catholic church*, Carlton 1969.

1357 FITZPATRICK (BRIAN). The British empire in Australia: an economic history, 1834–1939. Melb. 1941. 2nd edn. 1949.

Now dated, but still stimulating. See also Alan George Lewers Shaw, *The economic development of Australia*, 1944, 4th edn. 1960.

1358 BUTLIN (NOEL GEORGE). Investment in Australian economic development, 1861–1900. Camb. 1964.

Based on new statistical ser., notably those in his *Private capital formation in Australia: estimates, 1861–1900*, Canberra 1955, *Public capital formation in Australia: estimates, 1860–1900* [joint author H. de Meel], Canberra 1954, and *Australian domestic product, investment and foreign borrowing, 1861–1938/9*, Camb. 1962.

1359 COGHLAN (*Sir* TIMOTHY AUGUSTINE). Labour and industry in Australia: from the first settlement in 1788 to the establishment of the commonwealth in 1901. 4 v. 1918.

A very valuable quarry. See also his *A statistical survey of New South Wales, 1893–4*, Sydney 1895.

1360 DUNSDORFS (EDGARS). The Australian wheat-growing industry, 1788–1948. Melb. 1956.

1361 BARNARD (ALAN). The Australian wool market, 1840–1900. Carlton. 1958.

1362 DUNCAN (ROSS). The Northern Territory pastoral industry, 1863–1910. Melb. 1967.

1363 WATERSON (DUNCAN BRUCE). Squatter, selector and storekeeper: a history of the Darling Downs, 1859–93. Sydney. 1968.

1364 BUXTON (GORDON LESLIE). The Riverina, 1861–1891: an Australian regional study. Melb. 1967.

1365 BAILEY (JOHN DONNISON). Growth and depression: contrasts in the Australian and British economies, 1870–80. Canberra. 1956.

See also Ernst Arthur Boehm, *Prosperity and depression in Australia, 1887–1897*, Oxf. 1971.

1366 BLAINEY (GEOFFREY). The rush that never ended: a history of Australian mining. Parkville. 1963.

The Australian gold rushes. See also Norman Bartlett, *The gold seekers*, 1965.

1367 GOLLAN (ROBIN). The coalminers of New South Wales: a history of the union, 1860–1960. Melb. 1963.

1368 HALL (ALAN ROSS). The stock exchange of Melbourne and the Victorian economy, 1852–1900. Canberra. 1968.

1369 BUTLIN (SYDNEY JAMES). Australia and New Zealand Bank: the Bank of Australasia and the Union Bank of Australia Limited, 1828–1951. 1961.

Cp. Geoffrey Blainey, *Gold and paper: a history of the National Bank of Australasia Limited*, Melb. 1958.

1370 BAILEY (JOHN DONNISON). A hundred years of pastoral banking: a history of the Australian Mercantile Land & Finance Company, 1863–1963. Oxf. 1966.

1371 FREELAND (JOHN MAXWELL). Architecture in Australia: a history. Melb. etc. 1968.

See also his *Melbourne churches, 1836–1851: an architectural record*, Melb. 1963, and Sir Edward James Ranembe Morgan and Stephen Hamilton Gilbert, *Early Adelaide architecture, 1836–1886*, Melb. etc. 1970.

1372 BOYD (ROBIN). Australia's home: its origins, builders and occupiers. Carlton. 1952.

See also his *Victorian modern: one hundred and eleven years of modern architecture in Victoria, Australia*, Melb. 1947, and Max Dupain, *Georgian architecture in Australia . . .*, Sydney 1963.

1373 BASSETT (MARNIE MASSON). The Hentys: an Australian colonial tapestry. 1954.

1374 KIDDLE (MARGARET LOCH). Men of yesterday: a social history of the western district of Victoria, 1834–1890. Parkville. 1961.

1375 CHISHOLM. Caroline Chisholm. By Margaret Loch Kiddle. Melb. 1950. 2nd edn. Carlton. 1957.

The life of one of the emigrants' friends.

1376 AUSTIN (ALBERT GORDON). Australian education, 1788–1900: church, state and public education in colonial Australia. Melb. 1961.

See also his *Select documents in Australian education, 1788–1900*, Melb. 1963, and *George William Rusden and national education in Australia, 1849–62*, Carlton 1958, Ronald Fogarty, *Catholic education in Australia, 1806–1950*, 2 v. Carlton 1959, Sir Ernest Scott, *A history of the University of Melbourne*, Melb. 1936, and Geoffrey Blainey, *A centenary history of the University of Melbourne*, Melb. 1957.

1377 GREEN (HENRY MACKENZIE). A history of Australian literature, pure and applied: a critical review of all forms of literature produced in Australia from the first books published after the arrival of the First Fleet until 1950 . . . 2 v. Sydney. 1961.

1378  SMITH (BERNARD WILLIAM). Australian painting, 1788–1960. 1962.

Fuller than his *Place, taste and tradition: a study of Australian art since 1788*, Sydney 1945.

1379  ORCHARD (WILLIAM ARUNDEL). Music in Australia: more than 150 years of development. Melb. 1952.

1380  PRICE (*Sir* ARCHIBALD GRENFELL). White settlers and native peoples: an historical study of racial contacts between English-speaking whites and aboriginal peoples in the United States, Canada, Australia and New Zealand. Melb. 1950.

Raises interesting questions, chiefly about Australia.

1381  HASLUCK (PAUL MEERNAA CAEDWALLA). Black Australians: a survey of native policy in Western Australia, 1829–1897. Melb. 1942.

Better than Edmund John Buchanan Foxcroft, *Australian native policy: its history, especially in Victoria*, Melb. 1941.

1382  YARWOOD (ALEXANDER TURNBULL). Asian migration to Australia: the background to exclusion, 1896–1923. Melb. 1964.

See also the symposium ed. by him, *Attitudes to non-European immigration*, Melb. 1968, and Myra Willard, *History of the white Australia policy [to 1920]*, Melb. 1923, repr. Lond. 1967, N.Y. 1968.

(c) *New Zealand*

1383  NEW ZEALAND NATIONAL BIBLIOGRAPHY TO THE YEAR 1960. Ed. by Austin Graham Bagnall. 5 v. Wellington. 1970–.

Will repl. Thomas Morland Hocken, *A bibliography of the literature relating to New Zealand*, Wellington 1909, suppls. Auckland 1927, Dunedin 1938, and Arthur Harold Johnstone, *Canterbury books, 1847–1955: a bibliography*, Christchurch, N.Z. 1956. Current books are listed in *New Zealand national bibliography*, Wellington 1967+; reference books in John Harris, *Guide to New Zealand reference material . . .*, [Wellington] 1947, 2nd edn. 1950, suppls. 1951+; bibliogs. in New Zealand Library Assoc., *A bibliography of New Zealand bibliographies*, prelim. edn. Wellington 1967; theses in David Lloyd Jenkins, *Union list of theses of the University of New Zealand, 1910–54*, Wellington 1956; and official papers in Guy Hardy Scholefield, comp., *Union list of New Zealand official papers and British official papers relating to New Zealand*, Wellington 1938, and James Oakley Wilson, *A finding list of British parliamentary papers relating to New Zealand, 1817–1900*, Wellington 1960.

1384  WRITINGS ON NEW ZEALAND HISTORY. Publ. in Historical studies [Australia and New Zealand]. Melb. 1940+.

For economic hist. consult Frank Wakefield Holmes and Richard H. Carey, *A preliminary bibliography of New Zealand economics and economic history*, Wellington 1967. Historical theses are listed in *New Zealand j. of hist.*, Auckland 1967+, the leading New Zealand hist. j. There are good bibliogs. in *The Cambridge history of the British empire*, vol. VII, pt. II, *New Zealand*, Camb. 1933. Maori hist. is covered by Polynesian Soc., *Journal*, Wellington 1892+.

**1385** ALEXANDER TURNBULL LIBRARY. Union catalogue of New Zealand and Pacific manuscripts in New Zealand libraries. Interim edn. 2 v. Wellington. 1968–9.

See also **1317**.

**1386** NATIONAL ARCHIVES OF NEW ZEALAND. A review and summary of work. Wellington. 1966. Annual suppls.

Formerly the Dominion Archives, which publ. a number of prelim. inventories. The main printed source is the *Appendices to the journals of the House of Representatives*, Auckland etc. 1854+, which parallel the British parl. papers. Robert McNab, ed., *Historical records of New Zealand*, 2 v. Wellington 1908–14, is of little use.

**1387** McINTYRE (WILLIAM DAVID) and GARDNER (WILLIAM JAMES) *eds*. Speeches and documents on New Zealand history. Oxf. 1970.

**1388** McLINTOCK (ALEXANDER HARE) *ed*. An encyclopaedia of New Zealand. 3 v. Wellington. 1966.

Good, as is his edn. of *A descriptive atlas of New Zealand*, Wellington 1959, and *New Zealand official year book* [formerly *hand book*], Wellington 1892+.

**1389** SCHOLEFIELD (GUY HARDY) *comp*. A dictionary of New Zealand biography. 2 v. Wellington. 1940.

Office holders are listed in Scholefield's *New Zealand parliamentary record, 1840–1949*, Wellington 1950. *Who's who in New Zealand*, Wellington 1908+, covers minor figures.

**1390** SINCLAIR (KEITH). A history of New Zealand. Harmondsworth. 1959. 2nd edn. Lond. 1961.

The best general hist. To be suppl. by Robert McDonald Chapman and Keith Sinclair, eds., *Studies of a small democracy: essays in honour of Willis Airey*, Auckland 1963, and R. F. Watters, ed., *Land and society in New Zealand: essays in historical geography*, Wellington 1965. See also William Hosking Oliver, *The story of New Zealand*, 1963; William Pember Reeves, *The long white cloud: ao tea roa*, 1898, 4th edn. 1950; and (for an unorthodox and very Radical view) William Ball Sutch, *The quest for security in New Zealand*, Harmondsworth 1942, 2nd edn. Wellington 1966. Angus John Harrop, *England and New Zealand: from Tasman to the Taranaki war*, 1926, and *England and the Maori wars*, Lond. & Christchurch, N.Z. 1937, are of little value.

**1391** McLINTOCK (ALEXANDER HARE). Crown colony government in New Zealand. Wellington. 1958.

**1392** MORRELL (WILLIAM PARKER). The provincial system in New Zealand, 1852–76. 1932. 2nd edn. Christchurch, N.Z. 1964.

**1393** LIPSON (LESLIE). The politics of equality: New Zealand's adventures in democracy. Chicago. 1948.

An idiosyncratic constitutional hist. Needs to be suppl. by André Siegfried, *Democracy in New Zealand*, trans. by E. V. Burns, 1914, Reeves, *State experiments* (**1314**), James Edward Le Rossignol and William Downie Stewart, *State socialism in New Zealand*, 1910, and *Visit to New Zealand in 1898: Beatrice Webb's diary, with entries by Sidney Webb*, Wellington 1959. There is also useful material in Leicester Chisholm Webb,

Government in New Zealand, Wellington 1940. Sir James Hight and Harry Dean
Bamford, *The constitutional history and law of New Zealand*, Christchurch, N.Z. 1914,
is now badly dated.

**1394  MILNE (ROBERT STEPHEN). Political parties in New Zealand.
Oxf. 1966.**

Incl. a hist.

**1395  WILLIAMS (JOHN ADRIAN). Politics of the New Zealand Maori:
protest and co-operation, 1891–1909. Seattle & Auckland. 1969.**

**1396  SINCLAIR (KEITH). Imperial federation: a study of New Zealand
policy and opinion, 1880–1914. Commonwealth papers 2. 1955.**

See also Frederick Lloyd Whitfield Wood, 'Why did New Zealand not join the
Australian commonwealth in 1900–1901?', *N.Z. J. of Hist.* ii (1968), 115–29.

**1397  GODLEY. John Robert Godley of Canterbury. By Charles Edmund
Carrington. Christchurch [N.Z.]. 1950.**

Useful for the politics of the new settlements.

**1398  SCHOLEFIELD (GUY HARDY) ed. The Richmond–Atkinson papers.
2 v. Wellington. 1960.**

The only good collection of political and general corresp. covering the 1860s to 1890s.

**1399  SEDDON. King Dick: a biography of Richard John Seddon. By Randal
Mathew Burdon. Christchurch [N.Z.]. 1955.**

The only New Zealand prime minister of the period to make his mark abroad. Burdon
also wrote *The life and times of Sir Julius Vogel*, Christchurch, N.Z. 1948.

**1400  REEVES. William Pember Reeves: New Zealand Fabian. By Keith
Sinclair. Oxf. 1965.**

Brings out the links between Britain and N.Z. One of the few good N.Z. biogs.

**1401  BELL. The Right Honourable Sir Francis H. D. Bell: his life and times.
By William Downie Stewart. Wellington. 1937.**

Useful for the generation after Seddon. See also Downie Stewart's *William Rolleston:
a New Zealand statesman*, Christchurch etc. 1940.

**1402  MILLER (HAROLD). Race conflict in New Zealand, 1814–1865.
Auckland. 1966.**

A reworking of old themes, but well written.

**1403  SINCLAIR (KEITH). The origins of the Maori wars. Wellington. 1957.**

The chief book on the subject. See also Alan D. Ward, 'The origins of the Anglo-
Maori wars: a reconsideration', *N.Z. J. of Hist.* i (1967), 148–70, and Ian McLean
Wards, *The shadow of the land: a study of British policy and racial conflict in New Zealand,
1832–1852*, Wellington 1968.

**1404 DALTON (BRIAN JAMES).** War and politics in New Zealand, 1855–1870. Sydney. 1967.

A study of the transfer of responsibility for Maori affairs to N.Z. ministers. Not altogether satisfactory in emphasis.

**1405 COWAN (JAMES).** The New Zealand wars. 2 v. Wellington. 1922–3. 2nd edn. 2 v. 1955.

Still the basic book. Edgar Crawshaw Holt, *The strangest war: the story of the Maori wars, 1860–72*, 1962, is a popular account. Later military developments are covered in Charles Emil Dornbusch, *The New Zealand army: a bibliography*, Cornwallville, N.Y. 1961.

**1406 ROBSON (JOHN LOCHIEL)** *ed.* New Zealand: the development of its laws and constitution. 1954.

**1407 CONDLIFFE (JOHN BELL).** New Zealand in the making: a survey of economic and social development. 1930. 2nd edn. 1959.

Muriel Florence Lloyd Prichard, *An economic history of New Zealand to 1939*, Auckland & Lond. 1970, has fuller data. Colin George Frederick Simkin, *The instability of a dependent economy: economic fluctuations in New Zealand, 1840–1914*, 1951 and W. Rosenberg, 'Capital imports and growth—the case of New Zealand—foreign investment in New Zealand, 1840–1958', *Econ. J.* lxxi (1961), 93–113 are important studies.

**1408 MAY (PHILIP ROSS).** The West Coast gold rushes. Christchurch, N.Z. 1962. 2nd edn. 1967.

See also John Hearsey McMillan Salmon, *A history of goldmining in New Zealand*, Wellington 1963. For other sections of the New Zealand economy see H. G. Philpott, *A history of the New Zealand dairy industry, 1840–1935*, Wellington 1937, and B. A. Moore and John Saxon Barton, *Banking in New Zealand*, Wellington 1935. For pioneer rural life see Herbert Guthrie-Smith, *Tutira: the story of a New Zealand sheep station*, Edin. 1921. 3rd edn., 1953.

**1409 PURCHAS (HENRY THOMAS).** A history of the English church in New Zealand. Christchurch [N.Z.]. 1914.

See also the lives of Bishop Selwyn (**3685**), and Purchas's *Bishop Harper and the Canterbury settlement*, rev. edn. Christchurch, N.Z., 1909. For other churches see William Morley, *History of Methodism in New Zealand*, Wellington 1900, and John Rawson Elder, *The history of the Presbyterian church of New Zealand, 1840–1940*, Christchurch, N.Z. 1940.

**1410 McCORMICK (ERIC HALL).** Letters and art in New Zealand. Wellington. 1940. Rev. edn. [New Zealand literature: a survey.] Lond. 1959.

**1411 ROTH (HERBERT).** A bibliography of New Zealand education. Wellington. 1964.

For education generally see Arnold Everitt Campbell, *Educating New Zealand*, Wellington 1941; Arthur Gordon Butchers, *Young New Zealand: a history of the early contact of the Maori race with the European, and of the establishment of a national system of education for both races*, Dunedin 1929, cont. in *Education in New Zealand . . .*, Dunedin 1930; John Cawte Beaglehole, *The University of New Zealand: an historical study*,

Auckland & Lond. 1937, and *Victoria University college: an essay towards a history*, Wellington 1949; George Edward Thompson, *A history of the University of Otago, 1869–1919*, Dunedin [1919]; William Parker Morrell, *The University of Otago: a centennial history*, Dunedin 1969; Sir Charles Ernest Hercus and Sir Francis Gordon Bell, *The Otago Medical School under the first three deans*, Edin. & Lond. 1964; John Lithgow Ewing, *Origins of the New Zealand primary school curriculum, 1840–1878*, Wellington 1960; and John Mackey, *The making of a state education system: the passing of the New Zealand Education Act, 1877*, 1967.

**1412  McLINTOCK (ALEXANDER HARE).** The history of Otago: the origins and growth of a Wakefield class settlement. Dunedin. 1949.

Other good provincial studs. are Canterbury Centennial Assoc., *A history of Canterbury*, 3 v. Christchurch, N.Z. 1957–71, and Alister Donald McIntosh, *Marlborough: a provincial history*, Blenheim, N.Z. 1940. On local hist. see Ruth Allan, *The history of Port Nelson*, Wellington 1954, Basil Hillyer Howard, *Rakiura: a history of Stewart Island, New Zealand*, Dunedin 1940, Hensleigh Carthew Marryat Norris, *Armed settlers: the story of the founding of Hamilton, New Zealand, 1864–1874*, Hamilton, N.Z. 1956, and *Settlers in depression: a history of Hamilton, 1875–94*, Hamilton, N.Z., 1964, and William James Gardner, *The Amuri: a county history*, Culverden, N.Z., 1956.

## (d) *Pacific Islands*

**1413  LEESON (IDA)** *ed.* A bibliography of bibliographies of the South Pacific. 1954.

**1414  TAYLOR (CLYDE ROMER HUGHES)** *comp.* A Pacific bibliography . . . Polynesian Soc. memoirs 24. Wellington. 1951. 2nd edn. Oxf. 1965.

Excellent. See also Philip A. Snow, comp., *A bibliography of Fiji, Tonga and Rotuma: a preliminary working edition*, Canberra & Coral Gables, Fla. 1969, Floyd M. Cammack and Shiro Saito, *Pacific island bibliography*, N.Y. 1962, and Bernice P. Bishop Museum, *Dictionary catalog of the library*, 9 v. Boston 1964, suppls. 1967, 1969.

**1415  PRICE (*Sir* ARCHIBALD GRENFELL).** The western invasions of the Pacific and its continents: a study of moving frontiers and changing landscapes, 1513–1958. Oxf. 1963.

Suggestive rather than authoritative. Cp. Bernard William Smith, *European vision and the South Pacific, 1768–1850: a study in the history of art and ideas*, Oxf. 1960, which is beautifully illustr. Needs to be suppl. by anthropological studs. such as Ernest Beaglehole, *Social change in the South Pacific: Rarotonga and Aitutaki*, 1957, Raymond William Firth, *We, the Tikopia* . . ., 1957, and *Social change in Tikopia* . . ., 1959, and Herbert Ian Priestley Hogbin, *Experiments in civilization: the effects of European culture on a native community of the Solomon Islands*, 1939.

**1416  THE JOURNAL OF PACIFIC HISTORY.** Canberra. 1966+.

**1417  MORRELL (WILLIAM PARKER).** Britain in the Pacific islands. Oxf. 1960.

Largely repl. Jean Ingram Brookes, *International rivalry in the Pacific islands, 1800–1875*, Berkeley etc. 1941, and John Manning Ward, *British policy in the South Pacific, 1786–1893* . . ., Sydney 1948.

**1418  PARNABY (OWEN WILFRED).** Britain and the labor trade in the southwest Pacific. Durham, N.C. 1964.

1419  ROSS (ANGUS). New Zealand aspirations in the Pacific in the nineteenth century. Oxf. 1964.

1420  KOSKINEN (AARNE ANTTI). Missionary influence as a political factor in the Pacific islands. Helsinki. 1953.

For the Melanesian mission see Charles Elliot Fox, *Lord of the southern isles: being the story of the anglican mission in Melanesia, 1849–1949*, 1958, and Charlotte Mary Yonge, *Life of John Coleridge Patteson, missionary bishop of the Melanesian islands*, 2 v. 1874, 6th edn. 2 v. 1878.

1421  SCARR (DERYCK ANTONY). Fragments of empire: a history of the Western Pacific high commission, 1877–1914. Canberra. 1967.

1422  WEST (FRANCIS JAMES). Political advancement in the South Pacific: a comparative study of colonial practice in Fiji, Tahiti and American Samoa. Melb. 1961.

1423  LEGGE (JOHN DAVID). Britain in Fiji, 1858–1880. 1958.

Needs to be suppl. by McIntyre (**1243**). For this period there are substantial printed documentary sources in Arthur Hamilton Gordon, Baron Stanmore, *Fiji: records of private and public life, 1875–1880*, 4 v., priv. pr. 1897–1912, and *Letters and notes written during the disturbances in the Highlands . . . of Fiji, 1876*, 2 v., priv. pr. Edin. 1879. See also Evelyn Stokes, 'The Fiji cotton boom in the eighteen-sixties', *N.Z. J. Hist.* ii (1968), 165–77; Peter France, *The charter of the land: custom and colonization in Fiji*, Melb. 1969; Kenneth Lowell Oliver Gillion, *Fiji's Indian migrants: a history to the end of indenture in 1920*, Melb. 1962, and 'The sources of Indian emigration to Fiji', *Population Studs.* x (1956–7), 139–57; Ina Mary Cumpston, 'Sir Arthur Gordon and the introduction of Indians into the Pacific: the West Indian system in Fiji', *Pacific Hist. Rev.* xxv (1956), 369–88; and Adrian Curtis Mayer, *Indians in Fiji*, 1963.

1424  MASTERMAN (SYLVIA). The origins of international rivalry in Samoa, 1845–1884. 1934.

See also Richard Phillip Gilson, *Samoa, 1830 to 1900: the politics of a multi-cultural community*, Melb. etc. 1970; James Wightman Davidson, *Samoa mo Samoa: the emergence of the independent state of Western Samoa*, Melb. 1967; Robert Louis Stevenson, *A footnote to history: eight years of trouble in Samoa*, 1892; George Herbert Ryden, *The foreign policy of the United States in relation to Samoa*, New Haven, Conn. 1933; and P. M. Kennedy, 'The Royal Navy and the Samoan civil war, 1898–1899', *Canadian J. of Hist.* v (1970), 52–72.

1424a  RUTHERFORD (NOEL). Shirley Baker and the king of Tonga. Melbourne. 1971.

Good on missionary activity. See also Sir Basil Home Thomson, *The diversions of a prime minister*, Edin. & Lond. 1894, and *Savage Island: an account of a sojourn in Niué and Tonga*, 1902, and Sir Harry Charles Luke, *Queen Salote and her kingdom*, 1954.

1425  TATE (MERZE). 'Great Britain and the sovereignty of Hawaii'. *Pacific Hist. Rev.* xxxi (1962), 327–48.

1426  GORDON (DONALD CRAIGIE). The Australian frontier in New

Guinea, 1870–1885. Columbia Univ. Studs. in Hist., Econ, & Public Law 562. N.Y. 1951.

Needs revision. See also Paul Willem Van Der Veur, *Search for New Guinea's boundaries: from Torres Strait to the Pacific*, Canberra 1966, and *Documents and correspondence on New Guinea's boundaries*, Canberra 1966; John David Legge, *Australian colonial policy: a survey of native administration and European development in Papua*, Sydney 1956; Lucy Philip Mair, *Australia in New Guinea*, 1948; Francis James West, *Hubert Murray: the Australian proconsul*, Melb. 1968, and *Selected letters of Hubert Murray*, Melb. 1970; Lewis Lett, *Sir Hubert Murray of Papua*, 1949; and Sir John Hubert Plunkett Murray, *Papua: or, British New Guinea*, 1912, and *Review of the Australian administration in Papua from 1907 to 1920*, Port Moresby [1921].

## 5. BRITISH NORTH AMERICA (CANADA)

### (a) *General*

In addition to the works below, a file of the *Canadian Historical Review* should be consulted.

**1427** HAMELIN (JEAN), BEAULIEU (ANDRÉ), and BERNIER (BENÔIT) *comps*. Guide d'histoire du Canada. Québec. 1969.

A valuable guide to archives, bibliogs, librs., and the lit. of the subject.

**1428** TANGHE (RAYMOND). Bibliography of Canadian bibliographies. Toronto. 1960. Suppl. 1964.

The most important general lists of books are Toronto Public Library, *A bibliography of Canadiana: being items in the public library of Toronto, relating to the early history and development of Canada*, ed. by Frances Maria Staton and Marie Tremaine, Toronto 1934, suppl. ed. by G. M. Boyle, Toronto 1959; and *The Canadian catalogue of books published in Canada, about Canada, as well as those written by Canadians, with imprint, 1921–1949*, 2 v. Toronto 1959.

**1429** HARVARD UNIVERSITY LIBRARY. Canadian history and literature. Widener Libr. shelflist 20. Camb., Mass. 1968.

A good subject list.

**1430** CANADIANA: a list of publications of Canadian interest. 1950/51+. Ottawa. 1951+.

The official national bibliog. of current publs.

**1431** BISHOP (OLGA BERNICE). Publications of the government of the province of Canada, 1841–1867. National Libr. of Canada. Ottawa. 1963.

For later publs. see Marion Villiers Higgins, *Canadian government publications: a manual for librarians*, Amer. Libr. Assoc., Chicago 1935, and George Fletcher Henderson, comp., *Federal royal commissions in Canada, 1867–1966: a checklist*, Toronto 1967.

**1432** WATTERS (REGINALD EYRE). A check list of Canadian literature and background materials, 1628–1950. Humanities Research Council of Canada. Toronto. 1959.

See also William Matthews, *Canadian diaries and autobiographies*, Berkeley etc. 1950; Guy Sylvestre, Brandon Conron, and Carl F. Klink, eds., *Canadian writers: écrivains canadiens: a biographical dictionary*, Toronto 1964, new edn. Montreal 1966; and David M. Hayne and Marcel Tirol, comps., *Bibliographie critique du roman canadien-français*, *1837–1900*, Toronto 1968, Quebec 1969.

1433  CANADIAN LIBRARY ASSOCIATION. Canadian newspapers on microfilm. Ottawa. 1959+.

1434  BROWN (CHARLES RAYNOR), MAXWELL (P.A.), *and* MAXWELL (LESLIE F.) *comps*. Canadian and British–American colonial law, from earliest times to December 1956. A legal bibliog. of the British Commonwealth, vol. 3. 1957.

1435  UNION LIST OF MANUSCRIPTS in Canadian repositories: catalogue collectif des manuscrits des archives canadiennes. Ed. by Robert S. Gordon and others. Public Archives of Canada and Humanities Research Council of Canada. Ottawa. 1968.

The Public Archives of Canada also publ. an annual report and a *General inventory: manuscripts*, Ottawa 1971+, issued in pts. In addition to the federal archives there are substantial provincial archives, notably in Quebec, the only guide to which is usually a ser. of archivists' reports.

1436  ENCYCLOPEDIA CANADIANA. 10 v. Ottawa. 1957–8. New edn. 1968.

1437  STORY (NORAH). The Oxford companion to Canadian history and literature. Toronto & N.Y. 1967. Suppl. by William Toye. 1974.

Repl. Lawrence Johnstone Burpee, *The Oxford encyclopaedia of Canadian history*, 1926. See also Walter Spencer Avis and others, *A dictionary of Canadianisms on historical principles*, Toronto 1967, and François Joseph Audet, *Canadian historical dates and events*, *1492–1915*, Ottawa 1917.

1438  WRONG (GEORGE McKINNON) *and others*. Review of historical publications relating to Canada [1896–1918]. Univ. of Toronto Studs. in Hist. 22 v. Toronto. 1897–1919.

A valuable bibliog. survey. For hist. publs. 1919+, see 'Recent publications relating to Canada', *Canadian hist. rev.* 1+, 1920+. For theses see *Canadian historical review, Canadian theses in Canadian history and economics*, 1933+, Canada, Public Archives, *Register of post-graduate dissertations in progress in history and related subjects*, Ottawa 1966+, and Doris M. Cruger, comp., *A list of doctoral dissertations on Australia . . ., Canada . . ., New Zealand, covering 1933/34 through 1964/65*, Ann Arbor [Mich.] 1967.

1439  KERR (DONALD GORDON GRADY) *ed*. A historical atlas of Canada. Toronto. 1960. 2nd edn. Don Mills, Ontario. 1966.

See also D. G. G. Kerr and R. I. K. Davidson, *Canada: a visual history*, 1966.

1440  URQUHART (MALCOLM CHARLES) *and* BUCKLEY (KENNETH ARTHUR HAIG) *eds*. Historical statistics of Canada. Camb. and Toronto. 1965.

Covers 1867–1960.

1441 WALLACE (WILLIAM STEWART). The dictionary of Canadian biography. Toronto 1926. Rev. edn. 2 v. Toronto 1945. 3rd edn. [The Macmillan dictionary . . .] Lond. 1963.

See also Sir Charles George Douglas Roberts and Arthur Leonard Tunnell, eds., *A standard dictionary of Canadian biography: the Canadian who was who* [*1875–1937*], 2 v. Toronto 1934–8. An older work, William Lawson Grant, ed., *The makers of Canada series*, 26 v. 1926, incls. 29 biogs. For office holders see *Guide to Canadian ministries since confederation* . . ., Ottawa 1950, *The Canadian parliamentary guide* [*companion*] Quebec 1862+, and Narcisse Omer Coté, ed., *Political appointments: parliaments and the judicial bench in the Dominion of Canada, 1867 to 1895*, Ottawa 1896, suppl. for 1896–1917, Ottawa 1917.

1442 DICTIONARY OF CANADIAN BIOGRAPHY. *c.* 20 v. Toronto. 1966+.

Will repl. Wallace (1441), when complete.

1443 REID (JOHN HOTCHKISS STEWART), MCNAUGHT (KENNETH), *and* CROWE (HARRY S.) *comps.* A source-book of Canadian history: selected documents and personal papers. Toronto. 1959.

See also Kenneth Alexander MacKirdy, John Sargent Moir and Yves F. Zoltvany, eds., *Changing perspectives in Canadian history*, Notre Dame, Ind. 1968, two vols. in the Canadian hist. docs. ser., vol. II, Peter Busby Waite, ed., *Pre-confederation*, Scarborough, Ont. 1965, and vol. III, Robert Craig Brown and M. E. Prang, eds., *Confederation to 1949*, Scarborough, Ont. 1966, and John William Michael Bliss, ed., *Canadian history in documents, 1763–1966*, Toronto 1966.

1444 CHAMPLAIN SOCIETY. Publications. 1+. Toronto. 1907+.

The chief Canadian record publishing soc. The main ser. is suppl. by an *Ontario series*, 1+, Toronto 1957+. For the west there is Manitoba Record Soc., *Publications*, 1+, Altona 1965+, and Hudson's Bay Record Soc., *Publications*, 1+, 1938+.

1445 THE CANADIAN ANNUAL REVIEW OF PUBLIC AFFAIRS. Toronto. 1901–38.

A useful survey. For a statistically-based survey see Canada: Census and Statistics Office, *Canada year book*, 1905+, Ottawa 1906+, which repl. the *Statistical yearbook of Canada*, publ. by the Canadian Dept. of Agric. under different titles for 1885–1904.

1446 MORTON (WILLIAM LEWIS) *and* CREIGHTON (DONALD GRANT) *eds.* The Canadian centenary series. 17 v. Toronto. 1964–.

An up-to-date multi-vol. hist., which largely repl. Adam Shortt and Sir Arthur George Doughty, eds., *Canada and its provinces: a history of the Canadian people and their institutions*, 23 v. Toronto 1913–17. The vols. which cover 1851–1914 are 9. William Stewart MacNutt, *The Atlantic provinces: the emergence of colonial society, 1712–1857*, Toronto 1965; 10. James Maurice Stockford Careless, *The union of the Canadas: the growth of Canadian institutions, 1841–1857*, Toronto 1967; 12. William Lewis Morton, *The critical years: the union of British North America, 1857–1873*, Toronto 1964; 13. Peter Busby Waite, *Canada, 1874–1896: arduous destiny*, Toronto 1971; 16. Morris Zaslow, *The opening of the Canadian north, 1870–1914*, Toronto 1972.

1447 CREIGHTON (DONALD GRANT). Dominion of the north: a history of Canada. Boston. 1944. New edn. Toronto 1966.

A useful interpretative short hist. But see also John Bartlet Brebner, *Canada: a modern history*, Ann Arbor, Mich. 1960; George Ramsay Cook, John C. Ricker, and John Tupper Saywell, *Canada: a modern study*, Toronto 1967; James Maurice Stockford Careless, *Canada: a story of challenge*, Camb. 1953, 2nd edn. 1963; William Lewis Morton, *The kingdom of Canada: a general history from earliest times*, Toronto & Indianapolis 1963; George Parkin de Twenebroker Glazebrook, *A short history of Canada*, Oxf. 1950; Arthur Reginald Marsden Lower, *Colony to nation: a history of Canada*, Toronto 1946, 4th edn. Don Mills, Ontario 1964; and Edgar Wardwell McInnis, *Canada: a political and social history*, N.Y. & Toronto 1947, 3rd edn. 1969. McInnis is a good college textbook.

1448  CANADIAN HISTORICAL REVIEW. 1+. Toronto. 1920+.

The leading English-language hist. journ. See also Canadian Historical Assoc., *Annual report*, Toronto 1922+, which publ. conference papers, *Canadian j. of hist.*, Saskatoon 1966+, *Histoire sociale: revue canadienne*, Ottawa 1968+, *Journal of Canadian studies*, Peterborough, Ont. 1966+, and the regional hist. journs., notably Ontario Hist. Soc., *Papers and records*, later *Ontario history*, 1+, Toronto 1899+, *British Columbia historical quarterly*, 1+, Victoria, B.C. 1937+, *Alberta historical rev.*, 1+, Edmonton 1953+, *Acadiensis: j. of the hist. of the Atlantic region*, Fredericton, N.B. 1973+, *B.C. studies*, Vancouver 1968+, and *Saskatchewan hist.*, Saskatoon 1948+. The *University of Toronto quarterly*, 1+, Toronto 1931+, is more literary than historical in its interests, but it does contain useful articles, as do *The Dalhousie rev.*, 1+, Halifax 1921+, and *Queen's quarterly*, 1+, Kingston 1893+.

1449  REVUE D'HISTOIRE DE L'AMÉRIQUE FRANÇAISE. 1+. Montreal. 1947–8+.

The leading French-language hist. j. See also *Bulletin des recherches historiques*, 1+, Lévis etc 1895+. For 19th-cent. events *Revue canadienne*, Montreal 1864–1922, is useful.

1450  BREBNER (JOHN BARTLET). North Atlantic triangle: the interplay of Canada, the United States and Great Britain. New Haven & Toronto. 1945. Repr. N.Y. 1958. New edn. by Donald Grant Creighton. Toronto. 1966.

A stimulating interpretative essay. See also Marcus Lee Hansen and J. B. Brebner, *The mingling of the Canadian and American peoples*, New Haven [Conn.] 1940. For Canadian external relations see 1489–99.

1451  CARELESS (JAMES MAURICE STOCKFORD) *and* BROWN (ROBERT CRAIG) *eds.* The Canadians, 1867–1967. Toronto. 1967.

A useful symposium. But see also Ralph Flenley, ed., *Essays in Canadian history presented to George Mackinnon Wrong . . .*, Toronto 1939.

1452  SMITH (GOLDWIN). Canada and the Canadian question. 1891.

Sceptical about Canada's future: questions the basis of confederation.

1453  SIEGFRIED (ANDRÉ). The race question in Canada. 1907.

A remarkable survey by a famous French sociologist.

1454  MARTIN (CHESTER). Foundations of Canadian nationhood. Toronto. 1955.

Contrast with George Ramsay Cook, *Canada and the French-Canadian question*, Toronto 1966, and Donald Grant Creighton, *Canada's first century, 1867–1967*, Toronto 1970.

1455  KLINCK (CARL FREDERICK) *and others, eds.* Literary history of
Canada: Canadian literature in English. Toronto. 1965. Repr. with rev. 1966.

For painting see J. Russell Harper, *Painting in Canada: a history,* Toronto 1966.

(b) *Politics, External Relations, and Defence*

1456  STANLEY (GEORGE FRANCIS GILMAN). A short history of the
Canadian constitution. Toronto. 1969.

Intended to repl. William Paul McLure Kennedy, *The constitution of Canada: an introduction to its development and law,* 1922, 2nd edn. 1938. See also Robert MacGregor
Dawson, ed., *Constitutional issues in Canada, 1900–1931,* 1933, and *The development
of dominion status* (**1262**); Richard Arès, *Dossier sur le pact fédératif de 1867: la con-
fédération: pacte ou loi?* New edn. Montreal 1967; Paul Gérin-Lajoie, *Constitutional
amendment in Canada,* Toronto 1950; Margaret A. Banks, 'Privy Council, cabinet and
ministry in Britain and Canada: a story of confusion', *Canadian J. Econ. & Pol. Sci.*
xxxi (1965), 193–205, and Eugene Forsey, 'Meetings of the Queen's Privy Council for
Canada, 1867–1882', ibid. xxxii (1966), 488–98; John Tupper Saywell, *The office of
lieutenant-governor: a study in Canadian government and politics,* Toronto 1957; and
Norman Ward, *The Canadian House of Commons representation,* Toronto 1950. *The
Canadian parliamentary companion* [*guide*], Montreal etc. 1862+, gives biogs. of members. The standard contemp. handbook was Sir John George Bourinot, *How Canada is
governed* . . ., Boston etc. 1895, 3rd edn. Toronto 1897, to which Edward Porritt,
*Evolution of the dominion of Canada* . . ., N.Y. 1918, was a handy successor. A fuller
account was provided by Augustus Henry Frazer Lefroy, *Canada's federal system* . . .,
Toronto 1913, and *The law of legislative power in Canada,* Toronto 1897–8.

1457  KENNEDY (WILLIAM PAUL McCLURE) *ed.* Documents of the
Canadian constitution, 1759–1915. Toronto. 1918. 2nd edn. [Statutes, treaties,
and documents.] 1930.

Repl. Hugh Edward Egerton and William Lawson Grant, *Canadian constitutional
development, shown by selected speeches and dispatches,* 1907.

1458  OLLIVIER (MAURICE) *ed.* British North America Acts and selected
statutes . . . 1867–1962. Ottawa. 1962.

On confederation see also Sir Joseph Pope, ed., *Confederation: being a series of hitherto
unpublished documents bearing on the British North America Act,* Toronto 1895, new edn.
[*Documents on the confederation of British North America*] by Gerald Peter Browne,
Toronto 1969. The main source of docs. of the federal government is *Sessional papers
of the parliament of Canada,* 61 v. 1867–1925.

1459  OLLIVIER (MAURICE). Problems of Canadian sovereignty from the
British North America Act, 1867, to the Statute of Westminster, 1931.
Toronto. 1945.

See also *Report pursuant to resolution of the Senate to the Hon. the Speaker, by the parliamentary counsel, Mr. O'Connor, relating to the enactment of the British North America
Act, 1867, any lack of consonance between its terms and judicial construction of them and
cognate matters,* Government printer, Ottawa 1939; Gerald Peter Browne, *The Judicial
Committee and the British North America Act: an analysis of the interpretative scheme for
the distribution of legislative powers,* Toronto 1967; and Coen Gallatin Pierson, *Canada
and the Privy Council,* 1960.

1460  FARR (DAVID MORICE LEIGH). The Colonial Office and Canada,
1867–1887. Toronto. 1955.

For earlier years see James A. Gibson, 'The Duke of Newcastle and British North American affairs, 1859–64', *Canadian Hist. Rev.* xliv (1963), 142–56, and Peter Busby Waite, 'Edward Cardwell and confederation', ibid. xliii (1962), 17–41.

1461 ROWELL–SIROIS COMMISSION. Report of the royal commission on dominion–provincial relations. Rapport de la commission royale des relations entre le dominion et les provinces [Chairmen: Newton Wesley Rowell and Joseph Sirois]. 3 v. and appendixes. Ottawa. 1940.

Good. The appendixes incl. important hist. analyses. See also *Correspondence and reports of the minister of justice and orders-in-council re dominion and provincial legislation, 1867–1920,* Ottawa 1927.

1462 HODGETTS (JOHN EDWIN). Pioneer public service: an administrative history of the United Canadas, 1841–1867. Toronto. 1955.

1463 CREIGHTON (DONALD GRANT). The road to confederation: the emergence of Canada, 1863–1867. Toronto. 1964.

Good. Older books such as John Lyle Morison, *British supremacy & Canadian self-government, 1839–1854,* Glasgow & Toronto 1919, and Reginald George Trotter, *Canadian federation: its origins and achievement: a study in nation building,* Toronto 1924, are now out of date.

1464 WAITE (PETER BUSBY). The life and times of confederation, 1864–1867: politics, newspapers, and the union of British North America. Toronto. 1962. 2nd edn. 1967.

See also his edn. of *The confederation debates in the province of Canada, 1865,* Toronto 1963, which were originally publ. as *Parliamentary debates on the subject of the confederation of the British North American provinces: 3rd session, 8th provincial parliament of Canada,* Quebec 1865, repr. Ottawa 1951, index Ottawa 1951. Helen Elliot, comp., *Fate, hope and editorials: contemporary accounts and opinions in the newspapers, 1862–1873, microfilmed by the CLA/ACB microfilm project,* Canadian Libr. Assoc., Ottawa 1967, and George Ramsay Cook, ed., *Confederation,* Toronto 1967, cover other aspects of confederation.

1465 GARNER (JOHN). The franchise and politics in British North America, 1755–1867. Toronto. 1969.

1466 GILLIS (DUNCAN HUGH). Democracy in the Canadas, 1759–1867. Toronto. 1951.

1467 CORNELL (PAUL GRANT). The alignment of political groups in Canada, 1841–1867. Toronto. 1962.

See also Robert Craig Brown, ed., *Upper Canadian politics in the 1850s,* Toronto 1967.

1468 CLEVERDON (CATHERINE LYLE). The woman suffrage movement in Canada. Toronto. 1950.

1469 MORTON (WILLIAM LEWIS). The Progressive party in Canada. Toronto. 1950.

1470 GLAZEBROOK (GEORGE PARKIN DE TWENEBROKER). A history of Canadian political thought. Toronto. 1966.

1471   ABERDEEN. The Canadian journal of Lady Aberdeen, 1893–1898. Ed. by John Tupper Saywell. Champlain Soc. 38. Toronto. 1960.

For Aberdeen's career as governor-general see also **814**.

BLAKE. For the life of Edward Blake see **10367**.

1472   BORDEN. Sir Robert Laird Borden: his memoirs. Ed. by Henry Borden. 2 v. Toronto & N.Y. 1938. Abridged edn. [1969.] Cont. by Letters to limbo. Ed. by Henry Borden. Toronto. [1971.]

See also Harold A. Wilson, *The imperial policy of Sir Robert Borden*, Gainesville, Fla., 1966, and Heath N. Macquarrie, 'The formation of Borden's first cabinet', *Canadian J. Econ. & Pol. Sci.* xxiii (1957), 90–104, and 'Robert Borden and the election of 1911', ibid. xxv (1959), 271–86. Borden was prime minister of Canada, 1911–20.

1473   BROWN. Brown of the *Globe*. By James Maurice Stockford Careless. 2 v. Toronto. 1959–63.

Important for Toronto politics.

1474   CARTIER. Sir George Étienne Cartier, Bart: his life and times: a political history of Canada from 1814 until 1873. By John Boyd. Toronto. 1914.

1475   DAFOE. The politics of John W. Dafoe and the *Free Press*. By George Ramsay Cook. Toronto. 1963.

Important for Manitoba and Canadian politics. See also Murray Smith Donnelly, *Dafoe of the Free Press*, Toronto 1968, G. R. Cook, ed., *The Dafoe–Sifton correspondence, 1919–1927*, Manitoba Record Soc. public. 7, Altona, Manitoba 1966, and John Wesley Dafoe, *Clifford Sifton in relation to his times*, Toronto 1931.

1476   DUFFERIN. Dufferin–Carnarvon correspondence, 1874–1878. Ed. by Cornelis Willem de Kiewiet and Frank Hawkins Underhill. Champlain Soc. 33. Toronto. 1955.

See also Hariot Georgina Blackwood, Marchioness of Dufferin, *My Canadian journal, 1872–'78: extracts from my letters home written while Lord Dufferin was governor-general*, N.Y. 1891, William Leggo, *The history of the administration of the . . . Earl of Dufferin . . .*, Montreal 1878, and **1134**.

1477   ELGIN. The Elgin–Grey papers, 1846–1852. Ed. by Sir Arthur George Doughty. 4 v. Ottawa. 1937.

Elgin's official corresp. as governor. See also William Paul McClure Kennedy, *Lord Elgin*, Lond. & Toronto 1926, Sir John Bourinot, *Lord Elgin*, 1903, and **760**.

1478   GALT. The life and times of Sir Alexander Tilloch Galt. By Oscar Douglas Skelton. Toronto. 1920. New edn. by Guy MacLean. Toronto. 1966.

1479   HEAD. Sir Edmund Head: a scholarly governor. By Donald Gordon Grady Kerr. Toronto. 1954.

Useful for 1848–61.

1480 LANGEVIN. Hector-Louis Langevin, un père de la conféderation canadienne, 1826–1906. By Andrée Desilets. Quebec. 1969.

1481 LAURIER. Life and letters of Sir Wilfrid Laurier. By Oscar Douglas Skelton. 2 v. Toronto 1921. N.Y. 1922. New edn. by David M. L. Farr. 2 v. Toronto. 1965.

Still the best life, though needs to be suppl. by John Wesley Dafoe, *Laurier: a study in Canadian politics*, Toronto 1922, new edn. by Murray Smith Donnelly, Toronto 1963, and Sir John Stephen Willison, *Sir Wilfrid Laurier and the Liberal party: a political history*, 2 v. Lond. & Toronto 1903. Joseph Schull, *Laurier: the first Canadian*, Toronto & N.Y. 1965, is long, but more popular than scholarly. Laurent Olivier David, *Laurier: sa vie, ses oevres*, Beauceville 1919, is good for French Canada. For speeches see Sir Wilfrid Laurier, *Discours à l'étranger et au Canada*, Montreal 1909. Laurier was prime minister of Canada 1896–1911.

1482 MACDONALD. John A. Macdonald. By Donald Grant Creighton. 2 v. Toronto. 1952–5.

Good. Largely repl. Sir Joseph Pope, *Memoirs of the Right Honourable Sir John Alexander Macdonald, G.C.B., first prime minister of the Dominion of Canada . . .*, 2 v. Ottawa 1894, rev. edn. Toronto 1930, and *Correspondence of Sir John Macdonald . . .*, Toronto 1921. Macdonald was largely responsible for confederation, and was first prime minister.

1483 McGEE. The assassination of D'Arcy McGee. By Timothy Patrick Slattery. Toronto & Garden City, N.Y. 1968.

See also Josephine Phelan, *The ardent exile: the life and times of Thomas D'Arcy McGee*, Toronto 1951.

1484 MACKENZIE. Alexander Mackenzie, clear grit. By Dale C. Thomson. Toronto. 1960.

Largely repl. an early life by William Buckingham and Sir George William Ross, *The Hon. Alexander Mackenzie: his life and times*, 5th edn. Toronto 1892. Prime minister of Canada, 1873–8.

1485 MOWAT. Sir Oliver Mowat, Q.C., LL.D., G.C.M.G., P.C.: a biographical sketch. By Charles Robert Webster Biggar. 2 v. Toronto. 1905.

1486 RIEL. Louis Riel. By George Francis Gilman Stanley. Toronto. 1963.

The best biog. of the man who led two important rebellions in the north-west, for which see 1555.

1487 STRATHCONA. The life of Lord Strathcona and Mount Royal, G.C.M.G., G.C.V.O. By Beckles Willson. 2 v. Boston & N.Y. 1915.

Financier, railway promoter, and politician.

1488 TUPPER. Recollections of sixty years. By Sir Charles Tupper. 1914.

See also Edward Manning Saunders, ed., *The life and letters of the Rt. Hon. Sir Charles Tupper, Bart., K.C.M.G.*, 2 v. 1916; suppl. ed. by Sir Charles Hibbert Tupper, Toronto 1926. A leading politician, 1855–1900.

1489 CANADA: DEPARTMENT OF EXTERNAL AFFAIRS. Documents on Canadian external relations. 1+. Ottawa. 1967+.

An hist. ser. vol. I of which covers 1909–18. For treaties see Canada: Department of External Affairs, *Treaties and agreements affecting Canada in force between his majesty and the United States of America, with subsidiary documents, 1814–1913*, Ottawa 1915, new edn. [1814–1925] 1927. For numerous Anglo-American agreements concerning Canadian boundaries see also the indexes to the British parliamentary papers (33–4), and the works on the United States listed in Bemis and Griffin (2577).

1490 GLAZEBROOK (GEORGE PARKIN DE TWENEBROKER). A history of Canadian external relations. Toronto & N.Y. 1950. New edn. 2 v. Toronto. 1966.

Brief. See also Harold Gordon Skilling, *Canadian representation abroad: from agency to embassy*, Toronto 1945; John Semple Galbraith, *The establishment of Canadian diplomatic status at Washington*, Berkeley etc. 1951, and James Eayrs, 'The origins of Canada's Department of External Affairs', *Canadian J. Econ. & Pol. Sci.* xxv (1959), 102–28.

1491 SHIPPEE (LESTER BURRELL). Canadian–American relations, 1849–1874. New Haven [Conn.]. 1939.

Cont. by Charles Callan Tansill, *Canadian–American relations, 1875–1911*, New Haven, Conn. & Toronto 1943. Useful compilations, but, like James Morton Callahan, *American foreign policy in Canadian relations*, N.Y. 1937, repr. 1967, now somewhat dated. For a more up-to-date account see Gerald M. Craig, *The United States and Canada*, Camb., Mass. 1968, and Sydney F. Wise and Robert Craig Brown, *Canada views the United States: nineteenth-century political attitudes*, Toronto 1967. There are also a number of useful monographs on Canadian–American relations, notably Donald Frederick Warner, *The idea of continental union: agitation for the annexation of Canada to the United States, 1849–1893*, Mississippi Valley Hist. Assoc., Lexington 1960; Robin William Winks, *Canada and the United States: the civil war years*, Baltimore 1960; Goldwin Albert Smith, *The Treaty of Washington, 1871: a study in imperial history*, Ithaca, N.Y. 1941; James O. McCabe, *The San Juan water boundary question*, Toronto 1965; and James Morton Callahan, *The neutrality of the American lakes and Anglo-American relations*, Baltimore 1898.

1492 BROWN (ROBERT CRAIG). Canada's national policy, 1883–1900: a study in Canadian–American relations. Princeton [N.J.]. 1964.

Concerned with the issue of protection (which Brown defends). See also 1507.

1493 SHIELDS (R. A.). 'The Canadian treaty negotiations with France: a study in imperial relations, 1878–83'. *Inst. Hist. Res. Bull.* xl (1967), 186–202.

Shields has also publ. a ser. of other articles on the closely-interlocked questions of imperial relations, protection, and Franco-Canadian relations, notably 'Imperial policy and the Ripon circular of 1895', *Canadian Hist. Rev.* xlvii (1966), 119–35, 'Sir Charles Tupper and the Franco-Canadian treaty of 1895: a study of imperial relations', ibid. xlix (1968), 1–23, and 'Imperial reaction to the Fielding tariff of 1897', *Canadian J. Econ. & Pol. Sci.* xxxi (1965), 524–37.

1494 BERGER (CARL). The sense of power: studies in the ideas of Canadian imperialism, 1867–1914. Toronto. 1970.

An illuminating study of imperial propagandists. Berger also ed. a useful coll. of papers, *Imperial relations in the age of Laurier*, Toronto 1969. For the Round Table group see

James Eayrs, 'The Round Table movement in Canada, 1909–1920', *Canadian Hist. Rev.*
xxxviii (1957), 1–20, and Carroll Quigley, 'The Round Table groups in Canada, 1908–
38', ibid. xliii (1962), 204–24.

1495   PENLINGTON (NORMAN). Canada and imperialism, 1896–1899.
Toronto. 1965.

1496   STANLEY (GEORGE FRANCIS GILMAN) *and* JACKSON
(HAROLD McGILL). Canada's soldiers, 1604–1954: the military history
of an unmilitary people. Toronto. 1954. Rev. edn. 1960.

See also J. Mackay Hitsman, *Safeguarding Canada, 1763–1871*, Toronto 1968;
Charles Emil Dornbusch, *The Canadian army, 1855–1958: regimental histories and a
guide to the regiments*, Cornwallville, N.Y. 1959, 2nd edn. 1966; Desmond Morton,
*Ministers and generals: politics and the Canadian militia, 1868–1904*, Toronto 1970;
and Richard Arthur Preston, *Canada's RMC: a history of the Royal Military College*,
Toronto 1969.

1497   STACEY (CHARLES PERRY). Canada and the British army, 1846–
1871: a study in the practice of responsible government. 1936. Rev. edn.
Toronto. 1963.

For the Fenian invasions see **10341**.

1498   PRESTON (RICHARD ARTHUR). Canada and imperial defense;
a study of the origins of the British commonwealth's defense organization,
1867–1919. Durham, N.C. 1967.

1499   TUCKER (GILBERT NORMAN). The naval service of Canada: its
official history. 2 v. Ottawa. 1952.

See also Thomas A. Appleton, ed., *Usque ad mare: a history of the Canadian coast guard
and marine services*, Dept. of Transport, Ottawa, 1969.

(c) *Economic, Social, and Church History*

1500   INNIS (HAROLD ADAMS) *and* LOWER (ARTHUR REGINALD
MARSDEN). Select documents in Canadian economic history, 1783–1885.
Toronto. 1933.

1501   INNIS (HAROLD ADAMS). Essays in Canadian economic history.
Ed. by Mary Quayle Innis. Toronto. 1956.

In many ways the best book on Canadian economic hist. As a textbook William Thomas
Easterbrook and Hugh George Jeffrey Aitken, *Canadian economic history*, Toronto
1956, repr. 1968, is preferable to Mary Quayle Innis, *An economic history of Canada*,
Toronto 1935, new edn. 1954. Donald Grant Creighton, *British North America at
confederation: a study prepared for the royal commission on dominion–provincial relations*,
Ottawa 1963, is good for the economy in 1867, Albert Faucher, *Histoire économique
et unité canadienne*, Montreal 1970, is strong on Quebec, and Oscar Douglas Skelton,
*General economic history of the Dominion (1867–1912)*, Toronto 1913, is still sometimes
useful. For the movements of the economy see O. John Firestone, *Canada's economic
development, 1867–1953* . . ., Internat. Assoc. for Research in Income & Wealth,
Studies in Income & Wealth, ser. vii. 1958, Edward J. Chambers, 'Late nineteenth-
century business cycles in Canada', *Canadian J. Econ. & Pol. Sci.* xxx (1964), 391–412,

and K. A. J. Hay, 'Early twentieth-century business cycles in Canada', ibid. xxxii (1966), 354–65. For Canadian trade with the West Indies see **1578**.

1502  TUCKER (GILBERT NORMAN). The Canadian commercial revolution, 1845–1851. New Haven [Conn.]. 1936. Rev. edn. by Hugh G. J. Aitken. Toronto. 1964.

1503  McIVOR (RUSSEL CRAIG). Canadian monetary, banking and fiscal development. Toronto. 1958.

See also Kenneth Arthur Haig Buckley, *Capital formation in Canada, 1896–1930*, Toronto 1955, and Roeliff Morton Breckenridge, *The Canadian banking system, 1817–1890*, Amer. Econ. Assoc. N.Y. 1895.

1504  VILLARD (HAROLD GARRISON) *and* WILLOUGHBY (WESTEL WOODBURY). The Canadian budgetary system. Inst. for Government Research. N.Y. 1918.

See also Norman Ward, *The public purse: a study in Canadian democracy*, Toronto 1962.

1505  MACKINTOSH (WILLIAM ARCHIBALD). The economic background of dominion–provincial relations. Ed. by John Harkness Dales. Toronto. 1964.

Orig. publ. as Appendix III of the Rowell–Sirois report (**1461**). For details see also James Ackley Maxwell, *Federal subsidies to the provincial governments in Canada*, Camb., Mass. 1937.

1506  PERRY (JOHN HARVEY). Taxes, tariffs and subsidies: a history of Canadian fiscal development. 2 v. Toronto. 1955.

1507  MASTERS (DONALD CAMPBELL CHARLES). The reciprocity treaty of 1854: its history, its relation to British colonial and foreign policy and to the development of Canadian fiscal autonomy. 1937. New edn. Toronto. 1963.

Must be suppl. by Robert E. Ankli, 'The reciprocity treaty of 1854', *Canadian J. Econ.* iv (1971), 1–20. See also John Harkness Dales, *The protective tariff in Canada's development: eight essays . . . 1870–1955*, Toronto [1966], Edward Porritt, *Sixty years of protection in Canada, 1846–1907: where industry leans on the politician*, 1908, 2nd edn. Winnipeg 1913, and Lewis Ethan Ellis, *Reciprocity 1911: a study in Canadian–American relations*, New Haven, Conn. 1939.

1508  VINER (JACOB). Canada's balance of international indebtedness, 1900–1913: an inductive study in the theory of international trade. Camb., Mass. 1924.

See also Penelope Hartland, 'Canadian balance of payments since 1868' in *Trends in the American economy in the nineteenth century*, Nat. Bureau of Econ. Research, Studies in Income & Wealth, xxiv (1960), 717–55, and Matthew Simon, 'New British investment in Canada, 1865–1914', *Canadian J. Econ.* iii (1970), 238–54.

1509  FOWKE (VERNON CLIFFORD). Canadian agricultural policy: the historical pattern. Toronto. 1947.

See also his *The national policy and the wheat economy*, Toronto 1957.

1510 INNIS (HAROLD ADAMS). The cod fisheries: the history of an international economy. New Haven [Conn.] & Toronto. 1940. New edn. Toronto. 1954.
The Newfoundland fisheries.

1511 INNIS (HAROLD ADAMS). The fur trade of Canada. Univ. of Toronto Studs., Hist. & Econ. vol. V., no. 1. Toronto. 1927. New edn. Toronto. 1956.

1512 LOWER (ARTHUR REGINALD MARSDEN). The north American assault on the Canadian forest: a history of the lumber trade between Canada and the United States. Toronto. 1938. Repr. N.Y. 1968.

1513 McDOUGALL (DUNCAN M.). 'Canadian manufactured commodity output, 1870–1915'. *Canadian J. Econ.* iv (1971), 21–36.
See also Gordon W. Bertram, 'Economic growth in Canadian industry, 1870–1915: the staple model and the take-off hypothesis', *Canadian J. Econ. & Pol. Sci.* xxix (1963), 159–84. Samuel Delbert Clark, *The Canadian Manufacturers' Association: a study in collective bargaining and political pressure*, Univ. of Toronto Studs., Hist. & Econ. vii, Toronto 1939, is a useful study of the manufacturers' lobby.

1514 RITCHIE (THOMAS) *and others*. Canada builds, 1867–1967. Toronto. 1967.
A history of the Canadian building industry and of Canadian housing.

1515 GLAZEBROOK (GEORGE PARKIN DE TWENEBROKER). A history of transportation in Canada. Toronto. 1938. New edn. 2 v. Toronto. 1964.
For railways see also Canada: Bureau de Statistique, *Bibliographical list of references to Canadian railways, 1829–1938*, Ottawa 1938, and Leonard Bertram Irwin, *Pacific railways and nationalism in the Canadian–American northwest, 1845–1873*, Phila. 1939.

1516 HEDGES (JAMES BLAINE). Building the Canadian west: the land and colonization policies of the Canadian Pacific Railway. N.Y. 1939.
See also his *The federal railway land subsidy policy of Canada*, Camb., Mass. 1934.

1517 CURRIE (ARCHIBALD WILLIAM). The Grand Trunk Railway of Canada. Toronto. 1957.
For the system into which the Grand Trunk was absorbed see George Roy Stevens, *Canadian National Railways*, 2 v. Toronto 1960–2.

1518 INNIS (HAROLD ADAMS). A history of the Canadian Pacific Railway. Lond. & Toronto. 1923. Repr. Toronto. 1970.
See also Pierre Berton, *The national dream: the great railway, 1871–1881*, Toronto 1970 and *The last spike . . . , 1881–1885*, Toronto 1971.

1519 MOUNT STEPHEN. Awakening continent: the life of Lord Mount Stephen. By Heather Gilbert. Vol. 1. Aberdeen. 1965.
Manufacturer and president of Canadian Pacific Railway.

1520  CLARK (SAMUEL DELBERT). The social development of Canada:
an introductory study with select documents. Toronto. 1942.

1521  LOWER (ARTHUR REGINALD MARSDEN). Canadians in the
making: a social history of Canada. Toronto. 1958.

1522  MACDONALD (NORMAN). Canada: immigration and colonization,
1841–1903. Toronto. 1966.

See also James Pickett, 'An evaluation of estimates of immigration into Canada in the
late nineteenth century', *Canadian J. Econ. & Pol. Sci.* xxxi (1965), 499–508, and Mabel
F. Timlin, 'Canada's immigration policy, 1896–1910', ibid. xxvi (1960), 517–32. On
Canadian population see also Leon Edgar Truesdell, *The Canadian-born in the United
States: an analysis of the statistics of the Canadian element in the population of the United
States, 1850–1930*, New Haven [Conn.] & Toronto 1943, and Robert Hamilton
Coats and Murdoch Campbell MacLean, *The American-born in Canada: a statistical
interpretation*, New Haven [Conn.] 1943.

1523  LOGAN (HAROLD AMOS). Trade unions in Canada: their development and functioning. Toronto. 1948.

1524  WILSON (J. DONALD), STAMP (ROBERT M.), *and* AUDET
(LOUIS PHILIPPE). Canadian education: a history. Scarborough, Ontario.
1970.

See also Robert Craig Brown, ed., *Minorities, schools and politics*, Toronto 1969;
Charles Edward Phillips, *The development of education in Canada*, Toronto 1957;
Howard Adams, *The education of Canadians, 1800–1867: the roots of separatism*,
Montreal 1968; John George Hodgins, ed., *Documentary history of education in Upper
Canada from the passing of the Constitutional Act of 1791, to the close of Rev. Dr. Ryerson's administration of the Education department in 1876*, 28 v. Toronto 1894–1910,
with *An index to the material bearing on higher education . . .*, comp. by Robin Sutton
Harris and Constance Allen, Toronto 1966, and *The establishment of schools and colleges
in Ontario, 1792–1910*, 3 v., Toronto 1910; John Harold Putman, *Egerton Ryerson and
education in Upper Canada*, Toronto 1912; Charles Bruce Sissons, *Egerton Ryerson:
his life and letters*, 2 v. Toronto etc. 1937–47; and Francis Henry Johnson, *A history of
public education in British Columbia*, Vancouver 1964.

1525  HARRIS (ROBIN SUTTON) *and* TREMBLAY (ARTHUR). A
bibliography of higher education in Canada: bibliographie de l'enseignement
supérieur au Canada. Toronto. 1960. Suppl. etc. 1965.

The following hists. of English-speaking univs. are useful. *The University of Toronto
and its colleges, 1827–1906*, Toronto 1906; William Stewart Wallace, *A history of the
University of Toronto, 1827–1927*, Toronto 1927; Thomas Arthur Reed, ed., *A history
of the University of Trinity College, Toronto, 1852–1952*, Toronto 1952; Claude
Thomas Bissell, ed., *University College: a portrait, 1853–1953*, Toronto 1953; Charles
Bruce Sissons, *A history of Victoria University*, Toronto 1952; Cyrus John Macmillan,
*McGill and its story, 1821–1921*, 1921; Hugh MacLennan, ed., *McGill: the story of a
university*, 1960; Donald Campbell Masters, *Bishop's University: the first hundred
years*, Toronto 1950; Delano Dexter Calvin, *Queen's University at Kingston: the first
century of a Scottish-Canadian foundation, 1841–1941*, Kingston, Ontario 1941;
*Queen's University: a centenary volume, 1841–1941*, Toronto 1941; William Lewis
Morton, *One university: a history of the University of Manitoba, 1877–1952*, Toronto
1957; James John Talman and Ruth Davis Talman, *'Western'—1878–1953: being*

the history of the origins and development of the University of Western Ontario during its first seventy-five years, London, Ont. 1953.

1526   MOIR (JOHN SARGENT) *ed.* Church and state in Canada, 1627–1867: basic documents. Toronto. 1967.

1527   CLIFFORD (N. K.). 'Religion and the development of Canadian Society: an historiographical analysis'. *Church Hist.* xxxviii (1969), 506–23.

A valuable interpretative guide. Most discussion of Canadian church hist. turns on Samuel Delbert Clark, *Church and sect in Canada*, Toronto 1948, William Francis Ryan, *The clergy and economic growth in Quebec, 1896–1914*, Quebec 1966, and John Sargent Moir, *Church and state in Canada West: three studies in the relation of denominationalism and nationalism, 1841–1867*, Toronto 1959. The church and state question is further explored by Charles Bruce Sissons, *Church & state in Canadian education: an historical study*, Toronto 1959; Roy Clinton Dalton, *The Jesuits' estates question, 1760–1888: a study of the background for the agitation of 1889*, Toronto 1968; and Goldwin Sylvester French, *Parsons & politics: the rôle of the Wesleyan Methodists in Upper Canada and the Maritimes from 1780 to 1855*, Toronto 1962. It also figures largely in Donald Campbell Masters, *Protestant church colleges in Canada*, Toronto 1966. For the Anglican church see Philip Carrington, Archbishop of Quebec, *The Anglican church in Canada: a history*, Lond. & Toronto 1963; John Irwin Cooper, *The blessed communion: the origins and history of the diocese of Montreal, 1760–1960*, Montreal 1960; Spencer Ervin, *The political and ecclesiastical history of the Anglican church in Canada*, Ambler, Pa. 1967; Frank Alexander Peake, *The Anglican church in British Columbia*, Vancouver 1959, and *The bishop who ate his boots: a biography of Isaac O. Stringer*, Toronto 1966; and Alfred Henchman Crowfoot, *Benjamin Cronyn, first bishop of Huron*, Lond., Ontario 1957, and *This dreamer: life of Isaac Hellmuth, second bishop of Huron*, Vancouver 1963.

(d) *The Provinces*

1528   MORLEY (WILLIAM F. E.) *ed.* Canadian local histories to 1950: a bibliography. 1+ v. Toronto. 1967+.

Good. V. 1 covers the Atlantic provinces, v. 2 Quebec.

1529   WICKETT (SAMUEL MORLEY) *ed.* Municipal government in Canada. Univ. of Toronto Studies, Hist. and Econ. II. Toronto. 1907.

A series of short studies incl. a 'Bibliography of Canadian municipal government'.

1530   BISHOP (OLGA BERNICE). Publications of the governments of Nova Scotia, Prince Edward Island, New Brunswick, 1758–1952. Ottawa. 1957.

1531   RAWLYK (GEORGE A.) *ed.* Historical essays on the Atlantic provinces. Toronto. 1967.

See also William Menzies Whitelaw, *The maritimes and Canada before confederation*, Toronto 1934.

1532   PUBLIC ARCHIVES OF NOVA SCOTIA. Publications. 1+. Halifax. 1933+.

The ser. incl. Phyllis R. Blakeley, *Glimpses of Halifax, 1867–1900*, Halifax 1949; Charles Bruce Fergusson, ed., *The diary of Adolphus Gaetz* [1855–73], Halifax 1965;

*A directory of the members of the Legislative Assembly of Nova Scotia, 1758–1958*, Halifax 1958; and *Place names and places of Nova Scotia*, Halifax 1967.

1533  DUNN (CHARLES WILLIAM). Highland settler: a portrait of the Scottish gael in Nova Scotia. Toronto. 1953. Repr. 1968.

1534  TAYLOR (HUGH A.) *comp.* New Brunswick history: a checklist of secondary sources. Provincial Archives. Fredericton. 1971.

See also J. Russell Harper, comp., *Historical directory of New Brunswick newspapers and periodicals*, Fredericton 1961.

1535  MACNUTT (WILLIAM STEWART). New Brunswick: a history, 1784–1867. Toronto. 1963.

See also his *The Atlantic provinces* (**1446**).

1536  BOLGER (FRANCIS WILLIAM PIUS). Prince Edward Island and confederation, 1863–1873. Charlottetown [P.E.I.]. 1964.

For the constitutional development of Prince Edward Island see Frank MacKinnon, *The government of Prince Edward Island*, Toronto 1951. There is also a popular history, Lorne Clayton Callbeck, *The cradle of confederation: a brief history of Prince Edward Island from its discovery in 1534 to the present time*, Fredericton, N.B. 1964.

1537  CHADWICK (GERALD WILLIAM ST. JOHN). Newfoundland: island into province. Camb. 1967.

See also Gertrude E. Gunn, *The political history of Newfoundland, 1832–1864*, Toronto 1966; Robert Alexander Mackay, ed., *Newfoundland: economic, diplomatic and strategic studies*, 1946, and the documents in *In the Privy Council: in the matter of the boundary between the dominion of Canada and the colony of Newfoundland in the Labrador peninsula, between the dominion of Canada of the one part and the colony of Newfoundland of the other part*, 12 v. 1928. Domestic politics are the subject of E. C. Moulton, 'Constitutional crisis and civil strife in Newfoundland, February to November 1861', *Canadian Hist. Rev.* xlviii (1967), 251–72, and Harvey Mitchell, 'Canada's negotiations with Newfoundland, 1887–1895', ibid. xl (1959), 277–93, and 'The constitutional crisis of 1889 in Newfoundland', *Canadian J. Econ. & Pol. Sci.* xxiv (1958), 323–31.

1538  MARTIN (GÉRARD). Bibliographie sommaire du Canada-français, 1854–1954. Québec. 1954.

See also Philippe Garigue, *A bibliographical introduction to the study of French Canada*, Montreal 1956; Philippe Garigue and Raymonde Savard, comps., *Bibliographie du Québec (1955–1965)*, Montreal 1967; André Beaulieu and Jean Hamelin, *Les journaux du Québec de 1764 à 1964*, Québec 1965; André Beaulieu, Jean Charles Bonenfant and Jean Hamelin, *Répertoire des publications gouvernmentales du Québec, de 1867 à 1964*, Québec 1968; and André Beaulieu and William F. E. Morley, *La province du Québec*, Toronto 1971.

1539  COOKE (ALAN) *and* CARON (FABIEN). Bibliographie de la Péninsula du Québec–Labrador: bibliography of the Quebec–Labrador peninsula. Centre d'études nordique, Université Laval. 2 v. Boston. 1968.

The fullest list of books on French Canada.

1540  WADE (MASON). The French Canadians, 1760–1945. 1955. Rev. edn. 2 v. Toronto etc. 1968.

Must be suppl. by William Francis Ryan, *The clergy and economic growth in Quebec, 1896–1914,* Quebec 1966. For the English enclave in Quebec see John Irwin Cooper, *Montreal: a brief history,* Montreal 1970, and *The blessed communion: the origins and history of the diocese of Montreal, 1760–1960,* Montreal 1960.

**1541** SPENCER (LORAINE) *and* HOLLAND (SUSAN). Northern Ontario: a bibliography. Toronto. 1968.

**1542** MIDDLETON (JESSE EDGAR) *and* LANDON (FRED). The province of Ontario: a history, 1615–1927. 4 v. Toronto. [*c.* 1927.]
A quarry rather than a hist., as is Fred Landon, *Western Ontario and the American frontier,* Toronto & New Haven [Conn.] 1941, new edn. Toronto 1967. For records see Champlain Soc., *Ontario series,* 1+, Toronto 1957+.

**1543** GLAZEBROOK (GEORGE PARKIN DE TWENEBROKER). Life in Ontario: a social history. Toronto. 1968.
See also his *The story of Toronto,* Toronto 1971, and Ontario Hist. Soc. *Profiles of a province: studies in the history of Ontario . . .,* Toronto 1967.

**1544** JONES (ROBERT LESLIE). History of agriculture in Ontario, 1613–1880. Univ. of Toronto Studies, Hist. and Econ. XI. Toronto. 1946.

**1545** SPELT (JACOB). The urban development in South-Central Ontario. Assen [Netherlands]. 1955.

**1546** MASTERS (DONALD CAMPBELL CHARLES). The rise of Toronto, 1850–1890. Toronto. 1947.

**1547** PEEL (BRUCE BRADEN) *comp.* A bibliography of the prairie provinces to 1953. Toronto. 1956. Suppl. 1963.
See also Christine MacDonald, *Publications of the governments of the North-West Territories, 1876–1905, and of the province of Saskatchewan, 1905–1952,* Regina 1952, and *Historical directory of Saskatchewan newspapers, 1878–1950,* Saskatoon 1951.

**1548** MORTON (ARTHUR SILVER). A history of the Canadian west to 1870–71: being, a history of Rupert's land (the Hudson's Bay Company's territory) and of the North-West territory (including the Pacific slope). 1939.

**1549** ENGLAND (ROBERT). The colonization of western Canada: a study of contemporary land settlement (1896–1934). 1936.

**1550** MACKINTOSH (WILLIAM ARCHIBALD) *and* JOERG (WOLFGANG LOUIS GOTTFRIED) *eds.* Canadian frontiers of settlement. 8 v. Toronto. 1934–41.
Most of the ser. covers the period from *c.* 1910. It consists of two books by Mackintosh, *Prairie settlement, the geographical setting,* Toronto 1934, and *Economic problems of the prairie provinces,* Toronto 1935; Arthur Silver Morton, *History of prairie settlement,* Toronto 1938; Robert Welch Murchie, *Agricultural progress on the prairie frontier,* Toronto 1936; Arthur Reginald Marsden Lower, *Settlement and the forest frontier in eastern Canada,* bound with Harold Adams Innis, *Settlement and the mining frontier,* Toronto 1936; and three books by Carl Addington Dawson, *The settlement of the Peace*

*river country: a study of a pioneer area*, Toronto 1934, *Group settlement: ethnic communities in western Canada*, Toronto 1936, and [with Eva R. Younge] *Pioneering in the prairie provinces: the social side of the settlement process*, Toronto 1940.

1551  SHARP (PAUL FREDERICK). Whoop-up country: the Canadian–American west, 1865–1885. Minneapolis, Minn. 1955.

1552  GLUEK (ALVIN CHARLES) *Jr*. Minnesota and the manifest destiny of the Canadian northwest: a study in Canadian–American relations. Toronto. 1965.

1553  RICH (EDWIN ERNEST). The history of the Hudson's Bay Company, 1670–1870. 2 v. Hudson's Bay Record Soc. 1958–9.

1554  GALBRAITH (JOHN SEMPLE). The Hudson's Bay Company as an imperial factor, 1821–1869. Berkeley etc. 1957.

1555  STANLEY (GEORGE FRANCIS GILMAN). The birth of western Canada: a history of the Riel rebellions. 1936. New edn. Toronto. 1961.

To be read with his life of Riel (**1486**). There is a considerable literature on the Riel rebellions, and their background. See particularly A. I. Silver, 'French Canada and the prairie frontier, 1870–1890', *Canadian Hist. Rev.* 1 (1969), 11–36, Joseph Kinsey Howard, *Strange empire: a narrative of the northwest*, N.Y. 1952; Robert E. Lamb, *Thunder in the north: conflict over the Riel risings, 1870–1885*, N.Y. 1957, and *Alexander Begg's Red River journal and other papers relative to the Red River resistance of 1869–1870*, ed. by William Lewis Morton, Champlain Soc. 34, Toronto 1956. John Peter Turner, *The North-west mounted police, 1873–1893*, 2 v. Ottawa 1950, is too popular to be of much value.

1556  THOMAS (LEWIS HERBERT). The struggle for responsible government in the North-West Territories, 1870–97. Toronto. 1956.

1557  WRIGHT (JAMES FREDERICK CHURCH). Saskatchewan: the history of a province. Toronto. 1955.

1558  MORTON (WILLIAM LEWIS). Manitoba: a history. Toronto. 1957. 2nd edn. 1967.

Morton also ed. *Manitoba: the birth of a province*, Manitoba Record Soc. 1, Altona, Manitoba 1965.

1559  THOMAS (LEWIS GWYNNE). The liberal party in Alberta: a history of politics in the province of Alberta, 1905–1921. Toronto. 1959.

1560  MACGREGOR (JAMES GRIERSON). Edmonton: a history. Edmonton. 1967.

1561  SMITH (CHARLES WESLEY). Pacific Northwest Americana: a checklist of books and pamphlets relating to the history of the Pacific Northwest. 3rd edn. Portland, Oregon. 1950.

1562 HOLMES (MARJORIE C.). Publications of the government of British Columbia, 1871–1947. Victoria, B.C. 1950.

1563 ORMSBY (MARGARET ANCHORETTA). British Columbia: a history. Toronto. 1958.

See also Henry Forbes Angus, ed., *British Columbia and the United States: the north Pacific slope from fur trade to aviation*, Toronto & New Haven [Conn.] 1942, Walter Noble Sage, *Sir James Douglas and British Columbia*, Univ. of Toronto Studies, Hist. & Econ., vol. VI, no. 1, Toronto 1930 and Martin Robin, *The rush for spoils: the company province, 1871–1933*, Toronto 1972.

1564 MORRISON (DAVID R.). The politics of the Yukon territory, 1898–1909. Toronto. 1968.

## 6. British West Indies

1565 NEW YORK PUBLIC LIBRARY. List of works relating to the West Indies. N.Y. 1912.

See also Ann Duncan Brown, comp., *British possessions in the Caribbean area: a selected list of references*, U.S. Library of Congress, Wash. 1943, and Frank Cundall, *Bibliographia Jamaicensis . . .*, Kingston 1902, suppl. 1908, *Bibliography of the West Indies (excluding Jamaica)*, Kingston, 1909, and *Political and social disturbances in the West Indies: a brief account and bibliography*, 1906. Each of the West Indian colonies publ. a considerable number of official docs., incl. in the case of the bigger colonies, a local equivalent of *Hansard*. In addition annual reports from each colony were publ. as parl. papers.

1566 COMITAS (LAMBROS). Caribbeana, 1900–1965: a topical bibliography. Seattle. 1968.

For manuscripts see **2636**.

1567 GOVEIA (ELSA V.). A study on the historiography of the British West Indies to the end of the nineteenth century. Mexico. 1956.

Scholarly. Eric Eustace Williams, *British historians and the West Indies*, Port of Spain 1964, Lond. & N.Y. 1966, is polemical but entertaining.

1568 PARRY (JOHN HORACE) *and* SHERLOCK (PHILIP MANDERSON). A short history of the West Indies. 1956. 2nd edn. 1966.

A good general introduction. Cp. William Laurence Burn, *The British West Indies*, 1951, and David Alan Gilmour Waddell, *The West Indies & the Guianas*, Englewood Cliffs, N.J. 1967. Sir Alan Cuthbert Maxwell Burns, *History of the British West Indies*, 1954, 2nd edn. 1965, is fuller, and so is Gordon Kenneth Lewis, *The growth of the modern West Indies*, 1968, but neither do more than give a general outline hist.

1569 SOCIAL AND ECONOMIC STUDIES. 1+. Inst. Soc. & Econ. Res., Univ. of the West Indies. Kingston, Jamaica. 1953+.

The main source for articles about the 19th- and 20th-cent. British West Indies. But see also *Jamaica Hist. Rev.* 1+, Jamaica Hist. Soc., Kingston 1945–8+, and *J. of Caribbean Hist.* 1+, Dept. of Hist., Univ. of West Indies, Barbados 1970+.

1570 MATHIESON (WILLIAM LAW). The sugar colonies and governor Eyre, 1849–1866. 1936.

Now out of date but not repl.

1571 WRONG (HUME). Government of the West Indies. Oxf. 1923.

A constitutional hist.

1572 WILL (H. A.). Constitutional change in the British West Indies, 1880–1903: a study of movements for constitutional reform in Jamaica, British Guiana, and Trinidad, and of British policy towards them. Oxf. 1970.

See also his 'Problems of constitutional reform in Jamaica, Mauritius and Trinidad, 1880–1895', *Eng. Hist. Rev.* lxxxi (1966), 693–716, and 'Colonial policy and economic development in the British West Indies, 1895–1903', *Econ. Hist. Rev.* 2 ser. xxiii (1970), 129–47.

1573 BEACHEY (RAYMOND WENDELL). The British West Indies sugar industry in the late 19th century. Oxf. 1957.

See also Philip De Armond Curtin, 'The British sugar duties and West Indian prosperity', *J. Econ. Hist.* xiv (1954), 157–64; Deerr (**5687**); Samuel Berrick Saul, 'The British West Indies in depression, 1880–1914', *Inter-American Econ. Affairs*, xii (1958–9), no. 3, 3–25; and Michael Craton and James Walvin, *A Jamaican plantation: the history of Worthy Park, 1670–1970*, Lond. & Toronto 1971. For the recruitment of labour see G. W. Roberts and J. Byrne, 'Summary statistics of indenture and associated migration affecting the West Indies, 1834–1918', *Population Studs.* xx (1966–7), 125–34.

1574 SEWELL (WILLIAM GRANT). The ordeal of free labor in the British West Indies. N.Y. 1861.

The best contemp. account of the West Indies after emancipation. But see also Edward Bean Underhill, *The West Indies: their social and religious condition*, 1862. British attitudes were much influenced by the for the most part anti-negro account in James Anthony Froude, *The English in the West Indies: or, the bow of Ulysses*, 1888. Anthony Trollope, *The West Indies and the Spanish Main*, 1859, shared many of Froude's prejudices.

1575 BOYCE (*Sir* ROBERT WILLIAM). Health progress and administration in the West Indies. 1910.

1576 CALDECOTT (ALFRED). The church in the West Indies. 1898. Repr. 1970.

See also Frank Cundall, *The life of Enos Nuttall, archbishop of the West Indies*, 1922.

1577 ROYAL COMMISSION ON WEST INDIAN REVENUES. Report of the royal commission appointed . . . to inquire into the public revenues, expenditure, debts, and liabilities of the islands of Jamaica, Grenada, St. Vincent, Tobago, and St. Lucia, and the Leeward Islands . . . [Members: Colonel William Crossman and George Smyth Baden-Powell]. [C. 3840] H.C. (1884). XLVI, 1.

A useful source.

1578  WEST INDIA ROYAL COMMISSION. [Chairman: General Sir Henry Wylie Norman]. Report. [C. 8655] H.C. (1898). L, 1. Appendixes [C. 8656–7] H.C. (1898). L, 183, 397. [C. 8689, 8799] H.C. (1898). LI, 1, 431.

An examination of the economic prospects of the sugar colonies. See also *Royal Commission on trade relations between Canada and the West Indies* [Chairman: Lord Balfour of Burleigh]. *Report.* [Cd. 5369] H.C. (1910). XI, 159. Evidence: [Cd. 4991, Cd. 5370–1] H.C. (1910). XI, 225. On Canada there is also Peter K. Newman, 'Canada's role in West Indian trade before 1912', *Inter-American Econ. Affairs,* xiv (1960–1), no. 1, 25–49.

1579  CRATON (MICHAEL). A history of the Bahamas. 1962. 2nd edn. 1968.
Popular.

1580  CHANDLER (MICHAEL JOHN). A guide to records in Barbados. Oxf. 1965.
For articles see *Barbados Museum & Hist. Soc. J.* 1+, Bridgetown 1933+.

1581  HAMILTON (BRUCE). Barbados & the confederation question, 1871–1885. 1956.

1582  WILKINSON (HENRY CAMPBELL). Bermuda from sail to steam: the history of the island from 1784 to 1901. 2 v. 1972.
There is also a good hist. of the naval base, Roger Willock, *Bulwark of empire: Bermuda's fortified naval base, 1860–1920,* priv. pr. Princeton [N.J.] 1962. See also *Bermuda Hist. Q.* 1+, Hamilton 1944+.

1583  RODWAY (JAMES). Guiana: British, Dutch and French. 1912.
More general in coverage than his *History of British Guiana: from the year 1688 to the present time,* 3 v. Georgetown 1891–4, which is a useful source of facts. There are a number of good monographs on British Guiana, chief among them Sir Cecil Clementi, *A constitutional history of British Guiana,* 1937, and *The Chinese in British Guiana,* Georgetown 1915, and Dwarka Nath, *A history of Indians in British Guiana,* 1950. For the aboriginal population see Sir Everard Ferdinand im Thurn, *Among the Indians of Guiana . . .,* 1883.

1584  WADDELL (DAVID ALAN GILMOUR). British Honduras: a historical and contemporary survey. 1961.
A brief intro. There is some archive material in Sir John Alder Burdon, ed., *Archives of British Honduras:* vol. III *from 1841 to 1884,* 1935.

1585  HUMPHREYS (ROBERT ARTHUR). The diplomatic history of British Honduras, 1638–1901. 1961.
Good. On the Bay Islands see also D. A. G. Waddell, 'Great Britain and the Bay Islands, 1821–61', *Hist. J.* ii (1959), 59–77, and Colin C. Eldridge, 'The myth of mid-Victorian "separatism": the cession of the Bay Islands and the Ionian Islands in the early 1860's', *Victorian Studs.* xii (1968–9), 331–46.

1586  JAMAICA LIBRARY SERVICE. Jamaica: a select bibliography, 1900–1963. Kingston. 1963.
For earlier works consult Cundall (**1565**).

1587 CURTIN (PHILIP DE ARMOND). Two Jamaicas: the role of ideas in a tropical colony, 1830–1865. Camb., Mass. 1955.

A social and intellectual history of the colony after emancipation.

1588 EISNER (GISELA). Jamaica, 1830–1930: a study in economic growth. Manch. 1961.

A good analysis by an economist. But needs to be suppl. by Hall (**1589**).

1589 HALL (DOUGLAS GORDON HAWKINS). Free Jamaica, 1838–1865: an economic history. New Haven [Conn.]. 1959.

1590 SEMMEL (BERNARD). The governor Eyre controversy. 1962. Publ. in America as *Jamaican blood and Victorian conscience*. Boston. 1963. *Democracy versus empire* . . . Garden City, N.Y. 1969.

Eyre (for whose career outside and in Jamaica see also Dutton, **1300**) was, as acting-governor of Jamaica, over-zealous in suppressing a rising and became a centre of dispute in British politics. For the Jamaica rising see *Report of the Jamaica royal commission* [President: Sir Henry Storks], [3683] H.C. (1866). XXX, 489. Evidence: [3683–I] H.C. (1866). XXXI, 1. Papers laid before the commission by Eyre: [3682] H.C. (1866). XXX, 1. Eyre was dragged before the courts and an extensive literature developed. See particularly William Francis Finlason, *A history of the Jamaica case* . . ., 1868, 2nd edn. 1869, *Justice to a colonial governor* . . ., 1869, and *Report of the case of the Queen v. Edward John Eyre* . . ., 1868, Hamilton Hume, *The life of Edward John Eyre, late governor of Jamaica*, 1867, and Sydney Haldane Olivier, Baron Olivier, *The myth of governor Eyre*, 1933.

1591 BAKER (EDWARD CECIL). A guide to records in the Leeward Islands. Oxf. 1965.

1592 WOOD (DONALD). Trinidad in transition: the years after slavery. Lond. & N.Y. 1968.

Primarily concerned with race relations. See also Ina Mary Cumpston, 'Radicalism in Trinidad and Colonial Office reactions, 1855–6', *Inst. Hist. Res. Bull.* xxxvi (1963), 153–67.

1593 WILLIAMS (ERIC EUSTACE). History of the people of Trinidad and Tobago. Port of Spain. 1962. N.Y. 1964.

Patriotic and nationalist. Cp. Gertrude Carmichael, *The history of the West Indian islands of Trinidad and Tobago, 1498–1900*, 1961.

1594 BAKER (EDWARD CECIL). A guide to records in the Windward Islands. Oxf. 1968.

1595 DAVY (JOHN). The West Indies: before and since slave emancipation: comprising the Windward and Leeward Islands' military command: founded on notes and observations collected during a three years' residence. Dublin & Barbados. 1854.

A useful account of post-emancipation conditions.

## 7. BRITISH TERRITORIES IN AFRICA

### (a) *General*

The works of travellers, ethnographers, and anthropologists have been kept to a minimum in the list below in order to save space. They are, of course, indispensable for the study of modern Africa.

### (i) *Reference*

**1596  CONOVER (HELEN FIELD)** *ed.* Africa south of the Sahara: a selected, annotated list of writings. U.S. Library of Congress. Wash. 1963.

Suppl. by her *Serials for African studies*, U.S. Library of Congress, Wash. 1961. For bibliogs. see also South African Public Libr., *A bibliography of African bibliographies: covering Africa south of the Sahara*, 4th edn., Cape Town 1961, Jan Wepsiec, comp., *A checklist of bibliographies and serial publications for studies of Africa south of the Sahara*, Univ. of Chicago, Chicago 1956, Anthea Garling, *Bibliography of African bibliographies*, Camb. 1968, and John B. Webster, comp., *Reading list on African history*, Ibadan 1965.

**1597  STANDING CONFERENCE ON LIBRARY MATERIALS ON AFRICA (SCOLMA).** United Kingdom publications and theses on Africa, 1963+, Camb. 1966+.

**1598  GLAZIER (KENNETH M.)** *comp.* Africa south of the Sahara: a select and annotated bibliography, 1958–1963. Hoover Instn. Bibliog. ser. xvi. Stanford [Calif.]. 1964. Suppl. for 1964–8. Bibliog. ser. xlii. Stanford. 1969.

The fullest guide.

**1599  COLLISON (ROBERT LEWIS)** *comp.* The Scolma directory of libraries and special collections on Africa. Standing Conference on Library Materials on Africa. 1963. 2nd edn. 1967. 3rd edn. 1973.

On British libr. See also **2506.**

**1600  DUIGNAN (PETER).** Handbook of American resources for African studies. Hoover Instn. Bibliog. Ser. xxix. Stanford [Calif.]. 1967.

See also *United States and Canadian publications on Africa*, Wash. later Stanford [Calif.], annual 1960+; New York Public Library, Schomburg Collection, *Dictionary catalogue of the Schomburg collection of negro literature and history*, 9 v. Boston 1962, suppl. 2 v. Boston 1967; Harvard University Libr., *Widener library shelflist 35: African history and literatures . . .*, Camb., Mass. 1970; Northwestern University Library, *Catalogue of the African collection*, 2 v. Boston, 1962; Rozanne M. Barry, comp., *African newspapers in selected American libraries: a union list*, U.S. Library of Congress, 3rd edn. Wash. 1965; and Peter Duignan and Kenneth M. Glazier, *A checklist of serials for African studies based on the libraries of the Hoover Institution and Stanford University*, Stanford [Calif.] 1963. For Russian work see Mary Holdsworth, *Soviet African studies, 1918–1959: an annotated bibliography*, 2 pts. 1961.

**1601  STANDING CONFERENCE ON LIBRARY MATERIALS ON AFRICA (SCOLMA).** Theses on Africa accepted by universities in the United Kingdom and Ireland. Camb. 1964.

Cont. by **1597.** See also U.S. Library of Congress (African section), *A list of American* doctoral dissertations on Africa, Wash. 1962; Jochen Kohn Köhler, *Deutsche Disserta-tionen über Afrika: ein Verzeichnis für die Jahre, 1918–1959*, Deutsche Afrika-Gesellschaft, Bonn 1962; and Marion Dinstel, comp., *Boston university libraries: list of French doctoral dissertations on Africa, 1884–1961*, Boston 1966.

1602  PEARSON (JAMES DOUGLAS) *ed.* A guide to manuscripts and documents in the British Isles relating to Africa. Comp. by Noel Matthews and Mary Doreen Wainwright. 1971.

Indispensable. Suppl. by Louis Benson Frewer, comp., *Manuscript collections of Africana in Rhodes House Library, Oxford*, Oxf. 1968, and Scottish Record Office, *Material relating to Africa in the Scottish Record Office*, 2 pts., Edin. 1965.

1603  ANENE (JOSEPH CHRISTOPHER) *and* BROWN (GODFREY NORMAN) *eds.* Africa in the nineteenth and twentieth centuries: a handbook for teachers and students. Lond. & Ibadan. 1966.

1604  MITCHELL (ROBERT CAMERON) *and* TURNER (HAROLD W.) *comps.* A comprehensive bibliography of modern African religious movements. Evanston, Ill. 1966.

1605  COUCH (MARGARET) *comp.* Education in Africa: a select bibliography. Part 1. British and former British territories in Africa. Univ. of Lond. Inst. of Educ. Education Libraries Bull. Suppl. V. 1962.

See also Howard Drake, comp., *A bibliography of African education south of the Sahara*, Aberdeen 1942, and University of London, Institute of Education, *Catalogue of the collection of education in tropical areas*, 3 v. Boston 1964.

1606  COLONIAL OFFICE. Bibliography of published sources relating to African land tenure. 1950.

1607  MEEK (CHARLES KINGSLEY). Colonial law: a bibliography with special reference to native African systems of law and land tenure. 1948.

1608  SCHOOL OF ORIENTAL AND AFRICAN STUDIES (UNIVERSITY OF LONDON). Bibliography of African law. Pt. 1. East Africa. 1961.

1609  HAILEY (WILLIAM MALCOLM), *Baron Hailey.* An African survey: a study of the problems arising in Africa south of the Sahara. 1938. 4th edn. 1970.

The nearest thing to an encyclopedia of Africa.

1610  AFRICAN ABSTRACTS: a quarterly review of ethnographic, social and linguistic studies appearing in current periodicals. Internat. African Inst. 1950+.

The following are the principal general journs. relating to Africa: *Africa: j. of the Inst. of African Languages and Culture* [*Internat. African Inst.*], 1928+, *J. of the Royal African Soc.* [*African affairs*], 1901+, *African studies*, Johannesburg 1942+, *Journal of African administration*, 1949+, and *Journal of Modern African studies*, 1963+. For African hist. see *Journal of African history*, 1960+, and *African historical studies*, Boston 1968+.

**1611** HERTSLET (*Sir* EDWARD) *ed.* The map of Africa by treaty. 2 v. 1894. 3rd edn. 3 v. 1909. Repr. 3 v. 1967.

Standard. John Donnelly Fage, *An atlas of African history*, 1958, is a useful short handbook.

(ii) *Other works*

**1612** OLIVER (ROLAND ANTHONY) *and* FAGE (JOHN DONNELLY). A short history of Africa. Harmondsworth. 1962. 2nd edn. 1968.

The best short intro. Other useful short hists. incl. Roland Anthony Oliver and Anthony Atmore, *Africa since 1800*, 1967; Basil Davidson, *Guide to African history*, Lond. 1963, Garden City, N.Y. 1965, and *Africa: history of a continent*, 1966, new edn. [*Africa in history: themes and outlines*] Lond. 1968, N.Y. 1969; and Robert Irwin Rotberg, *A political history of tropical Africa*, N.Y. [1965]. Endre Sík, *The history of black Africa*, trans. by Sándor Simon, 2 v. Budapest 1966, is interesting as an east European study. Peter James Michael McEwan, ed., *Readings in African history*, 3 v. 1968, is a series of extracts from scholarly and other writings.

**1613** VANSINA (JAN), MAUNY (RAYMOND), *and* THOMAS (L. V.) *eds.* The historian in tropical Africa: studies presented and discussed at the Fourth International African Seminar at the University of Dakar, Senegal, 1961. 1964.

See also *Historians in tropical Africa: proceedings of the Leverhulme Inter-Collegiate History Conference held at the University College of Rhodesia and Nyasaland, September 1960*, Salisbury 1962, Terence Osborn Ranger, ed., *Emerging themes of African history*, Nairobi 1968, and John Donnelly Fage ed., *Africa discovers her past*, 1970.

**1614** PERHAM (*Dame* MARGERY FREDA) *and* SIMMONS (JACK). African discovery: an anthology of exploration . . . 1942. Repr. 1963.

Much the best general account. See also **1693** and **8561-83**.

**1615** JOHNSTON (*Sir* HARRY HAMILTON). A history of the colonization of Africa by alien races. Camb. 1899. 2nd edn. 1913. Repr. 1930. Repr. N.Y. 1966.

A pioneer work, reflecting a strong sense of the European mission to bring enlightenment to Africa. Sir Charles Prestwood Lucas, *The partition and colonization of Africa*, Oxf. 1922, is in the same vein, but adds little.

**1616** GANN (LEWIS HENRY) *and* DUIGNAN (PETER) *eds.* Colonialism in Africa, 1870-1960. Vol. 1. The history and politics of colonialism, 1870-1914. Camb. 1969.

A collection of articles, not held together by any common theme. For protest movements against colonialism see Robert Irwin Rotberg and Ali Al'Amin Mazrui, eds., *Protest and power in black Africa*, N.Y. 1970. Gann and Duignan also publ. a tendentious general work, *Burden of empire: an appraisal of western colonialism in Africa south of the Sahara*, N.Y. 1967, new edn. Lond. 1968.

**1617** KELTIE (*Sir* JOHN SCOTT). The partition of Africa. 1893. 2nd edn. 1895.

Old, but still useful. For modern books on the partition of West Africa see **1805-6**.

1618  GIFFORD (PROSSER) *and* LOUIS (WILLIAM ROGER) *eds.*
Britain and Germany in Africa: imperial rivalry and colonial rule. New
Haven [Conn.]. 1967.

A useful symposium suppl. by their *France and Britain in Africa*, New Haven 1972.
See also Fritz Schwarze, *Das deutsch-englisch Abkommen über die portugiesischen Kolonien
vom 30 August 1898*, Göttingen 1931, and the works at **1728**. For British relations
with other powers see Jean Darcy, *France et angleterre: cent années de rivalité coloniale:
l'Afrique*, Paris 1904; Carlo Giglio, *La politica africana dell' Inghilterra nel XIX secolo*,
Padua 1950; Eric Victor Axelson, *Portugal and the scramble for Africa, 1875–1891*,
Johannesburg 1967; and Richard James Hammond, *Portugal and Africa, 1815–1910:
a study in uneconomic imperialism*, Stanford 1966.

1619  HATCH (JOHN CHARLES). The history of Britain in Africa: from
the fifteenth century to the present day. 1969.

1620  CURTIN (PHILIP DE ARMOND). The image of Africa: British
ideas and action, 1780–1850. Madison, Wis. 1964.

A very revealing book, though too early. See also Dorothy O. Helly, ' "Informed
opinion" on tropical Africa in Great Britain, 1860–1890', *African Affairs*, lxviii (1969),
195–217, and Bernard Porter (**971**).

1621  ROBINSON (RONALD EDWARD) *and* GALLAGHER (JOHN
ANDREW) *assisted by* DENNY (ALICE). Africa and the Victorians: the
official mind of imperialism. Lond. & N.Y. 1961.

Important. For the ideas involved see also **953–84**.

1622  HOLMBERG (ÅKE). African tribes and European agencies: colonialism
and humanitarianism in British south and east Africa, 1870–1895. Göteborg.
1966.

Intended to suppl. Robinson and Gallagher (**1621**), by recounting what was happening
'on the ground' in Africa.

1623  LOUIS (WILLIAM ROGER). 'Sir Percy Anderson's grand African
strategy, 1883–1896'. *Eng. Hist. Rev.* lxxxi (1966), 292–314.

Anderson was head of the African department of the Foreign Office.

1624  GILLARD (D. R.). 'Salisbury's African policy and the Heligoland offer
of 1890'. *Eng. Hist. Rev.* lxxv (1960), 631–53.

The views in this article were attacked in George Neville Sanderson, 'The Anglo-
German Agreement of 1890 and the Upper Nile', *Eng. Hist. Rev.* lxxviii (1963), 49–
72, and defended by Gillard in 'Salisbury's Heligoland offer: the case against the "Witu
thesis" ', ibid. lxxx (1965), 538–52. See also Alexander Sydney Kanya-Forstner,'French
African policy and the Anglo-French agreement of 5 August 1890', *Hist. J.* xii (1969),
628–50.

1625  JOHNSTON. Sir Harry Johnston & the scramble for Africa. By Roland
Anthony Oliver. 1957.

Johnston and Lugard (**1626**), were the leading British proconsuls in post-partition
Africa, and their influence was felt all over the continent. There is an earlier life,
Alexander Johnston, *The life and letters of Sir Harry Johnston*, 1929.

1626   LUGARD. Lugard: the years of adventure, 1858–1898: the first part of the life of Frederick Dealtry Lugard, later Lord Lugard of Abinger. By Dame Margery Freda Perham. 1956. Cont. in Lugard: the years of authority, 1898–1945 . . . 1960.

Magisterial. Much better than Arthur Alexander Malcolm Thompson and Dorothy Middleton, *Lugard in Africa*, 1959. For special aspects of Lugard's work see **1771 1868**, and **1870**. For Lugard's distinguished journalist wife see Enid Moberley Bell, *Flora Shaw (Lady Lugard, D.B.E.)*, 1948.

1627   BUELL (RAYMOND LESLIE). The native problem in Africa. 2 v. N.Y. 1928. Repr. 2 v. Lond. 1965.

A pioneer and far-reaching account of the problems of 'native administration'. See also Lucy Philip Mair, *Native policies in Africa*, 1936, and Dame Margery Freda Perham, *Native administration in Nigeria*, 1937.

1628   LUGARD (FREDERICK JOHN DEALTRY), *Baron Lugard*. The dual mandate in British tropical Africa. Edin. & Lond. 1922. 5th edn. by Dame Margery Freda Perham. 1965.

The case for indirect rule at its most forceful.

1629   MOYSE-BARTLETT (HUBERT). The King's African Rifles: a study in the military history of east and central Africa, 1890–1945. Aldershot. 1956.

A useful hist. of a notable British regiment recruited in Africa.

1630   RAPHAEL (LOIS ALWARD CHILDS). The Cape-to-Cairo dream: a study in British imperialism. N.Y. 1936.

1631   WEINTHAL (LEO) *ed.* The story of the Cape to Cairo railway and river route, from 1887 to 1922. 5 v. 1923–6.

1632   FRANKEL (SALLY HERBERT). Capital investment in Africa: its course and effects. 1938.

1633   GROVES (CHARLES PELHAM). The planting of Christianity in Africa. 4 v. 1948–58. Repr. 4 v. 1964.

A general hist. of African missions. For new work on African missions see Society for African Church Hist., *Bulletin*, Nsukka etc. 1963+. Frank Deaville Walker, *The call of the dark continent: a study in missionary progress, opportunity and urgency*, 1910, is a good contemp. Wesleyan work. For the 20th cent. the most important work on African missions has been assoc. with Bengt Gustaf Malcolm Sundkler, whose *The Christian ministry in Africa*, Uppsala 1960, sums up much earlier work.

1634   JONES (THOMAS JESSE) *ed.* Education in Africa: a study of west, south and equatorial Africa, by the African Education Commission, under the auspices of the Phelps–Stokes Fund and foreign missionary societies of north America and Europe. N.Y. 1922.

Suppl. by his *Education in east Africa: a study of east, central and south Africa by the second African Education Commission . . .*, N.Y. 1925.

**1635** LLOYD (CHRISTOPHER). The navy and the slave trade: the suppression of the African slave trade in the nineteenth century. 1949. Repr. 1968.

See also **1732**. The dimensions of the transatlantic slave trade are discussed in Philip De Armond Curtin, *The Atlantic slave trade: a census*, Madison, Wis. 1969.

#### (b) *Egypt and the Sudan*

For the diplomatic background see Robinson and Gallagher, (**1621**), and Sanderson (**1703**).

##### (i) *Egypt*

**1636** PRATT (IDA AUGUSTA) *comp*. Modern Egypt: a list of references to material in the New York Public Library. N.Y. 1929.

Prince Ibrahim Hilmy, *The literature of Egypt and the Soudan from the earliest times to the year 1885 inclusive: a bibliography* . . ., 2 v. 1886–7, repr. 2 v. Nendeln, Liechtenstein 1966, adds little.

**1637** MAUNIER (RENÉ). Bibliographie économique, juridique et sociale de l'Égypte moderne (1798–1916). Cairo. 1918.

There is also Charles Davies Sherborn, comp., *Bibliography of scientific and technical literature relating to Egypt, 1800–1900*, Cairo 1910.

**1638** HOLT (PETER MALCOLM). Egypt and the fertile crescent, 1516–1922: a political history. Lond. & Ithaca, N.Y. 1966.

**1639** VATIKIOTIS (PANAYIOTIS JERASIMOF). The modern history of Egypt. Lond. & N.Y. 1969.

A useful 1-vol. hist. Robert O. Collins and Robert L. Tignor, *Egypt & the Sudan*, Englewood Cliffs, N.J. 1967, is a short but up-to-date general hist.

**1640** HOLT (PETER MALCOLM) *ed*. Political and social change in modern Egypt: historical studies from the Ottoman conquest to the United Arab Republic. Lond. & N.Y. 1968.

A very valuable symposium. See also **1652**.

**1641** ROWLATT (MARY). Founders of modern Egypt. 1962.

An account, based on family papers, of the occupation of 1882 and its background. For assessments of conditions in Egypt, before and after the British occupation, from the British point of view, see Sir Donald Mackenzie Wallace, *Egypt and the Egyptian question*, 1883; Sir Edward Dicey, *England and Egypt*, 1881, new edn. 1907, and *The story of the Khedivate*, 1902; William Blanchard Jerrold, ed., *Egypt under Ismail Pasha* . . ., 1879; and [Charles Frederic Moberly Bell], *Khedives and pashas: sketches of contemporary Egyptian rulers and statesmen*, 1884. For French views of the situation in Egypt see Georges Douin, *Histoire du règne du khédive Ismaïl*, 3 pts. in 6 v. Rome 1933–41; Achille Biovès, *Français et Anglais en Égypte, 1881–1882*, Paris 1910; and **1642**. For Italian views see Angelo Sammarco, *Histoire d'Égypte moderne depuis Mohammed Ali jusqu'à l'occupation britannique, 1801–1882, d'après les documents originaux égyptiens et étrangers*, Cairo 1937, and Lucien E. Roberts, 'Italy and the Egyptian question, 1878–1882', *J. Mod. Hist.* xviii (1946), 314–32. For a German view see Maximilian von Hagen, *England und Ägypten: Materialien zur Geschichte der britischen-Okkupation mit besonderer Rücksicht auf Bismarcks Ägypten-politik*, Bonn 1915. Mohammed

Sabry, *Épisode de la question d'Afrique: l'empire égyptien sous Ismaïl et l'ingérence anglo-française, 1863–1879* . . ., Paris 1933, and *Le genèse de l'esprit national égyptien, 1863–1882*, Paris 1924, and Pierre Crabitès, *Ismail: the maligned khedive*, 1933, add little.

**1642   LANDES (DAVID SAUL).** Bankers and pashas: international finance and economic imperialism in Egypt. 1958.
Chiefly on French financiers, but important for the financial background of the khedival regime.

**1643   BLUNT (WILFRID SCAWEN).** Secret history of the English occupation of Egypt: being, a personal narrative of events. 2 v. 1907.
The erratic but invaluable record of the chief British opponent of the occupation. Cont. by his *Gordon at Khartoum* (**1694**), and suppl. by his *Diaries* (**305**). For one of Blunt's allies see Alexander Meyrick Broadley, *How we defended Arabi and his friends: a story of Egypt and the Egyptians*, 1884.

**1644   MAURICE (*Sir* JOHN FREDERICK).** Military history of the campaign of 1882 in Egypt. War Office. 1887. New edn. 1908.
The best account of the campaign. But see also Caspar Frederick Goodrich, *Report of the British naval and military operations in Egypt, 1882*, 2 pts., U.S. Navy Department, War Ser. 3, Wash. 1883; Sir Charles Cameron, *A romance of war: or, how the cash goes in campaigning, compiled from evidence given before the select committee on the recent Egyptian campaign*, 1884; Sir William Francis Butler, *Journal of operations: expedition to Egypt, 1882*, 1883; George Lionel Brackenridge Killick, *The English army in Egypt, 1882* [bound with M. Vertray, *The French army in Egypt, 1798–1801*], [1899]; A German Field Officer, *The English military power and the Egyptian campaign of 1882*, 1883; Herman Vogt, *The Egyptian war of 1882*, 1883; Charles Royle, *The Egyptian campaigns, 1882 to 1885, and the events which led to them*, 2 v. 1886, rev. edn. 1900; William Stephen, ed., *Our Highlanders in Egypt: the great victory at Tel-el-Kebir, chiefly as described by themselves*, Edin. 1882, 2nd edn. 1882.

**1645   ABD AL-RAHMAN AL-RAFII.** Al-thaurat al-Arabiyah wa'l-ihtilal al-injlizi. [The Arabi revolt and the English occupation.] Cairo. 1937.
This work and Abd al-Rahman al-Rafii's '*Asr Isma'ili* [The period of Ismail Pasha], 2 pts. Cairo 1932, and *Misr wa'l-sudan fi awa'il 'abd al-ihtilal* [Egypt and the Sudan at the time of the British occupation, 1886–92], Cairo 1948, give an Egyptian nationalist view of the British occupation.

**1646   MARLOWE (JOHN).** Anglo-Egyptian relations, 1800–1953. 1954. 2nd edn. 1965.
Publ. in America as *A history of modern Egypt and Anglo-Egyptian relations* . . ., N.Y. 1954, 2nd edn. Hamden, Conn. 1965. See also T. B. Miller, 'The Egyptian question and British foreign policy, 1892–1894', *J. Mod. Hist.* xxxii (1960), 1–15.

**1647   FABUNMI (LAWRENCE APALARA).** The Sudan in Anglo-Egyptian relations: a case study in power politics, 1800–1956. 1960.
See also **1691**.

**1648   MATHEWS (JOSEPH JAMES).** Egypt and the formation of the Anglo-French entente of 1904. Phila. 1939.
See also Charles Louis de Saulses de Freycinet, *La question d'Égypte*, Paris 1905, and Étienne Velay, *Les rivalités franco-anglaises en Égypte, 1876–1904*, Nîmes 1904.

Italian influence is covered by Angelo Sammarco, *Gli Italiani in Egitto: il contributo italiano nella formazione dell'Egitto moderno*, Alexandria 1937.

**1649 BARING (EVELYN), Earl of Cromer. Modern Egypt. 2 v. 1908. New edn. 1911.**

A famous account of Egypt under British control, by the chief British representative. Cont. by George Ambrose Lloyd, Baron Lloyd of Dolobron, *Egypt since Cromer*, 2 v. 1933–4, repr. 2 v. N.Y. 1970. Two similar works were prepared earlier by English officials: Alfred Milner, Viscount Milner, *England in Egypt*, 1892, 11th edn. 1904, and Sir Auckland Colvin, *The making of modern Egypt*, 1906. Both are good reading. Sir Sidney James Mark Low, *Egypt in transition*, 1914, belongs to the same tradition. A more detached view may be found in Juliette Adam, formerly Lamber, *L'Angleterre en Égypte*, Paris 1922.

**1650 BARING (EVELYN), Earl of Cromer, and others. Report on the administration and condition of Egypt and the progress of reforms, dated March 29, 1891. [C. 6321] H.C. (1890–1). XCVII, 717.**

The first annual report to claim to cover more than finance. Subsequent reports styled *Report on the administration, finances and condition of Egypt . . .*, with some variations, to 1924+.

**1651 AFAF LUTFI AL-SAYYID. Egypt and Cromer: a study in Anglo-Egyptian relations. 1968.**

See also John Marlowe, *Cromer in Egypt*, 1970, and **1673**. Edward Roger John Owen, 'The influence of Lord Cromer's Indian experience on British policy in Egypt, 1883–1907', *St. Antony's papers 17: Middle Eastern affairs 4* (1965), 109–39, Robert L. Tignor, 'The "Indianization" of the Egyptian administration under British rule', *Amer. Hist. Rev.* lxviii (1962–3), 636–61, and Édouard Méra, *Une page de politique coloniale: Lord Cromer en Égypte, 1883–1907*, Paris 1913, deal with aspects of Cromer's policy.

**1652 TIGNOR (ROBERT L.). Modernization and British colonial rule in Egypt, 1882–1914. Princeton [N.J.]. 1966.**

**1653 LANDAU (JACOB M.). Parliaments and parties in Egypt, [1866–1924]. Tel Aviv. 1953. N.Y. 1954.**

Useful. There are no adequate monographs on the organization of the nationalist movement. Mahmud Yusuf Zayid, *Egypt's struggle for independence*, Beirut 1965, is only an outline, as is Mohammed Rifaat, *The awakening of modern Egypt*, 1947, repr. Lahore [1964].

**1654 HOURANI (ALBERT HABIB). Arabic thought in the liberal age, 1798–1939. 1962.**

The starting-point for any study of Egyptian thought.

**1655 AHMED (JAMAL MOHAMMED). The intellectual origins of Egyptian nationalism. 1960.**

See also Charles Clarence Adams, *Islam and modernism in Egypt: a study of the modern reform movement inaugurated by Muhammad Abduh*, 1933. For Muhammad Abduh see **1677**.

1656 SAFRAN (NADAV). Egypt in search of political community . . . Camb., Mass. 1961.

1657 ZIADEH (FARHAT JACOB). Lawyers, the rule of law and liberalism in modern Egypt. Stanford [Calif.]. 1968.

1658 O'ROURKE (VERNON ALFRED). The juristic status of Egypt and the Sudan. Baltimore [Md.]. 1935.

Better than Jules Cocheris, *La situation internationale de l'Égypte et du Sudan, juridique et politique*, Paris 1903.

1659 BRINTON (JASPER YEATES). The mixed courts of Egypt. New Haven [Conn.]. 1930. Rev. edn. 1968.

See also James Harry Scott, *The law affecting foreigners in Egypt as the result of the capitulations: with an account of their origin and development*, Edin. 1907, rev. edn. 1908, and Philippe Gémayel, *Un régime qui meurt: les capitulations en Égypte*, Paris 1938.

1660 CROUCHLEY (ARTHUR EDWIN). The economic development of modern Egypt. Lond. etc. 1938.

A brief outline hist. May be suppl. by his *The investment of foreign capital in Egyptian companies and public debt*, Cairo 1936; Abdel-Maksud Hamza, *The public debt of Egypt, 1854–1876*, Cairo 1944; Mohammed Ali Rifaat, *The monetary system of Egypt: an inquiry into its history and present working*, 1935; and Gabriel Baer, *A history of land ownership in modern Egypt, 1800–1950*, 1962.

1661 OWEN (EDWARD ROGER JOHN). Cotton and the Egyptian economy, 1820–1914: a study in trade and development. Oxf. 1969.

Good. See also his 'Lord Cromer and the development of Egyptian industry, 1883–1907', *Middle Eastern Studs.* ii (1965–6), 282–301. François Charles-Roux, *La production du coton en Égypte*, Paris 1908, is now out of date.

1662 SOCIETY OF COMPARATIVE LEGISLATION AND INTERNATIONAL LAW. The Suez canal: a selection of documents relating to the international status of the Suez canal and the position of the Suez Canal Company, Nov. 30, 1854–July 26, 1956. 1956.

1663 WILSON (*Sir* ARNOLD TALBOT). The Suez canal: its past, present and future. 1933. 2nd edn. Lond. & N.Y. 1939.

See also John Marlowe, *The making of the Suez canal*, 1964; Douglas Antony Farnie, *East and West of Suez: the Suez canal in history, 1854–1956*, Oxf. 1969; Charles William Hallberg, *The Suez canal: its history and diplomatic importance*, N.Y. 1931; Angelo Sammarco, *Suez: storia e problemi secondo documenti inediti egiziani ed europei*, Milan 1943, and K. Bell, 'British policy towards the construction of the Suez Canal, 1859–65', *Roy. Hist. Soc. Trans.*, 5 ser. 15 (1965) 121–44.

1664 WILLCOCKS (*Sir* WILLIAM). Egyptian irrigation. 1889. 3rd edn. by James Ireland Craig. 2 v. Lond. & N.Y. 1913.

By the chief British engineer in Egypt. See also his *The Nile in 1904*, 1904, and *Sixty years in the east* . . ., Edin. & Lond. 1935. For the Nile waters see also Harold Edwin Hurst, *The Nile: a general account of the river and the utilization of its waters*, 1952, rev. edn. 1957.

1665  SANDES (EDWARD WARREN CAULFEILD). The Royal Engineers in Egypt and the Sudan. Chatham. 1937.

1666  HEYWORTH-DUNNE (JAMES). An introduction to the history of education in modern Egypt. [1939.] Repr. 1968.

1667  GWYNNE. Pastor of the Nile: being, some account of the life and letters of Llewellyn H. Gwynne, C.M.G., C.B.E., D.D., LL.D., formerly bishop in Egypt and the Sudan . . . By Henry Cecil Jackson. 1960.

1668  MIKHAIL (KYRIAKOS). Copts and Moslems under British control: a collection of facts and a résumé of authoritative opinions on the Coptic question. 1911.

See also Jacob M. Landau, *The Jews in nineteenth-century Egypt* [in Hebrew], Jerusalem 1967.

1669  BOWMAN. Middle East window. By Humphrey Ernest Bowman. 1942.

Memoirs of a British official in Egypt, 1903–11, the Sudan, 1911–13, etc.

1670  BOYLE. Boyle of Cairo: a diplomatist's adventures in the middle east. By Clara Asch Boyle. Kendal. 1965.

An extended version of the Egyptian sections of Clara Boyle, *A servant of empire: a memoir of Harry Boyle,* 1938.

1671  CECIL. The leisure of an Egyptian official. By Lord Edward Herbert Gascoyne-Cecil. [1921.]

1672  COLES. Recollections and reflections by Coles Pasha [Charles Edward Coles], C.M.G., late inspector-general of prisons, Egypt. [1919.]

1673  CROMER. Lord Cromer: being the authorized life of Evelyn Baring, first Earl of Cromer. By Lawrence John Lumley Dundas, Marquess of Zetland. 1932.

There is also a poor life by Henry Duff Traill, *Lord Cromer: a biography,* 1897, and John Marlowe, *Cromer in Egypt,* 1970.

1674  KUSEL. An Englishman's recollections of Egypt, 1863 to 1887, with an epilogue dealing with the present time, 1914: by Baron de Kusel (Bey), sometime English Controller-General of Egyptian Customs, etc. Lond. & N.Y. 1915.

1675  MALET. Egypt, 1879–1883. By Sir Edward Malet. Ed. by Thomas Henry Sanderson, Baron Sanderson. Priv. pr. 1909.

Malet was British representative in Egypt in the years covered.

1676  MARSHALL. The Egyptian enigma, 1890–1928. By John Edwin Marshall. 1928.

The memoirs of an anti-Egyptian British official.

1677 MUHAMMAD ABDUH. Muhammad Abduh . . . By Uthman Amin. Trans. by Charles Wendell. Wash. 1953.

Largely repl. by Malcolm H. Kerr, *Islamic reform: the political and legal theories of Muhammud Abduh and Rashid Rida*, Berkeley, etc. 1966. See also Elie Kedourie, *Afghani and 'Abduh: an essay on religious unbelief and political activism in modern Islam*, 1966.

1678 MUHAMMAD FARID. Muhammad Farid ramz al-ikhlas wa'l-tadhiyah. [Muhammad Farid and his part in the social history of Egypt, 1908–1919.] By Abd al-Rahman al-Rafii. Cairo. 1948.

1679 MUSTAFA KAMIL. Mustafa Kamil bā'ith al-harakat al-wataniyah. [Mustafa Kamil, animator of the national movement.] By Abd al-Rahman al-Rafii. Cairo. 1939.

Mustafa Kamil publ. an interesting account of his views in French, *Égyptiens et Anglais*, Paris 1906. Fritz Steppat, *Nationalismus und Islam bei Mustafa Kamil: ein Beitrag zur Ideengeschichte der ägyptischen Nationalbewegung*, in *Die Welt des Islams*, new ser. iv, no. 4, Leiden 1956, is a handy short account.

1680 RUSSELL. Egyptian service, 1902–1946. By Sir Thomas Wentworth Russell. 1949.

1681 SA'D ZAGHLUL. Sa'd Zaghlul sirah wa-tahiyah. [Biography, etc. of Sa'd Zaghlul.] By Abbas Mahmud al-Aqqad. Cairo. 1936.

1682 STORRS. Orientations. By Sir Ronald Henry Amherst Storrs. 1937. New edn. 1943. [Publ. in N.Y. as The memoirs of Sir Ronald Storrs. 1937.]

1683 VIZETELLY. From Cyprus to Zanzibar by the Egyptian delta: the adventures of a journalist. By Edward Vizetelly. 1901.

Chiefly interesting on the early 1880s.

(ii) *The Sudan*

See also under Egypt. The reports of the British representatives in Egypt covered the Sudan, as did Cromer's *Modern Egypt* (**1649**).

1684 HILL (RICHARD LESLIE). A bibliography of the Anglo-Egyptian Sudan from the earliest times to 1937. 1939.

Cont. by Abdel Rahman El Nasri, *A bibliography of the Sudan, 1938–1958*, 1962. For later works see *Sudan notes and records*, 1+, Khartoum 1918+. The most important archive sources are Central Archives of the Republic of the Sudan in Khartoum and the Sudan Archive in the School of Oriental Studies, Durham. The British parl. papers (**30**) include correspondence and reports on the various Sudan campaigns.

1685 HILL (RICHARD LESLIE). A biographical dictionary of the Anglo-Egyptian Sudan. Oxf. 1951. 2nd edn. Lond. 1967.

1686 GLEICHEN (ALBERT EDWARD WILFRED), *Count, afterwards Lord, ed.* The Anglo-Egyptian Sudan: a compendium prepared by officers of the Sudan government. 2 v. H.M.S.O. 1905–6.

A detailed survey by the Intelligence Dept., which became a substitute for an encyclopedia: based on the earlier *Handbook of the Sudan*, 1898, ed. by Gleichen and printed at the War Office. The War Office also issued *Report on the Egyptian provinces of the Sudan, Red Sea and Equator*, 1883, 2nd edn. rev. up to July 1884, 1885, which also contains useful material.

1687 SUDAN INTELLIGENCE REPORTS, 1892–1903. Comp. by Egyptian Military Intelligence Dept., Cairo. Repr. Khartoum. 3 v. [1968.]

A summary of the intelligence files now in the Sudan government archives, which are the most important single source of information about conditions in the various parts of the Sudan during the period, 1892–1914.

1688 GOVERNOR-GENERAL OF THE SUDAN. Annual report. 1898–1951/2.

Publ. as a parl. paper, from 1898 to 1920, in the form of an annual report styled *Report by her majesty's agent and consul-general on the finances, administration and condition of Egypt and the Soudan in 1898+*.

1689 HOLT (PETER MALCOLM). A modern history of the Sudan: from the Funj sultanate to the present day. 1961. 2nd edn. 1963.

A good general hist. Other good general hists. written from a British point of view are Kenneth David Druitt Henderson, *Survey of the Anglo-Egyptian Sudan, 1898–1944*, 1946, and *Sudan republic*, 1965, and Sir Harold Alfred MacMichael, *The Anglo-Egyptian Sudan*, 1934, and *The Sudan*, 1954. There is also a good German survey, Walter Krämer, *Die koloniale Entwicklung des Anglo-Ägyptischen Sudans*, Berlin 1938. Alternative interpretations have been slow to emerge. See particularly Muddathir 'Abd Al-Rahim, (**1711**), and Mandour el-Mahdi, *A short history of the Sudan*, 1965. For the Arabs in the Sudan there are two good general works, Sir Harold Alfred MacMichael, *A history of the Arabs in the Sudan . . .*, 2 v. Camb. 1922, and John Spencer Trimingham, *Islam in the Sudan*, 1949. For the south, Mohamed Omer Beshir, *The southern Sudan: background to conflict*, 1968, is valuable. The best of the old imperialist hists. is Pierre Crabitès, *The winning of the Sudan*, 1934.

1690 SUDAN NOTES AND RECORDS. Khartoum. 1918+.

A good hist. journ. For anthropology and antiquities consult also *Kush: journal of the Sudan Antiquities Service*, Khartoum 1953+.

1691 HILL (RICHARD LESLIE). Egypt in the Sudan, 1820–1881. 1959.

A good survey. See also L. A. Fabunmi (**1647**), Muhammad Fu'ad Shukri, *The Khedive Ismail and slavery in the Sudan, 1863–1879: a history of the Sudan from the Egyptian conquest of 1820 to the outbreak of the Mahdiist rebellion in 1881, with special reference to British policy and the work of Sir Samuel Baker and Charles George Gordon*, Cairo 1930, and *Equatoria under Egyptian rule: the unpublished correspondence of Col. (afterwards Major-Gen.) C. G. Gordon, with Ismaïl, Khedive of Egypt and the Sudan, during the years 1874–1876*, Cairo 1953, Mohammed Sabry, *Le Soudan égyptien, 1821–1898*, Cairo 1947, and Richard Buchta, *Der Sudan unter ägyptischer Herrschaft . . .*, Leipzig 1888.

1692 GRAY ([JOHN] RICHARD). A history of the southern Sudan, 1839–1889. 1961.

**1693** MOOREHEAD (ALAN McCRAE). The White Nile. 1960. New edn. 1963.

A good popular account of Nile exploration. Suppl. by his (equally good) *The Blue Nile*, 1962, new edn. 1964. An older but good account was Sir Harry Hamilton Johnston, *The Nile quest* . . ., 1903. For the major explorers see **8575–83**. There are numerous minor travel books about the Nile and its tributaries which were still being explored down to 1914. Among the more useful are Wilhelm Johann Junker, *Travels in Africa during the years 1875–[86]*, trans. by Augustus Henry Keane, 3 v. 1890–2, David Charles Edward Ffrench Comyn, *Service and sport in the Sudan* . . ., 1911, Edward Fothergill, *Five years in the Sudan*, 1910, and the more comprehensive guidebooks such as Ernest Alfred Thompson Wallis Budge, *The Egyptian Sudan: its history and monuments*, 2 v. 1907, and Hermann Karl Wilhelm Kumm, *The Sudan: a short compendium of facts and figures about the land of darkness*, [1907] 2nd edn. [?1909].

**1694** GORDON. Gordon and the Sudan. By Bernard Meredith Allen. 1931.

The best book on the subject. Richard Leslie Hill, 'The Gordon literature', *Durham Univ. J.* new ser. xvi (1954–5), 97–103, is a thin essay. For lives of Gordon see also John Marlowe, *Mission to Khartum: the apotheosis of General Gordon*, 1969; Hugh Evelyn Wortham, *Gordon: an intimate portrait*, 1933; Pierre Crabitès, *Gordon, the Sudan and slavery*, 1933; John Buchan, Baron Tweedsmuir, *Gordon at Khartoum*, 1934; Godfrey Elton, Baron Elton, *General Gordon*, 1954; Charles Beatty, *His country was the world: a study of Gordon of Khartoum*, 1954; [Edward] Gerald French, *Gordon Pasha of the Sudan* . . ., Glasgow 1958; and Gerald Sparrow, *Gordon: mandarin and pasha*, 1962. For the policy behind the Gordon mission see Sanderson (**1703**) and Robinson, Gallagher, and Denny (**1621**). For Gordon's correspondence see George Birkbeck Norman Hill, ed., *Colonel Gordon in Central Africa, 1874–1879*, 1881, 2nd edn. 1884, *Letters of General C. G. Gordon to his sister M. A. Gordon*, 1888; Shukri, *Equatoria under Egyptian rule* (**1691**); and Demetrius Charles de Kavanagh Boulger, ed., *General Gordon's letters from the Crimea, the Danube and Armenia . . . 1854 to . . . 1858*, 1884. For events at Khartoum itself see Alfred Egmont-Hake, ed., *The journals of Major-Gen. C. G. Gordon, C.B., at Khartoum*, Lond., Boston, & N.Y. 1885, and reprs., Gordon's reports to Cairo publ. as C. P. Stone, ed., *Provinces of the equator: summary of letters and reports of the governor general*, 2 pts. Cairo 1874–7, and Frank Power, *Letters from Khartoum written during the siege*, 1885, 3rd edn. 1885. Wilfrid Scawen Blunt, *Gordon at Khartoum: being a personal narrative of events* . . ., 1911, is a cont. of his Egyptian journals (**1643**).

**1695** ZAGHI (CARLO). Gordon, Gessi e la riconquista del Sudan, 1874–1881: documenti inediti . . . Florence. 1947.

See also Romolo Gessi, *Seven years in the Soudan* . . ., ed. by Felice Gessi, 1892, Carlo Zaghi, *Vita di Romolo Gessi*, Milan 1939, and Luigi Messedaglia, *Uomini d'Africa: Messedaglia bey e gli altri collaboratori italiani di Gordon pascià*, Bologna 1935.

**1696** HOLT (PETER MALCOLM). The mahdist state in the Sudan, 1881–1898: a study of its origins, development and overthrow. Oxf. 1958. 2nd edn. 1970.

A good book based on sources set out by Holt in *Sudan notes and records*, xxxvi (1955), 71–80, *School of Oriental & African Studies Bull.* xviii (1956), 227–38, and *St Antony's papers 4: Middle Eastern affairs 1* (1958), 107–18. For the Mahdiya generally see Alan Buchan Theobald, *The Mahdiya: a history of the Anglo-Egyptian Sudan, 1881–1899*, 1951; Sir Francis Reginald Wingate, *Mahdiism and the Egyptian Sudan* . . ., Lond. & N.Y. 1891, 2nd edn. 1898, new edn. 1968; Gaston Dujarrie, *L'état mahdiste du Soudan*, Paris 1901; and Na'um Shuqair [Naum Shoucair Bey], *The history and geography of the Sudan* [In Arabic (*Ta'rikh al-Sudan* . . .)], Cairo 1903, part of which has been trans. into German in Ernst Ludwig Dietrich, 'Der Mahdi Mohammed Ahmad vom Sudan nach arabischen Quellen', *Der Islam*, xiv (1925), 197–288. There is a specialized literature on life under the Mahdiya written by Europeans, much of it summarized in Byron Farwell, *Prisoners of the Mahdi: the story of the Mahdist revolt from the fall of Khartoum to the reconquest of the Sudan by Kitchener fourteen years later, and of the daily lives and sufferings in captivity of three European prisoners, a soldier, a merchant and a priest*, 1967. The main works are Sir Francis Reginald Wingate, ed. and trans., *Ten years' captivity in the Mahdi's camp, 1882–1892: from the original manuscripts of Father Joseph Ohrwalder*, 1892, also available in German, 2 v. Leipzig etc. 1893; Sir Rudolf Carl Slatin, *Fire and sword in the Sudan: a personal narrative of fighting and serving the dervishes 1879–1895*, trans. by Sir Francis Reginald Wingate, Lond. & Camb. 1896; and Carl Neufeld, *A prisoner of the Khaleefa: twelve years' captivity at Omdurman*, 1899.

1697   WHITE (STANHOPE). Lost empire on the Nile: H. M. Stanley, Emin Pasha and the imperialists. Lond. & N.Y. 1969.

1698   EMIN. Emin Pasha: his life and work, compiled from his journals, letters, scientific notes and from official documents by Georg Schweitzer. Ed. by R. W. Felkin. 2 v. 1898. New edn. 2 v. N.Y. 1969.

Emin's real name was Eduard Carl Oscar Theodor Schnitzer. *Die Tagebücher von Dr. Emin Pascha*, ed. by Franz Stuhlmann, 6 v. Hamburg 1916–27, is an important doc. for the hist. of the southern Sudan, as is Georg Schweinfurth and others, eds., *Emin Pasha in Central Africa: being a collection of his letters and journals*, trans. by Mrs. R. W. Felkin, 1888. There are several popular lives. For Emin's unwilling 'rescue' see Sir Henry Morton Stanley, *In darkest Africa: or the quest, rescue and retreat of Emin, Governor of Equatoria*, 2 v. 1890; Sir John Scott Keltie, ed., *The Story of Emin's rescue as told in Stanley's letters*, Boston, N.Y. etc. 1890; Arthur J. Mounteney-Jephson, *Emin Pasha and the rebellion at the equator*, 1890; Dorothy Middleton and Maurice Denham Jephson, eds., *The diary of A. J. Mounteney Jephson: Emin Pasha relief expedition, 1887–1899*, Hakluyt Soc., Camb. 1969; and Iain R. Smith, *The Emin Pasha relief expedition, 1886–1890*, Oxf. 1972.

1699   OSMAN DIGNA. Osman Digna. By Henry Cecil Jackson. 1926.

1700   SLATIN. Slatin Pasha. By Richard Leslie Hill. 1965.

1701   SHIBEIKA (MEKKI E. T.). British policy in the Sudan, 1882–1902. 1952.

A good book by a distinguished Sudanese. Much better than Ettore Anchieri, *Storia della politica inglese nel Sudan, 1882–1938*, Milan 1939.

1702   ABBAS (MEKKI). The Sudan question: the dispute over the Anglo-Egyptian condominium, 1884–1951. 1952.

See also Gabriel Warburg, 'The Sudan, Egypt and Britain, 1899–1916', *Middle Eastern Studs.* vi (1970), 163–78, and **1647**.

1703   SANDERSON (GEORGE NEVILLE). England, Europe and the Upper Nile, 1882–99: a study in the partition of Africa. Edin. 1965.

An important study of the diplomacy of the Nile question, including the Fashoda incident.

1704 COLLINS (ROBERT OAKLEY). The southern Sudan, 1883–1898: a struggle for control. New Haven [Conn.]. 1962.
Cont. by his *Land beyond the rivers: the southern Sudan, 1898–1918,* New Haven, Conn. 1971.

1705 COLLINS (ROBERT OAKLEY). King Leopold, England and the Upper Nile, 1899–1909. New Haven [Conn.]. 1968.

1706 BUJAC ([JEAN LEOPOLD] ÉMILE). Égypte et Soudan. Précis de quelques campagnes contemporaines. III. Paris. [1899.]
A series of battle summaries covering the various Sudan campaigns.

1707 SYMONS (JULIAN). England's pride: the story of the Gordon relief expedition. 1965.
A popular account making use of such contemp. works as Wolseley's journals (**1708**); Sir Henry Edward Colvile, *History of the Sudan campaign,* 3 pts. War Office 1889 (the best military account); Sir William Francis Butler, *The campaign of the cataracts: being a personal narrative of the great Nile expedition of 1884–5,* 1887; John Colborne, *With Hicks Pasha in the Soudan: being an account of the Senaar campaign in 1883,* 1884, 2nd edn. 1885; Thomas Archer, *The war in Egypt and the Soudan . . .,* 4 v. [1885–7]; Sir Charles William Wilson, *From Korti to Khartum: a journal of the desert march . . .,* 1885, 4th edn. 1886; Ernest Gambier-Parry, *Suakin, 1885 . . .,* 1885, 2nd edn. 1886; J. L. Robertson, *Suakin expeditionary force, 1885 . . .,* 1885; William Harcourt Sawyer, *Diary of the Suakin expedition, 1885 . . .,* 1885; Emilius Albert De Cosson, *Days and nights of service with Sir Gerald Graham's field force at Suakin,* 1886; William Galloway, *The battle of Tofrek fought near Suakin, March 22nd, 1885 . . .,* 1887, Count, afterwards Lord, Albert Edward Wilfred Gleichen, *With the camel corps up the Nile,* 2nd edn. 1888; James Grant, *Cassell's history of the war in the Soudan,* 6 v. [1885–6]; W. Melville Pimblett, *Story of the Soudan War . . .,* 1885; and Augustus Blandy Wylde, *'83 to '87 in the Soudan . . .,* 2 v. 1888.

1708 WOLSELEY (GARNET JOSEPH), *Viscount Wolseley.* In relief of Gordon. Lord Wolseley's campaign journal of the Khartoum relief expedition, 1884–1885. Ed. by Adrian Preston. Lond. 1967. Rutherford, N.J. 1970.

1709 WAR OFFICE (INTELLIGENCE BRANCH). Reports on the Nile expedition, 1884–85, by officers who took part in the operations. 1885.
The War Office publ. a great deal of *Correspondence respecting the affairs of the Sudan* and *Correspondence respecting British military operations in the Soudan* and a number of reports, for which see the *General index* of parl. papers (**33**). Further reports for internal use are in the War Office Libr.

1710 CHURCHILL (*Sir* WINSTON LEONARD SPENCER-). The river war: an historical account of the reconquest of the Sudan. 1899. 2nd edn. 1902. Repr. 1951.
The best contemp. book about Kitchener's campaign, which attracted a considerable number of war correspondents. For other accounts see Andrew Hilliard Atteridge, *Towards Khartoum: the story of the Soudan war of 1896 . . .,* 1897; Sir Ernest Nathaniel Bennett, *The downfall of the dervishes, being a sketch of the final Sudan campaign of 1898,* 1898; Bennet Burleigh, *Khartoum campaign, 1898 . . .,* 1899, and *Sirdar and Khalifa . . .,* 1898; Edward Frederick Knight, *Letters from the Sudan . . ., 1896,* 1897; H. C. Seppings Wright, *Soudan, '96: the adventures of a war artist,* 1897; and Granville George

Algernon Egerton, *With the 72nd Highlanders in the Sudan campaign of 1898*, 1909. The most popular book at the time was George Warrington Steevens, *With Kitchener to Khartum*, Edin. & Lond. 1898, which sold prolifically. The Sudan campaign also led to the production of a number of general books, notably Henry Stamford Lewis Alford and William Dennistoun Sword, *The Egyptian Soudan: its loss and recovery*, 1898, and Henry Duff Traill, *England, Egypt and the Sudan*, 1900.

1711 MUDDATHIR 'ABD AL-RAHIM. Imperialism and nationalism in the Sudan: a study in constitutional and political development, 1899–1956. Oxf. 1969.

1712 WINGATE. Wingate of the Sudan: the life and times of General Sir Reginald Wingate . . . By Sir Ronald Evelyn Leslie Wingate. 1955.

Wingate was Governor-General of the Sudan, 1899–1916, and a remarkable man. See also Gabriel Warburg, *The Sudan under Wingate: administration in the Anglo-Egyptian Sudan, 1899–1916*, 1971. There are interesting contrasts with the life of a later Sudanese administrator in Kenneth David Druitt Henderson, *The making of the modern Sudan: the life and letters of Sir Douglas Newbold*, 1953.

1713 STONE (JOHN). Sudan economic development, 1899–1913. Khartoum. 1955.

1714 STONE (JOHN). The finance of government economic development in the Sudan, 1899 to 1913. Khartoum. 1954.

1715 MARTIN (PERCY FALCKE). The Sudan in evolution: a study of the economic, financial and administrative conditions of the Anglo-Egyptian Sudan. 1921.

See also Richard Leslie Hill, *Sudan transport: a history of railway, marine and river services . . .*, 1965; John Douglas Tothill, *Agriculture in the Sudan . . .*, 1948; John Harold George Lebon, *Land use in Sudan*, Bude, Cornwall 1965; and K. M. Barbour, 'Population shifts and changes in the Sudan since 1898', *Middle Eastern Studs.* ii (1965–6), 98–122.

1716 GARSTIN (*Sir* WILLIAM EDMUND). Report on the Sudan. [C. 9332] H.C. (1899). CXII, 925.

Garstin was chief engineer in Egypt and cont. his inquiries in reports on irrigation projects on the Upper Nile, publ. as [Cd. 672] H.C. (1901). XCI, 1149, and [Cd. 2165] H.C. (1904). CXI, 309.

1717 HILL (RICHARD LESLIE). 'Government and Christian missions in the Anglo-Egyptian Sudan, 1899–1914', *Middle Eastern Studs.* i (1964–5), 113–34.

1718 BESHIR (MOHAMED OMER). Educational development in the Sudan, 1898–1956. Oxf. 1969.

(c) *East and North-East Africa*

(i) *General*

1719 CONOVER (HELEN FIELD) *comp.* British east and central Africa . . . U.S. Libr. of Congress. Wash. 1942.

1720 THE HISTORY OF EAST AFRICA. Vol. I ed. by Roland Anthony Oliver and Gervase Mathew. Oxf. 1963. Vol. II ed. by Vincent Harlow and Elizabeth M. Chilver. Oxf. 1963.

Incl. good bibliogs.

1721 OGOT (BETHWELL ALLAN) *and* KIERAN (JOHN A.) *eds.* Zamani: a survey of East African history. Nairobi. 1968.

1722 INGHAM (KENNETH). A history of east Africa. 1962. 3rd edn. 1965.

A useful general hist. Zoë Marsh and G. W. Kingsnorth, *An introduction to the history of east Africa*, Camb. 1957, 3rd edn. 1965, and Zoë Marsh, ed., *East Africa through contemporary records*, Camb. 1961, are useful books for schools. Charles Granston Richards and James Burnip Place, eds., *East African explorers*, 1960, is a handy anthology.

1723 DAVIDSON (BASIL). A history of east and central Africa to the late nineteenth century. Garden City, N.Y. 1969.

1724 COUPLAND (*Sir* REGINALD). The exploitation of East Africa, 1856–1890: the slave trade and the scramble. 1939. 2nd edn. 1968.

Good. Cont. his *East Africa and its invaders: from the earliest times to the death of Seyyid Said in 1856*, Oxf. 1938, 2nd edn. 1961, which has been superseded by Christine Stephanie Nicholls, *The Swahili coast: politics, diplomacy and trade in the East African littoral, 1798–1856*, 1971.

1725 OLIVER (ROLAND ANTHONY). The missionary factor in East Africa. 1952. 2nd edn. 1965.

Good. The most interesting contemp. work was Sir [Henry] Bartle [Edward] Frere, *Eastern Africa as a field for missionary labour: four letters to the Archbishop of Canterbury*, 1874.

1726 BENNETT (NORMAN ROBERT). Studies in East African history. Boston. 1963.

See also the vol. ed. by Bennett entitled *Leadership in eastern Africa: six political biographies*, Boston 1968.

1727 BECK (ANN). A history of the British medical administration of east Africa, 1900–1950. Camb., Mass. 1970.

1728 JANTZEN (GÜNTHER). Ostafrika in der deutsch-englischen Politik, 1884–1890. Hamburg. 1934.

See also **1618** and Ralph Albert Austen, *Northwest Tanzania under German and British rule: colonial policy and tribal politics, 1889–1939*, New Haven [Conn.] 1968.

1728a GALBRAITH (JOHN SEMPLE). Mackinnon and East Africa, 1878–1895: a study in the 'New Imperalism'. Camb. 1972.

1729 LOWE (CEDRIC JAMES). 'Anglo-Italian differences over East Africa,

1892–1895, and their effects upon the Mediterranean entente'. *Eng. Hist. Rev.* lxxxi (1966), 315–36.

See also John Semple Galbraith, 'Italy, the British East Africa Company, and the Benadir coast, 1888–1893', *J. Mod. Hist.* xlii (1970), 549–63.

1730  LOUIS (WILLIAM ROGER). Ruanda-Urundi, 1884–1919. Oxf. 1963.

Good on British policy.

1731  GURNEY COMMITTEE ON EAST AFRICAN SLAVE TRADE. Report from the select committee on slave trade (east coast of Africa) [Chairman: Russell Gurney]. H.C. 420. (1871). XII, 1.

A useful inquiry backed by a series of diplomatic inquiries, reported on in Foreign Office docs. publ. as parl. papers.

1732  HUTCHINSON (EDWARD). The slave trade of East Africa. 1874.

See also his *The Victoria Nyanza as a field for missionary enterprise*, 1876, and *The lost continent: its re-discovery and recovery*, 1879. For the suppression of the slave trade see Coupland (1724); Sir John Charles Ready Colomb, *Slave catching in the Indian ocean: a record of naval experiences*, 1803, repr. N.Y. 1969; Lilian M. Russell (Mrs. Charles E. B. Russell), *General Rigby, Zanzibar and the slave trade, with journals, despatches, etc.*, ed. by his daughter, 1935; and Ernest Achey Loftus, ed., *Elton and the East African coast slave trade: being extracts from the diary of James Elton . . ., 1879*, 1958.

1733  MANGAT (JAGJIT S.). A history of the Asians in east Africa, c. 1886 to 1945. Oxf. 1969.

See also Robert G. Gregory, *India and East Africa: a history of race relations within the British empire, 1890–1939*, Oxf. 1971.

1734  FOSTER (HUBERT JOHN). Handbook of British East Africa, including Zanzibar, Uganda, and the territory of the Imperial British East Africa Company. War Office. 1893.

A rev. version was produced as *Precis of information concerning the British East Africa Protectorate and Zanzibar . . . Dec. 1900*, War Office, 1901, and Sir Edward Mabbott Woodward, *Precis of information concerning the Uganda Protectorate*, 1902.

1735  DRUMKEYS' YEAR BOOK FOR EAST AFRICA. Bombay. 1908–.

A semi-official directory. See also *Handbook for East Africa, Uganda & Zanzibar*, Mombasa 1906.

1736  CHURCHILL (*Sir* WINSTON LEONARD SPENCER-). My African journey. 1908.

(ii) *British Somaliland*

1737  LEWIS (IOAN MYRDDIN). The modern history of Somaliland: from nation to state. 1965.

Good. For background consult Angus Hamilton, *Somaliland*, 1911; Sir Douglas James Jardine, *The Mad Mullah of Somaliland*, 1923; Robert L. Hess, 'The "Mad Mullah" and northern Somalia', *J. African Hist.* v (1964), 415–33; and Henry A. Rayne, *Sun, sand and Somals: leaves from the notebook of a district commissioner in British Somaliland*, 1921.

1738  WAR OFFICE (GENERAL STAFF). Official history of the operations in Somaliland, 1901–04. 2 v. 1907.

See also Malcolm McNeill, *In pursuit of the 'Mad' Mullah: service and sport in the Somali protectorate*, 1902, and James Willes Jennings and Christopher Addison, Viscount Addison, *With the Abyssinians in Somaliland*, 1905.

1739  HORNBY (MONTAGUE LEYLAND) *ed.* Military report on Somaliland, 1907. War Office. 1907.

1740  CORFIELD. Richard Corfield of Somaliland. By Henry Francis Prevost Battersby. 1914.

(iii) *Ethiopia*

1741  WORK (ERNEST). Ethiopia: a pawn in European diplomacy. New Concord, Ohio. 1935.

The handiest general hist. is Arnold Hugh Martin Jones and Elizabeth Monroe, *A history of Abyssinia*, 1935, new edn. [*A history of Ethiopia*], 1955, 1960.

1742  JOURNAL OF ETHIOPIAN STUDIES. 1+. Addis Ababa. 1963+.

1743  JAENEN (CORNELIUS J.). 'Theodore II and British intervention in Ethiopia'. *Canadian J. of Hist.* i (1966), pt. 2, 26–56.

See also J. R. Hooker, 'The Foreign Office and the "Abyssinian captives" ', *J. African Hist.* ii (1961), 245–58.

1744  BEKE (CHARLES TILSTONE). The British captives in Abyssinia. 1865. 2nd edn. 1867.

1745  RASSAM (HORMUZD). Narrative of the British mission to Theodore, king of Abyssinia . . . 2 v. 1869.

1746  HOLLAND (TREVENEN JAMES) *and* HOZIER (*Sir* HENRY MONTAGUE). Record of the expedition to Abyssinia: compiled by order of the Secretary of State for War. 2 v. & maps. 1870.

See also Sir Clements Robert Markham, *A history of the Abyssinian expedition*, 1869; Sir Henry Morton Stanley, *Coomassie and Magdala: the story of two British campaigns in Africa*, 1874; Sir Henry Montague Hozier, *The British expedition to Abyssinia*, 1869; Sir Robert Phayre, *Abyssinian expedition: official journal of the reconnoitring party of the British force in Abyssinia . . .*, 1869; Henry St. Clair Wilkins, *Reconnoitring in Abyssinia . . .*, 1870, *The autobiography of Theophilus Waldmeier, missionary . . .*, 1886, new edn. by Stephen Hobhouse 1925; [W. W. Scott], *Letters from Abyssinia during the campaign of 1868; by a staff officer*, 1868; George Alfred Henty, *The march to Magdala*, 1868; A. F. Shepherd, *The campaign in Abyssinia*, Bombay 1868, and the life of Lord Napier of Magdala (**1184**). This model expedition is also discussed in Bond (**2698**), and Frederick Myatt, *The march to Magdala: the Abyssinian war of 1868*, 1970.

1747  CANDLISH COMMITTEE ON THE ABYSSINIAN WAR. Report from the select committee on the Abyssinian war [Chairman: John Candlish]. H.C. 380 (1868–9). VI, 1. Further report. H.C. 401 (1870). V, 1.

A full inquiry into the costs of the war.

1748 PORTAL (*Sir* GERALD HERBERT). An account of the English mission to King Johannis of Abyssinia in 1887. Winchester. [1888.]

1749 MARCUS (HAROLD G.). 'A background to direct British diplomatic involvement in Ethiopia, 1894–1896'. *J. Ethiopian Studs.* i (1963), 121–32.

Cont. in his 'Ethio-British negotiations concerning the western border with Sudan, 1896–1902', *J. African Hist.* iv (1963), 81–94, and 'A preliminary history of the Tripartite treaty of December 13, 1906', ibid. ii (1964), 21–40. See also George Neville Sanderson, 'The foreign policy of the Negus Menelik, 1896–1898', *J. African Hist.* v (1964), 87–97, with a rejoinder by Marcus, ibid. vii (1966), 117–22.

1750 GLEICHEN (ALBERT EDWARD WILFRID) *Count, afterwards Lord.* With the mission to Menelik, 1897. 1898.

### (iv) *Kenya*

1751 WEBSTER (JOHN B.) *and others, comps.* A bibliography on Kenya. Syracuse Univ. Eastern African Bibliog. Ser. 2. Syracuse, N.Y. 1967.

See also Robert G. Gregory, Robert M. Maxon, and Leon P. Spencer, *A guide to the Kenya National Archives . . .*, Syracuse, N.Y. 1968.

1752 BENNETT (GEORGE). Kenya: a political history: the colonial period. 1963.

The best short intro. Archibald Marshall MacPhee, *Kenya*, 1968, adds little.

1753 MUNGEAM (GORDON HUDSON). British rule in Kenya, 1895–1912: the establishment of administration in the East Africa protectorate. Oxf. 1966.

A sound scholarly monograph. Marjorie Ruth Dilley, *British policy in Kenya colony*, N.Y. 1937, 2nd edn. 1966; Charles William Hobley, *Kenya from chartered company to crown colony: thirty years of exploration and administration in British East Africa*, 1929, new edn. 1970; and Norman Maclean Leys, *Kenya*, 1924, 3rd edn. 1926, are also useful for pre-1914 British policy.

1754 ELIOT (*Sir* CHARLES NORTON EDGECUMBE). The East Africa protectorate. 1905. 3rd impr. 1966.

A good summary of the state of Kenya to 1904 by the leading British official in East Africa. See also the official *Report* of the colony, 1896+, John Walter Gregory, *The foundation of British East Africa*, 1901, and (for the chartered company) P. L. McDermott, comp., *British East Africa: or, Ibea: a history of the formation and work of the Imperial British East Africa Company . . .*, 1893, new edn. 1895, and Edward Reginald Vere-Hodge, *Imperial British East Africa Company . . .*, 1960.

1755 SORRENSON (MAURICE PETER KEITH). Origins of European settlement in Kenya. Nairobi. 1968.

An important pioneer study. See also his *Land reform in the Kikuyu country: a study in government policy*, Nairobi 1967.

1756 WARD (H. F.) *and* MILLIGAN (JOHN WILLIAMSON). Handbook of British East Africa, 1912–13. Lond. & Nairobi. 1912.

A useful reference manual.

1757  HILL (MERVYN FREDERICK). Permanent way: the story of the Kenya and Uganda railway . . . being the official history of the development of the transport system in Kenya and Uganda. 2 v. Nairobi 1950–9. 2nd edn. Nairobi 1961.

The most famous event in the construction of the railway is recorded in John Henry Patterson, *The man-eaters of Tsavo and other east African adventures*, 1907, numerous edns.

1758  HILL (MERVYN FREDERICK). Planters' progress: the story of coffee in Kenya. Nairobi. [1958.]

1759  FEARN (HUGH). An African economy: a study of the economic development of the Nyanza province of Kenya, 1903–1953. 1961.

1760  DELAMERE. White man's country: Lord Delamere and the making of Kenya. By Elspeth Josceline Huxley. 2 v. 1935. New edn. 2 v. 1953.

Vol. I covers the period to 1914.

1761  MEINERTZHAGEN. Kenya diary, 1902–1906. By Richard Meinertzhagen. Edin. & Lond. 1957.

1762  OGOT (BETHWELL ALLAN). History of the southern Luo. 2 v. Nairobi. 1967–.

1763  WELBOURN (FREDERICK BURKEWOOD) *and* OGOT (BETHWELL ALLAN). A place to feel at home: a study of two independent churches in Western Kenya. 1966.

1764  WEISBORD (ROBERT G.). African zion: the attempt to establish a Jewish colony in the East Africa protectorate, 1903–1905. Phila. 1968.

1765  FORAN (WILLIAM ROBERT). The Kenya Police, 1887–1960. 1962.

### (v) *Uganda*

1766  INGHAM (KENNETH). The making of modern Uganda. 1958.

Historical articles appear chiefly in *The Uganda J.*, 1+, 1934+.

1767  ADMIRALTY (NAVAL INTELLIGENCE DIVISION). A handbook of the Uganda protectorate. 1920.

The most useful general collection of data on the early 20th cent.

1768  MUKHERJEE (RAMAKRISHNA). The problem of Uganda: a study in acculturation. Berlin. 1956.

1769  LOW (DONALD ANTHONY) *and* PRATT (ROBERT CRANFORD). Buganda and British overrule, 1900–1955: two studies. 1960.

1770  BARBER (JAMES P.). Imperial frontier: a study of relations between the British and the pastoral tribes of North-East Uganda. Nairobi. 1968.

1771 LUGARD (FREDERICK JOHN DEALTRY), *Baron Lugard*. The rise of our East African empire: early efforts in Nyasaland and Uganda. 2 v. Edin. & Lond. 1893. Repr. 2 v. 1968.

A useful account. But Dame Margery Freda Perham and Mary Bull, eds., *The diaries of Lord Lugard: East Africa, 1889–1892*, 4 v. Lond. & Evanston, Ill. 1959–63, are also indispensable and good reading. For Lugard's career see **1626**.

1772 PORTAL (*Sir* GERALD HERBERT). The British mission to Uganda in 1893. Ed. by James Rennell Rodd, Baron Rennell. 1894. Repr. 1970.

For the political background of the Portal mission see Stansky (**520**), and Sir John Gray, 'Anglo-German relations in Uganda, 1890–1892', *J. African Hist.* i (1960), 281–98. For conditions in the countryside see Edward Coode Hore, *Tanganyika: eleven years in Central Africa*, 1892, 2nd edn. 1892, and Robert Pickering Ashe, *Chronicles of Uganda*, 1894, and *Two kings of Uganda . . .*, 1889.

1773 MACDONALD (*Sir* JAMES RONALD LESLIE). Soldiering and surveying in British East Africa, 1891–94. 1897.

One of a ser. of accounts of the opening up of Uganda written by military men. Other contemp. books were Sir Henry Edward Colvile, *The land of the Nile springs: being chiefly an account of how we fought Kabarega*, 1895; [Cecil Foster] Seymour Vandeleur, *Campaigning on the Upper Nile and Niger*, 1898 [for Vandeleur see also Sir Frederick Ivor Maxse, *Seymour Vandeleur . . .*, 1905]; Herbert Henry Austin, *With Macdonald in Uganda: narrative account of the Uganda mutiny and Macdonald expedition in the Uganda protectorate and the territories to the north*, 1903; and Arthur Blyford Thruston, *African incidents . . . with . . . an account of Major Thruston's last stay in 1897 in the protectorate, his death and the mutiny of the Uganda rifles*, 1900. For a recent assessment of military events see R. W. Beachey, 'Macdonald's expedition and the Uganda mutiny, 1897–98', *Hist. J.* x (1967), 237–54, and A. T. Matson, 'A further note on the Macdonald expedition', ibid. xii (1969), 155–7. John Vernon Wild, *The Uganda mutiny, 1897*, 1954, is only a pamphlet.

1774 JOHNSTON (*Sir* HARRY HAMILTON). The Uganda protectorate: an attempt to give some description of the physical geography, botany, zoology, anthropology, languages and history of the territories under British protection in East Central Africa . . . 2 v. 1902.

A useful survey. James Francis Cunningham, *Uganda and its peoples: notes on the protectorate of Uganda, especially the anthropology and ethnology of its indigenous races* 1905, is weak on British admin.

1775 JACKSON. Early days in East Africa. By Sir Frederick John Jackson. 1930. Repr. 1969.

1776 COOK. Uganda memories (1897–1940). By Sir Albert Ruskin Cook. Kampala. 1945.

1777 JONES (HERBERT GRESFORD), *bishop*. Uganda in transformation, 1876–1926. 1926.

Essentially an Anglican Church hist.

1778 TAYLOR (JOHN VERNON). The growth of the church in Buganda: an attempt at understanding. 1958.

1779 HANNINGTON. James Hannington, D.D., F.L.S., F.R.G.S., first Bishop of Eastern Equatorial Africa: a history of his life and work, 1847–85. By Edwin Collas Dawson. 1887.

Dawson also ed. *The last journals of Bishop Hannington* . . ., 1888.

1780 KIVEBULAYA. African saint: the story of Apolo Kivebulaya. By Anne Luck. 1963.

1781 MACKAY. A. M. Mackay: pioneer missionary of the Church Missionary Society to Uganda. By his sister J. W. H. Lond. & N.Y. 1896. Repr. 1904. New edn. 1970.

There are also a couple of popular lives: Mrs. Sophia Fahs, *Uganda's white man of work: a story of Alexander M. Mackay*, Boston 1907, and Constance Evelyn Padwick, *Mackay of the great lake*, 1917, rev. edn. 1948.

1782 PILKINGTON. Pilkington of Uganda. By Charles Forbes Harford Battersby, afterwards Harford. 1898. 2nd edn. 1899.

1783 TUCKER. Eighteen years in Uganda and East Africa. By Alfred Robert Tucker, bishop. 2 v. 1908. New edn. 1911.

See also Arthur Pearce Shepherd, *Tucker of Uganda: artist and apostle, 1849–1914*, 1929, and Christopher James Wilson, *Uganda in the days of Bishop Tucker*, 1955.

1784 GALE (HUBERT PHILIP PETER). Uganda and the Mill Hill fathers. 1959.

1785 THOONEN (JOHN P.). Black martyrs. 1941.

An important pioneer work. John Francis Faupel, *African holocaust: the story of the Uganda martyrs*, 1962, 2nd edn. 1965, is based on Thoonen.

(vi) *Zanzibar*

1786 GRAY (*Sir* JOHN MILNER). History of Zanzibar from the middle ages to 1856. 1962.

See also Coupland (**1724**).

1787 LYNE (ROBERT NUNEZ). Zanzibar in contemporary times: a short history of the southern east in the nineteenth century. 1905. Repr. N.Y. 1969.

Still the best account of 19th-cent. Zanzibar. There are also a number of good general descriptive works, notably Sir Richard Francis Burton, *Zanzibar: city, island & coast*, 2 v. 1872; Henry Stanley Newman, *Banani: the transition from slavery to freedom in Zanzibar and Pemba* [1898]; Francis Barrow Pearce, *Zanzibar: the island metropolis of eastern Africa*, 1920, 3rd impr. 1967; and William Harold Ingrams, *Zanzibar: its history and its people*, 1931, repr. 1967.

1788 GAVIN (R. J.). 'The Bartle Frere mission to Zanzibar, 1873'. *Hist. J.* v (1962), 122–48.

For later events see Emile De Groot, 'Great Britain and Germany in Zanzibar: consul Holmwood's papers, 1886–1887', *J. Mod. Hist.* xxv (1953), 120–38.

1789 HOLLINGSWORTH (LAWRENCE WILLIAM). Zanzibar under the Foreign Office, 1890–1913. 1953.

A useful monograph, to be suppl. by R. Oliver's *Sir Harry Johnston* (**1625**).

1790 WESTON. Frank, Bishop of Zanzibar: life of Frank Weston, D.D., 1871–1924. By Herbert Maynard Smith. 1926.

### (vii) *Mauritius*

1791 TOUSSAINT (AUGUSTE) *and* ADOLPHE (H.). Bibliography of Mauritius, 1502–1954: covering the printed record, manuscripts, archivalia and cartographic material. Mauritius Archives Dept. Port Louis. 1956.

1792 SOCIÉTÉ DE L'HISTOIRE DE L'ÎLE MAURICE. Dictionnaire de biographie mauricienne: dictionary of Mauritian biography. 5 v. in pts. St. Louis. 1941+. In progress.

1793 BARNWELL (PATRICK JOSEPH) *and* TOUSSAINT (AUGUSTE). A short history of Mauritius. 1949.

Short and weak, as is Derek Hollingworth, *They came to Mauritius: portraits of the eighteenth and nineteenth centuries*, 1965, which deals with visitors to the island. The best book on 19th-cent. admin. is Pope-Hennessy, *Verandah* (**1306**). For a description of the colony see Allister Macmillan, comp., *Mauritius . . .*, 1914.

1794 FRERE–WILLIAMSON COMMISSION ON TREATMENT OF IMMIGRANTS IN MAURITIUS. Report of the royal commissioners appointed to enquire into the treatment of immigrants in Mauritius [Commissioners: William Edward Frere and Victor Alexander Williamson]. [C. 1115] H.C. (1875). XXXIV, 1. Appendices. [C. 1115–I] H.C. (1875). XXXV, 1.

Full of data about conditions on the sugar estates.

1795 SWETTENHAM COMMISSION ON CONDITION AND RESOURCES OF MAURITIUS. Report of the Mauritius royal commission, 1909 [Chairman: Sir Frank Athelstane Swettenham]. [Cd. 5185] H.C. (1910). XLII, 1. Appendices. [Cd. 5186–7] H.C. (1910). XLII, 85, 671.

1796 RYAN. Mauritius and Madagascar: journals of an eight years' residence in the diocese of Mauritius and of a visit to Madagascar. By Vincent William Ryan, Bishop of Mauritius. 1864.

For mission life in Madagascar see further Thomas Trotter Matthews, *Thirty years in Madagascar*, Lond. & N.Y. 1904, 2nd edn. 1904. Matthews worked for the London Missionary Society.

### (d) *West Africa*
#### (i) *General*

There is no general bibliog. H. A. Rydings, comp., *The bibliographies of West Africa*, Ibadan 1961, has very little to report for British West Africa and is less useful than Dipeolu (**1840**).

1797 AJAYI (JACOB FESTUS ADE) *and* ESPIE (IAN) *eds*. A thousand years of West African history: a handbook for teachers and students. Ibadan & Lond. 1965. Rev. edn. 1969.

1798 GUIDES TO MATERIALS FOR WEST AFRICAN HISTORY IN EUROPEAN ARCHIVES. 1+. 1962+.

The ser. incl.: 1. Patricia Carson, *Materials for West African history in the archives of Belgium and Holland,* 1962; 2. Alan Frederick Charles Ryder, *Materials . . . in Portuguese archives,* 1965; 3. Richard Gray and David Chambers, *Materials . . . in Italian archives,* 1965; 4. Patricia Carson, *Materials . . . in French archives,* 1968; 5. Noel Matthews, *Materials . . . in the archives of the United Kingdom,* 1973.

1799 MACMILLAN (ALLISTER) *ed*. The red book of West Africa: historical and descriptive, commercial and industrial: facts, figures and resources. 1920. Repr. 1968.

See also Harry Osman Newland, *West Africa: a handbook of practical information for the official, planter, miner, financier & trader,* ed. by Percy Evans Lewin, 1922, *West African year-book,* 1901+, and Colonial Office, *West Africa pocket book: a guide for newly-appointed government officials,* 1905.

1800 NEWBURY (COLIN WALTER) *comp*. British policy towards West Africa: select documents. Vol. I. 1786–1874. Oxf. 1965. Vol. II. 1875–1914. Oxf. 1971.

1801 FAGE (JOHN DONNELLY). An introduction to the history of West Africa. Camb. 1955. 4th edn. [A history of West Africa.] 1969.

The standard general hist. See also John Spencer Trimingham, *A history of Islam in west Africa,* 1962.

1802 JOHNSTON (*Sir* HARRY HAMILTON). Pioneers in West Africa. 1912. Repr. N.Y. 1969.

Chiefly on explorers. Cecil Howard, ed., *West African explorers,* 1951, is a popular anthology.

1803 BOAHEN (ALBERT ADU). Britain, the Sahara and the western Sudan, 1788–1861. Oxf. 1964.

1804 CROWDER (MICHAEL). West Africa under colonial rule. Lond. & Evanston, Ill. 1968.

Good. See also M. Crowder and Obaro Ikime, eds., *West African chiefs: their changing status under colonial rule and independence,* N.Y. 1970, and M. Crowder, ed., *West African resistance: the military response to colonial occupation,* Lond. & N.Y. 1971.

1805 HARGREAVES (JOHN DESMOND). Prelude to the partition of West Africa. Lond. & N.Y. 1963.

Indispensable for the whole process of partition. See also Keltie (**1617**).

1806 CROWE (SIBYL EYRE). The Berlin West African conference 1884–1885. 1952.

1807  JULY (ROBERT WILLIAM). The origins of modern African thought: its development in West Africa during the nineteenth and twentieth centuries. Lond. & N.Y. 1968.

See also Henry Summerville Wilson, ed., *Origins of West African nationalism*, Lond., N.Y., etc. 1969, an anthology.

1808  OMU (FRED I. A.). 'The dilemma of press freedom in colonial Africa: the West African example'. *J. African Hist.* IX (1968), 279–98.

1809  ADDERLEY COMMITTEE ON WEST AFRICA. Report from the select committee on Africa (western coast) [Chairman: C. B. Adderley.] H.C. 412 (1865). V, 1.

A lengthy report on the desirability of extending or withdrawing from the West African settlements.

1810  HORTON (JAMES AFRICANUS BEALE). West African countries and peoples. 1868. New edn. by George Allcott Shepperson. Edin. 1969.

For Horton's life see Christopher Fyfe, *Africanus Horton, 1835–1883: West African scientist and patriot*, N.Y. 1972.

1811  KINGSLEY (MARY HENRIETTA). West African studies. 1899. Rev. edn. 1901. New edn. 1964.

See also her *The story of West Africa* [1899], and *Travels in West Africa, Congo Français, Corisco and Cameroons*, Lond. & N.Y. 1897, 2nd edn. abridged 1897, 3rd edn. N.Y. 1965. For Mary Kingsley herself see Stephen Lucius Gwynn, *The life of Mary Kingsley*, 1932, 2nd edn. 1933; Olwen Ward Campbell, *Mary Kingsley: a Victorian in the jungle*, 1957; Cecil Howard, *Mary Kingsley*, 1957; John Edgar Flint, 'Mary Kingsley: a reassessment', *J. African Hist.* iv (1963), 95–104; and Porter (**971**).

1812  MOREL (EDMUND DENE). Affairs of West Africa. 1902. New edn. 1968.

1813  GEORGE (CLAUDE). The rise of British West Africa: comprising the early history of the colony of Sierra Leone, the Gambia, Lagos, Gold Coast, etc., etc., with a brief account of climate, the growth of education, commerce and religion, and a comprehensive history of the Bananas and Bance islands and sketches of the constitution. 5 pts. 1902–3. Repr. 1904. Repr. 1968.

1814  BAILLAUD (ÉMILE). La politique indigène de l'Angleterre en Afrique occidentale. Paris. 1912.

1815  McPHEE (ALLAN). The economic revolution in British West Africa. 1926.

A useful work. Unfortunately Peter Tamas Bauer, *West African trade: a study of competition, oligopoly and monopoly in a changing economy*, Camb. 1954, is not historically oriented.

1816  WHITFORD (JOHN). Trading life in western and central Africa. Liverpool. 1877. New edn. 1967.

1817  MOLONEY (*Sir* CORNELIUS ALFRED). Sketch of the forestry of West Africa: with particular reference to its present principal commercial products. 1887.

1818  MOLONEY (*Sir* CORNELIUS ALFRED). West African fisheries: with particular reference to the Gold Coast colony. 1883.

1819  HAYWOOD (AUSTIN HUBERT WIGHTWICK) *and* CLARKE (FREDERICK ARTHUR STANLEY). The history of the Royal West African Frontier Force. Aldershot. 1964.

For surviving 17th- and 18th-cent. forts, see Arnold Walter Lawrence, *Trade castles & forts of West Africa*, 1963.

### (ii) *The Gambia*

1820  GAMBLE (DAVID P.). The Gambia: bibliography of the Gambia. Bathurst. 1967.

1821  GRAY (*Sir* JOHN MILNER). A history of the Gambia. Camb. 1940. New impr. 1966.

Harry Alfred Gailey, *A history of the Gambia*, 1964, concentrates on the period after 1889. [Lady] Bella Sidney Southorn, *The Gambia: the story of a ground nut colony*, 1952, adds little. The best contemp. account of the colony is Francis Bisset Archer, *The Gambia colony and protectorate: an official handbook*, 1906, repr. 1967. René Catala, 'La question de l'échange de la Gambie britannique contre les comptoirs français du Golfe de Guinée de 1866 à 1876', *Revue d'histoire des colonies*, xxx (1948), 114–37, deals with the diplomatic hist. of the colony.

### (iii) *Gold Coast (Ghana)*

1822  CARDINALL (*Sir* ALLAN WOLSEY) *comp.* A bibliography of the Gold Coast: issued as a companion volume to the census report of 1931. Accra. 1932.

Cont. by Albert Frederick Johnson, comp., *A bibliography of Ghana, 1930–1961*, Evanston, Ill. 1964. See also Julian W. Witherell and Sharon B. Lockwood, comps., *Ghana: a guide to official publications, 1872–1968*, U.S. Libr. of Congress, Wash. 1969.

1823  METCALFE (GEORGE EDGAR) *comp.* Great Britain and Ghana: documents of Ghana history, 1807–1957. 1964.

A useful selection.

1824  KIMBLE (DAVID). A political history of Ghana: the rise of Gold Coast nationalism, 1850–1928. Oxf. 1963.

1825  CLARIDGE (WILLIAM WALTON). A history of the Gold Coast and Ashanti. 2 v. 1915. 2nd edn. 2 v. 1964.

A useful quarry. Suppl. by William Ernest Frank Ward, *A history of the Gold Coast [Ghana]*, 1948, 4th edn. 1967. Freda Wolfson, ed., *Pageant of Ghana*, 1958, is a pleasant anthology of contemp. docs. John Donnelly Fage, *Ghana: a historical interpretation*, Madison, Wis. 1959, is a general essay. Ronald Edward Wraith, *Guggisberg*, 1967, though chiefly concerned with a later period, has interesting information. Historical scholarship can be followed in Hist. Soc. of Ghana [formerly Gold Coast and Togoland Hist. Soc.], *Transactions*, 1952+, Achimota, later Legon, 1953+, and *Ghana notes and queries*, Kumasi 1961+.

1826   REINDORF (CARL CHRISTIAN). The history of the Gold Coast and Asante . . . 1500 to 1860. Basle 1895. Repr. Basle. 1951. 2nd edn. Accra. 1966.

The useful work of a Swiss missionary. Alfred Burdon Ellis, *A history of the Gold Coast of West Africa*, 1893, repr. N.Y. 1969, covers the period to 1888. George Macdonald, *The Gold Coast past and present: a short description of the country and its people*, 1898, is useful for the 1890s. James Africanus Beale Horton, *Letters on the political condition of the Gold Coast since the exchange of territory between the English and Dutch governments, on January 1st, 1868 . . .*, 1870, is notable more for its author than for its contents.

1827   COOMBS (DOUGLAS STAFFORD). The Gold Coast, Britain & the Netherlands, 1850–1874. 1963.

See also D. E. K. Amenumey, 'The extension of British rule to Anlo (South East Ghana), 1850–1890', *J. African Hist.* ix (1968), 99–117.

1828   SAMPSON (MAGNUS JOHN). Gold Coast men of affairs, past and present. 1937. Repr. 1969.

1829   ELIAS (TASLIM OLAWALE). Ghana and Sierra Leone: the development of their laws and constitutions. The British Commonwealth: the development of its laws and constitution 10. 1962.

1830   DEBRUNNER (HANS WERNER). A history of Christianity in Ghana. Accra. 1967.

1831   SMITH (NOEL). The Presbyterian church of Ghana, 1835–1960: a younger church in a changing society. Accra. 1966.

1832   FREEMAN. Thomas Birch Freeman: West African pioneer. By Norman Allen Birtwistle. 1950.

See also Frank Deaville Walker, *Thomas Birch Freeman, the son of an African*, 1929.

1833   PRIESTLEY (MARGARET). West African trade and coast society: a family study. 1969.

1834   TORDOFF (WILLIAM). Ashanti under the Prempehs, 1888–1935. 1965.

Good. The works of Robert Sutherland Rattray are also useful for Ashanti hist., notably his *Ashanti*, Oxf. 1923, and *Ashanti law and constitution*, Oxf. 1929. For the devel. of Ashanti soc. see also Kofi Abrefa Busia, *The position of the chief in the modern political system of the Ashanti . . .*, 1951, repr. 1968, and Ivor Wilks, *The northern factor in Ashanti history*, Achimota 1961. Henry Ponting Northcott, *Report on the northern territories of the Gold Coast*, War Office, Intelligence Div. 1899, is a good official report.

1835   HAYFORD ([JOSEPH EPHRAIM] CASELY). Gold Coast native institutions: with thoughts upon a healthy imperial policy for the Gold Coast and Ashanti. 1903.

See also his *Ethiopia unbound: studies in race emancipation*, 1911, new edn. 1969, *The truth about the West African land question*, 1913, and *West African leadership* . . . ed. by Magnus John Sampson, Ilfracombe 1951.

1836 ELDRIDGE (COLIN C.). 'Newcastle and the Ashanti war of 1863–64: a failure of the policy of "anti-Imperialism" '. *Renaissance & Modern Studs.* xii (1968), 68–90.

1837 BRACKENBURY (*Sir* HENRY). The Ashanti war: a narrative prepared from the official documents . . . 2 v. Lond. & Edin. 1874. Repr. 2 v. 1968.

The fullest account of the 1873–4 expedition, though it should be suppl. by William David McIntyre, 'British policy in West Africa: the Ashanti expedition of 1873–4', *Hist. J.* v (1962), 19–46, and the works on Wolseley at **2834**. More popular accounts were also publ., notably Sir John Frederick Maurice, *The Ashantee war: a popular narrative by the Daily News special correspondent*, 1874; Frederick Boyle, *Through Fanteeland to Coomassie: a diary of the Ashantee expedition*, 1874; Sir William Francis Butler, *Akim-Foo: the history of a failure*, 1875; William Toke Dooner, *To Coomassie and back, 1873–74*, 1895, 2nd edn. 1895; William Winwood Reade, *The story of the Ashantee campaign*, 1874; Sir Henry Morton Stanley, *Coomassie and Magdala: the story of two British campaigns in Africa*, 1874; and the boy's book by George Alfred Henty, *The march to Coomassie*, 1874. The War office also sponsored a number of reports and colls. of corres. For medicine see Albert Augustus Gore, *A contribution to the medical history of our West African campaigns*, 1876.

1838 BADEN-POWELL (ROBERT STEVENSON SMYTH), *Baron Baden-Powell*. The downfall of Prempeh: a diary of life with the native levy in Ashanti, 1895–96 . . . 1896.

On the 1896 campaign see also Bennet Burleigh, *Two campaigns: Madagascar and Ashantee*, 1896.

1839 ARMITAGE (*Sir* CECIL HAMILTON) *and* MONTANARO (ARTHUR FORBES). The Ashanti campaign of 1900. 1901.

See also B. Wasserman, 'The Ashanti war of 1900: a study in cultural conflict', *Africa* xxxi (1961), 167–79, Harold C. J. Biss, *The relief of Kumasi* . . ., 1901, and Mary Alice Hodgson, Lady Hodgson, *The siege of Kumassi* . . ., 1901.

(iv) *Nigeria*

1840 DIPEOLU (J. O.) *comp.* Bibliographical sources for Nigerian studies. Evanston, Ill. 1966.

1841 CONOVER (HELEN FIELD) *comp.* Nigerian official publications, 1869–1959: a guide. U.S. Libr. of Congress. Wash. 1959.

1842 CROWDER (MICHAEL). The story of Nigeria. 1962.

Like Sir Alan Cuthbert Maxwell Burns, *History of Nigeria*, 1929, 7th edn. 1969, (publ. in N.Y. as *A short history of Nigeria*, 1962, rev. edn. 1966), an introduction to Nigerian hist. rather than a standard work. Other introductions incl. Thomas Lionel Hodgkin, *Nigerian perspectives: an historical anthology*, 1960; James Smoot Coleman, *Nigeria: background to nationalism*, Berkeley etc. 1958; Arthur Norton Cook, *British enterprise in Nigeria*, Phila. 1943; and John Edgar Flint, *Nigeria and Ghana*, Englewood Cliffs,

N.J. 1966. The leading hist. j. is Hist. Soc. of Nigeria, *Journal*, 1+, Ibadan 1956+. For boundaries see Joseph Christopher Anene, *The international boundaries of Nigeria: the framework of an emergent African nation*, 1970.

1843 KIRK-GREENE (ANTHONY HAMILTON MILLARD) *ed.* The principles of native administration in Nigeria: selected documents, 1900–1947. 1965.

1844 NICOLSON (I. F.). The administration of Nigeria, 1900–1960: men, methods and myths. 1970.

1845 ELIAS (TASLIM OLAWALE). Groundwork of Nigerian law. 1954. 2nd edn. [The Nigerian legal system.] 1963.

Incl a hist. For land law see Charles Kingsley Meek, *Land tenure and land administration in Nigeria and the Cameroons*, 1957.

1846 MOCKLER-FERRYMAN (AUGUSTUS FERRYMAN). British Nigeria: a geographical and historical description of the British possessions adjacent to the Niger river, West Africa. 1902.

1847 MOREL (EDMUND DENE). Nigeria: its peoples and its problems. 1911. 2nd edn. 1912. 3rd edn. 1968.

1848 GEARY (*Sir* [WILLIAM] NEVILL [MONTGOMERIE]). Nigeria under British rule. 1927. Repr. N.Y. 1965.

1849 DIKE (KENNETH ONWUKA). Trade and politics in the Niger delta, 1830–1885: an introduction to the economic and political history of Nigeria. Oxf. 1956.

A pioneer work, written from an African point of view.

1850 ANENE (JOSEPH CHRISTOPHER). Southern Nigeria in transition, 1885–1906: theory and practice in a colonial protectorate. Camb. 1966.

1851 JONES (GWILYM IWAN). The trading states of the Oil Rivers: a study of political development in Eastern Nigeria. 1963.

1852 IKIME (OBARO). Niger delta rivalry: Itsẹkiri–Urhobo relations and the European presence, 1884–1936. 1969.

See also his *Merchant prince of the Niger delta: the rise & fall of Nana Olomu, last governor of Benin river*, 1968, and Ebiegberi Joe Alagoa, *The small brave city-state: a history of Nembe Brass in the Niger Delta*, Ibadan & Madison, Wis. 1964.

1853 PEDRAZA (HOWARD J.). Borrioboola-Gha: the story of Lokoja, the first British settlement in Nigeria. 1960.

1854 RYDER (ALAN FREDERICK CHARLES). Benin and the Europeans, 1485–1897. 1970.

1855 BIOBAKU (SABURI OLADENI). The Egba and their neighbours, 1842–1872. Oxf. 1957.

1856 McINTYRE (WILLIAM DAVID). 'Commander Glover and the colony of Lagos, 1861–73'. J. African Hist. iv (1963), 57–79.

Suppl. by his *The imperial frontier* (**1243**). See also A. G. Hopkins, 'Economic imperialism in West Africa: Lagos, 1880–92', *Econ. Hist. Rev.* 2 ser. xxi (1968), 580–606.

1857 NEWBURY (COLIN WALTER). The western slave coast and its rulers: European trade and administration among the Yoruba and Adja speaking peoples of south-western Nigeria, southern Dahomey and Togo. Oxf. 1961.

A study centred on Lagos.

1858 KOPYTOFF (JEAN HERSKOVITS). A preface to modern Nigeria: the 'Sierra Leonians' in Yoruba, 1830–1890. Madison, Wis. 1965.

1859 AJAYI (JACOB FESTUS ADE) *and* SMITH (ROBERT SYDNEY). Yoruba warfare in the nineteenth century. Camb. 1964.

See also Stephen Adebanji Akintoye, *Revolution and power politics in Yorubaland, 1840–1893: Ibadan expansion and the rise of Ekitiparapo*, Lond. & N.Y. 1971.

1860 CHALMERS COMMITTEE ON LIQUOR TRADE IN SOUTHERN NIGERIA. Report of the committee of inquiry into the liquor trade in southern Nigeria [Chairman: Sir Mackenzie Chalmers]. [Cd. 4906] H.C. (1909). LX, 497. Minutes of evidence. [Cd. 4907] H.C. (1909). LX, 519.

1861 HEUSSLER (ROBERT). The British in northern Nigeria. 1968.

1862 ORR (*Sir* CHARLES WILLIAM JAMES). The making of northern Nigeria. 1911. 2nd edn. 1965.

A good account by a participant. Flora Louisa Shaw, afterwards Lugard, Baroness Lugard, *A tropical dependency: an outline of the ancient history of the western Soudan: with an account of the modern settlement of Northern Nigeria*, 1906, repr. N.Y. 1965; Olive Susan Miranda Temple, *Notes on the tribes, provinces, emirates and states of the northern provinces of Nigeria*, ed. by Charles Lindsay Temple, Cape Town 1919, 2nd edn. Lagos 1922, repr. Lond. 1965, N.Y. 1967; and Charles Lindsay Temple, *Native races and their rulers: sketches and studies of official life and administrative problems in Nigeria*, Cape Town & Lond. 1918, 2nd edn. Lond. 1968, Chicago 1969, include useful suppl. material.

1863 MUFFETT (DAVID JOSEPH MEAD). Concerning brave captains: being, a history of the British occupation of Kano and Sokoto and of the last stand of the Fulani forces. 1964.

See also H. F. Backwell, ed., *The occupation of Hausaland, 1900–1904: being a translation of Arabic letters found in the house of the wazir of Sokoto, Bohari in 1903*, Lagos 1927, repr. Lond. 1969.

1864 HOGBEN (SIDNEY JOHN) *and* KIRK-GREENE (ANTHONY HAMILTON MILLARD). The emirates of northern Nigeria: a preliminary survey of their historical traditions. 1966.

1865 SMITH (MICHAEL GARFIELD). Government in Zazzau, 1800–1950. 1960.

1866   JOHNSTON (HUGH ANTHONY STEPHENS). The Fulani empire of Sokoto. Lond., Ibadan, etc. 1967.

See also Murray Last, *The Sokoto caliphate*, 1967, and Rowland Adevemi Adeleye, *Power and diplomacy in Northern Nigeria, 1804–1906: the Sokoto caliphate and its enemies*, 1971.

1867   BULL (MARY). 'Indirect rule in Northern Nigeria, 1906–1911'. In Kenneth Ernest Robinson and Albert Frederick Madden, eds. Essays in imperial government presented to Margery Perham. Oxf. 1963.

A useful intro. See also Charles Kingsley Meek, *Law and authority in a Nigerian tribe: a study in indirect rule*, 1937.

1868   LUGARD (FREDERICK JOHN DEALTRY), *Baron Lugard*. Instructions to political and other officers on subjects chiefly political and administrative. 1906. 2nd edn. 1919. New edn. by Anthony Hamilton Millard Kirk-Greene. 1971.

1869   DIGBY COMMITTEE ON NORTHERN NIGERIAN LANDS. Report of the Northern Nigeria lands committee [Chairman: Sir Kenelm E. Digby]. [Cd. 5102] H.C. (1910). XLIV, 271. Minutes of evidence. [Cd. 5103] H.C. (1910). XLIV, 305.

1870   LUGARD. Lugard and the amalgamation of Nigeria: a documentary record: being a reprint of the report by Sir F. D. Lugard on the amalgamation of northern and southern Nigeria and administration, 1912–1919 . . . Ed. by Anthony Hamilton Millard Kirk-Greene. 1968.

1871   GOLDIE. Sir George Goldie and the making of Nigeria. By John Edgar Flint. 1960.

See also Dorothy Ashton Wellesley, Lady Wellesley, and Stephen Lucius Gwynn, *Sir George Goldie: founder of Nigeria: a memoir*, 1934.

1872   KIRK-GREENE (ANTHONY HAMILTON MILLARD). Adamawa past and present: an historical approach to the development of a northern Cameroons province. 1958.

1873   AJAYI (JACOB FESTUS ADE). Christian missions in Nigeria, 1841– 1891: the making of a new elite. 1965.

Good. Better than Emmanuel Ayankanmi Ayandele, *The missionary impact on modern Nigeria, 1842–1914: a political and social analysis*, 1966.

1874   GRIMLEY (JOHN B.) *and* ROBINSON (GORDON E.). Church growth in Central and Southern Nigeria. Grand Rapids, Mich. 1966.

1875   WEBSTER (JAMES BERTIN). The African churches among the Yoruba, 1888–1922. Oxf. 1964.

1876   CROWTHER (SAMUEL ADJAI) *bishop, and* TAYLOR (JOHN CHRISTOPHER). The gospel on the banks of the Niger: journals and notices of the native missionaries accompanying the Niger expedition of 1857–1859. 1859. Repr. 1968.

See also Jesse Page, *The black bishop: Samuel Adjai Crowther*, 1908, 2nd edn. 1910.

1877  WALKER (FRANK DEAVILLE). The romance of the Black River: the story of the C.M.S. Nigeria mission. 1930.

See also Dandeson Coates Crowther, *The establishment of the Niger Delta pastorate church, 1864–1892*, Liverpool 1907, Emmanuel M. Tobiah Epelle, *The church in the Niger Delta*, Aba 1955, and Frank Deaville Walker, *A hundred years in Nigeria: the story of the Methodist mission in the western Nigeria district, 1842–1942*, 1942.

1878  McFARLAN (DONALD MAITLAND). Calabar: the Church of Scotland mission, founded 1846. 1946. Rev. edn. 1957.

Thin. See also William Pringle Livingstone, *Mary Slessor of Calabar, pioneer missionary*, 3rd edn. 1916, 9th edn. 1917, and Carol Christian and Gladys Plummer, *God and one redhead: Mary Slessor of Calabar*, 1970.

1879  MABOGUNJE (AKINLAWON LAPIDO). Urbanisation in Nigeria. Lond. & N.Y. 1968.

1880  LLOYD (PETER CUTT) *and others, eds.* The city of Ibadan. 1967.

1881  CALVERT (ALBERT FREDERICK). Nigeria and its tin fields. 1910. New edn. 1912.

(v) *Sierra Leone*

1882  LUKE *formerly* LUKACH (*Sir* HARRY CHARLES). Bibliography of Sierra Leone. Oxf. 1910. 2nd edn. Lond. 1925.

1883  FYFE (CHRISTOPHER). A history of Sierra Leone. 1962. New edn. 1968.

One of the few good full-length hists. of a British colony. Suppl. by his *Sierra Leone inheritance*, 1964, a collection of docs., and *A short history of Sierra Leone*, 1962, new edn. 1967. See also John Peterson, *Province of freedom: a history of Sierra Leone, 1787–1870*, Lond. & Evanston, Ill. 1969. The leading hist. j. is *Sierra Leone studies*, Freetown 1919–39 (old ser.), 1953+ (new ser.). For biog. there is Sierra Leone Soc., *Eminent Sierra Leoneans (in the nineteenth century)*, Freetown 1961. Background material is to be found chiefly in travel books listed by Fyfe, among them Thomas Joshua Alldridge, *A transformed colony: Sierra Leone as it was and as it is: its progress, peoples, native customs and undeveloped wealth*, 1910, and Harry Osman Newland, *Sierra Leone: its people, products and secret societies . . .*, [1916]. For law see **1829**.

1884  PORTER (ARTHUR THOMAS). Creoledom: a study of the development of Freetown society. 1963.

See also Christopher Fyfe and Eldred Jones, eds., *Freetown: a symposium*, Freetown 1968.

1885  JOHNSON. Holy Johnson: pioneer of African nationalism, 1836–1917. By Emmanuel Ayankanmi Ayandele. 1970.

1886  JOHNSON (THOMAS SYLVESTER CLAUDIUS), *bishop*. The story of a mission: the Sierra Leone church: first daughter of the C.M.S. 1953.

See also [Bishop] Ernest Graham Ingham, *Sierra Leone after a hundred years*, 1894, repr. 1968, and Hollis R. Lynch, 'The native pastorate controversy and cultural ethno-centrism in Sierra Leone, 1871–1874', *J. African Hist.* v (1964), 395–413.

1887  HARGREAVES (JOHN DESMOND). 'The establishment of the Sierra Leone protectorate and the insurrection of 1898'. *Camb. Hist. J.* xii (1956), 56–80.

See also Charles Braithwaite Wallis, *The advance of our West African empire*, 1903, which is largely about the 1898 rising.

1888  CHALMERS (*Sir* DAVID PATRICK). Report by her majesty's commissioner and correspondence on the subject of the insurrection in the Sierra Leone protectorate. [C. 9388] H.C. (1899). LX, 1. Evidence etc. [C. 9391] H.C. (1899). LX, 183.

A full inquiry running to over 800 pages.

1889  COX-GEORGE (NOAH ARTHUR). Finance and development in West Africa: the Sierra Leone experience. 1961.

(e) *Central Africa*

(i) *General*

1890  SHEPPERSON (GEORGE ALLCOT). 'The literature of British Central Africa: a review article'. *Rhodes–Livingstone J.* xxiii (1958), 12–46.

1891  ROUSSEAU (MARGUERITE HELÈNE) *comp.* A bibliography of African education in the Federation of Rhodesia and Nyasaland (1890–1958). Cape Town. 1958. Repr. 1969.

1892  STOKES (ERIC) *and* BROWN (RICHARD) *eds.* The Zambesian past: studies in Central African history. Manch. 1966.

1893  RHODES–LIVINGSTONE INSTITUTE. Conference on the history of the Central African peoples: papers presented . . . Lusaka. 1963.

1894  CENTRAL AFRICA HISTORICAL ASSOCIATION. Local history series. 1+. Salisbury. 1960+.

1895  THE RHODES–LIVINGSTONE JOURNAL. Rhodes–Livingstone Inst., Lusaka. Oxf. etc. 1944–65.

Superseded by *African social research: the j. of the Inst. for Social Research, University of Zambia*, Lusaka 1966+.

1896  CAIRNS (H. ALAN C.). Prelude to imperialism: British reactions to Central African society, 1840–1890. 1965.

Publ. in N.Y. as *The clash of cultures: early race relations in Central Africa*, 1965. A very useful study.

1897 GANN (LEWIS HENRY). 'The end of the slave trade in British Central Africa, 1889–1912'. *Rhodes–Livingstone J.* xvi (1954), 27–51.

1898 RANGER (TERENCE OSBORN) *ed.* Aspects of Central African history. Lond. etc. 1968.

1899 WILLS (ALFRED JOHN). An introduction to the history of Central Africa. 1964. 2nd edn. 1967.

Largely an introductory account of European settlement. To be used with caution. P. E. N. Tindall, *A history of Central Africa*, 1968, covers much the same ground, as does Alexander John Hanna, *The story of the Rhodesias and Nyasaland*, 1960, 2nd edn. 1965.

1900 APTHORPE (RAYMOND) *ed.* From tribal rule to modern government. Rhodes–Livingstone Inst. Lusaka. 1959.

1901 MOIR (FREDERICK LEWIS MAITLAND). After Livingstone: an African trade romance. 1923.

A hist. of the African Lakes Corporation.

1902 WARHURST (PHILIP ROBERT). Anglo-Portuguese relations in south-central Africa, 1890–1900. 1962.

1903 ANSTEY (ROGER THOMAS). Britain and the Congo in the nineteenth century. Oxf. 1962.

See also his *King Leopold's legacy: the Congo under Belgian rule, 1908–1960*, 1966; Arthur Berriedale Keith, *The Belgian Congo and the Berlin Act*, Oxf. 1919; and Ruth M. Slade, *King Leopold's Congo: aspects of the development of race relations in the Congo Independent State*, 1962. For the French Congo see also Sylvanus John Sodienye Cookey, 'The concession policy in the French Congo and the British reaction, 1898–1906', *J. African Hist.* vii (1966), 263–78.

1904 COOKEY (SYLVANUS JOHN SODIENYE). Britain and the Congo question, 1885–1913. 1968.

A major source is *E. D. Morel's history of the Congo reform movement*, ed. by William Roger Louis and Jean Stengers, Oxf. 1968. Edmund Dene Morel himself publ. *The Congo slave state: a protest against the new African slavery . . .*, Liverpool 1903; *King Leopold's rule in Africa*, 1904; *Red rubber: the story of the rubber slave trade flourishing on the Congo in the year of grace 1906*, 1906, new edn. 1908; *The future of the Congo . . .*, 1909; and *Great Britain and the Congo: the pillage of the Congo basin*, 1909. For Morel's career generally see Frederick Seymour Cocks, *E. D. Morel: the man and his work*, 1920. The anti-slavery viewpoint is set out in Henry Richard Fox-Bourne, *Civilisation in Congoland: a story of international wrong-doing*, 1903. Publicity was given to the Congo by Roger Casement, on whom see William Roger Louis, 'Roger Casement and the Congo', *J. African Hist.* v (1964), 99–120, and **10408**. For some diplomatic consequences of the Congo question for Anglo-Belgian relations see **2369** and **1705**.

1905 TABLER (EDWARD C.) *ed.* Zambezia and Matabeleland in the seventies: the narrative of Frederick Hugh Barber, 1875 and 1877–78, and the journal of Richard Frewen, 1877–1878. Robins ser. 1. 1960.

Tabler also ed. other books of travels incl. *The far interior: chronicles of pioneering in the Matabele and Mashona countries, 1847–1879*, Cape Town 1955; *Trade and travel in early Barotseland: the diaries of George Westbeech, 1885–1888, and Captain Norman MacLeod, 1875–1876,* Robins ser. 2, 1963; and *The Zambezi papers of Richard Thornton, geologist to Livingstone's Zambezi expedition,* [1858–63], Robins ser. 4, 2 v. 1963. Other travel vols. incl. Joseph Thomson, *To the central African lakes and back: the narrative of the Royal Geographical Society's east central African expedition, 1878–80,* 2 v. 1881, new edn. 2 v. 1968, and the works at **1969–71.**

## (ii) *Missions*

1906  DU PLESSIS (JOHANNES). The evangelisation of pagan Africa: a history of Christian missions to the pagan tribes of Central Africa. Cape Town & Johannesburg. 1930.

1907  SMITH (EDWIN WILLIAM). The way of the white fields in Rhodesia: a survey of Christian enterprise in northern and southern Rhodesia. 1928.

1908  BOLINK (PETER). Towards church union in Zambia: a study of missionary co-operation and church union efforts in Central Africa. Amsterdam. 1967.

A general missionary hist., strongest on the 20th cent.

1909  ROTBERG (ROBERT IRWIN). Christian missionaries and the creation of northern Rhodesia, 1880–1924. Princeton [N.J.]. 1965.

1910  TAYLOR (JOHN VERNON) *and* LEHMANN (DOROTHEA A.). Christians of the copperbelt: the growth of the church in Northern Rhodesia. 1961.

1911  ANDERSON-MORSHEAD (ANNA ELIZABETH MARY) *cont. by* BLOOD (ARTHUR GORDON). The history of the Universities' Mission to Central Africa, 1859–[1957]. 1897. 6th edn. 3 v. 1955–62.

A handy work of pious hagiography. See also George Herbert Wilson, *The history of the Universities' Mission to Central Africa,* 1936.

1912  GELFAND (MICHAEL) *ed.* Gubulawayo and beyond: letters and journals of the early Jesuit missionaries to Zambesia (1879–1887). 1968.

For the White Fathers see Henry Pineau, *Évêque roi des brigands: Monseigneur Dupont, premier vicaire apostolique du Nyassa, 1850–1930,* Paris [1937].

1913  HETHERWICK (ALEXANDER). The romance of Blantyre [mission]: how Livingstone's dream came true. 1931.

See also his *The gospel and the African: the Croall lectures for 1930–1931 on the impact of the gospel on a central African people,* Edin. 1902, and **1923.**

1914  JACK (JAMES WILLIAM). Daybreak in Livingstonia: the story of the Livingstonia mission, British Central Africa. Edin. & Lond. 1901.

See also James Horne Morrison, *Streams in the desert: a picture of life in Livingstonia,* 1919, and the lives of Laws (**1927**), and Fraser (**1921**).

1915 SLADE (RUTH M.). English-speaking missions in the Congo Independent State, 1878–1908. Brussels. 1959.

See also **1903-4** and **1922**.

1916 FRIPP (CONSTANCE ELIZABETH) *and* HILLER (VYVIAN WILLIAM) *eds*. Gold and the gospel in Mashonaland, 1888: being, the journals of 1. the Mashonaland mission of Bishop Knight-Bruce 2. the concession journey of Charles Dunell Rudd. Central African Archives: Oppenheimer ser. 4. 1949.

1917 ARNOT. Garenganze: or, seven years' pioneer mission work in Central Africa. By Frederick Stanley Arnot. 1889. New edn. by Robert I. Rotberg. 1969.

Arnot also publ. *From Natal to the Upper Zambesi* . . ., 2nd edn. Glasgow 1883, *Bihé and Garenganze: or, four years further work and travel in central Africa*, 1893, and *Missionary travels in central Africa*, Bath 1914. For his life see Ernest Baker, *The life & explorations of Frederick Stanley Arnot: the authorised biography of a zealous missionary, intrepid explorer, & self-denying benefactor amongst the natives of Africa*, 1921.

1918 COILLARD. On the threshold of Central Africa: a record of twenty years' pioneering among the Barotsi of the Upper Zambesi . . . By François Coillard. Trans. by Catherine Winkworth Mackintosh. 1897. 2nd edn. 1902.

Long regarded as a missionary classic. H. Dieterlen, *François Coillard*, Paris 1921, is the standard biog. But see also Catherine Winkworth Mackintosh, *Coillard of the Zambesi: the lives of François and Christina Coillard of the Paris Missionary Society, in South and Central Africa (1858–1904)*, 1907, Édouard Favre, *François Coillard*, 3 v. Paris 1908–13, and James Thayer Addison, *François Coillard*, Hartford [Conn.] 1929.

1919 CRAWFORD. Dan Crawford, missionary and pioneer in Africa. By George Edwin Tilsley. Lond. & Edin. [*c*. 1929.]

1920 DOUGLAS. Arthur Douglas: missionary on Lake Nyasa: the story of his life. By Berkeley William Randolph. Westminster. 1912.

1921 FRASER. Donald Fraser of Livingstonia. By Agnes Renton Fraser. 1934.

1922 GRENFELL. George Grenfell and the Congo: a history and description of the Congo Independent State and adjoining districts . . . diaries and researches of the late Rev. George Grenfell . . . and records of the British Baptist Missionary Society. By Sir Harry Hamilton Johnston. 2 v. 1908.

See also Harry Lathey Hemmens, *George Grenfell: pioneer in Congo*, 1927.

1923 HETHERWICK. A prince of missionaries: the Rev. Alexander Hetherwick . . . By William Pringle Livingstone. [1931.]

1924 HINE. Days gone by: being, some account of past years, chiefly in Central Africa. By John Edward Hine, Bishop of Zanzibar etc. 1924.

1925  JOHNSON. My African reminiscences, 1875–1895. By William Percival Johnson. [1924.]

See also his *Nyasa: the great water: being a description of the lake and the life of the people,* 1922, and Bertram Herbert Barnes, *Johnson of Nyasaland: a study of the life and work of William Percival Johnson, D.D., archdeacon of Nyasa, missionary pioneer, 1876–1928,* 1933.

1926  KIRK. Kirk on the Zambesi: a chapter of African history. By Sir Reginald Coupland. Oxf. 1928. Repr. 1968.

See also Reginald Foskett, ed., *The Zambesi journal and letters of Dr. John Kirk, 1858–63,* 2 v. Edin. 1965, and Kirk's corresp. with Livingstone (**1928**).

1927  LAWS. Reminiscences of Livingstonia. By Robert Laws. Edin. & Lond. 1934.

See also William Pringle Livingstone, *Laws of Livingstonia: a narrative of missionary adventure and achievement,* 1921, and James Johnston, *Dr. Laws of Livingstonia . . .,* [1909] new edn. [*Robert Laws . . .*] [1935].

1928  LIVINGSTONE. Private journals of David Livingstone, 1851–1853. Ed. by Isaac Schapera. Lond. & Berkeley. 1960.

Suppl. by *The Zambezi expedition of David Livingstone, 1858–1863,* ed. by John Peter Richard Wallis, Central African Archives: Oppenheimer ser. 9, 2 v. 1956, and Horace Waller, *Last journals of David Livingstone in Central Africa, from 1865 to his death . . .,* 2 v. 1874. For Livingstone's correspondence see Isaac Schapera, ed., *David Livingstone: family letters, 1841–1856,* 2 v. 1959, and *Livingstone's missionary correspondence, 1841–1856,* 1961; David Chamberlin, ed., *Some letters from Livingstone, 1840–1872,* 1940; and Reginald Foskett, ed., *The Zambesi doctors: David Livingstone's letters to John Kirk, 1858–1872,* Edin. 1964. David Livingstone's most important works were, *Missionary travels and researches in South Africa: including a sketch of sixteen years' residence in the interior of Africa, and a journey from the Cape of Good Hope to Loanda, on the west coast; thence across the continent, down the river Zambesi, to the eastern ocean,* 1857, *Narrative of an expedition to the Zambesi and its tributaries, and of the discovery of the lakes Shirwa and Nyassa, 1858–1864,* [by David and Charles Livingstone] 1865, and *Dr. Livingstone's Cambridge lectures . . .,* ed. by William Monk, Camb. 1858, 2nd edn. 1860. For other works see Margaret Elizabeth Appleyard, *Dr. David Livingstone: a bibliography,* Cape Town 1949.

1929  LIVINGSTONE. David Livingstone: his life and letters. By George Fenn Seaver. 1957.

See also Sir Harry Hamilton Johnston, *Livingstone and the exploration of Central Africa,* 1889, repr. 1912; George Martelli, *Livingstone's river: a history of the Zambesi expedition, 1858–1864,* 1970; Sir Reginald Coupland, *Livingstone's last journey,* 1945; Frank Debenham, *The way to Ilala: David Livingstone's pilgrimage,* 1955; Michael Gelfand, *Livingstone the doctor: his life and travels: a study in medical history,* Oxf. 1957; Jack Simmons, *Livingstone and Africa,* 1955; James Irvine Macnair, ed., *Livingstone's travels,* 1954; and Sir Henry Morton Stanley, *How I found Livingstone . . .,* 1872, rev. edn. 1874.

1930  MACKENZIE. Memoir of Bishop Mackenzie. By Harvey Goodwin, bishop of Carlisle. Camb. 1864. 2nd edn. 1865.

There is also an attractive modern study, [William] Owen Chadwick, *Mackenzie's grave,* 1959. Charles Frederick Mackenzie was bishop in Central Africa.

1931 MAPLES. Journals and papers of Chauncy Maples, D.D., F.R.G.S., late Bishop of Likoma, Lake Nyasa, Africa. Ed. by Ellen Maples. 1899.

1932 MOFFAT. John Smith Moffat, C.M.G., missionary: a memoir. By Robert Unwin Moffat. 1921.

1933 MOFFAT. The Matabele journals of Robert Moffat, 1829–1860. Ed. by John Peter Richard Wallis. Government Archives of Southern Rhodesia: Oppenheimer ser. 1. 2 v. 1945.

Suppl. by J. P. R. Wallis, ed., *The Matabele mission: a selection from the correspondence of John and Emily Moffat, David Livingstone and others, 1858–1878,* Oppenheimer ser. 2., 1945. The principal biography is [William] Cecil Northcott, *Robert Moffat, pioneer in Africa, 1817–1870,* 1961.

1934 SCOTT. A hero of the dark continent: memoir of Rev. Wm. Affleck Scott . . . By William Henry Rankine. Edin. & Lond. 1896.

1935 SMYTHIES. The life of Charles Alan Smythies, bishop of the Universities' Mission to Central Africa. By Gertrude Ward. Ed. by E. F. Russell. 1898.

1936 STEERE. A memoir of Edward Steere . . . third missionary bishop in central Africa. By Robert Marshall Heanley. 1888. 2nd edn. 1890.

STEWART. For the Zambesi journal of James Stewart see **2019**.

1937 SWANN. Fighting the slave-hunters in central Africa: a record of twenty-six years . . . By Alfred James Swann. 1910.

1938 TOZER. Letters of Bishop Tozer and his sister . . . Ed. by Gertrude Ward. 1902.

1939 WADDELL. An artisan missionary on the Zambesi: being the life story of William Thomson Waddell, largely drawn from his letters and journals. By John MacConnachie. Edin. & Lond. 1910.

1940 WHITE. John White of Mashonaland. By Charles Freer Andrews. 1935.

### (iii) *Southern Rhodesia*

1941 CARPENTER (OLIVE) *comp.* The development of Southern Rhodesia from the earliest times to the year 1900: a bibliography. Cape Town. 1946. 4th impr. 1969.

See also Elizabeth Ann Bean, comp., *Political development in Southern Rhodesia, 1890–1953: a bibliography,* Cape Town 1969.

1942 BAXTER (T. W.) *and* BURKE (ERIC EDWARD). Guide to the historical manuscripts in the National Archives of Rhodesia. Salisbury. 1970.

See also T. W. Baxter, ed., *Guide to the public archives of Rhodesia,* vol. 1, *1890–1923,* Nat. Archives of Rhodesia, Salisbury 1969.

1943  GANN (LEWIS HENRY). A history of Southern Rhodesia: Vol. 1. early days to 1934. Lond. 1965. N.Y. 1969.

Useful bibliog. For hist. articles see Rhodesia Africana Soc. *Rhodesiana*, [Salisbury] 1956+.

1944  MASON (PHILIP). The birth of a dilemma: the conquest and settlement of Rhodesia. Inst. of Race Relations. 1958.

1945  SAMKANGE (STANLAKE JOHN THOMPSON). Origins of Rhodesia. [1887–93.] Lond., Nairobi, etc. 1969.

1946  TABLER (EDWARD C.) *comp*. Pioneers of Rhodesia. Cape Town. 1966.

A list of Europeans in the area 1836–80.

1947  HOLE (HUGH MARSHALL). The making of Rhodesia. 1926.

See also his *Old Rhodesian days*, 1928.

1948  HICKMAN (A. S.). Men who made Rhodesia: a register of those who served in the British South Africa Company's police. Salisbury. 1960.

1949  PALLEY (CLAIRE). The constitutional history and law of Southern Rhodesia, 1888–1965: with special reference to imperial control. Oxf. 1966.

1950  WILLSON (FRANCIS MICHAEL GLENN) *ed*. Source book of parliamentary elections and referenda in Southern Rhodesia, 1898–1962. Comp. by Gloria C. Passmore and Margaret T. Mitchell. Salisbury. 1963.

1951  THOMSON (HARRY CRAUFUIRD). Rhodesia and its government. 1898.

1952  RAYNER (WILLIAM). The tribe and its successors: an account of African traditional life and European settlement in southern Rhodesia. 1962.

1953  GLASS (STAFFORD). The Matabele war. 1968.

1954  WILLS (WILLIAM ARTHUR) *and* COLLINGRIDGE (LEONARD THOMAS) *and others*. The downfall of Lobengula: the cause, history and effect of the Matabeli war . . . 1894.

See also Sir John Christopher Willoughby, *Report on the campaign in Matabeleland*, 1894; Patrick William Forbes, *Report on the campaign in Matabeleland*, 1894; Archibald Ross Colquhoun, *Matabeleland: the war and our position in South Africa*, [1894]; Charles Henry Wynne Donovan, *With Wilson in Matabeleland* . . ., 1894; and Charles L. Norris Newman, *Matabeleland and how we got it* . . ., 1895.

1955  RANGER (TERENCE OSBORN). Revolt in Southern Rhodesia, 1896–7: a study in African resistance. Lond. & Evanston, Ill. 1967.

On the Matabele rising. See also Stafford Glass, *The Matabele war*, Harlow 1968; Apollon Borisovich Davidson, *Matabele i Mashona v bor'be protiv Angliiskoi kolonizatsii, 1888–1897*, Moscow 1958; Hugh Marshall Hole, *The passing of the black kings*, 1932;

and the ser. of contemp. reports, of which the most useful are Robert Stevenson Smyth Baden-Powell, Baron Baden-Powell, *The Matabele campaign, 1896,* 1897, 4th edn. 1901; Sir Edwin Alfred Hervey Alderson, *With the mounted infantry and the Mashona-land field force, 1896* . . ., 1898; Herbert Charles Onslow Plumer, Viscount Plumer, *An irregular corps in Matabeleland,* 1897; Frederick Courteney Selous, *Sunshine and storm in Rhodesia: being a narrative of events in Matabeleland* . . ., 1896; Francis William Sykes, *With Plumer in Matabeleland: an account of the operations of the Matabeleland Relief Force during the rebellion of 1896,* Westminster 1897; and David C. de Waal, *With Rhodes in Mashonaland,* trans. by J. H. Hofmeyr de Waal, Cape Town 1896.

1956  GELFAND (MICHAEL). Tropical victory: an account of the influence of medicine on the history of southern Rhodesia, 1890–1923. Cape Town, etc. 1953.

(iv) *Nyasaland and Northern Rhodesia (Malawi and Zambia)*

1957  BROWN (EDWARD E.), FISHER (CAROL A.), *and* WEBSTER (JOHN B.). A bibliography of Malawi. Syracuse, N.Y. 1965. Suppl. 1969.

1958  NYASALAND SOCIETY (HISTORICAL AND SCIENTIFIC SOCIETY OF MALAWI). [The Nyasaland] Journal. 1+. Blantyre. 1948+.

There is no satisfactory general hist. Frank Debenham, *Nyasaland: the land of the lake,* 1955, is a handy introductory sketch.

1959  HANNA (ALEXANDER JOHN). The beginnings of Nyasaland and north-eastern Rhodesia, 1859–95. Oxf. 1956.

1960  ROTBERG (ROBERT IRWIN). The rise of nationalism in central Africa: the making of Malawi and Zambia, 1873–1964. Camb., Mass. 1965.

1961  JOHNSTON (*Sir* HARRY HAMILTON). British Central Africa. 1897.

See also Sir Hector Livingston Duff, *Nyasaland under the Foreign Office,* 1903, 2nd edn. 1906.

1962  GELFAND (MICHAEL). Lakeside pioneers: socio-medical study of Nyasaland (1875–1920). Oxf. 1964.

1963  SHEPPERSON (GEORGE ALLCOT) *and* PRICE (THOMAS). Independent African: John Chilembwe and the origins, setting, and significance of the Nyasaland native rising of 1915. Edin. 1958.

An important study. See also George Simeon Mwase, *Strike a blow and die,* ed. by Robert Irwin Rotberg, Camb., Mass. 1967, the reminiscences of one who lived through the rising and knew Chilembwe.

1964  GANN (LEWIS HENRY). A history of Northern Rhodesia: early days to 1953. 1964.

Less detailed than his *The birth of a plural society: the development of Northern Rhodesia under the British South Africa Company, 1894–1914,* Manch. 1958.

1965  CAPLAN (GERALD L.). 'Barotseland's scramble for protection'.
*J. African Hist.* x (1969), 277–94.
See also his *The elites of Barotseland, 1878–1969: a political history of Zambia's western province,* Lond. & Berkeley 1970.

1966  GELFAND (MICHAEL). Northern Rhodesia in the days of the charter: a medical and social study, 1878–1924. Oxf. 1961.

1967  DAVIS (JOHN MERLE) *ed.* Modern industry and the African: an enquiry into the effect of the copper mines of Central Africa upon native society and the work of Christian missions. Int. Missionary Council. 1933.

1968  BARNES (JOHN ARUNDEL). Politics in a changing society: a political history of the Fort Jameson Ngoni. Cape Town. 1954.

1969  BAINES. The northern goldfields diaries of Thomas Baines . . . 1869–[1872]. Ed. by John Peter Richard Wallis. Government Archives of Southern Rhodesia. Oppenheimer ser. 3. 3 v. 1946.

1970  LEASK. The southern African diaries of Thomas Leask, 1865–1870. Ed. by John Peter Richard Wallis. Central African Archives: Oppenheimer ser. 8. 1954.

1971  STEVENSON-HAMILTON. The Barotseland journal of James Stevenson-Hamilton, 1898–1899. Ed. by John Peter Richard Wallis. Central African Archives: Oppenheimer ser. 7. 1953.
For earlier diaries see **1905.**

### (f) *South Africa*

South African history has since the Great Trek usually been written from a distinctively British or Afrikaner point of view. There are therefore two distinctive literatures relating to British involvement in South Africa, each of them embracing several schools of thought. An attempt has been made to represent all schools in this bibliog. For Afrikaner views see in particular Van Jaarsveld on Afrikaner historiography (**1983**), and Muller's history of South Africa (**1995**).

#### (i) *Reference*

1972  MUSIKER (REUBEN) *comp.* Guide to South African reference books. Cape Town. 1955. 4th edn. Cape Town. 1965.

1973  MENDELSSOHN (SIDNEY). Mendelssohn's South African bibliography . . . 2 v. 1910. Repr. 2 v. 1957.
A pioneer general bibliog. Suppl. by *Annual list of africana added to the Mendelssohn library,* Cape Town 1938–46, etc. George McCall Theal, *Catalogue of books and pamphlets relating to Africa south of the Zambesi . . . in the collection of George McCall Theal . . . ,* Cape Town 1912, repr. 1963, was another pioneer work. For books in German there is Otto Hartung Spohr, comp., *German Africana: German publications on South and South West Africa,* Pretoria 1968, which largely repl. Ludwig Bielschowsky, comp.,

List of books in German on South Africa and South West Africa, published up to 1914, in the South African Public Library, Cape Town, Cape Town, 1949, cont. by A. F. Plaat for 1914–50 (Cape Town 1951) and, for 1950–64, by Ellen Lisa Marianne Both (Cape Town 1969).

1974  NIENABER (PETRUS JOHANNES). Bibliografie van afrikaanse boeke (6 April 1861–6 April 1943). Johannesburg. 1943. 2nd edn. 1956. Suppls. to date.

1975  STATE LIBRARY. S.A.N.B.: Suid-Afrikaanse nasionale bibliografie: South African national bibliography. Pretoria. 1959+.

The official list of South African books.

1976  TAYLOR (LOREE ELIZABETH). South African libraries. 1967.

Elizabeth Ann Newenham, comp., *A bibliography of printed catalogues of the libraries of southern Africa, 1820–1920*, Johannesburg Public Libr. 1967, is a handy list.

1977  BOTHA (COLIN GRAHAM). The public archives of South Africa, 1652–1910. Cape Town. 1928.

A useful guide which needs revision. For early records there are useful suppls. to the South African archives in George McCall Theal, comp., *Records of south-eastern Africa collected in various libraries and archive departments in Europe*, 9 v. 1898–1903, and *Records of the Cape colony, copied for the Cape government from the manuscript documents in the Public Record Office, London*, 36 v. 1897–1905.

1978  SOUTH AFRICA (HOUSE OF ASSEMBLY). Index to the manuscript annexures and printed papers of the House of Assembly, including select committee reports and bills, and also to principal motions and resolutions and commission reports, 1910–1961. Cape Town. 1963.

1979  MALAN (STEPHANUS IMMELMAN) Union catalogue of theses and dissertations of the South African universities, 1942–1958. Potchefstroom. 1959. Annual suppls. 1959+.

1980  VARLEY (DONALD HAROLD) *ed*. Union list of South African newspapers. Cape Town. 1950.

1981  SAUL (CONSTANCE DAPHNE). South African periodical publications, 1800–1875: a bibliography. Cape Town. 1949. 3rd edn. Cape Town. 1964.

Cont. by J. I. Plowman for 1875–1910. Cape Town 1952. Periodicals are indexed in Johannesburg Public Libr., *Index to South African periodicals, 1940–1949*, 4 v. Johannesburg 1953, cont. for 1950–9 in 3 v. Johannesburg 1962, with annual suppls. 1960+.

1982  MULLER (CHRISTOFFEL FREDERIK JAKOBUS), VAN JAARS-VELD (FLORIS ALBERTUS), *and* VAN WIJK (THEO) *eds*. A select bibliography of South African history: a guide for historical research. Pretoria. 1966.

Indispensable.

1983  VAN JAARSVELD (FLORIS ALBERTUS). The Afrikaner's interpretation of South African history. Cape Town. 1964.

See also Leonard Monteath Thompson, 'Afrikaner nationalist historiography and policy of apartheid', *J. African Hist.* iii (1962), 125–41.

1984  KIERSEN (SYLVIA). English and Afrikaans novels on South African history [1488–1957]: a bibliography. Cape Town. 1958.

See also Jacobus Petrus Lodewicus Snyman, *A bibliography of South African novels in English published from 1880–1930*, Potchefstroom 1951.

1985  ROBERTS (ALFRED ADRIAN). A South African legal bibliography: being a bio-bibliographical survey and law-finder of the Roman and Roman-Dutch legal literature in Southern Africa, with an historical chart, notes on all the judges since 1828, and other appendices. Pretoria. 1942.

1986  NOBLE (FIONA VIRGINIA) *comp*. South African numismatics, 1652–1965: a bibliography. Cape Town. 1967.

1987  POTGIETER (DIRK JACOBUS) *and others, eds*. The encyclopaedia of southern Africa. In preparation.

Pending the completion of this work, consult Eric Rosenthal, comp., *Encyclopaedia of southern Africa*, Lond. & N.Y. 1961, 4th edn. 1967.

1988  DE KOCK (WILLEM JOHANNES) *ed*. The dictionary of South African biography. 1+. Cape Town. 1968+. In progress.

When complete will repl. Eric Rosenthal, comp., *Southern African dictionary of national biography*, 1966, which is simply a short handbook. For contemp. biog. dictionaries see *South African who's who*, Johannesburg, etc. 1907+, *Anglo-African who's who . . .*, 3 v. 1905–10, and *Men of the times . . .*, 2 v. Johannesburg 1905–6. For autobiogs. see Rowse Ushpol, *A select bibliography of South African autobiographies*, Cape Town 1959.

1989  VAN RIEBEECK SOCIETY FOR THE PUBLICATION OF SOUTH AFRICAN HISTORICAL DOCUMENTS. Publications. Cape Town. 1918+.

1990  SOUTH AFRICAN ARCHIVAL RECORDS [SUID-AFRIKAANSE ARGIEFSTUKKE]: published under the supervision of the Archives Commission by the publication section of the archives of the Union of South Africa. 4 ser. Cape Town. 1952+.

Each of the four ser. covers an indiv. province.

1991  EYBERS (GEORGE VON WELFLING) *ed*. Select constitutional documents illustrating South African history, 1795–1910. 1918.

See also Daniel Wilhelmus Krüger, ed., *South African parties and policies, 1910–1960: a select source book*, Cape Town & Lond. 1960.

1992  POLLOCK (NORMAN CHARLES) *and* AGNEW (SWANZIE). An historical geography of South Africa. 1963.

1993  WALKER (ERIC ANDERSON). Historical atlas of South Africa. Cape Town, Lond., etc. 1922.

1994  WILSON (MONICA HUNTER) *and* THOMPSON (LEONARD MONTEATH) *eds.* The Oxford history of South Africa. 2 v. Oxf. 1969–71.

A sound modern hist. which attains high scholarly standards. Largely repls. Eric Anderson Walker, ed., *Cambridge history of the British empire*: VIII. *South Africa*, Camb. 1936, 2nd edn. 1963, which has valuable bibliogs. Such old multi-vol. works as Duncan Campbell Francis Moodie, *The history of the battles and adventures of the British, the Boers and the Zulus, &c., in southern Africa, from the time of Pharaoh Necho to 1880*, 2 v. Cape Town 1888; George McCall Theal, *History of South Africa* [1505–1884], 11 v. 1888–1919, repr. in 11 v. Cape Town 1964; and Sir George Edward Cory, *The rise of South Africa . . . to 1857*, 5 v. 1910–30 [v. 6 in *Archives year book* II (1939), pt. 1], repr. in 6 v. Cape Town 1965, are to be used with great caution, though they are handy for facts.

1995  MULLER (CHRISTOFFEL FREDERIK JACOBUS) *ed.* Vyfhonderd jaar Suid-Afrikaanse geskiedenis. [Five hundred years of South African history.] Pretoria. 1968. 2nd edn. [In both Afrikaans and English.] 1969.

A good hist. by Afrikaner historians. Preferable to Andries Jacobus Hendrik Van der Walt, J. A. Wiid, and Albertus Lourens Geyer, eds., *Geskiedenis van Suid-Afrika*, 2 v. Cape Town 1951, 2nd edn. 2 v. 1955, rev. edn. 1 v. 1966.

1996  WALKER (ERIC ANDERSON). A history of South Africa. 1928. 3rd edn. [A history of southern Africa.] 1957.

The first good short hist. of South Africa. Now out of date but not adequately repl. by Leopold Marquard, *The story of South Africa*, 1955, 3rd edn. 1968, or Arthur Mervyn Keppel-Jones, *South Africa: a short history*, 1949, 4th edn. 1963.

1997  ARCHIVES YEAR BOOK FOR SOUTH AFRICAN HISTORY. 1+. Archives of the Union of South Africa. Cape Town. 1938+.

The best of the South African hist. js. See also *Africana notes and news*, 1+, Johannesburg 1943+, *Historia: amptelike orgaan van die Historiese Genootskap van Suid-Afrika* [History: official organ of the Historical Assoc. of South Africa], Pretoria 1952+, and *South African archives j.*, Pretoria 1959+.

1998  BAINES. Journal of residence in Africa, 1842–1853. By Thomas Baines. Ed. by Reginald Frank Kennedy. 2 v. Van Riebeeck Soc. 42, 45. Cape Town. 1961–4.

Better than the usual traveller's tales. Covers Kaffir warfare.

1999  TROLLOPE (ANTHONY). South Africa. 2 v. 1878.

Not one of his best works.

2000  BRYCE (JAMES). Impressions of South Africa. 1897. 3rd edn. 1899.

Interesting because of its author. Packed with misc. information. Other general books of the period worth consulting are William Basil Worsfold, *South Africa: a study in colonial administration and development*, 1895, 2nd edn. 1897, Sir Francis Edward Younghusband, *South Africa of to-day*, Lond. & N.Y. 1898, and Alfred Peter Hillier, *South African studies*, 1900.

2001 HAHLO (HERMAN ROBERT) *and* KAHN (ELLISON). The Union of South Africa: the development of its laws and constitution. 1960. Suppl. 1962.

Hahlo and Kahn also publ. *The South African legal system and its background*, Cape Town 1968. For the operation of the legal system see Sir John Gilbert Kotzé, *Biographical memoirs and reminiscences*, 2 v. Cape Town 1934-47, which is good. Kotzé was a judge in both the Transvaal (where he was dismissed) and the Cape. For the Transvaal see **2139**.

2002 GREEN (LESLIE PERCIVAL). History of local government in South Africa: an introduction. Cape Town. 1957.

(iii) *The Churches*

2003 BROWNLEE (MARGARET) *comp.* The lives and work of South African missionaries: a bibliography. Cape Town. 1952. 3rd impr. 1969.

For the bibliog. of Natal missions see **2116**.

2004 DU PLESSIS (JOHANNES). A history of Christian missions in South Africa. Lond., N.Y., etc. 1911. Repr. Cape Town. 1965.

See also **2165, 2170-1,** and **2191-2**.

2005 CARLYLE (JAMES EDWARD). South Africa and its mission fields. 1878.

2006 MAJEKE (NOSIPHO). The role of the missionaries in conquest. Johannesburg. 1952.

2007 DAVIES ([DANIEL] HORTON [MARLAIS]). Great South African Christians. Cape Town. 1951.

See also Horton Davies and Robert Henry Wishart Shepherd, comps., *South African missions, 1800-1950, an anthology,* 1954.

2008 LEWIS (CECIL) *and* EDWARDS (GERTRUDE ELIZABETH). Historical records of the Church of the Province of South Africa. 1934.

2009 HINCHLIFF (PETER BINGHAM). The Anglican church in South Africa: an account of the history and development of the Church of the Province of South Africa. 1963.

See also Sally-Ann Ledward, *The constitutional development of the Church of the Province of South Africa, 1848-1936: bibliography,* Cape Town 1957; Arthur Hamilton Baynes, Bishop of Natal, *South Africa,* 1908; and Augustus Theodore Wirgman, *The history of the English church and people in South Africa,* Lond. & N.Y. 1895, repr. N.Y. 1969. For the important anglican dioceses of Cape Town and Natal see **2092, 2095 2098, 2117-9**.

2010 CALLAWAY (GODFREY). Pioneers in Pondoland. Lovedale. [1938.]

2011 CALLAWAY. Godfrey Callaway: missionary in Kaffraria, 1892-1942: his life and writings. Ed. by Edward Douglas Sedding. 1945.

2012 CALLAWAY. Henry Callaway, M.D., D.D., first bishop for Kaffraria: his life-history and work: a memoir. By Marian S. Benham. Ed. by William Benham. 1896.

2013 CECILE. Mother Cecile in South Africa, 1883–1906: foundress of the Community of the Resurrection of our Lord. Comp. by a sister of the community [Sister Kate]. 1922.

2014 KEY. A shepherd of the Veld: Bransby Lewis Key, Bishop of St. John's, Kaffraria. By Godfrey Callaway. 1912.

2015 WHITE. John White of Mashonaland. By Charles Freer Andrews. 1935.

2016 WHITESIDE (JOSEPH). History of the Wesleyan Methodist church of South Africa. Lond. & Cape Town. 1906.

See also William Clifford Holden, *A brief history of Methodism and of the Methodist missions in South Africa*, 1877, and William Shaw, *The story of my mission in south-eastern Africa . . .*, 1860, and [William Binnington Boyce, ed.] *Memoir of the Rev. William Shaw . . .*, 1874.

2017 EVELEIGH (WILLIAM). The settlers and Methodism, 1820–1920 Cape Town. 1920.

2018 SHEPHERD (ROBERT HENRY WISHART). Lovedale, South Africa: the story of a century, 1841–1941. Lovedale, Cape Province. 1940.

A substantial work on a major Presbyterian mission. For one of the mission's best-known leaders, James Stewart, see **2019**. Stewart himself publ. *Lovedale past and present*, Lovedale 1887, and *Lovedale, South Africa*, Edin. 1894.

2019 STEWART. Stewart of Lovedale: the life of James Stewart, D.D., M.D. . . . By James Wells. 1908. 2nd edn. 1919.

See also John Peter Richard Wallis, ed., *The Zambesi journal of James Stewart, 1862–1863, with a selection from his correspondence*, Central African Archives: Oppenheimer ser. 6, 1952.

2020 MURRAY. The life of Andrew Murray of South Africa. By Johannes du Plessis. [1920.]

2021 TINDALL. The journal of Joseph Tindall, missionary in South West Africa, 1839–55. Ed. by Benjamin Arthur Tindall. Van Riebeeck Soc. 40. Cape Town. 1959.

2022 BROWN (WILLIAM ERIC). The Catholic church in South Africa: from its origins to the present day. Ed. by Michael Derrick. 1960.

2023 BATTS (H. J.). The story of 100 years, 1820–1920: being the history of the Baptist Church in South Africa. Cape Town. [1922.]

2024 SARON (GUSTAV) *and* HOTZ (LOUIS) *eds.* The Jews in South Africa: a history. Cape Town. 1955.

See also Louis Herrman, *A history of the Jews in South Africa from the earliest times to 1895*, Lond. & Cape Town 1930, rev. edn. Johannesburg 1935, and *The Cape Town Hebrew congregation, 1841–1941: a centenary history*, Cape Town 1941.

### (iv) *The Non-White Population*

2025 SCHAPERA (ISAAC). Select bibliography of South African native life and problems. 1941. Suppls. [1939–49.] 2nd edn. 2 pts. Cape Town. 1964. [1950–8.] 2 pts. Cape Town. 1958. [1958–63.] Cape Town. 1964.

2026 BROOKES (EDGAR HARRY). The history of native policy in South Africa from 1830 to the present day. Cape Town. 1924. 2nd edn. Pretoria. 1927.

A major work, which has not lost its value though some of its arguments were disavowed by the author in his *The colour problems of South Africa . . .*, Lovedale 1934. See also for Natal, David Welsh, *The roots of segregation: native policy in colonial Natal, 1845–1910*, Cape Town etc. 1971; E. H. Brookes and N. Hurwitz, *The native reserves of Natal*, Natal regional survey 7, Cape Town 1957; L. M. Young, *The native policy of Benjamin Pine in Natal, 1850–1855*, *Archives year book*, (1951), pt. 2, 209–346; and **2112–3**; for the Cape, J. W. Macquarrie, ed., *The reminiscences of Sir Walter Stanford*, Van Riebeeck Soc. 39, 43, Cape Town 1958–62, and **2086**; for the Transvaal **2140–1**; and for Basutoland, Bechuanaland, Swaziland, and Zululand, **2159–92**.

2027 MACMILLAN (WILLIAM MILLER). Bantu, Boer, and Briton: the making of the South African native problem. 1929. Rev. edn. Oxf. 1963.

A pioneering work in race relations. See also Edward Rudolph Roux, *Time longer than rope: a history of the black man's struggle for freedom in South Africa*, 1948, 2nd edn. Madison, Wis. 1964, and Ian Douglas MacCrone, *Race attitudes in South Africa: historical, experimental and psychological studies*, Lond. 1937, 2nd edn. Johannesburg 1957.

2028 SACKS (BENJAMIN). South Africa: an imperial dilemma: non-Europeans and the British nation, 1902–1914. Albuquerque, New Mexico. 1967.

For the very end of the period see also Colin Martin Tatz, *Shadow and substance in South Africa: a study in land and franchise policies affecting Africans, 1910–1960*, Pietermaritzburg 1962.

2029 SOUTH AFRICAN NATIVE AFFAIRS COMMISSION. Report of the South African native affairs commission, 1903–1905 [Chairman: Sir Godfrey Lagden]. [Cd. 2399] H.C. (1905). LV, 69.

A major survey whose minutes of evidence, etc. were publ. in 6 v. Cape Town 1904–5. See also Cape of Good Hope, *Report and proceedings . . . of the government commission on native laws and customs*, 2 v. Cape Town 1883, repr. 2 v. Shannon 1970.

2030 TRANSVAAL LABOUR COMMISSION. Reports of the Transvaal labour commission [Chairman: A. Mackie Niven]. [Cd. 1896] H.C. (1904). XXXIX, 137. Further reports. [Cd. 1894] H.C. (1904). XXXIX, 225. Minutes of evidence. [Cd. 1897] H.C. (1904). XXXIX, 283.

For the character of the crisis see D. J. N. Denoon, 'The Transvaal labour crisis, 1901–6', *J. African Hist.* viii (1967), 481–94.

2031 MARAIS (JOHANNES STEPHANUS). The Cape Coloured people, 1652–1937. 1939. 2nd edn. Johannesburg. 1957. Repr. 1968.

See also Sheila Caffyn Patterson, *Colour and culture in South Africa: a study of the status of the Cape Coloured people within the social structure of the Union of South Africa*, 1953, and Izak David Du Plessis, *The Cape Malays*, Cape Town 1944, 2nd edn. 1947.

2032 HUTTENBACK (ROBERT A.). Gandhi in South Africa: British imperialism and the Indian question, 1860–1914. Ithaca, N.Y. 1971.

See also his 'Indians in South Africa, 1860–1914: the British imperial philosophy on trial', *Eng. Hist. Rev.* lxxxi (1966), 173–91, and 'Some fruits of Victorian imperialism: Gandhi and the Indian question in Natal, 1893–99', *Victorian Studs.* xi (1967–8), 153–80; the works on Gandhi at **1087**; Iqbal Narain, *The politics of racialism: a study of the Indian minority in South Africa down to the Gandhi–Smuts agreement*, Agra 1962; Union of South Africa, *Report of the Indian enquiry commission* [Chairman: W. H. Solomon]. [Cd. 7265] H.C. (1914). XLIX, 1; Mabel Palmer, formerly Atkinson, *The history of the Indians in Natal*, Natal regional survey 10, Cape Town 1957; Leonard Monteath Thompson, *Indian immigration into Natal, 1860–1872*, Archives year book, (1952), pt. 2, 1–76; Mohandas Karamchand Gandhi, *Satyagraha in South Africa*, trans. by Valji Govindji Desai, Madras 1928, 2nd edn. Ahmedabad 1950, repr. Stanford, Calif. 1954; George Harold Calpin, *Indians in South Africa*, Pietermaritzburg 1949; and P. S. Aiyar, *Conflict of races in South Africa*, Durban [1946?].

(v) *Social and Economic History*

2033 DE KIEWIET (CORNELIS WILLEM). A history of South Africa, social & economic. Oxf. 1941.

A revision of his *A history of South Africa*, 1928. Good. Other general economic hists. are Michiel Hendrik De Kock, *Selected subjects in the economic history of South Africa*, Cape Town 1924, and *The economic development of South Africa*, Westminster 1935; David Martin Goodfellow, *A modern economic history of South Africa*, 1931; and (not so useful) Lilian Charlotte Anne Knowles and Charles Matthew Knowles, *The economic development of the British overseas empire*: Vol. III. South Africa, 1936. For documents D. Hobart Houghton and Jenifer Dagut, *Source material on the South African economy, 1860–1970*, 3 v. 1973, is now standard.

2034 SCHUMANN (CHRISTIAN GUSTAV WALDEMAR). Structural changes and business cycles in South Africa, 1806–1936. 1938.

2035 GOLDMANN (CHARLES SYDNEY) *and* KITCHIN (JOSEPH). South African mines: their position, results and developments; together with an account of diamond, land, finance, and kindred concerns. 3 v. Lond. & Johannesburg. 1895–6.

Statistics and plans. Repl. Goldmann's *The financial, statistical and general history of the gold and other companies of Witwatersrand, South Africa*, 1892. Very useful for British investment. For a technical description of the mines see Frederick Henry Hatch and J. A. Chalmers, *The goldmines of the Rand . . .*, 1895. There are numerous more or less popular books about the Rand goldfields, incl. James Gray, *Payable gold . . .*, Johannesburg 1937; James Gray and Ethel L. Gray, *A history of the discovery of the Witwatersrand goldfields*, Johannesburg 1940; D. Jacobsson, *Fifty golden years of the Rand, 1886–1936*, 1936; Alan Patrick Cartwright, *Gold paved the way: the story of the Gold Fields group of companies*, Lond. & N.Y. 1967; and Owen Letcher, *The gold mines of southern Africa . . .*, Johannesburg & Lond. 1936. On the diamond fields see Gardner F. Williams, *The diamond mines of South Africa . . .*, N.Y. 1902, new edn. 2 v. N.Y. 1906, and Theodore Reunert, *Diamonds and gold in South Africa*, 1893.

2036 FRANKEL (SALLY HERBERT). Investment and the return to equity capital in the South African gold mining industry, 1887–1965: an international comparison. Oxf. & Camb., Mass. 1967.

2037 EMDEN (PAUL HERMAN). Randlords. 1935.

A handy summary. See also Hedley Arthur Chilvers, *The story of De Beers*, 1939; Stanley Jackson, *The great Barnato*, 1970; Harry Raymond, *B. I. Barnato: a memoir*, 1897; Richard Lewinsohn, *Barney Barnato: from Whitechapel clown to diamond king*, trans. by Geoffrey Sainsbury, 1937; George Seymour Fort, *Alfred Beit: a study of the man and his work*, 1932; Leo Weinthal, ed., *Memories, mines and millions: being the life of Sir Joseph B. Robinson*, 1929; and Stanhope Joel, *Ace of diamonds: the story of Solomon Barnato Joel*, [1958].

2038 VAN DER POEL (JEAN). Railway and customs policies in South Africa, 1885–1910. 1933.

See also Merilyn V. Buckland, comp., *South African railways before 1910: a bibliography*, Cape Town 1964; Edward Donald Campbell, *The birth and development of the Natal railways*, Pietermaritzburg 1951; and Dirk Jacobus Coetzee, *Spoorwegontwikkeling in die Suid-Afrikaanse Republiek, 1872–1899*, [Railway development in the South African republic], Cape Town 1940. For shipping see **6089, 6097**, and for roads E. Joubert, *Road transportation in South Africa in the 19th century: a bibliography*, Cape Town 1955. Other sections of the South African economy are covered by Ernest Heinrich Daniel Arndt, *Banking and currency development in South Africa, 1652–1927*, Cape Town etc. 1928; James A. Henry, *The first hundred years of the Standard Bank . . .*, ed. by H. A. Siepman 1963; Patricia Dicey, *Wine in South Africa: a select bibliography*, Cape Town 1951; Robert Farquhar Osborn, *Valiant harvest: the founding of the South African sugar industry, 1848–1926*, Durban 1964; and Hendrik Bernardus Thom, *Die geskiedenis van die skaapboerdery in Suid-Afrika* [The history of sheep-farming in South Africa], Amsterdam 1936. See also Hurwitz, *Agriculture in Natal*, **2122**.

2039 HATTERSLEY (ALAN FREDERICK). An illustrated social history of South Africa. Cape Town. 1969.

(vi) *Education and Science*

2040 MALHERBE (ERNST GIDEON). Education in South Africa, 1652–1922: a critical survey of the development of educational administration in the Cape, Natal, Transvaal and the Orange Free State. Cape Town etc. 1925.

Once standard: still useful. To be suppl. by Frederick Charles Metrowich, *The development of higher education in South Africa, 1873–1927*, Cape Town 1929; A. K. Bot, *The development of education in the Transvaal, 1836–1951*, Pretoria 1951; Johannes Christiaan Coetzee, ed., *Onderwys in Suid Afrika, 1652–1956*, Pretoria 1958; and Louis S. Steenkamp, *Onderwys vir blankes in Natal 1824–1940 . . .* [Education for whites in Natal], Pretoria 1941. For the University of Natal see **2120**.

2041 VAN WYK (A. H. DU PREEZ). Die invloed van die Engelse skoolwese op die Kaapse skoolwese, 1806–1915. [The influence of the English school system on the Cape school system.] Pretoria. 1947.

Other useful monographs on British influence are Michiel Albertus Basson, *Die Britse invloed in die Transvaalse onderwys, 1836–1907* [British influence on Transvaal education], *Archives Year Book* xix (1956), pt. II, Izak Stephanus Johannes Venter, *Die Anglikaanse kerk en die onderwys in die Oranje-Vrystaat, 1854–1900* [The Anglican church and education in the Orange Free State], Pretoria 1959. The other side of the picture is given in Daniel Hendrik Cilliers, *Die stryd van die Afrikaanssprekende in Kaapland om sy eie skool, 1652–1939* [The struggle of the Afrikaans-speaking people in the Cape for their own schools], Cape Town 1953, and Jan Ploeger, *Onderwys en onderwysbeleid in die Suid-Afrikaanse Republiek onder ds. S.J. du Toit en dr. N. Mansvelt, 1881–1900* [Education and educational policy in the South African republic under the Rev. S. J. du Toit and Dr. N. Mansvelt], *Archives Year Book* (1952), pt. I.

2042  BURROWS (EDMUND HARTFORD). A history of medicine in South Africa up to the end of the nineteenth century. Cape Town & Amsterdam. 1958.

See also Charlotte Searle, *The history of the development of nursing in South Africa, 1652–1960: a socio-historical survey*, Cape Town 1965.

2043  FLINT (WILLIAM) *and* GILCHRIST (JOHN DOW FISHER) *eds.* Science in South Africa: a handbook and review. Cape Town. 1905.

2044  VAN DER MEULEN (JAN). Die europäische Grundlage der Kolonialarchitektur am Kap der Guten Hoffnung. 3 v. Marburg. 1962.

### (vii) *British Expansion and the Boer War*

2045  JACKSON (MABEL VIOLET). European powers and south-east Africa: a study of international relations on the south-east coast of Africa, 1796–1856. 1942.

2046  BIXLER (RAYMOND WALTER). Anglo-German imperialism in South Africa, 1880–1900. Baltimore [Md.]. 1932.

See also Cornelius D. Penner, *England, Germany and the Transvaal, 1895–1902*, Chicago 1937; William Osgood Aydelotte, *Bismarck and British colonial policy: the problem of southwest Africa, 1883–1885*, Phila. 1937; Jan Hendrik Esterhuyse, *Southwest Africa, 1880–1894: the establishment of German authority in South-west Africa*, Cape Town 1968; and Horst Drechsler, *Südwestafrika unter deutscher Kolonialherrschaft; der Kampf der Herero und Nama gegen den deutschen Imperialismus, 1884–1915*, Berlin 1966.

2047  GALBRAITH (JOHN SEMPLE). Reluctant empire: British policy on the South African frontier, 1834–54. Berkeley. 1963.

2048  HATTERSLEY (ALAN FREDERICK). The convict crisis and the growth of unity: resistance to transportation in South Africa and Australia, 1848–1853. Pietermaritzburg. 1965.

See also **2110**.

2049  DE KIEWIET (CORNELIS WILLEM). British colonial policy and the South African republics, 1848–1872. 1929.

Cont. in his *The imperial factor in South Africa: a study in politics and economics*, Camb. 1930, which goes down to 1885. Colwyn Edward Vulliamy, *Outlanders: a study of imperial expansion in South Africa, 1877–1902*, 1938, is sometimes useful.

2050  CAMPBELL (WALDEMAR B.). The South African frontier, 1865–1885: a study of expansion. *Archives Year Book.* (1959) pt. I.

See also **2141, 2143–7**.

2051 VAN JAARSVELD (FLORIS ALBERTUS). The awakening of Afrikaner nationalism, 1868–1881. Trans. by F. R. Metrowich. Cape Town. 1961.

To be suppl. by Thomas Rodney Hope Davenport, *The Afrikaner bond: the history of a South African political party, 1880–1911,* Cape Town 1966. There is a large and growing literature on Afrikaner nationalism, of which Sheila Caffyn Patterson, *The last trek: a study of Boer people and the Afrikaner nation,* 1957, and William Henry Vatcher, *White laager: the rise of Afrikaner nationalism,* Lond. & N.Y. 1965, are examples.

2052 GOODFELLOW (CLEMENT FRANCIS). Great Britain and South African confederation, 1870–1881. Cape Town. 1966.

2053 SCHREUDER (DERYCK MARSHALL). Gladstone and Kruger: Liberal government and colonial 'Home rule', 1880–85. 1969.

2054 LOVELL (REGINALD IVAN). The struggle for South Africa, 1875–1899: a study in economic imperialism. N.Y. 1934.

2055 VAN DER POEL (JEAN). The Jameson raid. Cape Town, etc. 1951.

Good. The raid is also the subject of another good book, Elizabeth Pakenham, Countess of Longford, *Jameson's raid,* 1960, and of a number of useful articles, notably Henry Ralph Winkler, 'Joseph Chamberlain and the Jameson raid', *Amer. Hist. Rev.* liv (1948–9), 841–9; Ethel M. Drus, 'A report on the papers of Joseph Chamberlain relating to the Jameson raid and the inquiry', *Inst. Hist. Res. Bull.* xxv (1952), 33–62, and 'The question of imperial complicity in the Jameson raid', *Eng. Hist. Rev.* lxviii (1953), 582–93; Vincent Todd Harlow, 'Sir Frederick Hamilton's narrative of events relative to the Jameson raid', *Eng. Hist. Rev.* lxxii (1957), 279–305; Geoffrey Blainey, 'Lost causes of the Jameson raid', *Econ. Hist. Rev.* 2 ser. xviii (1965), 350–66; and Christopher Montague Woodhouse, 'The missing telegrams and the Jameson raid', *History Today,* xii (1962), 395–404, 506–14. See also **2149–52.** Ann Moggridge, *The Jameson raid: an annotated bibliography,* Cape Town 1960, gives further reading. Hugh Marshall Hole, *The Jameson raid,* 1930, is now out of date. [Fydell] Edmund Garrett and E. J. Edwards, *The story of an African crisis: being, the truth about the Jameson raid and Johannesburg revolt of 1896, told with the assistance of the leading actors in the drama,* Westminster 1897, is good journalism.

2056 BUTLER (JEFFREY). The Liberal party and the Jameson raid. Oxf. 1968.

Thorough and up-to-date, largely based on MSS. See also Joseph O. Baylen, 'W. T. Stead's *History of the Mystery* and the Jameson raid', *J. Brit. Studs.* iv (1964–5), pt. 1, 104–32.

2057 JACKSON COMMITTEE ON THE JAMESON RAID. Special report from the select committee on British South Africa. [Chairman: W. L. Jackson]. H.C. 64 (1897). IX, 1. Second report. H.C. 311 (1897). IX, 5. Appendixes. H.C. 311–I (1897). IX, 607.

See also *Report of the select committee of the Cape of Good Hope House of Assembly on the Jameson raid into the territory of the South African republic* [C. 8380] H.C. (1897). LXII, 223.

2058 LE MAY (GODFREY HUGH LANCELOT). British supremacy in South Africa, 1899–1907. Oxf. 1965.

2059 MILNER. The Milner papers: South Africa, 1897–[1905]. Ed. by Cecil Headlam. 2 v. 1931–3.

See also Eric Stokes, 'Milnerism', *Hist. J.* v (1962), 47–60; Eric Anderson Walker, 'Lord Milner and South Africa', *British Academy Proc.* xxviii (1942), 155–78; Herbert William McCready, 'Sir Alfred Milner, the Liberal party and the Boer war', *Canadian J. of Hist.* ii (1967), pt. 1, 13–44; Lionel George Curtis, *With Milner in South Africa*, Oxf. 1951; William Basil Worsfold, *Lord Milner's work in South Africa from its commencement in 1897 to the peace of Vereeniging in 1902*, 1906; Ernest Bruce Iwan-Müller, *Lord Milner and South Africa*, 1902; and the books on Milner at **1305** and **2077**.

2060 HAFERKORN (HENRY ERNEST). The South African war, 1899–1902: a bibliography of books and articles in periodicals. U.S. Army Engineer School, Fort Humphreys [Va.]. 1924.

J. G. Kesting, *The Anglo-Boer war, 1899–1902: a bibliography*, Cape Town 1956, is confined to magazine articles publ. outside South Africa in 1899. The War Office Libr. *Subject index*, **2691**, is good on the Anglo-Boer war.

2061 CALDWELL (THEODORE C.) *ed.* The Anglo-Boer war: why was it fought? who was responsible? Boston. 1965.

A brief anthology of interpretations.

2062 MARAIS (JOHANNES STEPHANUS). The fall of Kruger's republic. Oxf. 1961.

A useful general account. For biog. sketches see Stuart Cloete, *African portraits: a biography of Paul Kruger, Cecil Rhodes and Lobengula, last king of the Matabele*, 1946. For the controversy about the war see John Semple Galbraith, 'The pamphlet campaign on the Boer War', *J. Mod. Hist.* xxiv (1952), 111–26, and Joseph O. Baylen, 'W. T. Stead and the Boer war: the irony of idealism', *Canadian Hist. Rev.* xl (1959), 304–14. The best pro-Boer work was perhaps Michael Davitt, *The Boer fight for freedom*, N.Y. 1902.

2063 SCHOLTZ (GERT DANIEL). Die oorsake van die tweede vryheids-oorlog, 1899–1902 [The causes of the Second War of Independence]. 2 v. Johannesburg. 1948–9.

See also Johann Hendrik Breytenbach, *Die tweede vryheidsoorlog* [The Second War of Independence], 2 v. Cape Town 1948–9.

2064 AMERY (LEOPOLD CHARLES MAURICE STENNET) *ed.* The *Times* history of the war in South Africa, 1899–1900. 7 v. 1900–9.

The best general hist. For regiments see John Stirling, *Our regiments in South Africa, 1899–1902: their record, based on the despatches*, Edin. & Lond. 1903.

2065 MAURICE (*Sir* JOHN FREDERICK) *and* GRANT (MAURICE HAROLD). History of the war in South Africa, 1899–1902. 4 v.+4 v. of maps. 1906–10.

The British official hist.

2066 SELBY (JOHN MILLIN). The Boer war: a study in cowardice and courage. 1969.

A straightforward popular survey. Edgar Crawshaw Holt, *The Boer war*, 1958, Rayne Kruger, *Goodbye, Dolly Gray: the story of the Boer war*, 1959, new edn. 1964, Noel

William Baring Pemberton, *Battles of the Boer war*, 1964, Brian Gardner, *The lion's cage*, 1969, and Christopher Martin, pseud. of Edwin Palmer Hoyt, *The Boer war*, N.Y. 1969, all cover much the same ground. Julian Symons, *Buller's campaign*, 1963, concentrates on the Natal war. Brian Gardner, *Mafeking: a Victorian legend*, 1966, Duncan William Grinnell-Milne, *Baden-Powell at Mafeking*, 1957, and Oliver Ransford, *The battle of Spion Kop*, 1969, are more specialized.

2067  GERMANY: GROSSER GENERALSTAB (KRIEGSGESCHICHT-LICHE ABTEILUNG). The German official account of the war in South Africa. Pt. 1. Trans. by Wallscourt Hely Hutchinson Waters. 1904. Pt. 2. Trans. by Hubert Du Cane. 1906. Repr. N.Y. 1969.

The best foreign account. Alfred Thayer Mahan, *The story of the war in South Africa, 1899–1900*, 1900, is an American account, Christiaan Rudolf De Wet, *Three years war, October 1899–June 1902*, Westminster 1902, a good Boer account, and Hippolyte Langlois, *Lessons from two recent wars . . .*, trans. for the War Office, Dept. of the General Staff, 1909, a French account.

2068  CHILDERS ([ROBERT] ERSKINE). War and the arme blanche. 1910.

One of the better books to come out of the war: see also his *In the ranks of the C.I.V. . .*, 1900. Henry Spenser Wilkinson, *Lessons of the war . . .*, Westminster 1900, also deals with the military consequences of the war. John Atkinson Hobson, *The war in South Africa: its causes and effects*, 1900, is important as the first step towards his *Imperialism: a study*, 1902. The effects of the war on non-combatants are well brought out in Emily Hobhouse, *The brunt of the war, and where it fell*, 1902, J. C. Otto, *Die Konsentrasie-kampe* [The concentration camps] Cape Town 1964, and Johannes Leon Hattingh, *Die Irenekonsentrasiekamp* [The Irene concentration camp], *Archives Year Book*, (1967), I, 72–201.

2069  ELGIN COMMISSION ON THE WAR IN SOUTH AFRICA. Report of his majesty's commissioners appointed to inquire into the military preparations and other matters connected with the war in South Africa [Chairman: Earl of Elgin]. [Cd. 1789] H.C. (1904). XL, 1. Minutes of evidence etc. [Cd. 1790–2] H.C. (1904). XL, 325. XLI, 1. XLII, 1.

A major post-mortem. Suppl. by *Report of the royal commission on war stores in South Africa* [Chairman: Sir George Farwell]. [Cd. 3127] H.C. (1906). LVII, 1. Minutes of evidence, etc. [Cd. 3128–31] H.C. (1906). LVII, 101. LVIII, 1. See also *Report of the royal commission appointed to consider and report upon the care and treatment of the sick and wounded during the South African campaign* [Chairman: Sir Robert Romer]. [Cd. 453] H.C. (1901). XXIX, 1. Minutes of evidence. [Cd. 454] H.C. (1901). XXIX, 79. Appendix. [Cd. 455] H.C. (1901). XXX, 1.

2070  REITZ (DENEYS). Commando: a Boer journal of the Boer war. 1929. Repr. 1948, etc.

A minor classic. There are large numbers of reports and journs. of war experiences, incl. John Frederic Charles Fuller, *The last of the gentlemen's wars: a subaltern's journal of the war in South Africa, 1899–1902*, 1937; Leopold Marquard, ed., *Letters from a Boer parsonage: letters of Margaret Marquard during the Boer War*, Cape Town etc. 1967; Sir Winston Leonard Spencer-Churchill, *Ian Hamilton's march: together with extracts from the diary of Lieut. H. Frankland, a prisoner of war at Pretoria*, 1900, and *London to Ladysmith via Pretoria*, 1900; Frederick David Baillie, *Mafeking: a diary of the siege*, 1900; Evelyn Oliver Ashe, *Besieged by the Boers: a diary of life and events in Kimberley during the siege*, 1900; Gustav Schoeman Preller, *Scheepers se dagboek en die stryd in Kaapland (1 Oktober 1901–18 Januarie 1902)* [Scheepers' diary and the struggle in Cape Colony], Cape Town, etc. 1938; Sir Ian Standish Monteith Hamilton, *Listening for the drums*, 1944; and Henry John May, *Music of the guns: based on two journals of the Boer War*, 1970.

2071 STIRLING (JOHN). The colonials in South Africa, 1899–1902: their record based on the despatches. Edin. & Lond. 1907.

See also J. Bufton, *Tasmanians in the Transvaal war*, 1905; W. Henderson, *The New South Wales contingents to South Africa . . .*, Sydney 1900; W. T. Reay, *Australians in the war . . .*, 1900; William Sanford Evans, *The Canadian contingents and Canadian imperialism: a story and a study*, 1901; Norman Penlington, *Canada and imperialism, 1896–1899*, Toronto 1965; Canada (Militia), *Organization, equipment, despatch and service of the Canadian contingents during the war in South Africa, 1899–1902*, 2 pts., Ottawa 1901–2; Henry H. S. Pearse, *The history of Lumsden's horse . . .*, 1903; and David Oswald William Hall, *New Zealanders in South Africa, 1899–1902*, 1950.

2072 GIROUARD (*Sir* EDOUARD PERCY CRANWILL). History of the railways during the war in South Africa, 1899–1902. 1903.

Cont. by Royal Engineers Inst., *Detailed history of the railways in the South African war, 1899–1902*, 2 v. Chatham 1904. For other specialized aspects of the war see Thomas Tendron Jeans, ed., *Naval brigades in the South African war, 1899–1900, written by officers attached to the various brigades*, 1901, 2nd edn. 1902; Joan Letitia Beckerling, comp., *The medical history of the Anglo-Boer war: a bibliography*, Cape Town 1967; Robert John Shaw Simpson, *The medical history of the war in South Africa: an epidemiological essay*, 1911; and Sir William Deane Wilson, *Report on the medical arrangements in the South African war*, 1904.

2072a PRICE (RICHARD). An imperial war and the British working class: working-class attitudes and reactions to the Boer War, 1899–1902. Lond. & Toronto. 1972.

2073 FERGUSON (JOHN HENRY). American diplomacy and the Boer war. Phila. 1939.

2074 KESTELL (JOHN DANIEL) *and* VAN VELDEN (D. E.). The peace negotiations between the governments of the South African republic and the Orange Free State and the representatives of the British government, which terminated in the peace concluded at Vereeniging on the 31st May 1902. Trans. by D. E. Van Velden. 1912. Originally publ. in Afrikaans. Pretoria & Amsterdam. 1909.

2075 PYRAH (GEOFFREY BARKER). Imperial policy and South Africa, 1902–1910. Oxf. 1955.

2076 THOMPSON (LEONARD MONTEATH). The unification of South Africa, 1902–1910. Oxf. 1960.

The indispensable work on the subject. See also his 'The colony of Natal and the "Closer Union movement"', *Butterworth's South African Law Rev.* (1955), 81–106, and Robert Henry Brand, Baron Brand, *The Union of South Africa*, Oxf. 1909.

2077 WORSFOLD (WILLIAM BASIL). The reconstruction of the new colonies under Lord Milner. 2 v. 1913.

Suppl. his *The Union of South Africa . . .*, 1912, and *Lord Milner's work in South Africa . . .*, 1906.

2078 NEWTON (ARTHUR PERCIVAL) *comp.* Select documents relating to the unification of South Africa. 2 v. 1924.

See also [Arthur Frederic] Basil Williams, ed., *The Selborne memorandum: a review of the mutual relations of the British South African colonies in 1907*, 1925.

2079 PRELLER (JOHANN F.) *ed.* Die konvensie-dagboek van sy edelagbare François Stephanus Malan, 1908–1909. [The convention journal of the Hon. F. S. Malan.] With English trans. by A. J. de Villiers. Van Riebeeck Soc. 32. Cape Town. 1951.

A useful journ. of the National Convention. See also Gysbert Reitz Hofmeyr, ed., *Minutes of proceedings with annexures (selected) of the South African National Convention 1908–1909*, Cape Town 1911.

2080 WALTON (*Sir* EDGAR HARRIS). The inner history of the national convention of South Africa . . . Cape Town etc. 1912.

2081 MANSERGH (PHILIP NICHOLAS SETON). South Africa, 1906–1961: the price of magnanimity. 1962.

2082 DAVENPORT (THOMAS ROONEY HOPE). 'The South African rebellion, 1914'. *Eng. Hist. Rev.* lxxviii (1963), 73–94.

See also Gerald Dennis Quinn, *The rebellion of 1914–1915: a bibliography*, Cape Town 1957; Stephanus Petrus Erasmus Boshoff, *Rebellie-sketse uit my dagboek, 1914–1915* [Rebellion sketches from my diary], Amsterdam etc. 1918; J. K. O'Connor, *The Afrikander rebellion: South Africa today*, 1915; Philip J. Sampson, *The capture of De Wet: the South African rebellion, 1914*, 1915; Gert Daniel Scholtz, *Die rebellie, 1914–1915*, Johannesburg 1942; and [Leo Fouché] *Report on the outbreak of the rebellion and the policy of the government with regard to its suppression* [Cd. 7874] H.C. (1914–16). XLV, 441.

*(viii) Individual Colonies and States*

*Cape Colony*

2083 CAPE OF GOOD HOPE. Index to the annexures and printed papers of the House of Assembly, and also of the principal resolutions adopted, and to the bills and printed select committee and commission reports, 1854–1897. Cape Town. 1899. Suppls. for 1898–1903 and 1904–10. Cape Town. 1903–10.

See also 1978.

2084 SOUTH AFRICA: STATE ARCHIVES. South African archival records: Kaap. 1+. Cape Town. 1957+.

So far covers only early council records.

2085 McCRACKEN (JOHN LESLIE). The Cape parliament, 1854–1910. Oxf. 1967.

An examination of a British institution transplanted. Supersedes Ralph Pilkington Kilpin, *The romance of a colonial parliament . . .*, 1930, new edn. [*The parliament of the Cape*] 1938. See also Leonard Monteath Thompson, *The Cape coloured franchise*, Johannesburg 1949; Stanley Trapido, 'The origins of the Cape franchise qualifications of 1853', *J. African Hist.* v (1964), 37–54, and Alan Kenneth Fryer, *The government of the Cape of Good Hope, 1825–54: the age of imperial reform*, *Archives year book*, (1964), pt. I, 1–156.

2086 DE KOCK (WILLEM JACOBUS). Ekstraterritoriale vraagstukke van die Kaapse regering (1872–1885) met besondere verwysing na die Transgariep en Betsjoeanaland [Extraterritorial problems of the Cape government . . . with special reference to Trans-Orange and Bechuanaland]. *Archives Year Book.* (1948). Pt. I, 1–306.

See also Anthonie Eduard Du Toit, *The Cape frontier: a study of native policy with special reference to the years 1847–1866*, Archives Year Book, (1954), pt. I, Jacobus Johannes Oberholster, *Die anneksasie van Griekwaland-Wes* [The annexation of Griqualand West], *Archives Year Book*, (1945), and **2026**.

2087 LE CORDEUR (BASIL ALEXANDER). The relations between the Cape and Natal, 1846–1879. *Archives year book.* (1965). Pt. I, 1–264.

For relations with the Orange Free State and South African Republic see **2130**.

2088 LAIDLER (PERCY WARD). The growth and government of Cape Town. Cape Town. 1939. Index by Vera Varley. Cape Town. 1961.

Full of misc. data. John R. Shorten, *Cape Town* . . ., Cape Town 1963, is stronger on the 20th cent.

2089 BURTON (ALFRED RICHARD EDWARD). Cape colony for the settler: an account of its urban and rural industries, their probable future development and extension. Lond. & Cape Town. 1903.

A handbook for settlers.

2090 DE VILLIERS. Lord De Villiers and his times: South Africa, 1842–1914. By Eric Anderson Walker. 1925.

2091 FRERE. The life and correspondence of Sir Bartle Frere, Bart., G.C.B., F.R.S., etc. By John Martineau. 2 v. 1895.

See also William Basil Worsfold, *Sir Bartle Frere: a footnote to the history of the British empire*, 1923, and Balkrishna Nilaji Pitalé, *The speeches and addresses of Sir Henry Bartle Edward Frere* . . ., Bombay 1870.

2092 GRAY. Life of Robert Gray, bishop of Cape Town and metropolitan of Africa. [By Henrietta Louisa Farrer, afterwards Lear.] Ed. by his son, Charles Norris Gray. 2 v. 1876. Abridged edn. 1 v. 1883.

Audrey Brooke, *Robert Gray, first bishop of Cape Town*, Cape Town 1947, adds little.

2093 HOFMEYR. The life of Jan Hendrik Hofmeyr: 'Onze Jan'. By Jan Hendrik Hofmeyr assisted by Francis William Reitz. Cape Town. 1913.

2094 JAMESON. The life of Jameson. By Sir Ian Duncan Colvin. 2 v. 1922.

See also **2055**.

2095 JONES. A father in god: the episcopate of William West Jones . . . archbishop of Cape Town and metropolitan of South Africa, 1874–1908. By Michael Henry Mansel Wood. 1913.

There is another useful life throwing light on the Anglican church after Gray, Henry Purefoy Barnett Clarke, *Life and times of Thomas Fothergill Lightfoot, B.D., archdeacon of Cape Town*, Lond. & Cape Town 1908.

2096 MALAN. Die Lewe van senator F. S. Malan: president van die senaat [The life of senator F. S. Malan, president of the senate]. By Bettie Cloete. Johannesburg. 1946.

2097 MERRIMAN. The life of John Xavier Merriman. By Sir Perceval Maitland Laurence. 1930.

See also Phyllis Lewsen, ed., *Selections from the correspondence of J. X. Merriman*, Van Riebeeck Soc. 41, 44, 47, 50, 4 v. Cape Town 1960–9, which is important for Cape politics and affairs, 1870–1924.

2098 MERRIMAN. The Cape journals of Archdeacon N. J. Merriman, 1848–1855. Ed. by D. H. Varley and H. M. Matthew. Van Riebeeck Soc. 37. Cape Town. 1957.

2099 MOLTENO. The dominion of Afrikanderdom: recollections, pleasant and otherwise. By Sir James Tennant Molteno. 1923.

Cont. in his *Further South African recollections*, 1926. Chiefly on Cape politics 1890–1910.

2100 MOLTENO. The life and times of Sir John Charles Molteno, K.C.M.G., first premier of Cape Colony: comprising a history of representative institutions and responsible government at the Cape and of Lord Carnarvon's confederation policy & of Sir Bartle Frere's high commissionership. By Percy Alport Molteno. 1900.

2101 RHODES. Rhodes: the colossus of southern Africa. By John Gilbert Lockhart and Christopher Montague Woodhouse. Lond. & N.Y. 1963.

Does not altogether repl. the official biog., Sir Lewis Michell, *The life of the Right Honourable Cecil John Rhodes, 1853–1902*, 2 v. 1910, 1-v. edn. 1912. There is a useful bibliog. repr. by the Central African Archives, from Central African Rhodes Centenary Exhibition, *The story of Cecil Rhodes . . . descriptive catalogue*, intro. by John Peter Richard Wallis, Bulawayo 1953, viz. E. E. Burke, *A bibliography of Cecil John Rhodes, 1853–1902*, Salisbury, Rhodesia 1953. Vindex [F. Verschoyle], ed., *Cecil Rhodes: his political life and speeches, 1881–1900*, 1900, is a collection of speeches. A number of short lives add a few extra glimpses of Rhodes at work, [Arthur Frederic] Basil Williams, *Cecil Rhodes*, 1921, new edn. 1938; Sarah Gertrude Millin, *Rhodes*, 1933, new edn. Cape Town, etc. 1952; Felix Gross, *Rhodes of Africa*, 1956; Sir Herbert Baker, *Cecil Rhodes: by his architect*, 1934; William Charles Franklyn Plomer, *Cecil Rhodes*, 1933; and John Eric Sidney Green, *Rhodes goes north*, 1936. Other recent books add little to the picture: among them are Brian Gardner, *The lion's cage*, 1969, and Brian Roberts, *Cecil Rhodes and the princess*, Lond. & Phila. 1969. The most illuminating early study of Rhodes is William Thomas Stead, ed., *The last will and testament of Cecil John Rhodes, with elucidatory notes: to which are added some chapters describing the political and religious ideas of the testator*, 1902.

2102 RUTHERFOORD. In mid-Victorian Cape Town: letters from Miss [Mary] Rutherfoord. Ed. by Joyce Murray. Cape Town. New edn. 1968.

2103 SCHREINER. W. P. Schreiner: a South African. By Eric Anderson Walker. 1937.

2104 SOUTHEY. The life and times of Sir Richard Southey, K.C.M.G., etc., formerly colonial secretary of the Cape Colony and lieut.-governor of Griqualand West. By Alexander Wilmot. 1904.

2105 STOCKENSTRÖM. The role of Sir Andries Stockenström in Cape politics, 1848–1856. By Andrew Hadley Duminy. *Archives Year Book.* (1960). Pt. II, 73–175.

*Natal*

2106 O'BYRNE (SHELAGH P. M.) *comp.* The colony of Natal to the Zulu war, 1843–1878: a bibliography. Cape Town. 1965.

Cont. by Jeanette A. Sumner, *Natal, 1881–1911: a bibliography*, Cape Town 1965.

2107 WEBB (COLIN DE BERRY) *comp.* A guide to the official records of the colony of Natal. Pietermaritzburg. 1965. 2nd edn. 1968.

South Africa: State Archives, *South Africa archival records: Natal, II+: records of the Natal executive council, 1846+*, Cape Town 1960+, prints a number of basic records.

2108 HATTERSLEY (ALAN FREDERICK) *comp.* More annals of Natal. 1936.

Docs. covering *c.* 1840–88. Suppl. by his *Later annals of Natal* [*c.* 1860–1900], 1938, and *The Natalians: further annals of Natal*, Pietermaritzburg 1940.

2109 BROOKES (EDGAR HARRY) *and* WEBB (COLIN DE BERRI). A history of Natal. Pietermaritzburg. 1965.

A good general hist. with extensive annotated bibliog. See also Thomas Rodney Hope Davenport, 'The responsible government issue in Natal, 1880–1882', *Butterworth's South African Law Rev.* (1957), 84–133, and Stanley Trapido, 'Natal's non-racial franchise, 1856', *African Studs.* xxii (1963), 22–32. For relations with the Cape see **2087**.

2110 HATTERSLEY (ALAN FREDERICK). The British settlement of Natal: a study in imperial migration. Camb. 1950.

Heather A. Simmonds, *European immigration into Natal, 1824–1910*, Cape Town 1964, is a handy bibliog. See also R. D. Reynolds, *The struggle against the introduction of convict and reformatory labour into Natal*, *Archives Year Book* (1967), pt. II, 70–133.

2111 HATTERSLEY (ALAN FREDERICK). Portrait of a colony: the story of Natal. Camb. 1940.

Colonial life, *c.* 1840–70. See also his *Portrait of a city* [Pietermaritzburg], Pietermaritzburg 1951, and *Pietermaritzburg panorama . . .*, Pietermaritzburg 1938. There are pleasant snippets of information in Barbara Isabella Buchanan, *Pioneer days in Natal*, Pietermaritzburg 1936, and *Natal memories*, Pietermaritzburg 1941.

2112 VAN ZYL (MATHYS CHRISTOFFEL). Die uitbreiding van Britse gesag oor die Natalse noordgrensgebiede, 1879–1897. [The extension of British authority over Natal's northern border territories, 1879–1897.] *Archives Year Book.* (1966). Pt. I.

For the earlier period there is Cornelis Janse Uys, *In the era of Shepstone: being a study of British expansion in South Africa (1842–77)*, Lovedale 1933, which is out of date, but useful for Natal native policy.

2113 MARKS (SHULA). Reluctant rebellion: the 1906–8 disturbances in Natal. 1970.

A careful study of an African rising for which see also **2189**. For native policy see **2026**.

2114 ROBINSON. A life time in South Africa: being the recollections of the first premier of Natal. By Sir John Robinson. 1900.

2115 BROOKS (HENRY). Natal: a history and description of the colony . . . Ed. by Robert James Mann. 1876.

2116 FROST (PAMELA JEAN) *comp.* A bibliography of missions and missionaries in Natal. Cape Town. 1969.

2117 BURNETT (BILL BENDYSHE). Anglicans in Natal. Durban. [1955.]

See also Alfred William Lovely Rivett, *Ten years' church work in Natal* [1855–65], 1890.

2118 COLENSO. The life of John William Colenso, D.D., Bishop of Natal. By [Sir] George William Cox. 2 v. 1888.

Still the fullest life. Wynn Rees, ed., *Colenso letters from Natal*, Pietermaritzburg 1958, is in effect a biog. based on Mrs. [Frances] Colenso's letters. Peter Bingham Hinchliff, *John William Colenso, bishop of Natal*, 1964, is an interpretative essay rather than a biog. Further references to Colenso are recorded in Barbara Davidson Fraser, *John William Colenso: a bibliography*, Cape Town 1952. Colenso publ. extensively while in Natal, e.g. *Natal sermons*, 4 pts. 1866–8, *Ten weeks in Natal: a journal of a first tour of visitation among the colonists and Zulu kafirs of Natal*, Camb. 1855, and his works in defence of African chiefs (**2182**). For his trial see *Trial of the Bishop of Natal for erroneous teaching before the metropolitan bishop of Cape Town . . .*, Cape Town 1863, and the life of Bishop Gray (**2092**).

2119 GREEN. Life of James Green, doctor of divinity: rector and dean of Maritzburg, Natal, from February 1849 to January 1906. By Augustus Theodore Wirgman. 2 v. 1909.

Colenso's principal opponent in Natal.

2120 BROOKES (EDGAR HARRY). A history of the University of Natal. Pietermaritzburg. 1966.

2121 UNIVERSITY OF NATAL. Natal regional survey. 13 v. 1951–7.

Incl. hist. data on the economy, population, etc.

2122 HURWITZ (N.). Agriculture in Natal, 1860–1950. Cape Town. 1957.

2123 DOBIE. John Shedden Dobie: South African journal, 1862–6. Ed. by Alan Frederick Hattersley. Van Riebeeck. Soc. 26. Cape Town. 1945.

The journal of a Natal pastoralist from Scotland.

2124 HOLT (H. P.). The mounted police of Natal. 1913.

2125 HENDERSON (W. P. M.). Durban: fifty years' municipal history. Durban. 1904.

2126 GORDON (RUTH EVANGELINE). Shepstone: the role of the family in the history of South Africa, 1820–1900. Cape Town. 1968.

*Orange Free State (Orange River Colony)*

2127 VAN SCHOOR (MARTHINUS CORNELIUS ELLNARIUS) *and* MALAN (STEPHANUS IMMELMAN). 'n bibliografie van werke oor die Oranje-Vrystaat vanaf die vroegste tye tot 1910. [A bibliography of works on the Orange Free State from the earliest times to 1910.] Bloemfontein. 1954.

See also Dorothy Mary Sinclair, comp., *Orange Free State goldfields: a bibliography*, Cape Town 1967.

2128 SOUTH AFRICA: STATE ARCHIVES. South African archival records: Oranje-Vrystaat [Orange Free State]. 1+. Cape Town. 1952+.

The vols. that have appeared so far cover *Notule van die volksraad van die Oranje-Vrystaat* ... [Minutes of the Volksraad of the Orange Free State], 1854+.

2129 FOURIE (PHILLIPUS COENRAAD). Die administrasie van die Oranje-Vrystaat tot 1859. *Archives Year Book* XXVI (1963). Pt. II, 159–246.

See also A. P. J. Van Rensburg, *Die rol deur landdroste, vrederegters en veldkornette in die distrik Bloemfontein vanaf 1854–1880 gespeel* [The role of landdrosts, justices of the peace and field-cornets in the district of Bloemfontein], *Archives Year Book* (1954), pt. II, 185–308.

2130 ATTREE (EILEEN M.). The closer union movements between the Orange Free State, South African Republic and Cape Colony (1838–1863). *Archives Year Book.* (1949). Pt. I, 303–77.

2131 VAN RENSBURG (A. P. J.). Die ekonomiese herstel van die Afrikaner in die Oranjerivier-Kolonie, 1902–1907 [The economic recovery of the Afrikaner in the Orange River Colony]. *Archives Year Book.* (1967). Pt. II, 134–342.

2132 BRAND. President Johannes Henricus Brand, 1823–1888. By Gert Daniel Scholtz. Johannesburg. 1957.

2133 COLLINS. 'Free Statia': reminiscences of a lifetime in the Orange Free State. By William W. Collins. Cape Town. 1907. Repr. 1965.

2134 DE WET. General de Wet: a biography. By Eric Rosenthal. Cape Town. 1946. 2nd edn. 1968.

There are two other lives: John Daniel Kestell, *Christiaan de Wet: 'n lewensbeskrywing* [C. de Wet: a biography], Cape Town 1920, and Marthinus Cornelius Ellnarius Van Schoor and others, *Christiaan Rudolph de Wet, 1854–1922*, Bloemfontein 1954, 2nd edn. 1964.

2135 HERTZOG. James Barry Munnik Hertzog. By Oswald Pirow. Cape Town. 1957. Lond. 1958.

See also M. J. Burger, *Generaal J. B. M. Hertzog: 'n bibliografie*, Cape Town 1953, and Christiaan Maurits Van Der Heever, *Generaal J. B. M. Hertzog*, Johannesburg 1946.

2136 STEYN. Marthinus Theunis Steyn: 'n lewensbeskrywing. [M. T. Steyn: a biography.] By Nicolaas Johannes Van der Merwe. 2 v. Cape Town etc. 1921.

See also A. Kieser, *President Steyn en die Krisisjare, 1896–1899* [President Steyn in the years of crisis], Cape Town [1939], and Jacobus Johannes Oberholster and Marthinus Cornelius Ellnarius Van Schoor, *President Steyn aan die woord: openbare geskrifte en toesprake van Marthinus Theunis Steyn* . . . [President Steyn speaks: public writings and speeches of Marthinus Theunis Steyn], Bloemfontein 1953.

*Transvaal (South African Republic)*

2137 SOUTH AFRICA: STATE ARCHIVES. South African archival records: Transvaal 1+. Cape Town. [1951+.]

The vols. which have appeared so far cover *Notule van die volksraad van die Suid-Afrikaanse republiek* . . . [Minutes of the Volksraad of the South African Republic.] 1844+.

2138 FISHER (WILLIAM EDWARD GARRETT). The Transvaal and the Boers: a short history of the South African republic: with a chapter on the Orange Free State. [1899.] Rev. edn. 1900.

See also John Nixon, *The complete story of the Transvaal from the 'Great Trek' to the Convention of London*, 1885.

2139 BOTHA (PHILIP R.). Die staatkundige ontwikkeling van die Suid-Afrikaanse Republiek onder Krüger en Leyds: Transvaal, 1844–1899. [Constitutional development of the South African republic under Krüger and Leyds.] Amsterdam. 1926.

A solid work, gradually being repl. by monographs such as Jacobus Stephanus Du Plessis, *Die ontstaan en ontwikkeling van die amp van die staatspresident in die Zuid-Afrikaansche Republiek (1858–1902)* [The origin and development of the office of state president in the South African republic], *Archives Year Book*, (1955), pt. 1; Leonard Monteath Thompson, 'Constitutional development in the South African republics', *Butterworth's South African Law Rev.* (1954), 49–72; Maria Johanna Hugo, *Die stemregvraagstuk in die Zuid-Afrikaansche Republiek* [The franchise question in the South African Republic], *Archives Year Book*, (1947), 1–196; A. Wypkema, *De invloed van Nederland op ontstaan en ontwikkeling van de staatsinstellingen der Z. A. republiek tot 1881* [The influence of Holland on the origin and development of the political institutions of the South African Republic], Pretoria 1939; Jacobus Johannes Van Heerden, *Die kommandant-generaal in die geskiedenis van die Suid-Afrikaanse Republiek* [The commandant-general in the history of the South African Republic], *Archives Year Book*, (1964), pt. II, 1–198; W. A. Kleynhaus, *Volksregering in die Zuid-Afrikaansche Republiek: die rol van memories* [Popular government in the South African republic: the role of memorials], Pretoria 1966; and Ellison Kahn, 'The history of the administration of justice in the South African Republic', *South African Law J.* lxxv (1958), 294–317, 397–417, lxxvi (1959), 46–57.

2140 VAN ROOYEN (T. S.). Die verhoudinge tussen die Boere, Engelse en naturelle in die geskiedenis van die Oos-Transvaal tot 1882. [The relations between Boers, English, and natives in the history of the Eastern Transvaal.] Archives Year Book. (1951). Pt. I.

See also Kenneth Wyndham Smith, *The campaigns against the Bapedi of Sekhukhune, 1877–1879*, *Archives Year Book* (1967), pt. II, 1–69.

2141  KISTNER (W.). The anti-slavery agitation against the Transvaal republic, 1852–1868. *Archives Year Book.* (1952). Pt. II, 193–278.

2142  KRÜGER (DANIEL WILHELMUS). Die weg na die see of die ooskus in die Boerebeleid voor 1877 met besondere verwysing na die verhouding tot die Portugese [The road to the sea: or the east coast in Boer policy before 1877, with special reference to relations with the Portuguese]. *Archives Year Book.* (1938). Pt. I, 31–232.

2143  RANSFORD (OLIVER). The battle of Majuba hill: the first Boer War. Lond. & N.Y. 1967.

2144  BELLAIRS (BLANCHE ST JOHN), *Lady Bellairs, ed.* The Transvaal war, 1880–1881. Edin. & Lond. 1885.

One of the better contemp. works. See also A. M. Davey, *The siege of Pretoria, 1880–1881, Archives Year Book* (1956), pt. I, 265–316; Thomas Fortescue Carter, *A narrative of the Boer war: its causes and results*, 1883, new edn. 1896; and Charles L. Norris Newman, *With the Boers in the Transvaal and Orange Free State in 1880–1*, 1882 2nd edn. 1896.

2145  LEYDS (WILLEM JOHANNES). The first annexation of the Transvaal. 1906.

Cont. by his *The Transvaal surrounded . . .*, 1919.

2146  PIETERSE (D. J.). Transvaal en Britse susereiniteit, 1881–1884. [Transvaal and British suzerainty.] *Archives Year Book.* (1940). Pt. I, 257–344.

2147  VAN DER WALT (HENDRIK ROELOF). Die Suid-Afrikaanse Republiek in die Britse buitelandse en koloniale beleid, 1881–1899. [The South African republic in British foreign and colonial policy.] *Archives Year Book.* (1963). Pt. I.

See also H. E. Werner Backeberg, *Die betrekkinge tussen die Suid-Afrikaanse Republiek en Duitsland tot na die Jameson inval (1852–1896)* [The relations between the South African republic and Germany until after the Jameson raid], *Archives Year Book* (1949), pt. I, 1–302, and J. A. Wiid, *Die Rolle der Burenrepubliken in der auswärtigen und kolonialen Politik des Deutschen Reiches in den Jahren 1883–1900*, Nuremberg 1927.

2148  NELL (P. R.). 'Die konsulêre en diplomatieke verteenwoordiging van die Suid-Afrikaanse Republiek in die buiteland [The consular and diplomatic representation of the South African republic abroad]'. *Historiese Studs.* vi (1945), 93–193.

2149  WILDE (RICHARD H.). Joseph Chamberlain and the South African Republic, 1895–1899: a study in the formulation of Imperial policy. *Archives Year Book.* (1956). Pt. I, 1–158.

2150  HOFMEYR (NICOLAAS JACOBUS). De Afrikaner-Boer en de Jameson-inval. [The Afrikaner Boer and the Jameson raid.] Cape Town & Amsterdam. 1896. New edn. 1897.

2151 RHOODIE (DENYS). Conspirators in conflict: a study of the Johannesburg Reform Committee and its role in the conspiracy against the South African Republic. Cape Town. 1967.

See also Cecil Theodore Gordon, *The growth of Boer opposition to Kruger, 1890–1895,* Cape Town & Lond. 1970.

2152 FITZPATRICK (*Sir* JAMES PERCY). The Transvaal from within: a private record of public affairs. 1899. New edn. 1900.

An entertaining account by one of the Uitlander leaders. See also his *South African memories,* ed. by G. H. Wilson, 1932, and John Peter Richard Wallis, *Fitz: the story of Sir Percy FitzPatrick,* 1955. For the Johannesburg situation before the Boer war see also Robert Crisp, *The outlanders: the men who made Johannesburg,* 1964; William Henry Somerset Bell, *Bygone days . . .,* 1933; John Hays Hammond, *Autobiography,* 2 v. N.Y. 1935; Sir Lionel Phillips, *Some reminiscences,* 1924; and **2030**.

2153 HYAM (RONALD). 'Smuts and the decision of the Liberal government to grant responsible government to the Transvaal, January and February 1906'. *Hist. J.* viii (1965), 380–98.

See also Bentley Brinkerhoff Gilbert, 'The grant of responsible government to the Transvaal: more notes on a myth', *Hist. J.* x (1967), 457–9; D. J. N. Denoon, ' "Capitalist influence" and the Transvaal government during the crown colony period', ibid. xi (1968), 301–31; Noel George Garson, ' "Het Volk": the Botha–Smuts party in the Transvaal, 1904–11', ibid. ix (1966), 101–32; and Ferdinand Vermooten, *Transvaal en die totstandkoming van die Unie van Suid-Afrika, 1906–1910* [Transvaal and the making of the Union of South Africa], *Archives Year Book* (1957), pt. 2, 1–262.

2154 BOTHA. General Louis Botha. By Frans Vredenrijk Engelenburg. Pretoria. 1928. Lond. 1929.

Elizabeth M. M. Clark, *Louis Botha: a bibliography,* Cape Town 1956, is a useful list. [Arthur Frederic] Basil Williams, *Botha, Smuts and South Africa,* 1946, helpfully suppls. Engelenburg. Sydney Charles Buxton, Earl Buxton, *General Botha,* 1924, is based on personal knowledge. Johannes Meintjes, *General Louis Botha: a biography,* 1970, is a new study.

2155 DE LA REY. De la Rey—lion of the west: a biography. By Johannes Meintjes. Johannesburg. 1966.

KOTZE. See **2001**.

2156 KRUGER. The memoirs of Paul Kruger, four times president of the South African republic: told by himself. 2 v. 1902.

Disappointing. Marjorie Juta, *The pace of the ox: the life of Paul Kruger,* 1937, is popular but convenient. F. P. Smit, *Die Staatsopvattinge van Paul Kruger* [*Paul Kruger's concept of the state*], Pretoria 1951, is a useful monograph. Daniel Wilhelmus Krüger, *Paul Kruger,* 2 v. Johannesburg 1961–3, is a good life in Afrikaans. Stephanus Petrus Engelbrecht, ed., *Paul Kruger's amptelike briewe* [Paul Kruger's official letters], Pretoria 1925, prints a selection.

2157 LEYDS. Correspondentie (1899–1902). By Willem Johannes Leyds. 9 v. The Hague. 1919–34.

See also **2145**.

2158  SMUTS. Smuts: the sanguine years, 1870–1919. By Sir William Keith Hancock. Camb. 1962.

The standard biog. Suppl. by W. K. Hancock and Jean van der Poel, eds., *Selections from the Smuts papers, 1886–[1919]*, 4 v. Camb. 1966. Sarah Gertrude Millin, *General Smuts*, 2 v. 1936, has been superseded. Jan Christiaan Smuts jr., *Jan Christian Smuts*, 1952, adds little.

*Basutoland, Bechuanaland, Swaziland (Lesotho, Botswana, Swaziland)*

2159  HALPERN (JACK). South Africa's hostages: Basutoland, Bechuanaland and Swaziland. Harmondsworth. 1965.

Incl. a short hist. Richard P. Stevens, *Lesotho, Botswana & Swaziland: the former High Commission territories in southern Africa*, 1967, has less hist.

2160  HYAM (RONALD). 'African interests and the South Africa Act, 1908–1910'. *Hist. J.* xiii (1970), 85–105.

Attacks the argument of Alan R. Booth, 'Lord Selborne and the British protectorates, 1908–10', *J. African Hist.* x (1969), 133–48, that the British government took little interest in the fate of the protectorates.

2161  TE GROEN (JULIE) *comp.* Bibliography of Basutoland. Cape Town. 1946. 3rd impr. 1964.

See also John B. Webster and Paulus Mohome, *A bibliography of Lesotho*, Syracuse, N.Y. 1968.

2162  THEAL (GEORGE McCALL) *ed.* Basutoland records [1833–1868]: copies of official documents ... 3 v. Cape Town. 1883. Repr. 3 v. in 4. Cape Town. 1964.

See also Basutoland Government Archives, *Catalogue*, in pts., Maseru 1962+.

2163  LAGDEN (*Sir* GODFREY YEATMAN). The Basutos: the mountaineers & their country: being, a narrative of events relating to the tribe from its formation early in the nineteenth century to the present day. 2 v. 1909.

Along with D. Fred Ellenberger and James Comyn Macgregor, *History of the Basuto: ancient and modern*, 1912, long the standard account of the hist. of Lesotho. G. Tylden, *The rise of the Basuto*, Cape Town etc. 1950, John Grenfell Williams, *Moshesh: the man on the mountain*, 1950, 2nd edn. 1959, and Peter Becker, *Hill of destiny: the life and times of Moshesh, founder of the Basotho*, 1969, add little. George McCall Theall, *A fragment of Basuto history, 1854 to 1871*, Cape Town 1886, was largely superseded by Lagden.

2164  GROBBELAAR (JOHANNES JACOBUS GABRIEL). Die Vrystaatse Republiek en die Basoetoe-vraagstuk [The Free State Republic and the Basuto question]. Archives year book II (1939). Pt. 2. Cape Town. 1939.

See also Jean Van der Poel, *Basutoland as a factor in South African politics, 1858–1870* Archives Year Book (1941), pt. 1, 171–228.

2165  GERMOND (ROBERT CHARLES) *comp.* Chronicles of Basutoland: a running commentary on the events of the years 1830–1902 by the French protestant missionaries in Southern Africa. Morija. 1967.

See also V. Ellenberger, *Centenary jubilee of the Basutoland mission, 1833–1933: a century of mission work in Basutoland (1833–1933)*, trans. by Edmond M. Ellenberger,

Morija 1938; Edwin William Smith, *The Mabilles of Basutoland*, 1939; H. Dieterlen, *Adolphe Mabille (1836–1894)*, Paris 1898, new edn. Paris [1930]; Eugène Casalis, *The Basutos: or, twenty-three years in South Africa*, 1861; and Théophile Jousse, *La mission française évangélique au sud de l'Afrique* . . ., Paris 1889. There are fewer works on English missions. See however John Widdicombe, *In the Lesuto: a sketch of African mission life* . . ., 1895, which largely repl. his *Fourteen years in Basutoland: a sketch of African mission life* . . ., 1892, and *Memories and musings* . . ., 1915.

2166  MIDDLETON (CORAL) *comp.* Bechuanaland: a bibliography. Cape Town. 1965.

See also Paulus Mohome and John B. Webster, comps., *A bibliography of Bechuanaland*, Syracuse, N.Y. 1966. Suppl. 1968.

2167  SILLERY (ANTHONY). The Bechuanaland protectorate. Cape Town. 1952.

For a general intro. see also Bertram Alfred Young, *Bechuanaland*, 1966, and Sidwell Mhaladi Gabatshwane, *Introduction to the Bechuanaland protectorate: history and administration*, Kanye, Bechuanaland 1957.

2168  SILLERY (ANTHONY). Founding of a protectorate: history of Bechuanaland, 1885–95. The Hague. 1965.

A scholarly monograph.

2169  KHAMA. Khama: king of the Bamangwato. By Julian Mockford. 1931.

See also Edwin Lloyd, *Three great African chiefs (Khâmé, Sebelé and Bathoeng)*, 1895, 2nd edn. 1895.

2170  MACKENZIE. Austral Africa: losing it or ruling it: being incidents and experiences in Bechuanaland, Cape Colony and England. By John Mackenzie. 2 v. 1887.

See also William Douglas Mackenzie, *John Mackenzie: South African missionary and statesman*, N.Y. & Lond. 1902.

2171  PRICE. Great lion of Bechuanaland: the life and times of Roger Price, missionary. By Edwin William Smith. 1957.

2172  WALLACE (CHARLES STEWART) *comp.* Swaziland: a bibliography. Johannesburg. 1967.

See also John B. Webster and Paulus Mohome, *A bibliography of Swaziland*, Syracuse, N.Y. 1968.

2173  MARWICK (BRIAN ALLAN). The Swazi: an ethnographic account of the natives of the Swaziland protectorate. Camb. 1940. New edn. Lond. 1966.

Dudley Barker, *Swaziland*, 1965, is a brief intro.

2174  GARSON (NOEL GEORGE). The Swaziland question and a road to the sea, 1887–1895. Archives Year Book. (1957). Pt. 2, 263–434.

There is some additional background material in Alan C. G. Best, *The Swaziland railway: a study in politico-economic geography*, East Lansing, Mich. 1966.

*Zululand*

2175  GALLOWAY (MARGARET HUME) *comp*. Zululand and the Zulus: a bibliography. Cape Town. 1944. 3rd edn. 1969.

2176  BRYANT (ALFRED T.). The Zulu people: as they were before the white man came. Pietermaritzburg. 1949. 2nd edn. 1967.

Like his *A history of the Zulu and neighbouring tribes*, Cape Town 1964, invaluable for the background to the Zulu kingdom. See also Eileen Jensen Krige, *The social system of the Zulus*, 1936, and John D. Omer-Cooper, *The Zulu aftermath: a nineteenth-century revolution in Bantu Africa*, Lond. & Evanston, Ill. 1966.

2177  MORRIS (DONALD ROBERT). The washing of the spears: a history of the rise of the Zulu nation under Shaka and its fall in the Zulu War of 1879. N.Y. 1965. Lond. 1966.

The fullest general hist.

2178  CETSHWAYO. The last Zulu king: the life and death of Cetshwayo. By C. T. Binns. 1963.

Cont. by his *Dinuzulu: the death of the house of Shaka*, 1968. A good modern account. See also James Young Gibson, *The story of the Zulus*, Pietermaritzburg 1903, new edn. Lond. etc. 1911.

2179  MOODIE (DUNCAN CAMPBELL FRANCIS) *ed*. John Dunn, Cetywayo and the three generals. By John Dunn. Pietermaritzburg. 1886.

See also Oliver Walker, *Proud Zulu* [Cetshwayo and John Dunn], 1949, and *Zulu royal feather* [life of Dunn], 1961, novels based on African life.

2180  FARRER (JAMES ANSON). Zululand and the Zulus: their history, beliefs, customs, military system . . . and missions to them. 1879. 3rd edn. 1879.

A survey *c*. 1824–77. Cp. Paul Deléage, *Trois mois chez les Zoulous* . . ., Paris 1879; *A lady's life and travels in Zululand and the Transvaal during Cetewayo's reign: being, the African letters and journals of the late Mrs. Wilkinson*, 1882; Thomas B. Jenkinson, *Amazulu: the Zulus, their past history, manners, customs and language* . . . *the Zulu war and Zululand since the war*, 1882, repr. N.Y. 1969; Josiah Tyler, *Forty years among the Zulus*, Boston 1891; and Bertram Mitford, *Through the Zulu country: its battlefields and its people*, 1883.

2181  WAR OFFICE (INTELLIGENCE BRANCH). Précis of information concerning the Zulu country [Zululand]. 1878. 6th edn. corr. to December 1894 by Captain Wemyss. 1895.

A handy guide. The last edn. is the fullest and best.

2182  COLENSO (JOHN WILLIAM) *bishop of Natal*. The course of political events in Zululand: official, colonial and Zulu statements. N.d.

See also J. W. Colenso, ed., *Cetshwayo's Dutchman: being the private journal of a white trader in Zululand during the British invasion*, 1880, *Three native accounts of the visit of the bishop of Natal in September and October, 1859 to Umpande, king of the Zulus*, Maritzburg 1860, and Florence Gregg, *The story of bishop Colenso, the friend of the Zulus*, 1892.

2183 COUPLAND (*Sir* REGINALD). Zulu battle piece: Isandhlwana. 1948.

The best account of Zulu warfare. There are a number of popular books, incl. Rupert Furneaux, *The Zulu war* . . ., 1963, and W. H. Clements, *The glamour and tragedy of the Zulu war*, 1936. See also F. W. D. Jackson, 'Isandhlwana, 1879: the sources re-examined', *Soc. Army Hist. Res. J.* xliii (1965), 30–43, 113–32, 169–83.

2184 FRENCH ([EDWARD] GERALD). Lord Chelmsford and the Zulu war. 1939.

2185 WAR OFFICE (INTELLIGENCE BRANCH). Narrative of the field operations connected with the Zulu war of 1879. 1881.

The Zulu war was reported on at length, both in books and in the press. See particularly Waller Ashe and Edmund Verney Wyatt Edgell, *The story of the Zulu campaign*, 1880; Sir Henry Hallam Parr, *A sketch of the kafir and Zulu wars* . . ., 1880; Alexander Wilmot, *History of the Zulu war*, 1880; William Edward Montague, *Campaigning in South Africa: reminiscences of an officer in 1879*, Edin. 1880; Charles L. Norris Newman, *In Zululand with the British throughout the war of 1879*, 1880; Edward Durnford, *A soldier's life and work in South Africa, 1872 to 1879: a memoir of the late colonel A. W. Durnford*, 1882; and W. H. Tomasson, *With the irregulars in the Transvaal and Zululand*, 1881. Katherine John, *The Prince Imperial*, 1939, is also good on the war, in which the prince was killed.

2186 COLENSO (FRANCES ELLEN) *and* DURNFORD (EDWARD). History of the Zulu war and its origin. 1880.

The ablest attack on British policy. Cont. by Frances Colenso's *The ruin of Zululand: an account of British doings in Zululand since the invasion of 1879: being, a sequel to the history of the Zulu War*, 2 v. 1884–5. See also Lady Florence Caroline Dixie, *A defence of Zululand and its king: echoes from the blue books* . . ., 1882, and *In the land of misfortune* . . ., 1882; William Clifford Holden, *British rule in South Africa: illustrated in the story of Kama and his tribe and of the war in Zululand*, 1879, repr. Pretoria 1969; and Thomas John Lucas, *The Zulus and the British frontiers*, 1879.

2187 HAGGARD (*Sir* HENRY RIDER). Cetywayo and his white neighbours: or, remarks on recent events in Zululand, Natal and the Transvaal. 1882. 2nd edn. 1888.

2188 BRAATVEDT (H. P.). Roaming Zululand with a native commissioner. Pietermaritzburg. 1949.

2189 STUART (JAMES). A history of the Zulu rebellion, 1906 and of Dinuzulu's arrest, trial and expatriation. 1913. N.Y. 1969.

See also Walter Bosman, *The Natal rebellion of 1906*, 1907, and **2113**.

2190 MKABI. Kwa-Zulu: Queen Mkabi's story. By Cecil Cowley. Cape Town. 1966.

2191 JOHNSON. Charles Johnson of Zululand. By Albert William Lee, Bishop of Zululand. 1930.

2192 LINDLEY. The life and times of Daniel Lindley (1801–1880): missionary to the Zulus: pastor of the voortrekkers . . . By Edwin William Smith. Lond. 1949. N.Y. [1952.]

Interesting as an example of Dutch Reformed Church missionary enterprise.

*Atlantic Islands*

2193 GOSSE (PHILIP). St Helena, 1502–1938. 1938.

Emily L. Jackson, *St Helena: the historic island from its discovery to the present date*, Lond. 1903, N.Y. 1905, is a useful descriptive work.

2194 BRANDER (JAN). Tristan da Cunha, 1506–1902. 1940. New edn. to 1950 in Dutch. Hoorn. 1952.

See also Margaret Mackprang Mackay, *Angry island: the story of Tristan da Cunha (1506–1963)*, 1963. Katherine Mary Barrow, *Three years in Tristan da Cunha*, 1910, is based on the diary of a missionary's wife.

## 8. COLONIES IN ASIA

### (a) *General*

2195 IRELAND (ALLEYNE). The far eastern tropics: studies in the administration of tropical dependencies: Hong Kong, British North Borneo, Sarawak, Burma, the Federated Malay States, the Straits Settlements, French Indo-China, Java, the Philippine Islands. Westminster. 1904. Boston & N.Y. 1905.

Lennox Algernon Mills, *British rule in eastern Asia: a study of contemporary government and economic development in British Malaya and Hong Kong*, 1942, repr. N.Y. 1970, covers some of the same ground forty years later, and is useful for comparisons. There is a good deal of econ. hist. in George Cyril Allen and Audrey Gladys Donnithorne, *Western enterprise in Indonesia and Malaya: a study in economic development . . .*, 1957.

2196 KING (FRANK HENRY HAVILAND). Money in British East Asia. Colonial office: colonial research publics. 19. H.M.S.O. 1957.

Largely hist.

### (b) *Ceylon*

2197 GOONETILEKE (H. A. I.) *comp.* A bibliography of Ceylon: a systematic guide to the literature of the land, people, history and culture published in western languages from the sixteenth century to the present day. 2 v. Zug, Switzerland. 1970.

Edith Williams Ware, comp., *Bibliography on Ceylon*, Coral Gables, Florida 1962, is a handy short guide. For Ceylon Government archives see **989**.

2198 LUDOWYK (EVELYN FREDERICK CHARLES). The modern history of Ceylon. Lond. & N.Y. 1966.

See also Lennox Algernon Mills, *Ceylon under British rule, 1795–1932 . . .*, 1933, and Garrett Champness Mendis, *Ceylon under the British*, Colombo 1944, 2nd edn. 1946. The leading Ceylon hist. js. are *Ceylon hist. j.*, 1+, Dehiwala 1951+, with monograph ser., 1+, 1966+, and *Ceylon j. of hist. & social studs.*, 1+, Peradeniya 1958+.

2199 TENNENT (*Sir* JAMES EMERSON). Ceylon: an account of the island, physical, historical and topographical, with notices of its natural history, antiquities and productions. 2 v. 1859. 5th edn. 1860.

The most useful contemp. reference works were John Ferguson, *Ceylon in 1883: describing the progress of the island since 1803, its present agricultural and commercial enterprises* . . ., 1883, new edns. 1884, 1887, 1893, 1896, 1903, and Alastair Mackenzie Ferguson and others, *The Ceylon directory* . . ., Colombo 1868+. For contemp. ideas see also [Royal] Asiatic Soc., Ceylon branch, *Journal*, Colombo 1845+.

2200 COLLINS (*Sir* CHARLES HENRY). Public administration in Ceylon. 1951.

A hist. See also Sir William Ivor Jennings and Henry Vijayakone Tambia, *The dominion of Ceylon: the development of its laws and constitution*, 1952; James Reginald Toussaint, *Annals of the Ceylon civil service*, Colombo 1935, the works of Leonard Woolf at **1309**; William Digby, *Forty years of official and unofficial life in an oriental crown colony: being, the life of Sir Richard F. Morgan, Kt., queen's advocate and acting chief justice of Ceylon*, 2 v. Madras 1879; and H. A. de S. Gunasekera, *From dependent currency to central banking in Ceylon: an analysis of monetary experience, 1825–1957*, 1962.

2201 HULUGALLE (HERBERT ALEXANDER JAYATILLEKE). British governors of Ceylon. Colombo. 1963.

See also S. V. Balasingham, *The administration of Sir Henry Ward, governor of Ceylon, 1855–1860, Ceylon Hist. J.* ii, Dehiwala 1968, B. Bastiampillai, *The administration of Sir William Gregory, governor of Ceylon, 1872–1877, Ceylon Hist. J.* xii, Dehiwala 1968, and Sir Joseph West Ridgeway, *Administration of the affairs of Ceylon, 1896 to 1903: a review*, Colombo 1903.

2202 DE SILVA (K.M.). Social policy and missionary organizations in Ceylon, 1840–1855. 1965.

Good. See also Sir James Emerson Tennent, *Christianity in Ceylon* . . ., 1850.

2203 BEVEN (FRANCIS LORENZ) *ed.* A history of the diocese of Colombo: a centenary volume. Colombo. 1946.

Detailed. See also John William Balding, *One hundred years in Ceylon: or, the centenary volume of the Church Missionary Society in Ceylon, 1818–1918*, Madras 1922, and Roland Potter Butterfield, *Padre Rowlands of Ceylon*, Edin. & Lond. [1930].

2204 GOONERATNE (YASMINE). English literature in Ceylon, 1815–1878. *Ceylon Hist. J.* xiv. Dehiwala. 1968.

See also K. H. M. Sumathipala, *History of education in Ceylon, 1796–1965* . . ., *Ceylon Hist. J.* xiii, Dehiwala 1968.

## (c) *Malaya*

2205 CHEESEMAN (HAROLD AMBROSE ROBINSON) *comp.* Bibliography of Malaya: being a classified list of books wholly or partly in English relating to the Federation of Malaya and Singapore. British Assoc. of Malaya. 1959.

Needs to be suppl. by B. Lim, comp., 'Malaya: a background bibliography', *Royal Asiatic Soc. (Malayan branch) J.* xxxv, pts. 2–3 (1962). See also Univ. of Singapore Libr. *Catalogue of the Malaysia/Singapore collection*, Boston, Mass. 1968, Kennedy Gordon Phillip Tregonning, ed., *Malaysian historical sources*, Singapore 1962, and Sir William George Maxwell and William Sumner Gibson, eds., *Treaties and engagements affecting the Malay states and Borneo*, 1924.

2206 BASTIN (JOHN) *and* WINKS (ROBIN WILLIAM) *comps.* Malaysia: selected historical readings. Kuala Lumpur etc. 1966.

2207 TREGONNING (KENNEDY GORDON PHILLIP). A history of modern Malaya. Singapore. 1964.

A straightforward account. Cp. Sir Richard Olof Winstedt, *Malaya and its history*, 1948, 6th edn. 1962, *Britain and Malaya, 1786–1941*, 1944, and *A history of Malaya*, rev. edn. Singapore 1962, and Neil Joseph Ryan, *The making of modern Malaysia . . .*, 3rd edn. Kuala Lumpur 1967. For articles and monographs the *Roy. Asiatic Soc. (Straits* [later *Malayan*, later *Malaysian*] *Branch) J.*, Singapore 1878+, is very good. See also *Journal of Southeast Asian hist.*, 1+, Singapore 1960+, John Sturgus Bastin and Roelof Roolvink, *Malayan and Indonesian studies: essays presented to Sir Richard Winstedt . . .*, Oxf. 1964, and Kenneth Gordon Phillip Tregonning, ed., *Papers on Malayan history*, Singapore 1962.

2208 MILLS (LENNOX ALGERNON). British Malaya, 1824–67. Ed. by Constance M. Turnbull. *Roy. Asiatic Soc. (Malayan Branch) J.* xxxiii, pt. 3 (1960). New edn. Kuala Lumpur. 1966.

Standard. See also Constance M. Turnbull, *The Straits Settlements, 1826–67: Indian presidency to crown colony*, 1972. There are also three other very good books on the period: Nicholas Tarling, *British policy in the Malay peninsula and archipelago 1824–1871*, *Roy. Asiatic Soc. (Malayan branch) J.* xxx, pt. 3 (1957), and *Piracy and politics in the Malay world: a study of British imperialism in nineteenth-century south-east Asia*, Melb. 1963, and Charles Donald Cowan, *Nineteenth-century Malaya: the origins of British political control*, 1961, and a useful contemp. survey, John Cameron, *Our tropical possessions in Malayan India: being a descriptive account of Singapore, Penang, Province Wellesley and Malacca: their peoples, products, commerce and government*, 1865. For the underpinnings of British rule see Patrick Morrah, 'The history of the Malayan police', *Roy. Asiatic Soc. (Malayan Branch) J.* xxxvi, pt. 2 (1968). For an interesting conflict of officials see Constance M. Turnbull, 'Governor Blundell and Sir Benson Maxwell: a conflict of personalities', ibid. xxx (1957), pt. 1, 134–63.

2209 PARKINSON (CYRIL NORTHCOTE). British intervention in Malaya, 1867–1877. Singapore. 1960.

2210 SADKA (EMILY). The protected Malay states, 1874–1895. Kuala Lumpur. 1968.

See also J. de Vere Allen, 'The Colonial Office and the Malay states, 1867–73', *Roy. Asiatic Soc. (Malayan Branch) J.* xxxvi (1963), pt. 1, 1–36.

2211 THIO (EUNICE). British policy in the Malay peninsula, 1880–1910. 2 v. Kuala Lumpur. 1969–.

See also her 'Britain's search for security in North Malaya, 1886–97', *J. Southeast Asian Hist.* x (1969), 279–303.

2212 CHAI (HON CHAN). The development of British Malaya, 1896–1909. Kuala Lumpur etc. 1964.

2213 SWETTENHAM (*Sir* FRANK ATHELSTANE). British Malaya: an account of the origin and progress of British influence in Malaya. 1906. 3rd edn. 1948.

A good account by a participant. See also his autobiography, *Footprints in Malaya . . .*, 1942, and Charles Donald Cowan, ed., 'Sir Frank Swettenham's Perak journals, 1874–1876', *Royal Asiatic Soc. (Malayan branch) J.* xxiv, pt. 4 (1951). The diaries of other contemp. administrators have been publ., incl. Emily Sadka, ed., 'The journal of Sir Hugh Low: Perak, 1877', ibid. xxvii, pt. 4 (1954), and Khoo Kay Kim, ed., 'Expedition to Trengganu and Kelantan: report by Hugh Clifford', ibid. xxxiv, pt. 1 (1961).

Sir Hugh Charles Clifford publ. a considerable number of Malayan sketches, based on his experiences as an administrator, among them *Bush-whacking, and other Asiatic tales and memories*, 1929; *The further side of silence*, 1916; *In a corner of Asia* . . ., 1899; *In court & kampong* . . ., 1897; and *Malayan monochromes*, 1913, and a selection of *Stories* ed. by William R. Roff, Kuala Lumpur etc. 1966. For Swettenham and Clifford see also James De Vere Allen, 'Two imperialists . . .', *Royal Asiatic Soc. (Malayan Branch) J.* xxxvii (1964), pt. 1, 41–73. For early 20th-cent. British views of Malaya see Arnold Wright, ed., *Twentieth-century impressions of British Malaya: its history, people, commerce, industries and resources*, 1908, Arnold Wright and Thomas H. Reid, *The Malay peninsula: a record of British progress in the middle east* . . ., 1912.

**2214 JACKSON (JAMES CHARLES).** Planters and speculators: Chinese and European agricultural enterprise in Malaya, 1786–1921, Kuala Lumpur & Lond. 1968.

For industry see Wong Lin Ken, *The Malayan tin industry to 1914*, Assoc. for Asian Studs. Monograph XIV, Tucson [Ariz.] 1965.

**2215 PURCELL (VICTOR WILLIAM WILLIAMS SAUNDERS).** The Chinese in Malaya . . . 1948.

See also Robert Nicholas Jackson, *Pickering: protector of Chinese*, Kuala Lumpur 1965, and *Immigrant labour and the development of Malaya, 1786–1920*, Government of Malaya, [Kuala Lumpur] 1961. On the large Indian population see Kernial Singh Sandhu, *Indians in Malaya: some aspects of their immigration and settlement (1786–1957)*, Camb. 1969, and Ravindra K. Jain, *South Indians on the plantation frontier in Malaya*, New Haven [Conn.] 1970.

**2216 MAKEPEACE (WALTER), BROOKE (GILBERT EDWARD),** *and* **BRADDELL (ROLAND ST. JOHN)** *eds.* One hundred years of Singapore: being some account of the capital of the Straits Settlements from its foundation by Sir Stamford Raffles on the 6th February 1819 to the 6th February 1919. 2 v. 1921.

See also Donald and Joanna Moore, *The first 150 years of Singapore*, Singapore 1969; Saw Swee Hock, 'Population trends in Singapore, 1819–1967', *J. Southeast Asian Hist.* x (1969), 36–49; Charles Burton Buckley, *An anecdotal history of old times in Singapore from . . . 1819 to . . . 1867*, 2 v. Singapore 1902, repr. 2 v. in 1, Kuala Lumpur 1965; Song Ong Siang, *One hundred years' history of the Chinese in Singapore* . . ., 1923, repr. Singapore 1967; Wong Lin Ken, *The trade of Singapore, 1819–69*, *Royal Asiatic Soc. (Malayan Branch) J.* xxxiii, pt. 4 (1960); Constance M. Turnbull, 'The European mercantile community in Singapore, 1819–1867', *J. Southeast Asian Hist.* x (1969), 12–35; and George Bogaars, *The Tanjong Pagar Dock Company, 1864–1905*, bound with Carl Alexander Gibson-Hill, *Singapore old strait and new harbour, 1300–1870*, Memoirs of the Raffles Museum 3, Singapore 1956. For Kuala Lumpur see John Michael Gullick, 'Kuala Lumpur, 1880–95', *Royal Asiatic Soc. (Malayan Branch) J.* xxviii, pt. 4 (1955).

## (d) *Other Colonies*

**2217 IRWIN (GRAHAM).** Nineteenth-century Borneo: a study in diplomatic rivalry. Verhandelingen van het Koninklijk Instituut voor Taal- Land- en Volkenkunde XV. The Hague. 1955.

Strongest on the early 19th cent. Needs to be suppl. by Leigh R. Wright, *The origins of British Borneo*, Hong Kong 1970. For Brunei see Peter Leys and Robert M. Pringle, 'Observations on the Brunei political system, 1883–1885', *Royal Asiatic Soc. (Malayan Branch) J.* xli (1968), pt. 2, 117–30, and Reginald Edwards Stubbs and D. E. Brown, 'Two Colonial Office memoranda on the history of Brunei', *ibid.* 83–116.

2218  RUNCIMAN (*Sir* STEVEN) *i.e.* RUNCIMAN (*Sir* JAMES COCHRAN STEVENSON). The white rajahs: the history of Sarawak from 1841 to 1946. Camb. 1960.

See also Sabine Baring-Gould and Charles Agar Bampfylde, *A history of Sarawak under its two white rajahs, 1839–1908*, 1909; Sir Charles Anthoni Johnson Brooke, *Ten years in Sarawak* . . ., 2 v. 1866; Gertrude Le Grand Jacob, *The raja of Sarawak: an account of Sir James Brooke* . . ., 2 v. 1876; Sir Spencer Buckingham St. John, *Rajah Brooke* . . ., 2 v. 1899; Emily Hahn, *James Brooke of Sarawak* . . ., 1953; Owen Rutter, ed., *Rajah Brooke & Baroness Burdett Coutts: consisting of the letters from Sir James Brooke, first white Rajah of Sarawak, to Miss Angela (afterwards Baroness) Burdett Coutts*, 1935; *Reports of the commissioners appointed to inquire into certain matters connected with the position of Sir James Brooke*. [1976] H.C. (1854–5). XXIX, 1; Otto C. Doering III, 'Government in Sarawak under Charles Brooke', *Royal Asiatic Soc. (Malayan Branch) J.* xxxix, pt. 2 (1966), 95–107; Jon M. Reinhardt, 'Administrative policy and practice in Sarawak: continuity and change under the Brookes', *J. Asian Studs.* xxix (1969–70), 851–62; Robert Pringle, *Rajahs and rebels: the Ibans of Sarawak under Brooke rule, 1841–1941*, 1970; Nicholas Tarling, *Britain, the Brookes and Brunei*, Kuala Lumpur etc. 1971; and Charles John Bunyon, *Memoirs of Francis Thomas McDougall, Bishop of Labuan and Sarawak* . . ., 1889.

2219  TREGONNING (KENNEDY GORDON PHILLIP). Under chartered company rule: North Borneo, 1881–1946. Singapore. 1958. 2nd edn. [A history of modern Sabah (North Borneo) 1881–1963.] 1965.

See also Owen Rutter, *British North Borneo: an account of its history, resources and native tribes* . . ., 1922, and John Semple Galbraith, 'The chartering of the British North Borneo Company', *J. British Studs.* iv (1964–5), pt. 2, 102–26.

2220  ENDACOTT (GEORGE BEER) *comp*. An eastern entrepot: a collection of documents illustrating the history of Hong Kong. Dept. of Technical Co-operation Overseas Research Public. 4. H.M.S.O. 1964.

2221  ENDACOTT (GEORGE BEER). A history of Hong Kong. 1958.

See also his *A biographical sketch-book of early Hong Kong*, Singapore 1962; *Government and people in Hong Kong, 1841–1962: a constitutional history*, Hong Kong 1964; and with Dorothy E. She, *The diocese of Victoria, Hong Kong: a hundred years of church history, 1849–1949*, Hong Kong 1949; G. B. Endacott and Arthur Hinton, *Fragrant Harbour: a short history of Hong Kong*, Hong Kong 1962, 2nd edn. 1968; Ernest John Eitel, *Europe in China: the history of Hong Kong from the beginning to the year 1882*, Lond. & Hong Kong 1895; Sir Charles Henry Collins, *Public administration in Hong Kong* . . ., 1952, and James William Norton Kyshe, *The history of the laws and courts of Hong Kong* . . ., 2 v. Lond. & Hong Kong 1898.

## D. FOREIGN COUNTRIES

### 1. THE FOREIGN OFFICE, DIPLOMATS, AND CONSULS

#### (a) *General*

(For Foreign Office Records see **909–11**.)

2222  SATOW (*Sir* ERNEST MASON). A guide to diplomatic practice. 2 v. 1917. 4th edn. 1964.

An invaluable guide. See also Sir Harold George Nicolson, *The evolution of diplomatic method*, Lond. & N.Y. 1954.

8223897                     K

**2223** TILLEY (*Sir* JOHN ANTHONY CECIL) *and* GASELEE (STEPHEN). The Foreign Office. Whitehall series. 1933.

A general hist. There are some additional details in Sir Spencer Walpole, *Foreign relations*, 1882.

**2224** JONES (RAY). The nineteenth-century Foreign Office: an administrative history. 1971.

**2225** GOSSES (FRANS). The management of British foreign policy before the first World War, especially during the period 1880–1914. Trans. by E. C. van der Gaaf. Leiden. 1948.

**2226** STEINER (ZARA SHAKOW). The Foreign Office and foreign policy, 1898–1914. Camb. 1969.

Good. See also her 'Grey, Hardinge and the Foreign Office, 1906–1910', *Hist. J.* x (1967), 415–39, 'The last years of the old Foreign Office, 1898–1905', ibid. vi (1963), 59–90, and Margaret Boveri, *Sir Edward Grey und das Foreign Office*, Berlin 1933.

**2227** CECIL (ALGERNON). British foreign secretaries, 1807–1916: studies in personality and policy. 1927.

Unimpressive. For individual foreign secretaries, viz. Granville, Malmesbury, Russell, Clarendon, Stanley (15th Earl of Derby), Salisbury, Northcote, Rosebery, Kimberley, Lansdowne, and Grey, consult the index.

**2228** KENNEDY (AUBREY LEO). Old diplomacy and new, 1876–1922: from Salisbury to Lloyd George. 1922.

For the case for a new diplomacy see Arthur Ponsonby, Baron Ponsonby, *Democracy and diplomacy: a plea for popular control of foreign policy*, 1915.

**2229** GALL (WILHELM). Sir Charles Hardinge und die englische Vorkriegspolitik, 1903–1910. Berlin. 1939.

**2230** HERTSLET (*Sir* EDWARD). Recollections of the old Foreign Office. 1901.

**2231** NIGHTINGALE (ROBERT T.) The personnel of the British Foreign Office and diplomatic service, 1851–1921. Fabian Tract no. 232. 1930.

See also Dale Allen Hartman, 'British and American ambassadors, 1893–1930: a study in comparative personnel', *Economica* xi (1931), 328–41. For military attachés see **2687**.

**2232** PLATT (DESMOND CHRISTOPHER ST MARTIN). The cinderella service: British consuls since 1825. 1971.

See also his 'The role of the British consular service in overseas trade, 1825–1914', *Econ. Hist. Rev.* 2 ser. xv (1962–3), 494–512. For the duties of consuls see also E. W. A. Tuson, *The British consul's manual: being, a practical guide for consuls, as well as for the merchant, ship-owner and master-mariner in all their consular transactions*, 1856.

**2233** WHEELER-HOLOHAN (AMBROSE VINCENT). The history of the king's messengers. Lond. 1935.

2234 THE FOREIGN OFFICE LIST [and diplomatic and consular year book]. Annual. 1852–1965.

2235 SELECT COMMITTEE ON DIPLOMATIC SERVICE. Report from the select committee on diplomatic service [Chairman: R. Monckton Milnes]. H.C. 459 (1861). VI, 1.

2236 SELECT COMMITTEE ON DIPLOMATIC AND CONSULAR SERVICES. Report from the select committee on diplomatic and consular services [Chairmen: E. P. Bouverie and G. Sclater-Booth]. H.C. 382 (1870). VII, 279. Further reports: H.C. 238 (1871). VII, 197; H.C. 380 (1871). 345; H.C. 314 (1872). VII, 403.

2237 SELECT COMMITTEE ON CONSULAR SERVICE AND AP-POINTMENTS. Report from the select committee on consular service and appointments [Chairman: R. Monckton Milnes]. H.C. 482 (1857–8). VIII, 1.

(b) *Biographies*

2238 FOREIGN OFFICE, diplomatic and consular sketches. Reprinted from Vanity Fair. 1883.

2239 VITZTHUM VON ECKSTÄDT (KARL FRIEDRICH), *Count*. St Petersburg and London in the years 1852–1864: reminiscences of Count Charles Frederick Vitzthum von Eckstaedt. Ed. by Henry Reeve. Trans. by Edward Fairfax Taylor. 2 v. 1887.

Vitzthum was Saxon minister in London, and also publ. *London, Gastein und Sadowa, 1864–1866* . . ., Stuttgart 1889. Other diplomats who recorded views about diplomatic life in London were Staal (**2339**), Cambon (**2288**), Bernstorff, Hatzfeldt, Eckhardtstein, and Lichnowsky (**2301**), and the Americans at **2616–31**.

2240 BUCHANAN. My mission to Russia, and other diplomatic memories. By Sir George William Buchanan. 2 v. 1923.

See also Amalie Dengler, *Der englische Botschafter Sir George Buchanan und seine Stellung zu Deutschland*, Berlin 1937.

2241 BUNSEN. Maurice de Bunsen: diplomat and friend. By Edgar Trevelyan Stratford Dugdale. 1934.

2242 CORBETT. Reminiscences, autobiographical and diplomatic. By Sir Vincent Edwin Corbett. 1927.

2243 DURAND. The Right Honourable Sir Mortimer Durand P.C., G.C.M.G., K.C.S.I., K.C.I.E.: a biography. By Sir Percy Molesworth Sykes. 1926.

2244 ELLIOT. Some revolutions and other diplomatic experiences. By Sir Henry George Elliot. Ed. by his daughter, Gertrude Elliot. 1922.

2245 GREGORY. On the edge of diplomacy: rambles and reflections, 1902–28. By John Duncan Gregory. 1929.

2246 HARDINGE. A diplomatist in Europe. 1927. A diplomatist in the East. 1928. By Sir Arthur Henry Hardinge.

2247 HARDINGE. Old diplomacy: the reminiscences of Lord Hardinge of Penshurst. [By Charles Hardinge, Baron Hardinge.] 1947.

See also **1136** for his Indian career and **2229** for his work in the Foreign Office.

2248 HOWARD. Theatre of life [1863–1936]. By Esmé William Howard, Baron Howard of Penrith. 2 v. 1935–6.

2249 LAW. The life of Sir Edward FitzGerald Law, K.C.S.I., K.C.M.G. Ed. by Sir Theodore Morison and George Thompson Hutchinson. 1911.

A diplomatic and economic agent with very varied service in the East.

2250 LAYARD. Sir A. Henry Layard, G.C.B., D.C.L.: autobiography and letters from his childhood until his appointment as H.M. ambassador at Madrid. Ed. by William Napier Bruce. 2 v. 1903.

See also Gordon Waterfield, *Layard of Nineveh*, 1963, and Nora Benjamin Kubie, *Road to Nineveh: the adventures and excavations of Sir Austin Henry Layard*, 1965.

2251 LOFTUS. The diplomatic reminiscences of Lord Augustus Loftus, 1837–18[79]. By Lord Augustus William Frederick Spencer Loftus. 4 v. in 2 ser. 1892–4.

2252 LYONS. Lord Lyons: a record of British diplomacy. By Thomas Wodehouse Legh, Baron Newton. 2 v. 1913.

2253 MORIER. Memoirs and letters of the Right Hon. Sir Robert Morier, G.C.B., from 1826 to 1876. By Mrs. Rosslyn Wemyss [Victoria Wemyss, Baroness Wester Wemyss]. 2 v. 1911.

Cont. by Agatha Ramm, *Sir Robert Morier, envoy and ambassador in the age of imperialism, 1876–1893*, 1973.

2254 NICOLSON. Sir Arthur Nicolson, Bart., first Lord Carnock: a study in the old diplomacy. By Sir Harold George Nicolson. 1930. [Publ. as Portrait of a diplomatist . . . Boston. 1930.]

2255 ONSLOW. Sixty-three years: diplomacy, the Great War and politics . . . By Richard William Alan Onslow, Earl of Onslow. 1944.

2256 PAUNCEFOTE. The life of Lord Pauncefote, first ambassador to the United States. By Robert Balmain Mowat. Boston & N.Y. 1929.

2257 RODD. Social and diplomatic memories [1884–1919]. By James Rennell Rodd, Baron Rennell. 3 v. 1922–5.

2258 SPRING RICE. The letters and friendships of Sir Cecil Spring Rice: a record. Ed. by Stephen Lucius Gwynn. 2 v. Lond., Boston, & N.Y. 1929.

2259 RUMBOLD. Recollections of a diplomatist. 2 v. 1902. Further recollections . . . 1903. Final recollections . . . 1905. By Sir Horace Rumbold.

2260 RUSSELL. Ambassador to Bismarck: Lord Odo Russell, first Baron Ampthill. By Winifred Annie Taffs. 1938.

See also **2301.**

2261 SATOW. The Rt. Hon. Sir Ernest Satow, G.C.M.G.: a memoir. By Bernard Meredith Allen. 1933.

See also Sir Ernest Mason Satow, *A diplomat in Japan* . . ., Lond. & Phila. 1921, new edn. Kuala Lumpur 1969.

2262 STRATFORD DE REDCLIFFE. The life of the Right Honourable Stratford Canning, Viscount Stratford de Redcliffe . . . By Stanley Lane Poole. 2 v. 1888.

See also James Henry Skene, *With Lord Stratford in the Crimean War*, 1883, Elizabeth Frances Malcolm Smith, *The life of Stratford Canning, Lord Stratford de Redcliffe*, 1933, and Leo Gerald Byrne, *The great ambassador: a study of the diplomatic career of the Right Honourable Stratford Canning, K.G., G.C.B., Viscount Stratford de Redcliffe, and the epoch during which he served as the British ambassador to the sublime porte of the Ottoman sultan*, Columbus, Ohio 1964. Stratford's main works are incl. in *The eastern question: by the late Viscount Stratford de Redcliffe . . . being a selection from his writings during the last five years of his life, with a preface by Arthur Penrhyn Stanley*, 1881.

2263 WHITE. Sir William White, K.C.B., K.C.M.G. for six years ambassador at Constantinople: his life and correspondence. By Henry Sutherland Edwards. 1902.

See also Smith (**2410**).

## 2. EUROPE

### (a) *General*

2264 BULLOCK (*Sir* ALAN LOUIS CHARLES) *and* TAYLOR (ALAN JOHN PERCIVALE) *eds*. A select list of books on European history, 1815–1914. 2nd edn. Oxf. 1957. Repr. 1960.

A very useful checklist, though confined to books in the main West-European languages. To be consulted for general hists. of Europe and national hists. not listed here. For commentaries see the bibliog. in Taylor (**925**). For diplomatic archives see Daniel Harrison Thomas and Lynn Marshall Case, *Guide to the diplomatic archives of western Europe*, Phila. 1959.

2265 JOLL (JAMES BYSSE) *ed*. Britain and Europe: Pitt to Churchill, 1793–1940. 1950. Repr. with revs. 1961.

Docs.

**2266  HERTSLET** (*Sir* EDWARD). The map of Europe by treaty, showing the various political and territorial changes which have taken place since the general peace of 1814. 4 v. 1875–91.

Gives treaty texts, 1814–91. See also Sir Augustus Henry Oakes and Robert Balmain Mowat, eds., *The great European treaties of the nineteenth century*, Oxf. 1918, repr. 1970.

**2267  SETON-WATSON** (ROBERT WILLIAM). Britain in Europe, 1789–1914: a survey of foreign policy. Camb. 1937.

Chiefly pre-1880. Good. Reginald Charles Birch, *Britain and Europe, 1871–1939*, Oxf. & N.Y. 1966, is a basic narrative and no more.

**2268  RAMSAY** (ANNA AUGUSTA WHITTALL). Idealism and foreign policy: a study of the relations of Great Britain with Germany and France, 1860–1878. 1925.

**2269  MILLMAN** (RICHARD). British foreign policy and the coming of the Franco-Prussian war. Oxf. 1965.

A careful up-to-date study. Repl. Kurt Rheindorf, *England und der deutsch-französische Krieg 1870/71: ein Beitrag zur englischen Politik in der Zeit des Überganges von Manchestertum zum Imperialismus*, Bonn & Leipzig 1923, and Dora Neill Raymond, *British policy and opinion during the Franco-Prussian war*, Columbia Univ. Studies in Hist., etc., 227, N.Y. 1921. See also Elisabeth Wentz, *Die Behandlung des deutsch-französischen Krieges 1870/71 in der englischen Presse: ein Beitrag zur Geschichte der Kriegsberichterstattung*, 2 v. Würzburg 1940.

**2270  MEDLICOTT** (WILLIAM NORTON). Bismarck, Gladstone and the concert of Europe. 1956.

Standard. Suppls. his *The Congress of Berlin and after* (**2406**).

**2271  PRIBRAM** (ALFRED FRANCIS). England and the international policy of the European great powers, 1871–1914. Oxf. 1931. Repr. Lond. 1966.

Useful but out of date. So is Hajo Brugmans, *De Buitenlandsche Politiek van het Britsche Rijk van omstreeks 1870 tot 1914*, Leiden 1926.

**2272  RÖMER** (KLAUS). England und die europäischen Mächte im Jahre 1887. Aarau. 1957.

A useful short thesis.

**2273  HENDERSON** (WILLIAM OTTO). Britain and industrial Europe, 1750–1870: studies in British influence on the industrial revolution in Western Europe. Liverpool. 1954.

### (b) *France*

**2274  FRANCE: MINISTÈRE DES AFFAIRES ÉTRANGÈRES: COMMISSION DE PUBLICATION DES DOCUMENTS RELATIFS AUX ORIGINES DE LA GUERRE DE 1914.** Documents diplomatiques français, 1871–1914. 41 v. Paris. 1929–59.

Arr. in three ser. covering 1871–1900 in 16 v., 1901–11 in 14 v., 1911–14 in 11 v. There is also a separate ser. publ. by le Ministère des Affaires Étrangères, *Les origines diplomatiques de la guerre de 1870–71: recueil de documents*, 29 v. Paris 1910–32.

2275 COVILLE (ALEXANDRE ALFRED) *and* TEMPERLEY (HAROLD WILLIAM VAZEILLE) *eds.* Studies in Anglo-French history during the eighteenth, nineteenth and twentieth centuries. Camb. 1935.

See also Jean Darcy, *France et Angleterre: cent années de rivalité coloniale*, Paris 1904.

2276 GREEN (FREDERICK CHARLES). A comparative view of French and British civilization (1850–1870). Lond. & Chicago. 1965.

Opens up a subject that needs developing. Christophe Campos, *The view of France: from Arnold to Bloomsbury*, 1965, is an exercise in literary criticism. For French thought see also Drescher (**226**). Works such as Sylvaine Marandon, *L'image de la France dans l'Angleterre victorienne, 1848–1900*, Paris 1967, and Catherine Irvine Gavin, *Britain and France: a study of twentieth-century relations: the entente cordiale*, 1941, provide little more than background.

2277 WILLSON (BECKLES). The Paris embassy: a narrative of Franco-British diplomatic relations, 1814–1920. 1927.

Popular. Sir Edward Charles Blount, *Memoirs*, ed. by Stuart Johnson Reid, 1902, and Sir Thomas Barclay, *Thirty years: Anglo-French reminiscences (1876–1906)*, 1914, are useful for diplomatic relations at the consular and commercial level. The great ambassadors of the period were Lord Cowley (**2278**) and Lord Lyons (**2252**).

2278 COWLEY. The Paris embassy during the second empire: selections from the papers of Henry Richard Charles Wellesley, 1st Earl Cowley, ambassador at Paris, 1852–1867. Ed. by Frederick Arthur Wellesley. 1928. N.Y. edn. [Secrets of the second empire.] 1929.

See also Sir Victor Alexander Augustus Henry Wellesley and Robert Edmonde Sencourt [pseud. of Robert Esmonde Gordon George] eds., *Conversations with Napoleon III: a collection of documents . . .*, 1934, and Mary Charlotte Mair Senior, afterwards Simpson, *Many memories of many people*, 1898. Some of the background to Cowley's embassy is given in Daniel Hamson Thomas, 'The reaction of the great powers to Louis Napoleon's rise to power in 1851', *Hist. J.* xiii (1970), 237–50, and Franklin Charles Palm, *England and Napoleon III . . .*, Durham, N.C. 1948.

2279 DUNHAM (ARTHUR LOUIS). The Anglo-French Treaty of Commerce of 1860 and the progress of the industrial revolution in France. Ann Arbor [Mich.]. 1930.

2280 HEARDER (HARRY). 'Napoleon III's threat to break off diplomatic relations with England during the crisis over the Orsini attempt in 1858'. *Eng. Hist. Rev.* lxxii (1957), 474–81.

2281 MOSSE (WERNER EUGEN). 'Public opinion and foreign policy: the British public and the war-scare of November 1870'. *Hist. J.* vi (1963), 38–58.

For British foreign policy and the Franco-Prussian war see **2269**.

2282 CARROLL (EBER MALCOLM). French public opinion and foreign affairs, 1870–1914. N.Y. & Lond. 1931. Repr. Hamden, Conn. 1964.

2283 BLOCH (CHARLES). Les relations entre la France et la Grande-Bretagne, 1871–1878. Paris. 1955.

See also Charles Gavard, *Un diplomate à Londres: lettres et notes, 1871–1877*, Paris

1895, trans. as *A diplomat in London: letters and notes, 1871–1877*, Lond. & N.Y. 1897, and Wilhelm Koelle, *Englische Stellungnahme gegenüber Frankreich, . . . 1870–71 . . . 1882 . . .*, Berlin 1934.

**2284 BROWN (ROGER GLENN).** Fashoda reconsidered: the impact of domestic politics on French policy in Africa, 1893–1898. Baltimore [Md.]. 1970.

Provides the French background to Sanderson (**1703**). See also John Desmond Hargreaves, '*Entente manquée:* Anglo-French relations, 1895–1896', *Camb. Hist. J.* xi (1953–5), 65–92; Lowell Joseph Ragatz, *The question of Egypt in Anglo-French relations, 1875–1904*, Edin. etc. 1922; Joseph James Mathews, *Egypt and the formation of the Anglo-French entente of 1904*, Phila. 1939; Kurt Biedermann, *Englisch-französische Beziehungen von Faschoda bis zur Konferenz von Algeçiras*, Jena 1932, Morrison Beall Giffen, *Fashoda: the incident and its diplomatic setting*, Chicago 1930, and Gabriel Hanotaux, *Fachoda*, Paris 1909.

**2285 ROLO (PAUL JACQUES VICTOR).** Entente cordiale: the origins and negotiation of the Anglo-French agreements of 8 April 1904. Lond. & N.Y. 1969.

**2286 ANDREW (CHRISTOPHER).** Théophile Delcassé and the making of the entente cordiale: a reappraisal of French foreign policy, 1898–1905. 1968.

**2287 NEILSON (FRANCIS).** 'Edward VII and the entente cordiale'. *Amer. J. of Econ. & Sociology*. xvi (1956–7), 353–68; xvii (1957–8), 87–100, 179–94.

**2288 CAMBON ([PIERRE] PAUL).** Correspondence, 1870–1924, avec un commentaire et des notes par Henri Cambon. 3 v. Paris. 1940–6.

Cambon was ambassador in London, 1898–1920, and the last two vols. are largely concerned with England. For Cambon's career see, *inter alia*, Weaver Keith Eubank, *Paul Cambon: master diplomatist*, Norman, Oklahoma 1960; Adrien Thierry, *L'Angleterre au temps de Paul Cambon*, Paris 1961; Anon., *Paul Cambon, ambassadeur de France, par un diplomate*, Paris 1937; Ludwig Zimmerman, *Paul Cambon: Schöpfer der Entente Cordiale mit England*, Studien zum Geschichtsbild 18, Göttingen [1965]; and R. B. Jones, 'Anglo-French negotiations, 1907: a memorandum by Sir Alfred Milner', *Inst. Hist. Res. Bull.* xxxi (1958), 224–7.

**2289 WILLIAMSON (SAMUEL RUTHVEN)** *Jr.* The politics of grand strategy: Britain and France prepare for war, 1904–1914. Camb., Mass. 1969.
Good.

## (c) *Germany*

**2290 GEBHARDT (BRUNO).** Handbuch der deutschen Geschichte. 8th edn. 4 v. Stuttgart. 1954–60. Repr. with rev. 4 v. 1963–4.

A good guide to German hist., incl. the complicated literature of the pre-war period. For Anglo-German lit. contacts see Bayard Quincy Morgan, *A bibliography of German literature in English translation*, Madison, Wisc. 1922, 2nd edn. [*A critical bibliography*] Stanford 1938, new edn. N.Y. 1965; Lillie Vinal Hathaway, *German literature of the mid-nineteenth century in England and America, as reflected in the journals, 1840–1914*, Boston 1935; and B. Q. Morgan and Alexander Rudolph Hohlfeld, eds., *German literature in British magazines, 1750–1860*, Madison, Wisc. 1949.

2291  BRANDENBURG (ERICH) *and others*, eds. Die auswärtige Politik Preussens, 1858–1871: diplomatische Aktenstücke. 9 v. Oldenburg. 1932–45.

With *Die grosse Politik* (**2292**), forms a wonderful coll. of docs.

2292  LEPSIUS (JOHANNES), MENDELSSOHN-BARTHOLDY (AL-BRECHT) *and* THIMME (FRIEDRICH) eds. Die grosse Politik der europäischen Kabinette, 1871–1914. 40 v. in 54. Berlin. 1922–7.

Indispensable docs. For the outbreak of war in 1914 see also Maximilian, Graf von Montgelas, and Walther Schücking, eds., *Die deutschen Dokumente zum Kriegsausbruch: vollständige Sammlung der von Karl Kautsky zusammengestellten* . . ., 4 v. Charlottenburg 1919, rev. edn. 1927, English trans. [*Outbreak of the World War: German documents collected by Karl Kautsky*], Carnegie Endowment for International Peace, N.Y. etc. 1924; Pius Dirr, ed., *Bayerische Dokumente zum Kriegsausbruch und zum Versailler Schuldspruch* . . ., Munich 1922; August Bach, ed., *Deutsche Gesandtschaftsberichte zum Kriegsausbruch, 1914* . . ., Berlin 1937; and Anon., *Official German documents relating to the World War*, Carnegie Endowment for International Peace, 2 v. N.Y. etc. 1923.

2293  DUGDALE (EDGAR TREVELYAN STRATFORD) *ed.* German diplomatic documents, 1871–1914. 4 v. Lond. & N.Y. 1928–31. Repr. N.Y. 1969.

Based on *Die grosse Politik* (**2292**).

2294  SCHENK (WILLY). Die deutsch-englische Rivalität vor dem Ersten Weltkrieg in der Sicht deutscher Historiker: Missverstehen oder Machtstreben? Aarau. 1967.

A useful historiographical study. The main 'revisionist' work in the field has been Fritz Fischer's *Germany's aims in the First World War*, N.Y. 1967, and *Krieg der Illusionen: die deutsche Politik von 1911 bis 1914*, Düsseldorf 1970, the challenge to which is discussed in Norman Stone, 'Gerhard Ritter and the First World War', *Hist. J.* xiii (1970), 158–71. The best works on Anglo-German diplomatic relations are those of Langer (**926–7**).

2295  SCHMITT (BERNADOTTE EVERLY). England and Germany, 1740–1914. Princeton [N.J.]. 1916.

May be suppl. by Lawrence Marsden Price, *The reception of English literature in Germany*, Berkeley 1932.

2296  SONTAG (RAYMOND JAMES). Germany and England: background of conflict, 1848–1898. N.Y. 1938. Repr. 1964, 1969.

Good.

2297  MOSSE (WERNER EUGEN). The European powers and the German question, 1848–71, with special reference to England and Russia. Camb. 1958.

See also his 'Queen Victoria and her ministers in the Schleswig-Holstein crisis, 1863–1864', *Eng. Hist. Rev.* lxxviii (1963), 263–83, and 'The crown and foreign policy: Queen Victoria and the Austro-Prussian conflict, March–May 1866', *Camb. Hist. J.* x (1950–2), 205–23. There are a considerable number of short theses and other works on the subject, incl. Horst Michael, *Bismarck, England und Europa (vorwiegend von 1866–1870): eine Studie zur Geschichte Bismarcks und der Reichsgründung*, Munich 1930; Marie Luise Picot, *England und Preussens deutsche Politik, 1856–1866*, [Münster]

1934; Ruth Kutsch, *Queen Victoria und die deutsche Einigung*, Berlin 1938; H. R. Fischer-Aue, *Die Deutschlandpolitik des Prinzgemahls Albert von England, 1848–1852*, Untersiemau bei Coburg & Hanover 1953; Hildegard Binder, *Queen Victoria und Preussen–Deutschland bis zum Ausschluss Österreichs, 1866*, Bottrop 1933; Gerhard Brüns, *England und der deutsche Krieg, 1866*, Berlin 1933; Christopher John Bartlett, 'Clarendon, the Foreign Office and the Hohenzollern candidature, 1868–1870', *Eng. Hist. Rev.* lxxv (1960), 276–84; and Werner Frauendienst, 'England und die deutsche Reichsgründung', *Berliner Monatshefte*, xix (1941), 77–102.

**2298  VALENTIN ([RUDOLF JOHAN MAXIMILIAN] VEIT). Bismarcks Reichsgründung im Urteil englischer Diplomaten. Amsterdam. [1937.]**

For the Franco-Prussian war see **2269**. See also Maximilian von Hagen, *Bismarck und England*, Stuttgart 1941, and *England und Ägypten: Materialien zur Geschichte der britischen Okkupation mit besonderer Rücksicht auf Bismarcks Ägyptenpolitik*, Bonn [1915]; Hans Rothfels, *Bismarcks englische Bündnispolitik*, Stuttgart, etc. 1924; Eva Maria Baum, *Bismarcks Urteil über England und die Engländer*, Munich 1936; Kurt Meine, *England und Deutschland in der Zeit des Überganges vom Manchestertum zum Imperialismus, 1871 bis 1876*, Berlin 1937; Wilhelm Schüssler, *Deutschland zwischen Russland und England: Studien zur Aussenpolitik des bismarckschen Reiches*, Leipzig 1940, 3rd edn. 1943; and Alexander von Taube, *Fürst Bismarck zwischen England und Russland: ein Beitrag zur Politik des Reichskanzlers in den Jahren von 1871 bis 1890*, Stuttgart 1923.

**2299  NIEDERHOMMERT (CHARLOTTE). Queen Viktoria und der deutsche Kronprinz Friedrich Wilhelm. Emsdetten. 1934.**

For the Empress Frederick see **329** and **349**.

**2300  BESELER (DORA HEDWIG VON). Der Kaiser im englischen Urteil. Stuttgart & Berlin. 1932.**

Horst Schneider, *Prinz Wilhelm von Preussen und England bis zur Thronbesteigung, 1859–1888*, Dresden 1935, is another brief thesis. For Wilhelm II and the English royal family see **337, 340** and Edward Legge, *King Edward, the Kaiser and the war*, 1917.

**2301  KNAPLUND (PAUL) ed. Letters from the Berlin embassy, 1871–1874, 1880–1885. Amer. Hist. Assoc. Annual Report 1942. Vol. II. Wash. 1944.**

Letters from Odo Russeli (**2260**), to Lord Granville. For German diplomats in London see Karl Ringhoffer, ed., *The Bernstorff papers: the life of Count Albrecht von Bernstorff*, trans. by Mrs Charles Edward Barrett-Lennard and M. W. Hoper, 2 v. Lond. & N.Y. 1908; Marie Luise Wolf, *Botschafter Graf Hatzfeldt: seine Tätigkeit in London, 1885–1901: Studie zur Geschichte der deutsch-englischen Beziehungen*, Speyer-am-Rhein 1935; Hermann, Freiherr von Eckhardtstein, *Ten years at the court of St James*, *1895–1905*, trans. by George Young, Lond. 1921, N.Y. 1922; Karl Max, Fürst von Lichnowsky, *My mission to London, 1912–1914*, Lond. & N.Y. 1918; and Edward Frederick Willis, *Prince Lichnowsky, ambassador of peace: a study of prewar diplomacy, 1912–1914*, Berkeley, etc. 1942.

**2302  HOFFMAN (ROSS JOHN SWARTZ). Great Britain and the German trade rivalry, 1875–1914. Phila. 1933.**

See also Barnard Ellinger, 'Value and comparability of English and German foreign trade statistics', *Manch. Stat. Soc. Trans.* (1903–4), 139–58, and Edgar Crammond, 'The economic relations of the British and German empires', *Royal Stat. Soc. J.* lxxvii (1913–14), 777–824. The main propagandist work of the period was Ernest Edwin Williams, *Made in Germany*, 1896.

2303  KANTOROWICZ (HERMANN). The spirit of British policy and the myth of the encirclement of Germany. Trans. by Walter Henry Johnston. 1931.

2304  HALE (ORON JAMES). Publicity and diplomacy, with special reference to England and Germany, 1890–1914. N.Y. & Lond. 1940.

Useful. Developed from his *Germany and the diplomatic revolution: a study in diplomacy and the press, 1904–1906*, Phila. 1931. Cp. Eber Malcolm Carroll, *Germany and the great powers, 1866–1914: a study in public opinion and foreign policy*, N.Y. 1938. There is a considerable lit. on the influence of the press in Anglo-German relations. Note, in particular, Manfred Sell, *Das deutsch-englische Abkommen von 1890 über Helgoland und die afrikanischen Kolonien im Lichte der deutschen Presse*, Berlin, etc. 1926; Karl Otto Herkenberg, *The Times und das deutsch-englische Verhältnis im Jahre 1898*, Berlin 1925; Werner Primke, *Die Politik der Times: von der Unterzeichnung des Jangtse-abkommens bis zum Ende der deutsch-englischen Bündnisbesprechungen (Oktober 1900 bis Mai 1901)*, Berlin 1936; Erich Voegtle, *Die englische Diplomatie und die deutsche Presse, 1898–1914: ein Beitrag zu den deutsch-englischen Beziehungen der Vorkriegszeit*, Würzburg 1936; Johannes Dreyer, *Deutschland und England in ihrer Politik und Presse im Jahre 1901*, Berlin 1934; Ludwig Stein, ed., *England & Germany: by leaders of public opinion in both empires* [repr. from *Nord und Süd*], 1912; Austin Harrison, *England & Germany* [repr. from *The Observer*], 1907; John Twells Brex, comp., '*Scare-mongerings' from the Daily Mail, 1896–1914: the paper that foretold the war*, 1914; and Leopold James Maxse, ed., '*Germany on the brain': or, the obsession of 'a crank': gleanings from the National review, 1899–1914*, 1915.

2305  ANDERSON (PAULINE RELYEA). The background of anti-English feeling in Germany, 1890–1902. Wash. 1939.

2306  MEINECKE (FRIEDRICH). Geschichte des deutsch-englischen Bündnisproblems, 1890–1901. Munich & Berlin. 1927.

A brilliant interpretative essay challenged by Gerhard Ritter, *Die Legende von der verschmähten englischen Freundschaft, 1898–1901*, Freiburg-im-Breisgau 1929. Ritter's views are supported by H. W. Koch, 'The Anglo-German alliance negotiations: missed opportunity or myth?', *History* liv (1969), 378–92. See also Norman Rich and M. H. Fisher, *The Holstein papers*, 4 v. Camb. 1955–63; Norman Rich, *Friedrich von Holstein: politics and diplomacy in the era of Bismarck and Wilhelm II*, 2 v. Camb. 1965; Heinrich, Freiherr von Hoyningen genannt Huene, *Untersuchungen zur Geschichte des deutsch-englischen Bündnisproblems, 1898–1901*, Breslau 1934; Walter Löding, *Die deutsch-englischen Bündnisverhandlungen, 1898 bis 1901, ihr Verlauf auf Grund der deutschen und der englischen Akten*, Hamburg 1929; Eugen Fischer, *Holsteins grosses Nein: die deutsch-englischen Bündnisverhandlungen von 1898–1901*, Berlin 1925; Heinrich Gustav Dittmar, *Die deutsch-englischen Beziehungen in den Jahren 1898/99: die Vorbesprechungen zu den Bündnisverhandlungen von 1900/01*, Cologne 1938; Fritz Schwarze, *Das deutsch-englische Abkommen über die portugiesischen Kolonien vom 30 August 1898*, Göttingen 1931; Wolfgang Herrmann, *Dreibund, Zweibund, England, 1890–1895*, Stuttgart 1929; Theodor A. Bayer, *England und der neue Kurs, 1890–1895: auf Grund unveröffent-lichter Akten*, Tübingen 1955; Ludwig Israel, *England und der orientalische Dreibund: eine Studie zur europäischen Aussenpolitik, 1887–1896*, Stuttgart 1937; G. S. Papado-poulos, 'Lord Salisbury and the projected Anglo-German alliance of 1898', *Inst. Hist. Res. Bull.* xxvi (1953), 214–18; and John Ashley Soames Grenville, 'Lansdowne's abortive project of 12 March 1901 for a secret agreement with Germany', ibid. xxvii (1954), 201–13. There is also an illuminating essay in Eckart Kehr, *Der Primat der Innenpolitik . . .*, ed. by Hans-Ulrich Wehler, Berlin 1965.

2307 WOODWARD (*Sir* ERNEST LLEWELLYN). Great Britain and the German navy. Oxf. 1935. Repr. Lond. & Hamden, Conn. 1964.

Standard. Covers 1898–1914. See also Fritz Strigel, *Die deutsch-englischen Flottenver-handlungen in den Jahren 1909–1911 unter Bethmann-Hollweg*, Lohr-am-Main 1935; Fritz Uplegger, *Die englische Flottenpolitik vor dem Weltkrieg, 1904–1909*, Stuttgart 1930; Ilse Metz, *Die deutsche Flotte in der englischen Presse: der Navy scare vom Winter 1904/05*, Berlin 1936; Wilhelm Widenmann, *Marine-attaché an der kaiserlich-deutschen Botschaft in London, 1907 bis 1912*, Göttingen 1952; and Hermann Wilhelm Erd-brügger, *England–Deutschland und die Zweite Haager Friedenskonferenz, 1907*, Borna-Leipzig 1935. For the understanding of German policy Eckart Kehr, *Schlachtflottenbau und Parteipolitik, 1894–1901: Versuch eines Querschnitts durch die innenpolitischen, sozialen und ideologischen Voraussetzungen des deutschen Imperialismus*, Berlin, 1930, repr. Vaduz 1965, is important.

2308 BECKER (WILLY). Fürst Bülow und England, 1897–1909. Greifswald. 1929.

See also Bernhard Heinrich Martin Carl, Fürst von Bülow, *Memoirs of Prince von Bülow*, trans. by Frederick Augustus Voigt, 4 v. Lond. & Boston 1931–2, *Letters of Prince von Bülow . . .*, trans. by Frederic Whyte, 1930, and Wilhelm Schüssler, *Die Daily-Telegraph Affaire: Fürst Bülow, Kaiser Wilhelm und die Krise des Zweiten Reiches, 1908*, Göttingen 1952.

2309 HAUSER (OSWALD). Deutschland und der englisch-russische Gegen-satz, 1900–1914. Göttingen. 1958.

See also **2240**.

2310 HENNING (HANS JOACHIM). Deutschlands Verhältnis zu England in Bethmann Hollwegs Aussenpolitik, 1909–1914. Cologne. 1962.

See also Alexander Kessler, *Das deutsch-englische Verhältnis vom Amtsantritt Bethmann Hollwegs bis zur Haldane-Mission*, Erlangen 1938.

2311 DRINGENBERG (HENNY). Die Mission Haldanes. Bonn. 1930.

See also the works on Haldane at **772**; Bernadotte Everly Schmitt, 'Lord Haldane's mission to Berlin in 1912', in Louis John Paetow, ed., *The crusades and other historical essays . . .*, N.Y. 1928, pp. 245–88; Franz Zorger, *Haldanes Mission im Jahre 1912: der letzte deutsch-englische Verständigungsversuch vor dem Weltkriege*, Frankfurt 1928; Bernhard Daniel Ernst Kraft, *Lord Haldanes Zending naar Berlijn in 1912: de Duitsch-Engelsche Onderhandelingen over de Vlootquaestie, 1905–1912*, Utrecht 1931; and Rudolf Meyer-Adams, *Die Mission Haldanes im Februar 1912 im Spiegel der deutschen Presse*, Bochum-Langendreer 1935.

2312 SAROLEA (CHARLES). The Anglo-German problem. Lond. etc. 1912. New edn. 1915.

An analysis of the hostility provoked by Germany. Cp. John Adam Cramb, *Germany and England*, Lond. & N.Y. 1914. There were also many overtly anti-German works, incl. William Nicholas Willis, *What Germany wants* [1912], and Demetrius Charles Boulger, *England's arch-enemy: a collection of essays forming an indictment of German policy during the last sixteen years*, 1914.

(d) *Italy*

2313 CURATO (FEDERICO) *and* GIARRIZZO (GIUSEPPI) *eds.* Docu-menti per la storia delle relazioni diplomatiche fra le grandi potenze europee e gli stati Italiani, 1814–1860. Parte seconda: documenti esteri. Le relazioni diplomatiche fra la Gran Bretagna e il regno di Sardegna. III ser. 1848–60. 8 v. Fonti per la Storia d'Italia, Istituto Storico Italiano per L'Età Moderna e Contemporanea. Rome. 1961–9.

The vols. to appear so far have been nos. 51, 52, 80, 88, 98, 59, 60, 61 of the whole ser. of the *Fonti*. They are suppl. by Federico Curato, ed., *Le relazioni diplomatiche fra la Gran Bretagna e il regno di Sardegna dal 1852 al 1856: il carteggio diplomatico di Sir James Hudson*, Istituto per la Storia del Risorgimento Italiano, Comitato di Torino, 2 v. Turin 1956.

2314 CURATO (FEDERICO) *ed*. Documenti per la storia delle relazioni diplomatiche fra gli stati Italiani e le grandi potenze europee, 1814–1860. parte prima: documenti italiani. Le relazioni diplomatiche fra il regno di Sardegna e la Gran Bretagna: III ser. 1848–1860. 1+ v. Fonti per la Storia d'Italia, Istituto Storico Italiano per L'Età Moderna e Contemporanea. Rome. 1955–.

The vols. to appear so far have been nos. 22, 23, 72, 73, and 98 of the *Fonti*.

2315 ITALY: MINISTERO DEGLI AFFARI ESTERI: COMMISSIONE PER LA PUBBLICAZIONE DEI DOCUMENTI DIPLOMATICI. I documenti diplomatici italiani. 1+. Rome. 1952+.

Arranged in 9 ser. of which the 1st covers 1861–70, the 2nd, 1870–96, the 3rd 1896–1907, and the 4th 1908–14.

2316 URBAN (MIRIAM BELLE). British opinion and policy on the unification of Italy, 1856–1961. Scottdale, Pa. 1938.

Partly repl. by Beales (**2318**). See also Adolfo Colombo, *L'Inghilterra nel Risorgimento italiano*, Milan 2nd edn. 1917; Horst Ley, *Die italienische Einigung und die englische Politik, 1859–1861*, Leipzig 1935; Wilhelm Franz Platz, *Die italienische Frage vom Pariser Friedenskongress bis zur Gründung des Königreiches im Spiegel englischer Politik, 1856–1861*, Marburg 1960; Alfredo Signoretti, *Italia e Inghilterra durante il Risorgimento*, Milan 1940; and Emilia Morelli, ed., *Italia e Inghilterra nella prima fase del Risorgimento . . .*, Rome 1952.

2317 RUDMAN (HARRY WILLIAM). Italian nationalism and English letters: figures of the Risorgimento and Victorian men of letters. Columbia Univ. Studs. in English, etc., 146. Lond. & N.Y. 1940.

2318 BEALES (DEREK EDWARD DAWSON). England and Italy, 1859–60. 1961.

See also Frederick Arthur Simpson, 'England and the Italian war of 1859', *Hist. J.* v (1962), 111–21, and Franco Valsecchi, 'L'Inghilterra e la questione italiana nel 1859: la missione Cowley (27 febbraio–10 marzo 1859)', *Archivio storico italiano* cxxvi (1968), 479–94.

2319 CAVOUR. Cavour e l'Inghilterra. Ed. by Vittorio Emanuele Tapparelli, marchese d'Azeglio. 2 v in 3. Bologna. 1933. Repr. 1961.

2320 MAZZINI. L'Inghilterra di Mazzini. By Emilia Morelli. Istituto per la Storia del Risorgimento Italiano, Biblioteca Scientifica, Ser. II, xxi. Rome. 1965.

Disappointing, as is her *Mazzini in Inghilterra*, Florence 1938. Eleanore F. Richards, ed., *Mazzini's letters to an English family, 1844–[1872]*, 3 v. 1920–2, is good on Mazzini's English contacts.

2321 TREVELYAN (GEORGE MACAULAY) *ed.* English songs of Italian freedom. 1911.

2322 ARNOLD (MATTHEW). England and the Italian question. 1859. New edn. by Merle Mowbray Bevington. Durham, N.C. 1953.

2323 GOPAL (SARVEPALLI). 'Gladstone and the Italian question'. *History* xli (1956), 113–21.

Largely repl. by Deryck Marshall Schreuder, 'Gladstone and Italian unification: the making of a Liberal?', *Eng. Hist. Rev.* lxxxv (1970), 475–501.

2324 ELLIOT (GEORGE FRANCIS STEWART). Sir James Hudson and Earl Russell: an historical rectification from authentic documents. 1866.

2325 LACAITA. An Italian Englishman: Sir James Lacaita, K.C.M.G., 1813–1895, senator of the kingdom of Italy. By Charles Lacaita. 1933.

Good. Jesse Myers, *Baron Ward and the dukes of Parma*, 1938, fails to do for Ward, who died in 1858, what has been done for Lacaita.

2326 DE CUGIS (CARLO) *ed.* England and Italy a century ago: a new turn in economic relations; catalogue of the exhibition held during the British week in Milan (9–17 October 1965). Milan. 1967.

2327 BLAKISTON (NOEL) *ed.* The Roman question: extracts from the despatches of Odo Russell from Rome, 1858–1870. 1962.

See also Sir Alec Walter George Randall, 'British diplomacy and the Holy See, 1555–1925', *Dublin Rev.* ccxxxiii (1959–60), 291–303, and 'A British agent at the Vatican: the mission of Odo Russell', ibid. 37–57, and Samuel Adrian Miles Adshead, 'Odo Russell and the first Vatican council', *J. Religious Hist.* ii (1962–3), 295–302.

2328 MOZLEY (THOMAS). Letters from Rome on the occasion of the oecumenical council, 1869–1870. 2 v. 1891.

Inaccurate, but useful as a reflection of contemp. prejudice.

2329 BERKELEY (GEORGE FITZHARDINGE). The Irish battalion in the papal army of 1860. Dublin etc. 1929.

2330 MARSDEN (ARTHUR). 'Salisbury and the Italians in 1896'. *J. Mod. Hist.* xl (1968), 91–117.

2331 GLANVILLE (JAMES LINUS). Italy's relations with England, 1896–1905. Baltimore [Md.]. 1934.

For later events see Richard Bosworth, 'Great Britain and Italy's acquisition of the Dodecanese, 1912–1915', *Hist. J.* xiii (1970), 683–705.

2332 SERRA (ENRICO). L'intesa mediterranea del 1902: una fase risolutiva nei rapporti italo-inglesi. Milan. 1957.

2333 ARTOM TREVES (GUILIANA). The golden ring: the Anglo-Florentines, 1847–62. Trans. by Sylvia Sprigge. 1956.

2334 WOLLASTON (GEORGE HYDE) *comp.* The Englishman in Italy: being a collection of verses written by some of those who have loved Italy. Oxf. 1909.

2335 LUCAS (MATILDA). Two Englishwomen in Rome, 1871–1900. 1938.

Incl. as a reminder that there was a considerable English colony in Italy.

#### (e) *Russia*

2336 MIDDLETON (KENNETH WILLIAM BRUCE). Britain and Russia: an historical essay. [1947.]

A general survey comparable with Sir John Arthur Ransome Marriott, *Anglo-Russian relations, 1689–1943,* 1944. Barbara Brightfield Jelavich, *A century of Russian foreign policy, 1814–1914,* Phila. 1964, is useful for background.

2337 U.S.S.R.: MINISTERSTVO INOSTRANNYKH DEL. Vneshniaia politika Rossii XIX i nachala XX veka: dokumenty rossiiskogo Ministerstva inostrannykh del. 1+. Moscow. 1960+.

Intended to cover the period 1801–1917 in 6 ser. As yet only the 1st ser. has begun to appear. Meanwhile there are fragments of another ser. for the early 20th cent. U.S.S.R.: Komissiia po Izdaniiu Dokumentov Epokhi Imperializma, *Mezhdunarodnye otnosheniia v epokhu imperializma: Dokumenty iz arkhivov tsarskogo i vremennogo pravitel'sty, 1878–1910 gg: relations internationales de l'époque de l'impérialisme,* 1+, Moscow 1930+. Other docs. incl. in *Krasny Arkhiv,* are summarized in Louise M. Boutelle and Gordon W. Thayer, eds., and Leonid S. Rubinchek, trans., *A digest of the Krasnyi arkhiv (Red archives): a historical journal of the central archive department of the U.S.S.R.,* 2 v. Cleveland 1947–55.

2338 LIEVEN. The Lieven–Palmerston correspondence, 1828–1856. Trans. & Ed. by Arthur Paul John Charles Gore, Viscount Sudley, afterwards Earl of Arran. 1943.

See also Ernest Anthony Smith, ed., *Letters of Princess Lieven to Lady Holland, 1847–1857,* Roxburghe club, 1956. Other works about Princess Lieven deal principally with events before 1851.

2339 STAAL. Correspondance diplomatique de M. de Staal, 1884–1900. Ed. by Baron Aleksandr Feliksovich Meyendorff. 2 v. Paris. 1929.

2340 NOVIKOFF. The M.P. for Russia: reminiscences & correspondence of Madame Olga Novikoff. Ed. by William Thomas Stead. 2 v. 1909.

See also [Ol'ga Alekseievna Novikova], *Russia and England from 1876 to 1880: a protest and an appeal, by O.K., author of 'Is Russia wrong?',* 1880, 2nd edn. 1880, and *Russian memories,* 1916. On Stead's connection with Russia see also Joseph O. Baylen, 'W. T. Stead and the Russian revolution of 1905', *Canadian J. of Hist.* ii (1967), pt. 1, 45–66.

2341  CHURCHILL (ROGERS PLATT). The Anglo-Russian convention of 1907. Cedar Rapids, Iowa. 1939.

See also Beryl J. Williams, 'The strategic background to the Anglo-Russian entente of August 1907', *Hist. J.* ix (1966), 360–73, Olga Crisp, 'The Russian liberals and the 1906 Anglo-French loan to Russia', *Slavonic & East European Rev.* xxxix (1960–1), 497–511, and Gerhard Richter, *Die russischen Motive bei dem englisch-russischen Abkommen (agreement) vom 31 August 1907*, Berlin 1937.

2342  HAUSER (OSWALD). Deutschland und der englisch–russische Gegensatz, 1900–1914. Göttingen. 1958.

See also Heinz Schulze, *Die englisch–russischen Beziehungen, 1903–1909*, Auma 1933, and Laszlo Eduard Ludwig Sluimers, *De Brits–Russische Entente van 31 Augustus 1907, gezien als verwezenlijking van Bismarcks Cauchemar des Coalitions*, Amsterdam 1957.

2343  IGNAT'EV (ANATOLII VENEDIKTOVICH). Russko-angliiskie otnosheniia nakanune pervoi mirovoi voiny, 1908–1914 gg. Moscow. 1962.

2344  BOARD OF TRADE. North Sea incident (21–22 October, 1904). Reports thereon by the commissioners appointed by the Board of Trade . . . [Sir Cyprian Bridge and Butler Aspinall]. [Cd. 2451] H.C. (1905). LXIV, 327.

On the attack by Russian naval vessels on British trawlers in the North Sea.

2345  OREL (HAROLD). 'English critics and the Russian novel, 1850–1917'. *Slavonic & East European Rev.* xxxiii (1954–5), 457–69.

For travellers' reactions to Russia see Harry W. Nerhood, *To Russia and return: an annotated bibliography of travelers' English-language accounts of Russia from the ninth century to the present*, Columbus, Ohio 1968.

### (f) *The Mediterranean and Morocco*

2346  MONK (WINSTON FRANCIS). Britain in the western Mediterranean. 1953.

William Leonard Langer, 'Tribulations of empire: the Mediterranean problem', *Foreign Affairs* xv (1936–7), 646–60, is a pleasant essay.

2347  LEE (DWIGHT ERWIN). Great Britain and the Cyprus convention policy of 1878. Camb., Mass. 1934.

See also William Norton Medlicott, 'The Gladstone government and the Cyprus convention, 1880–85', *J. Mod. Hist.* xii (1940), 186–208.

2348  RAYMOND (ANDRÉ). 'Salisbury and the Tunisian question, 1878–1880'. St. Antony's Papers 11: Middle Eastern affairs 2. (1961). 101–38.

See also Arthur Marsden, 'Britain and the "Tunis base", 1894–1899', *Eng. Hist. Rev.* lxxix (1964), 67–96, and *Britain and the end of the Tunis treaties, 1894–1897*, *Eng. Hist. Rev.* suppl. 1 (1965).

2349  LOWE (CEDRIC JAMES). Salisbury and the Mediterranean, 1886–1896. 1965.

2350 GRENVILLE (JOHN ASHLEY SOAMES). 'Goluchowski, Salisbury and the Mediterranean agreements, 1895–1897'. *Slavonic & East European Rev.* xxxvi (1957–8), 340–69.

2351 HALLMANN (HANS). Spanien und die französisch–englische Mittelmeer–Rivalität, 1898–1907: ein Beitrag zur Geschichte der entstehenden und sich festigenden Entente Cordiale. Stuttgart. 1937.

2352 HALPERN (PAUL G.). The Mediterranean naval situation, 1908–1914. Camb., Mass. 1971.

2353 MIÈGE (JEAN LOUIS). Le Maroc et l'Europe, 1830–1894. 5+ v. Paris. 1961+.
Careless about British influence, but full of matter.

2354 FLOURNOY (FRANCIS ROSEBRO). British policy towards Morocco in the age of Palmerston, 1830–1865. Baltimore [Md.]. 1935.

2355 HAY. A memoir of Sir John Drummond Hay, P.C., K.C.B., G.C.M.G., sometime minister at the court of Morocco: based on his journals and correspondence. Ed. by Louisa Annette Edla Brooks and Alice Emily Drummond-Hay. 1896.
Hay was British representative in Morocco, 1847–86.

2356 TAYLOR (ALAN JOHN PERCIVALE). 'British policy in Morocco, 1886–1902'. *Eng. Hist. Rev.* lxvi (1951), 342–74.
See also Christopher John Bartlett, 'Great Britain and the Spanish change of policy towards Morocco in June 1878', *Inst. Hist. Res. Bull.* xxxi (1958), 168–85; F. V. Parsons, 'The North-West Africa company and the British government, 1875–95', *Hist. J.* i (1958), 136–53; 'The "Morocco question" in 1884: an early crisis', *Eng. Hist. Rev.* lxxvii (1962), 659–83, and 'The proposed Madrid conference on Morocco, 1887–88', *Hist. J.* viii (1965), 72–94; and Stephen Bonsal, *Morocco as it is: with an account of Sir Charles Euan Smith's recent mission to Fez,* 1893.

2357 STUART (GRAHAM HENRY). The international city of Tangier. Stanford [Calif.]. 1931. 2nd edn. 1955.

2358 ANDERSON (EUGENE NEWTON). The first Moroccan crisis, 1904–1906. Chicago. 1930. Repr. Hamden, Conn. 1966.

2359 BARLOW (IMA CHRISTINA). The Agadir crisis. Chapel Hill, N.C. 1940.
All the studies of international affairs in the period deal extensively with the Agadir crisis. See also Joanne Stafford Mortimer, 'Commercial interests and German diplomacy in the Agadir crisis', *Hist. J.* x (1967), 440–56, and Walter Mann, *Die Agadir-krisis des Jahres 1911*, Giessen 1934.

2360 MOREL (EDMUND DENE). Morocco in diplomacy. 1912. 6th edn. [Ten years of secret diplomacy.] Manch. 1920.

2361 ABBOTT (WILBUR CORTEZ). An introduction to the documents relating to the international status of Gibraltar, 1704–1934. N.Y. 1934.

A useful bibliog. Several propagandist collections of docs. have been publ. in Spain in recent years, the fullest being, Spain: Ministerio de Asuntos Exteriores, *Documents on Gibraltar presented to the Spanish cortes by the Minister of foreign affairs*, 'non-official translation', Madrid 1965, 2nd edn. 1968.

2362 GARRATT (GEOFFREY THEODORE). Gibraltar and the Mediterranean. 1939.

See also Henry William Howes, *The Gibraltarian: the origin and development of the population of Gibraltar from 1704*, Colombo [1950].

2363 LAFERLA (ALBERT VICTOR). British Malta, 1800–1921. 2 v. [Vol. 2. ed. by G. Zarb Adami.] Valetta. 1938–47.

A useful hist. For background see Henry Seddall, *Malta: past and present . . .*, 1870, and Allister Macmillan, *Malta and Gibraltar illustrated . . .*, 1915.

2364 SMITH (HARRISON). Britain in Malta. Vol. I: Constitutional development of Malta in the nineteenth century. Vol. II. Italian influence on British policy in Malta, 1899–1903. 2 v. Malta. 1953.

2365 PRICE (CHARLES ARCHIBALD). Malta and the Maltese: a study in nineteenth-century migration. Melb. 1954.

Good on the Maltese econ. for which see also Nicola Zammit, *Malta and its industries* [Colonial and Indian Exhibition handbook], Malta 1886, and Paul Cassar, *Medical history of Malta*, 1964.

## (g) *Other European Countries*

2366 HIETSCH (OTTO) *ed.* Österreich und die angelsächsische Welt: Kulturbegegnungen und Vergleiche. 2 v. Vienna. 1961–8.

2367 PRIBRAM (ALFRED FRANCIS). Austria–Hungary and Great Britain, 1908–14. Trans. by Ian Fitzherbert Despard Morrow. 1951.

Makes use of the publ. docs. in Ludwig Bittner and others, eds. *Österreich–Ungarns Aussenpolitik von der bosnischen Krise 1908 bis zum Kriegsausbruch, 1914 . . ., 9 v.* Vienna 1930. See also F. R. Bridge, 'The British declaration of war on Austria–Hungary in 1914', *Slavonic & East European Rev.* xlvii (1969), 401–22.

2368 ACADEMIE ROYALE DE BELGIQUE (COMMISSION ROYALE D'HISTOIRE). Documents relatifs au statut international de la Belgique depuis 1830. 1+ v. Brussels. 1964+.

So far confined to post-1920 docs. For pre-1914 docs. the main source is the circulars issued by the Belgian Foreign office to Belgian representatives abroad and publ. by their German captors in Bernard Heinrich Schwertfeger, ed., *Zur europäischen Politik, 1897–1914: unveröffentlichte Dokumente . . ., 5 v.* Berlin 1919.

2369 LEFÈVRE (JOSEPH). L'Angleterre et la Belgique a travers les cinq derniers siècles. Brussels. 1946.

No more than an outline. On Belgium in international affairs see Daniel Hamson Thomas, 'The use of the Scheldt in British plans for the defence of Belgian neutrality,

1831–1914', *Revue belge de philologie et d'histoire*, xli (1963), 449–70; Gordon Alexander Craig, 'Great Britain and the Belgian railways dispute of 1869', *Amer. Hist. Rev.* l (1944–5), 738–61; Daniel H. Thomas, 'English investors and the Franco-Belgium railway crisis of 1869', *The historian* xxvi (1963–4), 228–43; M. P. Hornik, 'The Anglo-Belgian agreement of 12 May 1894', *Eng. Hist. Rev.* lvii (1942), 227–43; Robert Devleeshouwer, *Les Belges et le danger de guerre, 1910–1914*, Louvain & Paris 1958; Jonathan Helmreich, 'Belgian concern over neutrality and British intentions, 1906–1914', *J. Mod. Hist.* xxxvi (1964), 416–27; Charles Percy Sanger and Henry Tertius James Norton, *England's guarantee to Belgium and Luxemburg*, N.Y. 1915; and Carl Hosse, *Die englisch-belgischen Aufmarschpläne gegen Deutschland vor dem Weltkriege: eine militärische Studie über die 'Conventions anglo-belges' mit neuen Dokumenten*, Vienna 1930. For the Belgian Congo see **1903–4** and Mary Elizabeth Thomas, 'Anglo-Belgian military relations and the Congo question, 1911–1913', *J. Mod. Hist.* xxv (1953), 157–65.

**2370** PREVELAKIS (ELEUTHERIOS GEORGIOU). British policy towards the change of dynasty in Greece, 1862–1863. Athens. 1953.

For background see also James Johnston Auchmuty, *Sir Thomas Wyse, 1791–1862: the life and career of an educator and diplomat*, 1939. Wyse was British representative in Greece to 1860.

**2371** XENOS (STEPHANOS THEODOROU). East and west: a diplomatic history of the annexation of the Ionian Islands to the kingdom of Greece ... 1865.

Suppl. by Harold William Vazeille Temperley, 'Documents illustrating the cession of the Ionian Islands to Greece, 1848–70', *J. Mod. Hist.* ix (1937), 48–55 and Eldridge, **1585.**

**2372** JENKINS (ROMILLY JAMES HEALD). The Dilessi murders. 1961.

On the murder of a group of British travellers in Greece in 1870.

**2373** FOOT (MICHAEL RICHARD DANIELL). 'Great Britain and Luxemburg, 1867'. *Eng. Hist. Rev.* lxvii (1952), 352–79.

**2374** BESCHEIDEN BETREFFENDE DE BUITENLANDSE POLITIEK VAN NEDERLAND, 1848–1919. Publ. in Rijks Geschiedkundige Publicatiën Grote serie. v. 100+. The Hague. 1957+.

Publ. will be in 4 ser. The ser. for 1871–98 (second period) ed. by J. Woltring, and for 1899–1919 (third period), ed. by Cornelis Smit, have been begun. Vols. now cover 1871–90 and 1899–1914.

**2375** BROMLEY (JOHN SELWYN) *and* KOSSMANN (ERNST HEINRICH) *eds.* Britain and the Netherlands [in Europe and Asia]; papers delivered to the Oxford–Netherlands [Anglo-Dutch] Hist. Conference, 1959. Lond. 1960. Further conference papers were publ. Groningen 1964. Lond. 1968.

**2376** KNAPLUND (PAUL) *ed.* British views on Norwegian–Swedish problems, 1880–1895: selections from diplomatic correspondence. Oslo. 1952.

**2377** LINBERG (FOLKE). Scandinavia in great power politics, 1905–1908. Stockholm. 1958.

See also David Sweet, 'The Baltic in British diplomacy before the First World War', *Hist. J.* xiii (1970), 451–90.

2378 GOSSE (*Sir* EDMUND). Correspondence with Scandinavian writers. Ed. by Elias Bredsdorff. Copenhagen. 1960.

2379 BURCHARDT (CARL BIRCH). Norwegian life and literature: English accounts and views, especially in the 19th century. 1920.

2380 BREDSDORFF (ELIAS). H. C. Andersen og England. Copenhagen. 1954.

For other Anglo-Danish literary connections see Paul Krüger, ed., *Correspondance de Georg Brandes*, 4 v. Copenhagen 1952–66; Elias Bredsdorff, *Hans Andersen and Charles Dickens: a friendship and its dissolution*, Anglistica 7, Copenhagen 1956; Jens Christian Bay, ed., *Denmark in English and American literature: a bibliography*, Danish American Assoc., Chicago 1915; and Elias Bredsdorff, *Danish literature in English translation*, Copenhagen 1950.

2381 ALMADA (JOSÉ DE). A aliança inglesa: subsídios para o seu estudo. Ministério dos Negócios Estrangeiros. 2 v. Lisbon. 1946–7.

Something of a misc. There are no general books on Anglo-Portuguese relations of the high quality of those on Britain and Portugal in Africa (**1618**) and (**1902**). For 1847–53 there is a useful collection of docs., Ruben Andresen Leitao, *Novos documentos dos arquivos de Windsor para a história de Portugal no século XIX*, Coimbra 1958. Armando Marques Guedes, *A aliança inglêsa (notas de história diplomática)*, Lisbon 1938, new edn. 1943, adds little. The military aspects of Portuguese defence are covered in José Etevão de Moraes Sarmento, *The Anglo-Portuguese alliance and coast defence*, trans. by Alfred Francis Custance, 1908. Rose Macaulay, *They went to Portugal*, 1946, is a pleasant misc. about foreign visitors.

2382 WERTHEIM *afterwards* TUCHMAN (BARBARA). The lost British policy: Britain and Spain since 1700. 1938.

2383 CHECKLAND (SYDNEY GEORGE). The mines of Tharsis: Roman, French and British enterprise in Spain. 1967.

2384 LUNN (ARNOLD HENRY MOORE). Switzerland and the English. 1944.

Chiefly on alpine climbers. Suppl. by his anthology, *Switzerland in English prose and poetry*, 1947. See also Elisabeth Gertrud König, *John Ruskin und die Schweiz*, Schweizer anglistische Arbeiten 14, Berne 1943, and Hans Löhrer, *Die Schweiz im Spiegel englischer Literatur*, *1849–1875*, Zürcher Beiträge zur vergleichenden Literaturgeschichte 1, Zurich 1952.

2385 IMLAH (ANN GORDON). Britain and Switzerland, 1845–60: a study of Anglo-Swiss relations during some critical years for Swiss neutrality. Lond. & Hamden, Conn. 1966.

See also Edgar Bonjour, *Die Schweiz und England: ein geschichtlicher Rückblick*, Bern 1934, and Paul Flaad, *England und die Schweiz, 1848–1852* . . ., Zurich 1935.

386 BONJOUR (EDGAR). Englands Anteil an der Lösung des Neuenburger Konflikts, 1856/57. Basler Beiträge zur Geschichtswissenschaft 12. Basel. 1943.

2387 GENNER (LOTTI). Die diplomatischen Beziehungen zwischen England und der Schweiz von 1870 bis 1890: eine Untersuchung der englischen Gesandtschaftsberichte aus Bern. Basle & Stuttgart. 1956.

2388 UHL (OTHMAR). Die diplomatisch-politischen Beziehungen zwischen Grossbritannien und der Schweiz in den Jahrzehnten vor dem Ersten Weltkrieg, 1890–1914. Basler Beiträge zur Geschichtswissenschaft 83. Basle. 1961.

2389 GOSSMAN (NORBERT J.). 'British aid to Polish, Italian and Hungarian exiles, 1830–1870'. *South Atlantic Q.* lxviii (1969), 231–45.

2390 MOSSE (WERNER EUGEN). 'England and the Polish insurrection of 1863'. *Eng. Hist. Rev.* lxxi (1956), 28–55.

See also K. S. Pasieka, 'The British press and the Polish insurrection of 1863', *Slavonic & East European Rev.* xlii (1963–4), 15–37; Klaus Mühlmann, *England und die polnische Frage im Jahre 1863*, Würzburg 1934; Henryk Wereszycki, *Anglia a Polska w latach 1860–1865*, Lwów 1934; John F. Kutolowski, 'Mid-Victorian public opinion, Polish propaganda and the uprising of 1863', *J. British Studs.* viii (1968–9), pt. 2, 86–110; and Peter Brock, 'Polish democrats and English radicals, 1832–1862: a chapter in the history of Anglo-Polish relations', *J. Mod. Hist.* xxv (1953), 139–56, 'The Polish revolutionary commune in London', *Slavonic & East European Rev.* xxxv (1956–7), 116–28, and 'Joseph Cowen and the Polish exiles', ibid. xxxii (1953–4), 52–69.

## 3. THE NEAR AND MIDDLE EAST

### (a) *General*

2391 HUREWITZ (JACOB COLEMAN). Diplomacy in the near and middle east: a documentary record, 1535–1956. 2 v. Princeton [N.J.]. 1956.

Invaluable. See also Thomas Erskine Holland, ed., *The European concert in the eastern question: a collection of treaties and other public acts*, Oxf. 1885, and Vojislav M. Jovanović, comp., *Engleska bibliografija o istočnom pitanju u Evropi* [English bibliography on the eastern question in Europe], Srpska Krakjevska Akademija Spomenik, xlviii, 2 razdel 40, Belgrade 1908.

2392 ANDERSON (MATTHEW SMITH). The eastern question, 1774–1923: a study in international relations. Lond. & N.Y. 1966.

A handy guide to a tangled subject. Needs to be suppl. by Leften Stavros Stavrianos, *The Balkans since 1453*, N.Y. 1958. Mason Whiting Tyler, *The European powers and the near east, 1875–1908*, Minneapolis 1925, and Wade Dewood David, *European diplomacy in the near-eastern question, 1906–1909*, Urbana, Ill. 1940, merely add a few details. *Middle Eastern Studies*, 1+, 1964+, is the journ. with the most articles on the British presence in the Near East.

2393 BULLARD (*Sir* READER WILLIAM). Britain and the middle east from earliest times to 1950. 1951. 3rd edn. 1964.

Brief. See also Sarah Searight, *The British in the Middle East*, Lond. 1969, N.Y. 1970.

2394 HOSKINS (HALFORD LANCASTER). British routes to India. N.Y. 1928. Repr. 1966.

Still the most useful study of the subject.

2395 BAILEY (FRANK EDGAR). British policy and the Turkish reform movement: a study in Anglo-Turkish relations, 1826–1853. Camb., Mass. 1942.

2396 DAVISON (RODERIC HOLLETT). Reform in the Ottoman empire, 1856–1876. Princeton [N.J.]. 1963.

A remarkable work which sets the scene for international relations. See also Bernard Lewis, *The emergence of modern Turkey*, 1961, 2nd edn. 1968; Sir Harry Charles Luke, *The old Turkey and the new* . . ., new edn. 1955; Harold William Vazeille Temperley, 'British policy towards parliamentary rule and constitutionalism in Turkey, 1830–1914', *Camb. Hist. J.* iv (1933), 156–91; and Allan Cunningham, ' "Dragomania": the dragomans of the British embassy in Turkey', *St. Antony's Papers 11: Middle Eastern Affairs 2* (1961), 81–100.

2397 PHILLIPSON (COLEMAN) *and* BUXTON *afterwards* NOEL-BUXTON (NOEL EDWARD), *Baron Noel-Buxton*. The question of the Bosphorus and Dardanelles. 1917.

See also Neculai Dascovici, *La question du Bosphore et des Dardanelles*, Geneva 1915; Ettore Anchieri, *Costantinopoli e gli stretti nella politica russa ed europea dal Trattato di Qüciük Rainargi alla Convenzione di Montreux*, Milan 1948; James Thomson Shotwell and Francis Deák, *Turkey at the Straits: a short history*, N.Y. 1940; and B. A. Dranov, *Chernomorskie prolivy*, Moscow 1948.

2398 BLAISDELL (DONALD CHRISTY). European financial control in the Ottoman empire: a study of the establishment, activities and significance of the administration of the Ottoman public debt. N.Y. 1929.

See also Olive Anderson, 'Great Britain and the beginnings of the Ottoman public debt, 1854–55', *Hist. J.* vii (1964), 47–63.

2399 SOUSA (NASIM). The capitulatory regime of Turkey: its history, origin and nature. Baltimore [Md.]. 1933.

Sir Reader William Bullard, *Large and loving privileges: the capitulations in the Middle East and North Africa*, Glasgow 1960, is an introductory essay.

2400 GRAVES (PHILIP PERCEVAL). Briton and Turk. 1941.

Covers *c.* 1878–1941. Hostile to the Ottoman regime.

2401 JELAVICH (BARBARA). 'The British traveller in the Balkans: the abuses of Ottoman administration in the slavonic provinces'. *Slavonic & East European Rev.* xxxiii (1954–5), 396–413.

2402 MOSSE (WERNER EUGEN). 'England, Russia and the Rumanian revolution of 1866'. *Slavonic & East European Rev.* xxxix (1960–1), 73–94.

For background see also Thad Weede Riker, *The making of Roumania: a study of an international problem, 1856–1866*, 1931; William Gordon East, *The union of Moldavia and Wallachia: an episode in diplomatic history*, Camb. 1929, and E. D. Tappe, 'General Gordon in Rumania', *Slavonic & East European Rev.* xxxv (1956–7), 566–72, and 'Rumania after the union as seen by two English journalists', ibid. xxxix (1960–1), 198–215.

2403  BOURNE (KENNETH). 'Great Britain and the Cretan revolt, 1866–1869'. *Slavonic & East European Rev.* xxxv (1956–7), 74–94.

See also Maureen M. Robson, 'Lord Clarendon and the Cretan question, 1868–9' *Hist. J.* iii (1960), 38–55.

2404  SETON-WATSON (ROBERT WILLIAM). Disraeli, Gladstone and the Eastern Question: a study in diplomacy and party politics. 1935. Repr. 1962.

Must be suppl. by Shannon (**293**).

2405  HARRIS (DAVID). A diplomatic history of the Balkan crisis of 1875–1878: the first year. 2 v. Stanford [Calif.] & Lond. 1936.

His *Britain and the Bulgarian horrors of 1876*, Chicago 1939, has been repl. by Shannon (**293**). See also Mihailo D. Stojanovic, *The great powers and the Balkans, 1875–1878*, Camb. 1939, and Frederick J. Dwyer, 'R. A. Cross and the eastern crisis of 1875–8', *Slavonic & East European Rev.* xxxix (1960–1), 440–58. Other works are out of date, notably Rudolf Gerhard Liebold, *Die Stellung Englands in der russisch-türkischen Krise von 1875–78*, Wilkau 1930, Eugen Sauer, *Die Politik Lord Beaconsfields in der orientalischen Krisis, 1875–1878*, Tübingen 1934, and Walter George Wirthwein, *Britain and the Balkan crisis, 1875–1878*, Columbia Univ. Studs. in Hist. etc. 407, N.Y. 1935.

2406  MEDLICOTT (WILLIAM NORTON). The Congress of Berlin and after: a diplomatic history of the near eastern settlement, 1878–80. 1938. 2nd edn. Hamden, Conn. 1963.

Standard. Cont. in his *Bismarck, Gladstone and the concert of Europe* (**2270**); see also Foreign Office, *The Congress of Berlin, 1878*, Foreign Office peace handbook 154, 1920, and Alexander Novotny, *Quellen und Studien zur Geschichte des Berliner Kongresses, 1878*, vol. I, Graz-Köln 1950, which has details of the work of the Congress.

2407  CAMPBELL (GEORGE DOUGLAS), *Duke of Argyll*. The eastern question: from the treaty of Paris, 1856, to the treaty of Berlin, 1878, and to the second Afghan war. 2 v. 1879.

The best contemp. study. But see also Eastern Question Association, *Papers on the eastern question*, 1877, and Stratford Canning, Viscount Stratford De Redcliffe, *The eastern question: being a selection from his writings during the last five years of his life*, 1881.

2408  ANDERSON (DOROTHY PAULINE). The Balkan volunteers. 1968.

British relief work in the Near East, 1876–8. See also her *Miss Irby and her friends*, 1966.

2409  HORNIK (M. P.). 'The mission of Sir Henry Drummond Wolff to Constantinople, 1885–7'. *Eng. Hist. Rev.* lv (1940), 598–623.

See also Wolff's memoirs (**893**).

2410  SMITH (COLIN LEONARD). The embassy of Sir William White at Constantinople, 1886–1891. 1957.

See also **2263**.

2411  JEFFERSON (MARGARET M.). 'Lord Salisbury and the eastern question, 1890–1898'. *Slavonic & East European Rev.* xxxix (1960–1), 44–60.

Suppl. by her 'Lord Salisbury's conversations with the Tsar at Balmoral, 27 and 29 September 1896', ibid. 216–22. See also Hugo Preller, *Salisbury und die Türkische*

*Frage im Jahre 1895: eine Einzeluntersuchung zur Geschichte der deutsch-englischen Beziehungen der Vorkriegszeit,* Stuttgart 1930.

2412 MacCOLL (MALCOLM). The sultan and the powers. 1896.

A famous denunciation. Cp. George Douglas Campbell, Duke of Argyll, *Our responsibilities for Turkey: facts and memories of forty years,* 1896.

2413 PERRIS (GEORGE HERBERT). The eastern crisis of 1897 and British policy in the near east. 1897.

Thin.

2414 SCHRÖDER (WERNER). England, Europa und der Orient. Untersuchungen zur englischen Vorkriegspolitik in Vorgeschichte und Verlauf der Balkankrise 1912. Stuttgart. 1938.

2415 IGNATIEV (ANATOLII VENEDIKTOVICH). Russko-Angliiskie otnosheniia nakanune pervoi mirovoi voiny (1908–1914 gg). Moscow. 1962.

See also M. B. Cooper, 'British policy in the Balkans, 1908–9', *Hist. J.* vii (1964), 258–79. British views on the Balkans were greatly influenced by Mary Edith Durham, *Through the lands of the Serb,* 1904, *The burden of the Balkans . . .,* 1905, repr. 1912, *High Albania . . .,* 1909, and *Twenty years of Balkan tangle,* 1920, Henry Noel Brailsford, *Macedonia: its races and its future,* 1906, and Robert William Seton-Watson, *Corruption and reform in Hungary . . .,* 1911, and *Absolutism in Croatia,* 1912.

2416 HELMREICH (ERNST CHRISTIAN). The diplomacy of the Balkan wars, 1912–1913. Camb., Mass. 1938.

2417 CHAPMAN (MAYBELLE REBECCA KENNEDY). Great Britain and the Bagdad Railway, 1888–1914. Northampton, Mass. 1948.

On this topic see also Ravinder Kumar, 'The records of the government of India on the Berlin–Baghdad railway question', *Hist. J.* v (1962), 70–9; Edward Mead Earle, *Turkey: the great powers and the Bagdad railway: a study in imperialism,* N.Y. & Lond. 1923; John Baptist Wolf, *The diplomatic history of the Bagdad railroad,* Columbia, Mo. 1936; Bekir Sitki, *Das Bagdad-bahn problem, 1890–1903,* Freiburg-im-Breisgau 1935; Louis Ragey, *La question du chemin de fer de Baghdad, 1893–1914,* Paris 1936; and Grigorii L'vovich Bondarevskii, *Bagdadskaia doroga i proniknovenie germanskogo imperializma na Blizhnii Vostok, 1888–1903,* Tashkent 1955.

2418 LONGRIGG (STEPHEN HEMSLEY). Oil in the middle east: its discovery and development. 1954. 3rd edn. 1968.

2419 CUNNINGHAM (ALLAN). 'The wrong horse? a study of Anglo-Turkish relations before the First World War'. St. Antony's papers 17: Middle Eastern Affairs 4 (1965), 56–76.

See also Feroz Ahmad, 'Great Britain's relations with the Young Turks', *Middle Eastern Studs.* ii (1965–6), 302–29.

(b) *Crimean War*

2420 GOOCH (BRISON DOWLING). 'A century of historiography on the origins of the Crimean war'. *Amer. Hist. Rev.* lxii (1956–7), 33–58.

See also his 'The Crimean war in selected documents and secondary works since 1940',

*Victorian Studs.* i (1957-8), 271-9, and Edgar Hösch, 'Neuere Literatur (1940-1960) über den Krimkrieg', *Jahrbücher für Geschichte osteuropas*, new ser. ix (1961), 399-434.

2421 KINGLAKE (ALEXANDER WILLIAM). The invasion of the Crimea: its origin and an account of its progress down to the death of Lord Raglan. 8 v. Edin. & Lond. 1863-87.

Long regarded as authoritative, though written from an English Radical point of view. Needs replacing. More recent short accounts of the war, such as Colwyn Edward Vulliamy, *Crimea: the campaign of 1854-6* . . ., 1939, Peter Gibbs, *Crimean blunder: the story of war with Russia a hundred years ago*, Lond. & N.Y. 1960, and Kellow Chesney, *Crimean war reader*, 1960, have simply provided a short popular outline of events. The old blow-by-blow accounts, such as Edward Henry Nolan, *The illustrated history of the war against Russia*, 2 v. 1855-7, and Henry Tyrrell, *The history of the war with Russia* . . ., 6 v. 1855-8, were outmoded by Kinglake. There is little of value in Sir George Fletcher MacMunn, *The Crimea in perspective*, 1935.

2422 TEMPERLEY (HAROLD WILLIAM VAZEILLE). England and the Near East: the Crimea. 1936. Repr. Hamden, Conn. 1964.

A good diplomatic hist., to be suppl. by Gavin Burns Henderson, *Crimean war diplomacy and other historical essays*, Glasgow 1947, and Werner Eugen Emil Mosse, *The rise and fall of the Crimean system, 1855-71: the story of a peace settlement*, Lond. & N.Y. 1963, both of them misc. colls. of repr. papers. Temperley's 'The Treaty of Paris of 1856 and its execution', *J. Mod. Hist.* iv (1932), 387-414, 523-43, is also useful. Other works on diplomatic hist. incl. Edmond Bapst, *Les origines de la guerre de Crimée* . . ., Paris 1912; Vernon John Puryear, *England, Russia and the Straits question, 1844-1856*, Univ. of California Publs. in Hist. xx, Berkeley 1931, repr. Hamden, Conn. 1965, and *International economics and diplomacy in the Near East* . . ., *1834-53*, Stanford [Calif.] 1935; Heinrich Friedjung, *Der Krimkrieg und die österreichische Politik*, Stuttgart, etc., 1907, 2nd edn. 1911; Kurt Borries, *Preussen im Krimkrieg (1853-1856)* . . ., Stuttgart 1930; Ferencz Eckhart, *Die deutsche Frage und der Krimkrieg*, Berlin etc. 1913; Luigi Chiala, *L'alleanza di Crimea*, Rome 1879; Georg Franz, 'Der Krimkrieg: ein Wendepunkt des europäischen Schicksals', *Geschichte in Wissenschaft und Unterricht*, vii (1956), 448-63; and Franco Valsecchi, *L'alleanza di Crimea: il risorgimento e l'Europa*, Milan 1948. Vicomte Eugène de Guichen, ed., *La guerre de Crimée, (1854-1856) et l'attitude des puissances européennes*, Paris 1936, is an analysis of diplomatic correspondence.

2423 ANDERSON (OLIVE). A liberal state at war: English politics and economics during the Crimean war. Lond. & N.Y. 1967.

Important.

2424 MARTIN ([BASIL] KINGSLEY). The triumph of Lord Palmerston: a study of public opinion in England before the Crimean War. 1924. New edn. 1963.

Idiosyncratic. See also Alan John Percivale Taylor, 'John Bright and the Crimean war', *John Rylands Libr. Bull.* xxxvi (1953-4), 501-22.

2425 TARLÉ (EUGENII VIKTOROVICH). Krymskaia voina. 2 v. Moscow. 1941-3. New edns. 1944-5. 1950.

The standard Soviet account.

2426 [JOMINI (ALEXANDRE)]. Diplomatic study on the Crimean war (1852 to 1856): Russian official publication. 2 v. 1882.

The Russian answer to allied claims. For the Russian background of the war see Andrei Medardovich Zaionchkovskii, *Vostochnaia voina 1853–1856 gg. v sviazi s sovremennoi ei politicheskoi obstanovkoi*, 2 v. St. Petersburg 1908–13; Andrei Nikolaevich Shebunin, *Rossiia na Blizhnem vostoke*, Leningrad 1926; Sergei Mikhailovich Goriainov, *Le Bosphore et les Dardanelles: étude historique sur la question des détroits*, Paris 1910; and Nikolai Federovich Dubrovin, *Materialii dlia istorii Krymskoi voiny . . .*, 2 v. 1871.

2427 MACQUEEN (JAMES). The war: who's to blame? or, the Eastern question investigated from the official documents. 1854.

Cp. David Urquhart, *The war of ignorance and collusion . . .*, 1854. A. J. P. Taylor, *The trouble makers* (**931**), gives an account of the opponents of the war.

2428 PEMBERTON (NOEL WILLIAM BARING). Battles of the Crimean war. 1962.

A short and straightforward account that draws on a wide variety of memoirs and diaries. Cp. Peter Bawtree Gibbs, *The battle of the Alma*, 1963, John Selby, *The thin red line of Balaclava*, 1970, and Arthur James Barker, *The vainglorious war, 1854–56*, 1970.

2429 GOOCH (BRISON DOWLING). The new Bonapartist generals in the Crimean war: distrust and decision-making in the Anglo-French alliance. The Hague. 1959.

Good.

2430 SAYER (FREDERICK) ed. Despatches and papers relative to the campaign in Turkey, Asia Minor, and the Crimea, during the war with Russia in 1854, 1855 and 1856. 1857.

2431 HIBBERT (CHRISTOPHER). The destruction of Lord Raglan: a tragedy of the Crimean war, 1854–55. 1961.

Preferable to Cecil Blanche Woodham-Smith, *The reason why*, 1953, which makes a number of serious mistakes, but is excellent reading.

2432 HAMLEY (*Sir* EDWARD BRUCE). The war in the Crimea. 1891.

A good short account by a professional soldier, who had already made a literary name for himself with *The story of the campaign of Sebastopol: written in the camp*, 1855. For other soldierly reviews of the war see Sir John Miller Adye, *A review of the Crimean war . . .*, 1860; Sir George Brackenbury, *The campaign in the Crimea: a historical sketch . . .*, 2 v. 1855–6; Sir Howard Crawfurd Elphinstone and others, *Siege of Sebastopol . . .*, 3 v., War Office 1859; Thomas William John Connolly, *The history of the corps of Royal Sappers and Miners*, vol. I, 2nd edn. 1857; William Edmund Moyses Reilly, *Siege of Sebastopol: an account of the artillery operations conducted by the Royal Artillery and the Royal Naval Brigade before Sebastopol in 1854 and 1855*, 1859; Lord George Paget, *The Light Cavalry Brigade in the Crimea*, 1881; and Sir George Wentworth Alexander Higginson, *Seventy-one years of a guardsman's life*, 1916. The Russian view of the siege of Sebastopol is conveniently given in [Franz] Eduard von Todleben, ed., *La Défense de Sébastopol . . .*, 2 v. St. Petersburg 1863–74.

2433 RUSSELL (*Sir* WILLIAM HOWARD). The British expedition to the Crimea. 1858. Rev. edn. 1877.

The report of a famous war correspondent, based on his *The war: from the landing at Gallipoli to the death of Lord Raglan*, 1855, which consisted of despatches to *The Times*. These have been ed. by Nicolas Bentley as *Russell's despatches from the Crimea, 1854–1856*, 1966. An interesting parallel ser. written far from the scene of battle for the *New York Tribune*, is Karl Marx, *The Eastern question: a reprint of letters written 1853–1856 dealing with the events of the Crimean war*, ed. by Eleanor Marx Aveling and Edward Aveling, 1897, repr. N.Y. 1969.

**2434** ROEBUCK COMMITTEE ON THE ARMY BEFORE SEBASTOPOL. First report from the select committee on the army before Sebastopol [Chairman: J. A. Roebuck]. H.C. 86 (1854–5). IX, Pt. I, 1. Second report. H.C. 156 (1854–5). IX, Pt. I, 7. Third report. H.C. 218 (1854–5). IX, Pt. II, 1. Fourth report. H.C. 247 (1854–5). IX, Pt. III, 1. Fifth report. H.C. 318 (1854–5). IX, Pt. III, 365.

**2435** McNEILL (*Sir* JOHN) *and* TULLOCH (ALEXANDER MURRAY). Report of the commission of inquiry into the supplies of the British army in the Crimea. [2007] H.C. (1856). XX, 1. Appendix. [2007–I] H.C. (1856). XX, 497.

See also *Report of the board of general officers* [President: General Sir Alexander Woodford] *appointed to inquire into the statements contained in the reports of Sir John McNeill and Colonel Tulloch, and the evidence taken by them relative thereto, animadverting upon the conduct of certain officers on the general staff, and others in the army.* [2119] H.C. (1856). XXI, 1, and *Memorandum calling for explanations in regard to a section of the report of the board of general officers . . . together with the explanation.* H.C. 117 (1857 Sess. I). IX, 83. Tulloch also publ. *The Crimean commission and the Chelsea board . . .*, 1857. For the controversy see F. M., *Memoir of the Right Hon. Sir John McNeill, G.C.B., and of his second wife, Elizabeth Wilson*, 1910.

**2436** GERNSHEIM (HELMUT) *and* GERNSHEIM (ALISON) *eds.* Roger Fenton, photographer of the Crimean war: his photographs and his letters from the Crimea, with an essay on his life and work. 1954.

**2437** CUMMING (ALEXANDER) *and others*. Report upon the state of the hospitals of the British army in the Crimea and Scutari. [1920] H.C. (1854–5). XXXIII, 1.

**2438** SUTHERLAND (JOHN), RAWLINSON (ROBERT), *and* MILROY (GAVIN). Report to the Right Hon. Lord Panmure, G.C.B., &c., Minister at War, of the proceedings of the sanitary commission dispatched to the seat of war in the east, 1855–6. [2196–Sess. 1] H.C. (1857). IX, 241.

**2439** HALL. The life and letters of Sir John Hall, M.D., K.C.B., F.R.C.S. By Siddhi Mohan Mitra. 1911.

See also R. E. Barnsley, 'The diaries of John Hall . . .', *Soc. Army Hist. Res. J.* xli (1963), 3–18. Hall was in charge of the medical work in the war. For this see also the lives of Florence Nightingale (**7469**); Douglas Arthur Reid, *Memories of the Crimean war, January to June 1856 . . .*, 1911; Joseph O. Baylen and Alan Conway, eds., *Soldier-surgeon: the Crimean war letters of Dr. Douglas A. Reid, 1855–1856*, Knoxville, Tenn. 1968; Victor Bonham-Carter, ed., assisted by Monica Lawson, *Surgeon in the Crimea: the experiences of George Lawson recorded in letters to his family, 1854–1855*, 1968; and Frederick Robinson, M.D., *Diary of the Crimean war*, 1856.

**2440** BONNER-SMITH (DAVID) *and* DEWAR (ALFRED CHARLES) *eds.* Russian war, 1854: Baltic and Black Sea: official correspondence. Navy Records Soc. lxxxiii. 1943.

Cont. by Bonner-Smith's, *Russian war, 1855: Baltic: official correspondence.* Navy Records Soc. lxxiv, 1944, and Dewar's *Russian war, 1855: Black Sea: official correspondence*, Navy Records Soc. lxxxv, 1945. The naval campaign is covered in outline in Wilhelm Treue, *Der Krimkrieg und die Entstehung der modernen Flotten*, Göttingen 1954. But see also [Paul] Bernard Whittingham, *Notes on the late expedition against the Russian settlements in Siberia . . .*, 1856, Francis Marx, *The Pacific and the Amoor: naval, military and diplomatic operations from 1855 to 1861*, 1861, and John J. Stephan, 'The Crimean war in the far east', *Modern Asian Studs.* iii (1969), 257–77.

**2441** SLADE (*Sir* ADOLPHUS). Turkey and the Crimean war: a narrative of historical events. 1867.

See also Thomas Buzzard, *With the Turkish army in the Crimea and Asia Minor . . .*, 1915.

**2442** ALLEN (WILLIAM EDWARD DAVID) *and* MURATOFF (PAUL). Caucasian battlefields: a history of the wars on the Turko-Caucasian border, 1828–1921. Camb. 1953.

See also Laurence Oliphant, *The Trans-Caucasian campaign of the Turkish army under Omer Pasha*, Edin. & Lond. 1856.

**2443** SANDWITH (HUMPHRY). A narrative of the siege of Kars and of the six months resistance by the Turkish garrison under General Williams to the Russian army . . . 1856. 2nd edn. 1856.

A book that became famous. See also Sir Henry Atwell Lake, *Narrative of the defence of Kars, historical and military*, 1857, and *Kars and our captivity in Russia*, 1856. Sandwith became the subject of a good biog., Thomas Humphry Ward, *Humphry Sandwith: a memoir . . .*, 1884.

**2444** [CALTHORPE (SOMERSET JOHN GOUGH)]. Letters from headquarters: or, the realities of the war in the Crimea, by an officer on the staff. 2 v. 1856.

One of the better colls. of contemp. letters and diaries, of which there are many. Others incl. Hugh Wodehouse Pearse, ed., *The Crimean diary and letters of Lieut.-General Sir Charles Ash Windham, K.C.B. . . .*, 1897; Colin Frederick Campbell, *Letters from camp to his relations during the siege of Sebastopol*, 1894; [Sir Henry Hugh Clifford], *Henry Clifford, V.C.: his letters and sketches from the Crimea*, ed. by Cuthbert Fitzherbert, 1956; Arthur Henry Taylor, 'Letters from the Crimea', *Royal United Service Instn. J.* cii (1957), 79–85, 232–8, 399–405, 564–70; Frances Isabella Duberly, *Journal kept during the Russian war: from the departure of the army from England in April 1854 to the fall of Sebastopol*, 2nd edn. 1856; George Palmer Evelyn, *A diary of the Crimea*, ed. by Cyril Falls, 1954; Timothy Gowing, *A soldier's experience: or, a voice from the ranks . . .*, Nottingham 1902, re-edited by Kenneth Fenwick as *Voice from the ranks . . .*, 1954; Sir Daniel Lysons, *The Crimean war from first to last*, 1895; Richard Cunningham McCormick, *A visit to the camp before Sebastopol*, N.Y. 1855; Reynell Pack, *Sebastopol trenches and five months in them*, 1878; James Henry Skene, *With Lord Stratford in the Crimean war*, 1883; John Foster George Ross of Bladensburg, *The Coldstream guards in the Crimea*, 1897; and Sir Anthony Coningham Sterling, *The story of the Highland Brigade in the Crimea . . .*, 1895.

## (c) The Levant

**2445** VERNEY (NOEL) _and_ DAMBMANN (GEORGE). Les puissances étrangères dans le Levant, en Syrie et en Palestine. Paris etc. 1900.

**2446** ISEMINGER (GORDON L.). 'The old Turkish hands: the British Levantine consuls, 1856–1876'. _Middle East J._ xxii (1968), 297–316.

**2447** TIBAWI (ABDUL LATIF). British interests in Palestine, 1800–1901: a study of religious and educational enterprise. 1961.

Fuller on the period than Barbara Tuchman, _Bible and sword: England and Palestine from the bronze age to Balfour_, N.Y. 1956, repr. 1968.

**2448** WOLF (LUCIEN). Notes on the diplomatic history of the Jewish question, with texts of protocols, treaty stipulations and other public acts and official documents. Jewish Hist. Soc. 1919.

**2449** HYAMSON (ALBERT MONTEFIORE) _ed._ The British consulate in Jerusalem in relation to the Jews of Palestine, 1838–[1914]. Jewish Hist. Soc. 2 v. 1939–41.

See also his _British projects for the restoration of the Jews_, 1917.

**2450** STEIN (LEONARD JACQUES). The Balfour declaration. Lond. & N.Y. 1961.

In effect a hist. of the quest for a Palestinian Jewish national home.

**2451** WATSON (_Sir_ CHARLES MOORE). Palestine Exploration Fund: fifty years' work in the Holy Land: a record and a summary, 1865–1915. 1915.

## (d) The Russian Threat in Central Asia

**2452** HÖJER (TORVALD TORVALDSON). England, Ryssland och den centralasiatiska frågan, 1869–1885. Uppsala Universitets Årsskrift 1944: 7. Uppsala & Leipzig. 1944.

Preferable to Muhammad Anwar Khan, _England, Russia and Central Asia (a study in diplomacy), 1857–1878_, Peshawar 1963. But see also Archibald Paton Thornton, 'The re-opening of the "Central Asian question", 1864–9', _History_ xli (1956), 122–36, Barbara Jelavich, 'Great Britain and the Russian acquisition of Batum, 1878–1886', _Slavonic & East European Rev._ xlviii (1970), 44–66, and _Russia in the east, 1876–1880: the letters of A. G. Jomini to N. K. Giers_, Leiden 1959. For the lit. of Russian central Asia see Richard A. Pierce, comp., _Soviet central Asia: a bibliography_, 3 pts. Berkeley etc. 1966.

**2453** RAWLINSON (_Sir_ HENRY CRESWICKE). England and Russia in the east: a series of papers on the political and geographical condition of central Asia. 1875. Repr. N.Y. 1970.

A good contemp. study. See also Sir Frederic John Goldsmid, _Central Asia and its question . . ._, 1873, Thedor Thedorovich Martens, _Russia and England in central Asia_, 1879, and William Edward Baxter, _England and Russia in Asia_, 1885.

**2454** BOULGER (DEMETRIUS CHARLES DE KAVANAGH). England and Russia in Central Asia. 2 v. 1879.

Important as providing a basic stock of information about the subject. Suppl. by his *Central Asian portraits: the celebrities of the Khanates and the neighbouring states,* 1880, *Central Asian questions: essays on Afghanistan, China and Central Asia . . .,* 1885, and other works.

**2455** CURZON (GEORGE NATHANIEL), *Marquess Curzon of Kedleston.* Russia in Central Asia in 1889, and the Anglo-Russian question. 1889. Repr. 1967.

**2456** POPOWSKI (JOSEF). The rival powers in central Asia: or, the struggle between England and Russia in the east. Trans. by A. B. Brabant and ed. by C. E. D. Black. 1893.

**2457** COLQUHOUN (ARCHIBALD ROSS). Russia against India: the struggle for Asia. Lond. & N.Y. 1900.

**2458** CHIROL (*Sir* VALENTINE). The middle eastern question: or, some political problems of Indian defence. 1903.

**2459** CENTRAL ASIAN SOCIETY [Royal Central Asian Society]. Proceedings. 1904–13. Journal. 1+. 1914+.

Important for British ideas.

**2460** CHURCHILL (ROGERS PLATT). The Anglo-Russian convention of 1907. Cedar Rapids, Iowa. 1939.

Deals chiefly with Persia and Afghanistan. See also **2341**.

### (e) *The Arab Lands and the Persian Gulf*

**2461** LORIMER (JOHN GORDON) *comp.* Gazetteer of the Persian gulf, Oman and central Arabia. Ed. by Richard Lockington Birdwood. 2 v. Government of India. Calcutta. 1908–15. Repr. Shannon. 1971.

Suppl. by Samuel Barrett Miles, *The countries and tribes of the Persian gulf,* 2 v. 1919, 2nd edn. 1 v. 1966, which consists largely of notes taken by Miles as political agent at Muscat, and Sir Arnold Talbot Wilson, *The Persian gulf: an historical sketch from the earliest times to the beginning of the twentieth century,* Oxf. 1928. There are also a number of excellent reports, prepared for the government of India, notably a series of précis ed. by Jerome Anthony Saldanha, which are listed by Landen (**2471**) and Busch (**2466**). Though they cover a later period the Admiralty (Naval Intelligence Division) Geographical handbooks B.R. 524 (*Iraq and the Persian gulf, September 1944*) and B.R. 527 (*Western Arabia and the Red Sea, June 1946*) are extremely useful for geography.

**2462** KIERNAN (REGINALD HUGH). The unveiling of Arabia: the story of Arabian travel and discovery. 1937.

Popular, but handy. More useful than David George Hogarth, *The penetration of Arabia: a record of the development of western knowledge concerning the Arabian peninsula,* N.Y. 1904, Lond. 1905, which was written before the explorations of Gertrude Bell (**8576**). For the obverse of the picture see Ibrahim Abu-Lughod, *Arab rediscovery of Europe: a study in cultural encounters,* Princeton 1963, and Norman Daniel, *Islam, Europe and empire,* Edin. 1966.

2463 KELLY (JOHN BARRETT). Britain and the Persian gulf, 1795–1880. Oxf. 1968.

Good.

2464 BONDAREVSKII (GRIGORII L'VOVICH). Angliiskaia politika i mezhdunarodnye otnosheniia v basseine Persidskogo zaliva (konets XIX–nachalo XX v.). Moscow. 1968.

2465 KUMAR (RAVINDER). India and the Persian Gulf region, 1858–1907: a study in British imperial policy. 1965.

2466 BUSCH (BRITON COOPER). Britain and the Persian gulf, 1894–1914. Berkeley etc. 1967.

Good. John Marlowe, *The Persian gulf in the twentieth century*, 1962, is a general survey which adds little. Abdul Amir Muhammed Amin, *British interests in the Persian gulf*, Leiden 1967, gives an Arab view.

2467 PLASS (JENS B.). England zwischen Russland und Deutschland: der Persische Golf in der britischen Vorkriegspolitik, 1899–1907, dargestellt nach englischen Archivmaterial. Hamburg. 1966.

A diplomatic study. For the Baghdad railway see also 2417.

2468 COX. The life of Sir Percy Cox. By Philip Perceval Graves. 1941.

Cox and Wilson were the principal British officials in the Persian Gulf in the early 20th cent.

2469 WILSON. S. W. Persia: a political officer's diary, 1907–1914. By Sir Arnold Talbot Wilson. 1941.

Fuller than John Marlowe, *Late Victorian: the life of Sir Arnold Talbot Wilson, K.C.I.E., C.S.I., C.M.G., D.S.O., M.P.*, 1967.

2470 SALIH (ZAKI). Mesopotamia (Iraq), 1600–1914: a study in British foreign affairs. Baghdad. 1957. 2nd edn. [Britain and Mesopotamia.] 1966.

Not a good book. Needs to be suppl. by Stephen Hemsley Longrigg, *Four centuries of modern Iraq* [to 1900], Oxf. 1925, and *Iraq, 1900 to 1950: a political, social and economic history* . . ., 1953, 2nd edn. 1956.

2471 LANDEN (ROBERT GERAN). Oman since 1856: disruptive modernization in a traditional Arab society. Princeton. 1967.

Good: incl. an account of British influence.

2472 WINDER (RICHARD BAYLY). Saudi Arabia in the nineteenth century. 1965.

Little on foreign relations.

2473 MARSTON (THOMAS EWART). Britain's imperial role in the Red Sea area, 1800–1878. Hamden, Conn. 1961.

Careless, but incl. useful material. For Aden see also [Ottiwell Henry] Gordon Waterfield, *Sultans of Aden*, 1968, and Frederick Mercer Hunter, comp., *An account of the British settlement at Aden in Arabia*, 1877.

**2474** PLASS (JENS B.) *and* GEHRKE (ULRICH). Die Aden-Grenze in der Südarabienfrage, 1900–1967: die Adener Grenzkommission, 1901–1907. By Jens B. Plass. Überblick über die englisch-Jemenitischen Beziehungen unter dem Gesichtspunkt des Süd-Jemenanspruchs, 1900–1967. By Ulrich Gehrke. Schriften des Deutschen Orient-Instituts. Opladen. 1967.

**2475** RAMM (AGATHA). 'Great Britain and the planting of Italian power in the Red Sea, 1868–1885', *Eng. Hist. Rev.* lix (1944), 211–36.

See also Angelo Gianni, *Italia e Inghilterra alle porte del Sudan: la spedizione di Massaua (1885)*, Pisa 1940, **1695**, and **1729**.

### (f) Persia

**2476** RAMAZANI (ROUHOLLAH K.). The foreign policy of Iran: a developing nation in world affairs, 1500–1941. Charlottesville, Va. 1966.

Attempts a coherent interpretation. *The Cambridge history of Iran*, Camb. 1968–, will cover the ground more thoroughly. Peter Avery, *Modern Iran*, N.Y. 1965, is a convenient general hist. For works on the late 19th cent. Sir Arnold Talbot Wilson, *A bibliography of Persia*, Oxf. 1930, is still useful.

**2477** HERTSLET (*Sir* EDWARD) *ed.* Treaties, &c., concluded between Great Britain and Persia, and between Persia and other foreign powers, wholly or partially in force on the 1st April 1891. 1891.

**2478** GAIL (MARZIEH). Persia and the Victorians. 1951.

Superficial, but all there is on cultural reactions.

**2479** BUSHEV (P. P.). Gerat i anglo-iranskaia voina, 1856–1857 gg. Moscow. 1959.

**2480** OUTRAM (*Sir* JAMES). Lieut.-General Sir James Outram's Persian campaign in 1857: comprising general orders and despatches relating to the military operations in Persia from the landing at Bushire to the treaty of peace; also selections from his correspondence . . . 1860.

See also G. H. Hunt, *Outram & Havelock's Persian campaign* . . ., 1858, the life of Outram (**1186**), and Barbara English, *John Company's last war: a Victorian military adventure*, 1971.

**2481** THORNTON (ARCHIBALD PATON). 'British policy in Persia, 1858–1890'. *Eng. Hist. Rev.* lxix (1954), 554–79; lxx (1955), 55–71.

Sir Frederic John Goldsmid, ed., *Eastern Persia: an account of the journeys of the Persian boundary commission, 1870–71–72*, 2 v. 1876, gives some indication of the extent of British knowledge of Persia at the time.

**2482** KAZEMZADEH (FIRUZ). Russia and Britain in Persia, 1864–1914: a study in imperialism. New Haven [Conn.]. 1968.

Largely repl. Pio Carlo Terenzio, *La rivalité anglo-russe en Perse et en Afghanistan jusqu'aux accords de 1907*, Paris 1947, Wilhelm Hannekum, *Persien im Spiel der Mächte, 1900–1907: ein Beitrag zur Vorgeschichte des Weltkrieges*, Berlin 1938, and Anushirvan Bihnam, *Les puissances et la Perse, 1907–1921*, Montreux 1957.

2483 GREAVES (ROSE LOUISE). Persia and the defence of India, 1884–1892: a study in the foreign policy of the third Marquis of Salisbury. 1959.

2484 KEDDI (NIKKI R.). Religion and rebellion in Iran: the tobacco protest of 1891–1892. 1966.

See also his 'British policy and the Iranian opposition, 1901–1907', *J. Mod. Hist.* xxxix (1967), 266–82.

2485 BROWNE (EDWARD GRANVILLE). The Persian revolution, 1905–1909. Camb. 1910. Repr. Lond. & N.Y. 1966.

Good.

2486 CURZON (GEORGE NATHANIEL), *Marquess Curzon of Kedleston.* Persia and the Persian question. 2 v. Lond. & N.Y. 1892. Repr. 2 v. 1966.

The most important contemp. discussion of British interests. Cp. the much inferior Henry James Whigham, *The Persian problem: an examination of the rival positions of Russia and Great Britain in Persia* . . ., Lond. & N.Y. 1903.

### (g) *Afghanistan and the Indian Borderlands*

2487 SYKES (*Sir* PERCY MOLESWORTH). A history of Afghanistan. 2 v. 1940.

Useful as reflecting British ideas, but less good for Afghanistan than Sir William Kerr Fraser-Tytler, *Afghanistan: a study of political developments in Central Asia*, 1950, 3rd edn. 1967. See also Donald Newton Wilber, comp., *Annotated bibliography of Afghanistan*, N.Y. 1956, 3rd edn. New Haven [Conn.] 1968.

2488 HABBERTON (WILLIAM). Anglo-Russian relations concerning Afghanistan, 1837–1907. Urbana [Ill.]. 1937.

2489 IULDASHBAEVA (FATIMA KHODZHAMBERDYEVNA). Iz istorii angliiskoi kolonial'noi politiki v Afganistan i Srednei Azii, 70–80 gody XIX v. Tashkent. 1963.

For Russian views see also Naftula Aronovich Khalfin, *Proval britanskoi agressii v Afganistane, XIX v.–nachalo XX v.*, Moscow 1959, and Aleksandr Mikhailovich Osipov, ed., *Indiia i Afganistan: ocherki istorii i ekonomiki*, Moscow 1958.

2490 BELLEW (HENRY WALTER). Journal of a political mission to Afghanistan, in 1857, under Major (now Colonel) Lumsden: with an account of the country and people. 1862.

See also his *Afghanistan and the Afghans* . . ., 1879.

2491 THORNTON (ARCHIBALD PATON). 'Afghanistan in Anglo-Russian diplomacy, 1869–1873'. *Camb. Hist. J.* xi (1953–5), 204–18.

2492 COWLING (MAURICE JOHN). 'Lytton, the cabinet, and the Russians, August to November 1878'. *Eng. Hist. Rev.* lxxvi (1961), 59–79.

On the origins of the Afghan war.

2493 IAVORSKII (IVAN LAVROVICH). Reise der russischen Gesandt-schaft in Afghanistan und Buchara in den Jahren 1878–79. Trans. from the Russian by Ed. Petri. 2 v. Jena. 1885.

2494 RUSSIA: MINISTERSTVO INOSTRANNYKH DEL. Afganskoe razgranichenie: peregovory mezhdu Rossiei i Velikobritaniei, 1872–1885: délimitation afghane: négociations entre la Russie et la Grande Bretagne, 1872–1885. 2 v. in 1. St. Petersburg. 1886.

2495 INDIA: ARMY HEADQUARTERS (INTELLIGENCE BRANCH). The second Afghan war, 1878–80: abridged official account. 1908.

Originally pr. for internal use and comp. by S. Pasfield Oliver. This edn. rev. by Francis Gordon Cardew. On the campaign see Waller Ashe, ed., *Personal records of the Kandahar campaign: by officers engaged therein*, 1881; Joshua Duke, *Recollections of the Kabul campaign, 1879 & 1880*, 1883; Archibald Forbes, *The Afghan wars, 1839–42 and 1878–80*, Lond. & N.Y. 1892, 3rd edn. Lond. 1896; Henry Bathurst Hanna, *The second Afghan war, 1878–79–80: its causes, its conduct and its consequences*, 2 v. 1899–1904; Howard Hensman, *The Afghan war of 1879–80: being a complete narrative of the capture of Cabul, the siege of Sherpur*, etc., 1881; Augustus Le Messurier, *Kandahar in 1879* . . ., 1880; Reginald Colville William Reveley Mitford, *To Caubal with the cavalry brigade* . . ., 1881; Sydney Henry Shadbolt, *The Afghan campaigns of 1878–80*, 1882; the memoirs of Lord Roberts (**2825**); Maud Diver, *Kabul to Kandahar*, 1935; and Kally Prosono Dey, *The life and career of Major Sir Louis Cavagnari, C.S.I., K.C.B., British envoy at Cabul, together with a brief outline of the second Afghan war*, Calcutta 1881.

2496 SINGHAL (DAMODAR PRASAD). India and Afghanistan, 1876–1907: a study in diplomatic relations. St. Lucia, Queensland. 1963.

Dilip Kumar Ghose, *England and Afghanistan: a phase in their relations* [1876–87], Calcutta 1960, adds little. Sir Frank Noyce, *England, India and Afghanistan: an essay upon the relations, past and future, between Afghanistan and the British empire in India*, 1902, is a brief prize essay. George Bruce Malleson, *The Russo-Afghan question and the invasion of India*, 2nd edn. 1885, is an anti-Russian polemic.

2497 YATE (ARTHUR CAMPBELL). England and Russia face to face in Asia: travels with the Afghan boundary commission. Edin. & Lond. 1887.

See also Charles Edward Yate, *Northern Afghanistan: or, letters from the Afghan boundary commission*, Edin. & Lond. 1888.

2498 ADAMEC (LUDWIG W.). Afghanistan, 1900–1923: a diplomatic history. Berkeley etc. 1967.

2499 LYONS (JAMES GERVAIS). Afghanistan, the buffer state: Great Britain and Russia in Central Asia: a comprehensive treatise on the entire central Asian question. Madras & Lond. 1910.

2500 HOLDICH (*Sir* THOMAS HUNGERFORD). The Indian borderland, 1880–1900. 1901.

2501 CALLWELL (*Sir* CHARLES EDWARD). Campaigns and their lessons: Tirah, 1897. 1911.

2502 BRUCE. The forward policy and its results: or, thirty-five years' work amongst the tribes on our north-west frontier of India. By Richard Isaac Bruce. 1900.

See also Alice Maude Pennell, *Pennell of the Afghan frontier: the life of Theodore Leighton Pennell, M.D., B.Sc., F.R.C.S. . .*, 1914.

2503 GORDON. A varied life: a record of military and civil service, of sport and of travels in India, Central Asia and Persia, 1849–1902. By Sir Thomas Edward Gordon. 1906.

2504 SANDEMAN. Colonel Sir Robert Sandeman: his life and work on our Indian frontier. By Thomas Henry Thornton. 1895.

### 4. East and South-East Asia

#### (a) *General*

2505 PEARSON (JAMES DOUGLAS). Oriental and Asian bibliography: an introduction with some reference to Africa. 1966.

A general guide to Asian studies, to be suppl. by *Handbook of oriental history*, by members of the Department of Oriental History, School of Oriental and African Studies, University of London, ed. by Cyril Henry Philips, Royal Hist. Soc. 1951. See also Godfrey Raymond Nunn, comp., *Asia: a selected and annotated guide to reference works*, Camb., Mass. 1971, and Assoc. for Asian Studs., *Cumulative bibliography of Asian Studies, 1941–1965: author bibliography*, 4 v. Boston 1969. Current books and articles are listed in *The journal of Asian studies*, Ann Arbor [Mich.] 1941+. Other leading general Asian js. are *Modern Asian studies*, 1967+, *Journal of Southeast Asian Hist.*, Singapore 1960+, and *Journal of Asian history*, Wiesbaden 1967+. For south-east Asia there are some further good guides: Donald Clay Johnson, comp., *A guide to reference materials on southeast Asia . . .*, New Haven [Conn.] 1970, Stephen N. Hay and Margaret H. Case, *Southeast Asian history: a bibliographic guide*, N.Y. 1962, suppl. comp. by Gayle Morrison, Santa Barbara 1969, and Gerald H. Anderson, ed., *Christianity in Southeast Asia: a bibliographical guide . . .*, N.Y. and New Haven [Conn.] 1966. For theses see Barry Cambray Bloomfield, *Theses on Asia accepted by universities in the United Kingdom and Ireland, 1877–1964*, 1967.

2506 SCHOOL OF ORIENTAL AND AFRICAN STUDIES, UNIVERSITY OF LONDON. Library catalogue. 28 v. Boston. 1963. First Suppl. 16 v. Boston. 1968.

The fullest libr. cat. at present available. Lists by author and subject. SOAS also sponsored David E. Hall, ed., *Union catalogue of Asian publications 1965–1970*, Standing Conference of Nat. & Univ. Librs., 4 v. 1971. There is also a useful, though dated, subject cat. in vol. 4 of Lewin (**1213**). For an outline cat. of another big collection see Harvard Univ. Libr., *Widener library shelflist, 19: southern Asia: Afghanistan, Bhutan, Burma, Cambodia, Ceylon, India, Laos, Malaya, Nepal, Pakistan, Sikkim, Singapore, Thailand, Vietnam*, Camb., Mass. 1968. For other libr. see Robert Lewis Collison and Brenda E. Moon, *Directory of libraries and special collections on Asia and North Africa*, Standing Conference of Nat. & Univ. Librs., 1970.

2507 WINT (GUY). The British in Asia. 1947. Rev. edn. 1954.

George Woodcock, *The British in the far east*, 1969, is also useful, but not always accurate.

2508 CHIROL (*Sir* VALENTINE). The far eastern question. 1896.

A good contemp. analysis. See also Sir Henry Norman, *The peoples and politics of the far east* . . ., Lond. & N.Y. 1895, and George Nathaniel Curzon, Marquess Curzon of Kedleston, *Problems of the far east: Japan–Korea–China*, 1894, rev. edn. 1896.

2509 ROSE (SAUL). Britain and south-east Asia. 1962.

See also Daniel George Edward Hall, *A history of south-east Asia*, Lond. & N.Y. 1955, 3rd edn. 1968; Nicholas Tarling, *A concise history of Southeast Asia*, N.Y. 1966; D. G. E. Hall, ed., *Historians of south-east Asia*, 1961; and Victor William Williams Saunders Purcell, *The colonial period in south-east Asia*, N.Y. 1953, and *South and east Asia since 1800*, Camb. 1965.

## (b) *China*

2510 CORDIER (HENRI). Bibliotheca sinica: dictionnaire bibliographique des ouvrages relatifs à l'Empire Chinois. 2 v. Paris. 1881–5. suppl. 1895. 2nd edn. 4 v. Paris 1904–08. suppl. 1922–4.

Cont. by Yuan T'ung-li, *China in Western literature* . . ., New Haven 1958. See also John Lust, *Index sinicus: a catalogue of articles relating to China in periodicals and other collective publications, 1920–1955*, Camb. 1964, and Leonard H. D. Gordon and Frank Joseph Shulman, eds., *Doctoral dissertations on China: a bibliography of studies in western languages, 1945–1970*, Assoc. Asian Studs, Seattle 1972.

2511 TENG (SSU-YÜ), FAIRBANK (JOHN KING), *and* SUN (E-TU ZEN) *eds.* China's response to the west: a documentary survey, 1839–1923. Camb., Mass. 1950.

Suppl. by their *Research guide for China's response to the west: a documentary survey, 1839–1923*, Camb., Mass. 1954.

2512 HERTSLET (*Sir* EDWARD) *ed.* Treaties, &c., between Great Britain and China, and between China and foreign powers . . . 2 v. 1896. 3rd edn. [Hertslet's China treaties] 2 v. 1908.

See also John Van Antwerp Macmurray, ed., *Treaties and agreements with and concerning China, 1894–1919: a collection of state papers, private agreements and other documents, in reference to the rights and obligations of the Chinese government in relation to foreign powers* . . ., 2 v. N.Y. 1921.

2513 KING (FRANK HENRY HAVILAND) *and* CLARKE (PRESCOTT). A research guide to China-coast newspapers, 1822–1911. Camb., Mass. 1965.

The views of the European community are also reflected in Roy. Asiatic Soc. (North China Branch), *Transactions*, 1847–59, *Journal*, 1859–60, 1864+, Hong Kong 1848–59, Shanghai 1860, 1865+.

2514 IWAO (SEIICHI) *ed.* List of the Foreign Office records preserved in the Public Record Office in London relating to China and Japan. Tokyo. 1959.

See also Lo Hui-Min, *Foreign Office confidential papers relating to China and her neighbouring countries, 1840–1914, with an additional list, 1915–1937*, The Hague 1969.

2515 MARCHANT (LESLIE RONALD). A guide to the archives and records of Protestant Christian missions from the British Isles to China, 1796–1914. Nedlands, W. A. 1966.

2516   MORSE (HOSEA BALLOU). The international relations of the Chinese empire [1834–1911]. 3 v. 1911–18.

Still the fullest work on the subject. Vol. I is titled *Conflict*, vol. II *Submission*, vol. III *Subjection*. See also his *The trade and administration of the Chinese empire*, 1908, 3rd edn. 1921. See also Henri Cordier, *Histoire des relations de la Chine avec les puissances occidentales, 1860–1902*, 3 v. Paris 1901–2. For the Chinese background see also John King Fairbank, ed., *The Chinese world order: traditional China's foreign relations*, Camb., Mass. 1968, and Yen-P'ing Hao, *The comprador in nineteenth-century China: bridge between east and west*, Camb., Mass. 1970.

2517   FAIRBANK (JOHN KING). Trade and diplomacy on the China coast: the opening of the treaty ports, 1842–1854. 2 v. Camb., Mass. 1953. Repr. I v. 1964.

Standard.

2518   TAI (EN SAI). Treaty ports in China: a study in diplomacy. N.Y. 1918.

2519   MAYERS (WILLIAM FREDERICK), DENNYS (NICHOLAS BEL-FIELD), *and* KING (CHARLES). The treaty ports of China and Japan: a complete guide to the open ports of those countries ... forming a guide book and vade mecum for travellers, merchants and residents ... Ed. by N. B. Dennys. 1867.

2520   SELBY (JOHN MILLIN). The paper dragon: an account of the China wars, 1840–1900. 1968.

Popular, as is Edgar Crawshaw Holt, *The opium wars in China*, 1964.

2521   SARGENT (ARTHUR JOHN). Anglo-Chinese commerce and diplomacy (mainly in the nineteenth century). Oxf. 1907.

2522   OWEN (DAVID EDWARD). British opium policy in India and China. New Haven [Conn.]. 1934. Repr. Hamden, Conn. 1962.

Good. See also Wen-Tsao Wu, *The Chinese opium question in British opinion and action*, N.Y. 1928, and Frederick Storrs Turner, *British opium policy and its results to India and China*, 1876.

2523   COSTIN (WILLIAM CONRAD). Great Britain and China, 1833–1860. Oxf. 1937.

2524   FOX (GRACE ESTELLE). British admirals and Chinese pirates, 1832–1869. 1940.

2525   RAWLINSON (JOHN LANG). China's struggle for naval development, 1839–1895. Camb., Mass. 1967.

2526   BANNO (MASATAKA). China and the west, 1858–1861: the origins of the Tsungli Yamen. Camb., Mass. 1964.

Makes good use of Chinese sources.

2527 HSÜ (IMMANUEL CHUNG YÜEH). China's entrance into the family of nations: the diplomatic phase, 1858–1880 . . . Camb., Mass. 1960.

2528 TENG (SSU-YÜ). Historiography of the Taiping rebellion. Camb., Mass. 1962.

See also his *The Taiping rebellion and the western powers: a comprehensive survey*, Oxf. 1970, and James Chester Cheng, *Chinese sources for the Taiping rebellion, 1850–1864*, Hong Kong 1963.

2529 COHEN (PAUL ANDREW). China and Christianity: the missionary movement and the growth of Chinese anti-foreignism, 1860–1870. Camb., Mass. 1963.

See also Eugene Powers Boardman, *Christian influence upon the ideology of the Taiping rebellion, 1851–1864*, Madison, Wis. 1952, and John Stradbroke Gregory, 'British missionary reaction to the Taiping movement in China', *J. Religious Hist.* ii (1962–3), 204–18, and **2530**.

2530 GREGORY (JOHN STRADBROKE). Great Britain and the Taipings. N.Y. 1969.

2531 BRINE (LINDESAY). The Taeping rebellion in China: a narrative of its rise and progress, based on original documents and information obtained in China. 1862.

The best contemp. British study of the Taiping movement. See also [John Scarth] *Twelve years in China: the people, the rebels and the mandarins: by a British resident*, Edin. 1860; William Henry Sykes, *The Taeping rebellion in China: its origin, progress and present condition . . .*, 1863; Lin Le, pseud. of Augustus F. Lindley, *Ti-ping tien kwoh: the history of the Ti-ping revolution . . .*, 2 v. 1866, repr. N.Y. 1969; and Andrew Wilson, *England's policy in China*, Hong Kong 1860.

2532 GORDON. The 'ever-victorious army': a history of the Chinese campaign under Lt. Col. C. G. Gordon, C.B., R.E., and of the suppression of the Tai-ping rebellion. By Andrew Wilson. Edin. & Lond. 1868.

See also Samuel Mossman, ed., *General Gordon's private diary of his exploits in China*, 1885, Alfred Egmont Hake, *Events in the Taiping rebellion: being reprints of MSS. copied by General Gordon, C.B., in his own handwriting, with monograph, introduction and notes*, 1891, and *The story of Chinese Gordon*, 7th edn. 2 v. 1884–5, and Bernard Meredith Allen, *Gordon in China*, 1933. All exaggerate Gordon's importance. See Immanuel C. Y. Hsu, 'Gordon in China, 1880', *Pacific Hist. Rev.* xxxiii (1964), 147–66, for a later visit. For Gordon's career see also **1694**.

2533 MACARTNEY. The life of Sir Halliday Macartney, K.C.M.G., commander of Li Hung Chang's trained force in the Taeping rebellion, founder of the first Chinese arsenal, for thirty years councillor and secretary to the Chinese legation in London. By Demetrius Charles De Kavanagh Boulger. Lond. & N.Y. 1908.

2534 HURD (DOUGLAS). The Arrow war, an Anglo-Chinese confusion. 1856–1860. 1967.

2535 COOKE (GEORGE WINGROVE). China: being *The Times* special correspondence from China in the years 1857–58. 1858.

2536   WOLSELEY (GARNET JOSEPH), *Viscount Wolseley*. Narrative of the war with China in 1860: to which is added the account of a short residence with the Tai-ping rebels at Nankin and a voyage from thence to Hankow. 1862.

2537   GRANT (*Sir* JAMES HOPE). Incidents in the China war of 1860: compiled from the private journals of General Sir Hope Grant. By Sir Henry Knollys. Edin. & Lond. 1875.

Other js. incl. George Allgood, *China war, 1860: letters and journal* . . ., 1901; Robert James Leslie M'Ghee, *How we got to Pekin: a narrative of the campaign in China of 1860*, 1862; David Field Rennie, *The British arms in north China and Japan: Peking, 1860; Kagosima, 1862*, 1864; Robert Swinhoe, *Narrative of the north China campaign of 1860* . . ., 1861; and Sir Charles Pyndar Beauchamp Walker, *Days of a soldier's life* . . ., 1894.

2538   BONNER-SMITH (DAVID) *and* LUMBY (ESMOND WALTER RAWSON) *eds*. The second China war, 1856–60. Navy Records Soc. xcv. 1954.

2539   OLIPHANT (LAURENCE). Narrative of the Earl of Elgin's mission to China and Japan in the years 1857, '58, '59. 2 v. Edin. & Lond. 1859. New edn. 2 v. Kuala Lumpur & Lond. 1970.

See also Henry Brougham Loch, Baron Loch, *Personal narrative of occurrences during Lord Elgin's second embassy to China, 1860*, 1869, 3rd edn. 1900, and David Field Rennie, *Peking and the Pekingese during the first year of the British embassy at Peking* 2 v. 1865.

2540   OSBORN (SHERARD). The past and future of British relations in China. Edin. & Lond. 1860.

A general discussion of Anglo-Chinese relations.

2541   PELCOVITS (NATHAN ALBERT). Old China hands and the Foreign Office. N.Y. 1948.

British merchants in China and the Foreign office, c. 1861–1906.

2542   ALCOCK. The Englishman in China during the Victorian era, as illustrated in the career of Sir Rutherford Alcock, K.C.B., D.C.L., many years consul and minister in China and Japan. By Alexander Michie. 2 v. Edin. & Lond. 1900.

2543   HART. Hart and the Chinese customs. By Stanley Fowler Wright. Belfast. 1950.

Standard. Repl. the poor Juliet Bredon, *Sir Robert Hart: the romance of a great career*, Lond. & N.Y. 1909. For Hart's views see '*These from the land of Sinim*': *essays on the Chinese question*, 1901. For officials in the same tradition see Paul Henry King, *In the Chinese customs service: a personal record of forty-seven years* [1930], Charles Drage, *Servants of the dragon throne: being the lives of Edward and Cecil Bowra*, 1966, and Sir Cecil Maurice Bowra, *Memories, 1898–1939*, Lond. 1966, Camb., Mass. 1967. The London agent of Sir Robert Hart is the subject of *James Duncan Campbell: a memoir by his son Robert Ronald Campbell*, Camb., Mass. 1970.

2544 PARKES. The life of Sir Harry Parkes, K.C.B., G.C.M.G., sometime her majesty's minister to China and Japan. By Stanley Lane-Poole and others. 2 v. 1894.

See also Stanley Lane-Poole, *Sir Harry Parkes in China*, 1901.

2545 WANG (SHEN TSU). The Margary affair and the Chefoo agreement [of 1876]. 1940.

On the borders of China and Burma. For this period see also Victor Gordon Kiernan, 'Kashgar and the politics of Central Asia, 1868–1878', *Camb. Hist. J.* xi (1953–5), 317–42. For the borders of China, Tibet, and India see **2562–5**.

2546 KIERNAN (VICTOR GORDON). British diplomacy in China, 1880 to 1885. Camb. 1939.

2547 McCORDOCK (R. STANLEY). British far eastern policy, 1894–1900. Columbia Univ. Studs. in Hist., Econ. & Public Law 346. N.Y. 1931.

On China. See also F. Q. Quo, 'British diplomacy and the cession of Formosa, 1894–95', *Modern Asian Studs.* ii (1968), 141–54; Kazuo Kawai, 'Anglo-German rivalry in the Yangtze region, 1895–1902', *Pacific Hist. Rev.* viii (1939), 413–33; John Desmond Hargreaves, 'Lord Salisbury, British isolation and the Yangtze valley, June–September 1900', *Inst. Hist. Res. Bull.* xxx (1957), 62–75; and Philip Joseph, *Foreign diplomacy in China, 1894–1900: a study in political and economic relations with China*, 1928.

2548 YOUNG (L. K.). British policy in China, 1895–1902. Oxf. 1970.

2549 NISH (IAN HILL). 'The Royal Navy and the taking of Weihaiwei, 1898–1905'. *Mariner's Mirror* liv (1968), 39–54.

See also E-Tu Zen Sun, 'The lease of Wei Hai Wei', *Pacific Hist. Rev.* xix (1950), 277–83.

2550 WEHRLE (EDMUND S.). Britain, China and the anti-missionary riots, 1891–1900. Minneapolis. 1966.

2551 BERESFORD (CHARLES WILLIAM DE LA POER), *Baron Beresford*. The break-up of China: with an account of its present commerce, currency, waterways, armies, railways, politics and future prospects . . . Lond. & N.Y. 1899.

Cp. Archibald Ross Colquhoun, *China in transformation*, Lond. & N.Y. 1898, rev. edn. 1912.

2552 FLEMING ([ROBERT] PETER). The siege at Peking. 1959.

2553 PURCELL (VICTOR WILLIAM WILLIAMS SAUNDERS). The Boxer uprising: a background study. Camb. 1963.

See also Chester C. Tan, otherwise Chun-Lin Tan, *The Boxer catastrophe*, N.Y. 1955, which uses Chinese sources. Among earlier books see Paul Henry Clements, *The Boxer rebellion: a political and diplomatic review*, N.Y. 1915; Harry Craufuird Thomson, *China and the powers: a narrative of the outbreak of 1900*, 1902; Arthur Henderson Smith, *China in convulsion*, 2 v. N.Y. etc. 1901; Charles Cabry Dix, *The world's navies in the Boxer rebellion (China 1900)*, 1905; Arnold Henry Savage Landor, *China and the Allies*, 2 v. Lond. & N.Y. 1901; and Gordon Casserly, *The land of the Boxers: or, China under the allies*, 1903.

2554  LATOURETTE (KENNETH SCOTT). A history of Christian missions in China. 1929. Repr. Taipei. 1966.

A handy summary. See also Donald MacGillivray, ed., *A century of Protestant missions in China (1807–1907): being the centenary conference historical volume*, Shanghai 1907; Shirley Stone Garrett, *Social reformers in urban China: the Chinese Y.M.C.A., 1895–1926*, Camb., Mass. 1970; Helen Edith Legge, *James Legge: missionary and scholar*, 1905; Leslie Theodore Lyall, *A passion for the impossible: the China Inland Mission, 1865–1965*, 1965; Marshall Broomhall, *Martyred missionaries of the China Inland Mission: with a record of the perils & sufferings of some who escaped*, 1901; and Henry Raymond Williamson, *British Baptists in China, 1845–1952*, 1957. For the anti-missionary outbreaks and the literature they led to see Cohen (**2529**), and Wehrle (**2550**).

2555  WRIGHT (STANLEY FOWLER). China's struggle for tariff autonomy, 1843–1938. Shanghai. 1938. Repr. Taipei. 1966.

See also his *The origin and development of the Chinese customs service, 1843–1911*, priv. pr. Shanghai 1939, his life of Hart (**2543**); and *The collection and disposal of the maritime and native customs revenue since the revolution of 1911 . . .*, Shanghai, 2nd edn. 1927, 3rd edn. [*China's customs revenue*] 1935. For the tangled currency background see Frank Henry Haviland King, *Money and monetary policy in China, 1845–1895*, Camb., Mass. 1965. For the gabelle see Samuel Adrian Miles Adshead, *The modernization of the Chinese salt administration, 1900–1920*, Camb., Mass. 1970.

2556  CAMPBELL (PERSIA CRAWFORD). Chinese coolie emigration to countries within the British empire. 1923.

2557  SYKES (WILLIAM HENRY). 'Notes on the progress of the trade of England with China since 1833 and on its present condition and prospects'. *Stat. Soc. J.* xxv (1862), 3–19.

2558  CHECKLAND (SYDNEY GEORGE). 'An English merchant house [Rathbone Brothers] in China after 1842'. *Business Hist. Soc. Bull.* xxvii (1953), 158–89.

2559  LE FEVOUR (EDWARD). Western enterprise in late Ch'ing China: a selective survey of Jardine, Matheson and Company's operations, 1842–1895. Camb., Mass. 1968.

2560  SUN (E-TU ZEN). Chinese railways and British interests, 1898–1911. N.Y. 1954.

See also Percy Horace Braund Kent, *Railway enterprise in China: an account of its origin and development*, 1907.

2561  LIU (KWANG-CHING). Anglo-American steamship rivalry in China, 1862–1874. Camb., Mass. 1962.

### (c) *Other Countries*

2562  LAMB (ALASTAIR). Britain and Chinese central Asia: the road to Lhasa, 1767–1905. 1960.

See also his *The China–India border: the origins of the disputed boundaries*, 1964, Harry Verrier Holman Elwin, ed., *India's north-east frontier in the nineteenth century*, 1959, and Birendra Chandra Chakravorty, *British relations with the hill tribes of Assam since 1858*, Calcutta 1964.

2563   LAMB (ALASTAIR). The McMahon line: a study in the relations between India, China and Tibet, 1904 to 1914. 2 v. Lond. & Toronto. 1966.

2564   FLEMING ([ROBERT] PETER). Bayonets to Lhasa: the first full account of the British invasion of Tibet in 1904. 1961.

2565   HUSAIN (ASAD). British India's relations with the kingdom of Nepal, 1857–1947: a diplomatic history of Nepal. 1970.

See also his *Bibliography of Nepal*, vol. 1, 2nd edn. Kathmandu 1968, and Margaret Welpley Fisher, *Selected bibliography of source materials for Nepal*, Inst. Internat. Studs., Univ. of Calif., 2nd edn. Berkeley 1966.

2566   KIERNAN (VICTOR GORDON). 'Britain, Siam and Malaya, 1875–1885'. *J. Mod. Hist.* xxviii (1956), 1–20.

See also his 'The Kra canal projects of 1882–5; Anglo-French rivalry in Siam and Malaya', *History* xli (1956), 137–57.

2567   KLEIN (IRA). 'Salisbury, Rosebery and the survival of Siam'. *J. British Studs.* viii (1968–9). Pt. 1, 119–39.

See also his 'British expansion in Malaya, 1897–1902', *J. Southeast Asian Hist.* ix (1968), 53–68, and 'Britain, Siam and the Malay peninsula, 1906–1909', *Hist. J.* xii (1969), 119–36; Thamsook Numnonda, 'The Anglo-Siamese secret convention of 1897', *J. Siam Soc.* liii, pt. 1 (1965), 45–60; Eunice Thio on British expansion in Malaya (**2211**); and J. Chandran, 'British foreign policy and the extraterritorial question in Siam, 1891–1900', *Royal Asiatic Soc. (Malayan Branch) J.* xxxviii (1965), pt. 2, 290–313.

2568   LAMB (ALASDAIR). The mandarin road to old Hué: narratives of Anglo-Vietnamese diplomacy from the 17th century to the eve of the French conquest. 1970.

2569   BEASLEY (WILLIAM GERALD). Great Britain and the opening of Japan, 1834–1858. 1951.

For British records relating to Japan see **2514**. For the treaty ports of Japan see **2519**. For Lord Elgin's mission see **2539**, for Sir Rutherford Alcock see **2542**, and for Sir Harry Parkes see **2544**.

2570   FOX (GRACE ESTELLE). Britain and Japan, 1858–1883. Oxf. 1969.

See also Gordon Daniels, 'The British role in the Meiji restoration: a re-interpretative note', *Modern Asian Studs.* ii (1968), 291–313, and Charles Alfred Fisher, 'The Britain of the east? A study in the geography of imitation', ibid. 343–76.

2571   NISH (IAN HILL). The Anglo-Japanese alliance: the diplomacy of two island empires, 1894–1907. 1966.

Cont. by his *Alliance in decline: a study in Anglo-Japanese relations, 1908–23*, 1972. Such works as Chung Fu Chang, *The Anglo-Japanese alliance*, Baltimore 1931, Alfred Lewis Pinneo Dennis, *The Anglo-Japanese alliance*, Berkeley etc. 1923, Paul Minrath, *Das englisch-japanische Bündnis von 1902 . . .*, Stuttgart 1933, Hans Plehn, *Nach dem englisch japanischen Bündnis*, Berlin 1907, A. Galperin, *Anglo-iaponskii soiuz 1902–1921 gody*, Moscow 1947, are largely repl. by Nish. But not Zara Shakow Steiner, 'Great Britain and the creation of the Anglo-Japanese alliance', *J. Mod. Hist.* xxxi (1959), 27–36, and the life of Sir Ernest Satow (**2261**).

2572 LOWE (PETER). Great Britain and Japan, 1911–1915: a study of British far eastern policy. 1969.

See also his 'The British empire and the Anglo-Japanese alliance, 1911–15', *History* liv (1969), 212–25.

2573 SATOW (*Sir* ERNEST MASON). Korea and Manchuria between Russia and Japan, 1895–1904: the observations of Sir Ernest Satow. Ed. by George Alexander Lensen. Tallahassee, Fla. 1966.

2574 EDWARDS (E. W.). 'Great Britain and the Manchurian railways question, 1909–1910'. *Eng. Hist. Rev.* lxxxi (1966), 740–69.

2575 FULTON (AUSTIN). Through earthquake, wind and fire: church and mission in Manchuria, 1867–1950 . . . Edin. 1967.

Presbyterian missionary enterprise, Scottish, Irish, and English.

2576 TROLLOPE. Mark Napier Trollope, bishop in Corea, 1911–1930 . . . By Constance A. N. Trollope. 1936.

## 5. UNITED STATES

### (a) *General*

2577 BEMIS (SAMUEL FLAGG) *and* GRIFFIN (GRACE GARDNER). Guide to the diplomatic history of the United States, 1775–1921. Libr. of Congress. Wash. 1935. Repr. Gloucester, Mass. 1959, 1963.

Extraordinarily full on Anglo-American relations. Indispensable.

2578 CRICK (BERNARD ROWLAND) and ALMAN (MIRIAM) *eds.* A guide to manuscripts relating to America in Great Britain and Ireland. 1961.

See also Scottish Record Office, *Source list of manuscripts relating to the U.S.A. and Canada in private archives preserved in the Scottish Record Office*, List & Index Soc. special ser. 3, 1970.

2579 UNITED STATES (DEPARTMENT OF STATE). Papers relating to the foreign relations of the United States. 1870+.

Title became *Foreign relations of the United States*, 1933+. For docs. to 1861 see Adelaide Rosalie Hasse, *Index to United States documents relating to foreign affairs, 1828–1861*, 3 v. Wash. 1914–21. For those from 1861–8 see *Papers relating to foreign affairs*, Wash. 1861–8. See also William Stull Holt, *Treaties defeated by the Senate* . . ., Baltimore, Md. 1933.

2580 MOORE (JOHN BASSETT). History and digest of the international arbitrations to which the United States has been a party . . . 6 v. Wash. 1898.

2581 ALLEN (HARRY CRANBROOK). Great Britain and the United States: a history of Anglo-American relations (1783–1952). 1954. Rev. edn. of pt. 1. publ. as *The Anglo-American relationship since 1783*, Lond. 1959, and as *Conflict and concord* . . ., N.Y. 1960.

Standard. Allen, Bourne (**2582**), Campbell (**2602**), and Perkins (**2601**) cover the hist. of the period in considerable detail. The basis of American policy is set out in Dexter Perkins, *The Monroe doctrine, 1867–1907*, Baltimore, Md. 1937.

**2582** BOURNE (KENNETH). Britain and the balance of power in North America, 1815–1908. Berkeley. 1967.

A careful study of British anxieties about the possibility of war with the United States. A further book is badly needed on Anglo-American naval relations. Forrest Davis, *The Atlantic system: the story of Anglo-American control of the seas*, 1943, merely suggests that there is a topic to be explored.

**2583** MOWAT (ROBERT BALMAIN). The diplomatic relations of Great Britain and the United States. 1925.

The earliest comprehensive diplomatic hist. of the period. Suppl. by Mowat's *The American entente*, 1939, and *Americans in England*, Camb., Mass. 1935. Tends to reflect pre-war views such as those expressed in John Randolph Dos Passos, *The Anglo-Saxon century*, N.Y. 1903, Henry Cabot Lodge, *One hundred years of peace and the unification of the English-speaking people*, Lond. & N.Y. 1913, and William Archibald Dunning, *The British empire and the United States: a review of their relations during the century of peace following the treaty of Ghent*, N.Y. & Lond. 1914. See also Henry Green Hodges, *Diplomatic relations between the United States and Great Britain*, Boston 1930, and Sir Harry Ernest Brittain, *Pilgrim partners: forty years of British-American friendship*, 1942.

**2584** NEVINS ([JOSEPH] ALLAN) *ed.* America through British eyes. New edn. N.Y. 1948.

See also Walter Ernest Allen, comp., *Transatlantic crossing: American visitors to Britain and British visitors to America in the nineteenth century*, Lond. & N.Y. 1971, and the American works at **193–229**.

**2585** PELLING (HENRY MATHISON). America and the British left: from Bright to Bevan. 1956. N.Y. 1957.

See also George D. Lillibridge, *Beacon of freedom: the impact of American democracy upon Great Britain, 1830–1870*, Phila. 1954, Arthur Mann, 'British social thought and American reformers of the Progressive era', *Mississippi Valley Hist. Rev.* xlii (1955–6), 672–92, and *Speeches of John Bright, M.P., on the American question*, Boston 1865.

**2586** KELLEY (ROBERT LLOYD). The transatlantic persuasion: the liberal-democratic mind in the age of Gladstone. N.Y. 1969.

A pioneer interpretative work of Anglo-American hist. There are useful essays in Robert O. Mead, *Atlantic legacy: essays in American-European cultural history*, N.Y. & Lond. 1969.

**2587** ABEL (ANNIE HELOISE) *and* KLINGBERG (FRANK JOSEPH) *eds.* A side-light on Anglo-American relations, 1839–1858: furnished by the correspondence of Lewis Tappan and others with the British and Foreign Anti-Slavery Society. Lancaster, Pa. 1927.

2588  SOULSBY (HUGH GRAHAM). The right of search and the slave trade in Anglo-American relations, 1814–1862. Baltimore [Md.]. 1933.

See also Christine Bolt, *The anti-slavery movement and reconstruction: a study in Anglo-American co-operation, 1833–77*, 1969, and Oscar Maurer, '*Punch* on slavery and civil war in America, 1861–1865', *Victorian Studs.* i (1957–8), 5–28.

2589  BOURNE (KENNETH). 'The Clayton–Bulwer Treaty and the decline of British opposition to the territorial expansion of the United States, 1857–60'. *J. Mod. Hist.* xxxiii (1961), 287–91.

See also Richard Warner Van Alstyne, 'British diplomacy and the Clayton–Bulwer Treaty, 1850–60', *J. Mod. Hist.* xi (1939), 149–83, and 'Anglo-American relations, 1853–57', *Amer. Hist. Rev.* xlii (1936–7), 491–500, and Mario Rodriguez, 'The "Prometheus" and the Clayton–Bulwer Treaty', *J. Mod. Hist.* xxxvi (1964), 260–78.

2590  ADAMS (EPHRAIM DOUGLASS). Great Britain and the American civil war. 2 v. 1925. Repr. Gloucester, Mass. 1957.

Still the fullest work on the subject. See also Max Beloff, 'Great Britain and the American civil war', *History* xxxvii (1952), 40–8; Wilbur Devereux Jones, 'The British Conservatives and the American civil war', *Amer. Hist. Rev.* lviii (1952–3), 527–43; John O. Waller, 'John Stuart Mill and the American civil war', *N.Y. Public Libr. Bull.* lxvi (1962), 505–18, and 'Edward Dicey and the American negro in 1862 . . .', ibid. 31–45; Adelaide Weinberg, *John Elliot Cairnes and the American civil war: a study in Anglo-American relations*, 1970; Richard Greenleaf, 'British labor against American slavery', *Science & Society* xvii (1953), 42–58; Royden Harrison, 'British labour and American slavery', ibid. xxv (1961), 291–319, suppl. ibid. xxvii (1963), 465–73, and 'British labour and the confederacy . . .', *Int. Rev. Soc. Hist.* ii (1957), 78–105; and Eli Ginzberg, 'The economics of British neutrality during the American civil war', *Agric. Hist.* x (1936), 147–56. Among earlier works Brougham Villiers, pseud. of Frederick John Shaw, and Wilfrid Hugh Chesson, *Anglo-American relations, 1861–1865*, 1919, Fitzwilliam Sargent, *England, the United States and the southern confederacy*, 1863, 2nd edn. 1864, and Mountague Bernard, *A historical account of the neutrality of Great Britain during the American civil war*, 1870, are useful. The role of the Confederacy in Europe may be followed in Charles P. Cullop, *Confederate propaganda in Europe, 1861–1865*, Coral Gables, Fla. 1969, James Dunwody Bulloch, *The secret service of the Confederate states in Europe: or, how the Confederate cruisers were equipped*, 2 v. 1883, new edn. by Philip Van Doren Stern, Lond. & N.Y. 1959, and Samuel Bernard Thompson, *Confederate purchasing operations abroad*, Chapel, N.C. 1935.

2591  BONHAM (MILLEDGE LOUIS). The British consuls in the Confederacy. *Columbia Studs. in Hist., Econ. & Public Law* xliii. No. 3. N.Y. 1911.

2592  MERLI (FRANK J.). Great Britain and the Confederate navy, 1861–1865. Bloomington, Ind. 1970.

2593  JOHN (EVAN) *pseud. of* SIMPSON (EVAN JOHN). Atlantic impact, 1861. Lond. & N.Y. 1952.

The *Trent* case.

2594  VANDIVER (FRANK EVERSON) *ed.* Confederate blockade running through Bermuda, 1861–1865: letters and cargo manifests. Austin, Tex. 1947.

2595 JONES (WILBUR DEVEREUX). The confederate rams at Birkenhead: a chapter in Anglo-American relations. Confederate Centennial Studies 19. Tuscaloosa [Ala.]. 1961.

2596 POOLMAN (KENNETH EDWARD). The Alabama incident. 1958.

See also Douglas H. Maynard, 'Union efforts to prevent the escape of the Alabama' *Mississippi Valley Hist. Rev.* xli (1954–5), 41–60.

2597 SEMMES (RAPHAEL). Memoirs of service afloat during the war between the states. Baltimore [Md.]. 1869.

Commanded the *Alabama*. The *Alabama* section of the book was reissued in 1962, ed. by Philip Van Doren Stern, as *The Confederate raider Alabama . . .*, Bloomington, Ind. 1962. See also *The cruise of the Alabama and the Sumter: from the private journals and other papers of Commander R. Semmes, C.S.N., and other officers*, 2 v. 1864. Edward Carrington Boykin, *Ghost ship of the Confederacy: the story of the Alabama and her Captain Raphael Semmes*, N.Y. 1957, is based on the *Memoirs*.

2598 BALCH (THOMAS WILLING). The Alabama arbitration. Phila. 1900. Repr. Freeport, N.Y. 1969.

See also Maureen M. Robson, 'The Alabama claims and the Anglo-American reconciliation, 1865–71', *Canadian Hist. Rev.* xlii (1961), 1–22, and Adrian Cook, 'A lost opportunity in Anglo-American relations: the Alabama claims, 1865–1867', *Australian J. of Politics & Hist.* xii (1966), 54–65.

2599 GRENVILLE (JOHN ASHLEY SOAMES) *and* YOUNG (GEORGE BERKELEY). Politics, strategy and American diplomacy: studies in foreign policy, 1874–1917. New Haven [Conn.]. 1966.

2600 MOMMSEN (WOLFGANG). Die letzte Phase des britischen Imperialismus auf den amerikanischen Kontinenten, 1880–1896. Leipzig. 1933.

2601 PERKINS (BRADFORD). The great rapprochement: England and the United States, 1895–1914. N.Y. 1968.

Covers a wider field than the two Campbells (2602–3) and Neale (2606) whose monographic work is very good, and Richard Heathcote Heindel, *The American impact on Great Britain, 1898–1914: a study of the United States in world history*, Phila. 1940. For the development of American ideas it is necessary to consult Ernest Richard May, *Imperial democracy: the emergence of America as a great power*, N.Y. 1961, and *American imperialism: a speculative essay*, N.Y. 1968.

2602 CAMPBELL (ALEXANDER ELMSLIE). Great Britain and the United States, 1895–1903. 1960.

2603 CAMPBELL (CHARLES SOUTER). Anglo-American understanding, 1898–1903. Baltimore [Md.]. 1957.

2604 BLAKE (NELSON M.). 'The Olney–Pauncefote Treaty of 1897', *Amer. Hist. Rev.* l (1944–5), 228–43.

2605 GELBER (LIONEL MORRIS). The rise of Anglo-American friendship: a study in world politics, 1898–1906. 1938. New edn. Hamden, Conn. 1966.

An influential pioneer work, now corrected at many points by more recent scholarship.

2606 NEALE (ROBERT GEORGE). Britain and American imperialism, 1898–1900. Brisbane, Queensland. 1965. U.S. edn. [Great Britain and United States expansion: 1898–1900.] East Lansing, Mich. 1966.

See also Geoffrey Seed, 'British reactions to American imperialism reflected in journals of opinion, 1898–1900', *Pol. Sci. Q.* lxxiii (1958), 254–72.

2607 REUTER (BERTHA ANN). Anglo-American relations during the Spanish-American war. N.Y. 1924.

Out of date. See also E. Ranson, 'British military and naval observers in the Spanish–American war', *J. Amer. Studs.* iii (1969), 33–56.

2608 FERGUSON (JOHN HENRY). American diplomacy and the Boer war. Phila. 1939.

2609 TANSILL (CHARLES CALLAN). America and the fight for Irish freedom, 1866–1922: an old story based on new data. N.Y. 1957.

A partisan outline hist. Needs to be suppl. by Ward (2610), William D'Arcy, *The Fenian movement in the United States, 1858–1886*, Wash. 1947, and Brian Jenkins, *Fenians and Anglo-American relations during Reconstruction*, Ithaca, N.Y. 1969.

2610 WARD (ALAN J.). Ireland and Anglo-American relations, 1899–1921. 1969.

2611 IONS (EDMUND). James Bryce and American democracy, 1870–1922. Lond. 1968. N.Y. 1970.

2612 PIERCY (FREDERICK HAWKINS). Route from Liverpool to Great Salt Lake valley. 1955. New edn. by Fawn M. Brodie. Camb., Mass. 1962.

British Mormon migration.

2613 BAGWELL (PHILIP SIDNEY) *and* MINGAY (GORDON EDMUND). Britain and America, 1850–1939: a study of economic change. 1970.

See also Habbakuk, **4805**. For British investment in America and American investment in Britain see **4682**.

2614 CHAPMAN (*Sir* SYDNEY JOHN). The history of trade between the United Kingdom and the United States: with special reference to the effect of tariffs. 1899.

2615 OSS (SALOMON FREDERIK VAN). American railroads and British investors. 1893.

A useful guide, suppl. by the much fuller *American railroads as investments*, 1893. See also Dorothy R. Adler, *British investment in American railways, 1834–1898*, ed. by Muriel E. Hidy, Charlottesville, Va. 1970.

(b) *American Ministers and Ambassadors*

**2616 WILLSON (BECKLES).** America's ambassadors to England (1785–1928): a narrative of Anglo-American diplomatic relations. Lond. 1928. N.Y. 1929. Repr. Freeport, N.Y. 1969.

Suppl. by his *Friendly relations: a narrative of Britain's ministers and ambassadors to America (1791–1930)*, 1934. Emily Bax, *Miss Bax of the embassy*, Boston 1939, is full of the trivia of U.S. embassy life in London, 1902–14.

**2617 ADAMS.** Charles Francis Adams, 1807–1886. By Martin Bauml Duberman. Boston. 1961. Repr. Stanford [Calif.]. 1968.

Minister in London, 1861–8. See also *Charles Francis Adams, by his son Charles Francis Adams*, Lond., Boston, & N.Y. 1900, Arda Di Pace Donald, David Donald and others, eds., *Diary of Charles Francis Adams*, 4+ v. Camb. Mass. 1964+, and Worthington Chauncey Ford, ed., *A cycle of Adams letters, 1861–1865*, 2 v. 1921.

**2618 BAYARD.** The foreign policy of Thomas F. Bayard, 1885–1897. By Charles Callan Tansill. N.Y. 1940.

Ambassador in London, 1893–7.

**2619 BUCHANAN.** President James Buchanan: a biography. By Philip Shriver Klein. Univ. Park, Penn. 1962.

Minister in London, 1853–6. See also George Ticknor Curtis, *Life of James Buchanan* . . ., 2 v. N.Y. 1883, Rushmore G. Horton, *The life and public services of James Buchanan, late minister to England* . . ., N.Y. &c. 1856, and John Bassett Moore, ed., *The works of James Buchanan* . . ., 12 v. Phila. 1908–11.

**2620 CHOATE.** The life of Joseph Hodges Choate, as gathered chiefly from his letters . . . By Edward Sandford Martin. 2 v. Lond. & N.Y. 1920.

Ambassador in London, 1899–1905. See also Theron George Strong, *Joseph H. Choate* . . ., N.Y. 1917.

**2621 DALLAS.** Diary of George Mifflin Dallas, while United States minister to Russia, 1837 to 1839, and to England, 1856 to 1861. Ed. by Susan Dallas. Phila. 1892.

Minister in London 1856–61. See also Julia Dallas, ed., *A series of letters from London written during the years 1856, '57, '58, '59 and '60, by George Mifflin Dallas, then minister of the United States at the British court* . . ., Phila. 1869, also publ. as *Letters from London* . . ., 2 v. Lond. 1870.

**2622 HAY.** The life and letters of John Hay. By William Roscoe Thayer. 2 v. Lond., Boston, & N.Y. 1915.

Ambassador in London, 1897–8. See also *Letters of John Hay and extracts from diary*, selected by Henry Adams and ed. by Mrs. Hay, priv. pr. 3 v. Wash. 1908, repr. N.Y. 1969, Tyler Dennett, *John Hay: from poetry to politics*, N.Y. 1934, and George Monteiro, *Henry James and John Hay: the record of a friendship*, Providence, R.I. 1965.

**2623 JOHNSON.** Life of Reverdy Johnson. By Bernard Christian Steiner. Baltimore [Md.]. [1914.]

Minister in London 1868–9.

2624 LAWRENCE. Memoir of Abbott Lawrence. By Hamilton Andrews Hill. Priv. pr. Boston. 1883. 2nd edn. [public] Boston. 1884.

Minister in London 1849–52.

2625 LINCOLN. Robert Todd Lincoln: a man in his own right. By John S. Goff. Norman, Okla. 1968.

Minister in London, 1889–93.

2626 LOWELL. James Russell Lowell. By Martin Bauml Duberman. Boston. 1966.

Minister in London, 1880–5. See also Charles Eliot Norton, ed., *Letters of James Russell Lowell*, 2 v. Lond. & N.Y. 1893; Mark Antony De Wolfe Howe, ed., *New letters of James Russell Lowell*, N.Y. & Lond. 1932; Ferris Greenslet, *James Russell Lowell: his life and work*, Lond. & Boston 1905; Edward Everett Hale, the elder, *James Russell Lowell and his friends*, Lond. & Boston 1899; and Horace Elisha Scudder, *James Russell Lowell: a biography*, Boston & N.Y. 2 v. 1901. There are several collected edns. of his works.

2627 MOTLEY. John Lothrop Motley: a memoir. By Oliver Wendell Holmes, the elder. Lond. & Edin. 1878. Boston. 1879.

Minister in London, 1869–70. See also George William Curtis, ed. *The correspondence of John Lothrop Motley*, 2 v. Lond. & N.Y. 1889.

2628 PAGE. The life and letters of Walter H. Page. By Burton Jesse Hendrick. 3 v. Garden City, N.Y. 1922–5.

Ambassador in London, 1913–18.

2629 PHELPS. Orations & essays of Edward John Phelps, diplomat and statesman. Ed. by John Griffith McCullough, with a memoir by John W. Stewart. N.Y. & Lond. 1901.

Minister in London, 1885–9.

2630 REID. The life of Whitelaw Reid. By Royal Cortissoz. 2 v. N.Y. & Lond. 1921.

Ambassador in London, 1905–12. See also U.S. Libr. of Congress, MS. Divn. *Whitelaw Reid: a register of his papers in the Library of Congress*, Wash. 1958.

2631 WELSH. Letters of John Welsh, envoy extraordinary and minister plenipotentiary to the Court of St. James. Ed. by Edward Lowber Stokes. Phila. 1937.

Minister in London, 1877–9.

## 6. LATIN AMERICA

2632 HUMPHREYS (ROBERT ARTHUR). Latin American history: a guide to the literature in English. 1958. Repr. 1966 etc.

Largely repl. by Griffin (**2633**). Publ. work on Latin America is listed annually in *Handbook of Latin American studies . . .*, Camb., Mass., now Gainesville, Fla., 1936+. Articles on British involvement in Latin America have appeared most frequently in *The Hispanic American hist. rev.*, Baltimore &c. 1918+, *Inter-American Econ. Affairs*, Wash. 1947+, and *J. of Latin American Studs.*, 1969+.

2633  GRIFFIN (CHARLES CARROLL) *assisted by* WARREN (J. BENE-DICT) *comps*. Latin America: a guide to the historical literature. Conference on Latin American Hist. Austin, Texas. 1971.

See also Stojan Albert Bayitch, *Latin America and the Caribbean: a bibliographical guide to works in English*, Univ. of Miami School of Law, Interamerican Legal Studies 10, Coral Gables, Fla. & N.Y. 1967.

2634  NAYLOR (BERNARD). Accounts of nineteenth-century South America: an annotated check-list of works by British and United States observers. 1969.

2635  HILL (ROSCOE R.) *ed*. The national archives of Latin America. Camb., Mass. 1945.

2636  WALNE (PETER) *ed*. A guide to manuscript sources for the history of Latin America and the Caribbean in the British Isles. 1973.

See also Desmond Christopher St. Martin Platt, 'The British in South America: an archive report', *Inst. Hist. Res. Bull.* xxxviii (1965), 172–91.

2637  IRELAND (GORDON). Boundaries, possessions and conflicts in South America. Camb., Mass. 1938.

Suppl. by his *Boundaries, possessions and conflicts in Central and North America and the Caribbean*, Camb., Mass. 1941. Useful for boundary disputes between Britain and the Latin American republics.

2638  PLATT (DESMOND CHRISTOPHER ST. MARTIN). 'British diplomacy in Latin America since the emancipation'. *Inter-American Econ. Affairs* xxi (1967–8), 21–42.

See also his 'British bondholders in nineteenth-century Latin America: injury and remedy', *Inter-American Econ. Affairs* xiv (1960–1), no. 3, 3–44 and *Latin America and British trade, 1806–1914*, 1972.

2639  RIPPY (JAMES FRED). British investments in Latin America, 1822–1949: a case study in the operations of private enterprise in retarded regions. Minneapolis. 1959. Repr. Hamden, Conn. 1966.

A handy summary, but to be used with caution. For the Bank of London & South America see **4645**.

2640  WORTHINGTON (THOMAS). Reports received from Mr. T. Worthington, the special commissioner appointed by the Board of Trade to inquire into and report upon the conditions and prospects of British trade in certain South American countries. First and second reports [Chile] [C. 9100] H.C. (1899). XCVI, 447. Third report [Argentine] [C. 9101] H.C. (1899). XCVI, 487. Fourth and fifth reports [Brazil] [C. 9160 and C. 9161] H.C. (1899). XCVI, 533 and 561. Sixth report [Uruguay] [C. 9298] H.C. (1899). XCVI, 587.

For trade see also Thomas Whifield Keeble, *Commercial relations between British overseas territories and South America, 1806–1914: an introductory essay*, 1970.

2641 PLATT (DESMOND CHRISTOPHER ST. MARTIN). 'British agricultural colonization in Latin America'. *Inter-American Econ. Affairs* xviii (1964–5), No. 3, 3–38; xix (1965–6), No. 1, 23–42.

For the Welsh colony in Patagonia see **9721**.

2642 MULHALL (MICHAEL GEORGE). The English in South America. Lond. [& Buenos Aires]. 1878.

A substantial descriptive work by a prolific compiler of guide-books.

2643 FERNS (HENRY STANLEY). Britain and Argentina in the nineteenth century. Oxf. 1960.

A model of how such a book should be written.

2644 FORD (ALEC GEORGE). The gold standard, 1880–1914: Britain and Argentina. Oxf. 1962.

2645 HANSON (SIMON GABRIEL). Argentine meat and the British market: chapters in the history of the Argentine meat industry. Stanford [Calif.]. 1938.

2646 MANCHESTER (ALAN KREBS). British preeminence in Brazil: its rise and decline: a study in European expansion. Chapel Hill [N.C.]. 1933.

2647 BETHELL (LESLIE). The abolition of the Brazilian slave trade: Britain, Brazil and the slave trade question, 1807–1869. Camb. Latin Amer. Studs. 6. Camb. 1970.

2648 GRAHAM (RICHARD). Britain and the onset of modernization in Brazil, 1850–1914. Camb. Latin Amer. Studs. 4. Camb. 1968.

2649 GUATEMALA (MINISTRY OF FOREIGN AFFAIRS). White book: controversy between Guatemala and Great Britain relative to the convention of 1859 on territorial matters. Guatemala. 1938.

A coll. of docs. These are used for polemical purposes in José Luis Mendoza, *Britain and her treaties on Belize, British Honduras: Guatemala has the right to reinstate the entire territory of Belize*, trans. by Lilly de Jongh Osborne, Ministry for Foreign Affairs, Guatemala 1946, 2nd edn. 1959.

For the dispute with Britain over British Honduras see also **1585**.

2650 GRAJALES RAMOS (GLORIA) *comp*. México y la Gran Bretaña durante la intervención, 1861–1862. Secretaría de Relaciones Exteriores. Archivo histórico diplomático mexicano, 2 ser. 15. Mexico. 1962.

See also her *Guía de documentos para la historia de México en archivos ingleses (siglo XIX)*, Mexico 1969, and William Spence Robertson, 'The Tripartite Treaty of London', *Hispanic Amer. Hist. Rev.* xx (1940), 167–89.

2651 TISCHENDORF (ALFRED). Great Britain and Mexico in the era of Porfirio Díaz. Durham, N.C. 1961.

2652  CALVERT (PETER). The Mexican revolution, 1910–1914: the diplomacy of Anglo-American conflict. Camb. Latin Amer. Studs. 3. Camb. 1968.

2653  OPPENHEIM (LASSA FRANCIS LAWRENCE). The Panama canal conflict between Great Britain and the United States of America. Camb. 1913. 2nd edn. 1913.

2654  WILLIAMS (MARY WILHELMINE). Anglo-American Isthmian diplomacy, 1815–1915. Baltimore & Wash. 1916. Repr. N.Y. 1965. Repr. Gloucester, Mass. 1965.

Needs to be suppl. by John Ashley Soames Grenville, 'Great Britain and the Isthmian canal, 1898–1901', *Amer. Hist. Rev.* lxi (1955–6), 48–69.

2655  SCHMITT (PETER ADOLF). Paraguay und Europa: die diplomatischen Beziehungen unter Carlos Antonio López und Francisco Solano López, 1841–1870. Berlin. 1963.

2656  MATHEW (W. M.). 'The imperialism of free trade: Peru, 1820–70'. *Econ. Hist. Rev.* 2 ser. xxi (1968), 562–79.

See also his 'Peru and the British guano market, 1840–1870', *Econ. Hist. Rev.* 2 ser. xxiii (1970), 112–28.

2657  UNITED STATES COMMISSION ON BOUNDARY BETWEEN VENEZUELA AND BRITISH GUIANA. Report and accompanying papers. 4 v. Wash. 1897.

The 1st vol. is a hist. of the dispute. Both Venezuela and Great Britain printed voluminous materials for use in the dispute: *Venezuela–British Guiana boundary arbitration: the case of the United States of Venezuela . . .*, 3 v. N.Y. 1898, *Venezuela–British Guiana boundary arbitration: the counter case of the United States of Venezuela . . .*, 3 v. N.Y. 1898, and *British Guiana boundary: arbitration with the United States of Venezuela: the case on behalf of the government of Her Britannic Majesty*, 3 v. 1898. In addition the *Proceedings* of the arbitration tribunal were printed, *British Guiana–Venezuelan boundary: arbitration between the governments of Her Britannic Majesty and the United States of Venezuela*, 11 v. Paris 1899, and a host of correspondence, British, Venezuelan, and American.

2658  HUMPHREYS (ROBERT ARTHUR). 'Anglo-American rivalries and the Venezuela crisis of 1895'. *Royal Hist. Soc. Trans.* 5 ser. xvii (1967), 131–64. Repr. in R. A. Humphreys, *Tradition and revolt in Latin America and other essays*, 1969, 186–215.

See also Desmond Christopher St Martin Platt, 'The allied coercion of Venezuela, 1902–3: a reassessment', *Inter-Amer. Econ. Affairs* xv (1961–2), no. 4, 3–28; William Spence Robertson, 'The tripartite Treaty of London', *Hispanic Amer. Hist. Rev.* xx (1940), 167–89; Grover Cleveland, *The Venezuelan boundary controversy*, Princeton & Lond. 1913; and Walter La Feber, 'The background of Cleveland's Venezuelan policy: a reinterpretation', *Amer. Hist. Rev.* lxvi (1960–1), 947–67. There is a large literature on the Venezuelan arbitration, but most of it is of little value.

# IV

## THE ARMED FORCES

### A. GENERAL

2659 HIGHAM (ROBIN DAVID STEWART) *ed*. A guide to the sources of British military history. Berkeley & Los Angeles. 1971.

An outline bibliog. Needs to be suppl. by *Return giving in chronological order, according to the dates of publication of the reports, a list of all inquiries into naval and military affairs which have been held since the year 1900, the reports of which have been published as parliamentary papers*. H.C. 297 (1908). LXV, 727. For reference books see Hardin Craig, Jr., *A bibliography of encyclopaedias and dictionaries dealing with military, naval and maritime affairs, 1626–1965*, 3rd edn., Houston, Texas [Fondren Library, Rice University] 1965.

2660 PUBLIC RECORD OFFICE. List of papers of the Committee of Imperial Defence to 1914. P.R.O. handbooks 6. 1964.

2661 WOOD (*Sir* HENRY EVELYN) *ed*. British battles on land and sea: with a history of the fighting services and notes by the editor. 2 v. 1915.

Like his *Our fighting services and how they made the Empire*, 1916, intended for a popular audience. Interesting for contemp. flavour. Works with a more serious intention are, unfortunately, too weak on the period to merit incl.

2662 FLOURNOY (FRANCIS ROSEBRO). Parliament and war: the relation of the British parliament to the administration of foreign policy in connection with the initiation of war. 1927.

From the First Afghan war to World War I. A useful summary.

2663 GORDON (DONALD CRAIGIE). The dominion partnership in imperial defense, 1870–1914. Baltimore [Md.]. 1965.

For earlier discussions of the subject see *Report from the select committee on colonial military expenditure* [Chairman: Arthur Mills]. H.C. 423 (1861). XIII, 69, and *Report of the committee on expense of military defences in the colonies*. H.C. 282 (1860). XLI, 573. For Canada and imperial defence see **1498**.

2664 WILKINSON. Thirty-five years, 1874–1909. By Henry Spenser Wilkinson. 1933.

The memoirs of one of the few British academic writers on military topics.

2665 JOHNSON (FRANKLYN ARTHUR). Defence by committee: the British Committee of Imperial Defence, 1885–1959. 1960.

Not always reliable. Needs to be suppl. by Mackintosh (**2667**), Luke Trainor, 'The Liberals and the formation of imperial defence policy, 1892–5', *Inst. Hist. Res. Bull.* xlii (1969), 188–200, and Zara Shakow, 'The defence committee: a forerunner of the

Committee of Imperial Defence', *Canadian Hist. Rev.* xxxvi (1955), 36–44. John Patrick William Ehrman, *Cabinet government and war, 1890–1940*, Camb. 1958, is a short interpretative study.

2666 HARTINGTON COMMISSION ON CIVIL AND PROFESSIONAL ORGANISATION OF THE NAVAL AND MILITARY DEPARTMENTS. Preliminary and further reports (with appendices) of the royal commissioners appointed to enquire into the civil and professional administration of the naval and military departments and the relation of those departments to each other and to the Treasury [Chairman: Marquess of Hartington]. [C. 5979] H.C. (1890). XIX, 1.

An important inquiry into the feasibility of a new defence structure.

2667 MACKINTOSH (JOHN PITCAIRN). 'The role of the Committee of Imperial Defence before 1914'. *Eng. Hist. Rev.* lxxvii (1962), 490–503.

Two of the secretaries of the committee have lives: Lord Sydenham's memoirs (**1162**), and Stephen Wentworth Roskill, *Hankey: man of secrets*, 2 v. 1970.

2668 d'OMBRAIN (NICHOLAS). War machinery and high policy: defence administration in peacetime Britain, 1902–1914. 1973.

2669 WILLIAMSON (SAMUEL RUTHVEN) *Jr*. The politics of grand strategy: Britain and France prepare for war, 1904–1914. Camb., Mass. 1969.

An excellent study of British pre-war defence policy.

2670 HANKEY (MAURICE PASCAL ALERS), *Baron Hankey*. The supreme command, 1914–1918. 2 v. 1961.

Incl. an introductory section on pre-1914 developments. There is also a certain amount of pre-1914 material in Sir Ernest Llewellyn Woodward, *Great Britain and the war of 1914–1918*, Lond. & N.Y. 1967, Boston 1970, Paul Guinn, *British strategy and politics, 1914 to 1918*, Oxf. 1965, and popular works on the outbreak of war such as Barbara Tuchman, *The guns of August*, N.Y. 1962.

2671 COLOMB (*Sir* JOHN CHARLES READY). The defence of Great and Greater Britain: sketches of its naval, military and political aspects . . . 1880.

2672 HAMLEY (*Sir* EDWARD BRUCE). National defence: articles and speeches. Edin. & Lond. 1889.

2673 DILKE (*Sir* CHARLES WENTWORTH) *and* WILKINSON (HENRY SPENSER). Imperial defence. 1892. Rev. edn. 1897.

See also Dilke's 'Statistics of the defence expenditure of the chief military and naval powers', *Royal Stat. Soc. J.* liv (1891), 1–21.

2674 MAURICE (*Sir* [JOHN] FREDERICK). National defences. 1897.

2675 WILKINSON (HENRY SPENSER). War and policy: essays. 1900. New edn. 1910.

2676 CHILDERS ([ROBERT] ERSKINE). The riddle of the sands: a record of secret service recently achieved. 1903. Numerous edns.

A splendid novel about a German invasion of England.

2677 CALLWELL (*Sir* CHARLES EDWARD). Military operations and maritime preponderance: their relations and interdependence. Edin. & Lond. 1905.

See also his *The effect of maritime command on land campaigns since Waterloo*, Edin. & Lond. 1897.

2678 REPINGTON (CHARLES À COURT). Imperial strategy: by the military correspondent of *The Times*. 1906.

See also his *Essays and criticisms: by the military correspondent of* The Times, 1911. For his life before 1914 see his own *Vestigia* [: *reminiscences of peace and war*], Lond., Boston, & N.Y. 1919, and Mary Repington, *Thanks for the memory*, 1938.

2679 ASTON (*Sir* GEORGE GREY). Sea, land and air strategy: a comparison. Lond. & Boston. 1914.

2680 [ROYAL] UNITED SERVICE INSTITUTION. Journal. 1857+.

2681 NAVAL AND MILITARY MAGAZINE. 1827+.

Title became *The united service j.* etc., 1829–43, *Colburn's united service magazine*, 1843–90, *United service magazine*, 1890–1920, *The army quarterly*, 1920+.

2682 ARMY AND NAVY GAZETTE. 1860–1921.

Absorbed *The broad arrow: the naval and military gazette*, 1868–1917, and *The naval and military record*, Plymouth, etc. 1886–1936.

2683 CLARKE (IGNATIUS FREDERICK). Voices prophesying war, 1783–1984. 1966.

On books about conjectural wars and invasions. The most famous of these during the period was [Sir George Tomkyns Chesney] *The battle of Dorking: reminiscences of a volunteer*, Edin. & Lond. 1871, on which see Clarke's 'The battle of Dorking, 1871–1914', *Victorian studs.* viii (1964–5), 308–28. For other threats of the invasion of Britain see Sir Herbert William Richmond, *The invasion of Britain: an account of plans, attempts & counter measures from 1586 to 1918*, 1941.

2684 TATE (MERZE). The disarmament illusion: the movement for a limitation of armaments to 1907. N.Y. 1942.

2685 CARNEGIE ENDOWMENT FOR INTERNATIONAL PEACE. The proceedings of the Hague peace conferences: translation of the official texts. Ed. by James Brown Scott. The conference of 1899. N.Y. 1920. The conference of 1907. 3 v. N.Y. 1920–1. Index to the 4 v. N.Y. 1921.

The Carnegie Endowment also publ. *The reports to the Hague conferences of 1899 and 1907* . . ., Oxf. 1917, and *The Hague conventions and declarations of 1899 and 1907* . . ., N.Y. 1915, both ed. by James Brown Scott. On the Hague conferences see James Brown Scott, *The Hague peace conferences of 1899 and 1907* . . ., 2 v. Baltimore, Md. 1909, and Alexander Pearce Higgins, *The Hague peace conferences and other international conferences concerning the laws and usages of war: texts of conventions with commentaries*, Camb. 1909.

2686  TREBILCOCK (CLIVE). '"Spin-off" in British economic history: armaments and industry, 1760–1914.' *Econ. Hist. Rev.* 2 ser. xxii (1969), 474–90.

See also his 'A "special relationship"—government, rearmament, and the cordite firms', *Econ. Hist. Rev.* 2 ser. xix (1966), 364–79.

2687  VAGTS (ALFRED). The military attaché. Princeton. 1967.

2688  MILNE COMMITTEE ON ARMY AND NAVY MEDICAL OFFI-CERS. Report and evidence of the committee on the position, etc. of the medical officers of the army and navy presided over by Vice Admiral Sir A[lexander] Milne. H.C. 515 (1866). LX, 85.

Unusual, in being an inquiry on a two-service basis. See also **2763** and **2904**.

2689  CARTER (THOMAS). Medals of the British army and how they were won: the Crimean campaign. 1861. Rev. edn. [to 1892] by William Henry Long. 1893.

An attractive compilation eventually superseded by the works of the medal-collectors. See also D. Hastings Irwin, *War medals and decorations issued to the British military and naval forces and allies from 1588 to 1889*, 1890, 4th edn. [1588 to 1910] 1910; William Augustus Steward, *War medals and their history*, 1915, 2nd edn [*The ABC of war medals and decorations*] 1918; and Algernon Archibald Payne, *A handbook of British and foreign orders, war medals and decorations awarded to the army and navy, chiefly described from those in the collection of A. A. Payne . . .*, Sheffield 1911. There is a comprehensive modern handbook: Lawrence Lee Gordon, *British battles and medals: a description of every campaign medal and bar awarded from the Armada, 1588, to the India service medal, 1946 . . .*, Aldershot 1947, 2nd edn. 1950.

2690  CREAGH (*Sir* [GARRETT] O'MOORE) *and* HUMPHRIS (EDITH M.) *eds.* The V.C. and D.S.O.: a complete record of all those officers and men of his majesty's naval, military and air forces who have been awarded these decorations . . . with descriptions of the deeds and services which won the distinctions . . . 3 v. [1924.]

Sir John George Smyth, *The story of the Victoria Cross, 1856–1963*, 1963, is an outline hist.

## B. THE ARMY

### 1. GENERAL

2691  WAR OFFICE. Catalogue of the library. Comp. by F. S. Hudleston. 4 v. 1906–16. Annual suppls. 1912+.

The subject index is an invaluable working tool. The War Office Libr. also issues over 1,000 mimeographed subject lists which are of the greatest value. *The catalogue of the library of the Royal United Service Institution*, 2nd edn. 1908, and *The subject list of works on military and naval arts, in the library of the Patent Office*, 1907, contain some works not in the War Office Libr. For the pre-1914 period the General Staff issued *Recent publications of military interest*, 1907–11, cont. as *The army review*, 1911–14.

2692  PUBLIC RECORD OFFICE. List of War Office Records . . . Vol. I. P.R.O. Lists and indexes. No. XXVIII. 1908. Repr. N.Y. 1963.

Cont. by *Lists and indexes supplementary series, no. VIII: list of War Office records vol. I,*
*continuing lists and indexes no. XXVIII,* N.Y. 1968. For search purposes *An alphabetical*
*guide to certain War Office and other military records preserved in the Public Record Office,*
P.R.O. lists and indexes, no. LIII, 1931, repr. N.Y. 1963 may also be useful.

2693 WAR OFFICE. Army list: list of all officers of the army and the Royal
Marines. 1756+.

Became the *Monthly army list,* 1881+. Suppl. by *The new annual army list* [*Hart's army*
*list*], annual, 1839–1915, and *The official army list,* 1880–1913, cont. as *The quarterly*
*army list,* 1913–22. The landmarks in the career of each officer were noted in the short-
lived *Whitaker's naval and military directory and Indian army list,* 1898, 1900.

2694 FORTESCUE (*Sir* JOHN WILLIAM). A history of the British army
[to 1870]. 13 v. 1899–1930.

Standard, but deals with only part of the period: vol. XII covers 1839–52, vol. XIII
1852–70.

2695 BARNETT (CORELLI DOUGLAS). Britain and her army, 1509–1970,
a military, political and social survey. 1970.

A good short hist. Much wider in scope than Peter Young, *The British army,* 1967;
David Henry Cole and Edgar Charles Priestley, *An outline of British military history,*
*1660–1936,* 1939; Eric William Sheppard, *A short history of the British army to 1914,*
1926, 4th edn. 1950; and Sir George Compton Archibald Arthur, *From Wellington to*
*Wavell,* 1942. For interpretation see also John Frederic Charles Fuller, *The army in my*
*time,* 1935; and Peter Young and James Philip Lawford, eds., *History of the British*
*army,* 1970.

2696 SOCIETY FOR ARMY HISTORICAL RESEARCH. Journal. 1921+.

The main j. for army hist., but see also the Royal United Service Instn., *Journal* (**2680**)
and *The army quarterly,* 1920+.

2697 LUVAAS (JAY). The education of an army: British military thought,
1815–1940. Chicago. 1964. Lond. 1965.

See also H. Moyse-Bartlett, 'Military historiography, 1850–1860', *Soc. Army Hist. Res.*
*J.* xlv (1967), 199–213.

2698 BOND (BRIAN JAMES) *ed.* Victorian military campaigns. 1967.
Good.

2699 PRATT (EDWIN A.). The rise of rail power in war and conquest, 1833
to 1914. 1915.

## 2. MILITARY ADMINISTRATION

2700 OMOND (JOHN STUART). Parliament and the army, 1642–1904.
Camb. 1933.

The best intro. to army admin. But see also Constitutionalist, pseud. of Arthur Lawrence
Haliburton, Baron Haliburton, *Army administration in three centuries,* 1901.

2701 WHEELER (OWEN). The War Office: past and present. 1914.

The best account. But see also Hampden Charles Gordon, *The War Office*, Whitehall Ser. 1935. There is only a little pre-1914 material in Sir Sam Fay, *The War Office at war*, 1937, and Sir Guy Douglas Arthur Fleetwood Wilson, *Letters to somebody: a retrospect*, 1922.

2702 CAMBRIDGE. The royal George, 1819–1904: the life of H.R.H. Prince George, Duke of Cambridge. By Giles St. Aubyn. Lond. 1963. N.Y. 1964.

See also [James] Edgar Sheppard, *H.R.H. George, Duke of Cambridge: a memoir of his private life, based on the journals and correspondence of His Royal Highness*, 2 v. 1906, Joachim Hayward Stocqueler, pseud. of Joachim Heyward Siddons, *A personal history of the Horse Guards from 1750 to 1872*, 1873, and Brian James Bond, 'The retirement of the Duke of Cambridge', *Royal United Service Instn. J.* cvi (1961), 544–53. The Duke was commander-in-chief, 1856–95.

2703 CARDWELL. Lord Cardwell at the War Office: a history of his administration, 1868–1874. By Sir Robert Biddulph. 1904.

For a more recent view see Brian James Bond, 'The effect of the Cardwell reforms in army organization, 1874–1904', *Royal United Service Instn. J.* cv (1960), 515–24, and 'Prelude to the Cardwell reforms, 1856–68', ibid. cvi (1961), 229–36, and Albert V. Tucker, 'Army and society in England, 1870–1900: a reassessment of the Cardwell reforms', *J. British Studs.* ii (1962–3), pt. 2, 110–41.

2704 HALIBURTON. Lord Haliburton: a memoir of his public service. By James Beresford Atlay. 1909.

Served in the civil admin. of the army 1855–97.

2705 HAMER (WILLIAM SPENCER). The British army: civil–military relations, 1885–1905. 1970.

See also Albert V. Tucker, 'The issue of army reform in the unionist government, 1903–5', *Hist. J.* ix (1966), 90–100.

2706 DAWSON (ROBERT McGREGOR). 'The cabinet minister and administration: the British War Office, 1903–1916'. *Canadian J. Econ. & Pol. Sci.* v (1939), 451–78.

2707 BOND (BRIAN JAMES). 'Richard Burdon Haldane at the War Office, 1905–1912'. *Army Quart.* lxxxvi (1963), 33–43.

2708 TYLER (JOHN ECCLESFIELD). The British Army and the Continent, 1904–1914. 1938.

Largely repl. by Williamson (**2668**).

2709 HITTLE (JAMES DONALD). The military staff: its history and development. Harrisburg, Pa. 1944. 3rd edn. 1961.

See also War Office (General Staff), *Staff manual*, 1912.

2710 DE FONBLANQUE (EDWARD BARRINGTON). Treatise on the administration and organization of the British army, with especial reference to finance and supply. 1858. Repr. 1970.

2711 PETRIE (MARTIN) *comp.* Organization, composition, and strength of the army of Great Britain. War Office. 1863. 5th edn. [1868.]

A very useful official manual.

2712 CLODE (CHARLES MATHEW). The military forces of the crown: their administration and government. 2 v. 1869.

A legalistic 'constitutional hist.'. Suppl. by his *The administration of justice under military and martial law*, 1872, 2nd edn. 1874, *The statutory powers of her majesty's principal secretary of state for the War Department, ordnance branch*, 1879, and *The statutes relating to the War Office and to the army* . . ., 1880. All are mines of useful material. The main source for military law is *Manual of military law*, War Office, 1884, 6th edn. 1914. The principal contemp. textbook was Sisson Cooper Pratt, *Military law: its procedure and practice*, 1883, 19th edn. 1915.

2713 GOODENOUGH (*Sir* WILLIAM HOWLEY) *and* DALTON (JAMES CECIL). The army book for the British Empire: a record of the development and present composition of the military forces and their duties in peace and war. 1893.

Good.

2714 DUNCOMBE-JEWELL (LOUIS CHARLES RICHARD) *afterwards* CAMERON (LUDOVICK CHARLES RICHARD) *ed.* The handbook to British military stations abroad. 1898.

2715 SELECT COMMITTEE ON MILITARY ORGANIZATION, 1859–60. Report from the select committee on military organization [Chairman: Sidney Herbert and Sir James Graham]. H.C. 441 (1860). VII, 1.

An inquiry into the changes made in 1855.

2716 HARTINGTON COMMITTEE ON THE ORGANISATION OF THE WAR OFFICE. Copy of any report or reports recently made upon the organisation of the war office. H.C. 184 (1865). XXXI, 601.

Consists of four short reports by a committee presided over by Lord Hartington.

2717 NORTHBROOK COMMITTEE ON THE ARMY DEPART-MENTS. Reports of a committee appointed to inquire into the arrangements in force for the conduct of business in the army departments [Chairman: Lord Northbrook]. [C. 54] H.C. (1870). XII, 1.

2718 MEMORANDUM ON MILITARY ORGANIZATION, 1872. Memorandum by His Royal Highness the Field Marshal Commanding in Chief on the proposal of the Secretary of State for War for the organization of the various military land forces of the country, and report of a committee on the details involved therein. [C. 493] H.C. (1872). XXXVII, 383. Supplementary report of the committee. [C. 588] H.C. (1872). XIV, 63. Final report. [C. 712] H.C. (1873). XVIII, 1.

2719 AIREY COMMITTEE ON ARMY RE-ORGANIZATION. Report of a committee of general and other officers of the army on army re-organization

[President: Lord Airey]. [C. 2791] H.C. (1881). XXI, 185. Reports and other documents relating to army organization. [C. 2792] H.C. (1881). XXI, 1.

2720 CHURCHILL COMMITTEE ON ARMY AND NAVY ESTI-MATES. First report from the select committee on army and navy estimates [Chairman: Lord Randolph Churchill]. H.C. 216 (1887). VIII, 1. Appendix. H.C. 216–I (1887). VIII, 241. Second report. H.C. 223 (1887). VIII, 343. Appendix. H.C. 223–I (1887). VIII, 415. Third report. H.C. 232 (1887). VIII, 443. Appendix. H.C. 232–I (1887). VIII, 519. Fourth report. H.C. 239 (1887). VIII, 541. Fifth report. H.C. 259 (1887). VIII, 639. Appendix. H.C. 259–I (1887). VIII, 725.

The inquiry was cont. in the following session: First report. H.C. 120 (1888). VIII, 391. Second report. H.C. 212 (1888). VIII, 549. Third report. H.C. 225 (1888). VIII, 871. Fourth report. H.C. 269, H.C. 269–I, H.C. 269–II (1888). IX, 1, 247, 267. Fifth and final report. H.C. 285 (1888). IX, 325. Index. H.C. 285–I (1888). IX, 351.

2721 BRODRICK COMMITTEE ON DECENTRALISATION OF WAR OFFICE BUSINESS. Report of a committee appointed by the Secretary of State for War to consider the decentralisation of War Office business [Chairman: W. St. John Brodrick]. [C. 8934] H.C. (1898). XIII, 123.

2722 DAWKINS COMMITTEE ON WAR OFFICE ORGANISATION. Report of the committee appointed to inquire into War Office organisation [Chairman: Clinton E. Dawkins]. [Cd. 580] H.C. (1901). XL, 179. Minutes of evidence. [Cd. 581] H.C. (1901). XL, 207.

2723 ESHER COMMITTEE ON WAR OFFICE (RECONSTITUTION). Report of the War Office (reconstitution) committee [Chairman: Viscount Esher]. Part I. [Cd. 1932] H.C. (1904). VIII, 101. Part II. [Cd. 1968] H.C. (1904). VIII, 121. Part III. [Cd. 2002] H.C. (1904). VIII, 157.

2724 JACKSON COMMITTEE ON WAR OFFICE CONTRACTS. Report from the select committee on War Office contracts [Chairman: William Lawies Jackson]. H.C. 313 (1900). IX, 1.

2725 MONCK COMMITTEE ON BARRACK ACCOMMODATION. Report from an official committee on barrack accommodation for the army [Chairman: Viscount Monck]. H.C. 405 (1854–5). XXXII, 37.

See also *General report of the commission appointed for improving the sanitary condition of barracks and hospitals* [Chairman: John Sutherland]. [2839] H.C. (1861). XVI, 1. Appendixes. [3084] H.C. (1863). XIII, 117. [3207] H.C. (1863). XIII, 475, and *Report of a committee appointed by the Secretary of State for War to consider and report as to the measures that should be adopted in order to simplify and improve the system under which all works and buildings (other than fortifications) connected with the War department are constructed, repaired and maintained* . . . [Chairman: Percy Egerton Herbert]. [3041] H.C. (1862). XXXIII, 507.

2726 WILSON PATTEN COMMITTEE ON COURTS MARTIAL. First report of the commissioners appointed to inquire into the constitution and practice of courts martial in the army, and the present system of punishment for military offences [Chairman: John Wilson Patten]. [4114] H.C. (1868–9). XII, 131. Second report. [4114–I] H.C. (1868–9). XII, 141.

2727 PAULTON COMMITTEE ON EMPLOYMENT OF MILITARY IN CASES OF DISTURBANCES. Report of the select committee on employment of military in cases of disturbances [Chairman: J. M. Paulton]. H.C. 236 (1908). VII, 365.

### 3. RECRUITMENT AND TRAINING

2728 BOND (BRIAN JAMES). 'Recruiting the Victorian army, 1870–92'. *Victorian Studs.* v (1961–2), 331–8.

See also Sir Alexander Murray Tulloch, 'On the pay and income of the British soldier as compared with the rate of agricultural wages', *Stat. Soc. J.* xxvi (1863), 168–85.

2729 DE WATTEVILLE (HERMAN GASTON). The British soldier: his daily life from Tudor to modern times. 1954.

A social hist. of the army. Comparable popular works are Douglas Gordon Browne, *Private Thomas Atkins: a history of the British soldier from 1840 to 1940* [1940], and John Laffin, *Tommy Atkins: the story of the English soldier*, 1966. See also Eric William Sheppard, comp., *Red coat: an anthology of the British soldier during the last three hundred years*, 1952, and Tom Henderson McGuffie, comp., *Rank and file: the common soldier at peace and war, 1642–1914*, 1964.

2730 TREVELYAN (*Sir* CHARLES EDWARD). The purchase system in the British army. 1867. 2nd edn. 1867.

2731 SOMERSET COMMISSION ON PURCHASE AND SALE OF COMMISSIONS. Report of the commissioners appointed to inquire into the system of purchase and sale of commissions in the army [Chairman: Duke of Somerset]. [2267] H.C. (1857 Sess. 2). XVIII, I. Further papers. H.C. 498 (1857–8). XXXVII, 409. H.C. 71 (1859 Sess. 1). XV, 13. H.C. 114 (1859 Sess. 1). XV, 43. H.C. 172 (1859 Sess. 1). XV, 69. H.C. 173 (1859 Sess. 1). XV, 123.

See also *Army purchase commission: report of the Right Honble Edward Ellice, M.P., Lieut. General Edward Buckley Wynyard, C.B., and Major-General Sir Henry John Bentinck, K.C.B.* [2292] H.C. (1857–8). XIX, 233, and *Report of the commissioners appointed to inquire into certain memorials from officers in the army, with reference to the abolition of purchase* [Chairman: Sir William Milbourne James]. [C. 1018] H.C. (1874). XII, I.

2732 HERBERT COMMISSION ON PROMOTION AND RETIRE-MENT IN THE ARMY. Report of the commissioners appointed to inquire into the question of promotion and retirement in the higher ranks of the army, commencing with the rank of major [Chairman: Sidney Herbert]. [2418] H.C. (1857–8). XIX, 241.

2733 DALHOUSIE COMMISSION ON RECRUITING FOR THE ARMY. Report of the commissioners appointed to inquire into the recruiting for the army [Chairman: Earl of Dalhousie]. [3752] H.C. (1867). XV, I.

2734 CHILDERS COMMITTEE ON ARMY RETIREMENT. Report from the select committee on army (system of retirement) [Chairman: H. C. E. Childers]. H.C. 482 (1867). VII, 1.

2735 PENZANCE COMMISSION ON ARMY PROMOTION AND RETIREMENT. Report of the royal commission on army promotion and retirement [Chairman: Lord Penzance]. [C. 1569] H.C. (1876). XV, 77.

2736 AKERS-DOUGLAS COMMITTEE ON OFFICER TRAINING. Report of the committee appointed to consider the education and training of officers of the army [Chairman: Aretas Akers-Douglas]. [Cd. 982] H.C. (1902). X, 193. Evidence [Cd. 983] H.C. (1902). X, 347.
Important.

2737 WARD COMMITTEE ON PROVISION OF OFFICERS. Interim report of the War Office committee on the provision of officers (a) for service with the regular army in war, and (b) for the auxiliary forces [Chairman: Sir E. W. D. Ward]. [Cd. 3294] H.C. (1907). XLIX, 549. Minutes of evidence. [Cd. 3295] H.C. (1907). XLIX, 577.
See also *Report of the committee appointed . . . to enquire into the nature of the expenses incurred by officers of the army, and to suggest measures for bringing commissions within reach of men of moderate means* [Chairman: Lord Stanley]. [Cd. 1421] H.C. (1903). X, 535.

2738 GROVE COMMITTEE ON PROMOTIONS. Report of the War Office committee on promotion to colonel and general [Chairman: Sir Coleridge Grove]. [Cd. 2995] H.C. (1906). LXVII, 419.

2739 BOND (BRIAN JAMES). The Victorian army and the staff college, 1854–1914. 1972.
See also Sir Alfred Reade Godwin-Austen, *The staff and the staff college,* 1927, and Francis Coningsby Hannam Clarke, *Staff duties: a series of lectures . . .,* 1884, rev. edn. 1890.

2740 WHITE (ARCHIE CECIL THOMAS). The story of army education, 1643–1963. 1963.
See also T. A. Bowyer-Bower, 'Some sources for the history of education in the British army during the 19th century', *Brit. J. of Educational Studs.* iv (1955–6), 71–7.

2741 THOMAS (HUGH SWYNNERTON). The story of Sandhurst. 1961.
See also Sir John George Smyth, *Sandhurst: the history of the Royal Military Academy, Woolwich, the Royal Military College, Sandhurst, and the Royal Military Academy, Sandhurst, 1741–1961,* 1961.

2742 DUFFERIN COMMISSION ON MILITARY EDUCATION. First report of the royal commission appointed to inquire into the present state of military education and into the training of candidates for commissions in the army [Chairman: Lord Dufferin]. [4221] H.C. (1868–9). XXII, 1. Minutes of evidence. [C. 25] H.C. (1870). XXIV, 1. Analysis of evidence. [C. 25–I] H.C. (1870). XXIV, 585. Second report. [C. 214] H.C. (1870). XXIV, 701.

See also **2736**.

**2743** BAYNES (JOHN). Morale: a study of men and courage: the Second Scottish Rifles at the battle of Neuve Chapelle, 1915. 1967.

An unusual study of pre-war training and morale-building in a single regiment.

### 4. MAIN BRANCHES OF THE ARMY

**2744** WHITE (ARTHUR SHARPIN) *comp.* A bibliography of regimental histories of the British army. Soc. for Army Hist. Res. and Army Museum Ogilby Trust. 1965.

An invaluable guide to a large and perplexing literature. Omits Indian regiments. Henry Manners Chichester and George Burges-Short, *The records and badges of every regiment and corps in the British army*, 1895, 2nd edn. 1900, is a useful handbook. For changes of title see Arthur Swinson, ed., *A register of the regiments and corps of the British army*, 1972.

**2745** COOPER (LEONARD). British regular cavalry, 1644–1914. 1965.

A very brief outline. See also George Taylor Denison, *A history of cavalry from the earliest times, with lessons for the future*, 1877, 2nd edn. 1913.

**2746** BOND (BRIAN JAMES). 'Doctrine and training in the British cavalry, 1870–1914'. In Michael Eliot Howard, ed., *The theory and practice of war: essays presented to Captain B. H. Liddell Hart*. 1965. Pp. 95–125.

**2747** PORTER (WHITWORTH). History of the corps of Royal Engineers. 2 v. 1889. Suppl. [v. 3] by Sir Charles Moore Watson. 1915.

The R.E. publ. a *Journal*, Chatham 1870+, and *Papers* [subsequently *Professional papers*], London & Chatham 1837–1918. For the R.E. in India see **1171**, and in Egypt and the Sudan see **1665**.

**2748** LANSDOWNE COMMITTEE ON ROYAL ENGINEERS IN CIVIL DEPARTMENTS. Report of the committee appointed to enquire into the employment of officers, Royal Engineers, in the civil departments of the state, 1870 [Chairman: Marquess of Lansdowne]. [C. 276]. H.C. (1871). XIV, 139.

**2749** CALLWELL (*Sir* CHARLES) *and* HEADLAM (*Sir* JOHN EMERSON WHARTON). The history of the Royal Artillery from the Indian mutiny to the Great War. 3 v. Woolwich. 1931–40.

There is also John Kane and others, *List of officers of the Royal Regiment of Artillery from the year 1716 to the year 1899 . . .*, 4th edn. 1900, suppl. by Frederick Cyril Morgan, ed., *List of officers of the Royal Regiment of Artillery from June 1862 to June 1914 . . .*, Sheffield 1914.

**2750** MAURICE-JONES (KENNETH WYN). The history of coast artillery in the British army. 1959.

2751 AIREY COMMITTEE ON ARTILLERY ORGANIZATION. Report of the Adjutant-General [Sir Richard Airey] upon the organization of the Royal Artillery . . . [C. 561] H.C. (1872). XIV, 69.

The report and minutes of evidence of a War Office committee of inquiry, presided over by Airey. Full. See also *Report of a committee on the education of artillery officers* [President: Sir E. C. Warde]. [C. 258] H.C. (1871). XIV, 1, and *Report of the committee on the organization of the Royal Artillery*, 27th April, 1888 [Chairman: Lord Harris]. [C. 5491] H.C. (1888). XXV, 207.

2752 YOLLAND COMMISSION ON TRAINING OFFICERS FOR THE SCIENTIFIC CORPS. Report of the commissioners appointed to consider the best mode of re-organizing the system for training officers for the scientific corps; together with an account of foreign and other military education [Chairman: William Yolland]. [O. 52] H.C. (1857–Sess. 1). VI, 1. Appendix. [O. 53] H.C. (1857–Sess. 1). VI, 555.

On the engineers and artillery. See also *Report of a committee on the admission of university candidates to the scientific corps* [President: William Napier]. [C. 935] H.C. (1874). XII, 205.

2753 FORTESCUE (*Sir* JOHN WILLIAM) *and* BEADON (ROGER HAMMETT). The Royal Army Service Corps: a history of transport and supply in the British army. 2 v. Camb. 1930–1.

See also Fortescue's *A short account of canteens in the British army*, Camb. 1928, and Charles Henri Massé, *The predecessors of the Royal Army Service Corps* [to 1888], Aldershot 1948. The R.A.S.C. has publ. a *Journal*, Chatham etc. 1891+, and a *Quarterly*, Aldershot 1905+.

2754 STRATHNAIRN COMMISSION ON TRANSPORT AND SUPPLY DEPARTMENTS. Report of a committee appointed by the Secretary of State for War to enquire into the administration of the transport and supply departments of the army [President: Lord Strathnairn]. [3848] H.C. (1867). XV, 343.

See also David Bryce Burn, *Notes on transport and on camel corps*, War Office 1887.

2755 FORBES (ARTHUR). A history of the army ordnance services. 3 v. 1929.

Highly competent.

2756 HOGG (OLIVER FREDERICK GILLILAN). The Royal Arsenal: its background, origin and subsequent history. 2 v. 1963.

Good.

2757 GREY COMMITTEE ON FORTIFICATIONS. Report of the committee appointed to enquire into the construction, condition and cost of the fortifications erected, or in course of erection, under 30th & 31st Vict., and previous statutes [Chairman: Sir Frederick W. Grey]. [4135] H.C. (1868–9). XII, 433. Minutes of evidence. [4135–I] H.C. (1868–9). XII, 559.

2758 NALDER (REGINALD FRANCIS HEATON). The Royal Corps of Signals: a history of its antecedents and development (circa 1800–1955). 1958.

2759 FARMER (HENRY GEORGE). Military music and its story: the rise and development of military music. 1912.

See also his *History of the Royal Artillery Band, 1762–1953*, 1954, Percy Lister Binns, *A hundred years of military music: being, the story of the Royal Military School of Music, Kneller Hall*, Gillingham, Dorset 1959; and Lewis Winstock, *Songs & music of the redcoats: a history of the war music of the British army, 1642–1902*, 1970.

2760 NORRIS (GEOFFREY). The Royal Flying Corps: a history. 1965.

See also Henry Albert Jones and Sir Walter Raleigh, *The war in the air: being, the story of the part played in the Great War by the Royal Air Force*, 6 v. Oxf. 1922–37, and Peter M. H. Lewis, *Squadron histories, R.F.C., R.N.A.S., and R.A.F., 1912–59*, 1959, 2nd edn. 1968. For aircraft see **6380–402.**

2761 SMYTH (*Sir* JOHN GEORGE). In this sign conquer: the story of the army chaplains. 1968.

2762 PETERKIN (ALFRED), JOHNSTON (WILLIAM), *and* DREW (*Sir* ROBERT). Commissioned officers in the medical services of the British army, 1660–1960. 2 v. Wellcome Hist. Med. Libr. Hist. Monograph 14. 1968.

See also John Laffin, *Surgeons in the field*, 1970, and Richard L. Blanco, 'The attempted control of venereal disease in the army of mid-Victorian England', *Soc. Army Hist. Res. J.* 45 (1967), 234–41.

2763 STAFFORD COMMITTEE ON ARMY MEDICAL DEPART-MENT. Report from the select committee on medical department (army) [Chairman: Augustus Stafford]. H.C. 331 (1856). XIII, 359.

See also *Report of the committee appointed to enquire into the pay, status, and conditions of service of medical officers of the army and navy* [Chairman: Earl of Camperdown]. [C. 5810] H.C. (1889). XVII, 137, and *Report of committee appointed by the Secretary of State to consider the reorganization of the army medical services* [Chairman: W. St. John Brodrick]. [Cd. 791] H.C. (1902). X, 131 and **2688.**

2764 HAY (IAN) *pseud. of* BEITH (JOHN HAY). A hundred years of army nursing. 1953.

See also *Report of committee appointed by the Secretary of State to consider the reorganization of the army and Indian nursing service* [Chairman: W. St. John Brodrick]. [Cd. 792] H.C. (1902). X, 143.

2765 SMITH (*Sir* FREDERICK). A history of the Royal Army Veterinary Corps, 1796–1919. 1927.

Smith also publ. *A veterinary history of the war in South Africa, 1899–1902*, 1919.

2766 DUNLOP (*Sir* JOHN KINNINMONT). The development of the British army, 1899–1914: from the eve of the South African war to the eve of the Great War, with special reference to the territorial force. 1938.

See also Harold Trevor Baker, *The territorial force: a manual of its law, organisation and administration*, 1909, and Sir Henry Seton-Karr, *The call to arms, 1900–1901: or, a review of the Imperial yeomanry movement . . .*, 1902. There are no adequate accounts of the volunteer movement, but see Geoffrey Cousins, *The defenders: a history of the British volunteer*, 1968.

2767  RICHMOND COMMISSION ON THE MILITIA. Report of the commissioners appointed to inquire into the establishment, organization, government and direction of the militia of the United Kingdom [Chairman: Duke of Richmond]. [2553] H.C. (1859–Sess. 2). IX, 1.

A full inquiry. Further full investigations took place in 1876 (*Report of the committee appointed by the Secretary of State for War to enquire into certain questions that have arisen with respect to the militia and the present brigade depôt system* [Chairman: Frederick Stanley]. [C. 1654] H.C. (1877). XVIII, 29) and in 1889 (*Report of the committee appointed to enquire into certain questions that have arisen with respect to the militia* [Chairman: Lord Harris]. [C. 5922] H.C. (1890). XIX, 145).

2768  STANLEY COMMITTEE ON YEOMANRY CAVALRY. Report of the committee appointed by the Secretary of State for War to enquire into certain questions that have arisen with respect to the yeomanry cavalry [Chairman: The Hon. Frederick Stanley]. [C. 1352] H.C. (1875). XV, 87.

2769  EVERSLEY COMMISSION ON THE VOLUNTEER FORCE. Report of the commissioners appointed to inquire into the condition of the volunteer force in Great Britain [Chairman: Viscount Eversley]. [3053] H.C. (1862). XXVII, 89.

2770  BURY COMMITTEE ON THE VOLUNTEER FORCE. Reports of the committee appointed by the Secretary of State for War to enquire into the financial state and internal organization of the volunteer force in Great Britain [Chairman: Viscount Bury]. [C. 2235–I] H.C. (1878–9). XV, 181.

See also *Report from the select committee on Volunteer Acts* [Chairman: William Woodall]. H.C. 224 (1894). XV, 631.

2771  WILKINSON (HENRY SPENSER). Citizen soldiers: essays towards the improvement of the volunteer force. 1884. 2nd edn. 1894.

See also his *The volunteers and the national defence*, 1896.

2772  CARMAN (WILLIAM YOUNG). British military uniforms from contemporary pictures: Henry VII to the present day. 1957.

One of a host of books on uniforms of indiv. regiments etc. Cp. Cecil Constant Philip Lawson, *A history of the uniforms of the British army*, 5+ v., 1962+; Robert Money Barnes, *Military uniforms of Britain & the empire, 1742 to the present time*, Imperial services libr. IV, 1960, and *The British army of 1914: its history, uniforms & contemporary continental armies*, Imperial services libr. IX, 1968; R. M. Barnes and others, *The uniforms & history of the Scottish regiments: Britain—Canada—Australia—New Zealand —South Africa: 1625 to the present day* [1956]; and Hugh Cuthbert Basset Rogers, *The mounted troops of the British army, 1066–1945*, Imperial services libr. III, 1959. For prints see also R. G. Thurburn, ed., *Index to British military costume prints, 1500–1914*, 1972.

2773  ROADS (CHRISTOPHER HERBERT). The British soldier's firearm, 1850–1864. 1964.

For military weapons see also Charles John Ffoulkes and Edward Campbell Hopkinson, *Sword, lance & bayonet: a record of the arms of the British army & navy*, Camb. 1938, 2nd edn. Lond. & N.Y. 1967; Robert John Wilkinson Latham, *British military bayonets from 1700 to 1945*, 1967, and *British military swords from 1800 to the present day*, 1966;

Hans Busk, *The rifleman's manual: or, rifles and how to use them*, 2nd edn. 1858, 7th edn. 1860; Edmund George Barton Reynolds, *The Lee Enfield rifle*, 1960; and **5100**. For the equipment of horses see Geoffrey Tylden, *Horses and saddlery: an account of the animals used by the British and Commonwealth armies from the seventeenth century to the present day with a description of their equipment*, Army Museums Ogilby Trust, 1965.

2774 ROGERS (HUGH CUTHBERT BASSET). Troopships and their history. Imperial services libr. VII. 1963.

## 5. CONTEMPORARY STUDIES

2775 MARTIN (CHARLES). Constitution et puissance militaires comparées de la France et de l'Angleterre: l'armée britannique, son organisation, sa composition et son effectif, sa force et sa faiblesse, sa distribution entre la métropole et les colonies anglaises. Paris. 1863.

2776 SYKES (WILLIAM HENRY). 'Comparison of the organisation and cost in detail of the English and French armies'. *Stat. Soc. J.* xxvii (1864), 1–69.
An early attempt to cost the British army.

2777 HAMLEY (*Sir* EDWARD BRUCE). The operations of war explained and illustrated. Edin. & Lond. 1866. 5th edn. 2 v. 1900. New edn. 1907.
Long the standard textbook used in training. Cp. Robert Home, *A precis of modern tactics: compiled from the works of recent continental writers and the statistical department of the War office*, 1873, rev. edn. 1892, and Sir Charles Edward Callwell, *The tactics of to-day*, Edin. & Lond. 1900, 2nd edn. 1909, *The tactics of home defence*, Edin. & Lond. 1908, and *Small wars: their principles and practice*, War Office intelligence div., 1896, 3rd edn. 1906.

2778 HAVELOCK (*Sir* HENRY MARSHAM). Three main military questions of the day: I. a home reserve army. II. the more economic military tenure of India. III. cavalry as affected by breachloading arms. 1867.

2779 SYNGE (MILLINGTON HENRY). On the defence of England: a military sketch. Portsmouth. 1872.

2780 DILKE (*Sir* CHARLES WENTWORTH). The British army: by the author of 'Greater Britain'. 1888.

2781 WILKINSON (HENRY SPENCER). The brain of an army: a popular account of the German general staff. 1890. New edn. 1895.
Suppl. by *The brain of the navy*, 1895.

2782 MAURICE (*Sir* JOHN FREDERICK). War: reproduced with amendments from the article in the last edition of the *Encyclopaedia Britannica* to which is added an essay on military literature and a list of books with brief comments. 1891.

2783 HENDERSON (GEORGE FRANCIS ROBERT). The science of war: a collection of essays and lectures, 1892–1903. Ed. by Neill Malcolm. 1905.
One of the best books on warfare.

2784 AMERY (LEOPOLD CHARLES MAURICE STENNETT). The problem of the army. 1903.

One of a number of pamphlets prompted by the Boer War. Cp. 'Linesman', pseud. of Maurice Harold Grant, *The mechanism of war*, Edin. & Lond. 1902, and Thomas David Pilcher, *Some lessons from the Boer War, 1899–1902*, 1903.

2785 ARNOLD-FORSTER (HUGH OAKLEY). The army in 1906: a policy and a vindication. 1906.

Arnold-Forster was a prolific writer on military topics. See also his *Our home army: being a reprint of letters published in* The Times, 1892, *Army letters, 1897–98, reprinted . . . from* The Times, 1898, *The War Office, the army and the empire: a review of the military situation in 1900*, 1900, and *Military needs and military policy*, 1909.

2786 ROBERTS (FREDERICK SLEIGH), *Earl Roberts*. A nation in arms: speeches on the requirements of the British army . . . 1907.

A call for conscription. See also his *Fallacies and facts: an answer to 'Compulsory Service'*, 1911, *Lord Roberts' message to the nation*, 1912, and *Lord Roberts' campaign speeches*, 1913. The opposition to Roberts's views is best rep. by Sir Ian Standish Monteith Hamilton, *Compulsory service: a study of the question in the light of experience*, 1910. See also Theodore Ropp, 'Conscription in Great Britain, 1900–1914: a failure in civil–military communications?', *Military affairs* xx (1956), 71–6.

2787 HALDANE (RICHARD BURDON), *Viscount Haldane*. Army reform and other addresses. 1907.

The views of the Liberal Secretary of State.

2788 EDMONDS (*Sir* JAMES EDWARD) *and* OPPENHEIM (LASSA FRANCIS LAWRENCE). Land warfare: an exposition of the laws and usages of war on land, for the guidance of officers of His Majesty's Army. [1912.]

Helpful in defining a difficult subject.

2789 THE TIMES book of the army. 1914.

## 6. BIOGRAPHY

(in alphabetical order)

2790 TEMPLE (ARTHUR). Our living generals: twelve biographical sketches of distinguished soldiers. 1898.

2791 ADYE. Recollections of a military life. By Sir John Miller Adye. 1895.

2792 ALLENBY. Allenby. By [Robert] Brian Gardner. [1965.]

See also Archibald Percival Wavell, Earl Wavell, *Allenby, a study in greatness: the biography of Field Marshal Viscount Allenby of Megiddo and Felixstowe*, G.C.B., G.C.M.G., 1940, cont. in his *Allenby in Egypt*, 1943; an abridged version of the two vols. was publ. as *Allenby, soldier and statesman*, 1946; and Raymond Savage, *Allenby of Armageddon . . .*, 1925, repr. 1926, 1928.

2793 ARDAGH. The life of Major-General Sir John Ardagh. By his wife, Susan Harris, Countess of Malmesbury. 1909.

2794 BADEN-POWELL. Baden-Powell: the two lives of a hero. By William Hillcourt and Olave, Lady Baden Powell. 1964.

The official life. Robert Stephenson Smyth Baden-Powell, Baron Baden-Powell, himself publ. a number of autobiog. works, incl. *My adventures as a spy*, 1915, *Indian memories* . . ., 1915 [Phila. edn. *Memories of India*, 1915], and *Lessons from the 'varsity' of life*, 1933 [N.Y. edn. *Lessons of a lifetime*, 1933]. Ernest Edwin Reynolds, *Baden-Powell: a biography of Lord Baden-Powell of Gilwell* . . ., 1943, 2nd edn. 1957, is the best of a number of popular biogs. See also **7286**.

2795 BELL. Soldier's glory: being 'Rough notes of an old soldier'. By Sir George Bell. Ed. by Brian Stuart. 1956.

Typical of the class of minor military reminiscences. Cp. Sir Henry Brackenbury, *Some memories of my spare time*, Edin. & Lond. 1909, *Episodes and reflections: being, some records from the life of Major-General Sir Wyndham Childs* . . ., 1930; Sir Richard Harrison, *Recollections of a life in the British army during the latter half of the 19th century*, 1908; William Thomas Jervis-Waldy, *From eight to eighty: the life of a Crimean and Indian mutiny veteran*, 1914; William Munro, *Reminiscences of military service with the 93rd Sutherland Highlanders*, 1883, and *Records of service and campaigning in many lands*, 2 v. 1887.

2796 BIRDWOOD. Khaki and gown: an autobiography. By William Riddell Birdwood, Baron Birdwood. 1941. N.Y. 1957.

See also his *In my time: recollections and anecdotes*, 1946.

2797 BULLER. Life of General the Right Honourable Sir Redvers Buller, V.C., G.C.B., G.C.M.G. By Charles Henderson Melville. 2 v. 1923.

See also **2066**.

2798 BURGOYNE. Life and correspondence of Field Marshal Sir John Burgoyne, bart. By George Wrottesley. 2 v. 1873.

Wrottesley also ed. *The military opinions of General Sir John Fox Burgoyne* . . ., 1859.

2799 BUTLER. Sir William Butler: an autobiography. By Sir William Francis Butler. Ed. by Eileen Butler. Lond. & N.Y. 1911.

See also Edward Alexander McCourt, *Remember Butler: the story of Sir William Butler*, Lond. & Toronto 1967.

2800 CALLWELL. Stray recollections. By Sir Charles Edward Callwell. 2 v. 1923.

Callwell had earlier publ. *Service yarns and memories*, Edin. & Lond. 1912. He was a prolific writer, for whose works see index.

2801 CLARKE. Life of Lieutenant-General the Hon. Sir Andrew Clarke G.C.M.G., C.B., C.I.E., colonel-commandant of Royal Engineers, agent-general of Victoria, Australia. Ed. by Robert Hamilton Vetch. 1905.

Demonstrates the diverse opportunities open to an engineer officer in the colonies and at home.

2802  COLLEY. The life of Sir George Pomeroy-Colley, K.C.S.I., C.B., C.M.G., 1835–1881: including services in Kaffraria—in China—in Ashanti—in India and in Natal. By Sir William Francis Butler. 1899.

2803  COWANS. General Sir John Cowans, G.C.B., G.C.M.G., the quartermaster general of the Great War. By [Wellesley William] Desmond [Mountjoy] Chapman-Huston and Owen Rutter. 2 v. 1924.

2804  FRENCH. The life of Field Marshal Sir John French, first Earl of Ypres, K.P., G.C.B., O.M., G.C.V.O., K.C.M.G. By Edward Gerald Fleming French. 1931.

Gerald French also ed., *Some war diaries, addresses and correspondence of Field Marshal the Right Honble the Earl of Ypres*, 1937, and French's *1914*, Lond. & N.Y. 1919. French's war diaries, etc. have also been publ.

2805  FULLER. Memoirs of an unconventional soldier. By John Frederic Charles Fuller. 1936.

2806  GLEICHEN. A guardsman's memories: a book of recollections. By Lord [Albert] Edward [Wilfred] Gleichen. Edin. & Lond. 1932.

See also 1686 and 1707.

2807  GOUGH. Soldiering on: being the memoirs of General Sir Hubert Gough. 1954.

2808  GRENFELL. Memoirs of Field Marshal Lord Grenfell [Francis Wallace Grenfell, Baron Grenfell]. 1925.

2809  GRIERSON. The life of Lieut. General Sir James Moncrieff Grierson. By Duncan Stewart MacDiarmid. 1923.

2810  HAIG. Haig. By Alfred Duff Cooper, Viscount Norwich. 2 v. 1935–6.

See also John Charteris, [*Field Marshal Earl*] *Haig*, Lond. & N.Y. 1929; John Terraine, *Douglas Haig: the educated soldier*, 1963 [publ. in the U.S. as *Ordeal of victory*, Phila. 1963]; Robert Norman William Blake, ed., *The private papers of Douglas Haig, 1914–1919 . . .*, 1952; Sir George Compton Archibald Arthur, *Lord Haig*, 1928; Sir John Humphrey Davidson, *Haig: master of the field*, 1953; George Simpson Duncan, *Douglas Haig as I knew him*, 1966; and Dorothy Maud Vivian Haig, Countess Haig, *The man I knew*, Edin. & Lond. 1936.

2811  HAMILTON. The happy warrior: a life of General Sir Ian Hamilton, G.C.B., G.C.M.G., D.S.O. By Ian Bogle Monteith Hamilton. 1966.

2812  HAMLEY. The life of General Sir Edward Bruce Hamley, K.C.B., K.C.M.G. By Alexander Innes Shand. 2 v. Edin. & Lond. 1895.

2813  HART. Memoirs of Captain [Basil Henry] Liddell Hart. 2 v. Lond. 1965. 2 v. N.Y. [The Liddell Hart memoirs] 1965.

2814  KITCHENER. Kitchener: portrait of an imperialist. By Sir Philip Montefiore Magnus [-Allcroft]. 1958.

Sir George Compton Archibald Arthur, *Life of Lord Kitchener*, 3 v., 1920, is a useful quarry. Reginald Balliol Brett, Viscount Esher, *The tragedy of Lord Kitchener*, Lond. & N.Y. 1921, is perceptive. James Bacon Rye and H. G. Groser pieced together speeches for *Kitchener in his own words* [1917]. Sir Hedley Francis Le Bas, *The Lord Kitchener memorial book*, 1917, incls. his war speeches and tributes by distinguished people. His work in Palestine, 1874-8, is the subject of Samuel Daiches, *Lord Kitchener and his work in Palestine*, 1915. His Great War services lie outside the scope of this bibliog. There are many popular lives listed in the British Museum catalogue (5). See also Joseph O. Baylen, *Lord Kitchener and the viceroyalty of India, 1910*, Oklahoma State Univ., Soc. Sci. Ser. 12, Stillwater, Okla. [1964?].

**2815  LYTTELTON.** Eighty years: soldiering, politics, games. By Sir Neville Gerald Lyttelton. 1927.

**2816  McCALMONT.** The memoirs of Major General Sir Hugh McCalmont. Ed. by Sir Charles Edward Callwell. 1924.

**2817  MACREADY.** Annals of an active life. By Sir [Cecil Frederick] Nevil Macready. 2 v. Lond. 1924. N.Y. 1925.

**2818  MAUDE.** The life of Sir Stanley Maude, lieutenant general, K.C.B., C.M.G., D.S.O. By Sir Charles Edward Callwell. 1920.

**2819  MAURICE.** Sir Frederick Maurice: a record of his work and opinions: with eight essays on discipline and national efficiency. Ed. by Sir Frederick Barton Maurice. 1913.

**2820  MAXWELL.** General Sir John Maxwell. By Sir George Compton Archibald Arthur. 1932.

**2821  MAY.** Changes & chances of a soldier's life. By Sir Edward Sinclair May. 1925.

**2822  MEINERTZHAGEN.** Army diary, 1899-1926. By Richard Meinertzhagen. Edin. & Lond. 1960.

For his early years see his *Diary of a black sheep*, Edin. & Lond. 1964. Suppl. by his *Kenya diary, 1902–1906*, Edin. & Lond. 1957.

**2823  PARR.** Recollections and correspondence of Sir Henry Hallam Parr. Ed. by Sir Charles Fortescue-Brickdale. 1917.

**2824  RAWLINSON.** The life of General Lord Rawlinson of Trent from his journals and letters. Ed. by Sir Frederick Barton Maurice. Lond. 1928. Boston [Soldier, artist, sportsman . . .]. 1928.

**2825  ROBERTS.** Lord Roberts. By David Pelham James. 1954.

Frederick Sleigh Roberts, Earl Roberts himself publ. *Forty-one years in India: from subaltern to commander-in-chief*, 2 v. Lond. & N.Y. 1897, 34th edn. 1901. His *Letters written during the Indian mutiny*, were publ. in 1924. There are a number of short lives, of which Sir George William Forrest, *The life of Lord Roberts, K.G., V.C.*, Lond. 1914, N.Y. 1915, is the best.

2826  ROBERTSON. From private to field marshal. By Sir William Robert Robertson. Lond. & Boston. 1921.

See also his *Soldiers and statesmen, 1914–1918,* 2 v. Lond. & N.Y. 1926, and Victor Bonham-Carter, *Soldier true: the life and times of Field Marshal Sir William Robertson, G.C.B., G.C.M.G., K.C.V.O., D.S.O., 1860–1933,* 1963, publ. in N.Y. as *The strategy of victory, 1914–1918.*

2827  SMITH-DORRIEN. Smith-Dorrien. By Colin Robert Ballard. 1931.

See also Sir Horace Lockwood Smith-Dorrien, *Memories of forty-eight years' service,* Lond. & N.Y. 1925, and Alan Jack Smithers, *The man who disobeyed: Sir Horace Smith-Dorrien and his enemies,* 1970.

2828  SYKES. From many angles: an autobiography. By Sir Frederick Hugh Sykes. 1942.

2829  TOWNSHEND. Townshend of Kut: a biography of Major-General Sir Charles Townshend. By Arthur James Barker. 1967.

2830  WARREN. The life of General Sir Charles Warren, G.C.M.G., K.C.B., F.R.S., colonel commandant, royal engineers. By Watkin Wynn Williams. Oxf. 1941.

Warren himself publ. *On the veldt in the seventies,* 1902.

2831  WATSON. Watson pasha: a record of the life work of Sir Charles Moore Watson, K.C.M.G., C.B., M.A., colonel in the royal engineers. By Stanley Lane Poole and Walter William Skeat. 1919.

Like Sir C. W. Wilson, **2832**, noted for a distinguished career in the Middle east.

2832  WILSON. The life of Major-General Sir Charles William Wilson, royal engineers, K.C.B., K.C.M.G., F.R.S., D.C.L., LL.D., M.E. By Sir Charles Moore Watson. 1909.

2833  WILSON. Field Marshal Sir Henry Wilson, Bart., G.C.B., D.S.O., his life and diaries. By Sir Charles Edward Callwell. 2 v. Lond. & N.Y. 1927.

See also Basil Collier, *Brasshat: a biography of Field Marshal Sir Henry Wilson,* 1961, and Bernard Ash, *The lost dictator: a biography of Field-Marshal Sir Henry Wilson, Bart, G.C.B., D.S.O., M.P.,* 1968.

2834  WOLSELEY. The life of Lord Wolseley. By Sir Frederick Barton Maurice and Sir George Compton Archibald Arthur. 1924.

See also Garnet Joseph Wolseley, Viscount Wolseley, *The story of a soldier's life,* 2 v. Lond. & N.Y. 1903; *The letters of Lord and Lady Wolseley,* ed. by Sir George Compton Archibald Arthur, 1922; *In relief of Gordon: Lord Wolseley's campaign journal of the Khartoum relief expedition, 1884–1885,* ed. by Adrian Preston, 1967; and Joseph Herbert Lehmann, *All Sir Garnet: a life of Field Marshal Lord Wolseley,* 1964, publ. in Boston as *The model major-general . . .,* 1964.

2835  WOOD. From midshipman to field marshal. By Sir [Henry] Evelyn Wood. 2 v. Lond. & N.Y. 1906.

Wood also publ. *Winnowed memories,* 1917.

2836 YOUNGHUSBAND. A soldier's memories in peace and war. By Sir George John Younghusband. Lond. & N.Y. 1917.

Younghusband also publ. *Forty years a soldier*, 1923.

## C. ROYAL NAVY

### I. REFERENCE

2837 NATIONAL MARITIME MUSEUM. Catalogue of the library. 1+ v. H.M.S.O. 1968+.

Very full. Vols. 2–3 cover biog. The best bibliog. is Albion, **6023**. The Admiralty Library *Subject catalogue of printed books*, 1912, is much inferior to its War Office counterpart.

2838 PUBLIC RECORD OFFICE. List of Admiralty records preserved in the Public Record Office. P.R.O. Lists and indexes XVIII. 1904. Repr. N.Y. etc. 1963.

Cont. by P.R.O. Lists and indexes supplementary series VI, *List of Admiralty records* [to 1913], N.Y. etc. 1966–7.

2839 COLLEDGE (JAMES JOSEPH). Ships of the Royal Navy: an historical index. 2 v. Newton Abbot & N.Y. 1969–70.

2840 BRASSEY (THOMAS), *Earl Brassey*. The British navy: its strength, resources and administration. 5 v. 1882–3.

A comprehensive encyclopedia, strong on shipbuilding and naval administration.

2841 BRASSEY (THOMAS), *Earl Brassey*. The naval annual. Portsmouth. 1886+.

Title became *Brassey's naval [and shipping] annual*, 1915+. An indispensable directory and commentary on merchant and warlike shipping. There were also a number of short-lived handbooks such as *O'Byrne's naval annual . . .*, 1855, and *O'Byrne's naval manual . . .*, 1860.

2842 JANE (FREDERICK THOMAS). All the world's fighting ships. [Jane's fighting ships.] 1898+.

Reprs. of the 1898, 1906/7, and 1914 edns. were publ. in Newton Abbot, 1969–70. Deservedly famous.

2843 MANNING (THOMAS DAVYS) *and* WALKER (CHARLES FREDERICK). British warship names. 1959.

Gives details of ships with the same name.

2844 WARNER (OLIVER [MARTIN WILSON]). Battle honours of the Royal Navy. 1956.

Lists naval actions, 1588–1953.

**2845 THE NAVY LIST. 1805+.**

Title *The Royal Navy list, 1878–92, Lean's Royal Navy list, 1893–1901, The Royal Navy list,* 1901+. Lists naval officers.

**2846 NAVY RECORDS SOCIETY. Publications. 1894+.**

Publs. docs. on naval hist.

**2847 SOCIETY FOR NAUTICAL RESEARCH. The mariner's mirror: the journal of the Society for Nautical Research. 1911+.**

Covers the hist. of both Royal and merchant navies. See also *Maritime notes and queries,* 1873–1900, 1883–1901.

**2848 BATTENBERG *afterwards* MOUNTBATTEN (LOUIS ALEXANDER), *Marquess of Milford Haven*. British naval medals, commemorative medals, naval rewards, war medals, naval tokens, portrait medallions, &c. &c. 1919.**

**2849 NAVY LEAGUE. The Navy League annual. 1907–8+.**

A useful handbook. The Navy League, a body that campaigned for the preservation of British naval supremacy, also publ. *The Navy League journal,* 1895–1908, *Navy: organ of the Navy League,* 1909+, *The Navy League quarterly,* 1910+, and an *Annual report,* 1897+.

## 2. HISTORIES

**2850 LLOYD ([CHARLES] CHRISTOPHER). The nation and the navy: a history of naval life and policy. 1954. Rev. edn. 1961.**

A good straightforward chronological hist., comparable with Sir Geoffrey Arthur Romaine Callender, *The naval side of British history,* 1924, new edn. by Francis Harry Hinsley 1952, Michael Arthur Lewis, *The history of the British navy,* 1957, new edn. 1959, and William Cuthbert Brian Tunstall, *The realities of naval history,* 1936. Neither Stanley Hubert Bonnett, *The price of admiralty: an indictment of the Royal Navy, 1805–1966,* 1968, nor Leslie Gardiner, *The British admiralty,* Edin. & Lond. 1968, adds anything of value to Lloyd. On naval customs there is a popular introduction by [Forster] Delafield Arnold Forster, *The ways of the navy,* 1931.

**2851 LEWIS (MICHAEL ARTHUR). The navy of Britain: a historical portrait. 1948.**

A topic-by-topic treatment, useful for the various aspects of naval development.

**2852 CLOWES (*Sir* WILLIAM LAIRD) *ed*. The Royal Navy: a history from the earliest times to the present. 7 v. 1897–1903.**

A big general hist. to 1900, with contribs. by a wide variety of writers. Incls. much biog. data and details of ships and naval admin. Charles Napier Robinson, *The British fleet: the growth, achievements and duties of the navy of the empire,* 1894, and Frederick Thomas Jane, *The British battle fleet: its inception and growth throughout the centuries,* 1912, rev. edn. 2 v. 1915, are also useful.

**2853 RICHMOND (*Sir* HERBERT WILLIAM). Statesmen and sea power. Oxf. 1946. 2nd edn. 1947.**

British naval policy since Elizabeth I. Cp. Stephen Wentworth Roskill, *The strategy of sea power: its development and application,* 1962.

2854 GRAHAM (GERALD SANDFORD). The politics of naval supremacy: studies in British maritime ascendancy. Camb. 1965.

2855 BRODIE (BERNARD). Sea power in the machine age: major naval inventions and their consequences on international politics, 1814–1940. Princeton. 1941. 2nd edn. [1943.]

The best account of the transition to steam, steel, and modern technology. May be suppl. by Frederick Leslie Robertson, *The evolution of naval armament*, 1921, and William Hovgaard, *Modern history of warships: comprising a discussion of present standpoint and recent war experiences, for the use of students of naval construction, naval constructors, naval officers and others interested in naval matters*, Lond. & N.Y. 1920.

2856 ALBION (ROBERT GREENHALGH). Forests and sea power: the timber problem of the Royal Navy, 1652–1862. Camb., Mass. 1926. Repr. Hamden, Conn. 1965.

2857 BAXTER (JAMES PHINNEY) *3rd*. The introduction of the ironclad warship. Camb., Mass. 1933.

Good.

2858 WILSON (HERBERT WRIGLEY). Ironclads in action: a sketch of naval warfare from 1855 to 1895, with some account of the development of the battleship in England. 2 v. Lond. & Boston. 1896. 5th edn. 2 v. 1897.

A detailed account. See also his *Battleships in action*, 2 v. Lond. & Boston 1926, repr. Grosse Pointe, Mich. 1969.

2859 BARTLETT (CHRISTOPHER JOHN). Great Britain and sea power, 1815–53. Oxf. 1963.

2860 LEWIS (MICHAEL ARTHUR). The navy in transition, 1814–1864: a social history. 1965.

[Charles] Christopher Lloyd, *A short history of the Royal Navy, 1805 to 1918*, 1942, is much briefer.

2861 EARDLEY-WILMOT (*Sir* SYDNEY MAROW). The development of navies during the last half century. Lond. & N.Y. 1892.

Cp. Sir Nathaniel Barnaby, *Naval development in the century*, Nineteenth century ser. 1902.

2862 LLOYD ([CHARLES] CHRISTOPHER). The navy and the slave trade: the suppression of the African slave trade in the nineteenth century. 1949. Repr. 1968.

See also William Ernest Frank Ward, *The Royal Navy and the slaves: the suppression of the Atlantic slave trade*, 1969, and Hugh Graham Soulsby, *The right of search and the slave trade in Anglo-American relations, 1814–1862*, Baltimore, Md. 1933.

2863 PRESTON (ANTONY) *and* MAJOR (JOHN). Send a gunboat! A history of the gunboat and its role in British policy, 1854–1904. 1967.

2864 MARDER (ARTHUR JACOB). The anatomy of British sea power: a history of British naval policy in the pre-Dreadnought era, 1880–1905. N.Y. 1940. [British edn. entitled *British naval policy 1880–1905: the anatomy of British sea power.*] Lond. 1941. Repr. Lond. & Hamden, Conn. 1964.

Indispensable.

2865 SCHURMAN (DONALD MACKENZIE). The education of a navy: the development of British naval strategic thought, 1867–1914. Lond. & Chicago. 1965.

2866 WOODWARD (*Sir* ERNEST LLEWELLYN). Great Britain and the German navy. Oxf. 1935.

See also Paul Kluke, *Heeresaufbau und Heerespolitik Englands vom Burenkrieg bis zum Weltkrieg*, Munich 1932; Otto Ernst Schüddekopf, *Die Britische Marinepolitik: wehrgeographische und strategische Grundlagen, 1880 bis 1918*, Hamburg 1930; Fritz Uplegger, *Die englische Flottenpolitik vor dem Weltkrieg, 1904–1909*, Stuttgart 1938; Ruddock F. Mackay, 'The Admiralty, the German navy and the redistribution of the British fleet, 1904–1905', *Mariner's Mirror* 56 (1970), 341–6; and the works at **2307**.

2867 MARDER (ARTHUR JACOB). From the Dreadnought to Scapa Flow: the Royal Navy in the Fisher era, 1904–19. 5 v. 1961–70.

Excellent. Vol. 1 covers 1904–14, vol. 2, 1914–16. On the early battles of World War I there is also Geoffrey Martin Bennett, *Coronel and the Falklands*, 1962.

2868 GORDON (DONALD CRAIGIE). 'The Admiralty and dominion navies, 1902–1914'. *J. Mod. Hist.* xxxiii (1961), 407–22.

2869 CHURCHILL. Former naval person: Winston Churchill and the Royal Navy. By Sir Peter William Gretton. 1968.

Robert MacGregor Dawson, *Winston Churchill at the Admiralty, 1911–1915*, Toronto 1940, is a short essay, repr. from *Canadian J. Econ. & Pol. Sci.* vi (1940), 325–58.

2870 MOORE (*Sir* ALAN HILARY). Sailing ships of war, 1800–1860: including the transition to steam. Lond. & N.Y. 1926.

A picture book.

2871 PARKES (OSCAR). British battleships: 'Warrior', 1860, to 'Vanguard', 1950: a history of design, construction and armament. 1957.

Detailed and useful. There are also a number of more popular works incl. Richard Alexander Hough, *Dreadnought: a history of the modern battleship*, N.Y. 1964, Lond. 1965, 2nd edn. Lond. 1968, Randolph Pears, *British battleships, 1892–1957: the great days of the fleets*, 1957, and Donald George Frederick Wyville McIntyre, *The thunder of the guns: a century of battleships*, 1959.

2872 KEMP (PETER KEMP). H.M. destroyers. 1956.

See also Thomas Davys Manning, *The British destroyers*, 1961, which has many photographs.

2873 OSBON (G. A.). 'The Crimean gunboats'. *Mariner's Mirror* li (1965), 103–16, 211–20.

2874 ARMSTRONG (*Sir* GEORGE ELLIOT). Torpedoes and torpedo vessels. 1896. 2nd edn. 1901.

See also Allen Hoar, *The submarine torpedo boat: its characteristics and modern development*, N.Y. 1916.

2875 LIPSCOMB (FRANK WOODGATE). The British submarine. 1954.

There are a number of good contemp. works, notably Herbert C. Fyfe, *Submarine warfare: past, present, and future*, 1902, 2nd edn. 1907; Sir Alan Hughes Burgoyne, *Submarine navigation: past and present*, 2 v. Lond. & N.Y. 1903; Cyril Field, *The story of the submarine from the earliest ages to the present day*, 1908; Sir Murray Fraser Sueter, *The evolution of the submarine boat, mine and torpedo from the sixteenth century to the present time*, Portsmouth 1907, 2nd edn. 1908; and Charles William Domville-Fife, *Submarine engineering of today*, 1914, and *Submarines of the world's navies*, 1910.

2876 ADDISON (ALBERT CHRISTOPHER). The story of the *Birkenhead*: a record of British heroism. 1902.

The loss of a troop transport off South Africa in 1852. See also Scott Corbett, *Danger point: the wreck of the Birkenhead*, Boston 1962, and James Lennox Kerr, *The unfortunate ship: the story of H.M. troopship 'Birkenhead'*, 1960. For other celebrated naval disasters see Arthur Hawkey, *H.M.S. Captain*, 1963, and Richard Alexander Hough, *Admirals in collision*, 1959, repr. 1961. There are detailed reports of major disasters in the parl. papers.

2877 JARRETT (DUDLEY). British naval dress. 1960.

Sir Gerald Dickens, comp., *The dress of the British sailor*, Nat. Maritime Museum 1957, is a picture book.

## 3. NAVAL ADMINISTRATION

### (a) *General*

2878 MURRAY (*Sir* OSWYN ALEXANDER RUTHVEN). 'The Admiralty'. *Mariner's Mirror* xxiii (1937), 13–35, 129–47, 316–31; xxiv (1938), 101–4, 204–25, 329–52, 458–78; xxv (1939), 89–111, 216–28, 328–38.

A draft hist. intended for the Whitehall series. The sections from xxiv (1938), 458–78, onwards, deal with the 19th and 20th cents.

2879 BRIGGS (*Sir* JOHN HENRY). Naval administrations, 1827 to 1892: the experience of 65 years. Ed. by Lady Briggs. 1897.

An annotated list of office-holders and events. Briggs was chief clerk in the Admiralty.

2880 HAMILTON (*Sir* RICHARD VESEY). Naval administration: the constitution, character and functions of the Board of Admiralty and of the civil departments it directs. 1896.

A valuable guide.

2881 ASHWORTH (WILLIAM). 'Economic aspects of late Victorian naval administration'. *Econ. Hist. Rev.* 2 ser. xxii (1969), 491–505.

2882 MURRAY. The making of a civil servant: Sir Oswyn Murray, G.C.B., secretary of the Admiralty, 1917–1936. By his widow, Lady Mildred Octavia Murray. 1940.

Served in the Admiralty from 1897.

2883 WALKER. Thirty-six years [1895–1931] at the Admiralty. By Sir Charles Walker. [1934.]

2884 THOMAS (JAMES PURDON LEWES), *Viscount Cilcennin.* Admiralty House, Whitehall. 1960.

2885 HAMILTON COMMITTEE ON NAVAL ESTIMATES. Report of a committee appointed by the Treasury to inquire into the navy estimates, from 1852 to 1858, and into the comparative state of the navies of England and France [Chairman: George A. Hamilton]. H.C. 182 (1859–Sess. 1). XIV, 703.

See also William Henry Sykes, 'Organisation, strength and cost of the English and French navies in 1865', *Stat. Soc. J.* xxix (1866), 36–77.

2886 HENLEY COMMITTEE ON THE BOARD OF ADMIRALTY. Report from the select committee on the Board of Admiralty [Chairman: J. W. Henley]. H.C. 438 (1861). V, 1.

Discussed a number of general issues, incl. those raised in Sir Frederick William Grey, *On the organisation of the navy,* 1860, and Anon, *Admiralty administration: its faults and defaults,* 2nd edn. 1861. See also *Report from the select committee on Admiralty monies and accounts* [Chairman: Charles Seely]. H.C. 469 (1867–8). VI, 1.

2887 LORDS COMMITTEE ON THE BOARD OF ADMIRALTY. Report from the select committee of the House of Lords on the Board of Admiralty [Chairman: Duke of Somerset]. H.C. 180 (1871). VII, 1.

2888 GOSCHEN COMMITTEE ON ADMIRALTY EXPENDITURE. Report from the select committee on the Admiralty (expenditure and liabilities) [Chairman: G. J. Goschen]. H.C. 311 (1884–5). VII, 293.

See also **2720.**

2889 BOARD OF ADMIRALTY. A statement of Admiralty policy. [Cd. 2791] H.C. (1906). LXX, 445.

Lord Cawdor's scheme of reorganization.

(b) *Recruitment, Training, and Terms of Service*

2890 LEWIS (MICHAEL ARTHUR). England's sea officers: the story of the naval profession. [1939.]

See also **2860** and Geoffrey Penn, *Snotty: the story of the midshipman,* 1957.

2891 LLOYD ([CHARLES] CHRISTOPHER). 'The Royal Naval colleges at Portsmouth and Greenwich'. *Mariner's Mirror* lii (1966), 145–56.

See also Edward Phillips Statham, *The story of the Britannia: the training ship for naval cadets, with some account of previous methods of education and of the new scheme of 1903,* 1904, Edward Arthur Hughes, *The Royal Naval College, Dartmouth,* 1950, and **2894–5.**

**2892** WALPOLE COMMITTEE ON NAVY PROMOTION AND RETIREMENT. Report from the select committee on navy (promotion and retirement) [President: Spencer Horatio Walpole]. H.C. 501 (1863). X, 71. Full.

**2893** SHADWELL COMMITTEE ON THE HIGHER EDUCATION OF NAVAL OFFICERS. Report of the committee on the higher education of naval officers [President: Charles F. A. Shadwell]. [C. 203] H.C. (1870). XXV, 835.

See also *Report of the committee to inquire into the establishment of the Royal Naval College, Greenwich* [Chairman: The Revd. Osborne Gordon]. [C. 1733] H.C. (1877). XXI, 415, and *Report of the committee appointed by the Admiralty to inquire into the system of training naval cadets on board H.M.S. Britannia* [Chairman: Edward Bridges Rice]. [C. 1154] H.C. (1875). XV, 347.

**2894** LUARD COMMITTEE ON THE EDUCATION OF NAVAL EXECUTIVE OFFICERS. Report of the committee appointed by the Lords commissioners of the Admiralty to inquire into and report on the education of naval executive officers [Chairman: W. G. Luard]. [C. 4885] H.C. (1886). XIII, 315.

**2895** TRACEY COMMITTEE ON THE TRAINING OF JUNIOR NAVAL OFFICERS. Report of the committee appointed by the Lords commissioners of the Admiralty to inquire into and report on the training and examination of junior naval officers . . . [Chairman: Richard E. Tracey]. [Cd. 508] H.C. (1901). XLII, 621.

See also *Reports of departmental committees appointed to consider certain questions concerning the extension of the new scheme of training for officers of the navy, &c.* [Cd. 2841] H.C. (1906). LXX, 493, and *Reports of the committee appointed to enquire into the education and training of cadets, midshipmen, and junior officers of His Majesty's fleet* [Chairman: Sir Reginald Custance]. [Cd. 6703] H.C. (1913). XLIII, 579.

**2896** BOWEN (FRANK CHARLES). History of the Royal Naval Reserve. 1926.

A handy outline. See also *Report of the naval reserves committee* [Chairman: Sir Edward Grey]. [Cd. 1491] H.C. (1903). XL, 663.

**2897** LLOYD ([CHARLES] CHRISTOPHER). The British seaman, 1200–1860: a social history. 1968.

Like Peter Kemp Kemp, *The British sailor: a social history of the lower deck*, 1970, a good summary of a subject about which many bad books have been written, among them Charles Napier Robinson, *The British tar in fact and fiction* . . ., Lond. & N.Y. 1909, and John Laffin, *Jack Tar: the story of the British sailor*, 1969.

**2898** TAYLOR (R.). 'Manning the Royal Navy: the reform of the recruiting systems, 1852–1862'. *Mariner's Mirror* xliv (1958), 302–13; xlv (1959), 46–58.

**2899** HARDWICKE COMMITTEE ON MANNING THE NAVY. Report of the commissioners appointed to inquire into the best means of manning the

navy [Chairman: Earl of Hardwicke]. [2469] H.C. (1859–Sess. 1). VI, 1.
Dissent by W. S. Lindsay. H.C. 99 (1859–Sess. 1). XV, 417.

Full. See also *Copies of a correspondence between the Board of Treasury and the Board of Admiralty on the subject of the manning of the Royal Navy, together with copies of a report of a committee of naval officers and Her Majesty's order in council relating thereto.* [1628] H.C. (1852–3). LX, 9, and *Copies or extracts of the report and appendix of the committee of 1852 on manning the navy* [Chairman: Arthur Fanshawe]. H.C. 45 (1859–Sess. 2). XVII, 337.

2900 SUMMERS (DAVID LEWIS). H.M.S. Ganges, 1866–1966: one hundred years of training boys for the Royal Navy. Shotley Gate, Suffolk. 1966.

2901 HARBORD (JOHN BRADLEY). Report by the inspector of naval schools on the educational condition of seamen and marines and the working of elementary schools under the Lords commissioners of the Admiralty. [C. 3569] H.C. (1883). XVII, 105.

2902 PENN (GEOFFREY). Up funnel, down screw: the story of the naval engineer. 1955.

Some idea of what knowledge of steam engines was required in the middle of the 19th cent. can be gained from Thomas John Main and Thomas Brown, *The marine steam engine: designed chiefly for the use of officers of Her Majesty's navy,* 1849, 5th edn. 1865. On recruitment at that period see *Report of the committee appointed by the Lords commissioners of the Admiralty to consider the best means of securing the highest mechanical skill and scientific knowledge in the management of the various engines of Her Majesty's ships of war and the supply of engineer officers and engine room artificers for Her Majesty's navy* [Chairman: Sir A. Cooper Key]. [C. 1647] H.C. (1877). XXI, 1.

2903 FIELD (CYRIL). Britain's sea soldiers: a history of the Royal Marines . . . 3 v. Liverpool. 1924.

See also *Report of a departmental committee appointed to report upon promotion and retirement in the corps of Royal Marines* [Chairman: R. E. Welby]. H.C. 422 (1877). XXI, 347.

2904 LLOYD ([CHARLES] CHRISTOPHER) *and* COULTER (JACK LEONARD SAGAR). Medicine and the navy, 1200–1900. Vol. IV. 1815–1900. Edin. & Lond. 1963.

Completes a work started by John Joyce Keevil. There were two big committees of inquiry into the recruitment of medical officers during the period, the Milne committee (**2688**), on both army and naval medical officers, and the Hoskins commission, *Report to the Lords commissioners of the Admiralty of the committee on the rank, pay and position of naval medical officers* [President: A. H. Hoskins]. [C. 2928] H.C. (1881). XXII, 309. See also *Report to the Lords commissioners of the Admiralty of the committee on the training of naval medical officers* [President: A. W. Moore]. [C. 9515] H.C. (1899). LV, 593.

2905 ROSKILL (STEPHEN WENTWORTH) *ed.* Documents relating to the naval air service. 1+ v. Navy Records Soc. 113+. 1969+.

2906 KILLEN (JOHN). A history of marine aviation, 1911–68. 1969.

2907 BOWEN (FRANK CHARLES). His Majesty's coastguard: the story of this important naval force from the earliest times to the present day. [1928.]

See also Edward Keble Chatterton, *King's cutters and smugglers, 1700–1855*, 1912, and (much more important) *Report of the interdepartmental conference on the coast guard, 1907* [President: Reginald F. H. Henderson]. [Cd. 4091] H.C. (1908). XCVI, 143.

2908 SIGWART (EMIL EDWARD). Royal Fleet Auxiliary: its ancestry and affiliations, 1600–1968. 1969.

On naval supply.

(c) *Shipbuilding and Repair*

2909 POOL (BERNARD). 'Naval contracts after 1832'. *Mariner's Mirror* liv (1968), 209–26.

2910 HOBBES. Reminiscences [and notes] on seventy years' life, travel and adventure, military and civil, scientific and literary. By a retired officer of H.M.'s civil service [Robert George Hobbes]. 2 v. 1893–5.

Vol. I. 'Soldiering in India'. Vol. II. 'Civil service in Sheerness and Chatham dockyards: home and foreign travel'. A long and tedious book, but has material not available elsewhere.

2911 SEYMOUR COMMITTEE ON DOCKYARD APPOINTMENTS. Report from the select committee on dockyard appointments [Chairman: Lord Seymour]. H.C. 511 (1852–3). XXV, 1.

An inquiry into attempts by the Conservative secretary of the Admiralty in the Derby government to use dockyard patronage for the benefit of his party.

2912 SMITH COMMITTEE ON GUN AND MORTAR BOATS. Report from the select committee on navy (gun and mortar boats) [Chairman: Sir Frederick Smith]. H.C. 545 (1860). VIII, 1.

2913 RICARDO COMMISSION ON NAVY YARDS. Report of the commissioners appointed to inquire into the control and management of Her Majesty's naval yards [Chairman: John Lewis Ricardo]. [2790] H.C. (1861). XXVI, 1.

2914 PAGET COMMITTEE ON DOCKYARDS. First report from the select committee on dockyards [Chairman: Lord Clarence Paget]. H.C. 270 (1864). VIII, 7. Second report. H.C. 496 (1864). VIII, 75.

2915 DUFFERIN COMMISSION ON SHIP DESIGN. Report of the committee appointed by the Lords commissioners of the Admiralty to examine the designs upon which ships of war have recently been constructed [Chairman: Lord Dufferin]. [C. 477] H.C. (1872). XIV, 501. Evidence. [C. 477–I] H.C. (1872). XIV, 583. Dissenting report. [C. 489] H.C. (1872). XIV, 993.

2916 BRASSEY COMMITTEE ON DOCKYARD OFFICERS. Report of committee appointed to consider the entry, training and promotion of the professional officers of the dockyards and in the department of the Controller of the Navy [Chairman: Sir Thomas Brassey]. H.C. 277 (1883). XVII, 1.

2917 RAVENSWORTH COMMITTEE ON SHIPBUILDING CON-
TRACTS. Report of the committee appointed to inquire into the conditions
under which contracts are invited for the building or repairing of ships,
including their engines, for Her Majesty's navy, and into the mode in which
repairs and refits of ships are effected in Her Majesty's dockyards [Chairman:
Earl of Ravensworth]. [C. 4219] H.C. (1884–5). XIV, 125.

2918 COMMITTEES ON ADMIRALTY AND DOCKYARD ADMINIS-
TRATION. Reports of committees appointed to inquire into Admiralty and
dockyard administration and expenditure. [C. 4615] H.C. (1886). XIII, 139.
Further reports. [C. 4979] H.C. (1887). XVI, 333.

2919 FORWOOD COMMITTEE ON NAVAL PURCHASE AND CON-
TRACT SYSTEM. Report of the committee appointed by the Lords commissioners of the Admiralty to inquire into the system of purchase and
contract in the navy [Chairman: A. B. Forwood]. [C. 4987] H.C. (1887).
XVI, 531. Suppl. statement. [C. 5231] H.C. (1887). XVI, 707.

2920 ARNOLD-FORSTER COMMITTEE ON ARREARS OF SHIP-
BUILDING. Report of the committee appointed to inquire into the arrears
of shipbuilding [Chairman: H. O. Arnold-Forster]. [Cd. 1055] H.C. (1902).
LXI, 1.

### 4. Contemporary Studies

2921 BUSK (HANS). The navies of the world: their present state and future
capabilities. 1859.
Alarmist and anti-French.

2922 RUSSELL (JOHN SCOTT). The fleet of the future: iron or wood?
1861.
Russell also publ. *The fleet of the future in 1862: or, England without a fleet*, 1862. For
other contemp. discussions of the issue see Edward Pellew Halsted, *Iron-cased ships . . .*,
1861, and Sir Howard Douglas, *A treatise on naval gunnery*, 1820, 5th edn. 1860, and
*A postscript to the section on iron defences contained in the fifth edition of 'Naval gunnery'*,
1860, 2nd edn. 1861.

2923 REED (*Sir* EDWARD JAMES). Our ironclad ships: their qualities,
performances and cost . . . 1869.
By a famous shipbuilder, who also publ. *On the modifications which the ships of the Royal
Navy have undergone during the present century . . .*, 1859, and (with Edward Simpson)
*Modern ships of war*, 1888, and a good textbook on *Shipbuilding* (6132).

2924 KING (JAMES WILSON). Report of Chief Engineer J. W. King,
United States Navy, on European ships of war and their armament, naval
administration, and economy, marine constructions, torpedo warfare, dock-
yards, etc. U.S. 44th Congress, 2nd sess. Senate Exec. Doc. 27. 1877. 2nd edn.
Washington 1878. New edn. [The war-ships of Europe.] Portsmouth. 1878.
King also publ. *The war-ships and navies of the world*, Boston 1880.

2925 COLOMB (PHILIP HOWARD). Naval warfare: its ruling principles and practice, historically treated. 1891. 3rd edn. 1899.

A good technical discussion, comparable in its strategic thinking to the teaching of the American A. J. Mahan.

2926 WILKINSON (HENRY SPENSER). The command of the sea. 1894. 3rd edn. 1894.

See also his *The brain of the navy*, 1895.

2927 CLARKE (GEORGE SYDENHAM), *Baron Sydenham*. The navy and the nation: or, naval warfare and imperial defence. 1897.

2928 [DANSON (JOHN TOWNE).] Our commerce in war: and how to protect it. 1897.

Argues that Britain must renounce in advance the capture of enemy private property at sea.

2929 ATTWOOD (EDWARD LEWIS). War-ships: a text book of the construction, protection, stability, turning, etc., of war vessels. 1904. 6th edn. 1917.

Attwood, a naval architect, also publ. *The modern warship*, Camb. 1913, as well as a basic work long in use, *Text-book of theoretical naval architecture*, 1899, new [10th] edn. 1953.

2930 JANE (FREDERICK THOMAS). Heresies of sea power. 1906.

A counter to Mahan and other naval strategists.

2931 BRIDGE (*Sir* CYPRIAN ARTHUR GEORGE). The art of naval warfare: introductory observations. 1907.

2932 YEXLEY (LIONEL) *pseud. of* WOODS (JAMES). The inner life of the navy: being an account of the inner social life led by our naval seamen on board ships of war, together with a detailed account of the systems of victualling and uniform in vogue during the latter part of the nineteenth and the opening years of the twentieth century. 1908.

Yexley also publ. *Our fighting sea men*, 1911.

2933 LONDON NAVAL CONFERENCE, 1908–9. Proceedings of the international naval conference held in London, December 1908–February 1909. [Cd. 4555] H.C. (1909). LIV, 415. Correspondence & documents. [Cd. 4554] H.C. (1909). LIV, 305. Correspondence respecting the Declaration of London. [Cd. 5418] H.C. (1910). LXXIV, 133. [Cd. 5718] H.C. (1911). CIII, 113.

Largely concerned with the protection of commerce.

2934 BOWLES (THOMAS GIBSON). Sea law and sea power, as they would be affected by recent proposals: with reasons against those proposals. 1910.

2935 CORBETT (*Sir* JULIAN STAFFORD). Some principles of maritime strategy. 1911.

2936  CUSTANCE (*Sir* REGINALD NEVILLE). The ship of the line in battle. 1912.

A discussion of tactics based on the lessons of the Russo-Japanese war.

2937  BERESFORD (CHARLES WILLIAM DE LA POER), *Baron Beresford*. The betrayal: being, a record of facts concerning naval policy and administration, from the year 1902 to the present time. 1912.

Beresford's views were earlier considered in *Report of the sub-committee of the Committee of Imperial Defence appointed to inquire into certain questions of naval policy raised by Lord Charles Beresford* [Chairman: H. H. Asquith]. H.C. 256 (1909). LIV, 295.

## 5. BIOGRAPHY

2938  JAMESON (*Sir* WILLIAM SCARLETT). The fleet that Jack built: nine men who made a modern navy. 1962.

For the lighter side of the navy see Geoffrey Lyttelton Lowis, comp., *Fabulous admirals and some naval fragments . . .*, 1957.

2939  ASTON. Memoirs of a marine: an amphibiography. By Sir George Grey Aston. 1919.

2940  BACON. A naval scrap-book: first part, 1877–1900. By Sir Reginald Hugh Spencer Bacon. 1925.

Cont. in his *From 1900 onward*, 1940.

2941  BATTENBERG. Prince Louis of Battenberg: admiral of the fleet. By Mark Edward Frederic Kerr. 1934.

See also Brian Connell, *Manifest destiny: a study in five profiles of the rise and influence of the Mountbatten family*, 1953, Alden Hatch, *The Mountbattens . . .*, N.Y. 1965, Lond. 1966, and Edward H. Cookridge, pseud. of Edward Spiro, *From Battenberg to Mountbatten*, 1966.

2942  BEATTY. The life and letters of David, Earl Beatty. By William Scott Chalmers. 1951.

2943  BERESFORD. The memoirs of Admiral Lord Charles Beresford, written by himself. 2 v. Lond. & Boston 1914.

See also Geoffrey Martin Bennett, *Charlie B: a biography of Admiral Lord Beresford of Metemmeh and Curraghmore, G.C.B., G.C.V.O., LL.D., D.C.L.*, 1968.

2944  BRIDGE. Some recollections. By Sir Cyprian Arthur George Bridge. 1918.

2945  COOPER KEY. Memoirs of Admiral the Right Honble Sir Astley Cooper Key, G.C.B., D.C.L., F.R.S., &c. By Philip Howard Colomb. 1898.

Important for the development of steam.

2946  CRESWELL. Close to the wind: the early memoirs (1866–79) of Admiral Sir William [Rooke] Creswell. Ed. by Paul Thompson. 1965.

2947 DALRYMPLE-HAY. Lines from my log-books. By Sir John Charles Dalrymple-Hay. Edin. 1898.

2948 DE CHAIR. The sea is strong. By Sir Dudley Rawson Stratford De Chair. 1961.

2949 DUNDAS. An admiral's yarns: stray memories of 50 years. By Sir Charles Hope Dundas. 1922.

2950 EARDLEY-WILMOT. An admiral's memories: sixty-five years afloat and ashore. By Sir Sydney Marow Eardley-Wilmot. 1927.

2951 FISHER. Fear God and dread nought: the correspondence of Admiral of the Fleet Lord Fisher of Kilverstone. Ed. by Arthur Jacob Marder. 3 v. 1952–9.
Suppl. by Peter Kemp Kemp, ed., *The papers of Admiral Sir John Fisher*, 2+ v. Navy Records Soc. 102, 106+, 1960–4+. [John Arbuthnot Fisher, Baron] Fisher publ. *Memories* and *Records*, 2 v. Lond. & N.Y. 1920. The first life was Sir Reginald Hugh Spencer Bacon, *The life of Lord Fisher of Kilverstone*, 2 v. Lond. & N.Y. 1929. Richard Alexander Hough, *First sea lord: an authorized biography of Admiral Lord Fisher*, 1969, publ in N.Y. as *Admiral of the fleet . . .*, 1970, adds little to Marder. The best life is now Ruddock Finlay Mackay, *Fisher of Kilverstone*, Oxf. 1973.

2952 FITZGERALD. Memories of the sea. By Charles Cooper Penrose Fitzgerald. 1913.
Suppl. by his *From sail to steam: naval recollections, 1878–1905*, 1916.

2953 FLEET. My life, and a few yarns. By Henry Louis Fleet. 1922.
Fleet also publ. *An admiral's yarns*, 1910.

2954 FREMANTLE. The navy as I have known it, 1849–1899. By Sir Edmund Robert Fremantle. 1904.

2955 FREMANTLE. My naval career, 1880–1928. By Sir Sydney Robert Fremantle. 1949.
See also Ann Parry, comp., *The Admirals Fremantle*, 1971.

2956 HARRIS. From naval cadet to admiral: half a century of naval service and sport in many parts of the world. By Sir Robert Hastings Harris. 1913.

2957 JELLICOE. Jellicoe: a biography. By Alfred Temple Patterson. 1969.
Repl. Sir Reginald Hugh Spencer Bacon, *The life of John Rushworth, Earl Jellicoe*, 1936, and is based on Alfred Temple Patterson, ed., *The Jellicoe papers: selections from the private and official correspondence of Admiral of the Fleet Earl Jellicoe of Scapa*, 2 v., Navy Records Soc. 108, 111, 1966–8.

2958 KEPPEL. The beloved little admiral: the life and times of Admiral of the Fleet, the Hon. Sir Henry Keppel, G.C.B., O.M., D.C.L., 1809–1904. By Vivian Stuart [Violet Vivian Mann]. 1967.
Keppel himself publ. *A sailor's life under four sovereigns*, 3 v. 1899.

2959 KERR. Land, sea and air reminiscences. By Mark Edward Frederic Kerr. 1927.

2960 KEYES. Adventures ashore & afloat. By Roger John Brownlow Keyes, Baron Keyes. 1939.

Cont. in *The naval memoirs of Admiral of the Fleet Sir Roger Keyes* . . ., 2 v. Lond. & N.Y. 1934–5. See also Cecil Faber Aspinell-Oglander, *Roger Keyes: being, the biography of Admiral of the Fleet Lord Keyes of Zeebrugge and Dover*, 1951.

2961 LYONS. Life of Vice-Admiral Edmund, Lord Lyons: with an account of naval operations in the Black Sea and Sea of Azoff, 1854–6. By Sir Sydney Marow Eardley-Wilmot. 1898.

2962 MENDS. Life of Admiral Sir William Robert Mends, G.C.B., &c., &c., &c., late director of transports. By Bowen Stilon Mends. 1899.

Chiefly on the Crimean war.

2963 MORESBY. Two admirals: Admiral of the Fleet Sir Fairfax Moresby, G.C.B., K.M.T., D.C.L. (1786–1877) and his son John Moresby: a record of life and service in the British navy for a hundred years. By John Moresby. 1909.

2964 OLIVER. A great seaman: the life of Admiral of the Fleet Sir Henry F. Oliver. By Sir William Milburne James. 1956.

2965 PAGET. Autobiography and journals of Admiral Lord Clarence E. Paget, G.C.B. Ed. by Sir Arthur John Otway. 1896.

2966 SCOTT. Aim straight: a biography of Admiral Sir Percy Scott. By Peter Padfield. 1966.

See also Sir Percy Moreton Scott's own *Fifty years in the Royal Navy*, 1919. Scott was the navy's greatest gunnery expert.

2967 SEYMOUR. My naval career and travels. By Sir Edward Hobart Seymour. 1911.

2968 SULIVAN. Life and letters of the late Admiral Sir Bartholomew James Sulivan, K.C.B., 1810–1890. Ed. by Henry Norton Sulivan. 1896.

2969 TRYON. Life of Vice-Admiral Sir George Tryon, K.C.B. By Charles Cooper Penrose Fitzgerald. Edin. & Lond. 1898.

2970 WESTON. My life among the bluejackets. By Agnes Elizabeth Weston. 1909.

A pioneer of welfare for sailors. See also Jennie Chappell, *Agnes Weston: the sailors' friend* . . ., 1935.

2971 WILSON. Life of Admiral of the Fleet Sir Arthur Knyvet Wilson, Bart. . . . By Sir Edward Eden Bradford. 1923.

# V

# THE LEGAL SYSTEM

## A. GENERAL

### 1. BIBLIOGRAPHY

2973 FRIEND (WILLIAM LAWRENCE). Anglo-American legal bibliographies: an annotated guide. U.S. Libr. of Congress. Wash. 1944. Repr. 1966.

2974 HARVARD LAW SCHOOL LIBRARY. Annual legal bibliography . . . 1+. Camb. , Mass. 1961+.
Full and well arranged.

2975 JAMES (JOHN S.) and MAXWELL (LESLIE F.) comps. A legal bibliography of the British Commonwealth of Nations. Vol. 2: English law from 1801 to 1954, including Wales, the Channel Islands and the Isle of Man. 2nd edn. 1957.
A full list of short titles, the 1st edn., comp. by Leslie F. Maxwell, entitled *A bibliography of English law from 1801 to June 1932: volume III of Sweet and Maxwell's complete law book catalogue*, 1933. Companion vols. are *Sweet and Maxwell's guide to law reports and statutes* . . ., 1929, 3rd edn. 1959, and William Harold Maxwell, comp., *A complete list of British & colonial law reports & legal periodicals* . . ., 1913, 3rd edn. 1937. A useful guide to current textbooks, many of which have hist. introductions, is Univ. of London Inst. of Adv. Legal Studs., *A bibliographical guide to the law of the United Kingdom, the Channel Islands and the Isle of Man*, 1956.

2976 WINFIELD (*Sir* PERCY HENRY). The chief sources of English legal history. Camb., Mass. 1925.
Like Sir William Searle Holdsworth, *Sources and literature of English law*, Oxf. 1925, has little post-1850. Frederick Charles Hicks, *Materials and methods of legal research*, Rochester, N.Y., 1923, 3rd edn. 1943, and Arthur Sydney Beardsley, *Legal bibliography and the use of law books*, Chicago 1937, 2nd edn. N.Y. 1947, fill some of the gaps and have full bibliogs. There is a short guide to English law books in Miles Oscar Price and Harry Bitner, *Effective legal research: a practical manual of law books and their use*, N.Y. 1953. A useful adjunct is Univ. of London Inst. of Adv. Legal Studs., *A manual of legal citations*. Part I: *The British Isles*, 1959. Albert Kenneth Roland Kiralfy, *A source book of English law*, 1957, is of little value for the period, except as an indication of important pre-1850 cases.

2977 JELF (*Sir* ERNEST ARTHUR). Where to find your law . . . 1897. 3rd edn. 1907.
Discusses contemp. law books. Charles Carroll Soule, *Lawyer's reference manual of law books*, Boston, Mass. 1883, 2nd edn. 1884, and *Sweet and Maxwell's catalogue of modern law books, with a selection of such old works as are still of value*, 1895, are lists without comment.

2978 MIDDLE TEMPLE. A catalogue of printed books . . . Ed. by Cyril Edward Alfred Bedwell. 1914. Suppl. for 1914–24. 1925.

> The fullest of British general law libr. cats. Other libr. cats. of particular value are those of Harvard Univ. Law School, 2 v. Camb., Mass. 1909, Gray's Inn, 1906, Lincoln's Inn, 1859, suppl. 1890, the Law Society, 1891, suppl 1906, Manchester Law Libr., 8th edn. 1911, and Columbia Univ. Law Libr., 28 v. Boston 1968.

2979 BRITISH LIBRARY OF POLITICAL AND ECONOMIC SCIENCE (EDWARD FRY LIBRARY OF INTERNATIONAL LAW). Catalogue of books, pamphlets and other documents . . . Comp. by Bertie Mason Headicar. 1923.

2980 HARVARD LAW SCHOOL LIBRARY. Catalog of international law and relations. 20 v. N.Y. 1965–7.

2981 PUBLIC RECORD OFFICE. Guide to the contents of the Public Record Office. Vol. I Legal records, etc. 1963. Vol. III suppl. 1968.

> See also P.R.O., *List of Chancery rolls, 1199–1903*, P.R.O. Lists & Indexes XXVII, 1908, repr. N.Y. 1963.

## 2. GENERAL HISTORIES

No adequate general history of the period has yet appeared and few of the books cited below have much on the period after 1850.

2982 HOLDSWORTH (*Sir* WILLIAM SEARLE). A history of English law. 16 v. 1903–66.

Down to 1875.

2983 JENKS (EDWARD). A short history of English law from the earliest times to end of [1911]. 1912. 6th edn. 1949.

> Other useful short hists. are Harold Potter, *An historical introduction to English law and its institutions*, 1932, 4th edn. 1958; Albert Thomas Carter, *A history of English legal institutions*, 1902 [in editions since 1927 styled *A history of the English courts*]; and Edward Stanley Roscoe, *The growth of English law: being studies in the evolution of law and procedure in England*, 1911.

2984 HARDING (ALAN). A social history of English law. 1966.

2985 KEETON (GEORGE WILLIAMS) *and* LLOYD (DENNIS) *eds*. The United Kingdom: the development of its laws and constitutions. Vol. I. England and Wales, Northern Ireland, the Isle of Man. 1955.

2986 ALLEN (*Sir* CARLETON KEMP). Law in the making. 1927. 7th edn. 1964.

> The best general intro. to the hist. of law-making: strongest on the 20th cent.

2987 LEVY-ULLMANN (HENRI). The English legal tradition, its sources and history. Trans. by M. Mitchell. Rev. and ed. by Frederic M. Goadby. 1935.

> Little on the 19th cent.

2988 PLUCKNETT (THEODORE FRANK THOMAS). A concise history of the common law. Rochester, N.Y. 1929. 5th edn. Lond. 1956.

2989 RADZINOWICZ (*Sir* LEON). A history of English criminal law and its administration, from 1750 . . . 4+ v. 1948–.
Good.

2990 EDWARDS (JOHN LLEWELYN JONES). The law officers of the crown: a study of the offices of attorney general and solicitor general of England, with an account of the office of the director of public prosecutions of England. 1964.

2991 WINFIELD (*Sir* PERCY HENRY). The present law of abuse of legal procedure. Camb. 1921.
Cont. his *The history of conspiracy and abuse of legal procedure*, Camb. 1921, which goes up to the end of the 18th cent.

2992 FOX (*Sir* JOHN CHARLES). The history of contempt of court: the form of trial and the mode of punishment. Oxf. 1927.

2993 STOLJAR (SAMUEL JACOB). The law of agency: its history and present principles. 1961.

2994 KEETON (GEORGE WILLIAMS). Social change in the law of trusts. 1958.

2995 FIFOOT (CECIL HERBERT STUART). History and sources of the common law: tort and contract. 1949.

2996 WINFIELD (*Sir* PERCY HENRY). The province of the law of tort. Camb. 1931.

2997 JACKSON (RICHARD MEREDITH). The history of quasi-contract in English law. Camb. 1936.

2998 HOLDEN (JAMES MILNES). The history of negotiable instruments in English law. 1955.

2999 DIGBY (*Sir* KENELM EDWARD). An introduction to the history of the law of real property. Oxf. 1875. 5th edn. 1897.
See also 3284, 4230–6, 4251–8.

3000 WIENER (FREDERICK BERNAYS). Civilians under military justice: the British practice since 1689, especially in North America. Chicago. 1967.

3001 HILL (*Sir* GEORGE FRANCIS). Treasure trove in law and practice from the earliest times to the present day. Oxf. 1936.

**3002** AMES (JAMES BARR). Lectures on legal history and miscellaneous legal essays. Camb., Mass. 1913.

Incls. a number of 19th-cent. essays. So too do Ernst Freund and others, *Select essays in Anglo-American legal history by various authors, compiled and edited by a committee of the Association of American Law Schools*, 3 v. Boston, Mass. 1907–9; Sir Frederick Pollock, *Essays in the law*, 1922; Robert Alderson Wright, Baron Wright, *Legal essays and addresses*, Camb. 1939; and Frederick William Maitland, *Collected papers* (**3089**). James Bryce, Viscount Bryce, *Studies in history and jurisprudence*, 2 v. Oxf. 1901, is less directly useful but reflects the attitude of an important thinker to the legal problems of the day. There are some light-hearted essays on the period in Robert Edgar Megarry, *Miscellany-at-law* . . ., 1955.

**3003** HOLDSWORTH (*Sir* WILLIAM SEARLE). Essays in law and history. Ed. by Arthur Lehman Goodhart and Harold Greville Hanbury. Oxf. 1946.

Important.

### 3. Law in the Nineteenth Century and After

**3004** DICEY (ALBERT VENN). Lectures on the relation between law & public opinion in England during the nineteenth century. 1905. 2nd edn. 1914. New edn. by E. C. S. Wade. 1962.

A remarkable book which has shaped the outlook of all subsequent writers, although recently under attack. See **356**.

**3005** FIFOOT (CECIL HERBERT STUART). Judge and jurist in the reign of Victoria. 1959.

Also useful are Fifoot's *English law and its background*, 1932, and the final chapter of Sir William Searle Holdsworth, *Some makers of the English law*, Camb. 1938.

**3006** GOODHART (ARTHUR LEHMAN) *ed.* 'Survey of English law, 1885–1935'. *Law Q. Rev.* li (1935), 1–262.

**3007** RODGERS (WILLIAM BLAKE) *and others*. A century of law reform: twelve lectures on the changes in the law of England during the nineteenth century. 1901.

**3008** MAITLAND (FREDERIC WILLIAM). Justice and police. The English citizen series. 1885.

A popular intro. to the legal system. See also the posthumous edn. of his lectures on *Equity: also the forms of action at common law*, Camb. 1909, rev. edn. 1936.

**3009** FRANQUET DE FRANQUEVILLE (AMABLE CHARLES), *Comte.* Le système judiciaire de la Grande Bretagne . . . 2 v. Paris. 1893.

**3010** GRAVESON (RONALD HARRY) *and* CRANE (FRANCIS ROGER) *eds.* A century of family law, 1857–1957. 1957.

A thorough and comprehensive symposium.

3011 DE VILLIERS (JEAN ÉTIENNE REENEN). The history of the legislation concerning real and personal property in England during the reign of Queen Victoria . . . 1901.

3012 HOLDSWORTH (*Sir* WILLIAM SEARLE). Charles Dickens as a legal historian. New Haven [Conn.]. 1928.

There is something of the Dickens spirit in Gilbert Abbott à Beckett, *The comic Blackstone*, rev. and enl. by Arthur William à Beckett and illus. by Harry Furniss, 1887.

3013 PARRY (*Sir* EDWARD ABBOTT). The law and the poor. 1914.

3014 KEETON (GEORGE WILLIAMS). Trial by tribunal: a study of the development and functioning of the tribunal of inquiry. 1960.

3015 WATTS (W. H. S.). 'The administration of justice in Lancashire'. *Manch. Stat. Soc. Trans.* (1884–5), 105–26.

## 4. JURISPRUDENCE

3016 GOODHART (ARTHUR LEHMAN). English contributions to the philosophy of law. N.Y. 1949.

A useful outline. There is also a little on English law in Wolfgang Gaston Friedmann, *Legal theory*, 1944, 4th edn. 1960.

3017 JURIDICAL SOCIETY. Papers read before the Juridical Society. 1855–73. 4 v. 1858–74.

Incl. important papers by the leading legal writers of the day as well as by non-lawyers such as F. D. Maurice.

3018 MAINE (*Sir* HENRY JAMES SUMNER). Ancient law: its connection with the early history of society and its relation to modern ideas. 1861. 11th edn. 1887. Many modern edns. with commentaries.

Extremely influential.

3019 HOLMES (OLIVER WENDELL) *the younger*. The common law. Boston, Mass. 1881. Lond. 1887. New edn. by Mark De Wolfe Howe. Boston 1963.

3020 POLLOCK (*Sir* FREDERICK). Essays in jurisprudence and ethics. 1882.

Pollock's *Essays* (**3002**) and *An essay on possession in the common law* [Pt. III by Sir Robert Samuel Wright], Oxf. 1888, are also important. There is a useful comp. of Pollock's *Jurisprudence and legal essays*, ed. by Arthur Lehman Goodhart, 1961.

3021 VINOGRADOFF (*Sir* PAUL GAVRIILOVICH). Common sense in law. 1914. 3rd edn. ed. by Harold Greville Hanbury. 1959.

A successful popular intro. to jurisprudence.

3022  MARKBY (*Sir* WILLIAM). Elements of law: considered with reference to principles of general jurisprudence. Oxf. 1871. 6th edn. 1905.

One of the first adequate textbooks on the subject. Soon superseded by Sir Thomas Erskine Holland, *The elements of jurisprudence*, Oxf. 1880, 13th edn. 1924, Sir Frederick Pollock, *A first book of jurisprudence* . . ., 1896, 6th edn. 1929, and Sir John William Salmond, *Jurisprudence* . . ., 1902, 12th edn. 1966.

## 5. LAW LISTS AND DIRECTORIES

3023  THE LAW LIST. 1841+.

The lineal descendant of *Browne's general law list*, 1775–97, through *The new law list*, 1798–1802, and *Clarke's new law list*, 1803–40. From 1860 quasi-official.

3024  THE SOLICITORS' DIARY, almanac & legal directory . . . 1844+.

3025  THE LAWYER'S COMPANION AND DIARY for 1848+ . . . 1847+.

## 6. PERIODICALS

3026  JONES (LEONARD AUGUSTUS) *and others*. An index to legal periodical literature [1789–1922]. 4 v. Boston, Mass. 1888–1924.

The *Index to legal periodicals and law library journals*, 1908+, N.Y. 1909+, indexes current legal periodicals.

3027  A SURVEY OF LEGAL PERIODICALS: union catalogue of holdings in British libraries. Univ. of London. Inst. of Advanced Legal Studs. 2nd edn. 1957.

3028  THE LAW QUARTERLY REVIEW. 1885+.

The chief forum for the discussion of legal problems and legal hist. Index to 1957, 1957. The American counterpart is the *Harvard law review*, 1887+.

3029  THE LONDON GAZETTE. 1665+.

The official channel for communicating to the public changes in the law and official appointments.

3030  THE LAW TIMES. 1843+.

The other leading professional js. were *The law journal*, 1866+, *The law magazine* . . ., 1828–1915, and *The solicitor's journal* [until 1856 styled *The legal observer*], 1831+.

3031  SOCIETY OF COMPARATIVE LEGISLATION. Journal [of comparative legislation]. 1896–1951.

## 7. DICTIONARIES

3032  JOWITT (WILLIAM ALLEN), *Earl Jowitt, ed.* The dictionary of English law. 2 v. 1959.

A convenient up-to-date work with articles by experts.

3033 WHARTON (JOHN JANE SMITH). The law lexicon, or dictionary of jurisprudence . . . 1848. 14th edn. 1938.

The best of the older dictionaries. Also useful are Herbert Norman Mozley and George Crispe Whiteley, *A concise law dictionary*, 1876, 6th edn. 1950, Henry Gilbert Rawson, *The student's pocket law lexicon*, 1882, 8th edn. 1951, and Archibald Brown, *A new law dictionary and institute of the whole law* . . ., 1874, 2nd edn. 1880.

3034 STROUD (FREDERICK). The judicial dictionary of words and phrases judicially interpreted. 1890. 2nd edn. 3 v. 1903. Repr. in 1 v. 1913. 3rd edn. 4 v. 1952–3.

At some points much fuller than Jowitt (**3032**).

3035 NORTON-KYSHE (JAMES WILLIAM). The dictionary of legal quotations: or, selected dicta of English chancellors and judges from the earliest periods to the present time. 1904.

## 8. REPORTS AND DIGESTS

For lists of reports see *Sweet and Maxwell's guide to law reports* (**2975**). Micro-print reproductions of many of the earlier reports are now available.

3036 WALLACE (JOHN WILLIAM). The reporters: chronologically arranged, with occasional remarks upon their respective merits. 4th edn. Boston, Mass. 1882.

3037 FOX (*Sir* JOHN CHARLES). A handbook of English law reports from the last quarter of the eighteenth century to the year 1865, with biographical notes of judges and reporters. Part I: House of Lords, Privy Council, and Chancery reports. 1913.

Originally intended to be a complete revision of Wallace (**3036**).

3038 DIGEST OF LAW COMMISSION. [First] report of the digest of law commission [Chairman: Lord Westbury]. [3849] H.C. (1867). XIX, 65. Second report. [C. 121] H.C. (1870). XVIII, 231.

3039 WOODS (WILLIAM ANDREW GEORGE) *and* RITCHIE (JOHN). A digest of cases overruled, approved or otherwise dealt with, in the English and other courts. 3 v. 1907.

3040 PETERSDORFF (CHARLES ERDMAN). A practical and elementary abridgment of the cases argued and determined in the courts of King's Bench, Common Pleas, Exchequer, and at Nisi Prius; and of the Rules of Court . . . [from 1660]. 15 v. 1825–30. 2nd edn. 6 v. 1861–4. Suppls. 1870, 1871.

The pioneer modern abridgement.

3041 MEWS (JOHN) *ed.* The digest of English case law: containing the reported decisions of the superior courts . . . [to 1897]. 16 v. 1898, and suppls. Reissued [covering reports to 1910]. 16 v. 1911. 2nd edn. 24 v. 1925–8. Suppl. to 1939.

**3042**  RENTON (*Sir* ALEXANDER WOOD) *and others*. Encyclopaedia of the laws of England: being a new abridgement by the most eminent legal authorities. 12 v. 1897–8. Suppl. 1903. 2nd edn. 15 v. 1906–9 and suppls. 1914, 1917, 1919.

**3043**  HALSBURY'S LAWS OF ENGLAND. The laws of England: being a complete statement of the whole law of England. Prepared under the editorship of Hardinge Stanley Giffard, Earl of Halsbury. 31 v. 1907–17. 3rd edn. 1952+.

Forming with *The complete statutes of England, classified and annotated* [*Halsbury's statutes of England*], 40 v. 1929–47, 2nd edn. 1948+, and *Halsbury's statutory instruments*, 24 v. 1954–60+, a complete statement of the law in force in the 20th cent.

**3044**  POLLOCK (*Sir* FREDERICK) *ed*. The revised reports: being a republication of such cases in the English courts of common law and equity, from the year 1785, as are still of practical utility. 152 v. 1891–1920.

A selection of cases judged to be still of use to working lawyers. A similar comp. repr. cases from the *Law Times reports* only, is in course of publ. as *All England law reports reprint* . . ., *1843–1935*, 30 v. and index. 1957+.

**3045**  THE ENGLISH REPORTS. 176 v. 1900–32.

Repr. of selected English cases to 1865 with original notes: about 300 v. of reports not incl. in the selection.

**3046**  INCORPORATED COUNCIL OF LAW REPORTING. The law reports. 1865+.

Gradually established themselves as the best and fullest reports, without displacing the older reports issued by the *Law Journal, Law Times, Solicitors' Journal, The Times,* and *Weekly Reporter.*

### 9. STATUTES

The best introduction to the process of law-making is Allen, *Law in the making* (**2986**). Christopher John Hughes, *The British statute book*, 1957, deals only with the position in the 1950s.

**3047**  INDEX TO THE STATUTES, public and private, from 1801. Compiled by order of the Select Committee of the House of Lords. In two parts. 2 v. 1845, 1854, 1867. Suppls. to pt. 2 1878 and 1888.

A *Chronological table of the statutes and index to the statutes in force*, 2 v. 1870+, has been issued annually since 1898.

**3048**  INDEX TO LOCAL AND PERSONAL ACTS: consisting of classified lists of the local and personal and private acts and special procedure orders, 1801–1947. 1949.

**3049**  BOND (MAURICE FRANCIS). 'Acts of parliament'. *Archives* iii (1957–8), 201–18.

Classifies Acts of Parliament for the benefit of those using the MS. records of parl *Acts of Parliament: some distinctions in their nature and numbering*, House of Commons Libr. Document No. 1, 1955, classifies them for the benefit of those using printed versions of the Acts.

**3050** ILBERT (*Sir* COURTENAY PEREGRINE). The mechanics of law-making. N.Y. 1914.

A very useful work by the leading draftsman of his day.

**3051** THRING (HENRY), *Baron Thring*. Practical legislation: or, the composition and language of Acts of Parliament. 1878. 2nd edn. 1902.

Thring was largely responsible for great improvements in the drafting of legislation during the 1860s and 1870s.

**3052** ILBERT (*Sir* COURTENAY PEREGRINE). Legislative methods & forms. Oxf. 1901.

The first comprehensive work on the subject. Succeeded by Sir [William] Alison Russell, *Legislative and other forms*, 1924, 4th edn. 1938.

**3053** MAXWELL (*Sir* PETER BENSON). On the interpretation of statutes. 1875. 11th edn. 1962.

The best of the few rather poor legal textbooks on the subject. Also useful is Henry Hardcastle, *A treatise on the rules which govern the construction and effect of statutory law*, 1879, 7th edn. 1936.

**3054** STATUTE LAW REVISION BOARD. Report of Mr. Bellenden Ker to the Lord Chancellor on the proceedings of the board for the revision of the statute law. H.C. 301 (1854). XXIV, 153. Second report. H.C. 302 (1854). XXIV, 363. Third report. H.C. 302-1 (1854). XXIV, 407.

**3055** STATUTE LAW COMMISSION. Report from Her Majesty's commissioners for consolidating the statute law [1963]. H.C. (1854-5). XV, 829. Second report. [2045] H.C. (1856). XVIII, 861. Third report. [2219] H.C. (1857 Sess. 2). XXI, 203. Appendix to third report. [2219-I] H.C. (Sess. 2). XXI, 211. Minutes etc. H.C. 46 (1857-8). XLVII, 309. Fourth report. H.C. 78. (1859 Sess. 2). XIII, Pt. I, 1.

See also *Memorandum of the Attorney-General* [Sir Alexander Cockburn], *as to the plan of proceeding in consolidation of the statutes*. H.C. 211 (1856). L, 617.

**3056** MANNER AND LANGUAGE OF CURRENT LEGISLATION. Report from the select committee on the Statute Law Commission [Chairman: Matthew Talbot Baines]. H.C. 99 (1857 Sess. 1). II, 773.

The Statute Law Commission had recommended that greater attention be paid to the drafting of bills. The 1857 inquiry collected evidence but made no report. A later inquiry in 1875 collected further evidence and presented a valuable report: *Report from the select committee on Acts of Parliament* [Chairman: Spencer Horatio Walpole]. H.C. 280 (1875). VIII, 213.

**3057** CHITTY (JOSEPH), *the elder*. A collection of statutes of practical utility, with notes thereon . . . 2 v. 1829-37. 5th edn. 14 v. 1894-1902. 6th edn. 1911+.

See also *Halsbury's statutes of England* (**3043**).

**3058** THE STATUTES: revised edition [1236-1878]. 18 v. 1870-85. 3rd edn. 32 v. 1951.

## 10. STATUTORY INSTRUMENTS

See also Administrative Law (**3268**).

**3059** COMMITTEE ON MINISTERS' POWERS [Chairman: Earl of Donoughmore]. Report. [Cmd. 4060] H.C. (1931–2). XII, 341.
Incl. a good hist. summary.

**3060** CARR (*Sir* CECIL THOMAS). Delegated legislation. Camb. 1921.

**3061** CHEN (CHIH-MAI). Parliamentary opinion of delegated legislation. N.Y. 1933.

**3062** WILLIS (JOHN). The parliamentary powers of English government departments. Camb., Mass. 1933.

**3063** STATUTORY RULES AND ORDERS: revised statutory rules and orders other than those of a local, personal, or temporary character, issued prior to 1890, and now in force [ed. by Alexander Pulling]. 8 v. [1896]. Rev. edn. [to 1903.] 13 v. 1904. Annual suppl. Rev. edn. [Statutory instruments…] 1948+.
See also *Halsbury's statutory instruments* (**3043**).

## 11. IMPORTANT TRIALS

**3064** ATLAY (JAMES BERESFORD). Famous trials of the century. 1899.
Mainly repr. from the *Cornhill magazine*.

**3065** SMITH-HUGHES (JACK). Unfair comment upon some Victorian murder trials. 1951.

**3066** LAMBERT (RICHARD STANTON). When justice faltered: a study of nine peculiar murder trials. 1935.
Eight Victorian cases and one modern.

**3067** WOODRUFF (JOHN DOUGLAS). The Tichborne claimant: a Victorian mystery. 1957.
The most celebrated of Victorian court cases: a fraudulent claim to the estates of the Tichborne family and a baronetcy by a Wapping butcher, who secured great popular support and was backed by a number of important people. Other good accounts are James Beresford Atlay, *The Tichborne case* [1917], Frederic Herbert Maugham, Viscount Maugham, *The Tichborne case*, 1936, and Michael Gilbert, *The claimant*, 1957. The claimant's counsel in the final trial, Edward Vaughan Hyde Kenealy (**3160**) publ. *The trial at bar of Sir Roger C. D. Tichborne, Bart. in the Court of Queen's Bench at Westminster . . .*, 8 v. 1875–80, and *The Tichborne tragedy . . .*, 1913.

**3068** BESTERMAN (THEODORE). The Druce–Portland case. 1935.
Comparable with the Tichborne case. A fraudulent claim, supported by speculators, to the Duke of Portland's estates, 1896–1909.

3069 HODGE (HARRY) *ed.* Notable British trials. Edin. & Lond. 1921+.

The largest coll. of modern trials. Until 1921 there were two separate ser., *Notable Scottish trials*, Glasgow & Edin. 12 v. 1905–15, and *Notable English trials*, Edin. & Lond. 15 v. 1911–21. Of the English trials of the period incl. in the ser. only four are not murder trials: Harford Montgomery Hyde, ed., *The trials of Oscar Wilde*, 1948; George Williams Keeton and Sir John Cameron, eds., *The trials of Gustav Rau, Otto Monsson and Walter Smith: the 'Veronica' trial*, 1952; William Teignmouth Shore, ed., *The baccarat case: Gordon-Cumming* v. *Wilson and others*, 1932; and Eric Russell Watson, ed., *Adolf Beck* [1924].

## B. THE LEGAL PROFESSIONS

### 1. GENERAL

3070 ABEL-SMITH (BRIAN) *and* STEVENS (ROBERT) *assisted by* BROOKE (ROSALIND). Lawyers and the courts: a sociological study of the English legal system, 1750–1965. Lond & Camb., Mass. 1967.

The only systematic modern study of the subject.

3071 WILLIAMS (JOSHUA). Letters to John Bull, Esq., on lawyers and law reform. 1857.

3072 SAUNDERS (CORNELIUS THOMAS). The amalgamation of the two branches of the legal profession considered with a special reference to contemplated law reforms. 1870.

3073 [CHARLEY (*Sir* WILLIAM THOMAS).] The legal profession viewed in the light of its past history, its present state, and projected law reforms. By Doctor-in-iure-civili. 1873.

3074 [DE SOUZA (LOUIS).] The truth about the bar and about the solicitors: being an appeal from the factions in both professions to the discreet in each, and to all serious men. By Innes Lincoln, Esq. 1882.

3075 CARR (*Sir* CECIL THOMAS). A Victorian law reformer's correspondence. Selden Soc. lecture. 1955.

Letters of Charles Henry Bellenden Ker (26 pp.).

3076 DERRIMAN (JAMES PARKYNS). Pageantry of the law. 1955.

Not on the period, but useful for ceremonies.

3077 SHEARWOOD (JOSEPH ALEXANDER). Guide for candidates for the professions of barrister and solicitor. 2nd edn. 1887.

The first edn. was entitled *The student's guide to the bar, the solicitors' intermediate and final and the universities' law examinations . . .*, 1879.

## 2. LEGAL EDUCATION

### (a) *General*

3078   BLAND (DESMOND SPARLING) *comp.* A bibliography of the inns of court and chancery. Selden Soc. 1965.

3079   BOWER (LAURENCE CECIL BARTLETT). 'English legal training: a critical survey'. *Modern Law Rev.* xiii (1950), 137–205.

> The best of the few accounts of a much-neglected subject. See also Alfred Zantzinger Reed, *Training for the public profession of the law: historical development and principal contemporary problems of legal education in the United States, with some account of conditions in England and Canada*, N.Y. 1921, and George Henry Emmott, 'Legal education in England', *Report of the nineteenth annual meeting of the American Bar Assoc.*, Phila. 1896, pp. 605–17.

3080   SELECT COMMITTEE ON LEGAL EDUCATION. Report from the select committee on legal education [Chairman: Thomas Wyse]. H.C. 686 (1846). X, 1.

> This committee and the Inns of Court Inquiry Commission (**3081**) produced masses of evidence which is invaluable for the unreformed system of legal education.

3081   INNS OF COURT INQUIRY COMMISSION. Report of the commissioners appointed to inquire into the arrangements in the Inns of Court and Inns of Chancery, for promoting the study of the law and jurisprudence [Chairman: Sir William Page Wood]. [1998] H.C. (1854–5). XVIII, 345.

3082   COUNCIL OF LEGAL EDUCATION. Calendar. 1901+.

3083   SCOTT (JOHN). The inns of court: their functions and privileges. 1869.

3084   SAUNDERS (CORNELIUS THOMAS). The inns of court and legal education: pending legislation reviewed, with suggestions for the proper function of a law university . . . 1875.

3085   LAWSON (FREDERICK HENRY). The Oxford law school, 1850–1965. Oxf. 1968.

> See also Harold Greville Hanbury, *The Vinerian chair and legal education*, Oxf. 1958, Albert Venn Dicey, *Can English law be taught at the universities?*, 1883, and James Bryce, Viscount Bryce, *Legal studies in the university of Oxford*, 1893.

3086   CLARK (EDWIN CHARLES). Cambridge legal studies. Camb. 1888.

### (b) *Academic Lawyers and Legal Historians*

3087   HOLDSWORTH (*Sir* WILLIAM SEARLE). The historians of Anglo-American law. N.Y. 1928. Repr. Hamden, Conn. 1966.

> Particularly good on the 19th cent. See also Cecil Herbert Stuart Fifoot, *Law and history in the nineteenth century*, Selden Soc. Lecture, 1956.

ANSON. See **8084**.

3088 DICEY. Memorials of Albert Venn Dicey : being chiefly letters and diaries. Ed. by Sir Robert Sangster Rait. 1925.

MAINE. See 714.

3089 MAITLAND. Frederic William Maitland. By Cecil Herbert Stewart Fifoot. Camb., Mass. 1971.

Largely replaces Herbert Albert Laurens Fisher, *Frederic William Maitland, Downing Professor of the Laws of England: a biographical sketch*, 1910. Fisher also ed. *The collected papers of Frederic William Maitland* . . ., 3 v. Camb. 1911. A new edn. of Maitland's works is in progress. Helen Maud Cam, ed., *Selected historical essays of F. W. Maitland*, Camb. 1957, incl. a useful list of books and articles about Maitland. There is a good coll. of corresp., Cecil Herbert Stuart Fifoot, ed., *The letters of Frederic William Maitland*, Selden Soc. 1965. For assessment see James Reese Cameron, *Frederic William Maitland and the history of English law*, Norman, Okla. 1961, and Henry Esmond Bell, *Maitland: a critical examination and assessment*, Camb., Mass. 1965.

3090 POLLOCK. For my grandson : remembrances of an ancient Victorian. By Sir Frederick Pollock. 1933.

Many of Pollock's letters are pr. in the *The Pollock–Holmes letters: correspondence of Sir Frederick Pollock and Mr. Justice Holmes, 1874–1932*, ed. by Mark DeWolfe Howe, 2 v. Camb. 1942. 2v. Camb., Mass. [*Holmes-Pollock letters*] 1941, 2nd edn. lv. Camb., Mass. 1961.

## 3. JUDGES

### (a) *Collective Biography*

3091 FOSS (EDWARD). Biographia juridica. A biographical dictionary of the judges of England . . . 1066–1870. 1870.

His *The judges of England . . . 1066–1864*, 9 v. 1848–64, is fuller but arranged in chronological not alphabetical order. His *Tabulae Curiales: or, tables of the superior courts of Westminster hall, showing the judges who sat in them from 1066 to 1864; with the attorney- and solicitor-generals of each reign*, 1865, is a useful list.

3092 DEBRETT'S HOUSE OF COMMONS AND THE JUDICIAL BENCH. 1867–1931. Annual.

Incl. biogs. of county court judges, recorders, stipendiary magistrates, Scots, Irish, and colonial judges.

3093 MANSON (EDWARD). The builders of our law during the reign of Queen Victoria. 1895. 2nd edn. 1904.

3094 SMITH (FREDERICK EDWIN), *Earl of Birkenhead*. Fourteen English judges. 1926.

3095 A GENERATION OF JUDGES : by their reporter [William Foulkes]. 1886. 2nd edn. 1888.

Brief and outspoken biog. sketches. Much better than Charles Kingston, pseud. of Charles Kingston O'Mahony, *Famous judges and famous trials*, 1923, and similar journalistic compilations.

3096  HEUSTON (ROBERT FRANCIS VERE). 'Lord Halsbury's judicial appointments'. *Law Q. Rev.* lxxviii (1962), 504–32.

3097  GIBB (ANDREW DEWAR). Judicial corruption in the United Kingdom. Edin. 1957.

### (b) *Lord Chancellors*

3098  ATLAY (JAMES BERESFORD). The Victorian chancellors. 2 v. 1906–8.

3099  HEUSTON (ROBERT FRANCIS VERE). Lives of the lord chancellors, 1885–1940. Oxf. 1964.

An excellent cont. of Atlay.

3100  CAMPBELL (JOHN), *Baron Campbell*. Lives of Lord Lyndhurst and Lord Brougham, lord chancellors and keepers of the great seal of England. Ed. by Mary Scarlett Campbell [Mrs. Hardcastle]. 1869.

To be read with Edward Burtenshaw Sugden, Baron St. Leonards, *Misrepresentations in Campbell's 'Lives of Lyndhurst and Brougham' corrected*, 1869.

3101  RUSSELL (EDWARD FREDERICK LANGLEY), *Baron Russell of Liverpool*. The royal conscience. 1961.

Short popular lives of 13 lord chancellors.

3102  CAIRNS. Brief memories of Hugh McCalmont, first Earl Cairns. By [Katherine M. Marsh]. 1885.

Trifling.

3103  CAMPBELL. Life of John, Lord Campbell, Lord High Chancellor of Great Britain: consisting of a selection from his autobiography, diary and letters. Ed. by his daughter, Mary Scarlett Hardcastle. 2 v. 1881. 2nd edn. 2 v. 1881.

The only coll. of speeches is the early *Speeches of Lord Campbell, at the bar, and in the House of Commons . . .*, Edin. 1842.

HALDANE. See 772.

3104  HALSBURY. The Earl of Halsbury, Lord High Chancellor, 1823–1921. By Alice Wilson-Fox. 1929.

Thin and pedestrian.

3105  HATHERLEY. A memoir of the Right Hon. William Page Wood, Baron Hatherley, with selections from his correspondence. By William Richard Wood Stephens. 2 v. 1883.

3106  SELBORNE. Memorials. By Roundell Palmer, Earl of Selborne. 4 v. 1896–8.

Diffuse, but incl. useful material. Nominally in two pts. each of 2 v. Pt. 1 *Family and personal, 1766–1865*, Pt. 2 *Personal and political, 1865–1895*. For his papers see Edward Geoffrey Watson Bill, ed., *Catalogue of the papers of Roundell Palmer (1812–1895), first Earl of Selborne*, Lambeth Palace Libr., 1967.

3107 WESTBURY. The life of Richard, Lord Westbury, formerly Lord High Chancellor, with selections from his correspondence. By Thomas Arthur Nash. 2 v. 1888.

### (c) *Other Judges*

3108 ALDERSON. Selections from the charges and other detached papers of Baron Alderson: with an introductory notice of his life. By Sir Charles Henry Alderson. 1858.

3109 ALVERSTONE. Recollections of bench and bar. By Richard Everard Webster, Viscount Alverstone. 1914.

Dull and inaccurate.

3110 AVORY. Mr. Justice Avory. By Stanley Jackson. 1935.

One of three books publ. about the time of Avory's death in 1935. The others are Gordon Lang, *Mr. Justice Avory*, and Bernard O'Donnell, *The trials of Mr. Justice Avory*. None has any permanent value.

3111 BOWEN. Lord Bowen: a biographical sketch . . . By Sir Henry Stewart Cunningham. 1897.

3112 BRAMWELL. Some account of George William Wilshere, Baron Bramwell of Hever, and his opinions. By Charles Fairfield. 1898.

3113 COLERIDGE. Life and correspondence of John Duke, Lord Coleridge, Lord Chief Justice of England. By Ernest Hartley Coleridge. 2 v. 1904.

There is also *Forty years of friendship as recorded in the correspondence of John Duke, Lord Coleridge and Ellis Yarnall during 1856–1895*, ed. by Carlton Yarnall, 1911.

3114 COLERIDGE. This for remembrance. By Bernard John Seymour Coleridge, Baron Coleridge. 1925.

Incl. reminiscences of his father and grandfather, both, like himself, judges.

3115 DARLING. The life of Lord Darling . . . By Sir Derek Walker-Smith. 1938.

There are also two popular books: Evelyn Graham, pseud. of Netley Lucas, *Lord Darling and his famous trials*, 1929, and Dudley Raymond Barker, *Lord Darling's famous cases*, 1936.

3116 DAY. John C. F. S. Day; his forbears and himself; a biographical study by one of his sons [Arthur Francis Day]. 1916.

3117 FRY. A memoir of the Right Honourable Sir Edward Fry, G.C.B. . . . . By his daughter, Agnes Fry. Oxf. 1921.

3118   GORELL. John Gorell Barnes, first Lord Gorell, 1848–1913: a memoir. By James Edward Geoffrey De Montmorency. 1920.

3119   HAWKINS. The reminiscences of Sir Henry Hawkins, Baron Brampton. Ed. by Richard Harris. 2 v. 1904.

There are also some interesting anecdotes in Ernest Brown Bowen-Rowlands, *The life in the law of Sir Henry Hawkins (Baron Brampton) as related by him to the writer* [1907].

3120   HOBHOUSE. Lord Hobhouse; a memoir. By Leonard Trelawney Hobhouse and John Lawrence Le Breton Hammond. 1905.

JAMES. See **783**.

3121   KERR. Commissioner Kerr: an individuality. By George Pitt-Lewis. 1903.

Robert Malcolm Kerr was judge of the City of London court, 1859–1901.

3122   LYNDHURST. A life of Lord Lyndhurst, from letters and papers in possession of his family. By Sir Theodore Martin. 1883. 2nd edn. 1884.

3123   MACNAGHTEN. A selection of Lord Macnaghten's judgments, 1887–1912. Priv. pr. 1951.

3124   MOULTON. The life of Lord Moulton. By Hugh Fletcher Moulton. 1922.

3125   PARMOOR. A retrospect: looking back over a life of more than eighty years. By Charles Alfred Cripps, Baron Parmoor. 1936.

3126   PARRY. My own way: an autobiography. By Sir Edward Abbott Parry. 1932.

The only good life of a county court judge. Parry also publ. numerous books of essays incl. *What the judge saw . . .*, 1912, and *What the judge thought*, 1922.

3127   POLLOCK. Lord Chief Baron Pollock: a memoir . . . By Ernest Murray Pollock, Baron Hanworth. 1929.

3128   ROBSON. A Liberal attorney-general: being the life of Lord Robson of Jesmond (1852–1918) . . . By George Williams Keeton. 1949.

3129   ROLT. The memoirs of the Right Honourable Sir John Rolt, Lord Justice of the Court of Appeal in Chancery, 1804–1871. Ed. by Charles Thomas Le Quesne and others. Hon. Soc. of Inner Temple. 1939.

3130   RUSSELL. The life of Lord Russell of Killowen. By Richard Barry O'Brien. 1901.

**3131  SHAW.** Letters to Isabel. By Thomas Shaw, Baron Shaw of Dunfermline, later Baron Craigmyle. 1921. New edn. 1936.

Cont. in *The other bundle*, 1927, primarily a coll. of legal anecdotes. There is a brief biog., Alexander Shaw, Baron Craigmyle, *Thomas Shaw, first Lord Craigmyle: a monograph*, 1937.

**3132  STEPHEN.** The life of Sir James Fitzjames Stephen, Bart., K.C.S.I., a judge of the High Court of Justice. By Sir Leslie Stephen. 1895.

Leon Radzinowicz, *Sir James Fitzjames Stephen, 1829–1894, and his contribution to the development of criminal law*, Selden Soc. lecture, 1957, is a fine study and includes a full bibliog. of Stephen's works. For his political theory see **715**.

## 4. THE BAR

### (a) *General*

**3133  KELLY (BERNARD WILLIAM).** A short history of the English bar. 1908.

**3134  GENERAL COUNCIL OF THE BAR.** Annual statement. 1894–5+.

**3135  COX (EDWARD WILLIAM).** The advocate: his training, practice, rights and duties. 1852.

Sir Frederick John Wrottesley, *The examination of witnesses in court*, 1910, 2nd edn. 1931, is based on Cox.

**3136  WELLMAN (FRANCIS LEWIS).** The art of cross-examination. N.Y. 1903. New edn. 1923.

A minor classic by an able American lawyer. Wellman also publ. *Day in court: or the subtle art of great advocates*, N.Y. 1910.

**3137  KELLY (BERNARD WILLIAM).** Famous advocates and their speeches: British forensic eloquence, from Lord Erskine to Lord Russell of Killowen. 1921. 2nd edn. 1949.

There are many popular books of this sort, incl. Charlie Lewis Broad, *Advocates of the golden age: their lives and cases*, 1958.

**3138  PULLING (ALEXANDER).** The order of the coif. 1884.

A history of the serjeants-at-law.

**3139  SENIOR (WILLIAM).** Doctors' commons and the old court of admiralty: a short history of the civilians in England. 1922.

A thin sketch of a neglected subject.

**3140  CARR (*Sir* CECIL THOMAS).** Pension book of Clement's Inn. Selden Soc. 78. 1960.

Useful intro. on the dissolution of the Inns of Chancery and Serjeants' Inn.

**3141  BALL (*Sir* WILLIAM VALENTINE).** Lincoln's Inn: its history and traditions. 1947.

3142 ATKIN (JAMES RICHARD), *Baron Atkin, ed.* The moot book of Gray's Inn. 1924.

(b) *Collective Biography*

3143 FOSTER (JOSEPH). Men-at-the-bar: a biographical handlist of the members of the various Inns of Court, including Her Majesty's judges, etc. 1885.

Succeeded and expanded Charles Shaw, *The Inns of Court calendar: a record of the members of the English bar* . . ., 1877.

3144 MASTERS OF THE BENCH of the Hon. Society of the Inner Temple, 1450–1883, and Masters of the Temple, 1540–1883. 1883. Suppl. for 1883–1900. 1901.

3145 HUTCHINSON (JOHN). A catalogue of notable Middle Templars, with brief biographical notices. 1902.

3146 STURGESS (HERBERT ARTHUR CHARLIE) *comp.* Register of admissions to the Honourable Society of the Middle Temple: from the fifteenth century to the year 1944. 3 v. 1949.

3147 INGPEN (ARTHUR ROBERT) *ed.* The Middle Temple bench book: being a register of benchers of the Middle Temple from the earliest record to the present time . . . 1912. 2nd edn. by John Bruce Williamson. 1937. Suppl. to 1958.

3148 FOSTER (JOSEPH) *ed.* The register of admissions to Gray's Inn, 1521–1889 . . . 1889.

3149 THE RECORDS OF THE HONOURABLE SOCIETY OF LINCOLN'S INN. Vol. II. Admissions from A.D. 1800 to A.D. 1893, and chapel registers. 1896.

(c) *Individual Biography*

3150 BENJAMIN. Judah P. Benjamin: confederate statesman. By Robert Douthat Meade. N.Y. 1943.

Largely supplants a sound early biog., Pierce Butler, *Judah P. Benjamin*, Phila. 1907. Benjamin became one of the leaders of the English bar after the American civil war.

3151 CAVE. Lord Cave: a memoir. By Sir Charles Edward Mallet. 1931.

3152 CLARKE. The life of Sir Edward Clarke. By Sir Derek Walker-Smith and Edward Clarke. 1939.

To be read with Clarke's own *The story of my life*, 1918. He publ. 4 v. of speeches: *Public speeches, 1880–1890*, 1890; *Public speeches, 1890–1900*, 1900; *Speeches . . . chiefly forensic* . . . [1894]; *Selected speeches* . . ., 1908.

3153 HALL. The life of Sir Edward Marshall Hall. By Edward Marjoribanks. 1929.

Marjoribanks also publ. *Famous trials of Marshall Hall*, 1950.

3154 HARRIS. The autobiography of George Harris, LL.D., F.S.A. Priv. pr. 1888.

Best known as an antiquarian, Harris was an eminent provincial barrister.

3155 HASTINGS. Sir Patrick Hastings: his life and cases. By Harford Montgomery Hyde. 1960.

Patricia Hastings, *The life of Patrick Hastings*, 1959, and Hastings's own *Autobiography*, 1948, and *Cases in court*, 1949, are also valuable.

3156 HEWART. The chief: the biography of Gordon Hewart, Lord Chief Justice of England, 1922–40. By Robert Jackson. 1959.

3157 HILL. The recorder of Birmingham: a memoir of Matthew Davenport Hill, with selections from his correspondence. By his daughters, Rosamond Davenport Hill and Florence Davenport Hill. 1878.

3158 HUMPHREYS. Sir Travers Humphreys: a biography. By Douglas Gordon Browne. 1960.

Humphreys himself publ. *Criminal days: recollections and reflections*, 1946, and *A book of trials*, 1953, and there are popular lives by Stanley Jackson, 1952, and Carl Eric Bechhofer Roberts [Ephesian], 1936.

3159 ISAACS. Lord Reading and his cases: the study of a great career. By Sir Derek Walker-Smith. 1934.

For Isaacs's career generally see **782**.

3160 KENEALY. Memoirs of Edward Vaughan Kenealy, LL.D. By his daughter Arabella Kenealy. 1908.

3161 LOCKWOOD. Sir Frank Lockwood: a biographical sketch. By Augustine Birrell. 1898.

Lockwood was a noted caricaturist whose best work appears in *The Frank Lockwood sketch book: being a selection from the pen and ink drawings of the late Sir Frank Lockwood, Q.C., M.P.*, 1898.

3162 MUIR. Sir Richard Muir: a memoir of a public prosecutor: intimate revelations compiled from the papers of Sir Richard Muir, late senior counsel to the British Treasury. By Sidney Theodore Felstead. Ed. by Lady Muir. 1927.

## 5. SOLICITORS AND ATTORNEYS

3163 BIRKS (MICHAEL). Gentlemen of the law. 1960.

The first general hist., inevitably rather thin. Edmund Brown Viney Christian, *A short history of solicitors*, 1896, and *Solicitors: an outline of their history*, 1925, are only sketches. His *Leaves of the lower branch: the attorney in life and letters*, 1909, is fuller but intended chiefly to entertain.

3164  PULLING (ALEXANDER). A summary of the law of attorneys and solicitors. 1849. 3rd edn. 1862.

Later works incl. Charles Ford, *The Solicitors' Acts: with notes and comments*, 1877, Arthur Cordery, *The law relating to solicitors of the Supreme Court of Judicature*, 1878, 4th edn. 1935, and Archer Moresby White, *A treatise on the constitution and government of solicitors: their rights and duties*, 1894.

3165  INCORPORATED LAW SOCIETY. Law Society's registry. 1888–1902.

Cont. as *The Law Society's gazette [and register]*, 1903+. The Law Society (formerly the Law Institution) also publ. an *Annual report*, 1837+.

3166  PEARSON. The doings of a country solicitor . . . By Alexander Pearson. Priv. pr. Kendal. 1947.

3167  TAYLOR. Autobiography of a Lancashire lawyer: being the life and recollections of John Taylor, attorney-at-law, and first coroner of the borough of Bolton . . . Ed. by James Clegg. Bolton. 1883.

Uncommonly like *The diary of a nobody*.

3168  WINDER. A life's adventure. By Thomas H. Winder. Priv. pr. 1921.

A Bolton solicitor.

## 6. LEGAL GOSSIP

In the absence of adequate histories, volumes of gossipy reminiscences are of considerable importance, although there are numerous errors of fact in most of them and their organization is unhelpful. Only the best of the kind are included here.

3169  ABINGER. Forty years at the bar: being the memoirs of Edward Abinger . . . [1930].

3170  ASHLEY. My sixty years in the law. By Frederick William Ashley. 1936.

Ashley was clerk to Mr. Justice Avory for 54 years.

3171  ASHTON. As I went on my way. By Arthur Jacob Ashton. 1924.

Incl. one of the best accounts of the courts in the 1880s.

3172  BALLANTINE. Some experiences of a barrister's life. By Serjeant William Ballantine. 2 v. 1882.

Cont. in *The old world and the new*, 1884. Immensely popular in the 1880s and 1890s. Many edns.

3173  BELL. These meddlesome attorneys. By Edward Albert Bell. 1939.

3174  BIRON. Without prejudice: impressions of life and law. By Sir Henry Chartres Biron. 1936.

3175   BROWNE. Forty years at the bar. By John Hutton Balfour Browne. 1916.

Browne also publ. *Essays critical and political*, 2 v. 1907, and *Recollections, literary and political*, 1917.

3176   CRISPE. Reminiscences of a K.C. By Thomas Edward Crispe. [1909.]

3177   DICKENS. The recollections of Sir Henry [Fielding] Dickens. 1934.

3178   HOLLAMS. Jottings of an old solicitor. By Sir John Hollams. 1906.

3179   LEIGH. Bar, bat and bit: recollections and experiences of Sir Edward Chandos Leigh. Ed. by Francis Robert Bush. 1913.

3180   PLOWDEN. Grain or chaff? The autobiography of a police magistrate. By Alfred Chichele Plowden. 1903.

3181   POLAND. Seventy-two years at the bar: a memoir [of Sir Harry Bodkin Poland]. By Ernest Brown Bowen-Rowlands. 1924.

3182   PURCELL. Forty years at the criminal bar: experiences and impressions. By Edmund Desanges Purcell. 1916.

3183   ROBINSON. Bench and bar: reminiscences of one of the last of an ancient race. By [Serjeant] Benjamin Coulson Robinson. 1889. 3rd edn. 1891.

3184   THORPE. The still life of the Middle Temple, with some of its table talk: preceded by fifty years' reminiscences. By William George Thorpe. 1892.

3185   WILLIAMS. Leaves of a life: being the reminiscences of Montagu Williams, Q.C. 2 v. 1890.

Followed by *Later leaves: being the further reminiscences of Montagu Williams, Q.C.*, 1891.

## C. THE ORGANIZATION AND PROCEDURE OF THE COURTS

Harold Greville Hanbury, *English courts of law*, Home Univ. Libr., 1944, 4th edn. 1967, is a general introduction to the subject. George Drewry Squibb, *The high court of chivalry: a study of the civil law in England*, Oxf. 1959, deals with a court in abeyance throughout the period, but subsequently revived.

### I. General

3186   FRANQUET DE FRANQUEVILLE (AMABLE CHARLES), *Comte*. Le système judiciaire de la Grande Bretagne. 2 v. Paris. 1893.

De Franqueville also publ. *Le barreau anglais*, Paris 1889, and *Les avoués en Angleterre*, Paris 1890.

3187 GUEST (ANTONY). 'The state of the law courts'. 4 pts. *Strand Mag.*
i (1891), 402–9, 531–8, 638–47; ii (1891), 84–92.

3188 MACDONELL (*Sir* JOHN). 'Statistics of litigation in England and
Wales since 1859'. *Roy. Stat. Soc. J.* lvii (1894), 452–519.

Macdonell comp. most of the official statistics from 1894 to 1919. See also James T.
Hammick, 'On the judicial statistics of England and Wales, with special reference to
the recent returns relating to crime', *Stat. Soc. J.* xxx (1867), 375–426; William John
Bovill, 'On the statistics of civil procedure in English courts of law', ibid. 427–53;
F. H. Janson, 'Some statistics of the courts of justice and of legal procedure in England',
*Stat. Soc. J.* xxxvii (1874), 21–42; and Leone Levi, 'A survey of indictable and summary
jurisdiction offences in England and Wales, from 1857 to 1876 . . .', *Stat. Soc. J.* xliii
(1880), 423–56.

3189 COLLIER (ROBERT PORRETT), *Baron Monkswell*. A letter on reform
of the superior courts of common law, to the Right Hon. Lord John Russell.
1851. 2nd edn. 1852.

3190 COCKBURN (*Sir* ALEXANDER JAMES EDMUND). Our judicial
system: a letter to the Lord High Chancellor on the proposed changes in the
judicature of the country. 1870.

3191 COLERIDGE COMMISSION ON BRINGING TOGETHER ALL
THE SUPERIOR COURTS. Report of the commissioners appointed to
inquire into the expediency of bringing together into one place or neighbourhood all the superior courts of law and equity, the probate and divorce courts
and the High Court of Admiralty . . . [Chairman: Sir John Taylor Coleridge.]
[2710] H.C. (1860). XXXI, 89.

3192 ENGLISH AND IRISH LAW AND CHANCERY COMMISSION.
First report of Her Majesty's commissioners appointed to inquire into the
superior courts of common law and courts of chancery of England and Ireland.
[3238] H.C. (1863). XV, 463. Second report. [3674] H.C. (1866). XVII, 83.
Minority report. H.C. 285 (1867). XIX, 287.

3193 JUDICATURE COMMISSION: first report of the commissioners
[Chairman: Lord Cairns]. [4130] H.C. (1868–9). XXV, 1. Second report, pt. 1.
[C. 631] H.C. (1872). XX, 217. Pt. 2. [C. 631–I] H.C. (1872). XX, 245. Third
report. [C. 957] H.C. (1874). XXIV, 1. Appendix to the third report. [C. 957–I]
H.C. (1874). XXIV, 13. Fourth report. [C. 984] H.C. (1874). XXIV, 183.
Appendix to fourth report. [C. 984–I] H.C. (1874). XXIV, 191. Fifth and final
report. [C. 1090] H.C. (1874). XXIV, 307.

The most important of all inquiries into the judicial system.

3194 LEGAL DEPARTMENTS COMMISSION. First report of the commissioners appointed to inquire into the administrative departments of the
courts of justice [Chairman: Lord Lisgar]. [C. 949] H.C. (1874). XXIV, 557.
Second report. [C. 1107] H.C. (1874). XXIV, 583. Minutes of evidence.
[C. 1245] H.C. (1875). XXX, 163.

3195  JUDICATURE ACTS (LEGAL OFFICES) COMMITTEE. Report of the judicature acts (legal offices) committee [Chairman: Sir George Jussel]. [C. 2067] H.C. (1878). XXV, 5.

3196  SUPREME COURT OFFICE COMMITTEE. Copy of the report of the committee on the central office of the Supreme court of judicature [Chairman: Lord Coleridge]. H.C. 181 (1887). LXVII, 179.

## 2. APPEALS GENERALLY

3197  LORDS COMMITTEE ON APPELLATE JURISDICTION. Report from the select committee of the House of Lords on appellate jurisdiction [Chairman: Lord Hatherley]. H.C. 325 (1872). VII, 193.

3198  COURT OF CRIMINAL APPEAL (REPORT OF THE JUDGES). Return of the report of the judges in 1892 to the Lord Chancellor recommending the constitution of a court of appeal and revision of sentences in criminal cases. H.C. 127 (1894). LXXI, 173.

3199  MACQUEEN (JOHN FRASER). A practical treatise on the appellate jurisdiction of the House of Lords and Privy Council. 1842.

3200  WEBB (CHARLES LOCOCK). The practice of the Supreme Court of Judicature and of the House of Lords on appeals . . . 1877.

## 3. HOUSE OF LORDS

See also Gibb, *Law from over the border* (**9831**).

3201  LORDS COMMITTEE ON APPELLATE JURISDICTION OF THE HOUSE. Report from the select committee of the House of Lords appointed to inquire whether it is expedient to make any, and if so, what provision, for more effectually securing the efficient exercise of the functions of this house as a court of appellate jurisdiction . . . [Chairman: Lord Cranworth.] H.L. 46 (1856). XXIV, I.

3202  DENISON (CHARLES MARSH) *and* SCOTT (CHARLES HENDERSON). The practice & procedure of the House of Lords, in English, Scotch & Irish appeal cases under the Appellate Jurisdiction Act, 1876. 1879.

3203  MACQUEEN (JOHN FRASER). A letter to the Lord Lyndhurst on the House of Peers in its judicial character. 1856.

3204  GORDON (JOHN WILLIAM). The appellate jurisdiction of the House of Lords and of the full parliament. 1905.

A pamphlet occasioned by the decision in Free Church of Scotland *v.* Overtoun, 1904, suggesting an appeal from the House of Lords to the full parliament.

## 4. JUDICIAL COMMITTEE OF THE PRIVY COUNCIL

3205  MACPHERSON (WILLIAM). The practice of the Judicial Committee of Her Majesty's most honorable Privy Council. 1860. 2nd edn. 1873. Suppl. 1900. New edns. by Frank Safford and George Wheeler, 1901 and 1912.

3206  PALMER (ROUNDELL), *Earl of Selborne*. Judicial procedure in the Privy Council. Priv. pr. 1881. 2nd edn. 1891.

3207  MICHELL (EDWARD BLAIR) *and* MICHELL (RICHARD BROOKE). The practice and procedure in appeals from India to the Privy Council. Madras. 1876.

3208  BENTWICH (NORMAN DE MATTOS). The practice of the Privy Council in judicial matters . . . 1912. 3rd edn. 1937.

3209  HOLLANDER (BARNETT). Colonial justice: the unique achievement of the Privy Council's committee of judges. Camb. 1961.

## 5. CHANCERY

3210  CHANCERY COMMISSION. First report of Her Majesty's commissioners appointed to inquire into the process, practice, and system of pleading in the Court of Chancery, &c. [Chairman: Sir John Romilly]. [1437] H.C. (1852). XXI, 1. Suppl. to first report. [1454] H.C. (1852). XXI, 333. Second report. [1731] H.C. (1854). XXIV, 1. Third report. [2064] H.C. (1856). XXII, 1. Some additional matter is printed in H.C. 216 (1852). XLII, 541.

3211  CHANCERY EVIDENCE COMMISSION. Report of Her Majesty's commissioners appointed to inquire into the mode of taking evidence in Chancery, and its effects [Chairman: Lord Campbell]. [2698] H.C. (1860). XXXI, 279.

3212  CHANCERY FUNDS COMMISSION. Report of Her Majesty's commissioners appointed to inquire into the constitution of the Accountant-General's department of the Court of Chancery, the forms of business in use therein, and the provisions for the custody and management of the stocks and funds of the court [Chairman: Duke of Argyll]. [3280] H.C. (1864). XXIX, 1.

3213  DANIELL (EDMUND ROBERT). A treatise on the practice of the High Court of Chancery . . . 3 v. 1837–41. 8th edn. 2 v. 1914.

3214  GOLDSMITH (GEORGE). The doctrine and practice of equity; or, a concise outline of proceedings in the High Court of Chancery. 1838. 6th edn. 1871.

3215  AYCKBOURN (HUBERT). The new Chancery practice: being a condensed treatise on the practice of the Court of Chancery. 1844. 10th edn. 1880.

3216  ROBERTS (THOMAS ARCHIBALD). The principles of the High Court of Chancery and the powers and duties of its judges. 1852. 3rd edn. 1877.

3217  MORGAN (*Sir* GEORGE OSBORNE). Chancery acts & orders: being a collection of statutes and general orders, recently passed and made, for extending the jurisdiction and improving the practice of the Court of Chancery. 1858. 6th edn. 1885.

Morgan and Horace Davey, Baron Davey, also publ. *A treatise on costs in Chancery* ... 1865, 2nd edn. 1882.

## 6. COMMON LAW COURTS

3218  COMMON LAW COURTS COMMISSION. Copy of the first report of Her Majesty's commissioners for inquiring into the process, practice, and system of pleading in the superior courts of common law &c. [Chairman: Sir John Jervis]. [1389] H.C. (1851). XXII, 567. Second report. [1626] H.C. (1852–3). XL, 701.

3219  COMMON LAW (JUDICIAL BUSINESS) COMMISSION. Report from the common law (judicial business) commissioners [Chairman: Lord Campbell]. [2268] H.C. (1857 Sess. 2). XXI, 1.

3220  CAWDOR COMMITTEE ON THE KING'S BENCH DIVISION. Report from the joint select committee on the High Court of Justice (King's Bench Division) [Chairman: Earl Cawdor]. H.C. 333 (1909). VIII, 1.

3221  ROYAL COMMISSION ON DELAY IN THE KING'S BENCH DIVISION: First report of the commissioners [Chairman: Viscount St. Aldwyn]. [Cd. 6761] H.C. (1913). XXX, 683. Minutes of evidence. [Cd. 6762] H.C. (1913). XXX, 689. Second and final report. [Cd. 7177] H.C. (1914). XXXVII, 1. Minutes of evidence. [Cd. 7178] H.C. (1914). XXXVII, 49.

3222  SUTTON (RALPH). Personal actions at common law. 1929.

3223  ARCHBOLD (JOHN FREDERICK). The practice of the Court of King's Bench in personal actions, and ejectment. 2 v. 1819. 14th edn. 2 v. 1885.

3224  LUSH (*Sir* ROBERT). The practice of the superior courts of law at Westminster in actions and proceedings over which they have a common jurisdiction. 1840. 3rd edn. 1865.

3225  DAY (*Sir* JOHN CHARLES FREDERICK SIGISMUND). The Common Law Procedure Acts and other statutes relating to the practice of the superior courts of common law, and the rules of court. 1861. 4th edn. 1872.

3226  WILSON (ARTHUR). The Supreme Court of Judicature Acts, 1873 and 1875 ... 1875. 7th edn. 1888.

The most widely used of a number of textbooks on the subject. Other useful ones are John Mountney Lely and William Decimus Inglett Foulkes, *The Judicature Acts, 1873 and 1875 . . .*, 1875, 4th edn. 1883, and Sir James Fitzjames Stephen, *The Supreme Court of Judicature Acts, 1873, 1874, and 1875, consolidated*, 1875.

3227 INDERMAUR (JOHN). A manual of the practice of the Supreme Court of Judicature in the Queen's Bench, Common Pleas, Exchequer and Chancery Divisions . . ., 1878. 10th edn. 1919.

3228 THE ANNUAL PRACTICE OF THE SUPREME COURT. 2 v. 1883+.

*The yearly supreme court practice 1899–1944, was a rival publ.*

### 7. COMMERCIAL COURT

3229 MATHEW (*Sir* THEOBALD). The practice of the Commercial Court. 1902.

### 8. COUNTY COURTS

3230 SNAGGE (*Sir* THOMAS WILLIAM). The evolution of county courts. 1904.

3231 SMITH (HARRY). 'The resurgent county court in Victorian Britain'. *Amer. J. Legal Hist.* xiii (1969), 126–38.

3232 COUNTY COURTS COMMISSION. First report of the commissioners appointed to inquire into the state of the county courts . . . [Chairman: Sir John Romilly]. [1914] H.C. (1854–5). XVIII, 149.

3233 LORDS COMMITTEE ON COUNTY COURTS BILL. Report from the select committee of the House of Lords on the County Courts Bill [H.L.]. H.L. 61 (1878–9). VII, 1.

3234 COUNTY COURT PROCEDURE COMMITTEE. Report of the committee appointed by the Lord Chancellor to inquire into certain matters of county court procedure. [Chairman: Lord Gorell]. H.C. 71 (1909). LXXII, 311.

3235 THE COUNTY COURTS CHRONICLE. 47 v. 1847–1920.

3236 ARCHBOLD (JOHN FREDERICK). The practice of the new county courts. 1847. 10th edn. 1889.

*Merged in* The yearly county court practice, *1897+, with George Pitt-Lewis,* A complete practice of the county courts *. . ., 2 v. 1880, 4th edn. 1890.*

3237 POLLOCK (*Sir* CHARLES EDWARD). The practice of the county courts . . . 1851. 9th edn. 1880.

*Merged in* The annual county courts' practice, *1889+, with George Washington Heywood,* The common law and equity practice of the county courts, *1870, 4th edn. 1886.*

## 9. THE ADMIRALTY COURTS

3238  WISWALL (FRANK LAWRENCE). The development of Admiralty jurisdiction and practice since 1800. Camb. 1970.

3239  WILLIAMS (ROBERT GRIFFITH) *and* BRUCE (*Sir* GAINSFORD). The jurisdiction and practice of the High Court of Admiralty . . . 1868–9. 3rd edn. 1902.

3240  ROSCOE (EDWARD STANLEY). A treatise on the jurisdiction and practice of the Admiralty division of the High Court of Justice . . . 1878. 4th edn. 1920.

3241  ROSCOE (EDWARD STANLEY). A history of the English prize court. 1924.

Roscoe also publ. *Reports of prize cases . . . 1745 to 1859*, 2 v. 1905, and *Studies in the history of the Admiralty and prize courts*, 1932.

## 10. JUSTICES OF THE PEACE

3242  MOIR (ESTHER ALINE LOWNDES). The justice of the peace. Harmondsworth. 1969.

3243  LEE (JOHN MICHAEL). 'Parliament and the appointment of magistrates: the origin of advisory committees'. *Parliamentary affairs* xiii (1959–60), 85–94.

3244  JAMES COMMISSION ON THE SELECTION OF JUSTICES OF THE PEACE. Report of the royal commission on the selection of justices of the peace [Chairman: Lord James of Hereford]. [Cd. 5250] H.C. (1910). XXXVII, 647. Minutes of evidence. [Cd. 5358] H.C. (1910). XXXVII, 669.

3245  BURN (RICHARD). The justice of the peace and parish officer, upon a plan entirely new, and comprehending all the law to the present time. 2 v. 1755. 30th edn. 5 v. 1869.

An alphabetical digest which, becoming unwieldy, was eventually succeeded by *Stone's justice's manual* (**3247**). Used in conjunction with William Paley, *The law and practice of summary convictions on penal statutes by justices of the peace . . .*, 1814, 10th edn. 1953.

3246  ARCHBOLD (JOHN FREDERICK). The jurisdiction and practice of the court of Quarter Sessions . . . 1836. 6th edn. 1908.

Suppl. by his *The justice of the peace and parish officer . . .*, 3 v. 1840, and later edns. to 1930, and his *Jervis's Acts . . .*, 1848, 4th edn. 1868. See also Thomas Sirrell Pritchard, *The jurisdiction, practice and procedure of the Quarter Sessions in judicial matters*, 1875, 2nd edn. 1904.

3247  STONE (SAMUEL). The justice's pocket manual: or, guide to the ordinary duties of a justice of the peace . . . 1842. 28th edn. 1895. Annual 1897+.

Cited as *Stone's justice's manual*. Not to be confused with another contemporary textbook, John Stone, *The practice of the petty sessions: comprising all the proceedings . . .*

*before justices of the peace out of sessions,* 1836, 9th edn. 1882. Stone was suppl. by
George Colwell Oke, *The magisterial formulist: being a complete collection of forms and
precedents for practical use in all matters out of Quarter Sessions,* 1850, 17th edn. 1968;
William Cunningham Glen, *The acts regulating the duties of justices of the peace out of
sessions . . . known as Jervis's Acts* [later edns. styled *The Summary Jurisdiction Acts . . .*],
1857, 7th edn. 1894; William Knox Wigram, *The justice's notebook,* 1879, 15th edn.
1951; and Harold Wright, *The office of magistrate,* 1889, 9th edn. 1953.

3248  OKE (GEORGE COLWELL). The synopsis of summary convictions,
showing, at one view, the penalties, &c., for 1300 offences, when proceedings
must be commenced, what justices to convict . . . 1848. 14th edn. 2 v. 1893.

3249  THE JUSTICE OF THE PEACE. 1837+. Weekly.

3250  ALVERSTONE COMMITTEE ON LONDON QUARTER SES-
SIONS. Report of the departmental committee on the County of London
Quarter Sessions [Chairman: the Lord Chief Justice, Lord Alverstone]. [Cd.
4828] H.C. (1909). XXXI, 329. Minutes of evidence. [Cd. 4829] H.C. (1909).
XXXI, 371.

## 11. Metropolitan Magistrates

3251  BELPER COMMITTEE ON METROPOLITAN POLICE MAGIS-
TRATES &c. Report of the departmental committee appointed by the Secretary of State for the Home Department to inquire into the jurisdiction of the
metropolitan police magistrates and county justices respectively in the Metropolitan Police Court District [Chairman: Lord Belper]. [Cd. 374] H.C. (1900).
XL, 659.

3252  GREENWOOD (JAMES). The prisoner in the dock: my four years'
daily experiences in the London police courts. 1902.

See also Cecil Maurice Chapman, *Poor man's court of justice: twenty-five years as a
metropolitan magistrate,* 1925.

3253  GAMON (HUGH REECE PERCIVAL). The London police court:
to-day & to-morrow. 1907.

## 12. Coroners

3254  WELLINGTON (RICHARD HENSLOWE). The king's coroner.
Vol. I. A complete collection of the statutes relating to the office together with
a short history of the same. Vol. II. The practice and procedure in his judicial
and ministerial capacities. 2 v. 1905–6.

3255  SELECT COMMITTEE ON THE OFFICE OF CORONER. Report
from the select committee on the office of coroner [Chairman: Robert Lowe].
H.C. 193 (1860). XXII, 257.

3256  CORONERS COMMITTEE. First report of the departmental committee appointed to inquire into the law relating to coroners and coroners'

inquests, and into the practice of coroners' courts [Chairman: Sir Mackenzie Dalzell Chalmers]. Pt. I. [Cd. 4781] H.C. (1909). XV, 385; Pt. II. [Cd. 4782] H.C. (1909). XV, 389. Second report, Pt. I. [Cd 5004] H.C. (1910). XXI, 561; Pt. II. [Cd. 5139] H.C. (1910). XXI, 583; Pt. III. [Cd. 5492] H.C. (1911). XIII, 649. Special report on deaths resulting from anaesthetics. [Cd. 5111] H.C. (1910). XXI, 785. Special report on the use of flannelette for clothing. [Cd. 5376] H.C. (1910). XXI, 793.

3257   JERVIS (*Sir* JOHN). A practical treatise on the office and duties of coroners. 1829. 8th edn. 1946.

### 13. JURIES

3258   DEVLIN (PATRICK ARTHUR), *Baron Devlin*. Trial by jury. 1956.

3259   SELECT COMMITTEE ON SPECIAL AND COMMON JURIES. Report from the select committee on special and common juries [Chairman: Viscount Enfield]. H.C. 425 (1867). IX, 597. Further report. H.C. 401 (1867–8). XII, 677.

3260   SELECT COMMITTEE ON JURIES BILL. Report from the select committee on the Juries Bill [Chairman: Viscount Enfield]. H.C. 306 (1870). VI, 61.

There was a further select committee in 1872 [Chairman: Sir John Duke Coleridge]. H.C. 286 (1872). X, 563.

3261   JURY LAW AND PRACTICE COMMITTEE. Report of the departmental committee appointed to inquire into and report upon the law and practice with regard to the constitution, qualifications, selection, summoning, &c. of juries [Chairman: Lord Mersey]. [Cd. 6817] H.C. (1913). XXX, 403. Minutes of evidence. [Cd. 6818] H.C. (1913). XXX, 463.

3262   THE GRAND JURY: is it a system which it is necessary or desirable to abolish? By a member of the Inner Temple. 1852.

3263   ERLE (THOMAS WILLIAM). The jury laws and their amendment. 1882.

One of a number of pamphlets by Erle advocating reform of the jury system.

### D. THE MAIN BRANCHES OF THE LAW

3264   BULLEN (EDWARD) *and* LEAKE (STEPHEN MARTIN). Precedents of pleading in actions in the superior courts of common law. 1860. 10th edn. 1950.

With *Smith's leading cases* (3265) the working lawyer's chief guide to all branches of the law during the period. Henry John Stephen, *A treatise on the principles of pleading in civil actions* . . ., 1824, 7th edn. 1866, and Joseph Chitty, the younger, *Precedents in pleading* . . ., 2 pts. 1836–8, 3rd edn. 1867–8, were older books of the same type.

3265 SMITH (JOHN WILLIAM). A selection of leading cases in various branches of the law: with notes. 2 v. 1837–40. 13th edn. 2 v. 1929.

3266 STEPHEN (HENRY JOHN). New commentaries on the laws of England (partly founded on Blackstone). 4 v. 1841–5. 21st edn. 4 v. 1950.

A famous work which to a large extent displaced Blackstone.

3267 INDEMAUR (JOHN). Principles of the common law . . . 1876. 12th end. 1914.

Indemaur also publ. *An epitome of leading common-law cases*, 1873, 10th edn. 1921.

3268 ADMINISTRATIVE LAW. Albert Venn Dicey, 'The development of administrative law in England'. *Law Q. Rev.* xxxi (1915), 148–53. George Stuart Robertson, *The law and practice of civil proceedings by and against the crown and departments of the government*, 1908. William Alexander Robson, *Justice and administrative law* . . ., 1928, 3rd edn. 1951 [like Frederick John Port, *Administrative law*, 1929, publ. too late to give more than a general idea of the law before 1914, but a useful textbook].

See also Statutory instruments (**3059–63**).

3269 AGENCY. Joseph Story, judge, *Commentaries on the law of agency, as a branch of commercial and maritime jurisprudence, with occasional illustrations from the civil and foreign law*, Boston, Mass. 1839, 9th edn. 1882. William Evans, *A treatise upon the law of principal and agent in contract and tort*, 1878, 2nd edn. 1888. William Bowstead, *A digest of the law of agency*, 1896, 13th edn. 1968. S. J. Stoljar, *The law of agency* (**2993**).

3270 BANKRUPTCY. Chief Registrar of the Court of Bankruptcy, *General returns: . . . of all matters . . . within the Bankruptcy Act, 1861* . . ., H.C. 31 (1864). XLVIII, 303, and annually to 1870. Comptroller in Bankruptcy, *General report for the year ending 31st December 1870*, H.C. 210 (1871). LVIII, 1, and annually to 1880. Board of Trade, *Report under section 131 of the Bankruptcy Act, 1883*. [C. 4072] H.C. (1884). LXIII, 293, and annually to 1921. Richard Seyd, *Record of failures and liquidations in the financial, international, wholesale and manufacturing branches of commerce . . . in the United Kingdom, from January 1865 to July 1876* . . . [1876], new edn. [to 1884], [1885]. *Report of Her Majesty's commissioners appointed to inquire into the fees, funds, and establishments of the Court of Bankruptcy, and the operation of the Bankruptcy Law Consolidation Act, 1849* [Chairman: Spencer Horatio Walpole]. [1770] H.C. (1854). XXIII, I. *Report from the select committee on the Bankruptcy Act* [Chairman: George Moffatt]. H.C. 512 (1864). V, I. Further report. H.C. 144 (1865). XII, 589. Arthur James Johnes, *Remarks on the late report from the select committee on bankruptcy and the Bankruptcy Bill now pending, in a letter to Lord Brougham and Vaux*, Caernarvon, 1866. *Report to the Lord Chancellor of a committee appointed to consider the working of the Bankruptcy Act, 1869* [Chairman: Rupert Kettle]. H.C. 152 (1877). LXIX, 41. *Report of the committee appointed by the Board of Trade to inquire into the bankruptcy law and its administration* [Chairman: Montague J. Muir Mackenzie]. [Cd. 4068] H.C. (1908). XXXIV, 1. Minutes of evidence. [Cd. 4069] H.C. (1908). XXXIV, 49. John Frederick Archbold, *The law and practice in bankruptcy . . .*, 1825, 11th edn. 1856. A rev. edn. was publ. as *The law of bankruptcy and insolvency as founded on the recent statute*, 1861. William Downes Griffith, *The law and practice in bankruptcy . . . partly founded on the eleventh edition of Mr. Archbold's treatise . . .*, 2 v. 1867–9, took its place until the publication of Sir Roland Lomax Bowdler Vaughan Williams and Walter Vere Vaughan Williams, *The new law and practice of bankruptcy, comprising the Bankruptcy Act, the Debtors Act, and the Bankruptcy Repeal and Insolvent Court Act of 1869 . . .*, 1870, 18th edn. 1968. Other well-known textbooks were Richard Ringwood, *The principles of bankruptcy . . .*, 1879, 18th edn. 1947, Edward Thomas Baldwin, *A concise treatise upon the law of bankruptcy . . .*, 1879, 11th edn. 1915, and Lawford Yate Lee, *The law and practice of bankruptcy and imprisonment for debt*, 1871, 3rd edn. 1891, rev. edn. by Henry Wace, 1904.

3271   COMMERCIAL LAW. Leone Levi, *Commercial law, its principles and administration: or, the mercantile law of Great Britain compared with the codes and laws of commerce of the following mercantile countries: Anhalt, Austria, Baden, Bavaria . . . Wurtemberg . . .*, 2 v. 1850–2. *Report of the commissioners appointed to inquire and ascertain how far the mercantile laws in the different parts of the United Kingdom of Great Britain and Ireland may be advantageously assimilated, and also whether any and what alterations and amendments should be made in the law of partnership as regards the question of the limited or unlimited responsibility of partners* [Chairman: Thomas Berry Cusack Smith]. [1791] H.C. (1854). XXVII, 445. Second report. [1977] H.C. (1854–5). XVIII, 653. *Report from the select committee of the House of Lords on the Mercantile Law Amendment Bill* [*H.L.*] [Chairman: Lord Cranworth]. H.C. 294 (1856). XIV, 1. *Report from the select committee on tribunals of commerce &c.* [Chairman: Acton Smee Ayrton]. H.C. 413 (1857–8). XVI, 505. Repr. 1873. A further Select Committee under Ayrton's chairmanship gathered additional evidence in 1871: H.C. 409 (1871). XII, 523. Archibald John Wolfe, *Commercial laws of England, Scotland, Germany and France*, U.S. Dept. of Commerce, Special agents, ser. 97, Wash. 1915. J. M. Holden (**2998**). Ernest Vinter, *A treatise on the history and law of fiduciary relationship [and resulting trusts], together with a selection of selected cases*, 1932, 3rd edn. Camb. 1955. Joseph Chitty, the elder, *A treatise on the law of bills of exchange, checks on bankers, promissory notes, bankers' cash notes, and bank-notes*, 1799, 11th edn. 1878. Sir John Barnard Byles, *A practical treatise on the law of bills of exchange, promissory notes, bank-notes, bankers' cash notes & checks*, 1829, 22nd edn. 1965. John William Smith, *A compendium of mercantile law*, 1834, 13th edn. 1931. Sir Mackenzie Dalzell Edwin Stewart Chalmers, *A digest of the laws of bills of exchange, promissory notes and cheques*, 1878, 13th edn. 1964. Joseph Hurst and Lord [Edgar Algernon] Robert Gascoyne-Cecil, Viscount Cecil of Chelwood, *The principles of commercial law . . .*, 1891, 2nd edn. 1906. Joshua Slater, *The principles of mercantile law*, 1884, 3rd edn. 1907. Colin Blackburn, Baron Blackburn, *A treatise on the effect of the contract of sale, on the legal rights of property and* *possession in goods, wares and merchandize*, 1845, 3rd edn. 1910. Judah Philip Benjamin, *A treatise on the law of sale of personal property: with references to the American decisions and to the French code and civil law*, 1868, 8th edn. 1950. Sir Mackenzie Dalzell Edwin Stewart Chalmers, *The Sale of Goods Act, 1893, including the Factors Acts, 1889 and 1890*, 1894, 12th edn. 1945. Sir Thomas Edward Scrutton, *The contract of affreightment as expressed in charterparties and bills of lading*, 1886, 17th edn. 1964.

3272   COMPANY LAW. Laurence Cecil Bartlett Gower, *The principles of modern company law*, 1957, 3rd edn. 1969, incl. a hist. *Report from the select committee on Limited Liability Acts* [Chairman: Edward William Watkin]. H.C. 329 (1867). X, 393. *Report from the select committee on the Companies Acts, 1862 and 1867* [Chairman: Robert Lowe]. H.C. 365 (1877). VIII, 419. *Report of the inter-departmental committee appointed to inquire into the limits of the action of the Board of Trade as regards the liquidation of companies under the Companies (Winding-Up) Act, 1890* [Chairman: Sir John Rigby]. [C. 7221] H.C. (1893–4). LXXXI, 219. *Report of the departmental committee appointed by the Board of Trade to inquire what amendments are necessary in the acts relating to joint-stock companies incorporated with limited liability under the Companies Acts, 1862 to 1890* [Chairman: Lord Davey]. [C. 7779] H.C. (1895) LXXXVIII, 151. *Report from the select committee of the House of Lords on the Companies Bill* [*H.L.*] [Chairman: Lord Halsbury]. H.C. 342 (1896). IX, 171. Further reports. H.C. 384 (1897). X. 97; H.C. 392 (1898). IX, 19. Final report. H.C. 361 (1899). VIII, 527. *Report of the company law amendment committee* [Chairman: C. M. Warmington]. [Cd. 3052] H.C. (1906). XCVII, 199. Appendix. [Cd. 3053] H.C. (1906). XCVII, 249. Board of Trade, *First report under Section 29 of the Companies (Winding-Up) Act, 1890*. H.C. 159 (1893–4). LXXXI, 83. Annual. Charles Favell Forth Wordsworth, *The law relating to railway, bank, insurance, mining, and other joint-stock companies*, 1836, 10th edn. 1865. Henry Burton Buckley, Baron Wrenbury, *The law and practice under the Companies Acts, 1862, 1867, 1870, the Life Assurance Companies Acts, 1870, 1871, 1872, and other Acts relating to joint stock companies*, 1873, 13th edn. 1957. Seward William Brice, *A treatise on the doctrine of ultra vires: being an investigation of the principles which limit the capacities . . . of corporations, and . . . joint stock companies.* 1874. 3rd edn. 1893. Nathaniel Lindley, Baron Lindley, *A treatise on the law of companies considered as a branch of the law of partnership*, 1889, suppl. 1891, rev. edn. 2 v. 1902. [The fifth and sixth edns. of a section of his *Partnership* (**3291**).] Thomas Eustace Smith, *A summary of the law of companies*, 1878, 14th edn. 1929. Sir Francis Beaufort Palmer, *Private companies: or, how to convert your business into a private company, and the benefit of so doing*, 1877, 42nd edn. 1961. Henry Hurrell and Sir Clarendon Golding Hyde, *The law of directors and officers of joint stock companies*, 1884, 4th edn. 1905, and *The joint stock companies practical guide . . .*, 1889, 11th edn. 1920. William Frederick Hamilton, *A manual of company law for the use of directors and promoters*, 1891, 3rd edn. 1910. Sir Francis Beaufort Palmer, *The shareholders' and directors' legal companion: a manual of every-day law and practice . . .*, 1878, 36th edn. 1948. Palmer also publ. *Com-*

*pany precedents* . . ., 1877, 17th edn. 2 v. 1956–60, and *Company law* . . ., 1898, 21st edn. 1968.

3273 CONFLICT OF LAWS (PRIVATE INTERNATIONAL LAW). Geoffrey Chevalier Cheshire, *Private international law*, Oxf. 1935, 7th edn. 1965 [incl. a short hist.]. Joseph Story, judge, *Commentaries on the conflict of laws, foreign and domestic, in regard to contracts, rights and remedies, and especially in regard to marriages, divorces, wills, successions and judgments,* Boston, Mass. 1834, 8th edn. 1883. William Burge, *Commentaries on colonial and foreign laws generally, and on their conflict with each other, and with the law of England,* 4 v. 1838, new edn. 5 v. 1907–28 [the fullest work on the subject]. John Alderson Foote, *Foreign and domestic law: a concise treatise on private international jurisprudence, based on decisions in the English courts,* 1878, 5th edn. 1925. Sir Francis Taylor Piggott, *Foreign judgments,* Pt. I: '*Their effect in the English courts*', 1879, Pt. II: '*The effect of an English judgment abroad*', 1881, 3rd edn. 3 pts. 1908–10, and *Service out of the jurisdiction,* 1892. Albert Venn Dicey, *A digest of the law of England with reference to the conflict of laws* . . ., 1896, 8th edn. 1967.

3274 CONTRACT. R. M. Jackson (**2997**). Joseph Chitty, the younger, *A practical treatise on the law of contracts not under seal; and upon the usual defences to actions thereon,* 1826, 23rd edn. 1968. Charles Greenstreet Addison, *A treatise on the law of contracts and rights and liabilities ex contractu,* 1847, 11th edn. 1911. Sir Edward Fry, *A treatise on the specific performance of contracts, including those of public companies,* 1858, 6th edn. 1921. Stephen Martin Leake, *The elements of the law of contracts,* 1867, 8th edn. 1931. Sir Frederick Pollock, *Principles of contract at law and equity,* 1876, 13th edn. 1950 [a great landmark in the hist. of the subject]. Sir William Reynell Anson, *Principles of the English law of contract,* Oxf. 1879, 22nd edn. 1964. Gerard Brown Finch, *A selection of cases on the English law of contract,* Camb. 1886, 2nd edn. 1896.

3275 COPYRIGHT. S. Nowell-Smith, *International copyright law* (**5467**). *Copyright commission: the royal commissions and the report of the commissioners* [Chairman: Lord John Manners]. [C. 2036] H.C. (1878). XXIV, 163. Minutes of evidence. [C. 2036–I] H.C. (1878). XXIV, 253. *Report from the select committee of the House of Lords on the Copyright (Amendment) Bill* [H.L.] [Chairman: Lord Monkswell]. H.C. 385 (1897). X, 213. Further reports. H.C. 393 (1898). IX, 231; H.C. 362 (1899). VIII, 539; H.C. 377 (1900). VI, 621. Walter Arthur Copinger, *The law of copyright in works of literature and art* . . ., 1870, 10th edn. 1965. John Shortt, *The law relating to works of literature and art: embracing the law of copyright, the law relating to newspapers* . . ., *and the law of libel,* 1871, 2nd edn. 1884. Sir Thomas Edward Scrutton, *The laws of copyright: an examination of the principles which should regulate literary and artistic property in England and other countries,* 1883, 4th edn. 1903. Augustine Birrell, *Seven lectures on the law and history of copyright in books,* 1899. George Stuart Robertson, *The law of copyright,* Oxf. 1912.

3276   CRIMINAL LAW. Radzinowicz (**2989**). Sir James Fitzjames Stephen, *A history of the criminal law of England*, 3 v. 1883; *A general view of the criminal law of England*, 1863, 2nd edn. 1890; *A digest of the criminal law* . . ., 1877, 9th edn. 1950; and (with Herbert Stephen) *A digest of the law of criminal procedure* . . ., 1883. *A report on criminal procedure to the Lord Chancellor, by Charles Sprengal Greaves, Esq., one of Her Majesty's counsel.* H.C. 456. (1856). L, 79. *Criminal Code Bill commission: report of the royal commission appointed to consider the law relating to indictable offences* [Chairman: Lord Blackburn]. [C. 2345] H.C. (1878–9). XX, 169. Sir William Oldnall Russell, *A treatise on crimes and misdemeanors*, 2 v. 1819, 12th edn. 2 v. 1964. [The oldest of the textbooks in general use during the period.] John Frederick Archbold, *A summary of the law relative to pleading and evidence in criminal cases* . . ., 1822, 36th edn. 1966. Henry Roscoe, *A digest of the law of evidence in criminal cases*, 2 v. 1835, 16th edn. 1952. Seymour Frederick Harris, *Principles of the criminal law* . . . *with tables of offences and their punishments* . . ., 1877, 21st edn. 1968. The first really good textbook for students was Courtney Stanhope Kenny, *Outlines of criminal law* . . ., Camb. 1902, 19th edn. 1966. Kenny also publ. *A selection of cases illustrative of English criminal law*, Camb. 1901, 8th edn. 1935.

3277   DEBTORS. *Report from the select committee of the House of Lords on the Debtors Act* [Chairman: Viscount Cross]. H.L. 156 (1893–4). IX, 1. *Report from the select committee on debtors (imprisonment)* [Chairman: E. H. Pickersgill]. H.C. 239 (1909). VII, 281.

3278   DIVORCE. *First report of the commissioners appointed by Her Majesty to enquire into the law of divorce and more particularly into the mode of obtaining divorces a vinculo matrimonii* [Chairman: Lord Campbell]. [1604] H.C. (1852–3). XL, 249. *Report from the select committee of the House of Lords appointed to consider the law respecting the parties who are entitled or ought to be entitled to sue in the Divorce Court in England, and in the Court of Session in Scotland, for a dissolution of marriage.* H.L. 63 (1861). XXIV, 19. *Report of the royal commission on the laws of marriage* [Chairman: Lord Chelmsford]. [4059] H.C. (1867–8). XXXII, 1. *Report of the royal commission on divorce and matrimonial causes* [Chairman: Lord Gorell]. [Cd. 6478] H.C. (1912–13). XVIII, 143. Minutes of evidence. Vol. I. [Cd. 6479] H.C. (1912–13). XVIII, 359. Vol. II. [Cd. 6480] H.C. (1912–13). XIX, 1. Vol. III. [Cd. 6481] H.C. (1912–13). XX, 1. Appendixes [Cd. 6482] H.C. (1912–13). XX, 655. John Fraser Macqueen, *A practical treatise on divorce and matrimonial jurisdiction under the act of 1857* . . ., 1858, 2nd edn. 1860. George Browne, *A treatise on the principles and practice of the Court for Divorce and Matrimonial Causes*, 1864, 14th edn. 1952. William John Dixon, *Law, practice and procedure in divorce and other matrimonial causes*, 1883, 4th edn. 1908. Thomas W. H. Oakley, *Divorce practice* . . ., 1885, 7th edn. 1911. James Roberts, *Divorce bills in the imperial parliament*, Dublin 1906. See also 6927–8.

3279   EQUITY. Harold Potter, *An introduction to the history of equity, and its courts*, 1931. Sir Duncan Mackenzie Kerly, *An historical sketch of the equitable jurisdiction of the Court of Chancery* . . ., Camb. 1890. [The early hist. of equity is set out in a famous work, George Spence, *The equitable jurisdiction of the Court of Chancery* . . ., 2 v. 1846–9.] Sir Henry Wilmot Seton, *Forms of decrees in equity and of orders connected with them*, 1830, 7th edn. 3 v. 1912 [title varies]. Joseph Story, judge, *Commentaries on equity jurisprudence as administered in England and America*, 2 v. Boston, Mass. 1836, 14th edn. 2 v. 1918, English edn. 2 v. 1884, 3rd edn. 1920, and *Commentaries on equity pleadings and the incidents thereto, according to the practice of the courts of equity of England and America*, Boston 1838, 10th edn. 1892. Josiah William Smith, *A manual of equity jurisprudence as administered in England, founded on the commentaries of J. Story* . . ., 1845, 15th edn. 1900. Frederick Thomas White and Owen Davies Tudor, *A selection of leading cases in equity*, 2 v. 1849–50, 9th edn. 2 v. 1928. Edmund Henry Turner Snell, *The principles of equity, intended for the use of students and the profession*, 1868, 26th edn. 1966. Chaloner William Chute, *Equity under the Judicature Act: or the relation of equity to common law*, 1874. Charles Francis Trower, *A manual of the prevalence of equity under the 25th section of the Judicature Act, 1873, amended by the Judicature Act, 1875*, 1876. F. W. Maitland, *Equity* (**3008**).

3280 EVIDENCE. James Bradley Thayer, *A preliminary treatise on evidence at the common law*, Camb., Mass. 1898. Henry Roscoe, *A digest of the law of evidence on the trial of actions at nisi prius*, 1827, 20th edn. 2 v. 1934, and *A digest of the law of evidence in criminal cases*, 2 v. 1835, 16th edn. 1952. William Wills, *An essay on the rationale of circumstantial evidence* . . ., 1838, 6th edn. 1912. John Pitt Taylor, *A treatise on the law of evidence as administered in England, and Ireland* . . ., 2 v. 1848, 12th edn. 2 v. 1931. William Mawdesley Best, *A treatise on the principles of evidence and practice as to proofs in courts of common law: with elementary rules for conducting the examination and cross-examination of witnesses*, 1849, 12th edn. 1922. Edmund Powell, *The complete practice of the law of England according to the new statutes, rules and orders: the new practice of evidence*, 1855, 10th edn. 1921. Sir James Fitzjames Stephen, *A digest of the law of evidence*, 1876, 12th edn. 1948. Sidney Lovell Phipson, *The law of evidence* . . ., 1892, 9th edn. 1966. William Wills, *The theory and practice of the law of evidence*, 1894, 3rd edn. 1938. Sir William Ellis Hume-Williams and Sir Albert Sortain Romer Macklin, *The taking of evidence on commission* . . ., 1895, 2nd edn. 1903.

3281 EXTRADITION. Report from the select committee on extradition [Chairman: Edward Pleydell Bouverie]. H.C. 393 (1867–8). VII, 129. *Royal commission on extradition: report of the commissioners* [Chairman: Sir Alexander Cockburn]. [C. 2039] H.C. (1878). XXIV, 903. Sir Edward George Clarke, *A treatise upon the law of extradition: with the conventions upon the subject existing between England & foreign nations, and cases decided thereon*, 1867, 4th edn. 1903. Sir Henry Chartres Biron and Kenneth Edlmann Chalmers, *The law and practice of extradition*, 1903. Sir Francis Taylor Piggott, *Extradition: a treatise on the law relating to fugitive offenders*, 1910.

**3282  FAMILY LAW.** R. H. Graveson and F. R. Crane (**3010**) is the standard hist. of the subject. *Special report from the select committee on Married Women's Property Bill* [Chairman: George John Shaw-Lefevre]. H.C. 441 (1867–8). VII, 339. John Fraser Macqueen, *The rights and liabilities of husband and wife at law and in equity, as affected by modern statutes and decisions*, 1848–9, 4th edn 1905. John Richard Griffith, *The Married Women's Property Act, 1870 . . .,* 1871, 6th edn. 1891. James Thomas Hammick, *The marriage law of England: a practical guide to the legal requirements connected with . . . the matrimonial contract . . .,* 1873, 2nd edn. 1887. Sir Charles Montague Lush, *The law of husband and wife . . .,* 1884, 4th edn. 1933. Henry Thomas Banning, *A concise treatise on the law of marriage settlements,* 1884. Ralph Thicknesse, *A digest of the law of husband and wife as it affects property,* 1884, and *The Married Women's Property Act, 1882,* 1882. William Pinder Eversley, *The law of the domestic relations . . .,* 1885, 6th edn. 1951. Sir William Nevill Montgomerie Geary, *The law of marriage and family relations: a manual of practical law,* Lond. & Edin. 1892. Charles Crawley, *The law of husband and wife,* 1892. John Savill Vaizey, *A treatise on the law of settlements of property made upon marriage and other occasions,* 2 v. 1887. See also 6929.

**3283  INHERITANCE AND SUCCESSION.** Thomas Radford Potts, *Principles of the law of succession to deceased persons,* 1888. Sir William Searle Holdsworth and Charles William Vickers, *The law of succession, testamentary and intestate,* Oxf. 1899.

**LAND LAW.** See **2999, 4230–6, 4251–8.**

**3284  LANDLORD AND TENANT.** William Woodfall, *The law of landlord and tenant,* 1802, 27th edn. 1968. John William Smith, *The law of landlord and tenant,* 1855, 3rd edn. 1882. Walter Arthur Copinger and Joseph Edwin Crawford Munro, *The law of rents: with special reference to the sale of land in consideration of a rent charge or chief rent,* 1886. Walter Clode, *The law relating to tenement houses and flats . . .,* 1889. Edward Bullen, *A practical treatise on the law of distress for rent, and of things damage-feasant . . .,* 1842, 2nd edn. 1899.

**3285  LIBEL AND SLANDER.** *Report from the select committee on the law of libel* [Chairman: Sir John Holker]. H.C. 343 (1878–9). XI, 261. Further report. H.C. 284 (1880 Sess. 2). IX, 309. Thomas Starkie, *A treatise on the law of slander, libel . . .,* 1813, 7th edn. 1908. William Blake Odgers, *A digest of the law of libel and slander . . .,* 1881, 6th edn. 1929. Sir Hugh Fraser, *Principles and practice of the law of libel and slander, with suggestions on the conduct of a civil action . . .,* 1893, 7th edn. 1936. George Elliott, *The Newspaper Libel and Registration Act, 1881,* 1884. Sir Hugh Fraser, *The law of libel in its relation to the press, together with the Law of Libel Amendment Act, 1888, and all previous statutes bearing on the subject,* 1889. John Clement Carpenter Gatly, *Law and practice of libel and slander in a civil action . . .,* 1920, 6th edn. 1967. Harford Montgomery Hyde, *Their good names: twelve cases of libel and slander, with some introductory reflections on the law,* 1970.

3286 LIMITATION OF ACTIONS. Edward Burtenshaw Sugden, Baron St. Leonards, *An essay on the new statutes relating to limitations of time, estates tail, dower, descent* . . ., 1852. James Walter, *A manual of the statutes of limitation* . . ., 1860, 4th edn. 1883. Henry Thomas Banning, *A concise treatise on the statute law of limitation of actions*, 1877, 3rd edn. 1906.

3287 MARITIME LAW. Thomas Eustace Smith, *A summary of the law and practice in Admiralty*, 1880, 4th edn. 1892 [a brief handbook]. Charles Abbott, Baron Tenterden, *A treatise of the law relative to merchant ships and seamen*, 1802, 14th edn. 1901. James Lees, *The laws of shipping and insurance* . . ., 1840, 12th edn. 1903, and *The Merchant Shipping Act[s]*, 1855, 5th edn. 1893. David Maclachlan, *A treatise on the law of merchant shipping*, 1860, 7th edn. 1932. Thomas Gilbert Carver, *A treatise on the law relating to the carriage of goods by sea*, 1885, 9th edn. 1952. Owen Davies Tudor, *A selection of leading cases on mercantile and maritime law*, 1860, 3rd edn. 1884. William Schaw Lindsay, *Our navigation and mercantile marine laws* . . ., 1852, 2nd edn. 1853. Reginald Godfrey Marsden, *A digest of cases relating to shipping, admiralty and insurance law, from the reign of Elizabeth to the end of 1897*, 1899, 2nd edn. 1927, and *A treatise on the law of collisions at sea*, 1880, 11th edn. 1961. Albert Saunders, *Maritime law: illustrated by the history of a ship from and including the agreement to build her until she becomes a total loss*, 1901, 2nd edn. 1910, rev. edn. 1920. Joseph Kay, *The law relating to shipmasters and seamen* . . ., 2 v. 1875, 2nd edn. 1894. Henry John Wastell Coulson and Urquhart Atwell Forbes, *The law relating to waters, sea, tidal and inland*, 1880, 6th edn. 1952. Stuart Archibald Moore, *A history of the foreshore and the law relating thereto*, 1888.

3288 NATIONALITY. Clive Parry, *British nationality: including citizenship of the United Kingdom and colonies and the status of aliens*, 1951. Sir Francis Taylor Piggott, *Nationality: including naturalization and English law on the high seas and beyond the realm* . . ., 2 v. 1907. John Mervyn Jones, *British nationality law and practice*, Oxf. 1947, rev. edn. 1956.

3289 NATURALISATION. *Report of the royal commissioners for inquiring into the laws of naturalization and allegiance* [Chairman: Earl of Clarendon]. [4109] H.C. (1868–9). XXV, 607. *Report of the inter-departmental committee appointed by the Secretary of State for the Home Department to consider the doubts and difficulties which have arisen in connexion with the interpretation and administration of the acts relating to naturalization* . . . [Chairman: Sir Kenelm Edward Digby]. [Cd. 723] H.C. (1901). LIX. 351. John Cutler, *The law of naturalization, as amended by the Naturalization Acts, 1870*, 1871.

3290 OATHS. *Report of the oaths commission* [Chairman: Duke of Richmond]. [3885] H.C. (1867). XXXI, 1. Francis A. Stringer, *Oaths and affirmations in Great Britain and Ireland* . . ., [1889], 4th edn. 1928. Charles Ford, *A handbook for the use of commissioners for oaths in the Supreme Court of Judicature in England*, 1876, 8th edn. 1903.

3291 PARTNERSHIP. *Report from the select committee on trade partnerships* [Chairman: C. M. Norwood]. H.C. 228 (1972). XII, 109. *Report from the*

*select committee on Partnerships Bill* [Chairman: Charles James Monk]. H.C.
204 (1882). XII, 231. Nathaniel Lindley, Baron Lindley, *A treatise on the law
of partnership, including its application to joint-stock and other companies*, 3 v.
1860–3, 12th edn. [1962.] John Howell, *Partnership-law legislation and limited
liability in their relation to the panic of 1866*, 1869. Sir Frederick Pollock,
*A digest of the law of partnership*, 1877, 15th edn. 1952. Sir Arthur Underhill,
*The law of partnership: six lectures*, 1899, 8th edn. 1966.

3292 PATENTS. James Johnson, *The patentee's manual: being a treatise on the
law and practice of letters patent . . .*, 1853, 6th edn. 1890. Clement Higgins,
*A digest of the reported cases relating to the law and practice of letters patent for
inventions . . .*, 1875–80, 2nd edn. 1890, and *A concise treatise on the law and
practice of patents for inventions . . .*, 1884. William Norton Lawson, *The practice as to letters patent for inventions, copyright in designs, and registrations of
trade marks, under the Patents, Designs and Trade Marks Act, 1883 . . .*, 1884,
3rd edn. 1898. Robert Frost, *A treatise on the law and practice relating to letters
patent for inventions*, 1891, 4th edn. 1912, and *The Patents and Designs Act,
1907*, 1908. Sir Henry Harding Samuel Cunynghame, *English patent practice
. . .*, 1894. James Roberts, *The grant and validity of British patents for inventions*,
1903. James Roberts and Hugh Fletcher Moulton, *The Patents and Designs
Act, 1907*, 1907.

3293 PERSONAL PROPERTY. Joshua Williams, *Principles of the law of
personal property*, 1848, 18th edn. 1926. Louis Arthur Goodeve, *The modern
law of personal property*, 1887, 9th edn. 1949.

3294 PUBLIC INTERNATIONAL LAW. Henry Wheaton, *Elements of
international law: with a sketch of the history of the science*, 2 v. 1836, numerous
edns. Sir Robert Joseph Phillimore, *Commentaries upon international law*, 4 v.
1854–61, 3rd edn. 4 v. 1879–89. Sir Travers Twiss, *The law of nations considered as independent political communities*, Pt 1: On the rights and duties of
nations in time of peace, Pt 2: 'On the rights and duties of nations in time of
war', 2 v. Oxf. 1861–3. Mountague Bernard, *Four lectures on subjects connected
with diplomacy*, 1868. William Edward Hall, *International law*, Oxf. 1880, 8th
edn. 1924, *The rights and duties of neutrals*, 1874, and *A treatise on the foreign
powers and jurisdiction of the British Crown*, Oxf. 1894. Thomas Joseph
Lawrence, *Essays on some disputed questions in modern international law*, Camb.
1884, 2nd edn. 1885, and *A handbook of public international law*, Camb. 1885,
11th edn. 1938. William Pitt Cobbett, *Leading cases and opinions on international law*, 1885, 6th edn. 1947+. Sir Henry James Sumner Maine, *International law: the Whewell lectures . . .*, 1887, 1888. Lassa Francis Lawrence
Oppenheim, *International law: a treatise*, 2 v. 1905–6, 8th edn. 1955. Arnold
Duncan MacNair, Baron MacNair, ed., *International law opinions*, 3 v. Camb.
1956. *Report of the neutrality laws commissioners* [Chairman: Lord Cranworth].
[4027] H.C. (1867–8). XXXII, 265. Robert Plumer Ward, *A treatise on the
relative rights and duties of belligerent and neutral powers in maritime affairs*,
1801, new edn. 1875. John Hosack, *The rights of British and neutral commerce*,

*as affected by recent royal declarations and orders in council*, 1854. Sir Francis Taylor Piggott, *The Declaration of Paris, 1856: a study*, 1919. H. W. Halkin, 'The inner history of the declaration of Paris', *British year book of international law*, 1927, pp. 1–44. Olive Anderson, 'Some further light on the inner history of the Declaration of Paris', *Law Q. Rev.* lxxvi (1960), 379–85. David Urquhart, *The Declaration of Paris: a letter to Mr. Gregory on his motion of March 2, 1866, for sparing private property in war at sea*, 1866. Mountague Bernard, *A historical account of the neutrality of Great Britain during the American civil war*, 1870. Sir Francis Taylor Piggott, *Extraterritoriality: the law relating to consular jurisdiction and to residence in oriental countries*, 1892, rev. edn. 1907. Sir Douglas Owen, *Declaration of war: a survey of the position of belligerents and neutrals, with relative considerations of shipping and marine insurance during war*, 1889. Alexander Pearce Higgins, *War and the private citizen: studies in international law*, 1910. See also *Law officers' opinions to the Foreign Office* (**911**).

3295 REGISTRATION OF BIRTHS, DEATHS, AND MARRIAGES. William Cunningham Glen, *The law relating to the registration of births, deaths and marriages; the duties of registration officers, and the marriage of dissenters in England*, 1860, 2nd edn. 1875. Herbert Davey and Sydney Davey, *The statutes relating to the registration of births, deaths & marriages*, 1899.

3296 TORTS. C. H. S. Fifoot, *History and sources of the common law: tort and contract* (**2995**). P. H. Winfield, *The province of the law of tort* (**2996**). Sir Frederick Pollock, *The law of torts: a treatise on the principles and obligations arising from civil wrongs in the common law*, 1887, 15th edn. 1951 [the first satisfactory work on the subject]. The best of the earlier works were Melville Madison Bigelow, *Leading cases on the law of torts determined by the courts of America and England*, Boston, Mass. 1875, Charles Greenstreet Addison, *Wrongs and their remedies: being a treatise on the law of torts*, 1860, 8th edn. 1906, and Sir Arthur Underhill, *A summary of the law of torts . . .*, 1873, 16th edn. 1949. John Frederick Clerk and William Harry Barber Lindsell, *The law of torts*, 1889, 12th edn. 1961, covers much the same ground as Pollock. The best modern books on the subject are Sir John William Salmond, *The law of torts . . .*, 1907, 15th edn. 1969, and Sir Percy Henry Winfield, *A text-book of the law of tort*, 1937, 8th edn. 1967.

3297 TRUSTS. *Report from the select committee on trusts administration* [Chairman: Sir Robert T. Reid]. H.C. 248 (1895). XIII, 403. Thomas Lewin, *A practical treatise on the law of trusts and trustees*, 1837, 16th edn. 1964. Sir Arthur Underhill, *A concise manual of the law relating to private trusts and trustees*, 1878, 11th edn. 1959. Henry Godefroi, *A digest of the principles of the law of trusts and trustees*, 1879, 5th edn. 1927.

3298 WILLS. Sir Edward Vaughan Williams, *The law of executors and administrators*, 2 v. 1832, 14th edn. 2 v. 1960. Thomas Jarman, *A treatise on wills*, 2 v. 1844, 8th edn. 3 v. 1951. George Browne, *A treatise on the principles and practice of the Court of Probate, in contentious and non-contentious business,*

1873, 3rd edn. 1892, 4th edn. by Louis Diston Bowles and Thomas W. H. Oakley, 1906. Sir Henry Studdy Theobald, *A concise treatise on the construction of wills*, 1876, 12th edn. 1963. John Charles Henry Flood, *An elementary treatise on the law relating to wills of personal property, and some subjects appertaining thereto*, 1877, and *The pitfalls of testators: a few hints about the making of wills*, 1884. William John Dixon, *Probate and administration: law and practice in common form and contentious business*, 1880, 3rd edn. 1912. Sir James Wigram, *An examination of the rules of law, respecting the admission of extrinsic evidence in aid of the interpretation of wills . . .*, 1831, 5th edn. 1914.

# VI

## THE CHURCHES

### A. GENERAL

#### 1. REFERENCE

**3299** BARROW (JOHN GRAVES). A bibliography of bibliographies in religion. Ann Arbor [Mich.]. 1955.

To be used in conjunction with Wilbur Moorehead Smith, *A list of bibliographies of theological and biblical literature published in Great Britain and America, 1595–1931,* Coatesville, Pa. 1931, which has full notes but does not deal with hists.

**3300** RICHARDSON (ERNEST CUSHING) *and others, comps.* An alphabetical subject index and index encyclopaedia to periodical articles on religion, 1890–1899. N.Y. [1907.]

**3301** INTERNATIONAL BIBLIOGRAPHY OF THE HISTORY OF RELIGIONS for the year 1952+. Leiden. 1954+. Annual.

**3302** CHADWICK ([WILLIAM] OWEN). The history of the church: a select bibliography. Hist. Assoc. Helps for Students 66. 1962. Rev. edn. 1966.

See also the more systematic treatment of John Henry Somerset Kent, 'The study of modern ecclesiastical history since 1930' in Jean, Cardinal Daniélou and others, *The Pelican guide to modern theology,* vol. 2, *Historical theology,* Harmondsworth 1969.

**3303** REVUE D'HISTOIRE ECCLESIASTIQUE. Louvain. 1900+. Quart.

Contains an annual classified bibliog. of books and articles on church and general hist.

**3304** PURVIS (JOHN STANLEY). An introduction to ecclesiastical records. 1953.

**3305** HASTINGS (JAMES) *and others.* The encyclopaedia of religion and ethics. 13 v. Edin. 1908–26.

Full bibliogs. An admirable publ.

**3306** CROSS (FRANK LESLIE) *ed.* The Oxford dictionary of the Christian church. 1957. 2nd. edn. 1974.

**3307** HERBERT (ARTHUR SUMNER). Historical catalogue of printed editions of the English Bible, 1525–1961. 1968.

Repl. vol. I of Thomas Herbert Darlow and Horace Frederick Moule, comps., *Historical catalogue of the printed editions of holy scripture in the library of the British and Foreign Bible society,* 2 v. 1903–11. For background see Frederick Fyvie Bruce, *The English Bible: a history of translations,* 1961, rev. edn. 1970.

3308  CURTIS (WILLIAM ALEXANDER). A history of creeds and confessions of faith in Christendom and beyond. Edin. 1911.

A convenient handbook.

## 2. Histories

For denominational education see **7929–51.**

3309  LATOURETTE (KENNETH SCOTT). Christianity in a revolutionary
age: a history of Christianity in the nineteenth and twentieth centuries. 4 v.
N.Y. 1953–61.

Covers all churches. On a smaller scale Alexander Roper Vidler, *The church in an age
of revolution: 1789 to the present day,* 1962, covers the same ground.

3310  ELLIOTT-BINNS (LEONARD ELLIOTT). Religion in the Victorian
era. 1936. 3rd edn. 1953.

The best general outline, though not up to the standards of modern scholarship. Chadwick, **3505,** is better.

3311  SPINKS (GEORGE STEPHENS) *and others.* Religion in Britain since
1900. 1952.

May be suppl. by Otto Baumgarten, *Religiöses und kirchliches Leben in England,* Leipzig
& Berlin 1922.

3312  ADDISON (WILLIAM GEORGE CLIBBENS). Religious equality in
modern England, 1714–1914. 1944.

3313  KITSON CLARK (GEORGE SIDNEY ROBERTS). The English
inheritance: an historical essay. 1950.

A perceptive study of religion. For popular religion see Geoffrey Francis Andrew Best,
'Popular Protestantism in Victorian Britain', in Robert Robson, ed., *Ideas and Institutions* (**177**), 115–42.

3314  ROGERS (JAMES GUINNESS). The church systems of England in the
nineteenth century. 1881.

Strongly Nonconformist. Rogers's *Present-day religion and theology, including a review of
the down grade controversy,* 1888, includes some characteristic essays carrying the discussion a stage further.

3315  TULLOCH (JOHN). Movements of religious thought in Britain during
the nineteenth century. Lond. & N.Y. 1885.

One of the few attempts at a systematic analysis of ideas. By a leader of the Church of
Scotland.

3316  JOURNAL OF ECCLESIASTICAL HISTORY. 1+. 1950+.

The chief English j. in the field. Other js. that incl. articles on English religious hist.
are *Studies in church history,* 1+, Lond., then Leiden 1964+; *The journal of religious
history,* Sydney 1960–1+; *Church history,* American Soc. of Church Hist., Chicago
1932+; *Journal of theological studies,* 1899+; *Hibbert Journal,* 1902+, *The modern*

*churchman* . . ., 1911+; *The Harvard theological review*, N.Y. etc. 1908+; *Archives de sociologie des religions*, Paris 1956+; and *Numen: international review for the history of religions*, Internat. Assoc. for the Hist. of Religions, Leiden 1954+.

**3317** ANSON (PETER FREDERICK). Bishops at large: some autocephalous churches of the past hundred years and their founders. 1964.

**3318** SMITH (WARREN SYLVESTER). The London heretics, 1870–1914. 1967.

Good for out-of-the-way movements.

**3319** GAY (JOHN DENNIS). The geography of religion in England. 1971.

See also R. B. Walker, 'Religious changes in Liverpool in the nineteenth century', *J. Eccles. Hist.* xix (1968), 195–211, and Ian Sellers, 'Nonconformist attitudes in later nineteenth-century Liverpool', *Historic Soc. Lancs & Ches. Trans.* 114 (1962), 215–39.

### 3. CONTEMPORARY SURVEYS

**3320** CENSUS OF GREAT BRITAIN, 1851: religious worship, England and Wales: reports and tables. [1690] H.C. (1852–3). LXXXIX, 1.

The only official religious census. For comments on its preparation see Horace Mann, 'On the statistical position of religious bodies in England and Wales', *Stat. Soc. J.* xviii (1855), 141–59, Kenneth Stanley Inglis, 'Patterns of religious worship in 1851', *J. Eccles. Hist.* xi (1960), 74–86, David M. Thompson, 'The 1851 religious census: problems and possibilities', *Victorian Studs.* xi (1967–8), 87–97, and W. S. F. Pickering, 'The 1851 religious census: a useless experiment?', *Brit. J. Sociology* xviii (1967), 382–407.

**3321** DAVIES (CHARLES MAURICE). Unorthodox London: or phases of religious life in the metropolis. 2 ser. 1873–5. 1-v. edn. 1876. Repr. 1969.

Davies also publ. companion vols. on Anglican and non-Christian places of worship: *Orthodox London: or, phases of religious life in the Church of England*, 2 ser. 1874–5, 1-v. edn. 1876; *Heterodox London: or, phases of free thought in the metropolis*, 2 v. 1874; repr. 1 v. 1969; and *Mystic London: or, phases of occult life in the metropolis*, 1875. Popular journalism rather than careful surveys, they have the merits and defects of their origin. Cp. George Jennings Davies, *Successful preachers*, 1884.

**3322** BRITISH WEEKLY SURVEY. 'Our religious census of London'. *British Weekly*, 5, 12, 19, 26 Nov.; 3, 17 Dec. 1886.

The best of the early studs. sponsored by newspapers.

**3323** MUDIE-SMITH (RICHARD) ed. The religious life of London. 1904.

A census for the *Daily News* by C. F. G. Masterman and other young social workers. Good. For ideas see William Leonard Courtney, ed., *Do we believe? a record of a great correspondence in 'The Daily Telegraph'*, October, November, December, *1904*, 1905.

**3324** BOOTH (CHARLES). Life and labour of the people in London. Third ser.: religious influences. 7 v. 1902.

By far the best and most comprehensive survey ever made. For the other series see **9485**.

## 4. DOCTRINE

### (a) *Histories*

**3325 REARDON (BERNARD MORRIS GARVIN).** From Coleridge to Gore: a century of religious thought in Britain. 1971.

See also his *Religious thought in the nineteenth century, illustrated from writers of the period*, Camb. 1966, which is primarily concerned with the philosophy of religion and is not confined to Britain. Anthony Oliver John Cockshut, *Religious controversies of the nineteenth century: selected documents*, Lond. & Lincoln, Nebr. 1966, covers English ecclesiastical controversies inadequately.

**3326 STORR (VERNON FAITHFULL).** The development of English theology in the nineteenth century, 1800–1860. 1913.

**3327 ELLIOTT-BINNS (LEONARD ELLIOTT).** English thought, 1860–1900: the theological aspect. Lond. & Greenwich, Conn. 1956.

Continues Storr (**3326**), and supersedes Elliott-Binns's own *The development of English theology in the later nineteenth century*, 1952. For some shrewd contemporary comments see Richard Holt Hutton, *Essays on some of the modern guides to English thought in matters of faith*, 1887, new edn. 1888.

**3328 WEBB (CLEMENT CHARLES JULIAN).** A study of religious thought in England from 1850. Oxf. 1933.

Other useful general works are Stephen Charles Neill, bishop, *The interpretation of the New Testament, 1861–1961*, 1961; John Kenneth Mozley, *Some tendencies in British theology from the publication of Lux Mundi to the present day*, 1951; Herbert George Wood, *Belief and unbelief since 1850*, Camb., 1955; Joseph Hillis Miller, *The disappearance of God: five nineteenth-century writers*, Camb., Mass. 1963; John Stewart Lawton, *Conflict in Christology: a study of British and American Christology from 1889–1914*, 1947; John Dickie, *Fifty years of British theology: a personal retrospect*, Edin. 1937; and Rupert Eric Davies, *Religious authority in an age of doubt*, 1968.

**3329 DAVIES ([DANIEL] HORTON [MARLAIS]).** Worship and theology in England. Vol. IV. From Newman to Martineau, 1850–1900. Princeton & Lond. 1961.

Stimulating. See also Anthony Symondson, ed., *The Victorian crisis of faith*, 1970.

**3330 McDONALD (HUGH DERMOT).** Ideas of revelation: an historical study, A.D. 1700 to A.D. 1860. 1959.

Cont. in his *Theories of revelation: an historical study, 1860–1960*, 1963. See also Ernest Robert Sandeen, *The roots of fundamentalism: British and American millenarianism, 1800–1930*, Chicago 1970.

**3331 ROUSE (RUTH) and NEILL (STEPHEN CHARLES)** *eds.* A history of the ecumenical movement, 1517–1948. Lond. & Phila. 1954. 2nd edn. 1967.

Excellent on the 19th cent. Extensive bibliog. Henry Renaud Turner Brandreth, *Unity and reunion: a bibliography*, 1945, 2nd edn. 1948, should also be consulted.

**3332 TATLOW (TISSINGTON).** The story of the Student Christian Movement of Great Britain and Ireland. 1933.

See also Ruth Rouse, *The World's Student Christian Federation: a history of the first thirty years*, 1948. There is a useful life of one of the most attractive leaders of the movement, Constance Evelyn Padwick, *Temple Gairdner of Cairo*, 1929.

**3333** ROE (WILLIAM GORDON). Lamennais and England: the reception of Lamennais's religious ideas in England in the nineteenth century. Oxf. 1966.

(b) *Anglican Theology*

**3334** RAMSEY (ARTHUR MICHAEL), *Archbishop*. From Gore to Temple: the development of Anglican theology between 1889 and 1939. 1960.

**3335** COCKSHUT (ANTHONY OLIVER JOHN). Anglican attitudes: a study of Victorian religious controversies. 1959.

The Gorham case, *Essays and reviews* (**3341**) and Colenso (**2118**). For Gorham see also John Charles Somerset Nias, *Gorham and the Bishop of Exeter*, 1951.

**3336** MAURICE (FREDERICK DENISON). Theological essays. 1853. 3rd edn. 1871.

Maurice was perhaps the most interesting theologian of his day. For his life see **3721**.

**3337** PUSEY (EDWARD BOUVERIE). The presence of Christ in the Holy Eucharist: a sermon . . . Oxf. 1853.

Amplified in his *The doctrine of the real presence . . . vindicated in notes on a sermon, 'The presence of Christ in the Holy Eucharist'*, Oxf. 1855, and *The real presence . . . the doctrine of the English church . . .*, Oxf. 1857. Important for the attempts by the Oxford movement to restate Anglican doctrine. For replies see William Goode, *The nature of Christ's presence in the eucharist . . .*, 2 v. 1856, and *A supplement . . . containing . . . a reply to Dr. Pusey's answer . . .*, 1858, and John Harrison, *The fathers versus Dr. Pusey . . .*, Lond. & Edin. 1873. For Pusey's later thought see his *An Eirenicon*, pt. 1. 'The Church of England a portion of Christ's one Holy Catholic Church, and a means of restoring visible unity', pt. 2. 'First letter to the Very Rev. J. H. Newman, D.D. . . .', pt. 3. 'Is healthful reunion impossible? . . .', Oxf. & Lond. 1865–70.

**3338** JOWETT (BENJAMIN). The epistles of St. Paul to the Thessalonians, Galatians, Romans; with . . . critical notes and dissertations. 1855.

A broad church statement.

**3339** RIGG (JAMES HARRISON). Modern Anglican theology: chapters on Coleridge, Hare, Maurice, Kingsley, and Jowett, and on the doctrine of sacrifice and atonement. 1857. 3rd edn. 1880.

A Wesleyan analysis.

**3340** MANSEL (HENRY LONGUEVILLE). The limits of religious thought examined . . . Bampton lectures. Lond. & Oxf. 1858. 5th edn. 1867.

High church. Provoked two answers from Frederick Denison Maurice, *What is revelation?*, 1859, and *Sequel to the inquiry, What is revelation?*, 1860, which opened up a wide controversy.

3341 ESSAYS AND REVIEWS. 1860. 12th edn. 1865. Boston, Mass. edn. publ. as *Recent enquiries in theology* . . ., 1860, and reprints.

The first important Anglican response to biblical criticism and modern thought. Important and influential.

3342 FARRAR (ADAM STOREY). A critical history of free thought in reference to the Christian religion. Bampton lectures. 1862.

3343 ARNOLD (MATTHEW). St. Paul and Protestantism: with an introduction on puritanism and the Church of England. 1870. 3rd edn. 1875. Pop. edn. 1887.

Influential, though Arnold was no theologian.

3344 ARNOLD (MATTHEW). Literature & dogma: an essay towards a better apprehension of the Bible. 1873. 5th edn. 1876. Pop. edn. 1883.

Cont. in *God & the Bible* . . . *Literature & Dogma*, 1875, pop. edn. 1884. The Bible as literature.

3345 COLENSO (JOHN WILLIAM), *bishop*. The Pentateuch and book of Joshua critically examined. 7 pts. 1862–79.

The first modernist assault. For Colenso see **2118**.

3346 SEELEY (*Sir* JOHN ROBERT). Ecce Homo. 1866.

A bold attempt at a life of Christ, reflecting modernist views.

3347 LIDDON (HENRY PARRY). The divinity of our Lord and Saviour Jesus Christ. Bampton lectures. 1867.

3348 HORT (FENTON JOHN ANTHONY). The way, the truth and the life. Hulsean lectures. Camb. & Lond. 1871.

3349 LIGHTFOOT (JOSEPH BARBER). The apostolic fathers. 3 v. 1877–85. 2nd edn. 5 v. 1889–90.

English scholarship at last reaches German standards.

3350 FARRAR (FREDERICK WILLIAM). Eternal hope. 1878. New edn. 1892.

With his *Mercy and judgment* . . ., 1881, constitutes an attack on eternal punishment. The controversy which raged on the subject is discussed by James Hogg, ed., *The wider hope: essays and strictures on the doctrine and literature of future punishment* . . ., 1890.

3351 HATCH (EDWIN). The organization of the early Christian churches. Bampton lectures for 1880. Oxf. 1881. 3rd edn. 1888.

Cont. in his *The influences of Greek ideas and usages upon the Christian church*, ed. by Andrew Martin Fairbairn, Hibbert lectures for 1888, 1890. See also Frederick Robert Tennant, *The sources of the doctrines of the fall and original sin*, Camb. 1903.

3352 WESTCOTT (BROOKE FOSS). Christus consummator: some aspects of the work and person of Christ in relation to modern thought. 1886.

**3353** WARD (MARY AUGUSTA), *Mrs. Humphry Ward*. Robert Elsmere. 3 v. 1888.

Important as bringing religious doubts before a wide public.

**3354** GORE (CHARLES) *ed*. Lux mundi: a series of studies in the religion of the incarnation. 1889. 15th edn. 1904.

The first joint effort since *Essays and reviews* to attempt an up-to-date restatement of the Anglican position.

**3355** GORE (CHARLES). The incarnation of the Son of God. Bampton lectures. 1891.

Lucid high-churchmanship.

**3356** MASON (ARTHUR JAMES). The relation of confirmation to baptism ... 1891.

**3357** ANSWER of the Anglican archbishops of England to the apostolic letter of Pope Leo XIII on English ordinations. 1897.

For the background of the controversy over Leo XIII's rejection of the validity of Anglican orders see Arthur West Haddan, *Apostolical succession in the church of England*, 1869; Frederick George Lee, *The validity of the holy orders of the church of England maintained and vindicated*, 1869; Edward Denny, *Anglican orders and jurisdiction*, 1893; Edward Denny and Thomas Alexander Lacey, *De hierarchia anglicana: dissertatio apologetica* . . ., 1895; and Beresford James Kidd, *The later medieval doctrine of the eucharistic sacrifice*, Church Historical Soc. xlvi. 1898, repr. 1954. For a modern account see **3521**.

**3358** SWETE (HENRY BARCLAY) *ed*. Essays on some theological questions of the day. 1905.

**3359** SANDAY (WILLIAM). The life of Christ in recent research. Oxf. 1907.

**3360** STREETER (BURNETT HILLMAN) *ed*. Foundations: a statement of Christian belief in terms of modern thought, by seven Oxford men. 1912.

Provoked a considerable controversy. Frank Weston, Bishop of Zanzibar, *Ecclesia anglicana: for what does she stand? an open letter to the* . . . *Bishop of St. Albans* . . ., 1913, and Ronald Arbuthnott Knox, *Some loose stones*, 1913, are the best-known attacks. But see also Herbert Hensley Henson, *The creed in the pulpit* [1912].

**3361** PRINGLE-PATTISON *formerly* SETH (ANDREW). The idea of God in the light of recent philosophy. Oxf. 1917.

### (c) *Nonconformist Theology*

**3362** ROGERS (HENRY). The eclipse of faith. 1852.

Immensely popular: influenced Dale.

**3363** ARTHUR (WILLIAM). The tongue of fire: or, the true power of Christianity. 1856.

**3364** RIGG (JAMES HARRISON). Essays for the times on ecclesiastical and social subjects. 1866.

**3365** DALE (ROBERT WILLIAM). The atonement. 1875.

The most influential of Dale's many works. For his life see **3788**.

**3366** POPE (WILLIAM BURT). The person of Christ: dogmatic, scriptural, historical. 1875.

**3367** MARTINEAU (JAMES). Essays, reviews and addresses, selected and revised by the author. 4 v. 1890–1.

Martineau's main independent works were *Types of ethical theory*, 2 v. 1885, *A study of religion*, Oxf. 1888, and *The seat of authority in religion*, 1890. For his life see **3815**.

**3368** HORTON (ROBERT FORMAN). Inspiration and the Bible. 1887.

Followed by *Verbum Dei*, 1893. For his life see **3792**.

**3369** FAIRBAIRN (ANDREW MARTIN). The place of Christ in modern theology. 1893.

Extremely influential. His *Catholicism: Roman and Anglican*, 1899, is a clear statement of the nonconformist objection to the Oxford movement. See also **3783**.

**3370** BALLARD (FRANK). The miracles of unbelief. Edin. 1900.

**3371** BEET (JOSEPH AGAR). The immortality of the soul: a protest. 1901.

See also his *The last things*, 1897, 3rd edn. 1898, new edn. 1905.

**3372** HOLLOWELL (JAMES HIRST). What Nonconformists stand for. 1901. 2nd edn. 1904.

The first of three valuable works in a still-born ser., *The Free Church library*. The others are Robert Forman Horton, *The dissolution of dissent*, 1902, and Sir Joseph Compton Rickett, *The free-churchman of to-day*, 1902. Together they gave a good account of the Nonconformist standpoint at the turn of the century.

**3373** CAMPBELL (REGINALD JOHN). The new theology. 1907.

A strong plea for modernism.

**3374** FORSYTH (PETER TAYLOR). The person and place of Jesus Christ. 1909. 5th edn. 1946.

Followed by *The work of Christ*, 1910, repr. 1938. Forsyth's *Positive preaching and the modern mind*, 1907, 3rd edn. 1949, was also influential. See also **3789**.

**3375** SHILLITO (EDWARD). The hope and mission of the free churches. 1912.

**3376** KEEBLE (SAMUEL EDWARD). Christian responsibility for the social order. 1922.

Sums up his social philosophy. There is a brief life: Maldwyn Edwards, *S. E. Keeble, pioneer and prophet*, 1949.

## 5. THE CHURCHES AND SOCIAL PROBLEMS

### (a) *Histories*

Charles Booth's *Life and labour* (**3324**) includes an exhaustive account of social work by the churches in London. The Salvation Army was formed in part to deal with social outcasts (**7223–4**), and Evangelicals in all churches undertook much social work (**7204**).

**3377** INGLIS (KENNETH STANLEY). Churches and the working classes in Victorian England. Lond. & Toronto. 1963.

Good.

**3378** MAYOR (STEPHEN). The churches and the labour movement. 1967.

Opens up an important topic. Covers *c.* 1850–1914.

**3379** MARTIN (HUGH) *ed.* Christian social reformers of the nineteenth century. 1927.

**3380** WICKHAM (EDWARD RALPH), *bishop.* Church and people in an industrial city [Sheffield]. 1957.

**3381** SOLOWAY (RICHARD ALLEN). Prelates and people: ecclesiastical social thought in England, 1783–1852. 1969.

**3382** KITSON CLARK (GEORGE SIDNEY ROBERTS). Churchmen and the condition of England, 1832–1885: a study in the development of social ideas and practice from the old regime to the modern state. 1973.

**3383** WAGNER (DONALD O.). The Church of England and social reform since 1854. N.Y. 1930.

**3384** RECKITT (MAURICE BENINGTON). Maurice to Temple: a century of the social movement in the Church of England (1846–1946). Scott Holland Memorial lectures 1946. 1947.

See also his *Church and society in England from 1800,* 1940, vol. III of *The Church and the world,* ed. by Cyril Edward Hudson and M. B. Reckitt; M. B. Reckitt, ed., *For Christ and the people: studies of four socialist priests and prophets of the Church of England between 1870 and 1930,* 1968; and Cyril Kennard Gloyn, *The church in the social order: a study of Anglican social theory from Coleridge to Maurice,* Forest Grove, Oreg. 1942.

**3385** McENTEE (GEORGIANA PUTNAM). The social catholic movement in Great Britain. N.Y. 1927.

See also John Martin Cleary, *Catholic social action in Britain, 1909–1959: a history of the Catholic Social Guild,* Oxf. 1961.

**3386** CHRISTENSEN (TORBEN). Origin and history of Christian socialism, 1848–54. *Acta Theologica Danica* 3. Aarhus. 1962.

Much the best book on the subject. Largely supersedes Gilbert Clive Binyon, *The Christian socialist movement in England . . .,* 1931, Charles Earle Raven, *Christian socialism, 1848–1854,* 1920, and other earlier works. Philip N. Backstrom, Jr., 'The practical side of Christian socialism in Victorian England', *Victorian Studs.* vi (1962–3), 305–24, adds little.

**3387 KINGSLEY.** Charles Kingsley & Christian socialism. By Colwyn Edward Vulliamy. 1914.

See also Mauritz Kaufmann, *Charles Kingsley: Christian socialist and social reformer,* 1892, William Henry Brown, *Charles Kingsley: the work and influence of Parson Lot* Manch. 1924, and **8384**.

**3388 LUDLOW.** John Malcolm Ludlow: the builder of Christian socialism. By Neville Charles Masterman. Camb. 1963.

See also Peter R. Allen, 'F. D. Maurice and J. M. Ludlow: a reassessment of the leaders of Christian socialism', *Victorian Studs.* xi (1967–8), 461–82.

**MAURICE. See 3721.**

**3389 JONES (PETER D'ALROY).** The Christian-socialist revival, 1877–1914: religion, class and social conscience in late Victorian England. Princeton. 1967.

Detailed.

**3390 NEWSOME (DAVID).** 'The assault on mammon: Charles Gore and John Neville Figgis'. *J. Eccles. Hist.* xvii (1966), 227–41.

**3391 BARNETT.** Canon Barnett: his life, work and friends . . . By Dame Henrietta Octavia Weston Barnett. 2 v. 1918.

The maker of Toynbee Hall. Dame Henrietta also ed. *Worship and work: thoughts from the unpublished writings of the late Canon Samuel Augustus Barnett . . .,* 1913.

**3392 HEADLAM.** Stewart Headlam: a biography. By Frederick George Bettany. 1926.

Christian socialist.

**3393 NOEL.** An autobiography. By Conrad le Despencer Roden Noel. 1945.

See also Reginald Groves, *Conrad Noel and the Thaxted movement: an adventure in Christian socialism,* 1967.

(b) *Contemporary Works on Social Christianity*

**3394 HUGHES (THOMAS)** *and others.* Tracts for priests and people. By various authors. 1st ser. 1861. 2nd ser. 1862.

A Christian socialist collection in 15 pts. Hughes himself also wrote a popular work, *The manliness of Christ,* 1879.

**3395 GIRDLESTONE (E. D.).** Christian socialism versus present-day unsocialism. Limavady [N. Ire.]. 1887.

**3396 WESTCOTT (BROOKE FOSS).** Social aspects of Christianity. 1887.

See also his *Christian Social Union addresses,* 1903.

3397  HUGHES (HUGH PRICE). Social Christianity: sermons . . . 1889.

Hughes's other principal works were *The philanthropy of God*, 1890, *Ethical Christianity*, 1892, and *Essential Christianity*, 1894. For his life see **3837**.

3398  BOOTH (WILLIAM). In darkest England and the way out. [1890.]

A grandiose agricultural scheme by the founder of the Salvation Army.

3399  GORE (CHARLES). The social doctrine of the sermon on the mount. 1892.

Anticipates his *Christ and society*, 1928, *Christianity applied to the life of men and nations* . . ., 1920, and other works dealing with social problems. See also his *The sermon on the mount: a practical exposition*, 1896, 2nd edn. 1910.

3400  HEADLAM (STEWART DUCKWORTH). Christian socialism. Fabian Tract no. 42. 1892.

See also his *The socialist's church*, 1907, and **3406** and **3392**.

3401  CLIFFORD (JOHN). Socialism and the teaching of Christ . . . Fabian Tract no. 78. 1897.

See also his *Socialism and the churches*, Fabian Tract no. 139, 1908, *God's greater Britain: letters and addresses*, 1899, and the lives at **3769**.

3402  HAND (JAMES EDWARD) *ed.* Good citizenship: a book of twenty-three essays . . . on social, personal and economic problems and obligations. Preface by Charles Gore. 1899.

3403  HOCKING (WILLIAM JOHN) *ed.* The church and new century problems. 1901.

Papers by Westcott, Scott Holland, Gore, Barnett, and others.

3404  WOODWORTH (ARTHUR V.). Christian socialism in England. 1903.

3405  KEEBLE (SAMUEL EDWARD). The ideal of the material life, and other social addresses. [1908.]

See also his later *Christian responsibility for the social order*, 1922.

3406  HEADLAM (STEWART DUCKWORTH) *ed.* Socialism and religion. Fabian Socialist Series no. 1. 1908.

Essays by Headlam, Dearmer, Clifford, and Woolman.

3407  DEARMER (PERCY). The church and social questions. Lond. & Oxf. 1910.

See also his *The beginnings of the Christian Social Union*, 1912, and *Christian socialism practical Christianity*, Clarion Pamphlet no. 19, 1897.

3408  NOEL (CONRAD LE DESPENCER RODEN). Socialism in church history. 1910.

3409 ADDERLEY (JAMES GRANVILLE). The parson in socialism: jottings from my notebook. Leeds & Lond. 1910.

See also his collection of sermons, etc., *A new earth* . . ., 1903, and his memoirs (**3561**).

3410 PATON (JOHN BROWN), BUNTING (*Sir* PERCY WILLIAM), *and* GARVIE (ALFRED ERNEST) *eds*. Christ and civilization: a survey of the influence of the Christian religion upon the course of civilization. Ed. for the Nat. Council of the Evangelical Free Churches. 1910.

3411 HOLLAND (HENRY SCOTT). Scott Holland's goodwill: a reprint of Canon Holland's articles in *Goodwill*. Ed. by James Granville Adderley. [1919.]

Holland also contrib. much to *Economic Review* and *Commonwealth*, and publ. numerous works, incl. *Our neighbours: a handbook for the Christian Social Union* [1911]. For his life see **3712**.

## 6. Overseas Missions

Studies of mission activities in particular areas are incl. in the sections of the bibliog. relating to those areas, notably India and Africa.

3412 MISSIONARY RESEARCH LIBRARY, NEW YORK. Dictionary catalog. 17 v. Boston. 1967.

The catalogue of the chief missionary libr., which is associated with the Union Theological Seminary in New York. The libr. issues mimeographed subject bibliogs. from time to time. Among the most valuable are Missionary Research Libr., *Missionary biography: an initial bibliography*, N.Y. 1965, Gerald H. Anderson, ed., *Bibliography of the theology of missions in the twentieth century*, N.Y. 1958, 3rd edn. 1966, and Gerald H. Anderson, ed., *Christianity in Southeast Asia: a bibliographical guide* . . ., N.Y. 1966. There is also John T. Ma, ed., *Current periodicals in the Missionary Research Library: alphabetical list and indexes*, 2nd edn. N.Y. 1961.

3413 STREIT (ROBERT) *et al*. Bibliotheca missionum. Internationales Institut für Missionswissenschaftliche Forschung. Münster. 25+ v. 1916+.

Extraordinarily comprehensive, but difficult to use. For Catholics see also Unione Missionaria del Clero in Italia, *Bibliografia missionaria*, 24+ v, Rome 1935+.

3414 SINCLAIR (JOHN H.) *ed*. Protestantism in Latin America: a bibliographical guide . . . Hispanic American Inst., Austin, Texas. 1967.

3415 KEEN (ROSEMARY). A survey of the archives of selected [British] missionary societies. Hist. Manuscripts Commission. 1968.

3416 MARCHANT (LESLIE R.). A guide to the archives and records of Protestant Christian missions from the British Isles to China, 1796–1914. Nedlands, W.A., 1966.

3417 THE INTERNATIONAL REVIEW OF MISSIONS. Edin. etc. 1912+. Index. 1912–66.

Standard, though not academic. Incl. a current bibliog. of studs. relating to missions. There are occasional references to British missions in *Église vivante*, Louvain 1949+, *Evangelische Missions-Zeitschrift*, Stuttgart 1940+, and other European missionary js.

3418 NEWCOMB (HARVEY). Cyclopedia of missions; containing a comprehensive view of missionary operations throughout the world . . . N.Y. 1854. Rev. edn. 1855. 2nd rev. edn. 1860.

3419 BLISS (EDWIN MUNSELL). The encyclopaedia of missions: descriptive, historical, biographical, statistical . . . 2 v. N.Y. 1891. 2nd edn. N.Y. 1904.

3420 BEACH (HARLAN PAGE). A geography and atlas of Protestant missions: their environment, forces, distribution, methods, problems, results and prospects at the opening of the twentieth century. 2 v. N.Y. 1901–3.

Cont. as *World atlas of Christian missions* . . ., N.Y. 1911, and *World missionary atlas* . . ., N.Y. 1925. There is also much ill-organized information in James Shepard Dennis, *Christian missions and social progress: a sociological study of foreign missions*, 3 v. Edin., Lond., N.Y., & Chicago 1897–1906, and its statistical suppl., *Centennial survey of foreign missions*, Edin., Lond., N.Y., & Chicago 1902.

3421 GODDARD (BURTON L.) *and others, eds.* The encyclopedia of modern Christian missions: the agencies. Gordon Divinity School. Camden, N.J. 1967.

See also Stephen Charles Neill, bishop, Gerald H. Anderson, and John Goodwin, eds., *Concise dictionary of the Christian world mission*, 1971.

3422 LATOURETTE (KENNETH SCOTT). A history of the expansion of Christianity. 7 v. 1938–47.

Extraordinarily comprehensive. Vols. 4–6 cover the period. Stephen Charles Neill, *Christian missions*, Pelican history of the church v. 6, Harmondsworth 1964, is a convenient one-v. hist., with up-to-date bibliog.

3423 HOLMES (BRIAN) *ed.* Educational policy and the mission schools: case studies from the British Empire. Lond. & N.Y. 1967.

A valuable pioneer study.

3424 HOGG (WILLIAM RICHEY). Ecumenical foundations: a history of the International Missionary Council and its nineteenth-century background. N.Y. 1952.

A useful hist. of missionary conferences and co-operation.

3425 CANTON (WILLIAM). A history of the British and Foreign Bible Society. 5 v. 1904–10.

Cont. by James Moulton Roe, *A history of the British and Foreign Bible Society, 1905–1954*, 1965.

3426 THOMPSON (HENRY PAGET). Into all lands: the history of the Society for the Propagation of the Gospel in foreign parts, 1701–1950. 1951.

See also C. F. Pascoe, Two hundred years of the S.P.G., *1701–1900*, 2u. 1901.

3427 CLARKE (WILLIAM KEMP LOWTHER). A history of the S.P.C.K. 1959.

Consult also William Bird Allen and Edmund McClure, *Two hundred years: the history of the Society for promoting Christian Knowledge, 1698–1898*, 1898.

3428  STOCK (EUGENE). The history of the Church Missionary Society, its environment, its men and its work. 4 v. 1899–1916.

See also *The centenary volume of the Church Missionary Society for Africa and the East, 1799–1899*, 1902. Stock is being cont. by [George Henry] Gordon Hewitt, *The problems of success: a history of the Church Missionary Society, 1910–1942*, 2 v. 1971–.

3429  LOVETT (RICHARD). History of the London Missionary Society, 1795–1895. 2 v. 1899.

Cont. by Norman Goodall, *A history of the London Missionary Society, 1895–1945*, 1954. See also Charles Silvester Horne, *The story of the London Missionary Society, 1795–1894*, 1895, 2nd edn. 1904 (a brilliant essay), Alfred Thomas Stephen James, *Twenty-five years of the L.M.S., 1895–1920*, 1923, and the useful life of *Dr. Ralph Wardlaw Thompson*, secretary of the L.M.S., 1881–1916, by Basil Joseph Mathews, 1917.

3430  LORD (FRED TOWNLEY). Achievement: a short history of the Baptist Missionary Society, 1792–1942. [1942.]

Suppl. by Ernest Alexander Payne, *The great succession: leaders of the Baptist Missionary Society during the nineteenth century*, 1938, 2nd edn. 1946.

3431  BAND (EDWARD). Working his purpose out: the history of the English Presbyterian Mission, 1847–1947. 1948.

3432  FINDLAY (GEORGE GILLANDERS) *and* HOLDSWORTH (WILLIAM WEST). The history of the Wesleyan Methodist Missionary Society. 5 v. 1921–4.

3433  GIDNEY (WILLIAM THOMAS). The history of the London Society for promoting Christianity amongst the Jews, from 1809 to 1908. 1908.

There is also George Henry Stevens, '*Go, tell my brethren': a short popular history of church missions to Jews (1809 to 1959)*, 1959.

3434  STRONG (LEONARD ALFRED GEORGE). Flying angel: the story of the missions to seamen. 1956.

3435  LIVERPOOL CONFERENCE. Conference on missions held in 1860 at Liverpool: including the papers read, the deliberations, and the conclusions reached . . . edited by the secretaries of the conference. 1860.

The first of the great missionary conferences, whose reports are a major source for missionary hist.

3436  MILDMAY PARK CONFERENCE. Proceedings of the general conference on foreign missions held at the conference hall in Mildmay Park, London, in October 1878. Edited by the secretaries to the conference. 1879.

3437  CENTENARY CONFERENCE. Report of the centenary conference on the protestant missions of the world, held in Exeter Hall (June 9th–19th), London, 1888. Ed. by the Rev. James Johnston. 2 v. 1889.

Incl. 'A contribution towards a missionary bibliography', by the Rev. Samuel Macauley Jackson in vol. I, pp. 489–538.

3438 BARROWS (JOHN HENRY) *ed.* The world's parliament of religions: an illustrated and popular story of the world's first parliament of religions held in Chicago in connection with the Columbian exposition of 1893. 2 v. Lond. & Chicago 1893.

3439 SPOTTISWOODE (GEORGE ANDREW) *ed.* The official report of the missionary conference of the Anglican communion on May 28, 29, 30, 31 and June 1, 1894. 1894.

3440 WORLD MISSIONARY CONFERENCE, EDINBURGH, 1910: reports. 9 v. Edin. 1910.

Much the most important missionary conference ever held. Full and admirable reports. See also William Henry Temple Gairdner, *Edinburgh 1910: an account and interpretation of the World Missionary Conference*, Edin. 1910.

3441 ALLEN (ROLAND). Missionary methods: St. Paul's or ours? 1912. 5th edn. 1960.

One of the few good contemporary English works discussing missionary problems. Cp. Robert Needham Cust, *Essay on the prevailing methods of the evangelization of the non-Christian world*, 1894.

3442 LAMBERT (JOHN C.). The romance of missionary heroism: true stories of the intrepid bravery and stirring adventures of missionaries with uncivilized man, wild beasts and the forces of nature in all parts of the world. 1907.

Interesting, as reflecting the heroic stature of missionaries in the popular press. Lambert also publ. *Missionary heroes in Africa* . . ., 1909, *Missionary heroes in Asia* . . ., 1908, and *Missionary heroes in North & South America* . . ., 1913.

### 7. EVANGELISTS AND REVIVALISTS

3443 SCHARPFF (PAULUS). Geschichte der Evangelisation: dreihundert Jahre Evangelisation in Deutschland, Grossbritannien und U.S.A. Giessen & Basle. 1964.

3444 JOHNSON (HENRY). Stories of great revivals. 1906.

3445 FINNEY (CHARLES GRANDISON). Revivals of religion: lectures: with the author's final additions. Rev. by William Henry Harding. 1910. New edn. by William G. McLoughlin. Camb., Mass. 1960.

The great textbook of revivalism first publ. N.Y. &c. 1835. Finney's *Lectures on systematic theology* were also publ. in England in 1851.

3446 ORR (JAMES EDWIN). The second evangelical awakening in Britain. Lond. & Edin. 1949.

A good scholarly hist. of the revival of 1859.

3447 CLARK (RUFUS WHEELWRIGHT). The work of God in Great Britain under Messrs. Moody & Sankey, 1873–1875: with biographical sketches. Lond. & N.Y. 1875.

The most famous revivalists of their day.

3448 MACPHERSON (JOHN). Revival and revival work. 1875.

See also his *The Christian hero,* 1867, new edn. 1878, *Life and labours of Duncan Matheson,* 1871, and *Isabella Macpherson* [1889].

3449 HENRY WARD BEECHER IN ENGLAND, 1886: addresses, lectures, sermons, prayers, biographical sketch and portrait. [1887.]

3450 MACLEAN (JOHN KENNEDY). Triumphant evangelism: the three years' missions of Dr. Torrey and Mr. Alexander in Great Britain and Ireland. [1905.]

Maclean also publ. *Torrey and Alexander: the story of their lives* . . . [1905], and *Under two masters: the story of Jacoby, Dr. Torrey's assistant* . . . [1905]. See also William Thomas Stead, *The revival of 1905: 1. the revival in the west. 2. the Torrey and Alexander Mission. 3. the National Free Church missions,* 1905.

3451 EDDY. Eighty adventurous years: an autobiography. By George Sherwood Eddy. N.Y. 1955.

3452 MOODY. The life and work of Dwight Lyman Moody. By John Wilbur Chapman. [1900.]

See also John Charles Pollock, *Moody without Sankey: a new biographical portrait,* 1963.

3453 MOORHOUSE. Henry Moorhouse, the English evangelist. By John Macpherson. [1881.]

3454 MORGAN. A man of the word: life of G. Campbell Morgan. By Jill Morgan. 1951.

See also John Harries, *G. Campbell Morgan: the man and his ministry,* 1930, and *This was his faith: the expository letters of G. Campbell Morgan,* ed. by Jill Morgan, 1954.

3455 MORGAN. 'A veteran in revival': R. C. Morgan: his life and times. By his son, George Ernest Morgan. 1909. New edn. [Mighty days of revival.] [1922.]

3456 MÜLLER. George Müller: the modern apostle of faith. By Frederick G. Warne. N.Y. etc. 1898.

See also 7272.

3457 RADCLIFFE. Recollections of Reginald Radcliffe. By his wife, Jane Radcliffe. [1896.]

3458 SANKEY. My life and sacred songs. By Ira David Sankey. [2nd edn. of Sankey's story of the gospel hymns and of sacred songs and solos . . . Phila. 1906.] 1906.

3459   SMITH. Gipsy Smith, his life and work, by himself [i.e. Rodney Smith]. 1902.

There are two brief lives, both by Harold Murray, *Sixty years an evangelist*, 1937, and *Gipsy Smith: an intimate memoir*, Exeter 1947.

3460   VARLEY. Henry Varley's life story. By Henry Varley, the younger. [1916.]

3461   WEAVER. Richard Weaver's life story. By James Paterson. [1897.] Repr. 1913.

See also Richard Cope Morgan, *The life of Richard Weaver, the converted collier*, 1861, repr. [1906.]

## 8. Church Music and Hymnology

3462   HUTCHINGS (ARTHUR JAMES BRAMWELL). Church music in the nineteenth century. 1967. 2nd edn. 1969.

For organs and organists see **9280–1** and **9318**.

3463   PHILLIPS (CHARLES STANLEY). The singing church: an outline of the music sung by choir and people. 1945.

3464   RAINBOW (BERNARR). The choral revival in the Anglican church, 1839–1872. 1970.

3465   FELLOWES (EDMUND HORACE). English cathedral music from Edward VI to Edward VII. 1941. 2nd edn. 1969.

See also John Skelton Bumpus, *A history of English cathedral music, 1549–1889*, 2 v. 1908; Church Music Society, *Forty years of cathedral music, 1898–1938: a comparison of the repertoires of service music and anthems in regular use in thirty-four cathedrals and collegiate churches of England and Wales at these dates*, 1940; Harold Watkins Shaw, *The Three Choirs festival: the official history of the meetings of the three choirs of Gloucester, Hereford and Worcester, 1713–1953*, Worcester 1954; John Ebenezer West, *Cathedral organists*, 1899; and Noel Boston, *The musical history of Norwich cathedral*, Norwich 1963. For Roman Catholic cathedral music see Hilda Andrews, *Westminster retrospect: a memoir of Sir Richard Terry*, 1948.

3466   ROUTLEY (ERIK). The musical Wesleys [1703–1876]. Lond. & N.Y. 1968.

3467   CURWEN (JOHN SPENCER). Studies in worship music chiefly as regards congregational singing. 1st ser. [1880.] 3rd edn. [1901.] 2nd ser. [1885.]

3468   BOX (CHARLES). Church music in the metropolis: its past and present condition. 1884.

3469   MESSENGER (RUTH ELLIS) *and* PFATTEICHER (HELEN) *comps.* A short bibliography for the study of hymns. The papers of the Hymn Soc. XXV. N.Y. 1964.

For the hist. of hymnody see also the Hymn Soc. of America, *The hymn*, N.Y. 1949+, and *Papers*, 1930+, and Hymn Soc. of Great Britain and Ireland, *Bulletin*, Edin. 1937+.

3470 JULIAN (JOHN) *ed*. A dictionary of hymnology: setting forth the origin and history of Christian hymns of all ages and nations. 1892. 2nd edn. 1925. [3rd edn.] N.Y. 1957.

Indispensable.

3471 BENSON (LOUIS FITZGERALD). The English hymn: its development and use in worship. N.Y. 1915. Repr. Richmond, Va. 1962.

Standard. William Thomas Whitley, *Congregational hymn-singing* . . ., 1933, Benjamin Brawley, *History of the English hymn*, N.Y. etc. 1932, Charles Stanley Phillips, *Hymnody, past and present*, 1937, and similar works, add little. Samuel Willoughby Duffield, *English hymns: their authors and history*, N.Y. 1886, 3rd edn. 1888, is a curious collection of misc. information. William Garrett Horder, *The hymn lover: an account of the rise and growth of English hymnody*, 1890, 2nd edn. 1900, reflects late Victorian taste.

3472 LIGHTWOOD (JAMES THOMAS). Hymn tunes and their story. 1906.

3473 ROUTLEY (ERIK). The music of Christian hymnody: a study of the development of the hymn tune since the Reformation, with special reference to English protestantism. 1957.

3474 BRIDGES (ROBERT). A practical discourse on some principles of hymn singing. Repr. from the *J. of Theol. Studs*. Oxf. 1901.

See also Bridges's *The Yattenden hymnal*, Oxf. 1899 and later edns., and his *Collected essays*, nos. XXI–XXVI, Oxf. 1935.

3475 PITMAN (EMMA RAYMOND). Lady hymn writers. 1892.

3476 CLARKE (WILLIAM KEMP LOWTHER). A hundred years of Hymns ancient & modern. 1960.

The most widely-used of Anglican hymn-books. To be used with Maurice Frost, ed., *Historical companion to Hymns ancient & modern*, 1962, and *Hymns, ancient & modern: historical edition*, 1909. See also Edward Henry Bickersteth, bishop of Exeter, ed., *The hymnal companion to the Book of Common Prayer: annotated edition, with introduction and notes*, 1870, 3rd edn. 1890, and James King, *Anglican hymnology: being, an account of the 325 standard hymns of the highest merit according to the verdict of the whole Anglican church*, Lond. & Edin. 1885.

3477 MARTIN (HUGH) *ed*. The Baptist hymn book companion. 1962.

See also Carey Bonner, *Some Baptist hymnists from the seventeenth century to modern times*, 1937.

3478 PARRY (KENNETH LLOYD) *ed*. Companion to Congregational praise. 1953. Suppl. 1960.

3479 STEVENSON (GEORGE JOHN). The Methodist hymn book and its associations. Edin. 1870.

His *The Methodist hymn book, illustrated with biography, incident and anecdote*, 1883, is a greatly expanded and improved version of this earlier work. See also James Thomas Lightwood, *The music of the Methodist hymnbook: being the story of each tune, with biographical notices of the composers*, 1935, and John Telford, *The new Methodist hymn book: illustrated in history and experience*, 1934, which was a successor to his *The Methodist hymn book illustrated*, 1906, 2nd edn. 1909.

3480 STEPHENSON (HAROLD WILLIAM). Unitarian hymn writers. 1931.

William Copeland Bowie, ed., *The Unitarian faith in Unitarian hymns*, 1918, prints a few characteristic hymns with notes.

3481 SANKEY (IRA DAVID). Sacred songs and solos. 1873+.

The 1st edn. of 1873 had 23 pieces; by 1903 the number was 1200. By far the best-known book of its type. Many other revivalists had their own hymn-books, among them Richard Weaver, Joshua Poole, William Trotter, William Carter, Philip Phillips, and Thomas Alexander; and there were also publishers' comps.

3482 TREVOR (JOHN) *ed.* The Labour church hymnbook. 1892.

See also J. H. Belcher, W. Mitchell, and T. A. Pierce, *The Labour church hymnbook*, 1906, 2nd edn. 1907.

3483 ROUTLEY (ERIK). The English carol. 1958.

## B. CHURCH OF ENGLAND

### 1. REFERENCE

3484 WHITNEY (JAMES POUNDER). Bibliography of church history. 1923.

See also Dorothy M. Owen, *The records of the established church in England, excluding parochial records*, British Records Assoc. 1970.

3485 'EPISCOPAL AND ANGLICAN HISTORY, 1965+: an annotated bibliography'. *Hist. Mag. of the Protestant Episcopal Church* xxxv (1966)+.

3486 STOCKS (JOHN EDWARD). A chronological list of reports of committees of both houses of the convocation of Canterbury, 1847–1921. 1921.

3487 SMYTHE (PAUL RODNEY). A bibliography of Anglican modernism. Camb. 1947.

3488 HUGH, *Father*. Nineteenth century pamphlets at Pusey House: an introduction for the prospective user. 1961.

A guide to the indexes to some 18,500 pamphlets. The best coll. of its kind.

3489 OLLARD (SIDNEY LESLIE) *and others*. A dictionary of English church history. Lond. & Oxf. 1912. 3rd edn. 1948.

3490 LELY (JOHN MOUNTNEY). The Church of England position as appearing from statutes, articles, canons, rubrics, and judicial decisions . . . 1899.

3491 PHILLIMORE (*Sir* ROBERT JOSEPH). The ecclesiastical law of the Church of England. 2 v. 1873–6. 2nd edn. 2 v. 1895.

Standard. But see also the shorter and more specialized works of Henry William Cripps, *A practical treatise on the laws relating to the church and the clergy*, 1845, 8th edn. 1937;

John Henry Blunt, *The book of church law: being an exposition of the legal rights and duties of the parochial clergy and the laity of the Church of England*, 1872, 11th edn. 1921; Thomas Eustace Smith, *A summary of the law and practice in the ecclesiastical courts*, 1880, 7th edn. 1920; and Charles Grevile Prideaux, *A practical guide to the duties of churchwardens in the execution of their office*, 1841, 16th edn. 1895. Alfred Charles Heales, *The history and law of church seats or pews*, 2 v. 1872, is also useful.

3492 TALBOT (*Sir* GEORGE JOHN). Modern decisions on ritual and kindred subjects. 1894.

The most useful coll. For other colls. of reports see **2975**. Three cases are well reported in separate vols., Edmund Fitz Moore, ed., *The case of the Rev. G. C. Gorham against the bishop of Exeter . . .*, 1852, Thomas Walter Perry, ed., *Folkestone ritual case . . .*, 1878, and Edward Stanley Roscoe, ed., *The Bishop of Lincoln's case . . .*, 1889–91.

3493 THE OFFICIAL YEAR BOOK OF THE CHURCH OF ENGLAND. 1882+.

Individual dioceses also publ. year books, which are often fuller than either the *Official year book* or *Crockford*.

3494 CROCKFORD'S CLERICAL DIRECTORY. 1861+.

3495 THE CLERGY LIST. 1841–1917.

Similar in character to *Crockford*. Other directories such as *The clergy directory and parish guide*, 1872–1930, give only a small proportion of the information in the two major directories.

## 2. PERIODICALS

3496 CONVOCATION OF CANTERBURY. The chronicle of convocation: being a record of the proceedings of the convocation of Canterbury. 1858+. 1859+.

3497 CONVOCATION OF YORK. York journal of convocation: containing the acts and debates of both houses of the convocation of the province of York. 1861+.

3498 CHURCH CONGRESS. Authorised report of the Church Congress. 1861–1938. 1862–1938.

Speeches and debates on social and other questions. At first styled *Report of the proceedings . . . .*

3499 ECCLESIASTICAL COMMISSIONERS. Annual report for 1846+.

Important for church property.

3500 CHURCH ESTATES COMMISSIONERS. Annual report. 1852–1938/9.

3501 THE CHURCH QUARTERLY REVIEW. 1875–1968.

The most serious church j. Amalg. with the *London quarterly and Holborn rev.*, 1853–1968, as *The church quarterly*, 1968–71.

**3502 THE GUARDIAN. 1846–1951.**

The leading high-church periodical. *The church times*, 1863 +, *Church review*, 1861–1902, *The English churchman*, 1843 +, and *The literary churchman*, Oxf. 1855–92, were also high-church weeklies. *The ecclesiastic* (monthly, various titles), 1846–68, and *The Christian remembrancer* (quarterly), 1819–68, where short-lived js. of the same general tone. Of the general press the *Quarterly Review, Morning Post*, and *John Bull*, 1820–92, took a high-church line.

**3503 THE RECORD. 1828+.**

The leading evangelical paper. *The Rock*, 1868–1905, was more militant, the *Christian Observer*, 1802–77, less influential. *The leisure hour*, 1852–1905, was an evangelical mag. for the home.

### 3. HISTORIES

**3504 MOORMAN (JOHN RICHARD HUMPIDGE). A history of the church in England. 1953. 2nd edn. 1967.**

Replaces Henry Offley Wakeman, *An introduction to the history of the Church of England* . . ., 1896, rev. edn. 1914, and other outline hists. See also John McLeod Campbell, *Christian history in the making*, Westminster 1946, a popular outline of Anglican overseas expansion.

**3505 CHADWICK ([WILLIAM] OWEN). The Victorian church. 2 v. Vol. I. 1966. 2nd edn. 1970. Vol. II. 1970.**

The first major study. Needs to be suppl. for the broad church by Margaret Anne Crowther, *Church embattled: religious controversy in mid-Victorian England*, Newton Abbot & Hamden, Conn. 1970.

**3506 CORNISH (FRANCIS WARRE). History of the English church in the nineteenth century. 2 v. 1910. Vol. VIII of *A history of the English church*, ed. by William Richard Wood Stephens and William Hunt.**

Full, but dated. John Henry Overton, *The Anglican revival*, Victorian era ser., 1897, is also worth consulting; there is little on the period in his *The church in England*, 2 v. 1897. There is much revealing matter in the broad-church essays, Walter Lowe Clay, ed., *Essays on church policy*, 1868.

**3507 CARPENTER (SPENCER CECIL). Church and people, 1789–1889: a history of the Church of England from William Wilberforce to 'Lux Mundi'. 1933. New edn. 3 v. 1959.**

**3508 LLOYD (ROGER BRADSHAIGH). The Church of England in the twentieth century. 2 v. 1946–50. New edn. [The Church of England, 1900–1965.] 1 v. 1966.**

Often careless and journalistic. Anglo-Catholic.

**3509 MAKOWER (FELIX). The constitutional history and constitution of the Church of England. 1895.**

A full legal hist.

3510 BOWEN (DESMOND). The idea of the Victorian church: a study of the Church of England, 1833–1889. Montreal. 1968.

Anglo-Catholic in emphasis.

3511 NICHOLLS (DAVID). Church and state in Britain since 1820. Lond. & N.Y. 1967.

A brief documentary intro.

3512 BROSE (OLIVE JOHNSON). Church and parliament: the reshaping of the Church of England, 1828–1860. Stanford, Calif. 1959.

See also P. J. Welch, 'The revival of an active convocation of Canterbury (1852–1855)', *J. Eccles. Hist.* x (1959), 188–97, and James Wayland Joyce, *Acts of the church, 1531–1885: the Church of England her own reformer, as testified by the records of her convocation,* 1886.

3513 ELLIOT (ARTHUR RALPH DOUGLAS). The state and the church. 1882. 2nd edn. 1899.

Cyril Forster Garbett, Archbishop of York, *Church and state in England,* 1950, is also largely hist. Much of the contemp. literature on church and state was concerned with Wales and Ireland, for which see **9616** and **10497**. The Nonconformist case for disestablishment is set out in the works at **3741–7**.

3514 THOMPSON (KENNETH ALFRED). Bureaucracy and church reform: the organizational response of the Church of England to social change, 1800–1965. Oxf. 1970.

3515 BEST (GEOFFREY FRANCIS ANDREW). Temporal pillars: Queen Anne's Bounty, the ecclesiastical commissioners and the Church of England. Camb. 1964.

Good. Largely replaces Sir Lewis Tonna Dibdin and Stanford Edwin Downing, *The ecclesiastical commission: a sketch of its history and work,* 1919.

3516 PORT (MICHAEL HARRY). Six hundred new churches: a study of the Church Building Commission, 1818–1856, and its church building activities. Church Historical Soc. 1961.

For church building see also Basil Fulford Lowther Clarke, *Church builders of the nineteenth century: a study of the Gothic revival in England,* 1938, and *Anglican cathedrals outside the British Isles,* 1958.

3517 VIDLER (ALEXANDER ROPER). The orb and the cross: a normative study in the relations of church and state, with reference to Gladstone's early writings. 1945.

For Gladstone's views see also D. C. Lathbury, *Correspondence on church and religion of W. E. Gladstone* (**731**), M. D. Stephen, 'Liberty, church and state: Gladstone's relations with Manning and Acton, 1832–70', *J. Religious Hist.* i (1960–1), 217–32, 'Gladstone's ecclesiastical patronage, 1868–1874', *Hist. Studs. Aust. & N.Z.* xi (1964), 145–62, and 'Gladstone and the composition of the final court in ecclesiastical causes, 1850–73', *Hist. J.* ix (1966), 191–200, and Dudley Ward Rhodes Bahlman, 'The Queen, Mr. Gladstone and church patronage', *Victorian Studs.* iii (1959–60), 349–80. There is an interesting comparison with the views of J. R. Seeley, for whom see Richard Thomas Shannon, 'John Robert Seeley and the idea of a national church', in R. Robson, *Ideas and institutions* (**177**), 236–67.

**3518 HERKLOTS (HUGH GERARD GIBSON). Frontiers of the church: the making of the Anglican communion. 1961.**

Like his *The Church of England and the American Episcopal Church: from the first voyages of discovery to the first Lambeth conference,* [1966] merely opens the subject.

**3519 DAVIDSON (RANDALL THOMAS), *Baron Davidson, ed.* The six Lambeth conferences, 1867–1920. 1929.**

See also Alan Malcolm George Stephenson, *The first Lambeth conference, 1867,* 1967, and William Redmond Curtis, *The Lambeth conferences: the solution for pan-Anglican organization,* N.Y. 1942.

**3520 BILL (EDWARD GEOFFREY WATSON) *ed.* Anglican initiatives in christian unity . . . 1967.**

A useful ser. of hist. papers.

**3521 HUGHES (JOHN JAY). Absolutely null and utterly void: the papal condemnation of Anglican orders, 1896. Wash. & Lond. 1968.**

**3522 BROWN (CHARLES KENNETH FRANCIS). A history of the English clergy, 1800–1900. 1953.**

See also Arthur Tindal Hart and Edward Carpenter, *The nineteenth-century country parson, circa 1832–1900,* Shrewsbury 1954, and McClatchey, *Oxfordshire clergy* (**3627**). The best-known clerical diary is *Kilvert's diary: selections from the diary of the Rev. Francis Kilvert* [1870–9], ed. by William Plomer, 3 v. 1938–40, new edn. 3 v. 1960. But see also 3 books by or about Norfolk parsons: Augustus Jessopp, *The trials of a country parson,* 1890, Herbert Benjamin John Armstrong, ed., *A Norfolk diary: passages from the diary of the Rev. Benjamin John Armstrong M.A. (Cantab.), Vicar of East Dereham, 1850–88,* 1949, and *Further passages,* 1963, and [William] Owen Chadwick, *Victorian miniature,* 1960, an account of the relations between squire and parson of Ketteringham to 1864. There is an attractive account of an East end of London dock parish shortly before 1914 in Eileen Baillie, *The shabby paradise: the autobiography of a decade,* 1958. For houses see Alan Savidge, *The parsonage in England: its history and architecture,* 1964.

**3523 MAYOR (STEPHEN). 'Discussion of the ministry in late nineteenth-century Anglicanism'. *Church Quart.* ii (1969–70), 54–62.**

The appendix to Lightfoot's commentary on the Philippians, 1868, provoked a debate, for which see also Mayor's 'The Anglo-Catholic understanding of the ministry: some protestant comments', ibid. 152–9.

**3524 BULLOCK (FREDERICK WILLIAM BAGSHAWE). A history of training for the ministry of the Church of England in England and Wales from 1800 to 1874. St. Leonard's-on-Sea. 1955.**

**3525 CHADWICK ([WILLIAM] OWEN). The founding of Cuddesdon. Oxf. 1954.**

There are also useful hists. of other theological colleges: St. Aidan's Birkenhead, by Francis Bernhard Heiser, Chester 1947; St. Augustine's, Canterbury, by Robert James Edmund Boggis, Canterbury 1907; King's College, London, by Fossey John Cobb

Hearnshaw, 1929; Lichfield Theological College by Ernest Charles Inman, Lichfield 1928; London College of Divinity, by George Colliss Boardman Davies, 1963; Ridley Hall, Cambridge, by Frederick William Bagshawe Bullock, 2 v. Camb. 1941–53; and Wells Theological College by Edward Leighton Elwes, 1923.

3526 CUMING (GEOFFREY JOHN). A history of Anglican liturgy. Lond. & N.Y. 1969.

3527 BRICE (SEWARD WILLIAM). The law relating to public worship: with especial regard to matters of ritual and ornamentation . . . 1875.

3528 HARFORD (GEORGE) *and* STEVENSON (MORLEY) *assisted by* TYRER (J. W.) *eds*. The prayer book dictionary. 1912. Repr. 1925.

3529 JASPER (RONALD CLAUD DUDLEY). Prayer book revision in England, 1800–1900. 1954.

3530 MACKERNESS (ERIC DAVID). The heeded voice: studies in the literary status of the Anglican sermon, 1830–1900. Camb. 1959.

See also Charles Hugh Egerton Smyth, *The art of preaching: a practical survey of preaching in the Church of England*, 747–1939, 1940.

3531 ADDLESHAW (GEORGE WILLIAM OUTRAM) *and* ETCHELLS (FREDERICK). The architectural setting of Anglican worship: an inquiry into the arrangements for public worship in the Church of England from the Reformation to the present day. 1948. 2nd edn. 1956.

Cp. James Floyd White, *Protestant worship and church architecture: theological and historical considerations*, N.Y. 1964.

3532 PERKINS (JOCELYN HENRY TEMPLE). Westminster Abbey: its worship and ornaments. Alcuin Club (vols. xxxiii, xxxiv, and xxxviii). 3 v. 1938–52.

3533 WHITE (JAMES FLOYD). The Cambridge movement: the ecclesiologists and the Gothic revival. Camb. 1962.

4. THE OXFORD MOVEMENT AND AFTER

3534 SIMPSON (WILLIAM JOHN SPARROW). The history of the Anglo-Catholic revival from 1845. 1932.

Probably the best of a large number of short hists. But see also Herbert Leslie Stewart, *A century of Anglo-Catholicism*, Lond. & Toronto 1929. The important early years of the movement, dealt with in Richard William Church, *The Oxford movement: twelve years, 1833–1845*, 1891, 3rd edn. 1892, new edn. by Geoffrey Francis Andrew Best, Chicago 1970, David Newsome, *The parting of friends: a study of the Wilberforces and Henry Manning*, 1966, and [William] Owen Chadwick, ed., *The mind of the Oxford movement*, 1961, lie outside the period. There is a bibliog. of them in *Camb. Hist. Engl. Lit.* XII, 453–63. Other short hists. covering the period after 1851 include Charles Philip Stewart Clarke, *The Oxford movement and after*, Lond. & Oxf. 1932; Marcus FitzGerald Grain Donovan, *After the Tractarians: from the recollections of Athelstan Riley*, 1933; Sir [John Randolph] Shane Leslie, *The Oxford movement, 1833–1933*,

1933; James Lewis May, *The Oxford movement: its history and its future: a layman's estimate*, 1933; Desmond Morse-Boycott, *The secret history of the Oxford movement*, 1933; Sidney Leslie Ollard, *A short history of the Oxford movement* [1915]; and Paul Schaefer, *The Catholic regeneration of the Church of England*, trans. by Ethel Talbot Scheffauer, 1935. G. Wakeling, *The Oxford church movement: sketches and recollections*, 1895, is sometimes useful for basic facts.

3535 BRILIOTH (YNGVE). The Anglican revival: studies in the Oxford movement. 1925.

Good. See also his *Three lectures on evangelicalism and the Oxford movement*, 1934.

3536 VOLL (DIETER). Catholic evangelicalism: the acceptance of evangelical traditions by the Oxford movement during the second half of the nineteenth century. Trans. by Veronica Ruffer. 1936.

Important. The subject matter is best indicated by the title of the German edition: *Hochkirchlicher Pietismus* . . ., Munich 1960. Particularly interesting on G. H. Wilkinson (**3695**), Dolling (**3569**), and those assoc. with St Alban's, Holborn (**3552**). See also Trevor Dearing, *Wesleyan and Tractarian worship: an ecumenical study*, 1966, and Herbert Clegg, 'Evangelicals and Tractarians', *Hist. Mag. Protestant Episcopal Church* xxxv (1966), 111–53, 237–94; xxxvi (1967), 127–78.

3537 WEBB (CLEMENT CHARLES JULIAN). Religious thought in the Oxford movement. 1928.

3538 WILLIAMS (NORMAN POWELL) *and* HARRIS (CHARLES) *eds.* Northern Catholicism: centenary studies in the Oxford and parallel movements. 1933.

3539 THUREAU-DANGIN (PAUL). The English Catholic revival in the nineteenth century . . . Rev. and re-edited from a trans. by Wilfrid Ignatius Wilberforce. 2 v. 1914.

Deals with the influence of the Oxford movement on both the Church of England and English Roman Catholicism.

3540 WALSH (WALTER). The secret history of the Oxford movement. 1897. 5th edn. 1899.

Hostile. See also his *The history of the Romeward movement in the Church of England, 1833–1864*, 1900.

3541 HÄRDELIN (ALF). The tractarian understanding of the eucharist. Uppsala. 1965.

3542 BRANDRETH (HENRY RENAUD TURNER). The œcumenical ideals of the Oxford movement. 1947.

3543 PECK (WILLIAM GEORGE). The social implications of the Oxford movement. Hale lectures. N.Y. & Lond. 1933.

3544 BAKER (JOSEPH ELLIS). The novel and the Oxford movement. Princeton [N.J.]. 1932.

3545 ROBERTS (GEORGE BAYFIELD). The history of the English Church Union, 1859–1894. 1895.

The chief organ of the Anglo-Catholic movement.

3546 PURCHAS (JOHN) *ed.* Directorium Anglicanum: being a manual of directions for the right celebration of the Holy Communion. 1858.

Incl. along with the books that follow (**3547–51**) as indications of the type of handbook favoured by the champions of the Oxford movement. For doctrine see **3337, 3347, 3355.**

3547 WALKER (CHARLES) *ed.* The ritual reason why. 1867. 2nd edn. 1869. Rev. edns. by T. I. Ball. Oxf. 1901. Lond. & Oxf. 1908.

3548 CARTER (THOMAS THELLUSSON). The doctrine of confession in the Church of England. 1865.

3549 SHIPLEY (ORBY) *ed.* The church and the world: essays on questions of the day. 2 ser. 1866–7.

A ritualist manifesto.

3550 OLDKNOW (JOSEPH) *and* CRAKE (AUGUSTINE DAVID). The priest's book of private devotion: with prayers for the use of candidates for holy orders. Oxf. 1872. 2nd edn. Oxf. 1877. Enl. edn. Oxf. 1884. New edn. ed. by W. M. Richardson. 1891. Further edn. by J. Watkin Williams. 1897, etc.

A manual of high-church clerical piety.

3551 HOPE (ALEXANDER JAMES BERESFORD). Worship in the Church of England. 1874. 2nd edn. 1875.

3552 RUSSELL (GEORGE WILLIAM ERSKINE). Saint Alban the Martyr, Holborn: a history of fifty years. 1913. 2nd edn. 1913.

3553 ALLCHIN (ARTHUR MACDONALD). The silent rebellion: Anglican religious communities, 1845–1900. 1958.

3554 ANSON (PETER FREDERICK). The call of the cloister: religious communities and kindred bodies in the Anglican communion. 1955. Rev. edn. 1956. New edn. by A. W. Campbell. 1964.

A full directory of past and present communities.

3555 EMBRY (JAMES). The Catholic movement and the Society of the Holy Cross. 1931.

One of the few substantial accounts of an Anglican community. For sisterhoods see Thomas Jay Williams and Allan Walter Campbell, *The Park Village sisterhood*, 1965, and Sister Joanna, 'The deaconess community of St. Andrew', *J. Eccles. Hist.* xii (1961), 215–30.

3556 BIRKBECK (WILLIAM JOHN) *ed.* Russia and the English church during the last fifty years: containing a correspondence between Mr. William

Palmer, Fellow of Magdalen College, Oxford, and M. Khomiakoff, in the years 1844–1854. Eastern Church Assoc. 1895.

Vol. I of a projected ser. Vol. II in fact became, Athelstan Riley, ed., *Birkbeck and the Russian church: containing essays and articles by the late W. J. Birkbeck, M.A., F.S.A., written in the years 1888–1915,* Anglican and Eastern Church Assoc. 1917.

3557 BURGON (JOHN WILLIAM). Lives of twelve good men. 2 v. 1888.

Deservedly famous. Lives of Routh, Rose, Marriott, Hawkins, Wilberforce, Cotton, Greswell, Coxe, Mansel, Jacobson, Eden, and Higgins. See also Augustus Blair Donaldson, *Five great Oxford leaders,* 1900, which deals with Keble, Newman, Pusey, Liddon, and Church.

3558 WINDLE (*Sir* BERTRAM COGHILL ALAN). Who's who of the Oxford movement . . . N.Y. 1926.

3559 MIDDLETON (ROBERT DUDLEY). Magdalen studies. 1936.

Ten leaders of the Oxford movement: Routh, Bloxam, Bulley, William Palmer, Roundell Palmer, J. B. Mozley, Best, Sibthorpe, Bernard Smith, Bramley.

3560 MACKAY (HENRY FALCONER BARCLAY). Saints and leaders. 1928.

Incl. lives of Lowder, Dolling, King, Stanton, Benson, and Weston.

3561 ADDERLEY. In slums and society: reminiscences of old friends. By James Granville Adderley. 1916.

See also Thomas Primmitt Stevens, *Father Adderley,* 1943.

3562 AYCKBOWM. A valiant Victorian: the life and times of Mother Emily Ayckbowm, 1836–1900. By the Community of the Sisters of the Church. 1964.

3563 BENNETT. The story of W. J. E. Bennett . . . and of his part in the Oxford church movement of the nineteenth century. By Frederick Bennett. 1909.

William James Early Bennett was a centre of controversy, as the British Museum catalogue (5) shows. His most characteristic works are *The eucharist: its history, doctrine and practice . . .,* 1837, 2nd edn. 1846, and *A defence of the catholic faith . . .,* 1873, 2nd edn. 1873.

3564 BENSON. Father Benson, founder of the Cowley fathers. By Mildred Violet Woodgate. 1953.

See also Richard Meux Benson, *Letters . . .,* ed. by George Congreve and William Hawks Longridge, 2 v. Lond. & Oxf. 1916–20, *Spiritual letters . . .,* ed. by William Hawks Longridge, Lond. & Oxf. 1924, and *The religious vocation . . .,* ed. by Henry Power Bull and others, 1939.

3565 BUTLER. Life and letters of William John Butler, late dean of Lincoln . . . By Arthur John Butler. 1897.

3566 CARTER. Life and letters of Thomas Thellusson Carter . . . By William Henry Hutchings. 1903.

See also Jane Frances Mary Carter, *Life and work of the Rev. T. T. Carter . . .,* 1911.

**3567** CHURCH. Dean Church: the Anglican response to Newman. By Basil Alec Smith. 1958.

See also Mary C. Church, ed., *Life and letters of Dean Church*, 1894.

**3568** COLES, V. S. S. Coles: letters, papers, addresses, hymns and verses, with a memoir. Ed. by John Featherstonhaugh Briscoe. 1930.

**3569** DOLLING. The life of Father Dolling. By Charles Edward Osborne. 1903. Repr. 1903, 1905.

See also Robert William Radclyffe Dolling's own *Ten years in a Portsmouth slum*, 1896, Joseph Clayton, *Father Dolling: a memoir*, 1902, and Richard Thomsen, *Robert Dolling: et Blad af den engelske Statskirkes Historie i det 19 Aarhundrede*, Copenhagen 1908.

**3570** FIGGIS. John Neville Figgis: a study. By Maurice Grahame Tucker. 1950.

**3571** FRERE. Walter Howard Frere, Bishop of Truro. By Charles Stanley Phillips and others. 1947.

One of the founders of the Community of the Resurrection. See also Ronald Claud Dudley Jasper, ed., *Walter Howard Frere: his correspondence on liturgical revision and construction*, Alcuin Club 39, 1954, and John Henry Arnold and Edward Gerald Penfold Wyatt, eds., *Walter Howard Frere: a collection of his papers on liturgical and historical subjects*, Alcuin Club 35, 1940.

**3572** GILMORE. Isabella Gilmore: sister to William Morris. By Janet Grierson. 1962.

Deaconess in Southwark.

**3573** HALIFAX. Charles Lindley [Wood], Viscount Halifax. By John Gilbert Lockhart. 2 v. 1935–6.

The leading Anglo-Catholic layman at the end of the 19th cent. See also Sidney Dark, *Lord Halifax: a tribute*, 1934.

**3574** IGNATIUS. Father Ignatius of Llanthony: a Victorian. By Donald Attwater. 1931.

See also Arthur Calder-Marshall, *The enthusiast: an enquiry into the life, beliefs and character of the Rev. Joseph Leycester Lyne, alias Fr. Ignatius, O.S.B., Abbot of Elm Hill, Norwich, and Llanthony, Wales*, 1962.

**3575** KEBLE. A memoir of the Rev. John Keble. By Sir John Taylor Coleridge. Oxf. 1869. 3rd edn. 1870.

There are numerous popular lives, of which the best is Georgina Battiscombe, *John Keble: a study in limitations*, 1963.

**3576** KELLY. Herbert Kelly, S.S.M. No pious person: autobiographical recollections. Ed. by George Every. 1960.

Founder of the Society of the Sacred Mission, Kelham.

**3577** LEE. Dr. Lee of Lambeth: a chapter in parenthesis in the history of the Oxford movement. By Henry Renaud Turner Brandreth. [1952.]

3578 LIDDON. Life and letters of Henry Parry Liddon . . . By John Octavius Johnston. 1904.

3579 MACKONOCHIE. Alexander Heriot Mackonochie: a memoir. By Eleanor A. Towle. 1890.

See also Michael Reynolds, *Martyr of ritualism: Father Mackonochie of St. Alban's, Holborn*, 1965.

3580 MEYRICK. Memories of life at Oxford and experiences in Italy, Greece, Turkey, Germany, Spain and elsewhere. By Frederick Meyrick. 1905.

3581 MOZLEY. Reminiscences: chiefly of Oriel college and the Oxford movement. By Thomas Mozley. 2 v. 1882.

Largely on events before 1850, but still useful. Suppl. by his *Reminiscences: chiefly of towns, villages and schools*, 2 v. 1885. See also his *Letters from Rome* (**3924**).

3582 NEALE. John Mason Neale, D.D. a memoir. By Eleanor A. Towle. 1906.

See also Arthur Geoffrey Lough, *The influence of John Mason Neale*, 1962.

3583 OMMANNEY. Ommanney of Sheffield: memoirs of George Campbell Ommanney, vicar of St. Matthew's, Sheffield, 1882–1936. Ed. by Francis George Belton. 1936.

3584 PUSEY. Life of Edward Bouverie Pusey . . . By Henry Parry Liddon and others. 4 v. 1893–7.

The prophet of Anglo-Catholicism. Pusey's *Spiritual letters* . . ., ed. by John Octavius Johnstone and W. C. E. Newbolt, 1898, give a good idea of his teaching. George Leonard Prestige, *Pusey*, 1933, and George William Erskine Russell, *Dr. Pusey*, 1905 etc., are useful short lives.

3585 SELLON. Priscilla Lydia Sellon: the restorer after three centuries of the religious life in the English church. By Thomas Jay Williams. 1950.

3586 STANTON. Arthur Stanton: a memoir. By George William Erskine Russell. 1917.

3587 WAGGETT. Flame from an Oxford cloister: the life and writings of Philip Napier Waggett, 1862–1939. By John Charles Somerset Nias. 1961.

## 5. THE EVANGELICALS

3588 BALLEINE (GEORGE REGINALD). A history of the evangelical party in the Church of England. 1908. 3rd edn. 1951.

3589 ELLIOTT-BINNS (LEONARD ELLIOTT). The evangelical movement in the English churches. 1928.

See also K. Heasman, *Evangelicals in action* (**7204**), and Arthur Tappan Pierson, *Forward movements of the last half century* . . ., 1900. The best contemp. hist. was Handley Carr Glyn Moule, Bishop of Durham, *The evangelical school in the Church of England: its men and its work in the nineteenth century*, 1901.

3590 POLLOCK (JOHN CHARLES). The Keswick story: the authorized history of the Keswick convention. 1964.

See also Herbert Frederick Stevenson, ed., *Keswick's authentic voice: sixty-five dynamic addresses delivered at the Keswick convention, 1875–1947*, 1959, and *Keswick's triumphant voice: forty-eight outstanding addresses delivered at the Keswick convention, 1882–1962*, 1963, Charles Forbes Harford, ed., *The Keswick convention: its message, its method and its men* [1907], John Benjamin Figgis, *Keswick from within* . . ., 1914, and Alexander Smellie, *Evan Henry Hopkins: a memoir*, 1920.

3591 REYNOLDS (JOHN STEWART). The evangelicals at Oxford, 1735–1871: a record of an unchronicled movement. Oxf. 1953.

For events after 1871 see Arthur Cleveland Downer, *A century of evangelical religion in Oxford* [1938]. On Cambridge see John Charles Pollock, *A Cambridge movement* [a history of the Cambridge Inter-Collegiate Christian Union], 1953.

3592 POLLOCK (JOHN CHARLES). The good seed: the story of the Children's Special Service Mission and the Scripture Union. 1959.

3593 LOANE (MARCUS LAWRENCE). Makers of our heritage: a study of four evangelical leaders. 1967.

J. C. Ryle, H. C. G. Moule, E. A. Knox, H. W. K. Mowll.

3594 BLACKWOOD. Some records of the life of Stevenson Arthur Blackwood, K.C.B. Comp. by a friend and ed. by his widow, Harriet S. Blackwood. 1896.

3595 CHRISTOPHER. Canon Christopher of St. Aldate's, Oxford. By John Stewart Reynolds. Abingdon. 1967.

3596 FIGGIS. 'Figgis of Brighton': a memoir of a modern saint . . . By John Westbury Jones. 1917.

3597 GARRATT. Life and personal recollections of Samuel Garratt . . . Pt. I: a memoir, by his daughter Evelyn R. Garratt. Pt. II: personal recollections by himself. 1908.

3598 MACGREGOR. John MacGregor: 'Rob Roy' . . . By Edwin Hodder. 1894. Pop. edn. 1895.

3599 McNEILE. Hugh McNeile and Reformation truth: the characteristics of Romanism and Protestantism: with a biographical sketch by Charles Bullock. 1882.

3600 MARSH. The life of the Rev. William Marsh . . . By Catherine M. Marsh. 1867.

See also L. E. O'Rorke, *The life and friendships of Catherine Marsh* . . ., 1917.

3601 PENNEFATHER. The life and letters of Rev. William Pennefather . . . Ed. by Robert Braithwaite. 1878.

3602  RICHARDSON. Forty years' ministry in East London: memoir of the Rev. Thomas Richardson. By his wife, Anna S. Richardson. 1903.

3603  STOWELL. Memoirs of the life and labours of the Rev. Hugh Stowell. By John Buxton Marsden. 1868.

3604  VICARS. Memorials of Captain Hedley Vicars, 97th regiment . . . By Catherine M. Marsh. 1856. New edn. 1861.

Killed in the Crimea. For another Crimea victim see *Memoir of Captain M. M. Hammond*, by his brother, Egerton Douglas Hammond, Lond. & Edin. 1858.

### 6. OFFICIAL INQUIRIES

Each of these reports provoked an extensive pamphlet battle, for which see **3488**.

3605  RUSSELL COMMITTEE ON THE ECCLESIASTICAL COMMISSION. First report from the select committee on Ecclesiastical Commission, &c. [Chairman: Lord John Russell]. H.C. 174 (1856). XI, 1. Second report. H.C. 278 (1856). XI, 505. Third report. H.C. 369 (1856). XI, 509. Index. H.C. 369–I (1856). XI, 787.

There was a further select committee [Chairman: Henry Danby Seymour] in 1862–3 which publ. two highly critical reports: H.C. 470 (1862). VIII, 1, and H.C. 457 (1863). VI, 43.

3606  LORDS COMMITTEE ON SPIRITUAL INSTRUCTION. Report from the select committee of the House of Lords appointed to inquire into the deficiency of means of spiritual instruction and places of divine worship in the metropolis, and in other populous districts in England and Wales . . . [Chairman: Marquess of Salisbury]. H.C. 387 (1857–8). IX, 1.

Important.

3607  MARLBOROUGH COMMITTEE ON CHURCH RATES. Report from the select committee of the House of Lords appointed to inquire into the present operation of the law and practice respecting the assessment and the levy of church rates [Chairman: Duke of Marlborough]. H.C. 179 (1859 Sess. 2). V, 15. Further report. H.C. 154 (1860). XXII, 159.

3608  PLURALITIES RETURN, 1861. Returns of all clergymen holding more than one consecrated church or chapel, showing the full income derived from each . . . H.C. 517 (1861). XLVIII, 165.

3609  CLERICAL SUBSCRIPTIONS COMMISSION. Report of Her Majesty's commissioners appointed to consider the subscriptions, declarations, and oaths required to be made and taken by the clergy of the United Church of England and Ireland [Chairman: the Archbishop of Canterbury, C. T. Longley]. [3441] H.C. (1865). XV, 29.

3610  RITUAL COMMISSION. First report of the commissioners appointed to inquire into the rubrics, orders, and directions for regulating the course and conduct of public worship . . . [Chairman: the Archbishop of Canterbury; C. T. Longley, then A. C. Tait]. [3951] H.C. (1867). XX, 719. Second report. [4016] H.C. (1867-8). XXXVIII, 1. Third report. [C. 17] H.C. (1870). XIX, 437. Fourth report. [C. 218] H.C. (1870). XIX, 461.

3611 LORDS COMMITTEE ON CHURCH PATRONAGE. Report from the select committee of the House of Lords on church patronage [Chairman: the Bishop of Peterborough, W. C. Magee]. H.C. 289 (1874). VII, 301.

3612 SALT COMMITTEE ON PUBLIC WORSHIP FACILITIES BILL. Report from the select committee on Public Worship Facilities Bill [Chairman: Thomas Salt]. H.C. 331 (1875). XIV, 97.

3613 CLEVELAND COMMISSION ON SALE OF ECCLESIASTICAL BENEFICES. Report of the commissioners appointed to inquire into the law and existing practice as to the sale, exchange, and resignation of ecclesiastical benefices [Chairman: Duke of Cleveland]. [C. 2375] H.C. (1878-9). XX, 595. Minutes of evidence. [C. 2507] H.C. (1880). XVIII, 373.

3614 GORDON COMMITTEE ON ECCLESIASTICAL FEES. Report from the select committee on ecclesiastical and mortuary fees [Chairman: Sir Alexander Gordon]. H.C. 309 (1882). X, 1.

3615 ECCLESIASTICAL COURTS COMMISSION. Report of the commissioners appointed to inquire into the constitution and working of the ecclesiastical courts [Chairman: the Archbishop of Canterbury, E. W. Benson]. Vol. I. [C. 3760] H.C. (1883). XXIV, 1. Vol. II. [C. 3760-I] H.C. (1883). XXIV, 321.
Incl. an hist. appendix by Bishop Stubbs.

3616 ST. ALDWYN COMMISSION ON ECCLESIASTICAL DISCIPLINE. Report of the royal commission on ecclesiastical discipline [Chairman: Sir Michael Hicks-Beach, afterwards Viscount St. Aldwyn]. [Cd. 3040] H.C. (1906). XXXIII, 1. Minutes of evidence, etc. Vol. I. [Cd. 3069] H.C. (1906). XXXIII, 91. Vol. II. [Cd. 3070] H.C. (1906). XXXIII, 639. Vol. III. [Cd. 3071] H.C. (1906). XXXIV, 1. Vol. IV. [Cd. 3072] H.C. (1906). XXXIV, 417.
A comprehensive inquiry.

## 7. Diocesan and Local History

3617 HILL (GEOFFREY). English dioceses: a history of their limits from the earliest times to the present day. 1900.

3618 BRISTOL. Isabel M. Kirby, comp., *Diocese of Bristol: a catalogue of the records of the bishop and archdeacons and of the dean and chapter*, Bristol 1971.

3619 CANTERBURY. Edward Geoffrey Watson Bill, comp., *A catalogue of manuscripts in Lambeth palace library*, Oxf. 1973. Dorothy Gardiner, *The story of Lambeth palace: a historic survey*, 1930.

3620 CARLISLE. Charles Murray Lowther Bouch, *Prelates and people of the lake counties: a history of the diocese of Carlisle, 1133–1933,* Kendal [1948].

3621 CHICHESTER. Francis William Steer and Isabel M. Kirby, comps., *Diocese of Chichester: a catalogue of the records of the bishop, archdeacons and former exempt jurisdictions,* West Sussex County Council, Chichester 1966, and *Diocese of Chichester: a catalogue of the records of the dean and chapter, vicars choral, St. Mary's hospital, colleges and schools,* Chichester 1967. George Leyden Hennessy, comp., *Chichester diocese clergy lists: or, clergy succession from the earliest time to the year 1900,* 1900, suppl. 1901.

3622 EXETER. Robert James Edmund Boggis, *A history of the diocese of Exeter,* Exeter 1922. Arthur Warne, *Church and society in nineteenth-century Devon,* Newton Abbot 1969.

3623 GLOUCESTER. Isabel Madeline Kirby, comp., *Diocese of Gloucester: a catalogue of the records of the bishop and archdeacons,* Gloucester Corp., Gloucester 1968, and . . . *a catalogue of the records of the dean and chapter . . .,* Gloucester 1967.

3624 LONDON. George Leyden Hennessy, comp., *Novum repertorium ecclesiasticum parochiale Londinense: or, London diocesan clergy succession from the earliest time to the year 1898, with copious notes,* 1898. George Leonard Prestige, *St. Paul's in its glory: a candid history of the cathedral, 1831–1911,* 1955. Walter Robert Matthews and William Maynard Atkins, eds., *A history of St. Paul's Cathedral and the men associated with it,* 1957. P. J. Welch, 'The difficulties of church extension in Victorian London', *Church Quart. Rev.* clxvi (1965), 302–15. Charles Hugh Egerton Smyth, *Church and parish: studies in church problems, illustrated from the parochial history of St. Margaret's, Westminster,* 1955. Sir Nevile Rodwell Wilkinson, *The Guards' Chapel, 1838–1938.* [1938.]

3625 MANCHESTER. William Reginald Ward, 'The cost of establishment: some reflections on church building in Manchester', *Studies in Church Hist.* iii (1966), 277–89. Joseph Stanley Leatherbarrow, *Victorian period piece: studies occasioned by a Lancashire church* [Swinton]. 1954.

3626 NORWICH. Paul A. Welsby, 'Church and people in Victorian Ipswich', *Church Quart. Rev.* clxiv (1963), 207–17.

3627 OXFORD. Diana McClatchey, *Oxfordshire clergy, 1777–1869: a study of the established church and of the role of its clergy in local society,* Oxf. 1960. E. P. Baker, ed., *Bishop Wilberforce's visitation returns for the archdeaconry of Oxford in the year 1854,* Oxf. Record Soc. 35 [1954]. See also **3694.**

3628 PETERBOROUGH. Henry Isham Longden, *Northamptonshire and Rutland clergy from 1500* [to 1942]. 15 v. Northampton. 1938–43. Indexes etc. [vol. XVI] by P. I. King and J. Hotine, Northants Record Soc., 1952.

3629  ROCHESTER. Cecil Henry Fielding, ed., *The records of Rochester*, Dartford 1910.

3630  SALISBURY. William Henry Rich Jones, comp., *Fasti ecclesiae sarisberiensis: or, a calendar of the bishops, deans, archdeacons, and members of the cathedral body at Salisbury, from the earliest times to the present*, 2 pts. Salisbury 1879–81. Dora H. Robertson, *Sarum close: a history of the life and education of the cathedral choristers for 700 years*, 1938, 2nd edn. Bath 1969.

3631  SOUTHWELL. Keith Sydney Sayer Train, ed., *Lists of the clergy of central Nottinghamshire*, Thoroton Soc. record ser. xv, 3 pts., 1953–5, and *Lists of the clergy of North Nottinghamshire*, Thoroton Soc. record ser. xx, 1961.

3632  TRURO. Augustus Blair Donaldson, *The bishopric of Truro: the first twenty-five years, 1877–1902*, 1902.

3633  WINDSOR. John Neale Dalton, ed., *The manuscripts of St. George's chapel, Windsor Castle*, Windsor 1957. Sidney Leslie Ollard, *Fasti Wyndesorienses: the deans and canons of Windsor*, Windsor 1950.

## 8. BIOGRAPHY

### (a) *Collective biography*

3634  HEAD (FREDERICK WALDEGRAVE). Six great Anglicans: a study of the history of the Church of England in the nineteenth century. 1929.

Simeon, Keble, Hook, Robertson, Kingsley, Barnett.

3635  LOWNDES (FREDERIC SAWREY ARCHIBALD). Bishops of the day: a biographical dictionary of all the archbishops and bishops of the Church of England and of all churches in communion therewith throughout the world. 1897.

Entries on the pattern of *Men of the time* (74). Frederick Arnold, *Our bishops and deans*, 2 v. 1875, is of little value.

3636  ROGERS (JAMES GUINNESS). Anglican church portraits. 1876.

By a Nonconformist.

3637  RUSSELL (GEORGE WILLIAM ERSKINE) ed. Leaders of the Church, 1800–1900. 8 v. 1905–9.

A useful ser. with lives of Church, Maurice, Pusey, Wilberforce, Liddon, Gladstone, Westcott, and Keble.

3638  MENZIES (AMY CHARLOTTE), *Mrs. Stuart Menzies*. Sportsmen parsons in peace and war. [1919.]

(b) *Archbishops of Canterbury and York*

3639  BENSON. The life of Edward White Benson, sometime Archbishop of Canterbury [1883–96]. By his son, Arthur Christopher Benson. 2 v. 1899.

See also Edward Frederic Benson, *As we were: a Victorian peep-show*, 1930, and *Our family affairs, 1867–96*, 1920. Benson's papers are in the libr. of Trinity College, Camb.

3640  DAVIDSON. Randall Davidson, Archbishop of Canterbury [1903–28]. By George Kennedy Allen Bell. 2 v. 1935. 3rd edn. 1952.

3641  LANG. Cosmo Gordon Lang. By John Gilbert Lockhart. 1949.

Archbishop of York, 1909–28; Canterbury, 1928–42.

3642  MACLAGAN. Archbishop Maclagan: being a memoir of the Most Rev. the Rt. Hon. William Dalrymple Maclagan, D.D., Archbishop of York [1891–1908], and Primate of England. By Frederick Douglas How. [1911.]

3643  MAGEE. The life and correspondence of William Connor Magee, Archbishop of York [1891], Bishop of Peterborough [1868–91]. By John Cotter Macdonnell. 2 v. 1896.

3644  SUMNER. 'Social and economic theories and pastoral concerns of a Victorian archbishop [John Bird Sumner, Archbishop of Canterbury, 1848–62]'. By Robert S. Dell. *J. Eccles. Hist.* xvi (1965), 196–208.

3645  TAIT. Life of Archibald Campbell Tait, Archbishop of Canterbury [1868–82]. By Randall Thomas Davidson and William Benham. 2 v. 1891. 3rd edn. 2 v. 1891.

A good life not entirely repl. by the more scholarly Peter Timothy Marsh, *The Victorian church in decline: Archbishop Tait and the Church of England, 1868–1882*, 1969.

3646  FREDERICK TEMPLE. Memoirs of Archbishop Temple by seven friends. Ed. by Ernest Grey Sandford. 2 v. 1906.

Archbishop of Canterbury, 1896–1902.

3647  THOMSON. William Thomson, Archbishop of York [1862–90]: his life and times, 1819–90. By Harold Kirk-Smith. 1958.

There is also Ethel H. Thomson, *The life & letters of William Thomson, Archbishop of York*, 1919.

(c) *Diocesan bishops*

There is a full list of bishops in the Royal Historical Society's *Handbook of British chronology*.

3648  BICKERSTETH. The life of Edward Henry Bickersteth, D.D., bishop and poet: author of 'Peace, perfect peace', 'Yesterday, to-day and for ever', Bishop of Exeter, 1885–1900. By Francis Keyes Aglionby. 1907.

3649  BICKERSTETH. A sketch of the life and episcopate of the Right Reverend Robert Bickersteth, D.D., Bishop of Ripon, 1857–1884. By Montagu Cyril Bickersteth. 1887.

3650  BLOMFIELD. A memoir of Charles James Blomfield, Bishop of London [1828–56], with selections from his correspondence. Ed. by his son Alfred Blomfield. 2 v. 1863. 2nd edn. 1864.

See also P. J. Welch, 'Bishop Blomfield and church extension in London', *J. Eccles. Hist.* iv (1953), 203–13.

3651  BOYD-CARPENTER. The life and letters of William Boyd Carpenter, Bishop of Ripon [1884–1911]. By Henry Dewsbury Alves Major. 1925.

Boyd-Carpenter himself publ. *Some pages of my life*, 1911, and *Further pages from my life*, 1916.

3652  BROWNE. Edward Harold Browne, D.D., Lord Bishop of Winchester [1873–90], and Prelate of the Most Noble Order of the Garter: a memoir. By George William Kitchin. 1895.

3653  BROWNE. The recollections of a bishop. By George Forrest Browne. 1915.

Bishop of Bristol, 1897–1914.

3654  BURGE. Discourses and letters of Hubert Murray Burge, D.D., K.C.V.O., Bishop of Southwark, 1911–1919, Bishop of Oxford, 1919–1925. Ed. with a memoir by Percy Cuthbert Quilter, Baron Charnwood. 1930.

3655  BURROWS. Winfrid Burrows, 1858–1929: Bishop of Truro, 1912–1919, Bishop of Chichester, 1919–1929. By his daughter Mary Moore. 1932.

3656  CHAVASSE. Francis James Chavasse, Bishop of Liverpool [1900–23]. By John Bennett Lancelot. Oxf. 1929.

3657  CREIGHTON. Life and letters of Mandell Creighton, . . . Bishop of London [1897–1901]. By his widow, Louise Creighton. 2 v. 1904.

See also William Gordon Fallows, *Mandell Creighton and the English church*, 1964.

3658  DURNFORD. A memoir of Richard Durnford, D.D., sometime Bishop of Chichester [1870–95]. By William Richard Wood Stephens. 1899.

3659  FRASER. James Fraser, second Bishop of Manchester [1870–85]: a memoir: 1818–1885. By Thomas Hughes. 1887. New edn. 1888.

There is also an admirable account of his career as bishop, John William Diggle, *The Lancashire life of Bishop Fraser*, 1889, 6th edn. 1890, as well as a number of pamphlet lives.

3660  GOODWIN. Harvey Goodwin, Bishop of Carlisle [1869–91]: a biographical memoir. By Hardwicke Drummond Rawnsley. 1896.

3661 GORE. The life of Charles Gore, a great Englishman. By George Leonard Prestige. Lond. & Toronto. 1935.

Bishop of Worcester, 1901–5, Bishop of Birmingham, 1905–11, and Bishop of Oxford, 1911–19. Anon., 'Bishop Gore and the Church of England', *Edinburgh Rev.* ccvii (1908), 79–104; Gordon Crosse, *Charles Gore*, 1932; Albert Mansbridge, *Edward Stuart Talbot and Charles Gore*, 1935; Arthur Michael Ramsey, *Charles Gore and Anglican theology*, 1955; and James Anderson Carpenter, *Gore: a study in Liberal Catholic thought*, 1960, should also be consulted.

3662 GOTT. Letters of Bishop Gott, arranged by members of his family: with a biographical sketch by Arthur John Worlledge. 1918.

Bishop of Truro, 1891–1906.

3663 HAMILTON. Walter Kerr Hamilton, Bishop of Salisbury [1854–69]: a sketch reprinted, with additions and corrections, from 'The Guardian'. By Henry Parry Liddon. 1869. 3rd edn. 1890.

3664 HAMPDEN. Some memorials of Renn Dickson Hampden, Bishop of Hereford [1847–68]. By his daughter, Henrietta Hampden. 1871.

3665 HERVEY. A memoir of Lord Arthur Hervey, D.D., Bishop of Bath and Wells . . . [1869–94.] By John Frederick Arthur Hervey. Priv. pr. 1896.

3666 HICKS. The life and letters of Edward Lee Hicks, Bishop of Lincoln, 1910–1919. By John Henry Fowler. 1922.

3667 HOSKYNS. Sir Edwyn Hoskyns, Bishop of Southwell, 1904–1925 . . . By Edward Gordon Selwyn. 1926.

3668 HOW. Bishop Walsham How: a memoir. By Frederick Douglas How. 1898.

Bishop of Bedford, 1879–88; Wakefield, 1888–97.

3669 KING. Edward King, sixtieth Bishop of Lincoln [1885–1910]: a memoir. By George William Erskine Russell. 1912. 2nd edn. 1912.

Godfrey Elton, Baron Elton, *Edward King and our times*, 1958, and William Owen Chadwick, *Edward King, Bishop of Lincoln, 1885–1910*, Lincoln Minster pamphlets, 2 ser. 4 1968, are sympathetic modern accounts. See also Berkeley William Randolph and James Weston Townroe, *The mind and work of Bishop King*, Lond. & Oxf. [1918.]

3670 KNOX. Reminiscences of an octogenarian, 1847–1934. By Edmund Arbuthnott Knox. [1935.]

Bishop of Manchester, 1903–21.

3671 LIGHTFOOT. Lightfoot of Durham: memories and appreciations. Ed. by George Rodney Eden and Frederick Charles Macdonald. Camb. 1932.

Bishop of Durham, 1879–89.

3672 LONSDALE. The life of John Lonsdale, Bishop of Lichfield [1843–67]; with some of his writings. By Edmund Beckett Denison, Baron Grimthorpe. 1868.

3673 MACKARNESS. Memorials of the episcopate of John Fielder Mackarness, D.D., Bishop of Oxford from 1870 to 1888 . . . By Charles Coleridge Mackarness. Oxf. 1892.

3674 MOBERLY. Dulce Domum: George Moberly (D.C.L., Headmaster of Winchester College, 1835–1866, Bishop of Salisbury, 1869–1885) his family and friends. By his daughter Charlotte A. E. Moberly. 1911.

3675 MOORHOUSE. Bishop Moorhouse of Melbourne and Manchester . . . By Edith C. Rickards. 1920.
Bishop of Manchester, 1886–1903.

3676 MOULE. Handley Carr Glyn Moule, Bishop of Durham [1901–20]: a biography. By John Battersby Harford and Frederick Charles Macdonald. 1922.

3677 PAGET. Francis Paget: Bishop of Oxford [1901–11], Chancellor of the Order of the Garter, honorary student and sometime Dean of Christ Church. By Stephen Paget and John McLeod Campbell Crum. 1912.

3678 PERCIVAL. Life of Bishop Percival. By William Temple. 1921.
Bishop of Hereford, 1895–1917.

3679 PHILLPOTTS. Henry Phillpotts, Bishop of Exeter, 1778–1869. By George Colliss Boardman Davies. 1954.
Bishop of Exeter, 1830–69.

3680 POLLOCK. A twentieth-century bishop: recollections and reflections. By Bertram Pollock. 1944.
Bishop of Norwich, 1910–42.

3681 RIDDING. George Ridding, schoolmaster and bishop: forty-third headmaster of Winchester, 1866–1884, first Bishop of Southwell, 1884–1904. By his wife, Lady Laura Ridding. 1908.

3682 RIDGEWAY. Frederic Edward Ridgeway, Bishop of Salisbury [1911–21]: a memoir. By Ernest Cross. 1924.

3683 RYLE. A memoir of Herbert Edward Ryle, K.C.V.O., D.D., sometime Bishop of Winchester [1903–11] and Dean of Westminster. By Maurice Henry Fitzgerald. 1928.

3684 RYLE. John Charles Ryle, 1816–1900: a short biography. By Marcus Lawrence Loane. 1953.
Bishop of Liverpool, 1880–1900.

3685 SELWYN. Memoir of the life and episcopate of George Augustus Selwyn, D.D., Bishop of New Zealand, 1841–1867, Bishop of Lichfield, 1867–1878. By Henry William Tucker. 2 v. 1879.

There are also two single-vol. lives by George Herbert Curteis, *Bishop Selwyn of New Zealand and of Lichfield: a sketch of his life and work*, 1889, and John H. Evans, *Churchman militant: George Augustus Selwyn, Bishop of New Zealand and Lichfield*, Lond. & Wellington, 1964.

3686 SHEEPSHANKS. A bishop in the rough. [John Sheepshanks, Bishop of Norwich, 1893–1910.] Ed. by David Wallace Duthie. 1909.

3687 STUBBS. Charles William Stubbs, D.D., fourth Bishop of Truro [1906–12]. By Edward Harold Sedding. Plymouth. 1914.

STUBBS. See 8534.

3688 SUMNER. Life of Charles Richard Sumner, D.D., Bishop of Winchester, during a forty years' episcopate [1827–69]. By George Henry Sumner. 1876.

3689 TALBOT. Edward Stuart Talbot, 1844–1934. By Gwendolen Stephenson. 1936.

Bishop of Rochester, 1895–1905, Southwark, 1905–11, and Winchester, 1911–23. See also A. Mansbridge, *Talbot and Gore* (3661).

3690 THOROLD. The life and work of Bishop Thorold: Rochester 1877–91, Winchester 1891–95, Prelate of the Most Noble Order of the Garter. By Charles Hare Simpkinson. 1896.

3691 WATTS-DITCHFIELD. John Edwin Watts-Ditchfield, first Bishop of Chelmsford [1914–23]. By Ellis Norman Gowing. [1926.]

3692 WESTCOTT. Life and letters of Brooke Foss Westcott, D.D., D.C.L., sometime [1890–1901] Bishop of Durham. By his son, Arthur Westcott. 2 v. 1903.

See also Geoffrey Francis Andrew Best, *Bishop Westcott and the miners . . .*, Camb. 1967.

3693 WILBERFORCE. The life of the Right Reverend Ernest Roland Wilberforce, first Bishop of Newcastle-on-Tyne [1882–95], and afterward Bishop of Chichester [1895–1907]. By James Beresford Atlay. 1912.

3694 WILBERFORCE. Life of the Right Reverend Samuel Wilberforce, D.D., Lord Bishop of Oxford [1845–69] and afterwards of Winchester [1869–73]: with selections from his diary and correspondence. By Arthur Rawson Ashwell and Reginald Garton Wilberforce. 3 v. 1880–2. Rev. and abridged edn. in 1 v. 1888.

There is also a good modern biog., Standish Meacham, *Lord Bishop: the life of Samuel Wilberforce, 1805–1873*, Camb., Mass. 1970, and a good article, David H. Newsome, 'The churchmanship of Samuel Wilberforce', *Studies in Church Hist.* iii (1966), 23–47. Earlier short lives may now be disregarded. R. K. Pugh assisted by J. F. A. Mason, eds., *The letter books of Samuel Wilberforce, 1843–68*, Buckinghamshire and Oxfordshire Record Socs., 1970, suppl. an earlier vol. of visitation returns (3627).

3695  WILKINSON. Memoir of George Howard Wilkinson, Bishop of
St. Andrews, Dunkeld and Dunblane [1893–1907] and Primus of the Scottish
Church: formerly [1883–91] Bishop of Truro. By Arthur James Mason. 2 v.
1909. Abridged edn. 1910.

3696  WINNINGTON-INGRAM. Winnington-Ingram: the biography of
Arthur Foley Winnington-Ingram, Bishop of London, 1901–1939. By Spencer
Cecil Carpenter. 1949.

There are also two short lives, Charles Herbert, *Twenty-five years as Bishop of London*
[1926], and Percy Colson, *Life of the Bishop of London*, 1935, and Winnington-Ingram's
own *Fifty years work in London*, 1940.

3697  WORDSWORTH. Christopher Wordsworth: Bishop of Lincoln [1868–
85], 1807–1885. By John Henry Overton and Elizabeth Wordsworth. 1888.
New edn. 1890.

3698  JOHN WORDSWORTH. Life of Bishop John Wordsworth. By Edward
William Watson. 1915.

Bishop of Salisbury, 1885–1911.

### (d) *Other Prominent Churchmen*

3699  BAILLIE. My first eighty years. By Albert Victor Baillie. 1951.

3700  BARING-GOULD. Onward Christian Soldier: a life of Sabine Baring-
Gould, parson, squire, novelist, antiquary. By William Ernest Purcell. 1957.

There is also a new life, Bickford Holland Cohan Dickinson, *Sabine Baring-Gould:
squarson, writer and folklorist, 1834–1924*, Newton Abbot 1970. See also Baring-
Gould's *The church revival: thoughts thereon and reminiscences*, 1914, *Early reminiscences,
1834–1864*, 1923, and *Further reminiscences, 1864–1894*, 1925.

3701  BULL. Parson Bull of Byerley. By John Clifford Gill. 1963.

3702  BURGON. John William Burgon, late Dean of Chichester: a biography
. . . By Edward Meyrick Goulburn. 2 v. 1892.

3703  CARLILE. Wilson Carlile and the Church Army. By [Edgar Rowan].
1905. 3rd edn. 1928.

See also Sidney Dark, *Wilson Carlile: the laughing cavalier of Christ* [1945].

3704  COLENSO. The life of John William Colenso, D.D., Bishop of Natal.
By Sir George William Cox. 2 v. 1888.

See also 2118.

3705  DEARMER. The life of Percy Dearmer. By his wife Nancy Dearmer.
1940.

Champion of more attractive church services.

3706 DENISON. Fifty years at East Brent: the letters of George Anthony Denison, 1845–1896, Archdeacon of Taunton. Ed. by Louisa Evelyn Denison. 1902.

See also G. A. Denison, *Notes of my life, 1805–78*, Oxf. & Lond. 1878, and Denison's other voluminous writings.

3707 FARRAR. The life of Frederic William Farrar: sometime Dean of Canterbury. By Reginald Anstruther Farrar. 1904. Rev. edn. 1905.

3708 GREGORY. Robert Gregory, 1819–1911: being the autobiography of Robert Gregory, D.D., Dean of St. Paul's. Ed. by William Holden Hutton. 1912.

3709 HEADLAM. Arthur Cayley Headlam: life and letters of a bishop. By Ronald Claud Dudley Jasper. Lond. & N.Y. 1960.

3710 HENSON. Retrospect of an unimportant life. By Herbert Hensley Henson. 3 v. 1942–50.

There are two vols. of letters ed. by Evelyn Foley Braley, *Letters of Herbert Hensley Henson*, 1950, and *More letters . . .*, 1954.

3711 HOLE. The letters of Samuel Reynolds Hole, Dean of Rochester. Ed. by George Albemarle Bertie Dewar. Lond. & N.Y. 1907.

Hole himself publ. *The memories of Dean Hole*, 1892, and *More memories . . .*, 1894.

3712 HOLLAND. Henry Scott Holland, Hon. D.D. Aberdeen, Hon. D.Litt. Oxford, Regius Professor of Divinity in Oxford, Canon of St Paul's: memoir and letters. Ed. by Stephen Paget. 1921.

Scott Holland himself publ. *A bundle of memories*, 1915. See also Edward Lyttelton, *The mind and character of Henry Scott Holland*, Lond. & Oxf. 1926, and Sidney Leslie Ollard, ed., *A forty years' friendship: letters from the late Henry Scott Holland to Mrs. Drew*, Lond. & N.Y. 1919.

3713 HOOK. The life and letters of Walter Farquhar Hook, D.D., F.R.S. By William Richard Wood Stephens. 2 v. 1878.

See also Charles James Stranks, *Dean Hook*, 1954.

3714 HORT. Life and letters of Fenton John Anthony Hort . . . By Sir Arthur Fenton Hort. 2 v. 1896.

See also Ernest Gordon Rupp, *Hort and the Cambridge tradition . . .*, Camb. 1970.

3715 ILLINGWORTH. The life and work of John Richardson Illingworth, M.A., D.D., as portrayed by his letters. Ed. by his wife, Agnes Louisa Illingworth. 1917.

3716 INGE. Dean Inge. By Adam Fox. 1960.

Inge himself publ. *Diary of a dean: St Paul's, 1911–1934*, 1949, and *Vale*, 1934. See also Robert M. Helm, *The gloomy dean: the thought of William Ralph Inge*, Winston-Salem, N.C. 1962.

KINGSLEY. See **3386** and **8384**.

**3717** LAKE. Memorials of William Charles Lake, Dean of Durham, 1869–94. Ed. by his widow Katherine Lake. 1901.

**3718** LIDDELL. Henry George Liddell, D.D., Dean of Christ Church, Oxford: a memoir . . . By Henry Lewis Thompson. 1899.

**3719** MACCOLL. Malcolm MacColl: memoirs and correspondence. By George William Erskine Russell. 1914.

**3720** MANSEL. The religious philosophy of Dean Mansel. By Walter Robert Matthews. 1956.

Mansel's *Letters, lectures and reviews* . . ., were ed. by Henry William Chandler, 1873. See also Don Cupitt, 'Mansel's theory of regulative truth', *J. Theological Studs.* xviii (1967), 104–26.

**3721** MAURICE. The life of Frederick Denison Maurice . . . By Sir [John] Frederick Maurice. 2 v. 1884.

See also Herbert George Wood, *Frederick Denison Maurice*, Camb. 1950; Alexander Roper Vidler, *The theology of F. D. Maurice*, Lond. 1948, publ. in N.Y. as *Witness to the light: F. D. Maurice's message for today*, 1948, enl. edn. publ. as *F. D. Maurice and company: nineteenth-century studies*, 1966; Arthur Michael Ramsey, Archbishop of Canterbury, *F. D. Maurice and the conflicts of modern theology*, Camb. 1951; Olive Johnson Brose, *Frederick Denison Maurice: rebellious conformist*, Athens, Ohio 1971; and Torben Christensen, 'F. D. Maurice and the contemporary religious world', *Studies in Church Hist.* iii (1966), 69–90. There is a growing interest in Maurice's work as indicated by John Francis Porter and William J. Wolff, eds., *Towards the recovery of unity: the thought of Frederick Denison Maurice, edited from his letters* . . ., N.Y. 1964; John C. Haughey, *The ecclesiology of Frederick Denison Maurice*, Catholic Univ. of America, Studs. in Sacred Theology, 2 ser. 182, Wash. 1967, Walter Merlin Davies, *An introduction to F. D. Maurice's theology* . . ., 1964; Rolf Ahlers, *Die Vermittlungstheologie des Frederick Denison Maurice* [Hamburg 1967]; and Ellen Flesseman-Van Leer, *Die overmacht van de liefde: inleiding in de theologie van F. D. Maurice*, Wageningen 1968.

**3722** MILMAN. Henry Hart Milman, Dean of St. Paul's: a biographical sketch. By Arthur Milman. 1900.

**3723** MOZLEY. Letters of the Rev. J. B. Mozley, D.D., late Canon of Christ Church and Regius Professor of Divinity in the University of Oxford. Ed. by his sister, Anne Mozley. 1885.

**3724** PAGET. Henry Luke Paget: portrait and frame. By Elma Katie Paget. 1939.

**3725** RASHDALL. The life of Hastings Rashdall. By Percy Ewing Matheson. 1928.

**3726** STANLEY. The life and correspondence of Arthur Penrhyn Stanley, D.D., late Dean of Westminster. By Rowland Edmund Prothero, Baron Ernle. 2 v. 1893.

See also Albert Victor Baillie and [Henry] Hector Bolitho, *A Victorian dean: a memoir of Arthur Stanley, Dean of Westminster, with many new and unpublished letters*, 1930. Baillie also ed. the letters of Stanley's wife: *Letters of Lady Augusta Stanley, 1849–63*, 1927, and *Later letters . . ., 1864–76*, 1929.

3727   SUMNER. Memoir of George Henry Sumner, D.D., Bishop of Guildford. By Mary Elizabeth Sumner. Winchester. 1910.

3728   TEIGNMOUTH-SHORE. Some recollections. By Thomas Teignmouth-Shore. 1911.

Mainly extracts from the j. of a royal chaplain.

3729   TEMPLE. William Temple, Archbishop of Canterbury, his life and letters. By Frederic Athelwold Iremonger. 1948.

3730   TUCKWELL. Reminiscences of a radical parson. By William Tuckwell. 1905.

3731   WELLDON. Recollections and reflections. By James Edward Cowell Welldon [late Bishop of Calcutta]. 1915.

Welldon also publ. *Forty years on: lights and shadows*, 1935.

3732   WILKINSON. Twenty years of continental work and travel. By Thomas Edward Wilkinson. 1906.

## C. NONCONFORMITY

### 1. GENERAL

3733   POWELL (WILLIAM RAYMOND). 'The sources for the history of Protestant nonconformist churches in England'. *Inst. Hist. Res. Bull.* xxv (1952), 213–27. Suppl. by R. B. Rose, ibid. xxxi (1958), 79–83.

3734   DR. WILLIAMS'S LIBRARY, LONDON. Catalogue of the library in Red Cross Street, Cripplegate, founded pursuant to the will of the Reverend Daniel Williams, D.D., who died in the year 1716. 3 v. 1841–70. 2 suppls. to v. III 1878–85. Catalogue of accessions, 1900–50. 1955.

The main centre for nonconformist books and records. No printed catalogue for 1886–99.

3735   CLARK (HENRY WILLIAM). History of English nonconformity: from Wiclif to the close of the nineteenth century. 2 v. 1911–13.

Still the standard hist., but Charles Silvester Horne, *A popular history of the free churches*, with suppl. by Albert Peel, 1926, Horne's *Nonconformity in the XIXth century*, 1905, and Herbert S. Skeats and Charles Septimus Miall, *History of the free churches of England, 1688–1891*, 1894, are all useful. Ernest Alexander Payne, *The free church tradition in the life of England*, 1944, is a short popular introduction to the subject which reflects the changed attitude of mid-20th-cent. nonconformists to their hist. Harry

Francis Lovell Cocks, *The nonconformist conscience*, 1943, John Thomas Wilkinson, *1662 and after: three centuries of English nonconformity*, 1962, and [Daniel] Horton [Marlais] Davies, *The English free churches*, 1952, 2nd edn. 1963, are similar works.

3736 GRANT (JOHN WEBSTER). Free churchmanship in England, 1870–1940, with special reference to Congregationalism. [1955.]

An important pioneer work in changing conceptions of churchmanship. Good bibliog. Willis Borders Glover, *Evangelical nonconformists and the higher criticism in the nineteenth century*, 1954, is little more than an introductory sketch.

3737 JORDAN (EDWARD KENNETH HENRY). Free Church unity: a history of the Free Church Council movement, 1896–1941. 1956.

The principal source for the hist. of the movement is the *Proceedings*, 1896+, of the National Council of the Evangelical Free Churches (now the Free Church Federal Council), publ. since 1900 as *The Free Church year book and official report. The Free Church chronicle*, 1899–1934, and *The Free Churchman*, 1897+, are the chief organs of the movement.

3738 MANNING (BERNARD LORD). The Protestant dissenting deputies. Ed. by Ormerod Greenwood. Cambridge. 1952.

The oldest nonconformist representative body, by 1850 largely confined to evangelical Baptists and Congregationalists in London.

3739 BROCKETT (ALLAN). Nonconformity in Exeter, 1650–1875. Manch. 1962.

See also Alan Everitt, 'Nonconformity in country parishes', in Joan Thirsk, ed., *Land, church and people: essays presented to Professor H. P. R. Finberg*, suppl. to *Agric. Hist. Rev.* xviii (1970), 178–99.

3740 WILSON (BRYAN RONALD) *ed*. Patterns of sectarianism: organisation and ideology in social and religious movements. 1967.

A good set of essays on various nonconformist sects since 1850.

3741 WINSLOW (REGINALD). The law relating to Protestant nonconformists and their places of worship: being a legal handbook for nonconformists. 1886.

3742 SALTER (FRANK REYNER). Dissenters and public affairs in mid-Victorian England. Dr. Williams's Trust. 1967.

3743 DALE (ROBERT WILLIAM). The politics of nonconformity. Manch. 1871.

Dale's friend James Guinness Rogers publ. a similar statement, 'Political dissent', *Fortnightly Rev.* xxviii, n.s. xxii (1877), 811–26.

3744 INGHAM (S. M.). 'The disestablishment movement in England, 1868–74'. *J. Religious Hist.* iii (1964), 38–60.

See also Noel J. Richards, 'Disestablishment of the Anglican Church in England in the late nineteenth century: reasons for failure', *J. of Church & State* xii (1970), 193–212. See also the life of Edward Miall, **3752**.

3745 SOCIETY FOR THE LIBERATION OF RELIGION FROM STATE PATRONAGE AND CONTROL [The Liberation Society]. The liberator. 1855–1924.

The main source for the hist. of the nonconformist disestablishment campaign, but needs to be suppl. by Miall's journal, *The nonconformist*, 1841–79+. The only general account of the Society is *The 'Liberation Society' and its triennial conferences*, 1880. For the Liberation Society and Wales see Jones (**9592**).

3746 MIALL (CHARLES SEPTIMUS). The disestablishment question in relation to the Liberal Party and electoral action. 1877.

Advocates the abandonment of direct action by the Liberation Soc. in favour of converting the Liberal Party.

3747 RICHARD (HENRY) *and* WILLIAMS (JOHN CARVELL). Disestablishment. 1885.

The best summary of the Liberation Soc. programme. See also Robert William Dale, *Speeches on disestablishment*, 1875.

3748 A NONCONFORMIST MINISTER, *pseud*. Nonconformity and politics. 1909.

An eloquent plea for political neutrality.

3749 SHAKESPEARE (JOHN HOWARD). The churches at the cross roads: a study in church unity. 1918.

Marks the ending of the 'dissidence of dissent'.

3750 GRANT. The dissenting world: an autobiography. By Brewin Grant. Lond. & Sheffield. 1869.

A curious account of the difficulties of a working-class minister. See also his *The tyranny of modern nonconformity compared with papal supremacy*, 1874.

3751 KENT. The testament of a Victorian youth: an autobiography. By William Richard Gladstone Kent. 1938.

An excellent account of late Victorian nonconformity.

3752 MIALL. Life of Edward Miall, formerly member of parliament for Rochdale and Bradford . . . By Arthur Miall. 1884.

The great champion of disestablishment and political dissent and editor of *The nonconformist*. His successors were Henry Richard and John Carvell Williams.

3753 MORLEY. The life of Samuel Morley. By Edwin Hodder. 1887. 5th edn. 1889.

The most prominent nonconformist philanthropist of his day: steered a middle path in controversy.

3754 NICOLL. William Robertson Nicoll: life and letters. By Thomas Herbert Darlow. 1925.

A central nonconformist figure as editor of the *British Weekly*, 1886–1923.

**3755 PORRITT. The best I remember. By Arthur Porritt. 1922.**

Followed by *More and more of memories*, 1947. Porritt was editor of *The independent and nonconformist*, 1895–9, and *The Christian world*, 1899–1936.

**3756 RUTHERFORD (MARK) *pseud. of* WHITE (WILLIAM HALE). The autobiography of Mark Rutherford, dissenting minister. 1881.**

Followed by *Mark Rutherford's deliverance*, 1885, enl. edn. 1888. Semi-autobiographical. The most convincing account of the reaction of an intelligent nonconformist to his times.

## 2. BAPTISTS

**3757 STARR (EDWARD C.). A Baptist bibliography: being a register of printed material by and about Baptists; including works written against the Baptists. Hamilton, N.Y. 1947+. In progress.**

The only Baptist bibliog. dealing with the period.

**3758 THE BAPTIST MANUAL [HANDBOOK AND ALMANACK]. 1845+.**

The main source of statistical and biog. information.

**3759 BAPTIST HISTORICAL SOCIETY. Transactions. 7 v. 1908–20. Index by Douglas C. Sparkes. 1966.**

Cont. in *The Baptist quarterly, incorporating the transactions of the Baptist Historica Society*, 1922+. Prints source material.

**3760 UNDERWOOD (ALFRED CLAIR). A history of the English Baptists. 1947.**

William Thomas Whitley, *A history of British Baptists*, 1923, 2nd edn. 1932, though fuller, is not always reliable on the 19th cent. David Mervyn Himbury, *British Baptists: a short history*, 1962, is short. Baptist thought is discussed in Ernest Alexander Payne, *The fellowship of believers: Baptist thought and practice yesterday and today*, 1944; Henry Wheeler Robinson, *Baptist principles*, 1925, and *The life and faith of the Baptists*, 1927, rev. edn. 1946; Arthur Dakin, *The Baptist view of the church and ministry*, 1944; and Robert Clifford Walton, *The gathered community*, 1946.

**3761 PAYNE (ERNEST ALEXANDER). The Baptist Union: a short history. 1959.**

The best book on 19th- and 20th-cent. Baptists. Useful suppls. are Fred Townley Lord, *Baptist world fellowship: a short history of the Baptist World Alliance*, 1955, and William Charles Johnson, *Encounter in London: the story of the London Baptist association, 1865–1965*, 1965. John Brown, *The history of the Bedfordshire Union of Christians . . .*, 1896, cont. to 1946 by David Prothero, 1946, deals briefly with a union of Baptist and Congregational Churches.

**3762 PRICE (SEYMOUR JAMES). A popular history of the Baptist building fund: the centenary volume, 1824–1924. [1927.]**

**3763 BAPTISTS IN YORKSHIRE, LANCASHIRE, CHESHIRE, & CUMBERLAND. Baptist Hist. Soc. 1913.**

Brings together Cecil Edgar Shipley, ed., *The Baptists of Yorkshire*, 2nd edn. 1912, and William Thomas Whitley, *Baptists of North-West England, 1649–1913*, Lond. & Preston 1913. The fullest of the local hists. Charles Boardman Jewson, *The Baptists in Norfolk*, 1957, based on MS. hists. of all the Norfolk chapels by the Rev. M. F. Hewett in Norfolk City Libr., and Ernest Alexander Payne, *The Baptists of Berkshire through three centuries*, 1951, are recent attempts to avoid the chapel-by-chapel hist. represented by William Thomas Whitley, *The Baptists of London, 1612–1928*, 1928, Arthur Swainson Langley, *Birmingham Baptists, past and present* [1939], and Arthur Henry Stockwell, ed., *The Baptist churches of Lancashire* [1910]. For architecture there is Ralph Frederick Chambers, *The strict Baptist chapels of England*, 1952+, *Surrey and Hampshire*, 1952, *Sussex* [1954], *Kent* [1956], *The industrial Midlands* [1963], *Wiltshire and the West*, [1968].

**3764** PAUL (SYDNEY FRANK). Story of the gospel in England. 4 v. Ilfracombe. 1948–50.

See also Philpot (**3773**).

**3765** PAUL (SYDNEY FRANK). Further history of the Gospel Standard Baptists. 3 v. Brighton. 1951–8.

**3766** BARRETT (JOHN OLIVER). Rawdon College (Northern Baptist Education Society) 1804–1954: a short history. 1954.

There is also Charles Rignal, *Manchester Baptist College, 1866–1916* [1918].

**3767** BROWN. Hugh Stowell Brown: his autobiography, his commonplace book, and extracts from his sermons and addresses. Ed. by William Sproston Caine. 1887.

The leading Liverpool Baptist. Alexander Maclaren, who later occupied a similar position in Manchester, has three lives, by David Williamson, 1910, John Charles Carlile, 1901, and Frederick Abijah Rees, ed., Manch. 1906.

**3768** CARLILE. My life's little day. By John Charles Carlile. 1935.

Editor of the *Baptist times*.

**3769** CLIFFORD. Dr. John Clifford, C.H. Life, letters and reminiscences. By Sir James Marchant. 1924.

The official biog. of the most active Baptist of the late 19th and early 20th cents. There are earlier lives by Charles Thomas Bateman, 1902, and Dennis Crane [*God's soldier and the people's tribune*], 1908.

**3770** LANDELS. William Landels, D.D. A memoir. By Thomas Durley Landels. 1900.

**3771** MEYER. F. B. Meyer: a biography. By William Young Fullerton. [1929.]

There are also short lives by A. Chester Mann [pseud. of Philip Ilott Roberts], 1929, and M. Jennie Street, 1902.

**3772** MURSELL. James Philippo Mursell: his life and work. By Arthur Mursell. 1886.

3773 PHILPOT. Letters by the late Joseph Charles Philpot, M.A., formerly fellow of Worcester College, Oxon., and for twenty years editor of the 'Gospel Standard': with a brief memoir of his life and labours. Ed. by William Clayton Walters (afterwards Clayton) and Sarah L. Philpot. 1871.

To be read with Philpot's *Memoir of the late William Tiptaft*, 2nd edn. 1867, and *The seceders, 1829–1869, the story of a spiritual awakening, as told in the letters of J. C. Philpot . . . and of William Tiptaft*, 1930. Both were Anglicans who became Baptists.

3774 SPURGEON. Autobiography of Charles Haddon Spurgeon. Comp. by his wife, Susannah Spurgeon, and Joseph William Harrald. 4 v. 1897–1900.

Suppl. by *The letters of Charles Haddon Spurgeon, collected and collated by his son, Charles Spurgeon*, 1923. Part of the *Autobiography* has been repr. as *C. H. Spurgeon: the early years . . .*, 1962. There is no really adequate biog. of the most famous Baptist of the 19th cent., but Ernest Wallace Bacon, *Spurgeon: heir of the Puritans*, 1967, and John Charles Carlile, *C. H. Spurgeon: an interpretative biography*, 1933, are useful. The older lives by Godfrey Holden Pike, 1879, and Robert Shindler, 1892, are of little value. Spurgeon's own *The Metropolitan Tabernacle, its history and work*, 1876, remains the best account. The life of Spurgeon's brother, William Young Fullerton, *Thomas Spurgeon: a biography*, 1919, has much important Spurgeon material. Many of Spurgeon's sermons are still in print.

### 3. CONGREGATIONALISTS

3775 SURMAN (CHARLES EDWARD). A bibliography of Congregational church history, including numerous cognate Presbyterian/Unitarian records and a few Baptist. Typescript. Congregational Hist. Soc. 1947.

Intended to supplement rather than supplant two older bibliogs., Henry Martyn Dexter, *The Congregationalism of the last three hundred years, as seen in its literature*, N.Y. 1880, which gives a full list of all types of Congregational works up to 1879, and *A catalogue of the Congregational Library, Memorial Hall, London*, 2 v. 1895–1910.

3776 THE CONGREGATIONAL YEAR BOOK. 1846+.

The main source of statistical and biog. information. The main contemp. periodicals were the monthly *British quarterly review*, 1845–86, amalg. with *The Congregationalist*, 1872–86, as *The Congregational review*, 1887–91, and the weekly *English independent*, 1867–79, which incorp. *The patriot*, 1832–1866, *The British banner*, 1848–58, and *The British standard*, 1857–66, and merged with *The nonconformist*, 1841–79, as *The nonconformist and independent*, 1880–90, renamed *The independent and nonconformist*, 1890–7, *The independent*, 1898–1900, *The examiner*, 1900–6, and *The British Congregationalist*, 1906–15. These were gradually ousted by the commercially much more successful *The Christian world*, 1857+, and *British weekly*, 1886+. For the beginning of the period *The Christian witness and church members' magazine*, 1844–71, *The evangelical magazine*, 1793–1904, and *The eclectic review*, 1805–68, were important.

3777 JONES (ROBERT TUDUR). Congregationalism in England, 1662–1962. 1962.

Repl. Robert William Dale, *History of English Congregationalism*, 2nd edn. 1907. John Waddington, *Congregational history, 1850–1880*, 1880, is still useful. For articles see Congregational Hist. Soc., *Trans.*, 1901+.

3778 PEEL (ALBERT). These hundred years: a history of the Congregational Union of England and Wales, 1831–1931. 1931.

The best book on Congregationalism during the period. Suppl. by Albert Peel and Douglas Horton, *International Congregationalism*, 1949, and Albert Peel, ed., *Essays congregational and catholic* [1931.]

3779 DALE (ROBERT WILLIAM). Manual of Congregational principles. Congregational Union. 1884.

The only attempt at a nonconformist creed during the period. Because of objections to the section on the sacraments an abridged version was also publ. as *Congregational church polity*, 1885.

3780 COMPTON-RICKETT (*Sir* JOSEPH). Congregationalism and modern life. [1917.]

Like his *The Free Churchman of today*, 1902, contains a useful summary of the Congregationalist point of view at the time.

3781 CLARE (ALBERT). The City Temple, 1640–1940. The tercentenary commemoration volume. 1940.

The focal point of English Congregationalism. But see also Elaine Kaye, *The history of the King's Weigh House church*, 1968.

3782 NIGHTINGALE (BENJAMIN). Lancashire nonconformity, or, sketches, historical and descriptive of the Congregational and old Presbyterian churches in the county. 6 v. Manch. [1890–3.]

Suppl. by his *The story of the Lancashire Congregational Union, 1806–1906*, Manch., 1906, and William Gordon Robinson, *A history of the Lancashire Congregational Union, 1806–1956*, Manch. 1955. Parallel studs. are William Henry Summers, *History of the Congregational churches in the Berks, South Oxon. and South Bucks. Association . . .*, Newbury 1905; John Brown, *History of Congregationalism and memorials of the churches in Norfolk and Suffolk*, 1877; Richard Ball, *Congregationalism in Cornwall . . .*, 1955; Edward Edney Cleal, *The story of Congregationalism in Surrey*, 1908; William Densham and Joseph Ogle, *The story of the Congregational churches of Dorset . . .*, Bournemouth, 1899; Ernest Elliott, *A history of Congregationalism in Shropshire*, Oswestry [1898]; Arnold Gwynne Matthews, *The Congregational churches of Staffordshire . . .*, 1924; Frederick James Powicke, *A history of the Cheshire County Union of Congregational churches . . .*, Manch. 1907.

3783 WADSWORTH (KENNETH WRIGHT). Yorkshire United Independent College. Two hundred years of training for the Christian ministry by the Congregational churches of Yorkshire. 1954.

On the Congregational colleges in general there is [Samuel Newth], *The calendar of the Congregational colleges of England and Wales . . .* [1879], which includes syllabuses. William Boothby Selbie, *The life of Andrew Martin Fairbairn . . . first principal of Mansfield College, Oxford*, 1914, deals with many aspects of Congregational learning.

3784 PEEL (ALBERT). The Congregational two hundred, 1530–1948. 1948.

Repls. his *A hundred eminent Congregationalists, 1530–1924*, 1927. Notes give details of publ. biogs. There is unfortunately no adequate biog. of Sir Albert Spicer, the leading layman of his day: *Albert Spicer, 1847–1934: a man of his time by one of his family*, 1938, is only a sketch. Nor is there anything adequate on Sir Joseph Compton-Rickett, although Arthur Compton-Rickett, ed., *Joseph Compton-Rickett: a memoir*, Bournemouth 1922, is a useful beginning.

3785 ALLON. Henry Allon, D.D., pastor and teacher: the story of his ministry, with selected sermons and addresses. By William Hardy Harwood. 1894.

Albert Peel, ed., *Letters to a Victorian editor, Henry Allon, editor of the British quarterly review*, 1929, is important for his editorship of the *British quarterly*, 1877–86.

3786 BINNEY. Thomas Binney: his mind, life and opinions . . . By Edwin Paxton Hood. 1874.

See also Binney's *King's Weigh House chapel sermons*, 2nd ser. 1875, with memoir by Henry Allon.

3787 CAMPBELL. A spiritual pilgrimage. By Reginald John Campbell. 1916.

There are also two popular lives by Charles Thomas Bateman, 1903, and Albert H. Wilkerson, 1907. For Campbell's *The new theology*, 1907, see **3373**.

3788 DALE. The life of R. W. Dale of Birmingham. By Sir Alfred William Winterslow Dale. 1898.

A biog. worthy of the greatest Congregationalist of his day.

3789 FORSYTH. P. T. Forsyth: the man and his work. By William Lee Bradley. 1952.

To be read with Gwilym Oswald Griffith, *The theology of P. T. Forsyth*, 1948, John H. Rodgers, *The theology of P. T. Forsyth: the cross of Christ and the Revelation of God*, 1965, and Harry Escott, *Peter Taylor Forsyth, director of souls*, 1948.

3790 HALL. Newman Hall: an autobiography . . . By Christopher Newman Hall. 1898.

3791 HORNE. Pulpit, platform and parliament. By Charles Silvester Horne. 1913.

There is also a *Life* ed. by William Boothby Selbie, 1920. Horne's close friend, John Daniel Jones, also wrote an autobiography, *Three score years and ten*, 1940, and was the subject of a life, Arthur Porritt, *J. D. Jones of Bournemouth*, 1942.

3792 HORTON. An autobiography. By Robert Forman Horton. 1917.

Albert Peel and Sir John Arthur Ransome Marriott, *Robert Forman Horton*, 1937, is a good biog.

3793 JAMES. The life and letters of John Angell James, including an unfinished autobiography. By Robert William Dale. 1861.

There is also a life by John Campbell, 1860. *The works of John Angell James*, 17 v. 1860–4, were ed. by his son, Thomas Smith James.

3794 PARKER. A preacher's life: an autobiography and an album. By Joseph Parker. 1899.

There is a full life by William Adamson, Glasgow, 1902, and a brief life by Albert Dawson, 1901. Godfrey Holden Pike, *Dr. Parker and his friends*, 1904, is also useful.

3795 PATON. John Brown Paton, M.A., D.D., educational and social pioneer. By Sir James Marchant. 1909.

There is also a full life by John Lewis Alexander Paton, *John Brown Paton: a biography*, 1914.

3796 ROGERS. An autobiography. By James Guinness Rogers. 1903.

Edited *The Congregationalist*, 1879–86, and its successor, *The Congregational review*, 1887–91.

### 4. PRESBYTERIANS

3797 LEVI (LEONE). Digest of the actings and proceedings of the synod of the Presbyterian Church of England, 1836–1876. 1877. Minutes of the synod have been publ. since 1881.

For statistical and biog. information consult *Year book of the Presbyterian Church in England*, 1887–8+, styled *The Presbyterian year book*, 1890–1 to 1891–2, and *The official handbook*, 1892–3+.

3798 DRYSDALE (ALEXANDER HUTTON). History of the Presbyterians in England, their rise, decline and revival. 1889.

Suppl. by Samuel William Carruthers, *Fifty years, 1876–1926: being a brief survey of the work and progress of the Presbyterian Church of England since the Union*, 1926.

3799 PRESBYTERIAN HISTORICAL SOCIETY of England. Journal. 1914+.

3800 BLACK (KENNETH MACLEOD). The Scots churches in England. 1906.

3801 ORCHARD (WILLIAM EDWIN). From faith to faith: an autobiography of religious development. Lond. & N.Y. 1933.

### 5. UNITARIANS

3802 BOLAM (CHARLES GORDON) *and others*. The English Presbyterians: from Elizabethan Puritanism to modern Unitarianism. Lond. & Boston. 1968.

3803 GOW (HENRY). The Unitarians. 1928.

A general introduction. Earl Morse Wilbur, *A history of Unitarianism in Transylvania, England and America*, Camb., Mass. 1952, emphasizes the international connections of the movement.

3804 McLACHLAN (HERBERT). The Unitarian movement in the religious life of England. Vol. 1. Its contribution to thought and learning, 1700–1900. 1934.

The work of a notable scholar. See also his *Essays and addresses*, Manch. 1950.

3805 HOLT (RAYMOND VINCENT). The Unitarian contribution to social progress in England. 1938. 2nd edn. 1952.

**3806 UNITARIAN HISTORICAL SOCIETY.** Transactions. 1916–18+.

There is much misc. information in *The Essex Hall directory of ministers and congregations* . . ., 1904–6, subsequently publ. as *The Unitarian pocket book* . . ., 1907–11, and *Directory of Unitarian ministers* . . ., 1911+, and in *The Essex Hall year book*, 1894–1928. The main Unitarian organ was *The inquirer* 1842+, but see also *Unitarian herald*, March, 1861–89, and *Christian life*, 1876. 1929.

**3807 HOLT (ANNE DURNING).** Walking together: a study in Liverpool nonconformity, 1688–1938. 1938.

There is an account of Cross St. and Stand Chapels, Manchester, in McLachlan's *Essays and addresses* (**3804**). There are no adequate regional hists. Robert Travers Herford and Evan David Priestley Evans, *Historical sketch of the North and East Lancashire Unitarian Mission and its affiliated churches, 1859–1909*, Bury 1909, and the numerous works of George Eyre Evans (notably *Record of the provincial assembly of Lancashire and Cheshire*, Manch., 1896, *Vestiges of Protestant dissent* . . ., Liverpool 1897, *Midland churches* . . ., Dudley 1899, and *Antiquarian notes*, 4 v. 1898–1906) give little more than lists of dates and benefactions.

**3808 McLACHLAN (HERBERT).** The Unitarian Home Missionary College, 1854–1914: its foundation and development, with some account of the missionary activities of its members. 1915.

This college, now the Unitarian College, Manchester, has a famous libr. about which there are two books by McLachlan, *The story of a nonconformist library*, Manch., 1923 and *The Unitarian College library: its history, contents and character*, priv. pr. Manch. 1939.

**3809 MELLONE (SYDNEY HERBERT).** Liberty and religion: the first century of the British & Foreign Unitarian Association. 1925.

**3810 McLACHLAN (HERBERT).** Records of a family, 1800–1933: pioneers in education, social service and liberal religion. Manch. 1935.

On the Beard family.

**3811 BROOKE.** Life and letters of Stopford Brooke. By Lawrence Pearsall Jacks. 2 v. 1917.

**3812 CARPENTER.** Joseph Estlin Carpenter: a memorial volume . . . Ed. by Charles Harold Herford. 1929.

Herbert McLachlan, *Alexander Gordon (9 June 1841–21 February 1931): a biography with a bibliography*, Manch., 1932, is an account of another leading Unitarian scholar of comparable range.

**3813 CROSSKEY.** Henry William Crosskey, LL.D., F.G.S.: his life and work. By Richard Acland Armstrong. Birmingham. 1895.

**3814 HARGROVE.** From authority to freedom: the spiritual pilgrimage of Charles Hargrove. By Lawrence Pearsall Jacks. 1920.

**3815 MARTINEAU.** The life and letters of James Martineau, LL.D., S.T.D. By James Drummond and Charles Barnes Upton. 2 v. Lond. & N.Y. 1902.

Other works on Martineau are *Inter amicos: letters between James Martineau and William*

*Knight, 1869–72*, 1901; Joseph Estlin Carpenter, *James Martineau, theologian and teacher* . . ., 1905; Alexander Henry Gregan Craufurd, *Recollections of James Martineau* . . ., 1903; and Abraham Willard Jackson, *James Martineau: a biography and study*, 1900.

**3816  WICKSTEED.** Philip Henry Wicksteed: his life and work. By Charles Harold Herford. Lond. & Toronto. 1931.

There is a poor *Memoir* of Wicksteed's closest friend, Richard Acland Armstrong, by his son, George Gilbert Armstrong, 1906.

### 6. METHODISM

#### (a) *General*

There is no adequate Methodist bibliography but Frank Cumbers, *The Book Room* (**3826**), gives an account of the official or quasi-official publications of the various branches of Methodism. The main collections of tract material are in the Thomas Jackson collection at Richmond College, London, and the Hobile collection at Hartley Victoria College, Manchester.

**3817  MINUTES OF THE . . . CONFERENCE OF THE UNITED METHODIST CHURCH. 1907+.**

In all but name a post-union Methodist year-book and directory.

**3818  TOWNSEND (WILLIAM JOHN)** *and others.* A new history of Methodism. 2 v. 1909.

Useful bibliog. A new *New history* is in preparation. The first vol., Rupert Eric Davies and Ernest Gordon Rupp, eds., *A history of the Methodist Church in Great Britain*, 1965, covers the 18th cent. R. E. Davies, *Methodism*, Harmondsworth 1963, incl. a short hist.

**3819  CURRIE (ROBERT).** Methodism divided: a study in the sociology of ecumenicalism. 1968.

Good, as is John Henry Somerset Kent, *The age of disunity*, 1966.

**3820  WESLEY HISTORICAL SOCIETY.** Proceedings. Burnley, etc. 1897+.

**3821  TOWNSEND (WILLIAM JOHN).** The story of Methodist union. [1906.]

There is much useful material in *Proceedings of the first Methodist œcumenical conference*, 1881, and the *Proceedings* of the subsequent conferences.

**3822  REDFERN (WILLIAM).** Modern developments in Methodism. 1906.

**3823  TAYLOR (ERNEST RICHARD).** Methodism & politics, 1791–1851. Camb. 1935.

Good on Methodism in 1851.

**3824  WEARMOUTH (ROBERT FEATHERSTONE).** Methodism and the struggle of the working classes, 1850–1900. Leicester. 1954.

Makes too much of his subject, as also in his *Some working-class movements of the nineteenth century*, 1948, *The social and political influence of Methodism in the twentieth century*, 1957, and *Methodism and the trade unions*, 1959.

3825 EDWARDS (MALDWYN). Methodism and England: a study of Methodism in its social and political aspects during the period 1850–1932. 1943.
To be used with caution.

3826 CUMBERS (FRANK HENRY). The Book Room: the story of the Methodist Publishing House and Epworth Press. 1956.

3827 BRASH (WILLIAM BARDSLEY). The story of our colleges, 1835–1935: a centenary record of ministerial training in the Methodist church. 1935.
See also W. B. Brash and Charles James Wright, eds., *Didsbury College centenary, 1842–1942*, 1942, and Frank Henry Cumbers, ed., *Richmond College, 1843–1943*, 1944.

3828 SHAW (THOMAS). A history of Cornish Methodism. Truro. 1967.
Useful. See also the *Journal*, 1960+, and *Occasional publications*, 1960+, of the Cornish Methodist Hist. Assoc.

3829 TICE (FRANK). The history of Methodism in Cambridge. 1966.

(b) *Wesleyans*

3830 OSBORN (GEORGE). Outlines of Wesleyan bibliography; or, a record of Methodist literature from the beginning. 1869.

3831 MINUTES OF THE METHODIST CONFERENCES . . . held in London, by . . . J. Wesley . . . [1744–1857]. 1812–59.
Cont. as *Minutes of the conference* . . .

3832 HALL (JOSEPH) *comp.* Hall's circuits and ministers: an alphabetical list of the circuits of Great Britain, with the names of the ministers stationed in each circuit from 1765 to 1885. 2nd. edn. 1886. Rev. edn. by T. Galland Hartley. [1914.] Suppl. 1925.

3833 THE WESLEYAN METHODIST MAGAZINE. 1778+.
Began life as *The Arminian magazine*; title varies. The leading Wesleyan papers were *The Methodist recorder*, 1861+, and *The Methodist times*, 1885–1937.

3834 GRINDROD (EDMUND). A compendium of the laws and regulations of Wesleyan Methodism. 1842. 8th edn. 1865.

3835 SIMON (JOHN S.). A summary of Methodist law and discipline: being a new edition of 'The Large Minutes'. 1897. Rev. edns. 1907, 1915, etc.

3836 CHADWICK. Samuel Chadwick. By Norman Grove Dunning. 1933.
Edited *The joyful news*.

3837 CHAMPNESS. The life story of Thomas Champness. By Eliza M. Champness. [1907.]
Edited *The Methodist recorder*.

3838 HUGHES. The life of Hugh Price Hughes. By his daughter, Dorothea Price Hughes. 1904.
A major political figure and editor of *The Methodist times*. There is also a brief popular life by J. Gregory Mantle, 1901. See also John Henry Somerset Kent, 'Hugh Price

Hughes and the nonconformist conscience', in Gareth Vaughan Bennett and John Dixon Walsh, eds., *Essays in modern English church history in memory of Norman Sykes*, Lond. & N.Y. 1966, pp. 181–205.

3839 KELLY. Memories. By Charles Henry Kelly. 1910.

3840 LIDGETT. Reminiscences. By John Scott Lidgett. 1928.

Rupert Eric Davies, ed., *John Scott Lidgett: a symposium*, 1957, incl. some good essays.

3841 LUNN. Chapters from my life: with special reference to reunion. By Sir Henry Simpson Lunn. 1918.

A leading layman. Lunn also publ. *Nearing harbour*, 1934.

3842 McARTHUR. Sir William McArthur K.C.M.G. A biography, religious, parliamentary, municipal, commercial. By Thomas McCullagh. 1891.

A prominent Londonderry Wesleyan who became a leading figure in the City of London and in English Wesleyanism.

3843 MACDONALD. As a tale that is told: recollections of many years. By Frederic William Macdonald. 1919.

Macdonald also publ. *Reminiscences of my early ministry* [1913].

3844 PUNSHON. The life of William Morley Punshon, LL.D. By Frederic William Macdonald. 1887.

3845 RIGG. The life of James Harrison Rigg, D.D., 1821–1909. By John Telford. [1909.]

### (c) *Other Methodist Churches*

#### (i) *Bible Christians*

3846 SHAW (THOMAS). The Bible Christians, 1815–1907. Wesley Hist. Soc. 1965.

3847 BOURNE (FREDERICK WILLIAM). The Bible Christians: their origin and history. Manch. 1905.

3848 PYNE (RICHARD). The golden chain: the story of the Bible Christian Methodists from the formation of the first society in 1815 to the union of the denomination in 1907 with the Methodist New Connexion and the United Methodist Free Churches in forming the United Methodist Church. [1915.]

3849 MICHELL (WILLIAM JOHN). Brief biographical sketches of Bible Christian ministers and laymen, with portraits. 2 v. Jersey. 1905–6.

3850 THE BIBLE CHRISTIAN MAGAZINE ... Shebbear, etc. 1852–1907.

3851 BOURNE. Memorials of Frederick William Bourne. By William Balkwill Luke. 1906.

3852 BRAY. The King's son: or, a memoir of 'Billy' Bray . . . compiled chiefly from his own memoranda. By Frederick William Bourne. 1871. New edn. 1937.

### (ii) *Methodist New Connexion*

3853 MINUTES OF CONVERSATIONS between preachers and delegates [preachers and representatives from the societies in the Methodist New Connexion . . .] 1797–1907.

3854 CROWTHER (R. G.) *ed.* The centenary of the Methodist New Connexion. 1897.

3855 THE METHODIST NEW CONNEXION magazine and evangelical repository. Manch. etc. 1798–1907.

### (iii) *Primitive Methodists*

3856 GENERAL MINUTES made at the ... annual conference of the Primitive Methodist Connexion. 1820–1915.

Publ. 1916-32 as *The Primitive Methodist year book.*

3857 KENDALL (HOLLIDAY BICKERSTAFFE). History of the Primitive Methodist Connexion. 2 v. 1906. Rev. edn. 1919.

3858 PATERSON (W. M.). Northern Primitive Methodism. 1909.

Arthur H. Patterson, *From hayloft to temple: the story of Primitive Methodism in Yarmouth . . .*, 1903, is a quaint local hist.

3859 THE PRIMITIVE METHODIST [LEADER]. 1868–1925+.

Absorbed *The Primitive Methodist world*, Manch. 1883–1908.

3860 GUTTERY. The life of Arthur Thomas Guttery, D.D. By John George Bowran. [1922.]

3861 HARTLEY. The life of Sir William Hartley. By Arthur Samuel Peake. 1926.

3862 PEAKE. Arthur Samuel Peake, 1865–1929: essays in commemoration, and selections from his writings. Ed. by John Thomas Wilkinson. 1958.

See also Leslie Sillman Peake, *Arthur Samuel Peake: a memoir*, 1930.

(iv) *United Methodist Free Churches*

**3863  BECKERLEGGE (OLIVER AVEYARD). The United Methodist Free Churches: a study in freedom. 1957.**

See also Joseph Kirsop, *Historic sketches of Free Methodism*, 1885, the *Handbook* publ. by the U.M.F.C., and *The Wesleyan Methodist Association magazine*, 1838–57, cont. as *The United Methodist Free Churches magazine*, 1858–91, and *The Methodist monthly*, 1892–1907.

**3864  MINUTES OF PROCEEDINGS of the . . . annual conference of the United Methodist Free Churches. 1857–1906.**

(v) *United Methodists*

**3865  SMITH (HENRY), SWALLOW (JOHN EDWARD), *and* TREFFREY (WILLIAM). The story of the United Methodist Church. 1932.**

Covers the union of 1907 and ends with the wider union of 1932. The basic docs. are *Minutes of the . . . conference of the United Methodist Church*, 1907–32, and *Official handbook of the United Methodist Church conference*, Birmingham 1908–31.

(vi) *Wesleyan Reform Union*

**3866  JONES (WILLIAM HAROLD). History of the Wesleyan Reform Union. 1952.**

The Union publ. a *Year book*, Sheffield 1899+, *The Wesleyan Reform Union magazine*, 1861–5, and *Christian words*, 1866+.

7. SALVATION ARMY

**3867  SALVATION ARMY YEAR BOOK. 1906+.**

**3868  SANDALL (ROBERT) *and* WIGGINS (ARCHIBALD RAYMOND). The history of the Salvation Army. 1+. 1947+.**

The standard hist. Vols. 1–3 are by Sandall, vols. 4–5 by Wiggins. Vol. 5 reaches 1914. There are a number of short hists., incl. Bernard Watson, *A hundred years' war: the Salvation Army, 1865–1965*, 1964.

**3869  BOOTH (WILLIAM BRAMWELL). These fifty years. [1929.]**

A hist. of the Salvation Army to 1912. Largely autobiog.

**3870  RAILTON (GEORGE SCOTT). Heathen England, and what to do for it; being a description of the . . . godless condition of the . . . majority of the English nation, and of . . . an organization for its regeneration, consisting of working people under the superintendence of William Booth. 1877.**

Railton also publ. a number of hist. works incl. *Twenty-one years [of the] Salvation Army*, 1890.

**3871  BOOTH (WILLIAM). In darkest England and the way out. 1890.**

Provoked many curious attacks such as Samuel Horatio Hodges, *General Booth, 'The Family', and the Salvation Army, showing its rise, progress and moral and spiritual decline*, Manch. 1890.

3872 HAGGARD (*Sir* HENRY RIDER). Regeneration: being an account of the social work of the Salvation Army. 1910.

See also 7223-4.

3873 MANSON (JOHN). The Salvation Army and the public: a religious, social, and financial study. 1906. 2nd edn. 1908.

A hostile analysis.

3874 BOOTH. God's soldier: General William Booth. By St. John Greer Ervine. 2 v. Lond. & Toronto. 1934.

Other useful lives are those of Edward Harold Begbie, 2 v. 1920, and George Scott Railton, 2nd edn. 1912. There are also lives by William Thomas Stead, 1891; Thomas F. G. Coates, Lond. 1905, N.Y. 1906; A. M. Nicol [1911]; Charles Thomas Bateman [1914]; George Campbell Morgan, 1935; Minnie Lindsay Carpenter, 1957; and Richard Hugheson Collier [*General next to God* . . .], 1965.

3875 MRS. BOOTH. The life of Catherine Booth, the mother of the Salvation Army. By Frederick St. George de Lautour Booth-Tucker. 2 v. 1893.

See also Catherine Bramwell Booth, *Catherine Booth: the story of her loves*, 1970. There is also a life by William Thomas Stead, 1900, and a number of poor popular lives.

3876 BRAMWELL BOOTH. Echoes and memories. By William Bramwell Booth. 1925.

There is also a full life, Catherine Bramwell Booth, *Bramwell Booth*, 1933.

## 8. QUAKERS

3877 SMITH (JOSEPH). A descriptive catalogue of Friends' books, and books written by members of the Society of Friends. 2 v. 1862-7. Suppl. 1893.

Smith also publ. *Bibliotheca anti-Quakeriana*, 1873, and *Catalogue of books, relating to Friends* . . . A–Anonymous only. [1883.] There is no guide to the large coll. of MSS. in the libr. at Friends' House, London.

3878 EPISTLES from the yearly meeting of Friends, held in London, to the quarterly and monthly meetings in Great Britain, Ireland, and elsewhere; from 1681 to 1857. 2 v. 1858.

Distributed annually 1682+. The main source for Quaker hist. Suppl. by *Extracts from the minutes and proceedings of the yearly meeting of Friends* . . ., 1857+. [*Index* 1857-1906.]

3879 FRIENDS' HISTORICAL SOCIETY. Journal. 1903-4+.

Publ. monographs as suppls. The Friends' Historical Society of Philadelphia also publ. a *Bulletin*, 1906+, which is well indexed. Except for *The Friends' year book*, 1908-13, there is no general directory. *Annual monitor or new letter case and memorandum book or obituary of the members of the Society of Friends*, 1813 to 1919-20, *Index*, 1813-32, is the main source for biog. information. *The Friend*, 1843+, and *The British Friend*, Glasgow 1843-1913, are important js.

3880   JONES (RUFUS MATTHEW). The later periods of Quakerism. 2 v. 1921.

Vol. 2 deals with the 19th cent. For the end of the 19th cent. and the early 20th cent. Elfrida Vipont [Foulds], *The story of Quakerism*, 1954, 2nd edn. 1960, is useful.

3881   ISICHEI (ELIZABETH). Victorian Quakers. 1970.

3882   SOCIETY OF FRIENDS: LONDON YEARLY MEETING. London yearly meeting during 250 years. 1919.

Unfortunately Reginald Leslie Hine, *A mirror for the Society of Friends: being the story of the Hitchin Quakers*, 1929, the only good book on a local Quaker meeting, has little on the period after 1850.

3883   GRAHAM (JOHN WILLIAM). The faith of a Quaker. Camb. 1920.

Deals with both doctrine and hist. See also John Sykes, *The Quakers: a new look at their place in society*, 1958.

3884   HIRST (MARGARET E.). The Quakers in peace and war: an account of their peace principles and practice. Lond. & N.Y. 1923.

3885   GREEN (JOSEPH JOSHUA) *ed.* Quaker records: being, an index to 'The annual monitor', 1813–1892: containing over twenty thousand obituary notices of members of the Society of Friends, alphabetically & chronologically arranged, with references to 'The annual monitor'. 1894.

3886   MILLS (JOSEPH TRAVIS). John Bright and the Quakers. 2 v. 1935.

Important both for the Quakers and for Bright.

3887   EMDEN (PAUL HERMAN). Quakers in commerce: a record of business achievement. [1940.]

See also Arthur Raistrick, *Two centuries of industrial welfare: the London (Quaker) lead company, 1692–1905*, 1938.

3888   ROBINSON (WILLIAM) *ed.* Friends of a half century: fifty memorials with portraits of members of the Society of Friends, 1840–90. Lond. 1891.

### 9. BRETHREN

3889   COAD (FREDERICK ROY). A history of the Brethren movement: its origins, its worldwide development, and its significance for the present day. Exeter. 1968.

Like Harold Hamlyn Rowdon, *The origins of the Brethren, 1825–1850*, 1967, stronger on early hist. than on the late 19th cent.

3890   BEATTIE (DAVID JOHNSTONE). Brethren: the story of a great recovery. Kilmarnock. [1939].

A workmanlike general hist.

3891  NEATBY (WILLIAM BLAIR). A history of the Plymouth Brethren. 1901. 2nd edn. 1902.

Useful, but shows little sympathy for J. N. Darby and his supporters. Henry Allan Ironside, *A historical sketch of the Brethren movement: an account of its inception, progress and failures, and its lessons for present day believers*, Grand Rapids, Mich. 1942, is more sympathetic.

3892  NOEL (NAPOLEON). The history of the Brethren. Ed. by William F. Knapp. 2 v. Denver, Colo. 1936.

Full, but written in the turgid evangelical jargon of the early Brethren.

3893  TEULON (JOSIAH SANDERS). The history and teaching of the Plymouth Brethren. 1883.

A balanced Anglican view of the Brethren. There is an extreme evangelical attack in Henry Groves, *Darbyism: its rise and development, and a review of 'The Bethesda Question'*, Lond. & Bristol 1866.

3894  GOSSE (*Sir* EDMUND WILLIAM). Father and son. 1907.

A first-rate account of a Brethren household as well as a major autobiog.

3895  DARBY (JOHN NELSON). The collected writings . . . Ed. by William Kelly. 34 v. 1867–[1900?]. Index [1902].

W. G. Turner, *John Nelson Darby: a biography*, 1926, is a brief but useful official life.

3896  KELLY (WILLIAM). The revelation expounded by William Kelly. [1901.] 5th edn. 1922.

The best of Kelly's many works. There is no life.

## 10. OTHER SECTS

3897  WILSON (BRYAN RONALD). Sects and society: a sociological study of three religious groups in Britain. Lond. & Berkeley. 1961.

3898  MORAVIANS. *The Moravian almanack & year book . . .*, 1869+. John Taylor Hamilton, *A history of the church known as the Moravian Church, or the Unitas fratrum, or the Unity of the brethren, during the eighteenth and nineteenth centuries*, Moravian Hist. Soc. Trans. vi, Bethlehem, Pa. 1900. Joseph Edmund Hutton, *A history of the Moravian Church*, 1895. 2nd edn. 1909.

3899  IRVINGITES. Plato Ernest Shaw, *The Catholic Apostolic Church, sometimes called Irvingite: a historical study*, N.Y. 1946. Andrew Landale Drummond, *Edward Irving and his circle . . .*, 1937. Edward Miller, *The history and doctrines of Irvingism: or, of the so-called Catholic and Apostolic Church*, 2 v. 1878. Henry Charles Whitley, *Blinded eagle: an introduction to the life and teaching of Edward Irving*, 1955, and *Laughter in heaven*, 1962.

3900  SOUTHCOTTIANS. George Reginald Balleine, *Past finding out: the tragic story of Joanna Southcott and her successors*, 1956.

3901 JEZREELITES. Philip George Rogers, *The sixth trumpeter: the story of Jezreel and his tower*, 1963.

3902 MORMONS. Richard Louis Evans, *A century of 'Mormonism' in Great Britain: a brief summary of the activities of the Church of Jesus Christ of the Latter-Day Saints in the United Kingdom, with emphasis on its introduction one hundred years ago*, Salt Lake City, Utah 1937. Philip Arthur Michael Taylor, *Expectations westward: the Mormons and the emigration of their British converts in the nineteenth century*, Edin. & Lond. 1965, Ithaca, N.Y. 1966.

3903 CHRISTADELPHIANS. B. R. Wilson, *Sects and society* (**3897**). Robert Roberts, *Dr. Thomas: his life and work: a biography illustrative of the process by which the system of truth revealed in the Bible has been extricated in modern times from the observation of Romish and Protestant tradition*, Birmingham 1873, 3rd edn. 1954. Robert Roberts, *My days and my ways*, Birmingham n.d., and *Christendom astray from the Bible*, 1928, 3rd edn. 1933. W. Islip Collyer, *Robert Roberts: a study of life and character*, Birmingham 1948. Roberts ed. *The ambassador of the coming age*, 1864–8, and renamed it *The Christadelphian*, 1869+.

CHRISTIAN SCIENCE. See **3897** and **4047**.

3904 FREE CHURCH OF ENGLAND. Frank Vaughan, Bishop, *A history of the Free Church of England, otherwise called the Reformed Episcopal Church*, 1936, 2nd edn. Wallasey 1960. F. Somner Merryweather, *The Free Church of England: its history, doctrines and ecclesiastical polity . . .*, 1873. *The Free Church of England magazine and harbinger*, 1867–8. *The magazine of the Free Church of England and Lady Huntingdon's Connexion*, 1869–95.

3905 REFORMED EPISCOPAL CHURCH. *Constitutions and canons of the Reformed Episcopal Church in the United Kingdom . . .*, 1878, new edns. 1883, 1898. *Report of the proceedings of the general synod of the Reformed Episcopal Church . . .*, Taunton 1903–25. *Work and worship*, Taunton 1897–1915. *The Reformed Church record*, 1881–91.

3906 SEVENTH-DAY ADVENTISTS. Gideon David Hagstotz, *The Seventh-day Adventists in the British Isles, 1878–1933*, Columbia, Mo. 1935.

3907 DUTCH REFORMED CHURCH. Johannes Lindeboom, *Austin Friars: history of the Dutch Reformed Church in London, 1550–1950*, The Hague 1950.

3908 AGAPEMONITES. Ronald Matthews, 'Henry James Prince (1811–1899), John Hugh Smyth-Piggott (1852–1927), and the "Abode of Love"', in *English messiahs: studies of six English religious pretenders, 1656–1927*, 1936, pp. 161–95.

3909 LABOUR CHURCHES. Kenneth Stanley Inglis, 'The Labour church movement', *Int. Rev. Soc. Hist.* iii (1958), 445–60, with note by Henry Pelling, ibid. iv (1959), 111–12, and reply, 112–13. Stanley Pierson, 'John Trevor and the Labor church movement in England, 1891–1900', *Church Hist.* xxix (1960), 463–78. F. Reid, 'Socialist Sunday schools in Britain, 1892–1939', *Int. Rev. Soc. Hist.* xi (1966), 18–47. K. S. Inglis, *Churches and the working classes* (**3377**). John Trevor, *My quest for God*, 1897, 2nd edn. 1908. David Blythe Foster, *Socialism and the Christ*, Leeds 1921. *The Labour church record*, Bolton 1899–1901.

**3910  PENTECOSTALISM.** Nils Egede Bloch-Hoell, *The Pentecostal movement: its origin, development and distinctive character*, Oslo & Lond. 1964.

## D. ROMAN CATHOLICS

### I. GENERAL

**3911  THE CATHOLIC ENCYCLOPAEDIA.** 16 v. N.Y. 1907–14. Suppl. 1922.

The main Catholic reference work. Incl. useful bibliogs. Better for the period than the *New Catholic encyclopedia*, 15 v. N.Y. etc. 1967.

**3912  THE CATHOLIC DIRECTORY AND ANNUAL REGISTER.** 1838+.

See also *The Catholic who's who & year-book*, 1908+, 1907+. The leading Catholic js. of the period were the *Dublin review*, 1836+, *The tablet*, 1840+, and the *Rambler*, 1848–62.

**3913  CATHOLIC RECORD SOCIETY.** Publications. 1+. 1905+.

Nothing of note on the late 19th cent. so far.

**3914  THE CATHOLIC HISTORICAL REVIEW.** 1+. Washington. 1915+.

Covers British as well as American Catholic hist. *Recusant history: a journal of research in post-Reformation Catholic history in the British Isles*, Bognor Regis 1951+ intends to publ. 19th-cent. articles.

**3915  FLETCHER (JOHN R.).** 'Early Catholic periodicals in England'. *Dublin Rev.* cxcviii (1936), 284–310.

A full list to 1876.

**3916  BECK (GEORGE ANDREW),** *bishop, ed.* The English Catholics, 1850–1950: essays to commemorate the centenary of the restoration of the hierarchy of England and Wales. 1950.

A fine symposium. There is useful background material in Archbishop David Mathew, *Catholicism in England, 1535–1935: portrait of a minority, its culture and tradition*, 1936, and in Edward Ingram Watkin, *Roman Catholicism in England from the Reformation to 1950*, 1957. General hists. of Catholicism, like Henry Daniel-Rops, *The church in an age of revolution, 1789–1870*, trans. by John Warrington, Lond. & N.Y. 1965, have little on England.

3917 GWYNN (DENIS ROLLESTON). A hundred years of Catholic emancipation (1829–1929). 1929.

Much more penetrating than *Catholic emancipation, 1829 to 1929: essays by various writers*, 1929, but lacks the period flavour of Percy Hetherington Fitzgerald, *Fifty years of Catholic life and social progress under Cardinals Wiseman, Manning, Vaughan and Newman*, 2 v. 1901.

3918 HICKEY (JOHN). Urban Catholics: urban Catholicism in England from 1829 to the present day. Lond. & Dublin. 1967.

3919 NORMAN (EDWARD ROBERT). Anti-Catholicism in Victorian England. Lond. & N.Y. 1968.

3920 ALTHOLZ (JOSEF LEWIS). The Liberal Catholic movement in England: *The Rambler* and its contributors, 1848–64. 1962.

See also his 'The political behavior of the English Catholics, 1850–1867', *J. Brit. Studs.* iv (1964–5), pt. 1, 89–103, Damian McElrath, *The syllabus of Pius IX: some reactions in England*, Louvain 1964, and 'Richard Simpson and John Henry Newman: The Rambler, laymen and theology', *Catholic Hist. Rev.* lii (1966–7), 509–33 and Josef L. Altholz and Damian McElrath, eds., *The correspondence of Lord Acton and Richard Simpson*, 3 v. Camb. 1971.

3921 VIDLER (ALEXANDER ROPER). The modernist movement in the Roman Church: its origins & outcome. Camb. 1934.

Still in many ways the best book on the subject in English, but see also his *A variety of Catholic modernists*, Camb. 1970, the works at **3940a** and **3946**, and Michele Ranchetti, *The Catholic modernists: a study of the religious reform movement, 1864–1907*, trans. by Isabel Quigly, Lond. & N.Y. 1969. Of older books Alfred Fawkes, *Studies in modernism*, 1913, Alfred Leslie Lilley, *Modernism: a record and a review*, 1908, and Maude Dominica Mary Petre, *Modernism: its failure and its fruits*, 1918, are still useful, as is Herbert Leslie Stewart, *Modernism, past and present*, 1932. The modernist case is stated in George Tyrrell, trans. and Alfred Leslie Lilley, ed., *The programme of modernism: a reply to the encyclical of Pius X*, 1908, and Alfred Leslie Lilley, trans., *What we want: an open letter to Pius X*, 1907. There is a good bibliog. in J. Ratté, *Three modernists* (**3946**).

3922 LILLY (WILLIAM SAMUEL) *and* WALLIS (*Sir* JOHN EDWARD POWER). A manual of the law specially affecting Catholics. 1893.

Earlier manuals are Thomas Chisholm Anstey, *A guide to the laws of England affecting Roman Catholics*, 1842, suppl. 1850, and John Jane Smith Wharton, *The statute law now in force relating to Roman Catholics in England*, 1851. The various changes in the law are briefly recorded in James Paton, *British history and papal claims, from the Norman Conquest to the present day*, 2 v. 1893.

3923 BRADY (WILLIAM MAZIERE). Annals of the Catholic hierarchy in England and Scotland . . . 1585–1876. Rome 1877. Lond. 1883.

The 3rd vol. (repr.) of *The episcopal succession in England, Scotland and Ireland*, 3 v. Rome etc. 1876–7. Incl. many extracts from official records.

3924 BUTLER (EDWARD CUTHBERT). The Vatican Council: the story told from inside in Bishop Ullathorne's letters. 2 v. 1930.

Indispensable. Other important sources are the lives of Acton (**8517**) and Manning (**3943**), Johann Joseph Ignaz von Döllinger, *Briefwechsel 1820–1890: mit Lord Acton:*

*I. 1850–1869, II. 1869–70*, ed. by Victor Conzemius, Munich 1963–5, Thomas, Mozley, *Letters from Rome on the occasion of the œcumenical council, 1869–1870*, 2 v. 1891, and N. Blakeston, ed., *The Roman question* (**2327**). For Acton's role see J. Victor Conzemius, 'Lord Acton and the First Vatican Council', *J. Eccles. Hist.* xx (1969), 267–94. The most important of the contemporary English pamphlets on the subject was William Ewart Gladstone, *The Vatican decrees in their bearing on civil allegiance: a political expostulation*, 1874, for which see Morley's *Life of Gladstone* (**731**), II, 507–22, and Josef Lewis Altholz, 'Gladstone and the Vatican decrees', *The Historian* xxv (1962–3), 312–24.

**3925 BURKE (THOMAS).** Catholic history of Liverpool. Liverpool. 1910.

The only adequate district hist. Bernard Joseph Bogan, *The great link: a history of St. George's cathedral, Southwark, 1786–1948*, 1948, 2nd edn. 1958, is a good hist. of an indiv. church.

**3926 MURPHY (JOHN NICHOLAS).** Terra incognita: or, the convents of the United Kingdom. 1873. Rev. edn. 1876.

A quasi-official publ. with valuable statistics. See also *Report from the select committee on conventual and monastic institutions, &c.* [Chairman: C. P. Villiers.] H.C. 383 (1870). VII, 1. Further report. H.C. 315 (1871). VII, 181.

**3927 ANSON (PETER FREDERICK).** The religious orders and congregations of Great Britain and Ireland. Worcester. 1949.

A directory with brief hist. notes. Much fuller than Francesca Maria Steele, *Monasteries and religious houses of Great Britain & Ireland*, 1902, and *The convents of Great Britain and Ireland*, 1902, rev. edn. 1924. For insights into the life of an English monastery as seen by an outsider see Pierre Teilhard de Chardin, *Letters from Hastings, 1908–1912*, N.Y. 1968, Lond. 1969.

**3928 SUTCLIFFE (EDMUND FELIX).** Bibliography of the English province of the Society of Jesus, 1773–1953. 1957.

**3929 BASSET (BERNARD).** The English Jesuits from Campion to Martindale. 1967.

**3930 MILBURN (DAVID).** A history of Ushaw college: a study of the origin, foundation and development of an English Catholic seminary . . . Durham. 1964.

## 2. BIOGRAPHY

**3931 BROWN (STEPHEN JAMES)** *comp.* An index of Catholic biographies. Dublin. 1930. 2nd edn. 1935.

2nd edn. entitled *International index* . . . Invaluable.

**3932 GILLOW (JOSEPH).** A literary and biographical history, or bibliographical dictionary of English Catholics, from the breach with Rome in 1534 to the present time. 5 v. Lond. & N.Y. 1885–1902.

On the cardinals there are Charles Stuteville Isaacson, *The story of the English Cardinals*, 1907, George Coulehan Heseltine, *The English Cardinals . . .*, 1931, and Ernest Edwin Reynolds, *Three Cardinals: Newman, Wiseman, Manning*, 1958.

3933 GORMAN (WILLIAM JAMES GORDON). Converts to Rome: a biographical list of the more notable converts to the Catholic Church in the United Kingdom during the past 60 years . . . New edn. 1910.

First edn. 1884 based on an earlier work entitled *Rome's recruits*.

3934 GUMBLEY (WALTER) *comp*. Obituary notices of the English Dominicans, 1555–1952. 1955.

ACTON. See **8517**.

3935 BENSON. Confessions of a convert. By Robert Hugh Benson. 1913.

There is also a full *Life* by Cyril Charles Martindale, 2 v. 1916. and five vols. of tributes and reminiscences by Blanche Warre Cornish and others, 1915, Arthur Christopher Benson, 1915, Olive Katharine Parr, 1915, Reginald J. J. Watt, 1918, and Agnès de la Gorce, 1928. *Spiritual letters of Monsignor R. Hugh Benson to one of his converts*, 1915, has some characteristic letters.

3936 BOURNE. Francis, Cardinal Bourne. By Ernest Oldmeadow. 2 v. 1940–4.

3937 CONNELLY. The case of Cornelia Connelly. By Juliana Wadham. 1956.

Founder of the Society of the Holy Child.

3938 DE LISLE. Life and letters of Ambrose Phillipps de Lisle . . . By Edmund Sheridan Purcell. Ed. by Edwin de Lisle. 2 v. 1900.

3939 FABER. Father Faber. By Ronald Chapman. 1961.

GASQUET. For Cardinal Gasquet see **8523**.

3940 HEDLEY. The life of Bishop Hedley. By Joseph Anselm Wilson. 1930.

A useful comparison is with Henry Francis John Vaughan, ed., *Memoirs of Francis Kerrill Amherst, Lord Bishop of Northampton*, 1903, and Kathleen O'Meara, *Thomas Grant, first Bishop of Southwark*, 1886.

3940a von HÜGEL. Baron Friedrich von Hügel and the modernist crisis in England. By Lawrence F. Barmann. Camb. 1972.

For letters see Bernard Holland, ed., *Baron Friedrich von Hügel: selected letters, 1896–1924*, 1927, Gwendolen Maud Greene, ed., *Letters from Baron Friedrich von Hügel to a niece*, 1928, and Petre, *Von Hügel and Tyrell* (**3946**). See also Michael De La Bedoyère, *The life of Baron von Hügel*, 1951, Joseph P. Whelan, *The spirituality of Friedrich von Hügel*, 1971, Lester Vallis Lester-Garland, *The religious philosophy of Baron F. von Hügel*, 1933, Arthur Hazard Dakin, *Von Hügel and the supernatural*, 1934, Maurice Nédoncelle, *Baron Friedrich von Hügel: a study of his life and thought*, trans. by Marjorie Vernon, 1937, Gwendolen Maud Greene, *Two witnesses: a personal recollection of Hubert Parry and Friedrich von Hügel*, 1930, and Jean Steinmann, *Friedrich von Hügel: sa vie, son oevre et ses amitiés*, Paris 1962.

3941 LUCAS. The life of Frederick Lucas, M.P. By Edward Lucas. 2 v. 1886.

Lucas was founder of *The Tablet* and an influential figure in Irish Catholic politics. See also Christopher James Riethmüller, *Frederick Lucas: a biography*, 1862.

3942 McCABE. Twelve years in a monastery. By Joseph McCabe. 1897. 3rd edn. 1912.

The widely-read autobiog. of an ex-priest. McCabe also publ. *A candid history of the Jesuits*, 1913, *The decay of the Church of Rome*, 1909, 3rd edn. 1911, and much else.

3943 MANNING. Life of Cardinal Manning, Archbishop of Westminster. By Edmund Sheridan Purcell. 2 v. 1895. 2nd [expurgated] edn. 2 v. 1896. 4th edn. 1896.

Still the best life, although it provoked a storm when it first appeared and provided ammunition for Lytton Strachey (**239**). Sir [John Randolph] Shane Leslie, *Henry Edward Manning: his life and labours*, 1921, is the best modern life. Arthur Wollaston Hutton, *Cardinal Manning*, 1892, has a useful bibliog. of Manning's works and is still worth reading. Joseph Raymond Gasquet, *Cardinal Manning*, 1896, is an interesting reply to Purcell. Vincent Alan McClelland, *Cardinal Manning: his public life and influence, 1865–92*, 1962, and A. E. Dingle and Brian Howard Harrison, 'Cardinal Manning as temperance reformer', *Hist. J.* xii (1969), 485–510, are good studies of Manning's public career. John Fitzsimons, ed., *Manning: Anglican and Catholic*, 1951, and David Newsome, *The parting of friends: the Wilberforces and Henry Manning*, Lond. & Camb., Mass. [title: *The Wilberforces and Henry Manning*] 1966, are chiefly concerned with events before 1851.

3944 NEWMAN. The life of John Henry, Cardinal Newman: based on his private journals and correspondence. By Wilfrid Philip Ward. 2 v. 1912.

Standard for Newman's Catholic period. Suppl. by Newman's own *Apologia pro vita sua . . .*, 1864, best used in Wilfrid Ward, ed., *Newman's Apologia pro vita sua: the two versions of 1864 & 1865; preceded by Newman's and Kingsley's pamphlets*, Lond. & N.Y. 1913, and *Autobiographical writings by John Henry Newman*, ed. by Henry Tristram, Lond. & N.Y. 1956. There is a large and increasing literature relating to Newman which is best approached through three excellent monographs, Louis Bouyer, *Newman: his life and spirituality*, trans. by James Lewis May, 1958, Arthur Dwight Culler, *The imperial intellect: a study of Newman's educational ideal*, New Haven, Conn. & Lond. 1955, and Charles Stephen Dessain, *John Henry Newman*, 1968, 2nd edn. 1971. There is also a large eulogistic life, Meriol Trevor, *Newman*, vol. 1: 'The pillar of the cloud'; vol. 2: 'Light in winter', 2 v. 1962. Henri Bremond, *The mystery of Newman*, trans. by H. C. Corrance, 1907, has been influential in provoking discussion. *The letters of John Henry Newman*, ed. by Muriel Spark and Derek Stanford, 1957, is a particularly useful selection. A complete edn. of Newman's *Letters and diaries* is in progress, ed. by Charles Stephen Dessain. The first vol. appeared in 1961. There is a convenient select bibliog. of earlier works in James Munro Cameron, *John Henry Newman*, 1956. Many of Newman's works were re-ed. by Charles Frederick Harrold in *A new edition of the works of John Henry Newman*, 8 v. N.Y. 1947–9, which was originally intended to incl. all the works in 12 v. Harrold's *John Henry Newman: an expository and critical study of his mind, thought and art*, Lond. & N.Y. 1945, may be regarded as an introduction to this edition. 2 v. of Newman's unpubl. sermons have been publ. by the Birmingham Oratory under the titles *Faith and prejudice . . .*, 1956, and *Catholic sermons of Cardinal Newman*, 1957. 3 v. of unpubl. papers are also being printed, beginning with Placid Murray, ed., *Newman the Oratorian: his unpublished Oratory papers*, Dublin 1970. The contrast between J. H. Newman and his brother is brought out by William Robbins, *The Newman brothers: an essay in comparative intellectual biography*, Lond. & Camb., Mass. 1966. See also Vincent Ferrer Blehl and Francis Xavier Connolly, eds., *Newman's apologia: a classic reconsidered*, N.Y. 1964; John Coulson and Arthur Macdonald Allchin, eds., *The rediscovery of Newman: an Oxford symposium*, 1967; *John Henry Newman: centenary essays*, 1945; Heinrich Fries and Werner Becker, eds., *Newman Studien*, Nürnberg 1948+; James Munro Cameron, *The night battle*, 1962; Hugh A. MacDougall, *The Acton–Newman relations: the dilemma of Christian liberalism*, N.Y. 1962; Jan Hendrik

Walgrave, _Newman the theologian: the nature of belief and doctrine as exemplified in his life and works_, trans. by Arthur Vincent Littledale, 1960; John Coulson, _Newman and the common tradition: a study in the language of church and society_, Oxf. 1970, and _Newman: a portrait restored: an ecumenical revaluation_, 1965; Vincent Ferrer Blehl, 'Newman and the missing miter', _Thought_ xxxv (1960), 110–23; David. J. De Laura, 'Matthew Arnold and John Henry Newman . . .', _Texas Studies in Literature and Language_ vi (1965), 573–702; J. Derek Holmes, 'Cardinal Newman and the Affirmation Bill', _Hist. Mag. of the Protestant Episcopal Church_ xxxvi (1967), 87–97, and 'Newman, Froude and Pattison . . .', _J. Religious Hist._ iv (1966–7), 28–38, and Josef Lewis Altholz, 'Newman and history', _Victorian Studs._ vii (1963–4), 285–94, with reply by Holmes, ibid. viii (1964–5), 271–7. The best critical accounts of Newman, unaffected by hagiography, are Henri Bremond, _The mystery of Newman_, trans. by George Tyrrell, 1910, and Sir Geoffrey Faber, _Oxford apostles_, 1933.

3945 STUART. Life and letters of Janet Erskine Stuart, Superior General of the Society of the Sacred Heart, 1857–1914. By Maud Monahan. 1923. New edn. 1931.

3946 TYRRELL. Autobiography and life of George Tyrrell. Ed. by Maude Dominica Mary Petre. 2 v. 1912.

Tyrrell was the leading Catholic modernist, eventually excommunicated. Maude Petre, _Modernism: its failure and its fruits_ [1918], _George Tyrrell's letters_, 1920, and _Von Hügel and Tyrrell: the story of a friendship . . ._, 1937, complete the 'official' life. For commentary see John Ratté, _Three modernists: Alfred Loisy, George Tyrrell, William L. Sullivan_, N.Y. 1967, Lond. etc. 1968; Johannes Jacobus Stam, _George Tyrrell, 1861–1909_, Utrecht 1938; James Lewis May, _Father Tyrrell and the modernist movement_, 1932; and Alfred Loisy, _George Tyrrell et Henri Bremond_, Paris 1936. There are many polemical commentaries.

3947 ULLATHORNE. The autobiography of Archbishop Ullathorne, with selections from his letters. 2 v. 1891–2.

A new edn. with an introduction by Sir [John Randolph] Shane Leslie was publ. as _From cabin-boy to archbishop: the autobiography of Archbishop Ullathorne, printed from the original draft_, 1941. There is a good life, Edward Cuthbert Butler, _The life and times of Bishop Ullathorne, 1806–1889_, 2 v. 1926. See also 3924.

3948 VAUGHAN. Life of Cardinal Vaughan. By John George Snead-Cox. 2 v. 1910.

See also Arthur McCormack, _Cardinal Vaughan: the life of the third Archbishop of Westminster . . ._, 1966, and Sir [John Randolph] Shane Leslie, ed., _Letters of Herbert, Cardinal Vaughan, to Lady Herbert of Lea, 1867 to 1903_, 1942.

3949 WILFRID WARD. The Wilfrid Wards and the transition. By Maisie Ward. 2 v. 1934–7.
Exceptionally good.

3950 W. G. WARD. William George Ward and the Catholic revival. By Wilfrid Philip Ward. 1893. 2nd edn. 1912.
A sequel to his _William George Ward and the Oxford movement_, 1889, 2nd edn. 1890.

**3951 WISEMAN.** The life and times of Cardinal Wiseman. By Wilfrid Philip Ward. 2 v. 1897.

Arthur Brian Fothergill, *Nicholas Wiseman*, Lond. & Garden City, Kans. 1963, and Denis Rolleston Gwynn, *Cardinal Wiseman*, 1929, give alternative views. Wiseman's *The religious and social position of Catholics in England*, Dublin 1864, is still worth reading. R. J. Schiefen, 'Some aspects of the controversy between Cardinal Wiseman and the Westminster chapter', *J. Eccles. Hist.* xxi (1970), 128–48, deals with a tiresome controversy.

## E. JEWS

### I. GENERAL

**3952 ROTH (CECIL).** Magna bibliotheca Anglo-Judaica: a bibliographical guide to Anglo-Jewish history. New edn. Jewish Hist. Soc. 1937.

Based on Joseph Jacobs and Lucien Wolf, *Bibliotheca Anglo-Judaica*, 1888. Additional material was pr. in the *Journal of Jewish bibliography*, N.Y. 1938+. Cont. by Ruth Pauline Lehmann, *Nova bibliotheca Anglo-Judaica: a bibliographical guide to Anglo-Jewish history, 1937–1960*, Jewish Hist. Soc. 1961.

**3953 ENCYCLOPAEDIA JUDAICA.** 16 v. Jerusalem. 1971–2.

**3954 ROTH (CECIL).** A history of the Jews in England. Oxf. 1941. 3rd edn. 1964.

To 1858 only. There is a good account of the Jews after 1858 in Albert Montefiore Hyamson, *A history of the Jews in England*, 1908, 2nd edn. 1928. The following sets of essays are valuable supplements to Roth and Hyamson: Vivian David Lipman, ed., *Three centuries of Anglo-Jewish history: a volume of essays*, Jewish Hist. Soc., Camb. 1961; James Picciotto, *Sketches of Anglo-Jewish history*, rev. and ed. by Israel Finestein, 1956; Lucien Wolf, *Essays in Jewish history*, ed. by Cecil Roth, 1934; Cecil Roth, *Essays and portraits in Anglo-Jewish history*, Phila. 1962; and John M. Shaftesley, ed., *Remember the days: essays on Anglo-Jewish history presented to Cecil Roth by members of the council of the Jewish Historical Society of England*, 1966. See also Stephen Aris, *The Jews in business*, 1971.

**3955 JEWISH HISTORICAL SOCIETY OF ENGLAND.** Transactions. 1893–4+. 1895+.

The society publ. *Miscellanies*, 1925+, and *Publications*, 1901+. There is much misc. information in *The Jewish year book*, 1896+ (from 1911 *The Jewish Chronicle year book*), the *Jewish Chronicle*, 1841+, and *Jewish social studs.*, N.Y. 1939+.

**3956 LIPMAN (VIVIAN DAVID).** Social history of the Jews in England, 1850–1950. 1954.

See also Maurice Freedman, ed., *A minority in Britain: social studies of the Anglo-Jewish community*, 1955.

**3957 GARTNER (LLOYD P.).** The Jewish immigrant in England, 1870–1914. 1960.

See also John Adrian Garrard, *The English and immigration: a comparative study of the Jewish influx, 1880–1910*, 1971. Bernard Homa, *A fortress in Anglo-Jewry: the story of the Machzike Hadath*, 1953, is an account of the reaction of the stricter Jews among the immigrants to the state of British Jewry.

3958  RUSSELL (CHARLES) *and* LEWIS (HARRY SAMUEL). The Jew in London: a study of racial character and present-day conditions. Being two essays prepared for the Toynbee Trustees. 1900.

3959  EMANUEL (CHARLES HERBERT LEWIS). A century and a half of Jewish history: extracted from the minute books of the London Committee of Deputies of British Jews. 1910.

3960  HYAMSON (ALBERT MONTEFIORE). The Sephardim of England: a history of the Spanish and Portuguese Jewish community, 1492–1951. 1951.

See also Neville Jonas Laski, *The laws and charities of the Spanish and Portuguese Jews congregation of London*, 1952.

3961  ROTH (CECIL). The great synagogue, London, 1690–1940. 1950.

See also Cecil Roth, *Records of the western synagogue, 1761–1932*, 1932, Arthur Barnett, *The western synagogue through two centuries (1761–1961)*, 1961, and Cecil Roth, *Archives of the united synagogue: report and catalogue*, 1930.

3962  LEVY (ARNOLD). History of the Sunderland Jewish community [1755–1955]. 1956.

Cp. Ernest Krausz, *Leeds Jewry: its history and social structure*, Jewish Hist. Soc., Camb. 1964, Percy Selvin Goldberg, *The Manchester congregation of British Jews, 1857–1957*, Manch. 1957, and Philip Ettinger, *'Hope Place' in Liverpool Jewry*, Liverpool 1930.

3963  ROTH (CECIL) *ed.* Anglo-Jewish letters (1158–1917). 1938.

3964  MODDER (MONTAGU FRANK). The Jew in the literature of England to the end of the 19th century. Phila. 1939.

3965  HENRIQUES (HENRY STRAUS QUIXANO). The Jews and the English law. Oxf. 1908.

3966  HYAMSON (ALBERT MONTEFIORE). Jew's College, London, 1855–1955. 1955.

Israel Wolf Slotki, *Seventy years of Hebrew education, 1880–1950* . . ., Manch. 1950, is a very formal account of the Jewish schools in Manchester.

3967  DUNLOP (JOHN). Memories of gospel triumphs among the Jews during the Victorian era. 1894.

See also **3433.**

## 2. BIOGRAPHY

3968  EMDEN (PAUL HERMAN). Jews of Britain: a series of biographies. [1944.]

3969  HYAMSON (ALBERT MONTEFIORE) *and others.* Anglo-Jewish notabilities: their arms and testamentary dispositions. Jewish Hist. Soc. 1949.

3970 BOLITHO ([HENRY] HECTOR) *ed.* Twelve Jews. 1934.
Incl. sketches of Lord Bearsted, Disraeli, Epstein, and Ludwig Mond.

3971 ARTHUR COHEN. Arthur Cohen: a memoir by his daughter [Lucy Cohen] for his descendents. 1919.

3972 ISRAEL COHEN. A Jewish pilgrimage: the autobiography of Israel Cohen. 1956.
A first-rate account of the Zionist movement.

3973 LOUISA COHEN. Changing faces: a memoir of Louisa, Lady Cohen. By her daughter, Hannah Floretta Cohen. 1937.

3974 GOLDSMID. Memoir of Sir Francis Henry Goldsmid, Bart., Q.C., M.P. By David Woolf Marks and Albert Löwy. 1879. 2nd edn. enlarged 1882.

3975 LEVI. Story of my life. The first ten years of my residence in England, 1845–1855. By Leone Levi. Priv. pr. 1888.

3976 MONTEFIORE. Diaries of Sir Moses and Lady Montefiore, comprising their life and work as recorded in their diaries from 1812 to 1883. With the addresses and speeches of Sir Moses, his correspondence . . . Ed. by Louis Loewe. 2 v. Lond. & Chicago. 1890.
The best biogs. are those of Lucien Wolf, 1884, Paul Goodman, Phila. 1925, and Josephine Kamm, 1960.

3977 ROTHSCHILD. The reign of the house of Rothschild. By Egon Caesar Corti, Count Corti. Trans. by Brian and Beatrix Lunn. 1928.
See also Lucy Cohen, *Lady de Rothschild and her daughters, 1821–1931*, 1935.

3978 SALOMONS. David Salomons. By Albert Montefiore Hyamson. 1939.

3979 WEIZMANN. Trial and error: the autobiography of Chaim Weizmann. 1949.
See also Meyer Wolf Weisgal and Joel Carmichael, eds., *Chaim Weizmann: a biography by several hands*, N.Y. 1963, and M. W. Weisgal, ed., *The letters and papers of Chaim Weizmann*, 1+v. 1968+.

3980 WOLFF. Joseph Wolff: his romantic life and travels. By Hurly Pring Palmer. 1935.

## F. FREETHINKERS

3981 McCABE (JOSEPH). A rationalist encyclopaedia: a book of reference on religion, philosophy, ethics and science. 1948.

3982 BURY (JOHN BAGNELL). A history of freedom of thought. 1913. 2nd edn. 1952.

**3983** BENN (ALFRED WILLIAM). The history of English rationalism in the nineteenth century. 2 v. 1906.

Benn's *Modern England: a record of opinion and action from the time of the French Revolution to the present day*, 2 v. 1908, is an attempt at a political hist. on rationalist lines. There is little in Constance E. Plumptre, *On the progress of liberty of thought during Queen Victoria's reign*, 1902, or in John Edwin McGee, *History of the British secular movement*, ed. by Emanuel Haldeman-Julius, Girard, Kans. 1948.

**3984** ROBERTSON (JOHN MACKINNON). A history of freethought in the nineteenth century. 2 v. 1929. 2 v. N.Y. 1930.
Good.

**3985** EROS (JOHN). 'The rise of organized freethought in mid-Victorian England'. *Sociological Rev.* New ser. ii (1954), 98–120.

A useful intro. to the subject. See also Francis Barrymore Smith, 'The atheist mission, 1840–1900', in Robson, *Ideas and Institutions* (**177**), 205–35, and Susan Budd, 'The loss of faith: reasons for unbelief among members of the secular movement in England, 1850–1950', *Past & Present* 36 (1967), 106–25.

**3986** COCKSHUT (ANTHONY OLIVER JOHN). The unbelievers: English agnostic thought, 1840–90. 1964.

**3987** TRIBE (DAVID HAROLD). 100 years of freethought. 1967.

**3988** WHYTE (ADAM GOWANS). The story of the R[ationalist] P[ress] A[ssociation], 1899–1949. 1949.

See also Frederick James Gould, *The pioneers of Johnson's court: a history of the Rationalist Press Association from 1899 onward*, 1929, rev. edn. 1935.

**3989** GOULD (FREDERICK JAMES). The history of the Leicester secular society. Leicester. 1900.

**3990** DAVIES (CHARLES MAURICE). Heterodox London: or, phases of free thought in the metropolis. 2 v. 1874–5.

**3991** BONNER (HYPATIA BRADLAUGH). Penalties upon opinion: or, some records of the laws of heresy and blasphemy. 1912. 3rd edn. 1934.

**3992** THE AGNOSTIC ANNUAL. 1884+.

Title changed to *The RPA annual*, 1908–26, *The rationalist annual*, 1927+.

**3993** NATIONAL REFORMER. 1860–93.

The most famous atheist publ., the work of Charles Bradlaugh. For other secularist js. see *The freethinker*, 1881+, *The secular review*, 1876–7, merged with *The secularist*, 1876–7, as *The secular review [and secularist]*, 1877–88, which became *The agnostic j.*, 1889–1907, *The free review*, 1893–7, cont. as *The university magazine and free review*, 1897–1900, and *[Watt's] Literary guide [and rationalist review]*, 1885–1956, cont. as *The humanist*, 1956+.

3994 BRADLAUGH (CHARLES) *and others.* The freethinker's text-book. N.d.

A coll. of notable secularist pamphlets. Cp. Charles Bradlaugh and George Jacob Holyoake, *Secularism, scepticism and atheism,* 1870.

3995 BRADLAUGH (CHARLES). Humanity's gain from unbelief, and other selections from the works of Charles Bradlaugh. Ed. by Hypatia Bradlaugh Bonner. The thinkers library no. 4. [1929.]

3996 READE (WILLIAM WINWOOD). The martyrdom of man. Lond. & Edin. 1872. Many edns.

One of the books most widely admired by freethinkers before Haeckel (**4000**).

3997 BESANT (ANNIE). The gospel of atheism. 1877.

3998 FOOTE (GEORGE WILLIAM) *and* BALL (W. P.) *eds.* The Bible handbook for freethinkers and inquiring Christians. 3 pts. 1885–7. New edn. 1900.

3999 STEPHEN (*Sir* LESLIE). An agnostic's apology. 1893. 2nd edn. 1903.

4000 HAECKEL (ERNST HEINRICH PHILIPP AUGUST). The riddle of the universe at the close of the nineteenth century. Trans. by Joseph McCabe. 1900.

See also Joseph McCabe, *Haeckel's critics answered,* 1903, 2nd edn. 1910.

4001 ROBERTSON (JOHN MACKINNON). Christianity and mythology. 1900. 2nd edn. 1910.

4002 WHYTE (ADAM GOWANS). The religion of the open mind. 1913.

4003 FORESTER (GEORGE) *pseud. of* GREENWOOD (*Sir* GRANVILLE GEORGE). The faith of an agnostic: or, first essays in rationalism. 1902. 2nd edn. 1919.

4004 McCABE (JOSEPH). A biographical dictionary of modern rationalists. 1920.

4005 COURTNEY (JANET ELIZABETH). Freethinkers of the nineteenth century. 1920.

Joseph Mazzini Wheeler, *A biographical dictionary of freethinkers of all ages and nations,* 1889, was a more popular work. See also Frederick James Gould, *Chats with pioneers of modern thought,* 1898.

4006 KNICKERBOCKER (FRANCIS WENTWORTH). Free minds: John Morley and his friends. Camb., Mass. 1943.

4007 ROBERTSON (JOHN MACKINNON). Modern humanists: socio-logical studies of Carlyle, Mill, Emerson, Arnold, Ruskin, and Spencer. 1891. 4th edn. 1908.

Robertson's second thoughts are set out in *Modern humanists reconsidered*, 1927.

4008 BRADLAUGH. Charles Bradlaugh: a record of his life and work. By Hypatia Bradlaugh Bonner. 2 v. 1894. 2nd edn. 1895.

David Harold Tribe, *President Charles Bradlaugh, M.P.*, 1971, is the latest life. W. L. Arnstein, *The Bradlaugh case* (**472**), is a good account of one part of his parl. career. The Bradlaugh centenary vol., James Pinkerton Gilmour, ed., *Champion of liberty: Charles Bradlaugh*, 1933, incl. a selection of his works. There are also brief lives by Adolphe S. Headingley, 1880, 2nd edn. 1883, and John Mackinnon Robertson, 1894 and 1920, and Chapman Cohen, *Bradlaugh and Ingersoll: a centenary appreciation of two great reformers*, 1933. Bradlaugh was a prolific writer and speaker. There are collected edns. of his *Political essays*, 3 v. 1891, *Theological essays*, 2 v. 1883, and *Speeches*, 1890, 2nd edn. 1895.

4009 HOLYOAKE. Sixty years of an agitator's life. By George Jacob Holyoake. 2 v. 1892.

Holyoake also publ. *Bygones worth remembering*, 2 v. 1905. Joseph McCabe, *Life and letters of George Jacob Holyoake*, 2 v. 1908, is a useful life based on these 4 v. of memoirs. See also Charles William Frederick Goss, *A descriptive bibliography of the writings of George Jacob Holyoake* . . ., 1908.

4010 BONNER. Hypatia Bradlaugh Bonner: the story of her life. By Arthur Bonner and Charles Bradlaugh Bonner. 1942.

4011 COHEN. Almost an autobiography: the confessions of a freethinker. By Chapman Cohen. 1940.

4012 SPILLER (GUSTAV). The ethical movement in Great Britain: a docu-mentary history. 1934.

A useful handbook. There is little of value in most of the general works such as Leo Jacobs, *Three types of practical ethical movements of the past half century*, N.Y. 1922.

4013 SOCIETY OF ETHICAL PROPAGANDISTS, *eds*. Ethics and religion: a collection of essays by Sir John Seeley, Dr. Felix Adler, Mr. W. M. Salter, Prof. Henry Sidgwick, Prof. G. von Gizycki, Dr. Bernard Bosanquet, Mr. Leslie Stephen, Dr. Stanton Coit, and Prof. J. H. Muirhead. 1900.

4014 RATCLIFFE (SAMUEL KERKHAM). The story of South Place. 1955.

The centre of the ethical societies. There is also Moncure Daniel Conway, *Centenary history of the South Place Society*, 1894.

4015 COIT. Stanton Coit, 1857–1944: selections from his writings. Ed. by Harold John Blackham. 1948.

4016 CONWAY. Autobiography, memories and experiences of Moncure Daniel Conway. 2 v. 1904.

See also Mary Elizabeth Burtis, *Moncure Conway, 1832–1907*, New Brunswick, N.J. 1953. Conway was for many years minister at South Place (**4014**).

## G. OCCULTISTS

### 1. General

4017 FODOR (NANDOR). Encyclopaedia of psychic science. [1934.] New edn. by Leslie Shepard. N.Y. 1966.

The 1966 edn. has useful bibliogs.

4018 DAVIES (CHARLES MAURICE). Mystic London: or, phases of occult life in the metropolis. 1875.

### 2. Theosophists

4019 RANSOM (JOSEPHINE). A short history of the Theosophical Society. . . . Adyar. 1938.

4020 FIVE YEARS OF THEOSOPHY: mystical, philosophical, theosophical, historical and scientific essays, selected from *The Theosophist*. 1885.

The *Theosophist* was publ. 1879–1929+. The *Transactions* of the London lodge of the Theosophical Society were publ. for 1884–1906 in 1913–16.

4021 SINNETT (ALFRED PERCY). The occult world. 1881. 3rd edn. 1883.

Sinnett became prominent in the theosophist movement. His other works were *Esoteric Buddhism*, 1883, 6th edn. 1888, *The growth of the soul*, 1896, 2nd edn. 1905, and *Collected fruits of occult teaching*, 1919.

4022 BLAVATSKY (HELENA PETROVNA). The secret doctrine: the synthesis of science, religion and philosophy. 2 v. 1888. New edn. in 4 pts., Point Loma, Calif. 1925.

The most influential work in theosophy. Blavatsky's other main works were *Isis unveiled: a master-key to the mysteries of ancient and modern science and theology*, 2 v. N.Y. 1877, rev. edn. 4 pts., Point Loma, Calif. 1919, *The key to theosophy: being a clear exposition, in the form of question and answer of the ethics, science and philosophy, for the study of which the Theosophical Society has been founded*, 1889, new edn. Los Angeles 1920. A new coll. edn. of *H. P. Blavatsky: collected writings*, ed. by Boris de Zirkoff, is in progress, publ. in Los Angeles and Adyar, 8 v.+, 1950–60+.

4023 BESANT. The first five lives of Annie Besant. By Arthur Hobart Nethercot. Chicago. 1960. Lond. 1961.

Good. Cont. in Nethercot's *The last four lives of Annie Besant*, 1963. Mrs. Besant herself publ. *An autobiography*, 1893. For her works and career see also Theodore Besterman, *A bibliography of Annie Besant*, 1924, *Mrs Annie Besant: a modern prophet* [1934], and *The mind of Annie Besant*, 1927; Esther Bright, *Old memories and letters of Annie Besant*, 1936; and Gertrude Marvin Williams, *The passionate pilgrim: a life of Annie Besant*, N.Y. 1931, Lond. 1932.

4024 BLAVATSKY. Personal memoirs of H. P. Blavatsky. Ed. by Mary Katherine Neff. 1937.

Autobiog. fragments. Contemporary hostilities in the theosophical movement are reflected in Emma Coulomb, *Some account of my intercourse with Madame Blavatsky* from *1872 to 1884*, 1885, and Alfred Percy Sinnett, *Incidents in the life of Madame Blavatsky . . .*, 1886, new edn. 1913. More or less favourable accounts of Blavatsky are given in William Kingsland, *The real H. P. Blavatsky*, 1928, Charles James Ryan, *H. P. Blavatsky and the Theosophical movement*, Point Loma, Calif. 1937, Josephine Ransom, *Madame Blavatsky as occultist*, 1931, and Gertrude Marvin Williams, *Priestess of the occult: Madame Blavatsky*, N.Y. 1946. John Symonds, *Madame Blavatsky: medium and magician*, 1959 [publ. as *The lady with the magic eyes*, N.Y. 1960], is a good popular biog., which compares well with older books such as Carl Eric Bechhofer-Roberts, *The mysterious Madame: a life of Madame Blavatsky*, 1931. Eugene Rollin Corson, *Some unpublished letters of Helena Petrovna Blavatsky* [1929], is intended to clear Blavatsky's name.

4025 WOOD. 'Is this theosophy . . .?' By Ernest Egerton Wood. 1936.

## 3. Spiritualists and Magicians

4026 NELSON (GEOFFREY KENNETH). Spiritualism and society. 1969.

A sketchy account of spiritualism as a form of sectarian worship.

4027 HALL (TREVOR HENRY). The spiritualists: the story of Florence Cook and William Crookes. 1962.

One of a number of debunking books by Hall. For others see **4039**.

4028 DOYLE (*Sir* ARTHUR CONAN). The history of spiritualism. 2 v. 1926.

By a spiritualist. Joseph McCabe, *Spiritualism: a popular history from 1847*, 1920, is by a rationalist.

4029 PODMORE (FRANK). Modern spiritualism: a history and a criticism. 2 v. 1902. Repr. as Mediums of the 19th century. 2 v. N.Y. 1963.

See also his *The newer spiritualism*, 1910, and **4043**.

4030 MYERS (FREDERIC WILLIAM HENRY). Human personality and its survival of bodily death. 2 v. 1903. Abridged edns. 1919. N.Y. 1954.

A spiritualist classic.

4031 LODGE (*Sir* OLIVER JOSEPH). The survival of man: a study in unrecognised human faculty. 1909.

Lodge, a noted scientist, made the most far-reaching claims for spiritualism, based on pseudo-scientific analysis. See also his *My philosophy: representing my views on the many functions of the ether of space*, 1933.

4032 KING (FRANCIS). Ritual magic in England: 1887 to the present day. 1970.

See also R. G. Torrens, *The inner teachings of the Golden Dawn*, 1970.

4033 CROWLEY. The spirit of solitude: an autohagiography. By Aleister Crowley. 2 v. 1929.

Abridged edn. in 1 v. by John Symonds and Kenneth Grant, entitled *The confessions of Aleister Crowley*, 1969. The best life is that of John Symonds, *The great beast: the life of Aleister Crowley*, 1951. See also Symonds's *The magic of Aleister Crowley*, 1958, and Charles Richard Cammell, *Aleister Crowley, the man, the mage, the poet*, 1951.

4034 HOME. Incidents in my life. By Daniel Dunglas Home. 1st ser. 1863. 2nd edn. 1864. 2nd ser. 1872.

Home also publ. *Lights and shadows of spiritualism*, 1877, 2nd edn. 1878. See also Mrs. Home's *D. D. Home: his life and mission*, 1888, new edn. by Sir Arthur Conan Doyle, 1921, and *The gift of D. D. Home*, 1890, Jean Burton, *Heyday of a wizard: Daniel Home the medium*, N.Y. 1944, Lond. 1948, and Windham Thomas Wyndham-Quin, Earl of Dunraven, *Experiences in spiritualism with Mr. D. D. Home*, 1871, repr. Glasgow 1924.

4035 STEAD. My father: personal & spiritual reminiscences. By Estelle Wilson Stead. 1913. New edn. 1918.

William Thomas Stead's most important spiritualist work was *Letters from Julia . . .*, 1898, enlarged edn. publ. as *After death . . .*, 1914. He also ed. the most important spiritualist j., *Borderland*, 1893–7, which must be consulted by all interested in the subject. For Stead's journalistic career see **5459**.

## 4. PSYCHICAL RESEARCH

Supposedly occult phenomena attracted the attention of some of the leading scientists and philosophers of the day, who hoped to use wave theories borrowed from physics to explain psychical phenomena, or to demonstrate the existence of non-material forces in the world. Among those involved were J. J. Thompson, Lord Rayleigh, Sir William Crookes, Henry Sidgwick and his wife, A. J. Balfour, and (less discriminatingly) Sir Oliver Lodge. The Society for Psychical Research developed as a meeting-ground for spiritualists and non-spiritualist scientists.

4036 BESTERMAN (THEODORE). Library catalogue of the Society for Psychical Research. Glasgow. 1927. 4 suppls. covering 1927–33.

The fullest list of English researches. Suppl. by Fodor (**4017**).

4037 SALTER (WILLIAM HENRY). The Society for Psychical Research: an outline of its history. 1948.

The *Proceedings*, 1883+, and *Journal*, 1884+, of the soc. are the main source for contemp. experiments. *Presidential addresses to the Society for Psychical Research, 1882–1911*, Glasgow 1912, is the most useful of the misc. publs. of the soc. The scientific tradition of the soc. is now represented by *The journal of parapsychology*, Durham, N.C. 1937+.

4038 GAULD (ALAN). The founders of psychical research. 1968.

4039 HALL (TREVOR HENRY). The strange case of Edmund Gurney. 1964.

One of a ser. of debunking books by Hall. See also Hall and John Lorne Campbell, *Strange things: the story of Fr. Allan McDonald, Ada Goodrich Freer, and the Society for Psychical Research's inquiry into Highland second sight*, 1968, and **4027**.

4040 BARRETT (*Sir* WILLIAM FLETCHER). Psychical research. Home Univ. Libr. 1911.

This work and Barrett's *On the threshold of the unseen: an examination of the phenomena of spiritualism and of the evidence of survival after death*, 1917, rev. edn. 1917, give the best introductions to contemp. ideas of the subject.

4041 BROAD (CHARLIE DUNBAR). Lectures on psychical research: including the Perrott Lectures given in Cambridge University in 1959 and 1960. Lond. & N.Y. 1962.

4042 GURNEY (EDMUND), MYERS (FREDERIC WILLIAM HENRY), *and* PODMORE (FRANK). Phantasms of the living. v. 1. 1886.

One of the first and most ambitious reports of the psychical researchers. Soon discredited.

4043 PODMORE (FRANK). Apparitions and thought transference: an examination of the evidence for telepathy. 1889. New edn. 1915.

A careful account of contemp. experiments. Podmore's main work was on spiritualism, **4029**.

4044 BESTERMAN (THEODORE). Crystal-gazing: a study in the history, distribution, theory and practice of scrying. 1924.

4045 BARRETT (*Sir* WILLIAM FLETCHER) *and* BESTERMAN (THEODORE). The divining rod: an experimental and psychological investigation. 1926.

Excellent bibliog. Suppl. by Besterman's *Water-divining: new facts and theories*, 1938.

4046 BRAMWELL (JOHN MILNE). Hypnotism: its history, practice and theory. 1903. 3rd edn. 1913.

Bramwell was the leading practitioner of medical hypnosis and publ. other books on the subject.

4047 PODMORE (FRANK). Mesmerism and Christian science: a short history of mental healing. 1909.

4048 CARRINGTON (HEREWARD) *and* FODOR (NANDOR). The story of the poltergeist down the centuries. 1953.

Popular. But incls. chronological list of poltergeists.

## H. OTHER GROUPS

4049 HUMPHREYS (TRAVERS CHRISTMAS). The development of Buddhism in England. Being a history of the Buddhist movement in London and the provinces. 1937.

4050 BRITISH ISRAELITES. John Wilson, 'British Israelitism . . .' in B. R. Wilson, ed., *Patterns of sectarianism* (**3740**), 345–76. Mary Hazell Gayer, *The heritage of the Anglo-Saxon race*, 1928, 2nd edn. 1939. Henry Leighton Goudge, *The British Israel theory*, Lond. & Oxf. 1933. Bede Frost, i.e. Albert Ernest Frost, *Some modern substitutes for Christianity*, 1942.

# VII

## ECONOMIC HISTORY

### A. GENERAL

#### I. REFERENCE

4051 PALGRAVE (*Sir* ROBERT HENRY INGLIS) *ed*. Dictionary of political economy. 3 v. 1894–9. Rev. edn. by Henry Higgs. 1923–6. Repr. N.Y. 1963.

Convenient for many topics.

4052 URE (ANDREW). A dictionary of arts, manufactures and mines. 1839. 7th edn. by Robert Hunt and others. 4 v. 1875–8.

To be suppl. by Peter Lund Simmonds, ed., *Waterston's cyclopaedia of commerce*, 1863, George Guillinane André and Charles George Warnford Lock, eds., *Spon's encyclopaedia of the industrial arts, manufactures and commercial products*, 5 v. 1879–82, Charles Tomlinson, ed., *Cyclopaedia of useful arts . . .*, 2 v. 1852–4, new edn. 1870, John Weale, *Rudimentary dictionary of terms used in architecture, civil and naval, building and construction, early and ecclesiastical art, engineering . . .*, 2 v. 1849–50, 5th edn. 1876.

4053 AMERICAN ECONOMIC ASSOCIATION. Index of economic journals. 1886+. Homewood, Ill. 1961+.

Selective coverage only of British js.

4054 PUBLIC RECORD OFFICE. List of Board of Trade records, to 1913. P.R.O. Supplementary lists and indexes XI. N.Y. & Lond. 1964.

4055 PUBLIC RECORD OFFICE. List of the records of the Board of Customs and Excise from 1697. List and Index Soc. Vol. 20. 1967.

4056 COBB (HENRY STEPHEN). 'Sources for economic history amongst the parliamentary records in the House of Lords Record Office'. *Econ. Hist. Rev.* 2 ser. xix (1966), 154–74.

4057 BUSINESS ARCHIVES COUNCIL. The first five hundred: chronicles and house histories of companies and organisations in the Business Archives Library. 1959.

For London-based companies see also 9446, and Chartered Inst. of Secretaries, *A list of company histories in the Chartered Institute of Secretaries Library*, 1957. For Lancashire companies see 9540. Theodore Cardwell Barker and others, *Business history*, Hist. Assoc. Helps for students 59, 1960, is an excellent guide to the subject. The house js. of indiv. firms often publ. hist. material: for a list see British Association of Industrial Editors, *British house journals*, 1956.

4058 HISTORICAL MANUSCRIPTS COMMISSION (NATIONAL REGISTER OF ARCHIVES). Sources of business history in the National Register of Archives. 1+. 1964+. Irregular.

4059 COURT (WILLIAM HENRY BASSANO). British economic history, 1870–1914: commentary and documents. Camb. 1965.

An excellent coll. of docs.

4060 BRITISH AND FOREIGN TRADE AND INDUSTRY. Memoranda, statistical tables and charts, prepared in the Board of Trade, with reference to various matters bearing on British and foreign trade and industrial conditions. [First series] [Cd. 1761] H.C. (1903). LXVII, 253. Second series. [Cd. 2337] H.C. (1905). LXXXIV, 1. Index to both series. [Cd. 2669] H.C. (1905). LXXXIV, 669. Statistical tables for 1854 to 1908 cont. the above. [Cd. 4954] H.C. (1909). CII, 693.

A useful set of statistics, though the tables in Mitchell and [Deane (125) are often easier to use.

4061 BOARD OF TRADE. Memorandum on the comparative statistics of population, industry, and commerce in the United Kingdom and some leading foreign countries. [Cd. 1199] H.C. (1902). XCVIII, pt. II, 609.

See also *Charts . . . illustrating the statistics of trade, employment and conditions of labour in the United Kingdom prepared for the St. Louis exhibition*. [Cd. 2145] H.C. (1904). LXXIX, 495. For earlier comparative data see Georg Friedrich Kolb, *The condition of nations, social and political*, trans. by Emma Brewer and ed. by Edwin William Streeter, 1880, and Michael George Mulhall, *Industries and wealth of nations*, 1896.

4062 BOARD OF TRADE. Return for the United Kingdom for each of the years 1801, 1811, 1821, 1831, 1841, 1851, 1861, 1871, 1881, 1891, 1901, and 1902, showing condition of trade and people under various heads. H.C. 340 (1903). LXIV, 247.

Similar return with 1906+ substituted for 1902, H.C. 294 (1907). LXXVI, 1025, and irregularly to 1914. For fuller details see George Richardson Porter, *The progress of the nation in its various social and economic relations from the beginning of the nineteenth century*, ed. by Francis Wrigley Hirst, 1912.

4063 BOARD OF TRADE. Tables of revenue, population and commerce. 1833+.

Known as 'Porter's tables' because the ser. was inaugurated by G. R. Porter. Issued as parl. papers. See also **127**.

### 2. Histories

4064 THE CAMBRIDGE ECONOMIC HISTORY OF EUROPE. Vol. VI in 2 v. The industrial revolutions and after. Ed. by Hrothgar John Habakkuk and Moisei Postan. Camb. 1965.

A good up-to-date survey.

4065 POLLARD (SIDNEY) *and* CROSSLEY (DAVID WYATT). The wealth of Britain, 1085–1966. 1968.

The only 1-v. account of the whole of English econ. hist. aimed at the general reader. For schools Michael Walter Flinn, *An economic and social history of Britain, 1066–1939*, 1961, is useful.

4066 CARUS-WILSON (ELEANORA MARY) *ed.* Essays in economic history. 3 v. 1954–62.

Articles repr. from a variety of js. for the Econ. Hist. Soc.

4067 CLAPHAM (*Sir* JOHN HAROLD). An economic history of modern Britain. 3 v. Camb. 1926–38. 2nd edn. of v. 1. Camb. 1930. Repr. 1951–64.

Comprehensive. The starting-point for most subsequent discussions on the development of the economy.

4068 MATHIAS (PETER). The first industrial nation: an economic history of Britain, 1700–1914. Lond. & N.Y. 1969.

A straightforward short hist. William Henry Bassano Court, *A concise economic history of Britain from 1750 to recent times*, Camb. 1954, and reprs., is a good alternative. Eric John Hobsbawm, *Industry and empire: an economic history of Britain since 1750*, 1968, is a general survey. Michael Walter Flinn, *An economic and social history of Britain since 1700*, 1963, though designed for schools, is also a good book, and is suppl. by Flinn's *Readings in economic and social history*, 1964. Gwilym Peredur Jones and Arthur George Pool, *A hundred years of economic development in Great Britain*, Lond. & N.Y. 1940, and Walter Marcel Stern, *Britain yesterday and today: an outline economic history from the middle of the eighteenth century*, 1962, are generally less useful. Charles Ryle Fay, *Great Britain from Adam Smith to the present day: an economic and social survey*, 1928, 5th edn. 1950, is a stimulating work, now dated but worth consulting. Among older hists. the most interesting were William Cunningham, *The growth of English industry and commerce*, Camb. 1882, 5th edn. 2 v. in 3 1910–12, and Lujo Brentano, *Eine Geschichte der wirtschaftlichen Entwicklung Englands*, 3 v. in 4, Jena 1927–9.

4069 DEANE (PHYLLIS) *and* COLE (WILLIAM ALAN). British economic growth, 1688–1959. Camb. 1962. 2nd edn. 1967.

An important study. For commentary see especially J. F. Wright, *Econ. Hist. Rev.* 2 ser. xviii (1965), 397–412, and Brinley Thomas, 'The dimensions of British economic growth, 1688–1959', *Royal Stat. Soc. J.* ser. A. cxxvii (1964), 111–23. See also **4083–4**.

4070 PAGE (WILLIAM) *ed.* Commerce and industry: a historical review of the economic conditions of the British Empire from the Peace of Paris in 1815 to the declaration of war in 1914, based on parliamentary debates. 2 v. 1919.

Vol. II contains the main economic statistics of the period.

4071 MULHALL (MICHAEL GEORGE). Fifty years of national progress, 1837–1887. 1887.

4072 CHECKLAND (SYDNEY GEORGE). 'Growth and progress: the nineteenth-century view in Britain'. *Econ. Hist. Rev.* xii (1959–60), 49–62.

See also Pollard, *The idea of progress* (**8538**), and Reginald Earle Welby, Baron Welby, 'The progress of the United Kingdom from the war of the French revolution to 1913'. *Royal Stat. Soc. J.* lxxviii (1915), 1–31.

4073 BREBNER (JOHN BARTLET). 'Laissez-faire and state intervention in nineteenth-century Britain'. *J. Econ. Hist.* viii (1948), Suppl. 59–73. Repr. in Carus-Wilson (**4066**) III, 252–62.

An important revision article. See also R. L. Crouch, 'Laissez faire in nineteenth-century Britain: myth or reality?', *Manch. School* xxxv (1967), 199–215.

4074 ROSTOW (WALT WHITMAN). British economy of the nineteenth century. Oxf. 1948.

Stimulating essays which have set the tone for much subsequent debate, but are now regarded as over-simplified. For an attack on the book see John Saville, 'A comment . . .', *Past & Present* 6 (1954), 66–81.

4075 CHECKLAND (SYDNEY GEORGE). The rise of industrial society in England, 1815–1885. 1964.

A comprehensive survey, strong on economic organization. Jonathan David Chambers, *The workshop of the world: British economic history from 1820 to 1880*, 1961, is a good short hist.

4076 HUGHES (JONATHAN ROBERTS TYSON). Fluctuations in trade, industry and finance: a study of British economic development, 1850–1860. Oxf. 1960.

A good detailed analysis.

4077 KINDLEBERGER (CHARLES POOR). Economic growth in France and Britain, 1851–1950. Camb., Mass. 1964.

An important analysis of the literature of development.

4078 ASHWORTH (WILLIAM). An economic history of England, 1870–1939.

The best general work on the period. Derek Howard Aldcroft and Harry Ward Richardson, *The British economy, 1870–1939*, 1969, is a discussion of important issues. Ernest Henry Phelps Brown and Bernard Weber, 'Accumulation, productivity and distribution in the British economy, 1870–1938', *Econ. J.* lxiii (1953), 263–88, repr. in Carus-Wilson, *Essays* (4066) III, 280–301, has much useful data.

4079 SAVILLE (JOHN) ed. Studies in the British economy, 1870–1914. *Yorkshire Bull.*, special number, xvii (1965), no. 1.

4080 BROWN (ERNEST HENRY PHELPS) and HANDFIELD-JONES (S. J.). 'The climacteric of the 1890's: a study in the expanding economy'. *Oxf. Econ. Papers.* iv (1952), 266–307.

Raised important issues about the great depression, taken up by Dennis John Coppock, 'The climacteric of the 1890s: a critical note', *Manch. School* xxiv (1956), 1–31. See also Eric Milton Sigsworth and Janet Blackman, 'The home boom of the 1890s', *Yorkshire Bull.* xvii (1965), 75–97.

4081 BEALES (HUGH LANCELOT). 'The "great depression" in industry and trade'. *Econ. Hist. Rev.* v, pt. 1 (1934–5), 65–75.

Began the modern discussion of the subject. Repr. in Carus-Wilson, *Essays* (4066) I, 406–15. See also Walt Whitman Rostow, 'Explanations of the "great depression", 1873–96: an historian's view of modern monetary theory', *Econ. Hist.* iv (1938–40), 356–70; Albert Edward Musson, 'The great depression in Britain, 1873–1896: a reappraisal', *J. Econ. Hist.* xix (1959), 199–228; Dennis John Coppock, 'The causes of the great depression, 1873–96', *Manch. School* xxix (1961), 205–32, with reply by John Saville, ibid. xxxi (1963), 47–71; Coppock's 'British industrial growth during the "great depression", 1873–96: a pessimist's view', *Econ. Hist. Rev.* 2 ser. xvii (1964–5), 389–96; and Musson's 'British industrial growth, 1873–96: a balanced view', ibid.

397–403; Harry Ward Richardson, 'Retardation in Britain's industrial growth, 1870–1913', *Scot. J. Pol. Econ.* xii (1965), 125–49; John Robert Meyer, 'An input-output approach to evaluating British industrial production in the late nineteenth century', in Alfred Haskell Conrad and John Robert Meyer, *Studies in econometric history*, 1965, pp. 183–220; Donald F. Wahl, 'Capital, labor and energy requirements for United Kingdom foreign trade, 1907', *Explorations in entrepreneurial hist.* 2 ser. iii (1965–6), 39–49; Derek Howard Aldcroft, 'The entrepreneur and the British economy, 1870–1914', *Econ. Hist. Rev.* 2 ser. xvii (1964–5), 113–34; 'Technical progress and British enterprise, 1875–1914', *Business Hist.* viii (1966), 122–39, 'Factor prices and the rate of innovation in Britain, 1875–1914', ibid. ix (1967), 126–31, and 'British industry and foreign competition' in *The development of British industry* (**4752**); and Donald Nansen McCloskey, ed., *Essays on a mature economy: Britain after 1840: papers and proceedings of the MSSB conference on the new economic history of Britain, 1840–1930*, 1971.

4082 WILSON (CHARLES HENRY). 'Economy and society in late Victorian Britain'. *Econ. Hist. Rev.* 2 ser. xviii (1965), 183–98. Repr. in his Economic history and the historian: collected essays. 1969.

An attempt at a detached view of the controversy over the great depression. For other discussions of the controversy see William Ashworth, 'The late Victorian economy', *Economica* new ser. xxxiii (1966), 17–33, Samuel Berrick Saul, *The myth of the 'great depression', 1873–1896*, 1969, Alec George Ford, 'British economic fluctuations, 1870–1914', *Manch. School* xxxvii (1969), 99–129, Levine (**4755**), and Donald Nansen McCloskey, 'Did Victorian England fail?', *Econ. Hist. Rev.* 2 ser. xxiii (1970), 446–59.

### 3. NATIONAL INCOME

4083 FEINSTEIN (CHARLES HILLIARD). National income, expenditure and output of the United Kingdom, 1855–1965. Camb. 1972.

4084 DEANE (PHYLLIS). 'Contemporary estimates of national income in the second half of the nineteenth century'. *Econ. Hist. Rev.* 2 ser. ix (1956–7), 451–61.

A useful summary of the lit. of the subject, with a brief discussion of the rate of growth of the economy. See also Deane and Cole, *British Economic Growth* (**4069**), and Phyllis Deane, 'New estimates of gross national product for the United Kingdom, 1830–1914', *Rev. Income & Wealth* xiv (1968), 95–112.

4085 PREST (ALAN RICHMOND). 'National income of the United Kingdom, 1870–1946'. *Econ. J.* lviii (1948), 31–62.

4086 JEFFERYS (JAMES BAVINGTON) and WALTERS (DOROTHY). 'National income and expenditure of the United Kingdom, 1870–1952'. *Income and Wealth Ser.*, v (1956).

4087 BOWLEY (*Sir* ARTHUR LYON) and STAMP (JOSIAH CHARLES), *Baron Stamp*. Three studies on the national income. 1938.

A repr. of Bowley's *The division of the product of industry: an analysis of national income before the war*, Oxf. 1919, and *The change in the distribution of the national income, 1880–1913*, Oxf. 1920, and of Bowley and Stamp's *The national income, 1924: a comparative study of the income of the United Kingdom in 1911 and 1924*, Oxf. 1927. Bowley's *Wages and income in the United Kingdom since 1860* (**6539**), covers a wider range, as does Stamp's *British incomes and property: the application of official statistics to economic problems*, 1916.

4088  BAXTER (ROBERT DUDLEY). National income: the United Kingdom. 1868.

Cont. in his *Taxation of the United Kingdom*, 1869, and *National debts*, 1871. Baxter, the pathfinder in the field, is generally more reliable than Leone Levi, *Wages and earnings of the working classes* . . ., 1867, or the later survey publ. by Levi under the same title in 1885.

4089  GOSCHEN (GEORGE JOACHIM), *Viscount Goschen*. 'The increase of moderate incomes'. *Royal Stat. Soc. J.* 1 (1887), 589–612.

4090  SMART (WILLIAM). The distribution of income: being a study of what the national wealth is and of how it is distributed according to economic worth. 1899. 2nd edn. 1912.

4091  DOUGLAS (PAUL H.). 'An estimate of the growth of capital in the United Kingdom, 1865–1909'. *J. Econ. & Business Hist.* ii (1929–30), 659–84.

4092  LENFANT (J. H.). 'Great Britain's capital formation, 1865–1914'. *Economica* new ser. xviii (1951), 151–68.

4093  GIFFEN (*Sir* ROBERT). The growth of capital. 1889.

See also his 'Accumulations of capital in the United Kingdom in 1875–85', *Roy. Stat. Soc. J. liii* (1890), 1–35.

4094  DANIELS (GEORGE WILLIAM) *and* CAMPION (*Sir* HARRY). The distribution of national capital. Manch. 1936.

4095  HARRIS (WILLIAM J.) *and* LAKE (KENNETH A.). 'Estimates of the realisable wealth of the United Kingdom, based mostly on the estate duty returns'. *Roy. Stat. Soc. J.* lxix (1906), 709–32.

See also Bernard Mallet, 'A method of estimating capital wealth from the estate duty statistics', *Roy. Stat. Soc. J.* lxxi (1908), 65–84.

4096  LANGLEY (KATHLEEN M.). 'An analysis of the asset structure of estates, 1900–1949'. *Oxf. Inst. Stats. Bull.* xiii (1951), 339–56.

### 4. BOARD OF TRADE

The position of the Board of Trade was a difficult one. For overseas information it was largely dependent on the goodwill of the Foreign Office. At home it was largely a catch-all for miscellaneous statistical and regulatory functions. Its statistical dept. became famous as a result of the work of Sir Robert Giffen. Its railway department (for whose hist. see **6208**) and its harbour and marine department, were in effect quasi-independent offices. To these at the beginning of the 20th cent. were added further offices for administering labour exchanges and national insurance. Nevertheless the Board did exercise a general oversight over all aspects of the economy.

4097 PROUTY (ROGER). The transformation of the Board of Trade, 1830–1855: a study of the administrative reorganization in the heyday of laissez faire. 1957.

There is no general hist. of the Board. But there is much misc. information in Sir Hubert Llewellyn Smith, *The Board of Trade*, Whitehall ser. 1928. For records see **4054**.

4098 FARRER (THOMAS HENRY), *Baron Farrer*. The state in its relation to trade. 1883. New edn. 1902.

Publ. while Farrer was Perm. Sec. of the Board of Trade. Sums up the free trade policies of the period.

4099 BOARD OF TRADE ESTABLISHMENTS. Copy of correspondence between the Treasury and the Board of Trade relative to the establishment of the latter office, including a report by the Right Honourable Stephen Cave and Mr. G. Ward Hunt. H.C. 47 (1867). XXXIX, 213.

Incl. a description of the organization of the department.

4100 JERSEY COMMITTEE ON THE BOARD OF TRADE AND LOCAL GOVERNMENT BOARD. Report of the committee appointed to consider the position and duties of the Board of Trade and of the Local Government Board [Chairman: Earl of Jersey]. [Cd. 2121] H.C. (1904). LXXVIII, 439.

4101 FARRER. Some Farrer memorials: being a selection from the papers of Thomas Henry, first Lord Farrer, 1819–1899, on various matters . . . By his son Thomas Cecil Farrer, Baron Farrer. Priv. pr. 1923.

4102 MALLET. Sir Louis Mallet: a record of public service and political ideals. By Sir Bernard Mallet. 1905.

Sir Louis served at the Board of Trade, 1847–74.

### 5. PATENTS AND TRADE-MARKS

4103 MACHLUP (FRITZ) *and* PENROSE (EDITH). 'The patent controversy in the nineteenth century'. *J. Econ. Hist.* x (1950), 1–29.

On England, France, Germany, Holland, Switzerland, *c.* 1850–75.

4104 FOX (HAROLD GEORGE). Monopolies and patents: a study of the history and future of the patent monopoly. Toronto. 1947.

4105 LADAS (STEPHEN PERICLES). The international protection of industrial property. Camb., Mass. 1930.

A hist. of the International Union for the Protection of Industrial Property from 1883. Deals with international recognition of patent rights.

4106 BOEHM (KLAUS) *and* SILBERSTON (AUBREY). The British patent system. 1. Administration. Univ. of Camb. Dept. of Applied Econ. Monograph 13. Camb. 1967.

Little hist. but useful. Some of the hist. of the system may be found in Barbara M. D. Smith, 'Patents for invention: the national and local picture', *Business Hist.* iv (1961–2), 109–19, Allan A. Gomme, *Patents of invention: origin and growth of the patent system in Britain*, 1946, William Martin, *The English patent system*, 1904, and Kenneth Raydon Swan, *The law and commercial usage of patents, designs and trade marks*, 1908.

4107  HARDING (HERBERT). Patent Office centenary: a story of 100 years in the life and work of the Patent Office. 1953.

For the organization of the office in the 1850s see also *Report from the select committee on the Patent Office library and museums* [Chairman: Lewis Llewelyn Dillwyn]. H.C. 504. (1864). XII, 1; *Reports made to the commissioners of patents by Mr. Hindmarsh, Q.C., and Mr. Greenwood, Q.C., the commissioners appointed to institute inquiries in reference to the Patent Office accounts* . . . H.C. 173 (1865). XLIII, 495; and *Report from the select committee of the House of Lords appointed to inquire into all the circumstances connected with the resignation by Mr. Edmunds of the offices of clerk of the patents and clerk to the commissioners of patents* . . . [Chairman: Earl Granville]. H.C. 294 (1865). IX, 1. For the later organization of the office see the reports of the Stanley, Samuelson, and Herschell committees (**4111–13**).

4108  ROGERS (JAMES EDWIN THOROLD). 'On the rationale and working of the patent laws'. *Stat. Soc. J.* xxvi (1863), 121–42.

4109  MACFIE (ROBERT ANDREW) *ed.* Recent discussions on the abolition of patents for inventions in the United Kingdom, France, Germany and the Netherlands . . . 1869.

Macfie was the leading patent abolitionist. See also his *The patent question: a solution of difficulties by abolishing or shortening the inventor's monopoly and instituting national recompenses* [1863], *Copyright and patents for inventions: pleas and plans for cheaper books and greater industrial freedom* . . ., 1879, and other works. There is a reply to his *The patent question* in W. H. Bailey, *The patent laws defended* . . ., Manch. 1872. Other contemp. pamphlets on the subject incl. William Spence, *Patentable invention and scientific evidence* . . ., 1851, *Practical remarks on the law of patents*, 1852, 2nd edn. 1856, and *The public policy of a patent law* . . ., 1869, Henry Dircks, *The policy of a patent law* . . ., 1869, and Matthew A. Soul, *Reform of the patent law, a working man's question* . . ., 1869.

4110  LORDS COMMITTEE ON PATENT LAW AMENDMENT BILLS Report and minutes of evidence taken before the select committee of the House of Lords appointed to consider of the bill intituled 'An Act further to amend the law touching letters patent for inventions . . .' [Chairman: Earl Granville]. H.C. 486 (1851). XVIII, 233.

4111  STANLEY COMMISSION ON PATENT LAW. Report of the commissioners appointed to inquire into the working of the law relating to letters patent for inventions [Chairman: Lord Stanley]. [3419] H.C. (1864). XXIX, 321.

4112  SAMUELSON COMMITTEE ON LETTERS PATENT. Report from the select committee on letters patent [Chairman: Bernhard Samuelson]. H.C. 368 (1871). X, 603. Further report. H.C. 193 (1872). XI, 395.

4113 HERSCHELL COMMITTEE ON PATENT OFFICE. Report of the committee appointed by the Board of Trade to inquire into the duties, organisation and arrangements of the Patent Office under the Patents, Designs and Trade Marks Act, 1883, having special regard to the system of examination of the specifications which accompany applications for patents . . . [Chairman: Lord Herschell]. [C. 4968] H.C. (1887). LXVI, 495. Further report on trade marks and designs. [C. 5350] H.C. (1888). LXXXI, 37.

For patent agents see *Special report from the select committee on Patent Agents Bill* [Chairman: Thomas Henry Bolton]. H.C. 235. (1894). XIV, 247.

4114 HOPWOOD COMMITTEE ON DEVELOPMENT OF PATENT OFFICE. Report of the committee appointed by the Board of Trade to consider various suggestions which have been made for developing the benefits afforded by the Patent Office to inventors [Chairman: Francis John Stephens Hopwood]. [Cd. 210] H.C. (1900). XXVI, 821.

4115 FRY COMMITTEE ON PATENT ACTS. Report of the committee appointed by the Board of Trade to inquire into the working of the Patent Acts on certain specified questions [Chairman: Sir Edward Fry]. [Cd. 506] H.C. (1901). XXIII, 599. Appendix. [Cd. 530] H.C. (1901). XXIII, 611.

4116 PATENT OFFICE. The commissioners of patents' journal. 1854–83.

Cont. as *The official j. of the Patent Office*, 1884–8, and *The illustrated official j. (patents)*, 1889–1931. Suppl. by *The illustrated j. of patented inventions*, 1884–5, which became *The illustrated j. of the Patent Office*, 1886–9, and *The illustrated official j. (patents): abridgments of patented inventions*, 1889–1931. Further suppl. by *Reports of patent cases* [title varies], 1884+, 1889+, and *Trade marks j.: list of applications for the registration of trade marks . . .*, 1876+.

4117 WOODCROFT (BENNET). Subject matter index (made from titles only) of patents of invention from March 2, 1617 . . . to October 1, 1852 . . . Commissioners of Patents. 2 pts. 1854–7.

Woodcroft's *Alphabetical index . . .*, 1854, was repr. 1969. The ser. was cont. by Patent Office, *Subject-matter index of patents applied for and patents granted* [title varies], 1852+, 1855+.

4118 COMPTROLLER-GENERAL OF PATENTS. Report. 1884+.

4119 [CHARTERED] INSTITUTE OF PATENT AGENTS. Transactions. 1882+.

The Inst. also publ. *The register of patent agents . . .*, 1889+.

4120 SEBASTIAN (LEWIS BOYD). The law of trade marks and their registration, and matters connected therewith. 1878. 5th edn. 1911.

See also Sir Duncan Mackenzie Kerly, *The law of trade marks, trade-name and merchandise-marks*, 1894, 9th edn. 1966.

4121 ROEBUCK COMMITTEE ON TRADE MARKS BILL. Report from the select committee on Trade Marks Bill and Merchandize Marks Bill [Chairman: John Arthur Roebuck]. H.C. 212 (1862). XII, 431.

**4122 DE WORMS COMMITTEE ON MERCHANDISE MARKS ACT,** 1862. Special report from the select committee on Merchandise Marks Act (1862) Amendment Bill [Chairman: Baron Henry De Worms]. H.C. 203 (1887). X, 357.

**4123 DE WORMS COMMITTEE ON MERCHANDISE MARKS ACT,** 1887. Report from the select committee on Merchandise Marks Act, 1887 [Chairman: Baron Henry De Worms]. H.C. 334 (1890). XV, 19.

A careful inquiry. There was also a special inquiry into trade marks on files: *Special report from the select committee on Merchandise Marks (Files) Bill* [Chairman: Charles Henry Hopwood]. H.C. 335 (1895). XII, 11.

**4124 ONSLOW COMMITTEE ON MARKING OF FOREIGN AND COLONIAL PRODUCE.** Report from the select committee on marking of foreign meat, &c. [Chairman: Earl of Onslow.] H.C. 214 (1893–4). XII, 341. Further report. H.C. 293 (1894). XIV, 109.

**4125 FERGUSSON COMMITTEE ON MERCHANDISE MARKS.** Report from the select committee on merchandise marks [Chairman: Sir James Fergusson]. H.C. 346 (1897). XI, 29.

Comparable in scope with the report of the De Worms Committees.

**4126 CRIPPS COMMITTEE ON TRADE MARKS BILL.** Report and special report from the select committee on the Trade Marks Bill [Chairman: C. A. Cripps]. H.C. 231 (1905). VIII, 257.

Another careful inquiry.

## 6. EXHIBITIONS

International exhibitions were important as pace-setters in design and show-places of industry, and great runs of official catalogues and reports were publ. Works listed here give details of British exhibits at major industrial exhibitions. See also the works on the International Fisheries Exhibition (**5822**), and the Colonial and Indian Exhibition, **1223**.

**4127 LUCKHURST (KENNETH WILLIAM).** The story of exhibitions. 1951.

A useful summary. See also the list of 'International exhibitions [1851–1907]', *Royal Soc. of Arts J.* lv (1906–7), 1140–6, Sir Patrick Geddes, *Industrial exhibitions and modern progress*, Edin. 1887, and H. Georges Berger, *Les expositions universelles internationales...*, Paris 1902. British policy toward such exhibitions was discussed (belatedly) in *Report of the committee appointed by the Board of Trade to make enquiries with reference to the participation of Great Britain in great international exhibitions* [Chairman: Sir Alfred Bateman]. [Cd. 3772] H.C. (1908). XLIX, 1. Minutes of evidence. [Cd. 3773] H.C. (1908). XLIX, 71.

**4128 FAY (CHARLES RYLE).** Palace of industry, 1851: a study of the great exhibition and its fruits. Camb. 1951.

One of a number of popular books produced to commemorate the centenary of the exhibition. Others were Kenneth William Luckhurst, *The great exhibition of 1851*, 1951,

Yvonne Ffrench, *The great exhibition, 1851,* 1950, Patrick John Fielding Howarth, *The year is 1851,* 1951, Charles Harvard Gibbs-Smith, comp., *The great exhibition of 1851: a commemorative album,* V. & A. Museum, 1950. In addition Asa Briggs publ. a useful general pamphlet, *1851,* for the Hist. Assoc., 1951.
An earlier book, Christopher Bernard Hobhouse, *1851 and the Crystal Palace: being an account of the great exhibition and its contents . . .,* 1937, was reissued in a rev. edn., 1950. See also Audrey Short, 'Workers under glass in 1851', *Victorian Studs.* x (1966–7), 193–202, which deals with working-class attendance, and R. J. Morris, 'Leeds and the Crystal Palace', ibid. xiii (1969–70), 283–300.

4129 PEVSNER (*Sir* NIKOLAUS BERNHARD LEON). High Victorian design: a study of the exhibits of 1851. 1951.

4130 WYATT (*Sir* MATTHEW DIGBY). The industrial arts of the nineteenth century: a series of illustrations of the choicest specimens produced by every nation at the great exhibition of the works of industry. 2 v. in pts. 1851.

Dickinson Brothers also publ. *Dickinson's comprehensive pictures of the great exhibition of 1851 from the originals painted . . . for H.R.H. Prince Albert,* 2 v. 1854.

4131 WHEWELL (WILLIAM) *and others.* Lectures on the results of the great exhibition of 1851, delivered before the Society of Arts, Manufactures and Commerce at the suggestion of H.R.H. Prince Albert. 1852. 2nd ser. 1853.

A notable contemp. analysis. See also Charles Babbage, *The exposition of 1851 . . .,* 1851, repr. Farnborough 1969, Michel Chevalier, *Exposition universelle de Londres, considérée sous les rapports philosophique, technique, commercial et administratif au point de vue français,* Paris 1851.

4132 HUNT (ROBERT). ed. Hunt's handbook to the official catalogues: an explanatory guide to the natural productions and manufactures of the great exhibition of the industry of all nations, 1851. 2 v. 1851.

A guide to the exhibits and the numerous catalogues and reports. See also Royal Commission for the Great Exhibition, *Official descriptive and illustrated catalogue,* ed. by Robert Ellis, 5 v. 1851. Many other handbooks were issued, among them John Tallis, *Tallis's history and description of the Crystal Palace and the exhibition of the world's industry . . .,* 3 v. 1851, *Cyclopaedia of the great exhibition . . .,* 1851, and John Timbs, *The year book of facts: extra volume: the great exhibition of 1851,* 1851. One of them has been repr. as *The great exhibition, London 1851: the 'Art journal' illustrated catalogue of the industry of all nations,* Newton Abbot 1970.

4133 COMMISSIONERS FOR THE EXHIBITION OF 1851. First report of the commissioners for the exhibition of 1851 [Chairmen: The Prince Consort and others]. [1485] H.C. (1852). XXVI, 1. Second report. [1566] H.C. (1852–3). LIV, 407. Third report. [2065] H.C. (1856). XXIV, 501. Fourth report. [2819] H.C. (1861). XXII, 243. Fifth report. [3933] H.C. (1867). XXIII, 319. Sixth report. [2378] H.C. (1878–9). XXVII, 1, etc.

The committee responsible for the 1851 exhibition and subsequent disbursement of profits, which still continues. For the Crystal Palace see also *Report of the commissioners appointed to inquire into the cost and applicability of the exhibition building in Hyde Park* [Chairman: Lord Seymour]. [1453] H.C. (1852). XXVI, 275.

4134 PARIS UNIVERSAL EXHIBITION, 1855. Catalogue of the work exhibited in the British section. 1855.

See also J. J. Arnoux, ed., *Le travail universel: revue complète des œuvres de l'art et de l'industrie exposées à Paris en 1855*, 3 v. Paris 1856. and *Reports on the Paris universal exhibition.* [2049–I to III] H.C. (1856). XXXVI, pts. I–III. For the earlier New York exhibition see *New York Industrial Exhibition: general report of the British commissioners.* [1716] H.C. (1854). XXXVI, 1, and the parallel *Special reports.* [1717, 1718, 1793, 1801, 1830] H.C. (1854). XXXVI, 9. For the important 1867 Paris exhibition see *Reports on the Paris universal exhibition, 1867.* [3968, 3968–I to IV, 3969] H.C. (1867–8). XXX, pts. I–III, *Report from the select committee on Paris exhibition* [Chairman: A. H. Layard]. H.C. 433 (1867). X, 605, and *The report of Her Majesty's commissioners for the Universal Exhibition of Works of Industry, Agriculture and Fine Art, held at Paris in the year 1867.* [4195] H.C. (1868–9). XXIII, 15.

4135 WARING (JOHN BURLEY). Masterpieces of industrial art & sculpture at the international exhibition, 1862. 3 v. 1863.

On the London international exhibition of 1862. See also the *Official catalogue of the industrial department*, 1862, Daniel Kinnear Clark, *The exhibited machinery of 1862 . . .*, 1864, *The record of the international exhibition, 1862*, Glasgow &c. 1862, *The Art Journal illustrated catalogue of the international exhibition*, 1862, John Timbs, *The year book of facts in the international exhibition of 1862 . . .*, 1862, Society of Arts, *Reports by the juries on the subjects in the thirty-six classes into which the exhibition was divided*, 1863; and Michel Chevalier, ed., *Rapports des membres de la section française du jury international sur l'ensemble de l'exposition universelle de Londres de 1862*, 6 v. Paris 1862.

4136 COLE (*Sir* HENRY). A special report on the annual international exhibitions of the years 1871, 1872, 1873 & 1874 . . . [C. 2379] H.C. (1878–9). XXVII, 139.

4137 VIENNA UNIVERSAL EXPOSITION [WELTAUSSTELLUNG], 1873. The British section . . . 1873.

See also *Reports on the Vienna Universal Exhibition of 1873.* [C. 1072, C. 1072–I to III] H.C. (1874). LXXIII, pts. I–IV. For the Philadelphia Centennial Exhibition of 1876 see *Official catalogue of the British section*, 1876.

4138 PARIS EXHIBITION, 1878. Official catalogue of the British section. 1878. 2nd edn. 1878.

The most interesting British reaction was the Society for the Encouragement of Arts [Royal Society of Arts], *Artisan reports on the Paris universal exhibition of 1878*, 1879. See also *The Art Journal, the illustrated catalogue of the Paris international exhibition, 1878*, 1878; *Report of Her Majesty's commissioners for the Paris universal exhibition of 1878.* [C. 2588, C. 2588–I] H.C. (1880). XXXII, 1, XXXIII, 1; James Dredge, *The Paris international exhibition of 1878 . . .*, comp. from *Engineering*, 1878; Eugène Lacroix, *L'Angleterre et les Indes anglaises à l'exposition universelle de 1878*, Paris 1879; Clovis Lamarre, *Les pays étrangers et l'exposition de 1878*, 18 v. Paris 1878; and *Rapports sur l'exposition universelle de 1878*, 56 v. 1879–82. For the Paris exhibition of 1900 see *Report of His Majesty's commissioners for the Paris international exhibition, 1900.* [Cd. 629–30] H.C. (1901). XXXI, 1, 311.

4139 CHICAGO: WORLD'S COLUMBIAN EXPOSITION, 1893. Official catalogue of the British section. 1893.

See also Royal commission for the St. Louis Exhibition for 1904, *Report of His Majesty's commissioners . . .* [Cd. 2800] H.C. (1906). LIV, 297.

For official reports on other exhibitions see *Report of the royal commission for the Australian international exhibitions.* [C. 3099] H.C. (1882). XXVIII, 1; *Report of the royal commission for the Adelaide jubilee international exhibition of 1887.* [C. 5440] H.C. (1888). XXIV, 1; *Report of the royal commission for the Melbourne centennial exhibition of 1888.* [C. 5848] H.C. (1889). XXXIV, 473; Board of Trade, Exhibitions Branch, *Report on the Argentine centennial exhibitions, Buenos Aires, 1910.* [Cd. 5677] H.C. (1911). XXI, 813; and *Report of His Majesty's commissioners for the international exhibitions at Brussels, Rome & Turin, 1910 & 1911.* [Cd. 6609] H.C. (1912–13). XXII, 1.

## B. AGRICULTURE

### 1. GENERAL

#### (a) *Reference*

4140 PERKINS (WALTER FRANK). British and Irish writers on agriculture. Lymington. 1929. 3rd edn. 1939.

A general bibliog. without notes. For the older authors John Donaldson, *Agricultural biography: containing a notice of the life and writings of the British authors on agriculture...* 1854, is sometimes of use. For the most prolific recent writer on British agric. see G. E. Fussell: *a bibliography of his writings on agricultural history*, Univ. of Reading, Reading 1967.

4141 DENMAN (DONALD ROBERT) *and others.* Bibliography of rural land economy and landownership, 1900–1957: a full list of works relating to the British Isles and selected works from the United States and Western Europe. Univ. of Camb. Dept. of Estate Management, Camb. 1958.

4142 ROYAL AGRICULTURAL SOCIETY OF ENGLAND. Survey of agricultural libraries in England and Scotland. 1957.

The best libr. cat. is Royal Agric. Soc., *Catalogue of the library*, 1918. See also Southampton University Libr., *Catalogue of the Walter Frank Perkins agricultural library*, Southampton 1961, and the *Subject list of works on agriculture, rural economy and allied sciences in the library of the Patent Office*, 1905. For current textbooks the best guide is *A selected and classified list of books relating to agriculture, horticulture, etc., in the library of the Ministry of Agriculture, Fisheries and Food*, Ministry of Agric. *Bull.* 78, 4th edn. 1958.

4143 BUTTRESS (FREDERICK ARTHUR) *comp.* Agricultural periodicals of the British isles, 1681–1900, and their location. Camb. 1950.

4144 BURN (ROBERT SCOTT). Year-book of agricultural facts for 1859 [–62]. Edin. & Lond. 1860 [–63].

A survey of agric. literature.

4145 INTERNATIONAL INSTITUTE OF AGRICULTURE. The science and practice of farming during 1910 in Great Britain (England, Wales, Scotland) as seen through the scientific and agricultural press. Rome. 1910.

4146 LIST OF BOOKS AND ARTICLES ON AGRICULTURAL [AGRARIAN] HISTORY, 1952–3+. *Agric. Hist. Rev.* i+. 1953+. Annual.

4147 A CENTURY OF AGRICULTURAL STATISTICS: Great Britain, 1866–1966. H.M.S.O. 1968.

Weak on pre-1914 statistics.

4148 COPPOCK (JOHN TERENCE). 'The statistical assessment of British agriculture'. *Agric. Hist. Rev.* iv (1956), 4–21, 66–79.

The best intro. to the bibliog. of agric. statistics. But see also George Edwin Fussell, 'The collection of agricultural statistics in Great Britain: its origin and evolution', *Agric. Hist.* xviii (1944), 161–7. For some earlier commentaries see Sir James Caird, 'On the agricultural statistics of the United Kingdom', *Stat. Soc. J.* xxxi (1868), 127–45; xxxii (1869), 61–77, and Patrick George Craigie, 'Ten years' statistics of British agriculture, 1870–79', *Stat. Soc. J.* xliii (1880), 275–312, and 'Statistics of agricultural production', *Stat. Soc. J.* xlvi (1883), 1–47.

(b) *Histories*

For rural depopulation see **6941**. For agricultural marketing see **5878–911**.

4149 ORWIN (CHRISTABEL SUSAN) and WHETHAM (EDITH HOLT). History of British agriculture, 1846–1914. 1964.

The most up-to-date hist., but not very inspired. Prothero (**4150**) is still the best general intro. though outdated. There is little on the period in Jonathan David Chambers and Gordon Edmund Mingay, *The agricultural revolution, 1750–1880*, 1966, or in Michael Tracy, *Agriculture in Western Europe: crisis & adaptation since 1880*, 1964, but both are worth consulting. The relevant vol. of *The agrarian history of England and Wales*, ed. by Herbert Patrick Reginald Finberg, Camb., 7 v. 1967+, has not yet appeared.

4150 PROTHERO (ROWLAND EDMUND), *Baron Ernle*. English farming past and present. 1912. 6th edn. 1961.

A famous book. The 5th edn. rev. by Sir Alfred Daniel Hall was long standard, but did not reflect recent scholarly findings. The 6th edn. has a controversial bibliog. survey by O. R. McGregor. For an important review of the 6th edn. see Eric Lionel Jones, 'English farming before and during the nineteenth century', *Econ. Hist. Rev.* 2 ser. xv (1962–3), 145–52. Ernle's 'English agriculture in the reign of Queen Victoria', *Royal Agric. Soc. J.* lxii (1901), 1–39, is also useful. The other short hists. covering the whole hist. of English agric. add little: they incl. William Henry Ricketts Curtler, *A short history of English agriculture*, Oxf. 1909; Charles Stewart Orwin, *A history of English farming*, 1949; Mabel Elizabeth Seebohm, *The evolution of the English farm*, 1927, rev. edn. 1952; and Ralph Whitlock, *A short history of farming in Britain*, 1965.

4151 VENN (JOHN ARCHIBALD). Foundations of agricultural economics. Camb. 1923. 2nd edn. 1933.

A detailed analysis of trends in English agric., *c.* 1870–1922. There is a useful short account, covering some of the same ground, in [Sir Hubert Douglas Henderson and Paul Lamartine Yates] *British agriculture: the principles of future policy: a report of an enquiry organized by Viscount Astor and B. Seebohm Rowntree*, 1938.

4152 THOMPSON (FRANCIS MICHAEL LONGSTRETH). English landed society in the nineteenth century. Lond. & Toronto. 1963.

A first-rate account of 19th-cent. landed estates. See also his 'Land and politics in England in the nineteenth century', *Roy. Hist. Soc. Trans.* 5 ser. xv (1965), 23–44, and 'The second agricultural revolution, 1815–1880', *Econ. Hist. Rev.* 2 ser. xxi (1968), 62–77.

4153  GARNIER (RUSSELL MONTAGUE). History of the English landed interest: its customs, law and agriculture. 2 v. 1892–3.

An old-fashioned but still useful account of English landed soc., worth reading as a background to Thompson (**4152**). Sir John Arthur Ransome Marriott, *The English land system: a sketch of its historical evolution in its bearing upon national wealth and national welfare*, 1914, and Robert Trow-Smith, *Society and the land*, 1953, are shorter and more popular attempts at the same sort of analysis.

4154  JONES (ERIC LIONEL). Seasons and prices: the role of the weather in English agricultural history. 1964.

Based on Thomas Henry Baker, comp., *Records of the seasons . . .*, 1883, as is John M. Stratton, *Agricultural records, A.D. 220–1968*, ed. by Ralph Whitlock, 1970. See also Reginald H. Hooker, 'The weather and the crops in eastern England, 1885–1921', *Royal Met. Soc. Q. J.* xlviii (1922), 115–38; Gordon Manley, 'The range of variation of the British climate', *Geog. J.* cxvii (1951), 43–68', 'Temperature trend in Lancashire, 1753–1945', *Royal Met. Soc. Q. J.* lxxii (1946), 1–31, and 'The mean temperature of central England, 1698–1952', ibid. lxxix (1953), 242–61, 558–67; M. de Carle S. Salter, *The rainfall of the British Isles*, 1921; Charles Ernest Pelham Brooks and John Glasspoole, *British floods and droughts . . .*, 1928; the publs. of the British Rainfall Organization, notably *British rainfall . . .*, Met. Office, annual, 1862+; *Royal Met. Soc. Q. J.* 1873+; Met. Office, *Snowfall in the British Isles . . . 1876–1925 . . .*, 1938; and Charles Davison, *A history of British earthquakes*, Camb. 1924. For comparative purposes Emmanuel Le Roy Ladurie, *Histoire du climat depuis l'an mil*, Paris 1967, is useful. William Henry Beveridge, Baron Beveridge, 'Weather and harvest cycles', *Econ. J.* xxxi (1921), 429–52, and 'Wheat prices and rainfall in Western Europe', *Roy. Stat. Soc. J.* lxxxv (1922), 418–78, deal with long-term periodicity.

4155  FLAVIGNY (PIERRE). Le régime agraire en Angleterre au XIXᵉ siècle et la concentration de l'exploitation agricole. Thèse pour le doctorat. Paris. 1932.

A summary of the obvious sources, but useful for French work on English agric.

4156  DRESCHER (LEO). 'The development of agricultural production in Great Britain and Ireland from the early nineteenth century'. Trans. by William Otto Henderson and William Henry Chaloner. *Manch. School* xxiii (1955), 153–75. Commentary by Thomas William Fletcher. Ibid. 176–83.

The only index of agricultural production for the whole of the period. See also Eric Mervyn Ojala, 'Gross and net output of agriculture in the United Kingdom by groups of years, 1867 to 1943', publ. as an appendix to his *Agriculture and economic progress*, Agric. Research Inst. Oxf. 1952, pp. 191–217.

4157  MINCHINTON (WALTER EDWARD) *ed.* Essays in agrarian history: a collection of reprinted articles edited for the British Agricultural History Soc. 2 v. Newton Abbot. 1968.

Vol. II is chiefly devoted to the 19th cent. and incls. a number of important papers, many of them noted below.

4158  THE AGRICULTURAL HISTORY REVIEW. Reading. 1953+.

Incls. annual bibliog. of British agric. hist. There are also articles on Britain in *Agricultural history*, Agric. Hist. Soc., Chicago etc. 1927+.

4159 BELLERBY (JOHN ROTHERFORD) *and others*. Agriculture and industry: relative income. 1956.

Mainly since 1867. See also Bellerby's 'Distribution of farm income in the United Kingdom, 1867–1938', *J. & Proc. Agric. Econ. Soc.* x (1952–4), 127–44, rev. edn. in Minchinton, *Essays* (4157) II, 259–79. For 1851 see also his 'National and agricultural income, 1851', *Econ. J.* lxix (1959), 95–104.

4160 REW (*Sir* ROBERT HENRY). 'Farm revenue and capital'. *Roy. Agric. Soc. J.* lvi (3 ser. vi) (1895), 30–46.

4161 PALGRAVE (*Sir* ROBERT HARRY INGLIS). 'Estimates of agricultural losses in the United Kingdom during the last thirty years'. *Roy. Stat. Soc. J.* lxviii (1905), 50–80.

4162 ADAMS (LEONARD PALMER). Agricultural depression and farm relief in England, 1813–1852. 1932. Repr. 1965.

4163 FUSSELL (GEORGE EDWIN). 'English agriculture from Cobbett to Caird (1830–80)'. *Econ. Hist. Rev.* xv (1945), 79–85.

Cp. with Sir James Caird, 'Fifty years of progress of British agriculture', *Roy. Agric. Soc. J.* li (3 ser. i) (1890), 20–36. Fussell has also publ. a ser. of articles on 'high farming' 1840–80, which are listed in **4140**.

4164 FAIRLIE (SUSAN). 'The Corn Laws and British wheat production, 1829–76'. *Econ. Hist. Rev.* 2 ser. xxii (1969), 88–116.

See also her 'The nineteenth-century Corn Law reconsidered', *Econ. Hist. Rev.* 2 ser. xviii (1965), 562–75.

4165 JONES (ERIC LIONEL). 'The changing basis of English agricultural prosperity, 1852–73'. *Agric. Hist. Rev.* x (1962), 102–19. Repr. in Minchinton, *Essays* (4157) II, 217–37.

See also his *The development of English agriculture, 1815–1873*, 1968, a short summary of existing knowledge, and E. J. T. Collins and E. L. Jones, 'Sectoral advance in English agriculture, 1850–80', *Agric. Hist. Rev.* xv (1967), 65–81.

4166 FLETCHER (THOMAS WILLIAM). 'The great depression of English agriculture, 1873–1896'. *Econ. Hist. Rev.* 2 ser. xiii (1960–1), 417–32. Repr. in Minchinton, Essays (4157) II, 239–57.

Shows that depression was confined to corn-growing districts. Cp. John Terence Coppock, 'Agricultural changes in the Chilterns, 1875–1900', *Agric. Hist. Rev.* ix (1961), 1–16, and John Rowe, 'Cornish agriculture in the age of the great depression, 1875–1895', *Roy. Instn. Cornwall J.* new ser. iii (1959–60), 147–62.

Raymond Phineas Stearns, 'Agricultural adaptation in England, 1875–1900', *Agric. Hist.* vi (1932), 84–101 and 130–54, based largely on official papers, is more general. P. J. Perry, ed., *British agriculture, 1875–1914*, 1973, is a useful coll. of articles.

4167 BESSE (PIERRE). La crise et l'évolution de l'agriculture en Angleterre de 1875 à nos jours: essai d'histoire économique. Paris. 1910.

4168 AGRICULTURE IN THE TWENTIETH CENTURY: essays on research, practice and organisation, to be presented to Sir Daniel Hall. Oxf. 1939.

Sir Alfred Daniel Hall, *Agriculture after the war*, 1916, incls. a useful account of pre-1914 agric.

4169 GARNETT (FRANK WALLS). Westmorland agriculture, 1800–1900. Kendal. 1912.

The earliest county study. See also Joan Thirsk and Jean Imray, *Suffolk farming in the nineteenth century*, Suffolk Records Soc. I, Ipswich 1958; Robert Charles Gaut, *A history of Worcestershire agriculture and rural evolution*, Worcester 1939; Joan Thirsk, *English peasant farming: the agrarian history of Lincolnshire from Tudor to recent times*, 1957; and William George Hoskins, ed., *Studies in Leicestershire agrarian history*, Leicestershire Archaeol. Soc. 1949.

4170 WATSON (*Sir* JAMES ANDERSON SCOTT). The history of the Royal Agricultural Society of England, 1839–1939. 1940.

A full hist. of the chief agric. soc. Hists. of lesser socs. incl. Leonard Bull, *History of the Smithfield Club, from 1798 to 1925*, 1926; H. G. Shepard, *One hundred years of the Royal Jersey Agricultural and Horticultural Society, 1833–1933*, Jersey 1934; Norman Lancelot Pickerill and others, *Straight furrows: being a history of Collingham Farmers' Club*, Lincoln [1950]; and Prideaux George Selby, *The Faversham Farmers' Club and its members*, Faversham 1927. There is also the memoirs of a sec. of the Bath and West Soc., Thomas Forder Plowman, *Fifty years of a showman's life*, 1919.

4171 MATTHEWS (*Sir* ALFRED HERBERT HENRY). Fifty years of agricultural politics: being the history of the Central Chamber of Agriculture, 1865–1915. 1915.

Important for agricultural legislation and policy. Cont. by William Philip Jeffcock, *Agricultural politics, 1915–1935 . . .*, Ipswich 1937. There is no hist. of the National Farmers' Union. But see Kevin Fitzgerald, *Ahead of their time: a short history of the Farmers' Club, 1842–1967*, 1968.

4172 ELLIOTT (*Sir* THOMAS HENRY). 'The organisation and work of the Board of Agriculture and Fisheries'. In George Montagu Harris, ed. Problems of local government. 1911. Pp. 419–36.

(c) *Contemporary investigations*

(i) *Private*

4173 COLMAN (HENRY). The agriculture and rural economy of Great Britain and Ireland, from personal observation. 2nd edn. 2 v. 1849.

The best account of English farming at the beginning of the period: by an American.

4174 CAIRD (*Sir* JAMES). English agriculture in 1850–51. 1852. 2nd edn. by Gordon Edmund Mingay. 1968.

A famous ser. of reports repr. from *The Times*.

4175 OLMSTED (FREDERICK LAW). Walks and talks of an American farmer in England. N.Y. 1852. Rev. edn. Columbus, Ohio. 1859.

4176 GUILHAUD DE LAVERGNE (LOUIS GABRIEL LÉONCE). The rural economy of England, Scotland and Ireland. Trans. by 'a Scottish farmer'. 1855.

Good. See also Société d'Agriculture, Sciences et Arts de Meaux, *Agriculture anglaise: situation économique et agricole, modes de culture,* 1852, and Éduard Hartstein, *Fortschritte in der englischen und schottischen Landwirtschaft,* 2 v. Bonn 1854, 2nd edn. 3 v. Bonn 1855-60, which summarizes English writings on the subject.

4177 KOERNER (THEODOR). Die Landwirthschaft in Grossbritannien nach eigener Anschauung dargestellt als ein Beitrag zur Kenntniss ihrer gegenwärtigen Lage. Berlin. 1877.

British agriculture in 1875-6.

4178 ROYAL AGRICULTURAL SOCIETY. Memoir on the agriculture of England and Wales prepared . . . for the International Agricultural Congress, Paris, 1878. Ed. by Henry Michael Jenkins. 1878. Also issued as Pt. II of the *Roy. Agric. Soc. J.* xxxix (2 ser. iv) (1878), 267-910.

The best account of English agriculture at the beginning of the great depression.

4179 CRAIGIE (PATRICK GEORGE). 'The size and distribution of agricultural holdings in England and abroad'. *Roy. Stat. Soc. J.* l (1887), 86-142.

4180 HAGGARD (*Sir* HENRY RIDER). Rural England: being an account of agricultural and social researches carried out in the years 1901 & 1902. 2 v. 1902.

4181 PRATT (EDWIN A.). The organization of agriculture. 1904. 3rd edn. 1908.

Cont. in his *The transition in agriculture,* 1905, repr. 1909.

4182 HALL (*Sir* ALFRED DANIEL). A pilgrimage of British farming, 1910-12. 1913.

Repr. from *The Times.*

4183 LAND ENQUIRY COMMITTEE [Chairman: Sir Arthur Herbert Dyke Acland]. The land: the report of the Land Enquiry Committee. 2 v. 1913.

A factual inquiry sponsored by members of the Liberal ministry as a prelude to land reform. For the numerous attacks on its conclusions and methods see Denman (4141): the best is *Facts about the land . . .,* 1916, ed. by Rowland Edmund Prothero, Baron Ernle.

4184 THE LAND HUNGER: life under monopoly: descriptive letters and other testimonies from those who have suffered . . . Ed. by [Thomas Fisher Unwin and] Jane Cobden Unwin. 1913.

Propaganda for land reform based on letters received in response to an appeal in the press.

4185 HALL (*Sir* ALFRED DANIEL) *and* RUSSELL (*Sir* EDWARD JOHN). A report on the agriculture and soils of Kent, Surrey and Sussex. 1911.

This vol. and John Orr, *Agriculture in Oxfordshire* . . ., 1916, and *Agriculture in Berkshire* . . ., 1918, mark the introduction of modern scientific methods into agric. surveys.

(ii) *Official*

4186 AGRICULTURAL RETURNS of Great Britain . . . 1866+.

Issued as a parl. paper. Title changed to *Agricultural statistics*, 1902+. The main run of official statistics. There are parallel statistics for other countries in Int. Inst. of Agric., *Annuaire international de statistique agricole*, Rome 1910–11+, and the other publs. of the Institute.

4187 BOARD OF AGRICULTURE AND FISHERIES. Journal. 1894+. Suppls. 1908–17.

4188 RICHMOND COMMISSION ON AGRICULTURE. Preliminary report from Her Majesty's commissioners on agriculture [Chairman: Duke of Richmond]. [C. 2778] H.C. (1881). XV, 1. Minutes of evidence. Pt. I. [C. 2778–I] H.C. (1881). XV, 25. Pt. II. [C. 3096] H.C. (1881). XVII, 1. Final report. [C. 3309] H.C. (1882). XIV, 1. Minutes of evidence. Pt. III. [C. 3309–I] H.C. (1882). XIV, 45.

A full-scale investigation into all aspects of British agric. prompted by the agric. depression. Conclusions feeble, but information good. For the reports of the assistant-commissioners who collected evidence in Britain and overseas, and the digests of the commission's minutes of evidence see Ford, *Select List* (**31**), p. 30.

4189 SHAW-LEFEVRE COMMISSION ON AGRICULTURE. First report of Her Majesty's commissioners appointed to inquire into the subject of agricultural depression [Chairman: G. J. Shaw-Lefevre]. [C. 7400] H.C. (1894). XVI, pt. I, 1. Second report. [C. 7981] H.C. (1896). XVI, 413. Final Report. [C. 8540] H.C. (1897). XV, 1.

For minutes of evidence, appendixes, assistant-commissioners' reports, etc., see Ford, *Select list* (**31**), pp. 30–1.

4190 REW REPORT ON THE DECLINE IN AGRICULTURAL POPULATION. Board of Agriculture and Fisheries: report on the decline in the agricultural population of Great Britain, 1881–1906. [By Sir Robert Henry Rew.] [Cd. 3273] H.C. (1906). XCVI, 583.

4191 AGRICULTURAL OUTPUT. The agricultural output of Great Britain: report on enquiries made by the Board of Agriculture and Fisheries in connection with the Census of Production Act, 1906, relating to the total output of agricultural land, the number of persons engaged, and the motive power employed. [Cd. 6277] H.C. (1912–13). X, 529.

4192 PEAT COMMISSION ON AGRICULTURE, 1919–20. Interim report of His Majesty's commissioners appointed to inquire into the economic prospects of the agricultural industry in Great Britain [Chairman: Sir William Barclay Peat]. [Cmd. 473] H.C. (1919). VIII, 1. Minutes of evidence. Vols. I–IV. [Cmd. 345, Cmd. 365, Cmd. 391, Cmd. 445] H.C. (1919). VIII, 23. Vol. V. [Cmd. 665] H.C. (1920). IX, 1.

### (d) *Contemporary Comment*

**4193** CAIRD (*Sir* JAMES). The landed interest and the supply of food. 1878. 4th edn. 1880.

An important discussion of the state of agric. now regarded as a classic of high farming. See also his 'Opening address', *Stat. Soc. J.* xliv (1881), 629–43. For Caird's views see also his *High farming under liberal covenants the best substitution for protection*, Edin. 1849, and *High farming vindicated and further illustrated*, Edin. 1850.

**4194** ARNOLD (*Sir* ROBERT ARTHUR). Free land. 1880.

Forms with Brodrick (**4238**) and Shaw-Lefevre (**4195**) a complete statement of the attitude of the Liberal land reformers of the 1870s and 1880s. Joseph Kay, *Free trade in land*, 1879, is a similar book. See also *Programme of the Land Tenure Reform Association*, 1870, and Sir Arthur Underhill, '*Freedom of land*', *and what it implies*, 1882.

**4195** SHAW-LEFEVRE (GEORGE JOHN), *Baron Eversley*. English and Irish land questions: collected essays. 1881.

**4196** WALLACE (ALFRED RUSSEL). Land nationalization: its necessity and its aims: being a comparison of the system of landlord and tenant, with that of occupying ownership . . . 1882. 3rd edn. 1883.

See also E. E. Barry, *Nationalisation in British politics* (**588**), Gavin Brown Clark, *A plea for the nationalisation of the land*, 1881; Samuel Whitfield Thackeray, *The land and the community*, 1889; and Harold Cox, *Land nationalisation*, 1892, 2nd edn. [entitled *Land nationalisation and local taxation*] 1906.

**4197** NICHOLSON (JOSEPH SHIELD). Tenant's gain not landlord's loss, and some other economic aspects of the land question. Edin. 1883.

**4198** BEAR (WILLIAM E.). The British farmer and his competitors. Cobden Club. 1888.

A defence of free trade. See also his 'Agricultural depression at home and abroad', *Roy. Agric. Soc. J.* lv (3 ser. v) (1894), 673–95; 'Unfair competition', ibid. lvi (3 ser. vi) (1895), 243–57, and 'The recent trend of agricultural competition', ibid. lix (3 ser. ix) (1898), 59–68.

**4199** REW (*Sir* ROBERT HENRY). An agricultural faggot: a collection of papers on agricultural subjects. 1913.

A useful set of essays publ. at various times from 1888.

**4200** PROTHERO (ROWLAND EDMUND), *Baron Ernle*. The pioneers and progress of English farming. 1888.

A defence of the land system.

4201 CHANNING (FRANCIS ALLSTON), *Baron Channing*. The truth about agricultural depression: an economic study of the evidence of the Royal Commission. 1897.

Challenges the conclusions of the Shaw-Lefevre commission (**4189**).

4202 SHELDON (JOHN PRINCE). The future of British agriculture: how farmers may best be benefited. 1893.

A useful statement of the case for scientific agriculture.

4203 TARIFF COMMISSION. Report of the agricultural committee. 1906.

4204 NICHOLSON (JOSEPH SHIELD). The relations of rents, wages and profits in agriculture, and their bearing on rural depopulation. 1906.

4205 FORDHAM (MONTAGUE). Mother earth: a proposal for a permanent reconstruction of our country life. [1907.] 2nd edn. 1908.

Advocates a state marketing organization, land nationalization, and the formation of rural co-operatives. Fordham also publ. *Agriculture and the guild system*, 1923, and *The rebuilding of rural England*, 1924.

4206 CARPENTER (EDWARD) *and others*. Socialism and agriculture. Fabian Socialist Series no. 2. 1908.

4207 COOPER (*Sir* WILLIAM EARNSHAW). Britain for the Briton: co-operative working of agriculture and other industries a necessity: an earnest appeal for land, industrial, economic and other vital reforms. 1909.

The fullest of four books by Cooper of which *The murder of agriculture . . .*, 1908, is the best known.

4208 TURNOR (CHRISTOPHER HATTON). Land problems and national welfare. 1911.

A careful discussion by an improving landlord.

4209 MILLS (JOHN SAXON). England's foundation: agriculture and the state. 1911.

A call for state aid.

4210 TOLLEMACHE (BEVIL). The occupying ownership of land: an analysis of the position of the tenant farmer, and some suggestions on the reconstruction of village life and on the creation of the peasant owner, drawn from practical experience. 1913.

4211 GEORGE (DAVID LLOYD), *Earl Lloyd George*. The rural land problem: what it is: a speech delivered at Bedford, on October 11th, 1913. 1913.

Followed by *The rural land problem: the remedy: a speech delivered at Swindon, on October 18th 1913*, 1913. Two interesting replies were Ernest George Pretyman, *Reply to Mr. Lloyd George's Bedford speech*, 1913, and G. E. Raine, *Lloyd George and the land . . .*, 1914.

4212 HARBEN (HENRY DEVENISH). The rural problem. 1913.

The report of a Fabian Soc. committee.

4213 A UNIONIST AGRICULTURAL POLICY. By a group of Unionists. 1913.

4214 LONG (JAMES). Making the most of the land. 1913.

Long wrote as 'Merlin' of the *Field*.

4215 ROBERTSON SCOTT (JOHN WILLIAM). The land problem: an impartial survey. [1913.]

4216 HYDER (JOSEPH). The case for land nationalisation. Land Nationalisation Soc. [1913.]

4217 COLLINGS (JESSE). The colonization of rural Britain: a complete scheme for the regeneration of British rural life. 2 v. [1914.]

Collings had been campaigning for land reform since the 1880s. This work and his *Land reform: occupying ownership, peasant proprietary, and rural education* . . ., 1906, new edn. 1908, sum up his views.

4218 FOX (*Sir* FRANK). Our English land muddle: an Australian view. [1913.]

4219 ROYAL AGRICULTURAL SOCIETY OF ENGLAND *formerly* English Agricultural Society. Journal. 1839+.

The most important agricultural periodical. Two other agric. socs. publ. similar js.: the Bath and West and Southern Counties Soc. for the Encouragement of Agriculture, Arts, Manufactures and Commerce, whose j. in its modern form dates from 1853, and the Royal Highland and Agric. Soc. of Scotland. The Central Chamber of Agric., 1868+, the Farmers' Club, 1842+, the Land Agents' Soc., 1902+, and the Yorkshire Agric. Soc., Leeds 1837+, all publ. js. with shorter articles.

4220 THE BRITISH YEAR-BOOK OF AGRICULTURE & agricultural who's who. 1908–9 to 1913–14.

4221 AGRICULTURAL GAZETTE. 1844–1925.

The most convenient of the agric. newspapers to handle. *The Mark Lane express*, 1832–1929, was more Radical and often more influential. The other chief papers were *Farmer's magazine*, 1834–81, *Journal of agriculture*, 1843–68 (publ. as *The country gentleman's magazine*, 1868–82), *Estates gazette*, 1858+, *Scottish farmer and horticulturalist*, 1861+ [title changed to *The farmer*, 1865–89, *The farmer and stockbreeder*, 1889+], *Agricultural economist and horticultural review*, 1870–1916, *Livestock journal and fanciers' gazette*, publ. under various titles, 1874–1933, and *The dairy world and the British dairy farmer*, 1892–1939. The gardening periodicals (**4391**) also incl. much agric. material.

(e) *Taxation and other Charges*

4222 PELL (*Sir* ALBERT). 'Local taxation as it affects agriculture'. *Roy. Agric. Soc. J.* lvi (3 ser. vi) (1895), 621–35.

See also A. Dudley Clarke, 'Taxation on land', *Roy. Agric. Soc. J.* liv (3 ser. iv) (1893), 23–36, and Sir Robert Henry Rew, 'Local taxation in rural districts', ibid. lvii (3 ser. vii) (1896), 637–62.

4223 NICHOLSON (JOSEPH SHIELD). Rates and taxes as affecting agriculture. 1905.

4224 ARNOTT (JOHN). 'The land tax'. *Roy. Agric. Soc. J.* lxxx (1919), 133–45.

See also **4539–40**.

4225 ORR (JOHN). Taxation of land values as it affects landowners and others. 1912.

4226 ROSENBAUM (S.). 'Food taxation in the United Kingdom, France, Germany and the United States'. *Roy. Stat. Soc. J.* lxxi (1908), 319–60.

4227 MILLARD (PERCY WILLIAM). Tithes and variable rentcharges: some aspects of their history and development. 1933.

An introductory essay suppl. his *The law relating to tithe rentcharge and other payments in lieu of tithe*, 1912, 3rd edn. 1938. There is a good account of tithe hist. in *Report of the royal commission on tithe rentcharge in England and Wales* [Chairman: Sir John Fischer Williams]. [Cmd. 5095] H.C. (1935–6). XIV, 859. The main source is *Report of the commissioners appointed to inquire into the redemption of tithe rentcharge in England and Wales* [Chairman: Lord Basing]. [C. 6606] H.C. (1892). XLVII, 341: Minutes of evidence. [C. 6606–I] H.C. (1892). XLVII, 355. Details of tithes commuted before 1887 are given in H.C. 214 (1887). LXIV, 239. There is also a little information in *Report from the select committee on tithe (rentcharges)* [Chairman: Frederick A. Inderwick]. H.C. 340 (1881). XII, 383. See also **4249**.

4228 REW (*Sir* ROBERT HENRY). 'Farmers and railway rates'. *Roy. Agric. Soc. J.* lvi (3 ser. vi) (1895), 288–308.

A convenient intro. to a subject with an enormous literature.

4229 WILSON (*Sir* JAMES). 'The co-operative insurance of livestock in England and Wales'. *Roy. Stat. Soc. J.* lxxvii (1913–14), 145–56.

## 2. Land Tenures

### (a) *Land Laws*

4230 POLLOCK (*Sir* FREDERICK). The land laws. The English citizen series. 1883. 3rd edn. 1896.

A splendid work written for laymen. Sir Kenelm Edward Digby, *An introduction to the history of the law of real property*, Oxf. 1875, 5th edn. 1897, Alfred William Brian Simpson, *An introduction to the history of the land law*, 1961, Anthony Dalzell Hargreaves, *An introduction to the principles of land law*, 1936, 4th edn. 1963, and Sir William Searle Holdsworth, *An historical introduction to the land law*, Oxf. 1927, are fuller but less easy to use for non-lawyers.

4231 SCRUTTON (*Sir* THOMAS EDWARD). Land in fetters: or, the history and policy of the laws restraining the alienation and settlement of land in England. Camb. 1886.

4232 SHAW-LEFEVRE (GEORGE JOHN), *Baron Eversley*. Agrarian tenures: a survey of the laws and customs relating to the holding of land in

England, Ireland and Scotland, and of the reforms therein during recent years. 1893.

Incls. a discussion of proposed reforms.

4233 CADLE (CLEMENT). 'The farming customs and covenants of England'. *Roy. Agric. Soc. J.* xxix (new ser. iv) (1868), 144–76.

4234 KENNY (COURTNEY STANHOPE). The history of the law of primogeniture in England and its effect upon landed property. Camb. 1878.

Also issued with Sir Perceval Maitland Laurence, *The law and custom of primogeniture*, Camb. 1878, as *Two essays on the law of primogeniture*, 1878. See also Evelyn Cecil, Baron Rockley, *Primogeniture: a short history of its development in various countries and its practical effects*, 1895.

4235 WILLIAMS (JOSHUA). Principles of the law of real property. 1845. 24th edn. 1933.

Standard throughout the period as a legal textbook. Other useful textbooks are Louis Arthur Goodeve, *The modern law of real property*, 1883, 5th edn. 1906; William Douglas Edwards, *A compendium of the law of property in land*, 1888, 5th edn. 1922; Edward Jenks, *Modern land law*, Oxf. 1899; and Leonard Shelford, *The real property statutes . . .*, 1834, 9th edn. 1893, rev. edn. by Thomas Henry Carson, 1902, 3rd edn. 1927.

4236 DOWSON (*Sir* ERNEST MACLEOD) *and* SHEPPARD (VIVIAN LEE OSBORNE). Land registration. Colonial Office: Colonial Research Publ. 13. H.M.S.O. 1952.

A good comparative study. See also R. R. A. Walker, 'The genesis of land registration in England', *L.Q.R.* lv (1939), 547–51, and *Royal Commission on the Land Transfer Acts: second and final report of the commissioners* [Chairman: Viscount St. Aldwyn]. [Cd. 5483] H.C. (1911). XXX, 1, which incls. a hist. survey. The best textbook is Sir Howard Warburton Elphinstone, *A practical introduction to conveyancing and to . . . registration of land*, 1871, 7th edn. 1918.

## (b) *Land Ownership*

4237 DENMAN (DONALD ROBERT). Origins of ownership: a brief history of land ownership and tenure in England from earliest times to the modern era. 1958.

4238 BRODRICK (GEORGE CHARLES). English land and English land-lords: an enquiry into the origin and character of the English land system . . . 1881. Repr. 1968.

Still the only comprehensive book on the subject, but largely repl. by Thompson (**4152**).

4239 WHITTAKER (*Sir* THOMAS PALMER). The ownership, tenure, and taxation of land: some facts, fallacies and proposals, relating thereto. 1914.

An exhaustive discussion by a leading land reformer.

4240 RETURN OF OWNERS OF LAND, 1873. England and Wales (exclusive of the metropolis). Vol. I. [C. 1097] H.C. (1874). LXXII, pt. I, 1.

Vol. II. [C. 1097–I] H.C. (1874). LXXII, pt. II, 1. Summary. H.C. 335 (1876). LXXX, 1.

The so-called 'New Domesday Book'. To be used in conjunction with Bateman (**4241**) who corrects some of the innumerable errors. *A Summary digest . . .*, by Frederick Purdy was publ. by the Local Government Board, 1876.

4241 BATEMAN (JOHN). The great landowners of Great Britain and Ireland: a list of all owners of three thousand acres and upwards, worth £3,000 a year, in England, Scotland, Ireland & Wales, their acreage, income from land, college, club, and services, culled from the Modern Domesday book. 1878. 4th edn. with additional tables. 1883. Repr. Leicester. 1971.

An indispensable directory. Each edn. incls. new corrections supplied by landowners or their agents.

4242 CRAIGIE (PATRICK GEORGE). 'The size and distribution of agricultural holdings in England and abroad'. *Roy. Stat. Soc. J.* 1 (1887), 86–142.

4243 SPRING (DAVID). 'The English landed estate in the age of coal and iron, 1830–1880'. *J. Econ. Hist.* xi (1951), 3–24.

Important. See also Richard Perren, 'The landlord and agricultural transformation, 1870–1900', *Agric. Hist. Rev.* xviii (1970), 36–51, Francis Michael Longstreth Thompson, 'English landownership: the Ailesbury trust, 1832–56', *Econ. Hist. Rev.* 2 ser. xi (1958–9), 121–32, and 'The social distribution of landed property in England since the sixteenth century', *Econ. Hist. Rev.* 2 ser. xix (1966), 505–17, and Henry Durant, 'The development of landownership, 1873–1925, with special reference to Bedfordshire', *Sociological Rev.* xxviii (1936), 85–99.

4244 RUSSELL (HERBRAND ARTHUR), *Duke of Bedford*. A great agricultural estate: being the story of the origin and administration of Woburn and Thorney. 1897.

Should be cp. with Langford Lovell Frederick Rice Price, 'The estates of the colleges of Oxford and their management', *Roy. Stat. Soc. J.* lxxvi (1912–13), 787–90, and *Surveyors' Instn. Trans.* xlv (1912–13), 542–97, 'The accounts of the colleges of Oxford, 1893–1903 . . .', *Roy. Stat. Soc. J.* lxvii (1904), 585–652, 'The recent depression in agriculture as shown in the accounts of an Oxford college, 1876–90', ibid. lv (1892), 2–36, 'The colleges of Oxford and agricultural depression', ibid. lviii (1895), 36–69, James John Macgregor, 'The economic history of two rural estates in Cambridgeshire, 1870–1934', *Roy. Agric. Soc. J.* xcviii (1937), 142–61, and J. C. Steele 'The agricultural depression and its effects on a leading London hospital', *Roy. Stat. Soc. J.* lv (1892), 37–48.

4245 HAVINDEN (MICHAEL ASHLEY). Estate villages: a study of the Berkshire villages of Ardington and Lockinge. Museum of English Rural Life, Univ. of Reading. 1966.

An important study of large-scale estate farming.

4246 TAYLOR (HENRY CHARLES). The decline of landowning farmers in England. Bull. Univ. Wisconsin 96. Madison, Wis. 1904.

A thin account of an important subject, much better dealt with in Stanley George Sturmey, 'Owner farming in England and Wales, 1900 to 1950', *Manch. School* xxiii (1955), 245–68, repr. in Minchinton, *Essays* (**4157**) II, 281–306.

4247 THOMPSON (FRANCIS MICHAEL LONGSTRETH). 'The land market in the nineteenth century'. *Oxf. Econ. Papers* new ser. ix (1957), 285–308. Repr. in Minchinton, Essays (4157) II, 29–54.

See also C. M. Fordham, 'Some notes on values of agricultural land in the Midlands and Eastern counties between 1823 and 1947', *Land Agents' Soc. J.* xlviii (1949), 270–6, and Norton, Trist and Gilbert, 'A century of land values, England and Wales', *The Times*, 20 April 1889, repr. *Roy. Stat. Soc. J.* liv (1891), 528–32, and Carus-Wilson, *Essays* (4066) III, 128–31.

4248 THOMPSON (ROBERT J.). 'An enquiry into the rent of agricultural land in England and Wales during the nineteenth century'. *Roy. Stat. Soc. J.* lxx (1907), 587–616. Repr. in Minchinton, Essays (4157) II, 55–86.

See also David B. Grigg, 'A note on agricultural rent and expenditure in nineteenth-century England', *Agric. Hist.* xxxix (1965), 147–54.

4249 BELLERBY (JOHN ROTHERFORD). 'Gross and net farm rent in the United Kingdom, 1867–1938'. *Agric. Econ. Soc. J. Proc.* x (1952–4), 356–62.

Bellerby and F. D. W. Taylor also publ. 'Aggregate tithe rentcharge on farm land in the United Kingdom, 1867–1938', *J. Agric. Econ.* xi (1954–6), 197–202.

4250 RHEE (HANS ALBERT). 'The rent of agricultural land in England and Wales, 1870–1943'. Publ. in The rent of agricultural land in England and Wales, 1870–1946. Central Landowners' Assoc. 1949.

(c) *Tenant Farming*

4251 BEAR (WILLIAM E.). The relations of landlord and tenant in England and Scotland. Cobden Club. 1876.

Bear and Howard (4252) were among the chief spokesmen of the Farmers' Alliance which campaigned in the 1880s to improve the status of the tenant farmer.

4252 HOWARD (JAMES). The tenant farmers: land laws and landlords. 1879.

4253 DIXON (HENRY HALL). A treatise on the law of the farm; including the agricultural customs of England and Wales. 1858. 6th edn. 1904.

Written for agriculturalists.

4254 ADKIN (BENAIAH WHITLEY). A handbook of the law relating to landlord and tenant. 1907. 14th edn. 1955.

The best modern work on tenancies. Of other textbooks the best were Joseph Haworth Redman and George Edward Lyon, *A concise view of the law of landlord and tenant . . .*, 1876, 11th edn. 1951, Suppl. 1952, 1953; Edgar Foa, *The relationship of landlord and tenant*, 1891, 7th edn. 1947, and *An outline of the law of landlord and tenant*, 1906, 5th edn. 1934; John Mountney Lely and Sir Edward Robert Pearce-Edgcumbe, *Agricultural holdings: the Agricultural Holdings Act, 1883 . . .*, 1883, 5th edn. 1926; John Wynne Jeudwine, *The Agricultural Holdings (England) Act, 1883*, 1883, 6th edn. 1915; Aubrey John Spencer, *The Agricultural Holdings (England) Act, 1883*, 8th edn. 1931; and Thomas Chalice Jackson, *The Agricultural Holdings Act . . .*, 1912, 10th edn. 1949.

4255 BULLEN (EDWARD). A practical treatise on the law of distress for rent, and of things damage-feasant. 1842. 2nd edn. 1899.

The first book on the subject. George St. Leger Daniels, *A handbook of the law of distress*, 1894, 6th edn. 1932, is much easier to follow. The best lawyer's book is John Herbert Williams and Walter Baldwyn Yates, *The law of ejectment or recovery of possession of land*, 1894, 2nd edn. 1911.

4256 DENMAN (DONALD ROBERT). Tenant-right valuation in history and modern practice. Camb. 1942.

Incls. a short hist. The best contemp. textbooks were Tom Bright, *The agricultural & tenant-right valuer's assistant . . .*, 1886, 5th edn. 1910, and John William Willis Bund, *The law of compensation for unexhausted agricultural improvements . . .*, 1876, 3rd edn. 1904.

4257 HAVERSHAM COMMITTEE ON TENANT FARMERS AND SALES OF ESTATES. Report of the departmental committee appointed by the Board of Agriculture and Fisheries to inquire into the position of tenant farmers on the occasion of any change in the ownership of their holdings and to consider whether any legislation on the subject is desirable [Chairman: Lord Haversham]. [Cd. 6030]. H.C. (1912–13). XLVII, 337. Minutes of evidence. [Cd. 6031] H.C. (1912–13). XLVII, 379.

4258 SELECT COMMITTEE ON LAW OF DISTRESS. Report from the select committee on law of distress [Chairman: G. J. Goschen]. H.C. 284 (1882). VIII, 269.

A thorough investigation.

(d) *Small Holdings and Allotments*

4259 LEVY (HERMANN JOACHIM). Large and small holdings: a study of English agricultural economics. Trans. by Ruth Kenyon. Camb. 1911.

Standard. Arthur Henry Johnson, *The disappearance of the small landowner*, Oxf. 1909, 2nd edn. by Joan Thirsk 1963, has little on the period. Newlin Russell Smith, *Land for the small man: English and Welsh experience with publicly-supplied small holdings, 1860–1937*, N.Y. 1946, is disappointing.

4260 JEBB (LOUISA). The small holdings of England: a survey of various existing systems. 1907.

The best survey of 19th-cent. experiments. Jebb also publ. *The small holdings of England: an enquiry into the conditions of success*, 1906, *How landlords can create small holdings . . .*, 1907, and *The working of the Small Holdings Act, with suggestions for its amendment*, 1907. There is important additional material in Arthur Wilfred Ashby, *Allotments and small holdings in Oxfordshire: a survey . . .*, Oxf. 1917, and J. W. E. Jordan, *County Council smallholdings in Derbyshire*, Derbyshire County Council, Matlock 1961, and P. Searby, 'Great Dodford and the later history of the Chartist land scheme', *Agric. Hist. Rev.* xvi (1968), 32–45.

4261 READ (CLARE SEWELL). 'Large and small holdings: a comparative view'. *Roy. Agric. Soc. J.* xlviii (2 ser. xxiii) (1887), 1–28.

The first of a ser. of important articles in the *Journal*. The others are Sir John Bennet Lawes and Sir Joseph Henry Gilbert, 'Allotments and small holdings', liii (3 ser. iii)

(1892), 439–63; Thomas Stirton, 'Small holdings', lv (3 ser. v) (1894), 84–94; A. Dudley Clarke, 'Small holdings and their equipment', lvii (3 ser. vii) (1896), 264–92; and Patrick George Craigie, 'The place of the small holder in English agriculture', lxvii (1906), 1–19. These are much better than W. G. S. Adams, 'Some considerations relating to the position of the small holding in the United Kingdom', *Roy. Stat. Soc. J.* lxx (1907), 411–37.

4262 SPENCER (AUBREY JOHN). The Small Holdings Acts, 1892 . . . 1892. 3rd edn. 1927.

4263 LITTLE (JAMES BROOKE). The law of allotments for the poor . . . 1887. 2nd edn. 1895.

4264 IMPEY (FREDERICK). Three acres and a cow: successful small holdings and peasant proprietors . . . 1886.
One of the best statements of the case for small holdings.

4265 ONSLOW (WILLIAM HILLIER), *Earl of Onslow*. Landlords and allotments: the history and present condition of the allotment system. 1886.

4266 BEAR (WILLIAM E.). A study of small holdings. Cobden Club. 1893.
A careful investigation.

4267 GREEN (*Sir* JOHN LITTLE). Allotments and small holdings. 1896.

4268 LONG (JAMES). The small farm and its management. 1901. 2nd edn. 1920.
Long also publ. *Small holdings*, 1913.

4269 CADBURY (GEORGE) *and* BRYAN (TOM). The land and the landless. 1908.
Sets out at length the case for small holdings.

4270 PRATT (EDWIN A.). Small holders: what they must do to succeed: with a chapter on the revival of county life. 1909.

4271 PARKER (*Sir* GILBERT) *and* DAWSON (RICHARD). The land, the people and the state: a case for small ownership . . . 1910.

4272 NATIONAL CONGRESS ON RURAL DEVELOPMENT AND SMALL HOLDINGS. Report of proceedings held at the Crystal Palace, on 18th, 19th & 20th October 1911, in connection with the Small Holdings and Country Life section of the Festival of Empire. 1912.

4273 CHAMBERLAIN COMMITTEE ON SMALL HOLDINGS. Report from the select committee on small holdings [Chairman: Joseph Chamberlain]. H.C. 313 (1889). XII, 1. Further report. H.C. 223 (1890). XVII, 183.
See also *Report from the select committee on the Charitable Trust Acts* [Chairman: G. J. Shaw-Lefevre]. H.C. 33 (1884–5). VIII, 1, which dealt with allotments.

4274 ONSLOW COMMITTEE ON SMALL HOLDINGS. Report of the departmental committee appointed by the Board of Agriculture and Fisheries to inquire into and report upon the subject of small holdings in Great Britain [Chairman: Earl of Onslow]. [Cd. 3277] H.C. (1906). LV, 411. Minutes of evidence. [Cd. 3278] H.C. (1906). LV, 477.

4275 TURNOR COMMITTEE ON THE EQUIPMENT OF SMALL HOLDINGS. Report of the departmental committee appointed by the President of the Board of Agriculture and Fisheries to inquire and report as to buildings for small holdings in England and Wales [Chairman: Christopher Turnor]. [Cd. 6708] H.C. (1913). XV, 561.

Fuller than the *Report of the departmental committee . . . [on the] duration of buildings . . . for small holdings* [Chairman: Hon. E. J. Strutt]. [Cd. 6536] H.C. (1912–13). XLVI, 907.

4276 BOARD OF AGRICULTURE AND FISHERIES. Annual report of land division on proceedings under various Acts, for the years 1900 [–1937]. 1901–38.

### (e) *Co-operative and other Land Companies*

4277 SMITH (LOUIS PATRICK FREDERICK). The evolution of agricultural co-operation. Oxf. 1961.

4278 DIGBY (MARGARET). Agricultural co-operation in Great Britain. 1949. Rev. edn. by Sheila Gorst. Oxf. 1957.

4279 KINGSLEY (CHARLES). The application of associative principles and methods to agriculture. 1851.

4280 BRABROOK (*Sir* EDWARD WILLIAM). 'The co-operative land movement'. *Stat. Soc. J.* xxxvii (1874), 327–36.

4281 GREY (ALBERT), *Earl Grey*. 'Profit-sharing in agriculture'. *Roy. Agric. Soc. J.* lii (3 ser. ii) (1891), 771–93.

4282 HOBSON (JOHN ATKINSON) *ed*. Co-operative labour upon the land (and other papers): the report of a conference upon 'Land, co-operation and the unemployed', held at Holborn Town Hall in October 1894. 1895.

4283 AGRICULTURAL ORGANISATION SOCIETY. Annual report. 1901+. Leicester. 1902+.

The soc. also publ. *A.O.S. journal*, 1907–10, which became *Co-operation in agriculture*, 1910–15, and *Our land*, 1908–12.

4284 RADFORD (GEORGE). Agricultural co-operation. [1910.]
Repr. from *Our land*.

4285 WOLFF (HENRY WILLIAM). Co-operation in agriculture. 1912.

Wolff wrote many books advocating co-operative banks and German-style co-operative institutions.

4286 SALISBURY COMMITTEE ON LAND COMPANIES. Report from the select committee of the House of Lords appointed to consider whether it would not be desirable that the powers now vested in the companies for the improvement of land should be made a subject of general regulation [Chairman: Marquess of Salisbury]. H.C. 403 (1854–5). VII, 245.

4287 RITCHIE (JAMES EWING). Freehold land societies: their history, present position, and claims. [1853.]

An important short pamphlet.

4288 NATIONAL FREEHOLD LAND SOCIETY. The freeholder's circular. 1852–1906.

Title changed to *The national freehold land society*, 1885+.

### (f) *Copyhold and Customary Tenures*

4289 ADKIN (BENAIAH WHITLEY). Copyhold and other land tenures of England. 1907. 7th edn. 1928.

The best intro. to the subject.

4290 LORDS COMMITTEE ON COPYHOLD ENFRANCHISEMENT BILL. Report from the select committee of the House of Lords on the Copyhold Enfranchisement Bill [H.L.]. H.L. 128 (1887). IX, 9.

Voluminous.

4291 SCRIVEN (JOHN). A practical treatise on copyhold tenure and court keeping. 1816. 7th edn. 1896.

Standard. There are also two useful short textbooks, George Wingrove Cooke, *A treatise on the law and practice of copyhold enfranchisement*, 1852, 2nd edn. 1853, and Archibald Brown, *The law and practice on enfranchisements and commutations under the Copyhold Acts, 1841–1887 . . .*, 1888, 3rd edn. 1903.

4292 ELTON (CHARLES ISAAC). A treatise on the law of copyholds and customary tenures of land. 1874. 2nd edn. 1893. Suppl. 1898.

Elton also publ. *Custom and tenant right*, 1882, and *The tenures of Kent*, 1867.

### (g) *Commons and Enclosures*

4293 HOSKINS (WILLIAM GEORGE) *and* STAMP (*Sir* LAURENCE DUDLEY). The common lands of England & Wales. 1963.

4294 SCRUTTON (*Sir* THOMAS EDWARD). Commons and common fields: or, the history and policy of the laws relating to commons and enclosures in England. Camb. 1887.

4295 CURTLER (WILLIAM HENRY RICKETTS). The enclosure and redistribution of our land. Oxf. 1920.

A general hist. of enclosures. See also Gilbert Slater, *The English peasantry and the enclosure of common fields*, 1907; and Sir Edward Carter Kersey Gonner, *Common land*

*and inclosure*, 1912. Lists of enclosure awards for most counties have been publ. for the period up to 1868. See *Inst. Hist. Res. Bull.* xviii (1940–1), 97–101. For later enclosures there is a voluminous literature among the parl. papers: see *General index* (33).

4296  TOTTIE (JOHN WILLIAM). 'On the Inclosure Commission: its powers and the principles on which they have been exercised'. *Stat. Soc. J.* xxv (1862), 297–312.

4297  HUNTER (*Sir* ROBERT). 'The movements for the inclosure and pre-servation of open lands'. *Roy. Stat. Soc. J.* lx (1897), 360–427.

4298  SHAW-LEFEVRE (GEORGE JOHN), *Baron Eversley*. Commons, forests and footpaths: the story of the battle during the last forty-five years for public rights over the commons, forests and footpaths of England. 1910.

Important. Orig. publ. as *English commons and forests . . .*, 1894. See also William Henry Williams, *The Commons, Open Spaces & Footpaths Preservation Society, 1865–1965 . . .*, 1965.

4299  TAVENER (LAURENCE ELLIS). The common lands of Hampshire. Hampshire County Council. 1957.

For Cambridgeshire there is a shorter report by the Cambridgeshire Town Planning Dept., Camb. 1956.

4300  HART (CYRIL EDWIN). The commoners of Dean Forest. Gloucester. 1951.

See also his *The verderers and speech-court of the Forest of Dean*, Gloucester 1950.

4301  COWPER COMMITTEE ON INCLOSURE ACT, 1845. Report from the select committee on Inclosure Act [Chairman: William Francis Cowper]. H.C. 304 (1868–9). X, 327.

Discussed the making of better provision for public recreation and allotments for the labouring poor.

4302  ROYAL COMMISSION ON COMMON LAND, 1955–1958 [Chair-man: Sir William Ivor Jennings]. Report. [Cmd. 462]. H.C. (1957–8). X, 1.

Incls. a hist. by William George Hoskins.

4303  COOKE (GEORGE WINGROVE). The acts for facilitating the in-closure of commons in England and Wales: with a treatise on the law of rights of commons . . . 1846. 4th edn. 1864.

A short legal textbook. See also Charles Isaac Elton, *The law of common fields: a treatise on commons and waste lands . . .*, 1868.

4304  HUNTER (*Sir* ROBERT). The preservation of open spaces and of footpaths and other rights of way: a practical treatise on the law of the subject. 1896. 2nd edn. 1902.

A very fine piece of work, prepared chiefly for the use of the Commons Preservation Soc.

## 3. Farming Methods

For agricultural science see **8642–54**; for agricultural education see **8172**.

### (a) General

**4305** SPRING (DAVID). The English landed estate in the nineteenth century: its administration. Baltimore [Md.]. 1963.

**4306** TROW-SMITH (ROBERT). English husbandry: from the earliest times to the present day. 1951.

See also Thomas Barclay Hennell, *Change in the farm*, Camb. 1934, 2nd edn. 1936, George Edwin Fussell, *Farming technique from prehistoric to modern times*, 1966, and W. Harwood Long, 'The development of mechanisation in English farming', *Agric. Hist. Rev.* xi (1963), 15–26.

**4307** WATSON (*Sir* JAMES ANDERSON SCOTT) *and* HOBBS (MAY ELLIOT). Great farmers. 1937. Rev. edn. 1951.

Standard. The main source for the lives of agriculturalists is the series of obituaries publ. in the *Royal Agric. Soc. J.* and other agric. periodicals. Paolo E. Coletta, 'Philip Pusey: English country squire', *Agric. Hist.* xviii (1944), 83–91, is useful. Among farming memoirs, Arthur George Street's semi-fictional *Farmer's glory*, 1932, etc., is widely admired, and the following are good: Thomas Bedford Franklin, *Good pastures: some memories of farming fifty years ago* [at Towcester, Northants], Camb. 1944; Samuel George Kendall, *Farming memoirs of a west-country yeoman*, 1944; Arthur Granville Bradley, *Exmoor memories*, 1926, and *When squires and farmers thrived*, 1927; Sir Henry Rider Haggard, *A farmer's year: being his commonplace book for 1898*, 1899; Primrose McConnell, *The diary of a working farmer: being the true history of a year's farming in Essex*, 1906; and Maude Robinson, *A South Down farm in the sixties*, 1938, repr. 1947.

**4308** MORTON (JOHN CHALMERS). The Prince Consort's farms: an agricultural memoir. 1863.

One of the few detailed accounts of experimental farming. Thomas John Elliot, *The land question: its examination and solution from an agricultural point of view, as illustrated by twenty-three years' experience on the Wilton House home farm, near Salisbury, Wilts, by the Right Honourable the Lord Herbert and Lady Herbert of Lea*, 1884, gives detailed accounts of a model cereal farm run on similar lines. These farms belong to a different world from that of Chandos Wren Hoskyns, *Talpa: or, the chronicles of a clay farm: an agricultural fragment*, 1852, new [i.e. 7th] edn. 1903.

**4309** GAVIN (*Sir* WILLIAM). Ninety years of family farming: the story of Lord Rayleigh's and Strutt & Parker farms. 1967.

Important for late 19th- and 20th-cent. large-scale scientific farming.

**4310** PARKER (JOHN OXLEY). The Oxley Parker papers: from the letters and diaries of an Essex family of land agents in the nineteenth century. Colchester. 1964.

**4311** THOMPSON (FRANCIS MICHAEL LONGSTRETH). Chartered surveyors: the growth of a profession. 1968.

An important study of the main professional group of estate managers.

**4312  INSTITUTION OF SURVEYORS. Transactions. 1868–9+.**

The Institution (from 1881 Surveyors' Institution, now Royal Institution of Chartered Surveyors) also publ. *Professional notes* [later *Journal*], 1886–7+. These two publs. give a great deal of information about estate management. The *Land Agents' Soc. journal*, 1902+, and *The estate magazine* of the Country Gentlemen's Assoc., 1904+, serve a similar function. *The country gentlemen's catalogue . . .*, 1893–9, publ. as *The country gentlemen's estate book*, 1900–24, with monthly suppl. 1901–3, and *Farmer and Stockbreeder's year book*, publ. under various titles since 1879, have some additional material.

**4313  LAWES (*Sir* JOHN BENNET) *and* GILBERT (*Sir* JOSEPH HENRY). 'Rotation of crops'. *Roy. Agric. Soc. J.* lv (3 ser. v) (1894), 585–646.**

Comprehensive. See also W. J. Malden, 'Recent changes in farm practices', ibid. lvii (3 ser. vii) (1896), 22–39, and Gilbert Murray, 'Variations in the four-course system', ibid. liii (3 ser. iii) (1892), 291–306.

**4314  STAMP (*Sir* LAURENCE DUDLEY) *ed.* The land of Britain: the report of the land utilisation survey of Great Britain: reports. 92 pts. 1936–46.**

Mainly on the 1930s, but has some data for earlier periods. There is a general summary of the survey in Stamp's *The land of Britain: its use and misuse*, 1947, 2nd edn. 1950. See also Robin Hewitson Best, *The major land uses of Great Britain: an evaluation of the conflicting records and estimates of land utilization since 1900*, Wye College Studies 4, 1959, and Robin Hewitson Best and John Terence Coppock, *The changing use of land in Britain*, 1962.

**4315  FRANKLIN (THOMAS BEDFORD). British grasslands from earliest times to the present day. 1953.**

**4316  ORWIN (CHARLES STEWART) *and* ORWIN (CHRISTABEL SUSAN). The open fields. Oxf. 1938. 2nd edn. 1954.**

Little on the period, for which see rather their *The history of Laxton*, Oxf. 1935, which deals with an open-field village.

**4317  EVANS (GEORGE EWART). The horse in the furrow. 1960.**

A history of farming with the horse in parts of East Anglia. For the horse generally see **4357–60.**

**4318  PERCIVAL (JOHN). Wheat in Great Britain. 1934. 2nd edn. 1948.**

See also M. K. Bennett, 'British wheat yield per acre for seven centuries', *Econ. Hist.* iii (1934–7), no. 10, 12–29.

**4319  OLSON (MANCUR) *and* HARRIS (CURTIS C.). 'Free trade in "corn": a statistical study of the prices and production of wheat in Great Britain from 1873 to 1914'. *Q.J. Econ.* lxxiii (1959), 145–68.**

**4320  BEAVEN (EDWIN SLOPER). Barley: fifty years of observation and experiment. 1947.**

**4321  SALAMAN (REDCLIFFE NATHAN). The history and social influence of the potato. Camb. 1949. Repr. 1963.**

4322  BURTON (WILLIAM GLYNN). The potato: a survey of its history and of factors influencing its yield, nutritive value and storage. 1948.

Includes acreage statistics from 1866.

4323  LAWES (*Sir* JOHN BENNET) *and* GILBERT (*Sir* JOSEPH HENRY). 'The growth of sugar-beet, and the manufacture of sugar, in the United Kingdom'. *Roy. Agric. Soc. J.* lix (3 ser. ix) (1898), 344–70.

4324  FUSSELL (GEORGE EDWIN). The English dairy farmer, 1500–1900. 1966.

4325  LONG (JAMES). British dairy farming . . . 1885.

The best contemp. book on the subject. But see also Long's *The dairy farm*, 1889, 2nd edn. 1889, John Chalmers Morton, *Handbook of dairy husbandry*, 1860, and John Prince Sheldon, *Dairy farming: being the theory, practice and methods of dairying*, 1879–81, *The farm and the dairy*, 1889, 4th edn. 1908, *British dairying* . . ., 1893, 3rd edn. 1908, and *Dairying* . . . [1912].

4326  BANNISTER (RICHARD). Cantor lectures on our milk, butter and cheese supply. Soc. of Arts. 1888.

Discusses recent developments.

4327  WHETHAM (EDITH HOLT). 'The London milk trade, 1860–1900'. *Econ. Hist. Rev.* 2 ser. xvii (1964–5), 369–80.

4328  JENKINS (H. M.). 'Report on Cheshire dairy-farming'. *Roy. Agric. Soc. J.* xxxi (2 ser. vi) (1870), 163–73.

See also T. J. Young, 'Dairy husbandry in Lancashire and Cheshire', *Roy. Agric. Soc. J.* lxxvi (1915), 97–110.

4329  CHEKE (VALERIE ESSEX). The story of cheese-making in Britain. 1959.

Good. See also John Chalmers Morton, 'On cheese-making in home dairies and in factories', *Roy. Agric. Soc. J.* xxxvi (2 ser. xi) (1875), 261–300, and Gilbert Murray, 'The origin and progress of the factory system of cheese-making in Derbyshire', ibid. xxxii (2 ser. vii) (1871), 42–60. Books like Sir John Collings Squire, ed., *Cheddar gorge: a book of English cheeses*, 1937, have no value except as period pieces.

4330  FRASER (HENRY MALCOLM). History of bee-keeping in Britain. Bee Research Assoc. 1958.

4331  KAINS-JACKSON (CHARLES). 'Agricultural weights and measures'. *Roy. Agric. Soc. J.* lxvii (1906), 106–17.

### (b) *Contemporary Textbooks*

4332  STEPHENS (HENRY). The book of the farm: detailing the labours of the farmer, farm-steward, ploughman, shepherd, hedger, cattle-man, field-worker and dairy-maid . . . 3 v. Edin. 1844. 5th edn. by James Macdonald. 3 v. Edin. 1908–9.

A splendid work, much better than John Marius Wilson, ed., *The rural cyclopedia: or, a general dictionary of agriculture* . . ., 4 v. Edin. 1847–9, etc. John Chalmers Morton, ed., *A cyclopedia of agriculture* . . ., 2 v. Glasgow 1851–5, is a comparable work. There is much local information in William Lewis Rham, *The dictionary of the farm* . . ., rev. by William and Hugh Raynbird, 1853, etc.

4333  MORTON (JOHN LOCKHART). The resources of estates: being a treatise on the agricultural improvement and general management of landed property. 1858.

4334  MECHI (JOHN JOSEPH). How to farm profitably: or, the sayings and doings of Mr. Alderman Mechi. 1859. Enl. edn. 1864.

Cont. in *Profitable farming* . . ., 1872, and *How to farm profitably* . . . *third series*, 1876. The best-known of the many books publ. by benevolent eccentrics for the enlightenment of farmers.

4335  DONALDSON (JOHN). British agriculture: containing the cultivation of land, management of crops, and the economy of animals. 1860.

4336  COPLAND (SAMUEL). Agriculture, ancient and modern: a historical account of its principles and practice, exemplified in their rise, progress and development. 2 v. In pts. 1864–6.

4337  CURTIS (CHARLES EDWARD). Estate management: a practical handbook for landlords, stewards, and pupils. 1879. 6th edn. 1911.

A good short manual which is a useful intro. to all aspects of agric. It repl. Robert Erskine Brown, *The book of the landed estate* . . ., Edin. 1869, and other manuals.

4338  BURN (ROBERT SCOTT). The practical directory for the improvement of landed property, rural and suburban, and the economic cultivation of its farms. Edin. 1881.

Burn also publ. *Outlines of landed estates management*, 1877, 2nd edn. 1880, and *Outlines of modern farming*, 5 v. 1863–5, 7th edn., 5 v. 1889–1904.

4339  MORTON (JOHN CHALMERS) *ed.* Handbook of the farm series. 11 v. 1881–1912.

A ser. of short vols., written by experts, which deal with the soil, plants, equipment, and livestock of the farm.

4340  FREAM (WILLIAM). Elements of agriculture: a textbook prepared under the authority of the Royal Agricultural Society of England . . . 1892. 13th edn. 1955.

4341  WRIGHT (*Sir* ROBERT PATRICK) *ed.* The standard cyclopedia of modern agriculture and rural economy. By the most distinguished authorities and specialists. 12 v. 1908–11.

Better than its rival, Charles Edward Green and D. Young, eds., *Encyclopedia of agriculture*, 4 v. Edin. [1907–9.]

4342  McCONNELL (PRIMROSE). The complete farmer: a practical handbook on soils, crops, live stock, & farm equipment. 1910.

## (c) *Livestock*

For genetics see Ian Lauder Mason, *A world dictionary of breeds, types and varieties of livestock*, Commonwealth Agric. Bureaux, Farnham Royal, 1951, suppl. 1957. There are numerous articles on particular types of livestock in *Roy. Agric. Soc. J.* and *Bath & West Soc. J.*

4343  TROW-SMITH (ROBERT). A history of British livestock husbandry, 1700–1900. 1959.

4344  WHETHAM (EDITH HOLT). 'Livestock prices in Britain, 1851–93'. *Agric. Hist. Rev.* xi (1963), 27–35. Repr. in Minchinton (**4157**) II, 199–209.

See also her 'The changing cattle enterprises of England and Wales, 1870–1910', *Geographical J.* cxxix (1963), 378–80, repr. in Minchinton (**4157**) II, 211–15.

4345  FLETCHER (THOMAS WILLIAM). 'Lancashire livestock farming during the great depression'. *Agric. Hist. Rev.* ix (1961), 17–42.

4346  M'COMBIE (WILLIAM). Cattle and cattle-breeders. Edin. 1867. 4th edn. 1886.

M'Combie was the leading breeder of his day. The 4th edn. includes a memoir of him.

4347  HEAPE (WALTER). The breeding industry: its value to the country and its needs. Camb. 1906.

4348  YOUATT (WILLIAM). The complete grazier and farmer's and cattle breeder's assistant: a compendium of husbandry . . . 11th edn. by Robert Scott Burn. 1864. 13th edn. by William Fream. 1893. 15th edn. by William E. Bear. 1908.

This famous manual derives ultimately from Youatt's *Cattle: their breeds, management and diseases*, publ. by the Soc. for the Diffusion of Useful Knowledge, 1834. Comparable but shorter works are Duncan George Forbes Macdonald, *Cattle, sheep and deer* . . ., 1872, and Robert Oliphant Pringle, *The live-stock of the farm*, 1874, 3rd edn. 1886.

4349  WALLACE (ROBERT). Farm live stock of Great Britain. Edin. 1885. 5th edn. 1923.

The best of the late Victorian textbooks. But see also John Coleman, ed., *The cattle, sheep and pigs of Great Britain: being, a series of articles on the various breeds of the United Kingdom, their history, management, &c.*, 1887, 2nd edn. 1887, James Sinclair, ed., *Live-stock handbooks*, 6 v. 1893–7, and Sir Cadwaladr Bryner Jones, ed., *Live stock of the farm*, 6 v. 1915–16.

4350  LYDEKKER (RICHARD). The ox and its kindred. 1912.

Still the only general book on the hist. of the subject. Lydekker also publ. *The sheep and its cousins*, 1912.

4351  MACDONALD (JAMES) *and* SINCLAIR (JAMES). History of polled Aberdeen or Angus cattle. Edin. 1882. Rev. edn. 1910.

The first British breed hist., now superseded. The title of the 1910 edn. was *History of Aberdeen-Angus cattle*. Macdonald and Sinclair also publ. *History of Hereford cattle*, 1886, rev. edn. 1909, while Sinclair alone ed. *History of the Devon breed of cattle*, 1893, and *History of shorthorn cattle*, 1907. Later hists. incl. Isabella M. Bruce, *The history of the Aberdeenshire shorthorn*, Aberdeen 1923; George Kenneth Whitehead, *The ancient white cattle of Britain and their descendants*, 1953; Eric James Boston, ed., *Jersey cattle*, 1954; James Rust Barclay and Alexander Keith, *The Aberdeen-Angus breed: a history*, Aberdeen 1958; and John Keith Stanford, *British Friesians: a history of the breed*, 1956. In addition there are herd-books for many breeds.

4352 JONES (ERIC LIONEL). 'Hereford cattle and Ryeland sheep: economic aspects of breed changes, 1780–1870'. *Woolhope Naturalists Field Club Trans.* xxxviii (1964–6), 36–48.

4353 RYDER (M. L.). 'The history of sheep breeds in Britain'. *Agric. Hist. Rev.* xii (1964), 1–12, 65–82.

4354 DARBY (JOSEPH). 'The breeds of sheep and their adaptations to different districts in the South and West of England'. *Bath & West Soc. J.* 3 ser. iii (1871), 65–98.

4355 MALDEN (WALTER JAMES). British sheep and shepherding. [1915.]
Sums up the state of knowledge of sheep at the end of the period.

4356 SCOTT (JOHN) *and* SCOTT (CHARLES). Blackfaced sheep: their history, distribution and improvement: with methods of management and treatment of their principal diseases. Edin. 1888.
Other breed hists. incl. E. Walford Lloyd, *The Southdown sheep*, 1922, 4th edn. 1946.

4357 DE TRAFFORD (*Sir* HUMPHREY FRANCIS) *ed*. The horses of the British empire. 2 v. [1907.]
A good illustrated textbook. Samuel Sidney, *The book of the horse . . .*, 1873–5, rev. [4th] edn. 1892–3, was also very popular in its day. Vesey-Fitzgerald, *The book of the horse* (**7781**) deals chiefly with race-horses. The best contemp. work on horse management was Sir Frederick Wellington John FitzWygram, *Horses and stables*, 1869, 5th edn. 1901.

4358 PEASE (*Sir* ALFRED EDWARD). Horse-breeding for farmers. 1894.

4359 FAWCUS (HENRY E.). 'The horse-breeding industry in Yorkshire'. *Roy. Agric. Soc. J.* lxxii (1911), 85–116.

4360 LORDS COMMITTEE ON HORSES. Report from the select committee of the House of Lords on horses [Chairman: Lord Rosebery]. H.C. 325 (1873). XIV, 1.
Deals with the breeding and importation of working horses. The Royal Commission on Horse Breeding (whose reports are listed in Ford, *Breviate, 1900–16* (**32**), pp. 84–5) dealt only with the award of Queen's premiums at agric. shows.

(d) *Market Gardening, Fruit, and Hops*

4361 EVERSHED (HENRY). 'Market gardening'. *Roy. Agric. Soc. J.* xxxii (2 ser. vii) (1871), 420–36.

4362 DONALDSON (JOHN) *and* BURN (ROBERT SCOTT). Suburban farming: a treatise on the laying out and cultivation of farms adapted to the produce of milk, butter and cheese, eggs, poultry and pigs. 1877.

4363 WHITEHEAD (*Sir* CHARLES). 'Report upon the market-garden and market-garden farm competition, 1879'. *Roy. Agric. Soc. J.* xl (2 ser. xv) (1879), 832–68.

4364 JOURNAL OF HORTICULTURE, cottage gardener and country gentleman. 1861–1915.
Title varies: publ. as *The cottage gardener*, 1849–61. Useful for crops like potatoes.

4365 WHITEHEAD (*Sir* CHARLES). 'Fifty years of fruit farming'. *Roy. Agric. Soc. J.* l (2 ser. xxv) (1889), 156–80.
See also his 'Fruit-growing in Kent', *Roy. Agric. Soc. J.* xxxviii (2 ser. xiii) (1877), 92–121, and David Harvey, 'Fruit growing in Kent in the nineteenth century', *Archaeologia Cantiana* lxxix (1964), 95–108. John Wright, *Profitable fruit growing for cottagers & smallholders* . . ., 1889, 11th edn. 1920, was a popular handbook of the period.

4366 BEAR (WILLIAM E.). 'Flower and fruit farming in England'. Pt. I. *Roy. Agric. Soc. J.* lix (3 ser. ix) (1898), 286–316. Pt. II, ibid. 512–50. Pt. III, ibid. lx (3 ser. x) (1899), 30–86. Pt. IV, ibid. 267–313.

4367 EAGLE (EDGAR C.). 'Some light on the beginnings of the Lincolnshire bulb industry'. *Lincs. Historian.* i (1947–53), 220–9.

4368 UDALE (JAMES). 'Market gardening and fruit growing in the Vale of Evesham'. *Roy. Agric. Soc. J.* lxix (1908), 95–104.

4369 BARNARD (ALFRED). Orchards and gardens, ancient and modern: with a description of the orchards, gardens, model farms and factories owned by Mr. William Whiteley . . . 1895.

4370 GRIFFITH-BOSCAWEN COMMITTEE ON FRUIT INDUSTRY. Report of the departmental committee appointed by the Board of Agriculture and Fisheries to inquire into and report upon the fruit industry of Great Britain [Chairman: Arthur S. T. Griffith-Boscawen]. [Cd. 2589] H.C. (1905). XX, 541. Minutes of evidence. [Cd. 2719] H.C. (1906). XXIV, 1.

4371 HOGG (ROBERT) *and* BULL (HENRY GRAVES), *eds.* The Herefordshire pomona: containing coloured figures and descriptions of the most esteemed kinds of apples and pears. Woolhope Naturalists' Field Club. 2 v. Hereford. 1876–85.
See also Hogg's *The fruit manual: containing the descriptions & synonymes of the fruits and fruit trees commonly met with in* . . . *Great Britain*, 1860, 5th edn. 1884.

4372 PARKER (HUBERT HENRY). The hop industry. 1934.
Standard. There is a good illust. account of the industry in Sir Charles Whitehead, *Hops: from the set to the sky-lights*, 1881, and much hist. in his 'Fifty years of hop-farming', *Roy. Agric. Soc. J.* li (3 ser. i) (1890), 321–48, and 'Hop cultivation', ibid. liv (3 ser. iv) (1893), 217–62.

4373  DODSON COMMITTEE ON HOP DUTIES. Report from the select committee on hop duties [Chairman: J. G. Dodson]. H.C. 252 (1857–Sess. 2). XIV, 347.
Deals with all aspects of the hop industry.

4374  SHAW-LEFEVRE COMMITTEE ON THE HOP INDUSTRY. Report from the select committee on the hop industry [Chairman: G. J. Shaw-Lefevre]. H.C. 302 (1890). XIII, 275.
The committee first met in the previous session but presented only a formal report.

4375  COLLINS COMMITTEE ON THE HOP INDUSTRY. Report from the select committee on the hop industry [Chairman: Sir William Collins]. H.C. 213 (1908). VIII, 285.

4376  STOPES (HENRY). Malt and malting: an historical, scientific, and practical treatise, showing, as clearly as existing knowledge permits, what malt is, and how to make it. 1885.
Extensive bibliog. An invaluable work, well illustrated.

4377  WHITE (EDWARD SKEATE). The maltster's guide: being a history of the art of malting from the earliest ages: also a description of the various systems of malting, . . . the construction of malthouses, and an abstract of the whole of the malt laws. 1860.
A brief handbook.

4378  BARTTELOT COMMITTEE ON MALT TAX. Report from the select committee on malt tax [Chairman: Colonel Barttelot]. H.C. 470 (1867). XI, 1. Further report. H.C. 420 (1867–8). IX, 235.
A comprehensive survey.

(e) *Horticulture*

4379  ROYAL HORTICULTURAL SOCIETY. The Lindley library: catalogue of books, pamphlets, manuscripts and drawings. [Comp. by H. R. Hutchinson and ed. by E. W. Hamilton.] 1927.

4380  GOTHEIN (MARIE LUISE). A history of garden art. Trans. by Laura Archer-Hind. Ed. by Walter Page Wright. 2 v. 1928.
Good. There is also a little on the period in Derek Clifford, *A history of garden design*, 1962.

4381  HADFIELD (MILES). Gardening in Britain. 1960.
Now standard. Replaced Alicia Margaret Tyssen-Amherst (afterwards Cecil), Baroness Rockley, *A history of gardening in England*, 1895, 3rd edn. 1910, and Eleanour Sinclair Rohde, *The story of the garden*, 1932.

4382  FLETCHER (HAROLD ROY). The story of the Royal Horticultural Society, 1804–1968. Roy. Hort. Soc. 1969.
See also Andrew Murray, *The book of the Royal Horticultural Society, 1862–1836*, 1863.

4383 TAYLOR (GEOFFREY GORDON). Some nineteenth-century gardeners. 1951.

Like Miles Hadfield, *Pioneers in gardening*, 1955, and Ronald Webber, *The early horticulturalists*, Newton Abbot and N.Y. 1968, rather thin.

4384 TAYLOR (GEOFFREY GORDON). The Victorian flower garden. 1952.

There is a large contemp. literature, centring round William Robinson, *The English flower garden . . .*, 1883, 15th edn. 1933, Sir Reginald Theodore Blomfield, *The formal garden in England*, 1892, 3rd edn. 1901, and the works of Gertrude Jekyll (**4388**). For descriptions of gardens see George S. Elgood and Gertrude Jekyll, *Some English gardens*, 1904; Robert William Theodore Günther, *Oxford gardens . . .*, Oxf. 1912; Henry Avray Tipping, *English gardens*, 1925; William Robinson, *Gravetye manor . . .*, 1911; Henry Inigo Triggs, *Formal gardens . . .*, 1902; Thomas Hayton Mawson, *The art & craft of garden-making*, 1900, 5th edn. 1926.

4385 ALLEN (DAVID ELLISTON). The Victorian fern craze: a history of pteridomania. 1969.

4386 VEITCH (JAMES HERBERT). Hortus Veitchii: a history of the rise and progress of the nurseries of Messrs. James Veitch and Sons . . . Priv. pr. 1906.

4387 LOUDON. Lady with green fingers: the life of Jane Loudon. By Bea Howe. 1961.

Little on the period, but useful as social hist. and as background to the work of Gertrude Jekyll (**4388**).

4388 JEKYLL. Gertrude Jekyll: a memoir. By Francis Jekyll. 1934.

Bibliog. Miss Jekyll was the leading garden designer and theorist of her day. Some of her articles are in Francis Jekyll and George Crosbie Taylor, eds., *A gardener's testament: a selection of articles and notes*, 1937.

4389 MAWSON. The life & work of an English landscape architect: an autobiography. By Thomas Hayton Mawson. 1927.

4390 NICHOLSON (GEORGE) *ed.* The illustrated dictionary of gardening: a practical and scientific encyclopaedia of horticulture. 6 v. 1885–1904.

The fullest contemp. textbook, since repl. by Frederick James Chittenden, ed., *The Royal Horticultural Society dictionary of gardening*, 2nd edn. 4 v. and suppl. Oxf. 1956. Among older books see also Charles M'Intosh *The book of the garden*, 2 v. 1853–5, Robert Thompson, *The gardener's assistant: practical and scientific*, Glasgow 1859, 4th edn. 6 v. Lond. [1925], Frederick William Burbidge, *Horticulture*, 1877, and John Wright, *The flower grower's guide . . .*, 3 v. 1896–1901, new edn. 2 v. 1924.

4391 [ROYAL] HORTICULTURAL SOCIETY of London. Journal. 1846–55. 1866+.

The leading gardening j. The Soc. also publ. *Proceedings*, 1838–43, 1859–69. There is an index to *J. & Proc.*, 1838–1935. The other main contemp. periodicals were *The floricultural cabinet . . .*, 1833–59, cont. as *The gardeners' [weekly] magazine*, 1860–1916, *Gardeners' chronicle*, 1841+, *The cottage gardener . . .*, 1849–61, cont. as *The j. of horticulture . . .*, 1861–1915, *The floral world and garden guide*, 1858–80, *The garden*,

1871–1927, *Gardening* [*illustrated*], 1879+, *Amateur gardening*, 1884+, *The gardening world*, 1884–1909, *The horticultural advertiser*, Nottingham 1883+, and *The horticultural trade j.*, Burnley 1898+.

4392 INTERNATIONAL HORTICULTURAL EXHIBITION and Botanical Congress, 1866. Report of proceedings. [1867.]

A useful source. Cont. by Reginald Cory, comp., *The horticultural record . . . of flowers, plants, shrubs, groups, & rock gardens exhibited at the Royal International Horticultural Exhibition, 1912, accompanied by contributions on the progress of horticulture since the first great International Horticultural Exhibition of 1866*, 1914.

### (f) *Forestry*

4393 NISBET (JOHN). Our forests and woodlands. Haddon Hall Libr. 1900. Rev. edn. 1909.

A good starting-point. Bernhard Eduard Fernow, *A brief history of forestry in Europe, the United States and other countries*, Toronto [1909], rev. edn. [1911], and Sir William Somerville, 'Forestry in some of its economic aspects', *Roy. Stat. Soc. J.* lxxii (1909), 40–54, are also useful for background material.

4394 GRIGOR (JOHN). Arboriculture: or, a practical treatise on raising and managing forest trees and on the profitable extension of the woods and forests of Great Britain. Edin. 1868. 2nd edn. 1881.

4395 RATTRAY (JOHN) *and* MILL (HUGH ROBERT) *eds.* Forestry and forest products: prize essays of the Edinburgh International Forestry Exhibition, 1884. Edin. 1885.

4396 SCHLICH (*Sir* WILLIAM). The utility of forests and fundamental principles of sylviculture. 1889.

This book became the first v. of his *A manual of forestry*, first publ. under various titles in 5 v. by Schlich and William Rogers Fisher, 1889–96, and reissued in a uniform edn. 5 v. 1906–8. The manual then became the basis for Charles Oldham Hanson, *Forestry for woodmen*, Oxf. 1911, 3rd edn. 1934. Schlich's views on the need for more British forests are set out in his *Forestry in the United Kingdom* [1904].

4397 SIMPSON (JOHN). The new forestry: or, the continental system adapted to British woodlands and game preservation. Sheffield. 1900.

Simpson also publ. *British woods and their owners: with illustrations of British woods and continental state forestry*, Sheffield & Lond. 1909.

4398 NISBET (JOHN). The forester: a practical treatise on British forestry and arboriculture for landowners, land agents and foresters. 2 v. Edin. & Lond. 1905.

Based largely on German practice. Nisbet also publ. many other works on forestry. Percival Trentham Maw, *The practice of forestry: concerning also the financial aspect of afforestation*, Brockenhurst, Hants. 1909, is a shorter manual of the same sort.

4399 FORBES (ARTHUR C.). The development of British forestry. 1910.

Like Edward Percy Stebbing, *British forestry: its present position and outlook after the war*, 1916, discusses ways of improving British forestry. See also Forbes's *English estate forestry*, 1904.

4400 HOWARD (ALEXANDER LIDDON). A manual of the timbers of the world: their characteristics and uses. 1920. 3rd edn. 1948.

The standard modern work.

4401 ENGLISH ARBORICULTURAL SOCIETY [Royal English Forestry Soc.]. Transactions. 1884–1914.

Later transactions are in the *Quarterly J. of Forestry*, Newcastle 1907+, the chief forestry periodical. The best material on forestry is, however, in the *Scottish Arboric. Soc. Trans.* (**9970**) and the *Highland & Agric. Soc. Trans.* (**9964**).

4402 LUBBOCK COMMITTEE ON FORESTRY. Report from the select committee on forestry [Chairmen: Sir John Lubbock, Sir John Kennaway, and Sir Edmund Lechmere]. H.C. 287 (1884–5). VIII, 779. Further reports. H.C. 202 (1886–Sess. 1). IX, 689. H.C. 246 (1887). IX, 537.

4403 MUNRO-FERGUSON COMMITTEE ON BRITISH FORESTRY. Report of the departmental committee appointed by the Board of Agriculture to inquire and report upon British forestry [Chairman: R. C. M. Munro-Ferguson]. [Cd. 1319] H.C. (1902). XX, 1203. Minutes of evidence. [Cd. 1565] H.C. (1903). XVII, 717.

4404 GUEST COMMISSION ON COAST EROSION AND AFFORESTA-TION. Second report (on afforestation) of the royal commission appointed to inquire into and to report on certain questions affecting coast erosion, the reclamation of tidal lands and afforestation in the United Kingdom [Chairman: the Hon. Ivor Churchill Guest, later Lord Ashby St. Ledgers and Viscount Wimborne]. [Cd. 4460] H.C. (1909). XIV, 125. Minutes of evidence. [Cd. 4461] H.C. (1909). XIV, 185.

4405 ADVISORY COMMITTEE ON FORESTRY. Committee appointed by the Board of Agriculture and Fisheries to advise on matters relating to the development of policy: reports, July to October 1912 [Chairman: Sir Stafford Howard]. [Cd. 6713] H.C. (1913). XXV, 493.

### (g) *Farm Equipment and Improvements*

The principal sources are the reports of various trials of machinery organized by the agric. socs., and publ. in their journals.

4406 FUSSELL (GEORGE EDWIN). The farmer's tools, 1500–1900: the history of British farm implements, tools and machinery, before the tractor came. 1952.

4407 PIDGEON (DANIEL). 'The evolution of agricultural implements'. *Roy. Agric. Soc. J.* liii (3 ser. iii) (1892), 49–70, 238–58.

4408 SPENCER (ARTHUR JOHN) *and* PASSMORE (JOHN B.). Handbook of the collections illustrating agricultural implements & machinery . . . Science Museum. Lond. 1930.

4409 WRIGHT (PHILIP ARTHUR). Old farm implements. 1961.

4410 PASSMORE (JOHN B.). The English plough. 1930.

4411 SPENCE (CLARK CHRISTIAN). God speed the plow: the coming of steam cultivation to Great Britain. Urbana, Ill. 1960.

See also Harold Bonnett, *Saga of the steam plough*, 1965; John Algernon Clarke, 'Account of the application of steam power to the cultivation of the land', *Roy. Agric. Soc. J.* xx (1859), 174–228, cont. in his 'Five years' progress of steam cultivation', ibid. xxiv (1863), 362–419, 'Reports of the committee appointed to investigate the present state of steam cultivation', ibid. xxviii (2 ser. iii) (1867), 97–427, with a county-by-county survey; and Charles Gay Roberts, 'The influence of the wet season of 1872 on steam-cultivation', ibid. xxxv (2 ser. x) (1874), 173–211.

4412 WRIGHT (PHILIP ARTHUR). Old farm tractors. 1962.

4413 SLIGHT (JAMES) *and* BURN (ROBERT SCOTT). The book of farm implements and machines. Ed. by Henry Stephens. Edin. 1858.

4414 HARVEY (NIGEL). A history of farm buildings in England and Wales. Newton Abbot. 1970.

4415 STEPHENS (HENRY) *and* BURN (ROBERT SCOTT). The book of farm buildings: their arrangement and construction. Edin. & Lond. 1861.

Burn was the leading authority on the subject. See also his 'Brief hints on the construction and arrangement of farm buildings', *Bath & West Soc. J.* 3rd ser. i, pt. II (1870), 9–33, and John Bailey Denton, ed., *The farm homesteads of England: a collection of plans . . . selected from the most approved specimens of farm architecture*, 1864.

4416 TAYLOR (SAMUEL). Modern homesteads: a practical and illustrated treatise on the designing of farm buildings, farm houses and cottages for farm labourers. 1905.

4417 WINDER (THOMAS). Handbook of farm buildings, ponds, etc., and their appurtenances. Country Gent. Assoc. 1908.

4418 GRAHAM (PETER ANDERSON). Reclaiming the waste: Britain's most urgent problem. 1916.

4419 ADKIN (BENAIAH WHITLEY). Land drainage in Britain. 1933.

Incls. a hist. of land drainage.

4420 FUSSELL (GEORGE EDWIN). 'The evolution of field drainage'. *Bath & West Soc. J.* (6th ser. iv) (1929–30), 59–72.

4421 PHILLIPS (A. D. M.). 'Underdraining and the English claylands, 1850–80: a review'. *Agric. Hist. Rev.* xvii (1969), 44–55.

Discusses a ser. of articles: R. W. Sturgess, 'The agricultural revolution on the English clays', *Agric. Hist. Rev.* xiv (1966), 104–21; E. J. T. Collins and E. L. Jones, 'Sectoral advance in English agriculture, 1850–80', ibid. xv (1967), 65–81; R. W. Sturgess, 'The agricultural revolution on the English clays: a rejoinder', ibid. xv (1967), 82–7; and E. H. Whetham, 'Sectoral advance in English agriculture: a summary', ibid. xvi (1968), 46–8.

4422  LITTLE (HERBERT J.). 'Sewage farming'. *Roy. Agric. Soc. J.* xxxii (2 ser. vii) (1871). 389–420.

See also John Chalmers Morton, 'Half-a-dozen English sewage farms', *Roy. Agric. Soc. J.* xxxvii (2 ser. xii) (1876), 407–39.

4423  MATTHEWS (ERNEST ROMNEY). Coast erosion and protection. 1913. 3rd edn. 1934.

Important.

4424  ORWIN (CHARLES STEWART). The reclamation of Exmoor Forest. Oxf. 1929. Rev. edn. by Roger J. Sellick. Newton Abbot. 1970.

See also Edward Terence MacDermot, *The history of the forest of Exmoor*, Taunton 1911.

4425  WILLIAMS (MICHAEL). The draining of the Somerset levels. Camb. 1970.

4426  WELLS (WILLIAM). 'The drainage of Whittlesea Mere'. *Roy. Agric. Soc. J.* xxi (1860), 134–53.

See also his 'On the treatment of the reclaimed bog-land of Whittlesea Mere', ibid. xxxi (2 ser. vi) (1870), 203–8, and Richard B. Grantham, 'A description of the works for reclaiming and marling parts of the late Forest of Delamere in the county of Chester', ibid. xxv (1864), 369–81.

4427  MARTELLI (GEORGE). The Elveden enterprise: a story of the second agricultural revolution. 1952.

The reclamation of the breckland on the Iveagh estate, West Suffolk.

4428  SALISBURY COMMITTEE ON IMPROVEMENT OF LAND. Report from the select committee of the House of Lords on the improvement of land [Chairman: Marquess of Salisbury]. H.C. 326 (1873). XVI, 1.

4429  ANDREWS (GEORGE HENRY). Rudimentary treatise on agricultural engineering. 3 v. 1852–3.

4430  HOZIER (WILLIAM W.). Practical remarks on agricultural drainage . . . 1870.

4431  SCOTT (JOHN). The complete text-book of farm engineering: comprising, practical treatises on draining and embanking; irrigation and water supply; farm roads, fences and gates; farm buildings; barn implements and machines; field implements and machines; and agricultural surveying. 1885.

4432  BEAZELEY (ALEXANDER). The reclamation of land from tidal waters: a handbook for engineers, landed proprietors, and others interested in works of reclamation. 1900.

4433 GUEST COMMISSION ON COAST EROSION etc. First report of the royal commission appointed to enquire into and to report on certain questions affecting coast erosion and the reclamation of tidal lands in the United Kingdom [Chairman: the Hon. Ivor Churchill Guest, later Baron Ashby St. Ledgers and Viscount Wimborne]. [Cd. 3683] H.C. (1907). XXXIV, 1. Minutes of evidence. [Cd. 3684] H.C. (1907). XXXIV, 7. Second report. **4404**. Third report. [Cd. 5708] H.C. (1911). XIV, 1. Minutes of evidence. [Cd. 5709] H.C. (1911). XIV, 203.

## C. FINANCE, BANKING, ETC.

### 1. GENERAL

4434 MASUI (MITSUZO) *ed.* A bibliography of finance. Kobe [Japan]. 1935.

The first section is devoted to British books to 1900.

4435 GIFFEN (*Sir* ROBERT). 'A financial retrospect, 1861–1901'. *Roy. Stat. Soc. J.* lxv (1902), 47–75.

4436 BALOGH (THOMAS), *Baron Balogh*. Studies in financial organization. 1947. Repr. 1950.

Incls. an hist. retrospect on the major financial institutions.

### 2. PUBLIC FINANCE

#### (a) *General*

4437 REES (*Sir* JAMES FREDERICK). A short fiscal and financial history of England, 1815–1918. 1921.

The only hist. of the whole period.

4438 HICKS (URSULA KATHLEEN). British public finances: their structure and development, 1880–1952. 1954.

The standard short intro. to the recent hist. of the subject. See also her 'The budget as an instrument of policy, 1837–1953', *Three Banks Rev.* xviii (June 1953), 16–34.

4439 PEACOCK (ALAN TURNER) *and* WISEMAN (JACK). The growth of public expenditure in the United Kingdom. Nat. Bureau Econ. Res. Public. 72. Princeton. 1961.

Chiefly from 1890.

4440 BALFOUR (*Sir* GEORGE). 'On the budgets and accounts of England and France'. *Stat. Soc. J.* xxix (1866), 323–444.

4441 WILSON (ALEXANDER JOHNSTONE). The national budget: the national debt: taxes and rates. The English citizen series. 1882.

**4442  HIGGS (HENRY). The financial system of the United Kingdom. 1914.**

With his *National economy: an outline of public administration,* 1917, forms a full accoun of public finance in 1914. See also William Franklin Willoughby and others, *The system of financial administration of Great Britain: a report,* N.Y. 1917; Edward Hilton Young, Baron Kennet, *The system of national finance,* 1915, 3rd edn. 1936; and Charles Francis Bastable, *Public finance,* 1892, 3rd edn. 1903, the only adequate textbook publ. during the period.

**4443  DURELL (ARTHUR JAMES VAVASOR). The principles & practice of the system of control over parliamentary grants. Portsmouth. [1917.]**

The most useful general book. But see also Paul Einzig, *The control of the purse: progress and decline of parliament's financial control,* 1959, and Ernest Harold Davenport, *Parliament and the taxpayer* [1918]. Stanislaus Sussmann, *Das Budgetprivileg des Hauses der Gemeinen . . .,* Mannheim & Leipzig 1909, is of little value.

**4444  CHUBB (BASIL). The control of public expenditure: financial committees of the House of Commons. Oxf. 1952. 2nd edn. 1961.**

Detailed, *c.* 1861+.

**4445  BUXTON (SYDNEY CHARLES), *Earl Buxton.* Finance and politics: an historical study, 1783–1885. 2 v. 1888.**

Deals primarily with the annual budget. Suppl. by Sir Bernard Mallet, *British budgets, 1887–88 to 1912–13,* 1913, and Sir Bernard Mallet and Cecil Oswald George, *British budgets, second series, 1913–1914 to 1920–21,* 1929.

**4446  NORTHCOTE (STAFFORD HENRY), *Earl of Iddesleigh.* Twenty years of financial policy: a summary of the chief financial measures passed between 1842 and 1861, with a table of budgets. 1862.**

A fine lucid analysis. A useful comparison is with John Noble, *Fiscal legislation, 1842–1865: a review of the financial changes of that period, and their effects upon revenue, trade, manufactures and employment,* 1867, which is continued in his *National finance: a review of the policy of the last two parliaments, and of the results of modern fiscal legislation,* 1875, and in his *Fifty-three years' taxation and expenditure, 1827–28 to 1879–80,* 1882.

**4447  HIRST (FRANCIS WRIGLEY). Gladstone as financier and economist. 1931.**

The standard account of Gladstonian finance. Repl. Sydney Charles Buxton, Earl Buxton, *Mr. Gladstone as Chancellor of the Exchequer: a study,* 1901. For Gladstone's early budgets see William Ewart Gladstone, *The financial statements of 1853, 1860–1863: to which are added a speech on tax-bills, 1861, and on charities, 1863,* 1863.

**4448  STAMP (JOSIAH CHARLES), *Baron Stamp.* British incomes and property: the application of official statistics to economic problems. 1916.**

An explanation of the value of official statistics (chiefly those of taxation).

**4449  PUBLIC INCOME AND EXPENDITURE: return to an order of the Honourable the House of Commons dated 24 July 1866. Part II : Gross accounts of the United Kingdom, 1801–1869. H.C. 366–I (1868–9). XXXV, 483.**

An invaluable summary of the government accounts to 1869, annotated by Henry Williams Chisholm.

4450 APPROPRIATION ACCOUNTS of the sums granted by parliament for civil services and revenue departments . . . with the reports of the Comptroller- and Auditor-General thereon, for the year ending 31st March [1862+]. 1863+.

These annual accounts, entered in the *Indexes* to parliamentary papers (33) under 'Civil service and revenue departments' give the best picture of civil expenditure. But consult also the annual estimates and supplementary estimates. The army and navy accounts and estimates were publ. separately.

4451 PUBLIC ACCOUNTS COMMITTEE. Index to the reports from the committees of public accounts, prepared by the Comptroller- and Auditor-General. H.C. 86 (1888). LXXIX, 331.

Covers 1857 to 1887, with a reprint of the more important reports. Cont. to 1892 in H.C. 109 (1893–4). LXX, 281. Two subsequent vols. covering 1893–1900 and 1901–7 were publ. as *Handbook to the reports of the committees of public accounts*, vol. III as H.C. 81 (1901). LVIII, 161; and vol. IV as H.C. 382 (1908). LXXXVII, 463. Each vol. includes a cumulative index and is full of unexpected misc. information.

4452 PUBLIC ACCOUNTS COMMITTEE. Epitome of the reports from the committees of public accounts, 1857 to 1910; and of the Treasury minutes thereon. H.C. 36 (1911). XLV, 513.

Extracts from reports of the committees dealing with matters of current importance. A rev. (3rd) edn. covering 1857 to 1938 was publ. as H.C. 154 (1937–8). XXII, 1.

4453 BARING COMMITTEE ON PUBLIC MONIES. Report from the select committee on public monies [Chairman: Sir Francis Thornhill Baring]. H.C. 375 (1856). XV, 1. Further report. H.C. 107 (1857–Sess. I). II, 761. Final report. H.C. 279 (1857–Sess. II). IX, 495. Treasury Minutes. H.C. 94 (1857–8). XXXIV, 377.

Additional committees were appointed to consider contracts and misc. expenditure. See *Report from the select committee on contracts for public departments* [Chairman: William Monsell]. H.C. 362 (1856). VII, 117, and further reports [Chairmen: Colonels Dunne and Baldero] at H.C. 93 (1857–Sess. 1). II, 623; H.C. 269 (1857–Sess 2). XIII, 1; H.C. 319 (1857–8). VI, 1; H.C. 328 (1857–8). VI, 5; and H.C. 398, 418, and 438 (1857–8). VI, 473. Also *Report from the select committee on miscellaneous expenditure* [Chairman: Lord Harry Vane]. H.C. 483 (1860). IX, 473.

4454 CHILDERS COMMITTEE ON CIVIL SERVICES EXPENDITURE. First report from the select committee on civil services expenditure [Chairman: Hugh C. E. Childers]. H.C. 131 (1873). VII, 387. Second report. H.C. 248 (1873). VII, 391. Third report. H.C. 352 (1873). VII, 415.

The second round of the inquiry started by the Baring committee. Again suppl. by a committee on contracts: see *Report from the select committee on public departments (purchases, &c.)* [Chairman: John Holms]. H.C. 311 (1873). XVII, 1. Further report. H.C. 263 (1874). XI, 339.

4455 ROYAL COMMISSION ON THE FINANCIAL RELATIONS BETWEEN GREAT BRITAIN AND IRELAND. First report by Her Majesty's commissioners appointed to inquire into the financial relations between Great Britain and Ireland [Chairmen: Hugh C. E. Childers and The

O'Conor Don]. [C. 7720] H.C. (1895). XXXVI, 1. Minutes of evidence. [C. 7720–I] H.C. (1895). XXXVI, 5. Final report. [C. 8262] H.C. (1896). XXXIII, 59. Minutes of evidence. [C. 8008] H.C. (1896). XXXIII, 291.

A full inquiry. The way had been prepared by the *Select Committee on Financial Relations (England, Scotland, and Ireland)* [Chairman: George Joachim Goschen], which gathered a great deal of evidence, but presented only a formal report. The material gathered by this committee was publ. in 3 pts., as a *Report*, H.C. 412 (1890). XIII, 269, as *Memoranda and tables*, H.C. 329 (1890–1). XLVIII, 225, and as *Imperial revenue (collection and expenditure): memorandum by the Treasury*, H.C. 313 (1894). LI, 149.

4456 FERGUSSON COMMITTEE ON NATIONAL EXPENDITURE. Report from the select committee on national expenditure [Chairman: Sir James Fergusson]. H.C. 387 (1902). VII, 15. Further report. H.C. 242 (1903). VII, 483.

An inquiry into possible means of exercising a greater measure of parliamentary control over expenditure.

### (b) *Central Banking*

4457 MORGAN (EDWARD VICTOR). The theory and practice of central banking, 1797–1913. Camb. 1943.

A valuable survey.

4458 WOOD (ELMER). English theories of central banking control, 1819–1858, with some account of contemporary procedure. *Harvard Econ. Studs.* lxiv. Camb., Mass. 1939.

4459 SAYERS (RICHARD SIDNEY). Central banking after Bagehot. Oxf. 1957.

4460 STEPHENS (THOMAS ARTHUR). A contribution to the bibliography of the Bank of England. 1897.

4461 CLAPHAM (*Sir* JOHN HAROLD). The Bank of England: a history. 2 v. Camb. 1944.

Admirable. See also John Giuseppi, *The Bank of England: a history from its foundation in 1694*, Lond. & Chicago 1966; Wilfrid Marston Acres, *The Bank of England from within, 1694–1900*, 2 v. 1931; Herbert George De Fraine, *Servant of this house: life in the old Bank of England*, 1960; and R. O. Roberts, 'Bank of England branch discounting, 1826–59', *Economica* new ser. xxv (1958), 230–45. Two older works superseded by Clapham are occasionally useful, Andreas M. Andreades, *History of the Bank of England, 1640–1903*, trans. by Christabel Meredith, 1909, and Eugen von Philippovich, ed., *The history of the Bank of England and its financial services to the state* trans. by Christabel Meredith, U.S. Nat. Monetary Commission, Senate Doc. 591. (61st Congress 2nd Sess.), Wash. 1911.

4462 HAWTREY (*Sir* RALPH GEORGE). A century of bank rate. 1938.

4463 PALGRAVE (*Sir* ROBERT HARRY INGLIS). Bank rate and the money market in England, France, Germany, Holland and Belgium, 1844–1900. 1903.

4464 CRAMP (ALFRED BERNARD). Opinion on bank rate, 1822–60. 1962.

4465 SAYERS (RICHARD SIDNEY). Bank of England operations, 1890–1914. 1936.

4466 SEYD (ERNEST). 'Statistical critique on the operation of the Bank Charter Act of 1844, and suggestions for an improved system of issue'. *Stat. Soc. J.* xxxv (1872), 458–540.

One of the more sober contemp. analyses of a difficult topic. A variety of different views are reflected in Samuel Jones Loyd, Baron Overstone, *Lord Overstone on the Bank Act and the currency: correspondence between the Right Hon. Lord Overstone and Henry Brookes* . . ., 1862, Adolph Heinrich Gotthilf Wagner, *Die Geld- und Credittheorie der Peel'schen Bankacte*, Vienna 1862, Sir Robert Harry Inglis Palgrave, 'On the relation of the banking reserve of the Bank of England to the current rate of interest . . .', *Stat. Soc. J.* xxxvi (1873), 529–64, and Thomas William Huskinson, *The Bank of England's charters, the cause of our social distress*, 1912.

4467 CARDWELL COMMITTEE ON BANK ACTS. Report from the select committee on Bank Acts [Chairman: Edward Cardwell]. H.C. 220 and H.C. 220–I (1857-Sess. 2). X, pts. 1 and 2. Further report. H.C. 381 (1857–8). V, 1.

4468 NORTHCOTE COMMITTEE ON BANKS OF ISSUE. Report from the select committee on banks of issue [Chairman: Sir Stafford Northcote]. H.C. 351 (1875). IX, 1.

A useful inquiry. A summary was publ. by Sir Robert Harry Inglis Palgrave, *Analysis of the minutes of evidence taken before the select committee of the House of Commons on banks of issue, 1875*, priv. pr. 1876.

4469 JEVONS (WILLIAM STANLEY). 'On the frequent autumnal pressure in the money market, and the action of the Bank of England'. *Stat. Soc. J.* xxix (1866), 235–53.

4470 PATTERSON (ROBERT HOGARTH). 'On the rate of interest and the effects of a high bank-rate during commercial and monetary crises'. *Stat. Soc. J.* xxxiv (1871), 334–56.

See also Patterson's 'On our home monetary drains and the crisis of 1866', *Stat. Soc. J.* xxxiii (1870), 216–42, and Hammond Chubb, 'The Bank Act and the crisis of 1866', ibid. xxxv (1872), 171–95.

4471 WOLOWSKI (LOUIS FRANÇOIS MICHEL RAYMOND). La Banque d'Angleterre et les banques d'Écosse. Paris. 1867. Trans. by Robert Somers incl. in his The Scotch banks and the system of issue. Edin. 1873.

(c) *Money*

4472 MEYER (HERMANN HENRY BERNARD) *and* SLADE (WILLIAM ADAMS), *comps.* Select list of references on the monetary question. U.S. Libr. of Congress, division of bibliog. Wash. 1913. Suppl. 1914.

The best of a number of bibliogs. produced by the Libr. of Congress.

4473 BUTCHART (MONTGOMERY) *comp.* Money: selected passages presenting the concepts of money in the English tradition, 1640–1935. 1935.

4474 FEAVEARYEAR (*Sir* ALBERT EDGAR). The pound sterling: a history of English money. Oxf. 1931. 2nd edn. ed. by Edward Victor Morgan. Oxf. 1963.

Standard: largely concerned with the work of the Bank of England, for which see also **4461.** Richard Sidney Sayers, 'Monetary thought and monetary policy in England', *Econ. J.* lxx (1960), 710–24, is a useful summary. Thomas Southcliffe Ashton and Richard Sidney Sayers, eds., *Papers in English monetary history*, Oxf. 1953, incls. two chaps. on the period.

4475 WALTERS (ALAN ARTHUR). Money in boom and slump: an empirical inquiry into British experience since the 1880s. Inst. of Econ. Affairs. 1969. 2nd edn. 1970.

See also his 'Monetary multipliers in the U.K., 1880–1962', *Oxf. Econ. Papers* n.s. xviii (1966), 270–83, and N. J. Kavanagh and A. A. Walters, 'Demand for money in the U.K., 1877–1962: some preliminary findings', *Oxf. Inst. Stats. Bull.* xxviii (1966), 93–116. Peter Wilsher, *The pound in your pocket, 1870–1970*, 1970, is more popular.

4476 FETTER (FRANK WHITSON). Development of British monetary orthodoxy, 1799–1875. Camb., Mass. 1965.

A hist. of monetary theory. Charles Rist, *Histoire des doctrines relatives au crédit et à la monnaie depuis John Law jusqu'à nos jours*, Paris 1938, 2nd edn. [1951], English trans. by Jane Degras 1940, is handy for background.

4477 HEGELAND (HUGO). The quantity theory of money: a critical study of its historical development and interpretation and a restatement. Göteborg. 1951.

4478 ESHAG (EPRIME). From Marshall to Keynes: an essay on the monetary theory of the Cambridge school. Oxf. 1963.

4479 RUSSELL (HENRY BENAJAH). International monetary conferences: their purposes, character, and results; with a study of the conditions of currency and finance in Europe and America during intervening periods and in their relations to international action. N.Y. & Lond. 1898.

Full. The principal reports publ. in Britain were, International Statistical Congress, *Report of the proceedings . . . held in Berlin in September 1863 on the subject of international weights, measures and coins.* H.C. 268 (1864). LVIII, 737; Leone Levi and others, *Reports on the international conference of weights, measures and coins, held in Paris, June 1867.* [4021] H.C. (1867–8). XXVII, 801; *Report from the royal commission on international coinage* [Chairman: Viscount Halifax]. [4021] H.C. (1867–8). XXVII, 9; *Report of the commissioners appointed to represent Her Majesty's Government at the monetary conference held in Paris in August 1878* [Chairman: G. J. Goschen]. [C. 2196] H.C. (1878–9). XXI, 105; and *Paris International Monetary Conference, 1881: translation of the procès verbaux.* H.C. 409 (1881). LXXV, 1, with correspondence about the conference at H.C. 449 (1881). LXXV, 287, report of the official British delegate at H.C. 221 (1882). LIII, 797, and the report of the India Office [C. 3229] H.C. (1882). LIII, 777. Fuller reports were publ. by the United States authorities.

4480 SHRIGLEY (IRENE MAUD) *ed.* The price of gold: documents illustrating the statutory control through the Bank of England of the market price of gold, 1694–1931. 1935.

4481 MICHELL (H.). 'The gold standard in the nineteenth century'. *Canadian J. Econ. & Pol. Sci.* xvii (1951), 369–76.
An outline only.

4482 SAYERS (RICHARD SIDNEY). 'The question of the standard in the eighteen-fifties'. *Econ. Hist.* ii (1930–3), 575–601.

4483 GOODWIN (CRAUFURD D.). 'British economists and Australian gold'. *J. Econ. Hist.* xxx (1970), 405–26.
Good: useful bibliog. notes. For the consequences of new gold discoveries see also Robert Hogarth Patterson, *The new golden age and influence of the precious metals upon the world*, 2 v. Edin. & Lond. 1882, and Geoffrey Blainey, 'A theory of mineral discovery: Australia in the nineteenth century', *Econ. Hist. Rev.* 2 ser. xxiii (1970), 298–313.

4484 KOCH (FRIEDRICH). Der Londoner Goldverkehr: eine Volkswirtschaftliche Studie. Münchener Volkswirtschaftliche Studien 73. Stuttgart & Berlin. 1905.

4485 SCAMMEL (W. M.). 'The working of the gold standard [1870–1914]'. *Yorkshire Bull.* xvii (1965), 32–45.

4486 BEACH (WALTER EDWARDS). British international gold movements and banking policy, 1881–1913. Camb., Mass. 1935.
See also Alec George Ford, *The gold standard, 1880–1914: Britain and Argentina*, Oxf. 1962, and Arthur Irving Bloomfield, *Monetary policy under the international gold standard, 1880–1914*, Federal Reserve Bank of N.Y., N.Y. 1959, and *Short-term capital movements under the pre-1914 gold standard*, Princeton 1963.

4487 EINZIG (PAUL). The history of foreign exchange. Lond. & N.Y. 1962.

4488 DAVIS (LANCE EDWIN) *and* HUGHES (JONATHAN ROBERTS TYSON). 'A dollar–sterling exchange, 1803–1895'. *Econ. Hist. Rev.* 2 ser. xiii (1960–1), 52–78.

4489 GOSCHEN (GEORGE JOACHIM), *Viscount Goschen.* The theory of the foreign exchanges. 1861. 16th edn. 1894 etc.
A book that made its author famous. More humdrum guides were George Clare, *The ABC of the foreign exchanges: a practical guide*, 1893, 11th edn. 1951, and *A money-market primer and key to the exchanges*, 1891, 4th edn. 1936, and Hartley Withers, *Money changing: an introduction to foreign exchange*, 1913, 2nd edn. 1916.

4490 TATE (WILLIAM). A manual of foreign exchanges . . . 1829. 3rd edn. [The modern cambist] 1836. 28th edn. 1929.
The standard guide to currencies and bills of exchange for the whole world. Known as *Tate's modern cambist*.

4491 LECOFFRE (A.). Tables of exchange for the reduction of English money into eastern currencies . . . 1906.

Lecoffre also publ. *Tables of exchange* for Austria and Holland, 1899; France, Belgium, and Switzerland, 1879, 11th edn. 1906; Germany, 1896; and the United States, 3rd edn. 1909. There are also useful tables in John Henry Norman, *A ready reckoner of the world's foreign and colonial exchanges* . . ., 1893, 2nd edn. [*Norman's universal cambist*] 1897, with addenda [*Money's worth* . . .] 1899, and George Koscky, *Russisch-englische Valuta-Umrechnungs-Tabellen: tables of exchange between Russia and Great Britain* . . ., Lond. etc. 1908.

4492 SHAW (WILLIAM ARTHUR). The history of currency, 1252 to 1894: being an account of the gold and silver monies and monetary standards of Europe and America, together with an examination of the effects of currency and exchange phenomena on commercial and national progress and well-being. [1895.] 2nd edn. 1896.

A useful survey. Fuller for the period than Christopher Robert Josset, *Money in Britain: a history of the currencies of the British isles*, 1962.

4493 PECK (CHARLES WILSON). English copper, tin and bronze coins in the British Museum, 1558–1958. 1960. 2nd edn. 1964.

There are also handy guides to other coins: Herbert Allen Seaby, *British imperial silver coinage*, 1949, 3rd edn. [*The English silver coinage*] by Peter Alan Rayner, 1968, Peter Alan Rayner, *The designers and engravers of the English milled coinage, 1662–1953*, 1954, and Sir Geoffrey Edgar Duveen and Harry George Stride, *The history of the gold sovereign*, 1962. See also William John Davis, *The nineteenth-century token coinage of Great Britain, Ireland, the Channel Islands and the Isle of Man* . . ., 1904, repr. 1969.

4494 CRAIG (*Sir* JOHN HERBERT McCUTCHEON). The mint: a history of the London mint from A.D. 287 to 1948. Camb. 1953.

See also Sir John Frederick William Herschel, [*Report relating to the changes in and present state of the Royal Mint, with correspondence*] H.C. 76 (1852). XXVIII, 435. H.C. 310 (1852). XXVIII, 491.

4495 COPPIETERS (EMMANUEL). English bank note circulation, 1694–1954. Louvain. 1955.

For the mechanism of bank-note printing see A. D. Mackenzie, *The Bank of England note: a history of its printing*, Camb. 1953.

4496 CHALMERS (ROBERT), *Baron Chalmers*. A history of currency in the British colonies. [1893.]

Laurence Victor Waud Wright, *Colonial and commonwealth coins: a practical guide to the series*, 1959, is a convenient illustrated guide.

4497 BOWRING (*Sir* JOHN). The decimal system in numbers, coins and accounts: especially with reference to the decimalisation of the currency and accountancy of the United Kingdom. 1854.

4498 SELECT COMMITTEE ON DECIMAL COINAGE. Report from the select committee on decimal coinage [Chairmen: Henry Tufnell and William Brown]. H.C. 851 (1852–3). XXII, 387.

**4499** DECIMAL COINAGE COMMISSION. Preliminary report of the decimal coinage commissioners [Chairman: Lord Monteagle of Brandon]. [2212] H.C. (1857–Sess. 2). XIX, 1. Questions communicated by Lord Overstone. [2213] H.C. (1857–Sess. 2). XIX, 385. Answers to questions. [2297] H.C. (1857–8). XXXIII, 603. Final report. [2529] H.C. (1859–Sess. 2). XI, 1. Appendix. [2591] H.C. (1860). XXX, 387.

Lord Monteagle resigned while the commission was sitting, leaving only two commissioners, Lord Overstone and J. G. Hubbard to prepare the final report. The dominant figure was of course Lord Overstone.

**4500** LOYD (SAMUEL JONES), *Baron Overstone*. Tracts and other publications on metallic and paper currency. [Ed. by John Ramsay McCulloch.] 1857.

Coll. papers of 1837–48 of the most influential exponent of the 'currency school'. See also Denis Patrick O'Brien, ed., *The correspondence of Lord Overstone*, 3 v. Camb. 1971. For his ideas see also Lloyd Alvin Helms, *The contributions of Lord Overstone to the theory of currency and banking*, Urbana, Ill. 1939. Other contemp. pamphlets were James Maclaren, ed., *A sketch of the history of the currency: comprising a brief review of the opinions of the most eminent writers on the subject*, 1858, 2nd edn. 1879, and Edward Norton, *National finance and currency: the Bank Acts of 1797, 1819, and 1844, with the operation of gain or loss of gold, and panics in peace and war*, 1860, 3rd edn. 1873, and George Arbuthnot, *Sir Robert Peel's Act of 1844, regulating the issue of bank notes, vindicated*, 1857.

**4501** BAXTER (ROBERT). The panic of 1866: with its lessons on the Currency Act. 1866.

**4502** CHISHOLM (HENRY WILLIAMS). Report to the Comptroller-General of the Exchequer upon the trial of the pyx and the coinage subjected to this public trial. H.C. 293 (1866). XL, 61.

On the state of the coinage generally.

**4503** SEYD (ERNEST). Bullion and foreign exchanges theoretically and practically considered: followed by a defence of the double valuation, with special reference to the proposed system of universal coinage. 1868.

**4504** PRICE (BONAMY). The principles of currency: six lectures delivered at Oxford . . . Oxf. & Lond. 1869.

**4505** JEVONS (WILLIAM STANLEY). Money and the mechanism of exchange. 1875. 11th edn. 1896.

Important. See also his *Investigations in currency and finance*, ed. by Herbert Somerton Foxwell, 1884, abridged edn. 1909. Jevons's papers incl. 'On the variation of prices and the value of the currency since 1782', *Stat. Soc. J.* xxviii (1865), 294–320, and 'On the condition of the metallic currency of the United Kingdom, with reference to the question of international coinage', ibid. xxxi (1868), 426–64.

**4506** GOSCHEN COMMITTEE ON DEPRECIATION OF SILVER. Report from the select committee on depreciation of silver [Chairman: G. J. Goschen]. H.C. 338 (1876). VIII, 217.

Replies to inquiries in India and elsewhere were slow in coming in, and were publ. separately. See Ford, *Select list* (31), p. 28.

4507  BAGEHOT (WALTER). Some articles on the depreciation of silver, and on topics connected with it . . . 1877.

4508  MARTIN (JOHN BIDDULPH). 'Our gold coinage: an inquiry into its present defective condition, with a view to its reform'. *Inst. Bankers J.* iii (1882), 297–346.

4509  THE CURRENCY QUESTION before the British Association for the Advancement of Science, 57th meeting, Manchester, September 1887. Manch. 1887.

4510  GOLD AND SILVER COMMISSION. First report of the royal commission appointed to inquire into the recent changes in the relative values of the precious metals [Chairmen: A. J. Balfour and Lord Herschell]. [C. 5099] H.C. (1887). XXII, 1. Second report. [C. 5248] H.C. (1888). XLV, 1. Final report. [C. 5512] H.C. (1888). XLV, 285. Minutes of evidence, etc. [C. 5512–I] H.C. (1888). XLV, 455.

4511  NICHOLSON (JOSEPH SHIELD). A treatise on money: and, essays on present monetary problems. Edin. & Lond. 1888. 5th edn. 1901.

4512  PRICE (LANGFORD LOVELL FREDERICK RICE). Money and its relation to prices: being an inquiry into the causes, measurement and effects of changes in general prices. 1896. 4th edn. 1929.

4513  DARWIN (LEONARD). Bimetallism: a summary and examination of the arguments for and against a bimetallic system of currency. 1897.

A useful intro. to a subject that has been neglected by historians. Writings on the subject incl. Arthur James Balfour, Earl of Balfour, *Address . . . Mansion house, London, August 3, 1893*, 1893; Sir David Miller Barbour, *The theory of bimetallism and the effects of the partial demonetisation of silver on England and India*, Lond. & N.Y. [1886]; Sir Edward Robert Pearce Edgcumbe, *Popular fallacies regarding bimetallism*, 1896; Henry Hucks Gibbs, Baron Aldenham, *A colloquy on currency*, 1893, 3rd edn. 1894; Sir Robert Giffen, *The case against bimetallism*, 1892; Henry A. Miller, *Money and bimetallism . . .*, N.Y. & Lond. 1898; J. Barr Robertson, 'Some statistics bearing upon bimetallism', *Roy. Stat. Soc. J.* lviii (1895), 417–66; William Thomas Rothwell, *Bimetallism explained*, 1897; Samuel Smith, *The bi-metallic question*, 1887; and Francis Amasa Walker, *International bimetallism*, 1896. The Bimetallic League publ. a number of papers, 1895–7, and *The proceedings of the bimetallic conference held at Manchester, 4th and 5th April 1888*, Manch. 1888, and there was also a j. *The bimetallist . . .*, 1895–1901. The rival organization, the Gold Standard Defence Assoc., issued *The gold standard: a selection from the papers issued . . . in 1895–1898*, 1898.

4514  FARRER (THOMAS HENRY), *Baron Farrer*. Studies in currency, 1898: or, inquiries into certain modern problems connected with the standard of value and the media of exchange. Lond. & N.Y. 1898.

4515  UNITED STATES NATIONAL MONETARY COMMISSION. Publications. Wash. 1910–11.

The vols. covering Britain were *Interviews on the banking and currency systems of England, Scotland, France, Germany, Switzerland and Italy under the direction of the Hon. Nelson*

W. *Aldrich*, 61st Congress, 2nd Sess., Senate doc. 405, Wash. 1910, Hartley Withers and others, *The English banking system*, 61st Congress, 2nd Sess., Senate doc. 492, Wash. 1910, and Francis Wrigley Hirst and others, *Statistics for Great Britain, Germany and France, 1867–1909*, 61st Congress, 2nd Sess., Senate doc. 578, Wash. 1910. A very useful ser. of reports.

4516  PEASE (EDWARD REYNOLDS). Gold and state banking: a study in the economics of monopoly. Fabian Tract 164. 1912.

## (d) *Taxation*

### (i) *General*

4517  DOWELL (STEPHEN). A history of taxation and taxes in England from the earliest times to the present day. 4 v. 1884. 2nd edn. 4 v. 1888. Repr. 1965–6.

Still the only general hist. There is little of interest in Wilhelm Vocke, *Geschichte der Steuern des britischen Reichs . . .*, Leipzig 1868.

4518  ANDERSON (OLIVE). 'Loans versus taxes: British financial policy in the Crimean war'. *Econ. Hist. Rev.* 2 ser. xvi (1963–4), 314–27.

4519  LEVI (LEONE). On taxation: how it is raised and how it is expended. 1860.

4520  LEVI (LEONE). 'On the distribution and productiveness of taxes: with reference to the prospective ameliorations in the public revenue of the United Kingdom'. *Stat. Soc. J.* xxiii (1860), 37–65.

Cont. in his 'Statistics of the revenue of the United Kingdom from 1859–82, in relation to the distribution of taxation', *Stat. Soc. J.* xlvii (1884), 1–25. See also his *Estimate of the amount of taxation falling on the working classes of the United Kingdom: a report to M. T. Bass, Esq., M.P.*, 1873.

4521  PETO (*Sir* SAMUEL MORTON). Taxation: its levy and expenditure, past and future: being, an enquiry into our financial policy. 1863.

A survey, plus an attack on the income tax.

4522  BAXTER (ROBERT DUDLEY). The taxation of the United Kingdom. 1869.

A very handy analysis by a noted statistician. John Noble, *The Queen's taxes: an inquiry into the amount, incidence, & economic results of the taxation of the United Kingdom, direct and indirect*, 1870, though less well known, is also useful.

4523  SARGANT (WILLIAM LUCAS). Taxation: past, present and future. 1874.

4524  ELLIOTT (*Sir* THOMAS HENRY). 'The annual taxes on property and income'. *Roy. Stat. Soc. J.* l (1887), 293–315.

4525  WILLIAMS (W. M. J.). The king's revenue: being a handbook to the taxes and the public revenue. 1908.

Chiefly on 1898–1908. Williams also publ. *The expenditure and taxation of the United Kingdom, 1825–1900 . . .*, 1901.

4526  JONES (ROBERT). The nature and first principle of taxation. 1914.

4527  TAXES RETURN. Return showing for each year since 1823 the taxes in force in England and Wales, Scotland, and Ireland . . . H.C. 109 (1912–13). XLIX, 675. Suppl. H.C. 107 (1917–18). XIX, 495.

A useful outline table. For details see the numerous annual returns and the reports of the commissioners of Inland Revenue.

### (ii) *Income Tax*

4528  SABINE (BASIL ERNEST VYVYAN). A history of income tax. 1966.

A workmanlike hist.

4529  SELIGMAN (EDWIN ROBERT ANDERSON). The income tax: a study of the history, theory, and practice of income taxation at home and abroad. N.Y. 1911. 2nd edn. 1914.

The pioneer work in the field. See also his *Essays in taxation*, N.Y. 1895, 8th edn. 1913, *On the shifting and incidence of taxation*, Amer. Econ. Assoc. Publics. iv (1892) nos. 2–3, publ. independently N.Y. 1899, 5th edn. N.Y. [1932], and *Progressive taxation in theory and practice*, Amer. Econ. Assoc. Publics. ix (1894) nos. 1–2, 2nd edn. N.Y. 1908. Other comparative works such as Franz Meisel, *Britische und deutsche Einkommensteuer: ihre Moral und ihre Technik*, Tübingen 1925, are of little value for British hist.

4530  SHEHAB (FAKHRI). Progressive taxation: a study in the development of the progressive principle in the British income tax. Oxf. 1953.

A detailed hist.

4531  HUBBARD (JOHN GELLIBRAND), *Baron Addington*. How should an income tax be levied? Considered in a letter to the Right Honourable Benjamin Disraeli, M.P., Chancellor of the Exchequer. 1852.

A challenge to existing methods of taxation by the leading advocate of income tax reform. See also his *Reform or reject the income tax: objections to a reform of the income tax considered . . .*, 1853, and *Gladstone on the income tax: discussion on the income tax in the House of Commons on 25th April, 1884, with preface and historical sketch, including a proposed bill*, 1885. For other attacks on the income tax see Alexander Gibbon, *Taxation: its nature and properties: with remarks on the incidence and the expediency of the repeal of the income-tax*, 1851, 2nd edn. 1853, and *The income tax: its causes and incidence: shewing by analysis that it is a land-tax, a house-tax, a tax upon commodities, and a repudiation of public debt*, 1860, John Gorham Maitland, *Property and income taxes: the present state of the question*, 1853, and William Lucas Sargant, 'An indiscriminating income tax reconsidered', Stat. Soc. J. xxv (1862), 339–76. There is a little on this discussion in Olive Anderson, 'Wage earners and income tax: a mid-nineteenth-century discussion', Public Admin. xli (1963), 189–92.

4532  DOWELL (STEPHEN). The acts relating to the income tax . . . 1874. 9th edn. 1934.

The most useful general textbook.

4533 HUME COMMITTEE ON INCOME AND PROPERTY TAX. First report from the select committee on income and property tax [Chairman: Joseph Hume]. H.C. 354 (1852). IX, 1. Second report. H.C. 510 (1852). IX, 463.

The first of what was to be a ser. of inquiries. The committee first met in 1851, but had no time to get to work. See H.C. 563 (1851). X, 339.

4534 HUBBARD COMMITTEE ON INCOME AND PROPERTY TAX. Report from the select committee on income and property tax [Chairman: John Gellibrand Hubbard]. H.C. 503 (1861). VII, 1.

4535 RITCHIE COMMITTEE ON INCOME TAX. Report of the departmental committee on income tax [Chairman: Charles Thomson Ritchie]. [Cd. 2575] H.C. (1905). XLIV, 219. Minutes of evidence. [Cd. 2576] H.C. (1905). XLIV, 245.

4536 DILKE COMMITTEE ON INCOME TAX. Report from the select committee on income tax [Chairman: Sir Charles Dilke]. H.C. 365 (1906). IX, 659.

4537 COLWYN COMMISSION ON INCOME TAX. Report of the royal commission on the income tax [Chairman: Lord Colwyn]. [Cmd. 615] H.C. (1920). XVIII, 97. Minutes of evidence. [Cmd. 288, pts. 1–8] H.C. (1919). XXIII, pts. 1–2; and 2 v. publ. as non-parl. papers. 1920. Appendixes publ. as non-parl. paper. 1920.

Not directly concerned with pre-1914 situation, but incls. much valuable material.

### (iii) *Taxation of Land Values*

The old land tax (4539) had by the 1850s become little more than a relic of a bygone tax system, and attention was shifting to the rating system and local taxation generally, which was one of the main controversial issues of the 1860s and 1870s. In the 1880s there was a new shift of interest, chiefly within the sphere of local taxation, towards the taxation of urban land values (betterment) and the 'single tax' of Henry George (4553). Urban land values were considered by the Dilke commission on the housing of the working class in 1885 (7099), the select committee on town holdings of 1886–92 (4549), the Lords' betterment committee of 1894 (4550), the Balfour commission on local taxation of 1898–1901 (4569), the Kempe committee on local taxation of 1914 (4571), and the select committee on land values in 1919–20 (4551).

4538 PURDY (FREDERICK). 'The pressure of taxation on real property'. *Stat. Soc. J.* xxxii (1869), 308–24.

A useful link-up of local taxation and the land tax. See also 4222–5.

4539 CHANDLER (PRETOR WHITTY). The land tax: its creation and management . . . 1899.

4540  BOURDIN (MARK A.). An exposition of the land tax: its assessment and collection: and rights and advantages conferred by the Redemption Acts. 1854. 4th edn. 1894.

Another useful guide is R. Rice Davies, *A handy book of the land, assessed and income-tax laws: expressly prepared for the use of magistrates, clergymen, commissioners and clerks to commissioners of taxes . . .*, 1864.

4541  HALLGARTEN (ROBERT). Die communale Besteuerung des unverdienten Wertzuwachses in England. Münchener Volkswirtshaftliche Studien 32. Stuttgart. 1899.

A useful outline hist.

4542  SARGANT (CHARLES HENRY). Urban rating: being an inquiry into the incidence of local taxation in towns, with special reference to current proposals for change. 1890.

Deals chiefly with ground rents.

4543  FOX (ARTHUR WILSON). The rating of land values: notes upon the proposals to levy rates in respect of site values. 1906.

An analysis of proposals for taxation of site values, by the secretary of the Balfour commission on local taxation (**4569**).

4544  COX (HAROLD). Land nationalization and land taxation. 2nd edn. 1906.

The 1st edn., publ. as *Land nationalization*, 1892, was less concerned with land taxation. Cox was an ardent individualist and sec. of the Cobden Club.

4545  CHORLTON (JAMES DEWSBURY). The rating of land values. Manch. 1907.

A careful analysis.

4546  PIGOU (ARTHUR CECIL). The policy of land taxation. 1909.

Cautious advocacy, by a leading economist, of taxation of unimproved values.

4547  LAND UNION. The new land taxes and mineral rights duty: the Land Union's handbook on provisional valuations . . . [1912.]

An exposition of the land clauses of the 1910 budget by their leading opponent. See also United Committee for the Taxation of Land Values, *Land valuation: a reply to the Land Union 'guide'* [1912], *The Land Union's reasons for repeal of the new land taxes and land valuation*, 1910, and the other pamphlets publ. by the two organizations.

4548  TAXATION OF LAND, &c. Papers bearing on land taxes and on income tax, &c., in certain foreign countries, and on the working of taxation of site values in certain cities of the United States and in British colonies, together with extracts relative to land taxation and land valuation from the reports of royal commissions and parliamentary committees. [Cd. 4750] H.C. (1909). LXXI, 365.

Cont. in *Taxation of Land, &c: second series of memoranda and extracts relating to land taxation and land valuation prepared for the Chancellor of the Exchequer.* [Cd. 4845]

H.C. (1909). LXXI, 693. A valuable ser. of extracts from a wide variety of sources. For other reports on foreign countries and British colonies see *General index* (33) under 'Rates'.

4549  SELECT COMMITTEE ON TOWN HOLDINGS, 1886–92. Report from the select committee on town holdings [Chairmen: G. J. Goschen & Lewis Fry]. H.C. 213 (1886–Sess. 1). XII, 367. Further reports. H.C. 260 (1887). XIII, 41. H.C. 313 (1888). XXII, 1. H.C. 251 (1889). XV, 1. H.C. 341 (1890). XVIII, 1. H.C. 325 (1890–1). XVIII, 15. H.C. 214 (1892–Sess. 1). XVIII, 613.

Chiefly concerned with urban land-value taxation.

4550  LORDS BETTERMENT COMMITTEE. Report from the select committee of the House of Lords on town improvements (betterment). [Chairman: Lord Halsbury]. H.C. 292 (1894). XV, 235.

The Lords debates for the period also include much material on this subject. There is a discussion of the evidence gathered by the committee in W. H. S. Watts, 'Betterment, worsement, and recoupment', *Manch. Stat. Soc. Trans.* (1894–5), 1–32.

4551  SELECT COMMITTEE ON LAND VALUES. Report from the select committee on land values [Chairman: Sir Thomas Whittaker]. H.C. 243 (1919). V, 467. Reprinted with minutes of evidence. [Cmd. 556] H.C. (1920). XIX, 753.

The committee failed to agree, and presented only a formal report, but the minutes of evidence are valuable, and include an analysis of the effects of part I of the 1909–10 Lloyd George budget.

4552  SAWYER (ROLLIN ALGER). Henry George and the single tax: a catalogue of the collection in the New York Public Library. N.Y. 1927.

The standard bibliog. of Henry Georgeism. Articles on the single tax movement appear regularly in *American J. of Econ. & Sociology*, Lancaster, Penn. 1941+.

4553  GEORGE. Henry George. By Charles Albro Barker. N.Y. 1955.

The standard general biog. Henry George, Jr., *The life of Henry George*, 1900, Anna Angela George De Mille, *Henry George: citizen of the world*, ed. by Donald Cleavenger Shoemaker, Chapel Hill, N.C. 1950, and Arthur Birnie, *Single-tax George*, 1939, are other useful biogs. See also Albert Jay Nock, *Henry George: an essay*, N.Y. 1939, and George Raymond Geiger, *The philosophy of Henry George*, N.Y. 1933. The standard edn. of George's works is *The complete works of Henry George*, 10 v. Garden City, N.Y. 1906–11.

4554  GEORGE. Henry George in the British Isles. By Elwood Parsons Lawrence. East Lansing, Mich. 1957.

See also Lawrence's 'George, Chamberlain and the land tax: a chapter in British party politics', *Amer. J. of Econ. & Sociology* xiii (1953–4), 283–95, 401–13, and John Saville, 'Henry George and the British labour movement: a select bibliography with commentary', *Soc. for the Study of Labour Hist. Bull.* v (1962), 18–26, and 'Henry George and the British labour movement', *Science and Society* xxiv (1960), 321–33. Saville gives a valuable list of journal articles about George.

4555 NEILSON (FRANCIS). 'What *Progress and poverty* did for me'. *Amer. J. of Econ. & Sociology* xiv (1954–5), 101–10, 213–24.

Liberal M.P. and single-taxer. See also his 'Land values movement in Great Britain', *Amer. J. of Econ. & Sociology* xviii (1958–9), 225–42, and *My life in two worlds*, 2 v. Appleton, Wis. 1952–3. There is a bibliog. of Neilson's voluminous writings by Phyllis Evans in *Amer. J. of Econ. & Sociology* vi (1946–7), 309–20; xx (1960–1), 355–60.

4556 GEORGE (HENRY). Progress and poverty: an inquiry into the cause of industrial depressions and of increase of want with increase of wealth: the remedy. N.Y. 1880. Lond. 1881.

The basic doc. in the single-tax controversy. For British restatements of the single-tax case see Josiah Clement Wedgwood, Baron Wedgwood, *Real land reform*, Glasgow etc. 1908, and *Land values: why and how they should be taxed*, Letchworth 1911, and Charles Henry Chomley and Robert Leonard Outhwaite, *The essential reform: land values taxation in theory & practice*, 1909. There is also an interesting debate between Francis Neilson and Leopold Charles Maurice Stennett Amery, *The taxation of land values versus tariff reform*, Shrewsbury 1909. The best-known attacks on the single-tax are Arnold Toynbee, '*Progress and poverty*': a criticism of Mr. Henry George . . ., 1883; William Hurrell Mallock, *Poverty and progress: or, a brief enquiry into contemporary social agitation in England*, 1884; William Smart, *Taxation of land values and the single tax*, Glasgow 1900 (to which William Richard Lester, *Professor Smart and the single tax: a rejoinder*, Glasgow 1905, is a reply); and G. E. Raine, *The new land tax*, London Municipal Soc. [1909.]

4557 SCOTTISH SINGLE-TAX LEAGUE [*afterwards* United committee for the taxation of land values]. The single tax. 1894+.

Title changed to *Land values*, 1902, and *Land and liberty*, 1919. The chief organ of the British single-tax movement.

(iv) *Local Taxation and Finance*

Until the new Poor Law was firmly established, public interest tended to be concentrated on the poor rate. But soon thereafter attention quickly shifted to the burdens of local taxation falling on landed property because of the increase of rate-borne expenditure. A formidable movement demanding a change in the incidence of taxation developed, headed by the Central Chamber of Agriculture (**4171**). A hostile report by G. J. Goschen as President of the Poor Law Board did nothing to stem this, and in 1876 the Disraeli government made important concessions to the agricultural interest. Thereafter, attention shifted to the taxation of land values, but the grievances of the ratepayers continued to be investigated by select committees at regular intervals as a result of continued political pressure. Detailed *Local taxation returns* were publ. as parl. papers, 1862+.

4558 CANNAN (EDWIN). A history of local rates in England: five lectures. 1896. 2nd edn. 1912.

4559 GRICE (JAMES WATSON). National and local finance: a review of the relations between the central and local authorities in England, France, Belgium and Prussia during the nineteenth century. 1910.

Suppl. by Sidney James Webb, Baron Passfield, *Grants in aid: a criticism and a proposal*, 1911, 2nd edn. 1920.

4560  HENNOCK (ERNEST PETER). 'Finance and politics in urban local government in England, 1835–1900'. *Hist. J.* vi (1963), 212–25.

4561  BAKER (CHARLES ASHMORE). 'Population and costs in relation to city management'. *Roy. Stat. Soc. J.* lxxiv (1910–11), 73–9.

4562  PURDY (FREDERICK). 'Statistics of the English poor rate, before and since the passing of the Poor Law Amendment Act'. *Stat. Soc. J.* xxiii (1860), 286–329.

4563  AYRTON COMMITTEE ON POOR RATES ASSESSMENT. Report from the select committee on poor rates assessment, &c. [Chairman: Acton Smee Ayrton.] H.C. 342 (1867–8). XIII, 107.

A full inquiry. See also *Report from the select committee of the House of Lords appointed to consider the laws relating to parochial assessments* [Chairman: Lord Portman]. H.C. 022 of 1850 repr. as H.C. 0.113 (1867–8). XIII, 1.

4564  WILSON-PATTEN COMMITTEE ON COUNTY FINANCIAL ARRANGEMENTS. Report from the select committee on county financial arrangements [Chairman: John Wilson-Patten]. H.C. 421 (1867–8). IX, 1.

4565  GOSCHEN (GEORGE JOACHIM), *Viscount Goschen.* Report of the Right Honourable George J. Goschen, M.P., President of the Poor Law Board, to the Right Honourable the Lords Commissioners of Her Majesty's Treasury, on the progressive increase of local taxation, with especial reference to the proportion of local and imperial burdens borne by the different classes of real property in the United Kingdom as compared with the burdens imposed upon the same classes of property in other European countries. H.C. 470 (1870). LV, 177. Repr. as H.C. 201 (1893–4). LXXVII, 1.

Also repr. in Goschen's *Reports and speeches on local taxation*, 1872. A suppl. and commentary was provided by Henry Hartley Fowler as President of the Local Government Board in H.C. 168 (1893–4). LXXVII, 233.

4566  BAXTER (ROBERT DUDLEY). Local government and taxation and Mr. Goschen's report. 1874.

Attacks the Goschen report for maintaining that the existing arrangements were equitable. Originally sponsored by the Central Chamber of Agric. which also publ. Christian F. Gardner, *Local taxation: an essay on the injustices, inequalities and anomalies of the present poor rate assessment . . . prize essay* [1870]. See also Patrick George Craigie, 'The cost of English local government', *Stat. Soc. J.* xl (1877), 262–88.

4567  PALGRAVE (*Sir* ROBERT HARRY INGLIS). 'On the local taxation of Great Britain and Ireland'. *Stat. Soc. J.* xxxiv (1871), 111–235. Repr. 1871.

One of two surveys of the subject awarded the Tayler Prize. The other was John Scott, 'On local taxation', *Stat. Soc. J.* xxxiv (1871), 281–333. Later accounts of the subject covering much the same ground are George H. Pownall, 'Local taxation and government', *Manch. Stat. Soc. Trans.* (1884–5), 59–88; Edwin Guthrie, 'Local taxation', *Manch. Stat. Soc. Trans.* (1894–5), 93–122; John Cameron Graham, *Local and imperial taxation and local government*, 1894, 4th edn. 1906 (title varies); G. H.

Blunden, *Local taxation and finance*, 1895; Henry Hartley Fowler, Viscount Wolverhampton, 'Municipal finance and municipal enterprise', *Royal Stat. Soc. J.* lxiii (1900), 383–407; and John Row-Fogo, *An essay on the reform of local taxation in England*, 1902.

4568 GOSCHEN COMMITTEE ON LOCAL TAXATION. Report from the select committee on local taxation [Chairman: George Joachim Goschen]. H.C. 353 (1870). VIII, 9.

The Committee was primarily concerned, not with the Goschen report, but with whether or not local rates should be shared between owners and occupiers.

4569 BALFOUR COMMISSION ON LOCAL TAXATION. First report of Her Majesty's commissioners appointed to inquire into the subject of local taxation [Chairman: Lord Balfour of Burleigh]. [C. 9141] H.C. (1899). XXXV, 733. Second report. [C. 9142] H.C. (1899). XXXV, 795. Final report. (England and Wales) [Cd. 638] H.C. (1901). XXIV, 413. (Scotland) [Cd. 1067] H.C. (1902). XXXIX, 57. (Ireland) [Cd. 1068] H.C. (1902). XXXIX, 9. Special report on valuation in Ireland. [Cd. 973] H.C. (1902). XXXIX, 1.

The chief service of the Balfour commission was to gather a great deal of evidence, the most important of which was in a vol. of 250 pp., *Memoranda, chiefly relating to the classification and incidence of imperial and local taxes* [C. 9528] H.C. (1899). XXXVI, 673. This vol. incls. a Treasury report by Sir Edward W. Hamilton and the answers to a questionnaire submitted to leading economists and other experts. There are also 5 v. of minutes of evidence: [C. 8763] H.C. (1898). XLI, 417; [C. 9150] H.C. (1899). XXXVI, 1; [C. 9319] H.C. (1899). XXXVI, 361 (on Scotland); [Cd. 201] H.C. (1900). XXXVI, 329; [Cd. 383] H.C. (1900). XXXVI, 615; and 3 v. of Appendixes. [C. 8764] H.C. (1898). XLII, 1; [C. 8765] H.C. (1898). XLII, 339; and [Cd. 1221] H.C. (1902). XXXIX, 175. There is an index to the whole at [Cd. 1480] H.C. (1903). XXIII, 683.

4570 PRIMROSE COMMITTEE ON EDUCATION RATES. Report of the departmental committee on education rates [Chairman: Sir Henry William Primrose]. [Cd. 3313] H.C. (1907). XXI, 521.

4571 KEMPE COMMITTEE ON LOCAL TAXATION. First report of the departmental committee on local taxation [Chairman: Sir John Arrow Kempe]. [Cd. 6304] H.C. (1912–13). XXXVIII, 1. Appendixes. [Cd. 6303–I] and [Cd. 6303–II] H.C. (1912–13). XXXVIII, 5, 499. Final report. [Cd. 7315] H.C. (1914). XL, 537. Appendix. [Cd. 7316] H.C. (1914). XL, 663.

4572 LUMLEY (WILLIAM GOLDEN). The law of parochial assessments. 1844. 7th edn. 1882.

Suppl. by his *The Union Assessment Committee Act . . .*, 1862, 11th edn. 1895. See also Charles Penfold, *The principle and law of rating: to the relief of the poor, railway, gas, water and other similar companies . . .*, 1847, 8th edn. 1893, and Walter Cranley Ryde, *The law and practice of rating, both within and without the metropolis*, 1900, 9th edn. 1950.

4573 POYNTON (THOMAS LLEWELLYN). The Institute of Municipal Treasurers and Accountants: a short history, 1885–1960. 1960.

(v) *Other Taxes and Duties*

For trade and tariff policy see **5959–83**.

4574 CUSTOMS TARIFFS of the United Kingdom from 1800 to 1897: with some notes upon the history of the more important branches of receipt from the year 1660. [C. 8706] H.C. (1898). LXXXV, 1.

4575 HAMEL, *afterwards* DE HAMEL (FELIX JOHN). The Customs Duties Acts consolidated, by direction of the Lords commissioners of Her Majesty's Treasury. 1853. 3rd edn. [The law of the customs.] 1881.

See also Charles Newdigate Newdegate, *A collection of the customs' tariffs of all nations: based upon a translation of the work of M. Hübner, augmented by additional information, brought down to the end of the year 1854*, 1855, George D. Ham, *Ham's revenue and mercantile vade-mecum; an epitome of the laws, regulations, and practice of customs, inland revenue and mercantile marine . . .*, 1876, cont. in 2 pts. as *Ham's revenue and mercantile year book*, 1877–9, *Ham's year book*, 1880–1, and *Ham's customs year book*, 1882–1930, and Sir Nathaniel Joseph Highmore, *The customs laws . . .*, 1906, 3rd edn. 1922.

4576 HANSON (ALFRED). The acts relating to probate, legacy and succession duties. 1865. 9th edn. 1946.

See also Corrie Hudson, *A practical guide to the payment of legacy and succession duties,* 1867, 10th edn. 1896, and Robert Dymond, *The death duties: comprising estate, settlement estate, legacy, succession, and increment value duties . . .*, 1913, 12th edn. 1955.

4577 HARMAN (JOHN EUSTACE). The Finance Act, 1894 . . . so far as it relates to death duties . . . 1894. 4th edn. 1921.

4578 DOWELL (STEPHEN). A history and explanation of the stamp duties . . . 1873.

See also Thomas Brittain Vacher, *The Stamp Acts condensed and simplified . . .*, 4th edn. 1860, 7th edn. 1874, cont. by Gualter C. Griffith as *A digest of the stamp duties*, to 11th edn. 1894, and Sir Nathaniel Joseph Highmore, *The Stamp Act, 1891 . . .*, 1900, 4th edn. 1921.

4579 HIGHMORE (*Sir* NATHANIEL JOSEPH). The excise laws . . . 2 v. 1898. 3rd edn. 2 v. 1923.

A thorough survey.

(e) *National Debt*

Detailed figures relating to the management of the debt and to Treasury bills, consols, etc., were publ. every year as parl. papers.

4580 HARGREAVES (ERIC LYDE). The national debt. 1930.

The standard hist. There is an attractive chart showing in diagram form the growth of the national debt. publ. as *The Statist's history of the British debt . . .* by Richard Rous Mabson [1911].

4581 WILSON (*Sir* CHARLES RIVERS). Report by the secretary and comptroller general of the proceedings of the Commissioners for the Reduction of the National Debt, from 1786 to 31st March 1890. [C. 6539] H.C. (1890–1). XLVIII, 511.

Comprehensive. The commissioners also publ. detailed annual reports.

4582  HAMILTON (*Sir* EDWARD WALTER). Conversion and redemption: an account of the operations under the National Debt Conversion Act, 1888, and the National Debt Redemption Act, 1889. 1889.

4583  LEVI (LEONE). 'On the progress and economical bearings of the national debts in this and other countries'. *Stat. Soc. J.* xxv (1862), 313–38.

4584  SARGANT (WILLIAM LUCAS). An apology for sinking funds. 1868.

4585  BAXTER (ROBERT DUDLEY). National debts. 1871. 2nd edn. 1871.

### (f) *Revenue Administration*

The main sources are the annual reports of the Boards of Customs and of Inland Revenue.

4586  BOARD OF CUSTOMS. First report of the commissioners of Her Majesty's Customs on the customs. [2186] H.C. (1857–Sess. I). III, 301.

Incls. a hist. and a description of the work of the customs. There is no later hist. Sir James Ian Cormack Crombie, *Her Majesty's Customs and Excise*, New Whitehall Ser. 1962, incls. no hist.

4587  COMMITTEE OF LONDON MERCHANTS FOR REFORM OF THE BOARD OF CUSTOMS. A digest of the proceedings and reports of the Committee of London merchants for the reform of the Board of Customs. 1852.

Originally issued in 3 pts., 1851–2. Deals with all aspects of customs administration. For comment see James O'Dowd, *Customs' administrators and customs' reformers: or, 'The digest of the proceedings of the Charlotte Row Committee' examined*, 1851, expanded edn. 1853.

4588  MITCHELL COMMITTEE ON THE CUSTOMS. First report from the select committee on customs [Chairman: Thomas Alexander Mitchell]. H.C. 209 (1851). XI, pt. I, 1. Second report. H.C. 604. (1851). XI, pt. I, 169. Minutes of evidence etc. [unnumbered.] (1851). XI, pts. II–IV. Further report. H.C. 498 (1852). VIII, pts. I–II. Reply of Board of Customs etc. H.C. 379 (1852–3). XCIX, 161.

The fullest inquiry of the period.

4589  HORSFALL COMMITTEE ON INLAND REVENUE AND CUSTOMS ESTABLISHMENTS. Report from the select committee on Inland Revenue and Customs establishments [Chairman: Thomas Berry Horsfall]. H.C. 370 (1862). XII, 131. Further report. H.C. 424. (1863). VI, 303.

4590  CUSTOMS AND EXCISE AMALGAMATION COMMITTEE. Report of the committee on the amalgamation of the Customs and Excise departments [Chairman: Charles Edward Henry Hobhouse]. [Cd. 5830] H.C (1911). XV, 287. Minutes of evidence. [Cd. 5834] H.C. (1911). XV, 313.

Important for administration.

4591   CAWSTON COMMITTEE ON THE CUSTOMS WATERGUARD SERVICE. Report of the committee on the Customs waterguard service and the customs watchers [Chairman: J. W. Cawston]. [Cd. 6290] H.C. (1912– 13). XVII, 647. Minutes of evidence. [Cd. 6299] H.C. (1912–13). XVII, 671

Interesting, because it deals with one of the surviving areas of political patronage.

4592   BOARD OF INLAND REVENUE. First report of the commissioners of Inland Revenue on the inland revenue. [2199] H.C. (1857–Sess. I). IV, 65.

A full report on the work of the Inland Revenue and the taxes it administered. Suppl. by *Report of the commissioners of Inland Revenue on the duties under their management for the years 1856 to 1869* ... [C. 82 and C. 82–I] H.C. (1870). XX, 193, 377; and by *Twenty-eighth report of the commissioners* ... [C. 4474] H.C. (1884–5). XXII, 43; which carries the 1870 report down to 1884–5.

4593   GRIFFITH (LLEWELYN). A hundred years: the Board of Inland Revenue, 1849–1949. 1949.

A short pamphlet written for the Inland Revenue staff.

4594   OWENS (JOHN). Plain papers relating to the Excise branch of the Inland Revenue department from 1621 to 1878: or, a history of the excise. Linlithgow 1879.

A careful and comprehensive work.

4595   A CIVIL SERVANT. Our postal and revenue establishments: con- sidered with a view to utilising the former for the receipt and payment of revenue moneys, the granting of licenses, and sale of stamps in all provincial towns, and to a thorough amalgamation and consolidation of the surveying branches of these departments. 1866.

Chiefly devoted to a reprint of evidence given before the Horsfall Committee (**4589**).

### 3. BANKING AND THE MONEY MARKET

#### (a) *Banking*

##### (i) *General*

4596   WITHERS (HARTLEY) *and others*. The English banking system U.S. National Monetary commission. U.S. Senate 61st Congress Doc. no 492. Wash. 1910.

Good. For a German account see Edgar Jaffé, *Das englische Bankwesen*, Leipzig 1904 2nd edn. 1910.

4597   MINTS (LLOYD WYNN). A history of banking theory in Great Britain and the United States. Chicago. 1945.

Good.

**4598** BARNETT (ROBERT WILLIAM). 'The history of the progress and development of banking in the United Kingdom from the year 1800 to the present time'. *Inst. Bankers J.* i (1879–80), 592–674.

**4599** DUN (JOHN). 'The banking institutions, bullion reserves, and non-legal-tender note circulation of the United Kingdom statistically investigated'. *Stat. Soc. J.* xxxix (1876), 1–189.

**4600** DICK (JAMES). 'Banking statistics: a record of nine years' progress, 1874 to 1883'. *Inst. Bankers J.* v (1884), 317–69.

Cont. for 1884–91 in *Inst. Bankers J.* xiii (1892), 283–343, and for 1892–6 in ibid. xviii (1897), 179–226. Further cont. to 1911 by D. Drummond Fraser, 'Some modern phases of British banking, 1896–1911', ibid. xxxiv (1913), 82–111. William Howarth, *Banking statistics, 1885–1890*, 1891, is not nearly as systematic. John Biddulph Martin, 'On some effects of a crisis on the banking interest', *Stat. Soc. J.* xlii (1879), 663–700, is an attempt at a different type of statistical evaluation.

**4601** PALGRAVE (*Sir* ROBERT HARRY INGLIS). 'Notes on banking in Great Britain and Ireland, Sweden, Denmark and Hamburg . . . '. *Stat. Soc. J.* xxxvi (1873), 27–152. Repr. 1873.

**4602** GOODHART (CHARLES ALBERT ERIC). The business of banking, 1891–1914. 1972.

**4603** INSTITUTE OF BANKERS. The first fifty years of the Institute of Bankers, 1879–1929. 1929.

**4604** HIGONNET (RENÉ P.). 'Bank deposits in the United Kingdom, 1870–1914'. *Quart. J. Econ.* lxxi (1957), 329–67.

**4605** GREGORY (*Sir* THEODORE EMANUEL GUGENHEIM). Select statutes, documents and reports relating to British banking, 1832–1928. 2 v. 1929.

**4606** GILBART (JAMES WILLIAM). The history, principles and practice of banking. Rev. edn. by Ernest Sykes. 2 v. 1907.

A good edn., rev. down to 1907, of one of the classics of English banking, first publ. in 1834. The edns. of 1882 and 1934 are also useful. Gilbart's views are scattered over a considerable number of works which were reissued from time to time long after his death in 1863.

**4607** WILSON (ALEXANDER JOHNSTONE). Banking reform: an essay on prominent banking dangers and the remedies they demand. 1879.

A good discussion of contemp. banking problems.

**4608** THOMSON (WILLIAM). Dictionary of banking: a concise encyclopaedia of banking law and practice. 1911. 10th edn. 1952.

Much more comprehensive than most previous textbooks, such as Harry Tucker Easton, [*History and principles of*] banks and banking, 1896, 3rd edn. 1924, and *Money, exchange and banking in their practical, theoretical and legal aspects . . .*, 1905, 3rd edn. 1926;

the doctrinaire works of Henry Dunning Macleod, *The theory and practice of banking* . . . ,
2 v. 1855, 5th edn. 2 v. 1892–3, and 'Great Britain' in *A history of banking in all the leading nations*, 4 v. N.Y. 1896, vol. II, pp. 1–183; William John Lawson, *The history of
banking* . . . , 1850, 2nd edn. 1855, and *A handy book of the law of banking*, 1859, rev.
edn. 1871; Charles Franklin, *Chapters on the theory and history of banking* . . . , N.Y.
1891, 4th edn. 1926; and John Hutchison, *The practice of banking* . . . , 4 v. 1881–91.

**4609   GRANT (JAMES).** A treatise on the law relating to bankers and banking
. . . 1856. 7th edn. 1923.

Repl. as a legal textbook by Sir John Rahere Paget, *The law of banking*, 1904, 5th edn.
1947, which was based on *Legal decisions affecting bankers*, ed. by Paget, publ. by the
Inst. of Bankers, 1900. There is a brief account of legal cases in Frank D. Johnson,
*Notes on banking cases, 1787–1948*, 1949.

**4610   THE BANKING ALMANAC, DIRECTORY, YEAR BOOK AND
DIARY. 1845+.**

One of the best of all year-books. The leading banking periodicals were *The bankers'
magazine* . . . [title varies], 1844+, *Bankers' circular* [title varies], 1828–60, and Institute of Bankers, *Journal*, 1879+. *The Economist* also publ. a semi-annual banking
number. *The banker*, 1926+, and *The three banks review*, Edin. 1949+, publ. occasional
hist. articles.

### (ii) *Banks Trading in England*

**4611   BANKS OF ISSUE.** Return showing . . . the names of all banks of issue
. . . H.C. 490. (1865). XXX, 147.

The last full return, showing the note issue and other details for each bank.

**4612   SYKES (JOSEPH).** The amalgamation movement in English banking,
1825–1924. 1926.

There is a useful suppl. in Drummond Fraser, 'A decade of bank amalgamations, 1897–
1906', *Inst. Bankers J.* xxix (1908), 25–55.

**4613   PRICE (FREDERICK GEORGE HILTON).** A handbook of London
bankers . . . 1876. Rev. edn. 1890–1.

The rev. edn. is a useful directory to 1890. Price's *The Marygold by Temple Bar: being
a history of the site now occupied by No. 1, Fleet Street, the banking house of Messrs
Child & Co.*, 1902, unfortunately has little on the 19th cent.

**4614   MATTHEWS (PHILIP W.).** Handbook to the London bankers'
clearing house. 1910. 2nd edn. 1912.

See also his *The bankers' clearing house* . . . , 1921, and William Howarth, *Our clearing
system and clearing houses*, 1884, 4th edn. 1907. Ernest Seyd, *The London banking and
bankers' clearing house system* [1872], covers the same ground.

**4615   KIDDY (JOHN GEORGE).** The country banker's handbook to the
rules and practice of the Bank of England, the London Bankers' Clearing
House, the Stock Exchange . . . 1894. 8th edn. 1938.

A mine of useful information.

4616  FULFORD (ROGER THOMAS BALDWIN). Glyn's, 1753–1953: six generations in Lombard Street. 1953.

The only adequate hist. of one of the big private banks. Of the two hists. of Smiths's, Harry Tucker Easton, *The history of a banking house (Smith, Payne and Smiths)*, 1903, is rather better than John Alfred Stuart Leighton Leighton-Boyce, *Smiths the bankers, 1658–1958*, 1958, at least for the period of this bibliog. The other hists. are [Henry Peregrine Rennie Hoare] *Hoare's bank: a record, 1673–1932*, 1932, 2nd edn. [1672–1955] 1955, Ralph Mosley Robinson, *Coutts': the history of a banking house*, 1929, and John Biddulph Martin, '*The grasshopper' in Lombard Street* [Martin & Co.], 1892.

4617  LUBBOCK. Life of Sir John Lubbock, Lord Avebury . . . By Horace [Horatio] Gordon Hutchinson. 2 v. 1914.

Lubbock (of Robarts, Lubbock) dominated the bankers' clearing house, secured the introduction of bank holidays, and was, as well, scientist, best-selling author, and politician.

4618  CURRIE. Bertram Wodehouse Currie, 1827–1896: recollections, letters and journals. Ed. by Caroline Louisa Currie. 2 v. Priv. pr. Roehampton. 1901.

Currie (of Glyn, Mills) was one of the few private bankers apart from Lubbock to make a name for himself during the period.

4619  THOMAS (SAMUEL EVELYN). The rise and growth of joint-stock-banking. Vol. I. Britain to 1860. 1934. No more publ.

4620  HARR (LUTHER ARMSTRONG). Branch banking in England. Phila. 1929.

Demonstrates the need for a hist. but doesn't adequately fulfil this need.

4621  MATTHEWS (PHILIP W.) *and* TUKE (ANTHONY W.). History of Barclay's Bank Limited: including the many private and joint stock banks amalgamated and affiliated with it. 1926.

4622  GREGORY (*Sir* THEODORE EMANUEL GUGENHEIM). The Westminster Bank through a century. 2 v. 1936.

4623  WITHERS (HARTLEY). National Provincial Bank, 1833–1933. 1933.

4624  CRICK (WILFRID FRANK) *and* WADSWORTH (JOHN EDWIN). A hundred years of joint-stock banking. 1936.

The Midland Bank Limited.

4625  SAYERS (RICHARD SIDNEY). Lloyds Bank in the history of English banking. 1957.

Suppl. by *Reference notes*, 1957. There is a little background material in Samuel Lloyd, *The Lloyds of Birmingham . . .*, 1907, 3rd edn. 1909.

4626  CHANDLER (GEORGE). Four centuries of banking, as illustrated by the bankers, customers and staff associated with the constituent banks of Martins Bank Ltd. 2 v. 1964–8.

4627 RAE (GEORGE). The country banker: his clients, cares and work: from an experience of forty years. 1885. 7th edn. 1930.

A famous manual.

4628 JACKSON (FREDERICK HUTH). 'Some reflections on modern country banking'. *Inst. Bankers J.* xxxiv (1913), 512–22.

4629 TAYLOR (AUDREY MARY). Gilletts: bankers at Banbury and Oxford: a study in local economic history. Oxf. 1964.

4630 PHILLIPS (MABERLY). A history of banks, bankers & banking in Northumberland, Durham and North Yorkshire, illustrating commercial development of the north of England from 1755 to 1894 . . . 1894.

4631 CAVE (CHARLES HENRY). A history of banking in Bristol from 1750 to 1899 . . . Priv. pr. Bristol. 1899.

4632 GRINDON (LEOPOLD HARTLEY). Manchester banks and bankers: historical, biographical and anecdotal. Manch. 1877. 2nd edn. 1878.

4633 ROTH (HENRY LING). The genesis of banking in Halifax: with side lights on country banking. Halifax. 1914.

See also H. Pemberton, 'Two hundred years of banking in Leeds', *Thoresby Soc. Pubs.* xlvi (1957–61), 54–86.

4634 HICKS (C. E.). 'The Cornish banking crisis of 1879'. *Banker's Mag.* clxxiv (1952), 471–7.

4635 SAUNDERS (PHILIP THOMAS). Stuckey's Bank. Taunton. 1928.

4636 BIDWELL (WILLIAM HENRY). Annals of an East Anglian bank (Gurney and Co.). Norwich. 1900.

See also Ralph Hale Mottram, *Bowler hat: a last glance at the old country banking*, 1940, memoirs of Gurneys.

4637 [McBURNIE (JOHN M.).] The story of the Lancashire & Yorkshire Bank Limited, 1872–1922. Priv. pr. Manch. 1922.

4638 LEADER (ROBERT EADON). The Sheffield Banking Company Limited: an historical sketch, 1831–1916. Sheffield. 1916.

4639 BAROU (NOAH ISAACOVITCH). Co-operative banking. 1932.

A useful intro.

4640 DEVINE (HENRY C.). People's co-operative banks for workers in towns and small holders, allotment cultivators and others in country districts. 1908.

Incls. hists. of a number of small banks. Devine was sec. of the Urban Co-operative Banks Assoc.

**4641 LORDS COMMITTEE ON THRIFT AND CREDIT BANKS BILL.** Report from the select committee of the House of Lords on the Thrift and Credit Banks Bill [H.L.] [Chairman: Lord Mersey]. H.L. 96 (1910). IX, 170.

The committee was set up to consider a bill, promoted by Henry William Wolff, who was for many years the leading advocate in England of German-style credit banks. Wolff maintained that the hundreds of banks which already existed and were registered under the Friendly Socs. Act, 1896, were entitled to limited liability, and the committee agreed. See also Wolff's *Co-operative banking . . .*, 1907, and his many other works.

### (iii) *Banks Trading Overseas*

**4642 BASTER (ALBERT STEPHEN JAMES).** The international banks. 1935.

See also his 'The origins of British banking expansion in the Near East', *Econ. Hist. Rev.* v (1934–5), pt. 1, 76–86, **4643**, and P. L. Cottrell, 'London financiers and Austria, 1863–1875: the Anglo-Austrian Bank', *Business Hist.* xi (1969), 106–19.

**4643 BASTER (ALBERT STEPHEN JAMES).** The imperial banks. 1929.

**4644 LARKWORTHY (FALCONER).** Ninety-one years . . . Ed. by Harold Begbie. 1924.

Reminiscences of the London manager of the Bank of New Zealand, who later became head of the Ionian Bank. For the latter see *Ionian Bank Limited: a history*, 1953.

**4645 JOSLIN (DAVID MAELGWYN).** A century of banking in Latin America: to commemorate the centenary in 1962 of the Bank of London & South America Limited. 1963.

**4646 A BANKING CENTENARY:** Barclays Bank, Dominion, Colonial and Overseas, 1836–1936. Priv. pr. 1938.

**4647 MACKENZIE (*Sir* [EDWARD MONTAGUE] COMPTON).** Realms of silver: one hundred years of banking in the east. 1954.

A hist. of Chartered Bank of India, Australia, & China.

**4648 TYSON (GEOFFREY WILLIAM).** 100 years of banking in Asia and Africa, 1863–1963. Priv. pr. 1963.

National & Grindlays Bank.

**4649 SELECT COMMITTEE ON CHARTERED BANKS.** Report from the select committee on Chartered Banks (Colonial) Bill [Chairman: Robert Lowe]. H.C. 115 (1880). VIII, 175.

No report publ., but the evidence is useful for imperial banking.

**4650 HIDY (RALPH WILLARD)** *and* **HIDY (MURIEL E.).** 'Anglo-American merchant bankers and the railroads of the old northwest, 1848–1860'. *Business Hist. Rev.* xxxiv (1960), 150–69.

4651  HIDY (RALPH WILLARD). The house of Baring in American trade and finance: English merchant bankers at work, 1763–1861. *Harvard Studies in Business Hist.* 14. Camb., Mass. 1949.

An important pioneer hist.

4652  ANTONY GIBBS AND SONS LTD. Merchants and bankers: a brief record of Antony Gibbs & Sons and its associated houses' business during 150 years, 1808–1958. [1958.]

4653  ELLIS (AYTOUN). Heir of adventure: the story of Brown, Shipley & Co., merchant bankers, 1810–1960. Priv. pr. 1960.

4654  MORGAN, GRENFELL & CO. LTD. George Peabody & Co., J. S. Morgan & Co., Morgan Grenfell & Co., Morgan, Grenfell & Co. Ltd., 1838–1958. Priv. pr. Oxf. 1958.

### (iv) Savings Banks

4655  HORNE (H. OLIVER). A history of savings banks. 1947.

Standard. Full bibliog. To be suppl. by Albert Fishlow, 'The trustee savings banks, 1817–1861', *J. Econ. Hist.* xxi (1961), 26–40. William Lewins, *A history of banks for savings in Great Britain and Ireland* . . ., 1866; Archibald Granger Bowie, *The romance of the savings banks*, 1898; Samuel Smiles, *Thrift*, 1875; and Henry William Wolff, 'Savings banks at home and abroad', *Roy. Stat. Soc. J.* lx (1897), 278–349, are still useful for some aspects of the subject. The main run of statistics is the *Return for each savings bank* . . ., 1849+, publ. by the Treasury as parl. papers. The oversight of savings banks is reviewed in *Report from the inspection committee on trustee savings banks.* H.C. 40 (1893–4). LXXXIII, pt. 1, and successive annual reports to 1921.

4656  HOBSON (*Sir* OSCAR RUDOLF). The Post Office savings bank, 1861–1961. [1961.]

A short pamphlet. See also Henry Riseborough Sharman, *A handy book on post office savings banks* . . . [1861], and U.S. National Monetary commission, *Notes on the postal savings-bank systems of the leading countries*, U.S. Senate 61st Congress Doc. 658, Wash. 1910. The main source is the *Annual report* publ. by the Postmaster general, 1861+. Detailed accounts were publ. as parl. papers.

4657  SCRATCHLEY (ARTHUR). A practical treatise on savings banks: containing a review of their past history and present condition, and of legislation on the subject. 1860. 4th edn. 1868.

Superseded by Urquhart Atwell Forbes, *The law relating to trustee and post-office savings banks*, 1878, suppl. 1884, and *The statutory law relating to trustee savings banks* . . ., 1892. The first good textbook was John Young Watt, *The law of savings banks* . . ., 1905, 3rd edn. 2 v. 1948.

4658  ESTCOURT COMMITTEE ON SAVINGS BANKS. Report from the select committee on savings banks [Chairman: T. H. S. Sotheron Estcourt]. H.C. 441. (1857–8). XVI, 1.

The first of three major inquiries which are the main sources for savings banks.

4659 SHAW-LEFEVRE COMMITTEE ON TRUSTEE SAVINGS BANKS. Report from the select committee on trustee savings banks [Chairman: G. J. Shaw-Lefevre]. H.C. 406 (1888). XXIII, 1. Further report. H.C. 301. (1889). XVI, 1.

4660 HICKS BEACH COMMITTEE ON SAVINGS BANK FUNDS. Report from the select committee on savings bank funds [Chairman: Sir Michael Hicks Beach]. H.C. 282. (1902). IX, 1.

## (b) *The Money Market*

### (i) *General*

4661 POWELL (ELLIS THOMAS). The evolution of the money market (1385–1915): an historical and analytical study of the rise and development of finance as a centralised, co-ordinated force. 1915.

A good general survey. He also wrote *The mechanism of the city: an analytical survey of the business activities of the City of London*, 1910. Shizuya Nishimura, *The decline of inland bills of exchange in the London money market, 1855–1913*, Camb. 1971, is an important quantitative study.

4662 BAGEHOT (WALTER). Lombard Street: a description of the money market. 1873. Numerous edns.

Famous and well-written.

4663 CHECKLAND (SYDNEY GEORGE). 'The mind of the City, 1870–1914'. *Oxf. Econ. papers* new ser. ix (1957), 261–78.

4664 KING (WILFRID THOMAS COUSINS). History of the London discount market. 1936.

A useful survey. See also William McConnell Scammell, *The London discount market*, 1968. For a discount house see Richard Sidney Sayers, *Gilletts in the London money market, 1867–1967*, Oxf. 1968.

4665 CAM (GILBERT ARTHUR). 'A survey of the literature on investment companies, 1864–1957'. *Bull. N.Y. Publ. Libr.* lxii (1958), 57–74.

4666 MACDONALD (ROBERT A.). 'The rate of interest since 1844'. *Roy. Stat. Soc. J.* lxxv (1911–12), 361–79.

4667 NASH (ROBERT LUCAS). A short inquiry into the profitable nature of our investments: with a record of more than five hundred of our most important public securities during the twelve years 1870 to 1880. 1880. 3rd edn. 1881.

4668 FLUX (*Sir* ALFRED WILLIAM). 'The yield of high-class investments, 1896–1910'. *Manch. Stat. Soc. Trans.* (1910–11), 103–38.

See also his *The foreign exchanges . . .*, 1924.

4669 RUSSELL COMMITTEE ON MONEY LENDING. Report from the select committee on money lending [Chairman: T. W. Russell]. H.C. 364 (1897). XI, 405. Further report. H.C. 260 (1898). X, 101.

See also Joseph Bridges Matthews, *The law of money-lending, past and present: being a short history of the usury laws in England, followed by a treatise upon the Moneylenders Act, 1900*, 1906.

4670 AYRTON COMMITTEE ON PAWNBROKERS. Report from the select committee on pawnbrokers [Chairman: Acton Smee Ayrton]. H.C. 377 (1870). VIII, 391. Further report. H.C. 419 (1871). XI, 377.

Cont. by *Report from the select committee on the Pawnbrokers Bill* [Chairman: John Whitwell]. H.C. 288 (1872). XII, 1. Covers a neglected section of the money market.

#### (ii) *Overseas Borrowing*

See also under individual countries.

4671 JENKS (LELAND HAMILTON). The migration of British capital to 1875. N.Y. 1927. Repr. Lond. 1963.

An important pioneer study.

4672 FEIS (HERBERT). Europe the world's banker, 1870–1914: an account of European foreign investment and the connection of world finance with diplomacy before the war. New Haven [Conn.]. 1930. Rev. edn. N.Y. 1964.

4673 WYNNE (WILLIAM HARRIS). State insolvency and foreign bond-holders. Vol. 2. Selected case histories of governmental foreign bond defaults and debt readjustments. New Haven [Conn.]. 1951.

4674 HOBSON (CHARLES KENNETH). The export of capital. 1914.

An important thesis.

4675 CAIRNCROSS (*Sir* ALEXANDER KIRKLAND). Home and foreign investment, 1870–1913: studies in capital accumulation. Camb. 1953.

Very valuable. See also Alan Ross Hall, 'A note on the English capital market as a source of funds for home investment before 1914', *Economica* new ser. xxiv (1957), 59–66, with a reply by Cairncross, *Economica* new ser. xxv (1958), 142–6, and a counter by Hall, ibid. 339–43. Also J. S. Pesmazoglu, 'A note on the cyclical fluctuations of British home investment, 1870–1913', *Oxf. Econ. Papers* new ser. iii (1951), 39–61.

4676 HALL (ALAN ROSS) *ed.* The export of capital from Britain, 1870–1914. 1968.

An up-to-date analysis.

4677 FORD (ALEC GEORGE). 'The transfer of British foreign lending, 1870–1913'. *Econ. Hist. Rev.* 2 ser. xi (1958–9), 302–8.

A pioneer article that challenged accepted views, chiefly those of Albert H. Imlah, 'British balance of payments and export of capital, 1816–1913', *Econ. Hist. Rev.* 2 ser. v (1952–3), 208–39, and John Knapp, 'Capital exports and growth', *Econ. J.* lxvii (1957), 432–44.

4678 SEGAL (HARVEY H.). *and* SIMON (MATTHEW). 'British foreign capital issues, 1865–1894'. *J. Econ. Hist.* xxi (1961), 566–81.

4679 PAISH (*Sir* GEORGE). 'Great Britain's capital investments in other lands'. *Roy. Stat. Soc. J.* lxxii (1909), 465–80.

See also his 'Great Britain's capital investments in individual colonial and foreign countries', *Roy. Stat. Soc. J.* lxxiv (1910–11), 167–87, and Matthew Simon, 'The enterprise and industrial composition of new British portfolio foreign investment, 1865–1914', *J. Development Studs.* iii (1966–7), 280–92.

4680 LOWE COMMITTEE ON FOREIGN LOANS. Report from the select committee on loans to foreign states [Chairman: Robert Lowe]. H.C. 367 (1875). XI, 1. Special report. H.C. 152 (1875). XI, 1*.

Useful for the details of loan flotations. For a contemp. analysis see Hyde Clarke, 'On the debts of sovereign and quasi-sovereign states, owing by foreign countries', *Stat. Soc. J.* xli (1878), 299–341.

4681 HALL (ALAN ROSS). The London capital market and Australia, 1870–1914. Canberra. 1963.

See also the works of Butlin (1358).

4682 SPENCE (CLARK CHRISTIAN). British investments and the American mining frontier, 1860–1901. Ithaca, N.Y. 1958.

See also Roger Victor Clements, 'British investment in the Trans-Mississippi West, 1870–1914, its encouragement, and the metal mining interests', *Pacific Hist. Rev.* xxix (1960), 35–50, and 'British investment and American legislative restrictions in the Trans-Mississippi West, 1880–1900', *Mississippi Valley Hist. Rev.* xlii (1955–6), 207–28; Alfred Paul Tischendorf, 'Florida and the British investor, 1880–1914', *Florida Hist. Q.* xxxiii (1954–5), 120–9; Richard Graham, 'The investment boom in British–Texan cattle companies, 1880–1885', *Business Hist. Rev.* xxxiv (1960), 421–45; James Fred Rippy, 'British investments in Texas lands and livestock', *Southwestern Hist. Q.* lviii (1954–5), 331–41; Francis Edwin Hyde, 'British capital and American enterprise in the north-west', *Econ. Hist. Rev.* vi (1935–6), 201–8, and **9994**.

## 4. JOINT-STOCK COMPANIES AND THE STOCK EXCHANGE

4683 WILSON (ALEXANDER JOHNSTONE). A glossary of colloquial, slang and technical terms, in use on the Stock Exchange and in the money market. 1895.

Better than William George Cordingley, *Cordingley's dictionary of stock exchange terms*, 1901.

4684 HUNT (BISHOP CARLETON). The development of the business corporation in England, 1800–1867. Camb., Mass. 1936. Repr. N.Y. 1969.

On joint-stock companies generally.

4685 SHANNON (HERBERT AUSTIN). 'The coming of general limited liability'. *Econ. Hist.* ii (1930–3), 267–91. Repr. in Carus-Wilson, *Essays* (**4066**) 358–79.

Companion articles are his 'The first five thousand limited companies and their duration', *Econ. Hist.* ii (1930–3), 396–424, and 'The limited companies of 1866–1883',

*Econ. Hist. Rev.* iv (1932–4), 290–316, repr. in Carus-Wilson, *Essays* (**4066**) 380–405.
See also Geoffrey Todd, 'Some aspects of joint-stock companies, 1844–1900', *Econ.
Hist. Rev.* iv (1932–4), 46–71, John Saville, 'Sleeping partnership and limited liability,
1850–1856', ibid. 2 ser. viii (1955–6), 418–33, and Leone Levi, 'On joint-stock companies', *Stat. Soc. J.* xxxiii (1870), 1–41, cont. in his 'The progress of joint-stock companies with limited and unlimited liability in the United Kingdom during the fifteen
years, 1869–84', ibid. xlix (1886), 241–64.

4686   O'HAGAN. Leaves from my life. By H. Osborne O'Hagan. 2 v. [1929.]

The autobiog. of a successful company promoter. Ernest Terah Hooley, *Hooley's
confessions*, 1924, tells the story of a promoter who ended in gaol.

4687   MORGAN (EDWARD VICTOR) *and* THOMAS (WILLIAM
ARTHUR). The stock exchange: its history and functions. 1962. 2nd edn. 1971.

A good general hist. See also J. R. Killick and W. A. Thomas, 'The provincial stock
exchanges, 1830–1870', *Econ. Hist. Rev.* 2 ser. xxiii (1970), 96–111.

4688   DUGUID (CHARLES). The story of the stock exchange: its history
and postion. 1901.

A handy contemp. survey. Cp. Duguid's *The stock exchange*, 1904, 5th edn. 1926,
Hartley Withers, *Stocks and shares*, 1910, 4th edn. 1948; William Charles van Antwerp,
*The stock exchange from within*, N.Y. 1913; Francis Wrigley Hirst, *The stock exchange:
a short study of investment and speculation*, Home Univ. Libr. 1911, 4th edn. 1948;
and Godefroi Drew Ingall and George Withers, *The stock exchange*, 1904. For a later
work of the same type see Frederick Ernest Armstrong, *The book of the stock exchange:
a comprehensive guide to the theory and practice of stock and share transactions and to the
business of members of the London and provincial stock exchanges*, 1934, 4th edn. 1949.

4689   POLEY (ARTHUR PIERRE). The history, law and practice of the
stock exchange. 1907. 5th edn. 1932.

A legal guide. Repl. Rudolph Eyre Melsheimer and Walter Laurence, *The law and customs of the London stock exchange*, 1879, 4th edn. 1905.

4690   PLAYFORD (WALTER M.). Hints for investors: being an explanation
of the mode of transacting business on the stock exchange . . . 1882.

A useful explanation of the work of the exchange. Cp. William George Cordingley,
*Cordingley's guide to the stock exchange*, 1893, 13th edn. 1931.

4691   FENN (CHARLES). A compendium of the English and foreign funds.
1837. Cont. by various eds. as Fenn's compendium, or Fenn on the funds,
to 16th edn. 1898.

A famous handbook of securities.

4692   WILSON (ALEXANDER JOHNSTONE). Handbook for investors.
2 v. 1893.

4693   LONDON STOCK EXCHANGE COMMISSION. Report of the
commissioners [Chairman: Lord Penzance]. [C. 2157] H.C. (1878). XIX,
263. Minutes of evidence. [C. 2157–I] H.C. (1878). XIX, 295.

On the work of the exchange in general.

4694  SMITH (KATIE CHARLOTTE) *and* HORNE (GWENDOLEN F.). An index number of securities, 1867–1914. Lond. & Camb. Econ. Service Special Memo 37. 1934.

4695  JEFFERYS (JAMES BAVINGTON). 'The denomination and character of shares, 1855–1885'. *Econ. Hist. Rev.* xvi (1946), 45–55. Repr. in Carus-Wilson, Essays (**4066**) I, 344–58.

4696  ORMEROD (C. B.). Dow theory applied to the London stock exchange: including chapters on chart reading and a table giving details of all the primary bull and bear markets of the London and New York stock exchanges from 1873 to date. 1939.

4697  PARKINSON (HARGREAVES). Ordinary shares: a manual for investors. 1944. 3rd edn. 1949.

A guide covering 1870–1939.

4698  MATHIESON (FREDERICK COXHEAD). Mathieson's highest and lowest prices and dividends paid for the . . . years 1873–78. 1878. Suppls. for 1877–82, etc.

Mathieson's firm, F. C. Mathieson & Son, also publ. many other useful guides, incl. *Stock exchange values: a decade of finance, 1885 to 1895* . . ., 1895, and *Exchange ten-year record of prices and dividends* . . . *1897 to 1906*, and annually, 1907+.

4699  GIFFEN (*Sir* ROBERT). Stock exchange securities: an essay on the general causes of fluctuations in their prices. 1877. 2nd edn. 1879.

A well-known theoretical work. Cp. William Hickman Smith Aubrey, *Stock exchange investments: the theory, methods, practice and results*, 1896, and Sir Joseph Burn, *Stock exchange investments in theory and practice: with chapters on the constitution and operations of the Bank of England and the national and local debts of the United Kingdom* . . ., 1909.

4700  SCRATCHLEY (ARTHUR). On average investment trusts and companies dealing with stock exchange securities. Div. VI of Treatise on Associations for Provident Investment. 1875. Repr. N.Y. [*c.* 1950.]

The first known book on investment companies.

4701  THE STOCK EXCHANGE YEAR-BOOK AND DIARY. 1875+.

An invaluable guide to companies. For companies withdrawn from the year-book see *Register of defunct and other companies removed from the Stock exchange official year-book*, irregular, 1934+.

4702  JOINT-STOCK COMPANIES DIRECTORY. 1865. 1867.

A useful but isolated publ. Regular publ. commenced with *The directory of directors* . . ., 1880+, which is virtually an index to the *Stock exchange year-book* (**4701**). See also George Templeton, *The joint-stock directory of banking, financial, insurance, and other public companies for* [*1866–67*], 2 v. 1866–7.

#### 4703  LONDON WEEKLY STOCK AND SHARE LIST. 1869+.

Title changed to *Burdett's weekly official intelligence*, 1882–98, and *The stock exchange weekly official intelligence*, 1899+. Suppl. by *The stock exchange ten-year record of prices and dividends* . . . *1897–1906*, 1907, and *The stock exchanges (London and provincial) ten-year record* . . ., *1898–1907+*, 1908+, and by *The stock-exchange making-up price list*, 1876–1914.

#### 4704  INVESTORS' GUARDIAN. 1863+.

The most firmly established of 'financial' papers. But see also James Box Wetenhall, *The course of the exchange*, 1697–1908, *Investor's monthly manual*, 1864–1930, *The investors' review*, 1892+, *Financial [and mining] news*, 1884+, *The financier*, 1870–1924, *The financial times* [started as *London financial guide*], 1888+, *The financial chronicle* [submerged in *Gold*, 1895–7], 1886–1921, *Money market review*, 1860–1921, and *The Stock exchange*, 1887–1915.

## 5. INSURANCE

### (a) *General*

#### 4705  INSTITUTE OF ACTUARIES. Catalogue of the library. 1935. 5 suppls. 1935–40.

#### 4706  RAYNES (HAROLD ERNEST). A history of British insurance. 1948. 2nd edn. 1964.

#### 4707  COCKERELL (HUGH ANTHONY LEWIS). Sixty years of the Chartered Insurance Institute, 1897–1957. 1957.

#### 4708  SIMMONDS (REGINALD CLAUD). The Institute of Actuaries, 1848–1948: an account of the Institute of Actuaries during its first one hundred years. Camb. 1948.

#### 4709  ASSURANCE COMPANIES RETURN. Return of the names, place of business and objects of assurance companies completely registered from passing of the Act 7 & 8 Vict. c. 110 to this day . . . and, copy of every account registered by such companies. H.C. 178 (1856). LIX, 1. Suppls. H.C. 70 (1857–Sess. 1). XVI, 143 and H.C. 310 (1863). LXVIII, 1.

Full lists of all types of insurance company.

#### 4710  THE POST MAGAZINE ALMANACK and court and parliamentary register. 1842+.

The main insurance directory. But see also William White, *The assurance register: being a record of the progress and financial position of various life assurance associations . . . also the progress of fire insurance companies*, 1864–8, cont. as *The insurance register . . .*, 1869–1914, *The insurance blue book and insurance companion*, 1873+, and *The insurance year book*, 1886+.

#### 4711  POST MAGAZINE [AND INSURANCE MONITOR]. 1840+.

The oldest of the insurance js., of which there were many. Other important ones were *Assurance magazine*, 1850–67, cont. as *Journal of the Institute of Actuaries*, 1869+,

Federation of Insurance Institutes [Chartered Insurance Inst.], *Journal*, 1898+, Insurance Inst. of London., *Journal*, 1908+, [*Life assurance*] *agents' journal*, 1885–1947, Life Assurance Medical Officers' Assoc. [Assurance Medical Soc.], *Report of the proceedings* [*transactions*] 1894+, *The policy holder and insurance j.*, Manch. 1883+, and *Assure…*, Manch. 1889–1925.

**4712 INDIVIDUAL INSURANCE COMPANIES. ALLIANCE.** Sir William Schooling, *Alliance assurance, 1824–1924*, 1924. **COMMERCIAL UNION.** Edward George Downing Liveing, *A century of insurance: the Commercial Union group of insurance companies, 1861–1961 …*, 1961. **CO-OPERATIVE.** Ronald George Garnett, *A century of co-operative insurance: the Co-operative Insurance Society, 1867–1967: a business history*, 1968. **COUNTY.** Aubrey Noakes, *The County fire office, 1807–1957: a commemorative history*, 1957. **EQUITABLE.** Maurice Edward Ogborn, *Equitable assurances: the story of life assurance in the experience of the Equitable Life Assurance Society, 1762–1962*, 1962. **ESSEX AND SUFFOLK.** Bernard Drew, '*The fire office': being, the history of the Essex and Suffolk Equitable Insurance Society, Limited, 1802–1952*, 1952. **GENERAL ACCIDENT.** Irvine Egerton Gray, *A business epic, 1885–1935: General Accident Fire & Life Assurance Corporation* … [1935.] **LIVERPOOL, LONDON & GLOBE.** James Dyer Simpson, *1936 our centenary year: the Liverpool, London & Globe Insurance Company Ltd.*, 1936. **LONDON & LANCASHIRE.** Eric Vernon Francis, *London and Lancashire history: the history of the London and Lancashire Insurance Company, Limited*, priv. pr. [1962.] **NORWICH UNION.** Robert Norman William Blake, Baron Blake, *Esto perpetua: the Norwich Union Life Insurance Society Limited, an account of one hundred and fifty years of progress*, priv. pr., Norwich 1958. Sir [Charles] Robert Bignold, *Five generations of the Bignold family, 1761–1947, and their connection with the Norwich Union*, 1948. **PROVIDENT.** Francis Henry Sherriff, *From then till now: being, a short history of the Provident Mutual Life Assurance Association 1840–1940*, 1940. **PROVINCIAL.** Sir Samuel Haslam Scott and Francis Clayton Scott, *Personal account: some recollections of fifty years of the Provincial Insurance Company*, 1953. **PRUDENTIAL.** R. W. Barnard, *A century of service: the story of the Prudential, 1848–1948*, 1948. H. Plaisted, *Prudential, past and present …*, Cardiff 1916. **RAILWAY PASSENGERS.** Frederick Hayter Cox, *The oldest accident office in the world: being, the story of the Railway Passengers' Assurance Company, 1849–1949*, [1949]. **REFUGE.** Cyril Clegg, *Friend in deed: the history of a life assurance office: from 1858, as the Refuge Friend in Deed Life Assurance and Sick Friendly Society, to 1958, as the Refuge Assurance Company Limited* [1958]. **ROYAL EXCHANGE.** Barry Supple, *The Royal Exchange Assurance: a history of British insurance, 1720–1970*, Camb. 1970. **ROYAL LONDON.** Walter Gore Allen, *We, the undersigned: a history of the Royal London Mutual Insurance Society limited …, 1861–1961* [1961]. **SUN.** Peter George Muir Dickson, *The Sun insurance office, 1710–1960: the history of two and a half centuries of British insurance*, 1960. **VULCAN BOILER.** William Henry Chaloner, *Vulcan: the history of one hundred years of engineering and insurance, 1859–1959*, priv. pr. Manch. 1958. The best of these hists. are those of the Co-operative, the Royal Exchange, and the Sun. For Scottish companies see **9990.**

4713  WALFORD (CORNELIUS). The insurance cyclopaedia . . . 5 v. & 1 pt.
1870–8.

Invaluable, but covers only A–Her. Materials for the remaining vol. are in Chartered Insurance Inst. libr. Walford publ. much on insurance, incl. *The insurance guide and hand
book* . . ., 2 pts. 1857, 6th edn. 2 v. 1922; and *The insurance year book* . . ., 1870.

4714  THE STATIST. All about insurance: reprinted from 'The Statist';
with additions. 1904.

A good intro. Alexander Johnstone Wilson, *The business of insurance*, 1904, is a similar
work of narrower scope.

4715  PORTER (JAMES BIGGS). The laws of insurance: fire, life, accident
and guarantee . . . 1884. 8th edn. 1933.

One of the few general textbooks to become established. For earlier years see Samuel
Marshall, *A treatise on the law of insurance in four books* . . ., 2 v. 1802, 5th edn. 1865.
For the 20th cent. see Evan James MacGillivray, *Insurance law* . . ., 1912, 4th edn. 1953.
For fire and life insurance see Bunyon (**4725**).

4716  WILSON COMMITTEE ON ASSURANCE ASSOCIATIONS.
Report from the select committee on assurance associations [Chairman:
James Wilson]. H.C. 965. (1852–3). XXI, 1.

The only general inquiry.

(b) *Special Branches*

4717  DINSDALE (WALTER ARNOLD). History of accident insurance in
Great Britain. 1954.

4718  WILSON (*Sir* ARNOLD TALBOT) *and* LEVY (HERMANN JOA-
CHIM). Industrial assurance: an historical and critical study. 1937.

See also [Sidney James Webb, Baron Passfield] *Industrial assurance*, suppl. to *New
Statesman*, 13 March 1915.

4719  MORRAH (DERMOT MACGREGOR). A history of industrial life
assurance. 1955.

Superficial. See also *Report of the departmental committee appointed to consider the question of encouraging the life insurance system of the Post Office* [Chairman: Lord Farrer].
H.C. 311 (1908). XXV, 275, which considered the possibility of the P.O. insuring
under the Workmen's Compensation Acts.

4720  GOLDING (CECIL EDWARD) *and others*. A history of reinsurance:
with sidelights on insurance . . . 1927. 2nd edn. 1931.

4721  WITHERS (HARTLEY). Pioneers of British life assurance. Ed. by
Conan Nicholas. 1951.

Little on the period. See also Alexander Fingland Jack, *An introduction to the history of
life assurance*, 1912.

4722  BENTLEY (JOSEPH). The manual of life assurance and almanack for
1862: a complete work of instructive reference for the public . . . [1862.]

Bentley also publ. *Report to the Board of Trade on the life assurance companies and popular credit institutions of the United Kingdom*, 1856, *A second report* . . ., 2 pts. 1861, 3rd edn. 1861, and *A third report* . . ., 1866, and other pamphlets.

4723 JOHNSTON (JACK) *and* MURPHY (GEORGE WILLIAM). 'The growth of life assurance in U.K. since 1880'. *Manch. School* xxv (1957), 107–82.

A comprehensive statistical analysis.

4724 BOARD OF TRADE. Statements and abstracts of reports deposited with Board of Trade under the Life Assurance Companies Act, 1870. 1871+. 1872+.

Publ. as parl. papers.

4725 BUNYON (CHARLES JOHN). A treatise upon the law of life insurance. 1853. 5th edn. 1914.

See also Arthur Scratchley, *A treatise on life assurance societies, friendly societies and savings banks*, 4th edn. 1856, 13th edn. 1887. Bunyon also publ. *The law of fire insurance*, 1866, 7th edn. 1923.

4726 LORDS COMMITTEE ON OVERSEAS LIFE INSURANCE COM-PANIES. Report from the select committee of the House of Lords on life insurance companies [Chairmen: Lords Balfour, Burghclere, and Beauchamp]. H.L. 194. (1906). IX, 207.

Deals with the business in Britain of non-British companies.

4727 FINLAISON (ALEXANDER). Report and observations . . . relating to tontines and life annuities and to the duration of life among the nominees. H.C. 585. (1860). XL, 775.

An actuarial report on government life annuitants.

4728 WALFORD (CORNELIUS). 'Fires and fire insurance considered under their historical, financial, statistical and national aspects'. *Stat. Soc. J.* xl (1877), 347–424.

A valuable survey, based on the stamp returns. See also Samuel Brown, 'On the progress of fire insurance in Great Britain, as compared with other countries', *Stat. Soc. J.* (1857), 135–68.

4729 MAYWALD (K.). 'Fire insurance and the capital coefficient in Great Britain, 1866–1952'. *Econ. Hist. Rev.* 2 ser. ix (1956–7), 89–105.

4730 COODE (GEORGE). Report on fire insurance duties. [2168] H.C. (1857–Sess. 1). III, 643. Revised report. [3118] H.C. (1863). XXVI, 27.

The original report contained important errors of fact which occasioned a considerable outcry from the Assoc. for the Abolition or Reduction of the Duty on Fire Insurances. See *The fire insurance duty: history of the agitation for abolition or reduction, and reply to Mr. George Coode's blue book revised report*, 1863. The abolition of the duties as from 24 June 1869 ended an important ser. of statistics publ. by the Stamp Office (from 1856 Inland Rev.) of duty paid by each office.

4731  JACK (ALEXANDER FINGLAND). Fire insurance and the municipalities. 1914.

Discusses current fire insurance organization, company and municipal, and the case for
reorganizing fire insurance. Incls. useful statistics.

4732  WILLIAMS (BERTRAM). Specimens of British fire marks. [1934.]

The emblems erected by fire insurance companies on buildings insured by them.

4733  WRIGHT (CHARLES) *and* FAYLE (CHARLES ERNEST). A history
of Lloyd's: from the founding of Lloyd's coffee house to the present day. 1928.

Good for the development of marine insurance. See also Frederick Martin, *The history
of Lloyd's and of marine insurance in Great Britain*, 1876, David Eric Wilson Gibb,
*Lloyd's of London: a study in individualism*, 1957, the slight sketches of Henry M. Grey,
*Lloyd's: yesterday and to-day*, 1893, 3rd edn. 1926, and Ralph Straus, *Lloyd's: a historical sketch* [1937]. Charles Ernest Fayle, *Charles Wright: a memoir*, 1943, is a useful
life of a Lloyd's underwriter. There are also pamphlet hists. of a number of marine
insurance companies: *Thames & Mersey Marine Insurance Company Limited, 1860–
1960*, priv. pr. Liverpool 1960, *The British & Foreign Marine Insurance Company Limited,
1863–1963* [Liverpool 1963], and Union, Marine & General Insurance Co., Ltd., *Centennial story: the Union, Marine & General Insurance Company, Limited, 1863–1963*
[1963].

### 6. ACCOUNTANCY

4734  INSTITUTE OF CHARTERED ACCOUNTANTS. Catalogue of the
library. 1903. 2nd edn. 1913. 3rd edn. 1937. Suppl. 1939.

The earlier edns. are fuller than the later. See also Society of Incorporated Accountants,
*Catalogue of the library at Incorporated Accountants' Hall*, 1939. Institute of Chartered
Accountants, *Library catalogue*: Vol. 2. *The bibliography of book keeping*, 1937, is a full
chronological list. Thomas Beckett, *The accountant's assistant: an index to the accountancy lectures and leading articles reported in periodicals during the last thirty years of the
nineteenth century; to which is added a list of the principal treatises now in use . . .*, 1901,
is invaluable for contemp. works.

4735  STACEY (NICHOLAS ANTHONY HOWARD). English accountancy:
a study in social and economic history, 1800–1954. 1954.

A good outline hist. with bibliog. There is little in Beresford Worthington, *Professional
accountants: an historical sketch*, 1895. David Murray, *Chapters in the history of book-
keeping, accounting & commercial arithmetic*, Glasgow 1930, is useful only for its footnotes.

4736  LITTELTON (ANANIAS CHARLES) *and* YAMEY (BASIL SELIG)
*eds*. Studies in the history of accounting. 1956.

Two chaps. cover the period. An earlier symposium, Richard Brown, ed., *A history
of accounting and accountants*, Edin. 1905, is still useful, and has a convenient directory
of 'deceased Scottish accountants'.

4737  BRIEF (RICHARD P.). 'The origin and evolution of nineteenth-century
asset accounting'. *Business Hist. Rev.* xl (1966), 1–23.

See also his 'Nineteenth-century accounting error', *J. Accounting Res.* iii (1965), 12–13.

**4738** LISLE (GEORGE) *ed.* Encyclopaedia of accounting. 6 v. 1903–4.

The most comprehensive guide to the subject.

**4739** WITTY (RICHARD ALFRED). How to become a qualified accountant. 1906.

A useful guide to the profession.

**4740** HOWITT (*Sir* HAROLD GIBSON) *and others.* The history of the Institute of Chartered Accountants in England and Wales, 1880–1965, and of its founder accountancy bodies, 1870–1880: the growth of a profession and its influence on legislation and public affairs. 1966.

For other accounting bodies see Alexander Adnett Garrett, *History of the Society of Incorporated Accountants, 1885–1957,* Oxf. 1961, and Anon., *Fifty years: the story of the Association of Certified and Corporate Accountants, 1904–54,* 1954.

**4741** MURPHY (MARY E.). 'Lord Plender: a vignette of an accountant and his times, 1861–1948'. *Business Hist. Soc. Bull.* xxvii (1953), 1–25.

There is a short hist. of the origin of the firm: James Kilpatrick, *Deloitte, Plender, Griffiths & Co.: some notes on the early days of the firm,* 1942.

**4742** COOPER BROTHERS & Co. A history of Cooper Brothers & Co., 1854 to 1954. Priv. pr. [1954.]

One of the biggest firms.

**4743** JOURNAL OF ACCOUNTING RESEARCH. 1+. Chicago, etc. 1963+.

Incls. hist. articles. The main contemp. periodicals were *The accountant,* 1874+, and *The incorporated accountants' j.,* 1889–1938+. Other js. are listed in Stacey (**4735**).

## D. INDUSTRY

### 1. GENERAL

#### (a) *Reference*

**4744** FERGUSON (EUGENE SHALLCROSS). Bibliography of the history of technology. Camb., Mass. 1968.

**4745** BEALES (HUGH LANCELOT). 'Studies in bibliography. IV. The "basic" industries of England, 1850–1914'. *Econ. Hist. Rev.* v (1934–5), pt. 2, 99–112.

The only good general bibliog. There is little on England in Aksel Gustav Salomon Josephson, comp., *John Crerar Library: a list of books on the history of industry and the industrial arts,* Chicago 1915. For the industries of the West Riding there is a useful bibliog. for 1750 to 1914 by C. A. W. Ward (**4889**).

**4746** CARNEGIE LIBRARY, PITTSBURGH. Men of science and industry. Pittsburgh. 1915.

A guide to biogs. See also **4773–9**.

4747   COLE (W. A.). 'The measurement of industrial growth'. *Econ. Hist. Rev.* 2 ser. xi (1958–9), 309–15.

A bibliog. guide.

4748   U.S. COMMISSIONER OF LABOR. Sixth annual report, 1890: cost of production: iron, steel, coal, etc. Wash. 1891. U.S. House of Representatives Executive Doc. 265, 51st Congress 2nd Session. XXXVII, 1.

Comprehensive statistics of labour, cost of living, etc., for U.S. and Europe, running to 1404 pp.

4749   ORGANISATION FOR EUROPEAN ECONOMIC CO-OPERATION. Industrial statistics, 1900–1962 . . . Paris. 1964.

(b) *Histories and Studies*

4750   LANDES (DAVID SAUL). The unbound Prometheus: technological change and industrial development in western Europe from 1750 to the present. Camb. 1969.

Important for placing British and continental developments in context. For mid-20th-cent. industry the indispensable book is Duncan Lyall Burn, ed., *The structure of British industry: a symposium*, 2 v. Camb. 1958.

4751   HOFFMANN (WALTHER GUSTAV). British industry, 1700–1950. Trans. by William Otto Henderson and William Henry Chaloner. Oxf. 1955.

Good for statistics.

4752   ALDCROFT (DEREK HOWARD) *ed*. The development of British industry and foreign competition, 1875–1914: studies in industrial enterprise. 1968.

A good ser. of papers on indiv. industries.

4753   MARSHALL (ALFRED) *and* MARSHALL (MARY PALEY). The economics of industry. 1879.

The first work of economic analysis of the subject written in modern economic terms. Changing ideas, below the level of serious economic analysis are reflected in Henry Dyer, *The evolution of industry*, 1895, and David Hutchison MacGregor, *The evolution of industry* [1911].

4754   ASHWORTH (WILLIAM). 'Changes in the industrial structure, 1870–1914'. *Yorkshire Bull.* xvii (1965), 61–74.

4755   LEVINE (AARON LAWRENCE). Industrial retardation in Britain, 1880–1914. Lond. & N.Y. 1967.

See also 4078–82.

4756   RIDLEY (T. M.). 'Industrial production in the United Kingdom, 1900–1953'. *Economica* new ser. xxii (1955), 1–12.

John Wilkinson Foster Rowe, *The physical volume of production*, London & Cambridge Economic Service, special memorandum no. 8, 1924, gives index numbers of production from 1907 to the 1920s.

4757 SAUNDERS (C. T.). 'Consumption of raw materials in the United Kingdom, 1851–1950'. *Roy. Stat. Soc. J.* ser. A cxv (1952), 313–53.

4758 MAIZELS (ALFRED). Industrial growth and world trade: an empirical study of trends in production, consumption and trade in manufactures from 1899–1959, with a discussion of probable future trends. Camb. 1963.

For a correction of some of Maizels's statistics see A. G. Ford, 'A note on British export performance, 1899–1913', *Econ. Hist. Rev.* 2 ser. xxii (1969), 120–1, with acknowledgment by Maizels, ibid. 122.

4759 JONES (GEORGE THOMAS). Increasing returns: a study of the relation between the size and efficiency of industries, with special reference to the history of selected British & American industries, 1850–1910. Ed. by Colin Grant Clark. Camb. 1933.

Deservedly celebrated.

4760 VOGELSTEIN (THEODOR). Kapitalistische Organisationsformen in der modernen Grossindustrie. I: Organisationsformen der Eisenindustrie und Textilindustrie in England und Amerika. Leipzig. 1910.

4761 DUNNING (JOHN HARRY). American investment in British manufacturing industry. 1958.

See also his 'The growth of U.S. investment in U.K. manufacturing industry, 1856–1940', *Manch. School* xxiv (1956), 245–69, and, for American competition and example, Samuel Berrick Saul, 'The American impact on British industry, 1895–1914', *Business Hist.* iii (1960–1), 19–38, Mira Wilkins, *The emergence of multinational enterprise: American business abroad from the colonial era to 1914*, Camb., Mass. 1970, and **4805**.

4762 BRITISH STANDARDS INSTITUTION. Fifty years of British standards, 1901–1951. 1951.

4763 ALLEN (GEORGE CYRIL). The industrial development of Birmingham and the Black Country, 1860–1927. 1929. Repr. 1966.

A pioneer work of regional industrial hist. Can be suppl. by Samuel Timmins, ed., *The resources, products and industrial history of Birmingham and the Midland hardware district: a series of reports collected by the Local Industries Committee of the British Association at Birmingham in 1865*, 1866; William Highfield Jones, *Story of the japan, tinplate working, and iron brazier's trades, bicycle and galvanising trades, and enamel ware manufacture in Wolverhampton and district*, 1900; Jack Wilson Jones, *The history of the Black Country*, Birmingham [1905]; and M. J. Wise, 'On the evolution of the jewellery and gun quarters in Birmingham', *Inst. Brit. Geographers Trans.* xv (1951), 57–72.

4764 JEANS (JAMES STEPHEN). Notes on northern industries: written for the Iron and Steel Institute of Great Britain. [1878.]

Tyneside and Cleveland. See also William George Armstrong, Baron Armstrong, and others, eds., *The industrial resources of the district of the three northern rivers, the Tyne, Wear and Tees, including the reports on the local manufactures read before the British Association in 1863*, 1864 .

4765 HALL (PETER GEOFFREY). The industries of London since 1861. 1962.

Chiefly clothing, furniture, printing, and engineering. The main sources are the reports of Charles Booth (**9485**). But see also William Glenny Crory, *East London industries*, 1876, a good ser. of articles repr. from the *East London Observer*.

4766 PREST (JOHN MICHAEL). The industrial revolution in Coventry. 1960.

4767 MATHER (FREDERICK CLARE). After the canal duke: a study of the industrial estates administered by the trustees of the third Duke of Bridgewater in the age of railway building, 1825–1872. Oxf. 1970.

### (c) *Industrial Organization*

4768 FONG (H. D.) *otherwise* FANG (HSIEN-T'ING). Triumph of factory system in England. Tientsin. 1930.

4769 PAYNE (PETER LESTER). 'The emergence of the large-scale company in Great Britain, 1870–1914'. *Econ. Hist. Rev.* 2 ser. xx (1967), 519–42.

See also Lance Edwin Davis, 'The capital markets and industrial concentration: the U.S. and U.K., a comparative study', *Econ. Hist. Rev.* 2 ser. xix (1966), 255–72.

4770 MACROSTY (HENRY WILLIAM). The trust movement in British industry: a study of business organisation. 1907.

Still the best account. See also his *Trusts and the state: a sketch of competition*, Fabian Soc., 1901; George Reginald Carter, *The tendency towards industrial combination: a study of the modern movement towards industrial combination in some spheres of British industry* . . ., 1913; Hermann Joachim Levy, *Monopolies, cartels and trusts in British industry*, 1927; James Stephen Jeans, *Trusts, pools and corners as affecting commerce and industry: an inquiry into the principles and recent operation of combinations and syndicates to limit production and increase prices*, 1894; and Ministry of Reconstruction, *Report of committee on trusts* [Chairman: Edward Shortt]. [Cd. 9236] H.C. (1918). XIII, 789. For the international background see [Jeremiah Whipple Jenks] *Report of the Industrial Commission on industrial combinations in Europe*, vol. XVIII of the Commission's reports (57th Congress 1st Sess. House of Rep. Doc. 187) Wash. 1901, and *The trust problem*, N.Y. 1901, 5th edn. N.Y. 1922, Alfred Plummer, *International combines in modern industry*, 1934, 3rd edn. 1951, and Robert W. Liefmann, *Cartels, concerns and trusts*, 1932. Edward James Smith, *The new trades combination movement: its principles, methods and progress*, 1899, is a justification of combinations by one of their leaders.

4771 CHAPMAN (*Sir* SYDNEY JOHN) *and* ASHTON (THOMAS SOUTHCLIFFE). 'The sizes of businesses, mainly in the textile industries'. *Roy. Stat. Soc. J.* lxxvii (1913–14), 469–549.

See also Chapman and Marquis (**6717**).

4772 URWICK (LYNDALL FOWNES) *and* BRECH (EDWARD F. L.). The making of scientific management. 3 v. 1948–9.

Vol. II, *Management in British industry*, 1949, is a history. Vol. I, *Thirteen pioneers*, 1949, has a little on Britain. Vol. III is confined to the U.S.A. For background there is Sidney Pollard, *The genesis of modern management: a study of the industrial revolution in Great Britain*, Lond. & Camb., Mass. 1965.

## (d) *Industrial Biography*

**4773** ERICKSON (CHARLOTTE). British industrialists: steel and hosiery, 1850–1950. Camb. 1959.

**4774** SMILES (SAMUEL). Men of invention and industry. 1884.

One of Smiles's better books. Other writers such as James Burnley, *The romance of modern industry*, 1889, Alexander Hay Japp and Frederic Morell Holmes, *Successful business-men: short accounts of the rise of famous firms with sketches of the founders*, 1892, and George Barnett Smith, *Leaders of modern industry: biographical sketches*, 1894, who sought a popular market, never quite hit the right note.

**4775** JEANS (WILLIAM T.). The creators of the age of steel. 1884. 2nd edn. 1885.

**4776** FORTUNES MADE IN BUSINESS: a series of original sketches, biographical and anecdotic, from the recent history of industry and commerce. By various writers. 3 v. 1884–7.

A useful ser. of short hists. of indiv. firms prominent to *c.* 1870.

**4777** FORTUNES MADE IN BUSINESS. Life struggles of successful people. [1901–2.]

Illustr. Seems to be unconnected with the earlier ser. of the same name. Mainly concerned with firms and indivs. prominent at the end of the 19th cent.

**4778** MURPHY (WILLIAM S.). Captains of industry. Glasgow. [1903.]

**4779** MENZIES (AMY CHARLOTTE), *Mrs. Stuart Menzies*. Modern men of mark: the romantic life stories of Lord Armstrong, Sir Richard Burbidge, Lord Leverhulme . . . 1921.

## (e) *Descriptive Works and Inquiries*

**4780** STRAUSS (GUSTAVE LOUIS MAURICE) *and others*. England's workshops. 1867.

A short survey of firms manufacturing metal, chemical, glass, provisions, etc. Useful.

**4781** BEVAN (GEORGE PHILLIPS) *ed.* British manufacturing industries. 14 v. 1876–7. 2nd edn. 6 v. 1877–8.

A useful ser. covering a very wide range of industries in short books or long articles by experts.

**4782** [BOURNE (HENRY RICHARD FOX) *ed.*] Great industries of Great Britain. 3 v. 1877–80.

Illustr. articles by experts on the major industries, foreign rivalries, health, indiv. firms, and manufacturers. Publ. by Cassells. Order obscure.

**4783** IDDESLEIGH COMMISSION ON DEPRESSION OF TRADE AND INDUSTRY. First report of the royal commission appointed to inquire into the depression of trade and industry [Chairman: Earl of Iddesleigh].

[C. 4621] H.C. (1886). XXI, 1. Second report. Part I. [C. 4715] H.C. (1886). XXI, 231. Part II. [C. 4715–I] H.C. (1886). XXII, 1. Third report. [C. 4797] H.C. (1886). XXIII, 1. Final report. [C. 4893] H.C. (1886). XXIII, 507.

The official inquiry into the 'great depression', for later comments on which see **4079– 82.** Full of information about all sections of industry and trade.

4784  BAINES (TALBOT). The industrial north in the last decade of the nineteenth century. 1928.

Repr. from *The Times* with a memoir of Baines by Sir Hugh Bell.

4785  GALTON (FRANCIS W.) *ed.* Workers on their industries. 1894. Another edn. 1896.

4786  WELTON (THOMAS ABERCROMBIE). 'On forty years' industrial changes in England and Wales'. *Manch. Stat. Soc. Trans.* (1897–8), 153–243.

See also his 'On the 1891 census of occupations . . .', ibid. 245–66.

4787  WEBB (SIDNEY JAMES), *Baron Passfield, and* WEBB (BEATRICE). Problems of modern industry. 1898. New edn. 1902.

4788  ASHLEY (*Sir* WILLIAM JAMES) *ed.* British industries: a series of general reviews for business men and students. 1903. 2nd edn. 1907.

Articles by experts. Good.

4789  [MOSELY (ALFRED) *ed.*] Mosely industrial commission to the United States of America, Oct.–Dec., 1902: reports of the delegates. Manch. 1903.

Comparisons by a trade union delegation of conditions in Britain & U.S.

4790  COX (HAROLD) *ed.* British industries under free trade: essays by experts. 1903.

A free trade manifesto, but also a useful set of reports.

4791  TARIFF COMMISSION. Reports. 7 v. 1904–9.

Although intended to show the need for tariff reform, became a serious inquiry which produced much valuable material. The arrangement is: I The iron and steel trades; II The textile trades; III Agriculture; IV Engineering; V Pottery; VI Glass; VII Sugar and confectionery.

4792  SHADWELL (ARTHUR). Industrial efficiency: a comparative study of industrial life in England, Germany and America. 2 v. 1906. New edn. 1909.

4793  WILLIAMS (ARCHIBALD). How it is made: describing in simple language how various machines and many articles in common use are manufactured from the raw materials. [1907.]

A very elementary illustr. account of all branches of industry. The two main series of textbooks of this period, covering all industries in some detail, were the *Westminster series*, 20 v. 1907+, and *Pitman's common commodities of commerce series*, 1910+. For lists of books in these and other series see the appendixes to the *English catalogue* (8).

4794 FIRST CENSUS OF PRODUCTION. Final report of the first census of production of the United Kingdom (1907). [Cd. 6320] H.C. (1912–13). CIX, 1.

> A great statistical landmark. The *Final report* includes rev. versions of the *Preliminary reports*, which were publ. separately. For later reports see **34**.

4795 BALFOUR OF BURLEIGH COMMITTEE ON COMMERCIAL AND INDUSTRIAL POLICY. First report of the committee on commercial and industrial policy after the war [Chairman: Lord Balfour of Burleigh]. [Cd. 9035]. H.C. (1918). XIII, 239.

> Of little interest if taken alone, but intended to be a link between a host of committees whose reports are of value. Committees were appointed by the Board of Trade on (a) coal trade [Chairman: Lord Rhondda]. *Report*. [Cd. 9093] H.C. (1918). XIII, 321; (b) electrical trades [Chairman: Sir Charles A. Parsons]. *Report*. [Cd. 9072] H.C. (1918). XIII, 355; (c) engineering trades [Chairman: Sir Clarendon Golding Hyde]. *Report*. [Cd. 9073] H.C. (1918). XIII, 369; (d) iron and steel trades [Chairman: G. Scoby-Smith]. *Report*. [Cd. 9071] H.C. (1918). XIII, 423; (e) shipping and shipbuilding industries [Chairman: Sir Alfred A. Booth]. *Report*. [Cd. 9092] H.C. (1918). XIII, 473; (f) textile trades [Chairman: Henry Birchenough]. *Report*. [Cd. 9070] H.C. (1918). XIII, 643. A similar committee was appointed by the Minister of Munitions to consider the sulphuric acid and fertiliser trades [Chairman: Edward Shortt]. *Report*. [Cd. 8994] H.C. (1918). XIII, 629.

4796 MACLAREN (CHARLES BENJAMIN BRIGHT), *Baron Aberconway*. The basic industries of Great Britain: coal, iron, steel, engineering, ships: an historic and economic survey. 1927.

4797 BALFOUR COMMITTEE ON INDUSTRY AND TRADE. Factors in industrial and commercial efficiency: being, Part I of a survey of industries, with an introduction by the committee [Chairman: Sir Arthur Balfour, afterwards Lord Riverdale]. 1927. Part II [Further factors . . .]. 1928. Part III [Textile industries . . .]. 1928. Part IV [Metal industries]. 1928.

> An important inquiry publ. as a non-parl. official paper. Only the *Final report* [Cmd. 3282] H.C. (1928–9). VII, 413, was publ. as a parl. paper. For the committee's reports on industrial relations and overseas markets see **6503** and **5958**.

4798 SCHONFIELD (HUGH JOSEPH) *ed*. The book of British industries. 1933.

4799 FITZRANDOLPH (HELEN ELIZABETH) *and* HAY (MAVIS DORIEL). The rural industries of England & Wales: a survey made on behalf of the Agricultural Economics Research Institute, Oxford. Vol. I: Timber and underwood industries and some village workshops. Vol. II: Osier-growing and basketry and some rural factories. Vol. III: Decorative crafts and rural potteries. 3 v. 1926–7.

> See also H. D. Watts, 'Agricultural industries: the decline of the small business', *Business Hist.* ix (1967), 118–25, and John Geraint Jenkins, *Traditional country craftsmen*, 1965.

4800 PLUMMER (ALFRED). New British industries in the twentieth century: a survey of development and structure. 1937.

(f) *Technological Change*

See also **4744** and **5145-251**.

**4801**  SINGER (CHARLES) *and others, eds.* The history of technology. 5 v. Oxf. 1954-8.

Ambitious. Vol. V covers 1850-1900. For reviews see *Technology and culture* i (1959-60), 299-414.

**4802**  DERRY (THOMAS KINGSTON) *and* WILLIAMS (TREVOR ILLTYD). A short history of technology: from the earliest times to A.D. 1900. Oxf. 1960.

A short version of Singer (**4801**). There are many other short hists. Among them are Abbott Payson Usher, *A history of mechanical inventions*, N.Y. 1929, 2nd edn. Camb., Mass. 1954; Robert James Forbes, *Man the maker: a history of technology and engineering*, 1950, new edn. 1958; Heinz Gartmann, *Science as history: the story of man's technological progress* . . ., trans. by Alan G. Readett, 1960; Joachim Gustav Leithäuser, *Inventors of our world*, trans. by Michael Bullock, 1958; Egon Larsen, pseud. of Egon Lehrburger, *A history of invention*, 1961, and *Ideas and inventions*, 1960; Richard Shelton Kirby and others, *Engineering in history*, N.Y. 1956; Friedrich Klemm, *A history of Western technology*, trans. by Dorothea Waley Singer, 1959.

**4803**  CHALONER (WILLIAM HENRY) *and* MUSSON (ALBERT EDWARD). Industry and technology. 1963.

An unusually good picture-book.

**4804**  DUNSHEATH (PERCY) *ed.* A century of technology, 1851-1951. 1951.

**4805**  HABAKKUK (HROTHGAR JOHN). American and British technology in the nineteenth century: the search for labour-saving inventions. Camb. 1962.

For a full review by David Saul Landes see *Business Hist.* vii (1965), 15-33. For the better periodical articles on the subject see Samuel Berrick Saul, ed., *Technological change: the United States and Britain in the nineteenth century*, 1970.

**4806**  ARMYTAGE (WALTER HARRY GREEN). The rise of the technocrats: a social history. 1965.

**4807**  JEWKES (JOHN), SAWERS (DAVID), *and* STILLERMAN (RICHARD). The sources of invention. 1958.

On inventors since mid-19th cent. For the 19th cent. see William H. Doolittle, *Invention in the century*, Nineteenth cent. series 1903; Edward Wright Byrn, *The progress of invention in the nineteenth century*, N.Y. 1900; Robert Routledge, *Discoveries and inventions of the nineteenth century*, 1876, 14th edn. 1903; and John Timbs, *Wonderful inventions: from the mariner's compass to the electric telegraph cable*, 1868. For the 20th cent. see James Gerard Crowther, *Discoveries and inventions of the 20th century*, 1955, based on Edward Cressy, *Discoveries and inventions of the twentieth century* . . ., 1914, 3rd edn. 1930.

**4808**  BERNAL (JOHN DESMOND). Science and industry in the nineteenth century. 1953.

4809  SIMMONDS (PETER LUND). Science and commerce: their influence on our manufactures: a series of statistical essays and lectures describing the progressive discoveries of science, the advance of British commerce, and the conditions of our principal manufactures in the nineteenth century. 1872.

A useful contemp. work dealing with all branches of manufacturing.

4810  GIEDION (SIGFRIED). Mechanization takes command: a contribution to anonymous history. Oxf. & N.Y. 1948.

Mainly a hist. of industrial design.

### (g) *Factory Acts*

The main source of data on the subject is to be found in the reports of the factory inspectorate which were publ. as parl. papers (**33–4**).

4811  HUTCHINS (B. [i.e. ELIZABETH] LEIGH) *and* HARRISON, *afterwards* SPENCER (AMY). A history of factory legislation. 1903. 3rd edn. 1926.

Still the best general account.

4812  DJANG (TIEN KAI). Factory inspection in Great Britain. 1942.

A brief hist. and a survey of the 20th-cent. system.

4813  MESS (HENRY ADOLPHUS). Factory legislation and its administration, 1891–1924. 1926.

A useful independent account. See also Sir Duncan Wilson, 'Factory inspection: a thirty-five years retrospect', *Roy. Stat. Soc. J.* civ (1941), 209–24.

4814  WARD (JOHN TREVOR). The factory movement, 1830–1855. 1962.

A hist. of the movement for factory legislation.

4815  WARD (LEONARD). 'The effect, as shown by statistics, of British statutory regulations directed to the improvement of the hygienic conditions of industrial occupations'. *Roy. Stat. Soc. J.* lxviii (1905), 435–518.

4816  WOOD (GEORGE HENRY). 'Factory legislation considered with reference to the wages, &c., of the operatives protected thereby'. *Roy. Stat. Soc. J.* lxv (1902), 284–320.

4817  HOWELL (GEORGE). A handy-book of the labour laws . . . 1876. 3rd edn. 1895.

A pioneer work by a leading trade unionist. Suppl. by Herman Joseph Cohen and George Howell, *Trade union law and cases: a text-book relating to trade unions and to labour*, 1901, 2nd edn. 1907. Both were designed for trade-union use.

4818  AUSTIN (H. EVANS). The law relating to factories and workshops . . . 1895. 2nd edn. 1901.

A hist. to 1895 and an exposition. For other contemp. textbooks see Alexander Redgrave, *The Factory & Workshop Act, 1878* . . ., 1879; Eugene Mervyn Roe, *The Factory and Workshop Acts explained and simplified*, 1896; May Edith Abraham afterwards Tennant and Arthur Llewelyn Davies, *The law relating to factories and workshops* . . .,

1896, 6th edn. 1908; William Bowstead, *The law relating to factories and workshops* . . ., 1901; Richard Whately Cooke-Taylor, *The factory system and the factory acts*, 1894, 2nd edn. 1912; and Beatrice Webb, ed., *The case for the factory acts*, 1901, 2nd edn. 1902.

4819 ANDREWS (JOHN BERTRAM). British factory inspection: a century of progress in administration of labor laws. U.S. Dept. of Labor. Division of Labor Standards. Bull. no. 11. Wash. 1937.

One of a long ser. of foreign works on the British factory acts. See also Ernst, Baron von Plener, *The English factory legislation from 1802 till the present time*, trans. by Frederick L. Weinmann, 1873; Otto W. Weyer, *Die englische Fabrikinspektion* . . ., Tübingen 1888; Foy Spencer Baldwin, *Die englischen Bergwerksgesetze: ihre Geschichte von ihren Anfängen bis zum Gegenwart*, Munich 1894, and Henry Émile Barrault, *La réglementation du travail à domicile en Angleterre*, Paris 1906.

4820 FERGUSSON COMMITTEE ON FACTORY AND WORKSHOP ACTS. Report of the commissioners appointed to inquire into the working of the Factory and Workshops Acts, with a view to their consolidation and amendment [Chairman: Sir James Fergusson]. [C. 1443] H.C. (1876). XXIX, 1. Minutes of evidence. [C. 1443-I] H.C. (1876). XXX, 1.

The only thorough inquiry.

4821 MARTINEAU (HARRIET). The factory controversy: a warning against meddling legislation. Manch. 1855.

For the hostility of the classical economists to factory legislation see Mark Blaug, 'The classical economists and the factory acts: a re-examination', *Q. J. Econ.* lxxiii (1958), 211–26.

4822 JEANS (VICTORINE). Factory act legislation: its industrial and commercial effects, actual and prospective. Cobden prize essay for 1891. 1892.

4823 ANDERSON (*Dame* ADELAIDE MARY). Women in the factory: an administrative adventure, 1893 to 1921. 1922.

Based on factory inspectors' reports.

4824 SQUIRE. Thirty years in the public service: an industrial retrospect. By Rose Elizabeth Squire. 1927.

4825 TENNANT. May Tennant: a portrait. By Violet Rosa Markham. 1949.

The first woman factory inspector.

(h) *Industrial Archaeology*

4826 HUDSON (KENNETH). Industrial archaeology: an introduction. 1963. 2nd edn. 1966.

4827 PANNELL (JOHN PERCIVAL MASTERMAN). The techniques of industrial archaeology. Newton Abbot. 1966.

See also Kenneth Hudson, *A handbook for industrial archaeologists: a guide to fieldwork and research*, 1967, and Michael Rix, *Industrial archaeology*, Hist. Assoc. G65 1967.

4828 SMITH (NORMAN A. F.). Victorian technology and its preservation in modern Britain: a report submitted to the Leverhulme Trust. Leicester. 1970.

4829 INDUSTRIAL ARCHAEOLOGY: the journal of the history of industry and technology. 3+. Newton Abbot. 1966+. First publ. as *The j. of industrial archaeology*, 1–2, 1964–5.

4830 MARSHALL (JOHN DUNCAN) *and* DAVIES-SHIEL (MICHAEL). The industrial archaeology of the Lake counties (Cumberland, Westmorland and Lancashire north of the Sands). Newton Abbot. 1969.

4831 ASHMORE (OWEN). The industrial archaeology of Lancashire. Newton Abbot. 1969.

4832 NIXON (FRANK). The industrial archaeology of Derbyshire. Newton Abbot. 1969.

4833 SMITH (DAVID MARSHALL). The industrial archaeology of the East Midlands: Nottinghamshire, Leicestershire and the adjoining parts of Derbyshire. Dawlish. 1965.

4834 HUDSON (KENNETH). The industrial archaeology of southern England: Hampshire, Wiltshire, Dorset, Somerset and Gloucestershire west of the Severn. Dawlish. 1965. 2nd edn. Newton Abbot. 1968.

4835 JOHNSON (WILLIAM BRANCH). The industrial archaeology of Hertfordshire. Newton Abbot. 1970.

4836 BUCHANAN (ROBERT ANGUS) *and* COSSONS (NEIL). The industrial archaeology of the Bristol region. Newton Abbot. 1969.

4837 HARRIS (HELEN WARREN). The industrial archaeology of Dartmoor. Newton Abbot. 1968. 2nd edn. 1973.

4838 BOOKER (FRANK). The industrial archaeology of the Tamar Valley. Newton Abbot. 1967.

2. TEXTILES

(a) *General*

There is a good run of statistics in Mitchell and Deane (**125**) based on the official returns publ. annually throughout the period.

4839 PATENT OFFICE LIBRARY. Subject list of works on the textile industries and wearing apparel, including the culture and chemical technology of textile fibres, in the library of the Patent Office. 1919.
Still the best list.

4840 MURPHY (WILLIAM S.) *ed.* The textile industries: a practical guide to fibres, yarns & fabrics in every branch of the textile manufacture . . . 8 v. 1910–11.

A rather poor textile encyclopedia. See also his *Modern drapery and allied trades . . .*, 4 v. 1914.

4841 COMMITTEE ON INDUSTRY AND TRADE [Chairman: Sir Arthur Balfour, later Baron Riverdale]: survey of textile industries; cotton, wool, artificial silk: being, Part III of a survey of industries. 1928.

A useful survey.

4842 TEXTILE HISTORY. 1+. Newton Abbot. 1968+.

4843 MELLOR (JOHN HANSON) *and others.* A century of British fabrics, 1850–1950. Leigh-on-Sea. 1955.

On textile design. The best intro. to early-20th-cent. design is William Watson, *Textile design and colour: elementary weaves and figured fabrics*, 1912, 6th edn. 1954, and *Advanced textile design*, 1913, 3rd edn. 1947.

4844 LEWIS (FRANK). English chintz: a history of printed fabrics from earliest times until the present day. 1935. New edn. Leigh-on-Sea. 1942.

4845 KELLY'S DIRECTORY OF THE MANUFACTURERS OF TEXTILE FABRICS. 1880+. Irregular.

A splendid directory. Other useful directories incl. *The 'Textile Manufacturer' annual*, 1894–1918.

4846 WORRALL'S DIRECTORY OF THE MANUFACTURING DISTRICTS not included in Worrall's textile directories of Lancashire and Yorkshire. Oldham. 1889+.

To suppl. *The cotton spinner's and manufacturer's directory* . . ., Oldham 1882+, and *The Yorkshire textile directory* . . ., Oldham 1883+.

4847 TEXTILE INSTITUTE. Journal. Manch. 1910+.

Most textile js. concentrated on either wool or cotton. A few aspired to be more general, e.g. *The textile manufacturer*, Manch. 1874+; *Textile review*, 1883–97; *The textile mercury*, Manch. 1888+; *Journal of fabrics* [*Textile industries and journal of fabrics*], Bradford 1881–1903; *The textile recorder*, Manch. 1883+.

### (b) *Cotton*

#### (i) *General*

4848 WOODBURY (CHARLES JEPHTHA HILL). Bibliography of the cotton manufacture. 2 v. Waltham, Mass. 1909–10.

4849 SCHERER (JAMES AUGUSTIN BROWN). Cotton as a world power: a study in the economic interpretation of history. N.Y. 1916.

A general hist. of the cotton industry in all countries.

4850　THE COTTON SPINNERS AND MANUFACTURERS DIREC-
TORY and engineers and machine-makers advertiser for Lancashire. Oldham.
1882–1930+.

The leading cotton directory. See also *The textile year book* . . . [from 1909 *The cotton
year book*], Manch. 1906+.

4851　COTTON FACTORY TIMES. Manch. 1885–1937.

The most important periodical on cotton manufacturing, but see also *The textile mercury*, Manch. 1888+. For cotton supply see Liverpool Cotton Assoc., *Annual circular*.

4852　CHAPMAN (*Sir* SYDNEY JOHN). The Lancashire cotton industry:
a study in economic development. Manch. 1904.

The best general work on the subject. See also his 'The conditions and consequences of
market developments in the cotton trade', *Manch. Stat. Soc. Trans.* (1902–3), 49–67.
The fullest accounts of the 19th-cent. industry are in the contemp. works at **4870–87.**
Popular general hists. like Leonard Southerden Wood and Albert Wilmore, *The romance
of the cotton industry in England*, 1927, add nothing to Chapman. For the mid-20th-cent.
industry see Robert Robson, *The cotton industry in Britain*, 1957. Armin Spälty,
*Die Lage der Englischen Baumwollindustrie* . . ., Zurich 1936, is also useful.

4853　REDFORD (ARTHUR). Manchester merchants and foreign trade . . .
2 v. Manch. 1934–56.

A good hist. of the Manchester Chamber of Commerce, the chief organ of the cotton
industry. See also Roland Smith, 'The Manchester Chamber of Commerce and
the increasing foreign competition to Lancashire cotton textiles, 1873–96', *John Rylands
Libr. Bull.* xxxviii (1955–6), 507–34.

4854　SILVER (ARTHUR WISTAR). Manchester men and Indian cotton,
1847–1872. Manch. 1966.

See also Peter Harnetty, *Imperialism and free trade: Lancashire and India in the mid-
nineteenth century*, Vancouver 1972. There is a big literature on Lancashire and Indian
cotton. Some of the main works publ. after 1850 were (on cotton growing) John Forbes
Royle, *On the culture and commerce of cotton in India and elsewhere* . . ., 1851, Walter
Richard Cassels, *Cotton: an account of its culture in the Bombay presidency* . . ., Bombay
1862, James Talboys Wheeler, *Madras versus America: a handbook to cotton cultivation* . . .,
N.Y. 1866, and (on cotton manufacture) Manchester Chamber of Commerce, *Bombay
and Lancashire cotton spinning inquiry*, Manch. 1888.

4855　OGDEN (H. W.). 'The geographical basis of the Lancashire cotton
industry'. *Manch. Geographical Soc. J.* xliii (1928), 8–30.

See also John Jewkes, 'The localisation of the cotton industry', *Econ. Hist.* suppl. of
*Econ. J.* ii (1930–3), 91–106, and Joyce M. Bellamy, 'Cotton manufacture in Kingston-
upon-Hull', *Business Hist.* iv (1961–2), 91–108.

4856　BLAUG (MARK). 'The productivity of capital in the Lancashire cotton
industry during the nineteenth century'. *Econ. Hist. Rev.* 2 ser. xiii (1960–1),
358–81.

A careful analysis of the growth of the industry. For an important branch of the industry
see Roland Smith, 'An Oldham limited liability company, 1875–1896', *Business Hist.*
iv (1961–2), 34–53.

4857   SPENCER (JOSEPH). 'The growth of the cotton trade in Great Britain, America and the continent of Europe during the half century ending with the year 1875'. *Manch. Stat. Soc. Trans.* (1876–7), 231–40.

4858   SANDBERG (LARS G.). 'Movements in the quality of British cotton textile exports, 1815–1913'. *J. Econ. Hist.* xxviii (1968), 1–27.

4859   HENDERSON (WILLIAM OTTO). The Lancashire cotton famine, 1861–1865. Manch. 1934. 2nd edn. 1969.

The best single book on the subject, with extensive bibliog. But it is still necessary to consult Sir Robert Arthur Arnold, *The history of the cotton famine: from the fall of Sumter to the passing of the Public Works Act*, 1864, 2nd edn. 1865; John Watts, *The facts of the cotton famine*, 1866; Edwin Waugh, *Factory folk during the cotton famine*, Manch., 1881; Sir Robert Rawlinson, *Public works in Lancashire for the relief of distress ... 1863–66*, 1898; and Frederick Purdy, 'Extent of pauperism of the distressed unions of Lancashire ...', 1861–2', *Stat. Soc. J.* xxv (1862), 377–83. For more recent accounts see Barnard Ellinger, 'The cotton famine of 1861–4', *Econ. Hist.* suppl. of *Econ. J.* iii (1933–7), 152–67, Herbert William McCready, 'The cotton famine in Lancashire, 1863', *Historic Soc. Lancs & Ches. Trans.* cvi (1954), 127–33, and Eugene A. Brady, 'A reconsideration of the Lancashire cotton famine', *Agric. Hist.* xxxvii (1963), 156–62, with note by Morgan B. Sherwood, ibid. 163–5. For official reports on relief works during the famine see Ford, *Select List* (**31**).

4860   HELM (ELIJAH). 'The cotton trade of the United Kingdom during the seven years, 1862–68, as compared with the seven years, 1855–61; with remarks on the return of factories existing in 1868'. *Stat. Soc. J.* xxxii (1869), 428–37.

See also Helm's 'A review of the cotton trade of the United Kingdom during the seven years, 1862–1868', *Manch. Stat. Soc. Trans.* (1868–9), 67–94; Maurice Williams, *Seven years history of the cotton trade of Europe, 1861–68*, Liverpool 1868, and Sir William Bower Forwood, 'The influence of price upon the cultivation and consumption of cotton during the ten years, 1860–70', *Stat. Soc. J.* xxxiii (1870), 366–83.

4861   CAMPION (*Sir* HARRY). 'Pre-war fluctuations of profits in the cotton-spinning industry'. *Roy. Stat. Soc. J.* xcvii (1934), 626–32.

4862   CHAPMAN (*Sir* SYDNEY JOHN) *and* KNOOP (DOUGLAS). 'Dealings in futures on the cotton market'. *Roy. Stat. Soc. J.* lxix (1906), 321–64.

On the market for raw cotton see also Chapman and Knoop, 'Anticipation in the cotton market', *Econ. J.* xiv (1904), 541–54, Stanley Dumbell, 'The origin of cotton fixtures', *Econ. Hist.* suppl. to *Econ. J.* i (1926–9), 259–67, and W. W. Biggs, 'Cotton corners', *Manch. Stat. Soc. Trans.* (1894–5), 123–34.

4863   HUTTON (J. ARTHUR). 'The work of the British Cotton-growing Association'. *Manch. Stat. Soc. Trans.* (1903–4), 109–38.

4864   BOYSON (RHODES). The Ashworth cotton enterprise: the rise and fall of a family firm, 1818–1880. Oxf. 1970.

4865 MACARA. Sir Charles W. Macara, Bart.: a study of modern Lancashire. By William Haslam Mills. Manch. 1917. 2nd edn. 1917.

See also Macara's own *Recollections*, 1921, dealing mainly with his interest in social reform, for which see his *Social and industrial reform*, Manch. 1918, 8th edn. 1920.

4866 WESTON-WEBB. The autobiography of a British yarn merchant. By W. F. M. Weston-Webb. 1929.

Cotton in Manch. and in Europe.

4867 BLYTH (H. E.). Through the eye of a needle: the story of the English Sewing Cotton Company. Manch. 1947.

Cp. John Wanklyn McConnel, *A century of fine cotton spinning: McConnel & Co. . . . 1790–1906*, Manch. 1906, 2nd edn. 1913.

4868 ELLISON. Gleanings and reminiscences. By Thomas Ellison. Liverpool. 1905.

Cotton-broking in Liverpool.

4869 GIBB. Autobiography of a Manchester cotton manufacturer . . . By H. S. G. [i.e. Henry S. Gibb]. Manch. 1887.

Thin.

(ii) *Contemporary Studies*

4870 ELLISON (THOMAS). A hand-book of the cotton trade; or, a glance at the past history, present condition and future prospects of the cotton commerce of the world. 1858.

Good. For a contemp. account of the 'mission' of the cotton industry see John Baynes, *The cotton trade: two lectures . . . second. . . its mission, politically, socially, morally and religiously . . .*, Blackburn 1857.

4871 MANN (JAMES A.). The cotton trade of Great Britain: its rise, progress, & present extent, based upon the most carefully digested statistics, furnished by the several government departments, and most eminent commercial firms. Lond. & Manch. 1860.

4872 URE (ANDREW). The cotton manufacture of Great Britain investigated and illustrated. Rev. edn. By Peter Lund Simmonds. 2 v. 1861.

Orig. publ. 1836.

4873 DONNELL (EZEKIEL J.). Chronological and statistical history of cotton. N.Y. 1872.

American cotton exports and prices.

4874 LEIGH (EVAN). The science of modern cotton spinning: embracing, mill architecture, machinery for cotton ginning, opening, scutching, preparing and spinning, with all the latest improvements . . . 2 v. Manch. 1873. 4th edn. 1877.

Admirable illustrations.

4875  BARLOW (ALFRED). The history and principles of weaving by hand and by power . . . 1878. 2nd edn. 1879.

4876  MARSDEN (RICHARD). Cotton spinning: its development, principles and practice. 1884.

4877  ELLISON (THOMAS). The cotton trade of Great Britain: including, a history of the Liverpool cotton market and the Liverpool Cotton Brokers' Association. 1886. Repr. 1968.

4878  NASMITH (JOSEPH). Modern cotton spinning machinery: its principles and construction. Manch. 1890.

Good. See also his *Recent cotton-mill construction and engineering*, Manch. 1894, 3rd edn. 1909.

4879  MARSDEN (RICHARD). Cotton weaving: its development, principles and practice. 1895.

4880  SCHULZE-GAEVERNITZ (GERHART VON). The cotton trade in England and on the continent: a study in the field of the cotton industry. Trans. by Oscar S. Hall. Lond. & Manch. 1895.

4881  COTTON CLOTH FACTORIES COMMITTEE. Report of a committee appointed to inquire into the working of the Cotton Cloth Factories Act, 1889, &c. [Chairman: Sir Henry E. Roscoe]. [C. 8348] H.C. (1897). XVII, 61. Minutes of evidence. [C. 8349] H.C. (1897). XVII, 79.

4882  BEAUMONT (WILLIAM A.) *and* RICHMOND (H. S.). Report of two of H.M. Inspectors of factories appointed to inquire into and report upon the prevention of accidents from machinery in the manufacture of cotton. [C. 9456] H.C. (1899). XII, 345.

4883  OPPEL (ALBERT). Die Baumwolle: nach Geschichte, Anbau, Verarbeitung und Handel, sowie nach ihrer Stellung im Volksleben und in der Staatswirtschaft. Leipzig. 1902.

4884  CHAPMAN (*Sir* SYDNEY JOHN). The cotton industry and trade. 1905.

4885  TARIFF COMMISSION. Report of the tariff commission. Vol. 2. The textile trades. Part 1. The cotton industry. 1905.

For a reply see Sir Sydney John Chapman, *A reply to the report of the Tariff Commission on the cotton industry, written for the Free Trade League*, Manch. 1905.

4886  WHITTAM (WILLIAM). Report on England's cotton industry: with brief notes on other industries. U.S. Dept. of Commerce and Labor, Bureau of Manufactures. Special Agents' series no. 15. Wash. 1907.

4887 FREER-SMITH COMMITTEE ON HUMIDITY &c. IN COTTON WEAVING SHEDS. Report of the departmental committee on humidity and ventilation in cotton weaving sheds [Chairman: Sir Hamilton Freer-Smith]. [Cd. 4484] H.C. (1909). XV, 635. Minutes of evidence. [Cd. 4485] H.C. (1909). XV, 657. Second report. [Cd. 5566] H.C. (1911). XXIII, 807.

See also Frank Scudder, *Report on air tests in humid cotton weaving sheds.* [Cd. 2135] H.C. (1904). X, 629.

(c) *Wool*

4888 U.S. LIBRARY OF CONGRESS. Select list of references on wool, with special reference to the tariff. Wash. 1911. Suppl. 1913.

4889 WARD (CLIVE A. W.). A bibliography of the history of industry in the West Riding of Yorkshire, 1750–1914. *Leeds Philosophical & Literary Soc. Trans.* xiii, pt. 1. Leeds. 1968.

Covers all types of industry, but chiefly the woollen and related industries.

4890 THE YORKSHIRE TEXTILE DIRECTORY AND ENGINEERS AND MACHINE MAKERS ADVERTISER [The Yorkshire textile industry]. 1882+. Oldham. 1883+.

A useful directory. The other main reference works are *The wool yearbook & diary,* Manch. 1908–9+, and Bradford Chamber of Commerce, *Statistics relating to the worsted, woollen and artificial silk trades of the United Kingdom,* Bradford 1906+ [annual]. William White, comp., *White's 1853 Leeds & clothing districts of Yorkshire,* has been repr., Newton Abbot 1969.

4891 LIPSON (EPHRAIM). The history of the woollen and worsted industries. 1921. Repr. 1965.

The standard short hist. George Fraser Rainnie, ed., *The woollen and worsted industry: an economic analysis,* Oxf. 1965, is sometimes useful for perspective. Lipson also publ. *A short history of wool and its manufacture (mainly in England),* Melb. 1953. John James, *History of the worsted manufacture in England from the earliest times . . .,* Bradford & Lond. 1857, has little on the period. James Bonwick, *Romance of the wool trade,* 1887, has a certain period charm, but little more.

4892 BURNLEY (JAMES). The history of wool and wool combing. 1889.

Useful for inventions.

4893 DECHESNE (LAURENT). L'évolution économique et sociale de l'industrie de la laine en Angleterre. Paris. 1900.

Good.

4894 BEAUMONT (ROBERTS). Woollen and worsted cloth manufacture: being a practical treatise for the use of all persons employed in the manipulation of textile fabrics. 1888. 3rd edn. 1899.

For spinning see Walter S. Bright McLaren, *Spinning woollen and worsted: being a practical treatise for the use of all . . . engaged in these trades,* 1884, and Aldred Farrer Barker, *Woollen and worsted spinning,* 1922.

4895  CLAPHAM (*Sir* JOHN HAROLD). The woollen and worsted industries. 1907.

Standard on the Edwardian woollen industry. But see also Tariff Commission, *Report . . .* vol. 2. *The textile trades.* Part 2. *Evidence on the woollen industry,* 1905, and William Alexander Graham Clark, *Manufacture of woolen, worsted and shoddy in France and England and jute in Scotland,* U.S. Bureau of Manufactures: Special Agents series no. 25, Wash. 1908. There are also a number of general textbooks of about this date, such as John Mackie, *How to make a woollen mill pay,* 1904.

4896  BERESFORD (MARCUS WARWICK). The Leeds Chamber of Commerce. Leeds. 1951.

One of the main spokesmen of the West Riding woollen industry.

4897  CRUMP (WILLIAM BUNTING). 'The wool-textile industry of the Pennines in its physical setting'. *Textile Inst. J.* xxvi (1935), 367–74, 383–94.

4898  GLOVER (FREDERICK J.). 'The rise of the heavy woollen trade of the West Riding of Yorkshire in the nineteenth century'. *Business Hist.* iv (1961–2), 1–21.

4899  PANKHURST (KENNETH V.). 'Investment in the West Riding wool textile industry in the nineteenth century'. *Yorkshire Bull.* vii (1955), 93–116.

4900  SIGSWORTH (ERIC MILTON). 'The West Riding wool textile industry and the Great Exhibition'. *Yorkshire Bull.* iv (1952), 21–32.

4901  BAINES (EDWARD). 'On the woollen manufacture of England; with special reference to the Leeds clothing district'. *Stat. Soc. J.* xxii (1859), 1–34.

4902  CRUMP (WILLIAM BUNTING) *and* GHORBAL (SARAH GERTRUDE). History of the Huddersfield woollen industry. Tolson Memorial Museum handbook IX. Huddersfield. 1935.

Covers the period to 1851 only, but useful for background.

4903  SIGSWORTH (ERIC MILTON). Black Dyke Mills: a history, with introductory chapters on the development of the worsted industry in the nineteenth century. Liverpool. 1958.

The only good mill hist. George Arthur Greenwood. *Taylor of Batley: a story of 102 years,* 1957, deals with profit-sharing in a West Riding mill. See also the lives of Sir Titus Salt (**7072**), a philanthropic woollen manufacturer.

4904  SMITH. The master spinner: a life of Sir Swire Smith. By James Keighley Snowden. 1921.

A prominent Yorkshire manufacturer.

4905  MANN (JULIA DE LACY). The cloth industry of the west of England from 1640 to 1880. Oxf. 1971.

Dorothy M. Hunter, *The West of England woollen industry under protection and under free trade,* 1910, is good on the late 19th cent. Kenneth George Ponting, *A history of the West of England cloth industry,* 1957, has little on the period.

4906 TANN (JENNIFER). Gloucestershire woollen mills: industrial archaelogy. Newton Abbot. 1967.

4907 EDWARDS (J. K.). 'The decline of the Norwich textiles industry'. *Yorkshire Bull.* xvi (1964), 31–41.

4908 PLUMMER (ALFRED) *and* EARLY (RICHARD ELLIOTT). The blanket makers, 1669–1969: a history of Charles Early & Marriott (Witney) Limited. 1969.
In effect a hist. of the Witney blanket industry in Oxfordshire.

4909 MEADE-KING COMMITTEE ON WOOL SORTING. Report of the departmental committee appointed to inquire into the conditions of work in wool-sorting and other kindred trades [Chairman: William Oliver Meade-King]. [C. 8506] H.C. (1897). XVII, 1.

4910 HAMILTON (ARCHIBALD). 'On wool supply'. *Stat. Soc. J.* xxxiii (1870), 486–521.
See also A. Barnard, 'Wool buying in the nineteenth century: a case history', *Yorkshire Bull.* viii (1956), 1–12, and Board of Agriculture, *Report on the production of wool in Great Britain in 1905 and 1906,* 1907.

4911 PHILPOTT (B. P.). 'Fluctuations in wool prices, 1870–1953'. *Yorkshire Bull.* vii (1955), 1–28.
See also R. J. Thompson, 'Wool prices in Great Britain, 1883–1901', *Roy. Stat. Soc. J.* lxv (1902), 503–13.

4912 PONTING (KENNETH GEORGE). The wool trade: past and present. Manch. & Lond. 1961.
Deals mainly with marketing. See also John W. Turner, 'The position of the wool trade', *Roy. Agric. Soc. J.* 3 ser. vii (1896), 67–76.

4913 BARNARD (ALAN). The Australian wool market, 1840–1900. Melb. 1958.
Good on London wool market.

### (d) *Linen, Flax, and Jute*

4914 TARIFF COMMISSION. Report of the tariff commission. Vol. 2: The textile trades. Part 7: Evidence on the flax, hemp and jute industries. 1905.

4915 CLARK (WILLIAM ALEXANDER GRAHAM). Linen, jute and hemp industries in the United Kingdom, with notes on the growing and manufacture of jute in India. U.S. Bureau of Foreign & Domestic Commerce. Special Agents series 74. Wash. 1913.
One of the few works covering the three related industries.

4916 WARDEN (ALEXANDER JOHNSTON). The linen trade, ancient and modern. 1864. 2nd edn. 1867.

Still the best account. See also Dundee Trade Report Assoc., *Statistics of the linen trade*, Dundee 1855.

4917 MARSHALL (LESLIE C.). The practical flax spinner: being a description of the growth, manipulation and spinning of flax and tow. Lond., Manch., & N.Y. 1885.

A good textbook. Peter Sharp, *Flax, tow and jute spinning: a handbook* . . ., Dundee etc. 1882, 4th edn. 1907, is a shorter work of the same type.

4918 RIMMER (WILLIAM GORDON). Marshall's of Leeds: flax spinners, 1788–1886. Camb. 1960.

A good technical hist. of the greatest firm in the trade.

4919 SCIENCE MUSEUM LIBRARY. The history of flax growing in England and Scotland. Bibliog. ser. 534. 1940.

4920 DEMAN (E. F.). The flax industry: its importance and progress; also, its cultivation and management . . . 1852.

Rambling, but full of useful scraps of information. Cont. in his *A report of the last two years on the flax question*, 1854.

4921 EYRE (JOHN VARGAS). Report on the possibility of reviving the flax industry in Great Britain. *Board of Agric. J.* xxi (1914–15), suppl. 12. 1914.

4922 WOODHOUSE (THOMAS) *and* BRAND (ALEXANDER). A century's progress in jute manufacture, 1833–1933. Dundee. 1934.

There is useful background material in Richard Wolff, *Die Jute: ihre Industrie und volkswirtschaftliche Bedeutung*, Berlin 1913. The fullest contemp. textbook is William Leggatt, *The theory and practice of jute-spinning: being, a complete description of the machines used in the preparation and spinning of jute yarns* . . ., Dundee etc. 1893. See also William Fleming, 'On the manufacture of jute', *Inst. Mech. Eng. Proc.* for 1880, pp. 380–95.

(e) *Silk and Rayon*

4923 SILK AND MAN-MADE FIBRES LIBRARY. Catalogue. [1953.]

Good. Frederick Oliver Howitt, *Bibliography of the technical literature on silk* [1947], is too technical for most hist. purposes.

4924 SCHOBER (JOSEPH). Silk and the silk industry. Trans. by Ronald Cuthill. 1930.

General. Deals with artificial silk.

4925 WARNER (*Sir* FRANK). The silk industry of the United Kingdom: its origin and development. 1921.

A standard, old-fashioned, town-by-town hist. There is a considerable pamphlet literature calling for protection for the industry, of which James Salter-Whiter, *The silk industry of Great Britain and its revival*, priv. pr. 1882, is an example.

4926 TARIFF COMMISSION. Report of the tariff commission. Vol. 2: The textile trades. Part 6: Evidence on the silk industry. 1905.

4927 RAYNER (HOLLINS). Silk throwing and waste silk spinning. 1903. 2nd edn. 1921.

An illustrated account of the industry. See also Arnold Hard, 'Silk throwing in England: a short history', *Fibres and fabrics monthly* i (1940), 10–14, 40–3, 85–8, 152–5.

4928 CROZIER (MARY). An old silk family, 1745–1945: the Brocklehursts of Brocklehurst–Whiston Amalgamated Limited. 1947.

A hist. of one of the old-established Macclesfield firms. A co-op. rival is dealt with in William Henry Brown, *The silken glow of Macclesfield: with the jubilee history of the Macclesfield Silk Manufacturing Society Limited*, Manch. [1938.] Berisfords, *the ribbon people: jubilee, 1858–1958*, Congleton 1958, deals with a silk-ribbon maker.

4929 RAWLLEY (RATAN CHAND). The silk industry and trade: a study in the economic organization of the export trade of Kashmir and Indian silks, with special reference to their utilization in the British and French markets. 1919.

4930 HARD (ARNOLD HENRY). The story of rayon and other synthetic textiles. 1939.

See also Edwin John Beer, *The beginning of rayon*, Paignton 1962.

4931 COLEMAN (DONALD CUTHBERT). Courtaulds: an economic and social history. Vol. I: The nineteenth century, silk and crepe. Vol. II: Rayon. 2 v. Oxf. 1969.

A good professional hist. of the pioneering firm in the rayon industry. Repl. Cyril Henry Ward-Jackson, *A history of Courtaulds . . .*, priv. pr. 1941.

## (f) Hosiery and Lace

4932 BRISCOE (JOHN POTTER) *and* KIRK (S. J.) *comps.* Hosiery, lace, embroidery, &c. Nottingham Free Public Librs., Public Reference Libr. class list 20. Nottingham. 1896.

4933 WELLS (FREDERICK ARTHUR). The British hosiery trade: its history and organisation. 1935.

See also C. Erickson, *British industrialists: steel and hosiery* (**4773**); W. A. Edwards and G. F. Hardcastle, 'Hosiery dyeing and finishing, 1884–1934' in *Jubilee issue of the Soc. of Dyers and Colourists J., 1834–1934*, Bradford 1934, pp. 169–83; D. M. Smith, 'The British hosiery industry in the middle of the nineteenth century: an historical study in economic geography', *Inst. British Geographers Trans.* 32 (1963), 125–42, which deals with the situation in 1844; and Peter Head, 'Putting out in the Leicester hosiery industry in the middle of the nineteenth century', *Leicestershire Archaeol. & Hist. Soc. Trans.* xxxvii (1962), 44–59.

4934 TARIFF COMMISSION. Report of the tariff commission. Vol. 2: The textile trades. Part 3: Evidence on the hosiery industry. 1905.

4935  CHURCH (ROY ANTHONY). 'Technological change and the Hosiery Board of Conciliation and Arbitration, 1860–1884'. *Yorkshire Bull.* xv (1963), 52–60.

4936  WARDLE (PATRICIA). Victorian lace. 1968.

Lace of the main lace-producing countries.

4937  FELKIN (WILLIAM). A history of the machine-wrought hosiery and lace manufactures. 1867. Repr. with intro. by Stanley David Chapman. Newton Abbot. 1967.

Still the best hist. but must be suppl. by his 'The lace and hosiery trades of Nottingham', *Stat. Soc. J.* xxix (1866), 536–41; Walter Harry Green Armytage, 'A. J. Mundella and the hosiery industry', *Econ. Hist. Rev.* xviii (1948), 91–9; *Nottingham Daily Express, The lace trade in Nottingham and district*, Nottingham 1905; D. E. Varley, 'John Heathcoat, 1783–1861: founder of the machine-made lace industry', *Textile Hist.* i (1968), 2–45; Walter Gore Allen, *John Heathcoat and his heritage* [the Tiverton lace industry], 1958; and Jonathan David Chambers, *The memoir of a Nottingham lace merchant, William Cripps, 1798–1884*, repr. from *Business Hist. Soc. Bull.* xxiv (1950), 65–109. The main official source is Hugh Seymour Tremenheere, *Report . . . upon the expediency of subjecting the lace manufacture to the regulations of the Factory Acts.* [2797] H.C. (1861). XXII, 461.

4938  PALLISER (FANNY BURY). A history of lace. 1865. 4th edn. 1902.

Hand-woven lace. See also Catherine C. Channer and M. E. Roberts, *Lace making in the Midlands, past and present*, 1900, Thomas Wright, *The romance of the lace pillow: being, the history of lace-making in Bucks, Beds, Northants . . .*, Olney 1919, and *Report of Mr. Alan Cole, commissioner from the South Kensington Museum, on the present condition and prospects of the Honiton lace industry.* H.C. 124. (1888). LXXX, 493. There is little in Emily Nevill Jackson, *A history of hand-made lace*, 1900.

4939  TARIFF COMMISSION. Report of the tariff commission. Vol. 2: The textile trades. Part 4: Evidence on the lace industry. 1905.

4940  CLARK (WILLIAM ALEXANDER GRAHAM). Lace industry in England and France. U.S. Bureau of Manufactures special agents series 23. Wash. 1909.

### (g) *Other Textiles and Related Substances*

4941  WELLS (FREDERICK ARTHUR). Hollins & Viyella: a study in business history. Newton Abbot. 1968.

A firm which developed a range of special goods using different materials. There is also an earlier house history, Stanley C. Pigott, *Hollins: a study of industry, 1784–1949*, Nottingham 1949.

4942  TARIFF COMMISSION. Report of the tariff commission. Vol. 2: The textile trades. Part 5: Evidence on the carpet industry. 1905.

See also J. N. Bartlett, 'The mechanisation of the Kidderminster carpet industry', *Business Hist.* ix (1967), 49–69.

4943 CRONWRIGHT *afterwards* CRONWRIGHT-SCHREINER (SAMUEL CRON). The angora goat . . . 1898.

Incls. a section on the English industry and trade.

4944 JUBB (SAMUEL). The history of the shoddy trade: its rise, progress and present position. 1860. Repr. 1969.

A very minor classic. For the techniques of the industry see Norman Cecil Gee, *Shoddy and mungo manufacture: its development, ancillary processes, methods and machinery*, Manch. 1950.

4945 FISCHER (HUGO). Geschichte, Eigenschaften und Fabrikation des Linoleums: eine technologische Studie . . . Leipzig. 1888. 2nd edn. 1924.

For the lino industry see the hist. of Lancaster (**9540**), Muir (**10022**), M. W. Jones, *The history and manufacture of floorcloth and linoleum: a paper*, Bristol 1919, and Frederick Walton, *The infancy and development of linoleum floorcloth, by its inventor*, 1925.

4946 PAHL (JANICE). 'The rope and net industry of Bridport: some aspects of its history and geography'. *Dorset Nat. Hist. & Archaeol. Soc. Proc.* lxxxii (1960), 143–54.

### (h) Dyeing, Bleaching, etc.

4947 LAWRIE (LESLIE GORDON). A bibliography of dyeing and textile printing: comprising a list of books from the sixteenth century to the present time (1946). 1949.

Particularly useful for contemp. textbooks. For articles in periodicals see Hermann Henry Bernard Meyer, ed., *Library of Congress: list of references on dyestuffs: chemistry, manufacture, trade*, Wash. 1919, which is, however, weak on British books.

4948 RICHARDSON (HARRY WARD). 'The development of the British dyestuffs industry before 1939'. *Scot. J. Pol. Econ.* ix (1962), 110–29.

4949 ROWE (FREDERICK MAURICE). Two lectures on the development of the chemistry of commercial synthetic dyes, 1856–1938. Inst. of Chemistry. 1938.

The best technical account of the subject. See also his 'The life and work of Sir William Henry Perkin' in *Soc. of Dyers & Colourists J.* liv (1938), 551–62; Howard J. White, ed., *Proceedings of the Perkin centennial, 1855–1956: commemorating the discovery of aniline dyes*, American Assoc. of Textile Chemists and Colourists [1956]; *Manchester Guardian, The centenary of a great discovery: Sir William Henry Perkin's mauve*, Manch. 1956; *Perkin centenary, London: 100 years of synthetic dyestuffs*, Tetrahedron Suppl. 1 [1958]; and *American Dyestuff Reporter, Perkin centenary issue*, v. 45, no. 18 (27 August 1956).

4950 SOCIETY OF DYERS & COLOURISTS. The jubilee issue of the Journal of the Society of Dyers and Colourists, 1884–1934. Ed. by F. N. Rowe and E. Clayton. Bradford. 1934.

The *Proceedings* [later *Journal*] of the Soc. are an important source.

4951  DAWE (DONOVAN ARTHUR). Skilbecks; drysalters, 1650–1950. 1950.

Merchants of dyestuffs.

4952  HIGGINS (SYDNEY HERBERT). A history of bleaching. 1924.

4953  SYKES (*Sir* ALAN JOHN) *and others*. Concerning the bleaching industry. Manch. 1926.

A short hist. of the Bleachers' Assoc. Ltd. and its component firms.

4954  TURNBULL (GEOFFREY) *ed*. A history of the calico printing industry of Great Britain. Ed. by John G. Turnbull. Altrincham. 1951.

4955  POTTER. Edmund Potter and Dinting Vale. By J. G. Hurst. Manch. 1948.

A short biog. of the leading calico printer of the 1850s and 1860s.

4956  CALVERT (FREDERICK GRACE). Lectures on coal-tar colours and on recent improvements and progress in dyeing & calico printing, embodying copious notes taken at the International Exhibition of 1862, and illustrated with numerous specimens of aniline and other colours. Manch. [1862.]

One of many books on recent discoveries. Calvert also wrote a big book, *Dyeing and calico printing* . . ., ed. by John Stenhouse and Charles Edward Groves, 1876, 3rd edn. 1878. The lectures and papers of Sir William Henry Perkin, and his son William Henry Perkin, the younger, include much material not readily available elsewhere. For a list see works cited in *D.N.B.* (71) and Sir Robert Robinson, *Life and work of Prof. W. H. Perkin*, Chemical Soc., 1932. Of contemp. textbooks Sir William Crookes, *A practical handbook of dyeing and calico-printing*, 1874, is perhaps the most useful.

4957  O'NEILL (CHARLES). The practice and principles of calico printing, bleaching, dyeing, etc. Manch. 2 v. 1878.

The best of O'Neill's three books on the subject, with full bibliog. O'Neill also ed. *The textile colourist* . . ., 1876–7.

4958  TREMENHEERE (HUGH SEYMOUR). Report of the commissioner appointed to inquire how far it may be advisable to extend the provisions of the acts for the better regulation of mills and factories to bleaching works . . . [1943.] H.C. (1854–5). XVIII, 1.

4959  SELECT COMMITTEE ON BLEACHING AND DYEING WORKS. First report from the select committee on bleaching and dyeing works [Chairmen: Lord John Manners and John Morgan Cobbett]. H.C. 151. (1857–Sess. 2). XI, 1. Second report. H.C. 211 (1857–Sess. 2). XI, 259. Further report. H.C. 270 (1857–8). XI, 685.

4960  TREMENHEERE (HUGH SEYMOUR) *and* TUFNELL (EDWARD CARLETON). Report on the Printworks Act and on the Bleaching and Dyeing Works Acts. [4149] H.C. (1868–9). XIV, 777.

(i) *Clothing Industries*

4961  HALL (PETER GEOFFREY). 'The location of the clothing trades in London, 1861–1951'. *Inst. Brit. Geographers Trans.* xxviii (1960), 155–78.

For indiv. firms see *The draper's diary and year book*, 1886+, and *The draper's record*, 1887+.

4962  THOMAS (JOAN). A history of the Leeds clothing industry. *Yorkshire Bull.* occ. paper no. 1. 1965.

4963  RYOTT (DAVID). John Barran's of Leeds, 1851–1951. Leeds. 1951.

Clothing manufacturers. For Burtons, a major chain of manufacturers and drapers, see Ronald Redmayne, ed., *Ideals in industry: being the story of Montague Burton Ltd., 1900–1950*, Leeds 1950, reissued 1951. For a firm of Birmingham drapers there is John Wills, *Wilkinson and Riddell Limited, 1851–1951*, priv. pr., Birmingham 1951.

4964  DONY (JOHN GEORGE). A history of the straw hat industry. Luton. 1942.

Standard. See also Charles Freeman, *Luton and the hat industry*, Luton Museum 1953.

4965  SMITH (D. M.). 'The hatting industry in Denton, Lancashire'. *Indust. Archaeol.* iii (1966), 1–7.

3. MINING AND THE MINERAL INDUSTRIES

(a) *Reference*

4966  PATENT OFFICE LIBRARY. Subject list of works on the mineral industries and allied sciences . . . 1903. 2nd. edn. 3 pts. 1912.

The best of the contemp lists. But see also H. White and T. W. Newton, *A catalogue of the library of the Museum of Practical Geology and the Geological Survey*, 1878.

4967  NORTH OF ENGLAND INSTITUTE OF MINING AND MECHANICAL ENGINEERS. Subject-matter index of mining, mechanical and metallurgical literature. 1900–2. Newcastle-upon-Tyne. 1902–7.

4968  LIST of memoirs, maps, sections, &c., published by the Geological Survey of Great Britain and the Museum of Practical Geology to 31st December, 1936. H.M.S.O. 1937.

Cont. in H.M.S.O. Sectional list no. 45. 1961, and revisions. The memoirs include much important material.

4969  HUNT (ROBERT). Mining records: mineral statistics of the United Kingdom of Great Britain and Ireland for 1853 and 1854. Memoirs of the Geological Survey of Great Britain and of the Museum of Practical Geology. 1855.

Cont. annually to year 1881. Statistics for 1848–52 were publ. in Robert Hunt, *Records of the School of Mines and of Science applied to the arts*, Museum of Practical Geology and Geological Survey, vol. I, pt. IV (1853), 413–82. The ser. was cont. by Home

Office, Mines Dept., as *Mining and mineral statistics*, 1882–96, 1884–97, then as *Mines and quarries: general report and statistics*, 1897+, 1898+. For a discussion of the statistics see *Report of the departmental committee on mining and mineral statistics* [Chairman: Clement Le Neve Foster]. [C. 7609] H.C. (1895). XLII, 1.

4970 PATENT OFFICE. Abridgments of specifications. Class 85: mining, quarrying, tunnelling and well sinking. 1855–66 to 1926–30.

4971 H.M. INSPECTORS OF MINES. List of mines worked in the year 1888 [–1938] under the Coal Mines Regulation Act, 1887, the Metalliferous Mines Regulation Acts, 1872 and 1875, and the Slate Mines (Gunpowder) Act, 1882. 1889 [–1939].

Earlier lists are incl. in *Mining and mineral statistics* (**4969**), but not at such great length.

4972 HOME OFFICE (MINES DEPARTMENT). Catalogue of plans of abandoned mines. 5 v. 1928–31. Suppls. 1930, 1937, 1938, 1939.

4973 H.M. INSPECTORS OF MINES. Annual reports. 1854+.

Publ. as parl. papers until 1914 under various titles. There is a parallel ser. of reports on the mining districts by the commissioners under the Act 5 & 6 Vict. c. 99 for the years 1844 to 1858.

4974 H.M. INSPECTORS OF MINES. Summaries of the reports of the inspectors of mines and mineral statistics of the United Kingdom . . . including lists of mines and mineral works for 1883–[96]. 1884–97.

Useful for lists of mines, etc. Subsequent data incl. in *Mines and quarries* (**4969**).

4975 FOSTER (*Sir* CLEMENT LE NEVE). [First] annual general report upon the mineral industry of the United Kingdom of Great Britain and Ireland for the year 1894 [–98]. 1896–9.

For full list see *General index* (**33**).

4976 WHO'S WHO IN MINING AND METALLURGY. 1908+.

4977 THE MINING MANUAL. 1887+.

Absorbed *The mining yearbook*, 1901–12, and became *The mining manual and mining year book*, 1913–27. *The colliery year book and coal trades directory*, 1922+, is also a useful source of facts.

4978 NORTH OF ENGLAND INSTITUTE OF MINING [AND MECHANICAL] ENGINEERS. Transactions. Newcastle-upon-Tyne. 1852/53+.

The earliest of the society transactions devoted largely to mining. The others are South Wales Institute of Engineers, *Transactions [Proceedings]*, Cardiff 1857+; Midland Institute of Mining [Civil and Mechanical] Engineers, *Transactions &c.*, Barnsley etc. 1869–1936; Chesterfield and Derbyshire Institute of Mining, Civil and Mechanical Engineers [Chesterfield and Midland Counties Institution of Engineers] *Transactions*, 1871–91; North Staffordshire Institute of Mining and Mechanical Engineers, *Transactions*, Newcastle-under-Lyme 1873–96; West of Scotland Mining Institute [Mining Institute of Scotland], *Transactions*, Hamilton 1879+; Federated Institute [Institution] of Mining Engineers, *Transactions*, Newcastle-upon-Tyne etc. 1889+; Institution of Mining and Metallurgy, *Transactions*, 1892+; and National Association of Colliery Managers, *Transactions*, 1889–95, and *Minutes of proceedings*, 1903+.

4979   THE MINING JOURNAL [RAILWAY] AND COMMERCIAL GAZETTE. 1835+.

The most useful of the general mining newspapers. Covers all aspects of mining. Other useful papers are *The colliery guardian and journal of the coal and iron trades*, 1858+; *The iron and coal trades rev.*, 1866+; *The colliery manager . . .*, 1884–1904; *Coal and iron*, 1891–1924; *Mining [engineering]*, Wigan 1892–1916; *The quarry*, 1896–1938; *The coal merchant and shipper*, 1900+; and *The mining magazine*, 1909+.

(b) *General*

4980   SHEDDEN (CHARLES T.) *ed.* The Iron and Coal Trades Review: diamond jubilee issue, 1867–1927: a record of sixty years' progress in the coal, iron and steel industries; compiled by leading authorities. 1927.

Good. None of the popular general hists., such as John Bernard Mannix, *Mines and their story*, 1913, is of more than slight value.

4981   HUNT (ROBERT). 'The present state of the mining industries of the United Kingdom'. *Stat. Soc. J.* xix (1856), 201–18, 311–24.

4982   FORDYCE (WILLIAM). A history of coal, coke, coal-fields, progress of coal mining . . . iron, its ores, and processes of manufacture . . . Newcastle-upon-Tyne. 1860.

4983   MEADE (RICHARD). The coal and iron industries of the United Kingdom. 1882.

Full and valuable.

4984   HART (CYRIL EDWIN). The free miners of the royal forest of Dean and hundred of St. Briavels. Gloucester. 1953.

4985   IMPERIAL INSTITUTE (MINERAL RESOURCES BUREAU). Reports on the mineral industry of the British Empire and foreign countries: war period, 1913–19: coal, coke and by-products. 3 v. H.M.S.O. 1921–2.

The other mineral industries are covered in parallel reports.

4986   ROTHWELL (RICHARD PENNEFATHER) *and others, eds.* The mineral industry: its statistics, technology and trade, in the United States and other countries, from the earliest times to the end of 1892+. Statistical suppl. of the *Engineering and Mining Journal*. N.Y. 1893+.

4987   LOCK (CHARLES GEORGE WARNFORD). Mining and ore-dressing machinery: a comprehensive treatise dealing with the modern practice of winning both metalliferous and non-metalliferous minerals; including all the operations incidental thereto, and preparing the product for the market. 1890.

Well illus. Cornelius McLeod Percy publ. two similar but more theoretical works, *The mechanical engineering of collieries*, 2 v. 1882–5, and *The mechanical equipment of collieries*, Manch. 1905.

4988  FOSTER (*Sir* CLEMENT LE NEVE). The elements of mining and quarrying. 1903. 2nd edn. 1910.

See also his *A text-book of ore and stone mining*, 1894, 7th edn. 1910.

4989  HARDWICK (F. W.) *and* O'SHEA (L. T.). 'Notes on the history of the safety-lamp'. *Instn. Mining Engineers Trans.* li (1915–16), 548–718.

4990  SUTCLIFFE. Richard Sutcliffe: the pioneer of underground belt conveying. By Edward Davis Sutcliffe. 1939.

4991  ROSEN (GEORGE). The history of miners' diseases: a medical and social interpretation. N.Y. 1943.

4992  SORLEY (WILLIAM RITCHIE). Mining royalties and their effect on the iron and coal trades: report of an enquiry made for the Toynbee Trustees. 1889.

A useful intro. to a complicated subject dealt with at length by the Northbrook Commission (**4993**). Repr. from *Roy. Stat. Soc. J.* lii (1889), 60–98.

4993  NORTHBROOK COMMISSION ON MINING ROYALTIES. First report of the royal commission appointed to inquire into the subject of mining royalties [Chairman: Earl of Northbrook]. [C. 6195] H.C. (1890). XXXVI, 1. Second report. [C. 6331] H.C. (1890–1). XLI, 375. Third report. [C. 6529] H.C. (1890–1). XLI, 817. Fourth report. [C. 6979] H.C. (1893–4). XLI, 1. Final report. [C. 6980] H.C. (1893–4). XLI, 341.

4994  KENDALL COMMITTEE ON RATING OF MINES. Report from the select committee on rating of mines [Chairman: Nicholas Kendall]. H.C. 346 (1856). XVI, 1. Further report. H.C. 241 (1857 Sess. 2). XI, 533.

4995  BAINBRIDGE (WILLIAM). A practical treatise on the law of mines and minerals. 1841. 5th edn. 1900.

A solid textbook. See also Robert Porrett Collier, Baron Monkswell, *A treatise on the law relating to mines*, 1849, 2nd edn. 1855, Arundel Rogers, *The law relating to mines, minerals and quarries in Great Britain and Ireland . . .*, 1864, 2nd edn. 1876, and Robert Forster MacSwinney, *The law of mines, quarries and minerals*, 1884, 5th edn. 1922.

(c) *Coal*

4996  JEVONS (HERBERT STANLEY). The British coal trade. 1915. Repr. with intro. by Baron Frederick Duckham. Newton Abbot. 1969.

A good intro. to all aspects of the industry. Andrew Martin Neuman, *The economic organisation of the British coal industry*, 1934, and Sir Gilbert Stone, *The British coal industry*, 1919, cover much the same ground, but not so fully. William Arthur Bone, *Coal and its scientific uses*, 1918, rev. edn. 1936, is a useful suppl. Alan R. Griffin, *Coalmining*, 1971, deals with techniques.

4997  GALLOWAY (ROBERT LINDSAY). A history of coal-mining in Great Britain. 1882. 2nd edn. 1898. Repr. with intro. by Baron Frederick Duckham. Newton Abbot. 1969.

Suppl. by his *Annals of coal mining and the coal trade: the invention of the steam engine and the origin of the railway*, 2 v. 1898–1904, repr. 2 v. Newton Abbot 1971. The only attempt at a comprehensive hist. But see also Sir Thomas Edward Thorpe, ed., *Coal. its history and uses*, 1878.

4998 MINING ASSOCIATION OF GREAT BRITAIN. Historical review of coal mining. [1924.]

A useful symposium.

4999 GIBSON (FINLAY A.) *ed*. A compilation of statistics (technological, commercial and general) of the coal-mining industry of the United Kingdom, the various coalfields thereof, and the principal foreign countries of the world. Cardiff. 1922.

5000 THOMAS (DAVID ALFRED), *Viscount Rhondda*. 'The growth and direction of our foreign trade in coal during the last half century'. *Roy. Stat. Soc. J.* lxvi (1903), 439–522.

See also his *Some notes on the present state of the coal trade in the United Kingdom: with special reference to that of South Wales and Monmouthshire . . .*, Cardiff 1896.

5001 JEVONS (WILLIAM STANLEY). The coal question: an inquiry concerning the progress of the nation and the probable exhaustion of our coal mines. 1865. 3rd edn. 1906.

A sensational warning of the imminent exhaustion of coal supplies, but nonetheless the starting-point for much serious discussion. See Leonard H. Courtney, Baron Courtney of Penwith, 'Jevons' *Coal question*: thirty years after', *Roy. Stat. Soc. J.* lx (1897), 789–810, Richard Price-Williams, 'The coal question', ibid. lii (1889), 1–39, and George G. Chisholm, 'An examination of the coal and iron production of the principal coal and iron producing countries of the world, with reference to the English coal question', ibid. liii (1890), 561–604.

5002 HULL (EDWARD). The coal fields of Great Britain: their history, structure, and duration: with notices of the coal-fields of other parts of the world. 1861. 4th edn. 1881. 5th edn. 1905.

A geologist's account of coal resources. Suppl. by his *Our coal resources at the close of the nineteenth century*, 1897.

5003 RUOLZ-MONTCHAL (*Comte* HENRI DE). Question des houilles: mission de M. de Ruolz en France et en Angleterre. 3 v. Paris. 1872–3.

Incls. an important statistical survey.

5004 ARGYLL COMMISSION ON COAL IN THE UNITED KINGDOM. Report of the commissioners appointed to inquire into the several matters relating to coal in the United Kingdom [Chairman: Duke of Argyll]. Vol. I. [C. 435] H.C. (1871). XVIII, 1. Vol. II. [C. 435–I] H.C. (1871). XVIII, 199. Vol. III. [C. 435–II] H.C. (1871). XVIII, 815.

On the extent of coal resources.

5005 AYRTON COMMITTEE ON COAL. Report from the select committee on coal [Chairman: Acton Smee Ayrton]. H.C. 313. (1873.) X, 1.

Concerned with the contemp. high price and the scarcity of coal. Suppl. the investigations of the Argyll commission.

5006 ALLERTON COMMISSION ON COAL SUPPLIES. First report of the royal commission on coal supplies [Chairman: Lord Allerton]. [Cd. 1724] H.C. (1903). XVI, 1. Minutes of evidence, etc. [Cd. 1725] H.C. (1903). XVI, 9; [Cd. 1726] H.C. (1903). XVI, 381. Second report. [Cd. 1990] H.C. (1904). XXIII, 1. Minutes of evidence, etc. [Cd. 1991] H.C. (1904). XXIII, 7; [Cd. 1992] H.C. (1904). XXIII, 435. Final report. [Cd. 2353] H.C. (1905). XVI, 1. Minutes of evidence, etc. [Cd. 2362] H.C. (1905). XVI, 237. Appendixes. [Cd. 2363] H.C. (1905). XVI, 659. Plans. [Cd. 2364] H.C. (1905). XVI, 797. Specialized reports. [Cd. 2354–61] H.C. (1905). XVI, 45+. Consular reports on coal trade. [Cd. 2365] H.C. (1905). XVI, 819.

Important.

5007 ATKINSON (FRANK). The great northern coalfield, 1700–1900: illustrated notes on the Durham and Northumberland coalfield. Durham County Local Hist. Soc. 1966. Lond. 1968.

See also John Elliot McCutcheon, *A Wearside mining story: including an account of the sinking of Wearmouth pit, Co. Durham . . .*, Seaham 1960, *The Hartley colliery disaster, 1862*, Seaham 1963, and *Troubled seams: the story of a pit and its people*, Seaham [1955], David Spring, 'The Earls of Durham and the great northern coalfield, 1830–1880', *Canadian Hist. Rev.* xxxiii (1952), 237–53, and George C. Greenwell, *A glossary of terms used in the coal trade of Northumberland and Durham*, 1851, 3rd edn. 1888.

5008 GRIFFIN (ALAN R.). Mining in the east Midlands, 1550–1947. 1971.

5009 RITCHIE (ARTHUR EDWIN). The Kent coalfield: its evolution and development. [1919.]

For other local studs. see John Anstie, *The coal fields of Gloucestershire and Somersetshire, and their resources*, 1873; Thomas East Lones, *A history of mining in the Black Country*, Dudley 1898; Cornelius McLeod Percy, *Mining in the Victorian era: a popular record of coal-mining progress from 1837 to 1897*, Wigan 1897; Arthur John Taylor, 'The Wigan coalfield in 1851', *Historic Soc. Lancs & Ches.* cvi (1954), 117–26; and S. M. Hardy, 'The development of coal mining in a north Derbyshire village, 1635–1860', *Univ. Birmingham Hist. J.* v (1955–6), 147–66.

5010 BOYD (ROBERT NELSON). Coal mines inspection: its history and results. 1879.

Carried down to the 1890s in his *Coal pits and pitmen: a short history of the coal trade and the legislation affecting it*, 1892, 2nd edn. 1895, which is a rev. version of the earlier book.

5011 ATHERLEY-JONES (LLEWELLYN ARTHUR) *and* BELLOT (HUGH HALE LEIGH). The miner's guide to the Coal Mines Regulation Acts and the law of employers and workmen. 1904. 3rd edn. 1914.

A layman's guide. The best lawyers' books are Maskell William Peace, *The Acts for the regulation and inspection of mines . . .*, 1861, and *The Coal Mines Regulation Act . . .*,

1872, 3rd edn. 1888, John Coke Fowler, *Collieries and colliers: a handbook of the law and leading cases relating thereto*, 1861, 4th edn. 1884, and Benjamin Francis Williams and George Pitt-Lewis, *The Coal Mines Regulation Acts, 1887–1896* . . ., 1896, 2nd edn. 1897.

5012 **HEDLEY (JOHN).** A practical treatise on the working and ventilation of coal mines: with suggestions for improvements in mining. 1851.

Other useful textbooks incl. James Mather, *The coal mines: their dangers and means of safety* . . ., 1853, new edn. 3 pts. 1868; George C. Greenwell, *A practical treatise on mine engineering*, Newcastle 1855, 2nd edn. 1869; Sir Warrington Wilkinson Smyth, *A [rudimentary] treatise on coal and coal mining*, 1867, 8th edn. 1900; Sarah Jane Fitzgerald, *Coal and colliers: or, how we get the fuel for our fires*, 1881; Harrison Francis Bulman and Sir Richard Augustine Studdert Redmayne, *Colliery working and management*, 1896, 5th edn. 1951; and Sydney Ferris Walker, *Coal-cutting by machinery in the United Kingdom*, 1902, and *Electricity in mining*, 1907.

5013 **CAYLEY COMMITTEE ON COAL MINES.** Report from the select committee on coal mines [Chairman: Edward Stillingfleet Cayley]. H.C. 509 (1852). V, 1.

On explosions in coal mines.

5014 **HUTCHINS COMMITTEE ON ACCIDENTS IN COAL MINES.** First report from the select committee on accidents in coal mines [Chairman: Edward John Hutchins]. H.C. 691 (1852–3). XX, 1. Second report. H.C. 740 (1852–3). XX, 179. Third and fourth reports. H.C. 820 (1852–3). XX, 279. Committee reappointed in following session. First report. H.C. 169 (1854). IX, 1. Second report. H.C. 258 (1854). IX, 63. Third & fourth reports. H.C. 277 & 325 (1854). IX, 219.

See also Alan Bagot, *Accidents in mines: their causes and prevention*, 1878.

5015 **KINNAIRD COMMISSION ON HEALTH AND SAFETY IN MINES.** Report of the commissioners appointed to inquire into the condition of all mines in Great Britain to which the provisions of the Act 23 & 24 Vict. Cap. 151 do not apply, with reference to the health and safety of persons employed in such mines [Chairman: Lord Kinnaird]. [3389] H.C. (1864). XXIV, pt. 1, 371. Minutes of evidence. [3389] H.C. (1864). XXIV, pt. 2, 1. Epitome of evidence. [3389–I] H.C. (1864). XXIV, pt. 1, 431.

5016 **NEATE COMMITTEE ON MINES.** Report from the select committee on mines [Chairman: Charles Neate]. H.C. 431 (1866). XIV, 1. Further report. H.C. 496 (1867). XIII, 1.

On the administration of the Mines Acts. Cont. work of a select committee appointed the previous session which made no progress (See H.C. 398 (1865). XII, 605).

5017 **MONKSWELL–CUNYNGHAME COMMISSION ON MINES ACTS.** First report of the royal commission on mines [Chairmen: Lord Monkswell & Sir Henry H. S. Cunynghame]. [Cd. 3548] H.C. (1907). XIV, 1. Second report. [Cd. 4820] H.C. (1909). XXXIV, 599. Third report. [Cd. 5561]

H.C. (1911). XXXVI, 465. Special report on ventilation. [Cd. 4551] H.C. (1909). XXXIV, 913. Special report on accidents. [Cd. 4821] H.C. (1909). XXXIV, 1111.

A careful inquiry into mine-working and safety. For a list of minutes of evidence see Ford, *Breviate 1900–16* (32).

5018 MOTT (REGINALD ARTHUR) *and* GREENFIELD (GEOFFREY JAMES) *eds*. The history of coke making and of the Coke Oven Managers' Association. Coke Oven Managers' Assoc. Camb. 1936.

### (d) *Metalliferous Mining*

5019 HUNT (ROBERT). British mining: a treatise on the history, discovery, practical development and future prospects of metalliferous mines in the United Kingdom. 1884. 2nd edn. 1887.

A full general survey. See also John Robert Pike, *Britain's metal mines: a complete guide to their laws, usages, localities and statistics*, 1860.

5020 CUNYNGHAME COMMISSION ON METALLIFEROUS MINES. Royal commission on metalliferous mines and quarries: first report of the commissioners [Chairman: Sir Henry Hardinge Samuel Cunynghame]. [Cd. 6389] H.C. (1912–13). XLI, 543. Second report. [Cd. 7476] H.C. (1914). XLII, 27. Minutes of evidence. Vol. I. [Cd. 6390] H.C. (1912–13). XLI, 547. Vol. II. [Cd. 7477] H.C. (1914). XLII, 233. Vol. III. [Cd. 7478] H.C. (1914). XLII, 575.

The only major official inquiry.

5021 DAVIES (EDWARD HENRY). Machinery for metalliferous mines: a practical treatise for mining engineers, metallurgists and managers of mines. 1894. 2nd edn. 1902.

5022 DINES (HENRY GEORGE). The metalliferous mining region of south-west England. [Memoirs of the Geological Survey.] 2 v. 1956.

An excellent survey of all known mines. Joseph Henry Collins, 'Observations on the West of England mining region: being an account of the mineral deposits and economic geology of the region', *Roy. Geol. Soc. of Cornwall Trans.* xiv (1912), which runs to 683 pp., and was also publ. separately by the author, Plymouth 1912, and the earlier reports of the Geological Survey are also useful. For the Devon mines there is a useful bibliog., Josslyn Vere Ramsden, 'Notes on the mines of Devonshire', *Devonshire Assoc. Trans.* lxxxiv (1952), 81–104.

5023 SPARGO (THOMAS). The mines of Cornwall and Devon: statistics and observations: illustrated by maps, plans and sections of the several mining districts in the two counties. 1865. Cornwall section repr. 6 pts. Truro. 1959.

The best of a number of extremely valuable guides for investors. Similar are John Henry Murchison, *British mines considered as a means of investment . . .*, 1854, 4th edn. 1856, J. Williams, *The Cornwall and Devon mining directory classified in districts . . .*, Hayle 1861, 1862, 1870, Richard Tredinnick, *A review of Cornish and Devon mining enterprise, 1850 to 1856 inclusive*, 1857, and Charles Thomas, *Mining fields of the west*

. . ., 1867, repr. Truro 1967. There is some background information in John Batten, *The Stannaries Act, 1869* . . ., 1873, and *Special report and reports from the select committee on Stannaries Act (1869) Amendment Bill* [Chairman: Charles Acland]. H.C. 245 & 252 (1887), XII, 323.

5024 JENKIN (ALFRED KENNETH HAMILTON). Mines and miners of Cornwall. 11 pts. Truro. 1961–5.

A detailed hist. by districts dealing at length with the mid-19th-cent. boom. For Cornish mining see also Cornish Institute of Mining, Mechanical and Metallurgical Engineers, *Transactions*, Camborne 1913+; Cornwall Polytechnic Soc., *Reports*, Falmouth 1833+; [Royal] Geological Soc. of Cornwall, *Transactions*, Lond. & Penzance 1818+; Mining [Association and] Institute of Cornwall, *Proceedings* [later *Transactions*], Truro etc. 1876–93; and Royal Institution of Cornwall, *Annual report* [from 1864 *Journal*], 1818+. See also John R. Leifchild, *Cornwall: its mines and miners* . . ., 1855, Richard Tredinnick, *A review of Cornish copper mining enterprise, with a description of the most important dividend and progressive copper and tin mines of Cornwall and Devon, and a detailed account of the Buller and Basset District, May 1st, 1858*, 1858, and Denys Bradford Barton, *A guide to the mines of west Cornwall*, Truro 1963, 2nd edn. 1965. Roger Burt, ed., *Cornish mining: essays on the organisation of Cornish mines and the Cornish mining economy*, Newton Abbot 1969, reprints contemp. reports.

5025 BARTON (DENYS BRADFORD). Essays in Cornish mining history. 2 v. Truro. 1968–70.

5026 BARTON (DENYS BRADFORD). A history of tin mining and smelting in Cornwall. Truro. [1967.]

5027 BARTON (DENYS BRADFORD). A history of copper mining in Cornwall and Devon. Truro. 1961. 2nd edn. 1968.

Suppl. by his *A historical survey of the mines and mineral railways of East Cornwall and West Devon*, Truro [1964].

5028 BARTON (DENYS BRADFORD). The Cornish beam engine: a survey of its history and development in the mines of Cornwall and Devon from before 1800 to the present day. Truro. 1965. New edn. 1966.

5029 JENKIN (ALFRED KENNETH HAMILTON). The Cornish miner: an account of his life above and underground from early times. [1927.] 3rd edn. 1962.

See also Langford Lovell Frederick Rice Price, 'West Barbary: or, notes on the system of work and wages in the Cornish mines', *Roy. Stat. Soc. J.* li (1888), 494–566, repr. Lond. 1891, and John Scott Haldane, Joseph S. Martin, and R. Arthur Thomas, *Report to the Secretary of State for the Home Department on the health of Cornish miners*. [Cd. 2091] H.C. (1904). XIII, 693.

5030 GOODRIDGE (J. C.). 'Devon Great Consols: a study of Victorian mining enterprise'. *Devonshire Assoc. Trans.* xcvi (1964), 228–68.

The most famous Victorian mine in the west country, which figures in Trollope's *The three clerks*.

5031 SELLICK (ROGER). The west Somerset mineral railway and the story of the Brendon hills iron mines. Dawlish. 1962.

5032 O'NEAL (RICHARD ANTONY HUGH) *comp*. Derbyshire lead and lead mining: a bibliography. Derby County Libr. Matlock. 1956. 2nd edn. 1960.

5033 STOKES (ARTHUR HENRY). Lead and lead mining in Derbyshire. Peak District Mines Hist. Soc. Sheffield. 1964.

5034 GOUGH (JOHN WIEDHOFFT). The mines of Mendip. Oxf. 1930. Repr. Newton Abbot. 1968.
Chiefly lead.

5035 RAISTRICK (ARTHUR) *and* JENNINGS (BERNARD). A history of lead mining in the Pennines. 1965.
See also Christopher John Hunt, *The lead miners of the northern Pennines in the eighteenth and nineteenth centuries*, March, 1970.

5036 RAISTRICK (ARTHUR). Mines and miners of Swaledale. Clapham, Yorks. 1955.

(e) *Quarries*

5037 H.M. INSPECTORS OF MINES. Quarries: year 1895: list of quarries (under the Quarries Act) in the United Kingdom of Great Britain and Ireland, and the Isle of Man. 1896.
Publ. annually 1895–1937.

5038 QUARRY COMMITTEE. Report to Her Majesty's Principal Secretary of State for the Home Department on the conditions under which the quarrying of stone, ironstone, slate, and clay is conducted, with the object of diminishing any proved dangers to the life or health of the workpeople engaged therein by the Quarry Committee of Enquiry [Chairman: Frank N. Wardell]. [C. 7237] H.C. (1893–4). LXXIII, 1.

5039 GREENWELL (ALLAN) *and* ELSDEN (JAMES VINCENT). Practical stone quarrying: a manual for managers, inspectors, and owners of quarries and for students. 1913.
Good illustrations. See also E. Benfield, *Purbeck shop* (**5781**).

5040 DUNHAM (KINGSLEY CHARLES). Fluorspar. Memoirs of the Geol. Survey. Special Report, vol. IV. 4th edn. 1952.
A quarry-by-quarry survey.

4. THE METAL INDUSTRIES

(a) *General*

5041 PATENT OFFICE LIBRARY. Subject list of works on mineral industries . . . Part 2: Iron manufacture, alloys and metallography. Part 3: Metallurgy, non-ferrous and general, assaying, and fuel combustion. 2 pts. 1912.
See also Patent Office, *Abridgments of specifications: class 82: metals and alloys excepting iron and steel manufactures*, 1855/6–1926/30.

5042 PEDDIE (ROBERT ALEXANDER). Metallurgical bibliography, 1901–1906. 1907.

Cont. as *Engineering and metallurgical books, 1907–1911* . . ., 1912. See also *Metallurgical abstracts*, 1909+, publ. in *Inst. of Metals J.*, 1909+.

5043 RYLANDS' COAL, IRON, STEEL, TINPLATE, METAL, ENGINEERING, FOUNDRY, HARDWARE AND ALLIED TRADES DIRECTORY. 1881+.

The fullest directory. See also *Metal industry handbook and directory*, 1912+. There were a number of js. which also publ. occasional handbooks, incl. *The ironmonger and metal trades advertiser*, 1869+, which started life briefly as *Morgan's monthly circular* . . ., 1869, *The hardware trade journal*, 1873+, *The ironmongers' chronicle*, 1892–1932, styled *The hardwareman and ironmongers' chronicle*, 1912–32, and *The iron trade circular* . . ., Birmingham 1864–1915.

5044 INSTITUTE OF METALS. Journal. 1909+.

One of the first js. to break away from the preoccupation with iron of most contemp. periodicals, such as *Industries [and iron]*, 1886–1900. See also *Metal industry*, 1909+.

5045 AITCHISON (LESLIE). A history of metals. 2 v. 1960.
Good.

5046 DENNIS (WILLIAM HERBERT). A hundred years of metallurgy. 1963.

5047 AITCHISON (LESLIE). 'A hundred years of metallurgy, 1851–1951'. *Sheet Metal Industries* xxviii (1951), 405–24, 519–26, 530.

The pioneer writer of the period was John Percy whose *Metallurgy: the art of extracting metals from their ores and adapting them to various purposes of manufacture*, 4 v. 1861–80, was a standard textbook.

5048 HISTORICAL METALLURGY GROUP. Bulletin. 1963+.

5049 LARKE (EUSTACE C.). 'The rolling of metals and alloys: historical development of the rolling mill'. *Sheet Metal Industries* xxx (1953), 863–78, 989–98, 1081–91; xxxi (1954), 61–72, 241–8, 325–34, 338, 408, 411–25.

5050 HADFIELD (*Sir* ROBERT ABBOTT). Metallurgy and its influence on modern progress. 1925.

5051 KERSHAW (JOHN BAKER CANNINGTON). Electro metallurgy. 1908.

5052 JOHNSON. Percival Norton Johnson: the biography of a pioneer metallurgist. By Donald McDonald. 1951.

5053 JULIAN. Memorials of Henry Forbes Julian, member of the Institution of Mining and Metallurgy, joint author of 'Cyaniding gold and silver ores', who perished in the 'Titanic' disaster. By Hester Julian and others. 1914.

5054 ROBERTS-AUSTEN. Roberts-Austen: a record of his work: being, a selection of the addresses and metallurgical papers, together with an account of the researches of Sir William Chandler Roberts-Austen . . . Ed. by Sydney William Smith. 1914.

See also Roberts-Austen's *An introduction to the study of metallurgy*, 1891, 6th edn. 1910.

(b) *Iron and Steel*

(i) *General*

5055 IRON AND STEEL INSTITUTE. Abridged catalogue of the library. 1914.

The most useful general bibliog. An earlier *Catalogue* of 1884 lists a few additional pamphlets. For patents see Patent Office, *Abridgments of specifications: class 72: iron and steel manufacture*, 1855/6–1926/30.

5056 BIRCH (ALAN). The economic history of the British iron and steel industry, 1784–1879: essays in industrial and economic history, with special reference to the development of technology. 1967.

5057 BURNHAM (THOMAS HALL) *and* HOSKINS (GEORGE OWEN). Iron and steel in Britain, 1870–1930: a comparative study of the causes which limited the economic development of the British iron and steel industry. 1943.

See also Thomas J. Orsagh, 'Progress in iron and steel, 1870–1913', *Comparative Studs. in Sociology & Hist.* iii (1960–1), 216–30, Donald Nansen McCloskey, 'The British iron and steel industry, 1870–1914: a study of the climacteric in productivity', *J. Econ. Hist.* xxix (1969), 173–5, and P. L. Payne's account in Aldcroft **4752**.

5058 ROEPKE (HOWARD GEORGE). Movements of the British iron and steel industry, 1720 to 1951. *Illinois Studs. in the Soc. Sciences* xxxvi. Urbana, Ill. 1956.

5059 GALE (WALTER KEITH VERNON). Iron and steel. 1969.

A good technical hist. posing as an exercise in industrial archaeology. See also his *The British iron and steel industry: a technical history*, Newton Abbot 1967, and *The Black Country iron industry: a technical history*, 1966.

5060 MUSGRAVE (PETER WILLIAM). Technical change, the labour force and education: a study of the British and German iron and steel industries, 1860–1964. Oxf. 1967.

5061 CARR (JAMES CECIL) *and* TAPLIN (WALTER). History of the British steel industry. Oxf. & Camb., Mass. 1962.

Full and good, but must be suppl. by Burn (**5062**), Birch (**5056**), and Burnham and Hoskins (**5057**). There are pleasant pictures in Max Davies, *The story of steel*, 1950.

5062 BURN (DUNCAN LYALL). The economic history of steelmaking, 1867–1939: a study in competition. Camb. 1940. 2nd edn. 1961.

Good. See also W. A. Sinclair, 'The growth of the British steel industry in the late nineteenth century', *Scot. J. Pol. Econ.* vi (1959), 33–47, Michael Walter Flinn, 'British steel and Spanish ore, 1871–1914', *Econ. Hist. Rev.* 2 ser. viii (1955–6), 84–90, and Peter Temin, 'The relative decline of the British steel industry, 1880–1913', in Henry Rosovsky, ed., *Industrialization in two systems: essays in honour of Alexander Ger-schenkron*, N.Y. 1966, pp. 140–55.

**5063** IRON AND STEEL INSTITUTE. Transactions. 1869–70. Journal. 1871+.

Incls. historical articles. The other main society publs. were the British Iron Trade Assoc., *Annual report*, 1877–1906; South Staffordshire Institute of Iron and Steel Works Managers [Staffordshire Iron and Steel Institute], *Proceedings*, Brierley Hill 1879+; Cleveland Institution of Engineers, *Proceedings*, Middlesbrough 1864+; West of Scotland Iron and Steel Institute, *Journal*, Glasgow 1892+; South Wales Institute of Engineers, *Transactions*, Cardiff 1857–93, and *Proceedings*, Cardiff 1894+; Institution of Mechanical Engineers, *Proceedings*, 1847+; and Institution of Mining and Metallurgy, *Transactions*, 1892+.

**5064** THE IRON AND COAL TRADES REVIEW. 1866+.

The leading periodical for the iron industry. *The iron trade exchange* [later *The iron and steel trades j.*], 1849–1920, and *The foundry trade j.*, 1902+, are also useful.

**5065** JEANS (JAMES STEPHEN). The iron trade of Great Britain. 1906.

An excellent contemp. account of the iron and steel industries. See also his *Steel: its history, manufacture, properties and uses*, 1880, and the report he ed. for the British Iron Trade Assoc., *American industrial conditions and competition . . .*, 1902. Richard Meade, *The coal and iron industries of the United Kingdom . . .*, 1882; Sir Isaac Lowthian Bell, *The iron trade of the United Kingdom compared with that of the other chief iron-making nations*, 1886; J. D. Kendall, *The iron ores of Great Britain and Ireland . . .*, 1893; and George Griffiths, *Guide to the iron trade of Great Britain . . .*, 1873, repr. Newton Abbot 1967, are other good general surveys. Books publ. in the 1850s, such as Harry Scrivenor, *History of the iron trade*, 2nd edn. 1854, William Truran, *The iron manufacture of Great Britain . . .*, 1855, 2nd edn. 1862, and George Wilkie, *The manufacture of iron in Great Britain . . .*, Edin. 1857, are of limited value for the period.

**5066** FAIRBAIRN (*Sir* WILLIAM). Iron: its history, properties and processes of manufacture. Edin. 1861. 3rd edn. 1869.

A pioneer technical work to be read in conjunction with Fairbairn's other chief monographs (**5207**). Sir Isaac Lowthian Bell, *Principles of the manufacture of iron and steel . . .*, 1884, is in the same tradition. On metallurgy see also Hilary Bauerman, *A treatise on the metallurgy of iron . . .*, 1868, 6th edn. 1890, William Mattieu Williams, *Iron and steel manufacture*, Cantor lectures, 1876, Thomas Turner, *The metallurgy of iron and steel*, 1895, 5th edn. 1918, and *Lectures on iron-founding*, 1904, 2nd edn. 1911, and Frank William Harbord, *The metallurgy of steel . . .*, 1904, 7th edn. 1923. Joseph Gregory Horner, *Practical iron founding . . .*, 1889, 5th edn. 1930, was a well-known textbook.

**5067** GRUNER (LOUIS EMMANUEL) *and* LAN (C.). État présent de la metallurgie du fer en Angleterre. Paris. 1862.

The *Revue universelle des mines . . .*, Liège 1857–1914, publ. excellent articles on the British industry. Ludwig Beck, *Die Geschichte des Eisens in technischer- und kultur-geschichtlicher Beziehung*, 5 v. Brunswick 1884–1903, is also useful.

**5068** CREED (H. HERRIES) *and* WILLIAMS (WALTER VERE VAUGHAN). Handicraftsmen and capitalists: their organisation at home and abroad; republished from *The Times*; with . . . a sketch of English iron works. Birmingham. 1867.

Compares Belgian and English conditions. Gives useful details of British iron works.

**5069 HEWITT (ABRAM STEVENS).** Selected writings of Abram S. Hewitt. Ed. by Allan Nevins. N.Y. 1937.

Includes Hewitt's report on the European iron and steel industry of 1867 and his essay on Bessemer.

**5070 TARIFF COMMISSION.** Report of the tariff commission. Vol. I: The iron and steel trades. 1904.

**5071 BALFOUR COMMITTEE ON INDUSTRY AND TRADE.** Committee on Industry and Trade [Chairman: Sir Arthur Balfour, later Lord Riverdale]. Survey of metal industries: iron and steel, engineering, electrical manufacturing, shipbuilding, with a chapter on the coal industry: being, part IV of a survey of industries. H.M.S.O. 1928.

A careful inquiry.

**5072 HOSKISON (T. M.).** 'Northumberland blast furnace plants in the 19th century'. *Newcomen Soc. Trans.* xxv (1945-7), 73-82.

**5073 RICHARDSON (HARRY WARD)** *and* **BASS (J. M.).** 'The profitability of the Consett Iron Company before 1914'. *Business Hist.* vii (1965), 71-93.

**5074 HEAD (JEREMIAH).** 'On recent developments in the Cleveland iron and steel industries'. *Instn. Mech. Engineers Proc. for 1893.* Pp. 224-77.

Other articles in the same vol. deal with related topics. See also Addison Langhorne Steavenson, 'The last twenty years in the Cleveland mining district', *Iron & Steel Inst. J.* xliv (1893), 45-51; W. Hawdon, 'The iron and steel industries of the Cleveland district during the last quarter of a century', ibid. lxxviii (1908), 28-35; Bolckow, Vaughan & Co. Ltd., *Thomas & Gilchrist, Bolckow & Vaughan, 1879-1929*, Middlesbrough 1929; Lady Bell [i.e. Florence Eveleen Eleanor Bell], *At the works: a study of a manufacturing town* [Middlesbrough], 1907, repr. 1911; and Jeans (**5065**).

**5075 JONES (DANIEL).** 'The iron industry of South Staffordshire'. *Iron & Steel Inst. J.* xlviii (1895), 8-19.

**5076 BEAVER (STANLEY HENRY).** 'The development of the Northamptonshire iron industry, 1851-1930'. In London essays in geography. Ed. by Sir Laurence Dudley Stamp and Sidney William Wooldridge, 1951. Pp. 33-58.

See also W. H. Butlin, 'On the Northampton iron ore district', *Iron & Steel Inst. J.* (1883) i, 188-208.

**5077 POCOCK (D. C. D.).** 'Iron and steel at Scunthorpe'. *E. Midland Geographer* iii (1962-5), 124-38.

See also George Dove, 'The Frodingham iron field, North Lincolnshire', *Iron & Steel Inst. J.* (1876) ii, 318-26.

## (ii) *Biography*

5078 ERICKSON (CHARLOTTE). British industrialists: steel and hosiery, 1850–1950. Camb. 1958.

5079 JEANS (JAMES STEPHEN). Pioneers of the Cleveland iron trade. Middlesbrough. 1875.

5080 BESSEMER. Sir Henry Bessemer, F.R.S.: an autobiography. 1905.

The greatest name in the hist. of the industry during the period. See also W. M. Lord, 'The development of the Bessemer process in Lancashire, 1856–1900', *Newcomen Soc. Trans.* xxv (1945–7), 163–80, and 'Bessemer centenary, 1956', *Iron & Steel Inst. J.* clxxxiii (1956), 179–225.

5081 BREARLEY. Knotted story: autobiography of a steelmaker. By Harry Brearley. 1941.

5082 DALE. Sir David Dale: inaugural address delivered for the Dale Memorial Trust by the Right Honourable Sir Edward Grey, M.P., to which is prefixed a memoir by Howard Pease. 1911.

5083 HALL. 'Notes on the life and work of Joseph Hall'. By J. W. Hall. *Staffs. Inst. Steel & Iron Proc.* xxi (1915–16), 1–2; xxii (1916–17), 94–108.

5084 HEATH. The case of Josiah Marshall Heath, the inventor and introducer of the manufacture of welding cast steel from British iron. By Thomas Webster. 1856.

5085 MUSHET. The story of the Mushets. By Frederick Marmaduke Osborn. 1952.

5086 NASMYTH. An autobiography. By James Nasmyth. Ed. by Samuel Smiles. 1883.

5087 NEILSON. 'The life of James Beaumont Neilson, F.R.S., inventor of the hot blast in 1828'. By T. B. Mackenzie. *West of Scotland Iron & Steel Inst. Trans.* xxxvi (1928). Suppl.

5088 SIEMENS. The life of Sir William Siemens, F.R.S., D.C.L., L.L.D., Member of the Council of the Institution of Civil Engineers. By William Pole. 1888.

See also George Horatio Nelson, Baron Nelson, ed., *A collection of letters to Sir Charles William Siemens, 1823–1883 . . .*, 1953, and Edward Fisher Bamber, ed., *The scientific works of C. William Siemens, Kt., F.R.S., D.C.L., L.L.D., civil engineer,* 3 v. 1889.

5089 THOMAS. Memoir and letters of Sidney Gilchrist Thomas. By Robert William Burnie. 1891.

See also Lilian Gilchrist Thompson, *Sidney Gilchrist Thomas: an invention and its consequences,* 1940, Frank William Harbord, 'The Thomas-Gilchrist basic process, 1879–1937', *Iron & Steel Inst. J.* cxxxvi (1937), 77–95, and James Mitchell, 'Sidney Gilchrist Thomas: a commemorative lecture', ibid. clxv (1950), 1–8.

(iii) *Manufactured Iron and Steel Trades*

**5090  MINCHINTON (WALTER EDWARD).** The British tinplate industry: a history. Oxf. 1957.

Standard, with good bibliog. But see also Edward Henry Brooke, *Chronology of the tinplate works of Great Britain,* Cardiff 1944, with *Appendix,* Cardiff 1949, and *Monograph on the tinplate works of Great Britain,* Swansea 1932, John Harry Jones, *The tinplate industry: with special reference to its relations with the iron and steel industry: a study in economic organisation,* 1914, and Edgar Leigh Collis and J. Hilditch, *Report on the condition of employment in the manufacture of tinplates* . . . [Cd. 6394] H.C. (1912–13). XXVI, 105.

**5091  FORESTIER-WALKER (E. R.).** A history of the wire-rope industry of Great Britain. Sheffield. 1952.

See also [Henry Hurford Janes] *Rylands of Warrington, 1805–1955: the story of Rylands Brothers Limited* [1956], and Stuart Petre Brodie Mais, *A history of N. Greening & Sons Ltd., Warrington, England, from 1799 to 1949,* Warrington [1949].

**5092  LANGLEY (S. J.).** 'The Wednesbury tube trade'. *Univ. of Birmingham Hist. J.* ii (1949–50), 163–77.

**5093  WARREN (K.).** 'The Sheffield rail trade, 1861–1930: an episode in the locational history of the British steel industry'. *Inst. British Geographers Trans.* xxxiv (1964), 131–57.

**5094  COCHRANE (ALFRED).** The early history of Elswick . . . Newcastle-upon-Tyne. 1909.

The great Armstrong steel and armament works on Tyneside.

**5095  SCOTT (JOHN DICK).** Vickers: a history. 1962.

The Barrow equivalent of Armstrongs, with which Vickers were amalgamated.

**5096  IMPERIAL METAL INDUSTRIES (KYNOCH) LTD.** Under five flags: the story of the Kynoch works, Witton, Birmingham, 1862–1962. 1962.

**5097  MAXIM.** My life. By Sir Hiram Stevens Maxim. 1915.

The most famous gun-maker of the Edwardian period. See also Hiram Percy Maxim, *A genius in the family: Sir Hiram Stevens Maxim through a small son's eyes,* 1936, and Paul Fleury Mottelay, *The life and work of Sir Hiram Maxim . . .,* 1920.

**5098  ZAHAROFF.** The man behind the scenes: the career of Sir Basil Zaharoff, 'the Mystery Man of Europe'. By Richard Lewinsohn. 1929.

None of the other biogs. adds much to this popular account. But see Donald McCormick, *Pedlar of death: the life of Sir Basil Zaharoff,* 1965. Zaharoff was a middleman for the arms industry.

**5099  RILING (RAY). (RAYMOND LAWRENCE JOSEPH)** Guns and shooting: a selected chronological bibliography. N.Y. 1951.

5100 GREENER (WILLIAM WELLINGTON). The gun and its development . . . 1881. 9th edn. 1910.

A useful guide to small arms. Greener also publ. a number of other works, incl. *The breech-loader and how to use it* . . ., 1892, 9th edn. 1906, *Modern shotguns* . . ., 1888, 2nd edn. 1891, and *The British miniature rifle*, 1908. See also J. D. Goodman, 'On the progress of the small arms manufacture', *Stat. Soc. J.* xxviii (1865), 494–506, and Anthony William Finlay Taylerson, *The revolver, 1818–[1914]*, 3 v. 1966–70.

5101 ARTIFEX *and* OPIFEX, *pseuds*. The causes of decay in a British industry. 1907.

On the armaments industry, by two gun-manufacturers.

5102 NOEL-BAKER (PHILIP JOHN). The private manufacture of armaments. v. 1. 1936.

5103 BUTLER (RODNEY FAWCETT). This history of Kirkstall Forge through seven centuries, 1200–1945. York. 1945. 2nd edn. 1954.

5104 ROLT (LIONEL THOMAS CASWELL). Waterloo ironworks: a history of Taskers of Andover, 1809–1968. Newton Abbot. 1969.

5105 JOHN (ARTHUR HENRY) *ed.* The Walker family: iron founders and lead manufacturers, 1741–1893: minutes relating to Messrs. Samuel Walker & Co., Rotherham, iron founders and steel refiners, 1741–1829, and Messrs. Walkers, Parker & Co., lead manufacturers, 1788–1893. Council for the Preservation of Business Archives. 1951.

5106 CHURCH (ROY ANTHONY). Kenricks in hardware: a family business, 1791–1966. Newton Abbot. 1969.

5107 GALE (WALTER KEITH VERNON). The Black country iron industry: a technical history. 1966.

See also Allen, *The industrial development of Birmingham and the Black country* (4763).

5108 PORTER (J. H.). 'Management, competition and industrial relations: the Midlands manufactured iron trade, 1873–1914'. *Business Hist.* xi (1969), 37–47.

5109 RIMMINGTON (G. T.). 'Leicester foundries, 1845–1914'. *Leicestershire Archaeol. & Hist. Soc. Trans.* xl (1964–5), 63–8.

5110 WATSON (BERNARD WILLIAM). The Sheffield Assay Office register: a copy of the register of the persons concerned in the manufacture of silver wares, and of the marks entered by them from 1773 to 1907. Sheffield. 1911.

5111 VEITCH (HENRY NEWTON). Sheffield plate: its history, manufacture and art: with makers' names and marks . . . 1908.

To 1850 only, but useful.

5112 LLOYD (GODFREY ISAAC HOWARD). The cutlery trades: an historical essay in the economics of small-scale production. 1913. Repr. 1968.

5113 POLLARD (SIDNEY). Three centuries of Sheffield steel: the story of a family business. Sheffield. 1954.

A hist. of Marsh brothers, makers of files, razors, and hardware.

5114 BAILLIE (GRANVILLE HUGH). Watchmakers and clockmakers of the world. 1929. 2nd edn. 1947.

See also his *Clocks and watches: an historical bibliography*, 1951.

5115 BRITTEN (FREDERICK JAMES). The watch and clockmakers' handbook . . . 4th edn. 1881. 12th edn. 1920. 15th edn. 1955.

A useful handbook. For trade terms see also Eric Moore Bruton, *Dictionary of clocks and watches*, 1962.

5116 WARD (FRANCIS ALAN BURNETT) *comp.* Science Museum: handbook of the collections illustrating time measurement. 2 pts. 1936–7. 3rd edn. 2 pts. 1947–55.

To be suppl. by *The horological j.*, 1858+, which is full of useful data. See also Herbert Alan Lloyd, *Some outstanding clocks over seven hundred years, 1250–1950*, 1958, Willis Isbister Milham, *Time & timekeepers: including the history, construction, care and accuracy of clocks and watches*, N.Y. & Lond. 1923, and James Francis Kendal, *A history of watches and other timekeepers*, 1892. David Glasgow, *Watch and clock making*, 1885, is a conventional textbook. T. P. Hewitt, *English watchmaking under free trade*, Liverpool 1903, sets out the plight of the Prescot watchmakers.

5117 GILLGRASS (ALFRED). The book of Big Ben: the story of the great clock at Westminster. 1946.

See also 9201.

5118 ERAS (VINCENT J. M.). Locks and keys throughout the ages. Amsterdam. 1957.

5119 JONES (PETER D'ALROY) *and* SIMONS (ERIC NORMAN). Story of the saw . . . Spear & Jackson Limited. 1760–1960. Manch. 1961.

5120 CHURCH (ROY ANTHONY) *and* SMITH (BARBARA M. D.). 'Competition and monopoly in the coffin furniture industry, 1870–1915'. *Econ. Hist. Rev.* 2 ser. xix (1966), 621–41.

5121 MOXON (STANLEY). A Fox centenary: umbrella frames, 1848–1948. [1948.]

5122 LISTER (RAYMOND GEORGE). Decorative wrought ironwork in Great Britain. 1957.

Suppl. by his *Decorative cast ironwork in Great Britain*, 1960.

5123 CRITTALL. Fifty years of work and play. By Francis Henry Crittall. 1934.

Hardware dealer and window-maker.

### (c) *Other Metals*

There appears to be no hist. of Britannia metal, which had largely driven out pewter by 1850.

5124 STATISTISCHE ZUSAMMENSTELLUNGEN ÜBER ALUMINIUM, Blei, Kupfer, Nickel, Quecksilber, Silber, Zink und Zinn. Frankfurt-am-Main. 1890–1+.

5125 HILEY (EDGAR NATHANIEL). Brass saga. 1957.

5126 BEST (ROBERT HALL) *and others*. The brassworkers of Berlin and of Birmingham: a comparison: joint report. 3rd edn. 1905. 5th edn. 1910.

5127 BEST. Brass chandelier: a biography of Robert Hall Best of Birmingham by his son. By Robert Dudley Best. 1940.

5128 DAVIS. The life story of W. J. Davis, J.P.: the industrial problem: achievements and triumphs of conciliation. By William Arthur Dalley. Birmingham. 1914.

Factory inspector, and sec. of Nat. Soc. of Amalg. Brassworkers. William John Davis publ. *A short history of the brass trade*, 1892, but it is of little value.

5129 BROWN (NICOL) *and* TURNBULL (CHARLES CORBETT). A century of copper. 2 pts. 1899–1900. 2nd edn. of pt. 1. 1906.

A useful summary of statistics and events. Bertie Webster Smith, *Sixty centuries of copper*, Copper Development Assoc., 1965, is a popular leaflet.

5130 LEVY (DONALD M.). Modern copper smelting: being, lectures delivered at Birmingham University . . . with an introduction on the history, uses and properties of copper. 1912.

Good.

5131 PULSIFER (WILLIAM HENRY). Notes for a history of lead: and an inquiry into the development of the manufacture of white lead and lead oxides. N.Y. 1888.

Only a few pages relevant. For smelting see Henry Francis Collins, *The metallurgy of lead* . . ., 1899, 2nd edn. 1910.

5132 LEAD COMMITTEE. Report from the departmental committee on the various lead industries [Chairmen: James Henderson and Edward Gould]. [C. 7239] H.C. (1893–4). XVII, 717. Minutes of evidence. [C. 7239–I] H.C. (1893–4). XVII, 743.

5133 RAISTRICK (ARTHUR). Two centuries of industrial welfare: the London (Quaker) Lead Company, 1692–1905. 1938.

5134 CLOUGH (ROBERT TAYLOR). The lead smelting mills of the York-shire Dales: their architectural character, construction and place in the European tradition. Keighley. 1962.

Good.

5135 HEDGES (ERNEST SYDNEY). Tin in social and economic history. 1964.

5136 FLOWER (PHILIP WILLIAM). A history of the trade in tin: a short description of tin mining and metallurgy, a history of the origin and progress of the tin-plate trade, and a description of the ancient and modern processes of manufacturing tin-plates. 1880.

See also 5090.

5137 COCKS (EDWARD JOHN) *and* WALTERS (BERNHARDT). A his-tory of the zinc smelting industry in Britain. 1968.

Chiefly a post-1914 hist. of the Imperial Smelting Corp.

5138 WANG (CHUNG-YU). Antimony: its history, chemistry, mineralogy, geology, metallurgy, uses and preparation, analysis, production and valuation: with complete bibliographies . . . 1909. 3rd edn. 1952.

5139 DEL MAR (ALEXANDER). A history of the precious metals: from the earliest times to the present. 1880. 2nd edn. N.Y. 1902.

There is a bibliog. of 19th-cent. works on the subject in Sir Thomas Kirke Rose, *The precious metals: comprising gold, silver and platinum,* 1907, 6th edn. 1915. Rose also publ. *The metallurgy of gold,* 1894, 7th edn. 1897. See also Henry Francis Collins, *The metallurgy of lead and silver,* Vol. II: *Silver,* 1900.

5140 DE CASTRO (JOHN PAUL). The law and practice of hall-marking gold and silver wares. 1926. 2nd edn. 1935.

For the assay offices see *Report from the select committee on silver and gold wares* [Chair-man: James Wilson]. H.C. 190 (1856). XVI, 263, and *Report from the select committee on gold and silver (hall marking)* [Chairman: Sir Henry Jackson]. H.C. 328 (1878). XIII, 139. Further report. H.C. 191 (1878–9). X, 365.

5141 WILSON (RONALD ELIOT). Two hundred precious metal years: a history of the Sheffield Smelting Co. Ltd. 1760–1960. 1960.

5142 HOWARD-WHITE (FRANK BULLER). Nickel: an historical review. 1964.

5143 STURNEY (ALFRED CHARLES). The story of Mond nickel. 1951.

5144 McDONALD (DONALD). A history of platinum: from the earliest times to the eighteen-eighties. 1960.

## 5. THE ENGINEERING INDUSTRIES

### (a) *General*

**5145** DESCRIPTIVE INDEX OF CURRENT ENGINEERING LITERA-TURE. 1884–1891. Assoc. of Engineering Socs. Chicago. [1892.]

Cont. by *The engineering index*, publ. by *Engineering mag.*, 1892+. Cumulative vols. to 1905, then annual.

**5146** PEDDIE (ROBERT ALEXANDER). Engineering and metallurgical books, 1907–1911. 1912.

Books publ. in England.

**5147** HIGGINS (THOMAS JAMES). Biographies of engineers and scientists. *Illinois Inst. Techn. Research Bull.* vii. No. 1. 1949.

See also his 'Book-length biographies of engineers, metallurgists and industrialists', *Bull. of Bibliog.* xviii (1943–6), 206–10, 235–9; xix (1946–9), 10–12, 32, and 'The function of biography in engineering education', *J. Engineering Education* xxxii (1941–2), 82–92.

**5148** ARMYTAGE (WALTER HARRY GREEN). A social history of engineering. 1961. 3rd edn. 1970.

**5149** FLEMING (*Sir* ARTHUR PERCY MORRIS) *and* BROCKLE-HURST (HAROLD JOHN STANLEY). A history of engineering. 1925.

**5150** ROLT (LIONEL THOMAS CASWALL). Victorian engineering. 1970.

**5151** The ENGINEER. Centenary number: a study of the influences on engineering advancement, 1856–1956. 1956.

**5152** VERNON-HARCOURT (LEVESON FRANCIS). Achievements in engineering during the last half century. 1891.

**5153** BOOKER (PETER JEFFREY). A history of engineering drawing. 1963.

**5154** THE NEWCOMEN SOCIETY FOR THE STUDY OF THE HIS-TORY OF ENGINEERING AND TECHNOLOGY. Transactions. 1920–1+.

**5155** HUMBER (WILLIAM) *ed.* A record of the progress of modern engineer-ing: comprising civil, mechanical, marine, hydraulic, railway, bridge and other engineering works . . . 4 v. 1863–8.

An annual survey with more plates than text. Other general periodicals were primarily concerned with mechanical engineering, incl. *The engineers year book* . . ., 1894+; *The engineer*, 1856+; Society of Engineers, *Transactions*, 1861+; Civil and Mechanical Engineers' Soc., *Transactions*, 1872–1909; *Engineering: an illustrated weekly j.*, 1866+; and *The engineering times: a weekly illustrated newspaper of engineering and trade* . . ., 1898–1910.

5156 TARIFF COMMISSION. Report of the tariff commission. Vol. 4. The engineering industries: including structural, electrical, marine and ship-building, mechanical and general industrial engineering. 1909.

A comprehensive survey.

5157 SMILES (SAMUEL). Lives of the engineers: with an account of their principal works . . . 3 v. 1861–2. New edn. 5 v. 1874–91. Repr. 3 v. 1969.

Important for the hist. of self-improvement, but not without a little value for engineering too. Suppl. by his *Industrial biography: iron-workers and toolmakers*, 1863, new edn. 1879, and *Men of invention and industry*, 1884.

5158 ROLT (LIONEL THOMAS CASWALL). Great engineers. 1962.

5159 VINCENT (JAMES EDMUND). British engineers and allied professions in the twentieth century. Pike's new century series no. 24. Brighton. 1908.

A good illustrated *Who's who*.

5160 HALDANE (JOHN WILTON CUNINGHAME). Life as an engineer, its lights, shades and prospects. 1905.

One of a ser. of books by Haldane designed to popularize engineering. A sort of auto-biography. See also his *Civil and mechanical engineering popularly and socially considered*, 1887, 2nd edn. 1890, and Sir Arthur Percy Morris Fleming and Richard William Bailey, *Engineering as a profession: scope, training and opportunities for advancement*, 1913.

5161 ASSOCIATION OF CONSULTING ENGINEERS. Fifty years, 1913–63. [1963.]

(b) *Civil Engineering*

5162 INSTITUTION OF CIVIL ENGINEERS. Catalogue of the library. 1851. 3rd edn. 3 v. 1895. Subject index. 1904. Suppls. for 1895–1915.

Much the best list of books. *Catalogue of the Royal Engineers Corps library at the Horse Guards*, 1929, is, however, a good alternative for some branches of civil engineering.

5163 PANNELL (JOHN PERCIVAL MASTERMAN). An illustrated history of civil engineering. [1964.]

There are many other general popular hists., incl. Hans Straub, *A history of civil engineering: an outline from ancient to modern times*, trans. by Edwin Rockwell, 1952, repr. 1960, Charles Matthew Norrie, *Bridging the years: a short history of British civil engineering*, 1956, and Richard Shelton Kirby and Philip Gustave Laurson, *The early years of modern civil engineering*, New Haven, Conn. 1932, which is American-orientated.

5164 HAMILTON (STANLEY BAINES). 'The historical development of structural theory'. *Instn. Civil Engineers Proc.* (1952), vol. I, pt. III, 374–419.

5165 TIMOSHENKO (STEFAN PROKOFIEVITCH). History of strength of materials: with a brief account of the history of theory of elasticity and theory of structures. N.Y. 1953.

Good.

5166 MIDDLEMAS (ROBERT KEITH). The master builders: Thomas Brassey, Sir John Aird, Lord Cowdray, Sir John Norton-Griffiths. 1963.

5167 ABERNETHY. The life and work of James Abernethy, C.E., F.R.S.E., past president of the Institute of Civil Engineers. By John Scott Abernethy. 1897.

5168 ARROL. Sir William Arrol: a memoir. By Sir Robert Purvis. Edin. 1913.

5169 BRUNTON. John Brunton's book, being the memoirs of John Brunton, engineer . . . Intro. by Sir John Harold Clapham. Camb. 1939.

5170 COWDRAY. Weetman Pearson, first Viscount Cowdray, 1856–1927. By John Alfred Spender. 1930.
See also Desmond Young, *Member for Mexico: a biography of Weetman Pearson, first Viscount Cowdray*, 1966.

5171 FOWLER. The life of Sir John Fowler, engineer, Bart., K.C.M.G., etc. By Thomas Mackay. 1900.

5172 FOX. River, road and rail: some engineering reminiscences. By Sir Francis Fox. 1904.
See also his *Sixty-three years of engineering, scientific and social work*, 1924.

5173 HUNTER. A man and his times. By Charles Henry Wilson. 1962.
Sir Ellis Hunter of Dorman, Long.

5174 RENNIE. Autobiography of Sir John Rennie. 1875.

5175 SCOTT-MONCRIEFF. The life of Sir Colin C. Scott-Moncrieff . . . Ed. by his niece, Mary Albright Hollings. 1917.

5176 VIGNOLES. Life of Charles Blacker Vignoles . . . soldier and civil engineer, formerly lieutenant in H.M. 1st Royals, past president of the Institution of Civil Engineers: a reminiscence of early railway history. By Olinthus John Vignoles. 1889.

5177 PUBLIC WORKS, ROADS AND TRANSPORT CONGRESS AND EXHIBITION. British bridges: an illustrated technical and historical record. Ed. by S. M. Johnson and C. W. Scott-Giles. 1933.
A useful county-by-county survey. See also Eric Samuel de Maré, *The bridges of Britain*, 1954 and Percy Stuart Attwood Berridge, *The girder bridge: after Brunel and others*, 1969. There are also a number of books on indiv. bridges, incl. Charles Welch, *History of the Tower Bridge and of other bridges over the Thames built by the corporation of London* . . ., 1894, and W. W. Webb, *A complete account of the origin and progress of the Clifton suspension bridge over the River Avon*, Bristol 1864. For bridges generally see Hubert Shirley Smith, *The world's great bridges*, 1953, and Henry Grattan Tyrrell, *History of bridge engineering*, Chicago 1911. Arne Arthur Jakkula, 'A history of suspension bridges in bibliographical form', *Texas Agricultural and Mechanical College, Engineering Experimental Station Bull.*, no. 57 (4 ser. xii (1941), no. 7), is an excellent bibliog.

5178  WEALE (JOHN) *ed.* The theory, practice and architecture of bridges of stone, iron, timber and wire: with examples on the principles of suspension. 4 v. in 3. 1843–53. Repr. 1855–6.

A useful descriptive work. See also William Humber, *A complete treatise on cast and wrought iron bridge construction, including iron foundations,* 2 v. 1861, 3rd edn. 2 v. 1870; Sir Benjamin Baker, *Long-span railway bridges . . .,* 1867, rev. edn. 1873; William Cawthorne Unwin, *Wrought iron bridges and roofs . . .,* 1869; and Ewing Matheson, *Works in iron: bridge and roof structures,* 1873.

5179  TAY BRIDGE DISASTER. Report of the court of inquiry and report of Mr. Rothery, upon the circumstances attending the fall of a portion of the Tay Bridge on the 28th December 1879. [C. 2616] H.C. (1880). XXXIX, 1. Appendix and evidence. [C. 2616–I] H.C. (1880). XXXIX, 53.

Important for establishing stress resistance required in large bridges. For background see 10039.

5180  SANDSTRÖM (GÖSTA HERBERT EDWARD). The history of tunnelling: underground work through the ages. 1963.

5181  SIMMS (FREDERICK WALTER). Practical tunnelling . . . 1844. 4th edn. 1896.

A good professional account.

5182  WALKER (THOMAS ANDREW). The Severn Tunnel: its construction and difficulties, 1872–1887 . . . 1888. 3rd edn. 1891.

5183  KEEN (P. A.). 'The Channel tunnel project'. *J. Transport Hist.* iii (1957–8), 132–44.

A useful summary of a major subject. See also Reginald Arthur Ryves, *The Channel tunnel project: a brief history,* 1929; Thomas Whiteside, *The tunnel under the Channel,* 1962; *Report of the commissioners for the Channel tunnel and railway.* [C. 1576] H.C. (1876). XX, 13; *Report from the joint select committee of the House of Lords and the House of Commons on the Channel tunnel* [Chairman: Marquess of Lansdowne]. H.C. 248 (1883). XII, 1; and Anthony Stewart Travis, *Channel Tunnel, 1802–1967,* 1967.

5184  JOFFE (MARK) *ed.* Britain builds abroad: British constructional engineering in the service of world civilization, 1850–1950: a tribute . . . 1951.

5185  MATHESON (EWING). Aid book to engineering enterprise abroad. 2 pts. 1878–81. 3rd edn. 1898.

A handbook for the use of British engineers.

5186  CRESY (EDWARD). An encyclopaedia of civil engineering: historical, theoretical and practical . . . 2 v. 1847. 2nd edn. 2 v. 1856.

A very useful descriptive work.

5187  INSTITUTION OF CIVIL ENGINEERS. Minutes of proceedings, 1837–1934/35.

See also Institution of Civil Engineers, *The education and status of civil engineers in the United Kingdom and in foreign countries,* 1870. Among civil engineering js. of note were *Civil engineer and architect's j., scientific and railway gazette,* 1837–1868, *Civil engineering,* 1906+, and *Concrete and constructional engineering,* 1906+.

## (c) *Mechanical Engineering*

5188 INSTITUTION OF MECHANICAL ENGINEERS. Library catalogue [and] subject index of papers in the proceedings. 1876. 3rd edn. [Proceedings, 1847–87.] 1887.

5189 [HORNER (JOSEPH GREGORY).] Lockwood's dictionary of terms used in the practice of mechanical engineering . . . Ed. by a foreman pattern maker. 1888. 7th edn. 1952.

5190 HAWKINS (NEHEMIAH) *and others.* Hawkins' mechanical dictionary: a cyclopedia of words, terms, phrases and data used in the mechanic arts, trades and sciences. N.Y. & Lond. [1909.]

5191 HORNER (JOSEPH GREGORY) *ed.* The encyclopaedia of practical engineering and allied trades. 10 v. 1906–9.

5192 BURSTALL (AUBREY FREDERIC). A history of mechanical engineering. 1963. Repr. 1965.

5193 INSTITUTION OF MECHANICAL ENGINEERS. Engineering heritage: highlights from the history of mechanical engineering. 2 v. 1964–6.

Reprints hist. articles from *The chartered mechanical engineer.*

5194 PARSONS (ROBERT HODSON). A history of the Institution of Mechanical Engineers, 1847–1947. 1947.

See also Lionel Thomas Caswall Rolt, *The mechanicals: progress of a profession,* Instn. Mech. Eng. 1967.

5195 SAUL (SAMUEL BERRICK). 'The market and the development of the mechanical engineering industries in Britain, 1860–1914'. *Econ. Hist. Rev.* 2 ser. xx (1967), 111–30.

5196 BURN (DUNCAN LYALL). 'The genesis of American engineering competition, 1850–1870'. *Econ. Hist.,* suppl to *Econ. J.* ii (1930–3), 292–311.

5197 BAILEY (R. W.). 'The contribution of Manchester researches to mechanical science'. *Instn. Mech. Engineers Proc.* (1929), 613–75.

Useful bibliog. On Manchester see also William Henry Chaloner, 'James Galloway (1804–1894), engineer of Manchester and his reminiscences', *Lancs & Ches. Antiq. Soc. Trans.* lxiv (1954), 93–116. On Leeds there is A. H. Meysey-Thompson, 'On the history of engineering in Leeds', *Instn. Mech. Engineers Proc.,* (1882), 266–78, and Edwin Kitson Clark, *Kitsons of Leeds, 1837–1937: a firm and its folk by one of them* [1938]. On Ipswich there is Ipswich Engineering Soc., *The history of engineering in Ipswich, 1899–1949,* Ipswich 1950, and the history of Napiers (**5203**).

5198 EWING. The man of room 40: the life of Sir [James] Alfred Ewing. By Alfred Washington Ewing. [1939.]

See also Sir James Alfred Ewing's, *An engineer's outlook,* 1933, and Leslie Fleetwood Bates, *Sir Alfred Ewing . . . a pioneer in physics and engineering,* 1946.

5199  FAIRBAIRN. The life of Sir William Fairbairn. Ed. by William Pole. 1877. New edn. Newton Abbot. 1970.

5200  NASMYTH. James Nasmyth, engineer: an autobiography. Ed. by Samuel Smiles. 1883. Many edns.

See also Albert Edward Musson, 'James Nasmyth and the early growth of mechanical engineering', *Econ. Hist. Rev.* 2 ser. x (1957–8), 121–7 and R. Dickinson, 'James Nasmyth and the Liverpool iron trade', *Historic Soc. Lancs & Ches. Trans.* cviii (1956), 83–104.

5201  PARSONS. Charles Parsons, his life and work. By Rollo Appleyard. 1933.

The inventor of the Parsons turbine, for which see **5217**. Parsons's *Scientific papers and addresses* were ed. by the Hon. Geoffrey Lawrence Parsons, along with a memoir by Robert John Strutt, 4th Baron Rayleigh, Camb. 1934.

5202  TANGYE. Sir Richard Tangye. By Stuart Johnson Reid. 1908.

See also *The growth of a great industry: 'one and all': an autobiography of Sir Richard Tangye of the Cornwall works, Birmingham*, Birmingham 1902, new edn. [*The rise of a great industry*], 1905, and Rachel Elizabeth Waterhouse, *A hundred years of engineering craftsmanship: a short history tracing the adventurous development of Tangyes Limited, Smethwick, 1857–1957*, 1957.

5203  WILSON (CHARLES HENRY) *and* READER (WILLIAM). Men and machines: a history of D. Napier & Son, Engineers, Ltd., 1808–1958. 1958.

A good business hist. For other East Anglian firms see Peter Kemp Kemp, *The Bentall story: commemorating 150 years service to agriculture, 1805–1955*, 1955, Bernard Newman, *One hundred years of good company: published on the occasion of the Ruston centenary, 1857–1957* [1957], and Robert Stanley Lewis, *Eighty years of enterprise, 1869–1949: being, the intimate story of the Waterside works of Ransomes & Rapier Ltd. of Ipswich, England* [1951].

5204  INSTITUTION OF MECHANICAL ENGINEERS. Proceedings &c. Birmingham etc. 1847+.

The principal mechanical engineering j. See also *The engineer*, 1856+, *The English mechanic*, 1865–1926+, Manchester Assoc. of Employers, Foremen and Draughtsmen of the Mechanical Trades of Great Britain [Manchester Assoc. of Engineers], *Papers* [*Transactions*], Manch. 1866+, and the other journals cited at **5155**. There are also some interesting early engineering js. primarily designed for mechanics, incl. *The mechanics' magazine*, 1823–93, which was styled *Iron*, 1873–93, and Artizan Club, ed., *The artizan: a monthly j. of the operative arts*, 1843–71, 1844–72.

5205  DEMPSEY (GEORGE DRYSDALE). The machinery of the nineteenth century. 6 pts. 1852.

Descriptions of exhibits at the Great Exhibition.

5206  CLARK (DANIEL KINNEAR). The exhibited machinery of 1862: a cyclopaedia of the machinery represented at the International Exhibition. 1864.

5207  FAIRBAIRN (*Sir* WILLIAM). Treatise on mills and millwork. 2 pts 1861–3. 4th edn. 1878.

One of the classics of mechanical engineering: deals with the milling of wrought iron. See also his *Useful information for engineers* . . ., 1856, 4th edn. [now styled 'of first series'], 1864, 2nd series 1860, 3rd series 1866. For a later work in the same field see Joseph Gregory Horner, *Modern milling machines: their design, construction and working*, 1906. Horner also publ. treatises on *Engineers' turning* . . . [*Practical metal turning*], 1905, 4th edn. 1937; *English and American lathes* . . ., 1900; *Gear cutting* . . ., 1914; *Pattern making* . . ., 1885, 8th edn. 1950; *The principles of fitting* . . ., 1893, 4th edn. 1909; and other works.

5208  VICTORIA AND ALBERT MUSEUM *later* SCIENCE MUSEUM. Catalogue of the mechanical engineering collection in the science division . . . 1907–8. 6th edn. 1919.

5209  WOODBURY (ROBERT SMITH). History of the gear-cutting machine: a historical study in geometry and machines. Camb., Mass. 1958.

One of a ser. of studies designed to provide the basis for a hist. of tools. See also his *History of the grinding machine: a historical study in tools and precision production*, Camb., Mass. 1959, and *History of the milling machine: a study in technical development*, Camb., Mass. 1960. For the cutting of metals generally there is a very full bibliog., Orlan William Boston, *A bibliography on cutting of metals, 1864–1943*, N.Y. 1945.

5210  STEEDS (WILLIAM). A history of machine tools, 1700–1910. Oxf. 1969.

See also Samuel Berrick Saul, 'The machine tool industry in Britain to 1914', *Business Hist.* x (1968), 22–43; Lionel Thomas Caswall Rolt, *Tools for the job: a short history of machine tools*, 1965, publ. in America as *A short history of machine tools*, Camb., Mass. 1965; Joseph Gregory Horner, *Tools for engineers and woodworkers* . . ., 1905; Godfrey L. Carden, *Machine tool trade in Germany, France, Switzerland, Italy and the United Kingdom*, U.S. Dept. of Commerce and Labor, Bureau of Manufactures special agents series 26, Wash. 1909; Joseph Wickham Roe, *English and American tool builders*, New Haven, Conn. 1916; and K. R. Gilbert, comp., *The machine tool collection: catalogue of exhibits*, Science Museum 1966.

5211  PATENT OFFICE. Abridgments of specifications relating to air, gas, and other motive power engines, A.D. 1635–1866. 1873. Suppl. for 1867–76. 1881.

Cont. by the Patent Office, *Abridgments of specifications*, class 7 and class 10, 1855–1930. See also *Abridgments of specifications relating to agriculture: division III: agricultural and traction engines, A.D. 1618–1866*, 1884.

5212  DICKINSON (HENRY WINRAM). A short history of the steam engine. Camb. 1938. Repr. with intro. by Albert Edward Musson. 1963.

See also George Watkins, *The textile mill engine*, 1+ v., Newton Abbot 1970+.

5213  GARVEY (MICHAEL ANGELO). The silent revolution: or, the future effects of steam and electricity upon the condition of mankind. 1852.

Reflects contemporary enthusiasm for the 'age of steam'. Cp. Robert Henry Thurston, *A history of the growth of the steam engine*, 1878, 4th edn. 1897, new edn. Ithaca, N.Y. 1939, and Robert L. Galloway, *The steam engine and its inventors: a historical sketch*, 1881.

5214 TREDGOLD (THOMAS). The principles and practice and explanation of the construction of the steam engine, including pumping, stationary and marine engines . . . [Vol. III of Tredgold on the Steam Engine.] 1853.

A very full descriptive work. See also Robert Scott Burn, *The steam-engine, its history and mechanism: being, descriptions and illustrations of the stationary, locomotive and marine engine*, 1854, John Bourne, ed., *A treatise on the steam engine in its various applications to mines, mills, steam navigation, railways and agriculture*, 1850, 5th edn. 1861, John Bourne, comp., *A catechism of the steam engine*, 1847, new edn. 1885, and Daniel Kinnear Clark, *An elementary treatise on steam and the steam-engine, stationary and portable (being an extension of the elementary treatise on steam of Mr. John Sewell)*, 1875.

5215 CLARK (DANIEL KINNEAR). The steam engine: a treatise on steam engines and boilers. 4 v. 1890. 4 pts. in 2 v. 1892.

Comprehensive and authoritative for the second half of the 19th cent.

5216 POWLES (HENRY HANDLEY PRIDHAM). Steam boilers: their history and development; giving an account of the earliest known examples of steam generators down to the most modern steam boilers. 1905.

A good full account. For boilers see also W. H. Chaloner, *Vulcan boiler insurance* (4712).

5217 PARSONS (ROBERT HODSON). The development of the Parsons steam turbine. 1936.

For Sir Charles Parsons see 5201.

5218 GLYNN (JOSEPH). Rudimentary treatise on the power of water as applied to drive flour mills and to give motion to turbines and other hydrostatic engines . . . 1853.

A defence of water power against steam.

5219 CLARK (RONALD HARRY). The development of the English traction engine. Norwich. 1960.

A good general hist., strong on technicalities. See also William Jesse Hughes, *A century of traction engines: being an historical account of the rise and decline of an industry whose benefits to mankind were and are incalculable*, 1959, and the popular hist. by Philip Arthur Wright, *Traction engines*, 1959. For the manufacturers of these engines see Ronald Harry Clark, *Steam-engine builders of Norfolk*, Norwich 1948, *Steam-engine builders of Suffolk, Essex and Cambridgeshire*, Norwich 1950, *Steam engine builders of Lincolnshire*, Norwich 1955, and *Chronicles of a county works: being, a history of Messrs Charles Burrell & Sons, Ltd., of Thetford, the famous traction engine builders* [1952]. There are also a number of attractive picture albums.

5220 EVANS (ARTHUR F.). The history of the oil engine: a review in detail of the development of the oil engine from 1608 to the beginning of 1930: with an index of important patents. [1932.]

5221 CLERK (*Sir* DUGALD) *and* BURLS (GEORGE ARTHUR). The gas, petrol and oil engine. 2 v. 1909–13.

A good textbook, strong on recent developments. See also William Robinson, *Gas and petroleum engines*, 1890, 2nd edn. 1902, and Vivian Byam Lewes, *Liquid and gaseous fuels and the part they play in modern power production*, 1907.

5222  VALE (EDMUND). The Harveys of Hayle: engine builders, ship-wrights and merchants of Cornwall. Truro. [1967.]

5223  TRIPP (BASIL HOWARD). Renold chains: a history of the company and the rise of the precision chain industry, 1879–1955. 1956.

### (d) Gas Engineering

5224  CHESTER (WILLIAM REGINALD) *comp*. Bibliography of coal gas: a subject index to interesting matters published in connection with coal gas to end of year 1891. Nottingham. 1892.

5225  PATENT OFFICE. Abridgments of the specifications relating to the production and applications of gas (excepting gas engines) [1681–1858]. 1860. Suppl. for 1859–66. 1871. 2nd edn. 1875.

Cont. by *Abridgments of specifications*, classes 54–5, for 1855–1930.

5226  BRACKENBURY (CHARLES ERNEST). British progress in gas works' plant and machinery. 1905.

5227  BRITISH ASSOCIATION OF GAS MANAGERS [Institution of Gas Engineers]. Report of the proceedings . . . [Transactions.] 1863+.

The leading professional j. But see also Incorp. Instn. of Gas Engineers, *Transactions*, 1891–1902; *The j. of gas-lighting . . .*, 1849–1916; *The gas engineer* [title varies], 1876–1936; *Gas trade circular and review* [title varies], 1876–90; and *The gas world*, 1884+. The best of the contemp. professional works for historians are Samuel Hughes, *A treatise on gas works . . .*, 1853, 9th edn. 1904; Thomas Newbigging, *The gas managers' hand-book . . . [Handbook for gas engineers and managers]*, 1870, 8th edn. 1913; William Richards, *A practical treatise on the manufacture and distribution of coal gas*, 1877; Walter Grafton, *A handbook of practical gas-fitting . . .*, 1900, 2nd edn. 1907; and William Hosgood Young Webber, *Town gas . . .*, 1907.

5228  BRAUNHOLTZ (WALTER THEODORE KARL). The Institution of Gas Engineers: the first hundred years, 1863–1963. [1963.]

### (e) Electrical Engineering

5229  INSTITUTION OF ELECTRICAL ENGINEERS. Catalogue of the lending library. 1956. New edn. 1959 [1960].

5230  RONALDS (*Sir* FRANCIS). Catalogue of books and papers relating to electricity, magnetism, the electric telegraph, &c., including the Ronalds library . . . Ed. by Alfred James Frost. Soc. of Telegraph Engineers. 1880.

A big catalogue reflecting current knowledge.

5231  SCIENCE ABSTRACTS: Section B: electrical engineering abstracts. Instn. of Electrical Engineers. 1898+.

Started life as *Science abstracts: physics and electrical engineering, issued under the direction of the Institution of Electrical Engineers, the Physical Society of London*, 1898–1902.

5232 HARTLEY (FREDERIC ST. AUBYN) *comp.* Science Museum: catalogue of the collections with descriptive and historical notes: electrical engineering. 1927.

Useful illustrations. Cp. William Thomas O'Dea, comp., *Science Museum: handbook of the collections illustrating electrical engineering: 1. electric power*, 2 v. 1933.

5233 PATENT OFFICE. Abridgments of specifications relating to electricity and magnetism, their generation and applications. 1859. Suppls. for 1858–83.

5234 THE ELECTRICIAN'S DIRECTORY. 1883+.

Title varies. See also *Manual of electrical undertakings . . .*, 1896+, commonly styled *Garcke's manual.*

5235 MACLEAN (MAGNUS) *ed.* Modern electric practice. 6 v. 1904–5.

A handy encyclopedia. For amateurs Selimo Romeo Bottone publ. an attractive ser. of books, notably *Electrical instrument making for amateurs: a practical handbook*, 1888, 9th edn. 1920.

5236 SOCIETY OF TELEGRAPH ENGINEERS [Institution of Electrical Engineers]. Journal. 1872–1948+.

The leading professional j. See also *The electrician*, 1861–4, 1878–1952+; *Lightning*, 1891–1901, renamed *The electrical times*, 1902+; *Electric light*, 1882–3, renamed *The electrical engineer*, 1883–1912, when merged with *Electrical engineering: the engineering j. of the electric industry*, 1906–16; Association of Mining Electrical [and Mechanical] Engineers, *Proceedings* &c., 1909+; and Electrical Contractors' Assoc., *The electrical contractor . . .*, 1903–29+.

5237 DUNSHEATH (PERCY). A history of electrical engineering. 1962.

5238 HUGHES (THOMAS PARKE). 'British electrical industry lag, 1882–1888'. *Technology & Culture* iii (1962), 27–44.

5239 APPLEYARD (ROLLO). The history of the Institution of Electrical Engineers, 1871–1931. 1939.

See also Laurence Hudson Ashdown Carr, *The history of the north-western centre of the Institution of Electrical Engineers*, 1950.

5240 PARSONS (ROBERT HODSON). The early days of the power station industry. Camb. 1939.

5241 WORDINGHAM (CHARLES HENRY). Central electrical stations: their design, organisation and management. 1901. 2nd edn. 1903.

See also Frank Koester, *Steam-electric power plants: a practical treatise on the design of central light and power stations and their economical construction and operation*, N.Y. & Lond. 1908, and Edward Tremlett Carter, *Motive power and gearing for electrical machinery: a treatise on the theory and practice of the mechanical equipment of power stations for electric supply and for electric traction*, 1903, 2nd edn. 1905.

5242 HAY (ALFRED). Electrical distributing networks and transmission lines. 1910.

5243  HASLAM (ARTHUR PIRRIE). Electricity in factories & workshops: its cost and convenience: a handy book for power producers and power users. 1909.

A good illustrated guide.

5244  MELLANBY (JOHN). The history of electric wiring. 1957.

Good. See also William Thomson Anderson, *From factory to face: the history of a colliery cable* [1922], and Daniel Coyle and F. J. O. Howe, *Electric cables: their construction and cost,* 1909.

5245  BARHAM (GEORGE BASIL). The development of the incandescent electric lamp. 1912.

Useful for details. There is not much more in Maurice Solomon, *Electric lamps,* 1908, John W. Howell and Henry Schroeder, *History of the incandescent lamp,* 1927, G. Arncliffe Percival, *The electric lamp industry,* 1920, and General Electric Company, *The story of the lamp* [1924].

5246  BRIGHT (ARTHUR AARON). The electric lamp industry: technological change and economic development from 1800 to 1947. N.Y. 1949.

5247  WHITE (ADAM GOWANS). Forty years of electrical progress: the story of G.E.C. 1930.

5248  SCOTT (JOHN DICK). Siemens Brothers, 1858–1958: an essay in the history of industry. [1958.]

See also **5088.**

5249  DUMMELOW (JOHN). Metropolitan Vickers Electrical Company, 1899–1949. Manch. 1949.

5250  FERRANTI. The life and letters of Sebastian Ziani de Ferranti. By Gertrude Ziani de Ferranti and Richard Ince. 1934.

A useful life of an important pioneer.

5251  FLEMING. Fifty years of electricity: the memories of an electrical engineer. By Sir John Ambrose Fleming. 1921.

See also John Turner MacGregor-Morris, *The inventor of the valve: a biography of Sir Ambrose Fleming,* 1954.

## 6. CHEMICAL INDUSTRIES

### (a) *General*

The great centre of the chemical industry was the Mersey. See particularly Barker and Harris's history of St. Helens (**9540**).

5252  PATENT OFFICE LIBRARY. Subject list of works on chemical technology: including, oils, fats, soaps, candles and perfumery; paints, varnishes, gums, resins, india-rubber; paper and leather industries. 1911.

5253 THE CHEMICAL MANUFACTURERS' DIRECTORY OF GREAT BRITAIN AND IRELAND. 1866+.

Title varies.

5254 SOCIETY OF THE CHEMICAL INDUSTRY. Proceedings [Journal]. 1+. 1881+.

The main professional periodical. But see also *The chemical gazette*, 1842–59; *The chemical news*, 1859–1932; *Chemical trade j.*, *and chemical engineer*, Manch. etc. 1887+; and *Transactions of the Chemical Soc.* (**8690**). There is also much information in the transactions of the International Congress of Applied Chemistry, the first of whose meetings was held in Brussels in 1894.

5255 PARTINGTON (JAMES RIDDICK). Origins and development of applied chemistry. 1935.

5256 TAYLOR (FRANK SHERWOOD). A history of industrial chemistry. 1957.

There is some useful material in Archibald Clow and Nan Louise Clow, *The chemical revolution: a contribution to social technology*, 1952, which ostensibly ends *c.* 1830; and in Gustav Fester, *Die Entwicklung der chemischen Technik bis zu den Anfängen der Grossindustrie*, Berlin 1923. There is little in Trevor Illtyd Williams, *The chemical industry past and present*, Harmondsworth 1953.

5257 HARDIE (DAVID WILLIAM FERGUSON) *and* PRATT (JAMES DAVIDSON). A history of the modern British chemical industry. Oxf. 1966.

5258 MORGAN (*Sir* GILBERT THOMAS) *and* PRATT (DAVID DOIG). British chemical industry: its rise and development. 1938.

5259 MIALL (STEPHEN). A history of the British chemical industry. Soc. of Chemical Industry. 1931.

5260 HABER (LUDWIG FRITZ). The chemical industry during the nineteenth century: a study of the economic aspects of applied chemistry in Europe and North America. Oxf. 1958.

Useful. Cont. by his *The chemical industry, 1900–1930: international growth and technological change*, Oxf. 1971. See also H. W. Richardson, 'Chemicals', in D. H. Aldcroft, *The development of British industry* (**4752**).

5261 HARDIE (DAVID WILLIAM FERGUSON). A history of the chemical industry in Widnes. 1950.

5262 NORRIS (W. G.). Chemical service in defence of the realm: one hundred years of chemical inspection: the story of the chemical inspectorate. Ministry of Supply. 1957.

5263 KNAPP (FRIEDRICH LUDWIG). Chemical technology: or, chemistry applied to the arts and to manufactures. Ed. by Edmund Ronalds and Thomas Richardson. 3 v. 1848–51.

A useful guide to current practice *c.* 1850.

5264 MACLEOD (ROY MALCOLM). 'The Alkali Acts administration, 1863–84: the emergence of the civil scientist'. *Victorian Studs.* ix (1965–6), 85–112.

See also *Report from the select committee of the House of Lords on injury from noxious vapours* [Chairman: Earl of Derby]. H.C. 486 (1862). XIV, 1.

5265 KINGZETT (CHARLES THOMAS). The history, products and processes of the alkali trade, including the most recent improvements. 1877.

Useful for machinery illustrations.

5266 PARTINGTON (JAMES RIDDICK). The alkali industry. 1919. 2nd edn. 1925.

5267 DICKINSON (HENRY WINRAM). 'History of vitriol-making in England'. *Newcomen Soc. Trans.* xviii (1937–8), 43–60.

5268 GARDNER (WALTER MYERS) *ed*. The British coal-tar industry: its origin, development and decline. 1915.

See also Arthur George Green, *The relative progress of the coal tar industry in England and Germany*, 1901. Thomas Howard Butler, *The history of Wm Butler & Co. (Bristol) Ltd., 1843 to 1943*, Bristol 1943, is a good hist. of a tar distillery.

5269 WORDEN (EDWARD CHAUNCEY). Nitrocellulose industry: a compendium of the history, chemistry, manufacture, commercial application and analysis of nitrates, acetates and xanthates of cellulose as applied to the peaceful arts, with a chapter on gun cotton, smokeless powder and explosive cellulose nitrates . . . 2 v. 1911.

5270 PARTINGTON (JAMES RIDDICK) *and* PARKER (LESLIE HENRY). The nitrogen industry. 1922.

5271 ALLEN (JOHN FENWICK). Some founders of the chemical industry: men to be remembered. Manch. 1906.

5272 BRUNNER. Sir John Brunner, Radical plutocrat, 1842–1919. By Stephen Edward Koss. Camb. 1970.

Chiefly on Brunner as a politician. For his industrial career see **5276**.

5273 MOND. The life of Ludwig Mond. By John Michael Cohen. 1956.

5274 MUSPRATT. My life and work. By Edmund Knowles Muspratt. 1917.

5275 SWINDIN. Engineering without wheels: a personal history. By Norman Swindin. 1962.

5276 READER (WILLIAM JOSEPH). Imperial Chemical Industries: a history. Vol. I. The forerunners, 1870–1926. Oxf. 1970.

See also **5272–3**.

5277 FIFTY YEARS OF PROGRESS: the story of the Castner–Kellner Alkali Company: told to celebrate the fiftieth anniversary of its formation, 1895–1945. N.d.

(b) *Salt*

5278 CALVERT (ALBERT FREDERICK). Salt and the salt industry. [1919.] 2nd edn. [1929].

The best intro. to the industry.

5279 CALVERT (ALBERT FREDERICK). Salt in Cheshire. 1915.

Astonishingly comprehensive. See also K. L. Wallwork, 'The mid-Cheshire salt industry', *Geography*, xliv (1959), 171–86, and 'Subsidence in the mid-Cheshire industrial area', *Geogr. J.* cxxii (1956), 40–53, and William Henry Chaloner, 'Salt in Cheshire, 1600–1870', *Lancs. & Ches. Antiq. Soc. Trans.* lxxi (1961), 58–74, and 'William Furnival, H. E. Falk and the Salt Chamber of Commerce, 1815–1889: some chapters in the economic history of Cheshire', *Historic Soc. Lancs. & Ches. Trans.* cxii (1960), 121–45. For the North-east salt industry see Richard Grigg, 'On the Middlesbrough salt industry', *Instn. Mech. Engineers Proc.* (1893), 278–308, and John Marley, 'On the Cleveland and South Durham salt industry', *Fed. Inst. Mining Engineers Trans.* i (1889–90), 339–73.

5280 CALVERT (ALBERT FREDERICK). A history of the Salt Union: a record of 25 years of disunion and depreciation; compiled from official reports. 1913.

(c) *Soap and Perfumery*

5281 EDWARDS (HAROLD RAYMOND). Competition and monopoly in the British soap industry. Oxf. 1962.

5282 READER (WILLIAM JOSEPH). 'The United Kingdom Soapmakers' Association and the English soap trade, 1867–1896'. *Business Hist.* i (1958–9), 77–83.

5283 MUSSON (ALBERT EDWARD). Enterprise in soap and chemicals: Joseph Crosfield & Sons Ltd., 1815–1965. Manch. 1965.

5284 WILSON (CHARLES HENRY). The history of Unilever: a study in economic growth and social change. 2 v. 1954.

A model business hist. centring on Lever Brothers, for whose head see William Hulme Lever, Viscount Leverhulme, *Viscount Leverhulme*, 1927, and William Hesketh Lever, Viscount Leverhulme, *The six-hour day & other industrial questions*, ed. by Stanley Unwin, 1918.

5285 THE PERFUMERY AND ESSENTIAL OIL RECORD ANNUAL DIRECTORY AND BUYERS' GUIDE. 1914+.

5286 WYNNE-THOMAS (EDWARD). The house of Yardley, 1770–1953. 1953.

### (d) *Rubber and Plastics*

5287 YESCOMBE (ERNEST RAYMOND). Sources of information on the rubber, plastics and allied industries. Oxf. & N.Y. 1968.

The best starting-point, though technically orientated. For 19th- and early 20th-cent. books the Research Assoc. of British Rubber and Tyre Manufacturers, *Libr. catalogue*, Camb. 1927, is sometimes helpful.

5288 CRONSHAW (HARRY BRENAN) *ed.* Rubber industry: an encyclopaedia of the rubber industry in all its branches . . . [1936.]

Useful, though no longer technically acceptable. For recent knowledge consult Hermann Franz Mark, Norman G. Gaylord, and Norbert M. Bikales, eds., *Encyclopaedia of polymer science and technology, plastics, resins, rubbers, fibers*, 12 v. N.Y. & Lond. 1964+, and Siegfried Boström, ed., *Kautschuk-handbuch*, 5 v. and suppl., Stuttgart 1959–62.

5289 INTERNATIONAL RUBBER CONGRESS, LONDON. Official guide book and catalogue. 1911.

Reflects contemp. knowledge. See also Joseph Torrey and A. Staines Manders, eds., *The rubber industry: being the official report of the proceedings . . .*, 1911.

5290 PATENT OFFICE. Abridgments of the specifications relating to india rubber and gutta percha: including air, fire and waterproofing. 1859. 2nd edn. 1875.

Covers 1627–1857. Suppls. to 1930.

5291 WHO'S WHO IN THE RUBBER WORLD. 1914+.

5292 SCHIDROWITZ (PHILIP) *and* DAWSON (T. R.) *eds.* History of the rubber industry: compiled under the auspices of the Institution of the Rubber Industry. Camb. [1953.]

Includes a chronological bibliog.

5293 GEER (WILLIAM CHAUNCEY). The reign of rubber. N.Y. 1922.

A hist.

5294 WOODRUFF (WILLIAM). 'An inquiry into the origins of invention and the intercontinental diffusion of techniques of production in the rubber industry'. *Econ. Record* xxxviii (1962), 479–97.

5295 HANCOCK (THOMAS). Personal narrative of the origin and progress of the caoutchouc or india-rubber manufacture in England. 1857. Repr. 1920.

Also reprinted along with Charles Goodyear's *Gum-elastic and its varieties . . .*, 2 v. New Haven, Conn. 1853–5, by the American Chemical Soc., in *A centennial volume of the writings of Charles Goodyear and Thomas Hancock . . .*, [Boston] 1939.

5296 WOODRUFF (WILLIAM). The rise of the British rubber industry during the nineteenth century. Liverpool. 1958.

Good. Based chiefly on the records of Moulton & Co. of Bradford-on-Avon.

**5297  PAYNE (PETER LESTER).** Rubber and railways in the nineteenth century: a study of the Spencer papers. Liverpool. 1961.

See also his 'The role of the salesman and the commission agent in the early years of the British rubber mechanicals industry', *Explorations in entrepren. hist.* vii (1955), 205–14.

**5298  TERRY (HUBERT LANPHIER).** India-rubber and its manufacture: with chapters on gutta-percha and balata. 1907.

**5299  CHRISTY (CUTHBERT).** The African rubber industry and funtumia elastica—'Kickxia'. 1911.

**5300  SCHIDROWITZ (PHILIP).** Rubber: its production and its industrial uses. 1911. 3rd edn. 1920.

**5301  INDIA RUBBER AND GUTTA PERCHA** and electrical trades journal [India-rubber journal]. 1884+.

The leading British j.

**5302  KAUFMAN (MORRIS).** The first century of plastics: celluloid and its sequel. Plastics Inst. [1963.]

**5303  IMPERIAL CHEMICAL INDUSTRIES LTD. (PLASTICS DIVISION).** Landmarks in the history of the plastics industry (1862–1962). Welwyn Garden City. 1962.

### (e) *Petroleum and other Oils*

**5304  SWANSON (EDWARD BENJAMIN).** A century of oil and gas in books: a descriptive bibliography. N.Y. 1960.

See also Institute of Petroleum, *Library catalogue*, 1956.

**5305  PATENT OFFICE.** Abridgments of specifications relating to oils, animal, vegetable and mineral: including lubricants, candles and soaps, A.D. 1617–1863. 1865. 2nd edn. [to 1866.] 1873. Suppls. publ. as Abridgments . . . class 91, 1855–1930.

**5306  THE OIL, PETROLEUM AND BITUMEN MANUAL** [The oil and petroleum year book]. 1910–54.

**5307  PURDY (GORDON A.).** Petroleum: prehistoric to petrochemicals. Vancouver & N.Y. [1957.]

**5308  READER (WILLIAM JOSEPH).** 'Oil for the west of England, 1889–1896: a study in competition'. *Business Hist. Rev.* xxxv (1961), 28–42.

For petrol distribution see also **5914**.

**5309  MUNDELLA COMMITTEE ON PETROLEUM.** Report from the select committee on petroleum [Chairmen: A. J. Mundella and Jesse Collings].

H.C. 244 (1894). XIV, 503. Further reports. H.C. 311 (1896). XII, 1. H.C. 309 (1897). XIII, 109. H.C. 299 (1898). XI, 405.

Concerned with the danger of fire and explosion when handling petroleum and other inflammable liquids. See also *First report of the departmental committee on petroleum spirit* [Chairman: Sir Henry Hardinge Cunynghame]. [Cd. 5175] H.C. (1910). XLIV, 609. Minutes of evidence. [Cd. 5176] H.C. (1910). XLIV, 653. Final report. [Cd. 6565] H.C. (1912–13). XLII, 791. Minutes of evidence. [Cd. 6644] H.C. (1912–13). XLII, 799.

5310  CADMAN. Ambassador for oil: the life of John, first Baron Cadman. By John Herbert Shelley Rowland and John Basil Cope Cadman, Baron Cadman. 1960.

5311  PEARSON. For Weetman Pearson, Viscount Cowdray, a great figure in the industry, see **5170**.

5312  SAMUEL. Marcus Samuel, first Viscount Bearsted and founder of the 'Shell' Transport and Trading Company, 1853–1927. By Robert David Quixano Henriques. 1960.

5313  ANDERSON (JOHN RICHARD LANE). East of Suez: a study of Britain's greatest trading enterprise [British Petroleum]. 1969.

See also Marian Jack, 'The purchase of the British government's shares in the British Petroleum company, 1912–1914', *Past & Present* xxxix (1968), 139–68, and Henry Carpenter Longhurst, *Adventure in oil: the story of British Petroleum*, 1959.

5314  FORBES (ROBERT JAMES) *and* O'BEIRNE (DENIS R.). The technical development of Royal Dutch Shell, 1890–1940. Leiden. 1957.

5315  LIVEING (EDWARD GEORGE DOWNING). Pioneers of petrol: a centenary history of Carless, Capel and Leonard Ltd., 1859–1959. 1959.

5316  BRACE (HAROLD WITTY). History of seed crushing in Great Britain 1960.

5317  BUTT (JOHN). 'Technical change and the growth of the British shale-oil industry (1680–1870)'. *Econ. Hist. Rev.* 2 ser. xvii (1965), 511–21.

See also **10023**.

(f) *Matches, Fireworks, and Explosives*

5318  CHRISTY (ROBERT MILLER) *comp.* The Bryant & May Museum of fire-making appliances: catalogue of the exhibits. 1926.

5319  DIXON (WILLIAM HEPWORTH). The match industry: its origin and development. [1925.]

See also Bryant and May Ltd., *Making matches, 1861–1961*, . . ., 1961.

5320  THRELFALL (RICHARD EVELYN). The story of 100 years of phosphorus making, 1851–1951. Oldbury. 1951.

A competent hist. of Albright and Wilson.

5321 THORPE (*Sir* THOMAS EDWARD) *and others*. Reports to the secretary of state for the home department on the use of phosphorus in the manufacture of lucifer matches. [C. 9188] H.C. (1899). XII, 437.

Full. But see also the further report on Moreland & Co., Gloucester. [Cd. 3373] H.C. (1907). X, 441; and the general report on chemical works, **6830**.

5322 BROCK (ALAN ST. HILL). A history of fireworks. 1949.

5323 MUNROE (CHARLES EDWARD). Index to the literature of explosives. Baltimore. 1886. 2nd edn. 1893.

5324 PATENT OFFICE. Abridgments of specifications. Class 9: ammunition, torpedoes, explosives, and pyrotechnics. Decennial vols. covering 1855–1930.

5325 MARSHALL (ARTHUR). Dictionary of explosives. 1920.

5326 MARSHALL (ARTHUR). Explosives: their manufacture, properties, tests and history. 1915. 2nd edn. 3 v. 1917–32.

For contemp. practice see also Manuel Eissler, *A handbook of modern explosives: being a practical treatise on the manufacture and application of . . . explosive compounds . . .*, 1890, 2nd edn. 1897, Oscar Guttmann, *The manufacture of explosives: a theoretical and practical treatise on the history, the physical and chemical properties and the manufacture of explosives*, 2 v. 1895, and *The manufacture of explosives: twenty years' progress: four Cantor lectures . . .*, 1909, and S. J. von Romocki, *Geschichte der Explosivstoffe*, 2 v. Berlin 1895–6.

5327 HODGETTS (EDWARD ARTHUR BRAYLEY) *ed*. The rise and progress of the British explosives industry: publ. under the auspices of the VIIth International Congress of Applied Chemistry by its explosives section. Lond. & N.Y. 1909.

A solid work.

5328 IMPERIAL CHEMICAL INDUSTRIES LIMITED, and its founding companies. Vol. I. The history of Nobel's Explosives Company Limited and Nobel Industries Limited, 1871–1926. 1938.

See also **5276**.

### 7. Ceramics and Glass

#### (a) *General*

5329 CENTRAL SCHOOL OF SCIENCE & TECHNOLOGY, STOKE-ON-TRENT [North Staffordshire Technical College]. Catalogue of the ceramic library: including the Solon library, the Ceramic Society library [the library of the British Refractories Research Association], and the library of the pottery department of the school. Hanley. [1925.] Suppl. 1930.

A very full author list, particularly useful for catalogues and out-of-the-way pamphlets. A more recent list was issued as North Staffordshire Technical College, *Library catalogue*, Stoke-on-Trent 1960, Suppl. 1960.

5330 SOLON (LOUIS MARC EMMANUEL). Ceramic literature: an analytical index to the works published in all languages on the history and the technology of the ceramic art . . . 1910.

There are a few other items in South Kensington Museum (National Art Libr.) *Classed catalogue of printed books relating to ceramics*, 1895; Patent Office Library, *Subject list of works on the silicate industries (ceramics and glass)*, 1914; John Casper Branner, *A bibliography of clays and the ceramic arts*, new edn., Amer. Ceramic Soc., Columbus, Ohio 1906; and Jules François Félix Husson alias Fleury alias Champfleury, *Bibliographie céramique* . . ., Paris 1881.

5331 PATENT OFFICE. Abridgments of the specifications relating to pottery [1626–1861]. 1863. Suppl. 1862–6.

5332 RACKHAM (BERNARD). Catalogue of the Glaisher collection of pottery and porcelain in the Fitzwilliam Museum, Cambridge. 2 v. Camb. 1935.

The best coll. of English ceramics.

5333 GREEN (ARNOLD TREVOR) *and* STEWART (GERALD H.) *eds.* Ceramics: a symposium. British Ceramic Soc. Stoke-on-Trent. 1953.

Incls. useful hist. notes.

5334 SEARLE (ALFRED BROADHEAD). An encyclopaedia of the ceramic industries: being, a guide to the materials, methods of manufacture, means of recognition, and testing the various articles produced in the clayworking and allied industries. 3 v. 1929–30.

5335 NORTH STAFFORDSHIRE [BRITISH] CERAMIC SOCIETY. Transactions. Hanley. 1901+.

Incls. *British ceramic abstracts*, 1900+, also publ. separately. The American equiv. is American Ceramic Soc., *Ceramic abstracts*, Easton, Pa. etc. 1922–45, cont. in the Society's *Journal*, 1946+.

5336 THE POTTERY AND GLASS TRADES JOURNAL. 1878+.

Became *The pottery gazette and glass trades' journal*, 1879+. From 1881 issued *The pottery gazette . . . year book* under various titles.

(b) *Pottery and Porcelain*

5337 JEWITT (LLEWELLYNN FREDERICK WILLIAM). The ceramic art of Great Britain from pre-historic times down to the present day: being a history of the ancient and modern [pottery and] porcelain works of the kingdom and of their productions of every class. 2 v. 1878. Rev. edn. 1883.

Vol. 2 is still very useful. Needs to be suppl. by James F. Blacker, *Nineteenth-century English ceramic art* [1911], and *The ABC of English salt-glaze stoneware from Dwight to Doulton*, 1922.

5338 BEMROSE (GEOFFREY). Nineteenth-century English pottery and porcelain. 1952.

Written for collectors. To be used with Geoffrey Arthur Godden, *Victorian porcelain*, 1961, George Bernard Hughes, *Victorian pottery and porcelain*, 1959, and Hugh

George Wakefield, *Victorian pottery*, 1962. Among the more general books on pottery the following have a little on the period: William Bowyer Honey, *English pottery and porcelain*, 1933, 5th edn. 1962; Reginald George Haggar, *English country pottery*, 1950; George Bernard Hughes, *English and Scottish earthenware, 1660–1860*, 1961; and William Burton, *A history and description of English porcelain*, 1902.

5339  BALSTON (THOMAS). Staffordshire portrait figures of the Victorian age. 1958. Suppl. 1963.

See also Reginald George Haggar, *Staffordshire chimney ornaments*, 1955, and *English pottery figures, 1660–1860*, 1947, and Sir Herbert Edward Read, *Staffordshire pottery figures* [to 1850], 1929.

5340  CLARKE (HAROLD GEORGE). Under-glaze colour picture prints on Staffordshire pottery (the centenary pot lid book): an account of their origin and a descriptive catalogue . . . 1949.

Good. Clarke also publ. a companion vol. [*The pictorial pot-lid book*], 1955. For parallel developments see William Turner, *Transfer printing on enamels, porcelain and pottery*, 1907.

5341  GODDEN (GEOFFREY ARTHUR). Encyclopaedia of British pottery and porcelain marks. Lond. & N.Y. 1964.

5342  NEWCOMB (REXFORD). Ceramic whitewares: history, technology and applications. N.Y. 1947.

5343  TARIFF COMMISSION. Report of the tariff commission. Vol. 5: The pottery industries. 1907.

5344  THISTLETHWAITE (FRANK). 'The Atlantic migration of the pottery industry'. *Econ. Hist. Rev.* 2 ser. xi (1958), 264–78.

5345  RHEAD (GEORGE WOOLISCROFT) *and* RHEAD (FREDERICK ALFRED). Staffordshire pots & potters. 1906.

5346  GRAHAM (MALCOLM). Cup and saucer land: being a simple descriptive account of the present-day methods of earthenware production . . . [1908.]

5347  BARTON (RITA MARGARET). A history of the Cornish china-clay industry. Truro. [1966.]

5348  DOULTON. Sir Henry Doulton: the man of business as a man of imagination. By Sir Edmund William Gosse. Ed. by Desmond Eyles. 1970.

See also Desmond Eyles, *Royal Doulton, 1815–1965: the rise and expansion of the Royal Doulton potteries*, 1965, which is a substantial study.

5349  TAYLOR. Howson Taylor, master potter: a memoir, with appreciation of Ruskin pottery. By L. B. Powell. Birmingham. 1936.

5350  BEARD (CHARLES RELLY). A catalogue of the collection of Martin-ware formed by Mr. Frederick John Nettlefold: together with a short history of the firm of R. W. Martin and Brothers of Southall. Priv. pr. 1936.

5351　KELLY (ALISON). The story of Wedgwood. Rev. edn. 1962.

A brief intro. Little on the period. Nor is there much in William Bowyer Honey, *Wedgwood ware*, 1948, or Wedgwood Soc., *Proceedings*, 1956+.

5352　HOBSON (ROBERT LOCKHART). Worcester porcelain: a description of the ware from the Wall period to the present day. 1910.

For other factories see Arthur Hayden, *Spode & his successors . . ., 1765–1865*, 1925, and Richard William Binns, *Worcester china: a record of the work of forty-five years, 1852–1897*, ed. by Charles Fergus Binns, 1897. The other firm hists. are thin: Franklin Allen Barrett, *Caughley and Coalport porcelain*, Leigh-on-Sea 1951; Sir Edward Montague Compton Mackenzie, *The house of Coalport, 1750–1950* [1951]; Frank Brayshaw Gilhespy, *Crown Derby porcelain*, 1951; and Abraham Lomax, *Royal Lancastrian pottery, 1900–1938 . . .*, Bolton 1957.

### (c) *Glass*

5353　DUNCAN (GEORGE SANG) *comp*. Bibliography of glass: from the earliest records to 1940. Ed. by Violet Dimbleby. Soc. of Glass Technology. [1960.]

Comprehensive and well-organized. The Patent Office issued *Abridgments of specifications: class 56. Glass*, for 1855–1930.

5354　SOCIETY OF GLASS TECHNOLOGY. Journal. 1+. Sheffield. 1917+.

Includes hist. articles.

5355　POWELL (HARRY JAMES). Glass-making in England. Camb. 1923.

The best short account of the post-1870 industry is by Theodore Cardwell Barker in Aldcroft, *The development of British industry* (**4752**). See also William Ernest Stephen Turner, 'The British glass industry: its development and its outlook', *Soc. of Glass Technology J.* vi (1922), pt. 2, 108–46; Edward Meigh, *The development of the automatic glass bottle machine*, repr. from *Glass technology*, 1960; W. E. S. Turner, 'The early development of bottling machines in Europe', *Soc. Glass Technology J.* xxii (1938), pt. 2, 250–8; and R. S. Biram, 'The introduction of the Owens machine into Europe', *Soc. Glass Technology J.* xlii (1958), 19–45N.

5356　TARIFF COMMISSION. Report of the tariff commission. Vol. 6: The glass industry. 1907.

5357　GUTTERY (DAVID REGINALD). From broad-glass to cut crystal: a history of the Stourbridge glass industry. 1956.

Useful. See also John Northwood the younger, *John Northwood: his contribution to the Stourbridge flint-glass industry, 1850–1902*, Stourbridge 1958.

5358　BARKER (THEODORE CARDWELL). Pilkington Brothers and the glass industry. 1960.

One of the best business hists. See also James Frederick Chance, *A history of the firm of Chance Brothers and Co., glass & alkali manufacturers*, priv. pr. 1919.

5359　WAKEFIELD (HUGH GEORGE). Nineteenth-century British glass. 1961.

See also Geoffrey William Beard, *Nineteenth-century cameo glass*, Newport, Mon. 1956; E. M. Elville, *English and Irish cut glass, 1750–1950*, 1953, and *English table-glass*, 1951; Lionel Milner Angus-Butterworth, *British table and ornamental glass*, 1956; and William Bowyer Honey, *Glass* . . ., Victoria and Albert Museum 1946. For the early 20th cent. there is Ada Buch Polak, *Modern glass*, 1962, and Charles Guillaume Janneau, *Modern glass*, trans. by John Arnold Fleming, 1931.

**5360  WOODFORDE (CHRISTOPHER). English stained and painted glass. Oxf. 1954.**

See also Sir Herbert Edward Read, *English stained glass*, 1926, John Baker, *English stained glass* [1960], and Edward Liddall Armitage, *Stained glass: history, technology and practice*, 1959. The ideas of Charles Winston, whose *Memoirs illustrative of the art of glass-painting* . . ., 1865, appeared during the period, are reflected in the early-20th-cent. practice described in Ernest W. Twining, *The art and craft of stained glass*, 1928. The main periodical is British Soc. of Master Glass Painters, *Journal*, Exeter 1924+. See also **9232**.

## 8. COMMUNICATIONS INDUSTRIES

### (a) *Publishing and the Press*

#### (i) *General*

**5361  GLAISTER (GEOFFREY ASHALL). Glossary of the book: terms used in paper-making, printing, bookbinding and publishing . . . Lond. 1960. U.S. edn. entitled An encyclopedia of the book. Cleveland & N.Y. 1960.**

Includes a bibliog.

**5362  ALTICK (RICHARD DANIEL). The English common reader: a social history of the mass reading public, 1800–1900. Chicago. 1957.**

Useful for circulation figures. See also Guinevere L. Griest, *Mudie's circulating library and the Victorian novel*, Bloomington, Ind. 1970, Newton Abbot 1971.

**5363  MYERS (ROBIN). The British book trade from Caxton to the present day: a bibliographical guide based on the libraries of the National Book League and the St. Bride Institute. 1973.**

**5364  INNIS (HAROLD ADAMS). 'The English press in the nineteenth century: an economic approach'. *Univ. Toronto Q.* xv (1945–6), 37–53.**

With his 'The newspaper in economic development', *J. Econ. Hist.* ii (1942), suppl. 1–33, forms a valuable study of the economic background of British newspapers and magazines.

#### (ii) *Newspapers*

There is a full bibliog. in the *New Cambridge Bibliog. of English Literature* (**11**), vol. III. For lists see also **57–9**.

**5365  PEET (HUBERT W.). 'A bibliography of journalism'. Sell's world's press guide. 1915. Repr. 1915.**

Useful for the period. Other bibliogs. such as Carl Leslie Cannon, *Journalism: a bibliography*, N.Y. Public Libr. 1924, and Warren C. Price, *The literature of journalism: an annotated bibliography*, Minneapolis 1959, add little.

**5366  HERD (HAROLD).** The march of journalism: the story of the British press from 1622 to the present day. 1952.

The best outline hist. But see also [Edward] Francis Williams, Baron Francis Williams, *The right to know: the rise of the world press*, 1969. Fox Bourne, Grant, and Symon (**5367, 5369**) together give a more detailed account. For personalities see Thomas Hay Sweet Escott, *Masters of English journalism: a study of personal forces*, 1911.

**5367  BOURNE (HENRY RICHARD FOX).** English newspapers: chapters in the history of journalism. 2 v. 1887.

Still the standard hist. for its period. But should be used in conjunction with James Grant, *The newspaper press . . .*, 3 v. 1871–2, of which v. 3 deals with the English press c. 1870. Alexander Andrews, *History of British journalism from the foundation of the newspaper press in England, to the repeal of the Stamp Act in 1855*, 2 v. 1859, is of little value for the 1850s. Working-class papers are covered in Stephen Coltham, 'English working-class newspapers in 1867', *Victorian Studs.* xiii (1969–70), 159–80.

**5368  HATTON (JOSEPH).** Journalistic London . . . 1882.

A popular guide. Cp. Henry William Massingham, *The London daily press . . .*, 1892.

**5369  SYMON (JAMES DAVID).** The press and its story: an account of the birth and development of journalism up to the present day, with the history of all the leading newspapers . . . 1914.

The fullest English account of newspapers just before World War I. There is some (but not much) suppl. material in Sir Alfred Farthing Robbins, *The press* [1928]; William Ewert Berry, Viscount Camrose, *British newspapers and their controllers*, 1947; Kennedy Jones, *Fleet Street & Downing Street* [1920]; Rolfe Arnold Scott-James, *The influence of the press*, 1913; and Lucy Maynard Salmon, *The newspaper and authority*, N.Y. 1923.

**5370  GRÜNBECK (MAX).** Die Presse Grossbritanniens: ihr geistiger und wirtschaftlicher Aufbau. 2 v. Leipzig. 1936.

Vol. 1 covers the pre-war press. There are also two other useful foreign works, Theodor Lorenz, *Die englische Presse*, Halle 1907, and Mario Borsa, *Il giornalismo Inglese*, Milan 1910.

**5371  WADSWORTH (ALFRED POWELL).** 'Newspaper circulations, 1800–1954'. *Manch. Stat. Soc. Trans.* 1954–5.

Standard for the major papers.

**5372  COLLET (COLLET DOBSON).** History of the taxes on knowledge, their origin and repeal. 2 v. 1899. Abridged edn. 1933.

A hist. of the newspaper taxes.

**5373  MORISON (STANLEY).** The English newspaper: some account of the physical development of journals printed in London between 1622 & the present day. Sanders Lectures for 1931–32. Camb. 1932.

Ellic Howe, *Newspaper printing in the nineteenth century*, 1943, is an invaluable survey of its period in less than 50 pp.

**5374 DIBBLEE (GEORGE BINNEY). The newspaper. 1913.**

The fullest account of newspaper production. publ. before 1914. An earlier work, H. Yeo, *Newspaper management*, Manch. 1891, is a brief manual of costs and organization. The principal j. of newspaper management was *The newspaper owner and manager*, 1898+, styled *Master printer*, 1903–5, *The newspaper owner*, 1905–13, *The newspaper world*, 1913+, which is a useful quarry for newspaper hist.

**5375 WHORLOW (H.). The Provincial Newspaper Society, 1836–1886: a jubilee retrospect. 1886.**

Useful for provincial newspaper management. For newspaper co-operation see also George Scott, *Reporter anonymous: the story of the Press Association* [1968], and Thomas H. Hardman, *A parliament of the press: the first Imperial Press Conference*, 1909.

**5376 STOREY (GRAHAM). Reuters' century, 1851–1951. 1951.**

A hist. of the famous news agency. See also Sir Roderick Jones, *A life in Reuters*, 1951, and Henry Michael Collins, *From pigeon post to wireless*, 1925.

**5377 DAWSON (JOHN). Practical journalism: how to enter thereon and succeed: a manual for beginners and amateurs. [1885.] 2nd edn. 1904.**

Comparable manuals are Thomas Allen Reed, *The reporter's guide*, 1869, 3rd edn. 1892; John Beveridge Mackie, *Modern journalism: a handbook of instruction and counsel for the young journalist*, 1894; Ernest Phillips, *How to become a journalist: a practical guide to newspaper work* [1895]; Enoch Arnold Bennett, *Journalism for women: a practical guide*, 1898; and J. Henry Harris, *The young journalist: his work and how to learn it*, 1902. Arthur Lawrence, *Journalism as a profession*, 'The start in life series', 1903, with a chapter by Northcliffe, reflects the rising status of journalists. The principal journalists' papers and guides were *London, provincial and colonial press news*, 1866–1912, *Sell's dictionary of the world press* [*Sell's world press*], 1881/2–1921, and *The journalist*, 1886–1909.

**5378 DAILY MAIL. The mystery of the *Daily Mail*, 1896–1921. By Frederick Arthur Mackenzie. 1921.**

Only a sketch: there is no adequate hist.

**5379 DAILY NEWS. The *Daily News* jubilee: a political and social retrospect of fifty years of the Queen's reign. By Justin McCarthy and Sir John Richard Robinson. 1896.**

See also **5453**.

**5380 DAILY TELEGRAPH. Peterborough Court: the story of the *Daily Telegraph*. By Edward Frederick Lawson, Baron Burnham. 1955.**

**5381 LONDON GAZETTE. A history of the *London Gazette*, 1665–1965. By Phyllis Margaret Handover. 1965.**

**5382 MORNING POST. The *Morning Post*, 1772–1937: portrait of a newspaper. By Wilfrid Hindle. [1937.]**

For 1853–1908 the main source is Reginald Jaffray Lucas, *Lord Glenesk and the Morning Post*, 1910.

**5383 THE OBSERVER. The *Observer* and J. L. Garvin, 1908–1914. A study in a great editorship. By Alfred Manuel Gollin. 1960.**

5384  PALL MALL GAZETTE. The story of the *Pall Mall Gazette*, of its first editor, Frederick Greenwood, and of its founder, George Murray Smith. By John William Robertson Scott. 1950.

Suppl. by Robertson Scott's *The life and death of a newspaper* . . ., 1952, '*We*' *and Me: memories of four eminent editors* . . ., 1956, and *The day before yesterday* . . ., 1951, all ranging well beyond the *P.M.G.* in a gossipy way.

5385  THE TIMES. The history of *The Times*. [By Stanley Morison.] 5 v. 1935–52.

By far the best newspaper hist. A supplementary volume is *Printing* The Times, *since* . . . *1785*, 1953. William Dodgson Bowman, *The story of* The Times, 1931, is now out of date. For collections of *The Times* articles consult the index.

5386  BIRMINGHAM POST. The *Birmingham Post*, 1857–1957: a centenary retrospect. By Harold Richard Grant Whates. Birmingham. 1957.

5387  MANCHESTER GUARDIAN. *Guardian*: biography of a newspaper. By David Ayerst. 1971.

Replaced William Haslam Mills, *The* Manchester Guardian: *a century of history*, 1921. See also **5456**.

5388  SHEFFIELD DAILY TELEGRAPH. Reminiscences in the career of a newspaper: starting a 'daily' in the provinces. By William Shepherdson. 1876.

5389  WESTERN TIMES. The Cobbett of the West: a study of Thomas Latimer and the struggle between pulpit and press at Exeter. By Richard Stanton Lambert. 1939.

5390  YORKSHIRE POST. The *Yorkshire Post*: two centuries. By Mildred Ann Gibb and Frank Beckwith. Leeds. 1954.

(iii) *Periodicals*

For lists and indexes see **51–6**.

5391  ELLEGÅRD (ALVAR). The readership of the periodical press in mid-Victorian Britain. Göteborgs Universitets Årsskrift lxiii (1957), pt. 3.

5392  WHITE (CYNTHIA LESLIE). Women's magazines, 1693–1968. 1970.

5393  ACADEMY. The *Academy*, 1869–1879: Victorian intellectuals in revolt. By Diderik Roll-Hansen. *Anglistica* viii. Copenhagen. 1957.

5394  ATHENAEUM. The *Athenaeum*: a mirror of Victorian culture. By Leslie Alexis Marchand. Chapel Hill, N.C. 1941.

See also **5485**.

5395  ECONOMIST. The *Economist*, 1843–1943. A centenary volume. 1943.

5396  THE FIELD. *The Field*, 1853–1953: a centenary volume. By Robert Norman Rose. 1953.

5397 FORTNIGHTLY REVIEW. The party of humanity: the *Fortnightly Review* and its contributors, 1865–1874. By Edwin Mallard Everett. Chapel Hill, N.C. 1939.

5398 FRASER'S MAGAZINE. Rebellious Fraser's: Nol Yorke's magazine in the days of Maginn, Thackeray and Carlyle. By Miriam Mulford Hunt Thrall. N.Y. 1934.

5399 JEWISH CHRONICLE. The *Jewish Chronicle*, 1841–1941: a century of newspaper history. *Jewish Chronicle*. 1949.

5400 NEW STATESMAN. The *New Statesman*: the history of the first fifty years, 1913–1963. By Edward Solomon Hyams. 1963.

5401 PUNCH. A history of *Punch*. By Richard Geoffrey George Price. 1957.
For Victorian *Punch* it is still necessary to consult Marion Harry Spielmann, *The history of* Punch, 1895. The writers for *Punch* formed a distinct group. The best lives are Joseph Hatton, *With a show in the north: reminiscences of Mark Lemon*, 1871; George Somes Layard, *A great* Punch *editor: being, the life, letters and diaries of Shirley Brooks*, 1907; Sir Francis Cowley Burnand, *Records and reminiscences, personal and general*, 2 v., 1903, abridged edn. 1917; Arthur William à Beckett, *Green room recollections*, [Bristol] 1896, *The à Becketts of* Punch . . ., 1903, and *Recollections of a humorist . . .*, 1907; and Walter Copeland Jerrold, *Douglas Jerrold and* Punch, 1910.

5402 SATURDAY REVIEW. The *Saturday Review*, 1855–1868: representative educated opinion in Victorian England. By Merle Mowbray Bevington. Columbia Univ. Studs. in English and Comparative Lit. 154. N.Y. 1941.
James Grant, *The* Saturday Review: *its origin and progress . . .*, 1873, is an attack on its methods.

5403 SPECTATOR. The story of the *Spectator*, 1828–1928. By Sir William Beach Thomas. 1928.

5404 SPORTING TIMES. Old 'Pink 'Un' days. By John Bennion Booth. 1924.
The first of three vols., of which the others are *A 'Pink 'Un' remembers*, 1937, and *Sporting times: the 'Pink 'Un' world*, 1938.

5405 STRAND. The *Strand* magazine, 1891–1950. By Reginald Pound. Lond. 1966. U.S. edn. entitled Mirror of the century. Cranbury, N.J. 1967.

5406 YELLOW BOOK. A study in yellow: the *Yellow Book* and its contributors. By Katherine Lyon Mix. Lawrence, Kansas, & London. 1960.
Deals also with the *Savoy*.

(iv) *Biographies of Journalists, Editors, and Proprietors*

Most of the works listed are informative about social hist. generally as well as about the press.

5407   ADAMS. Memoirs of a social atom. By William Edwin Adams. 2 v. 1903.
Ed. *Newcastle Weekly Chronicle.*

5408   ANNAND. From smithy to senate: the life story of James Annand, journalist and politician. By George B. Hodgson. 1909.
Ed. *Newcastle Chronicle, Shields Daily Chronicle,* and *Leader.*

5409   ARMSTRONG. Memories of George Gilbert Armstrong, journalist politician, author, preacher. 1944.
Useful recollections of provincial papers and provincial Nonconformity.

5410   ARNOLD. William Thomas Arnold, journalist and historian. By Mary Augusta Ward [Mrs. Humphry Ward] and Charles Edward Montague. Manch. 1907.
Wrote for *Manchester Guardian.*

5411   BEAUMONT. A rebel in Fleet Street. By William Comyns Beaumont. [1944.]
Ed. *Bystander, Graphic,* and *London Magazine.*

5412   BENTLEY. Those days. By Edmund Clerihew Bentley. 1940.
Writer for *Daily News* and *Daily Telegraph.*

5413   BLANCHARD. The life and reminiscences of E. L. Blanchard: with notes from the diary of William Blanchard. Ed. by Clement William Scott and Cecil Howard. 2 v. 1891.
Ed. *New London Magazine.*

5414   BLOWITZ. My memoirs. By Henri Georges Stéphane Adolphe Opper de Blowitz. 1903.
Paris correspondent of *The Times.* See also Frank Giles, *A prince of journalists: the life and times of Henri Stefan Opper de Blowitz,* 1962.

5415   BOON. Victorians, Edwardians and Georgians: the impressions of a veteran journalist extending over forty years. By John Boon. 2 v. 1928.
Lobby correspondent of Exchange Telegraph.

5416   BOYD. A pelican's tale: fifty years of London and elsewhere. By Frank Mortimer Boyd. 1919.
Proprietor and editor of *The Pelican.* Boyd also ed. *Some pelican tails: true more or less,* 1901.

5417   CATLING. My life's pilgrimage. By Thomas Thurgood Catling. 1911.
Staff of *Lloyd's News.*

5418   CLARKE. William Clarke: a collection of his writings, with a biographical sketch. Ed. by Herbert Burrows and John Atkinson Hobson. 1908.
Liberal writer for the *Daily Chronicle,* etc.

**5419  COOK.** Sir Edward Cook, K.B.E.: a biography. By John Saxon Mills. 1921.

Ed. *Pall Mall Gazette, Westminster Gazette, Daily News.*

**5420  COURTNEY.** The making of an editor: W. L. Courtney, 1850–1928. By Janet Elizabeth Courtney. 1930.

Ed. *Fortnightly Review.*

**5421  CROSLAND.** The life and genius of T. W. H. Crosland. By William Sorley Brown. 1928.

Ed. *English Review.*

**5422  DELANE.** John Thaddeus Delane, editor of *The Times*: his life and correspondence. By Arthur Irwin Dasent. 2 v. 1908.

See also Sir Edward Tyas Cook, *Delane of* The Times, 1915.

**5423  DONALD.** Robert Donald: being the authorized biography of Sir Robert Donald, G.B.E., LL.D., journalist, editor and friend of statesmen. By Henry Archibald Taylor. [1934.]

Ed. *Daily Chronicle.*

**5424  EDWARDS.** Personal recollections. By Henry Sutherland Edwards. 1900.

First ed. of *The Graphic*, and writer on music.

**5425  ELIAS.** Viscount Southwood. By Rubeigh James Minney. 1954.

Established Odham's Press, which printed *John Bull, The People*, etc.

**5426  FYFE.** Sixty years of Fleet Street. By Henry Hamilton Fyfe. 1949.

Fyfe also publ. *My seven selves*, 1935. Wrote for *The Times, Daily Mail*, etc. Ed. *Morning Advertiser, Daily Mirror, Daily Herald.*

**5427  GARRETT.** Edmund Garrett: a memoir. By Sir Edward Tyas Cook. 1909.

Staff of *Pall Mall Gazette.*

**5428  GARVIN.** J. L. Garvin: a memoir. By Katharine Garvin. 1948.

Ed. *The Observer*, 1908–42. A quite inadequate life. But see also Gollin (**5383**).

**5429  GIBBS.** The pageant of the years: an autobiography. By Sir Philip Hamilton Gibbs. 1946.

Gibbs also publ. *Adventures in journalism*, 1923, *Crowded company*, 1949, and *Life's adventure*, 1957. Lit. ed. of *Daily Mail*, etc.

**5430  HAMMERTON.** Books and myself: memoirs of an editor. By Sir John Alexander Hammerton. [1944.]

Ed. provincial papers, *London Magazine*, publishers' series.

5431 HARRIS. Frank Harris. By Hugh Kingsmill [Lunn]. [1932.]

Ed. *Saturday Review*. See also Vincent Brome, *Frank Harris*, 1959; Samuel Roth, *The private life of Frank Harris*, 1931; Edward Merrill Root, *Frank Harris*, 1947; Harris's own *My life and loves*, ed. by John F. Gallagher, N.Y. 1963; Robert Harborough Sherard, *Bernard Shaw, Frank Harris & Oscar Wilde*, N.Y. 1937; and Kate Stephens, *Lies and libels of Frank Harris*, ed. by Gerrit and Mary Caldwell Smith, N.Y. 1929.

5432 HAYWARD. A selection from the correspondence of Abraham Hayward, Q.C., from 1834 to 1884, with an account of his early life. By Henry E. Carlisle. 2 v. 1886.

An influential figure who contrib. much to the periodical press, and enjoyed the friendship of many statesmen.

5433 HEALY. Confessions of a journalist. By Christopher Healy. 1904.

5434 HIGGINBOTTOM. The vivid life: a journalist's career. By Frederick James Higginbottom. 1934.

Strongest on Ireland in the 1880s. Ed. *Pall Mall Gazette*, 1900–12.

5435 HIGGINS. 'Jacob Omnium': essays on social subjects [by Matthew James Higgins], with a memoir by Sir William Stirling Maxwell. 1875.

5436 HUGHES. Press, platform and parliament. By Spencer Leigh Hughes ['Sub Rosa']. 1918.

Parl. correspondent of the *Morning Leader*.

5437 HUTCHEON. Gentleman of the press: memories and friendships of forty years. By William Hutcheon. 1933.

Staff of *Morning Post*.

5438 HUTTON. Richard Holt Hutton of the *Spectator*: a monograph. By John Hogben. Edin. 1899. 2nd edn. 1900.

5439 LUCAS. Reading, writing and remembering. By Edward Verrall Lucas. 1932.

Staff of *Globe, Academy, Punch*.

5440 LUCY. Sixty years in the wilderness: some passages by the way. By Sir Henry William Lucy. 1909.

Cont. in *Sixty years in the wilderness: more passages by the way*, 1912, *Nearing Jordan*, 1916, *The diary of a journalist*, 1920, and *The diary of a journalist: later entries*, 1922. Lucy was primarily a parl. reporter. See also **482**.

5441 MACKAY. Bohemian days in Fleet Street. [By William Mackay.] 1913.

One of the best vols. of general reminiscences.

5442 MASSINGHAM. Remembrance: an autobiography. By Harold John Massingham. [1941.]

Staff of *Morning Leader*, National Press Agency, *Athenaeum*.

5443   MILNE. A window in Fleet Street. By James Milne. 1931.
Lit. ed. *Daily Chronicle.*

5444   MONTAGUE. C. E. Montague: a memoir. By Oliver Elton. 1929.
Staff of *Manchester Guardian.*

5445   MURRAY. Recollections. By David Christie Murray. 1908.
Staff various papers and *Daily News.*

5446   NEVINSON. Fire of life. By Henry Woodd Nevinson. 1935.
The best of Nevinson's many vols. of reminiscences, being an abbrev. version of *Changes and chances,* 1923, *More changes, more chances,* 1925, and *Last changes, last chances,* 1928. Staff of *Daily Chronicle, The Nation,* etc.

5447   NORTHCLIFFE. Northcliffe. By Reginald Pound and [Arthur] Geoffrey [Annesley] Harmsworth. 1959.
The best life. Lists the many other lives, of which Henry Hamilton Fyfe, *Northcliffe: an intimate biography,* 1930, and Tom Clarke, *My Northcliffe diary,* 1931, and *Northcliffe in history . . .,* 1950, are particularly useful.

5448   O'SHEA. Leaves from the life of a special correspondent. By John Augustus O'Shea. 2 v. 1885.
Staff of *The Standard.*

5449   PARKER. Memory looks forward: an autobiography. By Eric Parker. [1937.]
Ed. *Country gentleman, Shooting, The Field.*

5450   PEARSON. The life of Sir Arthur Pearson. By Sidney Dark. 1922.
Founded *Pearson's Weekly, Daily Express,* etc.

5451   REID. Memoirs of Sir Wemyss Reid, 1842–1885. Ed. by Stuart Johnson Reid. 1905.
Ed. *Leeds Mercury, The Speaker.*

5452   RICHARDSON. From the City to Fleet Street: some journalistic experiences. By Joseph Hall Richardson. 1927.

5453   ROBINSON. Fifty years of Fleet Street: being the life and recollections of Sir John R. Robinson. Ed. by Frederick Moy Thomas. 1904.
Manager *Daily News.*

5454   RUSSELL. That reminds me—. By Edward Richard Russell, Baron Russell of Liverpool. 1899.
Ed. *Liverpool Daily Post.*

5455   SALA. The life and adventures of George Augustus Sala: written by himself. 2 v. 1895. 3rd edn. 2 v. 1895. Popular edn. 1896.

Sala also publ. *Things I have seen and people I have known*, 2 v. 1894. See also Ralph Straus, *Sala: the portrait of an eminent Victorian*, 1942. Contrib. to many papers 1848–94: on the staff of *Daily Telegraph*, 1857+.

5456   SCOTT. C. P. Scott of the *Manchester Guardian*. By John Lawrence Le Breton Hammond. 1934.

See also *C. P. Scott, 1846–1932: the making of the 'Manchester Guardian'*, Manch. 1946, and Scott's diaries (309).

5457   SPENDER. The fire of life: a book of memories. By Edward Harold Spender. [1926.]

5458   SPENDER. Life, journalism and politics. By John Alfred Spender. 2 v. 1927.

See also Henry Wilson Harris, *J. A. Spender . . .*, 1945. Ed. *Westminster Gazette*.

5459   STEAD. The life of William Thomas Stead. By Frederic Whyte. 2 v. 1925.

Estelle Wilson Stead, *My father . . .*, 1913, and Edith Katherine Harper, *Stead the man . . .*, 1914, are strongest on his spiritualist interests. Ed. *Northern Echo, Pall Mall Gazette, Review of Reviews*.

5460   STEED. Through thirty years, 1892–1922: a personal narrative. By Henry Wickham Steed. 2 v. 1924.

Staff of *The Times* 1896–1922, editor, 1919–22.

5461   STRACHEY. St. Loe Strachey: his life and his paper. By Amy Strachey. 1930.

[John] St. Loe Strachey himself publ. *The adventure of living: a subjective autobiography*, 1922, and *River of life*, 1924. Ed. *Cornhill Magazine, Spectator*.

5462   THOMAS. A traveller in news. By Sir William Beach Thomas. 1925.

Thomas also publ. *The way of a countryman*, 1944.

5463   WATSON. A newspaperman's memories. By Aaron Watson. [1925.]

Ed. *Echo, Shields Daily Gazette, Newcastle Leader*.

5464   WHYTE. A bachelor's London: memories of the day before yesterday, 1889–1914. By Frederic Whyte. 1931.

Publisher's reader and journalist.

5465   YATES. Edmund Yates: his recollections and experiences. 1884.

Ed. *Temple Bar*, founded *The World*.

### (v) *Publishers*

5466   BARNES (JAMES JOHN). Free trade in books: a study of the London book trade since 1800. Oxf. 1964.

See also Marjorie Plant, *The English book trade: an economic history of the making and sale of books*, 1939, 2nd edn. 1965.

5467 NOWELL-SMITH (SIMON HARCOURT). International copyright law and the publisher in the reign of Queen Victoria. Oxf. 1968.

5468 KINGSFORD (REGINALD JOHN LETHBRIDGE). The Publishers' Association, 1896–1946. Camb. 1970.

5469 BATSFORD. A Batsford century: the record of a hundred years of publishing and bookselling, 1843–1943. Ed. by Henry Hector Bolitho. 1943.

See also William Hanneford-Smith, *Recollections of a half-century's association with the house of Batsford, 1893–1943*, 1943.

5470 BEETON. Mrs. Beeton and her husband. By Nancy Brooker Spain. 1948. 3rd edn. [The Beeton story.] 1956.

See also Harford Montgomery Hyde, *Mr. and Mrs. Beeton*, 1951.

5471 BELL. George Bell, publisher: a brief memoir. By Edward Bell. Priv. pr. 1924.

5472 BENTLEY. A Victorian publisher: a study of the Bentley papers. By Royal Alfred Gettmann. Camb. 1960.

5473 BLACK. Adam & Charles Black, 1807–1957: some chapters in the history of a publishing house. 1957.

5474 BLACKIE. Blackie & Son, 1809–1959: a short history of the firm. By Agnes Anna Coventry Blackie. Edin. 1959.

5475 BLACKWOOD. The house of Blackwood, 1804–1954: the history of a publishing firm. By Frank D. Tredrey. Edin. 1954.

Largely based on Margaret Oliphant Oliphant and Mary Porter, *Annals of a publishing house*: vols. 1–2, *William Blackwood and his sons, their magazine and friends*, vol. 3, *John Blackwood*, 3 v., Edin. 1897–8. There is a catalogue of the papers of the firm publ. by the Nat. Libr. of Scotland.

5476 BODLEY HEAD. The early nineties: a view from the Bodley Head. By James G. Nelson. Camb., Mass. 1971.

5477 BURNS, OATES. The house of Burns and Oates. By Wilfred Wilberforce. [1908.]

5478 CAMBRIDGE UNIVERSITY PRESS. A history of the Cambridge University Press, 1521–1921. By Sir Sydney Castle Roberts. Camb. 1921.

See also Roberts's *The evolution of Cambridge publishing*, Camb. 1956.

5479 CASSELL. The house of Cassell, 1848–1958. By Simon Harcourt Nowell-Smith. 1958.

See also Godfrey Holden Pike, *John Cassell*, 1894.

5480 CHAMBERS. Story of a long and busy life. By William Chambers. Edin. 1882. 13th edn. Edin. 1884.

5481 CHAPMAN AND HALL. A hundred years of publishing: being the story of Chapman & Hall Ltd., 1830–1930. By Arthur Waugh. 1930.

See also Arthur Waugh, *One man's road* . . ., 1931.

5482 CHATTO AND WINDUS. A century of writers, 1855–1955: a centenary volume. Ed. by David Morrice Low and others. 1955.

5483 COLLINS. The house of Collins: the story of a Scottish family of publishers from 1789 to the present day. By David Edwin Keir. 1952.

5484 DENT. The house of Dent, 1888–1938. Being the memoirs of J[oseph] M[alaby] Dent. [1921.] New edn. with additional chapters . . . by Hugh Railton Dent. 1938.

5485 FRANCIS. John Francis, publisher of the *Athenaeum*: a literary chronicle of half a century. By John Collins Francis. 2 v. 1888.

5486 GRIFFIN. The centenary volume of Charles Griffin and Co., 1820–1920. 1920.

5487 HATCHARD. Piccadilly bookmen: memorials of the house of Hatchard. By Arthur Lee Humphreys. 1893.

5488 HEINEMANN. William Heinemann: a memoir. By Frederic Whyte. 1928.

5489 JARROLDS. The house of Jarrolds, 1823–1923, established 1770: a brief history of 100 years. 1924.

5490 KEGAN PAUL. Memories. By Charles Kegan Paul. 1899.

See also 5502.

5491 KNIGHT. Passages of a working life during half a century: with a prelude of early reminiscences. By Charles Knight. 3 v. 1864–5. Abridged edn. N.Y. 1874.

See also Alice Ada Clowes, *Charles Knight: a sketch, by his granddaughter*, 1892.

5492 LANE. John Lane and the nineties. By James Lewis May. 1936.

5493 LONGMANS. The house of Longman, 1724–1924. By Harold Cox and John E. Chandler. Priv. pr. 1925.

5494 MACMILLAN. The house of Macmillan, 1843–1943. By Charles Langbridge Morgan. 1943.

See also Simon Harcourt Nowell-Smith, ed., *Letters to Macmillan*, 1967, Thomas Hughes, *Memoir of Daniel Macmillan*, 1882, 2nd edn., 1883, and Charles Larcom Graves, *Life and letters of Alexander Macmillan*, 1910.

5495 MARSTON. After work: fragments from the workshop of an old publisher. By Edward Marston. 1904.

5496  MURRAY. At John Murray's: records of a literary circle, 1843–1892. By George Paston [pseud. of Emily Morse Symonds]. 1932.

See also Sir John Murray IV, *John Murray III, 1808–1892: a brief memoir*, 1919.

5497  NEWNES. The life of Sir George Newnes, Bart. By Hulda Friederichs. [1911.]

5498  OXFORD UNIVERSITY PRESS. There is no adequate hist.

5499  PITMAN. The life of Sir Isaac Pitman, inventor of phonography. By Alfred Baker. 1908. 2nd edn. 1930.

See also Pitman's own *The life and work of Sir Isaac Pitman*, 1894, David Abercrombie, *Isaac Pitman* . . ., 1937, and Alfred Pitman, *Half a century of commercial education and publishing*, priv. pr. Bath 1932.

5500  RICHARDS. Memories of a misspent youth, 1872–1896. By Franklin Thomas Grant Richards. 1932.

Cont. in *Author hunting* . . ., 1934. New edn. 1960.

5501  RIVINGTON. The publishing house of Rivington. By Septimus Rivington. 1894.

See also his *The publishing family of Rivington*, 1919, and Sir Charles John Holmes, *Self and partners: mostly self* . . ., 1936.

5502  ROUTLEDGE. The house of Routledge, 1834–1934; with a history of Kegan Paul, Trench, Trübner and other associate firms. By Frank Arthur Mumby. 1934.

See also **5490**.

5503  SHAYLOR. Sixty years a bookman: with other recollections and reflections. By Joseph Shaylor. 1923.

5504  SMITH, ELDER. The house of Smith, Elder. By Leonard Huxley. Priv. pr. 1923.

5505  SWAN SONNENSCHEIN. From Swan Sonnenschein to George Allen & Unwin Ltd. . . . By Frank Arthur Mumby and Frances Helena Swan Stallybrass. 1955.

5506  TINSLEY. Random recollections of an old publisher. By William Tinsley. 2 v. 1900.

See also Edmund Downey, *Twenty years ago* . . ., 1905.

5507  VIZETELLY. Glances back through seventy years: autobiographical and other reminiscences. By Henry Vizetelly. 1893.

5508  WARD, LOCK. Adventure in publishing: the house of Ward, Lock, 1851–1954. By Edward George Downing Liveing. 1954.

5509  WARNE. The house of Warne: one hundred years of publishing. By Arthur King and Albert Frederick Stuart. 1965.

(vi) *Printing*

There is a full bibliog. in the *New Cambridge Bibliog. of English Literature* (**II**).

5510  BIGMORE (EDWARD CLEMENTS) *and* WYMAN (CHARLES WILLIAM HENRY). A bibliography of printing with notes & illustrations. 3 v. 1880–6. Repr. N.Y. 1945.

Full. See also Horace Hart, *Bibliotheca typographica in usum eorum qui libros amant: a list of books about books*, Rochester, N.Y. 1933, and Sir Geoffrey Stewart Tomkinson, *A select bibliography of the principal modern presses, public and private, in Great Britain and Ireland*, 1928.

5511  HASLAM (GEORGE ERIC) *ed.* Manchester Public Libraries: reference library subject catalogue: section 655: printing. 2 v. in 1. Manch. 1961–3.

5512  ULRICH (CAROLYN FARQUHAR) *and* KÜP (KARL). Books and printing: a selected list of periodicals, 1800–1942. Woodstock, Vermont, & N.Y. 1943.

5513  PATENT OFFICE. Patents for inventions: abridgments of specifications relating to printing ... 1859. Suppl. [1858–61.] 1864. 2nd edn. [1858–66.] 1878. Suppl. [1867–76.] 1880. Repr. as James Harrison, ed., *Printing patent abridgments, 1617–1857*, Printing Hist. Soc. 1969.

See also the parallel vol. of *Abridgments of specifications relating to books ... 1768–1866*, 1870, cont. by *Abridgments of specifications, class 100, printing: letterpress and photographic, 1855–1930*, and *class 101, printing other than letterpress or photographic, 1855–1908*.

5514  STEINBERG (SIGFRIED HENRY). Five hundred years of printing. 1955. 2nd edn. Harmondsworth. 1961.

A handy outline hist. For the chronology of printing inventions see William Turner Berry and Herbert Edmund Poole, *Annals of printing: a chronological encyclopaedia from the earliest times to 1950*, 1966, which is fuller than Colin Clair, *A chronology of printing*, 1969. The chief hist. j. is Printing Historical Soc., *Journal*, 1965+.

5515  ROSNER (CHARLES). Printer's progress: a comparative survey of the craft of printing, 1851–1951. Lond. & Camb., Mass. 1951.

5516  TWYMAN (MICHAEL). Printing, 1770–1970: an illustrated history of its development and uses in England. 1970.

5517  CLAIR (COLIN). A history of printing in Britain. 1965.

On machinery and techniques. Earlier general hists. are all weak on the post-1851 period.

5518  HOEHNE (OTTO) *ed.* Geschichte der Setzmaschinen. Leipzig. 1925.

**5519** HANDOVER (PHYLLIS MARGARET). Printing in London from 1476 to modern times: competitive practice and technical invention in the trade of book and Bible printing, periodical production, jobbing, &c. Lond. & Camb., Mass. 1960.

On the economics of printing. For the printers themselves see **6821–9**.

**5520** ALFORD (BERNARD WILLIAM ERNEST). 'Business enterprise and the growth of the commercial letterpress industry, 1850–1914'. *Business Hist.* vii (1965), 1–14.

See also his 'Government expenditure and the growth of the printing industry in the nineteenth century' *Econ. Hist. Rev.* 2 ser. xvii (1964–5), 96–112.

**5521** JACKSON (HOLBROOK). The printing of books. 1938. 2nd edn. 1947.

Useful for late-19th-cent. printing.

**5522** McLEAN (RUARI). Victorian book design & colour printing. 1963. 2nd edn. 1972.

Good. Cont. by his *Modern book design: from William Morris to the present day*, 1958.

**5523** HARRISON (*Sir* CECIL REEVES) *and* HARRISON (HARRY GEORGE). The house of Harrison: being, an account of the family and firm of Harrison and Sons, printers to the King. 1914.

Other business hists. incl. H. J. Keefe, *A century in print: the story of Hazell's, 1839–1939*, 1939, and Lorna Houseman, *The house that Thomas built: the story of De la Rue*, 1968.

**5524** DOWDING (GEOFFREY). An introduction to the history of printing types: an illustrated summary of the main stages in the development of type design from 1440 up to the present day: an aid to type face identification. 1961.

Useful for type identification.

**5525** DAY (KENNETH). Book typography, 1815–1965: in Europe and the United States of America. Lond. & Chicago. 1966.

**5526** GRAY (NICOLETTE MARY). XIXth century ornamented types and title pages. 1938.

Fuller than Stanley Morison, *Four centuries of fine printing: upwards of six hundred examples of the work of presses established during the years 1500 to 1914*, 1924, 4th edn. 1960. See also Robert M. Burch, *Colour printing and colour printers*, 1910.

**5527** SOUTHWARD (JOHN). Progress in printing and the graphic arts during the Victorian era. 1897.

**5528** WYSE (HENRY T.). Modern type display and the use of type ornament. Edin. 1911.

**5529** LEWIS (JOHN NOEL CLAUDE). Printed ephemera: the changing uses of type and letterforms in English and American printing. Ipswich. 1962.

5530  SOUTHWARD (JOHN). Practical printing: a handbook of the art of typography. 1882. 5th edn. by A. Powell. 2 v. 1902.

Widely used. See also his *Modern printing: a handbook of the principles and practice of typography and the auxiliary arts*, 2 pts. 1898–9, 3rd edn. 2 v. 1915, 8th edn. Leicester 1954.

5531  WILSON (FREDERICK J. F.) *and* GREY (DOUGLAS). A practical treatise upon modern printing machinery and letterpress printing . . . 1888.

5532  JACOBI (CHARLES THOMAS). Printing: a practical treatise on the art of typography as applied more particularly to the printing of books. 1890. 6th edn. 1919.

See also his *The printer's handbook of trade recipes, hints & suggestions* . . ., 1887, 3rd edn. 1905, *The printer's vocabulary* . . ., 1888, and *Some notes on books and printing: a guide for authors and others*, 1892, 4th edn. 1912.

5533  THE TIMES printing number: reprinted from the 40,000th issue of *The Times*, Tuesday, September 10, 1912. 1912.

5534  THE PRINTER'S REGISTER. Gloucester etc. 1863+.

The oldest of the long-lived printing js. The others incl. *The British and colonial printer and stationer* . . . [now *Printing world*], 1878+, *The British printer*, Leicester etc. 1888+, and *The printing world*, 1891–1911.

5535  MARES (GEORGE CARL). The history of the typewriter: being an illustrated account of the origin, rise and development of the writing machine. 1909.

Good for the period. Modern hists. such as Richard Nelson Current, *The typewriter and the men who made it*, Urbana, Ill. 1954, add little.

5536  RICHARDS (GEORGE TILGHMAN). *comp.* Science Museum: handbook of the collection illustrating typewriters: a brief outline of the history and development of the correspondence typewriter . . . 1938. 2nd edn. 1964.

### (vii) *Papermaking*

For a longer list see *New Cambridge Bibliog. of English Literature* (**II**), 27–32.

5537  SURFACE (HENRY EARLE). Bibliography of the pulp and paper industries. U.S. Dept. of Agric. Forest Science Bull. 123. Wash. 1913.

See also Paper Makers' Assoc. of Great Britain, *Catalogue of the library*, 1934, Clarence Jay West, *Bibliography of pulp and paper making, 1900–1928*, Technical Assoc. of the Pulp & Paper Industry, N.Y. 1929, cont. as *Bibliography of [pulp and] paper making* . . ., N.Y. 1931–44.

5538  LABARRE (ÉMILE JOSEPH). A dictionary of paper and papermaking terms, with equivalents in French, German, Dutch and Italian: an experiment in technical lexicography with a historical study on paper and an introduction. Amsterdam. 1937.

Rev. edn. issued as *Dictionary and encyclopaedia of paper and papermaking*, Amsterdam 1952.

5539  HERRING (RICHARD). A practical guide to the varieties and relative values of paper, illustrated with samples of nearly every description and specially adapted to the use of merchants, shippers and the trade . . . 1860.

Excellent for identifying paper. See also his *Paper & paper making, ancient and modern*, 1855, 3rd edn. 1863. T. H. Saunders, *Illustrations of the British paper manufacture*, 1855, also gives samples.

5540  DIRECTORY OF PAPER MAKERS OF THE UNITED KINGDOM. 1876+.

See also *The paper mills directory*, 1860+; *The paper trade directory of Great Britain and the colonies*, 1886+; *The paper maker's monthly j.*, 1863–1932; *The paper and printing trades j.*, 1872–95; *The [world's] paper trade review*, 1879+; *Paper making and selling*, 1881+; *The papermaker and British paper trade j.*, 1891+; and *Papermaking*, 1895+.

5541  THE STATIONER'S HANDBOOK and guide to the paper trade. By a stationer. 1859. 17th edn. 1893.

See also *The stationer's and printer's annual trade book of reference*, 1895+.

5542  PATENT OFFICE. Abridgments of specifications relating to the manufacture of paper, pasteboard and papier mâché, [1665–1857]. 1858. Suppl. 1872. 2nd edn. 1876. Cont. by Abridgments of specifications, class 96. 1855–1930.

5543  HUNTER (DARD). Papermaking: the history and technique of an ancient craft. N.Y. 1943. 2nd edn. 1947.

An outline hist. of techniques.

5544  CLAPPERTON (ROBERT HENDERSON). Paper: an historical account of its making by hand from the earliest times down to the present day. Oxf. 1934.

5545  CLAPPERTON (ROBERT HENDERSON). The paper-making machine: its invention, evolution and development. Oxf. 1967.

5546  BETTENDORF (HARRY J.). Paperboard and paperboard containers: a history. Chicago. [1946.]

5547  COLEMAN (DONALD CUTHBERT). The British paper industry, 1495–1860: a study in industrial growth. Oxf. 1958.

5548  SPICER (*Sir* ALBERT DYKES). The paper trade: a descriptive and historical survey of the paper trade from the commencement of the nineteenth century. 1907.

See also the biog. of Sir Albert Spicer (**3784**). Contemp. textbooks like Robert Walter Sindall, *The manufacture of paper*, 1908, and *Paper technology* . . ., 1906, 3rd edn. 1920, and Harry Alfred Maddox, *Paper: its history, sources and manufacture*, 1916, 6th edn. 1939, are disappointingly thin.

5549  BOHN (HENRY GEORGE). The paper duty considered in reference to its action on the literature and trade of Great Britain: showing that its abolition on the terms now proposed in parliament would be prejudicial to both. 1860. 3rd edn. 1861.

See also the reply to Bohn by G. William Petter, *Some objections to the repeal of the paper duty considered* . . . [1860], Thomas Wrigley, *The case of the paper makers*, Bury [1865], and C. D. Collet, *History of the taxes on knowledge* (**5372**).

5550 SELECT COMMITTEE ON PAPER. Report from the select committee on paper (export duty on rags) [Chairman: Charles Buxton]. H.C. 467 (1861). XI, 267.

5551 ROYAL SOCIETY OF ARTS. Report of the committee on the deterioration of paper. 1898.

5552 EVANS (JOAN). The endless web: John Dickinson & Company, Ltd., 1804–1954. 1955.
An excellent business hist.

### (viii) *Bookbinding*

5553 PRIDEAUX (SARAH TREVERBIAN). A bibliography of bookbinding. 1892.
There are a few additional books in Anthony Robert Alwyn Hobson, *The literature of bookbinding*, Nat. Book League, Camb. 1954.

5554 DIEHL (EDITH). Bookbinding: its background and technique. 2 v. N.Y. 1946.
See also Douglas Leighton, *Modern bookbinding: a survey and a prospect*, 1935.

5555 SADLEIR (MICHAEL THOMAS HARVEY). The evolution of publishers' binding styles, 1770–1900. 1930.

5556 CARTER (JOHN WAYNFLETE). Binding variants in English publishing, 1820–1900. 1932.
See also his *Publishers' cloth: an outline history of publishers' binding in England, 1820–1900*, N.Y. 1935.

5557 MIDDLETON (BERNARD CHESTER). A history of English craft bookbinding technique. N.Y. & Lond. 1963.

5558 PRIDEAUX (SARAH TREVERBIAN). Modern bookbindings: their design and decoration. 1906.
See also her *Bookbinders and their craft*, 1923, Charles W. Woolnough, *The whole art of marbling as applied to book edges and paper*, 1853, 2nd edn. 1881, and Joseph William Zaehnsdorf, *The art of bookbinding*, 1880, 8th edn. 1914, and *Modern bookbindings and their designers: winter number of* The Studio, *1899–1900*, 1899.

5559 COCKERELL (DOUGLAS). Bookbinding and the care of books: a textbook for bookbinders and librarians. 1901. 5th edn. 1953.
A famous craftsman's manual.

5560 ROSNER (CHARLES). The growth of the book jacket. 1954.

5561 LORING (ROSAMOND BOWDITCH). Decorated book papers: being an account of their designs and fashions. Camb., Mass. 1942. Rev. edn. 1952.

5562 ADAMS (JOHN). The house of Kitcat: a story of bookbinding, 1789–1948. Priv. pr. 1948.

5563 DARLEY (LIONEL SEABROOK). Bookbinding then and now: a survey of the first hundred and seventy-eight years of James Burn & Company. 1959.

(b) *Postal Services*

(i) *General*

See also the lives of Henry Fawcett (**820**) and Henry Cecil Raikes (**824**), both active postmaster generals.

5564 ROBINSON (HOWARD). Britain's post office: a history of development from the beginnings to the present day. 1953.

The standard introduction to the subject. His *The British Post Office: a history*, Princeton, N.J. 1948, and Joseph Clarence Hemmeon, *The history of the British Post Office*, Camb., Mass. 1912, are fuller but have little more on the period. There are many popular hists. of which the best is Laurin Zilliacus, *Fom pillar to post: the troubled history of the mail*, 1956.

5565 THE POST OFFICE: an historical summary. Published by order of the Postmaster General. 1911.

Particularly useful for the end of the 19th cent.

5566 BENNETT (EDWARD). The Post Office and its story: an interesting account of the activities of a great government department. 1912.

A good popular account. Sir George Evelyn Pemberton Murray, *The Post Office*, Whitehall Series, 1927, gives a more official account of the department.

5567 LEWINS (WILLIAM). Her Majesty's Mails: an historical and descriptive account of the British Post Office. 1864. 2nd edn. 1865.

5568 TEGG (WILLIAM). Posts and telegraphs: past and present. 1878.

Cp. William Lynd, *The popular guide to the telegraph and postal service*, 1884.

5569 FOXELL (J. T.) *and* SPAFFORD (A. O.). Monarchs of all they surveyed: the story of the Post Office surveyors. 1952.

5570 BRUCE (*Sir* ROBERT). Postal organisation: with special reference to the London postal service. 1912.

Better than Robert Charles Tombs, *The London postal service of to-day*, 1891.

5571 TOMBS (ROBERT CHARLES). The Bristol Royal Mail: post, telegraph and telephone. Bristol. [1899.]

The only account of a provincial post office: by the Postmaster. His *The King's post* . . ., Bristol 1905, 2nd edn. 1906, also deals with the Bristol post office.

5572 SMITH (ALFRED DANIEL). The development of rates of postage: an historical and analytical study. 1917.

5573 STAFF (FRANK). The penny post, 1680–1918. 1964.

5574 WATSON (EDWARD). The Royal Mail to Ireland: or, an account of the origin and development of the post between London and Ireland through Holyhead, and the use of the line of communication by travellers. 1917.

See also *Report of the committee appointed by the Treasury to enquire into the acceleration of the Irish day mails.* [C. 9023] H.C. (1898). XXXIV, 299. Minutes of evidence. [C. 9024] H.C. (1898). XXXIV, 317.

5575 ROBINSON (HOWARD). Carrying British mails overseas. N.Y. 1964.

See also Frank Staff, *The transatlantic mail*, 1956, and Robert G. Greenhill, 'The state under pressure: the West Indian mail contract, 1905', *Business Hist.* xi (1969), 120–7.

5576 STAFF (FRANK). The picture postcard & its origins. 1966.

See also **9110**.

5577 BAINES. Forty years at the Post Office: a personal narrative. By Frederic Ebenezer Baines. 2 v. 1895.

5578 BLACKWOOD. Some records of the life of Stevenson Arthur Blackwood, K.C.B. Ed. by his widow Harriet Sydney, Lady Blackwood. 1896. Pop. edn. 1897.

See also Harry Buxton Forman, *A few words about the late Sir Arthur Blackwood, Secretary of the Post Office*, 1894.

5579 HENNIKER HEATON. The life and letters of Sir John Henniker Heaton, Bt. By his daughter, Mrs. Adrian [i.e. Rose] Porter. 1916.

Henniker Heaton was the great champion of the Imperial penny post and Post Office reform.

5580 HILL. The life of Sir Rowland Hill . . . and the history of penny postage. By Sir Rowland Hill and George Birkbeck Norman Hill. 2 v. 1880.

See also Eleanor C. Smyth, *Sir Rowland Hill: the story of a great reform: told by his daughter*, 1907, and Henry Warburton Hill, *Rowland Hill and the fight for the penny post* . . ., 1940.

5581 TROLLOPE. An autobiography. By Anthony Trollope. 2 v. 1883. Best edn. by Frederick Page. 1950.

Incls. an account of his work at the Post Office.

5582  GENERAL POST OFFICE. British postal guide: containing, the chief
public regulations of the Post Office. 1856+.

Title became *The postal guide* . . ., 1880+.

5583  THE BLACKFRIARS MAGAZINE. 1885+.

Title changed to *St. Martin's-le-Grand: the Post Office magazine*, 1890–1933, and *The
Post Office magazine*, 1934+.

(ii) *Official Reports and Inquiries*

The reports of committees on the Post Office were notoriously voluminous. Only
the more extensive are included here.

5584  POSTMASTER-GENERAL. Report upon the Post Office, 1854. [1913]
H.C. (1855). XX, 555.

Subsequent annual reports were issued in this form up to the 57th (1911). They were
then issued as the report for 1911–12, etc. until the report for 1915–16.

5585  MUNTZ COMMITTEE ON POSTAGE LABEL STAMPS. Report
from the select committee on postage label stamps [Chairman: G. F. Muntz].
H.C. 386 (1852). XV, 1.

5586  CANNING COMMITTEE ON CONTRACT PACKETS. Report of
the committee on contract packets [Chairman: Earl Canning]. [1660] H.C.
(1852–3). XCV, 137.

5587  HERBERT COMMITTEE ON COMMUNICATION BETWEEN
LONDON AND DUBLIN. Report from the select committee on communication between London and Dublin [Chairman: Henry Arthur Herbert]. H.C.
747 (1852–3). XXIV, 611.

5588  WILSON-PATTEN COMMITTEE ON CONVEYANCE OF MAILS
BY RAILWAYS. Report from the select committee on conveyance of mails by
railways [Chairman: J. Wilson-Patten]. H.C. 411 (1854). XI, 1.

5589  COBDEN COMMITTEE ON PACKET AND TELEGRAPHIC
CONTRACTS. Report from the select committee on packet and telegraphic
contracts [Chairman: Richard Cobden]. H.C. 180 (1859–Sess. 2). VI, 1.
Further reports in following session [Chairman: Andrew Murray Dunlop].
First report. H.C. 328 (1860). XIV, 1. Second report. H.C. 407 (1860). XIV,
525. Appendix to second report. H.C. 407–I (1860). XIV, 605. Third report.
H.C. 431 (1860). XIV, 637.

A careful and exhaustive inquiry.

5590  DENT COMMITTEE ON MAIL CONTRACTS. Report from the
select committee on mail contracts [Chairman: J. D. Dent]. H.C. 106 (1868–9).
VI, 265.

5591 POST OFFICE MONEY ORDER SYSTEM. Report of the committee of inquiry into the money order system of the Post Office, into the proposed scheme of Post Office notes, and as to postal drafts payable to order [Chairman: George Moore]. H.C. 289 (1877). XXVII, 261.

5592 FAWCETT COMMITTEE ON POST OFFICE ANNUITIES AND LIFE ASSURANCE. Report from the select committee on Post Office (annuities and life assurance policies) [Chairman: Henry Fawcett]. H.C. 138 (1882). XII, 383.

On the failure of a Post Office experiment. See also *Report of, and evidence taken by, the departmental committee on the encouragement of the life insurance system of the Post Office* [Chairman: Lord Farrer]. H.C. 311 (1908). XXV, 275.

5593 NORTON COMMITTEE ON POST OFFICE FACTORIES. Report of the departmental committee on Post Office factories, 1910–11 [Chairman: Captain Cecil Norton]. [Cd. 6027] H.C. (1912–13). XLIII, 303.

5594 BARING COMMITTEE ON LONDON POST OFFICE RAILWAY BILL. Report and special report from the select committee on the Post Office (London) Railway Bill [Chairman: Sir Godfrey Baring]. H.C. 218 (1913). X, 57.

Discussed the Post Office plans for a special underground railway, which was subsequently built.

(iii) *Postage and other Stamps*

5595 MARSHALL (CHAPMAN FREDERICK DENDY). The British Post Office from its beginnings to the end of 1925. 1926.

Primarily a philatelic work.

5596 PHILBRICK (FREDERICK ADOLPHUS) *and* WESTOBY (WILLIAM A. B.). The postage and telegraph stamps of Great Britain. Philatelic Soc. 1881.

Standard until superseded by Wright and Creeke (5597).

5597 WRIGHT (HASTINGS ELWIN) *and* CREEKE (ANTHONY BUCK). A history of the adhesive stamps of the British Isles available for postal and telegraphic purposes: compiled from official sources. Philatelic Soc. 1899.

Standard for many years. Succeeded by Seymour, 5598.

5598 SEYMOUR (JAMES BENJAMIN) *and others*. The stamps of Great Britain. Royal Philatelic Soc. 4 v. 1934–57. 3rd edn. 1967+.

Standard. But see Lowe, 5599.

5599 LOWE (ROBSON). The British postage stamp: being the history of the nineteenth-century postage stamps, based on the collection presented to the nation by Reginald M. Phillips of Brighton. National Postal Museum. 1968.

5600 EASTON (JOHN). The De La Rue history of British & foreign postage stamps, 1855 to 1901. Royal Philatelic Soc. 1958.
A full account of the work of the printers of most British stamps during the period.

5601 HENDY (JOHN GEORGE). The history of the postmarks of the British Isles, 1840 to 1876, compiled chiefly from official records. 1909.

5602 ALCOCK (RONALD CECIL) *and* HOLLAND (FRANCH CHARLES). The postmarks of Great Britain and Ireland: being, a survey of British postmarks from 1660 to 1940. 1940. Suppls. 1940+.

5603 EWEN (HERBERT L'ESTRANGE) *comp*. A history of railway letter stamps: describing all varieties issued by the railway companies of Great Britain and Ireland under the authority of the Postmaster-General. 1901.

5604 CUMMINGS (HAYMAN ALFRED JAMES). The college stamps of Oxford and Cambridge: a study of their history and use from 1870–1886. [1904.]

5605 HARDY (WILLIAM JOHN) *and* BACON (EDWARD DENNY). The stamp collector. 1898.
The first solid work devoted to the subject. Includes a hist.

5606 POSTAL HISTORY SOCIETY. Bulletin of the Postal History Society. 1936+.

### (c) *Telecommunications*
#### (i) *General*

5607 HARLOW (ALVIN FAY). Old wires and new waves: the history of the telegraph, telephone and wireless. 1936.
An elementary introduction.

5608 APPLEYARD (ROLLO). Pioneers of electrical communication. 1930.

5609 KING COMMITTEE ON POST OFFICE ACCOUNTS. Post Office: departmental committee on telegraph and telephone accounts [Chairman: C. A. King]. Reports and appendixes. [Cd. 4520] H.C. (1909). XXXVI, 377.

#### (ii) *Telegraphy*

For the technical literature of the subject see Society of Telegraph Engineers [Instn. of Electrical Engineers], *Journal*, 1872+.

5610 PATENT OFFICE. Abridgments of specifications. Class 40: electric telegraphs and telephones. Decennial vols. 1855–1908. From 1909 to 1930 cont. as class 40 (iii): telegraphs, electric.

5611 HUBBARD (GEOFFREY). Cooke and Wheatstone and the invention of the electric telegraph. 1965.

See also Jeffrey L. Kieve, *The electric telegraph: a social and economic history*, Newton Abbot 1973.

5612 LISTER (RAYMOND GEORGE). Private telegraph companies of Great Britain and their stamps. Camb. 1961.

5613 MEYER (HUGO RICHARD). The British state telegraphs: a study of the problem of a large body of civil servants in a democracy. N.Y. 1907.

5614 DURHAM (JOHN FRANCIS LANGTON). Telegraphs in Victorian London. Camb. [1959.]

5615 GOLDSMID (*Sir* FREDERIC JOHN). Telegraph and travel: a narrative of the formation and development of telegraphic communications between England and India. 1874.

5616 SABINE (ROBERT). The electric telegraph. 1867. 2nd edn. 1869.

A useful hist. reflecting mid-19th-cent. ideas. See also Dionysius Lardner, *The electric telegraph popularised*, 1855, 3rd edn. 1874; Taliaferro Preston Shaffner, *The telegraph manual: a complete history and description of the semaphoric, electric and magnetic telegraphs of Europe, Asia, Africa and America, ancient and modern*, N.Y. 1859; Robert Dodwell, *An illustrated handbook to the electric telegraph*, 1861, 2nd edn. 1862; and Richard Spelman Culley, *A handbook of practical telegraphy*, 1863, 8th edn. 1885. Sir William Henry Preece, *Recent advances in telegraphy*, 1879, is a good survey. Preece and Sir James Sivewright also publ. *Telegraphy*, 1876, new edn. 1914.

5617 HERBERT (THOMAS ERNEST). Telegraphy: a detailed exposition of the telegraph system of the British Post Office. 1906. 5th edn. 1930.

5618 BAKER (THOMAS THORNE). The telegraphic transmission of photographs. 1910.

5619 ELECTRIC TELEGRAPH COMPANIES, 1860. Returns of the names of all companies incorporated either by Act of Parliament or Royal Charter, or otherwise, with power to establish and manage lines of electric telegraphs ... H.C. 434 (1860). LXII, 189.

5620 ELECTRIC TELEGRAPHS RETURN, 1868. Returns of the names of all railway companies in the United Kingdom which construct or use electric telegraphs as part of their undertaking: of the number of miles of telegraph both authorised and constructed, and of the number of stations and places connected with such telegraphs: and, of the places of connection and the length of each submarine telegraph connected with any place in the United Kingdom. H.C. 416 (1867-8). XLI, 721.

5621 ANDERSON (*Sir* JAMES). 'Statistics of telegraphy'. *Stat. Soc. J.* xxxv (1872), 272–326.

5622 SCUDAMORE (FRANK IVES). Reports to the Postmaster General by Mr. Scudamore upon the proposal for transferring to the Post Office the control and management of the electric telegraphs of the United Kingdom. H.C. 202 (1867-8). XLI, 555.

5623 WARD HUNT COMMITTEE ON ELECTRIC TELEGRAPHS BILL. Special report from the select committee on the Electric Telegraphs Bill [Chairman: George Ward Hunt, Chancellor of the Exchequer]. H.C. 435 (1867-8). XI, 1.

This Bill provided for the Post Office takeover of telegraphs. A further bill was introduced in the following session to provide for a Post Office monopoly. See *Report from the select committee on Telegraph Bill* [Chairman: Marquess of Hartington]. H.C. 348 (1868-9). VI, 651. A further bill extending the Post Office monopoly to the Channel Islands and the Isle of Man was introduced in the following session. See *Report from the select committee on the Telegraphs Acts Extension Bill* [Chairman: Marquess of Hartington]. H.C. 336 (1870). X, 613.

5624 ELECTRIC AND INTERNATIONAL TELEGRAPH COMPANY. The government and the telegraphs: statement of the case of the Electric and International Telegraph Company against the government bill for acquiring the telegraphs. [1868.]

For the Post Office's reply see H.C. 272 (1867-8). XLI, 737.

5625 SCUDAMORE (FRANK IVES). Report by Mr. Scudamore on the re-organization of the telegraph system of the United Kingdom. [C. 304] H.C. (1871). XXXVII, 703.

The fullest of a number of reports on the nationalization of the telegraphs publ. as parl. papers. Suppl. by Scudamore's report on the financial results of nationalization. H.C. 378 (1871). XXXVII, 691.

5626 AUSTIN (ALFRED), WEAVER (H.) *and* ANDERSON (WILLIAM GEORGE). Report of a committee appointed by the Treasury to investigate the causes of the increased cost of the telegraph service since the acquisition of the telegraphs by the state. [C. 1309] H.C. (1875). XX, 643.

5627 PLAYFAIR COMMITTEE ON TELEGRAPH DEPARTMENT. Report from the select committee on Post Office (Telegraph Department) [Chairman: Lyon Playfair]. H.C. 357 (1876). XIII, 1.

5628 WILLIAMS (RICHARD PRICE). 'The question of the reduction of the present postal telegraph tariff'. *Stat. Soc. J.* xliv (1881), 1-23.

5629 REPORT FROM THE SELECT COMMITTEE ON TELEPHONE AND TELEGRAPH WIRES [Chairman: George Russell]. H.C. 188 (1884-5). XII, 101.

On danger from overhead wires.

(iii) *Submarine Telegraphy*

5630 SMITH (WILLOUGHBY). The rise and extension of submarine telegraphy. 1891.

A good introduction.

5631 BRIGHT (*Sir* CHARLES). Submarine telegraphs: their history, construction and working; founded in part on Wünschendorff's 'Traité de Télégraphie Sous-Marine' and compiled from authoritative and exclusive sources. 1898.

See also Bright's essays in his *Imperial telegraphic communication*, 1911.

5632 CLARKE (ARTHUR CHARLES). Voice across the sea. N.Y. 1958.

The story of deep-sea cable-laying, 1858–1958.

5633 MULLALY (JOHN). The laying of the cable: or, the ocean telegraph: being, a complete and authentic narrative of the attempt to lay the cable across the entrance to the gulf of St. Lawrence in 1855 and of the three Atlantic telegraph expeditions of 1857 and 1858 . . . N.Y. 1858.

See also Sir William Howard Russell, *The Atlantic telegraph*, 1865; Henry Martyn Field, *History of the Atlantic telegraph*, N.Y. 1866, rev. edn. 1893; Sir Charles Bright, *The story of the Atlantic cable*, 1903; and Charles Frederick Briggs and Augustus Maverick, *The story of the telegraph and a history of the great Atlantic cable . . .*, N.Y. 1858.

5634 GALTON COMMITTEE ON CABLE CONSTRUCTION. Report of the joint committee appointed by the Lords of the Committee of Privy Council for Trade and the Atlantic Telegraph Company to inquire into the construction of submarine telegraph cables [Chairman: Douglas Galton]. [2744] H.C. (1860). LXII, 591.

Comprehensive.

5635 BRIGHT. The life story of the late Sir Charles Tilston Bright, civil engineer: with which is incorporated the story of the Atlantic cable and the first telegraph to India and the colonies. By Edward Brailsford Bright and Sir Charles Bright. 2 v. 1899. Abridged edn. 1908.

5636 FIELD. Cyrus W. Field: his life and work, 1819–1892. Ed. by Isabella Field Judson. N.Y. 1896.

See also Philip Bayaud MacDonald, *A saga of the seas: the story of Cyrus W. Field and the laying of the first Atlantic cable*, N.Y. 1937.

5637 BALFOUR OF BURLEIGH COMMITTEE ON CABLE COMMUNICATIONS. First report of the inter-departmental committee on cable communications [Chairman: Lord Balfour of Burleigh]. [Cd. 958] H.C. (1902). XI, 171. First and second reports. [Cd. 1056] H.C. (1902). XI, 199. Minutes of evidence. [Cd. 1118] H.C. (1902). XI, 291.

A full inquiry into imperial cable communications.

5638   MARGERIE (MAXIME DE). Le réseau anglais de cables sous-marins. Paris. 1909.

The best general account of the British system.

5639   PARKINSON (JOSEPH CHARLES). The ocean telegraph to India: a narrative and a diary. 1870.

5640   JOHNSON (GEORGE) *ed.* The all red line: the annals and aims of the Pacific cable project. Ottawa. 1903.

See also Pacific Cable Committee [Chairman: Earl of Selborne]. *Report, minutes of proceedings, &c.* [C. 9247] H.C. (1899). LIX, 347, and the related correspondence at [C. 9283] H.C. (1899). LIX, 557.

5641   [LAWFORD (G. L.) *and* NICHOLSON (L. R.).] The Telcon story, 1850–1950. Telegraph Construction & Maintenance Co. Ltd. 1950.

A pioneer cable company. Ernest Slater, *One hundred years, 1837–1937: the story of Henleys* [1937], deals with another.

5642   LAMB COMMITTEE ON INJURIES TO CABLES. Report of inter-departmental committee on injuries to submarine cables [Chairman: Sir J. C. Lamb]. [Cd. 4331] H.C. (1908). XXV, 875.

Chiefly concerned with trawlers which damaged cables, and cable repairs.

### (iv)  *Telephone*

5643   BALDWIN (FRANCIS GEORGE C.). The history of the telephone in the United Kingdom. 1925.

J. H. Robertson, *The story of the telephone: a history of the telecommunications industry of Britain,* 1947, is a short popular account.

5644   KINGSBURY (J. E.). The telephone and telephone exchanges: their invention and development. 1915.

Full.

5645   HALLEWOOD (A.). 'The origin of the state telephone service in Britain'. *Oxford Econ. Papers* new ser. v (1953), 13–25.

5646   MEYER (HUGO RICHARD). Public ownership and the telephone in Great Britain: restriction of the industry by the state and the municipalities. N.Y. 1907.

5647   WEBB (HERBERT LAWS). The development of the telephone in Europe. [1911.]

An attack on state-ownership in Britain. See also his *The telephone service: its past, its present and its future,* 1904, a short description of the service.

5648   MORLEY COMMITTEE ON THE TELEPHONE SERVICE. Report from the select committee on the telephone service [Chairman: Arnold Morley]. H.C. 350 (1895). XIII, 21.

Minutes of evidence only. The subject was later referred to a further committee which met in 1898, and eventually reported at length. See *Report from the select committee on telephones* [Chairman: R. W. Hanbury]. H.C. 383 (1898). XII, 1. The Hanbury Committee took into account the evidence collected by two other committees as well as that collected by the Morley Committee: the *Special report and report from the select committee on Telegraphs Bill.* H.C. 278 (1892–Sess. 1). XVII, 729, which dealt with Post Office trunk telephone lines and arrangements with the telephone companies, and *Glasgow telephone inquiry, 1897: proceedings at inquiry into the telephone system in Glasgow . . . before Andrew Jameson, Esquire . . .* [C. 8769] H.C. (1898). XLIX, 25, and Jameson's *Report.* [C. 8768] H.C. (1898). XLIX, 1.

5649   STUART-WORTLEY COMMITTEE ON POST OFFICE TELE-PHONE AGREEMENT. Report from the select committee on Post Office (telephone agreement), 1905 [Chairman: C. B. Stuart-Wortley]. H.C. 271 (1905). VII, 113.

The licence of the National Telephone Company, being about to expire, the Post Office proposed to take over the service. The committee was primarily concerned with the details of the transaction.

5650   HERBERT (THOMAS ERNEST). The telephone system of the British Post Office: a practical handbook. 2nd edn. 1901. 3rd edn. 1904.

He also publ. *Telephony: an elementary exposition of the telephone system of the British Post Office*, 1923, 3rd edn. 2 v. 1948.

5651   AITKEN (WILLIAM). Aitken's manual of the telephone. 1911.
Useful illustrations.

### (v) *Wireless Telegraphy*

5652   FAHIE (JOHN JOSEPH). A history of wireless telegraphy, 1838–1899, including some bare-wire proposals for subaqueous telegraphs. Edin. & Lond. 1899. 2nd edn. 1901. 3rd edn. N.Y. 1902.

5653   BLAKE (GEORGE GASCOIGNE). History of radio-telegraphy and telephony. 1926.

5654   BRIGGS (ASA). The history of broadcasting in the United Kingdom. v. 1. 1961.

Standard. See also Stanley George Sturmey, *The economic development of radio*, 1958.

5655   HAWKS (ELLISON). Pioneers of wireless. 1927.

5656   FAHIE. A short account of the life and work of John Joseph Fahie. By Eric Stanley Whitehead. 1939.

A pioneer of wireless telegraphy.

5657   BAKER (WILLIAM JOHN). A history of the Marconi company. 1970.

For the company's work in marine communications see **6156**. For the Marconi scandal see **296** and *Reports from the select committee on Marconi's Wireless Telegraph Company, Limited, agreement* [Chairman: Sir Albert Spicer]. H.C. 351, 430, 515 & 515–I [all one paper] (1912–13). VIII, 27. Further reports. H.C. 152 and 185 (1913). VII, 95, 805.

5658 DICKSON-POYNDER COMMITTEE ON RADIOTELEGRAPHIC CONVENTION. Report from the select committee on radiotelegraphic convention [Chairman: Sir John Dickson-Poynder]. H.C. 246 (1907). VIII, 1.

An important inquiry into the scientific and diplomatic hist. of radiotelegraphy.

(d) *Advertising*

For advertising manuals and directories see **58**.

5659 PRESBREY (FRANK). The history and development of advertising. Garden City, N.Y. 1929.

A useful general study. Ernest Sackville Turner, *The shocking history of advertising*, 1952, and Henry Sampson, *A history of advertising from the earliest times*, 1874, add little.

5660 ELLIOT (BLANCHE BEATRICE). A history of English advertising. 1962.

5661 HIATT (CHARLES). Picture posters: a short history of the illustrated placard, with many reproductions of the most artistic examples in all countries. 1895.

A fine piece of work.

5662 SHELDON (CYRIL). A history of poster advertising: with a record of legislation and attempted legislation affecting outdoor advertising. 1937.

See also Edward McKnight Kauffer, *The art of the poster: its origin, evolution and purpose*, 1924.

5663 DE VRIES (LEONARD) *and others, comps.* Victorian advertisements: or, the art of the Victorian persuader. Lond. & Phila. 1968.

See also Bernard Richard Meirion Darwin, ed., *The Dickens advertiser: a collection of the advertisements in the original parts of novels by Charles Dickens*, 1930.

5664 LARWOOD (JACOB) *pseud. of* VON SCHEVICHAYEN (HERMAN DIEDERIK JOHAN) *and* HOTTEN (JOHN CAMDEN). The history of signboards from the earliest times to the present day. 1866. 3rd edn. 1867. New edn. 1951.

Suppl. by Sir Ambrose Heal, *London shop-signs: other than those given by Larwood & Hotten . . .*, 1939.

5665 CRAWFORD. There is a tide . . . the life and work of Sir William Crawford, K.B.E.: embodying an historical study of modern British advertising. By Godfrey Hope Saxon Mills. 1954.

5666 STEAD (WILLIAM). The art of advertising: its theory and practice fully described. [1899.]

5667 SCOTT (WALTER DILL). The psychology of advertising: a simple exposition of the principles of psychology in their relation to successful advertising. 1909. Rev. edn. 1932.

An American work issued by Pitmans, the commercial educational firm.

## 9. FOOD AND DRINK INDUSTRIES

### (a) *Food*

For food imports and the food distribution system see **5874–911**.

5668 PATENT OFFICE LIBRARY. Subject list of works on domestic economy, foods, and beverages, including the culture of cacao, coffee, barley, hops, sugar, tea, and the grape, in the library of the Patent Office. Patent Office Libr. Ser. no. 9. Bibliog. Series No. 6. 1902.

5669 LAW (JAMES THOMAS). Law's grocer's manual. Liverpool. [1896.] 4th edn. 1950.

An encyclopedia of commodities.

5670 DRUMMOND (*Sir* JACK CECIL) *and* WILBRAHAM (ANNE). The Englishman's food: a history of five centuries of English diet. 1939. Rev. edn. 1957.

Standard.

5671 BURNETT (JOHN). Plenty and want: a social history of diet in England from 1815 to the present day. 1966.

See also Theodore Cardwell Barker, John Crawford McKenzie, and John Yudkin, eds., *Our changing fare: two hundred years of British food habits*, 1966, and D. J. Oddy, 'Working-class diets in late nineteenth-century Britain', *Econ. Hist. Rev.* 2 ser. xxiii (1970), 314–23.

5672 McCOLLUM (ELMER VERNER). A history of nutrition: the sequence of ideas in nutrition investigation. Boston. [1957.]

5673 SMITH (EDWARD). Foods. 1873. 10th edn. 1890.

The first successful popular manual of nutrition, by a medical officer of health. Among similar works Sir Arthur Herbert Church, *Food . . .*, South Kensington Museum, 1876, 3rd edn. 1893, Sir Henry Thompson, *Food and feeding* [1880], 12th edn. 1910, and Alexander Wynter Blyth, *Foods: their composition and analysis . . ., with an introductory essay on the history of food adulteration*, 1882, 7th edn. 1927 are useful.

5674 CURTIS-BENNETT (*Sir* [FRANCIS] NOEL). The food of the people: being, the history of industrial feeding. 1949.

5675 DODD (GEORGE). The food of London: a sketch of the chief varieties of source of supply . . . 1856.

**5676** BURNETT (JOHN). 'The history of food adulteration in Great Britain in the nineteenth century, with special reference to bread, tea and beer'. *Inst. Hist. Res. Bull.* xxxii (1959), 104–9.

Draws attention to a valuable thesis. Frederick Arthur Filby, *A history of food adulteration and analysis*, 1934, has little on the period. The law is covered by Sir William James Bell, *The Sale of Food and Drugs Acts, 1875 and 1879*, 1886, 13th edn. 1956, and Thomas Charles Hunter Hedderwick, *The sale of food and drugs: the Acts of 1875 and 1879 . . .*, 1894, 2nd edn. 1900.

**5677** SCHOLEFIELD COMMITTEE ON FOOD ADULTERATION. First report from the select committee on adulteration of food, &c. [Chairman: William Scholefield.] H.C. 432 (1854–5). VIII, 221. Second report. H.C. 480. (1854–5). VIII, 373. Further report. H.C. 379 (1856). VIII, 1.

See also *Report from the select committee on Adulteration of Food Act (1872)* [Chairman: Clare Sewell Read]. H.C. 262 (1874). VI, 243.

**5678** FOSTER COMMITTEE ON FOOD ADULTERATION. Report from the select committee on food products adulteration [Chairmen: Sir Balthazar Walter Foster and Thomas Wallace Russell]. H.C. 253 (1894). XII, 1. Further report. H.C. 363 (1895). X, 73. Further report. H.C. 288 (1896). IX, 483.

**5679** STORCK (JOHN) *and* TEAGUE (WALTER DORWIN). Flour for men's bread: a history of milling. Minneapolis. 1952.

**5680** BENNETT (RICHARD) *and* ELTON (JOHN). History of corn-milling. 4 v. 1898–1904.

Useful for details. Joseph Rank Ltd., *The master millers: the story of the house of Rank . . .* [1955], and William Maddin Scott, ed., *A hundred years a-milling: commemorating an Ulster mill centenary*, Belfast 1951, 2nd edn. 1956, are the best of a number of very poor hists. of firms.

**5681** McCANCE (ROBERT ALEXANDER) *and* WIDDOWSON (ELSIE MARY). Breads: white and brown: their place in thought and social history. 1956.

**5682** ASHLEY (*Sir* WILLIAM JAMES). The bread of our forefathers: an inquiry in economic history. Oxf. 1928.

Famous, but virtually nothing on the period. There is only a little more in Ronald Sheppard and Edward Newton, *The story of bread*, 1957. The leading contemp. writer was William Jago whose *Cantor lectures on modern developments of bread-making*, 1890, and *The technology of bread-making . . .* (written with William C. Jago), 1911, new edn. 1921, are his best works. John Frank Rowe, *The Bread Acts . . .*, 1894, 2nd edn. 1912, is good for the law. The leading periodicals were Nat. Assoc. of Master Bakers, *The national association review*, Birmingham etc. 1887+, *Baker's record*, 1864+, *British miller and baker* [title varies], 1885+, and *Baker and confectioner*, 1892+.

**5683** BURNETT (JOHN). 'The baking industry in the nineteenth century'. *Business Hist.* v (1962–3), 98–108.

For a specialist side of the industry see J. E. Brownlow, 'The Melton Mowbray pork pie industry', *Leicestershire Archaeol. & Hist. Soc. Trans.* xxxix (1963–4), 36–48.

5684 VAN STUYVENBERG (J. H.) *ed*. Margarine: an economic, social and scientific history, 1869–1969. Liverpool. 1969.

5685 PLUNKETT COMMITTEE ON BUTTER REGULATIONS. Interim report of the departmental committee appointed by the Board of Agriculture . . . to inquire and report upon the desirability of regulations . . . for butter [Chairman: Horace Curzon Plunkett]. [Cd. 944] H.C. (1902). XX, 123. Minutes of evidence. [Cd. 1039] H.C. (1902). XX, 131. Final report. [Cd. 1749] H.C. (1903). XVII, 349. Minutes of evidence. [Cd. 1750] H.C. (1903). XVII, 379.

See also *Report from the select committee on butter trade* [Chairman: Sir Edward Strachey]. H.C. 245 (1906). VII, 1.

5686 LIBRARY OF CONGRESS. Select list of references on sugar, chiefly in its economic aspects. Wash. 1910.

See also Henry Ling Roth, *A guide to the literature of sugar . . .*, 1890. The main periodical was *Sugar cane . . .*, Manch. 1869–98, later *The international sugar j.*, 1899+.

5687 DEERR (NOEL). The history of sugar. 2 v. 1949–50.

Standard. William Reed, *The history of sugar and sugar-yielding plants . . .*, 1866, gives prices and consumption to 1864. George Martineau, *Sugar, cane and beet: an object lesson* [1910], 7th edn. 1938, is a useful short account of the industry and its hist.

5688 HUTCHESON (JOHN M.). Notes on the sugar industry of the United Kingdom. Greenock. 1901.

A short hist. from 1801 to 1900.

5689 CARDWELL COMMITTEE ON SUGAR DUTIES. Report from the select committee on sugar duties [Chairman: Edward Cardwell]. H.C. 390. (1862). XIII, 1.

5690 RITCHIE COMMITTEE ON SUGAR INDUSTRIES. Report from the select committee on sugar industries [Chairman: Charles Thomson Ritchie]. H.C. 321 (1878–9). XIII, 1. Further report. H.C. 106 (1880). XII, 477. Further report. H.C. 332 (1880). XII, 517.

5691 MARTINEAU (GEORGE). 'The statistical aspect of the sugar question'. *Royal Stat. Soc. J.* lxii (1899), 296–332.

See also his 'The Brussels sugar convention', *Econ. J.* xiv (1904), 34–46. Martineau was a staunch advocate of state assistance against foreign sugar bounties and set out his views in *Free trade in sugar: a reply to Sir Thomas Farrer*, 1888, and *A short history of sugar, 1856–1916: a warning*, 1917. For the sugar bounties controversy see also Brown (**5965**) and William Smart, *The sugar bounties: the case for and against government interference*, Edin. & Lond. 1887.

5692 TARIFF COMMISSION. Report of the tariff commission. Vol. 7: Sugar and confectionery. 1907.

5693 TATE. Henry Tate, 1819–1899: a biographical sketch. By Tom Jones. 1960.

Founder of Tate & Lyle Ltd., sugar refiners.

5694 CROOKES (*Sir* WILLIAM). On the manufacture of beet-root sugar in England and Ireland. 1870.

5695 WALLIS-TAYLER (ALEXANDER JAMES). Sugar machinery: a descriptive treatise devoted to the machinery and apparatus used in the manufacture of cane and beet sugars. 1895. 4th edn. 1924.

5696 HOLM (JOHN). Cocoa and its manufacture: with remarks on the Adulteration of Food Act, 1872. 1874.

5697 WILLIAMS (IOLO ANEURIN). The firm of Cadbury, 1831–1931. 1931.

Cocoa manufacturing. For illustrations see T. B. Rogers, *A century of progress, 1831–1931: Cadbury, Bournville,* 1931.

5698 DRUMMOND (*Sir* JACK CECIL) *and others.* Historic tinned foods. Int. Tin Research and Devel. Council. Public. no. 85. 1939.

There is little in Ernest Henry Taylor, ed., *The story of preserved foods,* Newcastle-upon-Tyne 1921, 2nd edn. 1922, or Stephen Potter, *The magic number: the story of '57* [a history of Heinz Canning Co.], 1959.

5699 BRANNT (WILLIAM THEODORE). A practical treatise on the manufacture of vinegar [with special consideration of wood vinegar and other by-products obtained in the destructive distillation of wood; the fabrication of acetates, cider and fruit-wines; preservation of fruits and vegetables by canning and evaporation, preparation of fruit-butters, jellies, marmalades, pickles, mustards, etc.; preservation of meat, fish and eggs]. Phila. 1890. 3rd edn. 1914.

5700 MACKINTOSH. John Mackintosh: a biography. By George W. Crutchley. 1921.

Maker of Mackintosh's toffee.

(b) *Tea, Coffee, etc.*

5701 UKERS (WILLIAM HARRISON). All about tea. 2 v. N.Y. 1935.

Extensive bibliog.

5702 ANTROBUS (HINSON ALLAN). A history of the Assam Company, 1839–1953. Priv. pr. Edin. 1957.

A good hist. of a major British tea-planting company. Antrobus also publ. *A history of the Jorehaut Tea Company Ltd., 1859–1946* [1948]. See also Sir Percival Joseph Griffiths *The history of the Indian tea industry,* 1967.

5703 TWINING (STEPHEN HERBERT). The house of Twining, 1706–1956: being a short history of the firm of R. Twining and Co. Ltd. [tea and coffee merchants.] 1956.

5704 MUELLER (WOLF). Bibliographie des Kaffee, des Kakao, der Schokolade, des Tee und deren Surrogate bis zum Jahre 1900. Bibliotheca Bibliographica XX. Bad Bocklet. 1960.

5705 UKERS (WILLIAM HARRISON). All about coffee. N.Y. 1922. 2nd edn. 1935.
Good bibliog.

5706 JACOB (HEINRICH EDUARD). The saga of coffee: the biography of an economic product. Trans. by Eden and Cedar Paul. 1935.

5707 LOCK (CHARLES GEORGE WARNFORD) *ed*. Coffee: its culture and commerce in all countries. 1888.

5708 OBERPARLEITER (KARL). Der Londoner Kaffeemarkt. Vienna. 1912.

5709 COMMISSIONERS OF PATENTS FOR INVENTIONS. Abridgments of specifications relating to unfermented beverages, aerated liquids, mineral waters, etc. A.D. 1774–1866. 1877. Suppl. 1867–76. 1883. Cont. by Abridgments of specifications, class 14. 1855–1930.

5710 KIRKBY (WILLIAM). The evolution of artificial mineral waters. Manch. 1902.
The best account.

5711 THE MINERAL WATER MAKER'S MANUAL. 1884+.

5712 THE BRITISH AND COLONIAL MINERAL WATER TRADE JOURNAL. Wigan etc. 1888+.
A useful trade j., but see also *United Kingdom mineral water trade review and guardian*, 1873+, *Drinks: a monthly review for aerated water manufacturers* . . ., 1884–93, *National mineral water trades recorder*, ?–1896, cont. as *Mineral water recorder*, 1896–9, and as *Aërator and bottler*, 1900.

### (c) *Alcoholic Beverages*

#### (i) *General*

5713 WILSON (GEORGE BAILEY). 'A statistical review of the variations during the last twenty years in the consumption of intoxicating drinks in the United Kingdom, and in convictions for offences connected with intoxication, with a discussion of the causes to which these variations may be ascribed'. [Howard Medal essay.] *Roy. Stat. Soc. J.* lxxv (1911–12), 183–247.
One of the few careful accounts of the subject. But see also the commentary by Augustus D. Webb, 'The consumption of alcoholic liquors in the United Kingdom', *Roy. Stat. Soc. J.* lxxvi (1912–13), 207–20. Further stats. are given in Wilson's astonishingly comprehensive *Alcohol and the nation* (**7523**).

5714 GARDNER (JOHN) *ed.* The brewer, distiller and wine manufacturer: giving full directions for the manufacture of beer, spirits, wines, liqueurs, etc., etc. Phila. 1883.

A handy popular guide, incl. delicacies such as caraway cordial and lovage cordial.

(ii) *Brewing and Beer*

5715 BIRD (WILLIAM HENRY). A catalogue of the library of the London section [of the Institute of Brewing]. 1914.

The only list of its period. The fullest bibliog. is Fritz Schoellhorn, *Bibliographie des Brauwesens*, Gesellschaft für die Geschichte und Bibliographie des Brauwesens, Berlin [1928], 10 suppls. 1929–41. See also Peter Mathias, 'Historical records of the brewing industry', *Archives* vii (1965–6), 2–10.

5716 [DUNCAN'S] MANUAL OF BRITISH & FOREIGN BREWERY COMPANIES. 1889+.

A directory of brewers and brewing. See also *The brewers' year book*, 1876+, and *The brewers' almanack and wine and spirit trade annual*, 1894+.

5717 [COUNTRY] BREWERS' SOCIETY. The brewing trade review: the official organ of the [Country] Brewers' Society. 1886+.

The country brewers' gazette, 1877–1904, was the Country Brewers' official organ until 1886. It was cont. as *The brewers' gazette and wine and spirits trades' chronicle*, 1905–31. The other main brewers' periodical was *The brewers' journal*, 1865+. Rival publs. were *The brewers' guardian*, 1871–1906, and *The brewers' weekly*, 1899–1901 [publ. 1901–6 as *The brewer and wine merchant*], which united in 1906 as *The brewer and wine merchant and brewers' guardian*, 1906+. From 1910 the Operative Brewers' Guild also publ. a *Journal*. The Brewers' Congress publ. *Proceedings*, 1885+, 1886+.

5718 MONCKTON (HERBERT ANTHONY). A history of English ale and beer. 1966.

5719 VAIZEY (JOHN ERNEST). The brewing industry, 1886–1951: an economic study. 1960.

For background consult Peter Mathias, *The brewing industry in England, 1700–1830*, Camb. 1959.

5720 BAKER (JULIAN LEVETT). The brewing industry. [1905.]

A good contemp. account.

5721 SIGSWORTH (ERIC MILTON). 'Science and the brewing industry, 1850–1900'. *Econ. Hist. Rev.* 2 ser. xvii (1964–5), 536–50.

5722 BARNARD (ALFRED). The noted breweries of Great Britain and Ireland. 4 v. 1889–91.

Most of the bigger breweries have issued a short hist. or a hist. brochure in recent years. Among the more valuable are Henry Hurford Janes, *Albion brewery, 1808–1958: the story of Mann, Crossman & Paulin Ltd.* [1959], and *The red barrel: a history of Watney, Mann*, 1963, Whitbread & Co. Ltd., *Whitbread's brewery*, 1947, Leonard Alfred George Strong, *A brewer's progress, 1757–1957: a survey of Charrington's brewery on the occasion of its bicentenary*, priv. pr. 1957, and Walter Pearce Serocold, ed., *The story of Watneys*, 1949. See also H[enry] S[topes], *Brewery companies*, 1895, 2nd edn. 1895.

5723 BIRD (WILLIAM HENRY). A history of the Institute of Brewing. 1955.

Founded as the Laboratory Club to assist working brewers. Publ. *Transactions*, 1887–94, and a *Journal*, 1895+.

5724 NEVILE. Seventy rolling years. By Sir Sydney Oswald Nevile. 1958.

The autobiog. of a working brewer. Good.

5725 PEMBROKE COMMITTEE ON BEER MATERIALS. Report of the departmental committee on beer materials [Chairman: Earl of Pembroke and Montgomery]. [C. 9171] H.C. (1899). XXX, 1. Minutes of evidence. [C. 9172] H.C. (1899). XXX, 17.

The only useful inquiry orientated towards the industry rather than towards temperance, the malt tax, or hops. The report of the Brewers' License Inquiry Committee [C. 2582] H.C. (1880). XVIII, 61, gathered little evidence.

5726 FAULKNER (FRANK). The theory and practice of modern brewing: a rewritten and much enlarged edition of 'The art of brewing' [publ. 1876. 3rd edn. 1879]. 1884. 2nd edn. 1888.

Standard until superseded by Walter John Sykes, *The principles and practice of brewing*, 1897, 3rd edn. 1907. Walter Alfred Riley, *Brewery by-products*, 1913, has some out-of-the-way technical information.

5727 SCARISBRICK (JOSEPH). Beer manual: historical & technical. Revenue ser. no. 1. Burton-on-Trent. 1890. 3rd edn. Wolverhampton. 1896.

Explains the operation of the beer duties.

### (iii) *Distilling*

5728 FORBES (ROBERT JAMES). Short history of the art of distillation: from the beginnings up to the death of Cellier Blumenthal. Leiden. 1948.

Standard for the techniques of distillation.

5729 NETTLETON (JOSEPH ALFRED). The manufacture of spirit: as conducted at the various distilleries of the United Kingdom. 1893.

5730 SCARISBRICK (JOSEPH). Spirit manual: historical and technical. Revenue ser. no. 2. Burton-on-Trent. 1891. 2nd edn. Wolverhampton. 1894.

Explains the operation of distilleries and the control exercised over them by the revenue authorities. A further manual deals with the technical aspects of hydrometry.

5731 SELECT COMMITTEE ON BRITISH AND FOREIGN SPIRITS [Chairman: Sir Lyon Playfair]. Report. H.C. 316 (1890). X, 489. Further report. H.C. 210 (1890–1). XI, 351.

Although chiefly concerned with problems of excise and bonded warehouses, the committee also investigated many other aspects of the distilling and spirit-importing industries.

5732 BALFOUR ([JOHN] PATRICK [DOUGLAS]), *Baron Kinross*. The kindred spirit: a history of gin and of the house of Booth. 1959.

A hist. of one of the best-known gin manufacturers.

5733 NETTLETON (JOSEPH ALFRED). The manufacture of whisky and plain spirit. Aberdeen. 1913.

5734 BARNARD (ALFRED). The whisky distilleries of the United Kingdom. 1887.

5735 JAMES COMMISSION ON WHISKEY AND OTHER POTABLE SPIRITS. Interim report of the royal commission of whiskey and other potable spirits [Chairman: Lord James of Hereford]. [Cd. 4180] H.C. (1908). LVIII, 415. Minutes of evidence. [Cd. 4181] H.C. (1908). LVIII, 421. Final report. [Cd. 4796] H.C. (1909). XLIX, 451. Minutes of evidence. [Cd. 4797] H.C. (1909). XLIX, 503. Index and digest. [Cd. 4876] H.C. (1909). XLIX, 785.

Appointed to consider whether the manufacture of Scotch and Irish whisky should be regulated in any way. Reported against regulation. The evidence is the main source for the history of the whisky industry.

5736 LOCKHART (*Sir* ROBERT HAMILTON BRUCE). Scotch: the whisky of Scotland in fact and story. 1951. New edn. 1959.

Ross Wilson, *Scotch made easy*, 1959, covers the same ground, but is rather less satisfactory. James Laver, *The house of Haig*, Markinch 1958, deals with one of the main manufacturers.

(iv) *Cider*

5737 STOPES (HENRY). Cider: the history, method of manufacture and properties of this national beverage. 1888.

5738 COOKE (CHARLES WALLWYN RADCLIFFE). A book about cider and perry. 1898.

Radcliffe Cooke was founder and president of the National Assoc. of English Cider-Makers.

5739 LLOYD (F. J.). Report on the results of investigations into cider-making, carried out on behalf of the Bath and West and Southern Counties Society in the years 1893–1902. Board of Agriculture and Fisheries. [Cd. 1868] H.C. (1904). XVI, 219.

The first serious scientific inquiry into cider-making. Led directly to the establishment of the National Fruit and Cider Institute and the Long Ashton experimental station.

(v) *Wines*

5740 SIMON (ANDRÉ LOUIS). Bibliotheca vinaria: a bibliography of books and pamphlets dealing with viticulture, wine-making, distillation, the management, sale, taxation, use and abuse of wines and spirits. 1913.

Simon also publ. after 1914 a large number of other books on wines, spirits, and liqueurs for connoisseurs, but they are of less interest to the historian than contemporary works like W. & A. Gilbey, *A treatise on wines and spirits of the principal producing countries*, 1869, and Henry Vizetelly, *The wines of the world* . . ., 1875.

5741 MAXWELL (*Sir* HERBERT EUSTACE). Half-a-century of successful trade: being a sketch of the rise and development of the business of W. & A. Gilbey, 1857–1907. Priv. pr. 1907.

There is also a good centenary hist., Alec [i.e. Alexander Raban] Waugh, *Merchants of wine: being, a centenary account of the fortunes of the house of Gilbey*, 1957. Herbert Warner Allen, *Number Three Saint James's Street: a history of Berry's the wine merchants*, 1950, and Godfrey Percival Harrison, *Bristol cream* [a history of John Harvey & Sons], 1955, are much poorer business hists., because the necessary documentation is lacking. Ian Maxwell Campbell, *Wayward tendrils of the vine*, 1948, and *Reminiscences of a vintner*, 1947, form a badly-written wine merchant's autobiog.

5742 ANSTEY COMMITTEE ON WINE DUTIES. Report from the select committee on import duties on wines [Chairman: Thomas Chisholm Anstey]. H.C. 495 (1852). XVII, pts. 1–2.

5743 CARTWRIGHT COMMITTEE ON WINE DUTIES. Report from the select committee on wine duties [Chairman: W. Cornwallis Cartwright]. H.C. 278 (1878–9). XIV, 203.

5744 HARPER'S MANUAL: the standard work of reference for the wine and spirit trade. 1914+.

A very good contemp. handbook. The leading contemp. periodicals were *The wine-trade review*, 1864+, *Harper's weekly gazette*, 1885–7, cont. as *The wine and spirit gazette*, 1888+, and *The wine, spirit and beer exchange & reporter*, 1887–92.

### (d) Catering and Innkeeping

5745 BITTING (KATHERINE GOLDEN). Gastronomic bibliography. San Francisco. 1939.

Standard, but deals chiefly with American books and American editions of British books. Other gastronomic bibliographies such as André Louis Simon, *Bibliotheca gastronomica* . . ., 1953, and Georges Vicaire, *Bibliographie gastronomique*, Paris 1890, repr. Lond. 1954, have very little on the period.

5746 WHO'S WHO IN THE HOTEL WORLD and hotel keeper's vade mecum. 1912+.

See also *Caterer and hotel keeper's gazette*, 1878+.

5747 LICENSED VICTUALLERS' YEAR BOOK. 1874+.

5748 LICENSED VICTUALLERS' OFFICIAL ANNUAL. 1893–1940.

The leading trade js. were *The licensed victuallers' guardian*, ?–1887, renamed *The weekly advertiser*, 1887–9, and the *Morning advertiser*, 1805+.

5749 FRANCATELLI (CHARLES ELMÉ). The modern cook: a practical guide to the culinary art in all its branches, adapted as well for the largest establishments as for the use of private families. 1846. Many editions to 1911.

Francatelli was for a time the Queen's cook. Of the other good cookery books of the period the following are typical: John Henry Walsh, ed., *The English cookery book . . .,* 1858, new edn. [*British cookery book*] 1883; Charles Elmé Francatelli, *The cook's guide and housekeeper's and butler's assistant . . .,* 1861, many edns. to 1888; Urbain Dubois, *Artistic cookery: a practical system suited for the use of the nobility and gentry . . .,* 1870; Eliza Acton, *The English bread-book . . .,* 1857; Mary Pope, *Novel dishes for vegetarian households . . .,* Bradford 1893; and, of course, Mrs. Beeton's, *Household management* (**7166**).

5750   SOYER. Memoirs of Alexis Soyer: with unpublished receipts and odds and ends of gastronomy. Ed. by F. Volant and J. R. Warren. 1859.

Cook, large-scale caterer, and expert on military diet. See also Helen Morris, *Portrait of a chef: the life of Alexis Soyer, sometime chef to the Reform Club,* Camb. 1938.

5751   THYNNE *afterwards* FIELDING (DAPHNE WINIFRED LOUISE), *Marchioness of Bath.* The duchess of Jermyn Street: the life and good times of Rosa Lewis of the Cavendish hotel. 1964.

See also Michael Harrison, *Rosa,* 1962, and Rosa Lewis, *The queen of cooks—and some kings: the story of Rosa Lewis,* recorded by Mary Lawton, N.Y. 1925. For other dining places see *London at dinner: where to dine in 1858,* Newton Abbot 1969, a repr. of *London at table . . .,* which went through several edns., Guy Deghy, *Paradise in the Strand: the story of Romano's,* 1958, and Guy Deghy and Keith Spencer Waterhouse, *Cafe Royal: ninety years of Bohemia,* 1955.

5752   MONCKTON (HERBERT ANTHONY). A history of the English public house. [1969.]

General. There are few serious works on the subject and the picture books and chatty popular accounts add little: George Long, *English inns and road-houses,* 1937, and Basil Oliver, *The renaissance of the English public house,* 1947, are better than most.

5753   KNOX (D. M.). 'The development of the tied house system in London'. *Oxf. Econ. Papers* new ser. x (1958), 66–83.

Important for control of public houses, on the licensing aspects of which see **7555–71**.

### 10. BUILDING INDUSTRY

See also Civil Engineering (**5162–87**) and Housing (**7078–117**).

#### (a) *General*

5754   PATENT OFFICE. Abridgments of specifications. Class 20: buildings and structures. 1855/66 to 1926/30.

5755   DAVEY (NORMAN). Building in Britain: the growth and organisation of the building processes in Britain from Roman times to the present day. 1964.

A short outline hist.

5756  LEWIS (JOHN PARRY). Building cycles and Britain's growth: incorporating material by the late Bernard Weber. 1965.

Standard. Specially strong on house building. For the statistical materials utilized see also Bernard Weber, 'A new index of residential construction and long cycles in house building in Great Britain, 1838–1950', *Scot. J. Pol. Econ.* ii (1955), 104–32; J. Parry Lewis, 'Indices of house building in the Manchester conurbation, South Wales and Great Britain, 1851–1913', ibid. viii (1961), 148–56; Samuel Berrick Saul, 'House building in England, 1890–1914', *Econ. Hist. Rev.* 2 ser. xv (1962–3), 119–37; A. G. Kenwood, 'Residential building activity in north-eastern England, 1853–1913', *Manch. School* xxxi (1963), 115–28; K. Maiwald, 'An index of building costs in the United Kingdom, 1845–1938', *Econ. Hist. Rev.* 2 ser. vii (1954–5), 187–203; and E. W. Cooney, 'Long waves in building in the British economy of the nineteenth century', *Econ. Hist. Rev.* 2 ser. xiii (1960–1), 257–69 (with a comment by A. R. Hall, ibid. 2 ser. xiv (1961–2), 330–2), and 'Capital exports and investment in building in Britain and the U.S.A., 1856–1914', *Economica* new ser. xvi (1949), 347–54. See also Hrothgar John Habakkuk, 'Fluctuations in house-building in Britain and the United States in the nineteenth century', *J. Econ. Hist.* xxii (1962), 198–230, and Janet Blackman and Eric Milton Sigsworth, 'The home boom of the 1890s', *Yorkshire Bull.* xvii (1965), 75–97.

5757  BOWLEY (MARIAN). The British building industry: four studies in response and resistance to change. Camb. 1966.

Chiefly post-1914, but has interesting earlier chaps.

5758  COONEY (E. W.). 'The origins of the Victorian master builders'. *Econ. Hist. Rev.* 2 ser. viii (1955–6), 167–76.

Almost entirely pre-1850.

5759  DYOS (HAROLD JAMES). 'The speculative builders and developers of Victorian London'. *Victorian Studs.* xi (1967–8), 641–90.

5760  JONES (JOHN REGINALD). The Welsh builders on Merseyside: annals and lives. 1946.

A biographical dictionary.

5761  INSTITUTE OF BUILDERS. Proceedings. 1887+.

Became the leading periodical in the field. *The builder*, 1842+, was chiefly for architects. For building see also Master Builders' Assoc., *Journal*, Liverpool etc. 1896+; *Freehold land times and building news* [became *Land and building news*, 1855–6, *The building news*, 1857–1926], 1854–1926; *Builder's weekly reporter* [became *Builder's reporter and engineering times*, 1886–1906], 1869–1906; *The builder's trade circular* [*The building world*], 1877–93, and *The [illustrated] carpenter and builder*, 1877+, and **5187**.

5762  SIMON (JAMES D.). The house-owner's estimator: or, 'What will it cost to build, alter or repair?': a price book adapted to the use of unprofessional people . . . 1874. 5th edn. 1900.

A useful layman's guide to building costs. The main professional guides were *The builder's price book* [*Laxton's builder's price book*], 1840+, and *The builder's and contractor's price-book* [*Lockwood & Co.'s builder's price-book*], 1856+.

5763 MAITLAND (FOWLER). Building estates: a rudimentary treatise on the development, sale, purchase, and general management of building land. 1883. 2nd edn. 1887.

One of the best of many similar handbooks. For the 20th cent. see Tom Bright, *The development of building estates: a practical handbook*, 1910.

5764 DOBSON (EDWARD). Rudiments of the art of building. 1849. 13th edn. 1890.

5765 EMDEN (ALFRED CHARLES RICHARD). The law relating to building leases and building contracts, the improvement of land by, and the construction of, buildings. 1882. 5th edn. 1932.

5766 CUBITT (HORACE WILLIAM) *and others*. Building in London: a treatise on the law and practice affecting the erection and maintenance of buildings in the metropolis. 1911.

5767 DEPARTMENTAL COMMITTEE ON BUILDING BYELAWS. Report of the departmental committee on building byelaws [Chairmen: J. Herbert Lewis and Stephen Walsh]. [Cd. 9213] H.C. (1918). VII, 1. Minutes of evidence. [Cd. 9214] H.C. (1918). VII, 53.

The committee was established in 1914, went into recess at the outbreak of war, and resumed in 1917.

5768 BUILDING ACCIDENTS COMMITTEE. Report of the departmental committee appointed to inquire into the dangers attendant on building operations [Chairman: William Dawkins Cramp]. [Cd. 3848] H.C. (1908). XI, 469.

A full inquiry.

5769 HAMILTON (S. B.). A short history of the structural fire protection of buildings, particularly in England. *Nat. Building Studs. Spec. Report* 27. 1958.

5770 EDWARDS (FREDERICK). Our domestic fireplaces: a treatise on the economical use of fuel. 2nd edn. 1865. New edn. 1870.

See also his *On the economical use of fuel and the prevention of smoke in domestic fireplaces* . . ., 1864, *A treatise on smoky chimneys, their cure and prevention* . . ., 1864, 7th edn. 1875, and *On the ventilation of dwelling-houses* . . ., 1868, 2nd edn. 1881. Edwards manufactured smokeless grates. For kitchen stoves see **7174–5**.

5771 CONSTANTINE (JOSEPH). Practical ventilation and warming: with illustrations and examples and suggestions on the construction and heating, etc. of disinfecting rooms and Turkish baths. 1881.

5772 THE PLUMBER AND DECORATOR AND JOURNAL OF GAS AND SANITARY ENGINEERING. 1879+.

A useful periodical covering many aspects of building.

## (b) *Materials*

5773 DAVEY (NORMAN). A history of building materials. 1961.

5774 BOWLEY (MARIAN). Innovations in building materials: an economic study. 1960.

5775 BRUCE (ALFRED) *and* SANDBANK (HAROLD). A history of prefabrication. N.Y. 1943.

5776 GLOAG (JOHN EDWARDS) *and* BRIDGWATER (DEREK LAWLEY). A history of cast iron in architecture. 1948.

A picture book. Standard. But see also Richard Herbert Sheppard, *Cast iron in building*, 1945. Among illustr. contemp. works Ewing Matheson, *Works in iron: bridge and roof structures*, 1873, 2nd edn. 1877, is outstanding. The pioneer work on the theory of the subject was Sir William Fairbairn, *On the application of cast and wrought iron to building purposes*, 1854, 4th edn. 1870.

5777 McGRATH (RAYMOND) *and* FROST (ALBERT CHILDERSTONE). Glass in architecture and decoration. 1937. New edn. 1961.

5778 THE TIMBER TRADES JOURNAL AND SAWMILL ADVERTISER. Jubilee issue, 1873–1923. 1923.

A useful short hist. See also *The 'Timber trades journal' wood trades directory*, 1888+.

5779 RURAL INDUSTRIES BUREAU. The thatcher's craft. 1961.

5780 DOBSON (CHARLES GEORGE). Roofing tiles and slates: an introduction to their origin, production and distribution. Building Industry Distributors Course B, no. 3. 1952.

See also his *Roof tiling . . .*, 1931, and *A century and a quarter: the story of the growth of our business* [*Hall & Co.*] *from 1824 to the present day*, 1951.

5781 BENFIELD (ERIC). Purbeck shop: a stoneworker's story of stone. Camb. 1940.

A rambling story of all aspects of the stone-cutting industry.

5782 PURCHASE (WILLIAM R.). Practical masonry: a guide to the art of stone cutting. 1896. 6th edn. 1928.

Cp. Edward Dobson, *A rudimentary treatise on masonry and stone cutting . . .*, 1849, 12th edn. 1903.

5783 DOBSON (EDWARD). A rudimentary treatise on the manufacture of bricks and tiles . . . 2 v. 1850. 14th edn. 1936.

Dobson also publ. *A rudimentary treatise on foundations and concrete works*, 1850, and *Rudiments of the art of building . . .*, 1849, 16th edn. 1923. See also Anon., *Bricks and brickmaking: an historical, technical and descriptive sketch*, Birmingham 1878.

5784 THE BRICK AND POTTERY TRADES JOURNAL. 1896–1924.

See also *Brick and tile gazette*, 1885–92.

5785 SPACKMAN (CHARLES). Some writers on lime and cement from Cato to the present time. Camb. 1929.

A comprehensive annotated bibliog.

5786 GOODING (P.) *and* HALSTEAD (P. E.). 'The early history of cement in England'. In Proc. of the Third Internat. Symposium on the Chemistry of Cement. Pp. 1–29. Cement & Concrete Assoc. 1952.

5787 DAVIS (*Sir* ARTHUR CHARLES). A hundred years of Portland cement, 1824–1924. 1924.

5788 SKEMPTON (ALEC WESTLEY). 'Portland cements, 1843–1887'. *Newcomen Soc. Trans.* xxxv (1962–3), 117–52.

5789 HAMILTON (S. B.). A note on the history of reinforced concrete in buildings. Nat. Building Stud. Spec. Report 24. 1956.

5790 LEA (FREDERICK MEASHAM) *and* DESCH (CECIL HENRY). The chemistry of cement and concrete. 1935. 2nd edn. 1956.

Includes a hist. Among contemp. textbooks the following are useful: David Butler Butler, *Portland cement . . .*, 1899, 3rd edn. 1913; Charles Fleming Marsh, *Reinforced concrete*, 1904, 4th edn. 1922; Albert Wells Buel and Charles Shattuck Hill, *Reinforced concrete construction*, 1905, 2nd edn. 1906; Harmon Howard Rice and William M. Torrance, *The manufacture of concrete blocks and their use in building construction*, 1906; and Oliver Wheatley, *Ornamental cement work*, 1912.

### (c) *Woodworking and Furniture-Making*

See also under Furnishings (**7152–64**).

5791 SHOREDITCH PUBLIC LIBRARIES. Furniture and allied trades: a catalogue of the books in the special collection. 1950.

5792 PATENT OFFICE. Abridgments of specifications. Class 145: wood and wood-working machinery. 1855–66 to 1926–30.

See also Patent Office, *Abridgments of specifications relating to furniture and upholstery, A.D. 1620–1866*, 1869, cont. by *Abridgments of specifications*, class 52, 1855–1930.

5793 LASLETT (THOMAS). Timber and timber trees: native and foreign. 1875. 2nd edn. 1894.

A professional manual. See also Bryan Latham, *Timber: its development and distribution: an historical survey*, 1957.

5794 LATHAM (BRYAN). History of the Timber Trade Federation of the United Kingdom: the first seventy years. 1965.

5795 BOULTON (*Sir* HAROLD EDWIN) *ed.* A century of wood preserving. 1930.

5796  GOODMAN (WILLIAM LOUIS). The history of woodworking tools. 1964.

See also his *British plane makers from 1700* [1968], and Thomas Hibben, *The carpenter's tool chest*, N.Y. & Lond. 1933.

5797  ROSE (WALTER). The village carpenter. Camb. 1937.

5798  NEWLANDS (JAMES). The carpenter and joiner's assistant. Glasgow. 1857–60. New edn. Lond. 1877–80.

5799  RIDDELL (ROBERT). The carpenter and joiner, stair-builder and hand-railer. Edin. [1870.]

5800  RICHARDS (JOHN). A treatise on the construction and operation of wood-working machines: including a history of the origin and progress of the manufacture of wood-working machinery. 1872.

5801  ELLIS (GEORGE). Modern practical carpentry for the use of workmen, builders, architects and engineers . . . 1906. 3rd edn. 1927.

Suppl. by his *Modern practical joinery . . .*, 1902, 5th edn. 1924.

5802  BOURNE (GEORGE) *pseud. of* STURT (GEORGE). The wheelwright's shop. Camb. 1923. Repr. 1934 etc.

5803  THE CABINET MAKER DIRECTORY AND YEAR BOOK. 1904+.

A directory of the furniture trade. The leading periodical was *The cabinet maker and complete house furnisher*, 1880+.

5804  OLIVER (JOHN LEONARD). The development and structure of the furniture industry. Oxf. 1966.

See also *Furniture history: the j. of the Furniture History Soc.*, 1+, 1965+.

5805  MAYES (LEONARD JOHN). The history of chairmaking in High Wycombe. 1960.

5806  HOPKINSON. Victorian cabinet-maker: the memoirs of James Hopkinson, 1819–1894. Ed. by Jocelyne Baty Goodman. 1968.

5807  WELLS (PERCY A.) *and* HOOPER (JOHN). Modern cabinet work, furniture & fitments: an account of the theory & practice in the production of all kinds of cabinet work & furniture, with chapters on the growth and progress of design and construction. 1909. 6th edn. 1952.

## 11. FISHERIES

The many branches of the fisheries industry were subjected to official economic and scientific investigations on an astonishingly large scale throughout the period. The reports of these investigations, international conferences, international agreements, conferences of local authorities, along with the annual reports of the

Inspectors of Sea Fisheries, 1886+, Salmon Fisheries, 1862+, and the various branches of the Scottish and Irish fisheries, form an enormous literature, which has never been systematically examined. Most of it is listed, in the *General index* (**33**) of parl. papers. Only a few major items are included here. Fishery statistics were incl. in the general *Statistical abstract*, **127**.

5808  DEAN (BASHFORD). A bibliography of fishes. Ed. by Charles Roches-ter Eastman and Eugene Willis Gudger. Amer. Museum of Nat. Hist. 3 v. N.Y. 1916–23.

Incls. works on fisheries and marine biology.

5809  THE BRITISH FISHERIES DIRECTORY, 1883–84. 1884.

5810  JENKINS (JAMES TRAVIS). The sea fisheries. 1920.

The best account of the early-20th-cent. industry. But needs to be suppl. by Johnstone (**5816**), Innis (**1510**), and Moore (**5818**). For fishing boats see Edgar James March, *Sailing trawlers: the story of deep-sea fishing with long line and trawl*, 1953.

5811  JENKINS (JAMES TRAVIS). The herring and the herring fisheries. 1927.

See also Arthur Michael Samuel, Baron Mancroft, *The herring: its effect on the history of Britain*, 1918; John Mitchell Mitchell, *The herring: its natural history and national importance*, Edin. 1864; John William De Caux, *The herring and the herring fishery . . .*, Norwich 1881; W. S. Miln, *An exposure of the position of the Scotch herring trade in 1885, and proposals for its reformation*, 1886; Albert E. Lark, 'The herring fishery', *Roy. Stat. Soc. J.* lxx (1907), 242–59; and W. C. Smith, *A short history of the Irish Sea herring fisheries during the eighteenth and nineteenth centuries*, Port Erin Biol. Station, Liverpool & Lond. 1923. For the boats used see Edgar James March, *Sailing drifters: the story of the herring luggers of England, Scotland and the Isle of Man*, 1952, repr. Newton Abbot 1969.

5812  JENKINS (JAMES TRAVIS). A history of the whale fisheries: from the Basque fisheries of the tenth century to the hunting of the finner whale at the present date. 1921.

Suppl. by his *Whales and modern whaling*, 1932.

5813  HOLDSWORTH (EDMUND WILLIAM HUNT). Deep-sea fishing and fishing boats: an account of the practical working of the various fisheries around the British Islands; with illustrations and descriptions of the boats, nets, and other gear in use. 1874.

The best book of its kind. Holdsworth also publ. a short account of *Sea fisheries*, bound with Archibald Young, *Salmon fisheries*, in Bevan's *British Industries* series (**4781**), 1877. This was reissued separately as *The sea fisheries of Great Britain and Ireland . . .*, 1883. Peter Lund Simmonds, *The commercial products of the sea: or, marine contributions to food, industry and art*, 1879, is a useful complementary work.

5814  SWITHINBANK (HAROLD) *and* BULLEN (GEORGE EBS-WORTH). The scientific and economic aspects of the Cornish pilchard fishery. 2 pts. St. Albans. 1913–14.

5815  GREEN (NEAL). Fisheries of the North Sea. 1918.
Thin, popular.

5816  JOHNSTONE (JAMES). British fisheries: their administration and their
problems: a short account of the origin and growth of British sea-fishery
authorities and regulations. 1905.

5817  FULTON (THOMAS WEMYSS). The sovereignty of the sea: an
historical account of the claims of England to the dominion of the British seas,
and of the evolution of the territorial waters, with special reference to the
rights of fishing and the naval salute. 1911.
Useful on fisheries conventions.

5818  MOORE (STUART ARCHIBALD) *and* MOORE (HUBERT
STUART). The history and law of fisheries. 1903.

5819  CUNNINGHAM (JOSEPH THOMAS). The natural history of the
marketable marine fishes of the British Isles. 1896.

5820  CUTTING (CHARLES LATHAM). Fish saving: a history of fish
processing from ancient to modern times. 1955.

5821  MATHER (E. J.). Nor'ard of the dogger: or, deep-sea trials and gospel
triumphs; being, the story of the initiation, struggles and successes of the
mission to deep-sea fishermen. 1887. Several edns. to 1931.
For the most successful of the missioners see James Lennox Kerr, *Wilfred Grenfell:
his life and work*, N.Y. 1959, *A Labrador doctor: the autobiography of Wilfred Thomason
Grenfell*, Lond. & Boston 1919, and revisions, and Norman Duncan, *Dr. Grenfell's
parish: the deep-sea fishermen*, N.Y. & Lond. 1905.

5822  GREAT INTERNATIONAL FISHERIES EXHIBITION, 1883.
Papers of the conferences . . . 45 v. 1883.
These papers, the 6 v. of *Handbooks*, the 14 v. of *The fisheries exhibition literature* . . .,
the *Official catalogue*, and other papers relating to the exhibition, are among the main
sources for the late-19th-cent. fishing industry in all countries.

5823  CAIRD COMMISSION ON SEA FISHERIES. Report of the commissioners appointed to inquire into the sea fisheries of the United Kingdom
[Chairman: Sir James Caird]. [3596] H.C. (1866). XVII, 571. Minutes of
evidence. [3596–I] H.C. (1866). XVIII, 1.
The first major report on the industry as a whole.

5824  BUCKLAND (FRANCIS TREVELYAN) *and* WALPOLE (*Sir*
SPENCER). Report by Frank Buckland, Esq., and Spencer Walpole, Esq.,
inspectors of fisheries for England and Wales, and commissioners for sea
fisheries, on the sea fisheries of England and Wales. [C. 2449] H.C. (1878–9).
XVII, 251.

5825  NORWOOD COMMITTEE ON SEA FISHING TRADE. Report of
a committee appointed under a minute of the Board of Trade, to inquire into

and report whether any and what legislation is desirable with a view to placing the relations between the owners, masters and crews of fishing vessels on a more satisfactory basis [Chairman: Charles Morgan Norwood]. [C. 3432] H.C. (1882). XVII, 665.

5826 DALHOUSIE COMMISSION ON TRAWLING. Report of the commissioners appointed to inquire and report upon the complaints that have been made by line and drift-net fishermen of injuries sustained by them in their calling owing to the use of the trawl net and beam trawl in the territorial waters of the United Kingdom [Chairman: Earl of Dalhousie]. [C. 4328] H.C. (1884–5). XVI, 471.

5827 HOWARD COMMITTEE ON INSHORE FISHERIES. Report of the departmental committee on inshore fisheries [Chairman: Sir Edward Stafford Howard]. [Cd. 7373] H.C. (1914). XXX, 481. Minutes of evidence. [Cd. 7374] H.C. (1914). XXX, 569.

5828 MACLEOD (ROY MALCOLM). 'Government and resource conservation: the Salmon Acts administration, 1860–1886'. *J. British Studs.* vii (1967–8), pt. 2, 114–50.

5829 JARDINE COMMISSION ON SALMON FISHERIES. Report of the commissioners appointed to inquire into salmon fisheries (England and Wales) [Chairman: Sir William Jardine]. [2768] H.C. (1861). XXIII, 67. Maps accomp. report. [2768–I] H.C. (1861). XXIII, 659.

5830 DODDS COMMITTEE ON SALMON FISHERIES. Report from the select committee on salmon fisheries [Chairman: Joseph Dodds]. H.C. 361 (1868–9). VII, 525. Further report. H.C. 368 (1870). VI, 371.

5831 ELGIN COMMISSION ON SALMON FISHERIES. Report of the commissioners on salmon fisheries [Chairman: Earl of Elgin]. Pt. I. Report and maps. [Cd. 1188] H.C. (1902). XIII, 1. Pt. II. Minutes of evidence. [Cd. 1269] H.C. (1902). XIII, 75. Pt. III. Appendix (England and Wales). [Cd. 1280] H.C. (1902). XIV, 1. Pt. IV. Appendix (Scotland). [Cd. 1281] H.C. (1902). XIV, 263.

A voluminous inquiry.

5832 THE FISH TRADES GAZETTE. 1883+.

The chief trade j.

## 12. Leather Industries

5833 U.S. LIBRARY OF CONGRESS. List of references on the leather industry: including history, production, uses, chemistry and economics. Wash. 1918.

Suppl. by a *List of references on tanning materials*, Wash. 1920, and *Leather and the leather industry: a list of recent books*, Wash. 1928, new edn. 1940.

5834 PATENT OFFICE. Abridgments of specifications relating to skins, hides and leather, A.D. 1627–1866. 1872. Cont. by Abridgments of specifications, class 76. 1855–1930.

5835 WATERER (JOHN W.). Leather in life, art and industry: being, an outline of its preparation and uses in Britain yesterday and today. 1946.

A useful introduction. Among js. *The leather trades circular*, 1867–97, and *Leather* [*The leather world*], 1909+, were prominent. William Gordon Rimmer, 'Leeds leather industry in the nineteenth century', *Thoresby Soc. Publs.* xlvi (1957–61), 119–64, is good.

5836 [TOMLINSON, RUTH.] Bibliographical index: boots and shoes, leather, rubber & other materials. Nat. Instn. of the Boot and Shoe Industry. 1936.

5837 ST. CRISPIN: a weekly journal devoted to the interest of boot and shoe makers. 1869–78.

Cont. as *The boot and shoe maker*, 1878–9, and *The boot and shoe trades j.*, 1880–1915+. Noted for its one-time editor, John Bedford Leno. Other periodicals were *Boot and shoe trades chronicle*, 1876–7, cont. as *Shoe and leather trades chronicle*, 1877–87, *The shoe and leather record*, 1886+, and *The shoe manufacturers monthly*, Leicester 1895+.

5838 WRIGHT (THOMAS). The romance of the shoe: being, the history of shoemaking in all ages and especially in England and Scotland. 1922.

One of a number of similar books. Ernest Bordoli, *Footwear down the ages*, Northampton 1933, is a poor pamphlet.

5839 HILLMANN (H. C.). 'Size of firms in the boot and shoe industry'. *Econ. J.* xlix (1939), 276–93.

To be suppl. by the account by P. Head in Aldcroft (4752).

5840 CHURCH (ROY ANTHONY). 'The effect of the American export invasion on the British boot and shoe industry, 1885–1914'. *J. Econ. Hist.* xxviii (1968), 223–54.

See also his 'Labour supply and innovation, 1800–1860: the boot and shoe industry', *Business Hist.* xii (1970), 25–45, and 'The British leather industry and foreign competition, 1870–1914', *Econ. Hist. Rev.* 2 ser. xxiv (1971), 543–70.

5841 BUTMAN (ARTHUR B.). Shoe and leather trades in the United Kingdom. U.S. Bureau of Manufactures. Special agents ser. 49. Wash. 1912.

Good.

5842 SPARKS (W. L.). The story of shoemaking in Norwich: from the earliest times to the present day. Northampton. 1949.

Other local hists. incl. Peter Geoffrey Hall, 'The East London footwear industry: an industrial quarter in decline', *East London papers* v (1962), 3–21, and P. R. Mounfield, 'The footwear industry of the East Midlands', *East Midland Geographer* iii (1962–5), 293–306, 394–413, 434–53; iv (1966–9), 8–23, 154–75, and 'The shoe industry in Staffordshire, 1767–1951', *North Staffordshire J. of Field Studs.* v (1965), 74–80, but the fullest accounts are in *V.C.H.* for Northamptonshire and Leicestershire.

**5843 BARBER (L. H.). Clarks of Street, 1825–1950. Street. 1950.**

A useful hist. of an important shoe firm. See also G. B. Sutton, 'The marketing of ready-made footwear in the nineteenth century: a study of the firm of C. & J. Clark', *Business Hist.* vi (1963–4), 93–112, and Kenneth Hudson, *Towards precision shoe-making: C. & J. Clark Limited and the development of the British shoe industry*, Newton Abbot 1968.

**5844 LENO (JOHN BEDFORD). The art of boot and shoe making: a practical handbook . . . 1885. New edn. 1949.**

The best-known of all contemp. text books; by a Radical poet. A good later textbook is Edward J. C. Swaysland, *Boot and shoe design and manufacture*, Northampton 1905. But Frank Plucknett, *Boot and shoe manufacture: a comprehensive and authoritative guide to the principles and methods employed in the manufacture of the different styles of modern footwear*, 1931, is also useful.

# E. COMMERCE

## 1. GENERAL

### (a) *Commerce Generally*

**5845 BOARD OF TRADE. British and foreign trade and industry: memoranda, statistical tables and charts, prepared in the Board of Trade with reference to various matters bearing on British and foreign trade and industrial conditions. [Cd. 1761] H.C. (1903). LXVII, 253. Second ser. [Cd. 2337] H.C. (1905). LXXXIV, 1. Index. [Cd. 2669] H.C. (1905). LXXXIV, 669. Statistical tables and charts . . . 1854–1908. [Cd. 4954] H.C. (1909). CII, 693.**

The handiest set of trade statistics, with details for all parts of the world. An earlier series was publ. in batches from 1879 onwards. For the character of trade statistics see Sir Robert Giffen, 'The use of import and export statistics', *Stat. Soc. J.* xlv (1882), 181–284, and *Report of the committee appointed by the Board of Trade to consider and report how far any change is desirable in the form in which the trade accounts of the United Kingdom are published* . . . [Chairman: Sir Robert Giffen]. [Cd. 4345] H.C. (1908). H.C. XXV, 1041. Minutes of evidence. [Cd. 4346] H.C. (1908). XXV, 1049.

**5846 WILLIAMSON (JEFFREY G.). 'The long swing: comparisons between British and American balance of payments, 1820–1913'. *J. Econ. Hist.* xxii (1962), 21–46.**

See also Ilse Mintz, *Trade balances during business cycles: U.S. and Britain since 1880* Nat. Bureau Econ. Research Occ. Paper 67, N.Y. 1959.

**5847 HABAKKUK (HROTHGAR JOHN). 'Free trade and commercial expansion, 1853–1870'. *Camb. Hist. British Empire* (1237). II. 751–805.**

**5848 LEWIS (*Sir* WILLIAM ARTHUR). 'World production, prices and trade, 1870–1960'. *Manch. School* xx (1952), 105–38.**

**5849 LEVI (LEONE). The history of British commerce and of the economic progress of the British nation, 1763–1870. 1872. 2nd edn. [1763–1878.] 1880.**

Largely replaced for contemporaries by Cunningham (4068), and Page (4070).

5850   HUGHES (JONATHAN ROBERTS TYSON). 'The commercial crisis of 1857'. *Oxf. Econ. Papers* new ser. viii (1956), 194–222.

See also the fuller analysis of commercial fluctuations, 1850–60, at **4076**.

5851   EVANS (DAVID MORIER). The history of the commercial crisis, 1857–58, and the stock exchange panic of 1859. 1859. Repr. N.Y. & Newton Abbot. 1969.

See also Clément Juglar, *Des crises commerciales et de leur retour périodique en France, en Angleterre, et aux États Unis*, Paris 1862, 2nd edn. 1889.

5852   EVANS (DAVID MORIER). Facts, failures and frauds: revelations financial, mercantile, criminal. 1859. Repr. 1968.

5853   BOURNE (STEPHEN). Trade, population and food: a series of papers on economic statistics. 1880.

5854   HYNDMAN (HENRY MAYERS). Commercial crises of the nineteenth century. 1892. 2nd edn. 1902.

5855   TUGAN-BARANOVSKII (MIKHAIL IVANOVICH). Promyshlennye krizisy: ocherk iz sotsial'noi istorii Anglii. 2nd edn. St. Petersburg. 1900.

Also avail. in French [where the author is called Michel Tougan-Baranowsky] as *Les crises industrielles en Angleterre*, trans. by Joseph Schapiro, Paris 1913, and in German as *Studien zur Theorie und Geschichte der Handelskrisen in England*, Jena 1901. Repr. Aalen, 1969.

5856   WOLFE (ARCHIBALD JOHN). Commercial organizations in the United Kingdom: with a description of British manufacturers' and employers' organizations. U.S. Dept. of Commerce special agents ser. 102. Wash. 1915.

5857   BASSETT (HERBERT HARRY) *ed.* Men of note in finance and commerce, with which is incorporated 'men of office'. A biographical business directory. 1901.

One of the best publs. of its kind. See also *The red book of commerce: or, who's who in business*, 1906–39 (which absorbed *Dod's business who's who*, 1910), and *The business world: men & methods of the new Georgian era: imperial interests . . .*, 1913, 1914.

(b) *Chambers of Commerce*

5858   PASCOE (CHARLES EYRE) *ed.* The Chambers of Commerce year book: a directory of places in the United Kingdom where they are instituted, and a record of their aims and work. Vol. I. 1908–9. York. 1909.

5859   ILERSIC (ALFRED ROMAN) *and* LIDDLE (PATRICIA FLORENCE BERTRAM). Parliament of commerce: the story of the Association of British Chambers of Commerce, 1860–1960. 1960.

5860 REDFORD (ARTHUR). Manchester merchants and foreign trade . . . Manch. 2 v. 1934–56.

A good hist. of the Manchester Chamber of Commerce.

5861 BERESFORD (MAURICE WARWICK). The Leeds Chambers of Commerce. Leeds. 1951.

5862 MARTIN (WILLIAM ALEXANDER GIBSON). A century of Liverpool's commerce. Liverpool. [1950.]

5863 LEICESTER AND COUNTY CHAMBER OF COMMERCE. Centenary, 1860–1960. Leicester. 1960.

5864 RIEMSDIJK (A. K. VAN). The Netherlands Chamber of Commerce in London, 1891–1951: a record of sixty years of trade promotion. 1953.

### (c) Prices

The best outline statistics are in Mitchell and Deane (**125**), pp. 465–500, where there is a cautionary note on the element of guesswork in the major statistical series. For the period after 1850 the best general indices are those of Rousseaux (**5873**), Sauerbeck (**5867**), and the Board of Trade (**5868**).

5865 LAYTON (WALTER THOMAS), *Baron Layton*. An introduction to the study of prices with special reference to the history of the nineteenth century. 1912. New edn. by Layton and Geoffrey Crowther. 1937.

5866 BROWN (ERNEST HENRY PHELPS) *and* HOPKINS (SHEILA V.). 'Seven centuries of the prices of consumables, compared with builders' wage-rates'. *Economica* new ser. xxiii (1956), 296–314.

5867 SAUERBECK (AUGUSTUS). The course of average prices of general commodities in England. 1908.

See also Sauerbeck's 'Prices of commodities and the precious metals', *Stat. Soc. J.* xlix (1886), 581–648, repr. in Carus-Wilson, *Essays* (**4066**), III, 68–127, with suppls. in *Stat. Soc. J.* lii (1889), 116–20, and liii (1890), 141–5, and 'Prices of commodities during the last seven years', *Roy. Stat. Soc. J.* lvi (1893), 215–47, a ser. cont. by *The Statist*. There are further statistics in R. H. Hooker, 'The course of prices at home and abroad, 1890–1910', *Roy. Stat. Soc. J.* lxxv (1911–12), 1–36.

5868 BOARD OF TRADE. Report on wholesale and retail prices in the United Kingdom in 1902: with comparative statistical tables for a series of years. H.C. 321 (1903). LXVIII, 1.

5869 TOOKE (THOMAS) *and* NEWMARCH (WILLIAM). A history of prices, and of the state of the circulation from 1792 to [1856]. 6 v. 1838–57. New edn. by Sir Theodore Emanuel Gugenheim Gregory. 6 v. 1928.

Cont. by Michael George Mulhall, *History of prices since the year 1850*, 1885.

5870 SILVERMAN (A. G.) 'Monthly index numbers of British export and import prices, 1880–1913'. *Rev. Econ. Stats.* xii (1930), 139–48.

5871 CRUMP (ARTHUR). An investigation into the causes of the great fall in prices which took place coincidently with the demonetisation of silver by Germany. 1889.

5872 DANSON (JOHN TOWNE). Economic and statistical studies, 1840–1890. 1906.

Incls. many useful diagrams showing commodity prices, etc. to 1890.

5873 ROUSSEAUX (PAUL). Les mouvements de fond de l'économie anglaise, 1800–1913. Univ. of Louvain. Brussels & Paris. 1938.

## 2. THE DOMESTIC MARKET

### (a) *Food Supply*

#### (i) *General*

5874 WALKER (FRANCES R.). 'Sources of food imports, 1855–1955'. Manch. Stat. Soc. Trans. (1958–9). Econ. Stats. Study Group. Pp. 16–20.

See also Stephen Bourne, 'The extent of food imports into the United Kingdom', *Manch. Stat. Soc. Trans.* (1892–3), 25–48, and 'Food products and their international distribution', *Stat. Soc. J.* xlvi (1883), 423–50, Richard F. Crawford, 'Notes on the food supply of the United Kingdom, Belgium, France and Germany', *Roy. Stat. Soc. J.* lxii (1899), 597–629, and Frank Harris Hitchcock, *Agricultural imports of the United Kingdom, 1896–1900*, U.S. Dept. of Agric. Div. of Foreign Markets Bull. 26, Wash. 1902.

5875 IMPORTED FOOD SUPPLIES. Return showing annually, for each year since 1870 . . . the imported quantities of (1) wheat, wheat meal and flour, (2) meat, including animals for food and (3) sugar retained for home consumption . . . H.C. 179 (1903). LXVIII, 513.

5876 REW (*Sir* ROBERT HENRY). 'Observations on the production and consumption of meat and dairy products'. *Roy. Stat. Soc. J.* lxvii (1904), 413–27.

Based on statistics collected by a committee and printed in *Roy. Stat. Soc. J.* lxv (1902), 367–71 and lxvii (1904), 368–412. See also Rew's 'The food production of British farms', *Roy. Agric. Soc. J.* lxiv (1903), 110–22, and 'The nation's food supplies', *Roy. Stat. Soc. j.* lxxvi (1912–13), 98–105.

5877 BALFOUR OF BURLEIGH COMMISSION ON FOOD AND RAW MATERIAL SUPPLY. Report of the royal commission on supply of food and raw material in time of war [Chairman: Lord Balfour of Burleigh]. Vol. I. Report. [Cd. 2643] H.C. (1905). XXXIX, 1. Vol. II. Minutes of evidence. [Cd. 2644] H.C. (1905). XXXIX, 217. Vol. III. Appendixes. [Cd. 2645] H.C. (1905). XL, 1.

An important reflection of contemporary anxieties. Covers all types of imported agricultural produce. The D'Abernon Commission on the natural resources of the dominions (**1226**), also produced a paper, *Food and raw material requirements of the United Kingdom*. [Cd. 8123] H.C. (1914–16). XIV, 371.

(ii) *The Agricultural Marketing System*
For the grocery trade see **5928–31**.

5878   TALLERMAN (D.). Farm produce realization. 1892.

An exhaustive critique of the agricultural marketing system. Cont. by his *Markets and marketing . . .*, 1899. Special aspects are dealt with in Sir Robert Henry Rew, 'The middleman in agriculture', *Roy. Agric. Soc. J.* liv (3 ser. iv) (1893), 59–76, and William E. Bear, 'Gambling in farm produce', ibid. 286–315.

5879   DODD (GEORGE). The food of London: a sketch of the chief varieties, sources of supply, probable quantities, modes of arrival, processes of manufacture, and machinery of distribution of the food for a community of two millions and a half. 1856.

See also W. W. Glenny, 'The fruit and vegetable markets of the metropolis', *Roy. Agric. Soc. J.* lvii (3 ser. vii) (1896), 53–67.

5880   BEAR (WILLIAM E.). 'The food supply of Manchester'. Pt. I. Vegetable produce. *Roy. Agric. Soc. J.* lviii (3 ser. viii) (1897), 205–28. Pt. II. Animal produce. Ibid. 490–515.

See also John Page, 'The sources of supply of the Manchester fruit and vegetable markets', *Roy. Agric. Soc. J.* xli (2 ser. xvi) (1880), 475–85.

5881   BLACKMAN (JANET). 'The food supply of an industrial town: a study of Sheffield's public markets, 1780–1900'. *Business Hist.* v (1962–3), 83–97.

5882   LINLITHGOW COMMITTEE ON DISTRIBUTION AND PRICES OF AGRICULTURAL PRODUCE. Ministry of Agriculture and Fisheries: departmental committee on distribution and prices of agricultural produce [Chairman: Marquess of Linlithgow]. Interim report on milk and milk products. [Cmd. 1854] H.C. (1923). IX, 41. Interim report on fruit and vegetables. [Cmd. 1892] H.C. (1923). IX, 151. Interim report on meat, poultry and eggs. [Cmd. 1927] H.C. (1923). IX, 297. Interim report on cereals, flour and bread. [Cmd. 1971] H.C. (1923). IX, 483. Final report. [Cmd. 2008] H.C. (1924). VII, 1.

Incls. a good deal of information relative to the pre-war position.

(iii) *The Corn Market*

5883   MALENBAUM (WILFRED). The world wheat economy, 1885–1939. Camb., Mass. 1953.

5884   BROOMHALL (GEORGE JAMES SHORT) *and* HUBBACK (JOHN H.). Corn trade memories: recent and remote. Liverpool. 1930.

5885   MACKENZIE (JOHN A. P.) *and* BAINES (*Sir* JERVOISE ATHELSTANE). 'Bibliography of the prices of cereals'. *Roy. Stat. Soc. J.* lxxi (1908), 178–206.

5886 LAWES (*Sir* JOHN BENNET) *and* GILBERT (*Sir* JOSEPH HENRY). 'Home produce, imports, consumption, and price of wheat, over forty harvest-years, 1852–53 to 1891–92'. *Roy. Agric. Soc. J.* liv (3 ser. iv) (1893), 77–132.

Based on a similar article on the years 1852–3 to 1879–80, *Stat. Soc. J.* xliii (1880), 313–31. See also their 'On the depression of corn prices and on the production of wheat in some of the chief exporting countries of the world', *Roy. Agric. Soc. J.* lvii (3 ser. vii) (1896), 723–37.

5887 OLSON (MANCUR LLOYD) *and* HARRIS (CURTIS C.). 'Free trade in "corn": a statistical study of the prices and production of wheat in Great Britain from 1873 to 1914'. *Quart. J. Econ.* lxxiii (1959), 145–68.

5888 ROTHSTEIN (MORTON). 'America in the international rivalry for the British wheat market, 1860–1914'. *Mississippi Valley Hist. Rev.* xlvii (1960–1), 401–18.

See also Rodman W. Paul, 'The wheat trade between California and the United Kingdom', *Mississippi Valley Hist. Rev.* xlv (1958–9), 391–412.

5889 CROOKES (*Sir* WILLIAM). The wheat problem: based on remarks made in the presidential address to the British Association at Bristol in 1898. 1899. 3rd edn. 1917.

Maintains that the world is running out of wheat, and Britain is likely to go short. See what is in effect a reply in Walter Thomas Layton, Baron Layton, 'Wheat prices and the world's production', *Roy. Agric. Soc. J.* lxx (1909), 99–110.

5890 BENNETT (RICHARD) *and* ELTON (JOHN). History of corn-milling. 4 v. 1898–1904.

5891 MORE COMMITTEE ON CORN AVERAGES. Report from the select committee on corn averages [Chairman: Jasper More]. H.C. 312 (1888). X, 1. Second report. H.C. 413 (1888). X, 207.

Discusses the value of the methods of calculating the official tables.

5892 MORE COMMITTEE ON CORN SALES. Report from the select committee on corn sales [Chairman: Jasper More]. H.C. 347 (1890–1). XII, 19. Further reports. H.C. 279 (1892–Sess. 1). XI, 475. H.C. 220 (1893–4). XI, 1.

A full discussion of corn weights and measures.

### (iv) *The Meat and Cattle Market*

5893 HOWARD (JAMES). Our meat supply. Bedford. 1876.

General comments by one of the farmers' champions.

5894 CHANNON (GEOFFREY). 'The Aberdeenshire beef trade with London: a study in steamship and railway competition, 1850–69'. *Transport Hist.* ii (1969), 1–24.

5895 CRAIGIE (PATRICK GEORGE). 'Twenty years' changes in our foreign meat supply'. *Roy. Agric. Soc. J.* xlviii (2 ser. xxiii) (1887), 465–500.

See also William David Zimmerman, 'Live cattle export trade between United States and Great Britain, 1868–1885', *Agric. Hist.* xxxvi (1962), 46–52, and Richard Perren, 'The North American beef and cattle trade with Great Britain, 1870–1914', *Econ. Hist. Rev.* 2 ser. xxiv (1971), 430–44.

5896 HOOKER (R. H.). 'The meat supply of the United Kingdom'. *Roy. Stat. Soc. J.* lxxii (1909), 304–76.

5897 MURRAY (KEITH ANDERSON HOPE), *Baron Murray of Newhaven*. Factors affecting the prices of livestock in Great Britain: a preliminary study. Agric. Econ. Inst. Oxf. 1931.

5898 WHETHAM (EDITH HOLT). 'Livestock prices in Britain, 1851–93'. *Agric. Hist. Rev.* xi (1963), 27–35. Repr. in Minchinton, *Essays* (**4157**).

See also her 'The changing cattle enterprises of England and Wales, 1870–1910', *Geog. J.* cxxix (1963), 378–80, repr. in Minchinton, *Essays* (**4157**).

5899 MACDONALD (WILLIAM). 'On the relative profits to the farmer from horse, cattle and sheep breeding, rearing and feeding in the United Kingdom'. *Roy. Agric. Soc. J.* xxxvii (2 ser. xii) (1876), 1–108.

5900 PUTNAM (GEORGE ELLSWORTH). Supplying Britain's meat. 1923.

Chiefly on chilled beef imports.

5901 CRITCHELL (JAMES TROUBRIDGE) *and* RAYMOND (JOSEPH). A history of the frozen meat trade: an account of the development and present-day methods of preparation, transport, and marketing of frozen and chilled meats. 1912.

See also R. Duncan, 'The demand for frozen beef in the United Kingdom, 1880–1940', *J. Agric. Econ.* xii (1956–7), 82–8; Patrick George Craigie, 'The growth and development of the trade in frozen mutton', *Roy. Agric. Soc. J.* l (2 ser. xxv) (1889), 203–40; R. Duncan, 'The Australian export trade with the United Kingdom in refrigerated beef, 1880–1940', *Business Archives & Hist.* ii (1962), 106–21; and Simon G. Hanson, *Argentine meat and the British market: chapters in the history of the Argentine meat industry*, Stanford, Calif. 1938. For the techniques of refrigeration see Alexander James Wallis-Tayler, *Refrigeration, cold storage and ice-making . . .*, 1902, 9th edn. 1950, and *Refrigerating and ice-making machinery . . .*, 1896, 3rd edn. 1902, and Sir James Alfred Ewing, *The mechanical production of cold*, Camb. 1908, 2nd edn. 1921.

5902 MONTAGU COMMITTEE ON METROPOLITAN FOREIGN CATTLE MARKET BILL. First report from the select committee on the Metropolitan Foreign Cattle Market Bill [Chairman: Lord Robert Montagu]. H.C. 227 (1867–8). XII, 1. Second report. H.C. 261 (1867–8). XII, 353. Third report. H.C. 303 (1867–8). XII, 479.

See also Robert Dudley Baxter, *The Foreign Cattle Market Bill*, 1869.

5903 CECIL COMMITTEE ON COMBINATIONS IN THE MEAT TRADE. Report of the departmental committee appointed to inquire into combinations in the meat trade [Chairman: Lord Robert Cecil]. [Cd. 4643] H.C. (1909). XV, 1. Minutes of evidence etc. [Cd. 4661] H.C. (1909). XV, 33.

See also *Commonwealth of Australia: report (with appendices) of the royal commission (Mr. Justice Street) on the meat export trade of Australia*. [Cd. 7896] H.C. (1914–16). XLVI, 1, on the virtual disappearance of American meat from the British market, leaving Australia and the Argentine as main suppliers. For later inquiries on the same subject see Ford, *Breviate, 1917–39* (32), pp. 118–22.

5904 REPORT ON THE MARKETING OF CATTLE AND BEEF in England and Wales. Ministry of Agric. & Fisheries. Econ. Ser. 20. 1929.

See also *Report on the trade in refrigerated beef, mutton and lamb*, Ministry of Agric. Econ. Ser. 6. 1925.

5905 CHAPLIN COMMITTEE ON TRANSATLANTIC CATTLE TRADE. Report of the departmental committee of the Board of Trade and the Board of Agriculture appointed by the President of the Board of Agriculture to inquire into and report upon the transatlantic cattle trade [Chairman: Henry Chaplin]. [C. 6350] H.C. (1890–1). LXXVIII, 269. Minutes of evidence. [C. 6350–I] H.C. (1890–1). LXXVIII, 291.

5906 HART DYKE COMMITTEE ON INLAND TRANSPORT OF CATTLE. Report of the departmental committee appointed by the Board of Agriculture to enquire into and report upon the inland transit of cattle [Chairman: Sir William Hart Dyke]. [C. 8928] H.C. (1898). XXXIV, 1. Minutes of evidence. [C. 8929] H.C. (1898). XXXIV, 29.

5907 CAMERON COMMITTEE ON ANIMALS CARRIED COASTWISE. Report of the departmental committee appointed by the Board of Agriculture to inquire into the transit by water and the embarkation and landing of animals carried coastwise [Chairman: Sir Charles Cameron]. [C. 7511] H.C. (1894). LXIX, 267. Minutes of evidence. [C. 7511–I] H.C. (1894). LXIX, 293.

5908 STRACHEY COMMITTEE ON EXPORT TRADE IN LIVE STOCK. Report of the departmental committee appointed to enquire and report as to the British export trade in live stock with the colonies and other countries [Chairman: Sir Edward Strachey]. [Cd. 5947] H.C. (1911). XXII, 359. Minutes of evidence. [Cd. 6032] H.C. (1912–13). XXV, 335.

### (v) *Other Agricultural Markets*

5909 COHEN (RUTH LOUISA). The history of milk prices: an analysis of the factors affecting the prices of milk and milk products. Oxf. 1936.

See also Sir Robert Henry Rew, 'An inquiry into the statistics of the production and consumption of milk and milk products in Great Britain', *Roy. Stat. Soc. J.* lv (1892), 244–78.

5910 THOMPSON (ROBERT JOHN). 'Wool prices in Great Britain, 1883–1901'. *Roy. Stat. Soc. J.* lxv (1902), 503–13.

5911 BROWN (*Sir* EDWARD). 'The marketing of poultry'. *Roy. Agric. Soc. J.* lix (3 ser. ix) (1898), 270–86.

See also Brown's 'The British egg supply', ibid. lxi (3 ser. xi) (1900), 605–45.

### (b) *The Coal Market and other Wholesale Markets*

5912 DOWLING (SYDNEY WILLIAM). The exchanges of London. 1929.

Not on the period but useful. Cp. Cuthbert Maughan, *Markets of London: a description of the way in which business is transacted in the principal markets and in many commodities,* 1931.

5913 SMITH (RAYMOND). Sea-coal for London: history of the coal-factors in the London market. 1961.

See also Elspet Fraser-Stephen, *Two centuries in the London coal trade: the story of Charringtons,* priv. pr. 1952, *Report from the select committee on coal duties (metropolis)* [Chairman: Sir John Shelley]. H.C. 916 (1852–3). XXII, 125, and *Report from the select committee on Coal Duties (London) Abolition Bill* [Chairman: Sir Lyon Playfair]. H.C. 228. (1889). IX, 473. For shipping of coals see *Report of the royal commissioners appointed to inquire into the spontaneous combustion of coal in ships* [Chairman: H. C. E. Childers]. [C. 1586] H.C. (1876). XLI, 1.

5914 DIXON (DONALD F.). 'Petrol distribution in the United Kingdom, 1900–1950'. *Business Hist.* vi (1963–4), 1–19.

### (c) *Retail Markets and Fairs*

5915 PEASE (JOSEPH GERALD) *and* CHITTY (HERBERT). A treatise on the law of markets and fairs: with the principal statutes relating thereto. 1899.

5916 DERBY COMMISSION ON MARKET RIGHTS AND TOLLS. First report of the royal commission on market rights and tolls [Chairman: Earl of Derby]. [C. 5550] H.C. (1888). LIII, 1. Minutes of evidence. [C. 5550–I to III] H.C. (1888). LIII, 237, LIV, 1, LV, 1. Reports of assistant commissioners (Ireland). [C. 5888, C. 5888–I] H.C. (1889). XXXVIII, 1, 429. Final report. [C. 6268] H.C. (1890–1). XXXVII, 1. Minutes of evidence etc. [C. 6268–I to VII] H.C. (1890–1). XXXVII, 243, XXXVIII to XLI.

A comprehensive survey of all the major and many of the minor markets.

5917 MINISTRY OF AGRICULTURE AND FISHERIES. Report on markets and fairs of England and Wales. Ministry of Agriculture Econ. Ser. 13–14, 19, 23, 26. 5 pts. 1927–30.

Part of a most valuable illustrated series of reports, which also incl. special reports on indiv. commodities: Wool (Econ. ser. 7, 1927), Potatoes (Econ. ser. 9, 1927), Eggs (Econ. ser. 10, 1927), Poultry (Econ. ser. 11, 1926), Pigs (Econ. ser. 12, 1927), Fruit (Econ. ser. 15, 1927), Milk (Econ. ser. 16, 1927), Pork and bacon (Econ. ser. 17, 1928), Wheat, barley, and oats (Econ. ser. 18, 1928), Cattle and beef (Econ. ser. 20, 1929), Preparation of fruit for market (Econ. ser. 21, 24, 1928–31), Dairy produce (Econ. ser. 22, 30, 1930–2), Vegetables (Econ. ser. 25, 1935), Honey and beeswax (Econ. ser. 28, 1931), and Sheep, mutton, and lamb (Econ. ser. 29, 1931).

5918 STERN (WALTER MARCEL). 'The baroness' market: the history of a noble failure'. *Guildhall Misc.* ii (1960–7), 353–66.

## (d) *Retail Shops*

5919 NYSTROM (PAUL HENRY) *comp.* Bibliography of retailing: a selected list of books, pamphlets and periodicals. Columbia Univ. School of Business. N.Y. 1928.

5920 DAVIS (DOROTHY). A history of shopping. 1966.

5921 JEFFERYS (JAMES BAVINGTON). Retail trading in Britain, 1850–1950. Camb. 1954.

5922 PASDERMADJIAN (HRANT). The department store: its origins, evolution and economics. 1954.

5923 SELFRIDGE. Selfridge: a biography. By Reginald Pound. 1960.
See also Alfred Harry Williams, *No name on the door: a memoir of Gordon Selfridge,* 1956.

5924 WHITELEY. The universal provider: a study of William Whiteley and the rise of the London department store. By Richard Stanton Lambert. 1938.

5925 BRIGGS (ASA). Friends of the people: the centenary history of Lewis's. 1956.
A good hist. of a chain of north-country department stores.

5926 REES (GORONWY). St. Michael: a history of Marks and Spencer. 1969.

5927 ADBURGHAM (ALISON) *ed.* Yesterday's shopping: the Army & Navy Stores catalogue, 1907. Newton Abbot. 1969.
Cp. *The country gentleman's catalogue,* 1894, repr. 1969.

5928 BLACKMAN (JANET). 'The development of the retail grocery trade in the nineteenth century'. *Business Hist.* ix (1967), 110–17.
There is a little background material in Joseph Aubrey Rees, *The grocery trade: its history and romance,* 2 v. 1910.

5929 PENNANCE (F. G.) *and* YAMEY (BASIL SELIG). 'Competition in the retail grocery trade, 1850–1939'. *Economica* new ser. xxii (1955), 303–17.

5930 MATHIAS (PETER). Retailing revolution: a history of multiple retailing in the food trades based upon the Allied Suppliers group of companies. 1967.

5931 WAUGH (ALEC) *pseud. of* WAUGH (ALEXANDER RABAN). The Lipton story: a centennial biography. 1951.
Provision stores founded by Sir Thomas Lipton.

5932 ADBURGHAM (ALISON). Shops and shopping, 1800–1914: where, and in what manner the well-dressed Englishwoman bought her clothes. 1964.

5933 PEEL (DEREK WILMOT DOUGLAS). A garden in the sky: the story of Barkers of Kensington, 1870–1957. 1960.

5934 DAN (HORACE) *and* WILLMOTT (EDMUND CHARLES MORGAN). English shop-fronts old and new: a series of examples by leading architects . . . 1907.

## 3. OVERSEAS TRADE

### (a) *General*

See also Shipping, **6023–192**.

5935 THE EXPORTERS' DIRECTORY [and year book of foreign trade]. 1878–81. 3 v. 1878–80.

A useful guide. See also *The mercantile year book and directory of exporters*, 1887+, *Kelly's directory of merchants, manufacturers and shippers*, 1877+, and other general commercial directories.

5936 BOARD OF TRADE (STATISTICAL DEPARTMENT). Annual statement of the trade and navigation of the United Kingdom with foreign countries and British possessions in the year 1853+. [1890] H.C. (1854–5). LI, 1+. Annual.

Shipping statistics appeared separately from 1871 (**6029**). For comments on and use of the statistics see Stephen Bourne, 'The official trade and navigation statistics', *Stat. Soc. J.* xxxv (1872), 196–217, and Yehuda Don, 'Comparability of international trade statistics: Great Britain and Austria-Hungary before World War I', *Econ. Hist. Rev.* 2 ser. xxi (1968), 78–92.

5937 THE BOARD OF TRADE JOURNAL of tariff and trade notices and miscellaneous commercial information. 1886+.

5938 D'ABERNON COMMISSION ON RESOURCES OF THE DOMI-NIONS. Memorandum and tables relating to the food and raw material requirements of the United Kingdom prepared by the Royal Commission on the Natural Resources, Trade, and Legislation of certain portions of His Majesty's Dominions. [Cd. 8123] H.C. (1914–16). XIV, 371.

A useful collection of import figures.

5939 LEVIN (JONATHAN VICTOR). The export economies: their pattern of development in historical perspective. Camb., Mass. 1960.

5940 SCHLOTE (WERNER). British overseas trade from 1700 to the 1930s. Trans. by William Otto Henderson and William Henry Chaloner. Oxf. 1952.

See also Robert E. Baldwin, 'Britain's foreign balance and terms of trade in the nineteenth century', *Explorations in Entrepreneurial Hist.* v (1952–3), 248–52.

**5941 IMLAH ALBERT HENRY).** Economic elements in the 'Pax Britannica': studies in British foreign trade in the nineteenth century. Camb., Mass. 1958.

Important. Includes material based on an important article by him, 'The terms of trade of the United Kingdom, 1798–1913', *J. Econ. Hist.* x (1950), 170–94.

**5942 KINDLEBERGER (CHARLES POOR).** 'Foreign trade and economic growth: lessons from Britain and France, 1850 to 1913'. *Econ. Hist. Rev.* 2 ser. xiv (1961–2), 289–305.

See also his *Economic growth in France and Britain, 1851–1950*, Camb., Mass. 1964.

**5943 SAUL (SAMUEL BERRICK).** Studies in British overseas trade, 1870–1914. Liverpool. 1960.

Good. See also his 'The export economy, 1870–1914' in *Yorkshire Bull.* xvii (1965), 5–18, and A. J. Brown, 'Britain in the world economy, 1870–1914', ibid. 46–60.

**5944 FORD (ALEC GEORGE).** 'Notes on the role of exports in British economic fluctuations, 1870–1914'. *Econ. Hist. Rev.* 2 ser. xvi (1963–4), 328–50.

**5945 ROSTOW (WALT WHITMAN).** 'The terms of trade in theory and practice'. *Econ. Hist. Rev.* 2nd ser. iii (1950–1), 1–20.

Cont. in his 'The historical analysis of the terms of trade', *Econ. Hist. Rev.* 2nd ser. iv (1951–2), 53–76. Began an important discussion on the whole topic reflected in Charles Poor Kindleberger, 'Industrial Europe's terms of trade on current account, 1870–1953', *Econ. J.* lxv (1955), 19–35, repr. in Carus-Wilson, *Essays* (**4066**), III, 302–17, and G. M. Maier, 'Long period determinants of Britain's terms of trade, 1880–1913', *Rev. Econ. Studs.* xx (1952–3), 115–30. These works were also influenced by discussions of trade cycles, notably in J. S. Pesmazoglu, 'Some international aspects of British cyclical fluctuations, 1870–1913', *Rev. Econ. Studs.* xvi (1948–50), 117–43.

**5946 BOURNE (STEPHEN).** 'The progress of our foreign trade, imports and exports, during the past twenty years'. *Stat. Soc. J.* xxxviii (1875), 215–39.

Cont. in his 'On variations in the volume and value of exports and imports of the United Kingdom in recent years', *Roy. Stat. Soc. J.* lii (1889), 399–428, and 'Progress of the external trade of the United Kingdom in recent years', ibid. lvi (1893), 185–207.

**5947 NEWMARCH (WILLIAM).** 'On the progress of the foreign trade of the United Kingdom since 1856, with especial reference to the effects produced upon it by the protectionist tariffs of other countries'. *Stat. Soc. J.* xli (1878), 187–282.

**5948 BOWLEY (*Sir* ARTHUR LYON).** A short account of England's foreign trade in the nineteenth century: its economic and social results. Lond. & N.Y. 1893. Rev. edn. 1905.

**5949 FLUX (*Sir* ALFRED WILLIAM).** 'The flag and trade: a summary review of the trade of the chief colonial empires'. *Roy. Stat. Soc. J.* lxii (1899), 489–522.

See also his 'The commercial supremacy of Great Britain', *Econ. J.* ix (1899), 173–83.

5950 TAUSSIG (FRANK WILLIAM). 'The change in Great Britain's foreign trade terms after 1900'. *Econ. J.* xxxv (1925), 1–10.

The work of a famous economist, whose *International trade*, N.Y. 1927, is also worth consulting.

5951 FORSTER COMMITTEE ON TRADE WITH FOREIGN NATIONS. Report from the select committee on trade with foreign nations [Chairman: W. E. Forster]. H.C. 493 (1864). VII, 279.

Discusses the role of the Foreign Office and Board of Trade in foreign trade. Trade statistics were discussed in *Report from the select committee on charges on foreign trade (Customs Act, 1860)* [Chairman: George Moffatt]. H.C. 429 (1862). XII, 1.

5952 OPINIONS of H.M. diplomatic and consular officers on British trade methods. [C. 9078] H.C. (1899). XCVI, 619.

Extracts from reports. For British consuls and foreign trade see **2232**.

5953 GIFFEN (*Sir* ROBERT). Report to the secretary of the Board of Trade on recent changes in the amount of the foreign trade of the United Kingdom and the prices of imports and exports. [C. 3079] H.C. (1881). LXXXIII, 149.

5954 JEANS (JAMES STEPHEN). England's supremacy: its sources, economics and dangers. 1885.

Good.

5955 GASTRELL (WILLIAM SHAW HARRISS). Our trade in the world in relation to foreign competition, 1885 to 1895. 1897.

5956 DRAGE (GEOFFREY). The imperial organization of trade. 1911.

A free-trade imperialist on the details of international and imperial trade. See also John Wilson Root, *The trade relations of the British empire*, Liverpool 1903.

5957 BERNHARDT (GASTON DE) *comp.* Handbook of commercial treaties, &c., between Great Britain and foreign powers. H.M.S.O. 1912.

A useful manual comp. in the Foreign office. For other collections of commercial treaties see **(920–2)**.

5958 BALFOUR COMMITTEE ON INDUSTRY AND TRADE. Committee on industry and trade [Chairman: Sir Arthur Balfour, later Lord Riverdale]. Survey of overseas markets: based on material, mainly derived from official sources, with regard to the conditions prevailing in various overseas markets which affect British export trade, together with statistical and other information, with an introduction by the committee. 1925.

(b) *Free Trade and Protection*

5959 McCORD (NORMAN) *comp.* Free trade: theory and practice from Adam Smith to Keynes. Newton Abbot. 1970.

A handy coll. of docs.

5960 FUCHS (CARL JOHANNES). The trade policy of Great Britain and her colonies since 1860. Trans. by Constance H. M. Archibald. 1905.

5961 DUNHAM (ARTHUR LOUIS). The Anglo-French treaty of commerce of 1860 and the progress of the industrial revolution in France. Ann Arbor [Mich.]. 1930.

5962 HOFFMAN (ROSS JOHN SWARTZ). Great Britain and the German trade rivalry, 1875–1914. Phila. 1933.

For other works on the topic see **2302**.

5963 CALKINS (W. N.). 'A Victorian free trade lobby'. *Econ. Hist. Rev.* 2 ser. xiii (1960–1), 90–104.

On the early hist. of the Financial Reform Assoc.

5964 A HISTORY OF THE COBDEN CLUB. By members of the club [i.e. Christopher John Laurence Brock and Sir Gilbert Hollinshead Blomfield Jackson]. 1939.

The leading free trade body of the late 19th cent. It publ. a ser. of leaflets, 1870–1920, and a number of substantial studs.

5965 BROWN (BENJAMIN HOUSTON). The tariff reform movement in Great Britain, 1881–1895. N.Y. 1943.

See also Sydney Henry Zebel, 'Fair trade: an English reaction to the breakdown of the Cobden treaty system', *J. Mod. Hist.* xii (1940), 161–85.

5966 U.S. LIBRARY OF CONGRESS. Select list of references on the British tariff movement (Chamberlain's plan). Wash. 1904. 2nd edn. 1906.

A brief bibliog.

5967 ZEBEL (SYDNEY HENRY). 'Joseph Chamberlain and the genesis of tariff reform'. *J. British Studs.* vii (1967–8), 131–57.

A useful intro. See also the lives of Joseph and Austen Chamberlain (**749–50**), Arthur Balfour (**727**), the Duke of Devonshire (**778**), and other prominent politicians, and Semmel, *Imperialism and social reform* (**969**).

5968 GOLLIN (ALFRED MANUEL). Balfour's burden: Arthur Balfour and imperial preference. 1965.

5969 FAWCETT (HENRY). Free trade and protection: an inquiry into the causes which have retarded the general adoption of free trade since its introduction into England. 1878.

One of the most widely quoted defences of free trade. For orthodox free-trade statements see Anthony John Mundella, 'What are the conditions on which the commercial and manufacturing supremacy of Great Britain depend, and is there any reason to think they have been, or may be endangered?', *Stat. Soc. J.* xli (1878), 87–112; Augustus Mongredien, *History of the free-trade movement in England*, 1881, new edn. 1897; Thomas Henry Farrer, Baron Farrer, *Free trade versus fair trade*, Cobden Club 1882, 3rd edn. 1886, new edn. 1904, and *The state in its relation to trade*, 1883, new edn. 1902; Charles Francis Bastable, *The theory of international trade, with some of its applications to economic policy*, Dublin & Lond. 1887, 4th edn. 1903; Henry Dunckley and others, *Richard Cobden and the jubilee of free trade*, 1896; George Armitage-Smith, *The free-trade movement and its results*, Victorian era ser., 1898, 2nd edn. 1903.

5970   ECROYD (WILLIAM FARRER). The policy of self-help: suggestions towards the consolidation of the empire and the defence of its industries and commerce: two letters . . . 1879. 4th edn. 1881.

The first move towards protection. Other attacks on free trade incl. Richard Gill, *Free Trade: an inquiry into the nature of its operation*, Edin. & Lond. 1887; Andrew Williamson, *British industries and foreign competition*, 1894; Edwin Burgis, *Perils to British trade: how to avert them*, 1895, 3rd edn. 1904; and Ernest Edwin Williams, *The case for protection*, 1899.

5971   CAILLARD (*Sir* VINCENT HENRY PENALVER). Imperial fiscal reform. 1903.

A careful protectionist before Chamberlain.

5972   CHAMBERLAIN (JOSEPH). Imperial union and tariff reform: speeches delivered from May 15 to November 4, 1903. 1903.

The start of the tariff reform movt. A parallel explanatory vol. was issued: Charles Anthony Vince, *Mr. Chamberlain's proposals: what they mean and what we shall gain by them*, 1903. To this George Herbert Perris, *The protectionist peril: an examination of Mr. Chamberlain's proposals*, 1903, was a quick response. A strident protectionist equivalent is Thomas Penn Gaskell, *Free trade: a failure from the first*, 1903.

5973   BALFOUR (ARTHUR JAMES). Fiscal reform: speeches delivered . . . from June 1880 to December 1905, together with a reprint of the pamphlet 'Economic notes on insular free trade' and letters from and to the Right Hon. Joseph Chamberlain, M.P. (September 1903). 1906.

5974   GILMOUR (THOMAS LENNOX) *ed.* All sides of the fiscal controversy: speeches . . . 1903.

5975   LUBBOCK (JOHN), *Baron Avebury*. Free trade. 1904.

The free-trade case. See also William Smart, *The return to protection: being, a re-statement of the case for free trade*, 1904, 2nd edn. 1906, and Sir Leo George Chiozza Money, *Elements of the fiscal problem*, 1903, and *Through preference to protection: an examination of Mr. Chamberlain's fiscal proposals*, 1903. Thomas Brassey, Earl Brassey, *Fifty years of progress and the new fiscal policy*, 1904, new edns. 1906, 1911, 1914, with varying titles, states the free-trade case for an independent commission of inquiry.

5976   ASHLEY (*Sir* WILLIAM JAMES). The tariff problem. 1903. 4th edn. 1920.

Perhaps the strongest case for a tariff system.

5977   TARIFF REFORM LEAGUE. A short handbook for speakers and students of the policy of preferential tariffs. 1904. 7th edn. 1912.

The League also publ. *Monthly notes on tariff reform*, 1904–14.

5978   TARIFF COMMISSION, 1904–7. Established by Joseph Chamberlain to report on the tariff question. Its reports, at **4791**, are a valuable source.

A free-trade equiv. on a much smaller scale was Cox, *British industries under free trade* (**4790**).

5979  ROBERTSON (JOHN MACKINNON). Trade and tariffs. 1908.
A confident restatement of the free-trade case. Cp. Russell Rea, *Free trade in being*, 1908.

5980  HILLIER (ALFRED PETER). The Commonweal: a study of the federal system of political economy. 1909.

5981  CUNNINGHAM (WILLIAM). The case against free trade. 1911.
See also Edwin Ernest Enever Todd, *The case against tariff reform: a reply to 'The case against free trade' by Archdeacon Cunningham*, 1911.

5982  DRAGE (GEOFFREY). The imperial organization of trade. 1911.
Useful for imperial trade connections.

5983  PEEL ([ARTHUR] GEORGE [VILLIERS]). The tariff reformers. 1913.

## F. TRANSPORT

### 1. GENERAL

5984  JOHNSON (LEONARD CHARLES). 'Historical records of the British Transport Commission'. *J. Transport. Hist.* i (1953–4), 82–96. Suppl. v (1961–2), 159–65.

5985  BOND (MAURICE FRANCIS). 'Materials for transport history among the records of parliament'. *J. Transport. Hist.* iv (1959–60), 37–52.

5986  SIMMONS (JACK). Transport museums in Britain and western Europe. 1970.

5987  PRATT (EDWIN A.). History of inland transport and communication. 1912. Repr. Newton Abbot. 1970.
Good. William T. Jackman, *The development of transportation in modern England*, 2 v. Camb. 1916, new edn. by William Henry Chaloner, Lond. 1962, has little post-1850. Of more popular books, Jack Simmons, *Transport* [1962], is the best. Thomas Burke, *Travel in England: from pilgrim and packhorse to light car and plane*, 1942, is typical of the popular hists. Of contemp. general surveys the most useful is Amable Charles, Comte Franquet de Franqueville, *Du régime des travaux publics en Angleterre: rapport addressé à M. le Ministre des Travaux Publics*, 4 v. Paris 1874, 2nd edn. 4 v. 1875.

5988  SHERRINGTON (CHARLES ELY ROSE). A hundred years of inland transport, 1830–1933. 1934. Repr. 1969.

5989  DYOS (HAROLD JOHN) *and* ALDCROFT (DEREK HOWARD). British transport: an economic survey from the seventeenth century to the twentieth. Leicester. 1969.
Good. Full bibliog.

5990 SAVAGE (CHRISTOPHER IVOR). An economic history of transport. 1959. 2nd edn. 1961.

5991 KIRKALDY (ADAM WILLIS) *and* EVANS (ALFRED DUDLEY). The history and economics of transport. 1915. 5th edn. 1931.
Very useful.

5992 HULTGREN (THOR). Transport and the state of trade in Britain. Nat. Bureau Econ. Res. Occasional Paper 40. N.Y. & Lond. 1953.

5993 JOURNAL OF TRANSPORT HISTORY. 1–7. Leicester. 1953/4–65/6. 2 ser. 1+. Leicester. 1971/2+.
For a time the only British j. in the field. See also *Transport history*, 1+, Newton Abbot 1968+.

5994 BARKER (THEODORE CARDWELL) *and* ROBBINS ([RICHARD] MICHAEL). A history of London Transport: passenger travel and the development of the metropolis. Vol. I: 'The nineteenth century'. 1963.
Good. See also G. A. Sekon, pseud. of George Augustus Nokes, *Locomotion in Victorian London*, 1938, and Owen James Morris, ed., *Fares please: the story of London's road transport*, 1953.

5995 LONDON COUNTY COUNCIL (Local Government and Statistical Department). Locomotive service: return of services and routes by tramways, omnibuses, steamboats, railways and canals in the County of London and in Extra-London. Part I. 1895.
Part II on railways and canals never publ.

5996 BOOTH (CHARLES). Improved means of locomotion as a first step towards the cure of the housing difficulties in London. 1901.

5997 HARPER (EDGAR J.). 'Statistics of London traffic'. *Roy. Stat. Soc. J.* lxvii (1904), 177–219.

5998 BROWNING HALL CONFERENCE. Report of the sub-committee on housing and locomotion in London, 1902–7: with an appendix on the conditions prevailing in Lewisham, Greenwich and Woolwich. 1907.

5999 BARBOUR COMMISSION ON LONDON TRANSPORT. Report of the royal commission appointed to inquire into and report upon the means of locomotion and transport in London [Chairman: Sir David Miller Barbour]. [Cd. 2597] H.C. (1905). XXX, 533. Minutes of evidence. [Cd. 2751–2. Cd. 2787. Cd. 2798–9. Cd. 2743–4] H.C. (1906). XL–XLVI.
A monumental inquiry.

## 2. CANALS AND WATERWAYS

6000 PERMANENT INTERNATIONAL ASSOCIATION OF NAVIGA-
TION CONGRESSES. Rivers, canals and ports: bibliographic notes giving
the list of the principal works which have appeared and of the articles published
in periodicals. 6 v. covering 1892–1931. Brussels. 1908–32.

Less valuable than the title suggests. A good canal bibliog. is badly needed. Chiefly
concerned to suppl. the work of the International Congress of Navigation, the first
session of which met in Brussels in 1885. The various publs. of the congresses (the
12th was held in Philadelphia in 1912), which were at first intended to confine themselves to inland navigation, include a good deal of valuable material, but little of it is on
Britain.

6001 HADFIELD ([ELLIS] CHARLES [RAYMOND]). British canals: an
illustrated history. 1950. 4th edn. 1969.

The standard introduction to the subject. But see also Lionel Thomas Caswall Rolt,
*Navigable waterways*, 1969, which is strong on canal engineering. Hugh McKnight,
*Canal and river craft in pictures*, Newton Abbot 1969, is a pleasant picture book.

6002 FORBES (URQUHART ATWELL) *and* ASHFORD (W. H. R.). Our
waterways: a history of inland navigation considered as a branch of water
conservancy. 1906.

6003 DE SALIS (HENRY RODOLPH). Bradshaw's canals and navigable
rivers of England and Wales: a handbook of inland navigation for manufacturers, merchants, traders and others; compiled after a personal survey of
the whole of the waterways. 1904. 3rd edn. 1928. 1904 edn. repr. Newton
Abbot. 1969.

6004 SELECT COMMITTEE ON CANALS. Report from the select committee on canals [Chairman: Thomas Salt]. H.C. 252 (1883). XIII, 1.

The work of this committee was continued in the next session: see *Report from the
select committee on the Canal Boats Act (1877) Amendment Bill* [Chairman: W. E.
Forster]. H.C. 263 (1884). VIII, 435.

6005 ROYAL SOCIETY OF ARTS. Report of the canal conference of 1888
. . . 1888.

6006 SHUTTLEWORTH COMMISSION ON CANALS AND INLAND
NAVIGATIONS. First report of the royal commission appointed to
inquire into and to report on the canals and inland navigations of the United
Kingdom [Chairman: Lord Shuttleworth]. [Cd. 3183] H.C. (1906). XXXII,
1. Minutes of evidence. [Cd. 3184] H.C. (1906). XXXII, 9. Second report.
[Cd. 3716] H.C. (1907). XXXIII, pt. 1, 1. Minutes of evidence and returns.
[Cd. 3717–19] H.C. (1907). XXXIII, pt. 1, 9, pt. 2, 1. Third report. [Cd.
4839]. H.C. (1909). XIII, 1. Accompanying documents. [Cd. 4940–1] H.C.
(1909). XIII, 9. Fourth and final report. [Cd. 4979] H.C. (1910). XII, 1.
Accompanying documents. [Cd. 5204] H.C. (1910). XII, 287. [Cd. 5083]
H.C. (1910). XII, 539. [Cd. 5447, 5626, 5653] H.C. (1910). XIII, 1, 19, 123.

6007 THACKER (FREDERICK SAMUEL). The Thames highway. Vol. I:
'A history of the inland navigation'. Vol. II: 'A history of the locks and weirs'.
2 v. 1914–20. Repr. 2 v. Newton Abbot. 1968.

See also Herbert Spencer, *London's canal: the history of the Regent's Canal*, 1961,
Paul Ashley Laurence Vine, *London's lost route to the sea: an historical account of the
inland navigations which linked the Thames to the English Channel*, Dawlish 1965, and
*London's lost route to Basingstoke*, Newton Abbot 1968.

6008 HADFIELD ([ELLIS] CHARLES [RAYMOND]). The canals of
southern England. 1955.

Part of a ser. intended to cover every region of the British Isles. The English vols. in
the ser. are Hadfield's *The canals of South Wales and the border*, Cardiff & Lond.
1960, *The canals of the east Midlands*, Newton Abbot 1966, 2nd edn. 1970, *The canals
of south-west England*, Newton Abbot 1967, *The canals of the west Midlands*, Newton
Abbot 1966, 2nd edn. 1969, *The canals of south and south-east England*, Newton Abbot
1969, and E. C. R. Hadfield and Gordon Biddle, *The canals of northwest England*, 2 v.
Newton Abbot 1970.

6009 HOUSEHOLD (HUMPHREY). The Thames & Severn Canal. Newton
Abbot. 1969.

One of a growing number of hists. for those who now use the canals for pleasure trips.
Cp. [Ellis] Charles [Raymond] Hadfield and John Norris, *Waterways to Stratford*,
Dawlish 1962, 2nd edn. Newton Abbot 1968, and Kenneth R. Clew, *The Kennet &
Avon canal: an illustrated history*, Newton Abbot 1968.

6010 LEECH (*Sir* BOSDIN THOMAS). History of the Manchester ship
canal from its inception to its completion: with personal reminiscences. 2 v.
1907.

6011 PORTEOUS (JOHN D.). 'A new canal port in the railway age: railway
projection to Goole, 1830–1914'. *Transport Hist.* ii (1969), 25–47.

6012 SMITH (GEORGE). Our canal population: the sad condition of the
women and children, with the remedy . . . 1875. 2nd edn. 1879.

Like Smith's *Canal adventures by moonlight*, 1881, and Mark Guy Pearse, *Rob Rat:
a story of barge life*, 1878, a plea for state regulation of conditions of employment on
canals. For Smith's campaign see Edwin Hodder, *George Smith of Coalville: the story
of an enthusiast*, 1896.

6013 MACLEOD (ROY MALCOLM). 'Social policy and the "floating population": the administration of the Canal Boats Acts, 1877–1899'. *Past & Present*
xxxv (1966), 101–32.

See also Seymour Albert Broadbridge, 'Living conditions on Midland canal boats',
*Transport Hist.* iii (1970), 36–51.

6014 WEBSTER (ROBERT GRANT). The law relating to canals: comprising
a treatise on navigable rivers and canals. 1885.

6015 JEANS (JAMES STEPHEN). Waterways and water transport in different countries: with a description of the Panama, Suez, Manchester,
Nicaraguan and other canals. 1890.

6016	INDUSTRIAL RIVERS of the United Kingdom: namely the Thames, Mersey, Tyne, Tawe, Clyde, Wear, Taff, Avon, Southampton Water, the Hartlepools, Humber, Neath, Port Talbot, and Caermarthen, the Liffey, Usk, Tees, Severn, Wyre and Lagan. By various well-known experts. 1891.

6017	BOWLES COMMISSION ON THE RIVER TYNE. Report of the commissioners appointed to inquire into the present state of the River Tyne [Chairman: Vice-Admiral William Bowles]. [1948] H.C. (1854–5). XXVIII, 1.
A useful general inquiry.

6018	DUCKHAM (BARON FREDERICK). The Yorkshire Ouse: the history of a river navigation. Newton Abbot. 1967.

6019	THOMPSON (HUBERT GORDON). The canal system of England: its growth and present condition, with particular reference to the cheap carriage of goods. Cobden Club. 1903.

6020	PALMER (J. E.). British canals: problems and possibilities. 1910.

6021	PRATT (EDWIN A.). Canals and traders: the argument pictorial as applied to the report of the Royal Commission on Canals and Waterways. 1910.
Like his *British canals: is their resuscitation practicable?*, 1906, a controversial work which includes much useful factual material. Based on **6006**.

6022	NETTLEFOLD (JOHN SUTTON). Garden cities and canals. 1914.
Wants a new deal for canals. Suggests new towns with new canals.

### 3. Shipping and Shipbuilding

#### (a) *Reference*

6023	ALBION (ROBERT GREENHALGH) *comp*. Naval & maritime history: an annotated bibliography. 4th edn. Mystic, Conn. 1972.
Much the best bibliog., but see also U.S. Library of Congress, *List of references on shipping and shipbuilding*, Wash. 1919. There is little in Rupert C. Jarvis, 'Sources for the history of ships and shipping', *J. Transport Hist.* iii (1957–8), 212–34, or Robert Craig, 'Shipping records of the nineteenth and twentieth centuries', *Archives* vii (1965–6), 191–8. The main hist. j. in the field is the *Mariner's mirror* (**2847**).

6024	LEWIS (CHARLES LEE). Books of the sea: an introduction to nautical literature. U.S. Naval Inst. Annapolis, Md. 1943.
Covers novels, short stories, poems, plays, memoirs, oceanography, etc., in a chatty way. Edwin Courtlandt Bolles, *The literature of sea travel since the introduction of steam, 1830–1930*, Phila. 1943, adds little.

6025	MASON (HERBERT B.) *ed*. Encyclopaedia of ships and shipping. 1908.
The most useful manual. For others see H. Craig, *A bibliography of encyclopaedias and dictionaries dealing with military, naval and maritime affairs* (**2659**).

6026  SMYTH (WILLIAM HENRY). The sailor's word-book: an alphabetical digest of nautical terms . . . rev. for the press by Sir Edward Belcher. 1867.

For later words see Frank Charles Bowen, *Sea slang: a dictionary of the old-timers' expressions and epithets*, 1929, and Wilfred Granville, *Sea slang of the twentieth century: the Royal Navy, merchant navy, yachtsmen, fishermen, bargemen, canalmen, miscellaneous*, 1949, 2nd edn. 1962.

6027  LLOYD'S REGISTER OF BRITISH AND FOREIGN SHIPPING . . . 1834+.

The chief directory of ships, shipowners, shipbuilders, ports, insurers, which grew remarkably thick over the years. A number of suppls. were also publ., notably *Annual summary of shipbuilding at home and abroad*, 1894–1923, *Shipbuilding returns* . . ., 1888+, *Lloyd's register of yachts*, 1878+, and *Lloyd's calendar*, 1898+. For the background of the *Register* see *Annals of Lloyd's Register* . . ., 1934; and George Blake, *Lloyd's register of shipping, 1760–1960*, 1960.

6028  LLOYD'S LIST. 1726+.

Useful for shipping movements. The *List* has a curious hist. It existed as an independent j. from 1726 to 1884 when it was absorbed by *Mitchell's maritime register*, 1856–84, in *The shipping gazette and Lloyd's list weekly summary*, 1884–1916, and by *Shipping and mercantile gazette*, 1838–84, as *Shipping and mercantile gazette and Lloyd's list*, 1884–1914. *Lloyd's list* re-emerged as an independent publ. in 1914. The other main shipping lists were *The general weekly shipping list and postal and mercantile directory*, 1853+, and [*Liverpool*] *journal of commerce*, Liverpool 1861+, which absorbed *Liverpool telegraph and shipping gazette* [*Liverpool shipping gazette*], Liverpool 1846–99.

6029  REGISTRAR GENERAL OF SHIPPING AND SEAMEN. Annual statement of the navigation and shipping of the United Kingdom for 1871+. 1872+.

The main run of shipping stats. Publ. as parl. papers. Suppl. by consolidated tables at irreg. intervals. See also *Merchant shipping, 1881–1911: tables showing the progress of merchant shipping in the United Kingdom and the principal maritime countries*, [Cd. 7033] H.C. (1913). LX, 15.

6030  THE DIRECTORY OF SHIPOWNERS, SHIPBUILDERS AND MARINE ENGINEERS. 1903+. Annual.

Very useful for shipowners in particular.

6031  LIVERPOOL SHIPPING WHO'S WHO: a complete directory, personal and official, to the shipping and allied trades in the ports of Liverpool and Manchester, 1909+. Liverpool. 1909+. Annual.

6032  TURNBULL'S SHIPPING REGISTER AND BRITISH AND FOREIGN MARITIME ADVERTISER. North Shields. 1882+.

An annual directory of shipping in the north-east of England.

6033  PHILIP (GEORGE) *ed.* Philip's mercantile marine atlas . . . 1904. 16th edn. 1959.

Includes much information about shipping lines.

**6034** THE 'SHIPPING WORLD' YEAR BOOK: a desk manual of trade, commerce and navigation. 1886+.

Title varies. Chiefly on ports, tariffs, rules, regulations, and technical services. See also G. D. Urquhart, comp., *Dues and charges on shipping in foreign ports: a manual of reference for the use of shipowners, shipbrokers and shipmasters*, 1869, 15th edn. 1914, and Hugh Owen, *Ship economics: providing practical aids for shipmasters in regard to repairs, maintenance, surveys and construction, including a glossary of technical terms*, 1911, 4th edn. 1939.

**6035** MERCANTILE YEAR BOOK [and directory of exporters]. 1887+.

A useful commercial directory angled towards overseas trade.

**6036** MERCHANT SHIPPING REGULATIONS. List of the principal regulations, orders, instructions and notices relating to merchant shipping which are now in force. 1909.

**6037** BOARD OF TRADE (NAVAL DEPARTMENT). Mercantile navy list. 1849+. 1850+. Annual.

Lists ships' officers.

**6038** THE SYREN [and shipping illustrated]. 1+. 1868+.

A good contemp. j. which dealt with all aspects of shipping. See also Shipmasters' Soc., *The British merchant service j.*, 1879–85.

**6039** THE SHIPPING WORLD AND HERALD OF COMMERCE. 1883+.

The chief j. of the commercial shippers.

**6040** PATENT OFFICE. Abridgments of specifications relating to masts, sails, rigging, &c.: including, apparatus for raising and lowering ships' boats, A.D. 1625–1866. 1874.

The Patent Office also issued numerous other *Abridgments* relating to ships, their propulsion and equipment.

### (b) *Official Reports*

**6041** JOCELYN COMMITTEE ON STEAM COMMUNICATIONS WITH INDIA. First report from the select committee on steam communications with India &c. [Chairman: Viscount Jocelyn]. H.C. 372 (1851). XXI, 1. Second report. H.C. 605 (1851). XXI, 655.

**6042** BOARD OF ORDNANCE COMMITTEE ON MERCANTILE STEAM NAVY. Report of the committee appointed by the Board of Ordnance to inquire into the capabilities of the mercantile steam navy for purposes of war. H.C. 687 (1852–3). LXI, 379.

**6043** O'CONNELL COMMITTEE ON EMIGRANT SHIPS. First report from the select committee on emigrant ships [Chairman: John O'Connell]. H.C. 163 (1854). XIII, 1. Second report. H.C. 349 (1854). XIII, 187.

6044 VILLIERS COMMITTEE ON SOUND DUES. Report from the select committee on sound dues [Chairman: C. P. Villiers]. H.C. 380 (1856). XVI, 519.

Useful for Baltic shipping.

6045 LINDSAY COMMITTEE ON TRANSPORT SERVICE. Report from the select committee on transport service [Chairman: William Schaw Lindsay]. H.C. 480 (1860). XVIII, 1. Further report. H.C. 380 (1861). XII, 377.

A full inquiry into the shipping of troops, convicts, emigrants, and stores.

6046 HORSFALL COMMITTEE ON MERCHANT SHIPPING. Report from the select committee on merchant shipping [Chairman: Thomas Berry Horsfall]. H.C. 530 (1860). XIII, 1.

6047 SOMERSET COMMISSION ON UNSEAWORTHY SHIPS. Royal commission on unseaworthy ships. Preliminary report of the commissioners [Chairman: Duke of Somerset]. [C. 853] H.C. (1873). XXXVI, 315. Minutes of evidence. [C. 853–I] H.C. (1873). XXXVI, 335. Final report. [C. 1027] H.C. (1874). XXXIV, 1.

6048 SELECT COMMITTEE ON MERCHANT SEAMEN BILL. Report from the select committee on Merchant Seamen Bill [Chairmen: Sir Charles Adderley and Edward Stanhope]. H.C. 205 (1878). XVI, 77.

6049 NORWOOD COMMISSION ON MEASUREMENT OF TON-NAGE. Report by Her Majesty's commissioners appointed to inquire into the present operation of the law for the measurement of tonnage [Chairman: Charles Morgan Norwood]. [C. 3074] H.C. (1881). XLIX, 1. Minutes of evidence. [C. 3074–I] H.C. (1881). XLIX, 43.

The fullest of a number of reports on the subject for which see Ford, *Select list* (31).

6050 ABERDEEN COMMISSION ON LOSS OF LIFE AT SEA. First report of the royal commission on loss of life at sea. [Chairman: Earl of Aberdeen]. [C. 4577] H.C. (1884–5). XXXV, 1. Final report. [C. 5227] H.C. (1887). XLIII, 1. Evidence etc. [C. 5227–I and II] H.C. (1887). XLIII, 55.

See also *Report from the select committee on saving life at sea* [Chairman: Lord Charles Beresford]. H.C. 249 (1887). XII, 1.

6051 SPENCER COMMITTEE ON LIGHT LOAD LINE. Report from the select committee of the House of Lords on light load line [Chairman: Earl Spencer]. H.C. 356 (1903). VI, 139.

6052 BONAR LAW COMMITTEE ON FOREIGN SHIPS. Report from the select committee on foreign ships (application of statutory powers) [Chairman: Andrew Bonar Law]. H.C. 299 (1904). VI, 121. Further report. H.C. 269 (1905). VII, 37.

6053 CECIL COMMITTEE ON STEAMSHIP SUBSIDIES. Report from the select committee on steamship subsidies [Chairman: Evelyn Cecil]. H.C. 300 (1901). VIII, 271. Further report. H.C. 385 (1902). IX, 297.

The Foreign Office also obtained for the Board of Trade a number of reports from diplomatic representatives, which were publ. as *Reports from Her Majesty's representatives abroad respecting bounties on ship-building, &c.* [Cd. 596] H.C. (1901). LXXX, 349, with a further ser. *Report on bounties and subsidies in respect of shipbuilding, shipping and navigation of foreign countries.* [Cd. 6899] H.C. (1913). XL, 1.

6054 CHAMBERLAIN COMMITTEE ON WAR RISKS. Report by the committee on a national guarantee for the war risks of shipping to the Lords Commissioners of His Majesty's Treasury [Chairman: Austen Chamberlain]. [Cd. 4161] H.C. (1908). LVIII, 1. Minutes of evidence. [Cd. 4162] H.C. (1908). LVIII, 53.

6055 COHEN COMMISSION ON SHIPPING RINGS. Report of the royal commission on shipping rings [Chairman: Arthur Cohen]. Vol. I. Report. [Cd. 4668] H.C. (1909). XLVII, 1. Vol. II. Appendixes. [Cd. 4669] H.C. (1909). XLVII, 127. Vol. III. Minutes of evidence. [Cd. 4670] H.C. (1909). XLVII, 357. Vol. IV. Minutes of evidence. [Cd. 4685] H.C. (1909). XLVIII, 1. Vol. V. Report of sub-commission in South Africa. [Cd. 4686] H.C. (1909). XLVIII, 393.

6056 BOOTH COMMITTEE ON SHIPPING AND SHIPBUILDING. Reports of the departmental committee appointed by the Board of Trade to consider the position of the shipping and shipbuilding industries after the war [Chairman: Sir Alfred A. Booth]. [Cd. 9092] H.C. (1918). XIII, 473.

### (c) Merchant Shipping

6057 THORNTON (ROLAND HOBHOUSE). British shipping. Camb. 1939. 2nd edn. 1959.

A good popular account of the hist. and organization of all aspects of the industry. Stanley George Sturmey, *British shipping and world competition*, 1962, is good, but has little on the period.

6058 COURSE (ALFRED GEORGE). The merchant navy: a social history. 1963.

A pleasant work, but not strong on the period.

6059 NORTH (DOUGLASS). 'Ocean freight rates and economic development, 1750–1913'. *J. Econ. Hist.* xviii (1958), 537–55.

See also the indices in L. Isserlis, 'Tramp shipping cargoes and freights', *Roy. Stat. Soc. J.* ci (1938), 53–146, Joseph Russell Smith, *The ocean carrier: a history and analysis of the service and a discussion of the rates of ocean transportation*, N.Y. 1908, and *The organization of ocean commerce*, Phila. 1905.

6060 FOULKE (ROBERT D.). 'Life in the dying world of sail, 1870–1910'. *J. British Studs.* iii (1963–4), pt. 1, 105–36.

6061   ALDCROFT (DEREK HOWARD). 'The depression in British ship-ping, 1901–1911'. *J. Transport Hist.* vii (1965–6), 14–23.

6062   GINSBURG (BENEDICT WILLIAM). 'Shipping subsidies'. *Roy. Stat. Soc. J.* lxiv (1901), 461–84.

For the literature of this subj. see U.S. Libr. of Congress, *A list of books, with references to periodicals, on mercantile marine subsidies*, Wash. 1900, 2nd edn. 1903. Royal Meeker, *History of shipping subsidies*, Amer. Econ. Assoc. Publs. 3rd ser., vol. vi, no. 3, N.Y. 1905, and Edwin Munroe Bacon, *Manual of ship subsidies: an historical summary of the systems of all nations*, Chicago 1911, have little on Britain. The Cecil committee pro-duced useful evidence on the subject (**6053**).

6063   PARKHURST (PETER GEORGE). Ships of peace: a record of some of the problems which came before the Board of Trade in connection with the British mercantile marine from early days to the year 1885: compiled from official records. Vol. I. Priv. pr. New Malden. 1962.

Chiefly post-1850.

6064   LINDSAY (WILLIAM SCHAW). History of merchant shipping and ancient commerce. 4 v. 1874–6.

The last 2 v. are largely based on Lindsay's own experience in shipping. Detailed for 1851–75. Lindsay's *Our merchant shipping: its present state considered*, 1860, and *Our navigation and mercantile marine laws . . .*, 1852, 2nd edn. 1853, are also useful.

6065   MACDONALD (ALEXANDER FRASER). Our ocean railways: or, the rise, progress and development of ocean steam navigation. 1893.

A general survey.

6066   JONES (R. J. CORNEWALL). The British merchant service: being a history of the British mercantile marine from the earliest times to the present day. 1898. Repr. 1969.

Still the best account of many aspects of the subject.

6067   BLACKMORE (EDWARD). The British mercantile marine: a short historical review, including the rise and progress of British shipping and com-merce, the education of the merchant officer, and duty and discipline in the merchant service. 1897.

Useful for the period 1875–95: a textbook for ships' officers.

6068   MICHON (GEORGES). Les grandes compagnies anglaises de naviga-tion. Paris. 1913.

Chiefly on government aid. See also Ambroise Victor Charles Colin, *La navigation commerciale au XIXe siècle*, Paris 1901, and René Verneaux, *L'industrie des transports maritimes au XIXe siècle et au commencement du XXe siècle*, 2 v. Paris 1903.

6069   KIRKALDY (ADAM WILLIS). British shipping: its history, organisa-tion and importance. 1914. Repr. Newton Abbot. 1970.

Strongest on the end of the 19th cent. Should be suppl. by Edgar Crammond, *The British shipping industry*, 1917, which gives useful statistics, and Sir Clement Wake-field Jones, *British merchant shipping*, 1922. The possible effects of war on British shipping are discussed in *Shipping and Mercantile Gazette* . . ., *The mercantile marine in war time*, 1902, Sir Douglas William Owen, *Ocean trade and shipping*, Camb. 1914, and the Chamberlain committee (**6054**).

6070 CHANDLER (GEORGE). Liverpool shipping: a short history. 1960.

See also John Willox, *The steam fleet of Liverpool* . . ., Liverpool 1865.

6071 BULLEN (FRANK THOMAS). The men of the merchant service: being, the polity of the mercantile marine . . . 1900.

An account of the work of each member of a ship's crew. See also Archibald Greig Cowie, *The sea services of the Empire as fields for employment*, 1903. James Fell, *British seamen in San Francisco, 1892–1898*, 1899, is a useful curiosity.

6072 CHADWICK (FRENCH ENSOR). Report on the training systems for the navy and mercantile marine of England, and of the naval training system of France, made to the Bureau of Equipment and Recruiting. U.S. Navy Dept. 46th Congress. 2nd Sess. U.S. Senate. doc. no. 52. Wash. 1880.

See also John Edward Masefield, *The Conway: from her foundation to the present day*, 1933, a hist. of the leading training establishment.

6073 PLIMSOLL. The Plimsoll Mark. By David Masters. 1955.

A life of Samuel Plimsoll dealing mainly with his campaign for greater safety at sea. See also Plimsoll's *Our seamen: an appeal*, 1873, Sir Westcott Abell, *The safe sea* (**6164**), and Henry Jeula, 'Shipping casualties' (**6165**).

6074 WALROND (MARY L.). Launching out into the deep: or, the pioneers of a noble effort. The Missions to Seamen. 1904.

[H. L. Elvin] *Hill of Ratcliff Highway: a memoir: the life and work of the Rev. George John Hill*, priv. pr. Camb. 1932, gives a short account of the Seamen's Christian Friend Soc. See also Maurice Rooke Kingsford, *The Mersey Mission to Seamen, 1856–1956*, 1957 and **5821**.

6075 MITCHELL (CHARLES SAMUEL). The long watch: a history of the Sailors' Children's Society, 1821–1961. Hull. 1961.

6076 HOLT. The diary of John Holt: with, the voyage of the 'Maria' by John Holt. Ed. by Cecil R. Holt. 1948.

Covers the years, *c*. 1862–72.

6077 CRUTCHLEY. My life at sea: being a 'yarn' loosely spun for the purpose of holding together certain reminiscences of the transition period from sail to steam in the British mercantile marine (1863–1894). By William Caius Crutchley. 1912.

The memoirs of a liner captain. The best of other similar memoirs are William R. Lord, *Real life at sea: being, the reminiscences of a sailor*, 1913, Andrew Shewan, *The great days of sail: some reminiscences of a tea-clipper captain*, ed. by Rex Clements, 1927, and George Sorrell, *The man before the mast: being, the story of twenty years afloat*, ed. by Cicely Fox Smith, 1928.

6078 WILL. Trading under sail off Japan, 1860–99: the recollections of Captain John Baxter Will, sailing-master & pilot. Ed. by George Alexander Lensen. Tokyo & Tallahassee, Fla. 1968.

A Scot from Dundee who became a navigational jack-of-all-trades.

### (d) *Shipowners and Shipping Routes*

6079 JONES (*Sir* CLEMENT WAKEFIELD). Pioneer shipowners. 2 v. Liverpool. 1935–8.

6080 POWELL (LESLIE HUGHES). A hundred years on: history of the Liverpool Steam Ship Owners Association, 1858–1958. Priv. pr. Liverpool. 1958.

6081 POWELL (LESLIE HUGHES). The Shipping Federation: a history of the first sixty years, 1890–1950. 1950.

6082 HARRIS (LEONARD). London General Shipowners' Society, 1911–1961. [1961.]

6083 ANDERSON. Arthur Anderson, a founder of the P. & O. Coy. By John Nicolson. Paisley. 1914. Rev. edn. Lerwick. 1932.

6084 BURNS. Sir George Burns, Bart: his times and friends. By Edwin Hodder. 1890.

6085 FORWOOD. Reminiscences of a Liverpool shipowner, 1850–1920. By Sir William Bower Forwood. Liverpool. 1920.

See also his *Recollections of a busy life . . .*, Liverpool 1910.

6086 JONES. Sir Alfred Lewis Jones, K.C.M.G.: a story of energy and success. By Alan Hay Milne. Liverpool. 1914.

6087 RUNCIMAN. Before the mast—and after: the autobiography of a sailor and shipowner. By Walter Runciman, Baron Runciman. 1924.

6088 SWIRE. The senior: John Samuel Swire, 1825–98: management in far eastern shipping trades. By Sheila Marriner and Francis Edwin Hyde. Liverpool. 1967.

6089 INDIVIDUAL SHIPPING LINES. ANCHOR: R. S. McLellan, *Anchor line, 1856–1956*, Glasgow 1956. BEN: George Blake, *The Ben line: the history of Wm. Thomson & Co. of Leith and Edinburgh and of the ships owned and managed by them, 1825–1955*, 1956. T. E. Milne, 'British shipping in the nineteenth century: a study of the Ben line papers', in P. L. Payne, ed., *Studies in Scottish business hist.* (**9958**), pp. 345–66. BOOTH: Arthur Henry John, *A Liverpool merchant house: being, the history of Alfred Booth & Company, 1863–1958*, 1959. BOWRING: Arthur C. Wardle, *Benjamin Bowring*

*and his descendants: a record of mercantile achievement*, 1938. BRISTOL CITY: John Charles Gathorne Hill, *Shipshape and Bristol fashion*, Liverpool [1952]. BRITISH INDIA: George Blake, *B.I. centenary, 1856–1956: the story of the British India Steam Navigation Company*, 1956. BROCKLEBANK: John Frederic Gibson, *Brocklebanks, 1770–1950*, 2 v. Liverpool 1953. CANADIAN PACIFIC: Frank Charles Bowen, *History of the Canadian Pacific line* [1928]. CORY: John Cory & Sons Ltd., *A century of family shipowning, John Cory and Sons, Limited, 1854–1954* [1954]. CUNARD: Franklin Lawrence Babcock, *Spanning the Atlantic*, 1931. Hilda Kay Grant, *Samuel Cunard: pioneer of the Atlantic steamship* [1967]. DONALDSON: Alastair Mactavish Dunnett, *The Donaldson line: a century of shipping, 1854–1954*, Glasgow 1960. GENERAL STEAM NAVIGATION: Leslie Cope Cornford, *A century of sea trading, 1824–1924: the General Steam Navigation Company, Limited* . . ., 1924. HARRISON: Francis Edwin Hyde and others, *Shipping enterprise and management, 1830–1939: Harrisons of Liverpool*, Liverpool 1967. Anon. *One hundred years of progress: a brief history of the Harrison line, 1853–1953*, 1953. HOLT: Francis Edwin Hyde and John Raymond Harris, *Blue funnel: a history of Alfred Holt and Company of Liverpool, from 1865 to 1914*, Liverpool 1956. HOULDERS: [Edward Frank Stevens] *One hundred years of Houlders: a record of the history of Houlder Brothers & Co. Ltd., from 1849 to 1950*, 1950. ISLE OF MAN: Arthur William Moore, *The Isle of Man Steam Packet Co. Ltd., 1830–1904*, Manch. 1904. ISMAY: See White Star. KILLICK, MARTIN & Co.: David Roy MacGregor, *The China bird: the history of Captain Killick and one hundred years of sail and steam*, 1961. MARINE NAVIGATION Co.: Alfred George Course, *Windjammers of the Horn: the story of the last British fleet of square-rigged sailing ships*, 1969. PACIFIC STEAM NAVIGATION: Arthur C. Wardle, *Steam conquers the Pacific: a record of maritime achievement, 1840–1940*, 1940. PENINSULAR & ORIENTAL: Boyd Cable, pseud. of Ernest Andrew Ewart, *A hundred years of the P & O: Peninsular and Oriental Steam Navigation Company, 1837–1937*, 1937. David Divine [Arthur Durham Divine], *These splendid ships: the story of the Peninsular and Oriental line*, 1960. RATHBONE: Sheila Marriner, *Rathbones of Liverpool, 1845–1873*, Liverpool 1961. ROYAL MAIL: Thomas Alexander Bushell, *'Royal Mail': a centenary history of the Royal Mail line, 1839–1939*, 1939. SHAW, SAVILL: Frank Charles Bowen, *The flag of the Southern Cross: the history of Shaw, Savill & Albion Co. Ltd., 1858–1939*, 1939. SOUTHAMPTON & ISLE OF WIGHT: Geoffrey William O'Connor, *The first hundred years, 1861–1961: Southampton, Isle of Wight & South of England Royal Mail Steam Packet Company, Limited* . . . [1962.] STEWART: Alfred George Course, *The wheel's kick and the wind's song: the story of the John Stewart line of sailing ships, 1877–1928*, 1950, 3rd edn. Newton Abbot 1968. UNION CASTLE: Marischal Murray, *Union Castle chronicle, 1853–1953*, 1953. WHITE STAR: Wilton Joseph Oldham, *The Ismay line: the White Star line and the Ismay family story*, Liverpool 1961. Roy Anderson, *White Star*, Prescot 1964. *The White Star line of mail steamers: official guide* . . ., n.d. WILLIAM WATKINS: Frank Charles Bowen, *A hundred years of towage: a history of Messrs. William Watkins Ltd., 1833–1933*, Gravesend 1933.
The above list includes few good scholarly hists. The best

are Hyde on the Harrisons, Hyde and Harris on the Holts, John on the Booths, and Marriner on the Rathbones, all of them Liverpool firms.

6090 TYLER (DAVID BUDLONG). Steam conquers the Atlantic. N.Y. & Lond. 1939.
A pioneer scholarly study to 1880.

6091 MURKEN (ERICH). Die grossen transatlantischen Linienreederei-Verbände, Pools und Interessengemeinschaften bis zum Ausbruch des Weltkrieges: ihre Entstehung und Wirksamkeit. Jena. 1922.

6092 BONSOR (NOEL REGINALD PIXELL). North Atlantic seaway: an illustrated history of the passenger services linking the old world with the new. Prescot. 1955. Suppl. 1960.

Detailed annals of all the Atlantic shipping companies, with notes on their ships. The pioneer work in this field was Arthur J. Maginnis, *The Atlantic ferry: its ships, men and working*, 1892, 3rd edn. 1908. There are many other general works of which the following are of some value: Henry Fry, *The history of North Atlantic steam navigation . . .*, 1896, repr. 1969; Charles Robert Vernon Gibbs, *Passenger liners of the western ocean . . . from 1838 to the present day*, 1952, 2nd edn. 1957; Hereward Philip Spratt, *Transatlantic paddle steamers*, Glasgow 1951, and *Outline history of transatlantic steam navigation, as illustrated by the collections at the Science Museum*, 1950; J. Austin, 'Liverpool and the Atlantic ferry', *Inst. Mech. Eng. Proc.* (1934), 83–117; and (6208). William Mack Angas, *Rivalry on the Atlantic*, N.Y. [1939], is stronger on design and machinery. Laurence Dunn, *North Atlantic liners, 1899–1913*, 1961, is a picture book full of data. The three best popular hists. are Charles Edward Lee, *The blue riband: the romance of the Atlantic ferry* [1930], Warren Armstrong, pseud. of William Edward Bennett, *Atlantic highway*, 1961, and Warren Stanley Tute, *Atlantic conquest: the ships and the men of the North Atlantic passenger services, 1816–1961*, 1962.

6093 ALBION (ROBERT GREENHALGH). 'Capital movement and transportation: British shipping and Latin America, 1806–1914'. *J. Econ. Hist.* xi (1951), 361–74.

6094 HYDE (FRANCIS EDWIN). 'The expansion of Liverpool's carrying trade with the Far East and Australia, 1860–1914'. *Roy. Hist. Soc. Trans.* 5 ser. 6 (1956), 139–60.

6095 HOSKINS (HALFORD LANCASTER). British routes to India. N.Y. 1928.

6096 LEUBUSCHER (CHARLOTTE). The West African shipping trade, 1909–1959. Leyden. 1963.

See also P. N. Davies, 'The African Steam Ship Company' in John Raymond Harris, ed., *Liverpool and Merseyside: essays in the economic and social history of the port and its hinterland*, 1969, pp. 212–38.

6097 MURRAY (MARISCHAL). Ships and South Africa: a maritime chronicle of the Cape with particular reference to mail and passenger liners from the early days of steam down to the present. 1933.

6098 LAWSON (WILLIAM). Pacific steamers: the history, rise and development of steamers on the Australian, New Zealand and Western American coasts. Glasgow. 1927.

There is also John M. Maber, *'White Star' to 'Southern Cross'*, Prescot 1967.

6099 HAMILTON (J. H.). The 'All-Red Route', 1893–1953: a history of the Trans-Pacific mail service between British Columbia, Australia, and New Zealand. Repr. from *British Columbia Hist. Q.* Jan.–Apr. 1956. [1959.]

6100 VEALE (ERNEST WILLIAM PARTINGTON). Gateway to the Continent: a history of cross-Channel travel. 1955.

One of a number of popular books on the subject. Cp. Rixon Bucknall, *Boat trains and Channel packets: the English short sea routes*, 1957.

6101 PIETERS (L. J.). 'A hundred years of sea-communication between England and the Netherlands'. *J. Transport Hist.* vi (1963–4), 210–21.

6102 BURBURE DE WESENBEEK (ALBERT DE). The centenary of the Ostend–Dover line, 1846–1946: a contribution to the history of the Anglo-Continental maritime relations by mailboat service since its origin. Trans. by Cuthbert Grasemann. Antwerp. [1946.]

6103 BURTT (FRANK). Steamers of the Thames and Medway. 1949.

Suppls. his *Cross-Channel and coastal paddle steamers*, 1934. For other such boats see Grahame Edgar Farr, *West-country passenger steamers*, 1956, Edward Charles Bexley Thornton, *South coast pleasure steamers*, Prescot 1962, new edn. 1969.

### (e) *Types of Ships*

6104 GLOVER (*Sir* JOHN). 'On the statistics of tonnage during the first decade under the navigation law of 1849'. *Stat. Soc. J.* xxvi (1863), 1–18.

Cont. for 1860–70 in *Stat. Soc. J.* xxxv (1872), 218–30; for 1870–80 in ibid. xlv (1882), 37–58; for 1880–90 in *Roy. Stat. Soc. J.* lv (1892), 205–35; and for 1891–1900 in ibid. lxv (1902), 1–41. The best run of stats.

6105 HUGHES (JONATHAN ROBERTS TYSON) *and* REITER (STANLEY). 'The first 1,945 British steamships'. *Amer. Stat. Assoc. J.* liii (1958), 360–81.

Stats. for 1814–60.

6106 MAYWALD (K.). 'The construction costs and the value of the British merchant fleet, 1850–1938'. *Scot. J. Pol. Econ.* iii (1956), 44–66.

6107 SMITH (EUGENE WALDO). Passenger ships of the world, past and present. Boston, Mass. 1963.

An annotated list of ships of all countries.

**6108  GIBBS (CHARLES ROBERT VERNON).** British passenger liners of the five oceans: a record of the British passenger lines and their liners from 1838 to the present day. 1963.

Fuller than Smith (**6107**). Lists ships and owners, and gives pictures of selected ships. Some of the same ground is covered by Bonsor (**6092**).

**6109  GRAHAM (GERALD SANDFORD).** 'The ascendancy of the sailing ship, 1850–85'. *Econ. Hist. Rev.* 2 ser. ix (1956–7), 74–88.

There is a large literature on the last days of the big sailing ships. For the technical side see Arthur Hamilton Clark, *The clipper ship era: an epitome of famous American and British clipper ships, their owners, builders, commanders and crews, 1843–1869*, N.Y. 1910. Many of the works of Alfred Basil Lubbock are devoted to the various classes of ship. See his 'Merchant-men under sail, 1815–1932', *Mariner's Mirror* xliii (1957), 3–18, *The China clippers*, Glasgow 1914, 4th edn. 1919, *The nitrate clippers*, Glasgow 1932, repr. 1953, *The colonial clippers*, Glasgow 1921, new edn. 1948, *The Western ocean packets*, Glasgow 1925, *The last of the windjammers*, 2 v. Glasgow 1927, *Coolie ships and oil sailers*, Glasgow 1935, *The log of the 'Cutty Sark'*, Glasgow 1924, *The Blackwall frigates*, Glasgow 1922, 2nd edn. 1950, and *Sail: the romance of the clipper ships*, ed. by Frederick Arthur Hook and Alexander Campbell, 3 v. 1927–36, abridged edn. 1948. David Roy Macgregor, *The tea clippers: an account of the China tea trade and of some of the British sailing ships engaged in it from 1849 to 1869*, 1952, is the best account of one class of ships. For the tea and wool races there is also the popular Cicely Fox Smith, *Ocean racers*, 1931. For the seamen who worked the ships see R. A. Fletcher, *In the days of the tall ships*, 1928, Charles William Domville-Fife, ed., *Square-rigger days: autobiographies of sail*, 1938, and the life and works of Joseph Conrad (**8351**).

**6110  GREENHILL (BASIL).** The merchant schooners: a survey of the history of the small fore and aft rigged merchant sailing ships of England and Wales in the years 1870–1940 . . . 2 v. 1951–7. Repr. 2 v. Newton Abbot. 1968.

On small ships, operating often from small ports, see also Michael Rome Bouquet, *No gallant ship: studies in maritime and local history*, 1959, Frank George Griffith Carr, *Vanishing craft: British coastal types in the last days of sail*, 1934, and *Sailing barges*, 1931, rev. edn. 1951, William James Slade, *Out of Appledore: the autobiography of a coasting shipmaster and shipowner in the last days of wooden sailing ships*, ed. by Basil Greenhill, 1959, and Edgar James March, *Spritsail barges of Thames and Medway*, 1948, repr. Newton Abbot 1969.

**6111  HORNELL (JAMES).** British coracles and Irish curraghs . . . Soc. for Nautical Res. 1938.

**6112  PREBLE (GEORGE HENRY).** A chronological history of the origin and development of steam navigation, 1543–1882. Phila. 1883.

**6113  FLETCHER (R. A.).** Steam ships: the story of their development to the present day. 1910.

Better than John Kennedy, *The history of steam navigation*, Liverpool 1903, Edward Keble Chatterton, *Steamships and their story*, 1910, and George Gibbard Jackson, *The ship under steam*, 1927. There is more on ship types in Harry Parker and Frank C. Bowen, *Mail and passenger steamships of the nineteenth century: the Macpherson collection* . . ., 1928. Keith Thomas Rowland, *Steam at sea: a history of steam navigation*, Newton Abbot 1970, is the most up-to-date survey of this type.

6114  HARDY (ALFRED CECIL). History of motorshipping: the story of fifty years of progress which have had a profound influence upon the development of sea transport during the twentieth century. 1955.

6115  COURSE (ALFRED GEORGE). The deep sea tramp. 1960.

6116  LISLE (B. ORCHARD). Tanker technique, 1700–1936. 1936.
Useful.

6117  BATESON (CHARLES). The convict ships, 1787–1868. Glasgow. 1959.

(f) *Ship Construction*

6118  INSTITUTE OF MARINE ENGINEERS. Library catalogue. 1935.
Neither this catalogue nor that of the Institution of Naval Architects, 1930, suppl. 1936, is very full for the period. Betty M. Cooper, comp., *Catalogue of the Scott collection of books, manuscripts, prints and drawings*, Instn. of Naval Arch. 1954, is also disappointing. For more recent books see British Shipbuilding Research Assoc., *Library catalogue*, 1948, suppl. 1948.

6119  PATENT OFFICE. Abridgments of the specifications relating to ship building, repairing, sheathing, launching, &c. 1862. Suppl. 1869.

6120  PEASE (FRED FORREST). Modern shipbuilding terms defined and illustrated . . . Phila. & Lond. [1918.]

6121  ABELL (*Sir* WESTCOTT STILE). The shipwright's trade. Camb. 1948.
A good general hist.

6122  POLLOCK (DAVID). The shipbuilding industry: its history, practice, science and finance. 1905.
Extremely useful for all aspects of the subject.

6123  SMITH (EDGAR CHARLES). A short history of naval and marine engineering. Camb. 1938.
Good. But see also A. L. Mellanby, 'Fifty years of marine engineering', *Inst. Mech. Eng. Proc.* cxliii (1940), 328–48, and R. W. Skelton, 'Progress in marine engineering', *Inst. Mech. Eng. Proc.* (1930), 3–67.

6124  GILFILLAN (S. COLUM). Inventing the ship: a study of the inventions made in her history between floating log and rotorships. Chicago. 1935.

6125  MACGREGOR (DAVID R.). 'Tendering and contract procedure in merchant shipyards in the middle of the nineteenth century'. *Mariner's Mirror* xlviii (1962), 241–64.

6126  POLLARD (SIDNEY). 'Laissez-faire and shipbuilding [1870–1914]'. *Econ. Hist. Rev.* 2 ser. v (1952–3), 98–115.
See also his 'British and world shipbuilding, 1890–1914: a study in comparative costs', *J. Econ. Hist.* xvii (1957), 426–44.

6127 BARNABY (KENNETH CLOVES). The Institution of Naval Architects, 1860–1960: an historical survey of the Institution's transactions and activities over 100 years. 1960.

6128 CURLING (BERNARD CHARLES). History of the Institute of Marine Engineers. 1961.

6129 CLOWES (GEOFFREY SWINFORD LAIRD). Sailing ships: their history and development as illustrated by the collection of ship-models in the Science Museum. Science Museum. 2 pts. 4th–5th edn. 1952–8.

One of a ser. of Science Museum handbooks on shipping. Earlier edns. are sometimes worth consulting. Current edns. of the other handbooks are Hereward Philip Spratt, *Handbook of the collections illustrating merchant steamers and motorships*, pt. 2, 1949, and *Handbook of the collections illustrating marine engineering*, pt. 2, 1953, and Ernest W. White, *British fishing-boats and coastal craft*, 2 pts. 1952–6.

6130 UNDERHILL (HAROLD ALONSO). Deep-water sail. Glasgow. 1952.

A detailed account covering 19th and 20th cents. See also his *Masting and rigging: the clipper ship and ocean carrier: with authentic plans, working drawings and details of the nineteenth- and twentieth-century sailing ship*, Glasgow 1946.

6131 HALDANE (JOHN WILTON CUNINGHAME). Steamships and their machinery: from first to last. 1893.

A non-technical guide, useful as an intro. See also Alfred Cecil Hardy, *From slip to sea: a chronological account of the construction of merchant ships from the laying of the keel plate to the trial trip*, Glasgow 1926.

6132 RUSSELL (JOHN SCOTT). The modern system of naval architecture. 3 v. 1864–5.

A magnificent work, long standard. The other leading contemp. works were James Peake, *Rudiments of naval architecture: or, an exposition of the elementary principles of the science and the practical application to naval construction*, 1851, 3rd edn. 1867; John Grantham, *Iron ship building: with practical illustrations*, 1858, 5th edn. 1868; Andrew Murray and others, *The theory and practice of ship-building*, Edin. 1861, 2nd edn. 1863; Sir William Fairbairn, *Treatise on iron ship building: its history and progress as comprised in a series of experimental researches on the laws of strain . . .*, 1865; Sir Edward James Reed, *Shipbuilding in iron and steel: a practical treatise, giving full details of construction*, 1868; Sir William Henry White, *A manual of naval architecture: for the use of officers of the Royal Navy, officers of the mercantile marine, yachtsmen, ship-owners and shipbuilders*, 1877, 5th edn. 1900; Samuel J. P. Thearle, *The modern practice of shipbuilding in iron and steel*, 2 v. 1886; and A. Campbell Holms, *Practical shipbuilding: a treatise on the structural design and building of modern steel vessels . . .*, 2 v. 1904, 3rd edn. 2 v. 1916.

6133 TREDGOLD (THOMAS). The principles and practice and explanation of the machinery used in steam navigation; examples of British and American vessels; and papers on the properties of steam . . . [vol. II of Tredgold on the steam engine.] Ed. by James Hann and Robert Armstrong. 2 pts. 1851. Suppl. 1858.

See also F. C. Marshall 'On the progress and development of the marine engine', *Inst. Mech. Eng. Proc.* (1881), 449–509; Albert Edward Seaton, 'The development of the marine engine and the progress made in marine engineering during the past fifteen years', *Iron & Steel Inst. J.* (1890), no. 2, 460–90; George Leonard Overton and Hereward Philip Spratt, comps., *Handbook of the collections illustrating marine engines*, Science Museum, 2 v. 1935–8; Stanley S. Cook, 'Sir Charles Parsons and marine propulsion', *Inst. Mech. Eng. Proc.* cxl (1938), 133–55; and Robert Hudson Parsons, *The development of the Parsons steam turbine*, 1936. The most useful contemp. textbooks are Albert Edward Seaton, *A manual of marine engineering*, 1883, 20th edn. 1928; Richard Sennett, *The marine steam engine: a treatise*, 1882, 14th edn. 1924; Sir William Allan, *The shipowners' and engineers' guide to the marine engine*, Sunderland 1880; George Charles Vincent Holmes, *Marine engines and boilers*, South Kensington Museum 1889; and Wilhelm Gentsch, *Steam turbines: their development, styles of build, construction and uses*, trans. by Arthur L. Liddell, 1906. For propellers see John Bourne, *A treatise on the screw propeller . . .*, 1852, 3rd edn. 1867; Albert Edward Seaton, *The screw propeller and other competing instruments for marine propulsion*, 1909; and Sydney Walker Barnaby, *Marine propellers*, 1885, 6th edn. 1921.

6134 McCARTHY (D. F.) *ed.* The engineer's guide to the royal and mercantile navies by a practical engineer. 3rd edn. 1864. 6th edn. 1869.

6135 HARDY (ALFRED CECIL). Oil ships and sea transport: a story of oil in relation to its effects on sea transportation. 1931.

See also his *History of motor shipping . . .*, 1955.

6136 HARDY (ALFRED CECIL). Bulk cargoes: a treatise on their carriage by sea and consequent effect on the design and construction of merchant ships. 1926.

6137 HOBART (HENRY METCALFE). The electric propulsion of ships. Lond. & N.Y. 1911.

6138 INSTITUTION OF NAVAL ARCHITECTS. Transactions. 1860+.

Three other professional institutes also publ. important *Transactions:* Institution of Engineers and Shipbuilders in Scotland, Glasgow 1857+ (Index 1857–1957 in vol. 100), North-East Coast Institution of Engineers and Shipbuilders, Newcastle-upon-Tyne 1884–5+, and Institute of Marine Engineers, Stratford etc. 1889–90+. The other engineering socs. (**5063, 5155, 5204**) also publ. articles on shipbuilding. The most important periodicals were *The marine engineer and naval architect . . .*, 1879+, *Marine engineering*, 1881–1928, *The shipbuilder [and marine engine builder]*, Newcastle-upon-Tyne 1906+, and *Shipbuilding and shipping record*, 1913+.

6139 DUGAN (JAMES). The great iron ship. [The Great Eastern.] 1953.

6140 POLLOCK (*Sir* DAVID). Modern shipbuilding and the men engaged in it: a record of recent progress . . . 1884.

Particularly useful for indiv. shipyards. There is also a good deal of useful material in the many books and pamphlets on private versus state shipbuilding, for instance Patrick Barry, *Dockyard economy and naval power*, 1863, and *The dockyards and the private shipyards of the Kingdom*, 1863.

6141 DOUGAN (DAVID). The history of North-east shipbuilding. 1968.

Chiefly post-1840. But not systematically arranged. See also Malcolm Dillon, *Some account of the works of Palmers Shipbuilding and Iron Company Ltd.*, Newcastle-on-Tyne 1900.

6142  BELLAMY (JOYCE M.). 'A Hull shipbuilding firm: the history of C. & W. Earle and Earle's Shipbuilding and Engineering Company Ltd.'. *Business Hist.* vi (1963–4), 27–47.

6143  GLOVER (JOHN). 'On the decline of shipbuilding on the Thames'. *Stat. Soc. J.* xxxii (1869), 288–92.

6144  BARNABY (KENNETH CLOVES). 100 years of specialized shipbuilding and engineering . . . John I. Thorneycroft centenary, 1964. 1964.

6145  ERICSSON. The life of John Ericsson. By William Conant Church. N.Y. & Lond. 2 v. 1890.

6146  FROUDE. The papers of William Froude, M.A., LL.D., F.R.S., 1810–1879, with a memoir by Sir Westcott Abell. Ed. by Arthur Dyce Duckworth. Inst. of Naval Architects. 1955. Suppl. 1957.

6147  HUNTER. The man who built the 'Mauretania': big ships and great ideals: the life story of Sir George B. Hunter. By Wilfrid Rutherford. 1934.

6148  RICHARDSON. Memoirs of John Wigham Richardson, 1837–1908. Priv. pr. Glasgow. 1911.

6149  WHITE. The life of Sir William White, K.C.B., F.R.S., LL.D., D.Sc. By Frederic Manning. 1923.

6150  YARROW. Alfred Yarrow, his life and work. By Eleanor Cecilia Yarrow. 1923.

### (g) *Navigation*

See also Oceanography (**8574**).

6151  HEWSON (JOSEPH BUSHBY). A history of the practice of navigation. Glasgow. 1951.

The best gen. hist. See also Rupert Thomas Gould, *The marine chronometer: its history and development*, 1923; Arthur Joseph Hughes, *The book of the sextant . . .*, Glasgow 1938, new edn. 1957; H. O. Hill and E. W. Paget-Tomlinson, *Instruments of navigation: a catalogue of the instruments at the National Maritime Museum, with notes upon their use*, 1958; and Marion Vernon Brewington, *The Peabody Museum collection of navigating instruments with notes on their makers*, Salem, Mass. 1963.

6152  COTTER (CHARLES HENRY). A history of nautical astronomy. 1968. Standard.

6153  DAY (*Sir* ARCHIBALD). The Admiralty hydrographic service, 1795–1919. Ministry of Defence. 1967.

Good. Mary Blewitt, *Surveys of the seas: a brief history of British hydrography*, 1957, is a popular handbook.

6154 ROBINSON (ADRIAN HENRY WARDLE). Marine cartography in Britain: a history of the sea chart to 1855. Leicester. 1962.

Confined to coastal charts.

6155 RITCHIE (GEORGE STEPHEN). The Admiralty chart: British naval hydrography in the nineteenth century. Lond. & N.Y. 1967.

6156 HANCOCK (HARRY EDGAR). Wireless at sea: the first fifty years: a history of the progress and development of marine wireless communications written to commemorate the jubilee of the Marconi International Marine Communication Company Limited. Chelmsford. 1950.

For the Marconi Company see also **5657**.

6157 MEAD (HILARY POLAND). Trinity House. 1947.

Includes much on lighthouses, pilots, etc.

6158 BOWEN (*Sir* JOHN POLAND). British lighthouses. 1947.

The best of many short hists. There is a little more in William Henry Davenport Adams, *Lighthouses and lightships* . . ., 1870, and Frederick Arthur Ambrose Talbot, *Lightships and lighthouses*, 1913. For lighthouse engineering see James Frederick Chance, *The lighthouse work of Sir James Chance, baronet*, 1902, and *Instn. Civil Engineers Proc.* (**5187**).

6159 MACLEOD (ROY MALCOLM). 'Science and government in Victorian England: lighthouse illumination and the Board of Trade, 1866–1886'. *Isis* lx (1969), 5–38.

6160 FARR (GRAHAME EDGAR). 'Bristol channel pilotage: historical notes on its administration and craft'. *Mariner's Mirror* xxxix (1953), 27–44.

6161 BLACHE (ÉDOUARD). Guide du capitaine sur les côtes de la Grande-Bretagne . . . 2 pts. Paris. 1862.

A useful guide. For a more detailed account see *Sailing directions (pilots)* publ. by the Admiralty Hydrographic Office.

6162 BALFOUR COMMISSION ON LIGHTHOUSE ADMINISTRATION. Report of the royal commission on lighthouse administration [Chairman: Gerald William Balfour]. [Cd. 3923] H.C. (1908). XLIX, 457. Minutes of evidence. [Cd. 3937] H.C. (1908). XLIX, 499.

Full. Includes hist. See also *Report of the commissioners appointed to inquire into the condition and management of lights, buoys and beacons* . . . [Chairman: William A. Baillie Hamilton]. [Cd. 2793] H.C. (1861). XXV, 1.

6163 DIGBY COMMITTEE ON PILOTAGE. Report of the departmental committee on pilotage [Chairman: Sir Kenelm Edward Digby]. [Cd. 5571]

H.C. (1911). XXXVIII, 89. Minutes of evidence. [Cd. 5572] H.C. (1911). XXXVIII, 213.

A full and lucid account. The Horsfall committee on Merchant shipping (**6046**), *Report and special report from the select committee on Pilotage Bill* [Chairman: George John Shaw Lefevre]. H.C. 343 (1870). IX, 1, and *Report from the select committee on pilotage* [Chairman: Lord Claud Hamilton]. H.C. 324 (1888). XIV, 85, also go into the subject in detail.

6164   ABELL (*Sir* WESTCOTT STILE). The safe sea. Liverpool. 1932.

The development of safety at sea.

6165   JEULA (HENRY). 'A few statistics relating to shipping casualties'. *Stat. Soc. J.* xxvii (1864), 222–33. Suppl. ibid. xxxi (1868), 418–25.

6166   McKEE (ALEXANDER). The golden wreck: the true story of a great maritime disaster. 1961.

The loss of the *Royal Charter* off Anglesey, 1859. There is a substantial literature on the loss of indiv. ships, of which Walter Lord, *A night to remember*, N.Y. 1955, Lond. 1956, on the loss of the *Titanic* in 1912, is a good example. Hanson Weightman Baldwin, *Sea fights and shipwrecks: true tales of the seven seas*, N.Y. 1955, Lond. 1956, is an amusing coll. of stories.

6167   LARN (RICHARD) *and* CARTER (CLIVE). Cornish shipwrecks. 3 v. Newton Abbot. 1969–71.

6168   LEWIS (RICHARD). History of the life-boat and its work. 1874. 2nd edn. 1874.

The first of a long ser. of useful but not altogether satisfactory short hists. The best of the others are Arthur Lincoln Haydon, *The book of the lifeboat . . .*, 1909; Sir John Cameron Lamb, *The lifeboat and its work*, 1911; Noel T. Methley, *The lifeboat and its story*, 1912; Alec John Dawson, *Britain's lifeboats: the story of a century of heroic service*, 1923; and Patrick John Fielding Howarth, *The lifeboat story*, 1957. The main source is *The life boat: the journal of the National Shipwreck Institution* [later Royal National Life-Boat Institution], 1852+, but see also James C. Dibdin and John Ayling Dibdin, eds., *The book of the life boat: with a complete history of the Lifeboat Saturday movement . . .*, Edin. 1894. Sir John Ghest Cumming and Charles Vince, eds., *The life-boat in verse: an anthology covering a hundred years*, 1938, is much better than one would expect. Cyril Jolly, *Henry Blogg of Cromer: the greatest of the lifeboat men*, 1958, unfortunately has little on the period.

6169   DARLING COMMITTEE ON THE R.N.L.I. Report from the select committee on the Royal National Lifeboat Institution [Chairman: Charles John Darling]. H.C. 317. (1897). XIV, 1.

Comprehensive.

6170   JEFFERY (SYDNEY). The Liverpool Shipwreck and Humane Society, 1839–1939. Liverpool. 1939.

(h) *Ports*

6171 OWEN (*Sir* DOUGLAS WILLIAM). Ports and docks: their history, working and national importance. 1904.

Still the best hist. Sir David John Owen, *The origin and development of the ports of the United Kingdom*, 1939, 2nd edn. 1948, is merely a short popular picture hist. There are some useful bibliog. notes in James Harold Bird, *The major seaports of the United Kingdom*, 1963, and Rupert C. Jarvis, 'Sources for the history of ports', *J. Transport Hist.* iii (1957–8), 76–93.

6172 KENWOOD (A. G.). 'Port investment in England and Wales, 1851–1913'. *Yorkshire Bull.* xvii (1965), 156–67.

6173 VERNON HARCOURT (LEVESON FRANCIS). Harbours and docks: their physical features, history, construction, equipment, and maintenance, with statistics as to their commercial development. 2 v. Oxf. 1885.

A very useful account, full of misc. information.

6174 SIMONIN (LOUIS). Les ports de la Grande-Bretagne: Glasgow Newcastle, Liverpool, Londres: le mouvement maritime. Paris. 1881.

6175 HARBOUR AUTHORITIES: Return from the authorities of harbours . . . of works executed within the last twenty years . . . H.C. 313 (1883). LXII, 433.

A return of 761 pp. Cont. for next 20 years by H.C. 325 (1903). LXIII, 189. For government expenditure on harbours, 1800–75, see H.C. 401 (1876). LXV, 541.

6176 THUBRON (ROBERT). The dock and port charges of Great Britain and Ireland. 1877. Suppl. 1881.

6177 COLSON (CLEMENT) *and* ROUME (——). 'L'organisation financière des ports maritimes de commerce en Angleterre'. Annales des Ponts et Chaussées. 6th ser. 8th year (1888). Pt. I pp. 61–284.

6178 PATENT OFFICE. Abridgments of specifications relating to harbours, docks, canals, &c., A.D. 1617–1866. 1876.

6179 ROYAL COMMISSION ON SHIPPING DUES. Report of the commissioners appointed to inquire into local charges upon shipping in the ports of the United Kingdom and Islands of Jersey, Guernsey, Alderney, Sark and Man [Chairman: J. H. T. Manners Sutton]. England: [1836] H.C. (1854). XXXVII, 1. Ireland: [1911] H.C. (1854–5). XXVII, 1. Scotland &c.: [1967] H.C. (1854–5). XXVII, 177.

Suppl. by *Report from the select committee on local charges upon shipping* [Chairman: Robert Lowe]. H.C. 332 (1856). XII, 1.

6180 RENNIE (*Sir* JOHN). The theory, formation and construction of British and foreign harbours. 2 v. 1851–4.

Rennie was a famous harbour constructor. See also his *Autobiography* (**5174**).

6181 WILSON COMMITTEE ON HARBOURS OF REFUGE. Report from the select committee on harbours of refuge [Chairman: James Wilson]. H.C. 262 (1857–Sess. 2). XIV, 1. Further report. H.C. 344 and 344–I (1857–8). XVII, 203.

The work of the committee cont. in *Report of the commissioners appointed to complete the inquiry in the terms recommended in the report of the select committee . . . on harbours of refuge* [Chairman: James Hope]. Vol. I. Report. [2506–I] H.C. (1859–Sess. I). X, pt. 1, 25. Vol. II. Minutes of evidence. [2506–II] H.C. (1859–Sess. I). X, pt. II, 1.

6182 CLANRICARDE COMMITTEE ON BREAKWATERS AND HAR-BOURS. Report from the select committee of the House of Lords appointed to inquire how far it may be practicable to afford better shelter for shipping upon our coasts . . . [Chairman: Marquess of Clanricarde (Lord Somerhill).] H.C. 544 (1860). XV, 45.

Cont. the work of the Hope Commission (6181). A Commons committee also took up the subject. See *Minutes of evidence taken before the select committee on the Piers and Harbours Bill* [Chairman: Henry Paull]. H.C. 448 (1860). XV, 327.

6183 MARJORIBANKS COMMITTEE ON HARBOUR ACCOMMODA-TION. Report from the select committee on harbour accommodation [Chairman: Edward Marjoribanks]. H.C. 255 (1883). XIV, 1. Further report. H.C. 290 (1884). XII, 1.

Another big report.

6184 BROODBANK (*Sir* JOSEPH GUINNESS). History of the port of London. 2 v. 1921.

Standard. There is a little more in Charles Capper, *The port and trade of London: historical, statistical, local and general*, 1862; Sir David John Owen, *The port of London, yesterday and today*, 1927; Alan Bell, *Port of London, 1909–34*, 1934; Sir Arthur Wynne Morgan Bryant, *Liquid history: to commemorate fifty years of the Port of London Authority, 1909–1959*, priv. pr. 1960; and Aytoun Ellis, *Three hundred years on London river: the Hay's Wharf story, 1651–1951*, 1952. For geography Llewellyn Rodwell Jones, *The geography of London river*, 1931, and James Harold Bird, *The geography of the port of London*, 1957, are good.

6185 REVELSTOKE COMMISSION ON THE PORT OF LONDON. Report of His Majesty's commissioners appointed to inquire into the subject of the administration of the Port of London [Chairman: Lord Revelstoke]. [Cd. 1151] H.C. (1902). XLIII, 1. Minutes of evidence. [Cd. 1152] H.C. (1902). XLIII, 201. Appendixes. [Cd. 1153] H.C. (1902). XLIV, 1.

Two large vols. See also *Report from the joint select committee of the House of Lords and the House of Commons on the Port of London Bill* [Chairman: Viscount Cross]. H.C. 288 (1903). VIII, 1. and the report of a similar committee [Chairman: Russell Rea]. H.C. 288. (1908). X, 1.

6186 MOUNTFIELD (STUART). Western gateway: a history of the Mersey Docks and Harbour Board. Liverpool. 1965.

Replaces Mersey Docks and Harbour Board, *Business in great waters: an account of the activities of the Mersey Docks and Harbour Board, 1858–1958*, Manch. 1958. But see also John S. Rees, *History of the Liverpool pilotage service: mentioning the local light-*

*houses and lightships*, Southport [1949], and Thomas Webster, ed., *The port and docks of Birkenhead: minutes of evidence and of proceedings of the Birkenhead and Liverpool Dock Bills in the sessions of 1848, 1850, 1851 & 1852*, 1853. New edn. 1873.

6187  NEALE (W. G.). At the port of Bristol. Vol. I. Members and problems, 1848–1899. Vol. II. The turn of the tide, 1900–1914. Port of Bristol Authority. Bristol. 1968–71.

6188  BALDWIN (CHRISTOPHER EDMUND). The history and development of the Port of Blyth. Newcastle-upon-Tyne. 1929. Enl. edn. 1929.

6189  HUGHES (B. CARLYON). The history of Harwich harbour: particularly, the work of the Harwich Harbour Conservancy Board, 1863–1939. Dovercourt. 1939.

6190  CLARK (EDWIN A. G.). The ports of the Exe estuary, 1660–1860: a study in historical geography. Exeter. 1960.

6191  PEARSE (RICHARD). The ports and harbours of Cornwall: an introduction to the study of eight hundred years of maritime affairs. St. Austell. 1963.

6192  BROOKFIELD (H. C.). 'Three Sussex ports, 1850–1950'. *J. Transport Hist.* ii (1955–6), 35–50.

Littlehampton, Shoreham, Newhaven. See also D. F. Gibbs, 'The rise of the port of Newhaven, 1850–1914', *Transport Hist.* iii (1970), 258–82.

## 4. RAILWAYS

### (a) *General*

#### (i) *Reference*

6193  OTTLEY (GEORGE) *comp.* A bibliography of British railway history. 1965.

Admirable. To be suppl. by a further vol. on serials and periodical articles.

6194  JOHNSON (LEONARD CHARLES). 'Historical records of the British Transport Commission'. *J. Transport Hist.* i (1953–4), 82–96. Suppl. v (1961–2), 159–65.

Deals with the main coll. of railway records. See also D. B. Wardle, 'Sources for the history of railways at the Public Record Office', ibid. ii (1955–6), 214–34, and Jack Simmons, 'Railway history in English local records', ibid. i (1953–4), 155–69.

6195  BRADSHAW'S RAILWAY ALMANACK, DIRECTORY, SHAREHOLDERS' GUIDE AND MANUAL FOR 1848 [–1923]. 1847–1923.

Title became *Bradshaw's general railway directory*, 1850–2, *Bradshaw's shareholders' guide*, 1853–62, and *Bradshaw's railway manual . . .*, 1863–1923. The 1869 vol. was repr. at Newton Abbot, 1969. A detailed record of each railway with lists of officials. Alternative manuals were *The Universal directory of railway officials*, 1894–1949, and *Railway yearbook*, 1898–1932, both of them useful.

6196  BRADSHAW'S RAILWAY GUIDE. Manch. etc. 1841–1961.

Title varies. Passenger train and steamship time-tables, publ. monthly. The August 1887 and April 1910 issues have been repr. at Newton Abbot, 1969. For the hist. of the guide see G. Royde Smith, *The history of Bradshaw: a centenary review of the origin and growth of the most famous guide in the world*, Lond. & Manch. 1939.

6197  BOARD OF TRADE. Railway returns for England and Wales, Scotland and Ireland. 1846–[1920].

Publ. as parl. papers.

6198  F. C. MATHIESON & SONS. Investors' handbook of railway statistics, 1877–1893. 1893.

Cont. annually to 1900. Cont. as *Twenty years' railway statistics*, annually 1901–15.

6199  ACWORTH (*Sir* WILLIAM MITCHELL). 'English railway statistics'. *Roy. Stat. Soc. J.* lxv (1902), 613–52.

W. M. Acworth and George Paish also publ. 'British railways: their accounts and statistics', *Roy. Stat. Soc. J.* lxxv (1911–12), 687–730. George L. Boag, *Manual of railway statistics*, 1912, is also useful.

6200  [CONNOLLY (W. PHILIP) *and* VINCENT (V. A.). *comps.*] British railways pre-grouping atlas and gazetteer. [1958.] Repr. 1960, 1963.

6201  THE RAILWAY MAGAZINE. 1835–1903.

Title became *Herepath's railway magazine commercial j. and scientific rev.*, 1841–1903. The oldest and long the best railway j. Eventually merged in *The railway times*, 1837–1914. The other leading j. was *Railway news and joint stock j.*, 1864–1918, which publ. a good commemorative vol., *The jubilee of the Railway news, 1864–1914: fifty years of railway progress*, 1914.

6202  THE RAILWAY MAGAZINE. 1897+.

In the 20th cent. pre-eminent among railway js. Henry Maxwell, ed., *Railway magazine miscellany, 1897–1919*, 1958, is a good coll. of extracts. A number of railway companies also issued mags., notably *Great western railway mag.*, 1898–1947.

### (ii) *Histories*

6203  SIMMONS (JACK). The railways of Britain: an historical introduction. 1961.

Brief but useful.

6204  ELLIS (CUTHBERT HAMILTON). British railway history: an outline from the accession of William IV to the nationalisation of railways. 2 v. 1954–9.

There are a number of other general hists. incl. William Henry Boulton, *The railways of Britain: their history, construction and working*, 1950, which cover the same ground less thoroughly.

6205  CARTER (ERNEST FRANK). An historical geography of the railways of the British Isles. 1959.

See also Eric L. Waugh, 'Railroads and the changing face of Britain, 1825–1901', *Business Hist. Rev.* xxx (1956), 274–96.

6206  ROBBINS ([RICHARD] MICHAEL). The railway age. 1962.

See also Cyril Bruyn Andrews, *The railway age*, Lond. 1937, N.Y. 1938, Harold James Perkin, *The age of the railway*, 1970, and R. M. Robbins, comp., *Points and signals: a railway historian at work*, 1967.

6207  SHERRINGTON (CHARLES ELY ROSE). The economics of rail transport in Great Britain. 2 v. 1928. 2nd edn. of vol. II. 1937.

Vol. I. is a good hist. covering all aspects of railway operation.

6208  PARRIS (HENRY WALTER). Government and the railways in nineteenth-century Britain. 1965.

Good on the hist. of the Railway dept. of the Board of Trade. There is little in Ching-Ch'un Wang, *Legislative regulation of railway finance in England*, Univ. of Illinois Studs. in the Soc. Sciences, vol. 7, 1–2, Urbana, Ill. 1918.

6209  CLEVELAND-STEVENS (EDWARD). English railways: their development and their relation to the state. 1915.

On railway amalgamations and state regulation. See also William Alexander Robertson, *Combination among railway companies*, 1912.

6210  REED (MALCOLM CHRISTOPHER) *ed.* Railways in the Victorian economy: studies in finance and economic growth. Newton Abbot. N.Y. 1969.

See also Gary Richard Hawke and M. C. Reed, 'Railway capital in the United Kingdom in the nineteenth century', *Econ. Hist. Rev.* 2 ser. xxii (1969), 269–86, A. G. Kenwood, 'Railway investment in Britain, 1825–1875', *Economica* new ser. xxxii (1965), 313–21, and Derek Howard Aldcroft, 'The efficiency and enterprise of British railways, 1870–1914', *Explorations in Entrepreneurial Hist.* v (1967–8), 158–74.

6211  HAWKE (GARY RICHARD). Railways and economic growth in England & Wales, 1840–1870. Oxf. 1970.

6212  BROADBRIDGE (SEYMOUR ALBERT). Studies in railway expansion and the capital market in England, 1825–1873. 1970.

See also Harold Pollins, 'Railway contractors and the finance of railway development in Britain', *J. Transport Hist.* iii (1957–8), 41–51, 103–10.

6213  LEWIN (HENRY GROTE). The railway mania and its aftermath, 1845–1882. 1936. Repr. Newton Abbot. 1968.

Full of useful data.

6214  HUDSON. The railway king, 1800–71: a study of George Hudson and the business morals of his time. By Richard Stanton Lambert. 1934.

Popular, but good on the railway mania.

**6215** CAMPBELL (CHARLES DOUGLAS). British railways in boom and depression: an essay in trade fluctuations and their effects, 1878–1930. 1932.

See also the 1st chapter of Derek Howard Aldcroft, *British railways in transition: the economic problems of British railways since 1914*, 1968, and his 'The efficiency and enterprise of British railways, 1870–1914', *Explorations in Entrepren. Hist.* 2 ser. v (1968), 158–74, and William Ramage Lawson, *British railways: a financial and commercial survey*, 1913.

**6216** BAGWELL (PHILIP SIDNEY). 'The railway interest: its organisation and influence, 1839–1914'. *J. Transport Hist.* vii (1965–6), 65–86.

See also Walter Harry Green Armytage, 'The railway rates question and the fall of the third Gladstone ministry', *Eng. Hist. Rev.* lxv (1965), 18–51, with a rebuttal by Philip Maynard Williams, 'Public opinion and the railway rates question in 1886', ibid. lxvii (1952), 37–73, and Geoffrey Alderman, 'The politics of the railway passenger duty', *Transport Hist.* iii (1970), 1–20, and *The railway interest*, Leicester 1973.

**6217** DYOS (HAROLD JAMES). 'Workmen's fares in South London, 1860–1914'. *J. Transport Hist.* i (1953–4), 3–19.

See also **6221, 5994–9** and **9466**.

**6218** BAGWELL (PHILIP SIDNEY). The Railway Clearing House in the British economy, 1842–1942. 1968.

*The Railway Clearing House handbook*, 1904, was repr. Newton Abbot 1970.

**6219** EWEN (HERBERT L'ESTRANGE). A history of railway letter stamps: describing all varieties issued by the railway companies of Great Britain and Ireland. 1901.

Suppl. by his *Railway newspaper and parcel stamps of the United Kingdom issued from 1855 to October 1906*, 1906. See also James Malcolm Campbell Watson, *Stamps and railways*, 1960.

**6220** DUCKWORTH (CHRISTIAN LESLIE DYCE) *and* LANGMUIR (GRAHAM EASTON). Railway & other steamers. Glasgow. 1948. Repr. 1968.

See also Baron Frederick Duckham, 'Railway steamship enterprise: the Lancashire and Yorkshire railway's east coast fleet, 1904–14', *Business Hist.* x (1968), 44–57.

**6221** KELLETT (JOHN REGINALD). The impact of railways on Victorian cities. Lond. & Toronto. 1969.

A careful and systematic study of an important topic. See also Harold James Dyos, 'Some social costs of railway building in London', *J. Transport Hist.* iii (1957–8), 23–30, and **5994–9, 6217, 9466**.

**6222** ELLIS (CUTHBERT HAMILTON). Royal journey: a retrospect of royal trains in the British Isles. 1953. New edn. 1960.

**6223** ELLIS (CUTHBERT HAMILTON). Model railways, 1838–1939. 1962.

(iii) *Contemporary Studies*

6224 SCRIVENOR (HARRY). The railways of the United Kingdom statistically considered in relation to their extent, amalgamations, debentures, financial position . . . 1849. Suppl. 1851.

Designed for investors, but useful for conditions in 1850. Cp. for the end of the century William J. Stevens, *Home railways as investments*, 1896, 2nd edn. 1897, and *Investment and speculation in British railways*, 1902, and *The British railway outlook*, 1906.

6225 WILLIAMS (FREDERICK SMEETON). Our iron roads: their history, construction and social influences. 1852. 7th edn. 1888.

A handy descriptive work. Cp. Dionysius Lardner, *Railway economy: a treatise on the new art of transport*, 1850, repr. N.Y. 1968, R. Bond, *Murray & Co.'s book of information for railway travellers and railway officials . . .*, 1865, and Joseph Parsloe, *Our railways: sketches, historical and descriptive, with practical information as to fares and rates, etc., and a chapter on railway reform*, 1878.

6226 HENLEY COMMITTEE ON RAILWAY AND CANAL BILLS. First report from the select committee on railway and canal bills [Chairman: J. W. Henley]. H.C. 79 (1852-3). XXXVIII, 1. Second to fifth reports. H.C. 170, 246, 310, 736 (1852-3). XXXVIII, 5, 175, 437, 447.

On amalgamation of bills, and the details of legislation. The cost of legislation was considered in *Report from the select committee on railway and canal legislation* [Chairman: J. Wilson Patten]. H.C. 411 (1857-8). XIV, I.

6227 STANLEY COMMITTEE ON RAILWAY COMPANIES' POWERS. Report from the select committee on railway companies' powers [Chairman: Lord Stanley]. H.C. 141 (1864). XI, 95.

On the railway companies' power to operate docks, piers, harbours, ferries, and steamships. For the borrowing powers of railway companies see *Report from the select committee of the House of Lords on railway companies' borrowing powers* [Chairman: Earl of Donoughmore (Viscount Hutchinson)]. H.C. 518 (1864). XI, 43.

6228 BAXTER (ROBERT DUDLEY). 'Railway extension and its results'. *Stat. Soc. J.* xxix (1866), 549-95. Repr. in Carus-Wilson, *Essays* (**4066**) III, 29-67.

6229 DEVONSHIRE COMMISSION ON RAILWAY CHARGES AND COSTS. Royal commission on railways: report of the commissioners. [Chairman: Duke of Devonshire]. [3844] H.C. (1867). XXXVIII, pt. 1, 1. Minutes of evidence. [3844-I] H.C. (1867). XXXVIII, pt. 1, 127. Appendixes. [3844-II, III] H.C. (1867). XXXVIII, pt. 2, 1, 579.

A general inquiry into railway charges and costs, which gathered much information. For further inquiries see *Report from the select committee on railways* [Chairman: Evelyn Ashley]. H.C. 374 (1881). XIII, 1. Appendix. H.C. 374-I (1881). XIV, 2. [On charges for conveyance of merchandise.] *Report from the select committee on railways (rates and fares)* [Chairman: Evelyn Ashley]. H.C. 317 (1882), XIII, 1. *First report from the select committee on railway rates and charges* [Chairman: G. J. Shaw Lefevre]. H.C. 385 (1893-4). XIV, I. Second report. H.C. 462 (1893-4). XIV, 535. [On the powers of railway companies to vary charges.] For detailed discussion of particular proposals see *Report from the joint select committee of the House of Lords and the House of Commons* on the Railway Rates and Charges Provisional Order Bills [Chairman: Duke of Richmond and Gordon]. H.C. 394 (1890–1). XIV, 1. Further report. H.C. 187 (1892). XV, 1.

6230 FORTESCUE COMMITTEE ON RAILWAY AMALGAMATION. Report from the joint committee . . . on railway companies' amalgamation [Chairman: Chichester Fortescue]. H.C. 364 (1872). XIII, pts. 1 & 2.

6231 MARTIN (*Sir* RICHARD BIDDULPH). 'Notes on the purchase of the railways by the state'. *Stat. Soc. J.* xxxvi (1873), 177–202. Discussion. Ibid. 203–55.

A celebrated discussion on nationalization. See also William Galt, *Railway reform: its importance and practicability considered as affecting the nation, the shareholders and the government*, 1864, 2nd edn. 1865, James Hole, *National railways: an argument for state purchase*, 1893, 2nd edn. 1895, and Edwin A. Pratt, *Railways and nationalisation*, 1908.

6232 COHN (GUSTAV). Untersuchungen über die englische Eisenbahnpolitik. 2 v. Leipzig. 1874–5.

Cont. in his *Die englische Eisenbahnpolitik der letzten zehn Jahre, 1873–1883*, Leipzig 1883. A famous account of the railway system. Better than such other foreign contemp. works as Hermann Schwabe, *Über das englische Eisenbahnwesen Reisestudien*, Berlin 1871, new edn. Vienna 1877, French edn. [*Étude sur les chemins de fer anglais*], Paris 1872; Felix Guttmann, *Der Gütertransport auf den Eisenbahnen Englands*, Bromberg 1876; Émile Malézieux, *Les chemins-de-fer anglais en 1873: rapport de mission par M. Malézieux*, Ministère des Travaux Publics, Paris 1874, 2nd edn. 1874; and Edward Bates Dorsey, *English and American railroads compared*, N.Y. 1887, repr. from *Amer. Soc. of Civil Engineers Trans.* xv (1886).

6233 RODWELL COMMITTEE ON RAILWAY PASSENGER DUTY. Report from the select committee on railway passenger duty [Chairman: B. B. Hunter Rodwell]. H.C. 312 (1876). XIII, 369.

6234 FOXWELL (ERNEST). 'English express trains: their average speed, &c, with notes on gradients, long runs, &c.'. *Stat. Soc. J.* xlvi (1883), 517–74. Repr. in his English express trains: two papers. 1884.

See also H. B. Willock, 'English express trains in 1871: and a comparison between them and those of 1883'. *Stat. Soc. J.* xlvii (1884), 259–99, and E. Foxwell and Thomas Cecil Farrer, *Express trains, English and foreign . . .*, 1889.

6235 JEANS (JAMES STEPHEN). 'On the cost and the conditions of working railway traffic in different countries'. *Stat. Soc. J.* xlix (1886), 693–720.

Repr. in his *Railway problems: an inquiry into the economic conditions of railway working in different countries*, 1887.

6236 ACWORTH (*Sir* WILLIAM MITCHELL). The railways of England . . . 1889. 5th edn. 1900. Repr. 1964.

Good. For this period see also Arthur Twining Hadley, *Railroad transportation: its history and its laws*, N.Y. & Lond. 1885, 15th impr. 1903, J. Pearson Pattinson, *British railways: their passenger services, rolling stock, locomotives, gradients and express speeds*, 1893 [Good for statistics], and John Fraser, *English railways statistically considered*, 1903.

6237  MAVOR (JAMES). 'The English railway rate question'. *Q. J. Econ.* viii (1893–4), 280–318, 403–15.

The most lucid account of the subject. See also R. Price-Williams, 'Railway rates and terminal charges', *Roy. Stat. Soc. J.* lix (1896), 485–516, Sir William Mitchell Acworth, *The railways and the traders: a sketch of the railway rates question in theory and practice*, 1891, new edn. 1906, and Edwin A. Pratt, *Railways and their rates . . .*, 1905, 2nd edn. 1906.

6238  PAISH (*Sir* GEORGE). The British railway position . . . reprinted from *The Statist*. 1902.

For railway economics see also Sir William Mitchell Acworth, *The elements of railway economics*, Oxf. 1905, new edn. 1924, Sir Sydney Charles Stuart Williams, *The economics of railway transport*, 1909, and Douglas Knoop, *Outline of railway economics*, 1913, 2nd edn. 1923. For indiv. companies Walter William Wall, *British railway finance: a guide to investors*, 1902, 2nd edn. [*How to invest in railways*] 1903, is useful.

6239  SELECT COMMITTEE ON WORKMEN'S TRAINS. Report from the select committee on workmen's trains [Chairman: Andrew Bonar Law]. H.C. 297 (1903). VIII, 591. Further reports [Chairman: Lt. Col. Bowles]. H.C. 305 (1904). VII, 699. H.C. 270 (1905). VIII, 501.

6240  JERSEY COMMITTEE ON AGRICULTURAL FREIGHT RATES. Report of the departmental committee appointed by the Board of Agriculture and Fisheries to inquire into and report whether preferential treatment is given by the railway companies in Great Britain to foreign and colonial, as compared with home, farm, dairy and market garden produce [Chairman: Earl of Jersey]. [Cd. 2959] H.C. (1906). LV, I. Minutes of evidence. [Cd. 2960] H.C. (1906). LV, 47.

6241  BOARD OF TRADE RAILWAY CONFERENCE. Report of the Board of Trade railway conference. [Cd. 4677] H.C. (1909). LXXVII, 135.

Appointed to review matters of common interest to the railway companies.

6242  GORDON (WILLIAM JOHN). Our home railways: how they began and how they are worked. 2 v. 1910. 2nd edn. 1918. Repr. 1963.

6243  REA COMMITTEE ON RAILWAY AMALGAMATIONS. Report of the departmental committee on railway agreements and amalgamations [Chairman: Russell Rea]. [Cd. 5631] H.C. (1911). XXIX, pt. II, 1. Evidence, etc. [Cd. 5927] H.C. (1911). XXIX, pt. II, 51.

A full inquiry of over 1,000 pp. into the virtues of competition and amalgamations.

6244  DEFRANCE (P.). Les chemins de fer de la Grande-Bretagne et de l'Irlande: étude au point de vue commercial et financier. Brussels & Paris. 1911.

See also Johann Frahm, *Das englische Eisenbahnwesen*, Berlin 1911.

6245  ROYAL ECONOMIC SOCIETY. The state in relation to railways: papers read at the congress of the Royal Economic Society, January 11th, 1912. 1912.

**6246** RAILWAY AND CANAL COMMISSION. Annual report. 50 v. 1890–1938/9.

Preceded by the reports of the Railway Commission, 14 v. 1875–88. Suppl. by reports by the Board of Trade, 1865+, and reports of the Railway Dept. of Board of Trade 1852–9.

## (b) *Regional and Company Histories*

Detailed regional and company bibliogs. are given by Ottley (**6193**), who lists the pamphlets and small booklets that exist in such profusion in this field.

**6247** A REGIONAL HISTORY OF THE RAILWAYS OF GREAT BRITAIN. Ed. by David St. John Thomas. 5+ v. London, Dawlish, or Newton Abbot. 1960+.

V. 1: David St. John Thomas, *The West Country*, 1960, new edn. Newton Abbot 1966, 2: Henry Patrick White, *Southern England*, 1961, 3rd edn. Newton Abbot 1969, 3: H. P. White, *Greater London*, 1963, 4: Kenneth Hoole, *North-East England*, Dawlish etc. [1965], 5: Donald Ian Gordon, *Eastern counties*, Newton Abbot 1968. This ser. is suppl. by another styled *Railway history in pictures*, 1+, Newton Abbot 1969+, of which the following have appeared: Henry Cyril Casserley and Colin Cresswell Dorman, *The Midlands*, Newton Abbot 1969, Kenneth Hoole, *North-East England*, Newton Abbot 1969, and John Clarke and John Allan Patmore, *North-West England*, Newton Abbot 1968. Peter Edward Baughan, *The railways of Wharfedale*, Newton Abbot 1969, is a good example of a more localized treatment.

**6248** COURSE (EDWIN ALFRED). London railways. 1962.

Good. See also Alan Arthur Chirm Jackson, *London's termini*, Newton Abbot 1969, Jack Simmons, *St. Pancras station*, 1968, and the works at **5994–9, 6217, 6221**.

**6249** JACKSON (ALAN ARTHUR CHIRM) *and* CROOME (DESMOND FELIX). Rails through the clay: a history of London's tube railways. 1962.

There are also a number of more popular works, incl. Frederick Henry Howson, *London's underground*, 1951, 3rd edn. 1962, John Robert Day, *The story of London's underground*, 1963, 2nd edn. 1969, and Hugh Douglas, *The underground story*, 1963.

**6250** LORDS COMMITTEE ON METROPOLITAN RAILWAYS. First report from the select committee of the House of Lords on metropolitan railway communication [Chairman: Earl Granville]. H.C. 500 (1863). VIII, 1. Second report. H.C. 500–I (1863). VIII, 5. Third report. H.C. 500–II (1863). VIII, 9.

See also *Report from the select committee appointed to join with a committee of the House of Lords on railway schemes (metropolis)* [Chairman: Earl Granville]. H.C. 87 (1864). XI, 241.

**6251** STANSFELD COMMITTEE ON METROPOLITAN ELECTRIC & CABLE RAILWAYS. Report from the joint select committee . . . on the electric and cable railways (metropolis) [Chairman: James Stansfeld]. H.C. 215 (1892). XII, 1.

See also *Report of the committee appointed by the Board of Trade to inquire into the system of ventilation of tunnels on the Metropolitan railway* [Chairman: F. A. Marindin].

[C. 8684] H.C. (1898). XLV, 135, and Jack Simmons, 'The pattern of tube railways in London: a note on the joint select committee of 1892', *J. Transport Hist.* vii (1965–6), 234–40.

**6252  NOCK (OSWALD STEVENS). The railway race to the north. [1959.] New edn. 1962.**

O. S. Nock and Eric Treacy also publ. *Main lines across the border,* 1960.

**6253  WHITEHOUSE (PATRICK BRUCE). On the narrow gauge. 1964.**

An intro. to narrow gauge railways. See also his *Narrow gauge album,* 1957, and Richard Bagnold Jones, *British narrow gauge railways,* 1958.

**6254  DAVIES (WILLIAM JAMES KEITH). Light railways: their rise and decline. 1964.**

**6255  TONKS (ERIC SIDNEY). The ironstone railways & tramways of the Midlands. 1959. 2nd impr. rev. 1961.**

**6256  CARTER (ERNEST FRANK). Britain's railway liveries: colours, crests and linings, 1825–1948. 1952. 2nd edn. 1963.**

Gives the colour schemes adopted by the companies.

**6257  DOW (GEORGE). Great Central. 3 v. 1959–65.**

A detailed hist.

**6258  ALLEN (CECIL JOHN). The Great Eastern railway. 1955. 3rd edn. 1961.**

**6259  WROTTESLEY (ARTHUR JOHN FRANCIS). The Midland & Great Northern joint railway. Newton Abbot. 1970.**

**6260  GRINLING (CHARLES HERBERT). The history of the Great Northern railway, 1845–1895. 1898. New edn. [1845–1902.] 1903. New edn. 1966.**

See also Oswald Stevens Nock, *The Great Northern railway,* 1958, and George Frederick Bird, *The locomotives of the Great Northern railway, 1847–1902,* 1903, new edn. [1847–1910] 1910.

**6261  MACDERMOT (EDWARD TERENCE). History of the Great Western railway. 2 v. in 3. 1927–31. Rev. edn. by Charles Ralph Clinker. 3 v. 1964.**

The G.W.R. was the most popular in the country and employed, *inter alia,* Brunel (**6292**), Gooch (**6293**), and Williams (**6308**). For its advertising see Roger Burdett Wilson, *Go Great Western: a history of Great Western railway publicity,* Newton Abbot 1970. For the hist. of the railway generally see G. A. Sekon, pseud. of George Augustus Nokes, *A history of the Great Western railway: being, the story of the broad gauge,* 1895; Archibald Williams, *Brunel and after: the romance of the Great Western railway,* 1925; the centenary number of the *Great Western railway mag.* (xlvii (1935), 439–540); Oswald Stevens Nock, *The Great Western railway in the nineteenth century* [1962], *The Great Western railway in the twentieth century* [1964], *The Great Western railway:*

*an appreciation*, Camb. 1951, *The GWR stars, castles & kings:* ... *1906–1930*, Newton Abbot 1970, and *Fifty years of Western express running*, Bristol 1954; Harold Holcroft, *An outline of Great Western locomotive practice, 1837–1947*, 1957; William Alfred Tuplin, *Great Western steam*, 1958, 2nd edn. 1965; Michael Harris, *Great Western coaches, 1890–1954*, Newton Abbot 1968; and David Edward Charles Eversley, 'The Great Western railway works, Swindon', in *Victoria history of the counties of England: Wiltshire*, IV, 207–19, and 'The Great Western railway and the Swindon works in the great depression', *Univ. of Birmingham Hist. J.* v (1955–6), 167–90.

6262  MARSHALL (JOHN). The Lancashire and Yorkshire railway. 2 v. Newton Abbot. 1969–70.

See also Thomas Normington, *The Lancashire & Yorkshire railway: being a full account of the rise and progress of this railway* . . ., Manch. 1898, Eric Mason, *The Lancashire & Yorkshire railway in the twentieth century*, 1954, 2nd edn. 1961, and Robert William Rush, *The Lancashire & Yorkshire railway and its locomotives, 1846–1923*, 1949.

6263  BOX (CHARLES EDMUND). The Liverpool overhead railway, 1893–1956. 1959. Rev. edn. 1962.

6264  STEEL (WILFRED L.). The history of the London & North Western railway. 1914.

See also Oswald Stevens Nock, *The London & North Western railway*, 1960, *The premier line: the story of London & North Western locomotives*, 1952, and *The LNWR precursor family* . . . [locomotives], Newton Abbot 1966; William Alfred Tuplin, *North Western steam*, 1963; Roger Bradshaigh Lloyd, *Railwaymen's gallery*, 1953; Charles Ralph Clinker, comp., *London and North Western railway: a chronology of opening and closing dates of lines and stations, including joint worked and associated undertakings, 1900 to 1960*, Dawlish 1961; Sir George Findlay, *The working and management of an English railway*, 1889, 5th edn. 1894; and David Stevenson, *Fifty years on the London & North Western railway* . . ., ed. by Leopold Turner, 1891. Chaloner's *Crewe* (**9525**), is largely concerned with the London & North Western railway workshops, as are Neele's reminiscences (**6294**).

6265  WILLIAMS (RONALD ALFRED). The London & South Western railway. Vol. 1. Newton Abbot 1968.

See also Sir Sam Fay, *A royal road: being the history of the London & South Western railway, from 1825 to the present time*, Kingston 1882, repr. 1883, Cuthbert Hamilton Ellis, *The South-Western railway: its mechanical history and background, 1838–1922*, 1956, and Jack Simmons, 'South-Western *v* Great Western: railway competition in Devon and Cornwall', *J. Transport Hist.* iv (1959–60), 13–36.

6266  ELLIS (CUTHBERT HAMILTON). The London, Brighton and South Coast railway: a mechanical history of the London & Brighton, the London & Croydon, and the London, Brighton & South Coast railways, from 1839 to 1922. 1960.

See also [Frank Burtt] *The locomotives of the London, Brighton & South Coast railway, 1839–1903*, 1903, John Nevil Maskelyne, *The locomotives of the London, Brighton and South Coast railway, 1903–1923*, 1928, and John Fraser, *English railways statistically considered*, 1903.

6267  BARNES (ERIC GEORGE). The rise of the Midland railway, 1844–1874. 1966.

Cont. in his *The Midland main line, 1875–1922*, 1969. Based on one of the good early hists., Frederick Smeeton Williams, *The Midland railway: its rise and progress: a narrative of modern enterprise*, 1876, 5th [?7th] edn. 1888, repr. Newton Abbot 1968. See also Clement Edwin Stretton, *The history of the Midland railway*, 1901, Cuthbert Hamilton Ellis, *The Midland railway*, 1953, 2nd edn. 1955, and Oswald Stevens Nock, *The Midland compounds*, Dawlish 1964. There is also Ronald Harry Clark, *A short history of the Midland & Great Northern Joint Railway*, Norwich 1967.

6268 MAGGS (COLIN GORDON). The Midland and South Western Junction railway. Newton Abbot. 1967.

6269 MACLEAN (JOHN S.). The Newcastle & Carlisle railway, 1825–1862 . . . Newcastle-upon-Tyne. 1948.

6270 TOMLINSON (WILLIAM WEAVER). The North Eastern railway: its rise and development. Newcastle-upon-Tyne. [1914.] Repr. Newton Abbot. 1967.

See also Cecil John Allen, *The North Eastern railway*, 1964, Robert Bell, *Twenty-five years of the North-Eastern railway, 1898–1922*, 1951, John S. Maclean, *The locomotives of the North-Eastern railway, 1854–1905*, Newcastle-upon-Tyne [1905], new edn. [1841–1922] 1925, further edn. Lond. 1944, and Oswald Stevens Nock, *Locomotives of the North Eastern railway*, 1954.

6271 MANIFOLD, *pseud of* HOLLICK (JOHN REGINALD) *and others*. The North Staffordshire railway. Ashbourne. 1952.

6272 MARSHALL (CHAPMAN FREDERICK DENDY). A history of the Southern railway . . . 1936. 2nd edn. by Roger Wakely Kidner. 2 v. 1963–4. Repr. 1 v. 1968.

See also Roger Wakely Kidner, *The Southern railway*, South Godstone 1958, Oswald Stevens Nock, *Southern steam*, Newton Abbot 1966, George Thomas Moody, *Southern electric: the history of the world's largest suburban electrified system*, 1957, 3rd edn. 1960, and Harold Holcroft, *Locomotive adventure: fifty years of steam*, 2 v. 1962–5.

6273 DAVIES (WILLIAM JAMES KEITH). The Ravenglass & Eskdale railway. Newton Abbot. 1968.

6274 PAAR (HAROLD WILLIAM). The Severn & Wye railway: a history of the railways of the Forest of Dean. Part I. Dawlish. 1963.

Cont. in his *The Great Western railway in Dean: a history of the railways of the Forest of Dean*, part II, Dawlish 1965.

6275 ATTHILL (ROBIN). The Somerset & Dorset railway. Newton Abbot. 1967.

Suppl. by his *The picture history of the Somerset and Dorset railway*, Newton Abbot 1970. Cp. Gordon Arthur Brown, J. D. C. Prideaux, and H. G. Radcliffe, *The Lynton and Barnstaple railway*, Dawlish 1964, rev. edn. Newton Abbot 1971.

6276 NOCK (OSWALD STEVENS). The South-Eastern and Chatham railway. [1961.]

Samuel Smiles was sec. of the South Eastern railway, 1854–66: see his autobiog. (8413).

6277 JEANS (JAMES STEPHEN). Jubilee memorial of the railway system: a history of the Stockton & Darlington railway and a record of its results. 1875.

A good account of the railway is also incl. in Tomlinson, *The North Eastern* (**6270**).

(c) *Railway Engineering*

(i) *Construction*

See also Civil Engineering (**5162–87**).

6278 FORWARD (ERNEST ALFRED) *comp*. Science Museum: catalogue of the collections in the Science Museum: Land transport IV; railway construction and working. 1927.

See also Brian Haresnape, *Railway design since 1830*, 2 v. 1968–9.

6279 PATENT OFFICE. Patents for inventions: abridgments of specifications relating to railways, A.D. 1770–1863. 2nd edn. 1873. Suppl. for 1867–76. 1884. Cont. by Abridgments of specifications, class 104. 1855–1930.

6280 BRASSEY. Life and labours of Mr. Brassey, 1805–1870. By Sir Arthur Helps. 1872. 7th edn. 1888. Repr. 1969.

Charles Walker, *Thomas Brassey: railway builder*, 1969, adds little, but is clear.

6281 FIRBANK. The life and work of Joseph Firbank, J.P., D.L., railway contractor. By Frederick McDermott. 1887.

6282 LOCKE. The Life of Joseph Locke, civil engineer. By Joseph Devey. 1862.

6283 PETO. Sir Morton Peto, a memorial sketch. By Sir Henry Peto. Priv. pr. 1893.

6284 STEPHENSON. George and Robert Stephenson: the railway revolution. By Lionel Thomas Caswall Rolt. 1960.

A straightforward account of two rather tight-lipped men. George Stephenson died in 1848, Robert in 1859. For Robert's life see also John Cordy Jeaffreson, *The life of Robert Stephenson*, 2 v. 1864.

6285 HADFIELD ([ELLIS] CHARLES [RAYMOND]). Atmospheric railways: a Victorian venture in silent speed. Newton Abbot. 1967.

6286 BARMAN (CHRISTIAN). An introduction to railway architecture. 1950.

6287 MEEK (CARROLL LOUIS VANDERSLICE). The railroad station: an architectural history. New Haven [Conn.] & Lond. 1957.

**6288 HASKOLL (W. DAVIS).** Railway construction: from the setting out of the centre line to the completion of the works . . . 2 v. 1857. 2 ser. 2 v. 1864.

A useful guide to contemp. practice. See also George Drysdale Dempsey, *The practical railway engineer: examples of the mechanical and engineering operations and structures combined in the making of a railway*, 1847, 4th edn. 1855; John Wolfe Barry, *Railway appliances: a description of details of railway construction subsequent to the completion of the earthworks and structures, including a short notice of railway rolling stock*, 1876, 6th edn. 1890; William Hemingway Mills, *Railway construction*, 1898; Cecil John Allen, *Modern British permanent way*, 1915; and William Henry Cole, *Notes on permanent-way material, platelaying and points and crossings*, 1890, 10th edn. 1940.

(ii) *Operation*

**6289 FINDLAY (*Sir* GEORGE).** The working and management of an English railway. 1889. 5th edn. 1894.

A very helpful account, based on long experience with the London & North Western. See also E. B. Ivatts, *Railway management at stations*, 1885, 5th edn. 1910.

**6290 MACAULAY (JOHN)** *ed.* Modern railway working: a practical treatise by engineering and administrative experts. 8 v. 1912–14.

Cp. two ser. of articles repr. from the *Railway news*, Charles Travis, David Ritchie Lamb, and John A. Jenkinson, *The elements of railway operating economics* . . ., 1913, and *Practical railway working* . . ., 1915. About the same time the North Eastern railway publ. Harry Mainwaring Hallsworth, *The elements of railway operating* [York 1914]. There is also Hugh Munro Ross, *British railways: their organisation and management*, 1904.

**6291 HOUGH (RICHARD ALEXANDER).** Six great railwaymen: Stephenson, Hudson, Denison, Huish, Stephen, Gresley. 1955.

**6292 BRUNEL.** Isambard Kingdom Brunel: a biography. By Lionel Thomas Caswall Rolt. 1957.

A straightforward modern biog. The starting-point for all Brunel studies is Isambard Brunel, *The life of Isambard Kingdom Brunel, civil engineer*, 1870. For the family generally see Celia Brunel Noble, *The Brunels, father and son*, 1938.

**6293 GOOCH.** Diaries of Sir Daniel Gooch, baronet: with an introductory note by Sir Theodore Martin. 1892. New edn. Ed. by Roger Burdett Wilson. Newton Abbot. 1972.

**6294 NEELE.** Railway reminiscences: notes and reminiscences of half-a-century's progress in railway working and of a railway superintendent's life, principally on the London & North Western railway. By George P. Neele. 1904.

**6295 TATLOW.** Fifty years of railway life in England, Scotland and Ireland. By Joseph Tatlow. 1920. 2nd edn. 1948.

**6296 TAYLOR.** Autobiography of Peter Taylor. Paisley. 1903.

8223897 A a

6297  FORWARD (ERNEST ALFRED) *comp.* Science Museum: catalogue of the collections of the Science Museum: land transport III: railway locomotives and rolling stock. 1923. New edn. 2 pts. 1931, 1951.

6298  PATENT OFFICE. Patents for inventions: abridgments of specifications: class 79: locomotives and motor vehicles for road and rail, period 1867–76. 1904.

Incl. as an indication of the type of handlist on railways publ. by the Patent Office.

6299  AHRONS (ERNEST LEOPOLD). The British steam railway locomotive, 1825–1925. 1927. Repr. 1961.

Very full. See also his *The development of British locomotive design* [1914]. There were some other good contemp. hists., notably G. A. Sekon, pseud. of George Augustus Nokes, *The evolution of the steam locomotive, 1803 to 1898*, 1899, 2nd edn. 1899; Clement Edwin Stretton, *The locomotive engine and its development: a popular treatise on the gradual improvements made in railway engines between 1803 and 1892* . . ., 1892, 6th edn. 1903; George Charles Montagu, *Ten years of locomotive progress* [1896–1906], 1907; and Clarence Edgar Allen, *The modern locomotive*, Camb. 1912.

6300  TUPLIN (WILLIAM ALFRED). British steam since 1900. 1969.

See also Edward Cecil Poultney, *British express locomotive development, 1896–1948*, 1952; Cecil John Allen, *Locomotive practice and performance in the twentieth century* [repr. from the *Railway mag.*], Camb. 1949; Oswald Stevens Nock, *Steam locomotive* . . ., 1957, and *Historical steam locomotives*, 1959; and Cecil John Allen, *The locomotive exchanges, 1870–1948*, 1949.

6301  HAUT (F. J. G.). The history of the electric locomotive. 1969.

For early ideas on the use of electricity see William Edward Langdon, *The application of electricity to railway working*, 1877, new edn. 1897.

6302  ELLIS (CUTHBERT HAMILTON). Twenty locomotive men. 1958.

See also Henry Anthony Vaughan Bulleid, *Master builders of steam*, 1963, and Oswald Stevens Nock, *The railway engineers*, 1957.

6303  BULLEID. Bulleid, last giant of steam. By Sean Day Lewis. 1964.

6304  GRESLEY. Nigel Gresley: locomotive engineer. By Francis Allen St. John Brown. 1961.

See also Oswald Stevens Nock, *The locomotives of Sir Nigel Gresley*, 1945.

6305  NOCK (OSWALD STEVENS). The locomotives of R. E. L. Maunsell, 1911–1937. Bristol. 1954.

For other locomotive designers see Paul Coulthard Dewhurst, 'The Fairlie locomotive', ed. by Harold Holcroft, *Newcomen Soc. Trans.* xxxiv (1961–2), 105–32; xxxix (1966–7), 1–34, and Richard L. Hills, 'Some contributions to locomotive development by Beyer, Peacock & Co.', ibid. xl (1967–8), 75–123.

6306  COOKE (CHARLES JOHN BOWEN) *and others.* Round the works of our great railways. By various authors. [1893.]

See also his *British locomotives* . . ., 1893, 3rd edn. 1900.

6307 HALDANE (JOHN WILTON CUNINGHAME). Railway engineering: mechanical and electrical. 1897.

A useful account of each railway works.

6308 WILLIAMS (ALFRED). Life in a railway factory [Swindon]. 1915. New edn. Newton Abbot. 1969.

See also Leonard Clark, *Alfred Williams: his life and work*, Oxf. 1945, repr. Newton Abbot 1969.

6309 BENNETT (ALFRED ROSLING). The chronicles of Boulton's siding. 1927.

Locomotives built by Boulton & Watt.

6310 WARREN (JAMES GRAEME HEPBURN). A century of locomotive building by Robert Stephenson & Co., 1823–1923. Newcastle-upon-Tyne. 1923. Repr. Newton Abbot. 1970.

6311 NORTH BRITISH LOCOMOTIVE COMPANY LTD. North British Locomotive: a catalogue of narrow gauge locomotives. Glasgow. 1912. Repr. Newton Abbot. 1970.

6312 TREDGOLD (THOMAS). The principles and practice and explanation of the machinery of locomotive engines in operation on the several lines of railway . . . forming the first volume of the new edition of Tredgold on the steam engine. Ed. by James Hann and Robert Armstrong. 1850.

6313 CLARK (DANIEL KINNEAR). Railway machinery: a treatise on the mechanical engineering of railways; embracing the principles and construction of rolling and fixed plant, illustrated by a series of plates on a large scale, and by numerous engravings in wood. Publ. in pts. 1851–5. Reissued 2 v. Glasgow. 1855.

See also his *Railway locomotives: their progress, mechanical construction and performance* . . ., publ. in pts. 1858–60, reissued 2 v. Glasgow 1860.

6314 COLBURN (ZERAH). Locomotive engineering and the mechanism of railways: a treatise on the principles and construction of the locomotive engine, railway carriages and railway plant . . . 2 v. Lond. & Glasgow. 1871.

6315 COOKE (CHARLES JOHN BOWEN). British locomotives: their history, construction and modern development. 1893. 3rd edn. 1900.

For locomotives in the 1890s see also Clement Edwin Stretton, *The locomotive engine and its development: a popular treatise* . . ., 1892, 6th edn. 1903, and William Frank Pettigrew, *A manual of locomotive engineering* . . ., 1899, 3rd edn. 1909.

6316 PRICE-WILLIAMS (RICHARD). 'On the serviceable life and average annual cost of locomotives in Great Britain'. *Instn. Civ. Eng. Proc.* clxxv (1908), 252–75.

6317 PATENT OFFICE. Patents for inventions: abridgements of specifications relating to carriages and other vehicles for railways, A.D. 1807–1866. 1871.

One of the biggest vols. publ. by the Patent Office. Cont. by *Abridgments of specifications,* class 103, 1855–1930.

6318 ELLIS (CUTHBERT HAMILTON). Railway carriages in the British isles from 1830 to 1914. 1965.

6319 LEE (CHARLES EDWARD). 'Passenger class distinctions'. *Inst. of Transport J.* xxi (1944), 756–60, 810–14; xxii (1944–5), 36–9, 61–3, 146–9. Rev. edn. publ. as Passenger class distinctions. 1946.

6320 CARTER (ERNEST FRANK). Britain's railway liveries: colours, crests and linings, 1825–1948. 1952. 2nd edn. 1963.

6321 MENCKEN (AUGUST). The railroad passenger car: an illustrated history of the first hundred years with accounts by contemporary passengers. Baltimore. [1957.]

6322 ESSERY (ROBERT JOHN), ROWLAND (DONALD PETER), and STEEL (WILLIAM OWEN). British goods wagons: from 1887 to the present day. Newton Abbot. 1970.

6323 WHITBREAD (J. R.). The railway policeman: the story of the constable on the track. 1961.

6324 PATENT OFFICE. Patents for inventions: abridgments of specifications relating to railway signals and communicating apparatus, A.D. 1840–1866. 1869. Cont. by Abridgments of specifications, class 105. 1855–1930.

6325 ROLT (LIONEL THOMAS CASWALL). Red for danger: a history of railway accidents and railway safety precautions. 1955. Repr. Newton Abbot. 1971.

There is a considerable literature on the subject, dominated by the extensive and beautifully-illustrated reports submitted to parliament after major accidents and publ. as parl. papers. See also Oswald Stevens Nock, *Fifty years of railway signalling: in celebration of the golden jubilee of the Institution of Railway Signal Engineers, 1912–1962,* 1962, John Thomas, *Obstruction—danger! stories of memorable railway disasters,* Edin. & Lond. 1937, and Richard Blythe, *Danger ahead: the dramatic story of railway signalling,* 1951.

For contemp. textbooks see Archibald Davis Dawnay, *A treatise upon railway signals and accidents,* 1874; Clement Edwin Stretton, *Safe railway working: a treatise on railway accidents, their cause and prevention, with a description of modern appliances and systems,* 1887, 3rd edn. 1893; Éduard Sauvage, *Le système anglais des signaux de chemins de fer,* Paris 1893; James Pigg, *Railway block signalling . . .,* 1899; C. B. Byles, *The first principles of railway signalling . . .,* 1910, 2nd edn. 1918; Henry Raynar Wilson, *The safety of British railways: or, railway accidents, how caused and how prevented,* 1909, and *Power railway signalling,* 1910; and Leonard P. Lewis, *Railway signal engineering: mechanical,* 1912, 3rd edn. 1932.

6326 BENTINCK COMMITTEE ON ACCIDENTS ON RAILWAYS. Report from the select committee on accidents on railways [Chairman: George P. Bentinck]. H.C. 362 (1857–8). XIV, 555.

See also *Report from the select committee of the House of Lords on the Regulation of Railways (Prevention of Accidents) Bill:* [*H.L.*] [Chairman: Duke of Somerset]. H.C. 148 (1873). XIV, 421; *Royal commission on railway accidents: report of the commissioners* [Chairman: Duke of Buckingham and Chandos]. [C. 1637] H.C. (1877). XLVIII, 1. Minutes of evidence. [C. 1637–I–II] H.C. (1877). XLVIII, 173; and *Report of the royal commission appointed to enquire into the causes of the accidents, fatal and non-fatal, to servants of railway companies and of truck owners* [Chairman: Lord James of Hereford]. [Cd. 41] H.C. (1900). XXVII, 1. Evidence etc. [Cd. 42] H.C. (1900). XXVII, 15. On the law relating to compensation for railway accidents see also *Report from the select committee on railway companies* [Chairman: T. C. Headlam]. H.C. 341 (1870). X, 207 .

## 5. ROAD TRANSPORT

6327 BALLEN (DOROTHY). Bibliography of road-making and roads in the United Kingdom. Lond. School of Econ. Studs. in Econ. Bibliogs. 3. 1914.

6328 PATENT OFFICE. Abridgments of specifications relating to roads and ways, A.D. 1619–1866. 1868. Cont. by Abridgments of specifications, class 107. 1855–1930.

6329 FORWARD (ERNEST ALFRED). *comp.* Catalogue of the collections of the Science Museum: land transport. 4 pts. 1923–7. New edn. [Handbook of the collections.] 1931–6.

6330 WEBB (SIDNEY JAMES), *Baron Passfield and* WEBB (BEATRICE). The story of the king's highway. English local government 5. 1913. Repr. 1963.

A brief but useful hist. of highway admin. See also John Tidd Pratt, *The law relating to highways . . .*, 1835, 19th edn. 1952.

6331 BIRD (ANTHONY COLE). Roads and vehicles. 1969.

A short technical hist. designed for a popular audience. Better than the considerable number of older general books about roads. But see W. Rees Jeffreys, *The king's highway: an historical and autobiographical record of the developments of the past sixty years,* 1949, and, for road making, Henry Law, *Rudiments of the art of constructing and repairing common roads: to which is prefixed a general survey of the principal metropolitan roads by Samuel Hughes,* 1850, 3rd edn. 1861–2, rev. edn. by David Kinnear Clark, publ. as *The construction of roads and streets . . .*, 2 pts. 1877, 8th edn. 1914, Henry Turlay Chapman, *Reminiscences of a highway surveyor, 1886–1932,* Maidstone 1932, and P. C. Cowan, 'Rural roads: with special reference to modern requirements', *Roy. Agric. Soc. J.* lxvii (1906), 20–45.

6332 SEARLE (MARK) *comp.* Turnpikes and toll-bars. 2 v. [1930.]

A comprehensive, toll road by toll road inquiry, attractively illustr. See also *Report from the select committee on turnpike trusts* [Chairman: George Clive]. H.C. 383 (1864). IX, 331, and John Edwin Bradfield, *Notes on toll reform and the turnpike & ticket system,* Toll Reform Central Office 1856, and *Turnpike abolition: free locomotion on roads and bridges: a letter addressed to Mr. Secretary Walpole,* 1867.

6333 SOMERSET COMMITTEE ON HIGHWAY ACTS. Report from the select committee of the House of Lords on Highway Acts [Chairman: Duke of Somerset]. H.C. 371 (1881). X, 1.

A comprehensive inquiry.

6334 GRANT LAWSON COMMITTEE ON HIGHWAYS. Report of the departmental committee appointed by the President of the Local Government Board to inquire into the subject of highway authorities and administration in England and Wales [Chairman: John Grant Lawson]. [Cd. 1793] H.C. (1904). XXIV, 279. Minutes of evidence. [Cd. 1794] H.C. (1904). XXIV, 295.

6335 ROAD BOARD. First report of the proceedings of the Road Board from 13th May 1910 to 30th June 1911. H.C. 292 (1911). XL, 713. Annual to 10th report. 1921.

6336 STRONG (LEONARD ALFRED GEORGE). The rolling road: the story of travel on the roads of Britain and the development of public passenger transport. 1956.

6337 BETT (WINGATE HENRY) *and* GILLHAM (JOHN C.). Great British tramway networks. 1940. 4th edn. 1967.

Lists all tramways.

6338 KLAPPER (CHARLES FREDERICK). The golden age of tramways. 1961.

See also Charles Edward Lee, 'The English street tramways of George Francis Train', *J. Transport Hist.* i (1953–4), 20–7, 97–108; John Horace Price, 'London's first electric tramway', ibid. iii (1957–8), 205–11; Selwyn Howard Pearce Higgins, *The Wantage tramway: a history of the first tramway to adopt mechanical traction*, Abingdon 1958; Ian Armour Yearsley, *The Manchester tram*, Huddersfield 1962; Roy Brook, *The tramways of Huddersfield: a history of Huddersfield corporation tramways, 1883–1940*, Huddersfield [1960]; Roger Thomas Baldwin Fulford, *Five decades of B.E.T.: the story of the British Electric Traction Company Limited*, 1946; and John Henry Cansdale, *Electric traction jubilee, 1896–1946: a brief survey of electric traction, with some account of the part played by the British Thomson–Houston Co. Ltd.*, 1946. Other works on tramways are listed in **6193**.

6339 SHAW–LEFEVRE COMMITTEE ON TRAMWAYS BILL. Report from the select committee on Tramways Bill [Chairman: G. J. Shaw-Lefevre]. H.C. 205 (1870). X, 691.

See also *Report from the joint select committee of the House of Lords and the House of Commons on tramways (metropolis)* [Chairman: Viscount Eversley]. H.C. 252 (1872). XII, 265.

6340 CAWLEY COMMITTEE ON LOCOMOTIVES ON ROADS. Report from the select committee on locomotives on roads [Chairman: Charles Edward Cawley]. H.C. 312 (1873). XVI, 477.

The first of a closely-related ser. of inquiries, viz. *Report from the select committee on tramways (use of mechanical power)* [Chairman: Thomas Salt]. H.C. 161 (1877). XVI,

445, *Report from the select committee on Tramways (Use of Mechanical Power) Bills* [Chairman: Arthur Peel]. H.C. 224 (1878). XVIII, 521, and *Report from the select committee of the House of Lords on tramways* [Chairman: Marquess of Ripon]. H.C. 148 (1878–9). XIV, 1.

6341 HOBHOUSE COMMITTEE ON TRACTION ENGINES ON ROADS. Report from the select committee on traction engines on roads [Chairman: Henry Hobhouse]. H.C. 272 (1896). XIV, 13.

6342 CLARK (DANIEL KINNEAR). Tramways: their construction and working . . . 1878. Suppl. 1882. 2nd edn. 1894.

Good.

6343 DUNCAN (WILLIAM WALLACE). Manual of tramway companies in the United Kingdom, together with traffic tables of the principal companies, and a map of those in London . . . 1877.

Cont. as *Duncan's manual of British and foreign tramway companies*, 1883–1905.

6344 RUSSELL COMMITTEE ON THE LONDON CAB SERVICE. The cab service of the metropolis: report of the committee of enquiry appointed by the Home Secretary [Chairman: George William Erskine Russell]. [C. 7607] H.C. (1895). XXXV, 1. Minutes of evidence. [C. 7607–I] H.C. (1895). XXXV, 21.

See also *Report from the select committee on Cabs and Omnibuses (Metropolis) Bill* [Chairman: Henry Norman]. H.C. 295 (1906). VII, 581, and *Report of the departmental committee on taxi-cab fares* [Chairman: Sir Archibald Williamson]. [Cd. 5782] H.C. (1911). XLI, 547. Minutes of evidence. [Cd. 5875] H.C. (1911). XLI, 561.

6345 HIBBS (JOHN). The history of British bus services. Newton Abbot. 1968.

Little more than an outline. Suppl. by his *The omnibus: readings in the history of road transport*, Newton Abbot 1971. See also Henry Charles Moore, *Omnibuses and cabs: their origin and history*, 1902. For indiv. companies see British Transport Commission, London Transport Executive, *London General: the story of the London bus, 1856–1956*, 1956; Roy Claude Anderson and Geoffrey George Alfred Frankis, *History of Royal Blue Express Services*, Newton Abbot & N.Y. 1970; John Tilling, *Kings of the highway*, 1957; and James Wentworth Day, *Wheels of service, 1898–1958: the story of P.M.T.* [1958.]

6346 DAVISON (CHARLES ST. CLAIR BUICK). History of steam road vehicles: mainly for passenger transport. Science Museum. 1953.

See also William Fletcher, *The history and development of steam locomotion on common roads*, 1891, and Charles Frederick T. Young, *The economy of steam power on common roads . . .*, 1861.

6347 SCIENCE MUSEUM. Some books on the history of the motor car. Science Libr. bibliog. ser. 749. 1957.

6348 BERSEY (WALTER C.) *and* FOUCARD (W. V.) *comps.* A list of motor cars [light cars and cycle cars] manufactured or sold in the United Kingdom, 1906–1911. 1911. New edns. (covering 1906–12, 1907–13, 1908–14, 1909–15) 1912–15.

**6349** CAUNTER (CYRIL FRANCIS). The history and development of light cars. Science Museum. 1957.

**6350** KARSLAKE (KENT) *and* POMEROY (LAURENCE). From veteran to vintage: a history of motoring and motorcars from 1884 to 1914. 1956.

One of a considerable number of general books intended for the vintage car enthusiast. Cp. Anthony Cole Bird, *The motor car, 1765–1914,* 1960; Lionel Thomas Caswall Rolt, *Horseless carriage: the motor car in England,* 1950; Timothy Robin Nicholson, ed., *The motor book: an anthology, 1895–1914,* 1962, and *The trailblazers: stories of the heroic age of transcontinental motoring, 1901–14,* 1958; David Scott-Moncrieff, *Veteran and Edwardian motor-cars,* 1955, rev. edn. 1961; Cecil Clutton and John Edward Gordon Stanford, *The vintage motor car,* 1954; St. John Cousins Nixon, *The antique automobile,* 1956; and Elizabeth Nagle, *Veterans of the road: the history of veteran cars and the Veteran Car Club of Great Britain,* 1955.

**6351** HOUGH (RICHARD ALEXANDER). A history of the world's sports cars. 1961.

See also Charles Jarrott, *Ten years of motors and motor racing,* 1906, 2nd edn. 1912.

**6352** NIXON (ST. JOHN COUSINS). Romance among cars. 1938.

The early hist. of the R.A.C. See also **7783.**

**6353** SAUL (SAMUEL BERRICK). 'The motor industry in Britain to 1914'. *Business Hist.* v (1962–3), 22–44.

**6354** AUSTIN. Lord Austin—the man. By Zita Elaine Lambert and Robert John Wyatt. 1968.

**6355** LANCHESTER. F. W. Lanchester: a life of an engineer. By Peter Wilfred Kingsford. 1960.

For his cars see Anthony Cole Bird, *Lanchester motor cars . . .,* 1965, and for his business career P. W. Kingsford, 'The Lanchester Engine Company Ltd., 1899–1904', *Business Hist.* iii (1960–1), 107–13.

**6356** MORRIS. The life of [William Morris] Lord Nuffield: a study in enterprise and benevolence. By Philip Walter Sawford Andrews and Elizabeth Brunner. Oxf. 1955.

**6357** JOHNSON. The hyphen in Rolls-Royce: a biography of Claude Johnson. By Wilton Joseph Oldham. 1967.

**6358** ROLLS. Rolls of Rolls-Royce: a biography of the Hon. C. S. Rolls. By Edward John Barrington Douglas-Scott-Montagu, Baron Montagu of Beaulieu and Michael Sedgwick. 1967.

There is also Laurence Walter Meynell, *Rolls: man of speed: a life of Charles Stewart Rolls and some account of the early days of motoring and flying,* 1953.

**6359** ROYCE. The life of Sir Henry Royce, Bart., M.I.E.E., M.I.M.E., with some chapters from the stories of the late Charles S. Rolls and Claude Johnson. By Sir Max Pemberton. 1934.

For Rolls-Royce cars see Anthony Cole Bird, *The Rolls-Royce motor car,* 1964. Harold Nockolds, *The magic of a name,* 1938, rev. edn. 1950, is a hist. of the firm.

6360 NIXON (ST. JOHN COUSINS). Daimler, 1896–1946: a record of fifty years of the Daimler company. 1947.

Nixon also publ. *Wolseley: a saga of the motor industry*, 1949.

6361 DUNLOP (JOHN BOYD). The history of the pneumatic tyre. Dublin. 1924.

By the inventor of the pneumatic tyre.

6362 DU CROS (*Sir* ARTHUR PHILIP). Wheels of fortune: a salute to pioneers. 1938.

A hist. of the pneumatic tyre in terms of the Du Cros family.

6363 HOBHOUSE COMMITTEE ON MOTOR CARS. Report of the departmental committee appointed by the President of the Local Government Board to inquire with regard to regulations for the purposes of section 12 of the Motor Car Act, 1903 [Chairman: Henry Hobhouse]. [Cd. 2069] H.C. (1904). LXXIX, 159. Minutes of evidence. [Cd. 2070] H.C. (1904). LXXIX, 175.

6364 SELBY COMMISSION ON MOTOR CARS. Report of the royal commission on motor cars [Chairman: Viscount Selby]. [Cd. 3080] H.C. (1906). XLVIII, 1. Minutes of evidence. [Cd. 3081] H.C. (1906). XLVIII, 89.

See also *Report of the committee on the horse-power rating of motor cars* [Chairman: Professor B. Hopkinson]. [Cd. 6414] H.C. (1912–13). XLII, 229. Minutes of evidence. [Cd. 6415] H.C. (1912–13). XLII, 237.

6365 YOUNG (ALEXANDER BELL FILSON). The complete motorist: being an account of the evolution and construction of the modern motor car. 1904. 8th edn. 1915.

6366 HOOPER (WILLIAM EDEN). The motor car in the first decade of the twentieth century: a souvenir and a historical survey of mechanical road locomotion in England from early times to the present day. Lond. & N.Y. 1908.

6367 BEAUMONT (WILLIAM WORBY). Motor vehicles and motors: their design, construction and working, by steam, oil and electricity. 1900. 2nd edn. 2 v. Lond. & Phila. 1902–6.

See also Gardner Dexter Hiscox, *Horseless vehicles, automobiles, motor cycles, operated by steam, hydrocarbon, electric and pneumatic motors: a practical treatise on the development, use and care of the automobile*, 1900; Rhys Jenkins, *Motor cars and the application of mechanical power to road vehicles* . . ., 1902; Alexander James Wallis Tayler, *Motor cars, or power carriages for common roads* . . ., 1897, and *Motor vehicles for business purposes* . . ., 1905; Louis Lockert, *Petroleum motor cars* . . ., 1898; and Rankin Kennedy, *The book of the motor car: a comprehensive and authoritative guide on the care, management, maintenance and construction of the motor car and motor cycle* . . ., 3 v. [1913.]

6368  OLIVER (GEORGE ARTHUR). A history of coachbuilding. 1962.

See also Hugh McCausland, *The English carriage*, 1948, and Marylian Watney, *The elegant carriage*, 1961.

6369  CAUNTER (CYRIL FRANCIS). The history and development of cycles as illustrated by the collection of cycles in the Science Museum. 2 pts. Science Museum. 1955–8.

Good. See also John Woodforde, *The story of the bicycle*, 1970.

6370  GREW (W. F.). The cycle industry: origin, history and latest developments. 1921.

See also Eric Weston Walford, *Early days in the British motor cycle industry: a brief history of the years before the arrival of the motor cycle press*, 1931. For a firm in the industry see Geoffrey Williamson, *Wheels within wheels: the story of the Starleys of Coventry*, 1966.

6371  HARRISON (A. E.). 'The competitiveness of the British cycle industry, 1890–1914'. *Econ. Hist. Rev.* 2 ser. xxii (1969), 287–303.

6372  SPENCER (CHARLES). The modern bicycle: containing instructions for beginners, choice of machine, hints on training, road book for England, Wales, etc. [1876.]

Cp. Alfred Dupont Chandler, *A bicycle tour in England and Wales, made in 1879 by the president, Alfred D. Chandler, and captain, John C. Sharp, jr., of the Suffolk bicycle club of Boston, Mass., with an appendix giving information on the use of the bicycle . . .*, Boston & Lond. 1881.

6373  PHILLIPS (ROBERT EDWARD). 'On the construction of modern cycles'. *Instn. Mechanical Engineers Proc.* (1885), 467–505.

A valuable, detailed paper.

6374  KEPPEL (WILLIAM COUTTS), *Viscount Bury, later Earl of Albemarle, and* HILLIER (GEORGE LACY). Cycling. Badminton Libr. 1887. 5th edn. 1895.

6375  WALLIS-TAYLER (ALEXANDER JAMES). Modern cycles: a practical handbook on their construction and repair. 1897.

6376  CYCLING. 1+. 1891+.

There were many cycling js. The most useful are *The cycle trader* [title varies], 1895+, *The cyclist* [title varies] 1879–1911, and *The cycle manufacturer*, 1898–9. '*The cyclist*' annual and year book, 1892–1900, was a useful compendium of facts.

6377  CAUNTER (CYRIL FRANCIS). The history and development of motor cycles, as illustrated by the collection of motor cycles in the Science Museum. 2 pts. Science Museum. 1955–8.

6378  TRAGATSCH (ERWIN). The world's motorcycles, 1894–1963: a record of 70 years of motorcycle production. 1964.

6379 CYCLE ENGINEERS' INSTITUTE. Proceedings. 1+. Birmingham. 1899+.

Became Automobile and Cycle Engineers' Inst., 1904–6, Incorporated Instn. of Automobile Engineers, 1906–10, and Institution of Automobile Engineers, 1911+. The main j. for the road vehicle constructors. But see also Birmingham Assoc. of Mechanical Engineers, *Proceedings*, Birmingham 1900+.

## 6. AIRCRAFT

6380 GAMBLE (WILLIAM BURT) *comp*. History of aeronautics: a selected list of references to material in the New York Public Library. N.Y. 1938.

Charles Harvard Gibbs-Smith, *The history of flying*, Nat. Book League reader guides 2 ser. 9, Camb. 1957, is a useful short hist.

6381 DAVY (MAURICE JOHN BERNARD) *comp*. Science Museum: handbook of the collections illustrating aeronautics. Pt. I: Heavier-than-air craft. 1929. Pt. II: Lighter-than-air craft. 1934. Pt. III: The propulsion of aircraft. 1930. 3rd edn. [Aeronautics.] 3 pts. 1949–50.

6382 JANE (FREDERICK T.). All the world's air-ships; aeroplanes and dirigibles; flying annual. 1909+.

Title became *All the world's aircraft*, 1912–29, *Jane's all the world's aircraft*, 1930+. The 1909 and 1913 edns. were repr. at Newton Abbot, 1969.

6383 STUBELIUS (SVANTE). Airship, aeroplane, aircraft: studies in the history of terms for aircraft in English. *Gothenberg Studs. in English* vii. Göteborg. 1958.

Cont. in his *Balloon, flying-machine, helicopter: further studies* . . ., Göteborgs Universitets Årsskrift lxvi, no. 5, Göteborg 1960.

6384 GIBBS-SMITH (CHARLES HARVARD). A history of flying. Lond. 1953. N.Y. 1954.

A useful handbook. Cp. Maurice John Bernard Davy, *Interpretative history of flight: a survey of the history and development of aeronautics* . . ., Science Museum 1937, 2nd edn. 1948, and C. H. Gibbs-Smith and others, *Aeronautics*, Science Museum 1966. There are many general hists. incl. Harry Harper, *The evolution of the flying machine: balloon, airship, aeroplane*, 1930, John Goldstrom, *A narrative history of aviation*, N.Y. 1950, and John Walter Edward Douglas-Scott-Montagu, Baron Montagu of Beaulieu, ed., *A short history of balloons and flying machines*, 1907.

6385 HODGSON (JOHN EDMUND). The history of aeronautics in Great Britain from the earliest times to the latter half of the nineteenth century. 1924.

See also Hartley Trevor Kemball Cook, ed., *The birth of flight: an anthology*, 1941.

6386 PENROSE (HARALD JAMES). British aviation: the pioneer years, 1903–1914. Lond. & N.Y. 1967.

See also R. Dallas Brett, *History of British aviation, 1908–1914*, 1933.

6387 BADEN-POWELL (BADEN FLETCHER SMYTH). Ballooning as a sport. 1907.

See also Henry Tracey Coxwell, *My life and balloon experiences, with a supplementary chapter on military ballooning*, 2 ser. 1887–9, and Charles Harvard Gibbs-Smith, *Ballooning*, 1948.

6388 CLARKE (BASIL ROBERTSON). The history of airships. 1961.

For contemp. accounts see A. Hildebrandt, *Airships past and present . . .*, trans. by W. H. Story, 1908, and George Whale, *British airships: past, present & future*, 1919. For military airships see Robin David Stewart Higham, *The British rigid airship, 1908–1931: a study in weapons policy*, 1961, and R. P. Hearne, *Aerial warfare . . .*, Lond. & N.Y. 1909, 2nd edn. [*Airships in peace & war*] 1910.

6389 GIBBS-SMITH (CHARLES HARVARD). The invention of the aeroplane, 1799–1909. 1966.

See also his *A directory and nomenclature of the first aeroplanes, 1809 to 1909*, Science Museum 1966, and *Sir George Cayley's aeronautics, 1796–1855*, Science Museum 1962.

6390 GIBBS-SMITH (CHARLES HARVARD). The aeroplane: an historical survey of its origins and development. Science Museum. 1960. Rev. edn. [Aviation.] 1970.

6391 LEWIS (PETER M. H.). British aircraft, 1809–1914. [1962.]

A useful list. See also his *The British fighter since 1912 . . .*, 1965.

6392 BOUGHTON (TERENCE BEVILLE ADAIR). The story of the British light aeroplane. [1963.]

6393 JACKSON (AUBREY JOSEPH). Avro aircraft since 1908. 1965.

For other manufacturers see his *Blackburn aircraft since 1909*, 1968, and Charles Ferdinand Andrews, *Vickers aircraft since 1908*, 1969.

6394 BRABAZON. The Brabazon story. By John Theodore Cuthbert Moore-Brabazon, Baron Brabazon of Tara. 1956.

6395 BRANCKER. Heavenly adventurer: Sefton Brancker and the dawn of British aviation. By Basil Collier. 1959.

See also Norman Macmillan, *Sir Sefton Brancker*, 1935.

6396 CODY. Pioneer of the air: the life and times of Col. S. F. Cody. By George Avon Broomfield. Aldershot. 1953.

6397 HAWKER. H. G. Hawker, airman: his life and work. By Muriel Hawker. 1922.

6398 GRAHAME-WHITE. Claude Grahame-White: a biography. By Graham Wallace. 1960.

6399 HURREN (BERNARD JOHN). Fellowship of the air: jubilee book of the Royal Aero Club, 1901–1951. 1951.

6400 LABORATORY OF THE AIR: an account of the Royal Aircraft Establishment of the Ministry of Supply. Farnborough. 1948.

6401 [ROYAL] AERONAUTICAL SOCIETY of Great Britain. The aeronautical j. 1897+.
Title varies.

6402 ADVISORY COMMITTEE FOR AERONAUTICS [Aeronautical Research Council] Reports. 1909–10+.
Publ. at first as parl. papers, beginning with [Cd. 5282] H.C. (1910). IX, 239.

## G. PUBLIC UTILITIES

### 1. MUNICIPAL ENTERPRISE

6403 MAXWELL (WILLIAM HENRY) *and* BROWN (JOHN THOMAS) *eds.* The encyclopaedia of municipal and sanitary engineering: a handy working guide in all matters connected with municipal and sanitary engineering and administration. Lond. & N.Y. 1910.
See also William Henry Maxwell, *British progress in municipal engineering: a series of three lectures . . .*, 1904.

6404 KNOOP (DOUGLAS). Principles and methods of municipal trading. 1912.
The best account of the subject.

6405 FINER (HERMAN). Municipal trading: a study in public administration. 1941.
Includes an outline hist.

6406 NATIONAL CIVIC FEDERATION (COMMISSION ON PUBLIC OWNERSHIP AND OPERATION). Municipal and private operation of public utilities. 3 v. N.Y. 1907.
The second vol. is devoted entirely to British experience and includes hists. of each type of municipally-owned public utility.

6407 SLEEMAN (J.). 'The rise and decline of municipal transport'. *Scot. J. Pol. Econ.* ix (1962), 46–64.

6408 VERMAUT (ROBERT). Les régies municipales en Angleterre. Univ. of Louvain. Courtrai. 1903.
A Belgian thesis with good bibliog. For an American account of the subject see Hugo Richard Meyer, *Municipal ownership in Great Britain*, N.Y. 1906; for two French accounts see Eugene Montet, *Étude sur le socialisme municipal anglais . . .*, Paris 1901, and Raymond Boverat, *Le socialisme municipal en Angleterre et ses résultats financiers*, Paris 1907; for a German account see C. Hugo, pseud. of Carl Hugo Lindemann, *Städteverwaltung und Munizipal-Sozialismus in England*, Stuttgart 1897.

6409 SHAW (GEORGE BERNARD). The common sense of municipal trading. 1904. 2nd edn. 1908.

Strong advocacy of municipal enterprise. A similar line is taken in Robert B. Suthers, *Mind your own business: the case for municipal management*, 1905, rev. edns. 1929, 1938, and A. Woodroofe Fletcher, 'Municipal trading', *Manch. Stat. Soc. Trans.* (1900–1), 85–106.

6410 DARWIN (LEONARD). Municipal trade: the advantages and disadvantages resulting from the substitution of representative bodies for private proprietors in the management of industrial undertakings. 1903.

Comprehensive. Unfavourable to municipal trading. Darwin also publ. *Municipal ownership: four lectures delivered at Harvard University, 1907*, 1907. A hostile view of municipal trading is also taken by John Lubbock, Baron Avebury, *On municipal and national trading*, 1906; Dixon Henry Davies, *The cost of municipal trading: a paper read before the Society of Arts, London, with the discussion thereon . . .*, 1903; Robert Percival Porter, *The dangers of municipal trading* [publ. in N.Y. as *The dangers of municipal ownership*], 1907; and W. G. Towler, *Socialism in local government*, London Municipal Soc., 1908, 2nd edn. 1924.

6411 MUNICIPAL CORPORATIONS (REPRODUCTIVE UNDERTAKINGS). Return of the water, gas, tramway, electric lighting, and other reproductive undertakings carried on by municipal boroughs. H.C. 88 (1899). LXXXIII, pt. I, 205. Further return. H.C. 398 (1902). XCIV, 113.

6412 MUNICIPAL TRADING RETURN. Return: municipal trading (United Kingdom). Pts. I–VI. H.C. 171 and H.C. 171, pts. I–V (1909). XC, 1.

Detailed accounts for 1902–6.

6413 CREWE COMMITTEE ON MUNICIPAL TRADING. Report from the joint select committee of the House of Lords and the House of Commons on municipal trading [Chairman: Earl of Crewe]. H.C. 305 (1900). VII, 183. Further report. H.C. 270 (1903). VII, 1.

Gives a full analysis of municipal trading accounts.

## 2. ELECTRICITY SUPPLY

See also Electrical engineering (5229–51).

6414 MACLAREN (MALCOLM). The rise of the electrical industry during the nineteenth century. Princeton. 1943.

6415 WHYTE (ADAM GOWANS). The electrical industry: lighting, traction and power. 1904.

There is a useful short account by Emile Garcke, *The progress of electrical enterprise: reprints of articles from the engineering supplement of* The Times *on British electrical industries*, 1907.

6416 SELF (*Sir* ALBERT HENRY) *and* WATSON (ELIZABETH M.). Electricity supply in Great Britain: its development and organization. 1952.

First two chapters deal with 19th-cent. developments to 1914.

6417 O'DEA (WILLIAM THOMAS). The social history of lighting. 1958.

6418 HIGGS (PAGET). The electric light in its practical application. 1879.

With his *Electric transmission of power: its present position and advantages*, 1879, a useful guide to mid-19th-cent. applications of electricity. See also James Dredge, ed., *Electric illumination*, 2 v. 1882–5, which is largely reproduced from *Engineering*, and Robert Hammond, *The electric light in our homes*, 1884.

6419 PLAYFAIR COMMITTEE ON LIGHTING BY ELECTRICITY. Report from the select committee on lighting by electricity [Chairman: Lyon Playfair]. H.C. 224 (1878–9). XI, 375.

An inquiry into systems in operation. Electrical undertakings were regulated in 1882. For the details of the bill see *Report from the select committee on Electric Lighting Bill* [Chairman: Edward Stanhope]. H.C. 227 (1882). X, 463. Annual reports on proceedings under the 1882 act were issued by the Board of Trade, 1883+, as parl. papers. For proposals to amend the 1882 act see the report of a Lords committee in 1886 (H.C. 252 (1886). VII, 401.), of a joint committee in 1893 (H.C. 331 (1893–4). XI, 609.), a joint committee on power stations in 1898 (H.C. 213 (1898). IX, 609), and a Lords committee on Supply of Electricity Bill in 1904 (H.C. 354 (1904). VII, 287).

6420 GIBBINGS (ALFRED HORSWILL). The commercial and business aspects of municipal electricity supply: a practical handbook . . . Bradford. 1899.

For municipal undertakings see also the commemorative brochures issued by many of them shortly before or after nationalization, and the *Journal* of the Instn. of Electrical Engineers (5236).

### 3. Gas Supply

6421 CHANTLER (PHILIP). The British gas industry: an economic study. Manch. 1938.

Not a hist. but has useful statistics. There is very little in Dean Chandler and A. Douglas Lacey, *The rise of the gas industry in Britain*, 1949, Sir [Edward Montague] Compton Mackenzie, *The vital flame*, 1947, or Thomas Newbigging, *A hundred years of gas enterprise*, 1901.

6422 SILVERTHORNE (ARTHUR). The transfer of gas-works to local authorities: with the latest statistics and analyses of working under municipal management, 1868–1878: also, the London gas supply, 1878 . . . New edn. 1878.

6423 BOARD OF TRADE. Annual return relating to all authorised gas undertakings in the United Kingdom. 1882–1921.

Two parallel series were also publ. as parl. papers, one on private gas works, the other on municipal. See also *The gas & water companies directory*, 1877–1930, and *The 'Gas world' year book*, 1898+.

6424 THE GAS WORLD. 1884+.

The best of contemp. js. Absorbed *Gas trade circular and review* [various titles], 1876–90.

6425　CHUBB (HARRY). 'The supply of gas to the metropolis'. *Stat. Soc. J.* xxxix (1876), 350–71.

6426　EVERARD (STIRLING). The history of the Gas Light and Coke Company, 1812–1949. 1949.

6427　HARRIS (STANLEY ARTHUR). The development of gas supply on north Merseyside, 1815–1949: a historical survey of the former gas undertakings of Liverpool, Southport, Prescot, Ormskirk and Skelmersdale. North-Western Gas Board. Liverpool. 1956.

### 4. WATER

6428　WALTERS (RUPERT CAVENDISH SKYRING). The nation's water supply. 1936.

A good account of water sources, with a short hist. of legislation and supply. Frederick William Robins, *The story of water supply*, 1946, is the only gen. hist. but quite inadequate for the period.

6429　BALDWIN-WISEMAN (WILLIAM RALPH). 'The increase in the national consumption of water'. *Roy. Stat. Soc. J.* lxxii (1909), 248–92.

6430　SILVERTHORNE (ARTHUR). London and provincial water supplies: with the latest statistics of metropolitan and provincial water works. 1884.

A directory of water undertakings with details of expenditure, etc. An earlier edn. was publ. as *The purchase of gas and water works . . .*, 1881.

6431　WATER UNDERTAKINGS RETURN, 1914. H.C. 395 (1914). LXXIX, 543.

The most comprehensive account of water undertakings and water supply in all parts of England and Wales. Useful hist. intro. For annual water statistics see *Water-works statistics*, 1881–94, and *The water companies' directory and statistics*, 1895–1915.

6432　RICHMOND COMMISSION ON WATER SUPPLY. Royal commission on water supply: report of the commissioners [Chairman: Duke of Richmond]. [4169] H.C. (1868–9). XXXIII, 1. Minutes of evidence. [4169–I] H.C. (1868–9). XXXIII, 133. Appendix, maps, etc. [4169–II] H.C. (1868–9). XXXIII, 625.

Voluminous. The only general inquiry into water supplies apart from the incomplete *Special report from the select committee on Waterworks Bill* [Chairman: John Arthur Roebuck]. H.C. 401 (1865). XII, 445.

6433　BRITISH ASSOCIATION OF WATERWORKS ENGINEERS. [Institution of Water Engineers.] Transactions. 1896–1945. Journal. 1945+.

The main professional body. Includes descriptions of the main waterworks. Much technical information on waterworks has also been publ. in *Instn. Mech. Engineers Proc.* (**5204**), *Instn. Civil Engineers Trans.* (**5187**), and other engineering js.

6434　DICKINSON (HENRY WILLIAM). Water supply of greater London: being, a series of articles originally published in *The Engineer* in 1948 and now revised and issued as a memorial volume . . . by the Newcomen Society. 1954.

The best general account. The 19th cent is covered in more detail in Henry Charles Richards and William Henry Christopher Payne, *The metropolitan water supply: being a compendium of the history, the law and the transactions relating to the metropolitan water companies* . . ., 1891, 2nd edn. [*London water supply*] 1899; Sir Francis John Bolton, *London water supply*, 1884, new edn. by Philip Arthur Scratchley, 1888; Arthur Shadwell, *The London water supply*, 1899, and in Reddaway (**9490**). The 20th cent. is covered by [Leonard J. Flowerdew and Geoffrey Clive Francis Berry] *London's water supply, 1903–1953: a review of the work of the Metropolitan Water Board* [1953]. There is little in Alfred Stanley Foord, *Springs, streams and spas of London* . . ., 1910. For statistics see *Annual return of metropolitan water statistics*, 1871+.

6435　GENERAL BOARD OF HEALTH. Report on the supply of water to the metropolis [1218] H.C. (1850). XXII, 1. Appendixes I–IV. [1281–4] H.C. (1850). XXII, 341.

The first of a ser. of major inquiries into London water. For a full list see **33**. Two other major reports are included here (**6436**) and (**6437**). For contemp. debate see Pedro Schwartz, 'John Stuart Mill and laissez-faire: London water', *Economica* new ser. xxxiii (1966), 71–83.

6436　BALFOUR COMMISSION ON METROPOLITAN WATER SUPPLY. Report of the royal commission appointed to inquire into the water supply of the metropolis [Chairman: Lord Balfour of Burleigh]. [C. 7172 and C. 7172–I to IV] H.C. (1893–4). XL, pts. 1–3.

6437　LLANDAFF COMMISSION ON METROPOLITAN WATER SUPPLY. First report of Her Majesty's commissioners appointed to inquire into the subject of the water supply within the limits of the metropolitan water companies [Chairman: Viscount Llandaff]. [C. 9122] H.C. (1899). XLI, 491. Final report. [Cd. 25] H.C. (1900). XXXVIII, pt. I, 1. Minutes of evidence. Vol. I. [Cd. 45] H.C. (1900). XXXVIII, pt. I, 95. Vol. II. [Cd. 198] H.C. (1900). XXXVIII, pt. II, 1. Appendixes. [Cd. 108] H.C. XXXIX, 1. Maps, plans, etc. [Cd. 267] H.C. (1900). XXXIX, 457.

5. Fire Fighting

6438　BLACKSTONE (GEOFFREY VAUGHAN). A history of the British fire service. 1957.

Standard. There is little on the period in Frederick Henry Radford, '*Fetch the engine . . .*': *the official history of the Fire Brigades Union*, 1951; or Charles Roetter, *Fire is their enemy*, 1962.

6439　WHILE (JOHN HENRY). Fifty years of fire fighting in London. 1931.

Hist. of the London Fire Brigade from 1861. See also Sir Eyre Massey Shaw, *Fire protection: a complete manual of the organization, machinery, discipline and general working of the fire brigade of London*, 1876, rev. edn. 1890, and *Fires and fire brigades*, 1884, the very full reports of the *Select committee on Metropolitan Fire Brigade* [Chairman: Sir Henry Selwin-Ibbetson]. H.C. 371 (1876). XI, 53 and H.C. 342 (1877). XIV, 37, and William Eric Jackson, *London's fire brigades*, 1966.

6440 THE FIREMAN and journal of the civil protective forces of the United Kingdom. 1+. 1877+.

6441 YOUNG (CHARLES FREDERICK T.). Fires, fire-engines and fire brigades: with a history of manual and steam fire engines, their construction, use and management. 1866.

Valuable for illustrations of equipment etc. See also the works of Sir Eyre Massey Shaw, notably *Fire protection* (**6439**), and, for the law, Hugh Orton Smith, *Fire brigades: England and Wales, their constitution, rights and responsibilities*, Lond. 1899, 3rd edn. Birmingham 1926.

6442 HANKEY COMMITTEE ON FIRES IN THE METROPOLIS. Report from the select committee on fires in the metropolis [Chairman: Thomson Hankey]. H.C. 221 (1862). IX, 1.

6443 M'LAGAN COMMITTEE ON FIRE PROTECTION. Report from the select committee on fire protection [Chairman: Peter M'Lagan]. H.C. 471 (1867). X, 1.

6444 COLLINGS COMMITTEE ON FIRE BRIGADES. Report from the select committee on fire brigades [Chairman: Jesse Collings]. H.C. 303 (1899). IX, 251. Further report. H.C. 278 (1900). VI, 943.

## H. LABOUR

### 1. GENERAL

#### (a) *Reference*

6445 A BIBLIOGRAPHY OF BRITISH LABOUR HISTORY. *Soc. for the Study of Labour Hist. Bull.* i (1960), 6–26; iii (1961), 16–52; iv (1962), 52–4; v (1962), 54–5, 62–70. In progress.

Covers publs. since 1945. The Bull. also publs. articles on major libr. colls. of labour literature and reports such as E. Loone, 'Soviet writings on British labour history publ. in 1945–1961: Pt. I. pre-1918 period', ibid. iii (1961), 53–8.

6446 INTERDEPARTMENTAL COMMITTEE ON SOCIAL AND ECONOMIC RESEARCH. Guides to official sources: No. 1. Labour statistics: material collected by the Ministry of Labour and National Service. Rev. edn. 1958.

A full account of 19th- and 20th-cent. stats. There is a convenient abstract of labour statistics in Mitchell and Deane (**125**).

6447 BRITISH LABOUR STATISTICS: historical abstract, 1886–1968. Dept. of Employment and Productivity. H.M.S.O. 1971.

6448 BOOTH (CHARLES). 'Occupations of the people of the United Kingdom, 1801–81'. *Stat. Soc. J.* xlix (1886), 314–435.

See also Clive Day, 'The distribution of industrial occupations in England, 1841–1861', *Connecticut Acad. of Arts & Sciences Trans.* xxviii (1927), 79–235, and Thomas Abercrombie Welton, 'On the English census of occupations, 1871', *Manch. Stat. Soc. Trans.* (1875–6), 51–110.

6449 BELLERBY (JOHN ROTHERFORD). 'The distribution of manpower in agriculture and industry, 1851–1951'. *Farm Economist* ix (1958–61), 1–11.

6450 WELTON (THOMAS ABERCROMBIE). 'The occupations of the people of England and Wales in 1911, from the point of view of industrial developments'. *Manch. Stat. Soc. Trans.* (1914–15), 47–176.

6451 BOWLEY (*Sir* ARTHUR LYON). 'The measurement of employment: an experiment'. *Roy. Stat. Soc. J.* lxxv (1911–12), 791–829.

6452 CHAPMAN (*Sir* SYDNEY JOHN) *and* SHIMMIN (ARNOLD NIXON). 'Industrial recruiting and the displacement of labour'. *Manch. Stat. Soc. Trans.* (1913–14), 93–147.

Changes in labour force of industries.

6453 COCKBURN COMMISSION ON LABOUR LAWS. First report of the commissioners appointed to inquire into the working of the Master and Servant Act, 1867, and the Criminal Law Amendment Act, 34 & 35 Vict. cap. 32, and for other purposes [Chairman: Sir Alexander Cockburn, L.C.J.]. [C. 1094] H.C. (1874). XXIV, 391. Second and final report. [C. 1157] H.C. (1875). XXX, 1. Appendix to second report. [C. 1157–I] H.C. (1875). XXX, 35.

A useful source for many aspects of labour. See also the earlier *Report from the select committee on master and servant.* [Chairman: John Morgan Cobbett.] H.C. 370 (1865). VIII, 1. This committee was reappointed in the following session with a new chairman, Lord Elcho, and made a further report, H.C. 449 (1866). XIII, 1.

6454 ROYAL COMMISSION ON LABOUR. First report of the royal commission on labour [Chairman: Duke of Devonshire]. [C. 6708] H.C. (1892). XXXIV, 1. Second report. [C. 6795] H.C. (1892). XXXVI, pt. 1. Third report. [C. 6894] H.C. (1893–4). XXXII, 1. Fourth report. [C. 7063] H.C. (1893–4). XXXIX, pt. 1. Fifth and final report. [C. 7421] H.C. (1894). XXXV, 9. Summaries, index, etc. [C. 7421–I] H.C. (1894). XXXV, 263.

An extraordinarily comprehensive inquiry. The commission appointed assistant commissioners and divided itself into groups to collect material. 10 v. of reports were publ. on labour conditions in the empire and overseas, in addition to those on Britain. The British evidence was divided as follows.
(*a*) AGRICULTURAL LABOUR. I. Regional reports on England in 6 pts. with an index. [C. 6894–I–VI, XIII] H.C. (1893–4). XXXV, 1+. II. Reports on Wales. [C. 6894–XIV] H.C. (1893–4). XXXVI, 1. III. Reports on Scotland. [C. 6894–XV–XVII] H.C. (1893–4). XXXVI, 203+. IV. Reports on Ireland. [C. 6894–XVIII–XXII] H.C. (1893–4). XXXVII, pt. I, 1+. V. General report, memoranda, tables &c. [C. 6894–XXIV–XXV] H.C. (1893–4). XXXVII, pt. II, 1+.
(*b*) WOMEN'S EMPLOYMENT. Reports. [C. 6894–XXIII] H.C. (1893–4). XXXVII, pt. I, 545.
(*c*) MINING, IRON, ENGINEERING, HARDWARE, SHIPBUILDING &c. Minutes of evidence &c. taken by Group A of the commission. 3 v. with digests. Vol. I. [6708–I, IV] H.C

(1892). XXXIV, 5+. Vol. II. [C. 6795–I, IV] (1892). XXXVI, pt. I, 5, pt. III, 1. Vol. III. [C. 6894–VII, X] H.C. (1893–4). XXXII, 5, 531. Answers to questions. [C. 6795–VII] H.C. (1892). XXXVI, pt. III, 533.

(*d*) AGRICULTURE, RAILWAYS, SHIPPING, CANALS, DOCKS, AND TRAMWAYS. Minutes of evidence &c. taken by Group B. 3 v. with digests. Vol. I. [C. 6708–II, V] H.C. (1892). XXXIV, 111, XXXV, 1. Vol. II. [C. 6795–II, V] H.C. (1892). XXXVI, pt. II, 1, pt. III, 197. Vol. III. [C. 6795–VIII, XI] H.C. (1893–4). XXXIII, 1, 681. Answers to questions. [C. 6795–VIII] H.C. (1892). XXXVI, pt. III, 1007.

(*e*) TEXTILE, CLOTHING, CHEMICAL, BUILDING, AND MISCELLANEOUS TRADES. Minutes of evidence &c. taken by Group C. 3 v. with digests. Vol. I. [C. 6708–II, VI] H.C. (1892). XXXIV, 209, XXXV, 711. Vol. II. [C. 6795–III, VI] H.C. (1892). XXXVI, pt. II, 441, pt. III, 369. Vol. III. [C. 6894–IX, XII] H.C. (1893–4). XXXIV, 1, 781. Answers to questions. [C. 6795–IX] H.C. (1892). XXXVI, pt. IV, 1.

In addition evidence was taken by the commission as a whole ([C. 7063–I] H.C. (1893–4). XXXIX, pt. I, 5. Digest. [C. 7063–II] H.C. (1893–4). XXXIX, pt. I, 629. Appendix. [C. 7063–IIIA] H.C. (1893–4). XXXIX, pt. I, 805) and collections of rules of associations ([C. 6795–XII] H.C. (1892). XXXVI, pt. V, 317) and technical terms ([C. 7063–VC] H.C. (1893–4). XXXVIII, 411) were issued, plus indexes in (1893–4). XXXVIII, and XXXIX, pt. I.

A guide to the whole work was publ. by Thomas George Spyers as *The labour question: an epitome of the evidence and the report of the Royal Commission on Labour*, 1894.

6455 BOARD OF TRADE (LABOUR DEPARTMENT). Report on the work of the Labour Department of the Board of Trade (1893–94): with supplement containing abstract of labour statistics. [C. 7565] H.C. (1894). LXXX, 397.

Cont. until *Twenty-second abstract of labour statistics, 1922–1936*. [Cmd. 5556] H.C. (1936–7). XXVI, 869. The *Eighteenth abstract . . . [1910–1925]*. [Cmd. 2740] H.C. (1926). XXIX, 1, and the *Nineteenth abstract . . .* [Cmd. 3140] H.C. (1928). XXV, 495, incl. particularly valuable retrospective statistical tables.

6456 BOARD OF TRADE. Directory of industrial associations in the United Kingdom, including employers' associations, trade unions, boards of conciliation and arbitration, and workmen's co-operative societies. [Cd. 120] H.C. (1900). LXXXIII, 231.

For later editions see 6446, p. 45.

6457 BOARD OF TRADE (LABOUR DEPARTMENT) [Ministry of Labour]. The labour gazette: the journal of the Labour Department of the Board of Trade. 1893+.

Styled *The Board of Trade labour gazette*, 1905–17, later titles vary.

### (b) *Histories*

6458 KUCZYNSKI (JURGEN). Die Geschichte der Lage der Arbeiter unter dem Kapitalismus. 37 v. in 39. Berlin. 1960–1.

Vols. 24–27 a and b deal with England, the colonies and dominions. Fuller than his *A short history of labour conditions under industrial capitalism*, vol. I. Great Britain and the empire, 2 pts. 1942–5.

6459 HOBSBAWM (ERIC JOHN ERNEST). Labouring men: studies in the history of labour. 1964.

A very important ser. of essays, incl. a number devoted to general issues.

6460 BRIGGS (ASA) *and* SAVILLE (JOHN) *eds.* Essays in labour history: in memory of G. D. H. Cole. 1960. Rev. edn. 1967.

See also the parallel vol. with the same eds., *Essays in Labour history, 1886–1923*, 1971.

6461 LUDLOW (JOHN MALCOLM) *and* JONES (LLOYD). The progress of the working class, 1832–1867. 1867.

6462 WEBB (SIDNEY JAMES), *Baron Passfield.* Labor in the longest reign (1837–1897). Fabian tract 75. 1897. 2nd edn. 1899.

6463 NOSTITZ-DRZEWIECKI (HANS GOTTFRIED VON). Das Aufsteigen des Arbeiterstandes in England: ein Beitrag zur sozialen Geschichte der Gegenwart. Jena. 1900.

6464 STEFFEN (GUSTAF FREDRIK). Studien zur Geschichte der englischen Lohnarbeiter mit besonderer Berücksichtigung der Veränderungen ihrer Lebenshaltungen. Stuttgart. 3 v. 1901–5.

6465 ANDERSON (OLIVE). 'Early experiences of manpower problems in an industrial society at war: Great Britain, 1854–56'. *Pol. Sci. Q.* lxxxii (1967), 526–45.

6466 OLIVER (*Sir* THOMAS) *ed.* Dangerous trades: the historical, social and legal aspects of industrial occupations as affecting health, by a number of experts. 1902.

A useful survey. See also Oliver's *Diseases of occupation, from the legislative, social and medical points of view*, 1908, 2nd edn. 1916. For official reports on particular dangerous trades see the *General index* to parl. papers (33).

6467 HANES (DAVID GORDON). The first British Workmen's Compensation Act, 1897. New Haven [Conn.]. 1968.

A sketch. See also W. C. Mallalieu, 'Joseph Chamberlain and workmen's compensation', *J. Econ. Hist.* x (1950), 45–57. For contemporary textbooks see Robert Metcalf Minton-Senhouse, *The Employers' Liability Act . . .*, 1892, 2nd edn. 1902, *The case law of the Workmen's Compensation Act, 1897 . . .*, 1899, 2nd edn. 1900, and *Digest of workmen's compensation cases*, 1903; R. M. Minton-Senhouse and George Frederick Emery, *Accidents to workmen . . .*, 1898, 2nd edn. 1902, and *A handbook to the Workmen's Compensation Act, 1897 . . .*, 1898, 2nd edn. 1899; Adshead Elliott, *The Workmen's Compensation Act*, 1900, 9th edn. 1926; and William Ellis Hill, *The law and practice relating to workmen's compensation and employers' liability*, 2 pts. 1898, 2nd edn. 1907.

6468 CALDWELL (J. A. M.). 'The genesis of the Ministry of Labour'. *Public Admin.* xxxvii (1959), 367–91.

6469 SEYMOUR (JOHN BARTON). The British employment exchange. 1928.

6470 BOARD OF TRADE. First report on the proceedings of the Board of Trade under Part II of the National Insurance Act, 1911. [Cd. 6965] H.C. (1913). XXXVI, 677.

On labour exchanges.

6471  HILTON (GEORGE WOODMAN). The truck system: including a history of the British truck acts, 1465–1960. Camb. 1960.

For data see particularly *Report of the truck committee* [Chairman: Thomas Shaw]. [Cd. 4442] H.C. (1908). LIX, 1. Minutes of evidence. [Cd. 4443–4] H.C. (1908). LIX, 147. [Cd. 4568] H.C. (1909). XLIX, 177.

6472  POLLARD (SIDNEY). A history of labour in Sheffield, 1850–1939. Liverpool. 1959.

The only general local hist. But see William Gordon Rimmer, 'Occupations in Leeds, 1841–1951', *Thoresby Soc. Publs.* 1 (1965–7), 158–79.

### (c) *Contemporary Commentary*

6473  SARGANT (WILLIAM LUCAS). Economy of the labouring classes. 1857.

6474  SMILES (SAMUEL). Workmen's earnings, strikes and savings. 1861.

6475  FAWCETT (HENRY). The economic position of the British labourer. Camb. 1865.

The stern views of classical political economy.

6476  THORNTON (WILLIAM THOMAS). On labour: its wrongful claims and rightful dues, its actual, present and possible future. 1869. 2nd edn. 1870.

6477  BEVAN (GEORGE PHILLIPS). The industrial classes and industrial statistics. Vol. 1. Mining metals, chemicals, ceramics, glass and paper. Vol. 2. Textiles and clothing, food, sundry industries. 2 v. 1876–7.

6478  WILLIAMS (HENRY LLEWELLYN). The worker's industrial index to London: showing where to go for work in all trades. Ed. by Alsager Hay Hill. 1881.

A penny pamphlet, useful for contemp. opinions, and for identifying localities.

6479  JEVONS (WILLIAM STANLEY). The state in relation to labour. 1866. 4th edn. by Francis Wrigley Hirst. 1910.

A famous economist on the labour question.

6480  LORDS COMMITTEE ON SWEATING. First report from the select committee of the House of Lords on the sweating system [Chairman: Earl of Dunraven]. H.C. 361 (1888). XX, 1. Second report. H.C. 448 (1888). XXI, 1. Third report. H.C. 165 (1889). XIII, 1. Fourth report. H.C. 331 (1889). XIV, pt. 1, 1. Fifth report. H.C. 169 (1890). XVII, 257.

A comprehensive inquiry. Chiefly on the boot and shoe, tailoring, cabinet, and upholstering trades. See also John Burnett, *Report to the Board of Trade on the sweating system in the East End of London* . . . H.C. 331 (1887). LXXXIX, 253.

6481  UNITED STATES CONSULAR REPORTS. Labor in Europe: reports from the consuls of the United States in the several countries of Europe on the rates of wages, cost of living to the laboring classes, past and present wages, &c., in their several districts, in response to a circular from the department of State. 48th Congress, 2nd sess. House Exec. Doc. 54, pts. 1–2. 2 v. Wash. 1884.

A similar report was publ. in 1879 as 46th Congress, 1st sess. House Exec. Doc. 5.

6482 SMITH (*Sir* HUBERT LLEWELLYN). Modern changes in the mobility of labour, especially between trade and trade. 1891.

6483 GORST (*Sir* JOHN ELDON). The labour question . . . Chatham. 1891.

Gorst was the most active of Lord Salisbury's ministers in labour matters and attended the international labour conference at Berlin, on which see [C. 5914] H.C. (1890). LXXXI, 529, [C. 6042] H.C. (1890). LXXXI, 537, and [C. 6371] H.C. (1890–1). LXXXIII, 139.

6484 WEBB (SIDNEY JAMES), *Baron Passfield and* COX (HAROLD). The eight-hours day. [1891.]

The first of a number of books that offered a careful description of the eight hours' movement. The others incl. John Rae, *Eight hours for work*, 1894, Sir Robert Abbott Hadfield and Henry De Beltgens Gibbins, *A shorter working day*, 1892, and John Mackinnon Robertson, *The eight hours question*, 1893. Sir William Mather, *The forty-eight hours week: a year's experiment and its results at the Salford Iron Works, Manchester* (*Mather & Platt, Ltd.*), Manch. 1894, was answered by James Stephen Jeans, *The eight hours' day in British engineering industries: an examination and criticism of recent experiments*, 1894. See also 6604.

6485 HOBHOUSE (LEONARD TRELAWNEY). The Labour movement. 1893. Rev. edn. 1912.

6486 DRAGE (GEOFFREY). The labour problem. 1896.

A handbook for politicians.

6487 ROUSIERS (PAUL DE). The labour question in Britain. Trans. by Fanny Louisa Dorothea Herbertson. 1896.

Publ. originally as *La question ouvrière en Angleterre*, Paris 1895.

6488 SHERARD (ROBERT HARBOROUGH). The white slaves of England: being, true pictures of certain social conditions in the kingdom of England in the year 1897. 1897.

On unhealthy or depressed trades, viz. alkali workers, nail-makers, slipper-makers and tailors, woolcombers, and white lead workers. See also his *The cry of the poor:* . . ., 1901, and *The child-slaves of Britain*, 1905.

6489 GREENWOOD (EDGAR). The employed: with observations by employers. 1903.

Advertisements for jobs and the public response to them.

6490 MASSINGHAM (HENRY WILLIAM) *ed.* Labour and protection: a series of studies. 1903.

6491 UNITED STATES COMMISSIONER OF LABOR. Eleventh special report: regulation and restriction of output. Prep. under the direction of Carroll Davidson Wright. Wash. 1904.

Full on British practices.

6492 CADBURY (EDWARD) *and* SHANN (GEORGE). Sweating. Social service handbooks 5. 1907. 2nd edn. 1908.

See also Constance Isabel Smith, *The case for wages boards*, 1908; Clementina Black, *Sweated industry and the minimum wage*, 1907; Richard Mudie-Smith, comp., *Handbook of the* Daily News *Sweated Industries Exhibition, May 1906*, 1906; Manchester Sweated Industries Exhibition, *Handbook*, Manch. 1906; Thomas Wright, ed., *Sweated labour and the Trade Boards Act*, Catholic Social Guild, 2nd edn. 1913; Paul Boyaval, *La lutte contre le sweating-system: le minimum légal de salaire: l'exemple de l'Australasie et de l'Angleterre*, Paris & Lille 1911; and Henry-Émile Barrault, *La réglementation du travail à domicile en Angleterre*, Paris 1906.

6493 WHITTAKER COMMITTEE ON HOME WORK. Report from the select committee on home work [Chairman: Sir Thomas Whittaker]. H.C. 290 (1907). VI, 55. Further report. H.C. 246 (1908). VIII, 1.

6494 CHARITY ORGANISATION SOCIETY (Special Committee on Unskilled Labour). Report and minutes of evidence, June 1908. 1908.

A careful inquiry.

6495 TUCKWELL (GERTRUDE MARY) *and* SMITH (CONSTANCE). The worker's handbook. 1908. New edn. 1910.

6496 VERNEY (HARRY). 'On the recent considerable increase in the number of reported accidents in factories'. *Roy. Stat. Soc. J.* lxxiii (1910), 95–118.

6497 TENNANT COMMITTEE ON FACTORY ACCIDENTS. Report of the departmental committee on accidents in places under the Factory and Workshop Acts [Chairman: H. J. Tennant]. [Cd. 5535] H.C. (1911). XXIII, 1. Evidence. [Cd. 5540] H.C. (1911). XXIII, 71.

6498 WARE (*Sir* FABIAN ARTHUR GOULSTONE). The worker and his country. 1912.

On the disillusionment of workers with representative government.

6499 WEBB (SIDNEY JAMES), *Baron Passfield and* FREEMAN (ARNOLD) *eds.* Seasonal trades. By various writers. 1912.

See also R. Williams, 'The organisation of the casual labour market', *Manch. Stat. Soc. Trans.* (1911–12), 37–60.

6500 [WHITE (ARNOLD HENRY) *ed.*] A day of my life: a description of the daily task and common round of working Britons at home and abroad. Written by themselves and arranged and revised by 'Vanoc' of the 'Referee'. 1912.

## 2. INDUSTRIAL RELATIONS

### (a) *General*

**6501 FLANDERS (ALLAN) *and* CLEGG (HUGH ARMSTRONG) *eds.*** The system of industrial relations in Great Britain: its history, law and institutions. Oxf. 1954.

A useful outline. See also Alan Fox, 'Industrial relations in nineteenth-century Birmingham', *Oxf. Econ. Papers* n.s. vii (1955), 57–70.

**6502 PHELPS BROWN (ERNEST HENRY).** The growth of British industrial relations: a study from the standpoint of 1906–1914. 1959.

An important study. See also Ronald V. Sires, 'Labor unrest in England, 1910–1914', *J. Econ. Hist.* xv (1955), 246–66.

**6503 BALFOUR COMMITTEE ON INDUSTRY AND TRADE.** Committee on industry and trade [Chairman: Sir Arthur Balfour]. Survey of industrial relations: based on material mainly derived from official sources, with regard to industrial remuneration, conditions, and relationships in Great Britain and certain other countries so far as available; together with statistical tables; with an introduction by the committee. 1926.

**6504 WEBB (SIDNEY JAMES), *Baron Passfield and* WEBB (BEATRICE).** Industrial democracy. 2 v. 1897. Rev. edn. 1920.

A celebrated survey with proposals for democratization.

**6505 SELLS (DOROTHY).** The British trade boards system. 1923.

The regulation of wages by trade boards after 1908.

**6506 CADBURY (EDWARD).** Experiments in industrial organization, 1912.

A study of industrial relations, dealing primarily with the education, health, pay, and organization of employees.

**6507 ASKWITH (GEORGE RANKEN), *Baron Askwith*.** Industrial problems and disputes. 1920.

All types of industrial disputes, 1889–1918. Good.

**6508 WELLS (HERBERT GEORGE) *and others*.** What the worker wants: the *Daily Mail* enquiry [into the causes of labour unrest]. [1912.]

**6509 CUNNINGHAM (WILLIAM).** The causes of labour unrest: and the remedies for it: the draft of a report. 1912.

**6510 BEVAN (GEORGE PHILLIPS).** 'The strikes of the past ten years'. *Stat. Soc. J.* xliii (1880), 35–54.

**6511 BOARD OF TRADE (LABOUR CORRESPONDENT).** Report on the strikes and lock-outs of 1888 . . . [C. 5809] H.C. (1889). LXX, 703.

Cont. annually to year 1913.

6512 KNOWLES (KENNETH GUY JACK CHARLES). Strikes: a study in industrial conflict: with special reference to British experience between 1911 and 1947. Oxf. 1952.

6513 PRIBIĆEVIĆ (BRANKO). The shop stewards' movement and workers' control, 1910–22. Oxf. 1959.

A useful pioneer study. See also Kendall (**589**).

6514 RUEGG (ALFRED HENRY). The laws regulating the relation of employer and workman in England. 1905.

## (b) *Industrial Conciliation and Arbitration*

6515 ALLEN (VICTOR LEONARD). 'The origins of industrial conciliation and arbitration'. *Int. Rev. Soc. Hist.* ix (1964), 237–54.

See also J. H. Porter, 'Wage bargaining under conciliation agreements, 1860–1914', *Econ. Hist. Rev.* 2 ser. xxiii (1970), 460–75.

6516 MACKENZIE (WILLIAM WARRENDER), *Baron Amulree*. Industrial arbitration in Great Britain. 1929.

Includes an outline hist.

6517 MACKINNON COMMITTEE ON COUNCILS OF CONCILIATION. Report from the select committee on masters and operatives (equitable councils of conciliation) [Chairman: William Alexander Mackinnon]. H.C. 343 (1856). XIII, 1.

The first careful consideration of the subject. A further committee under the same chairman came down strongly in favour of voluntary councils: *Report from the select committee on masters and operatives.* H.C. 307 (1860). XXII, 443.

6518 CROMPTON (HENRY). Industrial conciliation. 1876.

6519 PRICE (LANGFORD LOVELL FREDERICK RICE). Industrial peace: its advantages, methods and difficulties: a report of an inquiry made for the Toynbee Trustees. 1887.

See also his 'The relations between industrial conciliation and social reform', *Roy. Stat. Soc. J.* liii (1890), 290–302, and 'The position and prospects of industrial conciliation', ibid. 420–49.

6520 JEANS (JAMES STEPHEN). Conciliation and arbitration in labour disputes: a historical sketch and brief statement of the present position of the question at home and abroad. 1894.

6521 BOARD OF TRADE (COMMISSIONER FOR LABOUR). First report by the Board of Trade of proceedings under the Conciliation (Trade Disputes) Act, 1896. [C. 8533] H.C. (1897). LXXXIII, 643.

The first of a series of 14 annual reports, down to 1918, on trade disputes and attempts at conciliation by the Board of Trade.

6522 DALE (*Sir* DAVID). Thirty years' experience of industrial conciliation and arbitration. 1899.

See also J. H. Porter, 'David Dale and conciliation in the northern manufactured iron trade, 1869–1914', *Northern Hist.* v (1970), 157–71.

6523 PIGOU (ARTHUR CECIL). Principles and methods of industrial peace. 1905.

6524 KNOOP (DOUGLAS). Industrial conciliation and arbitration. 1905.
Detailed.

6525 BOARD OF TRADE (LABOUR DEPARTMENT). Report on rules of voluntary conciliation and arbitration boards and joint committees. [Cd. 3788] H.C. (1908). XCVIII, 1. Second report. [Cd. 5346] H.C. (1910). XX, 543.

6526 BOARD OF TRADE (LABOUR DEPARTMENT). Report on collective agreements between employers and workpeople in the United Kingdom. [Cd. 5366] H.C. (1910). XX, 1.

Prepared by D. F. Schloss. A comprehensive survey.

6527 INDUSTRIAL COUNCIL [Chairman: Sir George Askwith]. Report on enquiry into industrial agreements. [Cd. 6952] H.C. (1913). XXVIII, 1. Minutes of evidence. [Cd. 6953] H.C. (1913). XXVIII, 23.

6528 KROJANKER (GUSTAV). Die Entwicklung des Koalitionsrechts in England. Münchener Volkswirtschaftliche Studien 130. Stuttgart & Berlin. 1914.

(c) *Profit-sharing and Co-partnership*

6529 BOARD OF TRADE (LABOUR DEPARTMENT). Report by Mr. D. F. Schloss on profit-sharing. [C. 7458] H.C. (1894). LXXX, 575.

Good. Suppl. by *Report on 'Gain-sharing' and certain other systems of bonus on production* [C. 7848] H.C. (1895). LXXX, 103. There is also an earlier report, J. Lowry Whittle, *Report to the Board of Trade on Profit-sharing.* [C. 6267] H.C. (1890–1). LXXVIII, 15.

6530 BOARD OF TRADE (LABOUR DEPARTMENT). Report on profit-sharing and labour co-partnership in the United Kingdom. [Cd. 6496] H.C. (1912–13). XLIII, 853.

Covers events from 1894. Cont. in *Report on profit-sharing and labour co-partnership abroad.* [Cd. 7283] H.C. (1914). XLVI, 1.

6531 MINISTRY OF LABOUR (INTELLIGENCE AND STATISTICS DEPARTMENT). Report on profit-sharing and labour co-partnership in the United Kingdom. 1920.

Full bibliog.; cont. in *Ministry of Labour Gazette*, 1922–38.

**6532** CARPENTER (CHARLES CLAUDE). Industrial co-partnership: three papers, with chronological notes on British profit-sharing and co-partnership, 1829–1914. 1914.

A useful outline, but no better than Charles Ryle Fay, *Co-partnership in industry*, Camb. 1913, or Aneurin Williams, *Co-partnership and profit-sharing*, Home Univ. Libr. 1913. Other general books are Langford Lovell Frederick Rice Price, *Co-operation and co-partnership*, 1914, Frank Walter Raffety, *Partnership in industry*, 1928, and Nicolas Paine Gilman, *Profit-sharing between employer and employee . . .*, Boston & Lond. 1889. There is also material in Lloyd, *Labor copartnership* (**6854**).

**6533** TAYLOR (SEDLEY). Profit-sharing between capital and labour: six essays . . . to which is added a memorandum on the industrial partnership at the Whitwood Collieries (1865–1874) by Archibald Briggs and the late Henry Currer Briggs . . . 1884.

A pioneer statement of the case for profit-sharing. A similar book is Thomas William Bushill, *Profit-sharing and the labour question*, 1893. For the case against co-partnership see the Fabian attack, Edward Reynolds Pease, *Profit-sharing & co-partnership: a fraud or a failure?*, Fabian tract 170. 1913.

**6534** TAYLOR. Taylor of Batley: a story of 102 years. By George Arthur Greenwood. 1957.

For many years the leader of the co-partnership movement.

**6535** LABOUR CO-PARTNERSHIP. 1894+.

Title became *Co-partnership: publ. by the Labour Co-partnership Assoc. . . .*, 1907+. Absorbed *Profit-sharing and co-partnership*, 1912–13. The leading co-partnership j. See also the *Annual report of the Industrial Co-partnership Assoc.*, 1886–7+.

### 3. Earnings and Expenditure

**6536** U.S. LIBRARY OF CONGRESS. List of bibliographies on wages and salaries, with a section on bonus and profit-sharing systems. Wash. 1921.

**6537** HOPKINSON (A.) and BOWLEY (Sir ARTHUR LYON). 'Bibliography of wage statistics in the United Kingdom in the nineteenth century'. *Econ. Rev.* viii. (1898), 504–20.

**6538** BURNETT (JOHN). A history of the cost of living. Harmondsworth. 1969.

**6539** BOWLEY (Sir ARTHUR LYON). Wages in the United Kingdom in the nineteenth century: notes for the use of students on social and economic questions. Camb. 1900.

An important pioneering work, largely replaced for post-1860 by his *Wages and income in the United Kingdom since 1860*, Camb. 1937. Bowley also publ. many important papers, incl. 'Comparison of the changes in wages in France, the United States and the United Kingdom from 1840 to 1891', *Econ. J.* viii (1898), 474–89, and 'Changes in average wages (nominal and real) in the United Kingdom between 1860 and 1891', *Roy. Stat. Soc. J.* lviii (1895), 223–78. James Edwin Thorold Rogers, *Six centuries of work and wages: the history of English labour*, 2 v. 1884, and reprs. has little on the period.

6540 WOOD (GEORGE HENRY). 'The course of average wages between 1790 and 1860'. *Econ. J.* ix (1899), 588–92.

Cont. in 'Real wages and the standard of comfort since 1850', *Roy. Stat. Soc. J.* lxxii (1909), 91–103, repr. in Carus-Wilson, *Essays* (4066), III, 132–43, and his cotton wage statistics (**6719**).

6541 PREST (ALAN RICHMOND) *and* ADAMS (ARTHUR AVERY). Consumers' expenditure in the United Kingdom, 1900–1919. Camb. 1954.

6542 CHADWICK (DAVID). The expenditure of wages, 1839–1887. 1887.

Working-class budgets. See also Economic Club [i.e. Edith S. Collet and M. Robertson] *Family budgets: being the income and expenses of twenty-eight British households, 1891–1894*, 1896, Henry Higgs, 'Workmen's budgets', *Roy. Stat. Soc. J.* lvi (1893), 255–85, and Sir Robert Giffen, 'On the fall of prices of commodities in recent years', *Stat. Soc. J.* xlii (1879), 36–68, and 'Recent changes in prices and incomes compared', *Roy. Stat. Soc. J.* li (1888), 713–805.

6543 PHILLIPS (A. W.). 'The relation between unemployment and the rate of change of money wage rates in the United Kingdom, 1861–1957'. *Economica* new ser. xxv (1958), 283–99.

See also 'a further analysis' of the topic by Richard G. Lipsey, *Economica* new ser. xxvii (1960), 1–31.

6544 BROWN (ERNEST HENRY PHELPS) *and* BROWNE (MARGARET H.). A century of pay: the course of pay and production in France, Germany, Sweden, the United Kingdom and the United States of America, 1860–1960. 1969.

See also E. H. Phelps Brown and Sheila V. Hopkins, 'The course of wage-rates in five countries, 1860–1939', *Oxf. Econ. Papers* new ser. ii (1950), 226–96, 'Seven centuries of building wages', *Economica* new ser. xxii (1955), 195–206, and 'Seven centuries of the prices of consumables compared with builders' wage-rates', *Economica* new ser. xxiii (1956), 296–314.

6545 KNOWLES (KENNETH GUY JACK CHARLES) *and* ROBERTSON (DONALD JAMES). 'Differences between the wages of skilled and unskilled workers, 1880–1950'. *Oxf. Inst. Stats. Bull.* xiii (1951), 109–27.

6546 HINES (A. G.). 'Trade unions and wage inflation in the United Kingdom, 1893–1961'. *Rev. Econ. Studs.* xxxi (1964), 221–52.

An interesting theoretical exposition.

6547 ROUTH (GUY). Occupation and pay in Great Britain, 1906–1960. Nat. Inst. Econ. Soc. Res. Camb. 1965.

6548 INDUSTRIAL REMUNERATION CONFERENCE. The report of the proceedings and papers read . . . on the 28th, 29th, and 30th January 1885. 1885.

An important discussion of all aspects of the labour market.

6549 SCHLOSS (DAVID FREDERICK). Methods of industrial remuneration. 1892. 3rd edn. 1898.

Comprehensive.

6550 ASHLEY (*Sir* WILLIAM JAMES). The adjustment of wages: a study in the coal and iron industries of Great Britain and America. 1903.

6551 PRICE (LANGFORD LOVELL FREDERICK RICE). 'Sliding scales and other methods of wage arrangement in the North of England'. *Roy. Stat. Soc. J.* 1 (1887), 5–74.

6552 PETHICK-LAWRENCE (FREDERICK WILLIAM), *Baron Pethick-Lawrence.* Local variations in wages. Lond. School of Econ. Studs. in Econ. & Pol. Sci. 8. 1899.

6553 TUCKER (RUFUS S.). 'Real wages of artisans in London, 1729–1935'. *Amer. Stat. Assoc. J.* new ser. xxxi (1936), 73–84.

See also Frances Wood, 'The course of real wages in London, 1900–12'. *Roy. Stat. Soc. J.* lxxvii (1913–14), 1–55.

6554 CHADWICK (DAVID). 'On the rate of wages in Manchester and Salford, and the manufacturing districts of Lancashire, 1839–59'. *Stat. Soc. J.* xxiii (1860), 1–36.

6555 NICHOLSON (JOSEPH SHIELD). The effects of machinery on wages. Camb. 1878. New edn. Lond. 1892.

One of the few works to tackle this important question. Contemp. economists' ideas about wages are set out in Francis Amasa Walker, *The wages question: a treatise on wages and the wages class*, N.Y. 1876, Lond. 1877, new edns. 1886, 1888, Herbert Metford Thompson, *The theory of wages and its application to the eight hours question and other labour problems*, 1892, and Frank William Taussig, *Wages and capital: an examination of the wages fund doctrine*, 1896, repr. 1932. The humanitarian case for higher wages is reviewed in Philip Snowden, Viscount Snowden, *The living wage*, 1912. Later ideas of 19th-cent. wages are set out in John Wilkinson Foster Rowe, *Wages in practice and theory*, 1928.

6556 TAWNEY (RICHARD HENRY). Studies in the minimum wage: no. 1. The establishment of minimum rates in the chain-making industry under the Trade Boards Act of 1909. 1914.

Tawney also publ. no. 2 of the ser., *The establishment of the minimum rates in the tailoring industry* . . ., 1915. No. 3, *The establishment of legal minimum rates in the boxmaking industry* . . ., 1915, is by Mildred Emily Bulkley.

6557 McCULLOCH (JOHN RAMSAY). An essay on the circumstances which determine the rate of wages and the condition of the labouring classes. 1826. New edn. 1851. 2nd edn. 1854. New edn. 1868.

Reflects the views of the classical political economists. Henry Fawcett, *Labour and wages*, 1884, which consists of chapters repr. from his *Manual of political economy*, presents an even more rigid doctrine.

**6558** LEVI (LEONE). Wages and earnings of the working classes . . . 1867.

A later investigation was reported in a book of the same title publ. in 1885.

**6559** BRASSEY (THOMAS), *Earl Brassey*. Work and wages practically illustrated. 1872. 4th edn. 1873. New edn. 1916.

A privately-financed survey, giving international comparisons. See also his *Foreign work and English wages considered with reference to the depression of trade*, 1879.

**6560** JEANS (JAMES STEPHEN). 'On the comparative efficiency and earnings of labour at home and abroad'. *Stat. Soc. J.* xlvii (1884), 614–55.

Cont. in his 'On the recent movement of labour in different countries in reference to wages, hours of work and efficiency', *Roy. Stat. Soc. J.* lv (1892), 620–51.

**6561** CHAPMAN (*Sir* SYDNEY JOHN). Work and wages. 3 v. 1904–14.

Vol. 1 covers foreign competition, vol. 2 wages and employment, and vol. 3 social betterment. Cont. Brassey's work (**6559**).

**6562** BOARD OF TRADE. Returns of wages published between 1830 and 1886. [C. 5172] H.C. (1887). LXXXIX, 273.

**6563** GIFFEN (*Sir* ROBERT). Return showing the average number of hours worked as a week's work in the chief trade centres by the following industries in the years 1850, 1860, 1870, 1880 and 1890 . . . H.C. 375 (1890). LXVIII, 591.

**6564** ELLIOTT (*Sir* THOMAS HENRY). Report to the Board of Trade on the relation of wages in certain industries to the cost of production. [C. 6535] H.C. (1890–1). LXXVIII, 1051.

**6565** BOARD OF TRADE. General report on the wages of the manual labour classes in the United Kingdom, with tables of the average rates of wages and hours of labour of persons employed in several of the principal trades in 1886 and 1891. [C. 6889] H.C. (1893–4). LXXXIII, pt. II, 1.

**6566** BOARD OF TRADE. Report on wages and hours of labour: part I: changes in rates of wages and hours of labour in the United Kingdom in 1893. Part II: standard piece rates. Part III: standard time rates. [C. 7567-I-II] H.C. (1894). LXXXI, pt. II, 1.

The first of a ser. of annual reports down to 1914. Complete list in **6446**, p. 38.

**6567** GIFFEN (*Sir* ROBERT). Return of rates of wages paid by local authorities and private companies to police and to workpeople employed on roads, &c., and at gas and water works, with report thereon. [C. 6715] H.C. (1892). LXVIII, 719.

The Board of Trade is also said to have publ. *Rates of pay, hours of work, and other particulars with regard to labour employed by government departments in January 1893*, 1893.

6568 EARNINGS AND HOURS ENQUIRY, 1906–7. Report of an enquiry by the Board of Trade into the earnings and hours of labour of workpeople of the United Kingdom. I. Textile trades in 1906. [Cd. 4545] H.C. (1909). LXXX, 1. II. Clothing trades in 1906. [Cd. 4844] H.C. (1909). LXXX, 325. III. Building and woodworking trades in 1906. [Cd. 5086] H.C. (1910). LXXXIV, 1. IV. Public utility services in 1906. [Cd. 5196] H.C. (1910). LXXXIV, 229. V. Agriculture in 1907. [Cd. 5460] H.C. (1910). LXXXIV, 451. VI. Metal, engineering and shipbuilding trades in 1906. [Cd. 5814] H.C. (1911). LXXXVIII, 1. VII. Railway service in 1907. [Cd. 6053] H.C. (1912–13). CVIII, 1. VIII. Paper, printing, &c. trades; pottery, brick, glass and chemical trades; food, drink and tobacco trades; and miscellaneous trades in 1906. [Cd. 6556] H.C. (1912–13). CVIII, 289.

A vast inquiry covering some 3 million workers.

6569 WILSON FOX (ARTHUR). Report of an enquiry by the Board of Trade into working-class rents, housing and retail prices, together with the standard rates of wages prevailing in certain occupations in the principal industrial towns of the United Kingdom. [Cd. 3864] H.C. (1908). CVII, 319. Similar report for 1912 by F. H. McLeod. [Cd. 6955] H.C. (1913). LXVI, 393.

Parallel reports were issued on the cost of living in Germany ([Cd. 4032] H.C. (1908). CVIII, 1) and the United States ([Cd. 5609] H.C. (1911). LXXXVIII, 253).

6570 FAIR WAGES COMMITTEE. Report of the fair wages committee [Chairman: Sir George Herbert Murray]. [Cd. 4422] H.C. (1908). XXXIV, 551. Minutes of evidence. [Cd. 4423] H.C. (1908). XXXIV, 607.

## 4. UNEMPLOYMENT

6571 TAYLOR (FANNY ISABEL) *comp.* A bibliography of unemployment and the unemployed. Lond. School of Econ. 1909.

Cont. in British Library of Political & Econ. Science *Bulletin* 17, (1922), 22–8.

6572 HARRIS (JOSÉ). Unemployment and politics: a study in English social policy, 1886–1914. 1972.

6573 BOARD OF TRADE (LABOUR DEPARTMENT). Report on agencies and methods for dealing with the unemployed. [C. 7182] H.C. (1893–4). LXXXII, 377.

Suppl. by returns and notes in the *Labour gazette.* See also David Frederick Schloss, *Report to the Board of Trade on agencies and methods for dealing with the unemployed in certain foreign countries.* [Cd. 2304] H.C. (1905). LXXIII, 471, and *Labour bureaux . . . report made to the president of the Local Government Board by Arthur Lowry.* H.C. 86 (1906). CII, 363.

6574 BOARD OF TRADE (LABOUR DEPARTMENT). Second series of memoranda, statistical tables and charts . . . bearing on British and foreign trade and industrial conditions. [Cd. 2337] H.C. (1905). LXXXIV, 1.

Includes unemployment figures from the middle of the 19th cent. based on trade union membership. See also Marie Dessauer 'Unemployment records, 1848–59', *Econ. Hist. Rev.* x (1939–40), 38–43.

6575 HILL (ALSAGER HAY). The unemployed in great cities: with suggestions for the better organisation of labourers ... 1877.

Hill earlier publ. *Our unemployed: an attempt to point out some of the best means of providing occupation for distressed labourers*, 1868. With Allerdale Grainger he also ed. *The way to work: or, finger-posts on the road to employment*, 1877.

6576 HOBSON (JOHN ATKINSON). The problem of the unemployed: an enquiry and an economic policy. 1896.

The views of a radical economist. To be read with his *Problems of poverty: an inquiry into the industrial condition of the poor*, 1891.

6577 SELECT COMMITTEE ON DISTRESS FROM WANT OF EMPLOYMENT. First report from the select committee on distress from want of employment [Chairman: Sir Henry Campbell-Bannerman]. H.C. 111 (1895). VIII, 1. Second report. H.C. 253 (1895). VIII, 215. Third report. H.C. 365 (1895). IX, 1. Further committee [Chairman: T. W. Russell]. Report. H.C. 321 (1896). IX, 301.

6578 WOODWORTH (ARTHUR V.). Report of an inquiry into the condition of the unemployed, conducted under the Toynbee Trust, winter 1895–6 ... 1897.

6579 CHARITY ORGANISATION SOCIETY. Report of special committee on the relief of distress due to want of employment. 1904.

6580 ALDEN (*Sir* PERCY). The unemployed: a national question. 1905. 2nd edn. 1905.

See also his *The unemployable and the unemployed*, 1908, rev. edn. 1910.

6581 HATCH (*Sir* ERNEST FREDERICK GEORGE). A reproach to civilization: a treatise on the problem of the unemployed and some suggestions for a possible solution. 1906.

6582 JACKSON (*Sir* CYRIL) *and* PRINGLE (JOHN CHRISTIAN). Report on the effects of employment or assistance given to the unemployed since 1886 as a means of relieving distress outside the poor law ... [Cd. 4795] H.C. (1909). XLIV, 1.

A comprehensive survey for the Poor Law Commission. Similar reports were prepared on Scotland and Ireland. Jackson also publ. *Unemployment and the trade unions*, 1910.

6583 BEVERIDGE (WILLIAM HENRY), *Baron Beveridge*. Unemployment: a problem of industry. 1909. New edn. 1930.

Influenced his *Full employment in a free society: a report*, 1944.

6584 CHAPMAN (*Sir* SYDNEY JOHN) *and* HALLSWORTH (HARRY MAINWARING). Unemployment: the results of an investigation made in Lancashire, and an examination of the report of the Poor Law Commission. Manch. 1909.

**6585** SCHLOSS (DAVID FREDERICK). Insurance against unemployment. 1909.

A useful survey, as is Sir Ioan Gwilym Gibbon, *Unemployment insurance: a study of schemes of assisted insurance*, 1911. For national insurance see **7379–94**.

**6586** ROWNTREE (BENJAMIN SEEBOHM) *and* LASKER (BRUNO). Unemployment: a social study. 1911.

Based on York. See also Rowntree's *Poverty* **735**.

**6587** KELLOR (FRANCES ALICE). Out of work: a study of employment agencies. N.Y. 1904.

**6588** BOARD OF TRADE. Report on the state of employment in the United Kingdom in October 1914. [Cd. 7703] H.C. (1914–16). XXI, 25.

Similar reports were issued in December 1914 [Cd. 7755] H.C. (1914–16). XXI, 67, and February 1915 [Cd. 7850] H.C. (1914–16). XXI, 77.

## 5. TRADE UNIONS

**6589** DOLLÉANS (ÉDOUARD) *and* CROZIER (MICHEL). Mouvements ouvrier et socialiste: chronologie et bibliographie: Angleterre, France, Allemagne, États-Unis, 1750–1918. Paris. 1950.

See also Ruth Frow, Edmund Frow, and Michael Katanka, *The history of British trade unionism: a select bibliography*, Hist. Assoc. helps for students 76, 1969.

**6590** HOBSBAWM (ERIC JOHN ERNEST). 'Records of the trade union movement'. *Archives* iv (1959–60), 129–37.

**6591** GULICK (CHARLES ADAMS) *and others, comps*. History and theories of working-class movements: a select bibliography. Berkeley. 1955.

Periodical articles only. Strongest from *c*. 1895, as is Victor Leonard Allen, comp., *International bibliography of trade unionism*, 1968.

**6592** COLE (GEORGE DOUGLAS HOWARD) *and* FILSON (ALEXANDER WARNOCK) *comps*. British working-class movements: select documents, 1789–1875. 1951.

A useful general coll. Walter Milne-Bailey, ed., *Trade union documents*, 1929, adds surprisingly little.

**6592a** BELLAMY (JOYCE MARGARET) *and* SAVILLE (JOHN) *eds*. Dictionary of labour biography. 1+v. 1972+.

**6593** BOARD OF TRADE. Statistical tables and report on trade unions. [C. 5104] H.C. (1887). LXXXIX, 715.

The first of 17 reports covering 1887–1910. Title became [*Fourth*] *annual report on trade unions . . . for 1889 and 1890 . . .*, then [*Twelfth*] *report by the chief Labour correspondent of the Board of Trade on trade unions in 1899 . . .*, and finally *Report on trade unions in 1908–1910 with comparative statistics for 1901–1910*. [Cd. 6109] H.C. (1912–13). XLVII, 655.

6594 DAVIS (HORACE B.). 'The theory of union growth'. *Q.J. Econ.* lv (1940–1), 611–35.

See also P. E. Hart and Ernest Henry Phelps Brown, 'The sizes of trade unions: a study in the laws of aggregation', *Econ. J.* lxvii (1957), 1–15.

6595 PELLING (HENRY MATHISON). A history of British trade unionism. 1963.

A workmanlike hist. Better than [Edward] Francis Williams, Baron Francis Williams, *Magnificent journey: the rise of the trade unions,* 1954, and Robert Macey Rayner, *The story of trade unionism from the Combination Acts to the general strike,* 1929, or the Marxist George Allen Hutt, *British trade unionism: an outline history,* 1941, 5th edn. 1962, and Arthur Leslie Morton and George Tate, *The British labour movement, 1770–1920: a history,* 1956.

6596 WEBB (SIDNEY JAMES), *Baron Passfield, and* WEBB (BEATRICE). The history of trade unionism. With bibliog. by Robert Alexander Peddie. 1894. 3rd edn. 1911. New edn. without bibliog. 1920.

The great pioneer work on 19th-cent. trade unionism; now very dated, but still indispensable. See also their *Industrial democracy,* 2 v. 1897, new edn. 1920.

6597 COLE (GEORGE DOUGLAS HOWARD). A short history of the British working-class movement, 1789–1925. 3 v. 1925–7. New edn. [to 1947.] 1 v. 1948.

Wide ranging and often perceptive.

6598 HOBSBAWM (ERIC JOHN ERNEST). 'Trends in the British labour movement since 1850'. *Science & Society* xiii (1949), 289–312. Repr. in his Labouring men. 1964.

6599 GARBATI (IRVING). 'British trade unionism in the mid-Victorian era'. *Univ. of Toronto Q.* xx (1950–1), 69–84.

6600 COLTHAM (STEPHEN). 'George Potter, the Junta and the *Bee-hive*'. *Internat. Rev. Soc. Hist.* ix (1964), 391–432; x (1965), 23–65.

6601 McCREADY (HERBERT WILLIAM). 'British labour's lobby, 1867–75'. *Can. J. Econ. & Pol. Sci.* xxii (1956), 141–60.

6602 COLE (GEORGE DOUGLAS HOWARD). 'Some notes on British trade unionism in the third quarter of the nineteenth century'. *Int. Rev. for Soc. Hist.* ii (1937), 1–27. Repr. in Carus-Wilson, Essays (**4066**) III, 202–21.

See also A. E. P. Duffy, 'New unionism in Britain, 1889–1890: a reappraisal', *Econ. Hist. Rev.* 2 ser. xiv (1961–2), 306–19.

6603 CLEGG (HUGH ARMSTRONG), FOX (ALAN), *and* THOMPSON (ARTHUR FREDERICK). A history of British trade unions since 1889. V. 1. 1889–1910. Oxf. 1964.

The first vol. of a full general hist.

**6604** DUFFY (A. E. P.). 'The eight hours day movement in Britain, 1886–1893'. *Manch. School* xxxvi (1968), 203–22, 345–64.

See also **6484**.

**6605** ROBERTS (BENJAMIN CHARLES). The Trades Union Congress, 1868–1921. 1958.

Good. See also Albert Edward Musson, *The congress of 1868: the origins and establishment of the Trades Union Congress*, 1955, and William John Davis, *The British Trades Union Congress: history and recollections*, 2 v. 1910–16. 1968 produced a crop of centennial vols.: Lionel Birch, ed., *The history of the TUC, 1868–1968: a pictorial survey of a social revolution*, 1968, is a picture book; John Christopher Lovell and B. C. Roberts, *A short history of the T.U.C.*, 1968, is a useful hist.; Victor Leonard Allen, 'The centenary of the British Trades Union Congress, 1868–1968', *Socialist Register* (1968), 231–52, is an attempt at a Marxist commentary; and Edmund Frow and Michael Katanka, eds., *1868: year of the union: a documentary survey*, Edgware 1968, a misc. coll. of docs. An annual report of the Congress has been publ. since 1869 and lists of delegates since 1872. The parl. committee issued a separate report, 1872–1913.

**6606** TATE (GEORGE KENNETH) *ed.* London Trades Council, 1860–1950: a history. 1950.

An inadequate hist. of the main national trades union body before the rise of the T.U.C. See also John Corbett, *The Birmingham Trades Council, 1866–1966*, 1966.

**6607** HOBSBAWM (ERIC JOHN ERNEST). 'General labour unions in Britain, 1889–1914'. *Econ. Hist. Rev.* 2 ser. i (1948–9), 123–42. Repr. in his Labouring men. 1964.

**6608** CLEGG (HUGH ARMSTRONG). General union in a changing society: a short history of the National Union of General and Municipal Workers, 1889–1964. Oxf. 1964.

**6609** HYMAN (RICHARD). The Workers' Union, 1898–1929. Oxf. 1971.

**6610** COLLISON. The apostle of free labour: the life story of William Collison, founder and general secretary of the National Free Labour Association. Told by himself. 1913.

The organizer of the 'free labour' movement, on which see John Saville, 'Trade unions and free labour', in *Essays in labour hist.* (**6460**).

**6611** PELLING (HENRY MATHISON). 'The Knights of Labor in Britain, 1880–1901'. *Econ. Hist. Rev.* 2 ser. ix (1956–7), 313–31.

**6612** YEARLEY (CLIFTON K.). Britons in American labor: a history of the influence of the United Kingdom immigrants on American labor, 1820–1914. Baltimore [Md.]. 1957.

**6613** WOOD (GEORGE HENRY). 'Trade-union expenditure on unemployed benefits since 1860'. *Roy. Stat. Soc. J.* lxiii (1900), 81–92.

See also Edwin Leach Hartley, 'Trade union expenditure on unemployed benefit', *Roy. Stat. Soc. J.* lxvii (1904), 52–71, and Rosemary Hutt, 'Trade unions as friendly societies, 1912–1952', *Yorkshire Bull.* vii (1955), 69–87.

6614 CLEMENTS (ROGER VICTOR). 'British trade unions and popular political economy, 1850–1875'. *Econ. Hist. Rev.* 2 ser. xiv (1961–2), 93–104.

See also his 'Trade unions and emigration, 1840–80', *Population Studs.* ix (1955–6), 167–80, and Charlotte Erickson, 'The encouragement of emigration by British trade unions, 1850–1900', *Population Studs.* iii (1949–50), 248–73.

6615 POLLARD (SIDNEY). 'Trade unions and the labour market, 1870–1914'. *Yorkshire Bull.* xvii (1965), 98–112.

6616 WEARMOUTH (ROBERT FEATHERSTONE). Methodism and the trade unions. 1959.

6617 MOODY (THEODORE WILLIAM). 'Michael Davitt and the British labour movement, 1882–1906'. *Roy. Hist. Soc. Trans.* 5 ser. iii (1953), 53–76.

6618 HEDGES (ROBERT YORKE) *and* WINTERBOTHAM (ALLAN). The legal history of trade unionism. 1930.

See also Norman Arthur Citrine, *Trade union law*, 1950, 2nd edn. 1960, which includes an outline hist. Contemp. legal works on trade unionism included Sir William Erle, *The law relating to trade unions*, 1868, new edn. 1869; William Guthrie, *The law of trade unions in England and Scotland under the Trade Union Act, 1871*, Edin. 1873; Henry Frederick Alexander Davis, *The law and practice of friendly societies and trade unions . . .*, 1876; George Howell, *A handy book of the labour laws* [1876]; John Henry Greenwood, *The law relating to trade unions*, 1911; Henry Herman Schloesser, afterwards Sir Henry Slesser, and William Smith Clark, *The legal position of trade unions*, 1912, 2nd edn. 1913; and Herman Joseph Cohen, *Trade union law and cases . . .*, 1901, 3rd edn. 1913.

6619 NATIONAL ASSOCIATION FOR THE PROMOTION OF SOCIAL SCIENCE. Trades societies: report of the committee on trades societies . . . 1860.

An important pioneer inquiry.

6620 ERLE COMMISSION ON TRADES UNIONS. First report of the commissioners appointed to inquire into the organization and rules of trades unions and other associations [Chairman: Sir William Erle]. [3873] H.C. (1867). XXXII, 1. Second to Fourth reports. [3893, 3910, 3952] H.C. (1867). XXXII, 167, 197, 289. Fifth to Tenth reports. [3980-I-VI] H.C. (1867–8). XXXIX, 1+. Eleventh and final report. [4123] H.C. (1868–9). XXXI, 235, with Appendix. [4123-I] H.C. (1868–9). XXXI, 363.

On trade union outrages and the legal position of trade unions. To be read with *Report presented to the trades unions commissioners by the examiners* [Chairman: William Overend, Q.C.], *appointed to inquire into acts of intimidation, outrage or wrong alleged to have been promoted, encouraged or connived at by trades unions in the town of Sheffield*. [3952-I] H.C. (1867). XXXII, 397. Minutes of evidence. [3952-II] H.C. (1867). XXXII, 414, and a similar report on outrages in Manchester presented by another group of examiners [Chairman: P. A. Pickering Q.C.]. [3980] H.C. (1867–8). XXXIX, 571. For comment see Herbert William McCready, 'British labour and the Royal Commission on Trade Unions, 1867–9', *Univ. Toronto Q.* xxiv (1954–5), 390–409, and Sidney Pollard, 'The ethics of the Sheffield outrages', *Hunter Archaeol. Soc. Trans.* vii (1951–7), 118–39. Louis Philippe Albert d'Orléans, Comte de Paris, *The trades unions of England*, trans.

by Nassau John Senior and ed. by Thomas Hughes, 1869, is largely based on the commission's report.

**6621   JEVONS (WILLIAM STANLEY).** A lecture on trades' societies: their objects and policy. Manch. 1868.

A famous economist's reflections. Other contemp. works incl. James Ward, *Workmen and wages at home and abroad: or, the effects of strikes, combinations and trades' unions,* 1868; James Stirling, *[Trade] unionism . . .,* Glasgow 1869, 2nd edn. 1869; Charles Wilson Felt, *Free labour the first condition of free trade,* Manch. 1870; Robert Somers, *The trade unions: an appeal to the working classes and their friends,* 1876; and Lloyd Jones, *Trade unions . . .,* 1877.

**6622   BRENTANO (LUJO).** Die Arbeitergilden der Gegenwart. Leipzig. 2 v. 1871–2.

A deservedly famous pioneer study.

**6623   TRANT (WILLIAM).** Trades unions: their origin and objects, influence and efficacy. 1884.

A T.U.C. prize essay of 1873.

**6624   BURNETT (JOHN)** *and others.* The claims of labour: a course of lectures . . . on various aspects of the labour problem. Edin. 1886.

**6625   HOWELL (GEORGE).** The conflicts of capital and labour: historically and economically considered; being a history and review of the trade unions of Great Britain. 1878. 2nd edn. 1890.

A major source for the period. His *Trade unionism: new and old,* 1891, 2nd edn. 1894, and *Labour legislation, labour movements and labour leaders,* 1902, 2nd edn. 1905, are also important, although written from an old-fashioned point of view. Henry Herman Schloesser, afterwards Sir Henry Slesser, *Trade unionism,* 1913, 2nd edn. 1921, is avowedly based on Howell.

**6626   ROUSIERS (PAUL DE).** Le trade-unionisme en Angleterre. Paris. 1897. 2nd edn. 1904.

**6627   PRATT (EDWIN A.).** Trade unionism and British industry: a reprint of *The Times* articles on the crisis in British industry. 1904.

Alfred Henry Ruegg and Herman Joseph Cohen, *The present and future of trade unions,* 1906, is a discussion of trade union law.

**6628   DUNEDIN COMMISSION ON TRADE DISPUTES.** Report of the royal commission on trade disputes and trade combinations [Chairman: Andrew Graham Murray, later Lord Dunedin]. [Cd. 2825] H.C. (1906). LVI, 1. Minutes of evidence. [Cd. 2826] H.C. (1906). LVI, 137.

A general inquiry, hampered by the refusal of the trade unions to co-operate.

**6629   LLOYD (CHARLES MOSTYN).** Trade unionism. 1915. 3rd edn. 1928.

A good outline of the position of the trade unions in 1914.

6. WORKING WOMEN

(a) *General*

6630 PAPWORTH (LUCY WYATT) *and* ZIMMERN (DOROTHY M.). Women in industry: a bibliography. Women's Industrial Council. 1915.

See also McGregor's general bibliog. on women (**6986**).

6631 THE YEAR BOOK OF WOMEN'S WORK. 1875–1916.

Title became *The English woman's year-book and directory*, 1881–1916. Includes a long section on women's employment.

6632 HUTCHINS (B. [i.e. ELIZABETH] LEIGH). Women in modern industry. 1915.

Still the best general hist. Particularly useful for trade unions and factory legislation. There is a little additional material in Sylvia Anthony, *Women's place in industry and home*, 1932.

6633 HEWITT (MARGARET). Wives & mothers in Victorian industry: a study of the effects of the employment of married women in Victorian industry. 1958.

6634 NEFF (WANDA FRAIKEN). Victorian working women: an historical and literary study of women in British industries and professions, 1832–1850. Lond. & N.Y. 1929.

Not strictly on the period, but, like Ivy Pinchbeck, *Women workers and the industrial revolution, 1750–1850*, 1930, very useful.

6635 HAYNES (DOROTHY). 'A comparative study of the occupations of men and women, with special reference to their mutual displacement, from the census returns, 1861–1911'. *Women's Industrial News* xix (1915), 365–99. Bibliog. by Irene Hernaman. Ibid. 407–14.

6636 COLLET (CLARA ELIZABETH). Report . . . on the statistics of employment of women and girls. [C. 7564] H.C. (1894). LXXXI, pt. II, 845. Suppl. on flax and jute industries. [C. 8794] H.C. (1898). LXXXVIII, 305.

Based on the 1881 and 1891 censuses. Clara Elizabeth Collet also publ. 'The collection and utilisation of official statistics bearing on the extent and effects of the industrial employment of women', *Roy. Stat. Soc. J.* lxi (1898), 219–60. See also B. [i.e. Elizabeth] Leigh Hutchins 'A note on the distribution of women in occupations', *Roy. Stat. Soc. J.* lxvii (1904), 479–90, and 'Statistics of women's life and employment', ibid. lxxii (1909), 205–37.

6637 DISTRIBUTION OF WOMEN IN INDUSTRY. A study of the factors which have operated in the past and those which are operating now to determine the distribution of women in industry. [Cmd. 3508] H.C. (1929–30). XVII, 1019.

6638　WEBB (SIDNEY JAMES), *Baron Passfield*. 'The alleged differences in the wages paid to men and to women for similar work'. *Econ. J.* i (1891), 635–62.

6639　BOARD OF TRADE (LABOUR DEPARTMENT). Accounts of ex-expenditure of wage-earning women and girls. [Cd. 5963] H.C. (1911). LXXXIX, 531.

6640　BARTON (DOROTHEA M.). 'The course of women's wages'. *Roy. Stat. Soc. J.* lxxxii (1919), 508–44.

A coll. of 19th- and early 20th-cent. stats. Suppl. by her 'Women's minimum wages', ibid. lxxxiv (1921), 538–67.

### (b) *Contemporary Works*

See also the royal commission on the employment of women and children in agriculture (**6698**) and the reports on sweating (**6480**).

6641　JAMESON (ANNA BROWNELL). Sisters of charity: catholic and protestant, abroad and at home. 1855. 2nd edn. 1855.

Like her *The communion of labour* . . ., 1856, and Barbara Leigh Smith, afterwards Bodichon, *Women and work*, 1857, deals with the plight of the increasing number of unmarriageable women. Suggests that one possible escape is through charitable activities.

6642　[MILNE (JOHN DUGUID).] Industrial and social position of women in the middle and lower ranks. 1857. Rev. edn. 1870.

6643　BOUCHERETT (JESSIE). Hints on self-help: a book for young women. 1863.

Advice about behaviour plus information about occupations open to young women, chiefly of the respectable poor. Very improving.

6644　PARKES *afterwards* BELLOC (BESSIE RAYNER). Essays on woman's work. 1865.

A rather thin, feminist tract.

6645　THE ENGLISH WOMAN'S REVIEW of social and industrial questions. 1866–1910.

6646　JEUNE (SUSAN ELIZABETH MARY), *Baroness St. Helier, ed.* Ladies at work: papers on paid employments for ladies, by experts in the several branches. 1893.

A useful symposium.

6647　BULLEY (AGNES AMY) *and* WHITLEY (MARGARET). Women's work. 1894.

6648 BATESON (MARGARET). Professional women upon their professions: conversations recorded by Margaret Bateson. 1895. Cheap edn. 1897.

6649 BOUCHERETT (JESSIE) *and* BLACKBURN (HELEN) *eds.* The condition of working women and the Factory Acts. 1896.

Hostile on feminist grounds to special legislation for women.

6650 COLLET (CLARA ELIZABETH). Educated working women: essays on the economic position of women workers in the middle classes. 1902.

6651 MACDONALD (JAMES RAMSAY) *ed.* Women in the printing trades: a sociological study. 1904.

6652 CADBURY (EDWARD), MATHESON (M. CECILE), *and* SHANN (GEORGE). Women's work and wages: a phase of life in an industrial city. 1906.

A careful survey of Birmingham, especially its slums.

6653 MEYER (ADELE), *Mrs. Carl Meyer, afterwards Lady Meyer, and* BLACK (CLEMENTINA). Makers of our clothes: a case for trade boards: being the results of a year's investigation into the work of women in London in the tailoring, dressmaking and underclothing trades. 1909.

See also **6480**.

6654 BIRD (M. MOSTYN). Woman at work: a study of the different ways of earning a living open to women. 1911.

6655 MORLEY (EDITH JULIA) *ed.* Women workers in seven professions: a survey of their economic conditions and prospects. Fabian Women's Group. 1914.

The 7 professions are teaching, medicine, nursing, sanitary inspection, civil service, clerical and secretarial, and acting.

6656 BUTLER (C. VIOLET). Domestic service: an enquiry by the Women's Industrial Council. 1916.

### (c) *Trades Unions and other Organizations*

6657 BOONE (GLADYS). The women's trade union leagues in Great Britain and the United States of America . . . N.Y. 1942.

6658 DRAKE (BARBARA). Women in trade unions. Labour Research Dept. 1920.

Includes a short hist.

6659 HAMILTON (MARY AGNES). Women at work: a brief introduction to trade unionism for women. 1941.

Has some hist. material.

6660 BONDFIELD. A life's work. By Margaret Grace Bondfield. [1949.]

See also Mary Agnes Hamilton, *Margaret Bondfield*, 1924.

6661 MACARTHUR. Mary Macarthur: a biographical sketch. By Mary Agnes Hamilton. 1925.

The life of the leading woman trade unionist of the period.

6662 WOMEN'S PROTECTIVE AND PROVIDENT LEAGUE. The women's union journal: the organ of the Women's Protective and Provident League. 1876–90.

Cont. as *Quarterly report and review* . . ., 1891, and *The women's trades union review*, 1891–1919.

6663 NATIONAL UNION OF WOMEN WORKERS OF GREAT BRITAIN AND IRELAND [National Council of Women of Great Britain]. Handbook and report. 1890+.

Title varies. See also *Women workers: the quarterly mag. of the Birmingham Ladies' Union* . . ., 1891–1924.

6664 WOMEN'S INDUSTRIAL COUNCIL. Women's industrial news. 1895–1919.

An important source for statistical and other technical information.

### 7. WORKING CHILDREN

6665 THOMAS (MAURICE WALTON). Young people in industry, 1750–1945. 1945.

There is little on the period in George Lewis Phillips, *England's climbing boys: a history of the long struggle to abolish child labour in chimney sweeping*, Boston 1949.

6666 DUNLOP (OLIVE JOCELYN). English apprenticeship & child labour: a history. 1912.

See also Reginald Arthur Bray, *Boy labour and apprenticeship*, 1911.

6667 CHILDREN'S EMPLOYMENT COMMISSION. Children's Employment Commission (1862): first report of the commissioners [Chairman: Hugh Seymour Tremenheere]. [3170] H.C. (1863). XVIII, 1. Second and third reports. [3414, 3414-I] H.C. (1864). XXII, 1+. Fourth report. [3548] H.C. (1865). XX, 103. Fifth report. [3678] H.C. (1866). XXIV, 1. Sixth report. [3796] H.C. (1867). XVI, 67.

Wide-ranging. Covers, esp. in 6th report, agricultural labour, for which see also **6698**.

6668 CUNYNGHAME COMMITTEE ON EMPLOYMENT OF SCHOOL CHILDREN. Report of the inter-departmental committee on the employment of school children . . . [Chairman: H. H. S. Cunynghame]. [Cd. 849] H.C. (1902). XXV, 261. Minutes of evidence. [Cd. 895] H.C. (1902). XXV, 287.

6669 JACKSON (*Sir* CYRIL). Report on boy labour ... Royal Commission on the Poor Laws and Relief of Distress. Appendix XX. [Cd. 4632] H.C. (1909). XLIV, 921.

6670 SIMON COMMITTEE ON EMPLOYMENT OF CHILDREN ACT, 1903. Report of the departmental committee on the Employment of Children Act, 1903, appointed by His Majesty's principal secretary of state for the home department [Chairman: J. A. Simon, K.C.]. [Cd. 5229] H.C. (1910). XXVIII, 1. Minutes of evidence. [Cd. 5230] H.C. (1910). XXVIII, 25.

6671 BELLHOUSE COMMITTEE ON VAN AND WAREHOUSE BOYS. Report of the departmental committee on the hours and conditions of employment of van boys and warehouse boys ... [Chairman: Gerald Bellhouse.] [Cd. 6886] H.C. (1913). XXXIII, 463. Evidence. [Cd. 6887] H.C. (1913). XXXIII, 495.

6672 GREENWOOD (ARTHUR) *and* KETTLEWELL (JOHN E.). 'Some statistics of juvenile employment and unemployment'. *Roy. Stat. Soc. J.* lxxv (1911–12), 744–53.

See also Greenwood's *Juvenile labour exchanges and aftercare*, 1911.

6673 FREEMAN (ARNOLD). Boy life & labour: the manufacture of inefficiency. 1914.

Probably the best of a number of general studs. But see also John Howard Whitehouse, ed., *Problems of boy life*, 1912; J. H. Whitehouse, Geoffrey Gordon, and Norman Malcolmson, *Report of an enquiry into working boys' homes in London*, 1908; Mrs. Percy Alden [i.e. Margaret Elizabeth Alden], *Child life and labour*, Social service handbooks 6, 1908; Robert Harborough Sherard, *The child slaves of Britain*, 1905; and Margaret Neville Keynes, *The problem of boy labour in Cambridge*, Camb. 1911.

6674 KEELING (FREDERIC HILLERSDON). Child labour in the United Kingdom: a study of the development and administration of the law relating to the employment of children. 1914.

### 8. Particular Sectors of the Labour Market

#### (a) *Public Service*

6675 ROUTH (GUY). 'Civil service pay, 1875 to 1950'. *Economica* new ser. xxi (1954), 201–23.

6676 TWEEDMOUTH COMMITTEE ON POST OFFICE ESTABLISHMENTS ... Report of the inter-departmental committee on Post Office establishments [Chairman: Lord Tweedmouth]. H.C. 121 (1897). XLIV, 1. Minutes of evidence. H.C. 163 (1897). XLIV, 37.

Collected voluminous evidence.

6677 BRADFORD COMMITTEE ON POST OFFICE WAGES. Report and appendices of the committee appointed to enquire into Post Office wages

[Chairman: Sir Edward Bradford]. [Cd. 2170] H.C. (1904). XXXIII, 465. Minutes of evidence, etc. [Cd. 2171] H.C. (1904). XXXIII, 511.

6678 HOBHOUSE COMMITTEE ON POST OFFICE SERVANTS. Report from the select committee on Post Office servants [Chairman: Charles Hobhouse]. H.C. 266 (1907). VII, 299. Minutes of evidence. H.C. 380 (1906). XII, pt. I, 11 and Pt. II, 1.

6679 HOLT COMMITTEE ON POST OFFICE SERVANTS. Proceedings from the select committee on Post Office servants (wages and conditions of employment) [Chairman: R. D. Holt]. H.C. 268 (1913). X, 295. Minutes of evidence. H.C. 268 (1913). X, 1, XI, 1, XII, 1, and XIII, 1.

Produced an enormous volume of material. For official reactions to the report see [Cd. 7995] H.C. (1914–16). XXXII, 1009.

6680 SWIFT (HENRY G.). A history of postal agitation from fifty years ago till the present day. 1900. Rev. edn. Manch. & Lond. 1929.

See also John Golding, *75 years: a short history of the Post Office Engineering Union*, 1962.

6681 BAILEY COMMITTEE ON WORKMEN AT WOOLWICH ARSENAL. Report from the select committee on workmen (Woolwich arsenal) [Chairman: Sir Joseph Bailey]. H.C. 197 (1889). XVI, 531.

6682 HUMPHREYS (BETTY VANCE). Clerical unions in the civil service. Oxf. 1958.

6683 ALLEN (VICTOR LEONARD). 'The National Union of Police and Prison Officers'. *Econ. Hist. Rev.* 2 ser. xi (1958–9), 133–43.

(b) *Agriculture*

(i) *General*

For the decline in numbers of labourers see **6941–3**.

6684 HASBACH (WILHELM). A history of the English agricultural labourer, from the earliest times to 1894. Trans. by Ruth Kenyon. 1908. New edn. 1920.

Supplanted Russell Montague Garnier, *Annals of the British peasantry*, 1895, a rambling and inconclusive work.

6685 FUSSELL (GEORGE EDWIN). The English rural labourer: his house, furniture, clothing & food from Tudor to Victorian times. 1949.

6686 GREEN (FREDERICK ERNEST). A history of the English agricultural labourer, 1870–1920. 1920.

See also Eugene Mejer, *Agricultural labour in England and Wales*: Part I, '1900–1920' Nottingham Univ. School of Agric., Sutton Bonington, 1949.

6687  DUNLOP (OLIVE JOCELYN). The farm labourer: the history of a modern problem. 1913.

6688  SPRINGALL (LILLIE MARION). Labouring life in Norfolk villages, 1834–1914. 1936.

6689  GREY (EDWIN). Cottage life in a Hertfordshire village: how the agricultural labourer lived and fared in the late '60s and '70s. St. Albans. [1935.]

6690  GOSSET (ADELAIDE L. J.). Shepherds of Britain: scenes from shepherd life, past and present . . . 1911.

6691  JONES (ERIC LIONEL). 'The agricultural labour market in England, 1793–1872'. *Econ. Hist. Rev.* 2 ser. xvii (1964–5), 322–38.

6692  COLLINS (E. J. T.). 'Harvest technology and labour supply in Britain, 1790–1870'. *Econ. Hist. Rev.* 2 ser. xxii (1969), 453–73.

6693  HUNT (E. H.). 'Labour productivity in English agriculture, 1850–1914'. *Econ. Hist. Rev.* 2 ser. xx (1967), 280–92.

Includes a study of regional differences. There is further discussion of the topic in David Metcalf, 'Labour productivity . . . a theoretical comment', *Econ. Hist. Rev.* 2 ser. xxii (1969), 117–18, with reply by Hunt, ibid. 118–19, and Paul A. David, 'Labour productivity . . . some quantitative evidence of regional diffusion', ibid. 2 ser. xxiii (1970), 504–14, with reply by Hunt, ibid. 515–19.

6694  CLIFFORD (FREDERICK). 'The labour bill in farming'. *Roy. Agric. Soc. J.* xxxvi (2 ser. xi) (1875), 67–127.

6695  FOX (ARTHUR WILSON). 'Agricultural wages in England and Wales during the last half century'. *Roy. Stat. Soc. J.* lxvi (1903), 273–348.

To be read in conjunction with his official reports (**6696**), and with Sir Arthur Lyon Bowley, 'The statistics of wages in the United Kingdom during the last hundred years: Pt. I. Agricultural wages', *Roy. Stat. Soc. J.* lxi (1898), 702–22, William Henry Ricketts Curtler, 'Enquiry into the rate of wages per acre in England, 1913–14', *Int. Rev. Agric. Econ.* lxviii (1916), no. 8, 85–103, no. 10, 88–103, and Charles Stewart Orwin and B. I. Felton, 'A century of wages and earnings in agriculture', *Roy. Agric. Soc. J.* xcii (1931), 231–57.

6696  FOX (ARTHUR WILSON). Report by Mr. Wilson Fox on the wages and earnings of agricultural labourers in the United Kingdom. [Cd. 346] H.C. (1900). LXXXII, 557.

Includes a county-by-county survey of wage-rates since 1850. Continued in *Second report by Mr. Wilson Fox* . . . [Cd. 2376] H.C. (1905). XCVII, 335, and in *Earnings and hours enquiry: report of an enquiry by the Board of Trade into the earnings and hours of labour of workpeople of the United Kingdom: V. Agriculture in 1907.* [Cd. 5460] H.C. (1910). LXXXIV, 451.

6697 LENNARD (REGINALD VIVIAN). Economic notes on English agricultural wages. 1914.

For the position after the war see Board of Agriculture and Fisheries, *Wages and conditions of employment in agriculture*: I. *General report by Geoffrey Drage*. [Cmd. 24] H.C. (1919). IX, I. II: *Reports of investigators*. [Cmd. 25] H.C. (1919). IX, 207.

6698 [ROYAL] COMMISSION ON THE EMPLOYMENT OF CHILDREN, YOUNG PERSONS, AND WOMEN IN AGRICULTURE. First report of the commissioners [Hugh Seymour Tremenheere and Edward Carleton Tufnell]. [4068] H.C. (1867-8). XVII, I. Evidence. [4068-I] H.C. (1867-8). XVII, 237. Second report. [4202] H.C. (1868-9). XIII, I. Evidence. [4202-I] H.C. (1868-9). XIII, 231. Third report. [C. 70] H.C. (1870). XIII, I. Fourth report. [C. 221] H.C. (1870), XIII, 173.

Very full.

6699 KEBBEL (THOMAS EDWARD). The agricultural labourer: a short summary of his position . . . 1870. New edn. 1893.

See also John Dent Dent, 'The present condition of the English agricultural labourer, 1871', *Roy. Agric. Soc. J.* xxxii (2 ser. vii) (1871), 343–65.

6700 STRATTON (JOHN YOUNG). 'Farm labourers, their friendly societies and the poor law'. *Roy. Agric. Soc. J.* xxxi (2 ser. vi) (1870), 87–119.

Stratton also publ. 'Method of improving the labouring classes by altering the conditions of poor relief, and providing them with a system of insurance through the Post Office', *Roy. Agric. Soc. J.* xxxiii (2 ser. viii) (1872), 76–103, and 'Friendly societies, state action, and the poor law', ibid. xliii (2 ser. xviii) (1882), 153–86.

6701 HEATH (FRANCIS GEORGE). The English peasantry. 1874.

A good book, based partly on his even better book, *The 'romance' of peasant life in the West of England* . . ., 1872, new [3rd] edn. 1880.

6702 STUBBS (CHARLES WILLIAM), *bishop*. Village politics: addresses and sermons on the labour question. 1878.

6703 JEFFERIES ([JOHN] RICHARD). Hodge and his masters. 2 v. 1880. New edn. 1937.

Fiction, but of great importance in shaping opinion about village life.

6704 STUBBS (CHARLES WILLIAM), *bishop*. The land and the labourers: a record of facts and experiments in cottage farming and co-operative agriculture. 1884. 2nd edn. 1885.

6705 BEAR (WILLIAM E.). 'The farm labourers of England and Wales'. *Roy. Agric. Soc. J.* liv (3 ser. iv) (1893), 657–78.

6706 BAVERSTOCK (ALBAN HENRY). The English agricultural labourer. 1912.

6707 ROWNTREE (BENJAMIN SEEBOHM) *and* KENDALL (MAY). How the labourer lives: a study of the rural labour problem. 1913.

Includes household budgets and wage rates for 1912–13. See also C. Winckworth Allen, 'The housing of the agricultural labourer', *Roy. Agric. Soc. J.* lxxv (1914), 20–33; and A. Dudley Clarke, 'Cottages for rural labourers', ibid. lxv (1904), 125–47.

6708 HOLDENBY (CHRISTOPHER) *pseud. of* HATTON (RONALD GEORGE). Folk of the furrow. 1913.

Useful for the atmosphere of the period.

### (ii) *Trade Unions*

6709 FUSSELL (GEORGE EDWIN). From Tolpuddle to T.U.C. A century of farm labourers' politics. Slough. 1948.

Largely replaces Ernest Selley, *Village trade unions in two centuries*, 1919.

6710 GROVES (REGINALD). Sharpen the sickle! The history of the Farm Workers' Union. 1949.

6711 DUNBABIN (JOHN PAUL DELACOUR). 'The incidence and organization of agricultural trades unionism in the 1870s'. *Agric. Hist. Rev.* xvi (1968), 114–41.

6712 CLAYDEN (ARTHUR). The revolt of the field: a sketch of the rise and progress of the movement among the agricultural labourers known as the National Agricultural Labourers' Union. 1874.

An account of the great strikes and lock-outs of 1874. See also Frederick Clifford, *The agricultural lock-out, 1874*, Edin. & Lond. 1875.

6713 RUSSELL (REX C.) *pseud. of* RUSSELL (REGINALD CHARLES) *comp.* The revolt of the field in Lincolnshire: the origins and early history of farm-workers' trade unions. Lincolnshire County Committee: National Union of Agricultural Workers. Boston. 1956.

6714 ARCH. Joseph Arch: the story of his life told by himself. Ed. by Frances Evelyn Greville, Countess of Warwick. 1898.

The founder of the National Agricultural Union. See also Pamela Horn, *Joseph Arch, 1826–1919: the farm workers' leader*, Kineton 1971.

6715 EDWARDS. From crow-scaring to Westminster: an autobiography. By Sir George Edwards. 1922. Repr. 1957.

The pioneer of agricultural workers' unions in Norfolk.

### (c) *Textiles and Clothing*
#### (i) *General*

6716 GIFFEN (ROBERT). Return of rates of wages in the principal textile trades of the United Kingdom with report thereon. [C. 5807] H.C. (1889). LXX, 843.

Suppl. by *Return of rates of wages in the minor textile trades* . . . [C. 6161] H.C. (1890). LXVIII, 689. For further returns see **6568**.

6717  CHAPMAN (*Sir* SYDNEY JOHN) *and* MARQUIS (FREDERICK JAMES), *Earl of Woolton*. 'The recruiting of the employing classes from the ranks of the wage-earners in the cotton industry'. *Roy. Stat. Soc. J.* lxxv (1911–12), 293–306.

6718  PORTER (J. H.). 'Industrial peace in the cotton trade, 1875–1913'. *Yorkshire Bull.* xix (1967), 49–61.

6719  WOOD (GEORGE HENRY). The history of wages in the cotton trade during the past hundred years. Manch. 1910.

A famous pioneer work. Originally publ. as 'The statistics of wages in the United Kingdom during the nineteenth century: part xv. The cotton industry', *Roy. Stat. Soc. J.* lxxiii (1910), 39–58, 128–63, 283–315, 411–34, 585–626.

6720  JEWKES (JOHN) *and* GRAY (EDWARD MAYALL). Wages and labour in the Lancashire cotton spinning industry. Manch. 1935.

See also Edward Mayall Gray, 'Wage rates and earnings in cotton weaving', *Manch. Stat. Soc. Trans.* (1938–9). His *The weaver's wage . . .*, Manch. 1937, deals only with the 1930s.

6721  MERTTENS (FREDERICK). 'The hours and the cost of labour in the cotton industry at home and abroad'. *Manch. Stat. Soc. Trans.* (1893–4), 125–90.

6722  GIBSON (ROLAND). Cotton textile wages in the United States and Great Britain: a comparison of trends, 1860–1943. N.Y. 1948.

6723  BRIDGES (JOHN HENRY) *and* HOLMES (T.). Report to the Local Government Board on proposed changes in hours and ages of employment in textile factories. [C. 754] H.C. (1873). LV, 803.

Bridges and Edward Haydon Osborn also publ. *Report on the effects of heavy sizing in cotton weaving upon the health of the operatives employed.* [C. 3861] H.C. (1884). LXXII, 169.

6724  WARD. 'The diary of John Ward of Clitheroe, weaver, 1860–1864'. Ed. by Reginald Sharpe France. *Historic Soc. Lancs. & Ches. Trans.* cv (1953), 137–85.

Suppl. by Mary Brigg, ed., 'Life in East Lancashire, 1856–60: a newly-discovered diary of John O'Neil (John Ward), weaver of Clitheroe', ibid. cxx (1968), 87–133.

6725  CARNALL (GEOFFREY). 'Dickens, Mrs. Gaskell and the Preston strike [of 1853]'. *Victorian Studs.* viii (1964–5), 31–48.

6726  GUTTERIDGE. Lights and shadows in the life of an artisan. By Joseph Gutteridge. Coventry. 1893.

The autobiog. of a Coventry ribbon weaver, which is repr. in Valerie Edith Chancellor, ed., *Master and artisan in Victorian England: the diary of William Andrews and the autobiography of Joseph Gutteridge*, 1969, both of which deal with the silk industry.

6727 OSBORN (EDWARD HAYDON). Reports made by direction of the secretary of state by E. H. Osborn, Esq., one of H.M. Inspectors of factories upon the conditions of work, &c., in flax mills and linen factories in the United Kingdom. [C. 7287] H.C. (1893–4). XVII, 537.

A full report. Suppl. by a short report by Sir Hamilton P. Freer-Smith in 1904. [Cd. 1997] H.C. (1904). X, 465, and a further one under the Factory and Workshop Act, 1901, by G. A. Bonner, *Spinning and weaving flax and tow and all processes incidental thereto*. [Cd. 2851] H.C. (1906). XV, 943. See also *Report of the departmental committee on humidity and ventilation in flax mills and linen factories* [Chairman: Sir Hamilton P. Freer-Smith]. [Cd. 7433] H.C. (1914). XXXVI, 1. Minutes of evidence. [Cd. 7446] H.C. (1914). XXXVI, 107.

6728 DOBBS (SEALEY PATRICK). The clothing workers of Great Britain. 1928.

Little pre-1914.

6729 HIBBERT COMMITTEE ON ROYAL ARMY CLOTHING FACTORY. Report of a committee of inquiry into the wages of operatives, &c. (appointed by the War Office to inquire whether the rates of wages given to women employed in the Royal Army Clothing Factory are fair in comparison with those paid by the trade; and whether the complaints made by certain of the operatives as to harsh treatment on discharge have any foundation in fact) [Chairman: John T. Hibbert]. [C. 2433] H.C. (1878–9). XV, 1.

### (ii) *Trade Unions*

6730 TURNER (HERBERT ARTHUR). Trade union growth, structure and policy: a comparative study of the cotton unions. 1962.

A full hist. which raises important theoretical issues.

6731 HOPWOOD (EDWIN). A history of the Lancashire cotton industry and the Amalgamated Weavers' Association: the Lancashire Weavers' story. Amalg. Weavers Assoc. Manch. 1969.

6732 CUTHBERT (NORMAN H.). The Lace Makers' Society: a study of trade unionism in the British lace industry, 1760–1960. Nottingham. 1960.

6733 FOX (ALAN). A history of the National Union of Boot and Shoe Operatives, 1874–1957. Oxf. 1958.

Replaced [Edward Lawrence Poulton] *Fifty years: being, the history of the National Union of Boot & Shoe Operatives, 1874–1924*, 1924.

### (d) *Coal Mining*
#### (i) *General*

6734 WILLIAMS (JAMES ECCLES). 'Labour in the coalfields: a critical bibliography'. *Soc. for the Study of Labour Hist. Bull.* iv (1962), 24–32. Discussion. Ibid. v (1962), 44–54.

Chiefly on trades unions.

6735  TAYLOR (ARTHUR JOHN). 'Combination in the mid-nineteenth century coal industry'. *Roy. Hist. Soc. Trans.* 5 ser. iii (1953), 23–9.

See also D. Jeffrey Williams, *Capitalist combination in the coal industry,* 1924.

6736  TAYLOR (ARTHUR JOHN). 'Labour productivity and technological innovation in the British coal industry, 1850–1914'. *Econ. Hist. Rev.* 2 ser. xiv (1961–2), 48–70.

6737  RAYNES (JOHN R.). Coal and its conflicts: a brief record of the disputes between capital & labour in the coal-mining industry of Great Britain. 1928.

Mainly from 1890 to 1928. There is an interesting account of an important strike in Sir Dennis Holme Robertson, 'A narrative of the coal strike', *Econ. J.* xxii (1912), 365–87.

6738  McCORMICK (BRIAN J.) *and* WILLIAMS (JAMES ECCLES). 'The miners and the eight-hour day, 1863–1910'. *Econ. Hist. Rev.* 2 ser. xii (1959–60), 222–38.

See also Cornelius McLeod Percy, *Miners and the eight hours' movement,* Wigan 1891.

6739  REA COMMITTEE ON MINERS' EIGHT-HOUR DAY. First report of the departmental committee appointed to inquire into the probable economic effect of a limit of eight hours to the working day of coal miners [Chairman: Russell Rea]. [Cd. 3426] H.C. (1907). XIV, 525. Minutes of evidence. [Cd. 3427] H.C. (1907). XIV, 529 and [Cd. 3428] H.C. (1907). XV, 1. Final report. [Cd. 3505] H.C. (1907). XV, 261. Minutes of evidence etc. [Cd. 3506] H.C. (1907). XV, 349.

6740  ROWE (JOHN WILKINSON FOSTER). Wages in the coal industry. 1923.

A hist. See also Bowley (**6539**).

6741  RICHARDSON (THOMAS) *and* WALBANK (JOHN ARTHUR). Profits and wages in the British coal trade (1898 to 1910). Newcastle-upon-Tyne. 1911.

Advocates a minimum wage.

6742  GIFFEN (*Sir* ROBERT). Return of rates of wages in the mines and quarries in the United Kingdom, with report thereon. [C. 6455] H.C. (1890–1). LXXVIII, 569.

For later returns see **33–4**.

6743  HOOKER (R. H.). 'On the relation between wages and the numbers employed in the coal-mining industry'. *Roy. Stat. Soc. J.* lvii (1894), 627–42.

6744  ASHLEY (*Sir* WILLIAM JAMES). The adjustment of wages: a study in the coal and iron industries of Great Britain and America. 1903.

6745 MUNRO (JOSEPH EDWIN CRAWFORD). Sliding scales in the coal industry: a paper read before the British Association, section F, Aberdeen 1885. Manch. 1885.

See also his 'Sliding scales in the coal and iron industries from 1885 to 1889', *Manch. Stat. Soc. Trans.* (1889–90), 119–71.

6746 TREMENHEERE (HUGH SEYMOUR). Report of the commissioner appointed under the provisions of the Act 5 & 6 Vict. c. 99, to inquire into the operation of that Act, and into the state of the population in the mining districts, 1853. [1679] H.C. (1852–3). XL, 759.

The first of a ser. of annual reports, chiefly on the North-Eastern mining region, publ. until 1859.

6747 [LEIFCHILD (JOHN R.).] Our coal and our coal-pits: the people in them, and the scenes around them. By 'A traveller underground'. 2 pts. 1853. 2nd edn. 1857. Repr. 1968.

See also his *On coal at home and abroad: with relation to consumption, cost, demand and supply* . . . *being three articles contributed to the 'Edinburgh Review'*, 1873.

6748 GIRDLESTONE (CHARLES). The South Staffordshire colliery district: its evils and its cure: two letters . . . . Stourbridge. 1855.

A good pamphlet. Cp. with Ignotus, *The last thirty years in a mining district: or, scotching and the candle versus lamp and trades-unions*, 1867.

6749 NASSE (R.) *and* KRÜMMER (G.). Die Bergarbeiter-Verhältnisse in Grossbritannien. Saarbrücken. 1891.

6750 LLOYD (ALBERT LANCASTER) *comp.* Come all ye bold miners: ballads and songs of the coalfields. 1952.

(ii) *Trade Unions*

6751 GUGLIELMI (JEAN LOUIS). Naissance et formation des trade unions des mineurs en Grande-Bretagne, 1843–1919. Paris. 1952.

6752 ARNOT (ROBERT PAGE). The miners: a history of the Miners' Federation of Great Britain, 1889–1910. 1949.

Cont. in his *The miners: years of struggle* . . . [1910–30], 1953, and *The miners: in crisis and war* . . . [1930+], 1961.

6753 WELBOURNE (EDWARD). The miners' unions of Northumberland and Durham. Camb. 1923.

Covers the period to 1906–7. See also Richard Fynes, *The miners of Northumberland and Durham: a history of their social and political progress*, Blyth 1873, new edn. Sunderland 1923; John Wilson, *A history of the Durham Miners' Association, 1870–1904*, Durham 1907; Emil Auerbach, *Die Ordnung des Arbeitsverhältnisses in den Kohlengruben von Northumberland und Durham*, Schriften des Vereins für Sozialpolitik xlv, Leipzig 1890; and Sidney James Webb, Baron Passfield, *The story of the Durham miners (1662–1921)*, 1921. For the two most famous north-eastern miners' leaders, Thomas Burt and John Wilson, see (**6758**) and (**6759**). There is little on the pre-1914 period in John James Lawson, Baron Lawson, *Peter Lee*, 1936, repr. 1949.

6754 MACHIN (FRANK). The Yorkshire miners: a history. V. 1. Barnsley. 1958.

For the Lancashire miners see Raymond Challinor, *The Lancashire and Cheshire miners*, Newcastle-upon-Tyne 1972.

6755 WILLIAMS (JAMES ECCLES). The Derbyshire miners: a study in industrial and social history. 1962.

See also his 'The political activities of a trade union, 1906–1914', *Int. Rev. Soc. Hist.* ii (1957), 1–21.

6756 GRIFFIN (ALAN RAMSAY). The miners of Nottinghamshire: a history of the Nottinghamshire Miners' Association. Vol. I. 1881–1914. Nottingham. 1956.

Cont. in his *The miners of Nottinghamshire, 1914–1944 . . .*, 1962.

6757 HALLAM (WILLIAM) *ed.* Miners' leaders: thirty portraits and biographical sketches. 1894.

6758 BURT. Thomas Burt, M.P., D.C.L., pitman & privy councillor: an autobiography with supplementary chapters by Aaron Watson. 1924.

Watson also publ. *A great labour leader: being a life of the Right Hon. Thomas Burt, M.P.*, 1908. Burt led the Northumberland miners, 1865–1913, and was one of the first two working-class M.P.s in 1874.

6759 WILSON. Memories of a labour leader: the autobiography of John Wilson, J.P., M.P. 1910.

The leader of the Durham miners.

6760 SMITH. The man in the cap: the life of Herbert Smith. By John James Lawson, Baron Lawson. 1941.

The leader of the Yorkshire miners.

MABON. For the leader of the South Wales miners see (**9697**).

SMILLIE. For Robert Smillie, the leader of the Scottish miners, who became president of the Miners' Federation, 1912, see (**632**).

6761 HODGES. My adventures as a Labour leader. By Frank Hodges. [1925.]
Thin.

### (e) *Metals, Engineering, Building, and Ceramics*

6762 ODBER (A. J.). 'The origins of industrial peace: the manufactured iron trade of the North of England'. *Oxf. Econ. Papers* new ser. iii (1951), 202–20.

6763 PORTER (J. H.). 'Management, competition and industrial relations: the Midlands manufactured iron trade, 1873–1914'. *Business Hist.* xi (1969), 37–47.

6764 MUNRO (JOSEPH EDWIN CRAWFORD). 'Sliding scales in the iron industry'. *Manch. Stat. Soc. Trans.* (1885–6), 1–43.

See also his 'Sliding scales in the coal and iron industries from 1885 to 1889', ibid. (1889–90), 119–71.

6765 POLLARD (SIDNEY). 'Wages and earnings in the Sheffield trades, 1851–1914'. *Yorkshire Bull.* vi (1954), 49–64.

See also his 'Real earnings in Sheffield, 1851–1914', *Yorkshire Bull.* ix (1957), 54–62.

6766 BURNETT (JOHN). Report as to the condition of nail makers and small chain makers in South Staffordshire and East Worcestershire. H.C. 385 (1888). XCI, 459.

6767 TAWNEY (RICHARD HENRY). The establishment of minimum rates in the chain-making industry under the Trade Boards Act of 1909. 1914.

A survey.

6768 HATCH COMMITTEE ON CHECKWEIGHING IN IRON AND STEEL TRADES. Report of the departmental committee on checkweighing in the iron and steel trades [Chairman: Ernest F. G. Hatch]. [Cd. 3846] H.C. (1908). XI, 691. Minutes of evidence. [Cd. 3847] H.C. (1908). XI, 707.

The committee investigated trade union representations on the subject at considerable length. Similar committees, on checkweighing in chalk quarries and cement works and in limestone quarries and lime works, with the same chairman, are reported in [Cd. 4002] H.C. (1908). XI, 843.

6769 MAKEMSON (T.). The first half century: the history of the Institute of British Foundrymen, 1804–1954. 1954.

6770 [PUGH (*Sir* ARTHUR).] Men of steel: by one of them: a chronicle of eighty-eight years of trade unionism in the British iron and steel industry. Iron and Steel Trades Confed. 1951.

6771 OWEN (JACK). Ironmen: a short story of the history of the union. National Union of Blastfurnacemen, Ore Miners, Coke Workers and Kindred Trades. Middlesbrough. 1953.

6772 FYRTH (HUBERT JIM) *and* COLLINS (HENRY). The foundry workers: a trade union history. Manch. 1959.

6773 KIDD (A. T.). History of the Tin-Plate Workers and Sheet-Metal Workers and Braziers Societies. 1949.

6774 LUDLOW (JOHN MALCOLM FORBES). The master engineers and their workmen: three lectures on the relations of capital and labour . . . 1852.

6775 JEFFERYS (MARGOT) *and* JEFFERYS (JAMES BAVINGTON). 'The wages, hours and trade customs of the skilled engineer in 1861'. *Econ. Hist. Rev.* xvii (1947), 27–44.

6776 SPICER (ROBERT S.). British engineering wages. 1928.

Covers 1850–1927. See also Morris Lord Yates, *Wages and labour conditions in British engineering*, 1937.

6777 BURGESS (KEITH). 'Technological change and the 1852 lockout in the British engineering industry'. *Int. Rev. Soc. Hist.* xiv (1969), 215–36.

6778 CLARKE (R. O.). 'The dispute in the British engineering industry, 1897–98: an evaluation'. *Economica* new ser. xxiv (1957), 128–36.

6779 JEFFERYS (JAMES BAVINGTON). The story of the engineers, 1800–1945. 1946.

6780 MORTIMER (JAMES EDWARD). A history of the Association of Engineering and Shipbuilding Draughtsmen. Priv. pub. 1960.

Founded 1913.

6781 MINISTRY OF WORKS (CHIEF SCIENTIFIC ADVISER'S DIVISION, ECONOMICS RESEARCH SECTION). Wages, earnings and negotiating machinery in the building industry, 1886–1948. [1949.]

6782 DEARLE (NORMAN BURRELL). Problems of unemployment in the London building trades. Toynbee Trust essay. 1908.

6783 POSTGATE (RAYMOND WILLIAM). The builders' history. 1923.

A pioneer trade union hist. Suppl. by S. Higenbottam, *Our society* [Amalg. Soc. of Woodworkers]: *history*, Manch. 1939, and T. J. Connelly, *The Woodworkers, 1860–1960: Amalgamated Society of Woodworkers*, 1960.

6784 HILTON (WILLIAM SAMUEL). Foes to tyranny: a history of the Amalgamated Union of Building Trade Workers. 1963.

6785 NEWMAN (JAMES ROBERT). The N.A.O.P. heritage: a short historical review of the growth and development of the National Association of Operative Plasterers, 1860–1960. Wembley. 1960.

6786 FRENCH (JOHN OLIVER). Plumbers in unity: history of the Plumbing Trades Union, 1865–1965. 1965.

6787 BOCH (ROGER VON). Geschichte der Töpferarbeiter von Staffordshire im 19. Jahrhundert. Münchener Volkswirtschaftliche Studien no. 31. Stuttgart. 1899.

6788 POTTERIES COMMITTEE. Report to Her Majesty's principal secretary of state for the Home Department on the conditions of labour in potteries, the injurious effects upon the health of the workpeople, and the proposed remedies by the Potteries Committee of Enquiry [Chairman: Samuel W. May]. [C. 7240]. H.C. (1893–4). XVII, 41.

6789 OWEN (HAROLD). The Staffordshire potter. 1901.
A useful study of wages and living conditions.

6790 HATCH COMMITTEE ON DANGER FROM LEAD IN POT-
TERIES. Report of the departmental committee appointed to inquire into
the dangers attendant on the use of lead and the danger or injury to health
arising from dust and other causes in the manufacture of earthenware and
china . . . [Chairman: Sir Ernest F. G. Hatch.] [Cd. 5219] H.C. (1910).
XXIX, 85. Appendixes. [Cd. 5278] H.C. (1910). XXIX, 245. Minutes of
evidence. [Cd. 5385] H.C. (1910). XXIX, 385.
A good example of the type of technical inquiry which was carried on by the Home
Office in the decade before 1914. For other inquiries see 33–4.

6791 WARBURTON (WILLIAM HENRY). The history of trade-union
organisation in the North Staffordshire potteries. 1931.

(f) *Transport*

6792 JEUNE COMMITTEE ON MERCANTILE MARINE. Report of the
committee appointed by the Board of Trade to inquire into certain questions
affecting the mercantile marine [Chairman: Sir Francis Jeune]. [Cd. 1607]
H.C. (1903). LXII, 1. Minutes of evidence. [Cd. 1608) H.C. (1903). LXII, 15.
Appendixes. [Cd. 1609] H.C. (1903). LXII, 737.
On conditions for seamen on British ships and the growing use of lascars and foreign
seamen. There is also useful material in *Report of a committee appointed by the Board
of Trade on the question of continuous discharge certificates for seamen* [Chairman: the
Earl of Dudley]. [Cd. 133] H.C. (1900). LXXVII, 99. Minutes of evidence. [Cd. 136]
H.C. (1900). LXXVII, 107.

6793 KEARLEY COMMITTEE ON BOY SEAMEN. Report of the committee appointed by the Board of Trade to inquire into the supply & training
of boy seamen for the mercantile marine [Chairman: Hudson E. Kearley].
[Cd. 3722] H.C. (1907). LXXV, 167. Minutes of evidence. [Cd. 3723] H.C.
(1907). LXXV, 179.
A big inquiry.

6794 WILSON. My stormy voyage through life. By Joseph Havelock Wilson.
1925.
The leader of the National Sailors' and Firemen's Union.

6795 MOGRIDGE (BASIL). 'Militancy and inter-union rivalries in British
shipping, 1911–1929'. *Int. Rev. Soc. Hist.* vi (1961), 375–412.

6796 BOOTH (CHARLES). 'London riverside labour'. *Roy. Stat. Soc. J.*
lv (1892), 521–57.
See also George Pattison, 'Nineteenth-century dock labour in the port of London',
*Mariner's Mirror* lii (1966), 263–79.

6797   HATCH COMMITTEE ON DOCKPIECE-WORK. Departmental committee on the checking of piece-work wages in dock labour [Chairman: Ernest F. G. Hatch]. Report. [Cd. 4380] H.C. (1908). XXXIV, 467. Minutes of evidence. [Cd. 4381] H.C. (1908). XXXIV, 497.

6798   CLARKE (*Sir* EDWARD). Report upon the present disputes affecting transport workers in the port of London and in the Medway. [Cd. 6229] H.C. (1912–13). XLVII, 247.
The report of a court of inquiry.

6799   HOBSBAWM (ERIC JOHN ERNEST). 'National unions on the water-side'. Repr. in his Labouring men. 1964.

6800   LOVELL (JOHN CHRISTOPHER). Stevedores and dockers: a study of trade unionism in the port of London, 1870–1914. 1969.

6801   SMITH (*Sir* HUBERT LLEWELYN) *and* NASH (VAUGHAN). The story of the dockers' strike . . . [1889.]

6802   TILLETT (BENJAMIN). History of the London transport workers' strike, 1911. 1912.

6803   GOSLING. Up and down stream. By Harry Gosling. 1927.
The leader of the London lightermen.

6804   TILLETT. Memories and reflections. By Benjamin Tillett. 1931.
One of the most prominent leaders of the London dockers.

6805   SEXTON. Sir James Sexton, agitator: the life of the dockers' M.P. An autobiography. 1936.
The leader of the Liverpool dockers.

6806   BEVIN. The life and times of Ernest Bevin. Vol. I. Trade union leader, 1881–1940. By Sir Alan Louis Charles Bullock. 1960.
Useful on horse-transport workers.

6807   KINGSFORD (PETER WILFRED). Victorian railwaymen: the emergence and growth of railway labour, 1830–1870. 1970.
See also his 'Labour relations on the railways, 1835–1875', *J. Transport Hist.* i (1953–4), 65–81.

6808   HICKS BEACH COMMITTEE ON RAILWAY SERVANTS. Report from the select committee on railway servants (hours of labour) [Chairman: Sir Michael Hicks Beach]. H.C. 342 (1890–1). XVI, 1. Special report. H.C. 125 (1892–Sess. I). XVI, 1. Report. H.C. 246 (1892–Sess. I). XVI, 123.

6809   ASKWITH (GEORGE RANKEN), *Baron Askwith*. Report to the Board of Trade upon matters connected with the establishment and working of railway conciliation boards, set up in accordance with the agreement of the 6th November, 1907. [Cd. 4534] H.C. (1909). LXXVII, 73.

6810 HARREL COMMISSION ON RAILWAY CONCILIATION SCHEME. Report of the royal commission appointed to investigate and report on the working of the railway conciliation and arbitration scheme of 1907 [Chairman: Sir David Harrel]. [Cd. 5922] H.C. (1911). XXIX, pt. 1, 663. Evidence. [Cd. 6014] H.C. (1912–13). XLV, 87.

6811 KENNEY (ROWLAND). Men and rails. 1913.
On the exploitation of railwaymen since the founding of the railway system.

6812 GUPTA (P. S.). 'Railway trade unionism in Britain, c. 1880–1900'. *Econ. Hist. Rev.* 2 ser. xix (1966), 124–53.

6813 BAGWELL (PHILIP SIDNEY). The railwaymen: the history of the National Union of Railwaymen. 1963.
Full. See also his 'An early attempt at national organization of the railwaymen, 1865–1867', *J. Transport Hist.* iii (1957–8), 94–102, and George Douglas Howard Cole and Robert Page Arnot, *Trade unionism on the railways: its history and problems*, Fabian Research Dept., 1917.

6814 ALCOCK (GEORGE W.). Fifty years of railway trade unionism. 1922.
Useful for period flavour, as is also Alcock's, *The life of John H. Dobson, ex-organiser, National Union of Railwaymen*, 1921.

6815 McKILLOP (NORMAN). The lighted flame: a history of the Associated Society of Locomotive Engineers and Firemen. 1950.
Repl. John R. Raynes, *Engines and men: the history of the Associated Society of Locomotive Engineers and Firemen*, Leeds 1921.

6816 COLEMAN (TERRY). The railway navvies: a history of the men who made the railways. 1965.

6817 NATIONAL UNION OF VEHICLE BUILDERS. A hundred years of vehicle building, 1834–1934. Manch. [1934.]

(g) *Other Occupations*

6818 HOBSBAWM (ERIC JOHN ERNEST). 'British gas-workers, 1873–1914'. Repr. in his Labouring men. 1964.

6819 POPPLEWELL (FRANK). 'Seasonal fluctuations in employment in the gas industry'. *Roy. Stat. Soc. J.* lxxiv (1910–11), 693–730.

6820 MANSFIELD (FREDERICK JOHN). 'Gentlemen of the press!' Chronicles of a crusade. Official history of the National Union of Journalists. [1943.]
See also Clement James Bundock, *The National Union of Journalists: a jubilee history, 1907–1957,* 1957.

6821 CHILD (JOHN). Industrial relations in the British printing industry: the quest for security. 1967.

6822 HOWE (ELLIC). The British Federation of Master Printers, 1900–1950. 1950.

6823 BUNDOCK (CLEMENT JAMES). The story of the National Union of Printing, Bookbinding and Paper Workers. 1959.

6824 HOWE (ELLIC) *and* WAITE (HAROLD EDWARD). The London Society of Compositors: a centenary history. 1948.

6825 HOWE (ELLIC) *and* CHILD (JOHN). The Society of London Bookbinders, 1780–1951. 1952.

6826 HOWE (ELLIC) *ed.* The London compositor: documents relating to wages, working conditions and customs of the London printing trade, 1785–1900. Bibliog. Soc. 1947.

6827 MUSSON (ALBERT EDWARD). The Typographical Association: origins and history up to 1949. Oxf. 1954.

6828 GILLESPIE (SARAH C.). A hundred years of progress: the record of the Scottish Typographical Association, 1853 to 1952. Glasgow. 1953.

6829 MORAN (JAMES). Natsopa seventy-five years: the National Society of Operative Printers and Assistants, 1889–1964. 1964.

6830 CHEMICAL WORKS COMMITTEE OF INQUIRY. Report to Her Majesty's principal secretary of state for the home department on the conditions of labour in chemical works, the dangers to life and health of the workpeople employed therein, and the proposed remedies, by the chemical works committee of inquiry [Chairman: William Dawkins Cramp]. [C. 7235] H.C. (1893–4). XVII, 1. Further report on Lucifer match works. [C. 7236] H.C. (1893–4). XVII, 1197.

6831 STAFFORD (ANN) *pseud. of* PEDLAR (ANN). A match to fire the Thames. (The match girls' strike of 1888: the dockers' strike of 1889.) 1961.

6832 MARSHALL (DOROTHY). The English domestic servant in history. Hist. Assoc. General ser. G13. 1949.

6833 LAYTON (WALTER THOMAS), *Baron Layton.* 'Changes in the wages of domestic servants during fifty years'. *Roy. Stat. Soc. J.* lxxi (1908), 515–24.
See also Clara Elizabeth Collet, *Report on the money wages of indoor domestic servants.* [C. 9346] H.C. (1899). XCII, 1.

6834 TURNER (ERNEST SACKVILLE). What the butler saw: two hundred and fifty years of the servant problem. Lond. 1962. N.Y. 1963.

Popular. There are a number of servant memoirs, of which Eric Horne, *What the butler winked at* . . . [1923], and William Lanceley, *From hall-boy to house-steward*, 1925, are quite good.

6835 HOFFMAN (PHILIP CHRISTOPHER). They also serve: the story of the shop worker. 1949.

6836 SUTHERST (THOMAS). Death and disease behind the counter. 1884.

6837 HALLSWORTH (*Sir* JOSEPH) *and* DAVIES (RHYS JOHN). The working life of shop assistants: a study of conditions of labour in the distributive trades. Manch. 1910.

6838 PAINE (WILLIAM). Shop slavery and emancipation: a revolutionary appeal to the educated young men of the middle class. 1912.

6839 AVEBURY COMMITTEE ON EARLY CLOSING OF SHOPS. Report from the select committee of the House of Lords on early closing of shops [Chairman: Lord Avebury]. H.C. 369 (1901). VI, 1.

Recommended restrictions on the hours during which shops might open, in order to protect shop-workers.

6840 HUGHES (FRED). By hand and brain: the story of the Clerical and Administrative Workers' Union. 1953.

6841 WARD COMMITTEE ON EX-SOLDIERS AND SAILORS. Report of committee on civil employment of ex-soldiers and sailors [Chairman: Sir Edward Ward]. [Cd. 2991] H.C. (1906). XIV, 143. Minutes of evidence. [Cd. 2992] H.C. (1906). XIV, 221.

## I. CO-OPERATION

6842 ALLIANCE COOPÉRATIVE INTERNATIONALE. Bibliographie coopérative internationale. 1906.

See also John B. Smethurst, comp., *A bibliography of co-operative societies' histories*, Manch. [1973.] The main sources are the bulky *Proceedings* of the annual Co-operative Congress, Manch. 1869+, the Co-operative Wholesale Societies Ltd., *Annual*, Manch. 1883–1918, and the detailed stats. and lists of socs. publ. by the Chief Registrar of Friendly Societies.

6843 COLE (GEORGE DOUGLAS HOWARD). A century of co-operation. Manch. 1944. 2nd edn. 1946.

The best single book on the subject, but needs revision. See also Sidney Pollard, 'Nineteenth-century co-operation', in *Essays in labour hist.* (**6460**), Bert James Youngjohns, *Co-operation and the state, 1814–1914*, Loughborough 1954, and Desmond J. Flanagan, *1869–1969: a centenary story of the Co-operative Union of Great Britain and Ireland*, Manch. 1969.

6844 BONNER (ARNOLD). British co-operation: the history, principles and organisation of the British co-operative movement. Manch. 1961. Rev. edn. 1970.

A popular textbook for co-operators. Repl. Catherine Webb, ed., *Industrial co-operation* . . ., Manch. 1904, 10th edn. 1926, and Fred Hall and William Pascoe Watkins, *Co-operation* . . ., Manch. 1934. There are two outline hists. which cover the same ground, Paul Greer, *Co-operatives: the British achievement*, N.Y. 1955, and Jack Bailey, *The British co-operative movement*, 1955, 2nd edn. 1960.

6845 HOLYOAKE (GEORGE JACOB). The history of co-operation in England: its literature and its advocates. 2 v. Manch. 1875-7. Rev. edn. 2 v. 1906.

A first-hand account of great hist. importance. Holyoake also publ. *The co-operative movement to-day*, 1891; *Self-help by the people: history of co-operation in Rochdale*, 1858, 10th edn. 1893, and other local hists.

6846 POTTER, *afterwards* WEBB (BEATRICE). The co-operative movement in Great Britain. 1891. 4th imp. 1899. New edn. 1930.

The first reasonably dispassionate account of the movement. For other short accounts see Thomas Hughes and Edward Vansittart Neale, eds., *A manual for co-operators*, Manch. 1881; Sir Arthur Herbert Dyke Acland and Benjamin Jones, *Working-men co-operators* . . ., 1884, 9th edn. Manch. 1945; Ugo Rabbeno, *La cooperazione in Inghilterra* . . ., Milan 1885; and Joseph Cernesson, *Les sociétés coopératives anglaises*, Paris 1905.

6847 BOARD OF TRADE (LABOUR DEPARTMENT). Report on industrial and agricultural co-operative societies in the United Kingdom. [Cd. 698] H.C. (1901). LXXIV, 463. Further report. [Cd. 6045] H.C. (1912-13). LXXV, 441.

Careful reports, with bibliogs. The only other general inquiry was never completed, but took evidence. See *Report from the select committee on co-operative stores* [Chairman: Sir Massey Lopes]. H.C. 344 (1878-9). IX, 1.

6848 FAY (CHARLES RYLE). Co-operation at home and abroad: a description and analysis. Camb. 1908. 5th edn. 1948. Suppl. [vol. II] Camb. 1939. 2nd edn. 1948.

Fay and the Board of Trade reports together give a pretty full account of 20th-cent. co-operation. There is little more in Sidney James Webb, Baron Passfield, and Beatrice Webb, *The consumers' co-operative movement*, 1921, and Sir Alexander Morris Carr-Saunders and others, *Consumers' co-operation in Great Britain* . . ., 1938, rev. edn. 1942.

6849 HOOD (JULIA) *and* YAMEY (BASIL SELIG). 'The middle-class retailing societies in London, 1864-1900'. *Oxf. Econ. Papers* new ser. ix (1957), 309-22.

Chiefly on the Civil Service Supply Assoc.

6850 HOPKINS (O. T.). Working expenses in retail distributive co-operative societies: with a review of the changes during the period, 1897-1920, and of the causes affecting the same. Manch. 1921.

6851 HOUGH (JOHN ASPEY). Dividend on co-operative purchases: a study of dividend on purchases as an element in co-operative trading, with special reference to the British consumers' co-operative movement. Manch. 1936.

6852 REDFERN (PERCY). The new history of the C.W.S. Lond. & Manch. 1938.

Repl. his *The story of the C.W.S.: the jubilee history of the Co-operative Wholesale Society Limited, 1863–1913*, Manch. 1913.

6853 JONES (BENJAMIN). Co-operative production. 2 v. Oxf. 1894.

The best substitute for a hist. See also Co-operative Production Federation, *Co-operator's year book*, Leics. 1897+.

6854 LLOYD (HENRY DEMAREST). Labor copartnership: notes of a visit to co-operative workshops, factories and farms in Great Britain and Ireland, in which employer, employé and consumer share in ownership, management and results. N.Y. & Lond. 1898.

Very useful.

6855 BOARD OF TRADE (LABOUR DEPARTMENT). Report [by D. F. Schloss] on contracts given out by public authorities to associations of work-men. [C. 8233] H.C. (1896). LXXX, pt. II, 229.

6856 WEBB (CATHERINE). The woman with the basket: the history of the Women's Co-operative Guild, 1883–1927. Manch. 1927.

See also Margaret Llewelyn Davies, ed., *Life as we have known it: by co-operative working women*, 1931.

6857 GREENING. Edward Owen Greening: a maker of modern co-operation. By Tom Crimes. Manch. 1923.

6858 JACKSON. Service for democracy: or, fifty years with the C.W.S. By Edward Jackson. Manch. 1937.

6859 MAXWELL. Sir William Maxwell: a pioneer of national and inter-national co-operation. By Sydney R. Elliott. Manch. 1923.

6860 MITCHELL. John T. W. Mitchell: pioneer of consumers' co-operation. By Percy Redfern. Manch. 1923.

6861 NEALE. Memorial of Edward Vansittart Neale, general secretary of the Co-operative Union, 1875–1891. Comp. by Henry Pitman. Manch. 1894.

# VIII

## SOCIAL HISTORY

### A. GENERAL

6862   PERKIN (HAROLD JAMES). The origins of modern English society, 1780–1880. Lond. & Toronto. 1969.

One of the few general scholarly books of English social hist. Judith Ryder and Harold Silver, *Modern English society: history and structure, 1850–1970*, 1970, is interesting as the combined work of a sociologist and a historian. The *J. of social hist.*, 1+, Berkeley 1967+, is committed to developing the field.

6863   BEST (GEOFFREY FRANCIS ANDREW). Mid-Victorian Britain, 1851–1875. 1971.

The first vol. of a new series. Good.

6864   TREVELYAN (GEORGE MACAULAY). Illustrated English social history. Vol. IV. The nineteenth century. 1952.

Celebrated, but out of date. The first social hist. of the Victorian period was Henry Duff Traill and James Saumarez Mann, ed., *Social England: a record of the progress of the people in religion, laws, learning, arts, industry, commerce, science, literature and manners*: vol. VI: *from the battle of Waterloo to the general election of 1855*, 1897, illus. edn. 1904, which is in many ways inferior to the comparable works of Humphry Ward and Escott, **186.**

6865   FAY (CHARLES RYLE). Life and labour in the nineteenth century . . . Camb. 1920. 4th edn. 1947.

An interesting early attempt at a difficult genre. Cp. Thomas Kingston Derry and Thomas Leckie Jarman, *The making of modern Britain: life and work from George III to Elizabeth II*, 1956, Pauline Gregg, *A social and economic history of Britain, 1760–1950*, 1950, 6th edn. 1971, and William Joseph Reader, *Life in Victorian England*, 1964.

6866   COLE (GEORGE DOUGLAS HOWARD) *and* POSTGATE (RAYMOND). The common people, 1746–1938. New edn. [1746–1946.] 1946. Publ. in N.Y. as The British people.

A good socialist hist. Much influenced by the work of John Lawrence Le Breton Hammond and Lucy Barbara Hammond, whose chief work on the mid-19th cent. was *The age of the Chartists, 1832–1854: a study of discontent*, 1930, repr. Hamden, Conn. 1962. There is an interesting comparison with John Malcolm Ludlow and Lloyd Jones, *The progress of the working class, 1832–1867*, 1867.

6867   QUENNELL (MARJORIE) *and* QUENNELL (CHARLES HENRY BOURNE). A history of everyday things in England. Vol. IV. 1851–1914. 1931. 6th edn. 1960.

Popular, as is Peter Courtney Quennell, *Victorian panorama: a survey of life & fashion from contemporary photographs*, 1937, and Dorothy Constance Peel [Mrs. Charles Stuart Peel], *A hundred wonderful years: social and domestic life of a century, 1820–1920*, 1926.

6868 ADBURGHAM (ALISON) *ed.* A *Punch* history of manners and modes, 1841–1940. 1961.

Interesting. Cp. James Laver, *The age of optimism: manners and morals, 1848–1914,* 1966, the works at **151–3**, Edgar Royston Pike, ed., *Human documents of the Victorian golden age, 1850–1875,* 1967, publ. in N.Y. as *Golden times . . .,* and *Human documents of the age of the Forsytes,* 1969, publ. in N.Y. as *Busy times . . .,* 1970, and John Fletcher Clews Harrison, ed., *Society and politics in England, 1780–1960: a selection of readings and comments,* N.Y. 1965.

6869 BURNETT (JOHN). A history of the cost of living. Harmondsworth. 1969.

Sketchy. For diet see **5670–5**, and for budgets **6542**.

6870 MARSH (DAVID CHARLES). The changing social structure of England and Wales, 1871–1951. 1958.

A careful inquiry.

6871 THOMAS (DOROTHY SWAINE). Social aspects of the business cycle. Lond. & N.Y. 1925.

A well-known pioneering work, which has not been followed up.

6872 COLE (GEORGE DOUGLAS HOWARD). Studies in class structure. 1955.

6873 BLOOMFIELD (PAUL). Uncommon people: a study of England's élite. 1955.

See also Annan (**8296**).

6874 THORNTON (ARCHIBALD PATON). The habit of authority: paternalism in British history. Toronto & Lond. 1966.

6875 WINGFIELD-STRATFORD (ESMÉ CECIL). The squire and his relations. 1956.

6876 KIRBY (CHESTER). The English country gentleman: a study of nineteenth century types. [1937.]

6877 SANFORD (JOHN LANGTON) *and* TOWNSEND (MEREDITH WHITE). The great governing families of England. 2 v. 1865.

6878 [ESCOTT (THOMAS HAY SWEET).] Society in London: by a foreign resident. N.Y. 1885. Lond. 1886.

Followed by *Society in the new reign: by a foreign resident,* 1904, also publ. anonymously. Outspoken comment of the 'gossip column' type ranging over all sections of London 'society'. Escott also publ. *Social transformations of the Victorian age: a survey of court and country,* 1897, *Society in the country house,* 1907, and many other works on the functioning of 'society'.

**6879 BRUDENELL-BRUCE (CHANDOS SYDNEY CEDRIC),** *Marquess of Ailesbury.* The wardens of Savernake Forest. 1949.

A hist. of one section of the Brudenell family. For another see Joan Wake, *The Brudenells of Deene*, 1953. For upper-class families see also Aubrey Norris Newman, *The Stanhopes of Chevening: a family biography*, 1969, Averil Stewart, *Family tapestry* [on the Vivian family], 1961, Victor Bonham-Carter, *In a Liberal tradition: a social biography, 1700–1950* [on the Carter and Bonham-Carter families], 1960, Nancy Freeman Mitford, ed., *The Stanleys of Alderley: their letters between the years 1851–1865*, 1939, new edn. 1968, and Gervas Huxley, *Victorian duke: the life of Hugh Lupus Grosvenor, first Duke of Westminster*, 1967. For a working-class family see Clarice Stella Davies, *North-country bred: a working-class family chronicle*, 1963.

**6880 COOPER (DIANA OLIVIA WINIFRED MAUD),** *Viscountess Norwich.* The rainbow comes and goes. 1958.

One of the better autobiogs. of upper-class life. Others are Lady Clodagh De La Poer Anson, *Victorian days*, 1957; Lady Cynthia Mary Evelyn Asquith, *Haply I may remember*, 1950; Consuelo Vanderbilt Balsan, *The glitter and the gold*, N.Y. 1952, Lond. 1953; Edward Frederic Benson, *As we were: a Victorian peep-show*, 1930; Reginald Brabazon, Earl of Meath, *Memories of the nineteenth century*, 1923, and *Memories of the twentieth century*, 1924; William John Arthur Charles James Cavendish-Bentinck, Duke of Portland, *Men, women and things: memories . . .*, 1937; Lionel Evelyn Oswald Charlton, ed., *The recollections of a Northumbrian lady, 1815–1866: being the memoirs of Barbara Charlton . . .*, 1949; George Frederick Myddleton Cornwallis-West, *Edwardian hey-days: or, a little about a lot of things*, 1930; Charles Gordon, Marquess of Huntly, *Travels, sport and politics . . .*, 1887, *Milestones*, 1926, and *Auld acquaintance*, 1929; Sir Lawrence Evelyn Jones, *A Victorian boyhood*, 1955, *An Edwardian youth*, 1956, *Georgian afternoon*, 1958, and *I forgot to tell you*, 1959; Sonia Rosemary Keppel, *Edwardian daughter*, 1958; Lord Ronald Charles Sutherland-Leveson-Gower, *My reminiscences*, 2 v. 1883, rev. edn. 1895, and *Old diaries, 1881–1901*, 1902; Lady Sybil Marjorie Lubbock, ed., *A page from the past: memories of the Earl of Desart, by himself and his daughter*, 1936; William Angus Drogo Montagu, Duke of Manchester, *My candid recollections*, 1932; Eustace Sutherland Campbell Percy, Baron Percy of Newcastle, *Some memories*, 1958; Sir Osbert Sitwell, *Left hand, right hand!*, Boston 1944, Lond. 1945, *The scarlet tree*, 1946, and *Great morning*, 1948, and Anna Maria Diana Wilhelmina Stirling, *Life's little day: some tales and other reminiscences*, 1924, and *Life's mosaic: memories canny and uncanny*, 1934. A few biogs. catch the eccentricity of one section of upper-class life, notably Charles Henry Roberts, *The radical countess: the history of the life of Rosalind, Countess of Carlisle*, Carlisle 1962, Lady Dorothy Georgiana Henley, *Rosalind Howard, Countess of Carlisle*, 1958, and Douglas Sutherland, *The yellow earl: the life of Hugh Lowther, 5th Earl of Lonsdale, K.G., G.C.V.O., 1857–1944*, Lond. & N.Y. 1966. See also the lives of the society hostesses at **894–906**, and *The Amberley papers* (**828**).

**6881 RUSSELL.** Collections and recollections: by one who has kept a diary [George William Erskine Russell.] 1898. 7th edn. 1904. Second ser. 1918.

The leading gossip-writer of the Edwardian period. See also his *A Londoner's log-book, 1901–1902*, 1902, *One look back*, 1912, *Afterthoughts*, 1912, *Half-lengths*, 1913, *Politics and personalities and other essays*, 1917, *Sketches and snapshots*, 1910, *Seeing and hearing*, 1907, and *Social silhouettes*, 1906, and many other autobiog. essays. For other gossip see [Julia Clara Byrne, Mrs. William Pitt Byrne] *Gossip of the century: personal and traditional memories, social, literary, artistic, &c.*, 2 v. 1892, and *Social hours with celebrities: being, the third and fourth volumes of 'Gossip of the century'*, 2 v. 1898; the recollections of Lady Dorothy Nevill (**901**); the works of her son Ralph Henry Nevill, incl. *The gay Victorians*, 1930; Horace Wyndham, *Society sensations*, 1938, *Feminine frailty . . .*, 1929, *The Mayfair calendar . . .*, 1930, *Blotted 'scutcheons . . .* [1926], *Victorian sensations*, 1933, *Victorian parade*, 1934, and *Chorus to coronet*, 1951; Charles Kingston [O'Mahony],

Society sensations, 1922; and Michael Harrison, *Painful details: twelve Victorian scandals*, Lond. & Toronto 1962. The most famous trials involving 'society' were the Tichborne and Druce–Portland cases, **3067–8**.

6882 HAMILTON. The vanished pomps of yesterday. 1919. The days before yesterday. 1920. Here, there and everywhere. 1921. [Collected edn. publ. as My yesterdays, 1930.] By Lord Frederick Spencer Hamilton.

One of the better accounts of diplomatic and social life.

6883 BANKS (JOSEPH AMBROSE). 'The way they lived then: Anthony Trollope and the 1870s'. *Victorian Studs.* xii (1968–9), 177–200.

6884 MOERS (ELLEN). The dandy: Brummell to Beerbohm. 1960.

6885 VANITY FAIR: a weekly show of political, social and literary wares. 1868–1929.

The best-known of the 'society' js., famous for its cartoons by Ape, Spy, etc. The other leading society js. were *The world: a journal for men and women*, 1874–1922, and *Truth: a weekly journal*, 1877+.

6886 LEWIS (ROY) *and* MAUDE (ANGUS EDMUND UPTON). The English middle classes. 1949.

6887 READER (WILLIAM JOSEPH). Professional men: the rise of the professional classes in nineteenth-century England. Lond. & N.Y. 1967.

6888 MILLERSON (GEOFFREY). The qualifying associations: a study in professionalisation. 1964.

6889 CARR-SAUNDERS (*Sir* ALEXANDER MORRIS) *and* WILSON (PAUL ALEXANDER). The professions. Oxf. 1933.

See also 'English teachers and their professional organisation', *New Statesman*, suppls. 25 Sept., 2 Oct. 1915, and 'Professional associations', ibid. 21 Apr., 28 Apr. 1917.

6890 HARRISON (BRIAN HOWARD). 'The Sunday trading riots of 1855'. *Hist. J.* viii (1965), 219–45.

Useful for the opposition to Sabbatarianism.

6891 MARTIN (ERNEST WALTER). Where London ends: English provincial life after 1750: being, an account of the English country town and the lives, works, and development of provincial people through a period of two hundred years. 1958.

See also his *The secret people* (**7015**).

6892 LOCHHEAD (MARION CLELAND). Their first ten years: Victorian childhood. 1956.

See also her *Young Victorians*, 1959, and *The Victorian household*, 1964, Frederic Gordon Roe, *The Victorian child*, 1959, and Eleanor Farjeon, *A nursery in the nineties*, 1960.

6893 COMINOS (PETER T.). 'Late Victorian sexual respectability and the social system'. *Int. Rev. Soc. Hist.* viii (1963), 18–48, 216–50.

6894 PEARSALL (RONALD). The worm in the bud: the world of Victorian sexuality. 1969.

Poor. See also Steven Marcus, *The other Victorians: a study of sexuality and pornography in mid-nineteenth-century England*, N.Y. & Lond. 1966, Brian Howard Harrison, 'Underneath the Victorians', *Victorian Studs.* x (1966–7), 239–62, and **7494–521**.

6895 FRYER (PETER). Mrs. Grundy: studies in English prudery. 1963.

6896 CHESNEY (KELLOW). The Victorian underworld. 1970. Publ. in Boston as The anti-society: an account of the Victorian underworld. 1970.

6897 READE (BRIAN) *ed.* Sexual heretics: male homosexuality in English literature from 1850 to 1900: an anthology. 1970.

See also Timothy D'Arch Smith, *Love in earnest: some notes on the lives and writings of English Uranian poets from 1889 to 1930*, 1970, and Edward Carpenter, *Love's coming of-age* . . ., 1896, 12th edn. 1923.

# B. POPULATION

## 1. GENERAL

6898 ELDRIDGE (HOPE TISDALE). The materials of demography: a selected and annotated bibliography. Internat. Union for the Scientific Study of Population, etc. N.Y. 1959.

An annotated bibliog. with abstracts.

6899 POPULATION INDEX. 1+. Princeton, N.J. 1935+. Annual.

6900 INTERDEPARTMENTAL COMMITTEE ON SOCIAL AND ECONOMIC RESEARCH. Guides to official sources 2: census reports of Great Britain, 1801–1931. H.M.S.O. 1951.

A guide to the decennial census. On the use of census data see Edward Anthony Wrigley, ed., *Nineteenth-century society: essays in the use of quantitative methods for the study of social data*, Camb. 1972.

6901 REGISTRAR GENERAL OF BIRTHS, DEATHS AND MARRIAGES. Annual report. 1837/8–1920. 1839–1922.

On the publ. stats. see David Victor Glass, 'A note on the under-registration of births in Britain in the nineteenth century', *Population Studs.* v (1951–2), 70–88.

6902 HOLLINGSWORTH (THOMAS HENRY). Historical demography. Lond. & Ithaca, N.Y. 1969.

Useful for background. See also Edward Anthony Wrigley, *Population and history*, N.Y. 1969, David Victor Glass and David Edward Charles Eversley, eds., *Population in history: essays in historical demography*, Lond. & Chicago 1965, and E. A. Wrigley, ed., *An introduction to English historical demography: from the sixteenth to the nineteenth century*, Lond. & N.Y. 1966.

6903 VIVIAN (*Sir* PERCIVAL SYLVANUS). The story of the General Register Office and its origins, from 1538 to 1937. 1937.

6904 POPULATION STUDIES: a quarterly journal of demography. 1947+.
The main source of articles.

6905 MARSHALL (THOMAS HUMPHREY). 'The population of England and Wales from the industrial revolution to the world war'. *Econ. Hist. Rev.* v, no. II (1934-5), 65-78. Repr. in Carus-Wilson, Essays (**4066**) I, 331-43.
A famous survey. See also David Victor Glass, 'Population movements in England and Wales', in his *Population policies and movements in Europe*, Oxf. 1940, 2nd edn. Lond. & N.Y. 1967, pp. 1-85.

6906 LASLETT (PETER). 'Size and structure of the household in England over three centuries'. *Population Studs.* xxiii (1969), 199-223.
Cp. Hrothgar John Habakkuk, 'Family structure and economic change in nineteenth-century Europe', *J. Econ. Hist.* xv (1955), 1-12.

6907 MATRAS (JUDAH). 'Social strategies of family formation: data for British female cohorts born 1831-1906'. *Population Studs.* xix (1965-6), 167-81.

6908 FARRAG (ABDELMEGID M.). 'The occupational structure of the labour force: patterns and trends in selected countries'. *Population Studs.* xviii (1964-5), 17-34.

6909 BOOTH (CHARLES). 'Occupations of the people of the United Kingdom, 1801-81'. *Roy. Stat. Soc. J.* xlix (1886), 314-435.

6910 CANNAN (EDWIN). 'The changed outlook in regard to population, 1831-1931'. *Econ. J.* xli (1931), 519-33.
The great debates over population took place before 1850. See on them David Edward Charles Eversley, *Social theories of fertility and the Malthusian debate*, Oxf. 1959, Harold Anderson Boner, *Hungry generations: the nineteenth century case against Malthusianism*, N.Y. 1955, and David Victor Glass, *Introduction to Malthus*, Lond. & N.Y. 1953, which incl. full bibliog.

6911 MICKLEWRIGHT (FREDERICK HENRY AMPHLETT). 'The rise and decline of English neo-Malthusianism'. *Population Studs.* xv (1961-2), 32-51.

6912 BANKS (JOSEPH AMBROSE). Prosperity and parenthood: a study of family planning among the Victorian middle classes. 1954.
See also Joseph Ambrose Banks and Olive Banks, *Feminism and family planning in Victorian England*, Liverpool 1964, N.Y. 1964.

6913 BANKS (JOSEPH AMBROSE) *and* BANKS (OLIVE). 'The Brad-laugh–Besant trial and the English newspapers'. *Population Studs.* viii (1954–5), 22–34.

For the trial see also *In the High Court of Justice, Queen's Bench Division, June 18th, 1877: The Queen* v. *Charles Bradlaugh and Annie Besant* . . . [1877.] Annie Besant's views on marriage are set out in her *Marriage: as it was, as it is, and as it should be*, ed. by Asa K. O. Butts, N.Y. 1879. See also the lives of Besant (**4023**) and Bradlaugh (**4008**).

6914 SPENGLER (JOSEPH JOHN). '[Alfred] Marshall on the population question'. *Population Studs.* viii (1954–5), 264–87; ix (1955–6), 56–66.

6915 KUCZYNSKI (ROBERT RENÉ). 'The international decline of fertility'. In Lancelot Thomas Hogben, ed., Political arithmetic: a symposium on population studs. 1938. Pp. 47–72.

The same vol. incl. two important papers by David Victor Glass, 'Changes in fertility in England and Wales, 1851 to 1931', ibid. 161–212, and 'Marriage frequency and economic fluctuations in England and Wales, 1851 to 1934', ibid. 251–82. See also William Henry Beveridge, Baron Beveridge, 'The fall of fertility among European races', *Economica* v (1925), 10–27. The declining birth-rate also provoked a series of important contemp. statistical inquiries, notably Sir Arthur Newsholme and Thomas Henry Craig Stevenson, 'The decline of human fertility in the United Kingdom and other countries, as shown by corrected birth-rates', *Roy. Stat. Soc. J.* lxix (1906), 34–87; George Udny Yule, 'On the changes in the marriage- and birth-rates in England and Wales during the past half century: with an inquiry as to their probable causes', ibid. lxix (1906), 88–132; Reginald Dudfield, 'Some unconsidered factors affecting the birth-rate', ibid. lxxi (1908), 1–55; Sir Arthur Newsholme, *The declining birth-rate: its national and international significance*, 1911; and Sir Jervoise Athelstane Baines, 'The recent trend of population in England and Wales', *Roy. Stat. Soc. J.* lxxix (1916), 399–417. There was also a privately-sponsored National Birth-Rate Commission, whose proceedings were reported in [Sir James Marchant, ed.] *The declining birth rate: its causes and effects: being, the report of* . . . *the National Birth-Rate Commission* . . ., 1916. A second vol. was publ. as *Problems of population and parenthood: being, the second report of* . . . *the National Birth-Rate Commission* . . ., 1920.

6916 CARRIER (NORMAN HENRY). 'An examination of generation fertility in England and Wales'. *Population Studs.* ix (1955–6), 3–23.

6917 INNES (JOHN WARWICK). Class fertility trends in England and Wales, 1876–1934. Princeton. 1938.

6918 STEVENSON (THOMAS HENRY CRAIG). 'The fertility of various social classes in England and Wales from the middle of the nineteenth century to 1911'. *Roy. Stat. Soc. J.* lxxxiii (1920), 401–32.

See also David Heron, *On the relation of fertility in man to social status and on the changes in this relation that have taken place during the last fifty years*, University College, London, Nat. Deterioration Studs., 1906. For an early exercise in class demography see Charles Ansell, *On the rate of mortality at early periods of life, the age of marriage, the number of children to a marriage, the length of a generation and other statistics of families in the upper and professional classes*, 1874, an inquiry made for the National Life Assurance Soc.

**6919  HOLLINGSWORTH (THOMAS HENRY).** 'A demographic study of the British ducal families'. *Population Studs.* xi (1957–8), 4–26.

See also his *The demography of the British peerage*, suppl. to *Population studs.* xviii (1964–5), pt. 2. An early inquiry in the field was Arthur Hutcheson Bailey and Archibald Day, 'On the rate of mortality prevailing amongst the families of the peerage during the nineteenth century', *Stat. Soc. J.* xxvi (1863), 49–71.

**6920  BROWNLEE (JOHN).** 'The history of the birth and death rates in England and Wales taken as a whole from 1570 to the present time'. *Public Health* xxix (1916), 211–22, 228–38.

**6921  GALTON (FRANCIS).** 'The relative supplies from town and country families, to the population of future generations'. *Stat. Soc. J.* xxxvi (1873), 19–26.

**6922  SARGANT (WILLIAM LUCAS).** 'On the vital statistics of Birmingham and seven other large towns'. *Stat. Soc. J.* xxix (1866), 92–111.

Cp. William Tite, 'On the comparative mortality of London and Paris', *Stat. Soc. J.* xxvii (1864), 479–91.

**6923  STOLNITZ (GEORGE J.).** 'A century of international mortality trends'. *Population Studs.* ix (1955–6), 24–55; x (1956–7), 17–42.

**6924  LOGAN (WILLIAM PHILIP DOWIE).** 'Mortality in England and Wales from 1848 to 1947'. *Population Studs.* iv (1950–1), 132–78.

See also Sir William Palin Elderton and M. E. Ogborn, 'The mortality of adult males since the middle of the eighteenth century, as shown by the experience of life assurance companies', *Roy. Stat. Soc. J.* cvi (1943), 1–20; A. H. Gale, 'Variations in the mortality and incidence of the common infectious diseases of childhood over a century', *Roy. Soc. of Medicine Proc.* xxxvi (1943), 97–103; Hugh R. Jones, 'The perils and protection of infant life', *Roy. Stat. Soc. J.* lvii (1894), 1–98; Sir Arthur Newsholme, *Thirty-ninth annual report of Local Government Board, 1909–10, suppl. to the report of the Board's medical officer containing a report by the medical officer on infant and child mortality.* [Cd. 5263] H.C. (1910). XXXIX, 973; Noel A. Humphreys, 'Class mortality statistics', *Roy. Stat. Soc. J.* l (1887), 255–85; Thomas Abercrombie Welton, 'On certain changes in the English rates of mortality', ibid. xliii (1880), 65–83, and 'Local death-rates in England and Wales in the ten years 1881–90', ibid. lx (1897), 33–75; and F. S. Crum, 'Occupation mortality statistics of Sheffield, England, 1890–1907', *Amer. Stat. Assoc. Publ.* new ser. xi (1908–9), 309–18.

**6925  McKEOWN (THOMAS) *and* RECORD (R. G.).** 'Reasons for the decline of mortality in England and Wales during the nineteenth century'. *Population Studs.* xvi (1962–3), 94–122.

See also Noel A. Humphreys, 'The recent decline in the English death-rate and its effect upon the duration of life', *Stat. Soc. J.* xlvi (1883), 189–213; George Blundell Longstaff, 'The recent decline in the English death-rate considered in connection with the causes of death', *Stat. Soc. J.* xlvii (1884), 221–49; Sidney Phillips, 'A review of mortality statistics during the last half century', *Clinical J.* xxxii (1908), 55–61, 73–80; Sir Arthur Lyon Bowley, 'Death-rates, density, population and housing', *Roy. Stat. Soc. J.* lxxxvi (1923), 516–46; and Major Greenwood, 'English death-rates, past, present and future', ibid. xcix (1936), 674–707.

6926 ANDERSON (MICHAEL). Family structure in nineteenth-century Lancashire. Camb. 1972.

6927 McGREGOR (OLIVER ROSS). Divorce in England: a centenary study. 1957.

See also David Victor Glass, 'Divorce in England and Wales', *Sociological Rev.* xxvi (1934), 288–308, and Margaret K. Woodhouse, 'The Marriage and Divorce Bill of 1857', *Amer. J. Legal Hist.* iii (1959), 260–75. For divorce law and inquiries into divorce law see 3278. The case against the existing law was strongly stated in John Francis Stanley Russell, Earl Russell, *Divorce*, 1912.

6928 ROWNTREE (GRISELDA) *and* CARRIER (NORMAN HENRY). 'The resort to divorce in England and Wales, 1858–1957'. *Population Studs.* xi (1957–8), 188–233.

6929 JENKS (EDWARD). Husband & wife in the law. 1909.

A well-written handbook for the layman. For family law in detail see 3282.

6930 HUMPHREYS (NOEL A.) *ed.* Vital statistics: a memorial volume of selections from the reports and writings of William Farr. 1885.

Farr was the leading contemp. demographer. A similar coll. of papers was George Blundell Longstaff, *Studies in statistics: social, political and medical*, 1891.

6931 NEWSHOLME (*Sir* ARTHUR). The elements of vital statistics. 1889. New edn. 1923.

The best contemp. textbook.

6932 NEISON (FRANCIS G. P.). Contributions to vital statistics: being, a development of the rate of mortality and the laws of sickness from original and extensive data procured from friendly societies. 1845. 3rd edn. 1857.

A pioneer actuarial work.

6933 LEFFINGWELL (ALBERT). Illegitimacy and the influence of seasons on conduct: two studies in demography. Lond. & N.Y. 1892. 2nd edn. 1892.

See also W. G. Lumley, 'Observations upon the statistics of illegitimacy', *Stat. Soc. J.* xxv (1862), 219–74.

## 2. MIGRATION

### (a) *General*

6934 LEAK (HECTOR) *and* PRIDAY (T.). 'Migration from and to the United Kingdom'. *Roy. Stat. Soc. J.* xcvi (1933), 183–227.

Includes a general hist. survey. See also Sir Alexander Morris Carr-Saunders, 'Migration movements to and from the British Isles', *Sociological Rev.* xxix (1937), 232–42.

6935 THOMAS (BRINLEY). 'Migration and the rhythm of economic growth, 1830–1913'. *Manch. School* xix (1951), 215–71.

See also the fuller treatment at 6969.

6936 RAVENSTEIN (ERNEST GEORGE). 'The laws of migration'. *Stat. Soc. J.* xlviii (1885), 167–235; lii (1889), 241–305.

An attempt at a general theory.

6937 CAIRNCROSS (*Sir* ALEXANDER KIRKLAND). 'Internal migration in Victorian England'. *Manch. School* xvii (1949), 67–87.

See also C. T. Smith, 'The movement of population in England and Wales in 1851 and 1861', *Geog. J.* cxvii (1951), 200–10.

6938 FRIEDLANDER (D.) *and* ROSHIER (R. J.). 'A study of internal migration in England and Wales : Part I : geographical patterns of internal migration, 1851–1951'. *Population Studs.* xix (1965–6), 239–79.

6939 LAWTON (RICHARD). 'Population changes in England and Wales in the later nineteenth century: an analysis of trends by registration districts'. *Inst. British Geographers Trans.* xliv (1968), 55–74.

For population movements see also John William House, *North-eastern England: population movements and the landscape since the early 19th century*, King's College Dept. of Geography research ser. 1, Newcastle-upon-Tyne 1954, R. Lawton, 'Population movements in the west Midlands, 1841–1861', *Geography* xliii (1958), 164–77, and Henry Clifford Darby, 'The movement of population to and from Cambridgeshire between 1851 and 1861', *Geographical J.* ci (1943), 118–25.

6940 WELTON (THOMAS ABERCROMBIE). England's recent progress: an investigation of the statistics of migrations, mortality, &c. in the twenty years from 1881 to 1901, as indicating tendencies towards the growth or decay of particular communities. 1911.

The most extensive of Welton's many surveys of census data. See also his *Statistical papers based on the census of England and Wales, 1851, and relating to the occupations of the people and the increase of population, 1841–51*, 1860, 'On the distribution of population in England and Wales, and its progress in the period of ninety years from 1801 to 1891', *Roy. Stat. Soc. J.* lxiii (1900), 527–89, 'Bye-products of the census: a study of the recent migration of English people . . .', *Manch. Stat. Soc. Trans.* (1904–5), 1–39, and 'Note on urban and rural variations according to the English census of 1911', *Roy. Stat. Soc. J.* lxxvi (1912–13), 304–17. There is additional material in Richard Price Williams, 'On the increase of population in England and Wales', *Stat. Soc. J.* xliii (1880), 462–96.

6941 SAVILLE (JOHN). Rural depopulation in England and Wales, 1851–1951. 1957.

For rural population see also Lydia M. Marshall, *The rural population of Bedfordshire, 1671 to 1921*, Bedfordshire Hist. Record Soc. xvi, 1934.

6942 REW (*Sir* ROBERT HENRY). Board of Agriculture and Fisheries: report on the decline in the agricultural population of Great Britain, 1881–1906. [Cd. 3273] H.C. (1906). XCVI, 583.

For earlier accounts of the subject see Frederick Purdy, 'On the decrease of the agricultural population of England and Wales, 1851–61', *Stat. Soc. J.* xxvii (1864), 388–400, William Ogle, 'The alleged depopulation of the rural districts of England', ibid. lii (1889), 205–32, and George Blundell Longstaff, 'Rural depopulation', ibid. lvi (1893), 380–433.

6943 BOWLEY (*Sir* ARTHUR LYON). 'Rural population in England and Wales: a study of the changes of density, occupations and ages'. *Roy. Stat. Soc. J.* lxxvii (1913–14), 597–652.

6944 BANKS (JOSEPH AMBROSE). 'Population change and the Victorian city'. *Victorian Studs.* xi (1967–8), 277–89.

6945 SHANNON (HERBERT AUSTIN). 'Migration and the growth of London, 1841–91: a statistical note'. *Econ. Hist. Rev.* v (1934–5), no. 2, 79–86.

(b) *Immigration*

For Jewish immigration see (**3957**). Statistics of alien arrivals at British ports were publ. regularly as parl. papers from 1891.

6946 ROCHE (THOMAS WILLIAM EDGAR). The key in the lock: a history of immigration control in England, from 1066 to present day. 1969.

Little more than an outline. Bernard Gainer, *The alien invasion: the origins of the Aliens Act of 1905*, 1972, fills in some of the details.

6947 WILSON (FRANCESCA MARY). They came as strangers: the story of refugees to Great Britain. 1959.

6948 LEVI (LEONE). 'On the number, occupation and status of foreigners in England'. *Stat. Soc. J.* xxvii (1864), 558–65.

6949 CALCRAFT (HENRY GEORGE). Memorandum on the immigration of foreigners into the United Kingdom. Board of Trade. H.C. 112 (1887). LXXXIX, 223.

6950 MARRIOTT COMMITTEE ON MIGRATION OF FOREIGNERS. Report from the select committee on emigration and immigration (foreigners) [Chairman: Sir William Marriott]. H.C. 305 (1888). XI, 419. Further report. H.C. 311 (1889). X, 265.

6951 WILKINS (WILLIAM HENRY). The alien invasion. 1892.

Wilkins was sec. of the Assoc. for Preventing the Immigration of Destitute Aliens.

6952 WHITE (ARNOLD) *ed.* The destitute alien in Great Britain: a series of papers dealing with the subject of foreign pauper immigration. 1892. 2nd edn. 1905.

6953 BOARD OF TRADE. Reports on the volume and effects of recent immigration from eastern Europe into the United Kingdom. [C. 7406] H.C. (1894). LXVIII, 341.

6954 DRAGE (GEOFFREY). 'Alien immigration'. *Roy. Stat. Soc. J.* lviii (1895), 1–30.

6955 CUNNINGHAM (WILLIAM). Alien immigrants to England. 1897.

6956 EVANS-GORDON (WILLIAM EDEN). The alien immigrant. 1903.

6957 JAMES COMMISSION ON ALIEN IMMIGRATION. Report of the royal commission on alien immigration [Chairman: Lord James of Hereford]. [Cd. 1741] H.C. (1903). IX, 1. Minutes of evidence. [Cd. 1742] H.C. (1903). IX, 61. Appendix. [Cd. 1741–I] H.C. (1903). IX, 935. Index and analysis. [Cd. 1743] H.C. (1903). IX, 1041.

6958 HOME OFFICE. Aliens Act, 1905: Part I. A statement with regard to the expulsion of aliens. Part II. Fifth annual report of H.M. inspector under the act, for the year 1910. [Cd. 5789] H.C. (1911). X, 1.

For the working of the act see also Eugène Pépin, *La question des étrangers en Angleterre: L'Aliens Act de 1905, causes et résultats*, Paris 1913.

6959 LEHMANN COMMITTEE ON ALIEN RECEPTION. Report of the departmental committee appointed to advise the secretary of state as to the establishment of a receiving house for alien immigrants at the port of London [Chairman: R. C. Lehmann]. [C. 5575] H.C. (1911). X, 87. Minutes of evidence. [Cd. 5576] H.C. (1911). X, 99.

6960 LANDA (MYER JACK). The alien problem and its remedy. 1911.

6961 JACKSON (JOHN ARCHER). The Irish in Britain. Lond. & Cleveland [Ohio]. 1963.

Includes a good deal of hist. data about this important immigrant group. See also John Denvir, *The Irish in Britain from the earliest times to the fall and death of Parnell*, 1892, and Lynn H. Lees, 'Patterns of lower-class life: Irish slum communities in nineteenth-century London', in Stephan Albert Thernstrom and Richard Sennett, eds., *Nineteenth-century cities . . .*, New Haven, Conn. 1969, pp. 359–85.

6962 CURTIS (LEWIS PERRY) *Jr.* Anglo-Saxons and Celts: a study of anti-Irish prejudice in Victorian England. Bridgeport, Conn. 1968.

6963 PAULUCCI DI CALBOLI (RANIERO) *Marquis*. I girovaghi italiani in Inghilterra ed i suonatori ambulanti. Città di Castello. 1893.

(c) *Emigration*

6964 FERENCZI (IMRE) *and* WILLCOX (WALTER FRANCIS) *eds.* International migrations. 2 v. Nat. Bureau Econ. Res. N.Y. 1929–31.

Gives the basic statistics.

6965 CARRIER (NORMAN HENRY) *and* JEFFERY (JAMES R.). External migration 1814–1950: a study of the available statistics. General Register Office: Studies on Medical and Population Subjects. No. 6. 1953.

6966 BOARD OF TRADE. Statistical tables relating to emigration and immigration from and into the United Kingdom in the year 1876, with report . . . H.C. 5 (1877). LXXXV, 621. Annual.

Chiefly concerned with emigration. Separate tables were publ. for Ireland.

6967 CARROTHERS (WILLIAM ALEXANDER). Emigration from the British Isles: with special reference to the development of the overseas dominions. 1929.

A good but old-fashioned general hist. based on official records.

6968 PLANT (GEORGE FREDERIC). Oversea settlement: migration from the United Kingdom to the dominions. 1951.

A general survey of migration policy. The main government agencies were the Colonial Land and Emigration Commission, which issued 33 reports, 1842–73, publ. as parl. papers, and the Emigrants' Information Office, which issued annual reports, 1888–1914. For the Colonial Land and Emigration Commission see **6970** and **404**.

6969 THOMAS (BRINLEY). Migration and economic growth: a study of Great Britain and the Atlantic economy. Camb. 1954. 2nd edn. 1973.

An important work bearing on many aspects of the British economy.

6970 MACDONAGH (OLIVER ORMOND GERARD MICHAEL). 'The regulation of the emigrant traffic from the United Kingdom, 1842–55'. *Irish Hist. Studs.* ix (1954–5), 162–89.

For a more detailed account of the control of emigration see **404**, and Colonial Land and Emigration Commissioners, *Annual report*, 1842–73.

6971 ERICKSON (CHARLOTTE). 'The encouragement of emigration by British trade unions, 1850–1900'. *Population Studs.* iii (1949–50), 248–73.

See also Roger Victor Clements, 'Trade unions and emigration, 1840–80', ibid. ix (1955–6), 167–80.

6972 MONK (UNA BARBARA). New horizons: a hundred years of women's migration. H.M.S.O. 1963.

The Female Middle-Class Emigration Soc.

6973 BERTHOFF (ROWLAND TAPPAN). British immigrants in industrial America, 1790–1950. Camb., Mass. 1953.

Good. For a useful survey of emigration to the United States see Maldwyn Allen Jones, *American immigration*, Chicago 1960. Stanley Currie Johnson, *A history of emigration from the United Kingdom to North America, 1763–1912*, 1913, is still useful for statistics. There is little on the period in the works of Wilbur Stanley Shepperson, but there are some relevant passages in his *Emigration & disenchantment: portraits of Englishmen repatriated from the United States*, Norman, Okla. 1965, and *The promotion of British emigration by agents for American lands, 1840–1860*, Reno, Nev. 1954. Charlotte Erickson, *Invisible immigrants: the adaptation of English and Scottish immigrants to nineteenth-century America*, Lond. & Coral Gables, Fla., 1972, is based largely on letters.

6974 REYNOLDS (LLOYD GEORGE). The British immigrant: his social and economic adjustment in Canada. Toronto. 1935.

6975 HERBERT COMMITTEE ON PASSENGERS ACT. Report from the select committee on Passengers' Act [Chairman: Sidney Herbert]. H.C. 632 (1851). XIX, 1.

6976 COLONIAL OFFICE. Papers relative to emigration to the North American colonies. [1474] H.C. (1852). XXXIII, 559. Papers relative to emigration to the Australian colonies. [1489] H.C. (1852). XXXIV, 417.

6977 O'CONNELL COMMITTEE ON EMIGRANT SHIPS. First report from the select committee on emigrant ships [Chairman: John O'Connell]. H.C. 163 (1854). XIII, 1. Second report. H.C. 349 (1854). XIII, 187.

6978 COLONIAL OFFICE. Correspondence respecting emigration. [C. 335] H.C. (1871). XLVII, 693.

The replies to a letter of inquiry addressed to each colonial governor. For comment see *Report from Sir Clinton Murdoch, K.C.M.G., to Sir Frederic Rogers, Bart., K.C.M.G. . . . on the subject of emigration.* [C. 296] H.C. (1871). XLVII, 687.

6979 POZER COMMITTEE ON CANADIAN IMMIGRATION. First report of the select committee of the parliament of Canada on immigration and colonisation [Chairman: C. H. Pozer]. H.C. 275 (1875). LII, 105.

6980 DOYLE (ANDREW). Report to the Right Honourable the President of the Local Government Board by Andrew Doyle, Esquire, local government inspector, as to the emigration of pauper children to Canada. H.C. 9 (1875). LXIII, 255.

6981 BOARD OF TRADE. Reports with regard to the accommodation and treatment of emigrants on board Atlantic steam ships . . . [C. 2995] H.C. (1881). LXXXII, 93.

6982 LEVASSEUR (EMILE). 'Emigration in the nineteenth century'. *Stat. Soc. J.* xlviii (1885), 63–81.

6983 SELECT COMMITTEE ON COLONISATION. Report from the select committee on colonisation [Chairman: C. T. Ritchie]. H.C. 274 (1889). X, 1. Further report [Chairman: Sir James Fergusson]. H.C. 354 (1890). XII, 1. Further report. H.C. 152 (1890–1). XI, 571.

See also *Correspondence respecting a scheme of colonization referred in 1887 for the consideration of colonial governments.* [C. 5361] H.C. (1888). LXXIII, 1, and *Correspondence from colonial governments in answer to the memorandum by the parliamentary colonisation committee* . . . H.C. 106, 232, 314 (1889). LV, 27, 43, 65.

6984 TENNYSON COMMITTEE ON AGRICULTURAL SETTLEMENTS IN BRITISH COLONIES. Report of the departmental committee appointed to consider Mr. Rider Haggard's report on agricultural settlements in British colonies [Chairman: Lord Tennyson]. [Cd. 2978] H.C. (1906). LXXVI, 533. Minutes of evidence. [Cd. 2979] H.C. (1906). LXXVI, 579.

See also **4180, 7224** and **3872**.

6985 ROYAL COLONIAL INSTITUTE. Official report of the emigration conference, held on May 30–31, 1910, convened by the Royal Colonial Institute. 1910.

## C. STATUS OF WOMEN

For women's employment see **6630–64** and for women's suffrage see **676–90**.

**6986** McGREGOR (OLIVER ROSS). 'The social position of women in England, 1850–1914: a bibliography'. *Brit. J. of Sociology* vi (1955), 48–60.

An indispensable survey, with full commentary.

**6987** REISS (ERNA). Rights and duties of Englishwomen: a study in law and public opinion. Manch. 1934.

The most useful of the many general hists. of the status of women. Walter Lyon Blease, *The emancipation of English women*, 1910, rev. edn. 1913; George William Johnson, *The evolution of women from subjection to comradeship*, 1926; Irene Clephane, *Towards sex freedom*, 1935; Vera May Brittain, *Lady into woman: a history of women from Victoria to Elizabeth II*, 1953; Josephine Kamm, *Rapiers and battleaxes: the women's movement and its aftermath*, 1966; and Constance Rover, *Love, morals and feminists*, 1970, are similar works, all more or less unscholarly and feminist in their sympathies. Viola Klein, *The feminine character: history of an ideology*, 1946, is almost exclusively concerned with the mid-20th cent. John Langdon-Davies, *A short history of women*, 1928, is too short and general to be of any value. Except as general commentaries on social hist., the 19th-cent. gen. hists. of women are equally valueless. The best of them is Georgina Hill, *Women in English life from medieval to modern times*, 2 v. 1896. William L. O'Neill, ed., *The woman movement: feminism in the United States and England*, N.Y. & Lond., 1969, is a coll. of docs.

**6988** CROW (DUNCAN) The Victorian woman. 1971.

For background see also Janet Dunbar, *The early Victorian woman: some aspects of her life (1837–57)*, 1953.

**6989** ANDERSON (OLIVE). 'Women preachers in mid-Victorian Britain: some reflections on feminism, popular religion and social change'. *Hist. J.* xii (1969), 467–84.

An interesting pioneer study.

**6990** BEHRMAN (CYNTHIA FANSLER). 'The annual blister: a sidelight on Victorian social and parliamentary history'. *Victorian Studs.* xi (1967–8), 483–502.

Marriage with a deceased wife's sister.

**6991** BOTT (ALAN JOHN) *ed., and* CLEPHANE (IRENE) *comp.* Our mothers: a cavalcade in pictures, quotation and description of late Victorian women, 1870–1900. 1932.

See also Constance Rover, comp., *The 'Punch' book of women's rights*, 1967.

**6992** CUNNINGTON (CECIL WILLETT). Feminine attitudes in the nineteenth century. 1935.

A popular scissors-and-paste social hist.

**6993** LANG (ELSIE M.). British women in the twentieth century. 1929.

6994  PRATT (EDWIN A.). Pioneer women in Victoria's reign: being short histories of great movements. 1897.

Still the best account of the notable women of the 19th cent. Other useful biog. works are Frederick Douglas How, *Noble women of our time*, 1901, Margaret Emma Tabor, *Pioneer women*, 4 ser. 1925–33, and Janet Elizabeth Courtney, *The women of my time*, 1934.

6995  CHAPMAN (ANNIE BEATRICE WALLIS) *and* CHAPMAN (MARY WALLIS). The status of women under the English law: a compendious epitome of legislative enactments and social and political events arranged as a continuous narrative, with references to authorities and Acts of Parliament. 1909.

See also Ann Stafford, pseud. of Ann Pedlar, *The age of consent*, 1964.

6996  GEDDES (*Sir* PATRICK) *and* THOMSON (*Sir* JOHN ARTHUR). Sex. 1914.

See also Elizabeth Blackwell, *Counsel to parents on the moral education of the young in relation to sex*, 1878, 8th edn. 1913; Henry Havelock Ellis, *Man and woman . . .*, 1894; Jane Ellice Hopkins, *The power of womanhood: or, mothers and sons: a book for parents and those in loco parentis*, 1899, 16th edn. 1909; Edward Lyttelton, *Training of the young in laws of sex*, 1900; and H. Havelock Ellis, *The task of social hygiene*, Lond., Boston, & N.Y. 1912.

6997  BROWNLOW (JANE M. E.). Women's work in local government: England and Wales. 1911.

6998  COBBE (FRANCES POWER). Essays on the pursuits of women. 1863.

Essays incl. 'Social science congresses and women's part in them', 'What shall we do with our old maids?', and 'The education of women'. See also her *The duties of women: a course of lectures*, 1881.

6999  BUTLER (JOSEPHINE ELIZABETH) *ed.* Woman's work and woman's culture: a series of essays. 1869.

An important early symposium on the position of women.

7000  YONGE (CHARLOTTE MARY). Womankind. 1876.

A good example of what came to be thought of as 'the Victorian attitude' to women. Cp. John Maynard, *Matrimony: or, what marriage is and how to make the best life of it*, 1864, 2nd edn. 1866, Mary Taylor, *The first duty of women*, 1870, and Augusta Webster, *A housewife's opinions*, 1879.

7001  STANTON (THEODORE) *ed.* The woman question in Europe: a series of original essays. Lond. & N.Y. 1884.

Written for the American public.

7002  OSTROGORSKI (MOISEI YAKOVLEVICH). The rights of women: a comparative study in history and legislation. 1893.

7003  HIGGINSON (THOMAS WENTWORTH). Common sense about women. Boston & Lond. 1882.

7004 INTERNATIONAL CONGRESS OF WOMEN, 1899. International Council of Women: report of transactions of the second quinquennial meeting, held in London, July 1899. Ed. by Ishbel Maria Gordon, Marchioness of Aberdeen. 1900.

One of a ser. of 7 v. containing reports and papers delivered at the Congress. Other vols. are *Women in education, Women in industrial life, Women in politics, Women in the professions* (2 v.), and *Women in social life.* All were prepared under the general editorship of Lady Aberdeen. The papers are important sources of information about the period.

7005 STETSON *afterwards* GILMAN (CHARLOTTE PERKINS). Women and economics: a study of the economic relation between men and women as a factor in social evolution. Lond. & Boston. 1898. 5th edn. 1906.

The work of a strongly feminist American.

7006 SWINEY (FRANCES). The awakening of women [: or woman's part in evolution]. 1899. 3rd edn. [1908.]

A feminist tract on 'The normal superiority of the female in nature . . .'.

7007 STOPES (CHARLOTTE CARMICHAEL). British freewomen: their historical privilege. 1894. 3rd edn. 1907.

An attempt to show that the subjection of women is a modern phenomenon.

7008 MEAKIN (ANNETTE M. B.). Woman in transition. 1907.

A useful descriptive work.

7009 SALEEBY (CALEB WILLIAMS). Woman & womanhood: a search for principles. 1912.

A poor work, but full of period flavour.

7010 SNOWDEN (ETHEL), *Viscountess Snowden.* The feminist movement. [1913.]

Important for the connection between the Labour Party and feminism. See also her *The woman socialist,* 1907.

7011 STANWICK (HELENA MARIA). The future of the women's movement. 1913.

Strongly anti-militant.

7012 BAX (ERNEST BELFORT). The fraud of feminism. 1913.

More forceful, but no less hostile to feminism, than Ethel Colquhoun [Mrs. Archibald Colquhoun], *The vocation of woman,* 1913.

7013 FAIRFIELD (ZOË) *ed.* Some aspects of the women's movement Student Christian Movement. 1915.

Essays by Ernest Barker, Cecilia M. Ady, Clara E. Collet, Helen Wilson, Una M. Saunders, William Temple, and the editor.

## D. LIVING CONDITIONS

### 1. COUNTRY LIFE

#### (a) *General*

See also **6941** and **7087.**

**7014** FUSSELL (GEORGE EDWIN) *and* FUSSELL (KATHLEEN ROSEMARY). The English countryman: his life and work, A.D. 1500–1900. 1955.

The Fussells' *The English countrywoman: a farmhouse social history . . .*, 1953, is a companion vol. See also G. E. Fussell, *The English rural labourer: his house, furniture, clothing & food from Tudor to Victorian times*, 1949.

**7015** MARTIN (ERNEST WALTER). The secret people: English village life after 1750 . . . 1954.

Like Harold John Edward Peake, *The English village: the origin and decay of its community: an anthropological interpretation*, 1922, too general to be of much value. But see also George Ewart Evans, *The farm and the village*, 1969.

**7016** PULBROOK (ERNEST CRAPPING). English country life and work: an account of some past aspects and present features. 1923.

Chiefly useful for its photographs.

**7017** CUTTLE (GEORGE). The legacy of the rural guardians: a study of conditions in mid-Essex [1895–1929]. Camb. 1934.

**7018** DAVIES (MAUD FRANCES). Life in an English village: an economic and historical survey of the parish of Corsley in Wiltshire. 1909.

The only full hist. survey of an individual village. But see Havinden (**4245**) and Moreau (**9550**).

**7019** WILLIAMS (WILLIAM MORGAN). The sociology of an English village: Gosforth. 1956.

A pioneer study with much hist. background on this isolated Cumberland village.

#### (b) *Autobiographies and Biographies*

**7020** ASHBY. Joseph Ashby of Tysoe, 1859–1919: a study of English village life. By Mabel K. Ashby. Camb. 1961.

**7021** BRIDGES. Reminiscences of a country politician. By John Affleck Bridges. 1906.

Pleasant memoirs of country life. Bridges also publ. *A sportsman of limited income . . .*, 1910, and *Victorian recollections*, 1919.

**7022** KITCHEN. Brother to the ox: the autobiography of a farm labourer. By Fred Kitchen. 1940.

A splendid piece of work.

7023   STURT. A small boy in the sixties. By George Sturt. Camb. 1927.

Life in a Surrey village. See also *The journals of George Sturt, 'George Bourne', 1890–1902*, ed. by Geoffrey Grigson, 1941, and *The journals of George Sturt, 1890–1927, a selection*, ed. by Eric David Mackerness, 2 v. Camb. 1962. Sturt's other books on rural life (**7037**) publ. under the pseud. of George Bourne also have all the qualities of first-rate memoirs.

7024   THOMPSON. Lark rise to Candleford: a trilogy. By Flora Thompson. 1945.

North Oxfordshire village life at the end of the 19th cent. The best of many recent books of reminiscences of village life, which take on a fictional quality because of their distance from the period with which they deal.

7025   WILKINS. The autobiography of an English gamekeeper (John Wilkins of Stanstead, Essex). Ed. by Arthur H. Byng and Stephen M. Stephens. [1892.]

7026   WOOD. A Sussex farmer. By William Wood. 1938.

### (c) *Contemporary Works*

7027   JEFFERIES (JOHN RICHARD). The gamekeeper at home: sketches of natural history and rural life. 1877.

The first of Jefferies's successes. Nominally novels, his books differ little from colls. of essays on aspects of village life. His *The story of my heart: my autobiography*, 1883, 2nd edn. 1891, is a kind of fictionalized autobiog. *The gamekeeper at home* and *The amateur poacher*, 1879, are available together in a World's Classics edn. For his ideas see Philip Drew, 'Richard Jefferies and the English countryside', *Victorian Studs.* xi (1967–8), 181–206.

7028   KERRISON (*Sir* EDWARD CLARENCE). 'Village clubs'. *Roy. Agric. Soc. J.* xxxviii (2 ser. xiii) (1877), 375–93.

See also Arthur W. Ashby, 'Village clubs and associations', *Roy. Agric. Soc. J.* lxxv (1914), 1–20.

7029   JESSOPP (AUGUSTUS). Arcady: for better, for worse. 1887.

Essays on Norfolk village life, mainly repr. from the *Nineteenth century*. Jessopp was a prolific writer, and did much to establish a vogue for books on village life. Comparable works are Joseph Arthur Gibbs, *A Cotswold village . . .*, 1898, and Alfred Williams, *A Wiltshire village*, 1912.

7030   MILLIN (GEORGE FRANCIS). Life in our villages. By the special commissioner of the *Daily News*. 1891.

7031   KEBBEL (THOMAS EDWARD). The old and the new English country life. 1891.

7032   GRAHAM (PETER ANDERSON). The rural exodus: the problem of the village and the town. 1892.

Deals with all aspects of rural life.

7033    GREEN (*Sir* JOHN LITTLE). The rural industries of England. [1895.]

Based on an inquiry made about 1885. Green returned to the subject in *Village industries: a national obligation.* 1915.

7034    MILLIN (GEORGE FRANCIS). The village problem. 1903.

Suggests that the worst problems of village life, reported in his *Life in our villages* (**7030**), are being overcome.

7035    MANN (P. H.). 'Life in an agricultural village in England'. *Sociological Papers* 1904, 163–93.

7036    HEATH (FRANCIS GEORGE). British rural life and labour. 1911.

A good general survey. Heath's earlier books, *The English peasantry*, 1874, and *The romance of peasant life in the West of England*, 1872, 3rd edn. 1880, are also worth reading.

7037    BOURNE (GEORGE) *pseud. of* STURT (GEORGE). Change in the village. 1912. Repr. 1955.

Probably the best of Sturt's books, which, like Thomas Hardy's novels, are based on close observation of country life. Other important ones are *The wheelwright's shop*, Camb. 1923, *A farmer's life . . .*, 1922, *Memoirs of a Surrey labourer: a record of the last years of Frederick Bettesworth*, 1907, and *The Bettesworth book: talks with a Surrey peasant*, 1901. See also **7023**.

7038    DITCHFIELD (PETER HAMPSON). The cottages and the village life of rural England. 1912.

Like his *The charm of the English village*, 1900, typical of a large class of sentimental, illustrated books devoted to the picturesque qualities of the older villages. Chocolate-box illustrations by A. R. Quinton.

7039    GREEN (FREDERICK ERNEST). The tyranny of the countryside. 1913.

A radical attack on the social organization of English villages.

7040    BENNETT (*Sir* ERNEST NATHANIEL). Problems of village life. Home University Library. [1914.]

A valuable summary of the situation immediately before the outbreak of the 1914–18 war.

## 2. URBANIZATION

### (a) *General*

7041    GLASS (RUTH). 'Urban sociology in Great Britain: a trend report [i.e. a bibliography]'. *Current Sociology* iv (1955), no. 4, 5–76.

7042    CHALONER (WILLIAM HENRY). 'Writings on British urban history, 1934–1957 . . .'. *Vierteljahrschrift für Sozial- und Wirtschaftsgeschichte* xlv (1958), 76–87.

7043 DYOS (HAROLD JAMES) *ed.* The study of urban history: the proceedings of an international round-table conference . . . 1968.

An indication of the growing interest in urban hist. Cp. Oscar Handlin and John Burchard, eds., *The historian and the city*, Camb., Mass. 1963. See also *Urban history newsletter*, Leicester 1963+.

7044 SAVAGE (*Sir* WILLIAM GEORGE). The making of our towns. 1952.

7045 WEBER (ADNA FERRIN). The growth of cities in the nineteenth century: a study in statistics. N.Y. 1899. Repr. Ithaca, N.Y. 1963.

See also Thomas Abercrombie Welton, 'On the distribution, growth and decay of English towns in 1801, and since that date', *Manch. Stat. Soc. Trans.* (1901–2), 139–59, and F. Tillyard, 'English town development in the nineteenth century', *Econ. J.* xxiii (1913), 547–60.

7046 DYOS (HAROLD JAMES) *and* WOLFF (MICHAEL) *eds.* The Victorian city: images and realities. 2 v. Leicester. 1973.

7047 BRIGGS (ASA). Victorian cities. 1963.
Important.

7048 VICTORIAN STUDIES. Symposium on the Victorian city. *Victorian Studs.* xi (1967–8), 275–403, 627–730.

7049 CHADWICK (GEORGE FLETCHER). The park and the town: public landscape in the 19th and 20th centuries. Lond. & N.Y. 1966.

7050 FREEMAN (THOMAS WALTER). The conurbations of Great Britain. Manch. 1959.

7051 SELECT COMMITTEE ON TOWN HOLDINGS. Report from the select committee on town holdings [Chairmen: George Joachim Goschen and Lewis Fry]. H.C. 213 (1886). XII, 367. Further general reports. H.C. 260 (1887). XIII, 41; H.C. 313 (1888). XXII, 1; H.C. 251 (1889). XV, 1. Reports on taxation of ground rents and improved values. H.C. 341 (1890). XVIII, 1; H.C. 325 (1890–1). XVIII, 15; H.C. 214 (1892). XVIII, 613.

The only official inquiry into town development in general. The numerous contemp. works and inquiries on the taxation of land values (4538–57) also contain much of value.

7052 MASTERMAN (CHARLES FREDERICK GURNEY) *and others.* The heart of the empire: discussions of problems of modern city life in England: with an essay on imperialism. 1901. New edn. Lond. & N.Y. 1902.

7053 REEDER (D. A.). 'The politics of urban leaseholds in late Victorian England'. *Int. Rev. Soc. Hist.* vi (1961), 413–30.

7054 HOWARTH (EDWARD GOLDIE) *and* WILSON (MONA). West Ham: a study in social and industrial problems: being the report of the Outer London Inquiry Committee. 1907.

Incl. here as an example of many studs. of urban problems. The surveys of Rowntree (7351) and Booth (7353), were the most important conducted during the period. But see also 7197.

## (b) *Town Planning*

**7055 ASHWORTH (WILLIAM).** The genesis of modern British town planning: a study in economic and social history of the nineteenth and twentieth centuries. 1954.

See also Helen Rosenau, *The ideal city in its architectural evolution*, 1959; Cecil Stewart, *A prospect of cities: being, studies towards a history of town planning*, 1952; Walter Littlefield Creese, *The search for environment: the garden city, before and after*, New Haven, Conn. 1966; and David Victor Glass, *The town and a changing civilisation*, 1935. There are good pictures in Colin John Bell and Rose Bell, *City fathers: the early history of town planning in Britain*, 1969.

**7056 GEDDES.** Pioneer of sociology: the life and letters of Patrick Geddes. By Philip Mairet [i.e. Philippe Auguste Mairet]. 1957.

See also Philip Boardman, *Patrick Geddes: maker of the future*, Chapel Hill, N.C. 1944. Geddes was a leading exponent of town planning. See also **8545**.

**7057 HOWARD.** Sir Ebenezer Howard and the town planning movement. By Dugald Macfadyen. Manch. 1933.

**7058 HOWARD (*Sir* EBENEZER).** Tomorrow: a peaceful path to social reform. 1898.

The pioneer work in the field, reissued as *Garden cities of tomorrow*, 1902, new edn. 1946.

**7059 GEDDES (*Sir* PATRICK).** City development: a study of parks, gardens and culture-institutes: a report to the Carnegie Dunfermline Trust. Edin. 1904.

This and his *Cities in evolution: an introduction to the town planning movement and to the study of civics*, 1915, abridged edn. 1949, new edn. by Percy Johnson-Marshall 1968, are major landmarks in the literature of the subject.

**7060 SENNETT (ALFRED RICHARD).** Garden cities in theory and practice: being an amplification of a paper on the potentialities of applied science in a garden city . . . 2 v. 1905.

**7061 GARDEN CITY ASSOCIATION.** Town planning in theory and practice: a report of a conference arranged by the Garden City Association, held at the Guildhall, London, on October 25th, 1907, under the presidency of the Lord Mayor of London. [1908.]

**7062 NETTLEFOLD (JOHN SUTTON).** Practical housing. Letchworth. 1908.

A first-rate intro. to town planning, rather better than his *Practical town planning*, 1914. See also his *Garden cities and canals*, 1914.

**7063 TRIGGS (HENRY INIGO).** Town planning: past, present and possible. 1908.

**7064 UNWIN (*Sir* RAYMOND).** Town planning in practice: an introduction to the art of designing cities and suburbs. 1909. 2nd edn. 1932.

7065 COLE (THOMAS) *ed.* Housing and town planning conference held at the Institute, West Bromwich, July 5 and 6, 1911 . . . Instn. Municipal & County Engineers. 1911.

An important professional discussion of town planning. At a further conference at Great Yarmouth in 1913 the matter was taken up again and the meeting resulted in a second vol. of papers with the same title.

7066 MAWSON (THOMAS HAYTON). Civic art: studies in town planning, parks, boulevards and open spaces. 1911.

7067 WATERHOUSE (PAUL) *and* UNWIN (*Sir* RAYMOND). Old towns and new needs: also, the town extension plan. Warburton lectures for 1912. Manch. 1912.

7068 CULPIN (EWART GLADSTONE). The garden city movement up-to-date. Garden Cities and Town Planning Assoc. [1913.]

An intro. to the work and ideas of the Assoc. by its secretary. See also the Assoc.'s annual report, 1899+, and George Montagu Harris, *The garden city movement*, 1906.

7069 ALDRIDGE (HENRY R.). The case for town planning: a practical manual for the use of councillors, officers, and others engaged in the preparation of town planning schemes. Nat. Housing & Town Planning Council. [1915.]

7070 GARDEN CITIES ASSOCIATION [*later* Town and Country Planning Assoc.] The garden city. 1904+.

Title changed to *Garden cities and town planning*, 1908–32, *Town and country planning*, 1932+. The leading j. in the field. But see also *Town planning review*, Liverpool 1910+, Town Planning Inst., *Papers and discussions* [later *Journal*], 1914+, and Nat. Housing Reform Council, later Nat. Housing and Town Planning Council, *Annual report*, 1901+.

(c) *Experimental Towns and Villages*

7071 ASHWORTH (WILLIAM). 'British industrial villages in the nineteenth century'. *Econ. Hist. Rev.* 2 ser. iii (1950–1), 378–87.

For characteristic writings on the subject by reformers see Henry Solly, *Home colonisation: rehousing of the industrial classes: or, village communities v. town rookeries*, 1884, and *Industrial villages*, 1884, and James Edward Budgett Meakin, *Model factories and villages: ideal conditions of labour and housing*, 1905.

7072 HOLROYD (ABRAHAM). Saltaire, and its founder Sir Titus Salt, Bart. Saltaire. 1871. 2nd edn. 1871.

See also Robert Balgarnie, *Sir Titus Salt, baronet: his life and its lessons*, 1877, repr. Settle 1970. There are also a number of popular lives.

7073 PURDOM (CHARLES BENJAMIN). The garden city: a study in the development of a modern town [Letchworth]. 1913.

See also his *The building of satellite towns* . . ., 1925, rev. edn. 1949, which deals with Letchworth and Welwyn garden cities.

7074　BARNETT (*Dame* HENRIETTA OCTAVIA WESTON). The story of the growth of Hampstead garden suburb, 1907–1928. [1928.]

7075　THE BOURNVILLE VILLAGE TRUST, 1900–1955. Bournville. [1956.]

Apart from this hist. the Trust has publ. a number of other guides and brochures, *Bournville housing: a description of Cadbury Bros. Ltd., and the Bournville Trust*, 1922, *Sixty years of planning: the Bournville experiment* [1942], and *When we build again: a study based on research into conditions of living and working in Birmingham*, 1941.

7076　ONE MAN'S VISION: the story of the Joseph Rowntree Village Trust. 1954.

7077　GEORGE (WALTER LIONEL). Labour and housing at Port Sunlight. 1900.

### 3. Housing

#### (a) *General*

7078　WOOD (EDITH ELMER). Housing progress in Western Europe. N.Y. 1923.

Little more than an outline sketch. There is no general hist. of British housing. For housing generally see urban life (7041 ff.) and building (5754 ff.). For British housing statistics see L. R. Connor, 'Urban housing in England and Wales', *Roy. Stat. Soc. J.* xcix (1936), 1–50, Sir Robert Harry Inglis Palgrave, 'On the house accommodation of England and Wales, with reference to the census of 1871', *Stat. Soc. J.* xxxii (1869), 411–27, and Parry Lewis (5756).

7079　SINGER (HANS WOLFGANG). 'An index of urban land rents and house rents in England and Wales, 1845–1913'. *Econometrica* ix (1941), 221–30.

7080　WEBER (BERNARD). 'A new index of house rents for Great Britain, 1874–1913'. *Scot. J. Pol. Econ.* vii (1960), 232–7.

7081　HILL. Octavia Hill: a biography. By Enid Hester Chataway Moberly Bell. 1942.

Miss Hill was a leading housing and social reformer. See also Charles Edmond Maurice, ed., *Life of Octavia Hill: as told in her letters*, 1913, Emily Southwood Maurice, ed., *Octavia Hill: early ideals, from letters*, 1928, and William Thomson Hill, *Octavia Hill: pioneer of the National Trust and housing reformer*, 1956.

7082　JELLICOE. Basil Jellicoe. By [Archibald] Kenneth Ingram. 1936.

A champion of slum clearance.

#### (b) *Working-Class Housing*

7083　DEWSNUP (ERNEST RITSON). The housing problem in England: its statistics, legislation and policy. Manch. 1907.

Still the best book on the subject. But see John Nelson Tarn, *Working-class housing in nineteenth-century Britain*, 1971. Best read in conjunction with F. H. Millington, *The housing of the poor . . .*, Manch. 1891, Benjamin Seebohm Rowntree and Arthur Cecil Pigou, *Lectures on housing*, Manch. 1914, and John Frederick Joseph Sykes, *Public health and housing: the influence of the dwelling upon health in relation to the changing style of habitation*, 1901.

7084 CLARKE (JOHN JOSEPH). The housing problem: its history, growth, legislation and procedure. 1920.

7085 BARNES (HARRY). The slum, its story and solution. 1931.

7086 DYOS (HAROLD JAMES). 'The slums of Victorian London'. *Victorian Studs.* xi (1967–8), 5–40.

Good, with full bibliog. in notes. For London housing see also **7094**.

7087 WOODFORDE (JOHN). The truth about cottages: fifty types of cottages . . . 1969.

See also **7014–40** and **7117**.

7088 SAVAGE (*Sir* WILLIAM GEORGE). Rural housing. 1915.

Good. See also Sir John Little Green, *English country cottages: their condition, cost and requirements* [1899], Hugh Aronson, *Our village homes: present conditions & suggested remedies*, 1913, and William Walter Crotch, *The cottage homes of England: the case against the housing system in rural districts*, 2nd edn. 1901.

7089 SYKES (JOHN FREDERICK JOSEPH). 'The results of state, municipal, and organized private action on the housing of the working classes in London and in other large cities in the United Kingdom'. *Roy. Stat. Soc. J.* lxiv (1901), 189–253.

7090 U.S. BUREAU OF LABOR STATISTICS. Government aid to house owning and housing of working people in foreign countries. Bulletin 158. 63rd Congress, 3rd Sess. House doc. 1441. Wash. 1915.

7091 ALLAN (CHARLES EDWARD) *and* ALLAN (FRANCIS JOHN). The Housing of the Working Classes Act, 1890, and amending acts, annotated and explained . . . 1898. 4th edn. 1916.

7092 PARSONS (JAMES). Housing by voluntary enterprise: being chiefly an examination of the arguments concerning the provision of dwelling-houses by municipal authorities under Part III of the Housing of the Working Class Acts. 1903.

7093 NEWSHOLME (*Sir* ARTHUR). 'The vital statistics of Peabody Buildings and other artizans' and labourers' block dwellings'. *Roy. Stat. Soc. J.* liv (1891), 70–99.

See also John Nelson Tarn, 'The Peabody donation fund: the role of a housing society in the nineteenth century', *Victorian Studs.* x (1966–7), 7–38.

7094   LONDON COUNTY COUNCIL. Housing of the working classes in London: notes on the action taken between the years 1855 and 1912 for the better housing of the working classes in London . . . 1913.

Further details are given in another L.C.C. report, *The housing question in London* . . . [1901.] See also Hugh Quigley and Ismay Goldie, *Housing and slum clearance in London,* 1934.

7095   MANCHESTER CORPORATION HOUSING COMMITTEE. A short history of Manchester housing. Manch. 1947.

Similar hists. of municipal housing developments have been issued by many other municipalities.

7096   MARR (T. R.). Housing conditions in Manchester and Salford: a report prepared for the Citizens Association for the Improvement of the Unwholesome Dwellings and Surroundings of the People. Manch. 1904.

7097   FAIRBAIRN COMMISSION ON WARMING AND VENTILATION OF DWELLINGS. Report to the General Board of Health by the commissioners appointed to inquire into the warming and ventilation of dwellings [Chairman: William Fairbairn]. H.C. 320 (1857–Sess. 2). XLI, 309.

A pioneer study.

7098   CROSS COMMITTEE ON ARTIZANS' AND LABOURERS' DWELLINGS. Report from the select committee on artizans' and labourers' dwellings improvement [Chairman: Sir Richard Cross]. H.C. 358 (1881). VII, 395. Further report. H.C. 235 (1882). VII, 249.

The first official inquiry concerned with housing as distinct from public health.

7099   DILKE COMMISSION ON HOUSING OF THE WORKING CLASSES. First report of Her Majesty's commissioners for inquiring into the housing of the working classes [Chairman: Sir Charles Wentworth Dilke]. [C. 4402] H.C. (1884–5). XXX, 1. Minutes of evidence. [C. 4402–I] H.C. (1884–5). XXX, 87. Second report [on Scotland]. [C. 4409] H.C. (1884–5). XXXI, 1. Minutes of evidence. [C. 4409–I] H.C. (1884–5). XXXI, 15. Third report [on Ireland]. [C. 4547] H.C. (1884–5). XXXI, 187. Minutes of evidence. [C. 4547–I] H.C. (1884–5). XXXI, 203.

The most important official inquiry of the period. Two later inquiries dealt mainly with legislative problems: *Report from the joint select committee . . . on housing of the working classes* [Chairman: Earl of Camperdown]. H.C. 325 (1902). V, 801, and *Report . . . from the select committee on Housing of the Working Classes Acts Amendment Bill* [Chairman: Sir John Dickson-Poynder]. H.C. 376 (1906). IX, 1. But see also **7051**.

7100   BARRY (FREDERICK WILLIAM) *and* SMITH (PERCIVAL GORDON). Joint report . . . on back-to-back houses, February 1888. Local Government Board. 1888.

An important non-parl. paper. Cont. by L. W. Darra Mair, *Report on back-to-back houses . . . a report on relative mortality in through and back-to-back houses in certain towns in the West Riding of Yorkshire.* [Cd. 5314] H.C. (1910). XXXVIII, 893.

7101 HOLE (JAMES). The homes of the working classes: with suggestions for their improvement. 1866.

One of the best of a long ser. of good books on the subject. See also Octavia Hill, *Homes of the London poor*, 1875, new edn. 1883 and Thomas Locke Worthington, *The dwellings of the poor and weekly wage-earners in large towns*, 1893.

7102 MURPHY (*Sir* SHIRLEY FORSTER) *ed.* Our homes and how to make them healthy. 1883.

7103 BOWMAKER (EDWARD). The housing of the working classes. 1895.

7104 HAW (GEORGE). No room to live: the plaint of overcrowded London. Repr. from the *Daily News*. 1899. 2nd edn. 1900.

7105 FABIAN SOCIETY. The house famine and how to relieve it. 1900.

7106 THOMPSON (WILLIAM). The housing handbook: a practical manual for the use of officers, members, and committees of local authorities, ministers of religion, members of parliament, and all social or municipal reformers interested in the housing of the working classes. Nat. Housing Reform Council. 1903. Repr. with suppl. [Housing up-to-date.] 1907.
Good.

7107 ALDEN (*Sir* PERCY) *and* HAYWARD (EDWARD ERNEST). Housing. Social Service Handbooks no. 1. 1907.

7108 KAUFMAN (MAURITZ). The housing of the working classes and of the poor. Soc. Problems ser. 1907.

7109 HIGGS (MARY) *and* HAYWARD (EDWARD ERNEST). Where shall she live? The homelessness of the woman worker. Nat. Assoc. for Women's Lodging-homes. 1910.
Cont. in their *Where shall she live? The answer* . . ., 1914.

7110 SAYLE (ASHBURNHAM). The houses of the workers. Ed. by John A. Rosevear. 1924.
A good account of housing in 1919.

### (c) *House Design*

There is no adequate hist. Nathaniel Lloyd, *A history of the English house from primitive times to the Victorian period*, 1931, new edn. 1949, Robert Furneaux Jordan, *A picture history of the English house*, 1959, Andrew Henderson, *The family house in England*, 1964, and Martin Shaw Briggs, *The English farmhouse*, 1953, have only a few pages on the period. Books listed below give illustrations and descriptions of some of the better-class building of the period.

7111 DENTON (JOHN BAILEY) *ed.* The farm homesteads of England: a collection of plans of English homesteads existing in different parts of the

country, carefully selected from the most approved specimens of farm architecture, to illustrate the accommodation required under various modes of
husbandry . . . 1863.

7112 KERR (ROBERT). The gentleman's house: or, how to plan English
residences from the parsonage to the palace: with tables of accommodation and
cost and a series of selected plans. 1864. 3rd edn. 1871.

7113 RICHARDSON (CHARLES JAMES). Picturesque designs for mansions, villas, lodges, &c: with decorations, internal and external, suitable to
each style. 1870.

Also publ. in a popular edn. as *The Englishman's house from a cottage to a mansion:
a practical guide . . .*, 1870, 2nd edn. [1871.]

7114 WILKINSON (WILLIAM). English country houses: forty-five views
and plans of recently-erected mansions, private residences, parsonage houses,
farm-houses, lodges and cottages; with a practical treatise on house-building.
Lond. & Oxf. 1870. 2nd edn. [Sixty-one views] 1875.

7115 MUTHESIUS (HERMANN). Das Englische Haus: Entwicklung,
Bedingungen, Anlage, Aufbau, Einrichtung und Innenraum. 3 v. Berlin. 1904–5.
2nd edn. 3 v. 1908–11.

The fullest account of turn-of-the-century housing. See also Charles Holme, ed.,
*Modern British domestic architecture and decoration, The studio*, 1901; Mervyn Edmund
Macartney and others, *Recent English domestic architecture . . . being a special issue of the
Architectural Review*, Annual, 1908+; Walter Shaw Sparrow, ed., *The British home of
to-day: a book of modern domestic architecture & the applied arts*, 1904; Sir Banister
Flight Fletcher and Herbert Phillips Fletcher, *The English home*, 1910; and Sir Lawrence
Weaver, ed., *Small country houses of to-day* [1911], 3rd edn. 2 v. 1922, and *Small country
houses: their repair and enlargement*, 1914.

7116 WEAVER (*Sir* LAWRENCE). Houses and gardens by E. L. Lutyens.
1913. Rev. edn. 1925. Abridged edn. 1921.

See also 9204.

7117 MORRIS (GEORGE LL.) *and* WOOD (ESTHER). The country
cottage. 1906.

A handbook to all types of small houses. See also [John William Robertson Scott] *How
to build or buy a country cottage and fit it up . . . by Home Counties*, 1905; John Gordon
Allen, *The cheap cottage and small house: a manual of economical building*, 1912, 6th edn.
[1919]; Maurice Bingham Adams, ed., *Modern cottage architecture: illustrated from
works of well-known architects*, 1904, 2nd edn. 1912; Robert Alexander Briggs, *Homes
for the country: a series of designs . . .*, 1904; and Sir Lawrence Weaver, *The Country
Life book of cottages . . .*, 1913, 2nd edn. 1919.

(d) *Building Societies*

7118 THE BUILDING SOCIETIES' DIRECTORY AND ALMANACK.
1845–55.

*The building societies' year book*, 1927+, issued by the National Association of Building
Socs., has a useful biog. section.

**7119  THE BUILDING SOCIETIES' GAZETTE. 1869+.**

The main source for building soc. hist.

**7120  PRICE (SEYMOUR JAMES). Building societies: their origin and history. 1958.**

A full general hist. to the 1880s: thereafter primarily a hist. of the Building Societies' Association based on the records of the Association.

**7121  CLEARY (ESMOND JOHN). The building society movement. 1965.**

**7122  BELLMAN (*Sir* CHARLES HAROLD). Bricks and mortals: a study of the building society movement and the story of the Abbey National Society, 1849–1949. 1949.**

Supersedes his *The thrifty three millions: a study of the building society movement and the story of the Abbey Road Society*, 1935.

**7123  BROOKS (WILLIAM COLLIN). The first hundred years of the Woolwich Equitable Building Society. 1947.**

Other hists. of individual socs. include Sir Oscar Rudolf Hobson, *A hundred years of the Halifax: the history of the Halifax Building Society, 1853–1953*, 1953; Seymour James Price, *From Queen to Queen: the centenary story of the Temperance Permanent Building Society, 1854–1954* [1954]; George Elkington, *The National Building Society, 1849–1934*, Camb. 1935; Albert Mansbridge, *Brick upon brick: [Co-operative Permanent Building Society, 1884–1934]*, 1934; and C. J. Lowe, *A half-century record, 1850–1900* [of the Bristol and West Building Society], 1901.

**7124  DAVIS (HENRY FREDERICK ALEXANDER). Building societies: their theory, practice and management. 1887.**

See also *Special report and reports from the select committee on Building Societies (No. 2) Bill* [Chairman: Herbert Gladstone]. H.C. 297 (1893–4). IX, 363; a full inquiry.

**7125  BRABROOK (*Sir* EDWARD WILLIAM). Building societies. 1906.**

In many ways the best intro. to the subject, although very short. Brabrook was Chief Registrar of Friendly Socs.

**7126  HILL. The life of Sir Enoch Hill: the romance of the modern building society. By Reginald Kingsley Bacon. 1934.**

Hill served with the Leek United Building Soc., 1896–1903, and the Halifax Building Soc. from 1903.

**7127  DAVIS (HENRY FREDERICK ALEXANDER). The law of building and freehold land societies . . . 1870. 5th edn. 1931.**

**7128  WURTZBURG (EDWARD ALBERT). The acts relating to building societies. 1886. 10th edn. 1952.**

From the 2nd edn. 1892 entitled *The law relating to building societies*. More a lawyer's book than Davis (**7127**).

**7129  SCRATCHLEY (ARTHUR) *and* BRABROOK (*Sir* EDWARD WILLIAM). The law of building societies . . . 1875. 2nd edn. 1882.**

A brief popular handbook.

## 4. DOMESTIC ARRANGEMENTS

### (a) *General*

7130 GLOAG (JOHN EDWARDS). Victorian comfort: a social history of design from 1830–1900. 1961.

Deals with travel arrangements and pleasure as well as with domestic comfort.

7131 DUTTON (RALPH STAWELL). The Victorian home: some aspects of nineteenth-century taste and manners. 1954.

See also Robert Harling, *Home: a Victorian vignette*, 1938.

7132 LOCHHEAD (MARION CLELAND). The Victorian household. [1964.]

### (b) *Interior Decoration*

7133 DUTTON (RALPH STAWELL). The English interior, 1500 to 1900. 1948.

Like so many other general books dealing mainly with country houses, tails off after 1820. There is little more in Margaret Potter and Alexander Potter, *Interiors: a record of some changes in interior design and furniture of the English home from medieval times to the present day*, 1957, Arthur Stratton, *The English interior: a review of the decoration of English homes from Tudor times to the XIXth century* [1920], and Doreen Yarwood, *The English home: a thousand years of furnishing and decoration*, 1956.

7134 ALLSOPP (HAROLD BRUCE). Decoration and furniture. Vol. I. The English tradition. 1952.

7135 LICHTEN (FRANCES). Decorative art of Victoria's era. N.Y. 1950.

A good book designed chiefly for American readers.

7136 EDWARDS (HERBERT CECIL RALPH) *and* RAMSEY (LEONARD GERALD GWYNNE) *eds*. The Connoisseur period guides to the houses, decoration, furnishing and chattels of the classic periods: the early Victorian period, 1830–1860. 1958.

See also George Bernard Hughes and Therle Hughes, *After the regency, 1820–1860*, 1952.

7137 EASTLAKE (CHARLES LOCK). Hints on household taste in furniture, upholstery and other details. 1868. 4th edn. 1878.

An interesting comparison is with the far more general Ralph Nicholson Wornum, *Analysis of ornament: the characteristics of style: an introduction to the study of the history of ornamental art . . .*, 1856, 10th edn. 1896.

7138 LOFTIE (WILLIAM JOHN). A plea for art in the house: with special reference to the economy of collecting works of art and the importance of taste in education and morals. 1876.

The first vol. in the *Art at home series* which included three other good books on interior decoration: Rhoda and Agnes Garrett, *Suggestions for house decoration in painting*, *woodwork and furniture*, 1877, Mrs. M. J. Loftie, *The dining room*, 1876, and Mary Anne, Lady Barker afterwards Lady Broome, *The bedroom and the boudoir*, 1878.

7139  EDIS (*Sir* ROBERT WILLIAM). Decoration and furniture of town houses: a series of Cantor Lectures delivered before the Society of Arts, 1880, amplified and enlarged. 1881.

A treatise on the middle-class house. See also his *Healthy furniture and decoration*, Int. Health Exhib. 1884.

7140  HAWEIS (MARY ELIZA). The art of decoration. 1881. New edn. 1889.

7141  WATSON (ROSAMUND MARRIOTT). The art of the house. 1897.

7142  WHARTON (EDITH NEWBOLD) *and* CODMAN (OGDEN). The decoration of houses. 1898.

Deals only with country houses.

7143  DAY (LEWIS FOREMAN). Ornament & its application . . . 1904.

7144  ELDER-DUNCAN (JOHN HUDSON). The house beautiful and useful: being practical suggestions on furnishing and decoration. [1907.] New edn. 1911.

See also his *Country cottages and week-end homes*, 1906, 2nd edn. 1912, and Joseph Crouch and Edmund Butler, *The apartments of the house: their arrangement, furnishing and decoration*, 1900.

7145  DUVEEN (EDWARD JOSEPH). Colour in the home: with notes on architecture, sculpture, painting, and upon decoration and good taste. 1912.

7146  THE UNIVERSAL DECORATOR. 1 ser. 3 v. 1858–9. 2 ser. 1860. 3 ser. 3 v. 1861–3.

A vehicle for the illustrations of William Gibbs.

7147  THE JOURNAL OF DECORATIVE ART. Manch. 1881+.

*Decoration in painting, sculpture, architecture and art manufactures*, 1880–9, is a more recherché j.

7148  THE DECORATOR'S GAZETTE and plumber and gasfitter's review. 1884–1908.

Full of details about decoration and household management.

7149  THE HOUSE [BEAUTIFUL]. 1897–1905.

7150  THE DECORATOR: an illustrated monthly magazine for the house painting, decorating and kindred trades: official organ of the London Association of Master Decorators. 1902+.

See also *The decorators' and painters' magazine*, 1901–39, and *The decorator trade reference book and diary*, 1902+.

7151 'THE STUDIO' YEAR BOOK of decorative art. 1906+.

Devoted to 'the application of art to the decoration and general equipment' of the home.

(c) *Furnishings*

For furniture making see **5791–807**.

7152 JOEL (DAVID). The adventure of British furniture, 1851–1951. 1953.

A very useful introductory work. For the terms used see John Edwards Gloag, *A short dictionary of furniture* . . ., 1952. There are a number of general hists., none with much on the period, notably Frederick Litchfield, *Illustrated history of furniture from the earliest to the present time*, 1892, 7th edn. 1922.

7153 ROE (FREDERIC GORDON). Victorian furniture. [1952.]

Good. See also Robert Wemyss Symonds and Bruce Blundell Whineray, *Victorian furniture*, 1962, and Elizabeth Aslin, *Nineteenth-century English furniture*, 1962.

7154 TALBERT (BRUCE J.). Gothic forms applied to furniture, metal work and decoration for domestic purposes. Birmingham. 1867.

7155 YAPP (GEORGE WAGSTAFFE). Art industry: furniture, house fittings and decorations illustrative of the arts of the carpenter joiner . . . 1879.

7156 WATT (WILLIAM). Art furniture from designs by E. W. Godwin, F.S.A., and others: with hints and suggestions on domestic furniture and decoration. 1877.

A typical furniture-dealer's catalogue.

7157 FURNITURE AND DECORATION [Furniture record]. 1890+.

See also *The furniture gazette*, 1872–93.

7158 EDWARDS (HERBERT CECIL RALPH). A history of the English chair. Victoria & Albert Museum. 1951.

7159 ROE (FREDERIC GORDON). Windsor chairs. 1953.

7160 WRIGHT (LAWRENCE). Warm and snug: the history of the bed. 1962.

7161 TATTERSALL (CREASSEY EDWARD CECIL). A history of British carpets: from the introduction of the craft until the present day. Benfleet, Essex. 1934.

7162 ENTWISLE (ERIC ARTHUR). A literary history of wallpaper. 1960.

A comprehensive bibliog. with valuable illus. See also his *The book of wallpaper: a history and an appreciation*, 1954.

7163 SUGDEN (ALAN VICTOR) *and* EDMONDSON (JOHN LUDLAM). A history of English wallpaper, 1509–1914. [1926.]

The standard hist.

7164  JENNINGS (ARTHUR SEYMOUR). Wallpapers and wall coverings: a practical handbook for decorators, paperhangers, architects, builders and houseowners . . . 1903.

The only good contemp. manual. But see also James Arrowsmith, *The paperhanger's and upholsterer's guide* . . . [1854.]

### (d) *Domestic Economy*

7165  SHAW (ROBERT KENDALL) *comp.* Bibliography of domestic economy in English [1850–99]. N.Y. State Libr. Bull. 22. Albany, N.Y. 1901. Valuable.

7166  BEETON (ISABELLA MARY) *ed.* The book of household management. 1861. Frequent edns.

The best-known of all Victorian household guides.

7167  CASSELL'S HOUSEHOLD GUIDE: being a complete encyclopaedia of domestic and social economy, and forming a guide to every department of practical life. 4 v. issued in pts. [1869–71.] Many edns.

An illus. guide to all aspects of home life and associated problems (e.g. water supply), and to arts and crafts.

7168  HAMILTON (H. L.). Household management for the labouring classes. 1882.

7169  WALSH (JOHN HENRY). A manual of domestic economy: suited to families spending from £100 to £1000 a year. 2nd edn. 1857. New edn. 1889.

7170  HAWEIS (MARY ELIZA). The art of housekeeping . . . 1889.

7171  STACKPOOLE (FLORENCE). Handbook of housekeeping for small incomes. [1898.]

Includes guidance to house-hunters.

7172  MARKS (MONTAGUE) *ed.* The cyclopaedia of home arts. 1899.

Reissued as *The home arts self-teacher*, 1901. The sections dealing with fashionable hobbies such as poker-work, bent-iron work, and taxidermy were also reissued as *Home arts and crafts*, 1903.

7173  DAVIDSON (HUGH COLEMAN) *ed.* The book of the home: a practical guide to household management. 8 v. 1905.

A full guide for the middle-class household.

7174  WRIGHT (LAWRENCE). Home fires burning: the history of domestic heating and cooking. 1964.

7175  RAVETZ (ALISON). 'The Victorian coal kitchen and its reformers'. *Victorian Studs.* xi (1967–8), 435–60.

7176  WRIGHT (LAWRENCE). Clean and decent: the fascinating history of the bathroom & the water closet, and of sundry habits, fashions & accessories of the toilet, principally in Great Britain, France & America. 1960.

Popular, as are Geoffrey Ashe, *The tale of the tub: a survey of bathing through the ages*, 1950, and George Ryley Scott, *The story of baths and bathing*, 1939.

### 5. DRESS

7177  COLAS (RENÉ). Bibliographie générale du costume et de la mode: description des suites, recueils, séries, revues et livres français et étrangers relatifs au costume civil, militaire et religieux, aux modes, aux coiffures et aux divers accessoires de l'habillement . . . 2 v. Paris. 1933.

Standard, but now rather dated. Hilaire Hiler and Meyer Hiler, comps., *Bibliography of costume: a dictionary catalog of about eight thousand books and periodicals*, ed. by Helen Grant Cushing and Adah V. Morris, N.Y. 1939, is a good alternative. There is a convenient list of fashion magazines in Buck (**7182**).

7178  LELOIR (MAURICE). Dictionnaire du costume et de ses accessoires, des armes et des étoffes, des origines à nos jours. Paris. 1951.

7179  ASHDOWN (EMILY JESSIE). British costume during XIX centuries, civil and ecclesiastical. 1910. Repr. 1953.

The best of the many short general hists. of British costume, none of them of much value for the period. The most useful of the others are Iris Brooke, *A history of English costume*, 1937, 3rd edn. 1949, Nancy Bradfield, *Historical costumes of England from the eleventh to the twentieth century*, 1938, 2nd edn. 1958, Dion Clayton Calthrop, *English costume painted and described*, 1906, 2nd edn. 1907, and Georgiana Hill, *A history of English dress from the Saxon period to the present day*, 2 v. 1893.

See also Phillis Emily Cunnington and Catherine Lucas, *Occupational costume in England from the eleventh century to 1914*, 1967.

7180  LAVER (JAMES). Taste and fashion from the French Revolution until to-day. 1937. Rev. edn. 1945.

A useful guide to main trends, best used as background reading for Cunnington (**7181**). Laver's *Dress: how and why fashions in men's and women's clothes have changed during the past two hundred years*, 1950, adds little. But see his *Modesty in dress: an inquiry into the fundamentals of fashion*, Lond. & Boston 1969.

7181  CUNNINGTON (CECIL WILLETT) *and* CUNNINGTON (PHIL-LIS EMILY). Handbook of English costume in the nineteenth century. 1959.

Standard, although rivalled by Buck (**7182**). Much fuller than James Laver and Iris Brooke, *English costume in the nineteenth century*, 1929, Herbert Norris and Oswald Curtis, *Costume & fashion: v. 6: the nineteenth century*, 1933, and Dion Clayton Calthrop, *English dress from Victoria to George V*, 1934. Iris Brooke, *English costume, 1900–1950*, 1951, is so far the only attempt at a popular gen. hist. of post-Victorian costume.

7182  BUCK (ANNE MARY). Victorian costume and costume accessories. Lond. 1961. N.Y. 1962.

**7183 CUNNINGTON (CECIL WILLETT). English women's clothing in the nineteenth century. 1937.**

Cont. in his *English women's clothing in the present century*, 1952. These two books form a splendid comprehensive survey. A useful suppl. is Nancy Bradfield, *Costume in detail: women's dress, 1730–1930*, 1968. Ada S. Ballin, *The science of dress in theory and practice*, 1885, relates clothing to health. Mary Eliza Haweis, *The art of dress*, 1879, is another interesting contemp. work. Doris Langley Moore, *The woman in fashion*, 1949, Angus William Eden Holden, Baron Holden, *Elegant modes in the nineteenth century, from high waist to bustle*, 1935, and Aline Bernstein, *Masterpieces of women's costume of the 18th and 19th centuries*, N.Y. 1959, are of little value. For the greatest English couturier of the period, see Edith Saunders, *The age of Worth, couturier to the Empress Eugénie*, Lond. 1954, Bloomington, Ind. 1955.

**7184 GIBBS-SMITH (CHARLES HARVARD). The fashionable lady in the 19th century. Victoria and Albert Museum. 1960.**

An excellent coll. of fashion plates. Fashion plates have a whole lit. of their own. Isabel Stevenson Monro and Dorothy Elizabeth Cook, eds., *Costume index: a subject index to plates and to illustrated text*, N.Y. 1937, suppl. 1957, indexes illus. in books. Vyvyan Beresford Holland, *Hand-coloured fashion plates, 1770 to 1899*, 1955, and James Laver, *Fashions and fashion plates, 1800–1900*, 1943, are the most accessible colls. of reprints. Alison Gernsheim, *Fashion and reality*, 1963, is also a picture book.

**7185 WAUGH (NORAH). The cut of men's clothes, 1600–1900. 1964.**

Suppl. by her *The cut of women's clothes, 1600–1930*, 1968.

**7186 BROOKE (IRIS). English children's costume since 1775. 1930.**

See also Doris Langley Moore, *The child in fashion*, 1953, James Laver, ed., *Children's fashions in the nineteenth century*, 1951, Wallace Clare, *The historic dress of the English schoolboy*, 1 ser. 1940, and Phillis Emily Cunnington and Anne Mary Buck, *Children's costume in England . . .*, 1965.

**7187 HARRISON (MICHAEL). The history of the hat. 1960.**

**7188 CUNNINGTON (CECIL WILLETT) and CUNNINGTON (PHILLIS EMILY). The history of underclothes. 1952.**

Norah Waugh, *Corsets and crinolines*, 1954, is particularly useful for prices and fashions. See also Cecil Saint-Laurent, pseud. of Jacques Laurent, *A history of ladies underwear*, 1968.

**7189 VON BOEHN (MAX ULRIC). Modes & manners: ornaments, lace, fans, gloves, walking sticks, parasols, jewellery and trinkets. [1929.]**

For fans there is the monumental hist. by George Woolliscroft Rhead, *History of the fan*, 1910. On the umbrella see T. S. Crawford, *A history of the umbrella*, Newton Abbot & N.Y. 1970.

**7190 TUTE (WARREN STANLEY). The grey top hat: the story of Moss Bros. of Covent Garden. 1961.**

A hist. of the largest of the firms specializing in the hire of clothing.

## E. SOCIAL WELFARE

### 1. GENERAL

**7191 KEEBLE (SAMUEL EDWARD). The ABC annotated bibliography on social questions. 1907.**

See also William Dwight Porter Bliss, ed., *The encyclopedia of social reform* . . ., 1897, and *The new encyclopedia of social reform* . . ., 1908. A number of other contemp. works also attempt a survey of social questions incl. *The social science* ser. and the *Social questions of today* ser., S. E. Keeble, ed., *The citizen of tomorrow: a handbook on social questions* [1906], and Helen L. Kerr, *The path of social progress: a discussion of old and new ideas of social reform* . . ., Edin. 1912. Frederic Harrison, *National & social problems*, 1908, Samuel Augustus Barnett and Dame Henrietta Octavia Weston Barnett, *Towards social reform*, 1909, and Charles Frederick Gurney Masterman, *The condition of England*, 1909, new edn. 1960, reflect the anxiety of 1906–14 over the social question.

**7192 BRUCE (MAURICE). The coming of the welfare state. 1961.**

A good outline to be suppl. by Gilbert (**7379**). There are also a number of introductory hists. incl. Harold Ernest Raynes, *Social security in Britain: a history*, 1957, 2nd edn. 1960, Karl De Schweinitz, *England's road to social security* . . ., Phila. 1943, and William Hardy Wickwar and Kathleen Margaret Wickwar, *The social services: an historical survey*, 1936, new edn. 1949. Ernest Sackville Turner, *Roads to ruin: the shocking history of social reform*, 1950, is popular, Roy Lubove, ed., *Social welfare in transition: selected English documents, 1834–1909*, Pittsburgh 1966, an introductory coll. Robert Archey Woods, *English social movements*, N.Y. 1891, is a useful summary of the state of contemp. knowledge, to which Carlton Joseph Huntley Hayes, *British social politics: materials illustrating contemporary state action for the solution of social problems* [1905–12], Boston 1913, was a successor.

**7193 ROBERTS ([FREDERICK] DAVID). Victorian origins of the British welfare state. New Haven [Conn.]. 1960. Repr. Hamden, Conn. 1969.**

Useful for the situation in 1855.

**7194 MIDWINTER (ERIC CLARE). Social administration in Lancashire, 1830–1860: poor law, public health and police. Manch. 1969.**

**7195 INGLIS (KENNETH STANLEY). 'English nonconformity and social reform, 1880–1900'. *Past & Present* xiii (1958), 73–88.**

For Evangelicals and social problems see **7204**. For the Salvation Army see **7223–4**.

**7196 SOFFER (REBER NUSBAUM). 'The revolution in English social thought, 1880–1914'. *Amer. Hist. Rev.* lxxv (1970), 1938–64.**

See also Arthur Marwick, 'The Labour party and the welfare state in Britain, 1900–1948', *Amer. Hist. Rev.* lxxiii (1967–8), 380–403, and Charles Loch Mowat, 'Social legislation in Britain and the United States in the early twentieth century: a problem in the history of ideas', *Hist. Studs.* vii (1969), 81–96.

**7197 JONES (DAVID CARADOG). Social surveys. [1949.]**

An intro. to the surveys of Booth, Rowntree, and Bowley. There is little more in Alan Frank Wells, *The local social survey in Great Britain*, 1935. For earlier investigations see **8541**. For a general interpretation see Oliver Ross McGregor, 'Social research and social policy in the nineteenth century', *British J. Sociology* viii (1957), 146–57.

7198 ARMYTAGE (WALTER HARRY GREEN). Heavens below: utopian experiments in England, 1560–1960. 1961.

7199 NATIONAL ASSOCIATION FOR THE PROMOTION OF SOCIAL SCIENCE. Transactions. Annual 1857–84. 1886.

Important for many aspects of social welfare. For other contemp. colls. of papers on social problems see, *inter alia*, Lyon Playfair, Baron Playfair, *Subjects of social welfare*, 1889, and Bernard Bosanquet, ed., *Aspects of the social problem*, 1895.

## 2. PHILANTHROPY AND SOCIAL WORK

### (a) *General*

7200 CHARITY ORGANISATION SOCIETY. Catalogue of the library. 2 pts. 1893–4.

7201 OWEN (DAVID EDWARD). English philanthropy, 1660–1960. Camb., Mass. 1965.

A remarkably balanced survey. For a full review see Brian Howard Harrison, 'Philanthropy and the Victorians', *Victorian Studs.* ix (1966), 353–74.

7202 YOUNG (AGNES FREDA) *and* ASHTON (ELWYN THOMAS). British social work in the nineteenth century. 1956.

See also Marjorie Jean Smith, *Professional education for social work in Britain: an historical account*, Nat. Inst. for Social Work Training ser. 5, 1965, a new edn. of a booklet first publ. by the Family Welfare Assoc. in 1952.

7203 WOODROOFE (KATHLEEN). From charity to social work in England and the United States. 1962.

7204 HEASMAN (KATHLEEN JOAN). Evangelicals in action: an appraisal of their social work in the Victorian era. 1962.

See also John Christian Pringle, *Social work of the London churches: being some account of the Metropolitan Visiting and Relief Association, 1843–1937*, 1937.

7205 BEVERIDGE (WILLIAM HENRY), *Baron Beveridge*. Voluntary action: a report on methods of social advance. 1948.

Includes short hists. of the major charities and welfare organizations. Suppl. by *The evidence for voluntary action . . .*, ed. by Beveridge and Alan Frank Wells, 1949. See also Madeline Rooff, *Voluntary societies and social policy*, 1957, and Mary Morris, Baroness Morris, *Voluntary organisations and social progress*, 1955.

7206 BOURDILLON (ANNE FRANCES CLAUDINE) *ed.* Voluntary social services: their place in the modern state. 1945.

7207 CHARITY COMMISSION. Annual report. 1854+.

An important source. For the operation of the commission see *Report from the select committee on Charity Commission* [Chairman: John Ellis]. H.C. 221 (1894). XI, 1. For the possible extension of the Charitable Trusts Acts to cover allotments, etc., see *Report from the select committee on Charitable Trusts Acts* [Chairman: G. J. Shaw-Lefevre].

H.C. 306 (1884). IX, 1. Further report. H.C. 33 (1884–5). VIII, 1. For the law see Owen Davies Tudor, *The Charitable Trusts Act, 1853 . . .*, 1854, 5th edn. 1929, and Richard Edmund Mitchison, *Charitable trusts: the jurisdiction of the Charity Commission . . .*, 1887. For the principles involved see Courtney Stanhope Kenny, *The true principles of legislation with regard to property given for charitable and other public uses*, 1880, and Arthur Hobhouse, Baron Hobhouse, *The dead hand: addresses on the subject of endowments and settlements of property*, 1880.

7208  HENDERSON (CHARLES RICHMOND) *and others*. Modern methods of charity: an account of the systems of relief, public and private, in the principal countries having modern methods. N.Y. 1904.

See also George Milner Bell, ed., *Social service: a handbook for workers and visitors in London and other large towns*, 1908.

7209  MACKAY (THOMAS). The state and charity. 1898.

7210  GRAY (BENJAMIN KIRKMAN). Philanthropy and the state: or, social politics. Ed. by Eleanor Kirkman Gray and B. [i.e. Elizabeth] Leigh Hutchins. 1908.

7211  MOWAT (CHARLES LOCH). The Charity Organisation Society, 1869–1913: its ideas and work. 1961.

See also Kathleen Woodroofe, 'The Charity Organisation Society and the origins of social casework', *Hist. Studs. Aust. & N.Z.* ix (1959–61), 19–29. The soc. set the tone of debate about private versus public philanthropy. It publ. an annual *Report of the Council*, 1870+, *The Charity Organisation reporter*, 1872–84, *The Charity Organisation review*, 1885–1921, *Charity Organisation papers*, 1–20, 1881, rev. edn. 1896, repr. 1900, 1907, *C.O.S. occasional papers*, 4 ser. 1896, repr. 1900, 1905, 1907, 1913, and *The [annual] charities register* (**7214**). There is a list of misc. publs. in Mowat. For an account of the society's work by insiders see Charles Bertie Pulleine Bosanquet, *The organisation of charity: the history and mode of operation of the Charity Organisation Society*, 1874, Helen Dendy Bosanquet, *Social work in London, 1869 to 1912: a history of the Charity Organisation Society*, 1914, and the works of C. S. Loch (**7212**). Daniel Coit Gilman, ed., *The organization of charities: being a report of the sixth section of the International Congress of Charities, Corrections and Philanthropy, Chicago, June 1893*, 1894, is largely on C.O.S. lines.

7212  LOCH (*Sir* CHARLES STEWART). Charity organisation. 1890.

Loch was the leading light of the Charity Organisation Soc. (**7211**). For his ideas see also his *Charity and social life: a short study of religious and social thought in relation to charitable methods and institutions*, 1910, and the vol. he ed. called *Methods of social advance . . .*, 1904. For the views of Loch's colleagues see, *inter alia*, Helen Dendy Bosanquet, *Rich and poor*, Lond. & N.Y. 1896, 2nd edn. 1898, and *The strength of the people: a study in social economics*, Lond. & N.Y. 1902, 2nd edn. 1903, and the ser. ed. by Loch styled the *Charity organisation series*. For Lock's life see **7241**.

7213  LOW'S HANDBOOK TO THE CHARITIES OF LONDON. 1836+.

7214  THE [ANNUAL] CHARITIES REGISTER and digest: being, a classified register of charities in or available for persons in the metropolis. Charity Organisation Soc. 1882+. Annual.

7215  LOW (SAMPSON). The charities of London in 1852–3: presenting a report on the operation, resources and general condition of the charitable and religious institutions of London. 1854. New edn. 1862.

7216  BOSANQUET (CHARLES BERTIE PULLEINE). London: some account of its growth, charitable agencies and wants. 1868.

Good. See also his *A handy-book for visitors of the poor in London: with chapters on poor law, sanitary law and charities*, 1874.

7217  OWEN (DAVID EDWARD). 'The City parochial charities: the "dead hand" in late Victorian London'. *J. British Studs.* i (1961–2), 115–35.

There was a big inquiry into the city charities: see *Report of the Royal City parochial charities commission* [Chairman: Duke of Northumberland]. [C. 2522] H.C. (1880). XX, 1. Minutes of evidence, sub-commissioner's reports, and details of accounts. [C. 2522–I to III] H.C. (1880). XX, 51, 367, 735. See also *Report from the select committee on Parochial Charities (London) Bill and London Parochial Charities Bill* [Chairman: G. J. Shaw-Lefevre]. H.C. 205 (1882). XII, 1. Further report. H.C. 185 (1883). XIV, 515.

7218  WOODALL COMMITTEE ON ROYAL PATRIOTIC FUND. Report from the select committee on the Royal Patriotic Fund [Chairman: William Woodall]. H.C. 347 (1895). XII, 241. Further report. H.C. 368 (1896). XIII, 75.

7219  ROYAL HUMANE SOCIETY. Annual report: 1775+.

7220  BARRON (EDWARD EVELYN). The National Benevolent Institution, 1812–1936: a short account of its rise and progress extracted from the minutes. 1936.

7221  IMRAY (JEAN). The charity of Richard Whittington: a history of the trust administered by the Mercers' Company, 1424–1966. 1968.

7222  SIMEY (MARGARET BAYNE), *Lady Simey*. Charitable effort in Liverpool in the nineteenth century. Liverpool. 1952.

Good. See also Herbert Reginald Poole, *The Liverpool Council of Social Service, 1909–1959*, Liverpool 1960, and Anne Durning Holt, *A ministry to the poor: being the history of the Liverpool Domestic Mission Society, 1836–1936*, 1936.

7223  SEARCH ([MARION] PAMELA). Happy warriors: the story of the social work of the Salvation Army. 1956.

There are also hists. of a considerable number of local missions such as Elsbeth Platt, *The story of the Ranyard Mission, 1857–1937*, 1937.

7224  HAGGARD (*Sir* HENRY RIDER). Report on the Salvation Army colonies in the United States and at Hadleigh, England, with scheme of national land settlement. [Cd. 2562] H.C. (1905). LIII, 359.

Also publ. as *The poor and the land . . .*, 1905. See also **3872, 4180, 6984**.

7225  BROWN (JOHN). 'Charles Booth and labour colonies, 1889–1905'. *Econ. Hist. Rev.* 2 Ser. xxi (1968), 349–60.

BARNETT. For Canon Barnett and his wife see **7310**.

7226 BEDFORD. Peter Bedford, the Spitalfields philanthropist. By William Tallack. 1865. New edn. 1893.

7227 BOOTH. Charles Booth: social scientist. By Thomas Spensley Simey, Baron Simey, and Margaret Bayne Simey, Baroness Simey. 1960.

7228 BROWN. Mrs. John Brown, 1847–1935: an account of her social work in Lancashire and South Africa, of her memories of Lancashire folk and of her friendship with Olive Schreiner. Ed. by Angela James and Nina Hills. 1937.
Interesting for social work in Burnley and for the ideas of an interesting woman.

7229 BURDETT-COUTTS. Angela Burdett-Coutts and the Victorians. By Clara Burdett Patterson. 1953.
See also Edgar Johnson, ed., *Letters from Charles Dickens to Angela Burdett-Coutts, 1841–1865*, 1953.

7230 CADBURY. Life of George Cadbury. By Alfred George Gardiner. 1923.
See also Helen Cadbury Alexander, *Richard Cadbury of Birmingham*, 1906, Richenda Scott, *Elizabeth Cadbury, 1858–1951*, 1955, and Janet Payne Whitney, *Geraldine S. Cadbury, 1865–1941: a biography*, 1948.

7231 CARNEGIE. Andrew Carnegie. By Joseph Frazier Wall. Lond. and N.Y. 1970.
Repl. Burton Jesse Hendrick, *The life of Andrew Carnegie*, 2 v., Garden City, N.Y. 1932. See also John Charles Van Dyke, ed., *Autobiography of Andrew Carnegie*, 1920, and *Centenary of the birth of Andrew Carnegie: the British trusts and their work, with a chapter on the American foundations*, Edin. 1935.

7232 CARPENTER. The life and work of Mary Carpenter. By Joseph Estlin Carpenter. 1879.
See also Dame Millicent Garrett Fawcett, *Mary Carpenter*, 1912. Important for reformatories and child care.

7233 COBBE. Life of Frances Power Cobbe. By herself. 1894. New edn. 1904.

7234 DENISON. A brief record: being selections from letters and other writings of the late Edward Denison, M.P. for Newark. Ed. by Sir Baldwyn Leighton. Priv. pr. 1871. New edns. 1872, 1884.

7235 EDWARDS. J. Passmore Edwards, philanthropist . . . By Edwin Harcourt Burrage. 1902.
Edwards himself publ. *A few footprints*, 1905. J. J. Macdonald, *Passmore Edwards institutions: founding and opening ceremonies*, 1900, is an admirable album of architectural drawings.

7236 FOX. Francis William Fox: a biography. By James Edward Geoffrey de Montmorency. 1923.

7237   HILL. Octavia Hill: a biography. By Enid Hester Chataway Moberly Bell. 1942.
See also 7081.

7238   HOLE. Social reform in Victorian Leeds: the work of James Hole, 1820–1895. By John Fletcher Clews Harrison. Thoresby Soc. Leeds. 1954.

7239   JEBB. Rebel daughter of a country house: the life of Eglantyne Jebb, founder of the Save the Children Fund. By Francesca Mary Wilson. 1967.

7240   JOHNSON. George William Johnson: civil servant and social worker. By Alice Johnson. Priv. pr. Camb. 1927.

7241   LOCH. A great ideal and its champion: papers and addresses by the late Sir Charles Stewart Loch. 1923.
See also Mowat on the Charity Organisation Soc. (7211) and Loch's works (7212).

7242   LONSDALE. Recollections of Sophia Lonsdale. Comp. by Violet Martineau. 1936.

7243   MARSH. The life and friendships of Catherine Marsh. By L. E. O'Rorke. 1917.

7244   MEATH. The diaries of Mary, Countess of Meath. Ed. by Reginald Brabazon, Earl of Meath. 2 v. [1928–9.]

7245   MOORE. George Moore: merchant and philanthropist. By Samuel Smiles. 1878.

7246   MORLEY. The life of Samuel Morley. By Edwin Hodder. 1887.

7247   NUNN. Thomas Hancock Nunn: the life and work of a social reformer: written by his friends. 1942.

7248   PAGET. Lady Muriel: Lady Muriel Paget, her husband and her philanthropic work in central and eastern Europe. By Wilfrid Jasper Walter Blunt. 1962.

7249   PEABODY. The life of George Peabody. By Phebe Ann Hanaford. Boston. 1870. Repr. N.Y. 1970.

RATHBONE. For William Rathbone see 873.

7250   ROGERS. Reminiscences of William Rogers . . . Comp. by Robert Henry Hadden. 1888. 2nd edn. 1888.

7251   ROWNTREE. Social thought and social action: a study of the work of Seebohm Rowntree, 1871–1954. By Asa Briggs. 1961.
See also Anne Vernon, *A Quaker business man: the life of Joseph Rowntree, 1836–1925,* 1958, Elfrida Vipont [Foulds], *Arnold Rowntree: a life,* 1955, Phebe Doncaster, *John*

*Stephenson Rowntree: his life and work: memoir*, 1908, and S. Elizabeth Robson, *Joshua Rowntree . . .*, 1916.

7252  SHAFTESBURY. The life and work of the seventh Earl of Shaftesbury, K.G. By Edwin Hodder. 3 v. 1886. 1-v. edn. 1893.

The official biog. A good short life is John Lawrence Le Breton Hammond and Lucy Barbara Hammond, *Lord Shaftesbury*, 1923, 4th edn. 1936, repr. Lond. 1939, Hamden, Conn. 1969. Geoffrey Francis Andrew Best, *Shaftesbury*, 1964, is a perceptive sketch. Florence Mary Greir Higham, *Lord Shaftesbury: a portrait*, 1945, does little more than replace a long series of popular lives, none of them now worth reading. John Wesley Bready, *Lord Shaftesbury and social-industrial progress*, 1926, Edwin Hodder, *The seventh Earl of Shaftesbury, K.G., as social reformer*, 1897, and *A memoir of the Right Hon. Earl of Shaftesbury, K.G., compiled from original sources, under the direction of the editor of the 'Record'*, 1885, incl. useful information. There is also much of value in the 'Shaftesbury Lectures', which are publ. from time to time, and in Shaftesbury's *Speeches . . . upon subjects having relation chiefly to the claims and interests of the labouring class*, 1868.

7253  SOLLY. These eighty years: or the story of an unfinished life. By Henry Solly. 2 v. 1893.

7254  SOMERSET. Lady Henry Somerset. By Kathleen Fitzpatrick. 1923.

7255  TWINING. Recollections of life and work: being the autobiography of Louisa Twining. 1893.

7256  WATERLOW. The life of Sir Sydney H. Waterlow, Bart., London apprentice, Lord Mayor, captain of industry and philanthropist. By George Washburn Smalley. 1909.

### (b) *Child Care and Youth Work*

Much of the best material on this subject was publ. in the reports of bodies like the Boys' and Girls' Refuges and Homes and children's missions. See also children's employment, **6665–74**.

7257  McCLEARY (GEORGE FREDERICK). The early history of the infant welfare movement. 1933.

See also his *The maternity and child welfare movement*, 1935, and *Infantile mortality and infants' milk depôts*, 1905.

7258  ALLEN (ANNE) and MORTON (ARTHUR). This is your child: the story of the National Society for the Prevention of Cruelty to Children. 1961.

7259  WAUGH. The life of Benjamin Waugh. By Rosa Waugh, afterwards Hobhouse. 1913.

There is also an outline life, Rosa Waugh Hobhouse, *Benjamin Waugh: founder of the National Society for the Prevention of Cruelty to Children and framer of the 'children's charter'*, 1939.

7260  MONTAGUE (C. J.). Sixty years in waifdom: or, the ragged school movement in English history. 1904.

7261   WILLIAMSON (DAVID). Ninety not out: a record of ninety years' child welfare work of the Shaftesbury Society and R[agged] S[chool] U[nion]. 1934.

See also his *Lord Shaftesbury's legacy* . . . [1924], and V. I. Cuthbert, *Where dreams come true: a record of 95 years: the Shaftesbury homes and 'Arethusa' training ship* (*formerly the National Refuges for Homeless and Destitute Children*), 1937.
The Union publ. an annual report and *The Ragged School Union mag.*, 1849–75, cont. as *The Ragged School Union quart. record*, 1876–81, *In his name* . . ., 1888–1907, and *The Shaftesbury mag.*, 1908+.

7262   KIRK. Sir John Kirk: the life story of the children's friend. By David Williamson. [1922.]

See also John Stuart, *Mr. John Kirk, the children's friend* . . . [1907.] Kirk kept the Ragged School Union alive into the 20th cent.

7263   GORST (*Sir* JOHN ELDON). The children of the nation: how their health and vigour should be promoted by the state. 1906.

One of the best of a large class of books, which were widely read by contemporaries. See also Gertrude Mary Tuckwell, *The state and its children*, 1894, Third International Congress for the Welfare and Protection of Children, *Report of the proceedings*, ed. by Sir William Chance, 1902, and the report of a special conference convened by the British section of the Congress, *Legislation in regard to children* . . ., 1906.

7264   INGLIS (M. K.). The children's charter: a sketch of the scope and main provisions of the Children Act, 1908, containing suggestions for social workers throughout the kingdom. 1909.

7265   GREENWOOD (ARTHUR). The health and physique of school children. 1913.

See also his *Juvenile labour exchanges and after care*, 1911.

7266   BULKLEY (MILDRED EMILY). The feeding of school children. 1914.

See also Hilda Jennings, *The private citizen in public social work: an account of the voluntary children's care committee system in London*, 1930, Hilary Douglas Clerk Pepler, *The care committee, the child and the parent* . . .: *a history of the provision of meals to the children of poor parents and an account of children's care committees* . . ., 1912, and Maud Frances Davies, *School care committees: a guide to their work*, 1909.

7267   BEAVAN. Margaret Beavan of Liverpool: her character and work. By Ivy Ada Ireland. Liverpool. 1938.

Cared for invalid children.

7268   HILTON. Marie Hilton, her life and work, 1821–1896. By J. Deane Hilton. 1897.

Social worker and founder of crèches.

7269   McMILLAN. Margaret McMillan: prophet and pioneer: her life and work. By Albert Mansbridge. 1932.

See also George Alfred Norman Lowndes, *Margaret McMillan: 'the children's champion'*, 1960, Walter D'Arcy Cresswell, *Margaret McMillan: a memoir*, 1948, and the publ. 'Margaret McMillan lectures'. McMillan's best-known work is *The nursery school*, 1919.

7270  McMILLAN. The life of Rachel McMillan. By Margaret McMillan. 1927.

Useful on nursery schools.

7271  SUMNER. Mary Sumner: her life and work. Part I. Memoir. By Mary Bidder, afterwards Porter. Part II. A short history of the Mothers' Union. By Mary Underwood. Winchester. 1921. 2nd edn. of Pt. I. [1927.]

7272  MÜLLER (GEORG FRIEDRICH). The life of trust: being a narrative of the Lord's dealings with George Müller, written by himself. 2 pts. 1837–41. New edn. N.Y. 1878.

A full account of one of the most successful orphanages. See also G. F. Bergin, comp., *Autobiography of George Müller*, 1905; William Elfe Tayler, *Ashley Down: or, living faith in a living God: memorials of the new orphan houses on Ashley Down, Bristol, under the superintendence of George Müller*, 1861, rev. edn. [*The Bristol orphan houses . . .*] [1871]; Emma Raymond Pitman, *George Müller and Andrew Reed*, 1885; Andrew and Charles Reed, eds., *Memoirs of the life and philanthropic labours of Andrew Reed, with selections from his journals*, 2nd edn. 1863; Arthur Rendle Short, ed., *The diary of George Müller: selected extracts*, 1954, Nancy Garton, *George Müller and his orphans*, 1963, and **3456**.

7273  BIRT (LILIAN M.). The children's home-finder: the story of Annie Macpherson and Louisa Birt . . . 1913.

See also Clara M. S. Lowe, *God's answers: a record of Miss Annie Macpherson's work at the Home of Industry, Spitalfields, London, and in Canada*, 1882.

7274  WAIFS AND STRAYS SOCIETY. The first forty years: a chronicle of the Waifs & Strays Society. 1922.

7275  JEFFS (ERNEST H.). Motherless: the story of Robert Thomson Smith and the first homes for motherless children. [1930.]

7276  BARNARDO. Memoirs of the late Dr. Barnardo. By Mrs. Syrie Louise Barnardo and Sir James Marchant. 1907.

See also John Herridge Batt, *Dr Barnardo: the foster-father of 'nobody's children': a record and an interpretation*, 1904; John Wesley Bready, *Doctor Barnardo: physician, pioneer, prophet: child life yesterday and today*, 1930, repr. 1935; Arthur Edmund Williams, *Barnardo of Stepney: the father of nobody's children*, 1943, 3rd edn. 1966; Donald Frank William Ford, *Dr. Barnardo*, 1958; and A. R. Neuman, *Dr. Barnardo as I knew him: by one of his staff*, 1914. For an attack on the Barnardo homes in their early days, and its consequences, see George Reynolds, *Dr. Barnardo's homes: containing startling revelations*, 1877, and *The Charity Organisation Society and the Reynolds–Barnardo arbitration*, 1878.

7277  FEGAN. J. W. C. Fegan: a tribute. By William Young Fullerton [1930].

Established rescue homes for boys.

7278  SHARMAN. Charlotte Sharman: the romance of a great faith. By Marguerite Williams. [1931.]

Established children's homes.

7279 STEPHENSON. The life of the Reverend Thomas Bowman Stephenson, B.A., LL.D., D.D., founder of 'The Children's Home' and of the Wesley Deaconess Institute. By William Bradfield. 1913.

7280 PERCIVAL (ALICIA CONSTANCE). Youth will be led: the story of the voluntary youth organizations. 1951.

A useful general hist.

7281 EAGAR (WALDO McGILLYCUDDY). Making men: the history of boys' clubs and related movements in Great Britain. 1953.

See also Berman Paul Neuman, *The boys club in theory and practice*, 1900, Ernest Milbourne Swinnerton Pilkington, *An Eton playing field: a reminiscence of happy days spent at the Eton Mission*, 1896, Frank Whitbourn, *Lex: the biography of Alexander Devine, founder of Clayesmore School*, 1937, and Hector Graham Gordon Mackenzie, *Medical control in a boys' club: being, the record of the Hollington club clinic, 1909–1924*, 1925.

7282 STEVENSON (GEORGE JOHN). Historical records of the Young Men's Christian Association, from 1844 to 1884. [1884.]

There is no satisfactory later hist. But see the reminiscences of a national secretary, Sir Arthur Keysall Yapp, *In the service of youth*, 1927, and the life of Sir George Williams (**7283**).

7283 WILLIAMS. The life of Sir George Williams. By Sir John Ernest Hodder Williams. 1906. Rev. edn. [The father of the red triangle.] 1918.

7284 DUGUID (JULIAN). The blue triangle. 1955.

A history of the Y.W.C.A. See also Lucy M. Moor, *Girls of yesterday and to-day: the romance of the Y.W.C.A.*, 1910, Dame Emily Kinnaird, *Reminiscences*, 1925, the Y.W.C.A. *Annual report*, 1877+, and *The blue triangle*, 1884+.

7285 COLLIS (HENRY JOHN GURNEY), HURLL (ALFRED WILLIAM), *and* HAZLEWOOD (REX DENYS MICHAEL). B.-P.'s scouts: an official history of the Boy Scouts' Association. 1961.

See also Eileen Kirkpatrick Wade, *Twenty-one years of scouting: the official history of the boy scout movement from its inception*, 1929.

7286 BADEN-POWELL. Baden-Powell: a biography of Lord Baden-Powell of Gilwell. By Ernest Edwin Reynolds. 1942. 2nd edn. 1957.

See also Eileen Kirkpatrick Wade, *Olave Baden-Powell: the authorised biography of the world chief guide*, 1971, and **2794**.

7287 SMITH. William A. Smith of the Boys' Brigade. By Frederick P. Gibbon. [1934.]

See also Austin Edward Birch, *The story of the Boys' Brigade*, 1959, 2nd edn. 1965.

7288 CARPENTER (MARY). Reformatory schools for the children of the perishing and dangerous classes and for juvenile offenders. 1851.

A famous work. Mary Carpenter also publ. *Juvenile delinquents: their condition and treatment*, 1853, *The claims of ragged schools to pecuniary educational aid . . .*, 1859, *Our convicts*, 2 v. 1864, and *Reformatory prison discipline . . .*, 1872. For her life see **7232**.

7289 SYMONS (JELINGER COOKSON) *ed.* On the reformation of young offenders: a collection of papers, pamphlets and speeches on reformatories . . . 1855.

7290 REFORMATORY AND REFUGE UNION. The provincial reformatories and refuges: an authentic account of 58 institutions. 1857.
Suppl. by *The metropolitan reformatories* . . ., 4th edn. 1859.

7291 ADSHEAD (JOSEPH). 'On juvenile criminals, reformatories, and the means of rendering the perishing and dangerous classes serviceable to the state'. *Manch. Stat. Soc. Trans.* (1855–6), 67–122.
A useful survey. See also Thomas Barwick Lloyd Baker, 'Abstracts and inferences founded upon the official criminal returns of England and Wales for the years 1854–9, with special reference to the results of reformatories', *Stat. Soc. J.* xxiii (1860), 427–54, and Joseph Fletcher, 'Statistics of the farm school system of the continent, and of its applicability to the preventive and reformatory education of pauper and criminal children in England', *Stat. Soc. J.* xv (1852), 1–49.

7292 BAINES COMMITTEE ON CRIMINAL AND DESTITUTE CHILDREN. Report from the select committee on criminal and destitute juveniles [Chairman: M. T. Baines]. H.C. 515 (1852). VII, 1.
The inquiry was cont. by *Report from the select committee on criminal and destitute children* [Chairman: M. T. Baines]. H.C. 674 (1852–3). XXIII, 1. The two reports together make up a comprehensive study.

7293 NORTHCOTE COMMITTEE ON THE EDUCATION OF DESTITUTE CHILDREN. Report from the select committee on the education of destitute children [Chairman: Sir Stafford Northcote]. H.C. 460 (1861). VII, 395.

7294 HOME OFFICE. Reports to the secretary of state for the home department on the state of the law relating to the treatment and punishment of juvenile offenders. [C. 2808] H.C. (1881). LIII, 555.
Replies to an inquiry as to how the law might be amended.

7295 ABERDARE COMMISSION ON REFORMATORIES AND INDUSTRIAL SCHOOLS. Reformatories and Industrial Schools Commission: report of the commissioners [Chairman: Lord Aberdare]. [C. 3876] H.C. (1884). XLV, 1. Minutes of evidence. [C. 3876–I] H.C. (1884). XLV, 89.

7296 LUSHINGTON COMMITTEE ON REFORMATORY AND INDUSTRIAL SCHOOLS. Report to the secretary of state for the home department of the departmental committee on reformatory and industrial schools [Chairman: Sir Godfrey Lushington]. [C. 8204] H.C. (1896). XLV, 1. Evidence. [C. 8290] H.C. (1897). XLII, 1.
A monumental inquiry. See also Henry Michael Jenkins, 'Farming and agricultural training in reformatory and industrial schools: with notes on spade labour', *Roy. Agric. Soc. J.* xlvii (1886), 171–236.

7297  MORRISON (WILLIAM DOUGLAS). Juvenile offenders. 1896.

7298  WATSON (JOHN). 'Reformatory and industrial schools'. *Roy. Stat. Soc. J.* lix (1896), 255–312.

7299  BARRETT (ROSA MARY). 'The treatment of juvenile offenders: together with statistics of their numbers'. *Roy. Stat. Soc. J.* lxiii (1900), 183–261.

7300  COCHRANE COMMITTEE ON FUNDS FOR REFORMATORY AND INDUSTRIAL SCHOOLS. Report of the inter-departmental committee on the provision of funds for reformatory and industrial schools [Chairman: T. H. A. E. Cochrane]. [Cd. 3143] H.C. (1906). LIV, 1. Minutes of proceedings. [Cd. 3144] H.C. (1906). LIV, 55.

7301  MASTERMAN COMMITTEE ON REFORMATORY AND INDUSTRIAL SCHOOLS. Report of the departmental committee on reformatory and industrial schools [Chairman: C. F. G. Masterman]. [Cd. 6838] H.C. (1913). XXXIX, 1. Minutes of evidence. [Cd. 6839] H.C. (1913). XXXIX, 117.

7302  BARNETT (MARY G.). Young delinquents: a study of reformatory and industrial schools. 1913.

7303  INSPECTOR OF REFORMATORY AND INDUSTRIAL SCHOOLS. Annual report. 1857–1915.

7304  REFORMATORY AND REFUGE UNION. The reformatory and refuge journal. 1861–1939.

Title changed to *Seeking and saving*, 1900–39. For the work of the soc. see its jubilee report, *Fifty years' record of child saving & reformatory work, 1856–1906*, 1906, and Conference of Managers of Reformatory and Industrial Institutions, *Record of proceedings*, 1869+.

7305  APPROVED SCHOOLS GAZETTE. Stockport. 1906+.

7306  MADDISON (ARTHUR J. S.) *comp.* The law relating to child-saving and reformatory efforts: being extracts from acts of Parliament and other information. 1896. 4th edn. 1909.

7307  HOLLAND (ROBERT WOLSTENHOLME). The law relating to the child, its protection, education and employment. [1914.]

(c) *Settlements*

7308  KNAPP (JOHN MATTHEW) *ed.* The universities and the social problem: an account of the university settlements in East London. 1895.

See also Will Reason, ed., *University and social settlements*, 1898, which incl. a useful directory, and Arnold Freeman, *Education through settlements* [1919].

7309   PIMLOTT (JOHN ALFRED RALPH). Toynbee Hall: fifty years of social progress, 1884–1934. 1935.

See also Werner Picht, *Toynbee Hall and the English settlement movement*, rev. edn. trans. by Lillian A. Cowell, 1914.

7310   BARNETT. Canon Barnett: his life, work and friends. By his wife, Dame Henrietta Octavia Weston Barnett. 2 v. 1918. 2nd edn. 1919.

Founder of Toynbee Hall and sponsor of all kinds of social work. One of the most influential figures of his day.

7311   STOCKS (MARY DANVERS). Fifty years in Every Street: the story of the Manchester University Settlement. Manch. 1945. 2nd edn. 1956.

7312   [HOROBIN (*Sir* IAN MACDONALD).] Mansfield House University Settlement. 1925.

### (d) *Animal Welfare*

7313   HUME (ETHEL DOUGLAS). The mind-changers. 1939.

See also Dix Harwood, *Love for animals and how it developed in Great Britain*, N.Y. 1928.

7314   SALT. Salt and his circle. By Stephen Winsten. 1951.

Founder of the Humanitarian League, vegetarian, etc. See also Henry Stephens Salt, *Seventy years among savages*, 1921, *Company I have kept*, 1930, and *Humanitarianism: its general principles and progress*, 1891. There is some additional material in *Grace Hawkins, venturer for fellowship: compiled for the United Humanitarian League by two members of the Council*, 1941.

7315   SALT (HENRY STEPHENS) *ed.* Cruelties of civilization: a program of humane reform. 3 v. Humanitarian League. 1897.

7316   HUMANITARIAN LEAGUE. The humane review. 1900–1910. Quarterly.

The League also publ. *Humanity*, 1895–1902, *The humanitarian*, 1902–19, and an *Annual report*.

7317   TURNER (ERNEST SACKVILLE). All heaven in a rage. 1964.

On animal welfare. Popular.

7318   FAIRHOLME (EDWARD GEORGE) *and* PAIN (WELLESLEY). A century of work for animals: the history of the R.S.P.C.A., 1824–1924. 1924. 2nd edn. 1934.

See also the publs. of the [Royal] Society for the Prevention of Cruelty to Animals, notably *Animal world*, 1869–70+, and Arthur W. Moss, *Valiant crusade: the history of the R.S.P.C.A.*, 1961.

7319   BURTON (PERCY MERCERON) *and* SCOTT (GUY HARDEN GUILLUM). The law relating to the prevention of cruelty to animals . . . 1906.

**7320 SALT (HENRY STEPHENS)** *ed.* The new charter: a discussion of the rights of men and the rights of animals. 1896.

An interesting discussion. See also Salt's *Animals' rights considered in relation to social progress*, 1892, 5th edn. 1922, Edward Williams Byron Nicholson, *The rights of an animal: a new essay in ethics*, 1879, and the works at (**7314**). For examples of neglect of animals see Isabel M. Greg, *The present conditions of the cattle trade*, 1898, Isabel M. Greg and S. H. Towers, *Cattle ships and our meat supply*, 1894, and Sidney Trist, ed., *The under dog: a series of papers by various authors on the wrongs suffered by animals at the hand of man*, 1913.

**7321 SALT (HENRY STEPHENS)** *ed.* Killing for sport: essays by various writers. 1914.

**7322 WESTACOTT (EVALYN).** A century of vivisection and anti-vivisection: a study of their effect upon science, medicine and human life during the past hundred years. Romford. 1949.

**7323 OZER (MARK N.).** 'The British vivisection controversy'. *Bull. Hist. Med.* xl (1966), 158–67.

See also Lloyd G. Stevenson, 'Science down the drain: on the hostility of certain sanitarians to animal experimentation, bacteriology and immunology', *Bull. Hist. Med.* xxix (1955), 1–26.

**7324 CARDWELL COMMISSION ON VIVISECTION.** Report of the royal commission on the practice of subjecting live animals to experiments for scientific purposes [Chairman: Viscount Cardwell]. [C. 1397] H.C. (1876). XLI, 277. Digest of evidence. [C. 1397-I] H.C. (1876). XLI, 689.

See also *Royal commission on vivisection: first report of the commissioners* [Chairman: Viscount Selby]. [Cd. 3325] H.C. (1907). XLI, 645. Minutes of evidence. [Cd. 3326] H.C. (1907). XLI, 649. Second report. [Cd. 3461] H.C. (1907). XLI, 813. Minutes of evidence. [Cd. 3462] H.C. (1907). XLI, 817. Third report. [Cd. 3756] H.C. (1908). LVII, 279. Minutes of evidence. [Cd. 3757] H.C. (1908). LVII, 283. Fourth report. [Cd. 3954] H.C. (1908). LVII, 555. Minutes of evidence. [Cd. 3955] H.C. (1908). LVII, 559. Fifth report. [Cd. 4146] H.C. (1908). LVII, 875. Minutes of evidence. [Cd. 4147] H.C. (1908). LVII, 879. Sixth report. [Cd. 6112] H.C. (1912–13). XLVIII, 367. Appendix to sixth report. [Cd. 6113] H.C. (1912–13). XLVIII, 373. Final report. [Cd. 6114] H.C. (1912–13). XLVIII, 401.

**7325 RICHARDSON (*Sir* BENJAMIN WARD).** Biological experimentation: its function and limit . . . 1896.

See also Stephen Paget, *Experiments on animals*, 1900, 3rd edn. 1906. There is a vast anti-vivisection literature, of which the following are representative: Charles Adams, *The coward science . . .*, 1882; Philanthropos, *Physiological cruelty or, fact v. fancy: an inquiry into the vivisection question*, 1883; Brown Animal Sanatory Institution, *Man's injustice to animals*, 3rd edn. 1888; Mark Thornhill, *The clergy and vivisection* [1883]; Frances Power Cobbe, *The modern rack: papers on vivisection*, 1889; Edward Berdoe, *The healing art and the claims of vivisection*, 1890; Ouida [Louise de la Ramée], *The new priesthood*, 1893; G. M. Rhodes, comp., *The nine circles of the hell of the innocent, described from the reports of the presiding spirits*, 1892, 2nd edn. 1893; Stephen Smith, ed., *Fruitless experiment: an examination and critical analysis of the claims advanced on behalf of vivisection*, 1904; Albert Leffingwell, *The vivisection controversy: essays and criticisms*, 1908; Charles Richet, *The pros and cons of vivisection*, 1908; G. H. Bowker, ed., *Shaw on vivisection*, 1949; and Stephen William Buchanan Coleridge, *Vivisection: a heartless science*, 1916.

7326 HADWEN. Hadwen of Gloucester: man, medico, martyr. By Beatrice Ethel Kidd and M. Edith Richards. 1933.

7327 SALT (HENRY STEPHENS). The logic of vegetarianism: essays and dialogues. 1899. 2nd edn. 1906. Rev. edn. 1933.

## 3. POVERTY AND THE POOR LAW

7328 [THOMPSON (PAUL RICHARD) *ed.*] The Victorian poor. Victorian Soc. 1967.

7329 ROSE (MICHAEL EDWARD) *ed.* The English poor law, 1780–1930. 1971.

A book of docs.

7330 WEBB (SIDNEY JAMES), *Baron Passfield, and* WEBB (BEATRICE). English poor law history. English local government. Vols. VII–IX. 1927–9. 2nd edn. 1963.

Suppl. by their *English poor law policy*, English local government, vol. X, 1910, 2nd edn. 1963.

7331 RODGERS (BRIAN). The battle against poverty. 2 v. 1968–9.

Very brief, but a useful hist.

7332 MACKAY (THOMAS). A history of the English poor law from 1834 to the present time. 1899.

Continues Sir George Nicholls, *A history of the English poor law . . .*, 2 v. 1854, 2nd edn. 2 v. 1898. See also Mackay's *The English poor: a sketch of their social and economic history*, 1889.

7333 FOWLE (THOMAS WELBANKE). The poor law. English citizen series. 1881. 2nd edn. 1890. Repr. 1898.

7334 ASCHROTT (PAUL FELIX). The English poor law system, past and present. Trans. by Herbert Preston-Thomas. 1888. 2nd edn. 1902.

7335 CHADWICK. The life and times of Sir Edwin Chadwick. By Samuel Edwin Finer. 1952.

As executive head of the Poor Law Commission, Chadwick became the most notorious social reformer of his day. For his public health work see **7415**.

7336 ROBERTS ([FREDERICK] DAVID). 'How cruel was the Victorian Poor Law?' *Hist. J.* vi (1963), 97–107.

Chiefly pre-1850, as is Ursula Henriques, 'How cruel was the Victorian Poor Law?', ibid. xi (1968), 365–71.

7337 ROSE (MICHAEL EDWARD). 'The allowance system under the new Poor Law'. *Econ. Hist. Rev.* 2 ser. xix (1966), 607–20.

7338 MORGAN (JOHN S.). 'The break up of the poor law in Britain, 1907–47: an historical footnote'. *Canadian J. Econ. & Pol. Sci.* xiv (1948), 209–19.

7339 SHAW'S LOCAL GOVERNMENT MANUAL AND DIRECTORY FOR UNIONS. 1846+.

Began life as *Shaw's union officers' manual* . . ., 1846–75, and became *The local government manual and directory* in 1923. The fullest general directory. See also *The unions' and parish officers' year book* [*The local government officers' almanac and guide*], 1839–1922.

7340 POOR LAW BOARD [Local Government Board]. Annual report. 1848+.

The chief source for statistics, etc. See also Poor Law [District] Conferences, *Reports*, 1875–1930.

7341 THE POOR LAW OFFICERS' JOURNAL. Rochdale, etc. 1892–1929.

See also *Poor Law Unions' gazette*, 1857–1903, and *The Poor Law annual*, 1904/5–1929/30.

7342 GLEN (WILLIAM CUNNINGHAM). The General Consolidated Order issued by the Poor Law Commissioners, 24th July 1847, and the other general orders applicable to the unions to which that order is addressed: with a commentary and notes . . . 1847. 11th edn. 1898.

Title varies. A useful general textbook. Glen also ed. *The statutes in force relating to the poor, parochial unions and parishes*, 1857, and *The statutes in force relating to the poor laws* . . ., 3 v. 1873–9, cont. by Alexander Macmorran and Michael Stewart Johnstone, eds., *The Poor Law statutes* . . . *1879 to 1889*, 1890. See also James Brooke Little, *The Poor Law statutes: comprising the statutes in force relating to the poor* . . ., 3 v. 1901–2.

7343 MACKENZIE (WILLIAM WARRENDER), *Baron Amulree*. The overseers' handbook: being a statement of the duties and a summary of the law relating to overseers, churchwardens . . . 1889. 10th edn. 1932.

A good handbook. Suppl. by his *The poor law guardian: his powers and duties* . . ., 3rd edn. 1892, 4th edn. 1895. Arthur Frederick Vulliamy, *The duties of relieving officers and the administration of out-relief*, 1904, and *The law of settlement and removal of paupers*, 1895, 2nd edn. 1906, cover some additional ground.

7344 TWINING. Recollections of workhouse visiting and management during twenty-five years. By Louisa Twining. 1880.

7345 BAINES COMMITTEE ON POOR REMOVAL. Report from the select committee on poor removal [Chairman: Matthew Talbot Baines]. H.C. 396 (1854). XVII, 1. Further report. H.C. 308 (1854–5). XIII, 1.

See also *Report of George Coode, Esq., to the Poor Law Board on the law of settlement and removal of the poor* . . ., H.C. 675 (1851). XXVI, 171. Suppl. H.C. 493 (1854). LV, 345.

7346 VILLIERS COMMITTEE ON POOR RELIEF. First report from the select committee on poor relief (England) [Chairman: Charles Pelham Villiers].

H.C. 180 (1861). IX, 1. Second report. H.C. 323 (1861). IX, 199. Third to sixth reports. H.C. 474 to H.C. 474–III (1861). IX, 405. Committee re-appointed. First report. H.C. 181 (1862). X, 1. Second report. H.C. 321 (1862). X, 183. Third report. H.C. 468 (1862). X, 417. Further formal report. H.C. 383 (1863). VII, 459. Final report. H.C. 349 (1864). IX, 187.

The first full inquiry during the period. See also the earlier *Report from the select committee on irremovable poor* [Chairmen: T. H. Sotheron Estcourt, Earl of March, C. P. Villiers]. H.C. 374 (1857–8). XIII, 1. Further reports. H.C. 146 (1859–Sess. 2) VII, 1. H.C. 520 (1860). XVII, 1.

7347 PURDY (FREDERICK). 'The relative pauperism of England, Scotland and Ireland, 1851 to 1860'. *Stat. Soc. J.* xxv (1862), 27–49.

See also his 'Extent of pauperism in the distressed unions of Lancashire . . ., 1861–62', *Stat. Soc. J.* xxv (1862), 377–83.

7348 LOCH (*Sir* CHARLES STEWART). 'Statistics of population and pauperism in England and Wales, 1861–1901'. *Roy. Stat. Soc. J.* lxix (1906), 289–312.

7349 YULE (GEORGE UDNY). 'An investigation into the causes of changes in pauperism in England, chiefly during the last two intercensal decades'. *Roy. Stat. Soc. J.* lxii (1899), 249–86.

7350 HIBBERT COMMITTEE ON POOR LAW GUARDIANS. Report from the select committee on poor law guardians, &c. [Chairman: J. T. Hibbert]. H.C. 297 (1878). XVII, 263.

For the assessment of poor rates see 4558–72.

7351 ROWNTREE (BENJAMIN SEEBOHM). Poverty: a study of town life. 1901. 4th edn. 1902.

Like his *Unemployment* (6586) a study of social conditions in York. For other studs. of town social problems see Bowley (7352); Eglantyne Jebb, *Cambridge: a brief study in social questions*, Camb. 1906; Christina Violet Butler, *Social conditions in Oxford*, 1912; C. B. Hawkins, *Norwich: a social study*, 1910; and Sir Edward Goldie Howarth and Mona Wilson, *West Ham: a study in social and industrial problems: being the report of the Outer London inquiry committee*, 1907.

7352 BOWLEY (*Sir* ARTHUR LYON) *and* BURNETT-HURST (ALEX-ANDER ROBERT). Livelihood and poverty: a study in the economic conditions of working-class households in Northampton, Warrington, Stanley and Reading. 1915.

Incl. the data in Bowley's 'Working-class households in Reading', *Roy. Stat. Soc. J.* lxxvi (1912–13), 672–701.

7353 BOOTH (CHARLES). Life and labour of the people in London. 1 ser. Poverty. 4 v. 1902–3.

For details of Booth's other surveys see the index. Cp. Sir William Chance, 'A decade of London pauperism, 1891 to 1901', *Roy. Stat. Soc. J.* lxvi (1903), 534–70, and J. Basil Cook, 'An examination of the amount of in-door pauperism in three metropolitan boroughs, and of the causes which led to this pauperism', ibid. lxxi (1908), 147–74.

There are a number of selections from Booth, incl. Albert Fried and Richard Martin Elman, eds., *Charles Booth's London*, N.Y. 1967, Lond. 1969, and Harold W. Pfautz, ed., *Charles Booth on the city: physical pattern and social structure*, Chicago 1967.

7354 SHERARD (ROBERT HARBOROUGH). The cry of the poor: being, the true and faithful account of a three months' tour amongst the pariahs of the kingdoms of England, Scotland, and Ireland, during the last half year of the nineteenth century. 1901.

Slum life in the great cities.

7355 ROYAL COMMISSION ON THE POOR LAWS. Report of the royal commission on the poor laws and relief of distress [Chairman: Lord George Hamilton]. [Cd. 4499] H.C. (1909). XXXVII, 1. Index. [Cd. 4945] H.C. (1909). XXXVII, 1261.

For a summary of the report see Helen Dendy Bosanquet, *The Poor Law report of 1909* ..., 1909. For the setting up of the commission see John Brown, 'The appointment of the 1905 Poor Law Commission', *Inst. Hist. Res. Bull.* xlii (1969–70), 239–42. The commission also publ. reports on Ireland [Cd. 4630] H.C. (1909). XXXVIII, 1, and Scotland [Cd. 4922] H.C. (1909). XXXVIII, 95. Minutes of evidence and other data were issued as parl. papers in Vols. XXXIX–XLIV of 1909 and XLVI–LV of 1910.

7356 WEBB (SIDNEY JAMES), *Baron Passfield, and* WEBB (BEATRICE). English poor law policy. 1910. 2nd edn. 1963.

See also their *The break-up of the poor law* ..., 2 v. 1909, and *The prevention of destitution*, 1911.

7357 NATIONAL CONFERENCE ON THE PREVENTION OF DESTI- TUTION. Report of the proceedings. 2 v. 1911–12.

### 4. FRIENDLY SOCIETIES

7358 GOSDEN (PETER HENRY JOHN HEATHER). The friendly societies in England, 1815–1875. Manch. 1961.

Standard. There is no hist. of the post-1875 period, but see Bentley Brinkerhoff Gilbert, 'The decay of nineteenth-century provident institutions and the coming of old-age pensions in Great Britain', *Econ. Hist. Rev.* 2 ser. xvii (1964–5), 551–63.

7359 BRABROOK (*Sir* EDWARD WILLIAM). 'The relation of the state to thrift: ten years' statistics of friendly societies and similar institutions'. *Stat. Soc. J.* xlviii (1885), 21–44.

Cont. as 'The progress of friendly societies ... 1884–94', ibid. lviii (1895), 286–302; '1894–1904', ibid. lxviii (1905), 320–42, and '1904–1914', ibid. lxxviii (1915), 414–33. The main run of stats. See also Francis G. P. Neison, 'Some statistics of the affiliated orders of friendly societies (Odd Fellows and Foresters)', *Stat. Soc. J.* xl (1877), 42–89.

7360 HARDWICK (CHARLES). The history, present position, and social importance of friendly societies: including oddfellowship and other affiliated provident institutions of the working classes ... [Fly sheet gives title as Manual for patrons and members of friendly societies.] 1859. 3rd edn. [The history of friendly societies.] Manch. [1893.]

Valuable. Hardwick also publ. *The provident institutions of the working classes* . . ., Preston 1851, with useful tables, and a guide to friendly-soc. finance, *Insolvent sick and burial clubs: the causes and the cure: or, how to choose or found a reliable friendly society*, Manch. 1863.

7361 BAERNREITHER (JOSEPH MARIA). English associations of working men. Trans. by Alice Taylor. 1889.

Compares the situation in 1880 with that in 1844.

7362 WILKINSON (JOHN FROME). Mutual thrift. Social questions of to-day series. 1891.

A short hist. by a leading writer on friendly socs. See also his *The friendly society movement* . . ., 1886, *The mutual and provident institutions of the working classes*, 1888, and 'Some illustrations of friendly society finance', *Roy. Stat. Soc. J.* lviii (1895), 303–20.

7363 BRABROOK (*Sir* EDWARD WILLIAM). Provident societies and industrial welfare. Victorian era series. 1898.

By the Chief Registrar of Friendly Socs. Long the standard guide.

7364 ROBINSON (MARGARET FOTHERGILL). The spirit of association: being some account of the gilds, friendly societies, co-operative movement, and trade unions of Great Britain. 1913.

7365 BEVERIDGE (WILLIAM HENRY), *Baron Beveridge*. Voluntary action: a report on methods of social advance. 1948.

Suppl. by a vol. of reports ed. by Beveridge and Alan Frank Wells, *The evidence for voluntary action* . . ., 1949.

7366 WOLFSTIEG (AUGUST). Bibliographie der Freimaurerischen Literatur. Verein Deutscher Freimaurer. 3 v. 1911–13. 2nd edn. 4 v. Leipzig. 1923–6. Repr. 4 v. Hildesheim. 1964.

The fullest masonic bibliog. Needs to be suppl. by Sir Algernon Turnor Tudor-Craig, *Catalogue of manuscripts and library at Freemasons' Hall in the possession of the United Grand Lodge of England*, 1938, and Henry Josiah Whymper, *A catalogue of bibliographies, lists and catalogues of works on freemasonry*, 1891; and *Acts of Parliament referring to freemasonry*, 1892.

7367 GOULD (ROBERT FREKE). The history of freemasonry . . . 6 v. 1884–7. 3rd edn. by Herbert Poole. 4 v. N.Y. 1951.

Standard, but not very full on England. Needs to be suppl. by John Lane, *Masonic records, 1717–1886: comprising a list of all the lodges at home and abroad* . . ., 1886, suppl. 1887, 2nd edn. [to 1894] 1895, *Masonic year book*, 1775+, and *Who's who in freemasonry*, 1913–14. The many short hists. of English freemasonry like Albert Frederick Calvert, *The grand lodge of England, 1717–1917* . . ., 1917, have practically nothing on the period. There are hists. of many provincial lodges such as John Samuel Bedford Glasier, *History of Philanthropic Lodge, King's Lynn, No. 107*, priv. pr., King's Lynn 1911, and also hists. of freemasonry in many indiv. counties.

7368 MOFFREY (ROBERT WILLIAM). A century of oddfellowship: being, a brief record of the rise and progress of the Manchester Unity of the Independent Order of Oddfellows . . . Manch. 1910.

See also Francis G. P. Neison, *The Manchester Unity of Odd Fellows*, 1869.

7369 THORNLEY (JOHN). History of the Grand United Order of Odd-fellows [1838–1895]. 4 pts. Manch. 1911–13. Also issued in 1 vol. Manch. [1914.]

7370 FULLER (MARGARET DOROTHY). West Country friendly societies: an account of village benefit clubs and their brass pole heads. Univ. of Reading, Museum of English Rural Life. 1964.

Chiefly pre-1850.

7371 MORGAN (FREDERICK CHARLES). Friendly societies in Hereford-shire. Woolhope Naturalists' Field Club. Hereford. 1949.

7372 [CHIEF] REGISTRAR OF FRIENDLY SOCIETIES. Annual report. 1856+.

The main source for friendly soc. hist. There is an index for 1875–95 in H.C. 78 (1897). LXXXII, 663. From 1853 to 1875 there were also separate reports for Scotland and Ireland. For the year 1875 and subsequent years they were amalg. with the English reports. Full returns from registered socs. were publ. at irregular intervals from 1852 to 1930.

7373 SOTHERON COMMITTEE ON FRIENDLY SOCIETIES. Report from the select committee on friendly societies [Chairman: T. H. Sotheron afterwards Sotheron-Estcourt]. H.C. 531 (1852). V, 295.

The discussion of the consolidation of the friendly soc. laws begun by this committee was resumed in 1854 by another committee with the same chairman. See *Report from the select committee on Friendly Societies Bill.* H.C. 412 (1854). VII, 127.

7374 NORTHCOTE COMMISSION ON FRIENDLY SOCIETIES. First report of the commissioners appointed to inquire into friendly and benefit building societies [Chairman: Sir Stafford H. Northcote]. [C. 452] H.C. (1871). XXV, 1. Second report, on benefit building societies. Pt. I. [C. 514] H.C. (1872). XXVI, 1. Suppl. [C. 678] H.C. (1873). XXII, 285. Evidence. [C. 514–I] H.C. (1872). XXVI, 101. Index. [C. 514–II] H.C. (1872). XXVI, 745. Third report. [C. 842] H.C. (1873). XXII, 291. Fourth report etc. Pt. I. [C. 961] H.C. (1874). XXIII, pt. I, 1. Pt. II. [C. 961–I] H.C. (1874). XXIII, pt. I, 349. Assistant Commissioners' reports not included above. [C. 995 to C. 998] H.C. (1874). XXIII, pt. II, 1+.

The most extensive inquiry into the subject.

7375 MAXWELL COMMITTEE ON FRIENDLY SOCIETIES ACT, 1875. Report from the select committee on Friendly Societies Act, 1875 [Chairman: Sir Herbert Maxwell]. H.C. 304 (1889). X, 413.

The first full inquiry since the Northcote Commission. In the previous year a com-mittee with the same chairman had investigated the work of the collecting socs., such as the Royal Liver, but had no time to prepare a report. The evidence collected was issued as *Report from the select committee on friendly societies.* H.C. 389 (1888). XII, 119. Further minor inquiries were held in connection with the Industrial and Provident Societies Bill in 1894 (H.C. 330 (1893–4). XII, 289), and into the way in which some firms compelled employees to leave benefit socs. and join the firm's sick clubs ([C. 9203] H.C. (1899). XXXIII, 871).

7376 RYAN COMMITTEE ON APPROVED SOCIETY FINANCE.
Interim report of the departmental committee on approved society finance
and administration [Chairman: Sir Gerald H. Ryan]. [Cd. 8251] H.C. (1916).
XIV, 25. Further report. [Cd. 8396] H.C. (1916). XIV, 65. Final report.
[Cd. 8451] H.C. (1917–18). XVII, 395.

Deals with socs. approved under the National Insurance Acts.

7377 PRATT (JOHN TIDD). The law relating to friendly societies ... 1829.
15th edn. 1931.

The standard exposition of the law: the edns. from 1873 to 1897 were rev. by Sir Edward
William Brabrook. Frank Baden Fuller, *The law relating to friendly societies* ..., 1896,
4th edn. 1926, Nathaniel White, *A handy book on the law of friendly, industrial, and
provident, building and loan societies*, 1865, and Henry Frederick Alexander Davis, *The
law and practice of friendly societies* ..., 1876, are also useful. Pratt, as Registrar of
Friendly Socs., also publ. a number of short guides for the use of friendly soc. officers,
of which the best is *Suggestions for the establishment of friendly societies* ..., 1855.

7378 WATSON (*Sir* ALFRED WILLIAM). An account of an investigation
of the sickness and mortality experience of the I.O.O.F., Manchester Unity,
during the five years, 1893–1897. Manch. 1913.

The best of a very considerable number of works on friendly soc. finance. The tables
still form the basis of friendly soc. finance. See also his *Friendly society finance considered
in its actuarial aspect*, 1912. A number of actuarial reports were publ. by the Registrar
of Friendly Socs., several of them as parl. papers.

### 5. OLD AGE PENSIONS AND NATIONAL INSURANCE

7379 GILBERT (BENTLEY BRINKERHOFF). The evolution of national
insurance in Great Britain: the origins of the welfare state. 1966.

Standard. See also M. Bruce, *The coming of the welfare state* (**7192**), Richard William
Harris, *National health insurance in Great Britain, 1911–1946*, 1946, and Donald
McIntosh Johnson, *The British national health service*, 1962.

7380 COLLINS (DOREEN). 'The introduction of old-age pensions in Great
Britain'. *Hist. J.* viii (1965), 246–59.

See also Ronald V. Sires, 'The beginnings of British legislation for old-age pensions',
*J. Econ. Hist.* xiv (1954), 229–53, Francis Herbert Stead, *How old age pensions began to
be* [1909], and Sir Arnold Talbot Wilson and G. S. Mackay, *Old-age pensions: an
historical and critical study*, 1941.

7381 HOARE (HENRY JOSEPH). Old age pensions: their actual working and
ascertained results in the United Kingdom. 1915.

A careful study.

7382 STANHOPE/MAXWELL COMMITTEE ON NATIONAL PROVI-
DENT INSURANCE. Report from the select committee on national provident
insurance [Chairman: Hon. Edward Stanhope]. H.C. 270 (1884–5). X, 41.
Further reports [Chairman: Sir Herbert Maxwell]. H.C. 208 (1886). XI, 1.
H.C. 257 (1887). XI, 1.

Considered a national insurance scheme put forward by the Revd. William Lewery

Blackley, for whose views see Amalia Jeanne Josephine Blackley, ed., *Thrift & national insurance as a security against pauperism: with a memoir of the late Rev. Canon Blackley and a reprint of his essays*, 1906, and John Frome Wilkinson, *The Blackley national provident insurance scheme: a protest* . . . 1887.

7383 BOOTH (CHARLES). 'Enumeration and classification of paupers and state pensions for the aged'. *Roy. Stat. Soc. J.* liv (1891), 600–43.

Began the detailed consideration of schemes for old age pensions. Booth also publ. 'Statistics of pauperism in old age', *Roy. Stat. Soc. J.* lvii (1894), 235–45, *Pauperism; a picture, and endowment of old age; an argument*, 1892, *The aged poor in England and Wales* . . ., 1894, *Old age pensions and the aged poor: a proposal*, 1899, new edn. 1906, and 'Poor-law statistics as used in connection with the old-age pension question', *Econ. J.* ix (1899), 212–23.

7384 CHAMBERLAIN (JOSEPH). 'Old-age pensions'. *Nat. Rev.* xviii (1891–2), 721–39.

Outlines a scheme, on which see also his 'Old age pensions and friendly societies', *Nat. Rev.* xxiv (1894–5), 592–615.

7385 LOCH (*Sir* CHARLES STEWART). Old age pensions and pauperism: an inquiry as to the bearing of the statistics of pauperism, quoted by the Rt. Hon. J. Chamberlain, M.P., and others, in support of a scheme for national pensions. 1892.

Gives the Charity Organisation Soc. view.

7386 SPENDER (JOHN ALFRED). The state and pensions in old age. 1892.
A valuable inquiry.

7387 ABERDARE COMMISSION ON THE AGED POOR. Report of the royal commission on the aged poor . . . [Chairman: Lord Aberdare.] Report. [C. 7684] H.C. (1895). XIV, 1. Minutes of evidence. [C. 7684-I-II] H.C. (1895). XIV, 123, and XV, 1.

7388 ROTHSCHILD COMMITTEE ON OLD AGE PENSIONS. Report of the committee on old age pensions [Chairman: Lord Rothschild]. [C. 8911] H.C. (1898). XLV, 465.

Sir Henry Burdett submitted a scheme to the committee which he also set out in 'Old age pensions', *Roy. Stat. Soc. J.* lxi (1898), 597–624.

7389 CHAPLIN COMMITTEE ON AGED DESERVING POOR. Report from the select committee on aged deserving poor [Chairman: Henry Chaplin]. H.C. 296 (1899). VIII, 191.

The committee recommended a scheme which was referred to a departmental committee [Chairman: Sir Edward W. Hamilton], whose report is at [Cd. 67] H.C. (1900), X, 1. The subject was again considered in *Report and special report from the select committee on the Aged Pensioners Bill* [Chairman: Grant Lawson]. H.C. 276 (1903). V, 393.

7390 ROGERS (FREDERICK) *and* MILLAR (FREDERICK). Old age pensions: are they desirable and practical? 1903.

A useful survey. Rogers was an important advocate of pensions: for his life see his *Labour, life and literature: memories of sixty years,* 1913. See also Committee on Old Age Pensions, *Old age pensions: a collection of short papers,* 1903, William Sutherland, *Old-age pensions in theory and practice: with some foreign examples* [1907], Local Government Board, *Old age pensions: tables which have been prepared in connexion with the question of old age pensions, with a preliminary memorandum.* [Cd. 3618] H.C. (1907). LXVIII, 385, and *Old age pensions (non-contributory scheme): correspondence: copy of circular letter issued by the chief registrar to the principal friendly societies . . . together with abstract of their replies thereto.* H.C. 177 (1908). LXXXVIII, 367.

7391   CASSON (WILLIAM AUGUSTUS). Old-Age Pensions Act, 1908: together with the text of the regulations made thereunder and official circulars and instructions for the guidance of pension authorities by the Local Government Boards of England, Scotland and Ireland; annotated and explained, with historical introduction. 1908. 3rd edn. 1908.

7392   LLOYD GEORGE (DAVID), *Earl Lloyd George.* The people's insurance. 1911. 3rd edn. 1912.

Speeches, etc. by the minister responsible for the National Insurance Act, 1911 (**7394**).

7393   BRAITHWAITE (WILLIAM JOHN). Lloyd George's ambulance wagon: being the memoirs of William J. Braithwaite, 1911–1912. Ed. by Sir Henry Noel Bunbury. 1957.

On the making and admin. of the National Health Insurance Act. See also Richard William Harris, *Not so humdrum: the autobiography of a civil servant,* 1939.

7394   CARR (*Sir* ARTHUR STRETTELL COMYNS), GARNETT (WILLIAM HUBERT STUART), and TAYLOR (JAMES HENRY). National insurance. 1912. 4th edn. 1913.

An official summary of the National Insurance Act, 1911, on which see also Sir Leo George Chiozza Money, *Insurance versus poverty,* 1912; Orme Bigland Clarke, *The National Insurance Act, 1911: being, a treatise on the scheme of national health insurance and insurance against unemployment created by that act . . .,* 1912, 2nd edn. 1913; William Annan, *The duties of employers under the National Insurance Act, 1911* [1912]; Isaac Max Rubinow, *Social insurance,* 1913; and Sir Walter Addington Willis, *National health insurance through approved societies: being a practical legal treatise . . .* [1914.]

## 6. PUBLIC HEALTH

### (a) *General*

7395   FRAZER (WILLIAM MOWLL). A history of English public health, 1834–1939. 1950.

Standard. Strongest on the medical side. There are a number of other general works: Thomas Ferguson, 'Public health in Britain in the climate of the nineteenth century', *Population Studs.* xvii (1963–4), 213–24; John Hargreaves Harley Williams, *A century of public health in Britain, 1832–1929,* 1932; Sir Arthur Salusbury MacNalty, *The history of state medicine in England,* 1948; Sir Malcolm Alexander Morris, *The story of English public health,* 1919; Sir George Newman, *The building of a nation's health,* 1939; Major Greenwood, *Some British pioneers of social medicine,* 1948; and Colin Fraser Brockington, *A short history of public health,* 1956, 2nd edn. 1966. Sir John Alexander Charles, *Research and public health,* 1961, is also helpful.

**7396  BROCKINGTON (COLIN FRASER).** Public health in the nineteenth century. Edin. & Lond. 1965.

Chiefly on the medical officers of health to 1875. See also Edward Smith, *Manual for medical officers of health*, 1873, 2nd edn. 1874. For public health law see **7397**, and George Frederick Chambers, *A digest of the statutes relating to the public health* . . ., 2 v. 1873, 8th edn. 1887.

**7397  SIMON (*Sir* JOHN).** English sanitary institutions: reviewed in their course of development, and in some of their political and social relations. 1890. 2nd edn. 1897.

By the most notable of contemp. medical officers. See also Edward Seaton, ed., *Public health reports by Sir John Simon*, 2 v. 1887. There is an interesting later survey in L.G. Bannington, *English public health administration*, 1915, 2nd edn. 1929. For a wider view see Sir Andrew Balfour and Henry Harold Scott, *Health problems of the empire: past, present and future*, 1924.

**7398  NEWSHOLME (*Sir* ARTHUR).** Evolution of preventive medicine. Baltimore [Md.]. 1927.

Cont. in his *The story of modern preventive medicine: being a continuation of the evolution of preventive medicine*, Baltimore 1929. Useful as reflecting British official opinion. Newsholme also publ. *Medicine and the state: the relation between the private & official practice of medicine, with special reference to public health*, 1932. Cp. Sir George Newman, *The rise of preventive medicine*, 1932, *An outline of the practice of preventive medicine* . . . [Cmd. 363] H.C. (1919). XXXIX, 677, and *Health and social evolution*, 1931. For other gen. hists. of social medicine see George Rosen, *A history of public health*, N.Y. 1958, and René Sand, *The advance to social medicine*, 1952.

**7399  MACKINTOSH (JAMES MACALISTER).** Trends of opinion about the public health, 1901–51. 1953.

**7400  NEWSHOLME (*Sir* ARTHUR).** The Ministry of Health. Whitehall Series. 1925.

A hist. of the evolution of responsibility for public health. There is a great deal of misc. information in the Ministry's *First annual report* . . . *1919–20*. [Cmd. 913, 917, 923, 932] H.C. (1920). XVII, 49, 227, 283, 447.

**7401  HODGKINSON (RUTH GLADYS).** The origins of the National Health Service: the medical services of the new Poor Law, 1834–1871. Wellcome Hist. Medical Libr. Lond. & Berkeley [Calif.]. 1967.

See also James E. O'Neill, 'Finding a policy for the sick poor', *Victorian Studs.* vii (1963–4), 265–84, and Jeanne L. Brand, 'The parish doctor: England's poor law medical officers and medical reform, 1870–1900', *Bull. Hist. Med.* xxxv (1961), 97–122. There is a little more in Hugh James McCurrich, *The treatment of the sick poor of this country*, 1929, and Alfred Sheen, *The workhouse and its medical officer*, Cardiff 1875, 2nd edn. Bristol 1890.

**7402  HEASMAN (KATHLEEN JOAN).** 'The medical mission and the care of the sick poor in nineteenth-century England'. *Hist. J.* vii (1964), 230–45.

**7403  BRAND (JEANNE L.).** Doctors and the state: the British medical profession and government action in public health, 1870–1912. Baltimore [Md.]. 1965.

**7404** MACLEOD (ROY MALCOLM). 'The frustration of state medicine, 1880–1899'. *Medical Hist.* xi (1967), 15–40.

See also his 'Medico-legal issues in Victorian medical care', ibid. x (1966), 44–9.

**7405** BRIGGS (ASA). '"Middlemarch" and the doctors'. *Camb. J.* i (1947–8), 749–62.

**7406** BENJAMIN (BERNARD). 'The urban background to public health changes in England and Wales, 1900–50'. *Population Studs.* xvii (1963–4), 225–48.

Suppl. by Allen Daley and B. Benjamin, 'London as a case study', ibid. 249–62, and David Victor Glass, 'Some indicators of differences between urban and rural mortality in England and Wales and Scotland', ibid. 263–7.

**7407** JONES (KATHLEEN). Mental health and social policy, 1845–1959. 1960. Rev. edn. [A history of the mental health services.] 1972.

To be suppl. by William Llewelyn Parry-Jones, *The trade in lunacy: a study of private madhouses in England in the eighteenth and nineteenth centuries*, 1972. Among contemp. works consult Daniel Hack Tuke, *Chapters in the history of the insane in the British Isles*, 1882, and *Illustrations of the influence of the mind upon the body in health and disease*, 1872, 2nd edn. 1884, Sir John Charles Bucknill and Daniel Hack Tuke, *A manual of psychological medicine*, 1858, 4th edn. 1879, and Daniel Hack Tuke, ed., *A dictionary of psychological medicine*, 2 v. 1892. The leading contemp. j. was *The asylum j. of mental science*, 1855–7, cont. as *The j. of mental science*, 1858+.

On mental hospitals see Harold Capper Hunt, *A retired habitation: a history of the Retreat, York (mental hospital)*, 1932, and Edward Mansfield Brockbank, *A short history of Cheadle Royal: from its foundation in 1766 for the humane treatment of mental disease*, Manch. 1934.

A picturesque episode is recounted in Georgina Weldon, *How I escaped the mad doctors . . .*, 1882, Philip Treherne, *A plaintiff in person: life of Mrs. Weldon*, 1923, and Edward Grierson, *Storm bird: the strange life of Georgina Weldon*, 1959.

**7408** WALPOLE COMMITTEE ON LUNATICS. Report from the select committee on lunatics [Chairman: S. H. Walpole]. H.C. 204 (1859–Sess. 1). III, 75. Further reports. H.C. 156 (1859–Sess. 2). VII, 501. H.C. 495 (1860). XXII, 349.

See also *Report of the commission appointed by the Secretary of State for the Home Department to inquire into the subject of criminal lunacy* [Chairmen: Arthur W. Peel & Leonard H. Courtney]. [C. 3418] H.C. (1882). XXXII, 841, and *Report of the royal commission on the care of the feeble minded* [Chairmen: Marquess of Bath & Earl of Radnor]. [Cd. 4202] H.C. (1908). XXXIX, 159. Report of medical investigators. [Cd. 4220] H.C. (1908). XXXVIII, 351. Report on American instns. [Cd. 4221] H.C. (1908). XXXIX, 1. Minutes of evidence etc. [Cd. 4215–19] H.C. (1908). XXXV, 83, XXXVI–XXXVIII. The main official ser. of reports is the annual report of the Commissioners in Lunacy to 1914, cont. by the Board of Control, 1914+. The official statistics are examined in Noel A. Humphreys, 'Statistics of insanity in England: with special reference to its alleged increasing prevalence', *Roy. Stat. Soc. J.* liii (1890), 201–45, and 'The alleged increase of insanity', ibid. lxx (1907), 203–33, *Special report of the Commissioners in Lunacy to the Lord Chancellor on the alleged increase of insanity*. H.C. 87 (1897). XXXVIII, 1, and Sir Frederick Walker Mott, 'Is insanity on the increase?', *Sociological Rev.* vi (1913), 1–29.

**7409 EGERTON COMMISSION ON THE BLIND, DEAF AND DUMB.**
Report of the royal commission on the blind, the deaf and the dumb, &c. of the United Kingdom [Chairmen: Duke of Westminster and Lord Egerton of Tatton]. [C. 5781] H.C. (1889). XIX, 1. Appendix. [C. 5781–I] H.C. (1889). XIX, 131. Minutes of evidence. [C. 5781–II] H.C. (1889). XX, 1. Digest of evidence. [C. 5781–III] H.C. (1889). XX, 889.

The fullest report. There are also a number of brief reports on blind schools. [C. 4747] H.C. (1886). XXV, 553. [C. 4639] H.C. (1886). XXV, 563. [C. 4727] H.C. (1886). XXV, 571. [C. 8608] H.C. (1897). XXVII, 397. [C. 8985] H.C. (1898). XXIII, 229. [C. 9405] H.C. (1899). XXI, 327. [Cd. 600] H.C. (1901). XXI, 335. The next full report was *Report of the departmental committee on the welfare of the blind* [Chairman: W. Hayes Fisher]. [Cd. 8655] H.C. (1917–18). VII, 1. Minutes of evidence. [Cd. 8659] H.C. (1917–18). VII, 73. National Bureau for Promoting the General Welfare of the Deaf, *The deaf: handbook containing information relating to statistics and schools, missions, hospitals, charities and other institutions for the deaf*, 1913, is a useful handbook. For the hist. and lit. of deaf education see Pritchard (**7855**).

**7410 MILLARD (CHARLES KILLICK).** 'The movement in favour of voluntary euthanasia: an historical survey'. *Leicester Lit. & Phil. Soc. Trans.* xxxvii (1935–6), 32–47. Repr. Leicester. 1936.

**7411 JEPHSON (HENRY).** The sanitary evolution of London. 1907.

See also Donald Murray Connan, *A history of the public health department in Bermondsey*, Greenwich 1935.

**7412 HOPE (EDWARD WILLIAM).** Health at the gateway: problems and international obligations of a seaport city. Camb. 1931.

A hist. of the sanitation of Liverpool. See also Thomas Herbert Bickerton, *A medical history of Liverpool from the earliest days to the year 1920*, ed. by Herbert Richard Bickerton and Robert Merttins Bird McKenna, 1936, and **7416**.

**7413 MIDWINTER (ERIC CLARE).** 'Local boards of health in Lancashire, 1848–1858'. *Historic Soc. Lancs. & Ches. Trans.* cxvii (1965), 167–80.

See also J. R. Hunt, 'The Widnes local board of health, 1865–1892', ibid. cxix (1967), 213–24.

**7414 BAKER.** A battling life, chiefly in the civil service: an autobiography with fugitive papers on subjects of public importance. By Thomas Baker. 1885.

**7415 CHADWICK.** Edwin Chadwick and the public health movement, 1832–1854. By Richard Albert Lewis. 1952.

See also Dorsey Dee Jones, *Edwin Chadwick and the early public health movement in England*, Iowa 1931, and the standard life of Chadwick, **7335**.

**7416 DUNCAN.** Duncan of Liverpool: being an account of the work of Dr. W. H. Duncan, medical officer of health of Liverpool, 1847–63. By William Mowll Frazer. 1947.

7417  NEWSHOLME. Fifty years in public health: a personal narrative with comments. By Sir Arthur Newsholme. 1935.

Cont. in *The last thirty years in public health: recollections and reflections on my official and post-official life*, 1936. Good. Newsholme was chief medical officer of health.

7418  RICHARDSON. Vita medica: chapters of medical life and work. By Sir Benjamin Ward Richardson. 1897.

See also Sir Arthur Salusbury MacNalty, *A biography of Sir Benjamin Ward Richardson*, 1950.

7419  SIMON. Sir John Simon and English social administration, 1816–1904. By Royston James Lambert. 1964.

The best biog. in the field of public health.

7420  SMITH. Dr. Southwood Smith: a retrospect. By Gertrude Lewes. Edin. & Lond. 1898.

7421  LOCAL GOVERNMENT BOARD. Statistical memoranda and charts ... relating to public health and social conditions. [Cd. 4671] H.C. (1909). CIII, 669.

Covers 1850–1908 in detail.

7422  MEDICAL OFFICER OF THE PRIVY COUNCIL. Annual report. 1859+.

Cont. as reports of the medical officer of the [Privy Council and] Local Government Board, 1873+. For a list see Ernest Louis Marsh and Louis Godfrey Irvine, *Index to the reports of medical officers to the Privy Council and Local Government Board of England*, Glasgow [1895].

7423  [ROYAL] SANITARY INSTITUTE of Great Britain [Royal Society for the Promotion of Health]. Transactions. 1879–93. Journal. 1894+.

The Inst. also publ. conference papers and a number of other js.

7424  SOCIETY OF MEDICAL OFFICERS OF HEALTH. Public health. 1888+.

There were also a number of other professional js., incl. *The medical officer*, 1908+, Institute of Sanitary Engineers [Institution of Public Health Engineers], *Proceedings [Journal]*, 1897+, *The public health engineer*, 1897–1906, Sanitary Inspectors' Assoc., *Sanitary inspectors' journal*, 1895–1902, cont. as *Sanitary journal*, 1902–32, and *The sanitarian*, 1932+, and National Union of Sanitary Inspectors, *The sanitary inspector*, Liverpool 1899–1904. There is a useful year book, *The sanitary record and London medical record diary [and year book]*, publ. by a commercial j., *The sanitary record*, 1883–1916.

7425  PUBLIC HEALTH. Nat. Assoc. for the Promotion of Social Science Trans. Pt. IV. 1857–63. Pt. III. 1864–84. 1858–85.

A useful ser. of annual discussions.

7426  TROLLOPE COMMITTEE ON MEDICAL RELIEF. Report from the select committee on medical relief [Chairman: Sir John Trollope]. H.C. 348 (1854). XII, 431.

On Poor Law medical services. For medical relief see also J. Charles Steele, 'The charitable aspects of medical relief', *Roy. Stat. Soc. J.* liv (1891), 263–303.

7427  GENERAL BOARD OF HEALTH. Report of the General Board of Health on the administration of the Public Health Act and the Nuisances Removal and Diseases Prevention Acts, from 1848 to 1854. [1768] H.C. (1854). XXXV, 1.

See also *Report from the select committee on Public Health Bill and Nuisances Removal Amendment Bill* [Chairman: Sir Benjamin Hall]. H.C. 244 (1854–5). XIII, 413.

7428  RUMSEY (HENRY WYLDBORE). Essays on state medicine. 1856.

Rumsey also publ. a considerable number of other pamphlets.

7429  GREENHOW (EDWARD HEADLAM) *and* SIMON (*Sir* JOHN). Papers relating to the sanitary state of the people of England: being, the results of an inquiry into the different proportions of death produced by certain diseases in different districts in England . . . [by E. H. Greenhow and] an introductory report . . . [by J. Simon] on the preventability of certain kinds of premature death. [2415] H.C. (1857–8). XXIII, 267.

7430  STEWART (ALEXANDER PATRICK) *and* JENKINS (JOHN EDWARD). The medical and legal aspects of sanitary reform. 1867. 2nd edn. 1867. Repr. with intro. by Michael Walter Flinn. Leicester. 1969.

7431  ROYAL SANITARY COMMISSION. First report of the royal sanitary commission . . . [Chairman: Charles Bowyer Adderley]. [4218] H.C. (1868–9), XXXII, 301. Second report in 4 pts. [C. 281 to C. 281–II] H.C. (1871). XXXV, 1. [C. 1109] H.C. (1874). XXXI, 603.

Comprehensive. There is some additional matter in *First report from the select committee on sewage of towns* [Chairman: Dr. Brady]. H.C. 160 (1862). XIV, 321. Second report. H.C. 469 (1862). XIV, 439, Society of Arts, *Conference on the health and sewage of the towns, May 1876,* 1876, *Report of a committee appointed by the president of the Local Government Board to inquire into the several modes of treating town sewage* [Members: Robert Rawlinson and Clare Sewell Read]. [C. 1410] H.C. (1876). XXXVIII, 117, and Edward Crozier Sibbald Moore, *Sanitary engineering: a practical treatise on the collection, removal and final disposal of sewage,* 1898, 3rd edn. 2 v. 1909.

7432  BROWN COMMITTEE ON PUBLIC HEALTH ACT. Report from the Select Committee on Public Health Act (1875) Amendment Bill [Chairman: Alexander Brown]. H.C. 134 (1878). XVIII, 261.

7433  RICHARDSON (*Sir* BENJAMIN WARD). A ministry of health and other addresses. 1879.

Richardson was an active propagandist for a ministry of health. See also his *Hygeia: a city of health,* 1876. Cp. Fred Scott, 'The case for a ministry of health', *Manch. Stat. Soc. Trans.* (1902–3), 97–176.

7434 INTERNATIONAL HEALTH EXHIBITION, 1884. The Health Exhibition literature. 19 v. 1884.

The exhibition produced a ser. of 25 v. of *Handbooks*, 14 v. of *Conferences*, 37 v. of *Lectures*, and much else besides. Also a ser. of useful bibliogs. in the form of a *Catalogue of the International Health Exhibition Library*, 2 pts. 1884.

7435 WHITELEGGE (*Sir* BENJAMIN ARTHUR). Hygiene and public health. 1890. 13th edn. 1917.

Useful for contemp. knowledge.

7436 NEWSHOLME (*Sir* ARTHUR). 'A national system of notification and registration of sickness'. *Roy. Stat. Soc. J.* lix (1896), 1–28.

7437 IDDESLEIGH COMMISSION ON SEWAGE DISPOSAL. Interim report of the commissioners appointed in 1898 to inquire and report what methods of treating and disposing of sewage (including any liquid from any factory or manufacturing process) may be properly adopted [Chairman: Earl of Iddesleigh]. [Cd. 685, 686, 686–I] H.C. (1901), XXXIV, pts. 1 and 2. Second report. [Cd. 1178] H.C. (1902). XLIX, 1. Third report. [Cd. 1486] H.C. (1903). XXXI, 1. Minutes of evidence. [Cd. 1487] H.C. (1903). XXXI, 43. Fourth report on pollution of tidal waters. [Cd. 1883–6] H.C. (1904). XXXVII–XXXVIII. Fifth report. [Cd. 4278–86] H.C. (1908). LIII–LVI. Sixth report. [Cd. 4511] H.C. (1909). XLVI, 793. Seventh report. [Cd. 5542–3, 5543–I] H.C. (1911). XLI, 1. Eighth report. [Cd. 6464] H.C. (1912–13). XLVI, 613. Appendix. [Cd. 6943] H.C. (1913). XXXIX, 807. Ninth report. [Cd. 7819–20] H.C. (1914–16). XXXV, 333. Final report. [Cd. 7821] H.C. (1914–16). XXXV, 705.

A monumental inquiry.

7438 FITZROY COMMITTEE ON PHYSICAL DETERIORATION. Report of the interdepartmental committee on physical deterioration [Chairman: Sir Almeric W. FitzRoy]. [Cd. 2175] H.C. (1904). XXXII, 1. Minutes of evidence. [Cd. 2210] H.C. (1904). XXXII, 145. Appendix. [Cd. 2186] H.C. (1904). XXXII, 655.

A general investigation into the physical state of the nation. Includes valuable evidence. See Bentley Brinkerhoff Gilbert, 'Health and politics: the British physical deterioration report of 1904', *Bull. Hist. Med.* xxxix (1965), 145–53. There is some interesting additional data in Francis Warner, 'Results of an inquiry as to the physical and mental condition of fifty thousand children seen in one hundred and six schools', *Roy. Stat. Soc. J.* lvi (1893), 71–95; lix (1896), 125–62. For infant mortality see Sir Arthur Newsholme, *Thirty-ninth annual report of the Local Government Board, 1909–10: supplement to the report of the Board's medical officer containing a report by the medical officer on infant and child mortality.* [Cd. 5263] H.C. (1910). XXXIX, 973.

(b) *Infectious Diseases*

7439 CREIGHTON (CHARLES). A history of epidemics in Britain . . . 2 v. Camb. 1891–4. Repr. 1965.

Dated, but not supplanted. For a general coverage of infectious diseases see Sir Frank Macfarlane Burnet, *Natural history of infectious disease* [2nd edn. of his *Biological aspects of infectious disease*, Camb. 1940], Camb. 1953; Edward Wilberforce Goodall, *A short history of the epidemic infectious diseases*, 1934; Sir Henry Harold Scott, *Some notable epidemics*, 1934; Major Greenwood, *Epidemics and crowd diseases: an introduction to the study of epidemiology*, 1935; Geddes Smith, *Plague on us*, 1941; Walter Reginald Bett, ed., *The history and conquest of common diseases*, Norman, Okla. 1954; Ronald Hare, *Pomp and pestilence: infectious disease: its origins and conquest*, 1954.

7440  WINSLOW (CHARLES EDWARD AMORY). The conquest of epidemic disease: a chapter in the history of ideas. Princeton, N.J. 1944.

7441  ACKERKNECHT (ERWIN H.). 'Anticontagionism between 1821 and 1867'. *Bull. Hist. Med.* xxii (1948), 562–93.

See also Owsei Temkin, 'An historical analysis of the concept of infection' in Johns Hopkins Univ. Hist. of Ideas Club, *Studies in intellectual history*, Baltimore, Md. 1935, and Sir Jervoise Clarke Jervoise, *Infection*, 1882.

7442  PARISH (HENRY JAMES). A history of immunization. Edin. & Baltimore [Md.]. 1965.

7443  WOODWARK (*Sir* [ARTHUR] STANLEY). 'The rise and fall of certain diseases concurrently with the progress of hygiene and sanitation'. *Roy. Inst. Public Health J.* i (1938), 897–910.

7444  LONGMATE (NORMAN RICHARD). King cholera: the biography of a disease. [1966.]

7445  BRIGGS (ASA). 'Cholera and society in the nineteenth century'. *Past & Present* xix (1961), 75–96.

7446  ZINSSER (HANS). Rats, lice and history: being a study in biography which . . . deals with the life history of typhus fever. Boston & Lond. 1935.

7447  SHREWSBURY (JOHN FINDLAY DREW). A history of bubonic plague in the British isles. Camb. 1970.

See also Leonard Fabian Hirst, *The conquest of plague: a study of the evolution of epidemiology*, Oxf. 1953, a good book; Charles Frederic Mullett, *The bubonic plague and England: an essay in the history of preventive medicine*, Lexington, Ky., 1956; and Robert Bruce Low, ed., *Reports and papers on bubonic plague . . . an account of the progress and diffusion of plague throughout the world, 1898–1901, and of the measures employed in different countries for repression of this disease*. [Cd. 748] H.C. (1901). XXVII, I.

7448  PATRICK (ADAM). The enteric fevers, 1800–1920. Edin. 1955.

7449  ROLLESTON (JOHN DAVY). History of the acute exanthemata. 1937.

Small pox, chicken pox, scarlet fever, measles.

7450  NEWMAN (*Sir* GEORGE). On the history of the decline and final extinction of leprosy as an endemic disease in the British islands. 1895.

7451 NEWSHOLME (*Sir* ARTHUR). Epidemic diphtheria: a research on the origin and spread of the disease from an international standpoint. 1898.

See also Edward Wilberforce Goodall, Major Greenwood, and W. T. Russell, *Scarlet fever, diphtheria and enteric fever, 1895–1914: a clinical statistical study*, Medical Research Council, special report 137, 1929.

7452 LONDON SOCIETY FOR THE ABOLITION OF COMPULSORY VACCINATION. A catalogue of anti-vaccination literature. 1882.

Subsequent works were reviewed in the leading anti-vaccination j., *The vaccination inquirer and health review: the organ of the London Society for the Abolition of Compulsory Vaccination*, 1879+. The National Anti-Compulsory Vaccination League, *Occasional circular* [*Reporter*], Cheltenham 1874–84, *The Co-operator and anti-vaccinator*, Dewsbury & Lond. 1860–71, and *The anti-vaccinator and public health journal*, 1872–3, were other js.

7453 LAMBERT (ROYSTON JAMES). 'A Victorian national health service: state vaccination, 1855–71'. *Hist. J.* v (1962), 1–18.

7454 MACLEOD (ROY MALCOLM). 'Law, medicine and public opinion: the resistance to compulsory health legislation, 1870–1907'. *Public Law* (1967), 107–28, 189–211.

For contemp. opinion see William B. Carpenter, 'Smallpox and vaccination in 1871–1881', *Nineteenth Century* xi (1882), 526–46, and Peter Alfred Taylor, 'Anti-vaccination', ibid. 782–802. For Leicester, which was the centre of resistance, see Dale L. Ross, 'Leicester and the anti-vaccination movement, 1853–89', *Leicestershire Arch. & Hist. Soc. Trans.* xliii (1967–8), 35–44. See also Ann F. Beck, 'Issues in the anti-vaccination movement in England', *Medical Hist.* iv (1960), 310–21.

7455 GUY (WILLIAM AUGUSTUS).'Two hundred and fifty years of small-pox in London'. *Stat. Soc. J.* xlv (1882), 399–437.

7456 EDWARDES (EDWARD JOSHUA). A concise history of smallpox and vaccination in Europe. 1902.

7457 CROOKSHANK (EDGAR MARCH). History and pathology of vaccination. 2 v. 1889.

Gives useful information about the development of vaccination, as does Charles Creighton, *Jenner and vaccination: a strange chapter of medical history*, 1889. Both books were used to provide background for the battle over compulsory vaccination. The case against vaccination is set out in Charles Thomas Pearce, *Vital statistics: small pox and vaccination in the United Kingdom and continental countries and cities, with tables compiled from authentic sources*, 1882; Alfred Russel Wallace, *Forty-five years of registration statistics proving vaccination to be both useless and dangerous*, 1885, 2nd edn. by Alexander Wheeler, 1889, and *Vaccination a delusion: its penal enforcement a crime . . .*, 1898; Arthur Wollaston Hutton, *The vaccination question*, 1895; and Alexander Paul, *The vaccination problem in 1903 and the impracticability of compulsion*, 1903.

7458 HERSCHELL COMMISSION ON VACCINATION. First report of the royal commission appointed to inquire into the subject of vaccination [Chairman: Lord Herschell]. [C. 5845] H.C. (1889). XXXIX, 657. Second report. [C. 6066] H.C. (1890). XXXIX, 1. Third report. [C. 6192] H.C. (1890). XXXIX, 367. Fourth report. [C. 6527] H.C. (1890–1). XLIV, 735. Fifth report. [C. 6666] H.C. (1892). XLVII, 547. Sixth report. [C. 7993] H.C. (1896). XLVII, 1. Final report. [C. 8270] H.C. (1896). XLVII, 889. Appendixes. [C. 8609–15] H.C. (1897). XLV–XLVII.

See also *Report of the departmental committee appointed by the president of the Local Government Board to inquire into the subject of vaccination expenses* [Chairman: Evan Henry Llewellyn]. [Cd. 2420] H.C. (1905). XL, 385. Minutes of evidence. [Cd. 2421] H.C. (1905). XL, 413.

7459　KAYNE (GEORGE GREGORY). The control of tuberculosis in England, past and present. 1937.

See also *Interim report of the departmental committee on tuberculosis* [Chairman: Waldorf Astor]. [C. 6164] H.C. (1912–13). XLVIII, 1. Final report. [Cd. 6641] H.C. (1912–13). XLVIII, 29. Appendix. [Cd. 6654] H.C. (1912–13). XLVIII, 47, which incl. a useful summary of the provisions for dealing with the disease. There is also a vast technical lit.

(c) *Nursing*

7460　THOMPSON (ALICE MARY CHARLOTTE) *ed.* A bibliography of nursing literature, 1859–1960, with an historical introduction. Libr. Assoc. etc. 1968.

The main bibliog. is National League of Nursing Education: Department of Services to Schools of Nursing, *Bibliographies on nursing: books, pamphlets, articles, audio-visual aids*, 10 v. N.Y. 1952. For periodical articles see Yale University School of Nursing, *Nursing studies index*, ed. by Virginia Henderson, 1900+, 4+ v. Phila. 1963+.

7461　BURDETT (*Sir* HENRY CHARLES) *comp.* Burdett's official nursing directory. 1898–1903.

The leading nursing periodicals were *The nursing mirror*, 1886+, *The nursing record* [from 1902 *The British j. of nursing*], 1888+, and *Nursing times . . .*, 1905+.

7462　ABEL-SMITH (BRIAN). A history of the nursing profession. 1960.

Standard. Walter Reginald Bett, *A short history of nursing*, 1960; Richard Harrison Shryock, *The history of nursing: an interpretation of the social and medical factors involved*, Phila. 1959; Gladys Sellew and Celestine Joseph Nuesse, *A history of nursing*, St. Louis 1946, 2nd edn. 1951; Agnes Elizabeth Pavey, *The story of the growth of nursing as an art, a vocation and a profession*, 1938, 5th edn. 1960; Lucy Ridgely Seymer, *A general history of nursing*, 1932, 4th edn. 1957; Elizabeth Marion Jamieson and Mary F. Sewall, *Trends in nursing history: their relationship to world events*, Phila. & Lond. 5th edn. 1959; and Denis Gerard Murphy, *They did not pass by: the story of the early pioneers of nursing*, 1956; are all works designed primarily for the use of nurses and have few academic pretensions. Two older books are sometimes useful sources: Mary Adelaide Nutting and Lavinia L. Dock, *A history of nursing: the evolution of nursing systems from the earliest times to the foundation of the first English and American training schools for nurses*, 4 v. N.Y. & Lond. 1907–12 [vol. IV deals in fact with the previous 30 years], and Sarah A. Tooley, *The history of nursing in the British empire*, 1906.

7463　COPE (*Sir* [VINCENT] ZACHARY). A hundred years of nursing at St. Mary's hospital, Paddington. 1955.

7464　CHARLEY (IRENE HANNAH). The birth of industrial nursing: its history and development in Great Britain. 1954.

**7465** STOCKS (MARY DANVERS), *Baroness Stocks*. A hundred years of district nursing. 1960.

See also William Rathbone, *Sketch of the history and progress of district nursing . . .*, 1890, the life of Rathbone (**873**), and Jamieson Boyd Hurry, *District nursing on a provident basis*, 1898.

**7466** OLIVER (*Dame* BERYL). The British Red Cross in action. 1966.

**7467** FLETCHER (NIGEL CORBET). The St. John Ambulance Association: its history and its part in the ambulance movement. 1931.

See also Sir John Furley, *In peace and war: autobiographical sketches*, 1905 and Joan Clifford, *For the service of mankind: Furley, Lechmere and Duncan; St. John Ambulance founders*, 1971.

**7468** CAVELL. Edith Cavell. By Helen Judson. N.Y. 1941.

See also Herbert Leeds, *Edith Cavell: her life story: a Norfolk tribute*, 1915, and Sidney Theodore Felstead, *Edith Cavell: the crime that shook the world: written from the dossier of the German secret police and the personal narratives of survivors* [1940].

**7469** NIGHTINGALE. Florence Nightingale, 1820–1910. By Cecil Blanche Woodham-Smith. 1950.

Readable, but not always accurate. For criticism see William Howard Greanleaf, 'Biography and the "amateur" historian: Mrs. Woodham-Smith's "Florence Nightingale"', *Victorian Studs.* iii (1959–60), 190–202. The 'official' life is Sir Edward Tyas Cook, *The life of Florence Nightingale*, 2 v. 1913. See also Sir [Vincent] Zachary Cope, *Florence Nightingale and the doctors*, 1958, Ida Beatrice O'Malley, *Florence Nightingale, 1820–1856: a study of her life down to the end of the Crimean War*, 1932, William John Bishop and Sue Goldie, *A bio-bibliography of Florence Nightingale*, 1962, and the popular lives: Margaret Leland Goldsmith, *Florence Nightingale: the woman and the legend*, 1937, Lucy Ridgely Seymer, *Florence Nightingale*, 1950, Sarah A. Tooley, *The life of Florence Nightingale*, 1904, and Irene Cooper Willis, *Florence Nightingale: a biography*, 1931.

**7470** SEYMER (LUCY RIDGELY). Florence Nightingale's nurses: the Nightingale training school, 1860–1960. 1960.

See also M. Christabel Cadbury, *The story of a Nightingale nurse* [*Mary Cadbury*], *and kindred papers*, 1939.

**7471** O'NEILL (HANNAH COX) *and* BARNETT (EDITH A.). Our nurses and the work they have to do. [1888.]

**7472** TENNANT COMMITTEE ON REGISTRATION OF NURSES. Report from the select committee on registration of nurses [Chairman: H. J. Tennant]. H.C. 281 (1904). VI, 701. Further report. H.C. 263 (1905). VII, 733.

A useful coll. of data and a short report recommending registration.

**7473** FITZROY COMMITTEE ON MIDWIVES ACT. Report of the departmental committee appointed by the Lord President of the Council to consider the working of the Midwives Act, 1902 [Chairman: Sir Almeric W. FitzRoy]. [Cd. 4822] H.C. (1909). XXXIII, 19. Minutes of evidence. [Cd. 4823] H.C. (1909). XXXIII, 77.

An important report.

(d) *Hospitals*

**7474**  BIBLIOGRAPHIE D'HISTOIRE HOSPITALIÈRE. 1+. Paris. 1957+.

An annual bibliog. publ. originally by *Revue de l'assistance publique.*

**7475**  PINKER (ROBERT). English hospital statistics, 1861–1938. 1966.

**7476**  BURDETT'S HOSPITAL ANNUAL AND YEAR BOOK OF PHILANTHROPY. 1890–1930.

Established by Sir Henry Charles Burdett: title varies. The main periodicals were *Hospital*, 1886–1921, and *The hospital* [*gazette*], 1904+.

**7477**  ABEL-SMITH (BRIAN), *assisted by* PINKER (ROBERT). The hospitals, 1800–1948: a study in social administration in England and Wales. Lond. & Camb., Mass. 1964.

Standard. See also Courtney Dainton, *The story of England's hospitals*, 1961, Alva Delbert Evans and Louis G. Redmond Howard, *The romance of the British voluntary hospital movement*[1930], and Frederick Noel Lawrence Poynter, ed., *The evolution of hospitals in Britain*, 1964.

**7478**  CAMERON (HECTOR CHARLES). Mr. Guy's hospital, 1726–1948. 1954.

A thorough study. For other London hospitals see Maurice Davidson and Frederick George Rouvray, *The Brompton hospital . . .*, 1954; Thomas Twistington Higgins, '*Great Ormond Street*', *1852–1952*, 1954; Sir Gordon Morgan Holmes, *The National hospital, Queen Square, 1860–1948*, Edin. & Lond. 1954, and Anon., *Queen Square and the National Hospital, 1860–1960*, 1960; Eric Charles Oliphant Jewesbury, *The Royal Northern hospital, 1856–1956, . . .*, 1956; John Langdon-Davies, *Westminster hospital: two centuries of voluntary service, 1719–1948*, 1952; Sir Norman Moore, *The history of St. Bartholomew's hospital*, 2 v. 1918; Sir D'Arcy Power and Sir Holburt Jacob Waring, *A short history of St. Bartholomew's hospital, 1123–1923*, 1923; Archibald Edmund Clark-Kennedy, *The London: a study in the voluntary hospital system*, 2 v. 1962–3; Sir Ernest William Morris, *A history of the London hospital*, 2nd edn. 1910, 3rd edn. 1926; [Albert] Clifford Morson, ed., *St. Peter's hospital for stone, 1860–1960*, Edin. & Lond. 1960; Reginald Hugh Nichols and Francis Aslett Wray, *The history of the Foundling hospital*, 1935; Edward Geoffrey O'Donoghue, *The story of Bethlehem hospital from its foundation in 1247*, 1914; Frederick George Parsons, *The history of St. Thomas's hospital*, 3 v. 1932–6; Eilidh Margaret McInnes, *St. Thomas' hospital*, 1963; Hilary Aidan St. George Saunders, *The Middlesex hospital, 1745–1948*, 1949; Edward Treacher Collins, *The history & traditions of the Moorfields Eye Hospital . . .*, 1929; James Douglas Allan Gray, *The Central Middlesex hospital*, 1963; Brian Russell, ed., *St. John's hospital for diseases of the skin, 1863–1963*, Edin. & Lond. 1963.

**7479**  AYERS (GWENDOLINE MARGERY). England's first state hospitals and the Metropolitan Asylums Board, 1867–1930. Wellcome Inst. Hist. Med. Lond. & Berkeley [Calif.]. 1971.

Replaces Sir George Allan Powell, *The Metropolitan Asylums Board and its work, 1867–1930*, 1930.

**7480**  LONG (FRANK D.). King Edward's hospital fund for London: the story of its foundation and achievements, 1897–1942. 1942.

7481 BROCKBANK (WILLIAM). Portrait of a hospital, 1752–1948: to commemorate the bi-centenary of the Royal infirmary, Manchester. 1952.

Other good provincial hospitals covered incl. Stephen Towers Anning, *The General infirmary at Leeds*, 2 v., Edin. & Lond. 1963–6; Frank Harwood Jacob, *A history of the General hospital near Nottingham open to the sick and lame and poor of any county*, Bristol 1951; William Robinson, *The story of the Royal infirmary, Sunderland . . .*, Sunderland 1934; Rachel Elizabeth Waterhouse, *Children in hospital: a hundred years of child care in Birmingham*, 1962; Alexander George Gibson, *The Radcliffe infirmary*, 1926; John Daniel Leader, *Sheffield general infirmary, now the Sheffield Royal infirmary, 1797–1897 . . .*, Sheffield 1897; William Brockbank, *The honorary medical staff of the Manchester Royal Infirmary, 1830–1948*, Manch. 1965; Frederick Stancliffe Stancliffe, *The Manchester Royal Eye hospital, 1814–1964: a short history*, Manch. [1964]; John Harley Young, *St. Mary's hospitals, Manchester, 1790–1963*, Edin. & Lond. 1964.

7482 BELL (ENID HESTER CHATAWAY MOBERLY). The story of hospital almoners: the birth of a profession. 1961.

7483 NIGHTINGALE (FLORENCE). Notes on hospitals . . . 1859. 3rd edn. 1863.

A famous work. For her views on nursing see **7469**.

7484 BUCKLE (FLEETWOOD). Vital and economical statistics of the hospitals, infirmaries, etc., of England and Wales for the year 1863. 1865.

7485 THE LANCET. The *Lancet* sanitary commission for investigating the state of the infirmaries of workhouses: reports of the commissioners on metropolitan infirmaries. 1866.

On Poor Law hospitals. See also *Report of Dr. Edward Smith . . ., Poor Law inspector and medical officer to the Poor Law Board, on the metropolitan workhouse infirmaries and sick wards*. H.C. 372 (1866). LXI, 171, similar report by Dr. Smith on provincial workhouses. H.C. 4 (1867–8). LX, 325, and *Report of H. B. Farnell, Esquire, Poor Law inspector, on the infirmary wards of the several metropolitan workhouses and their existing arrangements*. H.C. 387 (1866). LXI, 389. There was also a later report, *British Medical Journal, The sick poor in workhouses: reports on the nursing and administration of provincial workhouses and infirmaries by a special commission of 'The British Medical Journal': with an appendix . . . and an introduction by Ernest Hart*, 2 ser. 1894–5.

7486 WARING (EDWARD JOHN). Cottage hospitals: their objects, advantages and management. 1867.

See also Sir Henry Charles Burdett, *The cottage hospital: its origin, progress, management and work*, 1877, 3rd edn. 1896, and R. M. S. McConaghey, 'The evolution of the cottage hospital', *Medical Hist.* xi (1967), 128–40.

7487 TAIT (ROBERT LAWSON). An essay on hospital mortality, based upon the statistics of the hospitals of Great Britain for fifteen years. 1877.

7488 OPPERT (FRANZ). Hospitals, infirmaries and dispensaries: their construction, interior arrangement and management. 1867. 2nd edn. 1883.

An influential work on hospital building.

7489 BLACHFORD COMMISSION ON SMALL-POX AND FEVER HOSPITALS. Report of the commissioners appointed to inquire respecting small-pox and fever hospitals [Chairman: Lord Blachford]. [C. 3314] H.C. (1882). XXIX, 1.

Careful. Suppl. by *Tenth annual report of the Local Government Board, 1880–81: supplement containing report and papers submitted by the Board's medical officer [George Buchanan] on the use and influence of hospitals for infectious diseases.* [C. 3290] H.C. (1882). XXX, pt. II, 1.

7490  BURDETT (*Sir* HENRY CHARLES). Hospitals and asylums of the world: their origin, history, construction, administration, management and legislation; with plans of the chief medical institutions . . . 4 v. and portfolio of plans. 1891–3.

See also his *Pay hospitals and paying wards throughout the world*, 1880, and *Hospitals and the state . . .*, 1881. There is also some comparative matter in William Gill Wylie, *Hospitals: their history, organization and construction*, N.Y. 1877.

7491  LORDS COMMITTEE ON METROPOLITAN HOSPITALS. Report from the select committee of the House of Lords on metropolitan hospitals, &c. [Chairman: Lord Sandhurst.] H.C. 392 (1890). XVI, 1. Second report. H.C. 457 (1890–1). XIII, 1. Third report. H.C. 321 (1892–Sess. I). XIII, 1. General index. H.C. 321–I (1892–Sess. I). XIII, 289.

A thorough inquiry.

7492  KERSHAW (RICHARD). Special hospitals: their origin, development and relationship to medical education. 1909.

7493  BRAUN (PERCY E.). 'The cost, conditions and results of hospital relief in London'. *Roy. Stat. Soc. J.* lxxii (1909), 1–30.

Suppl. by Stewart Johnson, 'An attempt to show from what class the out-patients of a voluntary hospital are drawn', *Roy. Stat. Soc. J.* lxxiv (1910–11), 630–40.

### (e) *Prostitution*

#### (i) *General*

There is no general hist., and the pamphlet literature of the subject is of rather poor quality.

7494  ACTON (WILLIAM). Prostitution considered in its moral, social and sanitary aspects in London and other large cities . . . 1857. 2nd edn. 1870.

A careful account by a surgeon.

7495  LOGAN (WILLIAM). The great social evil: its causes, extent, results and remedies. 1871.

7496  MERRICK (GEORGE PURNELL). Work among the fallen as seen in the prison cell. [1891.]

A report on the causes of prostitution.

7497  BLACKWELL (ELIZABETH). Essays in medical sociology. 2 v. 1902.

Includes two useful articles on prostitution.

**7498** MARTINDALE (LOUISA). Under the surface. 1912.
Suggests that economic independence and the vote will end prostitution.

**7499** READE (ALFRED ARTHUR). The tragedy of the streets. Wilmslow. [1913.]
A characteristic example of the pamphlet lit. produced by the well-intentioned lunatic fringe.

**7500** CREIGHTON (LOUISE). The social disease and how to fight it: a rejoinder. 1914.

**7501** FLEXNER (ABRAHAM). Prostitution in Europe. N.Y. 1914.
Chiefly concerned with the Continent.

**7502** ROYDEN (AGNES MAUDE) *ed.* Downward paths: an inquiry into the causes which contribute to the making of the prostitute. 1916.
A careful scientific inquiry confined to the previous five years.

**7503** MY SECRET LIFE. 11 v. in 2 v. N.Y. 1966.
An important anonymous erotic autobiog. with careful notes on the lives of prostitutes.

**7504** PEARL (CYRIL ALTSON). The girl with the swansdown seat. 1955.
A popular account of Catherine Walters, a society courtesan and her times. See also Henry Blyth, *Skittles, the last Victorian courtesan: the life and times of Catherine Walters,* 1970, and Wilfred Herbert Holden, *The pearl from Plymouth: Eliza Emma Crouch, alias Cora Pearl . . .,* 1970.

**7505** COLE (J. M.) *and* BACON (F. C.). Christian guidance of the social instincts: a survey of the church's work for social purity. 1928.

**7506** UNSWORTH (MADGE). Maiden tribute: a study in voluntary social service. 1949.
A hist. of the Salvation Army's work in reclaiming prostitutes and helping homeless women. An interesting comparison is with John Blackmore, *The London by moonlight mission . . .,* 1860. For other such missions see Mary H. Steer, *Opals from sand: a story of early days at the Bridge of Hope . . .* [1912], rev. edn. [*The Bridge of Hope mission*] 1929, and William J. Taylor, *The story of the homes . . .,* London Female Preventive & Reformatory Instn., 1907.

**7507** MADDISON (ARTHUR J. S.). Hints on rescue work: a handbook for missionaries. Reformatory and Refuge Union. 1898.
See also his *The law relating to child-saving and reformatory efforts . . .,* 1896, 4th edn. 1909, and Arthur Brinckman, *Notes on rescue work: a manual of hints to those who wish to reclaim the fallen,* 1885, rev. edn. 1894.

**7508** JARRETT. Rebecca Jarrett. By Josephine Elizabeth Butler. [1885.]
The life of a reformed prostitute.

7509  WAUGH. The life of Benjamin Waugh. By Rosa Waugh, afterwards
Hobhouse. 1913.

The life of an important social worker among prostitutes.

(ii) Contagious Diseases Acts

The best account of the campaign against the C.D. Acts is in the life of James
Stansfeld (**809**). See also the life of H. J. Wilson (**890**).

7510  SCOTT (BENJAMIN). A state iniquity: its rise, extension and overthrow: a concise history of the system of state-regulated and licensed vice . . .
1890.

Important. Includes a list of workers against the C.D. Acts, and a full bibliog. For a
cooler look at the subject see Robert Lawson, 'The operation of the Contagious Diseases
Acts among the troops in the United Kingdom and men of the Royal Navy on the Home
Station, from their introduction in 1864 to their ultimate repeal in 1884', *Roy. Stat. Soc.
J.* liv (1891), 31–62. Earlier statistical interests are reflected in Berkeley Hill, 'Statistical
results of the Contagious Diseases Acts', *Stat. Soc. J.* xxxiii (1870), 463–85, and James
Stansfeld, 'On the validity of the annual government statistics of the operation of the
Contagious Diseases Acts', *Stat. Soc. J.* xxxix (1876), 540–61. See also *The shield: the
Anti-Contagious Diseases Acts Association's weekly circular*, South Shields, later Lond.,
1870–86, cont. by successor socs., 1898+.

7511  AMOS (SHELDON). A comparative survey of laws in force for the
prohibition, regulation and licensing of vice in England and other countries.
1877.

Amos also publ. a number of pamphlets on the subject.

7512  BUTLER (JOSEPHINE ELIZABETH). Personal reminiscences of a
great crusade. 1896.

The campaign against the C.D. Acts as seen by its leader. See also her *Recollections of
George Butler*, 1892, and the five biogs. of Josephine Butler: Arthur Stanley George
Butler, *Portrait of Josephine Butler*, 1954; George William Johnson and Lucy A. Johnson, eds., *Josephine E. Butler* . . ., 1909; Ethel Mary Turner, *The Josephine Butler
centenary, 1828–1928: Josephine Butler an appreciation* [1927]; L. Hay-Cooper,
*Josephine Butler and her work for social purity*, 1922; and Glen Petrie, *A singular iniquity:
the campaigns of Josephine Butler*, 1971.

7513  VIVIAN COMMITTEE ON CONTAGIOUS DISEASES ACT, 1866.
Report from the select committee on Contagious Diseases Act (1866) [Chair-
man: J. C. W. Vivian]. H.C. 306 (1868–9). VII, 1.

7514  ROYAL COMMISSION ON CONTAGIOUS DISEASES ACTS.
Report of royal commission upon the administration and operation of the
Contagious Diseases Acts [Chairman: William Nathaniel Massey]. [C. 408]
H.C. (1871). XIX, 1. Minutes of evidence. [C. 408–I] H.C. (1871). XIX, 29.

7515  SELECT COMMITTEE ON CONTAGIOUS DISEASES ACTS.
Report from the select committee on the Contagious Diseases Acts [Chairman:
W. N. Massey]. H.C. 323 (1878–9). VIII, 397. Further reports. H.C. 114

(1880). VIII, 283. H.C. 308 (1880–Sess. 2). VIII, 361. H.C. 351 (1881). VIII, 193. H.C. 340 (1882). IX, 1.

A protracted and careful inquiry which led directly to the repeal of the Acts. During the 1882 session the committee was chaired by Arthur O'Shaughnessy.

7516 SYDENHAM COMMISSION ON VENEREAL DISEASES. Royal commission on venereal diseases: first report of the commissioners [Chairman: Lord Sydenham of Combe]. [Cd. 7474] H.C. (1914). XLIX, 109. Minutes of evidence. [Cd. 7475] H.C. (1914). XLIX, 113. Final report. [Cd. 8189] H.C. (1916). XVI, 1. Minutes of evidence. [Cd. 8190] H.C. (1916). XVI, 215.

See also R. W. Johnstone, *Report on venereal diseases*. [Cd. 7029] H.C. (1913). XXXII, 423.

### (iii) *White Slave Traffic*

The works cited below should be suppl. by the lives of W. T. Stead (**5459**).

7517 TERROT (CHARLES). The maiden tribute: a study of the white slave traffic of the nineteenth century. 1959.

Thin.

7518 CAIRNS COMMITTEE ON THE LAW RELATING TO THE PROTECTION OF YOUNG GIRLS. Report from the select committee of the House of Lords on the law relating to the protection of young girls [Chairman: Earl Cairns]. H.C. 448 (1881). IX, 355. Further report. H.C. 344 (1882). XIII, 823.

An important source for prostitution generally, as well as for the white slave traffic, chiefly to Belgium.

7519 COOTE (WILLIAM ALEXANDER). A vision and its fulfilment: being, the history of the origin of the work of the National Vigilance Association for the Suppression of the White Slave Traffic: with a record of visits paid to the capitals of Europe, and to America, Egypt, and South Africa, for the purpose of organising National Committees for the suppression of the traffic. [1910.]

See also William Alexander Coote, ed., *A romance of philanthropy: being, a record of some of the principal incidents connected with the exceptionally successful thirty years' work of the National Vigilance Association*, 1916, and *The white slave traffic*, 1910, rev. edn. 1916.

7520 DYER (ALFRED STACE). The European slave trade in English girls: a narrative of facts. 1880. 9th edn. 1885.

7521 WILLIS (WILLIAM NICHOLAS). The white slaves of London. [1912.]

A luridly got-up paperback, designed to sell rather than inform. Followed by *Why girls go wrong: how the white slave gangs work*, 1913, and *White slaves in a Piccadilly flat*, 1915. All of these books were reissued in 1949 for sale in the penny horror market. Willis and Olive Christian Mackirdy (formerly Malvery) also publ. *The white slave market*, 1912. Willis's *The life of Lena: a girl of London town* [1914], repr. 1949, purports to be a potted biog. of a white slave.

## 7. TEMPERANCE

### (a) *General*

7522 HARRISON (BRIAN HOWARD). 'Drink and sobriety in England, 1815–1872: a critical bibliography'. *Int. Rev. Soc. Hist.* xii (1967), 204–76.
Full on all aspects of the subject.

7523 WILSON (GEORGE BAILEY). Alcohol and the nation: a contribution to the study of the liquor problem in the United Kingdom from 1800 to 1935. 1940.

The best intro. to the temperance question and its statistics. For Wilson's own career in the United Kingdom Alliance see his *Looking back*, 1944.

7524 HARRISON (BRIAN HOWARD). Drink and the Victorians: the temperance question in England, 1815–1872. 1971.

The first serious hist. See also his 'The British prohibitionists, 1853–1872: a biographical analysis', *Int. Rev. Soc. Hist.* xv (1970), 375–467, and ' "A world of which we had no conception": Liberalism and the temperance press, 1830–1872', *Victorian Studs.* xiii (1969–70), 125–58, and B. H. Harrison and Barrie Trinder, *Drink and sobriety in an early Victorian country town: Banbury, 1830–1860*, 1969. Norman Richard Longmate, *The waterdrinkers: a history of temperance*, 1868, is popular.

7525 MATHIAS (PETER). 'The brewing industry, temperance and politics'. *Hist. J.* i (1958), 97–114.

7526 MACLEOD (ROY MALCOLM). 'The edge of hope: social policy and chronic alcoholism, 1870–1900'. *J. Hist. Med.* xxii (1967), 215–45.

7527 LORDS COMMITTEE ON INTEMPERANCE. First report from the select committee of the House of Lords on intemperance [Chairman: Duke of Westminster]. H.C. 171 (1877). XI, 1. Second report. H.C. 271 (1877). XI, 357. Third report. H.C. 418 (1877). XI, 759. Fourth report. H.C. 338 (1878). XIV, 1. [Final] report. H.C. 113 (1878–9). X, 469.

The first thorough investigation of the subject, but less far-reaching than the report of the Peel Commission (**7568**).

7528 ROWNTREE (JOSEPH) *and* SHERWELL (ARTHUR). The temperance problem and social reform. 1899. 9th edn. 1901.
A first-rate survey of the whole problem.

7529 SHADWELL (ARTHUR). Drink, temperance and legislation. 1902.

7530 SNOWDEN (PHILIP), *Viscount Snowden*. Socialism and the drink question. 1908.

7531 HORSLEY (*Sir* VICTOR ALEXANDER HADEN) *and* STURGE (MARY DARBY). Alcohol and the human body: an introduction to the study of the subject, and a contribution to national health. 1907. 6th edn. 1920.

This book and William Charles Sullivan, *Alcoholism: a chapter in social pathology*, 1906, were the main medical contributions to the serious discussion of the liquor problem inaugurated by Rowntree and Sherwell (**7528**). But see also Kate Mitchell, *The drink question: its social and medical aspects* [1890], 2nd edn. 1891. Horsley was the leading authority of the period on alcoholism. For his life see Stephen Paget, *Sir Victor Horsley: a study of his life and work*, 1919.

**7532** SELECT COMMITTEE ON HABITUAL DRUNKARDS. Report from the select committee on habitual drunkards [Chairman: Donald Dalrymple]. H.C. 242 (1872). IX, 417.

There were three further committees on the treatment of inebriates: *Report from the departmental committee on the treatment of inebriates* [Chairman: John Lloyd Wharton]. [C. 7008] H.C. (1893–4). XVII, 597; Minutes of evidence. [C. 7008–I] H.C. (1893–4). XVII, 607, *Report of the departmental committee appointed . . . to advise as to the regulations to be made under the Inebriates Act*, 1898 [Chairman: William Patrick Byrne]. [C. 9112] H.C. (1899). XII, 749, *Report of the departmental committee appointed to inquire into the operation of law relating to inebriates and to their detention in reformatories and retreats* [Chairman: Sir John Dickson-Poynder]. [Cd. 4438] H.C. (1908). XII, 817, Minutes of evidence. [Cd. 4439] H.C. (1908). XII, 861.

(b) *The Temperance and Prohibition Movements*

**7533** EDWARDS (WALTER N.). The temperance compendium: a cyclopaedia of the facts, figures and other useful data relating to the temperance question. 1906.

A poor substitute for a temperance encyclopedia.

**7534** CARTER (HENRY). The English temperance movement: a study in objectives. Vol. I. The formative period, 1830–1899. 1933.

Vol. II not publ. A controversial work, primarily concerned with the prohibitionist United Kingdom Alliance and the political side of the temperance movement.

**7535** COULING (SAMUEL). History of the temperance movement in Great Britain and Ireland from the earliest date to the present time: with biographical notices of departed temperance worthies. 1862.

The first full hist., written mainly for temperance workers. Succeeded by Burns (**7536** and Winskill (**7537**). James Samuelson, *The history of drink . . .*, 1878, 2nd edn. 1880, was an attempt to provide a background hist. for the use of the temperance movement.

**7536** BURNS (JAMES DAWSON). Temperance history: a consecutive narrative of the rise, development, and extension of the temperance reform. 2 v. issued in pts. 1889–91.

Burns also publ. *Temperance in the Victorian age, 1837–1897*, 1897.

**7537** WINSKILL (PETER TURNER). The temperance movement and its workers: a record of social, moral, religious and political progress. 4 v. Edin. 1890–2.

A very useful source. Winskill also publ. *The comprehensive history of the rise and progress of the temperance reformation from the earliest period to September 1881 . . .*, Warrington 1881.

7538 WOOLLEY (JOHN GRANVILLE) *and* JOHNSON (WILLIAM EUGENE). Temperance progress of the century. The nineteenth century series. 1905.

Mainly on the American side of the temperance movement.

7539 WINSKILL (PETER TURNER). Temperance standard bearers of the nineteenth century: a biographical and statistical temperance dictionary. 2 v. Manch. 1897–8.

Over 7,000 entries. Jabez Inwards, *Memorials of temperance workers* . . ., 1879, and James Dawson Burns, *Pen-pictures of some temperance notables*, 1895, have little more.

7540 HUDSON (THOMAS). Temperance pioneers of the West: personal and incidental experiences. 1887.

7541 LIVESEY. Autobiography of Joseph Livesey. Ed. by William Livesey. 1886.

The founder of teetotalism. See also James Weston, pseud. of Edward Step, ed., *Joseph Livesey, the story of his life, 1794–1884*, 1884, *The life and teachings of Joseph Livesey: comprising his autobiography with an introductory review of his labours* . . . *by John Pearce*, 1886, 2nd edn. 1887, and William Edward Armitage Axon, *Joseph Livesey, the pioneer of the temperance movement: his life and labours*, Manch. 1894.

7542 GOUGH. The autobiography of John B[artholomew] Gough: with a continuation of his life to the present time. 1855. Rev. edn. 1879.

The *Autobiography* was originally publ. in Boston, 1845. Gough was the best-known temperance orator of the period 1853–79. He also publ. *Sunlight and shadow: or, gleanings from my life-work* . . ., 1880, *Platform echoes: or, leaves from my note-book of forty years* . . ., 1885, and *Orations*, 1859, all of which ran to many edns., and many temperance addresses.

7543 GREGSON. Life of William Gregson, temperance advocate. By John George Shaw. Blackburn. 1891.

The best life of a rank-and-file professional temperance advocate. For a later man of the same type see *Memoirs of Henry Patterson, local preacher and temperance advocate, 1850–1939*, by his son, Gateshead 1941.

7544 LAWSON. Sir Wilfrid Lawson: a memoir. Ed. by George William Erskine Russell. 1909.

The parl. spokesman of the United Kingdom Alliance.

7545 LEES. Dr. Frederic Richard Lees, F.S.A. Edin.: a biography. By Frederic Lees. 1904.

Lees was famous as the ablest temperance and prohibitionist advocate of the late 19th cent. His *Selected works* were publ. in 12 v. 1884–94. Lees and James Dawson Burns publ. a much-admired work, *The temperance Bible commentary: giving at one view, version, criticism and exposition, in regard to all passages of Holy Writ bearing on 'Wine' and 'Strong drink'* . . ., 1868, 6th edn. 1894.

7546 BRITISH TEMPERANCE LEAGUE. The British temperance advocate. 1839+.

Title and place of publ. varies. The League also publ. an annual report, Sheffield 1835+.

7547   GOURLAY (WILLIAM). National Temperance: a jubilee biography of the National Temperance League, instituted 1856. 1906.

The National Temperance League publ. *Weekly record of the temperance movement,* *1856–1907,* entitled *The temperance record, 1870–1907, The medical temperance journal,* *1869–1919* [title varies], *The national temperance quarterly,* 1908+, *The National* *Temperance League annual,* 1881+, and an annual report.

7548   ELLISON (HENRY JOHN). The temperance reformation movement in the Church of England: its principles and progress. 1864. New edn. 1878.

Sets the background of the Church of England Temperance Society. The Soc. publ. *Sixty years old: a short history of a great work, 1862–1922,* 1922, *Church of England* *temperance magazine* [chronicle], *1862–1914, The illustrated temperance monthly,* 1890– 1914, and an annual report, 1863+. Ellison publ. a number of interesting works incl. *The people and the licensing laws,* 1871, and *Sermons and addresses on church temperance* *subjects,* 1895. Various church bodies considered the liquor question, beginning with a Province of Canterbury, Lower House of Convocation, *Report by the committee on* *intemperance,* 1869.

7549   MATHEW. Footprints of Father Theobald Mathew, O.F.M.Cap., apostle of temperance. By Father Augustine, O.F.M. Cap. Dublin. 1947.

The pioneer Catholic temperance worker. Consult also Patrick Rogers, *Father Theobald* *Mathew, apostle of temperance,* Dublin 1943, and John Francis Maguire, *Father Mathew:* *a biography,* 1863. There are many popular lives.

7550   BRIDGETT (THOMAS EDWARD). The discipline of drink: an historical inquiry into the principles and practice of the Catholic Church regarding the use, abuse, and disuse of alcoholic liquors. 1876.

See also Henry Edward Manning, cardinal, *The temperance speeches of Cardinal Man-* *ning,* ed. by Charles Kegan Paul, 1894, A. E. Dingle and B. H. Harrison, 'Cardinal Manning as temperance reformer' (**3943**), and the handbooks of the two chief Catholic temperance organizations, *The handbook of the League of the Cross,* 1876, and *The* *Pioneer temperance catechism,* 1911.

7551   TAYLER (ROBERT). The hope of the race. 1946.

A bad hist. of the U.K. Band of Hope Union, which publ. *Band of Hope chronicle,* 1877+, and other js. The founders of the soc. are commemorated in Henry Marles, *The life and labours of the Rev. Jabez Tunnicliff, minister of the Gospel at Call Lane* *Chapel, Leeds, and founder of the Band of Hope in England;* obtained from authentic documents, chiefly records made by himself, Lond. & Leeds 1865, Frederick Sherlock, *Ann Jane Carlile: a temperance pioneer,* 1897, and Richard Hayes Crofton, *Anne Jane* *Carlile and her descendants,* St. Leonards 1950.

7552   HAYLER (MARK HENRY CHAMBERS). The vision of a century, 1853–1953: the United Kingdom Alliance in historical retrospect. 1953.

The U.K. Alliance was the leading prohibitionist organization. It publ. a good news-paper, *Alliance news* [title varies], Manch. 1854+, *The Alliance year book and temperance* *reformers' handbook,* 1910+, *The Alliance temperance almanack,* 1911+, and the annual report of the executive committee. It also sponsored *Meliora: a quarterly review of social* *science,* 12 v., 1858–69. The leading figures in the Alliance were W. S. Caine, on whom see John Newton, *W. S. Caine, M.P.: a biography,* 1907; T. H. Green (**718**); William Hoyle, for whom see William Hoyle, *Wealth and social progress, in relation to thrift,* *temperance and trade,* Manch. 1887; Sir Wilfrid Lawson, for whom see George William Erskine Russell, ed., *Sir Wilfrid Lawson: a memoir,* 1909, and Robert Arthur Jameson, ed., *Wisdom, grave and gay: being, select speeches of Sir Wilfrid Lawson, Bart., M.P., chiefly on temperance and prohibition* . . ., 1889; Cardinal Manning (**7550**); F. W. Newman (**8429**); James Hayes Raper, for whom see J. Deane Hilton, *A brief memoir of James Hayes Raper, temperance reformer, 1820–1897*, 1898; and H. J. Wilson (**890**).

Characteristic statements of the Alliance's position are given in Frederic Richard Lees, *An argument, legal and historical, for the legislative prohibition of the liquor traffic*, 1856, William Sproston Caine, William Hoyle, and James Dawson Burns, *Local option*, 1885, and Henry Edward Manning, *The temperance reformation: the United Kingdom Alliance and 'local option': two speeches* . . ., 1882. William Stanley Jevons, 'On the United Kingdom Alliance and its prospects of success', *Manch. Stat. Soc. Trans.* (1875–6), 127–42, repr. in his *Methods of social reform* . . ., 1883, and William Hoyle, 'The prospects of the United Kingdom Alliance, with special reference to the objections of Professor Jevons', *Manch. Stat. Soc. Trans.* ibid. 173–96, debate the case against prohibition.

7553 HAYLER (GUY) *ed.* The prohibition movement: papers and proceedings of the National Convention for the Prohibition of the Liquor Traffic, Newcastle-upon-Tyne, April 3rd to 9th, 1897. Newcastle-upon-Tyne. 1897.

7554 THE LEES AND RAPER MEMORIAL LECTURES. [1898–1914.] [1905–14.]

An interesting series reflecting early 20th-cent. thought.

### (c) *Licensing Laws*

7555 WEBB (SIDNEY JAMES), *Baron Passfield and* WEBB (BEATRICE). The history of liquor licensing in England, principally from 1700 to 1830. 1903.

7556 MACKENZIE (FREDERICK ARTHUR). Sober by act of parliament. 1894.

A brief account of British and foreign legislation.

7557 CHAMBERLAIN (JOSEPH). Licensing reform and local option: a speech . . . Birmingham. 1876.

A strong plea for municipalization of the drink trade on the same lines as his 'The right method with the publicans', *Fortnightly Rev.* new ser. xix (1876), 631–51, and 'Municipal public-houses?', ibid. new ser. xxi (1877), 147–59.

7558 NATIONAL ASSOCIATION FOR THE PROMOTION OF SOCIAL SCIENCE. Conference on temperance legislation, London, 1886. 1886.

7559 PEASE (EDWARD REYNOLDS). The case for municipal drink trade. 1904. 2nd edn. 1908.

Pease was Secretary of the Fabian Soc.

7560 CUMMING (ALEXANDER NEILSON). Public-house reform: an explanation. 1901.

The case for public-house trusts.

7561 PEEL (*Sir* SIDNEY CORNWALLIS). Practical licensing reform. 1901.

Peel was sec. to the royal commission presided over by his father (**7568**).

7562   SANGER (CHARLES PERCY). The place of compensation in temperance reform. 1901.

7563   ROWNTREE (JOSEPH) *and* SHERWELL (ARTHUR). Public control of the liquor traffic: being a review of the Scandinavian experiments in the light of recent experience. 1903.

See also their *The British 'Gothenburg' experiments and public-house trusts,* 1901, and *Public interests or trade aggrandisement? an examination of some important issues raised by the Licensing Bill, 1904,* 1904, Edwin Goadsby, *The Gothenburg licensing system,* 1895, and Edwin A. Pratt, *Licensing and temperance in Sweden, Norway and Denmark,* 1907.

7564   VILLIERS COMMITTEE ON PUBLIC HOUSES. Report from the select committee on public houses, &c. [Chairman: C. P. Villiers.] H.C. 855 (1852–3). XXXVII, 1. Further report. H.C. 367 (1854). XIV, 231.

7565   BERKELEY COMMITTEE ON THE SALE OF BEER &c. ON THE LORD'S DAY. First report from the select committee on Sale of Beer, &c. Act [Chairman: the Hon. F. Henry F. Berkeley]. H.C. 407 (1854–5). X, 339. Second report. H.C. 427 (1854–5). X, 505.

The Sale of Beer, &c. Act, 1854, regulated the sale of intoxicants on Sundays. The committee recommended that the regulations should be relaxed. Later the topic was discussed by a further select committee: *Special report from the select committee on the Sale of Liquors on Sunday Bill* [Chairman: Sir James Fergusson]. H.C. 402 (1867–8). XIV, 1.

7566   LICENSING ACT, 1872. Reports from borough authorities in England and Wales relating to the Licensing Act, 1872. H.C. 160 (1874). LIV, 243.

7567   BURT COMMITTEE ON CLUBS REGISTRATION BILL. Report from the select committee on the Clubs Registration Bill [Chairman: Thomas Burt]. H.C. 314 (1893–4). X, 463.

Chiefly on clubs with liquor licenses.

7568   PEEL COMMISSION ON LIQUOR LICENSING LAWS. First report of the royal commission on liquor licensing laws [Chairman: Viscount Peel]. [C. 8355] H.C. (1897). XXXIV, 247. Second report. [C. 8523] H.C. (1897). XXXV, 1. Third report. [C. 8693] H.C. (1898). XXXVI, 1. Fourth report. [C. 8821] H.C. (1898). XXXVIII, 1. Fifth report. [C. 8979] H.C. (1898). XXXVIII, 9. Final report. [C. 9379] H.C. (1899). XXXV, 1. Evidence, appendixes, etc. General vols. [C. 8356] H.C. (1897). XXXIV, 253. [C. 8523–I] H.C. (1897). XXXV, 7. [C. 8694] H.C. (1898). XXXVI, 9. [C. 9075] H.C. (1899). XXXIV, 441. Special evidence etc. Clubs. [C. 8695] H.C. (1898). XXXVII, 1. Statistics. [C. 8696] H.C. (1898). XXXVII, 205. Scotland. [C. 8822] H.C. (1898). XXXVIII, 17. Ireland. [C. 8980] H.C. (1898). XXXVIII, 527. Précis of evidence and data. [C. 9076] H.C. (1899). XXXV, 395. Index. [C. 9379–I] H.C. (1899). XXXV, 591.

The first exhaustive investigation of the subject.

7569  PRATT (EDWIN A.). The licensed trade: an independent survey. 1907. 2nd edn. 1907.

7570  AMULREE COMMISSION ON LICENSING. Royal commission on licensing (England and Wales), 1929–31 [Chairman: Lord Amulree]. Report. [Cmd. 3988] H.C. (1931–2). XI, 573.

Minutes of evidence were publ. as non-parl. papers.

7571  PATERSON (JAMES). The Intoxicating Liquor Licensing Act, 1872, . . . 1872+.

Title became *The Licensing Acts*, 11th edn. 1896, 16th edn. 1905, publ. almost every year thereafter. The standard textbook. Other contemp. legal textbooks of note were John Mountney Lely and William Decimus Inglett Foulkes, *The Licensing Acts, 1828, 1869 & 1872* . . ., 1872, 3rd edn. 1887; George Crispe Whiteley, *The Licensing Acts, 1872– 1874* . . ., 1874, 3rd edn. 1901, cont. as *The Licensing Act, 1902* . . ., 1902, 4th edn. 1911; Robert Mortimer Montgomery, *The licensing laws, so far as they relate to the sale of intoxicating liquors*, 1895, 3rd edn. 1905, which became *Annual licensing practice*, 1911– 14; Henry Miles Finch, *The licensed victualler's handy guide to the licensing laws* . . ., 1903; and Sir Ernest Arthur Jelf and Sir Cecil James Barrington Hurst, *The law of innkeepers, under the custom of the realm of England, the common law, and the Innkeepers Acts, 1863 and 1878*, 1904.

## F. CRIME AND POLICE

### 1. GENERAL

7572  CUMMING (*Sir* JOHN GHEST). A contribution towards a biblio- graphy dealing with crime and cognate subjects. Receiver for Metropolitan Police Dist. 3rd edn. 1935.

Covers *c.* 1885–1935. Previous edns. were publ. in Calcutta. There is some further material in William H. Hewitt, *A bibliography of police administration, public safety and criminology, to July 1 1965*, Springfield, Ill. 1967.

7573  SCOTT (*Sir* HAROLD RICHARD). The concise encyclopedia of crime and criminals. Lond. & N.Y. 1961.

7574  RADZINOWICZ (*Sir* LEON). A history of English criminal law and its administration, from 1750. 4+ v. 1948+.

Covers all aspects of the subject. There is little more in Sir Leon Radzinowicz and James William Cecil Turner, eds., *Penal reform in England* . . ., 1940, 2nd edn. 1946, and Sir Edward Cecil George Cadogan, *The roots of evil: being, a treatise on the methods of dealing with crime and the criminal during the eighteenth and nineteenth centuries in relation to those of a more enlightened age*, 1937.

7575  TOBIAS (JOHN JACOB). Crime and industrial society in the 19th century. Lond. 1967. N.Y. 1968.

A useful pioneering study.

7576  WALKER (NIGEL). Crime and insanity in England: 1. the historical perspective. Edin. 1968.

Standard.

7577  GREENWOOD (MAJOR), MARTIN (W. J.), *and* RUSSELL (W. T.). 'Deaths by violence, 1837–1937'. *Roy. Stat. Soc. J.* civ (1941), 146–63.

There is a substantial lit. about murders and murder trials, for some of which see **3069**. There is a steady production of books such as Leonard W. Matters, *The mystery of Jack the Ripper*, 1929, new edn. 1948, William Stewart, *Jack the Ripper: a new theory*, 1939, George Donald King McCormick, *The identity of Jack the Ripper*, 1959, 2nd edn. 1970, and Tom A. Cullen, *Autumn of terror: Jack the Ripper, his crimes and times*, 1965, publ. in Boston as *When London walked in terror*, 1965.

7578  COLLINS (PHILIP ARTHUR WILLIAM). Dickens and crime. Camb. Studies in Criminology xvii. Lond. & N.Y. 1962. 2nd edn. 1964.

7579  IRVING (HENRY BRODRIBB). A book of remarkable criminals. 1918.

Incl. as representative of a class of popular books. Cp. Anon., *The master criminal: the life story of Charles Peace*, 1910, new edns. 1930, 1936, and William Teignmouth Shore, ed., *Trials of Charles Frederick Peace*, 1926. For the criminal in literature see Frank Wadleigh Chandler, *The literature of roguery*, 2 v. 1907.

7580  HINDE (RICHARD STANDISH ELPHINSTONE). The British penal system, 1773–1950. 1951.

7581  ROSE (ARTHUR GORDON). The struggle for penal reform: the Howard League and its predecessors. Lond. & Chicago. 1961.

See also William Tallack, *Howard letters and memories*, 1905.

7582  TUTTLE (ELIZABETH ORMAN). The crusade against capital punishment in Great Britain. Lond. & Chicago. 1961.

See also John Laurence, *A history of capital punishment, with special reference to . . . Great Britain*, 1932, and Horace William Bleackley, *The hangmen of England . . .*, 1929. The subject was discussed at length in *Report of the capital punishment commission* [Chairman: Duke of Richmond]. [3590] H.C. (1866). XXI, 1, and briefly in *Report from the select committee of the House of Lords appointed 'to take into consideration the present mode of carrying into effect capital punishments'* [Chairman: Samuel Wilberforce, Bishop of Oxford]. H.C. 366 (1856). VII, 9.

7583  HILL (FREDERIC). Crime: its amount, causes and remedies. 1853.

7584  HILL (MATTHEW DAVENPORT). Suggestions for the repression of crime, contained in charges delivered to grand juries of Birmingham . . . together with articles from reviews and newspapers . . . 1857.

7585  HILL (EDWIN). 'On the prevention of crime'. *Stat. Soc. J.* xxv (1862), 497–501.

7586  PUNISHMENT AND REFORMATION. Nat. Assoc. for the Promotion of Social Science Trans. Pt. III. 1857–1863. 1858–64.

7587  BAKER (THOMAS BARWICK LLOYD). 'War with crime': being a selection of reprinted papers on crime . . . Ed. by Herbert Philips and Edmund Verney. 1889.

7588  GROSVENOR (GEORGE). 'Statistics of the abatement of crime in England and Wales during the twenty years ended 1887–88'. *Roy. Stat. Soc. J.* liii (1890), 377–413.

7589  MORRISON (WILLIAM DOUGLAS). 'The interpretation of criminal statistics'. *Roy. Stat. Soc. J.* lx (1897), 1–24.

7590  HOLMES (THOMAS). Pictures and problems from London police courts. 1900.

One of a ser. of studs. by Holmes of petty criminals.

## 2. POLICE

7591  CRITCHLEY (THOMAS ALAN). A history of police in England and Wales, 900–1966. 1967.

See also his *The conquest of violence: order and liberty in Britain*, 1970, Charles Reith, *A new study of police history*, Edin. 1956, and Christopher Robert Druce Pulling, *Mr. Punch and the police*, 1964. The best contemp. account was Maitland, *Justice and police* (**3008**).

7592  HART (JENIFER MARGARET). 'The reform of the borough police, 1835–1856'. *Eng. Hist. Rev.* lxx (1955), 411–27.

See also her 'The County and Borough Police Act, 1856', *Public Admin.* xxxiv (1956), 405–17, and Henry Walter Parris, 'The Home Office and the provincial police in England and Wales, 1856–1870', *Public Law* (1961), 230–55, and 'Histories of provincial police forces in England and Wales', *Police J.* xxxiv (1961), 286–90.

7593  BROWNE (DOUGLAS GORDON). The rise of Scotland Yard: a history of the Metropolitan Police. 1956.

The older hists. such as George Dilnot, *The story of Scotland Yard*, 1926, rev. edn. [*Scotland yard . . .*] 1929, and Sir Basil Home Thomson, *The story of Scotland Yard*, Lond. 1935, Garden City, N.Y. 1936, add little, and there is also very little in contemp. works like Charles Tempest Clarkson and Joseph Hall Richardson, *Police!*, 1889. For one of the most important heads of the C.I.D. see the life of Sir Howard Vincent (**886**). The main official source is the annual report of the Commissioner of Police of the Metropolis, 1869+. See also **2830**.

7594  MOYLAN (*Sir* JOHN FITZGERALD). Scotland Yard and the Metropolitan Police. Whitehall ser. 1929. Rev. edn. 1934.

A department-by-department survey.

7595  MATHEW (*Sir* THEOBALD). The office and duties of the Director of Public Prosecutions. 1950.

For the career of an early director see **3162**. The subject of public prosecutions was considered by a number of committees. See notably *Report from the select committee on public prosecutors* [Chairman: John George Phillimore]. H.C. 206 (1856). VII, 347;

Report of the committee appointed to inquire into the office of Public Prosecutor [Chairman: Sir William V. Harcourt]. [C. 4016] H.C. (1884). XXIII, 309; *Report of the commissioners appointed to inquire into the costs of prosecutions, the expenses of coroners' inquests, &c.* [Chairman: Edward Cardwell]. [2575] H.C. (1859–Sess. 2). XIII, pt. 1, 13; *Report from the select committee on prosecution expenses* [Chairman: T. H. S. Sotheron Estcourt]. H.C. 401 (1862). XI, 1; *Report of the departmental committee appointed to inquire into the allowances to prosecutors and witnesses in criminal prosecutions* [Chairman: Sir John Edward Dorington]. [Cd. 1650] H.C. (1903). LVI, 357. Minutes of evidence. [Cd. 1651] H.C. (1903). LVI, 377; and *Report and special report from the select committee on Poor Prisoners' Defence Bill* [Chairman: W. Bousfield]. H.C. 264 (1903). VII, 583.

7596  GALTON (*Sir* FRANCIS). Finger prints. 1892. Suppl. 1892.

Suppl. by his *Finger print directories*, 1895. See also Sir William James Herschel, *The origin of finger printing*, 2 pts. 1916.

7597  DILNOT (GEORGE). Great detectives and their methods. [1927.]

There are a considerable number of detective autobiogs., most of them poor. See, *inter alia*, Andrew Lansdowne, *A life's reminiscences of Scotland Yard* [1890], new edn. 1893, Jerome Caminada, *Twenty-five years of detective life*, 2 v. Manch. 1895–1901, and John Sweeney, *At Scotland Yard: being the experiences during twenty-seven years' service of John Sweeney, late detective-inspector, Criminal Investigation Department, New Scotland Yard*, 1904, new edn. 1905.

7598  ANDERSON. The lighter side of my official life. By Sir Robert Anderson. 1910.

Chiefly on the secret service. See also his *Criminals and crime: some facts and suggestions*, 1907, and *Sidelights on the Home Rule movement*, 1906, new edn. 1907, abridged edn. [*A great conspiracy*] 1910.

7599  SMITH. From constable to commissioner . . . By Sir Henry Smith. 1910.

Head of the City of London police.

7600  H.M. INSPECTORS OF CONSTABULARY. Annual report. 1857+.

On the provincial police forces.

7601  RICE COMMITTEE ON POLICE. First report from the select committee on police [Chairman: Edward Royds Rice]. H.C. 603 (1852–3). XXXVI, 1. Second report. H.C. 715 (1852–3). XXXVI, 161.

7602  STUART-WORTLEY COMMISSION ON HYDE PARK RIOTS, 1855. Report of Her Majesty's commissioners appointed to inquire into the alleged disturbance of the public peace in Hyde Park on Sunday, July 1st, 1855; and the conduct of the Metropolitan Police in connexion with the same [Chairman: James Archibald Stuart-Wortley]. [2016] H.C. (1856). XXIII, 1.

See also 7635.

7603  CHILDERS COMMITTEE ON LONDON RIOT, 1886. Report of a committee to inquire and report as to the origin and character of the disturbances which took place in the metropolis on Monday, the 8th of February, and as to the conduct of the police authorities in relation thereto [Chairman: Hugh C. E. Childers]. [C. 4665] H.C. (1886). XXXIV, 381.

See also *Report of the committee appointed by the Secretary of State for the Home Department to inquire into the administration and organisation of the Metropolitan police force* [Chairman: Hugh C. E. Childers]. [C. 4894] H.C. (1886). XXXIV, 493.

7604 BRYNMOR JONES COMMISSION ON METROPOLITAN POLICE. Report of the royal commission upon the duties of the Metropolitan Police [Chairman: Sir David Brynmor Jones]. [Cd. 4156] H.C. (1908). L, 1. Minutes of evidence. [Cd. 4260–1] H.C. (1908). L, 501, LI, 1.

7605 HOBHOUSE COMMITTEE ON ORDER AT PUBLIC MEETINGS. Report of the departmental committee on the duties of the police with respect to the preservation of order at public meetings [Chairman: Henry Hobhouse]. [Cd. 4673] H.C. (1909). XXXVI, 83. Minutes of evidence. [Cd. 4674] H.C. (1909). XXXVI, 107.

## 3. PRISONS

7606 WEBB (SIDNEY JAMES), *Baron Passfield and* WEBB (BEATRICE). English prisons under local government. 1922.

Designed as an intro. to Hobhouse and Brockway (**7629**). There is little in gen. works like Derek Lionel Howard, *The English prisons: their past and their future*, 1960. However, Sir Lionel Wray Fox, *The modern English prison*, 1934, and *The English prison and borstal systems*, 1952, are quite good on recent hist., and William Branch-Johnson, *The English prison hulks . . .*, 1957, covers the first part of the period.

7607 RUGGLES-BRISE. Sir Evelyn Ruggles-Brise: a memoir of the founder of Borstal. Comp. by Sir [John Randolph] Shane Leslie. 1938.

Chairman of the Prison Commission. For his views see **7628.**

7608 CLAY. The prison chaplain: a memoir of John Clay: with selections from his reports and correspondence, and a sketch of prison discipline in England. By Walter Lowe Clay. Camb. 1861.

Clay was an influential figure. Many other chaplains publ. potboilers, e.g. Charles Bernard Gibson, *Life among convicts*, 2 v. 1863, and Eustace Jervis, *Twenty-five years in six prisons* [1925]. The best of the genre was John William Horsley, *I remember . . .*, 1911, *How criminals are made and prevented: a retrospect of forty years*, 1913, *Jottings from jail: notes and papers on prison matters*, 1887, and *Prisons and prisoners*, Lond. & N.Y. 1898.

7609 GRIFFITHS. Fifty years of public service. By Arthur George Frederick Griffiths. 1904.

Prison governor and inspector of prisons. He also publ. numerous other works incl. *Criminals I have known*, 1895, *Mysteries of police and crime . . .*, 2 v. 1898, new edn. 3 v. 1901–2, *Secrets of the prison-house . . .*, 2 v. 1894, and *Tales of a government official*, 1902.

7610 PRISON COMMISSION. Annual report. 1878+.

For earlier reports see H.M. Inspectors of Prisons, *Annual reports* [by regions], 1836–78, Surveyor-General of Prisons, *Reports*, irregular, 1850–1860/1, and Directors of Convict prisons, *Annual report*, 1850–1894/5.

7611 BAINES COMMITTEE ON TRANSPORTATION. First report from the select committee on transportation [Chairman: Matthew Talbot Baines]. H.C. 244 (1856). XVII, 1. Second report. H.C. 296 (1856). XVII, 189. Third report. H.C. 355 (1856). XVII, 397.

See also *Report from the select committee of the House of Lords appointed to inquire into the provisions and operation of the Act 16 & 17 Vict. cap. 99, intituled, 'An Act to substitute, in certain cases, other punishment in lieu of transportation'* [Chairman: Earl of Harrowby]. H.C. 404 (1856). XVII, 561; and *Report from the select committee on transportation* [Chairman: Hugh C. E. Childers]. H.C. 286 (1861). XIII, 505.

7612 MAYHEW (HENRY) and BINNY (JOHN). The criminal prisons of London and scenes of prison life. 1862.

A deservedly famous descriptive work. The nearest to a successful repetition of this sort of inquiry was George Chetwynd Griffith, *Sidelights on convict life*, 1903.

7613 GREY COMMISSION ON TRANSPORTATION AND PENAL SERVITUDE. Report of the commissioners appointed to inquire into the operation of the acts (16 & 17 Vict. c. 99 and 20 & 21 Vict. c. 3) relating to transportation and penal servitude [Chairman: Earl Grey]. [3190] H.C. (1863). XXI, 1. Minutes of evidence. [3190–I] H.C. (1863). XXI, 283.

A full inquiry. See also *Report from the select committee of the House of Lords on the present state of discipline in gaols and houses of correction* [Chairman: Earl of Carnarvon]. H.C. 499 (1863). IX, 1.

7614 CARPENTER (MARY). Our convicts. 2 v. 1864.

See also *Prison characters drawn from life, with suggestions for prison government: by a prison matron*, 2 v. 1866, and Charles Pennell Measor, *The convict service: a letter . . . on the administration, results, and expense of the present convict system, with suggestions*, 1861, *Criminal correction . . .*, 1864, and *The utilization of the criminal . . .*, 1869.

7615 INTERNATIONAL PENITENTIARY CONGRESS, 1872. Prisons and reformatories at home and abroad: being the transactions of the International Penitentiary Congress held in London, July 3–13, 1872. Ed. by Edwin Pears. 1872. Repr. 1912.

7616 TALLACK (WILLIAM). Defects in the criminal administration and penal legislation of Great Britain and Ireland, with remedial suggestions. 1872.

Tallack's first major work. For his subsequent career see **7581**.

7617 PENAL SERVITUDE ACTS COMMISSION. Report of the commissioners appointed to inquire into the working of the Penal Servitude Acts [Chairman: Earl of Kimberley]. [C. 2368] H.C. (1878–9). XXXVII, 1. Minutes of evidence. [C. 2368–I] H.C. (1878–9). XXXVII, 67. [C. 2368–II] H.C. (1878–9). XXXVIII, 1.

7618 A TICKET-OF-LEAVE MAN, *pseud.* Convict life: or, revelations concerning convicts and convict prisons. 1879. Rev. edn. 1880.

7619   DU CANE (*Sir* EDMUND FREDERICK). The punishment and prevention of crime. English citizen ser. 1885.

By the first chairman of the Prison Commission. See also his *An account of the manner in which sentences of penal servitude are carried out in England*, 1872, 3rd edn. 1872, new edn. 1882.

7620   ABERDARE COMMITTEE ON PRISON DRESS. Report of the committee of inquiry as to the rules concerning the wearing of prison dress, &c. [Chairman: Lord Aberdare]. [C. 5759] H.C. (1889). LXI, 269.

7621   SIGERSON (GEORGE). Political prisoners at home and abroad, with appendix on dietaries. 1890.

Provoked by the question of Irish political prisoners, on whom there was a whole series of official inquiries. They themselves publ. a good deal. See Jeremiah O'Donovan Rossa, *Irish rebels in English prisons: a record of prison life*, N.Y. 1882, Michael Davitt, *Leaves from a prison diary . . .*, 2 v. Lond. 1885, 1-v. edn. N.Y. 1886, and Thomas James Clarke, *Glimpses of an Irish felon's prison life*, Dublin & Lond. 1922.

7622   GLADSTONE COMMITTEE ON PRISONS. Report from the departmental committee on prisons [Chairman: Herbert J. Gladstone]. [C. 7702] H.C. (1895). LVI, 1. Minutes of evidence. [C. 7702–I] H.C. (1895). LVI, 55.

For implementation of the report see [C. 7996] H.C. (1896). XLIV, 177; [C. 7995] H.C. (1896). XLIV, 185; and [C. 8790] H.C. (1898), XLVII, 1.

See also *Report of the departmental committee on the education and moral instruction of prisoners in local and convict prisons* [Chairman: Robert Sidney Mitford]. [C. 8154] H.C. (1896). XLIV, 1. Minutes of evidence. [C. 8155] H.C. (1896). XLIV, 19. There is also useful material in George Purnell Merrick, *Report to Her Majesty's Commissioners of Prisons on the operations of discharged prisoners' aid societies*. [C. 8299] H.C. (1897). XL, 1, and Frederic John Mouat, 'On prison ethics and prison labour', *Roy. Stat. Soc. J.* liv (1891), 213–52.

7623   RUGGLES-BRISE (*Sir* EVELYN JOHN). Report to the Secretary of State for the Home Department on the proceedings of the fifth and sixth International Penitentiary Congresses. [Cd. 573] H.C. (1901). XXXIII, 1. Report on seventh congress. [Cd. 2849] H.C. (1906). LI, 299. Report on eighth congress. [Cd. 5593] H.C. (1911). XXXIX, 621.

Good for professional opinions. See also **7615** and **7628**.

7624   CARPENTER (EDWARD). Prisons, police and punishment: an inquiry into the causes and treatment of crime and criminals. 1905.

7625   QUINTON (RICHARD FRITH). The modern prison curriculum: a general review of our penal system. 1912.

See also his *Crime and criminals, 1876–1910*, 1910. James Devon, *The criminal & the community*, Lond. & N.Y. 1912, sets out the views of a Scottish prison medical officer.

7626   GORING (CHARLES BUCKMAN) *ed*. The English convict: a statistical study. 1913. Abridged edn. 1915.

An official report on anthropological lines.

7627 IVES (GEORGE CECIL). A history of penal methods: criminals, witches, lunatics. 1914.

A big, rambling discussion by a penal reformer.

7628 RUGGLES-BRISE (*Sir* EVELYN JOHN). The English prison system. 1921.

Important, as expounding the views of the head of the Prison Commission during most of the period. See also his *Prison reform at home and abroad: a short history of the international movement since the London Congress of 1872*, 1925, **7623** and **7607**.

7629 HOBHOUSE (STEPHEN) *and* BROCKWAY (ARCHIBALD FENNER), *Baron Brockway*. English prisons to-day: being the report of the Prison System Enquiry Committee. 1922.

A Labour Research Dept. venture, which gives much the best idea of the state of early 20th-cent. prisons.

7630 RHODES (ALBERT JOHN). Dartmoor prison: a record of 126 years of prisoner of war and convict life, 1806–1932. 1933.

## G. RECREATION

### 1. GENERAL

7631 HOLE (CHRISTINA). English sports and pastimes. 1949.

A gen. survey. Stella Margetson, *Leisure and pleasure in the nineteenth century*, 1969, is poor. Asa Briggs, *Mass entertainment: origins of a modern industry*, Adelaide 1960, is good but brief. Alan Delgado, *Victorian entertainment*, Newton Abbot 1971, is a brief intro. Laurence Whistler, *The English festivals*, 1947, has a few useful points.

7632 HERN (ANTHONY). The seaside holiday: the history of the English seaside resort. 1967.

Like John Alfred Ralph Pimlott, *The Englishman's holiday: a social history*, 1947, and *Recreations . . .*, 1968, H. G. Stokes, *The very first history of the English seaside*, 1947, and Ruth Manning-Sanders, *Seaside England*, 1951, just an intro. to an important subject.

7633 PUDNEY (JOHN). The Thomas Cook story. 1953.

The flavour of Victorian foreign travel is better caught by an earlier hist. of the firm, William Fraser Rae, *The business of travel: a fifty years record of progress . . .*, 1891.

7634 TRELAWNY COMMITTEE ON RECREATIONAL INSTITUTIONS. Report from the select committee on public institutions [Chairman: Sir John Trelawny]. H.C. 181 (1860). XVI, 1.

For bank holidays see *Report from the select committee on the Bank Holidays Bill* [Chairman: Sir Colman O'Loghlen]. H.C. 354 (1867–8). VII, 1.

7635 HARRISON (BRIAN HOWARD). 'Religion and recreation in nineteenth-century England'. *Past & Present* xxxviii (1967), 98–125.

See also his 'The Sunday trading riots of 1855', *Hist. J.* viii (1965), 219–45, and David Brooke, 'The opposition to Sunday railway services in north-east England, 1834–1914', *J. Transport Hist.* vi (1963–4), 95–109.

7636 GOMME (ALICE BERTHA), *Lady Gomme*. The traditional games of England, Scotland and Ireland: with tunes, singing in rhymes and methods of playing, according to the variants extant and recorded in different parts of the kingdom. 2 v. 1894–8.

7637 DITCHFIELD (PETER HAMPSON). Old English customs extant at the present time: an account of local observances, festival customs, and ancient ceremonies yet surviving in Great Britain. 1896.

7638 RUST (FRANCES). Dance in society: an analysis of the relationship between the social dance and society in England from the middle ages to the present day. Lond. & N.Y. 1969.

There is also a ser. of popular surveys, incl. Arthur Henry Franks, *Social dance: a short history*, 1963, Philip John Sampey Richardson, *The social dances of the nineteenth century in England*, 1960, and James Laver, ed., *Memorable balls*, 1954.

7639 STOTT (RAYMOND TOOLE). Circus and allied arts: a world bibliography, 1500–1957: based mainly on circus literature in the British Museum, the Library of Congress, the Bibliothèque Nationale and on his own collection. 3 v. Derby. 1958–62.

Stott also publ. *A bibliography of books on the circus in English, from 1773 to 1964*, Derby 1964.

7640 MANNING-SANDERS (RUTH). The English circus. 1952.

See also Rupert Croft-Cooke, ed., *The circus book* [1948], and *The circus has no home*, 1941, 2nd edn. 1950, and Maurice Willson Disher, *Greatest show on earth: as performed for over a century at Astley's (afterwards Sanger's) Royal Amphitheatre of Arts, Westminster Bridge Road*, 1937, and *Clowns & pantomimes*, 1925. The best of the many vols. of circus reminiscences are Charles W. Montague, *Recollections of an equestrian manager*, Edin. 1881, James Lloyd, *My circus life* . . ., 1925, George Sanger, *Seventy years a showman* . . . [1914], new edn. 1926, and G. Van Hare, *Fifty years of a showman's life* . . ., 1888, new edn. 1893.

7641 MANDER (RAYMOND) *and* MITCHENSON (JOE). British music hall: a story in pictures. 1965.

See also Maurice Willson Disher, *Winkles and champagne: comedies and tragedies of the music hall*, 1938; Archibald Haddon, *The story of the music hall: from cave of harmony to cabaret*, 1935; Walter James MacQueen Pope, *The melodies linger on: the story of the music hall*, 1950; Christopher Pulling, *They were singing: the old music-hall songs and what they sang about*, 1952; Harold Scott, *The early doors: origins of the music hall*, 1946; and **9337**.

7642 APPERSON (GEORGE LATIMER). The social history of smoking. [1914.]

See also Alfred Rive, 'The consumption of tobacco since 1600', *Econ. Hist.* suppl. to *Econ. J.* i (1926–9), 57–75, which incl. data from William Edward Armytage Axon, 'On the consumption of tobacco in the United Kingdom, 1801–70', *Stat. Soc. J.* xxxv (1872), 334–40. There is further data in Arthur Edmund Tanner, *Tobacco: from the grower to the smoker*, 1912, 5th edn. 1920, and *The tobacco laws and their administration: for the use of revenue officers*, Stroud 1898.

7643  WHITEHOUSE (FRANCIS REGINALD BEAMAN). Table games of Georgian and Victorian days. 1951.

See also William Prideaux Courtney, *English whist and English whist players*, 1894.

7644  CLARKE (SIDNEY W.) *and* BLIND (ADOLPHE). The bibliography of conjuring and kindred deceptions. 1920.

See also John Nevil Maskelyne, '*Sharps and flats*': *a complete revelation of the secrets of cheating at games of chance and skill*, 1894, 2nd edn. 1895, J. N. Maskelyne and David Devant, *Our magic: the art in magic, the theory of magic, the practice of magic*, Lond. & N.Y. [1912], and Jasper Maskelyne, *White magic: the story of Maskelynes*, 1936.

7645  SERGEANT (PHILIP WALSINGHAM). A century of British chess. 1934.

7646  BUDAY (GYÖRGY). The history of the Christmas card. 1954.

7647  STAFF (FRANK). The valentine and its origins. 1970.

7648  OPIE (IONA) *and* OPIE (PETER). The lore and language of schoolchildren. Oxf. 1959.

See also their *The Oxford dictionary of nursery rhymes*, Oxf. 1951.

7649  OPIE (IONA) *and* OPIE (PETER). Children's games in street and playground. Oxf. 1969.

See also Leslie Herbert Daiken, *Children's games throughout the year*, 1949, Alice Bertha Gomme, Lady Gomme, ed., *Children's singing games: with the tunes to which they are sung, pictured . . . by Winifred Smith*, 2 ser. [1894], and Daniel Parry-Jones, *Welsh children's games & pastimes*, Denbigh 1964.

7650  GREENE (VIVIEN). English dolls' houses of the eighteenth and nineteenth centuries. 1955.

## 2. Social Clubs

7651  ESCOTT (THOMAS HAY SWEET). Club makers and club members. [1914.]

The most useful of the gossipy books about Victorian clubs. Others are Arthur George Frederick Griffiths, *Clubs and clubmen*, 1907, George James Ivey, *The club directory: a general guide or index to the London and county clubs, and those of Scotland, Ireland and British colonial possessions, together with the English clubs in Europe, the United States and elsewhere . . .*, 1879, 2nd edn. [*Clubs of the world . . .*] 1880, and Ralph Henry Nevill, *London clubs: their history & treasures*, 1911.

7652  ARMY & NAVY. Cordell William Firebrace, *The Army and Navy Club*, *1837–1933*, 1934.

7653  ARTS. G. A. F. Rogers, *The Arts club and its members*, 1920.

7654  ATHENAEUM. Thomas Humphry Ward, *History of the Athenaeum*, *1824–1925*, 1926. Henry Richard Tedder, *The Athenaeum, 1824–1924*, 1924.

7655  BROOKS'S. *Memorials of Brooks's from the foundation of the club, 1764 to the close of the nineteenth century*, comp. from the records of the club, 1907.

CARLTON. See 553.

7656  CITY OF LONDON. J. Owen Unwin and others, *City of London club: centenary notes on its history and traditions, 1832–1932*. [1934.]

7657  THE CLUB. Sir Mountstuart Elphinstone Grant Duff, *The Club, 1764–1905*, 1905, new edn. by Reginald Earle Welby, Baron Welby and others [*Annals of The Club, 1764–1914*], 1914.

CONSTITUTIONAL. See 553.

7658  DEVONSHIRE. Henry Turner Waddy, *The Devonshire club and 'Crockfords'*, 1919.

7659  DILETTANTE. Sir Lionel Henry Cust, *History of the Society of Dilettante*, ed. by Sir Sidney Colvin, 1898, new edn. 1914.

7660  GARRICK. Guy Herman Sidney Boas, *The Garrick club, 1831–1947*, 1948. Percy Hetherington Fitzgerald, *The Garrick club*, 1904.

7661  GRILLIONS. [Sir Philip de Malpas Grey Egerton] *Grillion's club*, . . . 1880. *Grillion's club: a chronicle, 1812–1913*, Oxf. 1914.

7662  JUNIOR UNITED SERVICE. Sir Robert Hammill Firth, *The Junior: a history of the Junior United Service club, from its formation in 1827 to 1929*, 1929.

7663  NATIONAL SPORTING. Arthur Frederick Bettinson and William Outram Tristram, eds., *The National Sporting club, past and present*, 1901.

7664  ORIENTAL. Alexander Francis Baillie, *The Oriental club and Hanover Square*, 1901. Denys Mostyn Forrest, *The Oriental: life story of a West End club*, 1968.

REFORM. See 532.

7665  ROYAL SOCIETY. Sir Archibald Geikie, *Annals of the Royal Society Club: the record of a London dining club in the eighteenth & nineteenth centuries*, 1917.

7666   SAVAGE. Percy Venner Bradshaw, '*Brother savages and guests*': *a history of the Savage club, 1857–1957*, 1958.

7667   SAVILE. *The Savile club, 1868 to 1923*, priv. pr. Edin. 1923.

7668   TRAVELLERS'. Sir Almeric William FitzRoy, *History of the Travellers' club*, 1927.

7669   UNITED SERVICE. Sir Louis Charles Jackson, *History of the United Service club*, 1937.

7670   WHITE'S. Percy Colson, *White's, 1693–1950*, 1950. William Biggs Boulton, *History of White's*, 2 v. 1892.

### 3. Sports

#### (a) *General*

7671   HOWARD (HENRY CHARLES), *Earl of Suffolk and Berkshire*, PEEK (HEDLEY), *and* AFLALO (FREDERICK GEORGE) *comps.* The encyclopaedia of sport [and games]. 2 v. 1897–8. 2nd edn. 4 v. 1911.

The fullest such work. See also the much shorter Stonehenge, pseud. of John Henry Walsh, *Manual of British rural sports*, 1856, 16th edn. 1886, Anthony Trollope, ed., *British sports and pastimes*, 1868, and Henry Downes Miles, *English country life . . .*, 1873, new edn. [*British field sports . . .*] [1884].

7672   HARE (CHARLES ELAM). The language of sport. 1939. 2nd edn. [The language of field sports.] 1949.

7673   SOMERSET (HENRY CHARLES FITZROY), *Duke of Beaufort, and* WATSON (ALFRED EDWARD THOMAS) *eds.* The Badminton library of sports and pastimes. 27 v. 1886–1906.

Much the best of the contemp. ser. of books on sports. Most vols. incl. good bibliogs. Other ser. incl. Henry John Brinsley Manners, Duke of Rutland, and George Albermarle Bertie Dewar, eds., *The Haddon Hall library*, 9 v. 1899–1903; Horace Gordon Hutchinson and others, eds., *The Country Life library of sport*, 10 v. 1893–6; Alfred Edward Thomas Watson and others, *Fur, feather and fin series*, 12 v. 1893–1906; Sir Max Pemberton, ed., *The Isthmian library*, 11 v. 1896–9; and Frances Elizabeth Slaughter, ed., *The sportswoman's library*, 2 v. 1898.

7674   BELL'S LIFE IN LONDON AND SPORTING CHRONICLE. 1822–86.

Long the leading sporting paper. The 'quality' sporting papers were *The sporting magazine . . .*, 1792–1870; *The field*, 1853+ (for its hist. see **5396**); *Baily's* [*monthly*] *magazine of sports and pastimes*, 1860–1926; *The sporting gazette*, 1862–79, cont. as *The country gentleman*, 1880–1914; *Illustrated sporting and dramatic news*, 1874–1945; and *The Badminton magazine of sports and pastimes*, 1895–1923. There were also good sporting sections in *Country life*, 1897+, which began its career as *Racing illustrated*, 1895–6. For sports news the leading papers were *Sporting times*, 1865–1931 (for its hist. see **5404**), and *Sporting chronicle*, Manch. 1874+.

7675 TENNYSON (*Sir* CHARLES). 'They taught the world to play'. *Victorian Studs.* ii (1958–9), 211–22.

On the English example in sports.

7676 COOK (*Sir* THEODORE ANDREA). International sport: a short history of the Olympic movement from 1896 to the present day . . . 1909. New edn. 1910.

Useful for the British Olympic Assoc. But see also Frederick Annesley Michael Webster, *The evolution of the Olympic games, 1829 BC–1914 AD* [1914]. For international athletics see also Lawrence North Richardson, comp., *The history of the International Cross-Country Union, 1903 to 1953: jubilee souvenir* [1954].

7677 SPARROW (WALTER SHAW). British sporting artists . . . 1922.

See also **9107**.

7678 CUNNINGTON (PHILLIS EMILY) *and* MANSFIELD (ALAN). English costume for sports and outdoor recreation: from the sixteenth to the nineteenth centuries. London 1969. N.Y. 1970.

7679 BINNS (PERCY LESTER). The story of the Royal Tournament. Aldershot. 1952.

7680 THE SPORTFOLIO. Portraits and biographies of heroes and heroines of sport & pastime. 1896.

7681 ELLIOTT (ERNEST C.). Fifty leaders of British sport: a series of portraits . . . with biographical notes and a preface by Frederick George Aflalo. 1904.

7682 CROOME (ARTHUR CAPEL MOLYNEUX) *and others, eds.* Fifty years of sport at Oxford, Cambridge and the great public schools, arranged by the Right Hon. Lord Desborough. 3 v. 1913–22.

7683 COOK. The sunlit hours: a record of sport and life. By Sir Theodore Andrea Cook. 1925.

One of the few really influential sporting journalists. Edited *The field* from 1910.

### (b) *Cricket*

7684 KERR (DIANA RAIT) *comp.* Cricket: a catalogue of an exhibition of books, manuscripts and pictorial records preserved by the National Book League with the co-operation of the Marylebone Cricket Club. Nat. Book League. Camb. 1950.

Bibliogs. were publ. in *Wisden* (**7687**), in 1892, 1894, 1900, 1923. See also Gerald Brodribb, *Cricket in fiction: a bibliography*, Canford 1950; Ernest William Swanton, ed., *The world of cricket*, 1966; Eric Parker, *Between the wickets: an anthology of cricket*, 1926; Gerald Brodribb, ed., *The English game: a cricket anthology*, 1948, and *The book of cricket verse: an anthology*, 1953; and John Arlott, *Cricket*, 1953.

7685 LEWIS (W. J.) *ed.* The language of cricket: with illustrative extracts from the literature of the game. 1934.

7686 WEBBER (ROY) *comp.* The [Playfair] book of cricket records. 1951. New edn. 1961.

A useful coll. Cp. J. H. Lester, *Bat v. ball: the book of individual cricket records . . . 1864–1900*, 1900, and Sir Home Seton Charles Montagu Gordon, *Cricket form at a glance for sixty years, 1878–1937* [1938].

7687 WISDEN (JOHN). The cricketer's almanack for 1864+. Index, 1864–1943. 1944.

The cricketer's bible. On it see John Hadfield, *A Wisden century, 1850–1950*, 1950. The best cricket periodicals were *Cricket: a weekly record of the game*, 1882–1914, and *The cricket field: an illustrated record and review*, 1892–5.

7688 LILLYWHITE (FREDERICK) *comp.* Frederick Lillywhite's cricket scores and biographies of celebrated cricketers from 1746. 14 v. 1862–95.

Vols. 5–6 by Arthur Haygarth, vols. 7–13 styled *Marylebone Cricket Club cricket scores and biographies.* Cont. by Frederick Samuel Ashley-Cooper as *M.C.C. cricket scores and biographies.* Important for biographies of cricketers, 1878–98. See also *Cricket who's who*, 1909+.

7689 CAPLE (SAMUEL CANYNGE). The cricketer's who's who. 5 pts. Hunstanton. 1946–8.

Covers A–B, D–E.

7690 ALTHAM (HARRY SURTEES). A history of cricket. 1926. 2nd edn. [with Ernest William Swanton] 1938. New edn. 2 v. 1962.

Long standard. Now rivalled by Rowland Bowen, *Cricket: a history of its growth and development throughout the world*, 1970. See also Rowan Scrope Rait Kerr, *The laws of cricket: their history and growth*, 1950; Laurence Walter Meynell, *Famous cricket grounds*, 1951; George William Beldam and Charles Burgess Fry, *Great batsmen: their methods at a glance . . . illustrated by some 600 action photographs*, 1905, and *Great bowlers and fielders: their methods at a glance*, 1906; and Gerard Durani Martineau, *Bat, ball, wicket and all: an account of the origin and development of the implements, dress and appurtenances of the national game*, 1950, and *The valiant stumper: a history of wicket-keeping*, 1957. There are good illustr. in Horace Gordon Hutchinson, ed., *Cricket*, 1903. E. L. Roberts, *Cricket in England, 1894–1939*, 1946, is a handy summary.

7691 HARRIS (GEORGE ROBERT CANNING), *Baron Harris*, and ASHLEY-COOPER (FREDERICK SAMUEL). Lords & the M.C.C.: a cricket chronicle of 137 years . . . 1914.

Important for the centre of cricket. There is also a good hist., Sir Pelham Francis Warner, *Lords, 1787–1945*, 1946. Warner also publ. a detailed hist., *Gentlemen v. Players, 1806–1909*, 1950.

7692 WEBBER (ROY). The county cricket championship: a history of the competition from 1873 to the present day . . . 1957.

For the counties see, *inter alia*, Samuel Canynge Caple, *A history of the Gloucestershire Cricket Club, 1870–1948*, 1949; Archibald William Ledbrooke, *Lancashire county* cricket: the official history of the Lancashire County & Manchester Cricket Club, *1864–1953*, 1954; E. E. Snow, *A history of Leicestershire cricket*, Leicester 1949; William Justice Ford and Frederick Samuel Ashley-Cooper, *Middlesex County Cricket Club, 1864–1899 [1900–1920]*, 2 v. 1900–21; James Desmond Coldham, *Northamptonshire cricket: a history*, 1959; Richard Everard Webster, Viscount Alverstone, and Charles William Alcock, eds., *Surrey cricket: its history and associations . . .*, 1902; Louis Palgrave, *The story of the Oval and the history of Surrey cricket, 1902 to 1948*, 1949; John Norman Marshall, *Sussex cricket: a history*, 1959; George W. Egdell and Mickie F. K. Fraser, *Warwickshire County Cricket Club: a history*, Birmingham 1946; Wilfred Rowland Chignell, *A history of the Worcestershire County Cricket Club, 1844–1950*, Worcester [1951]; and Robert Stratten Holmes, *The history of Yorkshire county cricket, 1833–1903*, 1904, cont. by Alfred William Pullin, *History of Yorkshire county cricket, 1903–1923*, 1924. For university cricket at county level see Sir Pelham Francis Warner and Frederick Samuel Ashley-Cooper, *Oxford v. Cambridge at the wicket*, 1926; John Dover Betham, comp., *Oxford and Cambridge scores and biographies*, 1905; Geoffrey Arthur Bolton, *History of the O.U.C.C.*, Oxf. 1962; and William Justice Ford, *A history of the Cambridge University Cricket Club, 1820–1901*, 1902.

7693  ROE (W. NICHOLLS) *ed*. Public schools cricket, 1901–1950. 1951.

There are many hists. of indiv. clubs, both local and school. One of the better is Frederic Robert D'Oyly Monro, *A history of the Hampstead Cricket Club*, 1949.

7694  WEBBER (ROY) *comp*. The Playfair book of test cricket. 2 v. 1952–3.

There are numerous books on the development of international cricket. Among the more useful are E. L. Roberts, *Test cricket cavalcade, 1877–1947*, 1948; Ralph Hammond Barker and Irving Rosenwater, *England v. Australia: a compendium of test cricket between the countries 1877–1968*, 1969; John Arlott and Stanley Brogden, *The first test match: England v. Australia, 1877*, 1950; and Samuel Canynge Caple, *The Ashes at stake: memories of Anglo-Australian cricket*, Worcester 1961, *England v. the West Indies, 1895–1957*, Worcester, 1957, *The Springboks at cricket: England versus South Africa, 1888–1960*, Worcester 1960, *England versus India, 1886–1959*, Worcester 1959, and *The All-Blacks at cricket: the story of New Zealand cricket, 1860–1958*, Worcester 1958. The flavour of contemp. cricket tours is well caught by Frederick Lillywhite, *The English cricketers' trip to Canada and the United States*, 1860, Robert Allan Fitzgerald, *Wickets in the west: or, the twelve in America*, 1873, and Edward Humphrey Dalrymple Sewell, *Triangular cricket: being, a record of the greatest contest in the history of the game*, 1912.

7695  OLD EBOR *pseud. of* PULLIN (ALFRED WILLIAM). Talks with old English cricketers. 1900.

See also his *Alfred Shaw, cricketer: his career and reminiscences, . . .*, 1902, and Arthur Alexander Thomson, *Odd men in: a gallery of cricket eccentrics*, 1958, *Cricket: the golden ages*, 1961, and *Hirst and Rhodes*, 1959, which are all biog. in emphasis. For other minor biog. studs. see Walter Ambrose Bettesworth, *Chats on the cricket field . . .*, 1910, and *The Walkers of Southgate: a famous brotherhood of cricketers . . .*, ed. by E. T. Sacks, 1900; Charles William Alcock, ed., *Famous cricketers and cricket-grounds*, 1895; Alban George Moyes, *A century of cricketers*, 1950; Charles Burgess Fry, *Life worth living: some phases of an Englishman*, 1939; [Randolph Llewellyn Hodgson] *Cricket memories, by a country vicar*, 1930; and William E. Howard, *Fifty years' cricket reminiscences of a non-player*, Manch. 1928.

7696  BARLOW. Forty seasons of first-class cricket: being, the autobiography and reminiscences of R. G. Barlow. By Richard Gorton Barlow. Manch. 1908.

7697   GRACE. 'W.G.' Cricketing reminiscences and personal recollections. By William Gilbert Grace. 1899.

See also his *The history of a hundred centuries*, 1895, *Cricket*, Bristol 1891, and *W.G.'s little book*, 1909. There are many biogs. notably Bernard Richard Meirion Darwin, *W. G. Grace*, 1934, Clifford Bax, *W. G. Grace*, 1952, and Arthur Alexander Thomson, *The great cricketer*, 1957. Contemp. reaction is to be found in William Methven Brownlee, *W. G. Grace: a biography*, 1887, Acton Wye, *Dr. W. G. Grace*, 1901, and Martin Bladen Hawke, Baron Hawke, ed., *The memorial biography of Dr. W. G. Grace*, 1919. For W.G.'s cricketing brother see Frederick Samuel Ashley-Cooper, *Edward Mills Grace, cricketer*, 1916.

7698   HARRIS. A few short runs. By George Robert Canning Harris, Baron Harris. 1921.

7699   HAWKE. Recollections and reminiscences. By Martin Bladen Hawke, Baron Hawke. 1924.

7700   HOBBS. My cricket memories. By Sir John Berry Hobbs. 1924.

See also his *My life story*, 1935, and Ronald Charles Mason, *Jack Hobbs: a portrait of an artist as a great batsman*, 1960.

7701   JESSOP. A cricketer's log. By Gilbert Laird Jessop. 1922.

7702   LILLEY. Twenty-four years of cricket: recalling the most famous cricketers and their methods . . . By Arthur Augustus Lilley. 1912. New edn. 1914.

7703   MYNN. Alfred Mynn and the cricketers of his time. By Patrick Morrah. 1963.

7704   RHODES. Wilfred Rhodes, professional and gentleman. By Sidney Rogerson. 1960.

7705   WARNER. My cricketing life. By Sir Pelham Francis Warner. 1921.

Warner also publ. *Cricket reminiscences*, 1920, *Long innings*, 1951, *Cricket in many climes*, 1900, *How we recovered the Ashes*, 1904, and *The M.C.C. in South Africa*, 1906.

## (c) *Football*

7706   YOUNG (PERCY MARSHALL). A history of British football. 1968.

A simple outline as is Morris Marples, *A history of football*, 1954, and Denzil Batchelor, *Soccer: a history of Association football*, 1954.

7707   GREEN (GEOFFREY). The history of the Football Association. 1953.

The official hist. Sir Frederick Joseph Wall, *Fifty years of football*, 1935, adds little. But see Terence Delaney, *A century of soccer . . . a centenary publication of the Football Association*, 1963.

7708   GIBSON (ALFRED) *and* PICKFORD (WILLIAM). Association football & the men who have made it. 4 v. [1905–6.]

Cp. Aubrey Howard Fabian and Geoffrey Green, eds., *Association football*, 4 v. 1960.

**7709** GREEN (GEOFFREY). The official history of the F.A. cup. 1949. New edn. 1960.

**7710** CHURCHILL (REGINALD CHARLES). Sixty seasons of League football. 1958. New edn. [English League football.] 1961.

A club-by-club survey, with results from 1888. Charles E. Sutcliffe and others, comps., *The story of the Football League, 1888–1938*, Preston 1938, 2nd edn. 1939, is a solid official hist. For the regions see Charles E. Sutcliffe and F. Hargreaves, *History of the Lancashire Football Association, 1878–1928*, 1928, Arthur Appleton, *Hotbed of soccer: the story of football in the north-east*, 1960, and Lionel Francis, *Seventy-five years of Southern League football*, 1969.

**7711** YOUNG (PERCY MARSHALL). Manchester United. 1960.

A detailed hist. For other clubs see his *Bolton Wanderers*, 1961, *The Wolves: the first eighty years*, 1959, *Football in Sheffield*, 1962, and *Football on Merseyside*, 1963, Peter Morris, *Aston Villa: the history of a great football club, 1874–1960*, 1960, Ralph Leslie Finn, *A history of Chelsea Football Club*, 1969, and *Arsenal: Chapman to Mee*, 1969, and Denis Signy, *A history of Queen's Park Rangers Football Club*, 1969.

**7712** ROYDS (*Sir* PERCY). The history of the laws of Rugby football. Twickenham. 1949.

For a good contemp. description see Francis Marshall, ed., *Football: the Rugby Union game*, 1892, new edn. 1925.

**7713** OWEN (OWEN LLEWELLYN). The history of the Rugby Football Union. 1955.

See also Owen Llewellyn Owen, *The growth of a sporting venture: a history of the Eastern Counties' Rugby Union*, 1952; John Brinley George Thomas, *Great Rugger clubs*, 1962; Howard Percival Marshall and John Paul Jordan, *Oxford v. Cambridge: the story of the university Rugby match*, 1951; Walter Bernard Croxford, ed., *Rugby union in Lancashire and Cheshire*, Liverpool 1950; C. Berkeley Cowell and E. Watts Moses, *Durham County Rugby Union . . . 1876–1936*, Newcastle-upon-Tyne 1936; Emile De Lissa and others, comps., *Barbarian records: a complete record of the Barbarian Football Club, 1890–1932*, 1933, new edn. 1955; and Henry Blythe Thornhill Wakelam, *Harlequin story: the history of the Harlequin Football Club*, 1954.

**7714** MACKLIN (KEITH). The history of Rugby League football. 1962.

### (d) *Horse-racing*

**7715** COOK (*Sir* THEODORE ANDREA). A history of the English turf. 3 v. 1901–4.

Cont. by T. H. Browne, *History of the English turf, 1904–1930*, 2 v. 1931. Standard. For shorter accounts see Robert Rodrigo, *The racing game: a history of flat racing*, 1958, and Ernest A. Bland, ed., *Flat racing since 1900*, 1950. For royal horses see Michael Seth-Smith, *Bred for the purple: a history of the monarchy and the turf*, 1969.

**7716** THE RACING CALENDAR: containing an account of the plates matches and sweepstakes, run for in Great Britain and Ireland . . . 1773+. Annual.

Indispensable. Suppl. by *Steeple chases past for the season 1866–67+*, 1867+, and [*Ruff's*] *guide to the turf, or pocket racing companion*, 1842+. The leading racing js. were

*Racing times*, 1851–64, 1866–8, *The racing world*, 1887+, and *The jockey*, 1890+, but the best reports are usually in *The sporting times*, 1865–1931. For horses see **7781**. For the hist. of the *Racing calendar* see Charles Matthew Prior, *The history of the Racing Calendar and Stud Book from their inception in the eighteenth century* . . ., 1926.

**7717**  ROUS (HENRY JOHN). On the laws and practice of horse racing. 1850. 2nd edn. 1866.

Important for the regulation of racing.

**7718**  MORTIMER (ROGER). The Jockey Club. 1958.

The governing body for flat racing. There is little in Robert Black, *The Jockey Club and its founders*, 1891.

**7719**  MOORHOUSE (EDWARD). The romance of the Derby: into which are woven the facts and figures a sportsman requires . . . 2 v. 1908.

Each race is covered in more palatable form in Roger Mortimer, *The history of the Derby stakes*, 1962, and Vincent Robert Orchard, *The Derby stakes: a complete history from 1900 to 1953*, 1954. For other races see Joseph Smith Fletcher, *History of the St Leger stakes, 1776–1901*, 1902, new edn. 1926, Guy B. H. Logan, *The classic races of the turf*, 1931, and George Thomas Burrows, *Cheshire sports and sportsmen: including a history of the Chester cup*, Chester [1925].

**7720**  ELIOT (*Lady* [GERMAINE] ELIZABETH [OLIVE]). Portrait of a sport: a history of steeplechasing. 1957.

See also William Charles Arlington Blew, *A history of steeple-chasing*, 1901, and John Henry Peyto Verney, Baron Willoughby de Broke, ed., *Steeplechasing*, Lonsdale Libr. 32, 1954. On indiv. races see David Hoadley Munroe, *The Grand National, 1839–1931*, 1931, G. Finch Mason, *Heroes and heroines of the Grand National* . . ., 1907, 2nd edn. 1911, Thomas Henry Bird, *A hundred Grand Nationals*, 1937, and John Welcome, pseud. of John Needham Huggard Brennan, *The Cheltenham gold cup: the story of a great steeplechase*, 1957. For a more light-hearted organization see Charles Pascoe Hawkes, *Bench and bar in the saddle: the Pegasus Club during three reigns* . . ., 1928.

**7721**  CAWTHORNE (GEORGE JAMES) *and* HEROD (RICHARD S.). Royal Ascot: its history and its associations. 1900. New edn. 1902.

For Epsom see Edward Earle Dorling, *Epsom and the Dorlings*, 1939.

**7722**  ALLISON. My kingdom for a horse . . . By William Allison. 1919.

Better than his *Memories of men and horses*, 1922. Memoirs of a sports writer. The difference between competent and less than competent sports writing can be seen by comparing Allison's work with *A mingled yarn: the autobiography of Edward Spencer Mott* ('*Nathaniel Gubbins*'), 1898.

**7723**  ARCHER. The life of Fred Archer. By Edith M. Humphris. Ed. by Lord Arthur Hugh Grosvenor. 1923.

**7724**  ASTLEY. Fifty years of my life in the world of sport at home and abroad. By Sir John Dugdale Astley. 2 v. 1894.

**7725**  CHETWYND. Racing reminiscences and experiences of the turf. By Sir George Chetwynd. 2 v. 1891.

7726 CUSTANCE. Riding recollections and turf stories. [*c.* 1863–86.] By Henry Custance. 1894.

7727 DAWSON. The life of Matthew Dawson. By Edith M. Humphris. 1928.

7728 DIXON. Life and times of 'The Druid' (Henry Hall Dixon). By Francis Charles Lawley. 1895.

The most famous of contemp. racing journalists. See also John Bennion Booth, *Bits of character: a life of Henry Hall Dixon, 'The Druid'*, 1936. Dixon's works (republ. as *The Druid sporting library*, 5 v. 1895) deal mostly with pre-1850 events, but *Saddle and sirloin . . .*, 1870, is largely on the 1850s and 1860s.

7729 DIXON. From Gladiateur to Persimmon: turf memories of thirty years. By H. Sydenham Dixon. 1901.

Good for 1865–96. Dixon was a racing journalist.

7730 GOULD. The magic of sport: mainly autobiographical. By Nat[thaniel] Gould. 1909.

Gould was a racing novelist of some note in his day. See his *The double event . . .*, 1891, *Harry Dale's jockey 'Wild Rose' . . .*, 1893, and *The pace that kills*, 1899. There is a brief life, John Randall Swann, *Nat Gould: biography and appreciation* [1923].

7731 HODGMAN. Sixty years on the turf: the life and times of George Hodgman, 1840–1900. Ed. by Charles R. Warren. 1908.

7732 MORTON. My sixty years of the Turf: reminiscences of the joys and sorrows of a racing life. By Charles Morton. 1930.

7733 PORTER. John Porter of Kingsclere: an autobiography. Written in collaboration with Edward Moorhouse. 1919.

See also John Porter, *Kingsclere*, ed. by Byron Webber, 1896. Porter was a famous trainer.

7734 ROUS. Admiral Rous and the English turf, 1795–1877. By Thomas Henry Bird. 1939.

Rous was the dominant figure in English racing for a generation.

7735 SCOTT. Turf memories of sixty years. By Alexander Scott. Ed. by W. J. Collins. 1925.

7736 SIEVIER. Neck or nothing: the extraordinary life and times of Bob Sievier. By John Welcome, pseud. of John Needham Huggard Brennan. 1970.

7737 SYKES. Sykes of Sledmere: the record of a sporting family and famous stud. By John Freeman Fairfax-Blakeborough. 1929.

7738 WATSON. A sporting and dramatic career. By Alfred Edward Thomas Watson. 1918.

Watson was a general sports writer, who was effective editor of the Badminton Libr. (**7673**). But he chiefly wrote on horses, notably in *Racecourse and covert side*, 1883, *Racing and chasing . . .*, 1897, and *The turf*, 1898.

7739 YATES. Arthur Yates, trainer and gentleman rider: an autobiography, written in collaboration with Bruce Blunt. 1924.

7740 CURZON (LOUIS HENRY) *pseud. of* BERTRAM (JAMES GLASS). A mirror of the turf: or, the machinery of horse-racing revealed, showing the sport of kings as it is today. 1892.

Better than the usual run of 'revelations' and gossip. But see Thormanby, pseud. of W. Willmott Dixon, *Kings of the turf: memoirs and anecdotes of distinguished owners, backers, trainers and jockeys, who have figured on the British turf, with memorable achievements of famous horses,* 1898, and William Day, *Reminiscences of the turf . . .,* 1886, and *Turf celebrities I have known,* 1891.

### (e) *Hunting*

The literature of hunting is unmanageably large, because hunting men liked to publish their own memoirs and reminiscences of the hunts they rode with. Only a small selection is included here.

7741 HIGGINSON (ALEXANDER HENRY). 'Bibliography of books on hunting'. In *The book of the horse,* ed. by Brian Seymour Vesey-Fitzgerald. 1946. Pp. 807–66.

7742 HIGGINSON (ALEXANDER HENRY). British and American sporting authors: their writings and biographies. 1951.

On hunting. See also Edward William Dirom Cuming, *A fox-hunting anthology . . .,* 1928.

7743 BODKIN (THOMAS) *ed.* The noble science: John Leech in the hunting field. 1948.

7744 HIGGINSON (ALEXANDER HENRY). Two centuries of foxhunting. 1946.

Fuller than Patrick Reginald Chalmers, *History of hunting,* Lonsdale Libr. 1936, and other popular hists. But see also Arthur Wells Coaten, ed., *British hunting: a complete history of the national sport of Great Britain and Ireland from the earliest records* [1910], George F. Underhill, *Hunting and practical hints for hunting men,* 1897, and *A century of English fox hunting,* 1900, John Otho Paget, *Hunting,* 1900, and *Beagles and beagling,* 1923, and Ludovick Charles Richard Duncombe-Jewell, afterwards Cameron, *Otters and otter hunting,* 1908.

7745 BAILY'S FOX-HUNTING DIRECTORY. 1897+.

The best directory.

7746 BRITISH HUNTS AND HUNTSMEN: containing a short history of each fox and stag hunt in the British Isles, together with biographical records of masters past and present . . . profusely illustrated . . . Comp. in conjunction with *The Sporting Life.* 4 v. 1908–11.

7747 DE TRAFFORD (*Sir* HUMPHREY FRANCIS) *and others, eds.* The foxhounds of Great Britain and Ireland, their masters and huntsmen. 1906.

**7748** AFLALO (FREDERICK GEORGE) *ed.* The hunting library. 3 v. 1903.

Composed of Henry Anderson Bryden, *Hare hunting and harriers: with notices of beagles and basset hounds*, 1903, George F. Underhill, *Hunting and practical hints for hunting men*, 1897, and *The master of hounds*, 1903.

**7749** BRADLEY (CUTHBERT). The foxhound of the twentieth century: the breeding and work of the kennels of England . . . 1914.

The best work on the subject.

**7750** BROOKSBY *pseud. of* ELMHIRST (EDWARD PENNELL). The hunting countries of England: their facilities, character and requirements: a guide to hunting men. 2 v. 1878–82.

**7751** MENZIES (AMY CHARLOTTE) *Mrs. Stuart Menzies.* Women in the hunting field. 1913.

**7752** TROLLOPE (ANTHONY). Hunting sketches. 1865.

Trollope's novels are full of excellent hunting scenes.

**7753** BRADLEY (CUTHBERT). Good sport seen with some famous packs, 1885–1910 . . . [1910.]

Cont. in *Fox-hunting from shire to shire with many noted packs . . .*, 1912. Other books of hunting memoirs incl. Brooksby, pseud. of Edward Pennell Elmhirst, *The cream of Leicestershire: eleven seasons' skimmings: notable runs and incidents of the chase*, 1883, *The best season on record*, 1884, 2nd edn. 1885, and *The best of the fun, 1891–1897*, 1903, Henry S. Davenport, *Memories at random: Melton and Harborough*, 1926, John Malsbury Kirby Elliott, ed., *Fifty years' foxhunting with the Grafton and other packs of hounds*, 1900, and Sir Alfred Edward Pease, *Hunting reminiscences*, 1898, and *Half a century of sport*, 1932.

**7754** ELLIS (COLIN DARE BERNARD). Leicestershire and the Quorn hunt. Leicester. 1951.

For other county hists. see William Fawcett, *Hunting in Northumbria: being, the history of the Haydon hunt and many other packs*, 1927; James Fitzalan Hope, Baron Rankeillour, *History of hunting in Hampshire*, Winchester 1951; Henry Symonds, *Runs and sporting notes from Dorsetshire*, Blandford 1899; Richard Francis Ball and Tresham Gilby, *The Essex foxhounds: with notes upon hunting in Essex*, 1896; and Charles John Blagg, *A history of the North Staffordshire hounds and country, 1825 to 1902*, 1902.

**7755** FAIRFAX-BLAKEBOROUGH (JOHN FREEMAN). England's oldest hunt: being chapters in the history of the Bilsdale, Farndale and Sinnington hunts collected during several years. Northallerton. 1908.

For other hunting hists. see Thomas Guy Frederick Paget, *The Melton Mowbray of John Ferneley (1782–1860)*, Leicester 1931; William Charles Arlington Blew, *The Quorn hunt and its masters*, 1899; Robert Bingham Brassey, *Centenary of the Heythrop foxhounds, 1835–1935: hound breeding records covering 100 years*, 1936; Thomas Francis Dale, *The history of the Belvoir hunt*, 1899; Cuthbert Bradley, *The reminiscences of Frank Gillard, huntsman with the Belvoir hounds, 1886 to 1896*, 1898, and *Random recollections of the Belvoir hunt by a sportsman*, 1897; George Edwin Collins, *History of the Brocklesby hounds, 1700–1901*, 1902, *The Brocklesby hound lists, 1746–1925*, 2 v. 1904–26, *Farming and foxhunting: personal recollections of the Brocklesby hunt*, 1935, and *An undistinguished sportsman: the story of a humble follower of the sport of kings and a very gallant gentleman*, 1934; Thomas Francis Dale, *The eighth Duke of Beaufort and the Badminton hunt* . . ., 1901; William Scarth Dixon, *A history of the Bramham Moor hunt*, Leeds 1898, and *A history of the York and Ainsty hunt*, Leeds 1899; Herbert Francis Hore, *The history of the royal buckhounds*, Newmarket 1895; Thomas Lister, Baron Ribblesdale, *The Queen's hounds and stag-hunting recollections*, 1897; Sir Charles Mordaunt and Walter Robert Verney, *Annals of the Warwickshire hunt, 1795–1895, from authentic documents*, 2 v. 1896; 'Castor', *A century of fox hunting with the Warwickshire hounds* . . ., 1891; Henry Osmond Nethercote, *The Pytchley hunt: past and present: its history from its foundation* . . ., ed. by Charles Edmonds, 1888, 2nd edn. 1888; [Richard Ord] *The Sedgefield country in the seventies and eighties: with, the reminiscences of a first whipper in* [John Bevans], 1904; Thomas Guy Frederick Paget, *The history of the Althorp and Pytchley hunt, 1634–1920*, 1937; Sir Theophilus Henry Gresley Puleston, *A history of foxhunting in the Wynnstay Country and part of Shropshire: from the beginning of this century to the end of the season of 1884–85*, 1893; J. L. Randall, *A history of the Meynell hounds and country, 1780 to 1901*, 2 v. 1901; Francis Horner Reynard, *The Bedale hounds, 1832–1908*, Darlington 1908, and *Hunting notes from Holderness* . . ., c. 1920; Alys F. Serrell, *With hound and terrier in the field: hunting reminiscences* [of the Blackmore Vale hunt], ed. by Frances Elizabeth Slaughter, 1904; Frederick Cleave Loder Symonds and Edward Percy Crowdy, *A history of the Old Berks. hunt from 1760 to 1904*, 1905; and Arthur N. Walker, comp., *The Holcolme hunt*, Manch. 1937.

7756 EVERED (PHILIP). Stag hunting with the Devon and Somerset, 1887–1901: an account of the chase of the wild red deer on Exmoor. 1902.

See also Sir John William Fortescue, *Records of staghunting on Exmoor*, 1887, Fred Goss, *Memoirs of a stag harbourer: a record of twenty-eight years with the Devon and Somerset stag hounds, 1894–1921*, ed. by Herbert Campbell Thomson, 1931, and Edward Terence MacDermot, *The Devon and Somerset staghounds, 1907–1936*, 1936.

7757 KEMPSON (FREDERICK CLAUDE). The Trinity foot beagles: an informal record of Cambridge sport and sportsmen during the past fifty years. 1912.

7758 ANSTRUTHER THOMSON. Eighty years' reminiscences. By John Anstruther Thomson. 2 v. 1904.

See also his *Three great runs* . . ., 1889.

7759 FARQUHARSON. 'The Meynell of the West': being a biography of James John Farquharson, Esqre, master of fox hounds, 1806–1858. By Alexander Henry Higginson. 1936.

7760 OSBALDESTON. Squire Osbaldeston: his autobiography. Ed. by Edward William Dirom Cuming. 1926.

7761 MOLYNEUX. Thirty years a hunt servant: being the memoirs of Jack Molyneux. Ed. by John Freeman Fairfax-Blakeborough. 1935.

7762 RICHARDSON. The life of a great sportsman: John Maunsell Richardson. By Mary E. Richardson. 1919.

7763 SELBY LOWNDES. The hunting and sporting reminiscences of Henry William Selby Lowndes. Ed. by John Freeman Fairfax-Blakeborough. 1926.

## (f) *Other Sports*

**7764 HAMPTON (J. FITZGERALD).** Modern angling bibliography: books published on angling, fisheries, fish culture, from 1881 to 1945. 1947.

Useful, as is James Robb, *Notable angling literature* [1947]. The great bibliog. in the field is Thomas Westwood and Thomas Satchell, *Bibliotheca piscatoria: a catalogue of books on angling, the fisheries and fish culture*, 1883, suppl. by Robert Bright Marston, 1901. But Louise Rankin Albee, comp., *The Bartlett collection: a list of books on angling, fishes and fish culture in Harvard College Library*, Camb., Mass. 1896, has useful notes. Jonathan Couch, *A history of the fishes of the British islands*, publ. in pts. 1860–5, 4 v. 1868, has much misc. information. Walter Shaw Sparrow, *Angling in British art through five centuries*, 1923, is a helpful guide. Sir Herbert Eustace Maxwell and Frederick George Aflalo, eds., *The angler's library*, 6 v. 1897–9, is the fullest account of the subject; John Waller Hills, *A history of fly fishing for trout*, 1921, a convenient intro.

**7765 LONGMAN (CHARLES JAMES)** *and* **WALROND (HENRY).** Archery. Badminton Libr. 1894.

A good hist. with bibliog. Modern books, like Gordon Grimley, *The book of the bow*, 1958, and Edmund Holley Burke, *The history of archery*, 1958, are weak on the period.

**7766 WEBSTER (FREDERICK ANNESLEY MICHAEL).** Athletics of today: history, development and training. Lond. & N.Y. 1929.

Useful, though Sir Montague Shearman, *Athletics and football*, Badminton Libr. 1887, new edn. [*Athletics*] 1904, is fuller. See also Roberto L. Quercetani, *A world history of track and field athletics, 1864–1964*, 1964. *Athletic news*, Manch. 1875–1931, was the main newspaper of the sport. See also **7676**.

**7767 LINNEY (E. J.).** A history of the game of bowls. 1933.

Useful for the British Bowling Assoc. There are useful surveys of the state of the game in James M. Pretsell, *The game of bowls: past and present*, Edin. & Lond. 1908, James Alexander Manson, *The complete bowler: being, the history and practice of the ancient and royal game of bowls*, 1912, and George Thomas Burrows, *All about bowls: with hints for beginners*, 1915. Manson has records back to 1857.

**7768 MAGRIEL (PAUL DAVID).** Bibliography of boxing: a chronological check list of books in English published before 1900. New York Public Libr. 1948.

**7769 DEGHY (GUY).** Noble and manly: the history of the National Sporting Club. 1956.

The chief boxing organisation. For the club see also Arthur Frederick Bettinson and William Outram Tristram, eds., *The National Sporting Club, past and present*, 1901, A. F. Bettinson and Ben Bennison, *The home of boxing*, 1922, and Francis Archibald Kelhead Douglas, Marquess of Queensberry, *The sporting Queensberrys*, 1942.

**7770 LYNCH (JOHN GILBERT BOHUN).** Knuckles and gloves. 1922.

Useful, as is his *The complete amateur boxer*, 1913, 2nd edn. 1924, and *The prize ring*, 1925. There is a considerable literature devoted to indiv. contests. Cp. Henry Downes Miles, *Pugilistica: being one hundred and forty years of the history of British boxing . . . from . . . 1719 . . . to . . . 1863*, 3 v. 1880–1, Frederick W. J. Henning, *Fights for the championship: the men and their times . . .*, 2 v. 1902, and *Some recollections of the prize ring*, 1888, Charles Platt, *Famous fights and fighters* [1921], and Bernard John Angle, *My sporting memories*, 1925.

7771   LOVELOCK (JAMES). Caving. 1969.

7772   LILLIE (ARTHUR) *ed.* Croquet up to date: containing the ideas and teachings of the leading players and champions. 1900.

7773   LIGHTWOOD (JAMES THOMAS). The Cyclists' Touring Club: the romance of fifty years' cycling. 1928.

The *Cyclists' Touring Club gazette*, 1882+, is splendidly illus. For the famous socialist Clarion Club, see Tom Groom, *National Clarion Cycling Club: the fifty-year story of the club, 1894–1944*, 1944. For bicycles see **6369–79**.

7774   VESEY-FITZGERALD (BRIAN SEYMOUR). The domestic dog: an introduction to its history. 1957.

See also his comprehensive *The book of the dog*, 1948; Edward Cecil Ash, *Dogs: their history and development*, 2 v. 1927; John Meyrick, *House dogs and sporting dogs . . .*, 1861; Hugh Dalziel, *British dogs: their varieties, history, characteristics, breeding, management and exhibition*, publ. in pts. 1879–80, 2nd edn. 3 v. 1887–97; Rawdon B. Lee, *A history and description of the modern dogs of Great Britain and Ireland*, 3 v. 1893–4; *The Kennel Club stud book: a record of dog shows and field trials*, 1874+; Kennel Club, *The kennel gazette*, 1880+; Edward Cecil Ash, *The book of the greyhound*, 2 pts. 1933, 2nd edn. 1933; Freeman Lloyd, *The whippet and race dog . . .*, 1894; *The coursing calendar and review of the season*, 1857–1918; and *The greyhound stud book, established by authority of the National Coursing Club*, 1882+.

7775   DE BEAUMONT (CHARLES LOUIS LEOPOLD ALFRED). Modern British fencing: a history of the Amateur Fencing Association of Great Britain. [1949.]

See also Carl Albert Thimm, *A complete bibliography of fencing and duelling . . .*, 1896.

7776   BROWNING (ROBERT H.-K.). A history of golf: the royal and ancient game. 1955.

A straightforward account. See also Bernard Richard Meirion Darwin and others, *A history of golf in Britain*, 1952; Bernard Darwin, *The golf courses of the British Isles*, 1910, new edn. 1925; Charles Gordon Mortimer and Fred J. C. Pignon, *The story of the open golf championship, 1860–1950*, 1952; and Horace Gordon Hutchinson, *Fifty years of golf*, 1919. A good contemp. primer was James Braid, Edward Frederic Beacon, and Eustace Hamilton Miles, eds., *A book of golf*, 1903. Louie Mackern and M. Boys, *Our lady of the green: a book of ladies' golf*, 1899, and Mary E. L. Hezlet, *Ladies golf*, 1904, are interesting. Harry B. Wood, *Golfing curios and the like*, Manch. 1910, is useful for equipment and has a full bibliog. Cecil Hopkinson, *Collecting golf-books, 1743–1938*, 1938, and Peter Lawless, ed., *The golfer's companion*, 1937, are useful for golfing books.

7777   THE GOLFER'S HANDBOOK. Edin. 1898+. Annual.

One of a number of such works. Cp. *The golfer's yearbook*, later *Nisbet's golf yearbook*, 1905–1914, *The golfing annual*, 1887–1910, and *Ladies' Golf Union annual* [*yearbook*], Edin. & Lond. 1894+. *Who's who in golf and directory of golf-clubs and members*, 1908+, is also handy. *Golf* [from 1899 *Golf illustrated*], 1890+ ·and *Golfing . . .*, 1895+, were the two principal weeklies.

7778 SALMOND (JAMES BELL). The story of the R. & A.: being, the history of the first two hundred years of the Royal and Ancient Golf Club of St. Andrews. 1956.

See also Harry Stirling Crawfurd Everard, *A history of the Royal & Ancient Golf Club St. Andrews, from 1754–1900*, Edin. & Lond. 1907. Important for standards. See also Geoffrey Cousins, *Golfers at law*, 1958.

7779 LEACH (HENRY) *ed.* Great golfers in the making: being, autobiographical accounts of the early progress of the most celebrated players . . . [1907.]

See also Horace Gordon Hutchinson, *The book of golf and golfers*, 1899, George William Beldam, *Great golfers: their methods at a glance*, 1904, and Bernard Richard Meirion Darwin, *James Braid*, 1952.

7780 SMITH (J. NICHOLSON) *and* ROBSON (PHILIP APPLEBY). Hockey: historical and practical. 1899.

See also Eustace E. White, *The complete hockey player*, 1909, and W. A. Malherbe Chronological bibliography of hockey, rev. edn. Johannesberg 1965.

7781 VESEY-FITZGERALD (BRIAN SEYMOUR) *ed.* The book of the horse. 1946.

A useful comp. Cp. Sir Humphrey Francis De Trafford, ed., *The horses of the British empire*, 2 v. 1908, and Samuel Sidney, *The book of the horse* . . . [1873–5], 4th edn. [1892–3]. For horse-breeding see *The general stud book: containing . . . the pedigree of every horse* . . . 1803+, Judith Anne Dorothea Blunt-Lytton, Baroness Wentworth, *Thoroughbred racing stock and its ancestors* . . ., 1938, and *The authentic Arabian horse and his descendants* . . . 1945, 2nd edn. 1960, Wilhelm Friedrich Dünkelberg, *Das englische Vollblutpferd und seine Zuchtwahl* . . ., Brunswick 1902, and Paul Goldbeck, *Pferdezucht und Pferderassen Englands* . . ., Leipzig 1902. There are a number of hists. of indiv. horses, incl. Joscelyn Lechmere, *Pretty Polly: the history of her career on the turf*, 1907, and books of portraits of which the best is Thomas Henry Taunton, *Portraits of celebrated racehorses* [1702–1870] . . ., 4 v. 1887–8. Horse sales are covered in Vincent Robert Orchard, *Tattersalls two hundred years of sporting history*, 1954. Riding in William Sidney Felton, *Masters of equitation* . . ., 1962, Lida Louise Bloodgood, later Fleitmann, *The saddle of queens: the story of the side-saddle*, 1959, and William Scarth Dixon, *The complete horseman*, 1913, 4th edn. 1929.

7782 WALKERLEY (RODNEY LEWIS DE BURGH). Motor racing fact and figures. 1961.

For indiv. races see William Charles Boddy, *The history of Brooklands motor course*, 1957, Richard Alexander Hough, *Tourist trophy: the history of Britain's greatest motor race* 1957, and Charles Jarrott, *Ten years of motors and motor racing*, 1906, 4th edn. 1956. There are a number of useful vols. of reminiscences, incl. William Fletcher Bradley, *Motor racing memories, 1903–1921*, 1960, Selwyn Francis Edge, *My motoring reminiscences*, 1934, and Montague Graham White, *At the wheel* . . ., 1935. See also **6350**.

7783 KEIR (DAVID EDWIN) *and* MORGAN (BRYAN STANFORD). Golden milestone: 50 years of the A.A. 1955.

See also Royal Automobile Club, *Jubilee book, 1897–1947*, ed. by Dudley Noble, 1947. See also **6352**.

7784 ALPINE CLUB. Catalogue of books in the library. 1880. 4th edn. 1915.

See also Edward C. Porter, *Library of mountaineering and exploration and travel*, Chicago 1959, and Claire Éliane Engel, *La littérature alpestre en France et en Angleterre aux xviiie et xixe siècles*, Chambéry 1930.

7785 CLARK (RONALD WILLIAM) *and* PYATT (EDWARD CHARLES). Mountaineering in Britain: a history from the earliest times to the present day. 1957.

A good general hist. stronger on the period than Sir Arnold Henry Moore Lunn, *A century of mountaineering, 1857–1957*, Lond. 1957, N.Y. 1958, and Robert Lock Graham Irving, *A history of British mountaineering*, 1955. See also Clark's *The Victorian mountaineers*, 1953. Methods of mountaineering are described in Walter Parry Haskett Smith and Henry Chichester Hart, *Climbing in the British Isles*, 2 v. 1894–5, George Dixon Abraham, *The complete mountaineer* [1907], and Claude Ernest Benson, *British mountaineering*, 1909, 2nd edn. 1914.

7786 ENGEL (CLAIRE ÉLIANE). A history of mountaineering in the Alps. 1950.

See also her *They came to the hills*, 1952, Ronald William Clark, *The early alpine guides*, 1949, *The day the rope broke: the story of a great Victorian tragedy*, 1965, and *An eccentric in the Alps: the story of the Rev. W. A. B. Coolidge, the great Victorian mountaineer*, 1959, and Sir Arnold Henry Moore Lunn, ed., *The Englishman in the Alps: being a collection of English prose and poetry relating to the Alps*, Oxf. 1913, 2nd edn. 1927.

7787 MUMM (ARNOLD LOUIS) *ed.* The Alpine Club register. 3 v. 1923–8.

Covers 1857–90.

7788 THE ALPINE JOURNAL: a record of mountain adventure and scientific observation. By members of the Alpine Club. 1863+.

7789 MATHEWS (CHARLES EDWARD). The annals of Mont Blanc: a monograph. 1898.

An indication of the extraordinary attraction of the Alps for the Victorians, as are Albert Richard Smith, *The story of Mont Blanc*, 1853, Guido Rey, *The Matterhorn*, trans. by John Edward Caldwell Eaton, 1907, and such works as Frederic Harrison, *My Alpine jubilee, 1851–1907*, 1908; Charles Hudson and Edward Shirley Kennedy, *Where there's a will there's a way: an ascent of Mont Blanc by a new route and without guides*, 1856; Walter Landen, *Recollections of an old mountaineer*, 1910; Adolphus Warburton Moore, *The Alps in 1864: a private journal*, ed. by Sir Alexander Blackie William Kennedy, Edin. 1902; Albert Frederick Mummery, *My climbs in the Alps and Caucasus*, 1895; Claud Schuster, Baron Schuster, *Peaks and pleasant pastures*, 1911; Francis Fox Tuckett, *A pioneer in the High Alps: Alpine diaries and letters, 1856–1874*, ed. by Eliot Howard and William Augustus Brevoort Coolidge, 1920; and John Tyndall, *Hours of exercise in the Alps*, 1871, new edn. 1899.

The rival attractions of Norway are touched on in William Cecil Slingsby, *Norway, the northern playground: sketches of climbing and mountain exploration in Norway between 1872 and 1903*, 1904.

7790 WHYMPER (EDWARD). Scrambles amongst the Alps in the years 1860–69. 1871. 6th edn. by Henry Edmund Guise Tyndale. 1936.

A minor classic. See also Frank Sydney Smythe, *Edward Whymper*, 1940.

7791 LUNN (*Sir* ARNOLD HENRY MOORE). A history of ski-ing. 1927.

7792 DRYBROUGH (T. B.). Polo. 1898. Rev. edn. 1906.

7793 BRITTAIN (FREDERICK) *comp.* Oar, scull and rudder: a bibliography of rowing. 1930.

7794 CLEAVER (HYLTON REGINALD). A history of rowing. 1957.

For the Henley races see Richard Desborough Burnell, *Henley regatta: a history,* 1957, and Sir Theodore Andrea Cook, *Henley races: with details of regattas from 1903 to 1914 inclusive and a complete index of competitors and crews since 1839,* 1919, and *Rowing at Henley,* 1919. For Oxford v. Cambridge the most usable accounts are Richard Desborough Burnell, *The Oxford & Cambridge boat race, 1829–1953,* 1954, and Gordon Ross, *The boat race: the story of the first hundred races between Oxford and Cambridge,* 1954. Contemporaries used George Gilbert Treherne Treherne and John Haviland Dashwood Goldie, *Record of the university boat race, 1829–1880 . . .,* 1883, new edn. 1909, which was based on earlier work by William Fisher Macmichael and others.

7795 THE ROWING ALMANACK AND OARSMAN'S COMPANION. 1860+.

Includes annual bibliog. of publs.

7796 RILING (RAYMOND LAWRENCE JOSEPH). Guns and shooting: a selected chronological bibliography. N.Y. 1951.

7797 HUMPHRY (ALFRED PAGET) *and* FREMANTLE (THOMAS FRANCIS), *Baron Cottesloe.* History of the National Rifle Association, during its first fifty years, 1859 to 1909. Camb. 1914.

See also Howard Norman Cole, *The story of Bisley: a short history of the National Rifle Association and Bisley camp,* Aldershot 1960, and David Howie, *A history of the Queen's prize from 1860,* Glasgow 1901.

7798 TEGNER (HENRY STUART). The sporting rifle and its use in Britain. 1962.

See also John Henry Walsh, *The modern sportsman's gun and rifle . . .,* 2 v. 1882–4, George Teasdale Teasdale-Buckell, *Experts on guns and shooting,* 1900, and *The complete shot . . .,* 1907, 5th edn. 1924, and Hugh Alexander Macpherson, *A history of fowling,* Edin. 1897.

7799 PHILLIPPS-WOLLEY (*Sir* CLIVE) *and others.* Big game shooting. Badminton Libr. 2 v. 1894. 2nd edn. 2 v. 1895.

7800 FOSTER (FRED W.). A bibliography of skating. 1898.

7801 BROWN (NIGEL). Ice-skating: a history. 1959.

See also Alan Herbert Vawser Bloom, *The skaters of the Fens,* Camb. 1958.

7802 GREENWOOD (FRANCES ANDERSON). Bibliography of swimming. N.Y. 1940.

See also Ralph Thomas, *Swimming,* 1904.

7803 FOSTER (FRED. W.). A bibliography of lawn tennis, 1874–1897. Richmond. 1897.

7804 NOEL (EVAN BAILLIE) *and* CLARK (JAMES OSCAR MAX). A history of tennis. 2 v. 1924.

Standard. Morys George Lyndhurst Bruce, Baron Aberdare, *The story of tennis*, 1959, is a useful short hist. For the organization of tennis see George Whiteside Hillyard, *Forty years of first-class lawn tennis*, 1924, 2nd edn. 1925; Dennis C. Coombe, *A history of the Davis cup: being, the story of the international lawn tennis championship, 1900–48*, 1949; Lawn Tennis Assoc., *Handbook*, 1888+; and *Ayre's lawn tennis almanack*, 1910–38, and *Lawn tennis*, 1896+. John Moyer Heathcote and others, *Tennis*, Badminton Libr. 1890, is good for the old game. For illus. see George William Beldam and P. A. Vaile, *Great lawn tennis players: their methods illustrated*, 1905.

7805 GABE (JULIUS). Yachting: historical sketches of the sport. 1902.

Good for the period. There is little more in William Dodgson Bowman, *Yachting and yachtsmen* [1927], or Peter Stuart Heaton, *Yachting: a history*, 1955. But see Montague John Guest and William Biggs Boulton, *The Royal Yacht Squadron . . .*, 1903; John Black Atkins, *Further memorials of the Royal Yacht Squadron, 1901–1938*, 1939; [*Royal*] *Cruising Club j.*, 1888+; Alfred Fullerton Loomis, *Ocean racing: the great bluewater yacht races, 1866–1935*, 1936, rev. edn. 1946; Joan Evelyn Grigsby, *Annals of our royal yachts, 1604–1953*, 1953; Douglas Dixon, *The king's sailing master . . . Sir Philip Hunloke . . . with a history of yachting*, 1948; and Henry Coleman Folkard, *The sailing boat . . .*, 1853, 6th edn. 1906. *Hunt's yachting magazine*, 1852–87, *Hunt's universal yacht list*, annual, 1851–1914, *The yachtsman*, 1891+, and *The yachting world*, 1894+, were the leading contemp. periodicals.

## (g) The Game Laws

7806 KIRBY (CHESTER). 'The English game law system'. *Amer. Hist. Rev.* xxxviii (1932–3), 240–62.

Gives the 18th-cent. background. See also Charles Pocklington Chevenix Trench, *The poacher and the squire: a history of poaching and game preservation in England*, 1967. For 19th-cent. game laws it is necessary to consult the report of the Ward Hunt Committee (**7810**). There is no shortage of hostile radical pamphlets, incl. George John Shaw-Lefevre, Baron Eversley, *The game laws*, 1874, and J. Connell, *The truth about the game laws: a record of cruelty, selfishness and oppression*, Humanitarian League publ. new ser. 2, 1898.

7807 HAGGARD (LILIAS RIDER) *ed.* I walked by night: being the life & history of the king of the Norfolk poachers: written by himself. 1935.

One of the best books of a now-popular genre. See also Alfred Thomas Curtis, comp., *A poacher's tale . . .*, by Frederick James Speakman, 1960, and James Hawker, *A Victorian poacher: James Hawker's journal*, ed. by Garth Christian, 1961. Among older books J. Connell, *Confessions of a poacher*, 1901, is particularly good. On gamekeepers the best book is still [John] Richard Jefferies, *The gamekeeper at home*, 1878.

7808 OKE (GEORGE COLWELL). A handy book of the game and fishery laws: containing all the acts in force as to game, rabbits, private and salmon fisheries . . . 1861. 5th edn. 1912.

Standard. The fisheries section was publ. separately as *A handy book of the fishery laws . . .*, 1878, 4th edn. 1924. For birds there is also James Robert Vernam Marchant and

Watkin Watkins, *Wild Bird Protection Acts, 1880–1896,* 1897. For the law before 1861 see John Locke, *The game laws* . . ., 1836, 5th edn. 1866.

7809  EVERITT (NICHOLAS). Shots from a lawyer's gun. 1901. 6th edn. 1927.

A popular account of the game laws from the *Shooting times.* Charles Row, *A practical guide to the game laws,* 1907, 2nd edn. 1928, is better, but has less period flavour.

7810  WARD HUNT COMMITTEE ON GAME LAWS. Report from the select committee on game laws [Chairman: George Ward Hunt]. H.C. 337 (1872). X, 1. Further report. H.C. 285 (1873). XIII, 1.

The only thorough investigation of the subject.

7811  HERBERT COMMITTEE ON WILD BIRDS PROTECTION. Report from the select committee on wild birds protection [Chairman: Auberon Herbert]. H.C. 338 (1873). XIII, 647.

# IX

# INTELLECTUAL AND CULTURAL HISTORY

## A. EDUCATION

### 1. GENERAL

#### (a) *Reference*

7812  BARON (GEORGE). A bibliographical guide to the English educational system. 1951. 3rd edn. 1965.

Standard, but weak on hist. For 19th-cent. books Granville Stanley Hall and John M. Mansfield, *Hints towards a select and descriptive bibliography of education*, Boston 1886, repr. 1893, is useful, though inaccurate. For bibliogs. of educ. see Scottish Council for Research in Education, *Aids to educational research: comprising, bibliographies and plan of research*, rev. edn. Edin., 1956, and Walter Scott Monroe and Louis Shores, *Bibliographies and summaries in education to July 1935* . . ., N.Y. 1936. New works are listed in *The education index*, N.Y. 1929+, and *British education index*, 1954+. For articles see R. Szreter, 'The history of education in non-education periodicals, 1939–1967: a bibliography', *Brit. J. Educ. Studs.* xvi (1968), 318–28. For the policy of present American js. see William L. Camp, comp., *Guide to periodicals in education*, Metuchen, N.J. 1968.

7813  HIGSON (CONSTANCE WINIFRED JANE) *ed.* Sources for the history of education: a list of material (including school books) contained in the libraries of the institutes and schools of education, together with works from the libraries of the universities of Nottingham and Reading. Library Assoc. 1967.

A union list of books to 1870: government publs. to 1918.

7814  LONDON COUNTY COUNCIL. Education library catalogue. 1935. Suppl. 1935–45. 1948.

The best libr. cat. But see National Union of Teachers, *Library catalogue*, new edn. 1959, suppls. 1960+.

7815  WALLIS (PETER JOHN). Histories of old schools: a revised list for England and Wales. Univ. of Newcastle, Dept. of Educ. 1966.

A revision of a list orig. publ. in *Brit. J. Educ. Studs.* xiv (1965–6), 48–89, 224–65, no. 3, 74–82. See also his index of the *Educational register*, 1851–5, ibid. xiii (1964–5), 50–70.

7816  JACOBS (PHYLLIS M.). Registers of universities, colleges and schools of Great Britain and Ireland: a list. Repr. from *Inst. Hist. Res. Bull.* xxxvii (1964), 185–232.

7817  CHRISTOPHERS (ANN). An index to nineteenth-century British educational biography. Univ. of London Inst. of Educ. Educ. Librs. Bull. Suppl. 10. 1965.

7818 TROPP (ASHER). 'Some sources for the history of educational periodicals in England'. *British J. Educ. Studs.* vi (1957–8), 151–63.

7819 BLACKWELL (ANNIE MARGARET). A list of researches in education and educational psychology presented for higher degrees in the universities of the United Kingdom, Northern Ireland, and the Irish republic, from 1918 to 1948. Nat. Foundation for Educ. Research. 1950. Suppl. 1952+.

See also Walter Crosby Eells, *American dissertations on foreign education, 1884–1958*, Wash. 1959.

7820 PUBLIC RECORD OFFICE. Department of Education and Science class list. 4 pts. List and Index Soc. 21, 48, 71, and 78. 1967–72.

Suppl. by List & Index Soc., vol. 55, *Dept. of Educ. and Sci. Private Office Papers* (Ed. 24), 1970. For the reports of the Educ. Dept. see **7842**.

7821 WATSON (FOSTER) *ed.* The encyclopaedia and dictionary of education: a comprehensive, practical and authoritative guide on all matters connected with education, including educational principles and practice, various types of teaching institutions and educational systems throughout the world. 4 v. 1921–2.

Usually referred to as *Pitman's encyclopaedia of education.* Paul Monroe, ed., *A cyclopedia of education*, 5 v. N.Y. 1911–13, repr. 5 v. Detroit 1969, is in many ways a better work, but is less strong on British educ. Alfred Ewen Fletcher, ed., *Sonnenschein's cyclopaedia of education: a handbook of reference on all subjects connected with education . . .*, 1888, 3rd edn. 1906, was a popular 1-v. work.

7822 EDUCATION DEPARTMENT. Special report on educational subjects, 1896–7. [C. 8447] H.C. (1897). XXV, 1.

The first of a famous ser. of reports ranging over the whole of contemp. educ. at home and abroad, and constituting a sort of loosely-knit encyclopedia. Publ. as parl. papers. Repr. 1968.

7823 MACLURE (JOHN STUART) *comp.* Educational documents: England and Wales, 1816–1963. 1965. 2nd edn. 1968.

Replaces Arthur Francis Leach, comp., *Educational charters and documents, 598 to 1909*, Camb. 1911.

7824 GOSDEN (PETER HENRY JOHN HEATHER) *comp.* How they were taught: an anthology of contemporary accounts of learning and teaching in England, 1800–1950. Oxf. 1969.

A useful coll. For school horror stories see Geoffrey Frederick Lamb, *The happiest days*, 1959.

(b) *History*

7825 ARMYTAGE (WALTER HARRY GREEN). Four hundred years of English education. Camb. 1964. 2nd edn. 1970.

A useful intro. Stanley James Curtis, *History of education in Great Britain*, 1948, 7th edn. 1967, *An introductory history of English education since 1800*, 1960, 4th edn. 1966, and *Education in Britain since 1900*, 1952, S. J. Curtis and Myrtle E. A. Boultwood, *A short* history of educational ideas, 1953, 4th edn. 1965, Howard Clive Barnard, *A short history of English education from 1760 [to 1944]*, 1947, 2nd edn. 1961, and Bruno Dressler, *Geschichte der englischen Erziehung* . . ., Leipzig 1928, add little.

7826  ADAMSON (JOHN WILLIAM). English education, 1789–1902. Camb. 1930. Repr. Camb. 1965.

Long the best work on the period. Lawrence Stone, 'Literacy and education in England, 1640–1900', *Past & Present* xlii (1969), 69–139, develops a new perspective on the extent of literacy, on which see also Altick (**8298**).

7827  SIMON (BRIAN). Studies in the history of education, 1780–1870. 1960.

Cont. by his *Education and the Labour movement, 1870–1920*, 1965. Marxist. Strongest for the pre-1870 period.

7828  EAGLESHAM (ERIC JOHN ROSS). The foundations of twentieth-century education in England. Lond. & N.Y. 1967.

A major interpretative essay, which modifies many of the conclusions of earlier writers, incl. Simon (**7827**).

7829  LOWNDES (GEORGE ALFRED NORMAN). The silent social revolution: an account of the expansion of public education in England and Wales, 1895–1935. 1937. 2nd edn. 1969.

Standard.

7830  ROBERTS (ROBERT DAVIES) *ed.* Education in the nineteenth century . . . Camb. 1901.

A valuable symposium.

7831  MUSGRAVE (PETER WILLIAM). Society and education in England since 1800. 1968.

An interpretative essay. For non-English comparisons see Alexander Duncan Campbell Peterson, *A hundred years of education*, 1952.

7832  WEST (EDWIN GEORGE). Education and the state: a study in political economy. 1965. 2nd. edn. 1970.

Discusses the arguments for and against state educ., chiefly since 1870.

7833  MUSGROVE (FRANK). 'Middle-class education and employment in the nineteenth century'. *Econ. Hist. Rev.* 2 ser. xii (1959–60), 99–111.

Met by a critical note from Harold James Perkin, ibid. xiv (1961–2), 122–30, to which Musgrove replied, ibid. xiv (1961–2), 320–9. See also his 'Middle-class families and schools, 1780–1880: interaction and exchange of function between institutions', *Sociological Rev.* new ser. vii (1959), 169–78, repr. in Peter William Musgrave, ed., *Sociology, history and education: a reader*, 1970.

7834  ROACH (JOHN PETER CHARLES). Public examinations in England, 1850–1900. Camb. 1971.

An important study of trends in middle-class educ. Useful background material may be found in contemp. manuals, such as Arthur King, *Our sons: how to start them in life:*

*a manual of useful information respecting places of education, the modes of entrance to the professions, the civil service, and commercial employment* [1880], which attempts to describe English educ. as a competitive system.

7835  CLARKE (MARTIN LOWTHER). Classical education in Britain, 1500–1900. Camb. 1959.

See also Robert Maxwell Ogilvie, *Latin and Greek: a history of the influence of the classics on English life, 1600 to 1918*, Lond. & Hamden, Conn. 1964, and Elizabeth Rawson, *The Spartan tradition in European thought*, Oxf. 1969.

7836  WATSON (FOSTER). The beginnings of the teaching of modern subjects in England. 1909.

7837  PALMER (DAVID JOHN). The rise of English studies: an account of the study of English language and literature from its origins to the making of the Oxford English school. 1965.

See also Erik Frykman, *W. E. Aytoun: pioneer professor of English at Edinburgh, a study of his literary opinions and his contribution to the development of English as an academic discipline*, Göteborg 1963.

7838  CROMER COMMITTEE ON SCHOOL OF ORIENTAL STUDIES. Interim report and appendices regarding proposed school of oriental languages in London [Chairman: Earl of Cromer]. [Cd. 5967] H.C. (1911). XVIII, 707.

See also *Report of the committee appointed to consider the organisation of oriental studies in London* [Chairman: Lord Reay]. [Cd. 4560] H.C. (1909). XXV, 235. Evidence, etc. [Cd. 4561] H.C. (1909). XXXV, 397.

7839  ARMYTAGE (WALTER HARRY GREEN). The German influence on English education. Lond. & N.Y. 1969.

See also his *The French influence on English education*, Lond. & N.Y. 1968, *The Russian influence on English education*, Lond. & N.Y. 1969, and *The American influence on English education*, Lond. & N.Y. 1967. Like George Haines IV, *German influence upon English education and science, 1800–1866*, Connecticut College Monograph 6, New London, Conn. 1957, and *Essays on German influence . . ., 1850–1919*, Connecticut College Monograph 9, New London 1969, and Patience Hunkin, *Enseignement et politique en France et en Angleterre: étude historique et comparée des législations relatives à l'enseignement en France et en Angleterre depuis 1789*, Institut Pédagogique National, Paris 1962, these books merely open up an important topic without developing it fully. Thomas Leckie Jarman, *Landmarks in the history of education: English education as part of the European tradition*, 1951, 2nd edn. 1963, is a general hist. from ancient times, rather than a comparative study.

7840  BRITISH JOURNAL OF EDUCATIONAL STUDIES. 1952+.

The main source for bibliog. and hist. articles. Suppl. by *Journal of educational administration and history*, Leeds 1968+, *History of education quarterly*, Pittsburgh then N.Y. 1961+, and *Paedagogica historica*, Ghent 1961+.

7841  GOSDEN (PETER HENRY JOHN HEATHER). The development of educational administration in England and Wales. Oxf. 1966.

Suppl. by his *Educational administration in England and Wales: a bibliographical guide*, Leeds 1967. See also Sir Graham Balfour, *The educational systems of Great Britain and Ireland*, Oxf. 1898, 2nd edn. 1903, James Edward Geoffrey De Montmorency, *The progress of education in England: a sketch of the development of English educational organization from early times to the year 1904*, 1904, and Herbert Ward, *The educational system of England and Wales and its recent history*, Camb. 1935. Hist. of Educ. Soc., *Studies in the government and control of education since 1860*, 1970, is a set of five papers.

**7842 COMMITTEE OF COUNCIL ON EDUCATION** [Board of Education]. Minutes. 1839/40–1857/58. 1840–58. Annual report. 1858/59+. 1859+.

Detailed reports on the state of educ. publ. as parl. papers. The main source for primary and part-time educ. Until 1872/3 incl. Scotland as well as England and Wales. Suppl. by a ser. of *Statistics*, 1900+.

**7843 KAY-SHUTTLEWORTH** (*Sir* JAMES PHILLIPS). Four periods of public education, as reviewed in 1832, 1839, 1846 and 1862. 1862.

The founder of the Educ. Dept. on his work. See also **7866**. Christopher Duke, 'Robert Lowe: a re-appraisal', *Brit. Educ. Studs.* xiv (1965–6), 19–35, adds little to the general hists. on 1859–64. For the organization of the Educ. Dept. see also *Report from the select committee on education* [Chairman: Sir John Pakington]. H.C. 403 (1865). VI, 1. Further report. H.C. 392 (1866). VII, 115, and *Report from the select committee on education (inspectors' reports)* [Chairman: Edward Howes]. H.C. 468 (1864). IX, 13.

**7844 CRAIK** (*Sir* HENRY). The state in its relation to education. 1884. 3rd edn. 1914.

Reflects Educ. Dept. opinion.

**7845 BISHOP** (ANTHONY SAVELL). The rise of a central authority for English education. Camb. 1971.

See also Sir Lewis Amherst Selby-Bigge, *The Board of Education*, The Whitehall ser., 1927, new edn. 1934, and Peter Henry John Heather Gosden, 'The Board of Education Act, 1899', *Brit. J. Educ. Studs.* xi (1962–3), 44–60.

**7846 EAGLESHAM** (ERIC JOHN ROSS). From school board to local authority. 1956.

Educ. admin. at the end of the 19th cent. See also his *The foundations of twentieth-century education in England*, 1967, 'Controlling educational expenditure eighty years ago', *Brit. J. Educ. Studs.* v (1956–7), 119–30, 'Planning the Education Bill of 1902', ibid. ix (1960–1), 3–24, 'Implementing the Education act of 1902', ibid. x (1961–2), 153–75, and 'The centenary of Sir Robert Morant', ibid. xii (1963–4), 5–18, P. R. Sharp, 'The entry of county councils into English educational administration, 1889', *J. Educ. Admin. & Hist.* i. (1968–9), 14–22, and D. R. Pugh, 'The 1902 Education act: the search for a compromise', ibid. xvi (1968), 164–78. On the technical side of local authority admin. see Board of Educ., *Report of the consultative committee of the Board of Education upon the question of devolution by county education authorities* [Chairman: A. H. Dyke Acland]. [Cd. 3952] H.C. (1908). LXXXII, 439. K. M. Hughes, 'A political party and education: reflections on the Liberal party's educational policy, 1867–1902', *Brit. J. Educ. Studs.* viii (1959–60), 112–26, does little more than open up a neglected subject.

**7847 THE SCHOOL BOARD** [GOVERNMENT] CHRONICLE. 1871+.

For the local admin. of educ. see also *The school board gazette: the official record of the Association of School Boards of England and Wales*, 1899–1902 [cont. as *The London education gazette*, 1904–5, and *The London county council gazette*, 1905–40], and *Education . . . [the official organ of the Association of Education Committees]*, 1903+. The main directory was *The education authorities' directory*, 1903+.

7848 EDMUNDS (EDWARD LESLIE). The school inspector. 1962.

See also his 'School inspection: the contribution of religious denominations', *Brit. J. Educ. Studs.* vii (1958–9), 12–26, [H. F. Boothroyd] 'Some account of the origin and growth of the Board's inspectorate', *Report of the Board of Education for the year 1922–23.* [Cmd. 2179] pp. 9–45. H.C. (1924). IX, 15–70. Suppl. for Wales, *Education in Wales: report of the Board of Education under the Welsh Intermediate Education Act, 1889, for the year 1923.* [Cmd. 2130] pp. 6–15. H.C. (1924). IX, 190–9. Reports of the inspectors were publ. as parl. papers, 1839–1902. There are pleasant memoirs of school inspection in Edmund Mackenzie Sneyd Kynnersley, *H.M.I. some passages in the life of one of H.M. Inspectors of schools,* 1908, and *H.M.I.'s notebook: or, recreations of an inspector of schools,* 1930, but Frederick Herbert Spencer, *An inspector's testament,* 1938, is a very much better book.

7849 TROPP (ASHER). The school teachers: the growth of the teaching profession in England and Wales, from 1800 to the present day. 1957.

See also Sir Wilberforce Ross Barker, *The superannuation of teachers in England and Wales . . .,* 1926, and L. Fletcher, 'The development of periodicals addressed to teachers in Britain before 1870', *J. Educ. Admin. & Hist.* ii (1969–70), 9–19.

7850 THOMPSON (DONNA FAY). Professional solidarity among the teachers of England. N.Y. 1927.

On the National Union of Teachers, using its *Annual report,* 1871+, and *The schoolmaster . . .,* 1872+. A rival teachers' organization, the Assistant Masters' Association, publ. a *Circular to members,* 1898–1906, and *The A.M.A.: the journal of the Incorporated Association of Assistant Masters in Secondary Schools,* 1906+. For women teachers there was *The schoolmistress,* 1881–1935, *The woman teacher,* 1911–12, *The woman teacher's magazine,* 1909–13, and *[Woman] teachers' world,* 1911+.

7851 RICH (ROWLAND W.). The training of teachers in England and Wales during the nineteenth century. Camb. 1933.

See also Peter Sandiford, *The training of teachers in England and Wales,* Teachers Coll., Columbia Univ., contribs. to educ. 32, N.Y. 1910, and George Baron, 'The teachers' registration movement', *Brit. J. Educ. Studs.* ii (1953–4), 133–44. There are a number of useful hists. of teacher training colleges, among them Dorothy Dymond, ed., *The forge: the history of Goldsmiths' College, 1905–1955,* 1955, Roy Millington, *A history of the City of Sheffield Training College,* Sheffield 1955, and Frank Cyril Pritchard, *The story of Westminster College [Methodist], 1851–1951,* 1951. See also Leila Tomlinson, 'Oxford University and the training of teachers: the early years (1892–1921)', *Brit. J. Educ. Studs.* xvi (1968), 292–307, and N. R. Tempest, 'Some sources for the history of teacher training in England and Wales', *Brit. J. Educ. Studs.* ix (1960–1), 57–66.

7852 BOARD OF EDUCATION. General report on the instruction and training of pupil-teachers, 1903–1907, with historical introduction. [Cd. 3582] H.C. (1907). LXIV, 203.

A hist. and detailed analysis, educ. authority by educ. authority. A similar report was issued for Wales. [Cd. 3814] H.C. (1908). LXXXIII, 735.

7853 SEABORNE (MALCOLM VIVIAN JOHN). The English school: its architecture and organization, 1370–1870. 1971.

7854 DENT (HAROLD COLLETT). Part-time education in Great Britain: an historical outline. 1949.

7855 PRITCHARD (DAVID GWYN). Education and the handicapped, 1760–1960. Lond. & N.Y. 1963.

See also his 'Some sources for the history of the education of handicapped children in England and Wales', *Brit. J. Educ. Studs.* xi (1962–3), 167–76.

7856 RITCHIE (JOHN M.). Concerning the blind: being a historical sketch of organised effort on behalf of the blind in Great Britain . . . Edin. & Lond. 1930.

7857 MACLURE (JOHN STUART). One hundred years of London education, 1870–1970. 1970.

See also David Rubinstein, *School attendance in London, 1870–1904: a social history*, Hull & N.Y. 1969.

7858 WEBB (SIDNEY JAMES), *Baron Passfield*. London education. 1904.
A full survey.

7859 SPALDING (THOMAS ALFRED) *and* CANNEY (THOMAS STAN-LEY ALFRED). The work of the London School Board. [1900.]

A careful account prepared for the Paris exhibition. There are also two formal hists.: Hugh B. Philpott, *London at school: the story of the school board, 1870–1904*, 1904, and the *Final report of the board*, 1904. All are based on the *Minutes of proceedings* publ. by the Board, 60 v., 1870–1904. Thomas Gautrey, '*Lux mihi laus*': *school board memories*, 1937, and Charles Edward Baines Reed, *Memoir of Sir Charles Reed*, 1883, also deal with the London School Board.

7860 BINGHAM (JOHN HENRY). The period of the Sheffield School Board, 1870–1903: a record of the founding and career of the Board, and of progress in educational ideas, provision, practice and administration under the Board during that period. Sheffield. 1949.

7861 SIMON (BRIAN) *ed*. Education in Leicestershire, 1540–1940: a regional study. Leicester. 1968.

Good. For other local studs. see David Wardle, *Education and society in nineteenth-century Nottingham*, Camb. 1971; Rex C. Russell, pseud. of Reginald Charles Russell, *A history of schools and education in Lindsey, Lincs., 1800–1902*, 4+ pts., Lindsey County Council, 1965+; Thomas William Bamford, *The evolution of rural education: three studies of the East Riding of Yorkshire*, Hull 1965; Eric Clare Midwinter, 'The administration of public education in late Victorian Lancashire', *Northern Hist.* iv (1969), 184–96; J. R. Hunt, 'The Widnes School Board, 1874–1903', *Historic Soc. Lancs. & Ches. Trans.* cvi (1954), 145–7; and for Manchester, **7975.**

7862 LEESE (JOHN). Personalities and power in English education. Leeds. 1950.

Other gen. biog. studs. incl. Arthur Valentine Judges, ed., *Pioneers of English education* . . ., 1952, and 'The educational influence of the Webbs', *Brit. J. Educ. Studs.* x (1961–2), 33–48, and Frances Julia Wedgwood, *Nineteenth-century teachers and other essays*, 1909.

ARNOLD. For Matthew Arnold see **7878** and **8328.**

**7863 DICKENS.** Dickens and education. By Philip Arthur William Collins. 1963.

Better than John Manning, *Dickens on education*, Toronto 1959. See also **8354.**

**7864 FITCH.** Sir Joshua Fitch: an account of his life and work. By Alfred Leslie Lilley. 1906.

An important figure in the history of teacher training colleges, university, and women's education.

**7865 HUXLEY.** T. H. Huxley on education. By Cyril Bibby. Camb. 1971.

See also **8609.**

**7866 KAY-SHUTTLEWORTH.** The life and work of Sir James Kay-Shuttleworth. By Frank Smith. 1923.

The first head of the Educ. Dept. See also B. C. Bloomfield, 'Sir James Kay-Shuttleworth (1804–1877): a trial bibliography', *Brit. J. Educ. Studs.* ix (1960–1), 155–77, addenda, ibid. x (1961–2), 76–80, and **7843.**

**7867 KEKEWICH.** The Education Department and after. By Sir George William Kekewich. 1920.

Kekewich was head of the dept., 1890–1903.

**7868 LINGEN.** 'Ralph Lingen, secretary to the Education Department, 1849–1870'. *Brit. J. Educ. Studs.* xvi (1968), 138–63.

**7869 MASON.** The story of Charlotte Mason, 1842–1923. By Essex Cholmondeley. 1960.

Founder of Parents' Nat. Educ. Union which publ. *In Memoriam: Charlotte M. Mason,* 1923.

**7870 ROGERS.** Reminiscences of William Rogers, rector of St. Botolph, Bishopsgate. Comp. by Robert Henry Hadden. 1888.

An indefatigable educ. pioneer.

**7871 SADLER.** Michael Ernest Sadler (Sir Michael Sadler, K.C.S.I.), 1861–1943: a memoir. By his son Michael Thomas Harvey Sadleir. 1949.

One of the great figures in English educ. See also Lynda Grier, *Achievement in education: the work of Michael Ernest Sadler, 1885–1935,* 1952, and Daniel Norman Chester, 'Robert Morant and Michael Sadler', *Public. Admin.* xxviii (1950), 109–16.

**7872 SHAW.** [George Bernard] Shaw on education. By Louis Simon. N.Y. 1958.

### (c) *Contemporary Comment*

**7873 THE EDUCATIONAL TIMES.** 1847–1923+.

The longest-lived of the educ. periodicals. See also [*Quarterly*] *journal of education . . .,* 1867–1958, and *The Times educational supplement,* 1910+. Pt. II of the *Transactions* of the National Association for the Promotion of Social Science, 1857–84, also dealt with educ.

7874 SPENCER (HERBERT). Education: intellectual, moral and physical. 1861. 14th thousand. 1888.

7875 SENIOR (NASSAU WILLIAM). Suggestions on popular education. 1861.

7876 THRING (EDWARD). Education and school. Camb. & Lond. 1864. 2nd edn. 1867.

7877 MILL (JOHN STUART). Inaugural address delivered to the University of St. Andrews, Feb. 1st, 1867. 1867.

Mill's most famous venture into educ. theory. See also Francis Alexander Cavenagh, ed., *James & John Stuart Mill on education*, Camb. 1931 and **10136**.

7878 ARNOLD (MATTHEW). Matthew Arnold and the education of the new order: a selection of Arnold's writings on education. Ed. by Peter Smith and Geoffrey Summerfield. Camb. 1969.

Intended to suppl. his *Culture and anarchy*, ed. by John Dover Wilson, Camb. 1932, new edn. Camb. 1960. See also William Fraser Connell, *The educational thought and influence of Matthew Arnold*, 1950, and Leonard Huxley, ed., *Thoughts on education chosen from the writings of Matthew Arnold*, 1912. Arnold's *Schools and universities on the continent*, 1868, is one of the better English reactions to European educ.

7879 PLAYFAIR (LYON), *Baron Playfair*. On primary and technical education: two lectures. Edin. 1870.

7880 BARTLEY (*Sir* GEORGE CHRISTOPHER TROUT). The schools for the people: containing, the history, development and present working of each description of English school for the industrial and poorer classes. 1871.

The first work of its kind. Important. See also his *The educational condition and requirements of one square mile in the East-end of London: prepared at the request of the council of the Society of Arts, Manufactures and Commerce*, 2nd edn. 1870, which reports on a systematic inquiry.

7881 WIESE (LUDWIG ADOLF). German letters on English education written during an educational tour in 1876. Trans. by Leonhard Schmitz. Lond. 1877. N.Y. 1879.

A far-ranging survey by the author of an earlier study which made quite a stir, *German letters on English education*, trans. by William Delafield Arnold, 1854.

7882 ROBSON (EDWARD ROBERT). School architecture: being practical remarks on the planning, designing, building and furnishing of school houses. 1874. 2nd edn. 1877.

A good book, which reflects contemp. ideas.

7883 HERBERT (AUBERON EDWARD WILLIAM MOLYNEUX) *ed.* The sacrifice of education to examination: letters from 'all sorts and conditions of men'. 1889.

7884   LE CLERC (MAX). L'éducation des classes moyennes et dirigeantes en Angleterre. Paris. 1894.

See also his *Les professions et la société en Angleterre*, Paris 1894.

7885   WARE (*Sir* FABIAN ARTHUR GOULSTONE). Educational reform: the task of the Board of Education. 1900.

See also his *Educational foundations of trade and industry*, 1901. Cp. Henry Spencer Wilkinson, ed., *The nation's need: chapters on education*, 1903.

7886   LOCKYER (*Sir* JOSEPH NORMAN). Education and national progress: essays and addresses, 1870–1905. 1906.

See also **8737**.

7887   MAGNUS (*Sir* PHILIP). Educational aims and efforts, 1880–1910. 1910.

See also his *Industrial education*, **8166**. For Magnus's life see Frank Foden, *Philip Magnus: Victorian educational pioneer*, 1970.

## 2. Schools

### (a) *Public Schools*

7888   OGILVIE (VIVIAN). The English public schools. 1957.

Standard. Replaces a considerable number of general introductions of little value. A few are still worth consulting, e.g. Alfred Bowen Badger, *The public schools and the nation*, 1944.

7889   BAMFORD (THOMAS WILLIAM). Rise of the public schools: a study of boys' public boarding schools in England and Wales from 1837 to the present day. 1967.

7890   MACK (EDWARD CLARENCE). Public schools and British opinion 1780 to 1860: an examination of the relationship between contemporary ideas and the evolution of an English institution. 2 v. London. 1938–41. N.Y. 1939–41.

Good. Vol. 1 covers 1780–1860, vol. 2, 1860+. See also A. Jamieson, 'F. W. Farrar and novels of the public schools', *Brit. J. Educ. Studs.* xvi (1968), 271–8.

7891   NEWSOME (DAVID). Godliness & good learning: four studies on a Victorian ideal. 1961.

7892   WILKINSON (RUPERT HUGH). The prefects: British leadership and the public-school tradition: a comparative study in the making of rulers. 1964. Publ. in N.Y. as Gentlemanly power . . . 1964.

7893   PERCIVAL (ALICIA CONSTANCE). The origins of the Headmasters' Conference. 1969.

7894　HOW (FREDERICK DOUGLAS). Six great schoolmasters: Hawtrey, Moberly, Kennedy, Vaughan, Temple, Bradley. 1904.

For other great headmasters see the lives of Thring (**7925**), Sanderson (**7913**), Sewell (**7915**), and Peter Lyman Stansky, 'Lyttelton and Thring: a study in nineteenth-century education', *Victorian Studs.* v (1961–2), 205–23.

7895　CLARENDON COMMISSION ON THE PUBLIC SCHOOLS. Report of Her Majesty's commissioners appointed to inquire into the revenues and management of certain colleges and schools, and the studies pursued and instruction given therein [Chairman: Earl of Clarendon]. [3288] H.C. (1864) XX, 1 and XXI, 1.

Deals with Eton, Winchester, Westminster, Charterhouse, St. Paul's, Merchant Taylors', Harrow, Rugby, and Shrewsbury schools. See also *Report from the select committee of the House of Lords on the Public Schools Bill* [*H.L.*] [Chairman: Earl of Clarendon]. H.C. 481 (1865). X, 263.

7896　SCHOOLS INQUIRY COMMISSION. [TAUNTON COMMIS-SION.] Report of the commissioners [Chairman: Lord Taunton]. [3966] H.C. (1867–8). XXVIII, pt. I, 1. Minutes of evidence etc. [3966–I to XX] H.C. (1867–8). XXVIII, pts. II to XVII.

One of the most comprehensive inquiries of the period, running to 21 v., dealing with schools not investigated by the Newcastle (**7983**) or Clarendon (**7895**) commissions. See also *Christ's Hospital inquiry commission* [Chairman: Spencer H. Walpole]. *Report.* [C. 1849] H.C. (1877). XXVI, 39.

7897　THE PUBLIC SCHOOLS' YEAR BOOK [: the official book of reference of the Headmasters' Conference]. 1890+.

7898　PATON'S LIST OF SCHOOLS AND TUTORS: an aid to parents in the selection of schools. 1898/9+.

7899　ARDINGLY. Reginald Perry, *Ardingly, 1858–1946: a history of the school,* 1951.

7900　BROMSGROVE. Henry Edward McLaughlan Icely, *Bromsgrove school through four centuries,* Oxf. 1953.

7901　CHARTERHOUSE. Edward Mellor Jameson, *Charterhouse,* 1937. William Foster Veale, *From a new angle: reminiscences of Charterhouse, 1880–1945,* Winchester 1957.

7902　CITY OF LONDON. Aubrey Edward Douglas-Smith, *The City of London school,* Oxf. 1937, 2nd edn. 1965.

7903　CLIFTON. Octavius Francis Christie, *A history of Clifton College, 1860–1934,* 1935, and *Clifton schooldays, 1879–1885,* 1930. John Rickards Mozley, *Clifton memories,* Bristol 1927. *James M. Wilson: an autobiography, 1836–1931,* 1932. Nicholas Geoffrey Lemprière Hammond, ed., *Centenary essays on Clifton College,* Bristol 1962.

7904 ETON. Lewis Vernon Harcourt, Viscount Harcourt, *An Eton biblio-graphy*, 1898, new edn. 1902. [Maurice] Christopher Hollis, *Eton: a history*, 1960. Sir Henry Churchill Maxwell Lyte, *A history of Eton College* . . ., 1875, 4th edn. 1911. Lionel Stanley Rice Byrne and Ernest Lee Churchill, *Changing Eton: a survey of conditions based on the history of Eton since the royal commission of 1862–64*, 1937. Charles Robert Leslie Fletcher, *Edmond Warre, D.D., C.B., C.V.O., sometime headmaster and provost of Eton College*, 1922. Francis Warre Cornish, ed., *Extracts from the letters and journals of William Cory, author of Ionica*, 1897. Faith Compton Mackenzie, *William Cory: a biography* . . ., 1950. Reginald Baliol Brett, Viscount Esher, *Ionicus (William Cory)*, 1923. Arthur Campbell Ainger, *Memories of Eton sixty years ago*, 1917. Gilbert James Duke Coleridge, *Eton in the seventies*, 1912. Henry Stephens Salt, *Memories of bygone Eton*, 1928, and *The nursery of Toryism: reminiscences of Eton under Hornby*, 1911. Edward Lyttelton, *Memories and hopes*, 1925. Percy Lubbock, *Shades of Eton*, 1929. Hugh Vibart Macnaghten, *Fifty years of Eton in prose and verse*, 1924. Alfred Lubbock, *Memories of Eton and Etonians* . . ., 1899.

7905 FELSTED. Michael Romilly Craze, *The history of Felsted school, 1564–1947*, Ipswich 1955.

7906 HAILEYBURY. Lionel Sumner Milford, *Haileybury college: past and present*, 1909. Robert Leslie Ashcroft, *Haileybury, 1908–61* . . ., Haileybury 1961.

7907 HARROW. Edward Dalrymple Laborde, *Harrow school: yesterday and today*, 1948. Edmund Whytehead Howson and George Townsend Warner, eds., *Harrow school*, 1898. William Edward Bowen, *Edward Bowen: a memoir*, 1902. Edward Graham, *The Harrow life of Henry Montagu Butler*, 1920. *Robert Somervell: for thirty-three years assistant master and bursar at Harrow school: chapters of autobiography*, ed. by his sons, 1935. Charles Harry Powell Mayo, *Reminiscences of a Harrow master*, 1928. J. E. C. Welldon, *Recollections* (**3731**).

7908 LANCING. Basil Walter Thomas Handford, *Lancing: a history of SS. Mary and Nicolas College, Lancing, 1848–1930*, Oxf. 1933. Samuel Roebuck Brooke, *Sam Brooke's journal: the diary of a Lancing schoolboy, 1860–1865* . . ., Lancing 1953.

7909 MALVERN. Ralph Klaus Blumenau, *A history of Malvern College, 1865 to 1965*, 1965. Sydney Rhodes James, *Seventy years* . . ., 1926.

7910 MARLBOROUGH. Arthur Granville Bradley and others, *A history of Marlborough College during fifty years from its foundation to the present time*, 1893, rev. edn. 1923.

7911 MERCHANT TAYLORS'. Frederick William Marsden Draper, *Four centuries of Merchant Taylors' school, 1561–1961*, 1962.

7912  MILL HILL. Norman George Brett-James, *The History of Mill Hill school, 1807–1907*, 1909, rev. edn. 1938.

7913  OUNDLE. William George Walker, *A history of the Oundle schools*, 1956. Herbert George Wells, *The story of a great schoolmaster: being a plain account of the life and ideas of Sanderson of Oundle*, 1924.

7914  POCKLINGTON. Percy Cooper Sands and Christopher Matthew Haworth, *A history of Pocklington School, East Yorkshire, 1514–1950* [1951].

7915  RADLEY. Alfred Kenneth Boyd, *The history of Radley College, 1847–1947*, Oxf. 1948. Lionel James, *A forgotten genius: Sewell of St. Columba's and Radley*, 1945.

7916  REPTON. Bernard William Thomas, ed., *Repton, 1557 to 1957*, 1957.

7917  ROSSALL. John Frederick Rowbotham, *The history of Rossall school*, Manch. 1894, 2nd edn. 1901. William Furness, ed., *The centenary history of Rossall school*, Aldershot 1945.

7918  RUGBY. John Barclay Hope Simpson, *Rugby since Arnold: a history of Rugby school from 1842*, 1967. Thomas Hughes, *Tom Brown's school days: by an old boy*, 1857, 6th edn. with new preface, 1868. Claude Ronald Evers, *Rugby*, 1939.

7919  ST. PAUL'S. Cyril Moses Picciotto, *St. Paul's school*, 1939. Frank Reyner Salter, *St. Paul's school, 1909–1959*, 1959. Sir Michael Francis Joseph McDonnell, *The annals of St. Paul's school*, priv. pr. 1959.

7920  ST. PETER'S, YORK. Angelo Raine, *History of St. Peter's school, York . . .*, 1926.

7921  SEDBERGH. Henry Lowther Clarke, *History of Sedbergh school, 1525–1925*, Sedbergh 1925.

7922  SHERBORNE. Arthur Bellyse Gourlay, *A history of Sherborne school*, Winchester 1951.

7923  SHREWSBURY. James Basil Oldham, *A history of Shrewsbury school, 1552–1952*, Oxf. 1952.

7924  TONBRIDGE. David Churchill Somervell, *A history of Tonbridge school*, 1947. Septimus Rivington, *The history of Tonbridge school: from its foundation in 1553 . . .*, 1869, 4th edn. 1925.

7925  UPPINGHAM. Sir George Robert Parkin, *Edward Thring: headmaster of Uppingham school: life, diary and letters*, 2 v. 1898, abridged edn. 1900.

7926  WELLINGTON. David Newsome, *A history of Wellington College, 1859–1959*, 1959.

7927  WESTMINSTER. John Dudley Carleton, *Westminster* [*school: a history*], 1938, rev. edn. 1965. Lawrence Edward Tanner, *Westminster school*, 1934, 2nd edn. 1951.

7928  WINCHESTER. Christopher Wentworth Dilke, *Dr. Moberly's mint-mark: a study of Winchester College*, 1965. John D'Ewes Evelyn Firth, *Winchester College*, 1949. Lady Laura Elizabeth Ridding, *George Ridding* (**3681**). Thomas James Henderson Bishop and Rupert Wilkinson, *Winchester and the public school élite: a statistical analysis*, 1967.

### (b) Denominational Schools

7929  BOARD OF EDUCATION. A short list of books, pamphlets and papers, dealing with the subject of religious instruction in schools. [Cd. 3208] H.C. (1906). XC, 291.

A very useful bibliog. covering all countries. See also Board of Educ., *Statement showing syllabuses of religious instruction issued by diocesan and other associations for the use of Church of England schools*. [Cd. 3074] H.C. (1906). XC, 191.

7930  BEST (GEOFFREY FRANCIS ANDREW). 'The religious difficulties of national education in England, 1800–70'. *Camb. Hist. J.* xii (1956), 155–73.

See also Tom Fleming Kinloch, *Pioneers of religious education*, Oxf. 1939.

7931  MURPHY (JAMES). The religious problem in English education: the crucial experiment. Liverpool. 1959.

Liverpool's experiment with non-sectarian educ.

7932  CRUICKSHANK (MARJORIE). Church and state in English education, 1870 to the present day. 1963.

See also James Murphy, *Church, state and schools in Britain, 1800–1970*, 1971.

7933  SACHS (BENJAMIN). The religious issue in the state schools of England & Wales, 1902–1914: a nation's quest for human dignity. Albuquerque, New Mexico. 1961.

7934  ROGERS (ALAN). 'Churches and children: a study in the controversy over the 1902 Education Act'. *Brit. J. Educ. Studs.* viii (1959–60), 29–51.

Argues that the 1902 Act stemmed from religious and political, not educational, motives. See also Charmian Cannon, 'The influence of religion on educational policy, 1902–1944', ibid. xii (1963–4), 143–60.

7935  BURGESS (HENRY JAMES). Enterprise in education: the story of the work of the established church in the education of the people prior to 1870. 1958.

7936  BROWN (CHARLES KENNETH FRANCIS). The Church's part in education, 1833–1941, with special reference to the work of the National Society. 1942.

See also Robert Gregory, *Elementary education: some account of its rise and progress in England*, National Soc., 1895.

7937 CLARKE (WILLIAM KEMP LOWTHER). A history of the S.P.C.K. 1959.

A good short hist. For facts and dates it is still advisable to refer to William Osborn Bird Allen and Edmund McClure, *Two hundred years: the history of the Society for Promoting Christian Knowledge, 1698–1898*, 1898, and the annual reports of the Soc.

7938 BELL (ENID HESTER CHATAWAY MOBERLY). A history of the Church Schools Company, 1883–1958. 1958.

7939 HEENEY (BRIAN). Mission to the middle classes: the Woodard schools, 1848–91. Church Hist. Soc. 89. 1969.

See also Kenneth Escott Kirk, bishop, *The story of the Woodard schools*, 1937, rev. edn. 1952, and Sir John Lonsdale Otter, *Nathaniel Woodard: a memoir of his life*, 1925.

7940 DOCKING (J. W.). Victorian schools and scholars: Church of England elementary schools in nineteenth-century Coventry. Hist. Assoc. Coventry Branch. 1967.

7941 PRITCHARD (FRANK CYRIL). Methodist secondary education: a history of the contribution of Methodism to secondary education in the United Kingdom. 1949.

See also Arthur Glendinning Ives, *Kingswood school in Wesley's day and since*, 1970.

7942 STEWART (WILLIAM ALEXANDER CAMPBELL). Quakers and education, as seen in their schools in England. 1953.

A hist. of Quaker schools. See also Francis Edward Pollard, *A history of Sidcot School: a hundred years of West-country Quaker education, 1808–1908*, 1908, and Francis Edward Pollard, ed., *Bootham School*, 1926.

7943 BARNES (ARTHUR STAPLYTON). The Catholic schools of England. 1926.

See also Hubert Chadwick, *St. Omers to Stonyhurst: a history of two centuries*, 1962; Percy Hetherington Fitzgerald, *Stonyhurst memories: or, six years at school*, 1895; George Gruggen and Joseph Keating, *Stonyhurst: its past history and life in the present*, 1901; John Gerard, *Stonyhurst College . . .*, Belfast, etc. 1894; [Philip] Justin McCann and Columba Cary-Elwes, eds., *Ampleforth and its origins: essays . . .*, 1952; and Peter Levi, *Beaumont, 1861–1961*, 1961.

7944 MCCLELLAND (VINCENT ALAN). 'The Protestant Alliance and Roman Catholic schools, 1872–74'. *Victorian Studs.* viii (1964–5), 173–82.

7945 BATTERSBY (WILLIAM JOHN). The De La Salle Brothers in Great Britain: the story of a century of effort and achievement in the domain of English education. 1954.

Battersby has also publ. a life of the leading brother of the period, *Brother Potamian, educator and scientist*, 1953, and *St. Joseph's College, Beulah Hill, 1855–1955*, 1955, a hist. of the leading school founded by the brothers. See also his *History of the Institute of the Brothers of the Christian Schools in the nineteenth century, 1850–1900*, 1963.

7946 RICH (EDWIN ERNEST). 'Education and the dissenters: a sidelight on nineteenth-century political thought'. *Economica* x (1930), 188–99.

7947  NATIONAL EDUCATION LEAGUE. Monthly paper. 1869–77.

The organ of the nonconformist opponents of the 1870 Education Act. For their work see the lives of Dale (3788), Chamberlain (750), and Crosskey (3813).

7948  HOLLOWELL. James Hirst Hollowell and the movement for civic control in education. By William Evans and William Claridge. Manch. 1911.

Congregationalist minister and secretary of the Northern Counties Education League.

7949  MOORE (THOMAS). The education brief on behalf of voluntary schools. 1890.

A handbook for the advocates of voluntary schools.

7950  PASSIVE RESISTANCE LEAGUE. The crusader. 1903–07.

The organ of those who fought the 1902 Education Act. See also Charles Thomas Bateman, *For conscience sake: manual of the passive resistance movement*, 1903, and Edmund Charles Rawlings, *The free churchman's guide to the Education Act, 1902 . . .*, Nat. Council of the Evangelical Free Churches, 1903.

7951  FAIRBAIRN (ANDREW MARTIN). Education : national or denominational? 1902.

A prominent Nonconformist on the 1902 Act.

### (c) *Secondary Schools*

7952  TATE (WILLIAM EDWARD). 'Educational records: part II. Some sources for the history of English grammar schools'. *Brit. J. Educ. Studs.* i (1952–3), 164–75; ii (1953–4), 67–81, 145–65.

7953  DENT (HAROLD COLLETT). Secondary education for all: origins and developments in England. 1949.

7954  ARCHER (RICHARD LAWRENCE). Secondary education in the nineteenth century. Camb. 1921.

7955  GRAVES (JOHN TIARKS RANKE). Policy & progress in secondary education, 1902–42. 1943.

7956  KAZAMIAS (ANDREAS MICHAEL). Politics, society and secondary education in England. Phila. 1966.

The Bryce commission (7960), and after.

7957  DEMOGEOT (JACQUES CLAUDE) *and* MONTUCCI (HENRI) De l'enseignement secondaire en Angleterre et en Écosse: rapport addressé à Son Exc. M. le Ministre de l'Instruction Publique. Paris. 1868.

One of the best contemp. reports.

7958  ENDOWED SCHOOLS COMMISSION. Report of the Endowed Schools commissioners [Chairman: Lord Lyttelton] to the Lords of the committee of Her Majesty's Privy Council on Education. [C. 524] H.C. (1872). XXIV, 1. Further report. [C. 1142] H.C. (1875). XXVIII, 1.

See also *Report from the select committee on Endowed Schools Act (1869)* [Chairman: William Edward Forster]. H.C. 254 (1873). VIII, 299, *Report from the select committee on Endowed Schools Acts* [Chairman: Sir Lyon Playfair]. H.C. 191 (1886). IX, 1. Further report. H.C. 120 (1887). IX, 235, and Peter Gordon, 'Some sources for the history of the Endowed Schools Commission, 1869–1900', *Brit. J. Educ. Studs.* xiv (1965–6), no. 3, 59–73.

7959 ACLAND (*Sir* ARTHUR HERBERT DYKE) *and* SMITH (*Sir* HUBERT LLEWELLYN) *eds.* Studies in secondary education. 1892.

7960 BRYCE COMMISSION ON SECONDARY EDUCATION. Royal commission on secondary education: report of the commissioners [Chairman: James Bryce]. [C. 7862] H.C. (1895). XLIII, 1. Minutes of evidence &c. [C. 7862–I–VIII] H.C. (1895). XLIV–XLIX.

A far-reaching inquiry.

7961 SADLER (*Sir* MICHAEL ERNEST). Report on secondary education in Liverpool, including the training of teachers for public elementary schools. 1904. 2nd edn. [? 1904.]

Sadler also publ. parallel reports on secondary and higher educ. in *Sheffield*, 1903, *Derbyshire*, Derby 1905, *Essex*, Chelmsford 1906, *Huddersfield*, 1904, *Birkenhead*, 1904, *Newcastle-upon-Tyne*, Newcastle 1905, *Hampshire*, 1904, *Exeter*, 1905.

7962 LYTTELTON (EDWARD). Schoolboys and school work. 1909.

A plea for a broadening of the secondary school curriculum by the headmaster of Eton.

7963 BOARD OF EDUCATION. Report of the consultative committee on examinations in secondary schools [Chairman: A. H. Dyke Acland]. [Cd. 6004] H.C. (1911). XVI, 159.

A careful analysis of the existing system of examinations. See also Olive L. Banks, 'Morant and the secondary school regulations of 1904', *Brit. J. Educ. Studs.* iii (1954–5), 33–41.

7964 BINGLEY GRAMMAR. Edward Ernest Dodd, *A history of the Bingley grammar school, 1529–1929*, Bradford 1930.

7965 HULL GRAMMAR. John Lawson, *A town grammar school through six centuries: a history of Hull grammar school against its local background*, 1963.

7966 KING EDWARD'S, BIRMINGHAM. Thomas Winter Hutton, *King Edward's school, Birmingham, 1552–1952*, Oxf. 1952.

7967 LEEDS GRAMMAR. Aubrey Charles Price, *History of the Leeds grammar school*, 1919.

7968 MANCHESTER GRAMMAR. Alfred Alexander Mumford, *The Manchester grammar school, 1515–1915, a regional study of the advancement of learning in Manchester since the Reformation*, 1919. James Anson Graham and Brian Arthur Phythian, eds., *The Manchester grammar school, 1515–1965*, Manch. 1965.

7969  NOTTINGHAM HIGH. Adam Waugh Thomas, *A history of Nottingham high school, 1513–1953*, Nottingham 1957.

## (d) *Elementary Schools*

7970  PUGH (RALPH BERNARD). 'Educational records: I: sources for the history of English primary schools'. *Brit J. Educ. Studs.* i (1952–3), 43–51.

7971  BIRCHENOUGH (CHARLES). History of elementary education in England and Wales from 1800 to the present day. 1914. 3rd edn. 1938.

Fuller than Frank Smith, *A history of English elementary education, 1760–1902*, 1931. Both are largely repl. by Sturt (**7972**). There are a number of older works incl. Henry Holman, *English national education: a sketch of the rise of public elementary schools in England*, Victorian era series, 1898.

7972  STURT (MARY). The education of the people: a history of primary education in England and Wales in the nineteenth century. N.Y. 1966. London. 1967.

Standard. See also W. P. McCann, 'Elementary education in England and Wales on the eve of the 1870 Education Act', *J. Educ. Admin. & Hist.* ii (1969–70), 20–9, R. Szreter, 'The origins of full-time compulsory education at five', *Brit. J. Educ. Studs.* xiii (1964–5), 16–28, and David Wardle, *English popular education, 1780–1970*, Camb. 1970.

7973  RICH (ERIC). The Education Act, 1870. 1970.

A useful summary, but see also *Brit. J. Educ. Studs.* xviii, no. 2 (June 1970), which is largely devoted to commemorating the centenary of the Act. It includes the following articles: W. H. G. Armytage, 'The 1870 Education Act', 121–33; W. P. McCann, 'Trade unionists, artisans and the 1870 Education Act', 134–50; D. A. Turner, '1870: the state and the infant school system', 151–65; Nigel Middleton, 'The Education Act of 1870 as the start of the modern concept of the child', 166–79; and N. J. Richards, 'Religious controversy and the school boards, 1870–1902', 180–96, and 'Henry Edward Manning and the Education Bill of 1870', 197–212. The standard guide to the law of the Act was Sir Hugh Owen, *The Elementary Education Act, 1870 . . .*, 1870, 23rd edn. [*The Elementary Education Acts*] 1936.

7974  ADAMS (FRANCIS). History of the elementary school contest in England. 1882.

Important for the controversy that led to the 1870 Education Act.

7975  MALTBY (SAMUEL EDWIN). Manchester and the movement for national elementary education, 1800–1870. Manch. 1918.

For educ. in Manchester see also **7985**, Simon (**9422**), John Watts, 'Fifteen years of school board work in Manchester', *Manch. Stat. Soc. Trans.* (1885–6), 81–116, and 'Elementary education in Manchester', ibid. (1882–3), 1–28, and William Edward Armitage Axon, 'Education in Salford . . .', ibid. 189–210.

7976  SELLMAN (ROGER RAYMOND). Devon village schools in the nineteenth century. Newton Abbot. 1967.

7977 JOHNSON (MARION). Derbyshire village schools in the nineteenth century. Newton Abbot. 1970.

7978 PALLISER (RAY). 'Workhouse education in county Durham, 1834–1870'. *Brit. J. Educ. Studs.* xvi (1968), 279–91.

7979 BINNS (HENRY BRYAN). A century of education: being the centenary history of the British & Foreign School Society, 1808–1908. 1908.

7980 RAYMONT (THOMAS). A history of the education of young children 1937.

See also Robert Robertson Rusk, *A history of infant education*, 1933, and David Salmon and Winifred Hindshaw, *Infant schools: their history and theory*, 1904.

7981 CUSDEN (PHOEBE E.). The English nursery school. 1938.

See also Margaret McMillan, *The nursery school*, 1919, and Albert Mansbridge, *Margare McMillan, prophet and pioneer*, 1932.

7982 BRAMWELL (ROBERT DENIS). Elementary school work, 1900–1925. Univ. of Durham Inst. of Educ. 1961.

7983 NEWCASTLE COMMISSION ON POPULAR EDUCATION. Report of the commissioners appointed to inquire into the state of popular education in England [Chairman: Duke of Newcastle]. [2794–I] H.C. (1861). XXI, pt. I, 1. Reports of assistant commissioners &c. [2794–II–VI] H.C. (1861). XXI, pt. I–VI. Correspondence &c. H.C. 231 (1861). XLVIII, 295. H.C. 354 (1861). XLVIII, 307. H.C. 410 (1861). XLVIII, 341. H.C. 325 (1861). XLVIII, 305.

One of the great 19th-cent. inquiries.

7984 NORTHCOTE COMMITTEE ON EDUCATION OF DESTITUTE CHILDREN. Report from the select committee on the education of destitute children [Chairman: Sir Stafford Northcote]. H.C. 460 (1861). VII, 395.

See also *Reports made to the Poor Law Board on the education of pauper children, by W. H. T. Hawley, Esq., Robert Weale, Esq., Sir John Walsham, Bart., and Andrew Doyle, Esq., Poor Law inspectors.* H.C. 510 (1862). XLIX, pt. I, 513.

7985 EDUCATION DEPARTMENT. Return, confined to the municipal boroughs of Birmingham, Leeds, Liverpool, and Manchester, of all schools for the poorer classes of children . . . H.C. 91 (1870). LIV, 265.

A comprehensive ser. of reports on the schools of the big towns.

7986 MANN (HORACE). 'The resources of popular education in England and Wales: present and future'. *Stat. Soc. J.* xxv (1862), 50–71.

See also William Lucas Sargant, 'On the progress of elementary education', ibid. xxx (1867), 80–137.

7987  HAMILTON (ROWLAND). 'Popular education in England and Wales before and after the Elementary Education Act of 1870'. *Stat. Soc. J.* xlvi (1883), 283–349.

Cont. by Rowland Hamilton, 'Popular education in England and Wales since 1882', ibid. liii (1890), 50–112. See also Frederic J. Mouat, 'On the education and training of the children of the poor', ibid. xliii (1880), 183–250.

7988  ARNOLD (MATTHEW). Reports on elementary schools, 1852–1882. Ed. by Francis Richard John Sandford, Baron Sandford. 1889. New edn. 1908.

7989  EDUCATION DEPARTMENT. Report of F. J. Mouat, Esq., M.D., Local Government Board Inspector, and Captain J. D. Bowly, R.E., on the home and cottage system of training and educating the children of the poor . . . H.C. 285 (1878). LX, 297.

7990  CROSS COMMISSION ON ELEMENTARY EDUCATION. First report of the royal commission appointed to inquire into the working of the Elementary Education Acts, England and Wales [Chairman: Viscount Cross]. [C. 4863] H.C. (1886). XXV, 1. Second report. [C. 5056] H.C. (1887). XXIX, 1. Third report. [C. 5158] H.C. (1887). XXX, 1. Final report. [C. 5485] H.C. (1888). XXXV, 1. Digest of evidence. [C. 5329] H.C. (1888). XXXVII, 1. Appendixes. [C. 5485-I–IV] H.C. (1888). XXXV, 527, XXXVI, 1+.

For light relief there is also the foolish *Report of Dr. Crichton-Browne to the Education department upon the alleged over-pressure of work in public elementary schools* . . . H.C. 293 (1884). LXI, 259.

7991  MUNDELLA COMMITTEE ON EDUCATION OF CHILDREN IN INSTITUTIONS. Report of the departmental committee appointed by the Local Government Board to inquire into the existing systems for the maintenance and education of children under the charge of managers of district schools and boards of guardians in the metropolis and to advise as to any changes that may be desirable [Chairman: Anthony John Mundella]. [C. 8027] H.C. (1896). XLIII, 1. Minutes of evidence and appendixes. [C. 8032-3] H.C. (1896). XLIII, 189, 1037.

7992  CUNYNGHAME COMMITTEE ON EMPLOYMENT OF SCHOOL CHILDREN. Report of the inter-departmental committee on the employment of school children, appointed by H.M. Principal Secretary of State for the Home Department [Chairman: H. H. S. Cunynghame]. [Cd. 849] H.C. (1902). XXV, 261. Minutes of evidence. [Cd. 895] H.C. (1902). XXV, 287.

See also *Report of departmental committee appointed to inquire into the conditions of school attendance and child labour* [Chairman: William Tucker]. H.C. 311 (1893–4). LXVIII, 545, and *Report of the inter-departmental committee on partial exemption from school attendance* [Chairman: Charles Trevelyan]. [Cd. 4791] H.C. (1909). XVII, 731. Minutes of evidence. [Cd. 4887] H.C. (1909). XVII, 753.

7993  SIMPKINSON COMMITTEE ON MEDICAL INSPECTION AND FEEDING OF CHILDREN. Report of the inter-departmental committee on medical inspection and feeding of children attending public elementary schools

[Chairman: H. W. Simpkinson]. [Cd. 2779] H.C. (1906). XLVII, 1. Minutes of evidence. [Cd. 2784] H.C. (1906). XLVII, 157.

7994 BOARD OF EDUCATION. Reports on children under five years of age in public elementary schools by women inspectors of the Board of Education. [Cd. 2726] H.C. (1906). XC, 29.

See also Board of Education, *Report of the consultative committee upon the school attendance of children below the age of five.* [Cd. 4259] H.C. (1908). LXXXII, 527.

(e) *Experimental Schools*

7995 STEWART (WILLIAM ALEXANDER CAMPBELL) *and* McCANN (WILLIAM PHILIP). The educational innovators. Vol. I. 1750–1880. Vol. II. Progressive schools, 1881–1967. 2 v. 1967–8. New edn. [Progressives and Radicals in English education, 1750–1950.] 1 v. 1972.

See also Alice Woods, *Educational experiments in England*, 1920, *Co-education . . .*, 1903, and *Advance in co-education . . .*, 1919, L. B. Pekin, pseud. of Reginald Snell, *Progressive schools: their principles and practice*, 1934, and *Co-education in its historical and theoretical setting*, 1939, and William Boyd and Wyatt Trevelyan Rawson Rawson, *The story of the new education*, 1965.

7996 SELLECK (RICHARD JOSEPH WHEELER). The new education, 1870–1914. 1968.

7997 ABBOTSHOLME. Cecil Reddie, *Abbotsholme, 1889–1899: or, ten years' work in an educational laboratory*, 1900. Bernard Mordaunt Ward, *Reddie of Abbotsholme*, 1934.

7998 BEDALES. John Haden Badley, *Bedales: a pioneer school*, 1923, and *Memories and reflections*, 1955.

7999 SPRING GROVE. Cyril Bibby, 'A Victorian experiment in international education: the college at Spring Grove', *Brit. J. Educ. Studs.* v (1956–7), 25–36.

8000 SUMMERHILL. Alexander Sutherland Neill, *That dreadful school*, 1937, and *Summerhill: a radical approach to childrearing*, N.Y. 1960.

(f) *Girls' Schools*

8001 KAMM (JOSEPHINE). Hope deferred: girls' education in English history. 1965.

Like Dorothy Gardiner, *English girlhood at school: a study of women's education through twelve centuries*, 1929, and Alicia Constance Percival, *The English miss: today & yesterday: ideals, methods and personalities in the education and upbringing of girls during the last hundred years*, 1939, too general to be of much value.

8002 ZIMMERN (ALICE). The renaissance of girls' education in England: a record of fifty years' progress. 1898.

The best general survey of the period. See also Frances Evelyn Greville, Countess of Warwick, ed., *Progress in women's education in the British Empire*, 1898, the report of the education section of the Victorian Era Exhibition, 1897.

8003 SENIOR (JANE ELIZABETH), *Mrs. Nassau Senior.* 'Education of girls in pauper schools: report on'. Third annual report of the Local Government Board, 1873–4. [C. 1071] H.C. (1874). XXV, 311–94.

A famous report. For adverse comment see *Observations on the report of Mrs. Senior to the Local Government Board, as to the effect on girls of the system of education at pauper schools, by Edward Carleton Tufnell, Esquire, late Inspector of Poor Law Schools in the Metropolitan district.* H.C. 10 (1875). LXIII, 299, with reply by Mrs. Nassau Senior. H.C. 155 (1875). LXIII, 343. See also the corresp. in Dorothea M. Hughes, *Memoir of Jane Elizabeth Senior,* Boston 1916, which also reprints the *Report.*

8004 BURSTALL (SARA ANNIE). English high schools for girls: their aims, organisation and management. 1907.

See also *The girls' school year book: the official book of reference of the Association of Head Mistresses,* 1906+, 1905+, and S. A. Burstall and Mary Alice Douglas, eds., *Public schools for girls: a series of papers on their history, aims and schemes of study,* 1911.

8005 KAMM (JOSEPHINE). How different from us: a biography of Miss Buss & Miss Beale. 1958.

A duo-biog. of the founders of the modern girls' public school.

8006 MAGNUS (LAURIE). The jubilee book of the Girls' Public Day School Trust, 1873–1923. Camb. 1923.

8007 CLARKE (AMY KEY). A history of the Cheltenham Ladies' College, 1853–1953. 1953. 2nd edn. 1954.

Other useful school hists. are Mary Alice Douglas and Cecily Ray Ash, *The Godolphin School, 1726–1926,* 1928; Sara Annie Burstall, *The story of the Manchester High School for Girls, 1871–1911,* Manch. 1911; Ruby Margaret Scrimgeour, ed., *North London Collegiate School, 1850–1950 . . .,* 1950; [Mary] Rosalie Glynn Grylls, *Queen's College, 1848–1948,* 1948; Shirley C. Gordon, 'Studies at Queen's College, Harley Street, 1848–1868', *Brit. J. Educ. Studs.* iii (1954–5), 144–54; Helen Winifred Sturge and Theodora Clark, *The Mount school, York . . .,* 1931; Dorothy Eva De Zouche, *Roedean school, 1855–1955,* priv. pr., Brighton 1955; Julia Mary Grant and others, *St. Leonard's School, 1877–1927,* 1927; and Elsie Pike and Constance E. Curryer, eds., *The story of Walthamstow Hall: A century of girls' education,* 1938.

8008 BEALE. Dorothea Beale of Cheltenham. By Elizabeth Raikes. 1908.

See also Florence Cecily Steadman, *In the days of Miss Beale: a study of her work and influence* [at Cheltenham] [1931].

8009 BUSS. Frances Mary Buss and her work for education. By Annie E. Ridley. 1895. 2nd edn. 1896.

See also S. Grace Toplis, ed., *Leaves from the notebooks of Frances Mary Buss . . .,* 1896, and Sara Annie Burstall, *Frances Mary Buss: an educational pioneer,* 1938.

8010 BURSTALL. Retrospect & prospect: sixty years of women's education. By Sara Annie Burstall. 1933.

Mainly on educ. movements in Manchester, where Miss Burstall was headmistress of the Girls' High School.

8011 GRAY. 'And gladly wolde he lerne and gladly teche'—Chaucer: a book about learning and teaching. By Frances Ralph Gray. 1931.

Miss Gray was first High Mistress of St. Paul's Girls' High School.

8012 MERCIER. The life of Winifred Mercier. By Lynda Grier. 1937.

8013 WEST (KATHARINE). Chapter of governesses: a study of the governess in English fiction, 1800–1949. 1949.

See also Bea Howe, *A galaxy of governesses*, 1954, the most attractive of a number of reminiscences of governesses, and Governesses' Benevolent Instn., *Annual report*, 1843+.

8014 BOOTH (JAMES). On the female education of the industrial classes . . . 1855.

8015 SHIRREFF (EMILY ANNE ELIZA). Intellectual education and its influence on the character and happiness of women. 1858. New edn. 1862.

Books on the same lines are Sir Alexander Grant, *Happiness and utility as promoted by the higher education of women* . . ., Edin. 1872, and Emily Jane Pfeiffer, *Women and work* . . ., 1888.

8016 DAVIES (EMILY). Thoughts on some questions relating to women, 1860–1908 . . . Ed. by Emily Elizabeth Constance Jones. Camb. 1910.

8017 [SEWELL (ELIZABETH MISSING).] Principles of education drawn from nature and revelation and applied to female education in the upper classes. 2 v. 1865. Abridged edn. 1914.

8018 DAVIES (EMILY). The higher education of women. 1866.

8019 BEALE (DOROTHEA). On the education of girls . . . 1866.

8020 HODGSON (WILLIAM BALLANTYNE). The education of girls and the employment of women of the upper classes educationally considered: two lectures. 1869.

8021 BEALE (DOROTHEA) *ed.* Reports issued by the Schools' Enquiry Commission on the education of girls. [1869.]

8022 SHIRREFF (EMILY ANNE ELIZA). The work of the National Union [for improving the education of women of all classes]. 1872. 2nd edn. 1873.

The Union also issued useful pamphlets incl. Maria Georgina Shirreff, afterwards Grey, *Paper on the special requirements for improving the education of girls*, 1872, Mary Gurney, *Are we to have education for our middle-class girls?* . . ., 1872, and Isabella Todd, *The education of girls of the middle classes*, 1874.

8023 COBBE (FRANCES POWER). The duties of women: a course of lectures. 1881. Posthumous edn. 1905.

8024  BURGON (JOHN WILLIAM). To educate young women like young men, and with young men: a thing inexpedient and immodest: a sermon. Oxf. & Lond. [1884.]

8025  BREMNER (CHRISTINA SINCLAIR). Education of girls and women in Great Britain. 1897.

### 3. UNIVERSITY EDUCATION

#### (a) *General*

8026  GREEN (VIVIAN HUBERT HOWARD). The universities. Harmondsworth. 1969.

A handy outline. See also Harold Collett Dent, *Universities in transition: a survey of past, present and future*, 1961, and Robert Oliver Berdahl, *British universities and the state*, Berkeley [Calif.] & Lond. 1959.

8027  ASHBY (*Sir* ERIC). Universities: British, Indian, African; a study in the ecology of higher education. Lond. & Camb., Mass. 1966.

8028  ROACH (JOHN PETER CHARLES). 'Victorian universities and the national intelligentsia'. *Victorian Studs.* iii (1959–60), 131–50.

Important.

8029  McCLELLAND (VINCENT ALAN). English Roman Catholics and higher education, 1830–1903. Oxf. 1973.

8030  DAVIES (EMILY). Women in the universities of England and Scotland. Camb. 1896.

8030a  SANDERSON (MICHAEL). The universities and British industry, 1850–1970. 1973.

8031  HILL (ALEX) *ed.* [First] Congress of the universities of the Empire, 1912: report of the proceedings. 1912.

Marks the beginning of modern inter-univ. co-operation, on which see Sir Eric Ashby, *Community of universities: an informal portrait of the Association of Universities of the British Commonwealth, 1913–1963*, Camb. 1963.

8032  UNIVERSITIES BUREAU OF THE BRITISH EMPIRE. Year-book of the universities of the empire. 1914+.

The first systematic directory of British univs. Now styled *Commonwealth Universities Year Book. Minerva* . . ., Strasbourg etc., 1891+, is a much older directory but gives little or no information not in *Whitaker's almanack*.

8033  WILLIAMS (JAMES). The law of the universities. 1910.

8034  PROCTOR (MORTIMER ROBINSON). The English university novel. Berkeley, Calif. 1957.

8035   PETCH (JAMES ALEXANDER). Fifty years of examining: the Joint Matriculation Board, 1903–1953. 1953.

University entrance examinations for a syndicate of chiefly northern univs. For other univ. examinations for schools see **7834**.

### (b) *Educational Policy*

8036   McPHERSON (ROBERT GRIER). Theory of higher education in nineteenth-century England. Athens, Ga. 1959.

8037   WHEWELL (WILLIAM). Of a liberal education in general: and with particular reference to the leading studies of the University of Cambridge. 3 pts. 1845–52.

A discussion by an eminent philosopher–scientist of the subjects of study and the univs., the methods of tuition at Cambridge, and recent changes. Forms part of a sequence of major works on univ. educ. See also his *On the principles of English university education*, 1837, 2nd edn. 1838.

8038   HAMILTON (*Sir* WILLIAM). Discussions on philosophy and literature, education and university reform: chiefly from the *Edinburgh Review* . . . 1852. 3rd edn. 1866.

A vehement attack on the English univs. by the best-known Scottish philosopher of the time, for whom see **8456**.

8039   NEWMAN (JOHN HENRY), *Cardinal*. The idea of a university defined and illustrated. 1873.

The most influential of all essays on univ. educ. in the 19th cent., first publ. as *Discourses on the scope and nature of university education*, Dublin 1852, 2nd edn. Lond. 1859. The best edn. is that of Charles Frederick Harrold, N.Y. 1947. Newman also publ. *Lectures and essays on university subjects*, 1859. For a discussion of Newman's ideas see Fergal McGrath, *The consecration of learning: lectures on Newman's idea of a university*, Dublin & N.Y. 1962. See also **3944**.

8040   FARRAR (FREDERICK WILLIAM) *ed*. Essays on a liberal education. 1867. 2nd edn. 1868.

8041   PATTISON (MARK). Suggestions of academical organisation: with especial reference to Oxford. Edin. 1868.

For Pattison's ideas see **8045, 8068, 8082**, and **8087**.

8042   HUXLEY (THOMAS HENRY). 'A liberal education and where to find it'. Lay sermons, addresses and reviews. 1870. 3rd edn. 1895.

8043   DEMOGEOT (JACQUES CLAUDE) and MONTUCCI (HENRI). De l'enseignement supérieur en Angleterre et en Écosse: rapport addressé à Son Exc. M. le Ministre de l'Instruction Publique. Paris. 1870.

8044   WESTCOTT (BROOKE FOSS), *bishop*. On some points in the religious office of the universities. 1873.

8045 PATTISON (MARK) *and others*. Essays on the endowment of research. By various writers. 1876.

8046 LOCKYER (*Sir* JOSEPH NORMAN). Education and national progress: essays and addresses, 1870–1905. 1906.

8047 HALDANE (RICHARD BURDON), *Viscount Haldane*. Universities and national life: three [four] addresses to students. 1910. 2nd edn. 1911.

Haldane and Lockyer (**8046**) were among the few who gave much attention to the role of univs. at the end of the 19th and the beginning of the 20th cents. For his work for univ. reform see **8133** and the essay by Sir Douglas William Logan, *Haldane and the University of London*, 1960.

8048 MACLEAN (GEORGE EDWIN). Studies in higher education in England and Scotland: with suggestions for universities and colleges in the United States. U.S. Dept. of the Interior, Bureau of Education Bull. 1917, no. 16. Wash. 1917.

Suppl. by his *Studies in higher education in Ireland and Wales . . .*, Bull. 1917, no. 15, Wash. 1917.

### (c) *Oxford and Cambridge*

#### (i) *General*

8049 MANSBRIDGE (ALBERT). The older universities of England: Oxford & Cambridge. 1923.

A useful short intro.

8050 CAMPBELL (LEWIS). On the nationalisation of the old English universities. 1901.

A good account of univ. reform written from an Oxford point of view. Tillyard (**8051**) provides a Cambridge account.

8051 TILLYARD (ALFRED ISAAC). A history of university reform from 1800 A.D. to the present time . . . Camb. 1913.

8052 MAYOR (JOSEPH BICKERSTETH). Affiliation of local colleges to the universities of Oxford and Cambridge. 1874.

8053 VENN (JOHN ARCHIBALD). Oxford and Cambridge matriculations, 1544–1906: with a graphic chart illustrating the varying fortunes of the two universities. Camb. 1908. 2dn edn. Camb. 1930.

Some preliminary conclusions about Oxford and Cambridge students are set out in Charles Arnold Anderson and Miriam Schnaper, *School and society in England: social backgrounds of Oxford and Cambridge students*, Wash. 1952, and in Jenkins and Jones (**8093**).

8054 GREEN (VIVIAN HUBERT HOWARD). Religion at Oxford and Cambridge. 1964.

8055 ABRAHAMS (HAROLD MAURICE) *and* BRUCE-KERR (JOHN) *eds.* Oxford versus Cambridge: a record of inter-university contests, 1827–1930. 1931.

8056 BARKER. Age and youth: memories of three universities and father of the man. By Sir Ernest Barker. 1953.

Incls. his *Father of the man: memories of Cheshire, Lancashire and Oxford, 1874–1898* [1948].

8057 ROBERTS. Sherborne, Oxford and Cambridge: recollections of Mrs. Ernest Stewart Roberts. 1934.

8058 EWART COMMITTEE ON OXFORD AND CAMBRIDGE UNIVERSITIES EDUCATION BILL. Special report from the select committee on the Oxford and Cambridge Universities Education Bill [Chairman: William Ewart]. H.C. 497 (1867). XIII, 183.

The committee presented no report but gathered a great deal of misc. evidence.

8059 LORDS COMMITTEE ON UNIVERSITY TESTS. First report [1870 Session] from the select committee of the House of Lords on university tests [Chairman: Marquess of Salisbury]. H.C. 179 (1871). IX, 85. Further report [first of 1871 Session]. H.C. 179–I (1871). IX, 227. Final report [second of 1871 Session]. H.C. 237 (1871). IX, 593.

Deals with Oxford, Cambridge, and Durham, which alone confined their membership (in theory) to members of the Church of England.

8060 CLEVELAND COMMISSION ON OXFORD AND CAMBRIDGE PROPERTY. Report of the commissioners appointed to inquire into the property and income of the universities of Oxford and Cambridge, and of the colleges and halls therein [Chairman: Duke of Cleveland]. Vol. I. Report. [C. 856] H.C. (1873). XXXVII, pt. 1. Vol. II. Returns from the University of Oxford. [C. 856–I] H.C. (1873). XXXVII, pt. 2. Vol. III. Returns from the University of Cambridge. [C. 856–II] H.C. (1873). XXXVII, pt. 3.

8061 LAWSON COMMITTEE ON THE UNIVERSITIES AND COLLEGE ESTATES ACTS. Report of the departmental committee appointed by the Board of Agriculture to inquire into the working of the Universities and College Estates Acts, 1858 to 1880, and to report whether any, and if so what, amendments therein are desirable [Chairman: John Grant Lawson]. [C. 8646] H.C. (1897). XLV, 1. Minutes of evidence [C. 8647] H.C. (1897). XLV, 13.

8062 ASQUITH COMMISSION ON OXFORD AND CAMBRIDGE UNIVERSITIES [Chairman: H. H. Asquith]. Report. [Cmd. 1588] H.C. (1922). X, 27. Appendixes, incl. summaries of evidence, publ. as non-parl. papers.

8063 SHADWELL (LIONEL LANCELOT) *ed.* Enactments in parliament specially concerning the universities of Oxford and Cambridge, the colleges and halls therein, and the colleges of Winchester, Eton & Westminster. 4 v. Oxf. 1912.

(ii) *Oxford*

8064  CORDEAUX (EDWARD HAROLD) *and* MERRY (DENIS HARRY).
A bibliography of printed works relating to the University of Oxford. Oxf.
1968.

For the 19th cent. Grace M. Briggs, ed., *The Honnold Library: the William W. Clary
Oxford collection: a descriptive catalogue*, Claremont, Calif. 1956, and Catharine K.
Firman, ed., *A supplementary catalogue*, Claremont 1965, are often useful.

8065  MALLET (*Sir* CHARLES EDWARD). A history of the University of
Oxford. 3 v. 1924–7. Repr. Lond. & N.Y. 1968.

Standard. George Charles Brodrick, *A history of the University of Oxford*, 1886, is still
sometimes useful, and there are good photographs in Christopher Bernard Hobhouse,
*Oxford as it was and as it is today*, 1939, 5th edn. 1952. The history of the university is
also covered in vol. III of the Victoria County History of Oxfordshire. For curricula and
univ. officers consult the statutes and calendar of the university.

8066  WARD (WILLIAM REGINALD). Victorian Oxford [to *c.* 1880]. 1965.

Needs to be suppl. by the lives of the most influential figures at Oxford at the time,
Pusey (**3584**), Wilberforce (**3694**), and Liddon (**3578**), and by Burgon, *Twelve good men*
(**3557**).

8067  DAVIS (HENRY WILLIAM CARLESS). A history of Balliol College.
Rev. by Ralph Henry Carless Davis and Richard Hunt with suppl. by Sir
Harold Hartley and others. Oxf. 1963.

A good hist. There are lives of many of the masters of Balliol, notably those of Jowett
(**8086**), and the following: John William Mackail, *James Leigh Strachan-Davidson,
Master of Balliol: a memoir*, Oxf. 1925, and Mary Florence Smith, *Arthur Lionel Smith,
master of Balliol, 1916–1924* . . ., 1928. For other colleges see Robert Howard Hodgkin,
*Six centuries of an Oxford college: a history of the Queen's College, 1340–1940*, Oxf. 1949,
John Richard Magrath, *The Queen's College*, 2 v. Oxf. 1921, and (for women's colleges)
Gemma Bailey, ed., *Lady Margaret Hall: a short history, 1879–1923*, priv. pr. 1923, and
Muriel St. Clair Byrne and Catherine Hope Mansfield, *Somerville College, 1879–1921*,
Oxf. [1921]. There are outline hists. of other colleges in the *College history series*.

8068  GREEN (VIVIAN HUBERT HOWARD). Oxford common room:
a study of Lincoln College and Mark Pattison [1792–1884]. 1957.

Important for univ. politics and educ. policy. See also **8041**, **8045**, **8087**, and **8082**.

8069  BILL (EDWARD GEOFFREY WATSON) *and* MASON (JOHN
FREDERICK ARTHUR). Christ Church and reform, 1850–1867. Oxf. 1970.

8070  FIRTH (*Sir* CHARLES HARDING). The faculties and their powers:
a contribution to the history of university organization. Oxf. 1909.

See also Thomas Arnold, *The revival of the faculties of Oxford*, Oxf. & Lond. 1872.

8071  FIRTH (*Sir* CHARLES HARDING). Modern history in Oxford, 1841–
1918. Oxf. 1920.

See also his *Modern languages at Oxford, 1724–1929*, 1929, and *The school of English
language and literature: a contribution to the history of Oxford studies*, Oxf. 1909. For the
law at Oxford see **3085**, for music **9253**, for science **8152**, and for medicine **8842**.

**8072  ABBOTT (ROBERT LAMB).** The non-collegiate students: a brief sketch of their history. Oxf. 1894.

See also Reginald Robert Trotman and E. J. K. Garrett, *The non-collegiate students and St. Catherine's Society, 1868–1962*, Oxf. 1962; James Rumsey, *The unattached students of Oxford . . .*, Oxf. 1876; John William Burgon, *Our present lodging-house system immoral . . .*, Chichester 1876, and *The late vicar of S. Mary's in explanation . . .*, Oxf. 1876; Anon., *Saint and soubrette: or, chops and tomato sauce*, Oxf. 1876; and Edwin Hatch, *The proposed university hall*, Oxf. 1881.

**8073  ROGERS (ANNIE MARY ANNE HENLEY).** Degree by degrees: the story of the admission of Oxford women students to membership of the University. 1938.

See also Vera Mary Brittain, *The women at Oxford: a fragment of history*, 1960.

**8074  FOSTER (JOSEPH)** *comp.* Alumni oxonienses: the members of the University of Oxford, 1715–1886 . . . 4 v. 1887–8.

Suppl. by his *Oxford men, 1880–1892*, 1893, and *Oxford men & their colleges*, 1893. Printed lists of members also exist for most of the colleges.

**8075  ELTON (GODFREY),** *Baron Elton, ed.* The first fifty years of the Rhodes trust and the Rhodes scholarships, 1903–1953. Oxf. 1956.

See also Richard Frederick Scholz and Stanley Kuhl Hornbeck, *Oxford and the Rhodes scholarships*, 1907.

**8076  KNICKERBOCKER (WILLIAM SKINKLE).** Creative Oxford: its influence in Victorian literature. Syracuse, N.Y. 1925.

A general account of Oxford thought as found in the main printed sources. Not well done. Includes a list of Oxford novels. Most Oxford novels are poor, e.g. Cuthbert Bede, pseud. of Edward Bradley, *The adventures of Mr. Verdant Green, an Oxford freshman*, 1853, *The further adventures of Mr. Verdant Green . . .*, 1854, and *Mr. Verdant Green married and done for . . .*, 1857, and Thomas Hughes, *Tom Brown at Oxford*, 3 v. 1861.

**8077  MORRAH (HERBERT ARTHUR).** The Oxford Union, 1823–1923. 1923.

See also Christopher Hollis, *The Oxford Union* [1965].

**8078  HISCOCK (WALTER GEORGE)** *ed.* The Balliol rhymes. Oxf. 1955.

A celebrated example of Oxford humour.

**8079  BURROWS (MONTAGU).** Pass and class: an Oxford guide book through the courses of literae humaniores, mathematics, natural science, and law and modern history. 1860. 3rd edn. 1866.

The first of the Oxford handbooks for undergraduates. Comparable later works are Sir Algernon Methuen Marshall Stedman, afterwards Methuen, *Oxford: its social and intellectual life: with remarks and hints on expenses, the examinations, the selection of books, etc.*, 1878, new edn. 1887, and Joseph Wells, ed., *Oxford and Oxford life*, 1892. There are also a number of chatty books, which are sometimes useful, such as [Arthur Denis Godley], *Aspects of modern Oxford: by a mere don*, 1894.

8080   OXFORD UNIVERSITY COMMISSION. Report of Her Majesty's commissioners appointed to inquire into the state, discipline, studies and revenues of the university and colleges of Oxford [Chairman: Samuel Hinds, Bishop of Norwich]. [1482] H.C. (1852). XXII, 1.

8081   UNIVERSITY OF OXFORD COMMISSION [Chairman: Earl of Selborne]. Minutes of evidence &c. [C. 2868] H.C. (1881). LVI, 1.

A very useful compendium of evidence collected in Oxford. For the commission's work see Mountague Bernard, *A letter to the Right Hon. W. E. Gladstone on the statutes of the University of Oxford commission*, 1882.

8082   PATTISON (MARK). 'Oxford studies'. Essay IX in Oxford essays, contributed by members of the University, 1855. 1855.

Repr. in his *Essays*, ed. by Henry Nettleship, 2 v. Oxf. 1889. See also his *Suggestions of academical organisation* (**8041**). For other discussions of Oxford educ. see James Edwin Thorold Rogers, *Education in Oxford: its method, its aids and its rewards*, 1861; Goldwin Smith, *The reorganisation of the University of Oxford*, Oxf. 1868, and 'Oxford university reform', essay VII in *Oxford essays . . . 1858*, 1858; Walter Bagehot, *Oxford*, 1882, repr. as no. III in vol. III of his *Literary studies*, 1895; Percy Gardner, *Oxford at the crossroads: a criticism of the course of litterae humaniores in the University*, 1903; and George Nathaniel Curzon, Marquess Curzon of Kedleston, *Principles & methods of university reform: being a letter addressed to the University of Oxford*, Oxf. 1909.

8083   OXFORD UNIVERSITY GAZETTE. 1870+.

The official univ. j. More useful is *The Oxford magazine: a weekly newspaper and review*, 1883+. Before 1883 *The guardian* was virtually a weekly Oxford magazine.

8084   ANSON. A memoir of the Right Honourable Sir William Anson [Warden of All Souls and M.P.]. Ed. by Herbert Hensley Henson, bishop. Oxf. 1920.

8085   BRODRICK. Memories and impressions, 1831–1900. By George Charles Brodrick [Warden of Merton]. 1900.

8086   JOWETT. The life and letters of Benjamin Jowett, M.A. By Evelyn Abbott and Lewis Campbell. 2 v. 1897.

Suppl. by their *Letters of Benjamin Jowett, M.A.*, 1899. Sir Geoffrey Cust Faber, *Jowett: a portrait with background*, 1957, 2nd edn. 1958, is a good recent study. See also Lionel Arthur Tollemache, *Benjamin Jowett: a personal memoir*, 1895.

8087   PATTISON. Memoirs. By Mark Pattison. Ed. by Mrs. Emilia Frances Strong Pattison. 1885. Repr. 1970.

See also John Sparrow, *Mark Pattison and the idea of a university*, 1967; Lionel Arthur Tollemache, *Recollections of Pattison*, 1885; Green, *Oxford common room* (**8068**); and Pattison's works (**8041, 8045, 8082**). There is an account of Froude and Pattison in Cecil Stuart Emden, *Oriel papers*, Oxf. 1948.

8088   SMITH. Reminiscences. By Goldwin Smith. Ed. by Theodore Arnold Haultain. N.Y. 1910.

Haultain also ed. *A selection from Goldwin Smith's correspondence . . .*, N.Y. [1913] and publ. a biog., *Goldwin Smith: his life and opinions*, Lond. & N.Y. [1913]. The best account of Goldwin Smith is Elisabeth Wallace, *Goldwin Smith, Victorian Liberal*, Toronto 1957.

**8089 COURTNEY (JANET ELIZABETH).** An Oxford portrait gallery. 1931.

For other recollections of Oxford see, *inter alia*, Jacques Bardoux, *Memories of Oxford*, trans. by Sir Wilberforce Ross Barker, 1899; Sir Stephen Montagu Burrows, ed., *The autobiography of Montagu Burrows*, 1908; George Valentine Cox, *Recollections of Oxford*, 1868, 2nd edn. 1870; Eleanor Constance Lodge, *Terms and vacations*, ed. by Janet Spens, 1938; Sir John Arthur Ransome Marriott, *Memories of four score years . . .*, 1946; Sir Charles William Chadwick Oman, *Memories of Victorian Oxford . . .*, 1941; and William Tuckwell, *Reminiscences of Oxford*, 1900, 2nd edn. 1907. Few Oxford diaries have been publ., most of them of no great interest, but see Willie Elmhirst, *A freshman's diary, 1911–1912*, Oxf. 1969.

(iii) *Cambridge*

The standard hist. is vol. III of the *Victoria County History of Cambridgeshire*, but Winstanley (**8091**) is much fuller, on his period.

**8090 PEEK (HEATHER ELINOR)** *and* **HALL (CATHERINE PRISCILLA).** The archives of the University of Cambridge. Camb. 1962.

**8091 WINSTANLEY (DENYS ARTHUR).** Early Victorian Cambridge. Camb. 1940.

Cont. down to 1882 in *Later Victorian Cambridge*, Camb. 1947. These 2 v. give an admirable account of univ. life, but James Bass Mullinger, *A history of the University of Cambridge*, 1888, has still not been entirely superseded.

**8092 ROTHBLATT (SHELDON).** The revolution of the dons: Cambridge and society in Victorian England. Lond. & N.Y. 1968.

A pioneer study.

**8093 JENKINS (HESTER)** *and* **JONES (DAVID CARADOG).** 'Social class of Cambridge University alumni of the 18th and 19th centuries'. *Brit. J. Sociology* i (1950), 93–116.

**8094 EMERY (WILLIAM).** 'Expenses of university education at Cambridge: past and present'. *Stat. Soc. J.* xxvi (1863), 296–316.

**8095 WILLIS (ROBERT)** *and* **CLARK (JOHN WILLIS).** The architectural history of the University of Cambridge, and of the colleges of Cambridge and Eton. 4 v. Camb. 1886.

**8096 BURY (JOHN PATRICK TUER).** The College of Corpus Christi and of the Blessed Virgin Mary: a history from 1822 to 1952. Camb. 1952.

For other men's colls. see Arthur Gray and Frederick Brittain, *A history of Jesus College, Cambridge*, 1960; William Henry Samuel Jones, *The story of St. Catherine's College, Cambridge*, Camb. 1951; Edward Miller, *Portrait of a college: a history of the College of Saint John the Evangelist, Cambridge*, Camb. 1961; and the outline hists. in the *College history series*. For women's colls. see Barbara Stephen, *Girton College, 1869–1932*, Camb. 1933, and *Emily Davies and Girton College*, 1927; Muriel Clara Bradbrook, *'That infidel place': a short history of Girton College, 1869–1969 . . .*, 1969; Mary Agnes

Hamilton, *Newnham: an informal biography*, 1936, and *Remembering my good friends*, 1944; Blanche Athena Clough, *A memoir of Anne Jemima Clough*, 1897, new edn. 1903; and Alice Gardner, *A short history of Newnham college . . .*, Cambridge 1921.

**8097  VENN (JOHN) and VENN (JOHN ARCHIBALD)** *comps.* Alumni cantabrigienses: a biographical list of all known students, graduates and holders of office at the university of Cambridge from the earliest times to 1900. Part 2. 1752–1900. 6 v. Camb. 1940–54.

A splendid work. Other full registers are John James Withers, comp., *A register of admissions to King's College, Cambridge, 1797–1925, with short biographical notices*, 2nd edn. 1929, and John Venn, *Biographical history of Gonville and Caius college, 1349–[1932]*, 5 v. Camb. 1897–1948. See also Charles William Previté-Orton, comp., *Index to tripos lists, 1748–1910 . . .*, Camb. 1923, and Jack Weatherburn Goodison, *Catalogue of Cambridge portraits: I: the university collection*, Camb. 1955.

**8098  CRADOCK (PERCY)** *ed.* Recollections of the Cambridge Union, 1815–1939. Camb. 1953.

**8099  BROOKFIELD (FRANCES MARY).** The Cambridge 'Apostles'. 1906.

Useful for the earlier hist. to *c.* 1860 of this informal Cambridge society, later so influential.

**8100  BALL (WALTER WILLIAM ROUSE).** A history of the study of mathematics at Cambridge. Camb. 1889.

For other subjects see Thomas John Norman Hilken, *Engineering at Cambridge university, 1783–1965*, Camb. 1967, Eustace Mandeville Wetenhall Tillyard, *The muse unchained: an intimate account of the revolution in English studies at Cambridge*, Camb. 1958, and Anon., *A history of the Cavendish laboratory, 1871–1910*, 1910. Alexander Wood, *The Cavendish laboratory*, Camb. 1946, and Egon Larsen, *The Cavendish laboratory: nursery of genius*, 1962, are of little value. For music see **9253**, for medicine **8843**, and for law **3086**.

**8101  CAMBRIDGE UNIVERSITY COMMISSION.** Report of Her Majesty's commissioners appointed to inquire into the state, discipline, studies and revenues of the university and colleges of Cambridge [Chairman: John Graham, Bishop of Chester]. [1559] H.C. (1852–3). XLIV, 1.

Marks the beginning of modern Cambridge. For subsequent commissions see **8058–62.**

**8102  CLARK (JOHN WILLIS)** *ed.* Endowments of the University of Cambridge. Camb. 1904.

**8103  SEELEY (*Sir* JOHN ROBERT)** *ed.* The student's guide to the University of Cambridge. Camb. 1863. 5th edn. 1892.

Repl. by *The student's handbook to the University & Colleges of Cambridge*, Camb. 1902+. There are also numerous gossipy books such as Sir Charles Bruce Locker Tennyson, *Cambridge from within*, 1913.

**8104  EVERETT (WILLIAM).** On the Cam: lectures on the University of Cambridge in England. 1866.

Cp. another American account, Charles Astor Bristed, *Five years in an English university*, 2 v., N.Y. 1852, 3rd edn. 1873.

8105   CORNFORD (FRANCIS MACDONALD). Microcosmographia academica: being, a guide for the young academic politician. Camb. 1908. And reprs.

A celebrated piece of Cambridge trivia.

8106   CAMBRIDGE UNIVERSITY REPORTER. Camb. 1870+.

The official j. of the Univ. For univ. opinion consult *The Cambridge review: a journal of university life and thought*, Camb. 1879+, and, for literary work, Frederick Andrew Rice, ed., *The Granta and its contributors, 1889–1914*, 1924.

8107   AUSTEN LEIGH. Augustus Austen Leigh, Provost of King's College Cambridge: a record of college reform. Ed. by William Austen Leigh. 1906.

8108   BENSON. The diary of Arthur Christopher Benson. Ed. by Percy Lubbock. [1926.]

Deals mainly with his life at Magdalen College. Benson's numerous writings incl. other Cambridge material.

8109   BRADSHAW. A memoir of Henry Bradshaw, fellow of King's College, Cambridge, and university librarian. By Sir George Walter Prothero. 1888.

8110   BROWNING. Oscar Browning. By Hugh Evelyn Wortham. 1927. 2nd edn. [Victorian Eton and Cambridge: being, the life and times of Oscar Browning.] 1956.

Browning, in spite of numerous defects of character, was largely responsible for creating the Modern History School. He himself publ. *Memories of sixty years: at Eton, Cambridge and elsewhere*, 1910, and *Memories of later years*, 1923.

8111   BUTLER. Henry Montagu Butler, master of Trinity College, Cambridge, 1886–1918: a memoir. By Sir James Ramsay Montagu Butler. 1925.

See also Edward Graham, *The Harrow life of Henry Montagu Butler, D.D.*, 1920.

8112   JACKSON. Henry Jackson, O.M., vice-master of Trinity College & Regius Professor of Greek in the University of Cambridge: a memoir. By Reginald St. John Parry. Camb. 1926.

8113   JAMES. Eton and Kings: recollections, mostly trivial, 1875–1925. By Montague Rhodes James. 1926.

Samuel Gurney Lubbock, *A memoir of Montague Rhodes James, with a list of his writings by A. F. Scholfield*, Camb. 1939, and Gwendolen McBryde, ed., *Montague Rhodes James: letters to a friend*, 1956, add little on his Cambridge life.

8114   JEBB. Life and letters of Sir Richard Claverhouse Jebb. By his wife, Caroline Lane, Lady Jebb. Camb. 1907.

8115   JEBB. With dearest love to all: the life and letters of Lady Jebb. By Mary Reed Bobbitt. 1960.

A splendid evocation of the Cambridge scene.

8116   MARSHALL. What I remember. By Mary Paley Marshall. Camb. 1947.
The wife of Alfred Marshall (8489), and a Newnham don. An attractive book.

8117   MORGAN. Memoirs of Henry Arthur Morgan, master of Jesus College, Cambridge, 1885–1912. By his daughter, Iris L. Osborne Morgan. [1927.]

8118   RAVERAT. Period piece: a Cambridge girlhood. By Gwendolen Mary Raverat. 1952.
A deservedly famous book on the childhood of a don's daughter. Delightful reading.

8119   SIDGWICK. Mrs. Henry Sidgwick: a memoir. By her niece, Ethel Sidgwick. 1938.
As sister of A. J. Balfour, wife of Henry Sidgwick (8467), and principal of Newnham, a powerful Cambridge figure.

8120   STEPHEN. Leslie Stephen: his thought and character in relation to his time. By Noel Gilroy Annan, Baron Annan. 1951.
See also Sir Desmond MacCarthy, *Leslie Stephen*, Camb. 1937.

8121   THOMSON. Recollections and reflections. By Sir Joseph John Thomson. 1936.
Head of the Cavendish Laboratory and master of Trinity. See also 8726.

WHEWELL. See 8608.

### (d) *Modern Universities*

Lists of graduates, etc. have been publ. by most univs. or are incl. in their annual calendars.

8122   SILVER (HAROLD) *and* TEAGUE (S. JOHN) *comps*. The history of British universities, 1800–1969, excluding Oxford and Cambridge: a bibliography. Soc. for Research into Higher Educ. Monograph 13. 1970.

8123   ARMYTAGE (WALTER HARRY GREEN). Civic universities: aspects of a British tradition. 1955.
A useful gen. hist.

8124   UNIVERSITY COLLEGE REPORTS. Reports from university colleges participating, in accordance with the Treasury minute dated 1st July 1889, in the grant of £15,000 made by parliament for 'university colleges in Great Britain', 1894. [C. 7459] H.C. (1894). LXVI, 515.
The first of a ser. of reports which continued to 1913–14 and form the most useful single source for the hist. of the colleges before 1914. The reports of the government inspectors and the advisory committee appointed by the Treasury incl. very little additional material. These reports are listed in the *General index* to parl. papers (33) under 'Universities and colleges', and also in Berdahl (8026). There is a little additional information in *Treasury minute . . . on . . . a grant of £15,000 for university colleges in Great Britain.* H.C. 250 (1889). LIX, 351, and in *Report of the committee [on] compulsory retirement of*

*professors serving under the crown* [Chairman: Lord Playfair]. [C. 7889] H.C. (1895). LXXX, 317.

8125  BIRMINGHAM. Eric W. Vincent and Percival Hinton, *The University of Birmingham: its history and significance*, Birmingham 1947.

8126  BRISTOL. Basil Cottle and James Wilson Sherborne, *The life of a university*, Bristol 1951. New edn. 1959.

8127  DURHAM. Charles Edwin Whiting, *The University of Durham, 1832– 1932*, 1932. Joseph Thomas Fowler, *Durham University: earlier foundations and present colleges*, College History Series, 1904. *Report of the commissioners appointed for the purposes of the Durham University Act, 1861* [Chairman: the Bishop of Durham]. [3173] H.C. (1863). XVI, 1. Minutes of evidence. H.C. 77 (1863). XLVI, 275. *Royal Commission on the University of Durham* [Chairman: Lord Moyne]. Report. [Cmd. 4815]. H.C. (1934–5). VIII, 489.

8128  LEEDS. Arnold Nixon Shimmin, *The University of Leeds: the first half-century*, Camb. 1954. William Henry Draper, *Sir Nathan Bodington, first vice-chancellor of the University of Leeds: a memoir*, 1912.

8129  LEICESTER. Jack Simmons, *New university*, Leicester. 1958. Rev. edn. 1959.

8130  LONDON. Hugh Hale Bellot, *The University of London: a history*, 1969, repr. from vol. I of the *Victoria County History of Middlesex* (1969) which also contains brief accounts of the colleges. Sir William Henry Allchin, *An account of the reconstruction of the University of London*, 3 v. 1905–12. Karl Pearson, *The new University for London: a guide to its history and a criticism of its defects*, 1892. Thomas Lloyd Humberstone, *University reform in London*, 1926. Percy Dunsheath and Margaret Miller, *Convocation in the University of London: the first hundred years*, 1958. Mabel Helène, Lady Hartog, *P. J. Hartog: a memoir*, 1949.

8131  SELBORNE COMMISSION ON A NEW UNIVERSITY FOR LONDON. Report of the royal commissioners appointed to inquire whether any and what kind of new university or powers is or are required for the advancement of higher education in London [Chairman: Earl of Selborne]. [C. 5709] H.C. (1889). XXXIX, 323. Minutes of evidence. [C. 5709–I] H.C. (1889). XXXIX, 347.

8132  GRESHAM UNIVERSITY COMMISSION. The report of the commissioners appointed to consider the draft charter for the proposed Gresham University in London [Chairman: Earl Cowper]. [C. 7259] H.C. (1893–4). XXXI, 807. Minutes of evidence. [C. 7425] H.C. (1894). XXXIV, 1. Appendix and index. [C. 7425–I] H.C. (1894). XXXIV, 1229.

8133  HALDANE COMMISSION ON UNIVERSITY EDUCATION IN LONDON. Royal commission on university education in London: first report of the commissioners [Chairman: Richard Burdon Haldane]. [Cd. 5165] H.C. (1910). XXIII, 639. Minutes of evidence. [Cd. 5166] H.C. (1910). XXIII, 643. Second report. [Cd. 5527] H.C. (1911). XX, 1. Minutes of evidence. [Cd. 5528] H.C. (1911). XX, 5. Third report. [Cd. 5910] H.C. (1911). XX, 453. Minutes of evidence. [Cd. 5911] H.C. (1911). XX, 457. Fourth report. [Cd. 6015] H.C. (1912–13). XXII, 581. Fifth report. [Cd. 6311] H.C. (1912–13). XXII, 587. Appendix to fifth report. [Cd. 6312] H.C. (1912–13). XXII, 591. Final report. [Cd. 6717] H.C. (1913). XL, 297. Minutes of evidence. [Cd. 6718] H.C. (1913). XL, 543.

See also **8047**.

8134 HILTON YOUNG COMMITTEE ON THE UNIVERSITY OF LONDON. Report of the departmental committee on the University of London [Chairman: E. Hilton Young]. [Cmd. 2612] H.C. (1926). X, 241.

A review of the situation since the Haldane commission.

8135 LONDON (UNIVERSITY COLLEGE). Hugh Hale Bellot, *University College, London, 1826–1926,* 1929.

8136 LONDON (KING'S COLLEGE). Fossey John Cobb Hearnshaw, *The centenary history of King's College, London, 1828–1928,* 1929.

LONDON (BIRKBECK COLLEGE). See **8195**.

8137 LONDON (SCHOOL OF ECONOMICS). Sir Sydney Caine, *The history of the foundation of the London School of Economics and Political Science,* 1963. Janet Beveridge, Baroness Beveridge, *An epic of Clare Market: birth and early days of the London School of Economics,* 1960.

8138 LONDON (BEDFORD COLLEGE). Margaret Janson Tuke, *A history of Bedford College for women, 1849–1937,* 1939.

8139 LONDON (ROYAL HOLLOWAY COLLEGE). *The Royal Holloway College, 1887–1937,* 1937.

8140 LONDON (WESTFIELD COLLEGE). Catharine Beatrice Firth, *Constance Louisa Maynard, mistress of Westfield College: a family portrait,* 1949.

8141 LONDON (INSTITUTE OF EDUCATION). *Studies and impressions, 1902–1952,* Inst. of Educ. 1952.

8142 LONDON (SCHOOL OF PHARMACY). Thomas Edward Wallis, *History of the School of Pharmacy, University of London,* 1964.

8143 MANCHESTER. Henry Buckley Charlton, *Portrait of a university, 1851–1951: to commemorate the centenary of Manchester university,* Manch. 1951, 2nd edn. 1952. Joseph Thompson, *The Owens College: its foundation and growth, and its connection with the Victoria University, Manchester,* Manch. 1886. Edward Fiddes, *Chapters in the history of Owens College and of Man-*

*chester University, 1851–1914*, Manch. 1937. Sir Philip Joseph Hartog, ed., *The Owens College, Manchester* . . ., Manch. 1900. Mabel Tylecote, *The education of women at Manchester University, 1883 to 1933*, Manch. 1941. Ian Gabriel Gregory, ed., *In memory of Burlington Street: an appreciation of the Manchester University Unions, 1861–1957*, Manch. 1958. See also the lives of Roscoe (**8703**).

8144  NOTTINGHAM. Alfred Cecil Wood, *A history of the University College, Nottingham, 1881–1948*, Oxf. 1953.

8145  READING. William MacBride Childs, *Making a university: an account of the university movement at Reading*, 1933.

8146  SHEFFIELD. Arthur William Chapman, *The story of a modern university: a history of the University of Sheffield*, 1955.

8147  SOUTHAMPTON. Alfred Temple Patterson, *The University of Southampton: a centenary history of the evolution and development of the University of Southampton, 1862–1962*, Southampton 1962.

### 4. Scientific and Technical Education

8148  ARMYTAGE (WALTER HARRY GREEN). 'Some sources for the history of technical education in England'. *Brit. J. Educ. Studs.* v (1956–7), 72–9, 159–65; vi (1957–8), 64–73.

See also J. F. Kerr, 'Some sources for the history of the teaching of science in England', *Brit. J. Educ. Studs.* vii (1958–9), 149–60.

8149  ARGLES ([OWEN] MICHAEL [VENABLES]). South Kensington to Robbins: an account of English technical and scientific education since 1851. 1964.

See also Peter William Musgrave, 'Constant factors in the demand for technical education, 1860–1960', *Brit. J. Educ. Studs.* xiv (1965–6), 173–87.

8150  HUDSON (DEREK) *and* LUCKHURST (KENNETH WILLIAM). The Royal Society of Arts, 1754–1954. 1954.

The Soc. was interested in all types of educ., but chiefly in the fine arts and technology. The Society's main organ was a *Journal*, 1852+. There is an older hist., Sir Henry Trueman Wood, *A history of the Royal Society of Arts*, 1913.

8151  DEPARTMENT OF SCIENCE AND ART. First report. [1783] H.C. (1854). XXVIII, 269.

Cont. annually to 1899. For a full examination of the work of the dept. see *Report of the committee appointed to inquire into the distribution of science and art grants* [Chairman: Sir John E. Gorst]. [C. 8417] H.C. (1897). XXXIII, 421, and *Calendar, history and general summary of regulations of the Department of Science and Art, 1898*. [C. 8636] H.C. (1897). XXXII, 1.

8152   TURNER (DOROTHY MABEL). History of science teaching in England. 1927.

Inadequate. Consult also Charles Foster, 'One hundred years of science teaching in Great Britain', *Annals of Science* ii (1937), 335–44, George Haines IV, 'German influence upon scientific instruction in England, 1867–1887', *Victorian Studs.* i (1957–8), 215–44, and Frank Sherwood Taylor, 'The teaching of science at Oxford in the nineteenth century', *Annals of Science* viii (1952), 82–112. See also Florence Annie Yeldham, *The teaching of arithmetic through four hundred years, 1535–1935,* 1936.

8153   MILLIS (CHARLES THOMAS). Technical education: its development and aims. 1925.

Short and inadequate. Albert Abbott, *Education for industry and commerce in England,* 1933, is worse. But see **8030a.**

8154   COTGROVE (STEPHEN FREDERICK). Technical education and social change. 1958.

Raises interesting questions.

8155   BENNETT (CHARLES ALPHEUS). History of manual and industrial education up to 1870. Peoria, Ill. [1926.]

Cont. in his *History of manual and industrial education, 1870 to 1917,* Peoria 1937.

8156   MARTIN (THOMAS). The Royal Institution. 1942. 3rd edn. 1961.

8157   HALDANE COMMITTEE ON ROYAL COLLEGE OF SCIENCE. Preliminary report of the departmental committee on the Royal College of Science (including the Royal School of Mines) [Chairman: R. B. Haldane]. [Cd. 2610] H.C. (1905). LXI, 423. Final report. [Cd. 2872] H.C. (1906). XXXI, 391. Minutes of evidence. [Cd. 2956] H.C. (1906). XXXI, 431.

Important. Includes a short hist. and an international survey.

8158   ARMSTRONG. Henry Edward Armstrong, 1848–1937: the doyen of British chemists and pioneer of technical education. By John Vargas Eyre. 1958.

Armstrong was a pioneer of science educ. See particularly his *The teaching of scientific method, and other papers on education,* 1903, 2nd edn. 1910, repr. 1925.

8159   HOGG. Quintin Hogg: a biography. By Ethel May Hogg, afterwards Wood. 1904. Rev. edn. [The Polytechnic and its founder, Quintin Hogg.] 1932.

A good life of the founder of the Polytechnic. See also her *A history of the Polytechnic,* 1965. For other polytechnics see Edric Bayley, *The Borough polytechnic institute: its rise and development,* 1910, [William] Collin Brooks, *An educational adventure: a history of the Woolwich polytechnic,* Woolwich 1955, and Harold Arrowsmith, *Pioneering in education for the technologies: the story of Battersea college of technology,* Univ. of Surrey 1966.

8160   UNWIN. The life and work of William Cawthorne Unwin. By Edward George Walker. 1938. Repr. 1947.

A pioneer of engineering education.

8161  TWINING (THOMAS). Science for the people: a memorandum on various means for propagating scientific and practical knowledge among the working classes, and for thus promoting their physical, technical and social improvement. 1870.

Twining was a vice-president of the Society of Arts which earlier publ. *Report of the committee appointed by the council of the Society of Arts to inquire into the subject of industrial instruction, with the evidence on which the report is founded,* 1853. See also Charles, Chevalier de Cocquiel de Terherleir, *Industrial instruction in England: being, a report made to the Belgian government,* trans. by Peter Berlyn, 1853.

8162  SMITH (*Sir* SWIRE). Educational comparisons: or, remarks on industrial schools in England, Germany and Switzerland. 1873.

8163  DEVONSHIRE COMMISSION ON SCIENTIFIC INSTRUCTION. First report of the royal commission on scientific instruction and the advancement of science [Chairman: Duke of Devonshire]. [C. 318] H.C. (1871). XXIV, 643. First and second reports. [C. 536] H.C. (1872). XXV, 1. Third report. [C. 868] H.C. (1873). XXVIII, 637. Fourth report. [C. 884] H.C. (1874). XXII, 1. Fifth report. [C. 1087] H.C. (1874). XXII, 51. Minutes of evidence. [C. 958] H.C. (1874). XXII, 95. Sixth report. [C. 1279] H.C. (1875). XXVIII, 59. Seventh report. [C. 1297] H.C. (1875). XXVIII, 337. Eighth report. [C. 1298] H.C. (1875). XXVIII, 417. Minutes of evidence. [C. 1363] H.C. (1875). XXVIII, 473. Correspondence. [C. 422] H.C. (1871). LVI, 333.

See also *Report of a committee appointed by the council of the British Association for the Advancement of Science to consider the best means for promoting scientific education in schools.* H.C. 137 (1867–8). LIV, 1, and *Report from the select committee on scientific instruction* [Chairman: Bernhard Samuelson]. H.C. 432 (1867–8). XV, 1. The Taunton commission also publ. a short report on technical educ. [3898] H.C. (1867). XXVI, 261.

8164  LIVERY COMPANIES' COMMITTEE, 1878. Report on technical education. 1878.

Includes six reports of great interest by Sir William Armstrong, G. C. T. Bartley, Lt. Col. Donnelly, Douglas Galton, T. H. Huxley, and H. T. Wood.

8165  SAMUELSON COMMISSION ON TECHNICAL INSTRUCTION. First report of the royal commissioners on technical instruction [Chairman: Bernhard Samuelson]. [C. 3171] H.C. (1882). XXVII, 653. Second report. [C. 3981] H.C. (1884). XXIX, 1. Evidence, reports etc. [C. 3981–I–III] H.C. (1884). XXX–XXXI–I–II.

See also Francis Charles Montague, *Technical education: a summary of the report of the royal commission appointed to inquire into the state of technical education* [1887], and Maurice Vachon, *Rapport sur les musées et les écoles d'art industriel en Angleterre . . .,* Ministère de l'Instruction Publique, Paris 1890.

8166  MAGNUS (*Sir* PHILIP). Industrial education. 1888.

See also 7887.

8167  NATIONAL ASSOCIATION FOR THE PROMOTION OF TECHNICAL AND SECONDARY EDUCATION. Annual report. 1888+.

The assoc. also publ. *The record of technical and secondary education . . .,* 1891–1906.

**8168 OXFORD UNIVERSITY: DELEGATES FOR UNIVERSITY EXTENSION.** County councils and technical education: report on the peripatetic teaching in scientific and technical subjects carried on in various country districts under the supervision of the Oxford Delegates for University Extension acting in concert with the technical instruction committees of county councils during the winter, 1891–92. Oxf. 1892.

**8169 BELL (QUENTIN).** The schools of design. Lond. 1963. N.Y. 1964.

There is little in Frank Percival Brown, *South Kensington and its art training*, 1912, and Stuart MacDonald, *The history and philosophy of art education*, Lond & N.Y. 1970. But see **9015.**

**8170 NORTHCOTE COMMITTEE ON SCHOOLS OF ART.** Report from the select committee on schools of art [Chairman: Sir Stafford Northcote]. H.C. 466 (1864). XII, 187.

There is a useful handbook on the subject: John Charles Lewis Sparkes, *Schools of art: their origin, history, work and influence*, Internat. Health Exhib. 1884, and two handy articles, W. B. Stephens, 'The Victorian art schools and technical education: a case study, 1850–1889', *J. Educ. Admin. & Hist.* ii (1969–70), 13–19, and Gordon Sutton, 'The "art" of the Science and Art Department in English elementary schools', *Paedagogica Historica* v (1965), 455–75. See also *Report from the select committee on art union laws* [Chairman: Lord Robert Montagu]. H.C. 332 (1866). VII, 1.

**8171 CHAMBERS COMMITTEE ON ROYAL COLLEGE OF ART.** Report of the departmental committee on the Royal College of Art [Chairman: E. K. Chambers]. [Cd. 5810] H.C. (1911). XVIII, 549.

**8172 HALL (*Sir* ALFRED DANIEL).** 'The development of agricultural education in England and Wales'. *Roy. Agric. Soc. J.* lxxxiii (1922), 15–34.

See also *Agriculture in the twentieth century* (**4168**), the report of the Samuelson Commission (**8165**), and John Constable, ed., *Agricultural Education* [1863]. The main source is *Report of departmental commission on agricultural and dairy schools* [Chairman: Sir R. H. Paget]. [C. 5285] H.C. (1888). XXXII, 1. Final report. [C. 5313] H.C. (1888). XXXII, 11. Minutes of evidence. [C. 5313–I] H.C. (1888). XXXII, 27.

**8173 BROWN (KARL F.) *and* HASKELL (DANIEL CARL).** The shorthand collection in the New York public library: a catalogue of books, periodicals & manuscripts brought together by the National Shorthand Reporters' Association and the library. N.Y. 1935.

See also John Westby-Gibson, *The bibliography of shorthand*, 1887.

**8174 BUTLER (EDWARD HARRY).** The story of British shorthand. 1951.

See also Albert Navarre, *Histoire générale de la sténographie et de l'écriture à travers les âges*, Paris, 1909; Hans Fedor Clissold Glatte, *Shorthand systems of the world: a concise, historical and technical review of the development of handwriting and shorthand with hints for shorthand-typists*, Lond. 1957, 2nd edn. 1958, N.Y. 1959; Sir Isaac Pitman, *A history of shorthand* . . . [1884?], 4th edn. 1918; Thomas Anderson, *History of shorthand, with a review of its present condition and prospects in Europe and America*, 1882; Matthias Levy, *The history of short-hand writing: to which is prefixed the system used by the author*, 1862; and William Henry Gurney Salter, *A history of the Gurney system of shorthand*, Oxf. 1924.

8175 PITMAN. Life of Sir Isaac Pitman, inventor of phonography. By Alfred Baker. 1908. Repr. 1913. Rev. edn. 1930.

Incl. bibliog. of Pitman's works. See also **5499.**

8176 YOXALL (AILSA). A history of the teaching of domestic economy. 1912.

See also Helen Sillitoe, *A history of the teaching of domestic subjects*, 1933.

8177 McINTOSH (PETER CHISHOLM). Physical education in England since 1800. 1952.

### 5. ADULT AND FURTHER EDUCATION

#### (a) *General*

8178 KELLY (THOMAS) *ed.* A select bibliography of adult education in Great Britain: including works published to the end of the year 1950. Nat. Inst. of Adult Educ. 1952. 2nd edn. 1962.

8179 KELLY (THOMAS). A history of adult education in Great Britain. Liverpool. 1962. 2nd edn. 1970.

Standard. For different approaches to the subject rather than for facts see Raymond Charles Rowse, *An introduction to the history of adult education*, 1933, Harold Collett Dent, *Part-time education in Great Britain: an historical outline*, 1949, and Margaret Traube Hodgen, *Workers' education in England & the United States*, Lond. & N.Y. 1925. There is some background material in Philip Arthur William Collins, 'Dickens and adult education', *Brit. J. Educ. Studs.* iii (1954–5), 115–27.

8180 HARRISON (JOHN FLETCHER CLEWS). Learning and living, 1790–1960: a study in the history of the English adult education movement. 1961.

8181 SADLER (*Sir* MICHAEL ERNEST) *ed.* Continuation schools in England & elsewhere: their place in the educational system of an industrial and commercial state. Manch. 1907. 2nd edn. 1908.

Long the standard account and important for an understanding of the movement.

8182 MINISTRY OF RECONSTRUCTION (ADULT EDUCATION COMMITTEE). Interim report of the committee on adult education [Chairman: Arthur L. Smith]: industrial and social conditions in relation to adult education. [Cd. 9107] H.C. (1918). IX, 319. Second interim report: education in the army. [Cd. 9225] H.C. (1918). IX, 351. Third interim report: libraries and museums. [Cd. 9237] H.C. (1918). IX, 361. Final report. [Cmd. 321] H.C. (1919). XXVIII, 453.

The *Final report* includes a very full account of adult educ. up to 1918, as well as many important proposals for the future.

8183 BUISSON (FERDINAND ÉDOUARD) *ed.* L'éducation populaire des adultes en Angleterre: notices sur les principales institutions par des membres de leurs comités. Paris. 1896.

8184 BOARD OF EDUCATION. Report of the consultative committee [Chairman: Arthur H. D. Acland] on attendance, compulsory or otherwise, at continuation schools. [Cd. 4757] H.C. (1909). XVII, 1. Summaries of evidence. [Cd. 4758] H.C. (1909). XVII, 353.

8185 SANDHAGEN (ANTON). Ideen englischer Volkserziehung und Versuche zu ihrer Verwirklichung. Jena. 1911.
Mainly on the London Working-Men's College.

8186 GILLMAN (FREDERICK JOHN). The workers and education: a record of some present-day experiments. [1916.]

8187 PARRY (REGINALD ST. JOHN) *ed.* Cambridge essays on adult education. Camb. 1920.

8188 BULKELEY (JOHN PIERSON). Adult education: university extramural teaching in England and Wales. Bureau of Educ., India. Calcutta. 1922.
Not confined to univ. extension.

8189 YEAXLEE (BASIL ALFRED). Spiritual values in adult education: a study of a neglected aspect. 2 v. 1925.
The only major work on the theory of adult educ.

8190 MANSBRIDGE (ALBERT). Fellow-men: a gallery of England, 1876–1946. 1948.
Incl. sketches of many of the leading personalities in adult educ.

8191 BEGBIE (EDWARD HAROLD). Living water: being, chapters from the romance of the poor student. [1918.] Repr. 1970.
Brief biog. sketches of working-class students.

(b) *Mechanics' Institutes, Working-men's Colleges, etc.*

8192 HOLE (JAMES). An essay on the history and management of literary, scientific, and mechanics' institutions. Soc. of Arts. 1853.
A valuable critical survey. Cp. James William Hudson, *The history of adult education in which is comprised a full and complete history of the mechanics' and literary institutions athenaeums . . .*, 1851, and Thomas Edward Cliffe-Leslie, *An enquiry into the progress and present conditions of the mechanics' institutes*, 1852. For Hole see John Fletcher Clew Harrison, *Social reform in Victorian Leeds: the work of James Hole, 1820–1895*, Thoresby Soc. Leeds, 1954. Richard Dawes, *Mechanics' institutes and popular education*, 1856, is a shorter but comparable work.

8193 SOCIETY OF ARTS. Middle-class education and class instruction in mechanics' institutions. 1857.

8194 TRAICE (W. H. J.). Handbook of mechanics' institutions . . . 1856. 2nd edn. 1863.

8195 BURNS (CECIL DELISLE). A short history of Birkbeck College, University of London. 1924.

Founded 1823 as London Mechanics' Institution.

8196 WATERHOUSE (RACHEL ELIZABETH). The Birmingham and Midland Institute, 1854–1954. Birmingham. 1954.

8197 LOTT (FREDERICK BARNES). The story of the Leicester Mechanics' Institute, 1833–1871. Leicester. 1935.

8198 ORMEROD (HENRY ARDERNE). The Liverpool Royal Institution: a record and a retrospect. Liverpool. 1953.

8199 GARDINER (FREDERIC JOHN). The fiftieth birthday of a model institute, 1864–1914: an account of the origin and development of the Wisbech Working Men's Club and Institute. Wisbech. 1914.

8200 UNION OF LANCASHIRE AND CHESHIRE INSTITUTES. A hundred years of educational service, 1839–1939. Manch. 1939.

8201 SOLLY (HENRY). Working-men's social clubs and institutes . . . 1867. 2nd edn. Ed. by B. T. Hall. 1904.

Solly was the founder of the working-men's clubs movement, and a copious pamphleteer. The 2nd edn. incl. a good account of his work.

8202 HALL (BENJAMIN TOM). Our fifty years: the story of the Working Men's Club and Institute Union: together with brief impressions of the men of the movement. Working Men's Club and Institute Union. 1912. 2nd edn. [Our sixty years . . .] 1922.

Incl. a valuable biog. section. The Union publ. an *Annual report,* 1862+, and *The club and institute journal,* 1875+.

8203 SMITH (GEORGE CHARLES MOORE). The story of the People's College, Sheffield, 1842–1878. Sheffield. 1912.

The first working-men's college.

8204 MAURICE (FREDERIC DENISON). Learning and working. Lond. & Camb. 1855. New edn. by William Edward Styler. 1968.

Expounds Maurice's ideas for the [London] Working Men's College.

8205 HARRISON (JOHN FLETCHER CLEWS). A history of the Working Men's College, 1854–1954. 1954.

Full bibliog. There is a useful earlier hist., John Llewellyn Davies, ed., *The Working Men's College, 1854–1904: records of its history and its work for fifty years, by members of the college,* 1904. The College has issued an annual report since 1880 and a j. since 1890.

8206 ATKINS (E.) *ed.* The Vaughan Working-Men's College, Leicester, 1862–1912. Lond. & Leicester. 1912.

8207 CHADWICK (DAVID). On working-men's colleges. 1859.

8208 THE WORKING MEN'S COLLEGE MAGAZINE. 1859–62.
Useful for all the colleges.

### (c) *Literary and Philosophical Societies*

8209 KITSON CLARK (EDWIN). The history of 100 years of life of the Leeds Philosophical and Literary Society. Leeds. 1924.

8210 LOTT (FREDERICK BARNES). The centenary book of the Leicester Literary and Philosophical Society. Leicester. 1935.

8211 TIFFEN (HERBERT JOSEPH). A history of the Liverpool Institute Schools, 1825 to 1935. Liverpool. 1935.

8212 WATSON (ROBERT SPENCE). The history of the Literary and Philosophical Society of Newcastle-upon-Tyne, 1793–1896. 1897.

8213 TAIT (ARTHUR). History of the Oldham Lyceum, 1839–1897: with which is incorporated the history of the Oldham School of Science and Art, 1864–1892. Oldham. 1897.

8214 PORTER (WILLIAM SMITH). Sheffield Literary and Philosophical Society: a centenary restrospect, 1822–1922. Sheffield. 1922.

8215 BROWNE (HORACE BAKER). Chapters of Whitby history, 1823–1946: the story of the Whitby Literary and Philosophical Society and of Whitby Museum. Hull. 1946.

8216 JONES (JAMES P.). Historical sketch of the art and literary institutions of Wolverhampton. 1896.

8217 THE CITY OF LONDON COLLEGE, 1848–1948. 1948.

### (d) *University Extension and Tutorial Classes*

8218 DRAPER (WILLIAM HENRY). University extension: a survey of fifty years, 1873–1923. Camb. 1923.
See also Robert Davies Roberts, *Eighteen years of university extension*, Camb. 1891.

8219 MANSBRIDGE (ALBERT). University tutorial classes: a study in the development of higher education among working men and women. 1913.

8220 KELLY (THOMAS). Outside the walls: sixty years of university extension at Manchester, 1886–1946. Manch. 1950.

8221 STUART. Reminiscences. By James Stuart. Comp. by Helen Caroline Colman. Priv. pr. 1911. Public edn. 1912.

Stuart was the founder of university extension classes.

8222 HERVEY (*Lord* ARTHUR CHARLES). A suggestion for supplying the literary, scientific and mechanics' institutes of Great Britain and Ireland with lecturers from the universities. Camb. 1855.

The earliest proposal for extramural classes.

8223 PERCIVAL (JOHN), *bishop*. The connection of the universities and the great towns. 1873.

8224 MOULTON (RICHARD GREEN). The university extension movement. [1887.]

8225 OXFORD UNIVERSITY. Extension lectures: report of a conference in the examination schools, Oxford, of representatives of the local committees acting in concert with the committee of delegates of local examinations appointed to establish lectures and teaching in large towns, and of others interested in the extension of university teaching, April 20 & 21, 1887. Oxf. 1887.

See also **8168**.

8226 MACKINDER (*Sir* HALFORD JOHN) *and* SADLER (*Sir* MICHAEL ERNEST). University extension: has it a future? 1890. 3rd edn. 1891.

3rd edn. entitled *University extension: past, present and future.*

8227 OXFORD AND WORKING-CLASS EDUCATION: being the report of a joint committee of university and working-class representatives on the relation of the university to the higher education of work-people. Oxf. 1908. 2nd edn. 1909. Repr. 1951.

The basic doc. of the tutorial classes movement. For comment see James Bacon Rye, 'Oxford and the working-class', *Nineteenth Century* lxv (1909), 521–34, and Plebs League, *The burning question of education*, Oxf. 1909, 2nd edn. 1909, a plea for workers' control of workers' educ.

8228 ROBERTS (ROBERT DAVIES). University extension under the old and new conditions. Camb. 1908.

8229 UNIVERSITY EXTENSION [JOURNAL]. 1890–1926.

Title varies. A short-lived competitor was *Oxford University extension gazette*, 1890–7.

8230 CENTRAL JOINT ADVISORY COMMITTEE ON TUTORIAL CLASSES. Annual report. 1909–10+. 1910+.

There is also a valuable report by James Wycliffe Headlam, afterwards Sir J. W. Headlam-Morley and Leonard Trelawney Hobhouse, *Special report on certain tutorial classes in connection with the Workers' Educational Association*, Board of Educ. [1910.]

### (e) *Workers' Educational Association*

8231  STOCKS (MARY DANVERS). The Workers' Educational Association: the first fifty years. 1953.

Repl. Thomas William Price, *The story of the Workers' Educational Association from 1903 to 1924 . . .*, 1924, but not the more personal narrative of Albert Mansbridge (**8232**). The main sources are the reports of the Association to Promote the Higher Education of Working Men [from 1905 the Workers' Educational Assoc.], 1903–4+, 1904+, the reports of its district and branch organizations, and the numerous pamphlet hists. publ. by the branches. From 1908 the W.E.A. has publ. *The highway: a monthly journal of education for the people.*

8232  MANSBRIDGE (ALBERT). An adventure in working-class education: being, the story of the Workers' Educational Association, 1903–1915. 1920.

A hist. by the founder.

8233  SMITH (HENRY PERCIVAL). Labour and learning. Oxf. 1956.

An account of Oxford's connection with the W.E.A.

8234  TAWNEY (RICHARD HENRY). 'An experiment in democratic education'. *Political Q.* i (1914), 62–84.

The best statement of the aims and ideals of the W.E.A. before the 1914–18 war.

8235  MANSBRIDGE. The trodden road: experience, inspiration and belief. By Albert Mansbridge. 1940.

The autobiog. of the founder.

### (f) *Other Adult Education Movements*

8236  MARTIN (GEORGE CURRIE). The adult school movement: its origin and development. 1924.

Standard. See also John Wilhelm Rowntree and Henry Bryan Binns, *A history of the adult school movement*, 1903, and the publs. of the National Council of Adult School Unions, *Adult school year-book and directory*, 1911–1946/7, *Adult school lesson handbook*, 1911–45, and its annual report.

8237  TWIGG (HERBERT JAMES). An outline history of co-operative education. Manch. 1924.

A useful intro. See also A. Greenwood, *The educational department of the Rochdale Equitable Pioneers Society, Limited: its origin and development*, Manch. 1877, F. W. Peaples, *History of the educational department of the Bolton Co-operative Society, 1861–1914*, Manch. 1916, and the *Prospectus* of the education dept. of the Co-operative Union Ltd., Manch. 1898+.

8238  HAWKINS (THORNTON HORACE) *and* BRIMBLE (LIONEL JOHN FARNHAM). Adult education: the record of the British Army. 1947.

Little on the pre-1914 period.

8239  NATIONAL HOME READING UNION. The general readers' magazine. Camb. etc. 1889–91.

Cont. in 3 sections 1891–1914: reunited 1914–1925 as *The home reading magazine*. An important agency of adult educ. The Union issued an annual report to the year 1928–9.

**8240** BUXTON (CHARLES SYDNEY). 'Ruskin College: an educational experiment'. *Cornhill Mag.* xxv (1908), 192–200.

The best intro. to the subject. But see also *The story of Ruskin College, 1899–1949*, Oxf. 1949, rev. edn. 1955, and Henry Sanderson Furniss, Baron Sanderson, *Memories of sixty years*, 1931.

**8241** PLEBS LEAGUE. The 'Plebs' magazine. Oxf. etc. 1909+.

Useful for left-wing reactions to the adult educ. movement and for the origins of the National Council of Labour Colleges. See also **8227**.

**8242** PUMPHREY (MARY E.). Recollections of Fircroft: an experiment in adult education. Birmingham. 1952.

See also Herbert George Wood and Arthur E. Ball, *Tom Bryan: first warden of Fircroft*, 1922.

**8243** DAVIS (ROBERT) *ed.* Woodbrooke, 1903–1953: a brief history of a Quaker experiment in religious education. 1953.

See also Arnold Stephenson Rowntree, *Woodbrooke: its history and aims*, Birmingham 1923.

**8244** RICHARDS (DENIS). Offspring of the Vic: a history of Morley College. 1958.

Developed from an early social work centre sponsored by Samuel Morley (**3753**). There is additional material in Diana Hopkinson, *Family inheritance: a life of Eva Hubback* 1954, the life of a famous principal of Morley Coll.

## B. LIBRARIES AND MUSEUMS

### 1. GENERAL

The standard directory is *The libraries, museums and art galleries year book*, 1910+.

**8245** PAPWORTH (JOHN WOODY) and PAPWORTH (WYATT). Museums, libraries and picture galleries, public and private: their establishment, formation, arrangement and architectural construction . . . 1853.

Well illus.

**8246** TRELAWNY COMMITTEE ON PUBLIC INSTITUTIONS. Report from the select committee on public institutions [Chairman: Sir John Trelawny]. H.C. 181 (1860). XVI, 1.

On libraries, museums, etc.

**8247** GREGORY COMMITTEE ON THE BRITISH MUSEUM. Report from the select committee on the British Museum [Chairman: W. H. Gregory] H.C. 540 (1860). XVI, 173.

**8248** CHAMBERS (GEORGE FREDERICK). A digest of the law relating to public libraries and museums. 1874. 4th edn. 1899.

## 2. LIBRARIES

**8249** CANNONS (HARRY GEORGE TURNER). Bibliography of library economy: a classified index to the professional periodical literature in the English language, relating to library economy, printing, methods of publishing, copyright, bibliography, etc., 1876 to 1920. Amer. Lib. Assoc. 2nd edn. Chicago. 1927. Suppls. in progress.

**8250** THORNTON (JOHN LEONARD). A mirror for librarians: selected readings in the history of librarianship. Libr. Assoc. 1948. 2nd edn. [Selected Readings.] 1966.

Suppl. by his *Classics of librarianship: further selected readings in the history of librarianship*, Libr. Assoc. 1957.

**8251** PREDEEK (ALBERT). A history of libraries in Great Britain and North America. Trans. by Lawrence S. Thompson. Amer. Libr. Assoc. Chicago. 1947.

A general intro. like Raymond Irwin, *The English library: sources and history*, 1966.

**8252** LIBRARY ASSOCIATION (LIBRARY HISTORY GROUP). Library history . . . 1+ v. 1967+.

**8253** MUNFORD (WILLIAM ARTHUR) ed. Annals of the Library Association, 1877 to 1960. Libr. Assoc. 1965.

The Assoc. publ. the *Library Association year book*, 1891+, *The Library Assoc. record*, 1899+, *Monthly notes*, 1880–3, *The library chronicle*, 1884–8, *The library*, 1889+, and an *Annual Report*, 1878+.

**8254** GREENWOOD (THOMAS) *and others, comps.* Greenwood's library year book. 1897+.

Irregular. Title became *British library year book*, 1900–1, *The libraries, museums and art galleries year book*, 1910+.

**8255** THE LIBRARY WORLD. 1898+.

The other chief periodicals were those of the Library Assoc. (**8253**), *The library assistant*, 1898+, and *The librarian [and book world]*, 1910+.

**8256** CRASTER (*Sir* HERBERT HENRY EDMUND). History of the Bodleian Library, 1845–1945. Oxf. 1952.

**8257** GUPPY (HENRY). The John Rylands Library, Manchester, 1899–1924: a record of its history, with brief descriptions of the building and its contents. Manch. 1924.

**8258** BECKWITH (FRANK). The Leeds Library, 1768–1968. Priv. pr. Dewsbury. 1968.

8259 MINTO (JOHN). A history of the public library movement in Great Britain and Ireland. Libr. Assoc. 1932.

8260 MUNFORD (WILLIAM ARTHUR). Penny rate: aspects of British public library history, 1850–1950. Libr. Assoc. 1951. Repr. 1968.

8261 EDWARDS (EDWARD). Free town libraries: their formation, management and history: in Britain, France, Germany, & America . . . Lond. & N.Y. 1869.

Public librs. in Europe and the U.S. See also William Edward Armitage Axon, 'Statistical notes on the free town libraries of Great Britain and the continent', *Stat. Soc. J.* xxxiii (1870), 327–65, Thomas Greenwood, *Free public libraries* . . ., 1886, 4th edn. [*Public libraries: a history of the movement and a manual for the organization and management of rate-supported libraries*] 1891, John Joseph Ogle, *The free library: its history and present condition*, 1897, and William George Stewart Adams, *A report on library provision and policy*, Edin. 1915.

8262 KEELING (DENIS F.). 'British public library buildings, 1850–1870'. *Libr. Hist.* i (1967–9), 100–26.

See also Frank James Burgoyne, *Library construction: architecture, fittings and furniture,* 1897, Alfred Cotgreave, *Views and memoranda on public libraries*, 1901, Amian Lister Champneys, *Public libraries: a treatise on their design, construction and fittings*, 1907, and Sidney George Berriman and Kenneth Cecil Harrison, *British public library buildings*, 1966.

8263 BROWN. James Duff Brown, 1862–1914: portrait of a library pioneer. By William Arthur Munford. 1969.

8264 EDWARDS. Edward Edwards, 1812–1886: portrait of a librarian. By William Arthur Munford. Libr. Assoc. 1963.

See also Thomas Greenwood, *Edward Edwards: the chief pioneer of municipal public libraries*, 1902.

8265 EWART. William Ewart, M.P., 1798–1869: portrait of a radical. By William Arthur Munford. 1960.

The parl. champion of public librs.

8266 GREENWOOD. Shade-work: the story of Thomas Greenwood. By Grace Carlton. 1949.

Disappointing.

8267 PANIZZI. Prince of librarians: the life and times of Antonio Panizzi. By Edward Miller. 1967.

See also Louis Alexander Fagan, *The life of Sir Antony Panizzi, late principal librarian of the British Museum*, 2 v. 1880, and L. A. Fagan, ed. *Letters of Prosper Mérimée to Panizzi*, 2 v. 1881.

### 3. MUSEUMS

**8268**  SMITH (RALPH CLIFTON) *comp.* A bibliography of museums and museum work. Wash. 1928.

See also *Museums journal*, 1901+.

**8269**  MURRAY (DAVID). Museums: their history and their use . . . 3 v. Glasgow. 1904.

A full survey. See also Thomas Greenwood, *Museums and art galleries*, 1888, Bernard Douglas Taylor, *Municipal art galleries and art museums: their scope and value . . .*, Manch. 1912, and Sir Henry Alexander Miers, *A report on the public museums of the British isles (other than national museums)*, Carnegie U.K. Trustees, Edin. 1928. For a later assessment see Alma Stephanie Wittlin, *The museum: its history and its tasks in education*, 1949, and **141**.

**8270**  LOWE COMMITTEE ON SOUTH KENSINGTON MUSEUM. Report from the select committee on the South Kensington Museum [Chairman: Robert Lowe]. H.C. 504 (1860). XVI, 527.

**8271**  GORST–POWELL COMMITTEE ON MUSEUMS OF SCIENCE AND ART DEPARTMENT. First report from the select committee on museums of the Science and Art Department [Chairman: Sir John Gorst]. H.C. 223 (1897). XII, 1. Second report [Chairman: Sir Francis Sharp Powell vice Sir John Gorst, resigned]. H.C. 341 (1897). XII, 13. First report in 1898. H.C. 175 (1898). XI, 1. Second report. H.C. 327 (1898). XI, 9. Minute by the committee of council on education on the report. [C. 9163] H.C. (1899). LXXVI, 587.

A full but stormy inquiry. See also two earlier, shorter inquiries: *Report of the interdepartmental committee on the national science collections* [Chairman: Sir Frederick Bramwell]. H.C. 246 (1886). LI, 935, and *Report of the committee appointed by the Treasury to enquire into the science collections at South Kensington* [Chairman: John Evans]. [C. 5831] H.C. (1889). XXXIV, 281.

**8272**  BELL COMMITTEE ON SCIENCE MUSEUM. Report of the departmental committee on the Science Museum and the Geological Museum [Chairman: Sir Hugh Bell]. Pt. 1. [Cd. 5625] H.C. (1911). XVIII, 517. Pt. 2. [Cd. 6221] H.C. (1912–13). XXII, 375.

For the hist. of the museum see also Science Museum, *The Science Museum: the first hundred years*, 1957.

**8273**  ACLAND (*Sir* HENRY WENTWORTH) *and* RUSKIN (JOHN). The Oxford Museum. 1859. Rev. edn. 1893.

An important architectural and cultural landmark. See also Horace Middleton Vernon and Katharine Dorothea Vernon, *A history of the Oxford Museum*, 1909.

**8274**  CURTIS (WILLIAM HUGH). The Curtis Museum, Alton, Hampshire, 1855–1955: the first hundred years of a small museum. 1955.

## C. LITERARY CULTURE

### 1. REFERENCE

For the theatre see **9321–65**.

8275   HOWARD-HILL (TREVOR HOWARD) *comp.* Bibliography of British literary bibliographies. 3 v. Oxf. 1969+.

8276   THE NEW CAMBRIDGE BIBLIOGRAPHY OF ENGLISH LITERATURE. Ed. by George Watson. 4 v. Camb. 1969–74.

The Cambridge bibliography of English literature, 5 v. Camb. 1940–57, took a rather broader view of what constituted literature and will not be altogether replaced by the *New Cambridge bibliography*. For biogs. and autobiogs. see Matthews (**70**).

8277   KENNEDY (ARTHUR GARFIELD) *comp.* A concise bibliography for students of English. Stanford. 1940. 4th edn. 1960.

A useful handlist, fuller than Richard Daniel Altick and Andrew Wright, comps., *Selective bibliography for the study of English and American literature*, N.Y. 1960, 3rd edn. 1967, or Donald Frederic Bond, comp., *A reference guide to English studies*, Chicago 1962, 2nd edn. 1971. The most useful list for major authors is George Watson, comp., *The concise Cambridge bibliography of English literature, 600–1950*, Camb. 1958, 2nd edn. 1965. Frederick Wilse Bateson, *A guide to English literature*, Lond. & Garden City, N.Y. 1965, covers much the same ground but is more selective. Richard Daniel Altick, *The art of literary research*, N.Y. 1963, is a pleasant intro.

8278   ALLIBONE (SAMUEL AUSTIN) *comp.* A critical dictionary of English literature and British and American authors . . . 3 v. Phila. 1858–71. Suppl. by John Foster Kirk. 2 v. Phila. 1891. The whole repr. in 5 v. Detroit [Mich.] 1965.

Particularly useful for reviews of authors whose work was publ. in the 1850s. For later authors see Kunitz and Haycraft, *British authors of the nineteenth century* (**76**) and Elgin W. Mellown, comp., *A descriptive catalogue of the bibliographies of 20th century British writers*, Troy, N.Y. 1972.

8279   BIBLIOGRAPHY OF ENGLISH LANGUAGE AND LITERA-TURE, 1920+: comp. by members of the Modern Humanities Research Assoc. Camb. 1921+.

From 1923 *Annual bibliog. of English language and literature*. The English Assoc. publ. a fuller commentary as *The year's work in English studies*, 1919–20+.

8280   STEVENSON ([ARTHUR] LIONEL) *ed.* Victorian fiction: a guide to research. Camb., Mass. 1964.

To be suppl. by Lucien Leclaire, *A general analytical bibliography of the regional novelists of the British Isles, 1800–1950*, Clermont-Ferrand 1954, and William Freeman, *Dictionary of fictional characters*, 1963, suppl. by J. M. F. Leaper, 1965. Additional material may be found in Inglis Freeman Bell and Donald Baird, *The English novel, 1578–1956: a checklist of twentieth-century criticisms*, Denver, Colo. 1958; Ernest Albert Baker and James Packman, *A guide to the best fiction, English and American, including translations from foreign languages*, rev. edn., 1932, repr. N.Y. 1967; Daniel D. McGarry and Sarah Harriman White, *Historical fiction guide: annotated chronological*, *geographical and topical list of five thousand selected historical novels*, N.Y. 1963; Jonathan Nield, *A guide to the best historical novels and tales*, 1902, 5th edn. 1929; John Anthony Buckley and William Tom Williams, *A guide to British historical fiction*, 1912; and Jacques Souvage, *An introduction to the study of the novel . . .*, Ghent 1965. For detective fiction see Eric Osborne, comp., *Victorian detective fiction: a catalogue of the collection made by Dorothy Glover & Graham Greene*, 1966.

8281   FAVERTY (FREDERIC EVERETT) *ed.* The Victorian poets: a guide to research. Camb., Mass. 1956. 2nd edn. 1968.

See also Jerome Hamilton Buckley, *Victorian poets and prose writers*, N.Y. 1966, Joseph Marshall Kuntz, *Poetry explication: a checklist of interpretation since 1925 of British and American poems past and present*, rev. edn. Denver, Colo. 1962.

8282   ALTICK (RICHARD DANIEL) *and* MATTHEWS (WILLIAM R.) *comps.* Guide to doctoral dissertations in Victorian literature, 1886–1958. Urbana, Ill. 1960.

See also Lawrence Francis MacNamee, *Dissertations in English and American literature: theses accepted by American, British and German universities, 1865–1964*, N.Y. 1968.

8283   EHRSAM (THEODORE GEORGE), DEILY (ROBERT HOWARD), *and* SMITH (ROBERT METCALF) *comps.* Bibliographies of twelve Victorian authors. N.Y. 1936.

Arnold, Elizabeth Barrett Browning, Clough, FitzGerald, Hardy, Kipling, Morris, Christina and Dante Gabriel Rossetti, Stevenson, Swinburne, and Tennyson.

8284   SADLEIR (MICHAEL). XIX century fiction: a bibliographical record. 2 v. 1951.

A famous pioneering work. See also his *Excursions in Victorian bibliography*, 1922.

8285   CARTER (JOHN) *and* POLLARD (GRAHAM). An enquiry into the nature of certain nineteenth-century pamphlets. 1934. Working papers for a second edn. . . . 1+ v. Oxf. 1969+.

On the forgeries of Thomas J. Wise, for whom see William Burton Todd, ed., *Thomas J. Wise: centenary studies*, Austin, Tex. 1959, George Eric Haslam, ed., *Wise after the event: a catalogue of books . . .*, Manch. Public Libr. 1964, and Wilfred Partington, *Forging ahead: the true story of the upward progress of Thomas James Wise . . .*, N.Y. [1939], and *Thomas J. Wise in the original cloth . . .*, 1947.

8286   HARVEY (*Sir* PAUL) *comp.* The Oxford companion to English literature. Oxf. 1932. 4th edn. 1967.

The most convenient literary encyclopedia. Robin Myers, comp., *A dictionary of literature in the English language from Chaucer to 1940*, 2 v., Nat. Book League, Oxf. etc. 1970, is a list of authors and their works. Clarence Lewis Barnhart and William Darrach Halsey, eds., *The new century handbook of English literature*, N.Y. 1956, is also useful. Jyotish Chandra Ghosh and Elizabeth Gidley Withycombe, comps., *Annals of English literature*, Oxf. 1935, 2nd edn. by Robert William Chapman, Oxf. 1961, is important because it lists the publs. year by year. Robert Chambers, ed., *Cyclopaedia of English literature . . .*, 2 v. Edin. 1844, 4th edn. [*Chambers's cyclopaedia*] 1893, new edn. by David Patrick, 3 v. 1901–3, was the most popular of contemp. works.

8287 THE OXFORD DICTIONARY OF QUOTATIONS. Oxf. 1941. 2nd edn. 1953.

Good on the period. Bergen Evans, comp., *Dictionary of quotations*, N.Y. 1968, is comparable in scope. Edith Granger, ed., *An index to poetry and recitations . . .*, 5th edn. N.Y. 1962, suppl. 1967, indexes the contents of anthologies.

8288 BRUSSEL (ISIDORE ROSENBAUM). Anglo-American first editions. 1. 'East to west, 1826–1900'. 2. 'West to east, 1786–1930'. 2 v. 1935–6.

8289 KENNEDY (ARTHUR GARFIELD). A bibliography of writings on the English language from the beginning of printing to the end of 1922. Camb., Mass. 1927. Repr. 1967.

8290 BRIGHTFIELD (MYRON FRANKLIN) *comp.* Victorian England in its novels, 1840–1870. 4 v. Los Angeles. 1968.

A massive scissors-and-paste anthology, of 8,000 excerpts from 1,221 novels.

8291 GRAHAM (WALTER JAMES). English literary periodicals. N.Y. 1930. Repr. N.Y. 1966.

Also useful is Sheila A. Egoff, *Children's periodicals of the nineteenth century: a survey and bibliography*, Libr. Assoc. pamph. no. 8, 1951.

8292 CLARKE (IGNATIUS FREDERICK). The tale of the future: from the beginning to the present day: a check-list of those satires, ideal states, imaginary wars and invasions, all located in an imaginary future period, that have been published in the United Kingdom between 1644 and 1960. Libr. Assoc. 1961.

8293 THE CAMBRIDGE HISTORY OF ENGLISH LITERATURE. Ed. by Sir Adolphus William Ward and Alfred Rayney Waller. 15 v. Camb. 1907–27.

Out of date, but often useful as a source. Will probably be repl. by the *Oxford history of English literature*, ed. by Frank Percy Wilson and Bonamy Dobree, Oxf. 1945+. For the novel Ernest Albert Baker, *The history of the English novel*, 10 v. 1924–39, new edn. 11 v. N.Y. 1957–67, is encyclopedic. Albert Croll Baugh, ed., *A literary history of England*, N.Y. 1948, 2nd edn. Lond. & N.Y. 1967, includes a useful vol. on *The nineteenth century and after*. There is also George Sampson, *The concise Cambridge history of English literature*, Camb. 1941, 3rd edn. by Reginald Charles Churchill, 1970. Three older vols. sponsored by the Roy. Soc. of Lit. are interesting, John Drinkwater, ed., *The eighteen-sixties: essays by fellows of the Royal Society of Literature*, Camb. 1932, Harley Granville-Barker, ed., *The eighteen-seventies . . .*, Camb. 1929, and Walter De La Mare, ed., *The eighteen eighties . . .*, Camb. 1930.

8294 HUME (ABRAHAM). The learned societies and printing clubs of the United Kingdom . . . with a supplement . . . by A. I. Evans. 1853.

For the Roy. Soc. of Lit. see Sir Edward William Brabrook, *The Royal Society of Literature of the United Kingdom: a brief account of its origin and progress*, 2nd edn. 1897.

## 2. COMMENTARY

Other general works of interpretation are incl. at **171–90**.

8295  ALTICK (RICHARD DANIEL). 'The sociology of authorship: the social origins, education and occupations of 1,100 British writers, 1800–1935'. *New York Public Libr. Bull.* lxvi (1962), 389–404.

8296  ANNAN (NOEL GILROY), *Baron Annan.* 'The intellectual aristocracy'. In John Harold Plumb, ed., Studies in social history: a tribute to G. M. Trevelyan. 1955. Pp. 241–87.

> Good. A rather wider range is covered by Hyde Clarke, 'On the geographical distribution of intellectual qualities in England', *Stat. Soc. J.* xxxiv (1871), 357–73.

8297  GROSS (JOHN JACOB). The rise and fall of the man of letters: aspects of English literary life since 1800. Lond. 1969. Amer. edn. publ. as The rise and fall of the man of letters: a study of the idiosyncratic and the humane in modern literature. N.Y. 1969.

> See also Christopher Kent, 'Higher journalism and the mid-Victorian clerisy', *Victorian Studs.* xiii (1969–70), 181–98, René Wellek, *A history of modern criticism, 1750–1950*, 1955, and James Gordon Hepburn, *The author's empty purse and the rise of the literary agent*, 1968.

8298  ALTICK (RICHARD DANIEL). The English common reader: a social history of the mass reading public, 1800–1900. Chicago. 1957.

8299  CRUSE (AMY). The Victorians and their books. Lond. 1935. Publ. in Boston as The Victorians and their reading. 1935. Repr. 1962.

> Cont. in her *After the Victorians*, 1938.

8300  SAINTSBURY (GEORGE). A history of nineteenth-century literature, 1780–1895. 1896.

> Trenchant. Cp. Walter Bagehot, *Literary studies*, ed. by Richard Holt Hutton, 2 v. 1879, Gilbert Keith Chesterton, *The Victorian age in literature*, 1913, and Henry James, *Notes on novelists: with some other notes*, N.Y. 1914.

8301  BAKER (JOSEPH ELLIS) *ed.* The reinterpretation of Victorian literature. Princeton. 1950. New edn. N.Y. 1962.

8302  ROUTH (HAROLD VICTOR). Towards the twentieth century: essays in the spiritual history of the nineteenth century. Camb. 1937.

8303  DECKER (CLARENCE RAYMOND). The Victorian conscience. N.Y. 1952.

8304  BUCKLEY (JEROME HAMILTON). The triumph of time: a study of the Victorian concepts of time, history, progress and decadence. Camb., Mass. 1966.

> See also his *Victorian temper* (**173**).

8305 HOUGHTON (WALTER EDWARDS). 'Victorian anti-intellectualism'. *J. Hist. Ideas.* xiii (1952), 291–313.

See also his *Victorian frame of mind* (180).

8306 SUSSMAN (HERBERT LEWIS). Victorians and the machine: the literary response to technology. Camb., Mass. 1968.

8307 STEVENSON ([ARTHUR] LIONEL). Darwin among the poets. Chicago. 1932.

See also [John Nash] Douglas Bush, *Science and English poetry: a historical sketch, 1590–1950*, N.Y. 1950, Leo Justin Henkin, *Darwinism in the English novel, 1860–1910: the impact of evolution on Victorian fiction*, N.Y. 1940, George Roppen, *Evolution and poetic belief: a study in some Victorian and modern writers*, Oslo 1956, and Joseph Warren Beach, *The concept of nature in nineteenth-century English poetry*, N.Y. 1936, repr. 1956.

8308 DAVIES (HUGH SYKES) *ed.* The English mind: studies in the English moralists, presented to Basil Willey. Camb. 1964.

See also Willey's works at 174.

8309 NEFF (EMERY EDWARD). Carlyle and Mill: mystic and utilitarian. N.Y. 1924. 2nd edn. [Carlyle and Mill: an introduction to Victorian thought.] N.Y. 1926.

Cp. George Lewis Levine, *The boundaries of fiction: Carlyle, Macaulay, Newman,* Princeton 1968.

8310 WOODWARD (FRANCES JOYCE). The doctor's disciples: a study of four pupils of Arnold of Rugby: Stanley, Gell, Clough and William Arnold. 1954.

8311 DE LAURA (DAVID J.). Hebrew and Hellene in Victorian England: Newman, Arnold and Pater. Austin, Tex. 1969.

8312 HOLLOWAY (JOHN). The Victorian sage: studies in argument. 1953.

Arnold, Carlyle, Disraeli, George Eliot, Hardy, Newman.

8313 LEAVIS (FRANK RAYMOND). The great tradition: George Eliot, Henry James, Joseph Conrad. 1948.

8314 BUSH ([JOHN NASH] DOUGLAS). Mythology and the romantic tradition in English poetry. Camb., Mass. 1937. New edn. 1969.

See also Sir Cecil Maurice Bowra, *The romantic imagination*, Camb., Mass. 1949; John Francis Alexander Heath-Stubbs, *The darkling plain: a study of the later fortunes of romanticism in English poetry from George Darley to W. B. Yeats*, 1950; [John] Frank Kermode, *Romantic image*, Lond. & N.Y. 1957; Reginald Anthony Foakes, *The romantic assertion: a study in the language of nineteenth-century poetry*, New Haven, Conn. 1958; George Harry Ford, *Keats and the Victorians: a study of his influence and rise to fame, 1821–95*, New Haven 1944; Roland A. Duerksen, *Shelleyan ideas in Victorian literature*, The Hague 1966; Barbara Charlesworth, *Dark passages: the decadent consciousness in Victorian literature*, Madison, Wis. 1965; and Louise Michelle Rosenblatt, *L'idée de l'art pour l'art dans la littérature anglaise pendant la période victorienne*, Paris 1931.

**8315 HOUGH (GRAHAM). The last romantics. 1949.**

Morris, Pater, Rossetti, Ruskin, Yeats . . . See also Benjamin Ifor Evans, *English poetry in the later nineteenth century*, 1933, 2nd edn. Lond. & N.Y. 1966.

**8316 JACKSON (HOLBROOK). The eighteen-nineties: a review of art and ideas at the close of the nineteenth century. 1913. Frequent reprints.**

Still the most stimulating work of its kind. See also Albert John Farmer, *Le mouvement esthétique et 'décadent' en Angleterre, 1873–1900*, Paris 1931, Helmut E. Gerber, 'The nineties: beginning, end, or transition', in Richard Ellmann, ed., *Edwardians and late Victorians*, N.Y. 1960, pp. 50–79, Ian Fletcher, 'The 1890s: a lost decade', *Victorian Studs.* iv (1960–1), 345–54, and Derek Stanford, comp., *Critics of the nineties*, 1970.

**8317 LESTER (JOHN ASHBY). Journey through despair, 1880–1914: transformations in British literary culture. Princeton. 1968.**

Disappointing. See also **184–90.**

**8318 KISSANE (JAMES). 'Victorian mythology'. *Victorian Studs.* vi (1962–3), 5–28.**

**8319 BURROW (JOHN WYON). 'The uses of philology in Victorian England'. In Robert Robson, ed., Ideas and Institutions of Victorian Britain (177). 180–204.**

The Philological Soc. publ. *Proceedings*, 1842–53, and *Transactions*, 1854+. The greatest figure in philology was F. Max Müller (**8397**). See also Hans Aarsleff, *The study of language in England, 1780–1860*, Princeton 1967, and Elizabeth Mary Wright, *The story of Joseph Wright, man and scholar*, Oxf. 1934.

**8320 NINETEENTH-CENTURY FICTION. 1+. Berkeley etc. 1945+.**

Vols. 1–3 styled *The Trollopian*. Articles on the period are also publ. in *Victorian Studs.*, 1+, Bloomington, Ind. 1957+, *Victorian poetry: a critical journal of Victorian literature*, Morgantown, West Va., 1+, 1963+, and Modern Humanities Research Assoc., English X Group, *The Victorian newsletter*, 1+, N.Y. 1952+.

**8321 STARKIE (ENID). From Gautier to Eliot: the influence of France on English literature, 1851–1939. 1960.**

See also Ruth Zabriski Temple, *The critic's alchemy: a study of the introduction of French symbolism into England*, N.Y. 1953, Christophe Campos, *The view of France: from Arnold to Bloomsbury*, 1965, E. Hilda Dale, *La poéise française en Angleterre, 1850–1890*, Paris 1954, and **2276.**

**8322 MINER (EARL ROY). The Japanese tradition in British and American literature. Princeton. 1958.**

**8323 GOHDES (CLARENCE LOUIS FRANK). American literature in nineteenth-century England. N.Y. 1944.**

**8324 PHELPS (GILBERT). The Russian novel in English fiction. 1956.**

See also **2345**, Donald Lee Fanger, *Dostoevsky and romantic realism: a study of Dostoevsky in relation to Balzac, Dickens and Gogol*, Camb., Mass. 1965, and Helen Machnie, *Dostoevsky's English reputation, 1881–1935*, Northampton, Mass. 1939.

8325 FRANTZ (ADOLPH INGRAM). Half a hundred thralls to Faust: a study based on the British and American translations of Goethe's 'Faust', 1823–1949. Chapel Hill, N.C. 1949.

For Nietzsche see David S. Thatcher, *Nietzsche in England, 1890–1914: the growth of a reputation*, Toronto 1970, and Patrick Bridgwater, *Nietzsche in Anglosaxony: a study of Nietzsche's impact on English and American literature*, Leicester 1972.

8326 THOMAS (DONALD). A long time burning: the history of literary censorship in England. Lond. & N.Y. 1969.

There is also Noel Perrin, *Dr. Bowdler's legacy: a history of expurgated books*, Lond. & N.Y. 1969.

8327 THWAITE (MARY FLORENCE). From primer to pleasure: an introduction to the history of children's books from the invention of printing to 1900 . . . Libr. Assoc. 1963. Repr. 1966.

See also Judith St. John, comp., *The Osborne collection of early children's books, 1566– 1910: a catalogue* . . ., Toronto 1958; Leonard de Vries, *Flowers of delight culled from the Osborne collection* . . ., 1965; Frederick Joseph Harvey Darton, *Children's books in England: five centuries of social life*, Camb. 1932, 2nd edn. 1958; Percy Horace Muir, *English children's books, 1600 to 1900*, 1954; Cornelia Lynde Meigs and others, *A critical history of children's literature* . . ., N.Y. 1953; Roger Lancelyn Green, *Tellers of tales*, Leicester 1946; Gillian Avery, assisted by Angela Bull, *Nineteenth-century children: heroes and heroines in English children's stories, 1780–1900*, 1965; Rolf Hildebrandt, *Nonsense Aspekte der englischen Kinderliteratur*, Berlin 1970; William Oliver Guillemont Lofts and Derek John Adley, *The men behind boys' fiction*, 1970; and Ernest Sackville Turner, *Boys will be boys* . . ., rev. edn. 1957.

## 3. INDIVIDUAL AUTHORS

8328 ARNOLD. The bibliography of Matthew Arnold. Comp. by Thomas Burnett Smart. 1892.

To be suppl. by Faverty (**8281**). For letters see Arthur Kyle Davis, *Matthew Arnold's letters: a descriptive checklist*, Bibliog. Soc. of the Univ. of Virginia, Charlottesville 1968, George William Erskine Russell, ed., *Letters of Matthew Arnold, 1848–1888*, 2 v. 1895, and Harold Foster Lowry, ed., *The letters of Matthew Arnold to Arthur Hugh Clough*, 1932. H. F. Lowry, Karl Young, and Waldo Hilary Dunn, eds., *Note books of Matthew Arnold*, 1952, is important. William Earl Buckler, *Matthew Arnold's books: toward a publishing diary*, Geneva 1958, is useful for dating. For the poetry see Stephen Maxfield Parrish, *A concordance to the poems of Matthew Arnold*, Ithaca, N.Y. 1959. The nearest thing to a biog. is Louis Bonnerot, *Matthew Arnold, poète: essai de biographie psychologique*, Paris 1947. For commentary see particularly Lionel Trilling, *Matthew Arnold*, N.Y. 1939, new edn. 1949, and Arthur Dwight Culler, *Imaginative reason: the poetry of Matthew Arnold*, New Haven, Conn. 1966.

Other studies incl. Chauncey Brewster Tinker and H. F. Lowry, *The poetry of Matthew Arnold: a commentary*, 1940, repr. 1950; Edward Killoran Brown, *Matthew Arnold: a study in conflict*, Chicago 1948, and *Studies in the text of Matthew Arnold's prose works*, N.Y. 1969; Douglas Bush, *Matthew Arnold: a survey of his poetry and prose*, N.Y. 1971; Michael Thorpe, *Matthew Arnold*, 1969; David Gwilym James, *Matthew Arnold and the decline of English romanticism*, Oxf. 1961; Leon Gottfried, *Matthew Arnold and the romantics*, 1963; William Robbins, *The ethical idealism of Matthew Arnold: a study of the nature and sources of his moral ideas*, 1959; Robert Henry Super, *The time-spirit of Matthew Arnold*, Ann Arbor, Mich. 1970; Alan Roper, *Arnold's poetic landscapes*, Baltimore 1969; George Robert Stange, *Matthew Arnold:*

*the poet as humanist*, Princeton 1967; William Anthony Madden, *Matthew Arnold: a study of the aesthetic temperament in Victorian England*, Bloomington, Ind. 1967; Sir Edmund Kerchever Chambers, *Matthew Arnold: a study*, Oxf. 1947; Paull Franklin Baum, *Ten studies in the poetry of Matthew Arnold*, Durham, N.C. 1958; Warren De Witt Anderson, *Matthew Arnold and the classical tradition*, Ann Arbor, Mich. 1965; William Fraser Connell, *The educational thought and influence of Matthew Arnold*, 1950; Fred G. Walcott, *The origins of 'Culture & anarchy': Matthew Arnold & popular education in England*, Toronto 1970; Edward Alexander, *Matthew Arnold and John Stuart Mill*, N.Y. 1965; Patrick Joseph McCarthy, *Matthew Arnold and the three classes*, N.Y. 1964; Frederic Everett Faverty, *Matthew Arnold the ethnologist*, Evanston, Ill. 1951; Iris Esther Sells, *Matthew Arnold and France: the poet*, Camb. 1935, new edn. N.Y. 1970; Frank J. W. Harding, *Matthew Arnold, the critic, and France*, Geneva 1964; and John Henry Raleigh, *Matthew Arnold and American culture*, Berkeley etc. 1957. See also **7878**.

**8329 AUSTIN.** Alfred Austin: Victorian. By Norton Barr Crowell. Albuquerque, N. Mex. 1953.

There is also *The autobiography of Alfred Austin, poet laureate, 1835–1910*, 2 v. 1911.

**8330 BARNES.** The life of William Barnes, poet and philologist. By his daughter Lucy Baxter. Lond. & N.Y. 1887.

See also Giles Dugdale, *William Barnes of Dorset*, 1953; Trevor William Hearl, *William Barnes, 1801–1886, the schoolmaster: a study of education in the life and work of the Dorset poet*, Dorchester 1966; Florence Susan Hinchy, *The Dorset William Barnes*, Blandford 1966; Willis D. Jacobs, *William Barnes, linguist*, Albuquerque, N. Mex. 1952; and William Turner Levy, *William Barnes: the man and the poems*, Dorchester 1960.

**8331 BARRIE.** A bibliography of the writings of Sir James Matthew Barrie, Bart., O.M. By Herbert Garland. 1928.

Viola Meynell, ed., *Letters of J. M. Barrie*, Lond. 1942, N.Y. 1947, is the only coll. of letters. For his life see Janet Dunbar, *J. M. Barrie: the man behind the image*, Lond. & Boston 1970; Lady Cynthia Charteris Asquith, *Portrait of Barrie*, 1954; Frederick Joseph Harvey Darton, *J. M. Barrie*, 1928; Harry M. Geduld, *Sir James Barrie*, N.Y. 1971; Sir John Alexander Hammerton, *Barrie: the story of a genius*, Lond. & N.Y. 1929, and *J. M. Barrie and his books: biographical and critical studies*, 1900; and Denis George Mackail, *The story of J.M.B.: a biography*, 1941. On his work there is also Roger Lancelyn Green, *J. M. Barrie*, 1960, and *Fifty years of Peter Pan*, 1954, Henry Mackinnon Walbrook, *J. M. Barrie and the theatre*, 1922, and George Blake, *Barrie and the kailyard school*, 1951.

**8332 BEERBOHM.** A bibliography of the works of Max Beerbohm. By Albert Eugene Gallatin and Leslie Mahin Oliver. Camb., Mass. & Lond. 1952.

See also Jacob Gerhard Riewald, *Sir Max Beerbohm, man and writer: a critical analysis with a brief life and a bibliography*, The Hague 1953. For letters see Sir Rupert Hart-Davis, ed., *Max Beerbohm's letters to Reggie Turner*, Lond. 1964, Phila. 1965. For his life see Lord David Cecil, *Max: a biography*, Lond. 1964, Boston 1965, and Samuel Nathaniel Behrman, *Portrait of Max . . . .*, N.Y. 1960. For sketches see Sir R. Hart-Davis, comp., *A catalogue of the caricatures of Max Beerbohm*, Lond. & Camb., Mass. 1972.

**8333 BELLOC.** The English first editions of Hilaire Belloc . . . By Patrick Cahill. 1953.

See also Robert Speaight, ed., *Letters of Hilaire Belloc*, 1958, and *The life of Hilaire Belloc*, 1957, and Marie Adelaide Lowndes, *The young Hilaire Belloc*, N.Y. 1956.

**8334** BENNETT. Arnold Bennett, 1867–1931: a bibliography. By Norman Emery. Hanley. 1967.

The main biog. sources are Newman Flower, ed., *The journals of Arnold Bennett*, 3 v. 1932–3; Dorothy Cheston Bennett, ed., *Arnold Bennett: Florentine journal, 1st April–25th May 1910* . . ., 1967; James Gordon Hepburn, ed., *Letters of Arnold Bennett*, 1+ v. 1966+; Linette Fisher Brugmans, ed., *Correspondance André Gide–Arnold Bennett: vingt ans d'amitié littéraire, 1911–1931*, Geneva 1964; Harris Wilson, ed., *Arnold Bennett and H. G. Wells: a record of a personal and a literary friendship*, Lond. & Urbana, Ill. 1960; Richard Bennett, ed., *Arnold Bennett's letters to his nephew*, 1936; and Dorothy Cheston Bennett, *Arnold Bennett: a portrait done at home, together with 170 letters* . . ., 1935. The best biog. studs. are Walter Allen, *Arnold Bennett*, 1948, Frederick Joseph Harvey Darton, *Arnold Bennett*, 1915, James Gordon Hepburn, *The art of Arnold Bennett*, Bloomington, Ind. 1963, and Georges Lafourcade, *Arnold Bennett: a study*, 1939. Marguerite Bennett, *Arnold Bennett*, Lond. & N.Y. 1925, also publ. in England as *My Arnold Bennett*, 1931, is of little account. The process of re-discovering Arnold Bennett has led to the publication of a number of intro. works, incl. Reginald Pound, *Arnold Bennett: a biography*, 1952; Dudley Barker, *Writer by trade: a view of Arnold Bennett*, 1966; Oswald Harcourt Davis, *The master: a study of Arnold Bennett*, 1966; Ingo Pommerening, *Arnold Bennett als Literaturkritiker*, Giessen 1964; Louis Tillier, *Studies in the sources of Arnold Bennett's novels*, Paris 1969, and *Arnold Bennett et ses romans réalistes*, Paris 1968.

**8335** BORROW. A bibliography of the writings in prose and verse of George Henry Borrow. By Thomas James Wise. 1914.

See also William Ireland Knapp, *Life, writings and correspondence of George Borrow, 1803–1881* . . ., 2 v. Lond. & N.Y. 1899; Thomas Herbert Darlow, ed., *Letters of George Borrow to the British and Foreign Bible Society*, 1911; Clement King Shorter, *George Borrow and his circle* . . ., Lond., Boston, & N.Y. 1913; Martin Armstrong, *George Borrow*, 1950; René Fréchet, *George Borrow: vagabond polyglotte, agent biblique, écrivain*, Paris 1956; and Robert R. Meyers, *George Borrow*, N.Y. 1966.

**8336** BRIDGES. A bibliography of Robert Bridges. By George Leslie McKay. N.Y. 1933.

For letters see Robert Bridges, *Correspondence of Robert Bridges and Henry Bradley, 1900–1923*, Oxf. 1940, and Claude Colleer Abbott, ed., *The letters of Gerard Manley Hopkins to Robert Bridges*, 1935. For biog. see Edward Thompson, *Robert Bridges, 1844–1930*, 1945, Albert Joseph Guerard, *Robert Bridges: a study of traditionalism in poetry*, Camb., Mass. 1942, and Jean Georges Ritz, *Robert Bridges and Gerard Hopkins, 1863–1889: a literary friendship*, 1960.

**8337** BROOKE. A bibliography of Rupert Brooke. Comp. by Sir Geoffrey Langdon Keynes. 1954. 2nd edn. 1959.

For letters see Sir Geoffrey Langdon Keynes, ed., *The letters of Rupert Brooke*, 1968, and *Letters from America by Rupert Brooke*, intro. by Henry James, N.Y. 1916. For lives see Christopher Vernon Hassall, *Rupert Brooke: a biography*, 1964, Arthur Stringer, *Red wine of youth: a life of Rupert Brooke*, Indianapolis, Ind. 1948, Sir Edward Howard Marsh, *Rupert Brooke: a memoir*, Lond. & N.Y. 1918, and Michael Hastings, *The handsomest young man in England: Rupert Brooke*, 1967.

**8338** BROWN. Thomas Edward Brown, the Manx poet, 1830–1897: a bibliography. By William Cubbon. Douglas. 1934.

See also Sidney Thomas Irwin, ed., *Letters of Thomas Edward Brown*, 2 v. Westminster & N.Y. 1900, 4th edn. Liverpool 1952, Anon, *Thomas Edward Brown: a memorial volume, 1830–1930*, Camb. 1930, Samuel Norris, *Two men of Manxland:*

*Hall Caine, novelist, T. E. Brown, poet,* Douglas 1947, and Selwyn G. Simpson, *Thomas Edward Brown, the Manx poet: an appreciation,* Lond. etc. 1906.

8339  BROWNING. A bibliography of Elizabeth Barrett Browning. By Warner Jenkins Barnes. Austin, Tex. 1967.

To be suppl. by Faverty (**8281**), and Thomas James Wise, comp., *A bibliography of the writings in prose and verse of Elizabeth Barrett Browning,* priv. pr. 1918. For letters written in the period see Sir Frederic George Kenyon, ed., *The letters of Elizabeth Barrett Browning,* 2 v. 1897, 3rd edn. 1898, Leonard Huxley, ed., *Elizabeth Barrett Browning: letters to her sister, 1846–1859,* 1929, Richard Henry Stoddard, ed., *Letters of Elizabeth Barrett Browning addressed to Richard Hengist Horne,* 1877, and Paul Nissley Landis and Ronald Edward Freeman, eds., *Letters of the Brownings to George Barrett,* Urbana, Ill. 1958. For lives see Alethea Hayter, *Mrs. Browning: a poet's work and its setting,* 1962, and *Elizabeth Barrett Browning,* 1965, Dorothy Hewlett, *Elizabeth Barrett Browning: a life,* Lond. & N.Y. 1952, and Gardner Blake Taplin, *The life of Elizabeth Barrett Browning,* New Haven, Conn. 1957.

8340  BROWNING. Robert Browning: a bibliography, 1830–1950. Comp. by Leslie Nathan Broughton, Clark Sutherland Northup and Robert Pearsall. Ithaca, N.Y. 1953.

To be suppl. by Faverty (**8281**). For letters see Thurman Losson Hood, ed., *Letters of Robert Browning, collected by Thomas J. Wise,* New Haven, Conn. 1933; William Clyde De Vane and Kenneth Leslie Knickerbocker, ed., *New letters . . .,* New Haven 1950; Sir Frederic George Kenyon, ed., *Robert Browning and Alfred Domett,* 1906; Richard Curle, ed., *Robert Browning and Julia Wedgwood: a broken friendship as revealed by their letters,* 1937; Gertrude Reese Hudson, ed., *Browning to his American friends: letters between the Brownings, the Storys, and James Russell Lowell, 1841–1890,* N.Y. 1965; Edward C. McAleer, ed., *Dearest Isa: Robert Browning's letters to Isabella Blagden,* Austin, Tex. 1951, and *Learned lady: letters from Robert Browning to Mrs. Thomas FitzGerald, 1876–1889,* Camb., Mass. 1966; and Paul Nissley Landis and Ronald Edward Freeman, eds., *Letters of the Brownings to George Barrett,* Urbana, Ill. 1958.

For data see William Clyde De Vane, *A Browning handbook,* N.Y. 1935, 2nd edn. 1955, Alexandra Leighton Orr [Mrs. Sutherland Orr], *A handbook to the works of Robert Browning,* 1885, 6th edn. 1892, repr. 1937, N.Y. 1969, and Leslie Nathan Brown and Benjamin Franklin Stelter, *A concordance to the poems of Robert Browning,* 2 v. N.Y. 1925–6.

For lives see Alexandra Leighton Orr [Mrs. Sutherland Orr], *Life and letters of Robert Browning,* 1891, rev. edn. by Sir Frederic George Kenyon, 1908; Gilbert Keith Chesterton, *Robert Browning,* 1903; William Hall Griffin, *The life of Robert Browning . . .,* completed and ed. by Harry Christopher Minchin, Lond. & N.Y. 1910, 3rd edn. 1938; Betty Bergson Miller, *Robert Browning: a portrait,* 1952; Maisie Ward, *Robert Browning and his world,* 2 v. 1967–9; Lilian Whiting, *The Brownings: their life and art,* Boston 1911; and Roma Alvah King, *Robert Browning's finances from his own account book,* Waco, Tex. 1947.

For discussions of his work see *The Browning newsletter,* Waco, Tex. 1968+; Thomas Blackburn, *Robert Browning: a study of his poetry,* 1967; Leonard Burrows, *Browning the poet: an introductory study,* Nedlands, W. A. 1969; Philip Drew, ed., *Robert Browning: a collection of critical essays,* Lond. & Boston 1966; John Michael Cohen, *Robert Browning,* 1952, repr. 1954; William Clyde De Vane, *Browning's parleyings: the autobiography of a mind,* New Haven, Conn. 1927, repr. 1964; Park Honan, *Browning's characters: a study in poetic techniques,* New Haven 1961; Boyd Litzinger and Donald Smalley, eds., *Browning: the critical heritage,* 1970; Boyd Litzinger and Kenneth Leslie Knickerbocker, *The Browning critics,* Lexington, Ky. 1965; Boyd Litzinger, *Time's revenges: Browning's reputation as a thinker, 1889–1962,* Knoxville, Tenn. 1964; Hugh Martin, *The faith of Robert Browning,* 1963; Barbara Melchiori, *Browning's poetry of reticence,* Edin. 1968; Katherine H. Porter, *Through a glass darkly: spiritualism in the Browning circle*, Lawrence, Kans. 1958; William Ober Raymond, *The infinite moment, and other essays in Robert Browning*, Toronto 1950, 2nd edn. 1965; William David Shaw, *The dialectical temper: the rhetorical art of Robert Browning*, Ithaca, N.Y. 1968; Roma Alvah King, *The focusing artifice: the poetry of Robert Browning*, Athens, Ohio 1968, and *The bow and the lyre: the art of Robert Browning*, 1957; Clarence Rupert Tracy, ed., *Browning's mind and art: essays*, Edin. 1968; William Whitla, *The central truth: the incarnation in Robert Browning's poetry*, Toronto 1963; and Richard Daniel Altick and James F. Loucks, *Browning's Roman murder story: a reading of 'The ring and the book'*, Chicago 1968. For the Browning Soc. see William S. Peterson, *Interrogating the oracle: a history of the London Browning Society*, Athens, Ohio 1969.

8341 BUCHANAN. Robert Buchanan: some account of his life, his life's work and his literary friendships. By Harriett Jay. 1903.

BULWER-LYTTON. See 745.

8342 BUTLER. A bibliography of the writings of Samuel Butler, author of 'Erewhon', and of writings about him. By Alfred John Hoppé. 1925.

See also Stanley B. Harkness, *The career of Samuel Butler, 1835–1902: a bibliography*, 1955, Henry Festing Jones, ed., *The note-books of Samuel Butler . . .*, 1912, and Augustus Theodore Bartholomew, ed., *Further extracts from the note-books . . .*, 1934.

The first life was Henry Festing Jones, *Samuel Butler, author of 'Erewhon', 1835–1902: a memoir*, 2 v. 1919. See also Joseph Jay Jones, *The cradle of 'Erewhon': Samuel Butler in New Zealand*, Austin, Tex. 1959; George Douglas Howard Cole, *Samuel Butler* and '*The way of all flesh*', 1947, and *Samuel Butler*, 1948; Philip Henderson, *Samuel Butler: the incarnate bachelor*, 1953; Malcolm Muggeridge, *The earnest atheist: a study of Samuel Butler*, 1936; Philip Nicholas Furbank, *Samuel Butler, 1835–1902*, Camb. 1948; Lee Elbert Holt, *Samuel Butler*, N.Y. 1964; Basil Willey, *Darwin and Butler: two versions of evolution*, 1960; and Phyllis Greenacre, *The quest for the father: a study of the Darwin–Butler controversy as a contribution to the understanding of the creative individual*, N.Y. 1963.

8343 CALVERLEY. Calverley and some Cambridge wits of the nineteenth century. By Richard Basil Ince. 1929.

8344 CARLYLE. A bibliography of Thomas Carlyle's writings and ana. By Isaac Watson Dyer. Portland, Maine. 1928.

The standard colls. of letters will be Charles Richard Sanders, Kenneth Joshua Fielding, and others, eds., *The collected letters of Thomas and Jane Welsh Carlyle*, 1+, Durham, N.C. 1971+. The other major colls. of letters for the period are Edwin W. Marrs, jr., ed., *The letters of Thomas Carlyle to his brother Alexander, with related family letters*, Camb., Mass. 1968; Charles Eliot Norton, ed., *The correspondence of Thomas Carlyle and Ralph Waldo Emerson, 1834–1872*, 2 v. Boston 1883, suppl. Boston 1886, various edns.; Joseph Locke Slater, ed., *The correspondence of Emerson and Carlyle*, N.Y. 1964; Alexander James Carlyle, ed., *New letters of Thomas Carlyle*, 2 v. 1904; A. J. Carlyle, ed., *Letters of Thomas Carlyle to John Stuart Mill, John Sterling and Robert Browning*, Lond. & N.Y. 1923; and Trudy Bliss, ed., *Thomas Carlyle: letters to his wife*, Lond. & Camb., Mass. 1953. The official life, James Anthony Froude, *Thomas Carlyle: a history of his life in London, 1834–1881*, 2 v. Lond. & N.Y. 1884, was the subject of hot controversy, for which see Froude's *My relations with Carlyle*, N.Y. 1903, Alexander James Carlyle and Sir James Crichton-Browne, *The nemesis of Froude: a rejoinder to James Anthony Froude's 'My relations with Carlyle'*, N.Y. 1903, and Waldo Hilary Dunn, *Froude & Carlyle: a study of the Froude–Carlyle controversy*, 1930. The fullest life is David Alec Wilson, *Carlyle . . .*, 6 v. 1923–34. Emery Edward Neff, *Carlyle*, N.Y. [1932], and *Carlyle and Mill: mystic and utilitarian*, N.Y. 1924; Julian Symons, *Thomas*

*Carlyle: the life and ideas of a prophet,* 1952; Albert J. La Valley, *Carlyle and the idea of the modern . . .,* New Haven, Conn. 1968; Benjamin Harrison Lehman, *Carlyle's theory of the hero . . .,* Durham, N.C. 1928, repr. N.Y. 1966; and Eric Russell Bentley, *A century of hero worship: a study of the idea of heroism in Carlyle and Nietzsche,* Phila. & N.Y. 1944, 2nd edn. Boston 1957, publ. in Lond. as *The cult of the superman . . .,* 1944, are all useful.

For Mrs. Carlyle see James Anthony Froude, ed., *Letters and memorials of Jane Welsh Carlyle, prepared for publication by Thomas Carlyle,* 3 v. Lond. & N.Y. 1883; Alexander James Carlyle, ed., *New letters . . .,* 2 v. 1903; Leonard Huxley, ed., *Jane Welsh Carlyle: letters to her family, 1839–1863,* Lond. & N.Y. 1924; Lawrence Hanson, *Necessary evil: the life of Jane Welsh Carlyle,* 1952; Thea Holme, *The Carlyles at home,* 1965; and Annie Elizabeth Ireland (Mrs. Alexander Ireland), *Life of Jane Welsh Carlyle,* 1891.

8345   CARROLL. The Lewis Carroll handbook: being, a new version of 'A handbook of the literature of the Rev. C. L. Dodgson', by Sidney Herbert Williams . . . and Falconer Madan . . . comp. by Roger Lancelyn Green. 1962.

R. L. Green also ed. *The diaries of Lewis Carroll,* 2 v. Lond. 1953, N.Y. 1954. The official life was Stuart Dodgson Collingwood, *The life and letters of Lewis Carroll (Rev. C. L. Dodgson),* 1898. R. L. Green, *The story of Lewis Carroll,* 1949, and Derek Hudson, *Lewis Carroll,* 1954, are straightforward lives. Jean Gattégno, *Lewis Carroll,* Paris 1970, Helmut Gernsheim, *Lewis Carroll, photographer,* 1949, and Robert D. Sutherland, *Language and Lewis Carroll,* The Hague 1970, are useful monographs.

8346   CHESTERTON. G. K. Chesterton: a bibliography. By John Sullivan. 1958. Suppl. [Chesterton continued.] 1968.

See also Joseph W. Sprug, ed., *An index to G. K. Chesterton,* Wash. 1966. Chesterton himself publ. an *Autobiography,* Lond. & N.Y. 1936, new edn. by Anthony Burgess, 1969. His brother Cecil Edward publ. an anonymous study, *G. K. Chesterton: a criticism,* 1908. For the family see Ada Elizabeth Chesterton [Mrs. Cecil Chesterton], *The Chestertons,* 1941. For studs. see Christopher Hollis, *The mind of Chesterton,* 1970; Maisie Ward, *Gilbert Keith Chesterton,* N.Y. 1943, Lond. 1944, and *Return to Chesterton,* N.Y. 1952; Maurice Evans, *G. K. Chesterton . . .,* Camb. 1939; [Joseph] Hilaire [Pierre] Belloc, *On the place of Gilbert Chesterton in English letters,* 1940; and William B. Furlong, *GBS/GKC: Shaw and Chesterton: the metaphysical jesters,* Phila. 1970.

8347   CLOUGH. Arthur Hugh Clough, a descriptive catalogue: poetry, prose, biography and criticism. By Richard M. Gollin, Walter Edwards Houghton and Michael Timko. N.Y. Public Libr. N.Y. 1967.

To be suppl. by Faverty (**8281**). Clough's *Correspondence* was ed. by Frederick L. Mulhauser, 2 v. Oxf. 1957. The best studs. are Katharine Campbell Chorley, Baroness Chorley, *Arthur Hugh Clough: the uncommitted mind: a study of his life and poetry,* Oxf. 1962; Walter Edwards Houghton, *The poetry of Clough: an essay in revaluation,* New Haven, Conn. 1963; Michael Timko, *Innocent Victorian: the satiric poetry of Arthur Hugh Clough,* Athens, Ohio 1956; and Evelyn Barish Greenberger, *Arthur Hugh Clough: the growth of a poet's mind,* Camb., Mass. 1970. Paul Veyriras, *Arthur Hugh Clough, 1819–1861,* Paris 1964, is a big thesis.

8348   COLLINS. Wilkie Collins and Charles Reade: first editions (with a few exceptions) in the library at Dormy House, Pine Valley, New Jersey. Comp. by Morris Longstreth Parrish assisted by Elizabeth V. Miller. 1940.

The best studs. are Nuel Pharr Davis, *The life of Wilkie Collins,* Urbana, Ill. 1956, Kenneth Robinson, *Wilkie Collins: a biography,* 1951, and William Harvey Marshall, *Wilkie Collins,* N.Y. 1970.

8349  COLVIN. The Colvins and their friends. By Edward Verrall Lucas. 1928.

See also Sir Sidney Colvin, *Memories & notes of persons & places, 1852–1912*, 1921.

8350  CONAN DOYLE. A bibliographical catalogue of the writings of Sir Arthur Conan Doyle, M.D., LL.D., 1879–1928. By Harold Locke. Tunbridge Wells. 1928.

The best life is John Dickson Carr, *The life of Sir Arthur Conan Doyle*, 1949, but see also John Lamond, *Arthur Conan Doyle: a memoir*, 1931, Adrian Conan Doyle, *The true Conan Doyle*, 1945, Hesketh Pearson, *Conan Doyle*, Lond. & N.Y. 1961, and Pierre Nordon, *Conan Doyle*, trans. by Frances Partridge, 1966. For Doyle's detective Sherlock Holmes see [John] Michael [Drinkrow] Hardwick and Mollie Hardwick, *The Sherlock Holmes companion*, 1962; Orlando Park, *Sherlock Holmes, Esq., and John H. Watson, M.D.: an encyclopaedia of their affairs*, Evanston, Ill. 1962; *The Baker Street j.: an irregular quarterly of Sherlockiana*, N.Y. 1946+; William Stuart Baring-Gould, *The chronological Holmes: a complete dating of the adventures of Mr. Sherlock Holmes of Baker Street . . .*, 1955, and *Sherlock Holmes of Baker Street: the life of the world's first consulting detective*, N.Y. 1962; Sir Sydney Castle Roberts, *Holmes & Watson: a miscellany*, 1953; Trevor Henry Hall, *Sherlock Holmes: ten literary studies*, 1969, and *The late Mr. Sherlock Holmes and other literary studies*, 1971; Michael Harrison, *In the footsteps of Sherlock Holmes*, 2nd edn. 1959; Walter Klinefelter, *Sherlock Holmes in portrait and profile*, Syracuse, N.Y. 1963; and Harold Wilmerding Bell, ed., *Baker Street studies*, 1934, new edn. Morristown, N.J. 1955, and *Sherlock Holmes and Dr. Watson: the chronology of their adventures*, 1932.

8351  CONRAD. A bibliography of Joseph Conrad. Comp. by Theodore George Ehrsam. Metuchen, N.J. 1969.

To be suppl. by Bruce E. Teets and Helmut E. Gerber, comps. *Joseph Conrad: an annotated bibliography of writings about him*, De Kalb, Ill. 1971. Conrad himself publ. *Some reminiscences*, 1912, publ. in N.Y. 1912, and in later Lond. edns. as *A personal record*. For letters see *Joseph Conrad's letters to his wife*, priv. pr. 1927; Edward Garnett, ed., *Letters from Joseph Conrad, 1895 to 1924*, Lond. & Indianapolis, Ind. 1928; Richard Curle, ed., *Conrad to a friend: 150 selected letters from Joseph Conrad to Richard Curle*, 1928; John Archer Gee and Paul Jones Sturm, trans. and eds., *Letters of Joseph Conrad to Marguerite Poradowska, 1890–1920*, New Haven, Conn. 1940; René Rapin, ed., *Lettres de Joseph Conrad à Marguerite Poradowska*, Geneva 1966; William Blackburn, ed., *Joseph Conrad: letters to William Blackwood and David S. Meldrum*, Durham, N.C. 1958; Cedric Thomas Watts, ed., *Joseph Conrad's letters to R. B. Cunninghame Graham*, Camb. 1969; Zdzisław Najder, ed., *Conrad's Polish background: letters to and from Polish friends*, trans. by Halina Carroll, 1964; and Dale B. J. Randall, *Joseph Conrad and Warrington Dawson: the record of a friendship*, Durham, N.C. 1968. Frederick Robert Karl, *A reader's guide to Joseph Conrad*, N.Y. 1961, rev. edn. 1970, is useful. For Conrad's life see George Jean Aubry, *Joseph Conrad: life and letters*, 2 v. 1927, abridged edn. publ. as *The sea dreamer . . .*, trans. by Helen Seffa, Garden City, N.J. 1957; Mrs. Jessie Conrad, *Joseph Conrad as I knew him*, Lond. & Garden City, N.J. 1926; Borys Conrad, *My father*, Lond. & N.Y. 1970; Ford Madox Ford, *Joseph Conrad: a personal remembrance*, Lond. & Boston 1924; Jerry Allen, *The sea years of Joseph Conrad*, Garden City, N.J. 1965; and Bernard C. Meyer, *Joseph Conrad: a psychoanalytic biography*, Princeton 1967.

There is also a fast-growing body of criticism, much of it publ. since Albert Joseph Guerard, *Conrad the novelist*, Camb., Mass. 1958. Earlier works still of interest incl. Richard Curle, *Joseph Conrad: a study*, Garden City, N.Y. 1914, repr. N.Y. 1968, *Joseph Conrad and his characters: a study of six novels*, 1957, and *The last twelve years of Joseph Conrad*, Garden City, N.Y. 1928 repr. N.Y. 1968; Rodolphe Louis Mégroz, *Joseph Conrad's mind and method: a study of personality in art*, 1931, repr. N.Y. 1964;

Edward Crankshaw, *Joseph Conrad: some aspects of the art of the novel*, 1936, repr. N.Y. 1963; Muriel Clara Bradbrook *Joseph Conrad: Jozef Teodor Konrad Nalecz Korzeniowski: Poland's English genius*, Camb. 1941, repr. N.Y. 1965; Douglas John Hewitt, *Conrad: a reassessment*, Camb. 1952, 2nd edn. 1968; Paul Lazon Wiley, *Conrad's measure of man*, Madison, Wis. 1954; Thomas Colborn Moser, *Joseph Conrad: achievement and decline*, Camb., Mass. 1957; and Robert Fulton Haugh, *Joseph Conrad: discovery in design*, Norman, Okla. 1957.

Works publ. since 1958 incl. Osborn Andreas, *Joseph Conrad: a study in nonconformity*, N.Y. 1959; Jocelyn Baines, *Joseph Conrad: a critical biography*, 1960; Adam Gillon, *The eternal solitary: a study of Joseph Conrad*, N.Y. 1960; Robert Wooster Stallman, *The art of Joseph Conrad: a critical symposium*, East Lansing, Mich. 1960; Leo Gurko, *Joseph Conrad: giant in exile*, N.Y. 1962, and *The two lives of Joseph Conrad*, N.Y. 1965; Eloise Hay, *The political novels of Joseph Conrad: a critical study*, Chicago 1963; Ted Eugene Boyle, *Symbol and meaning in the fiction of Joseph Conrad*, The Hague 1965; Marvin Mudrick, ed., *Conrad: a collection of critical essays*, Englewood Cliffs, N.J. 1966; Edward William Said, *Joseph Conrad and the fiction of autobiography*, Camb., Mass. 1966; Norman Sherry, *Conrad's eastern world*, Camb. 1966, and *Conrad's western world*, Camb. 1971; Donald Charles Yelton, *Mimesis and metaphor: an inquiry into the genesis and scope of Conrad's symbolic imagery*, The Hague 1967; Avrom Fleishman, *Conrad's politics: community and anarchy in the fiction of Joseph Conrad*, Baltimore 1967; Claire Rosenfield, *Paradise of snakes: an archetypal analysis of Conrad's political novels*, Chicago 1967; Robert R. Hodges, *The dual heritage of Joseph Conrad*, The Hague 1967; John Innes Mackintosh Stewart, *Joseph Conrad*, N.Y. 1968; Paul Kirschner, *Conrad: the psychologist as artist*, Edin. 1968; John A. Palmer, *Joseph Conrad's fiction: a study in literary growth*, Ithaca, N.Y. 1968; Lawrence Graver, *Conrad's short fiction*, Berkeley 1969; Stanton de Voren Hoffman, *Comedy and form in the fiction of Joseph Conrad*, The Hague 1969; Robert F. Lee, *Conrad's colonialism*, The Hague 1969; Christopher Cooper, *Conrad and the human dilemma*, 1970; Wilfred S. Dowden, *Joseph Conrad: the imagined style*, Nashville, Tenn. 1970; Mohammad Yaseen, *Joseph Conrad's theory of fiction*, 2nd edn. Bombay & Lond. 1970; Leon F. Seltzer, *The vision of Melville and Conrad: a comparative study*, Athens, Ohio 1970; Royal Roussel, *The metaphysics of darkness: a study in the unity and development of Conrad's fiction*, Baltimore, Md. 1971; and Bruce Johnson, *Conrad's models of mind*, Minneapolis, Minn. 1971.

For Conrad's Polish connections see Gustav Morf, *The Polish heritage of Joseph Conrad*, 1930; Róza Jabłkowska, *Joseph Conrad, 1857–1924*, Wrocław 1961, and R. Jabłkowska, comp., *Joseph Conrad Korzeniowski*, Warsaw 1964; Barbara Kocówna, *Wspomnienia i studia o Conradzie*, Warsaw 1963, and *Polskość Conrada*, Warsaw 1967; Zdzisław Najder, *Nad Conradem*, Warsaw 1965, and *Conrad's Polish background . . .*, 1964; and Ludwik Krzyżanowski, ed., *Joseph Conrad: centennial essays*, Polish Inst. of Arts and Sciences in America, N.Y. 1960.

The Dept. of English, Univ. of Maryland, has publ. *Conradiana*, College Park, Md. 1968+.

**8352   CROSLAND.** The life and genius of T. W. H. Crosland. By William Sorley Brown. 1928.

**8353   DE LA MARE.** Walter de la Mare: a biographical and critical study. By Rodolphe Louis Mégroz. 1924.

See also Forrest Reid, *Walter de la Mare: a critical study*, 1929, Luce Bonnerot, *L'œuvre de Walter de la Mare: une aventure spirituelle*, Montreal 1969, Henry Charles Duffin, *Walter de la Mare: a study of his poetry*, 1949, and Doris Ross McCrosson, *Walter de la Mare*, 1966.

**8354   DICKENS.** The first editions of the writings of Charles Dickens and their values: a bibliography. By John C. Eckel. Lond. 1913. Rev. edn. N.Y. 1932.

See also Thomas Hatton and Arthur H. Cleaver, comps., *A bibliography of the periodical works of Charles Dickens, bibliographical, analytical and statistical*, 1933; British Museum, Dept. of Printed Books, *Dickens: an excerpt from the general catalogue of printed books in the British Museum*, 1960; Texas University, Humanities Research Center, *Catalogue of the Dickens collection at the University of Texas*, comp. by Mary Callista Carr, Austin, Tex. 1961, 2nd edn. 1968; William Miller, comp., *The Dickens student and collector: a list of writings relating to Charles Dickens and his works, 1836–1945*, Camb., Mass. 1946, suppl. 1947; and Moscow: Vsesoiuznaia Gosudarstvennaia Biblioteka Inostrannoi Literatury, *Charl'z Dikkens: bibliografiia russkikh perevodov i kriticheskoi literatury na russkom iazyke, 1838–1960*, Moscow 1962. Useful guides incl. Alexander John Philip, *A Dickens dictionary*, Gravesend 1909, 2nd edn. 1928, and [John] Michael [Drinkrow] Hardwick and Mollie Hardwick, *The Charles Dickens companion*, 1965. The official edn. of the letters was Georgina Hogarth and Mary Dickens, eds., *The letters of Charles Dickens*, 3 v. 1880–2. These were suppl. by a number of colls. such as Edgar Johnson, ed., *Letters from Charles Dickens to Angela Burdett-Coutts, 1841–65 . . .*, 1953, publ. in N.Y. as *The heart of Charles Dickens . . .*, 1952. The standard edn. will be the Pilgrim edn.: Madeline House and Graham Storey, eds., *Letters of Charles Dickens*, 1+ v. Oxf. 1965+.

The official life was John Forster, *The life of Charles Dickens*, 3 v. 1872–4. Edgar Johnson, *Charles Dickens: his tragedy and triumph*, 2 v. 1952, is a good modern life. See also Raymund Fitzsimons, *The Charles Dickens show: an account of his public readings, 1858–1870*, 1970.

For criticism see George Harry Ford and Lauriat Lane, eds., *The Dickens critics*, Ithaca, N.Y. 1962; George H. Ford, *Dickens and his readers: aspects of novel-criticism since 1836*, Princeton 1955; Philip Arthur William Collins, ed., *Dickens: the cultural heritage*, 1971; Kenneth Joshua Fielding, *Charles Dickens: a critical introduction*, 1958, 2nd edn. 1965; Stephen Wall, ed., *Charles Dickens: a critical anthology*, 1970; and John Jacob Gross and Gabriel Pearson, eds., *Dickens and the twentieth century*, Lond. & Toronto 1962.

Among important critical studs. are George Gissing, *Charles Dickens: a critical study*, 1898, and *The immortal Dickens*, Lond. 1925, first publ. as *Critical studies in the works of Charles Dickens*, N.Y. 1924; Gilbert Keith Chesterton, *Charles Dickens: a critical study*, N.Y. 1906; George Bernard Shaw, introductions to *Hard times*, Waverley edn. 1911, and *Great expectations*, Limited Edns. Club, 1937; Edmund Wilson, 'Dickens: the two Scrooges', in *The wound and the bow*, Boston 1941; Humphry House, *The Dickens world*, 1941, 2nd edn. 1942; John Butt and Kathleen Tillotson, *Dickens at work*, 1957; Philip Arthur William Collins, *Dickens and crime*, 1962, 2nd edn. 1964, and *Dickens and education*, Lond. & N.Y. 1963; Thomas Alfred Jackson, *Charles Dickens: the progress of a Radical*, 1937; Robert Garis, *The Dickens theatre: a reassessment of the novels*, Oxf. 1965; Steven Marcus, *Dickens: from Pickwick to Dombey*, 1965; Frank Raymond Leavis and Queenie Dorothy Leavis, *Dickens the novelist*, Lond. & N.Y. 1970; [William] John Lucas, *The melancholy man: a study of Dickens's novels*, 1970; Harvey Peter Sucksmith, *The narrative art of Charles Dickens: the rhetoric of sympathy and irony in his novels*, Oxf. 1970; Hillel Matthew Daleski, *Dickens and the art of analogy*, Lond. & N.Y. 1970; Barbara Hardy, *The moral art of Dickens*, 1970; Grahame Smith, *Dickens, money and society*, Berkeley 1968; Sylvère Monod, *Dickens the novelist*, Norman, Okla. 1968; Julian Symons, *Charles Dickens*, 1951; Angus Wilson, *The world of Charles Dickens*, Lond. & N.Y. 1970; Anthony Oliver John Cockshut, *The imagination of Charles Dickens*, 1961; and Robert Baker Partlow, jr., *Dickens the craftsman: strategies of presentation*, Carbondale, Ill. 1970.

The Dickens Fellowship has publ. *The Dickensian*, 1905+, *Dickens Studies*, since 1969, and *Dickens studies annual*, Boston, now Carbondale, Ill., 1965+.

8355 DOBELL. The life and letters of Sydney Dobell. Ed. by Emily Jolly. 2 v. 1878.

8356  DOBSON. University of London Library: catalogue of the collection of the works of Austin Dobson, 1840–1921. 1960.

For his life see Alban Dobson and others, *Austin Dobson . . .*, 1928, and *An Austin Dobson letter book*, Cleveland 1935.

8357  DOUGLAS. Bosie: the story of Lord Alfred Douglas, his friends and enemies. By Rupert Croft-Cooke. 1963.

See also *The autobiography of Lord Alfred Douglas*, 1929, Francis Archibald Kelhead Douglas, Marquess of Queensberry, and Percy Colson, *Oscar Wilde and the Black Douglas*, 1949, and Marie Carmichael Stopes, *Lord Alfred Douglas: his poetry and his personality*, 1949.

8358  DOWDEN. Letters of Edward Dowden and his correspondents. [Ed. by Elizabeth Dickinson Dowden and Hilda M. Dowden.] 1914.

8359  DOWSON. Ernest Dowson. By John Mark Longacre. Phila. 1944. 3rd edn. 1967.

See also Victor Gustave Plarr, *Ernest Dowson, 1888–1897: reminiscences, unpublished letters and marginalia . . .*, N.Y. 1914, Desmond Flower and Henry Maas, eds., *The letters of Ernest Dowson*, 1967, and Thomas Burnett Swann, *Ernest Dowson*, 1965.

8360  ELIOT. Victorian lady novelists: George Eliot, Mrs. Gaskell, the Brontë sisters: first editions in the library at Dormy House, Pine Valley, New York, comp. by Morris Longstreth Parrish. 1933.

See also Isadore Gilbert Mudge and Minnie Earl Sears, *A George Eliot dictionary: the characters and scenes of the novels, stories and poems, alphabetically arranged*, Lond. & N.Y. 1924. The standard edn. of letters is Gordon Sherman Haight, ed., *Letters of George Eliot*, 7 v. New Haven, Conn. 1954–6.
   The official life was John Walter Cross, *George Eliot's life as related in her letters and journals*, 3 v. 1885. The standard life is Gordon Sherman Haight, *George Eliot: a biography*, Lond. & N.Y. 1968. Useful biog. material is also incl. in Mary Hannah Deakin, *The early life of George Eliot*, Manch. 1913, Anna Theresa Kitchel, *George Lewes and George Eliot: a review of records*, N.Y. 1933, K. A. McKenzie, *Edith Simcox and George Eliot*, 1961, and Gordon S. Haight, *George Eliot & John Chapman: with Chapman's diaries*, New Haven, Conn. 1940, 2nd ed. Hamden, Conn. 1969.
   For criticism see Sir Leslie Stephen, *George Eliot*, 1902; Joan Bennett, *George Eliot: her mind and art*, Camb. 1948; Lawrence Hanson, *Marian Evans & George Eliot: a biography*, 1952; Barbara Hardy, *The novels of George Eliot: a study in form*, 1959; William John Harvey, *The art of George Eliot*, 1961; Ulrich Camillus Knoepflmacher, *George Eliot's early novels: the limits of realism*, Berkeley 1968; Henry Auster, *Local habitations: regionalism in the early novels of George Eliot*, Camb., Mass. 1970; Reva Stump, *Movement and vision in George Eliot's novels*, Seattle, Wash. 1959; Jerome Thale, *The novels of George Eliot*, N.Y. 1959; Bernard J. Paris, *Experiments in life: George Eliot's quest for values*, Detroit, Mich. 1965; John Philip Couch, *George Eliot in France: a French appraisal of George Eliot's writings, 1858–1960*, Chapel Hill, N.C. 1967; P. Bourl'honne, *George Eliot: essai de biographie intellectuelle et morale, 1819–1854*, Paris 1933; and Placide Gustave Maheu, *La pensée religieuse et morale de George Eliot: essai d'interprétation*, Paris 1958. For critical essays see Gordon S. Haight, ed., *A century of George Eliot criticism*, Boston 1965, Barbara Hardy, ed., *Critical essays on George Eliot*, 1970, and *Middlemarch: critical approaches to the novel*, 1967, and John Holmstrom and Laurence Lerner, eds., *George Eliot and her readers: a selection of contemporary reviews*, Lond. & N.Y. 1966.

**8361  ELLIS.** Havelock Ellis: a biography. By Arthur Calder-Marshall. 1959.

Havelock Ellis himself publ. *My life: autobiography*, Boston 1939. See also Joseph Ishill, ed., *The unpublished letters of Havelock Ellis to Joseph Ishill*, Berkeley Heights, N.J. 1954; Isaac Goldberg, *Havelock Ellis: a biographical and critical survey*, N.Y. 1926, which has a bibliog.; Joseph Ishill, ed., *Havelock Ellis: in appreciation . . .*, priv. pr. Berkeley Heights, N.J. 1929, which is a 70th-birthday tribute; Houston Peterson, *Havelock Ellis, philosopher of love*, Boston 1928; Françoise Delisle, *Friendship's odyssey*, 1946; and John Stewart Collis, *An artist of life . . .*, 1959, publ in N.Y. as *Havelock Ellis: artist of life . . .*, 1959.

**8362  FANE.** Julian Fane: a memoir. By Edward Robert Bulwer-Lytton, Earl of Lytton. 1871.

**8363  FITZGERALD.** Notes for a bibliography of Edward FitzGerald. By William Francis Prideaux. 1901.

To be suppl. by Faverty (**8281**). For letters see William Aldis Wright, ed., *Letters and literary remains of Edward FitzGerald*, 7 v. Lond. & N.Y. 1902–3, Francis Rickman Barton, ed., *Some new letters . . .*, 1923, publ. in N.Y. as *Edward FitzGerald and Bernard Barton*, 1924, Charlotte Quaritch Wrentmore, ed., *Letters from Edward FitzGerald to Bernard Quaritch, 1853 to 1883*, 1926, and Neilson Campbell Hannay and Catherine Bodham Johnson, eds., *A FitzGerald friendship, being hitherto unpublished letters from Edward Fitzgerald to William Bodham Donne*, 1932. John Michael Cohen, ed., *Letters of Edward FitzGerald*, Carbondale, Ill. 1960, and Joanna Richardson, ed., *Selected works*, Lond. & Camb., Mass. 1962, draw on Wright's edn.
The basic life is Thomas Wright, *The life of Edward FitzGerald*, 2 v. Lond. & N.Y. 1904. It must be suppl. by Alfred McKinley Terhune, *The life of Edward FitzGerald, translator of the Rubáiyát of Omar Khayyám*, New Haven, Conn. 1947, and Arthur John Arberry, *The romance of the Rubáiyát*, 1959.

**8364  FLECKER.** The life of James Elroy Flecker, from letters and materials provided by his mother. By Geraldine Emma Hodgson. Lond. & Boston. 1925.

There are some useful letters in *The letters of J. E. Flecker to Frank Savery*, 1926.

**8365  FORD.** Ford Madox Ford, 1873–1939: a bibliography of works and criticism. Comp. by David Dow Harvey. Princeton. 1962.

Richard M. Ludwig, ed., *Letters of Ford Madox Ford*, Princeton 1965, is the only coll. For biog. see Arthur Mizener, *The saddest story: a biography of Ford Madox Ford*, N.Y. 1971, Douglas Goldring, *The last pre-Raphaelite: a record of the life and writings of Ford Madox Ford*, 1948 [publ. in N.Y. as *Trained for genius*, 1949], and *South lodge: reminiscences of Violet Hunt, Ford Madox Ford, and the 'English Review' circle*, 1943. For criticism see Richard Allan Cassell, *Ford Madox Ford: a study of his novels*, Baltimore, Md. 1962; Richard Wald Lid, *Ford Madox Ford: the essence of his art*, Berkeley 1964; Carol Burke Ohmann, *Ford Madox Ford: from apprentice to craftsman*, Middletown, Conn. 1964; Frank MacShane, *The life and work of Ford Madox Ford*, 1965; Charles G. Hoffmann, *Ford Madox Ford*, N.Y. 1967; Ambrose Gordon, *The invisible tint: the war novels of Ford Madox Ford*, Austin, Tex. 1964; H. Robert Huntley, *The alien protagonist of Ford Madox Ford*, Chapel Hill, N.C. 1970; Norman Leer, *The hunted hero in the novels of Ford Madox Ford*, East Lansing, Mich. 1966; John Albert Meixner, *Ford Madox Ford's novels: a critical study*, Minneapolis, Minn. 1962; and Paul Lazon Wiley, *Novelist of three worlds: Ford Madox Ford*, Syracuse, N.Y. 1962.

**8366  FORSTER.** A bibliography of E. M. Forster. By Brownlee Jean Kirkpatrick. 1965.

Alfred Bonello, *An E. M. Forster dictionary*, Metuchen, N.J. 1971, is helpful. For criticism see Rose Macaulay, *The writings of E. M. Forster*, 1938; Lionel Trilling, *E. M.*

Forster, Norfolk, Conn. 1943, rev. edn. [*E. M. Forster: a study*] Lond. 1967; James McConkey, *The novels of E. M. Forster*, Ithaca, N.Y. 1957; John Bernard Beer, *The achievement of E. M. Forster*, 1962; Karl Watts Gransden, *E. M. Forster*, Edin. 1962, rev. edn. 1970; Wilfred Healey Stone, *The cave and the mountain: a study of E. M. Forster*, Stanford, Calif. 1966; Denis Godfrey, *E. M. Forster's other kingdom*, Edin. 1968; Laurence Brander, *E. M. Forster: a critical study*, 1968; John Keith Johnstone, *The Bloomsbury group: a study of E. M. Forster, Lytton Strachey, Virginia Woolf and their circle*, 1954; Frederick Campbell Crews, *E. M. Forster: the perils of humanism*, Princeton 1962; Alan Wilde, *Art and order: a study of E. M. Forster*, N.Y. 1964; David Shusterman, *The quest for certitude in E. M. Forster's fiction*, Bloomington, Ind. 1965; George H. Thomson, *The fiction of E. M. Forster*, Detroit, Mich. 1967; Norman Kelvin, *E. M. Forster*, Carbondale, Ill. 1967; Frederick Peter Woll McDowell, *E. M. Forster*, N.Y. 1969; and Martial Rose, *E. M. Forster*, 1970.

For colls. of criticism see Malcolm Bradbury, ed., *Forster: a collection of critical essays*, Englewood Cliffs, N.J. 1966; Oliver Stallybrass, ed., *Aspects of E. M. Forster: essays and recollections written for his ninetieth birthday, January 1, 1969*, 1969; K. Natwar-Singh, ed., *E. M. Forster: a tribute . . .*, N.Y. 1964; and Vasant Anant Shahane, ed., *Perspectives on E. M. Forster's 'A passage to India' . . .*, N.Y. 1968.

**8367  GALSWORTHY.** A bibliography of the works of John Galsworthy. By Harold Vincent Marrot. 1928.

See also Birmingham University Library, *John Galsworthy: catalogue of the collection*, Birmingham 1967. For letters see *Autobiographical letters: a correspondence with Frank Harris*, 1934; Edward Garnett, ed., *Letters from John Galsworthy, 1900–1932*, Lond. & N.Y. 1934; Asher Boldon Wilson, ed., *Letters to Leon Lion*, The Hague 1968; Mabel Edith Reynolds, *Memories of John Galsworthy, by his sister*, 1936; and Margaret Morris, *My Galsworthy story, including 67 hitherto unpublished letters*, 1967. For his life and work see Harold Vincent Marrot, *The life and letters of John Galsworthy*, 1935; Dudley Barker, *The man of principle: a view of Galsworthy*, 1963; Vida E. Markovic, *The reputation of Galsworthy in England, 1897–1950*, Belgrade 1969; Ralph Hale Mottram, *For some we loved: an intimate portrait of Ada and John Galsworthy*, 1956; Rudolf Helmut Sauter, *Galsworthy the man: an intimate portrait*, 1967; and Marianna Ivanovna Voropanova, *Dzhon Golsuorsi: ocherk zhizni i tvorchestva*, Krasnoiarsk 1968.

**8368  GARNETT.** The Garnett family. By Carolyn G. Heilbrun. Lond. & N.Y. 1961.

**8369  GASKELL.** Elizabeth Gaskell. By Gerald De Witt Sanders . . . with a bibliography by Clark Sutherland Northup. New Haven [Conn.]. 1929.

Includes the best bibliog. See also M. L. Parrish, *Victorian lady novelists* (**8360**), M. Sadleir, *Excursions* (**8284**), and John Albert Green, *A bibliographical guide to the Gaskell collection in the Moss Side library*, Manch. 1911. For letters see John Alfred Victor Chapple and Arthur Pollard, eds., *Letters of Elizabeth Cleghorn Gaskell*, Manch. 1966, Camb., Mass. 1967, and Jane Whitehill, ed., *Letters of Mrs. Gaskell and Charles Eliot Norton, 1855–1865*, 1932. For her life and work see Annette Brown Hopkins, *Elizabeth Gaskell, her life and work*, 1952; Arthur Pollard, *Mrs. Gaskell, novelist and biographer*, Manch. and Camb., Mass. 1966; John McVeagh, *Elizabeth Gaskell*, Lond. & N.Y. 1970; Margaret Ganz, *Elizabeth Gaskell: the artist in conflict*, N.Y. 1969; Esther Alice Chadwick, Mrs. Ellis H. Chadwick, *Mrs. Gaskell: haunts, homes and stories*, 1910, rev. edn. 1913; Elizabeth Sanderson Haldane, *Mrs. Gaskell and her friends*, 1930; Archie Stanton Whitfield, *Mrs. Gaskell: her life and work*, 1929; Aina Rubenius, *The woman question in Mrs. Gaskell's life and works*, Uppsala 1950; Edgar Wright, *Mrs. Gaskell: the basis for reassessment*, 1965; and John Geoffrey Sharps, *Mrs. Gaskell's observation and invention: a study of her non-biographic works*, Fontwell, Sussex 1970.

8370   GILBERT. A bibliography of Sir William Schwenck Gilbert: with bibliographical adventures in the Gilbert and Sullivan operas. By Townley Searle. 1931.

See also John Bush Jones, ed., *W. S. Gilbert: a century of scholarship and commentary*, N.Y. 1970. For lives see Sidney Dark and Rowland Grey, *W. S. Gilbert: his life and letters*, 1923, and Hesketh Pearson, *Gilbert: his life and strife*, Lond. & N.Y. 1957, and **9274–6.**

8371   GISSING. George Gissing: a critical biography. By Jacob Korg. Seattle. 1963.

See also Jacob Korg, ed., *George Gissing's commonplace book*, New York Public Libr. 1962. For letters see Algernon and Ellen Gissing, eds., *Letters of George Gissing to members of his family*, 1927, Royal Alfred Gettmann, ed., *George Gissing and H. G. Wells: their friendship and correspondence*, Lond. & Urbana, Ill. 1961; Pierre Coustillas, ed., *The letters of George Gissing to Gabrielle Fleury*, New York Public Libr. 1964, and Arthur C. Young, ed., *Letters to Eduard Bertz, 1887–1903*, New Brunswick, N.J. 1961.
    See also Frank Arthur Swinnerton, *George Gissing: a critical study*, 1912, 3rd edn., Port Washington, N.Y. 1966; Ruth Capers McKay, *George Gissing and his critic Frank Swinnerton*, 1933; Mabel Collins Donnelly, *George Gissing: grave comedian*, Camb., Mass. 1954; Oswald Harcourt Davis, *George Gissing: a study in literary leanings*, 1966; Samuel Vogt Gapp, *George Gissing, classicist*, Phila. 1936; Anton Weber, *George Gissing und die soziale Frage*, Leipzig 1932; Roger T. Gilmartin, *The social attitudes of George Gissing*, N.Y. 1953; and the *The Gissing newsletter*, Seattle, Wash. 1965+. Morley Roberts, *The private life of Henry Maitland . . .*, 1912, new edn. ed. by Morchard Bishop, pseud. of Oliver Stonor, 1958, is a novel based on Gissing's life.

8372   GOSSE. The life and letters of Sir Edmund Gosse. By Evan Edward Charteris. 1931.

The official life. See also University of Leeds, Brotherton Libr., *A catalogue of the Gosse correspondence in the Brotherton collection, consisting mainly of letters written to Sir Edmund Gosse in the period from 1867 to 1928*, Leeds 1950, and Euan Hillhouse Methven Cox, comp., *The library of Edmund Gosse . . .*, 1924. Paul F. Mattheisen and Michael Millgate, eds., *Transatlantic dialogue: selected American correspondence of Edmund Gosse*, Austin, Tex. 1965, is a handy edn. of letters. See also Linette Fisher Brugmans, ed., *The correspondence of André Gide and Edmund Gosse, 1904–1928*, N.Y. 1959. Gosse himself publ. a famous autobiog., *Father and son: biographical recollections*, 1907. For Gosse's Scandinavian connections see **2378.**

8373   HARDY. Thomas Hardy: a bibliographical study. By Richard Little Purdy. 1954.

Good. See also Carl Jefferson Weber, comp., *The first hundred years of Thomas Hardy, 1840–1940: a centenary bibliography of Hardiana*, Waterville, Maine 1942. For letters see Carl Jefferson Weber and Clara Carter Weber, comps., *Thomas Hardy's correspondence at Max Gate: a descriptive check list*, Waterville, Maine 1968, Evelyn Hardy, ed., *Notebooks . . . and some letters from Julia Augusta Martin*, 1955, and Carl Jefferson Weber, ed., *Letters transcribed from the original autographs now in the Colby College Library*, Waterville, Maine 1954, and '*Dearest Emmie*': *Thomas Hardy's letters to his first wife*, Lond. & N.Y. 1963. Claudius John Pakenham Beatty, ed., *The architectural notebook of Thomas Hardy*, Dorchester 1966, is brief but useful. Florence Emily Hardy, *The early life of Thomas Hardy, 1840–1891: compiled largely from contemporary notes, letters, diaries and biographical memoranda, as well as from oral information in conversations extending over many years*, Lond. & N.Y. 1928, cont. in *The later years of Thomas Hardy, 1892–1928*, Lond. & N.Y. 1930, the two repr. as *The life of Thomas Hardy, 1840–1928*, 1962, is generally regarded as a disguised autobiog. Harold Orel, ed.,

*Thomas Hardy: personal writings: prefaces, literary opinions, reminiscences,* Lawrence, Kans. 1966, is a useful biog. coll. William Archer, *Real conversations,* 1904; Vere Henry Collins, *Talks with Thomas Hardy at Max Gate, 1920–22,* 1928; Hermann Lea, *Thomas Hardy's Wessex,* 1913, repr. 1925, which was checked by Hardy himself; James Stevens Cox, *Monographs on the life, times and works of Thomas Hardy,* 1+, 1962+; Dulan Frier Barber, ed., *Concerning Thomas Hardy: a composite portrait from memory, based on material researched & collected by J. Stevens Cox,* 1968, and *The Thomas Hardy year book,* St. Peter Port, 1+, 1970+ incl. useful suppl. material. Carl Jefferson Weber, *Hardy of Wessex: his life and literary career,* N.Y. 1940, rev. edn. 1965, *Hardy and the lady from Madison Square,* Waterville, Maine 1952, and *Hardy in America: a study of Thomas Hardy and his American readers,* Waterville, Maine 1946, are sober. Lois Deacon, *Tryphena and Thomas Hardy,* 1962, and Lois Deacon and Terry Coleman, *Providence & Mr. Hardy,* 1966, are not.

For Hardy's work generally see Francis Bertram Pinion, *A Hardy companion: a guide to the works of Thomas Hardy and their background,* Lond. & N.Y. 1968; F. Outwin Saxelby, *A Thomas Hardy dictionary . . .,* Lond. & N.Y. 1911; Reginald Gordon Cox, ed., *Thomas Hardy: the critical heritage,* Lond. & N.Y. 1970; The Southern Review, *Thomas Hardy centennial issue,* vi, no. 1 (1940); Joseph Hillis Miller, *Thomas Hardy: distance and desire,* Camb., Mass. 1970; Roy Morrell, *Thomas Hardy: the will and the way,* Kuala Lumpur 1965; Joseph Warren Beach, *The technique of Thomas Hardy,* Chicago 1922, repr. N.Y. 1962; William Rutland Rutland, *Thomas Hardy: a study of his writings and their background,* Oxf. 1938; Lord [Edward Christian] David [Gascoyne-] Cecil, *Hardy, the novelist: an essay in criticism,* 1943; Edmund Charles Blunden, *Thomas Hardy,* 1941; Lionel Johnson, *The art of Thomas Hardy,* Lond. & N.Y. 1894, repr. 1923; Lascelles Abercrombie, *Thomas Hardy: a critical study,* 1912, repr. Lond. 1924, N.Y. 1964; Henry Charles Duffin, *Thomas Hardy: a study of the Wessex novels, the poems and 'The dynasts',* Manch. 1916, 3rd edn. 1937; Ernest Brennecke, *Thomas Hardy's universe: a study of a poet's mind,* 1924; Arthur Symons, *A study of Thomas Hardy,* 1927; Ruth Anita Firor, *Folkways in Thomas Hardy,* Phila. 1931; Joseph Hartmann, *Architektur in den Romanen Thomas Hardys,* Bochum-Langendreer 1934; Günther Wilmsen, *Thomas Hardy als impressionistischen Landschaftsmaler,* Marburg & Düsseldorf 1934; Amélie von Behr, *Der Typen-Konflikt in Thomas Hardys Romanen,* Marburg 1936; Harvey Curtis Webster, *On a darkling plain: the art & thought of Thomas Hardy,* Chicago 1947, repr. Hamden, Conn. 1964; Albert Joseph Guerard, *Thomas Hardy: the novels and stories,* Camb., Mass. 1949; Alice Reinhard-Stocker, *Charakterdarstellung und Schicksalsgestaltung in den Romanen Thomas Hardys,* Winterthur 1958; John Paterson, *The making of 'The return of the native',* Berkeley 1960; Albert Joseph Guerard, ed., *Hardy: a collection of critical essays,* Englewood Cliffs, N.J. 1963; Richard C. Carpenter, *Thomas Hardy,* N.Y. 1964; Laurence Lerner and John Holmstrom, eds., *Thomas Hardy and his readers: a selection of contemporary reviews,* 1968; Bert G. Hornback, *The metaphor of chance: vision and technique in the works of Thomas Hardy,* Athens, Ohio 1971; and Samuel Claggett Chew, *Thomas Hardy, poet and novelist,* Bryn Mawr, Penn. 1921, repr. N.Y. 1928, 1964.

Specifically for the poems, see James Osler Bailey, *The poetry of Thomas Hardy: a handbook and commentary,* Chapel Hill, N.C. 1970; Kenneth Marsden, *The poems of Thomas Hardy: a critical introduction,* 1969; James Granville Southworth, *The poetry of Thomas Hardy,* N.Y. 1947; Samuel Lynn Hynes, *The pattern of Hardy's poetry,* Chapel Hill, N.C. 1961; Amiya Chandra Chakravarty, *'The dynasts' and the post-war age in poetry: a study in modern ideas,* 1938, repr. N.Y. 1970; James Osler Bailey, *Thomas Hardy and the cosmic mind: a new reading of 'The dynasts',* Chapel Hill, N.C. 1956; Harold Orel, *Thomas Hardy's epic drama: a study of 'The dynasts',* Lawrence, Kans. 1963; Marguerite Roberts, *Hardy's poetic drama and the theatre: 'The dynasts' and 'The famous tragedy of the Queen of Cornwall',* N.Y. 1965; and Walter Francis Wright, *The shaping of 'The dynasts': a study in Thomas Hardy,* Lincoln, Nebr. 1967.

8374 HAWKER. The life and letters of R. S. Hawker, sometime vicar of Morwenstow. By his son-in-law Charles Edward Byles. Lond. & N.Y. 1905.

There is also Sabine Baring-Gould, *The vicar of Morwenstow: a life of Robert Stephen Hawker*, M.A., 1876, new edn. 1899, 8th edn. 1925, Margaret Florence Burrows, *Robert Stephen Hawker: a study of his thought and poetry*, Oxf. 1926, and Frederick George Lee, *Memorials of the late Rev. Robert Stephen Hawker*, M.A., *sometime vicar of Morwenstow in the diocese of Exeter*, 1876.

8375  HENLEY. William Ernest Henley: a study in the 'counter-decadence' of the 'nineties. By Jerome Hamilton Buckley. Princeton. 1945.

There is also John Connell, pseud. of John Henry Robertson, *W. E. Henley*, 1949, and Joseph M. Flora, *William Ernest Henley*, N.Y. 1970.

8376  HOPKINS. Works and criticism of Gerard Manley Hopkins: a comprehensive bibliography. By Edward H. Cohen. Wash. 1969.

See also Faverty (**8281**), and Ruth Seelhammer, *Hopkins collected at Gonzaga*, Chicago 1970. For his pr. papers see Humphry House, ed., *Note-books and papers . . .*, 1937, 2nd edn. [*Journals and papers*] completed by Graham Storey, 1959, and Claude Colleer Abbott, ed., *The letters of Gerard Manley Hopkins to Robert Bridges*, 1935, new edn. 1955, *The correspondence of Gerard Manley Hopkins and Richard Watson Dixon*, 1935, new edn. 1955, and *Further letters . . . including his correspondence with Coventry Patmore*, 1938, 2nd edn. 1956. For Hopkins's poems see Alfred Borrello, ed., *A concordance of the poetry in English of Gerard Manley Hopkins*, Metuchen, N.J. 1969, Robert J. Dilligan and Todd K. Bender, comps., *A concordance to the English poetry of Gerard Manley Hopkins*, Madison, Wis. 1970, and Donald McChesney, *A Hopkins commentary: an explanatory commentary on the main poems, 1876–89*, 1+ v., 1968+.

The best biog. study is Jean-Georges Ritz, *Le poète Gerard Manley Hopkins, S.J., 1844–1889: l'homme et l'œuvre*, Paris 1963. Ritz also publ. *Robert Bridges and Gerard Hopkins, 1863–1889: a literary friendship*, 1960. For Hopkins criticism see William Henry Gardner, *Gerard Manley Hopkins, 1844–1889, a study of poetic idiosyncrasy in relation to poetic tradition*, 2 v. New Haven, Conn. & Lond. 1944–9, 2nd edn. of v. 1 1958; Austin Warren and others, *Gerard Manley Hopkins by the Kenyon critics*, Norfolk, Conn. 1945; Wilhelmus Antonius Maria Peters, *Gerard Manley Hopkins: a critical essay towards the understanding of his poetry*, 1948, 2nd edn. Oxf. & N.Y. 1970; Geoffrey H. Hartman, ed., *Hopkins: a collection of critical essays*, Englewood Cliffs, N.J. 1966; Norman Weyand, ed., *Immortal diamond: studies in Gerard Manley Hopkins*, N.Y. 1949; Norman H. MacKenzie, *Hopkins*, Edin. 1968; Alfred Thomas, *Hopkins the Jesuit: the years of training*, 1969; Todd K. Bender, *Gerard Manley Hopkins: the classical background and critical reception of his work*, Baltimore, Md. 1966; Wendell Stacy Johnson, *Gerard Manley Hopkins: the poet as Victorian*, Ithaca, N.Y. 1968; Elizabeth Schneider, *The dragon in the gate: studies in the poetry of G. M. Hopkins*, Berkeley 1968; Alan Heuser, *The shaping vision of Gerard Manley Hopkins*, 1958, repr. Hamden, Conn. 1968; Robert Boyle, *Metaphor in Hopkins*, Chapel Hill, N.C. 1961; Robert Joseph Andreach, *Studies in structure: the stages of the spiritual life in four modern authors*, N.Y. 1964; David Anthony Downes, *Gerard Manley Hopkins: a study of his Ignatian spirit*, N.Y. n.d., and *Victorian portraits: Hopkins and Pater*, N.Y. 1965; Francis Noel Lees, *Gerard Manley Hopkins*, N.Y. 1966; Kurt R. Jankowsky, *Die Versauffassung bei Gerard Manley Hopkins, den Imagisten und T. S. Eliot*, Munich 1967; Peter Pasch *Wort und Sicht: Gerard Manley Hopkins visuelle Konzeption*, Tübingen 1968; Paul L. Mariani, *A commentary on the complete poems of Gerard Manley Hopkins*, Ithaca, N.Y. 1970; and Peter Milward, *A commentary on the sonnets of G. M. Hopkins*, 1970, and *A commentary on G. M. Hopkins' 'The wreck of the Deutschland'*, Tokyo 1968.

The Hopkins Soc. publ. *The Hopkins research bull.*, 1+, 1970+.

8377  HORNE. A concise bibliography of the complete works of Richard Henry (Hengist) Horne, 1802–1884. By Eri Jay Shumaker. Granville, Ohio. 1943.

For his life see Ann Blainey, *The farthing poet: a biography of Richard Hengist Horne, 1802–84, a lesser literary lion*, 1968, and Cyril Alston Pearl, *Always morning: the life of Richard Henry 'Orion' Horne*, Melb. 1960.

8378 HOUSMAN. A. E. Housman: an annotated hand-list. By John Carter and John Sparrow. 1952.

See also Andrew Sydenham Farrer Gow, *A. E. Housman: a sketch together with a list of his writings and indexes to his classical papers*, Camb. 1936. For letters see Henry Maas, ed., *The letters of A. E. Housman*, Camb., Mass. 1970, and Laurence Housman, *A.E.H.: some poems, some letters and a personal memoir*, 1937. For the poems see Clyde Kenneth Hyder, comp., *A concordance to the poems of A. E. Housman*, Lawrence, Kans. 1940. For his life and work see Norman Marlow, *A. E. Housman: scholar and poet*, 1958; Maude M. Hawkins, *A. E. Housman: man behind a mask*, Chicago 1958; George L. Watson, *A. E. Housman: a divided life*, 1957; Tom Burns Haber, *A. E. Housman*, N.Y. 1967; Christopher Bruce Ricks, ed., *A. E. Housman: a collection of critical essays*, Englewood Cliffs, N.J. 1968; Tom Burns Haber, comp., *The making of 'A Shropshire lad': a manuscript variorum*, Seattle, Wash. 1966; and Bobby Joe Leggett, *Housman's land of lost content: a critical study of 'A Shropshire lad'*, Knoxville, Tenn. 1970.

8379 HUGHES. Thomas Hughes: a life of the author of 'Tom Brown's schooldays'. By Edward Clarence Mack and Walter Harry Green Armytage. 1952.

For Hughes's works see M. L. Parrish, *Charles Kingsley and Thomas Hughes* (8384).

8380 HULME. T. E. Hulme. By Michael Roberts. 1938.

The only other biog. is Alun Richard Jones, *The life and opinions of T. E. Hulme*, 1960.

8381 JAMES. A bibliography of Henry James. By Leon Edel and Dan H. Laurence. 1957. 2nd edn. 1961.

For pr. papers see Francis Otto Matthiessen and Kenneth B. Murdock, eds., *The notebooks of Henry James*, N.Y. 1947; Percy Lubbock, ed., *The letters of Henry James*, 2 v. 1920; Leon Edel, ed., *Selected letters . . .*, 1956; and Leon Edel and Gordon Norton Ray eds., *Henry James and H. G. Wells: a record of their friendship, their debate on the art of fiction, and their quarrel*, Urbana, Ill. 1958. The best life is Leon Edel, *Henry James*, 5 v. Phila. 1953–70. For criticism see Roger Gard, comp., *Henry James: the critical heritage*, Lond. & N.Y. 1968. For James in England see Harford Montgomery Hyde, *Henry James at home*, Lond. & N.Y. 1969, Sir Geoffrey Langdon Keynes, *Henry James in Cambridge*, Camb. 1967, Janet Adam Smith, ed., *Henry James and Robert Louis Stevenson: a record of friendship and criticism*, 1948, and Millicent Bell, *Edith Wharton & Henry James: the story of their friendship*, N.Y. 1965. For James's works see Samuel Gorley Putt, *A reader's guide to Henry James*, 1966. Works on James exist in large numbers; most of them approach him as an American rather than an English writer.

8382 JOHNSON. Lionel Johnson (1867–1902), poète et critique. By Arthur W. Patrick. Paris. 1939.

8383 JONES. The life and letters of Henry Arthur Jones. By Doris Arthur Jones. Lond. 1930. Publ. in N.Y. as *Taking the curtain call*. 1930.

8384 KINGSLEY. Charles Kingsley and Thomas Hughes: first editions (with a few exceptions) in the library at Dormy House, Pine Valley, New Jersey. Comp. by Morris Longstreth Parrish. 1936.

Margaret Farrand Thorp, *Charles Kingsley, 1819–1875*, Princeton 1937, is a good biog. with extensive bibliog. Frances Eliza Kingsley, *Charles Kingsley: his letters and memories of his life*, 2 v. Lond. & N.Y. 1877, was the official life. Other letters are incl.

in Robert Bernard Martin, ed., *Charles Kingsley's American notes: letters from a lecture tour, 1874*, Princeton 1958. For other studies of his life and work see Stanley Everett Baldwin, *Charles Kingsley*, Ithaca, N.Y. 1934; Dame Una Pope-Hennessy, *Canon Charles Kingsley: a biography*, 1948; Robert Bernard Martin, *The dust of combat: a life of Charles Kingsley*, 1959; Guy Kendall, *Charles Kingsley and his ideas*, 1947; Fritz Köhler, *Charles Kingsley als religiöser Tendenz-schriftsteller*, Marburg 1912; Anna Jacobson, *Charles Kingsleys Beziehungen zu Deutschland*, Heidelberg 1917; Hilda Welte, *Das heroische Element bei Charles Kingsley*, Freiburg im Breisgau 1934; Bernardus Merker, *Die historischen Quellen zu Kingsleys Roman 'Hypatia'*, Würzburg 1908; Albert Nicol, *Charles Kingsley und die Geschichte*, Würzburg 1936; and G. Egner, pseud. of Patrick J. Fitzpatrick, *Apologia pro Charles Kingsley*, 1969. See also **3387.**

8385  KIPLING. Rudyard Kipling: a bibliographical catalogue. By James McGregor Stewart. Ed. by A. W. Yeats. Toronto. 1959.

Largely repl. Flora Virginia Livingston, *Bibliography of the works of Rudyard Kipling*, N.Y. 1927, suppl. Camb., Mass. 1938. The standard life is Charles Edmund Carrington, *Kipling: his life and work*, 1955, publ. as *The life of Rudyard Kipling*, Garden City, N.Y. 1955. But John Innes Mackintosh Stewart, *Rudyard Kipling*, N.Y. 1966, is also important. For Kipling's India see Louis L. Cornell, *Kipling in India*, Lond. & N.Y. 1966, Kanatur Bhaskara Rao, *Rudyard Kipling's India*, Norman, Okla. 1967, and (less good) Syed Sajjad Husain, *Kipling and India*, 1964. On Kipling's works see William Arthur Young, *A dictionary of the characters and scenes in the stories and poems of Rudyard Kipling, 1886–1911*, Lond. & N.Y. 1911, rev. edn. by John H. McGivering [*A Kipling dictionary*], 1967; Ralph Anthony Durand, *A handbook of the poetry of Rudyard Kipling*, Lond. & Garden City, N.Y. 1914; Edward Buxton Shanks, *Rudyard Kipling: a study in literature and political ideas*, 1940; Ann Matlack Weygandt, *Kipling's reading and its influence on his poetry*, Phila. 1939; Charles Hilton Brown, *Rudyard Kipling: a new appreciation*, 1945; Robert Charles Étienne Georges Escarpit, *Rudyard Kipling: servitudes et grandeurs imperiales*, Paris 1955; Joyce Marjorie Santzer Tompkins, *The art of Rudyard Kipling*, 1959; Carl Adolf Gottlieb Bodelsen, *Aspects of Kipling's art*, Manch. 1964; Thomas Rice Henn, *Kipling*, Edin. 1967; Roger Lancelyn Green, *Kipling and the children*, 1965; and Noel Gilroy Annan, Baron Annan, 'Kipling's place in the history of ideas', *Victorian Studs*. iii (1959–60), 323–48. Roger Lancelyn Green, ed., *Kipling: the critical heritage*, 1971, Andrew Rutherford, ed., *Kipling's mind and art*, Edin. 1964, and Elliot Lewis Gilbert, ed., *Kipling and the critics*, N.Y. 1965, are useful anthologies. The Kipling Soc. has publ. *The Kipling j.*, 1927+.

8386  LANG. Andrew Lang: a critical biography, with a short-title bibliography . . . By Roger Lancelyn Green. Leicester. 1946. N.Y. 1962.

See also Antonius Petrus Leonardus de Cocq, *Andrew Lang: a nineteenth-century anthropologist*, Tilburg 1968.

8387  LAWRENCE. A bibliography of D. H. Lawrence. By Warren Roberts. 1963.

The easiest bibliog. to use: but note also Lucy I. Edwards, comp., *D. H. Lawrence: a finding list: holdings in the city, county and university libraries of Nottingham*, Nottingham 1968, and Ernest Warnock Tedlock, jr., *The Frieda Lawrence collection of D. H. Lawrence manuscripts: a descriptive bibliography*, Albuquerque, N. Mex. 1948.

   For letters see Aldous Huxley, ed., *The letters of D. H. Lawrence*, Lond. & N.Y. 1932; Harry Thornton Moore, ed., *D. H. Lawrence's letters to Bertrand Russell*, N.Y. 1948, and *Collected letters*, 2 v. Lond. & N.Y. 1962; Ada Lawrence and George Stuart Gelder, eds., *Young Lorenzo: early life of D. H. Lawrence: containing hitherto unpublished letters, articles and reproductions of pictures*, Florence 1931, repr. N.Y. 1966; James Thompson Boulton, ed., *Lawrence in love: letters to Louie Burrows*, Nottingham

1968; and George J. Zytaruk, ed., *The quest for Rananim: D. H. Lawrence's letters to S. S. Koteliansky, 1914 to 1930*, Montreal 1970. There are also various selections.

For studies see Ronald Philip Draper, ed., *D. H. Lawrence: the critical heritage*, 1970; Reloy Garcia and James Karabatson, eds., *A concordance to the poetry of D. H. Lawrence*, Lincoln, Nebr. 1970; Stephen Potter, *D. H. Lawrence: a first study*, 1930; John Middleton Murry, *Son of woman: the story of D. H. Lawrence*, 1931, new edn. 1954, and *Reminiscences of D. H. Lawrence*, 1933; Catherine Carswell, *The savage pilgrimage: a narrative of D. H. Lawrence*, Lond. 1932; Dorothy Eugénie Brett, *Lawrence and Brett: a friendship*, Phila. 1933; Frieda Lawrence, '*Not I, but the wind*', N.Y. 1934, and *Memoirs and correspondence*, ed. by Ernest Warnock Tedlock, 1961; [Jessie Wood] *D. H. Lawrence: a personal record*, N.Y. 1936, 2nd edn. ed. by Jonathan David Chambers, Lond. 1965; Richard Aldington, *Portrait of a genius, but . . .*, Lond. & N.Y. 1950; Harry Thornton Moore, *The life and works of D. H. Lawrence*, Lond. & N.Y. 1951, 2nd edn. Lond. 1963, N.Y. [*D. H. Lawrence: his life and works*] 1964, and *Poste restante: a Lawrence travel calendar*, Berkeley 1956; Frank Raymond Leavis, *D. H. Lawrence, novelist*, 1955; Graham Hough, *The dark sun: a study of D. H. Lawrence*, 1956; Edward Nehls, ed., *D. H. Lawrence: a composite biography*, 3 v. Madison, Wis. 1957–9; Eliseo Vivas, *D. H. Lawrence: the failure and the triumph of art*, Evanston, Ill. 1960; Anthony Beal, *D. H. Lawrence*, Edin. 1961; Ernest Warnock Tedlock, jr., *D. H. Lawrence, artist & rebel: a study of Lawrence's fiction*, Albuquerque, N. Mex. 1963; Eugene Goodheart, *The utopian vision of D. H. Lawrence*, Chicago 1963; Julian Lane Moynahan, *The deed of life: the novels and tales of D. H. Lawrence*, Princeton 1963; Ronald Philip Draper, *D. H. Lawrence*, N.Y. 1964; Daniel Gillès, *D. H. Lawrence: ou, le puritain scandaleux*, Paris 1964; Helen Corke, *D. H. Lawrence: the Croydon years*, Austin, Tex. 1965; Hillel Matthew Daleski, *The forked flame: a study of D. H. Lawrence*, 1965; Ernest Warnock Tedlock, jr., ed., *D. H. Lawrence and 'Sons and lovers': sources and criticism*, N.Y. 1965; David James Gordon, *D. H. Lawrence as a literary critic*, New Haven, Conn. 1966; Keith Sagar, *The art of D. H. Lawrence*, Camb. 1966; Colin Campbell Clarke, *River of dissolution: D. H. Lawrence & English romanticism*, 1969; David Cavitch, *D. H. Lawrence and the new world*, 1969; Yudhishtar, *Conflict in the novels of D. H. Lawrence*, Edin. 1969; Émile Delavenay, *D. H. Lawrence: l'homme et la genèse de son œuvre: les années de formation, 1885–1919*, 2 v. Paris 1969, and *D. H. Lawrence and Edward Carpenter: a study in Edwardian transition*, N.Y. 1971; James C. Cowan, *D. H. Lawrence's American journey: a study in literature and myth*, Cleveland, Ohio 1970; Tom Marshall, *The psychic mariner: a reading of the poems of D. H. Lawrence*, N.Y. 1970; and Claude Negriolli, *La symbolique de D. H. Lawrence*, Paris 1970.

For work in progress see *The D. H. Lawrence news and notes*, 1+, University, Ala. 1959+, and *The D. H. Lawrence Rev.*, 1+, Fayetteville, Ark., 1968+.

**8388  LEAR. Edward Lear on my shelves. By William Bradhurst Osgood Field. Priv. pr. Munich. 1933.**

For js. see Lear's own edn. of *Journals of a landscape painter in Albania . . .*, 1851, repr. 1965, *Journals of a landscape painter in southern Calabria . . .*, 1852, repr. 1964, and *Journals of a landscape painter in Corsica*, 1870, Ray Murphy, ed., *Edward Lear's Indian journal: watercolours and extracts from the diary of Edward Lear, 1873–1875*, Lond. & N.Y. 1953, and Herbert Van Thal, ed., *Journals: a selection*, 1952. For letters see Lady Strachey, ed., *Letters of Edward Lear, author of 'The book of nonsense', to Chichester Fortescue, Lord Carlingford, and Frances, Countess Waldegrave*, 1907, 4th edn. 1909, cont. in *Later letters . . .*, 1911. For Lear's life see Angus Davidson, *Edward Lear, landscape painter and nonsense poet, 1812–1888*, Lond. 1938, N.Y. 1939, repr. Port Washington, N.Y. 1968, Joanna Richardson, *Edward Lear*, 1965, Philip Hofer, *Edward Lear as a landscape draughtsman*, Camb., Mass. 1967, and Vivien Noakes, *Edward Lear: the life of a wanderer*, 1968.

**8389  VERNON LEE (VIOLET PAGET). Vernon Lee: Violet Paget, 1856–1935. By Peter Gunn. 1964.**

8390 LE GALLIENNE. The quest of the golden boy: the life and letters of Richard Le Gallienne. By Richard Whittington-Egan and Geoffrey Smerdon. Lond. & Barre, Mass. 1960.

See also Robert J. C. Lingel, *A bibliographical checklist of the writings of Richard Le Gallienne*, Metuchen, N.J. 1926.

8391 MALLOCK. Memoirs of life and literature. By William Hurrell Mallock. Lond. & N.Y. 1920.

There is very little serious work on Mallock. But see John Lucas, 'Tilting at the moderns: W. H. Mallock's criticisms of the positivist spirit', *Renaissance & Modern Studs.* x (1966), 88–143, and Amy Belle Adams, *The novels of William Hurrell Mallock*, Orono, Maine 1934.

8392 MARTINEAU. Harriet Martineau: a bibliography of her separately-printed books. By Joseph Barry Rivlin. New York Public Libr. 1947.

For her life see her *Autobiography*, ed. by Maria Weston Chapman, 3 v. London. 1877, 2 v. Boston 1877, and Robert Kiefer Webb, *Harriet Martineau: Radical Victorian*, N.Y. 1957, which is superior to Vera Wheatley, *The life and work of Harriet Martineau*, 1957.

8393 MEREDITH. A bibliography of the writings in prose and verse of George Meredith. Comp. by Maurice Buxton Forman. Bibliog. Soc. 1922. Suppl. [Meredithiana . . .] 1924. Cont. by H. Lewis Sarvin in *Bulletin of Bibliog.* xxi (1953–6), 186–91, 215–16.

Clarence Lee Cline, ed., *The letters of George Meredith*, 3 v. Oxf. 1970, is now standard. There is no standard life, but see [Arthur] Lionel Stevenson, *The ordeal of George Meredith: a biography*, N.Y. 1953, and René Galland, *George Meredith: les cinquante premières années, 1828–1878*, Paris 1923. The best early criticism of Meredith was in George Macaulay Trevelyan, *The poetry and philosophy of George Meredith*, Lond. & N.Y. 1906, and Maurice Buxton Forman, ed., *George Meredith: some early appreciations*, 1909. For later comment see Norman Kelvin, *A troubled Eden: nature and society in the works of George Meredith*, Stanford, Calif. 1961, Gillian Beer, *Meredith: a change of masks*, 1970, and Victor Sawdon Pritchett, *George Meredith and English comedy*, 1970.

8394 MEYNELL. Alice Meynell: a memoir. By Viola Meynell. Lond. & N.Y. 1929.

See also Anne Kimball Tuell, *Mrs. Meynell and her literary generation*, N.Y. 1925.

8395 MILNES. Monckton Milnes: the flight of youth, 1851–1885. By James Pope-Hennessy. 1951.

See also Sir Thomas Wemyss Reid, *The life, letters and friendships of Richard Monckton Milnes, first Lord Houghton*, 2 v. 1890.

8396 MOORE. A bibliography of George Moore. By Edwin Gilcher. De Kalb, Ill. 1970.

For letters see Helmut E. Gerber, ed., *George Moore in transition: letters to T. Fisher Unwin and Lena Milman, 1894–1910*, Detroit, Mich. 1968, and Rupert Hart-Davis, ed., *George Moore: letters to Lady Cunard, 1895–1933*, 1957. For his life and work see Jean C. Noel, *George Moore: l'homme et l'œuvre, 1852–1933*, Paris 1966; John Freeman, *A portrait of George Moore in a study of his work*, 1922; Joseph Maunsell Hone, *The life of George Moore . . .*, Lond. & N.Y. 1936; Nancy Cunard, *GM: memories of George*

Moore, 1956; Alexander Norman Jeffares, *George Moore*, 1965; Georges Paul Collet, *George Moore et la France*, Geneva 1957; Herbert Zirker, *George Moore: Realismus und autobiographische Fiktion: Versuch zur Form der Autobiographie*, Cologne 1968; Malcolm Johnston Brown, *George Moore: a reconsideration*, Wash. 1955; Graham Owens, ed., *George Moore's mind and art: essays*, Edin. 1968; and Douglas A. Hughes, ed,. *The man of wax: critical essays on George Moore*, N.Y. 1971.

MORRIS. See **616.**

8397    MÜLLER. The life and letters of the Right Honourable Friedrich Max Müller. Ed. by his wife. 2 v. 1902.

Müller himself wrote *My autobiography: a fragment*, N.Y. 1901.

8398    PATER. Walter Pater: l'homme et l'œuvre. By Germaine d'Hangest. 2 v. Paris. 1961.

See also Lawrence Gove Evans, ed., *Letters of Walter Pater*, Oxf. 1970; Arthur Christopher Benson, *Walter Pater*, Lond. & N.Y. 1906; Thomas Wright, *The life of Walter Pater*, 2 v. 1907; Edward Thomas, *Walter Pater: a critical study*, N.Y. 1913; Arthur Symons, *A study of Walter Pater*, 1932; Lord [Edward Christian] David [Gascoyne-] Cecil, *Walter Pater: the scholar artist*, Camb. 1955; Edmund Chandler, *Pater on style . . .*, Copenhagen 1958; Wolfgang Iser, *Walter Pater: die Autonomie des Aesthetischen*, Tübingen 1960; David Anthony Downes, *Victorian portraits: Hopkins and Pater*, N.Y. 1965; Anthony Ward, *Walter Pater: the idea in nature*, 1966; Gordon McKenzie, *The literary character of Walter Pater*, Berkeley 1967; Gerald Cornelius Monsman, *Pater's portraits: mythic pattern in the fiction of Walter Pater*, Baltimore, Md. 1967; Richmond Crinkley, *Walter Pater: humanist*, Lexington, Ky. 1970, and De Laura (**8311**).

8399    PATMORE. Memoirs and correspondence of Coventry Patmore. By Basil Champneys. 2 v. 1900.

The official life. See also Derek Patmore, *The life and times of Coventry Patmore*, 1949, Frederick Page, *Patmore: a study in poetry*, 1933, John Cowie Reid, *The mind and art of Coventry Patmore*, 1957, and the correspondence with Hopkins (**8376**).

8400    PEACOCK. Peacock: his circle and his age. By Howard Mills. Camb. 1969.

See also Lionel Madden, *Thomas Love Peacock*, 1967, Carl Dawson, *Thomas Love Peacock*, 1968, and *His fine wit: a study of Thomas Love Peacock*, 1970, and John Boynton Priestley, *Thomas Love Peacock*, Lond. & N.Y. 1927.

8401    PINERO. Sir Arthur Pinero: a critical biography with letters. By Wilbur Dwight Dunkel. Chicago. 1941.

Poor. But Henry Hamilton Fyfe, *Sir Arthur Pinero's plays and players*, 1930, is no better.

8402    QUILLER-COUCH. Arthur Quiller-Couch: a biographical study of Q. By Frederick Brittain. Camb. 1947.

Incl. bibliog. Q. himself wrote *Memories & opinions: an unfinished autobiography*, ed. by Sir Sydney Castle Roberts, Camb. 1944.

8403    READE. Wilkie Collins and Charles Reade: first editions (with a few exceptions) in the library of Dormy House, Pine Valley, New Jersey. Comp. by Morris Longstreth Parrish. 1940.

See also Malcolm Elwin, *Charles Reade: a biography*, 1931, Charles L. Reade and Compton Read, comps., *Charles Reade, dramatist, novelist, journalist: a memoir*, 2 v. Lond. & N.Y. 1887, Wayne Burns, *Charles Reade: a study in Victorian authorship*, N.Y. 1961, and Albert Morton Turner, *The making of 'The cloister and the hearth'*, Chicago 1938.

8404 ROBERTSON. Thomas William Robertson: his plays and stagecraft. By Maynard Savin. Providence, R.I. 1950.

The first life was Thomas Edgar Pemberton, *The life and writings of T. W. Robertson*, 1893.

8405 ROLFE. A bibliography of Frederick Rolfe, Baron Corvo. Comp. by Cecil Woolf. 1957.

Woolf also ed. the centenary edn. of the *Letters*, 3+ v., 1959–62+. Alphonse James Albert Symons, *The quest for Corvo: an experiment in biography*, Lond. & N.Y. 1934, new edn. 1952, is deservedly famous. See also Cecil Woolf and Brocard Sewell, eds., *Corvo, 1860–1960: a collection of essays* . . ., Aylesford 1961, and Donald Weeks, *Corvo*, 1971.

8406 ROSSETTI. Christina Rossetti. By Lona Mosk Packer. Berkeley. 1963.

See also William Michael Rossetti, ed., *The family letters of Christina Georgina Rossetti* . . ., Lond. & N.Y. 1908, Fredegond Shove, *Christina Rossetti: a study*, N.Y. 1969, Georgina Battiscombe, *Christina Rossetti*, 1965, Mary Frances Sanders, *The life of Christina Rossetti*, 1930, and the works on D. G. Rossetti at **8407**.

8407 ROSSETTI. Bibliography of the works of Dante Gabriel Rossetti. By William Michael Rossetti. 1905.

See also Faverty (**8281**), and Paull Franklin Baum, ed., *Dante Gabriel Rossetti: an analytical list of manuscripts in the Duke University Library, with hitherto unpublished verse and prose*, Durham, N.C. 1931. For letters the standard edn. is Oswald Doughty and John Robert Wahl, ed., *Letters*, 5 v., Oxf. 1965+. Older colls. were Oswald Doughty, ed., *The letters of Dante Gabriel Rossetti to his publisher, F. S. Ellis*, 1928; William Michael Rossetti, comp., *Dante Gabriel Rossetti: his family letters*, 2 v. 1895, *Ruskin: Rossetti: Pre-Raphaelitism: papers 1854 to 1862*, Lond. & N.Y. 1899, and *Rossetti papers, 1862 to 1870* . . ., Lond. & N.Y. 1903; George Birkbeck Hill, ed., *Letters of Dante Gabriel Rossetti to William Allingham, 1854–1870*, N.Y. 1897; Paull Franklin Baum, ed., *Dante Gabriel Rossetti's letters to Fanny Cornforth*, Baltimore, Md. 1940; and Lona Mosk Packer, ed., *The Rossetti–Macmillan letters* . . ., Berkeley 1963.

The standard life is Oswald Doughty, *Dante Gabriel Rossetti: a Victorian romantic*, New Haven, Conn. 1949, publ. in Lond. as *A Victorian romantic* . . ., 1949, 2nd edn. 1960. For Rossetti's career see also Ross Douglas Waller, *The Rossetti family, 1824–1854*, Manch. 1932; Helen Maria Madox Rossetti Angeli, *Dante Gabriel Rossetti: his friends and enemies*, 1949; Henry Treffry Dunn, *Recollections of Dante Gabriel Rossetti and his circle (Cheyne Walk life)*, 1904; Sir Max Beerbohm, *Rossetti and his circle*, 1922; Sir Thomas Henry Hall Caine, *Recollections of Rossetti*, 1928; Gale Pedrick, *Life with Rossetti: or, no peacocks allowed*, 1964; and Henry Currie Marillier, *Dante Gabriel Rossetti: an illustrated memorial of his art and life*, 1899, 3rd edn. 1904. For his work see also William Michael Rossetti, *Dante Gabriel Rossetti as designer and writer*, 1889; Joseph Leopold Ford Hermann Madox Hueffer, *Rossetti: a critical essay on his art*, Lond. & N.Y. 1902; Arthur Christopher Benson, *Rossetti*, 1904; Jacques Savarit, *Tendances mystiques et ésotériques chez Dante-Gabriel Rossetti*, Paris 1961; Gordon H. Fleming, *Rossetti and the Pre-Raphaelite Brotherhood*, 1967; Robert De Sales Johnston, *Dante Gabriel Rossetti*, N.Y. 1969; Robert M. Cooper, *Lost on both sides: Dante Gabriel Rossetti, critic and poet*, Athens, Ohio 1970; David Arthur Sonstroem, *Rossetti and the fair lady*, Middletown, Conn. 1970; and the works on Pre-Raphaelitism at **9004–10** and **9078.**

8408   RUSKIN. A complete bibliography of the writings in prose and verse of
John Ruskin, LL.D., with a list of the more important Ruskiniana. Ed. by
Thomas James Wise. 2 v. 1893.

The standard edn. of the works is the Libr. edn., ed. by Sir Edward Tyas Cook and
Alexander Dundas Ogilvy Wedderburn, 39 v. 1903–12: vol. 39 is a *General index*, vols.
36–7 are a selection of letters. The *Diaries* were ed. by John Evans and John Howard
Whitehouse, 3 v. Oxf. 1956–9, but should be suppl. by Helen Gill Viljoen, ed., *The
Brantwood diary of John Ruskin* . . . [1876–84], New Haven, Conn. 1970. For letters
see Sir William Milburne James, ed., *The order of release: the story of John Ruskin,
Effie Gray and John Everett Millais, told for the first time in their unpublished letters*,
1947 N.Y. edn. entitled *John Ruskin and Effie Gray*, 1947; Mary Lutyens, ed., *Effie in
Venice: unpublished letters of Mrs. John Ruskin written from Venice between 1849–1852*,
1965, and *Millais and the Ruskins*, 1967; John Lewis Bradley, ed., *Ruskin's letters from
Venice, 1851–1852*, New Haven, Conn. 1955, and *The letters of John Ruskin to Lord
and Lady Mount Temple*, Columbus, Ohio 1964; Van Akin Burd, ed., *The Winnington
letters: John Ruskin's correspondence with Margaret Alexis Bell and the children at
Winnington Hall*, Camb., Mass. 1969; Margaret Elizabeth Spence, ed., *Dearest Mama
Talbot: a selection of letters written by John Ruskin to Mrs. Fanny Talbot*, 1966; Rayner
Unwin, ed., *The gulf of years: letters from John Ruskin to Kathleen Olander*, 1953;
Thomas James Wise, ed., *Letters from John Ruskin to Frederick J. Furnivall, M.A., Hon.
Dr. Phil., and other correspondents*, priv. pr. 1897, *Letters . . . to William Ward*, 2 v. priv.
pr. 1893, *Letters . . . to Ernest Chesnau*, priv. pr. 1894, *Letters . . . to Rev. J. P. Faunthorpe*,
2 v. priv. pr. 1895–6, *Letters to Rev. F. A. Malleson*, priv. pr. 1896, *Letters on art and
literature*, priv. pr. 1894, and *Letters upon subjects of general interest from John Ruskin to
various correspondents*, priv. pr. 1892; [Alexander Dundas Ogilvy Wedderburn, ed.]
*Arrows of the chace: being a collection of scattered letters, published chiefly in the daily
newspapers, 1840–1880, by John Ruskin*, 2 v. Orpington 1880; William Michael Rossetti,
ed., *Ruskin, Rossetti, Pre-Raphaelitism: papers 1854 to 1862*, Lond. & N.Y. 1899;
Charlotte Quaritch Wrentmore, ed., *Letters of John Ruskin to Bernard Quaritch, 1867–
1888*, 1938; and Anon., ed., *Letters to M. G. & H. G.*, Lond. & N.Y. 1903, *Letters of
John Ruskin to Charles Eliot Norton*, 2 v. Boston and N.Y. 1904, and *Letters to William
Ward . . .*, Boston 1922.

   The standard life is Sir Edward Tyas Cook, *The life of John Ruskin*, 2 v. 1911. See
also Helen Gill Viljoen, *Ruskin's Scottish heritage: a prelude*, Urbana, Ill. 1956; Frederic
Harrison, *John Ruskin*, 1902; Arthur Christopher Benson, *Ruskin: a study in personality*,
1911; Reginald Howard Wilenski, *John Ruskin: an introduction to further study of his
life and work*, 1933; Derrick Leon, *Ruskin: the great Victorian*, 1949; Peter Courtney
Quennell, *John Ruskin: the portrait of a prophet*, Lond. & N.Y. 1949; Joan Evans,
*John Ruskin*, 1954; John D. Rosenberg, *The darkening glass: a portrait of Ruskin's
genius*, N.Y. 1961; Quentin Bell, *Ruskin*, Edin. 1963; James S. Dearden, *Facets of
Ruskin: some sesquicentennial studies*, 1970; George P. Landow, *The aesthetic and critical
theories of John Ruskin*, Princeton 1971; Hélène Lemaître, *Les pierres dans l'œuvre de
Ruskin*, Caen 1965; Frank Daniel Curtin, *Aesthetics in English social reform: Ruskin and
his followers*, Ithaca, N.Y. 1940; Henry Andrews Ladd, *The Victorian morality of art:
an analysis of Ruskin's esthetic*, N.Y. 1932; Roger Breed Stein, *John Ruskin and aesthetic
thought in America, 1840–1900*, Camb., Mass. 1967; John Tyree Fain, *Ruskin and the
economists*, Nashville, Tenn. 1956; John Atkinson Hobson, *John Ruskin: social reformer*,
Boston 1898; Jacques Bardoux, *Le mouvement idéaliste et social dans la littérature anglaise
au XIXe siècle: John Ruskin*, Paris 1900; Hilda Boettcher Hagstotz, *The educational
theories of John Ruskin*, Lincoln, Nebr. 1942; William Jolly, *Ruskin on education: some
needed but neglected elements*, 1894; James S. Dearden, ed., *The professor: Arthur Severn's
memoir of John Ruskin*, 1967; and Elisabeth Gertrud Koenig, *John Ruskin und die
Schweiz*, Berne 1943.

8409   RUTHERFORD. Mark Rutherford: a biography of William Hale
White. By Catherine Macdonald Maclean. 1955.

See also Stephen Merton, *Mark Rutherford (William Hale White)*, N.Y. 1967; Irvin Stock, *William Hale White (Mark Rutherford): a critical study*, N.Y. 1956; Wilfred Healey Stone, *Religion and art of William Hale White (Mark Rutherford)*, Stanford, Calif. 1954; Dorothy Vernon White, *The Groombridge diary*, 1924; and Sir William Robertson Nicoll, *Memories of Mark Rutherford*, 1924.

**8410 SCHREINER.** Olive Emilie Albertina Schreiner, 1855–1920: bibliography. By E. Verster. Rondebosch. 1946.

For letters see Samuel Cron Cronwright-Schreiner, *The letters of Olive Schreiner, 1876–1920*, Lond. & Boston 1924. Cronwright-Schreiner also publ. *The life of Olive Schreiner*, Lond. & Boston 1924. Vera Buchanan-Gould, *Not without honour: the life and writings of Olive Schreiner*, 1948, and Johannes Meintjes, *Olive Schreiner: portrait of a South African woman*, Johannesburg 1965, give more popular accounts of her life. See also Marian Valerie Friedmann, *Olive Schreiner: a study in latent meanings*, Johannesburg 1955.

**8411 SHARP.** William Sharp—'Fiona Macleod', 1855–1905. By Flavia Alaya. Camb., Mass. 1970.

The official life was Elizabeth Amelia Sharp, comp., *William Sharp (Fiona Macleod): a memoir*, 1910.

**8412 SHAW.** Dictionary to the plays and novels of Bernard Shaw, with bibliography of his works and of the literature concerning him, with a record of the principal Shavian play productions. By Charlie Lewis Broad and Violet M. Broad. 1929.

For letters see Christopher St. John, ed., *Ellen Terry and Bernard Shaw: a correspondence*, N.Y. 1931; Charles Benjamin Purdom, ed., *Letters . . . to Granville Barker*, Lond. 1956, N.Y. 1957; Alan Holmes Dent, ed., *Bernard Shaw and Mrs. Patrick Campbell: their correspondence*, Lond. & N.Y. 1952; Clifford Bax, ed., *Florence Farr, Bernard Shaw and W. B. Yeats*, Dublin 1941, N.Y. 1942, Lond. 1946; and (most important) Dan H. Laurence, ed., *Collected letters, 1874–1897*, 1965, . . . *1898–1910*, 1972.

There is no standard life. Stanley Weintraub, ed., *Shaw: an autobiography, selected from his writings*, 2 v. N.Y. 1969–70, is a useful compilation. Allan Chappelow, *Shaw, 'the chucker-out': a biographical exposition and critique . . .*, 1969, and A. Chappelow, ed., *Shaw the villager and human being: a biographical symposium*, 1961, fill some of the gaps. Among useful works are Anthony Stenersen Abbott, *Shaw and Christianity*, N.Y. 1965; Eric Russell Bentley, *Bernard Shaw*, Norfolk, Conn. 1947, new edn. N.Y. 1959, Lond. 1950, 2nd edn. 1967; Roger Boxill, *Shaw and the doctors*, N.Y. 1969; Ivor Brown, *Shaw in his time*, 1965; Charles A. Carpenter, *Bernard Shaw & the art of destroying ideals: the early plays*, Madison, Wis. 1969; Gilbert Keith Chesterton, *George Bernard Shaw*, 1909; Louis Crompton, *Shaw, the dramatist*, Lincoln, Nebr. 1969; Richard Farr Dietrich, *Portrait of the artist as a young superman: a study of Shaw's novels*, Gainesville, Fla. 1969; Bernard Frank Dukore, *Bernard Shaw, director*, Seattle, Wash. 1971; Martin Ellehauge, *The position of Bernard Shaw in European drama and philosophy*, Copenhagen 1931; St. John Greer Ervine, *Bernard Shaw: his life, work and friends*, 1956; Harold Fromm, *Bernard Shaw and the theater in the nineties: a study of Shaw's dramatic criticism*, Lawrence, Kans. 1967; William B. Furlong, *GBS/GKC: Shaw and Chesterton, the metaphysical jesters*, Univ. Park, Pa. 1970; A. M. Gibbs, *Shaw*, Edin. 1969; *Frank Harris on Bernard Shaw: an unauthorised biography based on firsthand information*, 1931; Archibald Henderson, *Bernard Shaw: playboy and prophet*, N.Y. & Lond. 1932, rev. edn. [*Bernard Shaw: man of the century*] N.Y. 1956; William Irvine, *The universe of G. B. S.*, N.Y. 1949; Fritz Erwin Loewenstein, *Bernard Shaw through the camera . . .*, 1948; Desmond MacCarthy, *Shaw*, 1951, publ. in N.Y. as *Shaw's plays in review*, 1951; Raymond Mander and J. Mitchenson, *Theatrical companion to*

*Shaw: a pictorial record of the first performances of the plays of George Bernard Shaw*, 1954; Martin Meisel, *Shaw and the nineteenth-century theater*, Princeton 1963; Henry Louis Mencken, *George Bernard Shaw: his plays*, Boston & Lond. 1905, repr. New Rochelle, N.Y. 1969; Mina Moore, *Bernard Shaw et la France*, Paris 1933; Arthur Hobart Nethercot, *Men and supermen: the Shavian portrait gallery*, Camb., Mass. 1954; Richard Malin Ohmann, *Shaw: the style and the man*, Middletown, Conn. 1962; Hesketh Pearson, *Shaw: a full length portrait*, N.Y. 1942, Lond. [*Bernard Shaw: his life and personality*] 1942, and *G. B. S.: a postscript*, Lond. & N.Y. 1950; Charles Benjamin Purdom, *A guide to the plays of Bernard Shaw*, 1963; B. C. Rosset, *Shaw of Dublin: the formative years*, Univ. Park, Pa. 1964; Louis Simon, *Shaw on education*, N.Y. 1958; Colin Wilson, *Bernard Shaw: a reassessment*, Lond. & N.Y. 1969; Stephen Winsten, *Jesting apostle: the life of Bernard Shaw*, 1956; and Homer Edwards Woodbridge, *George Bernard Shaw, creative artist*, Carbondale, Ill. 1963. *The Shaw review*, 1+, University Park, Pa. 1951+, Shaw Soc., *The Shavian*, 1953+, and *The independent Shavian: j. of the New York Shavians*, N.Y. 1962+, all publ. articles.

8413   SMILES. Samuel Smiles and his surroundings. By Aileen Smiles. 1956.

See also Thomas Mackay, ed., *The autobiography of Samuel Smiles, LL.D.*, London & New York, 1905, and Kenneth Fielden, 'Samuel Smiles and self-help', *Victorian Studs.* xii (1968–9), 155–76.

8414   STEPHEN. Leslie Stephen: his thought and character in relation to his time. By Noel Gilroy Annan, Baron Annan. Lond. 1951. Camb., Mass. 1952.

Important. The official life was Frederic William Maitland, *The life and letters of Leslie Stephen*, 1906, repr. Lond. and Detroit, Mich. 1968. Stephen himself wrote *Some early impressions*, 1924. See also Regina Tangl, *Leslie Stephens Weltanschauung*, Hamburg 1961.

8415   STEVENSON. A Stevenson library: catalogue of a collection of writings by and about Robert Louis Stevenson, formed by Edwin J. Beinecke. Comp. by George Leslie McKay. 6 v. New Haven [Conn.]. 1951–64.

See also William Francis Prideaux, comp., *A bibliography of the works of Robert Louis Stevenson*, 1903, new edn. 1917. For letters see Sir Sidney Colvin, ed., *Vailima letters: being, correspondence addressed by Robert Louis Stevenson to Sidney Colvin, November 1890–October 1894*, 2 v. Lond. & Chicago 1895, and *The letters of Robert Louis Stevenson to his family and friends*, 2 v. Lond. & N.Y. 1899, 4th edn. with suppl. 1901, enlarged edn. [*The letters of Robert Louis Stevenson*] 4 v. 1911, Janet Adam Smith, ed., *Henry James and Robert Louis Stevenson: a record of friendship and criticism*, 1948, and John De Lancey Ferguson and Marshall Waingrow, eds., *R.L.S.: Stevenson's letters to Charles Baxter*, New Haven, Conn. 1956.

The basic life is Sir Graham Balfour, *The life of Robert Louis Stevenson*, 2 v. 1901. See also Edwin M. Eigner, *Robert Louis Stevenson and romantic tradition*, Princeton 1966; Joseph Chamberlain Furnas, *Voyage to windward: the life of Robert Louis Stevenson*, N.Y. 1951; Robert James Kiely, *Robert Louis Stevenson and the fiction of adventure*, Camb., Mass. 1965; Frank Arthur Swinnerton, *R. L. Stevenson: a critical study*, 1914, repr. Port Washington, N.Y. 1966; Gilbert Keith Chesterton, *Robert Louis Stevenson*, 1927; Doris Nellie Dalglish, *Presbyterian pirate: a portrait of Stevenson*, 1937; David Daiches, *Robert Louis Stevenson*, Norfolk, Conn. 1947; Malcolm Elwin, *The strange case of Robert Louis Stevenson*, 1950; Richard Aldington, *Portrait of a rebel: the life and work of Robert Louis Stevenson*, 1957; Elsie Caldwell, *Last witness for Robert Louis Stevenson*, Norman, Okla. 1960; Horst Dölvers, *Der Erzähler Robert Louis Stevenson: Interpretationen*, Berne 1969; and Harold Francis Watson, *Coasts of Treasure Island: a study of the backgrounds and sources for Robert Louis Stevenson's romance of the sea*, San Antonio, Tex. 1969.

8416 SURTEES. A Jorrocks handbook: a centenary dictionary of the characters, places, situations and allusions which occur in the Jorrocks novels and in the short stories by Robert Smith Surtees. By Robert Lewis Collison. 1964.

See also Frederick Watson, *Robert Smith Surtees: a critical study*, 1933, Leonard Cooper, R. S. Surtees, 1952, Anthony Bedford Steel, *Jorrocks's England*, 1932, Edward William Bovill, *The England of Nimrod and Surtees, 1815–1854*, 1959, and Horst Drescher, *Robert Smith Surtees: ein frühviktorianischer Erzähler*, Marburg 1961.

8417 SWINBURNE. A bibliography of the writings in prose and verse of Algernon Charles Swinburne. By Thomas James Wise. 2 v. 1919–20.

To be suppl. by Faverty (**8281**). The standard edn. of *The Swinburne letters* was ed. by Cecil Yelverton Lang, 6 v. New Haven, Conn. 1959–62. The *Complete works* were ed. by Sir Edmund William Gosse and Thomas James Wise, 20 v. 1925–7. Gosse also publ. *The life of Algernon Charles Swinburne*, Lond. & N.Y. 1917, incl. as vol. 19 of the *Complete works*, 1927. See also Jean Overton Fuller, *Swinburne: a critical biography*, 1968; Mollie Panter-Downes, *At The Pines: Swinburne and Watts-Dunton in Putney*, 1971; Clara Jane Watts-Dunton, *The home life of Swinburne*, 1922; Georges Lafourcade, *La jeunesse de Swinburne, 1837–1867*, 2 v. Paris 1928, and *Swinburne: a literary biography*, Lond. & N.Y. 1932; Clyde Kenneth Hyder, *Swinburne's literary career and fame*, Durham, N.C. 1933; John A. Cassidy, *Algernon C. Swinburne*, N.Y. 1964; Clyde Kenneth Hyder, ed., *Swinburne: the critical heritage*, 1970; William Rutland Rutland, *Swinburne: a nineteenth-century Hellene . . .*, Oxf. 1931; Thomas Edmund Connolly, *Swinburne's theory of poetry*, Albany, N.Y. 1964; Robert Louis Peters, *The crowns of Apollo: Swinburne's principles of literature and art: a study in Victorian criticism and aesthetics*, Detroit, Mich. 1965; and Christian Enzensberger, *Viktorianische Lyrik: Tennyson und Swinburne in der Geschichte der Entfremdung*, Munich 1969.

8418 SYNGE. The autobiography of J. M. Synge: constructed from the manuscripts by Alan Price. Dublin. 1965.

A brief fragment. For manuscripts see Trinity College, Dublin, Libr., *The Synge manuscripts in the library of Trinity College, Dublin: a catalogue prepared on the occasion of the Synge centenary exhibition, 1971*, Dublin 1971. For letters see Ann Saddlemyer, ed., *Letters to Molly: John Millington Synge to Maire O'Neill, 1901–1909*, Camb., Mass. 1971. The basic study is Maurice Bourgeois, *John Millington Synge and the Irish theatre*, 1913, repr. N.Y. 1965. The best life is David Herbert Green and Edward Millington Stephens, *J. M. Synge, 1871–1909*, N.Y. 1959. See also Daniel Corkery, *Synge and Anglo-Irish literature: a study*, Dublin and Cork 1931, repr. N.Y. 1965; Donna Lorine Gerstenberger, *John Millington Synge*, N.Y. 1964; Frank Laurence Lucas, *The drama of Chekhov, Synge, Yeats and Pirandello*, 1963; Alan Price, *Synge and Anglo-Irish drama*, 1961; Samuel Synge, *Letters to my daughter: memories of John Millington Synge*, Dublin & Cork [1932]; William Butler Yeats, *Synge and the Ireland of his time*, Dundrum 1911, and *The death of Synge . . .*, Dublin 1928; Robin Skelton, *J. M. Synge and his world*, N.Y. 1971; and Thomas R. Whitaker, comp., *Twentieth-century interpretations of 'The playboy of the western world': a collection of critical essays*, Englewood Cliffs, N.J., 1969.

8419 TAYLOR. Tom Taylor and the Victorian drama. By Winton Tolles. N.Y. 1940.

8420 TENNYSON. Alfred Tennyson: an annotated bibliography. Comp. by Sir Charles Tennyson and Christine Fall. Athens, Ga. 1967.

See also Faverty (**8281**), and Thomas James Wise, *A bibliography of the writings of Alfred, Lord Tennyson*, 2 v. priv. pr. 1908; Nancie Campbell, comp., *Tennyson in*

*Lincoln: a catalogue of the collections in the research centre*, v. 1+, Lincoln 1972+; Arthur Ernest Baker, *A Tennyson dictionary: the characters and place names contained in the poetical and dramatic works of the poet* . . ., Lond. & N.Y. 1916, and *A concordance to the poetical and dramatic works of Alfred, Lord Tennyson* . . ., 1914, repr. N.Y. 1966; Morton Luce, *A handbook to the works of Alfred, Lord Tennyson*, 1895, rev. edn. 1914; William Macneile Dixon, *A primer of Tennyson* . . ., 1896, 3rd edn. 1908; and George Edward Campion, comp., *A Tennyson dialect glossary: with the dialect poems*, Lincoln 1969.

The official life was Hallam Tennyson, Baron Tennyson, *Alfred, Lord Tennyson: a memoir by his son*, 2 v. Lond. & N.Y. 1897. Hallam Tennyson also ed. *Tennyson and his friends*, 1911. Family interest continues with Sir Charles Tennyson, *Alfred Tennyson*, 1949, *Six Tennyson essays*, 1954, *The Somersby Tennysons*, Tennyson Soc. Publs. 1, suppl. to *Victorian Studs.*, Bloomington, Ind. 1963, and Hope Dyson and Sir Charles Tennyson, eds., *Dear and Honoured Lady: the correspondence between Queen Victoria and Alfred Tennyson*, 1969.

For biog. and criticism see chiefly Jerome Hamilton Buckley, *Tennyson: the growth of a poet*, Camb., Mass. 1960; Joanna Richardson, *The pre-eminent Victorian: a study of Tennyson*, 1962; Valerie Pitt, *Tennyson laureate*, 1962; James D. Kissane, *Alfred Tennyson*, N.Y. 1970; John Davies Jump, ed., *Tennyson: the critical heritage*, Lond. & N.Y. 1967; and John Kilham, ed., *Critical essays on the poetry of Tennyson*, Lond. & N.Y. 1960. Other works incl. Stopford Augustus Brooke, *Tennyson: his art in relation to modern life*, Lond. & N.Y. 1896; Gilbert Keith Chesterton and Richard Garnett, *Tennyson*, 1903; Sir Harold George Nicolson, *Tennyson: aspects of his life, character and poetry*, Lond. & Boston, 1923; Hardwicke Drummond Rawnsley, *Memories of the Tennysons*, Glasgow 1900, 2nd edn. 1912; William Clark Gordon, *The social ideals of Alfred Tennyson as related to his time*, Chicago 1906; Charles Frederick Gurney Masterman, *Tennyson as a religious teacher*, 1900; Edna Moore Robinson, *Tennyson's use of the Bible*, Baltimore 1917; John Churton Collins, *Illustrations of Tennyson*, 1891; Wilfred Pirt Mustard, *Classical echoes in Tennyson*, 1904; Jelle Postma, *Tennyson as seen by his parodists*, Amsterdam 1926; Cornelia Geertrui Hendrika Japikse, *The dramas of Alfred Lord Tennyson*, 1926, repr. N.Y. 1966; Paull Franklin Baum, *Tennyson sixty years after*, Chapel Hill, N.C. 1948; Edward Dudley Hume Johnson, *The alien vision of Victorian poetry: sources of the poetic imagination in Tennyson, Browning and Arnold*, Princeton 1952; Christian Enzensberger, *Viktorianische Lyrik: Tennyson und Swinburne in der Geschichte der Entfremdung*, Munich 1969; William R. Brashear, *The living will: a study of Tennyson and nineteenth-century subjectivism*, The Hague 1969; Gerhard Joseph, *Tennysonian love: the strange diagonal*, Minneapolis, Minn. 1969; Andrew Cecil Bradley, *A commentary on Tennyson's 'In memoriam'*, 1901, 3rd. edn. 1910; Ralph Wilson Rader, *Tennyson's 'Maud': the biographical genesis*, Berkeley 1963; and John Kilham, *Tennyson and 'The princess': reflections of an age*, 1958.

The Tennyson Soc. publ. an annual *Tennyson research bull.*, 1+, Lincoln 1967+, and other reports and pamphlets.

8421   THACKERAY. A Thackeray library: first editions and first publications, portraits, water colors, etchings, drawings and manuscripts, collected by Henry Sayre Van Duzer. Priv. pr. N.Y. 1919.

See also Dudley Flamm, *Thackeray's critics: an annotated bibliography of British and American criticism, 1836–1901*, Chapel Hill, N.C. 1967, and Isadore Gilbert Mudge and Minnie Earl Sears, comps., *A Thackeray dictionary* . . ., Lond. & N.Y., 1910, repr. N.Y. 1962. The standard edn. of the letters is Gordon Norton Ray, ed., *The letters and private papers of William Makepeace Thackeray*, 4 v. Camb., Mass. 1945–6. The standard life is Gordon Norton Ray, *Thackeray*, 2 v. N.Y. 1955–8. Ray also publ. *The buried life: a study of the relation between Thackeray's fiction and his personal history*, Camb., Mass. 1952. The first big life was Lewis Melville, pseud. of Lewis Saul Benjamin, *William Makepeace Thackeray: a biography* . . ., 2 v. 1910. There is further biog. matter in Hester Ritchie, ed., *Letters of Anne Thackeray Ritchie* . . ., 1924; Anne Isabella Thackeray

Ritchie, *Chapters from some unwritten memoirs*, 1895; Sir William Wilson Hunter, *The Thackerays in India* . . ., 1897; James Grant Wilson, *Thackeray in the United States, 1852–3, 1855–6*, 2 v. 1904; and Eyre Crowe, *With Thackeray in America*, Lond. & N.Y. 1893.

For criticism see Anthony Trollope, *Thackeray*, 1879; George Edward Bateman Saintsbury, *A consideration of Thackeray*, 1931; Raymond Las Vergnas, *W. M. Thackeray, 1811–1863: l'homme, le penseur, le romancier*, Paris 1932; Malcolm Elwin, *Thackeray: a personality*, 1932; [Arthur] Lionel Stevenson, *The showman of 'Vanity fair': the life of William Makepeace Thackeray*, N.Y. 1947; John Young Thomson Greig, *Thackeray: a reconsideration*, 1950; John Wiltshire Loofbourow, *Thackeray and the form of fiction*, Princeton 1964; James Holbrook Wheetley, *Patterns in Thackeray's fiction*, Camb., Mass. 1969; Geoffrey Tillotson, *Thackeray the novelist*, Camb. 1954; Geoffrey Tillotson and Donald Hawes, eds., *Thackeray: the critical heritage*, Lond. & N.Y. 1968; and Alexander Welsh, ed., *Thackeray: a collection of critical essays*, Englewood Cliffs, N.J. 1968.

**8422 THOMAS.** Edward Thomas: a biography and a bibliography. By Robert Paul Eckert. 1937.

See also R. George Thomas, ed., *Letters from Edward Thomas to Gordon Bottomley*, 1968; William Cooke, *Edward Thomas: a critical biography, 1878–1917*, 1970; Henry Coombes, *Edward Thomas*, 1956; John Cecil Moore, *The life and letters of Edward Thomas*, 1939; and Helen Thomas, *As it was*, 1927, and *The childhood of Edward Thomas: a fragment of autobiography*, 1938.

**8423 THOMPSON.** Francis Thompson: man and poet. By John Cowie Reid. 1959.

To be suppl. by Myrtle Pihlman Pope, 'A critical bibliography of works by and about Francis Thompson', *N.Y. Public Libr. Bull.* lxii (1958), 571–6; lxiii (1959), 40–9, 155–61, 195–204. For letters see John Evangelist Walsh, ed., *The letters of Francis Thompson*, N.Y. 1969. For lives see also Everard Meynell, *The life of Francis Thompson*, 1913, rev. edn. 1926, which was a good official life; Viola Meynell, *Francis Thompson and Wilfrid Meynell: a memoir*, N.Y. 1953; Pierre Danchin, *Francis Thompson: la vie et l'œuvre d'un poète*, Paris 1959; Paul van Kuykendall Thomson, *Francis Thompson: a critical biography*, N.Y. 1961; and John E. Walsh, *Strange harp: strange symphony: the life of Francis Thompson*, N.Y. 1967.

**8424 THOMSON.** The life of James Thomson ('B. V.'): with a selection from his letters and a study of his writings. By Henry Stephens Salt. 1889.

See also Charles Vachot, *James Thomson, 1834–1882*, Paris 1964, Imogene B. Walker, *James Thomson (B. V.): a critical study*, Ithaca, N.Y. 1950, Kenneth Hugh Byron, *The pessimism of James Thomson (B. V.) in relation to his times*, The Hague 1965, Bertram Dobell, *The laureate of pessimism: a sketch of the life and character of James Thomson ('B.V.')* . . ., 1910, and William David Schaefer, *James Thomson, B.V.: beyond 'The city'*, Berkeley 1965.

**8425 TROLLOPE.** Trollope: a bibliography: an analysis of the history and structure of the works of Anthony Trollope . . . By Michael Sadleir. 1928. Addenda. 1934.

See also Winifred Gregory Gerould and James Thayer Gerould, *A guide to Trollope*, Princeton 1948. The *Letters* of Trollope were ed. by Bradford Allen Booth, 1951. Trollope himself wrote *An autobiography*, 2 v. 1883, the best edn. of which was ed. by Frederick Page, in *The Oxford Trollope*, 1950. Lucy Poate Stebbins and Richard Poate

Stebbins, *The Trollopes: the chronicles of a writing family*, N.Y. 1945, gives the family background. For criticism see Thomas Hay Sweet Escott, *Anthony Trollope: his work, associates and literary originals*, 1913; Michael Sadleir, *Anthony Trollope: a commentary*, 1927, new edn. 1945; Robert M. Polhemus, *The changing world of Anthony Trollope*, Berkeley 1968; Anthony Oliver John Cockshut, *Anthony Trollope: a critical study*, 1955; Bradford Allen Booth, *Anthony Trollope: aspects of his life and art*, Bloomington, Ind. 1958; Peter David Edwards, *Anthony Trollope*, 1968; Rafael Helling, *A century of Trollope criticism*, Helsinki 1956; Donald Arthur Smalley, ed., *Trollope: the critical heritage*, Lond. & N.Y. 1969, and *The Trollopian*, later *Nineteenth-century fiction*, 1+, Berkeley etc. 1945+.

8426  WELLS. H. G. Wells: a comprehensive bibliography. Comp. by the H. G. Wells Society. 1966. 2nd edn. 1968.

See also Geoffrey Harry Wells, *The work of H. G. Wells, 1887–1925: a bibliography, dictionary and subject-index*, 1926, repr. N.Y. 1968. For letters see Leon Edel and Gordon Norton Ray, eds., *Henry James and H. G. Wells: a record of their friendship, their debate on the art of fiction, and their quarrel*, Urbana, Ill. 1958, Harris Wilson, ed., *Arnold Bennett and H. G. Wells: a record of a personal and a literary friendship*, Urbana, Ill. 1960, and Royal Alfred Gettman, ed., *George Gissing and H. G. Wells: their friendship and correspondence*, 1961.

Wells himself publ. *Experiment in autobiography: discoveries and conclusions of a very ordinary brain (since 1866)*, 2 v. Lond. & N.Y. 1934. The latest life is Norman Mackenzie and Jeanne Mackenzie, *H. G. Wells: a biography*, Lond. & N.Y. 1973, which is fuller than Jean-Pierre Vernier, *H. G. Wells et son temps*, Univ. of Rouen 1971, which has a useful bibliog., and Lovat Dickson, *H. G. Wells: his turbulent life and times*, Lond. & N.Y. 1969. See also Patrick Parrinder, *H. G. Wells*, Edin. 1970; Iulii Iosifovich Kagarlitskii, *The life and thought of H. G. Wells*, trans. by Moura Budberg, 1966; Bernard Bergonzi, *The early H. G. Wells: a study of the scientific romances*, Manch. 1961; Mark Robert Hillegas, *The future as nightmare: H. G. Wells and the anti-utopians*, N.Y. 1967; Ingvald Raknem, *H. G. Wells and his critics*, Oslo [1962?]; and Kenneth B. Newell, *Structure in four novels by H. G. Wells*, The Hague 1968. George A. Connes, *A dictionary of the characters and scenes in the novels, romances and short stories of H. G. Wells*, Dijon 1926, is a useful handbook. The H. G. Wells Soc. publ. *The Wellsian*, Nottingham 1960+.

8427  WILDE. Bibliography of Oscar Wilde. By Stuart Mason, pseud. of Christopher Sclater Millard. 1914. New edn. 1967.

See also John Charles Finzi, comp., *Oscar Wilde and his literary circle: a catalog of manuscripts and letters in the William Andrews Clark Memorial Library, University of California at Los Angeles*, Berkeley 1957. Rupert Hart-Davis, ed., *The letters of Oscar Wilde*, 1962, is standard. For Wilde's life and work see Gustaaf Johannes Renier, *Oscar Wilde*, 1932; St. John Greer Ervine, *Oscar Wilde: a present-time appraisal*, 1951; André Paul Guillaume Gide, *Oscar Wilde: a study*, Oxf. 1905, new edn. 1951; Frances Winwar, pseud. of Frances Grebanier, *Oscar Wilde and the yellow nineties* [1940]; Hesketh Pearson, *The life of Oscar Wilde*, 1946 [N.Y. edn. publ. as *Oscar Wilde: his life and wit*, 1946]; Frank Harris, *Oscar Wilde: his life & confessions*, N.Y. 1918, new edn. 1938, repr. East Lansing, Mich. 1959; George Woodcock, *The paradox of Oscar Wilde*, 1949; Vyvyan Holland, *Oscar Wilde: a pictorial biography*, 1960, and *Son of Oscar Wilde*, 1954; Harford Montgomery Hyde, *Oscar Wilde: the aftermath*, Lond. & N.Y. 1963; Sebastian Juan Arbó, *Oscar Wilde*, Madrid 1960; and Philippe Jullian, *Oscar Wilde*, trans. by Violet Wyndham, Lond. & N.Y. 1969. For Wilde's family background see **10779** and **10798**, Epifanio San Juan, *The art of Oscar Wilde*, Princeton 1967, is a pioneer critical study. For other criticism see Karl E. Beckson, ed., *Oscar Wilde: the critical heritage*, N.Y. 1970, and Richard Ellmann, ed., *Oscar Wilde: a collection of critical essays*, Englewood Cliffs, N.J. 1969.

8428   YEATS. A bibliography of the writings of W. B. Yeats. By Allan Wade. 1951. 3rd edn. by Russell King Alspach. 1968.

See also K. P. S. Jochum, *W. B. Yeats's plays: an annotated checklist of criticism*, Saarbrücken 1966, Kenneth Gustav Walter Cross and R. T. Dunlop, *A bibliography of Yeats criticism, 1887–1965*, 1972, and Stephen Maxfield Parrish, ed., *A concordance to the poems of W. B. Yeats*, Ithaca, N.Y. 1963. Allan Wade, ed., *The Letters of W. B. Yeats*, 1954, is standard, but other earlier edns. may be found useful, incl. [Dorothy Violet Wellesley, Duchess of Wellington, ed.] *Letters on poetry from W. B. Yeats to Dorothy Wellesley*, 1940, Joseph Hone, ed., *J. B. Yeats: letters to his son, W. B. Yeats, and others, 1869–1922*, 1944, and Roger Joseph McHugh, ed., *Letters . . . to Katharine Tynan*, Dublin 1953. Roger Joseph McHugh, ed., *Ah, sweet dancer: W. B. Yeats, Margot Ruddock: a correspondence*, 1970, has appeared since the *Letters*. Yeats himself publ. *Autobiographies . . .*, 1926. For biog. and criticism see Harold Bloom, *Yeats*, 1970; Curtis Baker Bradford, *Yeats at work*, Carbondale, Ill. 1965; Richard Ellmann, *Yeats: the man and the masks*, N.Y. 1948, Lond. 1949, and *The identity of Yeats*, Lond. & N.Y. 1954; Edward Engelberg, *The vast design: patterns in W. B. Yeats's aesthetic*, Toronto 1964; Thomas Rice Henn, *The lonely tower: studies in the poetry of W. B. Yeats*, 1950, 2nd edn. 1966; Joseph Maunsell Hone, *W. B. Yeats, 1865–1939*, 1942, 2nd edn. 1962; Alexander Norman Jeffares, *A commentary on the collected poems of W. B. Yeats*, Stanford, Calif. 1968, *W. B. Yeats: man and poet*, 1949, repr. N.Y. 1966, and *The circus animals: essays on W. B. Yeats*, 1970; Louis MacNeice, *The poetry of W. B. Yeats*, 1941; Leonard Edward Nathan, *The tragic drama of William Butler Yeats: figures in a dance*, N.Y. 1965; Jon Stallworthy, *Between the lines: Yeats's poetry in the making*, Oxf. 1963; Donald T. Torchiana, *W. B. Yeats & Georgian Ireland*, Evanston, Ill. 1966; Phillip Le Duc Marcus, *Yeats and the beginning of the Irish renaissance*, Ithaca, N.Y. 1970; and Peter Ure, *Yeats*, Edin. 1963, and *Yeats the playwright . . .*, 1963.

The Yeats centenary saw the publ. of a number of symposia, among them Denis Donoghue and James Ronald Mulryne, eds., *An honoured guest: new essays on W. B. Yeats*, 1965, Alexander Norman Jeffares and Kenneth Gustav Walter Cross, eds., *In excited reverie: a centenary tribute to William Butler Yeats, 1865–1939*, 1965, Desmond Ernest Stewart Maxwell and Suheil Badi Bushrui, eds., *W. B. Yeats, 1865–1965: centenary essays on the art of W. B. Yeats*, Ibadan 1965, Liam Miller, ed., *Dolmen Press Yeats centenary papers, 1965*, 12 pts. in 2 v. Dublin 1965–8, and Robin Skelton and Ann Saddlemyer, eds., *The world of W. B. Yeats: essays in perspective*, Victoria, B.C. 1965, rev. edn. Seattle, Wash. 1967.

New essays are publ. in *Yeats studies: an international j.*, 1+, Shannon 1971+.

For special aspects of Yeats's work see Hazard Adams, *Blake and Yeats: the contrary vision*, Ithaca, N.Y. 1955, repr. N.Y. 1968; George Bornstein, *Yeats and Shelley*, Chicago 1970; Harbans Rai Bachchan, *W. B. Yeats and occultism: a study of his works in relation to Indian lore, the Cabbala, Swedenborg, Boehme and theosophy*, Delhi 1965; Birgit Bramsbäik, *The interpretation of the Cuchulain legend in the works of W. B. Yeats*, Uppsala 1950; Dorothy Mackenzie Hoare, *The works of Morris and Yeats in relation to early saga literature*, N.Y. 1971; Thomas R. Whitaker, *Swan and shadow: Yeats's dialogue with history*, Chapel Hill, N.C. 1964; Bernard Levine, *The dissolving image: the spiritual esthetic development of W. B. Yeats*, Detroit, Mich. 1970; Francis Alexander Charles Wilson, *W. B. Yeats and tradition*, 1958, and *Yeats's iconography*, 1960; Daniel Gerard Hoffman, *Barbarous knowledge: myth in the poetry of Yeats, Graves and Muir*, 1967; Suheil Badi Bushrui, *Yeats's verse-plays: the revisions, 1900–1910*, Oxf. 1965; Frank Lentricchia, *The gaiety of language: an essay on the radical poetics of W. B. Yeats and Wallace Stevens*, Berkeley 1968; Giorgio Melchiori, *The whole mystery of art: pattern into poetry in the work of W. B. Yeats*, 1960; David Ridgley Clark, *W. B. Yeats and the theatre of desolate reality*, Dublin 1965; John Rees Moore, *Masks of love and death: Yeats as dramatist*, Ithaca, N.Y. 1971; and Frank Laurence Lucas, *The drama of Chekhov, Synge, Yeats and Pirandello*, 1963.

8429 OTHER AUTHORS. AINSWORTH. Harold Locke, *A bibliographical catalogue of the published novels and ballads of William Harrison Ainsworth*, 1925, Stewart March Ellis, *William Harrison Ainsworth and his friends*, 2 v. Lond. & N.Y. 1910. ALLINGHAM. Helen Allingham and Dollie Radford, eds., *William Allingham: a diary*, 1907. BALLANTYNE. Eric Quayle, *R. M. Ballantyne: a bibliography of first editions*, 1968, and *Ballantyne, the brave: a Victorian writer and his family*, 1967. BARING. Dame Ethel Smyth, *Maurice Baring*, 1938. BESANT. Sir Walter Besant, *Autobiography*, Lond. & N.Y. 1902. BLACK-MORE. Waldo Hilary Dunn, *R. D. Blackmore: the author of 'Lorna Doone': a biography*, 1960. CAINE. Sir Thomas Henry Hall Caine, *My story*, Lond. & N.Y. 1909, Charles Frederick Kenyon, *Hall Caine: the man and the novelist*, 1901, Samuel Norris, *Two men of Manxland: Hall Caine, novelist, T. E. Brown, poet*, Douglas 1947. CLODD. Edward Clodd, *Memories*, 1916. COLLINS. Laurence Churton Collins, *Life and memoirs of John Churton Collins*, 1912. CORELLI. George Bullock, *Marie Corelli: the life and death of a best-seller*, 1940, Eileen Bigland, *Marie Corelli: the woman and the legend: a biography*, 1953, William Stuart Scott, *Marie Corelli: the story of a friendship*, 1955. CORY. See JOHNSON. DAVIDSON. James Benjamin Townsend, *John Davidson, poet of Armageddon*, New Haven, Conn. 1961. DOMETT. Ernest Alan Horsman, ed., *The diary of Alfred Domett, 1872–1885*, 1953, Sir Frederic George Kenyon, ed., *Robert Browning and Alfred Domett*, 1906. DOYLE. Sir Francis Hastings Doyle, *Reminiscences and opinions . . ., 1813–1885*, Lond. 1886, N.Y. 1887. EGERTON. Terence De Vere White, ed., *A leaf from the Yellow book: the correspondence of George Egerton* [Mary Chavelita Bright], 1958. FURNIVALL. *Frederick James Furnivall: a volume of personal record*, 1911. GATTY. Christabel Maxwell, *Mrs. Gatty and Mrs. Ewing*, 1949. GILFILLAN. Robert Addison Watson and Elizabeth Sophia Watson, *George Gilfillan: letters and journals*, 1892. GRAHAME. Peter Green, *Kenneth Grahame, 1859–1932: a study of his life, work and times*, 1959, Patrick Reginald Chalmers, *Kenneth Grahame: life, letters and unpublished work*, 1933. GREENAWAY. Marion Harry Spielmann and George Somes Layard, *Kate Greenaway*, 1905, Covelle Newcombe, *The secret door: the story of Kate Greenaway*, 1946. HAGGARD. James Edward Scott, *A bibliography of the works of Sir Henry Rider Haggard, 1856–1925*, 1947, Sir Henry Rider Haggard, *The days of my life: an autobiography*, ed. by Charles James Longman, 2 v. 1926, Morton Cohen, *Rider Haggard: his life and works*, 1960, 2nd edn. 1968, Lilias Rider Haggard, *The cloak that I left: a biography of the author, Henry Rider Haggard, K.B.E.*, 1951. HANNAY. George John Worth, *James Hannay: his life and works*, Univ. of Kansas Humanistic studs. 37, Lawrence, Kansas 1964, HENTY. George Manville Fenn, *George Alfred Henty: the story of an active life*, 1907. HIND. Charles Lewis Hind, *Naphtali: being influences and adventures while earning a living by writing*, 1926. HIRST. Francis Wrigley Hirst, *In the golden days*, 1947. HOBBES. [Pearl Mary-Teresa Craigie] *The life of John Oliver Hobbes (P. M.-T. Craigie) told in her correspondence with numerous friends, with a biographical sketch by her father* [John Morgan Richards], 1911. JOHNSON later CORY. Francis Warre Cornish, ed., *Extracts from the letters and journals of William Cory . . .*, Oxf. 1897, Faith Compton Mackenzie, *William Cory: a biography*, 1950, Reginald Baliol Brett, Viscount Esher, *Ionicus . . .*, Lond.

1923, N.Y. 1924. KER. John Henry Pyle Pafford, *W. P. Ker, 1855–1923: a bibliography*, 1950. KINGSTON. Maurice Rooke Kingsford, *The life, work and influence of William Henry Giles Kingston*, Toronto 1947. LE FANU. Nelson Browne, *Sheridan Le Fanu*, 1951. LINTON. George Somes Layard, *Mrs. Lynn Linton: her life, letters and opinions*, 1901. LOCKER-LAMPSON. Frederick Locker-Lampson, *My confidences: an autobiographical sketch, addressed to my descendants*, ed. by Augustine Birrell, 1896, Augustine Birrell, *Frederick Locker-Lampson: a character sketch*, 1920. MACDONALD. Greville Macdonald, *George MacDonald and his wife*, 1924, Robert Lee Wolff, *The golden key: a study of the fiction of George MacDonald*, New Haven, Conn. 1961. MORLEY. Henry Shaen Solby, *The life of Henry Morley, LL.D., Professor of English Language and Literature at University College, London*, 1898. NESBIT. Doris Langley Moore, *E. Nesbit: a biography*, 1933, new edn. Phila. 1966. Mary Noel Streatfield, *Magic and the magician: E. Nesbit and her children's books*, 1958. NEWMAN. Isabel Giberne Sieveking, *Memoir and letters of Francis W. Newman*, 1909. William Robbins, *The Newman brothers: an essay in comparative intellectual biography*, Camb., Mass. 1966. NORTON. Jane Gray Perkins, *The life of the Honourable Mrs. Norton*, 1909, Alice Acland, pseud. of Anne Marreco, *Caroline Norton*, 1948. OLIPHANT. Vineta Colby and Robert Alan Colby, *The equivocal virtue: Mrs. Oliphant and the Victorian literary market place*, Hamden, Conn. 1966. OUIDA. Elizabeth Lee, *Ouida: a memoir*, 1914, Yvonne Ffrench, *Ouida: a study in ostentation*, 1938, Eileen Bigland, *Ouida: the passionate Victorian*, 1951, Monica Stirling, *The fine and the wicked: the life and times of Ouida*, 1957. PALGRAVE. Gwenllian Florence Palgrave, *Francis Turner Palgrave: his journals and memories of his life*, 1899. PAYNE. Thomas Wright, *The life of John Payne*, 1919. PHILLPOTTS. Eden Phillpotts, *From the angle of 88*, 1951. POTTER. Jane Quinby, *Beatrix Potter: a bibliographical check list*, N.Y. 1954, Leslie Linder, *Beatrix Potter, 1866–1943: centenary catalogue*, 1966, Nat. Book League 1966, Margaret Lane, *The tale of Beatrix Potter: a biography*, 1946, rev. edn. 1968, Marcus Crouch, *Beatrix Potter*, 1960. RALEIGH. Gertrude, Lady Raleigh, ed., *The letters of Sir Walter Raleigh*, 2 v. 1926, 2nd edn. 1926. REID. Russell Burlingham, *Forrest Reid: a portrait and a study*, 1953. ROBINSON. Thomas Sadler, ed., *Diary, reminiscences and correspondence of Henry Crabb Robinson*, 3 v. 1869, 3rd edn. 2 v. 1872, Eluned Brown ed., *The London theatre, 1811–1866: selections from the diary of Henry Crabb Robinson*, 1966, John Milton Baker, *Henry Crabb Robinson . . .*, 1937, Edith Julia Morley, *The life and times of Henry Crabb Robinson*, 1935. Ros. Jack Loudan, *O rare Amanda: the life of Amanda McKittrick Ros*, 1954. ROSS. Margery Ross, ed., *Robert Ross, friend of friends: letters to Robert Ross, art critic and writer . . .*, 1952. SHORTER. *C.K.S.: an autobiography: a fragment*, ed. by John Malcolm Bulloch. Priv. pr. 1927. SIMS. George Robert Sims, *My life: sixty years' recollections of Bohemian London*, 1917. STOKER. Harry Ludlam, *A biography of Dracula: the life story of Bram Stoker* [1962]. STRACHEY. Michael Holroyd, *Lytton Strachey: a critical biography*, 2 v. Lond. 1967–8, N.Y. 1968, M. Holroyd, ed., *Lytton Strachey by himself: a self portrait*, Lond. & N.Y. 1971, Charles Richard Sanders, *Lytton Strachey: his mind and art*, New Haven, Conn. 1957. SYMONS. Roger Lhombreaud, *Arthur Symons: a critical biography*,

1963. THOMAS. Jevan Brandon Thomas, *Charley's aunt's father: a life of Brandon Thomas*, 1955. T. A. TROLLOPE. Thomas Adolphus Trollope, *What I remember*, 3 v. 1887–9. TUPPER. Derek Hudson, *Martin Tupper: his rise and fall*, 1949. WALPOLE. Rupert Hart-Davis, *Hugh Walpole: a biography*, 1952. MRS. HUMPHRY WARD. Janet Penrose Trevelyan, *The life of Mrs Humphry Ward*, Lond. & N.Y. 1923, and Mrs. Humphry Ward (Mary Augusta Ward), *A writer's recollections*, 2 v. Lond. & N.Y. 1918. WATTS-DUNTON. Thomas Hake and Arthur Compton-Rickett, *The life and letters of Theodore Watts-Dunton*, 2 v. 1916. WILTON. Mary Blamire Young, *Richard Wilton: a forgotten Victorian*, 1967. YONGE. Christabel Coleridge, *Charlotte Mary Yonge: her life and letters*, Lond. & N.Y. 1903, Georgina Battiscombe, *Charlotte Mary Yonge: the story of an uneventful life*, 1943, Margaret Mare and Alicia C. Percival, *Victorian best-seller: the world of Charlotte M. Yonge*, 1947, Georgina Battiscombe and Marghanita Laski, eds., *A chaplet for Charlotte Yonge . . .*, 1965. ZANGWILL. Joseph Leftwich, *Israel Zangwill*, N.Y. 1957, Maurice Wohlgelernter, *Israel Zangwill: a study*, N.Y. 1964.

# D. PHILOSOPHY AND THE SOCIAL SCIENCES

## 1. PHILOSOPHY

8430  MERZ (JOHN THEODORE). A history of European thought in the nineteenth century. 4 v. Edin. 1896–1914. Repr. N.Y. [1965.]

Still the best general survey. Frederick Charles John Paul Copleston, *A history of philosophy*. VIII: *Bentham to Russell*, 1966, is a Roman Catholic survey. There is much additional factual material in James Mark Baldwin, ed., *Dictionary of philosophy and psychology . . .*, 3 v. in 4, N.Y. & Lond. 1901–5, with new edn. of v. 2 publ. as Benjamin Rand, comp., *Bibliography of philosophy, psychology and cognate subjects*, 2 v. N.Y. 1928, and Paul Edwards, ed., *The encyclopedia of philosophy*, 8 v. N.Y. 1967.

8431  PASSMORE (JOHN ARTHUR). A hundred years of philosophy. 1957. 2nd edn. 1966.

Indispensable. Incl. excellent lists of books and articles. Centred on British philosophy. More technical than Arthur Kenyon Rogers, *English and American philosophy since 1900: a critical survey*, N.Y. 1922, Rudolph Metz, *A hundred years of British philosophy*, ed. by John Henry Muirhead, trans. by John Wilfred Harvey, Thomas Edmund Jessop and Henry Sturt, 1938, William Ritchie Sorley, *A history of English philosophy* [*to 1900*], Camb. 1920, rev. edn. 1965, and David Churchill Somervell, *English thought in the nineteenth century*, 1929, 6th edn. 1950. Geoffrey James Warnock, *English philosophy since 1900*, 1958, 2nd edn. 1969, is not so much about professional philosophy as about the movement of philosophical ideas. Leslie Allen Paul, *The English philosophers*, 1953, is an intro. to the great names. James Seth, *English philosophers and schools of philosophy*, 1912, adds little. Thomas Miller Forsyth, *English philosophy: a study of its method and general development*, 1910, is interesting for its period.

8432  ALBEE (ERNEST). A history of English utilitarianism. Lond. & N.Y. 1902. 2nd edn. 1957.

8433  LIARD (LOUIS). Les logiciens anglais contemporains. Paris. 1878. 5th edn. 1907.

8434 SIMON (WALTER MICHAEL). 'Auguste Comte's English disciples'. *Victorian Studs.* viii (1964–5), 160–72.

A useful intro. His *European positivism in the nineteenth century: an essay in intellectual history*, Ithaca, N.Y. 1963, covers the European origins of positivism, and his 'Herbert Spencer and the "social organism" ', *J. Hist. Ideas* xxi (1960), 294–9, covers Spencer's connections with the movement. The English positivists are also the subject of Sydney Eisen, 'Huxley and the positivists', *Victorian Studs.* vii (1963–4), 337–58, 'Herbert Spencer and the spectre of Comte', *J. Brit. Studs.* vii (1967–8), pt. 1, 48–67, 'Frederic Harrison and the religion of humanity', *South Atlantic Q.* lxvi (1967), 574–90, and 'Frederic Harrison and Herbert Spencer: embattled unbelievers', *Victorian Studs.* xii (1968–9), 33–56; Noel Gilroy Annan, Baron Annan, *The curious strength of positivism in English political thought*, 1959; John Edwin McGee, *A crusade for humanity: the history of organized positivism in England*, 1931; Susan Liveing, *A nineteenth century teacher: John Henry Bridges*, 1926, and *Recollections of John Henry Bridges, M.B.*, 1908; Frederick James Gould, *The life story of a humanist*, 1923; Malcolm Quin, *Memoirs of a positivist*, 1924; and **8457**.

8435 COLLINS (JAMES). 'Darwin's impact on philosophy'. *Thought* xxxiv (1959–60), 185–248.

See also John Passmore, 'Darwin's impact on British metaphysics', *Victorian Studs.* iii (1959–60), 41–54, and John Herman Randall, jr., 'The changing impact of Darwin on philosophy', *J. Hist. Ideas* xxii (1961), 435–62.

8436 BROWN (ALAN WILLARD). The Metaphysical Society: Victorian minds in crisis, 1869–1880. N.Y. 1947.

8437 PUCELLE (JEAN). L'idéalisme en Angleterre: de Coleridge à Bradley. Neuchâtel. 1955.

See also John Henry Muirhead, *The Platonic tradition in Anglo-Saxon philosophy: studies in the history of idealism in England and America*, Lond. & N.Y. 1931.

8438 MILNE (ALAN JOHN MITCHELL). The social philosophy of English idealism. 1962.

8439 SCHNEEWIND (JEROME B.). 'Moral problems and moral philosophy in the Victorian period'. *Victorian Studs.* ix (1965), suppl. 29–46.

8440 SIDGWICK (HENRY). Lectures on the ethics of T. H. Green, Mr. Herbert Spencer, and J. Martineau. 1902.

8441 WARNOCK (MARY). Ethics since 1900. 1960. 2nd edn. 1966.

8442 MUIRHEAD (JOHN HENRY) *ed.* Contemporary British philosophy: personal statements. 2 ser. 1924–5. Repr. 2 v. in 1. 1953.

Good for philosophers alive *c.* 1920.

8443 JOURNAL OF THE HISTORY OF IDEAS. Lancaster, Penn. etc. 1940+.

See also *J. hist. of philosophy*, Berkeley 1963+.

**8444  ALEXANDER.** Le système d'Alexander: exposé critique d'une théorie néo-réaliste du changement. By Philippe Devaux. Paris. 1929.

See also John William McCarthy, *The naturalism of Samuel Alexander*, 1948, and Bertram D. Brettschneider, *The philosophy of Samuel Alexander: idealism in 'Space, time and deity'*, N.Y. 1964.

**8445  BAIN.** Autobiography. By Alexander Bain. Ed. by William Leslie Davidson. Lond. etc. 1904.

**8446  BALFOUR.** Arthur James Balfour as philosopher and thinker: a collection of the more important and interesting passages in his non-political writings, speeches and addresses, 1879–1912. Ed. by Wilfred M. Short. 1912.

A reminder that Arthur Balfour was a major figure in contemp. philosophy.

**8447  BOSANQUET.** Bernard Bosanquet and his friends: letters illustrating the sources and development of his philosophical opinions. Ed. by John Henry Muirhead. 1935.

See also Charles Le Chevalier, *Éthique et idéalisme: le courant néo-hégélien en Angleterre: Bernard Bosanquet et ses amis*, Paris 1963, François Houang, otherwise Houang kia Tcheng, otherwise Chia-Cheng Huang, *Le néo-hégélianisme en Angleterre: la philosophie de Bernard Bosanquet, 1848–1923*, Paris 1954, and **719**.

**8448  BRADLEY.** F. H. Bradley. By Richard Wollheim. Harmondsworth. 1959. 2nd edn. 1969.

See also Garrett L. Vander Veer, *Bradley's metaphysics and the self*, New Haven, Conn. 1970; Sushil Kumar Saxena, *Studies in the metaphysics of Bradley*, Lond. & N.Y. 1967; Thomas Stearns Eliot, *Knowledge and experience in the philosophy of F. H. Bradley*, Lond. & N.Y. 1964; Ralph Withington Church, *Bradley's dialectic*, Lond. 1942, Ithaca, N.Y. 1948; Rudolf Kagey, *The growth of Bradley's logic*, N.Y. 1931; William Frederick Lofthouse, *F. H. Bradley*, 1949; and Ralph Gilbert Ross, *Scepticism and dogma: a study in the philosophy of F. H. Bradley*, N.Y. 1940.

**8449  CAIRD.** The life and philosophy of Edward Caird, LL.D., D.C.L., F.B.A., Professor of Moral Philosophy in the University of Glasgow and Master of Balliol College, Oxford. By Sir Henry Jones and John Henry Muirhead. Glasgow. 1921.

**8450  CALDERWOOD.** The life of Henry Calderwood. By William Leadbetter Calderwood and David Woodside. 1900.

**8451  DE MORGAN.** Memoir of Augustus De Morgan. By his wife Sophia Elizabeth De Morgan. 1882.

**8452  DICKINSON.** Goldsworthy Lowes Dickinson. By Edward Morgan Forster. Lond. & N.Y. 1934.

Dickinson's *A modern symposium*, 1905, new edns. by E. M. Forster, N.Y. 1962, Louis Filler, N.Y. 1963, is also interesting for the state of philosophy.

**8453  FERRIER.** James Frederick Ferrier. By Elizabeth Sanderson Haldane. Edin & Lond. 1899.

Ferrier's *Philosophical works* were publ. in 3 v., 1875.

**8454** FRASER. Biographia philosophica: a retrospect. By Alexander Campbell Fraser. Edin. & Lond. 1904. 2nd edn. 1905.

See also John Kellie, *Alexander Campbell Fraser: a sketch of his life and philosophical position,* Edin. 1909.

**8455** GREEN. Memoir of Thomas Hill Green, late fellow of Balliol College, Oxford, and Whyte's Professor of Moral Philosophy in the University of Oxford. By Richard Lewis Nettleship. 1906.

See also Jean Pucelle, *La nature et l'esprit dans la philosophie de T. H. Green: la renaissance de l'idéalisme en Angleterre au XIXe siècle,* 2 v. Louvain 1960–5, John Herman Randall, jr., 'T. H. Green: the development of English thought from J. S. Mill to F. H. Bradley', *J. Hist. Ideas* xxvii (1966), 217–44, and William Henry Fairbrother, *The philosophy of Thomas Hill Green,* 1896, 2nd edn. 1900. For Green's political ideas see **718**.

**8456** HAMILTON. Memoir of Sir William Hamilton, Bart. By John Veitch. Edin. & Lond. 1869.

See also John Stuart Mill, *An examination of Sir William Hamilton's philosophy and of the principal philosophical questions discussed in his writings,* 2 v. Lond. & Boston 1865, 6th edn. 1889; James Hutchison Stirling, *Sir William Hamilton: being the philosophy of perception: an analysis,* 1865; Henry Longueville Mansel, *The philosophy of the conditioned: comprising some remarks on Sir William Hamilton's philosophy, and on Mr. J. S. Mill's examination of that philosophy,* Lond. & N.Y. 1866; David Masson, *Recent British philosophy: a review, with criticisms, including some comments on Mr. Mill's answer to Sir William Hamilton,* 1865, 3rd edn. 1877; and Svend Valdemar Rasmussen, *The philosophy of Sir William Hamilton: a study,* Copenhagen 1925.

**8457** HARRISON. Autobiographic memoirs. By Frederic Harrison. 2 v. 1911.

See also Austin Harrison, *Frederic Harrison: thoughts and memories,* N.Y. 1927, and Frederic Harrison, *The creed of a layman: apologia pro fide mea,* 1907.

**8458** JONES. The life and letters of Sir Henry Jones, Professor of Moral Philosophy in the University of Glasgow. By Sir Hector James Wright Hetherington. 1924.

See also Thomas Jones, ed., *Old memories: autobiography of Sir Henry Jones,* 1922.

**8459** MACKENZIE. John Stuart Mackenzie. Ed. by his wife. 1936.

**8460** McTAGGART. J. McT. E. McTaggart. By Goldsworthy Lowes Dickinson. Camb. 1931.

See also Charlie Dunbar Broad, *Examination of McTaggart's philosophy,* 2 v. in 3. Camb. 1933–8.

**8461** MILL. Bibliography of the published writings of John Stuart Mill. Ed. by Ney Lannes MacMinn, John R. Hainds and James McNab McCrimmon. Evanston, Ill. 1945.

The prime source for Mill's life is his *Autobiography,* 1873, with new edn. based on the original MS. by John Jacob Coss, N.Y. 1924, and an early draft ed. by Jack Stillinger, Urbana, Ill. 1961. For letters see Hugh Samuel Robert Elliot, ed., *The letters of John Stuart Mill,* 2 v. 1910, Francis Edward Mineka and Dwight Lindley, eds., *Later letters of John Stuart Mill*, 4 v. Toronto 1972, and Friedrich August von Hayek, *John Stuart Mill and Harriet Taylor: their correspondence and subsequent marriage*, 1951. A new complete edn. of the *Collected works of John Stuart Mill*, ed. by F. E. L. Priestley, John Mercel Robson, and others, Toronto 1963 +, is in progress. News about Mill studs. is given in *The Mill newsletter*, Toronto 1965 +.

There is no standard life and there are few studs. on a scale commensurate with Mill's importance. On Mill's political and social thought see **713**. On his ideas generally see Alexander Bain, *John Stuart Mill: a criticism with personal recollections*, Lond. & N.Y. 1882; Leslie Stephen, *The English utilitarians: III John Stuart Mill*, 1900; Edward Alexander, *Matthew Arnold and John Stuart Mill*, N.Y. & Lond. 1965; Richard Paul Anschutz, *The philosophy of J. S. Mill*, Oxf. 1953; Karl Britton, *John Stuart Mill: an introduction to the life and teaching of a great pioneer of modern social philosophy and logic*, 1953; Maurice William Cranston, *John Stuart Mill*, 1958; Michael St. John Packe, *The life of John Stuart Mill*, 1954; Helmut Otto Pappe, *John Stuart Mill and the Harriet Taylor myth*, Parkville, Vict. 1960; John Collwyn Rees, *Mill and his early critics*, Leicester 1956; Alan Ryan, *The philosophy of John Stuart Mill*, N.Y. 1970; Thomas Woods, *Poetry and philosophy: a study in the thought of John Stuart Mill*, 1961; and Jerome B. Schneewind, ed., *Mill: a collection of critical essays*, Notre Dame, Ind. 1969.

**8462   MOORE.** The philosophy of G. E. Moore. Ed. by Paul Arthur Schilpp. Evanston, Ill. 1942. 2nd edn. N.Y. 1952.

A good exposition, incl. biog. data. See also Alan Richard White, *G. E. Moore: a critical exposition*, Oxf. 1958, E. D. Klemke, ed., *Studies in the philosophy of G. E. Moore*, Chicago 1969, and Alice Ambrose and Morris Lazerowitz, eds., *G. E. Moore: essays in retrospect*, N.Y. 1970.

**8463   MUIRHEAD.** John Henry Muirhead: reflections by a journeyman in philosophy on the movements of thought and practice in his time. Ed. by John Wilfred Harvey. 1942.

**8464   NETTLESHIP.** Philosophical lectures and remains of Richard Lewis Nettleship. Ed. by Andrew Cecil Bradley and Godfrey Rathbone Benson. 2 v. Lond. & N.Y. 1897.

**8465   RUSSELL.** The philosophy of Bertrand Russell. Ed. by Paul Arthur Schilpp. Evanston, Ill. 1944. 3rd edn. N.Y. 1951.

A useful intro. But see also Russell's *My philosophical development*, 1959, Alan Doward, *Bertrand Russell: a short guide to his philosophy*, 1951, and Barry Feinberg and others, comps., *A detailed catalogue of the archives of Bertrand Russell* [1967]. Russell himself publ. an *Autobiography*, 3 v. Lond. & Boston 1967–9, and *Portraits from memory, and other essays*, Lond. & N.Y. 1956. See also David Francis Pears, *Bertrand Russell and the British tradition in philosophy*, 1967, Lillian Woodworth Aiken, *Bertrand Russell's philosophy of morals*, N.Y. 1963, Jules Vuillemin, *Leçons sur la première philosophie de Russell*, Paris 1968, Robert J. Clack, *Bertrand Russell's philosophy of language*, The Hague 1969, Elizabeth Ramsden Eames, *Bertrand Russell's theory of knowledge*, 1969, and Alfred Jules Ayer, *Russell and Moore: the analytical heritage*, Camb., Mass. 1971. *Russell: the j. of the Bertrand Russell Archives*, 1 +, Hamilton, Ont. 1971 +, reports work in progress.

**8466   SCHILLER.** The pragmatic humanism of F. C. S. Schiller. By Reuben Abel. N.Y. 1955.

See also Kenneth Winetrout, *F. C. S. Schiller and the dimensions of pragmatism*, Columbus, Ohio 1967.

**8467** SIDGWICK. Henry Sidgwick: a memoir. By Arthur Sidgwick and Eleanor Mildred Sidgwick. 1906.

See also David Gwilym James, *Henry Sidgwick: science and faith in Victorian England*, 1971, Frank Herbert Hayward, *The ethical philosophy of Sidgwick*, 1901, the life of his wife (**8119**), and works on his political ideas at **721**.

**8468** SPENCER. An autobiography. By Herbert Spencer. 2 v. Lond. & N.Y. 1904.

David Duncan, *The life and letters of Herbert Spencer*, 2 v. Lond. & N.Y. 1908, is the official life. Judah Rumney, *Herbert Spencer's sociology: a study in the history of social theory, to which is appended a bibliography of Spencer and his work*, 1934, is useful for its bibliog. William Henry Hudson, *An introduction to the philosophy of Herbert Spencer*, N.Y. 1894, is useful. For Spencer's sociology, see **8548**.

**8469** STIRLING. James Hutchison Stirling: his life and work. By Amelia Hutchison Stirling. 1912.

**8470** WARD. The philosophy of James Ward. By Andrew Howson Murray. Camb. 1937.

**8471** WHITEHEAD. The philosophy of Alfred North Whitehead. Comp. by Paul Arthur Schilpp. Evanston, Ill. 1941. 2nd edn. N.Y. 1951.

A good coll. See also Wolfe Mays, *The philosophy of Whitehead*, 1959; Nathaniel Morris Lawrence, *Whitehead's philosophical development* . . ., Berkeley 1956; Dorothy Mary Emmet, *Whitehead's philosophy of organism*, 1932; William A. Christian, *An interpretation of Whitehead's metaphysics*, New Haven, Conn. 1959; Martin Jordan, *New shapes of reality: aspects of A. N. Whitehead's philosophy*, 1968; Paul Frederic Schmidt, *Perception and cosmology in Whitehead's philosophy*, New Brunswick, N.J. 1967; Ivor Leclerc, ed., *The relevance of Whitehead: philosophical essays in commemoration of the centenary of the birth of Alfred North Whitehead*, Lond. & N.Y. 1961; George Louis Kline, ed., *Alfred North Whitehead: essays on his philosophy*, Englewood Cliffs, N.J. 1963; Ivor Leclerc, *Whitehead's metaphysics: an introductory exposition*, 1958; Robert Moore Palter, *Whitehead's philosophy of science*, Chicago 1960; and Alix Parmentier, *La philosophie de Whitehead et le problème de Dieu*, Paris 1968.

## 2. Economics

**8472** BATSON (HAROLD EDWARD) *comp.* A select bibliography of modern economic theory, 1870–1920. Lond. School of Econ. Studs. in Econ. & Pol. Sci. Bibliogs. 6. 1930.

For j. articles see American Econ. Assoc., *Index of economic journals, 1886–1924+*, Homewood, Ill. 1961+.

**8473** BLACK (ROBERT DENIS COLLISON). A catalogue of pamphlets on economic subjects, published between 1750 and 1900, and now housed in Irish libraries. Belfast. 1969.

**8474** HUTCHISON (TERENCE WILMOT). A review of economic doctrines, 1870–1929. Oxf. 1953.

The best starting-point. But see also Sydney George Checkland, 'Economic opinion in England as Jevons found it', *Manch. School* xix (1951), 143–69, 'Growth and progress: the nineteenth-century view in Britain', *Econ. Hist. Rev.* 2 ser. xii (1959–60), 49–62, and 'The advent of academic economics in England', *Manch. School* xix (1951), 43–70, and Alfred William Coats, 'The historist reaction in English political economy, 1870–90', *Economica* 2 ser. xxi (1954), 143–53.

There are also useful sections in the general hists. of economic thought, notably Joseph Alois Schumpeter, *History of economic analysis*, ed. by Elizabeth Boody Schumpeter, N.Y. 1954, in the works of Lionel Charles Robbins, Baron Robbins, notably *The theory of economic policy in English classical political economy*, 1952, repr. 1965, *The theory of economic development in the history of economic thought*, Lond. & N.Y. 1968, and *The evolution of modern economic theory, and other papers in the history of economic thought*, 1970, and in George Joseph Stigler, *Essays in the history of economics*, Lond. 1964, Chicago 1965, Itla Myint, *Theories of welfare economics*, 1948, repr. N.Y. 1965, Narmadeshwar Jha, *The age of Marshall: aspects of British economic thought, 1890–1915*, Patna 1963, Eprime Eshag, *From Marshall to Keynes: an essay on the monetary theory of the Cambridge school*, Oxf. 1963, and John Andrew La Nauze, *Political economy in Australia: historical studies*, Carlton, Vict. 1949.

**8475  WINCH (DONALD).** Economics and policy: a historical study. 1969.

Good for the 20th cent.

**8476  HISTORY OF POLITICAL ECONOMY.** 1+. Durham, N.C. 1969+.

**8477  GRAMPP (WILLIAM DYER).** The Manchester school of economics. Stanford [Calif.] & Lond. 1960.

Chiefly pre-1850. See also Elisabeth Wallace, 'The political ideas of the Manchester school', *Univ. of Toronto Q.* xxix (1959–60), 122–38.

**8478  HOWEY (RICHARD S.).** The rise of the marginal utility school, 1870–1889. Lawrence, Kans. 1960.

See also Emil Kauder, *A history of marginal utility theory*, Princeton 1966.

**8479  LAWSON (WILLIAM RAMAGE).** British economics in 1904. Edin. & Lond. 1904. 2nd edn. 1906.

See also Alfred William Coats, 'Political economy and the tariff reform campaign of 1903', *J. of Law & Econ.* xi (1968), 181–229.

**8480  POLITICAL ECONOMY CLUB.** Minutes of proceedings, 1899–1920: roll of members and questions discussed, 1821–1920, with documents bearing on the history of the club. 1921.

Vol. VI of the club's *Proceedings*, which are a valuable and neglected source for the hist. of econ. thought. The first vol., covering 1821–82, is particularly interesting.

**8481  SMYTH (ROBERT LESLIE)** *ed.* Essays in economic method: selected papers read to section F of the British Association for the Advancement of Science, 1860–1913. 1962.

Suppl. by R. L. Smyth, ed., *Essays in the economics of socialism and capitalism: selected papers . . . 1886–1932*, 1964.

**8482  COATS (ALFRED WILLIAM).** 'The origins and early development of the Royal Economic Society'. *Econ. J.* lxxviii (1968), 349–71.

**8483  KEYNES (JOHN MAYNARD)** *Baron Keynes.* Essays in biography. Lond. & N.Y. 1933. New edn. 1951.

Includes good studs. of Marshall, Edgeworth, and F. P. Ramsey. Keynes's *Essays in persuasion,* Lond. & N.Y. 1931, and his other works on economics also incl. much material on the econ. ideas of the late 19th cent. The biogs. and studs. of Keynes's work also incl. material on the climate of econ. ideas in which he grew up.

**8484  ASHLEY.** William James Ashley: a life. By Anne Ashley. 1932.

**BAGEHOT. See 716.**

**8485  CUNNINGHAM.** William Cunningham: teacher and priest. By Audrey Cunningham. 1950.

**8486  HOBSON.** Confessions of an economic heretic. By John Atkinson Hobson. 1938.

See also Henry Noel Brailsford, *The life-work of J. A. Hobson,* 1948; Erwin Esser Nemmers, *Hobson and underconsumption,* Amsterdam 1956; William Tien-chên Liu, *A study of Hobson's welfare economics,* Peking 1934; Harvey Mitchell, 'Hobson revisited', *J. Hist. Ideas* xxvi (1965), 397–416; and the works on imperialism at **975;** and **529.**

**8487  HODGSKIN.** Thomas Hodgskin. By Élie Halévy. Trans. by Arnold Joseph Taylor. 1956.

There was an earlier work, Carl Koepp, *Das Verhältnis der Mehrwerttheorien von Karl Marx und Thomas Hodgskin,* Vienna 1911.

**8488  JEVONS.** Letters & journal of W. Stanley Jevons. Ed. by his wife, Harriet Ann Jevons. 1886.

Includes bibliog. See also Keynes, *Essays* (**8483**); Lionel Charles Robbins, Baron Robbins, 'The place of Jevons in the history of economic thought', *Manch. School* vii (1936), 1–17; Robert Denis Collison Black, 'W. S. Jevons and the economists of his time', *Manch. School* xxx (1962), 203–21, and 'Jevons and Cairnes', *Economica* new ser. xxvii (1960), 214–32; Rosamond Könekamp, 'William Stanley Jevons . . .', *Manch. School* xxx (1962), 251–73; and Wolfe Mays, 'Jevons' conception of scientific method', ibid. 223–49. R. D. Collison Black and Rosamond Könekamp are ed. *Papers and correspondence of William Stanley Jevons,* i + v. 1972+, which incl. a *Biography and personal journal,* 1972.

**8489  MARSHALL.** Memorials of Alfred Marshall. Ed. by Arthur Cecil Pigou. 1925.

Includes a good biog. by John Maynard Keynes. There is a considerable and growing lit. on Marshall's work. See particularly Herbert Joseph Davenport, *The economics of Alfred Marshall,* Ithaca, N.Y., & Lond. 1935; Hans Hirsch, *Alfred Marshalls Beitrag zur modernen Theorie der Unternehmung,* Berlin 1965; Talcott Parsons, 'Wants and activities in Marshall', *Q. J. Econ.* xlvi (1931–2), 101–40, and 'Economics and sociology: Marshall in relation to the thought of his time', ibid. 316–47; Arthur Cecil Pigou, *Marshall and current thought,* 1953; Gerald Frank Shove, 'The place of Marshall's *Principles* in the development of economic theory', *Econ. J.* lii (1942), 294–329; Jacob Viner, 'Marshall's economics: in relation to the man and to his time', *Amer. Econ. Rev.* xxxi (1941), 223–35; Milton Friedman, 'The Marshallian demand curve', *J. Pol. Econ.* lvii (1949), 463–95; G. Pursell, 'Unity in the thought of Alfred Marshall', *Q. J.*

*Econ.* lxxii (1958), 588–600; Douglas Chalmers Hague, 'Alfred Marshall and the competitive firm', *Econ. J.* lxviii (1958), 673–90; Alexander John Youngson, 'Marshall on economic growth', *Scottish J. Pol. Econ.* iii (1956), 1–18; James Nathaniel Wolfe, 'Marshall and the trade cycle', *Oxford Econ. Papers* new ser. viii (1956), 90–101; Herbert William McCready, 'Alfred Marshall and tariff reform . . .', *J. Pol. Econ.* lxiii (1955), 259–67; and the appropriate sections of Joseph Alois Schumpeter, *Ten great economists from Marx to Keynes*, 1952; Tapas Majumdar, *The measurement of utility*, 1958; and Clark Kerr, *Marshall, Marx and modern times: the multi-dimensional society*, Camb. 1969.

8490 SENIOR. Nassau Senior and classical economics. By Marian Bowley. 1937.

See also Samuel Leon Levy, *Nassau W. Senior, the prophet of modern capitalism*, Boston & Toronto 1943, rev. edn. [*Nassau W. Senior, 1790–1869*] Newton Abbot 1970.

8491 WILSON. The servant of all: pages from the family, social and political life of my father, James Wilson: twenty years of mid-Victorian life. By Emilie Isabel Barrington. 2 v. 1927.

Proprietor of the *Economist*, for whose views see Scott Gordon, 'The London *Economist* and the high tide of laissez faire', *J. Pol. Econ.* lxiii (1955), 461–88.

8492 MILL (JOHN STUART). Principles of political economy: with some of their applications to social philosophy. 2 v. 1848. Variorum edn. by Sir William James Ashley. 1909.

The most influential mid-19th-cent. economic work. For Mill's life see **8461**.

8493 GOSCHEN (GEORGE JOACHIM), *Viscount Goschen*. Essays and addresses on economic questions, 1865–1893. 1905.

8494 FAWCETT (HENRY). Manual of political economy. Lond. & Camb. 1863. 8th edn. 1907.

Long used as a textbook. For Fawcett's life see **820**.

8495 BAGEHOT (WALTER). Economic studies. Ed. by Richard Holt Hutton. 1880. 7th edn. 1908.

8496 GIFFEN (*Sir* ROBERT). Economic enquiries and studies. 2 v. 1904.

Giffen's other principal work was *Essays in finance*, 2 ser. 1880–6.

8497 JEVONS (WILLIAM STANLEY). The theory of political economy. 1871. 5th edn. with preface etc. by Herbert Stanley Jevons. N.Y. 1965.

8498 CAIRNES (JOHN ELLIOTT). Essays in political economy, theoretical and applied. 1873.

Shows Cairnes's methods of argument. His other econ. works were *The character & logical method of political economy . . .*, 1857, 2nd edn. 1875, repr. 1888, and *Some leading principles of political economy newly expounded*, 1874, new edn. 1884. There is no life, but see Adelaide Weinberg, *John Elliott Cairnes and the American Civil War: a study in Anglo-American relations*, 1970, and George O'Brien, 'J. S. Mill and J. E. Cairnes', *Economica* new ser. x (1943), 273–85.

8499 SIDGWICK (HENRY). The principles of political economy. 1883. 3rd edn. Lond. & N.Y. 1901.

For Sidgwick's econ. ideas see also Jack Melitz 'Sidgwick's theory of international values', *Econ. J.* lxxiii (1963), 431–41.

8500 MARSHALL (ALFRED). Principles of economics. 1890. 9th [variorum] edn. by Claude William Guillebaud. 2 v. 1961.

See also Marshall's *Official papers*, ed. by John Maynard Keynes, Baron Keynes, Roy. Econ. Soc. 1926.

8501 LESLIE (THOMAS EDWARD CLIFFE). Essays in political economy. 2nd edn. by John Kells Ingram and Charles Francis Bastable. Dublin. 1888. Orig. publ. as Essays in political and moral philosophy. Dublin. 1878.

8502 EDGEWORTH (FRANCIS YSIDRO). Papers relating to political economy. Roy. Econ. Soc. 3 v. 1925.

For Edgeworth see also Keynes, *Essays* (**8483**), and Sir Arthur Lyon Bowley, *F. Y. Edgeworth's contributions to mathematical statistics*, 1928.

8503 KEYNES (JOHN NEVILLE). The scope and method of political economy. 1891. 4th edn. 1917.

8504 WICKSTEED (PHILIP HENRY). The common sense of political economy, including a study of the human basis of economic law. 1910. New ed. with suppl. by Lionel Charles Robbins, Baron Robbins. 2 v. 1933.

For Wicksteed's life see **3816.**

8505 HOBSON (JOHN ATKINSON). The science of wealth. 1911.

For Hobson's other work see index.

### 3. HISTORY

There is an extensive bibliog. in *The New Cambridge Bibliog. of English Literature* (**8276**). Entries here have therefore been kept to a minimum.

8506 SHAW (WILLIAM ARTHUR) *comp.* A bibliography of the historical works of Dr. Creighton, late Bishop of London, Dr. Stubbs, late Bishop of Oxford, Dr. S. R. Gardiner and the late Lord Acton. Roy. Hist. Soc. 1903.

8507 GOOCH (GEORGE PEABODY). History and historians in the nineteenth century. 1913. Rev. edn. 1952.

8508 BUTTERFIELD (*Sir* HERBERT). Man on his past: the study of the history of historical scholarship. Camb. 1955. Boston. [1960.]

See also his *The Whig interpretation of history*, 1931, N.Y. 1951, and reprs., and 'Some trends in scholarship, 1868–1968, in the field of modern history', *Roy. Hist. Soc. Trans.* 5 ser. xix (1969), 159–84.

8509 KNOWLES (*Dom* MICHAEL DAVID). 'Some trends in scholarship, 1868–1968, in the field of medieval history', *Roy. Hist. Soc. Trans.* 5 ser. xix (1969), 139–57.

See also his *Great historical enterprises: problems in monastic history*, 1963.

8510 AUSUBEL (HERMAN), BREBNER (JOHN BARTLET), *and* HUNT (ERLING MESSER) eds. Some modern historians of Britain: essays in honor of R. L. Schuyler by some of his former students at Columbia university. N.Y. 1951.

There is a little more in John Rigby Hale, ed., *The evolution of British historiography from Bacon to Namier*, Cleveland, Ohio 1964.

8511 FORBES (DUNCAN). The Liberal anglican idea of history. Camb. 1952.

Good.

8512 DOCKHORN (KLAUS). Der deutsche Historismus in England: ein Beitrag zur englischen Geistesgeschichte des 19. Jahrhunderts . . . Ed. by George Peabody Gooch. Göttingen & Baltimore [Md.]. 1950.

For German views of England see Charles E. McClelland, *The German historians and England: a study in nineteenth-century views*, Camb. 1971.

8513 BEN-ISRAEL (HEDVA). English historians of the French revolution. Camb. 1968.

8514 CHANCELLOR (VALERIE EDITH). History for their masters: opinion in the English history textbook, 1800–1914. Bath. 1970.

See also G. M. D. Howat, 'The nineteenth-century history text-book', *Brit. J. Educ. Studs.* xiii (1964–5), 147–59.

8515 HUMPHREYS (ROBERT ARTHUR). The Royal Historical Society, 1868–1968. 1969.

For the publs. of the society see Milne (25).

8516 THE HISTORICAL ASSOCIATION, 1906–1956. 1957.

8517 ACTON. Lord Acton and his times. By Archbishop David Mathew. 1968.

Mathew also publ. *Acton: the formative years*, 1946. No one has yet written a successful life of Acton dealing with his many-sided career. Francis Aidan Gasquet (Cardinal Gasquet), ed., *Lord Acton and his circle*, 1906, for long standard, was very inaccurate (see A. Watkin and Sir Herbert Butterfield, 'Gasquet and the Acton–Simpson correspondence', *Camb. Hist. J.* x (1950–2), 75–105). For his political philosophy and historical work see George Eugene Fasnacht, *Acton's political philosophy: an analysis*, 1952, Gertrude Himmelfarb, *Lord Acton: a study in conscience and politics*, 1952, Sir Herbert Butterfield, *Lord Acton*, Hist. Assoc. G 9, 1948, and Lionel Kochan, *Acton on history*, 1964. There are three articles on Acton's parl. career by James Johnston Auchmuty, 'Acton's election as an Irish member of parliament', *Eng. Hist. Rev.* lxi (1946), 394–405, 'Acton as a member of the House of Commons', *Bull. Faculty of Arts, Farouk I Univ.*, Alexandria, v (1949), 31–46, and 'Acton, the youthful parliamentarian', *Hist. Studs. Australia & N.Z.* ix (1959–61), 131–9. Mary Drew, *Acton, Gladstone and others*, 1924, deals with an important friendship, Hugh A. MacDougall, *The Acton–Newman relations: the dilemma of Christian liberalism*, N.Y. 1962, with a strained relationship. Damian McElrath, *Lord Acton: the decisive decade, 1864–1874*, Louvain 1970, is a miscellany. For Acton's letters see *Selections from the correspondence of the first Lord Acton*, Vol. I: *Correspondence with Cardinal Newman, Lady Blennerhassett, W. E. Gladstone and others*, ed. by John Neville Figgis and Reginald Vere Laurence, 1917, *Letters of Lord Acton to Mary, daughter of the Right Hon. W. E. Gladstone*, ed. by Herbert Woodfield Paul, Lond. & N.Y. 1904, 2nd edn. 1906, [Johann Joseph Ignaz von Döllinger] *Briefwechsel mit Lord Acton . . .*, ed. by Victor Conzemius, 3 v. Munich 1963–71, and Josef Lewis Altholz and Damian McElrath, eds., *The correspondence of Lord Acton and Richard Simpson*, 3 v. Camb. 1971+.

8518  BUCKLE. A Victorian eminence: the life and works of Henry Thomas Buckle. By Giles St. Aubyn. 1958.

Largely an abstract of Alfred Henry Huth, *The life and writings of Henry Thomas Buckle*, 2 v. 1880, 1 v. N.Y. 1880, and sections of Helen Taylor, ed., *Miscellaneous and posthumous works of Henry Thomas Buckle*, 3 v. 1870, abridged edn. by Grant Allen, 1885. There is a good bibliog. study, John Mackinnon Robertson, *Buckle and his critics: a study in sociology*, 1895. See also Harold John Hanham, ed., *Henry Thomas Buckle on Scotland and the Scotch Intellect*, Chicago 1970.

8519  COULTON. Fourscore years: an autobiography. By George Gordon Coulton. Camb. 1943.

See also Sarah Campion, *Father: a portrait of G. G. Coulton at home*, 1948.

CREIGHTON. For Mandell Creighton's life see 3657, and for his works, 8506.

8520  FISHER. Herbert Fisher, 1865–1940: a short biography. By David Ogg. [1947.]

8521  FREEMAN. The life and letters of Edward Augustus Freeman, D.C.L., LL.D. By William Richard Wood Stephens. 2 v. Lond. & N.Y. 1895.

Includes a bibliog. See also his *The methods of historical study: eight lectures . . .*, 1886.

8522  FROUDE. James Anthony Froude: a biography. By Waldo Hilary Dunn. 2 v. Oxf. 1961–3.

Standard. Froude's work was much attacked in his lifetime, especially his work on Carlyle (for which see David Alec Wilson, *Mr. Froude and Carlyle*, 1898) and on the West Indies (for which see John Jacob Thomas, *Froudacity . . .*, new edn. 1969). Herbert Woodfield Paul, *The life of Froude*, 1905, is out of date. See also 8344.

8523  GASQUET. Cardinal Gasquet: a memoir. By Sir [John Randolph] Shane Leslie. 1953.

See also Dom David Knowles, *Cardinal Gasquet as an historian*, 1957.

8524  GREEN. John Richard Green. By William George Addison. 1946.

See also Sir Leslie Stephen, ed., *Letters of John Richard Green*, Lond. & N.Y. 1901. For Mrs. J. R. Green see 10767.

978 *Intellectual and Cultural History* 8525

**8525  GROTE.** Grote: a biography. By Martin Lowther Clarke. 1962.

See also Harriet [Lewin] Grote, *The personal life of George Grote* . . ., 1873, 2nd edn. 1873, and Arnaldo Momigliano, *George Grote and the study of Greek history* . . ., 1952.

**8526  HODGKIN.** Life and letters of Thomas Hodgkin. By Louise Creighton. 1917.

**8527  KINGLAKE.** A. W. Kinglake: a biographical and literary study. By William Tuckwell. 1902.

**8528  LECKY.** A memoir of the Right Hon. William Edward Hartpole Lecky, M.P., O.M., LL.D., D.C.L., Litt.D., member of the French Institute, and the British Academy. By his wife Elisabeth Lecky. Lond. & N.Y. 1909.

See also James Johnston Auchmuty, *Lecky: a biographical and critical essay*, Dublin, Lond., & N.Y. 1945, Harford Montgomery Hyde, ed., *A Victorian historian: private letters of W. E. H. Lecky, 1859–1878*, 1947, and Helen Mulvey, 'The historian Lecky: opponent of Irish home rule', *Victorian Studs.* i (1957–8), 337–51.

**8529  LODGE.** Sir Richard Lodge: a biography. By Margaret Beatrice Lodge. Edin. & Lond. 1946.

**8530  MACAULAY.** The life and letters of Lord Macaulay. By Sir George Otto Trevelyan. 2 v. Lond. & N.Y. 1876. Numerous edns.

The official life by Macaulay's nephew. There are several edns. of his speeches, the best being that corrected by himself and publ. in 1854, and there is a substantial lit. for which see *The New Cambridge Bibliog. of English Literature.* Useful studs. incl. John R. Griffin, *The intellectual milieu of Lord Macaulay*, Ottawa 1965, Dom David Knowles, *Lord Macaulay, 1800–1859*, Camb. 1960, Mark Almérias Thomson, *Macaulay*, Hist. Assoc. General Ser. 42, 1959, and John Harold Plumb, 'Thomas Babington Macaulay' in his *Men and places*, 1963, also publ. as *Men and centuries: essays*, Boston 1963, pp. 250–66. There is an excellent life covering Macaulay's public career: John Leonard Clive, *[Thomas Babington] Macaulay: the shaping of the historian*, N.Y. & Lond. 1973.

**MAINE.** See **714** and **1157.**

**MAITLAND.** See **3089.**

**8531  NAPIER.** Life of General Sir William Napier. Ed. by Henry Austin Bruce, Baron Aberdare. 2 v. 1864.

**8532  NEWMAN.** Cardinal Newman as an historian. By Thomas S. Bokenkotter. Louvain. 1959.

See also Josef Lewis Altholz, 'Newman and history', *Victorian Studs.* vii (1963–4), 285–94. For Newman generally see **3944.**

**8533  POWELL.** Frederick York Powell: a life and a selection from his letters and occasional writings. By Oliver Elton. 2 v. Oxf. 1906.

8534    STUBBS. Letters of William Stubbs, Bishop of Oxford, 1825–1901. Ed. by William Holden Hutton. 1904.

For Stubbs's works see **8506**. See also Helen Maud Cam, 'Stubbs seventy years after', *Camb. Hist. J.* ix (1947–9), 129–47, Sir John Goronwy Edwards, *William Stubbs*, Hist. Assoc. G 22, 1952, a short pamphlet, and N. J. Williams, 'Stubbs's appointment as regius professor, 1866', *Inst. Hist. Res. Bull.* xxxiii (1960), 121–5. For an attack on Stubbs see Henry Gerald Richardson and George Osborne Sayles, *The governance of medieval England . . .*, Edin. 1963.

8535    SYMONDS. John Addington Symonds: a biography. By Phyllis Marguerite Grosskurth. 1964.

See also Percy Lancelot Babington, comp., *Bibliography of the writings of John Addington Symonds*, 1925; Horatio Robert Forbes Brown, ed., *Letters and papers of John Addington Symonds*, Lond. & N.Y. 1923; Hubert M. Schueller and Robert L. Peters, eds., *The letters of John Addington Symonds*, 3 v., Detroit, Mich. 1967–9; Horatio Robert Forbes Brown, *John Addington Symonds: a biography compiled from his papers and correspondence*, 2 v. 1895, 2nd edn. 1903; Van Wyck Brooks, *John Addington Symonds: a biographical study*, N.Y. 1914; and Margaret Symonds, *Out of the past . . .*, 1925. For the background to his work see John Rigby Hale, *England and the Italian renaissance: the growth of interest in its history and art*, 1954.

### 4. SOCIOLOGY AND RELATED SUBJECTS

The fullest bibliog. is the *London bibliography of the social sciences* (**13**).

8536    ABRAMS (PHILIP). The origins of British sociology, 1834–1914: an essay with selected papers. Chicago. 1968.

There is a useful intro. to sociology generally in Geoffrey Duncan Mitchell, *A hundred years of sociology*, 1968, and *A dictionary of sociology*, 1968.

8537    BURROW (JOHN WYON). Evolution and society: a study in Victorian social theory. Camb. 1966.

8538    POLLARD (SIDNEY). The idea of progress: history and society. [1968.]

See also Morris Ginsberg, *The idea of progress: a revaluation*, Lond. & Boston 1953.

8539    McGREGOR (OLIVER ROSS). 'Social research and social policy in the nineteenth century'. *Brit. J. Sociology* viii (1957), 146–57.

8540    WELLS (ALAN FRANK). The local social survey in Great Britain. 1935.

8541    ASHTON (THOMAS SOUTHCLIFFE). Economic and social investigations in Manchester, 1833–1933: a centenary history of the Manchester Statistical Society. 1934.

For the Stat. Soc. of London, later Roy. Stat. Soc., see **8768**.

8542    RODGERS (BRIAN). 'The Social Science Association, 1857–1886'. *Manch. School* xx (1952), 283–310.

8543 SOCIOLOGICAL SOCIETY. Sociological papers. 3 v. 1904–6. Ledbury etc. 1905–7.

Cont. as *The sociological review: journal of the Sociological Society*, 1908+. *The British j. of sociology*, 1950+, carries occasional hist. papers.

8544 BOOTH. Charles Booth: social scientist. By Thomas Spensley Simey, Baron Simey, and Margaret Bayne Simey, Baroness Simey. 1960.

8545 GEDDES. Pioneer of sociology: the life and letters of Patrick Geddes. By Philip [i.e. Philippe Auguste] Mairet. 1957.

Geddes's style is best conveyed by Amelia Dorothy Defries, *The interpreter: Geddes: the man and his gospel*, 1927. For Geddes's work on town planning, etc., see **7056, 7059.**

8546 HOBHOUSE. L. T. Hobhouse: his life and work. By John Atkinson Hobson and Morris Ginsberg. 1931.

See also Victor Branford, 'The sociological work of Leonard Hobhouse', *Sociological Rev.* xxi (1929), 273–80.

8547 ROWNTREE. Social thought and social action: a study of the work of Seebohm Rowntree, 1871–1954. By Asa Briggs. 1961.

8548 SPENCER. Herbert Spencer: the evolution of a sociologist. By John David Yeadon Peel. Lond. & N.Y. 1971.

Good. See also **8468.**

8549 BLOXAM (GEORGE W.) *comp.* Index to the publications of the Anthropological Institute of Great Britain and Ireland . . . 1893.

Indexes the Ethnological Soc. of London, *Journal*, 1844–54, 1868–70, and *Transactions*, 1861–9, the Anthropological Soc. of London, *Memoirs*, 1863–9, *The anthropological rev.*, 1863–70, and *J. of anthropology*, 1870–1, and Roy. Anthropological Inst., *Journal*, 1871+.

8550 PENNIMAN (THOMAS KENNETH). A hundred years of anthropology. 1935. 2nd edn. 1952.

8551 HARRIS (MARVIN). The rise of anthropological theory: a history of theories of culture. Lond. & N.Y. 1968.

8552 BURROW (JOHN WYON). 'Evolution and anthropology in the 1860s: the Anthropological Society of London, 1863–71'. *Victorian Studs.* vii (1963–4), 137–54.

8553 FRAZER (*Sir* JAMES GEORGE). The golden bough: a study in comparative religion. 2 v. 1890. 2nd edn. 3 v. 1900. 3rd edn. 12 v. 1907–15. Suppl. by Aftermath . . . 1936.

One of the great books of the period. For contemp. comment see particularly Andrew Lang, *Magic and religion*, 1901.

8554 LOWIE (ROBERT HEINRICH). The history of ethnological theory. Lond. & N.Y. [1937.]

8555 MURPHREE (IDUS L.). 'The evolutionary anthropologists: the progress of mankind: the concepts of progress and culture in the thought of John Lubbock, Edward B. Tylor and Lewis H. Morgan'. *Amer. Phil. Soc. Proc.* cv (1961), 265–300.

See also Anthropological Soc. of Washington, *Evolution and anthropology: a centennial appraisal*, Wash. 1959.

8556 ODOM (HERBERT H.). 'Generalizations on race in nineteenth-century physical anthropology'. *Isis* lviii (1967), 4–18.

8557 FRAZER. A bibliography of Sir James George Frazer, O.M. . . . Comp. by Theodore Besterman. 1934.

Robert Angus Downie, *James George Frazer: the portrait of a scholar*, 1940, is the only biog. Downie also ed. *Anthologia anthropologica* . . ., 4 v. 1938–9, a coll. of Frazer's unpubl. work.

8558 BONSER (WILFRID). A bibliography of folklore as contained in the first eighty years of the publications of the Folk-lore Society. Folk-lore Soc. Publs. 121. 1961.

The Folk-lore Soc. publ. *The folk-lore record*, 1878–82, *The folk-lore j.*, 1883–90, and *Folk lore: a quarterly review of myth, tradition, institutions & customs*, 1890+.

8559 DORSON (RICHARD MERCER). The British folklorists: a history. 1968.

See also his *Peasant customs and savage myths: selections from the British folklorists*, 2 v. 1968.

8560 BRIGGS (KATHARINE MARY). A dictionary of British folk-tales in the English language. Pt. A. Folk narratives. Pt. B. Folk legends. 4 v. Lond. & Bloomington, Ind. 1970–1.

See also her *The fairies in [English] tradition and literature*, Lond. & Chicago 1967, and *Folk-tales of England*, ed. by Katharine M. Briggs and Ruth L. Tongue, Chicago & Lond. 1965.

## 5. GEOGRAPHY AND EXPLORATION

8561 WRIGHT (JOHN KIRTLAND) *and* PLATT (ELIZABETH TOWER) *comps.* Aids to geographical research: bibliographies, periodicals, atlases, gazetteers, and other reference books. American Geographical Soc. 2nd edn. N.Y. 1947.

8562 AMERICAN GEOGRAPHICAL SOCIETY. Research catalogue. 15 v. Boston. 1962.

8563 NATIONAL MARITIME MUSEUM. Catalogue of the library. Vol. I. Voyages and travel. 1968.

Important for exploration, because Edward Godfrey Cox, *A reference guide to the literature of travel* . . ., 3 v. Seattle, Wash. 1935–49, has little post-1800.

8564  DARTMOUTH COLLEGE LIBRARY. Dictionary catalogue of the Stefansson collection on the polar regions. 8 v. Boston. 1967.

See also Scott Polar Research Inst., *The polar record*, 1+, Camb. 1931+.

8565  ROYAL GEOGRAPHICAL SOCIETY. Hints to travellers, scientific and general. 1854. 11th edn. 2 v. 1935–8.

A useful handbook. See also George Robert Milne Murray, ed., *The Antarctic manual, for the use of the expedition of 1901*, Roy. Geog. Soc. 1901.

8566  FREEMAN (THOMAS WALTER). A hundred years of geography, 1961.

Fuller for the period than Robert Eric Dickinson and Osbert John Radcliffe Howarth, *The making of geography*, Oxf. 1933.

8567  BAKER (JOHN NORMAN LEONARD). A history of geographical discovery and exploration. 1931. 2nd edn. 1937. New edn. N.Y. 1967.

Standard. There is little more in Sir Percy Molesworth Sykes, *A history of exploration from the earliest times to the present day*, 1934, 3rd edn. 1949.

8568  ROYAL GEOGRAPHICAL SOCIETY. Journal. 1830–1880. Proceedings. 1855–92. Geographical journal. 1893+.

The leading contemp. j. For the hist. of the soc. see Hugh Robert Mill, *The record of the Royal Geographical Society, 1830–1930*, 1930, and Sir Clements Robert Markham, *The fifty years' work of the Royal Geographical Society*, 1881.

8569  ASSAD (THOMAS J.). Three Victorian travellers: Burton, Blunt, Doughty. Lond. 1964. N.Y. 1965.

8570  MIDDLETON (DOROTHY). Victorian lady travellers. Lond. & N.Y. 1965.

8571  DODGE (ERNEST STANLEY). Northwest by sea. N.Y. 1961.

8572  MARKHAM (*Sir* CLEMENTS ROBERT). The lands of silence: history of Arctic and Antarctic exploration. Ed. by Francis Henry Hill Guillemard. Camb. 1921.

8573  MIRSKY (JEANNETTE). To the north! The story of Arctic exploration. N.Y. & Lond. 1934. Rev. edn. [To the Arctic!] N.Y. 1948.

Engl. edn. entitled *Northern conquest*, 1934.

8574  COWEN (ROBERT CHURCHILL). Frontiers of the sea: the story of oceanographic exploration. 1960.

From 1872 on. See also Sir William Abbot Herdman, *Founders of oceanography and their work: an introduction to the science of the sea*, Lond. & N.Y. 1923, and Margaret Deacon, *Scientists and the sea, 1650–1900: a study of marine science*, Lond. & N.Y. 1971. For the pioneer exploration of the *Challenger* see Sir Charles Wyville Thomson, *The voyage of* the 'Challenger': the Atlantic: a preliminary account of the general results of the exploring voyage . . ., 2 v. Lond. 1877, 2 v. N. Y. 1878, and William James Joseph Spry, The cruise of Her Majesty's Ship 'Challenger': voyages over many seas, scenes in many lands, 1877. The scientific work of the expedition was publ. as Report on the scientific results of the voyage of H.M.S. Challenger during the years 1873–76 . . , prepared under the superintendence of the late Sir C. Wyville Thomson . . ., 40 v. in 44 and atlas in 6 v. 1880–95. An early voyage was reported by Sir Charles Wyville Thomson in a famous book, The depths of the sea: an account of the general results of the dredging cruises of H.M.SS. 'Porcupine' and 'Lightning' during the summers of 1868, 1869, and 1870 . . ., 1873, 2nd edn. 1874.

8575   BAKER. Sir Samuel Baker: a memoir. By Thomas Douglas Murray and Arthur Silva White. 1895.

See also Dorothy Middleton, Baker of the Nile, 1949. Baker's more important journeys are recorded in his The Nile tributaries of Abyssinia . . ., 1867, 4th edn. 1871, Ismailia . . ., 2 v. 1874, 2nd edn. 1879, and The Albert Nyanza, great basin of the Nile, and explorations of the Nile sources, 2 v. 1866.

8576   BELL. Gertrude Bell from her personal papers. By Elizabeth Burgoyne. 2 v. 1958–61.

See also Florence Eveleen Eleanore, Lady Bell, ed., The letters of Gertrude Bell, 2 v. 1927, [Florence] Elsa, Lady Richmond, ed., The earlier letters of Gertrude Bell, 1937, and Winifred Cotterill Donkin, comp., Catalogue of the Gertrude Bell collection in the library of King's College, Newcastle-upon-Tyne, Newcastle-upon-Tyne 1960.

8577   BURNABY. The true blue: the life and adventures of Colonel Fred Burnaby, 1842–85. By Michael Alexander. 1957.

Frederick Gustavus Burnaby was best known for his A ride to Khiva: travels and adventures in Central Asia, 1876. Earlier lives incl. James Redding Ware and R. K. Mann, The life and times of Fred Burnaby [1885], and Thomas Wright, The life of Colonel Fred Burnaby, 1908.

8578   BURTON. An annotated bibliography of Sir Richard Francis Burton. By Norman Mosley Penzer. 1923.

For his life see Isabel, Lady Burton, The life of Captain Sir Richard F. Burton, 2 v. 1893, and The romance of Isabel, Lady Burton, the story of her life, told in part by herself and in part by W. H. Wilkins, 2 v. 1897; Francis Hitchman, Richard F. Burton, K.C.M.G. his early, private and public life: with an account of his travels and explorations, 2 v. 1887; Georgiana M. Stisted, The true life of Capt. Sir Richard F. Burton . . . written by his niece . . . with the authority and approval of the Burton family, 1896; Thomas Wright, The life of Sir Richard Burton, 2 v. Lond. & N.Y. 1906; Fawn McKay Brodie, The devil drives: a life of Sir Richard Burton, London. & N.Y. 1967; Seton Dearden, The Arabian knight: a study of Sir Richard Burton [1936], publ. in N.Y. as Burton of Arabia [1937], rev. edn. Lond. 1953; Walter Phelps Dodge, The real Sir Richard Burton, 1907; Fairfax Davis Downey, Burton: Arabian nights adventurer, N.Y. 1931; Allen Edwardes, Death rides a camel: a biography of Sir Richard Burton, N.Y. 1963; Byron Farwell, Burton: a biography of Sir Richard Francis Burton, 1963; Hugh Joseph Schonfield, Richard Burton, explorer, 1936; John Norman Leonard Baker, 'Sir Richard Burton and the Nile sources', Eng. Hist. Rev. lix (1944), 49–61, and Jonathan Bishop, 'The identities of Sir Richard Burton: the explorer as actor', Victorian Studs. i (1957–8), 119–35.

8579  DOUGHTY. The life of Charles M. Doughty. By David George Hogarth. 1928.

See also Barker Fairley, *Charles M. Doughty: a critical study*, 1927.


8580  OLIPHANT. The life of Laurence Oliphant: traveller, diplomat and mystic. By Philip Henderson. 1956.


8581  SCOTT. Scott of the Antarctic. By Reginald Pound. 1966.

Robert Falcon Scott himself ed. *The voyage of the 'Discovery'*, 2 v. 1905. See also Leonard Huxley, ed., *Scott's last expedition* . . ., 2 v. Lond. & N.Y. 1913, incl. Scott's journals, which are also pr. in *Scott's last expedition: the personal journals of Captain R. F. Scott on his journey to the South Pole*, 1912, repr. 1925, new edn. 1964. Among lives are Stephen Lucius Gwynn, *Captain Scott*, Lond. 1929, N.Y. 1930, Martin Alexander Lindsay, *The epic of Captain Scott*, Lond. 1933, N.Y. 1934, and George Fenn Seaver, *Scott of the Antarctic: a study in character*, 1940. Members of the expedition also wrote accounts of their experiences, notably, Edward Ratcliffe Garth Russell Evans, Baron Mount-evans, *South with Scott*, 1921, Alexander Robert Ellis, ed., *Under Scott's command: Lashly's Antarctic diaries*, 1969, and Herbert George Ponting, *The great white south: being, an account of experiences with Captain Scott's South Pole expedition* . . ., 1921. Apsley Cherry-Garrard, *The worst journey in the world: Antarctic, 1910–1913: Scott's last expedition*, 2 v. 1922, 2nd edn. 1929, and reprs., is a moving account of the expedition. For Scott's companions see George Fenn Seaver, *Edward Wilson of the Antarctic: naturalist and friend*, Lond. & N.Y. 1937, and *'Birdie' Bowers of the Antarctic*, Lond. & N.Y. 1938.


8582  SHACKLETON. Shackleton. By Margery Lilian Edith Fisher and James Maxwell McConnell Fisher. 1957.

See also Hugh Robert Mill, *The life of Sir Ernest Shackleton* . . ., Lond. & Boston 1923, Frank Arthur Worsley, *Endurance: an epic of polar adventure*, 1931, and Alfred Lansing, *Endurance: Shackleton's incredible voyage*, Lond. & N.Y. 1959.


8583  STANLEY. Bibliographie de H. M. Stanley, 1841–1904. By Théodore Heyse. Brussels. 1961.

Dorothy, Lady Stanley, ed., *The autobiography of Sir Henry Morton Stanley*, Lond. & Boston 1909, Richard Stanley and Alan Neame, eds., *The exploration diaries of H. M. Stanley*, 1961, Albert Maurice, ed., *Lettres inédites*, Brussels 1955, English edn. publ. as *H. M. Stanley: unpublished letters*, Lond., Edin., & N.Y. 1957, and Belgium: Mini-stère des Affaires Africaines, Document Notte, *Stanley au Congo, 1879–1884*, ed. by Charles T. Notte, Brussels 1960, suppl. Stanley's travel writings. There are many poor popular lives incl. Frank Hird, *H. M. Stanley: the authorized life*, 1935, Ian Anstruther, *I presume: Stanley's triumph and disaster*, 1956, publ. in N.Y. as *Dr. Livingstone, I presume?*, 1957, Byron Farwell, *The man who presumed: a biography of Henry M. Stanley*, N.Y. 1957, Lond. 1958, and A. G. Feather, *Stanley's story* . . ., Phila. 1890, repr. Chicago 1969.


8584  YOUNGHUSBAND. Wonders of the Himalaya. By Sir Francis Edward Younghusband. 1924.

See also his *The light of experience* . . ., 1927, and George Fenn Seaver, *Francis Young-husband, explorer and mystic*, 1952. For earlier Himalayan climbing see Douglas William Freshfield, *Round Kanchenjunga* . . ., 1903, a minor classic of exploration.

# E. NATURAL SCIENCES

## 1. GENERAL

### (a) *Reference*

8585  SARTON (GEORGE). Horus: a guide to the history of science: a first guide for the study of science, with introductory essays on science and tradition. Waltham, Mass. 1952.

The best general bibliog; but weak on England. Needs to be suppl. by John Leonard Thornton and Robert Ian James Tully, *Scientific books, libraries, and collectors: a study of bibliography and the book trade in relation to science*, Libr. Assoc. 1954, 3rd edn. 1971. Other useful lists are John Crerar Libr., *A list of books on the history of science . . .*, Chicago 1911, suppls. 1916, 1942+; François Russo, comp., *Histoire des sciences et des techniques: bibliographie: ouvrage publié avec le concours du Centre National de la Recherche Scientifique et de l'Union Internationale d'Histoire des Sciences*, Paris 1954, 2nd edn. [*Éléments de bibliographie de l'histoire des sciences et des techniques*] Paris 1969; Heinrich Zeitlinger and Henry Cecil Sotheran, comps., *Bibliotheca chemico-mathematica: catalogue of works in many tongues on exact and applied science*, 2 v. 1921, suppls. 1932, 1937, 1952; and Patent Office Library, *Subject list of works on general science, physics, sound, music, light, microscopy, and philosophical instruments in the library . . .*, 1903.

8586  SARTON (GEORGE) *and others.* 'Critical bibliography of the history and philosophy of science and of the history of civilisation'. Publ. in *Isis.* Wondelgem-lez-Gand, etc. Annual. 1913+.

The best annual bibliog., which is cumulated in Magda Whitrow, ed., *Isis cumulative bibliography: a bibliography of the history of science . . ., 1913–65*, Hist. of Science Soc., 2 v. Chicago 1971.

8587  JEFFREYS (ALAN). 'Manuscript sources for the history of science'. *Archives* vii (1965–6), 75–9.

8588  BOLTON (HENRY CARRINGTON). A catalogue of scientific and technical periodicals, 1665 to 1882, together with chronological tables and a library check list. Smithsonian Instn. Wash. 1885. 2nd edn. [1665–1895.] Wash. 1897.

Useful for 19th-cent. periodicals. See also Roy. Soc. of London, *Catalogue of the periodical publications in the library . . .*, comp. by Luxmore Newcombe and Leonard Ellston, 1912, and *A world list of scientific periodicals published in the years 1900–1921*, 2 v. 1925–7, 4th edn. [1900–60], 3 v. 1963–5.

8589  ROYAL SOCIETY OF LONDON. Catalogue of scientific papers, 1800[–1900]. 19 v. 1867–1925. Subject index. 3 v. in 4 (incomplete). 1908–14.

The fullest and best of all lists of periodical articles. Cont. in *International catalogue of scientific literature . . .*, 1901[–14], 254 v. 1902–21.

8590  SCIENCE ABSTRACTS. Section A: Physics abstracts. Section B: Electrical engineering abstracts. 1898+.

Section A includes mathematics, astronomy, physics, biology, etc. Publ. undivided as *Science abstracts*, 1898–1902.

8591  DICTIONARY OF SCIENTIFIC BIOGRAPHY. Ed. by Charles Coulston Gillispie. 13 v. N.Y. 1970+.

A thoroughly professional work. The main biog. dictionary hitherto in use is Johann Christian Poggendorf and others, *Biographisch-literarisches Handwörterbuch zur Geschichte der exacten Wissenschaften*, 7 v. in 11+, Leipzig 1863–1955+. Major British scientists are covered fully in the *Proceedings* of the Royal Society of London down to 1932, with reprints in the Society's *Yearbook*, 1900–32, and in *Obituary notices of fellows of the Royal Society*, 9 v. 1932–54, cont. as *Biographical memoirs*, 1955+. There is an index to the obituaries of 1880–99 in vol. lxxv (1905) of the *Proceedings*. Lesser scientists are incl. in *Who's who in science*, 1912 and 1914. For shorter biogs. see also Trevor Illtyd Williams, ed., *A biographical dictionary of scientists*, Lond. & N.Y. 1969, and Allen George Debus, ed., *World who's who in science: a biographical dictionary of notable scientists from antiquity to the present*, Chicago 1968.

## (b) *General Histories*

8592  SINGER (CHARLES JOSEPH). A short history of scientific ideas to 1900. Oxf. 1959.

A useful gen. hist., on the whole easier to use than René Taton, ed., *A general history of the sciences*, 4 v. 1963–5, and John Desmond Bernal, *Science history*, 1954, 4th edn. Lond. & Camb., Mass. 1971.

8593  DAMPIER-WHETHAM (*Sir* WILLIAM CECIL). A history of science and its relations with philosophy & religion. Camb. 1929. 4th edn. 1948. Rev. edn. with postscript by I. Bernard Cohen. Camb. 1961.

8594  DINGLE (HERBERT) *ed*. A century of science, 1851–1951: written by specialist authors. 1951.

See also Charles Coulston Gillispie, *The edge of objectivity: an essay in the history of scientific ideas*, Princeton 1960, and [Horace] Romano Harré, ed., *Scientific thought, 1900–1960: a selective survey*, Oxf. 1969.

8595  WALLACE (ALFRED RUSSEL). The wonderful century: its successes and failures. Lond. & N.Y. 1898. New edn. [sub-title: the age of new ideas in science and invention.] 1903.

In many ways the most interesting work of its period, by a celebrated scientist. Sir John Arthur Thomson, *Progress of science in the century*, Nineteenth cent. ser. 1903, and Robert Henry Murray, *Science and scientists in the nineteenth century*, 1925, also reflect the views of late 19th-cent. scientists.

8596  SHARLIN (HAROLD I.). The convergent century: the unification of science in the nineteenth century. Lond. & N.Y. 1966.

8597  BUSH ([JOHN NASH] DOUGLAS). Science and English poetry: a historical sketch, 1590–1950. N.Y. 1950.

8598  CARDWELL (DONALD STEPHEN LOWELL). The organisation of science in England: a retrospect. 1957.

**8599 BECKER (BERNARD HENRY).** Scientific London. Lond. 1874. N.Y. 1875. Repr. 1968.

A useful account of the London scientific and engineering socs.

**8600 YEARBOOK OF THE SCIENTIFIC AND LEARNED SOCIETIES OF GREAT BRITAIN AND IRELAND. 1884–1939. 1951+.**

See also *Return showing all the government grants during the last fifty years towards establishing, endowing and maintaining the various scientific societies in England, Scotland and Ireland.* H.C. 358 (1906). LXV, 515.

**8601 LYONS (*Sir* HENRY GEORGE).** The Royal Society, 1660–1940: a history of its administration under its charters. Camb. 1944.

See also Edward Neville da Costa Andrade, *A brief history of the Royal Society*, 1960, *The record of the Royal Society of London for the Promotion of Natural Knowledge*, *1897*, 1897, 4th edn. 1940, which lists members and office-holders, Royal Society *Year book . . .*, 1896–7+; and the official biogs. of deceased fellows (**8591**).

**8602 HOWARTH (OSBERT JOHN RADCLIFFE).** The British Association for the Advancement of Science: a retrospect, 1831–1921. 1922. 2nd edn. [1831–1931.] 1931.

See also Sir Oliver Joseph Lodge, *Advancing science: being personal reminiscences of the British Association in the nineteenth century* [1869–1900], 1931.

**8603 JONES (HENRY BENCE).** The Royal Institution: its founder and its first professors. 1871.

See also Thomas Martin, *The Royal Institution*, 1942, 3rd edn. 1961, *The archives of the Royal Institution of Great Britain in facsimile: minutes of managers' meetings, 1799–1900*, 2 v. Menston 1971, the lives of Faraday (**8715**) and Tyndall (**8728**), and Denys Thompson, 'John Tyndall and the Royal Institution', *Annals of Science* xii (1957), 9–12.

**8604 CROWTHER (JAMES GERALD).** British scientists of the nineteenth century: Humphry Davy, Michael Faraday, James Prescott Joule, William Thomson, James Clerk Maxwell. Lond. N.Y. [Men of science . . .] 1936. New edn. 2 v. Harmondsworth. 1940–1.

See also his *British scientists of the twentieth century*, 1952, and *Statesmen of science . . .*, 1965.

**8605 HARRÉ ([HORACE] ROMANO)** *ed.* Some nineteenth-century scientists. Oxf. 1969.

**8606 GALTON (*Sir* FRANCIS).** English men of science: their nature and nurture. 1874. Repr. 1970.

**8607 MACLEOD (ROY MALCOLM).** 'The X club: a social network of science in late-Victorian England'. *Notes & records of the Royal Soc.* xxiv (1970), 305–22.

8608   WHEWELL. The life, and selections from the correspondence, of William Whewell, D.D., late Master of Trinity College, Cambridge. By Mrs. Stair Douglas [Janet Mary Douglas]. 1881. 2nd edn. 1882.

An eminent mathematician and philosopher, who pioneered the study of scientific method. Isaac Todhunter, *William Whewell, D.D.: an account of his writings, with selections from his literary and scientific correspondence*, 2 v. 1876, is a useful compilation. For his ideas see Curt John Ducasse, 'Whewell's philosophy of scientific discovery', *Philosophical Rev.* lx (1951), 59–69, 213–34, Edward W. Strong, 'William Whewell and John Stuart Mill: their controversy about scientific knowledge', *J. Hist. Ideas* xvi (1955), 209–31, and Robert Robson and Walter Farr Cannon, 'William Whewell, F.R.S. (1794–1866)', *Notes & Records of the Roy. Soc.* xix (1964), 168–91.

8609   HUXLEY. Life and letters of Thomas Henry Huxley. By Leonard Huxley. 2 v. 1900. 2nd edn. 3 v. 1903.

A good official biog. of the greatest public champion of science. For his work see Warren Royal Dawson, comp., *The Huxley papers: a descriptive catalogue of the correspondence, manuscripts and miscellaneous papers of the Right Hon. Thomas Henry Huxley, P.C., D.C.L., F.R.S., preserved in the Imperial College of Science and Technology, London,* 1946. See also Cyril Bibby, *T. H. Huxley: scientist, humanist and educator,* 1959, 'Huxley and the reception of the "Origin"', *Victorian Studs.* iii (1959–60), 76–86, and 'Thomas Henry Huxley and university development', ibid. ii (1958–9), 97–116, M. B. Crowe, 'Huxley and humanism', *Studies* xlix (1960), 249–60, and Ronald William Clark, *The Huxleys,* Lond. & N.Y. 1968.

### (c) *General Periodicals*

8610   ISIS: revue consacrée à l'histoire de la science. Wondelgem-lez-Gand, etc. 1913+.

The oldest hist. of science j. Suppl. by *Osiris: studies on the history and philosophy of science, and on the history of learning and culture,* Bruges 1936+.

8611   ANNALS OF SCIENCE: a quarterly review of the history of science since the Renaissance. 1+. 1936+.

8612   ROYAL SOCIETY OF LONDON. Notes and records. 1+. 1938+.

In effect an hist. j.

8613   HISTORY OF SCIENCE: an annual review of literature, research and teaching. 1+. Camb. 1962+.

Other hist. of science js. incl. *The British j. for the history of science,* British Soc. for the Hist. of Science, 1962+, *Hist. studs. in the physical sciences,* Amer. Phil. Soc., Phila. 1969+, *Studies in history and philosophy of science,* 1970+, *Archive for the history of the exact sciences,* Berlin 1960+, *Quellen und Studien zur Geschichte der Mathematik, Astronomie und Physik,* Berlin 1930+, *Centaurus: international magazine of the history of science and medicine,* Copenhagen 1950+, *British j. for the philosophy of science,* Edin. 1950+, and *Philosophy of science,* Baltimore, Md. 1934+.

8614   ROYAL SOCIETY OF LONDON Philosophical transactions . . . 1665+.

The leading scientific j. throughout the period. The other chief gen. scientific periodicals were Royal Institution of Great Britain, [*Notices of the*] *proceedings* . . ., 1851–4+, British Association for the Advancement of Science, *Report of the . . . meetings,* 1831/2–

1938, *Nature: a weekly j. of science*, 1869+, Royal Microscopical Soc. of London, *Transactions*, later *Monthly microscopical j.*, then *Journal*, 1844+, and *Quarterly j. of microscopical science*, 1852+, Royal Society of Edinburgh, *Proceedings*, Edin. 1832+, and *Transactions*, 1783+, Literary and Philosophical Soc. of Manch., *Memoirs*, 1785–1887, *Proceedings*, 1857–87, *Memoirs and procs.*, 1888+, and *Edinburgh philosophical j.*, later [*Quarterly*] *j. of science*, 1819+.


### (d) *Evolution*

8615   CARTER (GEORGE STUART). A hundred years of evolution. 1957.

8616   EISELEY (LOREN COREY). Darwin's century: evolution and the men who discovered it. Garden City, N.Y. 1958. Lond. 1959.

A general intro., better written and informed than William Irvine, *Apes, angels and Victorians: the story of Darwin, Huxley and evolution*, N.Y. 1955, Lond. edn. [. . .: *a joint biography of Darwin and Huxley*], 1955.

8617   GILLISPIE (CHARLES COULSTON). Genesis and geology: a study in the relations of scientific thought, natural theology and social opinion in Great Britain, 1790–1850. Camb., Mass. 1951. Repr. 1969.

Though covering ideas before 1851, indispensable for the 1850s as well. See also Reyer Hooykas, *Natural law and divine miracle: a historical–cultural study of the principle of uniformity in geology, biology and theology*, Leiden 1959; Francis Colin Haber, *The age of the world: Moses to Darwin*, Baltimore, Md. 1959; [Hiram] Bentley Glass, Owsei Temkin, and William Louis Straus, eds., *Forerunners of Darwin, 1745–1859*, Baltimore, Md. 1959; Milton Millhauser, *Just before Darwin: Robert Chambers and 'Vestiges'*, Middleton, Conn. 1959; Walter Farr Cannon, 'The uniformitarian–catastrophist debate', *Isis* li (1960), 38–55; and Roy Malcolm Macleod, 'Evolutionism and Richard Owen, 1830–1868: an episode in "Darwin's century" ', *Isis* lvi (1965), 259–80.

8618   DARWIN. The works of Charles Darwin: an annotated bibliographical handlist. By Richard Broke Freeman. 1965.

For works about Darwin see Bert James Loewenberg, 'Darwin and Darwin studies, 1959–63', *Hist. of Science* iv (1965), 15–54.

8619   CAMBRIDGE UNIVERSITY LIBRARY. Handlist of the Darwin papers at the University Library, Cambridge. Camb. 1960.

See also Henry William Rutherford, comp., *Catalogue of the library of Charles Darwin now in the Botany School, Cambridge*, Camb. 1908.

8620   DARWIN. The autobiography of Charles Darwin, 1809–1882, with original omissions restored. Ed. by [Emma] Nora, Lady Barlow. 1958.

8621   DARWIN. The life and letters of Charles Darwin: including an autobiographical chapter. By Sir Francis Darwin. 3 v. 1887. Repr. 2 v. N.Y. 1959.

A useful official biog. See also Gerhard Wichler, *Charles Darwin, the founder of the theory of evolution and natural selection*, Oxf. etc. 1961, and Francis Huxley, 'Charles Darwin: life and habit', *Amer. Scholar* xxviii (1959), 489–99; xxix (1960), 85–93. For the 'Beagle' expedition see Alan McCrae Moorehead, *Darwin and the Beagle*, 1969, and Harold Edward Leslie Mellersh, *FitzRoy of the Beagle*, 1968.

8622  DARWIN (CHARLES). The origin of species: a variorum text. Ed. by Morse Peckham. Phila. 1959.

8623  DE BEER (*Sir* GAVIN RYLANDS) *ed*. Darwin's notebooks on transmutation of species. British Museum (Natural Hist.) Bull., Hist. v. 2, nos. 2–5. 1960. Addenda. Hist. v. 2, no. 6. 1961.

Suppl. by [Emma] Nora, Lady Barlow, ed., *Darwin's ornithological notes*, British Museum (Natural Hist.) Bull., Hist. v. 2, no. 7, 1963.

8624  DE BEER (*Sir* GAVIN RYLANDS). Charles Darwin: evolution by natural selection. 1963.

See also his 'Further unpublished letters of Charles Darwin', *Annals of science* xiv (1958), 83–115, 'Some unpublished letters of Charles Darwin', *Notes and Records of the Royal Society* xiv (1959), 12–66, 'The origin of Darwin's ideas of evolution and natural selection', *Roy. Soc. Proc.*, section B, clv (1961), 321–38, 'Charles Darwin', *British Academy Proc.* xliv (1958), 163–83, and 'Mendel, Darwin and Fisher (1865–1965)', *Notes & Records of the Royal Soc.* xix (1964), 192–226; xxi (1966), 64–71.

8625  BARLOW ([EMMA] NORA), *Lady Barlow, ed*. Darwin and Henslow: the growth of an idea: letters, 1831–1860. 1967.

Other Darwin letters are incl. in Henrietta Emma Litchfield, ed., *Emma Darwin, wife of Charles Darwin: a century of family letters, 1792–1896*, priv. pr. 2 v. Camb. 1904, new edn. 1 v. 1915, and Robert M. Stecher, ed., 'The Darwin–Innes letters: the correspondence of an evolutionist with his vicar, 1868–1884', *Annals of Science* xvii (1961), 201–58. For Darwin's connections with his contemporaries see also Ernst Mayr, 'Agassiz, Darwin and evolution', *Harvard Libr. Bull.* xiii (1959), 165–94, Loren Corey Eiseley, 'Charles Darwin, Edward Blyth, and the theory of natural selection', *Amer. Phil. Soc. Proc.* ciii (1959), 94–158, and 'Darwin, Coleridge and the theory of unconscious creation', *Daedalus* xciv (1965), 588–602.

8626  HUXLEY (THOMAS HENRY). Darwiniana: essays. Collected essays. V. 2. Lond. & N.Y. 1893.

Important because of its author, for whom see **8609.**

8627  HIMMELFARB (GERTRUDE). Darwin and the Darwinian revolution. Garden City, N.Y. 1959.

Vigorous and controversial. Other re-interpretations incl. Walter Farr Cannon, 'The basis of Darwin's achievement: a revaluation', *Victorian Studs.* v (1961–2), 109–34, which links Darwin's ideas to natural theology in a novel way; Cyril Dean Darlington, *Darwin's place in history*, Oxf. 1959; Donald Fleming, 'Charles Darwin, the anaesthetic man', *Victorian Studs.* iv (1960–1), 219–36; and Geoffrey West, pseud. of Geoffrey H. Wells, *Charles Darwin, the fragmentary man*, 1937. For Darwin's impact on philosophy see **8435.** For Darwin's religion see Maurice Mandelbaum, 'Darwin's religious views', *J. Hist. Ideas* xix (1958), 363–78, and John C. Greene, 'Darwin and religion', in Harlow Shapley, ed., *Science ponders religion*, N.Y. 1960, pp. 254–76.

8628  BELL (PETER ROBERT) *ed*. Darwin's biological work: some aspects reconsidered. Camb. 1959.

See also Peter Vorzimmer, 'Charles Darwin and blending inheritance', *Isis* liv (1963), 371–90, and 'Darwin's ecology and its influence upon his theory', *Isis* lvi (1965), 148–55; Mary Alice Evans, 'Mimicry and the Darwinian heritage', *J. Hist. Ideas* xxvi (1965), 211–20; Sir Julian Sorell Huxley, 'The three types of evolutionary process',

_Nature_ clxxx (1957), 454–5, and 'The emergence of Darwinism', _Linnean Soc. J._ xliv (1958), 1–14; Sir Julian Sorell Huxley and Henry Bernard Davis Kettlewell, _Charles Darwin and his world_, 1965; Sir Julian Sorell Huxley assisted by Thomas Fisher, _The struggle for life: the living thoughts of Darwin_, Greenwich, Conn. 1963; and Paul Bigelow Sears, _Charles Darwin: the naturalist as a cultural force_, N.Y. 1950.

8629 ELLEGÅRD (HENRIK ALVAR). Darwin and the general reader: the reception of Darwin's theory of evolution in the British periodical press, 1859–1872. _Gothenburg Studs. in English_ viii. Göteborg. 1958. Also publ. as _Göteborgs Universitets Årsskrift_. v. 64. No. 7.

See also David L. Hull, _Darwin and his critics: the reception of Darwin's theory of evolution by the scientific community_, Camb., Mass. & Lond. 1973.

8630 GHISELIN (MICHAEL T.). The triumph of the Darwinian method. Berkeley. 1969.

8631 DE BEER (_Sir_ GAVIN RYLANDS) _ed._ Charles Darwin and Alfred Russel Wallace: evolution by natural selection. Camb. 1958.

See also De Beer's _A handbook on evolution_, British Museum (Natural Hist.), 1958, 2nd edn. 1959, and Bert James Loewenberg, _Darwin, Wallace and the theory of natural selection, including the Linnean Society papers_, New Haven, Conn. 1957, Camb., Mass. 1959.

8632 WALLACE. My life: a record of events and opinions. By Alfred Russel Wallace. 2 v. 1905. Abridged edn. 1908.

See also Wilma Beryl George, _Biologist philosopher: a study of the life and writings of Alfred Russel Wallace_, 1964, Sir James Marchant, _Alfred Russel Wallace: letters and reminiscences_, 2 v. 1916, Amabel Williams-Ellis, _Darwin's moon: a biography of Alfred Russel Wallace_, 1966, Carl Frederick Abel Pantin, 'Alfred Russel Wallace, F.R.S., and his essays of 1858 and 1855', _Notes & Records of the Roy. Soc._ xiv (1959), 67–84, and H. Lewis McKinney, 'Alfred Russel Wallace and the discovery of natural selection', _J. Hist. Medicine_ xxi (1966), 333–57.

8633 WILLEY (_Sir_ BASIL). Darwin and Butler: two versions of evolution. 1960.

See also Phyllis Greenacre, _The quest for the father: a study of the Darwin–Butler controversy as a contribution to the understanding of the creative individual_, N.Y. 1963.

8634 LUCAS (ERHARD). 'Marx' and Engels' Auseinandersetzung mit Darwin: zur Differenz zwischen Marx und Engels'. _Int. Rev. Soc. Hist._ ix (1964), 433–69.

See also Conway Zirkle, _Evolution, Marxian biology and the social scene_, Phila. 1959.

8635 BARZUN (JACQUES MARTIN). Darwin, Marx, Wagner: critique of a heritage. Boston. 1941. Lond. 1942. Rev. edn. Garden City, N.Y. 1958.

Incl. as an example of the type of exploratory essay now common. Other good examples of the type are Stanley Edgar Hyman, _The tangled bank: Darwin, Marx, Frazer and Freud as imaginative writers_, N.Y. 1962, and [Arthur] Lionel Stevenson, _Darwin among the poets_, Chicago 1932, repr. N.Y. 1963.

**8636  SEWARD** (*Sir* ALBERT CHARLES) *ed.* Darwin and modern science: essays in commemoration of the centenary of the birth of Charles Darwin and of the fiftieth anniversary of the publication of the *Origin of species*. Camb. 1909.

**8637  TAX** (SOL) *ed.* Evolution after Darwin. 3 v. Chicago. 1960.

One of the more useful products of the Darwin centenary. Others incl. special numbers of the *Antioch Rev.* xix (1959) no. 1 [styled '*The Origin of species: 100 years later*'], and *Victorian Studs.* iii (1959–60), pt. 1, American Phil. Soc., *Commemoration of the centennial of the publication of the Origin of species . . .*, *Amer. Phil. Soc. Proc.* ciii (1959) no. 2; Anthropological Soc. of Washington, *Evolution and anthropology: a centennial appraisal*, Wash. 1959, Samuel Anthony Barnett, ed., *A century of Darwin*, Lond. & Camb., Mass. 1958, Michael Parker Banton, ed., *Darwinism and the study of society: a centenary symposium*, Lond. & Chicago 1961, John Colton Greene, *The death of Adam: evolution and its impact on western thought*, Ames, Iowa 1959, and Gerhard Heberer and Franz Schwanitz, eds., *Hundert Jahre Evolutionsforschung: das wissenschaftliche Vermächtnis Charles Darwins*, Stuttgart 1960.

**8638  ALEKSEEV** (VALERII ANDREEVICH). Osnovy darvinizma: istoricheskoe i teoreticheskoe vvedenie. Moscow. 1964.

For another Russian view see Georgii Vasil'evich Platonov, *Darvin, darvinizm i filosofiia*, Moscow 1959. There was also an extensive Russian lit. on the Darwin centenary.

**8639  LACK** (DAVID LAMBERT). Evolutionary theory and Christian belief: the unresolved conflict. 1957. Rev. edn. 1961.

See also his *Darwin's finches . . .*, Camb. 1947, N.Y. 1961.

**8640  BATESON.** William Bateson, F.R.S., naturalist: his essays & addresses, together with a short account of his life by Beatrice Bateson. Camb. 1928.

Bateson's career as the principal proponent of Mendel's views may be followed in Reginald Crundall Punnett, ed., *Scientific papers of William Bateson*, 2 v. Camb. 1928, and in Bateson's *Mendel's principles of heredity: a defence*, Camb. 1902, and *Problems of genetics*, New Haven & Lond. 1913. Some early letters were publ. in Beatrice Bateson, ed., *Letters from the Steppe written in the years 1886–1887*, 1928.

　　　GALTON. See **8746–7.**

**8641  MIVART.** A conscience in conflict: the life of St. George Jackson Mivart. By Jacob William Gruber. N.Y. 1960.

Anti-evolutionist.

## 2. AGRICULTURAL SCIENCE

**8642  RUSSELL** (*Sir* EDWARD JOHN). A history of agricultural science in Great Britain, 1620–1954. 1966.

**8643  MOULTON** (FOREST RAY) *ed.* Liebig and after Liebig: a century of progress in agricultural chemistry. Amer. Assoc. Advancement of Science Publ. 16. Wash. 1942.

Unfortunately Charles Albert Browne, *A source book of agricultural chemistry*, Chronica Botanica, Waltham, Mass. 1944, only goes down to 1852.

**8644 THE JOURNAL OF AGRICULTURAL SCIENCE.** Camb. 1905–6+.

See also *The journal of the South-Eastern Agricultural College, Wye, Kent*, 1895–1913, 1923, 1927+, J. W. Hurst, ed., *The annual register of agricultural experiments: with full abstracts, 1913*, 1914, and *The farmer's annual register . . . 1915*, 1915.

**8645 JOHNSTON (JAMES FINLAY WEIR).** Elements of agricultural chemistry and zoology. Edin. 1842. 12th edn. 1881.

Long the standard textbook.

**8646 CONSTABLE (JOHN)** *and others.* Practice with science: a series of agricultural papers. 2 v. 1867–9.

A very good coll. of papers on many agric. subjects.

**8647 RONNA (ANTOINE CONSTANT COLOMB).** Chimie appliquée à l'agriculture: travaux et expériences du Dr. A. Voelcker, chimiste-conseil, directeur du laboratoire de la Société Royale d'Agriculture d'Angleterre. 2 pts. in 1. Paris. 1886–8.

**8648 HALL (*Sir* ALFRED DANIEL).** The book of the Rothamsted experiments. 1905. 2nd edn. 1917.

Rothamsted was the main British centre for agric. experiments and publ. a stream of reports in *The Rothamsted memoirs . . .*, Harpenden 1863+, and elsewhere. There is a useful short hist. in Sir Edward John Russell, 'Rothamsted and its experimental station', *Agric. Hist.* xvi (1942), 161–83. Fuller accounts are Sir John Bennet Lawes and Sir Joseph Henry Gilbert, 'The Rothamsted experiments . . .', *Highland & Agric. Soc. Trans.* 5 ser. vii (1895), 11–354, repr. Edin. 1895; Edwin Grey, *Rothamsted experimental station: reminiscences . . . 1872–1922*, Harpenden [1922]; Sir Edward John Russell, *The land called me: an autobiography*, 1956; Antoine Constant Colomb Ronna, *Rothamsted: trente années d'expériences agricoles . . .*, Paris 1877, 2nd edn. 1900; Sir Joseph Henry Gilbert, *Agricultural experiments at Rothamsted . . .*, U.S. Dept. of Agric. Office of Experimental Stations Bull. 22, Wash. 1895; and Bernard Shirley Dyer, *Results of investigations on the Rothamsted soils*, U.S. Dept. of Agric. Office of Exper. Sta. Bull. 106, Wash. 1902.

**8649 RUSSELL (*Sir* EDWARD JOHN)** *and* **VOELCKER (JOHN AUGUSTUS).** Fifty years of field experiments at the Woburn Experimental Station . . . 1936.

**8650 PAWSON (HENRY CECIL).** Cockle Park Farm: an account of the work of the Cockle Park Experimental Station from 1896 to 1956. 1960.

**8651 HALL (*Sir* ALFRED DANIEL).** 'The agricultural experiments of the late Mr. James Mason'. *Roy. Agric. Soc. J.* lxv (1904), 106–24.

**8652 ELLIOT (ROBERT HENRY).** The agricultural changes required by these times and laying-down land to grass. 2nd edn. Kelso. 1901.

First publ. 1888. Best known under its later title, *The Clifton Park system of farming . . .*, 4th edn. Lond. 1908, 5th edn. 1943.

**8653  HALL.** Daniel Hall: pioneer of scientific agriculture. By Harold Edward Dale. 1956.

Hall was the leading man in the generation after Lawes and Gilbert at Rothamsted. His *The soil . . .*, 1903, 5th edn. 1945, *Fertilisers and manures*, 1909, 4th edn. 1947, and *The feeding of crops and stock . . .*, 1911, 3rd edn. 1944, sum up the advances of half a century.

**8654  WHITEHEAD.** Retrospections. By Sir Charles Whitehead. Maidstone. [1908.]

### 3. BOTANY

See also Horticulture (**4379–92**).

**8655  LINNEAN SOCIETY OF LONDON.** Catalogue of the printed books and pamphlets in the library. New edn. 1925.

The most useful gen. list suppl. by a *Catalogue of the manuscripts . . .*, 1934+. See also Royal Botanic Gardens, Kew, *Catalogue of the library*, 1899, suppl. 1919, and *Catalogue of portraits of botanists*, comp. by James D. Milner, 1906, and Wilfrid Jasper Walter Blunt, *The art of botanical illustration*, 1950.

**8656  SACHS (FERDINAND GUSTAV JULIUS VON).** History of botany, 1530–1860. Trans. by Henry Edward Fowler Garnsey and Isaac Bayley Balfour. Oxf. 1890. Repr. 1906.

Cont. by Joseph Reynolds Green, *A history of botany, 1860–1900 . . .*, Oxf. 1909. There are good outlines in Robert John Harvey-Gibson, *Outlines of the history of botany*, 1919, and Howard Sprague Reed, *A short history of the plant sciences*, Waltham, Mass. 1942.

**8657  ROBERTS (HERBERT FULLER).** Plant hybridization before Mendel. Princeton. 1929.

Incl. a chapter on post-Mendelian development.

**8658  WEEVERS (THEODORUS).** Fifty years of plant physiology. [1895–1945.] Amsterdam. 1949.

**8659  BRETSCHNEIDER (EMILII VASILEVICH).** History of European botanical discoveries in China. 2 v. 1898. Repr. Leipzig. 2 v. 1935 and 1962.

Still the best account. Reviews the extensive lit. by English plant-hunters.

**8660  WHETZEL (HERBERT HICE).** An outline of the history of phytopathology. Phila. 1918.

**8661  GREEN (JOSEPH REYNOLDS).** A history of botany in the United Kingdom from the earliest times to the end of the 19th century. 1914.

**8662  GAGE (ANDREW THOMAS).** A history of the Linnean Society of London. 1938.

8663  BEAN (WILLIAM JACKSON). The Royal Botanic Gardens, Kew: historical and descriptive. 1908.

Standard. See also the lives of the two Hookers (**8673**). There is an outline hist. in William Bertram Turrill, *The Royal Botanic Gardens, Kew: past and present*, 1959.

8664  KENT (DOUGLAS H.) *and others*. British herbaria: an index to the location of herbaria of British vascular plants, with biographical references to their collectors. Botanical Soc. 1957.

8665  BRITTEN (JAMES) *and* BOULGER (GEORGE SIMONDS) *comps*. A biographical index of British and Irish botanists. 1893. Suppls. 1899, 1905. 2nd edn. ed. by Alfred Barton Rendle. 1931.

8666  OLIVER (FRANCIS WALL) *and others*. Makers of British botany: a collection of biographies of living botanists. Camb. 1913.

8667  NELMES (ERNEST) *and* CUTHBERTSON (WILLIAM) *eds*. Curtis's magazine dedications, 1827–1927: portraits and biographical notes. Roy. Hort. Soc. [1932.]

Each vol. of *Curtis's magazine* (**8674**) included a portrait and a biog. sketch of a botanist or horticulturalist to whom the vol. was dedicated.

8668  BABINGTON. Memorials, journal and botanical correspondence of Charles Cardale Babington. Ed. by Anna Maria Babington with memoir by John Eyton Bickersteth Mayor. Camb. 1897.

8669  BENTHAM. George Bentham. By Benjamin Daydon Jackson. 1906.

8670  BOWER. Sixty years of botany in Britain (1875–1935): impressions of an eye-witness. By Frederic Orpen Bower. 1938.

8671  FORREST. The journeys and plant introductions of George Forrest, V.M.H. Ed. by John Macqueen Cowan. Roy. Horticultural Soc. 1952.

8672  GRAY. Asa Gray, 1810–1888. By Anderson Hunter Dupree. Camb., Mass. 1959.

Gray, the leading American botanist of his time, was closely assoc. with the work of Hooker and other British botanists. See also Jane Loring Gray, ed., *Letters of Asa Gray*, 2 v. N.Y. & Lond. 1893, and Charles Sprague Sargent, ed., *Scientific papers of Asa Gray*, 2 v. Boston & Lond. 1889.

8673  HOOKER. Life and letters of Sir Joseph Dalton Hooker, O.M., G.C.S.I., based on materials collected and arranged by Lady Hooker. By Leonard Huxley. 2 v. 1917. Corrected edn. 2 v. 1918.

Important. Bibliog. See also William Bertram Turrill, *Joseph Dalton Hooker: botanist, explorer and administrator*, 1963, Frederic Orpen Bower, *Joseph Dalton Hooker*, 1919, Mea Allan, *The Hookers of Kew, 1785–1911*, 1967, and Sir Joseph Dalton Hooker, 'A sketch of the life and labours of Sir William Jackson Hooker', *Annals of Botany* xvi (1902), ix–ccxx.

8674   [CURTIS'S] BOTANICAL MAGAZINE. 1+. 1787+.

Taken over by Sir W. J. Hooker, 1858. Hooker had earlier publ. *Botanical miscellany*, 1830–4, cont. as *The j. of botany*, 1834–42, *The London j. of botany*, 1842–8, and *Hooker's j. of botany and Kew Garden miscellany*, 1849–57. The other leading botanical js. were Linnean Soc., *Proceedings*, 1838+, and *Journal*, 1855+, *The [Trimen's] journal of botany, British and foreign*, 1863–1942, *Annals of botany*, Oxf. 1887+, Royal Botanic Gardens, Kew, *Bulletin*, 1887+, and Royal Botanic Soc., *Quarterly record*, 1880–1909, cont. as *The botanical j.*, 1910–18.


4. CHEMISTRY

For the chemistry industry see 5252–328.


8675   CRANE (EVAN JAY) *and* PATTERSON (AUSTIN MCDOWELL). A guide to the literature of chemistry. N.Y. 1927.

See also Henry Carrington Bolton, ed., *A select bibliography of chemistry, 1492–1892*, Smithsonian Instn., Wash. 1893, suppls. 1899, 1904, and *Academic dissertations, 1492–1897*, Wash. 1901., Denis Ian Duveen, *Bibliotheca alchemica et chemica: an annotated catalogue of printed books on alchemy, chemistry and cognate subjects in the library of Denis I. Duveen*, 1949, and Patent Office Libr., *Subject list of the works on chemistry (including alchemy, electro-chemistry and radio-activity)*, 1911.

8676   PARTINGTON (JAMES RIDDICK). A history of chemistry. 4 v. 1961–4.

Standard. Partington's *A short history of chemistry*, 1937, 3rd edn. 1960, is also valuable.

8677   IHDE (AARON JOHN). The development of modern chemistry. N.Y. 1964.

8678   LEICESTER (HENRY MARSHALL). The historical background of chemistry. N.Y. & Lond. 1956.

A valuable adjunct to H. M. Leicester and Herbert S. Klickstein, *A source book in chemistry, 1400–1900*, N.Y. 1952.

8679   FINDLAY (ALEXANDER). A hundred years of chemistry. 1937. 3rd edn. 1965.

See also his *Chemistry in the service of man*, 1916, 8th edn. 1957, Arthur John Berry, *Modern chemistry: some sketches of its historical development*, Camb. 1948, and *From classical to modern chemistry: some historical sketches*, Camb. 1954. Contemp. views are reflected in Sir William Augustus Tilden, *A short history of the progress of scientific chemistry in our own times*, 1899, 2nd edn. 1913, and *Chemical discovery and invention in the twentieth century* [1917], 6th edn. 1936.

8680   CLOW (ARCHIBALD) *and* CLOW (NAN LOUISE). The chemical revolution: a contribution to social technology. 1952.

8681   CHYMIA: annual studies in the history of chemistry. Phila. 1948+.

8682   RAMSAY (*Sir* WILLIAM). The gases of the atmosphere: the history of their discovery. 1896. 4th edn. 1915.

See also Morris William Travers, *The discovery of the rare gases*, 1928.

8683  WEEKS (MARY ELVIRA). The discovery of the elements. *Journal of Chemical Educ..* Easton, Penn. 1933. 7th edn. 1968.

See also John Albert Newton Friend, *Man and chemical elements: from Stone-Age hearth to the cyclotron,* 1951, 2nd edn. 1961.

8684  RUSSELL (COLIN ARCHIBALD). The history of valency. Lond. & N.Y. 1970.

8685  WHITE (JOHN HENRY). The history of the phlogiston theory. 1932.

8686  SCHONLAND (*Sir* BASIL FERDINAND JAMIESON). The atomists, 1805–1933. Oxf. 1968.

See also George M. Fleck, 'Atomism in late nineteenth-century physical chemistry', *J. Hist. Ideas* xxiv (1963), 106–14, and David Marcus Knight, *Atoms and elements: a study of theories of matter in England in the nineteenth century,* 1967.

8687  BROCK (WILLIAM HODSON) *ed.* The atomic debates: Brodie and the rejection of the atomic theory: three studies. Leicester. 1967.

8688  THORPE (*Sir* THOMAS EDWARD) *ed.* A dictionary of applied chemistry. 3 v. 1890–3. 4th edn. 12 v. 1937–56.

8689  CHAPMAN (ALFRED CHASTON). The growth of the profession of chemistry during the past half century, 1877–1927. 1927.

See also Alexander Findlay and William Hobson Mills, *British chemists,* 1947, Richard Bertram Pilcher, *The profession of chemistry,* 1919, 4th edn. 1938, and *A list of official chemical appointments,* 2nd edn. 1908.

8690  MOORE (TOM SIDNEY) *and* PHILIP (JAMES CHARLES). The Chemical Society, 1841–1941: a historical review. 1947.

8691  PILCHER (RICHARD BERTRAM). The Institute of Chemistry of Great Britain and Ireland: history of the Institute, 1877–1914. 1914.

8692  PLIMMER (ROBERT HENRY ADERS). The history of the Biochemical Society, 1911–1949. Biochemical Soc. 1949.

8693  HIGGINS (THOMAS JAMES). 'Book-length biographies of chemists'. *School Science & Maths.* xliv (1944), 650–65.

8694  FARBER (EDUARD). Great chemists. N.Y. & Lond. 1961.

See also Sir William Augustus Tilden, *Famous chemists: the men and their work,* 1921, Günther Bugge, *Das Buch der grossen Chemiker . . .,* 2 v. Berlin [1929–30], repr. 1955, and Eduard Farber, *Nobel prize winners in chemistry, 1901–1950,* N.Y. 1953, rev. edn. 1963.

8695  ARMSTRONG. Henry Edward Armstrong, 1848–1937: the doyen of British chemists and pioneer of technical education. By John Vargas Eyre. 1958.

8696 CROOKES. The life of Sir William Crookes, O.M., F.R.S. By Edmund Edward Fournier D'Albe. 1923.

See also Frank Greenaway, 'A Victorian scientist: the experimental researches of Sir William Crookes, 1832–1919', *Royal Institution Proc.* xxxix (1962–3), pt. 2, 172–98.

8697 DEWAR. James Dewar, 1842–1923: a lecture. By Henry Edward Armstrong. 1924.

See also Helen Rose, Lady Dewar, and others, eds., *The collected papers of Sir James Dewar*, 2 v., Camb. 1927, and Henry Young, comp., *A record of the scientific work of Sir James Dewar*, 1933.

8698 FRANKLAND. Sketches from the life of Edward Frankland, born January 18th, 1825, died August 19th, 1899. Ed. by his daughters. 1902.

8699 HOPKINS. Hopkins & biochemistry, 1861–1947: papers concerning Sir Frederick Gowland Hopkins . . . Ed. by Noel Joseph Terence Montgomery Needham and Ernest Baldwin. 1949.

8700 ODLING. 'William Odling, 1829–1921'. By John L. Thornton and Anna Wiles. *Annals of Science* xii (1956), 288–95.

8701 PLAYFAIR. Memoirs and correspondence of Lyon Playfair, first Lord Playfair of St. Andrews . . . By Sir Thomas Wemyss Reid. 1899.

See also Imperial College of Science and Technology, *List of the papers and correspondence of Lyon Playfair . . . preserved in the Imperial College archives*, 1967.

8702 RAMSAY. Sir William Ramsay, K.C.B., F.R.S., memorials of his life and work. By Sir William Augustus Tilden. 1918.

See also Morris William Travers, *A life of Sir William Ramsay, K.C.B., F.R.S.*, 1956.

8703 ROSCOE. The life & experiences of Sir Henry Enfield Roscoe, D.C.L., LL.D., F.R.S., written by himself. 1906.

See also Sir Thomas Edward Thorpe, *The Right Honourable Sir Henry Enfield Roscoe, P.C., D.C.L., F.R.S.: a biographical sketch*, 1916.

## 5. NATURAL PHILOSOPHY

8704 WILSON (WILLIAM). A hundred years of physics. 1950.

A useful intro. An earlier essay in the genre was Sir Oliver Joseph Lodge, *A century's progress in physics*, 1927. There are many general hists. See also the works on the Cavendish laboratory at **8100**.

8705 DAMPIER-WHETHAM (*Sir* WILLIAM CECIL). The recent development of physical science. 1904. 5th edn. 1924.

Cp. Sir Arthur Schuster, *The progress of physics during the thirty-three years, 1875–1908*, Camb. 1911.

8706 WHITTAKER (*Sir* EDMUND TAYLOR). From Euclid to Eddington: a study of conceptions of the external world. Camb. 1949.

8707 WHITTAKER (*Sir* EDMUND TAYLOR). A history of the theories of aether and electricity from the age of Descartes to the close of the nineteenth century. 1910. Rev. edn. 2 v. 1951.

Very full.

8708 BRITISH ASSOCIATION FOR THE ADVANCEMENT OF SCIENCE. Reports of the committee on electrical standards: a record of the history of absolute units and of Lord Kelvin's work in connection with these. Ed. by Frank Edward Smith. Camb. 1913.

8709 MACFARLANE (ALEXANDER). Lectures on ten British physicists of the 19th century. N.Y. 1919.

8710 JEANS (WILLIAM T.). Lives of the electricians: Professors Tyndall, Wheatstone and Morse. 1887.

Good.

8711 MACDONALD (DAVID KEITH CHALMERS). Faraday, Maxwell and Kelvin. Garden City, N.Y. 1964. Lond. 1965.

8712 TRICKER (RONALD ALFRED RANSON). The contributions of Faraday and Maxwell to electrical science. Oxf. etc. 1966.

8713 HEATHCOTE (NIELS HUGH DE VAUDREY). Nobel prize winners in physics, 1901–1950. N.Y. 1953.

8714 EDDINGTON. The life of Arthur Stanley Eddington. By Allie Vibert Douglas. 1956.

See also Herbert Dingle, *The sources of Eddington's philosophy*, Camb. 1954, John William Yolton, *The philosophy of science of A. S. Eddington*, The Hague 1960, Johannes Witt-Hansen, *Exposition and critique of the conceptions of Eddington concerning the philosophy of physical science*, Copenhagen 1958, and Jacques Merleau-Ponty, *Philosophie et théorie physique chez Eddington*, Paris 1965.

8715 FARADAY. The life and letters of Faraday. By Henry Bence Jones. 2 v. 1870.

The official life. Thomas Martin, ed., *Faraday's diary: being the various philosophical notes of experimental investigation made by Michael Faraday, D.C.L., F.R.S., during the years 1820–1862 . . .*, 7 v. and index, 1932–6, and Alan Edward Jeffreys, *Michael Faraday: a list of his lectures and published writings*, Royal Instn. 1960, are important. For letters see Leslie Pearce Williams, ed., *The selected correspondence of Michael Faraday*, 2 v., Camb. 1971. There are a number of good biog. studs. incl. Silvanus Phillips Thompson, *Michael Faraday: his life and work*, Lond. & N.Y. 1898; Leslie Pearce Williams, *Michael Faraday: a biography*, Lond. & N.Y. 1965; James Kendall, *Michael Faraday: man of simplicity*, Lond. & N.Y. 1955; Sir Robert Abbott Hadfield, *Faraday and his metallurgical researches . . .*, 1931; Thomas Martin, *Faraday's discovery of electromagnetic induction*, 1949; and Joseph Agassi, *Faraday as a natural philosopher*, Chicago 1971.

8716 FORBES. Life and letters of James David Forbes, F.R.S., D.C.L., LL.D., late principal of the United College in the University of St. Andrews

. . . By John Campbell Shairp, Peter Guthrie Tait and Anthony Adams-Reilly. 1873.

See also [R.N. Smart, comp.] *An index to the correspondence and papers of James David Forbes (1809–1868)* . . ., St. Andrews Univ. Libr. 1968. Forbes did important work on glaciers and had a wide correspondence.

8717   JOULE. Memoirs of James Prescott Joule. By Osborne Reynolds. Manch. 1892.

8718   KELVIN. The life of William Thomson, Baron Kelvin of Largs. By Silvanus Phillips Thompson. 2 v. 1910.

See also Andrew Gray, *Lord Kelvin: an account of his scientific life and work*, 1908, and Alexander Russell, *Lord Kelvin*, 1938. There is also a considerable pamphlet lit. about him.

8719   LODGE. Past years: an autobiography. By Sir Oliver Joseph Lodge. 1931.

See also Theodore Besterman, *A bibliography of Sir Oliver Lodge, F.R.S.*, 1935, and John Arthur Hill, ed., *Letters from Sir Oliver Lodge* . . ., 1932.

8720   MAXWELL. The life of James Clerk Maxwell, with a selection from his correspondence . . . By Lewis Campbell and William Garnett. 1882. Abridged edn. 1884.

Good. See also Sir Joseph Larmor, ed., *Origins of Clerk Maxwell's electric ideas, as described in familiar letters to William Thomson*, Camb. 1937; Sir Richard Tetley Glazebrook, *James Clerk Maxwell and modern physics*, 1896; Sir Joseph John Thomson and others, *James Clerk Maxwell: a commemoration volume, 1831–1931: essays*, Camb. 1931; Cyril Domb, ed., *Clerk Maxwell and modern science: six commemorative lectures by Edward V. Appleton* [and others], 1963; Henry T. Bernstein, 'J. Clerk Maxwell on the history of the kinetic theory of gases, 1871', *Isis* liv (1963), 206–16; and I. B. Hopley, 'Clerk Maxwell's apparatus for the measurement of surface tension', *Annals of Science* xiii (1957), 180–7, 'Maxwell's determination of the number of electrostatic units in one electromagnetic unit of electricity', ibid. xv (1959), 91–108, and 'Maxwell's work on electrical resistance', ibid. xiii (1957), 265–72; xiv (1958), 197–210; xv (1959), 51–5.

8721   RAYLEIGH. [Life of] John William Strutt, third Baron Rayleigh, O.M., F.R.S. By Robert John Strutt, 4th Baron Rayleigh. 1924. Rev. edn. Madison, Wis. 1968.

See also Rayleigh's *Scientific papers*, 6 v. Camb. 1899–1920, repr. 3 v. N.Y. 1964.

8722   RUTHERFORD. Rutherford: being the life and letters of Lord Rutherford. By Arthur Stewart Eve. Camb. 1939.

The official life, suppl. by Sir James Chadwick, ed., *The collected papers of Lord Rutherford of Nelson*, 3 v. 1962–5. See also Lawrence Badash, ed., *Rutherford and Boltwood: letters on radioactivity*, New Haven, Conn. 1969; Edward Neville da Costa Andrade, *Rutherford and the nature of the atom*, Garden City, N.Y. 1964, Lond. 1965; John Bettely Birks, ed., *Rutherford at Manchester*, N.Y. 1963; and three Russian studs., Danül Semenovich Danin, *Rezerford*, Moscow 1966, Fedor Borisovich Kedrov, *Ernest Rezerford*, Moscow 1965, and Olga Andreevna Starosel'skaia-Nikitina, *Ernest Rezerford, 1871–1937*, Moscow 1967.

8723  STOKES. Memoir and scientific correspondence of the late Sir George Gabriel Stokes, Bart. Ed. by Sir Joseph Larmor. 2 v. Camb. 1907.

8724  SWAN. Sir Joseph Wilson Swan, F.R.S.: a memoir. By Mary Edmonds Swan and Kenneth Raydon Swan. 1929.

8725  TAIT. Life and scientific work of Peter Guthrie Tait . . . By Cargill Gilston Knott. Camb. 1911.

Forms v. 3 of Tait's *Scientific papers*, 3 v., Camb. 1898–1911.

8726  THOMPSON. Silvanus Phillips Thompson, D.Sc., LL.D., F.R.S., his life and letters. By Jane Smeal Thompson and Helen Gertrude Thompson. 1920.

8727  THOMSON. The life of Sir J. J. Thomson, O.M., sometime Master of Trinity College, Cambridge. By Robert John Strutt, Baron Rayleigh. Camb. 1942.

The official life. Sir Joseph John Thomson himself publ. *Recollections and reflections*, Lond. 1936, N.Y. 1937. See also Sir George Paget Thomson, *J. J. Thomson and the Cavendish laboratory in his day*, Lond. 1964, N.Y. 1965.

8728  TYNDALL. The life and work of John Tyndall. By Arthur Stewart Eve and Clarence Hamilton Creasey. 1945.

See also James Bryant Conant, *Pasteur's and Tyndall's study of spontaneous generation*, Camb., Mass. 1953.

### 6. OTHER SCIENCES

8729  BRITISH MUSEUM (NATURAL HISTORY). Catalogue of the books, manuscripts, maps and drawings . . . 5 v. 1903–15. Suppl. 3 v. 1922–40.

A splendid work covering biology, zoology, entomology, geology, palaeontology, botany, mineralogy, and natural history. The *List of accessions to the library*, 1955+, is a useful suppl.

8730  ROYAL ASTRONOMICAL SOCIETY. Catalogue of the library. 3 pts. 1886–1925.

8731  ABETTI (GIORGIO). The history of astronomy. Trans. by Betty Burr Abetti. 1954.

8732  JOURNAL FOR THE HISTORY OF ASTRONOMY. 1+. 1970+.

8733  WATERFIELD (REGINALD LAWSON). A hundred years of astronomy. 1938.

Cp. Angus Armitage, *A century of astronomy*, 1950, and Herbert Hall Turner, *Modern astronomy: being some account of the revolution of the last quarter of a century*, 1901.

8734 DREYER (JOHN LOUIS EMIL) *and* TURNER (HERBERT HALL) *eds.* History of the Royal Astronomical Society, 1820–1920. 1923.

8735 AIRY. Autobiography of Sir George Biddell Airy. Ed. by Wilfrid Airy. Camb. 1896.

8736 BALL. Reminiscences and letters of Sir Robert Ball. Ed. by his son, Sir William Valentine Ball. Lond. & Boston. 1915.

8737 LOCKYER. The life and work of Sir Norman Lockyer. By Thomazine Mary Lockyer and Winifred L. Lockyer. 1928.

See also **7886,** and Arthur Jack Meadows, *Science and controversy: a biography of Sir Norman Lockyer,* Lond. & Camb., Mass. 1972.

8738 SINGER (CHARLES JOSEPH). A history of biology. 1950.

A rev. edn. of his *A short history of biology: a general introduction to the study of living things,* Oxf. 1931, publ. in N.Y. as *The story of living things* . . ., N.Y. 1931, 3rd edn. 1962.

8739 DAWES (BENJAMIN). A hundred years of biology. 1952.

8740 JOURNAL OF THE HISTORY OF BIOLOGY. 1+. Camb., Mass. 1968+.

8741 GOSSE. A bibliography of the first editions of Philip Henry Gosse, F.R.S. By Peter Stageman. Camb. 1955.

See also Sir Edmund William Gosse, *The life of Philip Henry Gosse, F.R.S.,* 1890, and *Father and son* . . ., 1907.

8742 OWEN. The life of Richard Owen . . . By Richard Startin Owen. 2 v. 1894. Repr. Farnborough. 1970.

8743 ESSIG (EDWARD OLIVER). History of entomology. N.Y. 1931.

8744 NEAVE (SHEFFIELD AIREY). The history of the Entomological Society of London, 1833–1933. 1933.

8745 ORMEROD. Eleanor Ormerod, LL.D., economic entomologist: autobiography and correspondence. Ed. by Robert Wallace. 1904.

8746 BLACKER (CARLOS PATON). Eugenics: Galton and after. Camb., Mass. 1952.

See also Egon Sharpe Pearson, *Karl Pearson: an appreciation of some aspects of his life and work,* Camb. 1938, and Eugenics [Education] Soc., *Eugenics rev.,* 1+, 1909+.

8747 GALTON. The life, letters and labours of Francis Galton. By Karl Pearson. 3 v. in 4. Camb. 1914–30.

See also Sir Francis Galton, *Memories of my life,* 1908.

8748   GEIKIE (*Sir* ARCHIBALD). The founders of geology. 1897. 2nd edn. 1905. Repr. N.Y. 1962.

Still standard. There are also a number of more recent studs., incl. Cecil Jack Schneer, ed., *Towards a history of geology*, Camb., Mass. 1969, and John Challinor, comp., *The history of British geology: a bibliographical study*, Newton Abbot 1971.

8749   LA ROCQUE (AURÈLE) *ed*. Contributions to the history of geology. 3 v. Columbus, Ohio. 1964.

A useful handbook.

8750   FLETT (*Sir* JOHN SMITH). The first hundred years of the Geological Survey of Great Britain. 1937.

8751   WOODWARD (HORACE BOLINGBROKE). The history of the Geological Society of London. 1907.

8752   SWEETING (GEORGE SCOTLAND) *ed*. The Geologists' Association, 1858–1958: a history of the first hundred years. 1958.

8753   CHORLEY (RICHARD JOHN), DUNN (ANTHONY JARRETT), *and* BECKINSALE (ROBERT PERCY). The history of the study of landforms: or, the development of geomorphology. V. 1. Lond. & N.Y. 1964.

See also Gordon L. Davies, *The earth in decay: a history of British geomorphology, 1578–1878*, 1969.

8754   DAVISON (CHARLES). The founders of seismology. Camb. 1927.

8755   DAVISON (CHARLES). A history of British earthquakes. Camb. 1924.

8756   BONNEY. Memories of a long life. By Thomas George Bonney. Camb. 1921.

8757   GEIKIE. A long life's work: an autobiography. By Sir Archibald Geikie. 1924.

See also his *Scottish reminiscences*, Glasgow 1904.

8758   LYELL. Life, letters and journals of Sir Charles Lyell, Bart. Ed. by Katharine Murray Lyell. 2 v. 1881.

See also Sir Edward Battersby Bailey, *Charles Lyell*, Lond. 1962, N.Y. 1963, Thomas George Bonney, *Charles Lyell and modern geology*, Lond. & N.Y. 1895, and Leonard G. Wilson, ed., *Sir Charles Lyell's scientific journals on the species question*, New Haven, Conn. 1970.

8759   PRESTWICH. Life and letters of Sir Joseph Prestwich, Professor of Geology in the University of Oxford. By his wife Grace Anne, Lady Prestwich. Edin. & Lond. 1899.

8760   RAMSAY. Memoir of Sir Andrew Crombie Ramsay. By Sir Archibald Geikie. 1895.

8761   SARTON (GEORGE ALFRED LEON). The study of the history of mathematics. Camb., Mass. 1936. Repr. N.Y. 1957.

8762   CAJORI (FLORIAN). A history of mathematics. N.Y. 1894. 2nd edn. 1919.

Suppl. by his *A history of mathematical notations*, 2 v. Chicago 1928–9.

8763   HIGGINS (THOMAS JAMES). 'Biographies and collected works of mathematicians'. *Amer. Math. Monthly* li (1944), 433–45. Suppl. lvi (1949), 310–12.

8764   MACFARLANE (ALEXANDER). Lectures on ten British mathematicians of the nineteenth century. N.Y. 1916.

See also Ganesh Prasad, *Some great mathematicians of the nineteenth century: their lives and works*, 2 v. Benares 1933–4.

8765   BABBAGE. Passages from the life of a philosopher. By Charles Babbage. 1864. Repr. 1968.

For biog. data see also Maboth Moseley, *Irascible genius: a life of Charles Babbage, inventor*, 1964, and Philip Morrison and Emily Morrison, eds., *Charles Babbage and his calculating engines*, N.Y. 1961. For scientific papers see Henry Prevost Babbage, *Babbage's calculating engines . . .*, 1889.

8766   FUNKHOUSER (HOWARD GRAY). 'Historical development of the graphical representation of statistical data'. *Osiris* iii (1937), 269–404.

8767   FITZPATRICK (PAUL J.). 'Leading British statisticians of the nineteenth century'. *Amer. Stat. Assoc. J.* lv (1960), 38–70.

8768   MACROSTY (HENRY WILLIAM). Annals of the Royal Statistical Society, 1834–1934. 1934.

See also John Biddulph Martin, 'On some developments of statistical research and methods during recent years', *Roy. Stat. Soc. J.* lix (1896), 579–628.

8769   MULLENS (WILLIAM HERBERT) *and* SWANN (HARRY KIRKE). A bibliography of British ornithology from the earliest times to the end of 1912: including, biographical accounts of the principal writers and bibliographies of their published works. 1916–17. Suppl. 1923.

Suppl. by a county-by-county survey by Mullens and others, *A geographical bibliography of British ornithology from the earliest times to the end of 1918 . . .*, 1919–20. See also Reuben Myron Strong, *A bibliography of birds . . .*, 3 v. Field Museum of Nat. Hist., Chicago 1939–46.

8770   IRWIN (RAYMOND). British bird books: an index to British ornithology, A.D. 1481 to A.D. 1948. 1951.

8771   THE ZOOLOGICAL RECORD . . . being the record of zoological literature relating to the year 1864+. Zoological Soc. of London. 1865+.

8772   INDEX DES ZOOLOGISTES. Union Internationale des Sciences Biologiques/International Union of Biological Sciences. Paris. 1953. Suppl. 1959.

8773 MITCHELL (*Sir* PETER CHALMERS). Centenary history of the Zoological Society of London . . . 1929.

There is a chapter on zoological socs. in Geoffrey Schomberg, *British zoos: a study of animals in captivity*, 1957.

8774 BUCKLAND. Life of Frank Buckland. By George Cox Bompas. 1885.

8775 FLOWER. Sir William Henry Flower, K.C.B., F.R.S., LL.D., D.C.L., late director of the National History Museum and president of the Royal Zoological Society: a personal memoir. By Charles John Cornish. 1904.

See also Richard Lydekker, *Sir William Flower*, 1906.

8776 MITCHELL. My fill of days. By Sir Peter Chalmers Mitchell. 1937.

8777 NEWTON. Life of Alfred Newton, Professor of Comparative Anatomy, Cambridge University, 1866–1907 . . . By Alexander Frederick Richmond Wollaston. 1921.

8778 ROMANES. The life and letters of George John Romanes, M.A., LL.D., F.R.S. Ed. by his wife, Ethel Romanes. 1896.

8779 SHERBORN. Squire: memories of Charles Davies Sherborn. By John Roxborough Norman. 1944.

8780 WOLLASTON. Letters and diaries of A. F. R. Wollaston. Ed. by Mary Wollaston. Camb. 1933.

8781 TEGETMEIER. A veteran naturalist: being, the life and work of W. B. Tegetmeier . . . By E. W. Richardson. 1916.

8782 THOMPSON. D'Arcy Wentworth Thompson, the scholar naturalist, 1860–1948. By Ruth D'Arcy Thompson. 1958.

8783 WATERTON. The strange life of Charles Waterton, 1782–1865. By Richard Aldington. 1949.

See also Philip Gosse, *The squire of Walton Hall: the life of Charles Waterton . . .*, 1940, and R. A. Irwin, ed., *Letters of Charles Waterton . . .*, 1955.

## F. MEDICINE

### 1. GENERAL

#### (a) *Reference*

8784 GARRISON (FIELDING HUDSON) *and* MORTON (LESLIE THOMAS). A medical bibliography: a check-list of texts illustrating the history of the medical sciences. 1943. 2nd edn. 1954. 3rd edn. 1970.

The best guide to the subject. See also Lee Ash, *Serial publications containing medical classics: an index to citations in Garrison–Morton: with, the story of the Garrison–Morton bibliography of medical classics*, by Leslie Taylor Morton, New Haven, Conn. 1961.

**8785** WELLCOME HISTORICAL MEDICAL LIBRARY. A catalogue of printed books. v. 1+. 1962+.

Arranged chronologically. Nothing on the 19th cent. so far. Suppl. by Wellcome Historical Libr., *Catalogue of western manuscripts on medicine and science*, v. 1+, 1962+. For a famous private libr. of medical hist. see Sir William Osler, *Bibliotheca Osleriana: a catalogue of books illustrating the history of medicine and science, collected, arranged and annotated by Sir William Osler, and bequeathed to McGill University*, ed. by William Willoughby Francis, Reginald Harrison Hill, and Archibald Malloch, Oxf. 1929.

**8786** WELLCOME HISTORICAL MEDICAL LIBRARY. Current work in the history of medicine. 1954+.

See also United States: National Libr. of Medicine, *Bibliography of the history of medicine*, 1964+, Wash. 1966+.

**8787** THORNTON (JOHN LEONARD), MONK (AUDREY J.), and BROOKE (ELAINE S.). A select bibliography of medical biography. Libr. Assoc. 1961. 2nd edn. 1970.

See also New York Academy of Medicine, *Catalog of biographies in the library*, Boston, Mass. 1960.

**8788** GILBERT (JUDSON BENNETT). Disease and destiny: a bibliography of medical references to the famous: with additions and intro. by Gordon E. Mestler. 1962.

**8789** THORNTON (JOHN LEONARD). Medical books, libraries and collectors: a study of bibliography and the book trade in relation to the medical sciences. 1949. 2nd edn. 1966.

The American equivalent is John Ballard Blake and Charles Roos, eds., *Medical reference works, 1679–1966: a selected bibliography*, Amer. Libr. Assoc., Chicago 1967. See also Leslie Thomas Morton, *How to use a medical library* . . ., 1934, 5th edn. 1971, Libr. Assoc. (Medical Section), *Directory of medical libraries in the British Isles*, 1957, 3rd edn. 1969, and Medical Libr. Assoc., *Directory* . . ., Chicago 1966.

**8790** U.S. WAR DEPARTMENT: SURGEON-GENERAL'S OFFICE. Index-catalogue of the library of the Surgeon-General's office, United States Army. 14 v. Wash. 1880–95. 2 ser. 21 v. 1896–1916. 3 ser. 10 v. 1918–32. 4 ser. 11 v. [A–Mn] 1936–55. 5 ser. 3 v. 1959–61. Cont. by suppls. to U.S. Libr. of Congress, Catalog. 1950+.

The catalogue of the greatest medical libr. in the world, now styled the National Libr. of Medicine. Covers periodical articles as well as books.

**8791** INTERNATIONAL HEALTH EXHIBITION, LONDON, 1884. Catalogue of the International Health Exhibition Library. 1884.

A very useful list for those working on the period.

**8792** LE FANU (WILLIAM RICHARD). British periodicals of medicine: a chronological list. Baltimore [Md.]. 1938.

See also his *List of the transactions, periodicals and memoirs in the library of the Royal College of Surgeons of England*, 1890, 2nd edn. 1931, and *Index medicus: a monthly classified record of the current medical literature of the world*, N.Y. 1879–1927, which was succeeded by American Medical Assoc., *Quarterly cumulative index medicus*, Chicago 1927+.

8793 BRITTAIN (ROBERT PETER). Bibliography of medico-legal works in English. 1962.

8794 BISHOP (WILLIAM JOHN) *comp.* Bibliography of international congresses of medical sciences. Oxf. 1958.

(b) *Histories, etc.*

See also Public Health (**7395–521**).

8795 SINGER (CHARLES JOSEPH) *and* UNDERWOOD (EDGAR ASHWORTH). A short history of medicine. 2nd edn. Oxf. 1962.
The fullest hist. for the period. 1st edn. by Singer alone, Oxf. 1928. Frederick Noel Lawrence Poynter and Kenneth David Keele, *A short history of medicine*, 1961, is a handy outline. Ralph Hermon Major, *A history of medicine*, 2 v. Oxf. 1955, is also useful.

8796 SHRYOCK (RICHARD HARRISON). The development of modern medicine: an interpretation of the social and scientific factors involved. Phila. 1936. Lond. 1948.
A social hist. of medicine.

8797 GARRISON (FIELDING HUDSON). An introduction to the history of medicine: with medical chronology, bibliographic data . . . Phila. 1913. 4th edn. 1929. Repr. 1960.
A valuable miscellany.

8798 LLOYD (WYNDHAM EDWARD BUCKLEY). A hundred years of medicine. 1936. New edn. by Cushman Davis Haagensen, N.Y. 1943. 2nd edn. Lond. 1968.

8799 UNDERWOOD (EDGAR ASHWORTH) *ed.* Science, medicine and history: essays on the evolution of scientific thought and medical practice, written in honour of Charles Singer. 2 v. 1953.
A splendid symposium. Sir [Vincent] Zachary Cope, ed., *Sidelights on the history of medicine*, 1957, is a smaller general collection of the same type.

8800 MAJOR (RALPH HERMON). Classic descriptions of disease: with biographical sketches of the authors. Springfield, Ill. etc. 1932. 3rd edn. 1945. Repr. 1959.
A series of extracts covering all periods.

8801 WILLIAMS (GREER). Virus hunters. 1960.
A hist. of research on diseases.

8802 MEDICAL HISTORY: a quarterly journal devoted to the history and bibliography of medicine and the related sciences. 1957+.
Specializes in British medical hist.

8803 JOURNAL OF THE HISTORY OF MEDICINE AND ALLIED SCIENCES. 1+. New Haven, Conn. 1946+.

8804 BULLETIN OF THE HISTORY OF MEDICINE. American Assoc. for the History of Medicine and Johns Hopkins Institute of the Hist. of Medicine. 1+. Baltimore [Md.]. 1933+.

First publ. as Johns Hopkins Univ., Inst. of the Hist. of Medicine, *Bulletin*, 1933–8.

8805 ANNALS OF MEDICAL HISTORY. N.Y. 1917–42. Index. 1946.

8806 WELLCOME HISTORICAL MEDICAL MUSEUM. Catalogue of an exhibition illustrating medicine in 1850. 1950.

8807 POYNTER (FREDERICK NOEL LAWRENCE) *ed.* Medicine and science in the 1860s: proceedings of the sixth British Congress on the History of Medicine . . . 1968.

8808 JARAMILLO-ARANGO (JAIME). The British contribution to medicine. Edin. & Lond. 1953.

8809 NEUBURGER (MAX). British medicine and the Vienna school: contacts and parallels. 1943.

8810 ROWLETTE (ROBERT JAMES). The *Medical Press and Circular*, 1839–1939: a hundred years in the life of a medical journal. 1939.

See also R. J. Rowlette and others, 'The *Medical Press and Circular* Centenary Number, 1839–1939', *Medical Press and Circular* cci, no. 4 (25 Jan. 1939), 62–123.

8811 JEFFS (ERNEST H.). The doctor abroad: the story of the medical missions of the London Missionary Society. 1934. 3rd edn. 1945.

8812 COPE (*Sir* VINCENT ZACHARY). Some famous general practitioners and other medical historical essays. 1961.

8813 THE LANCET. 1823+.

The leading medical j. See also *The Dublin medical press*, subsequently *The [London] medical press and circular*, 1839+, *Provincial medical and surgical j.*, subsequently *The British medical journal*, Worcester then Lond. 1840+, the official j. of the British Medical Assoc., which started life as the Provincial Medical and Surgical Assoc., and *The medical chronicle: a monthly record of the progress of the medical sciences*, Manch. 1844–1916.

2. THE MEDICAL PROFESSION

(a) *General*

8814 POYNTER (FREDERICK NOEL LAWRENCE) *ed.* The evolution of medical practice in Britain. First British Congress on the Hist. of Medicine. 1961.

8815 TURNER (ERNEST SACKVILLE). Call the doctor: a social history of medical men. 1958.

Popular. Sir Norman Moore, *The physician in English history*, Camb. 1913, is a short lecture.

8816 BRIGHTFIELD (MYRON F.). 'The medical profession in early Victorian England, as depicted in the novels of the period, 1840–1870'. *Bull. Hist. Medicine* xxxv (1961), 238–56.

8817 HORNER (NORMAN GERALD). The growth of the general practitioner of medicine in England. 1922.

8818 BELL (ENID HESTER CHATAWAY MOBERLY). Storming the citadel: the rise of the woman doctor. 1953.

See also Louisa Martindale, *The woman doctor and her future*, 1922, and Alice Horlock Bennett, *English medical women: glimpses of their work in peace and war*, 1915.

8819 BRAND (JEANNE L.). Doctors and the state: the British medical profession and government action, 1870–1912. Baltimore [Md.]. 1965.

8820 FLEMMING (PERCY). 'Harley Street' from early times to the present day. 1939.

8821 MAPOTHER (EDWARD DILLON). The medical profession and its educational and licensing bodies. Dublin. 1868.

8822 DE STYRAP (JUKES). The young practitioner: with practical hints . . . 1890.

See also his *A code of medical ethics . . .*, 1878, 4th edn. 1895.

8823 DALE (WILLIAM). The state of the medical profession in Great Britain and Ireland: with remarks on the preliminary moral education of medical and surgical students . . . Lond. 1860. New edn. Dublin. 1875.

See also Isaac Ashe, *Medical politics . . .*, Dublin 1875, and *Medical education and medical interests*, Dublin 1868; Thomas Laffan, *The medical profession in the three kingdoms in 1879*, Dublin 1879, and *The medical profession in the three kingdoms in 1887*, Dublin 1888; Walter Rivington, *The medical profession [of the United Kingdom]*, Dublin 1879, new edn. 1888; Ebenezer Diver, *The young doctor's future: or, what shall be my practice? Being some account of medical appointments*, 1881, 2nd edn. 1885; Charles West, *The profession of medicine: its study and practice, its duties and rewards . . .*, 1850, new edn. 1896; Robert Saundby, *Medical ethics: a guide to professional conduct*, Bristol 1902, 2nd edn. Lond. 1907; and Sir Samuel Squire Sprigge, *Medicine and the public*, 1905.

8824 FORSTER COMMITTEE ON MEDICAL ACT. Special report from the select committee on the Medical Act (1858) Amendment (No. 3) Bill [Lords] [Chairman: William Edward Forster]. H.C. 320 (1878–9). XII, 1. Further report. H.C. 121 (1880). IX, 431.

An important source for the hist. of the medical profession. Needs to be read with the equally extensive evidence gathered by the Camperdown commission.

8825  CAMPERDOWN COMMISSION ON MEDICAL ACTS. Report of the royal commissioners appointed to inquire into the Medical Acts [Chairman: Earl of Camperdown]. [C. 3259–I] H.C. (1882). XXIX, 489.

8826  WEBB (SIDNEY JAMES), *Baron Passfield, and* WEBB (BEATRICE). The state and the doctor. 1910.

8827  THE [LONDON AND PROVINCIAL] MEDICAL DIRECTORY. 1845+.

Titled *The London medical directory*, 1845–7, *The medical directory* . . ., 1870+.

8828  THE MEDICAL REGISTER: pursuant to an act . . . to regulate the qualifications of practitioners in medicine and surgery. 1859+.

The official list drawn up by the General Council of Medical Education, now the British Medical Council.

8829  POWER (*Sir* D'ARCY) *ed*. British medical societies. 1939.

8830  LITTLE (ERNEST MUIRHEAD). History of the British Medical Association, 1832–1932. [1932.]

See also the life of Hastings (**8883**), Paul Vaughan, *Doctors' Commons: a short history of the British Medical Association*, 1959, and Alfred Cox, *Among the doctors* [1950].

8831  CLARK (*Sir* GEORGE NORMAN) *and* COOKE (ALEXANDER MACDOUGALL). A history of the Royal College of Physicians of London. 3 v. Oxf. 1964–72.

See also Gordon Ethelbert Ward Wolstenholme, ed., *The Royal College of Physicians of London: portraits*, 1964.

8832  COPE (*Sir* [VINCENT] ZACHARY). The Royal College of Surgeons of England: a history. 1959.

See also Sir Ernest Finch, ed., *The history of the College Council Club, 1869–1958*, 1960.

8833  WALL (CECIL). A history of the Worshipful Society of Apothecaries of London. Arranged by Hector Charles Cameron and ed. by Edgar Ashworth Underwood. Wellcome Hist. Medical Museum. New ser. 8+, v. 1+. 1963+.

8834  DAVIDSON (MAURICE). The Royal Society of Medicine: the realization of an ideal (1805–1955). 1955.

8835  MOORE (*Sir* NORMAN) *and* PAGET (STEPHEN). The Royal Medical and Chirurgical Society of London: centenary, 1805–1905. Aberdeen. 1905.

8836  SHARPEY-SCHAFER (*Sir* EDWARD ALBERT). History of the Physiological Society during its first fifty years, 1876–1926. 1927.

8837 FORBES (ROBERT). Sixty years of medical defence. 1948.

A hist. of the Medical Defence Union, 1885–1945.

8838 O'MALLEY (CHARLES DONALD) ed. The history of medical education. Berkeley etc. 1970.

8839 NEWMAN (CHARLES EDWARD). The evolution of medical education in the nineteenth century. 1957.

See also Sir Norman Moore, *The history of the study of medicine in the British Isles,* Oxf. 1908, and Herbert Junius Hardwicke, *Medical education and practice in all parts of the world,* 1880.

8840 BROCKBANK (EDWARD MANSFIELD). The foundation of provincial medical education in England, and of the Manchester school in particular. Manch. 1936.

Good. For other provincial medical schools see [Kenneth Douglas Wilkinson, ed.] *The history of the Birmingham medical school, 1825–1925,* Birmingham 1925; Arthur Alexander Gemmell, *The Liverpool medical school, 1834–1934: a brief record,* Liverpool 1934; George Grey Turner assisted by William Drewett Arnison, *The Newcastle-upon-Tyne school of medicine, 1834–1934,* Newcastle-upon-Tyne 1934; William Smith Porter, *The medical school in Sheffield, 1828–1928,* Sheffield 1928; and Liverpool School of Tropical Medicine, *Historical record, 1898–1920,* 1920.

8841 LYLE (HERBERT WILLOUGHBY). King's and some King's men: being a record of the medical department of King's College, London, from 1830 to 1909, and of King's College Hospital medical school from 1909 to 1934. 1935.

For other London medical schools see Sir [Vincent] Zachary Cope, *The history of St. Mary's hospital medical school: or, a century of medical education,* 1954, Sir Herbert Campbell Thomson, *The story of the Middlesex hospital medical school . . .,* 1935, and Sir Philip Heinrich Manson-Bahr, *History of the School of Tropical Medicine in London (1899–1949),* London School of Hygiene & Tropical Medicine Memoirs 11, 1956. See also **7478.**

8842 DAVIDSON (MAURICE). Medicine in Oxford: a historical romance. Oxf. 1953.

See also Hugh MacGregor Sinclair and Alastair Hamish Tearloch Robb-Smith, *A short history of anatomical teaching in Oxford,* Oxf. 1950.

8843 ROLLESTON (*Sir* HUMPHRY DAVY). The Cambridge medical school: a biographical history. Camb. 1932.

Sir Walter Langdon Brown, *Some chapters in Cambridge medical history,* Camb. 1946, adds a little.

8844 TURNER (GEORGE GREY). The Hunterian museum: yesterday and to-morrow. 1946.

(b) *Collective Biography*

8845 MUNK (WILLIAM) comp. The roll of the Royal College of Physicians of London . . . [1518–1825.] 3 v. 1878.

Suppl. by G. H. Brown, comp., *The lives of the fellows of the Royal College of Physicians of London, 1826–1925,* 1955.

8846  PLARR (VICTOR GUSTAVE). Plarr's lives of the fellows of The Royal College of Surgeons of England. Rev. by Sir D'Arcy Power, Walter George Spencer, and George Ernest Gask. Royal College of Surgeons. 2 v. 1930. Suppl. for 1930–51. 1953.

See also William Le Fanu, *A catalogue of the portraits and other paintings, drawings and sculpture in the Royal College of Surgeons of England*, 1960.

8847  HALE-WHITE (*Sir* WILLIAM). Great doctors of the nineteenth century. 1935.

There are also some 19th-cent. doctors in Sir D'Arcy Power, *British masters of medicine*, 1936, Major Greenwood, *The medical dictator and other biographical studies*, 1936, and George Thomas Bettany, *Eminent doctors: their lives and their work*, 2 v. 1885.

8848  BARKER (THOMAS HERBERT) *and others*. Photographs of eminent medical men of all countries: with brief analytical notices of their works. 2 v. 1865–8.

8849  LEYLAND (JOHN) *ed*. Contemporary medical men and their professional work: biographies of leading physicians and surgeons, with portraits, from the 'Provincial Medical Journal'. 2 v. Leicester. 1888.

8850  HIRSCH (AUGUST). Biographisches Lexikon der hervorragenden Ärzte aller Zeiten und Völker . . . 2nd edn. 5 v. & suppl. Berlin. 1929–35.

Down to 1880. Suppl. for 1880–1930 by Isidor Fischer, *Biographisches Lexikon der hervorragenden Ärzte der letzten fünfzig Jahre*, 2 v. Berlin 1932–3.

8851  BAILEY (HENRY HAMILTON) *and* BISHOP (WILLIAM JOHN). Notable names in medicine and surgery. 1944. 3rd edn. 1959.

The best of a large class of books. See also Webb Edward Haymaker, ed., *The founders of neurology: one hundred and thirty-three biographical sketches*, Springfield, Ill. 1953; Borden Smith Veeder, ed., *Pediatric profiles*, St. Louis, Mo. 1957; Lloyd Grenfell Stevenson, *Nobel prize winners in medicine and physiology, 1901–1950*, N.Y. 1953, new edn. to 1965 by Theodore Lionel Sourkes, 1967; William Stirling, *Some apostles of physiology: being an account of their lives and labours . . .*, 1902; M. E. M. Walker, *Pioneers of public health: the story of some benefactors of the human race*, Edin. 1930; and John Hargreaves Harley Williams, *Doctors differ: five studies in contrast . . .*, 1946.

8852  DOBSON (JESSIE). Anatomical eponyms: being a biographical dictionary of those anatomists whose names have become incorporated into anatomical nomenclature . . . 1946. 2nd edn. 1962.

8853  MONRO (THOMAS KIRKPATRICK). The physician as man of letters, science & action. Glasgow. 1933. 2nd edn. Edin. & Lond. 1951.

A biographical dictionary arranged by subject.

8854  FULTON (JOHN FARQUHAR). The great medical bibliographers: a study in humanism. Phila. 1951.

(c) *Individual Biography*

8855  ACLAND. Sir Henry Wentworth Acland, Bart., K.C.B., F.R.S., Regius Professor of Medicine in the University of Oxford: a memoir. By James Beresford Atlay. 1903.

8856  ADAMI. J. George Adami, Vice-Chancellor of the University of Liverpool, 1919–26, sometime Strathcona Professor of Pathology, McGill University, Montreal: a memoir by Marie Adami, with contributions from his friends. 1930.

8857  ALLBUTT. The Right Honourable Sir Thomas Clifford Allbutt . . .: a memoir. By Sir Humphrey Davy Rolleston. 1929.

8858  ANDERSON. Elizabeth Garrett Anderson, 1836–1917. By her daughter, Louisa Garrett Anderson. 1939.
See also Joan Grenville Manton, *Elizabeth Garrett Anderson,* 1958.

8859  BARCROFT. Joseph Barcroft, 1872–1947. By Kenneth James Franklin. Oxf. 1953.

8860  BARRY. The strange story of Dr. James Barry, army surgeon, Inspector-General of Hospitals, discovered on death to be a woman. By Isobel Rae. 1958.
See also Olger Raester and Jessica Grove, *Dr. James Barry: her secret story,* 1932.

8861  BEDDOE. Memories of eighty years. By John Beddoe. Bristol. 1910.

8862  BELL. Sir Charles Bell: his life and times. By Gordon Gordon-Taylor and Eldred Wright Walls. Edin., Lond., & Baltimore [Md.]. 1958.

8863  BLACKWELL. Pioneer work in opening the medical profession to women: autobiographical sketches. By Elizabeth Blackwell. 1895. New edn. [1914.]
See also Peggy Chambers, *A doctor alone: a biography of Elizabeth Blackwell, the first woman doctor, 1821–1910,* 1956; Ishbel Ross, *Child of destiny: the life story of the first woman doctor,* 1950; Laura Kerr, *Doctor Elizabeth,* N.Y. 1946; and Rachel Baker, *The first woman doctor: the story of Elizabeth Blackwell, M.D.,* 1939.

8864  BLAND-SUTTON. The story of a surgeon. By Sir John Bland-Sutton. 1930.
See also Walter Reginald Bett, *Sir John Bland-Sutton, 1855–1936,* Edin. 1956.

8865  BROADBENT. Life of Sir William Broadbent, physician extraordinary to H. M. Queen Victoria, physician in ordinary to the King and to the Prince of Wales. Ed. by Mary Ethel Broadbent. 1909.

8866  BRODIE. Autobiography. By Sir Benjamin Collins Brodie. Ed. by his son, Sir Benjamin Collins Brodie. 1865. 2nd edn. 1865.
See also Timothy Holmes, *Sir Benjamin Collins Brodie,* 1898.

8867   BROWNE. Sir George Buckston Browne. By Jessie Dobson and Sir Cecil Pembrey Grey Wakeley. Edin. 1957.

8868   BUDD. William Budd, M.D., Edin., F.R.S., the Bristol physician and epidemiologist [1811–80]. By Edward Wilberforce Goodall. Bristol. 1936.

8869   CHRISTISON. The life of Sir Robert Christison, Bart. Ed. by his sons. 2 v. Edin. 1885–6.

8870   CLARKE. Autobiographical recollections of the medical profession. By James Fernandez Clarke. 1874.

8871   CLARKE. William Fairlie Clarke: his life and letters, hospital sketches and addresses. By Eliza Ann Walker. 1885.

8872   CONOLLY. A memoir of John Conolly, M.D., D.C.L.: comprising a sketch of the treatment of the insane in Europe and America. By Sir James Clark. 1869.

8873   COX. William Sands Cox and the Birmingham medical school. By James Thomas Jackman Morrison. Birmingham. 1926.

8874   DAWSON. Dawson of Penn. By Francis Leslie Watson. 1950.

8875   DUNCAN. James Matthews Duncan: a sketch for his family. By Isabella Newlands. Priv. pr. 1891.

8876   EURICH. Dr. Eurich of Bradford. By Margaret Bligh. 1960.

8877   FLETCHER. The bright countenance: a personal biography of Walter Morley Fletcher. By Mary Frances, Lady Fletcher. 1957.

8878   GAIRDNER. Life of Sir William Tennant Gairdner, K.C.B., M.D., LL.D., F.R.S., Regius Professor of Practice of Medicine in the University of Glasgow. By George Alexander Gibson. 1912.

8879   GOWERS. Sir William Gowers, 1845–1915: a biographical appreciation. By Macdonald Critchley. 1949.

8880   HALFORD. The life of Sir Henry Halford, Bart. By William Munk. 1895.

8881   HALL. Memoirs of Marshall Hall. By his widow, Mrs. Charlotte Hall. 1861.

8882   HARLEY. George Harley, F.R.S.: the life of a London physician. Ed. by Ethel Brilliana Tweedie (Mrs. Alec Tweedie). 1899.

8883 HASTINGS. The life and times of Sir Charles Hastings, founder of the British Medical Association. By William Henry McMenemey. Edin. & Lond. 1959.

8884 HOLLAND. Recollections of past life. By Sir Henry Holland. 1872. 3rd edn. 1872.

See also his *Fragmentary papers* . . ., ed. by Francis James Holland, 1875.

8885 HORSLEY. Sir Victor Horsley: a study of his life and work. By Stephen Paget. 1919.

8886 HURST. A twentieth-century physician: being the reminiscences of Sir Arthur [Frederick] Hurst. 1949.

8887 HUTCHINSON. Jonathan Hutchinson: life and letters. By Herbert Hutchinson. 1946.

See also Joseph V. Klauder, 'Sir Jonathan Hutchinson', *Medical Life* xli (1934), 313–26.

8888 JEX-BLAKE. The life of Sophia Jex-Blake. By Margaret Georgina Todd. 1918.

A militant feminist who founded the London School of Medicine for Women.

8889 JONES. An autobiography. By Henry Bence Jones. 1929.

8890 JONES. The life of Robert Jones. By Frederick Watson. 1934.

8891 KEITH. An autobiography. By Sir Arthur Keith. 1950.

8892 LANE. Sir William Arbuthnot Lane, Bt.: an enquiry into the mind and influence of a surgeon. By Thomas Bramley Layton. 1956.

See also William Edward Tanner, *Sir W. Arbuthnot Lane: his life and work*, 1946.

8893 LISTER. A list of the original writings of Joseph, Lord Lister, O.M. Comp. by William Richard Le Fanu. Edin. & Lond. 1965.

8894 LISTER. Lord Lister. By Sir Rickman John Godlee. 1917. 3rd edn. Oxf. 1924.

See also [Sir Hector Clare Cameron, ed.] *The collected papers of Joseph, Baron Lister*, 2 v. Oxf. 1909, and *Reminiscences of Lister and of his work in the wards of the Glasgow Royal Infirmary, 1860–1869*, Glasgow 1927; Hector Charles Cameron, *Joseph Lister, the friend of man*, 1948; Charles John Samuel Thompson, *Lord Lister, the discoverer of antiseptic surgery*, 1934; Sir William Watson Cheyne, *Lister and his achievement*, 1925; John Rudd Leeson, *Lister as I knew him*, 1927; Douglas James Guthrie, *Lord Lister: his life and doctrine*, Edin. 1949; Rhoda Truax, *Joseph Lister: father of modern surgery*, Indianapolis, Ind., and N.Y. 1944, Lond. 1947; and Guy Theodore Wrench, *Lord Lister: his life and work*, 1913. There is also [Alfred Ernest Maylard and others] *Lister and the Lister ward in the Royal Infirmary of Glasgow: a centenary contribution*, Glasgow 1927.

8895 MACKENZIE. The beloved physician, Sir James Mackenzie: a biography. By Robert McNair Wilson. 1926.

8896 MACKENZIE. Sir Morell Mackenzie, physician and operator: a memoir compiled and edited from private papers and personal reminiscences. By Hugh Reginald Haweis. 1893. 2nd edn. 1894.

See also Robert Scott Stevenson, *Morell Mackenzie: the story of a Victorian tragedy,* 1946.

8897 MANSON. Patrick Manson, the father of tropical medicine. By Sir Philip Heinrich Manson-Bahr. 1962.

There is also Sir Philip Heinrich Manson-Bahr and Alfred William Alcock, *The life and work of Sir Patrick Manson,* 1927.

8898 MARSDEN. Surgeon compassionate: the story of Dr. William Marsden, founder of the Royal Free and Royal Marsden Hospitals. By Frieda Sandwith. 1960.

8899 MARTIN. Inspector-General Sir James Ronald Martin. By Sir Joseph Fayrer. 1897.

8900 MARTINDALE. A woman surgeon. By Louisa Martindale. 1951.

8901 MOYNIHAN. Berkeley Moynihan, surgeon. By Donald Scrimgeour Bateman. 1940.

8902 OSLER. The life of Sir William Osler. By Harvey Williams Cushing. 2 v. Oxf. 1925. New edn. 1940.

See also Maude Elizabeth Seymour Abbott, ed., *Classified and annotated bibliography of Sir William Osler's publications based on the chronological bibliography of Minnie Wright Blogg,* 2nd edn. Montreal 1939, Walter Reginald Bett, *Osler: the man and the legend,* 1951, Edith Gittings Reid, *The great physician: a short life of Sir William Osler,* N.Y. 1931, and Anne Wilkinson, *Lions in the way: a discursive history of the Oslers,* 1957.

8903 PAGET. Memoirs and letters of Sir James Paget. Ed. by Stephen Paget. 1901. 3rd edn. 1903.

8904 PARKER. William Kitchen Parker, F.R.S., sometime Hunterian Professor of Anatomy and Physiology in the Royal College of Surgeons of England: a biographical sketch. By Thomas Jeffery Parker. 1893.

8905 PHILIP. Sir Robert W. Philip, 1857–1939: memories of his friends and pupils one hundred years after his birth. Nat. Soc. for the Prevention of Tuberculosis. 1957.

8906 RICHARDSON. Vita medica: chapters of medical life and work. By Sir Benjamin Ward Richardson. 1897.

See also Sir Arthur Salusbury MacNalty, *A biography of Sir Benjamin Ward Richardson,* 1950.

8907 ROSS. Memoirs of Sir Ronald Ross: with a full account of the great malaria problem and its solution. 1923.

See also his *Studies on malaria*, 1928, Rodolphe Louis Mégroz, *Ronald Ross: discoverer and creator*, 1931, and John Rowland, *The mosquito man: the story of Sir Ronald Ross*, 1958.

8908 SANDERSON. Sir John Burdon Sanderson: a memoir. By [Lady] Ghetal Herschell Burdon Sanderson, completed by John Scott Haldane and Elizabeth Sanderson Haldane. Oxf. 1911.

8909 SEMON. The autobiography of Sir Felix Semon. Ed. by Henry Charles Gustavus Semon and Thomas A. McIntyre. [1926.]

8910 SHERRINGTON. Sherrington: physiologist, philosopher and poet. By Henry Cohen, Baron Cohen of Birkenhead. Liverpool. 1958.

8911 SIMPSON. Memoir of Sir James Young Simpson, Bart. By John Duns. Edin. 1873.

See also Henry Laing Gordon, *Sir James Young Simpson and chloroform (1811–1870)*, 1897 and **10068**.

8912 SMEE. Memoir of the late Alfred Smee: by his daughter [Elizabeth Mary Odling]: with a selection from his . . . writings. 1878.

8913 SMITH. Sir Grafton Elliot Smith: a biographical record by his colleagues. Ed. by Warren Royal Dawson. 1938.

8914 SOUTH. Memorials of John Flint South, collected by Charles Lett Feltoe. 1884.

8915 SYME. Memorials of the life of James Syme, Professor of Clinical Surgery in the University of Edinburgh. By Robert Paterson. Edin. 1874.

See also **10068**.

8916 TAIT. Lawson Tait, his life and work: a contribution to the history of abdominal surgery and gynaecology. By William John Stewart McKay. 1922.

See also Isaac Harvey Flack, *Lawson Tait, 1845–1899*, 1949.

8917 TAYLOR. The diary of a medical student during the mid-Victorian period, 1860–1864. By Shephard Thomas Taylor. Norwich. 1927.

8918 THOMAS. Hugh Owen Thomas: his principles and practice. By David McCrae Aitken. Oxf. 1935.

See also Abraham David Le Vay, *The life of Hugh Owen Thomas*, Edin. 1956, and Frederick Watson, *Hugh Owen Thomas: a personal study*, 1934.

8919 THOMPSON. The versatile Victorian: being, the life of Sir Henry Thompson, Bt., 1820–1904. By Sir [Vincent] Zachary Cope. 1951.

8920  THUDICHUM. Thudichum: chemist of the brain. By David Lion Drabkin. Phila. 1958.

8921  TURNER. Memoir of Thomas Turner, Esq., F.R.C.S., F.L.S. By a relative. Manch. 1875.

8922  WAKLEY. The life and times of Sir Thomas Wakley, founder and first editor of the 'Lancet', member of parliament for Finsbury and coroner for West Middlesex. By Sir Samuel Squire Sprigge. 1897.

See also Charles Wortham Brook, *Battling surgeon*, Glasgow 1945.

8923  WELLS. Spencer Wells: the life and work of a Victorian surgeon. By John Alfred Shepherd. Edin. & Lond. 1965.

8924  WRIGHT. Almroth Wright: provocative doctor and thinker. By Leonard Colebrook. 1954.

See also Colebrook's *Bibliography of the published writings of Sir Almroth E. Wright*, 1952.

### 3. The Main Branches of Medicine

8925  KEELE (KENNETH DAVID). The evolution of clinical methods in medicine. 1963.

8926  COPE (*Sir* [VINCENT] ZACHARY). A history of the acute abdomen. 1965.

See also his *Pioneers in acute abdominal surgery*, 1939.

8927  DUNCUM (BARBARA MARY). The development of inhalation anaesthesia, with special reference to the years, 1846–1900. Wellcome Hist. Medical Museum new ser. 2. 1947.

For background see Frederick Fox Cartwright, *The English pioneers of anaesthesia: Beddoes, Davy and Hickman*, Bristol 1952.

8928  SYKES (WILLIAM STANLEY). Essays on the first hundred years of anaesthesia. 2 v. Edin. & Baltimore [Md.]. 1960–1.

8929  BULLOCH (WILLIAM). The history of bacteriology. 1938. Repr. 1960.

8930  BALLANCE (*Sir* CHARLES ALFRED). A glimpse into the history of the surgery of the brain. 1922.

8931  HANDLEY (WILLIAM SAMPSON) *ed*. Cancer research at the Middlesex hospital, 1900–1924: retrospect and prospect. 1924.

8932  EAST (CHARLES FREDERICK TERENCE). The story of heart disease. [1958.]

8933 HIMES (NORMAN EDWIN). Medical history of contraception. Baltimore [Md.]. 1936. Repr. 1963.

8934 PUSEY (WILLIAM ALLEN). The history of dermatology. Springfield, Ill. & Lond. 1933.

8935 ROLLESTON (*Sir* HUMPHRY DAVY). The endocrine organs in health and disease: with an historical review. 1936.

8936 STEVENSON (ROBERT SCOTT) *and* GUTHRIE (DOUGLAS JAMES). A history of oto-laryngology. Edin. 1949.

8937 KERR (JOHN MARTIN MUNRO) *and others, eds.* Historical review of British obstetrics and gynaecology, 1800–1950. Edin. & Lond. 1954.

Standard. Harvey Graham, pseud. of Isaac Harvey Flack, *Eternal Eve,* 1950, is popular. See also Harold Speert, *Obstetric and gynecologic milestones: essays in eponymy,* N.Y. 1958, and John Harley Young, *Caesarian section: the history and development of the operation from earliest times,* 1944.

8938 DUKE-ELDER (*Sir* [WILLIAM] STEWART). A century of international ophthalmology (1857–1957): written at the request of the International Council of Ophthalmology. 1958.

8939 FOSTER (WILLIAM DEREK). A history of parasitology. Edin. & Lond. 1965.

8940 LONG (ESMOND RAY). A history of pathology. Baltimore [Md.] & Lond. 1928.

See also William Derek Foster, *A short history of clinical pathology,* Edin. & Lond. 1961.

8941 BROOKS (CHANDLER McCUSKEY) *and* CRANEFIELD (PAUL FREDERIC). The historical development of physiological thought: a symposium . . . N.Y. 1959.

8942 HUNTER (RICHARD ALFRED) *and* MACALPINE (IDA) *comps.* Three hundred years of psychiatry, 1535–1860: a history presented in selected English texts. 1963.

8943 ALEXANDER (FRANZ GABRIEL) *and* SELESNICK (SHELDON THEODORE). The history of psychiatry: an evaluation of psychiatric thought and practice from prehistoric times to the present. N.Y. 1966. Lond. 1967.

8944 LEIGH (DENIS). The historical development of British psychiatry. 3 v. Oxf. 1961+.

8945 FLUGEL (JOHN CARL). A hundred years of psychology, 1833–1933. 1933. 2nd edn. 1951.

8946   HEARNSHAW (LESLIE SPENCER). A short history of British psychology, 1840–1940. Lond. & N.Y. 1964.

8947   YOUNG (ROBERT MAXWELL). Mind, brain and adaptation in the nineteenth century: cerebral localization and its biological context from Gall to Ferrier. Oxf. 1970.

8948   SOFFER (REBER NUSBAUM). 'New elitism: social psychology in prewar England'. *J. British Studs.* viii (1968–9), pt. 2, 110–40.

8949   WALKER (NIGEL). A short history of psychotherapy in theory and practice. 1957.

8950   LIDDELL (EDWARD GEORGE TANDY). The discovery of reflexes. Oxf. 1960.

8951   ALLISON (RICHARD SYDNEY). Sea diseases: the story of a great natural experiment in preventive medicine in the Royal Navy. 1943.
For naval medicine see also **2904.**

8952   HURWITZ (ALFRED) *and* DEGENSHEIN (GEORGE AARON). Milestones in modern surgery. N.Y. & Lond. 1958.

8953   LASSEK (ARTHUR MARVEL). Human dissection: its drama and struggle. Springfield, Ill. 1958.
A hist. of dissection in medical schools.

8954   THOMPSON (CHARLES JOHN SAMUEL). The history and evolution of surgical instruments. N.Y. 1942.

8955   BISHOP (WILLIAM JOHN). A history of surgical dressings. Chesterfield. 1959.

8956   SCOTT (*Sir* HENRY HAROLD). A history of tropical medicine. 2 v. 1939.
See also **8897**, Sir Leonard Rogers, *Happy toil: fifty-five years of tropical medicine,* 1950, and Sir Neil Cantlie and George Fenn Seaver, *Sir James Cantlie: a romance in medicine,* 1939.

#### 4. RELATED ACTIVITIES

##### (a) *Dentistry*

8957   COLES (JAMES OAKLEY) *comp.* A list of works on dentistry, published between the years 1536 and 1882: with a catalogue of the periodical literature relating to the profession from 1839–1882. British Dental Assoc. 1883.
The fullest bibliog. is Bernhard Wolf Weinberger, comp., *Dental bibliography: index to the literature of dental science . . .*, N.Y. Acad. of Medicine Libr., 2nd edn. 2 v. N.Y. 1929–32.

8958　BLACK (ARTHUR DAVENPORT). Index of the perio dical dental literature published in the English language [1839–1936/8]. Dental I ndex Bureau, Buffalo & Amer. Dental Assoc., Chicago. 15 v. 1921–39.

8959　THE DENTISTS' REGISTER: published under the direction of the General Council of Medical Education. Annual. 1879+.

8960　WEINBERGER (BERNHARD WOLF). An introduction to the history of dentistry, with medical and dental chronology and bibliographic data. 2 v. St. Louis [Mo.]. 1948.

Vol. 2 covers the U.S. There is some further material in Charles Rudolph Edward Koch, ed., *History of dental surgery*, 3 v. Fort Wayne, Ind. 1910. Of the short hists. the best are probably Lilian Lindsay, *A short history of dentistry*, 1933, 2nd edn. 1938, and Edwin Maurice Smith, *A short history of dentistry*, 1958.

8961　CAMPBELL (JOHN MENZIES). From a trade to a profession: byways in dental history. 1958.

8962　BRITISH DENTAL ASSOCIATION. The jubilee book of the British Dental Association. 1930.

8963　HILL (ALFRED). The history of the reform movement in the dental profession in Great Britain during the last twenty years. 1877.

8964　TOMES. Sir John Tomes: a pioneer of British dentistry. By Sir [Vincent] Zachary Cope. 1961.

### (b) *Veterinary Medicine*

8965　ROYAL COLLEGE OF VETERINARY SURGEONS. Memorial library: catalogue of modern works, 1900–1954. 2nd edn. 1955. Suppls. 1957+.

8966　ROYAL COLLEGE OF VETERINARY SURGEONS. The register of veterinary surgeons from January 1794 to May 1858 inclusive. 1858. Publ. irregularly until 1884, annually 1884+.

Contemp. js. incl. *The veterinarian*, 1828–1902, *The veterinary j* . . ., later *The British veterinary j.*, 1875+, and *The veterinary record*, 1888+.

8967　FLEMING (GEORGE). Animal plagues: their history, nature and prevention. 2 v. 1871–82.

There is an enormous lit. on this subject. But see particularly James Howard, 'Foot-and-mouth disease: its history and teachings', *Roy. Agric. Soc. J.* xlvii (1886), 1–18.

8968　MINISTRY OF AGRICULTURE, FISHERIES AND FOOD. Animal health: a centenary, 1865–1965: a century of endeavour to control diseases of animals. H.M.S.O. 1965.

Comprehensive. See also British Veterinary Assoc., *A history of the overseas veterinary services*, pt. 1 ed. by Geoffrey Philip West, 1961.

8969 VETERINARY DEPARTMENT OF THE PRIVY COUNCIL. Report on the cattle plague in Great Britain during the years 1865, 1866, and 1867. [4060] H.C. (1867–8). XVIII, 219.

There is also a prelim. report on 1865–6 at [3653] H.C. (1866). LIX, 323. See also Arvel Benjamin Erickson, 'The cattle plague in England, 1865–1867', *Agric. Hist.* xxxv (1961), 94–103, Sherwin A. Hall, 'The great cattle plague of 1865', *Medical Hist.* vi (1962), 45–58, and John George Gamgee, *The cattle plague . . .*, 1866.

The cattle plague (rinderpest) set off a series of inquiries which elicited a great deal of material on the English cattle industry and the importation of cattle. The main reports are *Report from the select committee on trade in animals* [Chairman: T. Milner Gibson]. H.C. 427 (1866). XVI, 423; *First report of the commissioners appointed to inquire into the origin and nature, &c., of the cattle plague* [Chairman: Earl Spencer]. [3591] H.C. (1866). XXII, 1; *Second report.* [3600] H.C. (1866). XXII, 227; *Third report.* [3656] H.C. (1866). XXII, 321; *Report of the committee appointed by the Lord President of the Council to consider the powers entrusted to the Privy Council . . . and to suggest the best mode of carrying into effect the provisions . . . relative to the transit of animals by sea and land* [Chairman: Arthur Helps]. [C. 116] H.C. (1870). LXI, 1; *Report from the select committee on contagious diseases (animals)* [Chairman: W. E. Forster]. H.C. 353 (1873). XI, 189; *Report from the select committee on cattle plague and importation of livestock* [Chairman: Sir H. Selwin-Ibbetson]. H.C. 362 (1877). IX, 1; *Report from the select committee of the House of Lords on the Contagious Diseases (Animals) Bill* [Chairman: Duke of Richmond]. H.C. 154 (1878). XI, 71. See also the earlier *Report from the select committee on Cattle Diseases Prevention and Cattle &c. Importation Bills* [Chairmen: H. A. Bruce and T. G. Baring]. H.C. 431 (1864). VII, 1 and **8968**.

8970 WILSON COMMITTEE ON PLEURO-PNEUMONIA &c. Report of the departmental committee to inquire into pleuro-pneumonia and tuberculosis in the United Kingdom [Chairman: Jacob Wilson]. [C. 5461] H.C. (1888). XXXII, 267. Minutes of evidence. [C. 5461–I] H.C. (1888). XXXII, 295.

8971 FITZMAURICE COMMITTEE ON SWINE FEVER. Report of the departmental committee appointed by the Board of Agriculture to inquire into swine fever [Chairman: Lord Edmond Fitzmaurice]. [C. 6999] H.C. (1893–4). XXIII, 175. Minutes of evidence. [C. 6999–I] H.C. (1893–4). XXIII, 183.

8972 WHITMORE COMMITTEE ON DOG LAWS. Report of the departmental committee appointed by the Board of Agriculture to inquire into and report upon the working of the laws relating to dogs [Chairman: Charles Algernon Whitmore]. [C. 8320] H.C. (1897). XXXIV, 1. Minutes of evidence. [C. 8378] H.C. (1897). XXXIV, 17.

See also *Report from the select committee of the House of Lords on rabies in dogs* [Chairman: Viscount Cranbrook]. H.C. 322 (1887). XI, 451.

8973 HOPKINSON COMMITTEE ON PUBLIC VETERINARY SERVICES. Report of the departmental committee appointed by the President of the Board of Agriculture and Fisheries to inquire into the requirements of the public services with regard to officers possessing veterinary qualifications [Chairman: Sir Alfred Hopkinson]. [Cd. 6575] H.C. (1912–13). XLVIII, 251. Evidence. [Cd. 6652] H.C. (1912–13). XLVIII, 267.

(c) *Pharmacy*

8974 CRELLIN (JOHN KEITH). 'Pharmaceutical history and its sources in the Wellcome collections. 1. The growth of professionalism in nineteenth-century British pharmacy'. *Medical Hist.* xi (1967), 215–27. 2. 'Drug weighing in Britain, c. 1700–1900'. By J. K. Crellin and J. R. Scott. Ibid. xiii (1969), 51–67.

The leading contemp. js. were *The chemist and druggist*, 1859+, and *The British and colonial druggist* [*pharmacist*], 1884+, each of which issued a useful yearbook. For drug descriptions see the *British pharmacopoeia*, annual, 1858+.

8975 MATTHEWS (LESLIE GERALD). History of pharmacy in Britain. Edin. & Lond. 1962.

George Edward Trease, *Pharmacy in history*, 1964, is more general. Thomas Edward Wallis, *History of the School of Pharmacy, University of London*, 1964, covers the College of the Pharmaceutical Soc., 1842–1925. For the law see Hugh Hale Leigh Bellot, *The Pharmacy Acts, 1851 to 1908*, 1908. For a major supplier of pharmaceuticals see Ernest Charles Cripps, comp., *Plough Court: the story of a notable pharmacy, 1715–1927*, 1927, rev. edn. by [Wellesley William] Desmond [Mountjoy] Chapman–Huston, [*Through a city archway: the story of Allen and Hanburys, 1815–1954*], 1954.

8976 NORMAN COMMITTEE ON PATENT MEDICINES. Report from the select committee on patent medicines [Chairman: Sir Henry Norman]. H.C. 414 (1914). IX, 1.

A comprehensive inquiry.


## G. THE FINE ARTS

### 1. GENERAL

(a) *Reference*

8977 CHAMBERLIN (MARY WALLS) *comp.* Guide to art reference books. Amer. Libr. Assoc. Chicago. 1959.

8978 LUCAS (EDNA LOUISE) *comp.* Art books: a basic bibliography of the fine arts. Greenwich, Conn. 1968.

The South Kensington Museum publ. the fullest contemp. list, *The universal catalogue of books on art*, compiled for the use of the National Art Library and the schools of art of the United Kingdom, Science and Art Dept., 2 v. 1870, suppl. 1877. For colls. of photographs of works of art see UNESCO, *Répertoire international des archives photographiques d'œuvres d'art . . .*, 2 v. Paris 1950–4. For reproductions of paintings see UNESCO, *Catalogue de reproductions en couleur de peintures, 1860 à 1965 . . .*, Paris 1966.

8979 COURTAULD INSTITUTE OF ART (UNIVERSITY OF LONDON). Annual bibliography of the history of British art. 1934–7. Cont. as Bibliography of the history of British art . . . 1938–46. Camb. 1951–6.

Covers 1934–46. The best annual bibliog. is now *Répertoire d'art et d'archéologie d'épouillement des périodiques et des catalogues de ventes, bibliographie des ouvrages d'art français et étrangers*, 1+, Paris 1910+, which has national sub-headings. There is also

The art index: a cumulative author and subject index to a selected list of fine art periodicals, 1+, N.Y. 1929+, and Art. Inst. of Chicago: Ryerson Libr., *Index to art periodicals*, 11 v. Boston 1962.

8980  THE YEAR'S ART, 1880[–1947, 1968–69+]: a concise epitome of all matters relating to the arts of painting, sculpture, engraving and architecture and to schools of design, which have occurred during the year. 1880–1947. 1970+.

8981  ROBERTS (HELENE EMYLOU). 'British art periodicals of the eighteenth and nineteenth centuries'. *Victorian Periodicals Newsletter* ix (1970), 1–[183].
A valuable handlist.

8982  UNIVERSITY OF LONDON. Catalogue of books on archaeology and art and cognate works belonging to the Preedy Memorial Library and other collections in the university library. 3 v. 1935–7.

8983  THE METROPOLITAN MUSEUM OF ART, NEW YORK. Library catalogue. 25 v. Boston. 1960+.
The fullest general list.

8984  HISTORICAL MANUSCRIPTS COMMISSION. Architectural history and the fine and applied arts: sources in the National Register of Archives. 1+. 1970+.

8985  OSBORNE (HAROLD) *ed.* The Oxford companion to art. Oxf. 1970.
*The encyclopaedia of world art*, 14 v. N.Y. 1959–68, is fuller, but less orientated towards British art.

8986  THIEME (ULRICH) *and* BECKER (FELIX) *eds.* Allgemeines Lexikon der bildenden Künstler von der Antike bis zur Gegenwart . . . 37 v. Leipzig. 1908–50.
Cont. by Hans Vollmer, *Allgemeines Lexikon der bildenden Künstler des XX. Jahrhunderts*, 6 v. Leipzig 1953–62.

8987  BÉNÉZIT (EMMANUEL) *ed.* Dictionnaire critique et documentaire des peintres, sculpteurs, dessinateurs & graveurs de tous les temps et de tous les pays . . . Rev. edn. 8 v. Paris. 1948–55.
Thieme and Becker (**8986**) and Bénézit are fuller and more up-to-date than any British work.

8988  CLEMENT (CLARA ERSKINE) *and* HUTTON (LAURENCE). Artists of the nineteenth century and their works: a handbook containing two thousand and fifty biographical sketches. 2 v. Boston & N.Y. 1879. 7th edn. 1894. Repr. N.Y. 1969.

8989  BRYAN (MICHAEL). A biographical and critical dictionary of painters and engravers . . . 2 v. 1816. 2nd edn. by George Stanley. 1849. Suppl. on recent and living painters by Henry Ottley. 1866. New edn. by George Charles Williamson. 5 v. 1903–5. Repr. 1925–7 and 1964.

8990 GRAVES (ALGERNON) *comp.* A century of loan exhibitions, 1813–1912. 5 v. 1913–15. Repr. N.Y. 1965.

See also his *A dictionary of artists who have exhibited works in the principal London exhibitions from 1760 to 1893*, new edn. 1895, 3rd edn. 1901, repr. Bath 1969.

8991 GRAVES (ALGERNON) *comp.* The Royal Academy of Arts: a complete dictionary of contributors and their work from its foundation in 1769 to 1904. 8 v. 1905–6.

8992 GRAVES (ALGERNON) *comp.* The British Institution, 1806–1867: a complete dictionary of contributors and their work from the foundation of the Institution. 1908. Repr. Bath. 1969.

8993 NATIONAL GALLERY. Catalogue. 86th edn. 1929.

See also Martin Davies, *The British school*, 1966, 2nd edn. 1959, which was intended to replace the *Catalogue*.

8994 NATIONAL GALLERY OF BRITISH ART (TATE GALLERY). Descriptive and historical catalogue of the pictures and sculptures in the National Gallery of British Art. 7th edn. 1900. 25th edn. 1947.

8995 BRITISH MUSEUM (DEPARTMENT OF PRINTS AND DRAWINGS). Catalogue of drawings by British artists and artists of foreign origin working in Great Britain. Comp. by Laurence Binyon. 4 v. 1898–1907. New edn. in progress. 1960+.

### (b) *Other Works*

8996 BOASE (THOMAS SHERRER ROSS). English art, 1800–1870. Oxf. Hist. of Art 10. Oxf. 1959.

Standard.

8997 STEEGMAN (JOHN). Victorian taste: a study of the arts and architecture from 1830–1870. 1970.

First publ. as *Consort of taste, 1830–1870*, 1950. See also Winslow Ames, *Prince Albert and Victorian taste*, 1967.

8998 BELL (QUENTIN). Victorian artists. Lond. & Camb., Mass. 1967.

There is little on the period in Henry Currie Marillier, *The Liverpool school of painters: an account of the Liverpool Academy from 1810 to 1867, with memoirs of the principal artists*, 1904, George Pycroft, *Art in Devonshire, with the biographies of artists born in that county*, Exeter 1883, or Henry Cecil Hall, *Artists and sculptors of Nottingham and Nottinghamshire, 1750–1950: a biographical dictionary*, Nottingham 1953.

8999 PEVSNER (*Sir* NIKOLAUS BERNHARD LEON). Studies in art, architecture and design. 2 v. Lond. 1968. N.Y. 1969.

9000  PEVSNER (*Sir* NIKOLAUS BERNHARD LEON). High Victorian design: a study of the exhibits of 1851. 1951.

For the 1851 exhibition see also **4128-33**.

9001  WELBY (THOMAS EARLE). The Victorian romantics, 1850-70: the early work of Dante Gabriel Rossetti, William Morris, Burne-Jones, Swinburne, Simeon Solomon and their associates. 1929.

9002  BØE (ALF). From Gothic revival to functional form: a study in Victorian theories of design. Oslo studs. in English 6. Oslo, N.Y., & Oxf. 1957.

9003  MADSEN (STEPHAN TSCHUDI). Victoriansk Dekorativ Kunst, 1837-1901. Nordenfjeldske Kunstindustrimuseum Årbok 1952. Trondheim. 1953. Pp. 9-92.

9004  FREDEMAN (WILLIAM E.). Pre-Raphaelitism: a bibliocritical study. Camb., Mass. 1965.

9005  HUNT (WILLIAM HOLMAN). Pre-Raphaelitism and the Pre-Raphaelite brotherhood. 2 v. Lond. & N.Y. 1905-6. 2nd edn. 1914.

The basic work on the subject, by a participant. See also William Michael Rossetti, ed., *Pre-Raphaelite diaries and letters . . .*, 1900, and *Ruskin, Rossetti, Pre-Raphaelitism: papers, 1854 to 1862*, 1899, *Rossetti papers, 1862 to 1870*, Lond. & N.Y. 1903, and *The germ: thoughts towards nature in poetry, literature and art, being a facsimile reprint of the literary organ of the Pre-Raphaelite brotherhood, published in 1850, with an introduction . . .*, 1901; John Ruskin, *Pre-Raphaelitism*, 1851, new edn. 1862; Edward Young, *Pre-Raffaelitism: or, a popular enquiry into some newly-asserted principles connected with the philosophy, poetry, religion and revolution of art*, 1857; Joseph Leopold Ford Hermann Madox Hueffer [Ford Madox Ford], *The Pre-Raphaelite brotherhood: a critical monograph*, 1907; Percy H. Bate, *The English Pre-Raphaelite painters: their associates and successors*, 1899, 2nd edn. 1901; Hans Wolfgang Singer, *Der Prae-Raphaelitismus in England*, Munich 1912; and Francis Lawrence Bickley, *The Pre-Raphaelite comedy*, 1932.

9006  GAUNT (WILLIAM). The Pre-Raphaelite tragedy. 1942. Rev. edn. [The Pre-Raphaelite dream.] 1965.

9007  WELLAND (DENNIS SYDNEY REGINALD). The Pre-Raphaelites in literature and art. 1953.

9008  FLEMING (GORDON HOWARD). Rossetti and the Pre-Raphaelite brotherhood. 1967.

9009  HUNT (JOHN DIXON). The Pre-Raphaelite imagination, 1848-1900. Lond. 1968. Lincoln, Nebr. 1969.

9010  WATKINSON (RAYMOND). Pre-Raphaelite art and design. 1970.

See also Timothy Hilton, *The Pre-Raphaelites*, 1970, and John Nicoll, *The Pre-Raphaelites*, 1970.

9011 GAUNT (WILLIAM). Victorian Olympus. 1952.
On the classical revival of the 1870s and 1880s.

9012 NAYLOR (GILLIAN). The arts and crafts movement: a study of its sources, ideals and influence on design theory. 1971.

9013 ASLIN (ELIZABETH). The aesthetic movement: prelude to art nouveau. Lond. & N.Y. 1969.

9014 MADSEN (STEPHAN TSCHUDI). Sources of art nouveau. Trans. by Ragnar Christophersen. Oslo. 1956. N.Y. 1957.

9015 PEVSNER (*Sir* NIKOLAUS BERNHARD LEON). Academies of art: past and present. Camb. 1940.

9016 HUTCHISON (SIDNEY CHARLES). The history of the Royal Academy, 1768–1968. 1968.

9017 EVANS (JOAN). A history of the Society of Antiquaries. 1956.

9018 ROTHENSTEIN (*Sir* JOHN KNEWSTUB MAURICE). The Tate gallery. 1958. New edn. 1962.

9019 DAVIS (FRANK). Victorian patrons of the arts: twelve famous collections and their owners. 1963.

9020 REITLINGER (GERALD ROBERTS). The economics of taste: the rise and fall of picture prices, 1760–1960. 1961.
See also Algernon Graves, *Art sales from early in the eighteenth century to early in the 20th century (mostly old master and early English pictures)*, 3 v. 1918–21. For the leading sale-room see Percy Colson, *A story of Christie's*, 1950. For a leading art dealer see James Henry Duveen, *Collections & recollections: a century and a half of art deals*, 1934, *Secrets of an art dealer*, 1937, and *The rise of the house of Duveen*, 1957.

9021 KING (ANTHONY). 'George Godwin and the Art Union of London, 1837–1911'. *Victorian Studs.* viii (1964–5), 101–30.

9022 COCKERELL. Cockerell: Sydney Carlyle Cockerell, friend of Ruskin and William Morris and director of the Fitzwilliam Museum, Cambridge. By Wilfrid Jasper Walter Blunt. Lond. 1964. N.Y. & Toronto. 1965.

9023 DE MORGAN. William De Morgan and his wife. By Anna Maria Diana Wilhelmina Stirling. 1922.

9024 REDGRAVE. Richard Redgrave, C.B., R.A.: a memoir compiled from his diary. By Frances Margaret Redgrave. 1891.
Redgrave was one of the artist-administrators who became a force in the period. For others see Anne Pollen, *John Hungerford Pollen, 1820–1902*, 1912; L. M. Lamont, *Thomas Armstrong, C.B.: a memoir, 1832–1911*, 1912; Sir Charles John Holmes,

*Self and partners—mostly self* . . ., 1936; Dugald Sutherland Maccoll, *Confessions of a keeper and other papers, 1931;* William Minto, ed., *Autobiographical notes of the life of William Bell Scott and notices of his circle of friends, 1830–1882,* 2 v. 1892; and (for the career of her husband) Charles Eastlake Smith, ed., *Journals and correspondence of Lady Eastlake,* 2 v. 1895, and Marion Cleland Lochhead, *Elizabeth Rigby, Lady Eastlake,* 1961.

9025   THE STUDIO: an illustrated magazine of fine and applied art. 1893+.

The most historically-conscious of general art js. Noted for its *Special numbers* on contemp. artists, 1895+, and *The Studio yearbook of decorative art,* 1906–29+. British art is also covered in *The connoisseur* . . ., 1901+, *The Burlington magazine* . . ., 1903+, and *Country life,* all of which publ. occasional special numbers devoted to the period. *The art j.,* 1849–1912, *The portfolio* . . ., 1870–1907, *The magazine of art,* 1878–1904, and *The Royal Academy illustrated* [title varies], 1884+, were the best of contemp. js.

9026   ART. Nat. Assoc. for the Promotion of Social Science Trans. Pt. V. 1876–84. 1877–85.

See also [Edward] Dutton Cook, *Art in England: notes and studies,* 1869.

## 2. PAINTING

9027   GAUNT (WILLIAM). A concise history of English painting. Lond. & N.Y. 1964.

See also [Eric] Hesketh Hubbard, *A hundred years of British painting, 1851–1951,* 1951, and [Cyril] Anthony [George] Bertram, *A century of British painting, 1851–1951,* 1951. There is a good deal of background material in Richard Redgrave and Samuel Redgrave, *A century of British painters,* new edn. 1947. For miniatures see Daphne Foskett, *British portrait miniatures: a history,* 1963, and Basil Somerset Long, *British miniaturists,* 1929, repr. 1966.

9028   MAAS (JEREMY). Victorian painters. 1969.

A handbook for collectors. See also [Arthur] Graham Reynolds, *Painters of the Victorian scene,* 1953, and *Victorian painting,* Lond. 1966, N.Y. 1967, [Eric] Hesketh Hubbard, *Some Victorian draughtsmen,* Camb. 1944, and Raymond Lister, *Victorian narrative paintings,* Lond. & N.Y. 1966. For contemp. work see Sir Alfred George Temple, *The art of painting in the Queen's reign,* 1897, Sir Wyke Bayliss, *Five great painters of the Victorian era: Leighton, Millais, Burne-Jones, Watts, Holman Hunt,* 1902, and William Cosmo Monkhouse, *British contemporary artists,* N.Y. & Lond. 1899.
   For the lives of painters see Bryan (8989), Daphne Foskett, *A dictionary of British miniature painters,* 2 v. 1971, Maurice Harold Grant, *A dictionary of British landscape painters from the 16th century to the early 20th century,* Leigh-on-Sea 1952, and Sydney Herbert Pavière, *A dictionary of sporting painters,* Leigh-on-Sea 1965, *A dictionary of Victorian landscape painters,* Leigh-on-Sea 1968, and *A dictionary of Victorian painters,* Leigh-on-Sea 1969.

9029   IRONSIDE (ROBIN). Pre-Raphaelite painters. 1948.

See also 9004–10.

9030   HARDIE (MARTIN). Water-colour painting in Britain: Vol. III. 'The Victorian period'. Ed. by Dudley Snelgrove and others. 1968.

See also Herbert Minton Cundall, *A history of British water-colour painting: with biographical list of painters,* 1908, rev. edn. 1929, and Marcus Bourne Huish, *British water-colour art in the first year of the reign of King Edward the Seventh and during the century covered by the life of the Royal Society of Painters in Water Colours . . ., 1904.*

9031 CHESNEAU (ERNEST). The English school of painting. Trans. by Lucy N. Etherington. 1885. 3rd edn. 1887.

Orig. publ. in Paris in 1882, English edn. with preface by Ruskin. Cp. Robert de La Sizeranne, *English contemporary art*, trans. by H. M. Poynter, 1898.

9032 ROTHENSTEIN (*Sir* JOHN KNEWSTUB MAURICE). Modern English painters: Sickert to Smith. 1952.

See also his *Nineteenth-century painting: a study in conflict*, 1932, *The artists of the 1890s*, 1928, and *An introduction to English painting*, 1933, 5th edn. 1965.

9033 THE ROYAL ACADEMY ILLUSTRATED. Suppl. to The Magazine of Art. 1888–1915.

Title varies. Reflects contemp. preoccupations. Cp. Royal Academy of Arts, *Academy notes*, 1875–1907, Henry Blackburn, ed., *Academy sketches: containing illustrations from various exhibitions*, 1883–94, and the js. at **9025.**

9034 ROYAL ACADEMY OF ARTS. Winter exhibition, 1951–52: the first hundred years of the Royal Academy, 1769–1868. 1951.

Included to draw attention to the importance of exhibition catalogues for the study of painting. Recent exhibition catalogues are often of very high quality, particularly those comp. for Arts Council exhibitions, among them those on Watts (1954–5) and Whistler (1960), and those for the Walker Art Gallery, Liverpool, among them those on Millais (1967), Ford Madox Brown (1964), and Holman Hunt (1969).

9035 FIELD (GEORGE). Rudiments of the painter's art: or, a grammar of colouring. 1850. 2nd edn. 1858. New edns. 1870, 1875.

One of a number of successful contemp. guides to oil painting. Others incl. John Burnet, *A practical treatise on painting . . .*, 3 pts. 1822–7, new edns. 1850, 1880; Sir Arthur Herbert Church, *Colour: an elementary manual for students*, 1887, and *The chemistry of paints and painting*, 1890, 4th edn. 1915; John Collier, *A manual of oil painting*, 1886; Charles Martel, pseud. of Thomas Delf, *The principles of colouring in painting*, 1855, 14th edn. 1880; John Furnell, *Student's handbook of paints, colours, oils and varnishes*, Lond. & N.Y. 1903; Thomas John Gullick and John Timbs, *Painting popularly explained*, 1859, 4th edn. 1876; Sir Charles John Holmes, *Notes on the science of picture making*, Lond. & N.Y. 1909, 6th edn. 1927; George H. Hurst, *Painters' colours, oils and varnishes: a practical manual*, 1893, 5th edn. by Noel Heaton 1913, rev. edn. 1922; Arthur Pillans Laurie, *Facts about processes, pigments & vehicles: a manual for art students*, 1895; George Rowney & Co., *A guide to oil painting*, 37th edn. 1888; Henry Murray, *The art of portrait painting in oil colours . . .*, 1851, 41st edn. [1887], new edn. [1936]; and Solomon Joseph Solomon, *The practice of oil painting and of drawing as associated with it*, 1910, 2nd edn. 1911.

For mural painting see William Cave Thomas, *Mural or monumental decoration: its aims and methods . . .*, 1869, and Frederick Hamilton Jackson, *Mural painting*, 1904.

For water-colour painting see Alfred Lys Baldry, *The practice of water-colour painting, illustrated by the work of modern artists*, 1911; George Barnard, *The theory and practice of landscape painting in watercolours*, 1858, 1871; Thomas Hatton, *Hints for sketching in watercolours from nature*, 1853, 13th edn. 1896; Richard Pettigrew Leitch, *A course of water-colour painting*, 1873, 10th edn. 1887; Aaron Penley, *A system of water-colour painting*, 1850, 27th edn. 1869; Thomas Leeson Rowbotham and Thomas

Charles Leeson, *The art of landscape painting in water-colours*, 4th edn. 1851; and Sidney T. Whiteford, *A guide to figure painting in watercolours* [1870], 7th edn. 1885.

For sepia painting see Richard Pettigrew Leitch, *A course of sepia painting* [1875], 2nd ser. 1886.

9036 ALMA TADEMA. Lawrence Alma Tadema, R.A., a sketch of his life and work. Ed. by Frederic George Stephens. 1895.

See also Percy Cross Standing, *Sir Lawrence Alma-Tadema*, 1905, and George Moritz Ebers, *Lorenz Alma Tadema: his life and works* trans. by Mary Joanna Safford, N.Y. 1886.

9037 BAYLISS. Olives: the reminiscences of a president . . . By Sir Wyke Bayliss. Ed. by his wife. 1906.

9038 BOUGH. Sam Bough, R.S.A.: some account of his life and works. By Sidney Gilpin [pseud. of George Coward]. 1905.

9039 BRABAZON. Hercules Brabazon Brabazon, 1821–1906: his art and life. By Charles Lewis Hind. 1912.

9040 BRANGWYN. Frank Brangwyn and his work. By Walter Shaw Sparrow. 1910. New edn. to 1914. 1915.

See also William De Belleroche, *Brangwyn talks*, 1944, *Brangwyn's pilgrimage: the life story of an artist*, 1948, and **9114**.

9041 BROWN. Ford Madox Brown: a record of his life and work. By [Joseph Leopold] Ford [Hermann] Madox Hueffer. 1896.

Brown's diary for 1844–56 is incl. in W. M. Rossetti's *Pre-Raphaelite diaries* (**9005**).

9042 BURNE-JONES. Memorials of Edward Burne-Jones. By Georgiana, Lady Burne-Jones. 2 v. 1904.

See also Lord [Edward Christian] David [Gascoyne-] Cecil, *Visionary and dreamer: two poetic painters, Samuel Palmer and Edward Burne-Jones*, 1970, and Malcolm Bell, *Edward Burne-Jones: a record and a review*, 1892, new edn. 1899.

9043 BUTLER. An autobiography. By Elizabeth, Lady Butler. 1922.

See also her *From sketch-book and diary* . . ., 1909, and Wilfred Meynell, *The life and work of Lady Butler* . . ., 1898.

9044 CALLOW. William Callow, R.W.S., F.R.G.S.: an autobiography. Ed. by Herbert Minton Cundall. 1908.

9045 CONDER. The life and death of Conder. By Sir John Knewstub Maurice Rothenstein. 1938.

9046 COOPER. My life. By Thomas Sidney Cooper. 2 v. 1890. New edn. 1891.

9047 COPE. Reminiscences of Charles West Cope, R.A. By Charles Henry Cope. 1891.

9048　DAWSON. The life of Henry Dawson, landscape painter, 1811–1878 ...
Comp. by Alfred Dawson. 1891.

9049　FILDES. The life and work of Luke Fildes, R.A. By David Croal
Thomson. 1895.

9050　FORBES. Stanhope Alexander Forbes, A.R.A. and Elizabeth Stanhope
Forbes, A.R.W.S. By Mrs. Lionel Birch. 1906.

9051　FOSTER. Birket Foster, R.W.S. By Herbert Minton Cundall. 1906.

9052　FRITH. My autobiography and reminiscences. By William Powell Frith.
3 v. 1887–8. Abbrev. edn. by Nevile Wallis [A Victorian canvas]. 1957.

9053　HART. The reminiscences of Solomon Alexander Hart. Ed. by Alexander
Brodie. 1882.

9054　HERKOMER. Life and letters of Sir Hubert Herkomer. By John Saxon
Mills. 1923.

Sir Hubert von Herkomer himself publ. *The Herkomers*, 2 v. 1910–11, and *My school
and my gospel*, 1908. See also Alfred Lys Baldry, *Hubert von Herkomer: a study and a
biography*, 1901.

9055　HORSLEY. Recollections of a Royal Academician. By John Callcott
Horsley. Ed. by Mrs. Edmund [i.e. Mary Alice] Helps. 1903.

9056　HUGHES. My father [Edward Hughes] and I. By Alice Hughes. 1923.

9057　HOLMAN HUNT. Pre-Raphaelitism and the Pre-Raphaelite brotherhood. By William Holman Hunt. 2 v. Lond. & N.Y. 1905–6. 2nd edn. 1914.

Diana Holman-Hunt, *My grandfather: his wives and loves*, 1969, and *My grandmothers
and I*, 1960, 2nd edn. 1969, give a vivid account of the family. See also Alfred C. Gissing,
*William Holman Hunt: a biography*, 1936; Herbert Sussman, 'Hunt, Ruskin and "The
Scapegoat"', *Victorian Studs.* xii (1968–9), 83–90; Henry William Shrewsbury, *Brothers
in art: studies in William Holman Hunt . . . and John Everett Millais*, 1920; Mark
Wentworth Roskill, 'Holman Hunt's differing versions of "The Light of the world"',
*Victorian Studs.* vi (1962–3), 229–44; and Samuel J. Wagstaff, Jr., 'Some notes on
Holman Hunt (1827–1910) & the Lady of Shalott', *Wadsworth Athenaeum Bull.* 5 ser.
no. 11 (summer 1962), 1–21.

9058　JOHN. Chiaroscuro: fragments of autobiography. By Augustus Edwin
John. Lond. & N.Y. 1952.

See also Campbell Dodgson, *A catalogue of etchings by Augustus John, 1901–1914*, 1920.

9059　KNIGHT. Oil paint and grease paint: autobiography. By Dame Laura
Knight. 1936.

9060　LANDSEER. A catalogue of the works of . . . Sir Edwin Landseer.
Comp. by Algernon Graves. 1875.

There is no adequate life, though James Alexander Manson, *Sir Edwin Landseer, R.A.*,
1902, is useful.

9061   LAVERY. The life of a painter. By Sir John Lavery. 1940.

See also Walter Shaw Sparrow, *John Lavery and his work*, 1911.

9062   LEAR. Edward Lear as a landscape draughtsman. By Philip Hofer. Camb., Mass. 1967.

For Lear generally see **8388**.

9063   LEHMANN. An artist's reminiscences. By Rudolf Lehmann. 1894.

9064   LEIGHTON. The life, letters and work of Frederic Leighton. By Emilie Isabel Barrington, Mrs. Russell Barrington. 1906.

9065   LEITCH. William Leighton Leitch, landscape painter: a memoir. By Andrew MacGeorge. 1884.

9066   MARKS. Pen and pencil sketches. By Henry Stacy Marks. 2 v. 1894.

9067   MILLAIS. The life and letters of Sir John Everett Millais, president of the Royal Academy. By John Guille Millais. 2 v. 1899. 3rd edn. 1902. Abridged edn. 1905.

For Millais's private life see also Mary Lutyens, ed., *Millais and the Ruskins*, Lond. 1967, N.Y. 1968. For his work see also Marion Harry Spielmann, *Millais and his works: with special reference to the exhibition at the Royal Academy, 1898*, Edin. & Lond. 1898, Alfred Lys Baldry, *Sir John Everett Millais: his art and influence*, 1899, and Henry William Shrewsbury, *Brothers in art* (**9057**).

9068   MOORE. Albert Moore: his life and works. By Alfred Lys Baldry. 1894.

9069   NICHOLSON. William Nicholson. By Marguerite Steen. 1943.

9070   ORCHARDSON. The life of Sir William Quiller Orchardson, R.A. By Hilda Orchardson Gray. 1930.

9071   ORPEN. Sir William Orpen: artist & man. By Paul George Konody and Sidney Dark. 1932.

9072   PENNELL. The life and letters of Joseph Pennell. By Elizabeth Robins Pennell. 2 v. Boston. 1929. Lond. 1930.

9073   PETTIE. John Pettie, R.A., H.R.S.A. By Martin Hardie. 1908.

9074   PINWELL. George John Pinwell and his works. By George Charles Williamson. 1900.

9075   PRYDE. James Pryde, 1866–1941. By Derek Hudson. 1949.

9076   RICHMOND. The Richmond papers: from the correspondence and manuscripts of George Richmond, R.A., and his son Sir William Richmond. Ed. by Anna Maria Diana Wilhelmina Stirling. 1926.

9077 ROBERTSON. Time was: the reminiscences of W[alford] Graham Robertson. 1931.

See also Kerrison Preston, *Letters from Graham Robertson*, 1953.

9078 ROSSETTI. The paintings and drawings of Dante Gabriel Rossetti, 1828–1882: a catalogue raisonné. Comp. by Virginia Surtees. 2 v. Oxf. 1970.

Important. For Rossetti generally see **8407**.

RUSKIN. See **8408**.

9079 SARGENT. John S. Sargent: his life and work. By William Howe Downes. Boston. 1925. Lond. 1926.

See also Charles Merrill Mount, *John Singer Sargent: a biography*, 1957, and Richard Ormond, *Sargent: paintings, drawings, watercolours*, 1970.

9080 SICKERT. The life and opinions of Walter Richard Sickert. By Robert Emmons. 1941.

See also Lillian Browse, *Sickert*, 1960, Wendy Baron, *Sickert*, Lond. & N.Y. 1973, and Marjorie Lilly, *Sickert: the painter and his circle*, 1972.

9081 THOMPSON. The life and works of Jacob Thompson. By Llewellynn Frederick William Jewitt. 1882.

9082 THORNTON. The diary of an art student of the nineties. By Alfred Henry Robinson Thornton. 1938.

9083 TISSOT. 'Vulgar society': the romantic career of James Tissot, 1836–1902. By James Laver. 1936.

9084 WALKER. Life and letters of Frederick Walker, A.R.A. By John George Marks. 1896.

9085 WATTS. George Frederick Watts: the annals of an artist's life. By Mary S. Watts. 3 v. 1912.

See also Gilbert Keith Chesterton, *G. F. Watts*, 1904, and Ronald Chapman, *The laurel and the thorn: a study of G. F. Watts*, 1945.

9086 WHISTLER. The life of James McNeill Whistler. By Elizabeth Robins Pennell and Joseph Pennell. 2 v. 1908. Rev. edn. 1911.

See also Don Carlos Seitz, *Writings by & about James Abbott McNeill Whistler: a bibliography*, Edin. 1910, and *Whistler stories...*, N.Y. & Lond. 1913; Howard Mansfield, *A descriptive catalogue of the etchings and dry-points of James Abbott McNeill Whistler*, Chicago 1909; James Abbott MacNeill Whistler, *The gentle art of making enemies*, 1890, new edn. 1892; Elizabeth Robins Pennell and Joseph Pennell, eds., *The Whistler journal* . . ., Phila. 1921; Carl Paul Barbier, ed., *Correspondance Mallarmé–Whistler: histoire de la grande amitié de leurs dernières années*, Paris 1964; Walter Crane, ed., *William Morris to Whistler: papers and addresses on art and craft and the commonweal*, 1911; Donald Holden, *Whistler landscapes and seascapes*, N.Y. 1969; Elizabeth Robins Pennell, *Whistler the friend*, Phila. & Lond. 1930; Mortimer Menpes, *Whistler as I knew him*, 1904; Arthur Jerome Eddy, *Recollections and impressions of James A. McNeill*

*Whistler*, Phila. & Lond. 1903; James Laver, *Whistler*, 1930, 2nd edn. 1951; Hesketh Pearson, *The man Whistler*, 1952; Horace Victor Gregory, *The world of James McNeill Whistler*, N.Y. 1959, Lond. 1961; and Denys Sutton, *Nocturne: the art of James McNeill Whistler*, Lond. 1963, Phila. 1964.

## 3. ENGRAVINGS, PRINTS, ETC.

9087   LEVIS (HOWARD COPPOCK) *comp.* A descriptive bibliography of the most important books in the English language relating to the art & history of engraving and the collecting of prints. With supplement and index. 2 v. 1912–13.

9088   ABBEY (JOHN ROLAND). Life in England in aquatint and lithography, 1770–1860: architecture, drawing books, art collections, magazines, navy and army, panoramas, &c., from the library of J. R. Abbey: a bibliographical catalogue. 1953.

See also his *Scenery of Great Britain and Ireland in aquatint and lithography, 1775–1860* . . ., 1952, and *Travel in aquatint and lithography, 1770–1860* . . ., 2 v. 1956–7. A magnificent series in the grand manner.

9089   LEWIS (CHARLES THOMAS COURTNEY). The story of picture printing in England during the nineteenth century: or, forty years of wood and stone. [1928.]

See also Basil Gray, *The English print*, 1937.

9090   NEWBOLT (*Sir* FRANCIS GEORGE). The history of the Royal Society of Painter-Etchers and Engravers, 1880–1930. 1931.

9091   HIND (ARTHUR MAYGER). A short history of engraving & etching for the use of collectors and students . . . 1908. 3rd edn. 1923. Repr. N.Y. 1963.

Hind also comp. British Museum, Dept. of Prints and Drawings, *The processes and schools of engraving* . . ., 1914, 4th edn. 1952. John Herbert Slater, *Engravings and their value: a guide for the print collector*, 1891, 6th edn. 1929, and Hans Wolfgang Singer and William Strang, *Etching, engraving and other methods of printing pictures*, 1897, are useful guides.

9092   HIND (ARTHUR MAYGER). An introduction to a history of woodcut . . . 2 v. Boston & N.Y. 1935. Repr. 2 v. N.Y. 1963.

The best starting-point. General works such as Douglas Percy Bliss, *A history of wood engraving*, 1928, add little. But there is useful material in Harry Graham Carter, *Orlando Jewitt*, 1962; Bernard Sleigh, *Wood-engraving since eighteen-ninety*, 1932; Herbert Ernest Augustus Furst, *The modern woodcut: a study of the evolution of the craft*, 1924; Thomas Balston, *English wood engraving, 1900–1950*, 1951; and Malcolm Charles Salaman, *Modern woodcuts and lithographs by British and French artists*, Studio special no., 1919. Contemp. works illustr. the development of the craft include *The Cornhill gallery: containing one hundred engravings from drawings on wood* . . . [1864], and William James Linton, *Wood engraving: a manual of introduction*, 1884, and *The masters of wood engraving*, Lond. & New Haven, Conn. 1889.

9093   SPARROW (WALTER SHAW). A book of British etching from Francis Barlow to Francis Seymour Haden. 1926.

James Laver, *A history of British and American etching*, 1929, adds little. But see

Philip Gilbert Hamerton, *Etching and etchers*, Lond. 1868, 3rd edn. 1880, Boston 1883, and *The etcher's handbook* . . ., 1871, 3rd edn. 1881; Richard Samuel Chattock, *Practical notes on etching*, n.d., 3rd edn. 1886; John Ruskin, *Ariadne Florentina: six lectures on wood and metal engraving* . . ., 1890, and *The etcher: examples of the original etched work of modern artists*, monthly, 1879–83; Sir Frank Short, *On the making of etchings*, 1898, 4th edn. 1898; Sir Hubert von Herkomer, *Etching and mezzotint engraving: lectures delivered at Oxford*, 1892; Sir Frederick Wedmore, *Etching in England*, 1895; Hugh Paton, *Etching, drypoint, mezzotint: the whole art of the painter etcher: a practical treatise*, 1895, 2nd edn. 1909; Charles Holme, ed., *Modern etchings, mezzotints and dry prints*, Studio winter no., 1913, and Joseph Pennell, *Etchers and etching: chapters in the history of the art, together with technical explanations of modern artistic methods* [1920].

9094　GRANT (MAURICE HAROLD). A dictionary of British etchers. 1952.

9095　MAN (FELIX H.) *pseud. of* BAUMAN (HANS F. S.). 150 years of artists' lithographs, 1803–1953. 1953.

For contemp. examples see *The chromolithograph: a j. of art, decoration and the accomplishments*, 1867–9, and Joseph Pennell and Elizabeth Robins Pennell, *Lithography and lithographers: some chapters in the history of the art, with technical remarks and suggestions*, 1898, new edn. 1915.

9096　WHITMAN (ALFRED CHARLES). Nineteenth-century mezzotinters. 3 v. 1903–7.

9097　LOW (DAVID). British cartoonists, caricaturists and comic artists. 1942.

9098　JACKSON (EMILY NEVILL). The history of silhouettes. 1911.

9099　THE ARTIST & THE BOOK, 1860–1960, in western Europe and the United States. Museum of Fine Arts, Boston, and Harvard Coll. Libr. 1961.

A valuable exhibition catalogue. David Farrant Bland, *A history of book illustration: the illuminated manuscript and the printed book*, 1958, 2nd edn. 1970, is a useful general survey.

9100　TOOLEY (RONALD VERE). English books with coloured plates, 1790 to 1860: a bibliographical account of the most important books illustrated by English artists in colour aquatint and colour lithography. 1954.

Standard. Replaced his *Some English books with coloured plates* . . ., 1935.

9101　JAMES (PHILIP BRUTTON). English book illustration, 1800–1900. 1947.

9102　MUIR (PERCY HORACE). Victorian illustrated books. Lond. & N.Y. 1971.

9103　HARVEY (JOHN ROBERT). Victorian novelists and their illustrators. 1970.

See also Frederic George Kitton, *Dickens and his illustrators*, 1899.

9104 LAYARD (GEORGE SOMES). Tennyson and his Pre-Raphaelite illustrators: a book about a book. 1894.

9105 REID (FORREST). Illustrators of the sixties. 1928.

Cp. Joseph William Gleeson White, *English illustration: 'the sixties', 1855–70*, Westminster 1897. Developments in the following decade are reflected in Joseph William Comyns Carr, *Book illustration: old and new*, Cantor lectures, 1882, James Shirley Hodson, *An historical and practical guide to art illustration in connection with books, periodicals and general decoration: with specimens of the various methods*, 1884, and Sir Henry Trueman Wood, *Modern methods of illustrating books*, 1887.

9106 THORPE (JAMES). English illustration: the nineties. 1935.

For the period see also Walter Crane, *Of the decorative illustration of books, old and new*, 1896, 3rd edn. 1921, and Rose E. D. Sketchley, *English book illustration of today: appreciations of the work of living English illustrators, with lists of books*, 1903. What students were taught is indicated by Joseph Pennell, *Modern illustration*, 1895, and *The illustration of books* . . ., 1896.

9107 SILTZER (FRANK). The story of British sporting prints. 1925. 2nd edn. 1929.

See also **7677**.

9108 SLATER (JOHN HERBERT). Illustrated sporting books: a descriptive survey of a collection of English illustrated works of a sporting and racy character . . . 1899.

9109 CLARKE (HAROLD GEORGE). Under-glaze colour picture prints on Staffordshire pottery . . . 1955.

9110 CARLINE (RICHARD). Pictures in the post: the story of the picture postcard [and its place in the history of popular art]. Bedford. 1959. New edn. Lond. 1971.

See also Tonie Holt and Valmai Holt, *Picture postcards of the golden age: a collector's guide*, Lond. & Folsom, Pa. 1971 and **5576**. For cigarette cards see Alfred James Cruse, *Cigarette card cavalcade* . . ., 1948, 2nd edn. [*Cigarette card collecting*] 1951. For match-box labels see Alfred James Cruse, *Match-box labels of the world* . . ., 1946.

9111 BAXTER. Baxter colour prints: their history and methods of production. By Harold George Clarke. Leamington. 1919.

See also Charles Thomas Courtney Lewis, *George Baxter: the picture printer* [1924], *George Baxter, colour printer: his life and work: a manual for collectors*, 1908, and *The picture printer of the nineteenth century: George Baxter, 1804–1867*, 1911, Harold George Clarke, *Baxter colour prints, pictorially presented*, 12 pts. 1920–1, and H. G. Clarke and Joseph Harold Rylatt, *The centenary Baxter book* . . ., Leamington 1936.

9112 THE BAXTER TIMES: a journal for XIXth century print collectors. Leamington. 1923+.

Title became *The Baxter print collector and Baxter times*, 1925+.

9113  BEARDSLEY. Aubrey Beardsley: catalogue of drawings and bibliography. By Albert Eugene Gallatin. Priv. pr. N.Y. 1945.

See also A. E. Gallatin and Alexander D. Wainwright, *The Gallatin Beardsley collection in Princeton University Library: a catalogue*, Princeton 1952; Henry Maas, John Lindsay Duncan, and W. G. Good, eds., *The letters of Aubrey Beardsley*, Rutherford, N. J. 1970, Lond. 1971; Arthur Symons, *Aubrey Beardsley*, 1898, 2nd edn. 1905; Eberhard Hoelscher, *Aubrey Beardsley*, Hamburg 1949; Rainforth Armitage Walker, ed., *Letters from Aubrey Beardsley to Leonard Smithers*, 1937, *The best of Beardsley*, 1948, A *Beardsley miscellany*, 1949, and *How to detect Beardsley forgeries*, Bedford 1950; Robert Baldwin Ross, *Aubrey Beardsley*, 1909; [Chambers] Haldane [Cooke] Macfall, *Aubrey Beardsley: the man and his work*, 1928; and Stanley Weintraub, *Beardsley: a biography*, Lond. & N.Y. 1967. There are three useful colls. of his work: *The early work of Aubrey Beardsley*, 1899, 2nd edn. 1912, *The later work of Aubrey Beardsley*, 1900, 2nd edn. 1912, *The uncollected work of Aubrey Beardsley*, 1925.

BEERBOHM. See **8332**.

9114  BRANGWYN. The etchings of Frank Brangwyn, R.A.: a catalogue raisonné. By William Gaunt. 1926.

See also **9040**.

9115  CALDECOTT. The complete collection of pictures & songs by Randolph Caldecott, engraved and printed by Edmund Evans. 1887.

See also *The complete collection of Randolph Caldecott's contributions to 'The Graphic'*, printed by Edmund Evans, 1888, Henry George Blackburn, *Randolph Caldecott: a personal memoir of his early art career*, 1886, and Mary Gould Davis, *Randolph Caldecott, 1846–1886: an appreciation*, Phila. & N.Y. 1946.

9116  COUSINS. Samuel Cousins. By Alfred Charles Whitman. 1904.

9117  CRANE. An artist's reminiscences. By Walter Crane. 1907.

See also Gertrude C. E. Massé, *Bibliography of the first editions of books illustrated by Walter Crane*, 1923, and Paul George Konody, *The art of Walter Crane*, 1902.

9118  CRUIKSHANK. George Cruikshank: his life and work as a book illustrator. By Ruari McLean. 1948.

See also William Makepeace Thackeray, *An essay on the genius of George Cruikshank*, ed. by W. E. Church, 1884, William Blanchard Jerrold, *The life of George Cruikshank in two epochs*, 2 v. 1882, and Albert Mayer Cohn, *George Cruikshank: a catalogue raisonné of the work executed during the years 1806–1877 . . .*, 1924, and A *bibliographical catalogue of the printed works illustrated by George Cruikshank*, 1914.

9119  DALZIEL. The brothers Dalziel: a record of fifty years' work, in conjunction with many of the most distinguished artists of the period, 1840–1890 . . . By George Dalziel and Edward Dalziel. 1901.

9120  DOYLE. Richard Doyle, his life and work. By Daria Hambourg. 1948.

9121  DU MAURIER. George Du Maurier: the satirist of the Victorians: a review of his art and personality. By T. Martin Wood. 1913.

A notable book. See also Felix Moscheles, *In Bohemia with Du Maurier . . .*, Lond. 1896, N.Y. 1897, Du Maurier's own *Social pictorial satire*, 1898, and Derek Pepys Whiteley,

*George Du Maurier: his life and work,* 1948. For his life see Daphne Du Maurier, *The Du Mauriers,* 1937, and *The young George Du Maurier: a selection of his letters, 1860–67,* 1951, C. C. Hoyer-Millar, *George Du Maurier and others,* 1937, and Leonée Ormond, *George du Maurier,* Lond. & Pittsburgh 1969.

9122  FURNISS. The confessions of a caricaturist. By Harry Furniss. 2 v. 1901.

Furniss was a prolific author whose other works (see *Who was who*) are of little value, apart from *Our lady cinema* . . ., Bristol 1914, an early account of the film industry.

9123  GREENAWAY. Kate Greenaway. By Marion Harry Spielmann and George Somes Layard. 1905.

See also **8429.**

9124  HADEN. The engraved work of Sir Francis Seymour Haden. By Samuel Henry Nazeby Harrington. Liverpool. 1910.

See also Sir William Richard Drake, comp., *A descriptive catalogue of the etched work of Francis Seymour Haden,* 1880, suppl. by H. N. Harrington 1903, and Malcolm Charles Salaman, *The etchings of Sir Francis Seymour Haden, P.R.E.,* 1923.

9125  KEENE. The work of Charles Keene: with an introduction & comments on the drawings illustrating the artist's methods by Joseph Pennell, to which is added a bibliography of the books Keene illustrated and a catalogue of his etchings by W. H. Chesson. 1897.

See also George Somes Layard, *The life and letters of Charles Samuel Keene,* 1892, Derek Hudson, *Charles Keene,* 1947, and Sir Lionel Arthur Lindsay, *Charles Keene: the artists' artist,* 1934.

9126  LEECH. John Leech: his life and work. By William Powell Frith. 2 v. 1891.

See also Frederic George Kitton, *John Leech: artist and humourist* . . ., 1883, new edn. 1884, June Rose, *The drawings of John Leech,* 1950, and Thomas Bodkin, *The noble science: John Leech in the hunting field,* 1948, and *John Leech's pictures of life and character from the collection of Mr. Punch,* 3 v. 1886–7.

9127  LINTON. Threescore and ten years, 1820 to 1890: recollections. By William James Linton. N.Y. 1894. Lond. [Memories.] 1895.

9128  MAY. Phil May: master-draughtsman & humorist, 1864–1903. By James Thorpe. 1932. Abridged edn. 1948.

9129  PENNELL. The adventures of an illustrator: mostly in following his authors in America & Europe. By Joseph Pennell. Boston, Lond., etc. 1925.

See also Elizabeth Robins Pennell, *The life and letters of Joseph Pennell,* 2 v. Boston 1929, Lond. 1930.

9130  PHIZ. Phiz (Hablot K. Browne): a memoir, including a selection from his correspondence. By Frederic George Kitton. 1882.

See also David Croal Thomson, *Life and labours of Hablot Knight Browne: 'Phiz',* 1884, Edgar Athelstane Browne, *Phiz and Dickens as they appeared to Edgar Browne,* 1913, and Frank Raymond Leavis and Queenie Dorothy Leavis, *Dickens, the novelist,* 1970.

POTTER. For Beatrix Potter see **8429**.

9131   RACKHAM. Arthur Rackham: his life and work. By Derek Hudson. 1960.

9132   REED. Edward Tennyson Reed, 1860–1933: a memoir compiled by [Sir John Randolph] Shane Leslie from an incomplete autobiography . . . 1957.

9133   RICKETTS. Self-portrait: taken from the letters & journals of Charles Ricketts, R.A. Comp. by Thomas Sturge Moore. Ed. by Cecil Lewis. 1939.

9134   ROBINSON. My line of life. By William Heath Robinson. 1938.

9135   SANDYS. Reproductions of woodcuts by Frederick Sandys, 1860–1866. Ed. by Mary Sandys. Priv. pr. [1915.]

9136   SHIELDS. The life and letters of Frederic Shields. Ed. by Ernestine Mills. 1912.

9137   SHORT. The etched and engraved work of Frank Short. By Edward Fairbrother Strange. 1908.

9138   SIMPSON. The autobiography of William Simpson, R.I. (Crimean Simpson). Ed. by George Eyre-Todd. 1903.

9139   STRANG. The etchings of William Strang & Sir Charles Holroyd. By Campbell Dodgson. 1933.

See also [Laurence Binyon, ed.] *William Strang: catalogue of his etched work*, Glasgow 1906, 2nd edn. 1912, suppl. 1923.

9140   TENNIEL. Sir John Tenniel. By Frances Sarzano. 1948.

9141   THOMSON. Hugh Thomson: his art, his letters, his humour and his charm. By Marion Harry Spielmann and Walter Jerrold. 1931.

9142   WARD. Forty years of 'Spy'. By Sir Leslie R. P. Ward. 1915.

### 4. SCULPTURE

9143   GRANT (MAURICE HAROLD) *comp*. A dictionary of British sculptors from the XIIIth to the XXth century. 1953.

Little more than an annotated hist. Unfortunately Rupert Gunnis, comp., *Dictionary of British sculptors, 1660–1851*, 1953, rev. edn. 1968, has little on the period, but it is useful for mid-19th-cent. sculptors.

9144   UNDERWOOD (ERIC GORDON). A short history of English sculpture. 1933.

Not very full. See also Willliam Bell Scott, *The British school of sculpture . . .*, 1871, and Katharine Ada Esdaile, *English monumental sculpture since the renaissance*, 1927. For one episode John Frederick Physick, *The Wellington monument*, 1970, is good.

9145  SPIELMANN (MARION HARRY). British sculpture and sculptors of today. Lond. & N.Y. 1901.

See also Alexander Koch, ed., *Sculptures from 'Academy architecture', 1904–1908*, 1908. Earlier handbooks incl. Joseph Barlow Robinson, *Trade secrets: a collection of practical receipts for the use of sculptors, modellers, stone masons, builders, marble masons, polishers, etc.*, Derby 1862, and George Halse, *The modeller: a guide to the principles and practice of sculpture, for the use of students and amateurs* [1880].

9146  ADAMS-ACTON. Victorian sidelights from the papers of the late Mrs. Adams-Acton. By Anna Maria Diana Wilhelmina Stirling. 1954.

9147  EPSTEIN. Let there be sculpture: an autobiography. By Sir Jacob Epstein. 1940. New edn. [Epstein: an autobiography.] 1955.

9148  FOLEY. The works of John Henry Foley, R.A., sculptor ... By William Cosmo Monkhouse. [1875.]

9149  GIBSON. The biography of John Gibson, R.A., sculptor, Rome. Ed. by Thomas Matthews. 1911.

See also Elizabeth, Lady Eastlake, ed., *Life of John Gibson, R.A., sculptor*, 1870.

9150  GILBERT. Alfred Gilbert ... By Isabel G. McAllister. 1929.

See also Adrian Bury, *Shadow of Eros: a biographical and critical study of the life and works of Sir Alfred Gilbert*, 1952.

9151  GILL. Autobiography. By [Arthur] Eric [Rowton] Gill. 1940.

Evan Robertson Gill, comp., *Bibliography of Eric Gill*, 1953, and *The inscriptional work of Eric Gill: an inventory*, 1964, are comprehensive. Walter Hayward Shewring, ed., *Letters of Eric Gill*, Lond. 1947, N.Y. 1948, is the only coll. The standard life is Robert Speaight, *The life of Eric Gill*, 1966.

9152  JONES. Memoirs of a soldier artist ... By Adrian Jones. 1933.

9153  MOORE. Henry Moore, R.A. By Frank John Maclean. Lond. & N.Y. 1905.

Not to be confused with the great sculptor of the same name, who was b. 1898.

9154  SCOTT. Self-portrait of an artist: from the diaries and memoirs of Lady Kennet (Kathleen, Lady Scott). 1949.

9155  STEVENS. Alfred Stevens: architectural sculptor, painter and designer: a biography with new material. By Kenneth Romney Towndrow. 1939.

Full. Sir Walter Armstrong, *Alfred Stevens—a biographical study*, 1881, Hugh Stannus, *Alfred Stevens and his work ...*, 1891, and K. R. Towndrow, *The works of Alfred Stevens ... in the Tate Gallery*, 1950, are also useful.

9156  TWEED. John Tweed, sculptor: a memoir. By Lendal Tweed. 1936.

9157  WOOLNER. Thomas Woolner, R.A.: sculptor and poet: his life in letters. By his daughter, Amy Woolner. 1917.

## 5. ARCHITECTURE

9158  GUPPY (HENRY) *and* VINE (GUTHRIE) *eds.* A classified catalogue of the works on architecture and the allied arts in the principal libraries of Manchester and Salford . . . Manch. 1909.

Includes important books not in the librs. surveyed.

9159  ROYAL INSTITUTE OF BRITISH ARCHITECTS. Catalogue of the library . . . 2 v. 1937–8.

Suppl. by *Catalogue of the drawings collection*, v. 1+, Farnborough 1969+, and by the R.I.B.A., *Annual review of periodical articles*, 1+, 1965–6+. The best American libr. cats. are those of the Avery Memorial Architectural Libr. of Columbia Univ., which comprise a general *Catalog*, 2nd edn. 19 v. Boston 1968, *Avery index to architectural periodicals*, 12 v. Boston 1963, and *Avery obituary index of architects and artists*, Boston 1963.

9160  HARRIS (JOHN) comp. A catalogue of British drawings for architecture, decoration, sculpture and landscape gardening, 1550–1900, in American collections. Boston. 1971.

9161  GWILT (JOSEPH). An encyclopaedia of architecture, historical, theoretical and practical. 1842. [5th] edn. 1894.

Interesting as a reflection of contemp. taste. See also Architectural Publication Soc., *The dictionary of architecture*, 9 v. 1853–92. and Russell Sturgis, *A dictionary of architecture and building: biographical, historical and descriptive*, 3 v. N.Y. & Lond. 1901–2.

9162  PEVSNER (*Sir* NIKOLAUS BERNHARD LEON) *and others.* The buildings of England. 46 v. 1951–74.

A county-by-county survey publ. by Penguin Books, particularly strong on the Victorian period.

9163  WEALE (JOHN). Rudimentary dictionary of terms used in architecture, civil and naval, building and construction, early and ecclesiastical art. 1849–50. 5th edn. 1876.

9164  ROSCOE (EDWARD STANLEY). A digest of cases relating to the construction of buildings, the liability and rights of architects, surveyors and builders in relation thereto. 1879. 4th edn. 1900.

See also Alfred Emden, *The laws relating to building leases and building contracts*, 1882, 5th edn. 1932, and Alfred Arthur Hudson, *The law of building and engineering contracts*, 1891, 7th edn. 1946.

9165  THE BUILDER: an illustrated weekly magazine for the architect, engineer. 1842+.

The leading trade periodical throughout the period. The other major js. were *The architect*, 1869+, *The architectural review: for the artist and craftsman*, 1869+, *The British architect*, Manch. etc., 1874–1919, *The builders' journal and architectural record* [title *The architects' and builders' journal*, 1910–19, *The architects' j.*, 1919+], 1895+, Alexander Koch and Charles William English, eds., *Academy architecture and annual architectural review*, 1889–1931, and *British competitions in architecture*, 1905–13.

9166  HITCHCOCK (HENRY RUSSELL). Architecture: nineteenth and twentieth centuries. Pelican history of art. 1958.

The best outline hist., but should be suppl. by Sigfried Giedion, *Space, time and architecture: the growth of a new tradition*, trans. by Erwart Matthews, Camb., Mass. 1944, 4th edn. 1962; Sir Nikolaus Bernhard Leon Pevsner, *Pioneers of the modern movement from William Morris to Walter Gropius*, 1936, new edn. [*Pioneers of modern design*], 1960, and *The sources of modern architecture and design*, 1970; Robert Macleod, *Style and society: architectural ideology in Britain, 1835–1914*, 1971; Dennis Sharp, *Sources of modern architecture*, 1970; and Roy. Inst. of British Architects, *One hundred years of British architecture, 1851–1951*, 1951, which deal with the 'modern movement', and by the 17th edn. of Sir Banister Flight Fletcher, *A history of architecture on the comparative method*, 1961.

9167  SUMMERSON (*Sir* JOHN NEWENHAM) *ed.* Concerning architecture: essays on architectural writers and writing presented to Nikolaus Pevsner. 1970.

9168  SOCIETY OF ARCHITECTURAL HISTORIANS OF GREAT BRITAIN. Architectural history. York. 1958+. Annual.

See also *Journal of the Society of Architectural Historians*, Amherst, Mass. etc. 1941+. *Country life . . .*, 1897+, also publ. good hist. articles. The Victorian Soc., *Conference report*, 1963+, and other publs. also deal with Victorian buildings.

9169  HITCHCOCK (HENRY RUSSELL). Early Victorian architecture in Britain. 2 v. New Haven [Conn.]. 1954.

Monumental. James Fergusson, *History of the modern styles of architecture*, 1862, 3rd edn. 2 v. 1891, is a full contemp. account of the same period.

9170  JORDAN (ROBERT FURNEAUX). Victorian architecture. Harmondsworth. 1966.

The handiest introduction.

9171  FERRIDAY (PETER) *ed.* Victorian architecture. 1963.

A useful symposium.

9172  GOODHART-RENDEL (HARRY STUART). English architecture since the regency: an interpretation. 1953.

Deservedly famous. Sir Hugh Maxwell Casson, *An introduction to Victorian architecture*, 1948, Dudley Harbron, *Amphion: or, the nineteenth century*, 1930, and Sir John Betjeman, *First and last loves*, 1952, also offer convincing interpretations.

9173  CLARK (KENNETH MACKENZIE), *Baron Clark*. The Gothic revival: an essay in the history of taste. Lond. & N.Y. 1929. 3rd edn. Lond. 1962.

A lively short study. Needs to be suppl. by Charles Lock Eastlake, *A history of the Gothic revival: an attempt to show how the taste for medieval architecture which lingered in England during the last two centuries, has since been encouraged and developed*, 1872, repr. Leicester 1970, and Sir George Gilbert Scott, *Remarks on secular and domestic architecture: present and future*, 1857, 2nd edn. 1858. There are also some interesting passages, in Thomas Harris, *Victorian architecture . . .*, 1860, and *Three periods of English archi-*

*tecture*, 1894. The influence of the Ecclesiological Soc. was chiefly felt before 1850. For its work see James Floyd White, *The Cambridge movement: the ecclesiologists and the gothic revival*, Camb. 1962.

9174 CLARKE (BASIL FULFORD LOWTHER). Church builders of the nineteenth century: a study of the Gothic revival in England. 1938.

9175 SUMMERSON (*Sir* JOHN NEWENHAM). Victorian architecture: four studies in evaluation. N.Y. 1970.

Excellent. See also his *Heavenly mansions and other essays on architecture*, 1949.

9176 GLOAG (JOHN EDWARDS). Victorian taste: some social aspects of architecture and industrial design from 1820–1900. 1962.

Popular, but well illustr. See also his *Victorian comfort: a social history of design from 1830–1900*, 1961.

9177 PEVSNER (*Sir* NIKOLAUS BERNHARD LEON). Ruskin and Viollet-le-Duc: Englishness and Frenchness in the appreciation of Gothic architecture. 1970.

See also his *Some architectural writers of the nineteenth century*, Oxf. 1972. For non-Gothic influences see Joseph Mordaunt Crook, *The Greek revival: neo-classical attitudes in British architecture, 1760–1870*, 1972.

9178 GIROUARD (MARK). The Victorian country house. Oxf. 1971.

9179 RICHARDSON (*Sir* ALBERT EDWARD). Monumental classic architecture in Great Britain and Ireland during the eighteenth & nineteenth centuries. [1914.]

9180 MUTHESIUS (HERMANN). Die englische Baukunst der Gegenwart: Beispiele neuer englischer Profanbauten. Leipzig & Berlin. 1900–2.

Full on major buildings, 1875–98. See also his *Das englische Haus*..., 3 v. Berlin 1908–11.

9181 STEWART (CECIL). The stones of Manchester. 1956.

One of the best books on Victorian architecture. Suppl. by his *The architecture of Manchester: an index of the principal buildings and their architects, 1800–1900*, Manch. 1956. William Edward Armitage Axon, ed., *An architectural and general description of the town hall, Manchester*..., Manch. 1878, gives a detailed account of one of the greatest buildings of the period. Cp. James Quentin Hughes, *Seaport: architecture and townscape in Liverpool*, Liverpool 1964.

9182 BRIGGS (MARTIN SHAW). The architect in history. Oxf. 1927.

Popular, like his *Men of taste from Pharaoh to Ruskin*, 1947, and *Goths and vandals: a study of the destruction, neglect and preservation of historical buildings in England*, 1952.

9183 JENKINS (FRANK). Architect and patron: a survey of professional relations and practice in England from the sixteenth century to the present day. 1961.

9184 KAYE (BARRINGTON LAURENCE BURNETT). The development of the architectural profession in England: a sociological study. 1960.

9185 GOTCH (JOHN ALFRED) *ed.* The growth and work of the Royal Institute of British Architects, 1834–1934. 1934. Rev. edn. 1934.

See also Sir John Newenham Summerson, *The Architectural Association, 1847–1947,* 1947, and Charles McArthur Butler, *The Society of Architects . . .,* 1926, the former good, the latter a thin pamphlet. Each of these socs. publ. js. The R.I.B.A. publ. *Transactions* [later *Journal*], 1836+, and *Proceedings,* 1878–93, plus a *Kalendar,* 1885+. The A.A. publ. *Architectural Association notes* [later *Journal*], 1887+, which were suppl. by a *Sketch book,* 1867–1917, and a *Year book,* publ. under various names, 1875–1918. The S.A. publ. *Proceedings,* 1888+, which became *The journal of the Society of Architects,* 1893–1900, 1907–22, *The architects' magazine,* 1900–7, and *Architecture,* 1922–31.

9186 KERR (ROBERT). The consulting architect: practical notes on administrative difficulties and disputes. 1886.

A good guide to professional problems.

9187 SHAW (RICHARD NORMAN) *and* JACKSON (*Sir* THOMAS GRAHAM) *eds.* Architecture a profession or an art? Thirteen short essays on the qualifications and training of architects. 1892.

See also William Henry White, *The architect and his artists . . .,* 1892, and *Architecture and public buildings: their relation to school, academy and state in Paris and London,* 1884.

9188 TRAVERS (WALTER IRWIN). Architectural education: a history of the past and some criticism of the present system . . . with particular reference to the position of the universities. 1908.

9189 COLVIN (HOWARD MONTAGU). A biographical dictionary of English architects, 1660–1840. 1954.

Includes a few men still working in 1851.

9190 WHO'S WHO IN ARCHITECTURE: brief biographies and particulars of architects practising in the United Kingdom. 1914+.

Irregular.

9191 WILSON (T. BUTLER). Two Leeds architects: Cuthbert Broderick and George Carson. Leeds. 1937.

9192 BAKER. Architecture & personalities. By Sir Herbert Baker. 1944.

9193 BARRY. The life and works of Sir Charles Barry, R.A., F.R.S. By Alfred Barry. 1867. 2nd edn. 1870.

9194 BENTLEY. John Francis Bentley. By William Walter Scott Moncrieff. 1924.

See also Arthur Stanley George Butler, *John Francis Bentley, the architect of Westminster cathedral: an essay,* 1961.

9195 BLOMFIELD. Memoirs of an architect. By Sir Reginald Theodore Blomfield. 1932.

For his views see his *The mistress art,* 1908.

9196 BUTTERFIELD. William Butterfield. By Paul Thompson. 1971.

9197 DOBSON. Memoir of John Dobson of Newcastle-on-Tyne, member of the Royal Institute of British Architects: containing, some account of the revival of architecture in the north of England, with a list of his works. By his daughter, Margaret Jane Dobson. Lond. & Newcastle. 1885.

9198 FLETCHER. The architectural work of Sir Banister Fletcher . . . By William Hanneford-Smith. 1934.

9199 GIMSON. Ernest Gimson: his life and work. By William Richard Lethaby and others. Stratford-upon-Avon. 1924.

9200 GODWIN. The conscious stone: the life of Edward William Godwin. By Dudley Harbron. 1949.

9201 GRIMTHORPE. Lord Grimthorpe, 1816–1905. By Peter Ferriday. 1957.

9202 JACKSON. Recollections of Thomas Graham Jackson, 1835–1924. Ed. by Basil Hippisley Jackson. 1950.

9203 LORIMER. The work of Sir Robert Lorimer, K.B.E., A.R.A., R.S.A. By Christopher Edward Clive Hussey. [1932.]

9204 LUTYENS. The life of Sir Edwin Lutyens. By Christopher Edward Clive Hussey. Lond. & N.Y. 1950. Special edn. 1953.

Suppl. by Arthur Stanley George Butler and others, *The Lutyens memorial: the archi-tecture of Sir Edwin Lutyens*, 3 v. 1950. See also Robert Lutyens, *Sir Edwin Lutyens: an appreciation in perspective*, 1942 and **7116**.

9205 MACKINTOSH. Charles Rennie Mackintosh and the modern move-ment. By Thomas Howarth. 1952.

See also Robert Macleod, *Charles Rennie Mackintosh*, 1968, and the brochures and catalogue publ. on the occasion of the Mackintosh centenary, 1968.

9206 MAWSON. The life & work of an English landscape architect: an auto-biography. By Thomas Hayton Mawson. [1927.]

9207 NEWTON. The work of Ernest Newton, R.A. With a critical appreciation by William Godfrey Newton. 1925.

9208 PAXTON. The works of Sir Joseph Paxton, 1803–1865. By George Fletcher Chadwick. 1961.

Good. See also Violet Rosa Markham, *Paxton and the bachelor duke*, 1935, which deals with Paxton's career and personality. For the Crystal Palace see also **4128–33**, **9000**.

9209 SCOTT. Personal and professional recollections. By Sir George Gilbert Scott. Ed. by his son George Gilbert Scott. 1879.

9210 SHAW. Richard Norman Shaw, R.A., architect, 1831–1912: a study. By Sir Reginald Theodore Blomfield. 1940.

9211 STREET. Memoir of George Edmund Street, R.A., 1824–1881. By Arthur Edmund Street. 1888.

See also Georgiana Goddard King, ed., *George Edmund Street: unpublished notes and reprinted papers*, Hispanic Soc. of America, N.Y. 1916.

9212 TAYLOR. The autobiography of an octogenarian architect: being a record of his studies at home and abroad during 65 years . . . By George Ledwell Taylor. 2 v. 1870–2.

Little on the period, but catches the atmosphere of the lesser architect's practice.

9213 WEAVER. Lawrence Weaver. By [Bertram] Clough Williams-Ellis. 1933.

9214 WEBB. Philip Webb and his work. By William Richard Lethaby. 1935.

9215 WYATT. Matthew Digby Wyatt: the first Cambridge Slade Professor of Fine Art: an inaugural lecture. By Sir Nikolaus Bernhard Leon Pevsner. 1950.

## 6. OTHER ARTS

### (a) *Fine Books*

9216 STEELE (ROBERT REYNOLDS). The revival of printing: a bibliographical catalogue of works issued by the chief modern English presses. 1912.

See also Will Ransom, *Private presses and their books*, N.Y. 1929.

9217 WILLIAMS (*Sir* HAROLD HERBERT). Book clubs & printing societies of Great Britain and Ireland. 1929.

See also Charles Clive Bigham, Viscount Mersey, *The Roxburghe Club: its history and its members, 1812–1927*, 1928.

9218 SPARLING (HENRY HALLIDAY). The Kelmscott Press and William Morris, master craftsman. 1924.

See also Sir Sydney Carlyle Cockerell, ed., *A note by William Morris on his aims in founding the Kelmscott Press, together with a short description of the press*, Kelmscott 1898, Harry Buxton Forman, *The books of William Morris described . . .*, 1897, William Atkins, *William Morris: artist, printer and man of business*, 1918, and Raymond Watkinson, *William Morris as designer*, N.Y. 1967. For Morris see also **616.**

9219 COBDEN-SANDERSON. Cobden-Sanderson and the Doves press: the history of the press and the story of its types. By Alfred William Pollard and others. San Francisco. 1929.

See also *The journals of Thomas James Cobden-Sanderson, 1879–1922*, 1926, Edward Lorenzo de Coverly, *Cobden-Sanderson, bookbinder . . .*, 1951, and *Catalogue raisonné of the books printed at the Doves Press, 1900–1916*, 1916.

9220 ASHBEE (CHARLES ROBERT). The private press: a study in idealism: to which is added a bibliography of the Essex House Press. Broad Campden. 1909.

For other presses see *The Daniel Press: memorials of C. H. O. Daniel, with a bibliography of the press* [by Falconer Madan], *1845–1919*, Oxf. 1921; *C. H. St. J. Hornby, 25 June 1867–26 April 1946: an anthology of appreciations*, 1946; *A descriptive bibliography of the books printed at the Ashendene Press* [1895–1925], 1925; Thomas Sturge Moore, *A brief account of the origin of the Eragny Press*, 1903; and Charles de Sousy Rickett, *A bibliography of books printed between 1896 and 1903 by Hacon and Ricketts*, 1904.

(b) *Photography*

9221 BONI (ALBERT) *comp*. Photographic literature: an international bibliographic guide to general and specialized literature on photographic processes, techniques, theory, chemistry, physics, apparatus, materials & applications, industry, history, biography, aesthetics. N.Y. 1962.

The best libr. cat. is Royal Photographic Soc. of Great Britain, *Library catalogue*, 2 pts. 1939–52, suppls. 1952+.

9222 THOMAS (DAVID BOWEN). The Science Museum photography collection. H.M.S.O. 1970.

For other colls. see Nunn (140).

9223 GERNSHEIM (HELMUT) *and* GERNSHEIM (ALISON). The history of photography: from the earliest use of the camera obscura . . . up to 1914. 1955. 2nd edn. 1969.

See also their *L. J. M. Daguerre: the history of the diorama and the daguerreotype*, 1956, Helmut Gernsheim, *Creative photography: aesthetic trends, 1839–1960*, 1962, *Masterpieces of Victorian photography*, 1951, *Lewis Carroll, photographer*, 1949, and *Julia Margaret Cameron: pioneer of photography*, 1948, and Helmut and Alison Gernsheim, *Roger Fenton: photographer of the Crimean War*, Lond. & N.Y. 1954. See also Heinrich Schwarz, *David Octavius Hill: master of photography*, trans., by Helene E. Fraenkel, 1932, and Alex Strasser, ed., *Victorian photography* . . ., 1942.

9224 EMERSON (PETER HENRY). Naturalistic photography for students of the art. 1889. 3rd edn. 1899.

A famous contemp. guide. For the mechanics of photography see Bernard Edward Jones, ed., *Cassell's cyclopaedia of photography*, 1911. The *'Photographic News' almanac* [*Yearbook of photography*], 1859+, and The *'British journal' photographic almanac*, 1860+, both list societies. The best contemp. j. was *The British j. of photography*, 1854+, publ. originally as *The Liverpool photographic j.*

9225 THOMAS (DAVID BOWEN). The first negatives: an account of the discovery and early use of the negative–positive photographic process. Science Museum. 1964.

9226 COBURN. Alvin Langdon Coburn, photographer: an autobiography. Ed. by Helmut and Alison Gernsheim. Lond. & N.Y. 1966.

9227 TALBOT. William Henry Fox Talbot: father of photography. By Arthur Harold Booth. 1965.

9228  BRITISH EMPIRE FILM INSTITUTE. British Film Library: catalogue of books and publications in cinematography and allied subjects. 1928. 3rd edn. 1951

For the National Film Archive see **146**.

9229  LOW (RACHEL) *and* MANVELL (ROGER). The history of the British film. 3 v. 1948–9.

(c) *Minor Arts*

9230  GRIGSON (GEOFFREY EDWARD HARVEY) *comp.* English drawing from Samuel Cooper to Gwen John. 1955.

See also [Arthur] Graham Reynolds, *Nineteenth-century drawings, 1850–1900*, 1949, and Arts Council of Great Britain, *Three centuries of British water colours and drawings*, comp. by Brinsley Ford, 1951, and *Drawings & water-colours from the Whitworth Art Gallery, University of Manchester*, 1960. For the main coll. of British drawings see **8995**. Charles George Harper, *English pen artists of today: examples of their work with some criticisms and appreciations*, 1892, is a good contemp. work. Other handbooks incl. George Harley, *A guide to landscape drawing in pencil and chalk*, 1848, 8th edn. 1865; G. W. Caldwell Hutchinson, *Some hints on learning to draw* . . ., 1893; Mary Philadelphia Merrifield, *Handbook of light and shade, with especial reference to model drawing*, 1855, 14th edn. 1896; Henry Murray, *The art of painting and drawing in coloured crayons* . . ., 1865; Henry O'Neill, *A guide to pictorial art: how to use the black lead pencil, chalks and watercolours*, 1846, 5th edn. 1861; and William Walker, *Handbook of drawing*, 1879.

9231  GRANT (MAURICE HAROLD). 'Catalogue of British medals since 1760'. *British Numismatic J.* xxii (1936–7), 269–93; xxiii (1938–9), 119–52; xxiii (1939–40), 321–62; xxiii (1940–1), 449–80. The whole repr. with index and addenda. N.d.

See also Leonard Forrer, *Biographical dictionary of medallists, coin, gem, and seal-engravers, &c. ancient and modern, with references to their works, B.C. 500–A.D. 1900*, 8 v. 1902–30, and Frederick Parkes Weber, *Medals and medallions of the nineteenth century relating to England by foreign artists*, 2 pts. 1894–1907.

9232  DAY (LEWIS FOREMAN). Windows: a book about stained & painted glass. 1897. 3rd edn. 1909.

See also Bernard Rackham, comp., *Victoria and Albert Museum, Department of Ceramics: a guide to the collections of stained glass*, 1936, and **5360**.

9233  WEAVER (*Sir* LAWRENCE). English leadwork: its art & history. 1909.

9234  MORRIS (BARBARA J.). Victorian embroidery. Lond. 1962. N.Y. 1963.

See also Elizabeth Glaister, *Needlework*, Art at home ser. 1880; Alice Dryden, *Church embroidery*, 1911; Marian[ne] Margaret Cust, Viscountess Alford, *Needlework as art*, 1886; L. Higgin, *Handbook of embroidery*, ed. by Lady Marian Alford, Roy. Soc. of Art Needlework, 1880; and A. Grace I. Christie, *Embroidery and tapestry weaving* . . ., 1906.

9235  LELAND (CHARLES GODFREY). The minor arts: porcelain painting, wood carving, stencilling, modelling, mosaic work, &c. Art at home ser. 1880.

See also Sidney T. Whiteford, *A guide to porcelain painting* [1877], 6th edn. 1879, and Edward Henry Pinto, *Treen and other wooden bygones: an encyclopaedia and social history*, 1969.

## H. MUSIC

For church music see **3462–83.**

**9236** DUCKLES (VINCENT) *comp.* Music reference and research materials: an annotated bibliography. N.Y. 1964. 2nd edn. 1967.

A good annotated list. The best working bibliog. is Lionel Roy McColvin and Harold Reeves, *Music libraries . . .*, 2 v. 1937–8, rev. edn. by Jack Dove, 2 v. 1965. Imogen Fellinger, *Verzeichnis der Musikzeitschriften des 19. Jahrhunderts*, Regensburg 1968, is a list of periodicals arranged by date of first publ. James E. Matthew, *The literature of music*, 1896, is a useful contemp. manual. John Howard Davies, *Musicalia: sources of information in music*, Oxf. 1966, is useful for special colls. in Britain. New British books about music, are incl. in Council of the British National Bibliog., *British catalogue of music*, 1+,1957+.

**9237** NEW YORK PUBLIC LIBRARY: REFERENCE DEPARTMENT. Dictionary catalog of the music collection. 33 v. Boston. 1964. Suppls. 1966+.

The fullest catalogue. Indexes articles as well as books. The best British catalogue is Liverpool Public Librs. *Catalogue of the music library*, Liverpool 1954. For recordings see Robert Bauer, comp., *The new catalogue of historical records, 1898–1908/09*, 1947, and *Voices of the past: vocal recordings, 1898–1925*, 1+, Lingfield, Surrey 1957+.

**9238** GROVE (*Sir* GEORGE) *comp.* Grove's dictionary of music and musicians. 5th edn. by Eric Blom. 9 v. 1954. Suppl. 1961.

First publ. in 4 v. 1878–89. A mine of musical data. A more scholarly German equivalent is Friedrich Blume, ed., *Die Musik in Geschichte und Gegenwart: allgemeine Enzyklopädie der Musik . . .*, 14 v. Kassel 1949–68, suppls. in progress. Willi Apel, comp., *Harvard dictionary of music*, Camb., Mass. 1944, 2nd edn. 1969, is a 1-v. guide to musicology, Percy Alfred Scholes, comp., *The Oxford companion to music . . .*, 1938, 10th edn., ed. by John Owen Ward, 1970, a 1-v. guide to musicians and music.

**9239** BAKER (THEODORE) *comp.* A biographical dictionary of musicians. N.Y. 1900. 5th edn. N.Y. 1958.

To be suppl. by James Duff Brown and Stephen Samuel Stratton, *British musical biography: a dictionary of musical artists, authors and composers born in Britain and its colonies*, Birmingham 1897, and *Musical directory*, irregular 1870–1912, annual 1912+.

**9240** WYNDHAM (HENRY SAXE) *and* L'EPINE (GEOFFREY) *eds.* Who's who in music: a biographical record of contemporary musicians. 2 v. 1913–15.

**9241** NEW OXFORD HISTORY OF MUSIC. 11 v. 1954+. In progress.

The old *Oxford history of music*, 6 v. 1901–5, 2nd edn. 7 v. 1931–8, is also useful.

**9242** WALKER (ERNEST). A history of music in England. Oxf. 1907. 3rd edn. 1952.

**9243** YOUNG (PERCY MARSHALL). A history of British music. Lond. & N.Y. 1967.

**9244** MACKERNESS (ERIC DAVID). A social history of English music. Lond. & Toronto. 1964.

Too general to be of much value.

9245   ABRAHAM (GERALD ERNEST HEAL) *ed.* A hundred years of music. 1938. 2nd edn. 1949.

See also John Culshaw, *A century of music,* 1952, and **9287.**

9246   FULLER-MAITLAND (JOHN ALEXANDER). English music in the XIXth century. 1902.

See also his *A doorkeeper of music,* 1929.

9247   HOWES (FRANK). The English musical renaissance. 1966.

A helpful intro.

9248   FULLER-MAITLAND (JOHN ALEXANDER). The music of Parry and Stanford: an essay in comparative criticism. Camb. 1934.

9249   SHAW (GEORGE BERNARD). London music in 1888–89, as heard by Corno di Bassetto (later known as Bernard Shaw), with some further auto-biographical particulars. Lond. & N.Y. [1937.]

See also his *Music in London, 1890–94,* v. 19 of the Standard edn. of his work, 3 v. [1932], and *How to become a musical critic,* ed. by Dan H. Laurence, Lond. & N.Y. 1960.

9250   GALLOWAY (WILLIAM JOHNSON). Musical England. 1910.

See also Sydney Grew, *Our favourite musicians: from Stanford to Holbrooke,* Edin. & Lond. 1922, and *Favourite musical performers,* Edin. & Lond. 1923, Charles Larcom Graves, *Post-Victorian music, with other studies and sketches,* 1911, Charles Willeby, *Masters of contemporary music,* 1893, and Hermann Klein, *Thirty years of musical life in London, 1870–1900,* 1903.

9251   CLARK (RONALD WILLIAM). The Royal Albert hall. 1958.

There is also Robert Elkin, *Queen's Hall, 1893–1941,* 1944.

9252   CORDER (FREDERICK). A history of the Royal Academy of Music from 1822 to 1922. 1922.

See also Sir Alexander Campbell Mackenzie, *A musician's narrative,* 1927, and, for the Royal College, Henry Cope Colles, *The Royal College of Music: a jubilee record, 1883–1933,* 1933.

9253   SMITH (WILLIAM JAMES). Five centuries of Cambridge musicians, 1464–1964. Camb. 1964.

For Oxford see Sir Percy Carter Buck, John Henry Mee, and Francis Cunningham Woods, *Ten years of university music in Oxford: being, a brief record of the proceedings of the Oxford University Musical Union . . ., 1884–1894,* 1894, and Edgar Stephen Kemp and John Henry Mee, *Ten more years of university music in Oxford . . ., 1894–1904,* Oxf. 1904.

9254   NETTEL (REGINALD). Music in the five towns, 1840–1914: a study of the social influence of music in an industrial district . . . 1944.

For other districts see Joseph Sutcliffe Smith, *The story of music in Birmingham,* Birmingham 1945.

9255 NETTEL (REGINALD). The orchestra in England: a social history. 1946. 2nd edn. 1956.

9256 FOSTER (MYLES BIRKET). History of the Philharmonic Society of London, 1813–1912. Lond. & Toronto. 1912.

See also Robert Elkin, *Royal Philharmonic: the annals of the Royal Philharmonic Society* . . ., 1947.

9257 KENNEDY ([GEORGE] MICHAEL [SINCLAIR]). The Hallé tradition: a century of music. Manch. 1960.

Better than Clifford Burwyn Rees, *One hundred years of the Hallé*, 1957. For Sir Charles Hallé see Charles Émile Hallé and Marie Hallé, eds., *Life and letters of Sir Charles Hallé: being an autobiography, 1819–1860, with correspondence and diaries*, 1896, and Charles Rigby, *Sir Charles Hallé: a portrait for today*, Manch. 1952.

9258 SEARS (MINNIE EARL) *assisted by* CRAWFORD (PHYLLIS) *comps.* Song index: an index to more than 12,000 songs . . . N.Y. 1926. Suppl. N.Y. 1934.

See also Helen Grant Cushing, comp., *Children's song index: an index to more than 22,000 songs* . . ., N.Y. 1936.

9259 NETTEL (REGINALD). Sing a song of England: a social history of traditional song. 1954. Repr. Bath. 1970.

9260 DISHER (MAURICE WILLSON). Victorian song from dive to drawing room. 1955.

9261 SIMPSON (HAROLD). A century of ballads, 1810–1910: their composers and singers. 1910.

9262 DEAN-SMITH (MARGARET). A guide to English folk-song collections, 1822–1952, with an index to their contents, historical annotations and an introduction. Liverpool. 1954.

9263 HOWES (FRANK). Folk music of Britain: and beyond. 1969.

9264 LLOYD (ALBERT LANCASTER). Folk song in England. 1967.

See also his *Come all ye bold miners: ballads and songs of the coalfields*, 1952.

9265 SHARP (CECIL JAMES). English folk-song: some conclusions. 1907. 3rd edn. 1954.

By the pioneer of folk-song collection.

9266 YOUNG (PERCY MARSHALL). The choral tradition: an historical and analytical survey from the sixteenth century to the present day. 1962.

See also Arthur Mees, *Choirs & choral music*, 1901, John Spencer Curwen, *Memorials of John Curwen*, 1882, and Sir Alfred Herbert Brewer, *Memoirs of choirs and choristers: fifty years of music*, 1931.

9267  SPRITTLES (J.). 'Leeds musical festivals'. *Thoresby Soc. Publs.* xlvi (1957–61), 200–70.

See also Frederick R. Spark and Joseph Bennett, *History of the Leeds music festivals, 1858–1889* ..., Leeds 1892, 2nd. edn. 1892. For the Sheffield festivals see J. A. Rodgers, *Dr. Henry Coward, the pioneer chorus-master,* 1911, and Sir Henry Coward, *Reminiscences,* 1919.

9268  LOEWENBERG (ALFRED). Annals of opera, 1597–1940. Camb. 1943. 2nd edn. 2 v. Geneva. 1955.

Details of performances. For plots see Gustav Kobbé, comp., *The complete opera book ... the stories of the operas* ..., N.Y. & Lond. 1919, rev. edn. by George Henry Hubert Lascelles, Earl of Harewood, Lond. 1954 and 1963, and Mark Hugh Lubbock, *The complete book of light opera* ..., Lond. 1962, N.Y. 1963.

9269  ROSENTHAL (HAROLD DAVID) *and* WARRACK (JOHN). Concise Oxford dictionary of opera. N.Y. etc. 1964.

9270  WHITE (ERIC WALTER). The rise of English opera. 1951.

9271  ROSENTHAL (HAROLD DAVID). Two centuries of opera at Covent Garden. 1958.

See also Richard Northcott, *Records of the Royal Opera, Covent Garden, 1888–1921,* 1921.

9272  TEMPERLEY (NICHOLAS). 'The English romantic opera'. *Victorian Studs.* ix (1965–6), 293–301.

9273  MAURER (OSCAR). 'Punch and the opera war, 1847–1867'. *Texas Studs. in Lit. and Lang.* i (1959), 139–70.

9274  WALBROOK (HENRY MACKINNON). Gilbert & Sullivan opera: a history and a comment. 1922.

There is a large lit., as well as works on Gilbert (**8370**), and Sullivan (**9315**). See Audrey May Williamson, *Gilbert & Sullivan opera: a new assessment,* 1953; Leslie William Alfred Baily, *The Gilbert & Sullivan book,* 1952, 4th edn. 1956; Frederick Joseph Halton, *The Gilbert and Sullivan operas: a concordance,* N.Y. 1935; Raymond Mander and Joe Mitchenson, *A picture history of Gilbert and Sullivan,* 1962; and William Aubrey Cecil Darlington, *The world of Gilbert and Sullivan,* N.Y. 1951.

9275  DUNN (GEORGE E.). A Gilbert & Sullivan dictionary. 1936.

9276  ROLLINS (CYRIL BERNARD) *and* WITTS (RAWDON JOHN) *comps.* The D'Oyly Carte Opera company in Gilbert and Sullivan operas: a record of productions, 1875–1961. 1962.

See also Shafto Justin Adair FitzGerald, *The story of the Savoy opera: a record of events and productions,* 1924, Sir Henry Alfred Lytton, *The secrets of a Savoyard,* 1921, and *A wandering minstrel: reminiscences* ..., 1933, François Arsène Cellier and Cunningham Bridgeman, *Gilbert, Sullivan and D'Oyly Carte: reminiscences of the Savoy and Savoyards,* 1914, 2nd edn. 1927, and Rutland Barrington, *Rutland Barrington* ..., 1908, and *More Rutland Barrington,* 1911.

9277 FORRESTER (FELICITÉE SHEILA). Ballet in England: a bibliography and survey, *c.* 1700–June 1966. Libr. Assoc. 1968.

9278 GUEST (IVOR FORBES). The romantic ballet in England: its development, fulfilment and decline. 1954.

Guest also publ. *The dancer's heritage: a short history of ballet,* 1960, rev edn. 1962, *Fanny Cerrito: the life of a romantic ballerina,* 1956, *Victorian ballet-girl: the tragic story of Clara Webster,* 1957, and *Adeline Genée: a lifetime of ballet under six reigns; based on the personal reminiscences of Dame Adeline Genée-Isitt,* 1958.

9279 CLARKE (MARY). The Sadler's Wells ballet: a history and an appreciation. 1955.

9280 WILLIAMS (CHARLES FRANCIS ABDY). The story of the organ. 1903.

Suppl. by his *The story of organ music,* 1905.

9281 LEWIS (WALTER) *and* LEWIS (THOMAS). Modern organ building: being a practical explanation and description of the whole art of organ construction . . . 1911. 3rd edn. 1939.

9282 RUSSELL (JOHN FREDERICK) *and* ELLIOT (JOHN HAROLD). The brass band movement. 1936.

To follow events consult *The British bandsman,* 1887+. Title became *The orchestral times and bandsman,* 1891–2, *The British musician,* 1893–8, *The British bandsman,* 1899+.

9283 MORRIS (WILLIAM MEREDITH). British violin makers, classical and modern. 1904. 2nd edn. 1920.

Morris also publ. a good life, *Walter H. Mayson: an account of the life and work of a celebrated modern violin maker,* 1906. David Laurie, *Reminiscences of a fiddle dealer,* 1924, is interesting.

9284 MORRIS (ERNEST). The history and art of change-ringing. 1931.

9285 CLARK (JOHN ERNEST THOMAS). Musical boxes [: a history and an appreciation]. 1948. 3rd edn. 1961.

9286 HUMPHRIES (CHARLES) *and* SMITH (WILLIAM CHARLES). Music publishing in the British Isles, from the earliest times to the middle of the nineteenth century: a dictionary of engravers, printers, publishers, and music sellers . . . 1954.

See also William Boosey, *Fifty years of music,* 1931, Novello, Ewer & Co., *A short history of cheap music as exemplified in the records of the house of Novello, Ewer & Co. . . .,* Lond. & N.Y. 1887, Novello & Co., *A century and a half in Soho: short history of the firm of Novello, publishers and printers of music, 1811–1961* [1961], and Chappell & Co., *The Chappell centenary, 1811–1912* [1912].

9287  SCHOLES (PERCY ALFRED). The mirror of music, 1844–1944 : a century of musical life in Britain as reflected in the pages of the *Musical times.* 2 v. 1947.

Good. The *Musical times,* 1844+, was the leading musical j. of the day. But see also Edward Algernon Baughan, ed., *Sixty years of music: being the diamond jubilee number of the* Musical standard, 1897. Many of the music critics of the daily papers publ. memoirs, among them Henry Fothergill Chorley of the *Athenaeum,* whose *Autobiography, memoir and letters,* were ed. by Henry Gay Hewlett, 2 v. 1873, and whose *Thirty years' musical reminiscences,* 2 v. 1862, were ed. by Ernest Newman in 1 v. 1926, and James William Davison of *The Times* whose work was ed. by Henry Davison as *Music during the Victorian era: from Mendelssohn to Wagner: being the memories of J. W. Davison, forty years music critic of* The Times, 1912. See also Bernard Shaw's music criticism at **9249.**

9288  KING (ALEXANDER HYETT). Some British collectors of music, *c.* 1600–1960. Camb. 1963.

9289  ARDITI. My reminiscences. By Luigi Arditi. Ed. by the Baroness von Zelditz. 1896.

9290  BANTOCK. Granville Bantock. By Howard Ormond Anderton. Lond. & N.Y. 1915.

9291  BAX. Farewell, my youth. By Sir Arnold Edward Trevor Bax. 1943.

See also Robert Hoare Hull, *A handbook on Arnold Bax's symphonies,* 1932.

9292  BEECHAM. Sir Thomas Beecham: a memoir. By Neville Cardus. 1961.

See also Beecham's own *A mingled chime: leaves from an autobiography,* 1944, Charles Reid, *Thomas Beecham: an independent biography,* Lond. 1961, N.Y. 1962, Berta Geissmar, *The baton and the jackboot: recollections of musical life,* 1944, and **9313.**

9293  BENNETT. The life of William Sterndale Bennett. By James Robert Sterndale Bennett. Camb. 1907.

9294  BERLIOZ. Berlioz in London. By A. W. Ganz. 1950.

9295  BRIDGE. A Westminster pilgrim: being a record of service . . . By Sir John Frederick Bridge. 1919.

9296  COLERIDGE-TAYLOR. Samuel Coleridge-Taylor, musician: his life and letters. By William Charles Berwick Sayers. 1915. 2nd edn. 1927.

See also Jessie S. Fleetwood Coleridge-Taylor, *Genius and musician: personal reminiscences of my husband,* Bognor Regis & Lond. 1943.

9297  COWEN. My art and my friends. By Sir Frederick Hymen Cowen. 1913.

9298  DELIUS. Frederick Delius. By Sir Thomas Beecham. 1959.

See also Clare Delius, *Frederick Delius: memories of my brother,* 1935, and Eric Fenby, *Delius as I knew him,* 1939. There is little more in Philip Arnold Heseltine, *Frederick Delius,* 1923, 2nd edn 1952; Arthur James Bramwell Hutchings, *Delius: a critical biography,* 1948; Max Chop, *Frederick Delius,* Berlin 1907; Arthur Keith Holland, *The songs of Delius,* 1951; and Robert Hoare Hill, *Delius,* 1928.

9299 DOLMETSCH. Personal recollections of Arnold Dolmetsch. By Mabel Dolmetsch. 1957.

See also Robert Donington, *The work and ideas of Arnold Dolmetsch: the renaissance of early music*, Haslemere 1932.

9300 ELGAR. Portrait of Elgar. By Michael Kennedy. 1968. New edn. 1973.

Makes use of new material publ. in Percy Marshall Young, ed., *Letters of Edward Elgar and other writings*, 1956, and *Letters to Nimrod: Edward Elgar to August Jaeger, 1897–1908*, Lond. & N.Y. 1965. The basic life is Basil Maine, *Elgar: his life and works*, 2 v. 1933. Ernest Newman, *Elgar*, 1922, and Percy M. Young, *Elgar, O.M.: a study of a musician*, 1955, are good monographs. There are personal reminiscences in Dora M. Powell, *Edward Elgar: memories of a variation*, 1937, 3rd edn. 1949, and William Henry Reed, *Elgar as I knew him*, 1936. Other studs. incl. W. H. Reed, *Elgar*, 1939; A. J. Sheldon, *Edward Elgar*, 1932; Robert John Buckley, *Sir Edward Elgar*, Lond. & N.Y. 1905; John Fielder Porte, *Sir Edward Elgar*, Lond. & N.Y. 1921, and *Elgar and his music: an appreciative study*, 1933; and Diana Mary McVeagh, *Edward Elgar: his life and music*, 1955. Jerrold Northrop Moore, *Elgar: a life in photographs*, 1972, is pleasant.

9301 GERMAN. Edward German: an intimate biography. By William Herbert Scott. 1932.

9302 GODFREY. Memories and music: thirty-five years of conducting. By Sir Daniel Eyers Godfrey. 1924.

9303 GROVE. The life & letters of Sir George Grove, C.B. By Charles Larcom Graves. 1903.

9304 HENSCHEL. Musings & memories of a musician. By Sir George Henschel. 1918.

See also Helen Henschel, *When soft voices die: a musical biography*, 1944.

9305 HOLBROOKE. Josef Holbrooke and his work. By George Lowe. 1920.

See also *Josef Holbrooke: various appreciations by many authors*, 1937.

9306 HOLST. Gustav Holst. By Imogen Holst. 1938. 2nd. edn. 1969.

See also her *The music of Gustav Holst*, 1951, 2nd edn. 1968, Edmund Duncan Rubbra, *Gustav Holst*, 1947, and **9316**.

9307 JULLIEN. The life of Jullien: adventurer, showman-conductor, and establisher of the promenade concerts in England, together with the history of those concerts up to 1895. By Adam Von Ahn Carse. Camb. 1951.

9308 MACFARREN. George Alexander MacFarren: his life, works and influence. By Henry Charles Banister. 1891.

MacFarren's brother was also a well-known musician: see Walter Cecil MacFarren, *Memories: an autobiography*, 1905.

9309 PARRY. Hubert Parry: his life and works. By Charles Larcom Graves. 2 v. 1926.

There is little in Charles Willeby, *Charles Hubert Hastings Parry*, 1893, but see **9248** and Gwendolen Maud Greene, *Two witnesses: a personal recollection of Hubert Parry and Friedrich von Hügel*, 1930.

**9310  RONALD.** Myself and others: written lest I forget. By Sir Landon Ronald. [1931.]

See also his *Variations on a personal theme*, 1922.

**9311  SHARP.** Cecil Sharp. By Arthur Henry Fox-Strangways assisted by Maud Karpeles. 1933. 2nd edn. 1955.

**9312  SHAW.** Up to now. By Martin Shaw. 1929.

**9313  SMYTH.** Ethel Smyth. By Christopher Marie St. John. 1959.

Dame Ethel Mary Smyth publ. a ser. of autobiogs., *Impressions that remained*, 2 v. 1919, new edn. 1923, *Streaks of life*, 1921, new edn. 1924, *A final burning of boats*, 1928, *Beecham and Pharaoh* . . ., 1935, *As time went on*, 1936, and *What happened next*, 1940, also a number of autobiog. essays, incl. *Female pipings in Eden*, 1934.

**9314  STANFORD.** Charles Villiers Stanford. By Harry Plunket Greene. 1935.

Sir Charles Villiers Stanford himself publ. *Studies and memories*, 1908, *Pages from an unwritten diary*, 1914, and *Interludes, records and reflections*, 1922. See also John Fielder Porte, *Sir Charles V. Stanford*, Lond. & N.Y. 1921, and **9248.**

**9315  SULLIVAN.** The music of Arthur Sullivan. By Gervase Hughes. 1960.

See also Sirvart Poladian, *Sir Arthur Sullivan: an index to the texts of his vocal works*, Detroit [Mich.] 1961. The official life was Herbert Thomas Sullivan and Sir Walter Newman Flower, *Sir Arthur Sullivan: his life, letters & diaries*, 1927, 2nd edn. 1950. There are many other lives, incl. Arthur Lawrence, *Sir Arthur Sullivan: life story, letters and reminiscences*, 1899, Benjamin William Findon, *Sir Arthur Sullivan: his life and music*, 1904, and Henry Saxe Wyndham, *Arthur Seymour Sullivan, 1842–1900*, 1926. For Gilbert and Sullivan opera see **9274–6.**

**9316  VAUGHAN WILLIAMS.** R.V.W.: a biography of Ralph Vaughan Williams. By Ursula Vaughan Williams. 1965.

See also Ursula Vaughan Williams and Imogen Holst. eds., *Heirs and rebels: letters written to each other and occasional writings on music by Ralph Vaughan Williams and Gustav Holst*, 1959, Alan Edgar Frederic Dickinson, *Vaughan Williams*, 1963, [George] Michael [Sinclair] Kennedy, *The works of Ralph Vaughan Williams*, 1964, and James Churchill Jeanes Day, *Vaughan Williams*, 1961.

**9317  WOOD.** Sir Henry Wood: a biography. By Reginald Pound. 1969.

Sir Henry Joseph Wood himself publ. *My life of music*, 1938, and his widow, Jessie, Lady Wood, *The last years of Henry J. Wood*, 1954. There is also a British Broadcasting Corporation souvenir, *Sir Henry Wood: fifty years of the Proms*, comp. by Ralph Hill and Clifford Burwyn Rees, 1948.

**9318  ORGANISTS.** BATES. Frank Bates, *Reminiscences and autobiography of a musician in retirement*, Norwich 1930. DAVIES. Henry Cope Colles, *Walford Davies: a biography*, 1942. ELVEY. Mary, Lady Elvey, *Life and reminiscences of George Job Elvey*, 1894. HOLLINS. Alfred Hollins, *A blind musician looks back: an autobiography*, 1936. MINSHALL. Ebenezer Minshall, *Fifty years' reminiscences of a Free Church musician*, 1910. SPARK. William Spark, *Musical memories*, 1888, new edn. 1909, and *Musical reminiscences* . . ., 1892.

9319   SINGERS. Butt. Harriet Winifred Ponder, *Clara Butt: her life story*, 1928. Ffrangcon-Davies. Marjorie Ffrangcon-Davies, *David Ffrangcon-Davies: his life and book*, 1938. Garcia. Malcolm Sterling MacKinlay, *Garcia: the centenarian and his times*, Edin. & Lond. 1908. Kennedy-Fraser. Marjory Kennedy-Fraser, *A life of song*, 1929. Lind. Edward Charles Wagenknecht, *Jenny Lind*, Boston & N.Y. 1931. Joan Carroll Boone Bulman, *Jenny Lind: a biography*, 1956. Jenny Maria Catherine Maude, *The life of Jenny Lind: briefly told by her daughter*, 1926. Melba. Dame Nellie Melba, pseud. of Dame Helen Porter Armstrong, *Melodies and memories*, 1925. Agnes G. Murphy, *Melba: a biography*, 1909. Percy Colson, *Melba: an unconventional biography*, 1932. Joseph Wechsberg, *Red plush and black velvet: the story of Dame Nellie Melba and her times*, 1962. Novello. Averil Mackenzie-Grieve, *Clara Novello, 1818–1908*, 1955. Clara Anastasia Novello, *Reminiscences*, comp. by Contessa Valeria Cigliucci, 1910. Clara Novello-Davies, *The life I have loved*, 1940. Palmer. Bessie Palmer, *Musical recollections*, 1904. Patti. Hermann Klein, *The reign of Patti*, Lond. & N.Y. 1920. Reeves. John Sims Reeves, *Sims Reeves: his life and recollections* . . ., 1888, and *My jubilee: or, fifty years of artistic life*, 1889. Charles E. Pearce, *Sims Reeves: fifty years of music in England*, 1924. Santley. Sir Charles Santley, *Student and singer: the reminiscences of Charles Santley*, 1892, new edn. 1893, and *Reminiscences of my life*, 1909. Soldene. Emily Soldene, *My theatrical and musical recollections*, 1897. Whiffen. Blanche Whiffen, *Keeping off the shelf*, 1928. White. Maude Valérie White, *Friends and memories*, 1914, and *My Indian summer* . . ., 1932.

9320   INSTRUMENTALISTS. Dressel. Dettmar Dressel, *Up and down the scale: reminiscences*, 1937. Scott. Cyril Scott, *My years of indiscretion*, 1924. Verne. Mathilde Verne, *Chords of remembrance*, 1936. Whitehouse. William Edward Whitehouse, *Recollections of a violoncellist*, 1930.

# I. THEATRE

9321   ARNOTT (JAMES FULLARTON) *and* ROBINSON (JOHN WILLIAM). English theatrical literature, 1559–1900: a bibliography, incorporating Robert W. Lowe's 'A bibliographical account of English theatrical literature', published in 1888. Soc. for Theatre Research. 1970.

A full bibliog. to 1900, concentrating on the sources of theatrical hist. Reginald Clarence, comp., '*The stage' cyclopaedia: a bibliography of plays: an alphabetical list of plays and other stage pieces of which any record can be found since the commencement of the English stage* . . ., 1909, is a useful handbook. The fullest listing of books, plays, etc., is N.Y. Public Libr.: the Research Librs., *Catalog of the theatre and drama collections*: pt. 1, *Drama collection: author listing*, 6 v. Boston 1967, *Listing by cultural origin*, 6 v. Boston 1967. Pt. 2, *Theatre collection*, 9 v. Boston 1967. Robert William Lowe, *A bibliographical account of English theatrical literature from the earliest times to the present day*, 1888, and David F. Cheshire, *Theatre: history, criticism and reference*, 1967, are also useful.

   Ina Ten Eyck Firkins, comp., *Index to plays, 1800–1926*, N.Y. 1927, suppl. 1935, and Ruth Gibbons Thomson, comp., *Index to full-length plays, 1895 to 1925*, Boston 1956, are useful for tracing plays whose title is known.

**9322   LOEWENBERG (ALFRED).** The theatre of the British Isles excluding London: a bibliography. Soc. for Theatre Research. 1950.

Fuller than Arnott and Robinson (**9321**).

**9323   STRATMAN (CARL JOSEPH)** *comp.* A bibliography of British dramatic periodicals, 1720–1960. N.Y. Public. Libr. 1962.

See also his *Bibliography of English printed tragedy, 1565–1900*, Carbondale, Ill. 1966, and 'Dramatic play lists, 1591–1963', pt. 2, *New York Public Libr. Bull.* lxx (1966), 169–88.

**9324   HARTNOLL (PHYLLIS MAY)** *ed.* The Oxford companion to the theatre. 1951. 3rd edn. 1967.

See also Diana Howard, *London theatres and music halls, 1850–1950*, Libr. Assoc. 1970, which is a useful handbook.

**9325   THE GREEN ROOM BOOK,** or, Who's who on the stage. Annual. 1906–9.

Cont. as *Who's who in the theatre*, 1912+.

**9326   NICOLL (ALLARDYCE).** A history of late nineteenth-century drama, 1850–1900. 2 v. Camb. 1946. 2nd edn. 1959.

Standard. Forms v. 5 of his *A history of English drama, 1660–1900*. V. 6 is a *Short-title alphabetical catalogue of plays produced or printed in England*. The whole work is cont. by his *English drama, 1900–1930: the beginning of the modern period*, Camb. 1973. Must be suppl. by George Rignal Rowell, *The Victorian theatre: a survey*, 1956, rev. edn. Oxf. 1967. See also Gary J. Scrimgeour, 'Nineteenth-century drama', *Victorian Studs.* xii (1968–9), 91–100, a handy review of anthologies; Harry Bergholz, *Die Neugestaltung des modernen englischen Theaterwesens und ihre Bedeutung für den Spielplan*, Berlin 1933; Maurice Willson Disher, *Blood and thunder: mid-Victorian melodrama and its origins*, 1949, and *Melodrama: plots that thrilled . . .*, Lond. & N.Y. 1954; Albert Edward Wilson, *Edwardian theatre*, 1951; D. Forbes-Winslow, *Daly's: the biography of a theatre*, 1944; and the nostalgic works of Walter James Macqueen-Pope, *Carriages at eleven: the story of the Edwardian theatre*, 1947, *Shirtfronts and sables . . .*, 1953, *Ladies first: the story of woman's conquest of the British stage*, 1952, *The footlights flickered*, 1959, *St. James: theatre of distinction*, 1958, *Haymarket: theatre of perfection*, 1948, *Gaiety: theatre of enchantment*, 1949, *Theatre Royal, Drury Lane* [1945], *Pillars of Drury Lane*, 1955, and *Goodbye Piccadilly*, 1960. Arthur Colby Sprague, *Shakespeare and the actors: the stage business in his plays, 1660–1905*, Camb., Mass. 1944, covers an important special topic.

**9327   MORLEY (HENRY).** The journal of a London playgoer, from 1851 to 1866. 1866. New edn. 1891.

The more impressionistic reporting of the 1870s is represented by Edward Dutton Cook, *A book of the play . . .*, 1876, 3rd. edn. 1881, *Hours with the players*, 2 v. 1881, *On the stage . . .*, 2 v. 1883, and *Nights at the play: a view of the English stage*, 2 v. 1883. The actors of the 1880s and 1890s were the subjects of many gossipy books, among them Arthur Goddard, *Players of the period: a series of anecdotal, biographical and critical monographs of the leading English actors of the day*, 2 v. 1891, and Erskine Reid and Herbert Compton, *The dramatic peerage, 1892: personal notes and professional sketches of the actors and actresses of the London stage*, 1892.

**9328  ARCHER (WILLIAM).** English dramatists of today. 1882.

See also his *The theatrical 'World' for 1893* [-97], 5 v. 1894–8, *Study and stage: a year-book of criticism*, 1899, *Play-making: a manual of craftsmanship*, 1912, 3rd edn. 1926, *The old drama and the new: an essay in re-evaluation*, Camb., Mass. & Lond. 1923, and W. Archer and Harley Granville Barker, *A national theatre: scheme & estimates*, 1907. Archer was one of the leading critics of his day. For his life see Charles Archer, *William Archer: life, work and friendships*, Lond. & New Haven, Conn. 1931, Hans Schmid, *The dramatic criticism of William Archer*, Berne 1964, and John Mackinnon Robertson, ed., *William Archer as rationalist . . .*, 1925.

**9329  JONES (HENRY ARTHUR).** The renascence of the English drama: essays, lectures and fragments relating to the modern English stage, written and delivered in the years 1883–94. 1895.

See also his *The foundations of a national drama: a collection of lectures, essays and speeches, delivered and written in the years 1896–1912*, Lond. & N.Y. 1913, and the biog. at **8383**. For other contemp. comment see [Pierre Marie] Augustin Filon, *The English stage: being, an account of the Victorian drama*, trans. by Frederic Whyte, 1897, and Georges Bourdon, *Les théatres anglais*, Paris 1903.

**9330  SHAW (GEORGE BERNARD).** The quintessence of Ibsenism. 1891. 3rd edn. 1922.

See also his *Dramatic opinions and essays*, 2 v. 1907. His theatre criticism was collected for the Standard edn. of his works as *Our theatres in the nineties*, 3 v. 1932. John F. Matthews, ed., *Shaw's dramatic criticism, 1895–98: a selection*, N.Y. [1959], and E. J. West, ed., *Shaw on theatre*, N.Y. 1958, are selections. For Shaw's work generally see **8412**.

**9331  SCOTT (CLEMENT WILLIAM).** The drama of yesterday & today. 2 v. 1899.

Scott was a well-known critic. See also his *Some notable Hamlets of the present time . . .*, 1900, new edn. 1905, and *From 'The bells' to 'King Arthur': a critical record of the first-night productions at the Lyceum theatre from 1871 to 1895*, 1897. For his life see Margaret Scott, *Old days in Bohemian London: recollections of Clement Scott*, 1919.
Another influential critic of the same period, Arthur Bingham Walkley, publ. rather more in book form: *Playhouse impressions*, 1892, *Frames of mind*, 1899, *Dramatic criticism*, 1903, *Drama and life*, 1903, *Pastiche and prejudice*, 1921, *More prejudice*, 1923, and *Still more prejudice*, 1925. There are also some interesting fragments in Edward Ford-ham Spence, *Our stage and its critics*, 1910, and *Bar and buskin: being, memories of life, law and the theatre*, 1930.

**9332  CRAIG (EDWARD GORDON).** The art of the theatre. Edin. & Lond. 1905.

The first of the works that helped to make him famous. The others were *A living theatre . . .*, Florence 1913, *On the art of the theatre*, Lond. & Chicago 1911, repr. 1924, *Towards a new theatre . . .*, 1913, and *The theatre advancing*, 1921. For his life see **9348**.

**9333  MACCARTHY (*Sir* DESMOND).** The Court theatre, 1904–1907: a commentary and criticism. 1907. New edn. by Stanley Weintraub. Coral Gables, Fla. [1966.]

**9334  SOUTHERN (RICHARD).** Changeable scenery: its origin and development in the British theatre. 1952.

See also William Burt Gamble, comp., *The development of scenic art and stage machinery:*

*a list of references in the New York Public Library*, N.Y. 1920, rev. edn. 1928, and Erika Meier, *Realism and reality: the function of the stage directions in the 'New drama' from Thomas William Robertson to George Bernard Shaw*, Berne 1967.

9335   GOSCHEN COMMITTEE ON THEATRE LICENCES. Report from the select committee on theatrical licences and regulations [Chairman: George Joachim Goschen]. H.C. 373 (1866). XVI, 1.

See also *Report from the select committee on theatres and places of entertainment* [Chairman: David R. Plunket]. H.C. 240 (1892). XVIII, 1. The substantial earlier *Report from the select committee on public houses, &c.* [Chairman: Charles Pelham Villiers.] H.C. 855 (1852–3). XXXVII, 1. Further report. H.C. 367 (1854). XIV, 231, covers 'dancing, saloons, coffee houses, theatres, temperance hotels and places of public entertainment, by whatever name they are called', as well as public houses, hotels, and beershops.

9336   SAMUEL COMMITTEE ON STAGE CENSORSHIP. Report from the joint select committee of the House of Lords and the House of Commons on the stage plays (censorship) [Chairman: Herbert Samuel]. H.C. 303 (1909). VIII, 451.

For the administration of the censorship see James F. Stottlar, 'A Victorian stage censor: the theory and practice of William Bodham Donne', *Victorian Studs.* xiii (1969–70), 253–82.

9337   GEARY (*Sir* WILLIAM NEVILL MONTGOMERIE). The law of theatres and music-halls, including contracts and precedents of contracts. 1885.

The first satisfactory legal textbook. See also Edward Cutler, Thomas Eustace Smith, and Frederic E. Weatherly, *The law of musical and dramatic copyright*, 1890, 3rd edn. 1910, Clarence Hamlyn, *A manual of theatrical law . . .*, 1891, and Albert Ambrose Strong, *Dramatic and musical law . . .*, 1898, 3rd edn. 1910.

9338   THE ERA. 103 v. Weekly. 1838–1939.

The oldest theatrical j., suppl. by *The era almanack*, 1868–1919. Other major js. were *The [London] entr'acte*, 1870–1907, *The theatre*, 1877–97, *Dramatic notes*, 1879–92, and *The stage directory*, 1880–1, cont. as *The stage*, 1881+, which was suppl. by *The stage year book*, 1908+.

9339   PEARSON (HESKETH). The last actor-managers. 1950.

9340   ASCHE. Oscar Asche: his life. By himself. 1929.

9341   BANCROFT. Mr. & Mrs. Bancroft on and off the stage: written by themselves. [i.e. Sir Squire Bancroft Bancroft and Mary Effie, Lady Bancroft.] 2 v. 1888. 9th edn. 1891. Abridged edn. [Gleanings from on and off the stage.] 1892.

They also publ. *The Bancrofts: recollections of sixty years*, 1909. Sir Squire alone publ. *Empty chairs*, 1928.

9342   BAYLIS. Lilian Baylis. By Dame Sybil Thorndike and Arthur Russell Thorndike. 1938.

See also E. G. Harcourt Williams, ed., *Vic–Wells: the work of Lilian Baylis*, 1938, and *Old Vic saga*, 1949, and Cicely Mary Hamilton and Lilian Mary Baylis, *The Old Vic*, 1926.

9343 BENSON. My memoirs. By Sir Frank Robert Benson. 1930.

See also John Courtenay Trewin, *Benson and the Bensonians*, 1960, and Gertrude Constance, Lady Benson, *Mainly players: Bensonian memories*, 1926.

9344 BERTRAM. Behind the scenes: being the confessions of a strolling player. By Peter Paterson, pseud. of James Glass Bertram. Edin. 1858. 2nd edn. 1859.

Gives a good picture of the world of touring actors. See also his *Glimpses of real life . . .*, Edin. 1864, and *Some memories . . .*, Westminster 1893.

9345 BROOKFIELD. Random reminiscences. By Charles Hallam Elton Brookfield. 1902.

9346 CAMPBELL. My life and some letters. By Mrs. Patrick Campbell. [Beatrice Stella Cornwallis-West.] Lond. & N.Y. 1922.

See also Alan Holmes Dent, ed., *Bernard Shaw and Mrs. Patrick Campbell: their correspondence*, Lond. & N.Y. 1952, Alan Holmes Dent, *Mrs. Patrick Campbell*, 1961, and Richard Huggett, *The truth about Pygmalion*, 1969.

9347 CONQUEST. Conquest: the story of a theatre family. By Frances Fleetwood. 1953.

9348 CRAIG. Index to the story of my days: some memoirs of Edward Gordon Craig, 1872–1907. Lond. & N.Y. 1957.

See also Ifan Kyrle Fletcher, comp., *Edward Gordon Craig: a bibliography*, Soc. for Theatre Research, 1967, Edward Anthony Craig, *Gordon Craig: the story of his life*, Lond. & N.Y. 1968, Denis Bablet, *Edward Gordon Craig*, trans. by Daphne Woodward, N.Y. 1966, and Enid Rose, *Gordon Craig and the theatre: a record and an interpretation*, 1931.

9349 FORBES-ROBERTSON. A player under three reigns. By Sir Johnston Forbes-Robertson. 1925.

9350 HAWTREY. The truth at last from Charles Hawtrey. Ed. by William Somerset Maugham. 1924.

9351 HICKS. Seymour Hicks: twenty-four years of an actor's life. By Sir [Edward] Seymour Hicks. Lond. 1910. N.Y. 1911.

See also his *Between ourselves*, 1930, *Not guilty m'lud*, 1939, *Me and my missus: fifty years on the stage*, 1939, and *Vintage years: when King Edward the Seventh was Prince of Wales*, 1943.

9352 HORNIMAN. Miss Horniman and the Gaiety Theatre, Manchester. By Rex Pogson. 1952.

9353 IRVING. Henry Irving: the actor and his world. By Laurence Henry Forster Irving. Lond. 1951. N.Y. 1952.

See also Edward Henry Gordon Craig, *Henry Irving*, Lond. & N.Y. 1930; William Archer, *Henry Irving: actor and manager: a critical study* [1883]; Frederic Daly, pseud. of Louis Frederic Austin, *Henry Irving in England and America, 1838–84*, 1884;

Austin Brereton, *The life of Henry Irving*, 2 v. 1908; Percy Hetherington Fitzgerald, *Henry Irving: a record of twenty years at the Lyceum*, 1893, new edn. 1895, and *Sir Henry Irving: a biography*, Lond. & Phila. 1906; Bram [i.e. Abraham], Stoker, *Personal reminiscences of Henry Irving*, 2 v. 1906, rev. edn. 1 v. 1907.

9354  KEAN. The life and theatrical times of Charles Kean, F.S.A., including a summary of the English stage for the last fifty years, and a detailed account of the management of the Princess's Theatre, from 1850 to 1859. By John William Cole. 2 v. 1859. 2nd edn. 1860.

See also William Glasgow Bruce Carson, *Letters of Mr. and Mrs. Charles Kean relating to their American tours*, St. Louis 1945.

9355  KEMBLE. Affectionately yours, Fanny: Fanny Kemble and the theatre. By Henry Gibbs. 1947.

See also Frances Anne Kemble, *Further records, 1848–1883: a series of letters*, 2 v. Lond. 1890, 1 v. N.Y. 1891, Margaret Neilson Armstrong, *Fanny Kemble: a passionate Victorian*, N.Y. & Lond. 1938, and Robert Rushmore, *Fanny Kemble*, N.Y. 1970.

9356  KENDAL. Dame Madge Kendal. By herself. [Dame Margaret Shafto Grimston, called Madge Kendal.] 1933.

See also her *Dramatic opinions*, Lond. & Boston 1890, and Thomas Edgar Pemberton, *The Kendals: a biography*, Lond. & N.Y. 1900.

9357  LANGTRY. The days I knew. By Lillie Langtry. [Emilie Charlotte, Lady de Bathe.] Lond. & N.Y. 1925.

See also Pierre Sichel, *The Jersey lily: the story of the fabulous Mrs. Langtry*, Englewood Cliffs, N.J. 1958, publ. in Lond. as *The Jersey lily: a novel based on the life of Lily Langtry*, 1958.

9358  LLOYD. 'Our Marie': Marie Lloyd: a biography. By Naomi Ellington Jacob. 1936.

See also Walter James MacQueen Pope, *Queen of the music halls: being the dramatized story of Marie Lloyd*, 1957.

9359  MARTIN-HARVEY. The last romantic: the authorised biography of Sir John Martin-Harvey. By Maurice Willson Disher. 1948.

See also Sir John Martin-Harvey, *Autobiography*, 1933, and *The book of Martin Harvey* ... [1930.]

9360  POEL. William Poel and the Elizabethan revival. By Robert Speaight. Lond. & Camb., Mass. 1954.

9361  TEMPEST. Marie Tempest. By [Henry] Hector Bolitho. Lond. & Phila. 1936.

9362  TERRY. Ellen Terry's memoirs. With preface etc. by Edith Craig and Christopher St. John, pseud. of Christabel Marshall. N.Y. 1932. Lond. 1933. Orig. publ. as The story of my life. 1908. 2nd edn. 1922.

See also Christopher St. John, pseud. of Christabel Marshall, ed., *Ellen Terry and Bernard Shaw: a correspondence*, Lond. & N.Y. 1931, new edn. 1949; Edward Henry

Gordon Craig, *Ellen Terry and her secret self*, 1931; Roger Manvell, *Ellen Terry*, Lond. & N.Y. 1968; Thomas Edgar Pemberton, *Ellen Terry and her sisters*, Lond. & N.Y. 1902; and Clement William Scott, *Ellen Terry: an appreciation*, N.Y. 1900.

**9363　TREE. Beerbohm Tree: his life and laughter. By Hesketh Pearson. 1956.**

See also Sir Max Beerbohm, *Herbert Beerbohm Tree: some memories of him and of his art . . .*, 1920, and Sir Herbert Beerbohm Tree, *Thoughts and afterthoughts*, Lond. & N.Y. 1913.

**9364　VANBRUGH. To tell my story. By Dame Irene Vanbrugh. 1948.**

See also her sister, Violet Vanbrugh's *Dare to be wise*, 1925.

**9365　SPEAIGHT (GEORGE). The history of the English puppet theatre. Lond. & N.Y. 1955.**

See also his *Juvenile drama: the history of the English toy theatre*, 1946 rev. edn. [*The history of the English toy theatre*] 1969, and Albert Edward Wilson, *Penny plain, twopence coloured: a history of the juvenile drama*, 1932.

# X

# LOCAL HISTORY

## A. GENERAL

9366   HUMPHREYS (ARTHUR LEE) *comp*. A handbook to county bibliography: being a bibliography of bibliographies relating to the counties and towns of Great Britain and Ireland. 1917.

Now out-of-date. For recent works there is a bookseller's catalogue: Dillon's University Bookshop, *British local history: a selected bibliography*, n.d.

9367   GROSS (CHARLES) *comp*. A bibliography of British municipal history, including gilds and parliamentary representation. N.Y. 1897. Repr. Camb., Mass. 1915. 2nd edn. Leicester. 1966.

Cont. by Geoffrey Haward Martin and Sheila MacIntyre, comps., *A bibliography of British and Irish municipal history*, 1+ v., Leicester 1972+.

9368   KUHLICKE (FREDERICK WILLIAM) *and* EMMISON (FREDE-RICK GEORGE) *eds*. English local history handlist: a short bibliography and list of sources for the study of local history and antiquities. Hist. Assoc. Helps for Students 69. 4th edn. 1969.

A list of ancillary works. William Brewer Stephens, *Sources for English local history*, Manch. & Totowa, N.J., 1973, is fuller, but chiefly on earlier periods.

9369   POWELL (WILLIAM RAYMOND). Local history from blue books: a select list of the sessional papers of the House of Commons. Hist. Assoc. Helps for Students 64. 1962.

9370   HANHAM (HAROLD JOHN). 'Some neglected sources of biographical information: county biographical dictionaries, 1890–1937'. *Inst. Hist. Res. Bull.* xxxiv (1961), 55–66.

9371   EMMISON (FREDERICK GEORGE). Archives and local history. 1966.

9372   SOCIETY OF ARCHIVISTS. Journal. 1+. 1955+.

The j. of the local archivists. Includes regular articles on local archives, as does *Archives: the journal of the British Records Association*, 1+, 1969+. On the preservation of local records see Lilian Jane Redstone and Francis William Steer, eds., *Local records: their nature and care*, Soc. of Archivists, 1953.

9373   EMMISON (FREDERICK GEORGE) *and* GRAY (IRVINE EGER-TON). County records (quarter sessions, petty sessions, clerk of the peace and lieutenancy). Hist. Assoc. Helps for Students 62. 1961.

9374  WHITAKER (HAROLD) *comp.* A descriptive list of the printed maps of Cheshire, 1577–1900. Chetham Soc. New ser. cvi. Manch. 1942.

There are parallel lists for most counties, viz. *Cambridgeshire* by Sir Herbert George Fordham, Camb. 1908; *Gloucestershire* by Thomas Chubb, Bristol & Glos. Archaeol. Soc. 1913; *Hertfordshire* by Sir Herbert Fordham, 2 v. Hertford 1907–14; *Lancashire* by Harold Whitaker, Chetham Soc. new ser. ci, Manch. 1938; *Leicestershire* by Basil Lovibond Gimson and Percy Russell, Leicester 1947; *Norfolk* by Thomas Chubb and Arthur George Stephen, Norwich 1928; *Northamptonshire* by Harold Whitaker, Northamptonshire Record Soc. xiv, 1948; *Northumberland* by Harold Whitaker, Newcastle-upon-Tyne 1949; *Shropshire* by Geoffrey Charles Cowling, Salop County Council, Shrewsbury 1959; *Somersetshire* by Thomas Chubb, Somersetshire Archaeol. & Nat. Hist. Soc., Taunton 1914; *Surrey* by Henry Alexander Sharp, Croydon 1929; *Sussex* by Francis William Steer, Sussex Record Soc. lxvi, 1968; *Warwickshire* by Paul Dean Adshead Harvey and Harry Thorpe, Warwick County Council, Warwick 1959; *Wiltshire* by Thomas Chubb, Wiltshire Archaeol. & Nat. Hist. Mag. xxxvii, Devizes 1911; and *Yorkshire* by Harold Whitaker, Yorkshire Archaeol. Soc. lxxxvi, Wakefield 1933. There are also a number of important catalogues, notably Frederick George Emmison, ed., *Catalogue of maps in the Essex Record Office, 1566–1855* [*1566–1860*], Essex Record Office, Chelmsford 1947, repr. 1969, suppls. 1952, 1964, 1968, and Ruth Marion Turner, comp., *Maps of Durham, 1576–1872, in the university library, Durham,* Durham 1954. See also **129–37.**

9375  HOSKINS (WILLIAM GEORGE). Local history in England. 1959.

A good handbook, which is more concerned with the post-1850 period than works such as Francis Celoria, *Teach yourself local history,* 1959. See also Hoskins's *The making of the English landscape,* 1955, and *Fieldwork in local history,* 1967.

9376  THE AMATEUR HISTORIAN [: the quarterly journal of the Standing Conference for Local History]. 1952+.

Styled *The local historian,* viii+, 1968+. The only gen. j. for local historians. Too popular to be of much value.

9377  NORTHERN HISTORY: a review of the history of the north of England. 1+. Leeds. 1966+.

Strong on the period, with full annual bibliog.

9378  THE VICTORIA HISTORY OF THE COUNTIES OF ENGLAND. Ed. by William Page and others. 1900+.

*V.C.H.* aims to provide standard hists. of the parishes, towns, and counties of England. Execution is necessarily uneven in quality, and coverage of the 19th cent. is adequate only in the more recent vols.

9379  BRITISH ASSOCIATION FOR THE ADVANCEMENT OF SCIENCE. Handbooks and scientific surveys. 1860+.

A handbook has been produced in most years on the district where the B.A. has held its annual meeting. The early vols. have valuable descriptive articles: the later ones usually include helpful hist. articles.

9380  KELLY (FREDERICK) *and others.* Kelly's post office directories. 1845+.

Directories for individual counties and groups of counties, covering the whole of England by 1871. Reissued with revisions at irregular intervals. The introductory material at the head of each entry is usually the best extant description of the place dealt with.

**9381** WHITE (WILLIAM). White's directories and gazetteers. Sheffield. *c* 1845+.

Important for the 1850s. Reprs. are available.

**9382** MEASOM (GEORGE). The official illustrated guide to the South-Eastern Railway in all its branches. [1853.]

The first of a ser. of splendid cheaply-produced topographical vols. with illustrations of factories and other buildings, as well as scenery. The others cover the Great Northern, Manchester, Sheffield and Lincolnshire, and Midland [1857], the London and North-Western [1858], the London and South-Western [1858], the North-Western [1859], the Lancaster and Carlisle, Edinburgh and Glasgow, and Caledonian [1859], the Great Western [1860], the Bristol and Exeter, North and South Devon, Cornwall and South Wales [1861], and the North Eastern, North British etc. [1861]. Later guides issued by the railway companies are usually less informative.

**9383** MURRAY (JOHN) *publisher*. Murray's English handbooks. *c.* 1850+.

The best-known and most carefully produced of contemp. guide-books, issued at first for groups of counties, later for particular counties. The text of the later vols. is often not as full as that in *Kelly's directories* (**9380**). Other well-known nationally-produced guide-books like *Baedeker* and the *Little guides* give much less information on the period.

**9384** FAWCETT (CHARLES BUNGAY). Provinces of England: a study of some geographical aspects of devolution. 1919. Rev. edn. by William [David] Gordon East and S. W. Wooldridge. 1960.

The most convincing attempt at regionalization.

**9385** EAST (WILLIAM [DAVID] GORDON) *ed*. Regions of the British Isles. 1960+.

A geographical survey to be completed in 14 v. Vols. that have appeared incl. Arthur Eltringham Smailes, *North England*, 1960, Alfred Henry Shorter, William Lionel Desmond Ravenhill, and Kenneth John Gregory, *Southwest England*, 1969, Frank Walker, *The Bristol region*, 1973 and George Harry Dury, *The East Midlands and the Peak*, 1963. A similar ser., 'Regions of Britain', includes Arthur Raistrick, *The Pennine dales*, 1968, Roy Millward, *The Lake district*, 1970, John Richard Lane Anderson, *The upper Thames*, 1970, and Samuel Holroyd Burton, *The West country*, 1972.

## B. LOCAL GOVERNMENT

### I. GENERAL

The chief problems of local administration, public health, and poverty are dealt with at **7395–571** and **7328–57**. For local taxation see **4558–73**. For municipal trading see **6403–13**.

**9386** REDLICH (JOSEPH) *and* HIRST (FRANCIS WRIGLEY). Local government in England. 2 v. 1903. Vol. 2 repr. 1958.

Standard. Includes both a hist. and an analysis of contemp. local government. Heinrich Rudolf Gneist, *Self-government: Communalverfassungs- und Verwaltungsgerichte in England*, Berlin 1871, is an earlier account comparable in quality but narrower in scope.

**9387** SMELLIE (KINGSLEY BRYCE SPEAKMAN). A history of local government. 1946. 4th edn. 1968.

A sound outline hist. Two other useful short hists. deal mainly with the 20th cent.: John Joseph Clarke, *A history of local government of the United Kingdom*, 1955, and William Alexander Robson, *The development of local government*, 1931, 3rd edn. 1954.

**9388** GUTCHEN (ROBERT M.). 'Local improvements and centralization in nineteenth-century England'. *Hist. J.* iv (1961), 85–96.

**9389** LOCAL GOVERNMENT BOARD. Annual report. 48 v. 1871/2–1918/19.

The successor of the Poor Law Board (**7340**) and much concerned with poor law functions. Its regulations were publ. from time to time by commercial publishers, e.g., *The orders of the Local Government Board with circulars and other explanatory documents issued in relation to the orders* . . ., 1877.

**9390** KEITH-LUCAS (BRYAN). The English local government franchise: a short history. Oxf. 1952.

**9391** LIPMAN (VIVIAN DAVID). Local government areas, 1834–1945. Oxf. 1949.

**9392** MACKENZIE (WILLIAM JAMES MILLAR). Theories of local government. Greater London papers 2. London School of Econ. & Pol. Sci. 1961.

**9393** SMITH (JOSHUA TOULMIN). Local self-government and centralization: the characteristics of each and its practical tendencies . . . 1851.

Strongly for local self-government. For the centralist view see Sir Edwin Chadwick, *On the evils of disunity in central and local administration* . . ., 1885. For local boards see Anon., *The natural history of local boards, or, local government as it is*, 1888.

**9394** CHALMERS (*Sir* MACKENZIE DALZELL EDWIN STEWART). Local government. English citizen series. 1883.

Replaced in the ser. by William Blake Odgers, *Local government*, 1899, 2nd edn. 1907. Other useful textbooks incl. Sir Robert Samuel Wright and Henry Hobhouse, *An outline of local government and local taxation in England and Wales (excluding the Metropolis) together with some considerations for amendment*, 1884, 9th edn. 1950, and Herman Finer, *English local government*, 1933, 4th edn. 1950.

**9395** PROBYN (JOHN WEBB) *ed.* Local government and taxation: Cobden Club essays. 1875.

Probyn also ed. a further ser. of essays, *Local government and taxation in the United Kingdom: a series of essays published under the sanction of the Cobden Club*, 1882. Both vols. incl. valuable essays by reformers. A related vol. is William Rathbone and others, *Local government and taxation*, 1885. See also Ernest Abraham Hart, *Local government as it is and as it ought to be* . . ., 1885. For local taxation see **4558–73**.

**9396** MALTBIE (MILO ROY). English local government of to-day: a study of the relations of central and local government. N.Y. 1897.

A useful American thesis with good bibliog. For other comparative studs. see Sir Percy

Walter Llewellyn Ashley, *Local and central government: a comparative study of England, France, Prussia and the United States,* 1906, and the rather thin Pierre Arminjon, *L'administration local de l'Angleterre,* Paris 1895.

9397 GOMME (*Sir* GEORGE LAURENCE). Lectures on the principles of local government. 1897.

9398 HARRIS (GEORGE MONTAGU) *ed.* Problems of local government. 1911.

Papers on British local govt. for the first Internat. Congress of Administrative Sciences.

9399 STANSFELD COMMITTEE ON BOUNDARIES. Report from the select committee on boundaries of parishes, unions, and counties [Chairman: James Stansfeld]. H.C. 308 (1873). VIII, 1.

Useful as a guide to anomalies.

9400 GLEN (WILLIAM CUNNINGHAM). The law relating to public health and local government in relation to sanitary and other matters . . . 1858. 16th edn. 1952.

Glen and William Golden Lumley and Edmund Lumley, *The Public Health Act, 1875, annotated,* 1876, 12th edn. 8 v. 1950–7, were the standard works on local government law.

9401 SCHOLEFIELD (*Sir* JOSHUA) *ed.* Encyclopaedia of local government law. 7 v. 1905–8.

Replaced by Hugh Pattison Macmillan, Baron Macmillan, ed., *Local government law and administration in England and Wales,* 14 v. 1934–41, suppl. vols. in progress.

9402 THE COUNTY COMPANION, diary, statistical chronicle and magisterial and official directory . . . 1879–89.

Amalg. with *The municipal corporations' companion . . .,* 1877–89, as *The county councils and municipal corporations' companion . . .,* 1890–1914. See also *The county council year book,* 1890–2.

9403 KNIGHT'S OFFICIAL ADVERTISER of local management in England and Wales. 1855–72.

Became *The local government chronicle,* 1872+. See also *The metropolitan,* 1872–90, which became *The metropolitan [and provincial] local government j.,* 1891–2, and *The local government j.,* 1892+, and *Local government,* 1908+.

9404 ASSOCIATION OF MUNICIPAL AND SANITARY ENGINEERS AND SURVEYORS. [Institution of Municipal Engineers.] Proceedings [Journal]. 1875+.

Important for all types of local government activity. Includes hist. articles. The Association was known from 1890 to 1910 as Incorporated Assoc. of Municipal and County Engineers, and from 1910 to 1947 as Institution of Municipal and County Engineers. In 1919 it amalg. with an earlier Institution of Municipal Engineers, which publ. a *Journal,* 1909–19. See also Maxwell (**9432**).

## 2. THE COUNTY

### (a) *General*

9405 STEPHENS (*Sir* LEON EDGAR). The clerks of the counties, 1360–
1960. Soc. of Clerks of the Peace. 1961.
Includes lists of clerks.

9406 ATKINSON (GEORGE). A practical treatise on sheriff law . . . 1839.
6th edn. 1878.
Replaced by Cameron Churchill and Alexander Carmichael Bruce, *The law of the office
and duties of the sheriff*, 1879, 2nd edn. 1882, and Philip Edward Mather, *A compendium
of sheriff law, especially in relation to writs of execution*, 1894, 3rd edn. 1935.

9407 LORDS COMMITTEE ON HIGH SHERIFFS. Report from the
select committee of the House of Lords on high sheriffs [Chairman: Viscount
Cranbrook]. H.C. 257 (1888). XII, 209.
A useful source. There was a further Lords committee five years later: H.L. 304 (1893–4).
IX, 263.

### (b) *County Councils*

The main sources of county council hist., hitherto little used, are the printed
minutes and accounts publ. by most councils since 1890. There are good hists.
of two county councils: Cheshire by J. M. Lee (**9410**) and Wiltshire in the
*Victoria County History*.

9408 ENSOR (*Sir* ROBERT CHARLES KIRKWOOD). 'The supersession
of county government'. *Politica* i (1934–5), 425–42.
See also John Paul Delacour Dunbabin, 'The politics of the establishment of county
councils', *Hist. J.* vi (1963), 226–52, and 'Expectations of the new county councils and
their realization', ibid. viii (1965), 353–79.

9409 COUNTY COUNCILS ASSOCIATION. The jubilee of county councils, 1889–1939: fifty years of local government. 32 v. 1939.
A vol. was publ. for each county, pt. 1, the same for each vol., consisting of an historical
introduction, pt. 2, of an account of the work of each council in 1939, and of the growth
of the major services. Quality indifferent.

9410 LEE (JOHN MICHAEL). Social leaders and public persons: a study of
county government in Cheshire since 1888. Oxf. 1963.
Good.

9411 LOCAL GOVERNMENT BOUNDARIES COMMISSION. Report
of the boundary commissioners of England and Wales, 1888. [In 2 pts.] H.C.
360 (1888). LI, 1.
Recommendations for county boundaries.

9412 LOCAL GOVERNMENT ACT COMMISSION. Report of the commissioners under the Local Government Act, 1888 [Chairman: Earl of Derby]. [C. 6839] H.C. (1892). XXXVII, 1. Minutes of evidence. [C. 6839–I] H.C. (1892). XXXVII, 11.

Concerned with the administrative consequences of the creation of county councils and county boroughs.

9413 DEVONSHIRE COMMITTEE ON LOCAL GOVERNMENT ACTS. Report from the joint select committee of the House of Lords and the House of Commons on the Local Government Acts, 1888 and 1894, and the Local Government (Scotland) Acts, 1889 and 1894 (financial adjustments) [Chairman: Duke of Devonshire]. H.C. 246 (1911). VII, 1.

On problems that had arisen since the Derby commission.

9414 HOBHOUSE (HENRY) and FANSHAWE (EVELYN LEIGHTON) eds. The county councillor's guide: being, a handbook to the Local Government Act, 1888 . . . 1888.

9415 MACMORRAN (ALEXANDER). The Local Government Act, 1888, and the incorporated provisions of the Municipal Corporations Act, 1882. 1888. 3rd edn. 1898.

See also Frank Rowley Parker, *The election of county councils under the Local Government Act, 1888* . . ., 1888, 2nd edn. 1892. *Rogers on elections* (**691**) also deals extensively with local govt. elections.

9416 COUNTY COUNCIL ELECTIONS, 1889 (COST). Return showing . . . (1) the total number of electoral divisions (2) the names of the electoral divisions in which the elections of county councillors were contested . . . the number of county electors on the register, and the total number of votes polled . . . (3) the total number of county electors on the register . . . (4) the total cost of the elections . . . H.C. 247 (1889). LXV, 7.

A similar return for 1892 was publ. as H.C. 268 (1892). LXVIII, 85.

9417 COUNTY COUNCIL TIMES. 1889–1906.

Absorbed *The county council gazette*, 1889–90. See also *The county government review*, 1888–9, *The county council magazine*, 1889–91, and Association of County Councils [County Councils Assoc.], *Official journal* [*County councils gazette*], 1908+.

(c) *District Councils*

9418 WELTON (THOMAS ABERCROMBIE). 'On the smaller urban districts of England and Wales'. *Roy. Stat. Soc. J.* lxvii (1904), 1–45.

9419 MACMORRAN (ALEXANDER) and DILL (THOMAS REGINALD COLQUHOUN). The Local Government Act, 1894. 1894. 4th edn. 1907.

See also Frank Rowley Parker, *The election of guardians and district councillors under the Local Government Act, 1894* . . ., 1894, 2nd edn. 1899.

## 3. THE BOROUGH

9420  BROOKS (ROBERT CLARKSON). A bibliography of municipal administration and city conditions. Municipal affairs. Vol. I, no. 1. N.Y. 1897. Rev. edn. N.Y. 1901.

9421  LASKI (HAROLD JOSEPH) *and others.* A century of municipal progress, 1835–1935. 1935.
A useful symposium celebrating the centenary of the 1835 Municipal Corporations Act. See also Asa Briggs, *Victorian cities* (**7047**).

9422  REDFORD (ARTHUR) *and* RUSSELL (INA STAFFORD). The history of local government in Manchester. 3 v. 1939–40.
The best municipal hist. But see also Shena Dorothy Simon, Baroness Simon of Wythenshawe, *A century of city government: Manchester, 1838–1938*, 1938.

9423  WHITE (BRIAN DAVID). History of the corporation of Liverpool, 1835–1914. Liverpool. 1951.

9424  BUNCE (JOHN THACKRAY), VINCE (CHARLES ANTHONY), *and others.* History of the corporation of Birmingham: with a sketch of earlier government in the town. 6 v. Birmingham. 1878–1957.

9425  BEALEY (FRANK). 'Municipal politics in Newcastle-under-Lyme, 1835–1872'. *North Staffs. J. Field Studs.* iii (1963), 68–77. Cont. for 1872–1914. Ibid. v (1965), 64–73.

9426  JONES (GEORGE WILLIAM). Borough politics: a study of the Wolverhampton town council, 1888–1964. 1969.

9427  HENNOCK (ERNEST PETER). 'The social compositions of borough councils in two large cities, 1835–1914' in Harold James Dyos, ed., The study of urban history. Pp. 315–36.
His *Fit and proper persons: ideal and reality in nineteenth century urban government*, 1973, cont. this study of Birmingham and Leeds. Important.

9428  VINE (*Sir* JOHN RICHARD SOMERS). English municipal institutions; their growth and development from 1835 to 1879, statistically illustrated. 1879.

9429  DOLMAN (FREDERICK). Municipalities at work: the municipal policy of six great towns and its influence on their social welfare. 1895.
Deals with Birmingham, Manchester, Liverpool, Glasgow, Leeds, Bradford.

9430  SHAW (ALBERT). Municipal government in Great Britain. 1895.
A careful American report, with chapters on Glasgow, Manchester, Birmingham, London.

**9431** HAW (GEORGE). To-day's work: municipal government, the hope of democracy. 1901.

A left-wing boost for local govt. publ. by *The clarion*. Cp. Frederic Clemson Howe, *The British city: the beginnings of democracy*, 1907, one of a ser. of books by an American on the theme *The city: the hope of democracy*, 1905.

**9432** MAXWELL (WILLIAM HENRY). British progress in municipal engineering . . . 1904.

See also Henry Percy Boulnois, *The municipal and sanitary engineer's handbook*, 1883, 3rd edn. 1898, and *Reminiscences of a municipal engineer*, 1920, George A. Soper, *Modern methods of street cleaning*, N.Y. & Lond. 1909, and W. H. Maxwell and John Thomas Brown, *The encyclopaedia of municipal and sanitary engineering* . . ., 1910.

**9433** GRIFFITH (ERNEST STACEY). The modern development of city government in the United Kingdom and the United States. 2 v. 1927.

Mainly on the period after 1870.

**9434** GAUS (JOHN MERRIMAN). Great Britain: a study of civic loyalty. Chicago. 1929.

**9435** SELECT COMMITTEE ON MUNICIPAL CORPORATIONS (BOROUGH FUNDS) BILL. Report from the select committee on Municipal Corporations (Borough Funds) Bill [Chairman: J. T. Hibbert]. H.C. 177 (1872). XI, 627.

The bill (which was carried) proposed that a poll of ratepayers should be held before local authorities could embark on expensive schemes.

**9436** MUNICIPAL CORPORATIONS COMMISSION. Report of the commissioners appointed to inquire into municipal corporations not subject to the Municipal Corporations Acts (other than the City of London) [Chairman: Stephen Cave]. Pt. I: Report. [C. 2490] H.C. (1880). XXXI, 1. Pt. II: Minutes of evidence. [C. 2490–I] H.C. (1880). XXXI, 173.

On the surviving unreformed corporations (except the City of London).

**9437** ARNOLD (THOMAS JAMES). A treatise on the law relating to municipal corporations. 1851. 7th edn. 1935.

For municipal law see also Sir Christopher Rawlinson, *The Municipal Corporations Act 5 & 6 Will. IV. c. 76, and acts since passed for amending the same* . . ., 1842, 10th edn. 1910, and Joseph William Hume Williams and Sir John Richard Somers Vine, *The English municipal code: being the Municipal Corporations Act, 1882 . . . with historical introduction* . . ., 1882, 3rd edn. 1888.

**9438** MUNICIPAL EMPLOYEES. Return showing the number of persons in the employ of the London County Council and the council of each metropolitan borough, and of each county borough in England and Wales . . . H.C. 136 (1907). LXXII, 333.

9439 THE MUNICIPAL YEAR BOOK of the United Kingdom for 1897+. 1897+.

The first editor was Sir Robert Donald of the *Municipal j.* The best of such works. But see also *The municipal corporations' companion, diary and year book of statistics*, 1877–89, which was amalg. with *The county companion . . .*, 1879–89, as *The county councils and municipal corporations companion . . .*, 1890–1914, and *The [metropolitan and provincial] local government annual [and diary]*, 1892+.

9440 THE MUNICIPAL JOURNAL AND LONDON. 1893+.

First publ. as *London*, 1893–8, then as *London and municipal j.*, 1898, then as *Municipal j.* . . . See also *The municipal review*, 1883–91, and *The municipal officer*, 1899–1904, and its successor of the same name, 1911–14.

## 4. THE PARISH

9441 TATE (WILLIAM EDWARD). The parish chest: a study of the records of parochial administration in England. Camb. 1946. 3rd edn. 1969.

9442 SHAW (JAMES). The parochial lawyer: or, churchwarden and overseer's guide and assistant. 1829. 8th edn. 1895.

For other books on parish law see John Steer, *Parish law: being a digest of the law relating to parishes, churches, parish registers, ministers . . .*, 1830, 6th edn. 1899, Joshua Toulmin Smith, *The parish: its powers and obligations at law . . . its officers, and committees*, 1854, 2nd edn. 1857, and Frank Rowley Parker, *The election of parish councils under the Local Government Act, 1894*, 1894, and *The parish councillor: being a concise description of his powers, duties, and liabilities . . .*, 1895.

9443 THE PARISH COUNCILLOR. 1894–1904.

Became *The councillor [and guardian]*, 1896–1904. See also *The parish councils journal*, 1895–9, which became *The councils journal*, 1899–1909, and *The local government review*, 1909–14, and *The parish, district and town councils gazette*, 1894–5, which became *The councils gazette*, 1895–9.

## C. LONDON

### I. GENERAL

#### (a) *Reference*

9444 LONDON COUNTY COUNCIL. Members' Library catalogue. Vol. I. London history and topography. 1939.

There is no adequate bibliog. Stanley Rubinstein, *Historians of London . . .*, 1968, consists of chatty comments by a book collector.

9445 GOSS (CHARLES WILLIAM FREDERICK). The London directories, 1677–1855: a bibliography with notes on their origin and development. 1932.

9446 GUILDHALL LIBRARY. London business house histories: a handlist. [1964.]

9447  DARLINGTON (IDA) *ed.* Guide to the records in the London county record office. Pt. 1. Records of the predecessors of the London county council except the board of Guardians. London County Council. 1962.

For Corporation of London records see **9506.**

9448  KENT (WILLIAM RICHARD GLADSTONE). An encyclopaedia of London. 1937. Rev. edn. 1951. 3rd edn. by Godfrey Thompson. 1971.

9449  HAYES (JOHN) *comp.* Catalogue of oil paintings in the London Museum. 1970.

9450  KENT (WILLIAM RICHARD GLADSTONE). London worthies. 1939. Rev. edn. 1949.

A convenient handbook. James Ewing Ritchie, *Famous city men,* 1884, and *Debrett's City of London book,* 1922, are also useful.

9451  JELF (*Sir* ERNEST ARTHUR). Some London institutions of public importance in their legal aspect. Ed. by Alexander Cockburn McBarnet. 1903.

9452  DONALD (ROBERT) *ed.* The London manual and municipal year book, 1896/97–1908. 1896–1908.

9453  LONDON COUNTY COUNCIL. London statistics. 1890/91–1936/38. 41 v. 1896–1939.

An impressive series, suppl. by *Statistical abstract for London,* 1897+.

## (b) *Histories*

9454  RASMUSSEN (STEEN EILER). London: the unique city. Engl. trans. 1937. Rev. edn. 1948.

Good. Better than any of the gen. popular hists., of which the best is Christopher Trent, *Greater London: its growth and development through two thousand years,* 1965.

9455  OLSEN (DONALD J.). Town planning in London: the eighteenth & nineteenth centuries. New Haven [Conn.]. 1964.

9456  SHEPPARD (FRANCIS HENRY WOLLASTON). Mid-Victorian London, 1808–1870. Lond. & Berkeley. 1971.

9457  PEARSON (SIDNEY VERE). London's overgrowth and the causes of swollen towns. 1939.

9458  COPPOCK (JOHN TERENCE) *and* PRINCE (HUGH COUNSELL) *eds.* Greater London. 1964.

Essays in hist. geography. See also Centre for Urban Studies, *London: aspects of change,* Centre reports 3, by Ruth Glass and others, 1964.

9459 CLUNN (HAROLD PHILIP). The face of London: the record of a century's changes and development. 1932. Rev. edn. 1951.

See also his *London rebuilt, 1897–1927: an attempt to depict the principal changes which have taken place, with some suggestions for the future improvement of the metropolis*, 1927, Hermione Hobhouse, *Lost London: a century of demolition and decay*, 1971, Philip Norman, *London vanished and vanishing*, 1905, and Nicholas James Barton, *The lost rivers of London. . .*, Leicester & Lond. 1962.

9460 LONDON SURVEY COMMITTEE *and* LONDON COUNTY COUNCIL. The survey of London. 1900+.

A parish-by-parish hist. and survey, chiefly of buildings. Immensely thorough. For tracing notable buildings and people it is often useful to consult George Hamilton Cunningham, *London: being a comprehensive survey of the history, buildings and monuments, arranged under streets in alphabetical order*, 1927, Henry Benjamin Wheatley, *London, past and present . . .*, 3 v. 1891, and (for the City of London) Henry Andrade Harben, *A dictionary of London . . .*, 1917. Bryant Lillywhite, *London coffee-houses: a reference book of coffee houses of the seventeenth, eighteenth and nineteenth centuries*, 1963, is a useful handbook.

9461 GOMME (*Sir* GEORGE LAURENCE). London in the reign of Victoria (1837–1897). Victorian era series. 1898.

Better than other gen. surveys, incl. Aldon D. Bell, *London in the age of Dickens*, Norman, Okla. 1967, and Michael Harrison, *London by gaslight, 1861–1911*, 1963. But see also Henry Jephson, *The making of modern London*, 1910, and Sir Walter Besant and others, *The survey of London*, 10 v. 1902–12, which includes Besant's *London in the nineteenth century*, 1909. For public health see **7411.**

9462 PASQUET (DÉSIRÉ). Londres et les ouvriers de Londres. Paris. 1914.

See also François Bédarida, 'L'histoire sociale de Londres au XIXe siècle: sources et problèmes', *Annales: économies, sociétés, civilisations*, 15e année (1960), 949–62, and the works on housing at **708–3110.**

9463 PRICE-WILLIAMS (R.). 'The population of London, 1801–81'. *Stat. Soc. J.* xlviii (1885), 349–432.

See also Shannon, 'Migration and the growth of London' (**6945**).

9464 JONES (GARETH STEDMAN). Outcast London: a study in the relationship between classes in Victorian society. Oxf. 1971.

9465 EDWARDS (PERCY J.). History of London street improvements, 1855–1897. London County Council. 1898.

For London transport generally see **5994–9.**

9466 DYOS (HAROLD JAMES). 'Railways and the effect their building had on housing in Victorian London'. *J. Transport Hist.* ii (1955–6), 11–21, 90–100.

See also his 'Some social costs of railway building in London', *J. Transport Hist.* iii (1957–8), 23–30, and 'Workmen's fares in South London, 1860–1914', ibid. i (1953–4), 3–19. Also Sir Sidney James Mark Low, 'The rise of the suburb: a lesson of the census', *Contemp. Rev.* lx (1891), 545–58, and **5994–9, 6221,** and **9469.**

9467  BANFIELD (FRANK). The great landlords of London. 1890.

See also Michael Harrison, *Lord of London: a biography of the 2nd Duke of Westminster*, 1966. For the 1st Duke see **6879**.

9468  JOHNSON (DAVID J.). Southwark and the city. 1969.

9469  DYOS (HAROLD JAMES). Victorian suburb: a study of the growth of Camberwell. Leicester. 1961.

Important. The first serious study of London suburbia.

9470  ROSE (MILLICENT). The East End of London. 1951.

Useful. See also University House, *East London papers: a journal of history, social studies and the arts*, 1+, 1958+.

9471  HARLING (ROBERT) *comp*. The London miscellany: a nineteenth-century scrapbook. 1937.

There are also a number of colls. of photos., such as Sir John Betjeman, *Victorian and Edwardian London from old photographs*, 1969, Owen James Morris, *Grandfather's London* [*c*. 1885], 1956, and Leonora Collins, ed., *London in the nineties*, 1950, and of scrap-book-type reminiscences such as Alfred Rosling Bennett, *London and Londoners in the eighteen fifties and sixties*, 1924, and Frederick Willis, *101 Jubilee Road: a book of London yesterdays*, 1948, *Peace and dripping toast*, 1950, *London general*, 1953, and *A book of London yesterdays*, 1960. Kent's *The testament of a Victorian youth* (**3751**) is an excellent book, similar in scope.

9472  SCOTT (JAMES MAURICE). The book of Pall Mall. 1965.

One of a large number of popular books on the better-known parts of London. Others incl. Edwin Beresford Chancellor, *The pleasure haunts of London during four centuries*, 1925, *The annals of Fleet Street*, 1912, *The annals of the Strand*, 1912, and *Memorials of St. James's Street*, 1922; Arthur Irwin Dasent, *The history of St. James's Square*, 1895, *Piccadilly*, 1920, and *A history of Grosvenor Square*, 1935; William John Passingham, *London's markets: their origin and history* [1935]; and Leopold Wagner, *London inns and taverns*, 1924, and *More London inns and taverns*, 1925.

9473  CORPORATION OF LONDON (LIBRARY COMMITTEE). The Guildhall miscellany. 1+. 1952+.

A good hist. j. See also *East London papers* (**9470**).

### (c) *Contemporary Reports*

9474  WEALE (JOHN) *ed*. London exhibited in 1851: elucidating its natural and physical characteristics, antiquity and architecture, art, manufactures, trade, and organization; social, literary and scientific institutions; and numerous galleries of fine art. 1851. 2nd edn. 1852. 3rd edn. [A new survey of London] 2 v. 1853. Subsequent edns. in 'Bohn's illustrated library' entitled 'The pictorial handbook of London'. 1854+.

A good guide-book. Cp. it with Charles Knight, ed., *London*, 6 v. 1851, and *Knight's cyclopaedia of London, 1851*, 1851; and with George Walter Thornbury and Edward Walford, *Old and new London . . .*, 6 v. 1873–8, 2nd edn. 1897; W. W. Hutchings, *London town: past and present*, 2 v. 1909; John James Sexby, *The municipal parks, gardens and open spaces of London . . .*, 1898; and [William Spencer Clarke] *The suburban homes of London: a residential guide to the favourite London localities, their society, celebrities and associations . . ., 1881.*

9475 GODWIN (GEORGE). London shadows: a glance at the 'homes' of the thousands . . . 1854.

Cont. in *Town swamps and social bridges . . .*, 1859, and *Another blow for life*, 1864. Neatly-illus. popular accounts of slum life by the editor of the *Builder*. Cp. Thomas Beames, *The rookeries of London, past, present and prospective*, 1850, 2nd edn. 1852, repr. 1969; John Garwood, *The million-peopled city: or, one half of the people of London made known to the other half*, 1853; Charles Manby Smith, *Curiosities of London life: or, phases, physiological and social, of the great metropolis*, 1853, repr. 1971, and *The little world of London: or pictures in little of London life*, 1857; and George Augustus Sala, *Twice round the clock: or the hours of day and night in London*, 1859, repr. 1969.

9476 MAYHEW (HENRY). London labour and the London poor: a cyclopaedia of the condition and earnings of those that will work, those that cannot work, and those that will not work. 4 v. 1861–2. Repr. 1968.

Includes part of an abortive 1851 edn. There have been various edns. of extracts, notably Peter Quennell, ed., *London's underworld*, 1950, *Mayhew's London*, 1951, and *Mayhew's characters*, 1951. The most celebrated of early surveys: well illustrated.

9477 HOLLINGSHEAD (JOHN). Ragged London in 1861. 1861.

9478 GREENWOOD (JAMES). Unsentimental journeys: or, byways of the modern Babylon. 1867.

One of a ser. of journalistic sketches by Greenwood of various aspects of London life. See also his *A night in a workhouse* [1866], *The seven curses of London*, 1869, *In strange company: being the experiences of a roving correspondent*, 1873, 2nd edn. 1886, and *The wilds of London*, 1874. Greenwood also publ. much else.

9479 HILL (OCTAVIA). Homes of the London poor. 1875. 2nd edn. 1883. Repr. 1969.

9480 THOMPSON (JOHN) *and* SMITH (ADOLPHE). Street life in London. 1877. Repr. N.Y. 1968.

9481 [MEARNS (ANDREW).] The bitter cry of outcast London: an inquiry into the condition of the abject poor. London Congreg. Union. 1883. New edn. by Anthony S. Wohl. Leicester. 1970.

See also A. S. Wohl, 'The bitter cry of outcast London', *Int. Rev. Soc. Hist.* xiii (1968), 189–245.

9482 HARE (AUGUSTUS JOHN CUTHBERT). Walks in London. 2 v. 1878. 7th edn. 2 v. 1901.

A once-famous book.

9483 WHITE (ARNOLD). The problems of a great city. 1886. New edns. 1887, 1895.

**9484** [OGLE (WILLIAM).] Tabulation of the statements made by men living in certain selected districts of London in March 1887. [C. 5228.] H.C. (1887). LXXI, 303.

A pioneer social survey, not altogether successful.

**9485** BOOTH (CHARLES) *ed.* Life and labour of the people in London. 3 v. 1889–91. 2nd edn. 4 v. 1889–93. 3rd edn. 9 v. 1892–7. 4th edn. 17 v. 1902–3.

Extraordinarily comprehensive. The 4th edn. is divided into 3 ser.: 1. poverty, 4 v.; 2. industry, 5 v.; 3. religious influences, 8 v. For Booth's work generally see **7227** and **7353**. For surveys earlier than *Life and labour* see his 'The inhabitants of Tower Hamlets (school board division), their condition and occupations', *Roy. Stat. Soc. J.* l (1887), 326–401, repr. as *Conditions and occupations of the people of Tower Hamlets, 1886–7*, 1887, and 'Condition and occupations of the people of East London and Hackney, 1887', *Roy. Stat. Soc. J.* li (1888), 276–339.

**9486** WILLIAMS (MONTAGU STEPHEN). Round London: down East and up West. 1892.

**9487** SHERWELL (ARTHUR). Life in West London: a study and a contrast. 1897. 3rd edn. 1901.

**9488** PATERSON (ALEXANDER). Across the bridges: or, life by the South London riverside. 1911.

**9489** SMITH (*Sir* HUBERT LLEWELLYN) *ed.* The new survey of London life and labour. 9 v. 1930–5.

Includes useful retrospective material.

## 2. GOVERNMENT

### (a) *General*

For the London Fire Brigade see **6439** and for London Transport see **5994–9**.

**9490** ROBSON (WILLIAM ALEXANDER). The government and mis-government of London. 1939.

A convenient intro. See also Sir Percy Alfred Harris, *London and its government*, 1913, rev. edn. 1931; Henry Jephson, *The sanitary evolution of London* (**7411**); Thomas Fiddian Reddaway, 'London in the nineteenth century', *Nineteenth Century* cxlv (1949), 363–74; cxlvii (1950), 104–18; cxlviii (1950), 118–30; Joseph E. Nève, *L'administration d'une grande ville: Londres*, Academie Lovaniensis, Ghent and Lond. 1901; and Ludwig Sinzheimer, *Der Londoner Grafschaftsrat: ein Beitrag zur städtischen Sozialreform: erster Band: die Schlussperiode der Herrschaft der Mittelklasse in der Londoner Stadtverwaltung* [to 1888], Stuttgart 1900.

**9491** FIRTH (JOSEPH FIRTH BOTTOMLEY). Municipal London: or, London government as it is, and London under a municipal council. 1876.

A substantial survey. Firth was the leading spirit in the London Municipal Reform League, for which see John Lloyd, *London municipal government: history of a great reform, 1880–1888*, 1910. For propagandist works see Thomas Hare, *London municipal reform . . .*, 1882, George Whale, *Greater London and its government*, 1888, and Firth's other works, notably his *Reform of London government and of city guilds,* Imperial parl. ser., 1888.

9492 HUNT (*Sir* JOHN). London local government. 2 v. 1897.

A useful legal textbook suppl. by his *The London Government Act, 1899: the law relating to metropolitan boroughs and borough councils,* 1899, and *Metropolitan borough councils elections . . .,* 1900.

9493 AYRTON COMMITTEE ON METROPOLITAN LOCAL GOVERNMENT. First report from the select committee on Metropolitan local government, &c. [Chairman: Acton Smee Ayrton]. H.C. 186 (1866). XIII, 171. Second report. H.C. 452 (1866). XIII, 317.

The first thorough examination of the subject. The committee also sat in the following session and produced three further reports: H.C. 135 (1867). XII, 431; H.C. 268 (1867). XII, 435; and H.C. 301 (1867). XII, 481.

9494 COURTNEY COMMISSION ON THE AMALGAMATION OF THE CITY AND COUNTY OF LONDON. Reports of the commissioners appointed to consider the proper conditions under which the amalgamation of the City and the County of London can be effected, and to make specific and practical proposals for that purpose [Chairman: Leonard H. Courtney]. [C. 7493] H.C. (1894). XVII, 1. Minutes of evidence. [C. 7493–I] H.C. (1894). XVII, 37. Appendixes. [C. 7393–II] H.C. (1894). XVIII, I.

9495 ULLSWATER COMMISSION ON LONDON GOVERNMENT. Report of the commissioners appointed to inquire into the local government of Greater London [Chairman: Viscount Ullswater]. [Cmd. 1830] H.C. (1923). XII pt. 1, 567. Minutes of evidence in 7 pts. pr. as non-parl. papers.

Mainly useful as a quarry. The later Herbert Commission also includes some hist. material: *Royal commission on local government in Greater London, 1957–60* [Chairman: Sir Edwin S. Herbert]: *report.* [Cmnd. 1164] H.C. (1959–60). XVIII, 9.

9496 AYRTON COMMITTEE ON METROPOLIS LOCAL TAXATION. First report from the select committee on metropolis local taxation [Chairman: Acton Smee Ayrton]. H.C. 211 (1861). VIII, 1. Second report. H.C. 372 (1861). VIII, 135. Third report. H.C. 476 (1861). VIII, 381.

9497 METROPOLITAN BOARD OF WORKS COMMISSION. Interim report of the royal commissioners appointed to inquire into certain matters connected with the working of the Metropolitan Board of Works [Chairman: Lord Herschell]. [C. 5560] H.C. (1888). LVI, 1. Minutes of evidence. [C. 5560–I] H.C. (1888). LVI, 47. Final report [formal only]. [C. 5705] H.C. (1889). XXXIX, 319.

Chiefly concerned with maladministration and corruption.

(b) *County of London*

9498 GUILDHALL LIBRARY. The county of London: a select book list. Libr. Assoc. 1959.

9499 GIBBON (*Sir* IOAN GWILYM) *and* BELL (REGINALD WILLIAM). History of the London County Council, 1889–1939. 1939.

There is also a short pamphlet hist. by a chairman of the L.C.C., Albert Emil Davies, *The story of the London County Council*, 1925, and a useful account by a councillor of the first council, William Saunders, *History of the first London County Council, 1889–1890–1891*, 1892. William Eric Jackson, *Achievement: a short history of the London County Council*, 1965, is a continuation of Gibbon and Bell.

9500 LONDON COUNTY COUNCIL. A review of the . . . year's work of the council. 1890+.

The L.C.C. also publ. an *Annual report*, 1890+, and *London statistics*, 1890+.

9501 GOMME (*Sir* GEORGE LAURENCE) *and* BERRY (SEAGER) *comps*. London statutes: a collection of acts relating specially to the administrative county of London and of local and personal acts affecting the powers and duties of the London County Council, from 1750 to 1907. 2 v. 1907.

9502 HAWARD (*Sir* HARRY EDWIN). The London County Council from within: forty years' official recollections. 1932.

Haward was comptroller, 1893–1920, and electricity commissioner, 1920–30.

9503 GARDINER (ALFRED GEORGE). John Benn and the progressive movement. 1925.

The best biog. dealing with the L.C.C. But see also Elizabeth Balmer Baker and Philip John Noel-Baker, *J. Allen Baker, member of parliament: a memoir*, 1927, and Hope Costley White, *Willoughby Hyett Dickinson, 1859–1943: a memoir*, Gloucester 1956, for other Progressive members of the Council, and Ernest P. Woolf, *Thirty years of public life . . .*, 1913, for a Conservative local politician.

9504 WEBB (SIDNEY JAMES), *Baron Passfield*. The London programme. Social Science Series. 1891.

The best statement of the Progressive party programme. Webb's *London education*, 1904, is in a sense a supplement made necessary by the 1902 Education Act.

### (c) *City of London*

The main sources for the hist. of the City are the reports of four big inquiries, **9494, 9511, 9514,** and **9516,** but there is also an extensive pamphlet lit. devoted to attacks on the City, of which the best representative is Firth (**9491**). For the most effective reply see Scott (**9512**).

9505 SMITH (RAYMOND). The City of London: a select book list. National Book League. [1951.]

9506 JONES (PHILIP EDMUND) *and* SMITH (RAYMOND) *comps*. A guide to the records in the Corporation of London Records Office and the Guildhall Library muniment room. 1951.

The Guildhall Libr. has also publ. *Handlists* of local records, as follows: *Vestry minutes . . .*, 1958, *Churchwardens' accounts . . .*, 1960, *London rate assessments and inhabitants' lists*, 1961, *Parish registers*, 2 pts. in 1, 1964–6. In addition the libr. publ. hist. articles in *The Guildhall miscellany*, 1+, 1952+.

9507 WELCH (CHARLES). Modern history of the City of London: a record of municipal and social progress from 1760 to the present day. 1896.

See also *The corporation of London: its origin, constitution, powers and duties*, Corp. of London 1950, Alexander Pulling, *A practical treatise on the laws, customs and regulations of the City and Port of London*, 1842, 2nd edn. 1849, 2nd edn. rev. 1854, and Sydney Perks, *The history of the Mansion house*, Camb. 1922.

9508 BEAVEN (ALFRED BEAVEN). The aldermen of the City of London, temp. Henry III–1908. With notes on the parliamentary representation of the city, the aldermen and the livery companies, the aldermanic veto, aldermanic baronets, and knights, etc. 2 v. 1908–13.

9509 SEYD (RICHARD) *comp.* After the turtle: thirty-one years' ministerial policy as set forth at Lord Mayor's day banquets, from 1845 to 1878. 1878.

9510 TRELOAR (*Sir* WILLIAM PURDIE). A Lord Mayor's diary, 1906–7... 1920.

The best of such diaries. Sir Henry Aaron Isaacs, *Memoirs of my mayoralty*, priv. pr. [1890], is a comparable work. Pearse Morrison, *Rambling recollections*, 1905, is the memoirs of a common councillor for nearly 30 yrs. Alfred George Temple, *Guildhall memories*, 1918, is primarily concerned with the Guildhall Gallery of which Temple was director, but has reminiscences of City officials.

9511 LABOUCHERE COMMISSION ON THE CORPORATION OF LONDON. Report of the commissioners appointed to inquire into the existing state of the corporation of the City of London, and to collect information respecting its constitution, order, and government, &c. [Chairman: Henry Labouchere.] [1772] H.C. (1854). XXVI, I.

9512 SCOTT (BENJAMIN). A statistical vindication of the city of London: or, fallacies exploded and figures explained. 1867.

A defence of the city. There is a considerable polemical lit. See also William Gilbert, *The city: an inquiry into the corporation, its livery companies, and the administration of their charities and endowments*, 1877.

9513 CITY OF LONDON CORPORATION. Report of the city day census, 1881. 1881.

Issued to counteract the effect of the official census which was confined to those who slept in the city. Further reports were issued in 1891 and 1911.

9514 HARTINGTON COMMITTEE ON LONDON CORPORATION (CHARGES OF MALVERSION). Report from the select committee on London Corporation (charges of malversion) [Chairman: Marquess of Hartington]. H.C. 161 (1887). X, 13.

A full investigation of the campaign by the Court of Common Council, against London municipal reform, 1882–5.

9515 KAHL (WILLIAM FREDERICK). The development of London livery companies: an historical essay and a select bibliography. Kress Libr. Publ. 15. Boston, Mass. 1960. Suppl. *Guildhall miscellany* ii (1962), 99–126.

9516  LONDON LIVERY COMPANIES' COMMISSION. City of London livery companies' commission [Chairman: Earl of Derby]. Report and appendix. [C. 4073] H.C. (1884). XXXIX, pts. I–V.

Sir Lewis Tonna Dibdin, *The livery companies of London: being a review of the report of the London Livery Companies' Commission*, 1886, is a useful short analysis. For a reply see *The royal commission: the London city livery companies' vindication*, 1885.

9517  DITCHFIELD (PETER HAMPSON). The city companies of London and their good works: a record of their history, charity and treasure. 1904.

A useful company-by-company survey, fuller than William Carew Hazlitt, *The livery companies of the City of London . . .*, 1892, but, like it, based on the report of the Derby commission. Ditchfield also publ. *The story of the City companies*, 1926.

9518  ALFORD (BERNARD WILLIAM ERNEST) *and* BARKER (THEODORE CARDWELL). A history of the Carpenters' company. 1968.

One of the few company hists. to deal at all adequately with the 19th cent. See also Arnold Francis Steele, *The worshipful company of gardeners of London: a history of its revival, 1890–1960*, 1964; Cyprian Blagden, *The Stationers' company: a history*, Lond. & Camb., Mass. 1960; Thomas Girtin, *The golden ram: a narrative history of the Clothworkers' company, 1528–1958*, 2nd edn. 1958, and *The triple crowns: a narrative history of the Drapers' company, 1364–1964*, 1964; and Eric Bennett, *The worshipful company of wheelwrights of the City of London, 1670–1970*, Newton Abbot 1970.

(d) *Metropolitan Boroughs*

9519  HOPKINS (ALBERT BASSETT). The boroughs of the Metropolis: a handbook to local administration in London under the London Government Act, 1899. 1900.

9520  MANCHEE (WILLIAM HENRY). The Westminster city fathers (the burgess court of Westminster) 1585–1901. Being some account of their powers and domestic rule of the city prior to its incorporation in 1901. 1924.

## D. COUNTY AND LOCAL HISTORIES

This list is confined to general hists., and excludes those intended primarily for use in schools. For studs. of agriculture, industry, social problems, the Church, and local government in the localities, consult the index. For lists of county maps see **9374**.

9521  BEDFORDSHIRE. Lewis Ralph Conisbee, *A Bedfordshire bibliography: with some comments and biographical notes*, Beds. Hist. Record Soc. 1962, suppl. 1967. Bedfordshire County Council, *Guide to the Bedfordshire record office*, Bedford 1957, suppl. for 1957–62, 1963. Bedfordshire Hist. Record Soc., *Publications*, 1+, Apsley Guise etc. 1913+. Joyce Godber, *History of Bedfordshire, 1066–1888*, Bedfordshire County Council 1969. Lydia M. Marshall, *The rural population of Bedfordshire* (**6941**). William Austin, *The history of Luton and its hamlets*, 2 v. 1928.

9522   BERKSHIRE. Reading Public Librs., *Local collection: catalogue of books and maps relating to Berkshire*, Reading 1958, suppl. for 1956–66, 1967. Felix Hull, ed., *Guide to the Berkshire Record Office*, Reading 1952. Berkshire Archaeol. Soc., *The Berkshire archaeological journal* [formerly *The Berks, Bucks & Oxon archaeological journal*], 1+, Reading 1895+. Bromley Challenor, ed., *Selections from the municipal chronicles of the borough of Abingdon from A.D. 1555 to A.D. 1897*, Abingdon 1898. M. A. Havinden, *Estate villages . . . Ardington and Lockinge* (**4245**). A. L. Bowley, 'Working-class households in Reading' (**7352**).

9523   BUCKINGHAMSHIRE. Buckinghamshire Archaeological Soc. (Records branch), *Publications*, 1+, 1937+. *Records of Buckinghamshire: being the journal of the Architectural and Archaeological Society for the County of Buckingham*, 1+, Aylesbury etc. 1958+. Leslie Joseph Ashford, *The history of the borough of High Wycombe from its origins to 1880*, High Wycombe 1960. Leonard John Mayes, *The history of the borough of High Wycombe from 1880 to the present day*, High Wycombe 1960. John Gilbert Jenkins, *Chequers: a history of the prime minister's Buckinghamshire home*, 1967. Sir Sydney Frank Markham, *The nineteen hundreds: being the story of the Buckinghamshire towns of Wolverton and Stony Stratford during the years 1900–1911*, 1962.

9524   CAMBRIDGESHIRE AND ELY. Cambridge Antiquarian Soc., *Publications*, 1840–6+, Camb. 1846+. Enid Porter, *Cambridgeshire customs and folklore*, 1969. Samuel Henry Miller and Sydney Barber Josiah Skertchly, *The fenland past and present*, Wisbech & Lond. 1878. Charles Henry Cooper and John William Cooper, *Annals of Cambridge*, vol. V. '1850–1856', Camb. 1908. E. Jebb, *Cambridge: a brief study in social questions* (**7351**). Frederic John Gardiner, *History of Wisbech and the neighbourhood during the last fifty years, 1848–1898*, Wisbech & Lond. 1898. W. Wells, 'The drainage of Whittlesea Mere' (**4426**).

9525   CHESHIRE. Chester and North Wales Architectural, Archaeol. and Hist. Soc., *Journal*, 1849–85+. *The Cheshire sheaf: being local gleanings, historical & antiquarian, from many scattered fields, reprinted . . . from the Chester 'Courant'* [later 'Cheshire observer'], 1+, Chester 1880+. J. M. Lee, *Social leaders and public persons* (**9410**). Mass Observation [H. D. Willcock, ed.], *Browns and Chester: portrait of a shop, 1780–1946* [1947.] William Brewer Stephens, ed., *History of Congleton*, Manch. 1969. William Henry Chaloner, *Social and economic development of Crewe, 1780–1923*, Manch. 1950. Thomas Middleton, *History of Hyde and its neighbourhood*, Hyde 1932. Clarice Stella Davies, ed., *A history of Macclesfield*, Manch. 1961. Edward Cuthbert Woods and Percy Culverwell Brown, *The rise and progress of Wallasey: a history of the borough*, Wallasey 1929, 2nd edn. 1960. See also Lancashire (**9540**).

9526   CORNWALL. George Clement Boase and William Prideaux Courtney, *Bibliotheca cornubiensis: a catalogue of the writings, both manuscript and printed, of Cornishmen and of works relating to the county of Cornwall . . .*, 3 v. 1874–82.

George Clement Boase, *Collectanea cornubiensia: a collection of biographical and topographical notes relating to the county of Cornwall*, priv. pr. Truro 1890. Royal Institution of Cornwall, *Journal*, 1+, Truro 1864+. Frank Ernest Halliday, *A history of Cornwall*, 1959. William George Victor Balchin, *Cornwall: the history of the landscape*, 1954. R. Pearse, *The ports of Cornwall* (**6191**). Henry Leslie Douch, *Old Cornish inns and their place in the social history of the county*, Truro 1966. Henry Spencer Toy, *The history of Helston*, 1936. Gordon Forrester Matthews, *The Isles of Scilly: a constitutional, economic and social survey of the development of an island people, from early times to 1900*, 1960. Elisabeth Inglis-Jones, *Augustus Smith of Scilly*, 1969.

See also under Devon (**9529**).

9527  CUMBERLAND. Henry Wigston Hodgson, comp., *A bibliography of the history and topography of Cumberland & Westmorland*, Carlisle 1968. Fred Barnes and James Leslie Hobbs, eds., *Handlist of newspapers published in Cumberland, Westmorland and north Lancashire*, Cumb. & Westmorland Antiq. & Archaeol. Soc. Tract xiv, 1951. Cumb. and Westmorland Antiq. and Archaeol. Soc., *Transactions*, 1+, 1874+, *Tract series*, 1+, 1884+. W. M. Williams, *The sociology of an English village: Gosforth* (**7019**). Alan Harris, 'Millom: a Victorian new town', *Cumb. & Westmorland Antiq. & Archaeol. Soc. Trans.* new ser. lxvi (1966), 449–67. Thomas William Carrick, *History of Wigton (Cumberland) from its origin to the close of the nineteenth century*, Carlisle 1949.

9528  DERBYSHIRE. [James Ormerod] *Derbyshire: a select catalogue of books about the county*, Derby Public Libr. 1930. John Charles Cox, *Calendar of the records of the county of Derby*, 1899. Derbyshire Archaeological and Natural Hist. Soc., *Journal*, 1+, London & Derby 1879+. Robert Grundy Heape, *Buxton: under the Dukes of Devonshire*, 1948. A. W. Davison, *Derby: its rise and progress* [1833–1905], Lond. & Derby 1906. Anthony Harold Birch, *Small-town politics: a study of political life in Glossop*, 1959.

9529  DEVON. Devon and Cornwall Record Soc., *Publications*, 1+, Exeter 1906+. Devonshire Assoc. for the Advancement of Science, Literature and Art, *Report and transactions*, 1+, Plymouth etc. 1863+. *Devon [and Cornwall] notes and queries*, 1900–1+, Exeter 1901+. William George Hoskins, *Devon*, 1954. E. A. G. Clark, *The ports of the Exe estuary* (**6190**). William Crossing, *A hundred years on Dartmoor: historical notices of the forest and its purlieus during the nineteenth century . . .*, Plymouth 1901, 5th edn. 1902, new edn. by Brian Le Messurier, Newton Abbot 1967, and *Crossing's Dartmoor worker*, ed. by Brian Le Messurier, Newton Abbot 1966. Richard George Hansford Worth, *Dartmoor*, ed. by Guy Malcolm Spooner and F. S. Russell, Plymouth 1953, new edn. Newton Abbot 1967. William Francis Gardiner, *Barnstaple, 1837–97*, Barnstaple 1897. Percy Russell, *Dartmouth*, 1950. Robert Newton, *Victorian Exeter, 1837–1914*, Leicester 1968. Joyce Youings, *Tuckers Hall, Exeter: the history of a provincial city company through five centuries*, Exeter 1968. Eric Raymond Delderfield, *Exmouth milestones: a history*, Exmouth 1948. Albert John

Rhodes, *Newton Abbot: its history and development*: Mid-Devon Times *handbook*, Newton Abbot [1904]. Plymouth City Librs., *A guide to the archives department* Part I: 1. *Plymouth records*, Plymouth 1962, 2. *Plymouth city charters, 1439–1935* . . ., Plymouth 1962. Henry Francis Whitfield, *Plymouth and Devonport in times of war and peace*, Plymouth etc. 1900. Robert Alfred John Walling, *The story of Plymouth*, 1950. Frederick John Snell, *The chronicles of Twyford: being a new and popular history of the town of Tiverton* . . ., Tiverton 1892. Percy Russell, *A history of Torquay and the famous anchorage of Torbay*, Torquay Nat. Hist. Soc., Torquay 1960. Arthur Charles Ellis, *An historical survey of Torquay*, Torquay 1930. Percy Russell, *The good town of Totnes*, Devonshire Assoc., Exeter [1964].

9530 DORSET. Robert Douch, *A handbook of local history: Dorset*, Univ. of Bristol 1952, suppl. 1962. A. C. Cox, comp., *County of Dorset: index to the county records in the record room at the county offices and . . . at the shire hall, Dorchester*, Dorset Nat. Hist. & Archaeol. Soc., Dorchester 1938. Dorset Nat. Hist. and Archaeol. Soc., *Proceedings*, 1+, Sherborne etc. 1877+. Barbara Kerr, *Bound to the soil: a social history of Dorset, 1750–1918*, 1968. Harry Percy Smith, *The history of the borough and county of the town of Poole*, 2 v. Poole 1948–51. See also under Somerset (**9552**).

9531 DURHAM. Surtees Soc., *Publications*, 1+, 1835+. Architectural and Archaeol. Soc. of Durham and Northumberland, *Transactions*, 1+, Durham 1862+. Ellen Wilkinson, *The town that was murdered* [Jarrow], 1939. Charles Henry Gordon Hopkins, *Pallion, 1874–1954: church and people in a shipyard parish*, Sunderland [1954]. George B. Hodgson, *The borough of South Shields: from the earliest period to the close of the nineteenth century*, Newcastle-upon-Tyne 1903. J. W. Smith and T. S. Holden, *Where ships are born: Sunderland, 1346–1946: a history of shipbuilding on the river Wear*, Sunderland 1946. Robert Wood, *West Hartlepool: the rise and development of a Victorian new town*, Hartlepool 1967. Robert Martin, *Historical notes and personal recollections of West Hartlepool and its founder: with chronological notes*, West Hartlepool 1924.

9532 ESSEX. William Raymond Powell, ed., *The Victoria history of the counties of England: a history of the county of Essex: bibliography*, 1959, suppl. by John Gerard O'Leary, Dagenham 1962. Frederick George Emmison, ed., *Guide to the Essex record office*, 2 pts. Essex Record Office, Chelmsford 1946–8, 2nd edn. in 2 v. Chelmsford 1969. Frederick George Emmison, ed., *Catalogue of the Essex parish records, 1240–1894, with supplement on nonconformist, charities', societies', and schools' records, 1341–1903*, Essex Record Office, Chelmsford, 2nd edn. 1966. A. F. J. Brown, ed., *English history from Essex sources, 1750–1900*, Essex Record Office, Chelmsford 1952. Essex Archaeol. Soc., *Transactions*, 1855–8+, 1858+. G. Cuttle, *The legacy of the rural guardians . . . in mid-Essex* (**7017**). J. Oxley Parker, *The Oxley Parker papers* (**4310**). James Edwin Oxley, ed., *Barking vestry minutes and other parish documents*, Colchester 1955. Geoffrey Haward Martin, *The story of Colchester from Roman times to the* *present day*, Colchester 1959. [James Howson, comp.] *Essex and Dagenham: a catalogue of books, pamphlets and maps*, Dagenham Public Libr. 1957, 2nd edn. 1961. John Gerard O'Leary, *The book of Dagenham: a history*, Dagenham Public Librs., 3rd edn. 1964. Alfred Stokes, *East Ham from village to county borough*, 3rd edn. Stratford etc. 1933. B. C. Hughes, *The history of Harwich harbour* (**6189**). Frederick William Austen, *Rectors of two Essex parishes* [Stock Harvard and Ramsden Bellhouse] *and their times . . .*, Colchester 1943. Ivan George Sparkes, *The history of Thurrock: a guide and bibliography*, priv. pr. Upminster 1960. George Edward J. Roebuck, *The story of Walthamstow*, Walthamstow 1959. Donald McDougall, *Fifty years a borough, 1886–1936: the story of West Ham*, 1936. E. G. Howarth and M. Wilson, *West Ham* (**7054**).

9533 GLOUCESTERSHIRE. Roland Austin, comp., *Catalogue of the Gloucestershire collection: books, pamphlets and documents in the Gloucester public library, relating to the county, cities, towns and villages of Gloucestershire*, Gloucester 1928, suppl. by his *Catalogue of the Gloucestershire books collected by Sir Francis Hyett of Painswick*, Gloucester 1950. Irvine Egerton Gray and Alexander Thomas Gaydon, eds., *Gloucestershire quarter sessions archives, 1660–1889, and other official records*, Gloucestershire County Council, Gloucester 1958. Irvine Egerton Gray and Elizabeth Ralph, eds., *Guide to the parish records of the city of Bristol and the county of Gloucester*, Bristol & Glos. Archaeol. Soc. Records v, 1963. Bristol and Gloucestershire Archaeol. Soc., *Transactions*, 1+, 1876+; Records section, *Publications*, 1+, 1952+. Herbert Patrick Reginald Finberg, *Gloucestershire: the history of the landscape*, 1957. Gwen Hart, *A history of Cheltenham*, Leicester 1965. Paul Hawkins Fisher, *Notes and recollections of Stroud*, Stroud 1871, 2nd edn. 1891, cont. by John Libby, *Twenty years' history of Stroud, 1870–1890*, Stroud 1890.

9534 BRISTOL. Edward Robert Norris Mathews, ed., *Bristol bibliography: city and county of Bristol municipal public libraries: a catalogue of the books, pamphlets, collectanea, etc., relating to Bristol, contained in the central reference library*, Bristol 1916. Bristol Record Soc., *Publications*, 1+, Bristol 1930+. Elizabeth Ralph, ed., *Guide to the Bristol archives office*, Bristol 1972. Bryan Little, *The city and county of Bristol: a study in Atlantic civilisation*, 1954. John Latimer, *The annals of Bristol in the nineteenth century*, Bristol 1887, suppl. to 1900, 1902. Alfred Beaven Beaven, *Bristol lists: municipal and miscellaneous*, Bristol 1899. Reece Winstone, *Bristol as it was, 1874–1866* [*sic*], Bristol 1966, *Bristol as it was, 1879–1874*, Bristol 1965, 2nd edn. 1968, *Bristol in the 1880s*, Bristol 1962, and *Bristol in the 1890s*, Bristol 1960. W. G. Neale, *At the port of Bristol* (**6187**).

9535 HAMPSHIRE. Hampshire Field Club, *Papers and proceedings*, 1+, 1885–90+, Southampton 1890+. Howard Norman Cole, *The story of Aldershot: a history and guide to town and camp*, Aldershot 1951. Charles Henry Mate and Charles Riddle, *Bournemouth, 1810–1910 . . .*, Bournemouth 1910. David Sievewright Young, *The story of Bournemouth*, 1957. George Frederick Chambers, *East Bourne memories of the Victorian period, 1845 to 1901 . . .*,

Eastbourne 1910. Frank Woodgate Lipscomb, *Heritage of seapower: the story of Portsmouth*, 1967. Southampton Corporation, *Southampton records: guide to the records of the corporation and absorbed authorities in the civic record office*, Southampton 1964. University of Southampton, *Southampton record series*, 1+, Southampton 1951+. Alfred Temple Patterson, *A history of Southampton, 1700–1914*, 3 v. Southampton 1966 +. Francis John Monkhouse, ed., *Survey of Southampton and its region*, [British Assoc. handbook] Southampton 1964.

**9536  HEREFORDSHIRE.** Herefordshire County Librs. (Local History Section), *Herefordshire books: a select list of books in the local collection . . .*, Hereford 1955. Woolhope Naturalists' Field Club, *Transactions*, 1852–65+, Hereford 1867+. Woolhope Naturalists' Field Club, *Herefordshire: its natural history, archaeology and history: chapters written to celebrate the centenary of the Woolhope Naturalists' Field Club . . .*, Gloucester [1951]. William Collins, *Old and new Hereford*: Part II: *Modern Hereford with special reference to the development of its municipality*, Hereford 1911, and *The mayors of Hereford from . . . 1854*, Hereford 1910.

**9537  HERTFORDSHIRE.** Mary Florence Thwaite, comp., *Hertfordshire newspapers, 1772–1955*, Herts. Local Hist. Council, Hatfield 1956, and *Periodicals and transactions relating to Hertfordshire: a short guide and subject index*, Herts. Local Hist. Council, Hatfield 1959. William Le Hardy, ed., *Guide to the Hertfordshire record office*: Part I: *Quarter sessions and other records in the custody of the county*, Hertfordshire County Council, Hertford 1961. William John Hardy, ed., *Hertfordshire county records*. Vol. III: 'Notes and extracts from the sessions rolls, 1851 to 1894 . . .', Hertfordshire County Council, Hertford 1910. E. Grey, *Cottage life* [in Harpenden] (**6689**). Reginald Leslie Hine, *The history of Hitchin*, 2 v. 1927, and *Hitchin worthies: four centuries of English life*, 1932. Howard Frederick Hayllar, *The chronicles of Hoddesdon from the earliest time to the present day*, Hoddesdon [1948]. C. B. Purdom, *The garden city* [Letchworth] (**7073**). Frederick Brittain, *South Mymms: the story of a parish*, Camb. 1931. Guy Ewing, *Westmill: the story of a Herts parish*, Tunbridge Wells [1928].

**9538  HUNTINGDONSHIRE.** Huntingdonshire County Libr., *Catalogue of the local history collection*, Huntingdon 1950, 2nd edn. 1958. George Hugo Findlay, ed., *Guide to the Huntingdonshire record office*, Hunts. County Council, Huntingdon 1958.

**9539  KENT.** Archibald John Gritten, comp., *Catalogue of books, pamphlets and excerpts dealing with Margate, the Isle of Thanet and the county of Kent in the local collection of the borough of Margate public library*, Margate 1934. Kent County Libr., *Local history catalogue*, Gillingham 1951, suppl. 1955. Felix Hull, ed., *Guide to the Kent county archives office*, Kent County Council, Maidstone 1958. Felix Hull, ed., *A calendar of the White and Black books of the Cinque Ports, 1432–1955*, Hist. MSS. Commn. 1966. Kent Archaeol. Soc., *Archaeologia Cantiana . . .*, 1+, 1858+. Robert Borrowman, *Beckenham: past and present*, Beckenham 1910. Francis De Paula Castella, *Bexley Heath and*

*Welling: being a contribution to the history of the district*, Bexleyheath 1910. Brian Burch, comp., *A bibliography of printed material relating to Bromley, Hayes and Keston, in the county of Kent*, Bromley Public Libr. 1964. Edward Lee Stuart Horsburgh, *Bromley, Kent, from the earliest times to the present century*, 1929. James Presnail, *Chatham: the story of a dockyard town and the birthplace of the British navy*, 1952. Sidney Kilworth Keyes, *Dartford: some historical notes*, 2 v. Dartford 1933–8. John Bavington Jones, *Annals of Dover . . .*, Dover 1916, and *Dover: a perambulation of the town, fort and fortress*, Dover 1907. Alexander John Philip Wraysbury, *A history of Gravesend and its surroundings, from prehistoric times* [1954]. Frederick Francis Smith, *A history of Rochester* [1928]. Greenwich and Lewisham Antiquarian Soc., *Transactions*, 1+, 1907+. Arthur Henry Neve, *The Tonbridge of yesterday*, Tonbridge 1933, rev. edn. 1934. Robert Harold Goodsall, *Whitstable, Seasalter and Swalecliffe: the history of three Kent parishes*, Canterbury 1938. William Thomas Vincent, *The records of the Woolwich district*, 2 v. Woolwich [1888–90]. Edward Francis Ernest Jefferson, *The Woolwich story, 1890–1965*, Woolwich 1970.

9540   LANCASHIRE. Joint Committee on the Lancashire Bibliography, *A contribution towards a Lancashire bibliography. 1. Lancashire directories, 1684–1957*, comp. by George Henry Tupling and ed. by Sidney Horrocks, Manch. 1968. 2. Sidney Horrocks, comp., *Lancashire Acts of Parliament, 1266–1957*, Manch. 1969. 3 Sidney Horrocks, comp., *Lancashire business histories*, Manch. 1971. Reginald Ernest George Smith, ed., *Newspapers first published before 1900 in Lancashire, Cheshire and the Isle of Man: a union list of holdings in libraries and newspaper offices within the area*, Libr. Assoc. 1964. Reginald Sharpe France, ed., *Guide to the Lancashire record office*, Lancashire County Council, Preston 1948, 2nd edn. 1962. Lancashire and Cheshire Record Soc. [The Record Soc. for the Publication of original Documents relating to Lancashire and Cheshire], *Publications*, 1+, 1879+. Chetham Soc., *Remains historical and literary connected with the palatine counties of Lancaster and Chester*, 1+, 1844+. Historic Soc. of Lancashire and Cheshire, *Proceedings and papers*, 1848–9+, Liverpool 1849+. Lancashire and Cheshire Antiq. Soc., *Transactions*, 1+, 1883+, Manch. 1884+. Roy Millward, *Lancashire: an illustrated essay on the history of the landscape*, 1955. Sir Edward Baines, *The history of the county palatine and duchy of Lancaster* [to 1867], 3rd edn. by James Croston, 5 v. Manch. 1888–93. Winifred Mary Bowman, *England in Ashton-under-Lyne*, Ashton-under-Lyne 1960. Alan Harris, 'Askam iron: the development of Askam-in-Furness, 1850–1920', *Cumberland & Westmorland Antiq. & Archaeol. Soc. Trans.* new ser. lxv (1965), 381–407. George Calvert Miller, *Blackburn: the evolution of a cotton town . . .*, Blackburn 1951, and *Blackburn worthies of yesterday . . .*, Blackburn 1959. Harold Hamer, *Bolton, 1838–1938: a centenary record of municipal progress*, Bolton 1938. Walter Bennett, *The history of Burnley*, 4 v. Burnley 1946–51. Alan Harris, 'Carnforth, 1840–1900: the rise of a north Lancashire town', *Historic Soc. Lancs. & Ches. Trans.* cxii (1960), 105–19. Thomas Middleton, *The history of Denton and Haughton*, Hyde 1936. Robert Speake and F. R. Witty, *A history of Droylsden*, Stockport 1953. John Duncan Marshall, *Furness and the industrial revolution:*

an economic history of Furness (*1711–1900*) and of the town of Barrow (*1757–1897*) with an epilogue, Barrow-in-Furness Corp. 1958. Christopher Aspin, *Haslingden, 1800–1900: a history*, Haslingden 1962, 2nd edn. 1963. Ronald Cunliffe Shaw, *Kirkham in Amounderness: the story of a Lancashire community*, 1949. Anon., *Outlines of an economic history of Lancaster, 1800 to 1860*, pt. 2, Lancaster 1951. William Duncombe Pink, *Leigh municipal record, 1863–1907*, Leigh 1907. John Lunn, *Leigh: the historical past of a Lancashire borough*, Leigh [1958]. Walter Bennett, *The history of Marsden and Nelson*, Nelson 1957. R. G. Armstrong, 'The rise of Morecombe (1820–1862)', *Historic Soc. Lancs & Ches. Trans.* c (1948), 157–92. John Henry Lane, *Newton-in-Makerfield: its history, with some account of its people*, 2 v. Newton-le-Willows 1914–16. Hartley Bateson, *A centenary history of Oldham*, Oldham 1949. Anthony Hewitson, *History of Preston in the county of Lancaster, A.D. 705 to 1883*, Preston 1883. Rebe Prestwich Taylor, *Rochdale retrospect: a handbook*, ed. by Ernest Taylor, Rochdale 1956. Henry Brierley, *Rochdale reminiscences*, Rochdale 1923. Theodore Cardwell Barker and John Raymond Harris, *A Merseyside town in the industrial revolution: St. Helens, 1750–1900*, Liverpool 1954, new edn. 1959. Robert Roberts, *The classic slum: Salford life in the first quarter of the century*, Manch. 1971. Francis Arthur Bailey, *A history of Southport*, Southport 1955. George A. Carter and others, *Warrington hundred: a handbook*, 1947. George Edward Diggle, *A history of Widnes*, Widnes Corp. 1961.

9541   LIVERPOOL. George Chandler, *Liverpool*, 1957. John Raymond Harris, ed., *Liverpool and Merseyside: essays in economic and social history*, 1969. B. D. White, *History of the corporation of Liverpool* (**9423**). Sir James Allanson Picton, *Memorials of Liverpool*, rev. edn. 2 v. Liverpool 1903. Thomas Baines, *Liverpool in 1859*, 2 pts. Liverpool 1859. Ramsay Muir, *A history of Liverpool*, 1907. Liverpool Econ. and Stat. Soc., *Transactions*, 1903–14. See also the hist. of Liverpool Chamber of Commerce (**5862**), and Hope (**7412**), Frazer (**7416**) and Bickerton (**7412**) on medical matters. R. Lawton, 'The population of Liverpool in the mid-nineteenth century', *Historic Soc. Lancs. & Ches. Trans.* cvii (1955), 89–120. Margaret B. Simey, *Charitable effort in Liverpool* (**7222**). James Quentin Hughes, *Seaport: architecture and townscape in Liverpool*, Liverpool 1964. S. Mountfield, *Western gateway* (**6186**).

9542   MANCHESTER. Nicholas Joseph Frangopulo, *Rich inheritance: a guide to the history of Manchester*, Manch. Education Committee 1962. Francis Archibald Bruton, *A short history of Manchester and Salford*, 1924, 2nd edn. 1927. A. Redford, *The history of local government in Manchester* (**9422**). S. D. Simon, *A century of city government* (**9422**). Thomas Southcliffe Ashton, *Economic and social investigations in Manchester, 1833–1933*, 1934. Manchester Stat. Soc., *Transactions*, 1853–4+. City of Manchester, Librs. Committee, *Manchester review*, 1936+. A. Redford, *Manchester merchants* (**5860**). Cecil Stewart, *The stones of Manchester* (**9181**). Katherine Chorley, Baroness Chorley, *Manchester made them*, 1950. T. R. Marr, *Housing conditions in Manchester* (**7096**). Manchester Corp. Housing Committee, *A short history of Manchester housing* (**7095**).

9543 LEICESTERSHIRE. John Michael Lee, *Leicestershire history: a handlist to printed sources in the libraries of Leicester*, Vaughan College papers 4, Leicester 1958. Leicestershire Archaeol. [and Hist.] Soc., *Transactions*, 1+, Leicester 1866+. William George Hoskins, *Leicestershire: the history of the landscape*, 1955, *The midland peasant: the economic and social history of a Leicestershire village*, 1957, and *Studies in Leicestershire agrarian history*, 1949. John Michael Lee, 'The rise and fall of a market town: Castle Donington in the nineteenth century', *Leics. Archaeol. & Hist. Soc. Trans.* xxxii (1956), 52–80. Henry Hartopp, ed., *Register of the freemen of Leicester, 1770–1930 . . .*, Leicester Corp. 1933, and *Roll of the mayors of the borough and lord mayors of the city of Leicester, 1209 to 1935 . . .*, Leicester City Council, Leicester [1936]. Jack Simmons, 'Mid-Victorian Leicester', *Leicestershire Archaeol. & Hist. Soc. Trans.* xli (1965–6), 41–56. *Leicester Chamber of Commerce* (**5863**).

9544 LINCOLNSHIRE. Lincoln Record Soc., *Publications*, 1+, Lincoln 1911+. Lincolnshire Local Hist. Soc., *Lincolnshire history and archaeology*, 1+, 1966+. J. Thirsk, *English peasant farming . . . Lincolnshire* (**4169**). Frank Baker, *The story of Cleethorpes and the contribution of Methodism through two hundred years* [1954]. Edward Gillett, *A history of Grimsby*, 1970. Bob Lincoln, *The rise of Grimsby*, 2 v. 1913. Alan Rogers, ed., *The making of Stamford*, Leicester 1965.

9545 MIDDLESEX. Standing Joint Committee of the County of Middlesex, *Guide to the Middlesex sessions records, 1549–1889*, comp. by E. Doris Mercer, Greater London Record Office (Middlesex records), 1965. [Richard] Michael Robbins, *Middlesex*, 1953. William King Baker, *Acton, Middlesex*, Acton 1912, 2nd edn. 1913. Warwick Draper, *Chiswick*, 1923. Edith Jackson, *Annals of Ealing from the twelfth century to the present time*, 1898. Sir Cuthbert Wilfrid Whitaker, *An illustrated historical, statistical and topographical account of the urban district of Enfield*, 1911. Dame H. Barnett, *The story . . . of Hampstead garden suburb* (**7074**). Norman George Brett-James, *The story of Hendon: manor and parish* [1931]. John Henry Lloyd, *The history, topography and antiquities of Highgate in the county of Middlesex: with notes of the surrounding neighbourhood of Hornsey, Crouch End, Muswell Hill, etc.*, Highgate Lit. & Scientific Inst., 1888. Denys Lawrence Munby, *Industry and planning in Stepney*, Stepney Reconstruction Group, Toynbee Hall, 1951.

9546 NORFOLK. Norfolk Rec. Soc., *Publications*, 1+, Norwich 1931+. Charles Mackie, *Norfolk annals: a chronological record of remarkable events in the nineteenth century*, 2 v. Norwich 1901, cont. by Harold B. Jaffa in *Norfolk events, 1901–1938*, 2 v. Norwich [1939]. Hamon Le Strange, *Norfolk official lists . . .*, Norwich 1890. *The East Anglian handbook . . .*, Norwich 1866+. L. M. Springall, *Labouring life in Norfolk* (**6688**). Joseph Noel Thomas Boston and Eric Ivimey Puddy, *Dereham: the biography of a country town*, priv. pr. Dereham 1952. W. O. Chadwick, *Victorian miniature* [Ketteringham] (**3522**). Henry J. Hillen, *History of the borough of King's Lynn*, 2 v. Norwich 1907. C. B. Hawkins, *Norwich* (**7351**). Arthur Redvers Randell, *Sixty years a fenman*

[Wiggenhall St. Mary the Virgin], ed. by Enid Porter, 1966, *Fenland railway-man*, ed. by Enid Porter, 1968, *Fenland memories*, ed. by Enid Porter, 1969, and *Fenland molecatcher*, ed. by Enid Porter, 1970. Charles John Palmer, *The perlustration of Great Yarmouth, with Gorleston and Southtown*, 3 v. Great Yarmouth 1872–5.

9547 NORTHAMPTONSHIRE. Northamptonshire Record Soc., *Publications*, 1+, Northampton 1924+, and *Northamptonshire past & present*, 1+, 1948–53, 1957+. William Ryland Dent Adkins, *Our county: sketches in pen and ink of representative men of Northamptonshire*, 1893. Janet Howarth, 'The Liberal revival in Northamptonshire' (**652**).

9548 NORTHUMBERLAND. Basil Anderton, ed., *Newcastle-upon-Tyne Public Libraries Committee: local catalogue of material concerning Newcastle and Northumberland as represented in the central public library, Newcastle-upon-Tyne*, Newcastle-upon-Tyne 1932. Soc. of Antiquaries of Newcastle-upon-Tyne, *Archaeologia aeliana* . . ., 1+, Newcastle-upon-Tyne 1822+. Northumberland County History Committee, *A history of Northumberland*, 15 v. Newcastle-upon-Tyne 1893–1940. Robert William Johnson, *The making of the Tyne: fifty years' progress*, 1895. Richard Welford, *Men of mark twixt Tyne and Tweed*, 3 v. Newcastle-upon-Tyne 1895. Christopher Edmund Baldwin, *The history and development of the port of Blyth*, Newcastle-upon-Tyne 1929, enlarged edn. 1929. Sydney Middlebrook, *Newcastle-upon-Tyne: its growth and achievement*, Newcastle-upon-Tyne 1950, new edn. Wakefield 1968. Charles Henry Hunter Blair, *The mayors and lord mayors of Newcastle-upon-Tyne, 1216–1940, and the sheriffs of the county of Newcastle-upon-Tyne, 1399–1940*, Newcastle-upon-Tyne 1940. William Richardson, *History of the parish of Wallsend* . . ., Newcastle-upon-Tyne 1923.

9549 NOTTINGHAMSHIRE. Nottinghamshire County Libr., *Nottinghamshire: catalogue of the county library local history collection*, Nottingham 1953, 3rd edn. 1966. Peter Alexander Kennedy, ed., *Guide to the Nottinghamshire County Records Office*, Nottingham 1961. Thoroton Soc., *Record series*, 1+, Newark etc. 1903+, *Transactions*, 1+, 1898+. Robert Mellors, *Men of Nottingham and Nottinghamshire* . . ., Nottingham 1924. William Horner Groves, *The history of Mansfield*, Nottingham 1894. Cornelius Brown, *A history of Newark-on-Trent: being the life story of an ancient town*, 2 v. Newark 1904–7. Duncan Gray and Violet W. Walker, eds., *Records of the borough of Nottingham: being a series of extracts from the archives of the corporation of Nottingham*, vol. IX, '1836–1900', Nottingham 1956. Roy Anthony Church, *Economic and social change in a Midland town: Victorian Nottingham, 1815–1900*, 1966. Kenneth Charles Edwards, ed., *Nottingham and its region* [British Assoc. handbook], Nottingham 1966. Duncan Gray, *Nottingham through 500 years: a short history of town government*, Nottingham 1949, 2nd edn. 1960. Jonathan David Chambers and others, *A century of Nottingham history, 1851–1951*, Univ. of Nottingham 1952. J. D. Chambers, *Modern Nottingham in the making*, Nottingham 1945. Alfred Cecil Wood, 'Nottingham, 1835–65', *Thoroton Soc. Trans.* lix (1955), 1–83.

9550 OXFORDSHIRE. Edward Harold Cordeaux and Denis Harry Merry, eds., *A bibliography of printed works relating to Oxfordshire (excluding the University and City of Oxford)*, Oxf. Hist. Soc. new ser. xi, Oxf. 1955, with suppls. in *Bodleian Library Record*, 1958+. Peter Spencer Spokes, ed., *Summary catalogue of manuscripts in the Bodleian library relating to the city, county and university of Oxford: accessions from 1916 to 1962*, Oxf. Hist. Soc. new ser. xvii, Oxf. 1964. Oxfordshire County Record Office, *Summary catalogue of the privately deposited records . . .*, Oxf. 1966. Oxfordshire Record Soc., *Oxfordshire record series*, 1+, Oxf. 1919+. Alexander Frederick Martin and Robert Walter Steel, eds., *The Oxford region: a scientific and historical survey*, Oxf. 1954. Charles Fenby, *The other Oxford: the life and times of Frank Gray and his father*, 1970. Mary Sturge Gretton, *A corner of the Cotswolds through the nineteenth century*, 1914. William Potts, *A history of Banbury: the story of the development of a country town*, Banbury 1958, and *Banbury through one hundred years . . .*, Banbury 1942. Mary Sturge Gretton, *Burford past and present*, 1920, rev. edn. 1945. Reginald Ernest Moreau, *The departed village: Berrick Salome at the turn of the century*, 1968. Ruth Fasnacht, *A history of the city of Oxford*, Oxf. 1954. Oxford Architectural and Historical Soc., *Oxoniensia: a journal dealing with the archaeology, history and architecture of Oxford and its neighbourhood*, 1+, Oxf. 1936. Oxford Historical Soc., *Publications*, 1+, Oxf. 1885+. C. V. Butler, *Social conditions in Oxford* (**7351**). William Owen Hassall, *Wheatley records, 956–1956*, Oxfordshire Record Soc. xxxvii, Oxf. 1956. Sir Charles Edward Ponsonby, *Wootton: the history of an Oxfordshire parish*, 1947.

9551 SHROPSHIRE. Geoffrey Shaw Hewins, ed., *A bibliography of Shropshire*, 1922. Mary C. Hill, ed., *A guide to the Shropshire records, 1952*, Salop County Council, Shrewsbury 1952. Robert Lloyd Kenyon and Sir Offley Wakeman, eds., *Shropshire county records: orders of the Shropshire quarter sessions*, 4 v. in 2, Shrewsbury 1902–11. Shropshire Archaeol. [and Natural Hist.] Soc., *Transactions*, 1+, Shrewsbury etc. 1878+.

9552 SOMERSET. Somerset County Council (County Records Committee), *Interim handlist of Somerset quarter sessions documents and other official records preserved in the Somerset Record Office, Shire hall, Taunton*, Taunton 1947, and *A handlist of the records of the boards of guardians in the county of Somerset*, Taunton 1949. John Edward King, ed., *Inventory of parochial documents in the diocese of Bath and Wells and the county of Somerset*, Somerset County Council, Taunton 1938. Somerset Record Soc., *Publications*, 1+, 1887+. Somersetshire Archaeol. and Natural Hist. Soc., *Proceedings*, 1+, Taunton 1851+. *Notes & queries for Somerset and Dorset*, 1+, Sherborne etc. 1890+. Arthur Lee Humphreys, *Somersetshire parishes: handbook of historical references to all places in the county*, 2 v. 1906. C. S. Orwin, *The reclamation of Exmoor forest* (**4424**). Michael Williams, *The draining of the Somerset levels* (**4425**). Bath Public Librs., *Bath guides, directories and newspapers*, Bath 1962. Bryan Little, *The building of Bath, 47–1947: an architectural and social study*, 1947. Arthur Herbert Powell, *Bridgwater in the later days*, Bridgwater 1908.

9553  STAFFORDSHIRE. Rupert Simms, comp., *Bibliotheca staffordiensis: or, a bibliographical account of books and other printed matter relating to—printed or published in—or written by a native, resident, or person deriving a title from—any portion of the county of Stafford, giving a full collation and biographical notices of authors and printers*, Lichfield 1894. Stoke-on-Trent Public Librs., *Staffordshire directories: a union list* . . ., Stoke 1966. Staffordshire Record Soc. (William Salt Archaeol. Soc.), *Collections for a history of Staffordshire*, 1+, Birmingham etc. 1880+. *North Staffordshire journal of field studies*, Keele 1961+. Lichfield [and South Staffordshire] Archaeol. & Historical Soc., *Transactions*, 1+, 1959–60+. Ernest James Dalzell Warrillow, *A sociological history of the city of Stoke-on-Trent*, Hanley 1960, and *History of Etruria, Staffordshire, England, 1760–1951*, Hanley 1952. Henry Wood, *Borough by prescription: a history of the municipality of Tamworth*, Tamworth 1958. John Frederick Ede, *History of Wednesbury*, Wednesbury [1962]. For municipal politics in Newcastle-under-Lyme see **9425** and in Wolverhampton see **9426**.

9554  SUFFOLK. Suffolk Records Soc., *Publications*, 1+, 1958+. Suffolk Institute of Archaeology, *Proceedings*, 1+, 1848+. Walter Arthur Copinger, *The manors of Suffolk*, 7 v. Lond. & Manch. 1905–11. J. Thirsk and J. Imray, *Suffolk farming* (**4169**). John Glyde, *Suffolk in the nineteenth century: physical, social, moral, religious, and industrial*, Lond. & Ipswich 1856. Ambrose J. R. Waller, *The Suffolk story*, Ipswich 1957. Edwin Alvis Goodwyn, *A Suffolk town in mid-Victorian England: Beccles in the 1860s*, Beccles 1966. G. Martelli, *The Elveden enterprise* (**4427**). John Glyde, *The moral, social and religious condition of Ipswich in the middle of the nineteenth century* . . ., Ipswich 1850. Anon., *Public men of Ipswich and East Suffolk*, Ipswich 1875.

9555  SURREY. William Minet and Charles Joseph Courtney, comps., *A catalogue of the collection of works relating to the county of Surrey contained in the Minet public library*, 1901, suppl. 1923. Surrey Librarians' Group, *Surrey people: a union list of directories and allied material held in the libraries of Surrey*, Surrey County Libr., Esher 1965. Sir Hilary Jenkinson, Montague Spencer Giuseppi, and Dorothy L. Powell, *Guide to archives and other collections of documents relating to Surrey*, 7 v. Surrey County Council [also Surrey Record Soc. xxiii–xxiv, xxvii–xxix, xxxi–xxxii] 1925–31. Surrey Record Soc., *Publications*, 1+, 1916+. Surrey Archaeol. Soc., *Surrey archaeological collections relating to the history and antiquities of the county*, 1+, 1858+. Nigel Hal Longdale Temple, *Farnham inheritance*, Farnham 1956. William Hooper, *Reigate: its story through the ages: a history of the town and parish, including Redhill*, Guildford 1945. Rowley W. C. Richardson, *Surbiton: thirty-two years of local self-government, 1855–1887*, Surbiton 1888.

9556  SUSSEX. Eastbourne Public Librs., *Catalogue of the local collection, comprising books on Eastbourne and Sussex*, Eastbourne 1956. East Sussex County Council Record Office and West Sussex County Council Record Office, *A descriptive report on the quarter sessions, other official and ecclesiastical records in the custody of the county councils of East and West Sussex* . . ., Lewes

& Chichester 1954. This report has been suppl. by a notable series of catalogues of indiv. colls. deposited in the two record offices, which are listed in Kellaway (**19**). Francis William Steer, comp., *A catalogue of Sussex estate and tithe award maps*, Sussex Record Soc. lxii, 1962. Jane M. Coleman, ed., *Sussex poor law records*, West Sussex County Council, Chichester 1960. Sussex Record Soc., *Publications*, 1+, Lewes etc. 1902+. Sussex Archaeological Soc., *Sussex archaeological collections illustrating the history and antiquities of the county*, 1+, 1847+, and *Sussex notes and queries* . . ., 1926–7+, Lewes 1927+. H. C. Brookfield, 'Three Sussex ports' (**6192**). Clifford Musgrave, *Life in Brighton: from the earliest times to the present*, 1970. Edmund William Gilbert, *Brighton: old ocean's bauble*, 1954. Antony Dale, *Fashionable Brighton, 1820–1860*, 1948, 2nd edn. Newcastle-upon-Tyne 1967. West Sussex Record Office, *A descriptive list of the archives of the City of Chichester*, Chichester 1949. Chichester City Council, *Chichester papers*, 1+, Chichester 1955+. Wallace Henry Hills, *The history of East Grinstead*, East Grinstead 1906. John Manwaring Baines, *Historic Hastings*, Hasting 1955, 2nd edn. 1963. William Albery, *A millennium of facts in the history of Horsham and Sussex, 947–1947*, Horsham 1947. Lindsay Fleming, *History of Pagham in Sussex, illustrating the administration of an archiepiscopal hundred, the decay of manorial organisation, and the rise of a seaside resort* [Bognor], 3 v. priv. pr. Ditchling 1949–50. Leopold Amon Vidler, *A new history of Rye*, Hove 1934.

9557 WARWICKSHIRE. Roger Burdett Wilson, *A hand-list of books relating to the county of Warwick*, Birmingham 1955. Dugdale Soc., *Publications*, 1+, Oxford 1921+. John Corday Jeaffreson, ed., *A calendar of the books, charters, letters patent, deeds, rolls, writs and other writings in the cases and drawers of the new muniment room of St. Mary's hall*, Coventry Corp. 1896, suppl. 1931. Frederick Smith, *Coventry: six hundred years of municipal life*, Coventry 1945. J. Prest, *The industrial revolution in Coventry* (**4766**). Thomas Henry Simms, *The rise of a midland town: Rugby, 1800–1900*, Rugby 1949. Mabel K. Ashby, *Joseph Ashby of Tysoe, 1859–1959: a study of English village life*, Camb. 1961.

9558 BIRMINGHAM. Walter Powell and Herbert Maurice Cashmore, eds., *Birmingham public libraries: a catalogue of the Birmingham collection* . . ., Birmingham 1918, suppl. 1931. Birmingham Archaeological Soc. (Birmingham and Midland Inst.), *Transactions and proceedings*, 1870+, Birmingham etc. 1871+. Conrad Gill and Asa Briggs, *History of Birmingham* [vol. 1 to 1865 by Gill, vol. 2 1865–1938 by Briggs], 1952. The Birmingham vol. of the *Victoria County History* (**9378**). J. T. Bunce and others, *History of the corporation of Birmingham* (**9424**). John Henry Muirhead, ed., *Birmingham institutions: lectures given at the university*, Birmingham 1911, and *Nine famous Birmingham men*, Birmingham 1909. Bournville Village Trust, [*Bournville*] (**7075**).

WESTMORLAND. F. W. Garnett, *Westmorland agriculture* (**4169**). See also Cumberland.

9559 WILTSHIRE. Edward Hungerford Goddard, comp., *Wiltshire bibliography: a catalogue of printed books, pamphlets and articles bearing on the history,* topography and natural history of the county, Wilts. Educ. Committee 1929. Maurice Gilbert Rathbone, ed., *Guide to the records in the custody of the clerk of the peace for Wiltshire*, Wiltshire County Council, Trowbridge 1959. Pamela Stewart, ed., *Guide to county council, parish, poor law and other official records in the Wiltshire county record office*, Wiltshire County Council, Trowbridge 1961. Wiltshire Archaeol. and Natural Hist. Soc., *Wiltshire archaeological and natural history museum*, 1853+, Devizes 1854+, and (Records branch), *Publications*, 1+, 1939+. Maude F. Davies, *Life in an English village . . . Corsley* (**7018**). Alfred Redvers Stedman, *Marlborough and the Upper Kennet country*, Marlborough 1960. Leslie Valentine Grinsell and others, *Studies in the history of Swindon*, Swindon 1950.

9560 WORCESTERSHIRE. Worcestershire Historical Soc., *Bibliography of Worcestershire*: Part 1, *Acts of parliament relating to the county*, ed. by John Richard Burton and F. S. Pearson; Part 2, *Being a classified catalogue of books and other printed matter relating to the county of Worcester . . .*, comp. by John R. Burton; Part 3, *Works relating to the botany of Worcestershire*, comp. by John Humphreys, 3 pts. Worcs. Hist. Soc. ix, 1898–1907. Worcestershire Historical Soc., *Publications*, 1+, 1893+, and *Miscellany number one+*, Worcester 1960+. Worcestershire Archaeological Soc., *Transactions*, new ser. 1923–4+, Worcester 1924+. Edith Ophelia Browne and John Richard Burton, *Short biographies of the worthies of Worcestershire*, Worcester & Hereford 1916. R. C. Gaut, *A history of Worcestershire agriculture* (**4169**). George Chandler and Ian Campbell Hannah, *Dudley: as it was and as it is to-day*, 1949. Brian Stanley Smith, *A history of Malvern*, Leicester 1964.

9561 YORKSHIRE. George Eden Kirk, comp., *Yorkshire Archaeological Society: catalogue of the printed books and pamphlets in the library*, 2 v. Wakefield 1935–6, suppls. in the Society's *Journal*. Yorkshire Archaeological Soc., *The Yorkshire archaeological [and topographical] journal*, 1+, 1870+, and *Record series*, 1+, 1885+. Arthur Raistrick, *Old Yorkshire dales*, Newton Abbot 1967. Marie Hartley and Joan Ingilby, *Yorkshire village [Askrigg]*, 1953. Edward Ernest Dodd, *Bingley: a Yorkshire town through nine centuries*, Bingley 1958. Bradford Hist. and Antiq. Soc., *The Bradford antiquary*, new ser. 1+, Bradford 1900+. William Cudworth, *Historical notes on the Bradford corporation . . .*, Bradford 1881. Horace Hird, *How a city grows: historical notes on the city of Bradford*, Bradford 1966, and *Bradford in history . . .*, Bradford 1968. Reginald Mitchell, *Brighouse: portrait of a town*, Brighouse 1953. David Hey, *The village of Ecclesfield*, Huddersfield 1968. Halifax Antiquarian Soc., *Transactions*, Halifax 1901+. W. Haythornthwaite, *Harrogate story: from Georgian village to Victorian town*, Clapham, Yorks. 1954. Mary F. Jagger, *The history of Honley and its hamlets from the earliest time to the present*, Huddersfield 1914. Roy Brook, *The story of Huddersfield*, 1968. The Hull vol. of the *Victoria County History*, **9378**. Thoresby Soc., *Publications* [on Leeds], 1+, Leeds 1891+. Kenneth J. Bonser and Harold Nichols, *Printed maps and plans of Leeds, 1711–1900*, Thoresby Soc. *Publications* xlvii (1958), Leeds 1960. Asa Briggs, 'The building of Leeds town hall:

a study in Victorian civic pride', *Thoresby Soc. Publications*, xlvi (1957–61), 275–302. M. W. Beresford, *Leeds Chamber of Commerce* (**5861**). William Lillie, *The history of Middlesbrough: an illustration of the evolution of English industry*, Middlesbrough Corp. 1968. Sir Hugh Gilzean Reid, *Middlesbrough and its jubilee*, Middlesbrough 1881. Lady Bell, *At the works . . . Middlesbrough* (**5074**). Bernard Jennings, ed., *A history of Nidderdale*, Huddersfield 1967. A. Holroyd, *Saltaire* (**7072**). Arthur Rowntree, ed., *History of Scarborough*, 1931. John William Walker, *Wakefield: its work and people*, Wakefield 1934.

9562   SHEFFIELD. Sheffield Public Librs., *Basic books on Sheffield history*, Sheffield 1948, rev. edn. 1958. R. Meredith, ed., *Guide to the manuscript collections in the Sheffield City Libraries*, Sheffield 1956, suppl. 1962. Hunter Archaeological Soc. of Sheffield, *Transactions*, 1+, Sheffield 1914–18+. Mary Walton, *Sheffield: its story and its achievements*, 1948, 3rd edn. 1952. David Leslie Linton, ed., *Sheffield and its region: a scientific and historical survey*, Sheffield 1956. E. R. Wickham, *Church and people* (**3380**). S. Pollard, *A history of labour in Sheffield* (**6472**). James Hayton Stainton, *The making of Sheffield, 1865–1914*, Sheffield 1924. Joseph M. Furness, *Record of municipal affairs in Sheffield . . . 1843 . . . to 1893*, Sheffield 1893. Herbert Keeble Hawson, *Sheffield: the growth of a city, 1893–1926*, Sheffield 1968. John Daniel Leader, *The records of the burgery of Sheffield, commonly called the town trust*, Sheffield 1897, suppl. by Edward Bramley, 1957.

9563   YORK. George Benson, *An account of the city and county of the city of York: from the reformation to the year 1925*, York 1925, repr. 2 v. York 1968. Charles Brunton Knight, *A history of the city of York*, 1944. The York vol. of the *Victoria County History* (**9378**). John Bowes Morrell and Arthur George Watson, eds., *How York governs itself: civic government as illustrated by the county of the city of York*, 1928. B. S. Rowntree, *Poverty* (**7351**) and *Unemployment* (**6586**) both consist of surveys of York.

## E. ISLE OF MAN AND CHANNEL ISLANDS

### 1. ISLE OF MAN

9564   CUBBON (WILLIAM) *comp*. A bibliographical account of works relating to the Isle of Man, with biographical memoranda and copious literary references. 2 v. 1933–9.

See also the publs. and annual report of the Manx Soc. and the *Journal* of the Manx Museum, 1924+.

9565   MOORE (ARTHUR WILLIAM). A history of the Isle of Man. 2 v. 1900.

Standard. Moore also comp. *Manx worthies: or, biographies of notable Manx men and women*, Douglas 1901. There is a little additional material in William Cubbon, *Island heritage: dealing with some phases of Manx history*, Manch. 1952. The best short hist. is Robert Henry Kinvig, *A history of the Isle of Man*, Liverpool 1944, 2nd edn. 1950.

Aldo Pecora, *L'isola di Man*, Società Geografica Italiana, Rome 1955, has a few useful facts.

**9566  ISLE OF MAN NATURAL HISTORY AND ANTIQUARIAN SOCIETY.** Proceedings. Douglas. 1880+.

**9567  NORRIS (SAMUEL).** Manx memories and movements: a journalist's recollections. Douglas. 1938. 2nd edn. 1939.

Indispensable for the end of the 19th and the early 20th cent.

**9568  WALPOLE (*Sir* SPENCER).** The land of home rule. 1893.

Important for constitutional hist. See also Bertram Edward Sargeaunt, *An outline of the financial system of the Isle of Man government*, Douglas 1925. The statutes of the Isle of Man were publ. in 10 v., Douglas 1886–1925, with an index by Ramsey Bignall Moore, Douglas 1927.

**9569  ISLE OF MAN CONSTITUTION COMMITTEE.** Report of the departmental committee on the constitution, &c., of the Isle of Man [Chairman: Lord MacDonnell]. [Cd. 5950] H.C. (1911). XXIX, pt. I, 631. Minutes of evidence. [Cd. 6026] H.C. (1912–13). XXXIV, 585.

**9570  BIRCH (JACK WILLIAM).** The Isle of Man: a study in economic geography. Univ. of Bristol. Camb. 1964.

**9571  PEARSON (KEITH).** Isle of Man tramways. Newton Abbot. 1970.

## 2. Channel Islands

**9572  ANSTED (DAVID THOMAS)** *and* **LATHAM (ROBERT GORDON).** The Channel Islands. 1862. 3rd edn. 1893.

The most comprehensive account of the islands. There is little in John Uttley, *The story of the Channel Islands*, 1966.

**9573  JERSEY.** *Table des décisions de la cour royale, 1885–[1916]*, 5 v. Jersey 1896–1930. Société Jersiaise, *Bulletin*, 1875+, St. Helier 1897+. George Reginald Balleine, *The bailiwick of Jersey*, 1951, *A history of the island of Jersey from the cave men to the German occupation and after*, 1950, and *A biographical dictionary of Jersey* [1948]. *Who's who in Jersey*, St. Helier 1937. F. de L. Bois, *A constitutional history of Jersey*, Jersey 1970. *Report of the commissioners appointed to inquire into the civil, municipal and ecclesiastical laws of the island of Jersey* [Chairman: Sir John Wither Awdrey]. [2725] H.C. (1860). XXXI, 1. René Lemasurier, *Le droit de l'île de Jersey: la loi, la coutume et l'idéologie dans l'île de Jersey*, Univ. of Paris, Inst. de Droit Comparé, Paris 1956. Pierre Dalido, *Jersey: île agricole anglo-normande: étude de sociographie*, Vannes 1951. Joan Stevens, *Victorian voices*, Société Jersiaise, St. Helier 1969. Michael Ginns, *Transport in Jersey: an historical survey of transport facilities, . . . 1788–1961*, 1961.

9574 GUERNSEY. *Recueil d'ordonnances de la cour royale* . . ., St. Peter Port 1852+. *Recueil d'ordres en conseil d'un intérêt général, enregistrés sur les records de l'île de Guernsey*, 1800+, St. Peter Port 1903+. Guernsey Soc. of Natural Science [Société Gerneciaise], *Reports and transactions*, 1882+, St. Peter Port 1889+.

9575 SARK. Louis Selosse, *L'île de Sark: un état féodal au XXe siècle*, Lille 1928, 2nd edn. Lille 1929.

# XI

# WALES

Members of the nonconformist churches, which were the dominant force in Welsh life during the period, normally used the Welsh language rather than English, so many sources are inaccessible to those who do not read Welsh. These Welsh-language sources, like historical works wholly in Welsh, most of them listed in *A bibliography of the history of Wales* (**9576**), have regretfully been kept to a minimum in this bibliog.

## A. GENERAL

### 1. BIBLIOGRAPHIES AND GUIDES

**9576** UNIVERSITY OF WALES BOARD OF CELTIC STUDIES. A bibliography of the history of Wales. 2nd edn. Cardiff. 1962. Suppl. 1959–62. *Board of Celtic Studies Bull.* xx (1962–4), 126–64. Suppl. 1963–5. Ibid. xxii (1966–8), 49–70. Suppl. 1966–8. Ibid. xxiii (1968–70), 263–83.

Standard. Needs to be suppl. by the annual checklist of books and articles for 1959+ in *Welsh Hist. Rev.* (**9582**).

**9577** BIBLIOTHECA CELTICA: a register of publications relating to Wales and the Celtic peoples & languages. 1909+. Nat. Libr. of Wales. Aberystwyth. 1910+.

See also *Subject index to Welsh periodicals*, 1931+, Cardiff and Swansea 1933+, now publ. by Libr. Assoc., Wales & Mons. Branch, and *Handlist of Scottish and Welsh record publics.* (**9777**).

**9578** BALLINGER (*Sir* JOHN) *and* JONES (JAMES IFANO) *eds.* Cardiff Free Libraries: catalogue of printed literature in the Welsh department. Cardiff. 1898.

A useful list incl. newspapers, official reports, and pamphlets.

**9579** THOMAS (*Sir* DANIEL LLEUFER). Royal commission on land in Wales and Monmouthshire: bibliographical, statistical and other miscellaneous memoranda . . . [C. 8242] H.C. (1896). XXXIII, 555.

A comprehensive reference work covering all aspects of Welsh life.

**9580** NATIONAL LIBRARY OF WALES. Handlist of manuscripts. In pts. Aberystwyth. 1943+.

Issued as suppl. to *Nat. Libr. of Wales J.* (**9584**), which also prints notes on accessions. For the facilities of the National Libr. see William Llewelyn Davies, *The National Library of Wales: a survey of its history, its contents and its activities*, Aberystwyth 1937.

9581 JONES (THOMAS IEUAN JEFFREYS). Acts of parliament concerning Wales, 1714–1901. Univ. of Wales Bd. of Celtic Studs. Hist. & Law Series xvii. Cardiff. 1959.

Does not entirely supersede Ivor Bowen, ed., *The statutes of Wales . . .* 1908, which has a valuable intro.

## 2. PERIODICALS

9582 UNIVERSITY OF WALES BOARD OF CELTIC STUDIES. The Welsh history review Cylchgrawn hanes Cymru. 1+. Cardiff. 1960+.

The main hist. j. for the period, with annual checklist of publs.

9583 UNIVERSITY OF WALES BOARD OF CELTIC STUDIES. Bulletin. 1+. Lond. & Cardiff. 1921+.

9584 NATIONAL LIBRARY OF WALES. Journal. 1+. Aberystwyth. 1939–40+.

For scholarly bibliog. articles see also *Journal of the Welsh Bibliographical Society*, Aberystwyth etc. 1910+.

9585 HONOURABLE SOCIETY OF CYMMRODORION. Transactions. 1+. 1893+.

The Soc. also publ. *Y Cymmrodor*, 1877+. Both are indexed for 1877–1912.

9586 CAMBRIAN ARCHAEOLOGICAL ASSOCIATION. Archaeologia cambrensis . . . the journal of the Cambrian Archaeological Assoc. 1+. 1846+.

## 3. GENERAL HISTORY AND BIOGRAPHY

9587 WILLIAMS (DAVID). A history of modern Wales. 1950. Rev. edn. 1965.

The only adequate hist. But see also Sir John Rhys and Sir David Brynmor Jones, *The Welsh people . . .*, 1900, 4th edn. 1906, based on the hist. sections of the report of the Welsh Land Commission (9632), John Vyrnwy Morgan, *A study in nationality*, 1911, 2nd edn. 1912, and *The philosophy of Welsh history*, 1914, Arthur James Roderick, ed., *Wales through the ages*, 2 v. Llandybie 1959–60, a valuable series of broadcast talks by leading scholars, and *Aspects of Welsh history: selected papers of the late Glyn Roberts*, Cardiff 1969.

9588 BOWEN (EMRYS GEORGE) *ed*. Wales: a physical, historical and regional geography. 1957.

See also Harold Carter, *The towns of Wales: a study in urban geography*, Cardiff 1965, and Dorothy Sylvester, *The rural landscape of the Welsh borderland: a study in historical geography*, 1969.

9589 REES (WILLIAM). A historical atlas of Wales from early to modern times. Cardiff. 1951. New edn. Cardiff. 1959.

See also Melville Richards, *Welsh administrative and territorial units, medieval and modern*, Cardiff 1969.

9590 [JENKINS (ROBERT THOMAS) *and others, eds.*] The dictionary of Welsh biography down to 1940. Hon. Soc. of Cymmrodorion. 1959.

Indispensable. Each entry has full bibliog. For county families see also Thomas Nicholas, *Annals and antiquities of the counties and county families of Wales* . . ., 2 v. 1872, rev. edn. 1875. Some of the entries in Thomas Mardy Rees, *Notable Welshmen, 1700–1900* . . ., Caernarvon 1908, Thomas R. Roberts, *A dictionary of eminent Welshmen* . . ., Cardiff & Merthyr 1908, and Sir Thomas John Hughes, *Great Welshmen of modern days*, Cardiff 1931, are also useful.

9591 MORGAN (JOHN VYRNWY) *ed.* Welsh political and educational leaders of the Victorian era. 1908.

Suppl. by his *Welsh religious leaders in the Victorian era* . . ., 1905. See also John Austin Jenkins, ed., *South Wales and Monmouthshire at the opening of the twentieth century: contemporary biographies*, Pike's New Century Ser. 21, Brighton 1907, and *Who's who in Wales*, 1921.

## 4. POLITICS

9592 JONES (IEUAN GWYNEDD). 'The Liberation Society and Welsh politics, 1844 to 1868'. *Welsh Hist. Rev.* i (1960–3), 193–224.

Important for the connection between nonconformist disabilities and Welsh Liberalism. See also his 'Franchise reform and Glamorgan politics in the mid-nineteenth century', *Morgannwg* ii (1958), 47–64; 'The election of 1868 in Merthyr Tydfil . . .', *J. Mod. Hist.* xxxiii (1961), 270–86; 'Dr. Thomas Price and the election of 1868 in Merthyr Tydfil: a study in nonconformist politics', *Welsh Hist. Rev.* ii (1964–5), 147–72, 251–70; 'Merioneth politics in mid-nineteenth century: the politics of a rural economy', *Merioneth Hist. & Record Soc. J.* v (1965–8), 273–334; 'Cardiganshire politics in the mid-nineteenth century: a study of the elections of 1865 and 1868', *Ceredigion* v (1964–7), 14–41; and 'The elections of 1865 and 1868 in Wales, with special reference to Cardiganshire and Merthyr Tydfil', *Hon. Soc. Cymmrodorion Trans.* (1964), 41–68. For Merioneth elections see also D. G. Lloyd Hughes, 'David Williams, Castell Deudraeth, and the Merioneth elections of 1859, 1865 & 1868', *Merioneth Hist. & Record Soc. J.* v (1965–8), 335–51. For Denbighshire see Frank Price Jones, 'Politics in 19th-century Denbighshire', *Denbighshire Hist. Soc. Trans.* x (1961), 179–94, and for Monmouth dist. see Clifford Tucker, 'The representation of Monmouth district from the Great Reform Bill, 1832, to the Representation of the People Act, 1918', *Presenting Monmouthshire*, no. 18 (1964), 37–44; no. 21 (1966), 20–7; no. 25 (1968), 39–46.

9593 MORGAN (KENNETH OWEN). Wales in British politics, 1868–1922. Cardiff. 1963. 2nd edn. 1970.

The only comprehensive account of Welsh Liberalism. Good bibliog. See also his 'Gladstone and Wales', *Welsh Hist. Rev.* i (1960–3), 65–82; 'Liberals, nationalists and Mr. Gladstone', *Hon. Soc. Cymmrodorion Trans.* (1960), 36–52; 'The Liberal Unionists in Wales', *Nat. Libr. Wales J.* xvi (1969–70), 163–71; 'Democratic politics in Glamorgan, 1884–1914', *Morgannwg* iv (1960), 5–27; 'The Gower election of 1906', *Gower* xii (1959), 15–19; and 'Cardiganshire politics: the Liberal ascendancy, 1885–1923', *Ceredigion* v (1964–7), 311–46; Henry Pelling, 'Wales and the Boer war', *Welsh Hist. Rev.* iv (1968–9), 363–5, with reply by Morgan, ibid. 367–80; and Kevin R. Cox, 'Geography, social contexts and voting behavior in Wales, 1861–1951', in Erik Allardt and Stein Rokkan, eds., *Mass politics: studies in political sociology*, N.Y. & Lond. 1970, pp. 117–59.

9594 WILLIAMS (WILLIAM RETLAW). The parliamentary history of the principality of Wales, from the earliest times to the present day, 1541–1895:

comprising lists of the representatives chronologically arranged under counties, with biographical and genealogical notices . . . Brecknock. 1895.

9595  MAINWARING (THOMAS). Glimpses of Welsh politics. Llanelly. 1881.

9596  WILLIAMS (*Sir* THOMAS MARCHANT). The Welsh parliamentary party, 1894. Cardiff. 1894.

A series of portraits and biog. sketches.

9597  JONES (WILLIAM HUGHES). Wales drops the pilots. 1937.

On T. E. Ellis and Lloyd George, 1890–5.

9598  WILLIAMS (GLANMOR) *ed.* Merthyr politics: the making of a working-class tradition. Cardiff. 1966.

See also the articles by I. G. Jones at **9592**, Kenneth Owen Fox, 'Labour and Merthyr's khaki election of 1900', *Welsh Hist. Rev.* ii (1964–5), 351–66, and 'The Merthyr election of 1906', *Nat. Libr. Wales J.* xiv (1965–6), 237–41, and Tydfil Davies Jones, 'Poor law administration in Merthyr Tydfil union, 1834–1894', *Morgannwg* viii (1964), 35–62.

9599  AWBERY (STANLEY STEPHEN). Labour's early struggles in Swansea. Swansea. 1949.

See also Lawrence John Williams, 'The first Welsh "Labour" M.P.: the Rhondda election of 1885', *Morgannwg* vi (1962), 78–94. On rural Wales see Cyril Parry, 'The Independent Labour party and Gwynedd politics, 1900–20', *Welsh Hist. Rev.* iv (1968–9), 47–66, 'Fabianism and Gwynedd politics, 1890–1918', *Caernarvonshire Hist. Soc. Trans.* xxix (1968), 121–36, and *The Radical tradition in Welsh politics: a study of Liberal and Labour politics in Gwynedd, 1900–1920*, Univ. of Hull 1970.

9600  COUPLAND (*Sir* REGINALD). Welsh and Scottish nationalism: a study. 1954.

Mainly concerned with governmental devolution.

9601  JENKINS (ROBERT THOMAS). 'The development of nationalism in Wales'. *Sociological Rev.* xxvii (1935), 163–82.

See also Sir James Frederick Rees, 'Wales: the political problem', *Nineteenth century* cxlv (1949), 239–51; Edgar Leyshon Chappell, *Wake up Wales!, a survey of Welsh home rule activities*, 1943; David Myrddin Lloyd, ed., *The historical basis of Welsh nationalism*, Plaid Cymru, Cardiff 1950; and Glanmor Williams, 'The idea of nationality in Wales', *Camb. J.* vii (1953–4), 145–58. The main sources for political nationalism in English are Cymru Fydd Soc., *Home rule for Wales: what does it mean?*, 1888; Sir Thomas Marchant Williams, *Home rule for Wales*, Aberdare 1888; David Randall, David Lloyd George, and William John Parry, *Home rule bill for Wales*, Caernarvon 1890; *Cymru fydd gymru rydd: or, the national movement in Wales*, by a Celt, Caernarvon 1895; Charles Edward Breese, *Welsh nationality*, Caernarvon 1895; Thomas Darlington, *Welsh nationality and its critics . . .*, Wrexham 1895; Edward Thomas John, *Home rule for Wales*, Bangor 1912, and *Wales: its politics and economics . . .*, Cardiff 1919, and *Young Wales . . . the organ of the Cymru fydd movement*, Aberystwyth 1895–1904.

9602  WILLIAMS. The life and work of William Williams, M.P. for Coventry, 1835–1847, M.P. for Lambeth, 1850–1865. By Daniel Evans. Llandyssul. [1940.]

The rather ineffectual parliamentary spokesman of the London Welsh at the beginning of the period.

**9603 RICHARD.** Henry Richard, M.P.: a biography. By Charles Septimus Miall. 1889.

The leading Nonconformist spokesman of the 1860s. His *Letters on the social and political condition of the principality of Wales*, 1866, and *Letters and essays on Wales*, 1884, together with the symposium *Welsh nonconformity and the Welsh representation: papers and speeches* . . ., 1866, give the best account of the attitudes and objectives of the Nonconformist radicals who began to take over Welsh parliamentary representation in 1868. For Richard's work for the Peace Soc. see Lewis Appleton, *Memoirs of Henry Richard: the apostle of peace*, 1889. For his relations with Cobden see H. R. Evans, 'Henry Richard and Cobden's letters', *Hon. Soc. Cymmrodorion Trans.* (1960), 54–81.

**9604 GEE.** Cofiant Thomas Gee. By Thomas Gwynn Jones. Denbigh. 1913.

An English life of the great dissenting publisher is badly needed.

**9605 ELLIS.** The forerunner: the dilemmas of Tom Ellis, 1859–1899. By Neville Charles Masterman. Llandybie. 1972.

Thomas Iorworth Ellis, *Thomas Edward Ellis: cofiant*, 2 v. Liverpool 1944–8, incl. letters in English. Ellis's widow publ. his English *Speeches and addresses* . . ., Wrexham 1912. There is also Llewelyn Wyn Griffith, *Thomas Edward Ellis* . . ., Llandybie 1959. Ellis was leader of 'Young Wales' in the early 1890s and Liberal Chief Whip, 1894–9.

**9606 JONES.** 'Evan Pan Jones: land reformer'. By Peris Jones-Evans. *Welsh Hist. Rev.* iv (1968–9), 143–59.

**9607 LEWIS.** Syr Herbert Lewis, 1858–1933. Ed. by Kitty Idwal Jones. Cardiff. 1958.

Includes interesting letters in English. See also Sir Ben Bowen Thomas and W. Hugh Jones, 'Sir John Herbert Lewis: centenary tributes', *Flints. Hist. Soc. Publ.* xviii (1960), 131–55.

**9608 LLOYD GEORGE.** David Lloyd George: Welsh radical as world statesman. By Kenneth Owen Morgan. Cardiff. 1963.

The fullest account of Lloyd George and Wales is in William Watkin Davies, *Lloyd George, 1863–1914*, 1939. Herbert du Parcq, *Life of David Lloyd George*, 4 v. 1912–13, John Hugh Edwards and John Saxon Mills, *The life of David Lloyd George* . . ., 5 v. 1913–24, Sir Alfred Thomas Davies, *The Lloyd George I knew*, 1948, Thomas Jones, *Lloyd George*, 1951, and William George, *My brother and I*, 1958, also deal with Lloyd George's Welsh career.

## B. THE CHURCHES

### I. GENERAL

**9609 ROYAL COMMISSION ON THE CHURCH OF ENGLAND AND OTHER RELIGIOUS BODIES IN WALES AND MONMOUTHSHIRE.** Report of the commission [Chairman: Lord Justice Sir Roland Lomax Bowdler Vaughan-Williams]. [Cd. 5432] H.C. (1910). XIV, 1. Appendixes to the report. [Cd. 5432–I] H.C. (1910). XIV, 413. Minutes of evidence. [Cd. 5433–5] H.C. (1910). Vols. XV–XVII. Appendix on Church of England. [Cd. 5436] H.C. (1910). XVIII, 1. Appendix of Nonconformist county statistics. [Cd. 5437] H.C. (1910). XVIII, 247. Appendix on Nonconformist bodies. [Cd. 5438] H.C. (1910). XIX, 1. Index. [Cd. 5439] H.C. (1910). XIX, 185.

The 6 large vols. contain a systematic record of church life for which there is no English or Scottish equivalent. The statistics show a deceptively large Nonconformist majority because they refer to 1905, the year after the 1904 revival, when Nonconformist numbers were at the highest point they ever attained. For earlier figures see Ieuan Gwynedd Jones, 'Denominationalism in Caernarvonshire in the mid-nineteenth century as shown in the religious census of 1851', *Caernarvonshire Hist. Soc. Trans.* xxxi (1970), 78–114, and 'Denominationalism in Swansea and district: a study of the ecclesiastical census of 1851', *Morgannwg* xii (1968), 67–96.

## 2. Church of England in Wales

9610 DAVIES (JAMES CONWAY). 'The records of the church of Wales'. *Nat. Libr. Wales J.* iv (1945–6), 1–34.

Records the transfer of all the diocesan archives in Wales to the National Libr. of Wales.

9611 JONES (DAVID AMBROSE). A history of the Church in Wales. Carmarthen. 1926.

See also Alfred George Edwards, Bishop, *Landmarks in the history of the Welsh Church*, 1912, and the *Handbook* of the 1953 Welsh Church Congress.

9612 HISTORICAL SOCIETY OF THE CHURCH IN WALES. Journal. 1947+.

9613 THOMAS (DAVID RICHARD). Esgobaeth Llanelwy: the history of the diocese of St. Asaph; general, cathedral and parochial. New edn. 3 v. Oswestry. 1908–13.

Much the best diocesan hist. Covers contemp. conflicts. For other dioceses see Arthur Ivor Pryce, comp., *The diocese of Bangor during three centuries (seventeenth to nineteenth century inclusive): being, a digest of the registers of the bishops,* Cardiff 1929, William Hughes, *Recollections of Bangor cathedral,* 1904, and Thomas Baker, *Diocese of St. David's: particulars relating to endowments of livings,* 4 v. Carmarthen 1907. There is also Ebenezer Thomas Davies, ed., *The story of the church in Glamorgan, 1560–1960,* 1962.

9614 WILLS (WILTON D.). 'The established church in the diocese of Llandaff, 1850–70: a study of the evangelical movement in the South Wales coalfield'. *Welsh Hist. Rev.* iv (1968–9), 235–72.

9615 EDWARDS (HENRY THOMAS). Wales and the Welsh church: papers . . . with a biographical sketch of the author. 1889.

A coll. of pamphlets by an able churchman on the position of the church. See also William Latham Bevan, *The case of the church in Wales . . .,* 1886, and Arthur James Johnes, *An essay on the causes which have produced dissent from the established church in the principality of Wales,* new edn. 1870, the latter an 1832 pamphlet of great influence.

9616 MORGAN (KENNETH OWEN). Freedom or sacrilege? A history of the campaign for Welsh disestablishment. Penarth. 1966.

There is a good comprehensive account in P. M. H. Bell, *Disestablishment in Ireland and Wales* (**10497**). For the controversy over disestablishment see the *Memories* of A. G. Edwards (**9619**); Richard Warren Fowell and Sir Lewis Tonna Dibdin, *The Welsh disestablishment bill, 1909* . . ., Central Church Committee for Defence and Instruction, 1909; John James Fovargue Bradley, *The case against Welsh disendowment by a nonconformist minister*, 1911, and *Nonconformists and the Welsh Church Bill*, 1912; Sir David Brynmor Jones, ed., *The disestablishment and disendowment of the Church of England and Wales*, 1912; David Caird, *Church and state in Wales: a plain statement of the case for disestablishment*, Liberation Soc. 1912, 2nd edn. 1912; Henry James Clayton, *The indictment and defence of the church in Wales*, Central Church Committee 1911; Anthony Dell, *The church in Wales: a complete guide to the disestablishment question*, 1912; John Theodore Dodd, *Welsh disestablishment*, 1912; Alfred George Edwards, *A handbook of Welsh church defence*, 1894, 3rd edn. 1895; Howard Evans, *The case for disestablishment in Wales*, 1907; Griffith Jones, *The Welsh church bill controversy*, 1913; William George Arthur Ormsby-Gore, 4th Baron Harlech, *Welsh disestablishment and disendowment*, 1912; Arthur Wade Wade-Evans, *Papers for thinking Welshmen*, 1909; John Frome Wilkinson, *Disestablishment: Welsh and English*, 1894.

9617 MORGAN (JOHN). Four biographical sketches: Bishop Ollivant, Bishop Thirlwall, Rev. Griffith Jones, Vicar of Llanddowror, and Sir Thomas Phillips, Q.C. With a chapter on the Church in Wales. 1892.

9618 THIRLWALL. Connop Thirlwall, historian and theologian. By John Connop Thirlwall. 1936.

There are also 2 good colls. of letters: *Letters to a friend by Connop Thirlwall, late Lord Bishop of St. David's*, ed. by Arthur Penryn Stanley, 1881, new edn. 1882, and *Letters, literary and theological, of Connop Thirlwall, late Lord Bishop of St. David's*, ed. by John James Stewart Perowne and Louis Stokes, 1881. Perowne also ed. *Remains, literary and theological, of Connop Thirlwall, bishop of St. David's*, 3 v. 1877–8, and *Essays, speeches and sermons* . . ., 1880.

9619 EDWARDS. Memories. By Alfred George Edwards, Archbishop of Wales. 1927.

Bishop of St. Asaph, 1889–1934, and the leading figure in the Welsh church. The *Memories* give the best single account of the disestablishment controversy by a participant. There is a short essay on Edwards, George Geoffrey Lerry, *Alfred George Edwards, Archbishop of Wales*, Oswestry [1940].

9620 OWEN. The early life of Bishop Owen: a son of Lleyn. By Eluned Elizabeth Owen. Llandyssul. 1958.

Cont. in her *The later life of Bishop Owen* . . ., Llandyssul 1961.

9621 HARTWELL-JONES. A Celt looks at the world. By Griffith Hartwell-Jones. Ed. by Wyn Griffith. Cardiff. 1946.

### 3. PROTESTANT NONCONFORMITY

9622 REES (THOMAS). History of Protestant Nonconformity in Wales: from its rise to the present time. 1861. 2nd edn. 1883.

There is little on the period in this or in Howell Elvet Lewis, *Nonconformity in Wales*,

1904, and William Edwards, *Four centuries of nonconformist disabilities, 1509–1912*, 1912. A new hist. of Welsh Nonconformity in English is badly needed.

9623 PHILLIPS (THOMAS). The Welsh revival: its origin and development. 1860.

On the 1859 revival. See also John James Morgan, *The '59 revival in Wales: some incidents in the life and work of David Morgan, Ysbytty*, Mold 1909. There is an extensive Welsh-language lit. on this revival.

9624 MORGAN (JOHN VYRNWY). The Welsh religious revival, 1904–5: a restrospect and a criticism. 1909.

See also C. R. Williams, 'The Welsh religious revival, 1904–5', *Brit. J. Sociology* iii (1952), 242–59; William Thomas Stead, *The revival in the West: a narrative of facts*, 1905; Howell Elvet Lewis, *With Christ among the miners: incidents and impressions of the Welsh revival*, 1906; [Marie Henri] Joseph [Pierre Étienne] Rogues de Fursac, *Un mouvement mystique contemporain: le réveil religieux du Pays de Galles (1904–1905)*, Paris 1907; Robert Ellis, *Living echoes of the Welsh revival, 1904–5* [1951]; and Western Mail, *The religious revival in Wales, 1904* [1904]. Eifion Evans, *The Welsh revival of 1904*, 1969, is nostalgic.

9625 ROBERTS (JOHN). The Calvinistic Methodism of Wales. Caernarvon. 1934.

See also David Erwyd Jenkins, *Calvinistic Methodist holy orders*, Caernarvon 1911; William Williams, *Welsh Calvinistic Methodism: a historical sketch of the Presbyterian Church of Wales*, 1872, 2nd edn. 1884; Edward Griffiths, *Historical handbook to the Presbyterian Church of Wales, 1735–1905*, Wrexham n.d.; Robert Buick Knox, *Voices from the past: history of the English Conference of the Presbyterian Church of Wales, 1889–1938*, Llandyssul 1969; and Daniel Jenkins Williams, *One hundred years of Welsh Calvinistic Methodism in America*, Phila. 1937. The journal of the Welsh Calvinistic Methodist Soc., *Cylchgrawn Cymdeithas Hanes Methodistiaid Calfinaidd Cymru*, 1916+, is bilingual.

9626 YOUNG (DAVID). The origin and history of Methodism in Wales and the borders. 1893.

Includes Welsh chapels in England. See also Albert Hughes Williams, *Welsh Wesleyan Methodism, 1800–1858*, Bangor 1935.

9627 DAVIES (W. T. PENNAR). 'Episodes in the history of Brecknockshire dissent'. *Brycheiniog* iii (1957), 11–65.

9628 JONES (DAVID). Memorial volume of Welsh Congregationalists in Pennsylvania, U.S.A., their churches, periodical convocations, clergy and prominent lay members. Utica, N.Y. 1934.

### 4. ROMAN CATHOLIC CHURCH

9629 ATTWATER (DONALD). The Catholic church in modern Wales: a record of the past century. 1935.

See also Basil Hemphill, 'Bishop Joseph Brown, O.S.B., the modern apostle of Wales', *Studies* xxxix (1950), 31–9, and Anselm Wilson, *Life of Bishop Hedley* (**3940**).

## C. ECONOMIC HISTORY

### 1. Agriculture

9630 ASHBY (ARTHUR WILFRED) *and* EVANS (IFOR LESLIE). The agriculture of Wales and Monmouthshire. Cardiff. 1944.

The best intro. to the subject. See also George Edwin Fussell, 'Welsh farming in 1879', *Hon. Soc. Cymmrodorion Trans.* (1938), 247–55, and 'Glamorgan farming: an outline of its modern history', *Morgannwg* i (1957), 31–43, and J. Gibson, *Agriculture in Wales*, 1879. David Jenkins, *The agricultural community in South-West Wales at the turn of the twentieth century*, Cardiff 1971, is good for its period.

9631 WILLIAMS (DAVID). The Rebecca riots: a study in agrarian discontent. Cardiff. 1955.

Includes a valuable analysis of Welsh agric.

9632 ROYAL COMMISSION ON LAND IN WALES AND MONMOUTHSHIRE. First report of the royal commission on land in Wales and Monmouthshire [Chairman: Earl Carrington]. [C. 7439] H.C. (1894). XXXVI, 1. Minutes of evidence etc. [C. 7439–I] H.C. (1894). XXXVI, 9. [C. 7439–II] H.C. (1894). XXXVII, 1. [C. 7661] H.C. (1895). XI, 1. [C. 7757] H.C. (1895). XLI, 1. [Second] report. [C. 8221] H.C. (1896). XXXIV, 1. Minutes of evidence. [C. 8222] H.C. (1896). XXXV, 1. Appendixes. [C. 8242] H.C. (1896). XXXIII, 555.

The main source for Welsh land and agric. Sir Daniel Lleufer Thomas, *The Welsh land commission: a digest of its report*, 1896, is a useful guide. See also Brian Ll. James, 'The "great landowners" of Wales in 1873', *Nat. Libr. Wales J.* xiv (1965–6), 301–20.

9633 VINCENT (JAMES EDMUND). The land question in North Wales: being, a brief survey of the history, origin and character of the agrarian agitation and of the nature and effect of the proceedings of the Welsh land commission. 1896.

Vincent represented the landowners during the commission's hearings. See also his *The land question in South Wales: a defence of the landowners of South Wales and Monmouthshire*, 1897. For the background of the commission see the lives of Gee (**9604**), T. E. Ellis (**9605**), and Lloyd George (**9608**); Robert Albert Jones, *The land question and a land bill, with special reference to Wales*, North Wales Liberal Federation, Wrexham 1887; Thomas John Hughes, 'Adfyfyr', *Cymru Fydd: landlordism in Wales*, Cardiff 1887, and *Neglected Wales*, 1888; [James Edmund Vincent] *Tenancy in Wales: a reply to* '*Landlordism in Wales*', North Wales Property Defence Assoc., Caernarvon 1889, and *Letters from Wales . . . a series of letters in* The Times *dealing with the state of Wales in especial relation to the land, the church and the tithes*, 1889; Charles Morgan-Richardson, *Does Wales require a land bill?*, Cardiff 1893; George H. M. Owen, *The land agitation in Wales*, 1893; and *The Welsh Land Commission: leading articles and correspondence from* The Times, 1896.

9634 BOWEN (IVOR). The great enclosures of common lands in Wales. 1914.

See also Evan John Jones, 'The enclosure movement in Anglesey, 1788–1866', *Anglesey Antiq. Soc. Trans.* (1925), 21–58; (1926), 31–89.

9635 DAVIES (JAMES LLEFELYS). 'The livestock trade in West Wales in the nineteenth century'. *Aberystwyth Studs.* xiii (1934), 85–105.

9636 EDMUNDS (HENRY). 'History of the Brecknockshire Agricultural Society, 1755–1955'. *Brycheiniog* ii (1956), 26–65; iii (1957), 67–125.

9637 BRIDGE (JOHN). Report of an inquiry as to disturbances connected with the levying of tithe rentcharge in Wales. [C. 5195] H.C. (1887). XXXVIII, 291. Minutes of evidence. [C. 5195–I] H.C. (1887). XXXVIII, 301.

For this aspect of the land question see also the life of Gee (**9604**), Rowland Edmund Prothero, Baron Ernle, *The anti-tithe agitation in Wales*, 1889, John Lloyd, *Glebe lands and tithes in South Wales*, 1888, and Thomas Price, *The case of the tithes simply stated*, Rhyl 1887.

9638 WELSH LAND ENQUIRY COMMITTEE. [Chairman: Alfred Mond.] Welsh land: rural report. 1914.

Parallel to the English and Scottish enquiries, **4183, 9975.**

9639 HORACE PLUNKETT FOUNDATION. Agricultural co-operation in Scotland and Wales: a survey. 1933.

9640 ATTWOOD (EDWIN ARTHUR). Statutory small holdings in agriculture: a study in government policy with a special analysis of the administration and economic results of small holdings in Wales. Aberystwyth. 1958.

## 2. INDUSTRY

9641 THOMAS (BRINLEY) *ed.* The Welsh economy: studies in expansion. Cardiff. 1962.

A useful intro. See also Trevor Morgan Thomas, *The mineral wealth of Wales and its exploitation*, Edin. & Lond. 1961, and Evan John Jones, *Some contributions to the economic history of Wales*, 1928.

9642 MINCHINTON (WALTER EDWARD) *ed.* Industrial South Wales, 1750–1914: essays in Welsh economic history. 1969.

See also Sir James Frederick Rees, 'How South Wales became industrialised', publ. in his *Studies in Welsh hist. . . .*, Cardiff [1947], 2nd edn. Cardiff 1965, pp. 130–48, and Walter Edward Minchinton and others, 'The place of Brecknock in the industrialization of South Wales', *Brycheiniog* vii (1961), 1–70.

9643 REES (DAVID MORGAN). Mines, mills and furnaces: an introduction to industrial archaeology in Wales. Nat. Museum of Wales. 1969.

9644 LERRY (GEORGE GEOFFREY). 'The industries of Denbighshire from Tudor times to the present day'. *Denbighshire Hist. Soc. Trans.* vi (1957), 67–96; vii (1958), 38–66; viii (1959), 95–113; ix (1960), 146–73.

9645 NORTH (FREDERICK JOHN). Coal and the coalfields in Wales. Nat. Museum of Wales. Cardiff. 1926. 2nd edn. 1931.

A useful guide to resources, with bibliog. See also Henry Davies, *The South-Wales coalfield, its geology and mines*, Pontypridd 1901.

9646 MORRIS (JOHN HENRY) *and* WILLIAMS (LAWRENCE JOHN). The South Wales coal industry, 1841–1875. Cardiff. 1958.

An up-to-date account. See also Charles Wilkins, *The South Wales coal trade and its allied industries from the earliest days to the present time*, Cardiff 1888; David Edwards, 'History of the rise, progress, and present prospects of the coal trade, more particularly steam coal, in South Wales and Monmouthshire', *Roy. Nat. Eisteddfod of Wales Trans.* (1883), 481–505, John Williams, 'The coal resources of South Wales and Monmouthshire', ibid. 307–34; David Alfred Thomas, Viscount Rhondda, *Some notes on the present situation of the coal trade in the United Kingdom, with special reference to that of South Wales and Monmouthshire*, Cardiff 1896; Elizabeth Phillips, *A history of the pioneers of the Welsh coalfield*, Cardiff 1925; Anthony Edward Christian Hare, *The anthracite coal industry of the Swansea district*, Soc. & econ. survey of Swansea 5, Cardiff 1940; and William Gascoyne Dalziel, *Records of the several coal owners' associations in Monmouthshire and South Wales, 1866 to 1895*, 1895. For social hist. Chris Evans, *Industrial and social history of Seven Sisters*, Cardiff 1964, is particularly useful.

9647 LERRY (GEORGE GEOFFREY). The collieries of Denbighshire: past and present. [Wrexham.] 1946.

9648 NORTH (FREDERICK JOHN). Mining for metals in Wales. Nat. Museum of Wales. Cardiff. 1962.

9649 WILKINS (CHARLES). The history of the iron, steel, tinplate, and other trades of Wales: with descriptive sketches of the land and the people during the great industrial era under review. Merthyr Tydfil. 1903.

9650 JONES (*Sir* EDGAR REES). Toilers of the hills: an historical record in memory of those who worked through more than a century on iron, steel and tinplate in villages scattered among the Welsh hills and valleys. Pontypool. 1959.

9651 MINCHINTON (WALTER EDWARD). The British tinplate industry: a history. Oxf. 1957.

Largely on the Welsh industry. See also his 'The tinplate maker and technical change', repr. in **9642**, pp. 107–20, and **5090.**

9652 ADDIS (JOHN PHILIP). The Crawshay dynasty: a study in industrial organisation and development, 1765–1867. Cardiff. 1957.

9653 ELSAS (MADELEINE) *ed.* Iron in the making: Dowlais Iron Company letters, 1782–1860. Cardiff. 1960.

9654 CHAPPELL (EDGAR LEYSHON). Historic Melingriffith: an account of Pentyrch iron works and Melingriffith tinplate works. Cardiff. 1940.

9655 FRANCIS (GEORGE GRANT). The smelting of copper in the Swansea district, from the time of Elizabeth to the present day. Swansea. 1867. 2nd edn. Lond. 1881.

See also R. O. Roberts, 'The development and decline of the copper and other non-ferrous metal-smelting industries in South Wales', *Hon. Soc. Cymmrodorion Trans.* (1956), 78–115, repr. in **9642**, pp. 121–60.

9656 LEWIS (WILLIAM JOHN). Lead mining in Wales. Cardiff. 1967.

9657 NORTH (FREDERICK JOHN). The slates of Wales. Nat. Museum of Wales. Cardiff. 1925. 3rd edn. 1946.

See also Joseph Kellow, *The slate trade in North Wales* . . ., 1868; David Christopher Davies, *A treatise on slate and slate quarrying, scientific, practical, and commercial*, 1878, 2nd edn. 1880; W. D. Hobson, *Penrhyn quarry*, Bangor 1913; David Dylan Pritchard, *The slate industry of North Wales*, Denbigh 1946; the memoirs of Samuel Holland (**9664**); *Report of the departmental committee upon Merionethshire slate mines* [Chairman: Clement Le Neve Foster]. [C. 7692] H.C. (1895). XXXV, 393; and D. D. Pritchard, 'The expansionist phase in the history of the Welsh slate industry', *Caernarvonshire Hist. Soc. Trans.* x (1949), 65–78.

9658 RICHARDS (J. HAMISH) *and* LEWIS (JOHN PARRY). 'House-building in the South-Wales coalfield, 1851–1913'. *Manch. School* xxiv (1956), 289–301. Repr. in **9642**, pp. 235–48.

9659 JONES (IFANO). A history of printers and printing in Wales to 1810, and of successive and related printers to 1923. Cardiff. 1925.

9660 DAVIES (ALUN EIRUG). 'Paper mills and paper makers in Wales, 1700–1900'. *Nat. Libr. Wales J.* xv (1967–8), 1–30.

9661 PEATE (IORWERTH CYFEILIOG). Clock and watch makers in Wales. Nat. Museum of Wales. Cardiff. 1945. New edn. 1960.

9662 JONES (J. GERAINT). 'Rural industry in Cardiganshire'. *Ceredigion* vi (1968–71), 90–127.

See also his 'Technological improvement and social change in South Cardiganshire', *Agric. Hist. Rev.* xiii (1965), 94–105.

9663 DAVIES. Top sawyer: a biography of David Davies of Llandinam. By Ivor Thomas. 1938.

Railway contractor, M.P., coal-owner, and founder of Barry Dock.

9664 HOLLAND. The memoirs of Samuel Holland, one of the pioneers of the North Wales slate industry. Merioneth Hist. Rec. Soc. 1952.

9665 NIXON. John Nixon, pioneer of the steam and coal trade in South Wales: a memoir. By James Edmund Vincent. 1900.

9666 THOMAS. D. A. Thomas, Viscount Rhondda. By his daughter Margaret Haig Mackworth, Viscountess Rhondda, and others. 1921.

Colliery proprietor, M.P., and leader of the S. Wales coal industry.

9667 JONES (ANNA MARIA). The rural industries of England and Wales: a survey. Vol. IV. Wales. Oxf. 1927.

See also **9711** and Arthur Beacham, *Survey of industries in Welsh country towns: being the report of a survey carried out in 1946–7* . . ., 1951.

)668  JENKINS (JOHN GERAINT). The Welsh woollen industry. Welsh Folk Museum. Cardiff. 1969.

)669  THOMAS (*Sir* DANIEL LLEUFER). Memorandum on the woollen industries of Wales. Priv. pr. [1900.]

See also William P. Crankshaw, *Report on a survey of the Welsh textile industry made on behalf of the University of Wales*, Cardiff 1927.

)670  MATHESON (COLIN). Wales and the sea fisheries. Cardiff. 1929.

### 3. TRANSPORT

The chief railway systems in Wales, those of the Great Western Railway and the London and North Western Railway, are dealt with at **6261** and **6264.**

)671  HOWELLS (CLARENCE S.). Transport facilities in the mining and industrial districts of South Wales and Monmouthshire: their history and future development. Cardiff. 1911.

)672  JENKINS (JOHN GERAINT). Agricultural transport in Wales. Nat. Museum of Wales. Cardiff. 1962.

)673  HADFIELD ([ELLIS] CHARLES [RAYMOND]). The canals of South Wales and the border. Cardiff. 1960.

)674  THORNLEY (FRANK CROSSLEY). Past and present steamers of North Wales. Prescot. 1952. 2nd edn. 1962.

)675  CHAPPELL (EDGAR LEYSHON). History of the port of Cardiff. Cardiff. 1939.

)676  DAWSON (JAMES WILLIAM). Commerce and customs: a history of the ports of Newport and Caerleon. Newport. 1932.

A hist. of the local customs establishment.

)677  LLOYD (WYNNE LL.). Trade and transport: an account of the trade of the port of Swansea and the transport facilities and industry in the district. Soc. & Econ. survey of Swansea 6. Cardiff. 1960.

See also William Henry Jones, *History of the port of Swansea*, Carmarthen 1922.

)678  REES (*Sir* JAMES FREDERICK). The story of Milford (Milford Haven). Cardiff. 1954.

See also Elizabeth E. Peters, *The history of Pembroke Dock*, 1905.

)679  MORGAN (DAVID WILLIAM). Brief glory: the story of a quest. Liverpool. 1948.

Ships and shipbuilding at Aberdovey.

9680  HUGHES (HENRY). Immortal sails : a story of a Welsh port [Portmadoc] and some of its ships. [1946.]

9681  JONES (PHILIP N.). 'Workmen's trains in the South Wales coalfield, 1870–1926'. *Transport Hist.* iii (1970), 21–35.

9682  BARRIE (DEREK STIVEN MAXWELTON). The Taff Vale railway. Sidcup. 1939. 2nd edn. South Godstone. 1950.

Barrie has also publ. *The Rhymney railway*, South Godstone 1952, *The Brecon and Merthyr railway*, Lingfield 1957, and (with Charles Edward Lee) *The Sirhowy valley and its railways*, 1940. See also Richard James Rimell, *History of the Barry Railway Company, 1884–1921*, Cardiff 1923.

9683  BOYD (JAMES IAN CRAIG). The Festiniog railway : a history of the narrow gauge railway connecting the slate quarries of Blaenau Festiniog with Portmadoc, North Wales. 2 v. Lingfield. 1956–9. 2nd edn. 1960–2.

Boyd has also publ. *Narrow-gauge rails to Portmadoc: a historical survey of the Festiniog-Welsh Highland railway and its ancillaries*, South Godstone 1949, and *Narrow-gauge rails in Mid-Wales: a historical survey of the narrow gauge railways in Mid-Wales*, South Godstone 1952, 2nd edn. Lingfield 1965. See also Charles Edward Lee, *Narrow-gauge railways in North Wales*, 1945, and *The first passenger railway—the Oystermouth or Swansea and Mumbles line*, 1942, 2nd edn. South Godstone 1954, Lionel Thomas Caswall Rolt, *Railway adventure (Talyllin)*, 1953, 2nd edn. 1961, and Charles Ralph Clinker, *The Hay railway*, Dawlish 1960.

9684  DUNN (JOHN MAXWELL). The Chester and Holyhead railway. South Godstone. 1948.

9685  GASQUOINE (CHARLES PENRHYN). The story of the Cambrian : a biography of a railway. Oswestry. 1922.

Not entirely repl. by Rex Christiansen and Robert William Miller, *The Cambrian railways*, 2 v. Newton Abbot 1967–8. Roger Wakely Kidner, *The Cambrian railways*, South Godstone 1954, is slight.

9686  ROBERTSON. Henry Robertson : pioneer of railways into Wales. By George Geoffrey Lerry. Oswestry. 1949.

### 4. LABOUR

9687  THOMAS (*Sir* DANIEL LLEUFER). Labour unions in Wales. Priv. pr. Swansea. 1901.

9688  THOMAS (PHILIP SYDNEY). Industrial relations : a short study of the relations between employers and employed in Swansea and neighbourhood, from about 1800 to recent times. Soc. & Econ. survey of Swansea 3. Cardiff. 1940.

9689  COMMISSION OF ENQUIRY INTO INDUSTRIAL UNREST : Report of the commissioners for Wales, including Monmouthshire [Chairman : Sir Daniel Lleufer Thomas]. [Cd. 8668] H.C. (1917–18). XV, 83.

9690   EVANS (ERIC WYN). The miners of South Wales [to 1912]. Cardiff. 1961.

9691   EDWARDS (NESS). The history of the South Wales miners. 1926.

9692   EDWARDS (NESS). History of the South Wales Miners' Federation. Vol. 1. 1938.

See also Robert Page Arnot, *South Wales miners—glowyr de cymru—a history of the South Wales Miners' Federation, 1898–1914*, 1967, and John Edward Morgan, *A village workers' council and what it accomplished: being, a short history of the Lady Windsor Lodge*, S.W.M.F., Pontypridd [1956].

9693   MORRIS (JOHN HENRY) *and* WILLIAMS (LAWRENCE JOHN). 'The discharge note in the South Wales coal industry, 1841–1898'. *Econ. Hist. Rev.* 2 ser. x (1957–8), 286–93.

See also their 'The South Wales sliding scale, 1876–79: an experiment in industrial relations', *Manch. School* xxviii (1960), 161–76, repr. in **9642**, pp. 218–31, and L. J. Williams, 'The new unionism in South Wales, 1889–92', *Welsh Hist. Rev.* i (1960–3), 413–29, and 'The strike of 1898', *Morgannwg* ix (1965), 61–79.

9694   THOMAS (BRINLEY). 'The migration of labour into the Glamorganshire coalfield, 1861–1911'. *Economica* x (1930), 275–94. Repr. in **9642**, pp. 37–56.

9695   DALZIEL (ALEXANDER). The colliers' strike in South Wales: its cause, progress and settlement. Cardiff. 1872.

9696   EVANS (DAVID). Labour strife in the South Wales coalfield, 1910–1911: a historical and critical record of the Mid-Rhondda, Aberdare Valley and other strikes. Cardiff. 1911. Repr. 1962.

9697   MABON. Mabon: William Abraham, 1842–1922: a study in trade union leadership. By Eric Wyn Evans. Cardiff. 1959.

The leader of the South Wales miners.

9698   ROGERS (EMLYN). 'The history of trade unionism in the coalmining industry of North Wales to 1914'. *Denbighshire Hist. Soc. Trans.* xii (1963), 110–35; xiii (1964), 219–40; xiv (1965), 209–34; xv (1966), 132–57; xvi (1967), 100–27; xvii (1968), 147–76.

9699   PARRY. '"Quarryman's champion": the life and activities of William John Parry of Coetmor'. By J. Roose Williams. *Caernarvonshire Hist. Soc. Trans.* xxiii (1962), 92–115; xxiv (1963), 217–38; xxv (1964), 81–116; xxvi (1965), 107–56; xxvii (1966), 149–91.

9700   JONES (CHARLES SHERIDAN). What I saw at Bethesda. [1903.]

One of a number of publs. on the Penrhyn quarries dispute and its background. See also William John Parry, *The Penrhyn lock-out, 1900–1901*, 1901; General Federation of Trade Unions, *Report on the Penrhyn dispute*, Caernarvon 1901; [E. A. Young] *The Penrhyn quarries dispute*, 1903; North Wales Quarrymen's Union, *The struggle for the right of combination*, Caernarvon 1897; the report to the Labour Commission (**6454**); and William John Williams, *The royal commission on labour*, Caernarvon 1893.

## D. SOCIAL HISTORY

9701   THOMAS (*Sir* DANIEL LLEUFER) *and others*. Social problems in Wales. 1913.

There is little hist. material in Tom Brennan and E. W. Cooney, *The social pattern: a handbook of social statistics of South-West Wales*, Swansea 1950, and Tom Brennan, E. W. Cooney, and H. Pollins, *Social change in South-West Wales*, 1954.

9702   BALFOUR COMMISSION ON WELSH SUNDAY CLOSING. Report of the royal commission appointed to inquire into the operation of the Sunday Closing (Wales) Act, 1881 [Chairman: Lord Balfour of Burleigh]. [C. 5994] H.C. (1890). XL, 1. Minutes of evidence. [C. 5994–I] H.C. (1890). XL, 43.

A useful quarry for social hist.

9703   BORROW (GEORGE HENRY). Wild Wales: its people, language and scenery. 3 v. 1862. Numerous edns.

The most celebrated of all books about mid-19th-cent. Wales.

9704   WILLIAMS (DAVID). 'Rural Wales in the nineteenth century'. *Univ. College of Wales Agric. Soc. J.* xxxiv (1953), 5–16.

See also A. Bailey Williams, 'Some aspects of village culture in Montgomeryshire in the latter part of the 19th century', *Montgomerysh. Coll.* liii (1953–4), 96–109, and 'Customs and traditions connected with sickness, death and burial in Montgomeryshire in the late 19th century', ibid. lii (1951–2), 51–61, G. J. Lewis, 'The demographic structure of a Welsh rural village during the mid-nineteenth century', *Ceredigion* v (1964–7), 290–304, and Robert Alun Roberts, *Welsh home-spun: studies of rural Wales*, Newtown 1930.

9705   VAUGHAN (HERBERT MILLINGCHAMP). The South Wales squires: a Welsh picture of social life. 1926.

9706   JONES (THOMAS GWYNN). Welsh folklore and folk-custom. 1930.

9707   OWEN (TREFOR MEREDITH). Welsh folk customs. Nat. Museum of Wales. Cardiff. 1959.

See also **7649**.

9708   SOCIETY FOR FOLK-LIFE STUDIES. Folk life. 1+. Cardiff. 1963+.

Largely concentrates on Wales, Scotland, and Ireland. Replaced *Gwerin*, 1–3, Oxf. etc. 1956–62.

9709   PEATE (IORWERTH CYFEILIOG). The Welsh house: a study in folk culture. *Y Cymmrodor* xlvii, 1940. 2nd edn. 1944.

9710   TWISTON-DAVIES (*Sir* LEONARD) *and* LLOYD-JOHNES (HERBERT JOHNES). Welsh furniture: an introduction. Cardiff. 1950.

9711  PEATE (IORWERTH CYFEILIOG). National Museum of Wales: guide to the collection of Welsh bygones . . . Cardiff. 1929.

Suppl. by his *Guide to the collection illustrating Welsh folk-crafts and industries,* Cardiff 1935, 2nd edn. 1945. See also Owen Evan-Thomas, *Domestic utensils of wood, XVIth to XIXth centuries: a short history,* 1932.

9712  WILLIAMS (DAVID JOHN). The old farmhouse. Trans. by Waldo Williams. 1961.

A minor classic of country life, 1840–86.

9713  JONES. Old Memories: autobiography. By Sir Henry Jones. 1922.

See also Sir Hector James Wright Hetherington, *The life and letters of Sir Henry Jones, Professor of Moral Philosophy in the University of Glasgow,* 1924.

9714  JONES. Rhymney memories. By Thomas Jones. Newtown. 1938.

Cont. in his *Leeks and daffodils,* Newtown 1942, and *Welsh broth* [1951]. Together these 3 v. give an excellent account of South Wales life, c. 1890–1914.

9715  TURNER. The memories of Sir Llewelyn Turner: memories, serious and light, of the Irish rebellion of 1798, Welsh judicature and English judges, admirals and sea fights, municipal work and notable persons in North Wales, strange crimes and great events. Ed. by James Edmund Vincent. 1903.

9716  PARRY-JONES. Welsh country upbringing. By Daniel Parry-Jones. 1948. 2nd edn. 1949.

9717  BLACKWELL (HENRY) *comp.* A bibliography of Welsh Americana. *Nat. Libr. Wales J. Suppl.* ser. iii no. 1. 1942. Cont. by Idwal Lewis. *Nat. Libr. Wales J.* xi (1959–60), 371–81.

See also his *Welsh country characters,* 1952.

9718  CONWAY (ALAN) *ed.* The Welsh in America: letters from the immigrants. Minneapolis & Cardiff. 1961.

9719  HARRIES (FREDERICK JAMES). Welshmen and the United States. Pontypridd. 1927.

See also Edward George Hartmann, *Americans from Wales,* Boston 1967; David Williams, *Cymru ac America: Wales and America,* Cardiff 1946; Benjamin Williams Chidlaw, *The story of my life,* Phila. 1890; David Davies and Howell David Davies, *History of the Oshkosh Welsh settlement, 1847–1947,* Amarillo, Tex. 1947; Daniel Jenkins Williams, *The Welsh of Columbus, Ohio: a study in adaptation and assimilation,* Oshkosh, Wis. 1913; Stephen Riggs Williams, *The saga of Paddy's Run,* Oxf., Ohio 1945; and Wilbur Stanley Shepperson, *Samuel Roberts: a Welsh colonizer in civil-war Tennessee,* Knoxville, Tenn. 1961. Berthoff and others (**6973**) also deal with Wales.

9720  ROSSER (FREDERICK THOMAS). The Welsh settlement in Upper Canada. London, Ont. 1954.

9721 WILLIAMS (RICHARD BRYN). Y Wladfa. Cardiff. 1962.

On the Welsh in Patagonia. In Welsh. Valuable for exhaustive bibliog. of English and Welsh works. See also John E. Baur, 'The Welsh in Patagonia: an example of national-istic migration', *Hispanic Amer. Hist. Rev.* xxxiv (1954), 468–92.

9722 WILLIAMS (DAVID). 'Welsh settlers in Russia'. *Nat. Libr. Wales J.* iii (1943–4), 55–8.

## E. WELSH LANGUAGE AND CULTURE

There is some useful general information in Sir Harold Idris Bell, *The crisis of our time and other papers*, Llandybie 1954, and Sir Alfred Eckhard Zimmern, *My impression of Wales*, 1921. For the annual progress of the language see the reports of the National Eisteddfod Council [Association], 1860+.

9723 UNIVERSITY OF WALES (BOARD OF CELTIC STUDIES). Studia Celtica. 1+. Cardiff. 1966+.

9724 JENKINS (ROBERT THOMAS) *and* RAMAGE (HELEN MYFANWY). A history of the Honourable Society of Cymmrodorion and of the Gwyneddigion and Cymreigyddion Societies, 1751–1951. *Y Cymmrodor* l, 1951.

9725 WELSH IN EDUCATION AND LIFE: being, the report of the departmental committee appointed by the President of the Board of Education to inquire into the position of the Welsh language and to advise as to its promotion in the educational system of Wales. 1927.

Includes a good sketch of the hist. of the language. See also Emrys Jones, 'The changing distribution of the Celtic languages in the British isles', *Hon. Soc. Cymmrodorion Trans.* (1967), 22–38.

9726 SOUTHALL (JOHN EDWARD). Wales and her language: considered from a historical, educational and social standpoint . . . Newport. 1892.

See also his *Bilingual teaching in Welsh elementary schools*, Newport 1888.

9727 O'RAHILLY (CECILE). Ireland and Wales: their historical and literary connections. 1924.

9728 JONES (BRYNMOR) *comp.* A bibliography of Anglo-Welsh literature, 1900–1965. Library Assoc., Wales & Monmouthshire branch. Swansea. 1970.

9729 LEWIS (JOHN PARRY). 'The anglicization of Glamorgan'. *Morgannwg* iv (1960), 28–49.

9730 HARDING (F. J. W.). 'Matthew Arnold and Wales'. *Hon. Soc. Cymmro-dorion Trans.* (1963), 251–72.

9731  BALLINGER (*Sir* JOHN). The Bible in Wales: a study in the history of the Welsh people . . . 1906.

9732  BELL (*Sir* HAROLD IDRIS). The development of Welsh poetry. Oxf. 1936.

9733  CROSSLEY-HOLLAND (PETER) *ed.* Music in Wales. 1948.

See also John Graham, *A century of Welsh music*, 1923, and Frederic Griffith, ed., *Notable Welsh musicians of today: with portraits* . . ., 1896, 2nd edn. 1896.

9734  BELL (DAVID). The artist in Wales. 1957.

9735  REES (THOMAS MARDY). Welsh painters, engravers, sculptors, 1527–1911 . . . Caernarvon. [1912.]

9736  STEEGMAN (JOHN) *and others*. A survey of portraits in Welsh houses. Nat. Museum of Wales. Cardiff. 2 v. 1957–62.

9737  PRICE (CECIL). 'Some Welsh theatres, 1844–1870'. *Nat. Libr. Wales J.* xii (1961–2), 156–76.

See also his 'Portable theatres in Wales, 1843–1914', *Nat. Libr. Wales J.* ix (1955–6), 65–92.


### F. EDUCATION

There is no hist. The nearest approach is Ministry of Education, *Education in Wales, 1847 to 1947* [bilingual], 1948. The Board of Education Welsh Dept. began to issue an annual report in 1907.

9738  EVANS (DAVID). The Sunday schools of Wales . . . 1883.

9739  ELLIS (THOMAS IORWERTH). The development of higher education in Wales. Wrexham. 1935.

9740  WEBSTER (J. R.). 'The Welsh Intermediate Education Act of 1889'. *Welsh Hist. Rev.* iv (1968–9), 273–91.

The 1889 Act is also dealt with in Thomas Edward Ellis and Ellis Jones Griffith, *Intermediate and technical education* (*Wales*), 1889, and Emrys Evans and others, 'The Welsh Intermediate Education Act, 1889: addresses', *Hon. Soc. Cymmrodorion Trans.* (1939), 101–31. For the background of the Act see Rendel (**874**), D. L. Lloyd, *The missing link*, 1876, and Sir Thomas Marchant Williams, *The educational wants of Wales*, 1877.

9741  SALMON (DAVID). History of the Normal College for Wales. Swansea. 1902.

See also Llewelyn Morgan Rees and others, *Bangor Normal College, 1858–1958*, Conway 1958, and Thomas Halliwell, *Trinity College, Carmarthen, 1848–1948*, Carmarthen 1948.

9742  GITTINS (CHARLES EDWARD) *ed.* Pioneers of Welsh education. Swansea. 1964.

9743 DAVIES (EBENEZER THOMAS). Monmouthshire schools and education to 1870. Newport. 1957.

9744 DODD (CHARLES). Wrexham schools and scholars. Wrexham. 1924.

9745 TROTT (ARTHUR LUTHER). 'The implementation of the 1870 Elementary Education Act in Cardiganshire during the period 1870–1880, with particular reference to the borough of Cardigan and the parish of Lampeter'. *Ceredigion* iii (1956–9), 207–30.

See also his 'Aberystwyth school board and board school, 1870–1902', *Ceredigion* ii (1952–5), 3–17; and 'Church day schools in Aberystwyth . . .', ibid. 66–84.

9746 WILLIAMS (A. BAILEY). 'Education in Montgomeryshire in the late nineteenth century'. *Montgomeryshire Colls.* lii (1951–2), 83–106.

9747 WYNNE EVANS (LESLIE). Education in industrial Wales, 1700–1900: a study of the works schools system in Wales during the industrial revolution. Cardiff. 1971.

9748 WATKINS. A Welshman remembers: an autobiography. By Sir Percy Emerson Watkins. Cardiff. 1944.

Good on educ. admin. See also Sir Alfred Thomas Davies, *The Lloyd George I knew* (**9608**).

9749 ABERDARE COMMITTEE ON INTERMEDIATE AND HIGHER EDUCATION. Report of the committee appointed to inquire into the condition of intermediate and higher education in Wales [Chairman: Lord Aberdare]. [C. 3047] H.C. (1881). XXXIII, 1. Minutes of evidence. [C. 3047–I] H.C. (1881). XXXIII, 115.

The decisive report for the development of post-primary educ. in Wales. See also Ben Bowen Thomas, 'The establishment of the "Aberdare" departmental committee, 1880: some letters and notes', *Board of Celtic Studs. Bull.* xix (1960–2), 318–34.

9750 BRUCE COMMITTEE ON SECONDARY EDUCATION. Report of the departmental committee on the organisation of secondary education in Wales [Chairman: W. N. Bruce]. [Cmd. 967] H.C. (1920). XV, 489.

9751 ARCHDALL (HENRY KINGSLEY). St. David's College, Lampeter: its past, present and future. Lampeter. 1952.

9752 EVANS (*Sir* DAVID EMRYS). The University of Wales: a historical sketch. Cardiff. 1953.

See also William Cadwaladr Davies and William Lewis Jones, *The University of Wales and its constituent colleges*, 1905, and Sir Harry Rudolf Reichel, '*The university*' in *Wales* . . ., Newtown 1920.

9753 RALEIGH COMMITTEE ON THE UNIVERSITY OF WALES. Report to the Lords Commissioners of Her Majesty's Treasury of the committee on the University of Wales and the Welsh university colleges [Chairman:

Sir Thomas Raleigh]. [Cd. 4571] H.C. (1909). XIX, 663. Minutes of evidence. [Cd. 4572] H.C. (1909). XIX, 699.

9754 HALDANE COMMISSION ON UNIVERSITY EDUCATION IN WALES. First report of the royal commission on university education in Wales [Chairman: Viscount Haldane]. [Cd. 8500] H.C. (1917–18). XII, 1. Minutes of evidence. [Cd. 8507] H.C. (1917–18). XII, 5. Second report. [Cd. 8698] H.C. (1917–18). XII, 337. Minutes of evidence. [Cd. 8699] H.C. (1917–18). XII, 341. Final report. [Cd. 8991] H.C. (1918). XIV, 1. Minutes of evidence. [Cd. 8993] H.C. (1918). XIV, 115.

Full and valuable. The final report gives a full and candid analysis of the hist. and development of Welsh univ. educ.

9755 ELLIS (EDWARD LEWIS). The University College of Wales, Aberystwyth, 1872–1972. Oxf. 1972.

See also W. E. Davies, *Sir Hugh Owen: his life and life-work* 1885, Thomas Iorwerth Ellis, ed., *Thomas Charles Edwards: letters*, suppl. to *Nat. Library of Wales J.* iii. ser. 3–4, Aberystwyth 1952–3, E. L. Ellis, 'Some aspects of the early history of the University College of Wales', *Hon. Soc. Cymmrodorion Trans.* (1967), 203–19, and Iwan J. Morgan, ed., *The college by the sea: a record and a review*, Aberystwyth 1928.

9756 TROW (ALBERT HOWARD) *and* BROWN (D. J. A.). A short history of the University College of South Wales, Cardiff, 1883–1933. Cardiff. [1933.]

See also Katharine Viriamu Jones, *Life of John Viriamu Jones*, 1915, Neville Charles Masterman, *J. Viriamu Jones, 1856–1901, pioneer of the modern university: an appreciation*, Llandybie 1957, and Sir Edward Bagnall Poulton, *John Viriamu Jones and other Oxford memories*, 1911.

9757 REICHEL. Sir Harry Reichel, 1856–1931: a memorial volume. Ed. by Sir John Edward Lloyd. Cardiff. 1934.

Principal, Univ. College, Bangor.

## G. LOCAL HISTORY

9758 SOUTH WALES AND MONMOUTH RECORD SOCIETY. *Publications.* 1+. Cardiff. 1949+.

9759 ANGLESEY. Anglesey Antiquarian Society and Field Club. *Transactions.* 1+. Llangefni etc. 1913+.

9760 BRECON. Brecknock Society, *Brycheiniog*, 1+, Brecon 1956+.

9761 CAERNARVONSHIRE. William Ogwen Williams, ed., *Guide to the Caernarvonshire record office*, Caernarvon 1952. Arthur Herbert Dodd, *A history of Caernarvonshire, 1284–1900*, Caernarvonshire Hist. Soc. 1968. Caernarvonshire Hist. Soc., *Transactions*, 1+, Aberystwyth 1939+, and *Record series*, 1+, Caernarvon 1951+. Llandudno, [Colwyn Bay] and District Field Club, *Proceedings*, 1+, 1907–8+, Llandudno 1909+.

9762  CARDIGANSHIRE. Cardiganshire Antiq. Soc., *Ceredigion: the journal of the Cardiganshire Antiquarian Society*, 1+, 1950-1+. I. G. Jones and K. O. Morgan, 'Cardiganshire politics' (**9592-3**). J. G. Jones, 'Rural industry in Cardiganshire' (**9662**).

9763  CARMARTHENSHIRE. Carmarthenshire Antiq. Soc. and Field Club, *The Carmarthen antiquary: the transactions of the* . . ., 1+, 1941+. *The Carmarthenshire historian*, 1961+. Sir John Edward Lloyd, ed., *A history of Carmarthenshire*, 2 v. 1935-9. H. W. E. Davies, 'The development of the industrial landscape of Llanelly', *Geographical Studs.* iv (1957), 104-15.

9764  DENBIGHSHIRE. Denbighshire County Libr., *Bibliography of the county*: pt. 1. *Biographical sources*, Ruthin 1935; pt. 2. *Historical and topographical sources*, 2nd edn. Ruthin 1951, suppl. 1959; pt. 3. *Denbighshire authors and their work*, Ruthin 1937. Denbighshire Hist. Soc., *Transactions*, 1+, Conway 1952+. James Idwal Jones, *An atlas of Denbighshire*, Denbighshire Educ. Committee 1951. Hugh Ellis Hughes, ed., *Eminent men of Denbighshire*, Liverpool 1946. G. C. Lerry, 'The industries of Denbighshire' (**9644**) and *The collieries of Denbighshire* (**9647**). Ellis Wynne Williams, *Abergele: the story of a parish*, priv. pr. Abergele 1968. Norman Ralph Friedel Tucker, *Colwyn Bay: its origin and growth*, Colwyn Bay 1953. Arthur Herbert Dodd, ed., *A history of Wrexham, Denbighshire*, Wrexham 1957.

9765  FLINTSHIRE. Edward Rhys Harries, comp., *Bibliography of the county of Flint*: pt. 1. 'Biographical sources', Flint County Libr., Mold 1953. A. G. Veysey, ed., *Guide to the Flintshire record office*, Hawarden 1974. Flintshire Hist. Soc., *Publications*, 1+, Prestatyn 1911-25, 1951+.

9766  GLAMORGAN. Henry John Randall, ed., *A breviate of Glamorgan and other papers*, South Wales & Mons. Record Soc. 3. 1957. Glamorgan Local Hist. Soc., *Morgannwg: transactions of the* . . ., 1+, Cardiff 1957+. Gower Soc., *Gower: journal of the Gower Society*, Swansea 1948+. K. O. Morgan, 'Democratic politics in Glamorgan' (**9593**). G. E. Fussell, 'Glamorgan farming' (**9630**). David Rhys Phillips, *The history of the vale of Neath*, Swansea 1925. Neath Antiq. Soc., *Transactions*, 1+, 1930-1+. Evan David Lewis, *The Rhondda valleys: a study in industrial development, 1800 to the present day* [1959]. Henry John Randall, *Bridgend: the story of a market town*, Newport, Mon. 1955. John Hobson Matthews, ed., *Cardiff records: being materials for a history of the county borough from the earliest times*, 6 v. Cardiff 1898-1911. William Rees, *Cardiff: a history of the city*, Cardiff [1962], 2nd edn. 1969. Herbert Metford Thompson, *Cardiff* . . ., Cardiff 1930. E. L. Chappell, *History of the port of Cardiff* (**9675**). T. M. Hodges, 'The peopling of the hinterland of the port of Cardiff [1801-1914]', *Econ. Hist. Rev.* xvii (1947), 62-72, repr. in **9642**, pp. 3-18. Charles Wilkins, *The history of Merthyr Tydfil*, 1867, 2nd edn. 1908. Margaret Stewart Taylor, *County borough of Merthyr Tydfil, 1905-1955* . . ., Merthyr [1955]. G. Williams, *Merthyr politics* (**9598**). I. G. Jones, articles on Merthyr politics (**9592**). C. Evans, *Seven Sisters* (**9646**).

David Trevor Williams, *The economic development of Swansea and of the Swansea district to 1921*, Soc. & Econ. Survey of Swansea 4, Cardiff 1940. Glyn Roberts, *The municipal development of the borough of Swansea to 1900*, Soc. & Econ. Survey of Swansea 2, Cardiff 1940. S. S. Awbery, *Labour's early struggles in Swansea* (**9599**). A. E. C. Hare, *The anthracite coal industry of Swansea* (**9646**). G. G. Francis, *The smelting of copper in Swansea* (**9655**). W. L. Lloyd, *Trade . . . of Swansea* (**9677**).

9767 MERIONETH. Merioneth Hist. and Record Soc., *Journal*, 1+, Dolgelly 1949+. I. G. Jones, 'Merioneth politics' (**9592**). E. Rosalie Jones, *A history of Barmouth and its vicinity . . .*, Barmouth 1909.

9768 MONMOUTHSHIRE. W. H. Baker, ed., *Guide to the Monmouthshire record office*, Newport 1959. Sir Joseph Alfred Bradney, *A history of Monmouthshire, from the coming of the Normans into Wales down to the present time*, 4 v. in pts., 1904–32. *Presenting Monmouthshire: the journal of Monmouthshire Local History Council*, 1+, 1956+. Sir Leonard Twiston-Davies, *Men of Monmouthshire*, 2 v. Cardiff 1933. William John Townsend Collins, *Monmouthshire writers: a literary history and anthology . . .*, Newport 1945, and *More Monmouthshire writers . . .*, Newport 1948. Henry John Davis, *The rise and progress of Newport (Monmouthshire)*, 1891. Arthur Clark and others, *The story of Pontypool*, Pontypool 1958.

9769 MONTGOMERYSHIRE. [Powysland Club] *Montgomeryshire collections . . .*, 1+, 1868+. Ernest Richmond Horsfall Turner, *A municipal history of Llanidloes*, Llanidloes 1908. B. Bennett Rowlands, *A brief history of . . . Newtown, Montgomeryshire*, Newtown 1914.

9770 PEMBROKESHIRE. James Phillips, *The history of Pembrokeshire*, 1909. Pembrokeshire Local Hist. Soc., *The Pembrokeshire historian*, Haverfordwest 1959+. J. W. Phillips and Fred. J. Warren, *The history of Haverfordwest*, Haverfordwest 1914. J. F. Rees, *The story of Milford* (**9678**). Roscoe Howells, *The sounds between: the story of the islands of Skomer, Skokholm, Ramsey and Grassholm . . .*, Llandysul 1968.

9771 RADNORSHIRE. Radnorshire Society, *Transactions*, 1+, Llandrindod Wells 1931+. Jonathan Williams, *A general history of the county of Radnor . . .*, ed. by Edwin Davies, Brecon 1905.

# XII

## SCOTLAND

### A. GENERAL

#### 1. BIBLIOGRAPHY

9772  NATIONAL BOOK LEAGUE. Reader's guide to Scotland: a bibliography. Ed. by D. M. Lloyd. 1968.

See also Archibald Alexander McBeth Duncan, *An introduction to Scottish history for teachers*, Hist. Assoc. 1967.

9773  BLACK (GEORGE FRASER) *comp.* A list of works relating to Scotland. New York Public Libr. N.Y. 1916.

Much the fullest list. For Scottish bibliog. consult *The bibliotheck: a journal of bibliographical notes and queries mainly of Scottish interest*, Glasgow etc. 1956+.

9774  'A LIST of articles on Scottish history published during the year 1959+'. *Scot. Hist. Rev.* xxxix+. 1960+.

A useful annual checklist.

9775  MITCHELL (*Sir* ARTHUR) *and* CASH (CALEB GEORGE) *comps.* A contribution to the bibliography of Scottish topography. Scot. Hist. Soc. 2 ser. xiv–xv. 2 v. Edin. 1917.

Continued by Hancock (**9776**).

9776  HANCOCK (PHILIP DAVID) *comp.* A bibliography of works relating to Scotland, 1916–50. 2 v. Edin. 1959–60.

9777  GOULDESBROUGH (PETER) *and others, comps.* Handlist of Scottish and Welsh record publications. British Records Assoc. 1954.

See also Mullins, *Texts and calendars* (**23**).

9778  TERRY (CHARLES SANFORD) *comp.* A catalogue of the publications of Scottish historical and kindred clubs and societies, and of the volumes relative to Scottish history, issued by His Majesty's Stationery Office, 1780–1908. Glasgow & Aberdeen. 1909.

Cont. by Cyril Matheson, comp., *A catalogue of the publications of Scottish historical and kindred clubs and societies . . ., 1908–1927*, Aberdeen 1928.

9779  MITCHELL (*Sir* ARTHUR). 'A list of travels, tours, journeys, voyages, cruises, excursions, wanderings, rambles, visits, etc., relating to Scotland'. *Soc. Antiquaries Scotland Proc.* xxxv (1900–1), 431–638. Repr. Edin. 1902. Suppls. ibid. xxxix (1904–5), 500–27; xliv (1909–10), 390–405.

Down to 1909.

9780 FERGUSON (JOAN PRIMROSE SCOTT) *ed*. Scottish newspapers held in Scottish libraries. Scottish Central Libr. Edin. 1956.

9781 UNIVERSITY OF EDINBURGH LIBRARY. Catalogue of the printed books in the library of the University of Edinburgh . . . 3 v. Edin. 1918–23.

See also the Library's *Index to manuscripts*, 2 v. Boston 1964. The library is less strong in books and manuscripts of the post-1851 period than the National Libr. of Scotland, whose book catalogue is not being publ. and whose manuscript catalogue (**9783**) is slow to appear.

9782 LIVINGSTONE (MATTHEW). A guide to the public records of Scotland deposited in H.M. General Register House, Edinburgh. Edin. 1905.

Suppl. in *Scottish Hist. Rev.* xxvi (1947), 26–46. Current accessions are reported by the National Register of Archives (**38**) and in *Scottish Hist. Rev.* (**9804**). A new guide is in preparation. For private archives see *List of gifts and deposits in the Scottish Record Office*, 1+, H.M.S.O. Edin. 1972+, and National Register of Archives (Scotland), *Report*, 1946+.

9783 NATIONAL LIBRARY OF SCOTLAND. Catalogue of manuscripts acquired since 1925. 1+. Edin. 1938+.

Accessions are listed in the *Annual report* of the library and in National Libr. of Scotland, *Accessions, 1959–1964: manuscripts*, Edin. [1968.] John Mackechnie, comp., *Catalogue of Gaelic manuscripts in selected libraries in Great Britain and Ireland*, Boston 1972, is based on the National Libr. Coll.

## 2. REFERENCE

9784 THE NEW STATISTICAL ACCOUNT of Scotland: by the ministers of the respective parishes, under the superintendence of a committee of the Society for the Benefit of the Sons and Daughters of the Clergy. 15 v. Edin. & Lond. 1845.

An indispensable source for economic and social life covering all the counties of Scotland. *The third statistical account of Scotland*, Edin. & Lond. 1951+, in progress, also includes hist. material, though the coverage is patchy.

9785 GRANT (WILLIAM) *and others, eds*. The Scottish national dictionary: designed partly on regional lines and partly on historical principles, and containing all the Scottish words known to be in use or to have been in use since *c*. 1700. Edin. 1931–4+. In progress.

Replaces John Jamieson, *An etymological dictionary of the Scottish language*, new edn. 4 v. 1879–82, suppl. 1887.

9786 HENDERSON (JAMES MERCER). Scottish reckonings of time, money, weights and measures. Hist. Assoc. of Scotland. 1926.

9787 GROOME (FRANCIS HINDES) *ed*. Ordnance gazetteer of Scotland: a survey of Scottish topography, statistical, biographical and historical. 6 v. Edin. 1882–5. Repr. 3 v. Edin. 1886. New edn. 6 v. Lond. [1894–5.] New edn. 6 v. Glasgow. 1901.

9788 BARTHOLOMEW (JOHN GEORGE) *and others.* The Royal Scottish Geographical Society's atlas of Scotland: a series of sixty-two plates of maps and plans illustrating the topography, physiography, geology, natural history and climate of the country. Edin. 1895.

Replaced by his *The survey atlas of Scotland* . . ., Edin. 1912.

9789 OLIVER & BOYD'S [NEW] EDINBURGH ALMANAC and national repository for the year. 1837+. Edin. 1836+.

An official list and professional directory, plus a guide to the statutes and law cases of the previous year.

9790 FERGUSON (JOAN PRIMROSE SCOTT) *ed.* Scottish family histories held in Scottish libraries. Scottish Central Libr. Edin. 1960.

9791 STUART (MARGARET). Scottish family history: a guide to works of reference on the history and genealogy of Scottish families. Edin. & Lond. 1930.

9792 PAUL (*Sir* JAMES BALFOUR) *ed.* The Scots peerage: founded on Wood's edition of Sir Robert Douglas's peerage of Scotland; containing an historical and genealogical account of the nobility of that kingdom. 9 v. Edin. 1904–14.

9793 CHAMBERS (ROBERT) *and others.* A biographical dictionary of eminent Scotsmen . . . Rev. edn. 9 v. 1853–5.

Only of slight value for the period, as are Joseph Irving, *The book of Scotsmen eminent for achievements in arms and arts, church and state, law, legislation and literature, commerce, science, travel and philanthropy,* Paisley 1881, Jabez Marrat, *Northern lights: pen and pencil sketches of modern Scottish worthies,* 2nd edn. 1877, and William Anderson, *The Scottish nation: or, the surnames, families, literature, honours and biographical history of the people of Scotland,* 3 v. Edin. 1860–3.

9794 MEMOIRS AND PORTRAITS OF ONE HUNDRED GLASGOW MEN who have died during the last thirty years . . . 2 v. Glasgow. 1886.

Good, especially for industrial biog., as is James Stephen Jeans, *Western worthies: a gallery of biographical and critical sketches of west of Scotland celebrities,* Glasgow 1872.

9795 CARSWELL (DONALD). Brother Scots. 1927.

Lively, Lytton Strachey-like lives of Henry Drummond, Robertson Smith, J. S. Blackie, Keir Hardie, Lord Overtoun, Robertson Nicoll.

9796 KNIGHT (WILLIAM ANGUS). Some nineteenth-century Scotsmen: being personal recollections. Edin. & Lond. 1903.

9797 SCOTTISH NATIONAL PORTRAIT GALLERY. Illustrated catalogue. Edin. 1951.

9798 BLACK (GEORGE FRASER). The surnames of Scotland: their origin, meaning and history. New York Public Libr. 1946.

## 3. General and Political History

**9799 FERGUSON (WILLIAM).** Scotland: 1689 to the present. Edin. Hist. of Scotland IV. Edin. & Lond. 1968.

The best general hist. of the period. George Smith Pryde, *A new history of Scotland*, vol. II: *Scotland from 1603 to the present day*, 1962, is much inferior. The numerous short hists. of Scotland give only a few pages to the late Victorian period, but there are some interesting comments in Rosalind Mitchison, *A history of Scotland*, 1970, and Sir Robert Sangster Rait and George Smith Pryde, *Scotland*, 1934, 2nd edn. 1954. For economic hist. see **9955**. Few 19th-cent. gen. hists. and surveys have worn well. Henry Thomas Buckle, *The history of civilization in England*, vol. II 1861, new edn. [*Scotland and the Scotch intellect*] by Harold John Hanham, Chicago 1970, caused a great stir when publ. and is important for intellectual hist. Otherwise only George Douglas Campbell, Duke of Argyll, *Scotland as it was and as it is*, 2 v. Edin. 1887, and John Mackintosh, *The history of civilisation in Scotland*, rev. edn. 4 v. Paisley & Lond. 1892–6, now appear to be useful.

**9800 KELLAS (JAMES G.).** Modern Scotland: the nation since 1870. Lond. & N.Y. 1968.

A useful survey whose chief emphasis is on the 20th cent. The politics of the late 19th cent. are examined in more detail by Kellas in 'The Liberal party and the Scottish church disestablishment crisis', *Eng. Hist. Rev.* lxxix (1964), 31–46, 'The Liberal party in Scotland, 1876–1895', *Scot. Hist. Rev.* xliv (1965), 1–16, and 'The Mid-Lanark by-election (1888) and the Scottish Labour party (1888–1894)', *Parliamentary affairs* xviii (1964–5), 318–29; Alistair B. Cooke, 'Gladstone's election for the Leith district of burghs, July 1886', *Scot. Hist. Rev.* xlix (1970), 172–94; Derek William Urwin, 'The development of the Conservative party organisation in Scotland until 1912', *Scot. Hist. Rev.* xliv (1965), 89–111; and Donald C. Savage, 'Scottish politics, 1885–6', *Scot. Hist. Rev.* xl (1961), 118–35.

**9801 MINTO (CHARLES SINCLAIR).** Victorian & Edwardian Scotland from old photographs. 1970.

**9802 DONALDSON (GORDON).** The Scots overseas. 1966.

A useful survey of a neglected subject. See also George Fraser Black, *Scotland's mark on America*, N.Y. 1921; C. Dunn, *Highland settler* (**1533**); William Jordan Rattray, *The Scot in British North America*, 4 v. Toronto [1880–3]; William Wilfred Campbell and George Bryce, *The Scotsman in Canada . . .*, 2 v. Toronto & Lond. [1911]; and John Kenneth Galbraith, *The Scotch*, Boston 1964.

**9803 SCOTTISH HISTORY SOCIETY.** Publications. 1+. Edin. 1887+.

The chief Scottish record soc. With the 4th series, 1964+, publication of post-1832 records has begun in earnest.

**9804 SCOTTISH HISTORICAL REVIEW.** 1+. Edin. etc. 1903–28, 1947+.

The principal Scottish hist. j. Hist. articles also appear in University of Edinburgh, School of Scottish Studies, *Scottish studies*, 1+, Edin. 1957+; [Royal] Scottish Geographical Soc., *The Scottish geographical mag.*, 1+, Edin. 1885+; *Scottish j. of political economy*, 1+, Edin. 1954+; *Juridical rev.* (**9827**); *Folk life* (**9708**); *The Scottish genealogist: the quarterly j. of the Scottish Genealogical Soc.*, 1+, Edin. 1954+; and in the local js. listed under local hist. below.

**9805 HANHAM (HAROLD JOHN).** Scottish nationalism. Lond. & Camb., Mass. 1969.

See also Coupland, *Welsh and Scottish nationalism* (**9600**) and James Nathaniel Wolfe, ed., *Government and nationalism in Scotland: an enquiry by members of the University of Edinburgh*, Edin. 1969.

**9806 PRYDE (GEORGE SMITH).** Central and local government in Scotland since 1707. Hist. Assoc. 1960.

A brief intro. To be suppl. by Malcolm Ronald McLarty and George Campbell Henderson Paton, eds., *A source book and history of administrative law in Scotland*, Edin. etc. 1956; Day (**10188**) on the Highlands; Atkinson (**10165**) on local government; and Sir Francis James Grant, *Court of the Lord Lyon: list of His Majesty's officers of arms and other officials . . ., 1318–1945*, Scottish Record Soc. lxxvii, pt. cxlviii, Edin. 1946.

**9807 HANHAM (HAROLD JOHN).** 'The creation of the Scottish office, 1881–87'. *Juridical Rev.* new ser. x (1965), 205–44.

The story of the office is cont. in Sir David Milne, *The Scottish office and other Scottish government departments*, New Whitehall series, 1957, and in Wolfe (**9805**). For its initial functions see William Charles Smith, *The Secretary for Scotland: being a statement of the powers and duties of the new Scottish office . . .*, Edin. 1885.

**9808 SCOTCH OFFICES INQUIRY COMMISSION.** Report of the commissioners appointed by the Lords Commissioners of Her Majesty's Treasury to inquire into certain civil departments in Scotland [Chairman: Earl of Camperdown]. [C. 64]. H.C. (1870). XVIII, 1.

A report on government offices in Edinburgh. Later information is incl. in the reports of the Ridley and MacDonnell commissions (**395–6**), *Committee on Scottish administration* [Chairman: Sir John Gilmour]: *report*. [Cmd. 5563]. H.C. (1936–7). XV, 633, and *Royal commission on Scottish affairs, 1952–1954* [Chairman: Earl of Balfour]: *report*. [Cmd. 9212]. H.C. (1953–4). XIX, 1.

**9809 FERGUSSON (*Sir* JAMES).** The sixteen peers of Scotland: an account of the elections of the representative peers of Scotland, 1707–1959. Oxf. 1960.

**9810 NICOLSON (JAMES BADENACH).** A practical treatise on the law of parliamentary elections in Scotland, including the election of representative peers and members of parliament, and the registration of voters in counties and burghs. Edin. & Lond. 1865. 2nd edn. 1879.

Cont. in his *Analysis of recent statutes affecting parliamentary elections in Scotland*, Edin. & Lond. 1885. For other election manuals see **9816**.

**9811 BOUNDARY COMMISSION, 1885.** Report of the boundary commissioners for Scotland, 1885 [Chairman: John Lambert]. [C. 4288] H.C. (1884–5). XIX, 677.

**9812 FOSTER (JOSEPH).** Members of parliament, Scotland: including the minor barons, the commissioners for the shires, and the commissioners for the burghs, 1357–1882, on the basis of the parliamentary return 1880, with genealogical and biographical notes. Priv. pr. 1882. 2nd edn. 1882.

For election results see the general lists at **636** and T. Wilkie, *The representation of*

Scotland: parliamentary elections since 1832 . . ., Paisley etc. 1895. For local members see Alistair Norwich Tayler and Helen Agnes Henrietta Tayler, *Morayshire M.P.s since the Act of Union*, Elgin 1930.

**9813   McLAREN.** The life and work of Duncan McLaren. By John Beveridge Mackie. 2 v. 1888.

A leading Edinburgh Radical from the 1840s to the 1880s. Cp. Charles Cowan, *Reminiscences*, priv. pr. 1878.

**9814   LOWE.** Souvenirs of Scottish labour. By David Lowe. Glasgow. 1919.

Most Labour reminiscences are weak on events before 1914, as is Robert Keith Middlemas, *The Clydesiders: a left-wing struggle for parliamentary power*, 1965. But there is a little in William Martin Haddow, *My seventy years*, Glasgow 1943, Thomas Johnston, *Memories*, 1952, David Kirkwood, Baron Kirkwood, *My life of revolt*, 1935, and the lives of Keir Hardie (**623**).

## B. LAW

### 1. GENERAL

**9815   [McKECHNIE (HECTOR) *ed*.]** An introductory survey of the sources and literature of Scots law. Stair Soc. 1. Edin. 1936. Index by James Cowie Brown. Edin. 1939.

**9816   MAXWELL (LESLIE F.)** *and* **MAXWELL (WILLIAM HAROLD). *comps*.** A legal bibliography of the British Commonwealth of Nations. Vol. V. Scottish law . . . 2nd edn. 1957.

**9817   [PATON (GEORGE CAMPBELL HENDERSON) *ed*.]** An introduction to Scottish legal history. Stair Soc. 10. Edin. 1958.

**9818   COOPER (THOMAS MACKAY), *Lord Cooper*.** The Scottish legal tradition. Saltire Soc. 1949.

Repr. in his *Selected papers, 1922–54*, ed. by James Murray Cooper, 1957.

**9819   SMITH (THOMAS BROUN).** Scotland: the development of its laws and constitution. 1962.

First publ. in George W. Keeton, ed., *The British Commonwealth: the development of its laws and constitutions*, vol. I, 1955. See also Smith's *The doctrines of judicial precedent in Scots law*, Edin. 1952, and *British justice: the Scottish contribution*, 1961.

**9820   BELL (GEORGE JOSEPH).** Principles of the law of Scotland . . . 4th edn. Edin. 1839. 10th edn. 1899.

Bell's *Commentaries on the laws of Scotland . . .*, 5th edn. 2 v. Edin. 1826, 7th edn. 2 v. 1870, was also important. See also John Erskine, *The principles of the law of Scotland . . .*, Edin. 1754, 21st edn. Edin. 1911.

**9821   BELL (WILLIAM).** A dictionary and digest of the law of Scotland: with short explanations of the most ordinary English law terms. Edin. 1838. 7th edn. 1890.

**9822** ENCYCLOPAEDIA OF THE LAWS OF SCOTLAND. 14 v. Edin. 1896–1904. 3rd edn. 16 v. 1926–35.

**9823** THE SCOTS STATUTES REVISED: the public general statutes affecting Scotland, 1707[–1900]. 10 v. 1899–1902.

Cont. as *The Scots statutes, 1901[–22+]*. Edin. 1902–23+.

**9824** THE PUBLIC GENERAL STATUTES AFFECTING SCOTLAND from the beginning of the first parliament of Great Britain . . . [1707–1847.] 3 v. Edin. 1876. Annual vols. 1848+.

**9825** THE SCOTS DIGEST of appeals in the House of Lords from 1707 and of the cases decided in the supreme courts of Scotland, 1800–1873. 1 ser. 4 v. Edin. 1908–12. 2 ser. [1873–1904.] 2 v. Edin. 1905. 3 ser. [1905–15.] Edin. 1915. In progress.

Consult also 'The Faculty digest' of the Faculty of Advocates, publ. as *An analytical digest of cases decided in the supreme courts of Scotland and on appeal in the House of Lords, 1868 to 1922*, 6 v. Edin. 1924–6. Suppl. in progress.

**9826** THE SCOTTISH LAW LIST. Edin. 1848+.

Became *Index juridicus: the Scottish law list and directory*, in 1852: later titles vary. *The parliament house book*, Edin. 1870+, and *The Scottish law directory*, Edin. 1891+, are also legal directories.

**9827** THE JURIDICAL REVIEW: a journal of legal and political science. Edin. 1889+.

The main source for comment on Scottish and comparative law. See also *Journal of jurisprudence and Scottish law magazine*, 35 v. Edin. 1857–91; *The Scottish jurist [Reports of cases]* 46 v. Edin. 1829–73; *The Scottish law review and reports of cases in the sheriff courts*, Glasgow 1885+; with *Index* for 1885–1934, Edin. 1936; *The Scots law times*, Edin. 1893+; and *Scottish law journal and sheriff court record*, Glasgow 1858–61, cont. as *Scottish law magazine*, Glasgow 1862–7.

**9828** TOD (THOMAS MILLAR). The Scots black kalendar: a record of criminal trials and executions in Scotland, 1800–1910. Perth. 1938.

Murder cases. There are fuller reports of a few cases in the works of William Roughead, notably in his *Twelve Scots trials*, Edin. 1913.

## 2. THE ADMINISTRATION OF JUSTICE

**9829** OMOND (GEORGE WILLIAM THOMAS). The Lord advocates of Scotland: second series, 1834–1880. 1914.

Important for Scottish law and administration.

**9830** WILLOCK (IAN DOUGLAS). The origins and development of the jury in Scotland. Stair Soc. 23. Edin. 1966.

**9831** GIBB (ANDREW DEWAR). Law from over the border: a short account of a strange jurisdiction. Edin. 1950.

A nationalist attack on the subordination of the Scottish courts to the House of Lords.

9832 GRANT (*Sir* FRANCIS JAMES). The Faculty of Advocates in Scotland, 1532–1943, with genealogical notes. Scottish Record Soc. lxxvi, pt. cxlv. Edin. 1944.

A list of advocates. See also Alexander Arthur Grainger Stewart, *Portraits in the hall of the Parliament House in Edinburgh: with introduction and biographical notes*, Edin. 1907.

9833 THE SOCIETY OF WRITERS TO HIS MAJESTY'S SIGNET: with a list of members and abstracts of the minutes of the Society, the commissioners and the council, and the early history of the Scottish signet. Edin. 1936.

Replaced *A history of the Society of Writers to Her Majesty's Signet* . . ., Edin. 1890.

9834 HENDERSON (JOHN ALEXANDER) *ed.* History of the Society of Advocates in Aberdeen. New Spalding Club. xl. Aberdeen. 1912. Suppl. by Norman J. J. Walker. Aberdeen. 1939.

9835 BEGG (JOHN HENDERSON). A treatise on the law of Scotland relating to law agents . . . Edin. 1873. 2nd edn. 1883.

Includes a short hist. The Incorporated Soc. of Law Agents has publ. a report since 1885.

9836 COCKBURN. Journal of Henry Cockburn: being, a continuation of the memorials of his time, 1831–1854. 2 v. Edin. 1874.

Cockburn was the most literary of Scottish judges in the period, but his writings are scarcer after 1850. See also *Circuit journeys, by the late Lord Cockburn*, Edin. 1888, and *Letters chiefly connected with the affairs of Scotland from Henry Cockburn . . . to Thomas Francis Kennedy, M.P. . . . with other letters from eminent persons during the same period, 1818–1852*, 1874.

9837 INGLIS. John Inglis, Lord Justice-General of Scotland: a memoir. By James Crabb Watt. Edin. 1893.

Inglis was a great public figure and one of the most influential men of his day.

9838 GUTHRIE. Lord Guthrie: a memoir. By Robert Low Orr. 1923.

Legal adviser to the Free Church.

9839 ARDWALL. Andrew Jameson, Lord Ardwall. By John Buchan, Baron Tweedsmuir. Edin. & Lond. 1913.

Well-written and perceptive.

9840 MACMILLAN. A man of law's tale: the reminiscences of the Rt. Hon. Lord Macmillan. By Hugh Pattison Macmillan, Baron Macmillan. 1952.

Interesting on the Scottish Bar. There is relatively little legal matter in the other 20th cent. legal autobiogs., but the following are worth reading for general background: Archibald Crawford, *Guilty as libelled!*, 1938; Sir John Hay Athol Macdonald, Lord Kingsburgh, *Life jottings of an old Edinburgh citizen*, 1915; Lachlan McKinnon, *Recollections of an old lawyer*, Aberdeen 1935; *Memoirs of Lord Salvesen*, ed. by Harold Frederic Andorsen 1949; John Hay Shennan, *A judicial maid-of-all-work*, Edin. & Glasgow 1933; Charles Stewart, *Haud immemor: reminiscences of legal and social life in*

*Edinburgh and London, 1850–1900,* Edin. & Lond. 1901; and Thomas Shaw, Baron Shaw of Dunfermline, later Baron Craigmyle, *Letters to Isabel,* 1921, new edn. 1936, cont. in *The other bundle,* 1927.

9841 COLONSAY COMMISSION ON SCOTTISH COURTS. First report of the commissioners appointed to inquire into the courts of law in Scotland [Chairman: Lord Colonsay]. [4125] H.C. (1868–9). XXV, 29. Second report. [4188] H.C. (1868–9). XXV, 423. Third report. [C. 36] H.C. (1870). XVIII, 239. Fourth report. [C. 175] H.C. (1870). XVIII, 455. Appendix to fifth report. [C. 175–I] H.C. (1870). XVIII, 511. Fifth report. [C. 260] H.C. (1871). XX, 257.

A thorough survey and an important source.

9842 CLYDE COMMISSION ON THE COURT OF SESSION &c. Report of the royal commission on the court of session and the office of sheriff princi- pal ... [Chairman: Lord Clyde.] [Cmd. 2801] H.C. (1927). VIII, 1. Summary of evidence not publ.

There is some additional material on the sheriff courts in *Report of the departmental committee on sheriff court procedure* [Chairmen: Andrew Graham Murray and Charles Scott Dickson]. [Cd. 2287] H.C. (1905). LXIV, 451. The *Sixth Report* of the McDon- nell commission (**396**) and *Departmental committee on minor legal appointments in Scot- land: report of the committee appointed by the Secretary for Scotland* [Chairman: Lord Salvesen]. [Cd. 5602] H.C. (1911). XXXV, 665, *Minutes of evidence.* [Cd. 5603] H.C. (1911). XXXV, 693, also deal with the staffing of the Scottish courts.

## C. THE CHURCHES

### 1. GENERAL

9843 MACGREGOR (MALCOLM BLAIR). The sources and literature of Scottish church history. Glasgow. 1934.

Poor for the period.

9844 SCOTTISH CHURCH HISTORY SOCIETY. Records of the Church of Scotland preserved in the Scottish Record Office and General Register Office, Register House, Edinburgh. *Scot. Church Hist. Soc. Records.* Appen- dix to vol. xvi. Glasgow. 1967. Also publ. as Scottish Record Soc. xciv. 1967.

A preliminary list incl. records of the churches reunited with the Church of Scotland in 1929. For the records of the United Presbyterian Church transferred to the United Free Church and thence to the Church of Scotland see *Scot. Church Hist. Soc. Records* i (1925–6), 88–93.

9845 SCOTTISH CHURCH HISTORY SOCIETY. Records. 1+. Edin. etc. 1923–4+.

A general periodical on Scottish church hist. Covers all denominations. For Catholics see also *Innes Rev.* (**9930**).

9846 THE SCOTTISH CHURCH AND UNIVERSITY ALMANAC, 1880+. Edin. 1881+.

Lists the clergy of all denominations.

9847  BURLEIGH (JOHN HENDERSON SEAFORTH). A church history
of Scotland. 1960.

The best gen. hist. of the Presbyterian churches. See also Donald Macmillan, *Representative men of the Scottish church*, Edin. 1928. There are no good studies of church
doctrine and discipline, but see John Macleod, *Scottish theology in relation to church
history since the Reformation*, Edin. 1943, which is a partisan evangelical statement,
George Bain Burnet, *The holy communion in the reformed Church of Scotland, 1560–
1960*, Edin. 1960, and Ivo MacNaughton Clark, *A history of church discipline in Scotland*,
Aberdeen 1929. There are no specialized studies of late 19th-cent. church architecture,
but much of value is incl. in George Hay, *The architecture of Scottish post-reformation
churches, 1560–1843*, Oxf. 1957, and David MacGibbon and Thomas Ross, *The ecclesiastical architecture of Scotland from the earliest Christian times to the seventeenth century*,
3 v. Edin. 1896–7.

9848  FLEMING (JOHN ROBERT). A history of the church in Scotland,
1843–[1929]. 2 v. Edin. 1927–33.

The fullest account of the period, but needs revision. For disestablishment as a political
issue see Kellas's article at **9800**.

9849  SJÖLINDER (ROLF). Presbyterian reunion in Scotland, 1907–1921:
its background and development. Trans. by Eric J. Sharpe. Stockholm etc.
1962.

Good, with full bibliog. Largely replaces John Robert Fleming, *The story of church union
in Scotland: its origins and progress, 1560–1929* [1929].

9850  MECHIE (STEWART). The church and Scottish social development,
1780–1870. 1960.

Chiefly on the Church of Scotland and Free Church, but too brief to do more than open
up the subject. See also Lewis Legertwood Legg Cameron, *The challenge of need: a
history of social service by the Church of Scotland, 1869–1969*, Edin. 1971.

9851  MECHIE (STEWART). 'Education for the ministry in Scotland since
the Reformation'. *Scot. Church Hist. Soc. Records* xiv (1960–2), 115–33, 161–
78; xv (1963–5), 1–20.

See also Henry Martyn Beckwith Reid, *The divinity professors in the university of
Glasgow, 1640–1903*, Glasgow 1923, Gordon Quig, 'The divinity staff at Glasgow
university in 1903', *Scot. Church Hist. Soc. Records* iii (1929), 210–19, and the histories
of New College and Trinity College (**9893**).

9852  PATRICK (MILLAR). Four centuries of Scottish psalmody. Oxf. 1949.

See also James Love, *Scottish church music: its composers and sources*, Edin. & Lond.
1891.

9853  CENSUS OF GREAT BRITAIN, 1851. Religious worship and education: Scotland: reports and tables. [1764] H.C. (1854). LIX, 301.

9854  MACLAREN (A. ALLAN). 'Presbyterianism and the working class in
a mid-nineteenth century city [Aberdeen]'. *Scot. Hist. Rev.* xlvi (1967), 115–39.

Uses local records to suppl. the 1851 census.

9855 HOWIE (ROBERT). The churches and the churchless in Scotland: facts and figures. Glasgow. 1893.

See also William Simpson, *Facts and fictions concerning the Church of Scotland: being a critique of the Rev. Robert Howie's volume* . . ., Glasgow [1895].

9856 BRACKENRIDGE (R. DOUGLAS). 'The "Sabbath War" of 1865–66: the shaking of the foundations'. *Scot. Church Hist. Soc. Records* xvi (1966–8), 23–34.

The battle over the running of trains on Sunday.

9857 STANLEY (ARTHUR PENRHYN). Lectures on the history of the Church of Scotland, delivered in Edinburgh in 1872. 1872. 2nd edn. 1879.

An intelligent outsider's view of the Church, which aroused great controversy, for which see Robert Rainy, *Three lectures on the Church of Scotland, with especial reference to the Dean of Westminster's recent course* . . ., Edin. 1872.

9858 DIBELIUS (OTTO), *Bishop*. Das kirchliche Leben Schottlands. Studien zur praktischen Theologie. V. Pt. 2. Giessen. 1911.

9859 COUPER (WILLIAM JAMES). Scottish revivals. Dundee. 1918.

9860 HEWAT (ELIZABETH GLENDINNING KIRKWOOD). Vision and achievement, 1796–1956: a history of the foreign missions of the churches united in the Church of Scotland. 1960.

See also Albert Glenthorn Mackinnon, *Beyond the Alps: the story of the Scottish church in Italy and Malta*, Edin. [1937]; John McKerrow, *History of the foreign missions of the Secession and United Presbyterian Church*, Edin. 1867; Robert Hunter, *History of the missions of the Free Church of Scotland in India and Africa*, 1873; James Horne Morrison, *The Scottish churches' work abroad*, Edin. 1927, and *On the trails of the pioneers: a sketch of the missions of the United Free Church of Scotland*, 1913; David McDougall, *In search of Israel: a chronicle of the Jewish missions of the Church of Scotland*, 1941; and **3412–42**.

9861 SCOTTISH INSTITUTE OF MISSIONARY STUDIES. Bulletin. 1+. Edin. 1967+.

9862 LEADING ECCLESIASTICAL CASES decided in the Court of Session, 1849–1874. Edin. 1878.

A useful coll. See also A. Mitchell Hunter, 'The Cardross case', *Scot. Church Hist. Soc. Records* vii (1939–41), 247–58.

9863 INNES (ALEXANDER TAYLOR). The law of creeds in Scotland: a treatise on the legal relation of the churches in Scotland, established and not established, to their doctrinal confessions. Edin. & Lond. 1867. New edn. 1902.

## 2. The Church of Scotland

9864 THE PRINCIPALL ACTS OF THE SOLEMNE GENERALL ASSEMBLY of the kirk of Scotland. 1638+. Edin. 1639+.

Title varies. Annual from 1841.

9865 REPORTS ON THE SCHEMES OF THE CHURCH of Scotland. Edin. 1866–1930.

Gives details of the work of the General Assembly and its committees. For other debates in the Church see *Church congress held by order of the General Assembly: official report of the proceedings*, Edin. 1899+. The official j. of the Church is *Life and work: a parish magazine published under the supervision of a committee of the General Assembly of the Church of Scotland*, 1+, Edin. 1879+, which absorbed *The home and foreign missionary record* [*The Church of Scotland home and foreign missionary record*], 1839–1900. *Good words: a weekly magazine*, Edin. 1860–1911, was also closely assoc. with the Church.

9866 YEAR BOOK OF THE CHURCH OF SCOTLAND. 1+. Edin. 1886+.

Title *The book of the Church . . .*, 1889–99, *The Church of Scotland year-book*, 1900+. See also *The layman's book of the General Assembly, issued under the auspices of the Elders' Union of the Church of Scotland*, Edin. 1907+.

9867 SCOTT (HEW) *comp*. Fasti ecclesiae scoticanae: the succession of ministers in the Church of Scotland from the Reformation. Rev. edn. 8 v. Edin. 1914–50.

9868 HENDERSON (GEORGE DAVID). The claims of the Church of Scotland. 1951.

9869 MAXWELL (WILLIAM DELBERT). A history of worship in the Church of Scotland. 1955.

9870 HENDERSON (GEORGE DAVID). The Scottish ruling elder. [1935.]

9871 MECHIE (STEWART). The office of Lord High Commissioner. Edin. 1957.

9872 STORY (ROBERT HERBERT) *ed*. The Church of Scotland, past and present: its history, its relation to the law and the state, its doctrine, ritual, discipline and patrimony. 5 v. [1890–1.]

9873 MACGREGOR (MALCOLM BLAIR). Towards Scotland's social good: a hundred years of temperance work in the Church of Scotland. Edin. [*c*. 1950.]

9874 MAIR (WILLIAM). A digest of laws and decisions, ecclesiastical and civil, relating to the constitution, practice and affairs of the Church of Scotland. Edin. & Lond. 1887. 4th edn. 1923.

See also *The constitution and law of the Church of Scotland, by a member of the College of Justice*, Edin. 1884, new edn. 1886, William George Black, *A handbook of the parochial ecclesiastical law of Scotland*, Edin. 1888, 4th edn. 1928, and John Morison Duncan, *Treatise on the parochial ecclesiastical law of Scotland*, Edin. 1864, 3rd edn. 1903.

9875 CAIRD. Principal Caird. By Sir Charles Laing Warr. 1926.

For John Caird's views on a variety of subjects see his *University addresses . . .*, ed. by Edward Caird, Glasgow 1898, and *University sermons . . . 1873–1898*, Glasgow 1898.

9876 CHARTERIS. The life of Archibald Hamilton Charteris, D.D., LL.D. By the Hon. Arthur Gordon. 1912.

See also Kenneth D. MacLaren, *Memoir of the Reverend Professor Charteris . . .*, Lond. & Edin. 1914.

9877 COOPER. James Cooper . . . a memoir. By Henry Johnstone Wotherspoon. 1926.

9878 FLINT. The life of Robert Flint, D.D., LL.D. By Donald MacMillan. 1914.

9879 LEE. Life and remains of Robert Lee, D.D. . . By Robert Herbert Story. 2 v. 1870.

9880 LEES. The life of James Cameron Lees . . . By Norman Maclean. Glasgow. 1922.

9881 MACGREGOR. Life and letters of the Rev. James MacGregor, D.D. By Lady Frances Balfour. 1912.

9882 MACLEOD. Memorials of the Rev. Norman MacLeod (Senr.), D.D., Minister of St. Columba's church, Glasgow. By John N. MacLeod. Edin. 1898.

9883 MACLEOD. Memoir of Norman Macleod, D.D., minister of Barony parish, Glasgow, one of Her Majesty's chaplains . . . By Donald MacLeod. 2 v. 1876. 2nd edn. 1877.

9884 ROBERTSON. Life of the Rev. James Robertson. By Archibald Hamilton Charteris. Edin. & Lond. 1863.

9885 SCOTT. Dr. Archibald Scott of St George's, Edinburgh, and his times. By Christopher Nicholson Johnston, Lord Sands. Edin. & Lond. 1919.

STORY see **10135.**

9886 TULLOCH. A memoir of the life of John Tulloch. By Mrs. Margaret Oliphant Oliphant. Edin. 1888.

9887 WHITE. John White, C.H., D.D., LL.D. By Augustus Muir. 1958.

A leader of the ecumenical movement.

9888 WILLIAMSON. Life of Andrew Wallace Williamson, K.C.V.O., D.D. By Christopher Nicholson Johnston, Lord Sands. Edin. & Lond. 1929.

### 3. THE FREE CHURCH OF SCOTLAND

9889 FREE CHURCH OF SCOTLAND. Principal acts of the General Assembly. 1843+. Edin. 1851+.

Suppl. by *Assembly papers*, 1845–93, and *Assembly proceedings and debates*, 1843+. The official j. of the Church was *The home and foreign missionary record*, Edin. 1843+, whose title became *The home and foreign record* . . ., 1850–6, *The Free Church of Scotland weekly record*, 1861–2, *The Free Church of Scotland monthly* . . . [*record*], 1862–1900, and *The monthly record of the Free Church of Scotland*, 1900+. The most influential j. publ. in connection with the Church was Hugh Miller's *The witness*, Edin. 1840–64.

9890  EWING (WILLIAM) *ed.* Annals of the Free Church of Scotland, 1843–1900. 2 v. Edin. 1914.

Lists of ministers.

9891  WALKER (NORMAN LOCKHART). Chapters from the history of the Free Church of Scotland. Edin. and Lond. [1895.]

The 'official' hist. See also Robert Buchanan, 'Finance of the Free Church of Scotland', *Stat. Soc. J.* xxxiii (1870), 74–110.

9892  STEWART (ALEXANDER) *and* CAMERON (JOHN KENNEDY). The Free Church of Scotland, 1843–1910: a vindication. Edin. and Glasgow 1911.

A good hist. written for those who did not joint the United Free Church in 1900. Cameron also publ. *Scottish church union of 1900: reminiscences and reflections*, Inverness 1923, and *The clerkship of the General Assembly of the Free Church of Scotland*, Inverness 1938.

9893  WATT (HUGH). New College, Edinburgh: a centenary history. Edin. & Lond. 1946.

The chief Free Church college. For its Glasgow counterpart see Stewart Mechie, *Trinity College, Glasgow, 1856–1956* . . ., Glasgow 1956.

9894  MONCREIFF (*Sir* HENRY WELLWOOD). The Free Church principle: its character and history. Edin. 1883.

A clear statement of the Free Church position. Cp. Peter Bayne, *The Free Church of Scotland: her origin, founders and testimony*, Edin. 1893, 2nd edn. 1894.

9895  RAINY (ROBERT) *and others.* Church and state, chiefly in relation to Scotland. 1878.

An authoritative Free Church statement on the establishment.

9896  MONCREIFF (*Sir* HENRY WELLWOOD). The practice of the Free Church of Scotland in her several courts . . . Edin. 1871. 4th edn. 1886.

9897  ORR (ROBERT LOW) *ed.* The Free Church of Scotland appeals, 1903–1904: authorised report. Edin. & Lond. 1904.

9898  ELGIN COMMISSION ON THE PROPERTY OF THE FREE CHURCH. Report of the royal commission on churches (Scotland) [Chairman: the Earl of Elgin]. [Cd. 2494] H.C. (1905). XXIII, 113. Evidence etc. [Cd. 2495] H.C. (1905). XXIII, 139.

The commission was brought into being because of the dispute over the ownership of the property of the Free Church after its union with the United Presbyterian Church. For the subsequent allocation see *Report of the royal commissioners appointed under the Churches (Scotland) Act, 1905* [Chairman: the Earl of Elgin]. [Cd. 5060] H.C. (1910). XIII, 343; Proceedings etc. [Cd. 5061] H.C. (1910). XIII, 355.

9899 BEGG. Memoirs of James Begg, D.D., minister of Newington Free Church, Edinburgh. By Thomas Smith. 2 v. Edin. 1885–8.

9900 BONAR. Andrew A. Bonar, D.D. Diary and letters. Ed. by Marjory Bonar. 1894. Popular edn. 1910. New edn. 1961.

See also *Reminiscences of Andrew A. Bonar, D.D.*, ed. by Marjory Bonar, 1895, and, for his brother, *Horatius Bonar, D.D.: a memorial*, 1889.

9901 BUCHANAN. Robert Buchanan, D.D.: an ecclesiastical biography. By Norman Lockhart Walker, 1877.

9902 CANDLISH. Memorials of Robert Smith Candlish, D.D. By William Wilson. Edin. 1880.

9903 CUNNINGHAM. Life of William Cunningham, D.D. By Robert Rainy and James Mackenzie. Edin. & Lond. 1871.

9904 DODS. Early letters of Marcus Dods, D.D., late Principal of New College, Edinburgh, 1850–1864. Ed. by Marcus Dods, 1911.

Suppl. by *Later letters . . ., 1895–1909*, 1911. For other college principals see William Garden Blaikie, *David Brown, D.D., LL.D.: Professor and Principal of the Free Church College, Aberdeen*, 1898, Sir William Robertson Nicoll and James Alexander Robertson, eds., *Letters of Principal James Denney to W. Robertson Nicoll, 1893–1917*, 1920, James Moffatt, ed., *Letters of Principal James Denney to his family and friends*, 1922, and the lives of Cunningham, **9903**, Rainy, **9911**, and Whyte, **9913**.

9905 DRUMMOND. The life of Henry Drummond. By Sir George Adam Smith. 1899.

9906 DUNCAN. Life of the late John Duncan, LL.D. By David Brown. Edin. 1872. 2nd. edn. 1872.

See also William Angus Knight, comp., *Colloquia peripatetica* [(*deep-sea soundings*): *being notes of conversations by the late John Duncan with William Knight*], Edin. 1870, 6th edn. 1907. Duncan was the acknowledged 'saint' of the Free Church.

9907 GUTHRIE. Autobiography of Thomas Guthrie, and memoir by his sons, D. K. Guthrie and C. J. Guthrie. 2 v. Edin. 1874–5.

9908 INNES. Chapters of reminiscence. By Alexander Taylor Innes. 1913.

9909 KENNEDY. Life of John Kennedy, D.D. by Alexander Auld. 1887.

The greatest Highland preacher, *c.* 1850–80, and associate of Spurgeon. For other Highland ministers of note see William Keith Leask, *Dr. Thomas M'Lauchlan*, Edin. & Lond. 1905, Alexander MacRae, *The Life of Gustavus Aird, A.M., D.D., Creich, moderator of the Free Church of Scotland, 1888*, Stirling n.d., John Maclean, ed., *Donald Munro of Ferintosh and Rogart: a memorial volume*, 1939, Archibald Auld, *Memorials of Caithness ministers: being memoirs and sermons of Rev. W. Ross Taylor, D.D., Thurso, and Rev. Alexander Auld, Olrig, with brief notices of some of their co-presbyters*, Edin., 1911, John Macaskill, ed., *A Highland pulpit: being sermons of the late Rev. Murdoch Macaskill, with a biographical sketch*, Inverness, 1907, Alexander Mackenzie, *The Rev. John Mackay, M.A.: student, pastor, General Assembly's Highland evangelist*, Paisley 1921, and George Norman Macleod Collins, *Donald Maclean, D.D.*, Edin. 1944, and *John Macleod, D.D.*, Edin. 1951.

9910  MILLER. The life and letters of Hugh Miller. By Peter Bayne. 2 v. 1871.

Miller was the leading lay protagonist of the Free Church as editor of *The witness*. There are several collected edns. of his works.

9911  RAINY. The life of Principal Rainy. By Patrick Carnegie Simpson. 2 v. 1909. Popular edn. 1 v. n.d.

9912  ROBERTSON SMITH. The life of William Robertson Smith. By John Sutherland Black and George Chrystal. 1912.

Suppl. by their edn. of *Lectures & essays of William Robertson Smith*, 1912. Robertson Smith was the centre of conflict in the Free Church over the application of German philological scholarship to the Bible. He later became professor of Arabic at Cambridge. For his teacher see James Strahan, *Andrew Bruce Davidson, D.D., LL.D., D. Litt.*, 1917.

9913  WHYTE. The life of Alexander Whyte, D.D. By George Freeland Barbour. 1923.

### 4. The United Presbyterian Church

9914  UNITED PRESBYTERIAN CHURCH. Proceedings of the synod. Edin. 1848–1900.

The U.P. Church also publ. a *Missionary record*, 3 ser. 48 v. Edin. 1846–1900, and *The United Presbyterian magazine*, 1847–1900, cont. as *The Union magazine . . .*, 1901–4.

9915  BLAIR (WILLIAM). The United Presbyterian Church: a handbook of its history and principles. Edin. 1888.

See also Joseph H. Leckie, *Secession memories: the United Presbyterian contribution to the Scottish church*, Edin. 1926, and David Woodside, *The soul of a Scottish church: or, the contribution of the United Presbyterian church to Scottish life and religion*, Edin. [1918.]

9916  SMALL (ROBERT). History of the congregations of the United Presbyterian Church from 1733 to 1900. 2 v. Edin. 1904.

Intended to be a U.P. equiv. of Scott (**9867**), only rather fuller.

9917  CAIRNS. David Cairns: an autobiography. [By David Smith Cairns.] Some recollections of a long life and selected letters. Ed. by D. and Alison H. Cairns, with a memoir by D. M. Baillie. 1950.

9918  CAIRNS. Life and letters of John Cairns, D.D., LL.D. By Alexander Robertson MacEwen. 1895. 4th edn. 1898.

9919  CALDERWOOD. The life of Henry Calderwood, LL.D., F.R.S.E. . . . By William Leadbetter Calderwood and David Woodside. 1900.

9920  FERGUSON. Fergus Ferguson, D.D.: his theology and heresy trial: a chapter in Scottish church history. By Joseph H. Leckie. Edin. 1923.

9921 HUTTON. Life of George Clark Hutton, principal of the United Presbyterian College. By Alexander Oliver. Paisley. 1910.

9922 MACEWEN. Life and times of Alexander Robertson MacEwen, professor of church history, New College, Edinburgh. By David Smith Cairns. 1925.

### 5. THE UNITED FREE CHURCH

9923 PRINCIPAL ACTS OF THE UNITED FREE CHURCH OF SCOTLAND. Edin. 1901–29.

The United Free Church also publ. *Reports to the General Assembly*, Edin. 1901–29, *Proceedings and debates of the General Assembly*, Edin. 1901–29, and *Missionary record . . .*, Edin. 1901–29.

9924 LAMB (JOHN ALEXANDER) *ed.* The fasti of the United Free Church of Scotland, 1900–1929. Edin. 1956.

A suppl. to Scott (**9867**) and Ewing (**9890**).

9925 REITH (GEORGE MURRAY). Reminiscences of the United Free Church General Assembly (1900–1929). Edin. & Lond. 1933.

9926 BARR (JAMES). The United Free Church of Scotland. 1934.

By a supporter of the minority which refused to enter the union with the Church of Scotland in 1929. See also his *The Scottish church question*, 1920.

9927 MANUAL OF PRACTICE and procedure in the United Free Church of Scotland, prepared by a committee of the General Assembly. Edin. 1905.

### 6. THE ROMAN CATHOLIC CHURCH

9928 ANSON (PETER FREDERICK). The Catholic Church in modern Scotland, 1560–1937. 1937.

A rev. edn. to 1878 was publ. as *Underground Catholicism in Scotland, 1622–1878*, Montrose 1970. There are a few 19th-cent. references in Frederick Odo Blundell, *The Catholic Highlands of Scotland*, 2 v. Edin. 1909–17. The other gen. hists. have little on the 19th cent. though there is much in Handley on *The Irish in modern Scotland* (**10052**).

9929 THE CATHOLIC DIRECTORY for the clergy & laity of Scotland. Glasgow. 1828+.

9930 THE INNES REVIEW: SCOTTISH CATHOLIC HISTORICAL STUDIES. 1+. Glasgow. 1950+.

A remarkably good j. which has done much to encourage Catholic hist. studs.

9931 McCLELLAND (VINCENT ALAN). 'The Irish clergy and Archbishop Manning's apostolic visitation of the western district of Scotland, 1867'. *Catholic Hist. Rev.* liii (1967–8), 1–27, 229–50.

Important for Hiberno-Scottish relations in the church. For docs. see James F. Walsh, 'Archbishop Manning's visitation of the western district of Scotland', *Innes Rev.* xviii (1967), 3–18.

9932　CHISHOLM. A Highland bishop: the Rt. Rev. Aeneas Chisholm . . . Bishop of Aberdeen: a character sketch. By Alice Mary Fraser, Baroness Lovat. Edin. 1927.

## 7. THE EPISCOPAL CHURCH

9933　LOCHHEAD (MARION). Episcopal Scotland in the nineteenth century. 1966.

Opens up an important subject in an interesting way. Better for the period than Frederick Goldie, *A short history of the Episcopal Church in Scotland from the Reformation to the present time*, 1951. There are some gossipy bits of information in A. K. H. Boyd's works (**10136**). The Church issued a *Yearbook*, 1892–1918.

9934　PERRY (WILLIAM). The Oxford movement in Scotland. Camb. 1933.

9935　PERRY (WILLIAM). Guide to the Scottish prayer book. Camb. 1941.

See also his *The Scottish prayer book: its value & history*, Camb. 1929, and *The Scottish liturgy: its value and history*, 1917.

9936　COWAN (IAN BORTHWICK) *and* ERVIN (SPENCER). The Scottish Episcopal Church: the ecclesiastical history and polity. Ambler, Pa. 1966.

9937　FARQUHAR (GEORGE TAYLOR SHILLITO). History of the lay claims under the Scottish bishops, 1789–1905 . . . Dumfries. 1911.

9938　FARQUHAR (GEORGE TAYLOR SHILLITO). The episcopal history of Perth, 1689–1894. Perth. 1894.

9939　CAMPBELL. The Rt. Rev. Archibald Ean Campbell, D.D., late Bishop of Glasgow and Galloway: a memoir by various authors. Ed. by George Taylor Shillito Farquhar. Edin. 1924.

9940　FORBES. Alexander Penrose Forbes, Bishop of Brechin: the Scottish Pusey. By William Perry. 1939.

There is also a good early life, Donald John Mackey, *Bishop Forbes: a memoir*, 1888.

9941　FORBES. George Hay Forbes: a romance in scholarship. By William Perry. 1927.

9942　WORDSWORTH. The episcopate of Charles Wordsworth, Bishop of St. Andrews, Dunkeld and Dunblane, 1853–1892: a memoir . . . By [Bishop] John Wordsworth. 1899.

Bishop Wordsworth himself wrote *Annals of my early life, 1806 to 1846*, 1891, and *Annals of my life, 1847 to 1856*, ed. by William Earl Hodgson, 1893.

## 8. OTHER CHURCHES

9943　ESCOTT (HARRY). A history of Scottish congregationalism. Glasgow. 1960.

Good. Includes lists of ministers and a full bibliog.

9944  YUILLE (GEORGE) *ed.* History of the Baptists in Scotland from pre-Reformation times. Glasgow. 1926.

See also Derek Boyd Murray, *The first hundred years: the Baptist Union of Scotland,* Glasgow 1969, and *The Scottish Baptist year-book,* 1903+, Glasgow 1903+.

9945  SCOTT (DAVID). Annals and statistics of the Original Secession Church, till its disruption and union with the Free Church of Scotland in 1852. Edin. 1886.

Cont. by A. Macwhirter, 'The last Anti-Burghers: a footnote to secession history', *Scot. Church Hist. Soc. Records* viii (1942–4), 254–91.

9946  DAVIDSON (FRANCIS) *ed.* History and doctrine of the United Original Secession Church of Scotland. Edin. 1924.

9947  HUTCHISON (MATTHEW). The Reformed Presbyterian Church in Scotland: its origin and history, 1680–1876. Paisley. 1893.

9948  COUPER (WILLIAM JAMES). The Reformed Presbyterian Church in Scotland: its congregations, ministers, and students. *Scot. Church Hist. Soc. Records* ii. Edin. 1925.

A substantial survey. The records of the Church are listed in *Scot. Church Hist. Soc. Records* iii (1929), 220–4.

9949  HISTORY OF THE FREE PRESBYTERIAN CHURCH OF SCOTLAND, 1893–1933: compiled by a committee appointed by the synod of the Free Presbyterian Church. Glasgow. 1933. Repr. Dingwall. 1965.

9950  MACWHIRTER (ARCHIBALD). 'Unitarianism in Scotland'. *Scot. Church Hist. Soc. Records* xiii (1957–9), 101–43.

9951  LEVY (ARNOLD). The Origins of Scottish Jewry. Glasgow. 1959.

See also Levy's *The origins of Glasgow Jewry (1812–1895),* Glasgow 1949, and Salis Daiches, 'The Jew in Scotland', *Scot. Church Hist. Soc. Records* iii (1929), 196–209.

9952  BURNET (GEORGE BAIN). The story of Quakerism in Scotland, 1650–1850, with an epilogue of the period 1850–1950 by William Hutton Marwick. 1952.


## D. ECONOMIC AND SOCIAL HISTORY

### 1. ECONOMIC HISTORY

#### (a) *General*

9953  MARWICK (WILLIAM HUTTON) *comp.* 'A bibliography of Scottish economic history'. *Econ. Hist. Rev.* iii (1931–2), 117–37. Suppls. 2 ser. iv (1951–2), 376–82; 2 ser. xvi (1963–4), 147–54; 2 ser. xxiv (1971), 469–79.

There is also a full 'Bibliography of Scottish business history' by Marwick in Payne (**9958**).

9954  CAMPBELL (ROY HUTCHESON) *and* DOW (JAMES B. A.) *eds.*
Source book of Scottish economic and social history. Oxf. 1969.

9955  CAMPBELL (ROY HUTCHESON). Scotland since 1707: the rise of an industrial society. Oxf. & N.Y. 1965.
Standard.

9956  CAIRNCROSS (*Sir* ALEXANDER KIRKLAND) *ed.* The Scottish economy: a statistical account of Scottish life by members of the staff of Glasgow University. Camb. 1954.
Chiefly on the mid-20th-cent., but with some retrospective data.

9957  MARWICK (WILLIAM HUTTON). Economic developments in Victorian Scotland. 1936.
A useful compendium of facts. More useful than his *Scotland in modern times: an outline of economic and social development since the Union of 1707*, 1964.

9958  PAYNE (PETER LESTER) *ed.* Studies in Scottish business history. 1967.
Includes a survey of archives and a full bibliog.

9959  CRAMMOND (EDGAR). 'The economic position of Scotland and her financial relations with England and Ireland'. *Stat. Soc. J.* lxxv (1911–12), 157–82.
See also **4455**.

(b) *Agriculture*

For the Highlands see **10187–232**.

9960  SYMON (JAMES ALEXANDER). Scottish farming past and present. Edin. & Lond. 1958.
Standard. Thomas Bedford Franklin, *A history of Scottish farming*, 1952, is a useful introductory sketch. For statistics see George Houston, 'Agricultural statistics in Scotland before 1866', *Agric. Hist. Rev.* ix (1961), 93–7, and Edith Holt Whetham, 'Prices and production in Scottish farming, 1850–1870', *Scot. J. Pol. Econ.* ix (1962), 233–43. There are some interesting comments in H. M. Jenkins, 'Report on some features of Scottish agriculture', *Roy. Agric. Soc. J.* 2 ser. vii (1871), 145–219. For farm labour see **10103–4**.

9961  SCOTLAND. OWNERS OF LAND AND HERITAGES ... 1872–73. Return . . . [C. 899] H.C. (1874). LXXII, pt. III, 1. Summary. H.C. 335 (1876). LXXX, 1.
The Scottish section of the 'New Domesday Book' (**4240**).

9962  BOARD [DEPARTMENT] OF AGRICULTURE FOR SCOTLAND. Annual report. 1912+. Edin. 1913+.
Publ. as a parl. paper.

9963 BOARD OF AGRICULTURE FOR SCOTLAND. Agricultural statistics. 1912+. Edin. 1913+.

For earlier statistics see *Report of the Highland and Agricultural Society of Scotland to the Board of Trade, on the agricultual statistics of Scotland for the year 1854.* [1876] H.C. (1854–5). XLVII, 637. Further report. H.C. 343 (1854–5). XLVII, 657, and the statistical ser. for Great Britain **4147–8, 4186–7.**

9964 [ROYAL] HIGHLAND AND AGRICULTURAL SOCIETY OF SCOTLAND. Transactions. Edin. 3 ser. I–II. 1843–65. 4 ser. I–20. 1866–88. 5 ser. I–67. 1889–1955. 6 ser. I+. 1966+.

Much the most important agric. periodical. But see also *The North British agriculturalist,* Edin. 1849–1931, *Scottish farmer and horticulturalist,* 1861–5 [subsequently *The farmer,* 1865–89, and *The farmer and stock-breeder,* 1889+], *The Scottish agricultural gazette,* Edin. 1885–7, then *Farming world,* 1887–97.

9965 WILSON (JAMES). 'Farming in Aberdeenshire: ancient and modern'. *Highland & Agric. Soc. Trans.* 5 ser. xiv (1902), 76–102.

For articles on other counties, see the following: Argyll by Duncan Clerk, *Highland & Agric. Soc. Trans.* 4 ser. x (1878), 1–105; Ayrshire by Archibald MacNeilage, ibid. 5 ser. xviii (1906), 1–17, and James Alexander Symon, ibid. 6 ser. ii (1958), 55–62; Banffshire by James R. Barclay, ibid. 5 ser. xx (1908), 155–81; Berwickshire and Roxburghshire by James Sanderson, ibid. 3 ser. x (1861–3), 333–71, 397–405; Bute and Arran by Archibald MacNeilage, ibid. 4 ser. xiii (1881), 1–52; Caithness by James Macdonald, ibid. 4 ser. vii (1875), 166–257; Clackmannan and Kinross by James Tait, ibid. 4 ser. xv (1883), 50–65; Dumbarton by John MacNeilage, ibid. 4 ser. xviii (1886), 1–69; East Lothian by Robert Scot Skirving, *Roy. Agric. Soc. J.* 2 ser. i (1865), 99–113, and *Highland & Agric. Soc. Trans.* 4 ser. v (1873), 1–48; Edinburgh and Linlithgow by Thomas Farrall, ibid. 4 ser. ix (1877), 1–66; Elgin and Nairn by Alexander Macdonald, ibid. 4 ser. xvi (1884), 1–123; Fife by James Macdonald, ibid. 4 ser. viii (1876), 1–60, and Andrew S. Grant, ibid. 5 ser. xxiv (1912), 249–76; Forfar and Kincardine by James Macdonald, ibid. 4 ser. xiii (1881), 53–173; Inverness-shire by William Macdonald, ibid. 4 ser. iv (1872), 1–65; Kirkcudbright and Wigtownshire by Thomas MacLelland, ibid. 4 ser. vii (1875), 1–69; Lanarkshire by James Tait, ibid. 4 ser. xvii (1885), 1–91, and Archibald MacNeilage, ibid. 5 ser. xix (1907), 161–76; Orkney by Robert Oliphant Pringle, ibid. 4 ser. vi (1874), 1–68, and Thomas Farrall, ibid. 4 ser. vi (1874), 68–99; Peeblesshire by Lawrence Anderson, ibid. 4 ser. iv (1872), 226–40; Perthshire by A. S. Grant, ibid. 5 ser. xvi (1904), 92–127; Renfrewshire by Alexander Macdonald, ibid. 4 ser. xix (1887), 1–110; Ross-shire by James Macdonald, ibid. 4 ser. ix (1877), 67–209, and (on forestry) W. F. Gunn, ibid. 4 ser. xvii (1885), 133–202; Selkirkshire by Alexander Macdonald, ibid. 4 ser. xviii (1886), 69–124; Shetland by Henry Evershed, ibid. 4 ser. vi (1874), 187–228, and Robert Scot Skirving, ibid. 4 ser. vi (1874), 229–63; Stirling by James Tait, ibid. 4 ser. xvi (1884), 143–79, and by John Drysdale, ibid. 5 ser. xxi (1909), 74–101; Sutherland by Charles Gay Roberts, *Roy. Agric. Soc. J.* 2 ser. x (1879), 397–487, and James Macdonald, *Highland & Agric. Soc. Trans.* 4 ser. xii (1880), 1–90; Wigtownshire by William H. Ralston, ibid. 4 ser. xvii (1885), 92–133.

9966 WILSON (JOHN) *ed.* Report of the present state of the agriculture of Scotland. Highland and Agricultural Society of Scotland. Edin. 1878.

9967 FARRAN (CHARLES D'OLIVIER). The principles of Scots and English land law: a historical comparison. Edin. 1958.

9968 BROWN (JOHN). 'Scottish and English land legislation, 1905–11'. *Scot. Hist. Rev.* xlvii (1968), 72–85.

9969   HORACE PLUNKETT FOUNDATION. Agricultural co-operation in Scotland and Wales: a survey. 1933.

9970   ANDERSON (MARK LOUDEN). A history of Scottish forestry. Ed. by Charles J. Taylor. 2 v. 1967.

See also the Scottish Arboricultural Soc., later [Royal] Scottish Forestry Soc., *Transactions*, 1+, Edin. 1858–1926, cont. as *The Scottish forestry j.* 1927–46, and *Scottish forestry*, 1947+, and Alexander Smith, 'On Aberdeenshire woods, forests and forestry', *Highland & Agric. Soc. Trans.* 4 ser. vi (1874), 264–303.

9971   COX (EUAN HILLHOUSE METHVEN). A history of gardening in Scotland. 1935.

9972   DIXON (HENRY HALL). Field and fern: or, Scottish flocks and herds. 2 v. ['North' and 'South'] 1865.

A journalist's report.

9973   M'COMBIE (WILLIAM). Cattle and cattle breeders. Edin. & Lond. 1867. 4th edn. 1886.

9974   GILLESPIE (JOHN). 'The cattle industry in Scotland'. *Highland & Agric. Soc. Trans.* 5 ser. x (1898), 234–59.

9975   SCOTTISH LAND ENQUIRY COMMITTEE. Scottish land: the report of the Scottish Land Enquiry Committee [Chairman: J. Ian Macpherson]. 1914.

A compendium of misc. information on the same lines as the English and Welsh reports (**4183, 9638**).

9976   HOPE. George Hope of Fenton Barns: a sketch of his life, comp. by his daughter, Charlotte Hope. Edin. 1881.

The best-known tenant farmer of his day.

9977   ROYAL COMMISSION ON HYPOTHEC. Report of Her Majesty's commissioners appointed to consider the law relating to the landlord's right of hypothec in Scotland, in so far as regards agricultural subjects [Chairman: Sir William Gibson-Craig]. [3546] H.C. (1865). XVII, 413. Minutes of evidence. [3546–I] H.C. (1865). XVII, 441.

See also *Report from the select committee of the House of Lords on the law of hypothec in Scotland* [Chairman: the Earl of Airlie]. H.C. 367. H.C. (1868–9). IX, 305. Appendix H.C. 367–I. (1868–9). IX, 575.

## (c) *Fisheries*

See also the general works at **5808–32** and those on the Highlands at **10201** and **10204**.

9978   FISHERY BOARD FOR SCOTLAND. Annual report. 1882–1938. Edin. 1883–1939.

Replaced the *Annual report* of the Fishery Board (Scotland), 1872–1881, Edin. 1873–82.

9979 ANSON (PETER FREDERICK). Fishing boats and fishing folk on the east coast of Scotland. 1930.

Suppl. by his *Scots fisherfolk*, Saltire Soc., Banff 1950.

9980 PLAYFAIR COMMISSION ON SCOTTISH HERRINGS. Report of the royal commission on the operation of the acts relating to trawling for herring on the coasts of Scotland [Chairman: Lyon Playfair]. [3106] H.C. (1863). XXVIII, 139. Evidence. [3106–I] H.C. (1863). XXVIII, 177.

9981 BUCKLAND (FRANCIS TREVELYAN) *and* YOUNG (ARCHIBALD). Report of the special commissioners appointed to enquire into the effect of recent legislation on the salmon fisheries in Scotland. [C. 419] H.C. (1871). XXV, 489.

9982 BUCKLAND (FRANCIS TREVELYAN), WALPOLE (SPENCER), *and* YOUNG (ARCHIBALD). Report on the herring fisheries of Scotland. [C. 1979] H.C. (1878). XXI, 233.

9983 SUTHERLAND COMMITTEE ON NORTH SEA FISHING. Report of the Scottish departmental committee on the North Sea fishing industry [Chairman: Angus Sutherland]. [Cd. 7221] H.C. (1914). XXXI, 533. Minutes of evidence. [Cd. 7462] H.C. (1914). XXXI, 773.

## (d) *Finance and Commerce*

9984 KERR (ANDREW WILLIAM). History of banking in Scotland. Glasgow. 1884. 4th edn. Lond. 1926.

See also James Simpson Fleming, *Scottish banking: a historical sketch*, 3rd edn. Edin. 1877; Charles Alexander Malcolm, *The Bank of Scotland, 1695–1945*, Edin. 1948, and *The history of the British Linen Bank*, priv. pr. Edin. 1950; Neil Munro, *The history of the Royal Bank of Scotland, 1727–1927*, Edin. 1928; Sir Robert Sangster Rait, *The history of the Union Bank of Scotland*, Glasgow 1930; James Macarthur Reid, *The history of the Clydesdale Bank, 1838–1938*, Glasgow 1938; James Lawson Anderson, *The story of the Commercial Bank of Scotland . . . from 1810 to 1910*, priv. pr. Edin. 1910; Alexander Keith, *The North of Scotland Bank Limited, 1836–1936*, Aberdeen 1936; and Commercial Bank of Scotland, *Our bank: the story of the Commercial Bank of Scotland Ltd., 1810–1941*, Edin. 1942. There are useful statistics in Andrew William Kerr, *Scottish banking during the period of published accounts, 1865–1896*, 1898, and Charles William Boase, *A century of banking in Dundee: being the annual balance sheets of the Dundee Banking Company from 1764 to 1864*, Edin. 1864, 2nd edn. 1867.

9985 GRAHAM (WILLIAM). The one pound note in the rise and progress of banking in Scotland and its adaptability to England. Edin. 1886. 2nd edn. 1911.

See also William Baird, *The one pound note: its history, place and power in Scotland, and its adaptability for England*, Edin. 1885, 2nd. edn. Edin. 1901, and Robert Somers, *The Scotch banks and system of issue*, Edin. 1873.

9986 GASKIN (MAXWELL). 'Anglo-Scottish banking conflicts, 1874–1881'. *Econ. Hist. Rev.* 2 ser. xii (1959–60), 445–55.

9987 INSTITUTE OF BANKERS IN SCOTLAND. The Scottish bankers' magazine. Edin. 1909+.

See also *Scottish banking and insurance*, Edin. 1879–97, styled *The British economist*, 1887–8, *The North British economist*, 1889–95, and *Banking and insurance*, 1896–7.

9988 COUPER (CHARLES TENNANT). Report of the trial before the High Court of Justiciary, Her Majesty's Advocate against the directors and manager of the City of Glasgow Bank, and of the procedure upon the petition for bail . . . Edin. 1879. 2nd edn. 1879.

See also William Wallace, ed., *Trial of the City of Glasgow Bank directors*, Glasgow & Edin. 1905. For an earlier bank failure see *The Western Bank failure and the Scottish banking system: being the evidence thereon given before the select committee on the bank acts . . .*, Glasgow 1858, and Roy Hutcheson Campbell, 'Edinburgh bankers and the Western Bank of Scotland', *Scot. J. Pol. Econ.* ii (1955), 133–48.

9989 HENDERSON (THOMAS). The Savings Bank of Glasgow: one hundred years of thrift. Glasgow. 1936.

See also the valuable statististics in Payne (**9958**) and W. Meikle, *The Savings Bank of Glasgow: its origin and progress*, Glasgow 1898. For other savings banks see the bibliog. in Horne (**4655**).

9990 MAXWELL (*Sir* HERBERT EUSTACE). Annals of the Scottish Widows' Fund Life Assurance Society during one hundred years, 1815–1914. Edin. 1914.

See also Mary D. Steuart, *The Scottish Provident Institution, 1837–1937*, Edin. 1937, W. Schorling, *The Standard Life Assurance Company, 1825–1925*, Edin. 1925, and William Forbes Gray, *A brief chronicle of the Scottish Union & National Insurance Company, 1824–1924*, Edin. 1924.

9991 DAVIDSON (ANDREW RUTHERFORD). The history of the Faculty of Actuaries in Scotland, 1856–1956. Edin. 1956.

There is much valuable material in the *Transactions* of the Faculty (formerly styled the Actuarial Society of Edinburgh), Edin. 1878+, and in the *Transactions*, 1881–1923, of the Insurance and Actuarial Soc. of Glasgow.

9992 INSTITUTE OF CHARTERED ACCOUNTANTS OF SCOT-LAND. A history of the chartered accountants of Scotland from the earliest times to 1954 . . . Edin. 1954.

9993 MACMILLAN (DAVID STIRLING). 'The transfer of company control from Scotland to London in the nineteenth century: the case of the Scottish Australian Company, 1853'. *Business Hist.* xii (1970), 102–15.

9994 JACKSON (WILLIAM TURRENTINE). The enterprising Scot: investors in the American West after 1873. Edin. 1968.

9995 LAWSON (WILLIAM RAMAGE). The Scottish investors' manual: a review of the leading Scottish securities in 1883. Edin. 1884.

9996 GILBERT (JOHN CANNON). A history of investment trusts in Dundee, 1873–1938. 1939.

See also George Glasgow, *The Scottish investment trust companies*, 1932.

9997 GLASGOW STOCK EXCHANGE ASSOCIATION. Records of the Glasgow Stock Exchange Association, 1844–1926. Glasgow. 1927.

### (e) *Industry*

9998 BREMNER (DAVID). The industries of Scotland, their rise, progress and present condition. Edin. 1869. New edn. by John Butt and Ian L. Donnachie. Newton Abbot. 1969.

The best of contemp. works. See also *Notices of some of the principal manufacturers of the West of Scotland* (British Assoc. handbook), Glasgow 1876, *Glasgow and its environs: a literary, commercial and social review, past and present*, 1891, Angus McLean, ed., *Local industries of Glasgow and the West of Scotland* (British Assoc. handbook), Glasgow 1901, William S. Murphy, *Captains of industry* [on industries in or near Glasgow], Glasgow [1901], and the British Assoc. handbooks for Dundee (**10178**) and Glasgow (**10182**).

9999 SCOTTISH EXHIBITION OF HISTORY, ART AND INDUSTRY, GLASGOW 1911. Official catalogue: industrial section. Glasgow. 1911.

10000 BUTT (JOHN) *and others*. The industrial archaeology of Scotland. Newton Abbot. 1967.

Suppl. by John Butt, John R. Hume, and Ian L. Donnachie, *Industrial history in pictures: Scotland*, Newton Abbot 1968.

10001 ROBERTSON (A. J.). 'The decline of the Scottish cotton industry, 1860–1914'. *Business Hist.* xii (1970), 116–28.

10002 HENDERSON (WILLIAM OTTO). 'The cotton famine in Scotland and the relief of distress, 1862–1864'. *Scot. Hist. Rev.* xxx (1951), 154–64.

See also David Crabbe Carrie, *Dundee and the American civil war, 1861–65*, Abertay Hist. Soc., Dundee 1953.

10003 GAULDIE (ENID) *ed.* The Dundee textile industry, 1790–1885: from the papers of Peter Carmichael of Arthurstone. Scottish Hist. Soc. 4 ser. 6. Edin. 1969.

10004 LENMAN (BRUCE), LYTHE (CHARLOTTE), *and* GAULDIE (ENID). Dundee and its textile industry, 1850–1914. Abertay Hist. Soc. 14. Dundee. 1969.

Dundee was the centre of the linen and jute industries, for which see **4914–22**. For neighbouring Arbroath see W. H. K. Turner, *The textile industry of Arbroath since the early 18th century*, Abertay Hist. Soc., Dundee 1954.

10005 TURNER (W. H. K.). 'The textile industries of Dunfermline and Kirkcaldy, 1700–1900'. *Scot. Geog. Mag.* lxxiii (1957), 129–45.

See also Peter Kininmonth Livingstone, *Flax and linen in Fife through the centuries*, Kirkcaldy 1952, and A. Muir, *Nairns of Kirkcaldy* (**10022**).

10006  BLAIR (MATTHEW). The Paisley thread industry and the men who created and developed it: with notes concerning Paisley, old and new. Paisley. 1907.

See also his *The Paisley shawl and the men who produced it . . .*, Paisley 1904, and John Conran Irwin, *Shawls; a study in Indo-European influences*, Victoria & Albert Museum 1955.

10007  OLIVER (THOMAS). Development of the tweed trade. Galashiels. 1921.

See also his *Weaving and designing*, Galashiels 1907, and F. Thompson on Harris tweed (**10220**).

10008  CAIRNCROSS (*Sir* ALEXANDER KIRKLAND). 'The Glasgow building industry (1870–1914)'. *Rev. Econ. Studs.* ii (1934–5), 1–17.

10009  DIACK (WILLIAM). The Scottish granite industry. 1903.

10010  TATLOCK (R. R.). The past, present and prospective condition of some of the leading chemical industries of Glasgow and the West of Scotland. Glasgow. 1883.

10011  NETTLETON (JOSEPH ALFRED). The manufacture of whisky and plain spirit. Aberdeen. 1913.

10012  BARNARD (ALFRED). The whisky distilleries of the United Kingdom. 1887. Repr. Newton Abbot. 1969.

10013  JAMES COMMISSION ON WHISKEY AND OTHER POTABLE SPIRITS. Interim report of the royal commission of whiskey and other potable spirits [Chairman: Lord James of Hereford]. [Cd. 4180] H.C. (1908). LVIII, 415. Minutes of evidence. [Cd. 4181] H.C. (1908). LVIII, 421. Final report. [Cd. 4796] H.C. (1909). XLIX, 451. Minutes of evidence. [Cd. 4797] H.C. (1909). XLIX, 503. Index and digest. [Cd. 4876] H.C. (1909). XLIX, 785.

Appointed to consider whether the manufacture of Scotch and Irish whisky should be regulated in any way. Reported against regulation. The evidence is the main source for the hist. of the whisky industry.

10014  LOCKHART (*Sir* ROBERT HAMILTON BRUCE). Scotch: the whisky of Scotland in fact and story. 1951. New edn. 1959.

Ross Wilson, *Scotch made easy*, 1959, covers the same ground, but is rather less satisfactory. James Laver, *The house of Haig*, Markinch 1958, deals with one of the main manufacturers.

10015  [McKECHNIE (JAMES) *and* MACGREGOR (MURRAY).] A short history of the Scottish coal-mining industry. National Coal Board. 1958.

See also Andrew Storar Cunningham, *Mining in the 'kingdom' of Fife . . .*, Dunfermline & Edin. 1913, and *Mining in Mid and East Lothian . . .*, Edin. 1925.
    For geology see Robert Wilson Dron, *The coalfields of Scotland*, 1902, rev. edn. Glasgow 1921.

For machinery see Robert Lindsay Galloway, *Mining exhibition, 1885: review of the progressive improvement of mining in Scotland: official catalogue* . . ., Glasgow 1885.

For individual firms see John Lees Carvel, *The New Cumnock coal-field* . . ., priv. pr. Edin. 1946, and *One hundred years in coal: the history of the Alloa Coal Company*, priv. pr. Edin. 1944, Andrew Storar Cunningham, *The Fife Coal Company Ltd.* . . ., Leven 1922, and Augustus Muir, *The Fife Coal Company Limited: a short history*, Leven [1951].

10016 WEST OF SCOTLAND MINING INSTITUTE [from 1880 Mining Institute of Scotland]. Transactions. 1+. Hamilton. 1879+.

10017 CAMPBELL (ROY HUTCHESON). Carron Company. Edin. & Lond. 1961.

The pioneer Scottish ironworks. Cp. John Lees Carvel, *The Coltness Iron Company* . . ., Edin. 1948.

10018 GIBSON (I. F.). 'The establishment of the Scottish steel industry'. *Scot. J. Pol. Econ.* v (1958), 22–39.

10019 WEST OF SCOTLAND IRON AND STEEL INSTITUTE. Journal. 1+. Glasgow. 1892+.

10020 HARVEY (R.). Early days of engineering in Glasgow. Glasgow. 1919.

10021 SMITH (DAVID LARMER). The Dalmellington Iron Company and its engines and men. Newton Abbot. 1967.

10022 MUIR (AUGUSTUS). Nairns of Kirkcaldy: a short history of the company, 1847–1956. Camb. 1956.

Linoleum manufacturers.

10023 BUTT (JOHN). 'The Scottish oil mania of 1864–86'. *Scot. J. Pol. Econ.* xii (1965), 195–209.

See also his 'Technical change and the growth of the British shale-oil industry (1680–1870)', *Econ. Hist. Rev.* 2 ser. xvii (1964–5), 511–21.

10024 CARVEL (JOHN LEES). The Alloa glass work: an account of its development since 1750. Priv. pr. Edin. 1953.

10025 [BROGAN (COLM) *comp.*] James Finlay & Company Limited, manufacturers and East India merchants, 1750–1950. Glasgow. 1951.

An important business hist.

10026 CARVEL (JOHN LEES). One hundred years in timber: the history of the City Saw Mills, 1849–1949. Port Dundas, Glasgow. [1949.]

### (f) Transport

10027 SIMMONS (JACK). 'The Scottish records of the British Transport Commission'. *J. Transport Hist.* iii (1957–8), 158–67.

10028   LINDSAY (JEAN). The canals of Scotland. Newton Abbot. 1968.
A general hist. which needs to be suppl. by (**10029**).

10029   PRATT (EDWIN A.). Scottish canals and waterways. 1922.

10030   MASON (*Sir* THOMAS). 'The improvement of the River Clyde and harbour of Glasgow, 1873–1914'. *Inst. Civil Eng. Proc.* cc (1915), 101–35.
See also James Deas, *The River Clyde: an historical description of the rise and progress of the harbour of Glasgow, and of the improvement of the river from Glasgow to Port Glasgow*, Glasgow 1876, and William Forrest MacArthur, *History of Port Glasgow*, Glasgow 1932.

10031   SHIELDS (JOHN). Clyde built: a history of shipbuilding on the River Clyde. Glasgow. [1949.]
See also George Blake, *Down to the sea: the romance of the Clyde, its ships and shipbuilders*, 1937, 2nd edn. 1938; Scott's Shipbuilding and Engineering Co. Ltd., *Two centuries of shipbuilding by the Scotts at Greenock*, 3rd edn. priv. pr. Manch. 1950, 4th edn. [*Two hundred and fifty years . . .* ] 1961; John Lees Carvel, *A record of two hundred years of shipbuilding: Stephen of Linthouse, 1750–1950*, Glasgow 1951; Sir Allen John Grant, *Steel & ships: the history of John Brown's*, 1950; Alastair Borthwick, *Yarrow and Company Ltd: the first hundred years, 1865–1965*, Glasgow [1965]; and James Macarthur Reid, *James Lithgow, master of work*, 1964. For the 19th-cent. shipmasters see Alexander Balmain Brice, *The life of William Denny, shipbuilder, Dumbarton*, 1888, 2nd edn. 1889, James Robert Napier, *Memoir of David Elder*, Glasgow 1866, repr. 1891, and William John Macquorn Rankine, *A memoir of John Elder, engineer and shipbuilder*, Edin. 1871.

10032   WILLIAMSON (JAMES). The Clyde passenger steamer: its rise and progress during the nineteenth century, 1812–1901. Glasgow. 1904.
See also Alan D. Cuthbert, *Clyde Shipping Company Limited*, Glasgow 1956; Andrew McQueen, *Clyde river steamers of the last fifty years*, Glasgow 1923; Christian Leslie Dyce Duckworth and Graham Easton Langmuir, *Clyde river and other steamers*, 1937, *Clyde and other coastal steamers*, Glasgow 1939, and *West Highland steamers*, 1935, 3rd edn. Prescot 1967; and Alan James Stuart Paterson, *The golden years of the Clyde steamers, 1889–1914*, Newton Abbot 1969.

10033   FLINN (MICHAEL WALTER). 'The overseas trade of Scottish ports, 1900–1960'. *Scot. J. Pol. Econ.* xiii (1966), 220–37.

10034   CLARK (VICTORIA ELIZABETH). The port of Aberdeen: a history of its trade and shipping from the 12th century to the present day. Aberdeen. 1921.
See also Leslie Cope Cornford, *The sea carriers, 1825–1925: the Aberdeen line*, 1925, and Gordon Donaldson, *Northwards by sea*, Edin. 1966.

10035   THOMPSON (JOHN HORACE HANNAY) *and* RITCHIE (GEORGE G.). Dundee Harbour Trust centenary, 1830–1930: history and development of the harbour of Dundee. Dundee. 1930.
See also Thompson's *Granton Harbour, Edinburgh: a brief history . . .*, Edin. 1934.

10036 ACWORTH (*Sir* WILLIAM MITCHELL). The railways of Scotland: their present position, with a glance at their past and a forecast of their future. 1890.

See also James Mavor, *The Scottish railway strike: a history and criticism*, Edin. 1891.

10037 NOCK (OSWALD STEVENS). The Scottish railways. 1950. Rev. edn. 1961.

Chiefly technical. See also John Thomas, *A regional history of the railways of Great Britain*, v. 6, *Scotland: the Lowlands and the Borders*, Newton Abbot 1971, and *Scottish railway history in pictures*, Newton Abbot 1967. For individual railways see Cuthbert Hamilton Ellis, *The North British Railway*, 1955, 2nd edn. 1959; John Thomas, *The North British Railway*, 2 v. Newton Abbot 1969–70; O. S. Nock, *The Caledonian Railway* [1961]; O. S. Nock and Eric Treacy, *Main lines across the border*, 1960; William Mcilwraith, *The Glasgow and South Western Railway: its origin, progress and present position*, Glasgow 1880; Hugh Aymer Vallance, *The [history of the] Highland Railway*, 1938, 2nd edn. Dawlish 1963, 3rd edn. Newton Abbot 1969; O. S. Nock, *The Highland Railway*, 1965; Sir Charles Malcolm Barclay-Harvey, *A history of the Great North of Scotland Railway*, 1940, 2nd edn. 1950; H. A. Vallance, *The Great North of Scotland Railway*, Dawlish 1965; George Dow, *The story of the West Highland*, 2nd edn. 1947; John Thomas, *The West Highland Railway*, Newton Abbot 1965, *The Callander & Oban Railway*, Newton Abbot 1966, and *The Springburn story: the history of the Scottish railway metropolis*, Dawlish 1964; Nigel Stuart Cameron Macmillan, *The Campbeltown & Machrihanish light railway*, Newton Abbot 1970; David Larmer Smith, *The little railways of south-west Scotland*, Newton Abbot 1969; Alfred Derek Farr, *The Royal Deeside line*, Newton Abbot 1968; and Campbell Highet, *Scottish locomotive history, 1831–1923*, 1971.

10038 VAMPLEW (WRAY). 'Railway investment in the Scottish Highlands'. *Transport Hist.* iii (1970), 141–53.

See also his 'Railways and the transformation of the Scottish economy', *Econ. Hist. Rev.* 2 ser. xxiv (1971), 37–54.

10039 PREBBLE (JOHN EDWARD CURTIS). The high girders. 1956. N.Y. [Disaster at Dundee.] 1957.

On the Tay Bridge disaster. See also **5179**.

10040 PHILLIPS (PHILIP). The Forth Bridge in its various stages of construction, and compared with the most notable bridges of the world. Edin. 1889. 2nd edn. [1890.]

10041 SCOTTISH TRAMWAY MUSEUM SOCIETY. Publications. Glasgow. 1960+.

See also Anthony S. E. Browning, *Glasgow's trams, their history and a descriptive guide* . . ., Glasgow Art Gallery and Museum, Glasgow 1964; Alan W. Brotchie, *Tramways of the Tay valley* . . ., Dundee 1965; David Lawrie Thomson and David Edwin Sinclair, *The Glasgow subway*, Glasgow 1964; Ian Leslie Cormack, *Glasgow tramways, 1872–1962*, 1962; and David Lindsay George Hunter, 'The Edinburgh cable tramways', *J. Transport Hist.* i (1953–4), 170–84.

10042 HUNTER (DAVID LINDSAY GEORGE). Edinburgh's transport. Huddersfield. 1964.

10043 MACDONALD (ALEXANDER CRAIG), BROWNING (AN-
THONY S. E.) *and others*. Scottish cars: their history and a descriptive guide
to a few of those which survive. Glasgow Art Gallery and Museum. Glasgow.
1962.

10044 SMYTHE COMMISSION ON SCOTTISH ROADS. Report of the
commissioners for inquiring into matters relating to public roads in Scotland
[Chairman: William Smythe]. [2596] H.C. (1860). XXXVIII, 1. Evidence.
[2596–I] H.C. (1860). XXXVIII, 301.

10045 COMMITTEE ON RURAL TRANSPORT (SCOTLAND) [Chair-
man: Sir T. Carlaw Martin]. Report. [Cmd. 227] H.C. (1919). XXX, 77.
Suppl. [Cmd. 987] H.C. (1920). XXIV, 921.

10046 COOK (THOMAS). Cook's Scottish tourist official directory: a guide
to the system of tours in Scotland under the direction of the principal railway,
steamboat & coach companies commanding the Highland excursion traffic.
1861.

## 2. SOCIAL HISTORY

10047 KYD (JAMES GRAY). 'Scotland's population'. *Scot. Hist. Rev.* xxviii
(1949), 97–107.

Outlines only. See also Kyd's *Scottish population statistics; including Webster's analysis
of population, 1755*, Scot. Hist. Soc. 3 ser. xliv, Edin. 1952, and Richard H. Osborne,
'The movements of people in Scotland, 1851–1951', *Scot. Studs.* ii (1958), 1–46, and
'Scottish migration statistics: a note', *Scot. Geog. Mag.* lxxii (1956), 153–9. John W.
Paterson, 'Rural depopulation in Scotland: being an analysis of its causes and consequences', *Highland & Agric. Soc. Trans.* 5 ser. ix (1897), 236–78, is a useful contemp.
account. The main sources for Scottish population statistics are the *Annual report* of
the Registrar General for Scotland, Edin. 1855+, and the decennial Scottish census
returns.

10048 BEST (GEOFFREY FRANCIS ANDREW). 'The Scottish Victorian
city'. *Victorian Studs.* xi (1967–8), 329–58.

See also C. M. Allan, 'The genesis of British urban redevelopment: with special reference to Glasgow', *Econ. Hist. Rev.* 2 ser. xviii (1965), 598–613.

10049 GUTHRIE COMMITTEE ON HOUSE-LETTING IN SCOT-
LAND. Report of the departmental committee on house-letting in Scotland
[Chairman: Lord Guthrie]. [Cd. 3715] H.C. (1907). XXXVII, 1. Minutes of
evidence etc. [Cd. 3792] H.C. (1908). XLVII, 1.

Concerned with working-class housing. For statistics see *Return showing the housing
conditions of the people of Scotland* [Cd. 4016] H.C. (1908). XCIII, 445.

10050 BALLANTYNE COMMISSION ON HOUSING IN SCOTLAND.
Report of the royal commission on the housing of the industrial population of
Scotland, rural and urban [Chairman: Sir Henry Ballantyne]. [Cd. 8731] H.C.
(1917–18). XIV, 345. Special report on design, construction &c. of small
dwelling houses, by John Wilson. [Cd. 8760] H.C. (1917–18). XIV, 825.

An important source.

10051 DUNBAR (JOHN TELFER). History of Highland dress: a definitive study of the history of Scottish costume and tartan, both civil and military, including weapons. Edin. & Lond. 1962.

Beautifully illus. Deals with the widespread adoption of a formal system of Highland dress in the 19th cent. Richard Manisty Demain Grange, *A short history of the Scottish dress*, 1966, adds little.

10052 HANDLEY (JAMES EDMUND). The Irish in modern Scotland. Cork, etc. 1947.

Good.

10053 ALISON. Some account of my life and writings: an autobiography. By Sir Archibald Alison. Ed. by his daughter-in-law Lady [Jane R.] Alison. 2 v. Edin. & Lond. 1883.

Historian and sheriff of Lanarkshire. Useful on life in the west of Scotland.

10054 GEIKIE. Scottish reminiscences. By Sir Archibald Geikie. Glasgow. 1904.

Entertaining. For Geikie's career as a geologist see **8757.**

10055 PATON (DIARMID NOEL) *and others*. A study of the diet of the labouring classes in Edinburgh. [1902.]

See also Arthur Henderson Kitchin and Reginald Passmore, *The Scotsman's food: an historical introduction to modern food administration*, Edin. 1949, and Florence Marian McNeill, *The Scots kitchen: its traditions and lore . . .*, 1929, 2nd edn. 1963, and *The Scots cellar . . .*, 1956.

10056 FERGUSON (THOMAS). Scottish social welfare, 1864–1914. Edin. & Lond. 1958.

Cont. his *The dawn of Scottish social welfare: a survey from medieval times to 1863*, Edin. & Lond. 1948. See also **9850.**

10057 DUNDEE SOCIAL UNION (SOCIAL INQUIRY COMMITTEE). Report of investigation into social conditions in Dundee. Dundee. 1905.

See also the parallel *Report on housing and industrial conditions and medical inspection of school children*, Dundee 1905.

10058 WHITEHOUSE (JOHN HOWARD). Problems of a Scottish provincial town (Dunfermline). Birmingham & Lond. 1905.

10059 SUTHERLAND (WILLIAM). Social questions in Scotland. Glasgow. [1910.]

10060 EDINBURGH COUNCIL OF SOCIAL SERVICE. A social survey of the city of Edinburgh. Edin. 1926.

10061 COMRIE (JOHN DIXON). History of Scottish medicine to 1860. 1927. 2nd edn. 2 v. Wellcome Hist. Medic. Museum. 1932.

Standard. See also Clarendon Hyde Creswell, *The Royal College of Surgeons of Edinburgh: historical notes from 1505 to 1905*, priv. pr. Edin. 1926, John Ritchie, *History of the laboratory of the Royal College of Physicians of Edinburgh*, Edin. 1953, Royal College of Physicians of Edinburgh, *Historical sketch and laws of the Royal College of Physicians of Edinburgh from its institution to 1925*, Edin. 1925, and James Gray, *History of the Royal Medical Society, 1737–1937*, ed. by Douglas James Guthrie, Edin. 1952. For indiv. Scottish doctors see **8869, 8878, 8894, 8911, 8915, 10065-8.**

10062  SCOTTISH SOCIETY OF THE HISTORY OF MEDICINE. Report of proceedings. Edin. 1963-4+.

10063  TURNER (ARTHUR LOGAN). Story of a great hospital: the Royal Infirmary of Edinburgh, 1729–1929. Edin. & Lond. 1937.

Full. For other hospitals see Charles Cromhall Easterbrook, *The chronicle of Crichton Royal, 1833–1936: being the story of a famous mental hospital during its first century, and illustrating the evolution of the hospital care and treatment of mental invalids in Scotland* . . ., Dumfries 1940, Douglas James Guthrie and others, *The Royal Edinburgh Hospital for Sick Children, 1860–1960*, Edin. & Lond. 1960, and Archibald McClellan Wright Thomson, *The history of the Glasgow Eye Infirmary, 1824–1962*, Glasgow 1963.

10064  GUTHRIE (DOUGLAS JAMES). Extramural medical education in Edinburgh and the school of medicine of the royal colleges. Edin. & Lond. 1965.

10065  MACALISTER. Sir Donald Macalister of Tarbert. By his widow, Edith Florence Boyle [Lady] Macalister. 1935.

Physician and vice-chancellor of Glasgow Univ.

10066  MACEWEN. The life and teaching of Sir William MacEwen: a chapter in the history of surgery. By Alexander King Bowman. 1942.

10067  TURNER. Sir William Turner . . . a chapter in medical history. By Arthur Logan Turner. Edin. & Lond. 1919.

10068  WRIGHT-ST. CLAIR (REX EARL). Doctors Monro: a medical saga. Wellcome Hist. Med. Libr. 1964.

The story of an Edinburgh medical dynasty. Cp. Alfred Shepherd, *Simpson and Syme of Edinburgh*, Edin. 1969.

10069  BROTHERSTON (JOHN HOWIE FLINT). Observations on the early public health movement in Scotland. London School of Hygiene and Tropical Medic. Memoir 8. 1952.

10070  CHALMERS (ARCHIBALD KERR). The health of Glasgow, 1818–1925: an outline. Glasgow. 1930.

See also James Christie, ed., *The medical institutions of Glasgow* . . ., Glasgow 1888, James Burn Russell, *The evolution of the function of public health administration as illustrated by the sanitary history of Glasgow in the nineteenth century, and especially since 1854* . . ., Glasgow 1895, Archibald Kerr Chalmers, ed., *Public health administration in Glasgow: a memorial volume of the writings of James Burn Russell*, Glasgow 1905, and Sir Alexander Macgregor, *Public health in Glasgow, 1905–1946*, Edin. 1967.

10071 YOUNG (JOHN A.). Report on the evolution and development of public health administration in the city of Edinburgh from 1865 to 1919. Edin. 1919.

10072 KELSO (WILLIAM W.). Sanitation in Paisley: a record of progress, 1488–1920. Paisley. 1922.

10073 LOCH (CHARLES STEWART). 'Poor relief in Scotland: its statistics and development, 1791 to 1891'. *Stat. Soc. J.* lxi (1898), 271–365.

10074 CORMACK (ALEXANDER ALLAN). Poor relief in Scotland: an outline of the growth and administration of the poor laws in Scotland, from the middle ages to the present day. Aberdeen. 1923.

For background see also Sir George Nicholls, *A history of the Scotch poor law in connexion with the condition of the people*, 1856, Scotus, *The Scottish poor laws: examination of their policy, history and practical action*, Edin. 1870, and Thomas Ivory, ed., *Pauperism and the poor laws: the lectures delivered . . . under the auspices of the Chalmers Association in 1869–70*, Edin. 1870.

10075 BOARD OF SUPERVISION FOR THE RELIEF OF THE POOR and Public Health of Scotland. Annual report. Edin. 1847–95.

Publ. as a parl. paper. Cont. as *Annual report of the Local Government Board for Scotland*, Edin. 1894–1918/19. A useful source of local information.

10076 CRAUFURD COMMITTEE ON THE SCOTTISH POOR LAW. Report from the select committee on poor law (Scotland) [Chairman: E. H. J. Craufurd]. H.C. 301 (1868–9). XI, 1. Further reports. H.C. 357 (1870). XI, 1. H.C. 329 (1871). XI, 389.

10077 ROYAL COMMISSION ON THE POOR LAWS AND THE RELIEF OF DISTRESS [Chairman: Lord George Hamilton]. Report on Scotland. [Cd. 4922] H.C. (1909). XXXVIII, 95.

See also *Report of the departmental committee appointed by the Local Government Board for Scotland to inquire into the system of poor law medical relief and into the rules and regulations for the management of poorhouses* [Chairman: J. Patten MacDougall]. [Cd. 2008] H.C. (1904). XXXIII, 1. Evidence etc. [Cd. 2022] H.C. (1904). XXXIII, 137, and *Report on the methods of administering poor relief in certain large town parishes of Scotland*. [Cd. 2524] H.C. (1905). LXVIII, 433.

10078 POOR LAW MAGAZINE. Edin. 1858–1930.

10079 CAMERON COMMITTEE ON HABITUAL OFFENDERS. Report from the departmental committee on habitual offenders, vagrants, beggars, inebriates, and juvenile delinquents [Chairman: Sir Charles Cameron]. [C. 7753] H.C. (1895). XXXVII, 1. Minutes of evidence. [C. 7753–I] H.C. (1895). XXXVII, 65.

See also *Report of the departmental committee appointed by the Secretary for Scotland to report as to rules for inebriate reformatories under the Inebriates Act, 1898* [Chairman: Lt. Col. A. B. McHardy]. [C. 9175] H.C. (1899). XII, 775, and *Departmental committee on the operation in Scotland of the law relating to inebriates and their detention in reforma-*

*tories and retreats* [Chairman: Sir William Bilsland]. Report [Cd. 4766] H.C. (1909). XXVI, 573. Minutes of evidence. [Cd. 4767] H.C. (1909). XXVI, 601.

10080 ELGIN COMMITTEE ON SCOTTISH PRISONS. Report from the departmental committee on Scottish prisons [Chairman: the Earl of Elgin]. [Cd. 218] H.C. (1900). XLII, 89. Minutes of evidence. [Cd. 219] H.C. (1900). XLII, 119.

10081 ALLEN COMMITTEE ON SCOTTISH REFORMATORY AND INDUSTRIAL SCHOOLS. Report of the departmental committee on reformatory and industrial schools in Scotland [Chairman: A. Acland Allen]. [Cd. 7886] H.C. (1914–16). XXXIV, 491. Evidence. [Cd. 7887] H.C. (1914–16). XXXIV, 609.

10082 SCOTTISH TEMPERANCE LEAGUE. Scottish [temperance] review. 1845–63.

The League also publ. *The adviser*, 1847+, and a *Weekly journal*, 1857–61, which became the *League journal*, 1862–1902, and *The temperance leader and league journal*, 1903–22.

10083 CLERK COMMISSION ON SCOTTISH LICENSING. Report by Her Majesty's commissioners for inquiring into the licensing system and sale and consumption of excisable liquors in Scotland [Chairman: Sir George Clerk]. [2684 and 2684–I] H.C. (1860). XXXII, 1 and XXXIII, 1.

A thorough inquiry. See also *Report by the commissioners appointed to inquire into the laws regulating the sale and consumption of excisable liquors sold not for consumption on the premises in Scotland* [Chairman: Sir James Fergusson]. [C. 1941] H.C. (1878). XXVI, 1.

10084 ELLANGOWAN *pseud. of* BERTRAM (JAMES GLASS). Out of door sports in Scotland: deer stalking, grouse shooting, salmon fishing, golfing, curling, etc. . . . 2nd edn. 1890.

Cp. Herbert Byng Hall, *Scottish sports and pastimes*, 1851. For golf see 7776–9.

10085 GRANT (JOHN GORDON). The complete curler: being, the history and practice of the game of curling. 1914.

10086 MACDONALD (J. NINIAN). Shinty: a short history of the ancient Highland game. 1932.

10087 WHITTON (KENNETH) *and* JAMIESON (DAVID A.) *eds*. Fifty years of athletics: an historical record of the Scottish Amateur Athletic Association, 1883–1933. Edin. 1933.

See also David A. Jamieson, *Powderhall and pedestrianism: the history of a famous sports enclosure, 1870–1943*, Edin. & Lond. 1943.

10088 HAY (IAN) *pseud. of* BEITH (JOHN HAY). The Royal Company of Archers, 1676–1951. Edin. & Lond. 1951.

Chiefly post-1875, because Sir James Balfour Paul, *The history of the Royal Company of Archers, the Queen's body-guard for Scotland*, Edin. & Lond. 1875, covers earlier years.

10089 MACGREGOR (ARTHUR WALLACE) *ed.* Fifty years of lawn tennis in Scotland. Scottish Lawn Tennis Assoc. Edin. 1927.

10090 PHILLIPS (R. J.). The story of Scottish rugby. Edin. & Lond. 1925.

10091 HANDLEY (JAMES EDMUND). The Celtic story: a history of the Celtic Football Club. 1960.

For other Assoc. football clubs see John Fairgrieve, *The Rangers: a complete history of Scotland's greatest football club,* 1964, and Albert Mackie, *The Hearts: the story of the Heart of Midlothian F.C.,* 1959.

### 3. LABOUR HISTORY

10092 MACDOUGALL (IAN) *ed.* An interim bibliography of the Scottish working-class movement and of other labour records held in Scotland. Soc. for the Study of Labour Hist., Scottish Committee. Edin. 1965.

A checklist of libr. holdings. Up-to-date information about Scottish labour hist. is to be incl. in Scottish Labour Hist. Soc., *Journal,* 1+, Glasgow 1969+.

10093 MARWICK (WILLIAM HUTTON). A short history of labour in Scotland. Edin. & Lond. 1967.

Brief but chiefly post-1851. Thomas Johnston, *The history of the working classes in Scotland,* Glasgow 1920, is both polemical and thin on the period 1850–1900.

10094 BUCKLEY (KENNETH DONALD). Trade unionism in Aberdeen, 1878 to 1900. Edin. 1955.

See also **10100.**

10095 ARNOT (ROBERT PAGE). A history of the Scottish miners from the earliest times. 1955.

See also Alexander John Youngson Brown, 'Trade union policy in the Scots coalfields, 1855–1885', *Econ. Hist. Rev.* 2 ser. vi (1953), 35–50, and (**632**).

10096 GILLESPIE (SARAH CRAIG). A hundred years of progress: the record of the Scottish Typographical Association, 1853 to 1952. Glasgow. 1953.

10097 TUCKETT (ANGELA). The Scottish carter: the history of the Scottish Horse and Motormen's Association, 1898–1964. 1967.

Good. However, Hugh Lyon, *The history of the Scottish Horse and Motormen's Association, 1898–1919,* Glasgow 1919, is still worth consulting.

10098 HANDLEY (JAMES EDMUND). The navvy in Scotland. Cork. [*c.* 1970.]

10099 MACDOUGALL (IAN) *ed.* The minutes of Edinburgh Trades Council, 1859–1873. Scot. Hist. Soc. 4 Ser. 5. Edin. 1968.

The first transcript of the records of a trades council.

10100   DIACK (WILLIAM). History of the trades council and the trade union movement in Aberdeen. Aberdeen. 1939.

See also **10094**.

10101   MAXWELL (*Sir* WILLIAM). The history of co-operation in Scotland: its inception and its leaders. Glasgow. 1910.

See also James Lucas, *Co-operation in Scotland*, Manch. 1920, and A. Buchan, *History of the Scottish Co-operative Women's Guild, 1892–1913*, Glasgow 1913. For local societies see the lists in MacDougall (**10092**).

10102   FLANAGAN (JAMES A.). Wholesale co-operation in Scotland: the fruits of fifty years' efforts (1868–1918). An account of the Scottish Co-operative Wholesale Society . . . S.C.W.S. Glasgow. 1920.

10103   HOUSTON (GEORGE). 'Labour relations in Scottish agriculture before 1870'. *Agric. Hist. Rev.* vi (1958), 27–41.

See also Gwenllian Evans, 'Farm servants' unions in Aberdeenshire from 1870–1900', *Scot. Hist. Rev.* xxxi (1952), 29–40, and Richard Henderson, 'The farm-labourer's cottage', *Highland & Agric. Soc. Trans.* 5 ser. xiii (1901), 18–65.

10104   HOUSTON (GEORGE). 'Farm wages in central Scotland from 1814 to 1870'. *Roy. Stat. Soc. J.* Ser. A 118 (1955), 224–8.

Cont. by R. Molland and G. Evans, 'Scottish farm wages from 1870 to 1900', *Roy. Stat. Soc. J.* Ser. A 113 (1950), 220–7. For earlier treatments of the subject see Frederick Purdy, 'On the earnings of agricultural labourers in Scotland and Ireland', *Stat. Soc. J.* xxv (1862), 425–90, and Arthur Lyon Bowley, 'The statistics of wages in the United Kingdom during the last hundred years (Part II) Agricultural wages—Scotland', *Stat. Soc. J.* lxii (1899), 140–50.


## E. EDUCATION AND CULTURE

### 1. EDUCATION

10105   CRAIGIE (JAMES). A bibliography of Scottish education before 1872. Scot. Council for Res. in Educ. 60. 1970.

10106   SCOTLAND (JAMES). The history of Scottish education. 2 v. 1969.

Standard. But there is also useful material in Henry MacDonald Knox, *Two hundred and fifty years of Scottish education, 1696–1946*, Edin. 1953; John Kerr, *Scottish education, school and university, from early times to 1908*, Camb. 1910, 2nd edn. [to 1913] 1913; Alexander Morgan, *Rise and progress of Scottish education*, Edin. 1927, and *Makers of Scottish education*, 1929; and Robert Kiefer Webb, 'Literacy among the working classes in nineteenth-century Scotland', *Scot. Hist Rev.* xxxiii (1954), 100–14. There are many other short hists., none of them of any account, though they occasionally have a few useful paragraphs. Among them are George Stewart, *The story of Scottish education*, 1927; Alexander Wright, *The history of education and of the old parish schools in Scotland*, Edin. 1898; William John Gibson, *Education in Scotland: a sketch of the past and the present*, 1912; Thomas Pettigrew Young, *Histoire de l'enseignement primaire et secondaire en Écosse, plus spécialement de 1560 à 1872*, Paris 1907; and Mary Mackintosh, *Education in Scotland: yesterday and today*, Glasgow [1962].

10107  SELLAR (ALEXANDER CRAIG). Manual of the Education Act[s] for Scotland . . . Edin. & Lond. 1872. 7th edn. 1879. Rev. edns. by James Edward Graham, 1888, 1894, 1902, 1911.

10108  GRANT (JAMES). History of the burgh and parish schools of Scotland. Vol. I. Burgh schools. Glasgow & Lond. 1876.

Deals with the school system in the burghs before 1872. Vol. II was never issued.

10109  MASON (JOHN). A history of Scottish experiments in rural education, from the eighteenth century to the present day. Scot. Council for Res. in Educ. VII. 1935.

10110  BONE (THOMAS RENFREW). School inspection in Scotland, 1840–1966. Scot. Council for Res. in Educ. 57. [1968.]

Good.

10111  LAURIE (SIMON SOMERVILLE). Report to the trustees of the Dick Bequest on the rural public (formerly parochial) schools of Aberdeen, Banff and Moray, with special reference to the higher instruction in them. Edin. 1890.

On the most advanced part of the parochial school system. See also Laurie's *Report on education in the parochial schools of the counties of Aberdeen, Banff and Moray, addressed to the trustees of the Dick Bequest,* Edin. 1865, and Marjorie Cruickshank, 'The Dick Bequest: the effect of a famous nineteenth-century endowment on the parish schools of north-east Scotland, *Hist. of Ed. Q.* v (1965), 153–65. William Barclay, *The schools and schoolmasters of Banffshire,* Banff 1925, is a detailed study of each school under the system in Banff.

10112  STRONG (JOHN). A history of secondary education in Scotland: an account of Scottish secondary education from early times to the Education Act of 1908. Oxf. 1909.

10113  WADE (NEWMAN ATKINSON). Post-primary education in the primary schools of Scotland, 1872–1936. 1939.

10114  BOYD (WILLIAM). Education in Ayrshire through seven centuries. Scot. Council for Res. in Educ. XLV. 1961.

Covers the whole of the period. Other modern county studies stop at 1872: Ian James Simpson, *Education in Aberdeenshire before 1872,* Scot. Council for Res. in Educ. XXV, 1947, J. C. Jessop, *Education in Angus: an historical survey of education up to the act of 1872, from original and contemporary sources,* Scot. Council for Res. in Educ. II, 1931, and Andrew Bain, *Education in Stirlingshire from the Reformation to the Act of 1872,* Scot. Council for Res. in Educ. LI, 1965.

10115  CRAIK (*Sir* HENRY). Report on Highland schools. [C. 4261] H.C. (1884–5). XXVI, 527.

On Gaelic in the Highland schools see the reports of H. M. inspectors of schools at **10121,** and **10209.** See also Marjorie Cruickshank, 'Education in the Highlands and Islands of Scotland: an historical retrospect', *Paedagogica Historica* vii (1967), 361–77.

10116 KNOX (HENRY MACDONALD). 'Simon Somerville Laurie, 1829–1909'. *Brit. J. Educ. Studs.* x (1962), 138–52.

Includes bibliog. Laurie was the most important educational theorist in Scotland during the period.

10116a CRUICKSHANK (MARJORIE). A history of the training of teachers in Scotland. Scot. Council for Res. in Educ. 61. 1970.

10117 BONE (THOMAS RENFREW) *ed.* Studies in the history of Scottish education, 1872–1939. Scot. Council for Res. in Educ. LIV. 1967.

Includes studs. of Catholic elementary education in Glasgow, teachers and security of tenure, the Scottish leaving certificate, and the junior student system. Good.

10118 BELFORD (ALFRED J.). Centenary handbook of the Educational Institute of Scotland. Edin. 1946.

A useful hist. of the main teacher's organization.

10119 NISSEN (HARTVIG). Beskrivelse over Skotlands Almueskolevæsen tilligemed Forslag til forskjellige Foranstaltninger til en videre Udvikling af det norske Almueskolevæsen. Christiania [Oslo]. 1854.

For a summary see Lawrence Stenhouse, 'Hartvig Nissen's impressions of the Scottish educational system in the mid-nineteenth century', *Brit. J. Educ. Studs.* ix (1960–1), 143–54.

10120 ARGYLL COMMISSION ON THE SCHOOLS OF SCOTLAND. Education Commission (Scotland): first report by Her Majesty's commissioners appointed to inquire into the schools in Scotland [Chairman: the Duke of Argyll]. [3483] H.C. (1865). XVII, 1. Appendix to 1st report. [C. 3858] H.C. (1867). XXV, 981. Second report. [3845] H.C. (1867). XXV, 1. Statistical report on Lowland country districts. [3845–I] H.C. (1867). XXV, 305. Report on Glasgow. [3845–II] H.C. (1867). XXV, 345. Report on country districts. [3845–III] H.C. (1867). XXV, 509. Report on the Hebrides. [3845–IV] H.C. (1867). XXV, 777. Statistics on schools. [3845–V] H.C. (1867). XXVI, 1.

A major inquiry, for which see Marjorie Cruickshank, 'The Argyll commission report, 1865–8: a landmark in Scottish education', *Brit. J. Educ. Studs.* xv (1967), 133–47. The Argyll commission report was suppl. by the English Taunton commission (7896) which issued a 'Report on certain burgh schools, and other schools of secondary education, in Scotland' by Daniel Robert Fearon. [5966–V] H.C. (1867–8). XXVIII, pt. 5.

10121 COMMITTEE OF COUNCIL ON EDUCATION IN SCOTLAND [Scotch *subsequently* Scottish Education Department]. Report. 1873–4+. Edin. 1874+.

Publ. as a parl. paper. Suppl. (for 1874–9) by reports of the Board of Educ. for Scotland, and by occasional returns of schools in each district in Scotland, also publ. as parl. papers. For lists see *General index* (33). There is also Scottish material in the earlier general reports of the Committee of Council on Education for Great Britain (7842).

10122 COLEBROOKE COMMISSION ON EDUCATIONAL ENDOWMENTS (SCOTLAND). First report of the royal commissioners appointed to inquire into the endowed schools and hospitals (Scotland) [Chairman:

Sir Thomas Edward Colebrooke]. [C. 755] H.C. (1873). XXVII, 1. Second report. [C. 976] H.C. (1874). XVII, 111. Third report. [C. 1123] H.C. (1875). XXIX, 1. Appendixes to third report. [C. 1123-I-II] H.C. (1875). XXIX, 257, 695.

For subsequent commissions in the 1880s see *General Index* (33).

10123 PARKER COMMITTEE ON EDUCATION IN SCOTLAND. First and second reports of the committee appointed to inquire into certain questions relating to education in Scotland [Chairman: Charles Stuart Parker]. [C. 5336] H.C. (1888). XLI, 603. Third report with minutes of evidence. [C. 5425] H.C. (1888). XLI, 641.

Chiefly concerned with recruitment of teachers.

10124 CLARKE (JOHN). Short studies in education in Scotland. 1904.

One of the few contemp. studies of Scottish educ.

10125 KERR. Memories grave and gay: forty years of school inspection. By John Kerr. Edin. & Lond. 1902.

Kerr also publ. *Other memories . . .*, Edin. & Lond. 1904. Cp. John Wilson, *Tales and travels of a school inspector*, Glasgow 1908, and the memoirs of F. G. Rea (**10230**).

10126 MORGAN (ALEXANDER). Scottish university studies. 1933.

An introductory handbook. May be suppl. by John Robert Peddie, *The first 50 years: the Carnegie Trust for the Universities of Scotland, 1901–1951 . . .*, Edin. 1951.

10127 DAVIE (GEORGE ELDER). The democratic intellect: Scotland and her universities in the nineteenth century. Edin. 1961. 2nd edn. 1964.

A study of major importance for univ. hist.

10128 LORIMER (JAMES). The universities of Scotland: past, present and possible. Edin. 1854.

Suggests radically replanning the role of the Scottish univs. to make them a training-ground for statesmen. Cp. John Struthers, *How to improve the teaching of the Scottish universities*, Edin. 1859.

10129 ANDERSON (PETER JOHN) *ed.* Rectorial addresses delivered in the Universities of Aberdeen, 1835–1900. Aberdeen Univ. Studs. 6. Aberdeen. 1902.

An interesting reflection of contemp. ideas of what university students should be thinking about. See also William Angus Knight, ed., *Rectorial addressses delivered at the University of St. Andrews: Sir William Stirling-Maxwell, Bart. to the Marquess of Bute, 1863–1893*, 1894, and Archibald Stodart-Walker, ed., *Rectorial addresses delivered before the University of Edinburgh, 1859–1899*, 1900.

10130 SCOTTISH UNIVERSITIES COMMISSION, 1858. General report of the commissioners under the Universities (Scotland) Act, 1858 . . . [Chairman: John Inglis.] [3174] H.C. (1863). XVI, 335.

The commission was concerned with the detailed regulation of the Scottish univs.

**10131** SCOTTISH UNIVERSITIES COMMISSION, 1876. Report of the royal commissioners appointed to inquire into the Universities of Scotland [Chairman: Lord President John Inglis]. [C. 1935] H.C. (1878). XXXII, 1. Evidence. [C. 1935-I-III] H.C. (1878). XXXIII-XXXV.

A general inquiry into the state of the universities.

**10132** BURNET (JOHN). Higher education and the war. 1917.

Interesting reflections on Prussian and Scottish universities.

**10133** ABERDEEN UNIVERSITY. The fusion of 1860: a record of the centenary celebrations and a history of the united University of Aberdeen, 1860–1960. Ed. by William Douglas Simpson. Edin. 1963.

To be suppl. by Donald Ian Mackay, *Geographical mobility and the brain drain: a case study of Aberdeen university graduates, 1860–1960*, 1969. On the hist. and life of the university see also Peter John Anderson, ed., *Studies in the history and development of the University of Aberdeen . . .*, Aberdeen Univ. Studs. 19, Aberdeen 1906; Alexander Shewan, comp., *Meminisse juvat: being the autobiography of a class at King's College in the sixties . . .*, Aberdeen Univ. Studs. 15, Aberdeen 1905; Neil Nathaniel Maclean, *Life at a northern university*, Aberdeen 1874, 4th edn. 1917; and Peter John Anderson, comp., *Collections towards a bibliography of the universities of Aberdeen*, Edin. Bibliog. Soc., Edin. 1907. For members of the university see Peter John Anderson, ed., *Roll of alumni in arts of the University and King's College of Aberdeen, 1596–1860*, Aberdeen Univ. studs. 1, Aberdeen 1900; *Officers and graduates of University & King's College, Aberdeen MVD–MDCCCLX*, New Spalding Club 11, Aberdeen 1893; *Officers of the Marischal College and University of Aberdeen, 1593–1860*, Aberdeen 1897; and *Fasti academiae mariscallanae aberdonensis: selections from the records of the Marischal college and University, MDXCIII–MDCCCLX*, 3 v., New Spalding club, 4, 18–19, Aberdeen 1889–98; William Johnston, comp., *Roll of the graduates of the University of Aberdeen, 1860–1900*, Aberdeen Univ. Studs. 18, Aberdeen 1906; and Theodore Watt, comp., *Roll of the graduates of the University of Aberdeen, 1901–1925, with supplement, 1860–1900*, Aberdeen 1935. Famous members of the univ. are listed in W. E. McCulloch, *Viri illustres universitatum aberdonensium*, Aberdeen Univ. Studs. 88, Aberdeen 1923. Studies of univ. hist. are publ. in *Aberdeen Univ. Rev.*, 1+, Aberdeen 1913+.

**10134** EDINBURGH UNIVERSITY. The story of the University of Edinburgh during its first three hundred years. By Sir Alexander Grant. 2 v. 1884.

Full on the 19th cent. Cont. by Arthur Logan Turner, ed., *History of the University of Edinburgh, 1883–1933*, Edin. 1933. Better reading is David Bayne Horn, *A short history of the University of Edinburgh, 1556–1889*, Edin. 1967. The standard reference works are Alexander Morgan, ed., *University of Edinburgh: charters, statutes, and acts of the town council and the senatus, 1583–1858*, with hist. intro. by Robert Kerr Hannay, Edin. 1937, [David Laing, ed.] *A catalogue of the graduates in the faculties of arts, divinity and law of the University of Edinburgh since its foundation*, Edin. 1858, *Alphabetical list of graduates . . . from 1859 to 1888 . . .*, Edin. 1889, and David Talbot Rice and Peter McIntyre, comps., *The university portraits*, Edin. 1957. For rectorial addresses see **10129**. For medicine see **10061–8**. Historical studies appear in *University of Edinburgh J.*, 1+, Edin. 1925+.

**10135** GLASGOW UNIVERSITY. The University of Glasgow, 1451–1951: a short history. By John Duncan Mackie. Glasgow. 1954.

See also *University of Glasgow: old and new . . .*, Glasgow 1891, [J. B. Neilson, ed.] *Fortuna domus: a series of lectures delivered in the University of Glasgow in commemoration of the fifth century of its foundation*, Glasgow 1952, and David Murray, *Memories of the old College of Glasgow . . .*, Glasgow 1927. For principals of the university see the lives of Caird (**9875**), and MacAlister (**10065**), and Elma Story and Helen Constance Herbert Story, *Memoir of Robert Herbert Story, D.D., LL.D., principal and vice-chancellor of the University of Glasgow, one of His Majesty's chaplains in Scotland*, Glasgow 1909. For divinity professors see **9851**. For students see William Innes Anderson, ed., *The matriculation albums of the University of Glasgow from 1728 to 1858*, Glasgow 1913, and *A roll of the graduates of the University of Glasgow from 31st December, 1727, to 31st December, 1897, with short biographical notes*, Glasgow 1898. Historical articles appear in *The College courant: being, the j. of the Glasgow Univ. Graduates Assoc.*, 1+, Glasgow 1948+.

**10136  ST. ANDREWS UNIVERSITY.** The University of St. Andrews: a short history. By Ronald Gordon Cant. Edin. & Lond. 1946. 2nd edn. 1971.

See also Cant's *The college of St. Salvator . . .*, Edin. & Lond. 1950; James Bell Salmond, ed., *Veterum laudes: being a tribute to the achievements of the members of St. Salvator's College during five hundred years*, Edin. & Lond. 1950; Douglas Young, *St. Andrews* (**10181**), which is interesting on the post-1851 period; Anna Jean Mill, 'The first ornamental rector at St. Andrews University: John Stuart Mill', *Scot. Hist. Rev.* xliii (1964), 131–44; and William Angus Knight, *Principal Shairp & his friends*, 1888. Principal Sir James Donaldson's *Addresses delivered in the University of St. Andrews from 1886 to 1910*, Edin. 1911, is in effect a year-by-year survey, which is suppl. by *Votiva tabella: a memorial volume of St. Andrews university in connection with its quincentenary festival*, Univ. of St. Andrews 1911, and Andrew Kennedy Hutchinson Boyd, *Twenty-five years of St. Andrews: September 1865 to September 1890*, 2 v. 1892, *The last years of St. Andrews, September 1890 to September 1895*, 1896, and *St. Andrews and elsewhere*, 1894. For rectorial addresses see **10129**. For students see James Maitland Anderson, ed., *The matriculation roll of the University of St. Andrews, 1747–1897*, Edin. & Lond. 1905, and for univ. hist. *The Alumnus chronicle*, 1947+.

**10137  BLACKIE.** John Stuart Blackie: a biography. By Anna M. Stoddart. 2 v. Edin. & Lond. 1895. New edn. 1896.

The best-known Scottish professor of his day. Professor of Greek, writer, and propagandist. See also Archibald Stodart Walker, *The letters of John Stuart Blackie to his wife . . .*, Edin. & Lond. 1909, Blackie's own *Notes of a life*, ed. by A. S. Walker, 1910, and Howard Angus Kennedy, *Professor Blackie, his sayings and doings . . .*, 1895.

## 2. CULTURAL HISTORY

For medicine see **10061–72**.

**10138  ANNUAL BIBLIOGRAPHY OF SCOTTISH LITERATURE,** 1969+. Scottish Group of the University, College and Research Section of the Library Assoc. Publ. as suppl. to *The Bibliotheck*. Aberdeen. 1970+.

**10139  McCOSH (JAMES).** The Scottish philosophy: biographical, expository, critical, from Hutcheson to Hamilton. Lond. & N.Y. 1875. Repr. Hildesheim. 1966.

See also Selwyn Alfred Grave, *The Scottish philosophy of common sense*, Oxf. 1960.

**10140  MILLAR (JOHN HEPBURN).** A literary history of Scotland. Lond. & N.Y. 1903.

The most detailed account of 19th-cent. Scottish writers. For more general evaluations see William Power, *Literature & oatmeal: what literature has meant to Scotland*, 1935,

John Speirs, *The Scots literary tradition: an essay in criticism*, 1940, 2nd edn. 1962, Kurt Wittig, *The Scottish tradition in literature*, Edin. 1958, and George Blake, *Barrie and the Kailyard school*, 1951.

**10141** STUDIES IN SCOTTISH LITERATURE. 1+. Lubbock, Tex. 1963+.

**10142** MACLEAN (DONALD). Typographia Scoto-Gadelica: or, books printed in the Gaelic of Scotland from . . . 1567 to . . . 1914. Edin. 1915.

For works on Gaelic see **10209–14**.

**10143** COWAN (ROBERT McNAIR WILSON). The newspaper in Scotland: a study of its first expansion, 1815–1860. Glasgow. 1946.

See also *Scottish newspaper directory and guide to advertisers: a complete manual of the newspaper press*, 2nd edn. Edin. 1855.

**10144** EWING (ALEXANDER McLEAN). A history of the *Glasgow Herald*, 1783–1948. Priv. pr. Glasgow. [1949.]

See also Alexander Sinclair, *Fifty years of newspaper life, 1845–1895*, priv. pr. Glasgow [*c.* 1897].

**10145** MILLAR (ALEXANDER HASTIE). The *Dundee Advertiser*, 1801–1901: a centenary memoir. Dundee. 1901.

**10146** THE SCOTSMAN. The glorious privilege: the history of *The Scotsman*. Edin. & Lond. 1967.

See also Edinburgh Evening News, *Fifty years, 1873–1923*, Edin. 1923.

**10147** COOPER. An editor's retrospect: fifty years of newspaper work. By Charles Alfred Cooper. 1896.

Editor of *The Scotsman*.

**10148** WALLACE. Robert Wallace: life and last leaves. Ed. by John Campbell Smith and William Wallace. 1903.

Prominent churchman, editor of *The Scotsman*, and M.P.

**10149** FARMER (HENRY GEORGE). A history of music in Scotland. 1947.

See also Francis Collinson, *The traditional and national music of Scotland*, 1966.

**10150** NATIONAL GALLERY OF SCOTLAND. Catalogue of Scottish drawings. By Keith Kurt Andrews and James Rainey Brotchie. Edin. 1960.

**10151** CAW (*Sir* JAMES LEWIS). Scottish painting, past and present, 1620–1908. Edin. & Lond. 1908.

See also Sir Walter Armstrong, *Scottish painters: a critical study*, 1888; Robert Brydall, *Art in Scotland: its origin and progress*, Edin. & Lond. 1889; William Darling McKay, *The Scottish school of painting*, Lond. & N.Y. 1906; Caw's *Scottish portraits . . .*, 2 v. Edin. 1902–3; and Ian Finlay, *Art in Scotland*, 1948.

10152　RINDER (FRANK) *and others*. The Royal Scottish Academy, 1826–
1916: a complete list of the exhibited works by Raeburn and by academicians,
associates and hon. members . . . Glasgow. 1917.

10153　SCOTTISH EXHIBITION OF NATIONAL HISTORY, ART
AND INDUSTRY, GLASGOW 1911. Official catalogue of the fine art
section. Glasgow. 1911.

10154　CURSITER (STANLEY). Scottish art to the close of the nineteenth
century. Lond. & N.Y. 1949.

See also Sir Walter Armstrong, *The art of William Quiller Orchardson*, Lond. & N.Y.
1895; Sir James Lewis Caw, *William McTaggart, R.S.A. . . . a biography and an
appreciation*, Glasgow 1917, and *Sir James Guthrie, P.R.S.A., LL.D.: a biography . . .*,
1932, Alexander Joseph Finberg, ed., *The paintings of D. Y. Cameron*, 1919, and Frank
Rinder, *D. Y. Cameron . . .*, Glasgow 1912, 2nd edn. 1932.

10155　SCOTTISH ART AND LETTERS. 1+. Glasgow. 1944+.

10156　FINLAY (IAN). Scottish crafts. 1948.

10157　FLEMING (JOHN ARNOLD). Scottish pottery. Glasgow. 1923.

10158　WEST (THOMAS WILSON). A history of architecture in Scotland.
1967.

Poor, but the only book to cover the period. See also Andor Gomme and David Walker,
*Architecture of Glasgow*, 1968, which is fuller for that city.

10159　LORIMER. The work of Sir Robert Lorimer, K.B.E., A.R.A., R.S.A.
By Christopher Edward Clive Hussey. 1931.

10160　MACKINTOSH. Charles Rennie Mackintosh and the modern movement. By Thomas Howarth. 1952.

See also Robert Macleod, *Charles Rennie Mackintosh*, 1968, and Harry Jefferson
Barnes, comp., *Some examples of furniture by Charles Rennie Mackintosh in the Glasgow
School of Art collection*, Glasgow 1969.

10161　CLEMENT (ARCHIBALD GEORGE) *and* ROBERTSON (ROB-
ERT HUGH STANNUS). Scotland's scientific heritage. Edin. & Lond. 1961.

See also *Edinburgh's place in scientific progress: a handbook prepared in connection with
the 1921 meeting of the British Association*, Edin. 1921, and Alexander Findlay, *The
teaching of chemistry in the universities of Aberdeen*, Aberdeen 1935.

10162　FLETCHER (HAROLD ROY) *and* BROWN (WILLIAM HUN-
TER). The Royal Botanic Garden, Edinburgh, 1670–1970. H.M.S.O. 1970.


## F. LOCAL AND REGIONAL HISTORY

### I. GENERAL

10163　BARCLAY (JOHN BRUCE) *ed*. Local history in Scotland . . . Univ.
of Edinburgh Dept. of Adult Educ. Edin. 1966.

10164  BARTHOLOMEW (JOHN). Philip's handy atlas of the counties of Scotland. 1882.

Repl. by George Philip, ed., *Philip's handy administrative atlas of Scotland: a series of detailed county maps showing local government and parliamentary divisions* . . . [1909.]

## 2. LOCAL GOVERNMENT

For the Board of Supervision, later Local Government Board for Scotland, see **10075**.

10165  ATKINSON *afterwards* PALMER (MABEL). Local government in Scotland. Edin. & Lond. 1904.

The only systematic account of Scottish local government in the period. But see Henry Goudy and William Charles Smith, *Local government*, Edin. & Lond. 1880.

10166  SKELTON (JOHN). Report on local taxation in Scotland. [C. 7575] H.C. (1894). LXXIV, pt. II, 1.

10167  MARWICK (*Sir* JAMES DAVID). Observations on the law and practice in regard to municipal elections, and the conduct of the business of town councils and commissioners of police in Scotland. Edin. 1879.

See also his *Acts of parliament relating to municipal elections in the royal burghs of Scotland*, Edin. 1873, and the companion vols. dealing with *Police burghs*, Edin. 1873, and *Parliamentary burghs*, Edin. 1873.

10168  MUIRHEAD (JAMES). The law and practice relating to police government in burghs in Scotland . . . Glasgow. 1893. 3rd edn. 2 v. & suppl. 1924–35.

See also his *Bye-laws and standing orders for burghs in Scotland* . . ., Glasgow 1895, 'Burghs of barony and regality under the Burgh Police Act of 1892', *Scottish Law Rev.* ix (1893), 234–43, *The Town Councils (Scotland) Act, 1900*, Glasgow 1900, *The Burgh Police (Scotland) Act, 1903*, and the *Town Councils (Scotland) Act, 1903* . . ., Glasgow 1904.

10169  THE COUNCILLOR'S MANUAL: being a guide to Scottish local government. Edin. 1892. 13th edn. 1933.

10170  CHISHOLM (JOHN) *and* SHENNAN (JOHN HAY). Manual of the Local Government (Scotland) Act, 1889. Edin. 1889.

See also James Badenach Nicolson and William John Mure, *The county council guide for Scotland: a handbook to the Local Government (Scotland) Act, 1889*, Edin. 1889.

10171  SHENNAN (JOHN HAY). The parish councillor's handbook: being a digest of the Local Government (Scotland) Act, 1894. Edin. 1894. 5th edn. 1908.

See also Sir James Patten Macdougall and Sir James Miller Dodds, *The parish council guide for Scotland: a handbook of the Local Government (Scotland) Act, 1894*, Edin. 1894, James Edward Graham, *Manual of the acts relating to parish councils in Scotland*,

Edin. 1897, and *The law relating to the poor and to parish councils*, Edin. 1905, new edn. 1922, and Charles Cleveland Ellis, *The Local Government (Scotland) Act, 1894, and relative provisions of other statutes*, Edin. 1912.

10172 SHENNAN (JOHN HAY). Boundaries of counties and parishes in Scotland as settled by the boundary commissioners under the Local Government (Scotland) Act, 1889. Edin. 1892.

Shennan was secretary of the boundary commission.

10173 THE SANITARY JOURNAL FOR SCOTLAND. Glasgow. 1876+.

Title became *The sanitary j.*, 1878–1902, *The municipal record & sanitary j.*, 1902–3, and *The county & municipal record*, 1903+.

### 3. THE LOWLANDS

10174 ABERDEENSHIRE. James Fowler Kellas Johnstone and Alexander Webster Robertson, *Bibliographia aberdonensis: being, an account of books relating to or printed in the shires of Aberdeen, Banff, Kincardine, or written by natives or residents or by officers, graduates or alumni of the universities of Aberdeen*, 2 v. Aberdeen 1929–30. Fenton Wyness, *City by the grey North Sea: Aberdeen*, Aberdeen 1966. Alexander Keith, *A thousand years of Aberdeen*, Aberdeen 1972. William Carnie, *Reporting reminiscences*, 3 v. Aberdeen 1902–6. John Cranna, *Fraserburgh past and present*, Aberdeen 1914.

10175 AYRSHIRE. James Edward Shaw, *Ayrshire, 1745–1950: a social and industrial history of the county*, Ayrshire Archaeol. & Nat. Hist. Soc., Edin. & Lond. 1953. Ayrshire Archaeol. and Nat. Hist. Soc., *Collections*, 2 ser., Kilmarnock 1950+. John Strawhorn, *The new history of Cumnock*, Cumnock 1966.

10176 BERWICKSHIRE. Berwickshire Naturalists' Club, *History* [*Proceedings*], 1+, Alnwick, etc. 1831+.

10177 DUMFRIESSHIRE. Dumfriesshire and Galloway Nat. Hist. and Antiq. Soc., *Transactions and j. of proceedings*, 1862–3+.

10178 DUNDEE. Abertay Hist. Soc., *Publications*, 1+, Dundee 1953+. A. W. Paton and A. H. Millar, eds., *British Association, Dundee, 1912: handbook and guide to Dundee and district*, Dundee 1912. For Dundee harbour see **10035.**

10179 EAST LOTHIAN. James H. Jamieson and Eleanor Hawkins, *Bibliography of East Lothian*, E. Lothian Antiq. & Field Naturalists' Soc., Edin. 1936. East Lothian Antiq. & Field Naturalists' Soc., *Transactions*, 1+, Haddington 1924–5+. William Forbes Gray and James H. Jamieson, *East Lothian biographies*, E. Lothian Antiq. & Field Naturalists' Soc. Trans. iv, Haddington 1941.

10180   EDINBURGH AND LEITH. Edinburgh Corporation Libraries and Museums Committee, *Edinburgh, 1767–1967: a select list of books*, Edin. 1967. Robert Butchart, *Prints & drawings of Edinburgh: a descriptive account of the collection in the Edinburgh room of the central public library*, Edin. 1955. William Cowan, *The maps of Edinburgh, 1544–1929*, 2nd edn. by Charles Brodie Boog Watson, Edin. 1932. *The book of the Old Edinburgh Club*, 1+, Edin. 1908+. James Grant, *Cassell's old and new Edinburgh* . . ., 3 v. Edin. 1880–3. J. Brian Crossland, *Victorian Edinburgh*, Letchworth 1966. Marguerite Wood, *The lord provosts of Edinburgh, 1296 to 1932*, Edin. 1932. James Campbell Irons, *Leith and its antiquities from the earliest times to the close of the nineteenth century* . . ., 2 v. Edin. 1898.

10181   FIFE. Erskine Beveridge, comp., *A bibliography of works relating to Dunfermline and the west of Fife, including publications of writers connected with the district*, Edinburgh Bibliog. Soc. 5, Dunfermline 1901. J. H. Whitehouse, *Problems of a Scottish provincial town (Dunfermline)* (**10058**). James Houston Baxter, *Collections towards a bibliography of St. Andrews*, St. Andrews 1926. Douglas Young, *St. Andrews: town and gown, royal and ancient*, 1969.

10182   GLASGOW. Charles Allen Oakley, *The second city*, Glasgow & Lond. 1946, new edn. 1967. Ronald Miller and Joy Tivey, eds., *The Glasgow region: a general survey prepared for the meeting of the British Association*, Glasgow 1958. George Eyre-Todd, *Who's who in Glasgow*, Glasgow 1909. *Memoirs of one hundred Glasgow men* (**9794**). *The lord provosts of Glasgow from 1833 to 1902* . . ., Glasgow 1902. James Nicol, *Vital, social and economic statistics of the City of Glasgow, 1885–1891* . . ., Glasgow 1891. Sir James Bell and James Paton, *Glasgow: its municipal organization and administration*, Glasgow 1896. Glasgow Corporation, *Handbook on the municipal enterprises*, Glasgow 1904, and *Municipal Glasgow: its evolution and enterprises*, Glasgow 1914. Sir James David Marwick, *The River Clyde and the Clyde burghs: the city of Glasgow and its old relations with Rutherglen, Renfrew, Paisley, Dumbarton, Port Glasgow, Greenock, Rothesay and Irvine*, Glasgow 1909. For public health see **10070**. For the Clyde ports see **10030**. For architecture see **10158**.

10183   PEEBLESSHIRE. James Walter Buchan, ed., *A history of Peeblesshire*, 3 v. Glasgow 1925–7.

10184   RENFREWSHIRE. Robert Brown, *The history of Paisley from the Roman period down to 1884*, 2 v. Paisley 1886.

10185   ROSS-SHIRE. Robert William Munro and Jean Munro, *Tain through the centuries*, Tain town council 1966.

10186   ROXBURGHSHIRE. Hawick Archaeol. Soc., *Transactions*, 1+, Hawick 1863+.

## 4. The Highlands and Islands

There is a useful booklist, *The Highlands and islands of Scotland*, Nat. Book League 1967. For background consult Malcolm Gray, *The Highland economy, 1750–1850*, Edin. 1957. For Queen Victoria's life in the Highlands see **330**.

**10187** O'DELL (ANDREW CHARLES) *and* WALTON (KENNETH). The Highlands and islands of Scotland. Lond. & Edin. 1962.

A good historical geography, suppl. by David Turnock, *Patterns of Highland development*, 1970. For population trends see Frank Fraser Darling, ed., *West Highland survey: an essay in human ecology*, 1955. There is no gen. hist. of the Highlands during the period. Angus John Beaton, *The social and economic condition of the Highlands of Scotland since 1800*, Stirling 1906, is only a brief essay.

**10188** DAY (JOHN PERCIVAL). Public administration in the Highlands and islands of Scotland. 1918.

A comprehensive hist. of late-19th-cent. developments.

**10189** GRANT (ISABEL FRANCES). Highland folk ways. 1961.

An excellent intro. to rural life in the Highlands. See also Colin Sinclair, *The thatched houses of the old Highlands*, Edin. & Lond. 1953.

**10190** GRANT (ISABEL FRANCES). The Macleods: the history of a clan, 1200–1956. 1959.

The only good clan hist.

**10191** COLLIER (ADAM). The crofting problem. Camb. 1953.

A useful intro. See also Margaret M. Leigh, 'The crofting problem, 1790–1883', *Scot. J. Agric.* xi (1928), 4–21, 137–47, 261–73, 426–33; xii (1929), 34–9; P. T. Wheeler, 'Landownership and the crofting system in Sutherland since 1800', *Agric. Hist. Rev.* xiv (1966), 45–56; James R. Coull, 'Crofters' common grazings in Scotland', ibid. xvi (1968), 142–54; and M. L. Ryder, 'Sheep and clearances in the Scottish Highlands: a biologist's view', ibid. xvi (1968), 155–8.

**10192** HANHAM (HAROLD JOHN). 'The problem of Highland discontent, 1880–1885'. *Roy. Hist. Soc. Trans.* 5 ser. xix (1969), 21–65.

For the hagiography of the land movement see Joseph Gordon Macleod, *Highland heroes of the land reform movement*, Inverness n.d.

**10193** MACKENZIE (ALEXANDER). The history of the Highland clearances: containing a reprint of Donald Macleod's 'Gloomy memories of the Highlands'; Isle of Skye in 1882; and a verbatim report of the trial of the Braes crofters. Inverness. 1883.

A work of political polemic, but includes useful material. The 1883 edn. was the only complete one publ. Later edns. were pruned of their late-19th-cent. material. Suppl. by Mackenzie's articles in the *Celtic magazine* (**10211**).

**10194** CAMERON (JAMES). The old and the new Highlands & Hebrides, from the days of the great clearances to the Pentland Act of 1912. Kirkcaldy. 1912.

A journalist's reminiscences rather than a hist., but incl. useful material.

10195 McNEILL (*Sir* JOHN). Report to the Board of Supervision on the Western Highlands and Islands. [1397] H.C. (1851). XXVI, 899.

On the aftermath of the potato famine.

10196 LEVI (LEONE). 'On the economic condition of the Highlands and Islands of Scotland'. *Stat. Soc. J.* xxviii (1865), 372–401.

A useful survey. See also the rejoinder by George Douglas Campbell, Duke of Argyll, ibid. xxix (1866), 504–35.

10197 CAMPBELL (GEORGE DOUGLAS), *Duke of Argyll*. 'On the economic condition of the Highlands of Scotland'. *Nineteenth Century* xiii (1883), 173–98.

Contd. in his 'A corrected picture of the Highlands', *Nineteenth Century* xvi (1884), 681–701. A utilitarian view of the Highlands representing the intellectual opposition to Blackie's arguments (**10198**). See also [Lord Colin Campbell] *The crofter in history* by *Dalriad*, Edin. 1885. An alternative view is presented by J. A. Cameron, 'Storm-clouds in the Highlands', *Nineteenth Century* xvi (1884), 379–95. [Alexander Innes Shand,] *Letters from the Highlands*, Edin. & Lond. 1884, has details of estates.

10198 BLACKIE (JOHN STUART). The Scottish highlanders and the land laws: an historico-economical enquiry. 1885.

An attack on the Highland land system by one of its most popular opponents. See also his *Altavona*, Edin. 1882, and *The language and literature of the Scottish Highlands*, Edin. 1876.

10199 NAPIER COMMISSION ON HIGHLANDS AND ISLANDS. Report of Her Majesty's commissioners of inquiry into the condition of the crofters and cottars in the Highlands and Islands of Scotland [Chairman: Lord Napier and Ettrick]. Report. [C. 3980] H.C. (1884) XXXII, 1. Minutes of Evidence. [C. 3980-I–IV] H.C. (1884). XXXIII–XXXVI.

A monumental inquiry to be suppl. by the unpubl. papers of the Commission in the Scottish Record Office. Following on this report a number of acts were passed establishing permanent commissions. The Crofters' Commission issued an annual report from 1886–7 until it was succeeded by the Land Court (Scotland) in 1914; the Crofter Colonization Commissioners issued fifteen reports, 1890–1906, and the Congested Districts Board for Scotland issued fourteen reports, 1899–1913. For details see *General Index* (**33**).

10200 FRASER (ALEXANDER) *and* McNEILL (MALCOLM). Report to Her Majesty's Secretary for Scotland on the condition of the cottar population in the Lews. [C. 5265] H.C. (1888). LXXX, 639.

10201 WALPOLE COMMISSION ON WESTERN HIGHLANDS. Report of the commission appointed to inquire into certain matters affecting the interests of the population of the Western Highlands and Islands [Chairman: Spencer Walpole]. [C. 6138] H.C. (1890). XXVII, 651. Second report. [C. 6242] H.C. (1890–1). XLIV, 561.

On Highland fisheries.

10202   BRAND COMMISSION ON DEER FORESTS. Report of the royal commission (Highlands and Islands, 1892) [Chairman: Sheriff David Brand]. [C. 7681] H.C. (1895). XXXVIII, 1. Minutes of evidence. [C. 7668] H.C. (1895). XXXVIII, 95; [C. 7668-I-II] H.C. (1895). XXXIX, pts. I-II.
Fuller than the report of the 1873 committee (**7810**).

10203   CROFTERS COMMISSION. Report to the Secretary for Scotland by the Crofters Commission on the social condition of the people of Lewis in 1901, as compared with twenty years ago. [Cd. 1327] H.C. (1902). LXXXIII, 287.

10204   MANSFIELD COMMITTEE ON SUTHERLAND AND CAITHNESS FISHERIES. Report of the departmental committee on the sea fisheries of Sutherland & Caithness [Chairman: The Earl of Mansfield]. [Cd. 2557] H.C. (1905). XIII, 735. Minutes of evidence etc. [Cd. 2608] H.C. (1905). XIII, 751.

10205   DITTMAR (FREDERICK) *and* MILLAR (ALEXANDER B.). Report to the Local Government Board for Scotland on the sanitary condition of the Lews. [Cd. 2616] H.C. (1905). XXXIV, 767.

10206   LOCAL GOVERNMENT BOARD FOR SCOTLAND. Reports to the Local Government Board for Scotland on the burden of the existing rates and the general financial position of the Outer Hebrides. [Cd. 3014] H.C. (1906). CIV, 689.

10207   HIGHLANDS AND ISLANDS MEDICAL SERVICES COMMITTEE [Chairman: Sir John A. Dewar]. Report to the commissioners of His Majesty's Treasury. [Cd. 6559] H.C. (1912-13). XLII, 581. Minutes of evidence. [Cd. 6920] H.C. (1913). XXXVII, 213.

10208   SCOTT (WILLIAM ROBERT). Report to the Board of Agriculture for Scotland on home industries in the Highlands and Islands. [Cd. 7564] H.C. (1914). XXXII, 43.

10209   CAMPBELL (JOHN LORNE). Gaelic in Scottish education and life: past, present and future. Saltire Soc. Edin. 1945.
See also **10115.**

10210   MACNEILL (NIGEL). The literature of the Highlanders: a history of Gaelic literature from the earliest times to the present day. Inverness. 1892. 2nd edn. Stirling. 1929.

10211   GAELIC SOCIETY OF INVERNESS. Transactions. 1+. Inverness. 1871-2+.

The oldest of the socs. concerned with the preservation of Highland culture. See also Univ. of Aberdeen, Celtic Dept., *Scottish Gaelic studies*, Aberdeen 1926+, Gaelic Soc. of Glasgow, *Transactions*, 4 v. Glasgow 1887-1934, and *Gairm*, Glasgow 1952-70. Among older journals *The Celtic magazine*, 1-13, Inverness 1875-88, and *The Celtic monthly*, 1-25, Glasgow 1892-1917, were most useful. For other collectors of Gaelic see Hall and Campbell, *Strange things* (**4039**).

10212 CARMICHAEL (ALEXANDER). Carmina gadelica: hymns and incantations with illustrative notes, on words, rites and customs, dying and obsolete; orally collected in the Highlands of Scotland and translated into English. 6 v. Edin. 1900–71.

10213 CAMPBELL (JOHN FRANCIS). Popular tales of the West Highlands, orally collected, with a translation. 4 v. Edin. 1860. New edn. 4 v. Paisley etc. 1890–3.

Cont. in *More West Highland tales* . . ., ed. for the Scottish Anthropological and Folklore Soc., 2 v. Edin. & Lond. 1940–60.

10214 SHAW (MARGARET FAY). Folksongs and folklore of South Uist. 1955.

See also John Lorne Campbell, ed., *Hebridean folksongs: a collection of waulking songs by Donald MacCormick in Kilphedir in South Uist in the year 1893*, Oxf. 1969, and *Bàrdachd Mhgr Áilein air a deasachadh le Iain L. Caimbeul ('Fear Chanaidh'): the Gaelic poems of Fr Allan McDonald of Eriskay (1859–1905)*, Edin. 1965.

10215 ANDERSON (PETER JOHN). A concise bibliography of the printed & MS. material on the history, topography & institutions of the burgh, parish and shire of Inverness. Aberdeen Univ. Studs. lxxiii. Aberdeen. 1917.

10216 MOWAT (JOHN). A new bibliography of the county of Caithness . . . Wick. 1940.

The only reasonably up-to-date county bibliog.

10217 GASKELL (PHILIP). Morvern transformed: a Highland parish in the nineteenth century. Camb. 1968.

An admirable account of a parish taken over as a pleasure ground.

10218 GREGOR (MARY J. F.) *and* CRICHTON (RUTH MOREY). From croft to factory: the evolution of an industrial community in the Highlands [Kinlochleven]. 1946.

10219 MACKAY (NORMAN DOUGLAS). Aberfeldy, past and present: the story of a small Highland town . . . Aberfeldy. 1954.

10220 THOMPSON (FRANCIS). Harris and Lewis: Outer Hebrides. Newton Abbot. 1968.

A brief but useful historical and social survey. Suppl. by his *Harris tweed: the story of a Hebridean industry*, Newton Abbot & N.Y. 1969.

10221 GEDDES (ARTHUR). The isle of Lewis and Harris: a study in British community. Edin. 1955.

10222 CAMPBELL (JOHN LORNE) *ed.* The book of Barra: being, accounts of the island of Barra in the Outer Hebrides written by various authors at different times, together with unpublished letters and other matter relating to the island. 1936.

10223  MACLEAN (JOHN PATTERSON). History of the island of Mull, together with a narrative of Iona, the sacred isle, 2 v. Greenville, Ohio. 1923–5.

See also Peter Angus Macnab, *The isle of Mull*, Newton Abbot 1970.

10224  STEEL (TOM). The life and death of St Kilda. Nat. Trust for Scotland. 1965.

See also Francis Thompson, *St. Kilda and other Hebridean outliers*, Newton Abbot 1970.

10225  BARRON (JAMES). The northern Highlands in the nineteenth century: newspaper index and annals [to 1856]. 3 v. Inverness. 1903–13.

Of little value for the period.

10226  CAMPBELL. Reminiscences and reflections of an octogenarian Highlander. By Duncan Campbell. Inverness. 1910.

Good. Campbell edited the Conservative newspaper in Inverness.

10227  MACKENZIE. A hundred years in the Highlands. By Osgood Hanbury Mackenzie. 1921. New edn. 1949.

The reclamation of a West Highland wilderness and the making of a famous garden at Inverewe.

10228  MACLEAN. The former days. By Norman Maclean. 1945.

Life on Skye and the mainland. Cont. in *Set free* [1949], and *The years of fulfilment*, 1953, which deal chiefly with the Church of Scotland.

10229  MITCHELL. Reminiscences of my life in the Highlands (1883). By Joseph Mitchell. New edn. 2 v. Newton Abbot. 1971.

On Highland roads, railways, and families.

10230  REA. A school in South Uist: reminiscences of a Hebridean schoolmaster, 1890–1913. By Frederick G. Rea. Ed. by John Lorne Campbell. 1964.

A delightful account of island life by a Catholic schoolmaster from Birmingham.

10231  NICOLSON (NIGEL). Lord of the Isles: Lord Leverhulme in the Hebrides. 1960.

10232  M'CONNOCHIE (ALEXANDER INKSON). The deer & deer forests of Scotland: historical, descriptive, sporting . . . 1923.

See also **10084.**

# XIII

## IRELAND

### A. GENERAL

#### 1. REFERENCE

10233  EAGER (ALAN ROBERT). A guide to Irish bibliographical material: being, a bibliography of Irish bibliographies and some sources of information. Libr. Assoc. 1964.

10234  CARTY (JAMES). Bibliography of Irish history, 1870–1911. Nat. Libr. of Ireland. Dublin. 1940.

Cont. by his *Bibliography of Irish history, 1912–1921*, Nat. Libr. of Ireland, Dublin 1936. Carty also began the series of 'Writings on Irish history', 1936+, publ. in *Irish Hist. Studs.*, 1+, Dublin 1938+. These provide an invaluable guide to all aspects of Irish history. Edith Mary Johnston, *Irish history: a select bibliography*, Hist. Assoc. helps for students 73, 1969, is a useful handlist. Helen Frances Mulvey, 'Thirty years' work in Irish history, III: nineteenth-century Ireland, 1801–1914', *Irish Hist. Studs.* xvii (1970–1), 1–31, repr. in Theodore William Moody, ed., *Irish historiography, 1936–70*, Dublin 1972, is a good bibliog. discussion, covering the period better than her 'Modern Irish history since 1940: a bibliographical survey, 1600–1922', *The Historian* xxvii (1964–5), 516–59.

10235  NATIONAL LIBRARY OF IRELAND. Sources for the history of Irish civilisation: articles in Irish periodicals. 9 v. Boston. 1970.

A useful index. See also John Power, *List of Irish periodical publications—chiefly literary —from 1729 to the present time*, 1866.

10236  NATIONAL LIBRARY OF IRELAND. Manuscript sources for the history of Irish civilisation. Ed. by Richard James Hayes. 11 v. Boston. 1965.

Covers MSS. in 30 countries. For surveys of documents in private hands see, in particular, *Analecta Hibernica* xv (1944) and xx (1958), and subsequent suppls., *Irish Hist. Studs.* ix (1954–5), 28–52, and National Libr. of Ireland, *Report of the Council*, notably since the report for 1949–50.

10237  WOOD (HERBERT). A guide to the records deposited in the Public Record Office of Ireland. Dublin. 1919.

For lists of records salvaged after the destruction of the Record Office in 1922 see *56th Report of the Deputy Keeper of the Public Records, Ireland*, Dublin 1931, Herbert Wood, 'The public records of Ireland before and after 1922', *Roy. Hist. Soc. Trans.* 4 ser. xiii (1930), 17–49, and Margaret Griffith, 'A short guide to the Public Record Office of Ireland', *Irish Hist. Studs.* viii (1952–3), 45–58. The estimate of damage given in these reports is somewhat exaggerated. For the state of the Irish official records consult also the *Reports* of the Deputy Keeper of the Public Records in Ireland, Dublin 1869+, and of the Deputy Keeper of the Records of Northern Ireland, Belfast 1928+. The Northern Irish reports have full indexes of acquisitions and are good for private archives. The Northern Ireland report for 1960–5, Belfast 1968, is particularly full.

10238 IRISH MANUSCRIPTS COMMISSION. Catalogue of publications issued and in preparation, 1928–66. Dublin. 1966.

Reports of the Commission are also incl. in *Analecta Hibernica*, Dublin 1930+.

10239 EVANS (EDWARD). Historical and bibliographical account of almanacks, directories, etc. published in Ireland from the sixteenth century: their rise, progress and decay . . . Dublin. 1897.

10240 LEWIS (SAMUEL). A topographical dictionary of Ireland, comprising the several counties, cities, boroughs, corporate, market, and post towns, parishes and villages, with historical and statistical descriptions. 2 v. and atlas. 1837. 2nd edn. 2 v. and atlas. 1842. Repr. 1850.

Still the best Irish gazetteer. For admin. districts, etc., the following atlases are useful: John Bartholomew, comp., *Philip's handy atlas of the counties of Ireland*, rev. edn. 1882, George Philip and Son, publishers, *Philip's atlas and geography of Ireland* . . ., 1883, and *Philip's handy administrative atlas of Ireland* . . ., 1909.

10241 GRIMSHAW (THOMAS WRIGLEY). Facts and figures about Ireland. Part I. Comprising a summary and analysis of the principal statistics of Ireland for the fifty years, 1841–1890. Part II. Comprising comparative statistics of Irish counties; with tables of the principal statistics of the counties for each of the six decennial census years, 1841–1891, and summary and analysis. Dublin. 1893.

10242 ELMES (ROSALIND M.) *comp.* Catalogue of Irish topographical prints and original drawings. Nat. Libr. of Ireland. Dublin. 1943.

10243 THOM'S IRISH ALMANAC and official directory for 1844+. Dublin. 1844+.

Title changed to *Thom's official directory* . . ., 1881+, and then to *Thom's directory of Ireland*. Includes both lists of office-holders and a biog. dictionary of peers, M.P.s, Lords-Lieutenant, etc.

10244 CRONE (JOHN SMYTH). A concise dictionary of Irish biography. Dublin. 1928. Rev. and enl. edn. Dublin. 1937.

Too brief. Alfred John Webb, *A compendium of Irish biography* . . ., Dublin 1878, is an earlier attempt in the same vein. Better are the 4 v. in Pike's New Century series: *Dublin and County Dublin*, 1908, *Belfast and the province of Ulster*, 1909, *Ulster contemporary biographies*, 1910, and *Cork and County Cork*, 1911. Also useful for the end of the period are *Thom's Irish who's who*, Dublin 1923, *Who's who in Northern Ireland*, Belfast 1937, 1938, 1939, and Ernest Gaskell, *Ulster leaders: social and political*, [*c.* 1914].

10245 BURKE (*Sir* JOHN BERNARD) *and others*. A genealogical and heraldic history of the landed gentry of Ireland. 1899. 2nd edn. 1904. 3rd edn. 1912. 4th edn. 1958.

Irish genealogies were included in the United Kingdom *Landed gentry* (**86**) up to and incl. 1898 and in 1937.

10246 MACLYSAGHT (EDWARD). Irish families: their names, arms and origins. Dublin. 1957. Suppl. Dublin. 1964.

A remarkable miscellany, cont. by his *More Irish families*, Galway & Dublin 1960. For family pedigrees see Irish Genealogical Research Soc., *The Irish genealogist*, 1937–8+, and Margaret Dickson Falley, *Irish and Scotch-Irish ancestral research: a guide to the genealogical records, methods and sources in Ireland*, 2 v. priv. pr. Strasburg, Va. 1962.

10247 BURTCHAELL (GEORGE DAMES) *and* SADLEIR (THOMAS ULICK) *eds.* Alumni Dublinenses: a register of the students, graduates, professors, and provosts of Trinity college, in the University of Dublin [1593–1846]. 1924. New edn. [1593–1860.] Dublin. 1935.

To some extent an Irish Protestant *Who was who.*

10248 CURTIS (EDMUND) *and* McDOWELL (ROBERT BRENDAN) *eds.* Irish historical documents, 1172–1922. 1943. Repr. 1968.

James Carty, comp., *Ireland from the Great Famine to the Treaty, 1851–1921: a documentary record*, Dublin 1951, is fuller and well illus.

## 2. HISTORIES AND STUDIES

10249 BECKETT (JAMES CAMLIN). The making of modern Ireland, 1603–1923. 1966.

Much the best general hist. with handy bibliog. Beckett's *A short history of Ireland*, 1952, 3rd edn. 1966, is also the best intro. to Irish hist., though it should be suppl. by Theodore William Moody and Francis Xavier Martin, eds., *The course of Irish history*, Cork 1967; [Donat] Conor Cruise O'Brien, ed., *The shaping of modern Ireland*, Lond. & Toronto 1960; and other vols. in the series of Thomas Davis lectures, for a list of which for 1953–67 see *Irish. Hist. Studs.* xv (1966–7), 276–302. Edmund Curtis, *A History of Ireland*, 1936, 6th edn. 1950, long standard, adds little. Oliver MacDonagh, *Ireland*, Englewood Cliffs, N.J. 1968, is a good short, interpretative study. Sir James O'Connor, *History of Ireland, 1798–1924*, 2 v. 1925, and Patrick Sarsfield O'Hegarty, *A history of Ireland under the union, 1801 to 1922 . . .*, 1952, speak from different nationalist viewpoints. Godfrey Locker-Lampson, *A consideration of the state of Ireland in the nineteenth century*, 1907, William O'Connor Morris, *Ireland, 1798–1898*, 1898, Sir Thomas Wallace Russell, *Ireland and the empire: a review, 1800–1900*, 1901, and Sir Ernest Barker, *Ireland in the last fifty years (1866–1916)*, Oxf. 1917, 2nd edn. 1919, reflect bygone preoccupations but are useful reflections of contemp. ideas.

10250 LYONS (FRANCIS STEWART LELAND). Ireland since the famine: 1850 to the present. Lond. & N.Y. 1971.

Now standard for the period.

10251 IRISH HISTORICAL STUDIES . . . 1938–9+. Dublin. 1939+.

The principal Irish historical periodical. Publishes annual lists of 'Writings on Irish history' and 'Research on Irish history in Irish universities'. The following periodicals also publ. general historical articles: *Studies: an Irish quarterly review*, Dublin 1912+, Irish Conference of Historians, *Historical studies*, annual. Camb. 1959+, *Studia Hibernica*, Dublin 1961+, and the js. of the two universities in Dublin, *Hermathena . . .* [Trinity College], 1873+, Dublin 1874+, and *University Review* [National University], Dublin 1954+. Irish Manuscripts Commission, *Analecta Hibernica: including the reports of the Irish Manuscripts Commission*, Dublin 1930+, concentrates its attention on archive collections. Section C of the Royal Irish Academy, *Proceedings*, Dublin 1786+, and the Royal Soc. of Antiquaries of Ireland, *Transactions and journal*, Dublin 1849+, occasionally publ. papers on the period. There is a useful guide to local publs.: Seosamh Ó Dufaigh, 'Irish local historical and archaeological journals', *Éire-Ireland* v (1970), 90–9.

10252 FREEMAN (THOMAS WALTER). Ireland: its physical, historical, social and economic geography. 1950. 4th edn. [Ireland: a general and regional geography.] Lond. & N.Y. 1969.

10253 LABONNINIÈRE DE BEAUMONT (GUSTAVE DE). L'Irlande sociale, politique et religieuse. 2 v. Paris. 1839. Rev. edn. 2 v. 1863.

A famous work. The rev. edn. incl. a longish preface on the 1860s.

10254 PERRAUD (ADOLPHE LOUIS ALBERT), *Cardinal*. Ireland in 1862. Trans. from the French. Dublin. 1863.

10255 SENIOR (NASSAU WILLIAM). Journals, conversations and essays relating to Ireland. 2 v. 1868.

10256 WILKINSON (HENRY SPENSER). The eve of Home Rule: impressions of Ireland in 1886. 1886.

10257 MORRIS (WILLIAM O'CONNOR). Present Irish questions. 1901.

There is also a naïve chronicle of events in Michael John FitzGerald McCarthy, *Five years in Ireland, 1895–1900*, Dublin & Lond. 1901, 10th edn. 1903.

10258 PLUNKETT (*Sir* HORACE CURZON). Ireland in the new century. 1904.

10259 BROOKS (SYDNEY). The new Ireland. Dublin. 1907.

Reports for the *Daily Mail*. He also publ. *Aspects of the Irish question*, Dublin 1912.

10260 PAUL-DUBOIS (LOUIS FRANÇOIS ALPHONSE). Contemporary Ireland. Trans. by Thomas Michael Kettle. Dublin & N.Y. 1908.

Still the best general account of Edwardian Ireland. Cont. by his *The Irish struggle and its results*, trans. by Thomas Patrick Gill, 1934.

10261 THE TIMES. Ireland of today. 1913.

### 3. The Irish Abroad

For the Irish in England see **6961**, and in Scotland, **10052**.

10262 EMIGRATION STATISTICS of Ireland for the year 1876+. [C. 1700] H.C. (1877). LXXXV, 643. Annual for 1876–1920.

10263 KEEP (G. R. C.). 'Official opinion on Irish emigration in the later 19th century'. *Irish Eccles. Rec.* lxxxi (1954), 412–21.

For some of the consequences of emigration see **10679**.

10264 CALKIN (HOMER L.). 'The United States government and the Irish: a bibliographical study of research materials in the U.S. national archives'. *Irish Hist. Studs.* ix (1954–5), 28–52.

10265 SCHRIER (ARNOLD). Ireland and the American emigration, 1850–1900. Minneapolis. 1958.

10266 WITTKE (CARL). The Irish in America. Baton Rouge, La. 1956.

A basic outline, as is George Potter, *To the golden door: the story of the Irish in Ireland and America*, Boston & Toronto 1960. William Vincent Shannon, *The American Irish*, N.Y. 1963, rev. edn. 1966, is amusing, but adds little. Among contemp. books John Francis Maguire, *The Irish in America*, 1868, is probably the best. The American-Irish Hist. Soc., *Journal*, 1898–1914+, includes articles on the period. For the American Irish and Anglo-American relations see **2609–10**.

10267 HANDLIN (OSCAR). Boston's immigrants, 1790–1865: a study in acculturation. Camb., Mass. 1941. Rev. edn. [to 1880.] 1959.

Chiefly concerned with the Boston Irish. See also Nathan Glazer and Daniel Patrick Moynihan, *Beyond the melting pot: the Negroes, Puerto Ricans, Jews, Italians and Irish of New York city*, Camb., Mass. 1963, 2nd. edn. 1970; Robert Ernst, *Immigrant life in New York City, 1825–1863*, N.Y. 1949; Albon P. Man, 'The Irish in New York in the early eighteen sixties', *Irish. Hist. Studs.* vii (1950–1), 87–108; Richard J. Purcell, 'The New York commissioners of emigration and Irish immigrants, 1847–1860', *Studies* xxxvii (1948), 29–42; Earl Francis Niehaus, *The Irish in New Orleans, 1800–1860*, Baton Rouge, La. 1965; and Justille McDonald, *History of the Irish in Wisconsin in the nineteenth century*, Wash. 1954.

10268 BROWN (THOMAS NICHOLAS). Irish-American nationalism, 1870–1890. Phila. 1966.

Important. See also Florence Elizabeth Gibson, *The attitudes of the New York Irish toward state and national affairs, 1848–1892*, N.Y. 1951; Charles Callan Tansill, *America and the fight for Irish freedom, 1866–1922, an old story based on new data*, N.Y. 1957 and **10341**.

10269 LEVINE (EDWARD M.). The Irish and Irish politicians: a study of cultural and social alienation. Notre Dame [Ind.]. 1966.

See also Morris Robert Werner, *Tammany Hall*, Garden City, N.Y. 1928, [Theodore] Lothrop Stoddard, *Master of Manhattan: the life of Richard Croker*, N.Y. etc. 1931, and John Paul Bocock, 'The Irish conquest of our cities', *Forum* xvii (1894), 186–95.

10270 BROEHL (WAYNE G.) *Jr.* The Molly Maguires. Camb., Mass. 1964.

On Pennsylvania secret societies in the 1860s and 1870s.

10271 WARD (ALAN J.). Ireland and Anglo-American relations, 1899–1921. 1969.

There are some interesting comments in Sir [John Randolph] Shane Leslie, *The Irish issue in its American aspect: a contribution to the settlement of Anglo-American relations during and after the Great War*, N.Y. 1917.

10272 GREEN (JAMES J.). 'American Catholics and the Irish Land League, 1879–1882'. *Catholic Hist. Rev.* xxxv (1949–50), 19–42.

10273 SPALDING. The career of the Right Reverend John Lancaster Spalding, bishop of Peoria, as president of the Irish Catholic Colonization Association of the United States, 1879–1892. By Mary Evangela Henthorne. Urbana, Ill. 1932.

10274 DAVIN (NICHOLAS FLOOD). The Irishman in Canada. Toronto. 1877. Repr. Shannon. 1970.

See also the lives of D'Arcy McGee (**1483**), and Edward Blake (**10367**).

10275 KIERNAN (THOMAS JOSEPH). The Irish exiles in Australia. Dublin. 1954.

See also William Fielding Wannan, *The wearing of the green: the lore, literature, legend and balladry of the Irish in Australia*, ed. by Bill Wannan, Melb. 1965, and James Francis Hogan, *The Irish in Australia*, Dublin & Melb. 1887.

10276 MURRAY (THOMAS). The story of the Irish in Argentina. N.Y. 1919.

See also Santiago M. Ussher, *Los capellanes irlandeses en la colectividad hiberno-argentina durante el siglo XIX*, Buenos Aires 1954.

## B. POLITICAL AND ADMINISTRATIVE HISTORY

### 1. ANGLO-IRISH RELATIONS

10277 MANSERGH ([PHILIP] NICHOLAS [SETON]). Ireland in the age of reform and revolution: a commentary on Anglo-Irish relations and on political forces in Ireland, 1840–1921. 1940. New edn. [The Anglo-Irish question, 1840–1921 . . .] 1965.

The best interpretative essay.

10278 STRAUSS (ERICH). Irish nationalism and British democracy, 1801–1921. 1951.

Marxist; stimulating.

10279 McCAFFREY (LAWRENCE JOHN). The Irish question, 1800–1922. Lexington, Ky. 1968.

A good up-to-date survey. Patrick O'Farrell, *Ireland's English question: Anglo-Irish relations, 1534–1970*, 1971, gives the story a sharp nationalist twist.

10280 RUSSELL (*Sir* THOMAS WALLACE). Ireland and the empire: a review, 1800–1900. 1901.

Like Richard Barry O'Brien, *Fifty years of concessions to Ireland, 1831–1881*, 2 v. [1883–5], and Thomas Dunbar Ingram, *A history of the legislative union of Great Britain and Ireland*, Lond. & N.Y. 1887, 2nd edn. 1890, intended chiefly for polemical purposes.

10281 CURTIS (LEWIS PERRY) *Jr*. Anglo-Saxons and Celts: a study of anti-Irish prejudice in Victorian England. Bridgeport, Conn. 1968.

A useful study of British attitudes to Irish claims to self-government. See also his *Apes and angels: the Irishman in Victorian caricature*, Newton Abbot 1971.

10282 HERNON (JOSEPH M.). Celts, Catholics & copperheads: Ireland views the American civil war. Columbus, Ohio. 1968.

American conflicts seen in terms of 'the Irish question'.

10283 HAMMOND (JOHN LAWRENCE LE BRETON). Gladstone and the Irish nation. 1938. Repr. Lond. & Hamden, Conn. 1964.

Still the fullest account of Gladstone's Irish policy, but needs to be suppl. by George John Shaw-Lefevre, Baron Eversley, *Gladstone and Ireland: the Irish policy of parliament from 1850–1894*, 1912, and E. D. Steele, 'Gladstone and Ireland', *Irish Hist. Studs.* xvii (1970–1), 58–88.

10284 KAVANAGH. The incredible Mr. Kavanagh. By Donald McCormick. 1960.

The most unusual of the Anglo-Irish M.P.s of the 1860s and 1870s: legless, armless, and a reformer. See also Sarah Louisa Steele, *The Right Honourable Arthur MacMurrough Kavanagh: a biography*, Lond. & N.Y. 1891.

10285 CURTIS (LEWIS PERRY) *Jr.* Coercion and conciliation in Ireland, 1880–1892: a study in conservative unionism. Princeton [N.J.]. 1963.

Important. See also Owen Dudley Edwards, 'American diplomats and Irish coercion, 1880–1883', *J. Amer. Studs.* i (1967), 213–32.

10286 PHILLIPS (WALTER ALISON). The revolution in Ireland, 1906–1923. 1923. 2nd edn. 1926.

An important unionist study.

10287 GWYNN (DENIS ROLLESTON). The history of partition, 1912–1925. Dublin. 1950.

10288 BIRRELL. The chief secretary: Augustine Birrell in Ireland. By Leon Ó Broin. Lond. 1969. Hamden, Conn. 1970.

See also 740.

10289 CHURCHILL. Churchill and Ireland. By Mary Cogan Bromage. Notre Dame, Ind. 1964.

10290 RYAN (ALFRED PATRICK). Mutiny at the Curragh. 1956.

Needs to be suppl. by Sir James Fergusson, *The Curragh incident*, 1964.

## 2. Administration

10291 McDOWELL (ROBERT BRENDAN). The Irish administration, 1801–1914. 1964.

Standard. The main sources for admin. hist. are the annual reports of the various Irish offices and the reports of committees of inquiry. Charles O'Mahony, *The viceroys of Ireland . . .*, 1912, is a popular account of viceroys to 1911.

10292 INSTITUTE OF PUBLIC ADMINISTRATION OF IRELAND. Administration . . . 1+. Dublin. 1953+.

Includes hist. articles.

10293 ROBINSON. Memories, wise and otherwise. 1923. Further memories of Irish life. 1924. By Sir Henry Augustus Robinson.

Robinson was a noted raconteur and vice-president of the Local Government Board for Ireland, 1898–1922. Sir Nevile Rodwell Wilkinson, *To all and singular* [1926], the memoirs of Ulster King at Arms, has little on official life.

10294 HEADLAM. Irish reminiscences. By Maurice Francis Headlam. 1947. An official in Ireland from 1912.

10295 BAILEY (WILLIAM FREDERICK). Local & centralized government in Ireland: a sketch of the existing systems. 1888.

10296 O'BRIEN (RICHARD BARRY). Dublin Castle and the Irish people. Dublin. 1909. 2nd edn. 1912.

A full but hostile account of the Irish administration.

10297 MONCK COMMISSION ON CIVIL SERVICE IN IRELAND. Report of the commissioners appointed by the Lords Commissioners of Her Majesty's Treasury to enquire into the condition of the civil service in Ireland [Chairman: Lord Monck]. I. Local Government Board, General Register Office and general report. [C. 789] H.C. (1873). XXII, 1. II. Dublin Metropolitan Police. [C. 788] H.C. (1873). XXII, 69. III. Royal Irish Constabulary. [C. 831] H.C. (1873). XXII, 131. IV. Resident magistrates. [C. 923] H.C. (1874). XVI, 723.

There is also much material on Irish officialdom in the reports of general committees of inquiry into the United Kingdom civil service, notably **394–5**.

10298 BOARD OF WORKS (IRELAND) ENQUIRY COMMITTEE. Report of the committee appointed to inquire into the Board of Works, Ireland [Chairman: Viscount Crichton]. [C. 2060] H.C. (1878). XXIII, 1. Statement by Colonel McKerlie, head of the office. [C. 2080] H.C. (1878). XXIII, 357.

10299 MILITARY HISTORY SOCIETY OF IRELAND. The Irish sword . . . Dublin. 1952+.

The papers of the commander-in-chief in Ireland, 1780–1894, are now in the Nat. Libr. of Ireland.

### 3. UNIONISM

See also Curtis (**10285**).

10300 THORNLEY (DAVID). 'The Irish Conservatives and Home Rule, 1869–73'. *Irish Hist. Studs.* xi (1958–9), 200–22.

10301 HOLMES (HUGH). 'Ireland and party politics, 1885–7: an unpublished Conservative memoir'. Ed. by Alistair B. Cooke and John Russell Vincent. *Irish Hist. Studs.* xvi (1968–9), 321–38, 446–71.

**10302**  SAVAGE (DONALD C.). 'The origins of the Ulster Unionist party, 1885–6'. *Irish Hist. Studs.* xii (1960–1), 185–208.

See also David Savage, 'The Irish Unionists, 1867–1886', *Éire-Ireland* ii (1967), 86–101.

**10303**  BUCKLAND (PATRICK). Irish Unionism. 2 v. Dublin & N.Y. 1972–3.

Suppl. by his *Irish Unionism, 1885–1923: a documentary history*, Belfast 1973, and *Irish Unionism, 1885–1922*, Hist. Assoc. G 81, 1973. The 4 v. constitute a full study of the period 1886–1922.

**10304**  LYONS (FRANCIS STEWART LELAND). 'The Irish Unionist party and the devolution crisis of 1904–5'. *Irish Hist. Studs.* vi (1948–9), 1–22.

See also P. J. Buckland, 'The southern Irish Unionists, the Irish question, and British politics, 1906–14', *Irish Hist. Studs.* xv (1966–7), 228–55, and J. Ronan Fanning, 'The Unionist Party and Ireland, 1906–10', ibid. 147–71.

**10305**  STEWART (ANTHONY TERENCE QUINCEY). The Ulster crisis. 1967.

On 1910–18. See also the life of Carson (**10307**), and D. G. Boyce, 'British Conservative opinion, the Ulster question, and the partition of Ireland, 1912–21', *Irish Hist. Studs.* xvii (1970–1), 89–112.

**10306**  CRAWFORD (FREDERICK HUGH). Guns for Ulster. 1947.

By the organizer of the gun-running.

**10307**  CARSON. Carson: the life of Sir Edward Carson, Lord Carson of Duncairn. By Harford Montgomery Hyde. 1953.

The first full life was Edward Marjoribanks and Ian Duncan Colvin, *The life of Lord Carson*, 2 v. 1932–5, publ. in N.Y. as Edward Marjoribanks, *Carson the advocate*, 1932, and Ian Colvin, *Carson the statesman*, 1935. There were also contemp. polemical works incl. [Arthur] George [Villiers] Peel, *The reign of Sir Edward Carson*, 1914, and St. John Greer Ervine, *Sir Edward Carson and the Ulster movement*, Lond. & N.Y. 1916.

**10308**  CRAIG. Craigavon: Ulsterman. By St. John Greer Ervine. 1949.

**10309**  DUNRAVEN. Past times and pastimes. By Windham Thomas Wyndham-Quin, Earl of Dunraven. 2 v. 1922.

Conservative exponent of Irish devolution. Important for his *The crisis in Ireland: an account of the present condition of Ireland and suggestions towards reform*, Lond. & Dublin 1905, rev. and enlarged edn. publ. as *The outlook in Ireland: the case for devolution and conciliation*, Dublin & Lond. 1907.

**10310**  MIDLETON. Ireland—dupe or heroine. By William St. John Brodrick, Earl of Midleton. 1932.

Reflections on events of 1870–1911, by an active supporter of conciliation of the nationalists. See also his autobiography (**742**).

**10311**  SAUNDERSON. Colonel Saunderson, M.P.: a memoir. By Reginald Jaffray Lucas. 1908.

Veteran Ulster Tory.

10312 SMITH (GOLDWIN). Irish history and Irish character. Oxf. 1861.

An early attack on Irish character. Cp. his *Irish history and the Irish question,* 1905. Smith, and other pamphleteers, were answered by John Mackinnon Robertson, *The Saxon and the Celt: a study in sociology,* 1897.

10313 FITZGIBBON (GERALD). Ireland in 1868, the battle-field for English party strife: its grievances, real and factitious: remedies, abortive or mischievous. Dublin. 1868.

A defence of the Protestant ascendancy.

10314 DICEY (ALBERT VENN). England's case against home rule. 1886. 3rd edn. 1887.

The most famous unionist statement. Dicey also publ. *A leap in the dark: or, our new constitution,* 1893, 2nd edn. 1911, *A fool's paradise: being a constitutionalist's criticism of the Home Rule Bill of 1912,* 1913, and *The verdict: a tract on the political significance of the report of the Parnell commission,* 1890.

10315 IRISH LOYAL AND PATRIOTIC UNION. Notes from Ireland. 1886–1891.

Cont. to 1918 by the Irish Unionist Alliance. A Unionist propaganda sheet. Cp. Henry Brougham Leech, *1848 and 1887: the continuity of the Irish revolutionary movement . . .,* 1887, rev. edn. [*1848 and 1912*] 1912, a Unionist handbook, and Arthur St. George Patton, comp., *Speaker's handbook on the Irish question,* Liberal Unionist Assoc., 3rd edn. [1890.]

10316 NATIONAL RADICAL LEAGUE. A Unionist policy for Ireland . . . with a preface by the Rt. Hon. J. Chamberlain, M.P. 1888.

10317 GREY (HENRY GEORGE), *Earl Grey.* Ireland: the cause of its present condition, and the measures proposed for its improvement. 1888.

A discussion of Irish legislation since the Union by a veteran Whig.

10318 THE TIMES. Parnellism and crime. 1887.

Includes facsimiles of the famous forged letters. Led to the appointment of the Parnell commission (**10364**). *The Times* also publ. *Home Rule: a reprint from* The Times *of recent articles and letters,* 2 v. 1888, and *Parnellism and crime: O'Donnell* v. *Walter,* 1888.

10319 UNIONIST CONVENTION for the provinces of Leinster, Munster & Connaught (June, 1892): report of proceedings, lists of committees, delegates, etc. Dublin. [1893.]

Useful for southern Unionism.

10320 ANDERSON (*Sir* ROBERT). Sidelights on the Home Rule movement. 1906.

Abridged as *A great conspiracy,* 1909. Anderson was head of the British Secret Service and appeared as a witness against the Irish party before the Parnell commission. His memoirs (**408**), were debated in the House of Commons, 21 April 1910. See also *The Times,* 12 May 1910.

10321   ROSENBAUM (S.) *ed*. Against Home Rule: the case for the Union. 1912.

Essays by British and Irish Unionist leaders. See also James Henry Campbell, Baron Glenavy, ed., *A guide to the Home Rule Bill*, Union Defence League and National Unionist Assoc., priv. pr. 1912, and Frank Frankfort Moote, *The truth about Ulster*, 1914.

10322   GOOD (JAMES WINDER). Irish Unionism. Dublin & Lond. 1920.

10323   MACNEILL (RONALD), *Baron Cushendun*. Ulster's stand for union. 1922.

See also *The Ulster Liberal Unionist Association: a sketch of its history, 1885–1914: how it has opposed Home Rule, and what it has done for remedial legislation in Ireland*, Belfast [1914].

## 4. NATIONALISM

### (a) *General*

10324   SULLIVAN (TIMOTHY DANIEL) *and others*. Speeches from the dock: or, protests of Irish patriotism. New edn. to 1921. Ed. by Sean Ua Ceallaigh. Dublin. 1945.

The 23rd edn. was publ. in 1882: the book eventually ran through fifty edns. For nationalist oratory see also Thomas Michael Kettle, ed., *Irish orators and oratory*, 1915.

10325   SULLIVAN (ALEXANDER MARTIN), SULLIVAN (TIMOTHY DANIEL), *and* SULLIVAN (D. B.). Irish readings. 2 v. Dublin. 1904.

Extracts from speeches and statements by leading nationalists since *c*. 1870. Widely read in Ireland.

10326   ZIMMERMANN (GEORGES DENIS). Irish political street ballads and rebel songs, 1780–1900. Geneva. 1966. Dublin. 1967. Publ. as Songs of Irish rebellion . . . Hatboro, Pa. 1967.

10327   POLLARD (HUGH BERTIE CAMPBELL). The secret societies of Ireland: their rise and progress. 1922.

### (b) *The Irish Brigade and Tenant Right*

10328   WHYTE (JOHN HENRY). The Independent Irish party, 1850–9. 1958.

See also his *The Tenant league and Irish politics in the eighteen fifties*, Dublin Hist. Assoc., Dundalk 1963, repr. 1966, and 'Fresh light on Archbishop Cullen and the Tenant League', *Irish Eccles. Rec.* 5 ser. xcix (1963), 170–6, and K. Theodore Hoppen, 'Tories, Catholics and the general election of 1859', *Hist. J.* xiii (1970), 48–67.

10329   SULLIVAN (ALEXANDER MARTIN). New Ireland: political sketches and personal reminiscences of thirty years of Irish public life. 1877. 8th edn. Glasgow. 1882.

The first account of the politics of the 1850s and 1860s.

10330 DUFFY (*Sir* CHARLES GAVAN). The League of North and South: an episode in Irish history, 1850–1854. 1886.

Important. To be read in conjunction with his *Four years of Irish history, 1840–1850,* 1883, *Young Ireland: a fragment of Irish history,* Lond. & N.Y. 1880, rev. edn. 1896 and **10333.**

10331 DAUNT (WILLIAM JOSEPH O'NEILL). Eighty-five years of Irish history, 1800–1885. 2 v. 1886.

The Union as seen by an old O'Connellite. Suppl. by his *Essays on Ireland,* Dublin 1886.

10332 DAUNT. A life spent for Ireland: being selections from the journals of the late W. J. O'Neill Daunt. Ed. by his daughter, Alice Ismene O'Neill Daunt. 1896.

10333 DUFFY. My life in two hemispheres. By Sir Charles Gavan Duffy. 2 v. 1898.

See also Helen Frances Mulvey, 'Sir Charles Gavan Duffy: Young Irelander and imperial statesman', *Canadian Hist. Rev.* xxxiii (1952), 369–86, and León Ó Broin, *Charles Gavan Duffy, patriot and statesman: the story of Charles Gavan Duffy, 1816–1903,* Dublin 1967.

10334 GREGORY. Sir William Gregory, K.C.M.G., formerly member of parliament and sometime governor of Ceylon. An autobiography. Ed. by Isabella Augusta, Lady Gregory. 1894.

10335 LUCAS. The life of Frederick Lucas, M.P. By Edward Lucas. 2 v. 1886. 2nd edn. 1887.

Fuller than Christopher James Riethmüller, *Frederick Lucas: a biography,* 1862.

10336 MOORE. An Irish gentleman: George Henry Moore: his travel, his racing, his politics. By Maurice George Moore. 1913.

### (c) *Fenianism*

10337 CHOILLE (BREANDÁN MACGIOLLA). 'Fenian documents in the State Paper Office'. *Irish Hist. Studs.* xvi (1968–9), 258–84.

10338 MOODY (THEODORE WILLIAM) *ed.* The Fenian movement. Cork. 1968.

Incl. good bibliog. See also León Ó Broin, *Fenian fever: an Anglo-American dilemma,* 1971. There are also two other good series of essays: Maurice Harmon, ed., *Fenians and Fenianism: centenary essays,* Dublin & Seattle, Wash. 1968, and the special Fenian issue of *University Review* iv (1967), 203–82. John De Courcy Ireland, 'A preliminary study of the Fenians and the sea', *Éire-Ireland* ii (1967), 36–54, raises some interesting points.

10339 RYAN (DESMOND). The Phoenix flame: a study of Fenianism and John Devoy. 1937.

Useful, but overstresses the importance of Devoy. Diarmuid Lynch, *The I.R.B. and the 1916 insurrection . . .,* ed. by Florence O'Donoghue, Cork 1957, includes some useful material on the pre-1914 period.

10340   TYNAN (PATRICK JOSEPH PERCY). The Irish National Invincibles and their times . . . Chatham. 1894. N.Y. 1894.

10341   D'ARCY (WILLIAM). The Fenian movement in the United States, 1858–1886. Wash. 1947.

See also Brian Jenkins, *Fenians and Anglo-American relations during Reconstruction*, Ithaca, N.Y. 1969; Denis Rolleston Gwynn, *Thomas Francis Meagher*, Dublin 1961; Robert Greenleaf Athearn, *Thomas Francis Meagher: an Irish revolutionary in America*, Boulder, Colo. 1949; Paul John Jones, *The Irish brigade*, Wash. 1969; W. F. Lyons, *Brigadier-General Thomas Francis Meagher . . .*, N.Y. 1870; Meagher's own *Speeches on the legislative independence of Ireland*, N.Y. 1853; George P. Welch, 'The Fenian foray into Canada, May–June 1866', *An Cosantóir* xviii (1958), 268–90, 297–301; Harold A. Davis, 'The Fenian raid on New Brunswick', *Canadian Hist. Rev.* xxxvi (1955), 316–34; Hereward Senior, 'Quebec and the Fenians', ibid. xlviii (1967), 26–44; and Brian Jenkins, 'The British government, Sir John A. Macdonald, and the Fenian claims', ibid. xlix (1968), 142–59. For the rescue of Fenian prisoners from Australia by American Fenians, see Seán Ó Lúing, *Fremantle mission*, Tralee 1965.

10342   ROSE (PAUL). The Manchester martyrs: the story of a Fenian tragedy. 1970.

10343   CORFE (THOMAS HOWELL). The Phoenix park murders: conflict, compromise and tragedy in Ireland, 1879–1882. 1968.

10344   Ó FIAICH (TOMÁS). 'The clergy and Fenianism, 1860–70'. *Irish Eccles. Rec.* 5 ser. cix (1968), 81–103.

10345   RICE (CHARLES T.). 'Fenianism in Monaghan: memoir of James Blayney Rice: personalities of the Fenian movement, and interesting details of activities in Monaghan, 1865–85'. *Clogher Rec.* i (1956), 29–84.

See also Breandán MacGiolla Choille, 'Fenians, Rice and ribbonmen in county Monaghan, 1864–67', *Clogher Rec.* vi (1967), 221–52, and Seán Ó Lúing, 'A contribution to a study of Fenianism in Breifne', *Breifne* iii (1967), 155–74.

10346   CLARKE. Glimpses of an Irish felon's prison life. By Thomas James Clarke. Dublin. 1922.

See also Louis N. Le Roux, *Tom Clarke and the Irish freedom movement*, Dublin & Cork 1936.

10347   DENIEFFE. A personal narrative of the Irish Revolutionary Brotherhood. By Joseph Denieffe. N.Y. 1906. Repr. Shannon. 1969.

10348   DEVOY. Recollections of an Irish rebel: the Fenian movement, its origin and progress . . . By John Devoy. N.Y. 1929. Repr. Shannon. 1969.

Devoy's important corres. as American leader of the Irish underground movement is printed in William O'Brien and Desmond Ryan, *Devoy's postbag, 1871–1928*, 2 v. Dublin 1948–53. See also Seán Ó Lúing, *John Devoy*, Dublin 1961 and **10339**.

10349   KICKHAM. Life and times of Charles J. Kickham. By James J. Healy. Dublin. 1915.

10350 MARTIN. The life and letters of John Martin . . . By P. A. S[illard]. Dublin. 1893. 2nd edn. 1901.

10351 MITCHEL. Life of John Mitchel. By William Dillon. 2 v. 1888.

The authorized biog. See also Mitchel's *Jail journal* . . . of which the best edn. is that by Arthur Griffith, Dublin 1913, and 3 biog. sketches: Seamus MacCall, *Irish Mitchel: a biography*, 1938, Patrick Sarsfield O'Hegarty, *John Mitchel: an appreciation* . . ., Dublin 1917, and Émile Montégut, *John Mitchel: a study of Irish nationalism*, trans. by J. M. Hone, Dublin 1915. P. A. S[illard], *The life of John Mitchel*, Dublin 1889, and Louis J. Walsh, *John Mitchel*, Dublin & Cork, 1934, are of less value. There is a 'Bibliography of the writings of John Mitchel', by M. J. MacManus, *Dublin Mag.* new ser. xvi (1941), no. 2, 42–50.

10352 O'DONOVAN ROSSA. Ó Donnabháin Rosa. By Seán Ó Lúing. 1+ v. Dublin. 1969+.

See also Jeremiah O'Donovan Rossa, *O'Donovan Rossa's prison life: six years in English prisons*, N.Y. 1874, reissued as *Irish rebels in English prisons: a record of prison life*, N.Y. [1882], and as *My years in English jails*, Tralee 1967, and Margaret O'Donovan Rossa, *My father and mother were Irish*, N.Y. 1939.

10353 O'LEARY. Recollections of Fenians and Fenianism. By John O'Leary. 2 v. 1896. New edn. 2 v. Shannon. 1969.

See also Marcus Bourke, *John O'Leary: a study in Irish separatism*, Tralee 1967.

10354 RONEY. Frank Roney: Irish rebel and California labor leader: an autobiography. Ed. by Ira Brown Cross. Berkeley etc. 1931.

10355 RYAN. Fenian memories. By Mark Francis Ryan. Ed. by Thomas F. O'Sullivan. Dublin. 1945.

10356 STEPHENS. The Fenian chief: a biography of James Stephens. By Desmond Ryan. Dublin. [1967.]

See also D. R. Gwynn, 'James Stephens and the Fenian rising', *Old Kilkenny Rev.* xx (1968), 27–44.

(d) *The Home Rule Movement*

10357 McCAFFREY (LAWRENCE JOHN). Irish federalism in the 1870's: a study in conservative nationalism. *Amer. Phil. Soc. Trans.* new ser. 52, pt. 6. Phila. 1962.

See also his 'Home rule and the general election of 1874 in Ireland', *Irish Hist. Studs.* ix (1954–5), 190–212, and 'The Home Rule party and Irish nationalist opinion, 1874–1876', *Catholic Hist. Rev.* xliii (1957–8), 160–77.

10358 THORNLEY (DAVID). 'The Irish Home Rule party and parliamentary obstruction, 1874–87'. *Irish Hist. Studs.* xii (1960–1), 38–57.

10359 MOODY (THEODORE WILLIAM). 'The new departure in Irish politics, 1878–9'. In Henry Alfred Cronne, T. W. Moody, and David Beers

Quinn, eds., Essays in British and Irish history in honour of J. E. Todd. 1949. Pp. 303–33.

10360　O'BRIEN ([DONAT] CONOR CRUISE). Parnell and his party, 1880–90. Oxf. 1957. Repr. with revs. 1964.

Standard. See also his 'The machinery of the Irish parliamentary party, 1880–85', *Irish Hist. Studs.* v (1946–7), 55–85; Richard Hawkins, 'Gladstone, Forster and the release of Parnell, 1882–8', ibid. xvi (1968–9), 417–45; Walter Leonard Arnstein, 'Parnell and the Bradlaugh case', ibid. xiii (1962–3), 212–35; James J. Green, 'American Catholics and the Irish Land League, 1879–1882', *Catholic Hist. Rev.* xxxv (1949–50), 19–42; Robert Dudley Edwards, 'Parnell and the American challenge to Irish nationalism', *Univ. Rev.* ii (1958–[61]), 47–64; and Theodore William Moody, 'Parnell and the Galway election of 1886', *Irish Hist. Studs.* ix (1954–5), 319–38. A number of earlier books were based on first-hand knowledge, notably Thomas Power O'Connor, *The Parnell movement: with a sketch of Irish parties from 1843*, 1886, rev. edns. 1887, 1889; T. P. O'Connor and Robert McWade, *Gladstone, Parnell and the great Irish struggle*, Phila. etc. 1888; Frank Hugh O'Donnell, *A history of the Irish parliamentary party*, 2 v. Lond. & N.Y. 1910; and Michael MacDonagh, *The Home Rule movement*, Dublin & Lond. 1920. Michael John Fitzgerald McCarthy, *The Irish revolution*: Vol. I 'The murdering time, from the Land League to the first Home Rule Bill', Edin. & Lond 1912, is a unionist counterblast to these works. Michael Hurst, *Parnell and Irish nationalism*, 1968, adds little to O'Brien: see *Irish Hist. Studs.* xvi (1968–9), 230–6.

10361　ALTER (PETER), *pseud. of* BEER (FRITZ). Der Irische Nationalbewegung zwischen Parlament und Revolution: der konstitutionelle Nationalismus in Irland, 1800–1918. Munich etc. 1971.

10362　HAMER (DAVID ALAN). 'The Irish question and Liberal politics, 1880–1894'. *Hist. J.* xii (1969), 511–32.

See also Herbert William McCready, 'Home rule and the Liberal party, 1899–1906', *Irish Hist. Studs.* xiii (1962–3), 316–48.

10363　HOWARD (CHRISTOPHER HENRY DURHAM). 'Joseph Chamberlain, Parnell and the Irish "central board" scheme, 1884–85'. *Irish Hist. Studs.* viii (1952–3), 324–61.

Suppl. by his 'Documents relating to the Irish "central board" scheme, 1884–5', *Irish Hist. Studs.* viii (1952–3), 237–63. See also his 'Joseph Chamberlain, W. H. O'Shea and Parnell, 1884, 1891–2', *Irish Hist. Studs.* xiii (1962–3), 33–8, 'The Parnell manifesto of 21 November 1885 and the schools question', *Eng. Hist. Rev.* lxii (1947), 42–51, and ' "The man on the tricycle": W. H. Duignan and Ireland, 1881–5', *Irish Hist. Studs.* xiv (1964–5), 246–60.

10364　MOODY (THEODORE WILLIAM). '*The Times* versus Parnell and Co., 1887–90'. *Hist. Studs.* vi (1965), 147–82.

The report and minutes of evidence of the Parnell commission was printed as *Special Commission Act, 1888: reprint of the shorthand notes of the speeches, proceedings and evidence taken before the commissioners under the above-named act* [Chairman: Sir James Hannen], 12 v. H.M.S.O. 1890. The report was also printed as [C. 5891] H.C. (1890). XXVII, 477. There were also unofficial reports, incl. John Macdonald, *Diary of the Parnell commission, revised from the Daily News*, 1890, *The Special Commission Act, 1888: report of the proceedings before the commissioners appointed by the act, reprinted from* The Times, 4 v. 1890, *Parnellism and crime: the special commission: reprinted from* The Times, 35 pts. 1889–90. See also **10318**.

10365   LYONS (FRANCIS STEWART LELAND). The fall of Parnell, 1890–91. 1960.

Good. See also John Frederic Glaser, 'Parnell's fall and the nonconformist conscience', *Irish Hist. Studs.* xii (1960–1), 119–38; Lewis Perry Curtis, jr., 'Government policy and the Irish Party crisis, 1890–92', *Irish Hist. Studs.* xiii (1962–3), 295–315; Emmet Larkin, 'The Roman Catholic hierarchy and the fall of Parnell', *Victorian Studs.* iv (1960–1), 315–336, cont. as 'Mounting the counter-attack: the Roman Catholic hierarchy and the destruction of Parnellism', *Rev. of Politics* xxv (1963), 157–82; and Mark Tierney, ed., 'Dr. Croke, the Irish bishops and the Parnell crisis, 18 November 1890–21 April 1891', *Collectanea Hibernica* ii (1968), 111–48. Earlier accounts add little: they incl. Donal Sullivan, *The story of Room 15*, Dublin [1891], *The Parnellite split: or the disruption of the Irish parliamentary party: from* The Times, 1891, and *The story of the Parnell crisis . . .*, Pall Mall Gazette extra, 1891, and Margaret Leamy, *Parnell's faithful few*, N.Y. 1936.

10366   LYONS (FRANCIS STEWART LELAND). The Irish parliamentary party, 1890–1910. 1951.

See also his 'The machinery of the Irish parliamentary party in the general election of 1895', *Irish Hist. Studs.* viii (1952–3), 115–39, and 'The Irish parliamentary party and the Liberals in Mid-Ulster, 1894', *Irish Hist. Studs.* vii (1950–1), 191–5.

10367   BLAKE. Edward Blake, Irish nationalist: a Canadian statesman in Irish politics, 1892–1907. By Margaret A. Banks. Toronto. 1957.

See also D. C. Lyne, 'Irish-Canadian financial contributions to the Home Rule movement in the 1890s', *Studia Hibernica* x (1967), 182–206.

10368   BUTT. Isaac Butt and Home Rule. By David Thornley. 1964.

Standard. Terence de Vere White, *The road of excess*, Dublin [1946], is a general biog. See also Lawrence John McCaffrey, 'Isaac Butt and the Home Rule movement: a study in conservative nationalism', *Rev. of Politics* xxii (1960), 72–95.

10369   DAVITT. Michael Davitt, revolutionary agitator and labour leader. By Francis Sheehy Skeffington. 1908. Repr. 1967.

Inadequate. Davitt's own *The fall of feudalism in Ireland: or, the story of the Land League revolution*, 1904, and *Leaves from a prison diary: or, lectures to a 'solitary' audience*, 2 v. 1885, are much more important. The best modern account of Davitt is in a number of articles by Theodore William Moody: 'Michael Davitt, 1846–1906: a survey and appreciation', *Studies* xxxv (1946), 199–208, 325–34, 433–8, 'Michael Davitt in penal servitude, 1870–1877', *Studies* xxx (1941), 517–30; xxxi (1941), 16–30, 'Michael Davitt and the British labour movement, 1882–1906', *Roy. Hist. Soc. Trans.* 5 ser. iii (1953), 53–76, and 'Michael Davitt and the "pen" letter', *Irish Hist. Studs.* iv (1944–5), 224–53. Two older works are also useful: D. B. Cashman, *The life of Michael Davitt . . .*, Boston 1881, and M. M. O'Hara, *Chief and tribune: Parnell and Davitt*, Dublin 1919.

10370   DENVIR. The life story of an old rebel. By John Denvir. Dublin. 1910.

See also **6961.**

10371   DILLON. John Dillon: a biography. By Francis Stewart Leland Lyons. 1968.

A full modern biog. Standard.

**10372**  DUNLOP. Fifty years of Irish journalism. By Andrew Dunlop. Dublin. 1911.

Dunlop reported large numbers of nationalist meetings.

**10373**  HEALY. Letters and leaders of my day. By Timothy Michael Healy. 2 v. 1928.

Rambling, but has valuable letters. Liam O'Flaherty, *The life of Tim Healy*, 1927, and Maev Sullivan, *No man's man* (a political life to 1891 by his daughter), Dublin 1943, are biogs. Sir Dunbar Plunket Barton, *Timothy Healy: memories and anecdotes*, Dublin & Lond. 1933, is a pleasant trifle. Healy publ. a good deal, his most important works being, *A record of coercion: votes of Irish members for the enlightenment of Irish electors*, Dublin 1881, *A word for Ireland*, Dublin 1886, and *Why Ireland is not free: a study of twenty years in politics*, Dublin 1898.

**10374**  HORGAN. Parnell to Pearse: some recollections and reflections. By John Joseph Horgan. Dublin. 1948.

**10375**  KETTLE. The material for victory: being the memoirs of Andrew J. Kettle. Ed. by Laurence J. Kettle. Dublin. 1958.

**10376**  LYNCH. My life story. By Arthur Alfred Lynch. 1924.

Lynch became the central figure in a *cause célèbre* as a Nationalist M.P. who had fought against the British in the Boer War.

**10377**  McCARTHY. Our book of memories: letters of Justin McCarthy to Mrs. Campbell Praed. [1885–1911.] 1912.

McCarthy also wrote three pot-boilers: *Reminiscences*, 2 v. 1899, *The story of an Irishman*, 1904, and *Irish recollections* [1911].

**10378**  MacNEILL. What I have seen and heard. By John Gordon Swift MacNeill. 1925.

**10379**  O'BRIEN. The life of William O'Brien, the Irish nationalist: a biographical study of Irish nationalism, constitutional and revolutionary. By Michael MacDonagh. 1928.

Fuller and more attractive are O'Brien's own very partisan *Recollections* [1852–83], 1905, *Evening memories* [1883–90], Dublin 1920, *An olive branch in Ireland and its history* [1890–1910], 1910, and *The Irish revolution and how it came about* [1910–22], Dublin 1923. His wife Sophie O'Brien also publ. *My Irish friends*, Dublin and London [1937].

**10380**  O'CONNOR. T. P. O'Connor. By Henry Hamilton Fyfe. 1934.

O'Connor's own *Memoirs of an old parliamentarian*, 2 v. 1929, are disappointing.

**10381**  O'GORMAN MAHON. The O'Gorman Mahon: duellist, adventurer and politician. By Denis Rolleston Gwynn. 1934.

**10382**  O'MALLEY. Glancing back: 70 years' experiences and reminiscences of press man, sportsman and member of parliament. By William O'Malley. [1933.]

Reminiscences of a nationalist journalist.

10383 PARNELL. The life of Charles Stewart Parnell, 1846–1891. By Richard Barry O'Brien. 2 v. 1898. 1 v. 1910.

Still the best biog. The only fairly recent full-length lives in English are Joan Haslip, *Parnell: a biography*, 1936, and Jules Abels, *The Parnell tragedy*, Lond. & N.Y. 1966. Francis Stewart Leland Lyons, *Parnell*, Dublin Hist. Assoc. 1963, repr. 1965, is an excellent sketch. Mary McAuley Gillgannon, *Charles Stewart Parnell: political paradox*, N.Y. 1967, adds little. The lives by Thomas Sherlock (Boston 1881, Dublin 1882, repr. 1945), R. Johnston (1888), Thomas Power O'Connor (1891), and León Ó'Broin (Dublin 1937, in Irish) add little, but are worth reading. The semi-fictional and grossly inaccurate St. John Greer Ervine, *Parnell*, 1925, provoked rejoinders in William O'Brien, *The Parnell of real life*, 1926, and Henry Harrison, *Parnell vindicated: the lifting of the veil*, 1931. Harrison's views, set out briefly in his 'Parnell's vindication', *Irish. Hist Studs.* v (1947), 231–43, and at greater length in *Parnell, Joseph Chamberlain and Mr. Garvin*, 1938, and *Parnell, Joseph Chamberlain and 'The Times': a documentary record*, Belfast & Dublin 1953, are now generally accepted by Irish historians. Three members of Parnell's family publ. their recollections of him in old age, but all three make numerous mistakes. Katherine O'Shea (his wife), *Charles Stewart Parnell: his love story and political life*, 2 v. 1914, includes important letters. Emily Monroe Dickinson (his sister), *A patriot's mistake: being personal recollections of the Parnell family*, Dublin & Lond. 1905, is best on his last years. John Howard Parnell (his brother), *Charles Stewart Parnell: a memoir*, 1916, has little to recommend it. Special aspects of Parnell's career are dealt with in Sir Alfred Farthing Robbins, *Parnell: the last five years, told from within*, 1926, by a Liberal-Unionist journalist, M. M. O'Hara, *Chief and tribune: Parnell and Davitt*, Dublin & Lond. 1919, and Francis Stewart Leland Lyons, 'The economic ideas of Parnell', *Hist. Studs.* iii (1959), 60–78. There is only 1 v. of speeches, Jennie Wyse-Power, ed., *Words of the dead chief: being extracts from the public speeches and other pronouncements of Charles Stewart Parnell*, Dublin 1892.

10384 REDMOND. The life of John Redmond. By Denis Rolleston Gwynn. 1932.

Based on the Redmond papers. Supersedes Warre Bradley Wells, *John Redmond, a biography*, 1919, and Louis George Redmond-Howard, *John Redmond, the man and the demand: a biographical study in Irish politics*, 1910. There are 2 v. of collected speeches, *Historical and political addresses, 1883–1897*, Dublin 1898, and *Home Rule: speeches by John Redmond, M.P.* [1886–1909], ed. by Richard Barry O'Brien, 1910. There is no adequate life of Redmond's brother William, but there is a short pamphlet, *In memoriam: Major Willie Redmond . . .*, Dublin [1917].

10385 SHEEHAN. Ireland since Parnell. By Daniel Desmond Sheehan. 1921.

10386 A. M. SULLIVAN. A. M. Sullivan: a memoir. By Timothy Daniel Sullivan. Dublin. 1885.

There is also a vol. of speeches, ed. by T. D. Sullivan, *Speeches & addresses in parliament, on the platform, and at the bar, 1859 to 1881*, Dublin 1878, 4th. edn. 1886.

10387 T. D. SULLIVAN. Recollections of troubled times in Irish politics. By Timothy Daniel Sullivan. Dublin. 1905.

10388 BUTT (ISAAC). Home government for Ireland. Irish federalism! Its meaning, its objects, and its hopes. Dublin. 1874.

10389 BAGENAL (PHILIP HENRY). The Irish agitator in parliament and on the platform: a complete history of Irish politics for the year 1879; with a summary of conclusions and an appendix containing documents of political importance published during the year. Dublin. 1880.

10390  REID (ANDREW), *ed*. Ireland: a book of light on the Irish problem . . . 1886.

Papers by Thorold Rogers, Alfred Russel Wallace, W. S. Blunt, T. P. O'Connor, etc.

10391  BRYCE (JAMES), *Viscount Bryce, ed*. Handbook of Home Rule: being articles on the Irish question by the Right Hon. W. E. Gladstone, M.P., the Right Hon. John Morley, M.P., Lord Thring, James Bryce, M.P., Canon MacColl, E. L. Godkin, and R. Barry O'Brien. 1887.

10392  WILLIAMS ([ARTHUR FREDERIC] BASIL) *ed*. Home Rule problems . . . with a preface by Viscount Haldane. 1911.

Contributors include G. P. Gooch, W. P. Ryan, Erskine Childers, Frank McDermott.

10393  HOME RULE FROM THE TREASURY BENCH. Speeches during the first and second reading debates. 1912.

See also John Edward Redmond, *The Home Rule Bill*, 1912.

10394  MORGAN (JOHN HARTMAN) *ed*. The new Irish constitution: an exposition and some arguments. The Eighty Club. 1912.

See also Charles Roden Buxton, *The ABC Home Rule handbook*, Home Rule Council 1912, and [Edward] Harold Spender, *Home Rule*, 1912.

### (e) *Radical Nationalism in the Twentieth Century*

10395  PHILLIPS (WALTER ALISON). The revolution in Ireland, 1906–1923. Lond. & N.Y. 1923. 2nd edn. 1926.

A good Unionist account of events.

10396  CHOILLE (BREANDÁN MACGIOLLA) *ed*. Chief Secretary's Office, Dublin Castle: intelligence notes, 1913–16, preserved in the State Paper Office. Dublin. 1966.

10397  O'SULLIVAN (THOMAS F.). Story of the G.A.A. (Gaelic Athletic Association). Dublin. 1916.

See also Michael Tierney, 'What did the Gaelic League accomplish?' *Studies* lii (1963), 337–47, and León Ó Broin, 'The Gaelic League and the chair of Irish at Maynooth', ibid. 348–62.

10398  HENRY (ROBERT MITCHELL). The evolution of Sinn Féin. Dublin. 1920.

10399  JONES (FRANCIS P.). History of the Sinn Féin movement and the Irish rebellion of 1916. N.Y. 1917.

Quite detailed on Sinn Fein policy, for which see also *The Sinn Féin policy*, Dublin 1907.

10400 O'HEGARTY (PATRICK SARSFIELD). The victory of Sinn Féin: how it won it, and how it used it. Dublin. 1924.

See also his *Sinn Féin: an illumination*, Dublin 1919.

10401 CLARKSON (JESSE DUNSMORE). Labour and nationalism in Ireland. N.Y. 1925.

See also Cathal O'Shannon, ed., *Fifty years of Liberty hall*, Dublin 1959, and Arnold Wright, *Disturbed Dublin: the story of the great strike of 1913–14, with a description of the industries of the Irish capital*, 1914.

10402 LARKIN (EMMET). 'Socialism and catholicism in Ireland'. *Church Hist.* xxxiii (1964), 462–83.

10403 MARTIN (FRANCIS XAVIER) *ed*. The Irish volunteers, 1913–15: recollections and documents. Dublin. 1963.

See also Darrell Figgis, *Recollections of the Irish war*, 1927, James Robert White, *Misfit: an autobiography*, 1930, and Bulmer Hobson, *A short history of the Irish volunteers*, Dublin 1918.

10404 MARTIN (FRANCIS XAVIER) *ed*. The Howth gun-running and the Kilcoole gun-running, 1914: recollections and documents. Dublin. 1964.

See also *Royal commission into the circumstances connected with the landing of arms at Howth on July 26th 1914: report of commission* [Chairman: Lord Shaw]. [Cd. 7631] H.C. (1914–16). XXIV, 805. Minutes of evidence. [Cd. 7649] H.C. (1914–16). XXIV, 821, and Conor O'Brien, *From three yachts: a cruiser's outlook*, 1928.

10405 MARTIN (FRANCIS XAVIER) *ed*. Leaders and men of the Easter rising. Dublin. 1916. Lond. & Ithaca, N.Y. 1967.

Excellent biog. sketches.

10406 FOX (RICHARD MICHAEL). The history of the Irish Citizen Army. Dublin. 1943.

10407 FOX (RICHARD MICHAEL). Rebel Irishwomen. Dublin. 1935.

10408 CASEMENT. Roger Casement: a new judgment. By René MacColl. 1956.

See also Denis Rolleston Gwynn, *The life and death of Roger Casement*, Lond. 1930, N.Y. [*Traitor or patriot*] [1931]; Robert Monteith, *Casement's last adventure*, Dublin 1953; Geoffrey Vincent de Clinton Parmiter, *Roger Casement*, 1936; Charles E. Curry, *The Casement diaries and the Findlay affair*, Munich 1922; Herbert Owen Mackey, *The life and times of Roger Casement*, Dublin 1954, and *Roger Casement: the forged diaries*, Dublin 1966; Alfred Noyes, *The accusing ghost: or, justice for Casement*, 1957; and Harford Montgomery Hyde, ed., *Trial of Sir Roger Casement*, 1960. Casement's chief works were *The crime against Europe . . .*, Phila. 1915, new edn. by Herbert Owen Mackey, Dublin 1958, and the controversial diaries publ. by Peter Singleton-Gates and Maurice Girodias, as *The black diaries: an account of Roger Casement's life and times, with a collection of his diaries and public writings*, N.Y. 1959. The most recent life is Brian Inglis, *Roger Casement*, 1973.

**10409** COLLINS. Michael Collins. By Rex Taylor. 1958.

See also Frank O'Connor, pseud. of Michael Francis O'Donovan, *The big fellow: a life of Michael Collins*, Lond. 1937, N.Y. [*Death in Dublin*] 1937; Piaras Béaslai, *Michael Collins and the making of a new Ireland*, 2 v. 1926, abridged edn. Dublin etc. 1937; Eoin Neeson, *The life and death of Michael Collins*, Cork 1968; Batt O'Connor, *With Michael Collins in the fight for Irish independence*, 1929; and Desmond Ryan, *The invisible army: a story of Michael Collins*, 1932. The most recent life is Margery Forester, *Michael Collins: the lost leader*, 1971.

**10410** CONNOLLY. The life and times of James Connolly. By Charles Desmond Greaves. 1961.

A Marxist life of a revolutionary socialist and nationalist. See also Richard Michael Fox, *James Connolly: the forerunner*, Tralee 1946, and Nora O'Brien, *Portrait of a rebel father*, 1935. For his works see Desmond Ryan, ed., *James Connolly, his life, work & writings*, Dublin 1924, *Labour and Easter week* . . ., Dublin 1949, and *Socialism and nationalism: a selection from the writings of James Connolly*, Dublin 1948, Proinsias Mac-Aonghusa and Liam Ó'Réagáin, eds., *The best of Connolly*, Cork [1967], and Robert Lynd, ed., *Labour in Ireland: labour in Irish history: the reconquest of Ireland*, Dublin etc. 1917. There are also cheap edns. of most of the works.

**10411** DE VALERA. Eamon De Valera. By Francis Aungier Pakenham, Earl of Longford and Thomas Patrick O'Neill. 1970.

Séan O'Faoláin, *The life story of Eamon De Valera*, Dublin & Cork 1933, new edn. [*De Valera*] Harmondsworth 1939, is only an outline. See also David T. Dwane, *Early life of Eamon de Valera*, Dublin [1922]; Denis Rolleston Gwynn, *De Valera*, 1933; Mary Cogan Bromage, *De Valera and the march of a nation*, 1956; Katherine O'Doherty, *Assignment America: De Valera's mission to the United States*, N.Y. 1957; Patrick McCartan, *With De Valera in America*, Dublin 1932; and M. J. MacManus, *Eamon de Valera: a biography*, Dublin etc. 1944, various edns.

**10412** FITZGERALD. Memoirs of Desmond FitzGerald, 1913–1916. Ed. by Fergus FitzGerald and others. 1968.

**10413** GRIFFITH. Arthur Griffith. By Padraic Colum. Dublin. 1959. N.Y. [Ourselves alone: the story of Arthur Griffith and the origin of the Irish Free State.] 1959.

See also Séan Ó Lúing, *Art Ó Gríofa* . . ., Dublin 1953, James Stephens, *Arthur Griffith: journalist & statesman*, Dublin 1922 (good), and George A. Lyons, *Some recollections of Griffith & his times*, Dublin 1923.

**10414** HOBSON. Ireland yesterday and tomorrow. By Bulmer Hobson. Tralee. 1968.

**10415** HYDE. Douglas Hyde, President of Ireland. By Diarmid Coffey. Dublin. 1938.

Badly needs replacement.

**10416** LARKIN. James Larkin, Irish labour leader, 1876–1947. By Emmet Larkin. Camb., Mass. 1965.

Good: Larkin founded the Irish Transport & General Workers' Union. Richard Michael Fox, *Jim Larkin: the rise of the underman*, 1957, and [Donal Nevin, comp.] *1913: Jim Larkin and the Dublin lock-out*, Workers' Union of Ireland, Dublin 1964, are in the hagiographical tradition.

10417 MACBRIDE. A servant of the Queen: reminiscences. By Maud Gonne MacBride. 1938. New edn. Dublin. 1950.

10418 MARKIEVICZ. Constance de Markievicz in the cause of Ireland. By Jacqueline Van Voris. Amherst, Mass. 1967.

See also Anne Marreco, *The rebel countess: the life and times of Constance Markievicz*, 1967, and Séan O'Faoláin, *Constance Markievicz . . .*, 1934, rev. edn. 1968. Countess Markievicz publ. *A call to the women of Ireland*, Dublin 1909, repr. 1918, and *Prison letters*, Dublin 1934.

10419 O'HIGGINS. Kevin O'Higgins. By Terence de Vere White. 1948.

10420 PEARSE. Patrick H. Pearse. By Louis N. Le Roux. Trans. by Desmond Ryan. Dublin. 1932.

See also Desmond Ryan, *The man called Pearse*, Dublin 1919, Hedley McCay, *Padraic Pearse: a new biography*, Cork [1966], and Mary B. Pearse, *The home life of Patrick Pearse*, Dublin 1935. Philip Sarsfield O'Hegarty publ. a bibliog. of Pearse in *Dublin Mag.* vi (1931), no. 3, 44–9. Pearse's principal works were gathered in *Political writings and speeches*, Dublin 1952, and *Plays, stories and poems*, Dublin 1963.

## 5. ELECTIONS

10421 WHYTE (JOHN HENRY). 'The influence of the Catholic clergy on elections in nineteenth-century Ireland'. *Eng. Hist. Rev.* lxxv (1960), 239–59.

Suppl. by his 'Landlord influence at elections in Ireland, 1760–1885', *Eng. Hist. Rev.* lxxx (1965), 740–60, and Michael Hurst, 'Ireland and the Ballot Act of 1872', *Hist. J.* viii (1965), 326–52.

10422 HEAD (*Sir* FRANCIS BOND). A fortnight in Ireland. 1852. 2nd edn. 1852.

The Irish election of 1852, for which see also Terence P. Cunningham, 'The 1852 general election in county Cavan', *Breifne* iii (1966), 108–35, and the 'Burrowes–Hughes by-election', ibid. iii (1967), 175–217, James Lord, *Popery at the hustings*, 1852, A Barrister, *Observations on intimidation at elections in Ireland*, Dublin 1854, and Eladrius, *Thoughts on the late general election in Ireland*, Dublin 1853.

10423 CARLETON (JOHN WILLIAM). Compendium of the practice at elections . . . in Ireland. Dublin. 1847. 11th edn. 1892.

Probably the easiest textbook for ordinary use.

10424 PLUNKET COMMITTEE ON REGISTRATION OF VOTERS. Report from the select committee on registration of parliamentary voters (Ireland) [Chairman: David R. Plunket]. H.C. 261 (1874). XI, 167.

10425 IRISH BOUNDARY COMMISSION, 1885. Report of the boundary commissioners for Ireland, 1885 [Chairman: John Lambert]. [C. 4291] H.C. (1884–5). XIX, 499.

Further informal reports are in [C. 4374] H.C. (1884–5). XIX, 669, and an appendix in [C. 4354] H.C. (1884–5). LXII, 241.

## C. LAW, JUSTICE, AND POLICE

10426   O'HIGGINS (PAUL). 'A select bibliography of Irish legal history'. *Amer. J. Legal Hist.* iv (1960), 173–80; viii (1964), 261–3; xiii (1969), 233–41.

See also his *A bibliography of periodical literature relating to Irish law*, Belfast 1966.

10427   MAXWELL (LESLIE F.) *and* MAXWELL (W. HAROLD). A legal bibliography of the British Commonwealth of Nations. Vol. V. Irish law. 2nd edn. 1957.

First publ. by Leslie F. Maxwell as *A bibliography of Irish law from earliest times to December, 1935*, 1936.

10428   NORTHERN IRELAND. The statutes revised, Northern Ireland, A.D. 1226–1950 inclusive (as amended up to the end of 1954). Belfast. 16 v. 1956.

Vols. I–VIII cover Irish and U.K. statutes, 1226–1920, still in force. In addition *A chronological table of the statutes, 1226–1957*, Belfast 1958, and *An index*, have been publ.

10429   JUDICIAL STATISTICS OF IRELAND. (a) Civil. (b) Criminal. Annual. 1863–1919.

10430   DONALDSON (ALFRED GASTON). Some comparative aspects of Irish law. Camb. & Durham, N.C. 1957.

Francis Headon Newark, *Notes on Irish legal history*, Belfast 1960, 2nd edn. 1964, is a handy pamphlet.

10431   THE IRISH JURIST. Dublin. 1849–67. 1935+.

See also the *Northern Ireland legal quarterly*, Belfast 1936+. Both publ. hist. articles. For contemp. js. see *Irish law times and solicitors' j.*, Dublin 1867+. Official notices were publ. in *The Dublin gazette*, Dublin 1705+.

10432   McDOWELL (ROBERT BRENDAN). 'The Irish courts of law, 1801–1914'. *Irish Hist. Studs.* x (1957), 363–91.

Substantially the same as the relevant chapter of his *Irish administration* (**10291**), which also incl. a section on police and prisons.

10433   FITZGERALD COMMITTEE ON COURT OF CHANCERY (IRELAND) BILLS. Report from the select committee on Court of Chancery (Ireland) Bills [Chairman: John David FitzGerald]. H.C. 311 (1856). X, 1.

See also *Report of the commissioners appointed to inquire into the duties of the officers and clerks of the Court of Chancery, Ireland* [Chairman: Edward Litton]. [2473] H.C. (1859). XII, 361.

10434   HIGH COURT OF ADMIRALTY IN IRELAND COMMISSION. Report of Her Majesty's commissioners appointed to inquire into the High Court of Admiralty in Ireland [Chairman: Mr. Justice John David FitzGerald]. [3343] H.C. (1864). XXIX, 219.

10435 FERGUSON (WILLIAM DWYER) *and* FERGUSON (GEORGE NAPIER). A treatise on the Supreme Court of Judicature Act (Ireland), 1877 ... Dublin. 1878.

10436 CARLETON (JOHN WILLIAM). The jurisdiction and procedure of county courts in Ireland. 2 v. 1878. 2nd edn. 1891.

One of the simpler books on the subject.

10437 BODKIN (MATTHIAS McDONNELL). Famous Irish trials. Dublin. 1918. New edn. 1928.

10438 BAMFORD (FRANCIS) *and* BANKES (VIOLA). Vicious circle: the case of the missing Irish crown jewels. 1965.

10439 BALL (FRANCIS ELRINGTON). The judges in Ireland, 1221–1921. 2 v. 1926.

Standard. Oliver Joseph Burke, *The history of the Lord Chancellors of Ireland, from A.D. 1186 to A.D. 1874*, Dublin 1879, is also useful.

10440 BLACKBURNE. Life of the Right Hon. Francis Blackburne, late Lord Chancellor of Ireland, by his son, Edward Blackburne, one of Her Majesty's counsel in Ireland. 1874.

10441 BODKIN. Recollections of an Irish judge: press, bar and parliament. By Matthias McDonnell Bodkin. 1914.

10442 CURRAN. Reminiscences of John Adye Curran, K.C., late county court judge and chairman of quarter sessions. 1915.

10443 MORRIS. An Irishman and his family: Lord Morris and Killanin. By Maud Wynne. 1937.

10444 MORRIS. Memories and thoughts of a life. By William O'Connor Morris. 1895.

10445 NAPIER. The life of Sir Joseph Napier, Bart., ex-Lord Chancellor of Ireland: from his private correspondence. By Alexander Charles Ewald. 1887. Rev. edn. 1892.

There is also an edn. of *The lectures, essays and letters of the Right Hon. Sir Joseph Napier, bart.*, Dublin 1888.

10446 O'BRIEN. The reminiscences of the Right Hon. Lord O'Brien (of Kilfenora) Lord Chief Justice of Ireland. Ed. by his daughter, Georgina O'Brien. 1916.

10447 O'HAGAN. Selected speeches and arguments of the Right Hon. Thomas, Baron O'Hagan. Ed. by George Teeling. 1885.

A collection of *Occasional papers and addresses*, was publ. in 1884.

10448    PALLES. Christopher Palles, Lord Chief Baron of Her Majesty's Court of Exchequer in Ireland, 1874–1916: his life and times. By Vincent Thomas Hyginus Delany. Dublin. 1960.

10449    ROSS. The years of my pilgrimage: random reminiscences by the Rt. Hon. Sir John Ross, Bart., last Lord Chancellor of Ireland. 1924.

Cont. in his *Pilgrim scrip: more random reminiscences,* 1927. Ross also publ. *Essays and addresses,* 1930.

10450    SULLIVAN. Old Ireland: reminiscences of an Irish K.C. By Alexander Martin Sullivan. 1927.

10451    HEALY (MAURICE). The old Munster circuit. Dublin. 1939.

In the tradition of works such as James Roderick O'Flanaghan, *The Munster circuit . . .,* 1880, and *The Irish bar: comprising anecdotes, bon mots and biographical sketches . . .,* 1879, and Oliver Joseph Burke, *Anecdotes of the Connaught circuit . . .,* Dublin 1885.

10452    SMITH (GEORGE HILL). The north-east bar: a sketch, historical and reminiscent. Belfast. 1910.

See also his *Rambling reminiscences . . .,* Newry 1896, and Louis J. Walsh, *The yarns of a country attorney: being stories and sketches of life in rural Ulster,* Dublin 1917, *Old friends: being memories of men and places,* Dundalk 1934, and 'Our own wee town': *Ulster stories & sketches,* Dublin & Cork [1928].

10453    INCORPORATED LAW SOCIETY OF IRELAND. Calendar and law directory. Dublin. 1886+.

The Soc. has also publ. a Report of the Council, 1841+, and *The gazette of the Incorporated Law Society of Ireland,* Dublin 1907+.

10454    LEVINGE (EDWARD PARKYNS). The justice of the peace for Ireland: comprising the practice of indictable offences, and the proceedings preliminary and subsequent to convictions. Dublin. 1860. 4th edn. by Constantine Molloy. 1890. Rev. edn. 1910.

One of a number of handy manuals. See also Henry Humphreys, *The justice of the peace for Ireland . . .,* Dublin 1863, 9th edn. 1897, and Sir James O'Connor and others, *The Irish justice of the peace . . .,* Dublin 1911, 2nd. edn. 2 v. 1915. Returns of Irish J.P.'s were called for regularly in the House of Commons and were so arranged as to show religious affiliations.

10455    SELECT COMMITTEE ON GRAND JURY PRESENTMENTS (IRELAND). Report from the select committee on the grand jury presentments (Ireland) [Chairman: The O'Conor Don]. H.C. 392 (1867–8). X, 47.

10456    VANSTON (*Sir* GEORGE THOMAS BARRETT). The grand jury laws of Ireland . . . Dublin. 1883.

10457    SELECT COMMITTEE ON IRISH JURIES. First, second and special reports from the select committee on juries (Ireland) [Chairman: Marquess of Hartington]. H.C. 283 (1873). XV, 389.

The work of this committee was cont. in the following session. See *Report from the select committee on jury system (Ireland)* [Chairman: Sir Michael Hicks Beach]. H.C. 244 (1874). IX, 557.

10458 LORDS COMMITTEE ON IRISH JURY LAWS. Report from the select committee of the House of Lords on Irish jury laws [Chairman: Marquess of Lansdowne]. H.C. 430 (1881). XI, 1.

10459 ROYAL IRISH CONSTABULARY LIST AND DIRECTORY: containing lists of the constabulary departments, Dublin Metropolitan Police, resident magistrates, coastguard . . . Dublin. Half-yearly. 1840–1919.

10460 BROPHY (MICHAEL). Sketches of the Royal Irish Constabulary. 1886.

One of a number of such books. Cp. G. Garrow Green, *In the Royal Irish Constabulary*, 1905.

10461 LE CARON. Twenty-five years in the secret service: the recollections of a spy. By Henri Le Caron, pseud. of Thomas Beach. 1892.

10462 NAPIER COMMITTEE ON OUTRAGES IN IRELAND. Report from the select committee on outrages (Ireland) [Chairman: Joseph Napier]. H.C. 438 (1852). XIV, 1.

10463 MONTEAGLE COMMITTEE ON SUPPRESSION OF ILLICIT DISTILLATION. Report from the select committee of the House of Lords appointed to consider the consequences of extending the functions of the constabulary in Ireland to the suppression or prevention of illicit distillation [Chairman: Lord Monteagle of Brandon]. H.C. 53 (1854). X, 1.

An unexpectedly thorough inquiry.

10464 BELFAST RIOTS COMMISSION, 1857. Report of the commissioners of inquiry into the origin and character of the riots in Belfast in July and September, 1857 [Commissioners: David Lynch and Hamilton Smythe]. [2309] H.C. (1857–8). XXVI, 1.

10465 BELFAST POLICE COMMISSION, 1864. Report of the commissioners of inquiry, 1864, respecting the magisterial and police jurisdiction, arrangements and establishment of the borough of Belfast [Commissioners: Charles Robert Barry and Richard Dowse]. [3466] H.C. (1865). XXVIII, 1. Minutes of evidence. [3466–I] H.C. (1865). XXVIII, 27.

10466 CONSTABULARY (IRELAND) COMMISSION, 1866. Constabulary (Ireland): report of commissioners [Chairman: E. H. Knatchbull Hugessen]. [3658] H.C. (1866). XXXIV, 167.

10467 LONDONDERRY RIOTS COMMISSION, 1869. Report of the commissioners of inquiry, 1869, into the riots and disturbances in the City of Londonderry [Commissioners: William A. Exham and James Murphy]. [C. 5] H.C. (1870). XXXII, 411.

See also *Report of a commission appointed to inquire into certain disturbances which took place in the city of Londonderry on the 1st November 1883.* [Commissioners: Piers F. White and Edmund T. Bewley]. [C. 3954] H.C. (1884). XXXVIII, 515.

10468   WESTMEATH COMBINATIONS COMMITTEE. Report from the select committee on Westmeath, &c. (unlawful combinations) [Chairman: Marquess of Hartington]. H.C. 147 (1871). XIII, 547.

10469   MONCK COMMISSION ON THE CIVIL SERVICE IN IRE-LAND. Report of the commissioners appointed by the Lords Commissioners of Her Majesty's Treasury to enquire into the condition of the civil service in Ireland on the Royal Irish Constabulary [Chairman: Lord Monck]. [C. 831] H.C. (1873). XXII, 131. Similar report on Dublin Metropolitan Police. [C. 788] H.C. (1873). XXII, 69.

10470   O'SHAUGHNESSY COMMITTEE ON ROYAL IRISH CON-STABULARY, 1883. Royal Irish Constabulary: report of the committee of inquiry, 1883 [Chairman: Richard O'Shaughnessy]. [C. 3577] H.C. (1883). XXXII, 255. Minutes of evidence. [C. 3577–I] H.C. (1883). XXXII, 281.

There was a parallel inquiry on the Dublin police: *Dublin Metropolitan Police: report of the committee of inquiry, 1883* [Chairman: J. W. O'Donnell]. [C. 3576] H.C. (1883). XXXII, 1. Evidence. [C. 3576–I] H.C. (1883). XXXII, 35.

10471   BELFAST RIOTS COMMISSION, 1886. Report of the Belfast riots commissioners [Chairman: Sir John Charles Day]. [C. 4925] H.C. (1887). XVIII, 1. Minutes of evidence. [C. 4925–I] H.C. (1887). XVIII, 25. Minority report by Commander William B. McHardy. [C. 5029] H.C. (1887). XVIII, 631.

10472   VINCENT COMMITTEE ON ROYAL IRISH CONSTABULARY, 1901. Royal Irish Constabulary: report of the committee of inquiry, 1901 [Chairman: Sir Howard Vincent]. [Cd. 1087] H.C. (1902). XLII, 279. Minutes of evidence. [Cd. 1094] H.C. (1902). XLII, 313.

The inquiry was extended to cover the Dublin police. See *Dublin Metropolitan Police: report of the committee of enquiry, 1901* [Chairman: Sir Howard Vincent]. [Cd. 1088] H.C. (1902). XLII, 209. Minutes of evidence. [Cd. 1095] H.C. (1902). XLII, 227. There was a further inquiry in 1914. See *Royal Irish Constabulary and Dublin Metropolitan Police: report of the committee of inquiry, 1914* [Chairman: Sir David Harrel]. [Cd. 7421] H.C. (1914). XLIV, 247. Minutes of evidence. [Cd. 7637] H.C. (1914–16). XXXII, 359.

10473   GENERAL PRISONS BOARD (IRELAND). Annual report. Dublin. 1878–1920.

Superseded the reports of the Inspector General of Prisons, 1808–1877, and the Directors of Convict Prisons, 1854–77.

10474   CROSS COMMISSION ON IRISH PRISONS. Preliminary report of the royal commission appointed to inquire into the administration, discipline and condition of the prisons in Ireland, 1883 [Chairman: Sir Richard Assheton Cross]. [C. 3496] H.C. (1883). XXXII, 803. Second report. [C. 4145] H.C. (1884). XLII, 671. Reports. [C. 4233] H.C. (1884–5). XXXVIII, 1. Minutes of evidence. [C. 4233–I] H.C. (1884–5). XXXVIII, 259.

# D. THE CHURCHES

## 1. Roman Catholic Church

10475 ACTA ET DECRETA synodi plenariae episcoporum Hiberniae habitae apud Maynutiam, an. MDCCCLXXV. Dublin. 1877.

There is also a further coll. for the Maynooth synod of 1900, publ. in 2 v. Dublin 1906. There are also *Acta et decreta* and other similar vols. for each of the Irish provinces.

10476 CATHOLIC RECORD SOCIETY OF IRELAND. Archivium Hibernicum: or, Irish historical records. 1+. Maynooth. 1912+.

Weaker on the period than *Collectanea Hibernica: sources for Irish history*, 1+, Dublin 1958+.

10477 THE IRISH CATHOLIC DIRECTORY, ALMANAC AND REGISTRY. Dublin. 1835+.

There is also the *Complete Catholic directory, almanack and registry*, Dublin 1837+, whose title became *Battersby's registry for the Catholic world*, 1846–57, *Battersby's Catholic directory*, 1854–64, and *Catholic directory*, 1865+. For lists of bishops see 101.

10478 CORISH (PATRICK J.) *ed.* A history of Irish Catholicism. 6 v. Dublin. 1967+.

In process of issue in pts. Will constitute a good up-to-date hist. Vol. 5, pts. 2–3 by John Henry Whyte and Patrick J. Corish, 'Political problems, 1850–1878' has been publ.

10479 THE IRISH ECCLESIASTICAL RECORD. Dublin. 1864–1968.

Includes many hist. articles. Others are publ. in Irish Catholic Historical Committee [Society], *Proceedings*, Dublin 1955+, *Reportorium novum: Dublin diocesan historical record*, 1–3, Dublin 1955–64, *Seanchas ard mhacha: journal of the Armagh Diocesan Historical Society*, 1954–62, 1969+, *The Clogher record*, Drogheda 1953+, and *Breifne: journal of Cumann Seanchais Bhreifne*, 1+, Monaghan 1958+.

10480 BELLESHEIM (ALPHONS). Geschichte der katholischen Kirche in Irland von der Einführung des Christenthums bis auf die Gegenwart. 3 v. Mainz. 1890–1.

A good example of the older scholarship. See also Oliver Joseph Burke, *The history of the Catholic archbishops of Tuam from the foundation of the see to the death of the Most Rev. John MacHale, D.D., A.D. 1881*, Dublin 1882, Edward Alfred D'Alton, *History of the archdiocese of Tuam*, 2 v. Dublin 1928, and [Bishop] James Joseph MacNamee, *History of the diocese of Ardagh*, Dublin 1954.

10481 NORMAN (EDWARD ROBERT). The Catholic Church and Ireland in the age of rebellion, 1859–1873. 1965.

Full. See also his *The Catholic Church and Irish politics in the eighteen sixties*, Dublin Hist. Assoc., Dundalk 1965.

10482 MILLER (DAVID W.). Church, state and nation in Ireland, 1898–1921. Pittsburgh and Dublin. 1973.

10483 MACSUIBHNE (PEADAR). 'Ireland at the Vatican council'. *Irish Eccles. Rec.* xciii (1960), 209–22, 295–307.

10484 LARKIN (EMMET). 'Economic growth, capital investment and the Roman Catholic Church in nineteenth-century Ireland'. *Amer. Hist. Rev.* lxxii (1967), 852–84.

See also his article at **10402**.

10485 WHYTE (JOHN HENRY). 'The appointment of Catholic bishops in nineteenth-century Ireland'. *Catholic Hist. Rev.* xlviii (1962–3), 12–32.

10486 HEALY (JOHN), *Bishop.* Maynooth College: its centenary history, 1795–1895. Dublin. 1895.

See also Denis Meehan, *Window on Maynooth*, Dublin 1949, and Walter McDonald, *Reminiscences of a Maynooth Professor*, ed. by Denis Rolleston Gwynn, 1925. Patrick J. Hamell, 'Maynooth students and ordinations, 1795–1895: index', *Irish Eccles. Rec.*, 5 ser. cviii (1967), 353–71; 5 ser. cix (1968), 28–40, 122–34, 196–203, 256–64, 335–40, 407–16; 5 ser. cx (1968), 84–99, 173–82, 277–88, 381–6, covers A–M. A full index is to be publ. in book form.

10487 BROWN (STEPHEN JAMES MEREDITH) *comp.* An index of Catholic biographies. Dublin. 1930.

10488 BURKE. The life of the Very Rev. Thomas N. Burke, O.P. By William John Fitzpatrick. 2 v. 1885. New edn. 1894.

See also James Francis Cassidy, *The great Father Tom Burke*, Dublin 1947, and *The sermons, lectures and addresses delivered by the Very Rev. Thomas N. Burke . . . in the principal cities of the United States . . .*, N.Y. 1872.

10489 CULLEN. Life and work of Rev. James Aloysius Cullen, S.J. By Lambert A. J. McKenna. 1924.

One of the ablest of the Irish clergy.

10490 CULLEN. Paul Cullen and his contemporaries: with their letters from 1820–1902. Ed. by Peadar MacSuibhne. 3 v. Naas. 1961–5.

See also Michael J. Curran, 'Cardinal Cullen: biographical materials', *Reportorium Novum* i (1955–6), 213–27, Patrick J. Corish, 'Cardinal Cullen and Archbishop MacHale', *Irish Eccles. Rec.* xci (1959), 393–408, and 'Cardinal Cullen and the National Association of Ireland', *Reportorium Novum* iii (1961–4), 13–61, and Patrick Francis Moran, ed., *The pastoral letters and other writings of Cardinal Cullen, Archbishop of Dublin . . .*, 3 v. Dublin 1882.

10491 HEALEY. John Healey, Archbishop of Tuam. By Patrick J. Joyce. Dublin. 1931.

10492 MACHALE. John MacHale, Archbishop of Tuam: his life, times and correspondence. By [Bishop] Bernard O'Reilly. 2 v. N.Y. & Cincinnati [Ohio]. 1890.

There is also Nuala Costello, *John MacHale, Archbishop of Tuam*, Dublin & Lond. 1939.

10493   SULLIVAN. Father John Sullivan, S.J. By Fergal McGrath. 1941. 2nd edn. 1950.

See also Matthias Bodkin, *The port of tears: the life of Father John Sullivan, S.J.*, Dublin 1954.

10494   WALSH. William J. Walsh, Archbishop of Dublin. By Patrick J. Walsh. Dublin. 1928.

## 2. OTHER CHURCHES

10495   PHILLIPS (WALTER ALISON) *ed.* History of the Church of Ireland from the earliest times to the present day. 3 v. 1933–4.

The fullest general hist. John Thomas Ball, *The reformed Church of Ireland, 1537–1886*, 1886, 2nd edn. 1890, adds little and is unduly partisan. Thomas James Johnston, John Lubbock Robinson, and Robert Wyse Jackson, *A history of the Church of Ireland*, Dublin 1953, is a modern short hist. Donald Harman Akenson, *The Church of Ireland: ecclesiastical reform and revolution, 1800–1885*, New Haven 1971, is chiefly concerned with admin. questions. For misc. data consult *Irish Church directory*, Dublin 1862+.

10496   ESTABLISHED CHURCH (IRELAND) COMMISSION. Report of Her Majesty's commissioners on the revenues and condition of the established church (Ireland) [Chairman: Earl of Meath]. [4082] H.C. (1867–8). XXIV, 3. Appendix. [4082–I] H.C. (1867–8). XXIV, 651.

A careful survey of Irish church property.

10497   BELL (PHILIP MICHAEL HETT). Disestablishment in Ireland and Wales. Church Hist. Soc. 90. 1969.

Good. Replaced Anna Laura Evans, *The disestablishment of the Church of Ireland in 1869*, Lancaster, Pa. 1929. See also James Camlin Beckett, 'Gladstone, Queen Victoria and the disestablishment of the Irish church, 1868–9', *Irish Hist. Studs.* xiii (1962–3), 38–47, and Hugh Shearman, *How the Church of Ireland was disestablished*, Dublin 1970, and 'Irish church finances after disestablishment', in Henry Alfred Cronne, Theodore William Moody, and David Beers Quinn, eds., *Essays in British and Irish history in honour of James Eadie Todd*, 1949, pp. 278–302. The starting-point for the controversy about the Irish church in the period was Sir William Shee, *The Irish Church . . .*, Lond. & Dublin 1852, 2nd edn. 1863, a strong Roman Catholic attack. It was answered by Edward Adderley Stopford, *The income and requirements of the Irish church: being a reply to Serjeant Shee . . .*, Dublin 1853, and *A brief reply to the second edition of The Irish Church . . .*, Dublin 1864. The best defence of the Irish Church was *Essays on the Irish church by clergymen of the established church in Ireland*, Oxf. & Lond. 1868. See also John Pinnington, 'The Church of Ireland's apologetic position in the years before disestablishment', *Irish Eccles. Rec.* 5 ser. cviii (1967), 303–25. The Catholic disestablishment campaign in Ireland is covered in Patrick J. Corish, 'Cardinal Cullen and the National Association of Ireland', *Reportorium Novum* iii (1961–4), 13–61, and Mark Tierney, ed., 'Correspondence concerning the disestablishment of the Church of Ireland, 1862–1869', *Collectanea Hibernica* xii (1969), 102–91. The law of disestablishment is set out in William Leigh Bernard, *The Irish Church Acts, 1869 & 1872, and various statutes connected therewith . . .*, Dublin 1876.

10498   HURLEY (MICHAEL) *ed.* Irish Anglicanism, 1869–1969: essays on the role of Anglicanism in Irish life presented to the Church of Ireland on the occasion of the centenary of its disestablishment by a group of Methodist, Presbyterian, Quaker and Roman Catholic scholars. Dublin. 1970.

10499   LESLIE (JAMES BLENNERHASSETT). Catalogue of manuscripts in possession of the Representative Church Body . . ., Dublin. Dublin. 1938.

10500   LOVE (W. H.). The records of the archbishops of Armagh: being, an indexed catalogue of manuscripts, documents and books in the archiepiscopal registry of Armagh. Dundalk. 1965.

10501   COLE (JOHN HARDING). Church and parish records of the united diocese of Cork, Cloyne and Ross, comprising the eventful period in the church's history of the forty years from A.D. 1863, to the present time. Cork. 1903.
See also Charles Alexander Webster, *The diocese of Cork . . .*, Cork 1920.

10502   HEALY (JOHN). History of the diocese of Meath . . . 2 v. Dublin. 1908.

10503   LESLIE (JAMES BLENNERHASSETT). Derry clergy and parishes: being an account of the clergy of the Church of Ireland in the diocese of Derry from the earliest period, with historical notices of the several parishes, churches, etc. Enniskillen. 1937.
Leslie also publ. *Ardfert & Aghadoe clergy and parishes . . .*, Dublin 1940, *Armagh clergy and parishes . . .*, Dundalk 1911, suppl. 1948, *Clogher clergy and parishes . . .*, Enniskillen 1929, *Ferns clergy and parishes . . .*, Dublin 1936, *Ossory clergy and parishes . . .*, Enniskillen 1933, *Raphoe clergy and parishes . . .*, Enniskillen 1940, and with Henry Biddall Swanzy, *Biographical succession lists of the clergy of the diocese of Down*, Enniskillen 1936, and *Succession lists of the diocese of Dromore*, Belfast 1933. Hugh Jackson Lawlor, *The fasti of St. Patrick's Dublin . . .*, Dundalk 1930, covers the period; Henry Cotton, *Fasti ecclesiae Hibernicae . . .*, 5 v. and suppl. Dublin 1847–78, covers cathedral dignitaries to 1870.

10504   ALEXANDER. Primate Alexander, Archbishop of Armagh: a memoir. Ed. by Eleanor Alexander. 1913.

10505   BERNARD. Archbishop Bernard: professor, prelate and provost. By Robert Henry Murray. 1931.

10506   DALY. Memoir of the late Right Rev. Robert Daly, D.D., Lord Bishop of Cashel. By Mrs. Hamilton Madden. 1875.

10507   D'ARCY. The adventures of a bishop: a phase of Irish life: a personal and historical narrative. By Charles Frederick D'Arcy. 1934.

10508   GREGG. John Allen Fitzgerald Gregg, Archbishop. By George Fenn Seaver. Lond. & Dublin. 1963.

10509   KEENE. In loving memory: a sketch of the life of James Bennett Keene, D.D., Bishop of Meath. By his wife, Henrietta Sophia Bennett Keene. 1920.

10510  O'BRIEN. A memoir of the Right Rev. James Thomas O'Brien, late Lord Bishop of Ossory . . . By William George Carroll. Dublin. 1875.

10511  PLUNKET. William Conyngham Plunket, fourth Baron Plunket and sixty-first Archbishop of Dublin: a memoir. By Frederick Douglas How. 1900.

10512  REEVES. Life of the Rt. Rev. William Reeves. By Lady Mary Catherine Ferguson. Dublin. 1893.

10513  REICHEL. Sermons by Charles Parsons Reichel, D.D., D.Lit., sometime Bishop of Meath, with a memoir. By his son Henry Rudolf Reichel. 1899.

10514  TRENCH. The man of ten talents: a portrait of Richard Chevenix Trench, 1807–86, philologist, poet, theologian, archbishop. By John Bromley. 1959.

[Maria Trench, ed.] *Richard Chevenix Trench, archbishop: letters and memorials,* 2 v. 1888, is a source-book rather than a biog.

10515  WHATELY. Life and correspondence of Richard Whately, D.D., late Archbishop of Dublin. By Elizabeth Jane Whately. 2 v. 1866. 1-v. edn. 1868. New edn. 1875.

10516  WYNNE. The life of Frederick Richards Wynne, D.D., Bishop of Killaloe . . . By James Owen Hannay. 1897.

10517  BARKLEY (JOHN MONTEITH). A short history of the Presbyterian Church in Ireland. Belfast. 1960.

Useful for the 19th cent. James Ernest Davey, *1840–1940: the story of a hundred years: an account of the Irish Presbyterian Church from the formation of the General Assembly to the present time,* Belfast 1940, is a centenary brochure. The main source for the period is Presbyterian Church in Ireland, *Minutes of the General Assembly,* Belfast 1840+. For the pre-1850 period the indispensable account is James Seaton Reid, *History of the Presbyterian Church in Ireland . . .,* ed. by William Dool Killen, 3 v. Belfast 1867, and *History of congregations of the Presbyterian Church in Ireland . . .,* ed. by W. D. Killen, Belfast & Edin. 1886. James McConnell, *Presbyterianism in Belfast,* Belfast 1912, and Clarke Huston Irwin, *A history of Presbyterianism in Dublin and the south and west of Ireland,* 1890, are useful for local hist. For Presbyterian education see Robert Allen, *The Presbyterian College, Belfast, 1853–1953,* Belfast 1954. A. Albert Campbell, *Irish Presbyterian magazines, past and present: a bibliography,* Belfast 1919, is a handy list.

10518  JEFFERY (F.). Irish Methodism: an historical account of its traditions, theology and influence. Belfast. 1964.

See also Richard Lee Cole, *History of Methodism in Ireland: one Methodist church, 1860–1960,* Belfast 1960, which counts as v. 4 of Charles Henry Crookshank, *History of Methodism in Ireland,* 3 v. Belfast 1885–8, and *Wesley College, Dublin: an historical summary, 1845–1962,* Dublin 1963.

10519  GRUBB (ISABEL). Quakers in Ireland, 1654–1900. 1927.

See also Olive C. Goodbody, *Guide to Irish Quaker records, 1654–1860,* Irish MSS. Commission 1967, Isabel Grubb, *J. Ernest Grubb of Carrick-on-Suir,* Dublin 1928, and Charlotte Fell Smith, *James Nicholson Richardson of Bessbrook . . .,* 1925.

10520  GIBSON (WILLIAM). The year of grace: a history of the Ulster revival of 1859. Edin. 1860. New edn. 1909.

See also John T. Carson, *God's river in spate: the story of the religious awakening of Ulster in 1859*, Belfast 1958.

10521  DEWAR (MICHAEL WILLOUGHBY), BROWN (JOHN), *and* LONG (SAMUEL ERNEST). Orangeism: a new historical appreciation. Belfast. 1967.

Disappointing. John W. Boyle, 'The Belfast Protestant Association and the Independent Orange Order, 1901–10', *Irish Hist. Studs.* xiii (1962–3), 117–52, is much fuller for its subject.

10522  SHILLMAN (BERNARD). A short history of the Jews in Ireland. Dublin. 1945.


## E. ECONOMIC HISTORY

### 1. GENERAL

10523  PRENDEVILLE (P. L.). 'A select bibliography of Irish economic history. Part III: the nineteenth century'. *Econ. Hist. Rev.* iv (1932–4), 81–90.

10524  CULLEN (LOUIS MICHAEL). An economic history of Ireland since 1660. 1972.

See also L. M. Cullen, ed., *The formation of the Irish economy*, Cork [1969]. David Alfred Chart, *An economic history of Ireland*, Dublin 1920, new edn. 1942, is now out of date.

10525  BLACK (ROBERT DENIS COLLISON). Economic thought and the Irish question, 1817–1870. Camb. 1960.

See also his catalogue of economic writings (**8473**), E. D. Steele, 'J. S. Mill and the Irish question: the principles of political economy, 1848–1865', *Hist. J.* xiii (1970), 216–36, and 'Reform and the integrity of the empire, 1865–1870', ibid. xiii (1970), 419–50, and J. M. Goldstrom, 'Richard Whately and political economy in school books, 1833–80', *Irish Hist. Studs.* xv (1966–7), 131–46.

10526  STATISTICAL AND SOCIAL INQUIRY SOCIETY OF IRE-LAND: centenary volume, 1847–1947: with a history of the society by R. D. Collison Black . . . and indexes to the transactions of the society. Dublin. 1947.

Includes index to publs., and biog. sketches, 1847–1947. The publs. of the society, notably its journal, are of the greatest historical value. There is also economic matter in the publs. of the Royal Dublin Soc. (**10789**).

10527  SPROULL (JOHN). The resources and manufacturing industry of Ireland, as illustrated by the exhibition of 1853. Manch. 1854.

10528  HANCOCK (WILLIAM NEILSON). Report on the supposed progressive decline of Irish prosperity. Dublin. 1863.

A careful statistical analysis in the form of an official report.

10529  MURPHY (JOHN NICHOLAS). Ireland: industrial, political and social. 1870.

A careful account of the Irish economy.

10530  GIFFEN (*Sir* ROBERT). 'The economic value of Ireland to Great Britain'. *Nineteenth Century* xix (1886), 329–45.

10531  COYNE (WILLIAM P.) *ed.* Ireland, industrial and agricultural: handbook for the Irish pavilion, Glasgow International Exhibition, 1901. Dept. of Agriculture & Technical Instruction. Dublin etc. [1901.] 2nd edn. 1902.

A valuable account of Irish economic life. For interesting retrospective sketches see William Patrick O'Brien, *The great famine in Ireland and a retrospect of the fifty years, 1845–95, with a sketch of the present condition and future prospects of the congested districts,* Dublin 1896, William Frederick Bailey, 'Ireland since the famine . . .', *Stat. & Soc. Inquiry Soc. of Ireland J.* ii (1903), 129–54, and Edward J. Riordan, *Modern Irish trade and industry . . .,* 1920.

## 2. AGRICULTURE

### (a) *General*

10532  BUCKLEY (K.). 'The records of the Irish land commission as a source of historical evidence'. *Irish Hist. Studs.* viii (1952–3), 28–36.

10533  CROTTY (RAYMOND D.). Irish agricultural production: its volume and structure. Cork. 1966.

For comments see the review article by Joseph Lee in *Agric. Hist. Rev.* xvii (1969), 64–76.

10534  O'DONOVAN (JOHN). The economic history of live stock in Ireland. Dublin & Cork. 1940.

Standard.

10535  O'NEILL (THOMAS P.). 'From famine to near-famine, 1845–1879'. *Studia Hibernica* i (1961), 161–71.

10536  DE BURGH (ULICK H. HUSSEY) *comp.* The landowners of Ireland: an alphabetical list of the owners of estates of 500 acres or £500 valuation and upwards in Ireland . . . Dublin. 1878.

Based on **10557**.

10537  ROBINSON (O.). 'The London companies as progressive landlords in nineteenth-century Ireland'. *Econ. Hist. Rev.* 2 ser. xv (1962–3), 103–18.

10538  BAILEY (WILLIAM FREDERICK). The Irish Land Acts: a short sketch of their history and development. Dublin. 1917.

10539  MARTENS (HEINRICH). Die Agrarreformen in Irland: ihre Ursachen, ihre Durchführung, und ihre Wirkungen. Staats-und sozialwissenschaftliche Forschungen. Ed. by Gustav Schmoller and Max Sering. Vol. 177. Munich & Leipzig. 1915.

In many ways still the best account of the land reforms.

10540   POMFRET (JOHN EDWIN). The struggle for land in Ireland, 1800–1923. Princeton [N.J.]. 1930.

A good outline hist.

10541   HOOKER (ELIZABETH R.). Readjustments of agricultural tenure in Ireland. Chapel Hill [N.C.]. 1938.

10542   O'NEILL (BRIAN). The war for the land in Ireland. 1933.

A Marxist analysis.

10543   MONTROSE (JAMES LOUIS). 'The Landlord and Tenant Act of 1860'. *Irish Committee Hist. Sciences Bull.* i (1939).

10544   SHEARMAN (HUGH). 'State-aided land purchase under the disestablishment act of 1869'. *Irish Hist. Studs.* iv (1944–5), 58–80.

10545   BURN (WILLIAM LAURENCE). 'Free trade in land: an aspect of the Irish question'. *Roy. Hist. Soc. Trans.* 4 ser. xxxi (1949), 61–74. Repr. in Ian Ralph Christie, ed. Essays in modern history... Lond. & N.Y. 1968. Pp. 268–83.

10546   STEELE (E. D.). 'Ireland and the empire in the 1860s: imperial precedents for Gladstone's first Irish Land Act'. *Hist. J.* xi (1968), 64–83.

10547   PALMER (NORMAN DUNBAR). The Irish Land League crisis. New Haven [Conn.]. 1940.

Standard. Includes useful bibliog. of pamphlets.

10548   SOLOW (BARBARA LEWIS). The land question and the Irish economy, 1870–1903. Camb., Mass. 1971.

Questions the value of the Land Acts of 1870 and 1881.

10549   CONNELL (KENNETH HUGH). 'The land legislation and Irish social life'. *Econ. Hist. Rev.* 2 ser. xi (1958–9), 1–7.

10550   BUCKLEY (K.). 'The fixing of rents by agreement in Co. Galway, 1881–5'. *Irish Hist. Studs.* vii (1950–1), 147–79.

10551   DELANY (VINCENT THOMAS HYGINUS). 'Irish and Scottish land resettlement legislation'. *Internat. & Comparative Law Q.* 4 ser. viii (1959), 299–319.

10552   HORACE PLUNKETT FOUNDATION. Agricultural co-operation in Ireland: a survey. 1931.

See also Lionel Smith-Gordon and Laurence C. Staples, *Rural reconstruction in Ireland: a record of co-operative organisation,* 1917.

10553 PLUNKETT. Horace Plunkett: an Anglo-American Irishman. By Margaret Digby. Oxf. 1949.

Plunkett was Vice-President of the Dept. of Agriculture and Technical Instruction and the pioneer of Irish agricultural co-operation. There is little more on him in Rupert Metcalfe, *England and Sir Horace Plunkett* ..., 1933, and Edward E. Lysaght [MacLysaght], *Sir Horace Plunkett and his place in the Irish nation*, Dublin 1916.

10554 ANDERSON. With Horace Plunkett in Ireland. By Robert Andrew Anderson. 1935.

Anderson was sec. of the Irish Agric. Organisation Soc.

10555 MICKS (WILLIAM LAWSON). An account of the constitution, administration and dissolution of the Congested Districts Board for Ireland from 1891 to 1923. Dublin. 1925.

For the work of the Board see **10573-4.**

(b) *Official Reports*

See also the reports of the Richmond Commission (**4188**).

10556 AGRICULTURAL STATISTICS OF IRELAND. Annual. Dublin. 1847–1917.

Publ. as parl. papers. There was also an annual series of *General abstracts showing the acreage under crops and the number and description of livestock* ..., 1852–1920. For a summary see John Hooper, ed., *Agricultural statistics, 1847 to 1926*, Dept. of Industry and Commerce, Dublin 1930.

10557 OWNERS OF LAND IN IRELAND. Return of owners of land of one acre and upwards, in the several counties, counties of cities, and counties of towns in Ireland, showing the names of such owners arranged alphabetically in each county; their addresses—as far as could be ascertained—the extent in statute acres, and the valuation in each case; together with the number of owners in each county of less than one statute acre in extent; and the total area and valuation of such properties; and the grand total of area and valuation for all owners of property ... to which is added a summary for each province and for all Ireland. [C. 1492]. H.C. (1876). LXXX, 61. Suppl. [C. 2022]. H.C. (1878). LXXIX, 501.

See also **10536.**

10558 BRADY COMMISSION ON INCUMBERED ESTATES COURT. Report of Her Majesty's commissioners appointed to inquire into the Incumbered Estates Court . . . [Chairman: Maziere Brady, Lord Chancellor of Ireland.] [1938] H.C. (1854–5). XIX, 527.

10559 MAGUIRE COMMITTEE ON TENURE AND IMPROVEMENT OF LAND (IRELAND) ACT. Report from the select committee on Tenure and Improvement of Land (Ireland) Act [Chairman: John Francis Maguire]. H.C. 402 (1865). XI, 341.

See also *Report from the select committee of the House of Lords on the Tenure (Ireland) Bill [H.L.]* [Chairman: Marquess of Clanricarde (Lord Somerhill)]. H.C. 518 (1867). XIV, 423.

10560  HANCOCK (WILLIAM NEILSON). Two reports to the Irish government on the history of the landlord and tenant question in Ireland, with suggestions for legislation: first report made in 1859: second in 1866 . . . [4204] H.C. (1868–9). XXVI, 1.

10561  POOR LAW INSPECTORS (IRELAND). Reports from Poor Law inspectors in Ireland as to the existing relations between landlord and tenant in respect of improvements on farms, drainage, reclamation of land, fencing, planting, etc.; also as to the existence (and to what extent) of the Ulster tenant-right in their respective districts . . . [C. 31] H.C. (1870). XIV, 37.

10562  CHELMSFORD COMMITTEE ON IRISH LAND ACT, 1870. Report from the select committee of the House of Lords on the Landlord and Tenant (Ireland) Act, 1870 [Chairman: Lord Chelmsford]. H.C. 403 (1872). XI, 1.

10563  SHAW-LEFEVRE COMMITTEE ON IRISH LAND ACT, 1870. Report from the select committee on Irish Land Act, 1870 [Chairman: G. J. Shaw-Lefevre]. H.C. 328 (1877). XII, 1. Further report. H.C. 249 (1878). XV, 1.

10564  BESSBOROUGH COMMISSION ON IRISH LAND ACT, 1870. Report of Her Majesty's commissioners of inquiry into the working of the Landlord and Tenant (Ireland) Act, 1870, and the acts amending the same [Chairman: Earl of Bessborough]. [C. 2779] H.C. (1881). XVIII, 1. Digest of evidence, minutes of evidence etc. [C. 2779–I] H.C. (1881). XVIII, 73. [C. 2779–II] H.C. (1881). XIX, 1.

A comprehensive inquiry.

10565  IRISH LAND COMMISSIONERS. Annual report. 1881–1920.

10566  CAIRNS COMMITTEE ON IRISH LAND LAW. First report from the select committee of the House of Lords on Land Law (Ireland) [Chairman: Earl Cairns]. H.C. 249 (1882). XI, 1. Second report. H.C. 379 (1882). XI, 547. Third report. H.C. 204 (1883). XIII, 443. Fourth report. H.C. 279 (1883). XIII, 655.

10567  COWPER COMMISSION ON LAND ACTS OF 1881 AND 1885. Report of the royal commission on the Land Law (Ireland) Act, 1881, and the Purchase of Land (Ireland) Act, 1885 [Chairman: Earl Cowper]. [C. 4969] H.C. (1887). XXVI, 1. Minutes of evidence etc. [C. 4969–I–II] H.C. (1887). XXVI, 25, 1109. Report by Thomas Knipe. [C. 5015] H.C. (1887). XXVI, 1241.

10568 EVICTED TENANTS COMMISSION. Report of the evicted tenants commission [Chairman: Sir James Charles Mathew]. [C. 6935] H.C. (1893–4). XXXI, 13. Minutes of evidence. [C. 6935–I] H.C. (1893–4). XXXI, 111.

10569 MORLEY COMMITTEE ON IRISH LAND ACTS. Report from the select committee on Land Acts (Ireland) [Chairman: John Morley]. H.C. 310 (1894). XIII, 1.

10570 FRY COMMISSION ON THE IRISH LAND ACTS. Report of Her Majesty's commissioners of inquiry into the procedure and practice and the methods of valuation followed by the Land Commission, the Land Judge's Court, and the Civil Bill Courts in Ireland under the Land Acts and the Land Purchase Acts [Chairman: Sir Edward Fry]. [C. 8734] H.C. (1898). XXXV, 1. Minutes of evidence. [C. 8859] H.C. (1898). XXXV, 41. Appendixes. [C. 9107] H.C. (1899). XXXIV, 1.

10571 RUNCIMAN COMMITTEE ON FUNDS FOR IRISH LAND ACT, 1903. Report of the departmental committee appointed to enquire into Irish land purchase finance in connection with the provision of funds required for the purposes of the Irish Land Act, 1903 [Chairman: Walter Runciman]. [Cd. 4005] H.C. (1908). XXIII, 267.

10572 MURNAGHAN COMMITTEE ON AGRICULTURAL CREDIT IN IRELAND. Report of the departmental committee on agricultural credit in Ireland [Chairman: George Murnaghan]. [Cd. 7375] H.C. (1914). XIII, 1. Minutes of evidence. [Cd. 7376] H.C. (1914). XIII, 431.

10573 CONGESTED DISTRICTS BOARD FOR IRELAND. Annual Report. Dublin. 1892–1920.

10574 DUDLEY COMMISSION ON CONGESTION IN IRELAND. Royal Commission on congestion in Ireland: first report of the commissioners [Chairman: Earl of Dudley]. [Cd. 3266] H.C. (1906). XXXII, 617. Evidence. [Cd. 3267] H.C. (1906). XXXII, 621. Second report. [Cd. 3318] H.C. (1907). XXXV, 1. Evidence. [Cd. 3319] H.C. (1907). XXXV, 5. Third report. [Cd. 3413] H.C. (1907). XXXV, 333. Evidence. [Cd. 3414] H.C. (1907). XXXV, 337. Fourth report. [Cd. 3508] H.C. (1907). XXXVI, 1. Evidence. [Cd. 3509] H.C. (1907). XXXVI, 5. Fifth report. [Cd. 3629] H.C. (1907). XXXVI, 257. Evidence. [Cd. 3630] H.C. (1907). XXXVI, 261. Sixth report. [Cd. 3747] H.C. (1908). XXXIX, 697. Evidence. [Cd. 3748] H.C. (1908). XXXIX, 701. Seventh report. [Cd. 3784] H.C. (1908). XL, 1. Evidence. [Cd. 3785] H.C. (1908). XL, 5. Statistics. [Cd. 3786] H.C. (1908). XL, 431. Eighth report. [Cd. 3838] H.C. (1908). XLI, 1. Evidence. [Cd. 3839] H.C. (1908). XLI, 5. Ninth report. [Cd. 3844] H.C. (1908). XLI, 483. Evidence. [Cd. 3845] H.C. (1908). XLI, 487. Tenth report. [Cd. 4006] H.C. (1908). XLII, 1. Evidence. [Cd. 4007] H.C. (1908). XLII, 5. Eleventh report. [Cd. 4088] H.C. (1908). XLII, 583. Evidence. [Cd. 4089] H.C. (1908). XLII, 587. Final report. [Cd. 4097] H.C. (1908). XLII, 729. Index and digest. [Cd. 4098–9] H.C. (1908). XLIII, 1, 369.

The committee was peripatetic and each report represents a separate hearing.

10575 DEPARTMENT OF AGRICULTURE AND TECHNICAL IN-
STRUCTION (IRELAND). Annual report. 1900/1–1918/19.

See also Daniel Hoctor, *The department's story: a history of the Department of Agriculture*,
Dublin 1971, William P. Coyne, 'The work of the Irish agricultural department', *Roy.
Agric. Soc. J.* lxiii (1902), 370–80, and Sir Horace Plunkett, 'State aid to agriculture in
Ireland', ibid. lxxii (1911), 37–61.

10576 DIGBY COMMITTEE ON AGRICULTURE AND TECHNICAL
INSTRUCTION ACT. Department of Agriculture and Technical Instruction
(Ireland): report of the departmental committee of inquiry [Chairman: Sir
Kenelm Edward Digby]. [Cd. 3572] H.C. (1907). XVII, 799. Minority report.
[Cd. 3575] H.C. (1907). XVII, 963. Appendixes. [Cd. 3573–4] H.C. (1907).
XVIII, 1, 1051.

10577 ROBINSON COMMISSION ON FAIRS AND MARKETS IN
IRELAND. Report of the commissioners appointed to inquire into the state
of the fairs and markets in Ireland [Commissioner: Hercules G. R. Robinson].
[1674] H.C. (1852–3). XLI, 79. Minutes of evidence. [1910] H.C. (1854–5).
XIX, 1.

See also the report of the later United Kingdom commission on the subject, **5916.**

10578 DUNRAVEN COMMISSION ON HORSE BREEDING IN IRE-
LAND. Reports by the commissioners appointed to inquire into the horse
breeding industry in Ireland [Chairman: Earl of Dunraven]. [C. 8651] H.C.
(1898). XXXIII, 261. Minutes of evidence. [C. 8652] H.C. (1894). XXXIII,
295.

10579 CAMPBELL COMMISSION ON IRISH BUTTER INDUSTRY.
Report of the departmental committee on the Irish butter industry [Chairman:
John Ritch Campbell]. [Cd. 5092] H.C. (1910). VII, 835. Minutes of evidence.
[Cd. 5093] H.C. (1910). VIII, 1.

10580 CAMPBELL COMMITTEE ON THE IRISH FLAX-GROWING
INDUSTRY. Report of the departmental committee on the Irish flax-growing
industry [Chairman: John Ritch Campbell]. [Cd. 5502] H.C. (1911). XXVI, 1.
Minutes of evidence. [Cd. 5503] H.C. (1911). XXVI, 37.

10581 GILL COMMITTEE ON IRISH FORESTRY. Report of the departmental committee on Irish forestry [Chairman: Thomas Patrick Gill]. [Cd.
4027] H.C. (1908). XXIII, 601. Minutes of evidence. [Cd. 4028] H.C. (1908).
XXIII, 699.

(c) *Other Contemporary Works*

10582 THE IRISH FARMER'S GAZETTE and journal of practical horticulture. Dublin. 1842+.

Important. Title varies. Other important js. were *The Irish farming world*, Dublin 1888–
1920, and *The Irish homestead: the organ of Irish agricultural and industrial development*, Dublin 1895–1923.

10583  DE MOLEYNS (THOMAS). The landowner's and agent's practical guide. Dublin. 1860. 8th edn. 1899.

10584  SHEE (*Sir* WILLIAM). Papers, letters and speeches in the House of Commons, on the Irish land question, with a summary of its parliamentary history from the general election of 1852 to the close of the session of 1863. 1863.

10585  BUTT (ISAAC). The Irish people and the Irish land: a letter to Lord Lifford: with comments on the publications of Lord Dufferin and Lord Rosse. Dublin & Lond. 1867.

See also his *Land tenure in Ireland: a plea for the Celtic race*, Dublin 1866, 3rd edn. 1866. For Lord Lifford's views see James Hewitt, Viscount Lifford, *A plea for Irish landlords: a letter to Isaac Butt, Esq., Q.C.*, Dublin 1867.

10586  BLACKWOOD (FREDERICK TEMPLE HAMILTON-TEMPLE-), *Marquess of Dufferin and Ava*. Irish emigration and the tenure of land in Ireland. 1867.

A good statement of the landlord case.

10587  MILL (JOHN STUART). Chapters and speeches on the Irish land question. 1870.

See also his *England and Ireland*, 1868.

10588  LESLIE (THOMAS EDWARD CLIFFE). Land systems and industrial economy of Ireland, England, and continental countries. 1870.

Includes essays on the Irish land problem in 1867–70.

10589  MORRIS (WILLIAM O'CONNOR). Letters on the land question of Ireland. 1870.

Reports written as special commissioner for *The Times*. Morris publ. extensively on the land question, and also publ. *The Irish Land Act . . .*, Dublin 1870.

10590  LAVELLE (PATRICK). The Irish landlord since the revolution . . . Dublin. 1870.

Interesting as an attack on landlordism by a parish priest.

10591  PRINGLE (ROBERT OLIPHANT). 'A review of Irish agriculture: chiefly with reference to the production of live stock'. *Roy. Agric. Soc. J.* xxxiii (1872), 1–76.

See also his 'Illustrations of Irish farming', ibid. xxxiv (1873), 400–22, and 'Agricultural education in Ireland', ibid. 422–8.

10592  BALDWIN (THOMAS). Introduction to Irish farming. 1874.

An introductory textbook on better farming methods, covering much the same ground as his *Handy book of small farm management*, Dublin [1870], and *Introduction to practical farming, specially written for use in Irish national schools*, 1875, 18th edn. Dublin 1886.

10593  LAWSON (WILLIAM) *and others*. Ten years of gentleman-farming at Blennerhasset with co-operative objects. 1874. 2nd edn. 1875.

10594  O'BRIEN (RICHARD BARRY). The parliamentary history of the Irish land question from 1829 to 1869, and the origin and results of the Ulster custom. 1880.

The Parnellite view of the hist. of the land question.

10595  JONES. The life's work in Ireland of a landlord who tried to do his duty. By William Bence Jones. 1880.

A scientific landlord, extremely unpopular with the nationalists.

10596  TUKE (JAMES HACK). Irish distress and its remedies: the land question: a visit to Donegal and Connaught in the spring of 1880. 1880. 4th edn. 1880.

Tuke was the leading Quaker relief worker in Ireland. See **10686.**

10597  DUN (FINLAY). Landlords and tenants in Ireland. 1881.

Reports to *The Times*, 1880–1. Much of the best material on Ireland at this time appeared in newspapers. See also Charles Russell, Baron Russell of Killowen, *New views on Ireland: or, Irish land, grievances, remedies*, 1880, repr. from the *Daily Telegraph*, Bernard Henry Becker, *Disturbed Ireland: being, the letters written during the winter of 1880–81 by . . . special commissioner of the* Daily News, 1881, Edward Cant-Wall, *Ireland under the Land Act: letters contributed to the 'Standard' . . .*, 1882. There were also good reports in American papers, notably those incl. in David Bennett King, *The Irish question*, 1882.

10598  IRISH LAND COMMITTEE. The working of the land law act. Dublin. 1882.

No. XIV of a series of pamphlets.

10599  SHAW-LEFEVRE (GEORGE JOHN), *Baron Eversley*. Incidents of coercion: a journal of visits to Ireland in 1882 and 1888. 1888.

Cont. in his *Combination and coercion in Ireland [in 1889]: sequel to 'Incidents of coercion'*, 1890. He had already publ. *English and Irish land questions . . .*, 1881.

10600  BLUNT (WILFRID SCAWEN). The land war in Ireland, being a personal narrative of events . . . 1912.

Based on his diary, 1885–7.

10601  GEORGE (HENRY). The Irish land question . . . N.Y. 1881. 3rd edn. [The land question.] Lond. 1881.

10602  RECESS COMMITTEE. Report on the establishment of a department of agriculture and industries for Ireland. Dublin. 1896.

10603  COSBY (DUDLEY SYDNEY ASHWORTH). The Irish land problem and how to solve it: a defence of the Irish landlords. 1901.

Repr. from the *Westminster Rev.*

10604 JOHNSON (THOMAS). 'The Irish peat question'. *Roy. Dublin Soc. Econ. Proc.* i (1899–1909), 1–72.

See also Hugh Ryan, 'Reports upon the Irish peat industries', ibid. 371–420, 465–546.

10605 O'BRIEN (WILLIAM). The land conference and its critics. Dublin. 1904.

10606 HUSSEY. The reminiscences of an Irish land agent. By Samuel Murray Hussey. 1904.

10607 SCOTTISH COMMISSION ON AGRICULTURE. Revival of agriculture in Ireland: report of visit, 1906. Edin. 1907.

10608 BÉCHAUX (ÉTIENNE). La question agraire en Irlande au commencement du XXe siècle. Paris. 1906.

A full account up to the end of 1904.

10609 BONN (MORITZ JULIUS). Modern Ireland and her agrarian problem. Trans. by Thomas William Hazen Rolleston. Dublin. 1906.

10610 GINNELL (LAWRENCE). Land and liberty. Dublin. 1908.

An attack on the Land Purchase Act of 1903.

10611 NOLAN (FRANCIS) *and* KANE (ROBERT ROMNEY). The statutes relating to the law of landlord and tenant and land purchase in Ireland from 1860 to 1896 . . . 5th edn. Dublin. 1898.

A bulky, but useful legal manual. For technicalities of construction and the later land acts the standard work is Richard Robert Cherry and others, *The Irish land law and Land Purchase Acts* . . ., Dublin 1888, 3rd edn. 1903, suppls. 1906–10. For changes of tenancy, etc., consult Dodgson Hamilton Madden, *A practical treatise on the registration of deeds, conveyances and judgment-mortgages* . . ., Dublin 1868, 2nd edn. 1901, and *Land transfer and the registration of title in Ireland*, Dublin 1892. On early legislation there is Richard Charles Macnevin, *The practice of the Incumbered Estates Court in Ireland* . . ., Dublin 1850, 3rd edn. 1859. On later legislation there is a host of works, of which a sample only is given here. On the 1870 Act the best book is Alexander George Richey, *The Irish land laws*, 1880, but see Isaac Butt, *A practical treatise on the new law of compensation to tenants in Ireland, and other provisions of the Landlord and Tenant Act, 1870*, Dublin 1871; Dodgson Hamilton Madden, *The law and practice of the High Court of Justice in Ireland in relation to proceedings before the land judge* . . ., 1870, 3rd edn. 1889; Henry Dix Hutton, *Handy book of farm tenure and purchase under the Landlord and Tenant (Ireland) Act, 1870*, Dublin 1871, 3rd edn. 1872; and Robert Donnell, *Reports of one hundred & ninety cases in the Irish land courts* . . ., 2nd edn. Dublin 1876. Timothy Michael Healy, *The Land Law (Ireland) Act, 1881* . . ., Dublin 1882, is interesting chiefly because of its author. Sir George Fottrell and John George Fottrell, *Handbook of the law and practice in sales from landlord to tenant in Ireland*, Dublin 1884, and *Practical guide to the Land Purchase Acts (Ireland)* . . ., Dublin 1886, 4th edn. 1897, are rather technical. For later acts see Walter Acason, *Land purchase handbook: a popular guide to the Land Purchase Act, 1891* . . ., Dublin 1891; Sir Dunbar Plunket Barton and Richard Robert Cherry, *The Land Law (Ireland) Act, 1896* . . ., Dublin 1897; Thomas Joseph Campbell, *Irish land purchase: including the text of the Land Act, 1903* . . ., Dublin 1903, 3rd edn. 1904; and John George Fottrell and Frank Fottrell, *The Irish Land Act, 1903, explained* . . ., Dublin 1903, 4th edn. 1904.

## 3. FINANCE

10612  MURPHY (ALICE EFFIE). A history of the commercial and financial relations between England and Ireland from the period of the Restoration. 1903.

Good.

10613  KENNEDY (THOMAS). A history of the Irish protest against over-taxation from 1853 to 1897. Dublin. 1897.

For contemp. arguments about the subject see Thomas Lough, *England's wealth, Ireland's poverty*, 1896, 3rd edn. 1897; John Joseph Clancy, 'The financial grievance of Ireland', *Nineteenth Century* xl (1896), 982–94; Arthur James Balfour, Earl of Balfour, *Financial relations between Great Britain and Ireland* . . ., 1898; Thomas Michael Kettle, *Home Rule finance: an experiment in justice*, Dublin 1911; and Roy. Econ. Soc., *The fiscal relations of Great Britain & Ireland: papers read at the congress of the Royal Economic Society, January 10th, 1912*, 1912.

10614  DUNNE COMMITTEE ON TAXATION OF IRELAND. Report from the select committee on taxation of Ireland [Chairman: Colonel Dunne]. H.C. 513 (1864). XV, 1. Further report. H.C. 330. (1865.) XII, 1.

10615  CHILDERS COMMISSION ON FINANCIAL RELATIONS. First report by Her Majesty's commissioners appointed to inquire into the financial relations between Great Britain and Ireland [Chairmen: Hugh C. E. Childers and The O'Conor Don]. [C. 7720] H.C. (1895). XXXVI, 1. Minutes of evidence. [C. 7720–I] H.C. (1895). XXXVI, 5. [C. 8008] H.C. (1896). XXXII, 291. Final report. [C. 8262] H.C. (1896). XXXII, 59.

For figures see also *Taxes (England and Wales, Scotland and Ireland): return showing for each year since 1823 the taxes in force in England and Wales, Scotland and Ireland, separately, in cases where the taxes were not common to all three countries, or, where the same duties were in force in all three countries, but the rate of tax was different, specifying the principal rates and showing where available the amounts raised thereunder in each country.* H.C. 109 (1912–13). XLIX, 675.

10616  THE FREEMAN'S JOURNAL. The over-taxation of Ireland, a record of the city and county meetings; the declarations of public bodies, chambers of commerce, political conventions, and British statesmen on the financial relations between Great Britain and Ireland, with introduction, appendixes, and index. Dublin. 1898.

10617  PRIMROSE COMMITTEE ON IRISH FINANCE. Report by the committee on Irish finance [Chairman: Sir Henry Primrose]. [Cd. 6153] H.C. (1912–13). XXXIV, 5. Minutes of evidence. [Cd. 6799] H.C. (1913). XXX, 1.

A review of the whole field of Anglo-Irish finance, including the early Home Rule Bills and the Irish Councils Bill of 1907.

10618  DILLON (MALCOLM). The history and development of banking in Ireland from the earliest times to the present day. Lond. & Dublin. 1889.

Charles MacCarthy, *The law and practice of banking in Ireland* . . ., Dublin 1882, adds little.

10619 HALL (FREDERICK GEORGE) *and others*. The Bank of Ireland, 1783–1946. Dublin & Oxf. 1949.

The hist. narrative and appendixes, minus the biog. and architectural sections and the illustrations of this edn., were also issued as *History of the Bank of Ireland*, Dublin & Oxf. 1949.

10620 HILL (EDWIN DARLEY). The Northern Banking Company, Limited: an historical sketch commemorating a century of banking in Ireland by the first joint-stock bank established in that country, 1824–1924. Belfast. 1925.

Cp. Ulster Bank Limited, *Decades of the Ulster Bank, 1836–1964*, Belfast 1965, and Kenneth Milne, *A history of the Royal Bank of Ireland, Limited*, Dublin 1964.

10621 INSTITUTE OF BANKERS IN IRELAND. Journal. Dublin. 1898+.

10622 ROBINSON (HOWARD W.). A history of accountants in Ireland. Dublin. 1964.

### 4. INDUSTRY

10623 CRORY (WILLIAM GLENNY). Industry in Ireland. 1863.

Crory also publ. a sizeable pamphlet, *A treatise on industrial resources (still neglected) in Ireland . . .*, Dublin 1860.

10624 BEVAN (GEORGE PHILLIPS). 'The industrial resources of Ireland'. *Stat. Soc. J.* xliv (1881), 675–716.

10625 WILMOT COMMITTEE ON IRISH INDUSTRIES. Report from the select committee on industries (Ireland) [Chairman: Sir Eardley Wilmot]. H.C. 288 (1884–5). IX, 1.

A big vol. of evidence. There is also a pamphlet lit. designed, in the words of Robert Dennis, *Industrial Ireland: a practical and non-political view of 'Ireland for the Irish'*, 1887, 'to prove that Ireland may be made a prosperous industrial country'. Cp. *The Irish manufacturers' journal*, Dublin 1881–92, styled *Commercial Ireland*, 1889–92.

10626 THOM'S DIRECTORY OF MANUFACTURERS AND SHIPPERS OF IRELAND, 1908. Dublin. 1908. New edn. for 1909–10. 1910.

Includes a great deal of misc. material about aspects of the Irish economy. There is a good illustr. directory in *The industries of Ireland: Part 1. Belfast and towns of the north: the provinces of Ulster and Connaught: business men and mercantile interests, wealth and growth, historical, statistical, biographical*, 1891.

10627 GORDON (LIONEL SMITH-) *and* O'BRIEN (FRANCIS CRUISE). Co-operation in Ireland. Manch. 1921.

10628 LYNCH (PATRICK) *and* VAIZEY (JOHN). Guinness's brewery in the Irish economy, 1759–1876. Camb. 1960.

Important, as concerned with one of the few major industries in southern Ireland. The interpretation has been challenged in Joseph Lee, 'Money and beer in Ireland, 1790–1875', *Econ. Hist. Rev.* 2 ser. xix (1966), 183–90, to whom Lynch and Vaizey replied, ibid. 190–4.

10629  ARMSTRONG (D. L.). 'Social and economic conditions in the Belfast linen industry, 1850–1900'. *Irish Hist. Studs.* vii (1951), 235–69.

Conrad Gill, *The rise of the Irish linen industry*, Oxf. 1925, has little on the period. But see William Charley, *Flax and its products in Ireland*, 1862, and F. W. Smith, *The Irish linen-trade handbook and directory*, Belfast 1876.

10630  HATCH COMMITTEE ON NORTHERN IRISH LINEN. Committee of inquiry into the conditions of employment in the linen and other making-up trades of the North of Ireland [Chairman: Sir Ernest F. G. Hatch]. Report and evidence. [Cd. 6509] H.C. (1912–13). XXXIV, 365.

See also *Report of the departmental committee on humidity and ventilation in flax mills and linen factories* [Chairman: Sir Hamilton Freer-Smith]. [Cd. 7433] H.C. (1914). XXXVI 1. Minutes of evidence. [Cd. 7446] H.C. (1914]. XXXVI, 107.

10631  THE IRISH BUILDER. Dublin. 1867+.

Also publ. 1859–66 as *The Dublin builder*.

10632  COMMISSIONERS OF PUBLIC WORKS IN IRELAND. Annual report. 1831–1921.

10633  ALLPORT COMMISSION ON IRISH PUBLIC WORKS. First report of the royal commission on Irish public works [Chairman: Sir James Joseph Allport]. [C. 5038] H.C. (1887). XXV, 471. Appendix. [C. 5038–I] H.C. (1887). XXV, 509. Second report. [C. 5264] H.C. (1888). XLVIII, 143. Appendix. [C. 5264–I] H.C. (1888). XLVIII, 205.

10634  INSTITUTION OF CIVIL ENGINEERS OF IRELAND. Transactions. Dublin. 1844+.

10635  COE (W. E.). The engineering industry of the north of Ireland. Newton Abbot. 1969.

10636  GRIBBON (HENRY DERWENT). The history of water power in Ulster. Newton Abbot. 1969.

10637  HAMMOND (JOSEPH W.). 'The King's printers in Ireland, 1551–1919'. *Dublin Hist. Rec.* xi (1949–50), 29–31, 58–64, 88–96.

10638  BROWN (STEPHEN J.). 'The Dublin newspaper press: a bird's eye view, 1659–1916'. *Studies* xxv (1936), 109–22.

See also A. Albert Campbell, *Belfast newspapers, past and present*, Belfast 1921.

10639  WESTROPP (MICHAEL SEYMOUR DUDLEY). Irish glass: an account of glass-making in Ireland from the XVIth century to the present day. 1920.

10640  MEREDITH (LOUISA ANNE). The lacemakers: sketches of Irish character: with some account of the effort to establish lacemaking in Ireland. 1865.

**10641 INSPECTORS OF IRISH FISHERIES.** Annual report. 1853–1907.

Cont. by the *Report of the Department of Agriculture and Technical Instruction for Ireland on the sea and inland fisheries of Ireland,* annual, 1908–19.

**10642 CONNER (HENRY DANIEL).** Fisheries (Ireland) Acts: being the statutes relating to salmon, trout, pollen, eel, oyster and other fisheries in Ireland. Dublin. 1892. 2nd edn. 1908.

**10643 McMAHON COMMITTEE ON FISHERIES (IRELAND) BILL.** Report from the select committee on the Fisheries (Ireland) Bill [Chairman: Patrick McMahon]. H.C. 360 (1862). IX, 289.

**10644 BLAKE COMMITTEE ON SEA COAST FISHERIES BILL.** Report from the select committee on the Sea Coast Fisheries (Ireland) Bill [Chairman: John Aloysius Blake]. H.C. 443 (1867). XIV, 1.

**10645 BLAKE COMMISSION ON IRISH OYSTER FISHERIES.** Report on the coast and deep sea fisheries of Ireland by the royal commissioners on Irish oyster fisheries [Chairman: John Aloysius Blake]. [C. 226] H.C. (1870). XIV, 231.

See also *Report of the commission appointed to inquire into the methods of oyster culture in the United Kingdom and France, with a view to the introduction of improved methods of cultivation of oysters into Ireland.* [C. 224] H.C. (1870). XIV, 305.

**10646 WALKER COMMITTEE ON SALMON FISHERIES.** Report from the select committee on salmon fisheries (Ireland) [Chairman: Samuel Walker]. H.C. 271 (1884–5). XI, 29.

See also *Report from the select committee on the Salmon Fisheries (Ireland) Acts Amendment Bill* [Chairman: Sir John Whittaker Ellis]. H.C. 236 (1892). XVII, 1.

**10647 INSPECTORS OF IRISH FISHERIES.** Report on inquiries held by the inspectors of Irish fisheries into an alleged decrease in the supply of fish off certain parts of the coast of Ireland . . . [C. 5777] H.C. (1889). XXII, 253.

**10648 IRISH INLAND FISHERIES COMMISSION.** Irish Inland Fisheries Commission: report of the commissioners [Chairman: Lord Justice Samuel Walker]. [Cd. 448] H.C. (1901). XII, 1. Minutes of evidence. [Cd. 450] H.C. (1901). XII, 19. Documents etc. [Cd. 451] H.C. (1901). XII, 539. [Cd. 452] H.C. (1901). XII, 681.

**10649 HARREL COMMITTEE ON IRISH INLAND FISHERIES.** Report of the departmental committee on Irish inland fisheries [Chairman: Sir David Harrel]. [Cd. 6433] H.C. (1912–13). XXVII, 161. Minutes of evidence. [Cd. 6545] H.C. (1912–13). XXVII, 191.

## 5. TRANSPORT

**10650 FLANAGAN (PATRICK JOSEPH).** Transport in Ireland, 1880–1910. Dublin. 1969.

A picture-book drawing on the Lawrence coll. in the National Libr. of Ireland.

10651 McCUTCHEON (WILLIAM ALAN). The canals of the north of Ireland. Newton Abbot. 1965.

Suppl. by Vincent Thomas Hyginus Delany and Dorothy Ruth Delany, *The canals of the south of Ireland*. Newton Abbot 1966.

10652 MARMION (ANTHONY). The ancient and modern history of the maritime ports of Ireland. 1855. 4th edn. 1860.

10653 OWEN (*Sir* DAVID JOHN). A short history of the port of Belfast. Belfast. 1917.

10654 ANDERSON (ERNEST B.). Sailing ships of Ireland: a book for lovers of sail; being, a record of Irish sailing ships of the nineteenth century. Dublin. [1951.]

10655 COOKE (SHOLTO). The maiden city and the western ocean: a history of the shipping trade between Londonderry and North America in the nineteenth century. Dublin. 1960.

For contemp. works on the American shipping routes see *Report of the commissioners appointed to inquire as to the proposal for an Irish packet station* [Chairman: Earl Granville]. [1391] H.C. (1851). XXV, 251, *Report and the evidence taken before the commission appointed to inquire into the merits of the western harbours of Ireland for the purposes of transatlantic communication* [Chairman: Captain T. W. Beechey]. H.C. 22 (1852–3). XCV, 411, which deals with the relative merits of Galway Bay and the River Shannon for a packet station, Pliny Miles. *The social, political and commercial advantages of direct steam navigation and rapid postal intercourse between Europe amd America via Galway, Ireland*, 1858, 2nd edn. 1859, and *Report from the select committee on the Royal Atlantic Steam Navigation Company* [Chairman: William Henry Gregory]. H.C. 463 (1861). XII, 1.

10656 MCNEILL (DONALD BURGESS). Irish passenger steamship services. 2v. Newton Abbot. 1969–72.

10657 CLEMENTS (EDWARD). Report of the commissioner appointed to inquire into the turnpike trusts, Ireland, 1856. [2110] H.C. (1856). XIX, 601.

10658 CONROY (JOHN CHARLES). A history of railways in Ireland. 1928.

Standard. See also Irish Railway Record Soc., *Journal*, 1+, 1947+, and [William] Alan McCutcheon, *Railway history in pictures: Ireland*, 2 v. Newton Abbot 1969–71.

10659 MURRAY (KEVIN). The Great Northern Railway, Ireland: past, present & future. Dublin. 1944.

10660 PATTERSON (EDWARD MERVYN). A history of the narrow-gauge railways of north-east Ireland. 1. The Ballycastle railway. Dawlish. 1965. 2. The Ballymena lines. Newton Abbot. 1968.

Suppl. by his *A history of the narrow-gauge railways of north-west Ireland*. 1. *The county Donegal railways*, Dawlish [1964], 2nd edn. Newton Abbot 1969; 2. *The Londonderry & Lough Swilly railway*, Dawlish [1964], 2nd edn. Newton Abbot 1969. There are also a number of hists. of minor railways, such as Patrick Joseph Flanagan, *The Cavan & Leitrim railway*, Newton Abbot 1966.

10661 DEVONSHIRE COMMISSION ON RAILWAYS. Royal commission on railways: evidence and papers relating to railways in Ireland extracted from the proceedings of the commission [Chairman: Duke of Devonshire]. [3607] H.C. (1866). LXIII, 279.

10662 SPEARMAN COMMISSION ON IRISH RAILWAY WORKS. Report of the commissioners appointed to inspect the accounts and examine the works of railways in Ireland . . . [Chairman: Sir Alexander Y. Spearman]. [4018] H.C. (1867–8). XXXII, 469. Sections, etc. [4018–I] H.C. (1867–8). XXXII, 649. Second report. [4086] H.C. (1868–9). XVII, 459.

10663 FABIAN SOCIETY. State railways for Ireland. Fabian tract 98. 1899.

10664 SCOTTER COMMISSION ON IRISH RAILWAYS. Vice-regal commission on Irish railways, including light railways: first report of the commissioners [Chairman: Sir Charles Scotter]. [Cd. 3632] H.C. (1907). XXXVII, 45. Appendix. [Cd. 3633] H.C. (1907). XXXVII, 49. Second report. [Cd. 3895] H.C. (1908). XLVII, 327. Appendix. [Cd. 3896] H.C. (1908). XLVII, 331. Third report. [Cd. 4053] H.C. (1908). XLVIII, 1. Appendix. [Cd. 4054] H.C. (1908). XLVIII, 5. Fourth report. [Cd. 4204] H.C. (1908). XLVIII, 541. Appendixes. [Cd. 4205] H.C. (1908). XLVIII, 545. [Cd. 4481] H.C. (1909). XXVII, 199. Fifth and final report. [Cd. 5247] H.C. (1910). XXXVII, 1. Appendix. [Cd. 5248] H.C. (1910). XXXVII, 137.

6. LABOUR

10665 BOYLE (J. W.) *ed.* Leaders and workers. Cork. 1966.

10666 POOR LAW INSPECTORS (IRELAND). Reports from the Poor Law inspectors on the wages of agricultural labourers in Ireland. [C. 35] H.C. (1870). XIV, 1.

The main survey was that of the Labour commission (6454).

10667 REPORT and tables relating to Irish migratory agricultural and other labourers. Annual. 1880–1915.

See also J. H. Johnson, 'Harvest migration from nineteenth-century Ireland', *Inst. British Geographers Trans.* xli (1967), 97–112.

10668 RYAN (WILLIAM PATRICK). The Irish labour movement: from the 'twenties to our own day. Dublin & Lond. 1919.

10669 DUBLIN DISTURBANCES COMMISSION. Report of the Dublin disturbances commission [Members: Denis S. Henry and Samuel Lombard Brown]. [Cd. 7269] H.C. (1914). XVIII, 513. Minutes of evidence. [Cd. 7272] H.C. (1914). XVIII, 533.

For the background of the great strike of 1913–14 see 10416.

## F. SOCIAL HISTORY

### 1. GENERAL

10670  GRIMSHAW (THOMAS WRIGLEY). Facts and figures about Ireland. 2 pts. Dublin. 1893.

Pt. 1 consists of an analysis of Irish statistics, 1841–90, pt. 2 of statistics of indiv. counties. Grimshaw was Registrar-General for Ireland.

10671  MEENAN (JAMES FRANCIS) *and* WEBB (DAVID ALLARDICE) *eds*. A view of Ireland: twelve essays on different aspects of Irish life and the Irish countryside. British Assoc. Dublin. 1957.

10672  HOOTON (EARNEST ALBERT) *and* DUPERTUIS (CLARENCE WESLEY). The physical anthropology of Ireland. Camb., Mass. 1955.

10673  EVANS (EMYR ESTYN). Irish folk ways. Lond. & N.Y. 1957.

Replaced his *Irish heritage: the landscape, the people and their work*, Dundalk 1942. See also Conrad Maynadier Arensberg, *The Irish countryman: an anthropological study*, Lond. & N.Y. 1937, repr. Gloucester, Mass. 1959, C. M. Arensberg and Solon Toothaker Kimball, *Family and community in Ireland*, Camb., Mass. 1940, 2nd edn. 1968, and Jeremiah Curtin, comp., *Irish folk tales*, ed. by Séamus Ó'Dulearga, Folklore Soc. of Ireland, Dublin 1943.

10674  TRENCH (WILLIAM STEUART). Realities of Irish life. 1866. Repr. 1966.

10675  FENTON. It all happened: reminiscences of Seamus Fenton. Dublin. 1948.

One of the better vols. of reminiscences of rural life.

10676  BARLOW (JANE). Bog-land studies. 1892. 2nd edn. 1893.

Interesting as an attempt at a picture of the Irish peasantry in verse. George A. Birmingham, pseud. of James Owen Hannay, *The bad times*, 1908, is a novel intended to capture the atmosphere of the Land League period. But neither can compare in quality with the work of Somerville and Ross (**10677**).

10677  SOMERVILLE (EDITH ŒNONE) *and* ROSS (MARTIN) *pseud. of* MARTIN (VIOLET FLORENCE). The real Charlotte. 3 v. 1894.

A major work of art about Irish country life. Their *Some experiences of an Irish R.M.*, 1899, is also deservedly famous. For their lives see **10777**.

10678  CONNELL (KENNETH HUGH). Irish peasant society: four historical essays. Oxf. 1968.

Important. See also his 'Marriage in Ireland after the famine: the diffusion of the match', *Stat. & Soc. Inquiry Soc. of Ireland J.* xix (1955–6), 82–103. Repr. with revs. *Past & Present* xii (1957), 76–91. See also his 'Peasant marriage in Ireland: its structure and development since the famine', *Econ. Hist. Rev.* 2 ser. xiv (1961–2), 502–23, James H. Johnson, 'Marriage and fertility in nineteenth-century Londonderry', *Stat. & Soc. Inquiry Soc. of Ireland J.* xx (1959–60), 99–117, Brendan M. Walsh,

'Marriage rates and population pressure: Ireland, 1871 and 1911', *Econ. Hist. Rev.* 2 ser. xxiii (1970), 148–62, and Edward J. Coyne, 'Irish population problems: eighty years a-growing, 1871–1951', *Studies* xliii (1954), 151–67.

10679 COUSENS (S. H.) 'Emigration and demographic change in Ireland, 1851–1861'. *Econ. Hist. Rev.* 2 ser. xiv (1961–2), 275–88.

See also his 'The regional variations in population changes in Ireland, 1861–1881', ibid. 2 ser. xvii (1964–5), 301–21.

10680 REGISTRAR GENERAL FOR IRELAND. First annual report of the Registrar-General of Marriages, Births and Deaths in Ireland, 1864. [4137] (1868–9). XVI, 665. Annual to 1921.

10681 MATHESON (ROBERT E.). Special report on surnames in Ireland, with notes as to numerical strength, derivation, ethnology and distribution; based on information extracted from the indexes of the General Register office. Appendix to the twenty-ninth detailed annual report of the Registrar-General . . . [C. 7289] H.C. (1893–4). XXI, 507.

10682 BOWEN (MURIEL). Irish hunting. Tralee. 1955.

For cricket see William Patrick Hone, *Cricket in Ireland*, Tralee 1955.

## 2. SOCIAL WELFARE

10683 POOR LAW INSPECTORS (IRELAND). Report from Poor Law inspectors in Ireland . . . on the subject of labourers' dwellings in that country. [C. 764] H.C. (1873). XXII, 615.

For agricultural labourers' cottages see also *Report from the select committee on agricultural labourers (Ireland)* [Chairman: Samuel Walker]. H.C. 317 (1884). VIII, 245, and *Further report.* H.C. 32 (1884–5). VII, 559. Irish housing was also dealt with by the United Kingdom commission on the housing of the working classes (**7099**).

10684 O'CONOR COMMISSION ON WORKING-CLASS HOUSING IN DUBLIN. Report of the departmental committee appointed . . . to inquire into the housing conditions of the working classes in the city of Dublin [Chairman: Charles H. O'Conor]. [Cd. 7273] H.C. (1914). XIX, 61.

10685 DUBLIN MANSION HOUSE RELIEF COMMITTEE. The Irish crisis of 1879–80: proceedings of the Dublin Mansion House Relief Committee, 1880. Dublin. 1881.

Useful on Irish philanthropy.

10686 TUKE. James Hack Tuke: a memoir. By Sir Edward Fry. 1899.

Quaker relief worker. See also **10596**.

10687 DELANY (VINCENT THOMAS HYGINUS). The law relating to charities in Ireland. Dublin. 1956. Rev. edn. 1962.

10688 NICHOLLS (*Sir* GEORGE). A history of the Irish Poor Law: in connexion with the condition of the people. Dublin. 1856.

For the law relating to the poor see B. Banks, *Compendium of the Irish Poor Law* . . ., Dublin 1872, and Thomas A. Mooney, *Compendium of the Irish Poor Law*, Dublin 1887, suppl. 1898.

10689 LOCAL GOVERNMENT BOARD FOR IRELAND. Annual report. 1873–1919/20.

Replaced the annual report of the Poor Law Commission, 1847/8–1872. See also *Returns of local taxation in Ireland*, Annual, 1865–1918/19.

10690 CARDWELL COMMITTEE ON POOR RELIEF (IRELAND). Report from the select committee on poor relief (Ireland) [Chairman: Edward Cardwell]. H.C. 408 (1861). X, 1.

For destitute Irishmen in Britain see *Report from the select committee on poor removal* [Chairman: Thomas Salt]. H.C. 282 (1878–9). XII, 561.

10691 LORDS COMMITTEE ON IRISH POOR LAW GUARDIANS. Report from the select committee of the House of Lords on the Poor Law Guardians (Ireland) Bill [Chairman: Marquess of Waterford (Lord Tyrone)]. H.C. 297 (1884–5). X, 281.

10692 POOR RELIEF (IRELAND) INQUIRY COMMISSION [Commissioners: Christopher Talbot Redington and Henry A. Robinson]. Report and evidence. [C. 5043] H.C. (1887). XXXVIII, 1.

On the financing of the Poor Law.

10693 MICKS COMMISSION ON POOR LAW REFORM IN IRELAND. Report of the vice-regal commission on poor law reform in Ireland [Chairman: William Lawson Micks]. [Cd. 3202] H.C. (1906). LI, 349. Appendix. [Cd. 3203] H.C. (1906). LI, 441. Minutes of evidence. [Cd. 3204] H.C. (1906). LII, 1.

See also the relevant section of the United Kingdom Poor Law report, notably *Royal commission on the Poor Laws and the relief of distress* [Chairman: Lord George Hamilton]. *Report on Ireland*. [Cd. 4630] H.C. (1909). XXXVIII, 1.

10694 GRIMSHAW (THOMAS WRIGLEY) *and others*. Manual of public health for Ireland. Dublin. 1875.

See also Charles Philip Cotton, *The Irish Public Health Acts, 1878–90* . . ., Dublin 1891, suppls. 1892, 1896, and Sir George Thomas Barrett Vanston, *The law relating to public health in Ireland* . . ., Dublin 1913.

10695 CAMERON (*Sir* CHARLES ALEXANDER). A brief history of municipal health administration in Dublin. Dublin. 1914.

10696 DUBLIN PUBLIC HEALTH COMMISSION. Report of the committee appointed by the Local Government Board for Ireland to inquire into the public health of the City of Dublin [Chairman: Charles P. Cotton]. [Cd. 243] H.C. (1900). XXXIX, 681. Minutes of evidence. [Cd. 244] H.C. (1900). XXXIX, 707.

There is also an earlier inquiry: *Report of the royal commissioners appointed to inquire into the sewerage and drainage of the city of Dublin and other matters connected therewith* [Commissioners: Robert Rawlinson and Francis Xavier Frederick MacCabe]. [C. 2605] H.C. (1880). XXX, 1.

10697 BELFAST HEALTH COMMISSION [Chairman: Thomas Walter Harding]. Report to the Local Government Board for Ireland. [Cd. 4128] H.C. (1908). XXXI, 699.

10698 NAAS COMMITTEE ON DUBLIN HOSPITALS. Report from the select committee on Dublin hospitals [Chairman: Lord Naas]. H.C. 338 (1854). XII, 1.

See also *Report of the commissioners appointed to inquire into the hospitals of Dublin* [Chairman: Lord Talbot de Malahide]. [2063] H.C. (1856). XIX, 115, and *Dublin Hospitals Commission: report of the committee of inquiry, 1887* [Chairman: Sir Rowland Blennerhassett]. [C. 5042] H.C. (1887). XXXV, 1. Annual reports were also publ. as parl. papers.

10699 ABRAHAM (GEORGE WHITLEY). The law and practice of lunacy in Ireland . . . Dublin. 1886.

10700 REDINGTON COMMISSION ON LUNATIC ASYLUMS. Report of the commissioners of inquiry into the state of the lunatic asylums and other institutions for the custody and treatment of the insane in Ireland [Chairman: Sir Thomas Nicholas Redington]. Report. [2436] H.C. (1857–8). XXVII, 1. Evidence etc. [2436–II] H.C. (1857–8). XXVII, 159.

10701 POOR LAW AND LUNACY COMMISSION. Poor Law Union and Lunacy Inquiry Commission (Ireland) [Chairman: Major William Le Poer Trench]. Report and evidence. [C. 2239] H.C. (1878–9). XXXI, 1.

10702 MITCHELL COMMISSION ON LUNACY ADMINISTRATION. First and second reports of the committee appointed by the Lord Lieutenant of Ireland on lunacy administration (Ireland) [Chairman: Arthur Mitchell]. [C. 6434] H.C. (1890–1). XXXVI, 739.

10703 O'REILLY COMMITTEE ON SALE OF LIQUORS ON SUNDAY BILL. Report from the select committee on the Sale of Liquors on Sunday (Ireland) Bill [Chairman: Myles William O'Reilly]. H.C. 280 (1867–8). XIV, 547.

For later discussions see *Report from the select committee on the Sale of Intoxicating Liquors on Sunday (Ireland) Bill* [Chairman: Sir Michael Hicks Beach]. H.C. 198 (1877). XVI, 1; and *Report from the select committee on Sunday Closing Acts (Ireland)* [Chairman: Dodgson Hamilton Madden]. H.C. 255 (1888). XIX, 1.

## G. INTELLECTUAL AND CULTURAL HISTORY

### 1. EDUCATION

10704  AUCHMUTY (JAMES JOHNSTON). Irish education: a historical survey. Dublin & Lond. 1937.

A basic guide.

10705  ATKINSON (NORMAN). Irish education: a history of educational institutions. Dublin. 1969.

10706  ELLIS (WILLIAM EDWARD). [Ellis's] Irish educational directory and scholastic guide: containing full information as to the Irish universities and professional schools, and the institutions in Ireland for promoting intermediate and primary education, with complete alphabetical lists of Irish colleges and schools. Dublin. 1883–8.

See also *The Irish educational year book, who's who and diary*, Dublin etc. 1911+.

10707  AKENSON (DONALD HARMAN). The Irish education experiment: the national system of education in the nineteenth century. Lond. & Toronto. 1970.

10708  MURRAY (FRANCIS). 'Compulsory school attendance in Ireland'. *Irish Eccles. Rec.* lxiv (1944), 44–7, 191–7.

See also William Neilson Hancock, 'The feasibility of compulsory education in Ireland', *Stat. Soc. J.* xlii (1879), 456–72.

10709  MOORE (HENRY KINGSMILL). The work of the Incorporated Society for Promoting Protestant Schools in Ireland. Dundalk. 1938.

Moore also publ. *The centenary book of the Church of Ireland Training College, 1811–1911*, Dublin 1911.

10710  JAMIESON (JOHN). The history of the Royal Belfast Academical Institution. Belfast. 1959.

10711  COMMISSIONERS OF NATIONAL EDUCATION IN IRELAND. Annual report. Dublin. 1834–1919/20.

10712  COMMISSIONERS OF EDUCATION IN IRELAND. Annual report. Dublin. 1814–1920.

10713  LORDS COMMITTEE ON NATIONAL EDUCATION IN IRELAND. Report from the select committee of the House of Lords appointed to inquire into the practical working of the system of national education in Ireland [Chairman: Earl Granville]. H.C. 525 (1854). XV, pts. 1–2.

10714 SHERIDAN (JOHN E.). Report made to the Board of National Education on the subject of convent schools . . . H.C. 179 (1864). XLVI, 1.

See also the further docs. relating to convent schools in H.C. 391 (1864). XLVI, 49; H.C. 405 (1864). XLVI, 63; H.C. 430 (1864). XLVI, 299. There is a long series of returns in the parl. papers relating to convent and monastic education.

10715 MEMORIALS addressed to the Secretary of State for the House Department by Roman Catholic prelates in Ireland on the subject of university and national education in Ireland . . . H.C. 84 (1866). LV, 243.

10716 NATIONAL EDUCATION (IRELAND) CONSCIENCE CLAUSE. Correspondence in the year 1895 between the Irish government and the Commissioners of National Education for Ireland . . . H.C. 324 (1895). LXXVII, 527. Further correspondence. H.C. 89 (1896). LXVI, 1.

10717 POWIS COMMISSION ON PRIMARY EDUCATION (IRELAND). Royal commission of inquiry into primary education (Ireland) [Chairman: Earl of Powis]. Report. [C. 6] H.C. (1870). XXVIII, pt. 1. Appendix. [C. 6A] H.C. (1870). XXVIII, pt. 2, 1. Reports of assistant commissioners. [C. 6–I] H.C. (1870). XXVIII, pt. 2, 381. Minutes of evidence. [C. 6–II–VII] H.C. (1870). XXVIII, pts. 3–5.

The report incl. a quite detailed hist.

10718 BELMORE COMMISSION ON MANUAL AND PRACTICAL INSTRUCTION (IRELAND). Commission on manual and practical instruction in primary schools under the Board of National Education in Ireland [Chairman: Earl of Belmore]. First report. [C. 8383] H.C. (1897). XLIII, 1. Second report. [C. 8531] H.C. (1897). XLIII, 109. Minutes of evidence. [C. 8532] H.C. (1897). XLIII, 113. Third report. [C. 8618] H.C. (1897). XLIII, 401. Minutes of evidence. [C. 8619] H.C. (1897). XLIII, 405. Final report. [C. 8923] H.C. (1898). XLIV, 1. Minutes of evidence. [C. 8924] H.C. (1898). XLIV, 77. Appendixes. [C. 8925] H.C. (1898). XLIV, 531.

10719 DALE (FRANK HARRY). Report . . . on primary education in Ireland. [Cd. 1981] H.C. (1904). XX, 947.

10720 DILL COMMISSION ON PRIMARY EDUCATION (IRELAND). Vice-Regal committee of enquiry into primary education (Ireland), 1913 [Chairman: Sir Samuel Dill]. First report. [Cd. 6828] H.C. (1913). XXII, 231. Minutes of evidence. [Cd. 6829] H.C. (1913). XXII, 235. Second report. [Cd. 7228] H.C. (1914). XXVIII, 1. Minutes of evidence. [Cd. 7229] H.C. (1914). XXVIII, 5. Third report. [Cd. 7479] H.C. (1914). XXVIII, 583. Minutes of evidence. [Cd. 7480] H.C. (1914). XXVIII, 587. Final report. [Cd. 7235] H.C. (1914). XXVIII, 1081.

10721 INTERMEDIATE EDUCATION BOARD FOR IRELAND. Reports. Dublin. 1879–1920.

10722  PALLES COMMISSION ON INTERMEDIATE EDUCATION (IRELAND). Intermediate Education (Ireland) Commission: first report of the commissioners [Chairman: Lord Chief Baron Christopher Palles]. [C. 9116] H.C. (1899). XXII, 175. Appendix. [C. 9117] H.C. (1899). XXII, 183. Final report. [C. 9511] H.C. (1899). XXII, 629. Appendix [C. 9512–13] H.C. (1899). XXIII, 1, XXIV, 1.

10723  DALE (FRANK HARRY) *and* STEPHENS (T. A.). Report . . . on intermediate education in Ireland. [Cd. 2546] H.C. (1905). XXVIII, 709.

See also *Intermediate education (Ireland): copy of correspondence between the Irish government and the Commissioners of Intermediate Education for Ireland* . . . [Cd. 3213] H.C. (1906). XCI, 531.

10724  KILDARE COMMISSION ON ENDOWED SCHOOLS (IRE-LAND). Report of Her Majesty's commissioners appointed to inquire into the endowments, funds, and actual condition of all schools endowed for the purpose of education in Ireland [Chairman: Marquess of Kildare]. [2336] H.C. (1857–8). XXII, 1. Minority report [letter] by Archibald John Stephens. [2345] H.C. (1857–8). XLVI, 409. Evidence. [2336–II–IV] H.C. (1857–8). XXII, pts. 2–4.

10725  ROSSE COMMISSION ON ENDOWED SCHOOLS (IRELAND). Report of the commissioners appointed by His Excellency the Lord Lieutenant of Ireland to inquire into the endowments, funds, and actual condition of all schools endowed for the purpose of education in Ireland . . . [Chairman: Earl of Rosse.] [C. 2831] H.C. (1881). XXXV, 1. Evidence. [C. 2831–I] H.C. (1881). XXXV, 539.

10726  FITZGIBBON COMMISSION ON EDUCATIONAL ENDOW-MENTS (IRELAND). Educational Endowments (Ireland) Commission: final report of the commissioners [Chairman: Lord Justice Gerald FitzGibbon]. [C. 7517] H.C. (1894). XXX, pt. 1, 469.

10727  THE IRISH TEACHERS' JOURNAL. Dublin. 1867+.

Title became *The Irish school weekly*, 1904+.

10728  MOODY (THEODORE WILLIAM). 'The Irish university question in the nineteenth century'. *History* xliii (1958), 90–109.

See also Alfred O'Rahilly, 'The Irish university question', *Studies* l (1961), 225–70; 353–70; li (1962), 147–70, 209–36, and Patricia McCaffrey, 'The Wyndham university scheme, 1903–4', *Irish Eccles. Rec.* cx (1968), 329–49.

10729  WALSH (WILLIAM), *Archbishop of Dublin*. The Irish university question: the Catholic case: selections from the speeches and writings of the Archbishop of Dublin, with a historical sketch of the Irish university question. Dublin. 1897.

10730  ROBERTSON COMMISSION ON UNIVERSITY EDUCATION (IRELAND). Royal commission on university education in Ireland: first report of the commissioners [Chairman: Lord Robertson]. [Cd. 825] H.C. (1902). XXXI, 21. Minutes of evidence. [Cd. 826] H.C. (1902). XXXI, 29. Second report. [Cd. 899] H.C. (1902). XXXI, 459. Minutes of evidence. [Cd. 900] H.C. (1902). XXXI, 463. Third report. [Cd. 1228] H.C. (1902). XXXII, 1. Minutes of evidence. [Cd. 1229] H.C. (1902). XXXII, 5. Final report. [Cd. 1483] H.C. (1903). XXXII, 1. Appendix. [Cd. 1484] H.C. (1903). XXXII, 81.

10731 MAXWELL (CONSTANTIA ELIZABETH). A history of Trinity College, Dublin, 1591–1892. Dublin. 1946.

Cont. by Kenneth Claude Bailey, *A history of Trinity College, Dublin, 1892–1945*, Dublin 1947. See also Olive Purser, *Women in Dublin University, 1904–1954*, Dublin 1954. Biog. lists are given at **10247**. There is also a popular handbook, David Allardice Webb, ed., *Of one company: biographical studies of famous Trinity men, 1591–1951*, Dublin 1951. Hist. articles are publ. in *Hermathena*, 1873+.

10732 MAHAFFY. Mahaffy: a biography of an Anglo-Irishman. By William Bedell Stanford and Robert Brendan McDowell. 1970.

Trinity's most picturesque figure during the period.

10733 WHATELY COMMISSION ON THE UNIVERSITY OF DUBLIN. Dublin University Commission: report of Her Majesty's commissioners appointed to inquire into the state, discipline, studies and revenues of the University of Dublin and of Trinity College [Chairman: Richard Whately, Archbishop of Dublin]. [1637] H.C. (1852–3). XLV, 1.

10734 BELMORE COMMISSION ON TRINITY COLLEGE, DUBLIN. Dublin University Commission: report of Her Majesty's commissioners, appointed to inquire into certain matters relating to the College of the Holy and Undivided Trinity of Queen Elizabeth, near Dublin [Chairman: Earl of Belmore]. [C. 2045] H.C. (1878). XXIX, 59.

10735 FRY COMMISSION ON TRINITY COLLEGE, DUBLIN. Royal commission on Trinity College, Dublin, and the University of Dublin: first report of the commissioners [Chairman: Sir Edward Fry]. [Cd. 3174] H.C. (1906). LVI, 601. Appendix. [Cd. 3176] H.C. (1906). LVI, 607. Final report. [Cd. 3311] H.C. (1907). XLI, 1. Appendix. [Cd. 3312] H.C. (1907). XLI, 87.

See also the persuasive attack on Trinity by a Maynooth professor in Daniel Coghlan, *Trinity College and the Trinity commission*, Dublin 1908. For college estates see *Trinity College, Dublin, estates commission: report of the commissioners* [Chairman: Gerald FitzGibbon]. [Cd. 2526] H.C. (1905). XXVII, 81. Appendix. [Cd. 2527] H.C. (1905). XXVII, 157.

10736 A PAGE OF IRISH HISTORY: story of University College, Dublin, 1839–1959. Comp. by Fathers of the Society of Jesus. Dublin. 1960.

See also James Meenan, ed., *Centenary history of the Literary and Historical Society of University College, Dublin, 1855–1955*, Tralee [1956], and *University review: the official organ of the Graduates Association of the National University of Ireland*, 1+, Dublin 1954+, restyled *Irish University Review*, 1970+.

10737   McGRATH (FERGAL). Newman's university: idea and reality. N.Y. & Lond. 1951.

See also William J. Williams, 'Newman's Irish adventure', *Irish Theological Q.* xviii (1951), 270–302; Michael Tierney, ed., *Struggle with fortune: a miscellany for the centenary of the Catholic University of Ireland, 1854–1954*, Dublin 1954; Mary Vale, 'Origins of the Catholic University of Ireland, 1845–1854', *Irish Eccles. Rec.* lxxxii (1954–5), 1–16, 152–62, 226–41; and Donal Kerr, 'Dr. Quinn's school and the Catholic University, 1850–1867', *Irish Eccles. Rec.* cviii (1967), 89–101.

10738   MOODY (THEODORE WILLIAM) *and* BECKETT (JAMES CAMLIN). Queen's Belfast, 1845–1949: the history of a university. 2 v. 1959.

One of the best university hists.

10739   HOLMES (R. F. G.). Magee, 1865–1965: the evolution of the Magee colleges. Belfast. 1965.

10740   KILDARE COMMISSION ON SCIENCE AND ART DEPARTMENT IN IRELAND. Report from the commission on the Science and Art Department in Ireland [Chairman: Marquess of Kildare]. [4103-I] H.C. (1868–9). XXIV, 1. Minutes of evidence. [4103-I] H.C. (1868–9). XXIV, 43.

10741   WINDSOR COMMITTEE ON ROYAL HIBERNIAN ACADEMY, &c. Report by committee of inquiry into the work carried on by the Royal Hibernian Academy and Metropolitan School of Art, Dublin [Chairman: Lord Windsor]. [Cd. 3256] H.C. (1906). XXXI, 799.

10742   KILDARE COMMISSION ON THE QUEEN'S COLLEGES. The Queen's colleges commission: report of Her Majesty's commissioners appointed to inquire into the progress and condition of the Queen's colleges at Belfast, Cork and Galway [Chairman: Marquess of Kildare]. [2413] H.C. (1857–8). XXI, 101.

The various colleges also submitted annual reports to parliament, as did the chancellor or vice-chancellor of the Queen's University.

10743   CARTON COMMISSION ON THE QUEEN'S COLLEGES. Reports of the commissioners appointed by His Excellency John Poyntz, Earl Spencer, K.G., Lord Lieutenant of Ireland, to inquire into certain matters affecting the well-being and efficiency of the Queen's colleges in Ireland [Chairman: Richard P. Carton]. [C. 4313] H.C. (1884–5). XXV, 1.

10744   NEYLON (MAURA) *and* HENCHY (MONICA). Public libraries in Ireland. Univ. College, Dublin. 1966.

10745   KELHAM (BRIAN B.). 'The Royal College of Science for Ireland, 1867–1926'. *Studies* lvi (1967), 297–309.

10746   GREGORY COMMITTEE ON SCIENTIFIC INSTITUTIONS. Report from the select committee on scientific institutions (Dublin) [Chairman: W. H. Gregory]. H.C. 495 (1864). XIII, 1.

See also *Scientific institutions (Dublin): copy of any correspondence . . . on the proposed amalgamation of the Museum of Irish Industry and the Royal Dublin Society.* H.C. 401 (1863). XLVI, 603, and **10789**.

## 2. Literature and the Theatre

10747 HAYES (RICHARD JAMES) *and* Ó DONNCHADHA (BRIGHID) *i.e.* hAe (Risteárd de) *and* Ḋonnċaḋa (Briġianí) *comps.* Clār Litrideachta na nua-ghaedhilge, 1850–1936. 3 v. Dublin. 1938–40.

10748 BEST (RICHARD IRVINE). Bibliography of Irish philology and of printed Irish literature. Dublin. 1913. Suppl. for 1913–41. Dublin. 1942.

10749 BROWN (STEPHEN JAMES MEREDITH). Ireland in fiction: a guide to Irish novels, tales, romances and folk-lore. Dublin & Lond. 1916. New edn. 1919.

A useful bibliog. Brown also ed. *A guide to books on Ireland:* Part I: *Prose literature, poetry, music and plays*, Dublin & Lond. 1912.

10750 HYDE (DOUGLAS). A literary history of Ireland: from earliest times to the present day. Dublin. 1899. 4th edn. 1967.

There is also Frank O'Connor, pseud. of Michael Francis O'Donovan, *The backward look: a survey of Irish literature*, 1967, Stephen Lucius Gwynn, *Irish literature and drama in the English language: a short history*, 1936, and Robert Farren, *The course of Irish verse in England* [*English*], N.Y. 1947, Lond. 1948.

10751 HOWARTH (HERBERT). The Irish writers, 1880–1940: literature under Parnell's star. 1958.

10752 BOYD (ERNEST AUGUSTUS). Ireland's literary renaissance. Dublin etc. 1916. N.Y. 1922. Repr. Dublin. 1968.

10753 MORRIS (LLOYD R.). The Celtic dawn: a survey of the renascence in Ireland, 1889–1916. N.Y. 1917.

See also William Patrick Ryan, *The Irish literary revival: its history, pioneers and possibilities*, 1894.

10754 KAIN (RICHARD MORGAN). Dublin in the age of William Butler Yeats and James Joyce. Norman, Okla. 1962.

10755 QUINN. The man from New York: John Quinn and his friends. By Benjamin Laurence Reid. N.Y. 1968.

10756 MALONE (ANDREW E.). The Irish drama. 1929.

See also Peter Kavanagh, *The Irish theatre: being, a history of the drama in Ireland, from the earliest period up to the present day*, Tralee 1946.

10757 DUGGAN (GEORGE CHESTER). The stage Irishman: a history of the Irish play and stage characters from the earliest times. Dublin. 1937.

10758 ELLIS-FERMOR (UNA MARY). The Irish dramatic movement. 1939. 2nd edn. 1954.

10759   ROBINSON ([ESMÉ STUART] LENNOX). Ireland's Abbey Theatre: a history, 1899–1951. 1951.

See also William George Fay and Catherine Carswell, *The Fays of the Abbey Theatre: an autobiographical record*, 1935; Gerard Francis Arthur Fay, *The Abbey Theatre: cradle of genius*, 1958; Peter Kavanagh, *The story of the Abbey Theatre: from its origins in 1899 to the present*, N.Y. 1950; Sean McCann, ed., *The story of the Abbey Theatre*, 1967; James Flannery, *Miss Annie F. Horniman and the Abbey Theatre*, Dublin 1970; Máire Nic Shiubhaigh, *The splendid years: recollections as told to Edward Kenny, with appendices and lists of Irish Theatre plays, 1899–1916*, Dublin 1955; [Esmé Stuart] Lennox Robinson, ed., *The Irish theatre: lectures delivered during the Abbey Theatre festival held in Dublin in August 1938*, 1939; and Robert Goode Hogan and Michael J. O'Neill, eds., *Joseph Holloway's Abbey Theatre . . .*, Carbondale, Ill. 1967.

10760   RYAN (DESMOND). The sword of light: from the four masters to Douglas Hyde, 1636–1938. 1939.

A popular account of the revival of the Irish language. For a famous example of hostility to Irish, see Matthew Arnold, *On the study of Celtic literature*, 1867, for commentary on which see John Vincent Kelleher, 'Matthew Arnold and the Celtic revival', in Harry Levin, ed., *Perspectives in criticism*, Camb., Mass. 1950, pp. 197–221, and Frederic Everett Faverty, *Matthew Arnold the ethnologist*, Evanston, Ill. 1951.

10761   A. E. [RUSSELL]. Printed writings of George W. Russell (AE): a bibliography, with some notes on his pictures and portraits. . . . Comp. by Alan Denson. Evanston, Ill. 1961.

Alan Denson, ed., *Letters from AE*, 1961, is a handy selection. For his life see Darrell Figgis, *AE (George W. Russell): a study of a man and a nation*, Dublin & Lond. 1916, and John Eglinton, pseud. of William Kirkpatrick Magee, *A memoir of AE, George William Russell*, 1937.

10762   DE VERE. Aubrey de Vere: a memoir based on his unpublished diaries and correspondence. By Wilfrid Philip Ward. 1904.

See also Sister Paraclita Reilly, *Aubrey de Vere: Victorian observer*, Lincoln, Nebr. 1953, Dublin 1956.

10763   DUNSANY. Dunsany the dramatist. By Edward Hale Bierstadt. Boston. 1917. Rev. edn. 1920.

See also Hazel Smith, *Lord Dunsany, king of dreams: a personal portrait*, N.Y. 1959, and Mark Amory, *Biography of Lord Dunsany*, 1972.

10764   FERGUSON. Sir Samuel Ferguson in the Ireland of his day. By Lady [Mary Catharine] Ferguson. 2 v. Edin. & Lond. 1896.

10765   GILBERT. Life of Sir John T. Gilbert, LL.D., F.S.A., Irish historian and archivist, vice-president of the Royal Irish Academy, secretary of the Public Record Office of Ireland. By his wife, Rosa Mulholland, Lady Gilbert. 1905.

10766   GRAVES. To return to all that: an autobiography. By Alfred Perceval Graves. 1930.

10767   GREEN. Alice Stopford Green: a passionate historian. By Robert Brendan McDowell. Dublin. 1967.

10768 GREGORY. Lady Gregory: a literary portrait. By [Eileen] Elizabeth Coxhead. 1961. 2nd edn. 1966.

Lady Gregory (Isabella Augusta Gregory) herself publ. *Our Irish theatre: a chapter of autobiography*, Lond. & N.Y. 1914, repr. N.Y. 1965. See also [Esmé Stuart] Lennox Robinson, ed., *Lady Gregory's journals, 1916–1930*, Lond. & N.Y. 1946, and Ann Saddlemeyer, *In defence of Lady Gregory, playwright*, Dublin 1966.

10769 HYDE. A bibliography of Dr. Douglas Hyde. By Patrick Sarsfield O'Hegarty. Dublin. 1939.

There is no adequate biog. Diarmid Coffey, *Douglas Hyde, President of Ireland*, Dublin & Cork 1938, is only a sketch.

10770 MACDONAGH. Thomas MacDonagh: the man, the patriot, the writer. By Edd Winfield Parks and Aileen Wells Parks. Athens, Ga. 1967.

10771 MARTYN. Edward Martyn and the Irish revival. By Denis Rolleston Gwynn. 1930.

See also Sister Marie Thérèse Courtney, *Edward Martyn and the Irish theatre*, N.Y. 1956.

10772 O'GRADY. Standish James O'Grady, the man & the writer: a memoir by his son, Hugh Art O'Grady . . . Dublin. 1929.

10773 O'SHAUGHNESSY. Arthur O'Shaughnessy: his life and his work . . . By Louise Moulton. Camb. & Chicago. 1894.

10774 ROBINSON. Lennox Robinson. By Michael J. O'Neill. N.Y. 1964.

10775 ROLLESTON. Portrait of an Irishman: a biographical sketch of T. W. Rolleston. By Charles Henry Rolleston. 1939.

10776 SHAW. Shaw of Dublin: the formative years. By B. C. Rosset. Univ. Park, Penn. 1964.

For Shaw see also **8412.**

10777 SOMERVILLE AND ROSS. A bibliography of the first editions of the works of E. Œ. Somerville and Martin Ross. Comp. by Elizabeth Hudson. N.Y. 1942.

See also Maurice Collis, *Somerville and Ross: a biography*, 1968, and Geraldine Dorothy Cummins, *Dr. E. Œ. Somerville: a biography* . . . *with a new bibliography of first editions compiled by Robert Vaughan*, 1952.

SYNGE. See **8418.**

10778 TYNAN. Twenty-five years: reminiscences. By Katharine Tynan [Hinkson]. Lond. & N.Y. 1913.

10779 WILDE. Speranza: a biography of Lady Wilde. By Horace Wyndham. 1951.

See also **10798.**

YEATS. See **8428.**

### 3. OTHER ARTS AND SCIENCES

10780  STRICKLAND (WALTER G.). A dictionary of Irish artists. 2 v. Dublin & Lond. 1913.

10781  ARNOLD (BRUCE). A concise history of Irish art. N.Y. 1968.
Weak on the period.

10782  ELLIOTT (ROBERT). Art and Ireland. Dublin. 1906.
See also Sam Hanna Bell, ed., *The arts in Ulster: a symposium*, 1951.

10783  BODKIN (THOMAS). Four Irish landscape painters, George Barret, R.A., James A. O'Connor, Walter F. Osborne, R.H.A., Nathaniel Hone, R.H.A. Dublin & Lond. 1920.

10784  BODKIN (THOMAS). Hugh Lane and his pictures. Dublin. [1932.] 2nd edn. 1956.

10785  FLOOD (WILLIAM HENRY GRATTAN). A history of Irish music. Dublin. 1905. 3rd edn. 1913.
Not always reliable. See also Aloys Georg Fleischmann, ed., *Music in Ireland: a symposium*, Cork & Oxf. 1952.

10786  HENEBRY (RICHARD). A handbook of Irish music. Dublin, Lond., & N.Y. 1928.

10787  BALFE. A memoir of Michael William Balfe. By Charles Lamb Kenney. 1875.
See also William Alexander Barrett, *Balfe: his life and work*, 1882.

10788  STEWART. Memoir of Sir Robert P. Stewart, Kt., Mus.Doc., Professor of Music in the University of Dublin (1862–94). By Olinthus John Vignoles. 1898. 2nd edn. 1899.

10789  BERRY (HENRY FITZPATRICK). A history of the Royal Dublin Society. 1915.
The leading scientific instn. in Ireland, on which there is also a more popular hist., Terence De Vere White, *The story of the Royal Dublin Society*, Tralee 1955. It publ. a *Journal*, 1856+, which became *Scientific proceedings . . .*, 1878+, in addition to *Proceedings*, 1764–1893, *Scientific transactions*, 1877–1909, and *Economic proceedings*, 1899–1920, 1926+. For natural hist. see *The Irish naturalist . . .*, Dublin 1892–1924+. See also *Report upon the Royal Dublin Society, the Museum of Irish Industry, and the system of scientific instruction in Ireland, October, 1862* [Chairman: Francis Blackburne]. [3180] H.C. (1863). XVII, pt. 1, 1, and **10746**.

10790  HAMILTON. Life of Sir William Rowan Hamilton. By Robert Perceval Graves. 3 v. Dublin & Lond. 1882–9.
Hamilton was a distinguished mathematician.

10791 KANE. Sir Robert Kane, first president of Queen's College, Cork: a pioneer in science, industry & commerce. By Deasmumhan O'Raghallaigh. Cork. 1942.

See also Thomas Sherlock Wheeler, 'Sir Robert Kane: his life and work', in Roy. Dublin Soc., *The natural resources of Ireland* ..., Dublin [1944], 1–42, 'Sir Robert Kane: life and work', *Studies* xxxiii (1944), 158–68, 316–30, and Robert C. Simington and Thomas Sherlock Wheeler, 'Sir Robert Kane's soil survey of Ireland: the record of a failure', *Studies* xxxiv (1945), 539–51.

10792 FLEETWOOD (JOHN FINLAYSON). History of medicine in Ireland. Dublin. 1949.

See also Sir Charles Alexander Cameron, *History of the Royal College of Surgeons in Ireland and of the Irish schools of medicine: including numerous biographical sketches: also a medical bibliography*, Dublin 1886, new edn. 1916; John David Henry Widdess, *A history of the Royal College of Physicians of Ireland, 1654–1963*, Edin. 1963, and *A Dublin school of medicine and surgery: an account of the schools of surgery, Royal College of Surgeons, Dublin, 1789–1948*, Edin. 1949, 2nd edn. [*The Royal College of Surgeons in Ireland* ...] 1967; Thomas Percy Claude Kirkpatrick, *History of the medical teaching in Trinity College, Dublin, and of the School of Physic in Ireland*, Dublin 1912; Ronan O'Rahilly, *A history of the Cork medical school, 1849–1949*, Cork & Oxf. 1949; Nicholas Marshall Cummins, *Some chapters in Cork medical history*, Cork 1957; James Charles McWalter, *History of the Worshipful Company of Apothecaries in the City of Dublin*, Dublin 1916; and William Doolin and Oliver FitzGerald, eds., *What's past is prologue: a retrospect of Irish medicine* ..., Dublin 1952.

10793 THE DUBLIN MEDICAL PRESS. 1839+.

Became *The medical press and circular* ..., 1866+. The journal of the Irish Medical Association was issued as a suppl., 1867–70. *The Dublin j. of medical and chemical science*, (title varies), Dublin 1832+ also covers the period. The *Medical press and circular* publ. *The Irish medical student's guide* ..., Dublin 1872. There was also an *Irish medical directory*, Dublin, c. 1873–97.

10794 BROWNE (O'DONEL THORNLEY DODWELL). The Rotunda hospital, 1745–1945. Edin. 1947.

See also Thomas Percy Claude Kirkpatrick, *The book of the Rotunda hospital* ..., ed. by Henry Jellett, 1913, Samuel Frederick Adair, *Rotunda lying-in hospital* ..., Dublin 1892 and **10698**.

10795 CORRIGAN. 'Sir Dominic Corrigan'. By Eileen Dixon. *Dublin Hist. Rec.* viii (1945–6), 28–38, 67–75.

10796 CAMERON. Autobiography. By Sir Charles Alexander Cameron. Dublin. 1920.

The chatty memoirs of a popular doctor. He also publ. *Reminiscences*, Dublin & Lond. 1913.

10797 STOKES. William Stokes: his life and work, 1804–1878. By Sir William Stokes. 1898.

10798 WILDE, Victorian doctor: being the life of Sir William Wilde. By Thomas George Wilson. 1942.

See also Terence De Vere White, *The parents of Oscar Wilde: Sir William and Lady*

*Wilde*, 1967, Patrick Byrne, *The Wildes of Merrion Square: the family of Oscar Wilde*, 1953, and Eric Lambert, *Mad with much heart: a life of the parents of Oscar Wilde*, 1967. For Lady Wilde see **10779**.

10799  WINDLE. Sir Bertram Windle: Bertram Coghill Alan Windle, F.R.S., F.S.A., K.S.G., M.D., M.A., LL.D., Ph.D., Sc.D.: a memoir. By Monica Taylor. 1932.

# H. LOCAL HISTORY

10800  LINENHALL LIBRARY, BELFAST. Catalogue of the books in the Irish section. Belfast. 1917.

Catalogued under places as well as authors. Much the fullest work on Irish local hist. See also Thomas Patrick O'Neill, *Sources of Irish local history*, Libr. Assoc. of Ireland, Dublin 1958, and Belfast Public Librs., *Finding list of books added to the stock of the Irish and local history collection before 1956*, Belfast 1965.

10801  MEGHEN (P. J.). 'Central–local relationships in Ireland'. *Administration* xiii (1965), 107–22.

10802  WEBB (JOHN JOSEPH). Municipal government in Ireland, medieval & modern. Dublin. 1918.

Feeble. For the law see Sir George Thomas Barrett Vanston, *The law relating to municipal towns under the Towns Improvement (Ireland) Act, 1854*, Dublin 1900, and *The law relating to local government in Ireland: being the Local Government (Ireland) Act, 1898, and other statutes affecting county and district councils . . .*, 2 v. Dublin 1899–1905.

10803  HICKS BEACH COMMITTEE ON LOCAL GOVERNMENT AND TAXATION OF TOWNS. Report from the select committee on local government and taxation of towns (Ireland) [Chairman: Sir Michael Hicks Beach]. H.C. 352 (1876). X, 147. Further reports. H.C. 357 (1877). XII, 309. H.C. 268 (1878). XVI, 1. Reports of commissioners to examine localities. [C. 1696]. H.C. (1877). XXXIX, 1. [C. 1755]. H.C. (1877). XL, 1. [C. 1787– C. 1787–I]. H.C. (1877). XL, 225, 625. Special report by William P. O'Brien. [C. 1965] H.C. (1878). XXIII, 707.

Comprehensive. O'Brien's report gives a good account of the structure of Irish local government. For Irish local taxation see also the report of the United Kingdom Commission, **4569**.

10804  HAMILTON COMMITTEE ON COUNTY AND DISTRICT SURVEYORS. Report from the select committee on county and district surveyors, &c. (Ireland) [Chairman: George Alexander Hamilton]. H.C. 270 (1857–Sess. 2). IX, 55.

An interesting study of professionalization.

10805  FRENCH COMMITTEE ON GENERAL VALUATION (IRE-LAND). Report from the select committee on general valuation, &c. (Ireland) [Chairman: Colonel French.] H.C. 362 (1868–9). IX, 1.

For rating and valuation see also *Report from the select committee on law of rating (Ireland)*

[Chairman: Marquess of Hartington]. H.C. 423 (1871). X, 1. Further report. H.C. 187 (1872). XI, 361; *Report . . . of commissioners of inquiry into the collection of rates in the city of Dublin* [Chairman: Hugh Holmes]. [C. 2062] H.C. (1878). XXIII, 455; and *Report from the select committee on Irish Valuation Acts* [Chairman: Andrew Graham Murray]. H.C. 370 (1902). VI, 57. Further reports. H.C. 337 (1903). VI, 19; H.C. 130 (1904). VI, 271.

10806 MUNICIPAL BOUNDARIES COMMISSION (IRELAND) [Chairman: W. A. Exham, Q.C.]. I: Evidence on Dublin, Rathmines, Pembroke, Kilmainham, Drumcondra, Clontarf, Kingston, Blackrock, and Dalkey. [C. 2725] H.C. (1880). XXX, 327. II: Report on I. [C. 2827] H.C. (1881). L, 1. III: Report and evidence on other towns. [C. 3089] H.C. (1881). L, 65. Suppl. of maps. [C. 3089–I] H.C. (1881). L, 669. IV: Report and evidence on Cork and Belfast. [C. 3089–II] H.C. (1881). L, 877.

10807 HERON (R. FINLAY). The law and practice of municipal elections in Ireland . . . Dublin. 1891.

For the new county system see John Muldoon and George M'Sweeny, *A guide to the election of county and rural district councillors in Ireland . . .*, Dublin 1902.

10808 BELFAST BOROUGH COMMISSION. Report of the commissioners appointed to inquire into the state of the municipal affairs of the borough of Belfast [Commissioners: James Major and Christopher Copinger]. [2470] H.C. (1859–Sess. 1). XII, 305. Minutes of evidence. [2526] H.C. (1859–Sess. 2). X, 57.

Suppl. by *Minutes of evidence taken before the select committee on the Belfast Improvement (no. 2) Bill* [Chairman: James Milnes Gaskell]. H.C. 348. (1864). VI, 1. Belfast was constantly in trouble: see also **10464–5**, **10471**, and *Report from the select committee on the Belfast Corporation Bill and Londonderry Improvement Bill* [Chairman: Sir William Houldsworth]. H.C. 233 (1896). VIII, 283.

10809 LIBRARY ASSOCIATION: NORTHERN IRELAND BRANCH. Directory of Northern Ireland libraries. 1967.

10810 MOODY (THEODORE WILLIAM) *and* BECKETT (JAMES CAMLIN) *eds.* Ulster since 1800. 1 ser. A political and economic survey. 1954. 2 ser. A social survey. 1957.

For Ulster see also Thomas Macknight, *Ulster as it is: or, twenty-eight years' experience as an Irish editor*, 2 v. 1896, *Ulster j. of archaeology*, Belfast 1853–62, 1894–1911, 1938+, *Ulster folklife*, 1+, Belfast 1955+, Cuman Seanchais Chlochair, *Clogher record*, 1953+, Robert Magill Young, comp., *Belfast and the province of Ulster in the 20th century*, Pike's new century ser., Brighton 1909, James Barkley Woodburn, *The Ulster Scot: his history and religion*, 1914, and Hugh Smith Morrison, *Modern Ulster: its character, customs, politics and industries* [1920].

10811 BELFAST. James Camlin Beckett and Robin Edgar Glasscock, eds., *Belfast: the origin and growth of an industrial city*, 1967. Sir David John Owen, *History of Belfast*, Belfast 1921. Emrys Jones, *A social geography of Belfast*, 1960. Andrew Boyd, *Holy war in Belfast*, Tralee 1969. Robert William Magill Strain, *Belfast and its Charitable Society: a story of urban social development*, 1961. Charles Edward Bainbridge Brett, *Buildings of Belfast, 1700–1914*, 1967.

10812   CARLOW. Old Carlow Soc., *Carloviana . . .*, 1947+.

10813   CAVAN and LEITRIM. *Breifne: journal of Cumann Seanchais Bhreifne,* Monaghan 1958+.

10814   CORK. Cork Historical and Archaeological Soc., *Journal,* 1892+.

10815   DONEGAL. County Donegal Historical Soc., *Journal* [later *Donegal annual*], 1947+.

10816   DUBLIN. *Dublin historical record,* Dublin 1938–9+. Maurice James Craig, *Dublin, 1660–1860,* Dublin & Lond. 1952. John Hooper Harvey, *Dublin: a study in environment,* 1949. Richard Morgan Kain, *Dublin in the age of William Butler Yeats and James Joyce,* Norman, Okla. 1962. Page Lawrence Dickinson, *The Dublin of yesterday* [1904–14], 1929. Elizabeth Bowen, *The Shelbourne* [*hotel*]: *a centre in Dublin life for more than a century,* 1951.

10817   FERMANAGH. Peadar Livingstone, The Fermanagh story: a documented history of the County Fermanagh, from the earliest times to the present day. Enniskillen. 1969.

10818   GALWAY. Mary Kavanagh, *A bibliography of the county Galway,* Galway County Librs., Galway 1965. Galway Archaeol. and Hist. Soc., *Journal,* Galway 1900+, and *Galvia . . .,* Galway 1954+. Patrick Kevin Egan, *The parish of Ballinasloe: its history from the earliest times to the present day,* Dublin 1960.

10819   KERRY. Kerry Archaeol. and Hist. Soc., *Journal,* 1968+.

10820   KILDARE. Kildare County Archaeol. Soc., *Journal,* Dublin 1895+.

10821   KILKENNY. Kilkenny Archaeol. Soc., *Old Kilkenny review,* Kilkenny 1948+.

10822   LIMERICK. Roisin De Nais, *A bibliography of Limerick history and antiquities,* Limerick County Libr., Limerick [1963].

10823   LOUTH. County Louth Archaeol. Soc., *Journal,* Dundalk 1904+.

10824   MEATH. Meath Archaeol. and Hist. Soc., *Ríocht na midhe: records . . .,* Drogheda 1955+.

10825   NORTH MUNSTER. Thomond Archaeol. Soc., *North Munster antiquarian j.,* Limerick 1936+.

10826   QUEEN'S COUNTY [LAOIGHIS]. John O'Hanlon, Edward O'Leary, and Matthew Lalor, *History of the Queen's County . . .,* 2 v. Dublin 1907–14.

10827   SLIGO. John C. McTernan, *Historic Sligo: a bibliographical introduction to the antiquities and history, maps and surveys, MSS. and newspapers, historical families and notable individuals of county Sligo*, Sligo 1965. William Gregory Wood-Martin, *History of Sligo, county and town . . .* Vol. 3. *From 1688 to the present time*, Dublin 1892.

10828   WESTMEATH. Old Athlone Soc., *Journal*, Athlone 1969+.

10829   WEXFORD. Old Wexford Soc., *Journal*, Wexford 1968+.

# INDEX

Aarsleff, Hans: study of language, 8319

Abbas Mahmud al-Aqqad: Sa'd Zaghlul, 1681

Abbas, Mekki: Sudan question, 1702

Abbey, John Roland: aquatint and lithography, 9088

Abbey National Soc., 7122

Abbey Theatre, 10759

Abbott, Albert: educ. for industry and commerce, 8153

Abbott, Anthony Stenersen: Shaw and Christianity, 8412

Abbott, Charles, Baron Tenterden: merchant ships, 3287

Abbott, Claude Colleer: ed. G. M. Hopkins, 8336, 8376

Abbott, Evelyn: Benjamin Jowett, 8086

Abbott, Maude Elizabeth Seymour: ed. bibliog. of Osler, 8902

Abbott, Robert Lamb: non-collegiate students, 8072

Abbott, Wilbur Cortez: docs. on Gibraltar, 2361

Abd Al-Rahman Al-Rafii: Al-thawrah al-Arabiyah, 1645; 'Asr Isma'ili, 1645; Misr wa'l-Sudan, 1645; Muhammad Farid, 1678; Mustafa Kamil, 1679

Abdel Maksud Hamza: public debt of Egypt, 1660

Abdel Rahman El Nasri: bibliog. of Sudan, 1684

Abduh, Muhammad: life, 1677

Abdul Amir Muhammed Amin: British in Persian Gulf, 2466

à Beckett, Arthur William: ed. 3012; green room recollections, 5401; recollections, 5401; the à Becketts of *Punch*, 5401

à Beckett, Gilbert Abbott: comic Blackstone, 3012

Abel, Annie Heloise: ed. Anglo-American relations, 2587

Abel, Reuben: humanism of F. C. S. Schiller, 8466

Abel-Smith, Brian: hospitals, 7477; lawyers, 3070; nursing, 7462

Abell, Sir Westcott Stile: shipwright's trade, 6121; the safe sea, 6164; William Froude, 6146

Abels, Jules: Parnell tragedy, 10383

Aberconway, Baron: see Maclaren, Charles Benjamin Bright

Abercrombie, David: Isaac Pitman, 5499

Abercrombie, Lascelles: Hardy, 8373

Aberdare, Baron: see Bruce, Henry Austin, and Bruce, Morys George Lyndhurst

Aberdare Valley coal strike, 9696

Aberdeen: advocates, 9834; churches, 9854; hist., 10174; port, 10034; trade unions, 10094, 10100; univ., 10129, 10133, 10161; *univ. rev.*, 10133

Aberdeen, 4th Earl of: admin. of, 290; corresp., 725; life, 725

Aberdeen, 1st Marquess of: commission on loss of life at sea, 6050; more cracks, 814; we twa, 814

Aberdeen, Ishbel Maria Gordon, Marchioness of: Canadian journal, 1471; ed., 7004; Edward Marjoribanks, 811; life, 814; more cracks, 814; musings, 814; we twa, 814

Aberdeen-Angus cattle, 4351

Aberdeenshire: agric., 9965, 10103; beef & cattle, 4346, 4351, 5894, 9973; bibliog. 10174; educ., 10111, 10114; forestry, 9970

Aberdovey, 9679

Aberfeldy, 10219

Abergele, 9764

Abernethy, James: life, 5167

Abernethy, John Scott: James Abernethy, 5167

Abertay Hist. Soc.: *publs.* 10178

Aberystwyth: schools, 9745; univ. coll., 9755

Abetti, Betty Burr: trans., 8731

Abetti, Giorgio: astronomy, 8731

Abingdon: hist., 9522

Abinger, Edward: forty years, 3169

Abraham, George Dixon: complete mountaineer, 7785

Abraham, George Whitley: lunacy, 10699

Abraham, Gerald Ernest Heal: ed. hundred years of music, 9245

Abraham, May Edith: see Tennant, May Edith

Abrahams, Harold Maurice: ed. Oxf. v. Camb., 8055

Abramovitz, Moses: public employment, 362

Abrams, Philip: Brit. sociology, 8536

Abramsky, Chimen: Karl Marx, 569; lit. of 1st Internat., 569

T t

Caird, John: life, 9875; univ. addresses, 9875; univ. sermons, 9875

Cairncross, Sir Alexander Kirkland: ed. the Scottish economy, 9956; Glasgow building industry, 10008; home and foreign investment, 4675; internal migration, 6937

Cairnes, John Elliot: essays on political economy, 8498; method of political economy, 8498; principles of political economy, 8498; studs. of his work, 2590, 8488, 8498

Cairns, Alison H.: ed. David Cairns, 9917

Cairns, David Smith: Alexander Robertson MacEwen, 9922; autobiog., 9917

Cairns, H. Alan C.: prelude to imperialism (clash of cultures), 1896

Cairns, Hugh McCalmont Cairns, Earl: committees on: Irish Land Law, 10566; protection of young girls, 7518
life, 3102
judicature commission, 3193

Cairns, John: life, 9918

Caithness: agric., 9965; bibliog., 10216

Cajori, Florian: works on hist. of mathematics, 8762

Calabar mission, 1878

Calcraft, Henry George: immigration of foreigners, 6949

Calcutta: bishops of, 1039; Hist. Soc., 1009; municipality, 1116; rev., 995; univ., 1045

Caldecott, Alfred: church in the West Indies, 1576

Caldecott, Randolph: life, 9115; works, 9115

Calder-Marshall, Arthur: Havelock Ellis, 8361; the enthusiast, 3574

Calderwood, Henry: life, 8450, 9919

Calderwood, William Leadbetter: Henry Calderwood, 8450, 9919

Caldwell, Elsie: last witness for Stevenson, 8415

Caldwell, J. A. M.: Ministry of Labour, 6468

Caldwell, Theodore C.: ed. Anglo-Boer war, 2061

Caledonian railway, 10037

calico printing, 4954-7

Calkin, Homer L.: U.S. govt. and the Irish, 10264

Calkins, W. N.: a free-trade lobby, 5963

Callahan, James Morton: American foreign policy in Canadian relations, 1491; neutrality of the American lakes, 1491

Callander & Oban railway, 10037

Callaway, Godfrey: life, 2011; pioneers in Pondoland, 2010; shepherd of the Veld, 2014

Callaway, Henry, bishop: life, 2012

Callbeck, Lorne Clayton: cradle of confederation, 1536

Callender, Sir Geoffrey Arthur Romaine: naval side of British hist., 2850

Callow, William: autobiog., 9044

Callwell, Sir Charles Edward: effect of maritime command, 2677; hist. of Royal Artillery, 2749; Sir Stanley Maude, 2818; military operations, 2677; service yarns, 2800; small wars, 2777; stray recollections, 2800; tactics, 2777; Tirah, 2501; Sir Henry Wilson, 2833; ed. Sir Hugh McCalmont, 2816

Calpin, George Harold: Indians in South Africa, 2032

Calthorpe, Somerset John Gough: letters, 2444

Calthrop, Dion Clayton: Eng. costume, 7179; Eng. dress, 7181

Calverley, Charles Stuart: life, 8343

Calvert, Albert Frederick: grand lodge of England, 7367; Nigeria, 1881; salt, 5278; salt in Cheshire, 5279; Salt Union, 5280

Calvert, Frederick Grace: coal-tar colours, 4956; dyeing and calico printing, 4956

Calvert, Peter: Mexican revolution, 2652

Calvin, Delano Dexter: Queen's Univ., 1525

Calvinistic Methodism of Wales, 9625

Cam, Gilbert Arthur: investment companies, 4665

Cam, Helen Maud: ed. F. W. Maitland, 3089; Stubbs, 8534

Camberwell, 9469

Cambon, Henri: ed., 2288

Cambon, Pierre Paul: life and correspondence, 2288

Cambray, Philip George: Constitutional club, 553; dictionary of political phrases, 257; game of politics, 511

Cambrian Archaeol. Assoc.: *archaeologia cambrensis*, 9586

Cambrian railway, 9685

Cambridge: bibliog. of English lit., 11, 8276; econ. hist., 4064; *hist. j.*, 26; hist. of British foreign policy, 929; hist. of Eng. lit., 8293; hist. of India, 1007; hist. of Iran, 2476; hist. of the British Empire 1237, 1316, 1384; modern hist., 163

Cambridge Antiq. Soc.: *publs.*, 9524

Cambridge, City of, 7351, 9524

Cambridge, George, Duke of: life, 2702

*Cambridge rev.*, 8106

Cohen, Lucy: Arthur Cohen, 3971; Lady de Rothschild, 3977

Cohen, Morton: Rider Haggard, 8429

Cohen, Paul Andrew: China and Christianity, 2529

Cohen, Ruth Louisa: milk prices, 5909

Cohn, Albert Mayer: Cruickshank, 9118

Cohn, Bernard S.: Indian civil service recruitment, 1101

Cohn, Gustav: englische Eisenbahnpolitik, 6232

Coillard, François: life, 1918; on the threshold, 1918

coins, 4493, 4496, 4502

Coit, Stanton: selections from, 4015

Cokayne, George Edward: complete baronetage, 78; complete peerage, 77

coke making, 5018

Coke Oven Managers' Assoc., 5018

Colas, René: bibliographie du costume, 7177

Colborne, John: with Hicks Pasha, 1707

*Colburn's united service mag.*, 2681

Colburn, Zerah: locomotive engineering, 6314

Colby, Robert Alan: equivocal virtue, 8429

Colby, Vineta: equivocal virtue, 8429

Colchester, 9532

Coldham, James Desmond: Northamptonshire cricket, 7692

Cole, Alan: Honiton lace industry, 4938

Cole, Alan S.: Sir H. Cole, 410

Cole, David Henry: British military hist., 2695

Cole, George Douglas Howard: Brit. trade unionism, 6602; Brit. working-class movements, 6592, 6597; Brit. working class politics, 565; cent. of co-operation, 6843; essays in memory of, 566, 6460; hist. of socialist thought, 562; self-government in industry, 591; studs. in class structure, 6872; the common people, 6866; trade unionism on railways, 6813; works on Samuel Butler, 8342

Cole, Henrietta: Sir H. Cole, 410

Cole, Sir Henry: international exhibitions, 4136; life, 410

Cole, Howard Norman: Aldershot, 9535; story of Bisley, 7797

Cole, J. M.: Christian guidance, 7505

Cole, John Harding: records of Cork, Cloyne, and Ross, 10501

Cole, John William: Charles Kean, 9354

Cole, Margaret Isabel: Beatrice Webb, 608; ed. Beatrice Webb's diaries, 303; makers of the Labour movement, 592;

story of Fabian socialism, 582; Webbs and their work, 608

Cole, Richard Lee: Methodism in Ireland, 10518

Cole, Thomas: ed. housing and town planning conference, 7065

Cole, William Alan: Brit. econ. growth, 4069; measurement of indust. growth, 4747

Cole, William Henry: permanent-way material, 6288

Colebrook, Leonard: Almroth Wright, 8924

Colebrooke, Sir Thomas Edward: commission on educ. endowments (Scotland), 10122

Coleman, Donald Cuthbert: Brit. paper industry, 5547; Courtaulds, 4931

Coleman, James Smoot: Nigeria, 1842

Coleman, Jane M.: ed. Sussex poor law records, 9556

Coleman, John: ed. cattle, sheep, and pigs. 4349

Coleman, Peter: cartoons of Australian hist., 1318

Coleman, Terry: railway navvies, 6816; Providence & Hardy, 8373

Colenso, Frances Ellen: letters 2118; ruin of Zululand, 2186; Zulu war, 2186

Colenso, John William, bishop: letters, 2118; life, 2118, 3704; Pentateuch, 3345; trial, 2118; works publ. in Natal, 2118, 2182

Coleridge, Bernard John Seymour Coleridge, baron: this for remembrance, 3114

Coleridge, Christabel: Charlotte Mary Yonge, 8429

Coleridge, Ernest Hartley: Lord Coleridge, 3113

Coleridge, Gilbert James Duke: Eton in the seventies, 7904

Coleridge, John Duke Coleridge, baron: committees on: juries, 3260; Supreme court office, 3196

life and letters, 3113

Coleridge, Sir John Taylor: commission on superior courts, 3191; John Keble, 3575

Coleridge, Samuel Taylor: and Darwin, 8625

Coleridge, Stephen William Buchanan: vivisection, 7325

Coleridge-Taylor, Jessie S. Fleetwood: genius and musician, 9296

Coleridge-Taylor, Samuel: life, 9296

Coles, Charles Edward: recollections, 1672

Corke, Helen: Lawrence, 8387

Corkery, Daniel: Synge, 8418

Cormack, Alexander Allan: poor relief in Scotland, 10074

Cormack, Ian Leslie: Glasgow tramways, 10041

Corn: *see* Wheat

Cornell, Louis L.: Kipling in India, 8385

Cornell, Paul Grant: alignment of political groups in Canada, 1467

Cornford, Francis Macdonald: microcosmographia academica, 8105

Cornford, James Peters: adoption of mass organization, 545; aggregate election data, 545; parliamentary foundations of Hotel Cecil, 545; transformation of Conservatism, 545

Cornford, Leslie Cope: century of sea trading, 6089; sea carriers, 10034

Cornforth, Fanny: D. G. Rossetti's letters to, 8407

*Cornhill gallery*, 9092

*Cornhill mag.*, 5461

Cornish, Blanche Warre: R. H. Benson, 3935

Cornish, Charles John: W. H. Flower, 8775

Cornish, Francis Warre: ed. William Cory, 7904, 8429; hist. of English Church, 3506

Cornish Inst. of Mining: *trans.*, 5024

Cornish Methodist Hist. Assoc., 3828

Cornwall: agric., 4166; banks, 4634; china clay, 5347; Congregationalism, 3782; harbours, 6191; hist., 9526; M.P.s, 505; Methodism, 3828; mining, 5022–9; pilchard fishery, 5814; Polytechnic Soc., 5024; shipwrecks, 6167

Cornwallis-West, Beatrice Stella: *see* Campbell, Mrs. Patrick

Cornwallis-West, George Frederick Myddleton: autobiog., 6880

coroners, 3254–7

Corpus Christi College, Camb., 8096

Corrance, H. C.: trans., 3944

Corrigan, Sir Dominic: life, 10795

Corry, Montagu William Lowry-, Baron Rowton: ed. Disraeli speeches, 669

Corsley, 7018

Corson, Eugene Rollin: H. P. Blavatsky, 4024

Corti, Egon Caesar, Conte: English empress, 349; house of Rothschild, 3977

Cortissoz, Royal: W. Reid, 2630

Corvo, Baron: *see* Rolfe, Frederick

Cory, Sir George Edward: rise of South Africa, 1994

Cory, John, & Sons, 6089

Cory, Reginald: horticultural record, 4392

Cory, William: letters and journals, 7904, 8429; life, 7904, 8429

Cosby, Dudley Sydney Ashworth: Irish land problem, 10603

Coss, John Jacob: ed., 8461

Cossons, Neil: indust. archaeol. of Bristol region, 4836

cost of living, 6536–70

Costello, Nuala: John MacHale, 10492

Costelloe, Rachel: *see* Strachey, Ray

Costin, William Conrad: constit. docs., 253; Great Britain and China, 2523

Coté, Narcisse Omer: political appointments, 1441

Cotgreave, Alfred: public librs., 8262

Cotgrove, Stephen Frederick: technical educ., 8154

*Cottage gardener*, 4391, 4364

cottage hospitals, 7486

cottages, 7087–8, 7014–40, 7117

Cotter, Charles Henry: nautical astronomy, 6152

Cottesloe, Thomas Francis Fremantle, Baron: National Rifle Assoc., 7797

Cottle, Basil: life of a university, 8126

cotton: Egyptian, 1661; English industry, 4848–87, 6716–25; 6730–1; famine, 4859, 10002; Fijian, 1423; Indian, 1030–1, 1075; raw, 4854, 4862–3, 4868, 4877; Scottish industry, 10001–6

Cotton, Charles Philip: Dublin public health commission, 10696; Irish Public Health Acts, 10694

Cotton, George Edward Lynch, bishop: life, 1039

Cotton, Henry: fasti ecclesiae Hibernicae, 10503

Cotton, Sir Henry John Stedman: new India, 1017

Cotton, James Sutherland: imperial gazetteer of India, 997; India, 280; reports on Indian educ., 1045

*Cotton factory times*, 4851

*Cotton spinners and manufacturers directory*, 4850, 4846

*Cotton year book*, 4850

Cottrell, P. L.: Lond. financier and Austria, 4642

Couch, Jonathan: fishes, 7764

Couch, John Philip: George Eliot in France, 8360

Couch, Margaret: educ. in Africa, 1605

Couling, Samuel: temperance movement, 7535

Cruickshank, Marjorie: Argyll commission report, 10120; church and state in Eng. educ., 7932; educ. in Highlands, 10115; the Dick Bequest, 10111; training of teachers in Scotland, 10116a

Cruikshank, George: catalogues, 9118; life, 9118

Cruikshank, Robert James: roaring century, 151

Crum, F. S.: occupation mortality, 6924

Crum, John McLeod Campbell: Francis Paget, 3677

Crump, Arthur: causes of great fall in prices, 5871; political opinion, 268

Crump, William Bunting: Huddersfield woollen industry, 4902; wool-textile industry of the Pennines, 4897

Cruse, Alfred James: cigarette card cavalcade, 9110; match-box labels, 9110

Cruse, Amy: after the Victorians, 8299; Victorians and their books, 8299

Crutchley, George W.: John Mackintosh, 5700

Crutchley, William Caius: autobiog., 6077

Crystal Palace, 4128, 4132–3, 9208

Cubbon, William: bibliog. of Isle of Man, 9564; island heritage, 9565; Thomas Edward Brown, 8338

Cubitt, Horace William: building in London, 5766

Cuddesdon College, 3525

Cudworth, William: Bradford, 9561

Cullen, Rev. James Aloysius: life, 10489

Cullen, Louis Michael: econ. hist. of Ireland, 10524; ed. formation of Irish economy, 10524

Cullen, Paul: letters, 10490; life, 10490; studs., 10490, 10328

Cullen, Tom A.: autumn of terror, 7577; the empress Brown, 323

Culler, Arthur Dwight: imaginative reason, 8328; imperial intellect, 3944

Culley, Richard Spelman: practical telegraphy, 5616

Cullop, Charles P.: Confederate propaganda, 2590

Culpin, Ewart Gladstone: garden city movement, 7068

Culshaw, John: century of music, 9245

Cumberland: hist., 9527; industry, 4830; M.P.s, 505

Cumberland, Ernest Augustus, Duke of, 337

Cumberland & Westmorland Antiq. and Archaeol. Soc.: *tract series*, 9527; *transactions*, 9527

Cumbers, Frank Henry: book room, 3826; Richmond Coll., 3827

Cuming, Edward William Dirom: ed., 7760; fox-hunting anthology, 7742

Cuming, Geoffrey John: hist. of anglican liturgy, 3526

Cumming, Alexander: hospitals in the Crimea, 2437

Cumming, Alexander Neilson: public-house reform, 7560

Cumming, Sir John Ghest: bibliog. of crime, 7572; ed. life-boat in verse, 6168; political India, 1014

Cummings, Hayman Alfred James: college stamps, 5604

Cummins, Geraldine Dorothy: Dr. E. OE. Somerville, 10777

Cummins, Nicholas Marshall: Cork medical hist., 10792

Cumnock, 10015, 10175

Cumpston, Ina Mary: imperial problems, 1244; Indians overseas, 1013; Radicalism in Trinidad, 1592; Sir A. Gordon & Indians, 1423; some early Indian nationalists, 1072

*Cumulative book index*, 9

Cunard, Maud Alice, Lady: George Moore's letters to, 8396

Cunard, Nancy: George Moore, 8396

Cunard Steam Ship Co., 6089

Cundall, Frank: bibliographia Jamaicensis, 1565; bibliog., of the West Indies, 1565; Enos Nuttall, 1576; political & social disturbances, 1565

Cundall, Herbert Minton: Birket Foster, 9051; Brit. water-colour painting, 9030; ed., 9044

Cunningham, Allan: dragomania, 2396; wrong horse, 2419

Cunningham, Andrew Storar: Fife Coal Co. Ltd., 10015; mining in Fife, 10015; mining in Mid and East Lothian, 10015

Cunningham, Audrey: William Cunningham, 8485

Cunningham, George Hamilton: London, 9460

Cunningham, Sir Henry Stewart: Earl Canning, 1131; Lord Bowen, 3111

Cunningham, James Francis: Uganda, 1774

Cunningham, John: election law, 691

Cunningham, Joseph Thomas: marketable marine fishes, 5819

Cunningham, Terence P.: Burrowes-Hughes by-election, 10422; 1852 general election in county Cavan, 10422

X x

Feather, A. G.: Stanley's story, 8583
Feavearyear, Sir Albert Edgar: pound sterling, 4474
Feaver, George A.: Sir H. Maine, 714
Federated Inst. of Mining Engineers: *trans.*, 4978
Federated Malay States: *see* Malaya
Federation of Insurance Institutes: *journal*, 4711
Fegan, J. W. C.: life, 7277
Feiling, Sir Keith Grahame: Toryism, 547
Feinberg, Barry: archives of B. Russell, 8465
Feinstein, Charles Hilliard: nat. income, 4083
Feis, Herbert: Europe the world's banker, 4672
Felkin, Robert William: ed. & trans., 1698
Felkin, William: works on hosiery and lace manufactures, 4937
Fell, James: Brit. seamen in San Francisco, 6071
Fellinger, Imogen: Verzeichnis der Musik-zeitschriften, 9236
Fellowes, Edmund Horace: English cathedral music, 3465
Felstead, Sidney Theodore: Edith Cavell, 7468; Sir R. Muir, 3162
Felsted school, 7905
Felt, Charles Wilson: free labour, 6621
Feltoe, Charles Lett: J. F. South, 8914
Felton, B. I.: wages and earnings in agric., 6695
Felton, William Sidney: masters of equitation, 7781
Female Middle-Class Emigration Soc., 6972
Fenby, Charles: the other Oxf., 9550
Fenby, Eric: Delius, 9298
fencing, 7775
Fenianism, 10337–56
Fenland, 9524, 9546
Fenn, Charles: compendium of funds, 4691
Fenn, George Manville: George Alfred Henty, 8429
Fenton, Roger: photographs, 2436, 9223
Fenton, Seamus: reminiscences, 10675
Fenwick, Kenneth: ed., 2444
Ferenczi, Imre: ed. internat. migrations, 6964
Ferguson, Alastair Mackenzie: Ceylon directory, 2199
Ferguson, Eugene Shallcross: bibliog. of hist. of technology, 4744
Ferguson, Fergus: theology and heresy trial of, 9920

Ferguson, George Napier: Supreme Court of Judicature Act (Ireland), 10435
Ferguson, Joan Primrose Scott: ed. Scottish family hists., 9790; ed. Scottish newspapers, 9780
Ferguson, John: Ceylon, 2199
Ferguson, Sir John Alexander: bibliog. of Australia, 1316
Ferguson, John De Lancey: ed. Stevenson's letters, 8415
Ferguson, John Henry: Amer. diplomacy and the Boer war, 2073, 2608
Ferguson, Lady Mary Catharine: Sir Samuel Ferguson, 10764; William Reeves, 10512
Ferguson, Richard Saul: Cumberland and Westmorland M.P.s, 505
Ferguson, Sir Samuel: life, 10764
Ferguson, Thomas: public health, 7395; works on Scottish social welfare, 10056
Ferguson, William: Scotland, 9799
Ferguson, William Dwyer: Supreme Court of Judicature Act (Ireland), 10435
Fergusson, Charles Bruce: diary of A. Gaetz, 1532
Fergusson, James: hist. of modern styles of architecture, 9169
Fergusson, Sir James, 6th bt.:
  commission on excisable liquors, 10083
  committees on: colonisation, 6983; Factory and Workshop Acts, 4820; merchandise marks, 4125; national expenditure, 4456; Sale of Liquors on Sunday Bill, 7565
Fergusson, Sir James, 8th bt.: Curragh incident, 10290; sixteen peers of Scotland, 9809
Fermanagh, 10817
Ferneley, John, 7755
Fernow, Bernhard Eduard: forestry, 4393
ferns, 4385
Ferns, Henry Stanley: Britain and Argentina, 2643
Ferns, diocese, 10503
Ferranti, Gertrude Ziani de: S. Z. de Ferranti, 5250
Ferranti, Sebastian Ziani de: life, 5250
Ferriday, Peter: ed. Victorian architecture, 9171; Lord Grimthorpe, 9201
Ferrier, James Frederick: life, 8453; phil. works, 8453
Fester, Gustav: chemischen Technik, 5256
Festiniog railway, 9683
festschriften, 17
Fetter, Frank Whitson: Brit. monetary orthodoxy, 4476

industry, 5842; industries of Lond., 4765; location of clothing trades, 4961

Hall, Sherwin A.: great cattle plague, 8969

Hall, Sydney P.: sketches, 502

Hall, Trevor Henry: strange case of Edmund Gurney, 4039; strange things, 4039; the spiritualists, 4027; works on Sherlock Holmes, 8350

Hall, William Edward: foreign powers of Brit. crown, 3294; internat. law, 3294; neutrals, 3294

Hall & Co., 5780

Hallam, William: ed. miners' leaders, 6757

Hallberg, Charles William: Suez canal, 1663

Hallé, Sir Charles: autobiog., 9257; life, 9257

Hallé, Charles Émile: ed., 9257

Hallé, Marie: ed., 9257

Hallé orchestra, 9257

Hallewood, A.: state telephone service, 5645

Hallgarten, Robert: communale Besteuerung, 4541

Halliday, Frank Ernest: Cornwall, 9526

Halliwell, Thomas: Trinity Coll., Carmarthen, 9741

Hallmann, Hans: Spanien und die französisch-englische Mittelmeer-Rivalität, 2351

Hallsworth, Harry Mainwaring: railway operating, 6290; unemployment, 6584

Hallsworth, Sir Joseph: working life of shop assistants, 6837

Halpérin, Vladimir: Lord Milner and the empire, 1305

Halpern, Jack: S. Africa's hostages, 2159

Halpern, Paul G.: Mediterranean naval situation, 2352

Halsbury, Hardinge Stanley Giffard, Earl of: betterment committee, 4550; committee on companies bill, 3272; ed., 3043; judicial appointments, 3096; life, 3104

Halsbury's: laws of England, 3043; statutes of England, 3043; statutory instruments, 3043

Halse, George: modeller, 9145

Halsey, William Darrach: ed. new cent. handbook of Eng. lit., 8286

Halstead, P. E.: cement, 5786

Halsted, Edward Pellew: iron-cased ships, 2922

Halton, Frederick Joseph: Gilbert and Sullivan operas, 9274

Ham, George D.: revenue and mercantile year books, 4575

Hambly, G. R. S.: Richard Temple and the Punjab Tenancy Act, 1027

Hambourg, Daria: Richard Doyle, 9120

Hamburger, Joseph: intellectuals in politics, 707

Hamel (afterwards De Hamel), Felix John: Customs Duties Acts, 4575

Hamelin, Jean: guide d'histoire du Canada, 1427; journaux de Québec, 1538; publications gouvernmentales de Québec, 1538

Hamell, Patrick J.: Maynooth students, 10486

Hamer, David Alan: ed. radical programme, 525; Irish question and Liberal politics, 10362; John Morley, 797; liberal politics, 519

Hamer, Frederick E.: personal papers of Lord Rendel, 874

Hamer, Harold: Bolton, 9540

Hamer, Philip May: archives in U.S.A., 49

Hamer, William Spencer: Brit. army, 2705

Hamerton, Philip Gilbert: etcher's handbook, 9093; etching and etchers, 9093

Hamilton, N.Z., 1412

Hamilton, Angus: Somaliland, 1737

Hamilton, Archibald: wool supply, 4910

Hamilton, Bruce: Barbados, 1581

Hamilton, Charles Joseph: trade relations between England and India, 1032

Hamilton, Cicely Mary: Old Vic, 9342

Hamilton, Lord Claud: committee on pilotage, 6163

Hamilton, E. W.: ed., 4379

Hamilton, Sir Edward Walter: committee on aged deserving poor, 7389; conversion and redemption, 4582; diary, 302; local taxation, 4569

Hamilton, Sir Frederick: Jameson raid, 2055

Hamilton, Lord Frederick Spencer: autobiog., 6882

Hamilton, George Alexander: committees on: county and district surveyors (Ireland), 10804; naval estimates, 2885

Hamilton, Lord George Francis: commission on the poor laws, 7355, 10077, 10693; parliamentary reminiscences, 773

Hamilton, H. L.: household management, 7168

Hamilton, Sir Horace Perkins: Treasury control, 363

Hamilton, Ian Bogle Monteith: the happy warrior, 2811

Hamilton, Sir Ian Standish Monteith:

Kirk-Smith, Harold: William Thomson, 3647

Kirkaldy, Adam Willis: Brit. shipping, 6069; hist. and econ. of transport, 5991; trade and commerce of Brit. empire, 1229

Kirkby, William: artificial mineral waters, 5710

Kirkcaldy: textiles, 10005, 10022

Kirkcudbright, 9965

Kirkham-in-Amounderness, 9540

Kirkpatrick, Brownlee Jean: bibliog. of E. M. Forster, 8366

Kirkpatrick, Thomas Percy Claude: medical teaching in Trinity College, Dublin, 10792; Rotunda hospital, 10794

Kirkstall Forge, 5103

Kirkwood, David, Baron Kirkwood: autobiog., 9814

Kirschner, Paul: Conrad, 8351

Kirsop, Joseph: Free Methodism, 3863

Kisch, H. M.: letters, 1155

Kissane, James D.: Tennyson, 8420; Victorian mythology, 8318

Kistner, W.: anti-slavery in Transvaal, 2141

Kitcat, house of, 5562

Kitchel, Anna Theresa: George Lewes and George Eliot, 8360

Kitchen, Fred: autobiog., 7022

Kitchener, Herbert Horatio, Earl Kitchener: life, 2814; memo on Indian army, 1169; Sudan campaign, 1710

Kitchin, Arthur Henderson: Scotsman's food, 10055

Kitchin, George William: E. H. Browne, 3652

Kitchin, Joseph: S. African mines, 2035

Kitson Clark, Edwin: Kitsons of Leeds, 5719; Leeds Phil. and Lit. Soc., 8209

Kitson Clark, George Sidney Roberts: churchmen and condition of England, 3382; Eng. inheritance, 3313; expanding society, 171; festschift for, 177; making of Victorian England, 171; statesmen in disguise, 381

Kitsons of Leeds, 5197

Kitton, Frederic George: Dickens and his illustrators, 9103; John Leech, 9126; Phiz, 9130

Kivebulaya, Apolo: life, 1780

Klapper, Charles Frederick: golden age of tramways, 6338

Klauder, Joseph V.: Sir Jonathan Hutchinson, 8887

Klein, Hermann: reign of Patti, 9319; thirty years of musical life, 9250

Klein, Ira: Britain, Siam, &c., 2567; Brit. expansion in Malaya, 2567; Salisbury, Rosebery, & Siam, 2567; utilitarianism & agric. progress, 1024; Wilson v. Trevelyan, 1110

Klein, Philip Shriver: James Buchanan, 2619

Klein, Viola: feminine character, 6987

Klemke, E. D.: ed. studs. in G. E. Moore, 8462

Klemm, Friedrich: Western technology, 4802

Kleynhaus, W. A.: Volksregering in Z.A.R., 2139

Klickstein, Herbert S.: source book in chemistry, 8678

Klinck, Carl Frederick: Canadian writers, 1432; lit. hist. of Canada, 1455

Kline, George Louis: ed. Whitehead, essays, 8471

Klinefelter, Walter: Sherlock Holmes, 8350

Kling, Blair Bernard: the blue mutiny, 1069

Klingberg, Frank Joseph: ed. sidelight on Anglo-American relations, 2587

Kluke, Paul: Heeresaufbau, 2866

Knaplund, Paul: Britain, commonwealth, and empire, 1236; Brit. empire, 1236; ed. Brit. views on Norwegian–Swedish problems, 2376; ed. Gladstone–Gordon correspondence, 731; ed. letters from Berlin embassy, 769, 2301; ed. Sir E. Grey's speeches, 770; Gladstone and imperial policy, 1244; Gladstone's foreign policy, 934

Knapp, Friedrich Ludwig: chemical technology, 5263

Knapp, John: capital exports and growth, 4677

Knapp, John Matthew: ed. univs. and the social problem, 7308

Knapp, William F.: ed., 3892

Knapp, William Ireland: George Borrow, 8335

Kneller Hall: Military School of Music, 2759

Knibbs, Sir George Handley: local govt. in Australia, 1342

Knickerbocker, Francis Wentworth: free minds, 4006

Knickerbocker, Kenneth Leslie: works on R. Browning, 8340

Knickerbocker, William Skinkle: creative Oxf., 8076

Knight, Charles: autobiog., 5491; ed. Knight's cyclopaedia of Lond., 9474; ed. Lond., 9474; Eng. cyclopaedia, 108; life, 5491; national cyclopaedia, 112

Lawrence, Arnold Walter: trade castles, 1819

Lawrence, Arthur: journalism as a profession, 5377; Sir Arthur Sullivan, 9315

Lawrence, David Herbert: bibliog., 8387; letters, 8387; life, 8387; studs., 8387

*Lawrence, D. H., news and notes*, 8387

*Lawrence, D. H., rev.*, 8387

Lawrence, Elwood Parsons: George, Chamberlain, and the land tax, 4554; Henry George in the Brit. Isles, 4554

Lawrence, Frieda: memoirs and corresp., 8387; 'not I, but the wind', 8387

Lawrence, George: trans., 226

Lawrence, Sir Henry Montgomery: life, 1138

Lawrence, John Laird Mair, Baron Lawrence: life, 1138

Lawrence, Nathaniel Morris: Whitehead's phil. development, 8471

Lawrence, Thomas Joseph: essays, 3294; public internat. law, 3294

Lawrie, Leslie Gordon: bibliog. of dyeing and textile printing, 4947

Laws, Robert: life, 1927; reminiscences, 1927

Lawson, Cecil Constant Philip: hist. of uniforms, 2772

Lawson, Edward Frederick, Baron Burnham: Peterborough Court, 5380

Lawson, Frederick Henry: constit. cases, 261; Oxf. law school, 3085

Lawson, George: letters, 2439

Lawson, John: Hull grammar school, 7965

Lawson, John Grant: committees on: Aged Pensioners Bill, 7389; Univs. and Coll. Estates Acts, 8061

Lawson, John James, Baron Lawson: Herbert Smith, 6760; Peter Lee, 6753

Lawson, Monica, 2439

Lawson, Robert: Contagious Diseases Acts, 7510

Lawson, Sir Wilfrid: cartoons in rhyme, 315; memoir, 7544; speeches, 7552

Lawson, William: gentleman-farming, 10593

Lawson, William, of Wellington, N.Z.: Pacific steamers, 6098

Lawson, William John: hist. of banking, 4608; law of banking, 4608

Lawson, William Norton: patents, 3292

Lawson, William Ramage: Brit. econ. in 1904, 8479; Brit. railways, 6215; Scottish investors' manual, 9995

Lawton, John Stewart: conflict in Christology, 3328

Lawton, Mary: ed., 5751

Lawton, Richard: pop. changes, 6939; pop. movts. in west Midlands, 6939; pop. of Liverpool, 9541

*Lawyer's companion*, 3025

lawyers: English, 3070–7, 3087–185; Irish, 10439–53; Scottish, 9829, 9832–40

Laxton, 4316

Layard, Sir Austen Henry: autobiog., 2250; committee on Paris exhibition, 4134; life, 2250

Layard, George Somes: Charles Samuel Keene, 9125; Kate Greenaway, 8429, 9123; Mrs. Lynn Linton, 8429; Shirley Brooks, 5401; Tennyson, 9104

Layton, Thomas Bramley: Sir William Arbuthnot Lane, 8892

Layton, Walter Thomas, Baron Layton: changes in wages of domestic servants, 6833; prices, 5865; wheat prices and world's production, 5889

Lazerowitz, Morris: ed. G. E. Moore, essays, 8462

Lea, Frederick Measham: chemistry of cement and concrete, 5790

Lea, Hermann: Hardy's Wessex, 8373

Leach, Arthur Francis: educ. charters and docs., 7823

Leach, Edmund Ronald: ed., 1024, 1116, 1203

Leach, Henry: Duke of Devonshire, 778; ed. great golfers, 7779

lead, 5032–5, 5105, 5131–4, 5139, 9233, 9656

Leader, John Daniel: records of Sheffield, 9562; Sheffield infirmary, 7481

Leader, Robert Eadon: J. A. Roebuck, 876; Sheffield Banking Co., 4638

Leader, William: election manual, 693

*Leader, the*, 5408

League of Nations movement, 945

League of the Cross handbook, 7550

Leak, Hector: migration from and to U.K., 6934

Leake, Stephen Martin: contracts, 3274; pleading, 3264

Leamy, Margaret: Parnell's faithful few, 10365

*Lean's Royal Navy list*, 2845

Leaper, J. M. F.: suppl. to, 8280

Lear, Edward: as landscape draughtsman, 9062; bibliog., 8388; journals, 8388; journals, 8388; letters, 8388; life, 8388

leaseholds, 526, 7053

Leask, Thomas: diaries, 1970

Leask, William Keith: Thomas M'Lauchlan, 9909

leather industries, 5833–44

3 A

Merrifield, Mary Philadelphia: handbook of light and shade, 9230

Merriman, John Xavier: life, 2097

Merriman, N. J.: Cape journals, 2098

Merry, Denis Harry: bibliog., Univ. of Oxf., 8064; ed. bibliog. of Oxfordshire, 9550

Merryweather, F. Somner: Free Church of England, 3904

Mersey, Charles Clive Bigham, 2nd Viscount: Roxburghe Club, 9217; viceroys of India, 1130

Mersey, John Charles Bigham, 1st Viscount: committees on: jury law, 3261; Thrift and Credit Banks Bill, 4641

Mersey Docks & Harbour Board, 6186

Mersey Mission to Seamen, 6074

Merseyside: football, 7711; gas supply, 6427

Merthyr Tydfil: hist., 9766; politics, 9592, 9598

Merton, Stephen: Mark Rutherford, 8409

Merttens, Frederick: hours and cost of labour in cotton industry, 6721

Merz, John Theodore: European thought, 8430

Mesopotamia, 2461, 2470

Mess, Henry Adolphus: factory legislation, 4813

Messedaglia, Luigi: uomini d'Africa, 1695

Messenger, Ruth Ellis: bibliog. for the study of hymns, 3469

Mestler, Gordon E.: intro. to 8788

metal industries: general, 5041–54; iron and steel, 5055–123, 6763–72, 9649–54; other metals, 5124–44, 9655–6

*Metal industry*, 5044

*Metal industry handbook and directory*, 5043

metalliferous mining, 5019–36, 9648

*Metallurgical abstracts*, 5042

metallurgy, 5046–51

Metaphysical Soc., 8436

Metcalf, David: labour productivity, 6693

Metcalf, Thomas Richard: aftermath of revolt, 1052

Metcalfe, Agnes Edith: women's effort, 676

Metcalfe, George Edgar: Great Britain and Ghana, 1823

Metcalfe, Rupert: England and Sir Horace Plunkett, 10553

Methley, Noel T.: lifeboat and its story, 6168

Methodist:
  churches and trade unions, 6616
  churches in: Canada, 1527; England, 3817–66; Ireland, 10518; New Zealand, 1409; S. Africa, 2016–17; Wales, 9626

hymns, 3479
  *monthly*, 3863
  New Connexion, 3853–5
  Publishing House, 3826
  *recorder*, 3833, 3837
  schools, 7941
  *times*, 3833, 3838

Methuen, Sir Algernon: see Stedman, Sir Algernon Methuen Marshall

*Metropolitan [and provincial local govt. j.]*, 9403

Metropolitan Asylums Board, 7479

metropolitan magistrates, 3251–3

Metropolitan Museum of Art, New York: libr. catalogue, 8983

Metropolitan Police: and India, 1119; commission on, 7604; hist., 7593–4

Metropolitan Vickers Electrical Co., 5249

Metropolitan Visiting and Relief Assoc. 7204

Metropolitan Water Board, 6434

Metrowich, Frederick Charles: higher educ. in S. Africa, 2040

Metz, Ilse: deutsche Flotte, 2307

Metz, Rudolph: hundred years of Brit. phil., 8431

Mews, John: digest of Eng. case law, 3041

Mexico, 2650–2

Meyendorff, Baron Aleksandr Feliksovich: ed., 2339

Meyer, Adele (Mrs. Carl Meyer, *afterwards* Lady Meyer): makers of our clothes, 6653

Meyer, Bernard C.: Conrad, 8351

Meyer, Frederic Brotherton: life, 3771

Meyer, Hermann Henry Bernard: ed. dyestuffs, 4947; monetary question, 4472

Meyer, Hugo Richard: Brit. state telegraphs, 5613; municipal ownership, 6408; public ownership and telephone, 5646

Meyer, John Robert: input–output approach to Brit. indust. production, 4081

Meyer, Sir William: trans., 1127

Meyer-Adams, Rudolf: Mission Haldanes, 2311

Meyers, Robert R.: George Borrow, 8335

Meynell, Alice: life, 8394

Meynell, Everard: Francis Thompson, 8423

Meynell, Laurence Walter: famous cricket grounds, 7690; Rolls, 6358

Meynell, Viola: Alice Meynell, 8394; ed. letters of J. M. Barrie, 8331; Francis Thompson and Wilfrid Meynell, 8423

Meynell, Wilfrid: and Francis Thompson 8423; Lady Butler, 9043

3 C

Philanthropos: physiological cruelty, 7325
philanthropy, 7200–327, 10685–6
Philbrick, Frederick Adolphus: postage and telegraph stamps, 5596
Philharmonic Soc., 9256
Philip, Alexander John: Dickens dictionary, 8354
Philip, George: ed. Philip's handy admin. atlas of Scotland, 10164; ed. Philip's mercantile marine atlas, 6033
Philip, James Charles: Chemical Soc., 8690
Philip, Sir Robert W.: life, 8905
Philips, Cyril Henry: ed. evolution of India & Pakistan, 1003; ed. handbook of oriental hist., 2505; ed. historians of India, Pakistan, and Ceylon, 994
Philips, Herbert: ed., 7587
Philips' atlases, 638, 6033, 10164, 10240
Phillimore, John George: committee on public prosecutors, 7595
Phillimore, John Swinnerton: essays in Liberalism, 527
Phillimore, Sir Robert Joseph: eccles. law, 3491; internat. law, 3294
Phillimore, William Phillimore Watts: county pedigrees, 98; index to changes of name, 92
Phillipps-Wolley, Sir Clive: big game shooting, 7799
Phillips, A. D. M.: underdraining, 4421
Phillips, A. W.: unemployment and rate of change of money wage rates, 6543
Phillips, Charles Edward: devel. of educ. in Canada, 1524
Phillips, Charles Stanley: hymnody, 3471; singing church, 3463; W. H. Frere, 3571
Phillips, David Rhys: vale of Neath, 9766
Phillips, Elizabeth: pioneers of Welsh coalfield, 9646
Phillips, Ernest: how to become a journalist, 5377
Phillips, George Lewis: England's climbing boys, 6665
Phillips, Henry Arthur Deuteros: our admin. of India, 1126
Phillips, J. W.: Haverfordwest, 9770
Phillips, James: Pembrokeshire, 9770
Phillips, Sir Lionel: some reminiscences, 2152
Phillips, Maberly: banking in north of Eng., 4630
Phillips, Philip: Forth Bridge, 10040
Phillips, Philip, *missioner*, 3481
Phillips, Philip Lee: Library of Congress atlases, 135
Phillips, R. J.: Scottish rugby, 10090

Phillips, Reginald M.: stamp collection of, 5599
Phillips, Robert Edward: modern cycles, 6373
Phillips, Sidney: mortality stats., 6925
Phillips, Sir Thomas: life, 9617
Phillips, Thomas: Welsh revival, 9623
Phillips, Walter Alison: ed. Church of Ireland, 10495; revolution in Ireland, 10286, 10395
Phillipson, Coleman: Bosphorus and Dardanelles, 2397
Phillpot, Henry Roy Stewart: J. H. Thomas, 634
Phillpotts, Eden: from the angle of 88, 8429
Phillpotts, Henry, bishop: life, 3679; and Gorham case, 3335
Philological Soc., 117; *proceedings*, 8319; *trans.*, 8319
philology, 8319
philosophy, 8430–71
*Philosophy of science*, 8613
Philpot, Joseph Charles: letters, 3773; William Tiptoft, 3773
Philpot, Sarah L.: ed., 3773
Philpott, B. P.: fluctuations in wool prices, 4911
Philpott, H. G.: N.Z. dairy industry, 1408
Philpott, Hugh B.: final report of the board, 7859; Lond. at school, 7859
Phipson, Sidney Lovell: evidence, 3280
'Phiz': *see* Browne, Hablot K.
phlogiston theory, 8685
Phoenix park murders, 10343
phosphorus, 5320–1
*'Photographic news' almanac*, 9224
photographs, 56, 140, 143, 145, 424
photography, 9221–7
physical deterioration, 7438
physical educ., 8177
Physick, John Frederick: Wellington monument, 9144
physics, 8704–28
Physiological Soc., 8836
physiology, 8941
Phythian, Brian Arthur: ed., Manch. grammar school, 7968
Piccadilly theatre, 9326
Picciotto, Cyril Moses: St. Paul's school, 7919
Picciotto, James: sketches of Anglo-Jewish hist., 3954
Picht, Werner: Toynbee Hall, 7309
Pickerill, Norman Lancelot: Collingham Farmers' Club, 4170
Pickering, P. A.: trades unions in Manch., 6620

3 D

*Index*

3 F

Hanham (Ed)

(s) History. Bibliographies.

(i) England. History, 19th
century.